# BLACKSTONE'S
# CRIMINAL PRACTICE

# BLACKSTONE'S

# CRIMINAL PRACTICE

## 2022

### SUPPLEMENT 3

GENERAL EDITORS

DAVID ORMEROD CBE, QC (HON)

BARRISTER, BENCHER OF MIDDLE TEMPLE,
PROFESSOR OF CRIMINAL JUSTICE,
UNIVERSITY COLLEGE LONDON

DAVID PERRY QC

BARRISTER, 6KBW COLLEGE HILL

FOUNDING EDITOR

HIS HONOUR PETER MURPHY

SUPPLEMENT EDITOR

WILLIAM HAYS

BARRISTER, 6KBW COLLEGE HILL

ADVISORY EDITORIAL BOARD
THE RT HON SIR BRIAN LEVESON, THE HON SIR HENRY GLOBE,
HHJ SALLY CAHILL QC, HHJ MARTIN EDMUNDS QC,
HHJ RICHARD MARKS QC, HHJ JEFFREY PEGDEN QC,
HHJ HEATHER NORTON, HHJ MICHAEL HOPMEIER,
HHJ STEVEN EVERETT, HHJ JONATHAN COOPER,
HHJ DEBORAH TAYLOR, MICHAEL BOWES QC, HHJ ALISON LEVITT QC,
TIM OWEN QC, ROBERT SMITH QC,
ADRIAN WATERMAN QC, HH ERIC STOCKDALE

CONTRIBUTORS
PARAMJIT AHLUWALIA, DUNCAN ATKINSON QC, ALEX BAILIN QC,
DIANE BIRCH OBE, STEVEN BIRD, HHJ JONATHAN COOPER,
MRS JUSTICE CUTTS DBE, ANAND DOOBAY, HHJ STEVEN EVERETT,
RUDI FORTSON QC, DANIEL GODDEN, HHJ MARTIN EDMUNDS QC,
KATHERINE HARDCASTLE, WILLIAM HAYS, MICHAEL HIRST,
LAURA C. H. HOYANO, PETER HUNGERFORD-WELCH, PAUL JARVIS,
ADRIAN KEANE, SALLY KYD, KARL LAIRD, MICHAEL LEREGO QC,
RICHARD MCMAHON QC, ALEXANDER MILLS, VALSAMIS MITSILEGAS,
TIM MOLONEY QC, AMANDA PINTO QC, HH PETER ROOK QC,
RICHARD D. TAYLOR, MARK TOPPING, MARTIN WASIK CBE

OXFORD
UNIVERSITY PRESS

## Sentencing Guidelines

The Sentencing Guidelines reflect the text as set out on the Sentencing Council website. Previous PDF versions of Guidelines are now included on that website for archive purposes only by the Council and we have amended the Guidelines in this Supplement to reflect the official statement of the Guidelines which means that some previous explanatory material has been excised. The approach taken in the Supplement is that the Overarching Guidelines are set out first from SG1 to SG9, followed by the Magistrates' Court Sentencing Guidelines at SG10 and then the Sentencing Guidelines by Offence Type. For a more detailed note on the treatment and order of the Sentencing Guidelines please see section SG0. The approach we have taken is to include all Sentencing Guidelines triable on indictment only and triable either way in the Offence Types. Offences triable summarily are included in the Magistrates' Court Sentencing Guidelines along with a cross-reference for any offences triable either way to the location of that guideline within the Offence Types.

This Supplement includes updates to the text of *Blackstone's Criminal Practice 2022* taking account of legislative developments and leading cases since the publication of the 2022 edition. These updates are included at the start of the Supplement and follow the headings and the paragraph numbering used in the 2022 edition.

## Blackstone's Briefing and Fortnightly Updates

Please visit the *Blackstone's Criminal Practice 2022* companion website at www.oup.com/ blackstones/criminal to register for e-mail updates or to download the latest updates. *Blackstone's Briefing* includes analysis of key developments and feature articles. If you have any queries, please contact blackstonescriminal@oup.com.

# Contents

# Table of Cases

# Table of Statutes

# Table of Statutory Instruments

# Table of Guidelines

# Table of Protocols and Circulars

# Table of International Treaties and Conventions and other Legal Instruments

# Table of European Legislation

# SUPPLEMENT TO PART A
# CRIMINAL LAW

the throat which was the actual cause of death. Fulford LJ considered (at [38]) that the result would now be different:

> We are confident that post-*Jogee*, the two acquitted defendants in *Gamble*, if tried in England and Wales, would be guilty of murder and would be unable to rely on the concept of OSA … Save perhaps for exceptional circumstances which are not readily easy to envisage, there will be no need to direct the jury on the concept of OSA simply because the fatal injuries were inflicted using an entirely different kind of weapon or method of killing than that originally contemplated and/or the perpetrator intended to kill rather than to inflict really serious harm.

# Section A5     Inchoate Offences

## ENCOURAGING OR ASSISTING CRIME: SERIOUS CRIME ACT 2007

### *Actus Reus* Elements Common to Offences under Part 2

**A5.4**   In *Scott v DPP* [2022] EWHC 91 (Admin), [2022] 1 Cr App R 16 (319), the Divisional Court confirmed that an offence under the SCA 2007, Part 2, may be charged whether or not D is also complicit in a substantive offence as a result of D's encouragement or assistance. D may be guilty of a Part 2 offence even where D has assisted or encouraged the continuance of an ongoing offence that was already being committed by the principal offender(s). D cannot be guilty under Part 2 in respect of another person's past and completed offence, but save to that extent, said the Court (at [27]):

> Nothing in … part 2 of the Act would justify the conclusion that there is some temporal or other limit to the connection between the accused's and the principal's offending.

In *Scott v DPP*, D was accordingly guilty of an offence under s. 45 by communicating with a remand prisoner (S) via S's illicitly operated mobile phone. Merely by possessing this phone, S was committing an offence under the Prison Act 1952, s. 40D(3A), and the court upheld a finding at Stratford Magistrates' court that, by communicating with S via this phone, D was encouraging or assisting him to commit or continue committing that offence. There would after all be no point in S taking the risk of being caught with the mobile phone if nobody else was willing to communicate with him via that phone. It did not matter that S was already committing the s. 40D(3A) offence even before D's first call or communication, because it was an ongoing offence.

## CONSPIRACY TO DEFRAUD

### Definition

**A5.65**   In *Hunter* [2021] EWCA Crim 1785, [2022] 1 Cr App R 13 (188), the Court of Appeal considered the relationship between conspiracy to defraud and the statutory offence of fraudulent trading, contrary to the Companies Act 2006, s. 933(1). The appellants were convicted of fraudulent trading on the basis that their company, BZZ Ltd, was operated by them for a fraudulent purpose, namely that of evading lawful restrictions on the resale or touting of tickets for artistic and sporting events, and reselling tickets that were of doubtful validity, to the potential detriment of purchasers.

It was submitted on behalf of the appellants that the concept of fraud in the offence of fraudulent trading should be narrowly construed in line with common law conspiracy to defraud. They sought to rely on *Evans* [2014] 1 WLR 2817, in which it was held that if a case of conspiracy to defraud does not involve an agreement to defraud another by deception, it must at least involve an agreement dishonestly to prejudice or compromise a 'proprietary right' of the intended victim.

The Court of Appeal rejected the submission that the two offences should be construed as subject to the same limitations, but added (obiter) that even in the context of conspiracy to defraud, 'proprietary rights' should be construed very broadly and need not be confined to beneficial or equitable interests or to the kinds of interests that need to be shown to be able to launch a claim for an equitable tracing remedy (following *Hayes* [2015] EWCA Crim 46 at [33]).

## Section A6  Corporate Liability

### SPECIAL RULES OF ATTRIBUTION: STATUTORY CONSTRUCTION

Breaches of regulatory obligations under the Money Laundering Regulations 2007 (SI 2007 **A6.7** No. 2157) (since replaced by the Money Laundering, Terrorist Financing and Transfer of Funds (Information on the Payer) Regulations 2017 (SI 2017 No. 692)) which transposed the EU Third Money Laundering Directive into UK law, attract both civil penalties and criminal offences. They require regulated bodies to carry out initial and continuing customer due diligence (CDD) and, in some circumstances, enhanced CDD (regs. 8, 9 and 14). Unlike the substantive POCA 2002 money laundering offences, the prosecution does not need to prove that money laundering had occurred. Remarkably, 2021 was the first time the FCA used those criminal powers: for failing to monitor its customer over a period of three and a half years, the bank pleaded guilty and was fined almost £265 million (*FCA v NatWest Bank Plc*, unreported 13 December 2021, tinyurl.com/47vfk8zy).

### SENTENCING CORPORATE CRIMES

Further extended liability for the terms of DPAs occurred in *SFO v Amec Foster Wheeler Energy* **A6.22** *Ltd* [2021] Lloyd's Rep FC 353. John Wood Group plc, the purchaser of the company, its ultimate parent company, described as 'twice-removed' from the misconduct, assumed responsibility for AFWEL's obligations and payments under the DPA, agreed to co-operate with the SFO and other law enforcement agencies during the DPA and to report annually on enhancements to its world-wide compliance programme. The latter has far wider effect than a serious crime prevention order under s. 19 of the Serious Crime Act 2007.

## Section A7  Human Rights

### PUBLIC AUTHORITIES

#### Substantive Challenges to the Criminal Law

The decision of the Divisional Court in *DPP v Ziegler* [2019] EWHC 71 (Admin), [2020] QB **A7.32** 253, was the subject of an appeal to the Supreme Court. In *DPP v Ziegler* [2021] UKSC 23, [2022] AC 408, the Supreme Court held that in overturning the decision of the District Judge to acquit the protestors the Divisional Court had applied the wrong test. Applying the correct test, the Supreme Court concluded that the decision of the District Judge had not been wrong in law or one that no reasonable judge could have reached. Moreover, the Supreme Court added that in cases such as this even deliberate physically obstructive conduct on the part of protestors is capable of constituting a lawful excuse even where the impact on other highway users is more than *de minimis*. Accordingly, the appeal was allowed and the acquittals restored. There is nothing in the judgment of the Supreme Court to undermine the approach the Divisional Court suggested that the lower courts should take in future when trying cases such as this.

# Section A8    Territorial and Extraterritorial Jurisdiction

## TERRITORIAL JURISDICTION

### The General Rule

**A8.2**    Although, for most purposes, England and Wales form a single jurisdiction, the devolution of law-making powers to the Welsh Assembly and ministers has resulted in some distinctions. These can be seen primarily in regulatory matters (e.g. in secondary legislation concerning Covid restrictions or animal welfare (see **B20.19** in the main work)) but the Welsh Assembly has also enacted primary legislation dealing with mainstream criminal law. As of 21 March 2022, the common-law defence of 'reasonable punishment' has been abolished in relation to the corporal punishment of a child taking place in Wales (Children (Abolition of Defence of Reasonable Punishment) (Wales) Act 2020, ss. 1 and 5(2)). Smacking a child, even lightly, is therefore a criminal battery anywhere in Wales, even where it would be considered lawful in England.

# SUPPLEMENT TO PART B
# OFFENCES

# Section B1    Homicide and Related Offences

## DIMINISHED RESPONSIBILITY

### Basis of Defence

**Providing an Explanation for Acts and Omissions**    *Curran* [2021] EWCA Crim 1999 (at    **B1.29**
[37]–[39]) concerns the question of whether the partial defence of diminished responsibility
can still be relied upon where, in contrast to the typical situation, D does not admit the
commission of the *actus reus* of murder. Macur LJ took the view that such an admission will not
always be required since there may be cases where D relies on the partial defence but does not
give evidence at the trial. What is necessary, it seems, is (at [39]):

> … an evidential basis upon which the partial defence is mounted. Be that an account by the
> defendant in interview with police or psychiatrists or a contemporaneous narrative eyewitness
> account of the assault leading to death and which provides the context for a psychiatric opinion as
> to the impact of or link between the likely abnormality of mind and the assault.

That evidential basis was lacking in *Curran* (which was a historic case under the original version
of the Homicide Act 1957, s. 2(1)). The point (under the current version of s. 2(1)) would seem
to be that without evidence as to the nature of the acts or omissions of D in doing or being party
to the killing, the statutory question of whether D's abnormality of mental functioning
provides an explanation for those acts or omissions cannot be addressed.

## MANSLAUGHTER GENERALLY

### Voluntary and Involuntary Manslaughter

The variety of possible routes to a verdict of manslaughter and the potentially different views of    **B1.42**
the facts taken by the jury (or by different members of the same jury) can lead to difficulties in
sentencing and in relation to the normal rule requiring unanimity of verdicts. The issues are
discussed in detail in D Ormerod and R Taylor, 'Agreement and Disagreement in Murder and
Manslaughter Verdicts' [2022] Crim LR 179.

In summary, case law has shown that a number of different situations can arise. Where there are
various types of voluntary manslaughter (and thus partial defences to murder) in issue, a
conviction for manslaughter will normally still be safe even if the jury are split between different
partial defences, *provided* they are all agreed that there was at least an unlawful act causing death
(*Jones* (1999) *The Times*, 17 February 1999). Where however the choice is between two
different types of involuntary manslaughter, i.e. between unlawful act manslaughter and gross
negligence manslaughter, the more recent case of *Rebelo (No. 1)* [2019] EWCA Crim 633 shows
that the jury need to be all agreed on at least one of these alternatives in order to convict of
manslaughter (see the discussion by Leveson LJ at [28]–[29] especially).

A separate question arises where the issue is not whether a manslaughter verdict can be said to
be agreed upon and thus validly returned but instead is whether, where there is initially a
murder charge, the jury are all agreed that D is 'not guilty of murder'. Unless the jury are
discharged from returning a verdict on the murder charge, that is a requirement before an
alternative verdict of manslaughter can be returned (see the Criminal Law Act 1967, s. 6(2)(a)).
In relation to the 'not guilty of murder' question, the cases of *McCandless* [2001] NI 86 and
*McClenaghan* [2016] NICA 51 suggest that the jury must be all agreed on at least one of the
reasons for the offence not being murder but only manslaughter. The relevant question here is
not whether D is at least guilty of manslaughter but instead whether it is agreed that D is not
guilty of the more serious offence of murder. If there is not agreement by the jury on at least one
reason for being not guilty of murder, the question then will be whether there should be a retrial
for murder or whether the jury should be discharged from returning a verdict on the murder
charge (and in that case the agreed manslaughter verdict can be returned).

## CONSTRUCTIVE MANSLAUGHTER (KILLING BY AN UNLAWFUL ACT LIKELY TO CAUSE BODILY HARM)

### The Unlawful Act

**B1.57**   In *Nica* [2021] EWCA Crim 1790, the unlawful act was constituted by the offence of facilitating a breach or attempted breach of immigration law in circumstances known to D (concealment in an air-tight container lorry) objectively likely to cause some harm.

## MANSLAUGHTER BY GROSS NEGLIGENCE

### Further Clarification of the Ingredients of Gross Negligence Manslaughter

**B1.74**   **(v) The Breach of the Duty Caused or Made a Significant (i.e. More than Minimal) Contribution to the Death of the Victim**   *Wood Treatment Ltd* [2021] EWCA Crim 618 provides another example (following on from *Broughton* [2020] EWCA Crim 1093, [2021] 1 Cr App R 3 (25)) of the prosecution being unable to prove that D's breach of duty caused death where the only relevant evidence before the jury was that of experts whose evidence did not rule out a credible potential cause of death which was not attributable to D's negligence. D1 was a company and D2 its managing director who were charged with corporate manslaughter and gross negligence manslaughter respectively of four employees killed in an explosion at the company's wood mill. The explosion was so devastating that it was impossible to say what was its actual cause. The expert evidence was that there were four potential causes, three of which (scenarios 1, 2 and 4) related to the large quantities of settled dust in the mill which was clearly the fault of D1 and D2. Potential cause 3, however, related to the possible malfunction of machinery, quite independently of settled dust, as to which machinery failure the expert evidence did not show fault on the part of D1 and D2. Furthermore, the prosecution had not adduced any other evidence on which a reasonable jury could find there was fault in this respect. Even though potential causes 1 and 2 were the most likely of the four to have been the actual cause, the trial judge was found to have correctly ruled there was no case to answer as the prosecution had not adduced evidence to show that the accident was not due to cause 3 occurring without the requisite degree of fault on the part of D1 and D2.

As Edis LJ put it (at [38]):

> The problem in this case was that at the conclusion of the prosecution case there was no evidence which would enable them rationally to say that [the expert's] evidence about scenario 3 was wrong, and no evidence which would enable them to say that the negligent acts or omissions of [D1 or D2] had caused the explosion if it had resulted from a scenario 3 event.

*Walker* [2021] EWCA Crim 1956 provides another example of a similarly unsuccessful appeal against a terminating ruling relating to causation in homicide where 'a reasonable jury would not be able to disregard the unanimous expert evidence on the live issue, and consequently could not be sure that [the deceased's] intoxication had not caused the reduced level of consciousness which preceded the hypoxic ischaemic brain damage which led to death, despite evidence of causation [by D] of the head injury or the impact of manual strangulation' (at [29]).

# Section B2   Non-fatal Offences Against the Person

## RESISTING OR WILFULLY OBSTRUCTING A CONSTABLE, ETC.

### Elements

**B2.58**   *Rice v Connelly* [1966] 2 QB 414 was followed in *Neale v DPP* [2021] EWHC 658 (Admin), [2021] 2 Cr App R 9 (175), in which the Divisional Court quashed D's conviction for obstructing a constable by refusing to provide his name and address in order that the constable couldserve a fixed penalty notice on him for breach of the Health Protection (Coronavirus Restrictions) (Wales) Regulations 2020 (SI 2020 No. 353) as then in force. Steyn J said:

39.... The right to remain silent is of particular significance at common law. And an obligation on an individual to give his name and address to the police would also engage the individual's rights under Articles 6 and 8 of the ECHR.

40. In my judgment, it is clear that the Coronavirus Regulations did not impliedly require individuals to give their name and address to a police officer on request. Carefully defined powers have been conferred on police officers by statute and the court should be wary of expanding them by implication. Where the legislature has intended to give police officers the power to require a person to give his name and address and to impose a corresponding duty on the individual to give that information, it has done so expressly …

41. As the appellant was not legally obliged to give his name and address, it follows that his refusal was not 'wilful' within the meaning of s. 89(2) of the Police Act 1996.

## WOUNDING OR CAUSING GRIEVOUS BODILY HARM WITH INTENT

### Sentence

**Assessment of Harm**    In *O'Bryan* [2021] EWCA Crim 1472, the Court of Appeal considered the latest (July 2021) Sentencing Council guideline on sentencing for offences under the OAPA 1861, s. 18. It was submitted on behalf of the A-G that a sentence of four years' imprisonment (based on a starting point of six years) passed on an offender (D) who had pleaded guilty to causing grievous bodily harm with intent was unduly lenient, given that the offence involved a knife attack in which V suffered three wounds, requiring major emergency surgery (two operations) and multiple blood transfusions. The injuries, and the surgical and medical care required, are described in detail at [4]–[15]. In particular:    **B2.90**

10. … There was a stab wound to the abdomen; a large volume of blood in the abdominal cavity; a large blood clot at the back of the abdomen on the right side (a 'retroperitoneal haematoma'); injuries to an artery and vessels in the abdomen (a partially transected ileo-colic artery with active bleeding, and a divided right inferior epigastric vessels with active bleeding); an injury to the middle part of the small intestine ('divided jejunum') and 'associated through-and-through injury' to the small bowel mesentery with active bleeding. The stab tract to the abdomen had entered the area in the back of the abdomen behind the peritoneum (retroperitoneum) adjacent to the inferior vena cava (the largest vein of the human body) at the level of the lower pole of the right kidney, but there was no obvious injury to either structure.

These were very serious injuries and without emergency surgery V's life would no doubt have been endangered. Did it follow that the judge had been wrong to place those injuries within category 2 of the guideline, rather than category 1? Injuries that are 'particularly grave or life-threatening' belong in category 1. The Court of Appeal nevertheless held that the judge had been right:

34. [Counsel] was right in our view to accept that the phrase 'life-threatening injury' does not cover every wounding causing injury which, left untreated, might lead to death. Most non-superficial injuries caused by a knife, save perhaps to an arm or leg where no artery is severed, will lead to loss of blood which, if no intervention takes place, could lead to infection or death from loss of blood or the spreading of blood to neighbouring organs. The Guideline must be read as a whole, and it must always be remembered that firstly … the harm caused must be 'really serious' to come within the s 18 Guideline at all. Secondly, … the court should assess the level of harm caused with reference to the impact on the victim. Thirdly, apart from the reference to life-threatening injury, the cases placed within Category 1 are where 'particularly grave' injury is caused (as opposed to 'grave' injury, which is Category 2), or where the injury results in lifelong dependency on third party care or medical treatment; or where the injury is permanent and irreversible and will have a substantial and long term effect on the victim's ability to work or carry out normal day to day activities. In short, … Category 1 is reserved for cases of exceptional seriousness even within the class of s. 18 cases.

35. Since the Sentencing Council did not define life-threatening injury we think it would be unwise for us to attempt to give a comprehensive definition or to substitute wording of our own for that of the guideline. But we are satisfied that where more than two and a half hours elapsed between [V's] arrival at hospital and his operation, and there is no expert medical evidence that his life was in imminent danger, this is not a case which falls within the Sentencing Council's classification of life-threatening injury.

Nor was this a case involving an unprovoked attack on an innocent victim. D was described rather as 'the principal instigator of mutual violence'. He was of previous good character and had some other mitigation. Even so, the sentence was arguably lenient — an appeal by D against a five-year sentence would probably not have succeeded, said Bean LJ. But it was not an *unduly* lenient sentence, so the Court of Appeal declined to interfere with it.

B2.98    **Sentences above the Range**   In *Fleming* [2022] EWCA Crim 250, the Solicitor-General referred D's 18-year extended sentence (with a 14-year custodial element) to the Court of Appeal on the basis that it failed to give sufficient weight to the enormity of D's offending, in which he had inflicted catastrophic injuries on his partner V, who had learning and physical disabilities and was extremely vulnerable. V had suffered brain damage with internal bleeding, multiple facial fractures, corneal dislocation, rib fractures and extensive bruising. There were also old rib and cheek fractures, indicating that the assault had been culmination of a prolonged course of violent, controlling and coercive conduct against her. She was still in need of care nine months later.

The Court of Appeal agreed that a sentence outside the normal range was required. William Davis LJ said:

26. We are satisfied that the combination and nature of the culpability factors and the extreme nature of the harm suffered by [V] required the judge to move to the top of the category range before any consideration of factors increasing seriousness. It would not have been reasonable to do otherwise. That approach would not involve any departure from the guideline. Having reached that point the judge was obliged to give proper weight to the factors increasing seriousness and any mitigating factors. In reality there were no mitigating factors of any substance. The fact that the offender had not previously been sent to custody other than for a very short time had no impact when the instant offence was as serious as this one. The offender may have called for assistance but in reality this was only at the behest of the social worker. Any problems and difficulties which may have afflicted the offender could not be said to have had any relevance to his behaviour towards [V].

27. The factors increasing seriousness were substantial. Given the nature of the relationship between the offender and V, she was effectively defenceless in her own home. The violation of trust was acute. This was not a case of a sudden outburst of temper in an otherwise good relationship. As accepted on the offender's behalf there was a long history of violence and coercive behaviour on his part. He continued to behave in that way despite the intervention of social workers trying to act in the best interests of [V]. In his submissions to us, Mr Wells said that it may be that the offender 'thought that he could behave like he did'. That clearly was the case. It adds substantially to the overall seriousness of the case.

Giving due weight to the appalling injuries inflicted on V, the appropriate custodial term before mitigation, was 19½ years, with a four-year extended licence period.

## KIDNAPPING

### Sentence

B2.124    *A-G's Ref (No. 92 of 2014) (Gibney)* [2014] EWCA Crim 2713, [2015] 1 Cr App R (S) 44 (323) and *A-G's Refs (Nos. 102 and 103 of 2014) (Perkins)* [2014] EWCA Crim 2922, [2015] 1 Cr App R (S) 55 (389) were considered by the Court of Appeal in *Saqib* [2022] EWCA Crim 213, in which V was in effect taken hostage and subjected to gross ill-treatment. He was abducted in the street, driven off, and robbed. While detained, he was punched, strangled, threatened, burned with cigarettes and forced to consume alcohol and drugs. He was made to withdraw and transfer money from his bank account. Hilliard J said (at [27]):

In the absence of sentencing guidelines for kidnap, the judge's task was a difficult one. He approached it with great care. He correctly identified the significant features of the offending and the future risk posed by the appellant. In our judgment, … if this case had been contested the offences would have merited a custodial term in the region of 17 years' imprisonment.

## Actus Reus

In *Dean* [2021] EWCA Crim 1157, [2022] QB 140, the Court of Appeal considered the *actus* **B2.125** *reus* of kidnapping and whether it could take the form of a continuing offence.

D was convicted of kidnapping on the basis of joint enterprise. V had been seized by D's partner and other men, and bundled into a car of which D was the driver. He was viciously assaulted both in the back of the car and after being dragged out of it. On appeal, it was submitted that the kidnapping was complete before V was bundled into the car, and that D herself was guilty only of participating in an offence of false imprisonment.

The Court of Appeal rejected that submission on two grounds. The first was that the evidence pointed to D's involvement from the very beginning. CCTV showed her carefully positioning the car and waiting for the men to force V into it before driving off with them. The second was that kidnapping is a continuing offence. It may be *complete* as soon as V has been seized and carried away, but that does not mean it is all over or finished at that point.

The Court adopted the reasoning of the Supreme Court of Canada in *Vu* [2012] 2 SCR 411: kidnapping is an aggravated form of false imprisonment in which V is not only detained but carried away, and like false imprisonment it continues until V is rescued, or freed, or escapes. D relied on the Court's earlier decision in *Reid* (1973) 56 Cr App R 703, but the Court in *Dean* found nothing in that decision that was inconsistent with kidnapping being a continuing offence.

## CONTROLLING OR COERCIVE DOMESTIC ABUSE

### General

The Serious Crime Act 2015, s. 76A (inserted by the Domestic Abuse Act 2021, s. 74 and sch. **B2.191** 3, part 1) came into effect on 29 June 2021 (Domestic Abuse Act 2021, s. 90(2)).

## PUTTING PEOPLE IN FEAR OF VIOLENCE

### Sentence (Basic Offence)

In *White* [2021] EWCA Crim 1511, [2022] 4 WLR 10, D was convicted following summary **B2.218** trial of harassment causing fear of violence, contrary to the Protection from Harassment Act 1997, s. 4. The case was then sent to the Crown Court for sentencing, where the recorder held that the offence fell within category 2B of the sentencing guideline: D had demonstrated hostility based on V's sexual orientation and transgender identity and had made frequent death threats. V had suffered real distress affecting the way she lived. Ordinarily, D would have faced a sentence of 12 months' immediate imprisonment, but his mental health issues (including bipolar disorder) were such that the recorder accepted the recommendations of a pre-sentence report and instead imposed an 18-month community order with a 15-day rehabilitation activity requirement, 200 hours of unpaid work and a five-year restraining order. The Solicitor-General referred this sentence to the Court of Appeal as unduly lenient, arguing that it was a category 1A offence. While the Court rejected the category 1A submission, it held that since the offence had clearly crossed the custody threshold, the correct sentence was 12 months' imprisonment suspended for two years, together with the same rehabilitation and unpaid work requirements.

## Section B3    Sexual Offences

### SENTENCING UNDER THE SEXUAL OFFENCES ACT 2003

**Assessment of Harm Caused**

B3.9    **Victim is Particularly Vulnerable Due to Personal Circumstances**    A combination of factors applicable to the offending may bring V within the guideline rubric of being 'particularly vulnerable'. This was illustrated in *KC* [2019] EWCA Crim 1632, [2020] 1 Cr App R (S) 41 (296) and confirmed in *DP* [2022] EWCA Crim 57 where factors included a child in a familial relationship with her abuser who subjected her to grooming and thereafter sustained abuse over many months.

While it does not follow that whenever V is asleep, V is particularly vulnerable within the meaning of the guideline (*AWA* [2021] EWCA Crim 1877), that will often be the case (e.g. *AAO* [2021] EWCA Crim 1718). In *JB* [2020] EWCA Crim 1699, V was particularly vulnerable because she was asleep, and possibly under the influence of sedatives. In *Behdarvani-Aida* [2021] EWCA Crim 582, [2022] 1 Cr App R (S) 1 (1), V fell into this category as she was unconscious after taking GHB (gamma-hydroxybutyrate). In *Husband* [2021] EWCA Crim 1240, the Court of Appeal accepted that a victim of a sexual offence, who is asleep when the sexual activity begins, is particularly vulnerable for the purposes of the guidelines. V's personal circumstances are such that V does not know what is happening, is unable to protest and may not even be able to report what has happened after the offence. That is so whether V is simply asleep or is also, to a greater or lesser degree, intoxicated, although the latter may affect how quickly V may awake. The Court also accepted that a combination of factors may have the overall effect of justifying the assessment. However, on the facts of the case, the Court concluded that particular vulnerability due to personal circumstances was not the only conclusion open to the judge. The complainant was not in fact asleep, nor was she so intoxicated that she did not know what was happening. In *BN* [2021] EWCA Crim 1250, the Court of Appeal, when explicitly rejecting a submission that a sentencer can only find V to be particularly vulnerable where there is a combination of intoxication and sleep, observed that the Court found it difficult to see how a child or adult who is asleep when the activity begins, and therefore does not know what is happening and so is powerless to resist, can generally be said to be anything other than particularly vulnerable due to personal circumstances.

Particular vulnerability need not relate to V's ability to resist or protest. In *Saunders* [2022] EWCA Crim 264, the Court of Appeal held that the judge was entitled to take the view that the complainant's desire to preserve her virginity, and the religious importance to her of doing so, were personal circumstances which rendered her particularly vulnerable to suffer increased harm as result of the offence going well beyond the harm inevitably suffered by anyone losing their virginity in the distressing circumstances of rape by a drunken man.

### RAPE AND OTHER OFFENCES AGAINST CHILDREN AGED UNDER 13

**Rape of a Child under 13**

B3.85    **Sentence**    For a recent example of the application of the guideline in a successful application for an A-G's reference see *DP* [2022] EWCA Crim 57.

### SEX OFFENCES AGAINST CHILDREN AGED 13 TO 15

**Causing or Inciting a Child to Engage in Sexual Activity**

B3.113    **Sentence**    For recent examples of the application of *Privett* [2020] EWCA Crim 557, [2020] 2 Cr App R (S) 45 (315) and *Reed* [2021] EWCA Crim 572, [2021] 1 WLR 5429, see the increase in sentence following a reference by the A-G in *Thompson* [2021] EWCA Crim 1513; *Voicu* [2021] EWCA Crim 1095; *Croucher* [2021] EWCA Crim 1273; and *Buckley* [2021] EWCA Crim 1484.

## CARE WORKERS FOR PERSONS WITH A MENTAL DISORDER

### Care Workers: Causing or Inciting Sexual Activity

**Elements**    The word 'causes' should be given its ordinary meaning. The SOA 2003 requires **B3.224** D's conduct to be an operative cause of the prohibited activity. This means that a care worker making the arrangements for securing the services of a sex worker for a mentally disordered person under a care plan would be in peril of committing an offence under s. 39. By contrast, care workers who arrange contact between a mentally disordered person and spouse or partner aware that sexual activity may take place would be creating the circumstances for that activity rather than causing it in a legal sense. In *Secretary of State for Justice v A Local Authority* [2021] EWCA Civ 1527, [2022] 1 Cr App R 9 (127), the Court of Appeal (the Lord Chief Justice giving the leading judgment) allowed the appeal against a decision in the Court of Protection in respect of a preliminary issue in advance of a care plan by Hayden J in *A Local Authority v C* [2021] EWCOP 25, [2021] 1 WLR 5689. Hayden J had decided that the SOA 2003, s. 39, would not criminalise care workers were they to facilitate a 27-year-old man to visit a sex worker under a care plan in circumstances where he has capacity (within the meaning of the Mental Capacity Act 2005) to consent to sexual relations and decide to have a contact with a sex worker but not to make the arrangements himself. Hayden J had based his decision upon the reasoning that the intention of s. 39 is to protect vulnerable adults from others and not from themselves. As the Act is concerned to reduce the risk of sexual exploitation, not to repress autonomous sexual expression, he took the view that the ordinary meaning of 'causes' is restricted. A care worker who made all the arrangements for someone with a mental disorder in his or her care to have sex with a sex worker would not have 'caused' that person to engage in sexual activity because the actions would have been calculated to give voice to the person's autonomy in the sphere of sexual relations. The Court of Appeal, in rejecting this line of reasoning, explained that the legislative technique of the 2003 Act is to draw bright lines to reduce the risk of abuse of those who are vulnerable and elsewhere to draw bright lines because it is necessary for certainty. The Court acknowledged that a line must be drawn which, in one sense, is arbitrary because it does not concern itself with harm or possible exploitation in the individual case or with an individual's physical or psychological maturity. It provides certainty and reflects Parliament's view of the correct balance to strike in a sensitive matter of morality.

## OTHER OFFENCES

### Voyeurism

**Sentence**    In *Roddis* [2021] EWCA Crim 1583, the appellant had been sentenced to a total of **B3.303** four years' imprisonment for nine offences of voyeurism. The total sentence was comprised of eight consecutive sentences of six months' imprisonment with a further six months to run concurrently. The appellant had worked as a masseur between 2016 and 2019 and had secretly filmed his female clients when they were in a state of undress. A great many women had been filmed in this way and the counts faced by the appellant concerned women the authorities had been able to trace. Although the appeal was allowed to the extent that the overall sentence was reduced to one of three years, the Court observed:

> 13. We do not consider in cases of multiple offending, such as this, particularly in respect of many different victims over a very long period, that the sentence is or should be limited to the imposition of concurrent sentences, the total of which must be no greater than the statutory maximum for each offence. Of course, the sentencer is bound to have regard in sentencing to the level of the statutory maximum when he or she comes to determine what the level of sentence is, but it does not provide a ceiling in relation to multiple offending such as this.

**B**

Part B Offences

14. Consecutive offences were entirely appropriate in this case. Indeed, not only was the offending so serious that only an immediate custodial sentence was appropriate, but furthermore, a total sentence of three years is the least which could be justified. The sentences on all nine counts must be served consecutively, making a total of three years' imprisonment in this case.

## PROSECUTION OF HISTORIC SEXUAL OFFENCES

### Sentencing in Historic Sexual Cases

B3.375    **Immaturity**    The definitive guideline, *Sentencing Children and Young People* (see **SG8-1** *et seq.*) also adds an important element to the approach to be taken when sentencing in cases where D has crossed a significant age threshold between the date the offence was committed and the date of conviction. This situation continues to arise frequently in prosecutions of sexual offences whether historic or not. Paragraphs 6.1 to 6.3 (see **SG8-8**) set out the principles to be applied when an increase in the age of a child or young person results in the maximum sentence on the date of conviction being greater than that available on the date on which the offending was committed (primarily 12, 15 or 18 years old). Paragraph 6.2 provides guidance that in such situations the court should take as its starting point the sentence likely to have been imposed on the date at which the offence was committed. This includes young people who attain the age of 18 between the commission and the finding of guilt of the offence. When this occurs the purpose of sentencing adult offenders has to be taken into account. However, para. 6.3 states that when any significant age threshold is passed it will rarely be appropriate that a more severe sentence than the maximum the court could have imposed at the time the offence was committed should be imposed. However, a sentence at or close to that maximum may be appropriate.

In *Limon* [2022] EWCA Crim 39, [2022] 4 WLR 37, the Court of Appeal observed that this approach is not inconsistent with *Forbes* [2016] EWCA Crim 1388, [2017] 1 WLR 53 where the Court was considering whether sentences offended against the ECHR, Article 7(1). The guideline raises a different point. Even though a longer sentence would not offend against Article 7(1), it must, for reasons of fairness, be tempered by reference to the sentence which would have been passed at the time of the offending. In *Limon,* the appellant appealed against a total sentence of four years' imprisonment imposed following his conviction for eight historic child sex offences (indecent assault under the SOA 1956, s. 14). The offences had taken place when he was aged between 14 and 17 and the complainant was aged between six and nine. The maximum sentence for each offence for an adult would have been ten years whereas for a young offender at the time it was 12 months' detention. The Court of Appeal applied the principles in the *Sentencing Children and Young People* guideline, accepting that the passage of time had not imbued the appellant with any greater culpability or moral responsibility than at the time of the offence. The judge should have taken as his starting point the sentence likely to have been passed at the time of the offending, and the maximum sentence which could then have been imposed. The appellant was aged under 18 throughout the indictment period, indecent assault was not one of the grave crimes included within the CYPA 1933, s. 53 (now the SA 2020, s. 250), and throughout the indictment period the CJA 1982, ss. 1A and 1B, placed a limit of 12 months on the total term of detention that could be imposed on a young offender even if sentenced for multiple offences. Accordingly, the sentence was reduced to 12 months' imprisonment. The Court of Appeal noted that these principles will apply in cases where D is a young adult when convicted of offences committed as a child a comparatively short time earlier. He observed that there is no reason not to apply them also to a case in which many years have passed between the offending and the conviction, as in the case of *Limon.*

### Indecent Assault

B3.390    **Absence of Consent**    In *Brooks* [2021] EWCA Crim 1468, the Court of Appeal distinguished *Fairclough v Whipp* (1951) 35 Cr App R 138, in a case where the applicant's abuse of a complainant aged 13 to 15 included her performing oral sex upon him to the point of ejaculation. The trial judge had held that this did constitute an indecent assault under the SOA

1956, s. 14, on the basis that a slight application of force as the ejaculate comes into contact with parts of the mouth would be sufficient to constitute an assault. The Court of Appeal concluded the judge was correct in that the activity involved an unlawful application of force. In that event, it was unnecessary to establish a show or threat of force.

## Section B4    Theft, Handling Stolen Goods and Related Offences

### ROBBERY AND ASSAULT WITH INTENT TO ROB

#### Sentence

In *Keeling* [2022] EWCA Crim 178, V was sleeping at night in a camper van (no longer having    **B4.71** any other home) when D and his accomplices broke into it and violently robbed him. One of the issues before the Court of Appeal was whether this should be sentenced as a robbery in a dwelling, or in accordance with the guideline for *Robbery — Street and Less Sophisticated Commercial* (see **SG30-2**), the one applied at the Crown Court.

The Court of Appeal had no hesitation in preferring the former. Edis LJ said (at [28]):

> In our judgment … it is necessary to define carefully the meaning of the word 'dwelling', in circumstances where an offence is charged as involving a burglary of a dwelling. For the purposes of understanding the [robbery] guideline, however, a rather more robust approach should be taken. The court's task is to identify the seriousness of the offence by considering the culpability involved and the harm which it caused or might foreseeably have caused. As far as [V] is concerned, he was woken up while he was asleep in the bed where he slept every night for four months by three armed and masked men screaming at him, hitting him and demanding his money. For the purposes of assessing the seriousness of that offence, fine distinctions of law as to the meaning of the word dwelling are unhelpful. What happened to him was just as bad having happened in the back of the van which was his habitual resting place at night every night, as it would have been had he been at his home and had the same thing happened to him there. For that reason, when construing the guidelines, we have come to the conclusion, without hesitation, that the judge was wrong to apply the guideline for street and less sophisticated commercial robberies and that the appropriate guideline was that for robbery in a dwelling.

See also **B4.85** in this supplement.

### BURGLARY

#### Sentence

**Burglary from Dwellings**    As to the imposition of sentences outside the normal range in cases    **B4.81** of persistent offending, the Court of Appeal in *Murphy* [2022] EWCA Crim 240 observed:

> 19. …It would … have been appropriate to take into account the full detail of the long history of the commission of domestic burglaries by the appellant, who had plainly not been deterred despite a number of very significant sentences.

> 20 Cases such as *Marcantonio* [2012] EWCA Crim 1279 indicate that where there is a need to protect the public from recidivist offenders who commit burglaries whenever they are at liberty, and thus the protection of the public is the uppermost consideration in the court's mind, it may be appropriate to depart 'radically' from the relevant Guideline.

#### Elements Common to Both s. 9(1)(a) and (b)

**Meaning of 'Building' and 'Dwelling'**    In *Keeling* [2022] EWCA Crim 178 (see **B4.71** in this    **B4.85** supplement), the Court of Appeal was not required to decide whether the camper van in which V was living was a dwelling for the purposes of the substantive law relating to burglary, but since this van was V's only home at the time, it is submitted that it was very clearly an 'inhabited vehicle' and indeed a dwelling. The arguments adopted by the Court in favour of treating the case as one of robbery in a dwelling for the purposes of sentencing would have been equally valid had the offence charged been one of burglary.

## INSIDER DEALING

### Sentence

**B7.36**    Where an offence of insider dealing is committed on or after 1 November 2021 the maximum sentence is ten years' imprisonment (Financial Services Act 2021, s. 31(1) and (3) to (4), and Financial Services Act 2021 (Commencement No. 3) Regulations 2021 (SI 2021 No. 1173)).

## BANKRUPTCY OFFENCES

**B7.59**    With effect from 29 June 2021 the monetary conditions to be satisfied for a debt relief order have been increased by the Insolvency Proceedings (Monetary Limits) (Amendment) Order 2021 (SI 2021 No. 673), art. 2(2). The maximum amount of a person's debts is now £30,000, the maximum amount of monthly surplus income is £75 and the maximum total value of property is £2,000.

---

# Section B10    Terrorism, Piracy and Hijacking

## SUBSTANTIVE OFFENCES UNDER THE TERRORISM ACT 2000

### Wearing a Uniform

**B10.46**    **Elements**    In *Pwr v DPP* [2022] UKSC 2, [2022] 1 WLR 789, the Supreme Court confirmed the previous decision of the Divisional Court and expressly agreed with the judgment of Holroyde LJ (see *Pwr v DPP* [2020] EWHC 798 (Admin), [2020] 2 Cr App R 11 (165) at **B10.46** in the main work). The Supreme Court observed that there was a limited mental element to the crime in that D is required to know that he or she was wearing, carrying or displaying the relevant article. However, the strong common-law presumption of *mens rea* was rebutted by necessary implication through an examination of the words, context and purpose of s. 13(1). Section 13(1) is a strict liability offence. The Supreme Court observed that the words of s. 13(1), with an objective requirement of arousing a reasonable suspicion, do not readily lend themselves to the importation of a subjective element, such as knowledge or intention. Moreover, the context demonstrated that s. 13(1) would be redundant if there was a *mens rea* requirement because anyone who committed an offence under s. 13(1) would almost inevitably come within the terms of ss. 11 or 12 of the 2000 Act. Both those offences *do* require *mens rea* and the sentence for each has a much higher maximum. The purposes of s. 13(1) were to avoid others becoming aware of proscribed organisations and to avoid the public disorder that might result from reaction against displays of support for such organisations. Neither of those purposes are concerned with D's intention or knowledge. Thus, contrary to the submissions of counsel for the appellant (see [36]–[41]), the true construction of s. 13(1) does not require that D had *knowingly* or *intentionally* aroused reasonable suspicion that D was a member or supporter of a proscribed organisation; nor that D *intended* to express support for a proscribed organisation, or had *known* that the organisation in question was a proscribed organisation.

## SUBSTANTIVE OFFENCES UNDER THE TERRORISM ACT 2006

### Dissemination of Terrorist Publications

**B10.99**    **Sentence**    In *Nugent* [2021] EWCA Crim 1535, the Court of Appeal allowed a reference by the Solicitor-General of an unduly lenient sentence imposed in respect of offences contrary to s. 2 of the TA 2006 and s. 58 of the TA 2000. D had pleaded guilty to the offences. The Court noted that, with effect from 12 April 2019, the maximum penalty for s. 2 offences was increased from seven years to 15 years, and the maximum penalty for s. 58 offences was increased from ten years to 15 years. The sentencing guideline has not, however, been revised to reflect those increases and the sentencing judge therefore had to sentence without a guideline which reflected the powers available. Moreover, there was no guidance from the Court of Appeal on how the change to the maximum penalty affects the sentencing levels for these offences. Having reviewed the pre-guideline authorities relevant to the issue of how an increase in the statutory maximum sentence should be reflected in the sentence to be imposed by a judge, the Court observed:

> 23. In *R v Richardson & Others* [2006] EWCA Crim 3186; [2007] 2 Cr App R (S) 36, considering the impact of the then recent increase in the maximum sentence for causing death by dangerous driving, the Lord Chief Justice said this at [13]:
>
>> 'Consistently with our own analysis, the principle to be derived … is that the primary object of the increase in the maximum sentence was to address cases of the most serious gravity, so as to permit the sentence to be greater than before, and in an appropriate case to be as long as or longer than the previous maximum. However, even in such cases it was not intended that the increase in sentence should reflect the consequences of the increase from ten years to fourteen years in a strictly mathematical proportion. It has long been recognised that mathematics does not provide the appropriate answer to a sentencing decision. That said, appropriate proportionality between the huge variety of offences which come within the ambit of these crimes leads to the conclusion that if the level of sentence in cases of the utmost gravity is significantly increased (as it should be) there should be some corresponding increase in sentences immediately below this level of gravity, continuing down the scale to the cases where there are no aggravating features at all.'
>
> 24. In the pre-guideline era that was enough to address the effect of the increase in maximum sentences on the previous practice of the courts. In the modern era sentencing has become a much more structured process and it will be for the Sentencing Council in due course to consider what if any increases should be made to sentence ranges and starting points within the relevant guideline…. [W]e accept that where, as here, a maximum sentence has been very substantially changed and the guideline has yet to be updated, the sentencing court should reflect that fact, where necessary, by departing from the guideline in the interests of justice and imposing a sentence in the more serious cases which reflects that change. This will involve applying the structured process of the guideline and considering in particular the factors referred to in it. It will not, however, involve being constrained by the sentence ranges or starting points established under the previous maximum penalty.

In the case before the Court, the sentencing judge had increased the sentence to be imposed before deductions for personal mitigation and plea from four to six years. That was at the top of the existing range for section A1 offences, and very close to the old maximum sentence. The Court concluded that a proper sentence for all the offending before it would have been eight years, from which the Court deducted the six months which the judge allowed for personal mitigation and the one-third deduction for the guilty pleas. The Court therefore substituted concurrent special custodial sentences of six years comprising a custodial term of five years and a one-year extended licence.

---

## Section B12    Offences Relating to Weapons

### GENERAL DEFINITIONS

#### 'Lethal Barrelled Weapon': Elements

**Shot, Bullet, or Missile can be Discharged**    The Home Office published a revised *Guide on Firearms Licensing Law* (tinyurl.com/mu5knmx9) in December 2021 to include all legislative changes made since the guidance was last published in April 2016.    **B12.11**

#### Component Parts

**Accessory Designed or Adapted to Diminish Noise or Flash**    See B12.11 in this supplement concerning the revised Home Office guidance on firearms licensing law.    **B12.16**

#### Ammunition

See **B12.11** in this supplement concerning the revised Home Office guidance on firearms licensing law.    **B12.24**

## OFFENCES RELATING TO IMITATION FIREARMS

### Readily Convertible Imitation Firearms: Firearms Act 1982

B12.30 See **B12.11** in this supplement concerning the revised Home Office guidance on firearms licensing law.

### Offences Concerning 'Realistic Imitation Firearms'

B12.32 See **B12.11** in this supplement concerning the revised Home Office guidance on firearms licensing law.

B12.33 **Offences and Defences** See **B12.11** in this supplement concerning the revised Home Office guidance on firearms licensing law.

## POSSESSING ETC. FIREARM OR AMMUNITION WITHOUT FIREARM CERTIFICATE

### Firearm Certificates: General Matters

B12.42 See **B12.11** in this supplement concerning the revised Home Office guidance on firearms licensing law.

The Firearms Rules 1998 (SI 1998 No. 1941) were amended from 1 November 2021 by SI 2021 No. 1172. Pursuant to r. 2(2) of SI 2021 No. 1172, for the form in the 1998 Rules, sch. 1, part 1 (form of application for firearm and shotgun certificates, and firearm certificate), substitute the form in sch. 1 to SI 2021 No.1172. For the form in Part IV to the 1998 Rules, substitute the form in sch. 2 to SI 2021 No.1172. Pursuant to r. 2(3) of SI 2021 No. 1172, for the form in the 1998 Rules, sch. 5, part I (firearms dealers: application for registration or for new certificate of registration) substitute the form in sch. 3 to SI 2021 No. 1172.

## POSSESSING OR DISTRIBUTING PROHIBITED WEAPONS OR AMMUNITION

### Expressions in the Firearms Act 1968, s. 5

B12.66 **Meaning of Expanding Missiles** See **B12.11** in this supplement concerning the revised Home Office guidance on firearms licensing law.

### Specific Issues Associated with Particular Prohibited Weapons

B12.72 **Firearms Act 1968, s. 5(1)(a)** See **B12.11** in this supplement concerning the revised Home Office guidance on firearms licensing law.

### Imitation Firearms and the Firearms Act 1968, s. 5

B12.77 See **B12.11** in this supplement concerning the revised Home Office guidance on firearms licensing law.

## EXEMPTIONS: HANDLING PROHIBITED SMALL FIREARMS

B12.87 **Trophies of War: s. 5(1)(aba) Exemption** See **B12.11** in this supplement concerning the revised Home Office guidance on firearms licensing law.

B12.88 **Firearms of Historic Interest: s. 5(1)(aba) Exemption** See **B12.11** in this supplement concerning the revised Home Office guidance on firearms licensing law.

## SENTENCING FOR FIREARMS OFFENCES

The Sentencing Council's guideline, *Firearms Importation* (see **SG34-10**), covers importation    **B12.137**
of firearms and ammunition under two Customs and Excise Management Act 1979 offences:
improper importation of goods and fraudulent evasion of prohibition/restriction. It applies to
adult offenders sentenced in a magistrates' court or the Crown Court on or after 1 January
2022.

## MANUFACTURE, SALE, HIRE AND PURCHASE OF WEAPONS

With regard to a local weights and measures authority enforcing within its area s. 1 of the    **B12.200**
Crossbows Act 1987 (sale etc. of crossbows to persons under 18), see ss. 64 and 70 of the
Offensive Weapons Act 2019.

## MANUFACTURE, MARKETING, SALE, HIRE AND PURCHASE OF KNIVES

### Elements

It was held in *STC Ltd* [2021] EWCA Crim 1237, [2022] 1 Cr App R 10 (150), that the    **B12.213**
offences under the Knives Act 1997, ss. 1 and 2, are not principally about the nature or purpose
of the knife, but about the way in which it is marketed. The marketing must not contain any
'suggestion' that the knife is 'suitable' for hurting someone to any extent. These are low
thresholds. The knife does not have to be 'made or adapted for use in causing injury to any
person' (to cite the wording of the Prevention of Crime Act 1953). If it is, and the way that it
is marketed suggests that this is so, then the offence is committed. The very wide terms of s. 1(3)
and (4) make it clear that the court is entitled to look at the whole context and content of a
marketing exercise in deciding whether it suggests that a knife is suitable for combat. Nothing
in either subsection suggests that s. 1 is concerned only with words and not images. The reason
why ss. 1 and 2 are in different terms is because they regulate different things. The former deals
with the person who 'markets a knife' whereas the latter deals with a person who is not
marketing the knife, but publishing material in connection with the marketing of any knife
which may be being done by someone else. However, if a person commits an offence under s. 2
that does not mean that s. 1 does not apply as well.

## CAUSING EXPLOSION LIKELY TO ENDANGER LIFE OR PROPERTY

### Explosive Substance and Explosion

'**Explosive**'    In *Margelis* [2021] EWCA Crim 1215, [2022] QB 148, the Court of Appeal    **B12.244**
observed that it was held in *Wheatley* [1979] 1 WLR 144 that the Explosive Substances Act
1883 should be interpreted in the light of the definition of 'explosive' in the Explosives Act
1875, s. 3. That definition gives examples of substances which are to be regarded as explosive
and, in addition, extends to substances which are used or manufactured with a view to
producing 'a practical effect by explosion or a pyrotechnic effect'. The expression 'pyrotechnic
effect' is not defined in either the 1875 Act or the 1883 Act. However, the expression
'pyrotechnic article' has been defined in the Pyrotechnic Articles (Safety) Regulations 2015 (SI
2015 No. 1553), reg. 3. The Court regarded that definition as providing the most reliable test
of whether a substance was used or manufactured with a view to producing a pyrotechnic effect.
The expression 'pyrotechnic' has a recognised scientific meaning, and Parliament had this in
mind when it amended the 1875 Act by reference to the meaning set out in the 2015
Regulations. Accordingly, it can be said that a pyrotechnic effect occurs when, as a result of a
sudden triggering event, heat, light, sound, gas, smoke or a combination of these effects is
produced through a self-sustained exothermic (i.e. energy-releasing) chemical reaction. The
Court did not accept that an effect will qualify as pyrotechnic only if it involves a significant
amount of heat or light (such as is produced by a firework), or that it necessarily requires
particular danger to life or property.

## MAKING OR POSSESSION OF EXPLOSIVE UNDER SUSPICIOUS CIRCUMSTANCES

**B12.256**    For the meaning of 'explosive', see *Margelis* [2021] EWCA Crim 1215, [2022] QB 148, and **B12.244** in this supplement.

# Section B14    Offences Against the Administration of Justice

## CONTEMPT OF COURT IN RESPECT OF CRIMINAL PROCEEDINGS

### Appeals

**B14.131**    In *A-G v Crosland* [2021] UKSC 58, [2022] 1 Cr App R 15 (277), D leaked the temporarily embargoed contents of a draft Supreme Court judgment to the public in order to generate publicity for his opposition to it. A three-justice panel of the Supreme Court then considered an application by the A-G, and fined D for contempt. D appealed against that decision, and his appeal came before a different panel of the Supreme Court. But did the Supreme Court have jurisdiction to hear an appeal from itself?

Any such jurisdiction could only be statutory, and the only statutory provision dealing with appeals in contempt cases is the Administration of Justice Act 1960, s. 13, but s. 13 does not directly address the precise issue involved. Nor indeed do the Rules of the Supreme Court prescribe how such an appeal might be dealt with. Section 13 includes express provision as to appeals *to* the Supreme Court, but says nothing explicitly about appeals *from* that Court. Moreover it was submitted that the very concept of an appeal to a higher court in such circumstances was an impossibility.

The Supreme Court resolved this difficulty by construing s. 13 as providing a general right of appeal in contempt cases, subject to any limitations imposed by that section. The absence of any specific exclusionary reference to the Supreme Court was construed as meaning that there must indeed be such a right of appeal, and there was no conceptual impossibility in a decision by one panel of the court being reviewed by another, especially if the latter panel is an enlarged one (e.g. five justices instead of three).

# Section B16    Revenue, Customs and Social Security Offences

## IMPROPER IMPORTATION AND EXPORTATION OF GOODS

### Improper Importation of Goods

**B16.27**    **Procedure, Evidence and Penalties**    The amendments made to s. 50 of the Customs and Excise Management Act 1979 by the Offensive Weapons Act 2019 were brought into force on 14 July 2021 (see **B12.61** in the main work).

The definitive sentencing guideline, *Firearms — Importation* (see Supplement, **SG34-10**), effective from 1 January 2022, includes guidance on sentencing for importation of firearms.

In *McDonald* [2021] EWCA Crim 272, [2021] 2 Cr App R (S) 20 (173), D pleaded guilty to importing a flick knife with a 10cm blade. It was intercepted in a package addressed to him. He had ordered it in his own name and paid for it by credit card. The Court of Appeal reduced a sentence of 12 months' immediate imprisonment to eight months' imprisonment suspended for two years. The Court took a starting point of 15 months, which it reduced to 12 months in the light of personal mitigation and then by one third for the guilty plea.

### Offences in Relation to Exportation of Prohibited or Restricted Goods

The amendments made to s. 68 of the Customs and Excise Management Act 1979 by the **B16.33** Offensive Weapons Act 2019 were brought into force on 14 July 2021 (see **B12.61** in the main work).

## FRAUDULENT EVASION OF DUTY ('SMUGGLING')

### Sentence

The amendments made to s. 170 of the Customs and Excise Management Act 1979 by the **B16.41** Offensive Weapons Act 2019 were brought into force on 14 July 2021 (see **B12.61** in the main work).

The definitive sentencing guideline, *Firearms — Importation* (see Supplement, **SG34-10**), effective from 1 January 2022, includes guidance on sentencing for fraudulent evasion of a prohibition or restriction relating to firearms.

## SENTENCING GUIDELINES FOR REVENUE FRAUD

**Drug Smuggling**   In *Urban* [2021] EWCA Crim 627, a lorry driver brought 25kg of heroin, **B16.55** with an average purity of 54 to 55 per cent and a street value of £1.25 million, by ferry into Harwich. His role was significant. The Court of Appeal stated that the starting point should have been 14 years' imprisonment, rather than 16 years taken by the sentencing judge, and reduced the sentence of 12 years' imprisonment to ten and a half years.

## SOCIAL SECURITY OFFENCES

**Suspended Sentences**   In *Logan* [2021] EWCA Crim 1627, D pleaded guilty to five offences **B16.66** of failing to notify the change of her circumstances following her marriage in 2002. She obtained over £130,000 fraudulently over many years. The Court of Appeal regarded a sentence of nine months' immediate imprisonment as a correct application of the guidelines, but suspended the sentence to enable her, now aged 67, to receive treatment for cancer.

**Costs**   An offender may be ordered to pay costs under s. 18 of the Prosecution of Offences Act **B16.67** 1985 (see **D33.23** *et seq.* in the main work) incurred by the CPS and investigation costs incurred by the Department for Work and Pensions and HMRC (*Protheroe* [2021] EWCA Crim 315).

# Section B19    Offences Relating To Drugs

## CONTROLLED DRUGS

### 'Substances and Products' Specified as Controlled Drugs in Class A, B or C

Flualprazolam, flunitrazolam and norfludiazepam were inserted into the MDA 1971, sch. 2, **B19.9** part 3, as Class C controlled drugs with effect from 18 August 2021 (SI 2021 No. 868; and see Home Office Circular 006/2021).

From 13 April 2022, SI 2022 No. 322 reclassifies 1,4-Butanediol (1,4-BD), Gamma-butyrolactone (GBL) and 4-Hydroxy-nbutyric acid (GHB) from Class C to Class B drugs for the purposes of control under the MDA 1971.

B

Part B Offences

## OTHER OFFENCES RELATED TO MISUSE OF DRUGS

### Contravention of Directions, Notices or Regulations Relating to Controlled Drugs

**B19.120**    **Prison Act 1952 Offences**   In relation to drug testing in prisons and young offender institutions, see now the Prisons (Substance Testing) Act 2021 that came into force on 8 December 2021 (see SI 2021 No. 1280). Among other matters, the 2021 Act amends the Prison Act 1952, s. 16A(1), so that if an authorisation is in force for the prison, 'any prison officer may, at the prison, in accordance with prison rules, require any prisoner who is confined in the prison to provide a sample of urine for the purpose of ascertaining whether the prisoner has in their body any (a) controlled drug, (b) pharmacy medicine, (c) prescription only medicine, (d) psychoactive substance, or (e) specified substance'.

Section 2(3) and (4) of the 2021 Act amend the Prison Rules 1999, rr. 2, 50, 51, 52, and the Young Offender Institution Rules 2000, rr. 2, 53, 55, 56, by omitting references to 'specified drug' and to 'schedule 2'.

SI 2016 No. 583 and SI 2016 No. 945 are revoked (Prisons (Substance Testing) Act 2021, s. 2(5)). Consequential amendments are made to SI 2018 No. 960 and SI 2020 No. 1077.

From 8 December 2021, SI 2021 No. 1279 came into force (r. 1(3)). The latter amends the Rules of 1999 and 2000 so that 'tests can be carried out for the broader generic definition of psychoactive substances and "prescription only medicines" and "pharmacy medicines" introduced by the 2021 Act' (Explanatory Note).

---

# Section B22   Modern Slavery, Trafficking and Immigration Offences

## SLAVERY, SERVITUDE AND FORCED OR COMPULSORY LABOUR

### Procedure and Sentence

**B22.3**    The same sentencing guideline applies for both the Modern Slavery Act 2015, s. 1 (slavery, servitude and forced or compulsory labour) and s. 2 offences (human trafficking) (see **SG36-1**). The guideline came into force on 1 October 2021 and applies to adult offenders. The maximum sentence is life imprisonment, with a sentencing range from high level community order to 18 years' custody.

Under this guideline, where D uses violence or threats towards V's family (as well as towards V) this can be considered in assessing culpability. If D is a victim of trafficking related to the offence, this can be a factor in reflecting lower culpability.

- High culpability (A): leading role in offending, expectation of substantial financial gain, high degree of planning/premeditation. Use or threat of substantial degree of physical violence or sexual violence/abuse towards either V or V's family.
- Medium culpability (B): significant role in offending, involving others through coercion/ intimidation/exploitation or reward. Expectation of significant financial or other material advantage. Use or threat of some physical violence, or some sexual violence/abuse towards V or V's family and other threats towards V or V's family.
- Lower culpability (C): includes offenders engaged by pressure, coercion or intimidation or who have themselves been a victim of slavery or trafficking related to this offence. Performing limited function under direction, limited understanding or knowledge of offending, little or no planning and expectation of limited or no financial or other material advantage.

The harm caused is not always obvious in modern slavery and human trafficking offences and the court will consider all the facts, even if V is unwilling or unable to give evidence. The guideline recognises that loss of personal autonomy is an inherent feature in this type of offending. For example, V's apparent consent to treatment is treated with caution and absence of a victim personal statement should not be taken to indicate an absence of harm.

- Category 1: V exposed to a high risk of death.
- Category 2: serious physical or psychological harm that has a substantial and/or long-term effect; substantial and long-term impact on V's daily life after the offending has ceased; V deceived or coerced into sexual activity.
- Category 3: some physical or psychological harm; significant financial loss/disadvantage to V; exposure of V to additional risk of serious physical or psychological harm.
- Category 4: limited physical or psychological harm, or limited financial loss/disadvantage to V.

Aggravating factors increasing seriousness include where V has been forced to commit criminal offences when not taken into account in step 1 (regardless of whether V is able to raise a defence if charged). Factors reducing seriousness include where D has been a victim of slavery or trafficking in circumstances unrelated to the offence.

There are sentencing guidelines for the Modern Slavery Act 2015, s. 4 (committing an offence with intent to commit a human trafficking offence; see **SG36-3**) and s. 30 (breach of a slavery and trafficking prevention or risk order; see **SG36-4**).

## HUMAN TRAFFICKING

### Sentence

For the sentencing guidelines on *Modern Slavery Offences* see **B22.3** in this supplement and SG36-1 *et seq.*    **B22.8**

## CONSIDERATIONS PRIOR TO PROSECUTION OF VICTIMS OF TRAFFICKING OR SLAVERY

### Abuse of Process for Cases Following the Modern Slavery Act 2015

In *AAD* [2022] EWCA Crim 106, the Court of Appeal clarified that the two limb abuse of    **B22.19**
process jurisdiction remains available in all victim of trafficking cases following the Modern Slavery Act 2015. The Court found itself puzzled by *DS* [2020] EWCA Crim 285, [2021] 1 WLR 303. The abuse of process doctrine does not subvert the provisions of s. 45 of the Act, but rather complements it (at [118]). The jurisdiction was only 'special' on account of it being applied in the context of sensitivity that has to be applied to victim of trafficking prosecutions, having regard to international obligations and specific CPS Guidance (at [142]). The core requirements of unfairness, oppression and illegality (inherent in every case of limb 2 abuse) remain central to applications to stay in a victim of trafficking context.

Where the CPS had taken into account the relevant prosecutorial guidance and conclusive grounds decision and had a rational basis for departing from it, then there was no basis for abuse of process (at [119] and [142]). But if the CPS had failed unjustifiably to take into account the CPS Guidance or had no rational basis for departing from a favourable conclusive grounds decision, an abuse of process did exist. It would then be assessed by the Court by way of review on grounds corresponding to public law grounds (at [120] and [142]).

## STATUTORY DEFENCE UNDER THE IMMIGRATION AND ASYLUM ACT 1999, s. 31

### Article 31 of the Convention Relating to the Status of Refugees

**B22.92**　In *JM* [2021] EWCA Crim 1137, the Court of Appeal quashed a conviction for possession of a false identity document where D had been deprived of the statutory defence under s. 31. The substantial injustice test had been met, given the clear continuing impact of the conviction, such as refusal of visas to travel to the USA and UAE, and requirements to disclose the conviction under enhanced disclosure and barring scheme checks.

# SUPPLEMENT TO PART C
# ROAD TRAFFIC OFFENCES

# Section C1 Definitions and Basic Principles in Road Traffic Cases

## DEFINITIONS

### Road or Other Public Place

**Other Public Place**  In *Bowen v Isle of Wight Council* [2021] EWHC 3254 (Ch), [2022] RTR 7 (96), recognising that the inquiry is essentially a factual one, a comprehensive review of the authorities contained in this section of the main work, along with some additional cases, was undertaken in order to answer the question as to whether a cul-de-sac adjoining a public highway was a road for the purposes of the RTRA 1984, s. 142, albeit in the context of a civil claim.  **C1.16**

In *Brown v Fisk* [2021] EWHC 2769 (QB), a helpful review of the authorities on the distinction between a private and a public place was undertaken, leading to a reverse summary judgment being given in a civil case.  **C1.17**

# Section C2 Procedure and Evidence in Road Traffic Cases

## EVIDENCE

### Admissibility of Highway Code

Revisions were made to the Highway Code which became effective from 29 January 2022. The 'hierarchy of road users' introduced puts those most at risk in the event of a collision at the top, referring particularly to pedestrians, cyclists, horse riders and motorcyclists.  **C2.16**

# Section C3 Offences Relating to Driving Triable on Indictment

## CAUSING DEATH BY DANGEROUS DRIVING

### Elements

**Causal Link to Fatality**  The argument that a tyre blow-out broke the chain of causation between D's dangerous driving and a fatal collision was rejected in *Muhammed* [2021] EWCA Crim 802, [2021] 2 Cr App R 17 (324). D had attempted to argue that the facts of the case distinguished it from the Court's approach in *A* [2020] EWCA Crim 407, [2020] RTR 18 (217), meaning that D should not be liable as he could not be expected to foresee the exact event that led to the impact (when driving at over 100mph on a 16-year-old tyre). The Court confirmed that *A* is not confined to the actions of third parties. It advised that foreseeability of the intervening act may be tested by considering what sensible '*ex ante*' advice would be tendered to D on the risks inherent in the manner in which D was driving, including any number of unpredictable situations regarding road conditions, vehicle malfunctions or other road user behaviour.  **C3.15**

## CAUSING DEATH BY CARELESS DRIVING WHEN UNDER THE INFLUENCE OF DRINK OR DRUGS

### Sentence

In *Redding* [2021] EWCA Crim 1502, the Court of Appeal refused leave to refer as unduly lenient a sentence of two years' imprisonment suspended for two years after D changed his plea to guilty following an indication of sentence from the judge. Here the judge was clear that he had decided to depart from the sentencing guideline on the basis that D's consumption of drugs  **C3.26** had not impaired D's driving such as to be causative of the collision. The Court of Appeal stated (at [35]):

> The absence of impairment is but one factor which permits a sentence at the lower end of the range or possible departure from the Definitive Guideline. That said, nothing in this judgment should be read as asserting that the absence of impairment in itself provides a basis for departure from the relevant Definitive Guideline.

## CAUSING SERIOUS INJURY BY DANGEROUS DRIVING

### Sentence

**C3.38**   In *Brown (Dominic)* [2021] EWCA Crim 1963, the judge passed sentences based on a notional sentence (six years) that was in excess of the statutory maximum. This was an improper approach and the sentences were reduced accordingly, with the Court of Appeal finding that the notional starting point after trial should have been four years.

## DANGEROUS DRIVING

### Sentence

**C3.46**   At the Crown Court, while there is no separate sentencing guideline for dangerous driving, it was suggested in *Spencer* [2021] EWCA Crim 1901 that the Sentencing Council's guideline, *Causing Death by Dangerous Driving* (see Supplement, **SG22-2**), is of more assistance than the magistrates' courts guidelines to a judge assessing the seriousness of the offence when sentencing an offender for dangerous driving in the Crown Court.

# Section C6    Summary Traffic Offences

## CONTRAVENTION OF CONSTRUCTION AND USE REGULATIONS

### Elements

**C6.35**   In respect of an offence under the RTA 1988, s. 41D, reg. 110 prohibits driving whilst using a hand-held mobile telephone or a prescribed hand-held device. Prior to 25 March 2022, such use must have involved an 'interactive communication function'. Using the phone's camera function to film the scene of a collision was found not to satisfy this requirement in *DPP v Barreto* [2019] EWHC 2044 (Admin), [2020] 1 Cr App R 6 (142). However, it was held in *Bendt v CPS* [2022] EWHC 502 (Admin) that such communication need not be with another person; it was sufficient to satisfy the requirement of 'interactive communication' that D was using the Bluetooth function on his phone to communicate with the sound system in his car in order to play music. As of 25 March 2022 what is important is that the phone is hand-held and that it is in use. The Road Vehicles (Construction and Use) (Amendment) (No. 2) Regulations 2022 (SI 2022 No. 81) amend reg. 110 to remove the need for the device to perform an interactive communication function, in response to *Barreto*. The amendment to paragraph 6(c) provides the following examples of what amounts to 'using' a phone: illuminating the screen; checking the time; checking notifications; unlocking the device; making, receiving, or rejecting a telephone or internet-based call; sending, receiving or uploading oral or written content; sending, receiving or uploading a photo or video; utilising camera, video, or sound recording functionality; drafting any text; accessing any stored data such as documents, books, audio files, photos, videos, films, playlists, notes or messages; accessing an application; accessing the internet. However, reg. 110(5B) provides an exception to allow a phone to be used for contactless payment while the vehicle is stationary, ensuring that drivers who use their phones to pay for products in a 'drive-thru' do not commit the offence.

# Section C7   Sentencing

## GENERAL PRINCIPLES

### Forfeiture of Motor Vehicle

*Rutherford* [2021] EWCA Crim 394, [2021] 2 Cr App R (S) 41 (323), demonstrates how **C7.2** deprivation orders under the SA 2020, ss. 152 to 155 (see **E8.1** *et seq.*), can be applied.

## OBLIGATORY AND DISCRETIONARY DISQUALIFICATION

### Obligatory Disqualification

In the RTOA 1988, s. 34(4A) and (4AA), after the references to the provisions of the PCC(S)A **C7.8** 2000 there are added 'or section 166 of the Sentencing Code' and 'or section 164 of the Sentencing Code' respectively.

*Dana* [2021] EWCA Crim 1414 explains that, in the absence of special reasons being **C7.9** advanced, an appeal cannot lie against a disqualification that accords with the statutory minimum period found in the RTOA 1988, s. 34 (in that case, the offence was contrary to the RTA 1988, s. 1A, so a disqualification of two years plus the required extension was mandatory).

## PENALTY POINTS DISQUALIFICATION

In the RTOA 1988, s. 35, a new subsection (2A) is inserted, providing that 'A previous **C7.24** disqualification imposed on an offender for a fixed period is not to be taken into account for the purposes of subsection (2) if that period would have been less than 56 days but for an extension period added pursuant to section 35A or 35C or section 147A of the Powers of Criminal Courts (Sentencing) Act 2000'. Further, in s. 35(2A) and (5), after the references to the provisions of the PCC(S)A 2000 there are added 'or section 166 of the Sentencing Code' and 'or section 164 of the Sentencing Code' respectively.

## DISQUALIFICATION GENERALLY

### Interim Disqualification

The reference in the RTOA 1988, s. 26(1)(a) to 'section 6 of the Powers of Criminal Courts **C7.30** (Sentencing) Act 2000' should now be a reference to 'section 20 of the Sentencing Code'.

### Length of Disqualification

A succinct summary of the principles of disqualifying an offender is found in *Smith (David)* **C7.36** [2021] EWCA Crim 1263 (at [16]) and *Morrison* [2021] EWCA Crim 917, [2022] 1 Cr App R (S) 20 (180) (at [30]). *Campbell* [2021] EWCA Crim 1962, [2022] 1 Cr App R (S) 20 (180), further emphasises the desirability of advocates assisting judges by highlighting the relevance of applicable principles to determine the length of disqualification, while also reminding that there is no formula by which a court can measure the right length of disqualification; it is a judicial decision aimed at producing a result tailored to the offender and to the offence.

When substituting a suspended sentence on appeal for one of immediate imprisonment, the extension period will be adjusted to reflect the time already spent in custody (*Moorhouse* [2021] EWCA Crim 1894, [2022] RTR 14 (216)).

*Anderson* [2021] EWCA Crim 1796 repeats the principle that disqualification runs from the **C7.37** date the court imposes it and comments on the approach to the CAA 1981, s. 11(3), where impermissible consecutive disqualifications had been imposed. The primary period of disqualification for 31 months was regarded as being the ceiling beyond which the Court of Appeal could not adjust the disqualification taking effect following the appeal rather than by reference to the total disqualification originally imposed.

## ENDORSEMENT

**C7.47** An example of a court falling into error and both disqualifying and incorrectly endorsing penalty points for the same offence is *Beswick* [2021] EWCA Crim 1269. Summary offences are now committed to the Crown Court pursuant to the SA 2020.

## Section C8    Schedules 2 and 3 to the Road Traffic Offenders Act 1988

**C8.2** At the end of the table, add:

| (1)  **Provision creating offence** | (2)  **General nature of offence** |
| --- | --- |
| *Offence under the Heavy Commercial Vehicles in Kent (No. 1) Order 2019* | |
| Article 2(6) of the Heavy Commercial Vehicles in Kent (No. 1) Order 2019 | Driver of a heavy commercial vehicle in Kent failing to comply with or contravening a direction given, or requirement imposed, by a traffic officer. |

# SUPPLEMENT TO PART D
# PROCEDURE

D

Part D Procedure

# Section D1    Powers of Investigation

## POLICE POWERS IN THE INVESTIGATION OF CRIME

### Investigations by Non-police Officers

The Police, Crime, Sentencing and Courts Act 2022, s. 54, with effect from 28 June 2022, **D1.3** amends the PACE 1984 to insert a new s. 114C which empowers the Secretary of State to make regulations applying any provisions of the Act to the investigation of offences conducted by food crime officers of the Food Standards Agency.

## REASONABLE SUSPICION

In *Betaudier v A-G of Trinidad and Tobago* [2021] UKPC 7, information supporting a **D1.5** reasonable suspicion that soldiers had been involved in the offence of kidnapping had been provided by way of briefing to the police. These briefings did not specifically identify D (who was a soldier) as being involved in the offence of kidnapping. D was subsequently arrested on suspicion of kidnapping. The Privy Council found that while there were a number of factors which gave rise to the suspicion that D had been involved in some type of unlawful activity, they did not support a reasonable suspicion that he had been involved in the offence of kidnapping.

## POWERS OF ARREST: GENERAL PROVISIONS

### Legal Characteristics of Arrest

It was held in *DPP v Ahmed* [2021] EWHC 2122 (Admin), [2022] 1 Cr App R 1 (1), following **D1.15** *Mepstead v DPP* (1996) 160 JP 475 and *Pegram v DPP* [2019] EWHC 2673 (Admin), that the question of whether an application of force by a police constable is unlawful and constitutes an assault will depend on all the circumstances. The Administrative Court reiterated that not all unwanted touching, including where a constable puts his or her hands on a person without any intention of arresting the person, constitutes an assault.

### Resisting Arrest

In *Neale v DPP* [2021] EWHC 658 (Admin), [2021] 2 Cr App R 9 (175), it was held that there **D1.19** was no legal obligation on a person suspected of being in breach of the Health Protection (Coronavirus Restrictions) (Wales) Regulations 2020 (SI 2020 No. 353) to give his or her name and address when stopped by the police.

It was further held in *Campbell v CPS* [2020] EWHC 3868 (Admin), which was followed in *DPP v Ahmed* [2021] EWHC 2122 (Admin), [2022] 1 Cr App R 1 (1), that the expression 'in the execution of functions' which is found in the Assaults on Emergency Workers (Offences) Act 2018 is not to be construed in the same way as the expression 'in the execution of his duty' in the Police Act 1996. The Divisional Court ruled that the phrase used in the 2018 Act does not import a requirement that the emergency worker is acting lawfully. This decision was followed in *DPP v Ahmed* whereupon the Court gave further general guidance as to the term 'functions' (see **B2.49** in the main work).

## POWERS OF ARREST: GENERAL PROVISIONS

### Action following Arrest

The Police, Crime, Sentencing and Courts Act 2022, s. 45, will, from a date to be appointed **D1.20** make significant amendments to the statutory provisions surrounding} pre-charge bail.

# ARREST WITHOUT WARRANT

## Police Powers of Arrest

**D1.28**    **Necessity**   *Rashid v Chief Constable of West Yorkshire Police* [2020] EWHC 2522 (QB) followed *Metropolitan Police Commissioner v MR* [2019] EWHC 888 (QB). Lavender J accepted the trial judge's finding that while the officers honestly believed that arrest was necessary this was not based on reasonable grounds. The only real reason for arresting the claimant, rather than inviting him for interview, was that the police wanted to seize his mobile phone. However, the High Court decided that there was no reason why he could not be asked for it if attending voluntarily at a police station and then arrested if he refused to comply with the request.

# DETENTION AND TREATMENT OF SUSPECTS

## The Decision to Detain

**D1.48**    The Police, Crime, Sentencing and Courts Act 2022, sch. 4, para. 3, will, from a date to be appointed, amend the PACE 1984, s. 34 (limitations on police detention).

## Detention Time-limits

**D1.67**    The Police, Crime, Sentencing and Courts Act 2022, sch. 4, paras. 35 and 36, will, from a date to be appointed, amend the PACE 1984, ss. 41 (limits on periods of detention without charge) and 47 (bail after arrest).

# INTERROGATION OF SUSPECTS

**D1.80**    Version 4 of the 'Joint Interim Interview Protocol between the National Police Chiefs' Council, Crown Prosecution Service, Law Society, the Criminal Law Solicitors' Association and the London Criminal Courts Solicitors' Association' ('the Protocol') came into force on 4 October 2021 (tinyurl.com/mu9rr9dt). The default position is that advice is provided by legal representatives in person unless one of the following exceptions applies:

(a)   the detainee is either confirmed or believed to be Covid-positive;

(b)   the detainee exercises his or her right to speak to a named legal representative/firm or duty solicitor (where the duty solicitor is unable to make alternative arrangements for another representative to attend) and the legal representative/duty solicitor is confirmed Covid-positive or is self-isolating as per government advice;

(c)   some other exceptional reason applies where, in consultation with all relevant parties, it is the belief of the custody officer that due to those exceptional reasons it would not be practical, possible, or desirable for an in-person attendance by the legal adviser in that individual case to safely take place, having regard to any relevant health or safety issues arising, or likely to arise;

(d)   where in consultation with all relevant parties the custody officer agrees that the police in the individual case concerned are unable to meet the obligations set out in the Protocol at paras. 19 to 22.

## Powers to Require Attendance at Police Station

**D1.115**   The Police, Crime, Sentencing and Courts Act 2022, s. 53, with effect from 28 June 2022, amends the PACE 1984, sch. 2A, para. 16 (attendance at police station for fingerprinting and taking of samples: date and time of attendance).

# POWERS TO PHOTOGRAPH SUSPECTS

**D1.118**   The Police, Crime, Sentencing and Courts Act 2022, s. 52, with effect from 28 June 2022, extends the power to photograph suspects under the PACE 1984, s. 64A.

## VISUAL IDENTIFICATION AND RECOGNITION PROCEDURES

In cases of historical identification the question as to whether the VIPER procedure should **D1.127** consist of images of the suspect at the time the offence was allegedly committed, and images of comparators from the same period, or whether they should be contemporaneous is not expressly catered for within Code D. In *Crampton* [2020] EWCA Crim 1334, the Court of Appeal did not comment on the trial judge's decision that the use of contemporaneous images was acceptable.

### Types and Conduct of Identification Procedures

**Video Identification**   In *Smith (David James)* [2020] NICA 42, it was submitted that the **D1.138** PACE (Northern Ireland) Code of Practice, Code D, annex A, para. 7 (which is in similar terms to that of Code D, annex A, para. 7), had been breached due to the police's failure to give D's solicitor a 'reasonable opportunity' to view the images used in the VIPER procedure before those images were shown to a key identification witness. It was held, dismissing the appeal, that although there had been a 'very serious breach of an important safeguard' the breach of Code D did not have a significant adverse effect on the fairness of the proceedings or put D at any substantial disadvantage.

Furthermore, in *Dickens* [2020] EWCA Crim 1661, [2021] 1 WLR 2275, it was held that there was no breach of Code D where the police refused to show a witness the VIPER images again after a positive identification had already been made.

### Controlled Recognition Procedures under Code D, part 3(B)

An earlier version of the recording requirements set out in Code D, paras. 3.36 and 3.37, in **D1.143** respect of controlled recognition procedures was considered in *Yaryare* [2020] EWCA Crim 1314, [2020] 4 WLR 156, where it was held (at [90]) that a police officer viewing CCTV should record 'the moments … when they first begin to note similarities with a particular individual, along with any significant features that occur to them during the process of viewing' and 'any factors that tend to indicate the suspect does not match a particular individual who is being considered'.

### Uncontrolled Recognition Procedures under Code D, part 3(C)

Code D, part 3(C), does not expressly regulate the position where an informal identification on **D1.144** social media is made by a member of the public acting on their own account prior to police involvement. An identification made in such circumstances is to be treated the same as where there has been a street identification. Even if such an identification has been made it does not necessarily follow that pursuant to Code D, para. 3.12, no useful purpose would be served in holding an identification procedure (see *Crampton* [2020] EWCA Crim 1334 and the Association of Chief Police Officers of England, Wales and Northern Ireland guidance, *Internet social media and identification procedures* (July 2014)).

## VOICE IDENTIFICATION

In *Crow* [2021] EWCA Crim 617, the Court of Appeal held that any risks associated with voice **D1.146** identification can be met by providing the jury with an appropriately modified *Turnbull* warning. This warning should be more stringent than that provided in relation to visual identification.

## ENTRY AND SEARCH UNDER WARRANT

### Warrant Issued by a Justice of the Peace

The Police, Crime, Sentencing and Courts Act 2022, s. 55, with effect from 28 June 2022, **D1.151** introduces new provisions that permit a justice of the peace to issue a warrant authorising a constable to enter and searchpremises if there are reasonable grounds for believing that there is material on the premises that consists of, or may relate to the location of, relevant human remains. There is no requirement for a justice of the peace to be satisfied that there are reasonable grounds for believing that an indictable offence has been committed.

### Access to Excluded or Special Procedure Material

**D1.156**  The Police, Crime, Sentencing and Courts Act 2022, s. 56, with effect from 28 June 2022, makes provision for a constable to obtain access to excluded material or special procedure material that consists of, or may relate to the location of, relevant human remains.

### Search Warrant Issued by Judge

**D1.167**  **The Application**  In *R (AIG) v Metropolitan Police Commissioner* [2021] EWHC 584 (Admin), Swift J disagreed (at [12]) with the proposition of Marcus Smith J in *Competition and Markets Authority v Concordia International RX (UK) Ltd* [2018] EWHC 3448 (Ch) at [28] that the harm to the public interest in the administration of justice will always be greater in a case where the rule in *R (Haralambous) v St Albans Crown Court* [2018] UKSC 1, [2018] AC 236, applies than in a case where it does not. Swift J instead followed the decision of Chamberlain J in *R (Jordan) v Chief Constable of Merseyside Police* [2020] EWHC 2274 (Admin) at [17(c)] that the damage to the public interest caused by the disclosure and the damage to the administration of justice caused by the non-disclosure must be evaluated and weighed against each other on a case-by-case basis.

## SEIZURE OF, ACCESS TO AND RETENTION OF MATERIALS

### Powers of Seizure

**D1.178**  The Police, Crime, Sentencing and Courts Act 2022, s. 57, with effect from 28 June 2022, confers powers of seizure in connection with human remains or material relating to human remains.

## POLICE BAIL WITHOUT CHARGE

### Powers and Duties to Release with or without Bail

**D1.186**  The Police, Crime, Sentencing and Courts Act 2022, s. 45, will, from a date to be appointed, make significant amendments to the police's powers and duties under the PACE 1984 to release (with or without bail) persons arrested and taken to, or detained at, a police station in respect of an offence, but not charged.

## INTERCEPTION OF COMMUNICATIONS AND SURVEILLANCE

### Surveillance and Covert Human Intelligence Sources

**D1.201**  The Covert Human Intelligence Sources (Criminal Conduct) Act 2021 (Commencement and Transitional Provisions) Regulations 2021 (SI 2021 No. 605) bring the CHIS(CC)A 2021, ss. 1 to 8 and the schedule into force in three stages:

(a)  on 10 August 2021 for the purposes of criminal conduct authorisations granted by a person holding an office, rank or position with any intelligence service;

(b)  on 15 September 2021 for the purposes of criminal conduct authorisations granted by a person holding an office, rank or position with any police force; and

(c)  on 30 September 2021 for all remaining purposes.

Transitional provisions concerning the authorisation of criminal conduct under the RIPA 2000, s. 29 (which is amended by the CHIS(CC)A 2021) are contained in reg. 3.

## INVESTIGATORY POWERS UNDER THE CRIME (OVERSEAS PRODUCTION ORDERS) ACT 2019

### Definitions

The Police, Crime, Sentencing and Courts Act 2022, s. 51 and sch. 5, with effect from 28 June **D1.203**
2022, amend the meaning of 'electronic data' and 'excepted electronic data' so that the Crime
(Overseas Production Orders) Act 2019, s. 3(4), reads 'Where the person against whom an
overseas production order is sought is a telecommunications operator, this Act applies as if
references to excepted electronic data included electronic data that is communications data,
*other than communications data to which subsection 4(A) applies*'.

### Extraction of Information from Electronic Devices

The Police, Crime, Sentencing and Courts Act 2022, s. 37, will, from a date to be appointed, **D1.204A**
introduce new provisions which permit an authorised person to extract information stored on
an electronic device if the (a) user of the device has voluntarily provided the device to an
authorised person and (b) the user has agreed to the extraction of information from the device
by an authorised person.

## Section D2   The Decision to Prosecute and Diversion

### THE DECISION TO PROSECUTE

#### The Tests for Deciding Whether to Charge

**Evidential Stage**   See *R (End Violence Against Women Campaign) v DPP* [2021] EWCA Civ **D2.11**
350, [2021] 2 Cr App R 2 (14), for a discussion of the 'merits based approach' to the evidential
stage of the Full Code Test.

**Public Interest Stage**   The CPS published updated legal guidance on *Rape and Sexual Offences* **D2.12**
(21 May 2021, tinyurl.com/uspa2y6f), replacing the interim guidance published in October
2020. The guidance encourages police and prosecutors to take an 'offender-centric' approach to
case building, looking closely at the actions of the suspect before, during and after the alleged
assault. It includes guidance on reasonable lines of inquiry involving digital communication
data, setting out four principles for investigators to follow.

#### Judicial Review of Prosecution Decisions

**Decision Not to Prosecute**   The long-standing line of authority that the power to review a **D2.23**
decision not to prosecute should be exercised sparingly was confirmed in *R (Canham) v DPP*
[2021] EWHC 3361 (Admin). The fact that the ECHR, Article 2, was engaged in this case did
not require the court to take a different approach.

### DETENTION FOLLOWING CHARGE

#### Detention of Children after Charge

In *Archer v Metropolitan Police Commissioner* [2021] EWCA Civ 1662, [2022] 1 Cr App R 14 **D2.53**
(239), the Court of Appeal upheld the Divisional Court in finding that detention of children
under the PACE 1984, s. 38(1)(b), was not incompatible with the ECHR, Article 5, although
such detention should be the exception rather than the rule.

In *R (AR) v London Borough of Waltham Forest* [2021] EWCA Civ 1185, the Court of Appeal **D2.54**
(Civil Division) found that a local authority had breached its duty under the Children Act
1989, s. 21(2), by failing to have a reasonable system in place to enable the authority to respond
to requests by the police for secure accommodation under the PACE 1984, s. 38(6), where a
child is at risk of being detained overnight in police custody.

Part D Procedure

D

# Section D3  Courts, Parties and Abuse of Process

## PARTIES TO CRIMINAL PROCEEDINGS

### The Crown Prosecution Service

D3.51 **Review of CPS Decision Not to Prosecute**  In *R (Purvis) v DPP* [2020] EWHC 3573 (Admin), [2021] 1 Cr App R 20 (377), the Divisional Court reiterated (at [21]) that a decision not to prosecute is amenable to judicial review on only limited grounds, namely:

(a) application of an unlawful policy,

(b) failure to act in accordance with the Code for Crown Prosecutors or other guidance that prosecutors are required to follow, and

(c) reaching a decision at which no reasonable prosecutor could have arrived (irrationality, sometimes referred to as *Wednesbury* unreasonableness).

It is also made clear that the Court will be very slow to find such grounds to be made out (at [22]). The Court emphasised (at [23]) the need to 'respect the fact that the task of deciding when, and when not, to prosecute is primarily one for the prosecuting authority' and that the Court's function is one of review.

In *R (Joseph) v DPP* [2022] EWHC 131 (Admin), [2022] 1 Cr App R 17 (330), the Divisional Court reiterated (at [23]) that:

> … a public authority is bound to adhere to its lawfully adopted policy save where there is good reason for departing from it … The DPP must therefore have regard to and apply the Code and the relevant CPS policy guidance in making prosecutorial decisions unless there is good reason not to do so.

The Court also noted (at [27]) that, where policy guidance is set out in a number of documents (not just the Code), those documents 'must be construed together and in their context'. The Court also made the point (at [33]) that the CPS Code 'does not purport to be exhaustive in identifying the relevant considerations in any given case', and so it is legitimate for the decision-maker to take into account other factors that may properly be considered relevant. This means that the wording of the guidance should not be construed as if it were a statute; rather, decisions should be taken in the spirit of the guidance.

## ABUSE OF PROCESS: THE POWER TO STAY PROCEEDINGS

### Magistrates' Courts

D3.71 In *Mansfield v DPP* [2021] EWHC 2938 (Admin), [2022] 1 Cr App R 8 (110), the issue was whether the district judge was correct to hold that a magistrates' court had no jurisdiction to grant a stay on the basis of the second category of abuse of process. In reaching that conclusion, the district judge relied on *Nembhard v DPP* [2009] EWHC 194 (Admin) and *Woolls v North Somerset Council* [2016] EWHC 1410 (Admin), where it had been held that the magistrates' court lacks jurisdiction to determine an application based on the second category of abuse. These decisions were based in part on *Horseferry Road Magistrates' Court ex parte Bennett* [1994] 1 AC 42, where Lord Griffiths (at p. 64) affirmed the power of magistrates to exercise control over their proceedings through an abuse of process jurisdiction, but said that 'this power should be strictly confined to matters directly affecting the fairness of the trial of the particular accused with whom they are dealing' and that wider responsibility for upholding the rule of law (the second category of abuse of process) 'must be that of the High Court'. May J (at [20]) accepted the submission that 'it was evidently not Lord Griffiths' intention to exclude from the magistrates' jurisdiction all category 2 cases of abuse'. Rather, Lord Griffiths was excluding from consideration by magistrates' courts only a sub-set of cases in the second category. May J also noted *R (Kay) v Leeds Magistrates' Court* [2018] EWHC 1233 (Admin), [2018] 2 Cr App R 27 (425), where Sweeney J (at [30]) said that 'the wide category of cases over which the magistrates' court has jurisdiction includes investigation of the bona fides of the prosecution or of whether the prosecution has been instituted oppressively or unfairly'. May J concluded (at [31]) that *Nembhard* and *Woolls* 'mistakenly overstate the extent of the exception to the magistrates' jurisdiction identified by Lord Griffiths in *Bennett* and accepted the suggestion of the district judge in the case stated that there may have been an 'unintended elision' of the wider supervisory jurisdiction referred to in *Bennett* with the second category of abuse of process. The exception contemplated by Lord Griffiths in *Bennett* was in fact a very narrow one, and most cases falling within the second category of abuse arising in the magistrates' court 'will be suitable to be considered and determined in that jurisdiction'. It followed that 'the dicta in *Nembhard* and *Woolls* dealing with the scope of the magistrates' jurisdiction are wrong and should not be followed'.

May J, considering the scope of the sub-set of 'category 2' cases which are outside the magistrates' jurisdiction, referred to *Panday v Virgil* [2008] UKPC 24, [2008] 1 AC 1386, where Lord Brown of Eaton-under-Heywood said (at [34]):

> … their Lordships find it difficult to think of any situation save where, as in [*Bennett*] itself, the accused has been unlawfully brought within the jurisdiction, in which the magistrates would have to adjourn the proceedings in favour of a judicial review challenge. The rationale for that particular exception must be that unlawful extradition introduces into the case cross-border considerations which may be of a sensitive character and which certainly range far outside the prosecution process itself.

May J went on to suggest (at [34]) that:

> … the class of abuse case falling to be decided exclusively in the High Court would seem to be very narrow indeed, perhaps comprising only executive misconduct in relation to extradition, as occurred in *Bennett* itself. I would decline to attempt any more precise definition of the exception. What appears clear from the above review of the authorities, however, is that magistrates will be competent to investigate and determine a wide range of circumstances falling into category 2 arising from, and bearing upon the fairness of, the domestic criminal process.

### Failure to Disclose Evidence

*Salt* [2015] EWCA Crim 662, [2015] 1 WLR 4905 was cited in *Ahmed* [2021] EWCA Crim   **D3.88**
927, where a stay was granted on the basis of failings as regards disclosure. The Court of Appeal set the stay aside. The Court noted (at [79]) that it was not the case that the prosecution had simply avoided their responsibilities. Each of the extensive requests for disclosure went answered. However, the disclosure officer had been overly restrictive when identifying the items to be disclosed or areas that required further investigation, and failed correctly to categorise all of the unused material; moreover, the CPS reviewing lawyer had not reviewed the material with sufficient care, with the result that the disclosure officer's errors consequently went undetected. However, the Court went on to hold (at [83]) that these failings did not 'reach the level of grave executive misconduct which would undermine public confidence in the criminal justice system and bring it into disrepute' and were 'not at a level of seriousness that they [outweighed] the very strong public interest in the trial of grave offences'. The Court also took account of the failure of the defence to raise these matters with the judge until after the trial had commenced and the absence of an application for disclosure.

### Going Back on a Promise, Legitimate Expectation and Double Jeopardy

**Cautions**   *Mansfield v DPP* [2021] EWHC 2938 (Admin), [2022] 1 Cr App R 8 (110)   **D3.90**
involved the police giving an assurance which was then withdrawn. The Divisional Court took account of *Abu Hamza* [2006] EWCA Crim 2918, [2007] QB 659, where Lord Phillips CJ said (at [54]):

> [I]t is not likely to constitute an abuse of process to proceed with a prosecution unless (i) there has been an unequivocal representation by those with the conduct of the investigation or prosecution of a case that the defendant will not be prosecuted and (ii) that the defendant has acted on that representation to his detriment. Even then, if facts come to light which were not known when the representation was made, these may justify proceeding with the prosecution despite the representation.

May J observed (at [40]) that the matters identified by Lord Phillips were 'necessary pre-conditions before a court could find that there had been abuse'. However, satisfying those conditions is not necessarily sufficient, per se, to establish an abuse of process. The Court also rejected the suggestion that 'every case of a reneged-upon promise made by police and acted upon by the defendant must necessarily result in criminal proceedings having to be stayed for abuse', since each case must depend on its own facts.

In abuse cases falling within the first category (where the accused cannot have a fair trial), proceedings will be stayed on the basis of that finding; there is no question of balancing competing interests. However, where the second category of abuse is alleged, competing public interests may have to be balanced. Carrying out that balancing exercise, May J said that the 'key circumstance' telling against a stay in this case was the seriousness of the offence. However, against that were the facts that there was a breach of the promise given by the officer responsible for the charging decision; D's age (he was 18 at the time); and D had no previous convictions. May J did not regard as relevant the fact that the assurance was given by mistake, or that it was rectified later the same day (the correction did not happen until after D had been interviewed and had made full admissions), nor that D might have sought to have the evidence of the admissions excluded at trial.

May J concluded (at [45]) that:

> Weighing these factors in the balance I conclude that in the particular circumstances of this case the public interest in holding a state official to their promise outweighs the public interest in seeing that an offence, albeit in this case a serious one, is prosecuted.

### Bringing Justice into Disrepute

**D3.109**  **Private Prosecutions**  In *Asif v Ditta* [2021] EWCA Crim 1091, [2021] 2 Cr App R 21 (415), the Court of Appeal reiterated (at [75]) that a private prosecutor can have another motive as well as being motivated by a public interest factor. Mixed motives are not of themselves a bar to a private prosecution. The question is where the line is to be drawn between the public interest motivation and the other 'oblique' motive. It follows that a distinction is to be drawn between mixed motives and 'an oblique motive which is so dominant and so unrelated to the proceedings that it renders them an abuse of process' (at [78]). On the particular facts of the case, the private prosecution was held to be an abuse of process because it was 'being used for private tactical and oppressive reasons' (at [94]).

## OPEN JUSTICE

### Appeals against Derogations from Open Justice

**D3.142**  As regards applications to revoke a reporting direction order or to make an excepting direction, the position under the YJCEA 1999, s. 46, mirrors that under s. 45 (child witnesses), and so s. 159 does not confer a right of appeal against a decision to refuse a reporting direction, or a decision to discharge such an order, or the decision on the making of an excepting direction (*Re Pembrokeshire Herald* [2021] EWCA Crim 1165, [2021] 2 Cr App R 23 (455) at [29]). Moreover, the statutory power to revoke a reporting direction does not confer a freestanding right of appeal against such a direction. The remedy instead is to seek judicial review (at [28]).

---

# Section D7   Bail

## BAIL AND CUSTODY TIME-LIMITS

**D7.43**  In *R (Jabber) v Sheffield Crown Court* [2022] EWHC 516 (Admin), it was noted (at [48]) that a judge may grant bail as a matter of discretion because the custody time-limit is about to expire, even if the point has not yet been reached where release is required by reg. 6(6) of the 1987 Regulations. If the accused does not breach bail or commit another offence before the trial starts, the custody time-limit becomes irrelevant. The Court went on to hold (at [49]) that where bail is granted other than as a consequence of the expiry of the custody time-limit, the 'clock' is paused when the accused is released from custody. If the accused is brought back before the court because of a breach of bail or commission of a further offence, and is remanded in custody on the original offence, the custody time-limit clock restarts. The Court added that it follows that the prosecution are not required to seek an extension until such time as the restarted period is approaching its limit.

# Section D8    Assets Recovery

## INTRODUCTION

### Accredited Financial Investigators

The following statutory instruments were revoked from 28 June 2021 by the Proceeds of Crime   **D8.2**
Act 2002 (References to Financial Investigators) (England and Wales and Northern Ireland) Order 2021 (SI 2021 No. 640):

(a)   the Proceeds of Crime Act 2002 (References to Financial Investigators) Order 2009 (SI 2009 No. 975);
(b)   the Proceeds of Crime Act 2002 (References to Financial Investigators) (Amendment) Order 2009 (SI 2009 No. 2707);
(c)   the Proceeds of Crime Act 2002 (References to Financial Investigators) (England and Wales) Order 2015 (SI 2015 No. 1853);
(d)   the Proceeds of Crime Act 2002 (References to Financial Investigators) (Amendment) Order 2017 (SI 2017 No. 74);
(e)   the Proceeds of Crime Act 2002 (References to Financial Investigators) (Amendment) (England and Wales) Order 2018 (SI 2018 No. 318);
(f)   the Proceeds of Crime Act 2002 (References to Financial Investigators) (Amendment) (England and Wales) Order 2020 (SI 2020 No. 1078).

## HIGH COURT: CIVIL RECOVERY ORDERS

### Interim Orders

Note that SI 2005 No. 3382 was amended by SI 2008 No. 523.    **D8.7**

It was said in *SFO v Jammal* [2021] EWHC 1422 (Admin) that the decision whether to grant a property freezing order is discretionary, and that one key consideration will be whether there is a risk of dissipation of the assets in question (as explained by Collins J in *Nuttall v NCA* [2016] EWHC 1911 (Admin), [2016] 4 WLR 134 at [19]).

## MAGISTRATES' COURTS: SEIZURE, DETENTION AND FORFEITURE

### Search and Seizure of Cash

**Searches**   The Proceeds of Crime Act 2002 (Cash Searches: Code of Practice) Order 2021 (SI   **D8.13**
2021 No. 728) came into force on 28 June 2021. From that date, the revised code of practice entitled 'Code of Practice issued under section 292 of the Proceeds of Crime Act 2002 Recovery of Cash: Search Powers' (laid in draft before Parliament on 22 March 2021) came into operation. The Proceeds of Crime Act 2002 (Cash Searches: Code of Practice) Order 2018 (SI 2018 No. 83) is revoked.

### Forfeiture of Listed Assets

**Overview**   From 28 June 2021, SI 2018 No. 85 was revoked by SI 2021 No. 727. From that   **D8.27**
date, the revised code of practice entitled 'Code of Practice issued under section 303G of the Proceeds of Crime Act 2002 Recovery of Listed Assets: Search Powers' (laid in draft before Parliament on 22 March 2021) came into operation.

D

Part D Procedure

In the main work, for 'Magistrates' Courts (Detention and Forfeiture of Listed Assets) Rules 2017 (SI 2017 No. 1297)' read 'Magistrates' Courts (Detention and Forfeiture of Listed Assets) Rules 2017 (SI 2017 No. 1293)'.

### Forfeiture of Money Held in Bank Accounts

D8.34   **Freezing Orders**   From 28 June 2021, SI 2017 No. 1223 was amended by SI 2021 No. 639.

It was held in *R (Javadov) v Westminster Magistrates' Court* [2021] EWHC 2751 (Admin) that it is implicit in s. 303Z1(4) of the POCA 2002 that when an application for an account freezing order is made without notice, it is permissible — indeed, it will often be entirely appropriate — for the hearing to be in private.

## POWERS OF INVESTIGATION

### General

D8.37   **Investigations**   See the Proceeds of Crime Act 2002 (Investigations: Code of Practice) Order 2021 (SI 2021 No. 726) in force from 28 June 2021. From that date, the revised code of practice entitled 'Code of Practice issued under section 377 of the Proceeds of Crime Act 2002 Investigations' (laid in draft before Parliament on 22 March 2021) came into operation. SI 2018 No. 84 is revoked.

### Unexplained Wealth Orders

D8.55   The Economic Crime (Transparency and Enforcement) Act 2022, which effects changes to the regime for unexplained wealth orders, came into force on 15 May 2022 (SI 2022 No. 519). For further information see House of Commons research briefing (23 March 2022, tinyurl.com/469fake5).

## Section D12   Arraignment and Pleas

### AUTREFOIS ACQUIT AND AUTREFOIS CONVICT

### Scope of the Pleas

D12.26   **Findings that Cannot Form Basis of Plea for Autrefois Acquit**   In *Douglas* [2021] EWCA Crim 1193, [2022] 1 Cr App R 5 (70), the Court of Appeal upheld the refusal of the Crown Court to vacate D's guilty plea to unauthorised possession of a specified item inside a prison despite the fact that there had already been an independent prison adjudication in relation to the same conduct. The referral of the matter to the prison adjudication and thus adjudication itself had not been validly constituted and compliant with the applicable regulations, and therefore there was no valid earlier determination to prevent the Crown Court from sentencing D.

### CHANGE OF PLEA

### Ambiguous Pleas

D12.99   In *Atkinson* [2021] EWCA Crim 153, D had entered guilty pleas to assault but also asserted that she had acted in self-defence. The Court of Appeal held that guilty pleas were not ambiguous because the judge had clarified any ambiguity with her counsel before accepting the pleas, and established that her guilty pleas were genuine.

# Section D15   Trial on Indictment: General Matters and Pre-trial Procedure

## CUSTODY TIME-LIMITS

### Effect of Expiry of Custody Time-limit

In *R (Jabbar) v Sheffield Crown Court* [2022] EWHC 516 (Admin), it was underlined that once **D15.18**
a custody time-limit is not extended and expires, the custody time-limit regime ceases to
operate and will not apply to any further period of remand.

## PRE-TRIAL AND PLEA AND TRIAL PREPARATION HEARINGS

### Use of Live Links and Telephone Facilities for Pre-trial Hearings

The temporary modifications to the CDA 1998, ss. 57A to 57B and sch. 3A, to give the court **D15.40**
power to direct 'live link' attendance at 'preliminary hearings' made by the Coronavirus Act
2020, s. 54 and sch. 24, are superseded in the same terms by s. 200 of the Police, Crime,
Sentencing and Courts Act 2022 and the new CJA 2003, s. 51, with effect from 28 June 2022.
The new s. 51 permits the use of live links for pre-trial, trial and appeal proceedings, save for
limitations relating to juries. The test for a link being permitted is that its use is in the interests
of justice (s. 51(4)). Circumstances relevant to the direction to be made are identified in
s. 51(6), and include the availability and needs of the person being granted a link, how effective
their participation will be and the suitability of the facilities they will use.

## ATTENDANCE OF WITNESSES

### Live Link

**Further Use of Live Links in the Interests of Justice**   In *Louanjli* [2021] EWCA Crim 819, **D15.98**
the Court of Appeal declined to overturn its earlier decision in *Ukpabio* [2007] EWCA Crim
2108, [2008] 1 Cr App R 6 (101), which held that the Crown Court had no jurisdiction to
direct that D could give evidence via live link.

# Section D16   Trial on Indictment: The Prosecution Case

## EXAMINATION AND CROSS-EXAMINATION OF A WITNESS

### Cross-examination

The court has a discretion to limit cross-examination (CrimPR 3.13(d); see **R3.13**) and/or to **D16.33**
set a timetable for the evidence of witnesses (CrimPR 3.13(b)). The discretion to time-limit
cross-examination is intended to address the real issues in a just and proportionate manner
(*Lally* [2021] EWCA Crim 1372).

# Section D17   Trial on Indictment: The Defence Case

## THE DEFENCE CASE

### The Accused as a Witness

Beyond the procedural measures that address the use of live links for the accused, and see **D17.10**
CrimPR 3.8(5) and 18.14 (see **R3.8** and **R18.14**) and CrimPD V, paras. 18A.1 to 18A.2 (see
**CPD.18A**), the Court of Appeal in *Louanjli* [2021] EWCA Crim 819 restated the position that
the Crown Court had no inherent common-law jurisdiction to direct that D could give
evidence via live link.

## Section D18    Trial on Indictment: Procedure between Close of Defence Case and Retirement of Jury

### SUMMING-UP

#### Duties of Counsel in Relation to the Summing-up

**D18.23**    There is a duty on all counsel to focus during the summing-up on what is being said and to raise any material error or omission at the time (*Sakin* [2021] EWCA Crim 291).

#### Written Directions

**D18.24**    In *Grant* [2021] EWCA Crim 1243, the Court of Appeal emphasised again the importance of judges providing the jury with written directions of law, incorporating a route to verdict. The Court observed (at [44]) that such written directions should be expected 'in all cases save perhaps for the most straightforward'. In that regard, the *Crown Court Compendium* has been updated, as of August 2021.

#### Standard Directions

**D18.28**    **Separate Consideration of Counts and Defendants**    The importance of a direction, where there is more than one count on the indictment, to give separate consideration to each of them was underlined by the Court of Appeal in *Thomas* [2021] EWCA Crim 804, when the fact that such a direction was given was relied on, in rejecting a claim that verdicts returned were inconsistent.

**D18.29**    **Ingredients of Offence**    In *Chipunza* [2021] EWCA Crim 597, [2021] 2 Cr App R 6 (103), D was charged with burglary and the key question was whether D had entered a dwelling house. The appeal against conviction was allowed because the judge in summing up, having correctly identified that whether the premises were a dwelling was a question of fact, failed to remind the jury of any of the factors mitigating against that being the case. Where an ingredient of an offence is a question of factual interpretation, it is incumbent on the judge to remind the jury of those facts relied on by the defence as arguing against that ingredient being established.

**D18.32**    **Other Standard Directions**    In relation to the direction that should be given regarding lies, and the circumstances in which such a direction is appropriate, the Court of Appeal gave further guidance in *Pitcher* [2021] EWCA Crim 1013, [2021] 2 Cr App R 18 (335).

It was emphasised in *Hindle* [2021] EWCA Crim 1367 that whether such a warning was required as to the care to be taken with a potentially unreliable witness, in accordance with *Makanjuola* [1995] 3 All ER 730, was a matter for the judge's discretion, which was to be sparingly exercised.

#### Unanimity

**D18.44**    **Unanimity as to the Basis of a Guilty Verdict**    In *Chilvers* [2021] EWCA Crim 1311, [2022] 1 Cr App R 2 (12), it was contended on behalf of the appellant, who had been convicted of controlling or coercive behaviour, contrary to the SCA 2015, s. 76, that a direction in accordance with *Brown* (1984) 79 Cr App R 115 was necessary. The basis for this was that the particulars of offence alleged a series of ways in which it was asserted that the appellant had been controlling or coercive, and it was submitted that the jury needed to agree which of these were established before they could convict. The Court of Appeal restated that a *Brown* direction was only necessary where there was an appreciable risk that different members of a jury would find different matters proved as establishing an ingredient of the offence to each other, or to put it another way that the factual bases for the charge as indicted are 'individually coterminous' with an essential element of the offence. Where, however, individual particulars are not coterminous with an element of offence, and where the defence is the same in relation to each, then a *Brown* direction is not required. In the appellant's case, it was sufficient for the jury to be sure that he had repeatedly engaged in coercive or controlling behaviour, and thus a *Brown* direction was not required.

# Section D19   Trial on Indictment: Procedure Relating to Retirement of the Jury and Verdict

## RETIREMENT OF THE JURY

### Timing of Retirement

In *Abraham* [2021] EWCA Crim 1000, it was observed to be good practice to make clear to a **D19.4** jury retiring late in the day, or receiving a majority direction late in the day, that they are under no pressure of time.

### Prohibition of Further Evidence Once Jury Enclosed

In *Dunster* [2021] EWCA Crim 1555, [2022] 1 Cr App R 12 (174), the Court of Appeal **D19.12** upheld a conviction where, by agreement of the parties, the judge had answered a jury question relating to DNA evidence which provided additional detail from the expert that had not been included in agreed facts. The additional information was uncontroversial and anodyne, and if anything helped the appellant. It was however unwise for the judge to have acted thus.

# Section D23   Sentencing in the Magistrates' Court

## VARIATION OF SENTENCE UNDER THE MAGISTRATES' COURTS ACT 1980, s. 142

### Procedure

In *Turner* [2021] EWCA Crim 1376, [2021] 4 WLR 133, a Crown Court judge had failed to **D23.27** impose disqualification from driving in a case where such disqualification was obligatory. Disqualification was imposed 'administratively' after the sentencing hearing, when the need to disqualify was brought to the attention of the judge by the court staff. The Court of Appeal noted that this variation should have been carried out in open court, adding (at [45]) that the case demonstrated:

> … the need for matters to be dealt with in open court with the offenders or, at the very least, their properly instructed representatives present. Taking what might be called 'administrative short cuts', which avoid the inconvenience of re-listing a case or reconvening the court, by dealing with such matters 'administratively' without notice to offenders is not acceptable.

## COMMITTAL FOR SENTENCE

### Guilty Plea at 'Plea before Venue' and Committal for Sentence

In *Isleworth Crown Court and Uxbridge Magistrates' Court ex parte Buda* [2000] 1 Cr App R (S) **D23.38** 538, D was charged with being knowingly concerned in the fraudulent evasion of the prohibition on the importation of a Class A drug (cocaine). He pleaded guilty in the magistrates' court and was committed to the Crown Court for sentence. Following the committal, but before his appearance in the Crown Court, it was discovered that the packages had contained sodium bicarbonate, not cocaine. The Crown Court remitted the case to the magistrates' court. The Divisional Court held that the Crown Court had no power to do so. Moses J said that, in the normal case where there has been a decision to commit on the wrong view of the facts, the proper approach is to allow D to make an application to change plea (which would enable the Crown Court to remit the case to the magistrates' court). However, this would only be appropriate where the mistake is such as to give D a possible defence.

More importantly, if the case remains in the Crown Court, that court should of course sentence on the basis of the facts as they are known to be at the sentencing hearing (not as they were thought to be at the time of conviction or committal).

### Committal under the Sentencing Act 2020, s. 20

**D23.55**    In *Jex* [2021] EWCA Crim 1708, the Court of Appeal upheld a committal for sentence under the SA 2020, s. 20, which referred to the committal power in sch. 16, para. 11(2), when the offences so committed occurred during the operational period of a Crown Court suspended sentence order imposed at a time when the power to commit arose under the CJA 2003, sch. 12, para. 11(2) (i.e. prior to 1 December 2020).

---

# Section D24    Trial of Children and Young People

## MODE OF TRIAL AND PROCEDURE FOR PERSONS CLOSE TO 18TH BIRTHDAY

### Determining Age

**D24.66**    In *Mohammed* [2021] EWCA Crim 1375, a defence age report stated that D was 16; however, a report from a youth justice worker concluded that he was an adult aged between 22 and 26. The judge ruled that D was an adult. The Court of Appeal noted (at [58]) that the leading case on determination of age is *R (B) v London Borough of Merton* [2003] EWHC 1689 (Admin), [2003] 4 All ER 280, where Stanley Burnton J had said (at [36]–[37]):

> The assessment of age in borderline cases is a difficult matter, but it is not complex. It is not an issue which requires anything approaching a trial, and judicialisation of the process is in my judgment to be avoided. It is a matter which may be determined informally, provided safeguards of minimum standards of inquiry and of fairness are adhered to.
>
> … [E]xcept in clear cases, the decision maker cannot determine age solely on the basis of the appearance of the applicant. In general, the decision maker must seek to elicit the general background of the applicant, including his family circumstances and history, his educational background, and his activities during the previous few years. Ethnic and cultural information may also be important. If there is reason to doubt the applicant's statement as to his age, the decision maker will have to make an assessment of his credibility, and he will have to ask questions designed to test his credibility.

The Court in *Mohammed* went on to note (at [59]) that:

> Compliance with s. 99 [of the CYPA 1933] requires much more than superficial observation of the defendant in court. The court must be provided with all the relevant evidence. It is for the parties or relevant social services to carry out the appropriate investigations … Where there is real doubt as to the claimed age, the proper course is to give directions for an age assessment to be conducted.

The Court also referred to *L* [2013] EWCA Crim 991, [2013] 2 Cr App R 23 (247), where the Court of Appeal had said (at [22]) that, when the issue arises, much more is required than superficial observation of the defendant in court or in the dock to enable the judge to make an appropriate age assessment:

> The facial features of the defendant may provide a clue or two, but experience has shown that this is very soft evidence indeed and liable to mislead. What we do know is that young people mature at different ages, and that their early life experiences can sometimes leave them with a misleading appearance. We also appreciate that young people from an ethnic group with which the court is unfamiliar may seem older, or indeed younger, than those from ethnic groups with which the court has greater experience. Therefore, when an age issue arises, the court must be provided with all the relevant evidence which bears on it. Although the court may adjourn proceedings for further investigations to be conducted, these have to be undertaken by one or other or both sides, or by the relevant social services. The court is not vested with any jurisdiction, and is not provided with the resources to conduct its own investigations into the age of a potential defendant until after the investigation has completed its course, and the individual in question is brought before the court.

There was also reference to *R (M) v Hammersmith Magistrates' Court* [2017] EWHC 1359 (Admin), where Irwin LJ had said (at [16]):

> In cases where there is a real doubt as to the claimed age, the proper course is to make directions for an age assessment to be conducted. The relevant local authority, through the medium of the youth offending team or service, will usually be the appropriate avenue to pursue.

The Court emphasised (at [62]) that:

> ... the age assessment can be an informal one, although it must be procedurally fair, and a formal trial procedure is not necessary. Relevant to his decision was the fact that the Judge was very familiar with the appellant, having presided over his trial.

The Court went on to hold that the judge was fully entitled to conclude that D was an adult. The judge had made it clear that his conclusion was not based on simple visual assessment but also took account of matters such as D's mannerisms and abilities, as demonstrated during his evidence and trial. Further, the judge was entitled to take into account the lack of any documentation confirming D's claimed date of birth, and the discrepancies in the ages given by him or on his behalf. He was also entitled to give weight to the report produced by a youth justice worker, who had concluded that D's conversational abilities and traits were those of an adult, not a child. It followed, said the Court, that there was no basis to interfere with the judge's reasoned disagreement with the findings of the defence age report. See also E15.2 in this supplement.

# Section D25    Behaviour Orders: Civil Injunctions, CBOs, CPNs, PSPOs, Closure Notices, Closure Orders, SCPOs, VOOs, STROs, KCPOs, SPOs and DAPOs

## SERIOUS CRIME PREVENTION ORDERS

### Powers of the Crown Court

In *Adams* [2021] EWCA Crim 1525, [2022] 1 WLR 1736, the Court of Appeal held that the **D25.63** Crown Court had jurisdiction to make a SCPO even if D had been sentenced and the confiscation proceedings against D concluded before the application for a SCPO was made.

## KNIFE CRIME PREVENTION ORDERS

The Offensive Weapons Act 2019 (Commencement No. 2) (England and Wales) Regulations **D25.84** 2021 (SI 2021 No. 762) brought into force on 5 July 2021 the 14-month pilot for KCPOs. At the same time the government introduced Practitioners' Guidance on KCPOs (tinyurl.com/2w52ucm5).

# Section D26    Appeal to the Court of Appeal (Criminal Division) Following Trial on Indictment

## DECIDING OUTCOME OF APPEAL AND GIVING JUDGMENT

In *Field* [2022] EWCA Crim 316, the Court of Appeal emphasised that the power provided **D26.6** under CrimPR 36.15 (see **R36.15**) to reopen a ruling which determines a decision or reference was extremely limited. It could only be exercised in exceptional circumstances. If an application was made with the aim of requiring another constitution of the court to reconsider the merits of an appeal on the basis of claims of procedural unfairness or bias of the original constitution of the court which had no sustainable basis, that would constitute an abuse of process.

# Section D31    Extradition

## ARREST AND INITIAL HEARING

### Part 1

**D31.5**   In *R (Salomon) v Westminster Magistrates' Court* [2022] EWHC 83 (Admin), the Administrative Court considered the extent to which the accuracy and completeness of legal advice may affect the validity of consent to extradition under s. 45(1) of the Extradition Act 2003.

### Part 2

**D31.7**   The Administrative Court considered a challenge to identity in *Prendi (aka Kola) v Government of the Republic of Albania* [2021] EWHC 2625 (Admin).

## BARS TO EXTRADITION

### Extraneous Considerations

**D31.24**   When considering if the requested person might be prejudiced at trial, on account of one of the specified reasons, the court does not have to particularise precisely how the prejudice would arise or become manifest. It was sufficient, in *Government of Turkey v Tanis* [2021] EWHC 1675 (Admin), for the judge to have found that the judiciary in Turkey were not independent, the rule of law was not operating and the requested person would, given his particular profile, suffer prejudice at trial.

### Passage of Time

**D31.25**   In *Barber v Administrator of the Sovereign Base Areas of Akrotiri and Dhekelia, British Overseas Territory* [2021] EWHC 2858 (Admin), [2021] 4 WLR 138, the Administrative Court considered whether it would be oppressive to extradite a requested person in respect of historic allegations of sexual offences involving children when there had been a previous criminal investigation which had not resulted in a prosecution (see also *Madison v Government of Australia* [2021] EWHC 1900 (Admin) where the Court considered if it would be unjust to extradite for allegations of historic sexual offences).

### Forum

**D31.28**   In *Craig v HM Advocate* [2022] UKSC 6, [2022] 1 WLR 1270, the Supreme Court held that the extradition proceedings and extradition order were incompatible with the requested person's rights under Article 8 of the ECHR as the forum bar provisions had not been brought into force in Scotland.

It is for the court to determine the weight to be attached to the 'belief' of a prosecutor when having regard to this as a specified matter under s. 83A(3) of the 2003 Act and the court is entitled to disagree with the prosecutor's evaluation of the other specified matters (*Government of the USA v Osborne* [2022] EWHC 35 (Admin) at [75]).

If a requested person is interviewed by the police in the UK and answered questions anticipating that he or she would be prosecuted in the UK then this may form part of the person's connection to the UK for the purposes of s. 83A(3)(g) (*Osborne* at [90]).

## CONVICTION IN ABSENCE

**D31.31**   In deciding whether a requested person would be entitled to a retrial or (on appeal) a review amounting to a retrial under the Extradition Act 2003, s. 85(5), the court should consider whether the requesting territory has proved to the criminal standard that the requested person would be provided with the procedural rights identified in s. 85(8). This does not preclude a submission from the requested person that the retrial would involve a breach of other fair trial rights under Article 6 of the ECHR but they must then show they will be exposed to a real risk of being subjected to a flagrant denial of justice (*Kaderli v Turkey* [2022] EWHC 13 (Admin) at [59]–[61]).

In *Konczos v Law Court in Gyor (Hungary)* [2021] EWHC 3287 (Admin), the requested person had been discharged in relation to an EAW and then exercised his right to a retrial in the requesting territory after a second EAW had been issued but before it had been certified by the UK.

## PRIMA FACIE CASE

In *Government of India v Singh* [2021] EWHC 3333 (Admin), the Divisional Court held that the statements of two co-accused of the requested person were not admissible in considering whether there was a prima facie case as they were not competent or compellable witnesses.    **D31.32**

## HUMAN RIGHTS AND PROPORTIONALITY

In *Government of the USA v Assange* [2021] EWHC 3313 (Admin), [2022] 4 WLR 11, the Divisional Court considered the use of assurances and when the court should afford a requesting territory the opportunity to offer assurances (see also *Sula v Public Prosecutor of the Thessaloniki Court of Appeal, Greece* [2022] EWHC 230 (Admin) at [34]–[41]).    **D31.33**

In *Wozniak v District Court in Gniezno (Poland)* [2021] EWHC 2557 (Admin), the Administrative Court considered whether the developments concerning the rule of law in Poland meant that there was a real risk on account of systemic or generalised deficiencies that any trial would not be before an independent tribunal, which would be a flagrant violation of Article 6. The Court found that there was a real risk generally but held it then needed to carry out a specific and precise assessment of each requested person's case. The Court found it was not required to make inquiries of the requesting territory in order to carry out this assessment and that there was no evidence of a real risk for each of the requested persons.    **D31.34**

In *Amnott v Lord Advocate* [2022] HCJAC 6, the High Court of Justiciary considered whether a potential mandatory life sentence, without parole, for a lesser crime than murder constitutes a breach of Article 3 because it is grossly disproportionate and, in any event, not capable of being reduced.

In *Marosan v Court of Cluj-Napoca (Romania)* [2021] EWHC 3098 (Admin), [2022] 1 WLR 1759, the Administrative Court considered the position if a requested person had been detained both due to a Part 1 warrant and a UK criminal investigation but the period of detention had not been treated as 'time served' for any UK criminal sentence. The Court considered that it should treat this period as qualifying remand which would be deductible under Article 26 of the EAW Framework Decision when considering Article 8 of the ECHR and the proportionality of extradition.    **D31.35**

The Administrative Court considered the impact that the UK leaving the EU may have in relation to Article 8 in *Vajdik v Bratislava District Court (Slovakia)* [2022] EWHC 55 (Admin).

## SECRETARY OF STATE

The time permitted for the Secretary of State to make a decision on whether to order the requested person's extradition to a Part 2 territory can be extended by the court under s. 99(4) of the 2003 Act. When considering an application for an extension, the judge must decide, as the primary decision-maker, whether sufficient reason has been provided for the extension (*R (Lynch) v Westminster Magistrates' Court* [2022] EWHC 142 (Admin)).    **D31.40**

D

Part D Procedure

## APPEALS

### Notice of Application for Leave to Appeal

**D31.42**  In *Public Prosecutor's Office of the Athens Court of Appeal v O'Connor* [2022] UKSC 4, [2022] 1 WLR 903, the Supreme Court considered that if the requested person had done everything reasonably possible to ensure that notice of an application for leave to appeal was given as soon as it could be given then the High Court should entertain the application which had been given after the expiry of the permitted period due to the failings of the person's legal representative.

# SUPPLEMENT TO PART E
# SENTENCING

# Section E1　Sentencing: General Provisions

## SENTENCING GUIDELINES

As to the approach to be taken by a judge when passing sentence for an offence where the **E1.5** maximum sentence has recently been increased, but where the relevant Sentencing Council guideline has not yet been adjusted accordingly, including the requirement to depart from the guideline where appropriate, see *Nugent* [2021] EWCA Crim 1535, at **E13.3** and **B10.99** in this supplement.

In *Fleming* [2022] EWCA Crim 250, the Solicitor-General referred an extended sentence of 18 years including a 14-year custodial element imposed upon D, who had pleaded guilty to an offence under the OAPA 1861, s. 18, as being unduly lenient. D had been in a violent and coercive relationship with V, who had learning and physical disabilities and was extremely vulnerable. D committed a prolonged assault upon V causing her very serious and irreversible injury which would necessitate her receiving individual personal care for the rest of her life. The Court noted that the particular guideline specified an offence range of two to 16 years, but permitted (a) certain extreme culpability factors in a category A1 offence to attract a sentence above the category range, and (b) aggravating features in the case to justify a move above the category range. The Court held that, considered in the round, the overall seriousness of the case was such that the proper sentence before credit for plea was significantly above the A1 category range, and hence above the offence range. The Court made it clear that this approach was permitted by the terms of the guideline, and was therefore *not* a departure from the guideline. The extended sentence was increased to 21½, including a custodial term of 17½ years.

## REQUIRED REDUCTIONS IN SENTENCE

### Reduction in Sentence for Guilty Plea

The Court of Appeal in *Dale* [2022] EWCA Crim 207 clarified the position that an **E1.9** unequivocal indication can be made at the first stage of proceedings (entitling D to full credit for a plea of guilty) even though D indicates that the guilty plea is on a basis, and whether or not the details of that basis of plea are made available in the magistrates' court. Of course, if there is a subsequent *Newton* hearing, and D's version of the facts is not accepted, some of the reduction will be lost: see the Sentencing Council's guideline, *Reduction in Sentence for a Guilty Plea* (see **SG5-1**), para. F2.

In *Paddon* [2021] EWCA Crim 1485, D pleaded guilty to robbery two days after his second PTPH, and was accorded a 25 per cent reduction for his plea. On appeal D argued that he should have been accorded full credit because he entered a guilty plea as soon as the contents of a psychiatric report ordered on his behalf were made available to his legal advisers. D relied upon para. F1 of the guideline. The Court of Appeal rejected D's argument. It was noted that there was no issue here of fitness to plead such that a report was necessary before proper legal advice could be given. The suggested mental health issues arose from duress, but those were circumstances in which legal advice could have been given without waiting for the report. The decision not to accord full credit was upheld.

### Reduction in Sentence for Assistance by Offender

It was held by the Court of Appeal in *T* [2021] EWCA Crim 1474 that a judge must look at all **E1.11** the factors in the round when considering the extent of any reduction in sentence for information provided to the authorities. It was legitimate to consider the extent of any financial reward received by D, but unless that reward had been exceptionally generous, that factor should play only a small, if any, part in the judge's calculation of the appropriate discount.

## AGGRAVATING FACTORS

### Offence Committed on Bail

E1.14 It has been held to be an aggravating factor if D, being sentenced for two offences, committed the second offence (an aggravated vehicle-taking) after receiving a postal requisition in respect of the first offence (causing death by dangerous driving) (*Shaw* [2021] EWCA Crim 685, [2022] 1 Cr App R (S) 5 (33)). The Court of Appeal said there was no reason why these circumstances should be treated any differently from offending on bail.

## DUTY TO GIVE REASONS FOR, AND EXPLAIN EFFECT OF, SENTENCE

E1.24 For another example of a case where the sentencing remarks of the judge were so short as to be 'wholly inadequate' and failed to provide proper reasoning to support the sentence, see *Goodman* [2021] EWCA Crim 1466. The sentence was not located within the applicable guideline, and no explanation had been given for adjustments made for aggravating or mitigating factors, or reduction for plea. The Court of Appeal observed that these failings in themselves would not result in an appeal being successful — the issue was whether the sentence imposed was manifestly excessive.

---

# Section E13    Custodial Sentences: General Provisions

## MAXIMUM CUSTODIAL SENTENCES

### Changes to Maximum Sentences

E13.3 In *Nugent* [2021] EWCA Crim 1535, the Court of Appeal considered an application by the Solicitor-General in relation to D, who was sentenced as an offender of 'particular concern', following his guilty pleas to five offences of dissemination of terrorist publications and 13 offences of possession of information likely to be useful for terrorist purposes, to a sentence of 54 months, comprising a custodial term of 42 months and a one-year extended licence. The maximum sentences for the relevant offences had been increased (from seven to 15 years, and from ten to 15 years respectively) by the C-TBSA 2019, but at the time of sentencing the applicable Sentencing Council guideline on *Terrorism Offences* had not yet been adjusted to reflect those changes. Edis LJ said (at [24]) that:

> … where … a maximum sentence has been very substantially changed and the guideline has yet to be updated, the sentencing court should reflect that fact, where necessary, by departing from the guideline in the interests of justice and imposing a sentence in the more serious cases which reflects that change. This will involve applying the structured process of the guideline and considering in particular the factors referred to in it. It will not, however, involve being constrained by the sentence ranges or starting points established under the previous maximum penalty.

The Court increased the special custodial sentence to one of six years, with a custodial term of five years and a one-year extended licence.

### Limits on Imprisonment: Magistrates' Courts and the Crown Court when Limited to Magistrates' Courts' Powers

E13.5 In *Jex* [2021] EWCA Crim 1708, the Court of Appeal held that the clear meaning of the MCA 1980, s. 133, was that where the Crown Court was dealing on committal with two or more offences triable either way plus one or more summary offences, the total sentence could exceed six months but must not exceed 12 months. Crucially, however, it did not matter how the individual sentences were made up so that, for example, a ten-month sentence comprising a total of nine months in respect of the summary offences plus a total of one month in respect of two either-way offences, was within the terms of the section.

**Time Remanded in Custody to Count as Time Served**

E13.15 **Extradited Prisoners**    The Supreme Court in *R (Shields-McKinley) v Secretary of State for Justice* [2021] 1 WLR 4222 denied permission to appeal from the decision of the Court of Appeal (Civil Division) in that case ([2019] EWCA Civ 1954, [2020] QB 521).

# Section E14    Suspended Sentences

## POWER TO IMPOSE SUSPENDED SENTENCES

E14.3 In the list of factors indicating that it may be appropriate to suspend a custodial sentence, for 'realistic prospect of conviction' read 'realistic prospect of rehabilitation'.

# Section E15    Custodial Sentences: Detention and Custody of Offenders under 18

## DETERMINING THE AGE OF THE OFFENDER

E15.2 In *Mohammed* [2021] EWCA Crim 1375, the Court of Appeal reaffirmed the main principles applicable where the assessment of age is required (see also **D24.66** in this supplement). The Court said that this issue should not be approached as if it were a trial, and indeed can be determined informally, provided that minimum standards of inquiry and fairness are adhered to. Except in clear cases age cannot be determined on appearance alone. The decision-maker must seek out the background of the person concerned, including family circumstances and history. It is for the parties to carry out the appropriate investigations. If there is reason to doubt the applicant's account the decision-maker will have to test and assess credibility, in accordance with the decision in *R (B) v Merton London Borough Council* [2003] EWHC 1689 (Admin), [2003] 4 All ER 280, which remains the leading case in this area. Where there is real doubt the proper course is to direct that an age assessment is carried out by the local authority.

# Section E16    Life Sentences, Extended Sentences, Serious Terrorism Sentences and Custodial Sentences for Certain Offenders of 'Particular Concern'

## DISCRETIONARY LIFE SENTENCE OR CUSTODY FOR LIFE FOR OFFENCE NOT LISTED IN SCHEDULE 19

E16.7 The Court of Appeal confirmed in *Ahmed* [2021] EWCA Crim 1786 that the common-law discretionary life sentence of imprisonment remains available to a sentencing court, but is a sentence of last resort and should be used only in a rare case. The relevant test remains that set out in *Ali (Muzaffer)* [2019] EWCA Crim 856, [2019] 2 Cr App R (S) 43 (333) (in the main work). On the particular facts of *Ahmed*, a determined and persistent case of perverting the course of justice, the life sentence imposed by the judge had not been justified, and a determinate sentence of ten years was substituted.

## EFFECT OF LIFE SENTENCE: MINIMUM TERM OR WHOLE LIFE ORDER

**Section 323(2)(b)**

E16.34 In *Collins* [2021] EWCA Crim 1074, [2022] 1 Cr App R (S) 23 (205), D was convicted after trial of six offences including manslaughter and two dwelling-house burglaries. The judge

happened here. However, the Crown Court may decline to make a determination under section 10A at that stage, (see section 10A(1)) which would leave it to be dealt with at the enforcement stage, and an Enforcement Receiver may be appointed to litigate the issue. In the present case, no party sought the deferral of the matter to enforcement.

It was said by the Court of Appeal in *Ruto* [2021] EWCA Crim 1669 (at [17]–[18]) that the principle 'to be borne firmly in mind' by a judge when considering a disputed issue under the POCA 2002, s. 10A, is found in *Forte* [2020] EWCA Crim 1455 (at [12]):

> The lack of a prescriptive procedural structure means that judges dealing with the determination of the property rights of non-parties to confiscation proceedings under s10A of the Act will be careful to ensure that the procedures adopted are fair and enable an accurate determination of the issue. Article 6 of the EHCR applies to protect the fair trial rights of such people.

This principle extends beyond procedural fairness (per Edis LJ in *Ruto* at [18]):

> The court must also clearly be careful to apply the relevant law properly and to explain any decision to deprive a third party of property which he or she claims to own clearly. This does not mean that it is necessary in every case to give a long and complex ruling. It is not necessary to mention every piece of evidence or every point which has been argued. It is however necessary to make clear findings of fact and to explain why they were made.

### Stage Five — Proportionality

E19.64  **Tainted Gifts and Proportionality**   See *Waring* [2021] EWCA Crim 1369 in which *Hayes* [2018] EWCA Crim 682, [2018] 2 Cr App R (S) 27 (239) at [25] and *Morrison* [2019] EWCA Crim 351, [2019] 2 Cr App R (S) 25 (188) (among other cases) are cited. The Court of Appeal accepted that the category of cases that are disproportionate is not closed but the tainted gift regime 'is a severe one designed to encourage or coerce those who dissipate the proceeds of crime into making good the losses thereby caused' (per Simler LJ (at [31]).

## ENFORCEMENT, RECONSIDERATION AND APPEALS

### Enforcement

E19.74  **Default Term**   In *Collins v DPP* [2021] EWHC 634 (Admin), [2021] 1 WLR 3391, the Divisional Court rejected the argument that in a case where confiscation orders have been made in respect of a benefit jointly obtained by two or more defendants, but with a direction that the orders are not to be enforced to the extent that a sum has been recovered by way of satisfaction of another confiscation order made in relation to the same joint benefit (see *Ahmad* [2014] UKSC 36, [2015] AC 299), credit should be given to each defendant for time served in default of payment by any of his or her accomplices. Proportionality does not require the default term of imprisonment to be, effectively, shared. Since proportionality is defined in *Andrewes* [2020] EWCA Crim 1055 as being proportionate to the statutory purpose of the scheme of the POCA 2002, it cannot be relied upon to support an approach which would defeat that purpose.

### Appeals

E19.83  It was held in *Barnet London Borough Council v Kamyab (No. 3)* [2021] EWCA Crim 1209, [2022] 1 WLR 57 that although a right of appeal is given to a prosecutor by the POCA 2002, s. 31(4) and (5)(a) against an order in relation to D's interest in property under s. 10A of the Act (and a costs power is specifically conferred by s. 89(4) on any such appeal), no such power is conferred in relation to prosecution appeals under s. 31(1) or (2) of the Act.

# Section E21    Exclusions and Disqualifications

## SEXUAL HARM PREVENTION ORDERS

### Nature of Order

The Court of Appeal in *Hanson* [2021] EWCA Crim 1008, [2022] 1 Cr App R (S) 28 (250)  **E21.24**
upheld a SHPO lasting for 15 years in the case of a 27-year-old primary schoolteacher of
previous good character who pleaded guilty to sexual activity with a child and meeting a child
following sexual grooming. He met the child (aged 14) and had sexual intercourse with her. The
Court said that although other judges might have imposed a shorter order, SHPOs were dealing
with risk, the eventuation of which was necessarily unpredictable, and a cautious approach was
justified on the facts of the case.

## RESTRAINING ORDERS

### Restraining Order on Acquittal

In *Khan* [2021] EWCA Crim 1526, the CPS decided to offer no evidence against D but applied  **E21.33**
for a restraining order to be imposed following his acquittal. On the day of the hearing the
complainant was not present and D (who was to represent himself) did not arrive on time. The
judge adjourned for a short time but then proceeded in D's absence to hear the prosecution
case. D arrived two and a half hours late, shortly after the judge had imposed a restraining order
for ten years under the Protection from Harassment Act 1997, s. 5A. The restraining order was
quashed on appeal, the Court of Appeal finding that the judge had not assessed all relevant
factors before deciding to proceed in D's absence. D had not received a fair trial because he did
not hear the prosecution evidence, had no opportunity to cross-examine the police officer
witness, and was unable to offer his own evidence. The Court further noted that, while there
was no statutory power to remit the matter back to the Crown Court, it was open to the
prosecution to make a fresh application to that court under s. 5A.

# Section E23    Notification Requirements

## NOTIFICATION REQUIREMENTS UNDER THE SEXUAL
## OFFENCES ACT 2003

In *Smith (Kyle Damian)* [2021] EWCA Crim 716, the Court of Appeal held that the  **E23.1**
notification requirement — that D must provide to the police his name and any aliases —
includes the use of different names in different contexts, particularly any username, pseudonym
or 'handle' which D used on a social media platform. Failure to notify the police of such name
or names was a breach of the notification requirements under the Act.

# SUPPLEMENT TO PART F
# EVIDENCE

# Section F1    General Principles of Evidence in Criminal Cases

## JUDICIAL NOTICE

### Introduction

For a further example of jurors making proper use of their general or everyday knowledge, see    **F1.4**
also *STC Ltd* [2021] EWCA Crim 1237, [2022] 1 Cr App R 10 (150), where it was held that
on the question whether marketing material suggested that a Rambo knife was suitable for use
in causing injury, for the purposes of the Knives Act 1997, ss. 1 and 2, jurors were entitled to
use their own general knowledge of the prevalence of such knives being carried by street gangs
in London.

## CIRCUMSTANTIAL EVIDENCE

### Lies

**Situations where a *Lucas* Direction is Unnecessary**    Best practice suggests that where issues    **F1.30**
relating to both lies and a failure to mention facts in interview are combined, a tailored
direction is likely to assist the jury. However, giving both the conventional directions will not
necessarily render a conviction unsafe (*Dabycharun* [2021] EWCA Crim 1923).

## QUESTIONS OF LAW AND FACT

### In a Trial on Indictment: General Principles

**Construction of Words**    'Pyrotechnic effect' in the Explosives Act 1875, s. 3, is an expression    **F1.38**
on which a jury needs to be given assistance; it is not an ordinary expression on which jurors can
make up their own minds (*Margelis* [2021] EWCA Crim 1215, [2022] QB 148 at [51]).

---

# Section F2    Evidence Unlawfully, Improperly or Unfairly Obtained and the Discretion to Exclude Evidence

## PACE 1984, s. 78

### Scope for Exclusion Wider Than at Common Law

The mere fact that evidence of D's conduct might have a prejudicial effect is not a reason to    **F2.9**
exclude it under the PACE 1984, s. 78: see *Hunter* [2021] EWCA Crim 1785, [2022] 1 Cr App
R 13 (188), a case of fraudulent trading, in relation to evidence of 'ticket touting' for two highly
emotive events, a concert in memory of those killed in a terror bombing and a teenage cancer
trust concert.

### Application to Evidence Obtained Unlawfully, Improperly or Unfairly

**Prosecutions Founded on Entrapment**    Proceedings should not be stayed as an abuse of the    **F2.17**
court's process where an undercover officer has done nothing more than present D with an
unexceptional opportunity to commit a crime. *Kureembokus* [2021] EWCA Crim 828 provides
an illustration. D was charged, under the SOA 2003, s. 14, with arranging an act involving
penetrative sexual activity with a child under 16. An officer had used the Grindr app, posing as
a schoolboy under 16. Following a conversation with D, they used WhatsApp to arrange to
meet. Asked what he wanted to do, D said that he wanted to engage in oral and anal sex.

---

## Section F3    Burden and Standard of Proof and Presumptions

### STANDARD OF PROOF

**Usual Direction where Legal Burden on Prosecution**

F3.49    Further to *Broughton* [2020] EWCA Crim 1093, [2021] 1 Cr App R 3 (25), see also *Wood Treatment Ltd* [2021] EWCA Crim 618, where the case had been properly withdrawn from the jury on the basis that the jury would not have been able to be sure of guilt, because they would not have been able to rule out a realistic possibility consistent with innocence (see also **B1.74** in this supplement).

## Section F7    Cross-examination and Re-examination

### RULES GOVERNING CONDUCT OF CROSS-EXAMINATION

**Power of Judge to Impose Time-limits and Limit Cross-examination**

F7.20    For a further example of a limitation on the time given for cross-examination that had not resulted in any unfairness, see *Lally* [2021] EWCA Crim 1372.

### PROTECTION OF COMPLAINANTS IN PROCEEDINGS FOR SEXUAL OFFENCES

**Previous False Complaints**

F7.30    An application under both the YJCEA 1999, s. 41, and the CJA 2003, s. 100, may also be required in cases not involving previous false complaints (*GR* [2020] EWCA Crim 1742 at [51]).

F7.31    In *TG* [2020] EWCA Crim 939, it was held that there was no evidential basis for asserting that previous statements made by the complainant against her husband were untrue. She had not pursued her allegations, but had good reason for not doing so. Her husband had denied the allegations, but this did not mean that they were false. An officer was of the view, based on recollection alone, that there were major discrepancies in the complainant's account, but this was insufficient — what was required were objective discrepancies so stark as to indicate invention.

**Section 41(3) and (4): Evidence or a Question Relating to a Relevant Issue**

F7.34    In *GR* [2020] EWCA Crim 1742, B, one of the two complainants, alleged that A, the other complainant, had behaved in a sexual way towards him. A denied the behaviour and said that B had admitted to fabrication of the allegations. It was held that the principal purpose of seeking to admit this evidence was to undermine the credibility of both A and B and therefore s. 41(4) was clearly engaged.

**Section 41 and the Right to a Fair Trial**

F7.45    **Sexual Behaviour with Third Parties**    Further to the dictum of Laws LJ in *White* [2004] EWCA Crim 946, see also *Costanzo* [2021] EWCA Crim 615 at **F7.46** in this supplement.

**Section 41(5): Evidence or a Question Relating to Evidence Adduced by the Prosecution**

F7.46    In *Costanzo* [2021] EWCA Crim 615, the issue was whether sexual intercourse was consensual or the complainant lacked the capacity to consent. It was submitted that, in order to ensure a fair trial, the YJCEA 1999, s. 41(5), should be read down under the ECHR, Article 6, to admit evidence about the sexual behaviour of the complainant with men other than D. The Court of Appeal impliedly rejected this submission. It held that the subsection had no application to the case because, having regard to its terms, the evidence in question neither 'rebutted' nor 'explained' the evidence advanced by the prosecution.

# Section F11    Opinion Evidence

## EXPERT OPINION EVIDENCE

### Competence of Expert Witnesses

An individual does not become competent to give expert evidence simply because he or she is   **F11.4**
employed by a particular organisation. Thus in *Rogers v Hoyle* [2014] EWCA Civ 257, [2015]
QB 265 (see **F12.24**), the report relating to a plane crash was not admissible simply on the basis
that it was prepared by the Department of Transport's Air Investigation Branch, but because
that organisation uses experts in such fields as aeronautical engineering and wreckage analysis
(*AAD* [2022] EWCA Crim 106 at [96]–[99]).

In *AAD* [2022] EWCA Crim 106, the Court of Appeal gave the following guidance relating to   **F11.5**
cases involving victims of trafficking:

(1)   Earlier decisions conclusively confirm that a conclusive grounds decision by the Home
      Office Single Competent Authority as to whether D is a victim of human trafficking or
      modern slavery may be admissible on appeal, applying the test for fresh evidence in the
      Criminal Appeal Act 1968, s. 23.
(2)   As to the inadmissibility of such decisions at trial, and further to *Brecani* [2021] EWCA
      Crim 731, [2021] 2 Cr App R 12 (215), a trafficking expert may not express a view as to
      the plausibility and consistency of D's account or his or her vulnerability. Jurors are well
      placed to form their own conclusions on these issues. It does not matter that they lack
      first-hand experience of the circumstances of the offence. This applies to all criminal trials.
      Few jurors, for example, will have been subjected to duress leading to their participation in
      an armed robbery or will have found themselves caught up in a city centre riot. This does
      not require a witness to express a view whether D's account is consistent with how someone
      would behave if placed under such duress or caught up in such a riot.
(3)   However, in trafficking cases there may be discrete issues that require explanation by way
      of expert evidence, for example as to D's psychiatric or psychological state or the detailed
      mores of people-trafficking gangs operating in countries outside the court's own knowl-
      edge or experience. As to the former, the expert may express a view as to the detail and
      content of D's account as a necessary step to reaching a diagnosis; but as to the latter, no
      commentary by the expert is required as to the consistency of D's account.
(4)   Whether such expert evidence should be admitted at trial should be resolved by reference
      to the normal three-part test: (i) whether the evidence is relevant to a matter in issue; (ii)
      whether the witness is competent to give expert opinion evidence; and (iii) whether the
      information is outside the court's own knowledge and experience.

---

# Section F13    Character Evidence: Evidence of Bad Character of Accused

## EVIDENCE OF BAD CHARACTER UNDER THE CRIMINAL JUSTICE ACT 2003

### Bad Character

**'Has To Do With' Alleged Facts**    *Ditta* [2016] EWCA Crim 8, *Okokono* [2014] EWCA Crim   **F13.10**
2521 and *Lunkulu* [2015] EWCA Crim 1350 were considered in *Stanton* [2021] EWCA Crim
1075. The prosecution case was that D's motive for a burglary in which a vulnerable elderly
householder was murdered was to feed his drug habit, and they adduced evidence that, at
around this time, D had ceased to be able to access funds belonging to another elderly man
towards whom he had demonstrated a propensity to extortion and violence. The Court of
Appeal accepted that evidence of recent facts establishing a motive fell within the CJA 2003,
s. 98(a), as evidence having to do with the facts of the offence, and did not therefore require

justification under the gateways of s. 101. It is submitted that the case is one where the similarity of the facts establishing the motive were so striking that it would have been prudent, as commended in the *Crown Court Compendium*, ch. 12-1, to have had regard to the statutory safeguards attaching to the admission of evidence under s. 101. Had such safeguards been applied, however, the Court of Appeal is clear that the evidence would have been admissible under s. 101(1)(d).

It was not accepted that the trial judge should have excluded the evidence because it was prejudicial and 'scandalous'; the Court commented that such an argument has more force when the character evidence reveals conduct that is more reprehensible than the crime charged than when the charge is one of murder.

Section 98 was also held to have been engaged in *Oloyowang* [2021] EWCA Crim 1412. D was on trial for dangerous driving by speeding away from police officers attempting to stop his car. He denied that the driving was dangerous and claimed to be unaware that the men trying to stop him were police officers. Evidence was admitted that the context for the stop was the officers' suspicion that a drug deal was being conducted in the car. The Court of Appeal considered that the evidence fell within s. 98(a) as having to do with the alleged facts of the offence charged, and that the trial judge had rightly rejected a submission that to admit the evidence was unfair under the PACE 1984, s. 78.

The statement in *Sule* [2012] EWCA Crim 1130, [2013] 1 Cr App R 3 (42) that it would be 'irrational' to introduce a strict temporal requirement in respect of evidence relied upon to prove motive was applied in *Abdi* [2022] EWCA Crim 315, in which the prosecution relied on evidence that D had suffered gunshot wounds some months before and after the murder with which he was charged. The former was said to suggest D's likely motive of revenge linked to gang activity, and the latter that D himself was the target of revenge for the murder. The fact that D had not wanted to involve the police was also said to suggest that he had his own ways of exacting revenge (see, as to the gang aspects, **F13.49** in this supplement).

In *AAM* [2021] EWCA Crim 1720, the Court of Appeal considered the appropriateness of a specific direction against the misuse of evidence of reprehensible behaviour admitted by agreement under the CJA 2003, s. 98(a). D was charged with the rape of his wife, and the evidence in question related to his coercive and controlling behaviour. While the court endorsed the general approach to evidence of coercive control in *MA* [2019] EWCA Crim 178, and agreed that neither the fact that all the evidence was admitted under s. 98(a) nor the fact that it was admitted by agreement rendered a direction unnecessary; the purpose of the direction suggested in *MA* was to ensure that the jury did not use the particular evidence in an improper way. While the direction should still have been given, the only live issues were consent and reasonable belief in consent, to both of which the evidence was clearly relevant, and the judge's remaining directions were sufficient to ensure that the jury would have appreciated its significance and would not have relied on the evidence of coercive control unless they were sure about it. The conviction was therefore safe.

In *Spraggon* [2022] EWCA Crim 128, D was charged with sexual offences against boys in an orphanage where he had worked. Another man, M, had previously pleaded guilty to assaults some of which had taken place in a dormitory in which the two men were said by one witness to have 'divvied up' the boys. The trial judge refused to admit M's plea at D's trial, but admitted the account of the witness who had since died (see, as to the hearsay implications, **F17.4** in this supplement). The Court of Appeal held that the deceased witness's evidence 'had to do with' the facts of D's alleged offence, given that his actions were inextricably linked with those of M.

## EXPLANATORY EVIDENCE

### Introduction

**F13.28**   In *Dabycharun* [2021] EWCA Crim 1923, the Court of Appeal held that evidence of the circumstances in which D had been disqualified from driving were correctly admitted as explanatory evidence, in order to prevent the jury speculating about them, in a case where D was said to have driven his car at V and then referenced his disqualification in order to explain why he had initially falsely claimed not to have been driving. This would seem to fall short of the statutory requirement that other evidence in the case was 'impossible or difficult' to understand without it. The test was, it is submitted, correctly applied in *Ibrahim* [2021] EWCA Crim 1935, decided under the CJA 2003, s. 100, where evidence of the association of a non-defendant with a gang was said not to be explanatory. It lent considerable colour to his presence at the hospital where another gang member was being treated, and made it more likely that he would have shared knowledge of a planned revenge attack with his brother, the defendant, but it could not be described as evidence without which the jury would have had difficulty in understanding the case against the brother. (The evidence was held admissible on other grounds: see F.15.17 in this supplement.)

## EVIDENCE OF BAD CHARACTER ADDUCED BY PROSECUTION TO PROVE GUILT OR UNTRUTHFULNESS

### Criminal Justice Act 2003: Admissibility under s. 101(1)(d)

**Propensity and Other Evidence of Bad Character**    In *Everson* [2021] EWCA Crim 1178, D      **F13.38** was tried for murder of a man who had been killed by a shotgun. The prosecution case was based on circumstantial evidence, and reliance was placed on D's previous convictions for possession of firearms solely in order to undermine his claim that he had owned a shotgun only briefly and had disposed of it before the murder. On appeal it was contended that the trial judge should have specifically directed the jury not to treat the convictions as demonstrating a propensity to use firearms. However the judge's direction had correctly identified and made clear the limited purpose for which the jury could legitimately use the evidence, and it could not have assisted D for the judge to add that the jury could not use it for a different purpose, which no one had suggested.

**Propensity and Fairness**    The requirement in *Hanson* [2005] EWCA Crim 824, [2005] 1      **F13.41** WLR 3169 that evidence of bad character should not be used to bolster a weak case was considered in *Belhaj-Farhat* [2022] EWCA Crim 115 in the context of DNA evidence. Immediately following a burglary the occupier found a cigarette butt propped against the internal frame of the front door. DNA evidence linked the butt to D, who had no legitimate connection with the premises or the occupants. This was the only evidence apart from the evidence of D's previous convictions for burglaries. Applying *Tsekiri* [2017] EWCA Crim 40, [2017] 1 Cr App R 32 (479) (see **F19.31** in the main work) the Court of Appeal noted that the DNA match was strong, D was the sole contributor, and the circumstances in which the cigarette butt was found all formed part of the framework within which the trial judge had to consider the strength of the case. The case was not weak and the bad character evidence was rightly admitted.

### Identifying the Accused by Evidence of Bad Character under the Criminal Justice Act 2003, s. 101(1)(d)

The principles under which evidence of gang membership or affiliation can be used to link D      **F13.49** to a specific offence were applied in *Abdi* [2022] EWCA Crim 315. The case concerned an established rivalry between two local gangs, and there was evidence that the murder with which D was charged was committed by one gang and that V was a member of the other. There was one item of evidence that directly linked the two men, where D was pictured with another man who was wearing a jacket that had been taken from V. The remaining evidence consisted of D's appearance in videos making reference in drill or rap lyrics to shooting and stabbing, and of his postings linked to such material. The Court of Appeal accepted that such evidence was not conclusive of gang membership, but held that a jury was entitled to consider it, if appropriately directed to approach it with caution.

## EVIDENCE OF BAD CHARACTER ADDUCED BY A CO-ACCUSED

### Criminal Justice Act 2003: Evidence of Bad Character Going to Matter in Issue Between Co-accused

F13.68    **Substantial Probative Value**    In *Pallas* [2021] EWCA Crim 684, D1 and D2 were charged with murder and each accused the other of being responsible for stabbing V. Evidence was adduced on behalf of D2 that D1, while on remand for the murder, had stabbed a fellow prisoner in the eye. Although the evidence was disputed, if accepted it was of undoubted probative value in relation to the central issue at trial and was rightly admitted.

## EVIDENCE OF BAD CHARACTER TO CORRECT FALSE IMPRESSION OR COUNTER ATTACK ON ANOTHER'S CHARACTER

### 'Attack on Another Person's Character'

F13.90    **Discretion**    *Clarke* [2011] EWCA Crim 939 was further considered in *Colecozy-Rogers* [2021] EWCA Crim 1111. D was permitted, under the CJA 2003, s. 100 (see **F15** in the main work), to adduce evidence of V's violent, aggressive and volatile disposition to support D's defences of accident, self-defence and the lack of intent to cause serious injury. In response the prosecution relied, under the CJA 2003, s. 101(1)(g), on D's convictions for robbery. The Court of Appeal rejected a submission that the trial judge should have exercised discretion to exclude these convictions, approving a passage from *Clarke* where it was said that:

> Although the character is adduced initially for the purpose of allowing the jury to determine whether the particular attack is true, it will inevitably affect the jury's assessment of a defendant's credibility as a whole. The authorities demonstrate that under paragraph (g) all convictions are potentially relevant to assist the jury to assess the character of the accused, and it is not necessary, or at least not generally so, for detailed facts about the nature and circumstances of those convictions to be put before the jury.

The Court further approved the conventional direction given to the jury, that they were entitled to know the character of the person who alleged that the deceased had been the aggressor, and could decide whether the evidence helped in deciding whether D was telling the truth. The trial judge might have gone further in directing the jury not to treat the evidence as showing D's propensity to violence or untruthfulness, but there was no requirement to do so, and such a direction had not been suggested at trial.

A further submission, that the purpose of s. 101(1)(g) was limited to cases where the jury were required to decide between the testimony of an accused and a prosecution witness, was rejected. *Hearne* [2009] EWCA Crim 103 was not authority for such a rule. The purpose of gateway (g) is to show that the accused's evidence is not worthy of belief, whether the person whose character has been attacked gives evidence or not.

See also to the same effect, approving the decision in *Clarke*, *Hussain* [2021] EWCA Crim 870.

# Section F15    Character Evidence: Evidence of Bad Character of Persons Other than the Accused

## CRIMINAL JUSTICE ACT 2003, s.100: PURPOSE AND RELATIONSHIP WITH OTHER EVIDENTIARY RULES

### Relationship with other Evidential Rules

F15.5    Nothing in s. 100, or in the authorities, requires an accused person to meet the criminal standard of proof of the propensity of a person whose character is adduced under s. 100. In

*Labinjo-Halcrow* [2020] EWCA Crim 951, D claimed to have no recollection of killing V, but put forward the defence that she would have been acting in self-defence based on V's previous violence towards her. The jury were incorrectly directed that it was for D to make them 'sure' of V's previous misconduct. Authorities such as *Mitchell* [2016] UKSC 55, [2017] AC 571 (see F13.4 in the main work), requiring the prosecution to prove propensity to the criminal standard, have no application to evidence adduced on behalf of the defence.

## CRIMINAL JUSTICE ACT 2003, s.100: GATEWAYS TO ADMISSIBILITY

### Evidence of Substantial Probative Value in Relation to Matter in Issue of Substantial Importance

**Substantial Probative Value in Relation to Issues Other than Credibility**    In *Ibrahim* [2021]    **F15.17**
EWCA Crim 1935, D was convicted as a secondary party to the murder of a gang member killed in a revenge attack by a rival gang. D claimed to be an innocent passenger in the car that had hunted V down, and to have had no knowledge of the impending attack or the principal's intentions towards V. This was rebutted by evidence that D's brother H was a member of the gang responsible for the attack, and that he had a close association with one of the attackers, B. H had rushed to see B in hospital when B had been attacked by the other gang, and the evidence of his affiliation was held to have been rightly admitted to support the prosecution case that D would have been aware of the plan, especially as D lived with H, and had been involved in drug-dealing for B.

**Substantial Probative Value in Relation to Credibility**    In *Hussain* [2021] EWCA Crim 870,    **F15.18**
D's convictions for affray and causing grievous bodily harm with intent were quashed because evidence of the bad character of IS, a key prosecution witness, had been wrongly excluded. IS gave evidence that D had driven a car at IS's brother ES, causing him serious injury. There was a long-running feud between the extended families of IS and ES on the one hand, and D on the other. IS had a long record of offences including crimes of dishonesty that could not be described as minor, and other offences which linked him in a significant way to the family feud. The trial judge had limited the jury to a single relevant offence of perverting the course of justice, having taken the view that the other convictions could not be described as of 'substantial' probative value in light of the distracting satellite issues they would raise. The Court of Appeal considered that a significant number of the convictions were admissible under the CJA 2003, s. 100, as they were 'reasonably capable of materially assisting the jury in reaching a decision as to whether IS's evidence as to the identity of the driver of the car which severely injured his brother, as well as his account of his involvement in the feud, was worthy of belief'. The Court also noted that the judge had been hampered in the making of a difficult decision by a process of 'rolling disclosure' of the detail of IS's convictions.

**Substantial Probative Value of Previous Allegations and 'Satellite' Issues**    *Dizaei* [2013]    **F15.24**
EWCA Crim 88, [2013] 1 WLR 2257 and *Umo* [2020] EWCA Crim 284, [2021] 1 Cr App R 12 (240) were considered in *Bogdanovic* [2020] EWCA Crim 1229, where it was agreed that whether the evidential dispute is capable of resolution by the jury is an 'important factor' when considering an application under s. 100(1)(b). The same point was made in *GR* [2020] EWCA Crim 1742 (see **F7.34** in this supplement), where the conditions of s. 100 were not satisfied in relation to sexual allegations against his mother by B, one of two complainants, that his brother A, the other complainant, had behaved in a sexualised way towards B. There was a lack of clear evidence as to what A's response to the allegations was, and it was unlikely that the jury would ever have been able to resolve what the Court described as a 'tangle'. None of the material went to the central question of the boys' relationship with GR, and it was concluded that it was not of substantial probative value. See to the same effect *TG* [2020] EWCA Crim 939.

## Section F17   Exceptions to the Rule against Hearsay (Excluding Confessions)

### INTRODUCTION

**Overview of the Criminal Justice Act 2003: Hearsay Exceptions and Additional Safeguards**

F17.4   **The Four Exceptions and Additional Safeguards for Hearsay Evidence**   The six steps for admitting hearsay evidence laid down in *Riat* [2012] EWCA Crim 1509, [2013] 1 All ER 349 were applied in *Spraggon* [2022] EWCA Crim 128, with the comment from the Court of Appeal (at [11]) that 'the guidance in *Riat* is comprehensive and is applied up and down the country in Crown Courts every week to the benefit of the criminal justice system'. In *Spraggon*, D was charged with sexual offences against boys in an orphanage where he had worked in the 1960s. At the time of the trial the three main witnesses were dead and their evidence was given as hearsay. This evidence was held to have been rightly admitted, and the defence argument characterised as an attempt to revive the 'sole or decisive' rule which does not apply in English law, as *Riat* makes clear. Further, in setting out scrupulously the evidence bearing on the reliability of D's accusers, the trial judge had shown himself to be acutely aware of the steps to be taken to achieve a fair and balanced trial by testing the hearsay evidence.

### HEARSAY EXCEPTIONS: (2) HEARSAY ADMISSIBLE IN THE INTERESTS OF JUSTICE

**Relationship with Other Hearsay Exceptions**

F17.37   In *Inglis* [2021] EWCA Crim 1545, the Court of Appeal considered that the prosecution should not have relied on the CJA 2003, s. 114(1)(d), in order to admit first-hand hearsay evidence of witness intimidation contained in a text message which had been sent to the witness by D's nephew C, allegedly on D's behalf. No reason had been suggested why the prosecution could not call C, but as C previously declined to provide a statement, the Court surmised that they preferred not to take the risk inherent in doing so. That was not an appropriate reason for seeking to admit the text as hearsay under s. 114(1)(d).

---

## Section F18   The Rule Against Hearsay: Confessions

### DISCRETIONARY EXCLUSION UNDER THE POLICE AND CRIMINAL EVIDENCE ACT 1984, s. 78

**Exclusion of Subsequent Confession**

F18.55   In *T* [2022] EWCA Crim 108, the Court of Appeal held that *Neill* [1994] Crim LR 222 was not authority for the proposition that the inadmissibility of a confession led to the conclusion that a subsequent confession was also inadmissible: on the contrary, it decided that everything depended on the circumstances. Further, even if a subsequent confession to the same offence was inadmissible, it did not follow that confessions to other offences would also be ruled out.

---

# Section F20    Inferences from Silence and the Non-production of Evidence

## OUT-OF-COURT SILENCE UNDER THE 1994 ACT

### No Conviction etc. Wholly or Mainly on Silence

In *Bonsu* [2020] EWCA Crim 660, the Court of Appeal held that there is no need, when **F20.9** directing a jury on the CJPO 1994, s. 34, to tell them that they must consider that there is a case to answer at trial before they can draw adverse inferences from D's failure to answer questions at interview. Nothing in *Condron* [1997] 1 WLR 827 is to the contrary, nor was it material that such a direction is given where D declines to testify at trial, as the two cases are distinguishable (see **F20.49** in the main work).

### Facts which Should Have Been Mentioned

In both *Cousins* [2021] EWCA Crim 1664, [2022] 1 Cr App R 11 (165) and *Harewood* [2021] **F20.17** EWCA Crim 1936, the Court of Appeal considered the question whether an adverse inference direction could properly be given where no evidence was presented of specific questions asked of D at interview. In *Harewood* the Court relied on *Green* [2019] EWCA Crim 411, [2019] 4 WLR 80 (see **F20.14** in the main work) to demonstrate that the issue was not what questions had been asked, but whether D could reasonably have been expected to mention a fact *when* questioned. There was no requirement that the unmentioned fact was one about which the accused had specifically been asked a question. In both cases, prepared statements had been relied on, and the defendants had declined to answer further questions for the remainder of the interviews. In *Harewood* it was said that the jury were entitled to infer that the lengthy questioning would have descended to matters of detail, and the more central the facts that D failed to mention to the issues at trial, the stronger the inference that he might have been expected to mention them. But the operation of the CJPO 1994, s. 34, is not limited to 'central' or 'important' facts: rather there is a sliding scale between irrelevant and peripheral matters and those of sufficient importance to be mentioned. In *Cousins*, the inference that the facts could have been expected to be mentioned was properly open to the jury where D's account at his trial for rape included a detailed account of events that D himself claimed had been withheld at interview on legal advice. The trial judge considered that evidence of the questions put to D would have been desirable but was not necessary on the facts, and the Court of Appeal agreed. Neither decision prevents D from arguing that lack of disclosure or failure to question on a particular matter was the reason for D's failure to mention it, but the plausibility of such an explanation depends on the facts.

### Direction as to Permissible Inferences

**Relationship with *Lucas* Direction on Lies**    *Rana* [2007] EWCA Crim 380, [2011] 2 Cr App **F20.26** R 3 (35) was considered in *Dabycharun* [2021] EWCA Crim 1923. D was tried for wounding with intent by driving his car at V. At interview he falsely claimed not to have been driving, but at trial gave an account of how he had collided accidentally with V. His explanation for both the lie and the withholding of the defence was that he wished to conceal that fact that he had driven while disqualified. The trial judge gave both a full *Lucas* direction and a direction under the CJPO 1994, s. 34. The Court of Appeal noted that, as indicated in *Rana*, 'best practice suggests that where issues relating to both lies and a failure to mention matters in interview are combined, a tailored direction which overlaps both the lies direction and the section 34 direction is likely to be of more assistance to the jury'. Nevertheless, the conviction was not rendered unsafe by the giving of both directions.

# Codes of Practice under the Police and Criminal Evidence Act 1984

## PACE CODE A

### REVISED CODE OF PRACTICE FOR THE EXERCISE BY:

### POLICE OFFICERS OF STATUTORY POWERS OF STOP AND SEARCH

### POLICE OFFICERS AND POLICE STAFF OF REQUIREMENTS TO RECORD PUBLIC ENCOUNTERS

**Commencement—Transitional Arrangements**

This code applies to any search by a police officer and the recording of public encounters taking place after 00.00 on 19 March 2015.

## 1.0 General

1.01 This code of practice must be readily available at all police stations for consultation by police officers, police staff, detained persons and members of the public.

1.02 The notes for guidance included are not provisions of this code, but are guidance to police officers and others about its application and interpretation. Provisions in the annexes to the code are provisions of this code.

1.03 This code governs the exercise by police officers of statutory powers to search a person or a vehicle without first making an arrest. The main stop and search powers to which this code applies are set out in Annex A, but that list should not be regarded as definitive (see *Note 1*). In addition, it covers requirements on police officers and police staff to record encounters not governed by statutory powers (see *paragraphs 2.11* and *4.12*). This code does not apply to:

(a) the powers of stop and search under:
  (i) the Aviation Security Act 1982, section 27(2), and
  (ii) the Police and Criminal Evidence Act 1984, section 6(1) (which relates specifically to powers of constables employed by statutory undertakers on the premises of the statutory undertakers);

(b) searches carried out for the purposes of examination under Schedule 7 to the Terrorism Act 2000 and to which the Code of Practice issued under paragraph 6 of Schedule 14 to the Terrorism Act 2000 applies.

(c) the powers to search persons and vehicles and to stop and search in specified locations to which the Code of Practice issued under section 47AB of the Terrorism Act 2000 applies.

## 1 Principles governing stop and search

1.1 Powers to stop and search must be used fairly, responsibly, with respect for people being searched and without unlawful discrimination. Under the Equality Act 2010, section 149, when police officers are carrying out their functions, they also have a duty to have due regard to the need to eliminate unlawful discrimination, harassment and victimisation, to advance equality of opportunity between people who share a relevant protected characteristic and people who do not share it, and to take steps to foster good relations between those persons. (See *Notes 1* and *1A.*) The Children Act 2004, section 11, also requires chief police officers and other specified persons and bodies to ensure that in the discharge of their functions they have regard to the need to safeguard and promote the welfare of all persons under the age of 18.

1.2 The intrusion on the liberty of the person stopped or searched must be brief and detention for the purposes of a search must take place at or near the location of the stop.

1.3 If these fundamental principles are not observed the use of powers to stop and search may be drawn into question. Failure to use the powers in the proper manner reduces their effectiveness. Stop and search can play an important role in the detection and prevention of crime, and using the powers fairly makes them more effective.

1.4　The primary purpose of stop and search powers is to enable officers to allay or confirm suspicions about individuals without exercising their power of arrest. Officers may be required to justify the use or authorisation of such powers, in relation both to individual searches and the overall pattern of their activity in this regard, to their supervisory officers or in court. Any misuse of the powers is likely to be harmful to policing and lead to mistrust of the police. Officers must also be able to explain their actions to the member of the public searched. The misuse of these powers can lead to disciplinary action (see *paragraphs 5.5* and *5.6*).

1.5　An officer must not search a person, even with his or her consent, where no power to search is applicable. Even where a person is prepared to submit to a search voluntarily, the person must not be searched unless the necessary legal power exists, and the search must be in accordance with the relevant power and the provisions of this Code. The only exception, where an officer does not require a specific power, applies to searches of persons entering sports grounds or other premises carried out with their consent given as a condition of entry.

1.6　Evidence obtained from a search to which this Code applies may be open to challenge if the provisions of this Code are not observed.

## 2　Types of stop and search powers

2.1　This code applies, subject to paragraph 1.03, to powers of stop and search as follows:

(a)　powers which require reasonable grounds for suspicion, before they may be exercised; that articles unlawfully obtained or possessed are being carried such as section 1 of PACE for stolen and prohibited articles and section 23 of the Misuse of Drugs Act 1971 for controlled drugs;

(b)　authorised under section 60 of the Criminal Justice and Public Order Act 1994, based upon a reasonable belief that incidents involving serious violence may take place or that people are carrying dangerous instruments or offensive weapons within any locality in the police area, or that it is expedient to use the powers to find such instruments or weapons that have been used in incidents of serious violence;

(c)　*Not used.*

(d)　the powers in Schedule 5 to the Terrorism Prevention and Investigation Measures (TPIM) Act 2011 to search an individual who has not been arrested, conferred by:

(i)　paragraph 6(2)(a) at the time of serving a TPIM notice;

(ii)　paragraph 8(2)(a) under a search warrant for compliance purposes; and

(iii)　paragraph 10 for public safety purposes.

See *paragraph 2.18A.*

(e)　powers to search a person who has not been arrested in the exercise of a power to search premises (see Code B *paragraph 2.4*).

*(a)　Stop and search powers requiring reasonable grounds for suspicion — explanation*

*General*

2.2　Reasonable grounds for suspicion is the legal test which a police officer must satisfy before they can stop and detain individuals or vehicles to search them under powers such as section 1 of PACE (to find stolen or prohibited articles) and section 23 of the Misuse of Drugs Act 1971 (to find controlled drugs). This test must be applied to the particular circumstances in each case and is in two parts:

(i)　*Firstly*, the officer must have formed a genuine suspicion in their own mind that they will find the object for which the search power being exercised allows them to search (see *Annex A*, second column, for examples); and

(ii)　*Secondly*, the suspicion that the object will be found must be reasonable. This means that there must be an objective basis for that suspicion based on facts, information and/or intelligence which are relevant to the likelihood that the object in question will be found, so that a reasonable person would be entitled to reach the same conclusion based on the same facts and information and/or intelligence.

Officers must therefore be able to explain the basis for their suspicion by reference to intelligence or information about, or some specific behaviour by, the person concerned (see *paragraphs 3.8(d)*, *4.6* and *5.5*).

2.2A　The exercise of these stop and search powers depends on the likelihood that the person searched is in possession of an item for which they may be searched; it does not depend on the person concerned being suspected of committing an offence in relation to the object of the search. A police officer who has reasonable grounds to suspect that a person is in innocent possession of a stolen or prohibited article, controlled drug or other item for which the officer is empowered to search, may stop and search the person even though there would be no power of arrest. This would apply when a child under the age of criminal responsibility (10 years) is suspected of carrying any such item, even if they knew they had it. (See Notes *1B* and *1BA*.)

*Personal factors can never support reasonable grounds for suspicion*

2.2B Reasonable suspicion can never be supported on the basis of personal factors. This means that unless the police have information or intelligence which provides a description of a person suspected of carrying an article for which there is a power to stop and search, the following cannot be used, alone or in combination with each other, or in combination with any other factor, as the reason for stopping and searching any individual, including any vehicle which they are driving or are being carried in:

    (a) A person's physical appearance with regard, for example, to any of the 'relevant protected characteristics' set out in the Equality Act 2010, section 149, which are age, disability, gender reassignment, pregnancy and maternity, race, religion or belief, sex and sexual orientation (see *paragraph 1.1* and *Note 1A*), or the fact that the person is known to have a previous conviction; and

    (b) Generalisations or stereotypical images that certain groups or categories of people are more likely to be involved in criminal activity.

2.3 Reasonable suspicion may also exist without specific information or intelligence and on the basis of the behaviour of a person. For example, if an officer encounters someone on the street at night who is obviously trying to hide something, the officer may (depending on the other surrounding circumstances) base such suspicion on the fact that this kind of behaviour is often linked to stolen or prohibited articles being carried.

*Reasonable grounds for suspicion based on information and/or intelligence*

2.4 Reasonable grounds for suspicion should normally be linked to accurate and current intelligence or information, relating to articles for which there is a power to stop and search, being carried by individuals or being in vehicles in any locality. This would include reports from members of the public or other officers describing:

    • a person who has been seen carrying such an article or a vehicle in which such an article has been seen.

    • crimes committed in relation to which such an article would constitute relevant evidence, for example, property stolen in a theft or burglary, an offensive weapon or bladed or sharply pointed article used to assault or threaten someone or an article used to cause criminal damage to property.

2.4A Searches based on accurate and current intelligence or information are more likely to be effective. Targeting searches in a particular area at specified crime problems increases their effectiveness and minimises inconvenience to law-abiding members of the public. It also helps in justifying the use of searches both to those who are searched and to the public. This does not however prevent stop and search powers being exercised in other locations where such powers may be exercised and reasonable suspicion exists.

2.5 *Not used.*

*Reasonable grounds for suspicion and searching groups*

2.6 Where there is reliable information or intelligence that members of a group or gang habitually carry knives unlawfully or weapons or controlled drugs, and wear a distinctive item of clothing or other means of identification in order to identify themselves as members of that group or gang, that distinctive item of clothing or other means of identification may provide reasonable grounds to stop and search any person believed to be a member of that group or gang. (See *Note 9*.)

2.6A A similar approach would apply to particular organised protest groups where there is reliable information or intelligence:

    (a) that the group in question arranges meetings and marches to which one or more members bring articles intended to be used to cause criminal damage and/or injury to others in support of the group's aims;

    (b) that at one or more previous meetings or marches arranged by that group, such articles have been used and resulted in damage and/or injury; and

    (c) that on the subsequent occasion in question, one or more members of the group have brought with them such articles with similar intentions.

These circumstances may provide reasonable grounds to stop and search any members of the group to find such articles (see *Note 9A*). See also *paragraphs 2.12* to *2.18*, '*Searches authorised under section 60 of the Criminal Justice and Public Order Act 1994*', when serious violence is anticipated at meetings and marches.

*Reasonable grounds for suspicion based on behaviour, time and location*

2.6B Reasonable suspicion may also exist without specific information or intelligence and on the basis of the behaviour of a person. For example, if an officer encounters someone on the street at night who is obviously trying to hide something, the officer may (depending on the other surrounding circumstances) base such suspicion on the fact that this kind of behaviour is often linked to stolen or prohibited articles being carried. An officer who forms the opinion that a person is acting suspiciously or that they appear to be nervous must be able to explain, with reference to specific aspects of the person's behaviour or conduct which they have observed, why they formed that opinion (see *paragraphs 3.8(d)* and *5.5*). A hunch or instinct which cannot be explained or justified to an objective observer can never amount to reasonable grounds.

2.7  *Not used.*

2.8  *Not used.*

*Securing public confidence and promoting community relations*

2.8A All police officers must recognise that searches are more likely to be effective, legitimate and secure public confidence when their reasonable grounds for suspicion are based on a range of objective factors. The overall use of these powers is more likely to be effective when up-to-date and accurate intelligence or information is communicated to officers and they are well-informed about local crime patterns. Local senior officers have a duty to ensure that those under their command who exercise stop and search powers have access to such information, and the officers exercising the powers have a duty to acquaint themselves with that information (see *paragraphs 5.1 to 5.6*).

*Questioning to decide whether to carry out a search*

2.9  An officer who has reasonable grounds for suspicion may detain the person concerned in order to carry out a search. Before carrying out a search the officer may ask questions about the person's behaviour or presence in circumstances which gave rise to the suspicion. As a result of questioning the detained person, the reasonable grounds for suspicion necessary to detain that person may be confirmed or, because of a satisfactory explanation, be dispelled. (See *Notes 2* and *3*.) Questioning may also reveal reasonable grounds to suspect the possession of a different kind of unlawful article from that originally suspected. Reasonable grounds for suspicion however cannot be provided retrospectively by such questioning during a person's detention or by refusal to answer any questions asked.

2.10 If, as a result of questioning before a search, or other circumstances which come to the attention of the officer, there cease to be reasonable grounds for suspecting that an article of a kind for which there is a power to stop and search is being carried, no search may take place. (See *Note 3*.) In the absence of any other lawful power to detain, the person is free to leave at will and must be so informed.

2.11 There is no power to stop or detain a person in order to find grounds for a search. Police officers have many encounters with members of the public which do not involve detaining people against their will and do not require any statutory power for an officer to speak to a person (see *paragraph 4.12* and *Note 1*). However, if reasonable grounds for suspicion emerge during such an encounter, the officer may search the person, even though no grounds existed when the encounter began. As soon as detention begins, and before searching, the officer must inform the person that they are being detained for the purpose of a search and take action in accordance with paragraphs 3.8 to 3.11 under 'Steps to be taken prior to a search'.

*(b) Searches authorised under section 60 of the Criminal Justice and Public Order Act 1994*

2.12 Authority for a constable in uniform to stop and search under section 60 of the Criminal Justice and Public Order Act 1994 may be given if the authorising officer reasonably believes:

(a)  that incidents involving serious violence may take place in any locality in the officer's police area, and it is expedient to use these powers to prevent their occurrence;

(b)  that persons are carrying dangerous instruments or offensive weapons without good reason in any locality in the officer's police area; or

(c)  that an incident involving serious violence has taken place in the officer's police area, a dangerous instrument or offensive weapon used in the incident is being carried by a person in any locality in that police area, and it is expedient to use these powers to find that instrument or weapon.

2.13 An authorisation under section 60 may only be given by an officer of the rank of inspector or above and in writing, or orally if paragraph 2.12(c) applies and it is not practicable to give the authorisation in writing. The authorisation (whether written or oral) must specify the grounds on which it was given, the locality in which the powers may be exercised and the period of time for which they are in force. The period authorised shall be no longer than appears reasonably necessary to prevent, or seek to prevent incidents of serious violence, or to deal with the problem of carrying dangerous instruments or offensive weapons or to find a dangerous instrument or offensive weapon that has been used. It may not exceed 24 hours. An oral authorisation given where paragraph 2.12(c) applies must be recorded in writing as soon as practicable. (See *Notes 10* to *13.*)

2.14  An inspector who gives an authorisation must, as soon as practicable, inform an officer of or above the rank of superintendent. This officer may direct that the authorisation shall be extended for a further 24 hours, if violence or the carrying of dangerous instruments or offensive weapons has occurred, or is suspected to have occurred, and the continued use of the powers is considered necessary to prevent or deal with further such activity or to find a dangerous instrument or offensive weapon used that has been used. That direction must be given in writing unless it is not practicable to do so, in which case it must be recorded in writing as soon as practicable afterwards. (See *Note 12.*)

2.14A  The selection of persons and vehicles under section 60 to be stopped and, if appropriate, searched should reflect an objective assessment of the nature of the incident or weapon in question and the individuals and vehicles thought likely to be associated with that incident or those weapons (see *Notes 10* and *11*). The powers must not be used to stop and search persons and vehicles for reasons unconnected with the purpose of the authorisation. When selecting persons and vehicles to be stopped in response to a specific threat or incident, officers must take care not to discriminate unlawfully against anyone on the grounds of any of the protected characteristics set out in the Equality Act 2010. (See *paragraph 1.1.*)

2.14B  The driver of a vehicle which is stopped under section 60 and any person who is searched under section 60 are entitled to a written statement to that effect if they apply within twelve months from the day the vehicle was stopped or the person was searched. This statement is a record which states that the vehicle was stopped or (as the case may be) that the person was searched under section 60 and it may form part of the search record or be supplied as a separate record.

*Powers to require removal of face coverings*

2.15  Section 60AA of the Criminal Justice and Public Order Act 1994 also provides a power to demand the removal of disguises. The officer exercising the power must reasonably believe that someone is wearing an item wholly or mainly for the purpose of concealing identity. There is also a power to seize such items where the officer believes that a person intends to wear them for this purpose. There is no power to stop and search for disguises. An officer may seize any such item which is discovered when exercising a power of search for something else, or which is being carried, and which the officer reasonably believes is intended to be used for concealing anyone's identity. This power can only be used if an authorisation given under section 60 or under section 60AA, is in force. (See *Note 4.*)

2.16  Authority under section 60AA for a constable in uniform to require the removal of disguises and to seize them may be given if the authorising officer reasonably believes that activities may take place in any locality in the officer's police area that are likely to involve the commission of offences and it is expedient to use these powers to prevent or control these activities.

2.17  An authorisation under section 60AA may only be given by an officer of the rank of inspector or above, in writing, specifying the grounds on which it was given, the locality in which the powers may be exercised and the period of time for which they are in force. The period authorised shall be no longer than appears reasonably necessary to prevent, or seek to prevent the commission of offences. It may not exceed 24 hours. (See *Notes 10* to *13.*)

2.18  An inspector who gives an authorisation must, as soon as practicable, inform an officer of or above the rank of superintendent. This officer may direct that the authorisation shall be extended for a further 24 hours, if crimes have been committed, or are suspected to have been committed, and the continued use of the powers is considered necessary to prevent or deal with further such activity. This direction must also be given in writing at the time or as soon as practicable afterwards. (See *Note 12.*)

*(c)  Not used*

*(d)  Searches under Schedule 5 to the Terrorism Prevention and Investigation Measures Act 2011*

2.18A  Paragraph 3 of Schedule 5 to the TPIM Act 2011 allows a constable to detain an individual to be searched under the following powers:

    (i)  paragraph 6(2)(a) when a TPIM notice is being, or has just been, served on the individual for the purpose of ascertaining whether there is anything on the individual that contravenes measures specified in the notice;

(ii) paragraph 8(2)(a) in accordance with a warrant to search the individual issued by a justice of the peace in England and Wales, a sheriff in Scotland or a lay magistrate in Northern Ireland who is satisfied that a search is necessary for the purpose of determining whether an individual in respect of whom a TPIM notice is in force is complying with measures specified in the notice (see *paragraph 2.20*); and

(iii) paragraph 10 to ascertain whether an individual in respect of whom a TPIM notice is in force is in possession of anything that could be used to threaten or harm any person.

See *paragraph 2.1(e)*.

2.19 The exercise of the powers mentioned in *paragraph 2.18A* does not require the constable to have reasonable grounds to suspect that the individual:

(a) has been, or is, contravening any of the measures specified in the TPIM notice; or

(b) has on them anything which:

- in the case of the power in sub-paragraph (i), contravenes measures specified in the TPIM notice;
- in the case of the power in sub-paragraph (ii) is not complying with measures specified in the TPIM notice; or
- in the case of the power in sub-paragraph (iii), could be used to threaten or harm any person.

2.20 A search of an individual on warrant under the power mentioned in paragraph 2.18A(ii) must [be] carried out within 28 days of the issue of the warrant and:

- the individual may be searched on one occasion only within that period;
- the search must take place at a reasonable hour unless it appears that this would frustrate the purposes of the search.

2.21 *Not used.*

2.22 *Not used.*

2.23 *Not used.*

2.24 *Not used.*

2.24A *Not used.*

2.25 *Not used.*

2.26 The powers under Schedule 5 only allow a constable to conduct a search of an individual only for specified purposes relating to a TPIM notice as set out above. However, anything found may be seized and retained if there are reasonable grounds for believing that it is or it contains evidence of any offence for use at a trial for that offence or to prevent it being concealed, lost, damaged, altered, or destroyed. However, this would not prevent a search being carried out under other search powers if, in the course of exercising these powers, the officer formed reasonable grounds for suspicion.

*(e) Powers to search persons in the exercise of a power to search premises*

2.27 The following powers to search premises also authorise the search of a person, not under arrest, who is found on the premises during the course of the search:

(a) section 139B of the Criminal Justice Act 1988 under which a constable may enter school premises and search the premises and any person on those premises for any bladed or pointed article or offensive weapon;

(b) under a warrant issued under section 23(3) of the Misuse of Drugs Act 1971 to search premises for drugs or documents but only if the warrant specifically authorises the search of persons found on the premises; and

(c) under a search warrant or order issued under paragraph 1, 3 or 11 of Schedule 5 to the Terrorism Act 2000 to search premises and any person found there for material likely to be of substantial value to a terrorist investigation.

2.28 Before the power under section 139B of the Criminal Justice Act 1988 may be exercised, the constable must have reasonable grounds to suspect that an offence under section 139A or 139AA of the Criminal Justice Act 1988 (having a bladed or pointed article or offensive weapon on school premises) has been or is being committed. A warrant to search premises and persons found therein may be issued under section 23(3) of the Misuse of Drugs Act 1971 if there are reasonable grounds to suspect that controlled drugs or certain documents are in the possession of a person on the premises.

2.29 The powers in paragraph 2.27 do not require prior specific grounds to suspect that the person to be searched is in possession of an item for which there is an existing power to search. However, it is still necessary to ensure that the selection and treatment of those searched under these powers is based upon objective factors connected with the search of the premises, and not upon personal prejudice.

### 3 Conduct of searches

3.1 All stops and searches must be carried out with courtesy, consideration and respect for the person concerned. This has a significant impact on public confidence in the police. Every reasonable effort must be made to minimise the embarrassment that a person being searched may experience. (See Note 4.)

3.2 The co-operation of the person to be searched must be sought in every case, even if the person initially objects to the search. A forcible search may be made only if it has been established that the person is unwilling to co-operate or resists. Reasonable force may be used as a last resort if necessary to conduct a search or to detain a person or vehicle for the purposes of a search.

3.3 The length of time for which a person or vehicle may be detained must be reasonable and kept to a minimum. Where the exercise of the power requires reasonable suspicion, the thoroughness and extent of a search must depend on what is suspected of being carried, and by whom. If the suspicion relates to a particular article which is seen to be slipped into a person's pocket, then, in the absence of other grounds for suspicion or an opportunity for the article to be moved elsewhere, the search must be confined to that pocket. In the case of a small article which can readily be concealed, such as a drug, and which might be concealed anywhere on the person, a more extensive search may be necessary. In the case of searches mentioned in paragraph 2.1(b) and (d), which do not require reasonable grounds for suspicion, officers may make any reasonable search to look for items for which they are empowered to search. (See Note 5.)

3.4 The search must be carried out at or near the place where the person or vehicle was first detained. (See Note 6.)

3.5 There is no power to require a person to remove any clothing in public other than an outer coat, jacket or gloves, except under section 60AA of the Criminal Justice and Public Order Act 1994 (which empowers a constable to require a person to remove any item worn to conceal identity). (See Notes 4 and 6.) A search in public of a person's clothing which has not been removed must be restricted to superficial examination of outer garments. This does not, however, prevent an officer from placing his or her hand inside the pockets of the outer clothing, or feeling round the inside of collars, socks and shoes if this is reasonably necessary in the circumstances to look for the object of the search or to remove and examine any item reasonably suspected to be the object of the search. For the same reasons, subject to the restrictions on the removal of headgear, a person's hair may also be searched in public. (See paragraphs 3.1 and 3.3.)

3.6 Where on reasonable grounds it is considered necessary to conduct a more thorough search (e.g. by requiring a person to take off a T-shirt), this must be done out of public view, for example, in a police van unless paragraph 3.7 applies, or police station if there is one nearby (see Note 6.) Any search involving the removal of more than an outer coat, jacket, gloves, headgear or footwear, or any other item concealing identity, may only be made by an officer of the same sex as the person searched and may not be made in the presence of anyone of the opposite sex unless the person being searched specifically requests it. (See Code C Annex L and Notes 4 and 7.)

3.7 Searches involving exposure of intimate parts of the body must not be conducted as a routine extension of a less thorough search, simply because nothing is found in the course of the initial search. Searches involving exposure of intimate parts of the body may be carried out only at a nearby police station or other nearby location which is out of public view (but not a police vehicle). These searches must be conducted in accordance with paragraph 11 of Annex A to Code C except that an intimate search mentioned in paragraph 11(f) of Annex A to Code C may not be authorised or carried out under any stop and search powers. The other provisions of Code C do not apply to the conduct and recording of searches of persons detained at police stations in the exercise of stop and search powers. (See Note 7.)

*Steps to be taken prior to a search*

3.8 Before any search of a detained person or attended vehicle takes place the officer must take reasonable steps, if not in uniform (see *paragraph 3.9*), to show their warrant card to the person to be searched or in charge of the vehicle to be searched and whether or not in uniform, to give that person the following information:

(a) that they are being detained for the purposes of a search;

(b) the officer's name (except in the case of enquiries linked to the investigation of terrorism, or otherwise where the officer reasonably believes that giving their name might put them in danger, in which case a warrant or other identification number shall be given) and the name of the police station to which the officer is attached;

(c) the legal search power which is being exercised, and

   (d) a clear explanation of:
      (i) the object of the search in terms of the article or articles for which there is a power to search; and
      (ii) in the case of:
- the power under section 60 of the Criminal Justice and Public Order Act 1994 (see *paragraph 2.1(b))*, the nature of the power, the authorisation and the fact that it has been given;
- the powers under Schedule 5 to the Terrorism Prevention and Investigation Measures Act 2011 (see *paragraph 2.1(e)* and *2.18A*):
     – the fact that a TPIM notice is in force or, (in the case of paragraph 6(2)(a)) that a TPIM notice is being served;
     – the nature of the power being exercised.
     For a search under paragraph 8 of Schedule 5, the warrant must be produced and the person provided with a copy of it.
- all other powers requiring reasonable suspicion (see *paragraph 2.1(a)*), the grounds for that suspicion. This means explaining the basis for the suspicion by reference to information and/or intelligence about, or some specific behaviour by, the person concerned (see *paragraph 2.2*).
   (e) that they are entitled to a copy of the record of the search if one is made (see *section 4* below) if they ask within 3 months from the date of the search and:
      (i) if they are not arrested and taken to a police station as a result of the search and it is practicable to make the record on the spot, that immediately after the search is completed they will be given, if they request, either:
- a copy of the record, or
- a receipt which explains how they can obtain a copy of the full record or access to an electronic copy of the record, or
      (ii) if they are arrested and taken to a police station as a result of the search, that the record will be made at the station as part of their custody record and they will be given, if they request, a copy of their custody record which includes a record of the search as soon as practicable whilst they are at the station. (See *Note 16.*)

3.9 Stops and searches under the power mentioned in paragraph 2.1(b) may be undertaken only by a constable in uniform.

3.10 The person should also be given information about police powers to stop and search and the individual's rights in these circumstances.

3.11 If the person to be searched, or in charge of a vehicle to be searched, does not appear to understand what is being said, or there is any doubt about the person's ability to understand English, the officer must take reasonable steps to bring information regarding the person's rights and any relevant provisions of this Code to his or her attention. If the person is deaf or cannot understand English and is accompanied by someone, then the officer must try to establish whether that person can interpret or otherwise help the officer to give the required information.

## 4 Recording requirements

*(a) Searches which do not result in an arrest*

4.1 When an officer carries out a search in the exercise of any power to which this Code applies and the search does not result in the person searched or person in charge of the vehicle searched being arrested and taken to a police station, a record must be made of it, electronically or on paper, unless there are exceptional circumstances which make this wholly impracticable (e.g. in situations involving public disorder or when the recording officer's presence is urgently required elsewhere). If a record is to be made, the officer carrying out the search must make the record on the spot unless this is not practicable, in which case, the officer must make the record as soon as practicable after the search is completed. (See *Note 16.*)

4.2 If the record is made at the time, the person who has been searched or who is in charge of the vehicle that has been searched must be asked if they want a copy and if they do, they must be given immediately, either:
- a copy of the record, or
- a receipt which explains how they can obtain a copy of the full record or access to an electronic copy of the record

4.2A An officer is not required to provide a copy of the full record or a receipt at the time if they are called to an incident of higher priority. (See *Note 21.*)

*(b) Searches which result in an arrest*

4.2B If a search in the exercise of any power to which this Code applies results in a person being arrested and taken to a police station, the officer carrying out the search is responsible for ensuring that a record of the search is made as part of their custody record. The custody officer must then ensure that the person is asked if they want a copy of the record and if they do, that they are given a copy as soon as practicable. (See *Note 16*.)

*(c) Record of search*

4.3 The record of a search must always include the following information:

  (a) A note of the self defined ethnicity, and if different, the ethnicity as perceived by the officer making the search, of the person searched or of the person in charge of the vehicle searched (as the case may be) (see *Note 18*);

  (b) The date, time and place the person or vehicle was searched (see *Note 6*);

  (c) The object of the search in terms of the article or articles for which there is a power to search;

  (d) In the case of:

   • the power under section 60 of the Criminal Justice and Public Order Act 1994 (see *paragraph 2.1(b)*), the nature of the power, the authorisation and the fact that it has been given (see *Note 17*);

   • the powers under Schedule 5 to the Terrorism Prevention and Investigation Measures Act 2011 (see *paragraphs 2.1(e)* and *2.18A*):

    – the fact that a TPIM notice is in force or, (in the case of paragraph 6(2)(a)), that a TPIM notice is being served;

    – the nature of the power, and

    – for a search under paragraph 8, the date the search warrant was issued, the fact that the warrant was produced and a copy of it provided and the warrant must also be endorsed by the constable executing it to state whether anything was found and whether anything was seized, and

   • all other powers requiring reasonable suspicion (see *paragraph 2.1(a)*), the grounds for that suspicion.

  (e) subject to paragraph 3.8(b), the identity of the officer carrying out the search. (See *Note 15*.)

4.3A For the purposes of completing the search record, there is no requirement to record the name, address and date of birth of the person searched or the person in charge of a vehicle which is searched. The person is under no obligation to provide this information and they should not be asked to provide it for the purpose of completing the record.

4.4 Nothing in paragraph 4.3 requires the names of police officers to be shown on the search record or any other record required to be made under this code in the case of enquiries linked to the investigation of terrorism or otherwise where an officer reasonably believes that recording names might endanger the officers. In such cases the record must show the officers' warrant or other identification number and duty station.

4.5 A record is required for each person and each vehicle searched. However, if a person is in a vehicle and both are searched, and the object and grounds of the search are the same, only one record need be completed. If more than one person in a vehicle is searched, separate records for each search of a person must be made. If only a vehicle is searched, the self-defined ethnic background of the person in charge of the vehicle must be recorded, unless the vehicle is unattended.

4.6 The record of the grounds for making a search must, briefly but informatively, explain the reason for suspecting the person concerned, by reference to information and/ or intelligence about, or some specific behaviour by, the person concerned (see *paragraph 2.2*).

4.7 Where officers detain an individual with a view to performing a search, but the need to search is eliminated as a result of questioning the person detained, a search should not be carried out and a record is not required. (See *paragraph 2.10* and *Notes 3* and *22A*.)

4.8 After searching an unattended vehicle, or anything in or on it, an officer must leave a notice in it (or on it, if things on it have been searched without opening it) recording the fact that it has been searched.

4.9 The notice must include the name of the police station to which the officer concerned is attached and state where a copy of the record of the search may be obtained and how (if applicable) an electronic copy may be accessed and where any application for compensation should be directed.

4.10 The vehicle must if practicable be left secure.

4.10A *Not used.*

4.10B *Not used.*

*Recording of encounters not governed by statutory powers*

4.11  *Not used.*

4.12  There is no national requirement for an officer who requests a person in a public place to account for themselves, i.e. their actions, behaviour, presence in an area or possession of anything, to make any record of the encounter or to give the person a receipt. (See *paragraph 2.11* and *Notes 22A* and *22B.*)

4.12A  *Not used.*

4.13  *Not used.*

4.14  *Not used.*

4.15  *Not used.*

4.16  *Not used.*

4.17  *Not used.*

4.18  *Not used.*

4.19  *Not used.*

4.20  *Not used.*

## 5  Monitoring and supervising the use of stop and search powers

*General*

5.1  Any misuse of stop and search powers is likely to be harmful to policing and lead to mistrust of the police by the local community and by the public in general. Supervising officers must monitor the use of stop and search powers and should consider in particular whether there is any evidence that they are being exercised on the basis of stereotyped images or inappropriate generalisations. Supervising officers should satisfy themselves that the practice of officers under their supervision in stopping, searching and recording is fully in accordance with this Code. Supervisors must also examine whether the records reveal any trends or patterns which give cause for concern, and if so take appropriate action to address this.

5.2  Senior officers with area or force-wide responsibilities must also monitor the broader use of stop and search powers and, where necessary, take action at the relevant level.

5.3  Supervision and monitoring must be supported by the compilation of comprehensive statistical records of stops and searches at force, area and local level. Any apparently disproportionate use of the powers by particular officers or groups of officers or in relation to specific sections of the community should be identified and investigated.

5.4  In order to promote public confidence in the use of the powers, forces in consultation with police and crime commissioners must make arrangements for the records to be scrutinised by representatives of the community, and to explain the use of the powers at a local level. (See *Note 19.*)

*Suspected misuse of powers by individual officers*

5.5  Police supervisors must monitor the use of stop and search powers by individual officers to ensure that they are being applied appropriately and lawfully. Monitoring takes many forms, such as direct supervision of the exercise of the powers, examining stop and search records (particularly examining the officer's documented reasonable grounds for suspicion) and asking the officer to account for the way in which they conducted and recorded particular searches or through complaints about a stop and search that an officer has carried out.

5.6  Where a supervisor identifies issues with the way that an officer has used a stop and search power, the facts of the case will determine whether the standards of professional behaviour as set out in the Code of Ethics (see [https://www.college.police.uk/What-we-do/Ethics/Documents/Code_of_Eth ics.pdf]) have been breached and which formal action is pursued. Improper use might be a result of poor performance or a conduct matter, which will require the supervisor to take appropriate action such as performance or misconduct procedures. It is imperative that supervisors take both timely and appropriate action to deal with all such cases that come to their notice.

*Notes for Guidance*

**Officers exercising stop and search powers**

*1      This Code does not affect the ability of an officer to speak to or question a person in the ordinary course of the officer's duties without detaining the person or exercising any element of compulsion. It is not the purpose of the code to prohibit such encounters between the police and the community with the co-operation of the person concerned and neither does it affect the principle that all citizens have a duty to help police officers to prevent crime and discover offenders. This is a civic rather than a legal duty; but when a police officer is trying to discover whether, or by whom, an offence has been committed he or she may question any person from whom useful information might be obtained, subject to the restrictions imposed by Code C. A person's unwillingness to reply does not alter this entitlement, but in the absence of a power to arrest, or to detain in order to search, the person is free to leave at will and cannot be compelled to remain with the officer.*

1A  *In paragraphs 1.1 and 2.2, 'relevant protected characteristic' are: age, disability, gender reassignment, pregnancy and maternity, race, religion or belief, sex and sexual orientation.*

1B  *Innocent possession means that the person does [not] have the guilty knowledge that they are carrying an unlawful item which is required before an arrest on suspicion that the person has committed an offence in respect of the item sought (if arrest is necessary — see PACE Code G) and/or a criminal prosecution) can be considered. It is not uncommon for children under the age of criminal responsibility to be used by older children and adults to carry stolen property, drugs and weapons and, in some cases, firearms, for the criminal benefit of others, either:*

- *in the hope that police may not suspect they are being used for carrying the items; or*
- *knowing that if they are suspected of being couriers and are stopped and searched, they cannot be arrested or prosecuted for any criminal offence.*

*Stop and search powers therefore allow the police to intervene effectively to break up criminal gangs and groups that use young children to further their criminal activities.*

1BA  *Whenever a child under 10 is suspected of carrying unlawful items for someone else, or is found in circumstances which suggest that their welfare and safety may be at risk, the facts should be reported and actioned in accordance with established force safeguarding procedures. This will be in addition to treating them as a potentially vulnerable or intimidated witness in respect of their status as a witness to the serious criminal offence(s) committed by those using them as couriers. Safeguarding considerations will also apply to other persons aged under 18 who are stopped and searched under any of the powers to which this Code applies. See paragraph 1.1 with regard to the requirement under the Children Act 2004, section 11, for chief police officers and other specified persons and bodies, to ensure that in the discharge of their functions, they have regard to the need to safeguard and promote the welfare of all persons under the age of 18.*

2  *In some circumstances preparatory questioning may be unnecessary, but in general a brief conversation or exchange will be desirable not only as a means of avoiding unsuccessful searches, but to explain the grounds for the stop/search, to gain co-operation and reduce any tension there might be surrounding the stop/search.*

3  *Where a person is lawfully detained for the purpose of a search, but no search in the event takes place, the detention will not thereby have been rendered unlawful.*

4  *Many people customarily cover their heads or faces for religious reasons – for example, Muslim women, Sikh men, Sikh or Hindu women, or Rastafarian men or women. A police officer cannot order the removal of a head or face covering except where there is reason to believe that the item is being worn by the individual wholly or mainly for the purpose of disguising identity, not simply because it disguises identity. Where there may be religious sensitivities about ordering the removal of such an item, the officer should permit the item to be removed out of public view. Where practicable, the item should be removed in the presence of an officer of the same sex as the person and out of sight of anyone of the opposite sex (see Code C Annex L).*

5  *A search of a person in public should be completed as soon as possible.*

6  *A person may be detained under a stop and search power at a place other than where the person was first detained, only if that place, be it a police station or elsewhere, is nearby. Such a place should be located within a reasonable travelling distance using whatever mode of travel (on foot or by car) is appropriate. This applies to all searches under stop and search powers, whether or not they involve the removal of clothing or exposure of intimate parts of the body (see paragraphs 3.6 and 3.7) or take place in or out of public view. It means, for example, that a search under the stop and search power in section 23 of the Misuse of Drugs Act 1971 which involves the compulsory removal of more than a person's outer coat, jacket or gloves cannot be carried out unless a place which is both nearby the place they were first detained and out of public view, is available. If a search involves exposure of intimate parts of the body and a police station is not nearby, particular care must be taken to ensure that the location is suitable in that it enables the search to be conducted in accordance with the requirements of paragraph 11 of Annex A to Code C.*

7  *A search in the street itself should be regarded as being in public for the purposes of paragraphs 3.6 and 3.7 above, even though it may be empty at the time a search begins. Although there is no power to require a person to do so, there is nothing to prevent an officer from asking a person voluntarily to remove more than an outer coat, jacket or gloves in public.*

8  *Not used.*

9  *Other means of identification might include jewellery, insignias, tattoos or other features which are known to identify members of the particular gang or group.*

9A  *A decision to search individuals believed to be members of a particular group or gang must be judged on a case by case basis according to the circumstances applicable at the time of the proposed searches and in particular, having regard to:*

(a) the number of items suspected of being carried;

(b) the nature of those items and the risk they pose; and

(c) the number of individuals to be searched.

A group search will only be justified if it is a necessary and proportionate approach based on the facts and having regard to the nature of the suspicion in these cases. The extent and thoroughness of the searches must not be excessive.

The size of the group and the number of individuals it is proposed to search will be a key factor and steps should be taken to identify those who are to be searched to avoid unnecessary inconvenience to unconnected members of the public who are also present.

The onus is on the police to be satisfied and to demonstrate that their approach to the decision to search is in pursuit of a legitimate aim, necessary and proportionate.

### Authorising officers

10   The powers under section 60 are separate from and additional to the normal stop and search powers which require reasonable grounds to suspect an individual of carrying an offensive weapon (or other article). Their overall purpose is to prevent serious violence and the widespread carrying of weapons which might lead to persons being seriously injured by disarming potential offenders or finding weapons that have been used in circumstances where other powers would not be sufficient. They should not therefore be used to replace or circumvent the normal powers for dealing with routine crime problems. A particular example might be an authorisation to prevent serious violence or the carrying of offensive weapons at a sports event by rival team supporters when the expected general appearance and age range of those likely to be responsible, alone, would not be sufficiently distinctive to support reasonable suspicion (see paragraph 2.6). The purpose of the powers under section 60AA is to prevent those involved in intimidatory or violent protests using face coverings to disguise identity.

11   Authorisations under section 60 require a reasonable belief on the part of the authorising officer. This must have an objective basis, for example: intelligence or relevant information such as a history of antagonism and violence between particular groups; previous incidents of violence at, or connected with, particular events or locations; a significant increase in knife-point robberies in a limited area; reports that individuals are regularly carrying weapons in a particular locality; information following an incident in which weapons were used about where the weapons might be found or in the case of section 60AA previous incidents of crimes being committed while wearing face coverings to conceal identity.

12   It is for the authorising officer to determine the period of time during which the powers mentioned in paragraph 2.1(b) may be exercised. The officer should set the minimum period he or she considers necessary to deal with the risk of violence, the carrying of knives or offensive weapons, or to find dangerous instruments or weapons that have been used. A direction to extend the period authorised under the powers mentioned in paragraph 2.1(b) may be given only once. Thereafter further use of the powers requires a new authorisation.

13   It is for the authorising officer to determine the geographical area in which the use of the powers is to be authorised. In doing so the officer may wish to take into account factors such as the nature and venue of the anticipated incident or the incident which has taken place, the number of people who may be in the immediate area of that incident, their access to surrounding areas and the anticipated or actual level of violence. The officer should not set a geographical area which is wider than that he or she believes necessary for the purpose of preventing anticipated violence, the carrying of knives or offensive weapons, or for finding a dangerous instrument or weapon that has been used or, in the case of section 60AA, the prevention of commission of offences. It is particularly important to ensure that constables exercising such powers are fully aware of the locality within which they may be used. The officer giving the authorisation should therefore specify either the streets which form the boundary of the locality or a divisional boundary if appropriate, within the force area. If the power is to be used in response to a threat or incident that straddles police force areas, an officer from each of the forces concerned will need to give an authorisation.

14   Not used.

### Recording

15   Where a stop and search is conducted by more than one officer the identity of all the officers engaged in the search must be recorded on the record. Nothing prevents an officer who is present but not directly involved in searching from completing the record during the course of the encounter.

16    When the search results in the person searched or in charge of a vehicle which is searched being arrested, the requirement to make the record of the search as part of the person's custody record does not apply if the person is granted 'street bail' after arrest (see section 30A of PACE) to attend a police station and is not taken in custody to the police station An arrested person's entitlement to a copy of the search record which is made as part of their custody record does not affect their entitlement to a copy of their custody record or any other provisions of PACE Code C section 2 (Custody records).

17    It is important for monitoring purposes to specify when authority is given for exercising the stop and search power under section 60 of the Criminal Justice and Public Order Act 1994.

18    Officers should record the self-defined ethnicity of every person stopped according to the categories used in the 2001 census question listed in Annex B. The person should be asked to select one of the five main categories representing broad ethnic groups and then a more specific cultural background from within this group. The ethnic classification should be coded for recording purposes using the coding system in Annex B. An additional 'Not stated' box is available but should not be offered to respondents explicitly. Officers should be aware and explain to members of the public, especially where concerns are raised, that this information is required to obtain a true picture of stop and search activity and to help improve ethnic monitoring, tackle discriminatory practice, and promote effective use of the powers. If the person gives what appears to the officer to be an 'incorrect' answer (e.g. a person who appears to be white states that they are black), the officer should record the response that has been given and then record their own perception of the person's ethnic background by using the PNC classification system. If the 'Not stated' category is used the reason for this must be recorded on the form.

19    Arrangements for public scrutiny of records should take account of the right to confidentiality of those stopped and searched. Anonymised forms and/or statistics generated from records should be the focus of the examinations by members of the public.

20    Not used.

21    In situations where it is not practicable to provide a written copy of the record or immediate access to an electronic copy of the record or a receipt of the search at the time (see paragraph 4.2A above), the officer should consider giving the person details of the station which they may attend for a copy of the record. A receipt may take the form of a simple business card which includes sufficient information to locate the record should the person ask for copy, for example, the date and place of the search, and a reference number or the name of the officer who carried out the search (unless paragraph 4.4 applies).

22    Not used.

22A   Where there are concerns which make it necessary to monitor any local disproportionality, forces have discretion to direct officers to record the self-defined ethnicity of persons they request to account for themselves in a public place or who they detain with a view to searching but do not search. Guidance should be provided locally and efforts made to minimise the bureaucracy involved. Records should be closely monitored and supervised in line with paragraphs 5.1 to 5.4, and forces can suspend or re-instate recording of these encounters as appropriate.

22B   A person who is asked to account for themselves should, if they request, be given information about how they can report their dissatisfaction about how they have been treated.

## Definition of offensive weapon

23    'Offensive weapon' is defined as 'any article made or adapted for use for causing injury to the person, or intended by the person having it with him for such use by him or by someone else'. There are three categories of offensive weapons: those made for causing injury to the person; those adapted for such a purpose; and those not so made or adapted, but carried with the intention of causing injury to the person. A firearm, as defined by section 57 of the Firearms Act 1968, would fall within the definition of offensive weapon if any of the criteria above apply.

24    Not used.

25    Not used.

## Annex A

### Summary of Main Stop and Search Powers to Which Code A Applies

This table relates to stop and search powers only. Individual statutes below may contain other police powers of entry, search and seizure.

| Power | Object of Search | Extent of Search | Where exercisable |
|---|---|---|---|
| *Unlawful articles general* | | | |
| 1. Public Stores Act 1875, s. 6 | HM Stores stolen or unlawfully obtained | Persons, vehicles and vessels | Anywhere where the constabulary powers are exercisable |
| 2. Firearms Act 1968, s. 47 | Firearms | Persons and vehicles | A public place, or anywhere in the case of reasonable suspicion of offences of carrying firearms with criminal intent or trespassing with firearms |
| 3. Misuse of Drugs Act 1971, s. 23 | Controlled drugs | Persons and vehicles | Anywhere |
| 4. Customs and Excise Management Act 1979, s. 163 | Goods: (a) on which duty has not been paid; (b) being unlawfully removed, imported or exported; (c) otherwise liable to forfeiture to HM Revenue and Customs | Vehicles and vessels only | Anywhere |
| 5. Aviation Security Act 1982, s. 24B *Note: This power applies throughout the UK but the provisions of this Code will apply only when the power is exercised at an aerodrome situated in England and Wales.* | Stolen articles or articles made, adapted or intended for use in the course of/in connection with conduct which constitutes an offence in the part of the UK where the aerodrome is situated or would so do, if it occurred there. | Persons, vehicles, aircraft. Anything in or on a vehicle or aircraft. | Any part of an aerodrome. |
| 6. Police and Criminal Evidence Act 1984, s. 1 | Stolen goods; | Persons and vehicles. | Where there is public access. |
| | Articles made, adapted or intended for use in the course of or in connection with, certain offences under the Theft Act 1968, Fraud Act and Criminal Damage Act 1971; | Persons and vehicles. | Where there is public access. |
| | Offensive weapons, bladed or sharply-pointed articles (except folding pocket knives with a bladed cutting edge not exceeding 3 inches); | Persons and vehicles. | Where there is public access. |

| Power | Object of Search | Extent of Search | Where exercisable |
|---|---|---|---|
| | Fireworks: Category 4 (display grade) fireworks if possession prohibited, Adult fireworks in possession of a person under 18 in a public place. | Persons and vehicles. | Where there is public access. |
| 7. Sporting Events (Control of Alcohol etc.) Act 1985, s. 7 | Intoxicating liquor | Persons, coaches and trains | Designated sports grounds or coaches and trains travelling to or from a designated sporting event. |
| 8. Crossbows Act 1987, s. 4 | Crossbows or parts of crossbows (except crossbows with a draw weight of less than 1.4 kilograms) | Persons and vehicles | Anywhere except dwellings |
| 9. Criminal Justice Act 1988 s. 139B | Offensive weapons, bladed or sharply pointed article | Persons | School premises |
| *Evidence of game and wildlife offences* | | | |
| 10. Poaching Prevention Act 1862, s. 2 | Game or poaching equipment | Persons and vehicles | A public place |
| 11. Deer Act 1991, s. 12 | Evidence of offences under the Act | Persons and vehicles | Anywhere except dwellings |
| 12. Conservation of Seals Act 1970, s. 4 | Seals or hunting equipment | Vehicles only | Anywhere |
| 13. Protection of Badgers Act 1992, s. 11 | Evidence of offences under the Act | Persons and vehicles | Anywhere |
| 14. Wildlife and Countryside Act 1981, s. 19 | Evidence of wildlife offences | Persons and vehicles | Anywhere except dwellings |
| *Other* | | | |
| 15. Paragraphs 6 & 8 of Schedule 5 to the Terrorism Prevention and Investigation Measures Act 2011 | Anything that contravenes measures specified in a TPIM notice. | Persons in respect of whom a TPIM notice is being served or is in force | Anywhere |
| 16. Paragraph 10 of Schedule 5 to the Terrorism Prevention and Investigation Measures Act 2011 | Anything that could be used to threaten or harm any person. | Persons in respect of whom a TPIM notice is in force. | Anywhere |
| 17. *Not used* | | | |
| 18. *Not used* | | | |
| 19. Section 60 Criminal Justice and Public Order Act 1994 | Offensive weapons or dangerous instruments to prevent incidents of serious violence or to deal with the carrying of such items or find such items which have been used in incidents of serious violence | Persons and vehicles | Anywhere within a locality authorised under subsection (1) |

ANNEX B

SELF-DEFINED ETHNIC CLASSIFICATION CATEGORIES

**[Omitted.]**

ANNEX C

SUMMARY OF POWERS OF COMMUNITY SUPPORT OFFICERS TO SEARCH AND SEIZE

The following is a summary of the search and seizure powers that may be exercised by a community support officer (CSO) who has been designated with the relevant powers in accordance with Part 4 of the Police Reform Act 2002.

When exercising any of these powers, a CSO must have regard to any relevant provisions of this Code, including section 3 governing the conduct of searches and the steps to be taken prior to a search.

1. *Not used*

2. **Powers to search requiring the consent of the person and seizure**

A CSO may detain a person using reasonable force where necessary as set out in Part 1 of Schedule 4 to the Police Reform Act 2002. If the person has been lawfully detained, the CSO may search the person provided that person gives consent to such a search in relation to the following:

| Designation | Powers conferred | Object of Search | Extent of Search | Where Exercisable |
|---|---|---|---|---|
| 1. Police Reform Act 2002, Schedule 4, paragraphs 7 and 7A | (a) Criminal Justice and Police Act 2001, s. 12(2) | (a) Alcohol or a container for alcohol | (a) Persons | (a) Designated public place |
| | (b) Confiscation of Alcohol (Young Persons) Act 1997, s. 1 | (b) Alcohol | (b) Persons under 18 years old | (b) Public place |
| | (c) Children and Young Persons Act 1933, s. 7(3) | (c) Tobacco or cigarette papers | (c) Persons under 16 years old found smoking | (c) Public place |

3. **Powers to search not requiring the consent of the person and seizure**

A CSO may detain a person using reasonable force where necessary as set out in Part 1 of Schedule 4 to the Police Reform Act 2002. If the person has been lawfully detained, the CSO may search the person without the need for that person's consent in relation to the following:

| Designation | Power conferred | Object of Search | Extent of Search | Where Exercisable |
|---|---|---|---|---|
| Police Reform Act 2002, Schedule 4, paragraph 2A | Police and Criminal Evidence Act 1984, s. 32 | (a) Objects that might be used to cause physical injury to the person or the CSO.<br><br>(b) Items that might be used to assist escape. | Persons made subject to a requirement to wait. | Any place where the requirement to wait has been made |

4. **Powers to seize without consent**

This power applies when drugs are found in the course of any search mentioned above.

| Designation | Power conferred | Object of Seizure | Where Exercisable |
|---|---|---|---|
| Police Reform Act 2002, Schedule 4, paragraph 7B | Police Reform Act 2002, Schedule 4, paragraph 7B | Controlled drugs in a person's possession. | Any place where the person is in possession of the drug. |

Annex D – Deleted.

Annex E – Deleted.

Annex F Establishing Gender of Persons for the Purpose of Searching

See Code C *Annex L*

# PACE CODE B

## REVISED CODE OF PRACTICE FOR SEARCHES OF PREMISES BY POLICE OFFICERS AND THE SEIZURE OF PROPERTY FOUND BY POLICE OFFICERS ON PERSONS OR PREMISES

**Commencement—Transitional Arrangements**

This code applies to applications for warrants made after 00.00 on 27 October 2013 and to searches and seizures taking place after 0.00 on 27 October 2013.

### 1 Introduction

1.1 This Code of Practice deals with police powers to:
 • search premises
 • seize and retain property found on premises and persons
1.1A These powers may be used to find:
 • property and material relating to a crime
 • wanted persons
 • children who abscond from local authority accommodation where they have been remanded or committed by a court
1.2 A justice of the peace may issue a search warrant granting powers of entry, search and seizure, e.g. warrants to search for stolen property, drugs, firearms and evidence of serious offences. Police also have powers without a search warrant. The main ones provided by the Police and Criminal Evidence Act 1984 (PACE) include powers to search premises:
 • to make an arrest
 • after an arrest
1.3 The right to privacy and respect for personal property are key principles of the Human Rights Act 1998. Powers of entry, search and seizure should be fully and clearly justified before use because they may significantly interfere with the occupier's privacy. Officers should consider if the necessary objectives can be met by less intrusive means.
1.3A Powers to search and seize must be used fairly, responsibly, with respect for people who occupy premises being searched or are in charge of property being seized and without unlawful discrimination. Under the Equality Act 2010, section 149, when police officers are carrying out their functions, they also have a duty to have due regard to the need to eliminate unlawful discrimination, harassment and victimisation, to advance equality of opportunity between people who share a relevant protected characteristic and people who do not share it, and to take steps to foster good relations between those persons. (See *Note 1A*).
1.4 In all cases, police should therefore:
 • exercise their powers courteously and with respect for persons and property
 • only use reasonable force when this is considered necessary and proportionate to the circumstances
1.5 If the provisions of PACE and this Code are not observed, evidence obtained from a search may be open to question.

*Note for Guidance*

1A *In paragraph 1.3A, 'relevant protected characteristic' includes: age, disability, gender reassignment, pregnancy and maternity, race, religion/belief, sex and sexual orientation.*

### 2 General

2.1 This Code must be readily available at all police stations for consultation by:
 • police officers
 • police staff

- detained persons
- members of the public

2.2 The Notes for Guidance included are not provisions of this Code.

2.3 This Code applies to searches of premises:

(a) by police for the purposes of an investigation into an alleged offence, with the occupier's consent, other than:
- routine scene of crime searches;
- calls to a fire or burglary made by or on behalf of an occupier or searches following the activation of fire or burglar alarms or discovery of insecure premises;
- searches when paragraph 5.4 applies;
- bomb threat calls;

(b) under powers conferred on police officers by PACE, sections 17, 18 and 32;

(c) undertaken in pursuance of search warrants issued to and executed by constables in accordance with PACE, sections 15 and 16 (see *Note 2A*);

(d) subject to paragraph 2.6, under any other power given to police to enter premises with or without a search warrant for any purpose connected with the investigation into an alleged or suspected offence. (See *Note 2B*.)

For the purposes of this Code, 'premises' as defined in PACE, section 23, includes any place, vehicle, vessel, aircraft, hovercraft, tent or movable structure and any offshore installation as defined in the Mineral Workings (Offshore Installations) Act 1971, section 1. (See *Note 2D*.)

2.4 A person who has not been arrested but is searched during a search of premises should be searched in accordance with Code A. (See *Note 2C*.)

2.5 This Code does not apply to the exercise of a statutory power to enter premises or to inspect goods, equipment or procedures if the exercise of that power is not dependent on the existence of grounds for suspecting that an offence may have been committed and the person exercising the power has no reasonable grounds for such suspicion.

2.6 This Code does not affect any directions or requirements of a search warrant, order or other power to search and seize lawfully exercised in England or Wales that any item or evidence seized under that warrant, order or power be handed over to a police force, court, tribunal, or other authority outside England or Wales. For example, warrants and orders issued in Scotland or Northern Ireland (see *Note 2B(f)*) and search warrants and powers provided for in sections 14 to 17 of the Crime (International Co-operation) Act 2003.

2.7 When this Code requires the prior authority or agreement of an officer of at leastinspector or superintendent rank, that authority may be given by a sergeant or chief inspector authorised to perform the functions of the higher rank under PACE, section 107.5

2.8 Written records required under this Code not made in the search record shall, unless otherwise specified, be made:
- in the recording officer's pocket book ('pocket book' includes any official report book issued to police officers) or
- on forms provided for the purpose

2.9 Nothing in this Code requires the identity of officers, or anyone accompanying them during a search of premises, to be recorded or disclosed:

(a) in the case of enquiries linked to the investigation of terrorism; or

(b) if officers reasonably believe recording or disclosing their names might put them in danger.

In these cases officers should use warrant or other identification numbers and the name of their police station. Police staff should use any identification number provided to them by the police force. (See *Note 2E*.)

2.10 The 'officer in charge of the search' means the officer assigned specific duties and responsibilities under this Code. Whenever there is a search of premises to which this Code applies one officer must act as the officer in charge of the search. (See *Note 2F*.)

2.11 In this Code:

(a) 'designated person' means a person other than a police officer, designated under the Police Reform Act 2002, Part 4 who has specified powers and duties of police officers conferred or imposed on them. (See *Note 2G*.)

(b) any reference to a police officer includes a designated person acting in the exercise or performance of the powers and duties conferred or imposed on them by their designation.

(c) a person authorised to accompany police officers or designated persons in the execution of a warrant has the same powers as a constable in the execution of the warrant and the search and seizure of anything related to the warrant. These powers must be exercised in the company and under the supervision of a police officer. (See *Note 3C.*)

2.12 If a power conferred on a designated person:

(a) allows reasonable force to be used when exercised by a police officer, a designated person exercising that power has the same entitlement to use force;

(b) includes power to use force to enter any premises, that power is not exercisable by that designated person except:

(i) in the company and under the supervision of a police officer; or

(ii) for the purpose of:
- saving life or limb; or
- preventing serious damage to property.

2.13 Designated persons must have regard to any relevant provisions of the Codes of Practice.

*Notes for Guidance*

2A *PACE sections 15 and 16 apply to all search warrants issued to and executed by constables under any enactment, e.g. search warrants issued by a:*

(a) *justice of the peace under the:*
- *Theft Act 1968, section 26 – stolen property;*
- *Misuse of Drugs Act 1971, section 23 – controlled drugs;*
- *PACE, section 8 – evidence of an indictable offence;*
- *Terrorism Act 2000, Schedule 5, paragraph 1;*
- *Terrorism Prevention and Investigation Measures Act 2011, Schedule 5, paragraph 8(2)(b) search of premises for compliance purposes (see paragraph 10.1).*

(b) *Circuit judge under:*
- *PACE, Schedule 1;*
- *Terrorism Act 2000, Schedule 5, paragraph 11.*

2B *Examples of the other powers in paragraph 2.3(d) include:*

(a) *Road Traffic Act 1988, section 6E(1) giving police power to enter premises under section 6E(1) to:*
- *require a person to provide a specimen of breath; or*
- *arrest a person following:*
  - *a positive breath test;*
  - *failure to provide a specimen of breath;*

(b) *Transport and Works Act 1992, section 30(4) giving police powers to enter premises mirroring the powers in (a) in relation to specified persons working on transport systems to which the Act applies;*

(c) *Criminal Justice Act 1988, section 139B giving police power to enter and search school premises for offensive weapons, bladed or pointed articles;*

(d) *Terrorism Act 2000, Schedule 5, paragraphs 3 and 15 empowering a superintendent in urgent cases to give written authority for police to enter and search premises for the purposes of a terrorist investigation;*

(e) *Explosives Act 1875, section 73(b) empowering a superintendent to give written authority for police to enter premises, examine and search them for explosives;*

(f) *search warrants and production orders or the equivalent issued in Scotland or Northern Ireland endorsed under the Summary Jurisdiction (Process) Act 1881 or the Petty Sessions (Ireland) Act 1851 respectively for execution in England and Wales.*

(g) *Terrorism Prevention and Investigation Measures Act 2011, Schedule 5, paragraphs 5(1), 6(2)(b) and 7(2), searches relating to TPIM notices (see paragraph 10.1).*

2C *The Criminal Justice Act 1988, section 139B provides that a constable who has reasonable grounds to suspect an offence under the Criminal Justice Act 1988, section 139A or 139AA has or is being committed may enter school premises and search the premises and any persons on the premises for any bladed or pointed article or offensive weapon. Persons may be searched under a warrant issued under the Misuse of Drugs Act 1971, section 23(3) to search premises for drugs or documents only if the warrant specifically authorises the search of persons on the premises. Powers to search premises under certain terrorism provisions also authorise the search of persons on the premises, for example, under paragraphs 1, 2, 11 and 15 of Schedule 5 to the Terrorism Act 2000 and section 52 of the Anti-terrorism, Crime and Security Act 2001.*

2D *The Immigration Act 1971, Part III and Schedule 2 gives immigration officers powers to enter and search premises, seize and retain property, with and without a search warrant. These are similar to the powers available to police under search warrants issued by a justice of the peace and without a warrant under PACE, sections 17, 18, 19 and 32 except they only apply to specified offences under the Immigration Act 1971 and immigration control powers. For certain types of investigations and enquiries these powers avoid* the need for the Immigration Service to rely on police officers becoming directly involved. When exercising these powers, immigration officers are required by the Immigration and Asylum Act 1999, section 145 to have regard to this Code's corresponding provisions. When immigration officers are dealing with persons or property at police stations, police officers should give appropriate assistance to help them discharge their specific duties and responsibilities.

2E   The purpose of paragraph 2.9(b) is to protect those involved in serious organised crime investigations or arrests of particularly violent suspects when there is reliable information that those arrested or their associates may threaten or cause harm to the officers or anyone accompanying them during a search of premises. In cases of doubt, an officer of inspector rank or above should be consulted.

2F   For the purposes of paragraph 2.10, the officer in charge of the search should normally be the most senior officer present. Some exceptions are:

(a)  a supervising officer who attends or assists at the scene of a premises search may appoint an officer of lower rank as officer in charge of the search if that officer is:

• more conversant with the facts;

• a more appropriate officer to be in charge of the search;

(b)  when all officers in a premises search are the same rank. The supervising officer if available, must make sure one of them is appointed officer in charge of the search, otherwise the officers themselves must nominate one of their number as the officer in charge;

(c)  a senior officer assisting in a specialist role. This officer need not be regarded as having a general supervisory role over the conduct of the search or be appointed or expected to act as the officer in charge of the search.

Except in (c), nothing in this Note diminishes the role and responsibilities of a supervisory officer who is present at the search or knows of a search taking place.

2G   An officer of the rank of inspector or above may direct a designated investigating officer not to wear a uniform for the purposes of a specific operation.

## 3  Search warrants and production orders

### (a) Before making an application

3.1   When information appears to justify an application, the officer must take reasonable steps to check the information is accurate, recent and not provided maliciously or irresponsibly. An application may not be made on the basis of information from an anonymous source if corroboration has not been sought. (See *Note 3A*.)

3.2   The officer shall ascertain as specifically as possible the nature of the articles concerned and their location.

3.3   The officer shall make reasonable enquiries to:

(i)   establish if:

• anything is known about the likely occupier of the premises and the nature of the premises themselves;

• the premises have been searched previously and how recently;

(ii)  obtain any other relevant information.

3.4   An application:

(a)  to a justice of the peace for a search warrant or to a Circuit judge for a search warrant or production order under PACE, Schedule 1 must be supported by a signed written authority from an officer of inspector rank or above:

Note: If the case is an urgent application to a justice of the peace and an inspector or above is not readily available, the next most senior officer on duty can give the written authority.

(b)  to a circuit judge under the Terrorism Act 2000, Schedule 5 for:

• a production order;

• search warrant; or

• an order requiring an explanation of material seized or produced under such a warrant or production order, must be supported by a signed written authority from an officer of superintendent rank or above.

3.5   Except in a case of urgency, if there is reason to believe a search might have an adverse effect on relations between the police and the community, the officer in charge shall consult the local police/community liaison officer:

• before the search; or

• in urgent cases, as soon as practicable after the search

*(b)  Making an application*

3.6   A search warrant application must be supported in writing, specifying:
  (a)   the enactment under which the application is made (see *Note 2A*);
  (b)   (i)   whether the warrant is to authorise entry and search of:
        • one set of premises; or
        • if the application is under PACE section 8, or Schedule 1, paragraph 12, more than one set of specified premises or all premises occupied or controlled by a specified person, and
        (ii)   the premises to be searched;
  (c)   the object of the search (see *Note 3B*);
  (d)   the grounds for the application, including, when the purpose of the proposed search is to find evidence of an alleged offence, an indication of how the evidence relates to the investigation;
  (da) Where the application is under PACE section 8, or Schedule 1, paragraph 12 for a single warrant to enter and search:
        (i)   more than one set of specified premises; the officer must specify each set of premises which it is desired to enter and search;
        (ii)   all premises occupied or controlled by a specified person; the officer must specify;
        • as many sets of premises which it is desired to enter and search as it is reasonably practicable to specify;
        • the person who is in occupation or control of those premises and any others which it is desired to search;
        • why it is necessary to search more premises than those which can be specified, and
        • why it is not reasonably practicable to specify all the premises which it is desired to enter and search;
  (db) Whether an application under PACE section 8 is for a warrant authorising entry and search on more than one occasion, and if so, the officer must state the grounds for this and whether the desired number of entries authorised is unlimited or a specified maximum;
  (e)   That there are no reasonable grounds to believe the material to be sought, when making application to a:
        (i)   justice of the peace or a Circuit judge consists of or includes items subject to legal privilege;
        (ii)   justice of the peace, consists of or includes excluded material or special procedure material; Note: this does not affect the additional powers of seizure in the Criminal Justice and Police Act 2001, Part 2 covered in paragraph 7.7 (see *Note 3B*).
  (f)   if applicable, a request for the warrant to authorise a person or persons to accompany the officer who executes the warrant. (See *Note 3C*.)
3.7   A search warrant application under PACE, Schedule 1, paragraph 12(a), shall if appropriate indicate why it is believed service of notice of an application for a production order may seriously prejudice the investigation. Applications for search warrants under the Terrorism Act 2000, Schedule 5, paragraph 11 must indicate why a production order would not be appropriate.
3.8   If a search warrant application is refused, a further application may not be made for those premises unless supported by additional grounds.

*Notes for Guidance*

*3A    The identity of an informant need not be disclosed when making an application, but the officer should be prepared to answer any questions the magistrate or judge may have about:*
  • *the accuracy of previous information from that source, and*
  • *any other related matters*
*3B    The information supporting a search warrant application should be as specific as possible, particularly in relation to the articles or persons being sought and where in the premises it is suspected they may be found. The meaning of 'items subject to legal privilege', 'excluded material' and 'special procedure material' are defined by PACE, sections 10, 11 and 14 respectively.*
*3C    Under PACE, section 16(2), a search warrant may authorise persons other than police officers to accompany the constable who executes the warrant. This includes, e.g. any suitably qualified or skilled person or an expert in a particular field whose presence is needed to help accurately identify the material sought or to advise where certain evidence is most likely to be found and how it should be dealt with. It does not give them any right to force entry, but it gives them the right to be on the premises during the search and to search for or seize property without the occupier's permission.*

**4  Entry without warrant – particular powers**

*(a)  Making an arrest etc*

4.1     The conditions under which an officer may enter and search premises without a warrant are set out in PACE, section 17. It should be noted that this section does not create or confer any powers of arrest. See other powers in *Note 2B(a)*.

*(b)  Search of premises where arrest takes place or the arrested person was immediately before arrest*

4.2     When a person has been arrested for an indictable offence, a police officer has power under PACE, section 32 to search the premises where the person was arrested or where the person was immediately before being arrested.

*(c)  Search of premises occupied or controlled by the arrested person*

4.3     The specific powers to search premises which are occupied or controlled by a person arrested for an indictable offence are set out in PACE, section 18. They may not be exercised, except if section 18(5) applies, unless an officer of inspector rank or above has given written authority. That authority should only be given when the authorising officer is satisfied that the premises are occupied or controlled by the arrested person and that the necessary grounds exist. If possible the authorising officer should record the authority on the Notice of Powers and Rights and, subject to paragraph 2.9, sign the Notice. The record of the grounds for the search and the nature of the evidence sought as required by section 18(7) of the Act should be made in:
* the custody record if there is one, otherwise
* the officer's pocket book, or
* the search record

**5  Search with consent**

5.1     Subject to paragraph 5.4, if it is proposed to search premises with the consent of a person entitled to grant entry the consent must, if practicable, be given in writing on the Notice of Powers and Rights before the search. The officer must make any necessary enquiries to be satisfied the person is in a position to give such consent. (See *Notes 5A* and *5B*.)

5.2     Before seeking consent the officer in charge of the search shall state the purpose of the proposed search and its extent. This information must be as specific as possible, particularly regarding the articles or persons being sought and the parts of the premises to be searched. The person concerned must be clearly informed they are not obliged to consent, that any consent given can be withdrawn at any time, including before the search starts or while it is underway and anything seized may be produced in evidence. If at the time the person is not suspected of an offence, the officer shall say this when stating the purpose of the search.

5.3     An officer cannot enter and search or continue to search premises under paragraph 5.1 if consent is given under duress or withdrawn before the search is completed.

5.4     It is unnecessary to seek consent under paragraphs 5.1 and 5.2 if this would cause disproportionate inconvenience to the person concerned. (See *Note 5C*.)

*Notes for Guidance*

5A     *In a lodging house, hostel or similar accommodation, every reasonable effort should be made to obtain the consent of the tenant, lodger or occupier. A search should not be made solely on the basis of the landlord's consent.*

5B     *If the intention is to search premises under the authority of a warrant or a power of entry and search without warrant, and the occupier of the premises co-operates in accordance with paragraph 6.4, there is no need to obtain written consent.*

5C     *Paragraph 5.4 is intended to apply when it is reasonable to assume innocent occupiers would agree to, and expect, police to take the proposed action, e.g. if:*
* *a suspect has fled the scene of a crime or to evade arrest and it is necessary quickly to check surrounding gardens and readily accessible places to see if the suspect is hiding, or*
* *police have arrested someone in the night after a pursuit and it is necessary to make a brief check of gardens along the pursuit route to see if stolen or incriminating articles have been discarded.*

**6  Searching premises – general considerations**

*(a)  Time of searches*

6.1     Searches made under warrant must be made within three calendar months of the date the warrant is issued or within the period specified in the enactment under which the warrant is issued if this is shorter.

6.2    Searches must be made at a reasonable hour unless this might frustrate the purpose of the search.

6.3    When the extent or complexity of a search mean it is likely to take a long time, the officer in charge of the search may consider using the seize and sift powers referred to in section 7.

6.3A  A warrant under PACE, section 8 may authorise entry to and search of premises on more than one occasion if, on the application, the justice of the peace is satisfied that it is necessary to authorise multiple entries in order to achieve the purpose for which the warrant is issued. No premises may be entered or searched on any subsequent occasions without the prior written authority of an officer of the rank of inspector who is not involved in the investigation. All other warrants authorise entry on one occasion only.

6.3B  Where a warrant under PACE section 8, or Schedule 1, paragraph 12 authorises entry to and search of all premises occupied or controlled by a specified person, no premises which are not specified in the warrant may be entered and searched without the prior written authority of an officer of the rank of inspector who is not involved in the investigation.

*(b)  Entry other than with consent*

6.4    The officer in charge of the search shall first try to communicate with the occupier, or any other person entitled to grant access to the premises, explain the authority under which entry is sought and ask the occupier to allow entry, unless:
    (i)    the search premises are unoccupied;
    (ii)   the occupier and any other person entitled to grant access are absent;
    (iii)  there are reasonable grounds for believing that alerting the occupier or any other person entitled to grant access would frustrate the object of the search or endanger officers or other people.

6.5    Unless sub-paragraph 6.4(iii) applies, if the premises are occupied the officer, subject to paragraph 2.9, shall, before the search begins:
    (i)    identify him or herself, show their warrant card (if not in uniform) and state the purpose of, and grounds for, the search, and
    (ii)   Identify and introduce any person accompanying the officer on the search (such persons should carry identification for production on request) and briefly describe that person's role in the process.

6.6    Reasonable and proportionate force may be used if necessary to enter premises if the officer in charge of the search is satisfied the premises are those specified in any warrant, or in exercise of the powers described in paragraphs 4.1 to 4.3, and if:
    (i)    the occupier or any other person entitled to grant access has refused entry;
    (ii)   it is impossible to communicate with the occupier or any other person entitled to grant access; or
    (iii)  any of the provisions of paragraph 6.4 apply.

*(c)  Notice of Powers and Rights*

6.7    If an officer conducts a search to which this Code applies the officer shall, unless it is impracticable to do so, provide the occupier with a copy of a Notice in a standard format:
    (i)    specifying if the search is made under warrant, with consent, or in the exercise of the powers described in paragraphs 4.1 to 4.3. Note: the notice format shall provide for authority or consent to be indicated (see *paragraphs 4.3* and *5.1*);
    (ii)   summarising the extent of the powers of search and seizure conferred by PACE and other relevant legislation as appropriate;
    (iii)  explaining the rights of the occupier and the owner of the property seized;
    (iv)   explaining compensation may be payable in appropriate cases for damages caused entering and searching premises, and giving the address to send a compensation application (see *Note 6A*), and
    (v)    stating this Code is available at any police station.

6.8    If the occupier is:
    •  present; copies of the Notice and warrant shall, if practicable, be given to them before the search begins, unless the officer in charge of the search reasonably believes this would frustrate the object of the search or endanger officers or other people;
    •  not present; copies of the Notice and warrant shall be left in a prominent place on the premises or appropriate part of the premises and endorsed, subject to paragraph 2.9 with the name of the officer in charge of the search, the date and time of the search
    The warrant shall be endorsed to show this has been done.

circumstances. If it is necessary for security reasons or to maintain confidentiality officers may exclude interested persons from decryption or other processes which facilitate the examination but do not form part of it. (See *Note 7D.*)

7.9 It is the responsibility of the officer in charge of the investigation to make sure property is returned in accordance with sections 53 to 55. Material which there is no power to retain must be:
* separated from the rest of the seized property, and
* returned as soon as reasonably practicable after examination of all the seized property.

7.9A Delay is only warranted if very clear and compelling reasons exist, for example:
* the unavailability of the person to whom the material is to be returned, or
* the need to agree a convenient time to return a large volume of material

7.9B Legally privileged, excluded or special procedure material which cannot be retained must be returned:
* as soon as reasonably practicable, and
* without waiting for the whole examination.

7.9C As set out in section 58, material must be returned to the person from whom it was seized, except when it is clear some other person has a better right to it. (See *Note 7E.*)

7.10 When an officer involved in the investigation has reasonable grounds to believe a person with a relevant interest in property seized under section 50 or 51 intends to make an application under section 59 for the return of any legally privileged, special procedure or excluded material, the officer in charge of the investigation should be informed as soon as practicable and the material seized should be kept secure in accordance with section 61. (See *Note 7C.*)

7.11 The officer in charge of the investigation is responsible for making sure property is properly secured. Securing involves making sure the property is not examined, copied, imaged or put to any other use except at the request, or with the consent, of the applicant or in accordance with the directions of the appropriate judicial authority. Any request, consent or directions must be recorded in writing and signed by both the initiator and the officer in charge of the investigation. (See *Notes 7F* and *7G.*)

7.12 When an officer exercises a power of seizure conferred by sections 50 or 51 they shall provide the occupier of the premises or the person from whom the property is being seized with a written notice:
(i) specifying what has been seized under the powers conferred by that section;
(ii) specifying the grounds for those powers;
(iii) setting out the effect of sections 59 to 61 covering the grounds for a person with a relevant interest in seized property to apply to a judicial authority for its return and the duty of officers to secure property in certain circumstances when an application is made, and
(iv) specifying the name and address of the person to whom:
* notice of an application to the appropriate judicial authority in respect of any of the seized property must be given;
* an application may be made to allow attendance at the initial examination of the property.

7.13 If the occupier is not present but there is someone in charge of the premises, the notice shall be given to them. If no suitable person is available, so the notice will easily be found it should either be:
* left in a prominent place on the premises, or
* attached to the exterior of the premises.

*(c) Retention*

7.14 Subject to paragraph 7.15, anything seized in accordance with the above provisions may be retained only for as long as is necessary. It may be retained, among other purposes:
(i) for use as evidence at a trial for an offence;
(ii) to facilitate the use in any investigation or proceedings of anything to which it is inextricably linked (see *Note 7H*);
(iii) for forensic examination or other investigation in connection with an offence;
(iv) in order to establish its lawful owner when there are reasonable grounds for believing it has been stolen or obtained by the commission of an offence.

7.15 Property shall not be retained under paragraph 7.14(i), (ii) or (iii) if a copy or image would be sufficient.

*(d) Rights of owners etc*

7.16 If property is retained, the person who had custody or control of it immediately before seizure must, on request, be provided with a list or description of the property within a reasonable time.

7.17 That person or their representative must be allowed supervised access to the property to examine it or have it photographed or copied, or must be provided with a photograph or copy, in either case within a reasonable time of any request and at their own expense, unless the officer in charge of an investigation has reasonable grounds for believing this would:

(i)   prejudice the investigation of any offence or criminal proceedings; or

(ii)  lead to the commission of an offence by providing access to unlawful material such as pornography;

A record of the grounds shall be made when access is denied.

### Notes for Guidance

7A   *Any person claiming property seized by the police may apply to a magistrates' court under the Police (Property) Act 1897 for its possession and should, if appropriate, be advised of this procedure.*

7B   *The powers of seizure conferred by PACE, sections 18(2) and 19(3) extend to the seizure of the whole premises when it is physically possible to seize and retain the premises in their totality and practical considerations make seizure desirable. For example, police may remove premises such as tents, vehicles or caravans to a police station for the purpose of preserving evidence.*

7C   *Officers should consider reaching agreement with owners and/or other interested parties on the procedures for examining a specific set of property, rather than awaiting the judicial authority's determination. Agreement can sometimes give a quicker and more satisfactory route for all concerned and minimise costs and legal complexities.*

7D   *What constitutes a relevant interest in specific material may depend on the nature of that material and the circumstances in which it is seized. Anyone with a reasonable claim to ownership of the material and anyone entrusted with its safe keeping by the owner should be considered.*

7E   *Requirements to secure and return property apply equally to all copies, images or other material created because of seizure of the original property.*

7F   *The mechanics of securing property vary according to the circumstances; 'bagging up', i.e. placing material in sealed bags or containers and strict subsequent control of access is the appropriate procedure in many cases.*

7G   *When material is seized under the powers of seizure conferred by PACE, the duty to retain it under the Code of Practice issued under the Criminal Procedure and Investigations Act 1996 is subject to the provisions on retention of seized material in PACE, section 22.*

7H   *Paragraph 7.14 (ii) applies if inextricably linked material is seized under the Criminal Justice and Police Act 2001, sections 50 or 51. Inextricably linked material is material it is not reasonably practicable to separate from other linked material without prejudicing the use of that other material in any investigation or proceedings. For example, it may not be possible to separate items of data held on computer disk without damaging their evidential integrity. Inextricably linked material must not be examined, imaged, copied or used for any purpose other than for proving the source and/or integrity of the linked material.*

## 8 Action after searches

8.1   If premises are searched in circumstances where this Code applies, unless the exceptions in paragraph 2.3(a) apply, on arrival at a police station the officer in charge of the search shall make or have made a record of the search, to include:

(i)    the address of the searched premises;

(ii)   the date, time and duration of the search;

(iii)  the authority used for the search:
   - if the search was made in exercise of a statutory power to search premises without warrant, the power which was used for the search:
   - if the search was made under a warrant or with written consent;
      – a copy of the warrant and the written authority to apply for it, see *paragraph 3.4*; or
      – the written consent;
         shall be appended to the record or the record shall show the location of the copy warrant or consent;

(iv)   subject to paragraph 2.9, the names of:
   - the officer(s) in charge of the search;
   - all other officers and authorised persons who conducted the search;

(v)    the names of any people on the premises if they are known;

(vi)   any grounds for refusing the occupier's request to have someone present during the search, see *paragraph 6.11*;

(vii)  a list of any articles seized or the location of a list and, if not covered by a warrant, the grounds for their seizure;

(viii) whether force was used, and the reason;

(ix)   details of any damage caused during the search, and the circumstances;

(x)    if applicable, the reason it was not practicable;
   (a)   to give the occupier a copy of the Notice of Powers and Rights, see *paragraph 6.7*;

    (b)   before the search to give the occupier a copy of the Notice, see *paragraph 6.8*;

  (xi)   when the occupier was not present, the place where copies of the Notice of Powers and Rights and search warrant were left on the premises, see *paragraph 6.8.*

8.2   On each occasion when premises are searched under warrant, the warrant authorising the search on that occasion shall be endorsed to show:

   (i)   if any articles specified in the warrant were found and the address where found;

   (ii)   if any other articles were seized;

  (iii)   the date and time it was executed and if present, the name of the occupier or if the occupier is not present the name of the person in charge of the premises;

  (iv)   subject to *paragraph 2.9*, the names of the officers who executed it and any authorised persons who accompanied them, and

   (v)   if a copy, together with a copy of the Notice of Powers and Rights was:
- handed to the occupier, or
- endorsed as required by paragraph 6.8; and left on the premises and where.

8.3   Any warrant shall be returned within three calendar months of its issue or sooner on completion of the search(es) authorised by that warrant, if it was issued by a:
- justice of the peace, to the designated officer for the local justice area in which the justice was acting when issuing the warrant; or
- judge, to the appropriate officer of the court concerned.

## 9  Search registers

9.1   A search register will be maintained at each sub-divisional or equivalent police station. All search records required under paragraph 8.1 shall be made, copied, or referred to in the register. (See *Note 9A*.)

*Note for Guidance*

9A   *Paragraph 9.1 also applies to search records made by immigration officers. In these cases, a search register must also be maintained at an immigration office. (See also Note 2D.)*

## 10  Searches under Schedule 5 to the Terrorism Prevention and Investigation Measures Act 2011

10.1   This Code applies to the powers of constables under Schedule 5 to the Terrorism Prevention and Investigation Measures Act 2011 relating to TPIM notices to enter and search premises subject to the modifications in the following paragraphs.

10.2   In paragraph 2.3(d), the reference to the investigation into an alleged or suspected offence include the enforcement of terrorism prevention and investigation measures which may be imposed on an individual by a TPIM notice in accordance with the Terrorism Prevention and Investigation Measures Act 2011.

10.3   References to the purpose and object of the entry and search of premises, the nature of articles sought and what may be seized and retained include (as appropriate):

   (a)   in relation to the power to search without a search warrant in paragraph 5 (for purposes of serving TPIM notice), finding the individual on whom the notice is to be served.

   (b)   in relation to the power to search without a search warrant in paragraph 6 (at time of serving TPIM notice), ascertaining whether there is anything in the premises, that contravenes measures specified in the notice. (See *Note 10A*.)

   (c)   in relation to the power to search without a search warrant under paragraph 7 (suspected absconding), ascertaining whether a person has absconded or if there is anything on the premises which will assist in the pursuit or arrest of an individual in respect of whom a TPIM notice is force who is reasonably suspected of having absconded.

   (d)   in relation to the power to search under a search warrant issued under paragraph 8 (for compliance purposes), determining whether an individual in respect of whom a TPIM notice is in force is complying with measures specified in the notice. (See *Note 10A*.)

*Note for Guidance*

10A   *Searches of individuals under Schedule 5, paragraphs 6(2)(a) (at time of serving TPIM notice) and 8(2)(a) (for compliance purposes) must be conducted and recorded in accordance with Code A. (See Code A paragraph 2.18A for details.)*

# POLICE AND CRIMINAL EVIDENCE ACT 1984
## (PACE) — CODE C

## REVISED CODE OF PRACTICE FOR THE DETENTION, TREATMENT AND QUESTIONING OF PERSONS BY POLICE OFFICERS

**Commencement—Transitional Arrangements**

This Code applies to people in police detention after 00.00 on 21 August 2019, notwithstanding that their period of detention may have commenced before that time.

### 1 General

1.0    The powers and procedures in this Code must be used fairly, responsibly, with respect for the people to whom they apply and without unlawful discrimination. Under the Equality Act 2010, section 149 (Public sector Equality Duty), police forces must, in carrying out their functions, have due regard to the need to eliminate unlawful discrimination, harassment, victimisation and any other conduct which is prohibited by that Act, to advance equality of opportunity between people who share a relevant protected characteristic and people who do not share it, and to foster good relations between those persons. The Equality Act *also* makes it unlawful for police officers to discriminate against, harass or victimise any person on the grounds of the 'protected characteristics' of age, disability, gender reassignment, race, religion or belief, sex and sexual orientation, marriage and civil partnership, pregnancy and maternity, when using their powers. See *Notes 1A* and *1AA*.

1.1    All persons in custody must be dealt with expeditiously, and released as soon as the need for detention no longer applies.

1.1A  A custody officer must perform the functions in this Code as soon as practicable. A custody officer will not be in breach of this Code if delay is justifiable and reasonable steps are taken to prevent unnecessary delay. The custody record shall show when a delay has occurred and the reason. See *Note 1H*.

1.2    This Code of Practice must be readily available at all police stations for consultation by:
* police officers;
* police staff;
* detained persons;
* members of the public.

1.3    The provisions of this Code:
* include the Annexes
* do not include the Notes for Guidance *which* form guidance to police officers and others about its application and interpretation.

1.4    If at any time an officer has any reason to suspect that a person of any age may be vulnerable (see *paragraph 1.13(d)*), in the absence of clear evidence to dispel that suspicion, that person shall be treated as such for the purposes of this Code and to establish whether any such reason may exist in relation to a person suspected of committing an offence (see *paragraph 10.1* and *Note 10A*), the custody officer in the case of a detained person, or the officer investigating the offence in the case of a person who has not been arrested or detained, shall take, or cause to be taken, (see *paragraph 3.5* and *Note 3F*) the following action:
  (a)   reasonable enquiries shall be made to ascertain what information is available that is relevant to any of the factors described in *paragraph 1.13(d)* as indicating that the person may be vulnerable might apply;
  (b)   a record shall be made describing whether any of those factors appear to apply and provide any reason to suspect that the person may be vulnerable or (as the case may be) may not be vulnerable; and
  (c)   the record mentioned in sub-paragraph (b) shall be made available to be taken into account by police officers, police staff and any others who, in accordance with the provisions of this or any other Code, are required or entitled to communicate with the person in question. This would include any solicitor, appropriate adult and healthcare professional and is particularly relevant to communication by telephone or by means of a live link (see *paragraphs 12.9A* (interviews), *13.12* (interpretation), and *15.3C, 15.11A, 15.11B, 15.11C* and *15.11D* (reviews and extension of detention)).
  See *Notes 1G, 1GA, 1GB* and *1GC*.

1.5 Anyone who appears to be under 18, shall, in the absence of clear evidence that they are older, be treated as a juvenile for the purposes of this Code and any other Code. See *Note 1L*.

1.5A *Not used*.

1.6 If a person appears to be blind, seriously visually impaired, deaf, unable to read or speak or has difficulty orally because of a speech impediment, they shall be treated as such for the purposes of this Code in the absence of clear evidence to the contrary.

1.7 'The appropriate adult' means, in the case of a:
   (a) juvenile:
       (i)   the parent, guardian or, if the juvenile is in the care of a local authority or voluntary organisation, a person representing that authority or organisation (see *Note 1B*);
       (ii)  a social worker of a local authority (see *Note 1C*);
       (iii) failing these, some other responsible adult aged 18 or over who is *not*:
             • a police officer;
             • employed by the police;
             • under the direction or control of the chief officer of a police force; or
             • a person who provides services under contractual arrangements (but without being employed by the chief officer of a police force), to assist that force in relation to the discharge of its chief officer's functions, whether or not they are on duty at the time.
             See *Note 1F*.
   (b) a person who is vulnerable (see *paragraph 1.4* and *Note 1D*):
       (i)   a relative, guardian or other person responsible for their care or custody;
       (ii)  someone experienced in dealing with vulnerable persons but who is *not*:
             • a police officer;
             • employed by the police;
             • under the direction or control of the chief officer of a police force; or
             • a person who provides services under contractual arrangements (but without being employed by the chief officer of a police force), to assist that force in relation to the discharge of its chief officer's functions, whether or not they are on duty at the time.
       (iii) failing these, some other responsible adult aged 18 or over who is other than a person described in the bullet points in *sub-paragraph (b)(ii)* above.
             See *Note 1F*.

1.7A The role of the appropriate adult is to safeguard the rights, entitlements and welfare of juveniles and vulnerable persons (see *paragraphs 1.4* and *1.5*) to whom the provisions of this and any other Code of Practice apply. For this reason, the appropriate adult is expected, amongst other things, to:
   • support, advise and assist them when, in accordance with this Code or any other Code of Practice, they are given or asked to provide information or participate in any procedure;
   • observe whether the police are acting properly and fairly to respect their rights and entitlements, and inform an officer of the rank of inspector or above if they consider that they are not;
   • assist them to communicate with the police whilst respecting their right to say nothing unless they want to as set out in the terms of the caution (see *paragraphs 10.5* and *10.6*);
   • help them to understand their rights and ensure that those rights are protected and respected (see *paragraphs 3.15*, *3.17*, *6.5A* and *11.17*).

1.8 If this Code requires a person be given certain information, they do not have to be given it if at the time they are incapable of understanding what is said, are violent or may become violent or in urgent need of medical attention, but they must be given it as soon as practicable.

1.9 References to a custody officer include any police officer who, for the time being, is performing the functions of a custody officer.

1.9A When this Code requires the prior authority or agreement of an officer of at least inspector or superintendent rank, that authority may be given by a sergeant or chief inspector authorised to perform the functions of the higher rank under the Police and Criminal Evidence Act 1984 (PACE), section 107.

1.10 Subject to *paragraph 1.12*, this Code applies to people in custody at police stations in England and Wales, whether or not they have been arrested, and to those removed to a police station as a place of safety under the Mental Health Act 1983, sections 135 and 136, as amended by the Policing and Crime Act 2017 (see *paragraph 3.16*). *Section 15* applies solely to people in police detention, e.g. those brought to a police station under arrest or arrested at a police station for an offence after going there voluntarily.

1.11 No part of this Code applies to a detained person:
   (a) to whom PACE Code H applies because:

- they are detained following arrest under section 41 of the Terrorism Act 2000 (TACT) and not charged; or
- an authorisation has been given under section 22 of the Counter-Terrorism Act 2008 (CTACT) (post-charge questioning of terrorist suspects) to interview them.

(b)  to whom the Code of Practice issued under paragraph 6 of Schedule 14 to TACT applies because they are detained for examination under Schedule 7 to TACT.

1.12  This Code does not apply to people in custody:

(i)    arrested by officers under the Criminal Justice and Public Order Act 1994, section 136(2) on warrants issued in Scotland, or arrested or detained without warrant under section 137(2) by officers from a police force in Scotland. In these cases, police powers and duties and the person's rights and entitlements whilst at a police station in England or Wales are the same as those in Scotland;

(ii)   arrested under the Immigration and Asylum Act 1999, section 142(3) in order to have their fingerprints taken;

(iii)  whose detention has been authorised under Schedules 2 or 3 to the Immigration Act 1971 or section 62 of the Nationality, Immigration and Asylum Act 2002;

(iv)  who are convicted or remanded prisoners held in police cells on behalf of the Prison Service under the Imprisonment (Temporary Provisions) Act 1980;

(v)   Not used.

(vi)  detained for searches under stop and search powers except as required by Code A.

The provisions on conditions of detention and treatment in *sections 8* and *9* must be considered as the minimum standards of treatment for such detainees.

1.13  In this Code:

(a)  'designated person' means a person other than a police officer, who has specified powers and duties conferred or imposed on them by designation under section 38 or 39 of the Police Reform Act 2002;

(b)  reference to a police officer includes a designated person acting in the exercise or performance of the powers and duties conferred or imposed on them by their designation;

(c)  if there is doubt as to whether the person should be treated, or continued to be treated, as being male or female in the case of:

(i)    a search carried out or observed by a person of the same sex as the detainee; or

(ii)   any other procedure which requires action to be taken or information to be given that depends on whether the person is to be treated as being male or female;
then the gender of the detainee and other parties concerned should be established and recorded in line with *Annex L* of this Code.

(d)  'vulnerable' applies to any person who, because of a mental health condition or mental disorder (see *Notes 1G and 1GB*):

(i)    may have difficulty understanding or communicating effectively about the full implications for them of any procedures and processes connected with:
- their arrest and detention; or (as the case may be)
- their voluntary attendance at a police station or their presence elsewhere (see *paragraph 3.21*), for the purpose of a voluntary interview; and
- the exercise of their rights and entitlements.

(ii)   does not appear to understand the significance of what they are told, of questions they are asked or of their replies:

(iii)  appears to be particularly prone to:
- becoming confused and unclear about their position;
- providing unreliable, misleading or incriminating information without knowing or wishing to do so;
- accepting or acting on suggestions from others without consciously knowing or wishing to do so; or
- readily agreeing to suggestions or proposals without any protest or question.

(e)  'Live link' means:

(i)    for the purpose of *paragraph 12.9A;* an arrangement by means of which the *interviewing officer* who is not present at the police station where the detainee is held, is able to see and hear, and to be seen and heard by, the detainee concerned, the detainee's solicitor, appropriate adult and interpreter (as applicable) and the officer who has custody of that detainee (see *Note 1N*).

(ii)   for the purpose of *paragraph 15.9A;* an arrangement by means of which the *review officer* who is not present at the police station where the detainee is held, is able to see and hear, and to be seen and heard by, the detainee concerned and the detainee's solicitor, appropriate adult and interpreter (as applicable) (see *Note 1N*). The use of live link for decisions about detention under *section 45A of PACE* is subject to regulations made by the Secretary of State being in force.

(iii) for the purpose of *paragraph 15.11A*; an arrangement by means of which the *authorising officer* who is not present at the police station where the detainee is held, is able to see and hear, and to be seen and heard by, the detainee concerned and the detainee's solicitor, appropriate adult and interpreter (as applicable) (see *Note 1N*).

(iv) for the purpose of *paragraph 15.11C;* an arrangement by means of which the *detainee* when not present in the court where the hearing is being held, is able to see and hear, and to be seen and heard by, the court during the hearing (see *Note 1N*).

Note: Chief officers must be satisfied that live link used in their force area for the above purposes provides for accurate and secure communication between the detainee, the detainee's solicitor, appropriate adult and interpreter (as applicable). This includes ensuring that at any time during which the live link is being used: a person cannot see, hear or otherwise obtain access to any such communications unless so authorised or allowed by the custody officer or, in the case of an interview, the interviewer and that as applicable, the confidentiality of any private consultation between a suspect and their solicitor and appropriate adult is maintained.

1.14 Designated persons are entitled to use reasonable force as follows:

(a) when exercising a power conferred on them which allows a police officer exercising that power to use reasonable force, a designated person has the same entitlement to use force; and

(b) at other times when carrying out duties conferred or imposed on them that also entitle them to use reasonable force, for example:

- when at a police station carrying out the duty to keep detainees for whom they are responsible under control and to assist any police officer or designated person to keep any detainee under control and to prevent their escape;
- when securing, or assisting any police officer or designated person in securing, the detention of a person at a police station;
- when escorting, or assisting any police officer or designated person in escorting, a detainee within a police station;
- for the purpose of saving life or limb; or
- preventing serious damage to property.

1.15 Nothing in this Code prevents the custody officer, or other police officer or designated person (see *paragraph 1.13(a)*) given custody of the detainee by the custody officer, from allowing another person (see *(a)* and *(b)* below) to carry out individual procedures or tasks at the police station if the law allows. However, the officer or designated person given custody remains responsible for making sure the procedures and tasks are carried out correctly in accordance with the Codes of Practice (see *paragraph 3.5* and *Note 3F*). The other person who is allowed to carry out the procedures or tasks must be someone who *at that time*, is:

(a) under the direction and control of the chief officer of the force responsible for the police station in question; or

(b) providing services under contractual arrangements (but without being employed by the chief officer the police force), to assist a police force in relation to the discharge of its chief officer's functions.

1.16 Designated persons and others mentioned in *sub-paragraphs (a)* and *(b)* of *paragraph 1.15*, must have regard to any relevant provisions of the Codes of Practice.

1.17 In any provision of this or any other Code which allows or requires police officers or police staff to make a record in their report book, the reference to report book shall include any official report book or electronic recording device issued to them that enables the record in question to be made and dealt with in accordance with that provision. References in this and any other Code to written records, forms and signatures include electronic records and forms and electronic confirmation that identifies the person making the record or completing the form. Chief officers must be satisfied as to the integrity and security of the devices, records and forms to which this *paragraph* applies and that use of those devices, records and forms satisfies relevant data protection legislation.

*Notes for Guidance*

1A  *Although certain sections of this Code apply specifically to people in custody at police stations, a person who attends a police station or other location voluntarily to assist with an investigation should be treated with no less consideration, e.g. offered or allowed refreshments at appropriate times, and enjoy an absolute right* to obtain legal advice or communicate with anyone outside the police station or other location (see paragraphs 3.21 and 3.22).

1AA    In paragraph 1.0, under the Equality Act 2010, section 149, the 'relevant protected characteristics' are age, disability, gender reassignment, pregnancy and maternity, race, religion/belief and sex and sexual orientation. For further detailed guidance and advice on the Equality Act, see: https://www.gov.uk/guidance/equality-act-2010-guidance.

1B    A person, including a parent or guardian, should not be an appropriate adult if they:
  • are:
    – suspected of involvement in the offence;
    – the victim;
    – a witness;
    – involved in the investigation.
  • received admissions prior to attending to act as the appropriate adult.
  Note: If a juvenile's parent is estranged from the juvenile, they should not be asked to act as the appropriate adult if the juvenile expressly and specifically objects to their presence.

1C    If a juvenile admits an offence to, or in the presence of, a social worker or member of a youth offending team other than during the time that person is acting as the juvenile's appropriate adult, another appropriate adult should be appointed in the interest of fairness.

1D    In the case of someone who is vulnerable, it may be more satisfactory if the appropriate adult is someone experienced or trained in their care rather than a relative lacking such qualifications. But if the person prefers a relative to a better qualified stranger or objects to a particular person their wishes should, if practicable, be respected.

1E    A detainee should always be given an opportunity, when an appropriate adult is called to the police station, to consult privately with a solicitor in the appropriate adult's absence if they want. An appropriate adult is not subject to legal privilege.

1F    An appropriate adult who is not a parent or guardian in the case of a juvenile, or a relative, guardian or carer in the case of a vulnerable person, must be independent of the police as their role is to safeguard the person's rights and entitlements. Additionally, a solicitor or independent custody visitor who is present at the police station and acting in that capacity, may not be the appropriate adult.

1G    A person may be vulnerable as a result of a having a mental health condition or mental disorder. Similarly, simply because an individual does not have, or is not known to have, any such condition or disorder, does not mean that they are not vulnerable for the purposes of this Code. It is therefore important that the custody officer in the case of a detained person or the officer investigating the offence in the case of a person who has not been arrested or detained, as appropriate, considers on a case by case basis, whether any of the factors described in paragraph 1.13(d) might apply to the person in question. In doing so, the officer must take into account the particular circumstances of the individual and how the nature of the investigation might affect them and bear in mind that juveniles, by virtue of their age will always require an appropriate adult.

1GA    For the purposes of paragraph 1.4(a), examples of relevant information that may be available include:
  • the behaviour of the adult or juvenile;
  • the mental health and capacity of the adult or juvenile;
  • what the adult or juvenile says about themselves;
  • information from relatives and friends of the adult or juvenile;
  • information from police officers and staff and from police records;
  • information from health and social care (including liaison and diversion services) and other professionals who know, or have had previous contact with, the individual and may be able to contribute to assessing their need for help and support from an appropriate adult. This includes contacts and assessments arranged by the police or at the request of the individual or (as applicable) their appropriate adult or solicitor.

1GB    The Mental Health Act 1983 Code of Practice at page 26 describes the range of clinically recognised conditions which can fall with the meaning of mental disorder for the purpose of paragraph 1.13(d). The Code is published here: https://www.gov.uk/government/publications/code-of-practice-mental-health-act-1983.

1GC    When a person is under the influence of drink and/or drugs, it is not intended that they are to be treated as vulnerable and requiring an appropriate adult for the purpose of paragraph 1.4 unless other information indicates that any of the factors described in paragraph 1.13(d) may apply to that person. When the person has recovered from the effects of drink and/or drugs, they should be re-assessed in accordance with paragraph 1.4. See paragraph 15.4A for application to live link

1H    Paragraph 1.1A is intended to cover delays which may occur in processing detainees e.g. if:
  • a large number of suspects are brought into the station simultaneously to be placed in custody;

- *interview rooms are all being used;*
- *there are difficulties contacting an appropriate adult, solicitor or interpreter.*

1I    *The custody officer must remind the appropriate adult and detainee about the right to legal advice and record any reasons for waiving it in accordance with section 6.*

1J    *Not used.*

1K    *This Code does not affect the principle that all citizens have a duty to help police officers to prevent crime and discover offenders. This is a civic rather than a legal duty; but when police officers are trying to discover whether, or by whom, offences have been committed they are entitled to question any person from whom they think useful information can be obtained, subject to the restrictions imposed by this Code. A person's declaration that they are unwilling to reply does not alter this entitlement.*

1L    *Paragraph 1.5 reflects the statutory definition of 'arrested juvenile' in section 37(15) of PACE. This section was amended by section 42 of the Criminal Justice and Courts Act 2015 with effect from 26 October 2015, and includes anyone who appears to be under the age of 18. This definition applies for the purposes of the detention and bail provisions in sections 34 to 51 of PACE. With effect from 3 April 2017, amendments made by the Policing and Crime Act 2017 require persons under the age of 18 to be treated as juveniles for the purposes of all other provisions of PACE and the Codes.*

1M    *Not used.*

1N    *For the purpose of the provisions of PACE that allow a live link to be used, any impairment of the detainee's eyesight or hearing is to be disregarded. This means that if a detainee's eyesight or hearing is impaired, the arrangements which would be needed to ensure effective communication if all parties were physically present in the same location, for example, using sign language, would apply to the live link arrangements.*

## 2 Custody records

2.1A    When a person:

- is brought to a police station under arrest;
- is arrested at the police station having attended there voluntarily; or
- attends a police station to answer bail;

they must be brought before the custody officer as soon as practicable after their arrival at the station or if applicable, following their arrest after attending the police station voluntarily. This applies to both designated and non-designated police stations. A person is deemed to be 'at a police station' for these purposes if they are within the boundary of any building or enclosed yard which forms part of that police station.

2.1    A separate custody record must be opened as soon as practicable for each person brought to a police station under arrest or arrested at the station having gone there voluntarily or attending a police station in answer to street bail. All information recorded under this Code must be recorded as soon as practicable in the custody record unless otherwise specified. Any audio or video recording made in the custody area is not part of the custody record.

2.2    If any action requires the authority of an officer of a specified rank, subject to *paragraph 2.6A*, their name and rank must be noted in the custody record.

2.3    The custody officer is responsible for the custody record's accuracy and completeness and for making sure the record or copy of the record accompanies a detainee if they are transferred to another police station. The record shall show the:

- time and reason for transfer;
- time a person is released from detention.

2.3A    If a person is arrested and taken to a police station as a result of a search in the exercise of any stop and search power to which PACE Code A (Stop and search) or the 'search powers code' issued under TACT applies, the officer carrying out the search is responsible for ensuring that the record of that stop and search is made as part of the person's custody record. The custody officer must then ensure that the person is asked if they want a copy of the search record and if they do, that they are given a copy as soon as practicable. The person's entitlement to a copy of the search record which is made as part of their custody record is in addition to, and does not affect, their entitlement to a copy of their custody record or any other provisions of section 2 (Custody records) of this Code. (See Code A, *paragraph 4.2B* and the TACT search powers code *paragraph 5.3.5*).

2.4    The detainee's solicitor and appropriate adult must be permitted to inspect the whole of the detainee's custody record as soon as practicable after their arrival at the station and at any other time on request, whilst the person is detained. This includes the following *specific* records relating to the reasons for the detainee's arrest and detention and the offence concerned to which *paragraph 3.1(b)* refers:

(a) The information about the circumstances and reasons for the detainee's arrest as recorded in the custody record in accordance with *paragraph 4.3* of Code G. This applies to any further offences for which the detainee is arrested whilst in custody;

(b) The record of the grounds for each authorisation to keep the person in custody. The authorisations to which this applies are the same as those described at items *(i)(a)* to *(d)* in the table in *paragraph 2* of *Annex M* of this Code.

Access to the records in *sub-paragraphs (a)* and *(b)* is *in addition* to the requirements in *paragraphs 3.4(b), 11.1A, 15.0, 15,7A(c)* and *16.7A* to make certain documents and materials available and to provide information about the offence and the reasons for arrest and detention.

Access to the custody record for the purposes of this paragraph must be arranged and agreed with the custody officer and may not unreasonably interfere with the custody officer's duties. A record shall be made when access is allowed and whether it includes the records described in *sub-paragraphs (a)* and *(b)* above.

2.4A When a detainee leaves police detention or is taken before a court they, their legal representative or appropriate adult shall be given, on request, a copy of the custody record as soon as practicable. This entitlement lasts for 12 months after release.

2.5 The detainee, appropriate adult or legal representative shall be permitted to inspect the original custody record after the detainee has left police detention provided they give reasonable notice of their request. Any such inspection shall be noted in the custody record.

2.6 Subject to *paragraph 2.6A*, all entries in custody records must be timed and signed by the maker. Records entered on computer shall be timed and contain the operator's identification.

2.6A Nothing in this Code requires the identity of officers or other police staff to be recorded or disclosed:

(a) *Not used.*

(b) if the officer or police staff reasonably believe recording or disclosing their name might put them in danger.

In these cases, they shall use their warrant or other identification numbers and the name of their police station. See *Note 2A*.

2.7 The fact and time of any detainee's refusal to sign a custody record, when asked in accordance with this Code, must be recorded.

*Note for Guidance*

2A *The purpose of paragraph 2.6A(b) is to protect those involved in serious organised crime investigations or arrests of particularly violent suspects when there is reliable information that those arrested or their associates may threaten or cause harm to those involved. In cases of doubt, an officer of inspector rank or above should be consulted.*

## 3 Initial action

*(A) Detained persons — normal procedure*

3.1 When a person is brought to a police station under arrest or arrested at the station having gone there voluntarily, the custody officer must make sure the person is told clearly about:

(a) the following continuing rights, which may be exercised at any stage during the period in custody:

    (i) their right to consult privately with a solicitor and that free independent legal advice is available as in *section 6*;

    (ii) their right to have someone informed of their arrest as in *section 5*;

    (iii) their right to consult the Codes of Practice (see *Note 3D*); and

    (iv) if applicable, their right to interpretation and translation (see *paragraph 3.12*) and their right to communicate with their High Commission, Embassy or Consulate (see *paragraph 3.12A*).

(b) their right to be informed about the offence and (as the case may be) any further offences for which they are arrested whilst in custody and why they have been arrested and detained in accordance with *paragraphs 2.4, 3.4(a)* and *11.1A* of this Code and *paragraph 3.3* of Code G.

3.2 The detainee must also be given a written notice, which contains information:

(a) to allow them to exercise their rights by setting out:

    (i) their rights under *paragraph 3.1, paragraph 3.12* and *3.12A*;

    (ii) the arrangements for obtaining legal advice, see *section 6*;

    (iii) their right to a copy of the custody record as in *paragraph 2.4A*;

    (iv) their right to remain silent as set out in the caution in the terms prescribed in *section 10*;

    (v) their right to have access to materials and documents which are essential to effectively challenging the lawfulness of their arrest and detention for any offence and (as the case may be) any further offences for which they are arrested whilst in custody, in accordance with *paragraphs 3.4(b)*, *15.0*, *15.7A(c)* and *16.7A* of this Code;

(vi) the maximum period for which they may be kept in police detention without being charged, when detention must be reviewed and when release is required;

(vii) their right to medical assistance in accordance with *section 9* of this Code;

(viii) their right, if they are prosecuted, to have access to the evidence in the case before their trial in accordance with the Criminal Procedure and Investigations Act 1996, the Attorney General's Guidelines on Disclosure, the common law and the Criminal Procedure Rules; and

(b) briefly setting out their other entitlements while in custody, by:

    (i) mentioning:
- the provisions relating to the conduct of interviews;
- the circumstances in which an appropriate adult should be available to assist the detainee and their statutory rights to make representations whenever the need for their detention is reviewed.

    (ii) listing the entitlements in this Code, concerning;
- reasonable standards of physical comfort;
- adequate food and drink;
- access to toilets and washing facilities, clothing, medical attention, and exercise when practicable.
- Personal needs relating to health, hygiene and welfare concerning the provision of menstrual and any other health, hygiene and welfare products needed by the detainee in question and speaking about these in private to a member of the custody staff (see *paragraphs 9.3A* and *9.3B*).

See *Note 3A*.

3.2A The detainee must be given an opportunity to read the notice and shall be asked to sign the custody record to acknowledge receipt of the notice. Any refusal to sign must be recorded on the custody record.

3.3 *Not used.*

3.3A An 'easy read' illustrated version should also be provided if available (see *Note 3A*).

3.4 (a) The custody officer shall:
- record the offence(s) that the detainee has been arrested for and the reason(s) for the arrest on the custody record. See *paragraph 10.3* and Code G, *paragraphs 2.2 and 4.3*;
- note on the custody record any comment the detainee makes in relation to the arresting officer's account but shall not invite comment. If the arresting officer is not physically present when the detainee is brought to a police station, the arresting officer's account must be made available to the custody officer remotely or by a third party on the arresting officer's behalf. If the custody officer authorises a person's detention, subject to *paragraph 1.8*, that officer must record the grounds for detention in the detainee's presence and at the same time, inform them of the grounds. The detainee must be informed of the grounds for their detention before they are questioned about any offence;
- note any comment the detainee makes in respect of the decision to detain them but shall not invite comment;
- not put specific questions to the detainee regarding their involvement in any offence, nor in respect of any comments they may make in response to the arresting officer's account or the decision to place them in detention. Such an exchange is likely to constitute an interview as in *paragraph 11.1A* and require the associated safeguards in *section 11*.

Note: This sub-paragraph also applies to any further offences and grounds for detention which come to light whilst the person is detained.

See *paragraph 11.13* in respect of unsolicited comments.

(b) Documents and materials which are essential to effectively challenging the lawfulness of the detainee's arrest and detention must be made available to the detainee or their solicitor. Documents and materials will be 'essential' for this purpose if they are capable of undermining the reasons and grounds which make the detainee's arrest and detention *necessary*. The decision about whether particular documents or materials must be made available for the purpose of this requirement therefore rests with the custody officer who determines whether detention is necessary, in consultation with the investigating officer who has the knowledge of the documents and materials in a particular case necessary to inform that decision. A note should be made in the detainee's custody record of the *fact* that documents or materials have been made available under this sub-paragraph and when. The investigating officer should make a separate note of what is made available and how it is made available in a particular case. This sub-paragraph also applies (with modifications) for the purposes of *sections 15 (Reviews and extensions of detention)* and *16 (Charging detained persons)*. See *Note 3ZA* and *paragraphs 15.0 and 16.7A.*

3.5 The custody officer or other custody staff as directed by the custody officer shall:

(a) ask the detainee whether at this time, they:

   (i) would like legal advice, see *paragraph 6.5*;

   (ii) want someone informed of their detention, see *section 5*;

(b) ask the detainee to sign the custody record to confirm their decisions in respect of *(a)*;

(c) determine whether the detainee:

   (i) is, or might be, in need of medical treatment or attention, see *section 9*;

   (ii) is a juvenile and/or vulnerable and therefore requires an appropriate adult (see *paragraphs 1.4, 1.5,* and *3.15*);

   (iia) wishes to speak in private with a member of the custody staff who may be of the same sex about any matter concerning their personal needs relating to health, hygiene and welfare (see *paragraph 9.3A*)

   (iii) requires:

     • help to check documentation (see *paragraph 3.20*);

     • an interpreter (see *paragraph 3.12* and *Note 13B*).

(ca) if the detainee is a female aged 18 or over, ask if they require or are likely to require any menstrual products whilst they are in custody (see *paragraph 9.3B*). For girls under 18, see *paragraph 3.20A*;

(d) record the decision and actions taken as applicable in respect of *(c)* and *(ca)*.

Where any duties under this paragraph have been carried out by custody staff at the direction of the custody officer, the outcomes shall, as soon as practicable, be reported to the custody officer who retains overall responsibility for the detainee's care and treatment and ensuring that it complies with this Code. See *Note 3F*.

3.6 When the needs mentioned in *paragraph 3.5(c)* are being determined, the custody officer is responsible for initiating an assessment to consider whether the detainee is likely to present specific risks to custody staff, any individual who may have contact with detainee (e.g. legal advisers, medical staff) or themselves. This risk assessment must include the taking of reasonable steps to establish the detainee's identity and to obtain information about the detainee that is relevant to their safe custody, security and welfare and risks to others. Such assessments should therefore always include a check on the Police National Computer (PNC), to be carried out as soon as practicable, to identify any risks that have been highlighted in relation to the detainee. Although such assessments are primarily the custody officer's responsibility, it may be necessary for them to consult and involve others, e.g. the arresting officer or an appropriate healthcare professional, see *paragraph 9.13*.

Other records held by or on behalf of the police and other UK law enforcement authorities that might provide information relevant to the detainee's safe custody, security and welfare and risk to others and to confirming their identity should also be checked. Reasons for delaying the initiation or completion of the assessment must be recorded.

3.7 Chief officers should ensure that arrangements for proper and effective risk assessments required by *paragraph 3.6* are implemented in respect of all detainees at police stations in their area.

3.8 Risk assessments must follow a structured process which clearly defines the categories of risk to be considered and the results must be incorporated in the detainee's custody record. The custody officer is responsible for making sure those responsible for the detainee's custody are appropriately briefed about the risks. If no specific risks are identified by the assessment, that should be noted in the custody record. See *Note 3E* and *paragraph 9.14*.

3.8A The content of any risk assessment and any analysis of the level of risk relating to the person's detention is not required to be shown or provided to the detainee or any person acting on behalf of the detainee. But information should not be withheld from any person acting on the detainee's behalf, for example, an appropriate adult, solicitor or interpreter, if to do so might put that person at risk.

3.9 The custody officer is responsible for implementing the response to any specific risk assessment, e.g.:

• reducing opportunities for self harm;

• calling an appropriate healthcare professional;

• increasing levels of monitoring or observation;

• reducing the risk to those who come into contact with the detainee.

See *Note 3E.*

3.10 Risk assessment is an ongoing process and assessments must always be subject to review if circumstances change.

3.11 If video cameras are installed in the custody area, notices shall be prominently displayed showing cameras are in use. Any request to have video cameras switched off shall be refused.

*(B) Detained persons — special groups*

3.12 If the detainee appears to be someone who does not speak or understand English or who has a hearing or speech impediment, the custody officer must ensure:

(a) that without delay, arrangements *(see paragraph 13.1ZA)* are made for the detainee to have the assistance of an interpreter in the action under *paragraphs 3.1 to 3.5.* If the person appears to have a hearing or speech impediment, the reference to 'interpreter' includes appropriate assistance necessary to comply with *paragraphs 3.1 to 3.5.* See *paragraph 13.1C* if the detainee is in Wales. See *section 13* and *Note 13B*;

(b) that in addition to the continuing rights set out in *paragraph 3.1(a)(i)* to *(iv)*, the detainee is told clearly about their right to interpretation and translation;

(c) that the written notice given to the detainee in accordance with *paragraph 3.2* is in a language the detainee understands and includes the right to interpretation and translation together with information about the provisions in *section 13* and *Annex M*, which explain how the right applies (see *Note 3A*); and

(d) that if the translation of the notice is not available, the information in the notice is given through an interpreter and a written translation provided without undue delay.

3.12A If the detainee is a citizen of an independent Commonwealth country or a national of a foreign country, including the Republic of Ireland, the custody officer must ensure that in addition to the continuing rights set out in *paragraph 3.1(a)(i)* to *(iv)*, they are informed as soon as practicable about their rights of communication with their High Commission, Embassy or Consulate set out in *section 7.* This right must be included in the written notice given to the detainee in accordance with *paragraph 3.2.*

3.13 If the detainee is a juvenile, the custody officer must, if it is practicable, ascertain the identity of a person responsible for their welfare. That person:

• may be:
  – the parent or guardian;
  – if the juvenile is in local authority or voluntary organisation care, or is otherwise being looked after under the Children Act 1989, a person appointed by that authority or organisation to have responsibility for the juvenile's welfare;
  – any other person who has, for the time being, assumed responsibility for the juvenile's welfare.

• must be informed as soon as practicable that the juvenile has been arrested, why they have been arrested and where they are detained. This right is in addition to the juvenile's right in *section 5* not to be held incommunicado. See *Note 3C.*

3.14 If a juvenile is known to be subject to a court order under which a person or organisation is given any degree of statutory responsibility to supervise or otherwise monitor them, reasonable steps must also be taken to notify that person or organisation (the 'responsible officer'). The responsible officer will normally be a member of a Youth Offending Team, except for a curfew order which involves electronic monitoring when the contractor providing the monitoring will normally be the responsible officer.

3.15 If the detainee is a juvenile or a vulnerable person, the custody officer must, as soon as practicable, ensure that:

• the detainee is informed of the decision that an appropriate adult is required and the reason for that decision (see *paragraph 3.5(c)(ii)*) and;

• the detainee is advised:
  – of the duties of the appropriate adult as described in *paragraph 1.7A;* and
  – that they can consult privately with the appropriate adult at any time.

• the appropriate adult, who in the case of a juvenile may or may not be a person responsible for their welfare, as in *paragraph 3.13*, is informed of:
  – the grounds for their detention;
  – their whereabouts; and

• the attendance of the appropriate adult at the police station to see the detainee is secured.

3.16 It is imperative that a person detained under the Mental Health Act 1983, section 135 or 136, be assessed as soon as possible within the permitted period of detention specified in that Act. A police station may only be used as a place of safety in accordance with The Mental Health Act 1983 (Places of Safety) Regulations 2017. If that assessment is to take place at the police station, an approved mental health professional and a registered medical practitioner shall be called to the station as soon as possible to carry it out. See *Note 9D*. The appropriate adult has no role in the assessment process and their presence is not required. Once the detainee has been assessed and suitable arrangements made for their treatment or care, they can no longer be detained under section 135 or 136. A detainee must be immediately discharged from detention if a registered medical practitioner, having examined them, concludes they are not mentally disordered within the meaning of the Act.

3.17 If the appropriate adult is:
- already at the police station, the provisions of *paragraphs 3.1* to *3.5* must be complied with in the appropriate adult's presence;
- not at the station when these provisions are complied with, they must be complied with again in the presence of the appropriate adult when they arrive,

and a copy of the notice given to the detainee in accordance with *paragraph 3.2*, shall also be given to the appropriate adult.

3.17A The custody officer must ensure that at the time the copy of the notice is given to the appropriate adult, or as soon as practicable thereafter, the appropriate adult is advised of the duties of the appropriate adult as described in *paragraph 1.7A*.

3.18 *Not used.*

3.19 If the detainee, or appropriate adult on the detainee's behalf, asks for a solicitor to be called to give legal advice, the provisions of *section 6* apply (see *paragraph 6.5A* and *Note 3H*).

3.20 If the detainee is blind, seriously visually impaired or unable to read, the custody officer shall make sure their solicitor, relative, appropriate adult or some other person likely to take an interest in them and not involved in the investigation is available to help check any documentation. When this Code requires written consent or signing the person assisting may be asked to sign instead, if the detainee prefers. This paragraph does not require an appropriate adult to be called solely to assist in checking and signing documentation for a person who is not a juvenile, or is not vulnerable (see *paragraph 3.15* and *Note 13C*).

3.20A The Children and Young Persons Act 1933, section 31, requires that arrangements must be made for ensuring that a girl under the age of 18, while detained in a police station, is under the care of a woman. The custody officer must ensure that the woman under whose care the girl is, makes the enquiries and provides the information concerning personal needs relating to their health, hygiene and welfare described in *paragraph 9.3A* and menstrual products described in *paragraph 9.3B*. See *Note 3G*. The section also requires that arrangements must be made for preventing any person under 18, while being detained in a police station, from associating with an adult charged with any offence, unless that adult is a relative or the adult is jointly charged with the same offence as the person under 18.

*(C) Detained persons – Documentation*

3.20B The grounds for a person's detention shall be recorded, in the person's presence if practicable. See *paragraph 1.8*.

3.20C Action taken under *paragraphs 3.12* to *3.20A* shall be recorded.

*(D) Persons attending a police station or elsewhere voluntarily*

3.21 Anybody attending a police station or other location (see *paragraph 3.22* and *Note 3I*) voluntarily to assist police with the investigation of an offence may leave at will unless arrested. See *Notes 1A* and *1K*. The person may only be prevented from leaving at will if their arrest on suspicion of committing the offence is necessary in accordance with Code G. See Code G *Note 2G*.

*Action if arrest becomes necessary*

(a) If during a person's voluntary attendance at a police station or other location it is decided for any reason that their arrest is necessary, they must:
- be informed at once that they are under arrest and of the grounds and reasons as required by Code G, and
- be brought before the custody officer at the police station where they are arrested or (as the case may be) at the police station to which they are taken after being arrested elsewhere. The custody officer is then responsible for making sure that a custody record is opened and that they are notified of their rights in the same way as other detainees as required by this Code.

*(E)  Persons answering street bail*

3.25 When a person is answering street bail, the custody officer should link any documentation held in relation to arrest with the custody record. Any further action shall be recorded on the custody record in accordance with *paragraphs 3.20B* and *3.20C above*.

*(F)  Requirements for suspects to be informed of certain rights*

3.26 The provisions of this section identify the information which must be given to suspects who have been cautioned in accordance with *section 10* of this Code according to whether or not they have been arrested and detained. It includes information required by *EU Directive 2012/13* on the right to information in criminal proceedings. If a complaint is made by or on behalf of such a suspect that the information and (as the case may be) access to records and documents has not been provided as required, the matter shall be reported to an inspector to deal with as a complaint for the purposes of *paragraph 9.2*, or *paragraph 12.9* if the challenge is made during an interview. This would include, for example:

  (a)  in the case of a detained suspect:
- not informing them of their rights (see *paragraph 3.1*);
- not giving them a copy of the Notice (see *paragraph 3.2(a)*);
- not providing an opportunity to read the notice (see *paragraph 3.2A*);
- not providing the required information (see *paragraphs 3.2(a), 3.12(b)* and, *3.12A*);
- not allowing access to the custody record (see *paragraph 2.4*);
- not providing a translation of the Notice (see *paragraph 3.12(c)* and *(d)*); and

  (b)  in the case of a suspect who is not detained:
- not informing them of their rights or providing the required information (see *paragraphs 3.21(b)* to *3.21B*).

*Notes for Guidance*

3ZA  *For the purposes of paragraphs 3.4(b) and 15.0:*

    *(a)  Investigating officers are responsible for bringing to the attention of the officer who is responsible for authorising the suspect's detention or (as the case may be) continued detention (before or after charge), any documents and materials in their possession or control which appear to undermine the need to keep the suspect in custody. In accordance with Part IV of PACE, this officer will be either the custody officer, the officer reviewing the need for detention before or after charge (PACE, section 40), or the officer considering the need to extend detention without charge from 24 to 36 hours (PACE, section 42) who is then responsible for determining, which, if any, of those documents and materials are capable of undermining the need to detain the suspect and must therefore be made available to the suspect or their solicitor.*

    *(b)  the way in which documents and materials are 'made available', is a matter for the investigating officer to determine on a case by case basis and having regard to the nature and volume of the documents and materials involved. For example, they may be made available by supplying a copy or allowing supervised access to view. However, for view only access, it will be necessary to demonstrate that sufficient time is allowed for the suspect and solicitor to view and consider the documents and materials in question.*

3A   *For access to currently available notices, including 'easy-read' versions, see https://www.gov.uk/guidance/notice-of-rights-and-entitlements-a-persons-rights-in-police-detention.*

3B   *Not used.*

3C   *If the juvenile is in local authority or voluntary organisation care but living with their parents or other adults responsible for their welfare, although there is no legal obligation to inform them, they should normally be contacted, as well as the authority or organisation unless they are suspected of involvement in the offence concerned. Even if the juvenile is not living with their parents, consideration should be given to informing them.*

3D   *The right to consult the Codes of Practice does not entitle the person concerned to delay unreasonably any necessary investigative or administrative action whilst they do so. Examples of action which need not be delayed unreasonably include:*

- *procedures requiring the provision of breath, blood or urine specimens under the Road Traffic Act 1988 or the Transport and Works Act 1992;*
- *searching detainees at the police station;*
- *taking fingerprints, footwear impressions or non-intimate samples without consent for evidential purposes.*

3E   *The Detention and Custody Authorised Professional Practice (APP) produced by the College of Policing (see http://www.app.college.police.uk) provides more detailed guidance on risk assessments and identifies key risk areas which should always be considered. See Home Office Circular 34/2007 (Safety of solicitors and probationary representatives at police stations).*

3F   *A custody officer or other officer who, in accordance with this Code, allows or directs the carrying out of any task or action relating to a detainee's care, treatment, rights and entitlements to another officer or any other person, must be satisfied that the officer or person concerned is suitable, trained and competent to carry out the task or action in question.*

3G   *Guidance for police officers and police staff on the operational application of section 31 of the Children and Young Persons Act 1933 has been published by the College of Policing and is available at: https://www.app.college.police.uk/app-content/detention-and-custody-2/detainee-care/children-and-yo ung-persons/#girls.*

3H   *The purpose of the provisions at paragraphs 3.19 and 6.5A is to protect the rights of juvenile and vulnerable persons who may not understand the significance of what is said to them. They should always be given an opportunity, when an appropriate adult is called to the police station, to consult privately with a solicitor in the absence of the appropriate adult if they want.*

3I   *An interviewer who is not sure, or has any doubt, about whether a place or location elsewhere than a police station is suitable for carrying out a voluntary interview, particularly in the case of a juvenile or vulnerable person, should consult an officer of the rank of sergeant or above for advice. Detailed guidance for police officers and staff concerning the conduct and recording of voluntary interviews is being developed by the College of Policing.*

   *It follows a review of operational issues arising when voluntary interviews need to be arranged. The aim is to ensure the effective implementation of the safeguards in paragraphs 3.21 to 3.22B particularly concerning the rights of suspects, the location for the interview and supervision.*

3J   *For voluntary interviews conducted by non-police investigators, the provision of legal advice is set out by the Legal Aid Agency at paragraph 9.54 of the 2017 Standard Crime Contract Specification. This is published at https://www.gov.uk/government/publications/standard-crime-contract-2017 and the rules mean that a non-police interviewer who does not have their own statutory power of arrest would have to inform the suspect that they have a right to seek legal advice if they wish, but payment would be a matter for them to arrange with the solicitor.*

## 4  Detainee's property

*(A)  Action*

4.1   The custody officer is responsible for:

   (a)   ascertaining what property a detainee:

      (i)   has with them when they come to the police station, whether on:
         • arrest or re-detention on answering to bail;
         • commitment to prison custody on the order or sentence of a court;
         • lodgement at the police station with a view to their production in court from prison custody;
         • transfer from detention at another station or hospital;
         • detention under the Mental Health Act 1983, section 135 or 136;
         • remand into police custody on the authority of a court.

      (ii)   might have acquired for an unlawful or harmful purpose while in custody;

   (b)   the safekeeping of any property taken from a detainee which remains at the police station.

   The custody officer may search the detainee or authorise their being searched to the extent they consider necessary, provided a search of intimate parts of the body or involving the removal of more than outer clothing is only made as in *Annex A*. A search may only be carried out by an officer of the same sex as the detainee. See *Note 4A* and *Annex L*.

4.2   Subject to *paragraph 4.3A*, detainees may retain clothing and personal effects at their own risk unless the custody officer considers they may use them to cause harm to themselves or others, interfere with evidence, damage property, effect an escape or they are needed as evidence. In this event the custody officer may withhold such articles as they consider necessary and must tell the detainee why.

4.3   Personal effects are those items a detainee may lawfully need, use or refer to while in detention but do not include cash and other items of value.

4.3A For the purpose of *paragraph 4.2*, the reference to clothing and personal effects shall be treated as including menstrual and any other health, hygiene and welfare products needed by a detainee in question (see *paragraphs 9.3A* and *9.3B*) and a decision to withhold any such products must be subject to a further specific risk assessment.

*(B) Documentation*

4.4   It is a matter for the custody officer to determine whether a record should be made of the property a detained person has with him or had taken from him on arrest. Any record made is not required to be kept as part of the custody record but the custody record should be noted as to where such a record exists and that record shall be treated as being part of the custody record for the purpose of this and any other Code of Practice (see *paragraphs 2.4, 2.4A* and *2.5*). Whenever a record is made the detainee shall be allowed to check and sign the record of property as correct. Any refusal to sign shall be recorded.

4.5   If a detainee is not allowed to keep any article of clothing or personal effects, the reason must be recorded.

*Notes for Guidance*

4A   *PACE, Section 54(1) and paragraph 4.1 require a detainee to be searched when it is clear the custody officer will have continuing duties in relation to that detainee or when that detainee's behaviour or offence makes an inventory appropriate. They do not require every detainee to be searched, e.g. if it is clear a person will only be detained for a short period and is not to be placed in a cell, the custody officer may decide not to search them. In such a case the custody record will be endorsed 'not searched', paragraph 4.4 will not apply, and the detainee will be invited to sign the entry. If the detainee refuses, the custody officer will be obliged to ascertain what property they have in accordance with paragraph 4.1.*

4B   *Paragraph 4.4 does not require the custody officer to record on the custody record property in the detainee's possession on arrest if, by virtue of its nature, quantity or size, it is not practicable to remove it to the police station.*

4C   *Paragraph 4.4 does not require items of clothing worn by the person to be recorded unless withheld by the custody officer as in paragraph 4.2.*

## 5   Right not to be held incommunicado

*(A) Action*

5.1   Subject to *paragraph 5.7B*, any person arrested and held in custody at a police station or other premises may, on request, have one person known to them or likely to take an interest in their welfare informed at public expense of their whereabouts as soon as practicable. If the person cannot be contacted the detainee may choose up to two alternatives. If they cannot be contacted, the person in charge of detention or the investigation has discretion to allow further attempts until the information has been conveyed. See *Notes 5C* and *5D*.

5.2   The exercise of the above right in respect of each person nominated may be delayed only in accordance with *Annex B*.

5.3   The above right may be exercised each time a detainee is taken to another police station.

5.4   If the detainee agrees, they may at the custody officer's discretion, receive visits from friends, family or others likely to take an interest in their welfare, or in whose welfare the detainee has an interest. See *Note 5B*.

5.5   If a friend, relative or person with an interest in the detainee's welfare enquires about their whereabouts, this information shall be given if the suspect agrees and *Annex B* does not apply. See *Note 5D*.

5.6   The detainee shall be given writing materials, on request, and allowed to telephone one person for a reasonable time, see *Notes 5A* and *5E*. Either or both of these privileges may be denied or delayed if an officer of inspector rank or above considers sending a letter or making a telephone call may result in any of the consequences in:

   (a)   *Annex B, paragraphs 1* and *2* and the person is detained in connection with an indictable offence;

   (b)   *Not used.*

      Nothing in this paragraph permits the restriction or denial of the rights in *paragraphs 5.1* and *6.1*.

5.7   Before any letter or message is sent, or telephone call made, the detainee shall be informed that what they say in any letter, call or message (other than in a communication to a solicitor) may be read or listened to and may be given in evidence. A telephone call may be terminated if it is being abused. The costs can be at public expense at the custody officer's discretion.

5.7A  Any delay or denial of the rights in this section should be proportionate and should last no longer than necessary.

5.7B  In the case of a person in police custody for specific purposes and periods in accordance with a direction under the *Crime (Sentences) Act 1997, Schedule 1* (productions from prison etc.), the exercise of the rights in this section shall be subject to any additional conditions specified in the direction for the purpose of regulating the detainee's contact and communication with others whilst in police custody. See *Note 5F.*

*(B) Documentation*

5.8   A record must be kept of any:

(a)   request made under this section and the action taken;

(b)   letters, messages or telephone calls made or received or visit received;

(c)   refusal by the detainee to have information about them given to an outside enquirer. The detainee must be asked to countersign the record accordingly and any refusal recorded.

*Notes for Guidance*

5A   *A person may request an interpreter to interpret a telephone call or translate a letter.*

5B   *At the custody officer's discretion and subject to the detainee's consent, visits should be allowed when possible, subject to having sufficient personnel to supervise a visit and any possible hindrance to the investigation.*

5C   *If the detainee does not know anyone to contact for advice or support or cannot contact a friend or relative, the custody officer should bear in mind any local voluntary bodies or other organisations who might be able to help. Paragraph 6.1 applies if legal advice is required.*

5D   *In some circumstances it may not be appropriate to use the telephone to disclose information under paragraphs 5.1 and 5.5.*

5E   *The telephone call at paragraph 5.6 is in addition to any communication under paragraphs 5.1 and 6.1.*

5F   *Prison Service Instruction 26/2012 (Production of Prisoners at the Request of Warranted Law Enforcement Agencies) provides detailed guidance and instructions for police officers and Governors and Directors of Prisons regarding applications for prisoners to be transferred to police custody and their safe custody and treatment while in police custody.*

## 6  Right to legal advice

*(A) Action*

6.1   Unless *Annex B* applies, all detainees must be informed that they may at any time consult and communicate privately with a solicitor, whether in person, in writing or by telephone, and that free independent legal advice is available. See *paragraph 3.1, Notes 1I, 6B and 6J.*

6.2   *Not used.*

6.3   A poster advertising the right to legal advice must be prominently displayed in the charging area of every police station. See *Note 6H.*

6.4   No police officer should, at any time, do or say anything with the intention of dissuading any person who is entitled to legal advice in accordance with this Code, whether or not they have been arrested and are detained, from obtaining legal advice. See *Note 6ZA.*

6.5   The exercise of the right of access to legal advice may be delayed only as in *Annex B*. Whenever legal advice is requested, and unless *Annex B* applies, the custody officer must act without delay to secure the provision of such advice. If the detainee has the right to speak to a solicitor in person but declines to exercise the right the officer should point out that the right includes the right to speak with a solicitor on the telephone. If the detainee continues to waive this right, or a detainee whose right to free legal advice is limited to telephone advice from the Criminal Defence Service (CDS) Direct (see *Note 6B*) declines to exercise that right, the officer should ask them why and any reasons should be recorded on the custody record or the interview record as appropriate. Reminders of the right to legal advice must be given as in *paragraphs 3.5, 11.2, 15.4, 16.4, 16.5, 2B of Annex A, 3 of Annex K and 5 of Annex M* of this Code and Code D, *paragraphs 3.17(ii)* and *6.3*. Once it is clear a detainee does not want to speak to a solicitor in person or by telephone they should cease to be asked their reasons. See *Note 6K.*

6.5A   In the case of a person who is a juvenile or is vulnerable, an appropriate adult should consider whether legal advice from a solicitor is required. If such a detained person wants to exercise the right to legal advice, the appropriate action should be taken and should not be delayed until the appropriate adult arrives. If the person indicates that they do not want legal advice, the appropriate adult has the right to ask for a solicitor to attend if this would be in the best interests of the person and must be so informed. In this case, action to secure the provision of advice if so requested by the appropriate adult shall be taken without delay in the same way as when requested by the person. However, the person cannot be forced to see the solicitor if they are adamant that they do not wish to do so.

6.6   A detainee who wants legal advice may not be interviewed or continue to be interviewed until they have received such advice unless:

(a) *Annex B* applies, when the restriction on drawing adverse inferences from silence in *Annex C* will apply because the detainee is not allowed an opportunity to consult a solicitor; or

(b) an officer of superintendent rank or above has reasonable grounds for believing that:

    (i)   the consequent delay might:

- lead to interference with, or harm to, evidence connected with an offence;
- lead to interference with, or physical harm to, other people;
- lead to serious loss of, or damage to, property;
- lead to alerting other people suspected of having committed an offence but not yet arrested for it;
- hinder the recovery of property obtained in consequence of the commission of an offence.

See *Note 6A*

    (ii)  when a solicitor, including a duty solicitor, has been contacted and has agreed to attend, awaiting their arrival would cause unreasonable delay to the process of investigation.

Note: In these cases the restriction on drawing adverse inferences from silence in *Annex C* will apply because the detainee is not allowed an opportunity to consult a solicitor.

(c) the solicitor the detainee has nominated or selected from a list:

    (i)   cannot be contacted;

    (ii)  has previously indicated they do not wish to be contacted; or

    (iii) having been contacted, has declined to attend; and

- the detainee has been advised of the Duty Solicitor Scheme but has declined to ask for the duty solicitor;
- in these circumstances the interview may be started or continued without further delay provided an officer of inspector rank or above has agreed to the interview proceeding.

Note: The restriction on drawing adverse inferences from silence in *Annex C* will not apply because the detainee is allowed an opportunity to consult the duty solicitor;

(d) the detainee changes their mind about wanting legal advice or (as the case may be) about wanting a solicitor present at the interview and states that they no longer wish to speak to a solicitor. In these circumstances, the interview may be started or continued without delay provided that:

    (i)   an officer of inspector rank or above:

- speaks to the detainee to enquire about the reasons for their change of mind (see *Note 6K*), and
- makes, or directs the making of, reasonable efforts to ascertain the solicitor's expected time of arrival and to inform the solicitor that the suspect has stated that they wish to change their mind and the reason (if given);

    (ii)  the detainee's reason for their change of mind (if given) and the outcome of the action in (i) are recorded in the custody record;

    (iii) the detainee, after being informed of the outcome of the action in (i) above, confirms in writing that they want the interview to proceed without speaking or further speaking to a solicitor or (as the case may be) without a solicitor being present and do not wish to wait for a solicitor by signing an entry to this effect in the custody record;

    (iv) an officer of inspector rank or above is satisfied that it is proper for the interview to proceed in these circumstances and:

- gives authority in writing for the interview to proceed and, if the authority is not recorded in the custody record, the officer must ensure that the custody record shows the date and time of the authority and where it is recorded, and
- takes, or directs the taking of, reasonable steps to inform the solicitor that the authority has been given and the time when the interview is expected to commence and records or causes to be recorded, the outcome of this action in the custody record.

    (v)  When the interview starts and the interviewer reminds the suspect of their right to legal advice (see *paragraph 11.2*, Code E *paragraph 4.5* and Code F *paragraph 4.5*), the interviewer shall then ensure that the following is recorded in the written interview record or the interview record made in accordance with Code E or F:

- confirmation that the detainee has changed their mind about wanting legal advice or (as the case may be) about wanting a solicitor present and the reasons for it if given;
- the fact that authority for the interview to proceed has been given and, subject to *paragraph 2.6A*, the name of the authorising officer;

- that if the solicitor arrives at the station before the interview is completed, the detainee will be so informed without delay and *a break will be taken* to allow them to speak to the solicitor if they wish, unless *paragraph 6.6(a)* applies, and
- that at any time during the interview, the detainee may again ask for legal advice and that if they do, a break will be taken to allow them to speak to the solicitor, unless *paragraph 6.6(a), (b), or (c)* applies.

Note: In these circumstances, the restriction on drawing adverse inferences from silence in *Annex C* will not apply because the detainee is allowed an opportunity to consult a solicitor if they wish.

6.7 If *paragraph 6.6(a)* applies, where the reason for authorising the delay ceases to apply, there may be no further delay in permitting the exercise of the right in the absence of a further authorisation unless *paragraph 6.6(b), (c)* or *(d)* applies. If *paragraph 6.6(b)(i)* applies, once sufficient information has been obtained to avert the risk, questioning must cease until the detainee has received legal advice unless *paragraph 6.6(a), (b)(ii), (c)* or *(d)* applies.

6.8 A detainee who has been permitted to consult a solicitor shall be entitled on request to have the solicitor present when they are interviewed unless one of the exceptions in *paragraph 6.6* applies.

6.9 The solicitor may only be required to leave the interview if their conduct is such that the interviewer is unable properly to put questions to the suspect. See *Notes 6D* and *6E*.

6.10 If the interviewer considers a solicitor is acting in such a way, they will stop the interview and consult an officer not below superintendent rank, if one is readily available, and otherwise an officer not below inspector rank not connected with the investigation. After speaking to the solicitor, the officer consulted will decide if the interview should continue in the presence of that solicitor. If they decide it should not, the suspect will be given the opportunity to consult another solicitor before the interview continues and that solicitor given an opportunity to be present at the interview. See *Note 6E*.

6.11 The removal of a solicitor from an interview is a serious step and, if it occurs, the officer of superintendent rank or above who took the decision will consider if the incident should be reported to the Solicitors Regulatory Authority. If the decision to remove the solicitor has been taken by an officer below superintendent rank, the facts must be reported to an officer of superintendent rank or above, who will similarly consider whether a report to the Solicitors Regulatory Authority would be appropriate. When the solicitor concerned is a duty solicitor, the report should be both to the Solicitors Regulatory Authority and to the Legal Aid Agency.

6.12 'Solicitor' in this Code means:
- a solicitor who holds a current practising certificate;
- an accredited or probationary representative included on the register of representatives maintained by the Legal Aid Agency.

6.12A An accredited or probationary representative sent to provide advice by, and on behalf of, a solicitor shall be admitted to the police station for this purpose unless an officer of inspector rank or above considers such a visit will hinder the investigation and directs otherwise. Hindering the investigation does not include giving proper legal advice to a detainee as in *Note 6D*. Once admitted to the police station, *paragraphs 6.6* to *6.10* apply.

6.13 In exercising their discretion under *paragraph 6.12A*, the officer should take into account in particular:
- whether:
  - the identity and status of an accredited or probationary representative have been satisfactorily established;
  - they are of suitable character to provide legal advice, e.g. a person with a criminal record is unlikely to be suitable unless the conviction was for a minor offence and not recent.
- any other matters in any written letter of authorisation provided by the solicitor on whose behalf the person is attending the police station. See *Note 6F*.

6.14 If the inspector refuses access to an accredited or probationary representative or a decision is taken that such a person should not be permitted to remain at an interview, the inspector must notify the solicitor on whose behalf the representative was acting and give them an opportunity to make alternative arrangements. The detainee must be informed and the custody record noted.

6.15 If a solicitor arrives at the station to see a particular person, that person must, unless *Annex B* applies, be so informed whether or not they are being interviewed and asked if they would like to see the solicitor. This applies even if the detainee has declined legal advice or, having requested it, subsequently agreed to be interviewed without receiving advice. The solicitor's attendance and the detainee's decision must be noted in the custody record.

*(B) Documentation*

6.16 Any request for legal advice and the action taken shall be recorded.

6.17 A record shall be made in the interview record if a detainee asks for legal advice and an interview is begun either in the absence of a solicitor or their representative, or they have been required to leave an interview.

*Notes for Guidance*

6ZA *No police officer or police staff shall indicate to any suspect, except to answer a direct question, that the period for which they are liable to be detained, or if not detained, the time taken to complete the interview, might be reduced:*

- *if they do not ask for legal advice or do not want a solicitor present when they are interviewed; or*
- *if they have asked for legal advice or (as the case may be) asked for a solicitor to be present when they are interviewed but change their mind and agree to be interviewed without waiting for a solicitor.*

6A *In considering if paragraph 6.6(b) applies, the officer should, if practicable, ask the solicitor for an estimate of how long it will take to come to the station and relate this to the time detention is permitted, the time of day (i.e. whether the rest period under paragraph 12.2 is imminent) and the requirements of other investigations. If the solicitor is on their way or is to set off immediately, it will not normally be appropriate to begin an interview before they arrive. If it appears necessary to begin an interview before the solicitor's arrival, they should be given an indication of how long the police would be able to wait before 6.6(b) applies so there is an opportunity to make arrangements for someone else to provide legal advice.*

6B *A detainee has a right to free legal advice and to be represented by a solicitor. This Note for Guidance explains the arrangements which enable detainees to obtain legal advice. An outline of these arrangements is also included in the Notice of Rights and Entitlements given to detainees in accordance with paragraph 3.2. The arrangements also apply, with appropriate modifications, to persons attending a police station or other location (see paragraph 3.22 and Notes 3I and 3J) voluntarily who are cautioned prior to being interviewed. See paragraph 3.21.*

*When a detainee asks for free legal advice, the Defence Solicitor Call Centre (DSCC) must be informed of the request.*

*Free legal advice will be limited to telephone advice provided by CDS Direct if a detainee is:*

- *detained for a non-imprisonable offence;*
- *arrested on a bench warrant for failing to appear and being held for production at court (except where the solicitor has clear documentary evidence available that would result in the client being released from custody);*
- *arrested for drink driving (driving/in charge with excess alcohol, failing to provide a specimen, driving/in charge whilst unfit through drink), or*
- *detained in relation to breach of police or court bail conditions*

*unless one or more exceptions apply, in which case the DSCC should arrange for advice to be given by a solicitor at the police station, for example:*

- *the police want to interview the detainee or carry out an eye-witness identification procedure;*
- *the detainee needs an appropriate adult;*
- *the detainee is unable to communicate over the telephone;*
- *the detainee alleges serious misconduct by the police;*
- *the investigation includes another offence not included in the list,*
- *the solicitor to be assigned is already at the police station.*

*When free advice is not limited to telephone advice, a detainee can ask for free advice from a solicitor they know or if they do not know a solicitor or the solicitor they know cannot be contacted, from the duty solicitor.*

*To arrange free legal advice, the police should telephone the DSCC. The call centre will decide whether legal advice should be limited to telephone advice from CDS Direct, or whether a solicitor known to the detainee or the duty solicitor should speak to the detainee.*

*When a detainee wants to pay for legal advice themselves:*

- *the DSCC will contact a solicitor of their choice on their behalf;*
- *they may, when free advice is only available by telephone from CDS Direct, still speak to a solicitor of their choice on the telephone for advice, but the solicitor would not be paid by legal aid and may ask the person to pay for the advice;*
- *they should be given an opportunity to consult a specific solicitor or another solicitor from that solicitor's firm. If this solicitor is not available, they may choose up to two alternatives. If these alternatives are not available, the custody officer has discretion to allow further attempts until a solicitor has been contacted and agreed to provide advice;*

- *they are entitled to a private consultation with their chosen solicitor on the telephone or the solicitor may decide to come to the police station;*
- *If their chosen solicitor cannot be contacted, the DSCC may still be called to arrange free legal advice. Apart from carrying out duties necessary to implement these arrangements, an officer must not advise the suspect about any particular firm of solicitors.*

6B1 *Not used.*

6B2 *Not used.*

6C *Not used.*

6D *The solicitor's only role in the police station is to protect and advance the legal rights of their client. On occasions this may require the solicitor to give advice which has the effect of the client avoiding giving evidence which strengthens a prosecution case. The solicitor may intervene in order to seek clarification, challenge an improper question to their client or the manner in which it is put, advise their client not to reply to particular questions, or if they wish to give their client further legal advice. Paragraph 6.9 only applies if the solicitor's approach or conduct prevents or unreasonably obstructs proper questions being put to the suspect or the suspect's response being recorded. Examples of unacceptable conduct include answering questions on a suspect's behalf or providing written replies for the suspect to quote.*

6E *An officer who takes the decision to exclude a solicitor must be in a position to satisfy the court the decision was properly made. In order to do this they may need to witness what is happening.*

6F *If an officer of at least inspector rank considers a particular solicitor or firm of solicitors is persistently sending probationary representatives who are unsuited to provide legal advice, they should inform an officer of at least superintendent rank, who may wish to take the matter up with the Solicitors Regulation Authority.*

6G *Subject to the constraints of Annex B, a solicitor may advise more than one client in an investigation if they wish. Any question of a conflict of interest is for the solicitor under their professional code of conduct. If, however, waiting for a solicitor to give advice to one client may lead to unreasonable delay to the interview with another, the provisions of paragraph 6.6(b) may apply.*

6H *In addition to a poster in English, a poster or posters containing translations into Welsh, the main minority ethnic languages and the principal European languages should be displayed wherever they are likely to be helpful and it is practicable to do so.*

6I *Not used.*

6J *Whenever a detainee exercises their right to legal advice by consulting or communicating with a solicitor, they must be allowed to do so in private. This right to consult or communicate in private is fundamental. If the requirement for privacy is compromised because what is said or written by the detainee or solicitor for the purpose of giving and receiving legal advice is overheard, listened to, or read by others without the informed consent of the detainee, the right will effectively have been denied. When a detainee speaks to a solicitor on the telephone, they should be allowed to do so in private unless this is impractical because of the design and layout of the custody area or the location of telephones. However, the normal expectation should be that facilities will be available, unless they are being used, at all police stations to enable detainees to speak in private to a solicitor either face to face or over the telephone.*

6K *A detainee is not obliged to give reasons for declining legal advice and should not be pressed to do so.*

## 7 Citizens of independent Commonwealth countries or foreign nationals

*(A) Action*

7.1 A detainee who is a citizen of an independent Commonwealth country or a national of a foreign country, including the Republic of Ireland, has the right, upon request, to communicate at any time with the appropriate High Commission, Embassy or Consulate. That detainee must be informed as soon as practicable of this right and asked if they want to have their High Commission, Embassy or Consulate told of their whereabouts and the grounds for their detention. Such a request should be acted upon as soon as practicable. See *Note 7A.*

7.2 A detainee who is a citizen of a country with which a bilateral consular convention or agreement is in force requiring notification of arrest must also be informed that subject to *paragraph 7.4*, notification of their arrest will be sent to the appropriate High Commission, Embassy or Consulate as soon as practicable, whether or not they request it. A list of the countries to which this requirement currently applies and contact details for the relevant High Commissions, Embassies and Consulates can be obtained from the Consular Directorate of the Foreign and Commonwealth Office (FCO) as follows:
- from the FCO web pages:
  - *https://gov.uk/government/publications/table-of-consular-conventions-and-mandatory-notification-obligations,* and

      – *https://www.gov.uk/government/publications/foreign-embassies-in-the-uk*
- by telephone to 020 7008 3100,
- by email to *fcocorrespondence@fco.gov.uk.*
- by letter to the Foreign and Commonwealth Office, King Charles Street, London, SW1A 2AH.

7.3    Consular officers may, if the detainee agrees, visit one of their nationals in police detention to talk to them and, if required, to arrange for legal advice. Such visits shall take place out of the hearing of a police officer.

7.4    Notwithstanding the provisions of consular conventions, if the detainee claims that they are a refugee or have applied or intend to apply for asylum, the custody officer must ensure that UK Visas and Immigration (UKVI) (formerly the UK Border Agency) is informed as soon as practicable of the claim. UKVI will then determine whether compliance with relevant international obligations requires notification of the arrest to be sent and will inform the custody officer as to what action police need to take.

*(B) Documentation*

7.5    A record shall be made:
- when a detainee is informed of their rights under this section and of any requirement in *paragraph 7.2*;
- of any communications with a High Commission, Embassy or Consulate, and
- of any communications with UKVI about a detainee's claim to be a refugee or to be seeking asylum and the resulting action taken by police.

*Note for Guidance*

7A    *The exercise of the rights in this section may not be interfered with even though Annex B applies.*

## 8  Conditions of detention

*(A) Action*

8.1    So far as it is practicable, not more than one detainee should be detained in each cell. See *Note 8C*.

8.2    Cells in use must be adequately heated, cleaned and ventilated. They must be adequately lit, subject to such dimming as is compatible with safety and security to allow people detained overnight to sleep. No additional restraints shall be used within a locked cell unless absolutely necessary and then only restraint equipment, approved for use in that force by the chief officer, which is reasonable and necessary in the circumstances having regard to the detainee's demeanour and with a view to ensuring their safety and the safety of others. If a detainee is deaf or a vulnerable person, particular care must be taken when deciding whether to use any form of approved restraints.

8.3    Blankets, mattresses, pillows and other bedding supplied shall be of a reasonable standard and in a clean and sanitary condition. See *Note 8A*.

8.4    Access to toilet and washing facilities must be provided. This must take account of the dignity of the detainee. See *Note 8D*.

8.5    If it is necessary to remove a detainee's clothes for the purposes of investigation, for hygiene, health reasons or cleaning, removal shall be conducted with proper regard to the dignity, sensitivity and vulnerability of the detainee and replacement clothing of a reasonable standard of comfort and cleanliness shall be provided. A detainee may not be interviewed unless adequate clothing has been offered.

8.6    At least two light meals and one main meal should be offered in any 24-hour period. See *Note 8B*. Drinks should be provided at meal times and upon reasonable request between meals. Whenever necessary, advice shall be sought from the appropriate healthcare professional, see *Note 9A*, on medical and dietary matters. As far as practicable, meals provided shall offer a varied diet and meet any specific dietary needs or religious beliefs the detainee may have. The detainee may, at the custody officer's discretion, have meals supplied by their family or friends at their expense. See *Note 8A*.

8.7    Brief outdoor exercise shall be offered daily if practicable.

8.8    A juvenile shall not be placed in a police cell unless no other secure accommodation is available and the custody officer considers it is not practicable to supervise them if they are not placed in a cell or that a cell provides more comfortable accommodation than other secure accommodation in the station. A juvenile may not be placed in a cell with a detained adult.

*(B) Documentation*

8.9    A record must be kept of replacement clothing and meals offered.

8.10  If a juvenile is placed in a cell, the reason must be recorded.

8.11 The use of any restraints on a detainee whilst in a cell, the reasons for it and, if appropriate, the arrangements for enhanced supervision of the detainee whilst so restrained, shall be recorded. See *paragraph 3.9*.

*Notes for Guidance*

8A *The provisions in paragraph 8.3 and 8.6 respectively are of particular importance in the case of a person likely to be detained for an extended period. In deciding whether to allow meals to be supplied by family or friends, the custody officer is entitled to take account of the risk of items being concealed in any food or package and the officer's duties and responsibilities under food handling legislation.*

8B *Meals should, so far as practicable, be offered at recognised meal times, or at other times that take account of when the detainee last had a meal.*

8C *The Detention and Custody Authorised Professional Practice (APP) produced by the College of Policing (see http://www.app.college.police.uk) provides more detailed guidance on matters concerning detainee healthcare and treatment and associated forensic issues which should be read in conjunction with sections 8 and 9 of this Code.*

8D *In cells subject to CCTV monitoring, privacy in the toilet area should be ensured by any appropriate means and detainees should be made aware of this when they are placed in the cell. If a detainee or appropriate adult on their behalf, expresses doubt about the effectiveness of the means used, reasonable steps should be taken to allay those doubts, for example, by explaining or demonstrating the means used.*

## 9 Care and treatment of detained persons

*(A) General*

9.1 Nothing in this section prevents the police from calling an appropriate healthcare professional to examine a detainee for the purposes of obtaining evidence relating to any offence in which the detainee is suspected of being involved. See *Notes 9A* and *8C*.

9.2 If a complaint is made by, or on behalf of, a detainee about their treatment since their arrest, or it comes to notice that a detainee may have been treated improperly, a report must be made as soon as practicable to an officer of inspector rank or above not connected with the investigation. If the matter concerns a possible assault or the possibility of the unnecessary or unreasonable use of force, an appropriate healthcare professional must also be called as soon as practicable.

9.3 Subject to *paragraph 9.6* in the case of a person to whom The Mental Health Act 1983 (Places of Safety) Regulations 2017 apply, detainees should be visited at least every hour. If no reasonably foreseeable risk was identified in a risk assessment, see *paragraphs 3.6 to 3.10*, there is no need to wake a sleeping detainee. Those suspected of being under the influence of drink or drugs or both or of having swallowed drugs, see *Note 9CA*, or whose level of consciousness causes concern must, subject to any clinical directions given by the appropriate healthcare professional, see *paragraph 9.13*:
- be visited and roused at least every half hour;
- have their condition assessed as in *Annex H*;
- and clinical treatment arranged if appropriate.

See *Notes 9B*, *9C* and *9H*

9.3A *As soon as practicable after arrival at the police station, each detainee must be given an opportunity to speak in private with a member of the custody staff who if they wish may be of the same sex as the detainee (see paragraph 1.13(c)), about any matter concerning the detainee's personal needs relating to their health, hygiene and welfare that might affect or concern them whilst in custody. If the detainee wishes to take this opportunity, the necessary arrangements shall be made as soon as practicable. In the cases of a juvenile or vulnerable person, the appropriate adult must be involved in accordance with paragraph 3.17 and in the case of a girl under 18, see paragraph 3.20A (see Note 9CB).*

9.3B *Each female detainee aged 18 or over shall be asked in private if possible and at the earliest opportunity, if they require or are likely to require any menstrual products whilst they are in custody. They must be told that they will be provided free of charge and that replacement products are available. At the custody officer's discretion, detainees may have menstrual products supplied by their family or friends at their expense (see Note 9CC). For girls under 18, see paragraph 3.20A.*

9.4 When arrangements are made to secure clinical attention for a detainee, the custody officer must make sure all relevant information which might assist in the treatment of the detainee's condition is made available to the responsible healthcare professional. This applies whether or not the healthcare professional asks for such information. Any officer or police staff with relevant information must inform the custody officer as soon as practicable.

*(B)  Clinical treatment and attention*

9.5 The custody officer must make sure a detainee receives appropriate clinical attention as soon as reasonably practicable if the person:
   (a) appears to be suffering from physical illness; or
   (b) is injured; or
   (c) appears to be suffering from a mental disorder; or
   (d) appears to need clinical attention.

9.5A This applies even if the detainee makes no request for clinical attention and whether or not they have already received clinical attention elsewhere. If the need for attention appears urgent, e.g. when indicated as in *Annex H*, the nearest available healthcare professional or an ambulance must be called immediately.

9.5B The custody officer must also consider the need for clinical attention as set out in *Note 9C* in relation to those suffering the effects of alcohol or drugs.

9.6 *Paragraph 9.5* is not meant to prevent or delay the transfer to a hospital if necessary of a person detained under the Mental Health Act 1983, sections 135 and 136, as amended by the Policing and Crime Act 2017. See *Note 9D*. When an assessment under that Act is to take place at a police station (see *paragraph 3.16*) the custody officer must also ensure that in accordance with *The Mental Health Act 1983 (Places of Safety) Regulations 2017*, a health professional is present and available to the person throughout the period they are detained at the police station and that at the welfare of the detainee is checked by the health professional at least once every thirty minutes and any appropriate action for the care and treatment of the detainee taken.

9.7 If it appears to the custody officer, or they are told, that a person brought to a station under arrest may be suffering from an infectious disease or condition, the custody officer must take reasonable steps to safeguard the health of the detainee and others at the station. In deciding what action to take, advice must be sought from an appropriate healthcare professional. See *Note 9E*. The custody officer has discretion to isolate the person and their property until clinical directions have been obtained.

9.8 If a detainee requests a clinical examination, an appropriate healthcare professional must be called as soon as practicable to assess the detainee's clinical needs. If a safe and appropriate care plan cannot be provided, the appropriate healthcare professional's advice must be sought. The detainee may also be examined by a medical practitioner of their choice at their expense.

9.9 If a detainee is required to take or apply any medication in compliance with clinical directions prescribed before their detention, the custody officer must consult the appropriate healthcare professional before the use of the medication. Subject to the restrictions in *paragraph 9.10*, the custody officer is responsible for the safekeeping of any medication and for making sure the detainee is given the opportunity to take or apply prescribed or approved medication. Any such consultation and its outcome shall be noted in the custody record.

9.10 No police officer may administer or supervise the self-administration of medically prescribed controlled drugs of the types and forms listed in the Misuse of Drugs Regulations 2001, Schedule 2 or 3. A detainee may only self-administer such drugs under the personal supervision of the registered medical practitioner authorising their use or other appropriate healthcare professional. The custody officer may supervise the self-administration of, or authorise other custody staff to supervise the self-administration of, drugs listed in Schedule 4 or 5 if the officer has consulted the appropriate healthcare professional authorising their use and both are satisfied self-administration will not expose the detainee, police officers or anyone else to the risk of harm or injury.

9.11 When appropriate healthcare professionals administer drugs or authorise the use of other medications, supervise their self-administration or consult with the custody officer about allowing self-administration of drugs listed in Schedule 4 or 5, it must be within current medicines legislation and the scope of practice as determined by their relevant statutory regulatory body.

9.12 If a detainee has in their possession, or claims to need, medication relating to a heart condition, diabetes, epilepsy or a condition of comparable potential seriousness then, even though *paragraph 9.5* may not apply, the advice of the appropriate healthcare professional must be obtained.

9.13 Whenever the appropriate healthcare professional is called in accordance with this section to examine or treat a detainee, the custody officer shall ask for their opinion about:
   • any risks or problems which police need to take into account when making decisions about the detainee's continued detention;
   • when to carry out an interview if applicable; and
   • the need for safeguards.

9.14 When clinical directions are given by the appropriate healthcare professional, whether orally or in writing, and the custody officer has any doubts or is in any way uncertain about any aspect of the directions, the custody officer shall ask for clarification. It is particularly important that directions concerning the frequency of visits are clear, precise and capable of being implemented. See *Note 9F.*

*(C) Documentation*

9.15 A record must be made in the custody record of:

(a) the arrangements made for an examination by an appropriate healthcare professional under *paragraph 9.2* and of any complaint reported under that paragraph together with any relevant remarks by the custody officer;

(b) any arrangements made in accordance with *paragraph 9.5*;

(c) any request for a clinical examination under *paragraph 9.8* and any arrangements made in response;

(d) the injury, ailment, condition or other reason which made it necessary to make the arrangements in (*a*) to (*c*); See *Note 9G.*

(e) any clinical directions and advice, including any further clarifications, given to police by a healthcare professional concerning the care and treatment of the detainee in connection with any of the arrangements made in (*a*) to (*c*); See *Notes 9E* and *9F.*

(f) if applicable, the responses received when attempting to rouse a person using the procedure in *Annex H.* See *Note 9H.*

9.16 If a healthcare professional does not record their clinical findings in the custody record, the record must show where they are recorded. See *Note 9G.* However, information which is necessary to custody staff to ensure the effective ongoing care and well being of the detainee must be recorded openly in the custody record, see *paragraph 3.8* and *Annex G, paragraph 7.*

9.17 Subject to the requirements of *Section 4*, the custody record shall include:

- a record of all medication a detainee has in their possession on arrival at the police station;
- a note of any such medication they claim to need but do not have with them.

*Notes for Guidance*

9A   *A 'healthcare professional' means a clinically qualified person working within the scope of practice as determined by their relevant statutory regulatory body. Whether a healthcare professional is 'appropriate' depends on the circumstances of the duties they carry out at the time.*

9B   *Whenever possible, detained juveniles and vulnerable persons should be visited more frequently.*

9C   *A detainee who appears drunk or behaves abnormally may be suffering from illness, the effects of drugs or may have sustained injury, particularly a head injury which is not apparent. A detainee needing or dependent on certain drugs, including alcohol, may experience harmful effects within a short time of being deprived of their supply. In these circumstances, when there is any doubt, police should always act urgently to call an appropriate healthcare professional or an ambulance. Paragraph 9.5 does not apply to minor ailments or injuries which do not need attention. However, all such ailments or injuries must be recorded in the custody record and any doubt must be resolved in favour of calling the appropriate healthcare professional.*

9CA  *Paragraph 9.3 would apply to a person in police custody by order of a magistrates' court under the Criminal Justice Act 1988, section 152 (as amended by the Drugs Act 2005, section 8) to facilitate the recovery of evidence after being charged with drug possession or drug trafficking and suspected of having swallowed drugs. In the case of the healthcare needs of a person who has swallowed drugs, the custody officer, subject to any clinical directions, should consider the necessity for rousing every half hour. This does not negate the need for regular visiting of the suspect in the cell.*

9D   *Except as allowed for under The Mental Health Act 1983 (Places of Safety) Regulations 2017, a police station must not be used as a place of safety for persons detained under section 135 or 136 of that Act. Chapter 16 of the Mental Health Act 1983 Code of Practice (as revised), provides more detailed guidance about arranging assessments under the Mental Health Act and transferring detainees from police stations to other places of safety. Additional guidance in relation to amendments made to the Mental Health Act in 2017 are published at https://www.gov.uk/government/publications/mental-health-act-1983-implementing-changes-to-police-powers.*

9E   *It is important to respect a person's right to privacy and information about their health must be kept confidential and only disclosed with their consent or in accordance with clinical advice when it is necessary to protect the detainee's health or that of others who come into contact with them.*

9F   *The custody officer should always seek to clarify directions that the detainee requires constant observation or supervision and should ask the appropriate healthcare professional to explain precisely what action needs to be taken to implement such directions.*

*9G   Paragraphs 9.15 and 9.16 do not require any information about the cause of any injury, ailment or condition to be recorded on the custody record if it appears capable of providing evidence of an offence.*

*9H   The purpose of recording a person's responses when attempting to rouse them using the procedure in Annex H is to enable any change in the individual's consciousness level to be noted and clinical treatment arranged if appropriate.*

## 10  Cautions

*(A)   When a caution must be given*

10.1   A person whom there are grounds to suspect of an offence, see *Note 10A*, must be cautioned before any questions about an offence, or further questions if the answers provide the grounds for suspicion, are put to them if either the suspect's answers or silence, (i.e. failure or refusal to answer or answer satisfactorily) may be given in evidence to a court in a prosecution. A person need not be cautioned if questions are for other necessary purposes, e.g.:

(a)   solely to establish their identity or ownership of any vehicle;

(b)   to obtain information in accordance with any relevant statutory requirement, see *paragraph 10.9*;

(c)   in furtherance of the proper and effective conduct of a search, e.g. to determine the need to search in the exercise of powers of stop and search or to seek co-operation while carrying out a search; or

(d)   to seek verification of a written record as in *paragraph 11.13*.

(e)   *Not used.*

10.2   Whenever a person not under arrest is initially cautioned, or reminded that they are under caution, that person must at the same time be told they are not under arrest and must be informed of the provisions of *paragraphs 3.21 to 3.21B* which explain that they need to agree to be interviewed, how they may obtain legal advice according to whether they are at a police station or elsewhere and the other rights and entitlements that apply to a voluntary interview. See *Note 10C*.

10.3   A person who is arrested, or further arrested, must be informed at the time if practicable or, if not, as soon as it becomes practicable thereafter, that they are under arrest and of the grounds and reasons for their arrest, see *paragraph 3.4, Note 10B* and Code G, *paragraphs 2.2 and 4.3*.

10.4   As required by Code G, *section 3*, a person who is arrested, or further arrested, must also be cautioned unless:

(a)   it is impracticable to do so by reason of their condition or behaviour at the time;

(b)   they have already been cautioned immediately prior to arrest as in *paragraph 10.1*.

*(B)   Terms of the cautions*

10.5   The caution which must be given on:

(a)   arrest; or

(b)   all other occasions before a person is charged or informed they may be prosecuted; see *section 16*,

should, unless the restriction on drawing adverse inferences from silence applies, see *Annex C*, be in the following terms:

'You do not have to say anything. But it may harm your defence if you do not mention when questioned something which you later rely on in Court. Anything you do say may be given in evidence.'

Where the use of the Welsh Language is appropriate, a constable may provide the caution directly in Welsh in the following terms:

*'Does dim rhaid i chi ddweud dim byd. Ond gall niweidio eich amddiffyniad os na fyddwch chi'n sôn, wrth gael eich holi, am rywbeth y byddwch chi'n dibynnu arno nes ymlaen yn y Llys. Gall unrhyw beth yr ydych yn ei ddweud gael ei roi fel tystiolaeth.'*

See *Note 10G*.

10.6   *Annex C, paragraph 2* sets out the alternative terms of the caution to be used when the restriction on drawing adverse inferences from silence applies.

10.7   Minor deviations from the words of any caution given in accordance with this Code do not constitute a breach of this Code, provided the sense of the relevant caution is preserved. See *Note 10D*.

10.8   After any break in questioning under caution, the person being questioned must be made aware they remain under caution. If there is any doubt the relevant caution should be given again in full when the interview resumes. See *Note 10E*.

10.9 When, despite being cautioned, a person fails to co-operate or to answer particular questions which may affect their immediate treatment, the person should be informed of any relevant consequences and that those consequences are not affected by the caution. Examples are when a person's refusal to provide:
- their name and address when charged may make them liable to detention;
- particulars and information in accordance with a statutory requirement, e.g. under the Road Traffic Act 1988, may amount to an offence or may make the person liable to a further arrest.

*(C)  Special warnings under the Criminal Justice and Public Order Act 1994, sections 36 and 37*

10.10  When a suspect interviewed at a police station or authorised place of detention after arrest fails or refuses to answer certain questions, or to answer satisfactorily, after due warning, see *Note 10F*, a court or jury may draw such inferences as appear proper under the Criminal Justice and Public Order Act 1994, sections 36 and 37. Such inferences may only be drawn when:
(a)  the restriction on drawing adverse inferences from silence, see *Annex C*, does not apply; and
(b)  the suspect is arrested by a constable and fails or refuses to account for any objects, marks or substances, or marks on such objects found:
- on their person;
- in or on their clothing or footwear;
- otherwise in their possession; or
- in the place they were arrested;
(c)  the arrested suspect was found by a constable at a place at or about the time the offence for which that officer has arrested them is alleged to have been committed, and the suspect fails or refuses to account for their presence there.

When the restriction on drawing adverse inferences from silence applies, the suspect may still be asked to account for any of the matters in (*b*) or (*c*) but the special warning described in *paragraph 10.11* will not apply and must not be given.

10.11  For an inference to be drawn when a suspect fails or refuses to answer a question about one of these matters or to answer it satisfactorily, the suspect must first be told in ordinary language:
(a)  what offence is being investigated;
(b)  what fact they are being asked to account for;
(c)  this fact may be due to them taking part in the commission of the offence;
(d)  a court may draw a proper inference if they fail or refuse to account for this fact; and
(e)  a record is being made of the interview and it may be given in evidence if they are brought to trial.

*(D)  Juveniles and vulnerable persons*

10.11A  The information required in *paragraph 10.11* must not be given to a suspect who is a juvenile or a vulnerable person unless the appropriate adult is present.

10.12  If a juvenile or a vulnerable person is cautioned in the absence of the appropriate adult, the caution must be repeated in the appropriate adult's presence.

10.12A  *Not used.*

*(E)  Documentation*

10.13A record shall be made when a caution is given under this section, either in the interviewer's report book or in the interview record.

*Notes for Guidance*

*10A  There must be some reasonable, objective grounds for the suspicion, based on known facts or information which are relevant to the likelihood the offence has been committed and the person to be questioned committed it.*

*10B  An arrested person must be given sufficient information to enable them to understand that they have been deprived of their liberty and the reason they have been arrested, e.g. when a person is arrested on suspicion of committing an offence they must be informed of the suspected offence's nature, when and where it was committed. The suspect must also be informed of the reason or reasons why the arrest is considered necessary. Vague or technical language should be avoided.*

*10C  The restriction on drawing inferences from silence, see Annex C, paragraph 1, does not apply to a person who has not been detained and who therefore cannot be prevented from seeking legal advice if they want, see paragraph 3.21.*

*10D  If it appears a person does not understand the caution, the person giving it should explain it in their own words.*

*10E   It may be necessary to show to the court that nothing occurred during an interview break or between interviews which influenced the suspect's recorded evidence. After a break in an interview or at the beginning of a subsequent interview, the interviewer should summarise the reason for the break and confirm this with the suspect.*

*10F   The Criminal Justice and Public Order Act 1994, sections 36 and 37 apply only to suspects who have been arrested by a constable or an officer of Revenue and Customs and are given the relevant warning by the police or Revenue and Customs officer who made the arrest or who is investigating the offence. They do not apply to any interviews with suspects who have not been arrested.*

*10G   Nothing in this Code requires a caution to be given or repeated when informing a person not under arrest they may be prosecuted for an offence. However, a court will not be able to draw any inferences under the Criminal Justice and Public Order Act 1994, section 34, if the person was not cautioned.*

## 11   Interviews — general

*(A)   Action*

11.1A   An interview is the questioning of a person regarding their involvement or suspected involvement in a criminal offence or offences which, under *paragraph 10.1*, must be carried out under caution. Before a person is interviewed, they and, if they are represented, their solicitor must be given sufficient information to enable them to understand the nature of any such offence, and why they are suspected of committing it (see *paragraphs 3.4(a)* and *10.3*), in order to allow for the effective exercise of the rights of the defence. However, whilst the information must always be sufficient for the person to understand the nature of any offence (see *Note 11ZA*), this does not require the disclosure of details at a time which might prejudice the criminal investigation. The decision about what needs to be disclosed for the purpose of this requirement therefore rests with the investigating officer who has sufficient knowledge of the case to make that decision. The officer who discloses the information shall make a record of the information disclosed and when it was disclosed. This record may be made in the interview record, in the officer's report book or other form provided for this purpose. Procedures under the Road Traffic Act 1988, section 7 or the Transport and Works Act 1992, section 31 do not constitute interviewing for the purpose of this Code.

11.1   Following a decision to arrest a suspect, they must not be interviewed about the relevant offence except at a police station or other authorised place of detention, unless the consequent delay would be likely to:

(a)   lead to:
- interference with, or harm to, evidence connected with an offence;
- interference with, or physical harm to, other people; or
- serious loss of, or damage to, property;

(b)   lead to alerting other people suspected of committing an offence but not yet arrested for it; or

(c)   hinder the recovery of property obtained in consequence of the commission of an offence.

Interviewing in any of these circumstances shall cease once the relevant risk has been averted or the necessary questions have been put in order to attempt to avert that risk.

11.2   Immediately prior to the commencement or re-commencement of any interview at a police station or other authorised place of detention, the interviewer should remind the suspect of their entitlement to free legal advice and that the interview can be delayed for legal advice to be obtained, unless one of the exceptions in *paragraph 6.6* applies. It is the interviewer's responsibility to make sure all reminders are recorded in the interview record.

11.3   *Not used.*

11.4   At the beginning of an interview the interviewer, after cautioning the suspect, see *section 10*, shall put to them any significant statement or silence which occurred in the presence and hearing of a police officer or other police staff before the start of the interview and which have not been put to the suspect in the course of a previous interview. See *Note 11A*. The interviewer shall ask the suspect whether they confirm or deny that earlier statement or silence and if they want to add anything.

11.4A   A significant statement is one which appears capable of being used in evidence against the suspect, in particular a direct admission of guilt. A significant silence is a failure or refusal to answer a question or answer satisfactorily when under caution, which might, allowing for the restriction on drawing adverse inferences from silence, see *Annex C*, give rise to an inference under the Criminal Justice and Public Order Act 1994, Part III.

11.5   No interviewer may try to obtain answers or elicit a statement by the use of oppression. Except as in *paragraph 10.9*, no interviewer shall indicate, except to answer a direct question, what action will be taken by the police if the person being questioned answers questions, makes a statement or refuses to do either. If the person asks directly what action will be taken if they answer questions, make a statement or refuse to do either, the interviewer may inform them what action the police propose to take provided that action is itself proper and warranted.

11.6  The interview or further interview of a person about an offence with which that person has not been charged or for which they have not been informed they may be prosecuted, must cease when:

(a)  the officer in charge of the investigation is satisfied all the questions they consider relevant to obtaining accurate and reliable information about the offence have been put to the suspect, this includes allowing the suspect an opportunity to give an innocent explanation and asking questions to test if the explanation is accurate and reliable, e.g. to clear up ambiguities or clarify what the suspect said;

(b)  the officer in charge of the investigation has taken account of any other available evidence; and

(c)  the officer in charge of the investigation, or in the case of a detained suspect, the custody officer, see *paragraph 16.1*, reasonably believes there is sufficient evidence to provide a realistic prospect of conviction for that offence. See *Note 11B*.

This paragraph does not prevent officers in revenue cases or acting under the confiscation provisions of the Criminal Justice Act 1988 or the Drug Trafficking Act 1994 from inviting suspects to complete a formal question and answer record after the interview is concluded.

*(B)  Interview records*

11.7  (a)  An accurate record must be made of each interview, whether or not the interview takes place at a police station.

(b)  The record must state the place of interview, the time it begins and ends, any interview breaks and, subject to *paragraph 2.6A*, the names of all those present; and must be made on the forms provided for this purpose or in the interviewer's report book or in accordance with Codes of Practice E or F.

(c)  Any written record must be made and completed during the interview, unless this would not be practicable or would interfere with the conduct of the interview, and must constitute either a verbatim record of what has been said or, failing this, an account of the interview which adequately and accurately summarises it.

11.8  If a written record is not made during the interview it must be made as soon as practicable after its completion.

11.9  Written interview records must be timed and signed by the maker.

11.10  If a written record is not completed during the interview the reason must be recorded in the interview record.

11.11  Unless it is impracticable, the person interviewed shall be given the opportunity to read the interview record and to sign it as correct or to indicate how they consider it inaccurate. If the person interviewed cannot read or refuses to read the record or sign it, the senior interviewer present shall read it to them and ask whether they would like to sign it as correct or make their mark or to indicate how they consider it inaccurate. The interviewer shall certify on the interview record itself what has occurred. See *Note 11E*.

11.12  If the appropriate adult or the person's solicitor is present during the interview, they should also be given an opportunity to read and sign the interview record or any written statement taken down during the interview.

11.13  A record shall be made of any comments made by a suspect, including unsolicited comments, which are outside the context of an interview but which might be relevant to the offence. Any such record must be timed and signed by the maker. When practicable the suspect shall be given the opportunity to read that record and to sign it as correct or to indicate how they consider it inaccurate. See *Note 11E*.

11.14  Any refusal by a person to sign an interview record when asked in accordance with this Code must itself be recorded.

*(C)  Juveniles and vulnerable persons*

11.15  A juvenile or vulnerable person must not be interviewed regarding their involvement or suspected involvement in a criminal offence or offences, or asked to provide or sign a written statement under caution or record of interview, in the absence of the appropriate adult unless *paragraphs 11.1* or *11.18* to *11.20* apply. See *Note 11C*.

11.16  Juveniles may only be interviewed at their place of education in exceptional circumstances and only when the principal or their nominee agrees. Every effort should be made to notify the parent(s) or other person responsible for the juvenile's welfare and the appropriate adult, if this is a different person, that the police want to interview the juvenile and reasonable time should be allowed to enable the appropriate adult to be present at the interview. If awaiting the appropriate adult would cause unreasonable delay, and unless the juvenile is suspected of an offence against the educational establishment, the principal or their nominee can act as the appropriate adult for the purposes of the interview.

11.17 If an appropriate adult is present at an interview, they shall be informed:
- that they are not expected to act simply as an observer; and
- that the purpose of their presence is to:
  - advise the person being interviewed;
  - observe whether the interview is being conducted properly and fairly; and
  - facilitate communication with the person being interviewed.

See paragraph 1.7A.

11.17A The appropriate adult may be required to leave the interview if their conduct is such that the interviewer is unable properly to put questions to the suspect. This will include situations where the appropriate adult's approach or conduct prevents or unreasonably obstructs proper questions being put to the suspect or the suspect's responses being recorded (see *Note 11F*). If the interviewer considers an appropriate adult is acting in such a way, they will stop the interview and consult an officer not below superintendent rank, if one is readily available, and otherwise an officer not below inspector rank not connected with the investigation. After speaking to the appropriate adult, the officer consulted must remind the adult that their role under *paragraph 11.17* does not allow them to obstruct proper questioning and give the adult an opportunity to respond. The officer consulted will then decide if the interview should continue without the attendance of that appropriate adult. If they decide it should, another appropriate adult must be obtained before the interview continues, unless the provisions of *paragraph 11.18* below apply.

*(D)  Vulnerable suspects — urgent interviews at police stations*

11.18 The following interviews may take place only if an officer of superintendent rank or above considers delaying the interview will lead to the consequences in *paragraph 11.1(a)* to *(c)*, and is satisfied the interview would not significantly harm the person's physical or mental state (see *Annex G*):
- (a) an interview of a detained juvenile or vulnerable person without the appropriate adult being present (see *Note 11C*);
- (b) an interview of anyone detained other than in *(a)* who appears unable to:
  - appreciate the significance of questions and their answers; or
  - understand what is happening because of the effects of drink, drugs or any illness, ailment or condition;
- (c) an interview, without an interpreter having been arranged, of a detained person whom the custody officer has determined requires an interpreter (see *paragraphs 3.5(c)(ii)* and *3.12*) which is carried out by an interviewer speaking the suspect's own language or (as the case may be) otherwise establishing effective communication which is sufficient to enable the necessary questions to be asked and answered in order to avert the consequences. See *paragraphs 13.2* and *13.5*.

11.19 These interviews may not continue once sufficient information has been obtained to avert the consequences in *paragraph 11.1(a)* to *(c)*.

11.20 A record shall be made of the grounds for any decision to interview a person under *paragraph 11.18*.

*(E)  Conduct and recording of Interviews at police stations — use of live link*

11.21 When a suspect in police detention is interviewed using a live link by a police officer who is not at the police station where the detainee is held, the provisions of this section that govern the conduct and making a written record of that interview, shall be subject to *paragraph 12.9B* of this Code.

*(F)  Witnesses*

11.22 The provisions of this Code and Codes E and F which govern the conduct and recording of interviews do not apply to interviews with, or taking statements from, witnesses.

*Notes for Guidance*

*11ZA  The requirement in paragraph 11.1A for a suspect to be given sufficient information about the offence applies prior to the interview and whether or not they are legally represented. What is sufficient will depend on the circumstances of the case, but it should normally include, as a minimum, a description of the facts relating to the suspected offence that are known to the officer, including the time and place in question. This aims to avoid suspects being confused or unclear about what they are supposed to have done and to help an innocent suspect to clear the matter up more quickly.*

*11A  Paragraph 11.4 does not prevent the interviewer from putting significant statements and silences to a suspect again at a later stage or a further interview.*

11B   *The Criminal Procedure and Investigations Act 1996 Code of Practice, paragraph 3.5 states 'In conducting an investigation, the investigator should pursue all reasonable lines of enquiry, whether these point towards or away from the suspect. What is reasonable will depend on the particular circumstances.' Interviewers should keep this in mind when deciding what questions to ask in an interview.*

11C   *Although juveniles or vulnerable persons are often capable of providing reliable evidence, they may, without knowing or wishing to do so, be particularly prone in certain circumstances to providing information that may be unreliable, misleading or self- incriminating. Special care should always be taken when questioning such a person, and the appropriate adult should be involved if there is any doubt about a person's age, mental state or capacity. Because of the risk of unreliable evidence it is also important to obtain corroboration of any facts admitted whenever possible. Because of the risks, which the presence of the appropriate adult is intended to minimise, officers of superintendent rank or above should exercise their discretion under paragraph 11.18(a) to authorise the commencement of an interview in the appropriate adult's absence only in exceptional cases, if it is necessary to avert one or more of the specified risks in paragraph 11.1.*

11D   *Juveniles should not be arrested at their place of education unless this is unavoidable. When a juvenile is arrested at their place of education, the principal or their nominee must be informed.*

11E   *Significant statements described in paragraph 11.4 will always be relevant to the offence and must be recorded. When a suspect agrees to read records of interviews and other comments and sign them as correct, they should be asked to endorse the record with, e.g. 'I agree that this is a correct record of what was said' and add their signature. If the suspect does not agree with the record, the interviewer should record the details of any disagreement and ask the suspect to read these details and sign them to the effect that they accurately reflect their disagreement. Any refusal to sign should be recorded.*

11F   *The appropriate adult may intervene if they consider it is necessary to help the suspect understand any question asked and to help the suspect to answer any question. Paragraph 11.17A only applies if the appropriate adult's approach or conduct prevents or unreasonably obstructs proper questions being put to the suspect or the suspect's response being recorded. Examples of unacceptable conduct include answering questions on a suspect's behalf or providing written replies for the suspect to quote. An officer who takes the decision to exclude an appropriate adult must be in a position to satisfy the court the decision was properly made. In order to do this they may need to witness what is happening and give the suspect's solicitor (if they have one) who witnessed what happened, an opportunity to comment.*

## 12  Interviews in police stations

*(A)  Action*

*When interviewer and suspect are present at the same police station*

12.1  If a police officer wants to interview or conduct enquiries which require the presence of a detainee, the custody officer is responsible for deciding whether to deliver the detainee into the officer's custody. An investigating officer who is given custody of a detainee takes over responsibility for the detainee's care and safe custody for the purposes of this Code until they return the detainee to the custody officer when they must report the manner in which they complied with the Code whilst having custody of the detainee.

12.2  Except as below, in any period of 24 hours a detainee must be allowed a continuous period of at least 8 hours for rest, free from questioning, travel or any interruption in connection with the investigation concerned. This period should normally be at night or other appropriate time which takes account of when the detainee last slept or rested. If a detainee is arrested at a police station after going there voluntarily, the period of 24 hours runs from the time of their arrest and not the time of arrival at the police station. The period may not be interrupted or delayed, except:
   (a)   when there are reasonable grounds for believing not delaying or interrupting the period would:
        (i)    involve a risk of harm to people or serious loss of, or damage to, property;
        (ii)   delay unnecessarily the person's release from custody; or
        (iii)  otherwise prejudice the outcome of the investigation;
   (b)   at the request of the detainee, their appropriate adult or legal representative;
   (c)   when a delay or interruption is necessary in order to:
        (i)    comply with the legal obligations and duties arising under *section 15*; or
        (ii)   to take action required under *section 9* or in accordance with medical advice.
   If the period is interrupted in accordance with *(a)*, a fresh period must be allowed. Interruptions under *(b)* and *(c)* do not require a fresh period to be allowed.

12.3  Before a detainee is interviewed, the custody officer, in consultation with the officer in charge of the investigation and appropriate healthcare professionals as necessary, shall assess whether the detainee is fit enough to be interviewed. This means determining and considering the risks to the detainee's physical and mental state if the interview took place and determining what safeguards are needed to allow the interview to take place. See *Annex G*. The custody officer shall not allow a detainee to be interviewed if the custody officer considers it would cause significant harm to the detainee's physical or mental state. Vulnerable suspects listed at *paragraph 11.18* shall be treated as always being at some risk during an interview and these persons may not be interviewed except in accordance with *paragraphs 11.18 to 11.20*.

12.4 As far as practicable interviews shall take place in interview rooms which are adequately heated, lit and ventilated.

12.5 A suspect whose detention without charge has been authorised under PACE because the detention is necessary for an interview to obtain evidence of the offence for which they have been arrested may choose not to answer questions but police do not require the suspect's consent or agreement to interview them for this purpose. If a suspect takes steps to prevent themselves being questioned or further questioned, e.g. by refusing to leave their cell to go to a suitable interview room or by trying to leave the interview room, they shall be advised that their consent or agreement to be interviewed is not required. The suspect shall be cautioned as in *section 10*, and informed if they fail or refuse to co-operate, the interview may take place in the cell and that their failure or refusal to co-operate may be given in evidence. The suspect shall then be invited to co-operate and go into the interview room. If they refuse and the custody officer considers, on reasonable grounds, that the interview should not be delayed, the custody officer has discretion to direct that the interview be conducted in a cell.

12.6 People being questioned or making statements shall not be required to stand.

12.7 Before the interview commences each interviewer shall, subject to *paragraph 2.6A*, identify themselves and any other persons present to the interviewee.

12.8 Breaks from interviewing should be made at recognised meal times or at other times that take account of when an interviewee last had a meal. Short refreshment breaks shall be provided at approximately two hour intervals, subject to the interviewer's discretion to delay a break if there are reasonable grounds for believing it would:

(i)   involve a:
   • risk of harm to people;
   • serious loss of, or damage to, property;
(ii)  unnecessarily delay the detainee's release; or
(iii) otherwise prejudice the outcome of the investigation.
   See *Note 12B*.

12.9 If during the interview a complaint is made by or on behalf of the interviewee concerning the provisions of any of the Codes, or it comes to the interviewer's notice that the interviewee may have been treated improperly, the interviewer should:

(i)   record the matter in the interview record; and
(ii)  inform the custody officer, who is then responsible for dealing with it as in *section 9*.

*Interviewer not present at the same station as the detainee — use of live link*

12.9A Amendments to PACE, section 39, allow a person in police detention to be interviewed using a live link (see *paragraph 1.13(e)(i)*) by a police officer who is not at the police station where the detainee is held. Subject to *sub-paragraphs (a)* to *(f)* below, the custody officer is responsible for deciding on a case by case basis whether a detainee is fit to be interviewed (see *paragraph 12.3*) and should be delivered into the physical custody of an officer who is not involved in the investigation, for the purpose of enabling another officer who is investigating the offence for which the person is detained and who is not at the police station where the person is detained, to interview the detainee by means of a live link (see *Note 12ZA*).

(a)   The custody officer must be satisfied that the live link to be used provides for accurate and secure communication with the suspect. The provisions of *paragraph 13.13* shall apply to communications between the interviewing officer, the suspect and anyone else whose presence at the interview or, (as the case may be) whose access to any communications between the suspect and the interviewer, has been authorised by the custody officer or the interviewing officer.

(b)   Each decision must take account of the age, gender and vulnerability of the suspect, the nature and circumstances of the offence and the investigation and the impact on the suspect of carrying out the interview by means of a live link. For this reason, the custody officer must consider whether the ability of the particular suspect, to communicate confidently and effectively for the purpose of the interview is likely to be adversely affected or otherwise undermined or limited if the interviewing officer is not physically present and a live-link is used (see *Note 12ZB*). Although a suspect for whom an appropriate adult is required may be more

*(G)  Documentation*

13.11  The following must be recorded in the custody record or, as applicable, the interview record:
  (a)  Action taken to arrange for an interpreter, including the live-link requirements in *Annex N* as applicable;
  (b)  Action taken when a detainee is not satisfied about the standard of interpretation or translation provided, see *paragraphs 13.10A* and *13.10C*;
  (c)  When an urgent interview is carried out in accordance with *paragraph 13.2* or *13.5* in the absence of an interpreter;
  (d)  When a detainee has been assisted by an interpreter for the purpose of providing or being given information or being interviewed;
  (e)  Action taken in accordance with *Annex M* when:
    • a written translation of an essential document is provided;
    • an oral translation or oral summary of an essential document is provided instead of a written translation and the authorising officer's reason(s) why this would not prejudice the fairness of the proceedings (see *Annex M, paragraph 3*);
    • a suspect waives their right to a translation of an essential document (see *Annex M, paragraph 4*);
    • when representations that a document which is not included in the table is essential and that a translation should be provided are refused and the reason for the refusal (see *Annex M, paragraph 8*).

*(H)  Live-link interpretation*

13.12  In this section and in *Annex N*, 'live-link interpretation' means an arrangement to enable communication between the suspect and an interpreter who is not *physically* present with the suspect. The arrangement must ensure that anything said by any person in the suspect's presence and hearing can be interpreted in the same way as if the interpreter was physically present at that time. The communication must be by audio *and* visual means for the purpose of an interview, and for all other purposes it may be *either*, by audio and visual means, or by audio means *only*, as follows:
  (a)  **Audio and visual communication**
    This applies for the purposes of an interview conducted and recorded in accordance with Code E (Audio recording) or Code F (Visual recording) and during that interview, live link interpretation must *enable*:
    (i)   the suspect, the interviewer, solicitor, appropriate adult and any other person *physically* present with the suspect at any time during the interview and an interpreter who is not *physically* present, to *see* and *hear* each other; and
    (ii)  the interview to be conducted and recorded in accordance with the provisions of Codes C, E and F, subject to the modifications in Part 2 of *Annex N*.
  (b)  **Audio and visual or audio without visual communication.**
    This applies to communication for the purposes of any provision of this or any other Code except as described in (a), which requires or permits information to be given to, sought from, or provided by a suspect, whether orally or in writing, which would include communication between the suspect and their solicitor and/or appropriate adult, and for these cases, live link interpretation must:
    (i)   *enable* the suspect, the person giving or seeking that information, any other person *physically* present with the suspect at that time and an interpreter who is not so present, to either *see* and *hear* each other, or to *hear without seeing* each other (for example by using a telephone); and
    (ii)  enable that information to be given to, sought from, or provided by, the suspect in accordance with the provisions of this or any other Code that apply to that information, as modified for the purposes of the live-link, by Part 2 of *Annex N*.

13.12A  The requirement in *sub-paragraphs 13.12(a)(ii)* and *(b)(ii)*, that live-link interpretation must enable compliance with the relevant provisions of the Codes C, E and F, means that the arrangements must provide for any written or electronic record of what the suspect says in their own language which is made by the interpreter, to be securely transmitted without delay so that the suspect can be invited to read, check and if appropriate, sign or otherwise confirm that the record is correct or make corrections to the record.

13.13  Chief officers must be satisfied that live-link interpretation used in their force area for the purposes of *paragraphs 3.12(a)* and *(b)*, provides for accurate and secure communication with the suspect. This includes ensuring that at any time during which live link interpretation is being used: a person cannot see, hear or otherwise obtain access to any communications between the suspect and interpreter or communicate with the suspect or interpreter unless so authorised or allowed by the custody officer or, in the case of an interview, the interviewer and that as applicable, the confidentiality of any private consultation between a suspect and their solicitor and appropriate adult (see *paragraphs 13.2A, 13.6* and *13.9*) is maintained. See *Annex N paragraph 4*.

## Notes for Guidance

13A  *Chief officers have discretion when determining the individuals or organisations they use to provide interpretation and translation services for their forces provided that these are compatible with the requirements of the Directive. One example which chief officers may wish to consider is the Ministry of Justice commercial agreements for interpretation and translation services.*

13B  *A procedure for determining whether a person needs an interpreter might involve a telephone interpreter service or using cue cards or similar visual aids which enable the detainee to indicate their ability to speak and understand English and their preferred language. This could be confirmed through an interpreter who could also assess the extent to which the person can speak and understand English.*

13C  *There should also be a procedure for determining whether a suspect who requires an interpreter requires assistance in accordance with paragraph 3.20 to help them check and if applicable, sign any documentation.*

## 14  Questioning — special restrictions

14.1  If a person is arrested by one police force on behalf of another and the lawful period of detention in respect of that offence has not yet commenced in accordance with PACE, section 41, no questions may be put to them about the offence while they are in transit between the forces except to clarify any voluntary statement they make.

14.2  If a person is in police detention at a hospital, they may not be questioned without the agreement of a responsible doctor. See *Note 14A*.

## Notes for Guidance

14A  *If questioning takes place at a hospital under paragraph 14.2, or on the way to or from a hospital, the period of questioning concerned counts towards the total period of detention permitted.*

## 15  Reviews and extensions of detention

*(A)  Persons detained under PACE*

15.0  The requirement in *paragraph 3.4(b)* that documents and materials essential to challenging the lawfulness of the detainee's arrest and detention must be made available to the detainee or their solicitor, applies for the purposes of this section as follows:
   (a)  The officer reviewing the need for detention without charge (PACE, section 40), or (as the case may be) the officer considering the need to extend detention without charge from 24 to 36 hours (PACE, section 42), is responsible, in consultation with the investigating officer, for deciding which documents and materials are essential and must be made available.
   (b)  When *paragraph 15.7A* applies (application for a warrant of further detention or extension of such a warrant), the officer making the application is responsible for deciding which documents and materials are essential and must be made available *before* the hearing. See *Note 3ZA*.

15.1  The review officer is responsible under PACE, section 40 for periodically determining if a person's detention, before or after charge, continues to be necessary. This requirement continues throughout the detention period and, except when a telephone or a live link is used in accordance with *paragraphs 15.9* to *15.11C*, the review officer must be present at the police station holding the detainee. See *Notes 15A* and *15B*.

15.2  Under PACE, section 42, an officer of superintendent rank or above who is responsible for the station holding the detainee may give authority any time after the second review to extend the maximum period the person may be detained without charge by up to 12 hours. Except when a live link is used as in *paragraph 15.11A*, the superintendent must be present at the station holding the detainee. Further detention without charge may be authorised only by a magistrates' court in accordance with PACE, sections 43 and 44 and unless the court has given a live link direction as in *paragraph 15.11B*, the detainee must be brought before the court for the hearing. See *Notes 15C, 15D* and *15E*.

15.2A  An authorisation under section 42(1) of PACE extends the maximum period of detention permitted before charge for indictable offences from 24 hours to 36 hours. Detaining a juvenile or a vulnerable person for longer than 24 hours will be dependent on the circumstances of the case and with regard to the person's:
   (a)  special vulnerability;
   (b)  the legal obligation to provide an opportunity for representations to be made prior to a decision about extending detention;

    (c)  the need to consult and consider the views of any appropriate adult; and

    (d)  any alternatives to police custody.

15.3  Before deciding whether to authorise continued detention the officer responsible under *paragraph 15.1* or *15.2* shall give an opportunity to make representations about the detention to:

    (a)  the detainee, unless in the case of a review as in *paragraph 15.1*, the detainee is asleep;

    (b)  the detainee's solicitor if available at the time; and

    (c)  the appropriate adult if available at the time.

    See *Note 15CA.*

15.3A  Other people having an interest in the detainee's welfare may also make representations at the authorising officer's discretion.

15.3B  Subject to *paragraph 15.10*, the representations may be made orally in person or by telephone or in writing. The authorising officer may, however, refuse to hear oral representations from the detainee if the officer considers them unfit to make representations because of their condition or behaviour. See *Note 15C.*

15.3C  The decision on whether the review takes place in person or by telephone or by live link (see *paragraph 1.13(e)(ii)*) is a matter for the review officer. In determining the form the review may take, the review officer must always take full account of the needs of the person in custody. The benefits of carrying out a review in person should always be considered, based on the individual circumstances of each case with specific additional consideration if the person is:

    (a)  a juvenile (and the age of the juvenile); or

    (b)  a vulnerable person; or

    (c)  in need of medical attention for other than routine minor ailments; or

    (d)  subject to presentational or community issues around their detention.

15.4  Before conducting a review or determining whether to extend the maximum period of detention without charge, the officer responsible must make sure the detainee is reminded of their entitlement to free legal advice, see *paragraph 6.5*, unless in the case of a review the person is asleep. When determining whether to extend the maximum period of detention without charge, it should also be pointed out that for the purposes of *paragraph 15.2*, the superintendent or (as the case may be) the court, responsible for authorising any such extension, will not be able to use a live link unless the detainee has *received* legal advice on the use of the live link (see *paragraphs 15.11A(ii)* and *15.11C(ii)*) and given consent to its use (see *paragraphs 15.11A(iii)* and *15.11C(iii)*). The detainee must also be given information about how the live link is used.

15.4A  Following sections 45ZA and 45ZB of PACE, when the reminder and information concerning legal advice and about the use of the live link is given and the detainee's consent is sought, the presence of an appropriate adult is required if the detainee in question is a juvenile (see *paragraph 1.5*) or is a *vulnerable adult* by virtue of being a person aged 18 or over who, because of a mental disorder established in accordance *paragraphs 1.4* and *1.13(d)* or for *any other reason* (see *paragraph 15.4B*), may have difficulty understanding the purpose of:

    (a)  an authorisation under section 42 of PACE or anything that occurs in connection with a decision whether to give it (see *paragraphs 15.2* and *15.2A*); or

    (b)  a court hearing under section 43 or 44 of PACE or what occurs at the hearing it (see *paragraphs 15.2* and *15.7A*).

15.4B  For the purpose of using a live link in accordance with sections 45ZA and 45ZB of PACE to authorise detention without charge (see *paragraphs 15.11A* and *15.11C*), the reference to '*any other reason*' would extend to difficulties in understanding the purposes mentioned in *paragraph 15.4A* that might arise if the person happened to be under the influence of drink or drugs at the time the live link is to be used. This does not however apply for the purposes of *paragraphs 1.4* and *1.13(d)* (see *Note 1GC*).

15.5  If, after considering any representations, the review officer under *paragraph 15.1* decides to keep the detainee in detention or the superintendent under *paragraph 15.2* extends the maximum period for which they may be detained without charge, then any comment made by the detainee shall be recorded. If applicable, the officer shall be informed of the comment as soon as practicable. See also *paragraphs 11.4* and *11.13*.

15.6  No officer shall put specific questions to the detainee:

    •  regarding their involvement in any offence; or

    •  in respect of any comments they may make:

       –  when given the opportunity to make representations; or

      – in response to a decision to keep them in detention or extend the maximum period of detention.

Such an exchange could constitute an interview as in *paragraph 11.1A* and would be subject to the associated safeguards in *section 11* and, in respect of a person who has been charged, *paragraph 16.5*. See also *paragraph 11.13*.

15.7   A detainee who is asleep at a review, see *paragraph 15.1*, and whose continued detention is authorised must be informed about the decision and reason as soon as practicable after waking.

15.7A  When an application is made to a magistrates' court under PACE, section 43 for a warrant of further detention to extend detention without charge of a person arrested for an *indictable offence*, or under section 44, to extend or further extend that warrant, the detainee:

    (a)  must, unless the court has given a live link direction as in *paragraph 15.11C*, be brought to court for the hearing of the application (see *Note 15D*);

    (b)  is entitled to be legally represented if they wish, in which case, *Annex B* cannot apply; and

    (c)  must be given a copy of the information which supports the application and states:

        (i)   the nature of the offence for which the person to whom the application relates has been arrested;

        (ii)  the general nature of the evidence on which the person was arrested;

        (iii) what inquiries about the offence have been made and what further inquiries are proposed;

        (iv)  the reasons for believing continued detention is necessary for the purposes of the further inquiries;

Note: A warrant of further detention can only be issued or extended if the court has reasonable grounds for believing that the person's further detention is necessary for the purpose of obtaining evidence of an indictable offence for which the person has been arrested and that the investigation is being conducted diligently and expeditiously.

See *paragraph 15.0(b)*.

15.8   *Not used.*

*(B)  Review of detention by telephone or by using a live link (section 40A and 45A)*

15.9   PACE, section 40A provides that the officer responsible under section 40 for reviewing the detention of a person who has not been charged, need not attend the police station holding the detainee and may carry out the review by telephone.

15.9A  PACE, section 45A(2) provides that the officer responsible under section 40 for reviewing the detention of a person who has not been charged, need not attend the police station holding the detainee and may carry out the review using a live link. See *paragraph 1.13(e)(ii)*.

15.9B  A telephone review is not permitted where facilities for review using a live link exist and it is practicable to use them.

15.9C  The review officer can decide at any stage that a telephone review or review by live link should be terminated and that the review will be conducted in person. The reasons for doing so should be noted in the custody record. See *Note 15F*.

15.10  When a review is carried out by telephone or by using a live link, an officer at the station holding the detainee shall be required by the review officer to fulfil that officer's obligations under PACE, section 40 and this Code by:

    (a)  making any record connected with the review in the detainee's custody record;

    (b)  if applicable, making the record in (*a*) in the presence of the detainee; and

    (c)  for a review by telephone, giving the detainee information about the review.

15.11  When a review is carried out by telephone or by using a live link, or the requirement in *paragraph 15.3* will be satisfied:

    (a)  if facilities exist for the immediate transmission of written representations to the review officer, e.g. fax or email message, by allowing those who are given the opportunity to make representations, to make their representations:

        (i)   orally by telephone or (as the case may be) by means of the live link; or

        (ii)  in writing using the facilities for the immediate transmission of written representations; and

    (b)  in all other cases, by allowing those who are given the opportunity to make representations, to make their representations orally by telephone or by means of the live link.

*(C) Authorisation to extend detention using live link (sections 45ZA and 45ZB)*

15.11A  For the purpose of *paragraphs 15.2* and *15.2A*, a superintendent who is not present at the police station where the detainee is being held but who has access to the use of a live link (see *paragraph 1.13(e)(iii)*) may, using that live link, give authority to extend the maximum period of detention permitted before charge, if, and only if, the following conditions are satisfied:

(i)   the custody officer considers that the use of the live link is appropriate (see *Note 15H*);

(ii)  the detainee in question has requested and received legal advice on the use of the live link (see *paragraph 15.4*).

(iii) the detainee has given their consent to the live link being used (see *paragraph 15.11D*)

15.11B  When a live link is used:

(a)  the authorising superintendent shall, with regard to any record connected with the authori-sation which PACE, section 42 and this Code require to be made by the authorising officer, require an officer at the station holding the detainee to make that record in the detainee's custody record;

(b)  the requirement in *paragraph 15.3* (allowing opportunity to make representations) will be satisfied:

(i)   if facilities exist for the immediate transmission of written representations to the authorising officer, e.g. fax or email message, by allowing those who are given the opportunity to make representations, to make their representations:

• in writing by means of those facilities or
• orally by means of the live link; or

(ii)  in all other cases, by allowing those who are given the opportunity to make representa-tions, to make their representations orally by means of the live link.

(c)  The authorising officer can decide at any stage to terminate the live link and attend the police station where the detainee is held to carry out the procedure in person. The reasons for doing so should be noted in the custody record.

15.11C  For the purpose of *paragraph 15.7A* and the hearing of an application to a magistrates' court under PACE, section 43 for a warrant of further detention to extend detention without charge of a person arrested for an *indictable offence*, or under PACE, section 44, to extend or further extend that warrant, the magistrates' court may give a direction that a live link (see *paragraph 1.13(e)(iv)*) be used for the purposes of the hearing if, and only if, the following conditions are satisfied:

(i)   the custody officer considers that the use of the live link for the purpose of the hearing is appropriate (see *Note 15H*);

(ii)  the detainee in question has requested and received legal advice on the use of the live link (see *paragraph 15.4*);

(iii) the detainee has given their consent to the live link being used (see *paragraph 15.11D*); and

(iv)  it is not contrary to the interests of justice to give the direction.

15.11D  References in *paragraphs 15.11A(iii)* and *15.11C(iii)* to the consent of the detainee mean:

(a)  if detainee is aged 18 or over, the consent of that detainee;

(b)  if the detainee is aged 14 and under 18, the consent of the detainee and their parent or guardian; and

(c)  if the detainee is aged under 14, the consent of their parent or guardian.

15.11E  The consent described in *paragraph 15.11D* will only be valid if:

(i)   in the case of a detainee aged 18 or over *who is a vulnerable adult* as described in *paragraph 15.4A*), information about how the live link is used and the reminder about their right to legal advice mentioned in *paragraph 15.4* and their consent, are given in the *presence of the appropriate adult*; and

(ii)  in the case of a *juvenile:*

• if information about how the live link is used and the reminder about their right to legal advice mentioned in *paragraph 15.4* are given in the *presence of the appropriate adult* (who may or may not be their parent or guardian); and

• if the juvenile is aged 14 or over, their consent is given in the *presence of the appropriate adult* (who may or may not be their parent or guardian).

Note: If the juvenile is aged under 14, the consent of their parent or guardian is sufficient in its own right (see *Note 15I*)

*(D) Documentation*

15.12  It is the officer's responsibility to make sure all reminders given under *paragraph 15.4* are noted in the custody record.

15.13  The grounds for, and extent of, any delay in conducting a review shall be recorded.

15.14  When a review is carried out by telephone or video conferencing facilities, a record shall be made of:
   (a)  the reason the review officer did not attend the station holding the detainee;
   (b)  the place the review officer was;
   (c)  the method representations, oral or written, were made to the review officer, see *paragraph 15.11*.

15.15  Any written representations shall be retained.

15.16  A record shall be made as soon as practicable of:
   (a)  the outcome of each review of detention before or after charge, and if *paragraph 15.7* applies, of when the person was informed and by whom;
   (b)  the outcome of any determination under PACE, section 42 by a superintendent whether to extend the maximum period of detention without charge beyond 24 hours from the relevant time. If an authorisation is given, the record shall state the number of hours and minutes by which the detention period is extended or further extended.
   (c)  the outcome of each application under PACE, section 43, for a warrant of further detention or under section 44, for an extension or further extension of that warrant. If a warrant for further detention is granted under section 43 or extended or further extended under 44, the record shall state the detention period authorised by the warrant and the date and time it was granted or (as the case may be) the period by which the warrant is extended or further extended.

   Note: Any period during which a person is released on bail does not count towards the maximum period of detention without charge allowed under PACE, sections 41 to 44.

*Notes for Guidance*

15A  *Review officer for the purposes of:*
   • *PACE, sections 40, 40A and 45A means, in the case of a person arrested but not charged, an officer of at least inspector rank not directly involved in the investigation and, if a person has been arrested and charged, the custody officer.*

15B  *The detention of persons in police custody not subject to the statutory review requirement in paragraph 15.1 should still be reviewed periodically as a matter of good practice. Such reviews can be carried out by an officer of the rank of sergeant or above. The purpose of such reviews is to check the particular power under which a detainee is held continues to apply, any associated conditions are complied with and to make sure appropriate action is taken to deal with any changes. This includes the detainee's prompt release when the power no longer applies, or their transfer if the power requires the detainee be taken elsewhere as soon as the necessary arrangements are made. Examples include persons:*
   (a)  *arrested on warrant because they failed to answer bail to appear at court;*
   (b)  *arrested under the Bail Act 1976, section 7(3) for breaching a condition of bail granted after charge;*
   (c)  *in police custody for specific purposes and periods under the Crime (Sentences) Act 1997, Schedule 1;*
   (d)  *convicted, or remand prisoners, held in police stations on behalf of the Prison Service under the Imprisonment (Temporary Provisions) Act 1980, section 6;*
   (e)  *being detained to prevent them causing a breach of the peace;*
   (f)  *detained at police stations on behalf of Immigration Enforcement (formerly the UK Immigration Service);*
   (g)  *detained by order of a magistrates' court under the Criminal Justice Act 1988, section 152 (as amended by the Drugs Act 2005, section 8) to facilitate the recovery of evidence after being charged with drug possession or drug trafficking and suspected of having swallowed drugs.*

   *The detention of persons remanded into police detention by order of a court under the Magistrates' Courts Act 1980, section 128 is subject to a statutory requirement to review that detention. This is to make sure the detainee is taken back to court no later than the end of the period authorised by the court or when the need for their detention by police ceases, whichever is the sooner.*

15C  *In the case of a review of detention, but not an extension, the detainee need not be woken for the review. However, if the detainee is likely to be asleep, e.g. during a period of rest allowed as in paragraph 12.2, at the latest time a review or authorisation to extend detention may take place, the officer should, if the legal obligations and time constraints permit, bring forward the procedure to allow the detainee to make representations. A detainee not asleep during the review must be present when the grounds for their continued detention are recorded and must at the same time be informed of those grounds unless the review officer considers the person is incapable of understanding what is said, violent or likely to become violent or in urgent need of medical attention.*

15CA *In paragraph 15.3(b) and (c), 'available' includes being contactable in time to enable them to make representations remotely by telephone or other electronic means or in person by attending the station.*

*Reasonable efforts should therefore be made to give the solicitor and appropriate adult sufficient notice of the time the decision is expected to be made so that they can make themselves available.*

15D *An application to a Magistrates' Court under PACE, sections 43 or 44 for a warrant of further detention or its extension should be made between 10am and 9pm, and if possible during normal court hours. It will not usually be practicable to arrange for a court to sit specially outside the hours of 10am to 9pm. If it appears a special sitting may be needed outside normal court hours but between 10am and 9pm, the clerk to the justices should be given notice and informed of this possibility, while the court is sitting if possible.*

15E *In paragraph 15.2, the officer responsible for the station holding the detainee includes a superintendent or above who, in accordance with their force operational policy or police regulations, is given that responsibility on a temporary basis whilst the appointed long-term holder is off duty or otherwise unavailable.*

15F *The provisions of PACE, section 40A allowing telephone reviews do not apply to reviews of detention after charge by the custody officer. When use of a live link is not required, they allow the use of a telephone to carry out a review of detention before charge.*

15G *Not used.*

15H *In considering whether the use of the live link is appropriate in the case of a juvenile or vulnerable person, the custody officer and the superintendent should have regard to the detainee's ability to understand the purpose of the authorisation or (as the case may be) the court hearing, and be satisfied that the suspect is able to take part effectively in the process (see paragraphs 1.4(c)). The appropriate adult should always be involved.*

15I *For the purpose of paragraphs 15.11D and 15.11E, the consent required from a parent or guardian may, for a juvenile in the care of a local authority or voluntary organisation, be given by that authority or organisation. In the case of a juvenile, nothing in paragraphs 15.11D and 15.11E require the parent, guardian or representative of a local authority or voluntary organisation to be present with the juvenile to give their consent, unless they are acting as the appropriate adult. However, it is important that the parent, guardian or representative of a local authority or voluntary organisation who is not present is fully informed before being asked to consent. They must be given the same information as that given to the juvenile and the appropriate adult in accordance with paragraph 15.11E. They must also be allowed to speak to the juvenile and the appropriate adult if they wish. Provided the consent is fully informed and is not withdrawn, it may be obtained at any time before the live link is used.*

## 16 Charging detained persons

*(A) Action*

16.1 When the officer in charge of the investigation reasonably believes there is sufficient evidence to provide a realistic prospect of conviction for the offence (see *paragraph 11.6*), they shall without delay, and subject to the following qualification, inform the custody officer who will be responsible for considering whether the detainee should be charged. See *Notes 11B* and *16A*. When a person is detained in respect of more than one offence it is permissible to delay informing the custody officer until the above conditions are satisfied in respect of all the offences, but see *paragraph 11.6*. If the detainee is a juvenile or a vulnerable person, any resulting action shall be taken in the presence of the appropriate adult if they are present at the time. See *Notes 16B and 16C*.

16.1A Where guidance issued by the Director of Public Prosecutions under PACE, section 37A is in force the custody officer must comply with that Guidance in deciding how to act in dealing with the detainee. See *Notes 16AA and 16AB*.

16.1B Where in compliance with the DPP's Guidance the custody officer decides that the case should be immediately referred to the CPS to make the charging decision, consultation should take place with a Crown Prosecutor as soon as is reasonably practicable. Where the Crown Prosecutor is unable to make the charging decision on the information available at that time, the detainee may be released without charge and on bail (with conditions if necessary) under section 37(7)(a). In such circumstances, the detainee should be informed that they are being released to enable the Director of Public Prosecutions to make a decision under section 37B.

16.2 When a detainee is charged with or informed they may be prosecuted for an offence, see *Note 16B*, they shall, unless the restriction on drawing adverse inferences from silence applies, see *Annex C*, be cautioned as follows:

> '*You do not have to say anything. But it may harm your defence if you do not mention now something which you later rely on in court. Anything you do say may be given in evidence.*'

Where the use of the Welsh Language is appropriate, a constable may provide the caution directly in Welsh in the following terms:

> *'Does dim rhaid i chi ddweud dim byd. Ond gall niweidio eich amddiffyniad os na fyddwch chi'n sôn, yn awr, am rywbeth y byddwch chi'n dibynnu arno nes ymlaen yn y llys. Gall unrhyw beth yr ydych yn ei ddweud gael ei roi fel tystiolaeth.'*

*Annex C, paragraph 2* sets out the alternative terms of the caution to be used when the restriction on drawing adverse inferences from silence applies.

16.3    When a detainee is charged they shall be given a written notice showing particulars of the offence and, subject to *paragraph 2.6A*, the officer's name and the case reference number. As far as possible the particulars of the charge shall be stated in simple terms, but they shall also show the precise offence in law with which the detainee is charged. The notice shall begin:

> *'You are charged with the offence(s) shown below.'* Followed by the caution.

If the detainee is a juvenile, mentally disordered or otherwise mentally vulnerable, a copy of the notice should also be given to the appropriate adult.

16.4    If, after a detainee has been charged with or informed they may be prosecuted for an offence, an officer wants to tell them about any written statement or interview with another person relating to such an offence, the detainee shall either be handed a true copy of the written statement or the content of the interview record brought to their attention. Nothing shall be done to invite any reply or comment except to:

(a)    caution the detainee, *'You do not have to say anything, but anything you do say may be given in evidence.'*;

Where the use of the Welsh Language is appropriate, caution the detainee in the following terms:

> *'Does dim rhaid i chi ddweud dim byd, ond gall unrhyw beth yr ydych yn ei ddweud gael ei roi fel tystiolaeth.'*

and

(b)    remind the detainee about their right to legal advice.

16.4A    If the detainee:

- cannot read, the document may be read to them;
- is a juvenile, mentally disordered or otherwise mentally vulnerable, the appropriate adult shall also be given a copy, or the interview record shall be brought to their attention.

16.5    A detainee may not be interviewed about an offence after they have been charged with, or informed they may be prosecuted for it, unless the interview is necessary:

- to prevent or minimise harm or loss to some other person, or the public
- to clear up an ambiguity in a previous answer or statement
- in the interests of justice for the detainee to have put to them, and have an opportunity to comment on, information concerning the offence which has come to light since they were charged or informed they might be prosecuted

Before any such interview, the interviewer shall:

(a)    caution the detainee, *'You do not have to say anything, but anything you do say may be given in evidence.'*

Where the use of the Welsh Language is appropriate, the interviewer shall caution the detainee: *'Does dim rhaid i chi ddweud dim byd, ond gall unrhyw beth yr ydych yn ei ddweud gael ei roi fel tystiolaeth.'*

(b)    remind the detainee about their right to legal advice.

See *Note 16B*

16.6    The provisions of *paragraphs 16.2* to *16.5* must be complied with in the appropriate adult's presence if they are already at the police station. If they are not at the police station then these provisions must be complied with again in their presence when they arrive unless the detainee has been released. See *Note 16C*.

16.7    When a juvenile is charged with an offence and the custody officer authorises their continued detention after charge, the custody officer must make arrangements for the juvenile to be taken into the care of a local authority to be detained pending appearance in court *unless* the custody officer certifies in accordance with PACE, section 38(6), that:

(a)    for any juvenile; it is impracticable to do so and the reasons why it is impracticable must be set out in the certificate that must be produced to the court; or,

(b)   in the case of a juvenile of at least 12 years old, no secure accommodation is available and other accommodation would not be adequate to protect the public from serious harm from that juvenile. See *Note 16D.*

Note: Chief officers should ensure that the operation of these provisions at police stations in their areas is subject to supervision and monitoring by an officer of the rank of inspector or above. See *Note 16E.*

16.7A  The requirement in *paragraph 3.4(b)* that documents and materials essential to effectively challenging the lawfulness of the detainee's arrest and detention must be made available to the detainee and, if they are represented, their solicitor, applies for the purposes of this section and a person's detention after charge. This means that the custody officer making the bail decision (PACE, section 38) or reviewing the need for detention after charge (PACE, section 40), is responsible for determining what, if any, documents or materials are essential and must be made available to the detainee or their solicitor. See *Note 3ZA.*

*(B)  Documentation*

16.8  A record shall be made of anything a detainee says when charged.

16.9  Any questions put in an interview after charge and answers given relating to the offence shall be recorded in full during the interview on forms for that purpose and the record signed by the detainee or, if they refuse, by the interviewer and any third parties present. If the questions are audibly recorded or visually recorded the arrangements in Code E or F apply.

16.10  If arrangements for a juvenile's transfer into local authority care as in *paragraph 16.7* are not made, the custody officer must record the reasons in a certificate which must be produced before the court with the juvenile. See *Note 16D.*

*Notes for Guidance*

16A   *The custody officer must take into account alternatives to prosecution under the Crime and Disorder Act 1998 applicable to persons under 18, and in national guidance on the cautioning of offenders applicable to persons aged 18 and over.*

16AA  *When a person is arrested under the provisions of the Criminal Justice Act 2003 which allow a person to be re-tried after being acquitted of a serious offence which is a qualifying offence specified in Schedule 5 to that Act and not precluded from further prosecution by virtue of section 75(3) of that Act the detention provisions of PACE are modified and make an officer of the rank of superintendent or above who has not been directly involved in the investigation responsible for determining whether the evidence is sufficient to charge.*

16AB  *Where Guidance issued by the Director of Public Prosecutions under section 37B is in force, a custody officer who determines in accordance with that Guidance that there is sufficient evidence to charge the detainee, may detain that person for no longer than is reasonably necessary to decide how that person is to be dealt with under PACE, section 37(7)(a) to (d), including, where appropriate, consultation with the Duty Prosecutor. The period is subject to the maximum period of detention before charge determined by PACE, sections 41 to 44. Where in accordance with the Guidance the case is referred to the CPS for decision, the custody officer should ensure that an officer involved in the investigation sends to the CPS such information as is specified in the Guidance.*

16B   *The giving of a warning or the service of the Notice of Intended Prosecution required by the Road Traffic Offenders Act 1988, section 1 does not amount to informing a detainee they may be prosecuted for an offence and so does not preclude further questioning in relation to that offence.*

16C   *There is no power under PACE to detain a person and delay action under paragraphs 16.2 to 16.5 solely to await the arrival of the appropriate adult. Reasonable efforts should therefore be made to give the appropriate adult sufficient notice of the time the decision (charge etc.) is to be implemented so that they can be present. If the appropriate adult is not, or cannot be, present at that time, the detainee should be released on bail to return for the decision to be implemented when the adult is present, unless the custody officer determines that the absence of the appropriate adult makes the detainee unsuitable for bail for this purpose. After charge, bail cannot be refused, or release on bail delayed, simply because an appropriate adult is not available, unless the absence of that adult provides the custody officer with the necessary grounds to authorise detention after charge under PACE, section 38.*

16D   *Except as in paragraph 16.7, neither a juvenile's behaviour nor the nature of the offence provides grounds for the custody officer to decide it is impracticable to arrange the juvenile's transfer to local authority care. Impracticability concerns the transport and travel requirements and the lack of secure accommodation which is provided for the purposes of restricting liberty does not make it impracticable to transfer the juvenile. Rather, 'impracticable' should be taken to mean that exceptional circumstances render movement of the child impossible or that the juvenile is due at court in such a short space of time that transfer would deprive them of rest or cause them to miss a court appearance. When the reason for not transferring the juvenile is an imminent court appearance, details of the travelling and court appearance times which justify the decision should be included in the certificate. The availability of secure accommodation is only a factor in relation to a juvenile aged 12 or over when other local authority accommodation would not be adequate to protect the public from serious harm from them. The obligation to transfer a juvenile to local authority accommodation applies as much to a juvenile charged during the daytime as to a juvenile to be held overnight, subject to a requirement to bring the juvenile before a court under PACE, section 46.*

16E    *The Concordat on Children in Custody published by the Home Office in 2017 provides detailed guidance with the aim of preventing the detention of children in police stations following charge. It is available here: https://www.gov.uk/government/publications/concordat-on-children-in-custody.*

## 17  Testing persons for the presence of specified Class A drugs

*(A)  Action*

17.1  This section of Code C applies only in selected police stations in police areas where the provisions for drug testing under section 63B of PACE (as amended by section 5 of the Criminal Justice Act 2003 and section 7 of the Drugs Act 2005) are in force and in respect of which the Secretary of State has given a notification to the relevant chief officer of police that arrangements for the taking of samples have been made. Such a notification will cover either a police area as a whole or particular stations within a police area. The notification indicates whether the testing applies to those arrested or charged or under the age of 18 as the case may be and testing can only take place in respect of the persons so indicated in the notification. Testing cannot be carried out unless the relevant notification has been given and has not been withdrawn. See *Note 17F.*

17.2  A sample of urine or a non-intimate sample may be taken from a person in police detention for the purpose of ascertaining whether they have any specified Class A drug in their body only where they have been brought before the custody officer and:

(a)  either the arrest condition, see *paragraph 17.3*, or the charge condition, see *paragraph 17.4* is met;

(b)  the age condition see *paragraph 17.5*, is met;

(c)  the notification condition is met in relation to the arrest condition, the charge condition, or the age condition, as the case may be. (Testing on charge and/or arrest must be specifically provided for in the notification for the power to apply. In addition, the fact that testing of under 18s is authorised must be expressly provided for in the notification before the power to test such persons applies.). See *paragraph 17.1*; and

(d)  a police officer has requested the person concerned to give the sample (the request condition).

17.3  The arrest condition is met where the detainee:

(a)  has been arrested for a trigger offence, see *Note 17E*, but not charged with that offence; or

(b)  has been arrested for any other offence but not charged with that offence and a police officer of inspector rank or above, who has reasonable grounds for suspecting that their misuse of any specified Class A drug caused or contributed to the offence, has authorised the sample to be taken.

17.4  The charge condition is met where the detainee:

(a)  has been charged with a trigger offence, or

(b)  has been charged with any other offence and a police officer of inspector rank or above, who has reasonable grounds for suspecting that the detainee's misuse of any specified Class A drug caused or contributed to the offence, has authorised the sample to be taken.

17.5  The age condition is met where:

(a)  in the case of a detainee who has been arrested but not charged as in *paragraph 17.3*, they are aged 18 or over;

(b)  in the case of a detainee who has been charged as in *paragraph 17.4*, they are aged 14 or over.

17.6  Before requesting a sample from the person concerned, an officer must:

(a)  inform them that the purpose of taking the sample is for drug testing under PACE. This is to ascertain whether they have a specified Class A drug present in their body;

(b)  warn them that if, when so requested, they fail without good cause to provide a sample they may be liable to prosecution;

(c)  where the taking of the sample has been authorised by an inspector or above in accordance with *paragraph 17.3(b)* or *17.4(b)* above, inform them that the authorisation has been given and the grounds for giving it;

   (d)  remind them of the following rights, which may be exercised at any stage during the period in custody:

   (i)   the right to have someone informed of their arrest [see *section 5*];

   (ii)  the right to consult privately with a solicitor and that free independent legal advice is available [see *section 6*]; and

   (iii) the right to consult these Codes of Practice [see *section 3*].

17.7  In the case of a person who has not attained the age specified in section 63B(5A) of PACE—

   (a)  the making of the request for a sample under *paragraph 17.2(d)* above;

   (b)  the giving of the warning and the information under *paragraph 17.6* above; and

   (c)  the taking of the sample, may not take place except in the presence of an appropriate adult. See *Note 17G*.

17.8  Authorisation by an officer of the rank of inspector or above within *paragraph 17.3(b)* or *17.4(b)* may be given orally or in writing but, if it is given orally, it must be confirmed in writing as soon as practicable.

17.9  If a sample is taken from a detainee who has been arrested for an offence but not charged with that offence as in *paragraph 17.3*, no further sample may be taken during the same continuous period of detention. If during that same period the charge condition is also met in respect of that detainee, the sample which has been taken shall be treated as being taken by virtue of the charge condition, see *paragraph 17.4*, being met.

17.10 A detainee from whom a sample may be taken may be detained for up to six hours from the time of charge if the custody officer reasonably believes the detention is necessary to enable a sample to be taken. Where the arrest condition is met, a detainee whom the custody officer has decided to release on bail without charge may continue to be detained, but not beyond 24 hours from the relevant time (as defined in section 41(2) of PACE), to enable a sample to be taken.

17.11 A detainee in respect of whom the arrest condition is met, but not the charge condition, see *paragraphs 17.3* and *17.4*, and whose release would be required before a sample can be taken had they not continued to be detained as a result of being arrested for a further offence which does not satisfy the arrest condition, may have a sample taken at any time within 24 hours after the arrest for the offence that satisfies the arrest condition.

*(B) Documentation*

17.12 The following must be recorded in the custody record:

   (a)  if a sample is taken following authorisation by an officer of the rank of inspector or above, the authorisation and the grounds for suspicion;

   (b)  the giving of a warning of the consequences of failure to provide a sample;

   (c)  the time at which the sample was given; and

   (d)  the time of charge or, where the arrest condition is being relied upon, the time of arrest and, where applicable, the fact that a sample taken after arrest but before charge is to be treated as being taken by virtue of the charge condition, where that is met in the same period of continuous detention. See *paragraph 17.9*.

*(C) General*

17.13 A sample may only be taken by a prescribed person. See *Note 17C*.

17.14 Force may not be used to take any sample for the purpose of drug testing.

17.15 The terms 'Class A drug' and 'misuse' have the same meanings as in the Misuse of Drugs Act 1971. 'Specified' (in relation to a Class A drug) and 'trigger offence' have the same meanings as in Part III of the Criminal Justice and Court Services Act 2000.

17.16 Any sample taken:

   (a)  may not be used for any purpose other than to ascertain whether the person concerned has a specified Class A drug present in his body; and

   (b)  can be disposed of as clinical waste unless it is to be sent for further analysis in cases where the test result is disputed at the point when the result is known, including on the basis that medication has been taken, or for quality assurance purposes.

*(D) Assessment of misuse of drugs*

17.17 Under the provisions of Part 3 of the Drugs Act 2005, where a detainee has tested positive for a specified Class A drug under section 63B of PACE a police officer may, at any time before the person's release from the police station, impose a requirement on the detainee to attend an initial assessment of their drug misuse by a suitably qualified person and to remain for its duration. Where such a requirement is imposed, the officer must, at the same time, impose a second requirement on the detainee to attend and remain for a follow-up assessment. The officer must inform the detainee that the second requirement will cease to have effect if, at the initial assessment they are informed that a follow-up assessment is not necessary These requirements may only be imposed on a person if:

(a) they have reached the age of 18

(b) notification has been given by the Secretary of State to the relevant chief officer of police that arrangements for conducting initial and follow-up assessments have been made for those from whom samples for testing have been taken at the police station where the detainee is in custody.

17.18 When imposing a requirement to attend an initial assessment and a follow-up assessment the police officer must:

(a) inform the person of the time and place at which the initial assessment is to take place;

(b) explain that this information will be confirmed in writing; and

(c) warn the person that they may be liable to prosecution if they fail without good cause to attend the initial assessment and remain for its duration and if they fail to attend the follow-up assessment and remain for its duration (if so required).

17.19 Where a police officer has imposed a requirement to attend an initial assessment and a follow-up assessment in accordance with *paragraph 17.17*, he must, before the person is released from detention, give the person notice in writing which:

(a) confirms their requirement to attend and remain for the duration of the assessments; and

(b) confirms the information and repeats the warning referred to in *paragraph 17.18*.

17.20 The following must be recorded in the custody record:

(a) that the requirement to attend an initial assessment and a follow-up assessment has been imposed; and

(b) the information, explanation, warning and notice given in accordance with *paragraphs 17.17* and *17.19*.

17.21 Where a notice is given in accordance with *paragraph 17.19*, a police officer can give the person a further notice in writing which informs the person of any change to the time or place at which the initial assessment is to take place and which repeats the warning referred to in *paragraph 17.18(c)*.

17.22 Part 3 of the Drugs Act 2005 also requires police officers to have regard to any guidance issued by the Secretary of State in respect of the assessment provisions.

*Notes for Guidance*

17A *When warning a person who is asked to provide a urine or non-intimate sample in accordance with paragraph 17.6(b), the following form of words may be used:*

*'You do not have to provide a sample, but I must warn you that if you fail or refuse without good cause to do so, you will commit an offence for which you may be imprisoned, or fined, or both'.*

*Where the Welsh language is appropriate, the following form of words may be used:*

*'Does dim rhaid i chi roi sampl, ond mae'n rhaid i mi eich rhybuddio y byddwch chi'n cyflawni trosedd os byddwch chi'n methu neu yn gwrthod gwneud hynny heb reswm da, ac y gellir, oherwydd hynny, eich carcharu, eich dirwyo, neu'r ddau.'*

17B *A sample has to be sufficient and suitable. A sufficient sample is sufficient in quantity and quality to enable drug-testing analysis to take place. A suitable sample is one which by its nature, is suitable for a particular form of drug analysis.*

17C *A prescribed person in paragraph 17.13 is one who is prescribed in regulations made by the Secretary of State under section 63B(6) of the Police and Criminal Evidence Act 1984. [The regulations are currently contained in regulation SI 2001 No. 2645, the Police and Criminal Evidence Act 1984 (Drug Testing Persons in Police Detention) (Prescribed Persons) Regulations 2001.]*

17D *Samples, and the information derived from them, may not be subsequently used in the investigation of any offence or in evidence against the persons from whom they were taken.*

17E *Trigger offences are:*

1. *Offences under the following provisions of the Theft Act 1968:*

| | |
|---|---|
| *section 1* | *(theft)* |
| *section 8* | *(robbery)* |
| *section 9* | *(burglary)* |
| *section 10* | *(aggravated burglary)* |
| *section 12* | *(taking a motor vehicle or other conveyance without authority)* |
| *section 12A* | *(aggravated vehicle-taking)* |

        *section 22*         *(handling stolen goods)*
        *section 25*         *(going equipped for stealing etc.)*

2.   *Offences under the following provisions of the Misuse of Drugs Act 1971, if committed in respect of a specified Class A drug:–*

        *section 4*         *(restriction on production and supply of controlled drugs)*
        section 5(2)         *(possession of a controlled drug)*
        section 5(3)         *(possession of a controlled drug with intent to supply)*

3.   *Offences under the following provisions of the Fraud Act 2006: section 1 (fraud)*

        *section 6*         *(possession etc. of articles for use in frauds)*
        *section 7*         *(making or supplying articles for use in frauds)*

3A.  *An offence under section 1(1) of the Criminal Attempts Act 1981 if committed in respect of an offence under:*

   (a)  *any of the following provisions of the Theft Act 1968:*

        *section 1*         *(theft)*
        *section 8*         *(robbery)*
        *section 9*         *(burglary)*
        *section 22*         *(handling stolen goods)*

   (b)  *section 1 of the Fraud Act 2006 (fraud)*

4.   *Offences under the following provisions of the Vagrancy Act 1824:*

        *section 3*         *(begging)*
        *section 4*         *(persistent begging)*

17F  *The power to take samples is subject to notification by the Secretary of State that appropriate arrangements for the taking of samples have been made for the police area as a whole or for the particular police station concerned for whichever of the following is specified in the notification:*

   (a)  *persons in respect of whom the arrest condition is met;*

   (b)  *persons in respect of whom the charge condition is met;*

   (c)  *persons who have not attained the age of 18.*

  *Note: Notification is treated as having been given for the purposes of the charge condition in relation to a police area, if testing (on charge) under section 63B(2) of PACE was in force immediately before section 7 of the Drugs Act 2005 was brought into force; and for the purposes of the age condition, in relation to a police area or police station, if immediately before that day, notification that arrangements had been made for the taking of samples from persons under the age of 18 (those aged 14-17) had been given and had not been withdrawn.*

17G  *Appropriate adult in paragraph 17.7 means the person's–*

   (a)  *parent or guardian or, if they are in the care of a local authority or voluntary organisation, a person representing that authority or organisation; or*

   (b)  *a social worker of a local authority; or*

   (c)  *if no person falling within (a) or (b) above is available, any responsible person aged 18 or over who is not:*

     •  *a police officer;*

     •  *employed by the police;*

     •  *under the direction or control of the chief officer of police force; or*

     •  *a person who provides services under contractual arrangements (but without being employed by the chief officer of a police force), to assist that force in relation to the discharge of its chief officer's functions;*

  *whether or not they are on duty at the time.*

## ANNEX A

### INTIMATE AND STRIP SEARCHES

**A Intimate search**

1.   An intimate search consists of the physical examination of a person's body orifices other than the mouth. The intrusive nature of such searches means the actual and potential risks associated with intimate searches must never be underestimated.

*(a) Action*

2.   Body orifices other than the mouth may be searched only:

   (a)  if authorised by an officer of inspector rank or above who has reasonable grounds for believing that the person may have concealed on themselves:

*A3*    *If authority is given for a search under paragraph 2(a)(i), a registered medical practitioner or registered nurse shall be consulted whenever possible. The presumption should be that the search will be conducted by the registered medical practitioner or registered nurse and the authorising officer must make every reasonable effort to persuade the detainee to allow the medical practitioner or nurse to conduct the search.*

*A4*    *A constable should only be authorised to carry out a search as a last resort and when all other approaches have failed. In these circumstances, the authorising officer must be satisfied the detainee might use the article for one or more of the purposes in paragraph 2(a)(i) and the physical injury likely to be caused is sufficiently severe to justify authorising a constable to carry out the search.*

*A5*    *If an officer has any doubts whether to authorise an intimate search by a constable, the officer should seek advice from an officer of superintendent rank or above.*

*A6*    *In warning a detainee who is asked to consent to an intimate drug offence search, as in paragraph 2B, the following form of words may be used:*

> *'You do not have to allow yourself to be searched, but I must warn you that if you refuse without good cause, your refusal may harm your case if it comes to trial.'*

> *Where the use of the Welsh Language is appropriate, the following form of words may be used:*

> *'Nid oes rhaid i chi roi caniatâd i gael eich archwilio, ond mae'n rhaid i mi eich rhybuddio os gwrthodwch heb reswm da, y gallai eich penderfyniad i wrthod wneud niwed i'ch achos pe bai'n dod gerbron llys.'*

## ANNEX B

### DELAY IN NOTIFYING ARREST OR ALLOWING ACCESS TO LEGAL ADVICE

**A  Persons detained under PACE**

1.    The exercise of the rights in *Section 5* or *Section 6*, or both, may be delayed if the person is in police detention, as in PACE, section 118(2), in connection with an indictable offence, has not yet been charged with an offence and an officer of superintendent rank or above, or inspector rank or above only for the rights in *Section 5*, has reasonable grounds for believing their exercise will:
      (i)   lead to:
            • interference with, or harm to, evidence connected with an indictable offence; or
            • interference with, or physical harm to, other people; or
      (ii)  lead to alerting other people suspected of having committed an indictable offence but not yet arrested for it; or
      (iii) hinder the recovery of property obtained in consequence of the commission of such an offence.

2.    These rights may also be delayed if the officer has reasonable grounds to believe that:
      (i)   the person detained for an indictable offence has benefited from their criminal conduct (decided in accordance with Part 2 of the Proceeds of Crime Act 2002); and
      (ii)  the recovery of the value of the property constituting that benefit will be hindered by the exercise of either right.

3.    Authority to delay a detainee's right to consult privately with a solicitor may be given only if the authorising officer has reasonable grounds to believe the solicitor the detainee wants to consult will, inadvertently or otherwise, pass on a message from the detainee or act in some other way which will have any of the consequences specified under *paragraphs 1 or 2*. In these circumstances, the detainee must be allowed to choose another solicitor. See *Note B3*.

4.    If the detainee wishes to see a solicitor, access to that solicitor may not be delayed on the grounds they might advise the detainee not to answer questions or the solicitor was initially asked to attend the police station by someone else. In the latter case, the detainee must be told the solicitor has come to the police station at another person's request, and must be asked to sign the custody record to signify whether they want to see the solicitor.

5.    The fact the grounds for delaying notification of arrest may be satisfied does not automatically mean the grounds for delaying access to legal advice will also be satisfied.

6.    These rights may be delayed only for as long as grounds exist and in no case beyond 36 hours after the relevant time as in PACE, section 41. If the grounds cease to apply within this time, the detainee must, as soon as practicable, be asked if they want to exercise either right, the custody record must be noted accordingly, and action taken in accordance with the relevant section of the Code.

7.    A detained person must be permitted to consult a solicitor for a reasonable time before any court hearing.

**B  Not used**

**C  Documentation**

13.   The grounds for action under this Annex shall be recorded and the detainee informed of them as soon as practicable.

14.   Any reply given by a detainee under *paragraphs 6* or *11* must be recorded and the detainee asked to endorse the record in relation to whether they want to receive legal advice at this point.

**D  Cautions and special warnings**

15.   When a suspect detained at a police station is interviewed during any period for which access to legal advice has been delayed under this Annex, the court or jury may not draw adverse inferences from their silence.

*Notes for Guidance*

B1   *Even if Annex B applies in the case of a juvenile, or a vulnerable person, action to inform the appropriate adult and the person responsible for a juvenile's welfare, if that is a different person, must nevertheless be taken as in paragraph 3.13 and 3.15.*

B2   *In the case of Commonwealth citizens and foreign nationals, see Note 7A.*

B3   *A decision to delay access to a specific solicitor is likely to be a rare occurrence and only when it can be shown the suspect is capable of misleading that particular solicitor and there is more than a substantial risk that the suspect will succeed in causing information to be conveyed which will lead to one or more of the specified consequences.*

ANNEX C

RESTRICTION ON DRAWING ADVERSE INFERENCES FROM SILENCE AND TERMS OF
THE CAUTION WHEN THE RESTRICTION APPLIES

*(a)  The restriction on drawing adverse inferences from silence*

1.   The Criminal Justice and Public Order Act 1994, sections 34, 36 and 37 as amended by the Youth Justice and Criminal Evidence Act 1999, section 58 describe the conditions under which adverse inferences may be drawn from a person's failure or refusal to say anything about their involvement in the offence when interviewed, after being charged or informed they may be prosecuted. These provisions are subject to an overriding restriction on the ability of a court or jury to draw adverse inferences from a person's silence. This restriction applies:

   (a)   to any detainee at a police station, see *Note 10C*, who, before being interviewed, see *section 11* or being charged or informed they may be prosecuted, see *section 16*, has:

      (i)    asked for legal advice, see *section 6, paragraph 6.1*;

      (ii)   not been allowed an opportunity to consult a solicitor, including the duty solicitor, as in this Code; and

      (iii)  not changed their mind about wanting legal advice, see *section 6, paragraph 6.6(d)*.

      Note the condition in (ii) will:

      • apply when a detainee who has asked for legal advice is interviewed before speaking to a solicitor as in *section 6, paragraph 6.6(a)* or *(b)*;

      • not apply if the detained person declines to ask for the duty solicitor, see *section 6, paragraphs 6.6(c)* and *(d)*.

   (b)   to any person charged with, or informed they may be prosecuted for, an offence who:

      (i)    has had brought to their notice a written statement made by another person or the content of an interview with another person which relates to that offence, see *section 16, paragraph 16.4*;

      (ii)   is interviewed about that offence, see *section 16, paragraph 16.5*; or

      (iii)  makes a written statement about that offence, see *Annex D, paragraphs 4* and *9*.

*(b)  Terms of the caution when the restriction applies*

2.   When a requirement to caution arises at a time when the restriction on drawing adverse inferences from silence applies, the caution shall be:

   *'You do not have to say anything, but anything you do say may be given in evidence.'*

Where the use of the Welsh Language is appropriate, the caution may be used directly in Welsh in the following terms:

   *'Does dim rhaid i chi ddweud dim byd, ond gall unrhyw beth yr ydych chi'n ei ddweud gael ei roi fel tystiolaeth.'*

ANNEX E

SUMMARY OF PROVISIONS RELATING TO MENTALLY DISORDERED AND OTHERWISE
MENTALLY VULNERABLE PEOPLE

1.	If at any time, an officer has reason to suspect that a person of any age may be vulnerable (see *paragraph 1.13(d)*), in the absence of clear evidence to dispel that suspicion that person shall be treated as such for the purposes of this Code and to establish whether any such reason may exist in relation to a person suspected of committing an offence (see *paragraph 10.1* and *Note 10A*), the custody officer in the case of a detained person, or the officer investigating the offence in the case of a person who has not been arrested or detained, shall take, or cause to be taken, (see *paragraph 3.5* and *Note 3F*) the following action:

    (a)	reasonable enquiries shall be made to ascertain what information is available that is relevant to any of the factors described in *paragraph 1.13(d)* as indicating that the person may be vulnerable might apply;

    (b)	a record shall be made describing whether any of those factors appear to apply and provide any reason to suspect that the person may be vulnerable or (as the case may be) may not be vulnerable; and

    (c)	the record mentioned in sub-paragraph (b) shall be made available to be taken into account by police officers, police staff and any others who, in accordance with the provisions of this or any other Code, are entitled to communicate with the person in question. This would include any solicitor, appropriate adult and healthcare professional and is particularly relevant to communication by telephone or by means of a live link (see *paragraphs 12.9A* (interviews), *13.12* (interpretation), and *15.3C, 15.11A, 15.11B, 15.11C* and *15.11D* (reviews and extension of detention)).

	*See Notes 1G, E5, E6* and *E7.*

2.	In the case of a person who is vulnerable, 'the appropriate adult' means:

    (i)	a relative, guardian or other person responsible for their care or custody;

    (ii)	someone experienced in dealing with vulnerable persons but who is not:

      • a police officer;

      • employed by the police;

      • under the direction or control of the chief officer of a police force;

      • a person who provides services under contractual arrangements (but without being employed by the chief officer of a police force), to assist that force in relation to the discharge of its chief officer's functions, whether or not they are on duty at the time.

    (iii)	failing these, some other responsible adult aged 18 or over who is other than a person described in the bullet points in *sub-paragraph (ii)* above.

	See *paragraph 1.7(b)* and *Notes 1D* and *1F.*

2A	The role of the appropriate adult is to safeguard the rights, entitlements and welfare of 'vulnerable persons' (see *paragraph 1*) to whom the provisions of this and any other Code of Practice apply. For this reason, the appropriate adult is expected, amongst other things, to:

    • support, advise and assist them when, in accordance with this Code or any other Code of Practice, they are given or asked to provide information or participate in any procedure;

    • observe whether the police are acting properly and fairly to respect their rights and entitlements, and inform an officer of the rank of inspector or above if they consider that they are not;

    • assist them to communicate with the police whilst respecting their right to say nothing unless they want to as set out in the terms of the caution (see *paragraphs 10.5* and *10.6*); and

    • help them understand their rights and ensure that those rights are protected and respected (see *paragraphs 3.15, 3.17, 6.5A* and *11.17*).

	See *paragraph 1.7A.*

3.	If the custody officer authorises the detention of a vulnerable person, the custody officer must as soon as practicable inform the appropriate adult of the grounds for detention and the person's whereabouts, and secure the attendance of the appropriate adult at the police station to see the detainee. If the appropriate adult:

    • is already at the station when information is given as in *paragraphs 3.1* to *3.5* the information must be given in their presence;

    • is not at the station when the provisions of *paragraph 3.1* to *3.5* are complied with these provisions must be complied with again in their presence once they arrive.

	See *paragraphs 3.15* to *3.17*

4.  If the appropriate adult, having been informed of the right to legal advice, considers legal advice should be taken, the provisions of *section 6* apply as if the vulnerable person had requested access to legal advice. See *paragraphs 3.19, 6.5A* and *Note E1*.

5.  The custody officer must make sure a person receives appropriate clinical attention as soon as reasonably practicable if the person appears to be suffering from a mental disorder or in urgent cases immediately call the nearest appropriate healthcare professional or an ambulance. See Code C *paragraphs 3.16, 9.5* and *9.6* which apply when a person is detained under the Mental Health Act 1983, sections 135 and 136, as amended by the Policing and Crime Act 2017.

6.  *Not used.*

7.  If a vulnerable person is cautioned in the absence of the appropriate adult, the caution must be repeated in the appropriate adult's presence. See *paragraph 10.12*.

8.  A vulnerable person must not be interviewed or asked to provide or sign a written statement in the absence of the appropriate adult unless the provisions of *paragraphs 11.1* or *11.18* to *11.20* apply. Questioning in these circumstances may not continue in the absence of the appropriate adult once sufficient information to avert the risk has been obtained. A record shall be made of the grounds for any decision to begin an interview in these circumstances. See *paragraphs 11.1, 11.15* and *11.18* to *11.20*.

9.  If the appropriate adult is present at an interview, they shall be informed they are not expected to act simply as an observer and the purposes of their presence are to:
    • advise the interviewee;
    • observe whether or not the interview is being conducted properly and fairly;
    • facilitate communication with the interviewee.
    See *paragraph 11.17*.

10. If the detention of a vulnerable person is reviewed by a review officer or a superintendent, the appropriate adult must, if available at the time, be given an opportunity to make representations to the officer about the need for continuing detention. See *paragraph 15.3*.

11. If the custody officer charges a vulnerable person with an offence or takes such other action as is appropriate when there is sufficient evidence for a prosecution this must be carried out in the presence of the appropriate adult if they are at the police station. A copy of the written notice embodying any charge must also be given to the appropriate adult. See *paragraphs 16.1* to *16.4A*.

12. An intimate or strip search of a vulnerable person may take place only in the presence of the appropriate adult of the same sex, unless the detainee specifically requests the presence of a particular adult of the opposite sex. A strip search may take place in the absence of an appropriate adult only in cases of urgency when there is a risk of serious harm to the detainee or others. See *Annex A, paragraphs 5* and *11(c)*.

13. Particular care must be taken when deciding whether to use any form of approved restraints on a vulnerable person in a locked cell. See *paragraph 8.2*.

## Notes for Guidance

E1  The purpose of the provisions at paragraphs 3.19 and 6.5A is to protect the rights of a vulnerable person who does not understand the significance of what is said to them. A vulnerable person should always be given an opportunity, when an appropriate adult is called to the police station, to consult privately with a solicitor in the absence of the appropriate adult if they want.

E2  Although vulnerable persons are often capable of providing reliable evidence, they may, without knowing or wanting to do so, be particularly prone in certain circumstances to provide information that may be unreliable, misleading or self-incriminating. Special care should always be taken when questioning such a person, and the appropriate adult should be involved if there is any doubt about a person's mental state or capacity. Because of the risk of unreliable evidence, it is important to obtain corroboration of any facts admitted whenever possible.

E3  Because of the risks referred to in Note E2, which the presence of the appropriate adult is intended to minimise, officers of superintendent rank or above should exercise their discretion to authorise the commencement of an interview in the appropriate adult's absence only in exceptional cases, if it is necessary to avert one or more of the specified risks in paragraph 11.1. See paragraphs 11.1 and 11.18 to 11.20.

E4  When a person is detained under section 136 of the Mental Health Act 1983 for assessment, the appropriate adult has no role in the assessment process and their presence is not required.

E5  For the purposes of Annex E paragraph 1, examples of relevant information that may be available include:
    • the behaviour of the adult or juvenile;
    • the mental health and capacity of the adult or juvenile;
    • what the adult or juvenile says about themselves;
    • information from relatives and friends of the adult or juvenile;

- *information from police officers and staff and from police records;*
- *information from health and social care (including liaison and diversion services) and other professionals who know, or have had previous contact with, the individual and may be able to contribute to assessing their need for help and support from an appropriate adult. This includes contacts and assessments arranged by the police or at the request of the individual or (as applicable) their appropriate adult or solicitor.*

E6   *The Mental Health Act 1983 Code of Practice at page 26 describes the range of clinically recognised conditions which can fall with the meaning of mental disorder for the purpose of paragraph 1.13(d). The Code is published here: https://www.gov.uk/government/publications/code-of-practice-mental-health-act-1983.*

E7   *When a person is under the influence of drink and/or drugs, it is not intended that they are to be treated as vulnerable and requiring an appropriate adult for the purpose of Annex E paragraph 1 unless other information indicates that any of the factors described in paragraph 1.13(d) may apply to that person. When the person has recovered from the effects of drink and/or drugs, they should be re-assessed in accordance with Annex E paragraph 1. See paragraph 15.4A for application to live link.*

## Annex F

### *Not Used*

## Annex G

### Fitness to be Interviewed

1.   This Annex contains general guidance to help police officers and healthcare professionals assess whether a detainee might be at risk in an interview.
2.   A detainee may be at risk in a interview if it is considered that:
     (a)   conducting the interview could significantly harm the detainee's physical or mental state;
     (b)   anything the detainee says in the interview about their involvement or suspected involvement in the offence about which they are being interviewed **might** be considered unreliable in subsequent court proceedings because of their physical or mental state.
3.   In assessing whether the detainee should be interviewed, the following must be considered:
     (a)   how the detainee's physical or mental state might affect their ability to understand the nature and purpose of the interview, to comprehend what is being asked and to appreciate the significance of any answers given and make rational decisions about whether they want to say anything;
     (b)   the extent to which the detainee's replies may be affected by their physical or mental condition rather than representing a rational and accurate explanation of their involvement in the offence;
     (c)   how the nature of the interview, which could include particularly probing questions, might affect the detainee.
4.   It is essential healthcare professionals who are consulted consider the functional ability of the detainee rather than simply relying on a medical diagnosis, e.g. it is possible for a person with severe mental illness to be fit for interview.
5.   Healthcare professionals should advise on the need for an appropriate adult to be present, whether reassessment of the person's fitness for interview may be necessary if the interview lasts beyond a specified time, and whether a further specialist opinion may be required.
6.   When healthcare professionals identify risks they should be asked to quantify the risks. They should inform the custody officer:
     - whether the person's condition:
       – is likely to improve;
       – will require or be amenable to treatment; and
     indicate how long it may take for such improvement to take effect.
7.   The role of the healthcare professional is to consider the risks and advise the custody officer of the outcome of that consideration. The healthcare professional's determination and any advice or recommendations should be made in writing and form part of the custody record.
8.   Once the healthcare professional has provided that information, it is a matter for the custody officer to decide whether or not to allow the interview to go ahead and if the interview is to proceed, to determine what safeguards are needed. Nothing prevents safeguards being provided in addition to those required under the Code. An example might be to have an appropriate healthcare professional present during the interview, in addition to an appropriate adult, in order constantly to monitor the person's condition and how it is being affected by the interview.

## Annex H

### Detained Person: Observation List

1. If any detainee fails to meet any of the following criteria, an appropriate healthcare professional or an ambulance must be called.

2. When assessing the level of rousability, consider:

   *Rousability* — can they be woken?
   * go into the cell
   * call their name
   * shake gently

   *Response to questions* — can they give appropriate answers to questions such as:
   * What's your name?
   * Where do you live?
   * Where do you think you are?

   *Response to commands* — can they respond appropriately to commands such as:
   * Open your eyes!
   * Lift one arm, now the other arm!

3. Remember to take into account the possibility or presence of other illnesses, injury, or mental condition; a person who is drowsy and smells of alcohol may also have the following:
   * Diabetes
   * Epilepsy
   * Head injury
   * Drug intoxication or overdose
   * Stroke

## Annex I

*Not used*

## Annex J

*Not used*

## Annex K

### X-Rays and Ultrasound Scans

*(a) Action*

1. PACE, section 55A allows a person who has been arrested and is in police detention to have an X-ray taken of them or an ultrasound scan to be carried out on them (or both) if:

   (a) authorised by an officer of inspector rank or above who has reasonable grounds for believing that the detainee:
      (i) may have swallowed a Class A drug; and
      (ii) was in possession of that Class A drug with the intention of supplying it to another or to export; and

   (b) the detainee's appropriate consent has been given in writing.

2. Before an x-ray is taken or an ultrasound scan carried out, a police officer or designated detention officer must tell the detainee:-

   (a) that the authority has been given; and
   (b) the grounds for giving the authorisation.

3. Before a detainee is asked to give appropriate consent to an x-ray or an ultrasound scan, they must be warned that if they refuse without good cause their refusal may harm their case if it comes to trial, see *Notes K1* and *K2*. This warning may be given by a police officer or member of police staff. In the case of juveniles and vulnerable persons, the seeking and giving of consent must take place in the presence of the appropriate adult. A juvenile's consent is only valid if their parent's or guardian's consent is also obtained unless the juvenile is under 14, when their parent's or guardian's consent is sufficient in its own right. A detainee who is not legally represented must be reminded of their entitlement to have free legal advice, see Code C, *paragraph 6.5*, and the reminder noted in the custody record.

4. An x-ray may be taken, or an ultrasound scan may be carried out, only by a registered medical practitioner or registered nurse, and only at a hospital, surgery or other medical premises.

*(b) Documentation*

5.    The following shall be recorded as soon as practicable in the detainee's custody record:
    (a)    the authorisation to take the x-ray or carry out the ultrasound scan (or both);
    (b)    the grounds for giving the authorisation;
    (c)    the giving of the warning required by *paragraph 3*; and
    (d)    the fact that the appropriate consent was given or (as the case may be) refused, and if refused, the reason given for the refusal (if any); and
    (e)    if an x-ray is taken or an ultrasound scan carried out:
        • where it was taken or carried out;
        • who took it or carried it out;
        • who was present;
        • the result.

6      *Not used.*

## Notes for Guidance

K1    *If authority is given for an x-ray to be taken or an ultrasound scan to be carried out (or both), consideration should be given to asking a registered medical practitioner or registered nurse to explain to the detainee what is involved and to allay any concerns the detainee might have about the effect which taking an x-ray or carrying out an ultrasound scan might have on them. If appropriate consent is not given, evidence of the explanation may, if the case comes to trial, be relevant to determining whether the detainee had a good cause for refusing.*

K2    *In warning a detainee who is asked to consent to an X-ray being taken or an ultrasound scan being carried out (or both), as in paragraph 3, the following form of words may be used:*

> *'You do not have to allow an x-ray of you to be taken or an ultrasound scan to be carried out on you, but I must warn you that if you refuse without good cause, your refusal may harm your case if it comes to trial.'*

*Where the use of the Welsh Language is appropriate, the following form of words may be provided in Welsh:*

> 'Does dim rhaid i chi ganiatáu cymryd sgan uwchsain neu belydr-x (neu'r ddau) arnoch, ond mae'n rhaid i mi eich rhybuddio os byddwch chi'n gwrthod gwneud hynny heb reswm da, fe allai hynny niweidio eich achos pe bai'n dod gerbron llys.'

## ANNEX L

### ESTABLISHING GENDER OF PERSONS FOR THE PURPOSE OF SEARCHING

1.    Certain provisions of this and other PACE Codes explicitly state that searches and other procedures may only be carried out by, or in the presence of, persons of the same sex as the person subject to the search or other procedure or require action to be taken or information to be given which depends on whether the detainee is treated as being male or female. See *Note L1*.

2.    All such searches, procedures and requirements must be carried out with courtesy, consideration and respect for the person concerned. Police officers should show particular sensitivity when dealing with transgender individuals (including transsexual persons) and transvestite persons (see *Notes L2, L3 and L4*).

*(a) Consideration*

3.    In law, the gender (and accordingly the sex) of an individual is their gender as registered at birth unless they have been issued with a Gender Recognition Certificate (GRC) under the Gender Recognition Act 2004 (GRA), in which case the person's gender is their acquired gender. This means that if the acquired gender is the male gender, the person's sex becomes that of a man and, if it is the female gender, the person's sex becomes that of a woman and they must be treated as their acquired gender.

4.    When establishing whether the person concerned should be treated as being male or female for the purposes of these searches, procedures and requirements, the following approach which is designed to maintain their diginity, minimise embarrassment and secure their co-operation should be followed:
    (a)    The person must not be asked whether they have a GRC (see *paragraph 8*);
    (b)    If there is no doubt as to as to whether the person concerned should be treated as being male or female, they should be dealt with as being of that sex.

(c)  If at any time (including during the search or carrying out the procedure or requirement) there is doubt as to whether the person should be treated, or continue to be treated, as being male or female:

    (i)  the person should be asked what gender they consider themselves to be. If they express a preference to be dealt with as a particular gender, they should be asked to indicate and confirm their preference by signing the custody record or, if a custody record has not been opened, the search record or the officer's notebook. Subject to (ii) below, the person should be treated according to their preference except with regards to the requirements to provide that person with information concerning menstrual products and their personal needs relating to health, hygiene and welfare described in *paragraph 3.20A* (if aged under 18) and *paragraphs 9.3A* and *9.3B* (if aged 18 or over). In these cases, a person whose confirmed preference is to be dealt with as being male should be asked in private whether they wish to speak in private with a member of the custody staff of a gender of their choosing about the provision of menstrual products and their personal needs, notwithstanding their confirmed preference (see *Note L3A*).

    (ii)  if there are grounds to doubt that the preference in (i) accurately reflects the person's predominant lifestyle, for example, if they ask to be treated as a woman but documents and other information make it clear that they live predominantly as a man, or vice versa, they should be treated according to what appears to be their predominant lifestyle and not their stated preference;

    (iii)  If the person is unwilling to express a preference as in (i) above, efforts should be made to determine their predominant lifestyle and they should be treated as such. For example, if they appear to live predominantly as a woman, they should be treated as being female except with regard to the requirements to provide that person with information concerning menstrual products and their personal needs relating to health, hygiene and welfare described in *paragraph 3.20A* (if aged under 18) and *paragraphs 9.3A* and *9.3B* (if aged 18 or over). In these cases, a person whose predominant lifestyle has been determined to be male should be asked in private whether they wish to speak in private with a member of the custody staff of a gender of their choosing about the provision of menstrual products and their personal needs, notwithstanding their determined predominant lifestyle (see *Note L3A*); or

    (iv)  if none of the above apply, the person should be dealt with according to what reasonably appears to have been their sex as registered at birth.

5.  Once a decision has been made about which gender an individual is to be treated as, each officer responsible for the search procedure or requirement should where possible be advised before the search or procedure starts of any doubts as to the person's gender and the person informed that the doubts have been disclosed. This is important so as to maintain the dignity of the person and any officers concerned.

*(b) Documentation*

6.  The person's gender as established under *paragraph 4(c)(i)* to *(iv)* above must be recorded in the person's custody record or, if a custody record has not been opened, on the search record or in the officer's notebook.

7.  Where the person elects which gender they consider themselves to be under *paragraph 4(b)(i)* but, following *4(b)(ii)* is not treated in accordance with their preference, the reason must be recorded in the search record, in the officer's notebook or, if applicable, in the person's custody record.

*(c) Disclosure of information*

8.  Section 22 of the GRA defines any information relating to a person's application for a GRC or to a successful applicant's gender before it became their acquired gender as 'protected information'. Nothing in this Annex is to be read as authorising or permitting any police officer or any police staff who has acquired such information when acting in their official capacity to disclose that information to any other person in contravention of the GRA. Disclosure includes making a record of 'protected information' which is read by others.

*Notes for Guidance*

L1  *Provisions to which paragraph 1 applies include:*
- *In Code C; paragraphs 3.20A, 4.1 and Annex A paragraphs 5, 6, and 11 (searches, strip and intimate searches of detainees under sections 54 and 55 of PACE) and 9.3B;*
- *In Code A; paragraphs 2.8 and 3.6 and Note 4;*

- *In Code D; paragraph 5.5 and Note 5F (searches, examinations and photographing of detainees under section 54A of PACE) and paragraph 6.9 (taking samples);*
- *In Code H; paragraphs 3.21, 4.1 and Annex A paragraphs 6, 7 and 12 (searches, strip and intimate searches under sections 54 and 55 of PACE of persons arrested under section 41 of the Terrorism Act 2000) and 9.4B.*

L2     *While there is no agreed definition of transgender (or trans), it is generally used as an umbrella term to describe people whose gender identity (self-identification as being a woman, man, neither or both) differs from the sex they were registered as at birth. The term includes, but is not limited to, transsexual people.*

L3     *Transsexual means a person who is proposing to undergo, is undergoing or has undergone a process (or part of a process) for the purpose of gender reassignment, which is a protected characteristic under the Equality Act 2010 (see paragraph 1.0), by changing physiological or other attributes of their sex. This includes aspects of gender such as dress and title. It would apply to a woman making the transition to being a man and a man making the transition to being a woman, as well as to a person who has only just started out on the process of gender reassignment and to a person who has completed the process. Both would share the characteristic of gender reassignment with each having the characteristics of one sex, but with certain characteristics of the other sex.*

L3A    *The reason for the exception is to modify the same sex/gender approach for searching to acknowledge the possible needs of transgender individuals in respect of menstrual products and other personal needs relating to health, hygiene and welfare and ensure that they are not overlooked.*

L4     *Transvestite means a person of one gender who dresses in the clothes of a person of the opposite gender. However, a transvestite does not live permanently in the gender opposite to their birth sex.*

L5     *Chief officers are responsible for providing corresponding operational guidance and instructions for the deployment of transgender officers and staff under their direction and control to duties which involve carrying out, or being present at, any of the searches and procedures described in paragraph 1. The guidance and instructions must comply with the Equality Act 2010 and should therefore complement the approach in this Annex.*

## Annex M

### Documents and Records to be Translated

1.     For the purposes of Directive 2010/64/EU of the European Parliament and of the Council of 20 October 2010 and this Code, essential documents comprise records required to be made in accordance with this Code which are relevant to decisions to deprive a person of their liberty, to any charge and to any record considered necessary to enable a detainee to defend themselves in criminal proceedings and to safeguard the fairness of the proceedings. Passages of essential documents which are not relevant need not be translated. See *Note M1*.

2.     The table below lists the documents considered essential for the purposes of this Code and when (subject to *paragraphs 3* to *7*) written translations must be created and provided. See *paragraphs 13.12* to *13.14* and *Annex N* for application to live-link interpretation.

*Table of essential documents:*

| | Essential Documents for the Purposes of this Code | When Translation to be Created | When Translation to be Provided |
|---|---|---|---|
| (i) | The grounds for each of the following authorisations to keep the person in custody as they are described and referred to in the custody record:<br>(a) Authorisation for detention before and after charge given by the custody officer and by the review officer, see Code C, *paragraphs 3.4* and *15.16(a)*. | As soon as practicable after each authorisation has been recorded in the custody record. | As soon as practicable after the translation has been created, whilst the person is detained or afters they have been releases (see *Note M3*). |

| | Essential Documents for the Purposes of this Code | When Translation to be Created | When Translation to be Provided |
|---|---|---|---|
| | (b) Authorisation to extend detention without charge beyond 24 hours given by a superintendent, see Code C, *paragraph 15.16(b)*.<br>(c) A warrant of further detention issued by a magistrates' court and any extension(s) of the warrant, see Code C, *paragraph 15.16(c)*.<br>(d) An authority to detain in accordance with the directions in a warrant of arrest issued in connection with criminal proceedings including the court issuing the warrant. | | |
| (ii) | Written notice showing particulars of the offence charged required by Code C, *paragraph 16.3* or the offence for which the suspect has been told they may be prosecuted. | As soon as practicable after the person has been charged or reported. | |
| (iii) | Written interview records: Code C, 11.11, 13.3, 13.4 and Code E4.7<br>Written statement under caution:<br>Code C, *Annex D*. | To be created contemporaneously by the interpreter for the person to check and sign. | As soon as practicable after the person has been charged or told they may be prosecuted. |

3. The custody officer may authorise an oral translation or oral summary of documents (i) to (ii) in the table (but not (iii)) to be provided (through an interpreter) instead of a written translation. Such an oral translation or summary may only be provided if it would not prejudice the fairness of the proceedings by in any way adversely affecting or otherwise undermining or limiting the ability of the suspect in question to understand their position and to communicate effectively with police officers, interviewers, solicitors and appropriate adults with regard to their detention and the investigation of the offence in question and to defend themselves in the event of criminal proceedings. The quantity and complexity of the information in the document should always be considered and specific additional consideration given if the suspect is vulnerable or is a juvenile (see Code C, *paragraph 1.5*). The reason for the decision must be recorded (see *paragraph 13.11(e)*).

4. Subject to *paragraphs 5 to 7* below, a suspect may waive their right to a written translation of the essential documents described in the table but only if they do so voluntarily after receiving legal advice or having full knowledge of the consequences and give their unconditional and fully informed consent in writing (see *paragraph 9*).

5. The suspect may be asked if they wish to waive their right to a written translation and before giving their consent, they must be reminded of their right to legal advice and asked whether they wish to speak to a solicitor.

6. No police officer or police staff should do or say anything with the intention of persuading a suspect who is entitled to a written translation of an essential document to waive that right. See *Notes M2* and *M3*.

7. For the purpose of the waiver:
   (a) the consent of a vulnerable person is only valid if the information about the circumstances under which they can waive the right and the reminder about their right to legal advice mentioned in *paragraphs 3 to 5* and their consent is given in the presence of the appropriate adult.

(b) the consent of a juvenile is only valid if their parent's or guardian's consent is also obtained unless the juvenile is under 14, when their parent's or guardian's consent is sufficient in its own right and the information and reminder mentioned in *subparagraph (a)* above and their consent is also given in the presence of the appropriate adult (who may or may not be a parent or guardian).

8.      The detainee, their solicitor or appropriate adult may make representations to the custody officer that a document which is not included in the table is essential and that a translation should be provided. The request may be refused if the officer is satisfied that the translation requested is not essential for the purposes described in *paragraph 1* above.

9.      If the custody officer has any doubts about
- providing an oral translation or summary of an essential document instead of a written translation (see *paragraph 3*);
- whether the suspect fully understands the consequences of waiving their right to a written translation of an essential document (see *paragraph 4*), or
- about refusing to provide a translation of a requested document (see *paragraph 7*),

the officer should seek advice from an inspector or above.

*Documentation*

10.     Action taken in accordance with this Annex shall be recorded in the detainee's custody record or interview record as appropriate (see Code C *paragraph 13.11(e)*).

*Notes for Guidance*

M1   *It is not necessary to disclose information in any translation which is capable of undermining or otherwise adversely affecting any investigative processes, for example, by enabling the suspect to fabricate an innocent explanation or to conceal lies from the interviewer.*

M2   *No police officer or police staff shall indicate to any suspect, except to answer a direct question, whether the period for which they are liable to be detained or if not detained, the time taken to complete the interview, might be reduced:*
- *if they do not ask for legal advice before deciding whether they wish to waive their right to a written translation of an essential document; or*
- *if they decide to waive their right to a written translation of an essential document.*

M3   *There is no power under PACE to detain a person or to delay their release solely to create and provide a written translation of any essential document.*

Annex N

Live-Link Interpretation (Para. 13.12)

**Part 1: When the physical presence of the interpreter is not required.**

1.      EU Directive 2010/64 (see *paragraph 13.1*), Article 2(6) provides 'Where appropriate, communication technology such as videoconferencing, telephone or the Internet may be used, unless the physical presence of the interpreter is required in order to safeguard the fairness of the proceedings.' This Article permits, but does not require the use of a live-link, and the following provisions of this Annex determine whether the use of a live-link is appropriate in any particular case.

2.      Decisions in accordance with this Annex that the physical presence of the interpreter is not required and to permit live-link interpretation, must be made on a case by case basis. Each decision must take account of the age, gender and vulnerability of the suspect, the nature and circumstances of the offence and the investigation and the impact on the suspect according to the particular purpose(s) for which the suspect requires the assistance of an interpreter and the time(s) when that assistance is required (see *Note N1*). For this reason, the custody officer in the case of a detained suspect, or in the case of a suspect who has not been arrested, the interviewer (subject to *paragraph 13.1(b)*), must consider whether the ability of the particular suspect, to communicate confidently and effectively for the purpose in question (see *paragraph 3*) is likely to be adversely affected or otherwise undermined or limited if the interpreter is not physically present and live-link interpretation is used. Although a suspect for whom an appropriate adult is required may be more likely to be adversely affected as described, it is important to note that a person who does not require an appropriate adult may also be adversely impacted by the use of live-link interpretation.

3.      Examples of purposes referred to in *paragraph 2* include:
(a) understanding and appreciating their position having regard to any information given to them, or sought from them, in accordance with this or any other Code of Practice which, in particular, include:

- the caution (see *paragraphs C10.1* and *10.12*).
- the special warning (see *paragraphs 10.10* to *10.12*).
- information about the offence (see *paragraphs 10.3, 11.1A* and *Note 11ZA*).
- the grounds and reasons for detention (see *paragraphs 13.10* and *13.10A*).
- the translation of essential documents (see *paragraph 13.10B* and *Annex M*).
- their rights and entitlements (see *paragraph 3.12 and C3.21(b)*).
- intimate and non-intimate searches of detained persons at police stations.
- provisions and procedures to which Code D (Identification) applies concerning, for example, eye-witness identification, taking fingerprints, samples and photographs.

(b) understanding and seeking clarification from the interviewer of questions asked during an interview conducted and recorded in accordance with Code E or Code F and of anything else that is said by the interviewer and answering the questions.

(c) consulting privately with their solicitor and (if applicable) the appropriate adult (see *paragraphs 3.18, 13.2A, 13.6 and 13.9*):

    (i) to help decide whether to answer questions put to them during interview; and

    (ii) about any other matter concerning their detention and treatment whilst in custody.

(d) communicating with practitioners and others who have some formal responsibility for, or an interest in, the health and welfare of the suspect. Particular examples include appropriate healthcare professionals (see *section 9* of this Code), Independent Custody Visitors and drug arrest referral workers.

4. If the custody officer or the interviewer (subject to *paragraph 13.1(b)*) is satisfied that for a particular purpose as described in *paragraphs 2 and 3 above*, the live-link interpretation *would not* adversely affect or otherwise undermine or limit the suspect's ability to communicate confidently and effectively for *that* purpose, they must so inform the suspect, their solicitor and (if applicable) the appropriate adult. At the same time, the operation of live-link interpretation must be explained and demonstrated to them, they must be advised of the chief officer's obligations concerning the security of live-link communications under *paragraph 13.13* (see *Note N2*) and they must be asked if they wish to make representations that live-link interpretation should not be used or if they require more information about the operation of the arrangements. They must also be told that at any time live-link interpretation is in use, they may make representations to the custody officer or the interviewer that its operation should cease and that the physical presence of an interpreter should be arranged.

*When the authority of an inspector is required*

5. If

    (i) representations are made that live-link interpretation should not be used, or that at any time live-link interpretation is in use, its operation should cease and the physical presence of an interpreter arranged; and

    (ii) the custody officer or interviewer (subject to *paragraph 13.1(b)*) is unable to allay the concerns raised;

then live-link interpretation may not be used, or (as the case may be) continue to be used, unless authorised in writing by an officer of the rank of inspector or above, in accordance with *paragraph 6*.

6. Authority may be given if the officer is satisfied that for the purpose(s) in question at the time an interpreter is required, live-link interpretation is necessary and justified. In making this decision, the officer must have regard to:

(a) the circumstances of the suspect;

(b) the nature and seriousness of the offence;

(c) the requirements of the investigation, including its likely impact on both the suspect and any victim(s);

(d) the representations made by the suspect, their solicitor and (if applicable) the appropriate adult that live-link interpretation should not be used (see *paragraph 5*);

(e) the availability of a suitable interpreter to be *physically* present compared with the availability of a suitable interpreter for live-link interpretation (see *Note N3*); and

(f) the risk if the interpreter is not *physically* present, evidence obtained using link interpretation might be excluded in subsequent criminal proceedings; and

(g) the likely impact on the suspect and the investigation of any consequential delay to arrange for the interpreter to be *physically* present with the suspect.

7. For the purposes of Code E and live-link interpretation, there is no requirement to make a visual recording which shows the interpreter as viewed by the suspect and others present at the interview.

The audio recording required by that Code is sufficient. However, the authorising officer, in consultation with the officer in charge of the investigation, may direct that the interview is conducted and recorded in accordance with Code F. This will require the visual record to show the live-link interpretation arrangements and the interpreter as seen and experienced by the suspect during the interview. This should be considered if it appears that the admissibility of interview evidence might be challenged because the interpreter was not *physically* present or if the suspect, solicitor or appropriate adult make representations that Code F should be applied.

*Documentation*

8.    A record must be made of the actions, decisions, authorisations and outcomes arising from the requirements of this Annex. This includes representations made in accordance with *paragraphs 4* and *7*.

**Part 2: Modifications for live-link interpretation**

9.    The following modification shall apply for the purposes of live-link interpretation:

(a)  **Code C paragraph 13.3:**
For the third sentence, substitute: 'A clear legible copy of the complete record shall be sent without delay via the live-link to the interviewer. The interviewer, after confirming with the suspect that the copy is legible and complete, shall allow the suspect to read the record, or have the record read to them by the interpreter and to sign the copy as correct or indicate the respects in which they consider it inaccurate. The interviewer is responsible for ensuring that that the signed copy and the original record made by the interpreter are retained with the case papers for use in evidence if required and must advise the interpreter of their obligation to keep the original record securely for that purpose.';

(b)  **Code C paragraph 13.4:**
For sub-paragraph (b), substitute: 'A clear legible copy of the complete statement shall be sent without delay via the live-link to the interviewer. The interviewer, after confirming with the suspect that the copy is legible and complete, shall invite the suspect to sign it. The interviewer is responsible for ensuring that that the signed copy and the original record made by the interpreter are retained with the case papers for use in evidence if required and must advise the interpreter of their obligation to keep the original record securely for that purpose.';

(c)  **Code C paragraph 13.7:**
After the first sentence, insert: 'A clear legible copy of the certified record must be sent without delay via the live-link to the interviewer. The interviewer is responsible for ensuring that the original certified record and the copy are retained with the case papers for use as evidence if required and must advise the interpreter of their obligation to keep the original record securely for that purpose.'

(d)  **Code C paragraph 11.2, Code E paragraphs 3.4 and 4.3 and Code F paragraph 2.5 interviews**
At the beginning of each paragraph, insert: 'Before the interview commences, the operation of live-link interpretation shall be explained and demonstrated to the suspect, their solicitor and appropriate adult, unless it has been previously explained and demonstrated (see Code C *Annex N paragraph 4*).'

(e)  **Code E, paragraph 3.20 (signing master recording label)**
After the third sentence, insert, 'If live-link interpretation has been used, the interviewer should ask the interpreter to observe the removal and sealing of the master recording and to confirm in writing that they have seen it sealed and signed by the interviewer. A clear legible copy of the confirmation signed by the interpreter must be sent via the live-link to the interviewer. The interviewer is responsible for ensuring that the original confirmation and the copy are retained with the case papers for use in evidence if required and must advise the interpreter of their obligation to keep the original confirmation securely for that purpose.'

Note: By virtue of *paragraphs 2.1* and *2.3 of Code F*, this applies when a visually recording to which Code F applies is made.

*Notes for Guidance*

*N1*   *For purposes other than an interview, audio-only live-link interpretation, for example by telephone (see Code C, paragraph 13.12(b)) may provide an appropriate option until an interpreter is physically present or audio-visual live-link interpretation becomes available. A particular example would be the initial action required when a detained suspect arrives at a police station to inform them of, and to explain, the reasons for their arrest and detention and their various rights and entitlements. Another example would be to inform the suspect by telephone, that an interpreter they will be able to see and hear is being arranged.*

*In these circumstances, telephone live-link interpretation may help to allay the suspect's concerns and contribute to the completion of the risk assessment (see Code C, paragraph 3.6).*

N2  *The explanation and demonstration of live-link interpretation is intended to help the suspect, solicitor and appropriate adult make an informed decision and to allay any concerns they may have.*

N3  *Factors affecting availability of a suitable interpreter will include the location of the police station and the language and type of interpretation (oral or sign language) required.*


# PACE CODE D

# CODE OF PRACTICE FOR THE IDENTIFICATION OF PERSONS BY POLICE OFFICERS

### Commencement—Transitional Arrangements

This code has effect in relation to any identification procedure carried out after 00:00 on 23 February 2017.

## 1 Introduction

1.1  This Code of Practice concerns the principal methods used by police to identify people in connection with the investigation of offences and the keeping of accurate and reliable criminal records. The powers and procedures in this code must be used fairly, responsibly, with respect for the people to whom they apply and without unlawful discrimination. Under the Equality Act 2010, section 149 (Public sector Equality Duty), police forces must, in carrying out their functions, have due regard to the need to eliminate unlawful discrimination, harassment, victimisation and any other conduct which is prohibited by that Act, to advance equality of opportunity between people who share a relevant protected characteristic and people who do not share it, and to foster good relations between those persons. The Equality Act also makes it unlawful for police officers to discriminate against, harass or victimise any person on the grounds of the 'protected characteristics' of age, disability, gender reassignment, race, religion or belief, sex and sexual orientation, marriage and civil partnership, pregnancy and maternity when using their powers. See *Note 1A*.

1.2  In this Code, identification by an eye-witness arises when a witness who has seen the offender committing the crime and is given an opportunity to identify a person suspected of involvement in the offence in a video identification, identification parade or similar procedure. These eye-witness identification procedures which are in Part A of section 3 below, are designed to:
  • test the eye-witness' ability to identify the suspect as the person they saw on a previous occasion
  • provide safeguards against mistaken identification.
While this Code concentrates on visual identification procedures, it does not prevent the police making use of aural identification procedures such as a 'voice identification parade', where they judge that appropriate. See *Note 1B*.

1.2A In this Code, separate provisions in Part B of section 3 below, apply when any person, including a police officer, is asked if they recognise anyone they see in an image as being someone who is known to them and to test their claim that they recognise that person. These separate provisions are not subject to the eye-witnesses identification procedures described in *paragraph 1.2*.

1.2B Part C applies when a film, photograph or image relating to the offence or any description of the suspect is broadcast or published in any national or local media or on any social networking site or on any local or national police communication systems.

1.3  Identification by fingerprints applies when a person's fingerprints are taken to:
  • compare with fingerprints found at the scene of a crime
  • check and prove convictions
  • help to ascertain a person's identity.

1.3A Identification using footwear impressions applies when a person's footwear impressions are taken to compare with impressions found at the scene of a crime.

1.4  Identification by body samples and impressions includes taking samples such as a cheek swab, hair or blood to generate a DNA profile for comparison with material obtained from the scene of a crime, or a victim.

1.5  Taking photographs of arrested people applies to recording and checking identity and locating and tracing persons who:
  • are wanted for offences
  • fail to answer their bail.

1.6 Another method of identification involves searching and examining detained suspects to find, e.g., marks such as tattoos or scars which may help establish their identity or whether they have been involved in committing an offence.

1.7 The provisions of the Police and Criminal Evidence Act 1984 (PACE) and this Code are designed to make sure fingerprints, samples, impressions and photographs are taken, used and retained, and identification procedures carried out, only when justified and necessary for preventing, detecting or investigating crime. If these provisions are not observed, the application of the relevant procedures in particular cases may be open to question.

1.8 The provisions of this Code do not authorise, or otherwise permit, fingerprints or samples to be taken from a person detained solely for the purposes of assessment under section 136 of the Mental Health Act 1983.

*Note for Guidance*

1A *In paragraph 1.1, under the Equality Act 1949, section 149, the 'relevant protected characteristics' are: age, disability, gender reassignment, pregnancy and maternity, race, religion/belief, sex and sexual orientation. For further detailed guidance and advice on the Equality Act, see: https://www.gov.uk/guid ance/equality-act-2010-guidance.*

1B *See Home Office Circular 57/2003 'Advice on the use of voice identification parades'.*

## 2 General

2.1 This Code must be readily available at all police stations for consultation by:
   • police officers and police staff
   • detained persons
   • members of the public

2.2 The provisions of this Code:
   • include the Annexes
   • do not include the Notes for guidance.

2.3 Code C, *paragraph 1.4* and the *Notes for guidance* applicable to those provisions apply to this Code with regard to a suspected person who may be mentally disordered or otherwise mentally vulnerable.

2.4 Code C, *paragraphs 1.5* and *1.5A* and the *Notes for guidance* applicable to those provisions apply to this Code with regard to a suspected person who appears to be under the age of 18.

2.5 Code C, *paragraph 1.6* applies to this Code with regard to a suspected person who appears to be blind, seriously visually impaired, deaf, unable to read or speak or has difficulty communicating orally because of a speech impediment.

2.6 In this Code:
   • 'appropriate adult' means the same as in Code C, *paragraph 1.7*
   • 'solicitor' means the same as in Code C, *paragraph 6.12* and the *Notes for guidance* applicable to those provisions apply to this Code.
   • where a search or other procedure under this Code may only be carried out or observed by a person of the same sex as the person to whom the search or procedure applies, the gender of the detainee and other persons present should be established and recorded in line with *Annex L* of Code C.

2.7 References to a custody officer include any police officer who, for the time being, is performing the functions of a custody officer, see *paragraph 1.9* of Code C.

2.8 When a record of any action requiring the authority of an officer of a specified rank is made under this Code, subject to *paragraph 2.18*, the officer's name and rank must be recorded.

2.9 When this Code requires the prior authority or agreement of an officer of at least inspector or superintendent rank, that authority may be given by a sergeant or chief inspector who has been authorised to perform the functions of the higher rank under PACE, section 107.

2.10 Subject to *paragraph 2.18*, all records must be timed and signed by the maker.

2.11 Records must be made in the custody record, unless otherwise specified. In any provision of this Code which allows or requires police officers or police staff to make a record in their report book, the reference to 'report book' shall include any official report book or electronic recording device issued to them that enables the record in question to be made and dealt with in accordance with that provision. References in this Code to written records, forms and signatures include electronic records and forms and electronic confirmation that identifies the person completing the record or form. Chief officers must be satisfied as to the integrity and security of the devices, records and forms to which this *paragraph* applies and that use of those devices, records and forms satisfies relevant data protection legislation. (taken from *Code C, paragraph 1.17*).

2.12 If any procedure in this Code requires a person's consent, the consent of a:

- mentally disordered or otherwise mentally vulnerable person is only valid if given in the presence of the appropriate adult
- juvenile is only valid if their parent's or guardian's consent is also obtained unless the juvenile is under 14, when their parent's or guardian's consent is sufficient in its own right. If the only obstacle to an identification procedure in *section 3* is that a juvenile's parent or guardian refuses consent or reasonable efforts to obtain it have failed, the identification officer may apply the provisions of *paragraph 3.21* (suspect known but not available). See *Note 2A*.

2.13 If a person is blind, seriously visually impaired or unable to read, the custody officer or identification officer shall make sure their solicitor, relative, appropriate adult or some other person likely to take an interest in them and not involved in the investigation is available to help check any documentation. When this Code requires written consent or signing, the person assisting may be asked to sign instead, if the detainee prefers. This paragraph does not require an appropriate adult to be called solely to assist in checking and signing documentation for a person who is not a juvenile, or mentally disordered or otherwise mentally vulnerable (see *Note 2B* and Code C, *paragraph 3.15*).

2.14 If any procedure in this Code requires information to be given to or sought from a suspect, it must be given or sought in the appropriate adult's presence if the suspect is mentally disordered, otherwise mentally vulnerable or a juvenile. If the appropriate adult is not present when the information is first given or sought, the procedure must be repeated in the presence of the appropriate adult when they arrive. If the suspect appears deaf or there is doubt about their hearing or speaking ability or ability to understand English, the custody officer or identification officer must ensure that the necessary arrangements in accordance with Code C are made for an interpreter to assist the suspect.

2.15 Any procedure in this Code involving the participation of a suspect who is mentally disordered, otherwise mentally vulnerable or a juvenile must take place in the presence of the appropriate adult. See Code C, *paragraph 1.4*.

2.15A Any procedure in this Code involving the participation of a witness who is or appears to be mentally disordered, otherwise mentally vulnerable or a juvenile should take place in the presence of a pre-trial support person unless the witness states that they do not want a support person to be present. A support person must not be allowed to prompt any identification of a suspect by a witness. See *Note 2AB*.

2.16 References to:
- 'taking a photograph', include the use of any process to produce a single, still or moving, visual image
- 'photographing a person', should be construed accordingly
- 'photographs', 'films', 'negatives' and 'copies' include relevant visual images recorded, stored, or reproduced through any medium
- 'destruction' includes the deletion of computer data relating to such images or making access to that data impossible

2.17 This Code does not affect or apply to, the powers and procedures:
   (i) for requiring and taking samples of breath, blood and urine in relation to driving offences, etc, when under the influence of drink, drugs or excess alcohol under the:
   - Road Traffic Act 1988, sections 4 to 11
   - Road Traffic Offenders Act 1988, sections 15 and 16
   - Transport and Works Act 1992, sections 26 to 38;
   (ii) under the Immigration Act 1971, Schedule 2, paragraph 18, for taking photographs, measuring and identifying and taking biometric information (not including DNA) from persons detained or liable to be detained under that Act, Schedule 2, paragraph 16 (Administrative Provisions as to Control on Entry etc.); or for taking fingerprints in accordance with the Immigration and Asylum Act 1999, sections 141 and 142(4), or other methods for collecting information about a person's external physical characteristics provided for by regulations made under that Act, section 144;
   (iii) under the Terrorism Act 2000, Schedule 8, for taking photographs, fingerprints, skin impressions, body samples or impressions from people:
   - arrested under that Act, section 41,
   - detained for the purposes of examination under that Act, Schedule 7, and to whom the Code of Practice issued under that Act, Schedule 14, paragraph 6, applies ('the terrorism provisions')
   (iv) for taking photographs, fingerprints, skin impressions, body samples or impressions from people who have been:

- arrested on warrants issued in Scotland, by officers exercising powers mentioned in Part X of the Criminal Justice and Public Order Act 1994;
- arrested or detained without warrant by officers from a police force in Scotland exercising their powers of arrest or detention mentioned in Part X of the Criminal Justice and Public Order Act 1994.

Note: In these cases, police powers and duties and the person's rights and entitlements whilst at a police station in England and Wales are the same as if the person had been arrested in Scotland by a Scottish police officer.

2.18 Nothing in this Code requires the identity of officers or police staff to be recorded or disclosed:

(a) in the case of enquiries linked to the investigation of terrorism;

(b) if the officers or police staff reasonably believe recording or disclosing their names might put them in danger.

In these cases, they shall use their warrant or other identification numbers and the name of their police station. *See Note 2D.*

2.19 In this Code:

(a) 'designated person' means a person other than a police officer, who has specified powers and duties conferred or imposed on them by designation under section 38 or 39 of the Police Reform Act 2002;

(b) any reference to a police officer includes a designated person acting in the exercise or performance of the powers and duties conferred or imposed on them by their designation.

2.20 If a power conferred on a designated person:

(a) allows reasonable force to be used when exercised by a police officer, a designated person exercising that power has the same entitlement to use force;

(b) includes power to use force to enter any premises, that power is not exercisable by that designated person except:

(i) in the company, and under the supervision, of a police officer; or

(ii) for the purpose of:
- saving life or limb; or
- preventing serious damage to property.

2.21 In the case of a detained person, nothing in this Code prevents the custody officer, or other police officer or designated person given custody of the detainee by the custody officer for the purposes of the investigation of an offence for which the person is detained, from allowing another person (see *(a)* and *(b)* below) to carry out individual procedures or tasks at the police station if the law allows. However, the officer or designated person given custody remains responsible for making sure the procedures and tasks are carried out correctly in accordance with the Codes of Practice. The other person who is allowed to carry out the procedures or tasks must be *someone who at that time* is:

(a) under the direction and control of the chief officer of the force responsible for the police station in question; or;

(b) providing services under contractual arrangements (but without being employed by the chief officer [of] the police force), to assist a police force in relation to the discharge of its chief officer's functions.

2.22 Designated persons and others mentioned in *sub-paragraphs (a)* and *(b)* of *paragraph 2.21* must have regard to any relevant provisions of the Codes of Practice.

*Notes for Guidance*

2A     *For the purposes of paragraph 2.12, the consent required from a parent or guardian may, for a juvenile in the care of a local authority or voluntary organisation, be given by that authority or organisation. In the case of a juvenile, nothing in paragraph 2.12 requires the parent, guardian or representative of a local authority or voluntary organisation to be present to give their consent, unless they are acting as the appropriate adult under paragraphs 2.14 or 2.15. However, it is important that a parent or guardian not present is fully informed before being asked to consent. They must be given the same information about the procedure and the juvenile's suspected involvement in the offence as the juvenile and appropriate adult. The parent or guardian must also be allowed to speak to the juvenile and the appropriate adult if they wish. Provided the consent is fully informed and is not withdrawn, it may be obtained at any time before the procedure takes place.*

2AB    *The Youth Justice and Criminal Evidence Act 1999 guidance 'Achieving Best Evidence in Criminal Proceedings' indicates that a pre-trial support person should accompany a vulnerable witness during any identification procedure unless the witness states that they do not want a support person to be present. It states that this support person should not be (or not be likely to be) a witness in the investigation.*

2B    *People who are seriously visually impaired or unable to read may be unwilling to sign police documents. The alternative, i.e. their representative signing on their behalf, seeks to protect the interests of both police and suspects.*

2C    *Not used*

2D    *The purpose of paragraph 2.18(b) is to protect those involved in serious organised crime investigations or arrests of particularly violent suspects when there is reliable information that those arrested or their associates may threaten or cause harm to the officers. In cases of doubt, an officer of inspector rank or above should be consulted.*

### 3 Identification and recognition of suspects

**Part (A)** *Identification of a suspect by an eye-witness*

3.0    This part applies when an eye-witness has seen a person committing a crime or in any other circumstances which tend to prove or disprove the involvement of the person they saw in a crime, for example, close to the scene of the crime, immediately before or immediately after it was committed. It sets out the procedures to be used to test the ability of that eye-witness to identify a person suspected of involvement in the offence ('the suspect') as the person they saw on the previous occasion. This part does not apply to the procedure described in Part B (see *Note 3AA*) which is used to test the ability of someone who is not an eye-witness, to recognise anyone whose image they see.

3.1    A record shall be made of the description of the suspect as first given by the eye-witness .This record must:

(a)   be made and kept in a form which enables details of that description to be accurately produced from it, in a visible and legible form, which can be given to the suspect or the suspect's solicitor in accordance with this Code; and

(b)   unless otherwise specified, be made before the eye-witness takes part in any identification procedures under *paragraphs 3.5 to 3.10, 3.21, 3.23* or *Annex E* (Showing Photographs to Eye-Witnesses).

A copy of the record shall where practicable, be given to the suspect or their solicitor before any procedures under *paragraphs 3.5 to 3.10, 3.21 or 3.23* are carried out. See *Note 3E*.

3.1A  References in this Part:

(a)   to the identity of the suspect being 'known' mean that there is sufficient information known to the police to establish, in accordance with Code G (Arrest), that there are reasonable grounds to suspect a particular person of involvement in the offence;

(b)   to the suspect being 'available' mean that the suspect is immediately available, or will be available within a reasonably short time, in order that they can be invited to take part in at least one of the eye-witness identification procedures under *paragraphs 3.5 to 3.10* and it is practicable to arrange an effective procedure under *paragraphs 3.5 to 3.10*; and

(c)   to the eye-witness identification procedures under *paragraphs 3.5 to 3.10* mean:
- Video identification (*paragraphs 3.5 and 3.6*);
- Identification parade (*paragraphs 3.7 and 3.8*); and
- Group identification (*paragraphs 3.9 and 3.10*).

*(a) Cases when the suspect's identity is not known*

3.2    In cases when the suspect's identity is not known, an eye-witness may be taken to a particular neighbourhood or place to see whether they can identify the person they saw on a previous occasion. Although the number, age, sex, race, general description and style of clothing of other people present at the location and the way in which any identification is made cannot be controlled, the principles applicable to the formal procedures under *paragraphs 3.5 to 3.10* shall be followed as far as practicable. For example:

(a)   where it is practicable to do so, a record should be made of the eye-witness' description of the person they saw on the previous occasion, as in *paragraph 3.1(a)*, before asking the eye-witness to make an identification;

(b)   Care must be taken not [to] provide the eye-witness with any information concerning the description of the suspect (if such information is available) and not to direct the eyewitness' attention to any individual unless, taking into account all the circumstances, this cannot be avoided. However, this does not prevent an eye-witness being asked to look carefully at the people around at the time or to look towards a group or in a particular direction, if this appears necessary to make sure that the witness does not overlook a possible suspect simply because the eye-witness is looking in the opposite direction and also to enable the eye-witness to make comparisons between any suspect and others who are in the area;

(c) where there is more than one eye-witness, every effort should be made to keep them separate and eye-witnesses should be taken to see whether they can identify a person independently;

(d) once there is sufficient information to establish, in accordance with *paragraph 3.1A(a)*, that the suspect is 'known', e.g. after the eye-witness makes an identification, the provisions set out from *paragraph 3.4* onwards shall apply for that and any other eyewitnesses in relation to that individual;

(e) the officer or police staff accompanying the eye-witness must record, in their report book, the action taken as soon as practicable and in as much detail, as possible. The record should include:

    (i) the date, time and place of the relevant occasion when the eye-witness claims to have previously seen the person committing the offence in question or in any other circumstances which tend to prove or disprove the involvement of the person they saw in a crime (see *paragraph 3.0*); and

    (ii) where any identification was made:
- how it was made and the conditions at the time (e.g., the distance the eyewitness was from the suspect, the weather and light);
- if the eye-witness's attention was drawn to the suspect; the reason for this;
- and anything said by the eye-witness or the suspect about the identification or the conduct of the procedure.

See *Note 3F*.

3.3 An eye-witness must not be shown photographs, computerised or artist's composite likenesses or similar likenesses or pictures (including 'E-fit' images) if in accordance with *paragraph 3.1A*, the identity of the suspect is known and they are available to take part in one of the procedures under *paragraphs 3.5* to *3.10*. If the suspect's identity is not known, the showing of any such images to an eye-witness to see if they can identify a person whose image they are shown as the person they saw on a previous occasion must be done in accordance with *Annex E*.

*(b) Cases when the suspect is known and available*

3.4 If the suspect's identity is known to the police (see *paragraph 3.1A(a)*) and they are available (see *paragraph 3.1A(b)*), the identification procedures that may be used are set out in *paragraphs 3.5* to *3.10* below as follows:

(i) video identification;

(ii) identification parade; or

(iii) group identification.

*(i) Video identification*

3.5 A 'video identification' is when the eye-witness is shown images of a known suspect, together with similar images of others who resemble the suspect. *Moving* images must be used unless the conditions in *sub-paragraph (a)* or *(b)* below apply:

(a) this sub-paragraph applies if:

    (i) the identification officer, in consultation with the officer in charge of the investigation, is satisfied that because of aging, or other physical changes or differences, the appearance of the suspect has significantly changed since the previous occasion when the eye-witness claims to have seen the suspect (see *paragraph 3.0* and *Note 3ZA*);

    (ii) an image (moving or still) is available which the identification officer and the officer in charge of the investigation reasonably believe shows the appearance of the suspect as it was at the time the suspect was seen by the eye-witness; and

    (iii) having regard to the extent of change and the purpose of eye-witness identification procedures (see *paragraph 3.0*), the identification officer believes that that such an image should be shown to the eye-witness.

In such a case, the identification officer may arrange a video identification procedure using the image described in (ii). In accordance with the 'Notice to suspect' (see *paragraph 3.17(vi)*), the suspect must first be given an opportunity to provide their own image(s) for use in the procedure but it is for the identification officer and officer in charge of the investigation to decide whether, following (ii) and (iii), any image(s) provided by the suspect should be used.

A video identification using an image described above may, at the discretion of the identification officer be arranged in addition to, or as an alternative to, a video identification using *moving* images taken after the suspect has been given the information and notice described in *paragraphs 3.17* and *3.18*.

See *paragraph 3.21* and *Note 3D* in any case where the suspect deliberately takes steps to frustrate the eye-witness identification arrangements and procedures.

(b)  this sub-paragraph applies if, in accordance with *paragraph 2A* of *Annex A* of this Code, the identification officer does not consider that replication of a physical feature or concealment of the location of the feature can be achieved using a moving image. In these cases, still images may be used.

3.6   Video identifications must be carried out in accordance with *Annex A*.

*(ii)  Identification parade*

3.7   An 'identification parade' is when the eye-witness sees the suspect in a line of others who resemble the suspect.

3.8   Identification parades must be carried out in accordance with *Annex B*.

*(iii)  Group identification*

3.9   A 'group identification' is when the eye-witness sees the suspect in an informal group of people.

3.10  Group identifications must be carried out in accordance with *Annex C*.

*Arranging eye-witness identification procedures – duties of identification officer*

3.11  Except as provided for in *paragraph 3.19*, the arrangements for, and conduct of, the eyewitness identification procedures in *paragraphs 3.5* to *3.10* and circumstances in which any such identification procedure must be held shall be the responsibility of an officer not below inspector rank who is not involved with the investigation ('the identification officer'). The identification officer may direct another officer or police staff, see *paragraph 2.21*, to make arrangements for, and to conduct, any of these identification procedures and except as provided for in *paragraph 7* of *Annex A*, any reference in this section to the identification officer includes the officer or police staff to whom the arrangements for, and/or conduct of, any of these procedure has been delegated. In delegating these arrangements and procedures, the identification officer must be able to supervise effectively and either intervene or be contacted for advice. Where any action referred to in this paragraph is taken by another officer or police staff at the direction of the identification officer, the outcome shall, as soon as practicable, be reported to the identification officer. For the purpose of these procedures, the identification officer retains overall responsibility for ensuring that the procedure complies with this Code and in addition, in the case of detained suspect, their care and treatment until returned to the custody officer. Except as permitted by this Code, no officer or any other person involved with the investigation of the case against the suspect may take any part in these procedures or act as the identification officer.

This paragraph does not prevent the identification officer from consulting the officer in charge of the investigation to determine which procedure to use. When an identification procedure is required, in the interest of fairness to suspects and eye-witnesses, it must be held as soon as practicable.

*Circumstances in which an eye-witness identification procedure must be held*

3.12  If, before any identification procedure set out in *paragraphs 3.5* to *3.10* has been held
(a)   an eye-witness has identified a suspect or purported to have identified them; or
(b)   there is an eye-witness available who expresses an ability to identify the suspect; or
(c)   there is a reasonable chance of an eye-witness being able to identify the suspect,
and the eye-witness in (a) to (c) has not been given an opportunity to identify the suspect in any of the procedures set out in *paragraphs 3.5* to *3.10*, then an identification procedure shall be held if the suspect disputes being the person the eye-witness claims to have seen on a previous occasion (see *paragraph 3.0*), unless:
(i)   it is not practicable to hold any such procedure; or
(ii)  any such procedure would serve no useful purpose in proving or disproving whether the suspect was involved in committing the offence, for example
• where the suspect admits being at the scene of the crime and gives an account of what took place and the eye-witness does not see anything which contradicts that; or
• when it is not disputed that the suspect is already known to the eye-witness who claims to have recognised them when seeing them commit the crime.

3.13  An eye-witness identification procedure may also be held if the officer in charge of the investigation, after consultation with the identification officer, considers it would be useful.

*Selecting an eye-witness identification procedure*

3.14 If, because of *paragraph 3.12*, an identification procedure is to be held, the suspect shall initially be invited to take part in a video identification unless:
    (a)   a video identification is not practicable; or
    (b)   an identification parade is both practicable and more suitable than a video identification; or
    (c)   *paragraph 3.16* applies.
    The identification officer and the officer in charge of the investigation shall consult each other to determine which option is to be offered. An identification parade may not be practicable because of factors relating to the witnesses, such as their number, state of health, availability and travelling requirements. A video identification would normally be more suitable if it could be arranged and completed sooner than an identification parade. Before an option is offered the suspect must also be reminded of their entitlement to have free legal advice, see Code C, *paragraph 6.5*.

3.15 A suspect who refuses the identification procedure in which the suspect is first invited to take part shall be asked to state their reason for refusing and may get advice from their solicitor and/or if present, their appropriate adult. The suspect, solicitor and/or appropriate adult shall be allowed to make representations about why another procedure should be used. A record should be made of the reasons for refusal and any representations made. After considering any reasons given, and representations made, the identification officer shall, if appropriate, arrange for the suspect to be invited to take part in an alternative which the officer considers suitable and practicable. If the officer decides it is not suitable and practicable to invite the suspect to take part in an alternative identification procedure, the reasons for that decision shall be recorded.

3.16 A suspect may initially be invited to take part in a group identification if the officer in charge of the investigation considers it is more suitable than a video identification or an identification parade and the identification officer considers it practicable to arrange.

*Notice to suspect*

3.17 Unless *paragraph 3.20* applies, before any eye-witness identification procedure set out in *paragraphs 3.5* to *3.10* is arranged, the following shall be explained to the suspect:
    (i)     the purpose of the procedure (see *paragraph 3.0*);
    (ii)    their entitlement to free legal advice; see Code C, *paragraph 6.5*;
    (iii)   the procedures for holding it, including their right, subject to *Annex A, paragraph 9*, to have a solicitor or friend present;
    (iv)   that they do not have to consent to or co-operate in the procedure;
    (v)    that if they do not consent to, and co-operate in, a procedure, their refusal may be given in evidence in any subsequent trial and police may proceed covertly without their consent or make other arrangements to test whether an eye-witness can identify them, see *paragraph 3.21*;
    (vi)   whether, for the purposes of a video identification procedure, images of them have previously been obtained either:
       • in accordance with *paragraph 3.20*, and if so, that they may co-operate in providing further, suitable images to be used instead; or
       • in accordance with *paragraph 3.5(a)*, and if so, that they may provide their own images for the identification officer to consider using.
    (vii)  if appropriate, the special arrangements for juveniles;
    (viii) if appropriate, the special arrangements for mentally disordered or otherwise mentally vulnerable people;
    (ix)   that if they significantly alter their appearance between being offered an identification procedure and any attempt to hold an identification procedure, this may be given in evidence if the case comes to trial, and the identification officer may then consider other forms of identification, see *paragraph 3.21* and *Note 3C*;
    (x)    that a moving image or photograph may be taken of them when they attend for any identification procedure;
    (xi)   whether, before their identity became known, the eye-witness was shown photographs, a computerised or artist's composite likeness or similar likeness or image by the police, see *Note 3B*;
    (xii)  that if they change their appearance before an identification parade, it may not be practicable to arrange one on the day or subsequently and, because of the appearance change, the identification officer may consider alternative methods of identification, see *Note 3C*;

(xiii) that they or their solicitor will be provided with details of the description of the suspect as first given by any eye-witnesses who are to attend the procedure or confrontation, see *paragraph 3.1*.

3.18 This information must also be recorded in a written notice handed to the suspect. The suspect must be given a reasonable opportunity to read the notice, after which, they should be asked to sign a copy of the notice to indicate if they are willing to co-operate with the making of a video or take part in the identification parade or group identification. The signed copy shall be retained by the identification officer.

3.19 In the case of a detained suspect, the duties under *paragraphs 3.17* and *3.18* may be performed by the custody officer or by another officer or police staff not involved in the investigation as directed by the custody officer, if:

(a) it is proposed to release the suspect in order that an identification procedure can be arranged and carried out and an inspector is not available to act as the identification officer, see *paragraph 3.11*, before the suspect leaves the station; or

(b) it is proposed to keep the suspect in police detention whilst the procedure is arranged and carried out and waiting for an inspector to act as the identification officer, see *paragraph 3.11*, would cause unreasonable delay to the investigation.

The officer concerned shall inform the identification officer of the action taken and give them the signed copy of the notice. See *Note 3C*.

3.20 If the identification officer and officer in charge of the investigation suspect, on reasonable grounds that if the suspect was given the information and notice as in *paragraphs 3.17* and *3.18*, they would then take steps to avoid being seen by a witness in any identification procedure, the identification officer may arrange for images of the suspect suitable for use in a video identification procedure to be obtained before giving the information and notice. If suspect's images are obtained in these circumstances, the suspect may, for the purposes of a video identification procedure, co-operate in providing new images which if suitable, would be used instead, see *paragraph 3.17(vi)*.

*(c) Cases when the suspect is known but not available*

3.21 When a known suspect is not available or has ceased to be available, see *paragraph 3.1A*, the identification officer may make arrangements for a video identification (see *paragraph 3.5* and *Annex A*). If necessary, the identification officer may follow the video identification procedures using any suitable moving or still images and these may be obtained covertly if necessary. Alternatively, the identification officer may make arrangements for a group identification without the suspect's consent (see *Annex C, paragraph 34*). See *Note 3D*. These provisions may also be applied to juveniles where the consent of their parent or guardian is either refused or reasonable efforts to obtain that consent have failed (see *paragraph 2.12*).

3.22 Any covert activity should be strictly limited to that necessary to test the ability of the eyewitness to identify the suspect as the person they saw on the relevant previous occasion.

3.23 The identification officer may arrange for the suspect to be confronted by the eye-witness if none of the options referred to in *paragraphs 3.5* to *3.10* or *3.21* are practicable. A 'confrontation' is when the suspect is directly confronted by the eye-witness. A confrontation does not require the suspect's consent. Confrontations must be carried out in accordance with *Annex D*.

3.24 Requirements for information to be given to, or sought from, a suspect or for the suspect to be given an opportunity to view images before they are shown to an eye-witness, do not apply if the suspect's lack of co-operation prevents the necessary action.

*(d) Documentation*

3.25 A record shall be made of the video identification, identification parade, group identification or confrontation on forms provided for the purpose.

3.26 If the identification officer considers it is not practicable to hold a video identification or identification parade requested by the suspect, the reasons shall be recorded and explained to the suspect.

3.27 A record shall be made of a person's failure or refusal to co-operate in a video identification, identification parade or group identification and, if applicable, of the grounds for obtaining images in accordance with *paragraph 3.20*.

*(e) Not used*

3.28 *Not used.*

3.29 *Not used.*

*(f) Destruction and retention of photographs taken or used in eye-witness identification procedures*

3.30  PACE, section 64A, see *paragraph 5.12*, provides powers to take photographs of suspects and allows these photographs to be used or disclosed only for purposes related to the prevention or detection of crime, the investigation of offences or the conduct of prosecutions by, or on behalf of, police or other law enforcement and prosecuting authorities inside and outside the United Kingdom or the enforcement of a sentence. After being so used or disclosed, they may be retained but can only be used or disclosed for the same purposes.

3.31  Subject to *paragraph 3.33*, the photographs (and all negatives and copies), of suspects *not* taken in accordance with the provisions in *paragraph 5.12* which are taken for the purposes of, or in connection with, the identification procedures in *paragraphs 3.5 to 3.10, 3.21* or *3.23* must be destroyed unless the suspect:

(a)  is charged with, or informed they may be prosecuted for, a recordable offence;

(b)  is prosecuted for a recordable offence;

(c)  is cautioned for a recordable offence or given a warning or reprimand in accordance with the Crime and Disorder Act 1998 for a recordable offence; or

(d)  gives informed consent, in writing, for the photograph or images to be retained for purposes described in *paragraph 3.30*.

3.32  When *paragraph 3.31* requires the destruction of any photograph, the person must be given an opportunity to witness the destruction or to have a certificate confirming the destruction if they request one within five days of being informed that the destruction is required.

3.33  Nothing in *paragraph 3.31* affects any separate requirement under the Criminal Procedure and Investigations Act 1996 to retain material in connection with criminal investigations.

**Part (B)** *Recognition by controlled showing of films, photographs and images*

3.34  This Part of this section applies when, for the purposes of obtaining evidence of recognition, arrangements are made for a person, including a police officer, who is not an eye-witness (see *Note 3AA*):

(a)  to view a film, photograph or any other visual medium; and

(b)  on the occasion of the viewing, to be asked whether they recognise anyone whose image is shown in the material as someone who is known to them.

The arrangements for such viewings may be made by the officer in charge of the relevant investigation. Although there is no requirement for the identification officer to make the arrangements or to be consulted about the arrangements, nothing prevents this. See *Notes 3AA and 3G*.

3.35  To provide safeguards against mistaken recognition and to avoid any possibility of collusion, on the occasion of the viewing, the arrangements should ensure:

(a)  that the films, photographs and other images are shown on an individual basis;

(b)  that any person who views the material;

(i)  is unable to communicate with any other individual to whom the material has been, or is to be, shown;

(ii)  is not reminded of any photograph or description of any individual whose image is shown or given any other indication as to the identity of any such individual;

(iii)  is not . . . told whether a previous witness has recognised any one;

(c)  that immediately before a person views the material, they are told that:

(i)  an individual who is known to them may, or may not, appear in the material they are shown and that if they do not recognise anyone, they should say so;

(ii)  at any point, they may ask to see a particular part of the material frozen for them to study and there is no limit on how many times they can view the whole or any part or parts of the material; and

(d)  that the person who views the material is not asked to make any decision as to whether they recognise anyone whose image they have seen as someone known to them until they have seen the whole of the material at least twice, unless the officer in charge of the viewing decides that because of the number of images the person has been invited to view, it would not be reasonable to ask them to view the whole of the material for a second time. A record of this decision must be included in the record that is made in accordance with *paragraph 3.36*. (see *Note 3G*).

3.36  A record of the circumstances and conditions under which the person is given an opportunity to recognise an individual must be made and the record must include:

(a)  whether the person knew or was given information concerning the name or identity of any suspect;

    (b)  what the person has been told *before* the viewing about the offence, the person(s) depicted in the images or the offender and by whom;

    (c)  how and by whom the witness was asked to view the image or look at the individual;

    (d)  whether the viewing was alone or with others and if with others, the reason for it;

    (e)  the arrangements under which the person viewed the film or saw the individual and by whom those arrangements were made;

    (f)  subject to *paragraph 2.18*, the name and rank of the officer responsible for deciding that the viewing arrangements should be made in accordance with this Part;

    (g)  the date time and place images were viewed or further viewed or the individual was seen;

    (h)  the times between which the images were viewed or the individual was seen;

    (i)  how the viewing of images or sighting of the individual was controlled and by whom;

    (j)  whether the person was familiar with the location shown in any images or the place where they saw the individual and if so, why;

    (k)  whether or not, on this occasion, the person claims to recognise any image shown, or any individual seen, as being someone known to them, and if they do:

        (i)  the reason;

        (ii)  the words of recognition;

        (iii)  any expressions of doubt; and

        (iv)  what features of the image or the individual triggered the recognition.

3.37  The record required under *paragraph 3.36* may be made by the person who views the image or sees the individual and makes the recognition; and if applicable, by the officer or police staff in charge of showing the images to that person or in charge of the conditions under which that person sees the individual. The person must be asked to read and check the completed record and as applicable, confirm that it is correctly and accurately reflects the part they played in the viewing (see *Note 3H*).

**Part (C)**  *Recognition by uncontrolled viewing of films, photographs and images*

3.38  This Part applies when, for the purpose of identifying and tracing suspects, films and photographs of incidents or other images are:

    (a)  shown to the public (which may include police officers and police staff as well as members of the public) through the national or local media or any social media networking site; or

    (b)  circulated through local or national police communication systems for viewing by police officers and police staff; and the viewing is not formally controlled and supervised as set out in Part B.

3.39  A copy of the relevant material released to the national or local media for showing as described in *sub-paragraph 3.38(a)*, shall be kept. The suspect or their solicitor shall be allowed to view such material before any eye-witness identification procedure under *paragraphs 3.5 to 3.10, 3.21 or 3.23* of Part A are carried out, provided it is practicable and would not unreasonably delay the investigation. This paragraph does not affect any separate requirement under the Criminal Procedure and Investigations Act 1996 to retain material in connection with criminal investigations that might apply to *sub-paragraphs 3.38(a)* and *(b)*.

3.40  Each eye-witness involved in any eye-witness identification procedure under *paragraphs 3.5 to 3.10, 3.21 or 3.23* shall be asked, *after they have taken part*, whether they have seen any film, photograph or image relating to the offence or any description of the suspect which has been broadcast or published as described in *paragraph 3.38(a)* and their reply recorded. If they have, they should be asked to give details of the circumstances and subject to the eye-witness's recollection, the record described in *paragraph 3.41* should be completed.

3.41  As soon as practicable after an individual (member of the public, police officer or police staff) indicates in response to a viewing that they may have information relating to the identity and whereabouts of anyone they have seen in that viewing, arrangements should be made to ensure that they are asked to give details of the circumstances and, subject to the individual's recollection, a record of the circumstances and conditions under which the viewing took place is made. This record shall be made in accordance with the provisions of *paragraph 3.36* insofar as they can be applied to the viewing in question (*see Note 3H*).

### Notes for Guidance

*3AA*  *The eye-witness identification procedures in Part A should not be used to test whether a witness can recognise a person as someone they know and would be able to give evidence of recognition along the lines that 'On (describe date, time, location and circumstances) I saw an image of an individual who I recognised as AB.' In these cases, the procedures in Part B shall apply if the viewing is controlled and the procedure in Part C shall apply if the viewing is not controlled.*

3ZA  *In paragraph 3.5(a)(i), examples of physical changes or differences that the identification officer may wish to consider include hair style and colour, weight, facial hair, wearing or removal of spectacles and tinted contact lenses, facial injuries, tattoos and makeup.*

3A  *Except for the provisions of Annex E, paragraph 1, a police officer who is a witness for the purposes of this part of the Code is subject to the same principles and procedures as a civilian witness.*

3B  *When an eye-witness attending an identification procedure has previously been shown photographs, or been shown or provided with computerised or artist's composite likenesses, or similar likenesses or pictures, it is the officer in charge of the investigation's responsibility to make the identification officer aware of this.*

3C  *The purpose of paragraph 3.19 is to avoid or reduce delay in arranging identification procedures by enabling the required information and warnings, see sub-paragraphs 3.17(ix) and 3.17(xii), to be given at the earliest opportunity.*

3D  *Paragraph 3.21 would apply when a known suspect becomes 'unavailable' and thereby delays or frustrates arrangements for obtaining identification evidence. It also applies when a suspect refuses or fails to take part in a video identification, an identification parade or a group identification, or refuses or fails to take part in the only practicable options from that list. It enables any suitable images of the suspect, moving or still, which are available or can be obtained, to be used in an identification procedure. Examples include images from custody and other CCTV systems and from visually recorded interview records, see Code F Note for Guidance 2D.*

3E  *When it is proposed to show photographs to a witness in accordance with Annex E, it is the responsibility of the officer in charge of the investigation to confirm to the officer responsible for supervising and directing the showing, that the first description of the suspect given by that eye-witness has been recorded. If this description has not been recorded, the procedure under Annex E must be postponed, see Annex E, paragraph 2.*

3F  *The admissibility and value of identification evidence obtained when carrying out the procedure under paragraph 3.2 may be compromised if:*
    *(a)  before a person is identified, the eye-witness' attention is specifically drawn to that person; or*
    *(b)  the suspect's identity becomes known before the procedure.*

3G  *The admissibility and value of evidence of recognition obtained when carrying out the procedures in Part B may be compromised if, before the person is recognised, the witness who has claimed to know them is given or is made, or becomes aware of, information about the person which was not previously known to them personally but which they have purported to rely on to support their claim that the person is in fact known to them.*

3H  *It is important that the record referred to in paragraphs 3.36 and 3.41 is made as soon as practicable after the viewing and whilst it is fresh in the mind of the individual who makes the recognition.*

**4**  *Identification by fingerprints and footwear impressions*

**(A)**  *Taking fingerprints in connection with a criminal investigation*

**(a)**  *General*

4.1  References to 'fingerprints' means any record, produced by any method, of the skin pattern and other physical characteristics or features of a person's:
     (i)  fingers; or
     (ii)  palms.

**(b)**  *Action*

4.2  A person's fingerprints may be taken in connection with the investigation of an offence only with their consent or if *paragraph 4.3* applies. If the person is at a police station, consent must be in writing.

4.3  PACE, section 61, provides powers to take fingerprints without consent from any person aged ten or over as follows:
     (a)  under *section 61(3)*, from a person detained at a police station in consequence of being arrested for a recordable offence, see *Note 4A*, if they have not had their fingerprints taken in the course of the investigation of the offence unless those previously taken fingerprints are not a complete set or some or all of those fingerprints are not of sufficient quality to allow satisfactory analysis, comparison or matching.
     (b)  under *section 61(4)*, from a person detained at a police station who has been charged with a recordable offence, see *Note 4A*, or informed they will be reported for such an offence if they have not had their fingerprints taken in the course of the investigation of the offence unless those previously taken fingerprints are not a complete set or some or all of those fingerprints are not of sufficient quality to allow satisfactory analysis, comparison or matching.

(c)  under *section 61(4A)*, from a person who has been bailed to appear at a court or police station if the person:

    (i)   has answered to bail for a person whose fingerprints were taken previously and there are reasonable grounds for believing they are not the same person; or

    (ii)  who has answered to bail claims to be a different person from a person whose fingerprints were previously taken;

and in either case, the court or an officer of inspector rank or above, authorises the fingerprints to be taken at the court or police station (an inspector's authority may be given in writing or orally and confirmed in writing, as soon as practicable);

(ca)  under *section 61(5A)* from a person who has been arrested for a recordable offence and released if the person:

    (i)   is on bail and has not had their fingerprints taken in the course of the investigation of the offence, or;

    (ii)  has had their fingerprints taken in the course of the investigation of the offence, but they do not constitute a complete set or some, or all, of the fingerprints are not of sufficient quality to allow satisfactory analysis, comparison or matching.

(cb)  under *section 61(5B)* from a person not detained at a police station who has been charged with a recordable offence or informed they will be reported for such an offence if:

    (i)   they have not had their fingerprints taken in the course of the investigation; or

    (ii)  their fingerprints have been taken in the course of the investigation of the offence but either:

        • they do not constitute a complete set or some, or all, of the fingerprints are not of sufficient quality to allow satisfactory analysis, comparison or matching; or

        • the investigation was discontinued but subsequently resumed and, before the resumption, their fingerprints were destroyed pursuant to section 63D(3).

(d)  under *section 61(6)*, from a person who has been:

    (i)   convicted of a recordable offence; or

    (ii)  given a caution in respect of a recordable offence (see *Note 4A*) which, at the time of the caution, the person admitted;

      if, since being convicted or cautioned:

        • their fingerprints have not been taken; or

        • their fingerprints which have been taken do not constitute a complete set or some, or all, of the fingerprints are not of sufficient quality to allow satisfactory analysis, comparison or matching;

and in either case, an officer of inspector rank or above is satisfied that taking the fingerprints is necessary to assist in the prevention or detection of crime and authorises the taking;

(e)  under *section 61(6A)* from a person a constable reasonably suspects is committing or attempting to commit, or has committed or attempted to commit, any offence if either:

    (i)   the person's name is unknown to, and cannot be readily ascertained by, the constable; or

    (ii)  the constable has reasonable grounds for doubting whether a name given by the person as their name is their real name.

Note: fingerprints taken under this power are not regarded as having been taken in the course of the investigation of an offence. [See *Note 4C*]

(f)  under *section 61(6D)* from a person who has been convicted outside England and Wales of an offence which if committed in England and Wales would be a qualifying offence as defined by PACE, section 65A (see *Note 4AB*) if:

    (i)   the person's fingerprints have not been taken previously under this power or their fingerprints have been so taken on a previous occasion but they do not constitute a complete set or some, or all, of the fingerprints are not of sufficient quality to allow satisfactory analysis, comparison or matching; and

    (ii)  a police officer of inspector rank or above is satisfied that taking fingerprints is necessary to assist in the prevention or detection of crime and authorises them to be taken.

4.4  PACE, section 63A(4) and Schedule 2A provide powers to:

(a)  make a requirement (in accordance with *Annex G*) for a person to attend a police station to have their fingerprints taken in the exercise of one of the following powers (described in *paragraph 4.3* above) within certain periods as follows:

    (i)   *section 61(5A)* – Persons arrested for a recordable offence and released, see *paragraph 4.3(ca)*: In the case of a person whose fingerprints were taken in the course of the investigation but those fingerprints do not constitute a complete set or some, or all, of the fingerprints are not of sufficient quality, the requirement may not be made more than six months from the day the investigating officer was informed that the fingerprints previously taken were incomplete or below standard. In the case of a person whose fingerprints were destroyed prior to the resumption of the investigation, the requirement may not be made more than six months from the day on which the investigation resumed.

(ii) *section 61(5B)* – Persons not detained at a police station charged etc. with a recordable offence, see *paragraph 4.3(cb)*: The requirement may not be made more than six months from:

- the day the person was charged or informed that they would be reported,
- if fingerprints have not been taken in the course of the investigation of the offence; or
- the day the investigating officer was informed that the fingerprints previously taken were incomplete or below standard, if fingerprints have been taken in the course of the investigation but those fingerprints do not constitute a complete set or some, or all, of the fingerprints are not of sufficient quality; or
- the day on which the investigation was resumed, in the case of a person whose fingerprints were destroyed prior to the resumption of the investigation.

(iii) *section 61(6)* – Persons convicted or cautioned for a recordable offence in England and Wales, see *paragraph 4.3(d)*: Where the offence for which the person was convicted or cautioned is a qualifying offence (see *Note 4AB*), there is no time limit for the exercise of this power. Where the conviction or caution is for a recordable offence which is not a qualifying offence, the requirement may not be made more than two years from:

- in the case of a person who has not had their fingerprints taken since the conviction or caution, the day on which the person was convicted or cautioned, or, if later, the day on which Schedule 2A came into force (March 7, 2011), ; or
- in the case of a person whose fingerprints have been taken in the course of the investigation but those fingerprints do not constitute a complete set or some, or all, of the fingerprints are not of sufficient quality, the day on which an officer from the force investigating the offence was informed that the fingerprints previously taken were incomplete or below standard, or, if later, the day on which Schedule 2A came into force (March 7, 2011).

(iv) *section 61(6D)* – A person who has been convicted of a qualifying offence (see *Note 4AB*) outside England and Wales, see *paragraph 4.3(g)*: There is no time limit for making the requirement.

Note: A person who has had their fingerprints taken under any of the powers in section 61 mentioned in *paragraph 4.3* on two occasions in relation to any offence may not be required under Schedule 2A to attend a police station for their fingerprints to be taken again under section 61 in relation to that offence, unless authorised by an officer of inspector rank or above. The fact of the authorisation and the reasons for giving it must be recorded as soon as practicable.

(b) arrest, without warrant, a person who fails to comply with the requirement.

4.5 A person's fingerprints may be taken, as above, electronically.

4.6 Reasonable force may be used, if necessary, to take a person's fingerprints without their consent under the powers as in *paragraphs 4.3* and *4.4*.

4.7 Before any fingerprints are taken:

(a) without consent under any power mentioned in *paragraphs 4.3* and *4.4* above, the person must be informed of:

(i) the reason their fingerprints are to be taken;

(ii) the power under which they are to be taken; and

(iii) the fact that the relevant authority has been given if any power mentioned in *paragraph 4.3(c)*, *(d)* or *(f)* applies

(b) with or without consent at a police station or elsewhere, the person must be informed:

(i) that their fingerprints may be subject of a speculative search against other fingerprints, see *Note 4B*; and

(ii) that their fingerprints may be retained in accordance with *Annex F, Part (a)* unless they were taken under the power mentioned in *paragraph 4.3(e)* when they must be destroyed after they have being checked (see *Note 4C*).

*(c) Documentation*

4.8A A record must be made as soon as practicable after the fingerprints are taken, of:

- the matters in *paragraph 4.7(a)(i)* to *(iii)* and the fact that the person has been informed of those matters; and
- the fact that the person has been informed of the matters in *paragraph 4.7(b)(i)* and *(ii)*.

The record must be made in the person's custody record if they are detained at a police station when the fingerprints are taken.

4.8  If force is used, a record shall be made of the circumstances and those present.

4.9  *Not used*

**(B)** *Not used*

4.10  *Not used*
4.11  *Not used*
4.12  *Not used*
4.13  *Not used*
4.14  *Not used*
4.15  *Not used*

**(C)** *Taking footwear impressions in connection with a criminal investigation*

*(a) Action*

4.16  Impressions of a person's footwear may be taken in connection with the investigation of an offence only with their consent or if *paragraph 4.17* applies. If the person is at a police station consent must be in writing.

4.17  PACE, section 61A, provides power for a police officer to take footwear impressions without consent from any person over the age of ten years who is detained at a police station:

(a)  in consequence of being arrested for a recordable offence, see *Note 4A*; or if the detainee has been charged with a recordable offence, or informed they will be reported for such an offence; and

(b)  the detainee has not had an impression of their footwear taken in the course of the investigation of the offence unless the previously taken impression is not complete or is not of sufficient quality to allow satisfactory analysis, comparison or matching (whether in the case in question or generally).

4.18  Reasonable force may be used, if necessary, to take a footwear impression from a detainee without consent under the power in *paragraph 4.17*.

4.19  Before any footwear impression is taken with, or without, consent as above, the person must be informed:

(a)  of the reason the impression is to be taken;

(b)  that the impression may be retained and may be subject of a speculative search against other impressions, see *Note 4B*, unless destruction of the impression is required in accordance with *Annex F, Part B*.

*(b) Documentation*

4.20  A record must be made, as soon as possible, of the reason for taking a person's footwear impressions without consent. If force is used, a record shall be made of the circumstances and those present.

4.21  A record shall be made when a person has been informed under the terms of *paragraph 4.19(b)*, of the possibility that their footwear impressions may be subject of a speculative search.

### Notes for Guidance

4A  *References to 'recordable offences' in this Code relate to those offences for which convictions or cautions may be recorded in national police records. See PACE, section 27(4). The recordable offences current at the time when this Code was prepared, are any offences which carry a sentence of imprisonment on conviction (irrespective of the period, or the age of the offender or actual sentence passed) as well as the non-imprisonable offences under the Vagrancy Act 1824 sections 3 and 4 (begging and persistent begging), the Street Offences Act 1959, section 1 (loitering or soliciting for purposes of prostitution), the Road Traffic Act 1988, section 25 (tampering with motor vehicles), the Criminal Justice and Public Order Act 1994, section 167 (touting for hire car services) and others listed in the National Police Records (Recordable Offences) Regulations 2000 as amended.*

4AB  *A qualifying offence is one of the offences specified in PACE, section 65A. These include offences which involve the use or threat of violence or unlawful force against persons, sexual offences, offences against children and other offences, for example:*
- *murder, false imprisonment, kidnapping contrary to Common law*

- *manslaughter, conspiracy to murder, threats to kill, wounding with intent to cause grievous bodily harm (GBH), causing GBH and assault occasioning actual bodily harm contrary to the Offences Against the Person Act 1861;*
- *criminal possession or use of firearms contrary to sections 16 to 18 of the Firearms Act 1968;*
- *robbery, burglary and aggravated burglary contrary to sections 8, 9 or 10 of the Theft Act 1968 or an offence under section 12A of that Act involving an accident which caused a person's death;*
- *criminal damage required to be charged as arson contrary to section 1 of the Criminal Damage Act 1971;*
- *taking, possessing and showing indecent photographs of children contrary to section 1 of the Protection of Children Act 1978;*
- *rape, sexual assault, child sex offences, exposure and other offences contrary to the Sexual Offences Act 2003.*

4B     *Fingerprints, footwear impressions or a DNA sample (and the information derived from it) taken from a person arrested on suspicion of being involved in a recordable offence, or charged with such an offence, or informed they will be reported for such an offence, may be subject of a speculative search. This means the fingerprints, footwear impressions or DNA sample may be checked against other fingerprints, footwear impressions and DNA records held by, or on behalf of, the police and other law enforcement authorities in, or outside, the UK, or held in connection with, or as a result of, an investigation of an offence inside or outside the UK.*

4C     *The power under section 61(6A) of PACE described in paragraph 4.3(e) allows fingerprints of a suspect who has not been arrested, and whose name is not known or cannot be ascertained, or who gave a doubtful name, to be taken in connection with any offence (whether recordable or not) using a mobile device and then checked on the street against the database containing the national fingerprint collection. Fingerprints taken under this power cannot be retained after they have been checked. The results may make an arrest for the suspected offence based on the name condition unnecessary (see Code G, paragraph 2.9(a)) and enable the offence to be disposed of without arrest, for example, by summons/charging by post, penalty notice or words of advice. If arrest for a non-recordable offence is necessary for any other reasons, this power may also be exercised at the station. Before the power is exercised, the officer should:*
- *inform the person of the nature of the suspected offence and why they are suspected of committing it.*
- *give them a reasonable opportunity to establish their real name before deciding that their name is unknown and cannot be readily ascertained or that there are reasonable grounds to doubt that a name they have given is their real name.*
- *as applicable, inform the person of the reason why their name is not known and cannot be readily ascertained or of the grounds for doubting that a name they have given is their real name, including, for example, the reason why a particular document the person has produced to verify their real name, is not sufficient.*

4D     *Not used.*

5 *Examinations to establish identity and the taking of photographs*

**(A)** *Detainees at police stations*

*(a) Searching or examination of detainees at police stations*

5.1    PACE, section 54A(1), allows a detainee at a police station to be searched or examined or both, to establish:
       (a) whether they have any marks, features or injuries that would tend to identify them as a person involved in the commission of an offence and to photograph any identifying marks, see *paragraph 5.5*; or
       (b) their identity, see *Note 5A*.
       A person detained at a police station to be searched under a stop and search power, see Code A, is not a detainee for the purposes of these powers.

5.2    A search and/or examination to find marks under section 54A(1)(a) may be carried out without the detainee's consent, see *paragraph 2.12*, only if authorised by an officer of at least inspector rank when consent has been withheld or it is not practicable to obtain consent, see *Note 5D*.

5.3    A search or examination to establish a suspect's identity under section 54A (1) (b) may be carried out without the detainee's consent, see *paragraph 2.12*, only if authorised by an officer of at least inspector rank when the detainee has refused to identify themselves or the authorising officer has reasonable grounds for suspecting the person is not who they claim to be.

5.4    Any marks that assist in establishing the detainee's identity, or their identification as a person involved in the commission of an offence, are identifying marks. Such marks may be photographed with the detainee's consent, see *paragraph 2.12*; or without their consent if it is withheld or it is not practicable to obtain it, see *Note 5D*.

5.5 A detainee may only be searched, examined and photographed under section 54A, by a police officer of the same sex.

5.6 Any photographs of identifying marks, taken under section 54A, may be used or disclosed only for purposes related to the prevention or detection of crime, the investigation of offences or the conduct of prosecutions by, or on behalf of, police or other law enforcement and prosecuting authorities inside, and outside, the UK. After being so used or disclosed, the photograph may be retained but must not be used or disclosed except for these purposes, see *Note 5B*.

5.7 The powers, as in *paragraph 5.1*, do not affect any separate requirement under the Criminal Procedure and Investigations Act 1996 to retain material in connection with criminal investigations.

5.8 Authority for the search and/or examination for the purposes of *paragraphs 5.2* and *5.3* may be given orally or in writing. If given orally, the authorising officer must confirm it in writing as soon as practicable. A separate authority is required for each purpose which applies.

5.9 If it is established a person is unwilling to co-operate sufficiently to enable a search and/or examination to take place or a suitable photograph to be taken, an officer may use reasonable force to:
(a) search and/or examine a detainee without their consent; and
(b) photograph any identifying marks without their consent.

5.10 The thoroughness and extent of any search or examination carried out in accordance with the powers in section 54A must be no more than the officer considers necessary to achieve the required purpose. Any search or examination which involves the removal of more than the person's outer clothing shall be conducted in accordance with Code C, *Annex A, paragraph 11*.

5.11 An intimate search may not be carried out under the powers in section 54A.

*(b) Photographing detainees at police stations and other persons elsewhere than at a police station*

5.12 Under PACE, section 64A, an officer may photograph:
(a) any person whilst they are detained at a police station; and
(b) any person who is elsewhere than at a police station and who has been:
(i) arrested by a constable for an offence;
(ii) taken into custody by a constable after being arrested for an offence by a person other than a constable;
(iii) made subject to a requirement to wait with a community support officer under paragraph 2(3) or (3B) of Schedule 4 to the Police Reform Act 2002;
(iiia) given a direction by a constable under section 27 of the Violent Crime Reduction Act 2006.
(iv) given a penalty notice by a constable in uniform under Chapter 1 of Part 1 of the Criminal Justice and Police Act 2001, a penalty notice by a constable under section 444A of the Education Act 1996, or a fixed penalty notice by a constable in uniform under section 54 of the Road Traffic Offenders Act 1988;
(v) given a notice in relation to a relevant fixed penalty offence (within the meaning of paragraph 1 of Schedule 4 to the Police Reform Act 2002) by a community support officer by virtue of a designation applying that paragraph to him;
(vi) given a notice in relation to a relevant fixed penalty offence (within the meaning of paragraph 1 of Schedule 5 to the Police Reform Act 2002) by an accredited person by virtue of accreditation specifying that that paragraph applies to him; or
(vii) given a direction to leave and not return to a specified location for up to 48 hours by a police constable (under section 27 of the Violent Crime Reduction Act 2006).

5.12A Photographs taken under PACE, section 64A:
(a) may be taken with the person's consent, or without their consent if consent is withheld or it is not practicable to obtain their consent, see *Note 5E*; and
(b) may be used or disclosed only for purposes related to the prevention or detection of crime, the investigation of offences or the conduct of prosecutions by, or on behalf of, police or other law enforcement and prosecuting authorities inside and outside the United Kingdom or the enforcement of any sentence or order made by a court when dealing with an offence. After being so used or disclosed, they may be retained but can only be used or disclosed for the same purposes. See *Note 5B*.

5.13 The officer proposing to take a detainee's photograph may, for this purpose, require the person to remove any item or substance worn on, or over, all, or any part of, their head or face. If they do not comply with such a requirement, the officer may remove the item or substance.

5.14 If it is established the detainee is unwilling to co-operate sufficiently to enable a suitable photograph to be taken and it is not reasonably practicable to take the photograph covertly, an officer may use reasonable force, see *Note 5F.*

(a) to take their photograph without their consent; and

(b) for the purpose of taking the photograph, remove any item or substance worn on, or over, all, or any part of, the person's head or face which they have failed to remove when asked.

5.15 For the purposes of this Code, a photograph may be obtained without the person's consent by making a copy of an image of them taken at any time on a camera system installed anywhere in the police station.

*(c) Information to be given*

5.16 When a person is searched, examined or photographed under the provisions as in *paragraph 5.1* and *5.12*, or their photograph obtained as in *paragraph 5.15*, they must be informed of the:

(a) purpose of the search, examination or photograph;

(b) grounds on which the relevant authority, if applicable, has been given; and

(c) purposes for which the photograph may be used, disclosed or retained. This information must be given before the search or examination commences or the photograph is taken, except if the photograph is:

(i) to be taken covertly;

(ii) obtained as in *paragraph 5.15*, in which case the person must be informed as soon as practicable after the photograph is taken or obtained.

*(d) Documentation*

5.17 A record must be made when a detainee is searched, examined, or a photograph of the person, or any identifying marks found on them, are taken. The record must include the:

(a) identity, subject to *paragraph 2.18*, of the officer carrying out the search, examination or taking the photograph;

(b) purpose of the search, examination or photograph and the outcome;

(c) detainee's consent to the search, examination or photograph, or the reason the person was searched, examined or photographed without consent;

(d) giving of any authority as in *paragraphs 5.2* and *5.3*, the grounds for giving it and the authorising officer.

5.18 If force is used when searching, examining or taking a photograph in accordance with this section, a record shall be made of the circumstances and those present.

**(B)** *Persons at police stations not detained*

5.19 When there are reasonable grounds for suspecting the involvement of a person in a criminal offence, but that person is at a police station **voluntarily** and not detained, the provisions of *paragraphs 5.1* to *5.18* should apply, subject to the modifications in the following paragraphs.

5.20 References to the 'person being detained' and to the powers mentioned in *paragraph 5.1* which apply only to detainees at police stations shall be omitted.

5.21 Force may not be used to:

(a) search and/or examine the person to:

(i) discover whether they have any marks that would tend to identify them as a person involved in the commission of an offence; or

(ii) establish their identity, see *Note 5A*;

(b) take photographs of any identifying marks, see *paragraph 5.4*; or

(c) take a photograph of the person.

5.22 Subject to *paragraph 5.24*, the photographs of persons or of their identifying marks which are not taken in accordance with the provisions mentioned in *paragraphs 5.1* or *5.12*, must be destroyed (together with any negatives and copies) unless the person:

(a) is charged with, or informed they may be prosecuted for, a recordable offence;

(b) is prosecuted for a recordable offence;

(c) is cautioned for a recordable offence or given a warning or reprimand in accordance with the Crime and Disorder Act 1998 for a recordable offence; or

(d) gives informed consent, in writing, for the photograph or image to be retained as in *paragraph 5.6*.

5.23 When *paragraph 5.22* requires the destruction of any photograph, the person must be given an opportunity to witness the destruction or to have a certificate confirming the destruction provided they so request the certificate within five days of being informed the destruction is required.

5.24 Nothing in *paragraph 5.22* affects any separate requirement under the Criminal Procedure and Investigations Act 1996 to retain material in connection with criminal investigations.

*Notes for Guidance*

5A   The conditions under which fingerprints may be taken to assist in establishing a person's identity, are described in Section 4.

5B   Examples of purposes related to the prevention or detection of crime, the investigation of offences or the conduct of prosecutions include:

(a)   checking the photograph against other photographs held in records or in connection with, or as a result of, an investigation of an offence to establish whether the person is liable to arrest for other offences;

(b)   when the person is arrested at the same time as other people, or at a time when it is likely that other people will be arrested, using the photograph to help establish who was arrested, at what time and where;

(c)   when the real identity of the person is not known and cannot be readily ascertained or there are reasonable grounds for doubting a name and other personal details given by the person, are their real name and personal details. In these circumstances, using or disclosing the photograph to help to establish or verify their real identity or determine whether they are liable to arrest for some other offence, e.g. by checking it against other photographs held in records or in connection with, or as a result of, an investigation of an offence;

(d)   when it appears any identification procedure in section 3 may need to be arranged for which the person's photograph would assist;

(e)   when the person's release without charge may be required, and if the release is:

(i)   on bail to appear at a police station, using the photograph to help verify the person's identity when they answer their bail and if the person does not answer their bail, to assist in arresting them; or

(ii)   without bail, using the photograph to help verify their identity or assist in locating them for the purposes of serving them with a summons to appear at court in criminal proceedings;

(f)   when the person has answered to bail at a police station and there are reasonable grounds for doubting they are the person who was previously granted bail, using the photograph to help establish or verify their identity;

(g)   when the person arrested on a warrant claims to be a different person from the person named on the warrant and a photograph would help to confirm or disprove their claim;

(h)   when the person has been charged with, reported for, or convicted of, a recordable offence and their photograph is not already on record as a result of (a) to (f) or their photograph is on record but their appearance has changed since it was taken and the person has not yet been released or brought before a court.

5C   There is no power to arrest a person convicted of a recordable offence solely to take their photograph. The power to take photographs in this section applies only where the person is in custody as a result of the exercise of another power, e.g. arrest for fingerprinting under PACE, Schedule 2A, paragraph 17.

5D   Examples of when it would not be practicable to obtain a detainee's consent, see paragraph 2.12, to a search, examination or the taking of a photograph of an identifying mark include:

(a)   when the person is drunk or otherwise unfit to give consent;

(b)   when there are reasonable grounds to suspect that if the person became aware a search or examination was to take place or an identifying mark was to be photographed, they would take steps to prevent this happening, e.g. by violently resisting, covering or concealing the mark etc and it would not otherwise be possible to carry out the search or examination or to photograph any identifying mark;

(c)   in the case of a juvenile, if the parent or guardian cannot be contacted in sufficient time to allow the search or examination to be carried out or the photograph to be taken.

5E   Examples of when it would not be practicable to obtain the person's consent, see paragraph 2.12, to a photograph being taken include:

(a)   when the person is drunk or otherwise unfit to give consent;

(b)   when there are reasonable grounds to suspect that if the person became aware a photograph, suitable to be used or disclosed for the use and disclosure described in paragraph 5.6, was to be taken, they would take steps to prevent it being taken, e.g. by violently resisting, covering or distorting their face etc, and it would not otherwise be possible to take a suitable photograph;

(c)   when, in order to obtain a suitable photograph, it is necessary to take it covertly; and

(d)  *in the case of a juvenile, if the parent or guardian cannot be contacted in sufficient time to allow the photograph to be taken.*

5F    *The use of reasonable force to take the photograph of a suspect elsewhere than at a police station must be carefully considered. In order to obtain a suspect's consent and cooperation to remove an item of religious headwear to take their photograph, a constable should consider whether in the circumstances of the situation the removal of the headwear and the taking of the photograph should be by an officer of the same sex as the person. It would be appropriate for these actions to be conducted out of public view (see paragraph 1.1 and Note 1A).*

**6** *Identification by body samples and impressions*

**(A)** *General*

6.1   References to:

(a)  an 'intimate sample' mean a dental impression or sample of blood, semen or any other tissue fluid, urine, or pubic hair, or a swab taken from any part of a person's genitals or from a person's body orifice other than the mouth;

(b)  a 'non-intimate sample' means:

(i)   a sample of hair, other than pubic hair, which includes hair plucked with the root, see *Note 6A*;

(ii)  a sample taken from a nail or from under a nail;

(iii) a swab taken from any part of a person's body other than a part from which a swab taken would be an intimate sample;

(iv)  saliva;

(v)   a skin impression which means any record, other than a fingerprint, which is a record, in any form and produced by any method, of the skin pattern and other physical characteristics or features of the whole, or any part of, a person's foot or of any other part of their body.

**(B)** *Action*

*(a) Intimate samples*

6.2   PACE, section 62, provides that intimate samples may be taken under:

(a)  section 62(1), from a person in police detention only:

(i)   if a police officer of inspector rank or above has reasonable grounds to believe such an impression or sample will tend to confirm or disprove the suspect's involvement in a recordable offence, see *Note 4A*, and gives authorisation for a sample to be taken; and

(ii)  with the suspect's written consent;

(b)  section 62(1A), from a person not in police detention but from whom two or more non-intimate samples have been taken in the course of an investigation of an offence and the samples, though suitable, have proved insufficient if:

(i)   a police officer of inspector rank or above authorises it to be taken; and

(ii)  the person concerned gives their written consent. See *Notes 6B* and *6C*.

(c)  section 62(2A), from a person convicted outside England and Wales of an offence which if committed in England and Wales would be qualifying offence as defined by PACE, section 65A (see *Note 4AB*) from whom two or more non-intimate samples taken under section 63(3E) (see *paragraph 6.6(h)* have proved insufficient if:

(i)   a police officer of inspector rank or above is satisfied that taking the sample is necessary to assist in the prevention or detection of crime and authorises it to be taken; and

(ii)  the person concerned gives their written consent.

6.2A  PACE, section 63A(4) and Schedule 2A provide powers to:

(a)  make a requirement (in accordance with *Annex G*) for a person to attend a police station to have an intimate sample taken in the exercise of one of the following powers (see *paragraph 6.2*):

(i)   *section 62(1A)* – Persons from whom two or more non-intimate samples have been taken and proved to be insufficient, see *paragraph 6.2(b)*: There is no time limit for making the requirement.

(ii)  *section 62(2A)* – Persons convicted outside England and Wales from whom two or more non-intimate samples taken under section 63(3E) (see *paragraph 6.6(g)* have proved insufficient, see *paragraph 6.2(c)*: There is no time limit for making the requirement.

(b)  arrest without warrant a person who fails to comply with the requirement.

6.3   Before a suspect is asked to provide an intimate sample, they must be:

(a)  informed:

(i) of the reason, including the nature of the suspected offence (except if taken under *paragraph 6.2(c)* from a person convicted outside England and Wales.

(ii) that authorisation has been given and the provisions under which given;

(iii) that a sample taken at a police station may be subject of a speculative search;

(b) warned that if they refuse without good cause their refusal may harm their case if it comes to trial, see *Note 6D*. If the suspect is in police detention and not legally represented, they must also be reminded of their entitlement to have free legal advice, see Code C, *paragraph 6.5*, and the reminder noted in the custody record. If *paragraph 6.2(b)* applies and the person is attending a station voluntarily, their entitlement to free legal advice as in Code C, *paragraph 3.21* shall be explained to them.

6.4 Dental impressions may only be taken by a registered dentist. Other intimate samples, except for samples of urine, may only be taken by a registered medical practitioner or registered nurse or registered paramedic.

*(b) Non-intimate samples*

6.5 A non-intimate sample may be taken from a detainee only with their written consent or if *paragraph 6.6* applies.

6.6 A non-intimate sample may be taken from a person without the appropriate consent in the following circumstances:

(a) under *section 63(2A)* from a person who is in police detention as a consequence of being arrested for a recordable offence and who has not had a non-intimate sample of the same type and from the same part of the body taken in the course of the investigation of the offence by the police or they have had such a sample taken but it proved insufficient.

(b) Under *section 63(3)* from a person who is being held in custody by the police on the authority of a court if an officer of at least the rank of inspector authorises it to be taken. An authorisation may be given:

(i) if the authorising officer has reasonable grounds for suspecting the person of involvement in a recordable offence and for believing that the sample will tend to confirm or disprove that involvement, and

(ii) in writing or orally and confirmed in writing, as soon as practicable; but an authorisation may not be given to take from the same part of the body a further non-intimate sample consisting of a skin impression unless the previously taken impression proved insufficient

(c) under *section 63(3ZA)* from a person who has been arrested for a recordable offence and released if:

(i) in the case of a person who is on bail, they have not had a sample of the same type and from the same part of the body taken in the course of the investigation of the offence, or;

(ii) in any case, the person has had such a sample taken in the course of the investigation of the offence, but either:
 • it was not suitable or proved insufficient; or
 • the investigation was discontinued but subsequently resumed and before the resumption, any DNA profile derived from the sample was destroyed and the sample itself was destroyed pursuant to section 63R(4), (5) or (12).

(d) under *section 63(3A)*, from a person (whether or not in police detention or held in custody by the police on the authority of a court) who has been charged with a recordable offence or informed they will be reported for such an offence if the person:

(i) has not had a non-intimate sample taken from them in the course of the investigation of the offence; or

(ii) has had a sample so taken, but it was not suitable or proved insufficient, see *Note 6B*; or

(iii) has had a sample taken in the course of the investigation of the offence and the sample has been destroyed and in proceedings relating to that offence there is a dispute as to whether a DNA profile relevant to the proceedings was derived from the destroyed sample.

(e) under *section 63(3B)*, from a person who has been:

(i) convicted of a recordable offence; or

(ii) given a caution in respect of a recordable offence which, at the time of the caution, the person admitted;

if, since their conviction or caution a non-intimate sample has not been taken from them or a sample which has been taken since then was not suitable or proved insufficient and in either case, an officer of inspector rank or above, is satisfied that taking the fingerprints is necessary to assist in the prevention or detection of crime and authorises the taking;

(f)    under *section 63(3C)* from a person to whom section 2 of the Criminal Evidence (Amendment) Act 1997 applies (persons detained following acquittal on grounds of insanity or finding of unfitness to plead).

(g)    under *section 63(3E)* from a person who has been convicted outside England and Wales of an offence which if committed in England and Wales would be a qualifying offence as defined by PACE, section 65A (see *Note 4AB*) if:

     (i)    a non-intimate sample has not been taken previously under this power or unless a sample was so taken but was not suitable or proved insufficient; and

     (ii)    a police officer of inspector rank or above is satisfied that taking a sample is necessary to assist in the prevention or detection of crime and authorises it to be taken.

6.6A   PACE, *section 63A(4)* and *Schedule 2A* provide powers to:

(a)    make a requirement (in accordance with *Annex G*) for a person to attend a police station to have a non-intimate sample taken in the exercise of one of the following powers (see *paragraph 6.6* above) within certain time limits as follows:

     (i)    *section 63(3ZA)* – Persons arrested for a recordable offence and released, see *paragraph 6.6(c)*: In the case of a person from whom a non-intimate sample was taken in the course of the investigation but that sample was not suitable or proved insufficient, the requirement may not be made more than six months from the day the investigating officer was informed that the sample previously taken was not suitable or proved insufficient. In the case of a person whose DNA profile and sample was destroyed prior to the resumption of the investigation, the requirement may not be made more than six months from the day on which the investigation resumed.

     (ii)    *section 63(3A)* – Persons charged etc. with a recordable offence, see *paragraph 6.6(d)*: The requirement may not be made more than six months from:

- the day the person was charged or informed that they would be reported, if a sample has not been taken in the course of the investigation;
- the day the investigating officer was informed that the sample previously taken was not suitable or proved insufficient, if a sample has been taken in the course of the investigation but the sample was not suitable or proved insufficient; or
- the day on which the investigation was resumed, in the case of a person whose DNA profile and sample were destroyed prior to the resumption of the investigation.

     (iii)    *section 63(3B)* – Person convicted or cautioned for a recordable offence in England and Wales, see *paragraph 6.6(e)*: Where the offence for which the person was convicted etc. is also a qualifying offence (see *Note 4AB*), there is no time limit for the exercise of this power. Where the conviction etc. was for a recordable offence that is not a qualifying offence, the requirement may not be made more than two years from:

- in the case of a person whose sample has not been taken since they were convicted or cautioned, the day the person was convicted or cautioned, or, if later. the day Schedule 2A came into force (March 7 2011); or
- in the case of a person whose sample has been taken but was not suitable or proved insufficient, the day an officer from the force investigating the offence was informed that the sample previously taken was not suitable or proved insufficient or, if later, the day Schedule 2A came into force (March 7 2011).

     (iv)    *section 63(3E)* – A person who has been convicted of qualifying offence (see *Note 4AB*) outside England and Wales, see *paragraph 6.6(h)*: There is no time limit for making the requirement.

Note: A person who has had a non-intimate sample taken under any of the powers in section 63 mentioned in *paragraph 6.6* on two occasions in relation to any offence may not be required under Schedule 2A to attend a police station for a sample to be taken again under section 63 in relation to that offence, unless authorised by an officer of inspector rank or above. The fact of the authorisation and the reasons for giving it must be recorded as soon as practicable.

(b)    arrest, without warrant, a person who fails to comply with the requirement.

6.7   Reasonable force may be used, if necessary, to take a non-intimate sample from a person without their consent under the powers mentioned in *paragraph 6.6*.

6.8   Before any non-intimate sample is taken:

(a)    without consent under any power mentioned in *paragraphs 6.6* and *6.6A*, the person must be informed of:

     (i)    the reason for taking the sample;

     (ii)    the power under which the sample is to be taken;

(iii)   the fact that the relevant authority has been given if any power mentioned in *paragraph 6.6(b)*, *(e)* or *(g)* applies, including the nature of the suspected offence (except if taken under *paragraph 6.6(e)* from a person convicted or cautioned, or under *paragraph 6.6(g)* if taken from a person convicted outside England and Wales;

(b)   with or without consent at a police station or elsewhere, the person must be informed:

(i)   that their sample or information derived from it may be subject of a speculative search against other samples and information derived from them, see *Note 6E*, and

(ii)   that their sample and the information derived from it may be retained in accordance with *Annex F*, Part (a).

*(c)  Removal of clothing*

6.9   When clothing needs to be removed in circumstances likely to cause embarrassment to the person, no person of the opposite sex who is not a registered medical practitioner or registered health care professional shall be present, (unless in the case of a juvenile, mentally disordered or mentally vulnerable person, that person specifically requests the presence of an appropriate adult of the opposite sex who is readily available) nor shall anyone whose presence is unnecessary. However, in the case of a juvenile, this is subject to the overriding proviso that such a removal of clothing may take place in the absence of the appropriate adult only if the juvenile signifies in their presence, that they prefer the adult's absence and they agree.

*(c)  Documentation*

6.10   A record must be made as soon as practicable after the sample is taken of:
- The matters in *paragraph 6.8(a)(i)* to *(iii)* and the fact that the person has been informed of those matters; and
- The fact that the person has been informed of the matters in *paragraph 6.8(b)(i)* and *(ii)*.

6.10A   If force is used, a record shall be made of the circumstances and those present.

6.11   A record must be made of a warning given as required by *paragraph 6.3*.

6.12   *Not used*

*Notes for Guidance*

6A   *When hair samples are taken for the purpose of DNA analysis (rather than for other purposes such as making a visual match), the suspect should be permitted a reasonable choice as to what part of the body the hairs are taken from. When hairs are plucked, they should be plucked individually, unless the suspect prefers otherwise and no more should be plucked than the person taking them reasonably considers necessary for a sufficient sample.*

6B   *(a)  An insufficient sample is one which is not sufficient either in quantity or quality to provide information for a particular form of analysis, such as DNA analysis. A sample may also be insufficient if enough information cannot be obtained from it by analysis because of loss, destruction, damage or contamination of the sample or as a result of an earlier, unsuccessful attempt at analysis.*

*(b)  An unsuitable sample is one which, by its nature, is not suitable for a particular form of analysis.*

6C   *Nothing in paragraph 6.2 prevents intimate samples being taken for elimination purposes with the consent of the person concerned but the provisions of paragraph 2.12 relating to the role of the appropriate adult, should be applied. Paragraph 6.2(b) does not, however, apply where the non-intimate samples were previously taken under the Terrorism Act 2000, Schedule 8, paragraph 10.*

6D   *In warning a person who is asked to provide an intimate sample as in paragraph 6.3, the following form of words may be used:*

*'You do not have to provide this sample/allow this swab or impression to be taken, but I must warn you that if you refuse without good cause, your refusal may harm your case if it comes to trial.'*

6E   *Fingerprints or a DNA sample and the information derived from it taken from a person arrested on suspicion of being involved in a recordable offence, or charged with such an offence, or informed they will be reported for such an offence, may be subject of a speculative search. This means they may be checked against other fingerprints and DNA records held by, or on behalf of, the police and other law enforcement authorities in or outside the UK or held in connection with, or as a result of, an investigation of an offence inside or outside the UK.*

*See Annex F regarding the retention and use of fingerprints and samples taken with consent for elimination purposes.*

6F   *Samples of urine and non-intimate samples taken in accordance with sections 63B and 63C of PACE may not be used for identification purposes in accordance with this Code. See Code C Note for guidance 17D.*

## Annex A

### Video Identification

*(a) General*

1. The arrangements for obtaining and ensuring the availability of a suitable set of images to be used in a video identification must be the responsibility of an identification officer (see *paragraph 3.11* of this Code) who has no direct involvement with the case.

2. The set of images must include the suspect and at least eight other people who, so far as possible, and subject to *paragraph 7*, resemble the suspect in age, general appearance and position in life. Only one suspect shall appear in any set unless there are two suspects of roughly similar appearance, in which case they may be shown together with at least twelve other people.

2A If the suspect has an unusual physical feature, e.g., a facial scar, tattoo or distinctive hairstyle or hair colour which does not appear on the images of the other people that are available to be used, steps may be taken to:
   (a)  conceal the location of the feature on the images of the suspect and the other people; or
   (b)  replicate that feature on the images of the other people.
   For these purposes, the feature may be concealed or replicated electronically or by any other method which it is practicable to use to ensure that the images of the suspect and other people resemble each other. The identification officer has discretion to choose whether to conceal or replicate the feature and the method to be used.

2B If the identification officer decides that a feature should be concealed or replicated, the reason for the decision and whether the feature was concealed or replicated in the images shown to any eye-witness shall be recorded.

2C If the eye-witness requests to view any image where an unusual physical feature has been concealed or replicated without the feature being concealed or replicated, the identification officer has discretion to allow the eye-witness to view such image(s) if they are available.

3. The images used to conduct a video identification shall, as far as possible, show the suspect and other people in the same positions or carrying out the same sequence of movements. They shall also show the suspect and other people under identical conditions unless the identification officer reasonably believes:
   (a)  because of the suspect's failure or refusal to co-operate or other reasons, it is not practicable for the conditions to be identical; and
   (b)  any difference in the conditions would not direct an eye-witness' attention to any individual image.

4. The reasons identical conditions are not practicable shall be recorded on forms provided for the purpose.

5. Provision must be made for each person shown to be identified by number.

6. If police officers are shown, any numerals or other identifying badges must be concealed. If a prison inmate is shown, either as a suspect or not, then either all, or none of, the people shown should be in prison clothing.

7. The suspect or their solicitor, friend, or appropriate adult must be given a reasonable opportunity to see the complete set of images before it is shown to any eye-witness. If the suspect has a reasonable objection to the set of images or any of the participants, the suspect shall be asked to state the reasons for the objection. Steps shall, if practicable, be taken to remove the grounds for objection. If this is not practicable, the suspect and/or their representative shall be told why their objections cannot be met and the objection, the reason given for it and why it cannot be met shall be recorded on forms provided for the purpose. The requirement in *paragraph 2* that the images of the other people 'resemble' the suspect does not require the images to be identical or extremely similar (see *Note A1*).

8. Before the images are shown in accordance with *paragraph 7*, the suspect or their solicitor shall be provided with details of the first description of the suspect by any eye-witnesses who are to attend the video identification. When a broadcast or publication is made, as in *paragraph 3.38(a)*, the suspect or their solicitor must also be allowed to view any material released to the media by the police for the purpose of recognising or tracing the suspect, provided it is practicable and would not unreasonably delay the investigation.

9. No unauthorised people may be present when the video identification is conducted. The suspect's solicitor, if practicable, shall be given reasonable notification of the time and place the video identification is to be conducted. The suspect's solicitor may only be present at the video identification on request and with the prior agreement of the identification officer, if the officer is satisfied that the solicitor's presence will not deter or distract any eye-witness from viewing the

images and making an identification. If the identification officer is not satisfied and does not agree to the request, the reason must be recorded. The solicitor must be informed of the decision and the reason for it. and that they may then make representations about why they should be allowed to be present. The representations may be made orally or in writing, in person or remotely by electronic communication and must be recorded. These representations must be considered by an officer of at least the rank of inspector who is not involved with the investigation and responsibility for this may not be delegated under *paragraph 3.11*. If, after considering the representations, the officer is satisfied that the solicitor's presence will deter or distract the eye-witness, the officer shall inform the solicitor of the decision and reason for it and ensure that any response by the solicitor is also recorded. If allowed to be present, the solicitor is not entitled to communicate in any way with an eye-witness during the procedure but this does not prevent the solicitor from communicating with the identification officer. The suspect may not be present when the images are shown to any eye-witness and is not entitled to be informed of the time and place the video identification procedure is to be conducted. The video identification procedure itself shall be recorded on video with sound. The recording must show all persons present within the sight or hearing of the eye-witness whilst the images are being viewed and must include what the eye-witness says and what is said to them by the identification officer and by any other person present at the video identification procedure. A supervised viewing of the recording of the video identification proce-dure by the suspect and/or their solicitor may be arranged on request, at the discretion of the investigating officer. Where the recording of the video identification procedure is to be shown to the suspect and/or their solicitor, the investigating officer may arrange for anything in the recording that might allow the eye-witness to be identified to be concealed if the investigating officer considers that this is justified (see *Note A2*). In accordance with *paragraph 2.18*, the investigating officer may also arrange for anything in that recording that might allow any police officers or police staff to be identified to be concealed.

(b) *Conducting the video identification*

10.  The identification officer is responsible for making the appropriate arrangements to make sure, before they see the set of images, eye-witnesses are not able to communicate with each other about the case, see any of the images which are to be shown, see, or be reminded of, any photograph or description of the suspect or be given any other indication as to the suspect's identity, or overhear an eye-witness who has already seen the material. There must be no discussion with the eye-witness about the composition of the set of images and they must not be told whether a previous eye-witness has made any identification.

11.  Only one eye-witness may see the set of images at a time. Immediately before the images are shown, the eye-witness shall be told that the person they saw on a specified earlier occasion may, or may not, appear in the images they are shown and that if they cannot make an identification, they should say so. The eye-witness shall be advised that at any point, they may ask to see a particular part of the set of images or to have a particular image frozen for them to study. Furthermore, it should be pointed out to the eye-witness that there is no limit on how many times they can view the whole set of images or any part of them. However, they should be asked not to make any decision as to whether the person they saw is on the set of images until they have seen the whole set at least twice.

12.  Once the eye-witness has seen the whole set of images at least twice and has indicated that they do not want to view the images, or any part of them, again, the eye-witness shall be asked to say whether the individual they saw in person on a specified earlier occasion has been shown and, if so, to identify them by number of the image. The eye-witness will then be shown that image to confirm the identification, see *paragraph 17*.

13.  Care must be taken not to direct the eye-witness' attention to any one individual image or give any indication of the suspect's identity. Where an eye-witness has previously made an identification by photographs, or a computerised or artist's composite or similar likeness, they must not be reminded of such a photograph or composite likeness once a suspect is available for identification by other means in accordance with this Code. Nor must the eyewitness be reminded of any description of the suspect.

13A. If after the video identification procedure has ended, the eye-witness informs any police officer or police staff involved in the post-viewing arrangements that they wish to change their decision about their identification, or they have not made an identification when in fact they could have made one, an accurate record of the words used by the eye-witness and of the circumstances immediately after the procedure ended, shall be made. If the eyewitness has not had an opportunity to communicate with other people about the procedure, the identification officer has the discretion to allow the eye-witness a second opportunity to make an identification by repeating the video identification procedure using the same images but in different positions.

14. After the procedure, action required in accordance with *paragraph 3.40* applies.

*(c) Image security and destruction*

15. Arrangements shall be made for all relevant material containing sets of images used for specific identification procedures to be kept securely and their movements accounted for. In particular, no-one involved in the investigation shall be permitted to view the material prior to it being shown to any witness.

16. As appropriate, *paragraph 3.30* or *3.31* applies to the destruction or retention of relevant sets of images.

*(d) Documentation*

17. A record must be made of all those participating in, or seeing, the set of images whose names are known to the police.

18. A record of the conduct of the video identification must be made on forms provided for the purpose. This shall include anything said by the witness about any identifications or the conduct of the procedure and any reasons it was not practicable to comply with any of the provisions of this Code governing the conduct of video identifications. This record is in addition to any statement that is taken from any eye-witness after the procedure.

*Note for Guidance*

A1 *The purpose of the video identification is to test the eye-witness' ability to distinguish the suspect from others and it would not be a fair test if all the images shown were identical or extremely similar to each other. The identification officer is responsible for ensuring that the images shown are suitable for the purpose of this test.*

A2 *The purpose of allowing the identity of the eye-witness to be concealed is to protect them in cases when there is information that suspects or their associates, may threaten the witness or cause them harm or when the investigating officer considers that special measures may be required to protect their identity during the criminal process.*

ANNEX B

IDENTIFICATION PARADES

*(a) General*

1. A suspect must be given a reasonable opportunity to have a solicitor or friend present, and the suspect shall be asked to indicate on a second copy of the notice whether or not they wish to do so.

2. An identification parade may take place either in a normal room or one equipped with a screen permitting witnesses to see members of the identification parade without being seen. The procedures for the composition and conduct of the identification parade are the same in both cases, subject to *paragraph 8* (except that an identification parade involving a screen may take place only when the suspect's solicitor, friend or appropriate adult is present or the identification parade is recorded on video).

3. Before the identification parade takes place, the suspect or their solicitor shall be provided with details of the first description of the suspect by any witnesses who are attending the identification parade. When a broadcast or publication is made as in *paragraph 3.38(a)*, the suspect or their solicitor should also be allowed to view any material released to the media by the police for the purpose of identifying and tracing the suspect, provided it is practicable to do so and would not unreasonably delay the investigation.

*(b) Identification parades involving prison inmates*

4. If a prison inmate is required for identification, and there are no security problems about the person leaving the establishment, they may be asked to participate in an identification parade or video identification.

5. An identification parade may be held in a Prison Department establishment but shall be conducted, as far as practicable under normal identification parade rules. Members of the public shall make up the identification parade unless there are serious security, or control, objections to their admission to the establishment. In such cases, or if a group or video identification is arranged within the establishment, other inmates may participate. If an inmate is the suspect, they are not required to wear prison clothing for the identification parade unless the other people taking part are other inmates in similar clothing, or are members of the public who are prepared to wear prison clothing for the occasion.

*(c)  Conduct of the identification parade*

6.   Immediately before the identification parade, the suspect must be reminded of the procedures governing its conduct and cautioned in the terms of Code C, *paragraphs 10.5* or *10.6*, as appropriate.

7.   All unauthorised people must be excluded from the place where the identification parade is held.

8.   Once the identification parade has been formed, everything afterwards, in respect of it, shall take place in the presence and hearing of the suspect and any interpreter, solicitor, friend or appropriate adult who is present (unless the identification parade involves a screen, in which case everything said to, or by, any witness at the place where the identification parade is held, must be said in the hearing and presence of the suspect's solicitor, friend or appropriate adult or be recorded on video).

9.   The identification parade shall consist of at least eight people (in addition to the suspect) who, so far as possible, resemble the suspect in age, height, general appearance and position in life. Only one suspect shall be included in an identification parade unless there are two suspects of roughly similar appearance, in which case they may be paraded together with at least twelve other people. In no circumstances shall more than two suspects be included in one identification parade and where there are separate identification parades, they shall be made up of different people.

10.  If the suspect has an unusual physical feature, e.g., a facial scar, tattoo or distinctive hairstyle or hair colour which cannot be replicated on other members of the identification parade, steps may be taken to conceal the location of that feature on the suspect and the other members of the identification parade if the suspect and their solicitor, or appropriate adult, agree. For example, by use of a plaster or a hat, so that all members of the identification parade resemble each other in general appearance.

11.  When all members of a similar group are possible suspects, separate identification parades shall be held for each unless there are two suspects of similar appearance when they may appear on the same identification parade with at least twelve other members of the group who are not suspects. When police officers in uniform form an identification parade any numerals or other identifying badges shall be concealed.

12.  When the suspect is brought to the place where the identification parade is to be held, they shall be asked if they have any objection to the arrangements for the identification parade or to any of the other participants in it and to state the reasons for the objection. The suspect may obtain advice from their solicitor or friend, if present, before the identification parade proceeds. If the suspect has a reasonable objection to the arrangements or any of the participants, steps shall, if practicable, be taken to remove the grounds for objection. When it is not practicable to do so, the suspect shall be told why their objections cannot be met and the objection, the reason given for it and why it cannot be met, shall be recorded on forms provided for the purpose.

13.  The suspect may select their own position in the line, but may not otherwise interfere with the order of the people forming the line. When there is more than one witness, the suspect must be told, after each witness has left the room, that they can, if they wish, change position in the line. Each position in the line must be clearly numbered, whether by means of a number laid on the floor in front of each identification parade member or by other means.

14.  Appropriate arrangements must be made to make sure, before witnesses attend the identification parade, they are not able to:
     (i)    communicate with each other about the case or overhear a witness who has already seen the identification parade;
     (ii)   see any member of the identification parade;
     (iii)  see, or be reminded of, any photograph or description of the suspect or be given any other indication as to the suspect's identity; or
     (iv)   see the suspect before or after the identification parade.

15.  The person conducting a witness to an identification parade must not discuss with them the composition of the identification parade and, in particular, must not disclose whether a previous witness has made any identification.

16.  Witnesses shall be brought in one at a time. Immediately before the witness inspects the identification parade, they shall be told the person they saw on a specified earlier occasion may, or may not, be present and if they cannot make an identification, they should say so. The witness must also be told they should not make any decision about whether the person they saw is on the identification parade until they have looked at each member at least twice.

17.  When the officer or police staff (see *paragraph 3.11*) conducting the identification procedure is satisfied the witness has properly looked at each member of the identification parade, they shall ask

the witness whether the person they saw on a specified earlier occasion is on the identification parade and, if so, to indicate the number of the person concerned, see *paragraph 28*.

18.    If the witness wishes to hear any identification parade member speak, adopt any specified posture or move, they shall first be asked whether they can identify any person(s) on the identification parade on the basis of appearance only. When the request is to hear members of the identification parade speak, the witness shall be reminded that the participants in the identification parade have been chosen on the basis of physical appearance only. Members of the identification parade may then be asked to comply with the witness' request to hear them speak, see them move or adopt any specified posture.

19.    If the witness requests that the person they have indicated remove anything used for the purposes of *paragraph 10* to conceal the location of an unusual physical feature, that person may be asked to remove it.

20.    If the witness makes an identification after the identification parade has ended, the suspect and, if present, their solicitor, interpreter or friend shall be informed. When this occurs, consideration should be given to allowing the witness a second opportunity to identify the suspect.

21    After the procedure, action required in accordance with *paragraph 3.40* applies.

22.    When the last witness has left, the suspect shall be asked whether they wish to make any comments on the conduct of the identification parade.

*(d)  Documentation*

23.    A video recording must normally be taken of the identification parade. If that is impracticable, a colour photograph must be taken. A copy of the video recording or photograph shall be supplied, on request, to the suspect or their solicitor within a reasonable time.

24.    As appropriate, *paragraph 3.30* or *3.31*, should apply to any photograph or video taken as in *paragraph 23*.

25.    If any person is asked to leave an identification parade because they are interfering with its conduct, the circumstances shall be recorded.

26.    A record must be made of all those present at an identification parade whose names are known to the police.

27.    If prison inmates make up an identification parade, the circumstances must be recorded.

28.    A record of the conduct of any identification parade must be made on forms provided for the purpose. This shall include anything said by the witness or the suspect about any identifications or the conduct of the procedure, and any reasons it was not practicable to comply with any of this Code's provisions.

## Annex C

### Group Identification

*(a)  General*

1.    The purpose of this Annex is to make sure, as far as possible, group identifications follow the principles and procedures for identification parades so the conditions are fair to the suspect in the way they test the witness' ability to make an identification.

2.    Group identifications may take place either with the suspect's consent and co-operation or covertly without their consent.

3.    The location of the group identification is a matter for the identification officer, although the officer may take into account any representations made by the suspect, appropriate adult, their solicitor or friend.

4.    The place where the group identification is held should be one where other people are either passing by or waiting around informally, in groups such that the suspect is able to join them and be capable of being seen by the witness at the same time as others in the group. For example people leaving an escalator, pedestrians walking through a shopping centre, passengers on railway and bus stations, waiting in queues or groups or where people are standing or sitting in groups in other public places.

5.    If the group identification is to be held covertly, the choice of locations will be limited by the places where the suspect can be found and the number of other people present at that time. In these cases, suitable locations might be along regular routes travelled by the suspect, including buses or trains or public places frequented by the suspect.

6.    Although the number, age, sex, race and general description and style of clothing of other people present at the location cannot be controlled by the identification officer, in selecting the location the officer must consider the general appearance and numbers of people likely to be present. In particular, the officer must reasonably expect that over the period the witness observes the group,

they will be able to see, from time to time, a number of others whose appearance is broadly similar to that of the suspect.

7.  A group identification need not be held if the identification officer believes, because of the unusual appearance of the suspect, none of the locations it would be practicable to use, satisfy the requirements of *paragraph 6* necessary to make the identification fair.

8.  Immediately after a group identification procedure has taken place (with or without the suspect's consent), a colour photograph or video should be taken of the general scene, if practicable, to give a general impression of the scene and the number of people present. Alternatively, if it is practicable, the group identification may be video recorded.

9.  If it is not practicable to take the photograph or video in accordance with *paragraph 8*, a photograph or film of the scene should be taken later at a time determined by the identification officer if the officer considers it practicable to do so.

10.  An identification carried out in accordance with this Code remains a group identification even though, at the time of being seen by the witness, the suspect was on their own rather than in a group.

11.  Before the group identification takes place, the suspect or their solicitor shall be provided with details of the first description of the suspect by any witnesses who are to attend the identification. When a broadcast or publication is made, as in *paragraph 3.38(a)*, the suspect or their solicitor should also be allowed to view any material released by the police to the media for the purposes of identifying and tracing the suspect, provided that it is practicable and would not unreasonably delay the investigation.

12.  After the procedure, action required in accordance with *paragraph 3.40* applies.

*(b)  Identification with the consent of the suspect*

13.  A suspect must be given a reasonable opportunity to have a solicitor or friend present. They shall be asked to indicate on a second copy of the notice whether or not they wish to do so.

14.  The witness, the person carrying out the procedure and the suspect's solicitor, appropriate adult, friend or any interpreter for the witness, may be concealed from the sight of the individuals in the group they are observing, if the person carrying out the procedure considers this assists the conduct of the identification.

15.  The person conducting a witness to a group identification must not discuss with them the forthcoming group identification and, in particular, must not disclose whether a previous witness has made any identification.

16.  Anything said to, or by, the witness during the procedure about the identification should be said in the presence and hearing of those present at the procedure.

17.  Appropriate arrangements must be made to make sure, before witnesses attend the group identification, they are not able to:

    (i)   communicate with each other about the case or overhear a witness who has already been given an opportunity to see the suspect in the group;

    (ii)  see the suspect; or

    (iii) see, or be reminded of, any photographs or description of the suspect or be given any other indication of the suspect's identity.

18.  Witnesses shall be brought one at a time to the place where they are to observe the group. Immediately before the witness is asked to look at the group, the person conducting the procedure shall tell them that the person they saw on a specified earlier occasion may, or may not, be in the group and that if they cannot make an identification, they should say so. The witness shall be asked to observe the group in which the suspect is to appear. The way in which the witness should do this will depend on whether the group is moving or stationary.

*Moving group*

19.  When the group in which the suspect is to appear is moving, e.g. leaving an escalator, the provisions of *paragraphs 20* to *24* should be followed.

20.  If two or more suspects consent to a group identification, each should be the subject of separate identification procedures. These may be conducted consecutively on the same occasion.

21.  The person conducting the procedure shall tell the witness to observe the group and ask them to point out any person they think they saw on the specified earlier occasion.

22.  Once the witness has been informed as in *paragraph 21* the suspect should be allowed to take whatever position in the group they wish.

23.  When the witness points out a person as in *paragraph 21* they shall, if practicable, be asked to take a closer look at the person to confirm the identification. If this is not practicable, or they cannot

confirm the identification, they shall be asked how sure they are that the person they have indicated is the relevant person.

24.   The witness should continue to observe the group for the period which the person conducting the procedure reasonably believes is necessary in the circumstances for them to be able to make comparisons between the suspect and other individuals of broadly similar appearance to the suspect as in *paragraph 6*.

*Stationary groups*

25.   When the group in which the suspect is to appear is stationary, e.g. people waiting in a queue, the provisions of *paragraphs 26* to *29* should be followed.

26.   If two or more suspects consent to a group identification, each should be subject to separate identification procedures unless they are of broadly similar appearance when they may appear in the same group. When separate group identifications are held, the groups must be made up of different people.

27.   The suspect may take whatever position in the group they wish. If there is more than one witness, the suspect must be told, out of the sight and hearing of any witness, that they can, if they wish, change their position in the group.

28.   The witness shall be asked to pass along, or amongst, the group and to look at each person in the group at least twice, taking as much care and time as possible according to the circumstances, before making an identification. Once the witness has done this, they shall be asked whether the person they saw on the specified earlier occasion is in the group and to indicate any such person by whatever means the person conducting the procedure considers appropriate in the circumstances. If this is not practicable, the witness shall be asked to point out any person they think they saw on the earlier occasion.

29.   When the witness makes an indication as in *paragraph 28*, arrangements shall be made, if practicable, for the witness to take a closer look at the person to confirm the identification. If this is not practicable, or the witness is unable to confirm the identification, they shall be asked how sure they are that the person they have indicated is the relevant person.

*All cases*

30.   If the suspect unreasonably delays joining the group, or having joined the group, deliberately conceals themselves from the sight of the witness, this may be treated as a refusal to co-operate in a group identification.

31.   If the witness identifies a person other than the suspect, that person should be informed what has happened and asked if they are prepared to give their name and address. There is no obligation upon any member of the public to give these details. There shall be no duty to record any details of any other member of the public present in the group or at the place where the procedure is conducted.

32.   When the group identification has been completed, the suspect shall be asked whether they wish to make any comments on the conduct of the procedure.

33.   If the suspect has not been previously informed, they shall be told of any identifications made by the witnesses.

*(c)   Identification without the suspect's consent*

34.   Group identifications held covertly without the suspect's consent should, as far as practicable, follow the rules for conduct of group identification by consent.

35.   A suspect has no right to have a solicitor, appropriate adult or friend present as the identification will take place without the knowledge of the suspect.

36.   Any number of suspects may be identified at the same time.

*(d)   Identifications in police stations*

37.   Group identifications should only take place in police stations for reasons of safety, security or because it is not practicable to hold them elsewhere.

38.   The group identification may take place either in a room equipped with a screen permitting witnesses to see members of the group without being seen, or anywhere else in the police station that the identification officer considers appropriate.

39.   Any of the additional safeguards applicable to identification parades should be followed if the identification officer considers it is practicable to do so in the circumstances.

*(e)   Identifications involving prison inmates*

40.   A group identification involving a prison inmate may only be arranged in the prison or at a police station.

41.   When a group identification takes place involving a prison inmate, whether in a prison or in a police station, the arrangements should follow those in *paragraphs 37* to *39*. If a group identification takes place within a prison, other inmates may participate. If an inmate is the suspect, they do not have to wear prison clothing for the group identification unless the other participants are wearing the same clothing.

*(f) Documentation*

42.   When a photograph or video is taken as in *paragraph 8* or *9*, a copy of the photograph or video shall be supplied on request to the suspect or their solicitor within a reasonable time.

43.   *Paragraph 3.30* or *3.31*, as appropriate, shall apply when the photograph or film taken in accordance with *paragraph 8* or *9* includes the suspect.

44.   A record of the conduct of any group identification must be made on forms provided for the purpose. This shall include anything said by the witness or suspect about any identifications or the conduct of the procedure and any reasons why it was not practicable to comply with any of the provisions of this Code governing the conduct of group identifications.

## Annex D

### Confrontation by a Witness

1.   Before the confrontation takes place, the eye-witness must be told that the person they saw on a specified earlier occasion may, or may not, be the person they are to confront and that if they are not that person, then the witness should say so.

2.   Before the confrontation takes place the suspect or their solicitor shall be provided with details of the first description of the suspect given by any eye-witness who is to attend. When a broadcast or publication is made, as in *paragraph 3.38(a)*, the suspect or their solicitor should also be allowed to view any material released to the media for the purposes of recognising or tracing the suspect, provided it is practicable to do so and would not unreasonably delay the investigation.

3.   Force may not be used to make the suspect's face visible to the eye-witness.

4.   Confrontation must take place in the presence of the suspect's solicitor, interpreter or friend unless this would cause unreasonable delay.

5.   The suspect shall be confronted independently by each eye-witness, who shall be asked 'Is this the person?'. If the eye-witness identifies the person but is unable to confirm the identification, they shall be asked how sure they are that the person is the one they saw on the earlier occasion.

6.   The confrontation should normally take place in the police station, either in a normal room or one equipped with a screen permitting the eye-witness to see the suspect without being seen. In both cases, the procedures are the same except that a room equipped with a screen may be used only when the suspect's solicitor, friend or appropriate adult is present or the confrontation is recorded on video.

7.   After the procedure, action required in accordance with *paragraph 3.40* applies.

## Annex E

### Showing Photographs

*(a) Action*

1.   An officer of sergeant rank or above shall be responsible for supervising and directing the showing of photographs. The actual showing may be done by another officer or police staff, see *paragraph 3.11*.

2.   The supervising officer must confirm the first description of the suspect given by the eyewitness has been recorded before they are shown the photographs. If the supervising officer is unable to confirm the description has been recorded they shall postpone showing the photographs.

3.   Only one eye-witness shall be shown photographs at any one time. Each witness shall be given as much privacy as practicable and shall not be allowed to communicate with any other eye-witness in the case.

4.   The eye-witness shall be shown not less than twelve photographs at a time, which shall, as far as possible, all be of a similar type.

5.   When the eye-witness is shown the photographs, they shall be told the photograph of the person they saw on a specified earlier occasion may, or may not, be amongst them and if they cannot make an identification, they should say so. The eye-witness shall also be told they should not make a decision until they have viewed at least twelve photographs. The eye-witness shall not be prompted or guided in any way but shall be left to make any selection without help.

6.  If an eye-witness makes an identification from photographs, unless the person identified is otherwise eliminated from enquiries or is not available, other eye-witnesses shall not be shown photographs. But both they, and the eye-witness who has made the identification, shall be asked to attend a video identification, an identification parade or group identification unless there is no dispute about the suspect's identification.

7.  If the eye-witness makes a selection but is unable to confirm the identification, the person showing the photographs shall ask them how sure they are that the photograph they have indicated is the person they saw on the specified earlier occasion.

8.  When the use of a computerised or artist's composite or similar likeness has led to there being a known suspect who can be asked to participate in a video identification, appear on an identification parade or participate in a group identification, that likeness shall not be shown to other potential eye-witnesses.

9.  When an eye-witness attending a video identification, an identification parade or group identification has previously been shown photographs or computerised or artist's composite or similar likeness (and it is the responsibility of the officer in charge of the investigation to make the identification officer aware that this is the case), the suspect and their solicitor must be informed of this fact before the identification procedure takes place.

10. None of the photographs shown shall be destroyed, whether or not an identification is made, since they may be required for production in court. The photographs shall be numbered and a separate photograph taken of the frame or part of the album from which the eye-witness made an identification as an aid to reconstituting it.

*(b) Documentation*

11. Whether or not an identification is made, a record shall be kept of the showing of photographs on forms provided for the purpose. This shall include anything said by the eye-witness about any identification or the conduct of the procedure, any reasons it was not practicable to comply with any of the provisions of this Code governing the showing of photographs and the name and rank of the supervising officer.

12. The supervising officer shall inspect and sign the record as soon as practicable.

## Annex F

### Fingerprints, Samples and Footwear Impressions — Destruction and Speculative Searches

*Part A: Fingerprints and samples*

Paragraphs 1 to 12 summarise and update information which is available at: https://www.gov.uk/ gover nment/publications/protection-of-freedoms-act-2012-dna-and-fingerprintprovisions/protection-of-freedoms-act-2012-how-dna-and-fingerprint-evidence-is-protected-in-law

*DNA samples*

1.  A DNA sample is an individual's biological material, containing all of their genetic information. The Act requires all DNA samples to be destroyed within 6 months of being taken. This allows sufficient time for the sample to be analysed and a DNA profile to be produced for use on the database.

2.  The only exception to this is if the sample is or may be required for disclosure as evidence, in which case it may be retained for as long as this need exists under the Criminal Procedure and Investigations Act 1996.

*DNA profiles and fingerprints*

3.  A DNA profile consists of a string of 16 pairs of numbers and 2 letters (XX for women, XY for men) to indicate gender. This number string is stored on the National DNA Database (NDNAD). It allows the person to be identified if they leave their DNA at a crime scene.

4.  Fingerprints are usually scanned electronically from the individual in custody and the images stored on IDENT1, the national fingerprint database.

*Retention Periods: Fingerprints and DNA profiles*

5.  The retention period depends on the outcome of the investigation of the recordable offence in connection with which the fingerprints and DNA samples was taken, the age of the person at the time the offence was committed and whether the *recordable* offence is a qualifying offence and whether it is an excluded offence (see Table *Notes (a)* to *(c)*), as follows:

*Table – Retention periods*

(a) *Convictions*

| Age when offence committed | Outcome | Retention Period |
|---|---|---|
| Any age | Convicted or given a caution or youth caution for a recordable offence which is also a qualifying offence | INDEFINITE |
| 18 or over | Convicted or given a caution for a recordable offence which is NOT a qualifying offence | INDEFINITE |
| Under 18 | Convicted or given a youth caution for a recordable offence which is NOT a qualifying offence. | 1st conviction or youth caution – 5 years plus length of any prison sentence. Indefinite if prison sentence 5 years or more 2nd conviction or youth caution: Indefinite |

(b) *Non-Convictions*

| Age when offence committed | Outcome | Retention Period |
|---|---|---|
| Any age | Charged but not convicted of a recordable qualifying offence. | 3 years plus a 2 year extension if granted by a District Judge (or indefinite if the individual has a previous conviction for a recordable offence which is not excluded) |
| Any age | Arrested for, but not charged with, a recordable qualifying offence | 3 years if granted by the Biometrics Commissioner plus a 2 year extension if granted by a District Judge (or indefinite if the individual has a previous conviction for a recordable offence which is not excluded) |
| Any age | Arrested for or charged with a recordable offence which is not a qualifying offence. | Indefinite if the person has a previous conviction for a recordable offence which is not excluded otherwise NO RETENTION |
| 18 or over | Given Penalty Notice for Disorder for recordable offence | 2 years |

*Table Notes:*

(a)  *A 'recordable' offence is one for which the police are required to keep a record. Generally speaking, these are imprisonable offences; however, it also includes a number of non-imprisonable offences such as begging and taxi touting. The police are not able to take or retain the DNA or fingerprints of an individual who is arrested for an offence which is not recordable.*

(b)  *A 'qualifying' offence is one listed under section 65A of the Police and Criminal Evidence Act 1984 (the list comprises sexual, violent, terrorism and burglary offences).*

(c)  *An 'excluded' offence is a recordable offence which is not a qualifying offence, was committed when the individual was under 18, for which they received a sentence of fewer than 5 years imprisonment and is the only recordable offence for which the person has been convicted.*

*Speculative searches*

6.    Where the retention framework above requires the deletion of a person's DNA profile and fingerprints, the Act first allows a *speculative search* of their DNA and fingerprints against DNA and fingerprints obtained from crime scenes which are stored on NDNAD and IDENT1. Once the speculative search has been completed, the profile and fingerprints are deleted unless there is a match, in which case they will be retained for the duration of any investigation and thereafter in

accordance with the retention framework (e.g. if that investigation led to a conviction for a qualifying offence, they would be retained indefinitely).

*Extensions of retention period*

7.   For qualifying offences, PACE allows chief constables to apply for extensions to the given retention periods for DNA profiles and fingerprints if considered necessary for prevention or detection of crime.

8.   Section 20 of the Protection of Freedoms Act 2012 established the independent office of Commissioner for the Retention and Use of Biometric Material ('the 'Biometrics Commissioner'). For details, see https://www.gov.uk/government/organisations/biometrics-commissioner.

9.   Where an individual is arrested for, but not charged with, a qualifying offence, their DNA profile and fingerprint record will normally be deleted. However, the police can apply to the Biometrics Commissioner for permission to retain their DNA profile and fingerprint record for a period of 3 years. The application must be made within 28 days of the decision not to proceed with a prosecution.

10.  If the police make such an application, the Biometrics Commissioner would first give both them and the arrested individual an opportunity to make written representations and then, taking into account factors including the age and vulnerability of the victim(s) of the alleged offences, and their relationship to the suspect, make a decision on whether or not retention is appropriate.

11.  If after considering the application, the Biometrics Commissioner decides that retention is not appropriate, the DNA profile and fingerprint record in question must be destroyed.

12.  If the Biometrics Commissioner agrees to allow retention, the police will be able to retain that individual's DNA profile and fingerprint record for a period of 3 years from the date the samples were taken. At the end of that period, the police will be able to apply to a District Judge (Magistrates' Courts) for a single 2 year extension to the retention period. If the application is rejected, the force must then destroy the DNA profile and fingerprint record.

*Part B: Footwear impressions*

13.  Footwear impressions taken in accordance with section 61A of PACE (see *paragraphs 4.16 to 4.21*) may be retained for as long as is necessary for purposes related to the prevention or detection of crime, the investigation of an offence or the conduct of a prosecution.

*Part C: Fingerprints, samples and footwear impressions taken in connection with a criminal investigation from a person not suspected of committing the offence under investigation for elimination purposes.*

14.  When fingerprints, footwear impressions or DNA samples are taken from a person in connection with an investigation and the person is *not suspected of having committed the offence*, see *Note F1*, they must be destroyed as soon as they have fulfilled the purpose for which they were taken unless:

   (a)  they were taken for the purposes of an investigation of an offence for which a person has been convicted; and

   (b)  fingerprints, footwear impressions or samples were also taken from the convicted person for the purposes of that investigation.

   However, subject to *paragraph 14*, the fingerprints, footwear impressions and samples, and the information derived from samples, may not be used in the investigation of any offence or in evidence against the person who is, or would be, entitled to the destruction of the fingerprints, footwear impressions and samples, see *Note F2*.

15.  The requirement to destroy fingerprints, footwear impressions and DNA samples, and information derived from samples and restrictions on their retention and use in *paragraph 14* do not apply if the person gives their written consent for their fingerprints, footwear impressions or sample to be retained and used after they have fulfilled the purpose for which they were taken, see *Note F1*. This consent can be withdrawn at any time.

16.  When a person's fingerprints, footwear impressions or sample are to be destroyed:

   (a)  any copies of the fingerprints and footwear impressions must also be destroyed; and

   (b)  neither the fingerprints, footwear impressions, the sample, or any information derived from the sample, may be used in the investigation of any offence or in evidence against the person who is, or would be, entitled to its destruction.

## Notes for Guidance

F1  Fingerprints, footwear impressions and samples given voluntarily for the purposes of elimination play an important part in many police investigations. It is, therefore, important to make sure innocent volunteers are not deterred from participating and their consent to their fingerprints, footwear impressions and DNA being used for the purposes of a specific investigation is fully informed and voluntary. If the police or volunteer seek to have the fingerprints, footwear impressions or samples retained for use after the specific investigation ends, it is important the volunteer's consent to this is also fully informed and voluntary. The volunteer must be told that they may withdraw their consent at any time. The consent must be obtained in writing using current nationally agreed forms provided for police use according to the purpose for which the consent is given. This purpose may be either:
- DNA/fingerprints/footwear impressions — to be used only for the purposes of a specific investigation; or
- DNA/fingerprints/footwear impressions — to be used in the specific investigation **and** retained by the police for future use.

To minimise the risk of confusion:
- if a police officer or member of police staff has any doubt about:
  - how the consent forms should be completed and signed, or
  - whether a consent form they propose to use and refer to is fully compliant with the current nationally agreed form,

  the relevant national police helpdesk (for DNA or fingerprints) should be contacted.
- in each case, the meaning of consent should be explained orally and care taken to ensure the oral explanation accurately reflects the contents of the written form the person is to be asked to sign.

F2  The provisions for the retention of fingerprints, footwear impressions and samples in paragraph 15 allow for all fingerprints, footwear impressions and samples in a case to be available for any subsequent miscarriage of justice investigation.

## ANNEX G

### REQUIREMENT FOR A PERSON TO ATTEND A POLICE STATION FOR FINGERPRINTS AND SAMPLES (PARAGRAPHS 4.4, 6.2A AND 6.6A)

1.  A requirement under Schedule 2A for a person to attend a police station to have fingerprints or samples taken:
    (a) must give the person a period of at least seven days within which to attend the police station; and
    (b) may direct them to attend at a specified time of day or between specified times of day.
2.  When specifying the period and times of attendance, the officer making the requirements must consider whether the fingerprints or samples could reasonably be taken at a time when the person is required to attend the police station for any other reason. See *Note G1*.
3.  An officer of the rank of inspector or above may authorise a period shorter than 7 days if there is an urgent need for person's fingerprints or sample for the purposes of the investigation of an offence. The fact of the authorisation and the reasons for giving it must be recorded as soon as practicable.
4.  The constable making a requirement and the person to whom it applies may agree to vary it so as to specify any period within which, or date or time at which, the person is to attend. However, variation shall not have effect for the purposes of enforcement, unless it is confirmed by the constable in writing.

## Notes for Guidance

G1  The specified period within which the person is to attend need not fall within the period allowed (if applicable) for making the requirement.

G2  To justify the arrest without warrant of a person who fails to comply with a requirement, (see paragraphs 4.4(b) and 6.7(b) above), the officer making the requirement, or confirming a variation, should be prepared to explain how, when and where the requirement was made or the variation was confirmed and what steps were taken to ensure the person understood what to do and the consequences of not complying with the requirement.

## 4. Records of arrest

### (a) General

4.1    The arresting officer is required to record in his pocket book or by other methods used for recording information:
- the nature and circumstances of the offence leading to the arrest;
- the reason or reasons why arrest was necessary;
- the giving of the caution; and
- anything said by the person at the time of arrest.

4.2    Such a record should be made at the time of the arrest unless impracticable to do so. If not made at that time, the record should then be completed as soon as possible thereafter.

4.3    On arrival at the police station or after being first arrested at the police station, the arrested person must be brought before the custody officer as soon as practicable and a custody record must be opened in accordance with section 2 of Code C. The information given by the arresting officer on the circumstances and reason or reasons for arrest shall be recorded as part of the custody record. Alternatively, a copy of the record made by the officer in accordance with paragraph 4.1 above shall be attached as part of the custody record. See *paragraph 2.2* and *Code C paragraphs 3.4 and 10.3.*

4.4    The custody record will serve as a record of the arrest. Copies of the custody record will be provided in accordance with paragraphs 2.4 and 2.4A of Code C and access for inspection of the original record in accordance with paragraph 2.5 of Code C.

### (b) Interviews and arrests

4.5    Records of interview, significant statements or silences will be treated in the same way as set out in sections 10 and 11 of Code C and in Codes E and F (audio and visual recording of interviews).

### *Notes for Guidance*

1      *For the purposes of this Code, 'offence' means any statutory or common law offence for which a person may be tried by a magistrates' court or the Crown court and punished if convicted. Statutory offences include assault, rape, criminal damage, theft, robbery, burglary, fraud, possession of controlled drugs and offences under road traffic, liquor licensing, gambling and immigration legislation and local government byelaws. Common law offences include murder, manslaughter, kidnapping, false imprisonment, perverting the course of justice and escape from lawful custody.*

1A     *This code does not apply to powers of arrest conferred on constables under any arrest warrant, for example, a warrant issued under the Magistrates' Courts Act 1980, sections 1 or 13, or the Bail Act 1976, section 7(1), or to the powers of constables to arrest without warrant other than under section 24 of PACE for an offence. These other powers to arrest without warrant do not depend on the arrested person committing any specific offence and include:*
- *PACE, section 46A, arrest of person who fails to answer police bail to attend police station or is suspected of breaching any condition of that bail for the custody officer to decide whether they should be kept in police detention which applies whether or not the person commits an offence under section 6 of the Bail Act 1976 (e.g. failing without reasonable cause to surrender to custody);*
- *Bail Act 1976, section 7(3), arrest of person bailed to attend court who is suspected of breaching, or is believed likely to breach, any condition of bail to take them to court for bail to be re-considered;*
- *Children & Young Persons Act 1969, section 32(1A) (absconding) —arrest to return the person to the place where they are required to reside;*
- *Immigration Act 1971, Schedule 2 to arrest a person liable to examination to determine their right to remain in the UK;*
- *Mental Health Act 1983, section 136 to remove person suffering from mental disorder to place of safety for assessment;*
- *Prison Act 1952, section 49, arrest to return person unlawfully at large to the prison etc. where they are liable to be detained;*
- *Road Traffic Act 1988, section 6D arrest of driver following the outcome of a preliminary roadside test requirement to enable the driver to be required to provide an evidential sample;*
- *Common law power to stop or prevent a Breach of the Peace — after arrest a person aged 18 or over may be brought before a justice of the peace court to show cause why they should not be bound over to keep the peace — not criminal proceedings.*

1B     *Juveniles should not be arrested at their place of education unless this is unavoidable. When a juvenile is arrested at their place of education, the principal or their nominee must be informed. (From Code C Note 11D)*

2      *Facts and information relevant to a person's suspected involvement in an offence should not be confined to those which tend to indicate the person has committed or attempted to commit the offence. Before making*

*a decision to arrest, a constable should take account of any facts and information that are available, including claims of innocence made by the person, that might dispel the suspicion.*

2A  *Particular examples of facts and information which might point to a person's innocence and may tend to dispel suspicion include those which relate to the statutory defence provided by the Criminal Law Act 1967, section 3(1) which allows the use of reasonable force in the prevention of crime or making an arrest and the common law of self-defence. This may be relevant when a person appears, or claims, to have been acting reasonably in defence of themselves or others or to prevent their property or the property of others from being stolen, destroyed or damaged, particularly if the offence alleged is based on the use of unlawful force, e.g. a criminal assault. When investigating allegations involving the use of force by school staff, the power given to all school staff under the Education and Inspections Act 2006, section 93, to use reasonable force to prevent their pupils from committing any offence, injuring persons, damaging property or prejudicing the maintenance of good order and discipline may be similarly relevant. The Association of Chief Police Officers and the Crown Prosecution Service have published joint guidance to help the public understand the meaning of reasonable force and what to expect from the police and CPS in cases which involve claims of self defence. Separate advice for school staff on their powers to use reasonable force is available from the Department for Education*

2B  *If a constable who is dealing with an allegation of crime and considering the need to arrest becomes an investigator for the purposes of the Code of Practice under the Criminal Procedure and Investigations Act 1996, the officer should, in accordance with paragraph 3.5 of that Code, 'pursue all reasonable lines of inquiry, whether these point towards or away from the suspect. What is reasonable in each case will depend on the particular circumstances.'*

2C  *For a constable to have reasonable grounds for believing it necessary to arrest, he or she is not required to be satisfied that there is no viable alternative to arrest. However, it does mean that in all cases, the officer should consider that arrest is the practical, sensible and proportionate option in all the circumstances at the time the decision is made. This applies equally to a person in police detention after being arrested for an offence who is suspected of involvement in a further offence and the necessity to arrest them for that further offence is being considered.*

2D  *Although a warning is not expressly required, officers should if practicable, consider whether a warning which points out their offending behaviour, and explains why, if they do not stop, the resulting consequences may make their arrest necessary. Such a warning might:*
- *if heeded, avoid the need to arrest, or*
- *if it is ignored, support the need to arrest and also help prove the mental element of certain offences, for example, the person's intent or awareness, or help to rebut a defence that they were acting reasonably.*

    *A person who is warned that they may be liable to arrest if their real name and address cannot be ascertained, should be given a reasonable opportunity to establish their real name and address before deciding that either or both are unknown and cannot be readily ascertained or that there are reasonable grounds to doubt that a name and address they have given is their real name and address. They should be told why their name is not known and cannot be readily ascertained and (as the case may be) of the grounds for doubting that a name and address they have given is their real name and address, including, for example, the reason why a particular document the person has produced to verify their real name and/or address, is not sufficient.*

2E  *The meaning of 'prompt' should be considered on a case by case basis taking account of all the circumstances. It indicates that the progress of the investigation should not be delayed to the extent that it would adversely affect the effectiveness of the investigation. The arresting officer also has discretion to release the arrested person on 'street bail' as an alternative to taking the person directly to the station. See Note 2J.*

2F  *An officer who believes that it is necessary to interview the person suspected of committing the offence must then consider whether their arrest is necessary in order to carry out the interview. The officer is not required to interrogate the suspect to determine whether they will attend a police station voluntarily to be interviewed but they must consider whether the suspect's voluntary attendance is a practicable alternative for carrying out the interview. If it is, then arrest would not be necessary. Conversely, an officer who considers this option but is not satisfied that it is a practicable alternative, may have reasonable grounds for deciding that the arrest is necessary at the outset 'on the street'. Without such considerations, the officer would not be able to establish that arrest was necessary in order to interview.*

    *Circumstances which suggest that a person's arrest 'on the street' would not be necessary to interview them might be where the officer:*
- *is satisfied as to their identity and address and that they will attend the police station voluntarily to be interviewed, either immediately or by arrangement at a future date and time; and*

- *is not aware of any other circumstances which indicate that voluntary attendance would not be a practicable alternative. See paragraph 2.9(e)(i) to (v).*

*When making arrangements for the person's voluntary attendance, the officer should tell the person:*

- *that to properly investigate their suspected involvement in the offence they must be interviewed under caution at the police station, but in the circumstances their arrest for this purpose will not be necessary if they attend the police station voluntarily to be interviewed;*
- *that if they attend voluntarily, they will be entitled to free legal advice before, and to have a solicitor present at, the interview;*
- *that the date and time of the interview will take account of their circumstances and the needs of the investigation; and*
- *that if they do not agree to attend voluntarily at a time which meets the needs of the investigation, or having so agreed, fail to attend, or having attended, fail to remain for the interview to be completed, their arrest will be necessary to enable them to be interviewed.*

2G     *When the person attends the police station voluntarily for interview by arrangement as in Note 2F above, their arrest on arrival at the station prior to interview would only be justified if:*

- *new information coming to light after the arrangements were made indicates that from that time, voluntary attendance ceased to be a practicable alternative and the person's arrest became necessary; and*
- *it was not reasonably practicable for the person to be arrested before they attended the station.*

*If a person who attends the police station voluntarily to be interviewed decides to leave before the interview is complete, the police would at that point be entitled to consider whether their arrest was necessary to carry out the interview. The possibility that the person might decide to leave during the interview is therefore not a valid reason for arresting them before the interview has commenced. See Code C paragraph 3.21.*

2H     *The necessity criteria do not permit arrest solely to enable the routine taking, checking (speculative searching) and retention of fingerprints, samples, footwear impressions and photographs when there are no prior grounds to believe that checking and comparing the fingerprints etc. or taking a photograph would provide relevant evidence of the person's involvement in the offence concerned or would help to ascertain or verify their real identity.*

2I     *The necessity criteria do not permit arrest for an offence solely because it happens to be one of the statutory drug testing 'trigger offences' (see Code C Note 17E) when there is no suspicion that Class A drug misuse might have caused or contributed to the offence.*

2J     *Having determined that the necessity criteria have been met and having made the arrest, the officer can then consider the use of street bail on the basis of the effective and efficient progress of the investigation of the offence in question. It gives the officer discretion to compel the person to attend a police station at a date/time that best suits the overall needs of the particular investigation. Its use is not confined to dealing with child care issues or allowing officers to attend to more urgent operational duties and granting street bail does not retrospectively negate the need to arrest.*

3     *An arrested person must be given sufficient information to enable them to understand they have been deprived of their liberty and the reason they have been arrested, as soon as practicable after the arrest, e.g. when a person is arrested on suspicion of committing an offence they must be informed of the nature of the suspected offence and when and where it was committed. The suspect must also be informed of the reason or reasons why arrest is considered necessary. Vague or technical language should be avoided. When explaining why one or more of the arrest criteria apply, it is not necessary to disclose any specific details that might undermine or otherwise adversely affect any investigative processes. An example might be the conduct of a formal interview when prior disclosure of such details might give the suspect an opportunity to fabricate an innocent explanation or to otherwise conceal lies from the interviewer.*

4     *Nothing in this Code requires a caution to be given or repeated when informing a person not under arrest they may be prosecuted for an offence. However, a court will not be able to draw any inferences under the Criminal Justice and Public Order Act 1994, section 34, if the person was not cautioned.*

5     *If it appears a person does not understand the caution, the person giving it should explain it in their own words.*

6     *Certain powers available as the result of an arrest — for example, entry and search of premises, detention without charge beyond 24 hours, holding a person incommunicado and delaying access to legal advice — only apply in respect of indictable offences and are subject to the specific requirements on authorisation as set out in PACE and the relevant Code of Practice.*

## PACE CODE H

### REVISED CODE OF PRACTICE IN CONNECTION WITH: THE DETENTION, TREATMENT AND QUESTIONING BY POLICE OFFICERS OF PERSONS IN POLICE DETENTION UNDER SECTION 41 OF, AND SCHEDULE 8 TO, THE TERRORISM ACT 2000 THE TREATMENT AND QUESTIONING BY POLICE OFFICERS OF DETAINED PERSONS IN RESPECT OF WHOM AN AUTHORISATION TO QUESTION AFTER CHARGE HAS BEEN GIVEN UNDER SECTION 22 OF THE COUNTER-TERRORISM ACT 2008

[Code H is not reproduced. The full text of Code H is freely available at tinyurl.com/vt22x6g.]

# Attorney-General's Guidelines

## EXERCISE BY THE CROWN OF ITS RIGHT OF STAND BY

1. Although the law has long recognised the right of the Crown to exclude a member of a jury panel from sitting as a juror by the exercise in open court of the right to request a stand by or, if necessary, by challenge for cause, it has been customary for those instructed to prosecute on behalf of the Crown to assert that right only sparingly and in exceptional circumstances. It is generally accepted that the prosecution should not use its right in order to influence the overall composition of a jury or with a view to tactical advantage.

2. The approach outlined above is founded on the principles that:
   a. the members of a jury should be selected at random from the panel subject to any rule of law as to right of challenge by the defence, and
   b. the Juries Act 1974 identifies those classes of persons who alone are disqualified from or ineligible for service on a jury. No other class of person may be treated as disqualified or ineligible.

3. The enactment by Parliament of s. 118 of the Criminal Justice Act 1988 abolishing the right of defendants to remove jurors by means of peremptory challenge makes it appropriate that the Crown should assert its right to stand by only on the basis of clearly defined and restrictive criteria. Derogation from the principle that members of a jury should be selected at random should be permitted only where it is essential.

4. Primary responsibility for ensuring that an individual does not serve on a jury if he is not competent to discharge properly the duties of a juror rests with the appropriate court officer and, ultimately the trial judge. Current legislation provides, in ss. 9 to s.10 of the Juries Act 1974, fairly wide discretion to excuse, defer or discharge jurors.

5. The circumstances in which it would be proper for the Crown to exercise its right to stand by a member of a jury panel are:
   a. where a jury check authorised in accordance with the Attorney-General's Guidelines on Jury Checks reveals information justifying exercise of the right to stand by in accordance with para.11 of the guidelines below [under **Jury Checks**] and the Attorney-General personally authorises the exercise of the right to stand by; or
   b. where a person is about to be sworn as a juror who is manifestly unsuitable and the defence agree that, accordingly, the exercise by the prosecution of the right to stand by would be appropriate. An example of the sort of exceptional circumstances which might justify stand by is where it becomes apparent that, despite the provisions mentioned in para. 4 above, a juror selected for service to try a complex case is in fact illiterate.

## JURY CHECKS

1. The principles which are generally to be observed are:
   a. that members of a jury should be selected at random from the panel,
   b. the Juries Act 1974 identifies those classes of persons who alone are either disqualified from or ineligible for service on a jury; no other class of person may be treated as disqualified or ineligible,
   c. the correct way for the Crown to seek to exclude a member of the panel from sitting as a juror is by the exercise in open court of the right to request a stand by or, if necessary, to challenge for cause.

2. Parliament has provided safeguards against jurors who may be corrupt or biased. In addition to the provision for majority verdicts, there is the sanction of a criminal offence for a disqualified person to serve on a jury. The omission of a disqualified person from the panel is a matter for court officials—they will check criminal records for the purpose of ascertaining whether or not a potential juror is a disqualified person.

3. There are, however, certain exceptional types of case of public importance for which the provisions as to majority verdicts and the disqualification of jurors may not be sufficient to ensure the proper administration of justice. In such cases it is in the interests of both justice and the public that there should be further safeguards against the possibility of bias and in such cases checks which go beyond the investigation of criminal records may be necessary.

4. These classes of case may be defined broadly as (a) cases in which national security is involved and part of the evidence is likely to be heard in camera, and (b) security and terrorist cases in which a juror's extreme beliefs could prevent a fair trial.

5. The particular aspects of these cases which may make it desirable to seek extra precautions are:
   a. in security cases a danger that a juror, either voluntarily or under pressure, may make an improper use of evidence which, because of its sensitivity, has been given in camera,
   b. in both security and terrorist cases the danger that a juror's personal beliefs are so biased as to go beyond normally reflecting the broad spectrum of views and interests in the community to reflect the extreme views of sectarian interest or pressure group to a degree which might interfere with his fair assessment of the facts of the case or lead him to exert improper pressure on his fellow jurors.

6. In order to ascertain whether in exceptional circumstances of the above nature either of these factors might seriously influence a potential juror's impartial performance of his duties or his respecting the secrecy of evidence given in camera, it may be necessary to conduct a limited investigation of the panel. In general, such further investigation beyond one of criminal records made for disqualifications may only be made with the records of the police. However, a check may, additionally be made against the records of the Security Service. No checks other than on these sources and no general inquiries are to be made save to the limited extent that they may be needed to confirm the identity of a juror about whom the initial check has raised serious doubts.

7. No further investigation, as described in para. 6 above, should be made save with the personal authority of the Attorney-General on the application of the Director of Public Prosecutions and such checks are hereafter referred to as 'authorised checks'. When a chief officer of police or the prosecutor has reason to believe that it is likely that an authorised check may be desirable and proper in accordance with these guidelines, he should refer the matter to the Director of Public Prosecutions. In those cases in which the Director of Public Prosecutions believes authorised checks are both proportionate and necessary, the Director will make an application to the Attorney-General.

8. The Director of Public Prosecutions will provide the Attorney-General with all relevant information in support of the requested authorised checks. The Attorney-General will consider personally the request and, if appropriate, authorise the check.

9. The result of any authorised check will be sent to the Director of Public Prosecutions. The Director will then decide, having regard to the matters set out in para. 5 above, what information ought to be brought to the attention of prosecuting counsel. The Director will also provide the Attorney-General with the result of the authorised check.

10. Although the right of stand by and the decision to authorise checks are wholly within the discretion of the Attorney-General, when the Attorney-General has agreed to an authorised check being conducted, the Director of Public Prosecutions will write to the Presiding Judge for the area to advise him that this is being done.

11. No right of stand by should be exercised by counsel for the Crown on the basis of information obtained as a result of an authorised check save with the personal authority of the Attorney-General and unless the information is such as, having regard to the facts of the case and the offences charged, to afford strong reason for believing that a particular juror might be a security risk, be susceptible to improper approaches or be influenced in arriving at a verdict for the reasons given above.

12. Information revealed in the course of an authorised check must be considered in line with the normal rules on disclosure.

13. A record is to be kept by the Director of Public Prosecutions of the use made by counsel of the information passed to him and of the jurors stood by or challenged by the parties to the proceedings. A copy of this record is to be forwarded to the Attorney-General for the sole purpose of enabling him to monitor the operation of these guidelines.

14. No use of the information obtained as a result of an authorised check is to be made except as may be necessary in direct relation to or arising out of the trial for which the check was authorised. The information may, however, be used for the prevention of crime or as evidence in a future criminal prosecution, save that material obtained from the Security Service may only be used in those circumstances with the authority of the Security Service.

# ACCEPTANCE OF PLEAS AND THE PROSECUTOR'S ROLE IN THE SENTENCING EXERCISE

## A. Foreword

A1. Prosecutors have an important role in protecting the victim's interests in the criminal justice process, not least in the acceptance of pleas and the sentencing exercise. The basis of plea, particularly in a case that is not contested, is the vehicle through which the victim's voice is heard. Factual inaccuracies in pleas in mitigation cause distress and offence to victims, the families of victims and witnesses. This can take many forms but may be most acutely felt when the victim is dead and the family hears inaccurate assertions about the victim's character or lifestyle. Prosecution advocates are reminded that they are required to adhere to the standards set out in the Victim's Charter, which places the needs of the victim at the heart of the criminal justice process, and that they are subject to a similar obligation in respect of the Code of Practice for Victims of Crime.

A2. The principle of fairness is central to the administration of justice. The implementation of Human Rights Act 1998 in October 2000 incorporated into domestic law the principle of fairness to the accused articulated in the European Convention on Human Rights. Accuracy and reasonableness of plea plays an important part in ensuring fairness both to the accused and to the victim.

A3. The Attorney General's Guidelines on the Acceptance of Pleas issued on December 7, 2000 highlighted the importance of transparency in the conduct of justice. The basis of plea agreed by the parties in a criminal trial is central to the sentencing process. An illogical or unsupported basis of plea can lead to an unduly lenient sentence being passed, and has a consequential effect where consideration arises as to whether to refer the sentence to the Court of Appeal under section 36 of the Criminal Justice Act 1988.

A4. These Guidelines, which replace the Guidelines issued in October 2005, give guidance on how prosecutors should meet these objectives of protection of victims' interests and of securing fairness and transparency in the process. They take into account [CrimPD VII, Sentencing, paras. B.1 to B.27: see **CPD.VII.B**] and the guidance issued by the Court of Appeal (Criminal) Division in *R v Beswick* [1996] 1 Cr App R 343, *R v Tolera* [1999] 1 Cr App R 25 and *R v Underwood* [2005] 1 Cr App R 178. They complement the Bar Council Guidance on Written Standards for the Conduct of Professional Work issued with the 7th edition of the Code of Conduct for the Bar of England and Wales and the Law Society's Professional Conduct Rules. When considering the acceptance of a guilty plea prosecution advocates are also reminded of the need to apply 'The Farquharson Guidelines on The Role and Responsibilities of the Prosecution Advocate'.

A5. The Guidelines should be followed by all prosecutors and those persons designated under section 7 of the Prosecution of Offences Act 1985 (designated caseworkers) and apply to prosecutions conducted in England and Wales.

## B. General Principles

B1. Justice in this jurisdiction, save in the most exceptional circumstances, is conducted in public. This includes the acceptance of pleas by the prosecution and sentencing.

B2. The Code for Crown Prosecutors governs the prosecutor's decision-making prior to the commencement of the trial hearing and sets out the circumstances in which pleas to a reduced number of charges, or less serious charges, can be accepted.

B3. When a case is listed for trial and the prosecution form the view that the appropriate course is to accept a plea before the proceedings commence or continue, or to offer no evidence on the indictment or any part of it, the prosecution should whenever practicable speak to the victim or the victim's family, so that the position can be explained. The views of the victim or the family may assist in informing the prosecutor's decision as to whether it is the public interest, as defined by the Code for Crown Prosecutors, to accept or reject the plea. The victim or victim's family should then be kept informed and decisions explained once they are made at court.

B4. The appropriate disposal of a criminal case after conviction is as much a part of the criminal justice process as the trial of guilt or innocence. The prosecution advocate represents the public interest, and should be ready to assist the court to reach its decision as to the appropriate sentence. This will include drawing the court's attention to:
- any victim personal statement or other information available to the prosecution advocate as to the impact of the offence on the victim;
- where appropriate, to any evidence of the impact of the offending on a community;
- any statutory provisions relevant to the offender and the offences under consideration;

- any relevant sentencing guidelines and guideline cases; and
- the aggravating and mitigating factors of the offence under consideration.

B5.  The prosecution advocate may also offer assistance to the court by making submissions, in the light of all these factors, as to the appropriate sentencing range. In all cases, it is the prosecution advocate's duty to apply for appropriate ancillary orders, such as anti-social behaviour orders and confiscation orders. When considering which ancillary orders to apply for, prosecution advocates must always have regard to the victim's needs, including the question of his or her future protection.

## C.  The Basis of Plea

C1.  The basis of a guilty plea must not be agreed on a misleading or untrue set of facts and must take proper account of the victim's interests. An illogical or insupportable basis of plea will inevitably result in the imposition of an inappropriate sentence and is capable of damaging public confidence in the criminal justice system. In cases involving multiple defendants the bases of plea for each defendant must be factually consistent with each other.

C2.  When the defendant indicates an acceptable plea, the defence advocate should reduce the basis of the plea to writing. This must be done in all cases save for those in which the defendant has indicated that the guilty plea has been or will be tendered on the basis of the prosecution case.

C3.  The written basis of plea must be considered with great care, taking account of the position of any other relevant defendant where appropriate. The prosecution should not lend itself to any agreement whereby a case is presented to the sentencing judge on a misleading or untrue set of facts or on a basis that is detrimental to the victim's interests. There will be cases where a defendant seeks to mitigate on the basis of assertions of fact which are outside the scope of the prosecution's knowledge. A typical example concerns the defendant's state of mind. If a defendant wishes to be sentenced on this basis, the prosecution advocate should invite the judge not to accept the defendant's version unless he or she gives evidence on oath to be tested in cross-examination. [CrimPD VII, Sentencing, para. B.12: see **CPD.VII.B**] states that in such circumstances the defence advocate should be prepared to call the defendant and, if the defendant is not willing to testify, subject to any explanation that may be given, the judge may draw such inferences as appear appropriate.

C4.  The prosecution advocate should show the prosecuting authority any written record relating to the plea and agree with them the basis on which the case will be opened to the court. If, as may well be the case, the basis of plea differs in its implications for sentencing or the making of ancillary orders from the case originally outlined by the prosecution, the prosecution advocate must ensure that such differences are accurately reflected in the written record prior to showing it to the prosecuting authority.

C5.  It is the responsibility of the prosecution advocate thereafter to ensure that the defence advocate is aware of the basis on which the plea is accepted by the prosecution and the way in which the prosecution case will be opened to the court.

C6.  In all cases where it is likely to assist the court where the sentencing issues are complex or unfamiliar the prosecution must add to the written outline of the case which is served upon the court a summary of the key considerations. This should take the form of very brief notes on:

- any relevant statutory limitations
- the names of any relevant sentencing authorities or guidelines
- the scope for any ancillary orders (e.g. concerning anti-social behaviour, confiscation or deportation will need to be considered).
- The outline should also include the age of the defendant and information regarding any outstanding offences.

C7.  It remains open to the prosecutor to provide further written information (for example to supplement and update the analysis at later stages of the case) where he or she thought that likely to assist the court, or if the judge requests it.

C8.  When the prosecution advocate has agreed the written basis of plea submitted by the defence advocate, he or she should endorse the document accordingly. If the prosecution advocate takes issue with all or part of the written basis of plea, the procedure set out in [CrimPD VII, Sentencing, paras. B.11 to B.27: see **CPD.VII.B** (and in the CrimPR, r. 25.16: see **R25.16**)] should be followed. The defendant's basis of plea must be set out in writing identifying what is in dispute; the court may invite the parties to make representations about whether the dispute is material to sentence; and if the court decides that it is a material dispute, the court will invite further representations or evidence as it may require and decide the dispute in accordance with the principles set out in *R v Newton* 77 Cr App R13, CA. The signed original document setting out the disputed factual matters should be made available to the trial judge and thereafter lodged with the court papers, as it will form part of the record of the hearing.

- whether the behaviour could be prosecuted under statute—whether under the Fraud Act 2006 or another Act or as a statutory conspiracy; and
- whether the available statutory charges adequately reflect the gravity of the offence.

7. Statutory conspiracy to commit a substantive offence should be charged if the alleged agreement satisfies the definition in section 1 of the Criminal Law Act 1977, provided that there is no wider dishonest objective that would be important to the presentation of the prosecution case in reflecting the gravity of the case.

8. Section 12 of the Criminal Justice Act 1987 provides that common law conspiracy to defraud may be charged even if the conduct agreed upon will involve the commission of a statutory offence. However, Lord Bingham said in *R v Rimmington* and *R v Goldstein* [(2005) UKHL 63]:

   'I would not go to the length of holding that conduct may never be lawfully prosecuted as a generally-expressed common law crime where it falls within the terms of a specific statutory provision, *but good practice and respect for the primacy of statute do in my judgment require that conduct falling within the terms of a specific statutory provision should be prosecuted under that provision unless there is good reason for doing otherwise.*'

9. In the Attorney General's view the common law charge may still be appropriate in the type of cases set out in paragraphs 12–15, but in order to understand the circumstances under which conspiracy to defraud is used *prosecutors should make a record of the reasons for preferring that charge.*

### Records of decisions

10. Where a charge of common law conspiracy to defraud is proposed the case lawyer must consider and set out in writing in the review note:
    - how much such a charge will add to the amount of evidence likely to be called both by the prosecution and the defence; and
    - the justification for using the charge, and why specific statutory offences are inadequate or otherwise inappropriate.
    - Thereafter, and before charge, the use of this charge should be specifically approved by a supervising lawyer experienced in fraud cases. Equivalent procedures to ensure proper consideration of the charge and recording of the decision should be applied by all prosecuting authorities in their case review processes.

11. Information from these records will be collected retrospectively for the review to be conducted in 3 years. It will enable the identification of where and why the common law offence has been used. It could then also form the basis for any future work on whether, and if so how, to replace the common law or whether it can simply and safely be repealed. It is expected that in 3 years the Government will be able to review the situation in the light of the practical operation not only of the new fraud offences, but of other relevant changes. These include the Lord Chief Justice's protocol on the control and management of heavy fraud cases, and the sample count provisions in the Domestic Violence, Crime and Victims Act 2004. Any actual or proposed changes to the law on assisting and encouraging crime in the light of the Law Commission's study of that issue [Cm 6878, published in July 2006] will also be taken into account.

### A. Conduct that can more effectively be prosecuted as conspiracy to defraud

12. There may be cases where the interests of justice can only be served by presenting to a court an overall picture which cannot be achieved by charging a series of substantive offences or statutory conspiracies. Typically, such cases will involve some, but not necessarily all of the following:
    - evidence of several significant but different kinds of criminality;
    - several jurisdictions;
    - different types of victims, e.g. individuals, banks, web site administrators, credit card companies;
    - organised crime networks.

13. The proper presentation of such cases as statutory conspiracies could lead to:
    - large numbers of separate counts to reflect the different conspiracies;
    - severed trials for single or discrete groups of conspiracies;
    - evidence in one severed trial being deemed inadmissible in another.

14. If so, the consequences might be that no one court would receive a cohesive picture of the whole case which would allow sentencing on a proper basis. In contrast a single count of common law conspiracy to defraud might, in such circumstances, reflect the nature and extent of criminal conduct in a way that prosecuting the underlying statutory offences or conspiracies would fail to achieve.

**B.  Conduct that can only be prosecuted as conspiracy to defraud**

15.    Examples of such conduct might include but are not restricted to agreements to the following courses of action:
- The dishonest obtaining of land and other property which cannot be stolen such as intellectual property not protected by the Copyright, Designs and Patents Act 1988 and the Trademarks Act 1994, and other confidential information. The Fraud Act will bite where there is intent to make a gain or cause a loss through false representation, failure to disclose information where there is a legal obligation to do so, or the abuse of position;
- Dishonestly infringing another's right; for example the dishonest exploitation of another's patent in the absence of a legal duty to disclose information about its existence;
- Where it is intended that the final offence be committed by someone outside the conspiracy; and
- Cases where the accused cannot be proved to have had the necessary degree of knowledge of the substantive offence to be perpetrated;

# SECTION 18 RIPA: PROSECUTORS INTERCEPT GUIDELINES

1.    These guidelines concern the approach to be taken by prosecutors in applying section 18 of the Regulation of Investigatory Powers Act (RIPA) in England and Wales.

**Background**

2.    It has been long-standing Government policy that the fact that interception of communications has taken place in any particular case should remain secret and not be disclosed to the subject. This is because of the need to protect the continuing value of interception as a vital means of gathering intelligence about serious crime and activities which threaten national security. The Government judges that if the use of the technique in particular cases were to be confirmed, the value of the technique would be diminished because targets would either know, or could deduce, when their communications might be intercepted and so could take avoiding action by using other, more secure means of communication.

3.    In the context of legal proceedings, the policy that the fact of interception should remain secret is implemented by section 17 of RIPA. Section 17 provides that no evidence shall be adduced, question asked, assertion or disclosure made or other thing done in, for the purposes of, or in connection with, any legal proceedings which discloses the contents of a communication which has been obtained following the issue of an interception warrant or a warrant under the Interception of Communications Act 1985, or any related communications data ('protected information'), or tends to suggest that certain events have occurred.

4.    The effect of section 17 is that the fact of interception of the subject's communications and the product of that interception cannot be relied upon or referred to by either party to the proceedings. This is given further effect by sections 3(7), 7(6), 7A(9) and 9(9) of the Criminal Procedure and Investigations Act 1996 (as amended). This protects the continuing value of interception whilst also creating a 'level playing-field', in that neither side can gain any advantage from the interception. In the context of criminal proceedings, this means that the defendant cannot be prejudiced by the existence in the hands of the prosecution of intercept material which is adverse to his interests.

**Detailed Analysis**

**First Stage:  action to be taken by the prosecutor**

5.    Section 18(7)(a) of RIPA provides:

'Nothing in section 17(1) shall prohibit any such disclosure of any information that continues to be available for disclosure as is confined to … a disclosure to a person conducting a criminal prosecution for the purpose only of enabling that person to determine what is required of him by his duty to secure the fairness of the prosecution'.

If protected information is disclosed to a prosecutor, as permitted by section 18(7)(a), the first step that should be taken by the prosecutor is to review any information regarding an interception that remains extant at the time that he or she has conduct of the case.[1] In reviewing it, the prosecutor

---

[1] Section 15(1) of RIPA provides that it is the duty of the Secretary of State to ensure that arrangements are in place to ensure that (amongst other matters) intercept material is retained by the intercepting agencies only for as long as is necessary for any of the authorised purposes. The authorised purposes include retention which:

should seek to identify any information whose existence, if no action was taken by the Crown, might result in unfairness. Experience suggests that the most likely example of such potential unfairness is where the evidence in the case is such that the jury may draw an inference which intercept shows to be wrong, and to leave this uncorrected will result in the defence being disadvantaged.

6.　If in the view of the prosecutor to take no action would render the proceedings unfair, the prosecutor should, first consulting with the relevant prosecution agency, take such steps as are available to him or her to secure the fairness of the proceedings provided these steps do not contravene section 18(10). In the example given above, such steps could include:

　(i)　putting the prosecution case in such a way that the misleading inference is not drawn by the jury; or

　(ii)　not relying upon the evidence which makes the information relevant; or

　(iii)　discontinuing that part of the prosecution case in relation to which the protected information is relevant, by amending a charge or count on the indictment or offering no evidence on such a charge or count; or

　(iv)　making an admission of fact.[2]

There is no requirement for the prosecutor to notify the judge of the action that he or she has taken or proposes to take. Such a course should only be taken by the prosecutor if he considers it essential in the interests of justice to do so (see below).

### Second Stage: disclosure to the judge

7.　There may be some cases (although these are likely to be rare) where the prosecutor considers that he cannot secure the fairness of the proceedings without assistance from the relevant judge. In recognition of this, section 18(7)(b) of RIPA provides that in certain limited circumstances, the prosecutor may invite the judge to order a disclosure of the protected information to him.

8.　If the prosecutor considers that he requires the assistance of the trial judge to ensure the fairness of the proceedings, or he is in doubt as to whether the result of taking the steps outlined at para 6 above would ensure fairness, he must apply to see the judge *ex parte*. Under section 18(8), a judge shall not order a disclosure to him except where he is satisfied that the exceptional circumstances of the case make that disclosure essential in the interests of justice. Before the judge is in a position to order such disclosure the prosecutor will need to impart to the judge such information, but only such information, as is necessary to demonstrate that exceptional circumstances mean that the prosecutor acting alone cannot secure the fairness of the proceedings. Experience suggests that exceptional circumstances in the course of a trial justifying disclosure to a judge arise only in the following two situations:

### (1) Where the judge's assistance is necessary to ensure the fairness of the trial

This situation may arise in the example given at paragraph 5 above, where there is a risk that the jury might draw an inference from certain facts, which protected information shows would be the wrong inference, and the prosecutor is unable to ensure that the jury will not draw this inference by his actions alone. The purpose in informing the judge is so that the judge will then be in a position to ensure fairness by:

　(i)　summing up in a way which will ensure that the wrong inference is not drawn; or

　(ii)　giving appropriate directions to the jury; or

　(iii)　requiring the Crown to make an admission of fact which the judge thinks *essential in the interests of justice* if he is of the opinion that *exceptional circumstances* require him to make such a direction (section 18(9)). However, such a direction **must not** authorise or require anything to be done which discloses any of the contents of an intercepted communication or related data or tends to suggest that anything falling within section 17(2) has or may have occurred or be going to occur (section 18(10)). Situations where an admission of fact is required are likely to be rare. The judge must be of the view that proceedings could not be continued unless an

---

'is necessary to ensure that a person conducting a criminal prosecution has the information he needs to determine what is required of him by his duty to secure the fairness of the prosecution'. (section 15(4)(d))

2　This is acceptable as long as to do so would not contravene section 17 i.e. reveal the existence of an interception warrant. Prosecutors must bear in mind that such a breach might conceivably occur not only from the factual content of the admission, but also from the circumstances in which it is made.

admission of fact is made (and the conditions in section 18(9) are satisfied). There may be other ways in which it is possible for a judge to ensure fairness, such as those outlined at (i) and (ii) above.

In practice, no question of taking the action at (i)–(iii) arises if the protected information is already contained in a separate document in another form that has been or can be disclosed without contravening section 17(1), and this disclosure will secure the fairness of the proceedings.

### (2) Where the judge requires knowledge of the protected material for some other purpose

This situation may arise where, usually in the context of a PII application, the true significance of, or duty of disclosure in relation to, other material being considered for disclosure by a judge, cannot be appraised by the judge without reference to protected information. Disclosure to the judge of the protected information without more may be sufficient to enable him to appraise the material, but once he has seen the protected information the judge may also conclude that the conditions in section 18(9) are satisfied so that an admission of fact by the Crown is required in addition to or instead of disclosure of the non-protected material.

Another example is a case where protected information underlies operational decisions which are likely to be the subject of cross-examination and it is necessary to inform the judge of the existence of the protected information to enable him to deal with the issue when the questions are first posed in a way which ensures section 17(1) is not contravened.

### What if the actions of the prosecutor and/or the judge cannot ensure the fairness of the proceedings?

9.  There may be very rare cases in which no action taken by the prosecutor and/or judge can prevent the continuation of the proceedings being unfair, e.g. where the requirements of fairness could only be met if the Crown were to make an admission, but it cannot do so without contravening section 18(10). In that situation the prosecutor will have no option but to offer no evidence on the charge in question, or to discontinue the proceedings in their entirety.

### Responding to questions about interception

10. Prosecutors are sometimes placed in a situation in which they are asked by the court or by the defence whether interception has taken place or whether protected information exists. Whether or not interception has taken place or protected information exists, an answer in the following terms, or similar should be given:

> 'I am not in a position to answer that, but I am aware of sections 17 and 18 of the Regulation of Investigatory Powers Act 2000 and the Attorney General's Guidelines on the Disclosure of Information in Exceptional Circumstances under section 18'.

In a case where interception has taken place or protected information exists, an answer in these terms will avoid a breach of the prohibition in section 17 while providing assurance that the prosecutor is aware of his obligations.

11. For the avoidance of doubt, any notification or disclosure of information to the judge in accordance with paragraphs 7–10 must be *ex parte*. It will never be appropriate for prosecutors to volunteer, either *inter partes* or to the Court *ex parte*, that interception has taken place or that protected information exists, save in accordance with section 18 as elaborated in these Guidelines.

### Further Assistance

12. Should a prosecutor be unsure as to the application of these guidelines in any particular case, further guidance should be sought from those instructing him or her. In those cases where a prosecutor has been instructed by the Crown Prosecution Service, the relevant CPS prosecutor must seek appropriate guidance from Casework Directorate, CPS Headquarters, Ludgate Hill.

## THE PROSECUTOR'S ROLE IN APPLICATIONS FOR WITNESS ANONYMITY ORDERS ...

### A.  Foreword

A1.  Every defendant has a right to a fair trial. An important aspect of a fair trial is the right of the defendant to be confronted by, and to challenge, those who accuse him or her.

A2.  Making an application for a witness anonymity order is therefore a serious step, to be taken by the prosecutor only where there are genuine grounds to believe that the court would not otherwise hear evidence that should be available to it in the interests of justice; that other measures falling short of anonymity would not be sufficient; and that the defendant will have a fair trial if the order is made.

A3.    Anonymous witness testimony is not necessarily incompatible with Article 6, even when it is the sole or decisive evidence against the accused. But whether the measures used to allow a witness to give evidence anonymously in any particular case would make the trial unfair has to be evaluated with care on the facts of each case.

A4.    When assessing whether and in what terms to make an application for a witness anonymity order, prosecutors have overriding duties to be fair, independent and objective. These guidelines set out the overarching principles by which a prosecutor should consider, and if appropriate apply for, a witness anonymity order in accordance with the considerations set out in the Criminal Evidence (Witness Anonymity) Act 2008.

## B.    The Prosecutor's Duties

B1.    The effect of a witness anonymity order is to prevent the defendant from knowing the identity of a witness. Without this information the defendant's ability to investigate and challenge the accuracy or credibility of the witness's evidence may be limited.

B2.    When considering whether to make a witness anonymity order the court will consider to what extent the defendant needs to know the identity of the witness in order to challenge the witness's evidence effectively. This question will often be central to the question of whether, having regard to all the circumstances, the witness anonymity order sought would be consistent with a fair trial.

B3.    The prosecutor's role is:
- To act with scrupulous fairness.
- To examine with care, and probe where appropriate, the material provided in support of the application and the evidential basis for it. Prosecutors should in particular objectively assess any statement made by the witness or witnesses in question and the grounds on which it is based.
- To be satisfied before making the application that, viewed objectively, it can properly be said that the order is necessary and in the interests of justice and that the defendant can receive a fair trial.
- To put before the court all material that is relevant to the application. Courts will rely to a significant extent upon the prosecutor and the investigator to provide relevant material. Material will be relevant if the prosecutor relies upon it to support the application, or if it may tend to undermine or qualify the justification for making the order at all, or for making it in the form sought by the prosecutor. Material is particularly relevant if credibility is or may be in issue, for example if there is a known link between the witness and the defendant or a co-accused.
- To disclose as much relevant material to the defence as possible without identifying the witness, including material that may tend to cast doubt on the credibility, reliability or accuracy of the witness's evidence.

B4.    The role of the prosecutor as an independent and impartial minister of justice is of paramount importance. Applications should only be authorised by prosecutors at an appropriately senior level within the prosecuting authority.

B5.    The interests of justice include the interests of the victim or victims, the interests of the witness or witnesses, the interests of the defendant and any co-defendants and the wider public interest.

B6.    Prosecutors should take all necessary and reasonable steps consistent with a fair trial and the interests of justice to ensure the safety of a witness or the avoidance of real harm to the public interest or the protection of property.

## C.    Applications by Defendants

C1.    The Act permits a defendant (as well as a prosecutor) to apply for a Witness Anonymity Order. Prosecutors should respond to such applications independently and objectively. Prosecutors should examine critically, but fairly, the basis for any application and any material put forward in support of any application.

C2.    The prosecutor should provide the court with all material within the prosecutor's possession or control that is relevant to the defendant's application.

## D.    Appointment and Role of Special Counsel in Applications for Witness Anonymity

D1.    The Act makes no statutory provision for the appointment of Special Counsel.

D2.    A criminal court may invite the Attorney General to appoint Special Counsel.[3] However, in line with authority, such an appointment:

---

3 Most recently, *Shiv Malik and Manchester Crown Court and Chief Constable of Greater Manchester Police, Constable and Robinson Ltd and Attorney General as interested parties* [2008] EWHC 1362 (Admin).

- Should be regarded as '… exceptional, never automatic, a course of last and never first resort.' *R v H* and *R v C* [2004] UKHL 3. The need for Special Counsel has to be shown.
- The court will take account of the seriousness of the issue that the court has to determine in the particular case. Whether credibility is at issue is likely to be an important consideration. The court will also need to consider the extent to which Special Counsel could further the defendant's case.
- The court itself can be expected to perform a role of testing and probing the case which is presented on the application. When coupled with the prosecutor's duty to put all relevant material before the court, this may often be sufficient to enable a fair and informed decision to be reached without the need to appoint Special Counsel.

D3. Where appointed, the role of Special Counsel is to make representations on behalf of the accused in any closed proceedings.

D4. The Attorney General will consider each invitation to appoint Special Counsel on its merits, having regard to all the relevant circumstances of the case. In particular, in this context, to the basis of the application, whether it is opposed, the basis upon which it is opposed and the particular considerations that the court wishes Special Counsel to address.

D5. A prosecutor making an application for a witness anonymity order should always be prepared to assist the court to consider whether the circumstances are such that exceptionally the appointment of Special Counsel may be called for. When appropriate a prosecutor should draw to the attention of the court any aspect of an application for a witness anonymity order or any aspect of the case that may, viewed objectively, call for the appointment of Special Counsel.

D6. When a court decides to invite the Attorney General to appoint Special Counsel the prosecutor should (regardless of any steps taken by the court or any defendant) ensure that the Attorney General's Office is promptly notified; and assist in ensuring that the Attorney General receives all the information needed to take a decision.

D7. Where Special Counsel is appointed, he or she will initially be provided by the prosecutor with any open material made available to the accused regarding the application (and any other open material requested by Special Counsel). Special Counsel may then seek instructions from the defendant and his legal representatives. Only then will Special Counsel be provided by the prosecutor with the closed or un-redacted material provided to the court.

# PLEA DISCUSSIONS IN CASES OF SERIOUS OR COMPLEX FRAUD

## A. Foreword

A1. These Guidelines set out a process by which a prosecutor may discuss an allegation of serious or complex fraud with a person who he or she is prosecuting or expects to prosecute, or with that person's legal representative. They come into force on the 5th day of May 2009 and apply to plea discussions initiated on or after that date.

A2. The Guidelines will be followed by all prosecutors in England and Wales when conducting plea discussions in cases of serious or complex fraud. For the purposes of the Guidelines, fraud means any financial, fiscal or commercial misconduct or corruption which is contrary to the criminal law. Fraud may be serious or complex if at least two of the following factors are present:
- The amount obtained or intended to be obtained is alleged to exceed £500,000;
- There is a significant international dimension;
- The case requires specialised knowledge of financial, commercial, fiscal or regulatory matters such as the operation of markets, banking systems, trusts or tax regimes;
- The case involves allegations of fraudulent activity against numerous victims;
- The case involves an allegation of substantial and significant fraud on a public body;
- The case is likely to be of widespread public concern;
- The alleged misconduct endangered the economic well-being of the United Kingdom, for example by undermining confidence in financial markets.

Taking account of these matters, it is for the prosecutor to decide whether or not a case is one of fraud, and whether or not it is serious or complex.

A3. The decision whether a person should be charged with a criminal offence rests with the prosecutor. In selecting the appropriate charge or charges, the prosecutor applies principles set out in the Code for Crown Prosecutors ('the Code'). Charges should reflect the seriousness and extent of the offending, give the court adequate sentencing powers and enable the case to be presented in a clear and simple way. The Code also states that prosecutors should not go ahead with more charges to encourage a defendant to plead guilty to a few; equally, prosecutors should not charge a more serious offence to encourage a defendant to plead to a less serious one.

A4. Once proceedings are instituted, the accused may plead guilty to all of the charges selected. If the defendant will plead guilty to some, but not all, of the charges or to a different, possibly less serious charge, the Code states that a prosecutor is entitled to accept such pleas if he or she assesses that the court could still pass an adequate sentence. In taking these decisions the prosecutor also applies the Attorney General's Guidelines on the Acceptance of Pleas and the Prosecutor's Role in the Sentencing Exercise ('the Acceptance of Pleas Guidelines').

A5. The purpose of plea discussions is to narrow the issues in the case with a view to reaching a just outcome at the earliest possible time, including the possibility of reaching an agreement about acceptable pleas of guilty and preparing a joint submission as to sentence.

A6. The potential benefits of plea discussions are that:
- Early resolution of the case may reduce the anxiety and uncertainty for victims and witnesses, and provide earlier clarity for accused persons who admit their guilt (subject to the court's power to reject the agreement);
- The issues in dispute may be narrowed so that even if the case proceeds to trial, it can be managed more efficiently in accordance with Rule 3.2 of the Criminal Procedure Rules 2005. If pleas are agreed, litigation can be kept to a minimum.

A7. Where plea discussions take place prior to the commencement of proceedings, the charges brought by the prosecutor will reflect those agreed, rather than those that the prosecutor would necessarily have preferred if no agreement had been reached. Also, any criminal investigation may not be complete when these discussions take place. For these reasons it is important that the procedures followed should command public and judicial confidence; that any agreement reached is reasonable, fair and just; that there are safeguards to ensure that defendants are not under improper pressure to make admissions; and that there are proper records of discussions that have taken place.

A8. The Guidelines are not intended to prevent or discourage existing practices by which prosecutors and prosecuting advocates discuss cases with defence legal representatives after charge, in order to narrow the issues or to agree a basis of plea. Neither do they affect the existing practice of judicial sentence indications at the plea and case management hearing or later in accordance with the guidance in *R v Goodyear (Karl)* [2005] EWCA 888 (see also the Acceptance of Pleas Guidelines). They complement, and do not detract from or replace, the Code and the Acceptance of Pleas Guidelines, or any other relevant guidance such as the Prosecutor's Pledge, the Victim's Charter and the Code of Practice for Victims of Crime.

A9. Where a plea agreement is reached, it remains entirely a matter for the court to decide how to deal with the case.

## B. General Principles

B1. In conducting plea discussions and presenting a plea agreement to the court, the prosecutor must act openly, fairly and in the interests of justice.

B2. Acting in the interests of justice means ensuring that the plea agreement reflects the seriousness and extent of the offending, gives the court adequate sentencing powers, and enables the court, the public and the victims to have confidence in the outcome. The prosecutor must consider carefully the impact of a proposed plea or basis of plea on the community and the victim, and on the prospects of successfully prosecuting any other person implicated in the offending. The prosecutor must not agree to a reduced basis of plea which is misleading, untrue or illogical.

B3. Acting fairly means respecting the rights of the defendant and of any other person who is being or may be prosecuted in relation to the offending. The prosecutor must not put improper pressure on a defendant in the course of plea discussions, for example by exaggerating the strength of the case in order to persuade the defendant to plead guilty, or to plead guilty on a particular basis.

B4. Acting openly means being transparent with the defendant, the victim and the court. The prosecutor must:
- Ensure that a full and accurate record of the plea discussions is prepared and retained;
- Ensure that the defendant has sufficient information to enable him or her to play an informed part in the plea discussions;
- Communicate with the victim before accepting a reduced basis of plea, wherever it is practicable to do so, so that the position can be explained; and
- Ensure that the plea agreement placed before the court fully and fairly reflects the matters agreed. The prosecutor must not agree additional matters with the defendant which are not recorded in the plea agreement and made known to the court.

## C. Initiating Plea Discussions

*When and with whom discussions should be initiated and conducted*

C1. Where he or she believes it advantageous to do so, the prosecutor may initiate plea discussions with any person who is being prosecuted or investigated with a view to prosecution in connection with a serious or complex fraud, and who is legally represented. The prosecutor will not initiate plea discussions with a defendant who is not legally represented. If the prosecutor receives an approach from such a defendant, he or she may enter into discussions if satisfied that it is appropriate to do so.

C2. Where proceedings have not yet been instituted, the prosecutor should not initiate plea discussions until he or she and the investigating officer are satisfied that the suspect's criminality is known. This will not usually be the case until after the suspect has been interviewed under caution.

C3. The prosecutor should be alert to any attempt by the defendant to use plea discussions as a means of delaying the investigation or prosecution, and should not initiate or continue discussions where the defendant's commitment to the process is in doubt. The prosecutor should ensure that the position is preserved during plea discussions by, for example, restraining assets in anticipation of the making of a confiscation order. Where a defendant declines to take part in plea discussions, the prosecutor should not make a second approach unless there is a material change in circumstances.

*Invitation letter*

C4. In order to initiate the plea discussions, the prosecutor will send the defendant's representatives a letter which:
  • Asks whether the defence wish to enter into discussions in accordance with these Guidelines; and
  • Sets a deadline for a response from the defence.

*Terms and conditions letter*

C5. Where the defence agree to engage in plea discussions, the prosecutor should send them a letter setting out the way in which the discussions will be conducted. This letter should deal with:
  • The confidentiality of information provided by the prosecutor and defendant in the course of the plea discussions;
  • The use which may be made by the prosecutor of information provided by the defendant; and
  • The practical means by which the discussions will be conducted.

*Confidentiality and use of information*

C6. In relation to confidentiality, the prosecutor will indicate that he or she intends to provide an undertaking to the effect that the fact that the defendant has taken part in the plea discussions, and any information provided by the defence in the course of the plea discussions will be treated as confidential and will not be disclosed to any other party other than for the purposes of the plea discussions and plea agreement (applying these Guidelines), or as required by law. The undertaking will make it clear that the law in relation to the disclosure of unused material may require the prosecutor to provide information about the plea discussions to another defendant in criminal proceedings.

C7. The prosecutor will require the defendant's legal representative to provide an undertaking to the effect that information provided by the prosecutor in the course of the plea discussions will be treated as confidential and will not be disclosed to any other party, other than for the purposes of the plea discussion and plea agreement or as required by law.

C8. In relation to the use of information, the prosecutor will indicate that he or she intends to undertake not to rely upon the fact that the defendant has taken part in the plea discussions, or any information provided by the defendant in the course of the discussions, as evidence in any prosecution of that defendant for the offences under investigation, should the discussions fail. However, this undertaking will make it clear that the prosecutor is not prevented from:
  • Relying upon a concluded and signed plea agreement as confession evidence or as admissions;
  • Relying upon any evidence obtained from enquiries made as a result of the provision of information by the defendant;
  • Relying upon information provided by the defendant as evidence against him or her in any prosecution for an offence other than the fraud which is the subject of the plea discussion and any offence which is consequent upon it, such as money laundering; and
  • Relying upon information provided by the defendant in a prosecution of any other person for any offence (so far as the rules of evidence allow).

C9. In exceptional circumstances the prosecutor may agree to different terms regarding the confidentiality and use of information. However, the prosecutor must not surrender the ability to rely upon a concluded and signed plea agreement as evidence against the defendant. The prosecutor may reserve the right to bring other charges (additional to those to which the defendant has indicated a willingness to plead guilty) in specific circumstances, for example if substantial new information comes to light at a later stage, the plea agreement is rejected by the court, or the defendant fails to honour the agreement.

C10. Until the issues of confidentiality and use of information have been agreed to the satisfaction of both parties, and the agreement reflected in signed undertakings, the prosecutor must not continue with the substantive plea discussions.

### D. Conducting Plea Discussions

*Statement of case*

D1. Where plea discussions take place prior to proceedings being instituted, the prosecutor will provide a statement of case to the defence. This is a written summary of the nature of the allegation against the suspect and the evidence which has been obtained, or is expected to be obtained, to support it. The statement of case should include a list of the proposed charges. Material in support of the statement of case may also be provided, whether or not in the form of admissible evidence. However, the prosecutor is not obliged to reveal to the suspect all of the information or evidence supporting his case, provided that this does not mislead the suspect to his or her prejudice.

D2. Where plea discussions are initiated after proceedings have been commenced, but before the prosecutor has provided the defence with a case summary or opening note, the prosecutor may provide a statement of case to assist the defendant in understanding the evidence and identifying the issues.

*Unused material*

D3. These Guidelines do not affect the prosecutor's existing duties in relation to the disclosure of unused material. Where plea discussions take place prior to the institution of proceedings, the prosecutor should ensure that the suspect is not misled as to the strength of the prosecution case. It will not usually be necessary to provide copies of unused material in order to do this.

*Conducting and recording the discussions*

D4. Having provided the defence with the statement of case and supporting material, the parties will then be in a position to conduct the plea discussion proper. Whether this is done by correspondence, by face-to-face meetings or by a combination of the two is a matter for the parties to decide in the individual case.

D5. It is essential that a full written record is kept of every key action and event in the discussion process, including details of every offer or concession made by each party, and the reasons for every decision taken by the prosecutor. Meetings between the parties should be minuted and the minutes agreed and signed. Particular care should be taken where the defendant is not legally represented. The prosecutor should only meet with a defendant who is not legally represented if the defendant agrees to the meeting being recorded, or to the presence of an independent third party.

*Queen's Evidence*

D6. If the defendant offers at any stage to provide information, or to give evidence about the criminal activities of others, any such offer will be dealt with in accordance with sections 71 to 75 of the Serious Organised Crime and Police Act 2005 ('SOCPA'), the judgment of the Court of Appeal in *R v P, R v Blackburn* [2007] EWCA Crim 2290 and the guidance agreed and issued by the Director of Public Prosecutions, the Director of the Serious Fraud Office and the Director of Revenue and Customs Prosecutions.

*Discussion of pleas*

D7. In deciding whether or not to accept an offer by the defendant to plead guilty, the prosecutor will follow sections 7 and 10 of the Code relating to the selection of charges and the acceptance of guilty pleas. The prosecutor should ensure that:
- The charges reflect the seriousness and extent of the offending;
- They give the court adequate powers to sentence and impose appropriate post-conviction orders;
- They enable the case to be presented in a clear and simple way (bearing in mind that many cases of fraud are necessarily complex);
- The basis of plea enables the court to pass a sentence that matches the seriousness of the offending, particularly if there are aggravating features;

- The interests of the victim, and where possible any views expressed by the victim, are taken into account when deciding whether it is in the public interest to accept the plea; and
- The investigating officer is fully appraised of developments in the plea discussions and his or her views are taken into account.

D8.   In reaching an agreement on pleas, the parties should resolve any factual issues necessary to allow the court to sentence the defendant on a clear, fair and accurate basis. Before agreeing to proposed pleas, the prosecutor should satisfy him or herself that the Full Code Test as set out in the Code will be made out in respect of each charge. In considering whether the evidential stage of the test will be met, the prosecutor should assume that the offender will sign a plea agreement amounting to an admission to the charge.

*Discussion of sentence*

D9.   Where agreement is reached as to pleas, the parties should discuss the appropriate sentence with a view to presenting a joint written submission to the court. This document should list the aggravating and mitigating features arising from the agreed facts, set out any personal mitigation available to the defendant, and refer to any relevant sentencing guidelines or authorities. In the light of all of these factors, it should make submissions as to the applicable sentencing range in the relevant guideline. The prosecutor must ensure that the submissions are realistic, taking full account of all relevant material and considerations.

D10.  The prosecutor should bear in mind all of the powers of the court, and seek to include in the joint submission any relevant ancillary orders. It is particularly desirable that measures should be included that achieve redress for victims (such as compensation orders) and protection for the public (such as directors' disqualification orders, serious crime prevention orders or financial reporting orders).

D11.  Due regard should be had to the court's asset recovery powers and the desirability of using these powers both as a deterrent to others and as a means of preventing the defendant from benefiting from the proceeds of crime or funding future offending. The Proceeds of Crime Act 2002 requires the Crown Court to proceed to the making of a confiscation order against a convicted defendant who has benefited from his criminal conduct where the prosecutor asks the court to do so, or the court believes that it is appropriate to do so. Fraud is an acquisitive crime, and the expectation in a fraud case should be that a confiscation order will be sought by the prosecutor reflecting the full benefit to the defendant. However, in doing so it is open to the prosecutor to take a realistic view of the likely approach of the court to the determination of any points in dispute (such as the interest of a third party in any property).

D12.  In the course of the plea discussions the prosecutor must make it clear to the defence that the joint submission as to sentence (including confiscation) is not binding on the court.

*Liaison with another prosecutor or regulator*

D13.  The prosecutor may become aware that another prosecuting authority or regulatory body (either in England and Wales or elsewhere) has an interest in the defendant. The prosecutor should liaise with the other agency, in accordance with the Prosecutors' Convention and any other relevant agreement or guidance. The other agency may wish to take part in the plea discussions, or they may authorise the prosecutor to discuss with the defendant the matters which they are interested in, with a view to resolving all matters in one plea agreement. The prosecutor should warn the defendant that a plea agreement will not bind any other agency which is not a party to it.

## E.  The Written Plea Agreement

E1.   All matters agreed between the prosecutor and the defence must be reduced to writing as a plea agreement and signed by both parties. The plea agreement will include:
- A list of the charges;
- A statement of the facts; and
- A declaration, signed by the defendant personally, to the effect that he or she accepts the stated facts and admits he or she is guilty of the agreed charges.

E2.   Any agreement under the SOCPA regarding the giving of assistance to the prosecutor by the defendant should be in a separate document accompanying the plea agreement.

E3.   Once a plea agreement is signed in a case where proceedings have not yet been commenced, the prosecutor will review the case in accordance with the Code and, assuming the evidential stage of the Full Code Test is satisfied on the basis of the signed plea agreement and the other available evidence, will arrange for proceedings to be instituted by summons or charge.

E4.   In advance of the defendant's first appearance in the Crown Court, the prosecutor should send the court sufficient material to allow the judge to understand the facts of the case and the history of the plea discussions, to assess whether the plea agreement is fair and in the interests of justice, and to decide the appropriate sentence. This will include:

- The signed plea agreement;
- A joint submission as to sentence and sentencing considerations;
- Any relevant sentencing guidelines or authorities;
- All of the material provided by the prosecution to the defendant in the course of the plea discussions;
- Any material provided by the defendant to the prosecution, such as documents relating to personal mitigation; and
- The minutes of any meetings between the parties and any correspondence generated in the plea discussions.

E5.   It will then be for the court to decide how to deal with the plea agreement. In particular, the court retains an absolute discretion as to whether or not it sentences in accordance with the joint submission from the parties.

### F.  Failure of Plea Discussions

F1.   There are several circumstances in which plea discussions may result in an outcome other than the defendant pleading guilty in accordance with a plea agreement. The prosecutor or the defendant may break off the discussions. They may be unable to reach an agreement. They may reach an agreement, but intervening events may lead the prosecutor to decide that proceedings should not be instituted. Proceedings may be instituted but the court may reject the plea agreement. The defendant may decline to plead guilty in accordance with the plea agreement, either as a result of a sentence indication given under the procedure set out in *R v Goodyear*, or for some other reason.

F2.   If any of these situations arises, the prosecutor may wish for further enquiries to be made with a view to bringing or completing proceedings against the defendant. If proceedings have already been instituted, the prosecutor will use the appropriate means to delay them — either discontinuing under section 23 or 23A of the Prosecution of Offences Act 1985 or (if the indictment has already been preferred) applying for an adjournment or stay of the proceedings. The prosecutor and the defendant's representatives will continue to be bound by the preliminary undertakings made in relation to the confidentiality and use of information provided in the course of the plea discussions.

F3.   Where plea discussions have broken down for any reason, it will be rare that the prosecutor will wish to re-open them, but he or she may do so if there is a material change in circumstances which warrants it.

# DISCLOSURE

The Attorney-General's Guidelines on Disclosure for Investigators, Prosecutors and Defence Practitioners are reproduced later in this Supplement.

# The Code for Crown Prosecutors

*Reproduced under © Crown Copyright 2004 under the terms of the Open Government Licence v2.0.*

## Introduction

1.1 The Code for Crown Prosecutors (the Code) is issued by the Director of Public Prosecutions (DPP) under section 10 of the Prosecution of Offences Act 1985. This is the eighth edition of the Code and replaces all earlier versions.

1.2 The DPP is the head of the Crown Prosecution Service (CPS), which is the principal public prosecution service for England and Wales. The DPP operates independently, under the superintendence of the Attorney General who is accountable to Parliament for the work of the CPS.

1.3 The Code gives guidance to prosecutors on the general principles to be applied when making decisions about prosecutions. The Code is issued primarily for prosecutors in the CPS but other prosecutors follow the Code, either through convention or because they are required to do so by law.

1.4 In this Code:
- 'Suspect' is used to describe a person who is under consideration as the subject of formal criminal proceedings;
- 'Defendant' is used to describe a person who has been charged or summonsed;
- 'Offender' is used to describe a person who has admitted guilt as to the commission of an offence, or who has been found guilty in a court of law;
- 'Victim' is used to describe a person against whom an offence has been committed, or the complainant in a case being considered or prosecuted by the CPS.

## General Principles

2.1 The independence of the prosecutor is central to the criminal justice system of a democratic society. Prosecutors are independent from persons or agencies that are not part of the prosecution decision-making process. CPS prosecutors are also independent from the police and other investigators. Prosecutors must be free to carry out their professional duties without political interference and must not be affected by improper or undue pressure or influence from any source.

2.2 It is not the function of the CPS to decide whether a person is guilty of a criminal offence, but to make assessments about whether it is appropriate to present charges for the criminal court to consider. The CPS assessment of any case is not in any sense a finding of, or implication of, any guilt or criminal conduct. A finding of guilt can only be made by a court.

2.3 Similarly, a decision not to bring criminal charges does not necessarily mean that an individual has not been a victim of crime. It is not the role of the CPS to make such determinations.

2.4 The decision to prosecute or to recommend an out-of-court disposal is a serious step that affects suspects, victims, witnesses and the public at large and must be undertaken with the utmost care.

2.5 It is the duty of prosecutors to make sure that the right person is prosecuted for the right offence and to bring offenders to justice wherever possible. Casework decisions taken fairly, impartially and with integrity help to secure justice for victims, witnesses, suspects, defendants and the public. Prosecutors must ensure that the law is properly applied, that relevant evidence is put before the court and that obligations of disclosure are complied with.

2.6 Although each case must be considered on its own facts and on its own merits, there are general principles that apply in every case.

2.7 When making decisions, prosecutors must be fair and objective. They must not let any personal views about the ethnic or national origin, gender, disability, age, religion or belief, sexual orientation or gender identity of the suspect, defendant, victim or any witness influence their decisions. Neither must they be motivated by political considerations. Prosecutors must always act in the interests of justice and not solely for the purpose of obtaining a conviction.

2.8 Prosecutors must be even-handed in their approach to every case, and have a duty to protect the rights of suspects and defendants, while providing the best possible service to victims.

2.9 The CPS is a public authority for the purposes of current, relevant equality legislation. Prosecutors are bound by the duties set out in this legislation.

2.10 Prosecutors must apply the principles of the European Convention on Human Rights, in accordance with the Human Rights Act 1998, at each stage of a case. They must comply with any guidelines issued by the Attorney General and with the policies and guidance of the CPS issued on behalf of the DPP, unless it is determined that there are exceptional circumstances. CPS guidance contains further evidential and public interest factors for specific offences and offenders and is available for the public to view on the CPS website. Prosecutors must also comply with the Criminal

Procedure Rules and Criminal Practice Directions, and have regard to the Sentencing Council Guidelines and the obligations arising from international conventions.

2.11  The CPS prosecutes on behalf of some other Government departments. In such cases, prosecutors should have regard to any relevant enforcement policies of those departments.

2.12  Some offences may be prosecuted by either the CPS or by other prosecutors in England and Wales. When making decisions in these cases, CPS prosecutors may, where they think it appropriate, have regard to any relevant enforcement or prosecution policy or code of the other prosecutor.

2.13  Where the law differs in England and Wales prosecutors must apply the Code and have regard to any relevant policy, guidance or charging standard.

**The Decision Whether to Prosecute**

3.1  In more serious or complex cases, prosecutors decide whether a person should be charged with a criminal offence and, if so, what that offence should be. Prosecutors may also advise on or authorise out-of-court disposals as an alternative to prosecution. They make their decisions in accordance with this Code, the DPP's Guidance on Charging and any relevant legal guidance or policy. The police apply the same principles in deciding whether to start criminal proceedings against a person in those cases for which they are responsible.

3.2  The police and other investigators are responsible for conducting inquiries into any alleged crime and for deciding how to deploy their resources. This includes decisions to start or continue an investigation and on the scope of the investigation. Prosecutors should advise the police and other investigators about possible reasonable lines of inquiry, evidential requirements, pre-charge procedures, disclosure management and the overall investigation strategy. This can include decisions to refine or narrow the scope of the criminal conduct and the number of suspects under investigation. Such advice assists the police and other investigators to complete the investigation within a reasonable period of time and to build the most effective prosecution case.

3.3  Prosecutors cannot direct the police or other investigators. However, prosecutors must have regard to the impact of any failure to pursue an advised reasonable line of inquiry or to comply with a request for information, when deciding whether the application of the Full Code Test should be deferred or whether the test can be met at all.

3.4  Prosecutors should identify and, where possible, seek to rectify evidential weaknesses but, subject to the Threshold Test (see section 5), they should quickly stop cases which do not meet the evidential stage of the Full Code Test (see section 4) and which cannot be strengthened by further investigation, or where the public interest clearly does not require a prosecution (see section 4). Although prosecutors primarily consider the evidence and information supplied by the police and other investigators, the suspect or those acting on their behalf may also submit evidence or information to the prosecutor, before or after charge, to help inform the prosecutor's decision. In appropriate cases, the prosecutor may invite the suspect or their representative to do so.

3.5  Prosecutors should not start or continue a prosecution where their view is that it is highly likely that a court will rule that a prosecution is an abuse of its process, and stay the proceedings.

3.6  Prosecutors review every case they receive from the police or other investigators. Review is a continuing process and prosecutors must take account of any change in circumstances that occurs as the case develops. This includes what becomes known of the defence case, any further reasonable lines of inquiry that should be pursued, and receipt of any unused material that may undermine the prosecution case or assist the defence case, to the extent that charges should be altered or discontinued or the prosecution should not proceed. If a case is to be stopped, care should be taken when choosing the method of termination, as this can affect the victim's position under the Victims' Right to Review scheme. Wherever possible, prosecutors should consult the investigator when considering changing the charges or stopping the case. Prosecutors and investigators work closely together, but the final responsibility for the decision whether or not a case should go ahead rests with the CPS.

3.7  Parliament has decided that a limited number of offences should only be taken to court with the agreement of the DPP. These are called consent cases. In such cases the DPP, or a prosecutor acting on their behalf, applies the Code in deciding whether to give consent to a prosecution.

3.8  There are also certain offences that can only be taken to court with the consent of the Attorney General. Prosecutors must follow current guidance when referring any such cases to the Attorney General. Some offences require the consent of a Secretary of State before a prosecution is started. Prosecutors must obtain such consent prior to charge and apply any relevant guidance in these cases. Additionally, the Attorney General will be kept informed of certain cases as part of their superintendence of the CPS and accountability to Parliament for its actions.

## The Full Code Test

4.1    Prosecutors must only start or continue a prosecution when the case has passed both stages of the Full Code Test. The exception is when the Threshold Test may be applied (see section 5).

4.2    The Full Code Test has two stages: (i) the evidential stage; followed by (ii) the public interest stage.

4.3    The Full Code Test should be applied:

a.    when all outstanding reasonable lines of inquiry have been pursued; or

b.    prior to the investigation being completed, if the prosecutor is satisfied that any further evidence or material is unlikely to affect the application of the Full Code Test, whether in favour of or against a prosecution.

4.4    In most cases prosecutors should only consider whether a prosecution is in the public interest after considering whether there is sufficient evidence to prosecute. However, there will be cases where it is clear, prior to reviewing all the evidence, that the public interest does not require a prosecution. In these instances, prosecutors may decide that the case should not proceed further.

4.5    Prosecutors should only take such a decision when they are satisfied that the broad extent of the criminality has been determined and that they are able to make a fully informed assessment of the public interest. If prosecutors do not have sufficient information to take such a decision, the investigation should continue and a decision taken later in accordance with the Full Code Test set out in this section.

### The Evidential Stage

4.6    Prosecutors must be satisfied that there is sufficient evidence to provide a realistic prospect of conviction against each suspect on each charge.[*] They must consider what the defence case may be, and how it is likely to affect the prospects of conviction. A case which does not pass the evidential stage must not proceed, no matter how serious or sensitive it may be.

4.7    The finding that there is a realistic prospect of conviction is based on the prosecutor's objective assessment of the evidence, including the impact of any defence and any other information that the suspect has put forward or on which they might rely. It means that an objective, impartial and reasonable jury or bench of magistrates or judge hearing a case alone, properly directed and acting in accordance with the law, is more likely than not to convict the defendant of the charge alleged. This is a different test from the one that the criminal courts themselves must apply. A court may only convict if it is sure that the defendant is guilty.

4.8    When deciding whether there is sufficient evidence to prosecute, prosecutors should ask themselves the following:

### Can the evidence be used in court?

Prosecutors should consider whether there is any question over the admissibility of certain evidence. In doing so, prosecutors should assess:

• the likelihood of that evidence being held as inadmissible by the court; and
• the importance of that evidence in relation to the evidence as a whole.

### Is the evidence reliable?

Prosecutors should consider whether there are any reasons to question the reliability of the evidence, including its accuracy or integrity.

### Is the evidence credible?

Prosecutors should consider whether there are any reasons to doubt the credibility of the evidence.

### Is there any other material that might affect the sufficiency of evidence?

Prosecutors must consider at this stage and throughout the case whether there is any material that may affect the assessment of the sufficiency of evidence, including examined and unexamined material in the possession of the police, and material that may be obtained through further reasonable lines of inquiry.

### The Public Interest Stage

4.9    In every case where there is sufficient evidence to justify a prosecution or to offer an out-of-court disposal, prosecutors must go on to consider whether a prosecution is required in the public interest.

4.10    It has never been the rule that a prosecution will automatically take place once the evidential stage is met. A prosecution will usually take place unless the prosecutor is satisfied that there are public

---

[*] For the purposes of the Code for Crown Prosecutors, 'conviction' includes a finding that 'the person did the act or made the omission' in circumstances where the person is likely to be found not guilty on the grounds of insanity.

interest factors tending against prosecution which outweigh those tending in favour. In some cases the prosecutor may be satisfied that the public interest can be properly served by offering the offender the opportunity to have the matter dealt with by an out-of-court disposal rather than bringing a prosecution.

4.11 When deciding the public interest, prosecutors should consider each of the questions set out below in paragraphs 4.14 a) to g) so as to identify and determine the relevant public interest factors tending for and against prosecution. These factors, together with any public interest factors set out in relevant guidance or policy issued by the DPP, should enable prosecutors to form an overall assessment of the public interest.

4.12 The explanatory text below each question in paragraphs 4.14 a) to g) provides guidance to prosecutors when addressing each particular question and determining whether it identifies public interest factors for or against prosecution. The questions identified are not exhaustive, and not all the questions may be relevant in every case. The weight to be attached to each of the questions, and the factors identified, will also vary according to the facts and merits of each case.

4.13 It is quite possible that one public interest factor alone may outweigh a number of other factors which tend in the opposite direction. Although there may be public interest factors tending against prosecution in a particular case, prosecutors should consider whether nonetheless a prosecution should go ahead and those factors put to the court for consideration when sentence is passed.

4.14 Prosecutors should consider each of the following questions:

a) *How serious is the offence committed?*

- The more serious the offence, the more likely it is that a prosecution is required.
- When assessing the seriousness of an offence, prosecutors should include in their consideration the suspect's culpability and the harm caused, by asking themselves the questions at b) and c).

b) *What is the level of culpability of the suspect?*

- The greater the suspect's level of culpability, the more likely it is that a prosecution is required.
- Culpability is likely to be determined by:
    i. the suspect's level of involvement;
    ii. the extent to which the offending was premeditated and/or planned;
    iii. the extent to which the suspect has benefitted from criminal conduct;
    iv. whether the suspect has previous criminal convictions and/or out-of-court disposals and any offending whilst on bail or whilst subject to a court order;
    v. whether the offending was or is likely to be continued, repeated or escalated;
    vi. the suspect's age and maturity (see paragraph d below).
- A suspect is likely to have a much lower level of culpability if the suspect has been compelled, coerced or exploited, particularly if they are the victim of a crime that is linked to their offending.
- Prosecutors should also have regard to whether the suspect is, or was at the time of the offence, affected by any significant mental or physical ill health or disability, as in some circumstances this may mean that it is less likely that a prosecution is required. However, prosecutors will also need to consider how serious the offence was, whether the suspect is likely to re-offend and the need to safeguard the public or those providing care to such persons.

c) *What are the circumstances of and the harm caused to the victim?*

- The circumstances of the victim are highly relevant. The more vulnerable the victim's situation, or the greater the perceived vulnerability of the victim, the more likely it is that a prosecution is required.
- This includes where a position of trust or authority exists between the suspect and victim.
- A prosecution is also more likely if the offence has been committed against a victim who was at the time a person serving the public.
- It is more likely that prosecution is required if the offence was motivated by any form of prejudice against the victim's actual or presumed ethnic or national origin, gender, disability, age, religion or belief, sexual orientation or gender identity; or if the suspect targeted or exploited the victim, or demonstrated hostility towards the victim, based on any of those characteristics.
- Prosecutors also need to consider if a prosecution is likely to have an adverse effect on the victim's physical or mental health, always bearing in mind the seriousness of the offence, the availability of special measures and the possibility of a prosecution without the participation of the victim.
- Prosecutors should take into account the views expressed by the victim about the impact that the offence has had. In appropriate cases, this may also include the views of the victim's family.
- However, the CPS does not act for victims or their families in the same way as solicitors act for their clients, and prosecutors must form an overall view of the public interest.

d) *What was the suspect's age and maturity at the time of the offence?*

- The criminal justice system treats children and young people differently from adults and significant weight must be attached to the age of the suspect if they are a child or young person under 18.
- The best interests and welfare of the child or young person must be considered, including whether a prosecution is likely to have an adverse impact on their future prospects that is disproportionate to the seriousness of the offending. Prosecutors must have regard to the principal aim of the youth justice system, which is to prevent offending by children and young people. Prosecutors must also have regard to the obligations arising under the United Nations 1989 Convention on the Rights of the Child.
- Prosecutors should consider the suspect's maturity, as well as their chronological age, as young adults will continue to mature into their mid-twenties.
- As a starting point, the younger the suspect, the less likely it is that a prosecution is required.
- However, there may be circumstances which mean that, notwithstanding the fact that the suspect is under 18 or lacks maturity, a prosecution is in the public interest. These include where:
  - i. the offence committed is serious;
  - ii. the suspect's past record suggests that there are no suitable alternatives to prosecution; and
  - iii. the absence of an admission means that out-of-court disposals that might have addressed the offending behaviour are not available.

e) *What is the impact on the community?*

- The greater the impact of the offending on the community, the more likely it is that a prosecution is required.
- The prevalence of an offence in a community may cause particular harm to that community, increasing the seriousness of the offending.
- Community is not restricted to communities defined by location and may relate to a group of people who share certain characteristics, experiences or backgrounds, including an occupational group.
- Evidence of impact on a community may be obtained by way of a Community Impact Statement.

f) *Is prosecution a proportionate response?*

- In considering whether prosecution is proportionate to the likely outcome, the following may be relevant:
  - i. The cost to the CPS and the wider criminal justice system, especially where it could be regarded as excessive when weighed against any likely penalty. Prosecutors should not decide the public interest on the basis of this factor alone. It is essential that regard is also given to the public interest factors identified when considering the other questions in paragraphs 4.14 a) to g), but cost can be a relevant factor when making an overall assessment of the public interest.
  - ii. Cases should be prosecuted in accordance with principles of effective case management. For example, in a case involving multiple suspects, prosecution might be reserved for the main participants in order to avoid excessively long and complex proceedings.

g) *Do sources of information require protecting?*

- In cases where public interest immunity does not apply, special care should be taken when proceeding with a prosecution where details may need to be made public that could harm sources of information, ongoing investigations, international relations or national security. It is essential that such cases are kept under continuing review.

**The Threshold Test**

5.1 In limited circumstances, where the Full Code Test is not met, the Threshold Test may be applied to charge a suspect. The seriousness or circumstances of the case must justify the making of an immediate charging decision, and there must be substantial grounds to object to bail.

5.2 There must be a rigorous examination of the five conditions of the Threshold Test, to ensure that it is only applied when necessary and that cases are not charged prematurely. All five conditions must be met before the Threshold Test can be applied. Where any of the conditions are not met, there is no need to consider any of the other conditions, as the Threshold Test cannot be applied and the suspect cannot be charged.

*First condition—There are reasonable grounds to suspect that the person to be charged has committed the offence*

5.3 Prosecutors must be satisfied, on an objective assessment of the evidence, that there are reasonable grounds to suspect that the person to be charged has committed the offence. The assessment must consider the impact of any defence or information that the suspect has put forward or on which they might rely.

5.4    In determining whether there are reasonable grounds to suspect, prosecutors must consider all of the material or information available, whether in evidential format or otherwise. Prosecutors must be satisfied that the material to be relied on at this stage is capable of being:
   • put into an admissible format for presentation in court;
   • reliable; and
   • credible.

*Second condition—further evidence can be obtained to provide a realistic prospect of conviction*

5.5    Prosecutors must be satisfied that there are reasonable grounds to believe that the continuing investigation will provide further evidence, within a reasonable period of time, so that when all the evidence is considered together, including material which may point away from as well as towards a particular suspect, it is capable of establishing a realistic prospect of conviction in accordance with the Full Code Test.

5.6    The likely further evidence must be identifiable and not merely speculative.

5.7    In reaching this decision prosecutors must consider:
   • the nature, extent and admissibility of any likely further evidence and the impact it will have on the case;
   • the charges that all the evidence will support;
   • the reasons why the evidence is not already available;
   • the time required to obtain the further evidence, including whether it could be obtained within any available detention period; and
   • whether the delay in applying the Full Code Test is reasonable in all the circumstances.

*Third condition—The seriousness or the circumstances of the case justifies the making of an immediate charging decision*

5.8    The seriousness and the circumstances of the case should be assessed in relation to the alleged offending and should be linked to the level of risk created by granting bail.

*Fourth condition—There are continuing substantial grounds to object to bail in accordance with the Bail Act 1976 and in all the circumstances of the case it is proper to do so*

5.9    This determination must be based on a proper risk assessment, which reveals that the suspect is not suitable to be bailed, even with substantial conditions. For example, a dangerous suspect who poses a serious risk of harm to a particular person or the public, or a suspect who poses a serious risk of absconding or interfering with witnesses. Prosecutors should not accept, without careful enquiry, any unjustified or unsupported assertions about risk if release on bail were to take place.

*Fifth condition—It is in the public interest to charge the suspect*

5.10   Prosecutors must apply the public interest stage of the Full Code Test based on the information available at that time.

**Reviewing the Threshold Test**

5.11   A decision to charge under the Threshold Test must be kept under review. The prosecutor should be proactive to secure from the police the identified outstanding evidence or other material in accordance with an agreed timetable. The evidence must be regularly assessed to ensure that the charge is still appropriate and that continued objection to bail is justified. The Full Code Test must be applied as soon as the anticipated further evidence or material is received and, in any event, in Crown Court cases, usually before the formal service of the prosecution case.

**Selection of Charges**

6.1    Prosecutors should select charges which:
   • reflect the seriousness and extent of the offending;
   • give the court adequate powers to sentence and impose appropriate post-conviction orders;
   • allow a confiscation order to be made in appropriate cases, where a defendant has benefitted from criminal conduct; and
   • enable the case to be presented in a clear and simple way.

6.2    This means that prosecutors may not always choose or continue with the most serious charge where there is a choice and the interests of justice are met by selecting the lesser charge.

6.3    Prosecutors should never proceed with more charges than are necessary just to encourage a defendant to plead guilty to a few. In the same way, they should never proceed with a more serious charge just to encourage a defendant to plead guilty to a less serious one.

6.4   Prosecutors should not change the charge simply because of the decision made by the court or the defendant about where the case will be heard.

6.5   Prosecutors must take account of any relevant change in circumstances as the case progresses after charge.

## Out-of-Court Disposals

7.1   An out-of-court disposal may take the place of a prosecution if it is an appropriate response to the offender and/or the seriousness and consequences of the offending.

7.2   Prosecutors must follow any relevant guidance when asked to advise on or authorise an out-of-court disposal, including any appropriate regulatory proceedings, a punitive or civil penalty, or other disposal. They should ensure that the appropriate evidential standard for the specific out-of-court disposal is met including, where required, a clear admission of guilt, and that the public interest would be properly served by such a disposal.

## Court Venue

8.1   Prosecutors must have regard to the guidelines on sentencing and allocation when making submissions to the magistrates' court about where the defendant should be tried.

8.2   Speed must never be the only reason for asking for a case to stay in the magistrates' court. But prosecutors should consider the effect of any likely delay if a case is sent to the Crown Court, including the possible effect on any victim or witness.

8.3   Prosecutors should bear in mind that if confiscation proceedings are required, these may only take place in the Crown Court. Summary proceedings may be committed for that purpose, where appropriate.

### Venue for trial in cases involving Children and Young People

8.4   Prosecutors must bear in mind that children and young people (under 18s) should be tried in the youth court wherever possible. It is the court which is best designed to meet their specific needs. A trial of a child or young person in the Crown Court should be reserved for the most serious cases or where the interests of justice require a child or young person to be jointly tried with an adult.

## Accepting Guilty Pleas

9.1   Defendants may want to plead guilty to some, but not all, of the charges. Alternatively, they may want to plead guilty to a different, possibly less serious, charge because they are admitting only part of the crime.

9.2   Prosecutors should only accept the defendant's plea if:
   - the court is able to pass a sentence that matches the seriousness of the offending, particularly where there are aggravating features;
   - it enables the court to make a confiscation order in appropriate cases, where a defendant has benefitted from criminal conduct; and
   - it provides the court with adequate powers to impose other ancillary orders, bearing in mind that these can be made with some offences but not with others.

9.3   Particular care must be taken when considering pleas which would enable the defendant to avoid the imposition of a mandatory minimum sentence.

9.4   Prosecutors must never accept a guilty plea just because it is convenient.

9.5   In considering whether the pleas offered are acceptable, prosecutors should ensure that the interests and, where possible, the views of the victim, or in appropriate cases the views of the victim's family, are taken into account when deciding whether it is in the public interest to accept the plea. However, the decision rests with the prosecutor.

9.6   It must be made clear to the court on what basis any plea is advanced and accepted. In cases where a defendant pleads guilty to the charges but on the basis of facts that are different from the prosecution case, and where this may significantly affect sentence, the court should be invited to hear evidence to determine what happened, and then sentence on that basis.

9.7   Where a defendant has previously indicated that they will ask the court to take an offence into consideration when sentencing, but then declines to admit that offence at court, prosecutors will consider whether a prosecution is required for that offence. Prosecutors should explain to the defence advocate and the court that the prosecution of that offence may be subject to further review, in consultation with the police or other investigators wherever possible.

**Reconsidering a Prosecution Decision**

10.1 People should be able to rely on decisions taken by the CPS. Normally, if the CPS tells a suspect or defendant that there will not be a prosecution, or that the prosecution has been stopped, the case will not start again. But occasionally there are cases where the CPS will overturn a decision not to prosecute or to deal with the case by way of an out-of-court disposal or when it will restart the prosecution, particularly if the case is serious.

10.2 These cases include:
- cases where a further review of the original decision shows that it was wrong and, in order to maintain confidence in the criminal justice system, a prosecution should be brought despite the earlier decision;
- cases which are stopped so that further anticipated evidence, which is likely to become available in the fairly near future, can be collected and prepared. In these cases, the prosecutor will tell the defendant that the prosecution may well start again;
- cases which are not prosecuted or are stopped because of a lack of evidence but where more significant evidence is discovered later; and
- cases involving a death in which a review following the findings of an inquest concludes that a prosecution should be brought, notwithstanding any earlier decision not to prosecute.

10.3 Victims may seek a review of certain CPS decisions not to start a prosecution or to stop a prosecution, under the Victims' Right to Review Scheme.

# Disclosure

## ATTORNEY GENERAL'S GUIDELINES ON DISCLOSURE
## FOR INVESTIGATORS, PROSECUTORS
## AND DEFENCE PRACTITIONERS

**EFFECTIVE FROM 31st DECEMBER 2020**

**Foreword**

[Omitted.]

**Introduction**

These Guidelines are issued by the Attorney General for investigators, prosecutors and defence practitioners on the application of the disclosure regime contained in the Criminal Procedure and Investigations Act 1996 ('CPIA') Code of Practice Order 2020.

These Guidelines replace the existing Attorney General's Guidelines on Disclosure issued in 2013 and the Supplementary Guidelines on Digital Material issued in 2013, which is an annex to the general guidelines.

The Guidelines outline the high level principles which should be followed when the disclosure regime is applied throughout England and Wales. They are not designed to be an unequivocal statement of the law at any one time, nor are they a substitute for a thorough understanding of the relevant legislation, codes of practice, case law and procedure.

**Important principles**

**Investigators**

Pursue all reasonable lines of inquiry and keep a record of all material relevant to the case, including that which will not be used as evidence in the prosecution case. Investigators prepare disclosure schedules for review by the prosecution.

**Prosecution**

Engage with the investigators and advise on reasonable lines of inquiry. Ensure investigators provide disclosure schedules, and review these. Apply the test for disclosure set out in CPIA 1996.

**Defence**

Engage with prosecution (including pre-charge where appropriate). Serve a defence statement setting out the nature of the defence, and request any material which could reasonably assist their case. Participate in process for completing a disclosure management document.

**Prosecution advocates**

Review schedules and disclosed material, advise the prosecution where advice is sought and at any rate where deficiencies in disclosure are apparent.

**Ongoing evaluation**

Disclosure is subject to continuous review throughout the lifetime of a case. All parties should reassess as new information or material becomes available and the case progresses.

Disclosure process, with judicial oversight

**Example**

There will be cases where there is no requirement for the police to take the devices of a complainant/ witness or others at all, and no requirement for any examination to be undertaken.

Examples of this could include sexual offences committed opportunistically against strangers, or historic allegations where there is considered to be no prospect that the complainant's phone will contain any material relevant to the period in which the conduct is said to have occurred and/or the complainant through age or other circumstances did not have access to a phone at that time.

However, decisions will depend on the facts of the case in question. For example, in the case of a sexual offence committed opportunistically against a stranger, a mobile phone could contain first complaint evidence. Investigators should always carefully consider what is relevant for the case in question.

A case might, for example, involve a complainant contacting the police to make an allegation of an offence against a person they had met that same day. The suspect may accept that they met the complainant but deny the allegation. The complainant and suspect communicated on a single medium. The investigator may consider it is a reasonable line of enquiry to view the messages from the day on which the two persons met as, before and after, they are highly likely to be relevant. They may contain material about what was expected or not expected when complainant and suspect met, the nature of their relationship, and the response after they met, all of which may cast light on the complainant's account and the suspect's account. That is unlikely to require the investigator taking custody of the phone or obtaining a large volume of data. If, by way of example and contrast, the complainant alleged coercive and controlling behaviour over a period of years, including manipulative conduct over various platforms, a larger quantity of data may be relevant and require review and retention by the investigator by different means.

**The investigation**

14. Consideration of disclosure issues is an integral part of an investigation and is not something that should be considered in isolation.

15. Investigators should approach the investigation with a view to establishing what actually happened. They are to be fair and objective.

16. The following diagram illustrates how material that forms part of an investigation may be categorised and consequently treated. Further information on sensitive material can be found at paragraph 65.

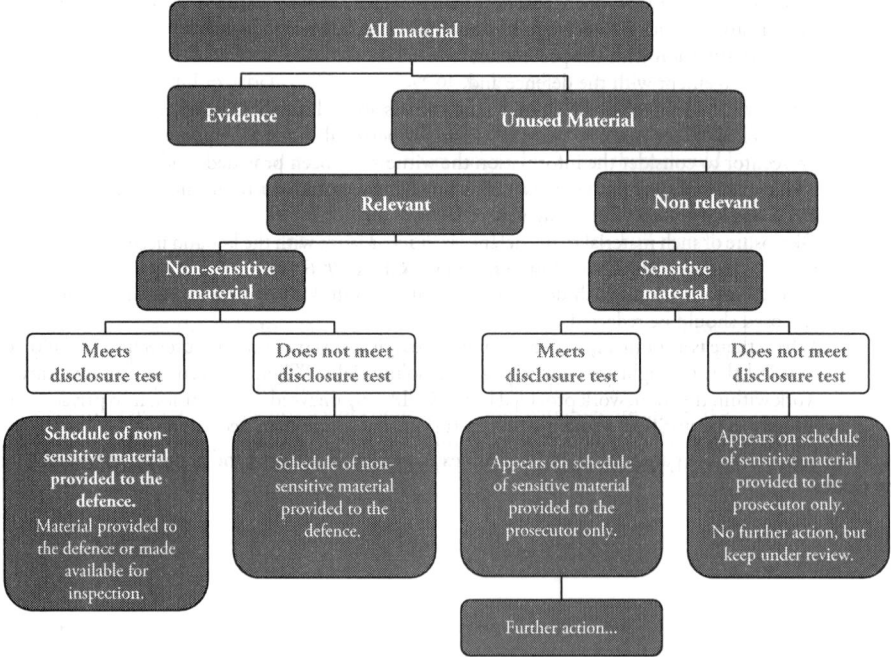

17. Investigators should ensure that all reasonable lines of inquiry are investigated, whether they point towards or away from the suspect. What is 'reasonable' will depend on the context of the case. A fair investigation does not mean an endless investigation. Investigators and disclosure officers must give thought to defining, and articulating the limits of the scope of their investigations. When assessing what is reasonable, thought should be given to what is likely to be obtained as a result of the line of inquiry and how it can be obtained. An investigator may seek the advice of the prosecutor when considering which lines of inquiry should be pursued where appropriate.

18. When conducting an investigation, an investigator should always have in mind their obligation to retain and record all relevant material[9]. Material which is presumed to meet the test for disclosure, as set out in paragraph 87 of these guidelines, must always be retained and recorded. All relevant material must be retained, whereas non-relevant material does not need to be retained.

## The definition of relevant material

Material may be relevant to an investigation if it appears to an investigator, or to the officer in charge of an investigation, or to the disclosure officer, that it has some bearing on any offence under investigation or any person being investigated, or on the surrounding circumstances of the case, unless it is incapable of having any impact on the case[10].

19. The decision as to relevance requires an exercise of judgment and, although some material may plainly be relevant or non-relevant, ultimately this requires a decision by the disclosure officer or investigator.

20. Disclosure officers and/or investigators must inspect, view, listen to, or search all relevant material. The disclosure officer must provide a personal declaration that this task has been completed. In some cases a detailed examination of every item of material seized would be disproportionate. In these cases the disclosure officer can apply search techniques using the principles contained in Annex A. Whatever the approach taken by disclosure officers in examining material, it is crucial that disclosure officers record their reasons for a particular approach in writing.

21. Disclosure officers should seek the advice and assistance of prosecutors when in doubt as to their responsibility as early as possible. They must deal expeditiously with requests by the prosecutor for further information on material, which may lead to disclosure.

22. Where prosecutors have reason to believe that the disclosure officer has not inspected, viewed, listened to or searched relevant material, or has not done so sufficiently or has not articulated a reason for doing so, they should raise this issue with the disclosure officer and request that it is addressed. Prosecutors should also assist disclosure officers and investigators in defining the parameters of review and the methodology to be adopted.

23. It may become apparent to an investigator that some material obtained in the course of an investigation, either because it was considered to be potentially relevant, or because it was inextricably linked to material that was relevant, is in fact incapable of impacting on the case[11]. It is not necessary to retain such material. However, the investigator should also exercise considerable caution in reaching that conclusion. The investigator should be particularly mindful of the fact that some investigations continue over some time. Material that is incapable of impact may change over time and it may not be possible to foresee what the issues in the case will be. The advice of the prosecutor may be sought where necessary. Ultimately, however, the decision on whether to retain material is one for the investigator, and should always be based on their assessment of the relevance of the material and the likelihood of it having any impact on the case in future.

24. Prosecutors must be alert to the need to provide advice to and, where necessary, probe actions taken by the investigator to ensure that disclosure obligations are capable of being met. This should include advice on potential further reasonable lines of inquiry. There should be no aspects of an investigation about which prosecutors are unable to ask probing questions.

25. In some investigations it may be appropriate for the officer in charge of the investigation to seek engagement with the defence at the pre-charge stage. This is likely to be where it is possible that such engagement will lead to the defence volunteering additional information which may assist in identifying new lines of inquiry. Annex B sets out the process for any such pre-charge engagement.

---

9 The CPIA Code paragraphs 4 and 5
10 The CPIA Code paragraph 2
11 The CPIA (section 23(1))

### Third party material

26.   Third party material is material held by a person, organisation, or government department other than the investigator and prosecutor, either within the UK or outside the UK. Third parties are not directly involved in the case in question, but may hold information relevant to it.

27.   The CPIA Code and these guidelines make clear the obligation on the investigator to pursue all reasonable lines of inquiry in relation to material held by third parties within the UK.

28.   It is for investigators, in consultation or discussion with prosecutors where appropriate, to pursue all reasonable lines of inquiry. Prosecutors can advise on additional reasonable lines of inquiry and should satisfy themselves that such reasonable lines of inquiry have been pursued.

29.   If as a result of the duty to pursue all reasonable lines of inquiry, the investigator or prosecutor obtains or receives material from a third party, then it must be dealt with in accordance with the CPIA 1996, (i.e. the prosecutor must disclose material if it meets the disclosure tests, subject to any public interest immunity claim). The person who has an interest in the material (the third party) may make representations to the court concerning public interest immunity (see section 16 of the CPIA 1996).

30.   Material not in the possession of an investigator or prosecutor falls outside the CPIA. In such cases these guidelines prescribe the approach to be taken to disclosure of material held by third parties.

### Material held by Government departments

31.   During an investigation or prosecution it may become apparent that a Government department or another Crown body has material that may be relevant to an issue in the case.

32.   The investigator or prosecutor should inform the Government department or Crown body at the earliest opportunity of the nature of the case and the relevant issues in the case, and ask whether it has any relevant material. They should assist the Government department or Crown body in understanding what may be relevant in the context of the case in question.

33.   Crown Servants have a duty to support the administration of justice and should take reasonable steps to identify and consider such material. This extends to revealing to the investigator or prosecutor the extent of the searches conducted and the existence of any information which they believe may be relevant to the issues in the case, to supply them with that information unless it is protected to the issues in the case, and to supply them with that information unless it is protected in law, subject to legal professional privilege or attracts public interest immunity.

34.   If access is denied to relevant material, the investigator or prosecutor should consider the reasons given by the Government department or Crown body and what, if any, further steps might be taken to obtain the material. The final decision on further steps rests with the prosecutor.

35.   Investigators and prosecutors cannot be regarded to be in constructive possession of material held by Government departments or Crown bodies simply by virtue of their status as Government departments or Crown bodies.

36.   The steps taken to identify and obtain relevant material held by a Government department or Crown body should be recorded by the investigator and the prosecutor.

37.   Where appropriate, the defence should be informed of the steps taken to obtain material and the results of the line of inquiry.

### Other domestic bodies

38.   An investigator, disclosure officer or a prosecutor may believe that a third party (for example a local authority, social services department, hospital, doctor, school, provider of forensic services, or CCTV operator) has material or information which might be relevant to the case. If so, then reasonable steps should be taken to secure and consider the material held by the third party where it appears that such material exists and that it may be relevant to an issue in the case.

39.   The investigator, disclosure officer or prosecutor should follow the steps in paragraphs 32, 34 and 36 above when engaging with the relevant domestic body.

40.   A third party has no obligation under the CPIA to reveal material to investigators or prosecutors. There is also no duty on the third party to retain material which may be relevant to the investigation and, in some circumstances, the third party may not be aware of the investigation or prosecution.

41.   If access to the material is refused and, despite the reasons given for refusal of access, it is still believed that it is reasonable to seek production of the material or information and that the requirements of

a witness summons[12,13] are satisfied (or any other relevant power), then the prosecutor or investigator should apply for the summons causing a representative of the third party to produce the material to court.

42. When the third party material in question is personal data, investigators and prosecutors must refer to paragraphs 11–13 of these guidelines to ensure that there is no unjust intrusion of privacy.

43. Further guidance and best practice on obtaining third party material can be found in the Joint Protocol on Third Party Material and Chapter 5 of the CPS Disclosure Manual.

44. The defence should be informed of what steps have been taken to obtain material and what the results of the inquiry have been.

### International enquiries

45. The obligations under the CPIA Code to pursue all reasonable lines of inquiry apply to material held overseas.

46. Where it appears that there is relevant material, the investigator or prosecutor must take reasonable steps to obtain it, either informally or by making use of the powers contained in the Crime (International Co-operation) Act 2003, the Criminal Justice (European Investigation Order) Regulations 2017 and any international conventions.

47. There may be cases where a foreign state or court refuses to make the material available to the investigator or prosecutor. There may be other cases where the foreign state, though willing to show the material to investigators, will not allow the material to be copied or otherwise made available and the courts of the foreign state will not order its provision.

48. It is for these reasons that there is no absolute duty on the prosecutor to disclose relevant material held overseas by entities not subject to the jurisdiction of the courts in England and Wales. However, consideration should be given to whether the type of material believed to be held can be provided to the defence.

49. The obligation on the investigator and prosecutor under the CPIA Code is to take reasonable steps. Where investigators are allowed to examine the files of a foreign state but are not allowed to take copies, take notes or list the documents held, there is no breach by the prosecution in its duty of disclosure by reason of its failure to obtain such material, provided reasonable steps have been taken to try and obtain it. Prosecutors have a margin of consideration as to what steps are appropriate in the particular case, but prosecutors must be alive to their duties and there may be some circumstances where these duties cannot be met. Whether or not a prosecutor has taken reasonable steps is for the court to determine in each case if the matter is raised.

50. Where it is apparent during the investigation that there may be relevant material held overseas then investigators and prosecutors should consider engaging with the defence at the pre-charge stage, applying the principles contained in Annex B, to ensure that all reasonable lines of inquiry are followed.

51. It is important that the position taken in relation to any material held overseas is clearly set out in a document such as a disclosure management document (DMD) so that the court and the defence know what the position is. Further information on DMDs can be found below, at paragraph 92.

52. In the DMD, investigators and prosecutors must record and explain the situation and set out, insofar as they are permitted by the foreign state, such information as they can and the steps they have taken to obtain it.

53. The defence should be informed of what steps have been taken to obtain material and what the results of the enquiry have been.

### Electronic material

54. The exponential increase in the use of technology in society means that many routine investigations are increasingly likely to have to engage with digital material of some form. It is not only in large and complex investigations where there may be large quantities of such material. When dealing with large quantities of digital material prosecutors and investigators should apply the principles contained in Annex A to these guidelines.

55. Where investigations involve a large quantity of digital material it may be impossible for investigators to examine every item of such material individually. Therefore there should be no expectation that this should happen. Investigators and disclosure officers will need to decide how best to pursue a reasonable line of inquiry in relation to the relevant digital material, and ensure that the extent and manner of the examination are appropriate to the issues in the case. In reaching any such decisions,

---

12 Criminal Procedure (Attendance of Witnesses) Act 1965, s 2
13 Magistrates Court Act 1980, s 97

investigators and disclosure officers must bear in mind the overriding obligation to ensure a fair trial of any suspect who is charged and the requirement to provide disclosure in the trial process.

56. Prosecutors and investigators must ensure that any line of inquiry pursued in relation to the digital devices of victims and witnesses are reasonable in the context of the likely issues in the case. Digital devices should not be obtained as a matter of course and the decision to obtain and examine a digital device will be a fact-specific decision to be made in each and every case[14]. Where digital devices are obtained, if it becomes apparent that they do not contain relevant material they should be returned at the earliest opportunity.

57. Prosecutors should be consulted, where appropriate, to agree a strategy for dealing with digital material. This strategy should be set out in a disclosure management document (DMD) and shared with the defence at the appropriate time.

### Revelation of material to a prosecutor

58. Prosecutors only have knowledge of the matters which are revealed to them by investigators and disclosure officers. The schedules are the means by which that revelation takes place. Therefore it is crucial that the schedules detail all of the relevant material and that the material is adequately described. This process will also enable defence practitioners to become appraised of relevant material at the appropriate stage of the investigation. More detail on what constitutes relevant material can be found here.

59. Schedules must be completed in a form which not only reveals sufficient information to the prosecutor, but which demonstrates a transparent and thinking approach to the disclosure exercise. The speed with which the schedule is produced should not reduce the quality of the material contained therein.

60. Descriptions on the schedules must be clear and accurate and must contain sufficient detail to enable the prosecutor to make an informed decision on disclosure. Abbreviations and acronyms should be avoided as they risk significant material being overlooked.

61. Investigators and disclosure officers must ensure that material which is presumed to meet the test for disclosure, as set out in paragraph 87 of these guidelines and paragraph 6.6 of the CPIA Code, is placed on the schedules. The requirement to schedule this material is in addition to the requirement to schedule all other relevant unused material.

62. Where relevant unused material has been omitted from the schedule or where material is not described sufficiently, and the prosecutor asks the disclosure officer to rectify the schedule, the disclosure officer must comply with this request in a timely manner.

63. Disclosure officers must bring to the prosecutor's attention any material which is potentially capable of meeting the test for disclosure. This material should be provided to the prosecutor along with the reasons why it is thought to meet the test.

64. Disclosure officers must also draw material to the attention of the prosecutor for consideration where they have doubt as to whether it might reasonably be considered capable of undermining the prosecution case or of assisting the case for the accused.

### Revelation of sensitive material

#### What is sensitive material?

65. Sensitive material is material that, if disclosed, would give rise to a **real** risk of **serious** prejudice to an **important** public interest. Investigators must ensure that all relevant unused sensitive material is retained, reviewed and revealed to the prosecutor. Sensitive material should be revealed to a prosecutor on a separate schedule to the non-sensitive material.

Examples of sensitive material can be found in paragraph 6.14 of the CPIA Code.

66. When making a decision about the sensitivity of an item, investigators should have regard to the types of material listed in paragraph 6.14 of the CPIA Code. The disclosure officer must ensure that the sensitive material schedule include the reasons why it is asserted that items on the schedule are considered sensitive.

67. Where a document contains a mix of sensitive and non-sensitive material, the sensitive material must be redacted, with a copy of the redacted document placed on the non-sensitive unused material schedule and the original placed on the sensitive schedule.

---

[14] *R v E* [2018] EWCA 2426 (Crim)

68. Investigators must ensure that the descriptions of sensitive unused material are sufficiently clear to enable the prosecutor to make an informed decision as to whether or not the material itself should be viewed, to the extent possible without compromising the confidentiality of the information.

69. Prosecutors must carefully review the sensitive unused material schedule in order to be satisfied that there are no omissions, that the items have been correctly identified as sensitive, and that the items are adequately described. If a prosecutor identifies that a schedule is inadequate, the investigator must provide an adequate schedule as soon as possible. This may involve items being moved from the sensitive unused material schedule to the non-sensitive unused material schedule.

### The timing of revelation

70. In order to support prosecutors' assessment of the impact of unused material on any proposed prosecution, it is essential that prosecutors are provided with the schedule of unused material at an early stage, as well as any material which the disclosure officer considers potentially capable of meeting the test for disclosure. This will allow for a thorough review of the case, and will enable the prosecutor to consider what the disclosure strategy should be.

71. The timing of revelation of material should be in accordance with paragraph 7.1 of the Code. The point at which the case file is submitted to the CPS will depend on the circumstances of the charging decision and on the anticipated plea:

   a. Where the police are seeking a charging decision under the Full Code Test from the CPS, and it is anticipated that the defendant will plead not guilty, the unused material schedules should be provided to the prosecutor by the disclosure officer at the same time as seeking this charging decision.

   b. Where the police have charged a suspect on the Full Code Test under the arrangements contained in the Director's Guidance on Charging, and a not guilty plea is anticipated, then the unused material schedule should be provided to the prosecutor at the point at which the case file is submitted to the CPS.

   c. In all other cases the disclosure officer must provide the schedules as soon as possible after a not guilty plea has either been indicated or entered.

72. There may be instances where an investigator is seeking a charging decision on the Full Code Test and anticipating a not guilty plea, but where it is not feasible to provide the unused material schedules to the prosecutor at the same time as seeking a charging decision. This may be the case where an arrest is not planned, and the suspect cannot be bailed.

73. For large and complex investigations, particularly those conducted by the Serious Fraud Office, it is recognised that the preparation of schedules continues beyond the point of charge due to the quantity and complexity of data to be analysed, and that it may not be feasible or necessary to provide the schedules at the same time that a charging decision is sought.

74. Disclosure officers should apply the criteria contained in the Director's Guidance on Charging when making a decision about a suspect's likely plea, and must follow any additional guidance provided by the prosecutor.

### The charging decision

75. Prosecutors must ensure that all reasonable lines of inquiry likely to affect the application of the Full Code Test have been pursued before the Test is applied, unless the prosecutor is satisfied that any further evidence or material is unlikely to affect the application of the Full Code Test[15]. The failure to pursue reasonable lines of inquiry may result in the application of the Full Code Test being deferred, or in a decision that the Test cannot be met.

76. If a decision is made to charge a case under the Threshold Test, then prosecutors and investigators need to be proactive in ensuring that any outstanding lines of inquiry are pursued and that the case is kept under continuous review.

### Common law disclosure

77. A prosecutor's statutory duty of disclosure applies from the point of a not guilty plea in the magistrates' court and from the point a case is sent to the Crown Court[16]. However prosecutors must also consider their duties under the common law, which apply at all stages of a case, from charge to sentence and post-conviction (see paragraphs 137 and 138), and regardless of anticipated or actual plea.

---

[15] Crown Prosecution Service, *The Code for Crown Prosecutors* paragraph 4.3
[16] Criminal Procedure and Investigations Act 1996 (CPIA 1996), s 1(1)(a) and (2)(cc)

78.   These duties may require the prosecutor to disclose material to the accused outside the statutory scheme in accordance with the interests of justice and fairness. An example of this is where it would assist the accused in the preparation of the defence case, prior to plea and regardless of anticipated plea. This would include material which would assist in the making of a bail application, material which may enable the accused to make an early application to stay the proceedings as an abuse of process, material which may enable the accused to make representations about the trial venue or a lesser charge, or material which would enable an accused to prepare for trial effectively[17].

### Initial disclosure

79.   The defence must be provided with copies of, or access to, any prosecution material not previously disclosed, which might reasonably be considered capable of undermining the case for the prosecution against the accused, or of assisting the case for the accused[18]. Paragraphs 100–107 of these Guidelines contain guidance as to when initial disclosure should be served.

80.   In order for the prosecutor to comply with their duty of initial disclosure they must analyse the case for the prosecution, the defence case, and the likely trial issues. A prosecutor can anticipate the likely issues on the basis of information available (such as any explanation provided by the accused in interview).

81.   The prosecutor must also encourage dialogue and prompt engagement with the defence about the likely issues for trial.

82.   The defence are under a duty to engage with the prosecutor in order to aid understanding about the defence case and the likely issues for trial at this early stage. This engagement assists in ensuring compliance with the overriding objective of the Criminal Procedure Rules[19],[20].

83.   Prosecutors must review schedules prepared by disclosure officers thoroughly at an early stage and must be alert to the possibility that relevant material may exist which has not been revealed to them or material included which should not have been. If no schedules are provided, if there are apparent omissions from the schedules, or if documents or other items are inadequately described or are unclear, the prosecutor must request properly completed schedules from the investigator. Investigators must comply with any such request. A log of such communications should be kept by the prosecutor.

84.   In deciding whether material satisfies the disclosure test, consideration should include:
   a.   The use that might be made of it in cross-examination;
   b.   Its capacity to support submissions that could lead to:
       i.   The exclusion of evidence;
       ii.   A stay of proceedings, where the material is required to allow a proper application to be made;
       iii.   A court or tribunal finding that any public authority had acted incompatibly with the accused's rights under the European Convention of Human Rights;
   c.   Its capacity to suggest an explanation or partial explanation of the accused's actions;
   d.   Its capacity to undermine the reliability or credibility of a prosecution witness;
   e.   The capacity of the material to have a bearing on scientific or medical evidence in the case.

85.   Material relating to the accused's mental or physical health, intellectual capacity, or to any ill treatment which the accused may have suffered when in the investigator's custody is likely to meet the test for disclosure.

86.   Material should not be viewed in isolation as, whilst items taken alone may not be reasonably considered capable of undermining the prosecution case or assisting the case for the accused, several items together can have that effect.

### Material which is likely to meet the test for disclosure

87.   The following material is likely to include information which meets the test for disclosure:
   a)   records which are derived from tapes or recordings of telephone messages (for example 999 calls) containing descriptions of an alleged offence or offender;
   b)   any incident logs relating to the allegation;
   c)   contemporaneous records of the incident, such as:

---

17  *R v DPP, ex p. Lee* [1999] 1 WLR 1950 [1962]–[1963]
18  CPIA 1996, s 3
19  The Criminal Procedure Rules 2020 SI No. 759 (L.19) (the CrimPR), part 1
20  *R v R and others* [2015] EWCA Crim 1941, [2016] 1 WLR 1872, paragraph [35]

- crime reports and crime report forms;
- an investigation log;
- any record or note made by an investigator (including police notebook entries and other handwritten notes) on which they later make a statement or which relates to contact with suspects, victims or witnesses;
- an account of an incident or information relevant to an incident noted by an investigator in manuscript or electronically;
- records of actions carried out by officers (such as house-to-house interviews, CCTV or forensic enquiries) noted by a police officer in manuscript or electronically;
- CCTV footage, or other imagery, of the incident in action;

d) the defendant's custody record or voluntary attendance record;

e) any previous accounts made by a complainant or by any other witnesses;

f) interview records (written records, or audio or video tapes, of interviews with actual or potential witnesses or suspects);

g) any material casting doubt on the reliability of a witness e. g. relevant previous convictions and relevant cautions of any prosecution witnesses and any co-accused.

88. This list is reflected in paragraph[s] 5.4 and 6.6 of the Code. This material, in addition to all other material which may be relevant to an investigation, must be **retained** and **listed** on the schedule by the investigator. It is likely that some of this material will need to be redacted (see paragraph 6(c) of the Code and paragraph 65 of these guidelines for redaction and revelation of sensitive material.)

89. As this material is likely to contain information which meets the test for disclosure, prosecutors should start their review of the material with a presumption that this material should be disclosed to the defence. However, in every instance the disclosure test should be applied in a thinking manner.

90. After applying the disclosure test, a prosecutor must record on the unused material schedule whether each item of this material does or does not meet the test for disclosure and they must record the reason for that decision.

91. This list of material is not intended to cause automatic disclosure – investigators and prosecutors should always apply the disclosure test and consider each list of material carefully in the context of the case in question.

## Disclosure management document (DMD)

### What is a disclosure management document?

92. A disclosure management document (DMD) outlines the strategy and approach taken in relation to disclosure and should be served to the defence and the court at an early stage. DMDs will require careful preparation and presentation which is tailored to the individual case. The investigator should provide information for use in the DMD and the prosecutor should prepare it.

93. A DMD is a living document which should be amended in light of developments in the case and kept up to date as the case progresses. DMDs are intended to assist the court in case management and will also enable the defence to engage from an early stage with the prosecution's proposed approach to disclosure.

94. DMDs may set out:

a. Where prosecutors and investigators operate in an integrated office, an explanation as to how the disclosure responsibilities have been managed.

b. A brief summary of the prosecution case and a statement outlining how the prosecutor's general approach will comply with the CPIA 1996 regime and these guidelines

c. The prosecutor's understanding of the defence case, including information revealed during interview. The prosecutor may wish to explain their understanding of what is in dispute and what is not in dispute, the lines of inquiry that have been pursued in light of these issues, and specific disclosure decisions that have been taken.

d. An outline of the prosecution's general approach to disclosure, which may include detail relating to:

    i. The lines of inquiry pursued, particularly those which may assist the defence.

    ii. The timescales for disclosure and, where relevant, how the review of unused material has been prioritised.

    iii. The method and extent of examination of digital material, in accordance with the Annex A to these guidelines.

    iv. Any potential video footage.

v. Any linked investigations, including an explanation of the nexus between investigations and any memoranda of understanding and disclosure agreements between investigators.
vi. Any third party material, including the steps taken to obtain the material.
vii. Any international material, including the steps taken to obtain the material.
viii. Credibility of prosecution witnesses (including professional witnesses).

95. In cases heard in the magistrates' court and the youth court, prosecutors should always consider whether or not a disclosure management document (DMD) would be beneficial. DMDs are most likely to be beneficial in cases with the following features:
   a. Substantial or complex third party material;
   b. Digital material in which parameters of search, examination or analysis have been set;
   c. Cases involving international enquiries;
   d. Cases where there are linked operations;
   e. Non-recent offending;
   f. Cases involving material held or sought by the investigation that is susceptible to a claim of legal professional privilege.
96. DMDs should be prepared in all Crown Court cases.
97. In order for the prosecutor to complete a DMD at an early stage, the investigator should, at the point of or prior to charge, provide written details as to the lines of inquiry that have been pursued.
98. Where a DMD has been prepared, it should be served at the same time as initial disclosure.
99. An example template for a DMD is contained in Annex C.

### The timing of initial disclosure

100. In all cases it is essential that the prosecution takes a grip on the case and its disclosure requirements at an early stage. Prosecutors must adopt a considered and appropriately resourced approach to providing initial disclosure. Initial disclosure in this context refers to the period post-charge; more detailed timings for this are set out below.

### Cases expected to be tried in the magistrates' courts

101. Where a case is charged on the Full Code Test and a not guilty plea is anticipated, initial disclosure should be served in advance of the first hearing.
102. Where a guilty plea was originally anticipated but a not guilty plea is entered then initial disclosure should be served as soon as possible after a not guilty plea is entered.
103. Where a case is charged on the Threshold Test, initial disclosure should be served as soon as possible after the Full Code Test is applied and in accordance with any order made by the court.

### Cases sent to the Crown Court for trial

104. Where it is expected that the accused will maintain a not guilty plea, it is encouraged as a matter of best practice for initial disclosure to be served prior to the Plea and Trial Preparation Hearing (PTPH).
105. It is accepted that it may not be appropriate or possible to serve initial disclosure prior to the PTPH for cases charged on the Threshold Test. Where initial disclosure has not been served at the PTPH it should be served as soon as possible after that hearing and in accordance with any direction made by the court.
106. In cases prosecuted by the Serious Fraud Office, or other similarly large or complex cases, it is accepted that full initial disclosure may not be capable of being served prior to the PTPH. In such cases, best practice is to adopt a phased approach to disclosure, ensuring that robust judicial case management during Further Case Management Hearings, and in line with the Criminal Procedure Rules and Criminal Practice Directions, manages the on-going disclosure process. Utilising an initial DMD at the PTPH which outlines the intended plan for onwards staged disclosure of remaining materials and associated schedules, can be an effective mechanism for this approach and is to adopted where possible.
107. Nothing in these guidelines should undermine the established principles of the Better Case Management Framework.

## Case management

108. In order for the statutory disclosure regime to work effectively all parties should ensure compliance with the Criminal Procedure Rules. The rules require the court to actively manage the case by identifying the real issues[21]. Each party is obliged to assist the court with this duty[22].

109. It is important that prosecutors keep a record of all correspondence which relates to disclosure and keep a record of any disclosure decisions made.

## Magistrates' court

110. Following a not guilty plea being entered in the magistrates' court, the defence must ensure that the trial issues are clearly identified both in court and on the preparation for effective trial form. Prosecutors should ensure that any issues of dispute that are raised are noted on file. The preparation for effective trial form should be carefully reviewed, alongside the DMD (where this is exists). Consideration of any issues raised in court or on the form will assist in deciding whether any further material undermines the prosecution case or assists the accused.

## Crown Court

111. A focus of the Plea and Trial Preparation Hearing (PTPH) must be on the disclosure strategy. This will involve the defence identifying the likely trial issues, a discussion of any additional lines of inquiry, and scrutiny of the DMD.

112. Prosecutors must ensure that the disclosure strategy and any disclosure decisions taken previously are reviewed in light of any issues raised at the PTPH and on the plea and trial preparation form.

113. Where the defence do not feel that the prosecution have adequately discharged their obligations then this must be brought to the court's attention at an early stage. The defence should be proactive in ensuring that any issue is addressed, and must not delay raising these issues until a late stage in the proceedings. The DMD may be relevant in any challenge raised.

114. Where any party has not complied with their obligations, the court will consider giving any direction appropriate to ensure compliance and progression of the case.

## Applications for non-disclosure in the public interest

115. The CPIA 1996 allows prosecutors to apply to the court for an order to withhold material which would otherwise fall to be disclosed if disclosure would give rise to a real risk of serious prejudice to an important public interest. Before making such an application, prosecutors should aim to disclose as much of the material as they properly can (for example, by giving the defence redacted or edited copies or summaries). Neutral material or material damaging to the defendant should not be disclosed, and should not be brought to the attention of the court. Only in truly borderline cases should the prosecution seek a judicial ruling on whether material in its possession should be disclosed.

116. Prior to the hearing, the prosecutor and the prosecution advocate must examine all material which is the subject matter of the application and make any necessary enquiries of the investigator. There is an additional duty of candour on the advocate at this hearing, given the defendant will not be present. In order to assist the court, it is best practice for the advocate to prepare a note that is either written in conjunction, or agreed with, the prosecutor and disclosure officer.

117. The investigator must also be frank with the prosecutor about the full extent of the sensitive material. Prior to or at the hearing the court must be provided with full and accurate information about the material.

118. The prosecutor and/or investigator should attend such applications. Section 16 of the CPIA 1996 allows a person claiming to have an interest in the sensitive material to apply to the court for the opportunity to be heard at the application.

119. The prosecutor should carefully consider the series of questions contained in paragraph 36 of *R v H and others* [2004] UKHL 3. These are the questions that the court must address before it makes a decision to withhold material. It is essential that these principles are scrupulously adhered to, to ensure that the procedure for examination of material in the absence of the accused is compliant with Article 6 of the ECHR.

120. If the prosecutor concludes that a fair trial cannot take place because material which satisfies the test for disclosure cannot be disclosed and that this cannot be remedied by an application for non-disclosure in the public interest, through altering the presentation of the case or by any other means, then they should not continue with the case.

---

[21] The CrimPR, rule 3.2(2)(a)
[22] The CrimPR, rule 3.3(1)(a)

### The defence statement

121. Defence statements are an integral part of the statutory disclosure regime. A defence statement should help to focus the attention of the prosecutor, court and co-defendants on the relevant issues in order to identify material which may meet the test for disclosure. The defence must serve their defence statement in a timely manner, in accordance with any court directions made.

122. There is no requirement for a defence statement to be served in the magistrates' court but it should be noted that if one is not provided the court does not have a power to hear an application for further prosecution disclosure under section 8 of the CPIA 1996.

123. Defence practitioners should ensure that defence statements are drafted in accordance with the requirements in the CPIA 1996[23]. Defence statements should not make general and unspecified allegations in order to seek far reaching disclosure[24] and should not describe the defence in ambiguous or limited terms (such as self-defence, mistaken identify, consent).

124. It is vital that prosecutors consider defence statements thoroughly. Prosecutors should challenge the lack of (in the Crown Court) or inadequate defence statements in writing, copying the document to the court and the defence and seeking directions from the court to require the provision of an adequate defence statement from the defence.

125. Prosecutors must send a copy of the defence statement to the investigator as soon as reasonably practicable after receipt and, at the same time, provide guidance to the disclosure officer about the key issues. The advice should contain guidance on whether any further reasonable lines of inquiry need to be pursued, guidance on what to look for when reviewing the unused material and guidance on what further material may need to be disclosed. On receipt of a defence statement, disclosure officers must re-review retained unused material and draw to the attention of the prosecutor any material which is potentially capable of meeting the test for disclosure and consider whether any further reasonable lines of inquiry need to be pursued. They should address the matters raised in guidance given by the prosecutor.

126. Defence requests for further disclosure should ordinarily only be answered by the prosecution if the request is relevant to, and directed to, an issue identified in the defence statement. If it is not, then a further or amended defence statement should be sought and obtained by the prosecutor before considering the request for further disclosure.

### Continuing disclosure

127. The obligation of continuing disclosure is crucial and particular attention must be paid to understanding the significance of developments in the case on the unused material and earlier disclosure decisions. After service of initial disclosure, a prosecutor must keep under review whether or not there is prosecution material which might reasonably be considered capable of undermining the case for the prosecution against the accused, or of assisting the case for the accused, which has not been previously been disclosed. This obligation is a continuous one[25], and it can be beneficial for it to take place in tranches, particularly in large and/or complex cases.

128. In particular, prosecutors should consider any issues raised by the defence at the first hearing in the magistrates' court or the PTPH in the Crown Court, as well as during any further hearings and after receipt of a defence statement. Any matters raised on the preparation for effective trial form or the PTPH form should also be carefully considered.

### Applications for disclosure under Section 8 of the CPIA

129. An application for disclosure can only be made if the defence have provided an adequate defence statement.

130. Any application for disclosure must describe the material which is subject to the application and explain why there is reasonable cause to believe that the prosecutor has the material and why it meets the test for disclosure.

131. Prosecutors must carefully review any application for disclosure and consider whether any items described in the application meet the test for disclosure. This may require the prosecutor asking the disclosure officer for copies of the items or inspecting the items.

### The trial

132. Prosecutors must ensure that advocates in court are provided with sufficient instructions regarding the disclosure strategy and any disclosure decisions taken.

---

[23] CPIA 1996, s 6A
[24] *R v H and others*
[25] CPIA 1996, s 7A

133. Prosecution advocates should ensure that all material which ought to be disclosed under the CPIA 1996 is disclosed to the defence. Prosecution advocates must ensure that they are fully informed about disclosure so that they are able to make decisions. Prosecution advocates must consider, in every case, whether they can be satisfied that they are in possession of all relevant documentation and that they have been fully instructed regarding disclosure matters. If the advocate considers that further information or action is required then written advice should be provided setting out the aspects that need clarification or action.

134. All decisions regarding disclosure must be kept under review until the conclusion of the trial, whenever possible in consultation with the reviewing prosecutor. The prosecution advocate must in every case specifically consider whether they can satisfactorily discharge the duty of continuing review on the basis of the material supplied already, or whether it is necessary to reconsider the unused material schedule and/or unused material.

135. Prosecution advocates must not abrogate their responsibility under the CPIA 1996 by disclosing material which does not pass the test for disclosure. This is especially so where it is proposed to disclose material engaging Article 8 rights.

136. There is no basis in practice or law for counsel-to-counsel disclosure. It is of critical importance that, even where prosecution counsel is advising and leading on disclosure, the duty to disclose material that meets the test for disclosure remains with the prosecutor. A record of material disclosed made must be kept, not least in the event of an appeal or a re-trial.

### Material relevant to sentence

137. At sentence, the prosecutor should disclose any material which might reasonably be considered capable of ensuring fairness in the sentencing process. This material could include information which might mitigate the seriousness of the offence or the level of the defendant's involvement.

### Post-conviction

138. Where, at any stage after the conclusion of the proceedings, material comes to light which might reasonably be considered capable of casting doubt upon the safety of the conviction, the prosecutor should disclose such material.

### Confiscation Proceedings

139. The disclosure regime in the CPIA ceases to have effect post-conviction and the continuing duty of disclosure does not apply to confiscation proceedings (see section 7A(1)(b) of the CPIA).

140. Part 2 of the Proceeds of Crime Act 2002 provides the legislative scheme for confiscation in the Crown Court following a conviction. The prosecutor is required to set out relevant matters in accordance with section 16 of the Proceeds of Crime Act 2002 apply and the disclosure requirements at common law also apply meaning that there may be a requirement to disclose material in the interests of justice and fairness in the proceedings.

## ANNEX A – DIGITAL MATERIAL

1. This annex is intended to supplement the Attorney General's Guidelines on Disclosure. It is not intended to be a detailed operational guide but is intended to set out a common approach to be adopted when seeking to obtain and handle digital material, whether that be from a suspect or from a complainant. This annex aims to set out how relevant material and consequently material satisfying the test for disclosure can best be identified, revealed and if necessary disclosed to the defence without imposing unrealistic or disproportionate demands on the investigator and prosecutor. This annex also seeks to recognise the considerations investigators and prosecutors should have when obtaining and handling sensitive personal information, in accordance with obligations under data protection legislation.

2. In cases involving large amounts of digital material, investigators should complete an investigation management document (IMD) which will inform the disclosure management document (DMD) that prosecutors should complete. The DMD allows prosecutors to be open and transparent with the defence and the court about how the prosecution has approached complying with its disclosure obligations in the specific context of the individual case.

3. In cases where there may be a large amount of digital material, the investigator should consult the prosecutor, ideally before it is seized, and in turn they may consider seeking the advice of a digital forensic specialist on the strategy for the identification and review of digital material, including potential timings for this.

4.    The defence must also play their part in defining the real issues in the case. This is required by the overriding objective of the Criminal Procedure Rules[26]. The defence should be invited by the prosecution at an early stage to participate in defining the scope of the reasonable searches that may be made of digital material in order to identify material that might reasonably be expected to undermine the prosecution case or assist the case for the defence.

5.    This approach enables the court to use its case management powers robustly to ensure that the prosecution's obligation of disclosure is discharged effectively.

### General principles for investigators

6.    These general principles must be followed by investigators in handling and examining digital material[27]:

   a.   No action should be taken which changes data on a device which may subsequently be relied upon in court.

   b.   If it is necessary to access original data then that data should only be accessed by someone who is competent to do so and is able to explain the relevance and implications of their actions to a court.

   c.   An audit trail should be kept of all processes followed. Another practitioner should be able to follow the audit trail and achieve the same results.

   d.   The investigator in charge of the investigation has responsibility for ensuring that the law and these principles are followed.

7.    Where an investigator has reasonable grounds for believing that digital material may contain material subject to legal professional privilege then this may not be seized unless the provisions of the Criminal Justice and Police Act 2001 apply. This is addressed in more detail later on in this Annex.

8.    The legal obligations in relation to seizure, relevance and retention are found in the Police and Criminal Evidence Act 1984, the Criminal Justice and Police Act 2001 and the Criminal Procedure and Investigations Act 1996.

### Obtaining devices by seizure or co-operation

9.    Digital material may be seized from suspects using legal powers but this material may be obtained from suspects and witnesses with their cooperation as well. Before searching a suspect's premises where digital material is likely to be found, consideration must be given to:

   a.   What sort of material is likely to be found, and in what volume;

   b.   Whether it is likely that relevant material at the location will be able to be viewed and copied; and

   c.   What should be seized.

10.   Investigators will need to consider the practicalities of requesting/seizing digital devices, especially where there are a large number of devices. They will also need to consider the effect that taking possession/seizure will have on a business, organisation or individual; and where it is not feasible to obtain an image of the digital material, the likely timescale for returning the obtained items.

11.   In deciding whether to obtain and retain digital material, it is important that the investigator either complies with the procedure under the relevant statutory authority, relying on statutory powers or a search warrant, or obtains the owner's permission.

12.   When seeking to obtain digital material, whether from a suspect or a witness/complainant, investigators should be guided by the principles set out in paragraphs 11–13 in the Attorney General's Guidelines. Any intrusion into the personal and private lives of individuals should be carried out only where deemed necessary and using the least intrusive means possible to obtain the material required, adopting an incremental approach. Further guidance has been published by the CPS which has been endorsed by the Court of Appeal [28]

13.   A computer hard drive is a single storage entity. This means that if any digital material found on the hard drive can lawfully be obtained or seized, the computer hard drive may, if appropriate, be seized or imaged. In some circumstances investigators may wish to image specific folders, files or categories of data where it is feasible to do so without seizing the hard drive or other media. Digital material may also be contained across a number of digital devices and so more than one device may be required in order to access the information sought.

---

[26] The CrimPR, part 1

[27] Association of Chief Police Officers, *ACPO Good Practice Guide for Digital Evidence* (2012), para 2.1

[28] CPS Guidance on 'Reasonable lines of Enquiry and Communications Evidence' and 'Disclosure—Guidance on Communications Evidence', endorsed in the case of *R v E* [2018] EWCA 2426 (Crim)

14.   Digital material must not be requested or seized if an investigator has reasonable grounds for
      believing it is subject to legal professional privilege, other than where sections 50 or 51 of the
      Criminal Justice and Police Act 2001 apply. If such material is seized it must be isolated from other
      seized material and any other investigation material in the possession of the investigation authority.

### The Police and Criminal Evidence Act 1984

15.   The Police and Criminal Evidence Act 1984 provides the power to seize anything from a suspect in
      the following circumstances:
      a.   Where a search has been authorised pursuant to a warrant – the search must fall within the scope
           of the warrant issued[29];
      b.   After arrest[30];
      c.   Where evidence or anything used in the commission of an offence is on a premises and it is
           necessary to seize it to prevent it being concealed, lost, altered or destroyed[31].
16.   An image of the digital material may be taken at the location of the search. Where an image is taken
      the original does not need to be seized. Where it is not possible to image the digital material it will
      need to be removed from the location for examination elsewhere. This allows the investigator to
      seize and sift material for the purpose of identifying material which meets the test of retention[32]. If
      digital material is seized in its original form, investigators must be prepared to copy or image the
      material for the owners of that material when reasonably practicable[33].

### The Criminal Justice and Police Act 2001

17.   The additional powers of seizure in sections 50 and 51 of the Criminal Justice and Police Act 2001
      (CJPA 2001) only extend the scope of existing powers of search and seizure under the Police and
      Criminal Evidence Act 1984 and other specified statutory authorities[34] where the relevant condi-
      tions and circumstances specified in the legislation apply.
18.   Investigators must be careful to only exercise powers under the CJPA 2001 when it is necessary and
      to not remove any more material than is justified. The removal of large volumes of material, much
      of which may not ultimately be retainable, may have serious consequences for the owner of the
      material, particularly when they are involved in business or other commercial activities.
19.   A written notice must be given to the occupier of the premises where items are seized under sections
      50 and 51[35].
20.   Until material seized under the CJPA 2001 has been examined, it must be kept securely and
      separately from any material seized under other powers. Any such material must be examined as
      soon as reasonably practicable to determine which elements may be retained and which should be
      returned. Consideration should be given as to whether the person from whom the property was
      seized, or a person with interest in the property, should be given an opportunity of being present or
      represented at the examination.

### Retention

21.   Where material is seized under the powers conferred by PACE 1984 the duty to retain it under the
      Code is subject to the provisions on retention under section 22 of PACE 1984. Material seized
      under sections 50 and 51 of the CJPA 2001 may be retained or returned in accordance with sections
      53 to 58 of the CJPA 2001. Where material is obtained through co-operation and not using powers
      conferred on investigators by legislation, these principles should also be observed, including
      retaining the material for only as long as is necessary (see paragraph 5(b) of the Code).
22.   Retention is limited to evidence and relevant material (as defined in the CPIA Code). Where either
      evidence or relevant material is inextricably linked to non-relevant material which it is not
      reasonably practicable to separate from the other linked material without prejudicing the use of that
      other material in any investigation or proceedings, that material can also be retained.
23.   However, inextricably linked material must not be examined, imaged, copied or used for any
      purpose other than for providing the source of or the integrity of the linked material.
24.   There are four categories of material that may be retained:

---

[29]  The Police and Criminal Evidence Act 1984 (PACE 1984), s 8
[30]  PACE 1984, s 18
[31]  PACE 1984, s 19
[32]  Special provision exists for investigators conducted by Her Majesty's Revenue and Customs in the application of their
powers under PACE 1984 (see s. 114(2)(b) of PACE and the CJPA)
[33]  The Home Office, *PACE 1984 Codes of Practice Code B* (2013), para 7.17
[34]  Criminal Justice and Police Act 2001 (CJPA 2001), Sch 1
[35]  CJPA 2001, s 52

    a. Material that is evidence or potential evidence in the case. Where material is retained for evidential purposes there will be a strong argument that the whole thing (or an authenticated image or copy) should be retained for the purpose of proving provenance and continuity.

    b. Where evidential material has been retained, inextricably linked non-relevant material which it is not reasonably practicable to separate can also be retained (PACE Code B paragraph 7).

    c. An investigator should retain material that is relevant to the investigation and required to be scheduled as unused material. This is broader than but includes the duty to retain material which may satisfy the test for prosecution disclosure. The general duty to retain relevant material is set out in the CPIA Code at paragraph 5.

    d. Material which is inextricably linked to relevant unused material which of itself may not be relevant material. Such material should be retained (PACE Code B paragraph 7).

25. The balance of any digital material should be returned in accordance with sections 53–55 of the CJPA 2001 if seized under that Act.

### Legal professional privilege

26. No digital material may be requested or seized which an investigator has reasonable grounds for believing to be subject to legal professional privilege (LPP), other than under the additional powers of seizure in the CJPA 2001.

27. The CJPA 2001 enables an investigator to seize relevant items which contain LPP material where it is not reasonably practicable on the search premises to separate LPP material from non-LPP material.

28. Where LPP material or material suspected of containing LPP is seized, it must be isolated from the other material which has been seized in the investigation. Where suspected LPP material is discovered when reviewing material, and it was not anticipated that this material existed, again it must be isolated from the other material and the steps outlined below taken. The prosecution will need to decide on a case by case basis if the material is LPP material or not – defence may be able to assist with this.

29. Where material has been identified as potentially containing LPP it must be reviewed by a lawyer independent of the prosecuting authority. No member of the investigative or prosecution team involved in either the current investigation or, if the LPP material relates to other criminal proceedings, in those proceedings should have sight of or access to the LPP material.

30. If the material is voluminous, search terms or other filters may have to be used to identify the LPP material. If so this will also have to be done by someone independent and not connected with the investigation.

31. It is essential that anyone dealing with LPP material maintains proper records showing the way in which the material has been handled and those who have had access to it, as well as decisions taken in relation to that material.

32. LPP material can only be retained in specific circumstances in accordance with section 54 of the CJPA 2001. It can only be retained where the property which comprises the LPP material has been lawfully seized and it is not reasonably practicable for the item to be separated from the rest of the property without prejudicing the use of the rest of the property. LPP material which cannot be retained must be returned as soon as practicable after the seizure without waiting for the whole examination of the seized material.

### Excluded and special procedure material

33. Similar principles to those that apply to LPP material apply to excluded or special procedure material[36],[37]. By way of example, this may include material a journalist holds in confidence from a source.

### Encryption

34. Part III of the Regulation of Investigatory Powers Act 2000 (RIPA 2000) and the Investigation of Protected Electronic Information Code of Practice govern encryption.

35. RIPA enables specified law enforcement agencies to compel individuals or companies to provide passwords or encryption keys for the purpose of rendering protected material readable. Failure to comply with RIPA 2000 Part III orders is a criminal offence. The Code of Practice provides guidance when exercising powers under RIPA, to require disclosure of protected electronic data in

---

[36] CJPA 2001, s 55
[37] Special provision exists for investigators conducted by Her Majesty's Revenue and Customs in the application of their powers under PACE 1984 (see s 114(2)(b) of PACE and the CJPA)

an intelligible form or to acquire the means by which protected electronic data may be accessed or put in an intelligible form.

### Sifting and examination

36. In complying with its duty of disclosure, the prosecution should follow the procedure as outlined below.

37. Where digital material is examined, the extent and manner of inspecting, viewing or listening will depend on the nature of the material and its form.

38. It is important for investigators and prosecutors to remember that the duty under the CPIA Code is to "pursue all reasonable lines of inquiry including those that point away from the suspect".

39. Lines of inquiry, of whatever kind, should be pursued only if they are reasonable in the context of the individual case. It is not the duty of the prosecution to comb through all the material in its possession (e.g. every word or byte of computer material) on the lookout for anything which might conceivably or speculatively undermine the case or assist the defence. The duty of the prosecution is to disclose material which might reasonably be considered capable of undermining its case or assisting the case for the accused which they become aware of, or to which their attention is drawn.

40. In some cases, the sift may be conducted by an investigator and/or disclosure officer manually assessing the content of the computer or other digital material from its directory and determining which files are relevant and should be retained for evidence or unused material.

41. In other cases, such an approach may not be feasible. Where there is a large volume of material, it is perfectly proper for the investigator and/or disclosure officer to search by sample, key words, or other appropriate search tools or analytical techniques to locate relevant passages, phrases and identifiers. For the avoidance of any doubt, mobile phones are capable of storing a large volume of material. Technology that takes the form of search tools which use unambiguous calculations to perform problem-solving operations, such as algorithms or predictive coding, are an acceptable method of examining and reviewing material for disclosure purposes.

42. In cases involving very large quantities of data, the person in charge of the investigation will develop a strategy setting out how the material should be analysed or searched to identify categories of data. This strategy may include an initial scoping exercise of the material obtained to ascertain the most effective strategy for reviewing relevant material. Any such strategy should be agreed with the prosecutor and communicated to the court and defence using a DMD

43. Where search terms are to be used, investigators and prosecutors should consider whether engagement with the defence at the pre-charge stage would assist in the identification of relevant search terms. It will usually be appropriate to provide to the accused and their legal representative with a copy of the reasonable search terms used, or to be used, and to invite them to suggest any further reasonable search terms. If search terms are suggested which the investigator or prosecutor believes will not be productive, for example where the use of common words is likely to identify a mass of irrelevant material, the investigator or prosecutor should discuss the issues with the defence in order to agree sensible refinements.

44. The digital strategy must be set out in an IMD and subsequently a DMD. This should include the details of any sampling techniques used (including key word searches) and how the material identified as a result was examined.

45. It may be necessary to carry out sampling and searches on more than one occasion, especially as there is a duty on the prosecutor to keep duties of disclosure under review. To comply with this duty, further sampling and searches may be appropriate (and should be considered) where:
    a. Further evidence or unused material is obtained in the course of the investigation; and/or
    b. The defence statement is served on the prosecutor; and/or
    c. The defendant makes an application under section 8 of the CPIA 1996 for disclosure; and/or
    d. The defendant requests that further sampling or searches be carried out (provided it is a reasonable line of inquiry).

### Record keeping

46. A record or log must be made of all digital material seized or imaged and subsequently retained as relevant to the investigation.

47. In cases involving large quantities of data where the person in charge of the investigation has developed a strategy setting out how the material should be analysed or searched to identify categories of data, a record should be made of the strategy and the analytical techniques used to search the data, including the software used. The record should include details of the person who has

carried out the process and the date and time it was carried out. In such cases the strategy should record the reasons why certain categories have been searched for (such as names, companies, dates etc.).

48.     It is important that any searching or analytical processing of digital material, as well as the data identified by that process, is properly recorded. So far as is practicable, what is required is a record of the terms of the searches or processing that has been carried out. This means that in principle the following details may be recorded:

   a.   A record of all searches carried out, including the date of each search and the person(s) who conducted it.

   b.   A record of all search words or terms used on each search. However, where it is impracticable to record each word or term it will usually be sufficient to record each broad category of search.

   c.   A log of the key judgements made while refining the search strategy in light of what is found, or deciding not to carry out further searches.

   d.   Where material relating to a "hit" is not examined, the decision not to examine should be explained in the record of examination or in a statement. For instance, a large number of "hits" may be obtained in relation to a particular search word or term, but material relating to the "hits" is not examined because they do not appear to be relevant to the investigation. Any subsequent refinement of the search terms and further hits should also be noted and explained as above.

49.     Just as it is not necessary for the investigator or prosecutor to produce records of every search made of hard copy material, it is not necessary to produce records of what may be many hundreds of searches or analyses that have been carried out on digitally stored material simply to demonstrate that these have been done. Instead, the investigator and the prosecutor should ensure that they are able to explain how the disclosure exercise has been approached and to give the accused or suspect's legal representative an opportunity to participate in defining the reasonable searches to be made, as described in the section on sifting/examination.

## Scheduling

50.     The disclosure officer should ensure that scheduling of relevant material is carried out in accordance with the CPIA Code of Practice. This may require each item of unused material to be listed separately on the unused material schedule and numbered consecutively (which may include numbering by volume and sub-volume). The description of each item should make clear the nature of the item and should contain sufficient detail to enable the prosecutor to decide whether they need to inspect the material before deciding whether or not it should be disclosed.

51.     It will generally be disproportionate in cases involving large quantities of digital data to list each item of material separately. Unless it is necessary or otherwise appropriate to separately list each item, the material should be listed in a block or blocks and described by quantity and generic title. Where the material is listed in a block or blocks, the search terms used and any items of material which might satisfy the disclosure test should be listed and described separately. In practical terms this will mean, where appropriate, cross referencing the schedules to the DMD.

52.     Where material has been listed in a block and metadata is available for the material within the block, consideration should be given to creating a file of that metadata and listing this separately and linked to the block listing to which it relates.

53.     Where continuation sheets of the unused material schedule are used, or additional schedules are sent subsequently, the item numbering must be, where possible, sequential to all other items on earlier schedules. This may include numbering by volume or sub-volume.

# ANNEX B – PRE-CHARGE ENGAGEMENT

## The scope of pre-charge engagement

1.     These Guidelines are intended to assist prosecutors, investigators, suspects and suspect's legal representatives who wish to enter into discussions about an investigation at any time after the first PACE interview, up until the commencement of criminal proceedings.

2.     These Guidelines are not intended to cover discussions regarding pleas to an allegation of serious or complex fraud. Nor do they apply to formal agreements relating to the provision of information or evidence about the criminal activities of others. In such cases, where appropriate, the parties should refer to the relevant guidance and follow the advised procedures:

   a.   In cases of serious or complex fraud, see the Attorney General's Guidelines on Plea discussions in cases of serious or complex fraud.

b.  In cases where the suspect wishes to enter into a formal agreement to provide information or evidence, see sections 71-75 of the Serious Organised Crime and Police Act (SOCPA) 2005 and the CPS legal guidance on SOCPA 2005 – Queen's Evidence.

## What is pre-charge engagement?

3.  Pre-charge engagement in these guidelines refers to voluntary engagement between the parties to an investigation after the first PACE interview, and before any suspect has been formally charged. Pre-charge engagement is a voluntary process and it may be terminated at any time. It does not refer to engagement between the parties to an investigation by way of further PACE interviews, and none of the guidance in this Annex is intended to apply to such circumstances. Should a defendant choose not to engage at this stage, that decision should not be held against him at a later stage in the proceedings.

4.  Pre-charge engagement may, among other things, involve:
    a.  Giving the suspect the opportunity to comment on any proposed further lines of inquiry.
    b.  Ascertaining whether the suspect can identify any other lines of inquiry.
    c.  Asking whether the suspect is aware of, or can provide access to, digital material that has a bearing on the allegation.
    d.  Discussing ways to overcome barriers to obtaining potential evidence, such as revealing encryption keys.
    e.  Agreeing any key word searches of digital material that the suspect would like carried out.
    f.  Obtaining a suspect's consent to access medical records.
    g.  The suspect identifying and providing contact details of any potential witnesses.
    h.  Clarifying whether any expert or forensic evidence is agreed and, if not, whether the suspect's representatives intend to instruct their own expert, including timescales for this.

5.  Pre-charge engagement is encouraged by the Code for Crown Prosecutors and may impact decisions as to charge[38].

## When is pre-charge engagement appropriate?

6.  It may take place whenever it is agreed between the parties that it may assist the investigation. Where a suspect is not yet represented, an investigator should take care to ensure that the suspect understands their right to legal advice before the pre charge engagement process commences. Sufficient time should be given to enable a suspect to access this advice if they wish to do so.

7.  Pre-charge engagement should not, however, be considered a replacement to a further interview with a suspect. Investigators and prosecutors should be conscious that adverse inferences under *section 34 of the Criminal Justice and Public Order Act 1994* are not available at trial where a suspect failed to mention a fact when asked about a matter in pre-charge engagement. An adverse inference may only be drawn where the suspect failed to mention a fact while being questioned under caution by a constable trying to discover whether or by whom the offence had been committed. Moreover, investigators and prosecutors should be aware of the advantages of holding a further formal interview, including the fact that suspects will have been appropriately cautioned and that any answers given will be recorded.

8.  Accordingly, investigators and prosecutors should not seek to initiate, or agree to, pre-charge engagement in respect of matters where they are likely to seek to rely on the contents of the suspect's answers as evidence at trial. Pre-charge engagement should not therefore be used for putting new summaries of the case to the defence, and where deemed necessary such accounts should be put to the suspect in a further interview.

9.  A no comment interview does not preclude the possibility of pre-charge engagement. When taking into account paragraph 8 above, while a no comment interview may limit the scope of any such discussions, pre-charge engagement may still be pursued where appropriate, but consideration should be given to a further PACE interview with the suspect before there is any agreement to engage in pre-charge engagement.

10. There are a number of potential benefits that may arise from pre-charge engagement:
    a.  Suspects who maintain their innocence will be aided by early identification of lines of inquiry which may lead to evidence or material that points away from the suspect or points towards another suspect.
    b.  Pre-charge engagement can help inform a prosecutor's charging decision. It might avoid a case being charged that would otherwise be stopped later in proceedings, when further information becomes available.

---

[38] The Code for Crown Prosecutors, paragraph 3.4

- Set out the method by which the defence will be given disclosure of material that satisfies the disclosure test explaining, if relevant, why the whole item is not being provided.
- What CCTV/multi-media evidence has been seized and how it has been examined?

*A suggested presentation and wording of the information is set out below:*

| Exhibit ref | Description | Inquiry undertaken | Result |
|---|---|---|---|
| AB/1 | I-phone seized from defendant | This telephone has been downloaded using the XRY software. This has resulted in 40,000 pages of data which includes telephone calls to and from the suspect, contact list, text messages, WhatsApp messages and internet search history. No further data has been downloaded from the phone.<br><br>The internet search history does not appear to be relevant to the issues in the case and has not been reviewed.<br><br>The contact list has been reviewed to identify whether the complainant is a contact, no further checks have been made.<br><br>The telephone call list has been reviewed for any contact between the suspect and complainant between dates x and Y. All identified contact has been produced as exhibit AB/2.<br><br>Text messages and WhatsApp messages have been searched using the following keywords [A, B, C, D] all responsive messages which correspond with thekeywords have been disclosed. | Relevant evidential material has been served.<br><br>Material which has been identified through keyword searching has been collated and scheduled. The defence are invited to identify any further keywords which might represent a reasonable line of inquiry. If further interrogation of the telephone is considered to be necessary the defence are invited to identify what enquiries should be undertaken and identify the relevance of such enquiries to the issues in this case. |
|  |  | No further checks have been conducted upon the phone. |  |

3.     Third Party Material

The prosecution believe that the following third parties have relevant non sensitive material that might satisfy the disclosure test if it were in the possession of the prosecution (e.g. Medical and dental records, Records held by other agencies, Records/material held by Social Services or local authority):

The reason for this belief is …

The type of relevant material is…

The following steps have been taken to obtain this material:

The defence have a critical role in ensuring that the prosecution are directed to material that meets the disclosure test. Any representations by the defence on the contents of this document, including identifying issues in the case and why material meets the test for disclosure should be received by *[insert date/ timescale]*

Signed:

Dated:

# CRIMINAL PROCEDURE RULES
# AND CRIMINAL PRACTICE DIRECTIONS

# Criminal Procedure Rules 2020 (SI 2020 No. 759 (L. 19)) and Criminal Practice Directions

Criminal Procedure Rules 2020 (SI 2020 No. 759) as amended by the Criminal Procedure (Amendment) Rules 2021 (SI 2021 No. 40), the Criminal Procedure (Amendment No. 2) Rules 2021 (SI 2021 No. 849), and the Criminal Procedure (Amendment) Rules 2022 (SI 2022 No. 45), the latest coming into force on 4 April 2022; and the Criminal Practice Directions October 2015 (as amended April 2016, November 2016, January 2017, April 2017, October 2017, April 2018, October 2018, April 2019, October 2019, May 2020, October 2020, and March 2022).

The Rules and the Practice Directions have been designed and structured to provide, in combination, an effective procedural framework, a key part of which has been arranging the Practice Directions so as to correspond so far as practicable with the related parts of the Criminal Procedure Rules. We have integrated the 2020 Rules (as amended by the 2021 and 2022 Amendment Rules) and the Practice Directions so far as possible and have included the twelfth amendment to the Practice Directions which has effect from 24 March 2022. At present the Practice Directions reference the Criminal Procedure Rules 2015 and those references have been included unedited. The text of the Rules is presented as laid, accompanied by a corresponding paragraph number (e.g., **R3.26** indicates **Rule 3.26; Commencement of preparatory hearing**). The text of the Practice Directions is displayed in grey boxes which, where possible, follow the text of the associated Rules. We have adopted a paragraph structure with the prefix CPD followed by the number used in the Practice Direction itself, or the Roman numeral section where there is no sequential numbering.

CRIMINAL PRACTICE DIRECTIONS   GENERAL MATTERS

**CPD I General matters A**                                                                                                   **CPD.0A**

0A.1   The Lord Chief Justice has power, including power under section 74 of the Courts Act 2003 and Part 1 of Schedule 2 to the Constitutional Reform Act 2005, to give directions as to the practice and procedure of the criminal courts. The following directions are given accordingly.

0A.2   These Practice Directions came into force on October 5, 2015 [2015] EWCA Crim 1567. Amendment Number 1 [2016] EWCA Crim 97 was issued by the Lord Chief Justice on 23rd March 2016 and came into force on the 4th April 2016. Amendment Number 2 [2016] EWCA Crim 1714 was issued by the Lord Chief Justice on 16th November 2016 and came into force on 16th November 2016. Amendment Number 3 [2017] EWCA Crim 30 was issued by the Lord Chief Justice on 31st January 2017 and came into force on 31st January 2017. Amendment Number 4 [2017] EWCA Crim 310 was issued by the Lord Chief Justice on 28th March 2017 and came into force on 3rd April 2017. Amendment Number 5 [2017] EWCA Crim 1076 was issued by the Lord Chief Justice on 27th July 2017 and came into force on 2nd October 2017. Amendment Number 6 [2018] EWCA Crim 516 was issued by the Lord Chief Justice on 21st March 2018 and came into force on 2nd April 2018. Amendment Number 7 [2018] EWCA Crim 1760 was issued by the Lord Chief Justice on 26th July 2018 and came into force on the 1st October 2018. Amendment Number 8 EWCA [2019] Crim 495 was issued by the Lord Chief Justice on 28th March 2019 and came into force on the 1st April 2019; Amendment Number 9 [2019] EWCA Crim 1603 was issued by the Lord Chief Justice on 10th October 2019 and came into force on 14th October 2019; Amendment Number 10 was issued by the Lord Chief Justice on 12th May 2020 and came into force on the 13th May 2020. Amendment Number 11 was issued by the Lord Chief Justice on 29th October 2020 and came into force on the 16th November 2020, and Amendment Number 12 was issued by the Lord Chief Justice on 23 March 2022 and came into force on the 24th March 2022.

0A.3   Annexes D and E to the Consolidated Criminal Practice Direction of 8th July, 2002, [2002] 1 W.L.R. 2870; [2002] 2 Cr. App. R. 35, as amended, which set out forms for use in connection with the Criminal Procedure Rules, remain in force. See also paragraph I 5A of these Practice Directions.

0A.4   These Practice Directions supplement many, but not all, Parts of the Criminal Procedure Rules, and include other directions about practice and procedure in the courts to which they apply. They are to be known as the Criminal Practice Directions 2015. They came into force on 5th October, 2015. They apply to all cases in all the criminal courts of England and Wales from that date.

0A.5   Consequent on the rearrangement of the Criminal Procedure Rules in the Criminal Procedure Rules 2015, S.I. 2015/1490:

(a) the content of these Practice Directions is arranged to correspond. Within each division of these Directions the paragraphs are numbered to correspond with the associated Part of the Criminal Procedure Rules 2015. Compared with the Criminal Practice Directions given in 2013, as amended, the numbering and content of some divisions is amended consequentially, as shown in this table:

| Derivations | |
| --- | --- |
| *Divisions of 2015 Directions* | *Divisions of 2013 Directions* |
| I General matters | I General matters; |
| II Preliminary proceedings | II Preliminary proceedings 16A–C |
| III Custody and bail | II Preliminary proceedings 9A, 10A, 14A–B |
| IV Disclosure | III Custody and bail |
| V Evidence | IV Disclosure |
| VI Trial | V Evidence |
| VII Sentencing | VI Trial |
| VIII Confiscation and related proceedings [empty] | VII Sentencing |
| IX Appeal | VIII Confiscation and related proceedings [empty] |
| X Costs [Criminal Costs Practice Direction] | X Appeal |
| XI Other proceedings | XI Costs [Criminal Costs Practice Direction] |
| XII General application | II Preliminary proceedings 6A, 17A–F; |
| XIII Listing | IX Contempt of court |
| | XII General application |
| | XIII Listing |

(b) the text of these Practice Directions is amended:
  (i) to bring up to date the cross-references to the Criminal Procedure Rules and to other paragraphs of these Directions which that text contains, and
  (ii) to adopt the abbreviation of references to the Criminal Procedure Rules ('CrimPR') for which rule 2.3(2) of the Criminal Procedure Rules 2015 provides.

**0A.6** In all other respects, the content of the Criminal Practice Directions 2015 reproduces that of the Criminal Practice Directions 2013, as amended.

## NOTE ON STATUTORY POWERS

The Criminal Procedure Rule Committee noted that in making the Rules listed in the first column of this table, it exercises also the powers listed in the corresponding entry in the second column—

| Rule | Power |
| --- | --- |
| 2.4, 2.5, 2.6, 2.7, 2.8 and 2.9 | Section 67B(1) of the Courts Act 2003[1] |
| 3.16 | Section 86A(2) of the Courts Act 2003[2] |
| 3.21 | Section 86A(2) of the Courts Act 2003 |
| 3.32 | Section 77(1) of the Senior Courts Act 1981[3] |
| 4.1 and 4.12 | Section 12(1) and (3) of the Road Traffic Offenders Act 1988[4] |
| 5.5 | Section 32(1) of the Criminal Appeal Act 1968[5] |
| Part 8 | Section 48(1) of the Criminal Law Act 1977[6] |
| 9.2 | Section 86A(2) of the Courts Act 2003 |
| Part 10 | Section 2 of the Indictments Act 1915[7] and section 2(6) of the Administration of Justice (Miscellaneous Provisions) Act 1933[8] |
| 14.6 | Section 5B(9) of the Bail Act 1976[9] |
| 16.4 | Section 9(2A) of the Criminal Justice Act 1967[10] |
| 19.3 | Section 81(1) of the Police and Criminal Evidence Act 1984[11] and section 20(3) of the Criminal Procedure and Investigations Act 1996[12] |
| 20.4 | Section 132(4) of the Criminal Justice Act 2003[13] |

| Rule | Power |
|------|-------|
| Part 23 | Sections 37(5) and 38(6) and (7) of the Youth Justice and Criminal Evidence Act 1999[14] |
| 24.11 | Section 52(4) of the Sentencing Act 2020[15] |
| 24.14 | Section 12(7ZA) of the Magistrates' Courts Act 1980[16] |
| 25.16 | Section 52(4) of the Sentencing Act 2020[17] |
| 28.4 | Section 385(7) of the Sentencing Act 2020 |
| 29.4 | Section 2 of the Commissioners for Oaths Act 1889[18] |
| 33.7, 33.37, 33.39 and 33.40 | Section 91 of the Proceeds of Crime Act 2002[19] |
| 33.47 | Section 52(1) of the Senior Courts Act 1981[20] |
| 34.11 | Sections 73(2) and 74(2), (3) and (4) of the Senior Courts Act 1981[21] |
| 36.8 | Section 87(4) of the Senior Courts Act 1981[22] |
| 37.6 | Section 49(1) of the Criminal Justice Act 2003 |
| 38.9 | Section 73(2) of the Criminal Justice Act 2003 |
| 40.8 | Section 159(6) of the Criminal Justice Act 1988[23] |
| 42.8 | Section 141(2) of the Sentencing Act 2020 |
| 42.14, 42.18, 42.19 and 42.20 | Section 91 of the Proceeds of Crime Act 2002 |
| 44.2 | Section 30(1) of the Criminal Justice Act 2003[24] and section 2 of the Commissioners for Oaths Act 1889[25] |
| 45.6 and 45.7 | Section 52(1) of the Senior Courts Act 1981 |
| 47.4 and 47.10; 47.24 and 47.30 | Paragraph 15A of Schedule 1 to the Police and Criminal Evidence Act 1984[26] |
| 47.4 and 47.11 to 47.16 inclusive | Paragraph 10(2) of Schedule 5, paragraph 14(2) of Schedule 5A, paragraph 4(1) of Schedule 6 and paragraph 5(1) of Schedule 6A to the Terrorism Act 2000[27] |
| 47.4 and 47.17 to 47.22 inclusive | Sections 351(2), 362(2), 369(2) and 375(1) of the Proceeds of Crime Act 2002[28] |
| 47.4 and 47.23 | Section 157(9) of the Extradition Act 2003[29] |
| 47.24 and 47.31 | Paragraph 11(5) of Schedule 5 to the Terrorism Act 2000[30] |
| 47.24 and 47.32 | Section 352(8) of the Proceeds of Crime Act 2002[31] |
| 47.24 and 47.33 | Section 160(10) of the Extradition Act 2003[32] |
| 47.35 and 47.38 | Section 59(13) of the Criminal Justice and Police Act 2001[33] |
| 47.49 | Section 74(3) of the Senior Courts Act 1981[34] |
| 47.63 to 47.68 | Sections 11(1) and 18(2) of the Crime (Overseas Production Orders) Act 2019[35] |
| 48.16 | Section 19 of the Criminal Procedure and Investigations Act 1996[36] |
| 50.17 | Section 67 of the Senior Courts Act 1981[37] |
| 50.23 | Sections 36A(4), 36B(3), 118A(4) and 118B(3) of the Extradition Act 2003[38] |
| 50.30 | Sections 19(3) and 66(1) of the Senior Courts Act 1981[39] |

[1] 2003 c. 39; section 67B was inserted by section 3 of, and paragraph 32 of the Schedule to, the Courts and Tribunals (Judiciary and Functions of Staff) Act 2018 (c. 33).

[2] 2003 c. 39; section 86A was inserted by section 162 of the Policing and Crime Act 2017 (c. 3).

[3] 1981 c. 54; section 77 was amended by section 15 of, and paragraph 11 of Schedule 2 to, the Criminal Justice Act 1987 (c. 38), section 168 of, and paragraph 18 of Schedule 9 to, the Criminal Justice and Public Order Act 1994 (c. 33), section 41 of, and paragraph 54 of Schedule 3 to, the Criminal Justice Act 2003 (c. 44) and article 3 of, and paragraph 11 and 13 of the Schedule to, SI 2004/2035. It is further amended by section 31 of, and paragraph 11 of Schedule 1 and Schedule 2 to, the Prosecution of Offences Act 1985 (c. 23) with effect from a date to be appointed.

[4] 1988 c. 53; section 12 was amended by article 3 of, and paragraphs 29 and 30 of the Schedule to, S.I. 2004/2035.

[5] 1968 c. 19.

[6] 1977 c. 45; section 48 was amended by paragraph 190 of Schedule 8 to the Courts Act 2003 (c. 39).

[7] 1915 c. 90; section 2 was amended by section 19 of the Criminal Justice Administration Act 1956 (c. 34) and sections 56 and 109 of, and paragraph 67 of Schedule 8 and Schedule 11 to, the Courts Act 2003 (c. 39).

[8] 1933 c. 36; section 2(6) was amended by Part IV of Schedule 11 to the Courts Act 1971 (c. 23), paragraph 1 of the Schedule to S.I. 2004/2035 and section 82 of the Deregulation Act 2015 (c. 20).

[9] 1976 c. 63; section 5B(9) was inserted by section 30 of the Criminal Justice and Public Order Act 1994 (c. 33) and amended by paragraph 183 of Schedule 8 to the Courts Act 2003 (c. 39).

[10] 1967 c. 80; section 9(2A) was inserted by section 80 of the Deregulation Act 2015 (c. 20).

[11] 1984 c. 60; section 81 was amended by paragraph 286 of Schedule 8 to, the Courts Act 2003 (c. 39).

[12] 1996 c. 25; section 20(3) was amended by paragraph 378 of Schedule 8 to, the Courts Act 2003 (c. 39).

[13] 2003 c. 44; section 132 was amended by article 3 of, and paragraphs 45 and 51 of the Schedule to, S.I. 2004/2035.

[14] 1999 c. 23; section 37(5) and section 38(6), (7) were amended by section 109 of, and paragraph 384 of Schedule 8 to, the Courts Act 2003 (c. 39).

[15] 2020 c. 17.

[16] 1980 c. 43; section 12(7ZA) was inserted by section 81 of the Deregulation Act 2015 (c. 20).

[17] 2020 c. 17.

[18] 1889 c. 10; section 2 was amended by section 59 of, and paragraph 15 of Schedule 11 to, the Constitutional Reform Act 2005 (c. 4).

[19] 2002 c. 29; section 91 was amended by section 109(1) of, and paragraph 410 of Schedule 8 to, the Courts Act 2003 (c. 39).

[20] 1981 c. 54; section 52 was amended by section 31 of, and Part II of Schedule 1 to, the Prosecution of Offences Act 1985 (c. 23), section 4 of the Courts and Legal Services Act 1990 (c. 41), article 3 and paragraphs 11 and 12(a) of the Schedule to S.I. 2004/2035 and section 59 of, and paragraph 26 of Schedule 11 to, the Constitutional Reform Act 2005 (c. 4).

[21] 1981 c. 54; section 73(2) was amended by article 3 of, and paragraphs 11 and 12(b) of the Schedule to, S.I. 2004/2035. Section 74(2) and (3) was amended by article 3 of, and paragraphs 11 and 12(c) of the Schedule to, S.I. 2004/2035.

[22] 1981 c. 54; section 87(4) was amended by articles 2 and 3 of, and paragraphs 11 and 17 of the Schedule to, S.I. 2004/2035.

[23] 1988 c. 33; section 159(6) was amended by S.I. 2004/2035.

[24] 2003 c. 44; section 30 was amended by article 3 of, and paragraphs 45 and 46 of the Schedule to, S.I. 2004/2035.

[25] 1889 c. 10; section 2 was amended by section 59 of, and paragraph 15 of Schedule 11 to, the Constitutional Reform Act 2005 (c. 4).

[26] 1984 c. 60; paragraph 15A of Schedule 1 was inserted by section 82 of the Deregulation Act 2015 (c. 20).

[27] 2000 c. 11; paragraph 10 of Schedule 5 was amended by section 109(1) of, and paragraph 389 of Schedule 8 to, the Courts Act 2003 (c. 39) and it is further amended by section 65 of, and paragraph 9 of Schedule 4 to, the Courts Act 2003 (c. 39), with effect from a date to be appointed. Paragraph 4 of Schedule 6 was amended by section 109(1) of, and paragraph 390 of Schedule 8 to, the Courts Act 2003 (c. 39). Schedule 6A was inserted by section 3 of, and paragraph 1(1) and (3) of Part 1 of Schedule 2 to, the Anti-terrorism, Crime and Security Act 2001 (c. 24).

[28] 2002 c. 29.

[29] 2003 c. 41; section 157(9) was inserted by section 174 of the Anti-social Behaviour, Crime and Policing Act 2014 (c. 12).

[30] 2000 c. 11; paragraph 11(5) of Schedule 5 was inserted by section 82 of the Deregulation Act 2015 (c. 20).

[31] 2002 c. 29; section 352(8) was inserted by section 82 of the Deregulation Act 2015 (c. 20).

[32] 2003 c. 41; section 160(10) was inserted by section 174 of the Anti-social Behaviour, Crime and Policing Act 2014 (c. 12).

[33] 2001 c. 16; section 59(13) was inserted by section 82 of the Deregulation Act 2015 (c. 20).

[34] 1981 c. 54; section 74(3) was amended by article 3 of, and paragraphs 11 and 12(c) of the Schedule to, S.I. 2004/2035. The Act's title was amended by section 59(5) of, and paragraph 1 of Schedule 11 to, the Constitutional Reform Act 2005 (c. 4).

[35] 2019 c. 5.

[36] 1996 c. 25; section 19 was amended by section 109 of, and paragraph 377 of Schedule 8 to, the Courts Act 2003 (c. 39), section 331 of, and paragraphs 20 and 34 of Schedule 36 to, the Criminal Justice Act 2003 (c. 44) and section 15 of, and paragraph 251 of Schedule 4 to, the Constitutional Reform Act 2005 (c. 4).

[37] 1981 c. 54.

[38] 2003 c. 41; sections 36A, 36B, 118A and 118B were inserted by section 161 of the Anti-social Behaviour, Crime and Policing Act 2014 (c. 12).

[39] 1981 c. 54.

CRIMINAL PROCEDURE RULES   PART 1   THE OVERRIDING OBJECTIVE

**R1.1**   **The overriding objective**

    **1.1**    (1)  The overriding objective of this procedural code is that criminal cases be dealt with justly.

          (2)  Dealing with a criminal case justly includes—

              (a)  acquitting the innocent and convicting the guilty;

              (b)  treating all participants with politeness and respect;

              (c)  dealing with the prosecution and the defence fairly;

              (d)  recognising the rights of a defendant, particularly those under Article 6 of the European Convention on Human Rights;

              (e)  respecting the interests of witnesses, victims and jurors and keeping them informed of the progress of the case;

              (f)  dealing with the case efficiently and expeditiously;

              (g)  ensuring that appropriate information is available to the court when bail and sentence are considered; and

              (h)  dealing with the case in ways that take into account—

> (i)   the gravity of the offence alleged,
> (ii)  the complexity of what is in issue,
> (iii) the severity of the consequences for the defendant and others affected, and
> (iv)  the needs of other cases.

### The duty of the participants in a criminal case

**R1.2**

1.2 (1) Each participant, in the conduct of each case, must—
> (a) prepare and conduct the case in accordance with the overriding objective;
> (b) comply with these Rules, practice directions and directions made by the court; and
> (c) at once inform the court and all parties of any significant failure (whether or not that participant is responsible for that failure) to take any procedural step required by these Rules, any practice direction or any direction of the court. A failure is significant if it might hinder the court in furthering the overriding objective.

(2) Anyone involved in any way with a criminal case is a participant in its conduct for the purposes of this rule.

### The application by the court of the overriding objective

**R1.3**

1.3 The court must further the overriding objective in particular when—
> (a) exercising any power given to it by legislation (including these Rules);
> (b) applying any practice direction; or
> (c) interpreting any rule or practice direction.

CRIMINAL PRACTICE DIRECTIONS    PART 1    THE OVERRIDING OBJECTIVE

### CPD I General matters 1A: The Overriding Objective

**CPD.1A**

1A.1 The presumption of innocence and an adversarial process are essential features of English and Welsh legal tradition and of the defendant's right to a fair trial. But it is no part of a fair trial that questions of guilt and innocence should be determined by procedural manoeuvres. On the contrary, fairness is best served when the issues between the parties are identified as early and as clearly as possible. As Lord Justice Auld noted, a criminal trial is not a game under which a guilty defendant should be provided with a sporting chance. It is a search for truth in accordance with the twin principles that the prosecution must prove its case and that a defendant is not obliged to inculpate himself, the object being to convict the guilty and acquit the innocent.

1A.2 Further, it is not just for a party to obstruct or delay the preparation of a case for trial in order to secure some perceived procedural advantage, or to take unfair advantage of a mistake by someone else. If courts allow that to happen it damages public confidence in criminal justice. The Rules and the Practice Direction, taken together, make it clear that courts must not allow it to happen.

CRIMINAL PROCEDURE RULES    PART 2    UNDERSTANDING AND APPLYING THE
RULES AND POWERS OF AUTHORISED COURT OFFICERS

### Understanding and applying the rules

### When the Rules apply

**R2.1**

2.1 (1) In general, the Criminal Procedure Rules apply—
> (a) in all criminal cases in magistrates' courts and in the Crown Court;
> (b) in extradition cases in the High Court; and
> (c) in all cases in the criminal division of the Court of Appeal.

(2) If a rule applies only in one or some of those courts, the rule makes that clear.

(3) These Rules apply on and after 5th October, 2020, but unless the court otherwise directs, they do not affect a right or duty existing under the Criminal Procedure Rules 2015[1].

(4) The following rules temporarily have effect as described beneath, subject to paragraphs (5) and (6) of this rule—
> (a) in this Part, rules 2.2 (Definitions), 2.7 (Exercise of functions of the Crown Court) and 2.8 (Exercise of functions of a magistrates' court) as if they were amended by rule 5 of the Criminal Procedure (Amendment No. 2) (Coronavirus) Rules 2020[2] ('the Coronavirus Rules');

---

[1] S.I. 2015/1490; amended by S.I. 2016/120, 2016/705, 2017/144, 2017/282, 2017/755, 2017/915, 2018/132, 2018/847, 2019/143, 2019/908, 2019/1119, 2020/32, 2020/417.
[2] S.I. 2020/417.

      (b)  in Part 3 (Case management)—

          (i)  rules 3.2 (The duty of the court), 3.3 (The duty of the parties) and 3.5 (The court's case management powers) as if they were amended by rule 6(a), (b) and (c) respectively of the Coronavirus Rules,

         (ii)  rule 3.8 (Case preparation and progression) as if it were amended by rule 6(d) of the Coronavirus Rules (which amended rule 3.9 of the Criminal Procedure Rules 2015), and

        (iii)  rule 3.10 (Directions for commissioning medical reports, other than for sentencing purposes) as if it were amended by rule 6(e) of the Coronavirus Rules (which amended rule 3.28 of the Criminal Procedure Rules 2015);

      (c)  in Part 5 (Forms and court records), rule 5.4 (Duty to make records) as if it were amended by rule 7 of the Coronavirus Rules;

      (d)  in Part 14 (Bail and custody time limits), rule 14.18 (Exercise of court's powers: extension of live link bail) as if it were amended by rule 8 of the Coronavirus Rules;

      (e)  in Part 18 (Measures to assist a witness or defendant to give evidence)—

          (i)  the heading to the Part as if it were amended by rule 9(a) of the Coronavirus Rules,

         (ii)  rules 18.1 (When this Part applies), 18.2 (Meaning of 'witness'), 18.4 (Decisions and reasons), 18.23 (Exercise of court's powers), 18.24 (Content of application for a live link direction), 18.25 (Application to discharge a live link direction, etc.) and 18.26 (Representations in response) as if they were amended by rule 9(b) to (h) respectively of the Coronavirus Rules, and

        (iii)  the note at the end of the Part as if it were amended by rule 9(i) of the Coronavirus Rules;

      (f)  in Part 24 (Trial and sentence in a magistrates' court), rule 24.11 (Procedure if the court convicts) as if it were amended by rule 10 of the Coronavirus Rules;

      (g)  in Part 25 (Trial and sentence in the Crown Court), rule 25.16 (Procedure if the court convicts) as if it were amended by rule 11 of the Coronavirus Rules;

      (h)  in Part 28 (Sentencing procedures in special cases), rule 28.8 (Directions for commissioning medical reports for sentencing purposes) as if it were amended by rule 12 of the Coronavirus Rules;

      (i)  in Part 47 (Investigation orders and warrants) the rules listed in rule 13 of the Coronavirus Rules as if they were amended by that rule; and

      (j)  in Part 50 (Extradition), rules 50.3 (Exercise of magistrates' court's powers) and 50.17 (Exercise of High Court's powers) as if they were amended by rule 14 of the Coronavirus Rules.

  (5)  The temporary amendments to rules 3.10 (Directions for commissioning medical reports, other than for sentencing purposes) and 28.8 (Directions for commissioning medical reports for sentencing purposes) to which paragraph (4) of this rule refers cease to have effect when paragraph 6 of Schedule 8 to the Coronavirus Act 2020[3] expires or is repealed.

  (6)  The other temporary amendments to which paragraph (4) of this rule refers cease to have effect when section 53 (and Schedule 23), section 54 (and Schedule 24) and section 55 (and Schedule 25) of the Coronavirus Act 2020 expire or are repealed.

*[Note. The rules replaced by the first Criminal Procedure Rules (the Criminal Procedure Rules 2005[4]) were revoked when those Rules came into force by provisions of the Courts Act 2003, the Courts Act 2003 (Consequential Amendments) Order 2004 and the Courts Act 2003 (Commencement No. 6 and Savings) Order 2004[5]. The first Criminal Procedure Rules reproduced the substance of all the rules they replaced.*

*The Criminal Procedure (Amendment No. 2) (Coronavirus) Rules 2020 made temporary amendments to the Criminal Procedure Rules 2015 in consequence of modifications to statutory provisions made by the Coronavirus Act 2020.]*

**R2.2**  **Definitions**

  2.2  (1)  In these Rules, unless the context makes it clear that something different is meant:

      'advocate' means a person who is entitled to exercise a right of audience in the court under section 13 of the Legal Services Act 2007[6];

      'authorised court officer' has the meaning given by rule 2.4;

---

[3] 2020 c. 7.
[4] S.I. 2005/384; amended by S.I. 2006/353, 2006/2636, 2007/699, 2007/2317, 2007/3662, 2008/2076, 2008/3269 and 2009/2087.
[5] S.I. 2004/2066.
[6] 2007 c. 29.

'business day' means any day except Saturday, Sunday, Christmas Day, Boxing Day, Good Friday, Easter Monday or a bank holiday;

'court' means a tribunal with jurisdiction over criminal cases. It includes a judge, recorder, District Judge (Magistrates' Court), lay justice and, when exercising their judicial powers, the Registrar of Criminal Appeals, and an authorised court officer;

'court officer' means the appropriate member of the staff of a court;

'justices' legal adviser' means a person authorised under section 28 of the Courts Act 2003[7] to give advice about law to justices of the peace;

'legal representative' means:

>    (i) the person for the time being named as a party's representative in any legal aid representation order made under section 16 of the Legal Aid, Sentencing and Punishment of Offenders Act 2012[8], or

>    (ii) subject to that, the person named as a party's representative in any notice for the time being given under rule 46.2 (Notice of appointment, etc. of legal representative: general rules) provided that person is entitled to conduct litigation in the court under section 13 of the Legal Services Act 2007;

'live link' means an arrangement by which a person can see and hear, and be seen and heard by, the court when that person is not in the courtroom;

'Practice Direction' means the Lord Chief Justice's Criminal Practice Directions, as amended, and 'Criminal Costs Practice Direction' means the Lord Chief Justice's Practice Direction (Costs in Criminal Proceedings), as amended;

'public interest ruling' means a ruling about whether it is in the public interest to disclose prosecution material under sections 3(6), 7A(8) or 8(5) of the Criminal Procedure and Investigations Act 1996[9]; and

'Registrar' means the Registrar of Criminal Appeals or a court officer exercising a function of the Registrar.

(2)   Definitions of some other expressions are in the rules in which they apply.

*[Note. The glossary at the end of the Rules is a guide to the meaning of certain legal expressions used in them.]*

### References to legislation, including these Rules    R2.3

2.3   (1)   In these Rules, where a rule refers to an Act of Parliament or to subordinate legislation by title and year, subsequent references to that Act or to that legislation in the rule are shortened: so, for example, after a reference to the Criminal Procedure and Investigations Act 1996[10] that Act is called 'the 1996 Act'; and after a reference to the Criminal Procedure and Investigations Act 1996 (Defence Disclosure Time Limits) Regulations 2011[11] those Regulations are called 'the 2011 Regulations'.

(2)   In the courts in which these Rules apply—

>    (a) unless the context makes it clear that something different is meant, a reference to the Criminal Procedure Rules, without reference to a year, is a reference to the Criminal Procedure Rules in force at the date on which the event concerned occurs or occurred;

>    (b) a reference to the Criminal Procedure Rules may be abbreviated to 'CrimPR'; and

>    (c) a reference to a Part or rule in the Criminal Procedure Rules may be abbreviated to, for example, 'CrimPR Part 3' or 'CrimPR 3.5'.

### Powers of authorised court officers

### Exercise of court's functions by authorised court officers: general rules    R2.4

2.4.—(1)   This rule and rules 2.5, 2.6, 2.7, 2.8 and 2.9 provide for the exercise of relevant judicial functions within the meaning of section 67A of the Courts Act 2003[12] —

>    (a) in a court in which these Rules apply;

>    (b) by a person authorised for the purpose by the Lord Chief Justice under section 67B of that Act[13].

---

[7] 2003 c. 39; section 28 is substituted by section 3 of, and paragraph 26 of the Schedule to, the Courts and Tribunals (Judiciary and Functions of Staff) Act 2018 (c. 33).

[8] 2012 c. 10.

[9] 1996 c. 25; section 7A was inserted by section 37 of the Criminal Justice Act 2003 (c. 44).

[10] 1996 c. 25.

[11] S.I. 2011/209.

[12] 2003 c. 39; section 67A is inserted by section 3 of, and paragraph 32 of the Schedule to, the Courts and Tribunals (Judiciary and Functions of Staff) Act 2018 (c. 33).

[13] 2003 c. 39; section 67B is inserted by section 3 of, and paragraph 32 of the Schedule to, the Courts and Tribunals (Judiciary and Functions of Staff) Act 2018 (c. 33).

(2) In this rule and in rules 2.5, 2.6, 2.7, 2.8 and 2.9—

(a) 'authorised court officer' means any such person;

(b) a reference to an authorised court officer who is legally qualified is a reference to one who has such qualifications as are for the time being prescribed by regulations made under section 28(3) of the Courts Act 2003.

(3) No court officer may—

(a) authorise a person's committal to prison;

(b) authorise a person's arrest (but that exclusion does not apply to the issue of a warrant of arrest, whether or not endorsed for bail, to secure that a person attends court proceedings relating to an offence of which the person has been accused or convicted in a case in which no objection is made by or on behalf of that person to the issue of the warrant);

(c) grant or withhold bail, except to the extent that rule 2.6 or rule 2.8 allows;

(d) adjudicate on guilt, or on the act or omission with which a defendant is charged, except to the extent of—

(i) acquitting a defendant against whom the prosecutor offers no evidence,

(ii) convicting a defendant who pleads guilty, or

(iii) giving a prosecutor permission to withdraw a case;

(e) determine the admissibility of evidence;

(f) set ground rules for the conduct of questioning where rule 3.8(6), (7) (directions for the appropriate treatment and questioning of a witness or the defendant) applies;

(g) make findings of fact for the purpose of sentence, defer or pass sentence, impose a penalty or commit a defendant to the Crown Court for sentence;

(h) make an order for a party or other person to pay costs, unless that party or person agrees;

(i) make any other order consequent upon acquittal, conviction or a finding that the accused did the act or made the omission charged, except to the extent that rule 2.8 allows;

(j) vary, discharge, remit, remove, revoke, review or suspend a sentence, penalty or other order consequent on acquittal or conviction, except to the extent that rule 2.8 allows;

(k) order the search, confiscation, restraint, detention or seizure of property except to the extent that rule 2.8 allows;

(l) determine an appeal or reference to an appeal court, or an application for permission to appeal or refer, except to the extent that rule 2.6 allows; or

(m) determine an allegation of contempt of court.

(4) An authorised court officer may exercise a relevant judicial function for which rule 2.5, 2.6, 2.7, 2.8 or 2.9 provides—

(a) only subject to the same conditions as apply to its exercise by the court or person whose function it is; and

(b) where a party affected by the exercise of that function is entitled to make representations before its exercise, only if each such party has had a reasonable opportunity to make such representations—

(i) in writing, or

(ii) at a hearing (whether or not that party in fact attends).

(5) Unless the context makes it clear that something different is meant, provision in rule 2.5, 2.6, 2.7, 2.8 or 2.9 permitting the exercise of a relevant judicial function by an authorised court officer includes a power to decline to exercise that function.

*[Note. Under section 67A of the Courts Act 2003, 'relevant judicial function' means a function of a court to which the general duty of the Lord Chancellor under section 1 of that Act applies and a judicial function of a person holding an office that entitles the person to exercise functions of such a court, but does not include in a court in which Criminal Procedure Rules apply—*

*(a) any function so far as its exercise involves authorising a person's committal to prison; or*

*(b) any function so far as its exercise involves authorising a person's arrest, except the issue of a warrant of arrest (whether or not endorsed for bail) to secure that a person attends court proceedings relating to an offence of which the person has been accused or convicted in a case in which no objection is made by or on behalf of that person to the issue of the warrant.*

*Under section 67B of the 2003 Act, in a court in which Criminal Procedure Rules apply the Rules may provide for the exercise of relevant judicial functions by persons who are appointed under section 2(1) of that Act and who satisfy any requirements specified in the Rules as to qualifications or experience. Such a person may exercise such a function only if authorised to do so by the Lord Chief Justice.*

*Section 28 of the 2003 Act provides for persons authorised by the Lord Chief Justice to give advice to justices of the peace about matters of law. Such a person may be authorised for that purpose only if appointed under section 2(1) of that Act and possessed of such qualifications as may be prescribed by regulations made under section 28. See also rule 2.2 (Definitions).]*

(e)   in some cases (destroying or damaging property; aggravated vehicle taking), whether the value involved is more or less than £5,000; and

(f)   in a case of low-value shoplifting, whether the defendant chooses Crown Court trial: see section 22A of the 1980 Act[5].

*Under paragraph 2(1) of Schedule 17 to the Crime and Courts Act 2013[6] and section 2 of the Administration of Justice (Miscellaneous Provisions) Act 1933[7], the Crown Court may give permission to serve a draft indictment where it approves a deferred prosecution agreement. See Part 11 for the rules about that procedure and Part 10 for the rules about indictments.*

*The procedure for applying for the permission of a High Court judge to serve a draft indictment is in rule 10.9 (Application to a High Court judge for permission to serve a draft indictment).*

*The Court of Appeal may order a retrial under section 8 of the Criminal Appeal Act 1968[8] (on a defendant's appeal against conviction) or under section 77 of the Criminal Justice Act 2003[9] (on a prosecutor's application for the retrial of a serious offence after acquittal). Section 8 of the 1968 Act, section 84 of the 2003 Act and rules 27.6 and 39.14 require the arraignment of a defendant within 2 months.]*

**R3.2    The duty of the court**

3.2    (1)   The court must further the overriding objective by actively managing the case.

(2)   Active case management includes—

(a)   the early identification of the real issues;

(b)   the early identification of the needs of witnesses;

(c)   achieving certainty as to what must be done, by whom, and when, in particular by the early setting of a timetable for the progress of the case;

(d)   monitoring the progress of the case and compliance with directions;

(e)   ensuring that evidence, whether disputed or not, is presented in the shortest and clearest way;

(f)   discouraging delay, dealing with as many aspects of the case as possible on the same occasion, and avoiding unnecessary hearings;

(g)   encouraging the participants to co-operate in the progression of the case; and

(h)   making use of technology.

(3)   The court must actively manage the case by giving any direction appropriate to the needs of that case as early as possible.

(4)   Where appropriate live links are available, making use of technology for the purposes of this rule includes directing the use of such facilities, whether an application for such a direction is made or not—

(a)   for the conduct of a pre-trial hearing, including a pre-trial case management hearing;

(b)   for the defendant's attendance at such a hearing—

(i)   where the defendant is in custody, or where the defendant is not in custody and wants to attend by live link, but

(ii)   only if the court is satisfied that the defendant can participate effectively by such means, having regard to all the circumstances including whether the defendant is represented or not; and

(c)   for receiving evidence under one of the powers to which the rules in Part 18 apply (Measures to assist a witness or defendant to give evidence).

---

[5]   1980 c. 43; section 22A was inserted by section 176 of the Anti-social Behaviour, Crime and Policing Act 2014 (c. 12) and amended by section 52 of the Criminal Justice and Courts Act 2015 (c. 2).

[6]   2013 c. 22.

[7]   1933 c. 36; section 2 was amended by Part IV of Schedule 11 to, the Courts Act 1971 (c. 23), Schedule 5 to, the Senior Courts Act 1981 (c. 54), Schedule 2 to the Prosecution of Offences Act 1985 (c. 23), paragraph 1 of Schedule 2 to the Criminal Justice Act 1987 (c. 38), paragraph 10 of Schedule 15 to the Criminal Justice Act 1988 (c. 33), paragraph 8 of Schedule 6 to the Criminal Justice Act 1991 (c. 53), Schedule 1 to the Statute Law (Repeals Act 1993, paragraph 17 of Schedule 1 to the Criminal Procedure and Investigations Act 1996 (c. 25), paragraph 5 of Schedule 8 to the Crime and Disorder Act 1998 (c. 37), paragraph 34 of Schedule 3 and Part 4 of Schedule 37 to the Criminal Justice Act 2003 (c. 44), paragraph 1 of the Schedule to S.I. 2004/2035, section 12 of, and paragraph 7 of Schedule 1 to, the Constitutional Reform Act 2005 (c. 4), sections 116 and 178 of, and Part 3 of Schedule 23 to, the Coroners and Justice Act 2009 (c. 25), paragraph 32 of Schedule 17 to the Crime and Courts Act 2013 (c. 22) and section 82 of the Deregulation Act 2015 (c. 20).

[8]   1968 c. 19; section 8 was amended by Section 12 of, and paragraph 38 of Schedule 2 to, the Bail Act 1976 (c. 63), section 56 of, and Part IV of Schedule 11 to, the Courts Act 1971 (c. 23), section 65 of, and paragraph 36 of Schedule 3 to, the Mental Health (Amendment) Act 1982 (c. 51), section 148 of, and paragraph 23 of Schedule 4 to, the Mental Health Act 1983 (c. 20), section 43 of the Criminal Justice Act 1988 (c. 33), section 168 of, and paragraph 19 of Schedule 10 to, the Criminal Justice and Public Order Act 1994 (c. 33), section 58 of the Access to Justice Act 1999 (c. 22), sections 41 and 332 of, and paragraph 43 of Schedule 3 to, and Part 4 of Schedule 37 to, the Criminal Justice Act 2003 (c. 44) and section 32 of, and paragraph 2 of Schedule 4 to, the Mental Health Act 2007 (c. 12).

[9]   2003 c. 44.

*[Note. See also—*

> *(a)  rule 2.4, which makes general rules about the exercise of judicial functions by authorised court officers;*
> *(b)  rule 3.6 (Application to vary a direction); and*
> *(c)  rule 50.4 (Case management in the magistrates' court and duty of court officer).]*

## Court's power to extend time under rule 2.6 or rule 2.7                        R2.10

**2.10.**—(1)  The court may extend (even after it has expired) a time limit under rule 2.6 (Exercise of functions of the High Court) or rule 2.7 (Exercise of functions of the Crown Court).

(2)  A party who wants an extension of time must—
   (a)  apply when serving the application for which it is needed; and
   (b)  explain the delay.

CRIMINAL PROCEDURE RULES   PART 3   CASE MANAGEMENT

**General rules**

## When this Part applies                                                        R3.1

**3.1**  (1)  Rules 3.1 to 3.15 apply to the management of each case in a magistrates' court and in the Crown Court (including an appeal to the Crown Court) until the conclusion of that case.

(2)  Rules 3.16 to 3.18 apply where the case must be tried in a magistrates' court, or the court orders trial there.
   (a)  the court sends the defendant for trial in the Crown Court; or
   (b)  the case is one to which rule 24.8 or rule 24.9 applies (Written guilty plea: special rules; Single justice procedure: special rules).

(3)  Rules 3.19 to 3.34 apply where—
   (a)  the defendant is sent to the Crown Court for trial;
   (b)  a High Court or Crown Court judge gives permission to serve a draft indictment; or
   (c)  the Court of Appeal orders a retrial.

*[Note. Rules that apply to procedure in the Court of Appeal are in Parts 36 to 42 of these Rules.*

*At the first hearing in a magistrates' court the court may (and in some cases must) order trial in that court, or may (and in some cases must) send the defendant to the Crown Court for trial under section 51 or 51A of the Crime and Disorder Act 1998[1]. See Part 9 (Allocation and sending for trial) for the procedure. The decision depends upon—*

> *(a)   the classification of the offence (and the general rule, subject to exceptions, is that an offence classified as triable only on indictment must be sent to the Crown Court for trial; an offence classified as triable only summarily must be tried in a magistrates' court; and an offence classified as triable either way, on indictment or summarily, must be allocated to one or the other court for trial, subject to the defendant's right to choose Crown Court trial: see in particular sections 50A, 51 and 51A of the 1998 Act[2] and section 19 of the Magistrates' Courts Act 1980[3] );*
> *(b)  the defendant's age (and the general rule, subject to exceptions, is that an offence alleged against a defendant under 18 must be tried in a magistrates' court sitting as a youth court: see in particular sections 24 and 24A of the 1980 Act[4]);*
> *(c)   whether the defendant is awaiting Crown Court trial for another offence;*
> *(d)   whether another defendant, charged with the same offence, is awaiting Crown Court trial for that offence;*

---

[1]  1998 c. 37; section 51 was substituted by paragraphs 15 and 18 of Schedule 3 to the Criminal Justice Act 2003 (c. 44) and amended by section 59 of, and paragraph 1 of Schedule 11 to, the Constitutional Reform Act 2005 (c. 4). Section 51A was inserted by paragraphs 15 and 18 of Schedule 3 to the Criminal Justice Act 2003 (c. 44) and amended by section 49 of, and paragraph 5 of Schedule 1 to, the Violent Crime Reduction Act 2006 (c. 38) and paragraph 6 of Schedule 21 to the Legal Aid, Sentencing and Punishment of Offenders Act 2012 (c. 10).

[2]  1998 c. 37; section 50A was inserted by paragraphs 15 and 17 of Schedule 3 to the Criminal Justice Act 2003 (c. 44).

[3]  1980 c. 43; section 19 was substituted by paragraphs 1 and 5 of Schedule 3 to the Criminal Justice Act 2003 (c. 44) and amended by sections 144, 177 and 178 of, and paragraph 4 of Schedule 17, paragraph 80 of Schedule 21 and Part 5 of Schedule 23 to, the Coroners and Justice Act 2009 (c. 25).

[4]  1980 c. 43; section 24 was amended by paragraph 47 of Schedule 14 to the Criminal Justice Act 1982 (c. 48), sections 17, 68 and 101 of, and paragraph 6 of Schedule 8 and Schedule 13 to, the Criminal Justice Act 1991 (c. 53), paragraph 40 of Schedule 10, and Schedule 11, to the Criminal Justice and Public Order Act 1994 (c. 33), sections 47 and 119 of, and paragraph 40 of Schedule 8, to the Crime and Disorder Act 1998 (c. 37), paragraph 64 of Schedule 9 to the Powers of Criminal Courts (Sentencing) Act 2000 (c. 6), section 42 of, and paragraphs 1 and 9 of Schedule 3, and Part 4 of Schedule 37, to the Criminal Justice Act 2003 (c. 44) and sections 49 and 65 of, and paragraph 1 of Schedule 1 and Schedule 5 to, the Violent Crime Reduction Act 2006 (c. 38). Section 24A was inserted by paragraphs 1 and 10 of Schedule 3 to the Criminal Justice Act 2003 (c. 44).

(10) In connection with the rules about costs (Part 45)—

    (a) making or varying an order for a party to pay costs, if both parties agree;

    (b) making or varying an order for another person to pay costs, if that person agrees; and

    (c) making a costs order to which rule 45.4 (Costs out of central funds) applies.

(11) In connection with the rules about other proceedings (Parts 46 to 50)—

    (a) making a legal aid representation order on an appeal against a refusal of legal aid (but a court officer may not decline to make such an order); and

    (b) determining an application for a change of legal representative.

(12) An authorised court officer who is not a justices' legal adviser may not exercise a function of the court in a case in which a District Judge (Magistrates' Courts), a lay justice or a justices' legal adviser so directs.

*[Note. See also—*

    *(a) rule 2.4, which makes general rules about the exercise of judicial functions by authorised court officers; and*

    *(b) rule 3.6 (Application to vary a direction).*

*Under section 148 of the Magistrates' Courts Act 1980[32], the expression 'magistrates' court' means any justice or justices of the peace acting under any enactment or by virtue of their commission or under the common law. For a court's power to try an allegation of an offence, see the note to rule 24.1 (Trial and sentence in a magistrates' court; When this Part applies).*

*Under section 50 of the Crime and Disorder Act 1998[33], where a defendant has been charged with an offence at a police station the magistrates' court before whom he or she appears or is brought for the first time in relation to the charge may consist of a single justice; and where on such an occasion the powers of a single justice are exercised by an authorised court officer that court officer may not remand the defendant in custody or, without the consent of the prosecutor and the defendant, remand the defendant on bail on conditions other than those (if any) previously imposed.*

*Under section 8B(3) of the Magistrates' Courts Act 1980[34], a magistrates' court may discharge or vary (or further vary) a pre-trial ruling within the meaning of section 8A of that Act[35] if the court has given the parties an opportunity to be heard and if, among other things, there has been a material change of circumstances since the ruling was made or, if a previous application has been made, since the application (or last application) was made.*

*Under section 53(4) of the Courts Act 2003[36], a court security officer acting in the execution of that officer's duty may remove any person from a courtroom at the request of a judge or a justice of the peace.]*

**R2.9** **Exercise of functions of a District Judge (Magistrates' Courts) in extradition cases**

2.9.—(1) This rule provides for the exercise by an authorised court officer of relevant judicial functions of a District Judge (Magistrates' Courts) in a case to which Part 50 (Extradition) applies.

(2) Subject to rule 2.4, an authorised court officer who is legally qualified may—

    (a) fix, cancel or vary the date, time or place for a hearing, including an extradition hearing; and

    (b) determine an application to extend a time limit set by a rule or by the court, unless the effect would be—

        (i) to affect the date of any hearing that has been fixed, including an extradition hearing, or

        (ii) significantly to affect the progress of the case in any other way.

(3) An authorised court officer who is not a justices' legal adviser may not exercise a function of the court in a case in which a District Judge (Magistrates' Courts) or a justices' legal adviser so directs.

---

[32] 1980 c. 43; section 148 was amended by section 109 of, and paragraph 248 of Schedule 8 to, the Courts Act 2003 (c. 39).

[33] 1998 c. 37; section 50 was amended by section 106 of, and Schedule 15 to, the Access to Justice Act 1999 (c. 22), sections 41 and 332 of, and paragraphs 15 and 16 of Schedule 3 and Part 4 of Schedule 37 to, the Criminal Justice Act 2003 (c. 44), regulation 8 of S.I. 2006/2493 and section 39 of, and paragraphs 46 and 47 of Schedule 5 to, the Legal Aid, Sentencing and Punishment of Offenders Act 2012 (c. 10). It is further amended by section 3 of, and paragraphs 20 and 22 of the Schedule to, the Courts and Tribunals (Judiciary and Functions of Staff) Act 2018 (c. 33).

[34] 1980 c. 43; section 8B was inserted by section 45 of, and Schedule 3 to, the Courts Act 2003 (c. 39) and amended by paragraph 51 of Schedule 3, and Part 4 of Schedule 37, to the Criminal Justice Act 2003 (c. 44).

[35] 1980 c. 43; section 8A was inserted by section 45 of, and Schedule 3 to, the Courts Act 2003 (c. 39) and amended by SI 2006/2493 and paragraphs 12 and 14 of Schedule 5 to the Legal Aid, Sentencing and Punishment of Offenders Act 2012 (c. 10).

[36] 2003 c. 39.

> (i)   the court officer, and
> (ii)  each other party (if any) affected by the decision; and
>
> (c)   in the application—
>   (i)   specify the decision in issue,
>   (ii)  explain why it is appropriate for the decision to be reconsidered and what decision the applicant thinks would be appropriate, and
>   (iii) ask for a hearing, if one is wanted, and explain why it is needed.

(6)  The judge may determine the application—
  (a)  at a hearing (which may be in public or private), or without a hearing;
  (b)  in the absence of—
    (i)   the applicant,
    (ii)  each other party (if any) affected by the decision.
(7)  But the judge must not determine the application in the absence of an affected party unless that party has had—
  (a)  such notice as the nature and urgency of the application permits; and
  (b)  a reasonable opportunity to make representations.

*[Note. See also—*

*(a)  rule 2.4, which makes general rules about the exercise of judicial functions by authorised court officers;*
*(b)  rule 2.10, which provides for extension of the time limit under this rule; and*
*(c)  rule 3.6 (Application to vary a direction).*

*For the constitution and powers of the Crown Court, see the note to rule 25.1 (Trial and sentence in the Crown Court; When this Part applies).]*

## Exercise of functions of a magistrates' court                                          R2.8

2.8.—(1)  This rule provides for the exercise by an authorised court officer of relevant judicial functions of a magistrates' court in a criminal cause or matter.
(2)  Subject to rule 2.4 and to paragraph (12) of this rule, an authorised court officer may—
  (a)  fix, cancel or vary the date, time or place for a hearing, including a trial, or adjourn a hearing;
  (b)  adjourn, remit or transfer proceedings from one local justice area to another;
  (c)  determine an application to extend a time limit set by a rule or by the court, unless the effect would be—
    (i)   to affect the date of any hearing that has been fixed, including a trial, or
    (ii)  significantly to affect the progress of the case in any other way;
  (d)  issue a summons at the request of a public prosecutor, or under section 16B of the Magistrates' Courts Act 1980[20] (Cases not tried in accordance with section 16A) or section 83 of that Act[21] (Process for securing attendance of offender);
  (e)  give a prosecutor permission to withdraw a case;
  (f)  grant bail where the defendant already is on bail and—
    (i)   the conditions, if any, to which that bail is subject will remain the same, or
    (ii)  bail conditions will be varied or imposed with both parties' agreement;
  (g)  give consent for another magistrates' court to deal with a defendant for an offence in respect of which the defendant, when an adult, was discharged conditionally;
  (h)  order a convicted defendant to produce his or her driving licence;
  (i)  require a statement of the defendant's assets and other financial circumstances;
  (j)  amend an attendance centre order to—
    (i)   vary the day or hour specified in that order for the defendant's first attendance, or
    (ii)  substitute an alternative centre;
  (k)  amend the local justice area or responsible officer named in an order of the court;
  (l)  amend a sentence or order by requiring it to be completed in Northern Ireland or Scotland;
  (m)  extend the time for service of a statutory declaration to which applies—
    (i)   rule 44.2 (Statutory declaration of ignorance of proceedings), or
    (ii)  rule 29.4 (Statutory declaration to avoid fine after fixed penalty notice);

---

[20]  1980 c. 43; section 16B was inserted by section 48 of the Criminal Justice and Courts Act 2015 (c. 2).
[21]  1980 c. 43; section 83 was amended by articles 46 and 47 of S.I. 2006/1737 and sections 97(2) and 106 of, and Part V (table 8) of Schedule 15 to, the Access to Justice Act 1999 (c. 22).

(b) unless the application is made at a hearing, serve the application on—
  (i) the court officer, and
  (ii) each other party (if any) affected by the decision; and
(c) in the application—
  (i) specify the decision in issue,
  (ii) explain why it is appropriate for the decision to be reconsidered and what decision the applicant thinks would be appropriate, and
  (iii) ask for a hearing, if one is wanted, and explain why it is needed.
(7) The judge may determine the application—
  (a) at a hearing (which may be in public or private), or without a hearing;
  (b) in the absence of—
    (i) the applicant,
    (ii) each other party (if any) affected by the decision.
(8) But the judge must not determine the application in the absence of an affected party unless that party has had—
  (a) such notice as the nature and urgency of the application permits; and
  (b) a reasonable opportunity to make representations.

*[Note. See also—*

  *(a) rule 2.4, which makes general rules about the exercise of judicial functions by authorised court officers;*

  *(b) rule 2.10, which provides for extension of the time limit under this rule;*

  *(c) rule 3.6 (Application to vary a direction); and*

  *(d) rule 50.18 (Case management in the High Court).*

*For the functions of the High Court for which this rule provides, see the introductory note to Section 3 of Part 50. See also rule 50.30 for the constitution of the High Court when exercising the powers to which that Section of that Part applies.*

*Under section 36 of the Extradition Act 2003, where an extradition order has been made under Part 1 of the Act and the outcome of an appeal by the defendant is that he or she is to be extradited then (a) the defendant must be removed to the requesting territory within 10 days starting with the day on which the decision of the relevant court on the appeal becomes final or proceedings on the appeal are discontinued, unless (b) the requesting authority and the High Court agree to postpone that starting date.]*

**R2.7**    **Exercise of functions of the Crown Court**

**2.7.**—(1) This rule provides for the exercise by an authorised court officer of relevant judicial functions of the Crown Court in a criminal cause or matter.
(2) Subject to rule 2.4 and to paragraph (3) of this rule, an authorised court officer may—
  (a) determine an application to extend a time limit set by a rule or by a judge, including a time limit for the conduct of confiscation proceedings, unless the effect would be—
    (i) to affect the date of any hearing that has been fixed, including a trial, or
    (ii) significantly to affect the progress of the case in any other way;
  (b) give a live link direction under section 57B, 57E or 57F of the Crime and Disorder Act 1998[19] (Use of live link at preliminary hearings where accused is in custody; Use of live link in sentencing hearings; Use of live link in certain enforcement hearings);
  (c) exercise the court's functions listed in rule 23.2 (Appointment of advocate to cross-examine witness) and select such an advocate as that rule describes (but a court officer may not decline to select such an advocate where that rule applies).
(3) An authorised court officer may not exercise a function of the court in a case in which a judge so directs.
(4) Paragraph (5) of this rule applies where a party or an advocate appointed under rule 23.2 (Appointment of advocate to cross-examine witness) wants a judge to reconsider a decision made by an authorised court officer.
(5) Such a party or advocate must—
  (a) apply for such a reconsideration as soon as reasonably practicable, and in any event no later than the earlier of—
    (i) the next hearing before a judge, or
    (ii) the tenth business day after the date on which notice of the decision is served on the applicant;
  (b) unless the application is made at a hearing, serve the application on—

---

[19] 1998 c. 37; sections 57A to 57E were substituted for section 57 as originally enacted by section 45 of the Police and Justice Act 2006 (c. 48). Sections 57B and 57E were amended, and section 57F was inserted, by section 106 of the Coroners and Justice Act 2009 (c. 25).

**Exercise of functions of the Court of Appeal**                                                    R2.5

2.5.—(1) This rule provides for the exercise by an authorised court officer of relevant judicial functions of—

    (a) the criminal division of the Court of Appeal; and

    (b) the Registrar of Criminal Appeals.

  (2) Subject to rule 2.4, an authorised court officer may exercise—

    (a) any function of the criminal division of the Court of Appeal that may be exercised by the Registrar of Criminal Appeals; and

    (b) any other judicial function of the Registrar.

  (3) Where an authorised court officer exercises a function of the court—

    (a) the same provision as that made by section 31A(4) or section 31C(3), as the case may be, of the Criminal Appeal Act 1968[14] applies as if that function had been exercised by the Registrar; and

    (b) rule 36.5 (Renewing an application refused by a judge or the Registrar) applies.

*[Note. See also rule 2.4, which makes general rules about the exercise of judicial functions by authorised court officers.*

*For the functions of the criminal division of the Court of Appeal that may be exercised by the Registrar of Criminal Appeals, see sections 31A and 31B of the Criminal Appeal Act 1968[15]. For other functions of the Registrar, see section 21 of that Act[16].*

*Sections 31A(4) and 31C(3) of the 1968 Act provide for the reconsideration by a judge of a decision by the Registrar to which those provisions apply.]*

**Exercise of functions of the High Court**                                                         R2.6

2.6.—(1) This rule provides for the exercise by an authorised court officer of relevant judicial functions of the High Court in relation to its jurisdiction under the Extradition Act 2003[17].

  (2) An authorised court officer may exercise any such function of the High Court to which the rules in Section 3 of Part 50 apply (Extradition; Appeal to the High Court), subject to—

    (a) rule 2.4; and

    (b) paragraph (3) of this rule.

  (3) No court officer may—

    (a) grant or withhold bail;

    (b) impose or vary a condition of bail; or

    (c) reopen a decision which determines an appeal or an application for permission to appeal, unless paragraph (4) applies.

  (4) If making a decision to which the parties have agreed in writing, an authorised court officer may—

    (a) give or refuse permission to appeal;

    (b) determine an appeal;

    (c) grant or withhold bail; or

    (d) impose or vary a condition of bail.

  (5) Paragraph (6) of this rule—

    (a) applies where a party wants a judge to reconsider a decision made by an authorised court officer;

    (b) does not apply where such an officer agrees to postpone the date on which the required period for extradition begins under section 36(3) of the Extradition Act 2003[18].

  (6) Such a party must—

    (a) apply for such a reconsideration as soon as reasonably practicable, and in any event no later than the earlier of—

      (i) the next hearing before a judge, or

      (ii) the fifth business day after the date on which notice of the decision is served on the applicant;

---

[14] 1968 c. 19; section 31A was inserted by section 6 of the Criminal Appeal Act 1995 (c. 35) and amended by sections 87 and 109 of, and Schedule 10 to, the Courts Act 2003 (c. 39) and paragraphs 86 and 88 of Schedule 36 to the Criminal Justice Act 2003 (c. 44). Section 31C was inserted by section 87 of the Courts Act 2003 (c. 39) and amended by sections 47 and 149 of, and paragraphs 1 and 12 of Schedule 8 and part 3 of Schedule 28 to, the Criminal Justice and Immigration Act 2008 (c. 4).

[15] 1968 c. 19; section 31B was inserted by section 87 of the Courts Act 2003 (c. 39).

[16] 1968 c. 19.

[17] 2003 c. 41.

[18] 2003 c. 41; section 36 was amended by section 40 of, and paragraph 81 of Schedule 9 to, the Constitutional Reform Act 2005 (c. 4).

(5) Where appropriate telephone facilities are available, making use of technology for the purposes of this rule includes directing the use of such facilities, whether an application for such a direction is made or not, for the conduct of a pre-trial case management hearing—

  (a) if telephone facilities are more convenient for that purpose than live links;

  (b) unless at that hearing the court expects to take the defendant's plea; and

  (c) only if—

    (i) the defendant is represented, or

    (ii) exceptionally, the court is satisfied that the defendant can participate effectively by such means without a representative.

*[Note. In relation to the defendant's attendance by live link at a pre-trial hearing, see sections 46ZA and 47 of the Police and Criminal Evidence Act 1984[10] and sections 57A to 57D and 57F of the Crime and Disorder Act 1998[11].*

*In relation to the giving of evidence by a witness and the giving of evidence by the defendant, see section 32 of the Criminal Justice Act 1988[12], sections 19, 24 and 33A of the Youth Justice and Criminal Evidence Act 1999[13] and section 51 of the Criminal Justice Act 2003[14]. Part 18 (Measures to assist a witness or defendant to give evidence) contains relevant rules.]*

## The duty of the parties                                                     R3.3

3.3  (1) Each party must—

  (a) actively assist the court in fulfilling its duty under rule 3.2, without or if necessary with a direction; and

  (b) apply for a direction if needed to further the overriding objective.

  (2) Active assistance for the purposes of this rule includes—

  (a) at the beginning of the case, communication between the prosecutor and the defendant at the first available opportunity and in any event no later than the beginning of the day of the first hearing;

  (b) after that, communication between the parties and with the court officer until the conclusion of the case;

  (c) by such communication establishing, among other things—

    (i) whether the defendant is likely to plead guilty or not guilty,

    (ii) what is agreed and what is likely to be disputed,

    (iii) what information, or other material, is required by one party of another, and why, and

    (iv) what is to be done, by whom, and when (without or if necessary with a direction);

  (d) reporting on that communication to the court—

    (i) at the first hearing, and

    (ii) after that, as directed by the court;

  (e) alerting the court to any reason why—

    (i) a direction should not be made in any of the circumstances listed in rule 3.2(4) or (5) (The duty of the court: use of live link or telephone facilities), or

    (ii) such a direction should be varied or revoked.

  (f) alerting the court to any potential impediment to the defendant's effective participation in the trial;

---

[10] 1984 c. 60; section 46ZA was inserted by section 46 of the Police and Justice Act 2006 (c. 48) and amended by section 107 of the Coroners and Justice Act 2009 (c. 25). Section 47 was amended by sections 27, 29 and 168 of, and Schedule 11 to, the Criminal Justice and Public Order Act 1994 (c. 33), section 46 of the Crime and Disorder Act 1998 (c. 37), section 109 of, and paragraph 283 of Schedule 8 to, the Courts Act 2003 (c. 39), sections 12 and 28 of, and paragraphs 1 and 10 of Schedule 1 and paragraphs 1 and 6 of Schedule 2 to, the Criminal Justice Act 2003 (c. 44), sections 10 and 46 of, and paragraphs 1, 6 and 11 of Schedule 6 to, the Police and Justice Act 2006 (c. 48) and section 1 of the Police (Detention and Bail Act 2011 (c. 9).

[11] 1998 c. 37; sections 57A to 57E were substituted for section 57 as originally enacted by section 45 of the Police and Justice Act 2006 (c. 48). Section 57A was amended by section 109 of the Coroners and Justice Act 2009 (c. 25) and section 105 of, and paragraphs 36 and 39 of Schedule 12 to, the Legal Aid, Sentencing and Punishment of Offenders Act 2012 (c. 10). Sections 57B, 57C and 57D were amended by section 106 of the Coroners and Justice Act 2009 (c. 25). Section 57F was inserted by section 109 of the Coroners and Justice Act 2009 (c. 25).

[12] 1988 c. 33; section 32 was amended by section 55 of the Criminal Justice Act 1991 (c. 53), section 29 of, and paragraph 16 of Schedule 2 to, the Criminal Appeal Act 1995 (c. 35), section 62 of the Criminal Procedure and Investigations Act 1996 (c. 25), section 67 of, and Schedule 6 and paragraph 3 of Schedule 7 to, the Youth Justice and Criminal Evidence Act 1999 (c. 23) and article 3 of, and paragraphs 24 and 26 of the Schedule to S.I. 2004/2035.

[13] 1999 c. 23; section 24 was amended by paragraph 385 of Schedule 8 to, and Schedule 10 to, the Courts Act 2003 (c. 39) and section 102(1) of the Coroners and Justice Act 2009 (c. 25). Section 33A was inserted by section 47 of the Police and Justice Act 2006 (c. 48).

[14] 2003 c. 44.

      (g)  alerting the court to any potential need for a witness to be accompanied while giving evidence, and in that event?

          (i)  identifying a proposed companion,

          (ii)  naming that person, if possible, and

         (iii)  explaining why that person would be an appropriate companion for the witness, including the witness' own views; and

      (h)  alerting the court to any related family proceedings or anticipated such proceedings as soon as reasonably practicable after becoming aware of them.

## R3.4  Case progression officers and their duties

3.4    (1)  At the beginning of the case each party must, unless the court otherwise directs—

      (a)  nominate someone responsible for progressing that case; and

      (b)  tell other parties and the court who that is and how to contact that person.

    (2)  In fulfilling its duty under rule 3.2, the court must where appropriate—

      (a)  nominate a court officer responsible for progressing the case; and

      (b)  make sure the parties know who that is and how to contact that court officer.

    (3)  In this Part a person nominated under this rule is called a case progression officer.

    (4)  A case progression officer must—

      (a)  monitor compliance with directions;

      (b)  make sure that the court is kept informed of events that may affect the progress of that case;

      (c)  make sure that he or she can be contacted promptly about the case during ordinary business hours;

      (d)  act promptly and reasonably in response to communications about the case; and

      (e)  if he or she will be unavailable, appoint a substitute to fulfil his or her duties and inform the other case progression officers.

## R3.5  The court's case management powers

3.5    (1)  In fulfilling its duty under rule 3.2 the court may give any direction and take any step actively to manage a case unless that direction or step would be inconsistent with legislation, including these Rules.

    (2)  In particular, the court may—

      (a)  nominate a judge, magistrate or justices' legal adviser to manage the case;

      (b)  give a direction on its own initiative or on application by a party;

      (c)  ask or allow a party to propose a direction;

      (d)  receive applications, notices, representations and information by letter, by telephone, by live link, by email or by any other means of electronic communication, and conduct a hearing by live link, telephone or other such electronic means;

      (e)  give a direction—

          (i)  at a hearing, in public or in private, or

         (ii)  without a hearing;

      (f)  fix, postpone, bring forward, extend, cancel or adjourn a hearing;

      (g)  shorten or extend (even after it has expired) a time limit fixed by a direction;

      (h)  require that issues in the case should be—

          (i)  identified in writing,

         (ii)  determined separately, and decide in what order they will be determined;

      (i)  specify the consequences of failing to comply with a direction.

      (j)  request information from a court dealing with family proceedings by—

          (i)  making the request itself, or

         (ii)  directing the court officer or a party to make the request on the criminal court's behalf; and

      (k)  supply information to a court dealing with family proceedings as if a request had been made under rule 5.8(7) (Request for information about a case) by—

         (i)  supplying the information itself, or

         (ii)  directing the court officer or a party to supply that information on the criminal court's behalf.

    (3)  A magistrates' court may give a direction that will apply in the Crown Court if the case is to continue there.

    (4)  The Crown Court may give a direction that will apply in a magistrates' court if the case is to continue there.

    (5)  Any power to give a direction under this Part includes a power to vary or revoke that direction.

    (6)  If a party fails to comply with a rule or a direction, the court may—

      (a)  fix, postpone, bring forward, extend, cancel or adjourn a hearing;

      (b)  exercise its powers to make a costs order; and

(c)  impose such other sanction as may be appropriate.

*[Note. Depending upon the nature of a case and the stage that it has reached, its progress may be affected by other Criminal Procedure Rules and by other legislation. The note at the end of this Part lists other rules and legislation that may apply.*

*See also rule 3.8 (Case preparation and progression).*

*The court may make a costs order under—*

   *(a)  section 19 of the Prosecution of Offences Act 1985[15], where the court decides that one party to criminal proceedings has incurred costs as a result of an unnecessary or improper act or omission by, or on behalf of, another party;*

   *(b)  section 19A of that Act[16], where the court decides that a party has incurred costs as a result of an improper, unreasonable or negligent act or omission on the part of a legal representative;*

   *(c)  section 19B of that Act[17], where the court decides that there has been serious misconduct by a person who is not a party.*

*Under some other legislation, including Parts 19, 20 and 21 of these Rules, if a party fails to comply with a rule or a direction then in some circumstances—*

   *(a)  the court may refuse to allow that party to introduce evidence;*

   *(b)  evidence that that party wants to introduce may not be admissible;*

   *(c)  the court may draw adverse inferences from the late introduction of an issue or evidence.*

*See also—*

   *(a)  section 81(1) of the Police and Criminal Evidence Act 1984[18] and section 20(3) of the Criminal Procedure and Investigations Act 1996[19] (advance disclosure of expert evidence);*

   *(b)  section 11(5) of the Criminal Procedure and Investigations Act 1996[20] (faults in disclosure by accused);*

   *(c)  section 132(5) of the Criminal Justice Act 2003[21] (failure to give notice of hearsay evidence).]*

### Application to vary a direction                                         R3.6

3.6   (1)  A party may apply to vary a direction if—

      (a)  the court gave it without a hearing;

      (b)  the court gave it at a hearing in that party's absence; or

      (c)  circumstances have changed.

     (2)  A party who applies to vary a direction must—

      (a)  apply as soon as practicable after becoming aware of the grounds for doing so; and

      (b)  give as much notice to the other parties as the nature and urgency of the application permits.

### Agreement to vary a time limit fixed by a direction                     R3.7

3.7   (1)  The parties may agree to vary a time limit fixed by a direction, but only if—

      (a)  the variation will not—

           (i)  affect the date of any hearing that has been fixed, or

           (ii) significantly affect the progress of the case in any other way;

      (b)  the court has not prohibited variation by agreement; and

      (c)  the court's case progression officer is promptly informed.

[15]  1985 c. 23; section 19 was amended by section 166 of the Criminal Justice Act 1988 (c. 33), section 45 of, and Schedule 6 to, the Legal Aid Act 1988 (c. 34), section 7 of, and paragraph 8 of Schedule 3 to, the Criminal Procedure (Insanity and Unfitness to Plead Act 1991 (c. 25), section 24 of, and paragraphs 27 and 28 of Schedule 4 to, the Access to Justice Act 1999 (c. 22), sections 40 and 67 of, and paragraph 4 of Schedule 7 to, the Youth Justice and Criminal Evidence Act 1999 (c. 23), section 165 of, and paragraph 99 of Schedule 9 to, the Powers of Criminal Courts (Sentencing Act 2000 (c. 6), section 378 of, and paragraph 107 of Schedule 16 to, the Armed Forces Act 2006 (c. 52), section 6 of, and paragraph 32 of Schedule 4 and paragraphs 1 and 5 of Schedule 27 to, the Criminal Justice and Immigration Act 2008 (c. 4) and paragraphs 22 and 23 of Schedule 5, and paragraphs 1 and 5 and Part 4 of Schedule 7, to the Legal Aid, Sentencing and Punishment of Offenders Act 2012 (c. 10).
[16]  1985 c. 23; section 19A was inserted by section 111 of the Courts and Legal Services Act 1990 (c. 41).
[17]  1985 c. 23; section 19B was inserted by section 93 of the Courts Act 2003 (c. 39).
[18]  1984 c. 60; section 81(1) was amended by section 109(1) of, and paragraph 286 of Schedule 8 to, the Courts Act 2003 (c.39).
[19]  1996 c. 25; section 20(3) was amended by section 109(1) of, and paragraph 378 of Schedule 8 to, the Courts Act 2003 (c.39).
[20]  1996 c. 25; section 11 was substituted by section 39 of the Criminal Justice Act 2003 (c. 44) and amended by section 60 of the Criminal Justice and Immigration Act 2008 (c. 4).
[21]  2003 c. 44.

Criminal Procedure Rules and Criminal Practice Directions

(2) The court's case progression officer must refer the agreement to the court if in doubt that the condition in paragraph (1)(a) is satisfied.

**R3.8    Case preparation and progression**

**3.8**    (1) At every hearing, if a case cannot be concluded there and then the court must give directions so that it can be concluded at the next hearing or as soon as possible after that.

(2) At every hearing the court must, where relevant—

(a) if the defendant is absent, decide whether to proceed nonetheless;

(b) take the defendant's plea (unless already done) or if no plea can be taken then find out whether the defendant is likely to plead guilty or not guilty;

(c) set, follow or revise a timetable for the progress of the case, which may include a timetable for any hearing including the trial or (in the Crown Court) the appeal;

(d) in giving directions, ensure continuity in relation to the court and to the parties' representatives where that is appropriate and practicable; and

(e) where a direction has not been complied with, find out why, identify who was responsible, and take appropriate action.

(3) In order to prepare for the trial, the court must take every reasonable step—

(a) to encourage and to facilitate the attendance of witnesses when they are needed; and

(b) to facilitate the participation of any person, including the defendant.

(4) Facilitating the participation of the defendant includes finding out whether the defendant needs interpretation because—

(a) the defendant does not speak or understand English; or

(b) the defendant has a hearing or speech disorder.

(5) Where the defendant needs interpretation—

(a) the court officer must arrange for interpretation to be provided at every hearing which the defendant is due to attend;

(b) interpretation may be by an intermediary where the defendant has a speech disorder, without the need for a defendant's evidence direction;

(c) on application or on its own initiative, the court may require a written translation to be provided for the defendant of any document or part of a document, unless—

(i) translation of that document, or part, is not needed to explain the case against the defendant, or

(ii) the defendant agrees to do without and the court is satisfied that the agreement is clear and voluntary and that the defendant has had legal advice or otherwise understands the consequences; and

(d) on application by the defendant, the court must give any direction which the court thinks appropriate, including a direction for interpretation by a different interpreter, where —

(i) no interpretation is provided,

(ii) no translation is ordered or provided in response to a previous application by the defendant, or

(iii) the defendant complains about the quality of interpretation or of any translation.

(6) Facilitating the participation of any person includes—

(a) giving directions for someone to accompany a witness while the witness gives evidence, including directions about seating arrangements for that companion; and

(b) giving directions for the appropriate treatment and questioning of a witness or the defendant, especially where the court directs that such questioning is to be conducted through an intermediary

(7) Where directions for appropriate treatment and questioning are required, the court must—

(a) invite representations by the parties and by any intermediary; and

(b) set ground rules for the conduct of the questioning, which rules may include—

(i) a direction relieving a party of any duty to put that party's case to a witness or a defendant in its entirety,

(ii) directions about the manner of questioning,

(iii) directions about the duration of questioning,

(iv) if necessary, directions about the questions that may or may not be asked,

(v) directions about the means by which any intermediary may intervene in questioning, if necessary,

(vi) where there is more than one defendant, the allocation among them of the topics about which a witness may be asked, and

(vii) directions about the use of models, plans, body maps or similar aids to help communicate a question or an answer.

Criminal Procedure Rules and Criminal Practice Directions

*[Note. Part 18 (Measures to assist a witness or defendant to give evidence) contains rules about an application for a defendant's evidence direction under (among other provisions) sections 33BA and 33BB of the Youth Justice and Criminal Evidence Act 1999[22].*

*Where a trial in a magistrates' court will take place in Wales, a participant may use the Welsh language: see rule 3.18. Where a trial in the Crown Court will take place in Wales and a participant wishes to use the Welsh language, see rule 3.34.]*

## Ground rules hearing                                                                    R3.9

**3.9**  (1)  This rule applies where the court exercises the powers to which rule 3.8(6) and (7) apply (directions for appropriate treatment and questioning of a witness or defendant).

(2)  At a pre-trial case management hearing convened for the purpose—

   (a)  the parties and any intermediary must—

   (i)  attend, unless the court otherwise directs, and

   (ii)  actively assist the court in setting ground rules and giving directions;

   (b)  the court must—

   (i)  discuss proposed ground rules and directions with the parties and any intermediary,

   (ii)  set ground rules for the conduct of questioning of the witness or defendant, as applicable, and

   (iii)  give such other directions as may be required to facilitate the effective participation of that witness or defendant; and

   (c)  despite rule 3.14(b) (court officer's duty to make a record of directions), the court may require the parties—

   (i)  to make a record of those ground rules and directions, and

   (ii)  to serve that record on each other, on any intermediary and on the court officer.

(3)  In setting such ground rules and giving such directions, the court must have regard to—

   (a)  any intermediary's report;

   (b)  the parties' representations; and

   (c)  such other information or advice as the court requires.

(4)  The ground rules for questioning set by the court may include any listed in rule 3.8(7)(b).

(5)  The directions given by the court may include any about—

   (a)  the timetable for the submission of proposed questions;

   (b)  the timetable for the trial, including the taking of breaks during proceedings;

   (c)  seating arrangements in the court room for the defendant, the defendant's advocate and legal representative, any intermediary and any parent, guardian or other companion of the defendant; and

   (d)  any explanation to be given to the jury, if there is one, of—

   (i)  the witness' or the defendant's communication needs and behaviour, as applicable, and

   (ii)  the role of the intermediary, if there is one.

*[Note. See also rule 3.16 (Pre-trial hearings in a magistrates' court: general rules) and rule 3.21 (Pre-trial hearings in the Crown Court: general rules).]*

## Directions for commissioning medical reports, other than for sentencing purposes    R3.10

**3.10**  (1)  This rule applies where, because of a defendant's suspected mental ill-health—

   (a)  a magistrates' court requires expert medical opinion about the potential suitability of a hospital order under section 37(3) of the Mental Health Act 1983[23] (hospital order without convicting the defendant);

   (b)  the Crown Court requires expert medical opinion about the defendant's fitness to participate at trial, under section 4 of the Criminal Procedure (Insanity) Act 1964[24]; or

   (c)  a magistrates' court or the Crown Court requires expert medical opinion to help the court determine a question of intent or insanity,

      other than such opinion introduced by a party.

(2)  A court may exercise the power to which this rule applies on its own initiative having regard to—

---

[22]  1999 c. 23; sections 33BA and 33BB are inserted by section 104 of the Coroners and Justice Act 2009 (c. 25), with effect from a date to be appointed.

[23]  1983 c. 20; section 37(3) was amended by sections 1 and 55 of, and paragraphs 1 and 7 of Schedule 1 and Schedule 11 to, the Mental Health Act 2007 (c. 12).

[24]  1964 c. 84; section 4 was substituted, together with section 4A, for section 4 as originally enacted, by section 2 of the Criminal Procedure (Insanity and Unfitness to Plead Act 1991 (c. 25), and amended by section 22 of the Domestic Violence, Crime and Victims Act 2004 (c. 28).

      (a) an assessment of the defendant's health by a mental health practitioner acting independently of the parties to assist the court;

      (b) representations by a party; or

      (c) observations by the court.

(3) A court that requires expert medical opinion to which this rule applies must—

      (a) identify each issue in respect of which the court requires such opinion and any legislation applicable;

      (b) specify the nature of the expertise likely to be required for giving such opinion;

      (c) identify each party or participant by whom a commission for such opinion must be prepared, who may be—

        (i) a party (or party's representative) acting on that party's own behalf,

        (ii) a party (or party's representative) acting on behalf of the court, or

        (iii) the court officer acting on behalf of the court;

      (d) where there are available to the court arrangements with the National Health Service under which an assessment of a defendant's mental health may be prepared, give such directions as are needed under those arrangements for obtaining the expert report or reports required;

      (e) where no such arrangements are available to the court, or they will not be used, give directions for the commissioning of an expert report or expert reports, including—

        (i) such directions as can be made about supplying the expert or experts with the defendant's medical records,

        (ii) directions about the other information, about the defendant and about the offence or offences alleged to have been committed by the defendant, which is to be supplied to each expert, and

        (iii) directions about the arrangements that will apply for the payment of each expert;

      (f) set a timetable providing for—

        (i) the date by which a commission is to be delivered to each expert,

        (ii) the date by which any failure to accept a commission is to be reported to the court,

        (iii) the date or dates by which progress in the preparation of a report or reports is to be reviewed by the court officer, and

        (iv) the date by which each report commissioned is to be received by the court; and

      (g) identify the person (each person, if more than one) to whom a copy of a report is to be supplied, and by whom.

(4) A commission addressed to an expert must—

      (a) identify each issue in respect of which the court requires expert medical opinion and any legislation applicable;

      (b) include—

        (i) the information required by the court to be supplied to the expert,

        (ii) details of the timetable set by the court, and

        (iii) details of the arrangements that will apply for the payment of the expert;

      (c) identify the person (each person, if more than one) to whom a copy of the expert's report is to be supplied; and

      (d) request confirmation that the expert from whom the opinion is sought—

        (i) accepts the commission, and

        (ii) will adhere to the timetable.

*[Note. See also rule 28.8 (Directions for commissioning medical reports for sentencing purposes).*

*The court may request a medical examination of the defendant and a report under—*

      *(a) section 4 of the Criminal Procedure (Insanity) Act 1964, under which the Crown Court may determine a defendant's fitness to plead;*

      *(b) section 35 of the Mental Health Act 1983[25], under which the court may order the defendant's detention in hospital to obtain a medical report;*

      *(c) section 36 of the 1983 Act[26], under which the Crown Court may order the defendant's detention in hospital instead of in custody pending trial or sentence;*

---

[25] 1983 c. 20; section 35 was amended by sections 1(4) and 10(1) and (2) of, and paragraphs 1 and 5 of Schedule 1 to, the Mental Health Act 2007 (c. 12) and section 208(1) of, and paragraphs 53 and 54 of Schedule 21 to, the Legal Services Act 2007 (c. 29).

[26] 1983 c. 20; section 36 was amended by sections 1(4), 5(1) and (2) and 10(1) and (3) of, and paragraphs 1 and 6 of Schedule 1 to, the Mental Health Act 2007 (c. 12) and section 208(1) of, and paragraphs 53 and 55 of Schedule 21 to, the Legal Services Act 2007 (c. 29).

(d) *section 37 of the 1983 Act[27], under which the court may order the defendant's detention and treatment in hospital, or make a guardianship order, instead of disposing of the case in another way (section 37(3) allows a magistrates' court to make such an order without convicting the defendant if satisfied that the defendant did the act or made the omission charged);*

(e) *section 38 of the 1983 Act[28], under which the court may order the defendant's temporary detention and treatment in hospital instead of disposing of the case in another way;*

(f) *section 157 of the Criminal Justice Act 2003[29], under which the court must usually obtain and consider a medical report before passing a custodial sentence if the defendant is, or appears to be, mentally disordered;*

(g) *section 207 of the 2003 Act[30] (in the case of a defendant aged 18 or over), or section 1(1)(k) of the Criminal Justice and Immigration Act 2008[31] (in the case of a defendant who is under 18), under which the court may impose a mental health treatment requirement.*

*For the purposes of the legislation listed in (a), (c), (d) and (e) above, the court requires the written or oral evidence of at least two registered medical practitioners, at least one of whom is approved as having special experience in the diagnosis or treatment of mental disorder. For the purposes of (b), (f) and (g), the court requires the evidence of one medical practitioner so approved.*

*Under section 11 of the Powers of Criminal Courts (Sentencing) Act 2000[32], a magistrates' court may adjourn a trial to obtain medical reports.*

*Part 19 (Expert evidence) contains rules about the content of expert medical reports.*

*For the authorities from whom the court may require information about hospital treatment or guardianship, see sections 39 and 39A of the 1983 Act[33].*

*The Practice Direction includes a timetable for the commissioning and preparation of a report or reports which the court may adopt with such adjustments as the court directs.*

*Payments to medical practitioners for reports and for giving evidence are governed by section 19(3) of the Prosecution of Offences Act 1985[34] and by the Costs in Criminal Cases (General) Regulations 1986[35], regulation 17 (Determination of rates or scales of allowances payable out of central funds), regulation 20 (Expert witnesses, etc.) and regulation 25 (Written medical reports). The rates and scales of allowances payable under those Regulations are determined by the Lord Chancellor.]*

---

[27] 1983 c. 20; section 37 was amended by sections 55 and 56 of, and paragraph 12 of Schedule 4 and Schedule 6 to, the Crime (Sentences Act 1997 (c. 43), section 67 of, and paragraph 11 of Schedule 4 to, the Youth Justice and Criminal Evidence Act 1999 (c. 23), paragraph 90 of Schedule 9 to the Powers of Criminal Courts (Sentencing Act 2000 (c. 6), section 304 of, and paragraphs 37 and 38 of Schedule 32 to, the Criminal Justice Act 2003 (c. 44), sections 49 and 65 of, and paragraph 2 of Schedule 1 and Schedule 5 to, the Violent Crime Reduction Act 2006 (c. 38), sections 1, 4, 10, 55 and paragraphs 1 and 7 of Schedule 1, and Part 1 of Schedule 11 to, the Mental Health Act 2007 (c. 12), sections 6 and 149 of, and paragraph 30 of Schedule 4, and Schedule 28 to, the Criminal Justice and Immigration Act 2008 (c. 4), sections 122 and 142 of, and paragraph 1 of Schedule 19 and paragraph 2 of Schedule 26 to, the Legal Aid, Sentencing and Punishment of Offenders Act 2012 (c. 10) and section 28 of, and paragraph 1 of Schedule 5 to, the Criminal Justice and Courts Act 2015 (c. 2). It is further amended by section 148 of, and paragraph 8 of Schedule 26 to, the Criminal Justice and Immigration Act 2008 (c. 4) with effect from a date to be appointed.

[28] 1983 c. 20; section 38 was amended by section 49(1) of the Crime (Sentences Act 1997 (c. 43), sections 1(4) and 10(1) and (5) of, and paragraphs 1 and 8 of Schedule 1 to, the Mental Health Act 2007 (c. 12) and section 208(1) of, and paragraphs 53 and 56 of Schedule 21 to, the Legal Services Act 2007 (c. 29).

[29] 2003 c. 44; section 157 was amended by section 38 of the Health and Social Care Act 2012 (c. 7).

[30] 2003 c. 44; section 207 was amended by article 4(2) of, and paragraph 7 of Schedule 5 to, S.I. 2009/1182, article 14(a and (b of, and Part 1 of Schedule 5 to, S.I. 2010/813, section 72 of the Health and Social Care Act 2012 (c. 7), section 73 of the Legal Aid, Sentencing and Punishment of Offenders Act 2012 (c. 10) and section 62 of, and paragraph 48 of Schedule 5 to, the Children and Social Work Act 2017 (c. 16).

[31] 2008 c. 4.

[32] 2000 c. 6.

[33] 1983 c. 20; section 39 was amended by sections 2(1) and 5(1) of, and paragraph 107 of Schedule 1 and Schedule 3 to, the Health Authorities Act 1995 (c. 17), section 2(5) of, and paragraphs 42 and 46 of Schedule 2 to, the National Health Service Reform and Health Care Professions Act 2002 (c. 17), section 31(1) and (2) of the Mental Health Act 2007 (c. 12), article 3 of, and paragraph 13 of the Schedule to, S.I. 2007/961 and section 55 of, and paragraphs 24 and 28 of Schedule 5 to, the Health and Social Care Act 2012 (c. 7). Section 39A was inserted by section 27(1) of the Criminal Justice Act 1991 (c. 53).

[34] 1985 c. 23; section 19(3) was amended by section 166 of the Criminal Justice Act 1988 (c. 33), section 7 of, and paragraph 8 of Schedule 3 to, the Criminal Procedure (Insanity and Unfitness to Plead Act 1991 (c. 25), sections 40 and 67 of, and paragraph 4 of Schedule 7 to, the Youth Justice and Criminal Evidence Act 1999 (c. 23), section 165 of, and paragraph 99 of Schedule 9 to, the Powers of Criminal Courts (Sentencing Act 2000 (c. 6) and section 378 of, and paragraph 107 of Schedule 16 to, the Armed Forces Act 2006 (c. 52).

[35] S.I. 1986/1335; regulation 17 was amended by regulations 2 and 13 of S.I. 2008/2448, regulation 20 was amended by regulations 2 and 14 of S.I. 2008/2448 and by regulations 4 and 7 of S.I. 2012/1804, and regulation 25 was amended by regulations 2 and 10 of S.I. 2009/2720.

Criminal Procedure Rules and Criminal Practice Directions

(f) unless the defendant pleads guilty, the court must satisfy itself that there has been explained to the defendant, in terms the defendant can understand (with help, if necessary), that at the trial—

    (i) the defendant will have the right to give evidence after the court has heard the prosecution case,

    (ii) if the defendant does not attend, the trial is likely to take place in the defendant's absence, and

    (iii) where the defendant is released on bail, failure to attend court when required is an offence for which the defendant may be arrested and punished and bail may be withdrawn.

(4) A pre-trial case management hearing must be in public, as a general rule, but all or part of the hearing may be in private if the court so directs.

(5) The court—

    (a) at the first hearing in the case must require a defendant who is present to provide, in writing or orally, his or her name and date of birth, unless already provided under rule 9.2 (Allocation and sending for trial; Exercise of magistrates' court's powers); and

    (b) at any subsequent hearing may require such a defendant to provide that information by those means.

[*Note. Under sections 8A and 8B of the Magistrates' Courts Act 1980[36], a pre-trial ruling about the admissibility of evidence or any other question of law is binding unless it later appears to the court in the interests of justice to discharge or vary that ruling.*

*Under section 86A of the Courts Act 2003[37], Criminal Procedure Rules must specify stages of proceedings at which the court must require the information listed in rule 3.16(5) and may specify other stages of proceedings when such requirements may be imposed. A person commits an offence if, without reasonable excuse, that person fails to comply with such a requirement, whether by providing false or incomplete information or by providing no information.*]

### R3.17 Place of magistrates' court trial

**3.17** The court officer must arrange for a magistrates' court trial to take place in a courtroom provided by the Lord Chancellor, unless—

    (a) the court otherwise directs; or

    (b) the case is one to which rule 24.9 (Single justice procedure: special rules) applies.

[*Note. See section 3 of the Courts Act 2003[38] and section 16A of the Magistrates' Courts Act 1980[39].*

*In some circumstances the court may conduct all or part of the hearing outside a courtroom. The members of the court may discuss the verdict and sentence outside the courtroom.*]

### R3.18 Use of Welsh language at magistrates' court trial

**3.18** Where a magistrates' court trial takes place in Wales—

    (a) any party or witness may use the Welsh language; and

    (b) if practicable, at least one member of the court must be Welsh-speaking.

[*Note. See section 3 of the Courts Act 2003[40] and section 22 of the Welsh Language Act 1993[41].*]

### Preparation for trial in the Crown Court

### R3.19 Service of prosecution evidence

**3.19** This rule applies where—

    (a) a magistrates' court sends the defendant to the Crown Court for trial; and

    (b) the prosecutor serves on the defendant copies of the documents containing the evidence on which the prosecution case relies.

(2) The prosecutor must at the same time serve copies of those documents on the Crown Court officer.

---

[36] 1980 c. 43; section 8A was inserted by section 45 of, and Schedule 3 to, the Courts Act 2003 (c. 39) and amended by SI 2006/2493 and paragraphs 12 and 14 of Schedule 5 to the Legal Aid, Sentencing and Punishment of Offenders Act 2012 (c. 10). Section 8B was inserted by section 45 of, and Schedule 3 to, the Courts Act 2003 (c. 39) and amended by paragraph 51 of Schedule 3, and Part 4 of Schedule 37, to the Criminal Justice Act 2003 (c. 44).

[37] 2003 c. 39; section 86A was inserted by section 162 of the Policing and Crime Act 2016 (c. 3).

[38] 2003 c. 39.

[39] 1980 c. 43; section 16A was inserted by section 48 of the Criminal Justice and Courts Act 2015 (c. 2).

[40] 2003 c. 39.

[41] 1993 c. 38.

*[Note. See the Crime and Disorder Act 1998 (Service of Prosecution Evidence) Regulations 2005[42]. The time for service of the prosecution evidence is prescribed by regulation 2. It is—*

    *(a) not more than 50 days after sending for trial, where the defendant is in custody; and*

    *(b) not more than 70 days after sending for trial, where the defendant is on bail.]*

**Application to dismiss offence sent for Crown Court trial**    **R3.20**

3.20  (1)  This rule applies where a defendant wants the Crown Court to dismiss an offence sent for trial there.

    (2)  The defendant must—
        (a)  apply in writing—
            (i)  not more than 20 business days after service of the prosecution evidence, and
            (ii)  before the defendant's arraignment under rule 3.32 (Arraigning the defendant on the indictment);
        (b)  serve the application on—
            (i)  the Crown Court officer, and
            (ii)  each other party; and
        (c)  in the application—
            (i)  explain why the prosecution evidence would not be sufficient for the defendant to be properly convicted,
            (ii)  ask for a hearing, if the defendant wants one, and explain why it is needed,
            (iii)  identify any witness whom the defendant wants to call to give evidence in person, with an indication of what evidence the witness can give,
            (iv)  identify any material already served that the defendant thinks the court will need to determine the application, and
            (v)  include any material not already served on which the defendant relies.

    (3)  A prosecutor who opposes the application must—
        (a)  serve notice of opposition, not more than 10 business days after service of the defendant's notice, on—
            (i)  the Crown Court officer, and
            (ii)  each other party; and
        (b)  in the notice of opposition—
            (i)  explain the grounds of opposition,
            (ii)  ask for a hearing, if the prosecutor wants one, and explain why it is needed,
            (iii)  identify any witness whom the prosecutor wants to call to give evidence in person, with an indication of what evidence the witness can give,
            (iv)  identify any material already served that the prosecutor thinks the court will need to determine the application, and
            (v)  include any material not already served on which the prosecutor relies.

    (4)  The court may determine an application under this rule—
        (a)  at a hearing, in public or in private, or without a hearing; and
        (b)  in the absence of—
            (i)  the defendant who made the application, and
            (ii)  the prosecutor, if the prosecutor has had at least 10 business days in which to serve notice opposing the application.

    (5)  The court may—
        (a)  shorten or extend (even after it has expired) a time limit under this rule; and
        (b)  allow a witness to give evidence in person even if that witness was not identified in the defendant's application or in the prosecutor's notice.

*[Note. Under paragraph 2 of Schedule 3 to the Crime and Disorder Act 1998[43], on an application by the defendant the Crown Court must dismiss an offence charged if it appears to the court that the evidence would not be sufficient for the applicant to be properly convicted.]*

### Preparation for trial in the Crown Court

**Pre-trial hearings in the Crown Court: general rules**    **R3.21**

3.21  (1)  The Crown Court—
        (a)  may, and in some cases must, conduct a preparatory hearing where rule 3.22 applies;
        (b)  must conduct a plea and trial preparation hearing; and

---

[43] 1998 c. 37; paragraph 2 of Schedule 3 was amended by paragraphs 15 and 20 of Schedule 3, paragraph 73 of Schedule 36 and Part 4 of Schedule 37 to the Criminal Justice Act 2003 (c. 44) and SI 2004/2035.

(c) may conduct a further pre-trial case management hearing (and if necessary more than one such hearing) only where—
  (i) the court anticipates a guilty plea,
  (ii) it is necessary to conduct such a hearing in order to give directions for an effective trial, or
  (iii) such a hearing is required to set ground rules for the conduct of the questioning of a witness or defendant.

(2) At the plea and trial preparation hearing the court must—
  (a) satisfy itself that there has been explained to the defendant, in terms the defendant can understand (with help, if necessary), that the defendant will receive credit for a guilty plea;
  (b) take the defendant's plea in accordance with rule 3.24 (Arraigning the defendant on the indictment) or if no plea can be taken then find out whether the defendant is likely to plead guilty or not guilty;
  (c) unless the defendant pleads guilty, satisfy itself that there has been explained to the defendant, in terms the defendant can understand (with help, if necessary), that at the trial—
    (i) the defendant will have the right to give evidence after the court has heard the prosecution case,
    (ii) if the defendant does not attend, the trial may take place in the defendant's absence,
    (iii) if the trial takes place in the defendant's absence, the judge may inform the jury of the reason for that absence, and
    (iv) where the defendant is released on bail, failure to attend court when required is an offence for which the defendant may be arrested and punished and bail may be withdrawn; and
  (d) give directions for an effective trial.

(3) A pre-trial case management hearing—
  (a) must be in public, as a general rule, but all or part of the hearing may be in private if the court so directs; and
  (b) must be recorded, in accordance with rule 5.5 (Recording and transcription of proceedings in the Crown Court).

(4) Where the court determines a pre-trial application in private, it must announce its decision in public.

(5) The court—
  (a) at the first hearing in the Crown Court must require a defendant who is present—
    (i) to provide, in writing or orally, his or her name and date of birth, or
    (ii) to confirm that information by those means, where the information was given to the magistrates' court which sent the defendant for trial; and
  (b) at any subsequent hearing may require such a defendant to provide or confirm that information by those means.

*[Note. See also the general rules in the first section of this Part (rules 3.1 to 3.15) and the other rules in this section.*

*The Practice Direction lists the circumstances in which a further pre-trial case management hearing is likely to be needed in order to give directions for an effective trial.*

*There are rules relevant to applications which may be made at a pre-trial hearing in Part 6 (Reporting, etc. restrictions), Part 14 (Bail and custody time limits), Part 15 (Disclosure), Part 17 (Witness summonses, warrants and orders), Part 18 (Measures to assist a witness or defendant to give evidence), Part 19 (Expert evidence), Part 20 (Hearsay evidence), Part 21 (Evidence of bad character), Part 22 (Evidence of a complainant's previous sexual behaviour) and Part 23 (Restriction on cross-examination by a defendant).*

*On an application to which Part 14 (Bail and custody time limits) applies, rule 14.2 (exercise of court's powers under that Part) may require the defendant's presence, which may be by live link. Where rule 14.10 applies (Consideration of bail in a murder case), the court officer must arrange for the Crown Court to consider bail within 2 business days of the first hearing in the magistrates' court.*

*Under section 40 of the Criminal Procedure and Investigations Act 1996[44], a pre-trial ruling about the admissibility of evidence or any other question of law is binding unless it later appears to the court in the interests of justice to discharge or vary that ruling.*

*Under section 86A of the Courts Act 2003[45], Criminal Procedure Rules must specify stages of proceedings at which the court must require the information listed in rule 3.21(5). A person commits an offence if, without reasonable excuse, that person fails to comply with such a requirement, whether by providing false or incomplete information or by providing no information.]*

---

[44] 1996 c. 25.
[45] 2003 c. 39; section 86A was inserted by section 162 of the Policing and Crime Act 2017 (c. 3).

**Preparatory hearing**                                                                 **R3.22**

3.22  (1)  This rule applies where the Crown Court—

(a)  can order a preparatory hearing, under—

(i)   section 7 of the Criminal Justice Act 1987[46] (cases of serious or complex fraud), or

(ii)  section 29 of the Criminal Procedure and Investigations Act 1996[47] (other complex, serious or lengthy cases);

(b)  must order such a hearing, to determine an application for a trial without a jury, under—

(i)   section 44 of the Criminal Justice Act 2003[48] (danger of jury tampering), or

(ii)  section 17 of the Domestic Violence, Crime and Victims Act 2004[49] (trial of sample counts by jury, and others by judge alone); and

(c)  must order such a hearing, under section 29 of the 1996 Act, where section 29(1B) or (1C) applies (cases in which a terrorism offence is charged, or other serious cases with a terrorist connection).

(2)  The court may decide whether to order a preparatory hearing—

(a)  on an application or on its own initiative;

(b)  at a hearing (in public or in private), or without a hearing; and

(c)  in a party's absence, if that party—

(i)   applied for the order, or

(ii)  has had at least 10 business days in which to make representations.

*[Note. See also section 45(2) of the Criminal Justice Act 2003 and section 18(1) of the Domestic Violence, Crime and Victims Act 2004.*

*At a preparatory hearing, the court may—*

*(a)  require the prosecution to set out its case in a written statement, to arrange its evidence in a form that will be easiest for the jury (if there is one) to understand, to prepare a list of agreed facts, and to amend the case statement following representations from the defence (section 9(4) of the 1987 Act, section 31(4) of the 1996 Act); and*

*(b)  require the defence to give notice of any objection to the prosecution case statement, and to give notice stating the extent of agreement with the prosecution as to documents and other matters and the reason for any disagreement (section 9(5) of the 1987 Act, section 31(6), (7), (9) of the 1996 Act).*

*Under section 10 of the 1987 Act[50], and under section 34 of the 1996 Act[51], if either party later departs from the case or objections disclosed by that party, then the court, or another party, may comment on that, and the court may draw such inferences as appear proper.]*

**Application for preparatory hearing**                                                 **R3.23**

3.23  (1)  A party who wants the court to order a preparatory hearing must—

(a)  apply in writing—

(i)   as soon as reasonably practicable, and in any event

(ii)  not more than 10 business days after the defendant pleads not guilty; and

(b)  serve the application on—

(i)   the court officer, and

(ii)  each other party.

(2)  The applicant must—

(a)  if relevant, explain what legislation requires the court to order a preparatory hearing; or

(b)  explain—

(i)   what makes the case complex or serious, or makes the trial likely to be long,

(ii)  why a substantial benefit will accrue from a preparatory hearing, and

(iii) why the court's ordinary powers of case management are not adequate.

(3)  A prosecutor who wants the court to order a trial without a jury must explain—

(a)  where the prosecutor alleges a danger of jury tampering—

(i)   what evidence there is of a real and present danger that jury tampering would take place,

---

[46]  1987 c. 38; section 7 is amended by paragraph 30 of Schedule 9 to the Criminal Justice and Public Order Act 1994 (c. 33), sections 72 and 80 of, paragraph 2 of Schedule 3 to, and Schedule 5 to, the Criminal Procedure and Investigations Act 1996 (c. 25) and sections 45 and 310 of, and paragraphs 52 and 53 of Schedule 36 to, the Criminal Justice Act 2003 (c. 44).

[47]  1996 c. 25; section 29 is amended by sections 45, 309 and 310 of, and paragraphs 65 and 66 of Schedule 36 to, the Criminal Justice Act 2003 (c. 44) and section 16 of the Terrorism Act 2006 (c. 11).

[48]  2003 c. 44.

[49]  2004 c. 28.

[50]  1987 c. 38; section 10 is amended by section 72 of, and paragraph 5 of Schedule 3 to, the Criminal Procedure and Investigations Act 1996 (c. 25), and paragraphs 52 and 55 of Schedule 36 to the Criminal Justice Act 2003 (c. 44).

[51]  1996 c. 25; section 34 is amended by paragraphs 65 and 68 of Schedule 36 to the Criminal Justice Act 2003 (c. 44).

(ii)  what steps, if any, reasonably might be taken to prevent jury tampering, and

(iii)  why, notwithstanding such steps, the likelihood of jury tampering is so substantial as to make it necessary in the interests of justice to order such a trial; or

(b)  where the prosecutor proposes trial without a jury on some counts on the indictment—

(i)  why a trial by jury involving all the counts would be impracticable,

(ii)  how the counts proposed for jury trial can be regarded as samples of the others, and

(iii)  why it would be in the interests of justice to order such a trial.

**R3.24**    **Application for non-jury trial containing information withheld from a defendant**

**3.24**    (1)  This rule applies where—

(a)  the prosecutor applies for an order for a trial without a jury because of a danger of jury tampering; and

(b)  the application includes information that the prosecutor thinks ought not be revealed to a defendant.

(2)  The prosecutor must—

(a)  omit that information from the part of the application that is served on that defendant;

(b)  mark the other part to show that, unless the court otherwise directs, it is only for the court; and

(c)  in that other part, explain why the prosecutor has withheld that information from that defendant.

(3)  The hearing of an application to which this rule applies—

(a)  must be in private, unless the court otherwise directs; and

(b)  if the court so directs, may be, wholly or in part, in the absence of a defendant from whom information has been withheld.

(4)  At the hearing of an application to which this rule applies—

(a)  the general rule is that the court will receive, in the following sequence—

(i)  representations first by the prosecutor and then by each defendant, in all the parties' presence, and then

(ii)  further representations by the prosecutor, in the absence of a defendant from whom information has been withheld; but

(b)  the court may direct other arrangements for the hearing.

(5)  Where, on an application to which this rule applies, the court orders a trial without a jury—

(a)  the general rule is that the trial will be before a judge other than the judge who made the order; but

(b)  the court may direct other arrangements.

**R3.25**    **Representations in response to application for preparatory hearing**

**3.25**    (1)  This rule applies where a party wants to make representations about—

(a)  an application for a preparatory hearing;

(b)  an application for a trial without a jury.

(2)  Such a party must—

(a)  serve the representations on—

(i)  the court officer, and

(ii)  each other party;

(b)  do so not more than 10 business days after service of the application; and

(c)  ask for a hearing, if that party wants one, and explain why it is needed.

(3)  Where representations include information that the person making them thinks ought not be revealed to another party, that person must—

(a)  omit that information from the representations served on that other party;

(b)  mark the information to show that, unless the court otherwise directs, it is only for the court; and

(c)  with that information include an explanation of why it has been withheld from that other party.

(4)  Representations against an application for an order must explain why the conditions for making it are not met.

**R3.26**    **Commencement of preparatory hearing**

**3.26**    At the beginning of a preparatory hearing, the court must—

(a)  announce that it is such a hearing; and

(b)  take the defendant's plea under rule 3.32 (Arraigning the defendant on the indictment), unless already done.

*[Note. See section 8 of the Criminal Justice Act 1987[52] and section 30 of the Criminal Procedure and Investigations Act 1996[53].]*

**Defence trial advocate**                                                      R3.27

3.27  (1)  The defendant must notify the court officer of the identity of the intended defence trial advocate—

   (a)  as soon as practicable, and in any event no later than the day of the plea and trial preparation hearing; and

   (b)  in writing, or orally at that hearing.

   (2)  The defendant must notify the court officer in writing of any change in the identity of the intended defence trial advocate as soon as practicable, and in any event not more than 5 business days after that change.

**Application to stay case for abuse of process**                              R3.28

3.28  (1)  This rule applies where a defendant wants the Crown Court to stay the case on the grounds that the proceedings are an abuse of the court, or otherwise unfair.

   (2)  Such a defendant must—

   (a)  apply in writing—

      (i)  as soon as practicable after becoming aware of the grounds for doing so,

      (ii)  at a pre-trial hearing, unless the grounds for the application do not arise until trial, and

      (iii)  in any event, before the defendant pleads guilty or the jury (if there is one) retires to consider its verdict at trial;

   (b)  serve the application on—

      (i)  the court officer, and

      (ii)  each other party; and

   (c)  in the application—

      (i)  explain the grounds on which it is made,

      (ii)  include, attach or identify all supporting material,

      (iii)  specify relevant events, dates and propositions of law, and

      (iv)  identify any witness the applicant wants to call to give evidence in person.

   (3)  A party who wants to make representations in response to the application must serve the representations on—

   (a)  the court officer; and

   (b)  each other party,

   not more than 10 business days after service of the application.

**Application for joint or separate trials, etc.**                             R3.29

3.29  (1)  This rule applies where a party wants the Crown Court to order—

   (a)  the joint trial of—

      (i)  offences charged by separate indictments, or

      (ii)  defendants charged in separate indictments;

   (b)  separate trials of offences charged by the same indictment;

   (c)  separate trials of defendants charged in the same indictment; or

   (d)  the deletion of a count from an indictment.

   (2)  Such a party must—

   (a)  apply in writing—

      (i)  as soon as practicable after becoming aware of the grounds for doing so, and

      (ii)  before the trial begins, unless the grounds for the application do not arise until trial;

   (b)  serve the application on—

      (i)  the court officer, and

      (ii)  each other party; and

   (c)  in the application—

      (i)  specify the order proposed, and

      (ii)  explain why it should be made.

   (3)  A party who wants to make representations in response to the application must serve the representations on—

   (a)  the court officer; and

   (b)  each other party,

   not more than 10 business days after service of the application.

---

[52]  1987 c. 38.
[53]  1996 c. 25.

(4) Where the same indictment charges more than one offence, the court may exercise its power to order separate trials of those offences if of the opinion that—

(a) the defendant otherwise may be prejudiced or embarrassed in his or her defence (for example, where the offences to be tried together are neither founded on the same facts nor form or are part of a series of offences of the same or a similar character); or

(b) for any other reason it is desirable that the defendant should be tried separately for any one or more of those offences.

*[Note. See section 5 of the Indictments Act 1915[54]. Rule 10.2 (The indictment: general rules) governs the form and content of an indictment.*

*Any issue arising from a decision under this rule may be subject to appeal to the Court of Appeal. Part 37 (Appeal to the Court of Appeal against ruling at preparatory hearing), Part 38 (Appeal to the Court of Appeal against ruling adverse to prosecution) and Part 39 (Appeal to the Court of Appeal about conviction or sentence) each contains relevant rules. The powers of the Court of Appeal on an appeal to which Part 39 applies are set out in sections 2, 3 and 7 of the Criminal Appeal Act 1968[55].]*

**R3.30** **Order for joint or separate trials, or amendment of the indictment**

**3.30** (1) This rule applies where the Crown Court makes an order—

(a) on an application under rule 3.29 applies (Application for joint or separate trials, etc.); or

(b) amending an indictment in any other respect.

(2) Unless the court otherwise directs, the court officer must endorse any paper copy of each affected indictment made for the court with—

(a) a note of the court's order; and

(b) the date of that order.

**R3.31** **Application for indication of sentence**

**3.31** (1) This rule applies where a defendant wants the Crown Court to give an indication of the maximum sentence that would be passed if a guilty plea were entered when the indication is sought.

(2) Such a defendant must—

(a) apply in writing as soon as practicable; and

(b) serve the application on—

(i) the court officer, and

(ii) the prosecutor.

(3) The application must—

(a) specify—

(i) the offence or offences to which it would be a guilty plea, and

(ii) the facts on the basis of which that plea would be entered; and

(b) include the prosecutor's agreement to, or representations on, that proposed basis of plea.

(4) The prosecutor must—

(a) provide information relevant to sentence, including—

(i) any previous conviction of the defendant, and the circumstances where relevant, and

(ii) any statement of the effect of the offence on the victim, the victim's family or others; and

(b) identify any other matter relevant to sentence, including—

(i) the legislation applicable,

(ii) any sentencing guidelines, or guideline cases, and

(iii) aggravating and mitigating factors.

(5) The hearing of the application—

(a) may take place in the absence of any other defendant; and

(b) must be attended by—

(i) the applicant defendant's legal representatives (if any), and

(ii) the prosecution advocate.

**R3.32** **Arraigning the defendant on the indictment**

**3.32** (1) In order to take the defendant's plea, the Crown Court must—

(a) obtain the prosecutor's confirmation, in writing or orally—

(i) that the indictment (or draft indictment, as the case may be) sets out a statement of each offence that the prosecutor wants the court to try and such particulars of the

---

[54] 1915 c. 90; section 5 was amended by section 12 of, and paragraph 8 of Schedule 2 to, the Bail Act 1976 (c. 63), section 31 of, and Schedule 2 to, the Prosecution of Offences Act 1985 (c. 23) and section 331 of, and paragraph 40 of Schedule 36 to, the Criminal Justice Act 2003 (c. 44).

[55] 1968 c. 19; section 2 was amended by section 2 of the Criminal Appeal Act 1995 (c. 35). Section 3 was amended by section 316 of the Criminal Justice Act 2003 (c. 44). Section 7 was amended by sections 43 and 170 of, and Schedule 16 to, the Criminal Justice Act 1988 (c. 33) and paragraph 44 of Schedule 36 to the Criminal Justice Act 2003 (c. 44).

conduct constituting the commission of each such offence as the prosecutor relies
upon to make clear what is alleged, and

    (ii) of the order in which the prosecutor wants the defendants' names to be listed in the
indictment, if the prosecutor proposes that more than one defendant should be tried
at the same time;

(b) ensure that the defendant is correctly identified by the indictment or draft indictment;

(c) satisfy itself that there has been explained to the defendant, in terms the defendant can
understand (with help, if necessary), each allegation against him or her; and

(d) in respect of each count—

    (i) read the count aloud to the defendant, or arrange for it to be read aloud or placed
before the defendant in writing,

    (ii) ask whether the defendant pleads guilty or not guilty to the offence charged by that
count, and

    (iii) take the defendant's plea.

(2) Where a count is read which is substantially the same as one already read aloud, then only the
materially different details need be read aloud.

(3) Where a count is placed before the defendant in writing, the court must summarise its gist aloud.

(4) In respect of each count in the indictment—

(a) if the defendant declines to enter a plea, the court must treat that as a not guilty plea unless
rule 25.10 applies (Defendant unfit to plead);

(b) if the defendant pleads not guilty to the offence charged by that count but guilty to
another offence of which the court could convict on that count—

    (i) if the prosecutor and the court accept that plea, the court must treat the plea as one
of guilty of that other offence, but

    (ii) otherwise, the court must treat the plea as one of not guilty; and

(c) if the defendant pleads a previous acquittal or conviction of the offence charged by that
count—

    (i) the defendant must identify that acquittal or conviction in writing, explaining the
basis of that plea, and

    (ii) the court must exercise its power to decide whether that plea disposes of that count.

(5) In a case in which a magistrates' court sends the defendant for trial, the Crown Court must take
the defendant's plea—

(a) not less than 10 business days after the date on which that sending takes place, unless the
parties otherwise agree; and

(b) more than 80 business days after that date, unless the court otherwise directs (either before
or after that period expires).

*[Note. See section 6 of the Criminal Law Act 1967[56], section 77 of the Senior Courts Act 1981[57] and section
122 of the Criminal Justice Act 1988[58]. Part 10 contains rules about the content and service of indictments: see
in particular rule 10.2 (The indictment: general rules).*

*Under section 6(2) of the 1967 Act, on an indictment for murder a defendant may instead be convicted of
manslaughter or another offence specified by that provision. Under section 6(3) of that Act, on an indictment for
an offence other than murder or treason a defendant may instead be convicted of another offence if—*

    *(a) the allegation in the indictment amounts to or includes an allegation of that other offence; and*

    *(b) the Crown Court has power to convict and sentence for that other offence.]*

**Place of Crown Court trial**                                                               **R3.33**

3.33 (1) Unless the court otherwise directs, the court officer must arrange for a Crown Court trial to
take place in a courtroom provided by the Lord Chancellor.

(2) The court officer must arrange for the court and the jury (if there is one) to view any place
required by the court.

*[Note. See section 3 of the Courts Act 2003[59] and section 14 of the Juries Act 1974[60].*

*In some circumstances the court may conduct all or part of the hearing outside a courtroom.]*

---

[56] 1967 c. 58; section 6 was amended by paragraph 41 of Schedule 36 to the Criminal Justice Act 2003 (c. 44) and section 11
of the Domestic Violence, Crime and Victims Act 2004 (c. 28).
[57] 1981 c. 54; section 77 was amended by section 15 of, and paragraph 11 of Schedule 2 to, the Criminal Justice Act 1987 (c.
38), section 168 of, and paragraph 18 of Schedule 9 to, the Criminal Justice and Public Order Act 1994 (c. 33), section 41 of,
and paragraph 54 of Schedule 3 to, the Criminal Justice Act 2003 (c. 44) and article 3 of, and paragraphs 11 and 13 of the
Schedule to, SI 2004/2035. It is further amended by section 31 of, and paragraph 11 of Schedule 1 and Schedule 2 to, the
Prosecution of Offences Act 1985 (c. 23) with effect from a date to be appointed.
[58] 1988 c. 33.
[59] 2003 c. 39.
[60] 1974 c. 23; section 14 was amended by paragraph 173 of Schedule 8 to the Courts Act 2003 (c. 39).

Criminal Procedure Rules and Criminal Practice Directions

**R3.34** **Use of Welsh language at trial**

**3.34** Where a Crown Court trial will take place in Wales and a participant wishes to use the Welsh language—

  (a) that participant must serve notice on the court officer, or arrange for such a notice to be served on that participant's behalf—

    (i) at or before the plea and trial preparation hearing, or

    (ii) in accordance with any direction given by the court; and

  (b) if such a notice is served, the court officer must arrange for an interpreter to attend.

*[Note. See section 22 of the Welsh Language Act 1993[61].]*

**Other provisions affecting case management**
*Case management may be affected by the following other rules and legislation:*

**Criminal Procedure Rules**
*Part 8 Initial details of the prosecution case*
*Part 9 Allocation and sending for trial*
*Part 10 The indictment*
*Part 15 Disclosure*
*Parts 16 – 23: the rules that deal with evidence*
*Part 24 Trial and sentence in a magistrates' court*
*Part 25 Trial and sentence in the Crown Court*

**Regulations**
*The Prosecution of Offences (Custody Time Limits) Regulations 1987[62]*
*The Crime and Disorder Act 1998 (Service of Prosecution Evidence) Regulations 2005[63]*
*The Criminal Procedure and Investigations Act 1996 (Defence Disclosure Time Limits) Regulations 2011[64]*

**Acts of Parliament**
*Sections 10 and 18, Magistrates' Courts Act 1980[65]: powers to adjourn hearings*
*Sections 128 and 129, Magistrates' Courts Act 1980[66]: remand in custody by magistrates' courts*
*Sections 19 and 24A, Magistrates' Courts Act 1980[67] and sections 51 and 51A, Crime and Disorder Act 1998[68]*
*: allocation and sending for trial*
*Section 2, Administration of Justice (Miscellaneous Provisions) Act 1933[69]: procedural conditions for trial in the Crown Court*

---

[61] 1993 c. 38.

[62] S.I. 1987/299; amended by sections 71 and 80 of, and paragraph 8 of Schedule 5 to, the Criminal Procedure and Investigations Act 1996 (c. 25) and S.I. 1989/767, 1991/1515, 1995/555, 1999/2744, 2000/3284, 2012/1344.

[63] S.I. 2005/902; amended by S.I. 2012/1345.

[64] S.I. 2011/209.

[65] 1980 c. 43; section 10 was amended by section 59 of, and paragraph 1 of Schedule 9 to, the Criminal Justice Act 1982 (c. 48), section 68 of, and paragraph 6 of Schedule 8 to, the Criminal Justice Act 1991 (c. 53) and section 47 of the Crime and Disorder Act 1998 (c. 37). Section 18 was amended by section 59 of, and paragraph 1 of Schedule 9 to, the Criminal Justice Act 1982 (c. 48), section 68 of, and paragraph 6 of Schedule 8 to, the Criminal Justice Act 1991 (c. 53), section 49 of the Criminal Procedure and Investigations Act 1996 (c. 25), and paragraphs 1 and 4 of Schedule 3 to the Criminal Justice Act 2003 (c. 44).

[66] 1980 c. 43; section 128 was amended by section 59 to, and paragraphs 2, 3 and 4 of Schedule 9 to, the Criminal Justice Act 1982 (c. 48), section 48 of the Police and Criminal Evidence Act 1984 (c. 60), section 170(1) of, and paragraphs 65 and 69 of Schedule 15 to, the Criminal Justice Act 1988 (c. 33), section 125(3) of, and paragraph 25 of Schedule 18 to, the Courts and Legal Services Act 1990 (c. 41), sections 49, 52 and 80 of, and Schedule 5 to, the Criminal Procedure and Investigations Act 1996 (c. 25), paragraph 75 of Schedule 9 to the Powers of Criminal Courts (Sentencing) Act 2000 (c. 6) and paragraph 51 of Schedule 3 and Part 4 of Schedule 37 to the Criminal Justice Act 2003 (c. 44). It is modified by section 91(5) of the Legal Aid, Sentencing and Punishment of Offenders Act 2012 (c. 10). Section 129 was amended by paragraph 51 of Schedule 3 to the Criminal Justice Act 2003 (c. 44).

[67] 1980 c. 43; section 19 was substituted by paragraphs 1 and 5 of Schedule 3 to the Criminal Justice Act 2003 (c. 44) and amended by sections 144, 177 and 178 of, and paragraph 4 of Schedule 17, paragraph 80 of Schedule 21 and Part 5 of Schedule 23 to, the Coroners and Justice Act 2009 (c. 25).

[68] 1998 c. 37; section 51 was substituted by paragraphs 15 and 18 of Schedule 3 to the Criminal Justice Act 2003 (c. 44) and amended by section 59 of, and paragraph 1 of Schedule 11 to, the Constitutional Reform Act 2005 (c. 4). Section 51A was inserted by paragraphs 15 and 18 of Schedule 3 to the Criminal Justice Act 2003 (c. 44) and amended by section 49 of, and paragraph 5 of Schedule 1 to, the Violent Crime Reduction Act 2006 (c. 38) and paragraph 6 of Schedule 21 to the Legal Aid, Sentencing and Punishment of Offenders Act 2012 (c. 10).

[69] 1933 c. 36; section 2 was amended by Part IV of Schedule 11 to, the Courts Act 1971 (c. 23), Schedule 5 to, the Senior Courts Act 1981 (c. 54), Schedule 2 to the Prosecution of Offences Act 1985 (c. 23), paragraph 1 of Schedule 2 to the Criminal Justice Act 1987 (c. 38), paragraph 10 of Schedule 15 to the Criminal Justice Act 1988 (c. 33), paragraph 8 of Schedule 6 to the Criminal Justice Act 1991 (c. 53), Schedule 1 to the Statute Law (Repeals) Act 1993, paragraph 17 of Schedule 1 to the Criminal Procedure and Investigations Act 1996 (c. 25), paragraph 5 of Schedule 8 to the Crime and Disorder Act 1998 (c. 37), paragraph 34 of Schedule 3 and Part 4 of Schedule 37 to the Criminal Justice Act 2003 (c. 44), paragraph 1 of the Schedule

*Sections 8A and 8B, Magistrates' Courts Act 1980[70]: pre-trial hearings in magistrates' courts*
*Section 7, Criminal Justice Act 1987[71]; Parts III and IV, Criminal Procedure and Investigations Act 1996:*
*pre-trial and preparatory hearings in the Crown Court*
*Section 9, Criminal Justice Act 1967[72]: proof by written witness statement*
*Part 1, Criminal Procedure and Investigations Act 1996[73]: disclosure.]*

CRIMINAL PRACTICE DIRECTIONS   PART 3   CASE MANAGEMENT

**CPD I General matters 3A: Case Management**                                           **CPD.3A**

**3A.1**  CrimPR 1.1(2)(e) requires that cases be dealt with efficiently and expeditiously. CrimPR 3.2 requires the court to further the overriding objective by actively managing the case, for example:

   a)   When dealing with an offence which is triable only on indictment the court must ask the defendant whether he or she intends to plead guilty at the Crown Court (CrimPR 9.7(5));

   b)   On a guilty plea, the court must pass sentence at the earliest opportunity, in accordance with CrimPR 24.11(9)(a) (magistrates' courts) and 25.16(7)(a) (the Crown Court).

**3A.2**  Given these duties, magistrates' courts and the Crown Court therefore will proceed as described in paragraphs 3A.3 to 3A.28 below. The parties will be expected to have prepared in accordance with CrimPR 3.3(1) to avoid unnecessary and wasted hearings. They will be expected to have communicated with each other by the time of the first hearing; to report to the court on that communication at the first hearing; and to continue thereafter to communicate with each other and with the court officer, in accordance with CrimPR 3.3(2).

**3A.3**  There is a Preparation for Effective Trial form for use in the magistrates' courts, and a Plea and Trial Preparation Hearing form for use in the Crown Court, each of which must be used as appropriate in connection with CrimPR Part 3: see paragraph 5A.2 of these Practice Directions. Versions of those forms in pdf and Word, together with guidance notes, are available on the Criminal Procedure Rules pages of the Ministry of Justice website.

**Case progression and trial preparation in magistrates' courts**

**3A.4**  CrimPR 8.3 applies in all cases and requires the prosecutor to serve:

   i.    a summary of the circumstances of the offence;

   ii.   any account given by the defendant in interview, whether contained in that summary or in another document;

   iii.  any written witness statement or exhibit that the prosecutor then has available and considers material to plea or to the allocation of the case for trial or sentence;

   iv.   a list of the defendant's criminal record, if any; and

   v.    any available statement of the effect of the offence on a victim, a victim's family or others.

   The details must include sufficient information to allow the defendant and the court at the first hearing to take an informed view:

   i.    on plea;

   ii.   on venue for trial (if applicable);

   iii.  for the purposes of case management; or

   iv.   for the purposes of sentencing (including committal for sentence, if applicable).

to S.I. 2004/2035, section 12 of, and paragraph 7 of Schedule 1 to, the Constitutional Reform Act 2005 (c. 4), sections 116 and 178 of, and Part 3 of Schedule 23 to, the Coroners and Justice Act 2009 (c. 25), paragraph 32 of Schedule 17 to the Crime and Courts Act 2013 (c. 22) and section 82 of the Deregulation Act 2015 (c. 20).

[70]  1980 c. 43; section 8A was inserted by section 45 of, and Schedule 3 to, the Courts Act 2003 (c. 39) and amended by SI 2006/2493 and paragraphs 12 and 14 of Schedule 5 to the Legal Aid, Sentencing and Punishment of Offenders Act 2012 (c. 10). Section 8B was inserted by section 45 of, and Schedule 3 to, the Courts Act 2003 (c. 39) and amended by paragraph 51 of Schedule 3, and Part 4 of Schedule 37, to the Criminal Justice Act 2003 (c. 44).

[71]  1987 c. 38; section 7 was amended by section 168(1) of, and paragraph 30 of Schedule 9 to, the Criminal Justice and Public Order Act 1994 (c. 33), section 80 of, and paragraph 2 of Schedule 3 and Schedule 5 to, the Criminal Procedure and Investigations Act 1996 (c. 25) and sections 45 and 310 of, and paragraphs 52 and 53 of Schedule 36 to, the Criminal Justice Act 2003 (c. 44). The amendment made by section 45 of the Criminal Justice Act 2003 (c. 44) is in force for certain purposes; for remaining purposes it has effect from a date to be appointed.

[72]  1967 c. 80; section 9 was amended by section 56 of, and paragraph 49 of Schedule 8 to, the Courts Act 1971 (c. 23), section 168 of, and paragraph 6 of Schedule 9 to, the Criminal Justice and Public Order Act 1994 (c. 33), section 69 of the Criminal Procedure and Investigations Act 1996 (c. 25), regulation 9 of, and paragraph 4 of Schedule 5 to, S.I. 2001/1090, paragraph 43 of Schedule 3 and Part 4 of Schedule 37 to the Criminal Justice Act 2003 (c. 44), section 26 of, and paragraph 7 of Schedule 2 to, the Armed Forces Act 2011 (c. 18) and section 80 of the Deregulation Act 2015 (c. 20). It is further amended by section 72 of, and paragraph 55 of Schedule 5 to, the Children and Young Persons Act 1969 (c. 54) and section 65 of, and paragraph 1 of Schedule 4 to, the Courts Act 2003 (c. 39), with effect from dates to be appointed.

[73]  1996 c. 25.

*Defendant in custody*

**3A.5**  If the defendant has been detained in custody after being charged with an offence which is indictable only or triable either way, at the first hearing a magistrates' court will proceed at once with the allocation of the case for trial, where appropriate, and, if so required, with the sending of the defendant to the Crown Court for trial. The court will be expected to ask for and record any indication of plea and issues for trial to assist the Crown Court.

**3A.6**  If the offence charged is triable only summarily, or if at that hearing the case is allocated for summary trial, the court will forthwith give such directions as are necessary, either (on a guilty plea) to prepare for sentencing, or for a trial.

*Defendant on bail*

**3A.7**  If the defendant has been released on bail after being charged, the case must be listed for the first hearing 14 days after charge, or the next available court date thereafter when the prosecutor anticipates a guilty plea which is likely to be sentenced in the magistrates' court. In cases where there is an anticipated not guilty plea or the case is likely to be sent or committed to the Crown Court for either trial or sentence, then it must be listed for the first hearing 28 days after charge or the next available court date thereafter.

*Guilty plea in the magistrates' courts*

**3A.8**  Where a defendant pleads guilty or indicates a guilty plea in a magistrates' court the court should consider whether a pre-sentence report — a stand down report if possible — is necessary.

*Guilty plea in the Crown Court*

**3A.9**  Where a magistrates' court is considering committal for sentence or the defendant has indicated an intention to plead guilty in a matter which is to be sent to the Crown Court, the magistrates' court should request the preparation of a pre-sentence report for the Crown Court's use if the magistrates' court considers that:

    (a)  there is a realistic alternative to a custodial sentence; or

    (b)  the defendant may satisfy the criteria for classification as a dangerous offender; or

    (c)  there is some other appropriate reason for doing so.

**3A.10**  When a magistrates' court sends a case to the Crown Court for trial and the defendant indicates an intention to plead guilty at the Crown Court, then that magistrates' court must set a date for a Plea and Trial Preparation Hearing at the Crown Court, in accordance with CrimPR 9.7(5)(a)(i).

*Case sent for Crown Court trial: no indication of guilty plea*

**3A.11**  In any case sent to the Crown Court for trial, other than one in which the defendant indicates an intention to plead guilty, the magistrates' court must set a date for a Plea and Trial Preparation Hearing, in accordance with CrimPR 9.7(5)(a)(ii). The Plea and Trial Preparation Hearing must be held within 28 days of sending, unless the standard directions of the Presiding Judges of the circuit direct otherwise. Paragraph 3A.16 below additionally applies to the arrangements for such hearings. A magistrates' court may give other directions appropriate to the needs of the case, in accordance with CrimPR 3.5(3), and in accordance with any standard directions issued by the Presiding Judges of the circuit.

*Defendant on bail: anticipated not guilty plea*

**3A.12**  Where the defendant has been released on bail after being charged, and where the prosecutor does not anticipate a guilty plea at the first hearing in a magistrates' court, then it is essential that the initial details of the prosecution case that are provided for that first hearing are sufficient to assist the court, in order to identify the real issues and to give appropriate directions for an effective trial (regardless of whether the trial is to be heard in the magistrates' court or the Crown Court). In these circumstances, unless there is good reason not to do so, the prosecution should make available the following material in advance of the first hearing in the magistrates' court:

    (a)  A summary of the circumstances of the offence(s) including a summary of any account given by the defendant in interview;

    (b)  Statements and exhibits that the prosecution has identified as being of importance for the purpose of plea or initial case management, including any relevant CCTV that would be relied upon at trial and any Streamlined Forensic Report;

    (c)  Details of witness availability, as far as they are known at that hearing;

    (d)  Defendant's criminal record;

    (e)  Victim Personal Statements if provided;

    (f)  An indication of any medical or other expert evidence that the prosecution is likely to adduce in relation to a victim or the defendant;

    (g)  Any information as to special measures, bad character or hearsay, where applicable.

**3A.13** In addition to the material required by CrimPR Part 8, the information required by the Preparation for Effective Trial form must be available to be submitted at the first hearing, and the parties must complete that form, in accordance with the guidance published with it. Where there is to be a contested trial in a magistrates' court, that form includes directions and a timetable that will apply in every case unless the court otherwise orders.

**3A.14** Nothing in paragraph 3A.12-3A.13 shall preclude the court from taking a plea pursuant to CrimPR 3.9(2)(b) at the first hearing and for the court to case manage as far as practicable under Part 3 CrimPR.

*Exercise of magistrates' court's powers*

**3A.15** In accordance with CrimPR 9.1, sections 49, 51(13) and 51A(11) of the Crime and Disorder Act 1998, and sections 17E, 18(5) and 24D of the Magistrates' Courts Act 1980 a single justice can:
   a)   allocate and send for trial;
   b)   take an indication of a guilty plea (but not pass sentence);
   c)   take a not guilty plea and give directions for the preparation of trial including:
       i.    timetable for the proceedings;
       ii.   the attendance of the parties;
       iii.  the service of documents;
       iv.   the manner in which evidence is to be given.

**Case progression and trial preparation in the Crown Court**

*Plea and Trial Preparation Hearing*

**3A.16** In a case in which a magistrates' court has directed a Plea and Trial Preparation Hearing, the period which elapses between sending for trial and the date of that hearing must be consistent within each circuit. In every case, the time allowed for the conduct of the Plea and Trial Preparation Hearing must be sufficient for effective trial preparation. It is expected in every case that an indictment will be lodged at least 7 days in advance of the hearing. Please see the Note to the Practice Direction.

**3A.17** In a case in which the defendant, not having done so before, indicates an intention to plead guilty to his representative after being sent for trial but before the Plea and Trial Preparation Hearing, the defence representative will notify the Crown Court and the prosecution forthwith. The court will ensure there is sufficient time at the Plea and Trial Preparation Hearing for sentence and a Judge should at once request the preparation of a pre-sentence report if it appears to the court that either:
   (a)   there is a realistic alternative to a custodial sentence; or
   (b)   the defendant may satisfy the criteria for classification as a dangerous offender; or
   (c)   there is some other appropriate reason for doing so.

**3A.18** If at the Plea and Trial Preparation Hearing the defendant pleads guilty and no pre-sentence report has been prepared, if possible the court should obtain a stand down report.

**3A.19** Where the defendant was remanded in custody after being charged and was sent for trial without initial details of the prosecution case having been served, then at least 7 days before the Plea and Trial Preparation Hearing the prosecutor should serve, as a minimum, the material identified in paragraph 3A.12 above. If at the Plea and Trial Preparation Hearing the defendant does not plead guilty, the court will be expected to identify the issues in the case and give appropriate directions for an effective trial. Please see the Note to the Practice Direction.

**3A.20** At the Plea and Trial Preparation Hearing, in addition to the material required by paragraph 3A.12 above, the prosecutor must serve sufficient evidence to enable the court to case manage effectively without the need for a further case management hearing, unless the case falls within paragraph 3A.21. In addition, the information required by the Plea and Trial Preparation Hearing form must be available to the court at that hearing, and it must have been discussed between the parties in advance. The prosecutor must provide details of the availability of likely prosecution witnesses so that a trial date can immediately be arranged if the defendant does not plead guilty.

*Further case management hearing*

**3A.21** In accordance with CrimPR 3.13(1)(c), after the Plea and Trial Preparation Hearing there will be no further case management hearing before the trial unless:
   (i)   a condition listed in that rule is met; and
   (ii)  the court so directs, in order to further the overriding objective.
   The directions to be given at the Plea and Trial Preparation Hearing therefore may include a direction for a further case management hearing, but usually will do so only in one of the following cases:
   (a)   Class 1 cases;
   (b)   Class 2 cases which carry a maximum penalty of 10 years or more;

(c)  cases involving death by driving (whether dangerous or careless), or death in the workplace;

(d)  cases involving a vulnerable witness;

(e)  cases in which the defendant is a child or otherwise under a disability, or requires special assistance;

(f)  cases in which there is a corporate or unrepresented defendant;

(g)  cases in which the expected trial length is such that a further case management hearing is desirable and any case in which the trial is likely to last longer than four weeks;

(h)  cases in which expert evidence is to be introduced;

(i)  cases in which a party requests a hearing to enter a plea;

(j)  cases in which an application to dismiss or stay has been made;

(k)  cases in which arraignment has not taken place, whether because of an issue relating to fitness to plead, or abuse of process or sufficiency of evidence, or for any other reason;

(l)  cases in which there are likely to be linked criminal and care directions in accordance with the 2013 Protocol.

(m) cases in which a substantial quantity of unused prosecution material has been disclosed, or will be disclosed, or in which the disclosure of such material raises complex questions of law or procedure.

**3A.22**  If a further case management hearing is directed, a defendant in custody will not usually be expected to attend in person, unless the court otherwise directs.

*Compliance hearing*

**3A.23**  If a party fails to comply with a case management direction, that party may be required to attend the court to explain the failure. Unless the court otherwise directs a defendant in custody will not usually be expected to attend. See paragraph 3A.26-3A.28 below.

*Conduct of case progression hearings*

**3A.24**  As far as possible, case progression should be managed without a hearing in the courtroom, using electronic communication in accordance with CrimPR 3.5(2)(d). Court staff should be nominated to conduct case progression as part of their role, in accordance with CrimPR 3.4(2). To aid effective communication the prosecution and defence representative should notify the court and provide details of who shall be dealing with the case at the earliest opportunity.

**Completion of Effective Trial Monitoring form**

**3A.25**  It is imperative that the Effective Trial Monitoring form (as devised and issued by Her Majesty's Courts and Tribunals Service) is accurately completed by the parties for all cases that have been listed for trial. Advocates must engage with the process by providing the relevant details and completing the form.

**Compliance courts**

**3A.26**  To ensure effective compliance with directions of the courts made in accordance with the Criminal Procedure Rules and the overriding objective, courts should maintain a record whenever a party to the proceedings has failed to comply with a direction made by the court. The parties may have to attend a hearing to explain any lack of compliance.

**3A.27**  These hearings may be conducted by live link facilities or via other electronic means, as the court may direct.

**3A.28**  It will be for the Presiding Judges, Resident Judge and Justices' Clerks to decide locally how often compliance courts should be held, depending on the scale and nature of the problem at each court centre.

**CPD.3B**  **CPD I General matters 3B: Pagination and Indexing of Served Evidence**

**3B.1**  The following directions apply to matters before the Crown Court, where

(a)  there is an application to prefer a bill of indictment in relation to the case;

(b)  a person is sent for trial under section 51 of the Crime and Disorder Act 1998 (sending cases to the Crown Court), to the service of copies of the documents containing the evidence on which the charge or charges are based under Paragraph 1 of Schedule 3 to that Act; or

(c)  a defendant wishes to serve evidence.

**3B.2**  A party who serves documentary evidence in the Crown Court should:

(a)  paginate each page in any bundle of statements and exhibits sequentially;

(b)  provide an index to each bundle of statements produced including the following information:

   i.    the name of the case;

   ii.   the author of each statement;

   iii.  the start page number of the witness statement;

   iv.   the end page number of the witness statement.

    (c)  provide an index to each bundle of documentary and pictorial exhibits produced, including the following information:
        i.   the name of the case
        ii.  the exhibit reference;
        iii. a short description of the exhibit;
        iv. the start page number of the exhibit;
        v.   the end page number of the exhibit;
        vi. where possible, the name of the person producing the exhibit should be added.

3B.3  Where additional documentary evidence is served, a party should paginate following on from the last page of the previous bundle or in a logical and sequential manner. A party should also provide notification of service of any amended index.

3B.4  The prosecution must ensure that the running total of the pages of prosecution evidence is easily identifiable on the most recent served bundle of prosecution evidence.

3B.5  For the purposes of these directions, the number of pages of prosecution evidence served on the court includes all
    (a)  witness statements;
    (b)  documentary and pictorial exhibits;
    (c)  records of interviews with the defendant; and
    (d)  records of interviews with other defendants which form part of the served prosecution documents or which are included in any notice of additional evidence,
    but does not include any document provided on CD-ROM or by other means of electronic communication.

## CPD I General matters 3C: Abuse of Process Stay Applications                     CPD.3C

3C.1  In all cases where a defendant in the Crown Court proposes to make an application to stay an indictment on the grounds of abuse of process, written notice of such application must be given to the prosecuting authority and to any co-defendant as soon as practicable after the defendant becomes aware of the grounds for doing so and not later than 14 days before the date fixed or warned for trial ('the relevant date'). Such notice must:
    (a)  give the name of the case and the indictment number;
    (b)  state the fixed date or the warned date as appropriate;
    (c)  specify the nature of the application;
    (d)  set out in numbered sub-paragraphs the grounds upon which the application is to be made;
    (e)  be copied to the chief listing officer at the court centre where the case is due to be heard.

3C.2  Any co-defendant who wishes to make a like application must give a like notice not later than seven days before the relevant date, setting out any additional grounds relied upon.

3C.3  In relation to such applications, the following automatic directions shall apply:
    (a)  the advocate for the applicant(s) must lodge with the court and serve on all other parties a skeleton argument in support of the application, at least five clear working days before the relevant date. If reference is to be made to any document not in the existing trial documents, a paginated and indexed bundle of such documents is to be provided with the skeleton argument;
    (b)  the advocate for the prosecution must lodge with the court and serve on all other parties a responsive skeleton argument at least two clear working days before the relevant date, together with a supplementary bundle if appropriate.

3C.4  All skeleton arguments must specify any propositions of law to be advanced (together with the authorities relied upon in support, with paragraph references to passages relied upon) and, where appropriate, include a chronology of events and a list of dramatis personae. In all instances where reference is made to a document, the reference in the trial documents or supplementary bundle is to be given. Paragraphs XII D.17 to D.23 of these Practice Directions set out the general requirements for skeleton arguments.

3C.5  The above time limits are minimum time limits. In appropriate cases, the court will order longer lead times. To this end, in all cases where defence advocates are, at the time of the preliminary hearing or as soon as practicable after the case has been sent, considering the possibility of an abuse of process application, this must be raised with the judge dealing with the matter, who will order a different timetable if appropriate, and may wish, in any event, to give additional directions about the conduct of the application. If the trial judge has not been identified, the matter should be raised with the Resident Judge.

expertise, location and availability. Registered Intermediaries are accredited by the WIS and bound by Codes of Practice and Ethics issued by the Ministry of Justice (which oversees the WIS).

**3F.9** Having identified a Registered Intermediary, the WIS does not provide funding. The party appointing the Registered Intermediary is responsible for payment at rates specified by the Ministry of Justice.

**3F.10** Further information is in *The Registered Intermediary Procedural Guidance Manual* (Ministry of Justice, 2015) and *Intermediaries: Step by Step* (see 3F.3 above).

Link to publication

- http://www.theadvocatesgateway.org/images/procedures/registered-intermediary-procedural-guidance-manual.pdf

*Intermediaries for defendants*

**3F.11** Statutory provisions providing for defendants to be assisted by an intermediary when giving evidence (where necessary to ensure a fair trial) are not in force (because s.104 Coroners and Justice Act 2009, which would insert ss. 33BA and 33BB into the YJCEA 1999, has yet to be commenced).

**3F.12** The court may direct the appointment of an intermediary to assist a defendant in reliance on its inherent powers (*C v Sevenoaks Youth Court* [2009] EWHC 3088 (Admin)). There is however no presumption that a defendant will be so assisted and, even where an intermediary would improve the trial process, appointment is not mandatory (*R v Cox* [2012] EWCA Crim 549). The court should adapt the trial process to address a defendant's communication needs (*R v Cox* [2012] EWCA Crim 549). It will rarely exercise its inherent powers to direct appointment of an intermediary but where a defendant is vulnerable or for some other reason experiences communication or hearing difficulties, such that he or she needs more help to follow the proceedings than her or his legal representatives readily can give having regard to their other functions on the defendant's behalf, then the court should consider sympathetically any application for the defendant to be accompanied throughout the trial by a support worker or other appropriate companion who can provide that assistance. This is consistent with CrimPR 3.9(3)(b) (see paragraph 3D.2 above); consistent with the observations in *R v Cox* (see paragraph 3D.4 above), *R (OP) v Ministry of Justice* [2014] EWHC 1944 (Admin) and *R v Rashid* [2017] EWCA Crim 2; and consistent with the arrangements contemplated at paragraph 3G.8 below.

**3F.13** The court may exercise its inherent powers to direct appointment of an intermediary to assist a defendant giving evidence or for the entire trial. Terms of appointment are for the court and there is no illogicality in restricting the appointment to the defendant's evidence (*R v R* [2015] EWCA Crim 1870), when the 'most pressing need' arises (*OP v Secretary of State for Justice* [2014] EWHC 1944 (Admin)). Directions to appoint an intermediary for a defendant's evidence will thus be rare, but for the entire trial extremely rare, keeping in mind paragraph 3F.12 above.

**3F.14** An application for an intermediary to assist a defendant must be made in accordance with Part 18 of the Criminal Procedure Rules. In addition, where an intermediary report is available (see 3F.4 above), it should be provided with the application.

**3F.15** The WIS is not presently available to identify intermediaries for defendants (although in *OP v Secretary of State for Justice* [2014] EWHC 1944 (Admin), the Ministry of Justice was ordered to consider carefully whether it were justifiable to refuse equal provision to witnesses and defendants with respect to their evidence). 'Non-registered intermediaries' (intermediaries appointed other than through the WIS) must therefore be appointed for defendants. Although training is available, there is no accreditation process for non-registered intermediaries and rates of payment are unregulated.

**3F.16** Arrangements for funding of intermediaries for defendants depend on the stage of the appointment process. Where the defendant is publicly funded, an application should be made to the Legal Aid Agency for prior authority to fund a pre-trial assessment. If the application is refused, an application may be made to the court to use its inherent powers to direct a pre-trial assessment and funding thereof. Where the court uses its inherent powers to direct assistance by an intermediary at trial (during evidence or for the entire trial), court staff are responsible for arranging payment from Central Funds. Internal guidance for court staff is in *Guidance for HMCTS Staff: Registered and Non-Registered Intermediaries for Vulnerable Defendants and Non-Vulnerable Defence and Prosecution Witnesses* (Her Majesty's Courts and Tribunals Service, 2014).

**3F.17** The court should be satisfied that a non-registered intermediary has expertise suitable to meet the defendant's communication needs.

**3F.18** Further information is in *Intermediaries: Step by Step* (see 3F.3 above).

*Ineffective directions for intermediaries to assist defendants*

3F.19   Directions for intermediaries to help defendants may be ineffective due to general unavailability, lack of suitable expertise, or non-availability for the purpose directed (for example, where the direction is for assistance during evidence, but an intermediary will only accept appointment for the entire trial).

3F.20   Intermediaries may contribute to the administration of justice by facilitating communication with appropriate defendants during the trial process. A trial will not be rendered unfair because a direction to appoint an intermediary for the defendant is ineffective. 'It would, in fact, be a most unusual case for a defendant who is fit to plead to be so disadvantaged by his condition that a properly brought prosecution would have to be stayed' because an intermediary with suitable expertise is not available for the purpose directed by the court (*R v Cox* [2012] EWCA Crim 549).

3F.21   Faced with an ineffective direction, it remains the court's responsibility to adapt the trial process to address the defendant's communication needs, as was the case prior to the existence of intermediaries (*R v Cox* [2012] EWCA Crim 549). In such a case, a ground rules hearing should be convened to ensure every reasonable step is taken to facilitate the defendant's participation in accordance with CrimPR 3.9. At the hearing, the court should make new, further and/ or alternative directions. This includes setting ground rules to help the defendant follow proceedings and (where applicable) to give evidence.

3F.22   For example, to help the defendant follow proceedings the court may require evidence to be adduced by simple questions, with witnesses being asked to answer in short sentences. Regular breaks may assist the defendant's concentration and enable the defence advocate to summarise the evidence and take further instructions.

3F.23   Further guidance is available in publications such as *Ground Rules Hearings and the Fair Treatment of Vulnerable People in Court* (Toolkit 1; The Advocate's Gateway, 2015) and *General Principles from Research — Planning to Question a Vulnerable Person or Someone with Communication Needs* (Toolkit 2(a); The Advocate's Gateway, 2015). In the absence of an intermediary, these publications include information on planning how to manage the participation and questioning of the defendant, and the formulation of questions to avert misunderstanding (for example, by avoiding 'long and complicated questions ... posed in a leading or 'tagged' manner' (*R v Wills* [2011] EWCA Crim 1938, [2012] 1 Cr App R 2)).

Links to publications
   • https://www.theadvocatesgateway.org/images/toolkits/1-ground-rules-hearings-and-the-fair-treatment-of-vulnerable-people-in-court-2019.pdf
   • https://www.theadvocatesgateway.org/images/toolkits/2-general-principles-from-research-policy-and-guidance-planning-to-question-a-vulnerable-person-or-someone-with-communication-needs-2019.pdf

*Intermediaries for witnesses and defendants under 18*

3F.24   Communication needs (such as short attention span, suggestibility and reticence in relation to authority figures) are common to many witnesses and defendants under 18. Consideration should therefore be given to the communication needs of all children and young people appearing in the criminal courts and to adapting the trial process to address any such needs. Guidance is available in publications such as *Planning to Question a Child or Young Person* (Toolkit 6; The Advocate's Gateway, 2015) and *Effective Participation of Young Defendants* (Toolkit 8; The Advocate's Gateway, 2013).

Links to publications
   • https://www.theadvocatesgateway.org/images/toolkits/6-planning-to-question-a-child-or-young-person-141215.pdf
   • https://www.theadvocatesgateway.org/images/toolkits/8-effective-participation-of-young-defendants-2017.pdf

3F.25   For the reasons set out in 3F.5 above, the appropriateness of an intermediary assessment for witnesses and defendants under 18 must be decided with care. Whilst there is no presumption that they will be assessed by an intermediary (to evaluate their communication needs prior to trial) or assisted by an intermediary at court (for example, if / when giving evidence), the decision should be made on an individual basis in the context of the circumstances of the particular case.

3F.26   Assessment by an intermediary should be considered for witnesses and defendants under 18 who seem liable to misunderstand questions or to experience difficulty expressing answers, including those who seem unlikely to be able to recognise a problematic question (such as one that is misleading or not readily understood), and those who may be reluctant to tell a questioner in a position of authority if they do not understand.

*Attendance at ground rules hearing*

**3F.27**  Where the court directs questioning will be conducted through an intermediary, CrimPR 3.9 requires the court to set ground rules. The intermediary should be present at the ground rules hearing to make representations in accordance with CrimPR 3.9(7)(a).

*Listing*

**3F.28**  Where the court directs an intermediary will attend the trial, their dates of availability should be provided to the court. It is preferable that such trials are fixed rather than placed in warned lists.

*Photographs of court facilities*

**3F.29**  Resident Judges in the Crown Court or the Chief Clerk or other responsible person in the magistrates' courts should, in consultation with HMCTS managers responsible for court security matters, develop a policy to govern under what circumstances photographs or other visual recordings may be made of court facilities, such as a live link room, to assist vulnerable and child witnesses to familiarise themselves with the setting, so as to be enabled to give their best evidence. For example, a photograph may provide a helpful reminder to a witness whose court visit has taken place sometime earlier. Resident Judges should tend to permit photographs to be taken for this purpose by intermediaries or supporters, subject to whatever restrictions the Resident Judge or responsible person considers to be appropriate, having regard to the security requirements of the court.

**CPD.3G**   **CPD I General matters 3G: Vulnerable Defendants**

**Before the trial, sentencing or appeal**

**3G.1**  If a vulnerable defendant, especially one who is young, is to be tried jointly with one who is not, the court should consider at the plea and case management hearing, or at a case management hearing in a magistrates' court, whether the vulnerable defendant should be tried on his own, but should only so order if satisfied that a fair trial cannot be achieved by use of appropriate special measures or other support for the defendant. If a vulnerable defendant is tried jointly with one who is not, the court should consider whether any of the modifications set out in this direction should apply in the circumstances of the joint trial and, so far as practicable, make orders to give effect to any such modifications.

**3G.2**  It may be appropriate to arrange that a vulnerable defendant should visit, out of court hours and before the trial, sentencing or appeal hearing, the courtroom in which that hearing is to take place so that he or she can familiarise him or herself with it.

**3G.3**  Where an intermediary is being used to help the defendant to communicate at court, the intermediary should accompany the defendant on his or her pre-trial visit. The visit will enable the defendant to familiarise him or herself with the layout of the court, and may include matters such as: where the defendant will sit, either in the dock or otherwise; court officials (what their roles are and where they sit); who else might be in the court, for example those in the public gallery and press box; the location of the witness box; basic court procedure; and the facilities available in the court.

**3G.4**  If the defendant's use of the live link is being considered, he or she should have an opportunity to have a practice session.

**3G.5**  If any case against a vulnerable defendant has attracted or may attract widespread public or media interest, the assistance of the police should be enlisted to try and ensure that the defendant is not, when attending the court, exposed to intimidation, vilification or abuse. Section 41 of the Criminal Justice Act 1925 prohibits the taking of photographs of defendants and witnesses (among others) in the court building or in its precincts, or when entering or leaving those precincts. A direction reminding media representatives of the prohibition may be appropriate. The court should also be ready at this stage, if it has not already done so, where relevant to make a reporting restriction under section 39 of the Children and Young Persons Act 1933 or, on an appeal to the Crown Court from a youth court, to remind media representatives of the application of section 49 of that Act.

**3G.6**  The provisions of the Practice Direction accompanying Part 6 should be followed.

**The trial, sentencing or appeal hearing**

**3G.7**  Subject to the need for appropriate security arrangements, the proceedings should, if practicable, be held in a courtroom in which all the participants are on the same or almost the same level.

3G.8    Subject again to the need for appropriate security arrangements, a vulnerable defendant, especially if he is young, should normally, if he wishes, be free to sit with members of his family or others in a like relationship, and with some other suitable supporting adult such as a social worker, and in a place which permits easy, informal communication with his legal representatives. The court should ensure that a suitable supporting adult is available throughout the course of the proceedings.

3G.9    It is essential that at the beginning of the proceedings, the court should ensure that what is to take place has been explained to a vulnerable defendant in terms he or she can understand and, at trial in the Crown Court, it should ensure in particular that the role of the jury has been explained. It should remind those representing the vulnerable defendant and the supporting adult of their responsibility to explain each step as it takes place and, at trial, explain the possible consequences of a guilty verdict and credit for a guilty plea. The court should also remind any intermediary of the responsibility to ensure that the vulnerable defendant has understood the explanations given to him/her. Throughout the trial the court should continue to ensure, by any appropriate means, that the defendant understands what is happening and what has been said by those on the bench, the advocates and witnesses.

3G.10   A trial should be conducted according to a timetable which takes full account of a vulnerable defendant's ability to concentrate. Frequent and regular breaks will often be appropriate. The court should ensure, so far as practicable, that the whole trial is conducted in clear language that the defendant can understand and that evidence in chief and cross-examination are conducted using questions that are short and clear. The conclusions of the 'ground rules' hearing should be followed, and advocates should use and follow the 'toolkits' as discussed above.

3G.11   A vulnerable defendant who wishes to give evidence by live link, in accordance with section 33A of the Youth Justice and Criminal Evidence Act 1999, may apply for a direction to that effect; the procedure in CrimPR 18.14 to 18.17 should be followed. Before making such a direction, the court must be satisfied that it is in the interests of justice to do so and that the use of a live link would enable the defendant to participate more effectively as a witness in the proceedings. The direction will need to deal with the practical arrangements to be made, including the identity of the person or persons who will accompany him or her.

3G.12   In the Crown Court, the judge should consider whether robes and wigs should be worn, and should take account of the wishes of both a vulnerable defendant and any vulnerable witness. It is generally desirable that those responsible for the security of a vulnerable defendant who is in custody, especially if he or she is young, should not be in uniform, and that there should be no recognisable police presence in the courtroom save for good reason.

3G.13   The court should be prepared to restrict attendance by members of the public in the courtroom to a small number, perhaps limited to those with an immediate and direct interest in the outcome. The court should rule on any challenged claim to attend. However, facilities for reporting the proceedings (subject to any restrictions under section 39 or 49 of the Children and Young Persons Act 1933) must be provided. The court may restrict the number of reporters attending in the courtroom to such number as is judged practicable and desirable. In ruling on any challenged claim to attend in the courtroom for the purpose of reporting, the court should be mindful of the public's general right to be informed about the administration of justice.

3G.14   Where it has been decided to limit access to the courtroom, whether by reporters or generally, arrangements should be made for the proceedings to be relayed, audibly and if possible visually, to another room in the same court complex to which the media and the public have access if it appears that there will be a need for such additional facilities. Those making use of such a facility should be reminded that it is to be treated as an extension of the courtroom and that they are required to conduct themselves accordingly.

## CPD I General matters 3H: Wales and the Welsh Language: Devolution Issues    CPD.3H

3H.1    These are the subject of Practice Direction: (Supreme Court) (Devolution Issues) [1999] 1 WLR 1592; [1999] 3 All ER 466; [1999] 2 Cr App R 486, to which reference should be made.

## CPD I General matters 3J: Wales and the Welsh Language: Applications for Evidence to be Given in    CPD.3J
## Welsh

3J.1    If a defendant in a court in England asks to give or call evidence in the Welsh language, the case should not be transferred to Wales. In ordinary circumstances, interpreters can be provided on request.

Criminal Procedure Rules and Criminal Practice Directions

**CPD.3K**    CPD I General matters 3K: Wales and the Welsh Language: Use of the Welsh Language in Courts in Wales

**3K.1**    The purpose of this direction is to reflect the principle of the Welsh Language Act 1993 that, in the administration of justice in Wales, the English and Welsh languages should be treated on a basis of equality.

*General*

**3K.2**    It is the responsibility of the legal representatives in every case in which the Welsh language may be used by any witness or party, or in any document which may be placed before the court, to inform the court of that fact, so that appropriate arrangements can be made for the listing of the case.

**3K.3**    Any party or witness is entitled to use Welsh in a magistrates' court in Wales without giving prior notice. Arrangements will be made for hearing such cases in accordance with the 'Magistrates' Courts' Protocol for Listing Cases where the Welsh Language is used' (January 2008) which is available on the Judiciary's website: https://www.judiciary.gov.uk/publications/mags-cts-protocol -for-listing-cases-in-welsh-language/. See also CrimPR 24.14.

**3K.4**    If the possible use of the Welsh language is known at the time of sending or appeal to the Crown Court, the court should be informed immediately after sending or when the notice of appeal is lodged. Otherwise, the court should be informed as soon as the possible use of the Welsh language becomes known.

**3K.5**    If costs are incurred as a result of failure to comply with these directions, a wasted costs order may be made against the defaulting party and / or his legal representatives.

**3K.6**    The law does not permit the selection of jurors in a manner which enables the court to discover whether a juror does or does not speak Welsh, or to secure a jury whose members are bilingual, to try a case in which the Welsh language may be used.

*Preliminary and plea and case management hearings*

**3K.7**    An advocate in a case in which the Welsh language may be used must raise that matter at the preliminary and/or the plea and case management hearing and endorse details of it on the advocates' questionnaire, so that appropriate directions may be given for the progress of the case.

*Listing*

**3K.8**    The listing officer, in consultation with the resident judge, should ensure that a case in which the Welsh language may be used is listed
(a)  wherever practicable before a Welsh speaking judge, and
(b)  in a court in Wales with simultaneous translation facilities.

*Interpreters*

**3K.9**    Whenever an interpreter is needed to translate evidence from English into Welsh or from Welsh into English, the court listing officer in whose court the case is to be heard shall contact the Welsh Language Unit who will ensure the attendance of an accredited interpreter.

*Jurors*

**3K.10**    The jury bailiff, when addressing the jurors at the start of their period of jury service, shall inform them that each juror may take an oath or affirm in Welsh or English as he wishes.

**3K.11**    After the jury has been selected to try a case, and before it is sworn, the court officer swearing in the jury shall inform the jurors in open court that each juror may take an oath or affirm in Welsh or English as he wishes. A juror who takes the oath or affirms in Welsh should not be asked to repeat it in English.

**3K.12**    Where Welsh is used by any party or witness in a trial, an accredited interpreter will provide simultaneous translation from Welsh to English for the jurors who do not speak Welsh. There is no provision for the translation of evidence from English to Welsh for a Welsh speaking juror.

**3K.13**    The jury's deliberations must be conducted in private with no other person present and therefore no interpreter may be provided to translate the discussion for the benefit of one or more of the jurors.

*Witnesses*

**3K.14**    When each witness is called, the court officer administering the oath or affirmation shall inform the witness that he may be sworn or affirm in Welsh or English, as he wishes. A witness who takes the oath or affirms in Welsh should not be asked to repeat it in English.

*Opening / closing of Crown Courts*

**3K.15**    Unless it is not reasonably practicable to do so, the opening and closing of the court should be performed in Welsh and English.

*Role of Liaison Judge*

**3K.16**   If any question or problem arises concerning the implementation of these directions, contact should in the first place be made with the Liaison Judge for the Welsh language through the Wales Circuit Office:

   HMCTS WALES / GLITEM CYMRU

   3rd Floor, Churchill House / 3ydd Llawr T Churchill

   Churchill Way / Ffordd Churchill

   Cardiff / Caerdydd

   CF10 2HH

   029 2067 8300

**CPD I General Matters 3L: Security of Prisoners at Court**                                    **CPD.3L**

**3L.1**   High-risk prisoners identified to the court as presenting a significant risk of escape, violence in court or danger to those in the court and its environs, and to the public at large, will as far as possible, have administrative and remand appearances listed for disposal by way of live link. They will have priority for the use of video equipment.

**3L.2**   In all other proceedings that require the appearance in person of a high-risk prisoner, the proceedings will be listed at an appropriately secure court building and in a court with a secure (enclosed or ceiling-high) dock.

**3L.3**   Where a secure dock or live link is not available the court will be asked to consider an application for additional security measures, which may include:

   (a)   the use of approved restraints (but see below at 3L.6);

   (b)   the deployment of additional escort staff;

   (c)   securing the court room for all or part of the proceedings;

   (d)   in exceptional circumstances, moving the hearing to a prison.

**3L.4**   National Offender Management Service (NOMS) will be responsible for providing the assessment of the prisoner and it is accepted that this may change at short notice. NOMS must provide notification to the listing officer of all Category A prisoners, those on the Escape-list and Restricted Status prisoners or other prisoners who have otherwise been assessed as presenting a significant risk of violence or harm. There is a presumption that all prisoners notified as high-risk will be allocated a hearing by live link and/or secure dock facilities. Where the court cannot provide a secure listing, the reasons should be provided to the establishment so that alternative arrangements can be considered.

*Applications for use of approved restraints*

**3L.5**   It is the duty of the court to decide whether a prisoner who appears before them should appear in restraints or not. Their decision must comply with the requirements of the European Convention on Human Rights, particularly Article 3, which prohibits degrading treatment, see *Ranniman v Finland* (1997) 26 EHRR 56.

**3L.6**   No prisoner should be handcuffed in court unless there are reasonable grounds for apprehending that he will be violent or will attempt to escape. If an application is made, it must be entertained by the court and a ruling must be given. The defence should be given the opportunity to respond to the application: proceeding in the absence of the defendant or his representative may give rise to an issue under Article 6(1) of the European Convention on Human Rights: *R v Rollinson* (1996) 161 JP 107, CA. If an application is to be made ex parte then that application should be made inter partes and the defence should be given an opportunity to respond.

*Additional security measures*

**3L.7**   It may be in some cases that additional dock officers are deployed to mitigate the risk that a prisoner presents. When the nature of the risk is so serious that increased deployment will be insufficient or would in itself be so obtrusive as to prejudice a fair trial, then the court may be required to consider the following measures:

   (a)   reconsider the case for a live link hearing, including transferring the case to a court where the live link is available;

   (b)   transfer the case to an appropriately secure court;

   (c)   the use of approved restraints on the prisoner for all or part of the proceedings;

   (d)   securing the court room for all or part of the proceedings; and

   (e)   the use of (armed) police in the court building.

3L.8　The establishment seeking the additional security measures will submit a Court Management Directions Form setting out the evidence of the prisoners identified risk of escape or violence and requesting the courts approval of security measures to mitigate that risk. This must be sent to the listing officer along with current, specific and credible evidence that the security measures are both necessary and proportionate to the identified risk and that the risk cannot be managed in any other way.

3L.9　If the court is asked to consider transfer of the case, then this must be in accordance with the Listing and Allocation Practice Direction XIII F.11-F.13 post. The listing officer will liaise with the establishment, prosecution and the defence to ensure the needs of the witnesses are taken into account.

3L.10　The Judge who has conduct of the case must deal with any application for the use of restraints or any other security measure and will hear representations from the Crown Prosecution Service and the defence before proceeding. The application will only be granted if:

(a)　there are good grounds for believing that the prisoner poses a significant risk of trying to escape from the court (beyond the assumed motivation of all prisoners to escape) and/or risk of serious harm towards those persons in court or the public generally should an escape attempt be successful; and

(b)　where there is no other viable means of preventing escape or serious harm.

*High-risk prisoners giving evidence from the witness box*

3L.11　High-risk prisoners giving evidence from the witness box may pose a significant security risk. In circumstances where such prisoners are required to move from a secure dock to an insecure witness box, an application may be made for the court to consider the use of additional security measures including:

(a)　the use of approved restraints;

(b)　the deployment of additional escort staff or police in the courtroom or armed police in the building. The decision to deploy an armed escort is for the Chief Inspector of the relevant borough: the decision to allow the armed escort in or around the court room is for the Senior Presiding Judge (see below);

(c)　securing the courtroom for all or part of the proceedings;

(d)　giving evidence from the secure dock; and

(e)　use of live link if the prisoner is not the defendant.

**CPD.3M**　**CPD I General Matters 3M: Procedure for Application for Armed Police Presence in the Royal Courts of Justice, Crown Courts and Magistrates' Court Buildings**

3M.1　This Practice Direction sets out the procedure for the making and handling of applications for authorisation for the presence of armed police officers within the precincts of any Crown Court and magistrates' court buildings at any time. It applies to an application to authorise the carriage of firearms or tasers in court for security purposes. It does not apply to officers who are carrying CS spray or PAVA incapacitant spray, which is included in the standard equipment issued to officers in some forces and therefore no separate authorisation is required for its carriage in court. Likewise, no separate authorisation is required for officers carrying tasers as part of their operational equipment where they are attending court on routine court business or to give evidence. If, however, the carrying of tasers is part of a tactical deployment for security purposes then an application must be made in accordance with the following provisions to ensure the court is aware of the arrangements sought.

3M.2　This Practice Direction applies to all cases in England and Wales in which a police unit intends to request authorisation for the presence of armed police officers in the Crown Court or in the magistrates' court buildings at any time and including during the delivery of prisoners to court.

3M.3　This Practice Direction allows applications to be made for armed police presence in the Royal Courts of Justice.

*Emergency situations*

3M.4　This Practice Direction does not apply in an emergency situation. In such circumstances, the police must be able to respond in a way in which their professional judgment deems most appropriate.

*Designated court centres*

3M.5　Applications may only be made for armed police presence in the designated Crown Court and magistrates' court centres (see below). This list may be revised from time to time in consultation with the Association of Chief Police Officers (ACPO) and HMCTS. It will be reviewed at least every five years in consultation with ACPO armed police secretariat and the Presiding Judges.

**3M.6**   The Crown Court centres designated for firearms deployment are:
  (a)   Northern Circuit: Carlisle, Chester, Liverpool, Preston, Manchester Crown Square & Manchester Minshull Street.
  (b)   North Eastern Circuit: Bradford, Leeds, Newcastle upon Tyne, Sheffield, Teesside and Kingston-upon-Hull.
  (c)   Western Circuit: Bristol, Winchester and Exeter.
  (d)   South Eastern Circuit (not including London): Canterbury, Chelmsford, Ipswich, Luton, Maidstone, Norwich, Reading and St Albans.
  (e)   South Eastern Circuit (London only): Central Criminal Court, Woolwich, Kingston and Snaresbrook.
  (f)   Midland Circuit: Birmingham, Northampton, Nottingham and Leicester.
  (g)   Wales Circuit: Cardiff, Swansea and Caernarfon.
**3M.7**   The magistrates' courts designated for firearms deployment are:
  (a)   South Eastern Circuit (London only): Westminster Magistrates' Court and Belmarsh Magistrates' Court.

*Preparatory work prior to applications in all cases*

**3M.8**   Prior to the making of any application for armed transport of prisoners or the presence of armed police officers in the court building, consideration must be given to making use of prison video link equipment to avoid the necessity of prisoners' attendance at court for the hearing in respect of which the application is to be made.

**3M.9**   Notwithstanding their designation, each requesting officer will attend the relevant court before an application is made to ensure that there have been no changes to the premises and that there are no circumstances that might affect security arrangements.

*Applying in the Royal Courts of Justice*

**3M.10**  All applications should be sent to the Listing Office of the Division in which the case is due to appear. The application should be sent by email if possible and must be on the standard form.

**3M.11**  The Listing Office will notify the Head of Division, providing a copy of the email and any supporting evidence. The Head of Division may ask to see the senior police officer concerned.

**3M.12**  The Head of Division will consider the application. If it is refused, the application fails and the police must be notified.

**3M.13**  In the absence of the Head of Division, the application should be considered by the Vice-President of the Division.

**3M.14**  The relevant Court Office will be notified of the decision and that office will immediately inform the police by telephone. The decision must then be confirmed in writing to the police.

*Applying to the Crown Court*

**3M.15**  All applications should be sent to the Cluster Manager and should be sent by email if possible and must be on the standard form.

**3M.16**  The Cluster Manager will notify the Presiding Judge on the circuit and the Resident Judge by email, providing a copy of the form and any supporting evidence. The Presiding Judge may ask to see the senior police officer concerned.

**3M.17**  The Presiding Judge will consider the application. If it is refused the application fails and the police must be informed.

**3M.18**  If the Presiding Judge approves the application it should be forwarded to the secretary in the Senior Presiding Judge's Office. The Senior Presiding Judge will make the final decision. The Presiding Judge will receive written confirmation of that decision.

**3M.19**  The Presiding Judge will notify the Cluster Manager and the Resident Judge of the decision. The Cluster Manager will immediately inform the police of the decision by telephone. The decision must then be confirmed in writing to the police.

*Urgent applications to the Crown Court*

**3M.20**  If the temporary deployment of armed police arises as an urgent issue and a case would otherwise have to be adjourned; or if the trial judge is satisfied that there is a serious risk to public safety, then the Resident Judge will have a discretion to agree such deployment without having obtained the consent of a Presiding Judge or the Senior Presiding Judge. In such a case:
  (a)   the Resident Judge should assess the facts and agree the proposed solution with a police officer of at least Superintendent level. That officer should agree the approach with the Firearms Division of the police.
  (b)   if the proposed solution involves the use of armed police officers, the Resident Judge must try to contact the Presiding Judge and/or the Senior Presiding Judge by email and telephone. The Cluster Manager should be informed of the situation.

(c) if the Resident Judge cannot obtain a response from the Presiding Judge or the Senior Presiding Judge, the Resident Judge may grant the application if satisfied:
  (i) that the application is necessary;
  (ii) that without such deployment there would be a significant risk to public safety; and
  (iii) that the case would have to be adjourned at significant difficulty or inconvenience.

**3M.21** The Resident Judge must keep the position under continual review, to ensure that it remains appropriate and necessary. The Resident Judge must make continued efforts to contact the Presiding Judge and the Senior Presiding Judge to notify them of the full circumstances of the authorisation.

*Applying to the magistrates' courts*

**3M.22** All applications should be directed, by email if possible, to the Office of the Chief Magistrate, at Westminster Magistrates' Court and must be on the standard form.

**3M.23** The Chief Magistrate should consider the application and, if approved, it should be forwarded to the Senior Presiding Judge's Office. The Senior Presiding Judge will make the final decision. The Chief Magistrate will receive written confirmation of that decision and will then notify the requesting police officer and, where authorisation is given, the affected magistrates' court of the decision.

*Urgent applications in the magistrates' courts*

**3M.24** If the temporary deployment of armed police arises as an urgent issue and a case would otherwise have to be adjourned; or if the Chief Magistrate is satisfied that there is a serious risk to public safety, then the Chief Magistrate will have a discretion to agree such deployment without having obtained the consent of the Senior Presiding Judge. In such a case:
  (a) the Chief Magistrate should assess the facts and agree the proposed solution with a police officer of at least Superintendent level. That officer should agree the approach with the Firearms Division of the police.
  (b) if the proposed solution involves the use of armed police officers, the Chief Magistrate must try to contact the Senior Presiding Judge by email and telephone. The Cluster Manager should be informed of the situation.
  (c) if the Chief Magistrate cannot obtain a response from the Senior Presiding Judge, the Chief Magistrate may grant the application if satisfied:
    (i) that the application is necessary;
    (ii) that without such deployment there would be a significant risk to public safety; and
    (iii) that the case would have to be adjourned at significant difficulty or inconvenience.

**3M.25** The Chief Magistrate must keep the position under continual review, to ensure that it remains appropriate and necessary. The Chief Magistrate must make continued efforts to contact the Senior Presiding Judge to notify him of the full circumstances of the authorisation.

**CPD.3N**    **CPD I General Matters 3N: Use of Live Link and Telephone Facilities**

**3N.1** Where it is lawful and in the interests of justice to do so, courts should exercise their statutory and other powers to conduct hearings by live link or telephone. This is consistent with the Criminal Procedure Rules and with the recommendations of the President of the Queen's Bench Division's *Review of Efficiency in Criminal Proceedings* published in January 2015. Save where legislation circumscribes the court's jurisdiction, the breadth of that jurisdiction is acknowledged by CrimPR 3.5(1), (2)(d).

**3N.2** It is the duty of the court to make use of technology actively to manage the case: CrimPR 3.2(1), (2)(h). That duty includes an obligation to give directions for the use of live links and telephone facilities in the circumstances listed in CrimPR 3.2(4) and (5) (pre-trial hearings, including pre-trial case management hearings). Where the court directs that evidence is to be given by live link, and especially where such a direction is given on the court's own initiative, it is essential that the decision is communicated promptly to the witness: CrimPR 18.4. Contrary to a practice adopted by some courts, none of those rules or other provisions require the renewal of a live link direction merely because a trial has had to be postponed or adjourned. Once made, such a direction applies until it is discharged by the court, having regard to the relevant statutory criteria.

**3N.3** It is the duty of the parties to alert the court to any reason why live links or telephones should not be used where CrimPR 3.2 otherwise would oblige the court to do so; and, where a direction for the use of such facilities has been made, it is the duty of the parties as soon as practicable to alert the court to any reason why that direction should be varied CrimPR 3.3(2)(e) and 3.6.

**3N.4** The word 'appropriate' in CrimPR 3.2(4) and (5) is not a term of art. It has the ordinary English meaning of 'fitting', or 'suitable'. Whether the facilities available to the court in any particular case can be considered appropriate is a matter for the court, but plainly to be appropriate such facilities must work, at the time at which they are required; all participants must be able to hear and, in the case of a live link, see each other clearly; and there must be no extraneous noise, movement or other distraction suffered by a participant, or transmitted by a participant to others. What degree of protection from accidental or deliberate interception should be considered appropriate will depend upon the purpose for which a live link or telephone is to be used. If it is to participate in a hearing which is open to the public anyway, then what is communicated by such means is by definition public and the use of links such as Skype or Facetime, which are not generally considered secure from interception, may not be objectionable. If it is to participate in a hearing in private, and especially one at which sensitive information will be discussed – for example, on an application for a search warrant – then a more secure service is likely to be required.

3N.5   There may be circumstances in which the court should not require the use of live link or telephone facilities despite their being otherwise appropriate at a pre-trial hearing. In every case, in deciding whether any such circumstances apply the court will keep in mind that, for the purposes of what may be an essentially administrative hearing, it may be compatible with the overriding objective to proceed in the defendant's absence altogether, especially if he or she is represented, unless, exceptionally, a rule otherwise requires. The principle that the court always must consider proceeding in a defendant's absence is articulated in CrimPR 3.9(2)(a). Where at a pre-trial hearing bail may be under consideration, the provisions of CrimPR 14.2 will be relevant.

3N.6   Such circumstances will include any case in which the defendant's effective participation cannot be achieved by his or her attendance by such means, and CrimPR 3.2(4) and (5) except such cases from the scope of the obligation which that rule otherwise imposes on the court. That exception may apply where (this list is not exhaustive) the defendant has a disorder or disability, including a hearing, speech or sight impediment, or has communication needs to which the use of a live link or telephone is inimical (whether or not those needs are such as to require the appointment of an intermediary); or where the defendant requires interpretation and effective interpretation cannot be provided by live link or telephone, as the case may be. In deciding whether to require a defendant to attend a first hearing in a magistrates' court by live link from a police station, the court should take into account any views expressed by the defendant, the terms of any mental health or other medical assessment of the defendant carried out at the police station, and all other relevant information and representations available. No single factor is determinative, but the court must keep in mind the terms of section 57C(6A) of the Crime and Disorder Act 1998 (Use of live link at preliminary hearings where accused is at police station) which provides that 'A live link direction under this section may not be given unless the court is satisfied that it is not contrary to the interests of justice to give the direction.'

3N.7   Finally, that exception sometimes may apply where the defendant's attendance in person at a pre-trial hearing will facilitate communication with his or her legal representatives. The court should not make such an exception merely to allow client and representatives to meet if that meeting can and should be held elsewhere. However, there will be cases in which defence representatives reasonably need to meet with a defendant, to take his or her instructions or to explain events to him or her, either shortly before or immediately after a pre-trial hearing and in circumstances in which that meeting cannot take place effectively by live link.

3N.8   Nothing prohibits the member or members of a court from conducting a pre-trial hearing by attending by live link or telephone from a location distant from all the other participants. Despite the conventional view that the venue for a court hearing is the court room in which that hearing has been arranged to take place, the Criminal Procedure Rules define 'court' as 'a tribunal with jurisdiction over criminal cases. It includes a judge, recorder, District Judge (Magistrates' Court), lay justice and, when exercising their judicial powers, the Registrar of Criminal Appeals, a justices' clerk or assistant clerk.' Neither CrimPR 3.25 (Place of trial), which applies in the Crown Court, nor CrimPR 24.14 (Place of trial), which applies in magistrates' courts, each of which requires proceedings to take place in a courtroom provided by the Lord Chancellor, applies for the purposes of a pre-trial hearing. Thus for the purposes of such a hearing there is no legal obstacle to the judge, magistrate or magistrates conducting it from elsewhere, with other participants assembled in a courtroom from which the member or members of the court are physically absent. In principle, nothing prohibits the conduct of a pre-trial hearing by live link or telephone with each participant, including the member or members of the court, in a different location (an arrangement sometimes described as a 'virtual hearing'). This is dependent upon there being means by which that hearing can be witnessed by the public – for example, by public attendance at a courtroom or other venue from which the participants all can be seen and heard (if by live link), or heard (if by telephone). The principle of open justice to which paragraph 3N.17 refers is relevant.

3N.9   Sections 57A to 57F of the Crime and Disorder Act 1998 allow a defendant who is in custody to enter a plea by live link, and allow for such a defendant who attends by live link to be sentenced. In appropriate circumstances, the court may allow a defendant who is not in custody to enter a plea by live link; but the same considerations as apply to sentencing in such a case will apply: see paragraph 3N.13 beneath.

**3N.10** The Crime and Disorder Act 1998 does not allow for the attendance by live link at a contested trial of a defendant who is in custody. The court may allow a defendant who wishes to do so to observe all or part of his or her trial by live link, whether she or he is in custody or not, but (a) such a defendant cannot lawfully give evidence by such means unless he or she satisfies the criteria prescribed by section 33A of the Youth Justice and Criminal Evidence Act 1999 and the court so orders under that section (see also CrimPR 18.14–18.17); (b) a defendant who is in custody and who observes the trial by live link is not present, as a matter of law, and the trial must be treated as taking place in his or her absence, she or he having waived the right to attend; and (c) a defendant who has refused to attend his or her trial when required to do so, or who has absconded, must not be permitted to observe the proceedings by live link.

**3N.11** Paragraphs I 3D to 3G inclusive of these Practice Directions (Vulnerable people in the courts; Ground rules hearings to plan the questioning of a vulnerable witness or defendant; Intermediaries; Vulnerable defendants) contain directions relevant to the use of a live link as a special measure for a young or otherwise vulnerable witness, or to facilitate the giving of evidence by a defendant who is likewise young or otherwise vulnerable, within the scope of the Youth Justice and Criminal Evidence Act 1999. Defence representatives and the court must keep in mind that special measures under the 1999 Act and CrimPR Part 18, including the use of a live link, are available to defence as well as to prosecution witnesses who meet the statutory criteria. Defence representatives should always consider whether their witnesses would benefit from giving evidence by live link and should apply for a direction if appropriate, either at the case management hearing or as soon as possible thereafter. A defence witness should be afforded the same facilities and treatment as a prosecution witness, including the same opportunity to make a pre-trial visit to the court building in order to familiarise himself or herself with it. Where a live link is sought as a special measure for a young or vulnerable witness or defendant, CrimPR 18.10 and 18.15 respectively require, among other things, that the applicant must identify someone to accompany that witness or defendant while they give evidence; must name the person, if possible; and must explain why that person would be an appropriate companion for that witness. The court must ensure that directions are given accordingly when ordering such a live link. Witness Service volunteers are available to support all witnesses, prosecution and defence, if required.

**3N.12** Under sections 57A and 57D or 57E of the Crime and Disorder Act 1998 the court may pass sentence on a defendant in custody who attends by live link. The court may allow a defendant who is not in custody and who wishes to attend his or her sentencing by live link her or him by such means. Factors of which the court will wish to take account in exercising its discretion include, in particular, the penalty likely to be imposed; the importance of ensuring that the explanations of sentence required by CrimPR 24.11(9), in magistrates' courts, and in the Crown Court by CrimPR 25.16(7), can be given satisfactorily, for the defendant, for other participants and for the public, including reporters; and the preferences of the maker of any Victim Personal Statement which is to be read aloud or played pursuant to paragraph VII F.3(c) of these Practice Directions.

*Youth defendants*

**3N.13** In the youth court or when a youth is appearing in the magistrates' court or the Crown Court, it will usually be appropriate for the youth to be produced in person at court. This is to ensure that the court can engage properly with the youth and that the necessary level of engagement can be facilitated with the Youth Offending Team worker, defence representative and/or appropriate adult responsible for the youth's care. The court should deal with any application for use of a live-link on a case-by-case basis, after consultation with the parties and the Youth Offending Team. Such hearings that may be appropriate, include, onward remand hearings at which there is no bail application or case management hearings, particularly if the youth is already serving a custodial sentence.

**3N.14** It rarely will be appropriate for a youth to be sentenced over a live link. However, notwithstanding the court's duties of engagement with a youth, the overriding welfare principle and the statutory responsibility of the youth offending worker to explain the sentence to the youth, after consultation with the parties and the Youth Offending Team, there may be circumstances in which it may be appropriate to sentence a youth over the live-link: a) If the youth is already serving a custodial sentence and the sentence to be imposed by the court is bound to be a further custodial sentence, whether concurrent or consecutive; b) If the youth is already serving a custodial sentence and the court is minded to impose a non-custodial sentence which will have no material impact on the sentence being served; c) The youth is being detained in a secure establishment at such a distance from the court that the travelling time from one to the other will be significant so

Criminal Procedure Rules and Criminal Practice Directions

as to materially affect the welfare of the youth; d) The youth's condition – whether mental or otherwise – is so disturbed that his or her production would be a significant detriment to his or her welfare.

3N.15    Arrangements must be made in advance of any live link hearing to enable the youth offending worker to be at the secure establishment where the youth is in custody. In the event that such arrangements are not practicable, the youth offending worker must have sufficient access to the youth via the live link booth before and after the hearing.

*Conduct of participants*

3N.16    Where a live link is used, the immediate vicinity of the device by which a person attends becomes, temporarily, part of the courtroom for the purposes of that person's participation. That person, and any advocate or legal representative, custodian, court officer, intermediary or other companion, whether immediately visible to the court or not, becomes a participant for the purposes of CrimPR 1.2(2) and is subject to the court's jurisdiction to regulate behaviour in the courtroom. The substance and effect of this direction must be drawn to the attention of all such participants.

*Open justice and records of proceedings*

3N.17    The principle of open justice to which CrimPR 6.2(1) gives effect applies as strongly where electronic means of communication are used to conduct a hearing as it applies in other circumstances. Open justice is the principal means by which courts are kept under scrutiny by the public. It follows that where a participant attends a hearing in public by live link or telephone then that person's participation must be, as nearly as may be, equally audible and, if applicable, equally visible to the public as it would be were he or she physically present. Where electronic means of communication are used to conduct a hearing, records of the event must be maintained in the usual way: CrimPR 5.4. In the Crown Court, this includes the recording of the proceedings: CrimPR 5.5.

## CPD I General matters 3P: Commissioning Medical Reports

*General observations*

3P.1    CrimPR 24.3 and 25.10 concern procedures to be followed in magistrates' courts and in the Crown Court respectively where there is doubt about a defendant's mental health and, in the Crown Court, the defendant's capacity to participate in a trial. CrimPR 3.28 governs the procedure where, on the court's own initiative, a magistrates' court requires expert medical opinion about the potential suitability of a hospital order under section 37(3) of the Mental Health Act 1983 (hospital order without convicting the defendant), the Crown Court requires such opinion about the defendant's fitness to participate at trial, under section 4 of the Criminal Procedure (Insanity) Act 1964, or either a magistrates' court or the Crown Court requires such opinion to help the court determine a question of intent or insanity.

3P.2    Rule 3.28 governs the procedure to be followed where a report is commissioned at the instigation of the court. It is not a substitute for the prompt commissioning of a report or reports by a party or party's representatives where expert medical opinion is material to that party's case. In particular, those representing a defendant may wish to obtain a medical report or reports wholly independently of the court. Nothing in these directions, therefore, should be read as discouraging a party from commissioning a medical report before the case comes before the court, where that party believes such a report to be material to an issue in the case and where it is possible promptly to commission it. However, where a party has commissioned such a report then if that report has not been received by the time the court gives directions for preparation for trial, and if the court agrees that it seems likely that the report will be material to what is in issue, then when giving directions for trial the court should include a timetable for the reception of that report and should give directions for progress to be reviewed at intervals, adopting the timetable set out in these directions with such adaptations as are needed.

3P.3    In assessing the likely materiality of an expert medical report to help the court assess a defendant's health and capacity at the time of the alleged offence or the time of trial, or both, the court will be assisted by the parties' representations; by the views expressed in any assessment that may already have been prepared; and by the views of practitioners in local criminal justice mental health services, whose assistance is available to the court under local liaison arrangements.

3P.4    Where the court requires the assistance of such a report then it is essential that there should be (i) absolute clarity about who is expected to do what, by when, and at whose expense; and (ii) judicial directions for progress with that report to be monitored and reviewed at prescribed intervals, following a timetable set by the court which culminates in the consideration of the report at a hearing. This is especially important where the report in question is a psychiatric assessment of the defendant for the preparation of which specific expertise may be required which is not readily available and because in some circumstances a second such assessment, by another medical practitioner, may be required.

*Timetable for the commissioning, preparation and consideration of a report or reports*

**3P.5**     CrimPR 3.28 requires the court to set a timetable appropriate to the case for the preparation and reception of a report. That timetable must not be in substitution for the usual timetable for preparation for trial but must instead be incorporated within the trial preparation timetable. The fact that a medical report is to be obtained, whether that is commissioned at a party's instigation or on the court's own initiative, is never a reason to postpone a preparation for trial or a plea and trial preparation hearing, or to decline to give the directions needed for preparation for trial. It follows that a trial date must be set and other directions given in the usual way.

**3P.6**     In setting the timetable for obtaining a report or reports the court will take account of such representations and other information that it receives, including information about the anticipated availability and workload of medical practitioners with the appropriate expertise. However, the timetable ought not be a protracted one. It is essential to keep in mind the importance of maintaining progress: in recognition of the defendant's rights and with respect for the interests of victims and witnesses, as required by CrimPR Part 1 (the overriding objective). In a magistrates' court account must be taken, too, of section 11 of the Powers of Criminal Courts (Sentencing) Act 2000, which limits the duration of each remand pending the preparation of a report to 3 weeks, where the defendant is to be in custody, and to 4 weeks if the defendant is to be on bail.

**3P.7**     Subject, therefore, to contrary judicial direction the timetable set by the court should require:

(a)   the convening of a further pre-trial case management hearing to consider the report and its implications for the conduct of the proceedings no more than 6 – 8 weeks after the court makes its request in a magistrates' court, and no more than 10 – 12 weeks after the request in the Crown Court (at the end of Stage 2 of the directions for pre-trial preparation in the Crown Court);

(b)   the prompt identification of an appropriate medical practitioner or practitioners, if not already identified by the court, and the despatch of a commission or commissions accordingly, within 2 business days of the court's decision to request a report;

(c)   acknowledgement of a commission by its recipient, and acceptance or rejection of that commission, within 5 business days of its receipt;

(d)   enquiries by court staff to confirm that the commission has been received, and to ascertain the action being taken in response, in the event that no acknowledgement is received within 10 business days of its despatch;

(e)   delivery of the report within 5 weeks of the despatch of the commission;

(f)   enquiries into progress by court staff in the event that no report is received within 5 weeks of the despatch of the commission.

**3P.8**     The further pre-trial case management hearing that is convened for the court to consider the report should not be adjourned before it takes place save in exceptional circumstances and then only by explicit judicial direction the reasons for which must be recorded. If by the time of that hearing the report is available, as usually should be the case, then at that hearing the court can be expected to determine the issue in respect of which the report was commissioned and give further directions accordingly. If by that time, exceptionally, the report is not available then the court should take the opportunity provided by that hearing to enquire into the reasons, give such directions as are appropriate, and if necessary adjourn the hearing to a fixed date for further consideration then. Where it is known in advance of that hearing that the report will not be available in time, the hearing may be conducted by live link or telephone: subject, in the defendant's case, to the same considerations as are identified at paragraph 3N.6 of these Practice Directions. However, it rarely will be appropriate to dispense altogether with that hearing, or to make enquiries and give further directions without any hearing at all, in view of the arrangements for monitoring and review that the court already will have directed and which, by definition therefore, thus far will have failed to secure the report's timely delivery.

**3P.9**     Where a requirement of the timetable set by the court is not met, or where on enquiry by court staff it appears that the timetable is unlikely to be met, and in any instance in which a medical practitioner who accepts a commission asks for more time, then court staff should not themselves adjust the timetable or accede to such a request but instead should seek directions from an appropriate judicial authority. Subject to local judicial direction, that will be, in the Crown Court, the judge assigned to the case or the resident judge and, in a magistrates' court, a District Judge (Magistrates' Courts) or justice of the peace assigned to the case, or the Justices' Clerk, an assistant clerk or other senior legal adviser. Even if the timetable is adjusted in consequence:

(a)   the further pre-trial case management hearing convened to consider the report rarely should be adjourned before it takes place: see paragraph 3O.13 [*sic*: 3P.8] above;

(b) directions should be given for court staff henceforth to make regular enquiries into progress, at prescribed intervals of not more than 2 weeks, and to report the outcome to an appropriate judicial authority who will decide what further directions, if any, to give.

3P.10 Any adjournment of a hearing convened to consider the report should be to a specific date: the hearing should not be adjourned generally, or to a date to be set in due course. The adjournment of such a hearing should not be for more than a further 6 – 8 weeks save in the most exceptional circumstances; and no more than one adjournment of the hearing should be allowed without obtaining written or oral representations from the commissioned medical practitioner explaining the reasons for the delay.

*Commissioning a report*

3P.11 Guidance entitled 'Good practice guidance: commissioning, administering and producing psychiatric reports for sentencing' prepared for and published by the Ministry of Justice and HM Courts and Tribunals Service in September 2010 contains material that will assist court staff and those who are asked to prepare such reports:

http://www.ohrn.nhs.uk/resource/policy/GoodPracticeGuidePsychReports.pdf

The guidance includes standard forms of letters of instruction and other documents.

3P.12 CrimPR 3.28 requires the commissioner of a report to explain why the court seeks the report and to include relevant information about the circumstances. The HMCTS Guidance contains forms for judicial use in the instruction of court staff, and guidance to court staff on the preparation of letters of instruction, where a report is required for sentencing purposes. Those forms and that guidance can be adapted for use where the court requires a report on the defendant's fitness to participate, in the Crown Court, or in a magistrates' court requires a report for the purposes of section 37(3) of the Mental Health Act 1983.

3P.13 The commission should invite a practitioner who is unable to accept it promptly to nominate a suitably qualified substitute, if possible, and to transfer the commission to that person, reporting the transfer when acknowledging the court officer's letter. It is entirely appropriate for the commission to draw the recipient's attention to CrimPR 1.2 (the duty of the participants in a criminal case) and to CrimPR 19.2(1)(b) (the obligation of an expert witness to comply with directions made by a court and at once to inform the court of any significant failure, by the expert or another, to take any step required by such a direction).

3P.14 Where the relevant legislation requires a second psychiatric assessment by a second medical practitioner, and where no commission already has been addressed to a second such practitioner, the commission may invite the person to whom it is addressed to nominate a suitably qualified second person and to pass a copy of the commission to that person forthwith.

*Funding arrangements*

3P.15 Where a medical report has been, or is to be, commissioned by a party then that party is responsible for arranging payment of the fees incurred, even though the report is intended for the court's use. That must be made clear in that party's commission.

3P.16 Where a medical report is requested by the court and commissioned by a party or by court staff at the court's direction then the commission must include (i) confirmation that the fees will be paid by HMCTS, (ii) details of how, and to whom, to submit an invoice or claim for fees, and (iii) notice of the prescribed rates of fees and of any legislative or other criteria applicable to the calculation of the fees that may be paid.

*Remand in custody*

3P.17 Where the defendant who is to be examined will be remanded in custody then notice that directions have been given for a medical report or reports to be prepared must be included in the information given to the defendant's custodian, to ensure that the preparation of the report or reports can be facilitated. This is especially important where bail is withheld on the ground that it would be otherwise impracticable to complete the required report, and in particular where that is the only ground for withholding bail.

**CPD I General matters 3Q: Failure to Comply with Requirement to Give Name, Date of Birth And**   **CPD.3Q**
**Nationality**

3Q.1 Section 86A of the Courts Act 2003 requires a magistrates' court and the Crown Court to require a defendant to provide his or her name, date of birth and nationality in the circumstances and at the times set out in CrimPR 3.13(5) and 3.27(5). Section 86A(3) of the Act makes it an offence for the defendant without reasonable excuse to fail to comply with such a requirement, whether by providing false or incomplete information or by providing no information. A person guilty of such an offence is liable on summary conviction to imprisonment for a term not exceeding 6 months, or to a fine, or both. It follows that a prosecution for failure to comply with a section 86A requirement may be brought by any of the procedures for which CrimPR Part 7 provides (Starting a prosecution in a magistrates' court) in the same way as any other allegation of a summary offence.

3Q.2    It does not follow, however, that every such allegation first must be reported to the police. Where the defendant's conduct evinces guilt, especially if the defendant refuses altogether to give the information required, such conduct undermines the administration of justice and the authority of the court. In principle, it should be dealt with at once. Section 86A(6) of the Act provides that, 'The criminal court before which a person is required to provide his or her name, date of birth and nationality may deal with any suspected offence under subsection (3) at the same time as dealing with the offence for which the person was already before the court'. In such a case, therefore, a magistrates' court may invite the prosecutor to institute proceedings orally, there and then, pursuant to section 1 of the Magistrates' Courts Act 1980 and CrimPR Part 7, and may there and then try the alleged offence in accordance with the rules in CrimPR Part 24 (Trial and sentence in a magistrates' court). A defendant should be allowed a reasonable opportunity to reflect and to take legal advice, from a duty solicitor if the defendant has no legal representative in the prosecution for the main offence. After that, unless the defendant then pleads guilty the prosecutor must call such evidence as may be convenient and sufficient, in the prosecutor's view, formally to prove the allegation; and the defendant may present evidence, for example of reasonable excuse, and may make representations in accordance with those rules.

3Q.3    Given that the Act expressly contemplates a prompt determination by the court before which there occurs an ostensible failure to comply with a section 86A requirement, rarely will it be necessary or appropriate to adjourn the trial of that allegation to a differently constituted court unless there emerges such a dispute of fact about what has occurred in the sight and hearing of the court as to disqualify the first bench from determining that dispute with perceived impartiality. In that rare event the trial of the allegation must be heard, the same day, by a different bench.[74] In any other event the constitution before whom the alleged offence under section 86A(3) has occurred usually should try the allegation, usually the same day.

3Q.4    If in the circumstances contemplated in the preceding paragraph a different bench convicts the defendant of the section 86A(3) offence, and if the defendant is convicted by the first bench of the offence for which the defendant was already before the court, then the court which passes sentence for that main offence should pass sentence also under section 86A(3). However, an offence under section 86A(3) is one that stands apart from the proceedings in the course of which it was committed the seriousness of which can be reflected by an appropriate and, generally, separate penalty.

3Q.5    Whether an alleged contravention of a section 86A requirement is dealt with the same day or later, after investigation by the police, no member of the court before whom the alleged contravention occurs should participate in the proceedings as the complainant or as a witness. Nor will it be appropriate to invite the defendant's representative, if any, to give evidence of what that representative may have witnessed in the court room. It is unexceptionable for court staff, including a legal adviser in a magistrates' court, to be asked to give evidence of what has taken place.

3Q.6    The offence contrary to section 86A(3) of the 2003 Act is one to which the time limit imposed by section 127 of the Magistrates' Courts Act 1980 applies, namely that a magistrates' court may not try an information unless that information was laid within 6 months from the time when the offence was committed. Where the court does not adopt the procedure described in paragraphs 3Q.2 and 3Q.3 above the alleged offence must be reported promptly to allow it to be investigated and, if appropriate, prosecuted in time.

**CPD.3R**    **CPD I General matters 3R: Hearing to Inform the Court of Sensitive Material**

3R.1    CrimPR 3.29 (Hearing to inform the court of sensitive material) governs the procedure that must be followed where a prosecutor has, or is aware of, sensitive material to which the prosecutor does not think the obligation to disclose applies but of the existence of which the prosecutor thinks it necessary to inform the court in order to mitigate the risks listed in that rule.

---

[74] The risk is that a constitution which witnesses a defendant's refusal to give the information required will not be perceived to adjudicate impartially on a contention that, as a matter of fact, and against the prosecution evidence, the defendant was not asked for the information or did not refuse to give it. If that were the defence then the court would, of course, offer the defendant a renewed opportunity to comply with the requirement and only if that further opportunity were declined would the prosecution for the section 86A(3) offence be adjourned to a different bench. Such circumstances may be expected to arise only wholly exceptionally.

**3R.2**    Examples of such material were given by the Court of Appeal in *R* v *Ali* [2019] EWCA Crim 1527. Examples include information about the activities of a defendant or witness, or about a person to whom the evidence in the case refers, or information to the effect that the prosecution evidence omits matters irrelevant to the trial, derived from observations, for example, which is of sensitivity in some other respect. These are, however, only examples and other material may come within the scope of the rule.

**3R.3**    In the Crown Court a hearing to which rule 3.29 applies must be recorded: CrimPR 5.5 (Recording and transcription of proceedings in the Crown Court). It is very likely that the hearing will be conducted in private (see CrimPR 3.29(4)) and very likely that it will take place in a private room rather than in the courtroom. The recording therefore should be made using a suitable and suitably secure device, and it should be stored securely. In some circumstances that may require arrangements for the storage of the recording to be dealt with in accordance with CrimPR 3.29(4)(c)(ii) (storage by an appropriate person other than the court officer). Such storage arrangements are likely also to apply to any written material provided to the court under CrimPR 3.29(3)(c).

CRIMINAL PROCEDURE RULES    PART 4    SERVICE OF DOCUMENTS

**When this Part applies**        R4.1

**4.1**    (1)   The rules in this Part apply—
> (a)   to the service of every document in a case to which these Rules apply; and
> (b)   for the purposes of section 12 of the Road Traffic Offenders Act 1988[1], to the service of a requirement to which that section applies.

     (2)   The rules apply subject to any special rules in other legislation (including other Parts of these Rules) or in the Practice Direction.

     (3)   In this Part, 'the relevant court office' means—
> (a)   in relation to a case in a magistrates' court or in the Crown Court, an office—
>> (i)   at which that court's business is administered, and
>> (ii)   the address or electronic address of which is advertised by the Lord Chancellor at the date of service as that at which that type of document must be served;
>
> (b)   in relation to an application to a High Court judge for permission to serve a draft indictment—
>> (i)   in London, the Queen's Bench Listing Office, Royal Courts of Justice, Strand, London WC2A 2LL,
>> (ii)   elsewhere, the office at which court staff administer the business of any court then constituted of a High Court judge, and
>> (iii)   in either case, the electronic address which is advertised by the Lord Chancellor at the date of service as that at which such an application must be served;
>
> (c)   in relation to an extradition appeal case in the High Court—
>> (i)   the Administrative Court Office, Royal Courts of Justice, Strand, London WC2A 2LL, and
>> (ii)   the electronic address which is advertised by the Lord Chancellor at the date of service as that at which that type of document must be served; and
>
> (d)   where the recipient is the Registrar of Criminal Appeals—
>> (i)   the Criminal Appeal Office, Royal Courts of Justice, Strand, London WC2A 2LL, and
>> (ii)   the electronic address which is advertised by the Lord Chancellor at the date of service as that at which that type of document must be served.

*[Note. Section 12 of the Road Traffic Offenders Act 1988 allows the court to accept the documents to which it refers as evidence of a driver's identity where a requirement to state that identity has been served under section 172 of the Road Traffic Act 1988[2] or under section 112 of the Road Traffic Regulation Act 1984[3].]*

**Methods of service**        R4.2

**4.2**    (1)   A document may be served by any of the methods described in rules 4.3 to 4.6 (subject to rules 4.7 and 4.10), or in rule 4.8.

     (2)   Where a document may be served by electronic means under rule 4.6, the general rule is that the person serving it must use that method.

---

[1] 1988 c. 53; section 12 was amended by article 3 of, and paragraphs 29 and 30 of the Schedule to, S.I. 2004/2035.
[2] 1988 c. 52; section 172 was substituted by section 21 of the Road Traffic Act 1991 (c. 40) and amended by paragraph 24 of Schedule 3 to the Vehicle Excise and Registration Act 1994 (c. 22) and the Statute Law (Repeals) Act 2004 (c. 14).
[3] 1984 c. 27; section 112 was amended by section 102 of, and Schedule 17 to, the Local Government Act 1985 (c. 51) and section 4 of, and paragraph 6 of the Schedule to, the Parking Act 1989 (c. 16).

**R4.3**    **Service by handing over a document**

4.3    (1)  A document may be served on—
- (a)  an individual by handing it to him or her;
- (b)  a corporation by handing it to a person holding a senior position in that corporation;
- (c)  an individual or corporation who is legally represented in the case by handing it to that legal representative;
- (d)  the prosecution by handing it to the prosecutor or to the prosecution representative; and
- (e)  the court officer or the Registrar of Criminal Appeals by handing it to a court officer with authority to accept it at the relevant court office.

(2)  If an individual is under 18, a copy of a document served under paragraph (1)(a) must be handed to his or her parent, or another appropriate adult, unless no such person is readily available.

(3)  Unless the court otherwise directs, for the purposes of paragraph (1)(c) or (d) (service by handing a document to a party's representative) 'representative' includes an advocate appearing for that party at a hearing.

*[Note. Some legislation treats a body that is not a corporation as if it were one for the purposes of rules about service of documents. See for example section 143 of the Adoption and Children Act 2002[4].]*

**R4.4**    **Service by leaving or posting a document**

4.4    (1)  A document may be served by addressing it to the person to be served and leaving it at the appropriate address for service under this rule, or by sending it to that address by first class post or by the equivalent of first class post.

(2)  The address for service under this rule on—
- (a)  an individual is an address where it is reasonably believed that he or she will receive it;
- (b)  a corporation is its principal office, and if there is no readily identifiable principal office then any place where it carries on its activities or business;
- (c)  an individual or corporation who is legally represented in the case is that legal representative's office;
- (d)  the prosecution is the prosecutor's office;
- (e)  the court officer or the Registrar of Criminal Appeals is the relevant court office.

*[Note. In addition to service in England and Wales for which these rules provide, service outside England and Wales may be allowed under other legislation. See—*

- *(a)  section 39 of the Criminal Law Act 1977[5] (service of summons, etc. in Scotland and Northern Ireland);*
- *(b)  section 1139(4) of the Companies Act 2006[6] (service of copy summons, etc. on company's registered office in Scotland and Northern Ireland);*
- *(c)  sections 3, 4, 4A and 4B of the Crime (International Co-operation) Act 2003[7] (service of summons, etc. outside the United Kingdom) and rules 49.1 and 49.2; and*
- *(d)  section 1139(2) of the Companies Act 2006 (service on overseas company).]*

**R4.5**    **Service by document exchange**

4.5    (1)  This rule applies where—
- (a)  the person to be served—
  - (i)   has given a document exchange (DX) box number, and
  - (ii)  has not refused to accept service by DX; or
- (b)  the person to be served is legally represented in the case and the legal representative has given a DX box number.

(2)  A document may be served by—
- (a)  addressing it to that person or legal representative, as appropriate, at that DX box number; and
- (b)  leaving it at—
  - (i)   the document exchange at which the addressee has that DX box number, or
  - (ii)  a document exchange at which the person serving it has a DX box number.

(3)  Where the person to be served under this rule is the court officer, the address for service is the relevant court office.

---

[4]  2002 c. 38.

[5]  1977 c. 45; sub-section (1) was substituted by section 331 of, and paragraph 6 of Schedule 36 to, the Criminal Justice Act 2003 (c. 44). Sub-section (3) was amended by section 83 of, and paragraph 79 of Schedule 7 to, the Criminal Justice (Scotland) Act 1980 (c. 62).

[6]  2006 c. 46.

[7]  2003 c. 32; sections 4A and 4B were inserted by section 331 of, and paragraph 16 of Schedule 36 to, the Criminal Justice Act 2003 (c. 44).

### Service by electronic means

4.6  (1)  This rule applies where—

    (a)  the person to be served—

      (i)   has given an electronic address and has not refused to accept service at that address, or

      (ii)  is given access to an electronic address at which a document may be deposited and has not refused to accept service by the deposit of a document at that address; or

    (b)  the person to be served is legally represented in the case and the legal representative—

      (i)   has given an electronic address, or

      (ii)  is given access to an electronic address at which a document may be deposited.

   (2)  A document may be served—

    (a)  by sending it by electronic means to the address which the recipient has given; or

    (b)  by depositing it at an address to which the recipient has been given access and—

      (i)   in every case, making it possible for the recipient to read the document, or view or listen to its content, as the case may be,

      (ii)  unless the court otherwise directs, making it possible for the recipient to make and keep an electronic copy of the document, and

      (iii) notifying the recipient of the deposit of the document (which notice may be given by electronic means).

   (3)  Where the person to be served under this rule is the court officer, the address for service is the relevant court office.

   (4)  Where a document is served under this rule the person serving it need not provide a paper copy as well.

### Documents that must be served by specified methods

4.7  (1)  An application or written statement, and notice, under rule 48.9 alleging contempt of court may be served—

    (a)  on an individual, only under rule 4.3(1)(a) (by handing it to him or her); and

    (b)  on a corporation, only under rule 4.3(1)(b) (by handing it to a person holding a senior position in that corporation).

   (2)  For the purposes of section 12 of the Road Traffic Offenders Act 1988[8], a notice of a requirement under section 172 of the Road Traffic Act 1988[9] or under section 112 of the Road Traffic Regulation Act 1984[10] to identify the driver of a vehicle may be served—

    (a)  on an individual, only by post under rule 4.4(1) and (2)(a); and

    (b)  on a corporation, only by post under rule 4.4(1) and (2)(b).

### Service by person in custody

4.8  (1)  A person in custody may serve a document by handing it to the custodian addressed to the person to be served.

   (2)  The custodian must—

    (a)  endorse it with the time and date of receipt;

    (b)  record its receipt; and

    (c)  forward it promptly to the addressee.

### Service by another method

4.9  (1)  The court may allow service of a document by a method—

    (a)  other than those described in rules 4.3 to 4.6 and in rule 4.8; and

    (b)  other than one specified by rule 4.7, where that rule applies.

   (2)  An order allowing service by another method must specify—

    (a)  the method to be used; and

    (b)  the date on which the document will be served.

### Documents that may not be served on a legal representative

4.10  Unless the court otherwise directs, service on a party's legal representative of any of the following documents is not service of that document on that party—

    (a)  a summons, requisition, single justice procedure notice or witness summons;

    (b)  notice of an order under section 25 of the Road Traffic Offenders Act 1988[11];

---

[8]  1988 c. 53; section 12 was amended by article 3 of, and paragraphs 29 and 30 of the Schedule to, S.I. 2004/2035.

[9]  1988 c. 52; section 172 was substituted by section 21 of the Road Traffic Act 1991 (c. 40) and amended by paragraph 24 of Schedule 3 to the Vehicle Excise and Registration Act 1994 (c. 22) and the Statute Law (Repeals) Act 2004 (c. 14).

[10]  1984 c. 27; section 112 was amended by section 102 of, and Schedule 17 to, the Local Government Act 1985 (c. 51) and section 4 of, and paragraph 6 of the Schedule to, the Parking Act 1989 (c. 16).

[11]  1988 c. 53; section 25 was amended by section 90 of, and paragraphs 140 and 142 of Schedule 13 to, the Access to Justice Act 1999 (c. 22), section 165 of, and paragraph 118 of Schedule 9 to, the Powers of Criminal Courts (Sentencing) Act 2000 (c. 6) and section 109 of, and paragraph 311 of Schedule 8 to, the Courts Act 2003 (c. 39).

(c) a notice of registration under section 71(6) of that Act[12],

(d) notice of a hearing to review the postponement of the issue of a warrant of detention or imprisonment under section 77(6) of the Magistrates' Courts Act 1980[13],

(e) notice under section 86 of that Act[14] of a revised date to attend a means inquiry;

(f) any notice or document served under Part 14 (Bail and custody time limits);

(g) notice under rule 24.15(a) of when and where an adjourned hearing will resume;

(h) notice under rule 28.5(3) of an application to vary or discharge a compensation order;

(i) notice under rule 28.10(2)(c) of the location of the sentencing or enforcing court;

(j) a collection order, or notice requiring payment, served under rule 30.2(a); or

(k) an application or written statement, and notice, under rule 48.9 alleging contempt of court.

### R4.11   Date of service

4.11 (1) A document served under rule 4.3 or rule 4.8 is served on the day it is handed over.

(2) Unless something different is shown, a document served on a person by any other method is served—

(a) in the case of a document left at an address, on the next business day after the day on which it was left;

(b) in the case of a document sent by first class post or by the equivalent of first class post, on the second business day after the day on which it was posted or despatched;

(c) in the case of a document served by document exchange, on the second business day after the day on which it was left at a document exchange allowed by rule 4.5;

(d) in the case of a document served by electronic means —

(i) on the day on which it is sent under rule 4.6(2)(a), if that day is a business day and if it is sent by no later than 2.30pm that day (or 4.30pm that day, in an extradition appeal case in the High Court or 5pm that day if it is an application for permission to refer a sentencing case to which Part 41 (Reference to the Court of Appeal of point of law or unduly lenient sentencing) applies),

(ii) on the day on which notice of its deposit is given under rule 4.6(2)(b), if that day is a business day and if that notice is given by no later than 2.30pm that day (or 4.30pm that day, in an extradition appeal case in the High Court, or 5pm that day if it is an application for permission to refer a sentencing case to which Part 41 (Reference to the Court of Appeal of point of law or unduly lenient sentencing) applies), or

(iii) otherwise, on the next business day after it was sent or such notice was given; and

(e) in any case, on the day on which the addressee responds to it, if that is earlier.

(3) Unless something different is shown, a document produced by a computer system for dispatch by post is to be taken as having been sent by first class post, or by the equivalent of first class post, to the addressee on the business day after the day on which it was produced.

(4) Where a document is served on or by the court officer or the Registrar of Criminal Appeals, 'business day' does not include a day on which the relevant court office is closed.

### R4.12   Proof of service

4.12 The person who serves a document may prove that by signing a certificate explaining how and when it was served.

### R4.13   Court's power to give directions about service

4.13 (1) The court may specify the time as well as the date by which a document must be—

(a) served under rule 4.3 (Service by handing over a document) or rule 4.8 (Service by person in custody); or

(b) sent or deposited by electronic means, if it is served under rule 4.6.

(2) The court may treat a document as served if the addressee responds to it even if it was not served in accordance with the rules in this Part.

CRIMINAL PROCEDURE RULES    PART 5    FORMS AND COURT RECORDS

### Forms

### R5.1   Applications, etc. by forms or electronic means

5.1 (1) This rule applies where a rule, a practice direction or the court requires a person to—

(a) make an application or give a notice;

---

[12] 1988 c. 53; section 71(6) was amended by section 109 of, and paragraph 317 of Schedule 8 to, the Courts Act 2003 (c. 39).

[13] 1980 c. 43; section 77(6) was substituted by section 109 of, and paragraph 218 of Schedule 8 to, the Courts Act 2003 (c. 39).

[14] 1980 c. 43; section 86 was amended by section 51(2) of the Criminal Justice Act 1982 (c. 48) and section 97(3) of the Access to Justice Act 1999 (c. 22).

     (b) supply information for the purposes of case management by the court; or

     (c) supply information needed for other purposes by the court.

  (2) Unless the court otherwise directs, such a person must—

     (a) use such electronic arrangements as the court officer may make for that purpose, in accordance with those arrangements; or

     (b) if no such arrangements have been made, use the appropriate form set out in the Practice Direction or the Criminal Costs Practice Direction, in accordance with those Directions.

## Forms in Welsh                                                          R5.2

**5.2** (1) Any Welsh language form set out in the Practice Direction, or in the Criminal Costs Practice Direction, is for use in connection with proceedings in courts in Wales.

  (2) Both a Welsh form and an English form may be contained in the same document.

  (3) Where only a Welsh form, or only the corresponding English form, is served—

     (a) the following words in Welsh and English must be added:

"Darperir y ddogfen hon yn Gymraeg / Saesneg os bydd arnoch ei heisiau. Dylech wneud cais yn ddi-oed i (swyddog y llys) (rhodder yma'r cyfeiriad)

This document will be provided in Welsh / English if you require it. You should apply immediately to (the court officer) (address)"; and

     (b) the court officer, or the person who served the form, must, on request, supply the corresponding form in the other language to the person served.

## Signature of forms                                                      R5.3

**5.3** (1) This rule applies where a form provides for its signature.

  (2) Unless other legislation otherwise requires, or the court otherwise directs, signature may be by any written or electronic authentication of the form by, or with the authority of, the signatory.

*[Note. Section 7 of the Electronic Communications Act 2000[1] provides for the use of an electronic signature in an electronic communication.]*

## Court records
## Duty to make records                                                    R5.4

**5.4** (1) For each case, as appropriate, the court officer must record, by such means as the Lord Chancellor directs—

     (a) each charge or indictment against the defendant;

     (b) the defendant's plea to each charge or count;

     (c) each acquittal, conviction, sentence, determination, direction or order;

     (d) each decision about bail;

     (e) the power exercised where the court commits or adjourns the case to another court—

       (i) for sentence, or

       (ii) for the defendant to be dealt with for breach of a community order, a deferred sentence, a conditional discharge, or a suspended sentence of imprisonment, imposed by that other court;

     (f) the court's reasons for a decision, where legislation requires those reasons to be recorded;

     (g) any appeal;

     (h) each party's presence or absence at each hearing;

     (i) any consent that legislation requires before the court can proceed with the case, or proceed to a decision;

     (j) in a magistrates' court—

       (i) any indication of sentence given by the court, and

       (ii) the registration of a fixed penalty notice for enforcement as a fine, and any related endorsement on a driving record;

       (iii) the power exercised where the court sends the defendant to the Crown Court for trial for an offence,

       (iv) any statement made by the court under section 70(5) of the Proceeds of Crime Act 200[2] (statement that if the court were not committing the defendant for consideration of a confiscation order then it would have committed the defendant to the Crown Court for sentence for an offence under section 14, 16 or 16A of the Sentencing Act 2020[3]),

[1] 2000 c. 7.

[2] 2002 c. 29; section 70 was amended by section 41 of, and paragraph 75 of Schedule 3 to, the Criminal Justice Act 2003 (c. 44), section 410 of, and paragraphs 181 and 195 of Schedule 24 to, the Sentencing Act 2020 (c. 17) and section 46 of, and paragraph 19 of Schedule 13 to, the Counter-Terrorism and Sentencing Act 2021 (c. 11).

[3] 2020 c. 17; section 16A was inserted by section 46 of, and paragraph 26 of Schedule 13 to, the Counter-Terrorism and Sentencing Act 2021 (c. 11).

        (v)   any opinion given by the court under section 18(4) or 19(3) of the Sentencing Act 2020 (opinion that if the court were not committing the defendant for sentence under section 18 or 19 of the 2020 Act then it could, or would be required to, commit the defendant to the Crown Court for sentence for the offence under one of sections 14, 15, 16, 16A or 17 of that Act), and

        (vi)  the exercise of a power to which paragraph (3) applies (judges exercising powers of District Judges (Magistrates' Courts));

    (k)   in the Crown Court, any request for assistance or other communication about the case received from a juror;

    (l)   the identity of—

        (i)   the prosecutor,

        (ii)  the defendant,

        (iii) any other applicant to whom these Rules apply,

        (iv) any interpreter or intermediary,

        (v)   the parties' legal representatives, if any, and

        (vi)  the judge, magistrate or magistrates, justices' legal adviser or other person who made each recorded decision;

    (m)  where a defendant is entitled to attend a hearing, any agreement by the defendant to waive that right; and

    (n)   where interpretation is required for a defendant, any agreement by that defendant to do without the written translation of a document.

  (2)  Such records must include—

    (a)   each party's and representative's address, including any electronic address and telephone number available;

    (b)   the defendant's date of birth, if available; and

    (c)   the date of each event and decision recorded.

  (3)  Where a judge acting under section 66 of the Courts Act 2003[4] (Judges having powers of District Judges (Magistrates' Courts)) exercises the power of a magistrates' court, the court officer then assisting that judge must—

    (a)   record, by such means as the Lord Chancellor directs, the magistrates' court power exercised by that judge; and

    (b)   as soon as practicable arrange the transmission to the magistrates' court of—

        (i)   that record, and

        (ii)  a record of the circumstances in which that power was exercised.

*[Note. For the duty to keep court records, see sections 5 and 8 of the Public Records Act 1958[5].*

*Requirements to record the court's reasons for its decision are contained in: section 5 of the Bail Act 1976[6]; section 47(1) of the Road Traffic Offenders Act 1988[7]; sections 20, 33A and 33BB of the Youth Justice and Criminal Evidence Act 1999[8]; section 174 of the Criminal Justice Act 2003[9]; and rule 6.8.*

*The prosecution of some offences requires the consent of a specified authority. Requirements for the defendant's consent to proceedings in his or her absence are contained in sections 23 and 128 of the Magistrates' Courts Act 1980[10].*

---

[4]  2003 c. 39; section 66 was amended by section 32 of, and paragraph 6 of Schedule 2 to, the Armed Forces Act 2011 (c. 18) and section 61 of, and paragraph 90 of Schedule 10 and paragraph 4 of Schedule 14 to, the Crime and Courts Act 2013 (c. 22).

[5]  1958 c. 51; section 5 was amended by sections 67 and 86 of, and paragraph 2 of Schedule 5 to, the Freedom of Information Act 2000 (c. 36); and section 8 was amended by sections 27 and 35 of, and Schedule 2 to, the Administration of Justice Act 1969 (c. 58), section 1 of, and paragraph 19 of Schedule 2 to, the Administration of Justice Act 1970 (c. 31), section 56 of, and Schedule 11 to, the Courts Act 1971 (c. 23), section 152 of, and Schedule 7 to, the Senior Courts Act 1981 (c. 54) and sections 56 and 59 of, and Schedule 11 to, the Constitutional Reform Act 2005 (c. 4).

[6]  1976 c. 63; section 5 was amended by section 65 of, and Schedule 12 to, the Criminal Law Act 1977 (c. 45), section 60 of the Criminal Justice Act 1982 (c. 48), paragraph 1 of Schedule 3 to the Criminal Justice and Public Order Act 1994 (c. 33), paragraph 53 of Schedule 9 to the Powers of Criminal Courts (Sentencing) Act 2000 (c. 6), section 129(1) of the Criminal Justice and Police Act 2001 (c. 16), paragraph 182 of Schedule 8 to the Courts Act 2003 (c. 39), paragraph 48 of Schedule 3, paragraphs 1 and 2 of Schedule 36, and Parts 2, 4 and 12 of Schedule 37 to the Criminal Justice Act 2003 (c. 44) and section 208 of, and paragraphs 33 and 35 of Schedule 21 to, the Legal Services Act 2007 (c. 27).

[7]  1988 c. 53.

[8]  1999 c. 23; section 20(6) was amended by paragraph 384(a) of Schedule 8 to the Courts Act 2003 (c. 39); section 33A was inserted by section 47 of the Police and Justice Act 2006 (c. 48). Section 33BB is inserted by section 104(1) of the Coroners and Justice Act 2009, with effect from a date to be appointed.

[9]  2003 c. 44; section 174 was substituted by section 64 of the Legal Aid, Sentencing and Punishment of Offenders Act 2012 (c. 10).

[10]  1980 c. 43; section 23 was amended by section 125 of, and paragraph 25 of Schedule 18 to, the Courts and Legal Services Act 1990 (c. 41) and paragraphs 1 and 8 of Schedule 3 to the Criminal Justice Act 2003 (c. 44). Section 128 was amended by section 59 to, and paragraphs 2, 3 and 4 of Schedule 9 to, the Criminal Justice Act 1982 (c. 48), section 48 of the Police and

*In the circumstances for which it provides, section 20 of the Magistrates' Courts Act 1980[11] allows the court to give an indication of whether a custodial or non-custodial sentence is more likely in the event of a guilty plea at trial in that court.*

*See also rule 9.11(3). Rules 3.16 and 9.13 provide for sentencing indications in other circumstances in magistrates' courts.*

*Under section 66 of the Courts Act 2003, every holder of a judicial office listed in that section has the powers of a justice of the peace who is a District Judge (Magistrates' Courts) in relation to criminal causes and matters. The list includes Circuit judges and judges of the High Court and Court of Appeal.]*

**Recording and transcription of proceedings in the Crown Court**                           **R5.5**

5.5    (1)    Where someone may appeal to the Court of Appeal, the court officer must—
        (a)    arrange for the recording of the proceedings in the Crown Court, unless the court otherwise directs; and
        (b)    arrange for the transcription of such a recording if—
            (i)    the Registrar wants such a transcript, or
            (ii)    anyone else wants such a transcript (but that is subject to the restrictions in paragraph (2)).
    (2)    Unless the court otherwise directs, a person who transcribes a recording of proceedings under such arrangements—
        (a)    may only supply a transcript of a recording of a hearing in private to—
            (i)    the Registrar, or
            (ii)    an individual who was present at that hearing;
        (b)    if the recording of a hearing in public contains information to which reporting restrictions apply, may only supply a transcript containing that information to—
            (i)    the Registrar, or
            (ii)    a recipient to whom that supply will not contravene those reporting restrictions; but
        (c)    subject to paragraph (2)(a) and (b), must supply any person with any transcript for which that person asks—
            (i)    in accordance with the transcription arrangements made by the court officer, and
            (ii)    on payment by that person of any fee prescribed.
    (3)    A party who wants to hear a recording of proceedings must—
        (a)    apply—
            (i)    in writing to the Registrar, if an appeal notice has been served where Part 36 applies (Appeal to the Court of Appeal: general rules), or
            (ii)    orally or in writing to the Crown Court officer;
        (b)    explain the reasons for the request; and
        (c)    pay any fee prescribed.
    (4)    If the Crown Court or the Registrar so directs, the Crown Court officer must allow that party to hear a recording of—
        (a)    a hearing in public; and
        (b)    a hearing in private, if the applicant was present at that hearing.

*[Note. See also section 32 of the Criminal Appeal Act 1968[12].*

*For the circumstances in which reporting restrictions may apply, see the provisions listed in the note to rule 6.1. In summary, reporting restrictions prohibit the publication of the information to which they apply where that publication is likely to lead members of the public to acquire the information concerned.]*

**Custody of case materials**                                                             **R5.6**

5.6    Unless the court otherwise directs, in respect of each case the court officer may—
    (a)    keep any evidence, application, representation or other material served by the parties; or
    (b)    arrange for the whole or any part to be kept by some other appropriate person, subject to—
        (i)    any condition imposed by the court, and
        (ii)    the rules in Part 34 (Appeal to the Crown Court) and Part 36 (Appeal to the Court of Appeal: general rules) about keeping exhibits pending any appeal.

Criminal Evidence Act 1984 (c. 60), section 170(1) of, and paragraphs 65 and 69 of Schedule 15 to, the Criminal Justice Act 1988 (c. 33), section 125(3) of, and paragraph 25 of Schedule 18 to, the Courts and Legal Services Act 1990 (c. 41), sections 49, 52 and 80 of, and Schedule 5 to, the Criminal Procedure and Investigations Act 1996 (c. 25), paragraph 75 of Schedule 9 to the Powers of Criminal Courts (Sentencing) Act 2000 (c. 6) and paragraph 51 of Schedule 3 and Part 4 of Schedule 37 to the Criminal Justice Act 2003 (c. 44). It is modified by section 91(5) of the Legal Aid, Sentencing and Punishment of Offenders Act 2012 (c. 10).

[11] 1980 c. 43; section 20 was amended by section 100 of, and paragraph 25 of Schedule 11 to, the Criminal Justice Act 1991 (c. 53), paragraph 63 of Schedule 9 to the Powers of Criminal Courts (Sentencing) Act 2000 (c. 6) and paragraphs 1 and 6 of Schedule 3 to the Criminal Justice Act 2003 (c. 44).

[12] 1968 c. 19.

### Access to information in court records

**R5.7**  **The open justice principle**

5.7   (1)  Where rules 5.8, 5.9, 5.10 and 5.11 apply, as well as furthering the overriding objective in accordance with rules 1.2 and 1.3 the court officer and the court must have regard to the importance of—
   (a)  dealing with criminal cases in public;
   (b)  allowing a public hearing to be reported to the public; and
   (c)  the rights of a person affected by a direction or order made, or warrant issued, by the court to understand why that decision was made.

   (2)  In rules 5.10 and 5.11 this requirement is called 'the open justice principle'.

**R5.8**  **Request for information about a case**

5.8   (1)  This rule applies where anyone, including a member of the public or a reporter, requests information about a case.

   (2)  A person requesting information must—
   (a)  ask the court officer;
   (b)  specify the information requested; and
   (c)  pay any fee prescribed.

   (3)  The request—
   (a)  may be made orally or in writing, and need not explain why the information is requested, if this rule requires the court officer to supply that information; but
   (b)  must be in writing, unless the court otherwise permits, and must explain why the information is requested, if this rule does not so require.

   (4)  Subject to paragraph (5), the court officer must supply to the person making the request—
   (a)  the date of a hearing in public;
   (b)  each alleged offence and any plea entered;
   (c)  the court's decision—
      (i)  at a hearing in public,
      (ii)  about bail, or
      (iii)  about the committal, sending or transfer of the case to another court;
   (d)  whether the case is under appeal;
   (e)  the outcome of the case;
   (f)  the identity of—
      (i)  the prosecutor,
      (ii)  the defendant, including the defendant's date of birth,
      (iii)  the parties' representatives, including their addresses, and
      (iv)  the judge, magistrate or magistrates, or justices' legal adviser by whom a decision at a hearing in public was made;
   (g)  such other information about the case as is required by arrangements to which paragraph (6)(c) refers; and
   (h)  details of any reporting or access restriction ordered by the court.

   (5)  The court officer must not supply the information requested if—
   (a)  the supply of that information is prohibited by a reporting restriction;
   (b)  that information is—
      (i)  the date of a hearing in public of which a party has yet to be notified, or
      (ii)  a recording arranged under rule 5.5 (Recording and transcription of proceedings in the Crown Court), or a copy or transcript of such a recording;
   (c)  that information concerns a trial in which the verdict was more than 6 months ago; or
   (d)  that information is not readily available to the court officer (for example, because of the location or conditions of its storage).

   (6)  Where the court officer must supply the information requested the supply may be—
   (a)  by word of mouth;
   (b)  in writing, including by written certificate or extract from a court record; or
   (c)  by such other arrangements as the Lord Chancellor directs, including supply by electronic means.

   (7)  Where this rule does not require the court officer to supply the information requested then unless that information can be supplied under rule 5.9—
   (a)  the court officer must refer the request to the court; and
   (b)  rule 5.10 applies.

*[Note. See also rule 5.7 (The open justice principle).]*

**Request for information by a party or person directly affected by a case** R5.9

5.9 (1) This rule applies where a party, or a person directly affected by a direction or order made or warrant issued by the court, wants information about their case.

(2) Such a party or person must—

(a) ask the court officer;

(b) specify the information requested; and

(c) pay any fee prescribed.

(3) The request—

(a) may be made orally or in writing, and need not explain why the information is requested, if this rule requires the court officer to supply that information; but

(b) must be in writing, unless the court otherwise permits, and must explain why the information is requested, if this rule does not so require.

(4) Subject to paragraph (5), the court officer must supply to the party or person making the request—

(a) information about the terms of any direction or order made, or warrant issued, which was—

(i) served on, or addressed or directed to, that party or person, or

(ii) made on an application by that party or person; and

(b) information received from that party or person (which might be, for example, to establish what information the court holds, or in case of a loss of that information by the party or person making the request).

(5) The court officer must not supply the information requested if that information—

(a) concerns the grounds on which a direction or order was made, or a warrant issued, in the absence of the party or person making the request;

(b) is a recording arranged under rule 5.5 (Recording and transcription of proceedings in the Crown Court), or a copy or transcript of such a recording; or

(c) is not readily available to the court officer (for example, because of the location or conditions of its storage).

(6) Where the court officer must supply the information requested the supply may be, at the choice of the party or person making the request—

(a) by word of mouth;

(b) in writing, including by written certificate or extract from a court record; or

(c) by a copy of a document served by, or on, that party or person (but not of a document not so served).

(7) Where this rule does not require the court officer to supply the information requested—

(a) the court officer must refer the request to the court; and

(b) rule 5.10 applies.

*[Note. See also rule 5.7 (The open justice principle).]*

**Request for information determined by the court** R5.10

5.10 (1) This rule applies where the court officer refers to the court a request for information under rule 5.8 (Request for information about a case) or rule 5.9 (Request for information by a party or person directly affected by a case).

(2) The court officer must—

(a) serve the request on—

(i) the applicant for any direction, order or warrant that the request concerns which was made or issued in the absence of the party or person making the request, and

(ii) anyone else, and to such extent, as the court directs; and

(b) notify the party or person making the request of—

(i) the date of its service under this rule, and

(ii) the identity of each person served with it, if the court so directs.

(3) If a party or person served with the request objects to the supply of information requested the objector must—

(a) give notice of the objection not more than 20 business days after service of the request, or within any longer period allowed by the court;

(b) serve that notice on the court officer and on the party or person making the request; and

(c) if the objector wants a hearing, explain why one is needed.

(4) A notice of objection must explain—

    (a) whether the objection is to the supply of the whole of the information requested, or only to the supply of a specified part or specified parts;

    (b) whether the objection applies without limit of time, or only for a specified period (for example, until a date or event specified by the objector); and

    (c) the grounds of the objection.

(5) Where a notice of objection includes material that the objector thinks ought not be revealed to the party or person making the request, the objector must—

    (a) omit that material from the notice served on that party or person;

    (b) mark the material to show that it is only for the court; and

    (c) with that material include an explanation of why it has been withheld.

(6) The court must not determine the request, and information requested must not be supplied, until—

    (a) each party or person served with the request has had at least 20 business days, or any longer period allowed by the court, in which to object or make other representations; and

    (b) the court is satisfied that in all the circumstances every such party or person has had a reasonable opportunity to do so.

(7) The court may determine the request—

    (a) without a hearing; or

    (b) at a hearing, which—

        (i) may be in public or private, but

        (ii) must be in private, unless the court otherwise directs, where the request concerns a direction, order or warrant made or issued in the absence of the party or person making the request.

(8) Where a notice of objection includes material that the objector thinks ought not be revealed to the party or person making the request—

    (a) any hearing of the request may take place, wholly or in part, in the absence of the party or person making it; and

    (b) at any such hearing the general rule is that the court must consider, in the following sequence—

        (i) representations first by the party or person making the request and then by the objector, in the presence of both, and then

        (ii) further representations by the objector, in the absence of the party or person making the request

but the court may direct other arrangements for the hearing.

(9) In deciding whether to order the supply of the information requested the court must have regard to—

    (a) the open justice principle;

    (b) any reporting restriction;

    (c) rights and obligations under other legislation;

    (d) the importance of any public interest in the withholding of that information, or in its supply only in part or subject to conditions (which public interest might be, for example, in preventing injustice, protecting others' rights, protecting the confidentiality of a criminal investigation or protecting national security); and

    (e) the extent to which that information is otherwise available to the party or person making the request.

(10) Where the court orders the supply of the information requested the supply may be, at the court's direction—

    (a) by word of mouth;

    (b) in writing, including by written certificate or extract from a court record; or

    (c) by a copy of a document.

*[Note. See also rule 5.7 (The open justice principle).*

*The court's decision under this rule may be affected by—*

    *(a) a reporting restriction imposed by legislation or by the court (Part 6 lists the reporting restrictions that might apply);*

    *(b) Articles 6, 8 and 10 of the European Convention on Human Rights;*

    *(c) the Rehabilitation of Offenders Act 1974[13] (section 5 of the Act[14] lists sentences and rehabilitation periods);*

---

[13] 1974 c. 53.

(d) section 18 of the Criminal Procedure and Investigations Act 1996[15], which affects the supply of information about material, other than evidence, disclosed by the prosecutor;

(e) Part 3 of the Data Protection Act 2018[16] (sections 43(3) and 117 of which make exceptions for criminal proceedings from some other provisions of that Act); and

(f) sections 33, 34 and 35 of the Legal Aid, Sentencing and Punishment of Offenders Act 2012[17], which affect the supply of information about applications for legal aid.]

**Publication of information about court hearings**                                                       **R5.11**

5.11  (1)  Where a case is due to be heard in public, the court officer must—
       (a)  publish the information listed in paragraph (2)—
            (i)   if that information is available to the court officer, and
            (ii)  unless the publication of that information is prohibited by a reporting restriction; and
       (b)  publish that information for no longer than 5 business days—
            (i)   by notice displayed somewhere prominent in the vicinity of a court room in which the hearing is due to take place, and
            (ii)  by such arrangements as the Lord Chancellor directs, including arrangements for publication by electronic means, but only to the extent needed to comply with the open justice principle.
       (2)  The information that paragraph (1) requires the court officer to publish is—
            (a)  the date, time and place of the hearing;
            (b)  the identity of the defendant; and
            (c)  such other information as it may be practicable to publish concerning—
                 (i)    the type of hearing,
                 (ii)   the identity of the prosecutor,
                 (iii)  the identity of the court,
                 (iv)   the offence or offences alleged, and
                 (v)    whether any reporting or access restriction applies.
       (3)  Where a case is ready to be tried without a hearing under rule 24.9 (Single justice procedure: special rules), the court officer must—
            (a)  publish the information listed in paragraph (4) if—
                 (i)   the information is available to the court officer, and
                 (ii)  the publication of the information is not prohibited by a reporting restriction; and
            (b)  publish that information for no longer than 5 business days by such arrangements as the Lord Chancellor directs, including arrangements for publication by electronic means, but only to the extent needed to comply with the open justice principle.
       (4)  The information that paragraph (3) requires the court officer to publish is—
            (a)  the identity of the defendant;
            (b)  the identity of the prosecutor;
            (c)  the offence or offences alleged; and
            (d)  whether any reporting restriction applies.

[Note. See also rule 5.7 (The open justice principle).]

**Request for written certificate or extract for use in evidence, etc.**                                  **R5.12**

5.12  (1)  This rule applies where legislation—
       (a)  allows a certificate of conviction or acquittal, or an extract from records kept by the court officer, to be introduced in evidence in criminal proceedings; or
       (b)  requires such a certificate or extract to be supplied by the court officer to a specified person for a specified purpose.
       (2)  A person who wants such a certificate or extract must—
            (a)  apply in writing to the court officer;
            (b)  specify the certificate or extract required;
            (c)  explain under what legislation and for what purpose it is required; and
            (d)  pay any fee prescribed.
       (3)  If the application satisfies the requirements of that legislation, the court officer must supply the certificate or extract requested—

[14]  1974 c. 53; section 5 was amended by section 15 of, and paragraphs 77 and 78 of Schedule 4 to, the Constitutional Reform Act 2005 (c. 4) and by sections 126 and 139 of, and paragraph 2 of Schedule 21 to, the Legal Aid, Sentencing and Punishment of Offenders Act 2012 (c. 10).
[15]  1996 c. 25.
[16]  2018 c. 12.
[17]  2012 c. 10.

(a) to a party; and

(b) unless the court otherwise directs, to any other applicant.

*[Note. Under sections 73 to 75 of the Police and Criminal Evidence Act 1984[18], a certificate of conviction or acquittal, and certain other details from records to which this Part applies, may be admitted in evidence in criminal proceedings.*

*Under section 115 of the Crime and Disorder Act 1998[19], information from records to which this Part applies may be obtained by specified authorities for the purposes of that Act.*

*Under section 92 of the Sexual Offences Act 2003[18], a certificate which records a conviction for an offence and a statement by the convicting court that that offence is listed in Schedule 3 to the Act is evidence of those facts for certain purposes of that Act.*

*A certificate of conviction or acquittal, and certain other information, required for other purposes, may be obtained from the Secretary of State under sections 112, 113A and 113B of the Police Act 1997[19].*

*This rule applies where certificates or extracts from court records are required for use in evidence or for some other purpose specified in legislation. Where this rule does not apply, information about a case may be obtained under rule 5.8.]*

CRIMINAL PRACTICE DIRECTIONS    PART 5    FORMS AND COURT RECORDS

**CPD.5A**    **CPD I General matters 5A: Forms**

5A.1    The forms at Annex D to the Consolidated Criminal Practice Direction of 8th July 2002 [2002] 1 WLR 2870; [2002] 2 Cr App R 35, or forms to that effect, are to be used in the criminal courts, in accordance with CrimPR 5.1.

5A.2    The forms at Annex E to that Practice Direction, the case management forms, must be used in the criminal courts, in accordance with that rule.

5A.3    The table at the beginning of each section of each of those Annexes lists the forms and:

(a) shows the Rule in connection with which each applies;

(b) describes each form.

5A.4    The forms may be amended or withdrawn from time to time, or new forms added, under the authority of the Lord Chief Justice.

**CPD.5B**    **CPD I General matters 5B: Access to Information Held by the Court**

5B.1    Open justice, as Lord Justice Toulson re-iterated in the case of *R (Guardian News and Media Ltd) v City of Westminster Magistrates' Court* [2012] EWCA Civ 420, [2013] QB 618, is a 'principle at the heart of our system of justice and vital to the rule of law'. There are exceptions but these 'have to be justified by some even more important principle'. However, the practical application of that undisputed principle, and the proper balancing of conflicting rights and principles, call for careful judgments to be made. The following is intended to provide some assistance to courts making decisions when asked to provide the public, including journalists, with access to or copies of

---

[18] 1984 c. 60; section 73 was amended by section 90(1) of, and paragraphs 125 and 128 of Schedule 13 to, the Access to Justice Act 1999 (c. 22), paragraph 285 of Schedule 8 to the Courts Act 2003 (c. 39) and paragraph 13 of Schedule 17 to the Coroners and Justice Act 2009 (c. 25); and section 74 was amended by paragraph 85 of Schedule 36, and Part 5 of Schedule 37, to the Criminal Justice Act 2003 (c. 44) and paragraph 14 of Schedule 17 to the Coroners and Justice Act 2009 (c. 25).

[19] 1998 c. 37; section 115 was amended by paragraphs 150 and 151 of Schedule 7 to the Criminal Justice and Court Services Act 2000 (c. 43), paragraph 35 of Schedule 1 to S.I. 2000/90, section 97 of the Police Reform Act 2002 (c. 30), paragraph 25 of Schedule 1 to S.I. 2002/2469, section 219 of the Housing Act 2004 (c. 34), section 22 of, and paragraphs 1 and 7 of Schedule 9 to, the Police and Justice Act 2006 (c. 48), paragraph 29 of the Schedule to S.I. 2007/961, section 29 of the Transport for London Act 2008 (c. i), paragraph 13 of Schedule 2 to S.I. 2008/912, paragraphs 109 and 111 of Schedule 2 to S.I. 2010/866 and paragraphs 83 and 90 of Schedule 5 to the Health and Social Care Act 2012 (c. 7).

[18] 2003 c. 42.

[19] 1997 c. 50; section 112 was amended by section 50 of the Criminal Justice and Immigration Act 2008 (c. 4), sections 93, 97 and 112 of, and Part 8 of Schedule 8 to, the Policing and Crime Act 2009 (c. 26) and sections 80 and 84 of the Protection of Freedoms Act 2012 (c. 9). Section 113A was added by section 163(2) of the Serious Organised Crime and Police Act 2005 (c. 15), modified by regulation 4 of S.I. 2010/1146, and amended by paragraph 14 of Schedule 9 to the Safeguarding Vulnerable Groups Act 2006 (c. 47), section 50 of the Criminal Justice and Immigration Act 2008 (c. 4), sections 97 and 112 of, and Part 8 of Schedule 8 to, the Policing and Crime Act 2009 (c. 26), sections 80 and 115 of, and paragraphs 35 and 36 of Schedule 9 and Part 5 of Schedule 10 to, the Protection of Freedoms Act 2012 (c. 9), articles 2 and 3 of S.I. 2009/203 and articles 36 and 37 of S.I. 2012/3006. Section 113B was added by section 163(2) of the Serious Organised Crime and Police Act 2005 (c. 15), modified by regulations 5 to 7 of S.I. 2010/1146, and amended by paragraph 14 of Schedule 9 to the Safeguarding Vulnerable Groups Act 2006 (c. 47), paragraph 149 of Schedule 16 to the Armed Forces Act 2006 (c. 52), section 50 of the Criminal Justice and Immigration Act 2008 (c. 4), sections 97 and 112 of, and Part 8 of Schedule 8 to, the Policing and Crime Act 2009 (c. 26), sections 79, 80, 82 and 115 of, and paragraphs 35 and 37 of Schedule 9 and Parts 5 and 6 of Schedule 10 to, the Protection of Freedoms Act 2012 (c. 9), articles 2 and 4 of S.I. 2009/203, regulation 8 of S.I. 2010/1146 and articles 36, 37 and 39 of S.I. 2012/3006.

information and documents held by the court, or when asked, exceptionally, to forbid the supply of transcripts that otherwise would have been supplied. It is not a prescriptive list, as the court will have to consider all the circumstances of each individual case.

5B.2   It remains the responsibility of the recipient of information or documents to ensure that they comply with any and all restrictions such as reporting restrictions (see Part 6 and the accompanying Practice Direction).

5B.3   For the purposes of this direction, the word document includes images in photographic, digital including DVD format, video, CCTV or any other form.

5B.4   Certain information can and should be provided to the public on request, subject to any restrictions, such as reporting restrictions, imposed in that particular case. CrimPR 5.5 governs the supply of transcript of a recording of proceedings in the Crown Court. CrimPR 5.8(4) and 5.8(6) read together specify the information that the court officer will supply to the public; an oral application is acceptable and no reason need be given for the request. There is no requirement for the court officer to consider the non-disclosure provisions of the Data Protection Act 1998 as the exemption under section 35 applies to all disclosure made under 'any enactment ... or by the order of a court', which includes under the Criminal Procedure Rules.

5B.5   If the information sought is neither transcript nor listed at CrimPR 5.8(6), rule 5.8(7) will apply, and the provision of information is at the discretion of the court. The following guidance is intended to assist the court in exercising that discretion.

5B.6   A request for access to documents used in a criminal case should first be addressed to the party who presented them to the court or who, in the case of a written decision by the court, received that decision. Prosecuting authorities are subject to the Freedom of Information Act 2000 and the Data Protection Act 1998 and their decisions are susceptible to review.

5B.7   If the request is from a journalist or media organisation, note that there is a protocol between the NPCC, the CPS and the media entitled 'Publicity and the Criminal Justice System':
www.cps.gov.uk/publications/agencies/mediaprotocol.html
www.cps.gov.uk/publication/publicity-and-criminal-justice-system
There is additionally a protocol made under CrimPR 5.8(5)(b) between the media and HMCTS:
www.newsmediauk.org/write/MediaUploads/PDF%20Docs/Protocol_for_Sharing_Court_Do
cuments.pdf
This Practice Direction does not affect the operation of those protocols. Material should generally be sought under the relevant protocol before an application is made to the court.

5B.8   An application to which CrimPR 5.8(7) applies must be made in accordance with rule 5.8; it must be in writing, unless the court permits otherwise, and 'must explain for what purpose the information is required.' A clear, detailed application, specifying the name and contact details of the applicant, whether or not he or she represents a media organisation, and setting out the reasons for the application and to what use the information will be put, will be of most assistance to the court. Applicants should state if they have requested the information under a protocol and include any reasons given for the refusal. Before considering such an application, the court will expect the applicant to have given notice of the request to the parties.

5B.9   The court will consider each application on its own merits. The burden of justifying a request for access rests on the applicant. Considerations to be taken into account will include:
   i.    whether or not the request is for the purpose of contemporaneous reporting; a request after the conclusion of the proceedings will require careful scrutiny by the court;
   ii.   the nature of the information or documents being sought;
   iii.  the purpose for which they are required;
   iv.   the stage of the proceedings at the time when the application is made;
   v.    the value of the documents in advancing the open justice principle, including enabling the media to discharge its role, which has been described as a 'public watchdog', by reporting the proceedings effectively;
   vi.   any risk of harm which access to them may cause to the legitimate interests of others; and
   vii.  any reasons given by the parties for refusing to provide the material requested and any other representations received from the parties.

Further, all of the principles below are subject to any specific restrictions in the case. Courts should be aware that the risk of providing a document may reduce after a particular point in the proceedings, and when the material requested may be made available.

*Documents read aloud in their entirety*

5B.10  If a document has been read aloud to the court in its entirety, it should usually be provided on request, unless to do so would be disruptive to the court proceedings or place an undue burden on the court, the advocates or others. It may be appropriate and convenient for material to be provided electronically, if this can be done securely.

**5B.11** Documents likely to fall into this category are:
    i.    Opening notes;
    ii.    Statements agreed under section 9 of the Criminal Justice Act 1967, including experts' reports, if read in their entirety;
    iii.    Admissions made under section 10 of the Criminal Justice Act 1967.

*Documents treated as read aloud in their entirety*

**5B.12** A document treated by the court as if it had been read aloud in public, though in fact it has been neither read nor summarised aloud, should generally be made available on request. The burden on the court, the advocates or others in providing the material should be considered, but the presumption in favour of providing the material is greater when the material has only been treated as having been read aloud. Again, subject to security considerations, it may be convenient for the material to be provided electronically.

**5B.13** Documents likely to fall into this category include:
    i.    Skeleton arguments;
    ii.    Written submissions;
    iii.    Written decisions by the court.

*Documents read aloud in part or summarised aloud*

**5B.14** Open justice requires only access to the part of the document that has been read aloud. If a member of the public requests a copy of such a document, the court should consider whether it is proportionate to order one of the parties to produce a suitably redacted version. If not, access to the document is unlikely to be granted; however open justice will generally have been satisfied by the document having been read out in court.

**5B.15** If the request comes from an accredited member of the press (see *Access by reporters* below), there may be circumstances in which the court orders that a copy of the whole document be shown to the reporter, or provided, subject to the condition that those matters that had not been read out to the court may not be used or reported. A breach of such an order would be treated as a contempt of court.

**5B.16** Documents in this category are likely to include:
    i.    Section 9 statements that are edited.

*Jury bundles and exhibits (including video footage shown to the jury)*

**5B.17** The court should consider:
    i.    whether access to the specific document is necessary to understand or effectively to report the case;
    ii.    the privacy of third parties, such as the victim (in some cases, the reporting restriction imposed by section 1 of the Judicial Proceedings (Regulation of Reports) Act 1926 will apply (indecent or medical matter));
    iii.    whether the reporting of anything in the document may be prejudicial to a fair trial in this or another case, in which case whether it may be necessary to make an order under section 4(2) of the Contempt of Court Act 1981.

The court may order one of the parties to provide a copy of certain pages (or parts of the footage), but these should not be provided electronically.

*Statements of witnesses who give oral evidence*

**5B.18** A witness statement does not become evidence unless it is agreed under section 9 of the Criminal Justice Act 1967 and presented to the court. Therefore the statements of witnesses who give oral evidence, including ABE interview and transcripts and experts' reports, should not usually be provided. Open justice is generally satisfied by public access to the court.

*Confidential documents*

**5B.19** A document the content of which, though relied upon by the court, has not been communicated to the public or reporters, nor treated as if it had been, is likely to have been supplied in confidence and should be treated accordingly. This will apply even if the court has made reference to the document or quoted from the document. There is most unlikely to be a sufficient reason to displace the expectation of confidentiality ordinarily attaching to a document in this category, and it would be exceptional to permit the inspection or copying by a member of the public or of the media of such a document. The rights and legitimate interests of others are likely to outweigh the interests of open justice with respect these documents.

**5B.20**  Documents in this category are likely to include:
  i.   Pre-sentence reports;
  ii.  Medical reports;
  iii. Victim Personal Statements;
  iv.  Reports and summaries for confiscation.

*Prohibitions against the provision of information*

**5B.21**  Statutory provisions may impose specific prohibitions against the provision of information. Those most likely to be encountered are listed in the note to CrimPR 5.8 and include the Rehabilitation of Offenders Act 1974, section 18 of the Criminal Procedure and Investigations Act 1996 ('unused material' disclosed by the prosecution), sections 33, 34 and 35 of the Legal Aid, Sentencing and Punishment of Offenders Act 2012 ('LASPO Act 2012') (privileged information furnished to the Legal Aid Agency) and reporting restrictions generally.

**5B.22**  Reports of allocation or sending proceedings are restricted by section 52A of the Crime and Disorder Act 1998, so that only limited information, as specified in the statute, may be reported, whether it is referred to in the court room or not. The magistrates' court has power to order that the restriction shall not apply; if any defendant objects the court must apply the interests of justice test as specified in section 52A. The restriction ceases to apply either after all defendants indicate a plea of guilty, or after the conclusion of the trial of the last defendant to be tried. If the case does not result in a guilty plea, a finding of guilt or an acquittal, the restriction does not lift automatically and an application must be made to the court.

**5B.23**  Extradition proceedings have some features in common with committal proceedings, but no automatic reporting restrictions apply.

**5B.24**  Public Interest Immunity and the rights of a defendant, witnesses and victims under Article 6 and 8 of the European Convention on Human Rights may also restrict the power to release material to third parties.

*Other documents*

**5B.25**  The following table indicates the considerations likely to arise on an application to inspect or copy other documents.

| Document | Considerations |
| --- | --- |
| Charge sheet Indictment | The alleged offence(s) will have been read aloud in court, and their terms must be supplied under CrimPR 5.8(4) |
| Material disclosed under CPIA 1996 | To the extent that the content is deployed at trial, it becomes public at that hearing. Otherwise, it is a criminal offence for it to be disclosed: section 18 of the 1996 Act. |
| Written notices, applications, replies (including any application for representation) | To the extent that evidence is introduced, or measures taken, at trial, the content becomes public at that hearing. A statutory prohibition against disclosure applies to an application for representation: sections 33, 34 and 35 of the LASPO Act 2012. |
| Written decisions by the court, other than those read aloud in public or treated as if so read | Such decisions should usually be provided, subject to the criteria listed in CrimPR 5.8(4)(a) (and see also paragraph 5B.31 below). |
| Sentencing remarks | Sentencing remarks should usually be provided to the accredited Press, if the judge was reading from a prepared script which was handed out immediately afterwards; if not, then permission for a member of the accredited Press to obtain a transcript should usually be given (see also paragraphs 5B.26 and 29 below). |
| Official recordings | See CrimPR 5.5. |
| Transcript | See CrimPR 5.5 (and see also paragraphs 5B.32 to 36 below). |

*Access by reporters*

**5B.26**  Under CrimPR Part 5, the same procedure applies to applications for access to information by reporters as to other members of the public. However, if the application is made by legal representatives instructed by the media, or by an accredited member of the media, who is able to produce in support of the application a valid Press Card (http://www.ukpresscardauthority.co. uk/) then there is a greater presumption in favour of providing the requested material, in recognition of the press' role as 'public watch dog' in a democratic society (*Observer and Guardian v United Kingdom* (1992) 14 EHRR 153, Times November 27, 1991). The general principle in those circumstances is that the court should supply documents and information unless there is a good reason not to in order to protect the rights or legitimate interests of others and the request will not place an undue burden on the court *R* (*Guardian News and Media Ltd*) at [87]. Subject to that, the paragraphs above relating to types of documents should be followed.

**5B.27** Court staff should usually verify the authenticity of cards, checking the expiry date on the card and where necessary may consider telephoning the number on the reverse of the card to verify the card holder. Court staff may additionally request sight of other identification if necessary to ensure that the card holder has been correctly identified. The supply of information under CrimPR 5.8(7) is at the discretion of the court, and court staff must ensure that they have received a clear direction from the court before providing any information or material under rule 5.8(7) to a member of the public, including to the accredited media or their legal representatives.

**5B.28** Opening notes and skeleton arguments or written submissions, once they have been placed before the court, should usually be provided to the media. If there is no opening note, permission for the media to obtain a transcript of the prosecution opening should usually be given (see below). It may be convenient for copies to be provided electronically by counsel, provided that the documents are kept suitably secure. The media are expected to be aware of the limitations on the use to which such material can be put, for example that legal argument held in the absence of the jury must not be reported before the conclusion of the trial.

**5B.29** The media should also be able to obtain transcripts of hearings held in open court directly from the transcription service provider, on payment of any required fee. The service providers commonly require the judge's authorisation before they will provide a transcript, as an additional verification to ensure that the correct material is released and reporting restrictions are noted. However, responsibility for compliance with any restriction always rests with the person receiving the information or material: see CPD I General Matters 6B beneath.

**5B.30** It is not for the judge to exercise an editorial judgment about 'the adequacy of the material already available to the paper for its journalistic purpose' (*Guardian* at 82) but the responsibility for complying with the Contempt of Court Act 1981 and any and all restrictions on the use of the material rests with the recipient.

*Written decisions*

**5B.31** Where the Criminal Procedure Rules allow for a determination without a hearing there may be occasions on which it furthers the overriding objective to deliver the court's decision to the parties in writing, without convening a public hearing at which that decision will be pronounced: on an application for costs made at the conclusion of a trial, for example. If the only reason for delivering a decision in that way is to promote efficiency and expedition and if no other consideration arises then usually a copy of the decision should be provided in response to any request once the decision is final. However, had the decision been announced in public then the criteria in CrimPR 5.8(4)(a) would have applied to the supply of information by the court officer; and ordinarily those same criteria should be applied by the court, therefore. Moreover, where considerations other than efficiency and expedition have influenced the court's decision to reach a determination without convening a hearing then those same considerations may be inimical to the supply of the written decision to any applicant other than a party. Reporting restrictions may be relevant, for example; as may the considerations listed in paragraph 5B.9 above. In such a case the court should consider supplying a redacted version of the decision in response to a request by anyone who is not a party; or it may be appropriate to give the decision in terms that can be supplied to the public, supplemented by additional reasons provided only to the parties.

*Transcript*

**5B.32** CrimPR 5.5 does not require an application to the court for transcript, nor does the rule anticipate recourse to the court for a judicial decision about the supply of transcript in any but unusual circumstances. Ordinarily it is the rule itself that determines the circumstances in which the transcriber of a recording may or may not supply transcript to an applicant.

**5B.33** Where reporting restrictions apply to information contained in the recording from which the transcript is prepared then unless the court otherwise directs it is for the transcriber to redact that transcript where redaction is necessary to permit its supply to that applicant. Having regard to the terms of the statutes that impose reporting restrictions, however, it is unlikely that redaction will be required frequently. Statutory restrictions prohibit publication 'to the public at large or any section of the public', or some comparable formulation. They do not ordinarily prohibit a publication constituted only of the supply of transcript to an individual applicant. However, any reporting restrictions will continue to apply to a recipient of transcript, and where they apply the recipient must be alerted to them by the endorsement on the transcript of a suitable warning notice, to this or the like effect:

'WARNING: reporting restrictions may apply to the contents transcribed in this document, particularly if the case concerned a sexual offence or involved a child. Reporting restrictions prohibit the publication of the applicable information to the public or any section of the public, in writing, in a broadcast or by means of the internet, including social media. Anyone who receives a copy of this transcript is responsible in law for making sure that applicable restrictions are not breached. A person who breaches a reporting restriction is liable to a fine and/or imprisonment. For guidance on whether reporting restrictions apply, and to what information, ask at the court office or take legal advice.'

**5B.34** Exceptionally, court staff may invite the court to direct that transcript must be redacted before it is supplied to an applicant, or that transcript must not be supplied to an applicant pending the supply of further information or assurances by that applicant, or at all, in exercise of the judicial discretion to which CrimPR 5.5(2) refers. Circumstances giving rise to concern may include, for example, the occurrence of events causing staff reasonably to suspect that an applicant intends or is likely to disregard a reporting restriction that applies, despite the warning notice endorsed on the transcript, or reasonably to suspect that an applicant has malicious intentions towards another person. Given that the proceedings will have taken place in public, despite any such suspicions, cogent and compelling reasons will be required to deny a request for transcript of such proceedings and the onus rests always on the court to justify such a denial, not on the applicant to justify the request. Even where there are reasons to suspect a criminal intent, the appropriate course may be to direct that the police be informed of those reasons rather than to direct that the transcript be withheld. Nevertheless, it may be appropriate in such a case to direct that an application for the transcript should be made which complies with paragraph 5B.8 above (even though that paragraph does not apply); and then for the court to review that application with regard to the considerations listed in paragraph 5B.9 above (but the usual burden of justifying a request under that paragraph does not apply).

**5B.35** Some applicants for transcript may be taken to be aware of the significance of reporting restrictions, where they apply, and, by reason of such an applicant's statutory or other public or quasi-public functions, in any event unlikely to contravene any such restriction. Such applicants include public authorities within the meaning of section 6 of the Human Rights Act 1998 (a definition which extends to government departments and their agencies, local authorities, prosecuting authorities, and institutions such as the Parole Board and the Sentencing Council) and include public or private bodies exercising disciplinary functions in relation to practitioners of a regulated profession such as doctors, lawyers, accountants, etc. It would be only in the most exceptional circumstances that a court might conclude that any such body should not receive unredacted transcript of proceedings in public, irrespective of whether reporting restrictions do or do not apply.

**5B.36** The rule imposes no time limit on a request for the supply of transcript. The assumption is that transcript of proceedings in public in the Crown Court will continue to be available for as long as relevant records are maintained by the Lord Chancellor under the legislation to which CrimPR 5.4 refers.

## CPD I General matters 5C: Issue of Medical Certificates

**CPD.5C**

**5C.1** Doctors will be aware that medical notes are normally submitted by defendants in criminal proceedings as justification for not answering bail. Medical notes may also be submitted by witnesses who are due to give evidence and jurors.

**5C.2** If a medical certificate is accepted by the court, this will result in cases (including contested hearings and trials) being adjourned rather than the court issuing a warrant for the defendant's arrest without bail. Medical certificates will also provide the defendant with sufficient evidence to defend a charge of failure to surrender to bail.

**5C.3** However, a court is not absolutely bound by a medical certificate. The medical practitioner providing the certificate may be required by the court to give evidence. Alternatively the court may exercise its discretion to disregard a certificate which it finds unsatisfactory: *R v Ealing Magistrates' Court ex parte Burgess* [2001] 165 JP 82.

**5C.4** Circumstances where the court may find a medical certificate unsatisfactory include:

(a) where the certificate indicates that the defendant is unfit to attend work (rather than to attend court);

(b) where the nature of the defendant's ailment (e.g. a broken arm) does not appear to be capable of preventing his attendance at court;

(c) where the defendant is certified as suffering from stress/anxiety/depression and there is no indication of the defendant recovering within a realistic timescale.

5C.5 It therefore follows that the minimum standards a medical certificate should set out are:

(a) the date on which the medical practitioner examined the defendant;

(b) the exact nature of the defendant's ailments;

(c) if it is not self-evident, why the ailment prevents the defendant attending court;

(d) an indication as to when the defendant is likely to be able to attend court, or a date when the current certificate expires.

5C.6 Medical practitioners should be aware that when issuing a certificate to a defendant in criminal proceedings they make themselves liable to being summonsed to court to give evidence about the content of the certificate, and they may be asked to justify their statements.

CRIMINAL PROCEDURE RULES   PART 6   REPORTING, ETC. RESTRICTIONS
### General rules

**R6.1   When this Part applies**

6.1   (1) This Part applies where the court can—

(a) impose a restriction on—

(i) reporting what takes place at a public hearing, or

(ii) public access to what otherwise would be a public hearing;

(b) vary or remove a reporting or access restriction that is imposed by legislation;

(c) withhold information from the public during a public hearing;

(d) order a trial in private; or

(e) allow there to take place during a hearing—

(i) sound recording, or

(ii) communication by electronic means.

(2) This Part does not apply to arrangements required by legislation, or directed by the court, in connection with—

(a) sound recording during a hearing, or the transcription of such a recording; or

(b) measures to assist a witness or defendant to give evidence.

*[Note. The court can impose reporting restrictions under—*

*(a) section 4(2) of the Contempt of Court Act 1981[1] (postponed report of public hearing);*

*(b) section 11 of the Contempt of Court Act 1981 (matter withheld from the public during a public hearing);*

*(c) section 58 of the Criminal Procedure and Investigations Act 1996[2] (postponed report of derogatory assertion in mitigation);*

*(d) section 45 of the Youth Justice and Criminal Evidence Act 1999[3] (identity of a person under 18);*

*(e) section 45A of the Youth Justice and Criminal Evidence Act 1999[4] (identity of a witness or victim under 18);*

*(f) section 46 of the Youth Justice and Criminal Evidence Act 1999[5] (identity of a vulnerable adult witness);*

*(g) section 82 of the Criminal Justice Act 2003[6] (order for retrial after acquittal); or*

*(h) section 75 of the Serious Organised Crime and Police Act 2005[7] (identity of a defendant who assisted the police).*

[1] 1981 c. 49.
[2] 1996 c. 25.
[3] 1999 c. 23.
[4] 1999 c. 23; section 45A was inserted by section 78 of the Criminal Justice and Courts Act 2015 (c. 2).
[5] 1999 c. 23.
[6] 2003 c. 44.
[7] 2005 c. 15.

*There are reporting restrictions imposed by legislation that the court can vary or remove, under—*

    (a)   *section 49 of the Children and Young Persons Act 1933[8] (youth court proceedings);*

    (b)   *section 8C of the Magistrates' Courts Act 1980[9] (pre-trial ruling in magistrates' courts);*

    (c)   *section 11 of the Criminal Justice Act 1987[10] (preparatory hearing in the Crown Court);*

    (d)   *section 1 of the Sexual Offences (Amendment) Act 1992[11] (identity of complainant of sexual offence);*

    (e)   *section 37 of the Criminal Procedure and Investigations Act 1996[12] (preparatory hearing in the Crown Court);*

    (f)   *section 41 of the Criminal Procedure and Investigations Act 1996[13] (pre-trial ruling in the Crown Court);*

    (g)   *section 52A of, and paragraph 3 of Schedule 3 to, the Crime and Disorder Act 1998[14] (allocation and sending for trial proceedings);*

    (h)   *section 47 of the Youth Justice and Criminal Evidence Act 1999[15] (special measures direction);*

    (i)   *section 141F of the Education Act 2002[16] (restrictions on reporting alleged offences by teachers);*

    (j)   *section 71 of the Criminal Justice Act 2003[17] (prosecution appeal against Crown Court ruling); and*

    (k)   *section 4A of, and paragraph 1 of Schedule 1 to, the Female Genital Mutilation Act 2003[18] (identity of person against whom a female genital mutilation offence is alleged to have been committed).*

*There are reporting restrictions imposed by legislation that the court has no power to vary or remove, under—*

    (a)   *section 1 of the Judicial Proceedings (Regulation of Reports) Act 1926[19] (indecent or medical matter);*

    (b)   *section 2 of the Contempt of Court Act 1981[20] (risk of impeding or prejudicing active proceedings).*

[8] 1933 c. 12; section 49 was substituted by section 49 of the Criminal Justice and Public Order Act 1994 (c. 33) and amended by section 45 of the Crime (Sentences) Act 1997 (c. 43), section 119 of, and paragraph 1 of Schedule 8 to, the Crime and Disorder Act 1998 (c. 37), section 165 of, and paragraph 2 of Schedule 9 to, the Powers of Criminal Courts (Sentencing) Act 2000 (c. 6), paragraph 2 of Schedule 32 to, the Criminal Justice Act 2003 (c. 44), sections 208 and 210 of, and paragraphs 15 and 19 of Schedule 21, and Schedule 23 to, the Legal Services Act 2007 (c. 29) and section 6 of, and paragraphs 1, 3 and 100 of Schedule 4 to, the Criminal Justice and Immigration Act 2008 (c. 4). It is further amended by section 48 of, and paragraphs 1 and 3 of Schedule 2 to, the Youth Justice and Criminal Evidence Act 1999 (c. 23), section 74 of, and paragraph 5 of Schedule 7 to, the Criminal Justice and Court Services Act 2000 (c. 43) and sections 6 and 149 of, and paragraphs 1 and 3 of Schedule 4 and Schedule 28 to, the Criminal Justice and Immigration Act 2008 (c. 4), with effect from dates to be appointed.

[9] 1980 c. 43; section 8C was inserted by section 45 of, and Schedule 3 to, the Courts Act 2003 (c. 39) and amended by paragraphs 12 and 15 of Schedule 5 to the Legal Aid, Sentencing and Punishment of Offenders Act 2012 (c. 10).

[10] 1987 c. 38; section 11 was amended by paragraphs 1 and 6 of Schedule 3 to the Criminal Procedure and Investigations Act 1996 (c. 25), section 24 of, and paragraphs 38 and 40 of Schedule 4 to, the Access to Justice Act 1999 (c. 22), section 311 of, and paragraph 58 of Schedule 3 and Part 4 of Schedule 37 to, the Criminal Justice Act 2003 (c. 44) and section 40(4) of, and paragraph 46 of Schedule 9 to, the Constitutional Reform Act 2005 (c. 4).

[11] 1992 c. 34; section 1 was amended by section 48 of, and paragraphs 6 and 7 of Schedule 2 to, the Youth Justice and Criminal Evidence Act 1999 (c. 23).

[12] 1996 c. 25; section 37 was amended by section 24 of, and paragraph 49 of Schedule 4 to, the Access to Justice Act 1999 (c. 22), section 311 of the Criminal Justice Act 2003 (c. 44) and section 40(4) of, and paragraph 61 of Schedule 9 to, the Constitutional Reform Act 2005 (c. 4).

[13] 1996 c. 25; section 41 was amended by section 311 of the Criminal Justice Act 2003 (c. 44).

[14] 1998 c. 37; section 52A was inserted by paragraphs 15 and 19 of Schedule 3 to the Criminal Justice Act 2003 (c. 44) and amended by paragraphs 46 and 47 of Schedule 5 to the Legal Aid, Sentencing and Punishment of Offenders Act 2012 (c. 10). Paragraph 3 of Schedule 3 was amended by section 24 of, and paragraphs 53 and 55 of Schedule 4 to, the Access to Justice Act 1999 (c. 22), paragraphs 68 and 71 of Schedule 3 to the Criminal Justice Act 2003 (c. 44) and paragraphs 46 and 50 of Schedule 5 to the Legal Aid, Sentencing and Punishment of Offenders Act 2012 (c. 10).

[15] 1999 c. 23; section 47 was amended by section 52 of, and paragraph 37 of Schedule 14 to, the Police and Justice Act 2006 (c. 48).

[16] 2002 c. 32; section 141F was inserted by section 13 of the Education Act 2011 (c. 21).

[17] 2003 c. 44; section 71 was amended by section 40(4) of, and paragraph 82 of Schedule 9 to, the Constitutional Reform Act 2005 (c. 4) and paragraph 65 of Schedule 5 to the Legal Aid, Sentencing and Punishment of Offenders Act 2012 (c. 10).

[18] 2003 c. 31; section 4A and Schedule 1 were inserted by section 71 of the Serious Crime Act 2015 (c. 9).

[19] 1926 c. 61; section 1 was amended by sections 38 and 46 of the Criminal Justice Act 1982 (c. 48), paragraph 2 of Schedule 8 to the Family Law Act 1996 (c. 27) and paragraph 8 of Schedule 27 to the Civil Partnership Act 2004 (c. 33). It is further amended by paragraph 7 of Schedule 26 to the Criminal Justice Act 2003 (c. 44), with effect from a date to be appointed.

[20] 1981 c. 49; section 2 was amended by paragraph 31 of Schedule 20 to the Broadcasting Act 1990 (c. 42).

Criminal Procedure Rules and Criminal Practice Directions

*Access to a youth court is restricted under section 47 of the Children and Young Persons Act 1933[21]. See also rule 24.2 (Trial and sentence in a magistrates' court – general rules).*

*Under section 36 of the Children and Young Persons Act 1933[22], no-one under 14 may be present in court when someone else is on trial, or during proceedings preliminary to a trial, unless that person is required as a witness, or for the purposes of justice, or the court permits.*

*The court can restrict access to the courtroom under—*

    (a)   *section 8(4) of the Official Secrets Act 1920[23], during proceedings for an offence under the Official Secrets Acts 1911 and 1920;*

    (b)   *section 37 of the Children and Young Persons Act 1933[24], where the court receives evidence from a person under 18;*

    (c)   *section 75 of the Serious Organised Crime and Police Act 2005[25], where the court reviews a sentence passed on a defendant who assisted an investigation.*

*The court has an inherent power, in exceptional circumstances—*

    (a)   *to allow information, for example a name or address, to be withheld from the public at a public hearing;*

    (b)   *to restrict public access to what otherwise would be a public hearing, for example to control disorder;*

    (c)   *to hear a trial in private, for example for reasons of national security.*

*Under section 9(1) of the Contempt of Court Act 1981[26], it is a contempt of court without the court's permission to—*

    (a)   *use in court, or bring into court for use, a device for recording sound;*

    (b)   *publish a recording of legal proceedings made by means of such a device; or*

    (c)   *use any such recording in contravention of any condition on which permission was granted.*

*Under section 41 of the Criminal Justice Act 1925[27], it is an offence to take or attempt to take a photograph, or with a view to publication to make or attempt to make a portrait or sketch, of any judge, juror, witness or party, in the courtroom, or in the building or in the precincts of the building in which the court is held, or while that person is entering or leaving the courtroom, building or precincts; or to publish such a photograph, portrait or sketch.*

*Section 32 of the Crime and Courts Act 2013[28] (Enabling the making, and use, of films and other recordings of proceedings) allows for exceptions to be made to the prohibitions imposed by section 9 of the 1981 Act and section 41 of the 1925 Act.*

*By reason of sections 15 and 45 of the Senior Courts Act 1981[29], the Court of Appeal and the Crown Court each has an inherent power to deal with a person for contempt of court for disrupting the proceedings. Under section 12 of the Contempt of Court Act 1981[30], a magistrates' court has a similar power.*

*See also—*

    (a)   *rule 5.5, under which the court officer must make arrangements for recording proceedings in the Crown Court;*

---

[21] 1933 c. 12; section 47 was amended by Parts II and III of Schedule 7 to the Justices of the Peace Act 1949 (c. 101), paragraph 40 of Schedule 11 to the Criminal Justice Act 1991 (c. 53), sections 47(7) and 120(2) of, and Schedule 10 to, the Crime and Disorder Act 1998 (c. 37) and paragraphs 15 and 18 of Schedule 21 to the Legal Services Act 2007 (c. 29). It is further amended by paragraph 2 of Schedule 4 to the Youth Justice and Criminal Evidence Act 1999 (c. 23), with effect from a date to be appointed.

[22] 1933 c. 12; section 36 was amended by section 73 of, and Part III of Schedule 15 to, the Access to Justice Act 1999 (c. 22).

[23] 1920 c. 75; section 8 was amended by section 32 of the Magistrates' Courts Act 1980 (c. 43).

[24] 1933 c. 12; section 37 was amended by paragraphs 15 and 16 of Schedule 21 to the Legal Services Act 2007 (c. 29) and is further amended by paragraph 2 of Schedule 4 to the Youth Justice and Criminal Evidence Act 1999 (c. 23), with effect from a date to be appointed.

[25] 2005 c. 15.

[26] 1981 c. 49.

[27] 1925 c. 86; section 41 was amended by section 56(4) of, and Part IV of Schedule 11 to, the Courts At 1971 (c. 23), sections 38 and 46 of the Criminal Justice Act 1982 (c. 48) and section 47 of the Constitutional Reform Act 2005 (c. 4).

[28] 2013 c. 22.

[29] 1981 c. 54.

[30] 1981 c. 49; section 12 was amended by section 78 of, and Schedule 16 to, the Criminal Justice Act 1982 (c. 48), section 17(3) of, and Part I of Schedule 4 to, the Criminal Justice Act 1991 (c. 53); section 65(3) and (4) of, and paragraph 6(4) of Schedule 3 to, the Criminal Justice Act 1993 (c. 36) and section 165 of, and paragraph 83 of Schedule 9 to, the Powers of Criminal Courts (Sentencing) Act 2000 (c. 6).

(b) *Part 18, which applies to live links and other measures to assist a witness or defendant to give evidence;*

(c) *rule 45.10, which applies to costs orders against a non-party for serious misconduct; and*

(d) *Part 48, which contains rules about contempt of court.]*

### Exercise of court's powers to which this Part applies                          **R6.2**

6.2 (1) When exercising a power to which this Part applies, as well as furthering the overriding objective, in accordance with rule 1.3, the court must have regard to the importance of—

  (a) dealing with criminal cases in public; and

  (b) allowing a public hearing to be reported to the public.

 (2) The court may determine an application or appeal under this Part—

  (a) at a hearing, in public or in private; or

  (b) without a hearing.

 (3) But the court must not exercise a power to which this Part applies unless each party and any other person directly affected—

  (a) is present; or

  (b) has had an opportunity—

   (i) to attend, or

   (ii) to make representations.

*[Note. See also section 121 of the Magistrates' Courts Act 1980[31] and rule 24.2 (general rules about trial and sentence in a magistrates' court).]*

### Court's power to vary requirements under this Part                            **R6.3**

6.3 (1) The court may—

  (a) shorten or extend (even after it has expired) a time limit under this Part;

  (b) require an application to be made in writing instead of orally;

  (c) consider an application or representations made orally instead of in writing; and

  (d) dispense with a requirement to—

   (i) give notice, or

   (ii) serve an application.

 (2) Someone who wants an extension of time must—

  (a) apply when making the application or representations for which it is needed; and

  (b) explain the delay.

#### Reporting and access restrictions

### Reporting and access restrictions                                            **R6.4**

6.4 (1) This rule applies where the court can—

  (a) impose a restriction on—

   (i) reporting what takes place at a public hearing, or

   (ii) public access to what otherwise would be a public hearing; or

  (b) withhold information from the public during a public hearing.

 (2) Unless other legislation otherwise provides, the court may do so—

  (a) on application by a party; or

  (b) on its own initiative.

 (3) A party who wants the court to do so must—

  (a) apply as soon as reasonably practicable;

  (b) notify—

   (i) each other party, and

   (ii) such other person (if any) as the court directs;

  (c) specify the proposed terms of the order, and for how long it should last;

  (d) explain—

   (i) what power the court has to make the order, and

   (ii) why an order in the terms proposed is necessary;

  (e) where the application is for a reporting direction under section 45A of the Youth Justice and Criminal Evidence Act 1999[32] (Power to restrict reporting of criminal proceedings for lifetime of witnesses and victims under 18), explain—

   (i) how the circumstances of the person whose identity is concerned meet the conditions prescribed by that section, having regard to the factors which that section lists; and

---

[31] 1980 c. 43; section 121 was amended by section 61 of the Criminal Justice Act 1988 (c. 33), section 92 of, and paragraph 8 of Schedule 11 to, the Children Act 1989 (c. 41), section 109 of, and paragraph 237 of Schedule 8 and Schedule 10 to, the Courts Act 2003 (c. 39).

[32] 1999 c. 23; section 45A was inserted by section 78 of the Criminal Justice and Courts Act 2015 (c. 2).

(ii) why such a reporting direction would be likely to improve the quality of any evidence given by that person, or the level of co-operation given by that person to any party in connection with the preparation of that party's case, taking into account the factors listed in that section; and

(f) where the application is for a reporting direction under section 46 of the Youth Justice and Criminal Evidence Act 1999[33] (Power to restrict reports about certain adult witnesses in criminal proceedings), explain—

(i) how the witness is eligible for assistance, having regard to the factors listed in that section, and

(ii) why such a reporting direction would be likely to improve the quality of the witness' evidence, or the level of co-operation given by the witness to the applicant in connection with the preparation of the applicant's case, taking into account the factors which that section lists.

*[Note. Under section 45A(10) or section 46(9) of the Youth Justice and Criminal Evidence Act 1999, if the conditions prescribed by those sections are met the court may make an excepting direction dispensing, to any extent specified, with the restrictions imposed by a reporting direction made under those sections.]*

**R6.5  Varying or removing restrictions**

6.5 (1) This rule applies where the court can vary or remove a reporting or access restriction.

(2) Unless other legislation otherwise provides, the court may do so—

(a) on application by a party or person directly affected; or

(b) on its own initiative.

(3) A party or person who wants the court to do so must—

(a) apply as soon as reasonably practicable;

(b) notify—

(i) each other party, and

(ii) such other person (if any) as the court directs;

(c) specify the restriction; and

(d) explain, as appropriate, why it should be varied or removed.

(4) A person who wants to appeal to the Crown Court under section 141F of the Education Act 2002[34] must—

(a) serve an appeal notice on—

(i) the Crown Court officer, and

(ii) each other party;

(b) serve on the Crown Court officer, with the appeal notice, a copy of the application to the magistrates' court;

(c) serve the appeal notice not more than 15 business days after the magistrates' court's decision against which the appellant wants to appeal; and

(d) in the appeal notice, explain, as appropriate, why the restriction should be maintained, varied or removed.

(5) Rule 34.11 (Constitution of the Crown Court) applies on such an appeal.

*[Note. Under section 141F(7) of the Education Act 2002, a party to an application to a magistrates' court to remove the statutory restriction on reporting an alleged offence by a teacher may appeal to the Crown Court against the decision of the magistrates' court. With the Crown Court's permission, any other person may appeal against such a decision.]*

**R6.6  Trial in private**

6.6 (1) This rule applies where the court can order a trial in private.

(2) A party who wants the court to do so must—

(a) apply in writing not less than 5 business days before the trial is due to begin; and

(b) serve the application on—

(i) the court officer, and

(ii) each other party.

(3) The applicant must explain—

(a) the reasons for the application;

(b) how much of the trial the applicant proposes should be in private; and

(c) why no measures other than trial in private will suffice, such as—

(i) reporting restrictions,

(ii) an admission of facts,

---

[33] 1999 c. 23.
[34] 2002 c. 32; section 141F was inserted by section 13 of the Education Act 2011 (c. 21).

        (iii) the introduction of hearsay evidence,

        (iv) a direction for a special measure under section 19 of the Youth Justice and Criminal Evidence Act 1999,

        (v) a witness anonymity order under section 86 of the Coroners and Justice Act 2009, or

        (vi) arrangements for the protection of a witness.

  (4) Where the application includes information that the applicant thinks ought not be revealed to another party, the applicant must—

     (a) omit that information from the part of the application that is served on that other party;

     (b) mark the other part to show that, unless the court otherwise directs, it is only for the court; and

     (c) in that other part, explain why the applicant has withheld that information from that other party.

  (5) The court officer must at once—

     (a) display notice of the application somewhere prominent in the vicinity of the courtroom; and

     (b) give notice of the application to reporters by such other arrangements as the Lord Chancellor directs.

  (6) The application must be determined at a hearing which—

     (a) must be in private, unless the court otherwise directs;

     (b) if the court so directs, may be, wholly or in part, in the absence of a party from whom information has been withheld; and

     (c) in the Crown Court, must be after the defendant is arraigned but before the jury is sworn.

  (7) At the hearing of the application—

     (a) the general rule is that the court must consider, in the following sequence—

        (i) representations first by the applicant and then by each other party, in all the parties' presence, and then

        (ii) further representations by the applicant, in the absence of a party from whom information has been withheld; but

     (b) the court may direct other arrangements for the hearing.

  (8) The court must not hear a trial in private until—

     (a) the business day after the day on which it orders such a trial, or

     (b) the disposal of any appeal against, or review of, any such order, if later.

## Representations in response                                              R6.7

6.7  (1) This rule applies where a party, or person directly affected, wants to make representations about an application or appeal.

  (2) Such a party or person must—

     (a) serve the representations on—

        (i) the court officer,

        (ii) the applicant,

        (iii) each other party, and

        (iv) such other person (if any) as the court directs;

     (b) do so as soon as reasonably practicable after notice of the application; and

     (c) ask for a hearing, if that party or person wants one, and explain why it is needed.

  (3) Representations must—

     (a) explain the reasons for any objection; and

     (b) specify any alternative terms proposed.

## Order about restriction or trial in private                             R6.8

6.8  (1) This rule applies where the court—

     (a) orders, varies or removes a reporting or access restriction; or

     (b) orders a trial in private.

  (2) The court officer must—

     (a) record the court's reasons for the decision; and

     (b) as soon as reasonably practicable, arrange for notice of the decision to be—

        (i) displayed somewhere prominent in the vicinity of the courtroom, and

        (ii) communicated to reporters by such other arrangements as the Lord Chancellor directs.

### Sound recording and electronic communication

## Sound recording and electronic communication                           R6.9

6.9  (1) This rule applies where the court can give permission to—

     (a) bring into a hearing for use, or use during a hearing, a device for—

Criminal Procedure Rules and Criminal Practice Directions

         (i)   recording sound, or

         (ii)   communicating by electronic means; or

     (b)   publish a sound recording made during a hearing.

(2)   The court may give such permission—

     (a)   on application; or

     (b)   on its own initiative.

(3)   A person who wants the court to give such permission must—

     (a)   apply as soon as reasonably practicable;

     (b)   notify—

         (i)   each party, and

         (ii)   such other person (if any) as the court directs; and

     (c)   explain why the court should permit the use or publication proposed.

(4)   As a condition of the applicant using such a device, the court may direct arrangements to minimise the risk of its use—

     (a)   contravening a reporting restriction;

     (b)   disrupting the hearing; or

     (c)   compromising the fairness of the hearing, for example by affecting—

         (i)   the evidence to be given by a witness, or

         (ii)   the verdict of a jury.

(5)   Such a direction may require that the device is used only—

     (a)   in a specified part of the courtroom;

     (b)   for a specified purpose;

     (c)   for a purpose connected with the applicant's activity as a member of a specified group, for example representatives of news-gathering or reporting organisations; or

     (d)   at a specified time, or in a specified way.

## R6.10   Forfeiture of unauthorised sound recording

**6.10**   (1)   This rule applies where someone without the court's permission—

     (a)   uses a device for recording sound during a hearing; or

     (b)   publishes a sound recording made during a hearing.

(2)   The court may exercise its power to forfeit the device or recording—

     (a)   on application by a party, or on its own initiative; and

     (b)   provisionally, despite rule 6.2(3), to allow time for representations.

(3)   A party who wants the court to forfeit a device or recording must—

     (a)   apply as soon as reasonably practicable;

     (b)   notify—

         (i)   as appropriate, the person who used the device, or who published the recording, and

         (ii)   each other party; and

     (c)   explain why the court should exercise that power.

*[Note. Under section 9(3) of the Contempt of Court Act 1981[35], the court can forfeit any device or recording used or made in contravention of section 9(1) of the Act.]*

## CRIMINAL PRACTICE DIRECTIONS    PART 6    REPORTING, ETC. RESTRICTIONS

**CPD.6A**   **CPD II Preliminary proceedings 6A: Unofficial Sound Recording of Proceedings**

**6A.1**   Section 9 of the Contempt of Court Act 1981 contains provisions governing the unofficial use of equipment for recording sound in court.

Section 9(1) provides that it is a contempt of court:

     (a)   to use in court, or bring into court for use, any tape recorder or other instrument for recording sound, except with the permission of the court;

     (b)   to publish a recording of legal proceedings made by means of any such instrument, or any recording derived directly or indirectly from it, by playing it in the hearing of the public or any section of the public, or to dispose of it or any recording so derived, with a view to such publication;

     (c)   to use any such recording in contravention of any conditions of leave granted under paragraph (a).

These provisions do not apply to the making or use of sound recordings for purposes of official transcripts of the proceedings, upon which the Act imposes no restriction whatever.

---

[35]   1981 c. 49.

**6A.2** The discretion given to the court to grant, withhold or withdraw leave to use equipment for recording sound or to impose conditions as to the use of the recording is unlimited, but the following factors may be relevant to its exercise:

   (a) the existence of any reasonable need on the part of the applicant for leave, whether a litigant or a person connected with the press or broadcasting, for the recording to be made;

   (b) the risk that the recording could be used for the purpose of briefing witnesses out of court;

   (c) any possibility that the use of the recorder would disturb the proceedings or distract or worry any witnesses or other participants.

**6A.3** Consideration should always be given whether conditions as to the use of a recording made pursuant to leave should be imposed. The identity and role of the applicant for leave and the nature of the subject matter of the proceedings may be relevant to this.

**6A.4** The particular restriction imposed by section 9(1)(b) applies in every case, but may not be present in the mind of every applicant to whom leave is given. It may therefore be desirable on occasion for this provision to be drawn to the attention of those to whom leave is given.

**6A.5** The transcript of a permitted recording is intended for the use of the person given leave to make it and is not intended to be used as, or to compete with, the official transcript mentioned in section 9(4).

**6A.6** Where a contravention of section 9(1) is alleged, the procedure in section 2 of Part 48 of the Rules should be followed. Section 9(3) of the 1981 Act permits the court to 'order the instrument, or any recording made with it, or both, to be forfeited'. The procedure at CrimPR 6.10 should be followed.

### CPD II Preliminary proceedings 6B: Restrictions on Reporting Proceedings       **CPD.6B**

**6B.1** Open justice is an essential principle in the criminal courts but the principle is subject to some statutory restrictions. These restrictions are either automatic or discretionary. Guidance is provided in the joint publication, *Reporting Restrictions in the Criminal Courts* issued by the Judicial College, the Newspaper Society, the Society of Editors and the Media Lawyers Association. The current version is the fourth edition and has been updated to be effective from May 2015.

**6B.2** Where a restriction is automatic no order can or should be made in relation to matters falling within the relevant provisions. However, the court may, if it considers it appropriate to do so, give a reminder of the existence of the automatic restriction. The court may also discuss the scope of the restriction and any particular risks in the specific case in open court with representatives of the press present. Such judicial observations cannot constitute an order binding on the editor or the reporter although it is anticipated that a responsible editor would consider them carefully before deciding what should be published. It remains the responsibility of those reporting a case to ensure that restrictions are not breached.

**6B.3** Before exercising its discretion to impose a restriction the court must follow precisely the statutory provisions under which the order is to be made, paying particular regard to what has to be established, by whom and to what standard.

**6B.4** Without prejudice to the above paragraph, certain general principles apply to the exercise of the court's discretion:

   (a) The court must have regard to CrimPR Parts 6 and 18.

   (b) The court must keep in mind the fact that every order is a departure from the general principle that proceedings shall be open and freely reported.

   (c) Before making any order the court must be satisfied that the purpose of the proposed order cannot be achieved by some lesser measure e.g., the grant of special measures, screens or the clearing of the public gallery (usually subject to a representative(s) of the media remaining).

   (d) The terms of the order must be proportionate so as to comply with Article 10 ECHR (freedom of expression).

   (e) No order should be made without giving other parties to the proceedings and any other interested party, including any representative of the media, an opportunity to make representations.

   (f) Any order should provide for any interested party who has not been present or represented at the time of the making of the order to have permission to apply within a limited period e.g., 24 hours.

   (g) The wording of the order is the responsibility of the judge or Bench making the order: it must be in precise terms and, if practicable, agreed with the advocates.

   (h) The order must be in writing and must state:

      (i) the power under which it is made;

      (ii) its precise scope and purpose; and

      (iii) the time at which it shall cease to have effect, if appropriate.

Criminal Procedure Rules and Criminal Practice Directions

(i) The order must specify, in every case, whether or not the making or terms of the order may be reported or whether this itself is prohibited. Such a report could cause the very mischief which the order was intended to prevent.

6B.5 A series of template orders have been prepared by the Judicial College and are available as an appendix to the Crown Court Bench Book Companion; these template orders should generally be used.

6B.6 A copy of the order should be provided to any person known to have an interest in reporting the proceedings and to any local or national media who regularly report proceedings in the court.

6B.7 Court staff should be prepared to answer any enquiry about a specific case; but it is and will remain the responsibility of anyone reporting a case to ensure that no breach of any order occurs and the onus rests on such person to make enquiry in case of doubt.

**CPD.6C** **CPD I General Matters 6C: Use of live text-based forms of communication (including *Twitter*) from court for the purposes of fair and accurate reporting**

6C.1 This part clarifies the use which may be made of live text-based communications, such as mobile email, social media (including *Twitter*) and internet-enabled laptops in and from courts throughout England and Wales. For the purpose of this part these means of communication are referred to, compendiously, as 'live text-based communications'. It is consistent with the legislative structure which:

(a) prohibits:

(i) the taking of photographs in court (section 41 of the Criminal Justice Act 1925);

(ii) the use of sound recording equipment in court unless the leave of the judge has first been obtained (section 9 of the Contempt of Court Act 1981); and

(b) requires compliance with the strict prohibition rules created by sections 1, 2 and 4 of the Contempt of Court Act 1981 in relation to the reporting of court proceedings.

*General Principles*

6C.2 The judge has an overriding responsibility to ensure that proceedings are conducted consistently, with the proper administration of justice, and to avoid any improper interference with its processes.

6C.3 A fundamental aspect of the proper administration of justice is the principle of open justice. Fair and accurate reporting of court proceedings forms part of that principle. The principle is, however, subject to well-known statutory and discretionary exceptions. Two such exceptions are the prohibitions, set out in paragraph 6C.1(a), on photography in court and on making sound recordings of court proceedings.

6C.4 The statutory prohibition on photography in court, by any means, is absolute. There is no judicial discretion to suspend or dispense with it. Any equipment which has photographic capability must not have that function activated.

6C.5 Sound recordings are also prohibited unless, in the exercise of its discretion, the court permits such equipment to be used. In criminal proceedings, some of the factors relevant to the exercise of that discretion are contained in paragraph 6A.2. The same factors are likely to be relevant when consideration is being given to the exercise of this discretion in civil or family proceedings.

*Use of Live Text-based Communications: General Considerations*

6C.6 The normal, indeed almost invariable, rule has been that mobile phones must be turned off in court. There is however no statutory prohibition on the use of live text-based communications in open court.

6C.7 Where a member of the public, who is in court, wishes to use live text-based communications during court proceedings an application for permission to activate and use, in silent mode, a mobile phone, small laptop or similar piece of equipment, solely in order to make live text-based communications of the proceedings will need to be made. The application may be made formally or informally (for instance by communicating a request to the judge through court staff).

6C.8 It is presumed that a representative of the media or a legal commentator using live text-based communications from court does not pose a danger of interference to the proper administration of justice in the individual case. This is because the most obvious purpose of permitting the use of live text-based communications would be to enable the media to produce fair and accurate reports of the proceedings. As such, a representative of the media or a legal commentator who wishes to use live text-based communications from court may do so without making an application to the court.

6C.9 When considering, either generally on its own motion, or following a formal application or informal request by a member of the public, whether to permit live text-based communications, and if so by whom, the paramount question for the judge will be whether the application may interfere with the proper administration of justice.

6C.10 In considering the question of permission, the factors listed in paragraph 6A.2 are likely to be relevant.

6C.11    Without being exhaustive, the danger to the administration of justice is likely to be at its most acute in the context of criminal trials e.g., where witnesses who are out of court may be informed of what has already happened in court and so coached or briefed before they then give evidence, or where information posted on, for instance, *Twitter* about inadmissible evidence may influence members of the jury. However, the danger is not confined to criminal proceedings; in civil and sometimes family proceedings, simultaneous reporting from the courtroom may create pressure on witnesses, by distracting or worrying them.

6C.12    It may be necessary for the judge to limit live text-based communications to representatives of the media for journalistic purposes but to disallow its use by the wider public in court. That may arise if it is necessary, for example, to limit the number of mobile electronic devices in use at any given time because of the potential for electronic interference with the court's own sound recording equipment, or because the widespread use of such devices in court may cause a distraction in the proceedings.

6C.13    Subject to these considerations, the use of an unobtrusive, hand-held, silent piece of modern equipment, for the purposes of simultaneous reporting of proceedings to the outside world as they unfold in court, is generally unlikely to interfere with the proper administration of justice.

6C.14    Permission to use live text-based communications from court may be withdrawn by the court at any time.

**CPD I General matters 6D: Taking Notes in Court**                                                      CPD.6D

6D.1    As long as it does not interfere with the proper administration of justice, anyone who attends a court hearing may quietly take notes, on paper or by silent electronic means. If that person is a participant, including an expert witness who is in the courtroom under CrimPR 24.4(2)(a)(ii) or 25.11(2)(a)(ii), note taking may be an essential aid to that person's own or (if they are a representative) to their client's effective participation. If that person is a reporter or a member of the public, attending a hearing to which, by definition, they have been admitted, note taking is a feature of the principle of open justice. The permission of the court is not required, and the distinctions between members of the public and others which are drawn at paragraphs 6C.7 and 6C.8 of these Practice Directions do not apply.

6D.2    However, where there is reason to suspect that the taking of notes may be for an unlawful purpose, or that it may disrupt the proceedings, then it is entirely proper for court staff to make appropriate enquiries, and ultimately it is within the power of the court to prohibit note taking by a specified individual or individuals in the court room if that is necessary and proportionate to prevent unlawful conduct. If, for example, there is reason to believe that notes are being taken in order to influence the testimony of a witness who is due to give evidence, perhaps by briefing that witness on what another witness has said, then because such conduct is unlawful (it is likely to be in contempt of court, and it may constitute a perversion of the course of justice) it is within the court's power to prohibit such note taking. If there is reason to believe that what purports to be taking notes with an electronic device is in fact the transmission of live text-based communications from court without the permission required by paragraph 6C.7 of these Practice Directions, or where permission to transmit such communications has been withdrawn under paragraph 6C.14, then that, too, would constitute grounds for prohibiting the taking of such notes.

6D.3    The existence of a reporting restriction, without more, is not a sufficient reason to prohibit note taking (though it may need to be made clear to those who take notes that the reporting restriction affects how much, if any, of what they have noted may be communicated to anyone else). However, if there is reason to believe that notes are being taken in order to facilitate the contravention of a reporting restriction then that, too, would constitute grounds for prohibiting such note taking.

**CPD I General matters 6E: Access to Courts**                                                           CPD.6E

*Proceedings before the Crown Court*

6E.1    The right of the public to access court rooms to observe proceedings is a fundamental part of open justice, and good practice will ensure that the public are able to view proceedings quietly, and without causing interruption, as far as is possible.

6E.2    However, as observed in *R (O'Connor) v Aldershot Magistrates' Court* [2017] 1 WLR 2833 'The right to attend a public court hearing and to enter the court building for that purpose is not unqualified.' The court has an inherent power to restrict public access to the courtroom where it is necessary to do so in the interests of justice, for example to prevent disorder.

6E.3    During criminal proceedings in a Crown Court there are some specific parts of proceedings whereby it may be appropriate for a judge to restrict movement in the public gallery. As observed by Bean LJ in *R (on the application of Ewing) v Isleworth Crown Court* [2019] EWHC 288 (Admin) this is to ensure that during 'these sensitive moments, generally of brief duration, it is necessary for the court to be still so that the process can take place without distraction and in a manner which preserves the dignity and solemnity of the proceedings'. It is expected that during the following parts of the proceedings, access may be restricted to prevent comings and goings in the public gallery:

I. Arraignment;
II. Empanelling and swearing in of the jury;
III. Oath taking or affirmation;
IV. Return of verdict by a jury;
V. Passing of sentence by a Judge.

**6E.4** In the *Ewing* judgment the Administrative Court made clear that it would be unlawful to issue a blanket policy that restricted access during other parts of the proceedings. Unless the judge has specifically directed restrictions to access to the public gallery for good reason in a particular case, then at all other times, it is expected that the public can enter and leave the courtroom as they require, provided they do so quietly and without disrupting proceedings.

CRIMINAL PROCEDURE RULES    PART 7    STARTING A PROSECUTION IN A
MAGISTRATES' COURT

**R7.1 When this Part applies**

7.1 (1) This Part applies in a magistrates' court where—

(a) a prosecutor wants the court to issue a summons or warrant under section 1 of the Magistrates' Courts Act 1980[1];

(b) a prosecutor with the power to do so issues—

(i) a written charge and requisition, or

(ii) a written charge and single justice procedure notice under section 29 of the Criminal Justice Act 2003[2]; or

(c) a person who is in custody is charged with an offence; or

(d) the prosecutor alleges an offence against a defendant who is due to attend, or attends, the court in response to another allegation.

(2) In this Part, 'authorised prosecutor' means a prosecutor authorised under section 29 of the Criminal Justice Act 2003 to issue a written charge and requisition or single justice procedure notice.

*[Note. Under section 1 of the Magistrates' Courts Act 1980, on receiving a formal statement (described in that section as an 'information') alleging that someone has committed an offence, the court may issue—*

*(a) a summons requiring that person to attend court; or*

*(b) a warrant for that person's arrest, if—*

*(i) the alleged offence must or may be tried in the Crown Court,*

*(ii) the alleged offence is punishable with imprisonment, or*

*(iii) the person's address cannot be established sufficiently clearly to serve a summons or requisition.*

*The powers of the court to which this Part applies may be exercised by a single justice of the peace.*

*Under section 29 of the Criminal Justice Act 2003, a prosecutor authorised under that section may issue a written charge alleging that someone has committed an offence, and either—*

*(a) a requisition requiring that person to attend court; or*

*(b) a notice that the single justice procedure under section 16A of the Magistrates' Courts Act 1980[3] and rule 24.9 of these Rules applies.*

---

[1] 1980 c. 43; section 1 was amended by section 68 of, and paragraph 6 of Schedule 8 to, the Criminal Justice Act 1991 (c. 53), sections 43 and 109 of, and Schedule 10 to, the Courts Act 2003 (c. 39), section 31 of, and paragraph 12 of Schedule 7 to, the Criminal Justice Act 2003 (c. 44) and section 153 of the Police Reform and Social Responsibility Act 2011. It is further amended by paragraphs 7 and 8 of Schedule 36 to, the Criminal Justice Act 2003 (c. 44), with effect from a date to be appointed.
[2] 2003 c. 44; section 29 has been brought into force for certain purposes only (see S.I. 2007/1999, 2008/1424, 2009/2879, 2010/3005, 2011/2188, 2012/825 and 2014/633). It was amended by section 50 of, and paragraph 130 of Schedule 4 to, the Commissioners for Revenue and Customs Act 2005 (c. 11), section 59 of, and paragraph 196 of Schedule 4 to, the Serious Organised Crime and Police Act 2005 (c. 15), section 15 of, and paragraph 187 of Schedule 8 to, the Crime and Courts Act 2013 (c. 22), S.I. 2014/834 and section 46 of the Criminal Justice and Courts Act 2015 (c. 2).
[3] 1980 c. 43; section 16A was inserted by section 48 of the Criminal Justice and Courts Act 2015 (c. 2).

*Section 30 of the 2003 Act[4] contains other provisions about written charges, requisitions and single justice procedure notices.*

*A person detained under a power of arrest may be charged if the custody officer decides that there is sufficient evidence to do so. See sections 37 and 38 of the Police and Criminal Evidence Act 1984[5].]*

## Application for summons, etc.                          R7.2

7.2    (1)   A prosecutor who wants the court to issue a summons must—

           (a)   serve on the court officer a written application; or

           (b)   unless other legislation prohibits this, present an application orally to the court, with a written statement of the allegation or allegations made by the prosecutor.

     (2)   A prosecutor who wants the court to issue a warrant must—

           (a)   serve on the court officer—

                (i)   a written application, or

                (ii)   a copy of a written charge that has been issued; or

           (b)   present to the court either of those documents.

     (3)   An application for the issue of a summons or warrant must—

           (a)   set out the allegation or allegations made by the applicant in terms that comply with rule 7.3(1) (Allegation of offence in application or charge); and

           (b)   demonstrate—

                (i)   that the application is made in time, if legislation imposes a time limit, and

                (ii)   that the applicant has the necessary consent, if legislation requires it.

     (4)   As well as complying with paragraph (3), an application for the issue of a warrant must—

           (a)   demonstrate that the offence or offences alleged can be tried in the Crown Court;

           (b)   demonstrate that the offence or offences alleged can be punished with imprisonment; or

           (c)   concisely outline the applicant's grounds for asserting that the defendant's address is not sufficiently established for a summons to be served.

     (5)   Paragraph (6) applies unless the prosecutor is—

           (a)   a public authority within the meaning of section 17 of the Prosecution of Offences Act 1985[6]; or

           (b)   a person acting—

                (i)   on behalf of such an authority, or

                (ii)   in that person's capacity as an official appointed by such an authority.

     (6)   Where this paragraph applies, as well as complying with paragraph (3), and with paragraph (4) if applicable, an application for the issue of a summons or warrant must—

           (a)   concisely outline the grounds for asserting that the defendant has committed the alleged offence or offences;

           (b)   disclose—

                (i)   details of any previous such application by the same applicant in respect of any allegation now made, and

                (ii)   details of any current or previous proceedings brought by another prosecutor in respect of any allegation now made; and

           (c)   include a statement that to the best of the applicant's knowledge, information and belief—

                (i)   the allegations contained in the application are substantially true,

                (ii)   the evidence on which the applicant relies will be available at the trial,

---

[4] 2003 c. 44; section 30 has been brought into force for certain purposes only (see S.I. 2007/1999, 2008/1424, 2009/2879, 2010/3005, 2011/2188, 2012/825 and 2014/633). It was amended by article 3 of, and paragraphs 45 and 46 of the Schedule to, S.I. 2004/2035 and section 47 of the Criminal Justice and Courts Act 2015 (c. 2).

[5] 1984 c. 60; section 37 was amended by section 108(7) of, and Schedule 15 to, the Children Act 1989 (c. 41), sections 72 and 101(2) of, and Schedule 13 to, the Criminal Justice Act 1991 (c. 53), sections 29(4) and 168(3) of, and Schedule 11 to, the Criminal Justice and Public Order Act 1994 (c. 33), section 28 of, and paragraphs 1 and 2 of Schedule 2 to, the Criminal Justice Act 2003 (c. 44), section 23(1) of, and paragraphs 1 and 2 of Schedule 1 to, the Drugs Act 2005 (c. 17) and sections 11 and 52 of, and paragraph 9 of Schedule 14 to, the Police and Justice Act 2006 (c. 48).

Section 38 was amended by section 108(5) of, and paragraph 53 of Schedule 13 to, the Children Act 1989 (c. 41), section 59 of the Criminal Justice Act 1991 (c. 53), sections 24, 28 and 168(2) of, and paragraph 54 of Schedule 10 to, the Criminal Justice and Public Order Act 1994 (c. 33), section 57 of the Criminal Justice and Court Services Act 2000 (c. 43), section 5 of, and paragraph 44 of Schedule 32 and paragraph 5 of Schedule 36 to, the Criminal Justice Act 2003 (c. 44), section 23 of, and paragraphs 1 and 3 of Schedule 1 to, the Drugs Act 2005 (c. 17) and paragraph 34 of Schedule 11 to the Legal Aid, Sentencing and Punishment of Offenders Act 2012 (c. 10).

[6] 1985 c. 23; section 17 was amended by section 40 of, and paragraph 41 of Schedule 9 to, the Constitutional Reform Act 2005 (c. 4) and paragraphs 1 and 4 and Part 4 of Schedule 7 to the Legal Aid, Sentencing and Punishment of Offenders Act 2012 (c. 10).

Criminal Procedure Rules and Criminal Practice Directions

        (iii)   the details given by the applicant under paragraph (6)(b) are true, and

        (iv)   the application discloses all the information that is material to what the court must decide

(7)    Where the statement required by paragraph (6)(c) is made orally—

     (a)    the statement must be on oath or affirmation, unless the court otherwise directs; and

     (b)    the court must arrange for a record of the making of the statement.

(8)    An authorised prosecutor who issues a written charge must notify the court officer immediately.

(9)    A single document may contain—

     (a)    more than one application; or

     (b)    more than one written charge.

(10)    Where an offence can be tried only in a magistrates' court, then unless other legislation otherwise provides—

     (a)    a prosecutor must serve an application for the issue of a summons or warrant on the court officer or present it to the court; or

     (b)    an authorised prosecutor must issue a written charge, not more than 6 months after the offence alleged.

(11)    Where an offence can be tried in the Crown Court then—

     (a)    a prosecutor must serve an application for the issue of a summons or warrant on the court officer or present it to the court; or

     (b)    an authorised prosecutor must issue a written charge, within any time limit that applies to that offence.

(12)    The court may determine an application to issue or withdraw a summons or warrant—

     (a)    without a hearing, as a general rule, or at a hearing (which must be in private unless the court otherwise directs);

     (b)    in the absence of—

        (i)   the prosecutor,

        (ii)   the defendant; and

     (c)    with or without representations by the defendant.

(13)    If the court so directs, a party to an application to issue or withdraw a summons or warrant may attend a hearing by live link or telephone.

*[Note. In some legislation, including the Magistrates' Courts Act 1980, an application for the issue of a summons or warrant is described as an 'information' and serving an application on the court officer or presenting it to the court is described as 'laying' that information.*

*The time limits for serving or presenting an application and for issuing a written charge are prescribed by section 127 of the Magistrates' Courts Act 1980[7] and section 30(5) of the Criminal Justice Act 2003[8].*

*In section 17 of the Prosecution of Offences Act 1985 'public authority' means (a) a police force as defined by that Act, (b) the Crown Prosecution Service or any other government department, (c) a local authority or other authority or body constituted for purposes of the public service or of local government, or carrying on under national ownership any industry or undertaking or part of an industry or undertaking, or (d) any other authority or body whose members are appointed by Her Majesty or by any Minister of the Crown or government department or whose revenues consist wholly or mainly of money provided by Parliament.*

*Part 46 (Representatives) contains rules allowing a member, officer or employee of a prosecutor, on the prosecutor's behalf, to—*

     *(a)   serve on the court officer or present to the court an application for the issue of a summons or warrant; or*

     *(b)   issue a written charge and requisition.*

*See Part 3 for the court's general powers of case management, including power to consider applications and give directions for (among other things) the amendment of an allegation or charge and for separate trials.*

*See also Part 32 (Breach, revocation and amendment of community and other orders). Rule 32.2(2) (Application by responsible officer) applies rules 7.2 to 7.4 to the procedure with which that rule deals.*

*The Practice Direction sets out a form of application for use in connection with rule 7.2(6).]*

**R7.3**    **Allegation of offence**

7.3    (1)   An allegation of an offences in an application for the issue of a summons or warrant or in a charge must contain—

[7]   1980 c. 43.

[8]   2003 c. 44; section 30(5) was amended by section 47 of the Criminal Justice and Courts Act 2015 (c.2).

Criminal Procedure Rules and Criminal Practice Directions

     (a)  a statement of the offence that—
        (i)  describes the offence in ordinary language, and
        (ii)  identifies any legislation that creates it; and
     (b)  such particulars of the conduct constituting the commission of the offence as to make clear what the prosecutor alleges against the defendant, including the value of any damage or theft alleged where that value is known and where it affects the exercise of the court's powers.

(2)  More than one incident of the commission of the offence may be included in the allegation if those incidents taken together amount to a course of conduct having regard to the time, place or purpose of commission.

(3)  Where rule 7.1(1)(d) applies (additional allegation in existing prosecution), the prosecutor must—
     (a)  set out the additional allegation in terms that comply with paragraph (1);
     (b)  as soon as practicable—
        (i)  serve the additional allegation on the court officer and the defendant, or
        (ii)  present the additional allegation orally to the court, with a written statement of that allegation;
     (c)  demonstrate that the allegation is made in time, if legislation imposes a time limit; and
     (d)  demonstrate that the prosecutor has the necessary consent, if legislation requires it.

*[Note. In some circumstances the court may allow the prosecutor to amend an allegation of an offence, including to allege a different offence. In those circumstances the allegation may be amended after any time limit for prosecuting the different offence has expired if the amendment is based on substantially the same facts as the allegation first made. See Part 3 for the court's general powers of case management, including power to consider an application and give directions for (among other things) the amendment of an allegation.]*

**Summons, warrant and requisition**                                                                                   **R7.4**

7.4  (1)  A summons, warrant or requisition may be issued in respect of more than one offence.

(2)  A summons or requisition must—
     (a)  contain notice of when and where the defendant is required to attend the court;
     (b)  specify each offence in respect of which it is issued;
     (c)  in the case of a summons, identify—
        (i)  the court that issued it, unless that is otherwise recorded by the court officer, and
        (ii)  the court office for the court that issued it; and
     (d)  in the case of a requisition, identify the person under whose authority it is issued.

(3)  A summons may be contained in the same document as an application for the issue of that summons.

(4)  A requisition may be contained in the same document as a written charge.

(5)  Where the court issues a summons—
     (a)  the prosecutor must—
        (i)  serve it on the defendant, and
        (ii)  notify the court officer; or
     (b)  the court officer must—
        (i)  serve it on the defendant, and
        (ii)  notify the prosecutor.

(6)  Where an authorised prosecutor issues a requisition that prosecutor must—
     (a)  serve on the defendant—
        (i)  the requisition, and
        (ii)  the written charge; and
     (b)  serve a copy of each on the court officer.

(7)  Unless it would be inconsistent with other legislation, a replacement summons or requisition may be issued without a fresh application or written charge where the one replaced—
     (a)  was served under rule 4.4 (Service by leaving or posting a document); but
     (b)  is shown not to have been received by the addressee.

(8)  Where a summons or requisition is served on a defendant under 18—
     (a)  the prosecutor or court officer who serves it must serve a copy on a parent or guardian of the defendant as well, and
     (b)  if the court requires the parent or guardian to attend, the copy may impose that requirement or a separate summons or requisition may be issued for that purpose.

*[Note. Part 13 contains other rules about warrants.]*

*Section 47 of the Magistrates' Courts Act 1980[9] and section 30(5) of the Criminal Justice Act 2003 make special provision about time limits under other legislation for the issue and service of a summons or requisition, where service by post is not successful.*

*Under section 34A of the Children and Young Persons Act 1933[10] unless the court is satisfied that it would be unreasonable to require such attendance having regard to the circumstances of the case (i) the court may require the parent or guardian of a defendant under 18 to attend court with the defendant, and (ii) the court must do so if the defendant is under 16.]*

CRIMINAL PRACTICE DIRECTIONS    PART 7    STARTING A PROSECUTION
IN A MAGISTRATES' COURT

**CPD.7A**

**CPD II Preliminary proceedings 7A: First Court Attendance after Charge and Detention**

7A.1   A defendant who has been kept in police detention after being charged with an offence must be brought before a magistrates' court as soon as practicable and in any event no later than the first subsequent court sitting: section 46 of the Police and Criminal Evidence Act 1984. If no magistrates' court is due to sit on the day on which the defendant is charged, or on the next day which is not a Sunday, Christmas Day or Good Friday, then the Act requires the police custody officer to inform the court's designated officer of the defendant's detention, and requires the designated officer to arrange for a magistrates' court to sit.

7A.2   The 1984 Act thus imposes duties on the police and on HM Courts and Tribunals Service. In *R (on the application of H (A Child)) v Clerk to Teesside Justices* [2000] 10 WLUK 532 the High Court observed,

> "it is incumbent on justices and their clerks, however busy their courts may be, to ensure that they are able to receive persons in custody up to the end of normal court hours, at least, in order to comply with section 46 …, unless some exceptional circumstance intervenes to make that impossible in any particular case".

7A.3   To comply with those duties arrangements must be made to allow courts to receive such defendants during the course of a sitting day if the available time allows for the hearing of all cases to be concluded by 4.30pm, or later if, and only if, some disability or vulnerability of the defendant so requires. In practice, to allow sufficient time for consultation with a legal representative and for the subsequent hearing, the defendant must have been brought to the court building, or given access to a live link to the court, by no later than 3.30pm. To that end, Judicial Business Groups must ensure that effective practical arrangements have been made between police forces, HMCTS, the Crown Prosecution Service and prisoner escort contractors for the prompt transmission of information about defendants held for production before the court.

7A.4   On a Saturday or bank holiday normal court hours may differ from court to court based on likely caseload. Those hours must be determined by the HMCTS Head of Legal Operations in consultation with the judiciary and other agencies. In accordance with the court's observations in the *Teesside Justices' Clerk* case, all magistrates' courts should sit until at least 11.30 a.m. to receive defendants to whom these directions apply unless arrangements have been made for such defendants to be dealt with by another court, either by attendance in person or by live link.

7A.5   For the purposes of section 46 of the 1984 Act the designated officer is the HMCTS Director of Operations, by whom the exercise of that statutory function is delegated to members of court staff. When informing such a delegate of a defendant's detention the police custody officer must at the same time supply the following, usually by electronic means:

(a)   confirmation that:
    (i)   the defendant has been charged,
    (ii)   the case file is complete and available,
    (iii)   any interpreter required is available,
    (iv)   any appropriate adult or local authority officer responsible for the defendant's care has been notified and is available,
    (v)   the defendant's legal representative has been notified and is available, and
    (vi)   the CPS or other relevant prosecuting authority has been notified;

(b)   the custody officer's proposal for the means by which the defendant should attend court, whether by live link or in person, and, if the latter, then whether by police transport or by prisoner escort contractor transport; and

---

[9]   1980 c. 43; section 47 was amended by section 109(1) of, and paragraph 207 of Schedule 8 to, the Courts Act 2003 (c. 39).
[10]   1933 c. 12; section 34A was inserted by section 56 of the Criminal Justice Act 1991 (c. 53) and amended by section 107 of, and paragraph 1 of Schedule 5 to, the Local Government Act 2000 (c. 22) and regulations 3 and 5 of S.I. 2016/413.

(c) details of:
    (i) any physical or mental disability or other vulnerability (whether by reason of age or other circumstance) of the defendant of which police officers are aware, in particular where any such might be thought to make the use of live link inappropriate, and
    (ii) the expected time of arrival at court, if the defendant is to be brought to court in person.
No court should be expected to hear a case in respect of which such information is missing or incomplete, or in respect of which such arrangements have not been made.

**7A.6** The designated officer's delegates must liaise with staff at the court buildings to which defendants in police detention may be brought. Each such delegate must be sufficiently experienced to be able to assess, swiftly and accurately, the availability of courts sitting in those buildings, and of sufficient seniority to take the decisions required by these directions. Each must be in a position to assess
    (i) the availability of court members, of legal advisers, of prosecutors and of the other staff needed to deal with an unexpected case,
    (ii) the potential effect of an unexpected case on other cases awaiting hearing that day, including the risk of a less urgent case being adjourned, perhaps not for the first time, in consequence of accommodating the unexpected hearing,
    (iii) the likely length of the unexpected hearing, and
    (iv) the significance of the age and any disability or other vulnerability of the unexpected defendant.

**7A.7** The delegate to whom a police custody officer reports a defendant's detention must decide whether, and if so how, when and where, to accommodate that defendant's case within the period to which paragraph 7A.3 or 7A.4 refers, having regard to the availability and content of the information to which paragraph 7A.5 refers and to the considerations listed in paragraph 7A.6. The decision must be informed by the views of those court members and legal advisers who may be affected, as listing is a judicial responsibility and function. It may be necessary for the delegate to take such steps as arranging for the unexpected case to be heard by live link; reorganising courts sitting in the court building to which the defendant is due to be brought; adjourning other cases; calling upon additional resources; or making arrangements with the delegate at another court building for the unexpected case to be heard by a court sitting there, by live link if appropriate. It may be necessary for the court that hears the unexpected case to impose a timetable for representations or to restrict the decisions that will be taken immediately. If it will not be possible to hear within the period to which paragraph 7A.3 or 7A.4 refers every case due to be heard that day at the court building to which the defendant is to be brought then every effort must be made to ensure that the cases of all defendants in custody, whether in that court building or attending by live link, still can be heard within that period. The delegate for that building must ensure that the police, the staff responsible for the court's own cells and the relevant prisoner escort contractor all are aware of the arrangements that have been made. If the prosecuting authority is not the CPS then that delegate must ensure that that other authority will arrange for a representative to attend, in person or by live link, to assist the court.

**7A.8** If after conducting the assessment required by paragraph 7A.6 and taking the steps to which paragraph 7A.7 refers the designated officer's delegate finds it impossible to accommodate an unexpected case within the period to which paragraph 7A.3 or 7A.4 refers then arrangements must be made to hear the case on the next sitting day and the police custody officer must promptly be so informed.

CRIMINAL PROCEDURE RULES    PART 8    INITIAL DETAILS OF THE PROSECUTION CASE

**When this Part applies**  R8.1

8.1 This Part applies in a magistrates' court.

**Providing initial details of the prosecution case**  R8.2

8.2 (1) The prosecutor must serve initial details of the prosecution case on the court officer—
    (a) as soon as practicable; and
    (b) in any event, no later than the beginning of the day of the first hearing.
  (2) Where a defendant requests those details, the prosecutor must serve them on the defendant—
    (a) as soon as practicable; and
    (b) in any event, no later than the beginning of the day of the first hearing.
  (3) Where a defendant does not request those details, the prosecutor must make them available to the defendant at, or before, the beginning of the day of the first hearing.

**R8.3 Content of initial details**

8.3   Initial details of the prosecution case must include—

(a) where, immediately before the first hearing in the magistrates' court, the defendant was in police custody for the offence charged—

(i) a summary of the circumstances of the offence, and

(ii) the defendant's criminal record, if any; or

(b) where paragraph (a) does not apply—

(i) a summary of the circumstances of the offence,

(ii) any account given by the defendant in interview, whether contained in that summary or in another document,

(iii) any written witness statement or exhibit that the prosecutor then has available and considers material to plea, or to the allocation of the case for trial, or to sentence,

(iv) the defendant's criminal record, if any, and

(v) any available statement of the effect of the offence on a victim, a victim's family or others.

**R8.4 Use of initial details**

8.4   (1) This rule applies where—

(a) the prosecutor wants to introduce information contained in a document listed in rule 8.3; and

(b) the prosecutor has not—

(i) served that document on the defendant, or

(ii) made that information available to the defendant.

(2) The court must not allow the prosecutor to introduce that information unless the court first allows the defendant sufficient time to consider it.

### CRIMINAL PRACTICE DIRECTIONS   PART 8   INITIAL DETAILS OF THE PROSECUTION CASE

**CPD.8A CPD II Preliminary proceedings 8A: Defendant's Record**

*Copies of record*

8A.1 The defendant's record (previous convictions, cautions, reprimands, etc) may be taken into account when the court decides not only on sentence but also, for example, about bail, or when allocating a case for trial. It is therefore important that up to date and accurate information is available. Previous convictions must be provided as part of the initial details of the prosecution case under CrimPR Part 8.

8A.2 The record should usually be provided in the following format:

Personal details and summary of convictions and cautions — Police National Computer ['PNC'] Court/Defence/Probation Summary Sheet;

Previous convictions — PNC Court/Defence/Probation printout, supplemented by Form MG16 if the police force holds convictions not shown on PNC;

Recorded cautions — PNC Court/Defence/Probation printout, supplemented by Form MG17 if the police force holds cautions not shown on PNC.

8A.3 The defence representative should take instructions on the defendant's record and if the defence wish to raise any objection to the record, this should be made known to the prosecutor immediately.

8A.4 It is the responsibility of the prosecutor to ensure that a copy of the defendant's record has been provided to the Probation Service.

8A.5 Where following conviction a custodial order is made, the court must ensure that a copy is attached to the order sent to the prison.

*Additional information*

8A.6 In the Crown Court, the police should also provide brief details of the circumstances of the last three similar convictions and/or of convictions likely to be of interest to the court, the latter being judged on a case-by-case basis.

8A.7 Where the current alleged offence could constitute a breach of an existing sentence such as a suspended sentence, community order or conditional discharge, and it is known that that sentence is still in force then details of the circumstances of the offence leading to the sentence should be included in the antecedents. The detail should be brief and include the date of the offence.

8A.8 On occasions the PNC printout provided may not be fully up to date. It is the responsibility of the prosecutor to ensure that all of the necessary information is available to the court and the Probation Service and provided to the defence. Oral updates at the hearing will sometimes be necessary, but it is preferable if this information is available in advance.

CRIMINAL PROCEDURE RULES    PART 9    ALLOCATION AND SENDING FOR TRIAL

### General rules

**When this Part applies**                                                   R9.1

**9.1**  (1)  This Part applies to the allocation and sending of cases for trial under—

(a)  sections 17A to 26 of the Magistrates' Courts Act 1980[1]; and

(b)  sections 50A to 52 of the Crime and Disorder Act 1998[2].

(2)  Rules 9.6 and 9.7 apply in a magistrates' court where the court must, or can, send a defendant to the Crown Court for trial, without allocating the case for trial there.

(3)  Rules 9.8 to 9.14 apply in a magistrates' court where the court must allocate the case to a magistrates' court or to the Crown Court for trial.

(4)  Rule 9.15 applies in a magistrates' court where, after applying other rules in this Part, the court can commit for sentence to the Crown Court a defendant who pleads guilty to an offence related to one sent for trial there.

*[Note. At the first hearing in a magistrates' court the court may (and in some cases must) order trial in that court, or may (and in some cases must) send the defendant to the Crown Court for trial under section 51 or 51A of the Crime and Disorder Act 1998[3]. The decision depends upon—*

*(a)  the classification of the offence (and the general rule, subject to exceptions, is that an offence classified as triable only on indictment must be sent to the Crown Court for trial; an offence classified as triable only summarily must be tried in a magistrates' court; and an offence classified as triable either way, on indictment or summarily, must be allocated to one or the other court for trial, subject to the defendant's right to choose Crown Court trial: see in particular sections 50A, 51 and 51A of the 1998 Act[4] and section 19 of the Magistrates' Courts Act 1980[5]);*

*(b)  the defendant's age (and the general rule, subject to exceptions, is that an offence alleged against a defendant under 18 must be tried in a magistrates' court sitting as a youth court: see in particular sections 24 and 24A of the 1980 Act[6];*

*(c)  whether the defendant is awaiting Crown Court trial for another offence;*

*(d)  whether another defendant, charged with the same offence, is awaiting Crown Court trial for that offence;*

*(e)  in some cases (destroying or damaging property; aggravated vehicle taking), whether the value involved is more or less than £5,000; and*

*(f)  in a case of low-value shoplifting, whether the defendant chooses Crown Court trial: see section 22A of the 1980 Act[7].*

*The court's powers of sending and allocation, including its powers (i) to receive a defendant's indication of an intention to plead guilty (see rules 9.7, 9.8 and 9.13) and (ii) to give an indication of likely sentence (see rule 9.11), may be exercised by a single justice: see sections 51 and 51A(11) of the 1998 Act, and sections 17E, 18(5) and 24D of the 1980 Act[8].]*

---

[1]  1980 c. 43; sections 17A, 17D, 17E, 18 to 21 and 23 to 26 were inserted or amended by Schedule 3 to the Criminal Justice Act 2003 (c. 44).

[2]  1998 c. 37; sections 50A to 52 were inserted or amended by Schedule 3 to the Criminal Justice Act 2003 (c. 44).

[3]  1998 c. 37; section 51 was substituted by paragraphs 15 and 18 of Schedule 3 to the Criminal Justice Act 2003 (c. 44) and amended by section 59 of, and paragraph 1 of Schedule 11 to, the Constitutional Reform Act 2005 (c. 4). Section 51A was inserted by paragraphs 15 and 18 of Schedule 3 to the Criminal Justice Act 2003 (c. 44) and amended by section 49 of, and paragraph 5 of Schedule 1 to, the Violent Crime Reduction Act 2006 (c. 38) and paragraph 6 of Schedule 21 to the Legal Aid, Sentencing and Punishment of Offenders Act 2012 (c. 10).

[4]  1998 c. 37; section 50A was inserted by paragraphs 15 and 17 of Schedule 3 to the Criminal Justice Act 2003 (c. 44).

[5]  1980 c. 43; section 19 was substituted by paragraphs 1 and 5 of Schedule 3 to the Criminal Justice Act 2003 (c. 44) and amended by sections 144, 177 and 178 of, and paragraph 4 of Schedule 17, paragraph 80 of Schedule 21 and Part 5 of Schedule 23 to, the Coroners and Justice Act 2009 (c. 25).

[6]  1980 c. 43; section 24 was amended by paragraph 47 of Schedule 14 to the Criminal Justice Act 1982 (c. 48), sections 17, 68 and 101 of, and paragraph 6 of Schedule 8 and Schedule 13 to, the Criminal Justice Act 1991 (c. 53), paragraph 40 of Schedule 10, and Schedule 11, to the Criminal Justice and Public Order Act 1994 (c. 33), sections 47 and 119 of, and paragraph 40 of Schedule 8, to the Crime and Disorder Act 1998 (c. 37), paragraph 64 of Schedule 9 to the Powers of Criminal Courts (Sentencing) Act 2000 (c. 6), section 42 of, and paragraphs 1 and 9 of Schedule 3, and Part 4 of Schedule 37, to the Criminal Justice Act 2003 (c. 44) and sections 49 and 65 of, and paragraph 1 of Schedule 1 and Schedule 5 to, the Violent Crime Reduction Act 2006 (c. 38). Section 24A was inserted by paragraphs 1 and 10 of Schedule 3 to the Criminal Justice Act 2003 (c. 44).

[7]  1980 c. 43; section 22A was inserted by section 176 of the Anti-social Behaviour, Crime and Policing Act 2014 (c. 12) and amended by section 52 of the Criminal Justice and Courts Act 2015 (c. 2).

[8]  1980 c. 43; section 17E was inserted by paragraphs 1 and 3 of Schedule 3 to the Criminal Justice Act 2003 (c. 44). Section 18 was amended by section 59 of, and paragraph 1 of Schedule 9 to, the Criminal Justice Act 1982 (c. 48), section 68 of, and paragraph 6 of Schedule 8 to, the Criminal Justice Act 1991 (c. 53), section 49 of the Criminal Procedure and Investigations Act 1996 (c. 25), and paragraphs 1 and 4 of Schedule 3 to the Criminal Justice Act 2003 (c. 44). Section 24D was inserted by paragraphs 1 and 10 of Schedule 3 to the Criminal Justice Act 2003 (c. 44).

**R9.2**  **Exercise of magistrates' court's powers**

**9.2**  (1)  This rule applies to the exercise of the powers to which rules 9.6 to 9.14 apply.

(2)  The general rule is that the court must exercise its powers at a hearing in public, but it may exercise any power it has to—

(a)  where rule 9.7 (Sending for Crown Court trial) applies, if the defendant is represented;

(b)  withhold information from the public; or

(c)  order a hearing in private.

(3)  The general rule is that the court must exercise its powers in the defendant's presence, but it may exercise the powers to which the following rules apply in the defendant's absence on the conditions specified—

(a)  where rule 9.7 (Sending for Crown Court trial) applies, if the defendant is represented;

(b)  where rule 9.8 (Adult defendant: request for plea), rule 9.9 (Adult defendant: guilty plea) or rule 9.13 (Young defendant) applies, if—

(i)  the defendant is represented, and

(ii)  the defendant's disorderly conduct makes his or her presence in the courtroom impracticable;

(c)  where rule 9.10 (Adult defendant: not guilty plea) or rule 9.11 (Adult defendant: allocation for magistrates' court trial) applies, if—

(i)  the defendant is represented and waives the right to be present, or

(ii)  the defendant's disorderly conduct makes his or her presence in the courtroom impracticable; and

(d)  where rule 9.15 (Committal for sentence for offence related to an offence sent for trial) applies, unless—

(i)  it appears to the court to be contrary to the interests of justice to do so, and

(ii)  the court considers that there is an acceptable reason for the defendant's absence.

(4)  The court—

(a)  at the first hearing in the case must require a defendant who is present to provide, in writing or orally, his or her name and date of birth;

(b)  at any subsequent hearing may require such a defendant to provide that information by those means; and

(c)  may exercise its power to adjourn—

(i)  if either party asks, or

(ii)  on its own initiative.

(5)  Where the court on the same occasion deals with two or more offences alleged against the same defendant, the court must deal with those offences in the following sequence—

(a)  any to which rule 9.6 applies (Prosecutor's notice requiring Crown Court trial);

(b)  any to which rule 9.7 applies (sending for Crown Court trial, without allocation there), in this sequence—

(i)  any the court must send for trial, then

(ii)  any the court can send for trial; and

(c)  any to which rule 9.14 applies (Allocation and sending for Crown Court trial).

(6)  Where the court on the same occasion deals with two or more defendants charged jointly with an offence that can be tried in the Crown Court then in the following sequence—

(a)  the court must explain, in terms each defendant can understand (with help, if necessary), that if the court sends one of them to the Crown Court for trial then the court must send for trial in the Crown Court, too, any other of them—

(i)  who is charged with the same offence as the defendant sent for trial, or with an offence which the court decides is related to that offence,

(ii)  who does not wish to plead guilty to each offence with which he or she is charged, and

(iii)  (if that other defendant is under 18, and the court would not otherwise have sent him or her for Crown Court trial) where the court decides that sending is necessary in the interests of justice

even if the court by then has decided to allocate that other defendant for magistrates' court trial; and

(b)  the court may ask the defendants questions to help it decide in what order to deal with them.

(7)  After following paragraph (5), if it applies, where the court on the same occasion—

(a)  deals with two or more defendants charged jointly with an offence that can be tried in the Crown Court;

(b)  allocates any of them to a magistrates' court for trial; and

(c)  then sends another one of them to the Crown Court for trial,

the court must deal again with each one whom, on that occasion, it has allocated for magistrates' court trial.

*[Note. See sections 50A, 51, 51A and 52 of the Crime and Disorder Act 1998[9] and sections 17A, 17B, 17C, 18, 23, 24A, 24B and 24C of the Magistrates' Courts Act 1980[10].*

*Under sections 57A to 57E of the 1998 Act[11], the court may require a defendant to attend by live link a hearing to which this Part applies.*

*Where a defendant waives the right to be present then the court may nonetheless require his or her attendance by summons or warrant: see section 26 of the 1980 Act[12].*

*Under section 52A of the 1998 Act[13], reporting restrictions apply to the proceedings to which rules 9.6 to 9.14 apply.*

*Under section 86A of the Courts Act 2003[14], Criminal Procedure Rules must specify stages of proceedings at which the court must require the information listed in rule 9.2(4) and may specify other stages of proceedings when such requirements may be imposed. A person commits an offence if, without reasonable excuse, that person fails to comply with such a requirement, whether by providing false or incomplete information or by providing no information.*

*Part 46 contains rules allowing a representative to act on a defendant's behalf for the purposes of these Rules.*

*Part 3 contains rules about the court's powers of case management.]*

## Matters to be specified on sending for trial                                    R9.3

9.3   (1)   Where the court sends a defendant to the Crown Court for trial, it must specify—
        (a)   each offence to be tried;
        (b)   in respect of each, the power exercised to send the defendant for trial for that offence; and
        (c)   the Crown Court centre at which the trial will take place.
    (2)   In a case in which the prosecutor serves a notice to which rule 9.6(1)(a) applies (notice requiring Crown Court trial in a case of serious or complex fraud), the court must specify the Crown Court centre identified by that notice.
    (3)   In any other case, in deciding the Crown Court centre at which the trial will take place, the court must take into account—
        (a)   the convenience of the parties and witnesses;
        (b)   how soon a suitable courtroom will be available; and
        (c)   the directions on the allocation of Crown Court business contained in the Practice Direction.

*[Note. See sections 51 and 51D of the Crime and Disorder Act 1998[15].]*

## Duty of justices' legal adviser                                                 R9.4

9.4   (1)   This rule applies—
        (a)   only in a magistrates' court; and
        (b)   unless the court—
            (i)   includes a District Judge (Magistrates' Courts), and
            (ii)   otherwise directs.
    (2)   On the court's behalf, a justices' legal adviser may—
        (a)   read the allegation of the offence to the defendant;
        (b)   give any explanation and ask any question required by the rules in this Part; and
        (c)   make any announcement required by the rules in this Part, other than an announcement of—

---

[9]  1998 c. 37; section 52 was amended by paragraphs 68 and 69 of Schedule 3 to the Criminal Justice Act 2003 (c. 44).

[10]  1980 c. 43; sections 17A, 17B and 17C were inserted by section 49 of the Criminal Procedure and Investigations Act 1996 (c. 25). Section 17A was amended by paragraph 62 of Schedule 9 to the Powers of Criminal Courts (Sentencing Act 2000 (c. 6) and paragraphs 1 and 2 of Schedule 3 to the Criminal Justice Act 2003 (c. 44). Section 23 was amended by section 125 of, and paragraph 25 of Schedule 18 to, the Courts and Legal Services Act 1990 (c. 41) and paragraphs 1 and 8 of Schedule 3 to the Criminal Justice Act 2003 (c. 44). Sections 24A, 24B and 24C were inserted by paragraphs 1 and 10 of Schedule 3 to the Criminal Justice Act 2003 (c. 44).

[11]  1998 c. 37; sections 57A to 57E were substituted for section 57 as originally enacted by section 45 of the Police and Justice Act 2006 (c. 48), and amended by sections 106, 109 and 178 of, and Part 3 of Schedule 23 to, the Coroners and Justice Act 2009 (c. 25). Section 57A was further amended by paragraphs 36 and 39 of Schedule 12 to the Legal Aid, Sentencing and Punishment of Offenders Act 2012 (c. 10).

[12]  1980 c. 43; section 26 was amended by paragraphs 1 and 12 of Schedule 3 to the Criminal Justice Act 2003 (c. 44).

[13]  1998 c. 37; section 52A was inserted by paragraphs 15 and 19 of Schedule 3 to the Criminal Justice Act 2003 (c. 44) and amended by paragraphs 46 and 47 of Schedule 5 to the Legal Aid, Sentencing and Punishment of Offenders Act 2012 (c. 10).

[14]  2003 c. 39; section 86A was inserted by section 162 of the Policing and Crime Act 2017 (c. 3).

[15]  1998 c. 37; section 51D was inserted by paragraphs 15 and 18 of Schedule 3 to the Criminal Justice Act 2003 (c. 44) and amended by section 59 of, and paragraph 1 of Schedule 11 to, the Constitutional Reform Act 2005 (c. 4).

        (i)   the court's decisions about allocation and sending,

        (ii)  any indication by the court of likely sentence, or

        (iii) sentence.

   (3)  A justices' legal adviser must—

      (a)  assist an unrepresented defendant;

      (b)  give the court such advice as is required to enable it to exercise its powers; and

      (c)  if required, attend the members of the court outside the courtroom to give such advice, but inform the parties of any advice so given.

*[Note. For the functions of a justices' legal adviser, see sections 28 and 29 of the Courts Act 2003[16].]*

## R9.5  Duty of magistrates' court officer

9.5   (1)  The magistrates' court officer must—

      (a)  serve notice of a sending for Crown Court trial on—

        (i)   the Crown Court officer, and

        (ii)  the parties;

      (b)  in that notice record—

        (i)   the matters specified by the court under rule 9.3 (Matters to be specified on sending for trial),

        (ii)  any decision by the defendant under rule 9.7 (Sending for Crown Court trial) to require Crown Court trial for low-level shoplifting,

        (iii) any indication given by the defendant under rule 9.7 of intended guilty plea

        (iv) any decision by the defendant under rule 9.11 (Adult defendant: allocation to magistrates' court for trial) to decline magistrates' court trial,

        (v)  any opinion stated by the court under rule 9.15 (Committal for sentence for offence related to an offence sent for trial), and

        (vi) the date on which any custody time limit will expire;

      (c)  record any indication of likely sentence to which rule 9.11 or rule 9.13 applies; and

      (d)  give the court such other assistance as it requires.

   (2)  The magistrates' court officer must include with the notice served on the Crown Court officer—

      (a)  the initial details of the prosecution case served by the prosecutor under rule 8.2;

      (b)  a record of any—

        (i)   listing or case management direction affecting the Crown Court,

        (ii)  direction about reporting restrictions,

        (iii) decision about bail, for the purposes of section 5 of the Bail Act 1976[17],

        (iv) recognizance given by a surety, or

        (v)  representation order; and

      (c)  if relevant, any available details of any—

        (i)   interpreter,

        (ii)  intermediary, or

        (iii) other supporting adult, where the defendant is assisted by such a person.

*[Note. See sections 51 and 51D of the Crime and Disorder Act 1998[18], and section 20A of the Magistrates' Courts Act 1980[19].]*

### Sending without allocation for Crown Court trial

## R9.6  Prosecutor's notice requiring Crown Court trial

9.6   (1)  This rule applies where a prosecutor with power to do so requires a magistrates' court to send for trial in the Crown Court—

      (a)  a case of serious or complex fraud; or

      (b)  a case which will involve a child witness.

---

[16]  2003 c. 39; section 28 was amended by section 15 of, and paragraphs 308 and 327 of Schedule 4 to, the Constitutional Reform Act 2005 (c. 4).

[17]  1976 c. 63; section 5 was amended by section 65 of, and Schedule 12 to, the Criminal Law Act 1977 (c. 45), section 60 of the Criminal Justice Act 1982 (c. 48), paragraph 1 of Schedule 3 to the Criminal Justice and Public Order Act 1994 (c. 33), paragraph 53 of Schedule 9 to the Powers of Criminal Courts (Sentencing Act 2000 (c. 6), section 129(1) of the Criminal Justice and Police Act 2001 (c. 16), paragraph 182 of Schedule 8 to the Courts Act 2003 (c. 39), paragraph 48 of Schedule 3, paragraphs 1 and 2 of Schedule 36, and Parts 2, 4 and 12 of Schedule 37 to the Criminal Justice Act 2003 (c. 44) and section 208 of, and paragraphs 33 and 35 of Schedule 21 to, the Legal Services Act 2007 (c. 27).

[18]  1998 c. 37; section 51 was substituted and section 51D inserted by paragraphs 15 and 18 of Schedule 3 to the Criminal Justice Act 2003 (c. 44). They were amended by section 59 of, and paragraph 1 of Schedule 11 to, the Constitutional Reform Act 2005 (c. 4).

[19]  1980 c. 43; section 20A was inserted by paragraphs 1 and 6 of Schedule 3 to the Criminal Justice Act 2003 (c. 44).

(2) The prosecutor must serve notice of that requirement—

    (a) on the magistrates' court officer and on the defendant; and

    (b) before trial in a magistrates' court begins under Part 24 (Trial and sentence in a magistrates' court).

(3) The notice must identify—

    (a) the power on which the prosecutor relies; and

    (b) the Crown Court centre at which the prosecutor wants the trial to take place.

(4) The prosecutor—

    (a) must, when choosing a Crown Court centre, take into account the matters listed in rule 9.3(3) (court deciding to which Crown Court centre to send a case); and

    (b) may change the centre identified before the case is sent for trial.

*[Note. Under section 51B of the Crime and Disorder Act 1998[20], the Director of Public Prosecutions or a Secretary of State may require the court to send a case for trial in the Crown Court if, in that prosecutor's opinion, the evidence of the offence charged—*

    *(a) is sufficient for the person charged to be put on trial for the offence; and*

    *(b) reveals a case of fraud of such seriousness or complexity that it is appropriate that the management of the case should without delay be taken over by the Crown Court.*

*Under section 51C of the Crime and Disorder Act 1998[21], the Director of Public Prosecutions may require the court to send for trial in the Crown Court a case involving one of certain specified violent or sexual offences if, in the Director's opinion—*

    *(a) the evidence of the offence would be sufficient for the person charged to be put on trial for that offence;*

    *(b) a child would be called as a witness at the trial; and*

    *(c) for the purpose of avoiding any prejudice to the welfare of the child, the case should be taken over and proceeded with without delay by the Crown Court.*

*'Child' for these purposes is defined by section 51C(7) of the 1998 Act.]*

### Sending for Crown Court trial

**R9.7**

**9.7** (1) This rule applies where a magistrates' court must, or can, send a defendant to the Crown Court for trial without first allocating the case for trial there.

(2) The court must read the allegation of the offence to the defendant.

(3) The court must explain, in terms the defendant can understand (with help, if necessary)—

    (a) the allegation, unless it is self-explanatory;

    (b) that the offence is one for which the court, as appropriate—

        (i) must send the defendant to the Crown Court for trial because the offence is one which can only be tried there or because the court for some other reason is required to send that offence for trial,

        (ii) may send the defendant to the Crown Court for trial if the magistrates' court decides that the offence is related to one already sent for trial there; or

        (iii) (where the offence is low-value shoplifting and the defendant is 18 or over) must send the defendant to the Crown Court for trial if the defendant wants to be tried there; and

    (c) that reporting restrictions apply, which the defendant may ask the court to vary or remove.

(4) In the following sequence, the court must then—

    (a) invite the prosecutor to—

        (i) identify the court's power to send the defendant to the Crown Court for trial for the offence, and

        (ii) make representations about any ancillary matters, including bail and directions for the management of the case in the Crown Court;

    (b) invite the defendant to make representations about—

        (i) the court's power to send the defendant to the Crown Court, and

        (ii) any ancillary matters;

    (c) (where the offence is low-value shoplifting and the defendant is 18 or over) offer the defendant the opportunity to require trial in the Crown Court; and

    (d) decide whether or not to send the defendant to the Crown Court for trial.

(5) If the court sends the defendant to the Crown Court for trial, it must—

    (a) ask whether the defendant intends to plead guilty in the Crown Court and—

[20] 1998 c. 37; section 51B was inserted by paragraphs 15 and 18 of Schedule 3 to the Criminal Justice Act 2003 (c. 44) and amended by section 50 of, and paragraph 69 of Schedule 4 to, the Commissioners for Revenue and Customs Act 2005 (c. 11) and paragraphs 46 and 48 of Schedule 5 to the Legal Aid, Sentencing and Punishment of Offenders Act 2012 (c. 10).

[21] 1998 c. 37; section 51C was inserted by paragraphs 15 and 18 of Schedule 3 to the Criminal Justice Act 2003 (c. 44) and modified by section 63 of, and paragraph 36 of Schedule 6 to, the Serious Crime Act 2007 (c. 27).

        (i)  if the answer is 'yes', make arrangements for the Crown Court to take the defendant's plea as soon as possible, or

       (ii)  if the defendant does not answer, or the answer is 'no', make arrangements for a case management hearing in the Crown Court; and

   (b)  give any other ancillary directions.

*[Note. See sections 51, 51A and 51E of the Crime and Disorder Act 1998[22], and sections 22A and 24A of the Magistrates' Courts Act 1980[23].*

*See also Part 6 (Reporting, etc. restrictions).]*

### Allocation for magistrates' court or Crown Court trial

**R9.8**   **Adult defendant: request for plea**

**9.8**   (1)  This rule applies where—

   (a)  the defendant is 18 or over; and

   (b)  the court must decide whether a case is more suitable for trial in a magistrates' court or in the Crown Court.

   (2)  The court must read the allegation of the offence to the defendant.

   (3)  The court must explain, in terms the defendant can understand (with help, if necessary)—

   (a)  the allegation, unless it is self-explanatory;

   (b)  that the offence is one which can be tried in a magistrates' court or in the Crown Court;

   (c)  that the court is about to ask whether the defendant intends to plead guilty;

   (d)  that if the answer is 'yes', then the court must treat that as a guilty plea and must sentence the defendant, or commit the defendant to the Crown Court for sentence;

   (e)  that if the defendant does not answer, or the answer is 'no', then—

       (i)  the court must decide whether to allocate the case to a magistrates' court or to the Crown Court for trial,

       (ii)  the value involved may require the court to order trial in a magistrates' court (where the offence is one to which section 22 of the Magistrates' Courts Act 1980[24] applies), and

       (iii)  if the court allocates the case to a magistrates' court for trial, the defendant can nonetheless require trial in the Crown Court (unless the offence is one to which section 22 of the Magistrates' Courts Act 1980 applies and the value involved requires magistrates' court trial); and

   (f)  that reporting restrictions apply, which the defendant may ask the court to vary or remove.

   (4)  The court must then ask whether the defendant intends to plead guilty.

*[Note. See section 17A of the Magistrates' Courts Act 1980[25].*

*For the circumstances in which a magistrates' court may (and, in some cases, must) commit a defendant to the Crown Court for sentence after that defendant has indicated an intention to plead guilty where this rule applies see sections 18 and 20 of the Sentencing Act 2020[26].*

*See also Part 6 (Reporting, etc. restrictions).]*

**R9.9**   **Adult defendant: guilty plea**

**9.9**   (1)  This rule applies where—

   (a)  rule 9.8 applies; and

   (b)  the defendant indicates an intention to plead guilty.

   (2)  The court must exercise its power to deal with the case—

   (a)  as if the defendant had just pleaded guilty at a trial in a magistrates' court; and

   (b)  in accordance with rule 24.11 (Procedure if the court convicts).

---

[22] 1998 c. 37; section 51 was substituted, and sections 51A and 51E inserted, by paragraphs 15 and 18 of Schedule 3 to the Criminal Justice Act 2003 (c. 44). Section 51 was amended by section 59 of, and paragraph 1 of Schedule 11 to, the Constitutional Reform Act 2005 (c. 4). Section 51A was amended by section 49 of, and paragraph 5 of Schedule 1 to, the Violent Crime Reduction Act 2006 (c. 38) and paragraph 6 of Schedule 21 to the Legal Aid, Sentencing and Punishment of Offenders Act 2012 (c. 10).

[23] 1980 c. 43; section 24A was inserted by paragraphs 1 and 10 of Schedule 3 to the Criminal Justice Act 2003 (c. 44). Section 22A was inserted by section 176 of the Anti-social Behaviour, Crime and Policing Act 2014 (c. 12).

[24] 1980 c. 43; section 22 was amended by sections 38 and 170(2) of, and Schedule 16 to, the Criminal Justice Act 1988 (c. 33), section 68 of, and paragraph 6 of Schedule 8 to, the Criminal Justice Act 1991 (c. 53), section 2(2) of the Aggravated Vehicle Taking Act 1992 (c. 11) and sections 46 and 168(3) of, and Schedule 11 to, the Criminal Justice and Public Order Act 1994 (c. 33).

[25] 1980 c. 43; section 17A was inserted by section 49 of the Criminal Procedure and Investigations Act 1996 (c. 25) and amended by paragraph 62 of Schedule 9 to the Powers of Criminal Courts (Sentencing Act 2000 (c. 6) and paragraphs 1 and 2 of Schedule 3 to the Criminal Justice Act 2003 (c. 44).

[26] 2020 c. 17.

*[Note. See section 17A of the Magistrates' Courts Act 1980.]*

**Adult defendant: not guilty plea**                                                    R9.10

**9.10** (1) This rule applies where—
    (a) rule 9.8 applies; and
    (b) the defendant—
        (i) indicates an intention to plead not guilty, or
        (ii) gives no indication of intended plea.
(2) In the following sequence, the court must then—
    (a) where the offence is one to which section 22 of the Magistrates' Courts Act 1980 applies, explain in terms the defendant can understand (with help, if necessary) that—
        (i) if the court decides that the value involved clearly is less than £5,000, the court must order trial in a magistrates' court,
        (ii) if the court decides that it is not clear whether that value is more or less than £5,000, then the court will ask whether the defendant agrees to be tried in a magistrates' court, and
        (iii) if the answer to that question is 'yes', then the court must order such a trial and if the defendant is convicted then the maximum sentence is limited;
    (b) invite the prosecutor to—
        (i) identify any previous convictions of which it can take account, and
        (ii) make representations about how the court should allocate the case for trial, including representations about the value involved, if relevant;
    (c) invite the defendant to make such representations;
    (d) where the offence is one to which section 22 of the Magistrates' Courts Act 1980 applies—
        (i) if it is not clear whether the value involved is more or less than £5,000, ask whether the defendant agrees to be tried in a magistrates' court,
        (ii) if the defendant's answer to that question is 'yes', or if that value clearly is less than £5,000, order a trial in a magistrates' court,
        (iii) if the defendant does not answer that question, or the answer is 'no', or if that value clearly is more than £5,000, apply paragraph (2)(e); and
    (e) exercise its power to allocate the case for trial, taking into account—
        (i) the adequacy of a magistrates' court's sentencing powers,
        (ii) any representations by the parties, and
        (iii) any allocation guidelines issued by the Sentencing Council.

*[Note. See sections 17A, 18, 19, 22 and 24A of the Magistrates' Courts Act 1980[27].*

*Under section 22 of the 1980 Act, some offences, which otherwise could be tried in a magistrates' court or in the Crown Court, must be tried in a magistrates' court in the circumstances described in this rule.*

*The convictions of which the court may take account are those specified by section 19 of the 1980 Act.*

*The Sentencing Council may issue allocation guidelines under section 122 of the Coroners and Justice Act 2009[28]. The definitive allocation guideline which took effect on 1st March, 2016 provides:*

*(1) In general, either way offences should be tried summarily unless—*
    *(a) the outcome would clearly be a sentence in excess of the court's powers for the offence(s) concerned after taking into account personal mitigation and any potential reduction for a guilty plea; or*
    *(b) for reasons of unusual legal, procedural or factual complexity, the case should be tried in the Crown Court. This exception may apply in cases where a very substantial fine is the likely sentence. Other circumstances where this exception will apply are likely to be rare and case specific; the court will rely on the submissions of the parties to identify relevant cases.*
*(2) In cases with no factual or legal complications the court should bear in mind its power to commit for sentence after a trial and may retain jurisdiction notwithstanding that the likely sentence might exceed its powers.*

---

[27] 1980 c. 43; section 18 was amended by section 59 of, and paragraph 1 of Schedule 9 to, the Criminal Justice Act 1982 (c. 48), section 68 of, and paragraph 6 of Schedule 8 to, the Criminal Justice Act 1991 (c. 53), section 49 of the Criminal Procedure and Investigations Act 1996 (c. 25), and paragraphs 1 and 4 of Schedule 3 to the Criminal Justice Act 2003 (c. 44). Section 19 was substituted by paragraphs 1 and 5 of Schedule 3 to the Criminal Justice Act 2003 (c. 44) and amended by sections 144, 177 and 178 of, and paragraph 4 of Schedule 17, paragraph 80 of Schedule 21 and Part 5 of Schedule 23 to, the Coroners and Justice Act 2009 (c. 25).
[28] 2009 c. 25.

Criminal Procedure Rules and Criminal Practice Directions

(3) *Cases may be tried summarily even where the defendant is subject to a Crown Court Suspended Sentence Order or Community Order.*

(4) *All parties should be asked by the court to make representations as to whether the case is suitable for summary trial. The court should refer to definitive guidelines (if any) to assess the likely sentence for the offence in the light of the facts alleged by the prosecution case, taking into account all aspects of the case including those advanced by the defence, including any personal mitigation to which the defence wish to refer.*

*Where the court decides that the case is suitable to be dealt with in the magistrates' court, it must warn the defendant that all sentencing options remain open and, if the defendant consents to summary trial and is convicted by the court or pleads guilty, the defendant may be committed to the Crown Court for sentence.]*

### R9.11   Adult defendant: allocation for magistrates' court trial

9.11  (1) This rule applies where—

   (a) rule 9.10 applies; and

   (b) the court allocates the case to a magistrates' court for trial.

(2) The court must explain, in terms the defendant can understand (with help, if necessary) that—

   (a) the court considers the case more suitable for trial in a magistrates' court than in the Crown Court;

   (b) if the defendant is convicted at a magistrates' court trial, then in some circumstances the court may commit the defendant to the Crown Court for sentence;

   (c) if the defendant does not agree to a magistrates' court trial, then the court must send the defendant to the Crown Court for trial; and

   (d) before deciding whether to accept magistrates' court trial, the defendant may ask the court for an indication of whether a custodial or non-custodial sentence is more likely in the event of a guilty plea at such a trial, but the court need not give such an indication.

(3) If the defendant asks for such an indication of sentence and the court gives such an indication—

   (a) the court must then ask again whether the defendant intends to plead guilty;

   (b) if, in answer to that question, the defendant indicates an intention to plead guilty, then the court must exercise its power to deal with the case—

      (i) as if the defendant had just pleaded guilty to an offence that can be tried only in a magistrates' court, and

      (ii) in accordance with rule 24.11 (Procedure if the court convicts); and

   (c) if, in answer to that question, the defendant indicates an intention to plead not guilty, or gives no indication of intended plea, in the following sequence the court must then—

      (i) ask whether the defendant agrees to trial in a magistrates' court,

      (ii) if the defendant's answer to that question is 'yes', order such a trial, and

      (iii) if the defendant does not answer that question, or the answer is 'no', apply rule 9.14.

(4) If the defendant asks for an indication of sentence but the court gives none, or if the defendant does not ask for such an indication, in the following sequence the court must then—

   (a) ask whether the defendant agrees to trial in a magistrates' court;

   (b) if the defendant's answer to that question is 'yes', order such a trial; and

   (c) if the defendant does not answer that question, or the answer is 'no', apply rule 9.14.

*[Note. See section 20 of the Magistrates' Courts Act 1980[29].*

*For the circumstances in which a magistrates' court may (and, in some cases, must) commit a defendant to the Crown Court for sentence after that defendant has been convicted at a magistrates' court trial, see sections 14, 15, 17 and 20 of the Sentencing Act 2020[30].*

*For the circumstances in which an indication of sentence to which this rule applies restricts the sentencing powers of a court, see section 20A of the 1980 Act[31].*

*Where the court orders trial in a magistrates' court, see also rules 3.16 to 3.18 about preparation for trial.]*

---

[29]  1980 c. 43; section 20 was amended by section 100 of, and paragraph 25 of Schedule 11 to, the Criminal Justice Act 1991 (c. 53), paragraph 63 of Schedule 9 to the Powers of Criminal Courts (Sentencing Act 2000 (c. 6) and paragraphs 1 and 6 of Schedule 3 to the Criminal Justice Act 2003 (c. 44).

[30]  2020 c. 17.

[31]  1980 c. 43; section 20A was inserted by paragraphs 1 and 6 of Schedule 3 to the Criminal Justice Act 2003 (c. 44).

**Adult defendant: prosecutor's application for Crown Court trial**                R9.12

9.12  (1)  This rule applies where—
    (a)  rule 9.11 applies;
    (b)  the defendant agrees to trial in a magistrates' court; but
    (c)  the prosecutor wants the court to exercise its power to send the defendant to the Crown Court for trial instead.

    (2)  The prosecutor must—
    (a)  apply before trial in a magistrates' court begins under Part 24 (Trial and sentence in a magistrates' court); and
    (b)  notify—
      (i)  the defendant, and
      (ii)  the magistrates' court officer.

    (3)  The court must determine an application to which this rule applies before it deals with any other pre-trial application.

*[Note. See sections 8A and 25 of the Magistrates' Courts Act 1980[32]. Under section 25(2B), the court may grant an application to which this rule applies only if it is satisfied that the sentence which a magistrates' court would have power to impose would be inadequate.]*

**Young defendant**                R9.13

9.13  (1)  This rule applies where—
    (a)  the defendant is under 18; and
    (b)  the court must decide whether to send the defendant for Crown Court trial instead of ordering trial in a youth court.

    (2)  The court must read the allegation of the offence to the defendant.

    (3)  The court must explain, in terms the defendant can understand (with help, if necessary)—
    (a)  the allegation, unless it is self-explanatory;
    (b)  that the offence is one which can be tried in the Crown Court instead of in a youth court;
    (c)  that the court is about to ask whether the defendant intends to plead guilty;
    (d)  that if the answer is 'yes', then the court must treat that as a guilty plea and must sentence the defendant, or commit the defendant to the Crown Court for sentence;
    (e)  that if the defendant does not answer, or the answer is 'no', then the court must decide whether to send the defendant for Crown Court trial instead of ordering trial in a youth court;
    (f)  that before answering and at any time until the court decides whether to send the defendant for Crown Court trial or order trial in a youth court—
      (i)  the defendant may ask the court for an indication of whether a custodial or non-custodial sentence is more likely in the event of a guilty plea there and then, but
      (ii)  the court need not give such an indication; and
    (g)  that reporting restrictions apply, which the defendant may ask the court to vary or remove.

    (4)  The defendant may then ask the court for such an indication of sentence,

    (5)  Whether the defendant asks for and the court gives such an indication or not, the court must then ask whether the defendant intends to plead guilty.

    (6)  If the defendant's answer to that question is 'yes', the court must exercise its power to deal with the case—
    (a)  as if the defendant had just pleaded guilty at a trial in a youth court; and
    (b)  in accordance with rule 24.11 (Procedure if the court convicts).

    (7)  If the defendant does not answer that question, or the answer is 'no', in the following sequence the court must then—
    (a)  invite the prosecutor to make representations about whether Crown Court or youth court trial is more appropriate;
    (b)  invite the defendant to make such representations; and
    (c)  exercise its power to allocate the case for trial in the Crown Court or a youth court, taking into account—
      (i)  the offence and the circumstances of the offence,
      (ii)  the suitability of a youth court's sentencing powers,

---

[32]  1980 c. 43; section 8A was inserted by section 45 of, and Schedule 3 to, the Courts Act 2003 (c. 39) and amended by SI 2006/2493 and paragraphs 12 and 14 of Schedule 5 to the Legal Aid, Sentencing and Punishment of Offenders Act 2012 (c. 10). Section 25 was amended by section 31 of, and paragraph 3 of Schedule 1 and Schedule 2, to the Prosecution of Offences Act 1985 (c. 23), paragraph 6 of Schedule 8 to the Criminal Justice Act 1991 (c. 53), paragraphs 1 and 5 of Schedule 1 to the Criminal Procedure and Investigations Act 1996 (c. 25), section 42 of the Criminal Justice Act 2003 (c. 44) and paragraphs 1 and 11 of Schedule 3, and Part 4 of Schedule 37, to the Criminal Justice Act 2003 (c. 44).

(iii) where the defendant is jointly charged with an adult, whether it is necessary in the interests of justice for them to be tried together in the Crown Court, and

(iv) any representations by the parties.

*[Note. See section 24A of the Magistrates' Courts Act 1980[33].*

*For the circumstances in which a magistrates' court may (and, in some cases, must) commit a defendant who is under 18 to the Crown Court for sentence after that defendant has indicated a guilty plea, sections 16, 17, 19 and 20 of the Sentencing Act 2020[34].*

*Where the court orders trial in a youth court, see also rules 3.16 to 3.18 about preparation for trial.]*

### R9.14    Allocation and sending for Crown Court trial

**9.14**   (1)   This rule applies where—

     (a)   under rule 9.10 or rule 9.13, the court allocates the case to the Crown Court for trial;

     (b)   under rule 9.11, the defendant does not agree to trial in a magistrates' court; or

     (c)   under rule 9.12, the court grants the prosecutor's application for Crown Court trial.

   (2)   In the following sequence, the court must—

     (a)   invite the prosecutor to make representations about any ancillary matters, including bail and directions for the management of the case in the Crown Court;

     (b)   invite the defendant to make any such representations; and

     (c)   exercise its powers to—

       (i)   send the defendant to the Crown Court for trial, and

       (ii)   give any ancillary directions.

*[Note. See sections 21 and 24A of the Magistrates' Courts Act 1980[35] and section 51 of the Crime and Disorder 1998[36]. See also rule 9.3 (matters to be specified on sending for trial).]*

### R9.15    Committal for sentence for offence related to an offence sent for trial

**(1)**    This rule applies where—

     (a)   on a previous occasion the court has sent the defendant to the Crown Court for trial for an offence in exercise of a power to which rule 9.7, 9.13 or 9.14 applies;

     (b)   on the present occasion, under rule 9.9 or 9.13 the defendant indicates an intention to plead guilty to, and is convicted of, an offence which the court decides is related to the offence for which the defendant was previously sent for trial;

     (c)   the court decides to commit the defendant to the Crown Court for sentence for the related offence under—

       (i)   section 18 of the Sentencing Act 2020[37], if the defendant is over 18, or

       (ii)   section 19 of the 2020 Act[38], if the defendant is under 18; and

     (d)   in the court's opinion, if it were not committing the defendant for sentence under section 18 or 19 of the 2020 Act then it could, or would be required to, commit the defendant to the Crown Court for sentence for the related offence under—

       (i)   section 14 or 15 of that Act, if the defendant is over 18, or

       (ii)   section 16, 16A or 17 of that Act[39], if the defendant is under 18.

   (2)   The court must state that opinion for the Crown Court.

*[Note. See sections 18(4) and 19(3) of the Sentencing Act 2020 for the court's powers to state the opinion to which this rule refers.*

*Under section 51E of the Crime and Disorder Act 1998[40]—*

[33] 1980 c. 43; section 24A was inserted by paragraphs 1 and 10 of Schedule 3 to the Criminal Justice Act 2003 (c. 44).

[34] 2020 c. 1.

[35] 1980 c. 43; section 21 was amended by paragraphs 1 and 7 of Schedule 3 to the Criminal Justice Act 2003 (c. 44).

[36] 1998 c. 37; section 51 was substituted by paragraphs 15 and 18 of Schedule 3 to the Criminal Justice Act 2003 (c. 44) and amended by section 59 of, and paragraph 1 of Schedule 11 to, the Constitutional Reform Act 2005 (c. 4).

[37] 2020 c. 17.

[38] 2020 c. 17; section 19 was amended by section 46 of, and paragraph 26 of Schedule 13 to, the Counter-Terrorism and Sentencing Act 2021 (c. 11).

[39] 2020 c. 17; section 16A was inserted by section 46 of, and paragraph 26 of Schedule 13 to, the Counter-Terrorism and Sentencing Act 2021 (c. 11).

[40] 1998 c. 37; section 51E was substituted by paragraphs 15 and 18 of Schedule 3 to the Criminal Justice Act 2003 (c. 44).

(a) *an offence classified as triable either way is related to an offence for which a defendant has been sent for trial in the Crown Court if both offences are based on the same prosecution evidence (and see rule 10.2(4)(c) in the rules about indictments); and*

(b) *an offence classified as triable only summarily is related to an offence for which a defendant has been sent for trial in the Crown Court if both offences arise out of the same or connected circumstances.*

*Under section 51 of the 1998 Act*[41]—

(a) *if a magistrates' court sends a defendant to the Crown Court for trial for an offence and on the same occasion deals with a related offence then the general rule is that the court must send the defendant to the Crown Court for trial for the related offence, too; but*

(b) *if the court sends a defendant to the Crown Court for trial for an offence on one occasion and on a later occasion deals with a related offence then it may send the defendant to the Crown Court for trial for the related offence, too, or it may finish dealing with that offence itself and, if it convicts the defendant, may commit the defendant for sentence to the Crown Court instead.*

*For the circumstances in which a magistrates' court may (and, in some cases, must) commit a defendant to the Crown Court for sentence or for the making of other orders beyond a magistrates' court's powers, see sections 14, 15, 16, 16A, 17, 18, 19, 20 and 24 of the Sentencing Act 2020 and paragraph 11 of Schedule 16 to that Act. See also rules 24.11 (Procedure if the court convicts) and 28.12 (Sentencing, etc. after committal to the Crown Court). The note to rule 28.12 summarises the statutory provisions that apply.]*

## CRIMINAL PRACTICE DIRECTIONS    PART 9    ALLOCATION AND SENDING FOR TRIAL

**CPD II Preliminary proceedings 9A: Allocation (Mode of Trial)**    CPD.9A

**9A.1** Courts must follow the Sentencing Council's guideline on Allocation (mode of trial) when deciding whether or not to send defendants charged with 'either way' offences for trial in the Crown Court under section 51(1) of the Crime and Disorder Act 1998.

## CRIMINAL PROCEDURE RULES    PART 10    THE INDICTMENT

**When this Part applies**    R10.1

**10.1** This Part applies where—

(a) a magistrates' court sends a defendant to the Crown Court for trial under section 51 or section 51A of the Crime and Disorder Act 1998[1];

(b) a prosecutor wants a High Court judge's permission to serve a draft indictment;

(c) the Crown Court approves a proposed indictment under paragraph 2 of Schedule 17 to the Crime and Courts Act 2013[2] and rule 11.4 (Deferred prosecution agreements: Application to approve the terms of an agreement);

(d) a prosecutor wants to re-institute proceedings in the Crown Court under section 22B of the Prosecution of Offences Act 1985[3]; or

(e) the Court of Appeal orders a retrial, under section 8 of the Criminal Appeal Act 1968[4] or under section 77 of the Criminal Justice Act 2003[5].

[41] 1998 c. 37; section 51 was substituted by paragraphs 15 and 18 of Schedule 3 to the Criminal Justice Act 2003 (c. 44) and amended by section 52 of the Criminal Justice and Courts Act 2015 (c. 2).

[1] 1998 c. 37; section 51 was substituted by paragraphs 15 and 18 of Schedule 3 to the Criminal Justice Act 2003 (c. 44) and amended by section 59 of, and paragraph 1 of Schedule 11 to, the Constitutional Reform Act 2005 (c. 4). Section 51A was inserted by paragraphs 15 and 18 of Schedule 3 to the Criminal Justice Act 2003 (c. 44) and amended by section 49 of, and paragraph 5 of Schedule 1 to, the Violent Crime Reduction Act 2006 (c. 38) and paragraph 6 of Schedule 21 to the Legal Aid, Sentencing and Punishment of Offenders Act 2012 (c. 10).

[2] 2013 c. 22.

[3] 1985 c. 23; section 22B was inserted by section 45 of the Crime and Disorder Act 1998 (c. 37) and amended by paragraph 17 of Schedule 36 to the Criminal Justice Act 2003 (c. 44) and section 112 of, and Part 13 of Schedule 8 to, the Policing and Crime Act 2009 (c. 26).

[4] 1968 c. 19; section 8 was amended by Section 12 of, and paragraph 38 of Schedule 2 to, the Bail Act 1976 (c. 63), section 56 of, and Part IV of Schedule 11 to, the Courts Act 1971 (c. 23), section 65 of, and paragraph 36 of Schedule 3 to, the Mental Health (Amendment) Act 1982 (c. 51), section 148 of, and paragraph 23 of Schedule 4 to, the Mental Health Act 1983 (c. 20), section 43 of the Criminal Justice Act 1988 (c. 33), section 168 of, and paragraph 19 of Schedule 10 to, the Criminal Justice and Public Order Act 1994 (c. 33), section 58 of the Access to Justice Act 1999 (c. 22), sections 41 and 332 of, and paragraph 43 of Schedule 3 to, and Part 4 of Schedule 37 to, the Criminal Justice Act 2003 (c. 44) and section 32 of, and paragraph 2 of Schedule 4 to, the Mental Health Act 2007 (c. 12).

[5] 2003 c. 44.

*[Note. See also sections 3, 4 and 5 of the Indictments Act 1915[6] and section 2 of the Administration of Justice (Miscellaneous Provisions) Act 1933[7]. Under section 2(1) of the 1933 Act, a draft indictment (in the Act, a 'bill of indictment') becomes an indictment when it is 'preferred' in accordance with these rules. See rule 10.2.*

*Part 3 contains rules about the court's general powers of case management, including power to consider applications and give directions for (among other things) the amendment of an indictment and for separate trials under section 5 of the Indictments Act 1915. See in particular rule 3.29 (Application for joint or separate trials, etc.).*

*Under section 51D of the Crime and Disorder Act 1998[8], the magistrates' court must notify the Crown Court of the offence or offences for which the defendant is sent for trial. Part 9 (Allocation and sending for trial) contains relevant rules.*

*A Crown Court judge may approve a proposed indictment on approving a deferred prosecution agreement. Part 11 (Deferred prosecution agreements) contains relevant rules.*

*A prosecutor may apply to a High Court judge for permission to serve a draft indictment under rule 10.9.*

*Under section 22B of the Prosecution of Offences Act 1985, one of the prosecutors listed in that section may re-institute proceedings that have been stayed under section 22(4) of that Act[9] on the expiry of an overall time limit (where such a time limit has been prescribed). Section 22B(2) requires the service of a draft indictment within 3 months of the date on which the Crown Court ordered the stay, or within such longer period as the court allows.*

*The Court of Appeal may order a retrial under section 8 of the Criminal Appeal Act 1968 (on a defendant's appeal against conviction) or under section 77 of the Criminal Justice Act 2003 (on a prosecutor's application for the retrial of a serious offence after acquittal). Section 8 of the 1968 Act and section 84 of the 2003 Act require the arraignment of a defendant within 2 months. See also rules 27.7 and 39.14.*

*Where a magistrates' court sends a defendant to the Crown Court for trial under section 51 or 51A of the Crime and Disorder Act 1998, in some circumstances the Crown Court may try the defendant for other offences: see section 2(2) of the Administration of Justice (Miscellaneous Provisions) Act 1933 (indictable offences founded on the prosecution evidence), section 40 of the Criminal Justice Act 1988[10] (specified summary offences founded on that evidence) and paragraph 6 of Schedule 3 to the Crime and Disorder Act 1998 (power of Crown Court to deal with related summary offence sent to that court). An offence of theft under section 1 of the Theft Act 1968 which is low-value shoplifting under section 22A of the Magistrates' Courts Act 1980[11] is a summary offence unless the defendant chooses to be tried in the Crown Court.]*

---

[6] 1915 c. 90; section 4 was amended by section 83 of, and Part I of Schedule 10 to, the Criminal Justice Act 1948 (c. 58) and section 10 of, and Part III of Schedule 3 to, the Criminal Law Act 1967 (c. 58). Section 5 was amended by section 12 of, and paragraph 8 of Schedule 2 to, the Bail Act 1976 (c. 63), section 31 of, and Schedule 2 to, the Prosecution of Offences Act 1985 (c. 23) and section 331 of, and paragraph 40 of Schedule 36 to, the Criminal Justice Act 2003 (c. 44).

[7] 1933 c. 36; section 2 was amended by Part IV of Schedule 11 to, the Courts Act 1971 (c. 23), Schedule 5 to, the Senior Courts Act 1981 (c. 54), Schedule 2 to the Prosecution of Offences Act 1985 (c. 23), paragraph 1 of Schedule 2 to the Criminal Justice Act 1987 (c. 38), paragraph 10 of Schedule 15 to the Criminal Justice Act 1988 (c. 33), paragraph 8 of Schedule 6 to the Criminal Justice Act 1991 (c. 53), Schedule 1 to the Statute Law (Repeals) Act 1993, paragraph 17 of Schedule 1 to the Criminal Procedure and Investigations Act 1996 (c. 25), paragraph 5 of Schedule 8 to the Crime and Disorder Act 1998 (c. 37), paragraph 34 of Schedule 3 and Part 4 of Schedule 37 to the Criminal Justice Act 2003 (c. 44), paragraph 1 of the Schedule to S.I. 2004/2035, section 12 of, and paragraph 7 of Schedule 1 to, the Constitutional Reform Act 2005 (c. 4), sections 116 and 178 of, and Part 3 of Schedule 23 to, the Coroners and Justice Act 2009 (c. 25), paragraph 32 of Schedule 17 to the Crime and Courts Act 2013 (c. 22) and section 82 of the Deregulation Act 2015 (c. 20).

[8] 1998 c. 37; section 51D was inserted by paragraphs 15 and 18 of Schedule 3 to the Criminal Justice Act 2003 (c. 44) and amended by section 59 of, and paragraph 1 of Schedule 11 to, the Constitutional Reform Act 2005 (c. 4).

[9] 1985 c. 23; section 22 was amended by paragraph 104 of Schedule 15 to the Criminal Justice Act 1988 (c. 33), section 43 of the Crime and Disorder Act 1998 (c. 37), paragraph 36 of Schedule 11 to the Criminal Justice Act 1991 (c. 53), paragraph 27 of Schedule 9 to the Criminal Justice and Public Order Act 1994 (c. 33), section 71 of the Criminal Procedure and Investigations Act 1996 (c. 25), section 67(3) of the Access to Justice Act 1999 (c. 22), section 70 of, and paragraph 57 of Schedule 3 and paragraphs 49 and 51 of Schedule 36 to, the Criminal Justice Act 2003 (c. 44), section 59 of, and paragraph 1 of Schedule 11 to, the Constitutional Reform Act 2005 (c. 4) and paragraph 22 of Schedule 12 to the Legal Aid, Sentencing and Punishment of Offenders Act 2012 (c. 10).

[10] 1988 c. 33; section 40 was amended by section 4 of, and paragraph 39 of Schedule 3 to, the Road Traffic (Consequential Provisions) Act 1988 (c. 54), section 168 of, and paragraph 35 of Schedule 9 to, the Criminal Justice and Public Order Act 1994 (c. 33), section 47 of, and paragraph 34 of Schedule 1 to, the Criminal Procedure and Investigations Act 1996 (c. 25), section 119 of, and paragraph 66 of Schedule 8 to, the Crime and Disorder Act 1998 (c. 37) and paragraph 60 of Schedule 3 and Part 4 of Schedule 37 to the Criminal Justice Act 2003 (c. 44).

[11] 1980 c. 43; section 22A was inserted by section 176 of the Anti-social Behaviour, Crime and Policing Act 2014 (c. 12).

**The indictment: general rules**                                                **R10.2**

10.2 (1) The indictment on which the defendant is arraigned under rule 3.32 (Arraigning the defendant on the indictment) must be in writing and must contain, in a paragraph called a 'count'—

(a) a statement of the offence charged that—

(i) describes the offence in ordinary language, and

(ii) identifies any legislation that creates it; and

(b) such particulars of the conduct constituting the commission of the offence as to make clear what the prosecutor alleges against the defendant.

(2) More than one incident of the commission of the offence may be included in a count if those incidents taken together amount to a course of conduct having regard to the time, place or purpose of commission.

(3) The counts must be numbered consecutively.

(4) An indictment may contain—

(a) any count charging substantially the same offence as one for which the defendant was sent for trial;

(b) any count contained in a draft indictment served with the permission of a High Court judge or at the direction of the Court of Appeal; and

(c) any other count charging an offence that the Crown Court can try and which is based on the prosecution evidence that has been served, including a summary offence to which section 40 of the Criminal Justice Act 1988 applies.

(5) For the purposes of section 2 of the Administration of Justice (Miscellaneous Provisions) Act 1933—

(a) a draft indictment constitutes a bill of indictment; and

(b) the draft, or bill, is preferred before the Crown Court and becomes the indictment—

(i) where rule 10.3 applies (Draft indictment generated electronically on sending for trial), immediately before the first count (or the only count, if there is only one) is read to or placed before the defendant to take the defendant's plea under rule 3.32(1)(d),

(ii) when the prosecutor serves the draft indictment on the Crown Court officer, where rule 10.4 (Draft indictment served by the prosecutor after sending for trial), rule 10.5 (Draft indictment served by the prosecutor with a High Court judge's permission), rule 10.7 (Draft indictment served by the prosecutor on re-instituting proceedings) or rule 10.8 (Draft indictment served by the prosecutor at the direction of the Court of Appeal) applies, or

(iii) when the Crown Court approves the proposed indictment, where rule 10.6 applies (Draft indictment approved by the Crown Court with deferred prosecution agreement).

(6) An indictment must be in one of the forms set out in the Practice Direction unless—

(a) rule 10.3 applies; or

(b) the Crown Court otherwise directs.

(7) Unless the Crown Court otherwise directs, the court officer must—

(a) endorse any paper copy of the indictment made for the court with—

(i) a note to identify it as a copy of the indictment, and

(ii) the date on which the draft indictment became the indictment under paragraph (5); and

(b) where rule 10.4, 10.5, 10.7 or 10.8 applies, serve a copy of the indictment on all parties.

(8) The Crown Court may extend the time limit under rule 10.4, 10.5, 10.7 or 10.8, even after it has expired.

[*Note. Under section 2(6) of the Administration of Justice (Miscellaneous Provisions) Act 1933, Criminal Procedure Rules may provide for the manner in which and the time at which 'bills of indictment' are to be 'preferred'.*

*Under rule 3.29 (Application for joint or separate trials, etc.), the court may order separate trials of counts in the circumstances listed in that rule.*]

**Draft indictment generated electronically on sending for trial**                 **R10.3**

10.3 (1) Unless the Crown Court otherwise directs before the defendant is arraigned, this rule applies where—

(a) a magistrates' court sends a defendant to the Crown Court for trial;

(b) the magistrates' court officer serves on the Crown Court officer the notice required by rule 9.5 (Duty of magistrates' court officer); and

        (c)  by means of such electronic arrangements as the court officer may make for the purpose, there is presented to the Crown Court as a count—

           (i)  each allegation of an indictable offence specified in the notice, and

          (ii)  each allegation specified in the notice to which section 40 of the Criminal Justice Act 1988 applies (specified summary offences founded on the prosecution evidence).

  (2)  Where this rule applies—

      (a)  each such allegation constitutes a count;

      (b)  the allegation or allegations so specified together constitute a draft indictment;

      (c)  before the draft indictment so constituted is preferred before the Crown Court under rule 10.2(5)(b)(i) the prosecutor may substitute for any count an amended count to the same effect and charging the same offence;

      (d)  if under rule 3.19 (Service of prosecution evidence) the prosecutor has served copies of the documents containing the evidence on which the prosecution case relies then, before the draft indictment is preferred before the Crown Court under rule 10.2(5)(b)(i), the prosecutor may substitute or add—

          (i)  any count charging substantially the same offence as one specified in the notice, and

         (ii)  any other count charging an offence which the Crown Court can try and which is based on the prosecution evidence so served; and

      (e)  a prosecutor who substitutes or adds a count under paragraph (2)(c) or (d) must serve that count on the Crown Court officer and the defendant.

*[Note. An 'indictable offence' is (i) an offence classified as triable on indictment exclusively, or (ii) an offence classified as triable either on indictment or summarily. See also the note to rule 9.1 (Allocation and sending for trial: When this Part applies).*

*Section 40 of the Criminal Justice Act 1988 lists summary offences which may be included in an indictment if the charge—*

      *(a)  is founded on the same facts or evidence as a count charging an indictable offence; or*

      *(b)  is part of a series of offences of the same or similar character as an indictable offence which is also charged.]*

## R10.4   Draft indictment served by the prosecutor after sending for trial

**10.4**  (1)  This rule applies where—

      (a)  a magistrates' court sends a defendant to the Crown Court for trial; and

      (b)  rule 10.3 (Draft indictment generated electronically on sending for trial) does not apply.

  (2)  The prosecutor must serve a draft indictment on the Crown Court officer not more than 20 business days after serving under rule 3.19 (Service of prosecution evidence) copies of the documents containing the evidence on which the prosecution case relies.

## R10.5   Draft indictment served by the prosecutor with a High Court judge's permission

**10.5**  (1)  This rule applies where—

      (a)  the prosecutor applies to a High Court judge under rule 10.9 (Application to a High Court judge for permission to serve a draft indictment); and

      (b)  the judge gives permission to serve a proposed indictment.

  (2)  Where this rule applies—

      (a)  that proposed indictment constitutes the draft indictment; and

      (b)  the prosecutor must serve the draft indictment on the Crown Court officer not more than 20 business days after the High Court judge's decision.

## R10.6   Draft indictment approved with deferred prosecution agreement

**10.6**  (1)  This rule applies where—

      (a)  the prosecutor applies to the Crown Court under rule 11.4 (Deferred prosecution agreements: Application to approve the terms of an agreement); and

      (b)  the Crown Court approves the proposed indictment served with that application.

  (2)  Where this rule applies, that proposed indictment constitutes the draft indictment.

## R10.7   Draft indictment served by the prosecutor on re-instituting proceedings

**10.7**  (1)  This rule applies where the prosecutor wants to re-institute proceedings in the Crown Court under section 22B of the Prosecution of Offences Act 1985.

  (2)  The prosecutor must serve a draft indictment on the Crown Court officer not more than 3 months after the proceedings were stayed under section 22(4) of that Act[12].

---

[12]  1985 c. 23; section 22(4) was amended by section 43 of the Crime and Disorder Act 1998 (c. 37).

**Draft indictment served by the prosecutor at the direction of the Court of Appeal**                    **R10.8**

10.8   (1)   This rule applies where the Court of Appeal orders a retrial.

(2)   The prosecutor must serve a draft indictment on the Crown Court officer not more than 28 days after that order.

**Application to a High Court judge for permission to serve a draft indictment**                          **R10.9**

10.9   (1)   This rule applies where a prosecutor wants a High Court judge's permission to serve a draft indictment.

(2)   Such a prosecutor must—

(a)   apply in writing;

(b)   serve the application on—

(i)   the court officer, and

(ii)   the proposed defendant, unless the judge otherwise directs; and

(c)   ask for a hearing, if the prosecutor wants one, and explain why it is needed.

(3)   The application must—

(a)   attach—

(i)   the proposed indictment,

(ii)   copies of the documents containing the evidence on which the prosecutor relies, including any written witness statement or statements complying with rule 16.2 (Content of written witness statement) and any documentary exhibit to any such statement,

(iii)   a copy of any indictment on which the defendant already has been arraigned, and

(iv)   if not contained in such an indictment, a list of any offence or offences for which the defendant already has been sent for trial;

(b)   include—

(i)   a concise statement of the circumstances in which, and the reasons why, the application is made, and

(ii)   a concise summary of the evidence contained in the documents accompanying the application, identifying each passage in those documents said to evidence each offence alleged by the prosecutor and relating that evidence to each count in the proposed indictment; and

(c)   contain a statement that, to the best of the prosecutor's knowledge, information and belief—

(i)   the evidence on which the prosecutor relies will be available at the trial, and

(ii)   the allegations contained in the application are substantially true

unless the application is made by or on behalf of the Director of Public Prosecutions or the Director of the Serious Fraud Office.

(4)   A proposed defendant served with an application who wants to make representations to the judge must—

(a)   serve the representations on the court officer and on the prosecutor;

(b)   do so as soon as practicable, and in any event within such period as the judge directs; and

(c)   ask for a hearing, if the proposed defendant wants one, and explain why it is needed.

(5)   The judge may determine the application—

(a)   without a hearing, or at a hearing in public or in private; and

(b)   with or without receiving the oral evidence of any proposed witness.

(6)   At any hearing, if the judge so directs a statement required by paragraph (3)(c) must be repeated on oath or affirmation.

(7)   If the judge gives permission to serve a draft indictment, the decision must be recorded in writing and endorsed on, or annexed to, the proposed indictment.

*[Note. See section 2(6) of the Administration of Justice (Miscellaneous Provisions) Act 1933[13].]*

CRIMINAL PRACTICE DIRECTIONS   PART 10   THE INDICTMENT

**CPD II Preliminary proceedings 10A: Preparation and Content of the Indictment**                         **CPD.10A**

*Preferring the indictment*

**10A.1**   Section 2 of the Administration of Justice (Miscellaneous Provisions) Act 1933 allows Criminal Procedure Rules to 'make provision … as to the manner in which and the time at which bills of indictment are to be preferred'. CrimPR 10.2(5) lists the events which constitute preferment for the purposes of that Act. Where a defendant is contemplating an application to the Crown Court

Criminal Procedure Rules and Criminal Practice Directions

---

[13]   1933 c. 36; section 2(6) was amended by Part IV of Schedule 11 to the Courts Act 1971 (c. 23), paragraph 1 of the Schedule to S.I. 2004/2035 and section 82 of the Deregulation Act 2015 (c. 20).

to dismiss an offence sent for trial, under the provisions to which CrimPR 9.16 applies, or where the prosecutor is contemplating discontinuance, under the provisions to which CrimPR Part 12 applies, the parties and the court must be astute to the effect of the occurrence of those events: the right to apply for dismissal is lost if the defendant is arraigned, and the right to discontinue is lost if the indictment is preferred.

*Printing and signature of indictment*

**10A.2** Neither Section 2 of the Administration of Justice (Miscellaneous Provisions) Act 1933 nor the Criminal Procedure Rules require an indictment to be printed or signed. Section 2(1) of the Act was amended by section 116 of the Coroners and Justice Act 2009 to remove the requirement for signature. For the potential benefit of the Criminal Appeal Office, CrimPR 10.2(7) requires only that any paper copy of the indictment which for any reason in fact is made for the court must be endorsed with a note to identify it as a copy of the indictment, and with the date on which the indictment came into being. For the same reason, CrimPR 3.22 requires only that any paper copy of an indictment which in fact has been made must be endorsed with a note of the order and of its date where the court makes an order for joint or separate trials affecting that indictment or makes an order for the amendment of that indictment in any respect.

*Content of indictment; joint and separate trials*

**10A.3** The rule has been abolished which formerly required an indictment containing more than one count to include only offences founded on the same facts, or offences which constitute all or part of a series of the same or a similar character. However, if an indictment charges more than one offence, and if at least one of those offences does not meet those criteria, then CrimPR 3.21(4) cites that circumstance as an example of one in which the court may decide to exercise its power to order separate trials under section 5(3) of the Indictments Act 1915. It is for the court to decide which allegations, against whom, should be tried at the same time, having regard to the prosecutor's proposals, the parties' representations, the court's powers under the 1915 Act (see also CrimPR 3.21(4)) and the overriding objective. Where necessary the court should be invited to exercise those powers. It is generally undesirable for a large number of counts to be tried at the same time and the prosecutor may be required to identify a selection of counts on which the trial should proceed, leaving a decision to be taken later whether to try any of the remainder.

**10A.4** Where an indictment contains substantive counts and one or more related conspiracy counts, the court will expect the prosecutor to justify their joint trial. Failing justification, the prosecutor should be required to choose whether to proceed on the substantive counts or on the conspiracy counts. In any event, if there is a conviction on any counts that are tried, then those that have not been proceeded with can remain on the file marked 'not to be proceeded with without the leave of the court or the Court of Appeal'. In the event that a conviction is later quashed on appeal, the remaining counts can be tried.

**10A.5** There is no rule of law or practice which prohibits two indictments being in existence at the same time for the same offence against the same person and on the same facts. However, the court will not allow the prosecutor to proceed on both indictments. They cannot be tried together and the court will require the prosecutor to elect the one on which the trial will proceed. Where different defendants have been separately sent for trial for offences which properly may be tried together then it is permissible to join in one indictment counts based on the separate sendings for trial even if an indictment based on one of them already exists.

*Draft indictment generated electronically on sending for trial*

**10A.6** CrimPR 10.3 applies where court staff have introduced arrangements for the charges sent for trial to be presented in the Crown Court as the counts of a draft indictment without the need for those charges to be rewritten and served a second time on the defendant and on the court office. Where such arrangements are introduced, court users will be informed (and the fact will become apparent on the sending for trial).

**10A.7** Now that there is no restriction on the counts that an indictment may contain (see paragraph 10A.3 above), and given the Crown Court's power, and in some cases obligation, to order separate trials, few circumstances will arise in which the court will wish to exercise the discretion conferred by rule 10.3(1) to direct that the rule will not apply, thus discarding such an electronically generated draft indictment. The most likely such circumstance to arise would be in a case in which prosecution evidence emerging soon after sending requires such a comprehensive amendment of the counts as to make it more convenient to all participants for the prosecutor to prepare and serve under CrimPR 10.4 a complete new draft indictment than to amend the electronically generated draft.

*Draft indictment served by the prosecutor*

**10A.8** CrimPR 10.4 applies after sending for trial wherever CrimPR 10.3 does not. It requires the prosecutor to prepare a draft indictment and serve it on the Crown Court officer, who by CrimPR

10.2(7)(b) then must serve it on the defendant. In most instances service will be by electronic means, usually by making use of the Crown Court digital case system to which the prosecutor will upload the draft (which at once then becomes the indictment, under section 2 of the Administration of Justice (Miscellaneous Provisions) Act 1933 and CrimPR 10.2(5)(b)(ii)).

10A.9     The prosecutor's time limit for service of the draft indictment under CrimPR 10.4 is 28 days after serving under CrimPR 9.15 the evidence on which the prosecution case relies. The Crown Court may extend that time limit, under CrimPR 10.2(8). However, under paragraph CrimPD I 3A.16 of these Practice Directions the court will expect that in every case a draft indictment will be served at least 7 days before the plea and trial preparation hearing, whether the time prescribed by the rule will have expired or not.

*Amending the content of the indictment*

10A.10    Where the prosecutor wishes to substitute or add counts to a draft indictment, or to invite the court to allow an indictment to be amended, so that the draft indictment, or indictment, will charge offences which differ from those with which the defendant first was charged, the defendant should be given as much notice as possible of what is proposed. It is likely that the defendant will need time to consider his or her position and advance notice will help to avoid delaying the proceedings.

*Multiple offending: count charging more than one incident*

10A.11    CrimPR 10.2(2) allows a single count to allege more than one incident of the commission of an offence in certain circumstances. Each incident must be of the same offence. The circumstances in which such a count may be appropriate include, but are not limited to, the following:

   (a)  the victim on each occasion was the same, or there was no identifiable individual victim as, for example, in a case of the unlawful importation of controlled drugs or of money laundering;

   (b)  the alleged incidents involved a marked degree of repetition in the method employed or in their location, or both;

   (c)  the alleged incidents took place over a clearly defined period, typically (but not necessarily) no more than about a year;

   (d)  in any event, the defence is such as to apply to every alleged incident. Where what is in issue differs in relation to different incidents, a single 'multiple incidents' count will not be appropriate (though it may be appropriate to use two or more such counts according to the circumstances and to the issues raised by the defence).

10A.12    Even in circumstances such as those set out above, there may be occasions on which a prosecutor chooses not to use such a count, in order to bring the case within section 75(3)(a) of the Proceeds of Crime Act 2002 (criminal lifestyle established by conviction of three or more offences in the same proceedings): for example, because section 75(2)(c) of that Act does not apply (criminal lifestyle established by an offence committed over a period of at least six months). Where the prosecutor proposes such a course, it is unlikely that CrimPR Part 1 (the overriding objective) will require an indictment to contain a single 'multiple incidents' count in place of a larger number of counts, subject to the general principles set out at paragraph 10A.3.

10A.13    For some offences, particularly sexual offences, the penalty for the offence may have changed during the period over which the alleged incidents took place. In such a case, additional 'multiple incidents' counts should be used so that each count only alleges incidents to which the same maximum penalty applies.

10A.14    In other cases, such as sexual or physical abuse, a complainant may be in a position only to give evidence of a series of similar incidents without being able to specify when or the precise circumstances in which they occurred. In these cases, a 'multiple incidents' count may be desirable. If on the other hand the complainant is able to identify particular incidents of the offence by reference to a date or other specific event, but alleges that in addition there were other incidents which the complainant is unable to specify, then it may be desirable to include separate counts for the identified incidents and a 'multiple incidents' count or counts alleging that incidents of the same offence occurred 'many' times. Using a 'multiple incidents' count may be an appropriate alternative to using 'specimen' counts in some cases where repeated sexual or physical abuse is alleged. The choice of count will depend on the particular circumstances of the case and should be determined bearing in mind the implications for sentencing set out in *R v Canavan; R v Kidd; R v Shaw* [1998] 1 WLR 604, [1998] 1 Cr App R 79, [1998] 1 Cr App R (S) 243. In *R v A* [2015] EWCA Crim 177, [2015] 2 Cr App R (S) 115(12) the Court of Appeal reviewed the circumstances in which a mixture of multiple incident and single incident counts might be appropriate where the prosecutor alleged sustained sexual abuse.

*Multiple offending: trial by jury and then by judge alone*

**10A.15**  Under sections 17 to 21 of the Domestic Violence, Crime and Victims Act 2004, the court may order that the trial of certain counts will be by jury in the usual way and, if the jury convicts, that other associated counts will be tried by judge alone. The use of this power is likely to be appropriate where justice cannot be done without charging a large number of separate offences and the allegations against the defendant appear to fall into distinct groups by reference to the identity of the victim, by reference to the dates of the offences, or by some other distinction in the nature of the offending conduct alleged.

**10A.16**  In such a case, it is essential to make clear from the outset the association asserted by the prosecutor between those counts to be tried by a jury and those counts which it is proposed should be tried by judge alone, if the jury convict on the former. A special form of indictment is prescribed for this purpose.

**10A.17**  An order for such a trial may be made only at a preparatory hearing. It follows that where the prosecutor intends to invite the court to order such a trial it will normally be appropriate to proceed as follows. A draft indictment in the form appropriate to such a trial should be served with an application under CrimPR 3.15 for a preparatory hearing. This will ensure that the defendant is aware at the earliest possible opportunity of what the prosecutor proposes and of the proposed association of counts in the indictment.

**10A.18**  At the start of the preparatory hearing, the defendant should be arraigned on all counts in Part One of the indictment. Arraignment on Part Two need not take place until after there has been either a guilty plea to, or finding of guilt on, an associated count in Part One of the indictment.

**10A.19**  If the prosecutor's application is successful, the prosecutor should prepare an abstract of the indictment, containing the counts from Part One only, for use in the jury trial. Preparation of such an abstract does not involve 'amendment' of the indictment. It is akin to where a defendant pleads guilty to certain counts in an indictment and is put in the charge of the jury on the remaining counts only.

**10A.20**  If the prosecutor's application for a two stage trial is unsuccessful, the prosecutor may apply to amend the indictment to remove from it any counts in Part Two which would make jury trial on the whole indictment impracticable and to revert to a standard form of indictment. It will be a matter for the court whether arraignment on outstanding counts takes place at the preparatory hearing, or at a future date.

**CPD.10B**  **CPD II Preliminary proceedings 10B: Voluntary Bills of Indictment**

**10B.1**  Section 2(2)(b) of the Administration of Justice (Miscellaneous Provisions) Act 1933 and paragraph 2(6) of Schedule 3 to the Crime and Disorder Act 1998 allow the preferment of a bill of indictment by the direction or with the consent of a judge of the High Court. Bills so preferred are known as 'voluntary bills'.

**10B.2**  Applications for such consent must comply with CrimPR 10.3.

**10B.3**  Those requirements should be complied with in relation to each defendant named in the indictment for which consent is sought, whether or not it is proposed to prefer any new count against him or her.

**10B.4**  The preferment of a voluntary bill is an exceptional procedure. Consent should only be granted where good reason to depart from the normal procedure is clearly shown and only where the interests of justice, rather than considerations of administrative convenience, require it.

**10B.5**  Prosecutors must follow the procedures prescribed by the rule unless there are good reasons for not doing so, in which case prosecutors must inform the judge that the procedures have not been followed and seek leave to dispense with all or any of them. Judges should not give leave to dispense unless good reasons are shown.

**10B.6**  A judge to whom application for consent to the preferment of a documents submitted by the prosecutor and any written submissions made by the prospective defendant, and may properly seek any necessary amplification. CrimPR 10.3(4)(b) allows the judge to set a timetable for representations. The judge may invite oral submissions from either party, or accede to a request for an opportunity to make oral submissions, if the judge considers it necessary or desirable to receive oral submissions in order to make a sound and fair decision on the application. Any such oral submissions should be made on notice to the other party and in open court unless the judge otherwise directs.

CRIMINAL PROCEDURE RULES    PART 11    DEFERRED PROSECUTION AGREEMENTS

## When this Part applies                                                    R11.1

**11.1**  (1)  This Part applies to proceedings in the Crown Court under Schedule 17 to the Crime and Courts Act 2013.[1]

(2)  In this Part—

(a)  'agreement' means a deferred prosecution agreement under paragraph 1 of that Schedule;

(b)  'prosecutor' means a prosecutor designated by or under paragraph 3 of that Schedule; and

(c)  'defendant' means the corporation, partnership or association with whom the prosecutor proposes to enter, or enters, an agreement.

*[Note. Under Schedule 17 to the Crime and Courts Act 2013, a designated prosecutor may make a deferred prosecution agreement with a defendant, other than an individual, whom the prosecutor is considering prosecuting for an offences or offences listed in that Schedule. Under such an agreement, the defendant agrees to comply with its terms and the prosecutor agrees that, if the Crown Court approves those terms, then paragraph 2 of the Schedule will apply and —*

*(a)  the prosecutor will serve a draft indictment charging the defendant with the offence or offences the subject of the agreement;*

*(b)  the prosecution will be suspended under that paragraph, and the suspension may not be lifted while the agreement is in force; and*

*(c)  no-one may prosecute the defendant for the offence or offences charged while the agreement is in force, or after it expires if the defendant complies with it.*

*The Code for prosecutors issued under paragraph 6 of that Schedule contains guidance on the exercise of prosecution functions in relation to a deferred prosecution agreement.]*

## Exercise of court's powers                                               R11.2

**11.2**  (1)  The court must determine an application to which this Part applies at a hearing, which—

(a)  must be in private, under rule 11.3 (Application to approve a proposal to enter an agreement);

(b)  may be in public or private, under rule 11.4 (Application to approve the terms of an agreement), rule 11.6 (Application to approve a variation of the terms of an agreement) or rule 11.9 (Application to postpone the publication of information by the prosecutor); and

(c)  must be in public, under rule 11.5 (Application on breach of agreement) or rule 11.7 (Application to lift suspension of prosecution), unless the court otherwise directs.

(2)  If at a hearing in private to which rule 11.4 or rule 11.6 applies the court approves the agreement or the variation proposed, the court must announce its decision and reasons at a hearing in public.

(3)  The court must not determine an application under rule 11.3, rule 11.4 or rule 11.6 unless—

(a)  both parties are present;

(b)  the prosecutor provides the court with a written declaration that, for the purposes of the application—

(i)  the investigator enquiring into the alleged offence or offences has certified that no information has been supplied which the investigator knows to be inaccurate, misleading or incomplete, and

(ii)  the prosecutor has complied with the prosecution obligation to disclose material to the defendant; and

(c)  the defendant provides the court with a written declaration that, for the purposes of the application—

(i)  the defendant has not supplied any information which the defendant knows to be inaccurate, misleading or incomplete, and

(ii)  the individual through whom the defendant makes the declaration has made reasonable enquiries and believes the defendant's declaration to be true.

(4)  The court must not determine an application under rule 11.5 or rule 11.7—

(a)  in the prosecutor's absence; or

(b)  in the absence of the defendant, unless the defendant has had at least 20 business days in which to make representations.

(5)  If the court approves a proposal to enter an agreement—

(a)  the general rule is that any further application to which this Part applies must be made to the same judge; but

---

[1]  2013 c. 22.

        (b) the court may direct other arrangements.

(6) The court may adjourn a hearing—

        (a) if either party asks, or on its own initiative; and

        (b) in particular, if the court requires more information about—

            (i) the facts of an alleged offence,

            (ii) the terms of a proposal to enter an agreement, or of a proposed agreement or variation of an agreement, or

            (iii) the circumstances in which the prosecutor wants the court to decide whether the defendant has failed to comply with the terms of an agreement.

(7) The court may—

        (a) hear an application under rule 11.4 immediately after an application under rule 11.3, if the court approves a proposal to enter an agreement; and

        (b) hear an application under rule 11.7 immediately after an application under rule 11.5, if the court terminates an agreement.

*[Note. See paragraphs 7(4), 8(5), (6) and 10(5), (6) of Schedule 17 to the Crime and Courts Act 2013.*

*The Code for prosecutors issued under paragraph 6 of that Schedule contains guidance on fulfilling the prosecution duty of disclosure.]*

### R11.3    Application to approve a proposal to enter an agreement

**11.3** (1) This rule applies where a prosecutor wants the court to approve a proposal to enter an agreement.

(2) The prosecutor must—

        (a) apply in writing after the commencement of negotiations between the parties but before the terms of agreement have been settled; and

        (b) serve the application on—

            (i) the court officer, and

            (ii) the defendant.

(3) The application must—

        (a) identify the parties to the proposed agreement;

        (b) attach a proposed indictment setting out such of the offences listed in Part 2 of Schedule 17 to the Crime and Courts Act 2013 as the prosecutor is considering;

        (c) include or attach a statement of facts proposed for inclusion in the agreement, which must give full particulars of each alleged offence, including details of any alleged financial gain or loss;

        (d) include any information about the defendant that would be relevant to sentence in the event of conviction for the offence or offences;

        (e) specify the proposed expiry date of the agreement;

        (f) describe the proposed terms of the agreement, including details of any—

            (i) monetary penalty to be paid by the defendant, and the time within which any such penalty is to be paid,

            (ii) compensation, reparation or donation to be made by the defendant, the identity of the recipient of any such payment and the time within which any such payment is to be made,

            (iii) surrender of profits or other financial benefit by the defendant, and the time within which any such sum is to be surrendered,

            (iv) arrangement to be made in relation to the management or conduct of the defendant's business,

            (v) co-operation required of the defendant in any investigation related to the offence or offences,

            (vi) other action required of the defendant,

            (vii) arrangement to monitor the defendant's compliance with a term,

            (viii) consequence of the defendant's failure to comply with a term, and

            (ix) prosecution costs to be paid by the defendant, and the time within which any such costs are to be paid;

        (g) in relation to those terms, explain how they comply with—

            (i) the requirements of the code issued under paragraph 6 of Schedule 17 to the Crime and Courts Act 2013, and

            (ii) any sentencing guidelines or guideline cases which apply;

        (h) contain or attach the defendant's written consent to the proposal; and

        (i) explain why—

            (i) entering into an agreement is likely to be in the interests of justice, and

            (ii) the proposed terms of the agreement are fair, reasonable and proportionate.

(4) If the proposed statement of facts includes assertions that the defendant does not admit, the application must—

    (a) specify the facts that are not admitted; and

    (b) explain why that is immaterial for the purposes of the proposal to enter an agreement.

*[Note. See paragraphs 5 and 7 of Schedule 17 to the Crime and Courts Act 2013.]*

**Application to approve the terms of an agreement**          **R11.4**

**11.4** (1) This rule applies where—

    (a) the court has approved a proposal to enter an agreement on an application under rule 11.3; and

    (b) the prosecutor wants the court to approve the terms of the agreement.

(2) The prosecutor must—

    (a) apply in writing as soon as practicable after the parties have settled the terms; and

    (b) serve the application on—

        (i) the court officer, and

        (ii) the defendant.

(3) The application must—

    (a) attach the agreement;

    (b) indicate in what respect, if any, the terms of the agreement differ from those proposed in the application under rule 11.3;

    (c) contain or attach the defendant's written consent to the agreement;

    (d) explain why—

        (i) the agreement is in the interests of justice, and

        (ii) the terms of the agreement are fair, reasonable and proportionate;

    (e) attach a draft indictment, charging the defendant with the offence or offences the subject of the agreement; and

    (f) include any application for the hearing to be in private.

(4) If the court approves the agreement and the draft indictment, the court officer must—

    (a) endorse any paper copy of the indictment made for the court with—

        (i) a note to identify it as the indictment approved by the court, and

        (ii) the date of the court's approval; and

    (b) treat the case as if it had been suspended by order of the court.

*[Note. See paragraph 8 of Schedule 17 to the Crime and Courts Act 2013. See also rule 11.9 (Application to postpone the publication of information by the prosecutor).*

*Under paragraph 2(1) of Schedule 17 to the 2013 Act and section 2 of the Administration of Justice (Miscellaneous Provisions) Act 1933[2], the draft indictment to which this rule applies becomes an indictment when the court approves the agreement and consents to the service of that draft. Part 10 contains rules about indictments.*

*Under paragraph 2(2) of Schedule 17 to the 2013 Act, on approval of the draft indictment the proceedings are automatically suspended.*

*Under paragraph 13(2) of Schedule 17 to the 2013 Act, where the court approves an agreement the statement of facts contained in that agreement is to be treated as an admission by the defendant under section 10 of the Criminal Justice Act 1967[3] (proof by formal admission) in any criminal proceedings against the defendant for the alleged offence.]*

**Application on breach of agreement**          **R11.5**

**11.5** (1) This rule applies where—

    (a) the prosecutor believes that the defendant has failed to comply with the terms of an agreement; and

    (b) the prosecutor wants the court to decide—

---

[2] 1933 c. 36; section 2 was amended by Part IV of Schedule 11 to, the Courts Act 1971 (c. 23), Schedule 5 to, the Senior Courts Act 1981 (c. 54), Schedule 2 to the Prosecution of Offences Act 1985 (c. 23), paragraph 1 of Schedule 2 to the Criminal Justice Act 1987 (c. 38), paragraph 10 of Schedule 15 to the Criminal Justice Act 1988 (c. 33), paragraph 8 of Schedule 6 to the Criminal Justice Act 1991 (c. 53), Schedule 1 to the Statute Law (Repeals) Act 1993, paragraph 17 of Schedule 1 to the Criminal Procedure and Investigations Act 1996 (c. 25), paragraph 5 of Schedule 8 to the Crime and Disorder Act 1998 (c. 37), paragraph 34 of Schedule 3 and Part 4 of Schedule 37 to the Criminal Justice Act 2003 (c. 44), paragraph 1 of the Schedule to S.I. 2004/2035, section 12 of, and paragraph 7 of Schedule 1 to, the Constitutional Reform Act 2005 (c. 4), sections 116 and 178 of, and Part 3 of Schedule 23 to, the Coroners and Justice Act 2009 (c. 25), paragraph 32 of Schedule 17 to the Crime and Courts Act 2013 (c. 22) and section 82 of the Deregulation Act 2015 (c. 20).

[3] 1967 c. 80.

Criminal Procedure Rules and Criminal Practice Directions

       (i)   whether the defendant has failed to comply, and

       (ii)  if so, whether to terminate the agreement, or to invite the parties to agree proposals to remedy that failure.

(2)  The prosecutor must—

    (a)  apply in writing, as soon as practicable after becoming aware of the grounds for doing so; and

    (b)  serve the application on—

       (i)   the court officer, and

       (ii)  the defendant.

(3)  The application must—

    (a)  specify each respect in which the prosecutor believes the defendant has failed to comply with the terms of the agreement, and explain the reasons for the prosecutor's belief; and

    (b)  attach a copy of any document containing evidence on which the prosecutor relies.

(4)  A defendant who wants to make representations in response to the application must serve the representations on—

    (a)  the court officer; and

    (b)  the prosecutor,

not more than 20 business days after service of the application.

*[Note. See paragraph 9 of Schedule 17 to the Crime and Courts Act 2013. See also rule 11.9 (Application to postpone the publication of information by the prosecutor).]*

**R11.6**    **Application to approve a variation of the terms of an agreement**

**11.6**   (1)  This rule applies where the parties have agreed to vary the terms of an agreement because—

    (a)  on an application under rule 11.5 (Application on breach of agreement), the court has invited them to do so; or

    (b)  variation of the agreement is necessary to avoid a failure by the defendant to comply with its terms in circumstances that were not, and could not have been, foreseen by either party at the time the agreement was made.

(2)  The prosecutor must—

    (a)  apply in writing, as soon as practicable after the parties have settled the terms of the variation; and

    (b)  serve the application on—

       (i)   the court officer, and

       (ii)  the defendant.

(3)  The application must—

    (a)  specify each variation proposed;

    (b)  contain or attach the defendant's written consent to the variation;

    (c)  explain why—

       (i)   the variation is in the interests of justice, and

       (ii)  the terms of the agreement as varied are fair, reasonable and proportionate; and

    (d)  include any application for the hearing to be in private.

*[Note. See paragraph 10 of Schedule 17 to the Crime and Courts Act 2013. See also rule 11.9 (Application to postpone the publication of information by the prosecutor).]*

**R11.7**    **Application to lift suspension of prosecution**

**11.7**   (1)  This rule applies where—

    (a)  the court terminates an agreement before its expiry date; and

    (b)  the prosecutor wants the court to lift the suspension of the prosecution that applied when the court approved the terms of the agreement.

(2)  The prosecutor must—

    (a)  apply in writing, as soon as practicable after the termination of the agreement; and

    (b)  serve the application on—

       (i)   the court officer, and

       (ii)  the defendant.

(3)  A defendant who wants to make representations in response to the application must serve the representations on—

    (a)  the court officer; and

    (b)  the prosecutor,

not more than 20 business days after service of the application.

*[Note. See paragraphs 2(3) and 9 of Schedule 17 to the Crime and Courts Act 2013.]*

**Notice to discontinue prosecution**

11.8  (1)  This rule applies where an agreement expires—
    (a)  on its expiry date, or on a date treated as its expiry date; and
    (b)  without having been terminated by the court.
  (2)  The prosecutor must—
    (a)  as soon as practicable give notice in writing discontinuing the prosecution on the indictment approved by the court under rule 11.4 (Application to approve the terms of an agreement); and
    (b)  serve the notice on—
      (i)  the court officer, and
      (ii)  the defendant.

*[Note. See paragraph 11 of Schedule 17 to the Crime and Courts Act 2013.]*

**Application to postpone the publication of information by the prosecutor**

11.9  (1)  This rule applies where the prosecutor—
    (a)  makes an application under rule 11.4 (Application to approve the terms of an agreement), rule 11.5 (Application on breach of agreement) or rule 11.6 (Application to approve a variation of the terms of an agreement);
    (b)  decides not to make an application under rule 11.5, despite believing that the defendant has failed to comply with the terms of the agreement; or
    (c)  gives a notice under rule 11.8 (Notice to discontinue prosecution).
  (2)  A party who wants the court to order that the publication of information by the prosecutor about the court's or the prosecutor's decision should be postponed must—
    (a)  apply in writing, as soon as practicable and in any event before such publication occurs;
    (b)  serve the application on—
      (i)  the court officer, and
      (ii)  the other party; and
    (c)  in the application—
      (i)  specify the proposed terms of the order, and for how long it should last, and
      (ii)  explain why an order in the terms proposed is necessary.

*[Note. See paragraph 12 of Schedule 17 to the Crime and Courts Act 2013.*

*Part 6 of these Rules contains rules about applications for a restriction on reporting what takes place at a public hearing, or public access to what otherwise would be a public hearing.]*

**Duty of court officer, etc.**

11.10  (1)  Unless the court otherwise directs, the court officer must—
    (a)  arrange for the recording of proceedings on an application to which this Part applies; and
    (b)  arrange for the transcription of such a recording if—
      (i)  a party wants such a transcript, or
      (ii)  anyone else wants such a transcript (but that is subject to the restrictions in paragraph (2)).
  (2)  Unless the court otherwise directs, a person who transcribes a recording of proceedings under such arrangements—
    (a)  must not supply anyone other than a party with a transcript of a recording of—
      (i)  a hearing in private, or
      (ii)  a hearing in public to which reporting restrictions apply; but
    (b)  subject to that, must supply any person with any transcript for which that person asks—
      (i)  in accordance with the transcription arrangements made by the court officer, and
      (ii)  on payment by that person of any fee prescribed.
  (3)  The court officer must not identify either party to a hearing in private under rule 11.3 (Application to approve a proposal to enter an agreement) or rule 11.4 (Application to approve the terms of an agreement)—
    (a)  in any notice displayed in the vicinity of the courtroom; or
    (b)  in any other information published by the court officer.

**Court's power to vary requirements under this Part**

11.11  (1)  The court may—
    (a)  shorten or extend (even after it has expired) a time limit under this Part; and
    (b)  allow there to be made orally—
      (i)  an application under rule 11.4 (Application to approve the terms of an agreement), or
      (ii)  an application under rule 11.7 (Application to lift suspension of prosecution)

where the court exercises its power under rule 11.2(7) to hear one application immediately after another.

(2) A party who wants an extension of time must—

    (a) apply when serving the application or notice for which it is needed; and

    (b) explain the delay.

CRIMINAL PROCEDURE RULES    PART 12    DISCONTINUING A PROSECUTION

**R12.1**    **When this Part applies**

**12.1**   (1) This Part applies where—

    (a) the Director of Public Prosecutions can discontinue a case in a magistrates' court, under section 23 of the Prosecution of Offences Act 1985;[1] or

    (b) the Director of Public Prosecutions, or another public prosecutor, can discontinue a case sent for trial in the Crown Court, under section 23A of the Prosecution of Offences Act 1985.[2]

   (2) In this Part, 'prosecutor' means one of those authorities.

*[Note. Under section 23 of the Prosecution of Offences Act 1985, the Director of Public Prosecutions may discontinue proceedings in a magistrates' court, before the court—*

    *(a) sends the defendant for trial in the Crown Court; or*

    *(b) begins to hear the prosecution evidence, at a trial in the magistrates' court.*

*Under section 23(4) of the 1985 Act, the Director may discontinue proceedings where a person charged is in custody but has not yet been brought to court.*

*Under section 23 of the 1985 Act, the defendant has a right to require the proceedings to continue. See rule 12.3.*

*Under section 23A of the 1985 Act, the Director of Public Prosecutions, or a public authority within the meaning of section 17 of that Act[3], may discontinue proceedings where the defendant was sent for trial in the Crown Court under section 51 of the Crime and Disorder Act 1998[4]. In such a case—*

    *(a) the prosecutor must discontinue before a draft indictment becomes an indictment under rule 10.2(5); and*

    *(b) the defendant has no right to require the proceedings to continue.*

*Where a prosecution does not proceed, the court has power to order the payment of the defendant's costs out of central funds. See rule 45.4.]*

**R12.2**    **Discontinuing a case**

**12.2**   (1) A prosecutor exercising a power to which this Part applies must serve notice on—

    (a) the court officer;

    (b) the defendant; and

    (c) any custodian of the defendant.

   (2) Such a notice must—

    (a) identify—

      (i) the defendant and each offence to which the notice relates,

      (ii) the person serving the notice, and

      (iii) the power that that person is exercising; and

    (b) explain—

      (i) in the copy of the notice served on the court officer, the reasons for discontinuing the case,

      (ii) that the notice brings the case to an end,

      (iii) if the defendant is in custody for any offence to which the notice relates, that the defendant must be released from that custody, and

      (iv) if the notice is under section 23 of the 1985 Act, that the defendant has a right to require the case to continue.

---

[1] 1985 c. 23; section 23 was amended by section 119 of, and paragraph 63 of Schedule 8 to, the Crime and Disorder Act 1998 (c. 37), paragraph 290 of Schedule 8 to the Courts Act 2003 (c. 39) and paragraph 57 of Schedule 3 to the Criminal Justice Act 2003 (c. 44).

[2] 1985 c. 23; section 23A was inserted by section 119 of, and paragraph 64 of Schedule 8 to, the Crime and Disorder Act 1998 (c. 37) and amended by paragraph 57 of Schedule 3, and Part 4 of Schedule 37, to the Criminal Justice Act 2003 (c. 44).

[3] 1985 c. 23; section 17 was amended by section 40 of, and paragraph 41 of Schedule 9 to, the Constitutional Reform Act 2005 (c. 4) and paragraphs 1 and 4 of Part 4 of Schedule 7 to the Legal Aid, Sentencing and Punishment of Offenders Act 2012 (c. 10).

[4] 1998 c. 37; section 51 was substituted by paragraphs 15 and 18 of Schedule 3 to the Criminal Justice Act 2003 (c. 44) and amended by section 59 of, and paragraph 1 of Schedule 11 to, the Constitutional Reform Act 2005 (c. 4).

(3)  Where the defendant is on bail, the court officer must notify—
    (a)  any surety; and
    (b)  any person responsible for monitoring or securing the defendant's compliance with a condition of bail.

## Defendant's notice to continue

R12.3

12.3  (1)  This rule applies where a prosecutor serves a notice to discontinue under section 23 of the 1985 Act.
    (2)  A defendant who wants the case to continue must serve notice—
      (a)  on the court officer; and
      (b)  not more than 25 business days after service of the notice to discontinue.
    (3)  If the defendant serves such a notice, the court officer must—
      (a)  notify the prosecutor; and
      (b)  refer the case to the court.

CRIMINAL PROCEDURE RULES     PART 13     WARRANTS FOR ARREST,
DETENTION OR IMPRISONMENT

*[Note. Part 30 contains rules about warrants to take goods to pay fines, etc.]*

## When this Part applies

R13.1

13.1  (1)  This Part applies where the court can issue a warrant for arrest, detention or imprisonment.
    (2)  In this Part, 'defendant' means anyone against whom such a warrant is issued.

## Terms of a warrant for arrest

R13.2

13.2  A warrant for arrest must require each person to whom it is directed to arrest the defendant and—
    (a)  bring the defendant to a court—
      (i)  specified in the warrant, or
      (ii)  required or allowed by law; or
    (b)  release the defendant on bail (with conditions or without) to attend court at a date, time and place—
      (i)  specified in the warrant, or
      (ii)  to be notified by the court.

*[Note. The principal provisions under which the court can issue a warrant for arrest are—*

    *(a)  section 4 of the Criminal Procedure (Attendance of Witnesses) Act 1965[1];*
    *(b)  section 7 of the Bail Act 1976[2];*
    *(c)  sections 1 and 97 of the Magistrates' Courts Act 1980[3]; and*
    *(d)  sections 79, 80 and 81(4), (5) of the Senior Courts Act 1981[4].*

*See also section 27A of the Magistrates' Courts Act 1980[5] (power to transfer criminal proceedings) and section 78(2) of the Senior Courts Act 1981[6] (adjournment of Crown Court case to another place).]*

## Terms of a warrant for detention or imprisonment

R13.3

13.3  (1)  A warrant for detention or imprisonment must—
    (a)  require each person to whom it is directed to detain the defendant and—
      (i)  take the defendant to any place specified in the warrant or required or allowed by law, and
      (ii)  deliver the defendant to the custodian of that place; and

[1]  1965 c. 69; section 4 was amended by section 56 of, and paragraph 45 of Schedule 8 to, the Courts Act 1971 (c. 23) and sections 65, 66, 67 and 80 of, and Schedule 5 to, the Criminal Procedure and Investigations Act 1996 (c. 25).
[2]  1976 c. 63; section 7(1A) and (1B) were inserted section 198 of the Extradition Act 2003 (c. 41).
[3]  1980 c. 43; section 1 was amended by section 68 of, and paragraph 6 of Schedule 8 to, the Criminal Justice Act 1991 (c. 53), sections 43 and 109 of, and Schedule 10 to, the Courts Act 2003 (c. 39), section 31 of, and paragraph 12 of Schedule 7 to, the Criminal Justice Act 2003 (c. 44) and section 153 of the Police Reform and Social Responsibility Act 2011. It is further amended by paragraphs 7 and 8 of Schedule 36 to, the Criminal Justice Act 2003 (c. 44), with effect from a date to be appointed. Section 97 was amended by sections 13 and 14 of, and paragraph 7 of Schedule 2 to, the Contempt of Court Act 1981 (c. 47), section 31 of, and paragraph 2 of Schedule 4 to, the Criminal Justice (International Co-operation) Act 1990 (c. 5), sections 17 and 65 of, and paragraph 6 of Schedule 3 and Part I of Schedule 4 to, the Criminal Justice Act 1991 (c. 53), section 51 of the Criminal Procedure and Investigations Act 1996 (c. 25) and section 169 of the Serious Organised Crime and Police Act 2005 (c. 15).
[4]  1981 c. 54; section 80 was amended by paragraph 54 of Schedule 3 to the Criminal Justice Act 2003 (c. 44).
[5]  1980 c. 43; section 27A was inserted by section 46 of the Courts Act 2003 (c. 39).
[6]  1981 c. 54.

          (b) require that custodian to detain the defendant, as ordered by the court, until in accordance with the law—
            (i) the defendant is delivered to the appropriate court or place, or
            (ii) the defendant is released.

    (2) Where a magistrates' court remands a defendant to police detention under section 128(7)[7] or section 136[8] of the Magistrates' Courts Act 1980, or to customs detention under section 152 of the Criminal Justice Act 1988[9], the warrant it issues must—
          (a) be directed, as appropriate, to—
            (i) a constable, or
            (ii) an officer of Her Majesty's Revenue and Customs; and
          (b) require that constable or officer to detain the defendant—
            (i) for a period (not exceeding the maximum permissible) specified in the warrant, or
            (ii) until in accordance with the law the defendant is delivered to the appropriate court or place.

    (3) Where a magistrates' court sentences a defendant to imprisonment or detention and section 11(3) of the Magistrates' Courts Act 1980[10] applies (custodial sentence imposed in the defendant's absence), the warrant it issues must—
          (a) require each person to whom the warrant is directed—
            (i) to arrest the defendant and bring him or her to a court specified in the warrant, and
            (ii) unless the court then otherwise directs, after that to act as required by paragraph (1)(a) of this rule; and
          (b) require the custodian to whom the defendant is delivered in accordance with that paragraph to act as required by paragraph (1)(b) of this rule.

*[Note. Under section 128(7) of the Magistrates' Courts Act 1980, a magistrates' court can remand a defendant to police detention for not more than 3 clear days, if the defendant is an adult, or for not more than 24 hours if the defendant is under 18.*

*Under section 136 of the 1980 Act, a magistrates' court can order a defendant's detention in police custody until the following 8am for non-payment of a fine, etc.*

*Under section 152 of the Criminal Justice Act 1988, a magistrates' court can remand a defendant to customs detention for not more than 192 hours if the defendant is charged with a drug trafficking offence.]*

**R13.4**   **Information to be included in a warrant**

**13.4**  (1) A warrant must identify—
          (a) each person to whom it is directed;
          (b) the defendant against whom it was issued;
          (c) the reason for its issue;
          (d) the court that issued it, unless that is otherwise recorded by the court officer; and
          (e) the court office for the court that issued it.

    (2) A warrant for detention or imprisonment must contain a record of any decision by the court under—
          (a) section 91 of the Legal Aid, Sentencing and Punishment of Offenders Act 2012[11] (remands of children otherwise than on bail), including in particular—
            (i) whether the defendant must be detained in local authority accommodation or youth detention accommodation,
            (ii) the local authority designated by the court,
            (iii) any requirement imposed by the court on that authority,
            (iv) any condition imposed by the court on the defendant, and
            (v) the reason for any such requirement or condition;

---

[7] 1980 c. 43; section 128(7) was amended by section 48 of the Police and Criminal Evidence Act 1984 (c. 60). It is modified by section 91(5) of the Legal Aid, Sentencing and Punishment of Offenders Act 2012 (c. 10).

[8] 1980 c. 43; section 136 was amended by section 77 of, and paragraph 58 of Schedule 14 to, the Criminal Justice Act 1982 (c. 48), section 68 of, and paragraph 6 of Schedule 8 to, the Criminal Justice Act 1991(c. 53), section 95(2) of the Access to Justice Act 1999 (c. 22) and section 165(1) of, and paragraph 78 of Schedule 9 to, the Powers of Criminal Courts (Sentencing) Act 2000 (c. 6). It is further amended by sections 74 and 75 of, and paragraphs 58 and 68 of Schedule 7, and Schedule 8 to, the Criminal Justice and Court Services Act 2000 (c. 43), with effect from a date to be appointed.

[9] 1988 c. 33; section 152 was amended by paragraphs 1 and 17 of Schedule 11 to, the Proceeds of Crime Act 2002 (c. 29) and section 8 of the Drugs Act 2005 (c. 17).

[10] 1980 c. 43; section 11(3) was amended by section 123 of, and paragraph 1 of Schedule 8 to, the Criminal Justice Act 1988 (c. 33), section 168 of, and paragraph 39 of Schedule 10 to, the Criminal Justice and Public Order Act 1994 (c. 33), section 119 of, and paragraph 39 of Schedule 8 to, the Crime and Disorder Act 1998 (c. 37), section 304 of, and paragraphs 25 and 26 of Schedule 32 to, the Criminal Justice Act 2003 (c. 44) and section 54 of the Criminal Justice and Immigration Act 2008 (c. 4).

[11] 2012 c. 10.

(b)  section 80 of the Magistrates' Courts Act 1980[12] (application of money found on defaulter to satisfy sum adjudged); or

(c)  section 82(1) or (4) of the 1980 Act[13] (conditions for issue of a warrant).

(3)  A warrant for detention or imprisonment must include such an indication of the defendant's physical and mental health as may be needed to alert those to whom the warrant is directed—

(a)  to any vulnerability of the defendant; and

(b)  to any risk to others that may be posed by the defendant.

(4)  The indication required by paragraph (3) may be given by reference to an accompanying document.

(5)  A warrant that contains an error is not invalid, as long as—

(a)  it was issued in respect of a lawful decision by the court; and

(b)  it contains enough information to identify that decision.

*[Note. See sections 93(7) and 102(5) of the Legal Aid, Sentencing and Punishment of Offenders Act 2012. Under section 91 of the Act, instead of granting bail to a defendant under 18 the court may—*

*(a)  remand him or her to local authority accommodation and, after consulting with that authority, impose on the defendant a condition that the court could impose if granting bail; or*

*(b)  remand him or her to youth detention accommodation, if the defendant is at least 12 years old and the other conditions, about the offence and the defendant, prescribed by the Act are met.*

*Under section 80 of the Magistrates' Courts Act 1980, the court may decide that any money found on the defendant must not be applied towards payment of the sum for which a warrant is issued under section 76 of that Act (enforcement of sums adjudged to be paid).*

*See section 82(6) of the 1980 Act. Under section 82(1) and (4), the court may only issue a warrant for the defendant's imprisonment for non-payment of a sum due where it finds that the prescribed conditions are met.*

*Under section 123 of the 1980 Act[14], "no objection shall be allowed to any … warrant to procure the presence of the defendant, for any defect in it in substance or in form …".]*

### Execution of a warrant                                                                   R13.5

**13.5**  (1)  A warrant may be executed—

(a)  by any person to whom it is directed; or

(b)  if the warrant was issued by a magistrates' court, by anyone authorised to do so by section 125[15] (warrants), 125A[16] (civilian enforcement officers) or 125B[17] (execution by approved enforcement agency) of the Magistrates' Courts Act 1980.

(2)  The person who executes a warrant must—

(a)  explain, in terms the defendant can understand, what the warrant requires, and why;

(b)  show the defendant the warrant, if that person has it; and

(c)  if the defendant asks—

(i)  arrange for the defendant to see the warrant, if that person does not have it, and

(ii)  show the defendant any written statement of that person's authority required by section 125A or 125B of the 1980 Act.

---

[12]  1980 c. 43; section 80 was amended by section 33(1) of, and paragraph 83 of Schedule 2 to, the Family Law Reform Act 1987 (c. 42) and section 62(3) of, and paragraphs 45 and 49 of the Tribunals, Courts and Enforcement Act 2007 (c. 15).

[13]  1980 c. 43; section 82 was amended by section 77 of, and paragraph 52 of Schedule 14 to, the Criminal Justice Act 1982 (c. 48), sections 61 and 123 of, and paragraphs 1 and 2 of Schedule 8 to, the Criminal Justice Act 1988 (c. 33), section 55 of and paragraph 10 of Schedule 4 to the Crime (Sentences) Act 1997 (c. 43), paragraph 220 of Schedule 8 to the Courts Act 2003 (c. 39), section 62 of, and paragraphs 45 and 51 of Schedule 13 to, the Tribunals, Courts and Enforcement Act 2007 (c. 15) and section 179 of the Anti-social Behaviour, Crime and Policing Act 2014 (c. 12) and section 54 of, and paragraphs 2 and 3 of Schedule 12 to, the Criminal Justice and Courts Act 2015 (c. 2). It is further amended by paragraphs 58 and 63 of Part II of Schedule 7 to the Criminal Justice and Court Services Act 2000 (c. 43) and Part 7 of Schedule 37 to the Criminal Justice Act 2003 (c. 44), with effect from dates to be appointed.

[14]  1980 c. 43.

[15]  1980 c. 43; section 125 was amended by section 33 of the Police and Criminal Evidence Act 1984 (c. 60), section 65(1) of the Criminal Justice Act 1988 (c. 33), sections 95(1), 97(4) and 106 of, and Part V of Schedule 15 and Table (8) to, the Access to Justice Act 1999 (c. 22), section 109(1) of, and paragraph 238 of Schedule 8 to, the Courts Act 2003 (c. 39) and sections 62(3), 86 and 146 of and paragraphs 45 and 57 of Schedule 23 to, the Tribunals, Courts and Enforcement Act 2007 (c. 15).

[16]  1980 c. 43; section 125A was inserted by section 92 of the Access to Justice Act 1999 (c. 22) and amended by articles 46 and 52 of S.I. 2006/1737 and article 8 of, and paragraph 5 of the Schedule to, S.I. 2007/2128 and section 62 of, and paragraphs 45 and 58 of Schedule 13 to, the Tribunals, Courts and Enforcement Act 2007 (c. 15).

[17]  1980 c. 43; section 125A was inserted by section 92 of the Access to Justice Act 1999 (c. 22) and amended by articles 46 and 52 of S.I. 2006/1737 and article 8 of, and paragraph 5 of the Schedule to, S.I. 2007/2128 and section 62 of, and paragraphs 45 and 58 of Schedule 13 to, the Tribunals, Courts and Enforcement Act 2007 (c. 15).

Criminal Procedure Rules and Criminal Practice Directions

(3) The person who executes a warrant of arrest that requires the defendant to be released on bail must—

    (a) make a record of—

        (i) the defendant's name,

        (ii) the reason for the arrest,

        (iii) the defendant's release on bail, and

        (iv) when and where the warrant requires the defendant to attend court; and

    (b) serve the record on—

        (i) the defendant, and

        (ii) the court officer.

(4) The person who executes a warrant of detention or imprisonment must—

    (a) take the defendant—

        (i) to any place specified in the warrant, or

        (ii) if that is not immediately practicable, to any other place at which the defendant may be lawfully detained (and the warrant then has effect as if it specified that place);

    (b) obtain a receipt from the custodian; and

    (c) notify the court officer that the defendant has been taken to that place.

*[Note. Under section 125 of the Magistrates' Courts Act 1980, a warrant issued by a magistrates' court may be executed by any person to whom it is directed or by any constable acting within that constable's police area.*

*Certain warrants issued by a magistrates' court may be executed anywhere in England and Wales by a civilian enforcement officer, under section 125A of the 1980 Act; or by an approved enforcement agency, under section 125B of the Act. In either case, the person executing the warrant must, if the defendant asks, show a written statement indicating: that person's name; the authority or agency by which that person is employed, or in which that person is a director or partner; that that person is authorised to execute warrants; and, where section 125B applies, that the agency is registered as one approved by the Lord Chancellor.*

*See also section 125D of the 1980 Act[18], under which—*

    *(a) a warrant to which section 125A applies may be executed by any person entitled to execute it even though it is not in that person's possession at the time; and*

    *(b) certain other warrants, including any warrant to arrest a person in connection with an offence, may be executed by a constable even though it is not in that constable's possession at the time.]*

## R13.6    Warrants that cease to have effect on payment

13.6 (1) This rule applies to a warrant issued by a magistrates' court under any of the following provisions of the Magistrates' Courts Act 1980—

    (a) section 76[19] (enforcement of sums adjudged to be paid);

    (b) section 83[20] (process for securing attendance of offender);

    (c) section 86[21] (power of magistrates' court to fix day for appearance of offender at means inquiry, etc.);

    (d) section 136[22] (committal to custody overnight at police station for non-payment of sum adjudged by conviction).

*[Note. See sections 79[23] and 125(1) of the Magistrates' Courts Act 1980.]*

(2) The warrant no longer has effect if—

    (a) the sum in respect of which the warrant was issued is paid to the person executing it;

    (b) that sum is offered to, but refused by, that person; or

---

[18] 1980 c. 43; section 125D was inserted by section 96 of the Access to Justice Act 1999 (c. 22) and amended by sections 62 and 146 of, and paragraphs 45 and 61 of Schedule 13 to, the Tribunals, Courts and Enforcement Act 2007 (c. 15).

[19] 1980 c. 43: section 76 was amended by section 7 of the Maintenance Enforcement Act 1991 (c. 17); section 78 of, and Schedule 16 to, the Criminal Justice Act 1982 (c. 48), and section 62(3) of, and paragraphs 45 and 46 of Schedule 13 to, the Tribunals, Courts and Enforcement Act 2007 (c. 15).

[20] 1980 c. 43; section 83 was amended by articles 46 and 47 of S.I. 2006/1737 and sections 97(2) and 106 of, and Part V (table 8) of Schedule 15 to, the Access to Justice Act 1999 (c. 22).

[21] 1980 c. 43; section 86 was amended by section 51(2) of the Criminal Justice Act 1982 (c. 48) and section 97(3) of the Access to Justice Act 1999 (c. 22).

[22] 1980 c. 43; section 82 was amended by section 77 of, and paragraph 52 of Schedule 14 to, the Criminal Justice Act 1982 (c. 48), sections 61 and 123 of, and paragraphs 1 and 2 of Schedule 8 to, the Criminal Justice Act 1988 (c. 33), section 55 of and paragraph 10 of Schedule 4 to the Crime (Sentences) Act 1997 (c. 43), paragraph 220 of Schedule 8 to the Courts Act 2003 (c. 39), section 62 of, and paragraphs 45 and 51 of Schedule 13 to, the Tribunals, Courts and Enforcement Act 2007 (c. 15), section 179 of the Anti-social Behaviour, Crime and Policing Act 2014 (c. 12) and section 54 of, and paragraphs 2 and 3 of Schedule 12 to, the Criminal Justice and Courts Act 2015 (c. 2). It is further amended by paragraphs 58 and 63 of Part II of Schedule 7 to the Criminal Justice and Court Services Act 2000 (c. 43) and Part 7 of Schedule 37 to the Criminal Justice Act 2003 (c. 44), with effect from dates to be appointed.

[23] 1980 c. 43; section 79 was amended by paragraph 219 of Schedule 8 to the Courts Act 2003 (c. 39) and section 62 of, and paragraphs 45, 47 and 48 of Schedule 13 to, the Tribunals, Courts and Enforcement Act 2007 (c. 15).

(c) that person is shown a receipt for that sum given by—
  (i) the court officer, or
  (ii) the authority to which that sum is due.

## Warrant issued when the court office is closed    R13.7

13.7 (1) This rule applies where the court issues a warrant when the court office is closed.

(2) The applicant for the warrant must, not more than 72 hours later, serve on the court officer—
  (a) a copy of the warrant; and
  (b) any written material that was submitted to the court.

CRIMINAL PROCEDURE RULES    PART 14    BAIL AND CUSTODY TIME LIMITS

**General rules**

## When this Part applies    R14.1

14.1 (1) This Part applies where a magistrates' court or the Crown Court can—
  (a) grant or withhold bail, or impose or vary a condition of bail; and
  (b) where bail has been withheld, extend a custody time limit.

(2) Rules 14.18, 14.19 and 14.20 apply where a magistrates' court can authorise an extension of the period for which a defendant is released on bail before being charged with an offence.

(3) In this Part, 'defendant' includes a person who has been granted bail by a police officer.

*[Note. See in particular—*

*(a) the Bail Act 1976[1];*

*(b) section 128 of the Magistrates' Courts Act 1980[2] (general powers of magistrates' courts in relation to bail);*

*(c) section 81 of the Senior Courts Act 1981[3] (general powers of the Crown Court in relation to bail);*

*(d) section 115 of the Coroners and Justice Act 2009[4] (exclusive power of the Crown Court to grant bail to a defendant charged with murder);*

*(e) section 22 of the Prosecution of Offences Act 1985[5] (provision for custody time limits);*

*(f) the Prosecution of Offences (Custody Time Limits) Regulations 1987[6] (maximum periods during which a defendant may be kept in custody pending trial); and*

*(g) sections 47ZF and 47ZG of the Police and Criminal Evidence Act 1984[7] (extensions by court of pre-charge bail time limit).*

*At the end of this Part there is a summary of the general entitlement to bail and of the exceptions to that entitlement*

---

[1] 1976 c. 63.

[2] 1980 c. 43; section 128 was amended by section 59 to, and paragraphs 2, 3 and 4 of Schedule 9 to, the Criminal Justice Act 1982 (c. 48), section 48 of the Police and Criminal Evidence Act 1984 (c. 60), section 170(1) of, and paragraphs 65 and 69 of Schedule 15 to, the Criminal Justice Act 1988 (c. 33), section 125(3) of, and paragraph 25 of Schedule 18 to, the Courts and Legal Services Act 1990 (c. 41), sections 49, 52 and 80 of, and Schedule 5 to, the Criminal Procedure and Investigations Act 1996 (c. 25), paragraph 75 of Schedule 9 to the Powers of Criminal Courts (Sentencing) Act 2000 (c. 6) and paragraph 51 of Schedule 3 and Part 4 of Schedule 37 to the Criminal Justice Act 2003 (c. 44). It is modified by section 91(5) of the Legal Aid, Sentencing and Punishment of Offenders Act 2012 (c. 10).

[3] 1981 c. 54; section 81(1) was amended by sections 29 and 60 of the Criminal Justice Act 1982 (c. 48), section 15 of, and paragraph 2 of Schedule 12 to, the Criminal Justice Act 1987 (c. 38), section 168 of, and paragraph 19 of Schedule 9 and paragraph 48 of Schedule 10 to, the Criminal Justice and Public Order Act 1994 (c. 33), section 119 of, and paragraph 48 of Schedule 8 and Schedule 10 to, the Crime and Disorder Act 1998 (c. 37), section 165 of, and paragraph 87 of Schedule 9 and Schedule 12 to, the Powers of Criminal Courts (Sentencing) Act 2000 (c. 6), paragraph 54 of Schedule 3, paragraph 4 of Schedule 36 and Part 4 of Schedule 37 to the Criminal Justice Act 2003 (c. 44), articles 2 and 6 of S.I. 2004/1033 and section 177(1) of, and paragraph 76 of Schedule 21 to, the Coroners and Justice Act 2009 (c. 25).

[4] 2009 c. 25.

[5] 1985 c. 23; section 22 was amended by paragraph 104 of Schedule 15 to the Criminal Justice Act 1988 (c. 33), section 43 of the Crime and Disorder Act 1998 (c. 37), paragraph 36 of Schedule 11 to the Criminal Justice Act 1991 (c. 53), paragraph 27 of Schedule 9 to the Criminal Justice and Public Order Act 1994 (c. 33), section 71 of the Criminal Procedure and Investigations Act 1996 (c. 25), section 67(3) of the Access to Justice Act 1999 (c. 22), section 70 of, and paragraph 57 of Schedule 3 and paragraphs 49 and 51 of Schedule 36 to, the Criminal Justice Act 2003 (c. 44), section 59 of, and paragraph 1 of Schedule 11 to, the Constitutional Reform Act 2005 (c. 4) and paragraph 22 of Schedule 12 to the Legal Aid, Sentencing and Punishment of Offenders Act 2012 (c. 10).

[6] S.I. 1987/299; amended by sections 71 and 80 of, and paragraph 8 of Schedule 5 to, the Criminal Procedure and Investigations Act 1996 (c. 25) and S.I. 1989/767, 1991/1515, 1995/555, 1999/2744, 2000/3284, 2012/1344.

[7] 1984 c. 60; sections 47ZF and 47ZG were inserted by section 63 of the Policing and Crime Act 2017 (c. 3).

**R14.2**     **Exercise of court's powers: general**

**14.2**  (1)  The court must not make a decision to which this Part applies unless—

     (a)  each party to the decision and any surety directly affected by the decision—

        (i)  is present, in person or by live link, or

        (ii)  has had an opportunity to make representations;

     (b)  on an application for bail by a defendant who is absent and in custody, the court is satisfied that the defendant—

        (i)  has waived the right to attend, or

        (ii)  was present when a court withheld bail in the case on a previous occasion and has been in custody continuously since then;

     (c)  on a prosecutor's appeal against a grant of bail, application to extend a custody time limit or appeal against a refusal to extend such a time limit—

        (i)  the court is satisfied that a defendant who is absent has waived the right to attend, or

        (ii)  the court is satisfied that it would be just to proceed even though the defendant is absent; and

     (d)  the court is satisfied that sufficient time has been allowed—

        (i)  for the defendant to consider the information provided by the prosecutor under rule 14.5(2), and

        (ii)  for the court to consider the parties' representations and make the decision required.

 (2)  The court may make a decision to which this Part applies at a hearing, in public or in private.

 (3)  The court may determine without a hearing an application to vary a condition of bail if—

     (a)  the parties to the application have agreed the terms of the variation proposed; or

     (b)  on an application by a defendant, the court determines the application no sooner than the fifth business day after the application was served.

 (4)  The court may adjourn a determination to which this Part applies, if that is necessary to obtain information sufficient to allow the court to make the decision required.

 (5)  At any hearing at which the court makes one of the following decisions, the court must announce in terms the defendant can understand (with help, if necessary), and by reference to the circumstances of the defendant and the case, its reasons for—

     (a)  withholding bail, or imposing or varying a bail condition;

     (b)  granting bail, where the prosecutor opposed the grant; or

     (c)  where the defendant is under 18—

        (i)  imposing or varying a bail condition when ordering the defendant to be detained in local authority accommodation, or

        (ii)  ordering the defendant to be detained in youth detention accommodation.

 (6)  At any hearing at which the court grants bail, the court must—

     (a)  tell the defendant where and when to surrender to custody; or

     (b)  arrange for the court officer to give the defendant, as soon as practicable, notice of where and when to surrender to custody.

 (7)  This rule does not apply on an application to a magistrates' court to authorise an extension of pre-charge bail.

*[Note. See section 5 of the Bail Act 1976 and sections 93(7) and 102(4) of the Legal Aid, Sentencing and Punishment of Offenders Act 2012[8].*

*Under sections 57A and 57B of the Crime and Disorder Act 1998[9], a defendant is to be treated as present in court when, by virtue of a live link direction within the meaning of those provisions, he or she attends a hearing through a live link.*

*Under section 91 of the 2012 Act, instead of granting bail to a defendant under 18 the court may—*

     *(a)  remand him or her to local authority accommodation and, after consulting with that authority, impose on the defendant a condition that the court could impose if granting bail; or*

     *(b)  remand him or her to youth detention accommodation, if the defendant is at least 12 years old and the other conditions, about the offence and the defendant, prescribed by the Act are met.*

*See also rule 14.18 (Exercise of court's powers: extension of pre-charge bail).]*

---

[8]  2012 c. 10.

[9]  1998 c. 37; sections 57A to 57E were substituted for section 57 as originally enacted by section 45 of the Police and Justice Act 2006 (c. 48), and amended by sections 106, 109 and 178 of, and Part 3 of Schedule 23 to, the Coroners and Justice Act 2009 (c. 25). Section 57A was further amended by paragraphs 36 and 39 of Schedule 12 to the Legal Aid, Sentencing and Punishment of Offenders Act 2012 (c. 10).

**Duty of justices' legal adviser**

**14.3** (1)  This rule applies—

 (a)  only in a magistrates' court; and

 (b)  unless the court—

 (i)  includes a District Judge (Magistrates' Courts), and

 (ii)  otherwise directs.

 (2)  A justices' legal adviser must—

 (a)  assist an unrepresented defendant;

 (b)  give the court such advice as is required to enable it to exercise its powers; and

 (c)  if required, attend the members of the court outside the courtroom to give such advice, but inform the parties of any advice so given.

*[Note. For the functions of a justices' legal adviser, see sections 28 and 29 of the Courts Act 2003[10].]*

**General duties of court officer**

**14.4** (1)  The court officer must arrange for a note or other record to be made of—

 (a)  the parties' representations about bail; and

 (b)  the court's reasons for a decision—

 (i)  to withhold bail, or to impose or vary a bail condition,

 (ii)  to grant bail, where the prosecutor opposed the grant or,

 (iii)  on an application to which rule 14.19 applies (Application to authorise extension of pre-charge bail).

 (2)  The court officer must serve notice of a decision about bail on—

 (a)  the defendant (but, in the Crown Court, only where the defendant's legal representative asks for such a notice, or where the defendant has no legal representative);

 (b)  the prosecutor (but only where the court granted bail, the prosecutor opposed the grant, and the prosecutor asks for such a notice);

 (c)  a party to the decision who was absent when it was made;

 (d)  a surety who is directly affected by the decision;

 (e)  the defendant's custodian, where the defendant is in custody and the decision requires the custodian—

 (i)  to release the defendant (or will do so, if a requirement ordered by the court is met), or

 (ii)  to transfer the defendant to the custody of another custodian; and

 (f)  the court officer for any other court at which the defendant is required by that decision to surrender to custody.

 (3)  Where the court postpones the date on which a defendant who is on bail must surrender to custody, the court officer must serve notice of the postponed date on—

 (a)  the defendant; and

 (b)  any surety.

 (4)  Where a magistrates' court withholds bail in a case to which section 5(6A)[11] of the Bail Act 1976 applies (remand in custody after hearing full argument on an application for bail), the court officer must serve on the defendant a certificate that the court heard full argument.

 (5)  Where the court determines without a hearing an application to which rule 14.21 applies (Application to authorise extension of pre-charge bail), the court officer must—

 (a)  if the court allows the application, notify the applicant; and

 (b)  if the court refuses the application, notify the applicant and the defendant.

*[Note. See section 5 of the Bail Act 1976[12]; section 43 of the Magistrates' Courts Act 1980[13]; and section 52 of the Mental Health Act 1983[14].]*

[10]  2003 c. 39; section 28 was amended by section 15 of, and paragraphs 308 and 327 of Schedule 4 to, the Constitutional Reform Act 2005 (c. 4).

[11]  1976 c. 63; section 5(6A) was inserted by section 60 of the Criminal Justice Act 1982 (c. 48) and amended by section 165 of, and paragraph 53 of Schedule 9 to, the Powers of Criminal Courts (Sentencing) Act 2000 (c. 6) and by paragraph 48 of Schedule 3, paragraphs 1 and 2 of Schedule 36, and Part 4 of Schedule 37 to the Criminal Justice Act 2003 (c. 44).

[12]  1976 c. 63; section 5 was amended by section 65 of, and Schedule 12 to, the Criminal Law Act 1977 (c. 45), section 60 of the Criminal Justice Act 1982 (c. 48), paragraph 1 of Schedule 3 to the Criminal Justice and Public Order Act 1994 (c. 33), paragraph 53 of Schedule 9 to the Powers of Criminal Courts (Sentencing) Act 2000 (c. 6), section 129(1) of the Criminal Justice and Police Act 2001 (c. 16), paragraph 182 of Schedule 8 to the Courts Act 2003 (c. 39), paragraph 48 of Schedule 3, paragraphs 1 and 2 of Schedule 36, and Parts 2, 4 and 12 of Schedule 37 to the Criminal Justice Act 2003 (c. 44) and section 208 of, and paragraphs 33 and 35 of Schedule 21 to, the Legal Services Act 2007 (c. 27).

[13]  1980 c. 43; section 43 was substituted by section 47 of the Police and Criminal Evidence Act 1984 (c. 60) and amended by paragraph 43 of Schedule 10 to the Criminal Justice and Public Order Act 1994 (c. 33) and paragraph 206 of Schedule 8 to the Courts Act 2003 (c. 39).

[14]  1983 c. 20; section 52 was amended by paragraph 55 of Schedule 3 and Schedule 37 to the Criminal Justice Act 2003 (c. 44), section 11 of the Mental Health Act 2007 (c. 12) and paragraphs 53 and 57 of Schedule 21 to the Legal Services Act 2007 (c. 29).

## Bail

**R14.5**　**Prosecutor's representations about bail**

14.5　(1)　This rule applies whenever the court can grant or withhold bail.

(2)　The prosecutor must as soon as practicable—

(a)　provide the defendant with all the information in the prosecutor's possession which is material to what the court must decide; and

(b)　provide the court with the same information.

(3)　A prosecutor who opposes the grant of bail must specify—

(a)　each exception to the general right to bail on which the prosecutor relies; and

(b)　each consideration that the prosecutor thinks relevant.

(4)　A prosecutor who wants the court to impose a condition on any grant of bail must—

(a)　specify each condition proposed; and

(b)　explain what purpose would be served by such a condition.

*[Note. A summary of the general entitlement to bail and of the exceptions to that entitlement is at the end of this Part.]*

**R14.6**　**Reconsideration of police bail by magistrates' court**

14.6　(1)　This rule applies where—

(a)　a party wants a magistrates' court to reconsider a bail decision by a police officer after the defendant is charged with an offence; and

(b)　a defendant wants a magistrates' court to reconsider a bail condition imposed by a police officer before the defendant is charged with an offence.

(2)　An application under this rule must be made to—

(a)　the magistrates' court to whose custody the defendant is under a duty to surrender, if any; or

(b)　any magistrates' court acting for the police officer's local justice area, in any other case.

(3)　The applicant party must—

(a)　apply in writing; and

(b)　serve the application on—

(i)　the court officer,

(ii)　the other party, and

(iii)　any surety affected or proposed.

(4)　The application must—

(a)　specify—

(i)　the decision that the applicant wants the court to make,

(ii)　each offence charged, or for which the defendant was arrested, and

(iii)　the police bail decision to be reconsidered and the reasons given for it;

(b)　explain, as appropriate—

(i)　why the court should grant bail itself, or withdraw it, or impose or vary a condition, and

(ii)　if the applicant is the prosecutor, what material information has become available since the police bail decision was made;

(c)　propose the terms of any suggested condition of bail; and

(d)　if the applicant wants an earlier hearing than paragraph (7) requires, ask for that, and explain why it is needed.

(5)　A prosecutor who applies under this rule must serve on the defendant, with the application, notice that the court has power to withdraw bail and, if the defendant is absent when the court makes its decision, order the defendant's arrest.

(6)　A party who opposes an application must—

(a)　so notify the court officer and the applicant at once; and

(b)　serve on each notice of the reasons for opposition.

(7)　Unless the court otherwise directs, the court officer must arrange for the court to hear the application as soon as practicable and in any event—

(a)　if it is an application to withdraw bail, no later than the second business day after it was served; and

(b)　in any other case, no later than the fifth business day after it was served.

(8)　The court may—

(a)　vary or waive a time limit under this rule;

(b)　allow an application to be in a different form to one set out in the Practice Direction; and

(c)　if rule 14.2 allows, determine without a hearing an application to vary a condition.

*[Note. The Practice Direction sets out a form of application for use in connection with this rule.*

*Under section 5B of the Bail Act 1976[15]—*

> *(a)  where a defendant has been charged with an offence which can be tried in the Crown Court; or*
> *(b)  in an extradition case,*

*on application by the prosecutor a magistrates' court may withdraw bail granted by a constable, impose conditions of bail, or vary conditions of bail. See also sections 37, 37C(2)(b), 37CA(2)(b), 46A and 47(1B) of the Police and Criminal Evidence Act 1984[16].*

*Under section 43B of the Magistrates' Courts Act 1980[17], where a defendant has been charged with an offence, on application by the defendant a magistrates' court may grant bail itself, in substitution for bail granted by a custody officer, or vary the conditions of bail granted by a custody officer. See also sections 37, 37C(2)(b), 37CA(2)(b), 46A and 47(1C), (1D) of the Police and Criminal Evidence Act 1984[18].*

*Under section 47(1E) of the Police and Criminal Evidence Act 1984[19], where a defendant has been released on bail by a custody officer without being charged with an offence, on application by the defendant a magistrates' court may vary any conditions of that bail. See also sections 37, 37C(2)(b), 37CA(2)(b), 46A and 47(1C) of the Act.]*

### Notice of application to consider bail

**R14.7**

14.7  (1)  This rule applies where—

    (a)  in a magistrates' court—

        (i)  a prosecutor wants the court to withdraw bail granted by the court, or to impose or vary a condition of such bail, or

        (ii)  a defendant wants the court to reconsider such bail before the next hearing in the case; and

    (b)  in the Crown Court,

        (i)  a party wants the court to grant bail that has been withheld, or to withdraw bail that has been granted, or to impose a new bail condition or to vary a present one, or

        (ii)  a prosecutor wants the court to consider whether to grant or withhold bail, or impose or vary a condition of bail, under section 88 or section 89 of the Criminal Justice Act 2003[20] (bail and custody in connection with an intended application to the Court of Appeal to which Part 27 (Retrial after acquittal) applies).

    (2)  Such a party must—

    (a)  apply in writing;

    (b)  serve the application on—

        (i)  the court officer,

        (ii)  the other party, and

        (iii)  any surety affected or proposed; and

    (c)  serve the application not less than 2 business days before any hearing in the case at which the applicant wants the court to consider it, if such a hearing is already due.

---

[15]  1976 c. 63; section 5B was inserted by section 30 of the Criminal Justice and Public Order Act 1994 (c. 33) and amended by section 129(3) of the Criminal Justice and Police Act 2001 (c. 16), section 109 of, and paragraph 183 of Schedule 8 and Schedule 10 to, the Courts Act 2003 (c. 39) and section 198 of the Extradition Act 2003 (c. 41).

[16]  1984 c. 60; section 37 was amended by section 108(7) of, and Schedule 15 to, the Children Act 1989 (c. 41), sections 72 and 101(2) of, and Schedule 13 to, the Criminal Justice Act 1991 (c. 53), sections 29(4) and 168(3) of, and Schedule 11 to, the Criminal Justice and Public Order Act 1994 (c. 33), section 28 of, and paragraphs 1 and 2 of Schedule 2 to, the Criminal Justice Act 2003 (c. 44), section 23(1) of, and paragraphs 1 and 2 of Schedule 1 to, the Drugs Act 2005 (c. 17) and sections 11 and 52 of, and paragraph 9 of Schedule 14 to, the Police and Justice Act 2006 (c. 48). Section 37C was inserted by section 28 of, and paragraphs 1 and 3 of Schedule 2 to, the Criminal Justice Act 2003 (c. 44). Section 37CA was inserted by section 10 of, and paragraphs 1 and 8 of Schedule 6 to, the Police and Justice Act 2006 (c. 48). Section 46A was inserted by section 29 of the Criminal Justice and Public Order Act 1994 (c. 33), and amended by section 28 of, and paragraphs 1 and 5 of Schedule 2 to, the Criminal Justice Act 2003 (c. 44), sections 10 and 46 of, and paragraphs 1 and 7 of Schedule 6 to, the Police and Justice Act 2006 (c. 48) and sections 107 and 178 of, and Part 3 of Schedule 3 to, the Coroners and Justice Act 2009 (c. 25). Section 47(1B) was inserted by section 28 of, and paragraphs 1 and 6 of Schedule 2 to, the Criminal Justice Act 2003 (c. 44) and amended by section 10 of, and paragraphs 1 and 11 of Schedule 6 to, the Police and Justice Act 2006 (c. 48).

[17]  1980 c. 43; section 43B was inserted by section 27 of, and paragraph 3 of Schedule 3 to, the Criminal Justice and Public Order Act 1994 (c. 33).

[18]  1984 c. 60; section 47(1C) and (1D) were inserted by section 28 of, and paragraphs 1 and 6 of Schedule 2 to, the Criminal Justice Act 2003 (c. 44), and section 47(1C) was amended by section 10 of, and paragraphs 1 and 11 of Schedule 6 to, the Police and Justice Act 2006 (c. 48).

[19]  1984 c. 60; section 47(1E) was inserted by section 28 of, and paragraphs 1 and 6 of Schedule 2 to, the Criminal Justice Act 2003 (c. 44).

[20]  2003 c. 44; section 88 is amended by section 148 of, and paragraphs 59 and 63 of Schedule 26 to, the Criminal Justice and Immigration Act 2008 (c. 4), with effect from a date to be appointed. Section 89 was amended by section 59 of, and paragraph 1 of Schedule 11 to, the Constitutional Reform Act 2005 (c. 4). It is further amended by section 148 of, and paragraphs 59 and 63 of Schedule 26 to, the Criminal Justice and Immigration Act 2008 (c. 4), with effect from a date to be appointed.

(3) The application must—
    (a) specify—
        (i) the decision that the applicant wants the court to make,
        (ii) each offence charged, and
        (iii) each relevant previous bail decision and the reasons given for each;
    (b) if the applicant is a defendant, explain—
        (i) as appropriate, why the court should not withhold bail, or why it should vary a condition, and
        (ii) what further information or legal argument, if any, has become available since the most recent previous bail decision was made;
    (c) if the applicant is the prosecutor, explain—
        (i) as appropriate, why the court should withdraw bail, or impose or vary a condition, and
        (ii) what material information has become available since the most recent previous bail decision was made;
    (d) propose the terms of any suggested condition of bail; and
    (e) if the applicant wants an earlier hearing than paragraph (6) requires, ask for that, and explain why it is needed.

(4) A prosecutor who applies under this rule must serve on the defendant, with the application, notice that the court has power to withdraw bail and, if the defendant is absent when the court makes its decision, order the defendant's arrest.

(5) A party who opposes an application must—
    (a) so notify the court officer and the applicant at once; and
    (b) serve on each notice of the reasons for opposition.

(6) Unless the court otherwise directs, the court officer must arrange for the court to hear the application as soon as practicable and in any event—
    (a) if it is an application to grant or withdraw bail, no later than the second business day after it was served; and
    (b) if it is an application to impose or vary a condition, no later than the fifth business day after it was served.

(7) The court may—
    (a) vary or waive a time limit under this rule;
    (b) allow an application to be in a different form to one set out in the Practice Direction, or to be made orally; and
    (c) if rule 14.2 allows, determine without a hearing an application to vary a condition.

*[Note. The Practice Direction sets out a form of application for use in connection with this rule,*

*In addition to the court's general powers in relation to bail—*

    *(a) under section 3(8) of the Bail Act 1976(), on application by either party the court may impose a bail condition or vary a condition it has imposed. Until the Crown Court makes its first bail decision in the case, a magistrates' court may vary a condition which it imposed on committing or sending a defendant for Crown Court trial.*
    *(b) under section 5B of the Bail Act 1976(), where the defendant is on bail and the offence is one which can be tried in the Crown Court, or in an extradition case, on application by the prosecutor a magistrates' court may withdraw bail, impose conditions of bail or vary the conditions of bail.*
    *(c) under sections 88 and 89 of the Criminal Justice Act 2003, the Crown Court may remand in custody, or grant bail to, a defendant pending an application to the Court of Appeal for an order for retrial under section 77 of that Act.*

*Under Part IIA of Schedule 1 to the Bail Act 1976(), if the court withholds bail then at the first hearing after that the defendant may support an application for bail with any argument as to fact or law, whether or not that argument has been advanced before. At subsequent hearings, the court need not hear arguments which it has heard previously.]*

**R14.8**    **Defendant's application or appeal to the Crown Court after magistrates' court bail decision**

14.8 (1) This rule applies where a defendant wants to—
    (a) apply to the Crown Court for bail after a magistrates' court has withheld bail; or
    (b) appeal to the Crown Court after a magistrates' court has refused to vary a bail condition as the defendant wants.

(2) The defendant must—
    (a) apply to the Crown Court in writing as soon as practicable after the magistrates' court's decision; and
    (b) serve the application on—

    (i)  the Crown Court officer,

    (ii)  the magistrates' court officer,

    (iii) the prosecutor, and

    (iv) any surety affected or proposed.

(3)  The application must—

    (a)  specify—

        (i)  the decision that the applicant wants the Crown Court to make, and

        (ii)  each offence charged;

    (b)  explain—

        (i)  as appropriate, why the Crown Court should not withhold bail, or why it should vary the condition under appeal, and

        (ii)  what further information or legal argument, if any, has become available since the magistrates' court's decision;

    (c)  propose the terms of any suggested condition of bail;

    (d)  if the applicant wants an earlier hearing than paragraph (6) requires, ask for that, and explain why it is needed; and

    (e)  on an application for bail, attach a copy of the certificate of full argument served on the defendant under rule 14.4(4).

(4)  The magistrates' court officer must as soon as practicable serve on the Crown Court officer—

    (a)  a copy of the note or record made under rule 14.4(1) in connection with the magistrates' court's decision; and

    (b)  the date of the next hearing, if any, in the magistrates' court.

(5)  A prosecutor who opposes the application must—

    (a)  so notify the Crown Court officer and the defendant at once; and

    (b)  serve on each notice of the reasons for opposition.

(6)  Unless the Crown Court otherwise directs, the court officer must arrange for the court to hear the application or appeal as soon as practicable and in any event no later than the business day after it was served.

(7)  The Crown Court may vary a time limit under this rule.

*[Note. The Practice Direction sets out a form of application for use in connection with this rule.*

*Under section 81 of the Senior Courts Act 1981[21], the Crown Court may grant bail in a magistrates' court case in which the magistrates' court has withheld bail.*

*Under section 16 of the Criminal Justice Act 2003[22], a defendant may appeal to the Crown Court against a bail condition imposed by a magistrates' court only where—*

    *(a)  the condition is one that the defendant must—*

        *(i)   live and sleep at a specified place, or away from a specified place,*

        *(ii)  give a surety or a security,*

        *(iii) stay indoors between specified hours,*

        *(iv) comply with electronic monitoring requirements, or*

        *(v)  make no contact with a specified person; and*

    *(b)  the magistrates' court has determined an application by either party to vary that condition.*

*In an extradition case, where a magistrates' court withholds bail or imposes bail conditions, on application by the defendant the High Court may grant bail, or vary the conditions, under section 22 of the Criminal Justice Act 1967[23]. For the procedure in the High Court, see Schedule 1 to the Civil Procedure Rules 1998 (RSC Order 79)[24].]*

[21]  1981 c. 54; section 81(1) was amended by sections 29 and 60 of the Criminal Justice Act 1982 (c. 48), section 15 of, and paragraph 2 of Schedule 12 to, the Criminal Justice Act 1987 (c. 38), section 168 of, and paragraph 19 of Schedule 9 and paragraph 48 of Schedule 10 to, the Criminal Justice and Public Order Act 1994 (c. 33), section 119 of, and paragraph 48 of Schedule 8 and Schedule 10 to, the Crime and Disorder Act 1998 (c. 37), section 165 of, and paragraph 87 of Schedule 9 and Schedule 12 to, the Powers of Criminal Courts (Sentencing) Act 2000 (c. 6), paragraph 54 of Schedule 3, paragraph 4 of Schedule 36 and Part 4 of Schedule 37 to the Criminal Justice Act 2003 (c. 44), articles 2 and 6 of S.I. 2004/1033 and section 177(1) of, and paragraph 76 of Schedule 21 to, the Coroners and Justice Act 2009 (c. 25).

[22]  2003 c. 44.

[23]  1967 c. 80; section 22 was amended by section 56 of, and paragraph 48 of Schedule 8 and Schedule 11 to, the Courts Act 1971 (c. 23), section 12 of, and paragraphs 36 and 37 of Schedule 2 and Schedule 3 to, the Bail Act 1976 (c. 63), section 65 of, and Schedules 12 and 13 to, the Criminal Law Act 1977 (c. 45), paragraph 15 of Schedule 10 to the Criminal Justice and Public Order Act 1994 (c. 33), sections 17 and 332 of, and Schedule 37 to, the Criminal Justice Act 2003 (c. 44) and section 42 of, and paragraph 27 of Schedule 13 to, the Police and Justice Act 2006 (c. 48).

[24]  S.I. 1998/3132; Schedule 1 RSC Order 79 was amended by S.I. 1999/1008, 2001/256, 2003/3361 and 2005/617.

**R14.9**   **Prosecutor's appeal against grant of bail**

**14.9**  (1)  This rule applies where a prosecutor wants to appeal—

(a)  to the Crown Court against a grant of bail by a magistrates' court, in a case in which the defendant has been charged with, or convicted of, an offence punishable with imprisonment; or

(b)  to the High Court against a grant of bail—

(i)  by a magistrates' court, in an extradition case, or

(ii)  by the Crown Court, in a case in which the defendant has been charged with, or convicted of, an offence punishable with imprisonment (but not in a case in which the Crown Court granted bail on an appeal to which paragraph (1)(a) applies).

(2)  The prosecutor must tell the court which has granted bail of the decision to appeal—

(a)  at the end of the hearing during which the court granted bail; and

(b)  before the defendant is released on bail.

(3)  The court which has granted bail must exercise its power to remand the defendant in custody pending determination of the appeal.

(4)  The prosecutor must serve an appeal notice—

(a)  on the court officer for the court which has granted bail and on the defendant; and

(b)  not more than 2 hours after telling that court of the decision to appeal.

(5)  The appeal notice must specify—

(a)  each offence with which the defendant is charged;

(b)  the decision under appeal;

(c)  the reasons given for the grant of bail; and

(d)  the grounds of appeal.

(6)  On an appeal to the Crown Court, the magistrates' court officer must, as soon as practicable, serve on the Crown Court officer—

(a)  the appeal notice;

(b)  a copy of the note or record made under rule 14.4(1) (record of bail decision); and

(c)  notice of the date of the next hearing in the court which has granted bail.

(7)  If the Crown Court so directs, the Crown Court officer must arrange for the defendant to be assisted by the Official Solicitor in a case in which the defendant—

(a)  has no legal representative; and

(b)  asks for such assistance.

(8)  On an appeal to the Crown Court, the Crown Court officer must arrange for the court to hear the appeal as soon as practicable and in any event no later than the second business day after the appeal notice was served.

(9)  The prosecutor—

(a)  may abandon an appeal to the Crown Court without the court's permission, by serving a notice of abandonment, signed by or on behalf of the prosecutor, on—

(i)  the defendant,

(ii)  the Crown Court officer, and

(iii)  the magistrates' court officer

before the hearing of the appeal begins; but

(b)  after the hearing of the appeal begins, may only abandon the appeal with the Crown Court's permission.

(10) The court officer for the court which has granted bail must instruct the defendant's custodian to release the defendant on the bail granted by that court, subject to any condition or conditions of bail imposed, if—

(a)  the prosecutor fails to serve an appeal notice within the time to which paragraph (4) refers; or

(b)  the prosecutor serves a notice of abandonment under paragraph (9).

*[Note. See section 1 of the Bail (Amendment) Act 1993*[25]*. The time limit for serving an appeal notice is prescribed by section 1(5) of the Act. It may be neither extended nor shortened.*

*For the procedure in the High Court, see Schedule 1 to the Civil Procedure Rules 1998 (RSC Order 79, rule 9) and the Practice Direction which supplements that Order. Under those provisions, the prosecutor must file in the High Court, among other things—*

---

[25]  1993 c. 26; section 1 was amended by sections 200 and 220 of, and Schedule 4 to, the Extradition Act 2003 (c. 41), section 18 of the Criminal Justice Act 2003 (c. 44), section 15 of, and paragraph 231 of Schedule 4 to, the Constitutional Reform Act 2005 (c. 4), section 42 of, and paragraph 28 of Schedule 13 to, the Police and Justice Act 2006 (c. 48) and paragraph 32 of Schedule 11 to the Legal Aid, Sentencing and Punishment of Offenders Act 2012 (c. 10).

(a)  a copy of the appeal notice served by the prosecutor under rule 14.9(4);

(b)  notice of the Crown Court decision to grant bail served on the prosecutor under rule 14.4(2); and

(c)  notice of the date of the next hearing in the Crown Court.]

### Consideration of bail in a murder case

**R14.10**

14.10 (1)  This rule applies in a case in which—

    (a)  the defendant is charged with murder; and

    (b)  the Crown Court has not yet considered bail.

    (2)  The magistrates' court officer must arrange with the Crown Court officer for the Crown Court to consider bail as soon as practicable and in any event no later than the second business day after—

    (a)  a magistrates' court sends the defendant to the Crown Court for trial; or

    (b)  the first hearing in the magistrates' court, if the defendant is not at once sent for trial.

[Note. See section 115 of the Coroners and Justice Act 2009[26].]

### Condition of residence

**R14.11**

14.11 (1)  The defendant must notify the prosecutor of the address at which the defendant will live and sleep if released on bail with a condition of residence—

    (a)  as soon as practicable after the institution of proceedings, unless already done; and

    (b)  as soon as practicable after any change of that address.

    (2)  The prosecutor must help the court to assess the suitability of an address proposed as a condition of residence.

### Electronic monitoring requirements

**R14.12**

14.12 (1)  This rule applies where the court imposes electronic monitoring requirements, where available, as a condition of bail.

    (2)  The court officer must—

    (a)  inform the person responsible for the monitoring ('the monitor') of—

        (i)  the defendant's name, and telephone number if available,

        (ii)  each offence with which the defendant is charged,

        (iii)  details of the place at which the defendant's presence must be monitored,

        (iv)  the period or periods during which the defendant's presence at that place must be monitored, and

        (v)  if fixed, the date on which the defendant must surrender to custody;

    (b)  inform the defendant and, where the defendant is under 16, an appropriate adult, of the monitor's identity and the means by which the monitor may be contacted; and

    (c)  notify the monitor of any subsequent—

        (i)  variation or termination of the electronic monitoring requirements, or

        (ii)  fixing or variation of the date on which the defendant must surrender to custody.

[Note. Under section 3(6ZAA) of the Bail Act 1976[27], the conditions of bail that the court may impose include requirements for the electronic monitoring of a defendant's compliance with other bail conditions, for example a curfew. Sections 3AA and 3AB of the 1976 Act[28] set out conditions for imposing such requirements.

Under section 3AC of the 1976 Act[29], where the court imposes electronic monitoring requirements they must provide for the appointment of a monitor.]

### Accommodation or support requirements

**R14.13**

14.13 (1)  This rule applies where the court imposes as a condition of bail a requirement, where available, that the defendant must—

    (a)  reside in accommodation provided for that purpose by, or on behalf of, a public authority; or

    (b)  receive bail support provided by, or on behalf of, a public authority.

---

[26]  2009 c. 25.

[27]  1976 c. 63; 1976 c. 63; section 3(6ZAA) was substituted, with sub-section (6ZAB), for sub-section (6ZAA) as inserted by section 131 of the Criminal Justice and Police Act 2001 (c. 16) by section 51 of, and paragraphs 1 and 2 of Schedule 11 to, the Criminal Justice and Immigration Act 2008 (c. 4) and amended by paragraphs 1 and 3 of Schedule 11 to the Legal Aid, Sentencing and Punishment of Offenders Act 2012 (c. 10).

[28]  1976 c. 63; section 3AA was inserted by section 131 of the Criminal Justice and Police Act 2001 (c. 16) and amended by sections 51 and 149 of, and paragraphs 1 and 3 of Schedule 11 to, and Part 4 of Schedule 28 to, the Criminal Justice and Immigration Act 2008 (c. 4) and paragraph 4 of Schedule 11 to the Legal Aid, Sentencing and Punishment of Offenders Act 2012 (c. 10).

[29]  1976 c. 63; section 3AC was inserted by section 51 of, and paragraphs 1 and 4 of Schedule 11 to, the Criminal Justice and Immigration Act 2008 (c. 4) and amended by paragraphs 1 and 7 of Schedule 11 to the Legal Aid, Sentencing and Punishment of Offenders Act 2012 (c. 10).

(2)  The court officer must—

    (a)  inform the person responsible for the provision of any such accommodation or support ('the service provider') of—

        (i)  the defendant's name, and telephone number if available,

        (ii)  each offence with which the defendant is charged,

        (iii)  details of the requirement,

        (iv)  any other bail condition, and

        (v)  if fixed, the date on which the defendant must surrender to custody;

    (b)  inform the defendant and, where the defendant is under 16, an appropriate adult, of—

        (i)  the service provider's identity and the means by which the service provider may be contacted, and

        (ii)  the address of any accommodation in which the defendant must live and sleep; and

    (c)  notify the service provider of any subsequent—

        (i)  variation or termination of the requirement,

        (ii)  variation or termination of any other bail condition, and

        (iii)  fixing or variation of the date on which the defendant must surrender to custody.

## R14.14  Requirement for a surety or payment, etc.

14.14 (1)  This rule applies where the court imposes as a condition of bail a requirement for—

    (a)  a surety;

    (b)  a payment; or

    (c)  the surrender of a document or thing.

(2)  The court may direct how such a condition must be met.

(3)  Unless the court otherwise directs, if any such condition or direction requires a surety to enter into a recognizance—

    (a)  the recognizance must specify—

        (i)  the amount that the surety will be required to pay if the purpose for which the recognizance is entered is not fulfilled, and

        (ii)  the date, or the event, upon which the recognizance will expire;

    (b)  the surety must enter into the recognizance in the presence of—

        (i)  the court officer,

        (ii)  the defendant's custodian, where the defendant is in custody, or

        (iii)  someone acting with the authority of either; and

    (c)  the person before whom the surety enters into the recognizance must at once serve a copy on—

        (i)  the surety, and

        (ii)  as appropriate, the court officer and the defendant's custodian.

(4)  Unless the court otherwise directs, if any such condition or direction requires someone to make a payment, or surrender a document or thing—

    (a)  that payment, document or thing must be made or surrendered to—

        (i)  the court officer,

        (ii)  the defendant's custodian, where the defendant is in custody, or

        (iii)  someone acting with the authority of either; and

    (b)  the court officer or the custodian, as appropriate, must serve immediately on the other a statement that the payment, document or thing has been made or surrendered.

(5)  The custodian must release the defendant when each requirement ordered by the court has been met.

*[Note. See also section 119 of the Magistrates' Courts Act 1980[30].]*

## R14.15  Forfeiture of a recognizance given by a surety

14.15 (1)  This rule applies where the court imposes as a condition of bail a requirement that a surety enter into a recognizance and, after the defendant is released on bail,—

    (a)  the defendant fails to surrender to custody as required, or

    (b)  it appears to the court that the surety has failed to comply with a condition or direction.

(2)  The court officer must serve notice on—

    (a)  the surety; and

    (b)  each party to the decision to grant bail,

of the hearing at which the court will consider the forfeiture of the recognizance.

(3)  The court must not forfeit the recognizance less than 5 business days after service of notice under paragraph (2).

---

[30]  1980 c. 43; section 119 was amended by section 77 of, and paragraph 55 of Schedule 14 to, the Criminal Justice Act 1982 (c. 48).

*[Note. If the purpose for which a recognizance is entered is not fulfilled, that recognizance may be forfeited by the court. If the court forfeits a surety's recognizance, the sum promised by that person is then payable to the Crown. See also section 120 of the Magistrates' Courts Act 1980[31].]*

## Application to extend a custody time limit    R14.16

**14.16** (1) This rule applies where the prosecutor gives notice of application to extend a custody time limit.

(2) The court officer must arrange for the court to hear that application as soon as practicable after the expiry of—

    (a) 5 days from the giving of notice, in the Crown Court; or

    (b) 2 days from the giving of notice, in a magistrates' court.

(3) The court may shorten a time limit under this rule.

*[Note. See regulation 7 of the Prosecution of Offences (Custody Time Limits) Regulations 1987[32].*

*Under regulations 4 and 5 of the 1987 Regulations[33], unless the court extends the time limit the maximum period during which the defendant may be in pre-trial custody is—*

    *(a) in a case which can be tried only in a magistrates' court, 56 days pending the beginning of the trial;*

    *(b) in a magistrates' court, in a case which can be tried either in that court or in the Crown Court—*

        *(i) 70 days, pending the beginning of a trial in the magistrates' court, or*

        *(ii) 56 days, pending the beginning of a trial in the magistrates' court, if the court decides on such a trial during that period;*

    *(c) in the Crown Court, pending the beginning of the trial, 182 days from the sending of the defendant for trial, less any period or periods during which the defendant was in custody in the magistrates' court.*

*Under section 22(3) of the Prosecution of Offences Act 1985[34], the court cannot extend a custody time limit which has expired, and must not extend such a time limit unless satisfied—*

    *(a) that the need for the extension is due to—*

        *(i) the illness or absence of the accused, a necessary witness, a judge or a magistrate,*

        *(ii) a postponement which is occasioned by the ordering by the court of separate trials in the case of two or more defendants or two or more offences, or*

        *(iii) some other good and sufficient cause; and*

    *(b) that the prosecution has acted with all due diligence and expedition.]*

## Appeal against custody time limit decision    R14.17

**14.17** (1) This rule applies where—

    (a) a defendant wants to appeal to the Crown Court against a decision by a magistrates' court to extend a custody time limit; or

    (b) a prosecutor wants to appeal to the Crown Court against a decision by a magistrates' court to refuse to extend a custody time limit.

(2) The appellant must serve an appeal notice—

    (a) on—

        (i) the other party to the decision,

        (ii) the Crown Court officer, and

        (iii) the magistrates' court officer;

    (b) in a defendant's appeal, as soon as practicable after the decision under appeal; and

    (c) in a prosecutor's appeal—

        (i) as soon as practicable after the decision under appeal, and

        (ii) before the relevant custody time limit expires.

(3) The appeal notice must specify—

---

[31] 1980 c. 43; section 120 was amended by section 55 of the Crime and Disorder Act 1998 (c. 37) and section 62 of, and paragraphs 45 and 56 of Schedule 13 to, the Tribunals, Courts and Enforcement Act 2007 (c. 15).

[32] S.I. 1987/299; regulation 7 was amended by S.I. 1989/767.

[33] S.I. 1987/299; regulation 4 was amended by section 71 of the Criminal Procedure and Investigations Act 1996 (c. 25) and S.I. 1989/767, 1991/1515, 1999/2744. Regulation 5 was amended by sections 71 and 80 of, and paragraph 8 of Schedule 5 to, the Criminal Procedure and Investigations Act 1996 (c. 25) and S.I. 1989/767, 1991/1515, 2000/3284, 2012/1344.

[34] 1985 c. 23; section 22 was amended by paragraph 104 of Schedule 15 to the Criminal Justice Act 1988 (c. 33), section 43 of the Crime and Disorder Act 1998 (c. 37), paragraph 36 of Schedule 11 to the Criminal Justice Act 1991 (c. 53), paragraph 27 of Schedule 9 to the Criminal Justice and Public Order Act 1994 (c. 33), section 71 of the Criminal Procedure and Investigations Act 1996 (c. 25), section 67(3) of the Access to Justice Act 1999 (c. 22), section 70 of, and paragraph 57 of Schedule 3 and paragraphs 49 and 51 of Schedule 36 to, the Criminal Justice Act 2003 (c. 44), section 59 of, and paragraph 1 of Schedule 11 to, the Constitutional Reform Act 2005 (c. 4) and paragraph 22 of Schedule 12 to the Legal Aid, Sentencing and Punishment of Offenders Act 2012 (c. 10).

(a) each offence with which the defendant is charged;

(b) the decision under appeal;

(c) the date on which the relevant custody time limit will expire;

(d) on a defendant's appeal, the date on which the relevant custody time limit would have expired but for the decision under appeal; and

(e) the grounds of appeal.

(4) The Crown Court officer must arrange for the Crown Court to hear the appeal as soon as practicable and in any event no later than the second business day after the appeal notice was served.

(5) The appellant—

(a) may abandon an appeal without the Crown Court's permission, by serving a notice of abandonment, signed by or on behalf of the appellant, on—

    (i) the other party,

    (ii) the Crown Court officer, and

    (iii) the magistrates' court officer

before the hearing of the appeal begins; but

(b) after the hearing of the appeal begins, may only abandon the appeal with the Crown Court's permission.

*[Note. See section 22(7), (8), (9) of the Prosecution of Offences Act 1985[35].]*

### Extension of bail before charge

**R14.18**    **Exercise of court's powers: extension of pre-charge bail**

**14.18** (1) The court must determine an application to which rule 14.19 (Application to authorise extension of pre-charge bail) applies—

(a) without a hearing, subject to paragraph (2); and

(b) as soon as practicable, but as a general rule no sooner than the fifth business day after the application was served.

(2) The court must determine an application at a hearing where—

(a) if the application succeeds, its effect will be to extend the period for which the defendant is on bail to less than 12 months from the day after the defendant's arrest for the offence and the court considers that the interests of justice require a hearing;

(b) if the application succeeds, its effect will be to extend that period to more than 12 months from that day and the applicant or the defendant asks for a hearing; or

(c) it is an application to withhold information from the defendant and the court considers that the interests of justice require a hearing.

(3) Any hearing must be in private.

(4) Subject to rule 14.20 (Application to withhold information from the defendant), at a hearing the court may determine an application in the absence of—

(a) the applicant; and

(b) the defendant, if the defendant has had at least 5 business days in which to make representations.

(5) If the court so directs, a party to an application may attend a hearing by live link or telephone.

(6) The court must not authorise an extension of the period for which a defendant is on bail before being charged unless—

(a) the applicant states, in writing or orally, that to the best of the applicant's knowledge and belief—

    (i) the application discloses all the information that is material to what the court must decide, and

    (ii) the content of the application is true; or

(b) the application includes a statement by an investigator of the suspected offence that to the best of that investigator's knowledge and belief those requirements are met.

(7) Where the statement required by paragraph (6) is made orally—

(a) the statement must be on oath or affirmation, unless the court otherwise directs; and

(b) the court must arrange for a record of the making of the statement.

(8) The court may shorten or extend (even after it has expired) a time limit imposed by this rule or by rule 14.19 (Application to authorise extension of pre-charge bail).

*[Note. For the definition of 'defendant' for the purposes of this rule and rules 14.19 and 14.20, see rule 14.1(3).*

---

[35] 1985 c. 23; section 22(7) and (8) was amended by section 43 of the Crime and Disorder Act 1998 (c. 37).

Sections 47ZA and 47ZB of the Police and Criminal Evidence Act 1984[36] limit the period during which a defendant who has been arrested for an offence may be on bail after being released without being charged. That period ('the applicable bail period') is—

(a)  3 months from the day after the day on which the defendant was arrested (the defendant's 'bail start date') in 'an SFO case' (that is, a case investigated by the Serious Fraud Office);

(b)  28 days from the defendant's bail start date in 'a standard case' (that is, 'an FCA case', meaning a case investigated by the Financial Conduct Authority, or any other non-SFO case).

Under sections 47ZC and 47ZD of the 1984[37] Act, in a standard case the applicable bail period may be extended on the authority of a police officer of the rank of superintendent or above until the end of 3 months from the bail start date.

Under sections 47ZC and 47ZE of the Act[38], if the case is designated by a qualifying prosecutor as exceptionally complex (a 'designated case') the applicable bail period may be extended, in an SFO case, or further extended, in a standard case, on the authority of one of the senior officers listed in section 47ZE, until the end of 6 months from the bail start date.

Under section 47ZF of the Act[39], on an application made before the date on which the applicable bail period ends by a member of the Serious Fraud Office, a member of staff of the Financial Conduct Authority, a constable or a Crown Prosecutor, a magistrates' court may authorise an extension of that period—

(a)  from a previous total of 3 months to a new total of 6 months or, if the investigation is unlikely to be completed or a police charging decision made within a lesser period, a new total of 9 months;

(b)  from a previous total of 6 months to a new total of 9 months or, if the investigation is unlikely to be completed or a police charging decision made within a lesser period, a new total of 12 months,

where the conditions listed in that section are met.

Under section 47ZG of the Act[40], on a further such application (of which there may be more than one) a magistrates' court may authorise a further extension of the applicable bail period, on each occasion by a further 3 months or, if the investigation is unlikely to be completed or a police charging decision made within a lesser period, a further 6 months, where the conditions listed in that section are met.

Under section 47ZL of the Act[41], the running of the applicable bail period does not begin (in the case of a first release on bail) or is suspended (in any other case) where—

(a)  the defendant is released on bail to await a charging decision by the Director of Public Prosecutions under section 37B of the Act; or

(b)  following arrest for breach of such bail the defendant is again released on bail.

The court's authority therefore is not required for an extension of an applicable bail period the running of which is postponed or suspended pending a Director's charging decision. However—

(a)  time runs in any period during which information requested by the Director is being obtained; and

(b)  if the Director requests information less than 7 days before the applicable bail period otherwise would end then the running of that period is further suspended until the end of 7 days beginning with the day on which the Director's request is made.

See also section 47ZI of the Police and Criminal Evidence Act 198[42] (Sections 47ZF to 47ZH: proceedings in magistrates' courts). The requirement for the court except in specified circumstances to determine an application without a hearing is prescribed by that section. Under that section the court must comprise a single justice of the peace unless a hearing is convened, when it must comprise two or more justices.]

[36]  1984 c. 60; sections 47ZA and 47ZB were inserted by section 63 of the Policing and Crime Act 2017 (c. 3).

[37]  1984 c. 60; sections 47ZC and 47ZD were inserted by section 63 of the Policing and Crime Act 2017 (c. 3).

[38]  1984 c. 60; section 47ZE was inserted by section 63 of the Policing and Crime Act 2017 (c. 3).

[39]  1984 c. 60; section 47ZF was inserted by section 63 of the Policing and Crime Act 2017 (c. 3).

[40]  1984 c. 60; section 47ZG was inserted by section 63 of the Policing and Crime Act 2017 (c. 3).

[41]  1984 c. 60; section 47ZL was inserted by section 63 of the Policing and Crime Act 2017 (c. 3).

[42]  1984 c. 60; section 47ZI was inserted by section 63 of the Policing and Crime Act 2017 (c. 3).

**R14.19**    **Application to authorise extension of pre-charge bail**

**14.19** (1)   This rule applies where an applicant wants the court to authorise an extension of the period for which a defendant is released on bail before being charged with an offence.

(2)   The applicant must—

   (a)   apply in writing before the date on which the defendant's pre-charge bail is due to end;

   (b)   demonstrate that the applicant is entitled to apply as a constable, a member of staff of the Financial Conduct Authority, a member of the Serious Fraud Office or a Crown Prosecutor;

   (c)   serve the application on—

      (i)   the court officer, and

      (ii)   the defendant; and

   (d)   serve on the defendant, with the application, a form of response notice for the defendant's use.

(3)   The application must specify—

   (a)   the offence or offences for which the defendant was arrested;

   (b)   the date on which the defendant's pre-charge bail began;

   (c)   the date and period of any previous extension of that bail;

   (d)   the date on which that bail is due to end;

   (e)   the conditions of that bail; and

   (f)   if different, the bail conditions which are to be imposed if the court authorises an extension, or further extension, of the period for which the defendant is released on pre-charge bail.

(4)   The application must explain—

   (a)   the grounds for believing that, as applicable—

      (i)   further investigation is needed of any matter in connection with the offence or offences for which the defendant was released on bail, or

      (ii)   further time is needed for making a decision as to whether to charge the defendant with that offence or those offences;

   (b)   the grounds for believing that, as applicable—

      (i)   the investigation into the offence or offences for which the defendant was released on bail is being conducted diligently and expeditiously, or

      (ii)   the decision as to whether to charge the defendant with that offence or those offences is being made diligently and expeditiously; and

   (c)   the grounds for believing that the defendant's further release on bail is necessary and proportionate in all the circumstances having regard, in particular, to any conditions of bail imposed.

(5)   The application must—

   (a)   indicate whether the applicant wants the court to authorise an extension of the defendant's bail for 3 months or for 6 months; and

   (b)   if for 6 months, explain why the investigation is unlikely to be completed or the charging decision made, as the case may be, within 3 months.

(6)   The application must explain why it was not made earlier where—

   (a)   the application is made before the date on which the defendant's bail is due to end; but

   (b)   it is not likely to be practicable for the court to determine the application before that date.

(7)   A defendant who objects to the application must—

   (a)   serve notice on—

      (i)   the court officer, and

      (ii)   the applicant, not more than 5 business days after service of the application; and

   (b)   in the notice explain the grounds of the objection.

*[Note. The Practice Direction sets out forms of application and response notice for use in connection with this rule.*

*See sections 47ZF (Applicable bail period: first extension of limit by the court), 47ZG (Applicable bail period: subsequent extensions of limit by the court) and 47ZJ (Sections 47ZF and 47ZG: late applications to magistrates' court) of the Police and Criminal Evidence Act 1984[43].*

---

[43] 1984 c. 60; section 47ZJ was inserted by section 63 of the Policing and Crime Act 2017 (c. 3).

*The time limit for making an application is prescribed by section 47ZF(2) and by section 47ZG(2) of the 1984 Act. It may be neither extended nor shortened. Under section 47ZJ(2) of the Act, if it is not practicable for the court to determine the application before the applicable bail period ends then the court must determine the application as soon as practicable. Under section 47ZJ(3), the applicable bail period is treated as extended until the application is determined. Under section 47ZJ(4), if it appears to the court that it would have been reasonable for the application to have been made in time for it to be determined by the court before the end of the applicable bail period then the court may refuse the application.]*

### Application to withhold information from the defendant                          R14.20

14.20 (1)  This rule applies where an application to authorise an extension of pre-charge bail includes an application to withhold information from the defendant.

  (2)  The applicant must—
      (a)  omit that information from the part of the application that is served on the defendant;
      (b)  mark the other part to show that, unless the court otherwise directs, it is only for the court; and
      (c)  in that other part, explain the grounds for believing that the disclosure of that information would have one or more of the following results—
          (i)  evidence connected with an indictable offence would be interfered with or harmed,
          (ii)  a person would be interfered with or physically injured,
          (iii)  a person suspected of having committed an indictable offence but not yet arrested for the offence would be alerted, or
          (iv)  the recovery of property obtained as a result of an indictable offence would be hindered.

  (3)  At any hearing of an application to which this rule applies—
      (a)  the court must first determine the application to withhold information, in the defendant's absence and that of any legal representative of the defendant; and
      (b)  if the court allows the application to withhold information, then in the following sequence—
          (i)  the court must consider representations first by the applicant and then by the defendant, in the presence of both, and
          (ii)  the court may consider further representations by the applicant in the defendant's absence and that of any legal representative of the defendant, if satisfied that there are reasonable grounds for believing that information withheld from the defendant would be disclosed during those further representations.

  (4)  If the court refuses an application to withhold information from the defendant, the applicant may withdraw the application to authorise an extension of pre-charge bail.

*[Note. See sections 47ZH and 47ZI(5), (6), (8) of the Police and Criminal Evidence Act 1984[44] (withholding sensitive information; proceedings in magistrates' courts: determination of applications to withhold sensitive information).]*

### *Summary of the general entitlement to bail and of the exceptions*

*The court must consider bail whenever it can order the defendant's detention pending trial or sentencing, or in an extradition case, and whether an application is made or not. Under section 4 of the Bail Act 1976[45], the general rule, subject to exceptions, is that a defendant must be granted bail. Under Part IIA of Schedule 1 to the Act[46], if the court decides not to grant the defendant bail then at each subsequent hearing the court must consider whether to grant bail.*

*Section 3 of the Bail Act 1976[47] allows the court, before granting bail, to require a surety or security to secure the defendant's surrender to custody; and allows the court, on granting bail, to impose such requirements as appear to the court to be necessary—*

---

[44]  1984 c. 60; sections 47ZH and 47ZI were inserted by section 63 of the Policing and Crime Act 2017 (c. 3).

[45]  1976 c. 63; section 4 was amended by section 154 of, and paragraph 145 of Schedule 7 to, the Magistrates' Courts Act 1980 (c. 43), section 168 of, and paragraphs 32 and 33 of Schedule 10 to, the Criminal Justice and Public Order Act 1994 (c. 33), section 58 of the Criminal Justice and Court Services Act 2000 (c. 43), sections 198 and 220 of, and Schedule 4 to, the Extradition Act 2003 (c. 41), section 304 of, and paragraphs 20 and 22 of Schedule 32 to, the Criminal Justice Act 2003 (c. 44), section 42 of, and paragraph 34 of Schedule 13 to, the Police and Justice Act 2006 (c. 48), sections 6 and 148 of, and paragraphs 23 and 102 of Schedule 4 and Part 1 of Schedule 28 to, the Criminal Justice and Immigration Act 2008 (c. 4) and paragraph 19 of Schedule 7, and Schedule 8, to the Policing and Crime Act 2009 (c. 26).

[46]  1976 c. 63; Schedule 1, Part IIA was added by section 154 of the Criminal Justice Act 1988 (c. 33).

[47]  1976 c. 63; section 3 was amended by section 65 of, and Schedule 12 to, the Criminal Law Act 1977 (c. 45), section 34 of the Mental Health (Amendment) Act 1982 (c. 51), paragraph 46 of Schedule 4 to the Mental Health Act 1983 (c. 20), section 15 of, and paragraph 9 of Schedule 2 to, the Criminal Justice Act 1987 (c. 38), section 131 of the Criminal Justice Act 1988

    (a)   to secure that the defendant surrenders to custody;

    (b)   to secure that the defendant does not commit an offence while on bail;

    (c)   to secure that the defendant does not interfere with witnesses or otherwise obstruct the course of justice whether in relation to the defendant or any other person;

    (d)   for the defendant's own protection or, if a child or young person, for the defendant's welfare or in the defendant's own interests;

    (e)   to secure the defendant's availability for the purpose of enabling enquiries or a report to be made to assist the court in dealing with the defendant for the offence;

    (f)   to secure that before the time appointed for surrender to custody the defendant attends an interview with a legal representative.

Under section 3 of the Bail Act 1976, a person granted bail in criminal proceedings is under a duty to surrender to custody as required by that bail. Under section 6 of the Act, such a person who fails without reasonable cause so to surrender commits an offence and, under section 7, may be arrested.

Exceptions to the general right to bail are listed in Schedule 1 to the Bail Act 1976[48]. They differ according to the category of offence concerned. Under section 4(2B) of the 1976 Act[49], in an extradition case there is no general right to bail where the defendant is alleged to have been convicted in the territory requesting extradition.

Under Part I of Schedule 1 to the 1976 Act, where the offence is punishable with imprisonment, and is not one that can be tried only in a magistrates' court, or in an extradition case—

    (a)   the defendant need not be granted bail if the court is satisfied that—

        (i)   there are substantial grounds for believing that, if released on bail (with or without conditions), the defendant would fail to surrender to custody, would commit an offence, or would interfere with witnesses or otherwise obstruct the course of justice,

        (ii)   there are substantial grounds for believing that, if released on bail (with or without conditions), the defendant would commit an offence by engaging in conduct that would, or would be likely to, cause physical or mental injury to an associated person (within the meaning of section 33 of the Family Law Act 1996[50]), or cause that person to fear injury,

        (iii)   the defendant should be kept in custody for his or her own protection or welfare, or

        (iv)   it has not been practicable, for want of time since the institution of the proceedings, to obtain sufficient information for the court to take the decisions required;

    (b)   the defendant need not be granted bail if it appears to the court that the defendant was on bail at the time of the offence (this exception does not apply in an extradition case);

    (c)   the defendant need not be granted bail if, having been released on bail in the case on a previous occasion, the defendant since has been arrested for breach of bail;

    (d)   the defendant need not be granted bail if in custody pursuant to a sentence;

    (e)   the defendant need not be granted bail if it appears to the court that it would be impracticable to complete enquiries or a report for which the case is to be adjourned without keeping the defendant in custody;

(c. 33), sections 27 and 168 of, and paragraph 12 of Schedule 9 and Schedule 11 to, the Criminal Justice and Public Order Act 1994 (c. 33), sections 54 and 120 of, and paragraph 37 of Schedule 8 and Schedule 10 to, the Crime and Disorder Act 1998 (c. 37), paragraph 51 of Schedule 9 to the Powers of Criminal Courts (Sentencing) Act 2000 (c. 6), section 131 of the Criminal Justice and Police Act 2001 (c. 16), sections 13 and 19 of, and paragraph 48 of Schedule 3 and Schedule 37 to, the Criminal Justice Act 2003 (c. 44), paragraphs 33 and 34 of Schedule 21 to the Legal Services Act 2007 (c. 29) and paragraphs 1 and 2 of Schedule 11, paragraphs 1 and 2 of Schedule 12, to the Criminal Justice and Immigration Act 2008 (c. 4) and paragraphs 1 to 4 of Schedule 11, and paragraphs 14 and 15 of Schedule 12, to the Legal Aid, Sentencing and Punishment of Offenders Act 2012 (c. 10).

[48] 1976 c. 63; Schedule 1 was amended by section 34 of the Mental Health (Amendment) Act 1982 (c. 51), sections 153, 154 and 155 of the Criminal Justice Act 1988 (c. 33), paragraph 22 of Schedule 11 to the Criminal Justice Act 1991 (c. 53), section 26 of the Criminal Justice and Public Order Act 1994 (c. 33), paragraph 38 of Schedule 8 to the Crime and Disorder Act 1998 (c. 37), paragraph 54 of Schedule 9 to the Powers of Criminal Courts (Sentencing) Act 2000 (c. 6), sections 129 and 137 of, and Schedule 7 to, the Criminal Justice and Police Act 2001 (c. 16), section 198 of the Extradition Act 2003 (c. 41), sections 13, 14, 15, 19 and 20 of, and paragraphs 20 and 23 of Schedule 32 and paragraphs 1 and 3 of Schedule 36 to, the Criminal Justice Act 2003 (c. 44), paragraph 40 of the Schedule to S.I. 2005/886, paragraph 78 of Schedule 16, and Schedule 17, to the Armed Forces Act 2006 (c. 52), paragraphs 1, 4, 5 and 6 of Schedule 12 to the Criminal Justice and Immigration Act 2008 (c. 4), section 114 of the Coroners and Justice Act 2009 (c. 25) and paragraphs 10 to 31 of Schedule 11, and paragraphs 14 and 17 of Schedule 12, to the Legal Aid, Sentencing and Punishment of Offenders Act 2012 (c. 10).

[49] 1976 c. 63; section 4(2B) was inserted by section 198 of the Extradition Act 2003 (c. 41) and amended by paragraph 34 of Schedule 13 to the Police and Justice Act 2006 (c. 48).

[50] 1996 c. 27; section 33 was amended by section 82 of, and paragraph 4 of Schedule 9 to, the Civil Partnership Act 2004 (c. 33).

(f)  the defendant may not be granted bail if charged with murder, unless the court is of the opinion that there is no significant risk of the defendant committing an offence while on bail that would, or would be likely to, cause physical or mental injury to some other person;

(g)  the defendant in an extradition case need not be granted bail if he or she was on bail on the date of the alleged offence and that offence is not one that could be tried only in a magistrates' court if it were committed in England or Wales.

Exceptions (a)(i), (b) and (c) do not apply where—

(a)  the defendant is 18 or over;

(b)  the defendant has not been convicted of an offence in those proceedings; and

(c)  it appears to the court that there is no real prospect that the defendant will be sentenced to a custodial sentence in those proceedings.

In deciding whether an exception to the right to bail applies the court must have regard to any relevant consideration, including—

(a)  the nature and seriousness of the offence, and the probable method of dealing with the defendant for it;

(b)  the character, antecedents, associations and community ties of the defendant;

(c)  the defendant's record of fulfilling obligations imposed under previous grants of bail; and

(d)  except where the case is adjourned for enquires or a report, the strength of the evidence of the defendant having committed the offence.

Under Part IA of Schedule 1 to the 1976 Act, where the offence is punishable with imprisonment, and is one that can be tried only in a magistrates' court—

(a)  the defendant need not be granted bail if it appears to the court that—

(i)  having previously been granted bail in criminal proceedings, the defendant has failed to surrender as required and, in view of that failure, the court believes that, if released on bail (with or without conditions), the defendant would fail to surrender to custody, or

(ii)  the defendant was on bail on the date of the offence and the court is satisfied that there are substantial grounds for believing that, if released on bail (with or without conditions), the defendant would commit an offence while on bail;

(b)  the defendant need not be granted bail if the court is satisfied that—

(i)  there are substantial grounds for believing that, if released on bail (with or without conditions), the defendant would commit an offence while on bail by engaging in conduct that would, or would be likely to, cause physical or mental injury to some other person, or cause some other person to fear such injury,

(ii)  the defendant should be kept in custody for his or her own protection or welfare, or

(iii)  it has not been practicable, for want of time since the institution of the proceedings, to obtain sufficient information for the court to take the decisions required;

(c)  the defendant need not be granted bail if in custody pursuant to a sentence;

(d)  the defendant need not be granted bail if, having been released on bail in the case on a previous occasion, the defendant since has been arrested for breach of bail, and the court is satisfied that there are substantial grounds for believing that, if released on bail (with or without conditions), the defendant would fail to surrender to custody, would commit an offence, or would interfere with witnesses or otherwise obstruct the course of justice.

Exceptions (a) and (d) do not apply where—

(a)  the defendant is 18 or over;

(b)  the defendant has not been convicted of an offence in those proceedings; and

(c)  it appears to the court that there is no real prospect that the defendant will be sentenced to a custodial sentence in those proceedings.

Under Part II of Schedule 1 to the 1976 Act, where the offence is not punishable with imprisonment—

(a)  the defendant need not be granted bail if it appears to the court that having previously been granted bail in criminal proceedings, the defendant has failed to surrender as required and, in view of that failure, the court believes that, if released on bail (with or without conditions), the defendant would fail to surrender to custody;

(b)  the defendant need not be granted bail if the court is satisfied that the defendant should be kept in custody for his or her own protection or welfare;

(c)  the defendant need not be granted bail if in custody pursuant to a sentence;

(d) *the defendant need not be granted bail if, having been released on bail in the case on a previous occasion, the defendant since has been arrested for breach of bail, and the court is satisfied that there are substantial grounds for believing that, if released on bail (with or without conditions), the defendant would fail to surrender to custody, would commit an offence, or would interfere with witnesses or otherwise obstruct the course of justice;*

(e) *the defendant need not be granted bail if, having been released on bail in the case on a previous occasion, the defendant since has been arrested for breach of bail, and the court is satisfied that there are substantial grounds for believing that, if released on bail (with or without conditions), the defendant would commit an offence while on bail by engaging in conduct that would, or would be likely to, cause physical or mental injury to an associated person (within the meaning of section 33 of the Family Law Act 1996), or to cause that person to fear such injury.*

*Exceptions (a) and (d) apply only where—*

(a) *the defendant is under 18; and*

(b) *the defendant has been convicted in those proceedings.*

*Further exceptions to the general right to bail are set out in section 25 of the Criminal Justice and Public Order Act 1994[51], under which a defendant charged with murder, attempted murder, manslaughter, rape or another sexual offence specified in that section, and who has been previously convicted of such an offence, may be granted bail only if there are exceptional circumstances which justify it.*

### CRIMINAL PRACTICE DIRECTIONS    PART 14 BAIL AND CUSTODY TIME LIMITS

**CPD.14A**    **CPD III Custody and bail 14A: Bail Before Sending for Trial**

**14A.1** Before the Crown Court can deal with an application under CrimPR 14.8 by a defendant after a magistrates' court has withheld bail, it must be satisfied that the magistrates' court has issued a certificate, under section 5(6A) of the Bail Act 1976, that it heard full argument on the application for bail before it refused the application. The certificate of full argument is produced by the magistrates' court's computer system, Libra, as part of the GENORD (General Form of Order). Two hard copies are produced, one for the defence and one for the prosecution. (Some magistrates' courts may also produce a manual certificate which will usually be available from the justices' legal adviser at the conclusion of the hearing; the GENORD may not be produced until the following day.) Under CrimPR 14.4(4), the magistrates' court officer will provide the defendant with a certificate that the court heard full argument. However, it is the responsibility of the defence, as the applicant in the Crown Court, to ensure that a copy of the certificate of full argument is provided to the Crown Court as part of the application (CrimPR 14.8(3)(e)). The applicant's solicitors should attach a copy of the certificate to the bail application form. If the certificate is not enclosed with the application form, it will be difficult to avoid some delay in listing.

*Venue*

**14A.2** Applications should be made to the court to which the defendant will be, or would have been, sent for trial. In the event of an application in a purely summary case, it should be made to the Crown Court centre which normally receives Class 3 work. The hearing will be listed as a chambers matter, unless a judge has directed otherwise.

**CPD.14B**    **CPD III Custody and bail 14B: Bail: Failure to Surrender and Trials in Absence**

**14B.1** The failure of defendants to comply with the terms of their bail by not surrendering, or not doing so at the appointed time, undermines the administration of justice and disrupts proceedings. The resulting delays impact on victims, witnesses and other court users and also waste costs. A defendant's failure to surrender affects not only the case with which he or she is concerned, but also the court's ability to administer justice more generally, by damaging the confidence of victims, witnesses and the public in the effectiveness of the court system and the judiciary. It is,

---

[51] 1994 c. 33; section 25 was amended by section 56 of the Crime and Disorder Act 1998 (c. 37), paragraph 160 of Schedule 9 to the Powers of Criminal Courts (Sentencing) Act 2000 (c. 6), paragraph 32 of Schedule 6 to the Sexual Offences Act 2003 (c. 42), paragraph 67 of Schedule 32 and Schedule 37 to the Criminal Justice Act 2003 (c. 44), article 16 of S.I. 2008/1779, paragraph 3 of Schedule 17, and Schedule 23, to the Coroners and Justice Act 2009 (c. 25) and paragraph 33 of Schedule 11 to the Legal Aid, Sentencing and Punishment of Offenders Act 2012 (c. 10).

therefore, most important that defendants who are granted bail appreciate the significance of the obligation to surrender to custody in accordance with the terms of their bail and that courts take appropriate action, if they fail to do so.

**14B.2** A defendant who will be unable for medical reasons to attend court in accordance with his or her bail must obtain a certificate from his or her general practitioner or another appropriate medical practitioner such as the doctor with care of the defendant at a hospital. This should be obtained in advance of the hearing and conveyed to the court through the defendant's legal representative. In order to minimise the disruption to the court and to others, particularly witnesses if the case is listed for trial, the defendant should notify the court through his legal representative as soon as his inability to attend court becomes known.

**14B.3** Guidance has been produced by the British Medical Association and the Crown Prosecution Service on the roles and responsibilities of medical practitioners when issuing medical certificates in criminal proceedings. Judges and magistrates should seek to ensure that this guidance is followed. However, it is a matter for each individual court to decide whether, in any particular case, the issued certificate should be accepted. Without a medical certificate or if an unsatisfactory certificate is provided, the court is likely to consider that the defendant has failed to surrender to bail.

**14B.4** If a defendant fails to surrender to his or her bail there are at least four courses of action for the courts to consider taking:
(a)   imposing penalties for the failure to surrender;
(b)   revoking bail or imposing more stringent conditions;
(c)   conducting trials in the absence of the defendant; and
(d)   ordering that some or all of any sums of money lodged with the court as a security or pledged by a surety as a condition on the grant of bail be forfeit.
The relevant sentencing guideline is the Definitive Guideline Fail to Surrender to Bail. Under section 125(1) of the Coroners and Justice Act 2009, for offences committed on or after 6 April 2010, the court must follow the relevant guideline unless it would be contrary to the interests of justice to do so. The guideline can be obtained from the Sentencing Council's website: https://www.sentencingcouncil.org.uk/

**CPD III Custody and bail 14C: Penalties for Failure to Surrender**                    CPD.14C

*Initiating Proceedings — Bail granted by a police officer*

**14C.1** When a person has been granted bail by a police officer to attend court and subsequently fails to surrender to custody, the decision whether to initiate proceedings for a section 6(1) or section 6(2) offence will be for the police/prosecutor and proceedings are commenced in the usual way.

**14C.2** The offence in this form is a summary offence although section 6(10) to (14) of the Bail Act 1976, inserted by section 15(3) of the Criminal Justice Act 2003, disapplies section 127 of the Magistrates' Courts Act 1980 and provides for alternative time limits for the commencement of proceedings. The offence should be dealt with on the first appearance after arrest, unless an adjournment is necessary, as it will be relevant in considering whether to grant bail again.

*Initiating Proceedings — Bail granted by a court*

**14C.3** Where a person has been granted bail by a court and subsequently fails to surrender to custody, on arrest that person should normally be brought as soon as appropriate before the court at which the proceedings in respect of which bail was granted are to be heard. (There is no requirement to lay an information within the time limit for a Bail Act offence where bail was granted by the court).

**14C.4** Given that bail was granted by a court, it is more appropriate that the court itself should initiate the proceedings by its own motion although the prosecutor may invite the court to take proceedings, if the prosecutor considers proceedings are appropriate.

*Timing of disposal*

**14C.5** Courts should not, without good reason, adjourn the disposal of a section 6(1) or section 6(2) Bail Act 1976 offence (failure to surrender) until the conclusion of the proceedings in respect of which bail was granted but should deal with defendants as soon as is practicable. In deciding what is practicable, the court must take into account when the proceedings in respect of which bail was granted are expected to conclude, the seriousness of the offence for which the defendant is already being prosecuted, the type of penalty that might be imposed for the Bail Act offence and the original offence, as well as any other relevant circumstances.

**14C.6** If the Bail Act offence is adjourned alongside the substantive proceedings, then it is still necessary to consider imposing a separate penalty at the trial. In addition, bail should usually be revoked in the meantime. Trial in the absence of the defendant is not a penalty for the Bail Act offence and a separate penalty may be imposed for the Bail Act offence.

*Conduct of Proceedings*

**14C.7** Proceedings under section 6 of the Bail Act 1976 may be conducted either as a summary offence or as a criminal contempt of court. Where proceedings are commenced by the police or prosecutor, the prosecutor will conduct the proceedings and, if the matter is contested, call the evidence. Where the court initiates proceedings, with or without an invitation from the prosecutor, the court may expect the assistance of the prosecutor, such as in cross-examining the defendant, if required.

**14C.8** The burden of proof is on the defendant to prove that he had reasonable cause for his failure to surrender to custody (section 6(3) of the Bail Act 1976).

*Sentencing for a Bail Act offence*

**14C.9** A defendant who commits an offence under section 6(1) or section 6(2) of the Bail Act 1976 commits an offence that stands apart from the proceedings in respect of which bail was granted. The seriousness of the offence can be reflected by an appropriate and generally separate penalty being imposed for the Bail Act offence.

**14C.10** As noted above, there is a sentencing guideline on sentencing offenders for Bail Act offences and this must be followed unless it would be contrary to the interests of justice to do so. Where the appropriate penalty is a custodial sentence, consecutive sentences should be imposed unless there are circumstances that make this inappropriate.

*Arrest for breach of bail*

**14C.11** A defendant who has been released on bail but subsequently arrested for breach of a bail condition, or for failure to surrender to the court, actual or anticipated, must be brought before a magistrates' court (or a Crown Court judge, if the defendant is charged with murder) as soon as practicable and in any event within 24 hours of arrest. This does not apply to a defendant who is arrested within 24 hours of the next court hearing which that defendant is due to attend: such a defendant must be produced at that hearing instead. The period of 24 hours does not include Sunday, Christmas Day or Good Friday: see section 7 of the Bail Act 1976.

**14C.12** Paragraphs II 7A.2 to 7A.8 of these Practice Directions apply to such a defendant as they do to one charged and brought before the court under section 46 of the Police and Criminal Evidence Act 1984, except for the requirements listed at paragraph II 7A.5(a)(i) and (ii) (requirements for confirmation of charge and preparation of case file), which must be read as if they required confirmation that (i) the allegation or allegations of breach of bail have been reduced to writing, and (ii) that allegation or those allegations, and any supporting documents, are complete and available. If the requirements of paragraph 7A.5, as thus read, are met, then the court before which the defendant is brought should take all the appropriate next steps in the case, including the taking of the defendant's plea; allocation and sending for trial, if applicable; and, if possible, sentencing; and should do so even if the defendant had been released on bail by a different court.

*Voluntary attendance at a court after failure to attend*

**14C.13** The court may consider taking any of the following courses of action where
    (i)  a defendant has failed to attend a court at the appointed time, (ii) a warrant has been issued for the defendant's arrest for that failure, and (iii) the defendant subsequently attends voluntarily at some other time, or indicates a wish to do so, for example by making telephone enquiries of court staff:
        (a)  if the defendant is present, the court may arrange for the execution there and then of the warrant;
        (b)  if the defendant is present, the court may deal there and then with the case as if consequent on the execution of the warrant;
        (c)  the court may arrange a resumed hearing in the defendant's case at the next convenient opportunity, while warning the defendant that the warrant remains liable to be executed in the meantime; and
        (d)  the court may withdraw the warrant and arrange a resumed hearing in the defendant's case at the next convenient opportunity. The court should not withdraw an outstanding warrant unless the defendant provides evidence of an established current residential address, a telephone number and, if available, an email or other established electronic address.

**14C.14** If an outstanding warrant is executed there and then, or if the court decides to deal at once with the defendant as if consequent on arrest, then paragraphs 14C.11 and 14C.12 apply and, consequently, paragraphs II 7A.2 to 7A.8 of these Practice Directions. However, if the defendant has not been arrested then the designated officer's delegate is under no such statutory duty as otherwise would apply to make efforts to accommodate the defendant's case and no step should be taken that disadvantages other cases awaiting hearing that day. In particular, it is only in exceptional circumstances that efforts should be made to accommodate a defendant who attends voluntarily and unexpectedly at a court building on any day other than a weekday on which a court is sitting at that building, or later than 12 noon on any such day.

14C.15   If an outstanding warrant for the defendant's arrest for failure to attend is either executed or withdrawn, court staff must ensure that this is recorded promptly in national police records.

## CPD III Custody and bail 14D: Relationship between the Bail Act Offence and Further Remands on Bail or in Custody

CPD.14D

14D.1   The court at which the defendant is produced should, where practicable and legally permissible, arrange to have all outstanding cases brought before it (including those from different courts) for the purpose of progressing matters and dealing with the question of bail. This is likely to be practicable in the magistrates' court where cases can easily be transferred from one magistrates' court to another. Practice is likely to vary in the Crown Court. If the defendant appears before a different court, for example because he is charged with offences committed in another area, and it is not practicable for all matters to be concluded by that court then the defendant may be remanded on bail or in custody, if appropriate, to appear before the first court for the outstanding offences to be dealt with.

14D.2   When a defendant has been convicted of a Bail Act offence, the court should review the remand status of the defendant, including the conditions of that bail, in respect of all outstanding proceedings against the defendant.

14D.3   Failure by the defendant to surrender or a conviction for failing to surrender to bail in connection with the main proceedings will be significant factors weighing against the re-granting of bail.

14D.4   Whether or not an immediate custodial sentence has been imposed for the Bail Act offence, the court may, having reviewed the defendant's remand status, also remand the defendant in custody in the main proceedings.

## CPD III Custody and bail 14E: Trials in Absence

CPD.14E

14E.1   Paragraphs VI 24C and 25B of these Practice Directions (Trial adjournment in magistrates' courts; Trial adjournment in the Crown Court) include guidance on the circumstances in which the court should proceed with or adjourn a trial from which the defendant absents himself or herself voluntarily.

## CPD III Custody and bail 14F: Forfeiture of Monies Lodged as Security or Pledged by a Surety/ Estreatment of Recognisances

CPD.14F

14F.1   A surety undertakes to forfeit a sum of money if the defendant fails to surrender as required. Considerable care must be taken to explain that obligation and the consequences before a surety is taken. This system, in one form or another, has great antiquity. It is immensely valuable. A court concerned that a defendant will fail to surrender will not normally know that defendant personally, nor indeed much about him. When members of the community who do know the defendant say they trust him to surrender and are prepared to stake their own money on that trust, that can have a powerful influence on the decision of the court as to whether or not to grant bail. There are two important side-effects. The first is that the surety will keep an eye on the defendant, and report to the authorities if there is a concern that he will abscond. In those circumstances, the surety can withdraw. The second is that a defendant will be deterred from absconding by the knowledge that if he does so then his family or friends who provided the surety will lose their money. In the experience of the courts, it is comparatively rare for a defendant to fail to surrender when meaningful sureties are in place.

14F.2   Any surety should have the opportunity to make representations to the defendant to surrender himself, in accordance with their obligations.

14F.3   The court should not wait or adjourn a decision on estreatment of sureties or securities until such time, if any, that the bailed defendant appears before the court. It is possible that any defendant who apparently absconds may have a defence of reasonable cause to the allegation of failure to surrender. If that happens, then any surety or security estreated would be returned. The reason for proceeding is that the defendant may never surrender, or may not surrender for many years. The court should still consider the sureties' obligations if that happens. Moreover, the longer the matter is delayed the more probable it is that the personal circumstances of the sureties will change.

14F.4   The court should follow the procedure at CrimPR 14.15. Before the court makes a decision, it should give the sureties the opportunity to make representations, either in person, through counsel or by statement.

14F.5   The court has discretion to forfeit the whole sum, part only of the sum, or to remit the sum. The starting point is that the surety is forfeited in full. It would be unfortunate if this valuable method of allowing a defendant to remain at liberty were undermined. Courts would have less confidence in the efficacy of sureties. It is also important to note that a defendant who absconds without in

Criminal Procedure Rules and Criminal Practice Directions

any way forewarning his sureties does not thereby release them from any or all of their responsibilities. Even if a surety does his best, he remains liable for the full amount, except at the discretion of the court. However, all factors should be taken into account and the following are noted for guidance only:

i)    The presence or absence of culpability is a factor, but is not in itself a reason to reduce or set aside the obligations entered into by the surety.

ii)   The means of a surety, and in particular changed means, are relevant.

iii)  The court should forfeit no more than is necessary, in public policy, to maintain the integrity and confidence of the system of taking sureties.

**CPD.14G**    **CPD III Custody and bail 14G: Bail During Trial**

**14G.1**  The following should be read subject to the Bail Act 1976.

**14G.2**  Once a trial has begun the further grant of bail, whether during the short adjournment or overnight, is in the discretion of the trial judge or trial Bench. It may be a proper exercise of this discretion to refuse bail during the short adjournment if the accused cannot otherwise be segregated from witnesses and jurors.

**14G.3**  An accused who was on bail while on remand should not be refused bail during the trial unless, in the opinion of the court, there are positive reasons to justify this refusal. Such reasons might include:

(a)   that a point has been reached where there is a real danger that the accused will abscond, either because the case is going badly for him, or for any other reason;

(b)   that there is a real danger that he may interfere with witnesses, jurors or co-defendants.

**14G.4**  Once the jury has returned a guilty verdict or a finding of guilt has been made, a further renewal of bail should be decided in the light of the gravity of the offence, any friction between co-defendants and the likely sentence to be passed in all the circumstances of the case.

**CPD.14H**    **CPD III Custody and bail 14H: Crown Court Judge's Certification of Fitness to Appeal and Applications to the Crown Court for Bail Pending Appeal**

**14H.1**  The trial or sentencing judge may grant a certificate of fitness for appeal (see, for example, sections 1(2) (b) and 11(1A) of the Criminal Appeal Act 1968); the judge in the Crown Court should only certify cases in exceptional circumstances. The Crown Court judge should use the Criminal Appeal Office Form C (Crown Court Judge's Certificate of fitness for appeal) which is available to court staff on the HMCTS intranet.

**14H.2**  The judge may well think it right to encourage the defendant's advocate to submit to the court, and serve on the prosecutor, before the hearing of the application, a draft of the grounds of appeal which he will ask the judge to certify on Form C.

**14H.3**  The first question for the judge is then whether there exists a particular and cogent ground of appeal. If there is no such ground, there can be no certificate; and if there is no certificate there can be no bail. A judge should not grant a certificate with regard to sentence merely in the light of mitigation to which he has, in his opinion, given due weight, nor in regard to conviction on a ground where he considers the chance of a successful appeal is not substantial. The judge should bear in mind that, where a certificate is refused, application may be made to the Court of Appeal for leave to appeal and for bail; it is expected that certificates will only be granted in exceptional circumstances.

**14H.4**  Defence advocates should note that the effect of a grant of a certificate is to remove the need for leave to appeal to be granted by the Court of Appeal. It does not in itself commence the appeal. The completed Form C will be sent by the Crown Court to the Criminal Appeal Office; it is not copied to the parties. The procedures in CrimPR Part 39 should be followed.

**14H.5**  Bail pending appeal to the Court of Appeal (Criminal Division) may be granted by the trial or sentencing judge if they have certified the case as fit for appeal (see sections 81(1)(f) and 81(1B) of the Senior Courts Act 1981). Bail can only be granted in the Crown Court within 28 days of the conviction or sentence which is to be the subject of the appeal and may not be granted if an application for bail has already been made to the Court of Appeal. The procedure for bail to be granted by a judge of the Crown Court pending an appeal is governed by CrimPR Part 14. The Crown Court judge should use the Criminal Appeal Office Form BC (Crown Court Judge's Order granting bail) which is available to court staff on the HMCTS intranet.

**14H.6**  The length of the period which might elapse before the hearing of any appeal is not relevant to the grant of a certificate; but, if the judge does decide to grant a certificate, it may be one factor in the decision whether or not to grant bail. If bail is granted, the judge should consider imposing a condition of residence in line with the practice in the Court of Appeal (Criminal Division).

CRIMINAL PROCEDURE RULES   PART 15   DISCLOSURE

**When this Part applies**                                                R15.1

15.1   This Part applies in a magistrates' court and in the Crown Court where Parts I and II of the Criminal Procedure and Investigations Act 1996 apply.

*[Note. A summary of the disclosure requirements of the Criminal Procedure and Investigations Act 1996 is at the end of this Part.]*

**Prosecution disclosure**                                                R15.2

15.2   (1)   This rule applies in the Crown Court where, under section 3 of the Criminal Procedure and Investigations Act 1996[1], the prosecutor—

   (a)   discloses prosecution material to the defendant; or

   (b)   serves on the defendant a written statement that there is no such material to disclose.

   (2)   The prosecutor must at the same time so inform the court officer.

*[Note. See section 3 of the Criminal Procedure and Investigations Act 1996 and paragraph 10 of the Code of Practice accompanying the Criminal Procedure and Investigations Act 1996 (Code of Practice) Order 2015[2].]*

**Prosecutor's application for public interest ruling**                   R15.3

15.3   (1)   This rule applies where—

   (a)   without a court order, the prosecutor would have to disclose material; and

   (b)   the prosecutor wants the court to decide whether it would be in the public interest to disclose it.

   (2)   The prosecutor must—

   (a)   apply in writing for such a decision; and

   (b)   serve the application on—

      (i)   the court officer,

      (ii)   any person who the prosecutor thinks would be directly affected by disclosure of the material, and

      (iii)   the defendant, but only to the extent that serving it on the defendant would not disclose what the prosecutor thinks ought not be disclosed.

   (3)   The application must—

   (a)   describe the material, and explain why the prosecutor thinks that—

      (i)   it is material that the prosecutor would have to disclose,

      (ii)   it would not be in the public interest to disclose that material, and

      (iii)   no measure such as the prosecutor's admission of any fact, or disclosure by summary, extract or edited copy, adequately would protect both the public interest and the defendant's right to a fair trial;

   (b)   omit from any part of the application that is served on the defendant anything that would disclose what the prosecutor thinks ought not be disclosed (in which case, paragraph (4) of this rule applies); and

   (c)   explain why, if no part of the application is served on the defendant.

   (4)   Where the prosecutor serves only part of the application on the defendant, the prosecutor must—

   (a)   mark the other part, to show that it is only for the court; and

   (b)   in that other part, explain why the prosecutor has withheld it from the defendant.

   (5)   Unless already done, the court may direct the prosecutor to serve an application on—

   (a)   the defendant; and

   (b)   any other person who the court considers would be directly affected by the disclosure of the material.

   (6)   The court must determine the application at a hearing which—

   (a)   must be in private, unless the court otherwise directs; and

   (b)   if the court so directs, may take place, wholly or in part, in the defendant's absence.

   (7)   At a hearing at which the defendant is present—

   (a)   the general rule is that the court must consider, in the following sequence—

      (i)   representations first by the prosecutor and any other person served with the application, and then by the defendant, in the presence of them all, and then

      (ii)   further representations by the prosecutor and any such other person in the defendant's absence; but

   (b)   the court may direct other arrangements for the hearing.

---

[1]   1996 c. 25; section 3 was amended by section 82 of, and paragraph 7 of Schedule 4 to, the Regulation of Investigatory Powers Act 2000 (c. 23) and section 32 and section 331 of, and paragraphs 20 and 21 of Schedule 36 to, the Criminal Justice Act 2003 (c. 44).

[2]   S.I. 2015/861.

(8) The court may only determine the application if satisfied that it has been able to take adequate account of—

    (a) such rights of confidentiality as apply to the material; and

    (b) the defendant's right to a fair trial.

(9) Unless the court otherwise directs, the court officer—

    (a) must not give notice to anyone other than the prosecutor—

        (i) of the hearing of an application under this rule, unless the prosecutor served the application on that person, or

        (ii) of the court's decision on the application; and

    (b) may—

        (i) keep a written application or representations, or

        (ii) arrange for the whole or any part to be kept by some other appropriate person, subject to any conditions that the court may impose.

*[Note. The court's power to order that it is not in the public interest to disclose material is provided for by sections 3(6), 7(6) (where the investigation began between 1ˢᵗ April, 1997 and 3ʳᵈ April, 2005) and 7A(8) (where the investigation began on or after 4ᵗʰ April, 2005) of the Criminal Procedure and Investigations Act 1996[3].*

*See also sections 16 and 19 of the 1996 Act[4].]*

## R15.4   Defence disclosure

15.4 (1) This rule applies where—

    (a) under section 5 or 6 of the Criminal Procedure and Investigations Act 1996[5], the defendant gives a defence statement; and

    (b) under section 6C of the 1996 Act[6], the defendant gives a defence witness notice.

(2) The defendant must serve such a statement or notice on—

    (a) the court officer; and

    (b) the prosecutor.

*[Note. The Practice Direction sets out forms of—*

    *(a) defence statement; and*

    *(b) defence witness notice.*

*Under section 5 of the 1996 Act, in the Crown Court the defendant must give a defence statement. Under section 6 of the Act, in a magistrates' court the defendant may give such a statement but need not do so.*

*Under section 6C of the 1996 Act, in the Crown Court and in magistrates' courts the defendant must give a defence witness notice indicating whether he or she intends to call any witnesses (other than him or herself) and, if so, identifying them.]*

## R15.5   Defendant's application for prosecution disclosure

15.5 (1) This rule applies where the defendant—

    (a) has served a defence statement given under the Criminal Procedure and Investigations Act 1996; and

    (b) wants the court to require the prosecutor to disclose material.

(2) The defendant must serve an application on—

    (a) the court officer; and

    (b) the prosecutor.

(3) The application must—

    (a) describe the material that the defendant wants the prosecutor to disclose;

    (b) explain why the defendant thinks there is reasonable cause to believe that—

        (i) the prosecutor has that material, and

        (ii) it is material that the Criminal Procedure and Investigations Act 1996 requires the prosecutor to disclose; and

---

[3] 1996 c. 25; section 7 was repealed by sections 331 and 332 of, and paragraphs 20 and 25 of Schedule 36 and Part 3 of Schedule 37 to, the Criminal Justice Act 2003 (c. 44), with transitional provisions for certain offences in article 2 of S.I. 2005/1817. Section 7A was inserted by section 37 of the Criminal Justice Act 2003 (c. 44).

[4] 1996 c. 25; section 16 was amended by section 331 of, and paragraphs 20 and 32 of Schedule 36 to, the Criminal Justice Act 2003 (c. 44). Section 19 was amended by section 109 of, and paragraph 377 of Schedule 8 to, the Courts Act 2003 (c. 39), section 331 of, and paragraphs 20 and 34 of Schedule 36 to, the Criminal Justice Act 2003 (c. 44) and section 15 of, and paragraph 251 of Schedule 4 to, the Constitutional Reform Act 2005 (c. 4).

[5] 1996 c. 25; section 5 was amended by section 33 of, and paragraph 66 of Schedule 3, paragraphs 20 and 23 of Schedule 36 and Parts 3 and 4 of Schedule 37 to, the Criminal Justice Act 2003 (c. 44). It was further amended by section 119 of, and paragraph 126 of Schedule 8 to, the Crime and Disorder Act 1998 (c. 37) in respect of certain proceedings only.

[6] 1996 c. 25; section 6C was inserted by section 34 of the Criminal Justice Act 2003 (c. 44).

    (c) ask for a hearing, if the defendant wants one, and explain why it is needed.

(4) The court may determine an application under this rule—

    (a) at a hearing, in public or in private; or

    (b) without a hearing.

(5) The court must not require the prosecutor to disclose material unless the prosecutor—

    (a) is present; or

    (b) has had at least 10 business days in which to make representations.

*[Note. The Practice Direction sets out a form of application for use in connection with this rule.*

*Under section 8 of the Criminal Procedure and Investigations Act 1996[7], a defendant may apply for prosecution disclosure only if the defendant has given a defence statement.]*

## Review of public interest ruling

**R15.6**

**15.6** (1) This rule applies where the court has ordered that it is not in the public interest to disclose material that the prosecutor otherwise would have to disclose, and—

    (a) the defendant wants the court to review that decision; or

    (b) the Crown Court reviews that decision on its own initiative.

(2) Where the defendant wants the court to review that decision, the defendant must—

    (a) serve an application on—

        (i) the court officer, and

        (ii) the prosecutor; and

    (b) in the application—

        (i) describe the material that the defendant wants the prosecutor to disclose, and

        (ii) explain why the defendant thinks it is no longer in the public interest for the prosecutor not to disclose it.

(3) The prosecutor must serve any such application on any person who the prosecutor thinks would be directly affected if that material were disclosed.

(4) The prosecutor, and any such person, must serve any representations on—

    (a) the court officer; and

    (b) the defendant, unless to do so would in effect reveal something that either thinks ought not be disclosed.

(5) The court may direct—

    (a) the prosecutor to serve any such application on any person who the court considers would be directly affected if that material were disclosed; and

    (b) the prosecutor and any such person to serve any representations on the defendant.

(6) The court must review a decision to which this rule applies at a hearing which—

    (a) must be in private, unless the court otherwise directs; and

    (b) if the court so directs, may take place, wholly or in part, in the defendant's absence.

(7) At a hearing at which the defendant is present—

    (a) the general rule is that the court must consider, in the following sequence—

        (i) representations first by the defendant, and then by the prosecutor and any other person served with the application, in the presence of them all, and then

        (ii) further representations by the prosecutor and any such other person in the defendant's absence; but

    (b) the court may direct other arrangements for the hearing.

(8) The court may only conclude a review if satisfied that it has been able to take adequate account of—

    (a) such rights of confidentiality as apply to the material; and

    (b) the defendant's right to a fair trial.

*[Note. The court's power to review a public interest ruling is provided for by sections 14 and 15 of the Criminal Procedure and Investigations Act 1996[8]. Under section 14 of the Act, a magistrates' court may reconsider an order for non-disclosure only if a defendant applies. Under section 15, the Crown Court may do so on an application, or on its own initiative.*

*See also sections 16 and 19 of the 1996 Act.]*

---

[7] 1996 c. 25; section 8 was amended by section 82 of, and paragraph 7 of Schedule 4 to, the Regulation of Investigatory Powers Act 2000 (c. 23) and section 38 of the Criminal Justice Act 2003 (c. 44).

[8] 1996 c. 25; section 14 was amended by section 331 of, and paragraphs 20 and 30 of Schedule 36 to, the Criminal Justice Act 2003 (c. 44) and section 15 was amended by section 331 of, and paragraphs 20 and 31 of Schedule 36 to, the Criminal Justice Act 2003 (c. 44).

**R15.7**    **Defendant's application to use disclosed material**

15.7   (1)   This rule applies where a defendant wants the court's permission to use disclosed prosecution material—

     (a)   otherwise than in connection with the case in which it was disclosed; or

     (b)   beyond the extent to which it was displayed or communicated publicly at a hearing.

  (2)   The defendant must serve an application on—

     (a)   the court officer; and

     (b)   the prosecutor.

  (3)   The application must—

     (a)   specify what the defendant wants to use or disclose; and

     (b)   explain why.

  (4)   The court may determine an application under this rule—

     (a)   at a hearing, in public or in private; or

     (b)   without a hearing.

  (5)   The court must not permit the use of such material unless—

     (a)   the prosecutor has had at least 20 business days in which to make representations; and

     (b)   the court is satisfied that it has been able to take adequate account of any rights of confidentiality that may apply to the material.

*[Note. The court's power to allow a defendant to use disclosed material is provided for by section 17 of the Criminal Procedure and Investigations Act 1996[9].]*

**R15.8**    **Unauthorised use of disclosed material**

15.8   (1)   This rule applies where a person is accused of using disclosed prosecution material in contravention of section 17 of the Criminal Procedure and Investigations Act 1996.

  (2)   A party who wants the court to exercise its power to punish that person for contempt of court must comply with the rules in Part 48 (Contempt of court).

  (3)   The court must not exercise its power to forfeit material used in contempt of court unless—

     (a)   the prosecutor; and

     (b)   any other person directly affected by the disclosure of the material.

     is present, or has had at least 14 days in which to make representations.

*[Under section 18 of the 1996 Act, the court can punish for contempt of court any other use of disclosed prosecution material. See also section 19 of the 1996 Act.]*

**R15.9**    **Court's power to vary requirements under this Part**

15.9   The court may—

     (a)   shorten or extend (even after it has expired) a time limit under this Part;

     (b)   allow a defence statement, or a defence witness notice, to be in a different written form to one set out in the Practice Direction, as long as it contains what the Criminal Procedure and Investigations Act 1996 requires;

     (c)   allow an application under this Part to be in a different form to one set out in the Practice Direction, or to be presented orally; and

     (d)   specify the period within which—

        (i)   any application under this Part must be made, or

        (ii)   any material must be disclosed, on an application to which rule 15.5 applies (Defendant's application for prosecution disclosure).

### Summary of disclosure requirements of Criminal Procedure and Investigations Act 1996

*The Criminal Procedure and Investigations Act 1996 came into force on 1st April, 1997. It does not apply where the investigation began before that date. With effect from 4th April, 2005, the Criminal Justice Act 2003 made changes to the 1996 Act that do not apply where the investigation began before that date.*

*In some circumstances, the prosecutor may be required to disclose material to which the 1996 Act does not apply: see sections 1 and 21[10].*

---

[9]   1996 c. 25; section 17 was amended by section 331 of, and paragraphs 20 and 33 of Schedule 36 to, the Criminal Justice Act 2003 (c. 44).

[10]   1996 c. 25; section 1 was amended by section 119 of, and paragraph 125 of Schedule 8 to, the Crime and Disorder Act 1998 (c. 37), paragraph 66 of Schedule 3 and Part 4 of Schedule 37 to the Criminal Justice Act 2003 (c. 44) and paragraph 37 of Schedule 17 to the Crime and Courts Act 2013 (c. 22). It was amended in respect of certain proceedings only by section 119 of, and paragraph 125(a) of Schedule 8 to, the Crime and Disorder Act 1998 (c. 37). It is further amended by section 9 of the Sexual Offences (Protected Material) Act 1997 (c. 39), with effect from a date to be appointed. Section 21 was amended by paragraph 66 of Schedule 3 to the Criminal Justice Act 2003 (c. 44).

Part I of the 1996 Act contains sections 1 to 21A. Part II, which contains sections 22 to 27, requires an investigator to record information relevant to an investigation that is obtained during its course. See also the Criminal Procedure and Investigations Act 1996 (Code of Practice) (No. 2) Order 1997[11], the Criminal Procedure and Investigations Act 1996 (Code of Practice) Order 2005[12] and the Criminal Procedure and Investigations Act 1996 (Code of Practice) Order 2015[13] issued under sections 23 to 25 of the 1996 Act.

### Prosecution disclosure

Where the investigation began between 1st April, 1997, and 3rd April, 2005, sections 3 and 7 of the 1996 Act require the prosecutor—

  (a)  to disclose material not previously disclosed that in the prosecutor's opinion might undermine the case for the prosecution against the defendant—
    (i)  in a magistrates' court, as soon as is reasonably practicable after the defendant pleads not guilty, and
    (ii)  in the Crown Court, as soon as is reasonably practicable after the case is committed or transferred for trial, or after the evidence is served where the case is sent for trial; and
  (b)  as soon as is reasonably practicable after service of the defence statement, to disclose material not previously disclosed that might be reasonably expected to assist the defendant's case as disclosed by that defence statement; or in either event
  (c)  if there is no such material, then to give the defendant a written statement to that effect.

Where the investigation began on or after 4th April, 2005, sections 3 and 7A of the 1996 Act[14] require the prosecutor—

  (a)  to disclose prosecution material not previously disclosed that might reasonably be considered capable of undermining the case for the prosecution against the defendant or of assisting the case for the defendant—
    (i)  in a magistrates' court, as soon as is reasonably practicable after the defendant pleads not guilty, or
    (ii)  in the Crown Court, as soon as is reasonably practicable after the case is committed or transferred for trial, or after the evidence is served where the case is sent for trial, or after a count is added to the indictment; and in either case
  (b)  if there is no such material, then to give the defendant a written statement to that effect; and after that
  (c)  in either court, to disclose any such material—
    (i)  whenever there is any, until the court reaches its verdict or the prosecutor decides not to proceed with the case, and
    (ii)  in particular, after the service of the defence statement.

Sections 2 and 3 of the 1996 Act define material, and prescribe how it must be disclosed.

In some circumstances, disclosure is prohibited by section 17 of the Regulation of Investigatory Powers Act 2000.

The prosecutor must not disclose material that the court orders it would not be in the public interest to disclose: see sections 3(6), 7(6) and 7A(8) of the 1996 Act.

Sections 12 and 13 of the 1996 Act prescribe the time for prosecution disclosure. Under paragraph 10 of the Code of Practice accompanying the Criminal Procedure and Investigations Act 1996 (Code of Practice) Order 2015, in a magistrates' court the prosecutor must disclose any material due to be disclosed at the hearing where a not guilty plea is entered, or as soon as possible following a formal indication from the accused or representative that a not guilty plea will be entered at that hearing.

See also sections 1, 4 and 10 of the 1996 Act.

### Defence disclosure

Under section 5 of the 1996 Act[15], in the Crown Court the defendant must give a defence statement. Under section 6 of the Act, in a magistrates' court the defendant may give such a statement but need not do so.

---

[11]  S.I. 1997/1033; this Order was revoked by S.I. 2005/985.

[12]  S.I. 2005/985.

[13]  S.I. 2015/861.

[14]  1996 c. 25; section 3 was amended by section 82 of, and paragraph 7 of Schedule 4 to, the Regulation of Investigatory Powers Act 2000 (c. 23) and section 32 and section 331 of, and paragraphs 20 and 21 of Schedule 36 to, the Criminal Justice Act 2003 (c. 44). Section 7A was inserted by section 37 of the Criminal Justice Act 2003 (c. 44).

[15]  1996 c. 25; section 5 was amended by section 33 of, and paragraph 66 of Schedule 3, paragraphs 20 and 23 of Schedule 36 and Parts 3 and 4 of Schedule 37 to, the Criminal Justice Act 2003 (c. 44). It was further amended by section 119 of, and paragraph 126 of Schedule 8 to, the Crime and Disorder Act 1998 (c. 37) in respect of certain proceedings only.

Under section 6C of the 1996 Act[16], in the Crown Court and in magistrates' courts the defendant must give a defence witness notice indicating whether he or she intends to call any witnesses (other than him or herself) and, if so, identifying them.

The time for service of a defence statement is prescribed by section 12 of the 1996 Act[17] and by the Criminal Procedure and Investigations Act 1996 (Defence Disclosure Time Limits) Regulations 2011[18]. It is—

    (a)  in a magistrates' court, not more than 14 days after the prosecutor—
        (i)  discloses material under section 3 of the 1996 Act, or
        (ii)  serves notice that there is no such material to disclose;
    (b)  in the Crown Court, not more than 28 days after either of those events, if the prosecution evidence has been served on the defendant.

The requirements for the content of a defence statement are set out in—

    (a)  section 5 of the 1996 Act, where the investigation began between 1$^{st}$ April, 1997 and 3$^{rd}$ April, 2005;
    (b)  section 6A of the 1996 Act[19], where the investigation began on or after 4$^{th}$ April, 2005. See also section 6E of the Act[20].

Where the investigation began between 1$^{st}$ April, 1997 and 3$^{rd}$ April, 2005, the defence statement must—

    (a)  set out in general terms the nature of the defence;
    (b)  indicate the matters on which the defendant takes issue with the prosecutor, and, in respect of each, explain why;
    (c)  if the defence statement discloses an alibi, give particulars, including—
        (i)  the name and address of any witness whom the defendant believes can give evidence in support (that is, evidence that the defendant was in a place, at a time, inconsistent with having committed the offence),
        (ii)  where the defendant does not know the name or address, any information that might help identify or find that witness.

Where the investigation began on or after 4$^{th}$ April, 2005, the defence statement must—

    (a)  set out the nature of the defence, including any particular defences on which the defendant intends to rely;
    (b)  indicate the matters of fact on which the defendant takes issue with the prosecutor, and, in respect of each, explain why;
    (c)  set out particulars of the matters of fact on which the defendant intends to rely for the purposes of the defence;
    (d)  indicate any point of law that the defendant wants to raise, including any point about the admissibility of evidence or about abuse of process, and any authority relied on; and
    (e)  if the defence statement discloses an alibi, give particulars, including—
        (i)  the name, address and date of birth of any witness whom the defendant believes can give evidence in support (that is, evidence that the defendant was in a place, at a time, inconsistent with having committed the offence),
        (ii)  where the defendant does not know any of those details, any information that might help identify or find that witness.

The time for service of a defence witness notice is prescribed by section 12 of the 1996 Act and by the Criminal Procedure and Investigations Act 1996 (Defence Disclosure Time Limits) Regulations 2011. The time limits are the same as those for a defence statement.

A defence witness notice that identifies any proposed defence witness (other than the defendant) must—

    (a)  give the name, address and date of birth of each such witness, or as many of those details as are known to the defendant when the notice is given;

---

[16] 1996 c. 25; section 6C was inserted by section 34 of the Criminal Justice Act 2003 (c. 44).
[17] 1996 c. 25; section 12 was amended by sections 331 of, and paragraphs 20 and 28 of Schedule 36 to, the Criminal Justice Act 2003 (c. 44).
[18] S.I. 2011/209.
[19] 1996 c. 25; section 6A was inserted by section 33 of the Criminal Justice Act 2003 (c. 44) and amended by section 60 of the Criminal Justice and Immigration Act 2008 (c. 4).
[20] 1996 c. 25; section 6E was inserted by section 36 of the Criminal Justice Act 2003 (c. 44).

(b)  *provide any information in the defendant's possession which might be of material assistance in identifying or finding any such witness in whose case any of the details mentioned in paragraph (a) are not known to the defendant when the notice is given; and*

(c)  *amend any earlier such notice, if the defendant—*

   (i)  *decides to call a person not included in an earlier notice as a proposed witness,*

   (ii)  *decides not to call a person so included, or*

   (iii)  *discovers any information which the defendant would have had to include in an earlier notice, if then aware of it.*

*Under section 11 of the 1996 Act*[21]*, if a defendant—*

(a)  *fails to disclose what the Act requires;*

(b)  *fails to do so within the time prescribed;*

(c)  *at trial, relies on a defence, or facts, not mentioned in the defence statement;*

(d)  *at trial, introduces alibi evidence without having given in the defence statement—*

   (i)  *particulars of the alibi, or*

   (ii)  *the details of the alibi witness, or witnesses, required by the Act; or*

(e)  *at trial, calls a witness not identified in a defence witness notice,*

*then the court or another party at trial may comment on that, and the court may draw such inferences as appear proper in deciding whether the defendant is guilty.*

*Under section 6E(2) of the 1996 Act, if before trial in the Crown Court it seems to the court that section 11 may apply, then the court must warn the defendant.*

### CRIMINAL PRACTICE DIRECTIONS   PART 15   DISCLOSURE

**CPD IV Disclosure 15A: Disclosure of Unused Material**                    CPD.15A

15A.1  Disclosure is a vital part of the preparation for trial, both in the magistrates' courts and in the Crown Court. All parties must be familiar with their obligations, in particular under the Criminal Procedure and Investigations Act 1996 as amended and the Code issued under that Act, and must comply with the relevant judicial protocol and guidelines from the Attorney-General. These documents have recently been revised and the new guidance will be issued shortly as *Judicial Protocol on the Disclosure of Unused Material in Criminal Cases* and the *Attorney-General's Guidelines on Disclosure*. The new documents should be read together as complementary, comprehensive guidance. They will be available electronically on the respective websites.

15A.2  In addition, certain procedures are prescribed under CrimPR Part 15 and these should be followed. The notes to Part 15 contain a useful summary of the requirements of the CPIA 1996 as amended.

### CRIMINAL PROCEDURE RULES   PART 16   WRITTEN WITNESS STATEMENTS

**When this Part applies**                    R16.1

16.1  This Part applies where a party wants to introduce a written witness statement in evidence under section 9 of the Criminal Justice Act 1967[1].

*[Note. Under section 9 of the Criminal Justice Act 1967, if the conditions specified in that section are met the written statement of a witness is admissible in evidence to the same extent as if that witness gave evidence in person.]*

**Content of written witness statement**                    R16.2

16.2  The statement must contain—

   (a)  at the beginning—

      (i)  the witness' name, and

---

[21]  1996 c. 25; section 11 was substituted by section 39 of the Criminal Justice Act 2003 (c. 44) and amended by section 60(2) of the Criminal Justice and Immigration Act 2008 (c. 4).

[1]  1967 c. 80; section 9 was amended by section 56 of, and paragraph 49 of Schedule 8 to, the Courts Act 1971 (c. 23), section 168 of, and paragraph 6 of Schedule 9 to, the Criminal Justice and Public Order Act 1994 (c. 33), section 69 of the Criminal Procedure and Investigations Act 1996 (c. 25), regulation 9 of, and paragraph 4 of Schedule 5 to, S.I. 2001/1090, paragraph 43 of Schedule 3 and Part 4 of Schedule 37 to the Criminal Justice Act 2003 (c. 44), section 26 of, and paragraph 7 of Schedule 2 to, the Armed Forces Act 2011 (c. 18) and section 80 of the Deregulation Act 2015 (c. 20). It is further amended by section 72 of, and paragraph 55 of Schedule 5 to, the Children and Young Persons Act 1969 (c. 54) and section 65 of, and paragraph 1 of Schedule 4 to, the Courts Act 2003 (c. 39), with effect from dates to be appointed.

           (ii)   the witness' age, if under 18;

    (b)   a declaration by the witness that—

           (i)   it is true to the best of the witness' knowledge and belief, and

           (ii)   the witness knows that if it is introduced in evidence, then it would be an offence wilfully to have stated in it anything that the witness knew to be false or did not believe to be true;

    (c)   if the witness cannot read the statement, a signed declaration by someone else that that person read it to the witness; and

    (d)   the witness' signature.

*[Note. The Practice Direction sets out a form of written statement for use in connection with this rule.]*

## R16.3 Reference to exhibit

**16.3**     Where the statement refers to a document or object as an exhibit, it must identify that document or object clearly.

*[Note. See section 9(7) of the Criminal Justice Act 1967([2]).]*

## R16.4 Written witness statement in evidence

**16.4**  (1)   A party who wants to introduce in evidence a written witness statement must—

    (a)   before the hearing at which that party wants to introduce it, serve a copy of the statement on—

           (i)   the court officer, and

           (ii)   each other party; and

    (b)   at or before that hearing, serve on the court officer the statement or an authenticated copy.

  (2)   If that party relies on only part of the statement, that party must mark the copy in such a way as to make that clear.

  (3)   A prosecutor must serve on a defendant, with the copy of the statement, a notice—

    (a)   of the right to object to the introduction of the statement in evidence instead of the witness giving evidence in person;

    (b)   of the time limit for objecting under this rule; and

    (c)   that if the defendant does not object in time, the court—

           (i)   can nonetheless require the witness to give evidence in person, but

           (ii)   may decide not to do so.

  (4)   A party served with a written witness statement who objects to its introduction in evidence must—

    (a)   serve notice of the objection on—

           (i)   the party who served it, and

           (ii)   the court officer; and

    (b)   serve the notice of objection not more than 5 business days after service of the statement unless—

           (i)   the court extends that time limit, before or after the statement was served,

           (ii)   rule 24.8 (Written guilty plea: special rules) applies, in which case the time limit is the later of 5 business days after service of the statement or 5 business days before the hearing date, or

           (iii)   rule 24.9 (Single justice procedure: special rules) applies, in which case the time limit is 15 business days after service of the statement.

  (5)   The court may exercise its power to require the witness to give evidence in person—

    (a)   on application by any party; or

    (b)   on its own initiative.

  (6)   A party entitled to receive a copy of a statement may waive that entitlement by so informing—

    (a)   the party who would have served it; and

    (b)   the court.

*[Note. The Practice Direction sets out a form of written witness statement and a form of notice for use in connection with this rule.*

*Under section 9(2A) of the Criminal Justice Act 1967[3], Criminal Procedure Rules may prescribe the period within which a party served with a written witness statement must object to its introduction in evidence, subject to a minimum period of 7 days from its service.*

---

[2] 1967 c. 80.
[3] 1967 c. 80; section 9(2A) was inserted by section 80 of the Deregulation Act 2015 (c. 20).

*Under section 133 of the Criminal Justice Act 2003[4], where a statement in a document is admissible as evidence in criminal proceedings, the statement may be proved by producing either (a) the document, or (b) (whether or not the document exists) a copy of the document or of the material part of it, authenticated in whatever way the court may approve. By section 134 of the 2003 Act, 'document' means anything in which information of any description is recorded.]*

CRIMINAL PRACTICE DIRECTIONS    PART 16    WRITTEN WITNESS STATEMENTS

**CPD V Evidence 16A: Evidence by Written Statement**                         CPD.16A

16A.1   Where the prosecution proposes to tender written statements in evidence under section 9 of the Criminal Justice Act 1967, it will frequently be necessary for certain statements to be edited. This will occur either because a witness has made more than one statement whose contents should conveniently be reduced into a single, comprehensive statement, or where a statement contains inadmissible, prejudicial or irrelevant material. Editing of statements must be done by a Crown Prosecutor (or by a legal representative, if any, of the prosecutor if the case is not being conducted by the Crown Prosecution Service) and not by a police officer.

*Composite statements*

16A.2   A composite statement giving the combined effect of two or more earlier statements must be prepared in compliance with the requirements of section 9 of the 1967 Act; and must then be signed by the witness.

*Editing single statements*

16A.3   There are two acceptable methods of editing single statements. They are:
   (a)  By marking copies of the statement in a way which indicates the passages on which the prosecution will not rely. This merely indicates that the prosecution will not seek to adduce the evidence so marked. The original signed statement to be tendered to the court is not marked in any way.
       The marking on the copy statement is done by lightly striking out the passages to be edited, so that what appears beneath can still be read, or by bracketing, or by a combination of both. It is not permissible to produce a photocopy with the deleted material obliterated, since this would be contrary to the requirement that the defence and the court should be served with copies of the signed original statement.
       Whenever the striking out/bracketing method is used, it will assist if the following words appear at the foot of the frontispiece or index to any bundle of copy statements to be tendered:
       *'The prosecution does not propose to adduce evidence of those passages of the attached copy statements which have been struck out and/or bracketed (nor will it seek to do so at the trial unless a notice of further evidence is served)'.*

   (b)  By obtaining a fresh statement, signed by the witness, which omits the offending material, applying the procedure for composite statements above.

16A.4   In most cases where a single statement is to be edited, the striking out/bracketing method will be the more appropriate, but the taking of a fresh statement is preferable in the following circumstances:
   (a)  When a police (or other investigating) officer's statement contains details of interviews with more suspects than are eventually charged, a fresh statement should be prepared and signed, omitting all details of interview with those not charged except, insofar as it is relevant, for the bald fact that a certain named person was interviewed at a particular time, date and place.
   (b)  When a suspect is interviewed about more offences than are eventually made the subject of charges, a fresh statement should be prepared and signed, omitting all questions and answers about the uncharged offences unless either they might appropriately be taken into consideration, or evidence about those offences is admissible on the charges preferred. It may, however, be desirable to replace the omitted questions and answers with a phrase such as: *'After referring to some other matters, I then said, "........."'*, so as to make it clear that part of the interview has been omitted.
   (c)  A fresh statement should normally be prepared and signed if the only part of the original on which the prosecution is relying is only a small proportion of the whole, although it remains desirable to use the alternative method if there is reason to believe that the defence might itself wish to rely, in mitigation or for any other purpose, on at least some of those parts which the prosecution does not propose to adduce.

[4] 2003 c. 44.

Criminal Procedure Rules and Criminal Practice Directions

(d) When the passages contain material which the prosecution is entitled to withhold from disclosure to the defence.

16A.5 Prosecutors should also be aware that, where statements are to be tendered under section 9 of the 1967 Act in the course of summary proceedings, there will be a need to prepare fresh statements excluding inadmissible or prejudicial material, rather than using the striking out or bracketing method.

16A.6 Whenever a fresh statement is taken from a witness and served in evidence, the earlier, unedited statement(s) becomes unused material and should be scheduled and reviewed for disclosure to the defence in the usual way.

## CPD.16B    CPD V Evidence 16B: Video Recorded Evidence in Chief

16B.1 The procedure for making an application for leave to admit into evidence video recorded evidence in chief under section 27 of the Youth Justice and Criminal Evidence Act 1999 is given in CrimPR Part 18.

16B.2 Where a court, on application by a party to the proceedings or of its own motion, grants leave to admit a video recording in evidence under section 27(1) of the 1999 Act, it may direct that any part of the recording be excluded (section 27(2) and (3)). When such direction is given, the party who made the application to admit the video recording must edit the recording in accordance with the judge's directions and send a copy of the edited recording to the appropriate officer of the Crown Court and to every other party to the proceedings.

16B.3 Where a video recording is to be adduced during proceedings before the Crown Court, it should be produced and proved by the interviewer, or any other person who was present at the interview with the witness at which the recording was made. The applicant should ensure that such a person will be available for this purpose, unless the parties have agreed to accept a written statement in lieu of attendance by that person.

16B.4 Once a trial has begun, if, by reason of faulty or inadequate preparation or for some other cause, the procedures set out above have not been properly complied with and an application is made to edit the video recording, thereby necessitating an adjournment for the work to be carried out, the court may, at its discretion, make an appropriate award of costs.

## CPD.16C    CPD V Evidence 16C: Evidence of Audio and Video Recorded Interviews

16C.1 The interrogation of suspects is primarily governed by Code C, one of the Codes of Practice under the Police and Criminal Evidence Act 1984 ('PACE'). Under that Code, interviews must normally be contemporaneously recorded. Under PACE Code E, interviews conducted at a police station concerning an indictable offence must normally be audio-recorded. In practice, most interviews are audio-recorded under Code E, or video-recorded under Code F, and it is best practice to do so. The questioning of terrorism suspects is governed separately by Code H. The Codes are available electronically on the Home Office website.

16C.2 Where a record of the interview is to be prepared, this should be in accordance with the current national guidelines, as envisaged by Note 5A of Code E.

16C.3 If the prosecution wishes to rely on the defendant's interview in evidence, the prosecution should seek to agree the record with the defence. Both parties should have received a copy of the audio or video recording, and can check the record against the recording. The record should be edited (see below) if inadmissible matters are included within it and, in particular if the interview is lengthy, the prosecution should seek to shorten it by editing or summary.

16C.4 If the record is agreed there is usually no need for the audio or video recording to be played in court. It is a matter for the discretion of the trial judge, but usual practice is for edited copies of the record to be provided to the court, and to the jury if there is one, and for the prosecution advocate to read the interview with the interviewing officer or the officer in the case, as part of the officer's evidence in chief, the officer reading the interviewer and the advocate reading the defendant and defence representative. In the magistrates' court, the Bench sometimes retire to read the interview themselves, and the document is treated as if it had been read aloud in court. This is permissible, but CrimPR 24.5 should be followed.

16C.5 Where the prosecution intends to adduce the interview in evidence, and agreement between the parties has not been reached about the record, sufficient notice must be given to allow consideration of any amendment to the record, or the preparation of any transcript of the interview, or any editing of a recording for the purpose of playing it in court. To that end, the following practice should be followed:

(a) Where the defence is unable to agree a record of interview or transcript (where one is already available) the prosecution should be notified at latest at the Plea and Case Management Hearing ('PCMH'), with a view to securing agreement to amend. The notice should specify the part to which objection is taken, or the part omitted which the defence consider should be included. A copy of the notice should be supplied to the court within the period specified above. The PCMH form inquires about the admissibility of the defendant's interview and shortening by editing or summarising for trial.

(b) If agreement is not reached and it is proposed that the audio or video recording or part of it be played in court, notice should be given to the prosecution by the defence as ordered at the PCMH, in order that the advocates for the parties may agree those parts of the audio or video recording that should not be adduced and that arrangements may be made, by editing or in some other way, to exclude that material. A copy of the notice should be supplied to the court.

(c) Notice of any agreement reached should be supplied to the court by the prosecution, as soon as is practicable.

16C.6    Alternatively, if, the prosecution advocate proposes to play the audio or video recording or part of it, the prosecution should at latest at the PCMH, notify the defence and the court. The defence should notify the prosecution and the court within 14 days of receiving the notice, if they object to the production of the audio or video recording on the basis that a part of it should be excluded. If the objections raised by the defence are accepted, the prosecution should prepare an edited recording, or make other arrangements to exclude the material part; and should notify the court of the arrangements made.

16C.7    If the defendant wishes to have the audio or video recording or any part of it played to the court, the defence should provide notice to the prosecution and the court at latest at the PCMH. The defence should also, at that time, notify the prosecution of any proposals to edit the recording and seek the prosecution's agreement to those amendments.

16C.8    Whenever editing or amendment of a record of interview or of an audio or video recording or of a transcript takes place, the following general principles should be followed:

(i) Where a defendant has made a statement which includes an admission of one or more other offences, the portion relating to other offences should be omitted unless it is or becomes admissible in evidence;

(ii) Where the statement of one defendant contains a portion which exculpates him or her and partly implicates a co-defendant in the trial, the defendant making the statement has the right to insist that everything relevant which is exculpatory goes before the jury. In such a case the judge must be consulted about how best to protect the position of the co-defendant.

16C.9    If it becomes necessary for either party to access the master copy of the audio or video recording, they should give notice to the other party and follow the procedure in PACE Code E at section 6.

16C.10    If there is a challenge to the integrity of the master recording, notice and particulars should be given to the court and to the prosecution by the defence as soon as is practicable. The court may then, at its discretion, order a case management hearing or give such other directions as may be appropriate.

16C.11    If an audio or video recording is to be adduced during proceedings before the Crown Court, it should be produced and proved in a witness statement by the interviewing officer or any other officer who was present at the interview at which the recording was made. The prosecution should ensure that the witness is available to attend court if required by the defence in the usual way.

16C.12    It is the responsibility of the prosecution to ensure that there is a person available to operate any audio or video equipment needed during the course of the proceedings. Subject to their other responsibilities, the court staff may be able to assist.

16C.13    If either party wishes to present audio or video evidence, that party must ensure, in advance of the hearing, that the evidence is in a format that is compatible with the court's equipment, and that the material to be used does in fact function properly in the relevant court room.

16C.14    In order to avoid the necessity for the court to listen to or watch lengthy or irrelevant material before the relevant part of a recording is reached, counsel shall indicate to the equipment operator those parts of a recording which it may be necessary to play. Such an indication should, so far as possible, be expressed in terms of the time track or other identifying process used by the interviewing police force and should be given in time for the operator to have located those parts by the appropriate point in the trial.

16C.15    Once a trial has begun, if, by reason of faulty preparation or for some other cause, the procedures above have not been properly complied with, and an application is made to amend the record of interview or transcript or to edit the recording, as the case may be, thereby making necessary an adjournment for the work to be carried out, the court may make at its discretion an appropriate award of costs.

**16C.16** Where a case is listed for hearing on a date which falls within the time limits set out above, it is the responsibility of the parties to ensure that all the necessary steps are taken to comply with this Practice Direction within such shorter period as is available.

CRIMINAL PROCEDURE RULES    PART 17    WITNESS SUMMONSES, WARRANTS AND ORDERS

**R17.1**  **When this Part applies**

**17.1** (1) This Part applies in magistrates' courts and in the Crown Court where—

   (a) a party wants the court to issue a witness summons, warrant or order under—
   
      (i) section 97 of the Magistrates' Courts Act 1980[1],
      
      (ii) paragraph 4 of Schedule 3 to the Crime and Disorder Act 1998[2],
      
      (iii) section 2 of the Criminal Procedure (Attendance of Witnesses) Act 1965[3], or
      
      (iv) section 7 of the Bankers' Books Evidence Act 1879[4];
      
   (b) the court considers the issue of such a summons, warrant or order on its own initiative as if a party had applied; or
   
   (c) one of those listed in rule 17.7 wants the court to withdraw such a summons, warrant or order.

(2) A reference to a 'witness' in this Part is a reference to a person to whom such a summons, warrant or order is directed.

*[Note. A magistrates' court may require the attendance of a witness to give evidence or to produce in evidence a document or thing by a summons, or in some circumstances a warrant for the witness' arrest, under section 97 of the Magistrates' Courts Act 1980 or under paragraph 4 of Schedule 3 to the Crime and Disorder Act 1998. The Crown Court may do so under sections 2, 2D, 3 and 4 of the Criminal Procedure (Attendance of Witnesses) Act 1965. Either court may order the production in evidence of a copy of an entry in a banker's book without the attendance of an officer of the bank, under sections 6 and 7 of the Bankers' Books Evidence Act 1879. See section 2D of the Criminal Procedure (Attendance of Witnesses) Act 1965 for the Crown Court's power to issue a witness summons on the court's own initiative.*

*See Part 3 for the court's general powers to consider an application and to give directions.]*

**R17.2**  **Issue etc. of summons, warrant or order with or without a hearing**

**17.2** (1) The court may issue or withdraw a witness summons, warrant or order with or without a hearing.

(2) A hearing under this Part must be in private unless the court otherwise directs.

*[Note. If rule 17.5 applies, a person served with an application for a witness summons will have an opportunity to make representations about whether there should be a hearing of that application before the witness summons is issued.]*

**R17.3**  **Application for summons, warrant or order: general rules**

**17.3** (1) A party who wants the court to issue a witness summons, warrant or order must apply as soon as practicable after becoming aware of the grounds for doing so.

(2) A party applying for a witness summons or order must—

   (a) identify the proposed witness;
   
   (b) explain—
   
      (i) what evidence the proposed witness can give or produce,
      
      (ii) why it is likely to be material evidence, and
      
      (iii) why it would be in the interests of justice to issue a summons, order or warrant as appropriate.

---

[1] 1980 c. 43; section 97 was amended by sections 13 and 14 of, and paragraph 7 of Schedule 2 to, the Contempt of Court Act 1981 (c. 47), section 31 of, and paragraph 2 of Schedule 4 to, the Criminal Justice (International Co-operation) Act 1990 (c. 5), sections 17 and 65 of, and paragraph 6 of Schedule 3 and Part I of Schedule 4 to, the Criminal Justice Act 1991 (c. 53), section 51 of the Criminal Procedure and Investigations Act 1996 (c. 25) and section 169 of the Serious Organised Crime and Police Act 2005 (c. 15).

[2] 1998 c. 37; paragraph 4 of Schedule 3 was amended by paragraphs 15, 20, 68 and 72 of Schedule 3 to the Criminal Justice Act 2003 (c. 44), section 169 of the Serious Organised Crime and Police Act 2005 (c. 15), article 3 of, and paragraphs 35 and 37 of the Schedule to, S.I. 2004/2035 and article 2 of, and paragraph 61 of the Schedule to, S.I. 2005/886.

[3] 1965 c. 69; section 2 was substituted, together with sections 2 A to 2E, by section 66 of the Criminal Procedure and Investigations Act 1996 (c. 25) and amended by section 119 of, and paragraph 8 of Schedule 8 to, the Crime and Disorder Act 1998 (c. 37), section 109 of, and paragraph 126 of Schedule 8 to, the Courts Act 2003 (c. 39), paragraph 42 of Schedule 3 and Part 4 of Schedule 37 to the Criminal Justice Act 2003 (c. 44), section 169 of the Serious Organised Crime and Police Act 2005 (c. 15) and paragraph 33 of Schedule 17 to the Crime and Courts Act 2013 (c. 22).

[4] 1879 c. 11; section 6 has been amended; none is relevant to these rules.

(3) A party applying for an order to be allowed to inspect and copy an entry in bank records must—
  (a) identify the entry;
  (b) explain the purpose for which the entry is required; and
  (c) propose—
    (i) the terms of the order, and
    (ii) the period within which the order should take effect, if 3 days from the date of service of the order would not be appropriate.
(4) The application may be made orally unless—
  (a) rule 17.5 applies; or
  (b) the court otherwise directs.
(5) The applicant must serve any order made on the witness to whom, or the bank to which, it is directed.

*[Note. The court may issue a warrant for a witness' arrest if that witness fails to obey a witness summons directed to him: see section 97(3) of the Magistrates' Courts Act 1980, paragraph 4(5) of Schedule 3 to the Crime and Disorder Act 1998 and section 4 of the Criminal Procedure (Attendance of Witnesses) Act 1965. Before a magistrates' court may issue a warrant under section 97(3) of the 1980 Act, the witness must first be paid or offered a reasonable amount for costs and expenses.]*

**Written application: form and service**                                                              **R17.4**

17.4 (1) An application in writing under rule 17.3 must be in the form set out in the Practice Direction, containing the same declaration of truth as a witness statement.
  (2) The party applying must serve the application—
    (a) in every case, on the court officer and as directed by the court; and
    (b) as required by rule 17.5, if that rule applies.

*[Note. Declarations of truth in witness statements are required by section 9 of the Criminal Justice Act 1967[5]. Section 89 of the 1967 Act[6] makes it an offence to make a written statement under section 9 of that Act which the person making it knows to be false or does not believe to be true.]*

**Application for summons to produce a document, etc.: special rules**                                  **R17.5**

17.5 (1) This rule applies to an application under rule 17.3 for a witness summons requiring the proposed witness—
    (a) to produce in evidence a document or thing; or
    (b) to give evidence about information apparently held in confidence, that relates to another person.
  (2) The application must be in writing in the form required by rule 17.4.
  (3) The party applying must serve the application—
    (a) on the proposed witness, unless the court otherwise directs; and
    (b) on one or more of the following, if the court so directs—
      (i) a person to whom the proposed evidence relates, and
      (ii) another party.
  (4) The court must not issue a witness summons where this rule applies unless—
    (a) everyone served with the application has had at least 10 business days in which to make representations, including representations about whether there should be a hearing of the application before the summons is issued; and
    (b) the court is satisfied that it has been able to take adequate account of the duties and rights, including rights of confidentiality, of the proposed witness and of any person to whom the proposed evidence relates.
  (5) This rule does not apply to an application for an order to produce in evidence a copy of an entry in bank records.

*[Note. Under section 2A of the Criminal Procedure (Attendance of Witnesses) Act 1965[7]), a witness summons to produce a document or thing issued by the Crown Court may require the witness to produce it for inspection by the applicant before producing it in evidence.]*

[5]  1967 c. 80; section 9 was amended by section 56 of, and paragraph 49 of Schedule 8 to, the Courts Act 1971 (c. 23), section 168 of, and paragraph 6 of Schedule 9 to, the Criminal Justice and Public Order Act 1994 (c. 33), section 69 of the Criminal Procedure and Investigations Act 1996 (c. 25), regulation 9 of, and paragraph 4 of Schedule 5 to, S.I. 2001/1090, paragraph 43 of Schedule 3 and Part 4 of Schedule 37 to the Criminal Justice Act 2003 (c. 44), section 26 of, and paragraph 7 of Schedule 2 to, the Armed Forces Act 2011 (c. 18) and section 80 of the Deregulation Act 2015 (c. 20). It is further amended by section 72 of, and paragraph 55 of Schedule 5 to, the Children and Young Persons Act 1969 (c. 54) and section 65 of, and paragraph 1 of Schedule 4 to, the Courts Act 2003 (c. 39), with effect from dates to be appointed.
[6]  1967 c. 80; section 89 was amended by section 154 of, and Schedule 9 to, the Magistrates' Courts Act 1980 (c. 43).
[7]  1965 c. 69; section 2A was substituted, together with sections 2, 2 B, 2D and 2E, for existing section 2 by section 66(1) and (2) of the Criminal Procedure and Investigations Act 1996 (c. 25).

**R17.6**   **Application for summons to produce a document, etc.: court's assessment of relevance and confidentiality**

17.6   (1)   This rule applies where a person served with an application for a witness summons requiring the proposed witness to produce in evidence a document or thing objects to its production on the ground that—

(a)   it is not likely to be material evidence; or

(b)   even if it is likely to be material evidence, the duties or rights, including rights of confidentiality, of the proposed witness or of any person to whom the document or thing relates, outweigh the reasons for issuing a summons.

(2)   The court may require the proposed witness to make the document or thing available for the objection to be assessed.

(3)   The court may invite—

(a)   the proposed witness or any representative of the proposed witness; or

(b)   a person to whom the document or thing relates or any representative of such a person, to help the court assess the objection.

**R17.7**   **Application to withdraw a summons, warrant or order**

17.7   (1)   The court may withdraw a witness summons, warrant or order if one of the following applies for it to be withdrawn—

(a)   the party who applied for it, on the ground that it no longer is needed;

(b)   the witness, on the grounds that he was not aware of any application for it, and—

(i)   he cannot give or produce evidence likely to be material evidence, or

(ii)   even if he can, his duties or rights, including rights of confidentiality, or those of any person to whom the evidence relates, outweigh the reasons for the issue of the summons, warrant or order; or

(c)   any person to whom the proposed evidence relates, on the grounds that he was not aware of any application for it, and—

(i)   that evidence is not likely to be material evidence, or

(ii)   even if it is, his duties or rights, including rights of confidentiality, or those of the witness, outweigh the reasons for the issue of the summons, warrant or order.

(2)   A person applying under the rule must—

(a)   apply in writing as soon as practicable after becoming aware of the grounds for doing so, explaining why he wants the summons, warrant or order to be withdrawn; and

(b)   serve the application on the court officer and as appropriate on—

(i)   the witness,

(ii)   the party who applied for the summons, warrant or order, and

(iii)   any other person who he knows was served with the application for the summons, warrant or order.

(3)   Rule 17.6 applies to an application under this rule that concerns a document or thing to be produced in evidence.

*[Note. See sections 2B, 2C and 2E of the Criminal Procedure (Attendance of Witnesses) Act 1965[8] for the Crown Court's powers to withdraw a witness summons, including the power to order costs.]*

**R17.8**   **Court's power to vary requirements under this Part**

17.8   (1)   The court may—

(a)   shorten or extend (even after it has expired) a time limit under this Part; and

(b)   where a rule or direction requires an application under this Part to be in writing, allow that application to be made orally instead.

(2)   Someone who wants the court to allow an application to be made orally under paragraph (1)(b) of this rule must—

(a)   give as much notice as the urgency of his application permits to those on whom he would otherwise have served an application in writing; and

(b)   in doing so explain the reasons for the application and for wanting the court to consider it orally.

---

[8]   1965 c. 69; sections 2B, 2C and 2E were substituted with section 2 and 2A, for the existing section 2 by section 66(1) and (2) of the Criminal Procedure and Investigations Act 1996 (c. 25) and amended by section 109 of, and paragraph 126 of Schedule 8 to, the Courts Act 2003 (c. 39).

CRIMINAL PRACTICE DIRECTIONS    PART 17    WITNESS SUMMONSES,
WARRANTS AND ORDERS

### CPD V Evidence 17A: Wards of Court and Children Subject to Current Family Proceedings

**CPD.17A**

17A.1    Where police wish to interview a child who is subject to current family proceedings, leave of the Family Court is only required where such an interview may lead to a child disclosing information confidential to those proceedings and not otherwise available to the police under Working Together to Safeguard Children (March 2013), a guide to inter-agency working to safeguard and promote the welfare of children: www.workingtogetheronline.co.uk/chapters/contents.html

17A.2    Where exceptionally the child to be interviewed or called as a witness in criminal proceedings is a Ward of Court then the leave of the court which made the wardship order will be required.

17A.3    Any application for leave in respect of any such child must be made to the court in which the relevant family proceedings are continuing and must be made on notice to the parents, any actual carer (e.g., relative or foster parent) and, in care proceedings, to the local authority and the guardian. In private proceedings the Family Court Reporter (if appointed) should be notified.

17A.4    If the police need to interview the child without the knowledge of another party (usually a parent or carer), they may make the application for leave without giving notice to that party.

17A.5    Where leave is given the order should ordinarily give leave for any number of interviews that may be required. However, anything beyond that actually authorised will require a further application.

17A.6    Exceptionally the police may have to deal with complaints by or allegations against such a child immediately without obtaining the leave of the court as, for example:

(a)    a serious offence against a child (like rape) where immediate medical examination and collection of evidence is required; or

(b)    where the child is to be interviewed as a suspect.

When any such action is necessary, the police should, in respect of each and every interview, notify the parents and other carer (if any) and the Family Court Reporter (if appointed). In care proceedings the local authority and guardian should be notified. The police must comply with all relevant Codes of Practice when conducting any such interview.

17A.7    The Family Court should be appraised of the position at the earliest reasonable opportunity by one of the notified parties and should thereafter be kept informed of any criminal proceedings.

17A.8    No evidence or document in the family proceedings or information about the proceedings should be disclosed into criminal proceedings without the leave of the Family Court.

CRIMINAL PROCEDURE RULES    PART 18    MEASURES TO ASSIST A
WITNESS OR DEFENDANT TO GIVE EVIDENCE OR OTHERWISE PARTICIPATE

### General rules

**When this Part applies**

**R18.1**

18.1    This Part applies—

(a)    where the court can give a direction (a 'special measures direction'), under section 19 of the Youth Justice and Criminal Evidence Act 1999[1], on an application or on its own initiative, for any of the following measures—

(i)    preventing a witness from seeing the defendant (section 23 of the 1999 Act),

(ii)    allowing a witness to give evidence by live link (section 24 of the 1999 Act[2]),

(iii)    hearing a witness' evidence in private (section 25 of the 1999 Act[3]),

(iv)    dispensing with the wearing of wigs and gowns (section 26 of the 1999 Act),

(v)    admitting video recorded evidence (sections 27 and 28 of the 1999 Act[4]),

(vi)    questioning a witness through an intermediary (section 29 of the 1999 Act[5]),

(vii)    using a device to help a witness communicate (section 30 of the 1999 Act);

(b)    where the court can vary or discharge such a direction, under section 20 of the 1999 Act[6];

---

[1]    1999 c. 23.

[2]    1999 c. 23; section 24 was amended by paragraph 385 of Schedule 8 to, and Schedule 10 to, the Courts Act 2003 (c. 39) and section 102(1) of the Coroners and Justice Act 2009 (c. 25).

[3]    1999 c. 23; section 25 was amended by paragraphs 1 and 3 of the Schedule to S.I. 2013/554 and section 46 of the Modern Slavery Act 2015 (c. 30).

[4]    1999 c. 23; section 27 was amended by paragraph 384 of Schedule 8 to the Courts Act 2003 (c. 39), paragraph 73 of Schedule 3 and Part 4 of Schedule 37 to the Criminal Justice Act 2003 (c. 44) and sections 102(2), 103(1), (3), (4) and (5), 177(1) and (2) and 178 of, and paragraph 73 of Schedule 21, paragraph 23 of Schedule 22 and Part 3 of Schedule 23 to, the Coroners and Justice Act 2009 (c. 25).

[5]    1999 c. 23; section 29 was amended by paragraph 384(d) of Schedule 8 to the Courts Act 2003 (c. 39).

[6]    1999 c. 23; section 20(6) was amended by paragraph 384(a) of Schedule 8 to the Courts Act 2003 (c. 39).

    (c) where the court can give, vary or discharge a direction (a 'defendant's evidence direction') for a defendant to give evidence—

        (i) by live link, under section 33A of the 1999 Act[7], or

        (ii) through an intermediary, under sections 33BA and 33BB of the 1999 Act[8];

    (d) where the court can—

        (i) make a witness anonymity order, under section 86 of the Coroners and Justice Act 2009[9], or

        (ii) vary or discharge such an order, under section 91, 92 or 93 of the 2009 Act;

    (e) where the court can give or discharge a direction (a 'live link direction'), on an application or on its own initiative, for a witness to give evidence by live link under—

        (i) section 32 of the Criminal Justice Act 1988[10], or

        (ii) sections 51 and 52 of the Criminal Justice Act 2003[11];

    (f) (i) appoint an intermediary to facilitate a defendant's effective participation in that defendant's trial, when the defendant gives evidence or at any other time, or

        (ii) vary or discharge such an appointment; and

    (g) where the court can exercise any other power it has to give, make, vary, rescind, discharge or revoke a direction for a measure to help a witness to give evidence or to help a defendant to participate in that defendant's trial.

*[Note. At the end of this Part there is a summary of the circumstances in which a witness or defendant may be eligible for the assistance of one of the measures to which this Part applies.]*

**R18.2    Meaning of 'witness'**

**18.2**    In this Part, 'witness' means anyone (other than a defendant) for whose benefit an application, direction or order is made.

**R18.3    Meaning of 'intermediary' and 'intermediary's report'**

**18.3**    (a) 'intermediary' means a person who is—

        (i) approved by the court for the purposes of section 29 of the Youth Justice and Criminal Evidence Act 1999[12] (Examination of witness through intermediary),

        (ii) approved by the court for the purposes of section 33BA of the 1999 Act[13] (Examination of accused through intermediary),

        (iii) asked to assess a defendant's communication needs, or

        (iv) appointed by the court to facilitate a defendant's effective participation in the trial, when the defendant gives evidence or at any other time, where otherwise that defendant's communication needs would impede such participation; and

    (b) a reference to 'an intermediary's report' means a report by such a person which complies with rule 18.32.

**R18.4    Making an application for a direction or order**

**18.4**    A party who wants the court to exercise its power to give or make a direction or order must—

    (a) apply in writing as soon as reasonably practicable, and in any event not more than—

        (i) 20 business days after the defendant pleads not guilty, in a magistrates' court, or

        (ii) 10 business days after the defendant pleads not guilty, in the Crown Court; and

    (b) serve the application on—

        (i) the court officer, and

        (ii) each other party.

---

[7] 1999 c. 23; section 33A was inserted by section 47 of the Police and Justice Act 2006 (c. 48).

[8] 1999 c. 23; sections 33BA and 33BB are inserted by section 104 of the Coroners and Justice Act 2009 (c. 25), with effect from a date to be appointed.

[9] 2009 c. 25.

[10] 1988 c. 33; section 32 was amended by section 55 of the Criminal Justice Act 1991 (c. 53), section 29 of, and paragraph 16 of Schedule 2 to, the Criminal Appeal Act 1995 (c. 35), section 62 of the Criminal Procedure and Investigations Act 1996 (c. 25), section 67 of, and Schedule 6 and paragraph 3 of Schedule 7 to, the Youth Justice and Criminal Evidence Act 1999 (c. 23) and paragraphs 24 and 26 of the Schedule to S.I. 2004/2035.

[11] 2003 c. 44.

[12] 1999 c. 23; section 29 was amended by paragraph 384 of Schedule 8 to the Courts Act 2003 (c. 39).

[13] 1999 c. 23; section 33BA is inserted by section 104(1) of the Coroners and Justice Act 2009 (c. 25), with effect from a date to be appointed.

*[Note. See also rule 18.10 (Content of application for a special measures direction), rule 18.15 (Content of application for a defendant's evidence direction), rule 18.19 (Content and conduct of application for a witness anonymity order) rule 18.24 (Content of application for a live link direction) and rule 18.27 ((Appointment of intermediary to facilitate a defendant's participation.*

*The Practice Direction sets out forms for use in connection with—*

*(a) an application under rule 18.10 for a special measures direction;*

*(b) an application under rule 18.24 for a live link direction (otherwise than as a special measures direction).]*

**Decisions and reasons**                                                                    **R18.5**

18.5  (1)  A party who wants to introduce the evidence of a witness who is the subject of an application, direction or order must—

(a)  inform the witness of the court's decision as soon as reasonably practicable; and

(b)  explain to the witness the arrangements that as a result will be made for him or her to give evidence.

(2)  The court must—

(a)  promptly determine an application; and

(b)  allow a party sufficient time to comply with the requirements of—

(i)  paragraph (1), and

(ii)  the code of practice issued under section 32 of the Domestic Violence, Crime and Victims Act 2004[14].

(3)  The court must announce, at a hearing in public before the witness gives evidence or the defendant's trial begins (as the case may be), the reasons for a decision—

(a)  to give, make, vary or discharge—

(i)  a special measures direction for a witness, or

(ii)  a direction to help a defendant to participate in that defendant's trial; or

(b)  to refuse to do so.

(4)  Where the court can give, vary or rescind a live link direction the court must—

(a)  announce the reasons for a decision not to give such a direction; and

(b)  in the case of a live link direction for a sentencing hearing, announce the reasons for a decision to rescind that direction.

(5)  Where the court gives a direction for everyone taking part in a hearing to do so by live link the court must announce the reasons for a decision—

(a)  not to direct that the proceedings are to be broadcast, within the meaning of section 85A of the Courts Act 2003[15] (Enabling the public to see and hear proceedings); or

(b)  not to direct that a recording of the proceedings is to be made, within the meaning of that section of that Act

*[Note. See sections 20(5), 33A(8) and 33BB(4) of the Youth Justice and Criminal Evidence Act 1999[16], sections 57B(6), 57E(8) and 57F(9) of the Crime and Disorder Act 1998 and section 51(8) of the Criminal Justice Act 2003.*

*Under section 32 of the Domestic Violence, Crime and Victims Act 2004, the Secretary of State for Justice must issue a code of practice as to the services to be provided by specified persons to a victim of criminal conduct.]*

*Under section 85A of the Courts Act 2003, if the court directs that proceedings are to be conducted wholly by live video or live audio link the court may direct (i) that the proceedings are to be broadcast for the purpose of enabling members of the public to see and hear, or to hear, those proceedings (as the case may be), and (ii) that a recording of the proceedings is to be made for the purpose of enabling the court to keep an audio-visual, or audio, record of the proceedings (as the case may be).]*

**Court's power to vary requirements under this Part**                                        **R18.6**

18.6  (1)  The court may—

(a)  shorten or extend (even after it has expired) a time limit under this Part; and

(b)  allow an application or representations to be made in a different form to one set out in the Practice Direction, or to be made orally.

(2)  A person who wants an extension of time must—

---

[14]  2004 c. 28; section 32 was amended by article 8 of, and paragraph 10 of the Schedule to, S.I. 2007/2128.

[15]  2003 c. 39; section 85A was temporarily inserted by section 55 of, and paragraph 1 of Schedule 25 to, the Coronavirus Act 2020 (c. 7).

[16]  1999 c. 23; section 20 was amended by paragraph 384(a) of Schedule 8 to the Courts Act 2003 (c. 39). Section 33A was inserted by section 47 of the Police and Justice Act 2006 (c. 48). Section 33BB is inserted by section 104 of the Coroners and Justice Act 2009 (c. 25), with effect from a date to be appointed.

      (a)   apply when serving the application or representations for which it is needed; and

      (b)   explain the delay.

**R18.7**    **Custody of documents**

    **18.7**    Unless the court otherwise directs, the court officer may—

      (a)   keep a written application or representations; or

      (b)   arrange for the whole or any part to be kept by some other appropriate person, subject to any conditions that the court may impose.

**R18.8**    **Exercise of court's powers**

    **18.8**    The court may decide whether to give, vary or discharge a special measures direction—

      (a)   at a hearing, in public or in private, or without a hearing; and

      (b)   in a party's absence, if that party—

         (i)   applied for the direction, variation or discharge, or

        (ii)   has had at least 10 business days in which to make representations.

**R18.9**    **Special measures direction without application**

    **18.9**    (1)   This rule applies where—

      (a)   a party notifies the court that a witness is eligible for assistance under section 16 or section 17 of the Youth Justice and Criminal Evidence Act 1999;

      (b)   the notice is given at—

         (i)   a preparation for trial hearing in a magistrates' court, or

        (ii)   a plea and trial preparation hearing in the Crown Court; and

      (c)   no other party opposes the giving of a special measures direction for the benefit of that witness.

    (2)   The court may exercise its power to give a special measures direction without requiring an application under rule 18.10.

    (3)   The party who gives the notice must—

      (a)   provide any information that the court may need to assess—

         (i)   the measure or measures likely to maximise so far as practicable the quality of the witness' evidence, and

        (ii)   the witness' own views; and

      (b)   where a direction provides for video recorded evidence to be admitted under section 27 or section 28 of the Youth Justice and Criminal Evidence Act 1999, as soon as reasonably practicable serve such evidence on—

         (i)   the court officer, and

        (ii)   each other party.

*[Note. Under sections 21 and 22 of the Youth Justice and Criminal Evidence Act 1999, a 'child witness' is one who is under 18, and a 'qualifying witness' is one who was a child witness when interviewed.*

*Under those sections, the 'primary rule' requires the court to give a direction—*

    *(a)   for the evidence of a child witness or of a qualifying witness to be admitted—*

    *(b)   by means of a video recording of an interview with the witness, in the place of examination-in-chief, and*

    *(c)   after that, by live link; or*

    *(d)   if one or both of those measures is not taken, for the witness while giving evidence to be screened from seeing the defendant.*

*The primary rule always applies unless—*

    *(a)   the witness does not want it to apply, and the court is satisfied that to omit a measure usually required by that rule would not diminish the quality of the witness' evidence; or*

    *(b)   the court is satisfied that to direct one of the measures usually required by that rule would not be likely to maximise, so far as practicable, the quality of the witness' evidence.]*

**R18.10**    **Content of application for a special measures direction**

    **18.10**    An applicant for a special measures direction must—

      (a)   explain how the witness is eligible for assistance;

      (b)   explain why special measures would be likely to improve the quality of the witness' evidence;

      (c)   propose the measure or measures that in the applicant's opinion would be likely to maximise, so far as practicable, the quality of that evidence;

      (d)   report any views that the witness has expressed about—

         (i)   his or her eligibility for assistance,

        (ii)   the likelihood that special measures would improve the quality of his or her evidence, and

        (iii)   the measure or measures proposed by the applicant;

(e)  in a case in which a child witness or a qualifying witness does not want the primary rule to apply, provide any information that the court may need to assess the witness' views;

(f)  in a case in which the applicant proposes that the witness should give evidence by live link—

(i)  identify someone to accompany the witness while the witness gives evidence,

(ii)  name that person, if possible, and

(iii)  explain why that person would be an appropriate companion for the witness, including the witness' own views;

(g)  in a case in which the applicant proposes the admission of video recorded evidence, identify—

(i)  the date and duration of the recording, and

(ii)  which part the applicant wants the court to admit as evidence, if the applicant does not want the court to admit all of it;

(h)  attach any other material on which the applicant relies; and

(i)  if the applicant wants a hearing, ask for one, and explain why it is needed.

*[Note. The Practice Direction sets out a form of application for use in connection with this rule.]*

## Application to vary or discharge a special measures direction

R18.11

18.11 (1)  A party who wants the court to vary or discharge a special measures direction must—

(a)  apply in writing, as soon as reasonably practicable after becoming aware of the grounds for doing so; and

(b)  serve the application on—

(i)  the court officer, and

(ii)  each other party.

(2)  The applicant must—

(a)  explain what material circumstances have changed since the direction was given (or last varied, if applicable);

(b)  explain why the direction should be varied or discharged; and

(c)  ask for a hearing, if the applicant wants one, and explain why it is needed.

*[Note. Under section 20 of the Youth Justice and Criminal Evidence Act 1999, the court can vary or discharge a special measures direction—*

*(a)  on application, if there has been a material change of circumstances; or*

*(b)  on the court's own initiative.]*

## Application containing information withheld from another party

R18.12

18.12 (1)  This rule applies where—

(a)  an applicant serves an application for a special measures direction, or for its variation or discharge; and

(b)  the application includes information that the applicant thinks ought not be revealed to another party.

(2)  The applicant must—

(a)  omit that information from the part of the application that is served on that other party;

(b)  mark the other part to show that, unless the court otherwise directs, it is only for the court; and

(c)  in that other part, explain why the applicant has withheld that information from that other party.

(3)  Any hearing of an application to which this rule applies—

(a)  must be in private, unless the court otherwise directs; and

(b)  if the court so directs, may be, wholly or in part, in the absence of a party from whom information has been withheld.

(4)  At any hearing of an application to which this rule applies—

(a)  the general rule is that the court must consider, in the following sequence—

(i)  representations first by the applicant and then by each other party, in all the parties' presence, and then

(ii)  further representations by the applicant, in the absence of a party from whom information has been withheld; but

(b)  the court may direct other arrangements for the hearing.

*[Note. See section 20 of the Youth Justice and Criminal Evidence Act 1999.]*

## Representations in response

R18.13

18.13 (1)  This rule applies where a party wants to make representations about—

(a)  an application for a special measures direction;

(b)  an application for the variation or discharge of such a direction; or

(c)  a direction, variation or discharge that the court proposes on its own initiative.

(2) Such a party must—
    (a) serve the representations on—
        (i) the court officer, and
        (ii) each other party;
    (b) do so not more than 10 business days after, as applicable—
        (i) service of the application, or
        (ii) notice of the direction, variation or discharge that the court proposes; and
    (c) ask for a hearing, if that party wants one, and explain why it is needed.

(3) Where representations include information that the person making them thinks ought not be revealed to another party, that person must—
    (a) omit that information from the representations served on that other party;
    (b) mark the information to show that, unless the court otherwise directs, it is only for the court; and
    (c) with that information include an explanation of why it has been withheld from that other party.

(4) Representations against a special measures direction must explain, as appropriate—
    (a) why the witness is not eligible for assistance;
    (b) if the witness is eligible for assistance, why—
        (i) no special measure would be likely to improve the quality of the witness' evidence,
        (ii) the proposed measure or measures would not be likely to maximise, so far as practicable, the quality of the witness' evidence, or
        (iii) the proposed measure or measures might tend to inhibit the effective testing of that evidence; and
    (c) in a case in which the admission of video recorded evidence is proposed, why it would not be in the interests of justice for the recording, or part of it, to be admitted as evidence.

(5) Representations against the variation or discharge of a special measures direction must explain why it should not be varied or discharged.

*[Note. Under sections 21 and 22 of the Youth Justice and Criminal Evidence Act 1999, where the witness is a child witness or a qualifying witness the special measures that the court usually must direct must be treated as likely to maximise, so far as practicable, the quality of the witness' evidence, irrespective of representations to the contrary.]*

**Defendant's evidence directions**

**R18.14    Exercise of court's powers**

18.14 The court may decide whether to give, vary or discharge a defendant's evidence direction—
    (a) at a hearing, in public or in private, or without a hearing; and
    (b) in a party's absence, if that party—
        (i) applied for the direction, variation or discharge, or
        (ii) has had at least 10 business days in which to make representations.

**R18.15    Content of application for a defendant's evidence direction**

18.15 An applicant for a defendant's evidence direction must—
    (a) explain how the proposed direction meets the conditions prescribed by the Youth Justice and Criminal Evidence Act 1999;
    (b) in a case in which the applicant proposes that the defendant give evidence by live link—
        (i) identify a person to accompany the defendant while the defendant gives evidence, and
        (ii) explain why that person is appropriate; and
    (c) ask for a hearing, if the applicant wants one, and explain why it is needed.

*[Note. See sections 33A and 33BA of the Youth Justice and Criminal Evidence Act 1999.]*

**R18.16    Application to vary or discharge a defendant's evidence direction**

18.16 (1) A party who wants the court to vary or discharge a defendant's evidence direction must—
    (a) apply in writing, as soon as reasonably practicable after becoming aware of the grounds for doing so; and
    (b) serve the application on—
        (i) the court officer, and
        (ii) each other party.

(2) The applicant must—
    (a) on an application to discharge a live link direction, explain why it is in the interests of justice to do so;
    (b) on an application to discharge a direction for an intermediary, explain why it is no longer necessary in order to ensure that the defendant receives a fair trial;

     (c)   on an application to vary a direction for an intermediary, explain why it is necessary for the direction to be varied in order to ensure that the defendant receives a fair trial; and

     (d)   ask for a hearing, if the applicant wants one, and explain why it is needed.

*[Note. See sections 33A(7) and 33BB of the Youth Justice and Criminal Evidence Act 1999.]*

**Representations in response**                                                                                    R18.17

**18.17** (1)  This rule applies where a party wants to make representations about—

     (a)   an application for a defendant's evidence direction;

     (b)   an application for the variation or discharge of such a direction; or

     (c)   a direction, variation or discharge that the court proposes on its own initiative.

   (2)  Such a party must—

     (a)   serve the representations on—

        (i)   the court officer, and

        (ii)   each other party;

     (b)   do so not more than 10 business days after, as applicable—

        (i)   service of the application, or

        (ii)   notice of the direction, variation or discharge that the court proposes; and

     (c)   ask for a hearing, if that party wants one, and explain why it is needed.

   (3)  Representations against a direction, variation or discharge must explain why the conditions prescribed by the Youth Justice and Criminal Evidence Act 1999 are not met.

**Witness anonymity orders**

**Exercise of court's powers**                                                                                    R18.18

**18.18** (1)  The court may decide whether to make, vary or discharge a witness anonymity order—

     (a)   at a hearing (which must be in private, unless the court otherwise directs), or without a hearing (unless any party asks for one); and

     (b)   in the absence of a defendant.

   (2)  The court must not exercise its power to make, vary or discharge a witness anonymity order, or to refuse to do so—

     (a)   before or during the trial, unless each party has had an opportunity to make representations;

     (b)   on an appeal by the defendant to which applies Part 34 (Appeal to the Crown Court) or Part 39 (Appeal to the Court of Appeal about conviction or sentence), unless in each party's case—

        (i)   that party has had an opportunity to make representations, or

        (ii)   the appeal court is satisfied that it is not reasonably practicable to communicate with that party;

     (c)   after the trial and any such appeal are over, unless in the case of each party and the witness—

        (i)   each has had an opportunity to make representations, or

        (ii)   the court is satisfied that it is not reasonably practicable to communicate with that party or witness.

**Content and conduct of application for a witness anonymity order**                                 R18.19

**18.19** (1)  An applicant for a witness anonymity order must—

     (a)   include in the application nothing that might reveal the witness' identity;

     (b)   describe the measures proposed by the applicant;

     (c)   explain how the proposed order meets the conditions prescribed by section 88 of the Coroners and Justice Act 2009[17];

     (d)   explain why no measures other than those proposed will suffice, such as—

        (i)   an admission of the facts that would be proved by the witness,

        (ii)   an order restricting public access to the trial,

        (iii)   reporting restrictions, in particular under sections 45, 45A or 46 of the Youth Justice and Criminal Evidence Act 1999[18],

        (iv)   a direction for a special measure under section 19 of the Youth Justice and Criminal Evidence Act 1999,

        (v)   introduction of the witness' written statement as hearsay evidence, under section 116 of the Criminal Justice Act 2003[19], or

        (vi)   arrangements for the protection of the witness;

     (e)   attach to the application—

---

[17] 2009 c. 25.

[18] 1999 c. 23; section 45A was inserted by section 78 of the Criminal Justice and Courts Act 2015 (c. 2).

[19] 2003 c. 44.

Criminal Procedure Rules and Criminal Practice Directions

(i) a witness statement setting out the proposed evidence, edited in such a way as not to reveal the witness' identity,

(ii) where the prosecutor is the applicant, any further prosecution evidence to be served, and any further prosecution material to be disclosed under the Criminal Procedure and Investigations Act 1996, similarly edited, and

(iii) any defence statement that has been served, or as much information as may be available to the applicant that gives particulars of the defence; and

(f) ask for a hearing, if the applicant wants one.

(2) At any hearing of the application, the applicant must—

(a) identify the witness to the court, unless at the prosecutor's request the court otherwise directs; and

(b) present to the court, unless it otherwise directs—

(i) the unedited witness statement from which the edited version has been prepared,

(ii) where the prosecutor is the applicant, the unedited version of any further prosecution evidence or material from which an edited version has been prepared, and

(iii) such further material as the applicant relies on to establish that the proposed order meets the conditions prescribed by section 88 of the 2009 Act.

(3) At any such hearing—

(a) the general rule is that the court must consider, in the following sequence—

(i) representations first by the applicant and then by each other party, in all the parties' presence, and then

(ii) information withheld from a defendant, and further representations by the applicant, in the absence of any (or any other) defendant; but

(b) the court may direct other arrangements for the hearing.

(4) Before the witness gives evidence, the applicant must identify the witness to the court—

(a) if not already done;

(b) without revealing the witness' identity to any other party or person; and

(c) unless at the prosecutor's request the court otherwise directs.

**R18.20**    **Duty of court officer to notify the Director of Public Prosecutions**

18.20 The court officer must notify the Director of Public Prosecutions of an application, unless the prosecutor is, or acts on behalf of, a public authority.

**R18.21**    **Application to vary or discharge a witness anonymity order**

18.21 (1) A party who wants the court to vary or discharge a witness anonymity order, or a witness who wants the court to do so when the case is over, must—

(a) apply in writing, as soon as reasonably practicable after becoming aware of the grounds for doing so; and

(b) serve the application on—

(i) the court officer, and

(ii) each other party.

(2) The applicant must—

(a) explain what material circumstances have changed since the order was made (or last varied, if applicable);

(b) explain why the order should be varied or discharged, taking account of the conditions for making an order; and

(c) ask for a hearing, if the applicant wants one.

(3) Where an application includes information that the applicant thinks might reveal the witness' identity, the applicant must—

(a) omit that information from the application that is served on a defendant;

(b) mark the information to show that it is only for the court and the prosecutor (if the prosecutor is not the applicant); and

(c) with that information include an explanation of why it has been withheld.

(4) Where a party applies to vary or discharge a witness anonymity order after the trial and any appeal are over, the party who introduced the witness' evidence must serve the application on the witness.

*[Note. Under sections 91, 92 and 93 of the Coroners and Justice Act 2009, the court can vary or discharge a witness anonymity order—*

*(a) on an application, if there has been a material change of circumstances since it was made or previously varied; or*

*(b) on the court's own initiative, unless the trial and any appeal are over.]*

### Representations in response

R18.22

18.22 (1) This rule applies where a party or, where the case is over, a witness, wants to make representations about—

    (a) an application for a witness anonymity order;

    (b) an application for the variation or discharge of such an order; or

    (c) a variation or discharge that the court proposes on its own initiative.

  (2) Such a party or witness must—

    (a) serve the representations on—

      (i) the court officer, and

      (ii) each other party;

    (b) do so not more than 10 business days after, as applicable—

      (i) service of the application, or

      (ii) notice of the variation or discharge that the court proposes; and

    (c) ask for a hearing, if that party or witness wants one.

  (3) Where representations include information that the person making them thinks might reveal the witness' identity, that person must—

    (a) omit that information from the representations served on a defendant;

    (b) mark the information to show that it is only for the court (and for the prosecutor, if relevant); and

    (c) with that information include an explanation of why it has been withheld.

  (4) Representations against a witness anonymity order must explain why the conditions for making the order are not met.

  (5) Representations against the variation or discharge of such an order must explain why it would not be appropriate to vary or discharge it, taking account of the conditions for making an order.

  (6) A prosecutor's representations in response to an application by a defendant must include all information available to the prosecutor that is relevant to the conditions and considerations specified by sections 88 and 89 of the Coroners and Justice Act 2009.

### Live link directions

*[Note. The rules in this Section do not apply to an application for a special measures direction allowing a witness to give evidence by live link: as to which, see rules 18.8 to 18.13.]*

### Exercise of court's powers

R18.23

18.23 The court may decide whether to give or discharge a live link direction—

    (a) at a hearing, in public or in private, or without a hearing; and

    (b) in a party's absence, if that party—

      (i) applied for the direction or discharge, or

      (ii) has had at least 10 business days in which to make representations in response to an application by another party.

### Content of application for a live link direction

R18.24

An applicant for a live link direction must—

    (a) unless the court otherwise directs, identify the place from which the witness will give evidence;

    (b) if that place is in the United Kingdom, explain why it would be in the interests of the efficient or effective administration of justice for the witness to give evidence by live link;

    (c) if the applicant wants the witness to be accompanied by another person while giving evidence—

      (i) name that person, if possible, and

      (ii) explain why it is appropriate for the witness to be accompanied; and

    (d) ask for a hearing, if the applicant wants one, and explain why it is needed.

*[Note. See section 32 of the Criminal Justice Act 1988[20] and section 51 of the Criminal Justice Act 2003.*

*The Practice Direction sets out a form of application for use in connection with this rule.]*

---

[20] 1988 c. 33; section 32 was amended by section 55 of the Criminal Justice Act 1991 (c. 53), section 29 of, and paragraph 16 of Schedule 2 to, the Criminal Appeal Act 1995 (c. 35), sections 67 and 68 of, and Schedule 6 to, the Youth Justice and Criminal Evidence Act 1999 (c. 23) and article 3 of, and paragraph 26 of the Schedule to, S.I. 2004/2035. It is temporarily omitted by section 87 of, and paragraph 10 of Schedule 23 to, the Coronavirus Act 2020 (c. 7).

Criminal Procedure Rules and Criminal Practice Directions

**R18.25**　**Application to discharge a live link direction**

18.25 (1) A party who wants the court to discharge a live link direction must—

    (a) apply in writing, as soon as reasonably practicable after becoming aware of the grounds for doing so; and

    (b) serve the application on—

        (i) the court officer, and

        (ii) each other party.

    (2) The applicant must—

    (a) explain what material circumstances have changed since the direction was given;

    (b) explain why it is in the interests of justice to discharge the direction; and

    (c) ask for a hearing, if the applicant wants one, and explain why it is needed.

    (3) An applicant for the variation or revocation of a European investigation order made on an application under rule 18.24 must demonstrate that the applicant is, as the case may be—

    (a) the person who applied for the order;

    (b) a prosecuting authority; or

    (c) any other person affected by the order.

    (4) Where the court varies or revokes such an order, the court officer must promptly notify the appropriate authority in the participating State in which the measure or measures are to be carried out.

*[Note. See section 32(4) of the Criminal Justice Act 1988[21] and section 52(3) of the Criminal Justice Act 2003[22].]*

**R18.26**　**Representations in response**

18.26 (1) This rule applies where a party wants to make representations about an application for a live link direction or for the discharge of such a direction.

    (2) Such a party must—

    (a) serve the representations on—

        (i) the court officer, and

        (ii) each other party;

    (b) do so not more than 10 business days after service of the application; and—

    (c) ask for a hearing, if that party wants one, and explain why it is needed.

    (3) Representations against a direction or discharge must explain, as applicable, why the conditions prescribed by the Criminal Justice Act 1988 or the Criminal Justice Act 2003 are not met.

Intermediary for a defendant

**R18.27**　**Appointment of intermediary to facilitate a defendant's participation**

18.27 (1) The court must exercise its power to appoint an intermediary to facilitate a defendant's effective participation in the trial where—

    (a) the defendant's ability to participate is likely to be diminished by reason of—

        (i) age, if the defendant is under 18, or

        (ii) mental disorder (as defined in section 1(2) of the Mental Health Act 1983[23]), a significant impairment of intelligence and social functioning, or a physical disability or disorder; and

    (b) the appointment is necessary for that purpose.

    (2) In determining whether such an appointment is necessary, who to appoint and the duration or purpose of the appointment, the court must have regard to—

    (a) the defendant's communication needs as reported to the court;

    (b) the recommendations in any intermediary's report received by the court;

    (c) any views that the defendant has expressed about—

        (i) receiving the assistance of an intermediary,

        (ii) other measures or arrangements to facilitate the defendant's effective participation in the trial;

    (d) the likely impact of the defendant's age, if under 18, level of intellectual ability or social functioning on the ability to—

---

[21] 1988 c. 33; section 32(4) was amended by article 3 of, and paragraph 26 of the Schedule to, S.I. 2004/2035.

[22] 2003 c. 44; section 52 is temporarily omitted by section 87 of, and paragraph 2 of Schedule 23 to, the Coronavirus Act 2020 (c. 7).

[23] 1983 c. 20; section 1(2) was amended by sections 1, 55 and 56 of, and Schedule 11 to, the Mental Health Act 2007 (c. 12).

        (i)   give evidence, and

        (ii)  understand what is said and done by the court and other participants;

   (e)  the likely impact on such participation and on such understanding of any mental disorder or other significant impairment of intelligence or social functioning;

   (f)  the adequacy of arrangements for questioning the defendant in the absence of an intermediary;

   (g)  any assistance that the defendant has received in the past—

        (i)   while giving evidence in legal proceedings,

        (ii)  while being questioned during the investigation of an alleged offence, or

        (iii) as a defendant in a criminal case;

   (h)  any assessment of the defendant's health by a mental health practitioner acting independently of the parties to assist the court;

   (i)  any expert medical opinion that the court may have received; and

   (j)  any other matter that the court thinks relevant.

(3) The court may exercise its power to appoint an intermediary—

   (a)  for the duration of every hearing that the defendant is due to attend;

   (b)  for the duration of any specified such hearing or hearings, or for the duration of a specified part of such a hearing; or

   (c)  for a specified purpose during a hearing.

(4) Unless the court otherwise directs, the appointment of an intermediary extends to facilitating the defendant's communication with that defendant's legal representatives for the duration and for the purpose of the appointment.

(5) The court may decide whether to appoint an intermediary to facilitate a defendant's effective participation in the trial and whether to vary or discharge any such appointment—

   (a)  on application or on the court's own initiative;

   (b)  at a hearing, in public or in private, or without a hearing; and

   (c)  in a party's absence, if that party—

        (i)   applied for the appointment, variation or discharge, or

        (ii)  has had at least 10 business days in which to make representations.

(6) The court must not exercise its power to vary or discharge a direction for the appointment of an intermediary unless satisfied that—

   (a)  since the direction was made—

        (i)   the defendant's communication needs have changed materially, or

        (ii)  any other material circumstance has changed materially; and

   (b)  the defendant will be able to participate effectively in the trial despite the variation or discharge of the direction.

### Application to vary or discharge the appointment of an intermediary for a defendant      R18.28

**18.28** (1) A party who wants the court to vary or discharge the appointment of an intermediary to facilitate a defendant's effective participation in the trial must—

   (a)  apply in writing, as soon as reasonably practicable after becoming aware of the grounds for doing so; and

   (b)  serve the application on—

        (i)   the court officer, and

        (ii)  each other party.

(2) The applicant must—

   (a)  explain how the criteria listed in rule 18.27(7) are met (variation or discharge of appointment); and

   (b)  ask for a hearing, if the applicant wants one, and explain why it is needed.

### Representations in response to application or proposal      R18.29

**18.29** (1) This rule applies where a party wants to make representations about—

   (a)  an application or proposal for the appointment of an intermediary to facilitate a defendant's effective participation in the trial; or

   (b)  an application or proposal for the variation or discharge of such an appointment.

(2) Such a party must—

   (a)  serve the representations on—

        (i)   the court officer, and

        (ii)  each other party;

    (b) do so not more than 10 business days after, as applicable—
        (i) service of the application, or
        (ii) notice of the appointment, variation or discharge that the court proposes; and
    (c) ask for a hearing, if that party wants one, and explain why it is needed.
(3) Representations against such an appointment, variation or discharge must explain why the criteria that apply are not met.

### Duties of intermediaries

**R18.30**   **Intermediary's duty to the court**

**18.30** (1) This rule applies to an intermediary who accepts—
    (a) approval by the court for the purposes of section 29 of the Youth Justice and Criminal Evidence Act 1999[24] (Examination of witness through intermediary);
    (b) approval by the court for the purposes of section 33BA of the 1999 Act[25] (Examination of accused through intermediary); or
    (c) appointment by the court to facilitate a defendant's effective participation in the trial, when the defendant gives evidence or at any other time.
(2) The intermediary must help the court to achieve the overriding objective—
    (a) to the best of the intermediary's skill and understanding by—
        (i) communicating to the witness or defendant (as the case may be) questions put to them,
        (ii) communicating to the questioner and the court the replies, and
        (iii) explaining such questions and answers so that they can be understood;
    (b) by assessing continually the witness' or the defendant's (as the case may be) ability to participate effectively and intervening if necessary;
    (c) where the intermediary is appointed to facilitate a defendant's effective participation, by explaining to the defendant, in terms the defendant can understand, what is said and done by the court and other participants; and
    (d) by actively assisting the court in fulfilling its duties under rule 3.2 (Case management; The duty of the court) and rule 3.9 (Case management; Ground rules hearing), in particular by—
        (i) complying with directions made by the court, and
        (ii) at once informing the court of any significant failure (by the intermediary or another) to take any step required by such a direction.
(3) This duty overrides any obligation to the witness or to the defendant (as the case may be), or to the person by whom the intermediary is paid.

### Declaration by intermediary

**R18.31**   **18.31** (1) This rule applies where—
    (a) a video recorded interview with a witness is conducted through an intermediary; or
    (b) the court directs the examination of a witness or defendant through an intermediary.
(2) The intermediary must make a declaration—
    (a) before such an interview begins; and
    (b) before the examination begins (even if such an interview with the witness was conducted through the same intermediary).
(3) The declaration must be in these terms, or in any corresponding terms that the intermediary declares to be binding—

"I swear by Almighty God [*or* I solemnly, sincerely and truly declare and affirm] that I shall faithfully communicate questions and answers and make true explanation of all matters and things required of me according to the best of my skill and understanding."

### Content of intermediary's report

**R18.32**   **18.32** (1) An intermediary's report must, in every case—
    (a) give details of the intermediary's qualifications, relevant experience and any accreditation;
    (b) identify the commissioner of the report;

---

[24] 1999 c. 23; section 29 was amended by paragraph 384 of Schedule 8 to the Courts Act 2003 (c. 39).
[25] 1999 c. 23; section 33BA is inserted by section 104(1) of the Coroners and Justice Act 2009 (c. 25), with effect from a date to be appointed.

(c)   identify those from whom the intermediary has obtained information material to the report;

(d)   list the documents received or inspected by the intermediary which contained such information and give an indication of their content;

(e)   give the date or dates on which the intermediary met the witness or defendant, as the case may be, for the purpose of preparing the report;

(f)   describe the nature and duration of the intermediary's assessment, or assessments, of the witness or defendant;

(g)   by reference to examples drawn from the intermediary's assessment of the witness or defendant explain why in this particular case intermediary assistance is necessary;

(h)   include an evaluation of—

(i)   the impact of any condition or conditions which, whether in isolation or together, may adversely affect the witness' or the defendant's ability to communicate, and

(ii)   the extent, if any, to which that impact may be exacerbated by the trial;

(i)   if the intermediary is not able to reach an evaluation without qualifying it, state the qualification;

(j)   report the views of the witness or defendant, as the case may be, on receiving the assistance of an intermediary;

(k)   include in a summary of the intermediary's conclusions any recommendation, with reasons, for—

(i)   the approval or appointment of an intermediary,

(ii)   the manner and duration of any questioning of the witness or defendant, as the case may be, and

(iii)   arrangements for the way in which the intermediary, if approved or appointed, should participate; and

(l)   contain a statement that the intermediary—

(i)   understands an intermediary's duty to the court, and

(ii)   will comply with that duty if approved or appointed.

(2)   Where the intermediary is asked to evaluate a defendant's communication needs the report must also—

(a)   include an evaluation of the extent to which any measures or arrangements beside the appointment of an intermediary will facilitate the defendant's effective participation in the trial; and

(b)   in the summary of the intermediary's conclusions include any recommendation, with reasons, for—

(i)   the duration and purpose of any appointment of an intermediary, and

(ii)   other measures or arrangements to help the defendant to participate effectively in the trial

## Summary of eligibility for measures to which this Part applies

### Special measures direction

Under section 16 of the Youth Justice and Criminal Evidence Act 1999[26], a witness is eligible for the assistance of a special measures direction given under section 19 of that Act if—

(a)   the witness is under 18; or

(b)   the witness has—

(i)   a mental disorder, or a significant impairment of intelligence and social functioning, or

(ii)   a physical disability or disorder

and the court considers that the completeness, coherence and accuracy (the 'quality') of evidence given by the witness is likely to be diminished by reason of those circumstances.

Under section 17 of the 1999([27]) Act, a witness is eligible for such assistance if—

(a)   the court is satisfied that the quality of evidence given by the witness is likely to be diminished because of his or her fear or distress in connection with giving evidence, taking account particularly of—

(i)   the circumstances of the offence,

(ii)   the witness' age, social and cultural background, ethnic origins, domestic and employment circumstances, religious beliefs or political opinions,

---

[26]   1999 c. 23.

[27]   1999 c. 23; section 17 was amended by section 99 of the Coroners and Justice Act 2009 (c. 25), paragraphs 1 and 2 of the Schedule to S.I. 2013/554 and section 46 of the Modern Slavery Act 2015 (c. 30).

(iii) any behaviour towards the witness on the part of the defendant, the defendant's family or associates, or any other potential defendant or witness, and

(iv) the witness' own views;

(b) the witness is the complainant in respect of a sexual offence, and has not declined such assistance; or

(c) the offence is one of a list of offences involving weapons, and the witness has not declined such assistance.

Section 28 of the 1999 Act (video recorded cross-examination or re-examination) is not yet in force. With that exception, all the special measures listed in rule 18.1 potentially are available where the witness is eligible for assistance under section 16 of the Act. Those numbered (i) to (v) are available where the witness is eligible for assistance under section 17.

As a general rule, but with exceptions, the court must give a special measures direction—

(a) under section 21 or 22 of the 1999 Act[28], where the witness—

(i) is under 18, or

(ii) was under that age when interviewed whether or not an application for a direction is made;

(b) under section 22A of the 1999 Act[29], where an application is made in the Crown Court for the evidence of a witness who is the complainant of a sexual offence to be admitted by means of a video recording of an interview with the witness in the place of examination-in-chief.

### Defendant's evidence direction

Under section 33A of the 1999 Act[30], the court can allow a defendant to give evidence by live link, or (when the Coroners and Justice Act 2009 comes into force) under section 33BA[31] can allow a defendant to give evidence through an intermediary, if—

(a) the defendant—

(i) is under 18, and the defendant's ability to participate effectively as a witness giving oral evidence is compromised by his or her level of intellectual ability or social functioning; or

(ii) suffers from a mental disorder or some other significant impairment of intelligence and social functioning and cannot participate effectively as a witness giving oral evidence for that reason;

(b) the use of a live link—

(i) would enable the defendant to participate more effectively, and

(ii) is in the interests of justice;

(c) the examination of the defendant through an intermediary is necessary to ensure that the defendant receives a fair trial.

### Witness anonymity order

Under section 86 of the Coroners and Justice Act 2009[32], a witness anonymity order is an order that specifies measures to be taken to ensure that the identity of a witness is not disclosed, such as withholding the witness' name from materials disclosed to a party to the proceedings, the use of a pseudonym, the screening of the witness from view, the modulation of the witness' voice, and the prohibition of questions that might reveal his or her identity. Before making such an order, the court must—

(a) be satisfied that three conditions prescribed by the Act are met (section 88 of the 2009 Act); and

(b) have regard to considerations specified by the Act (section 89 of the 2009 Act).

### Live link direction

Under section 32 of the Criminal Justice Act 1988, the court can allow a witness who is outside the United Kingdom to give evidence by live link—

(a) in proceedings in a youth court, or on appeal from such proceedings; or

(b) at a trial in the Crown Court, or on appeal from such a trial.

---

[28] 1999 c. 23; sections 21 and 22 were amended by sections 98, 100 and 178 of, and Part 3 of Schedule 23 to, the Coroners and Justice Act 2009 (c. 25).

[29] 1999 c. 23; section 22A was inserted by section 101 of the Coroners and Justice Act 2009 (c. 25).

[30] 1999 c. 23; section 33A was inserted by section 47 of the Police and Justice Act 2006 (c. 48).

[31] 1999 c. 23; section 33BA is inserted by section 104 of the Coroners and Justice Act 2009 (c. 25), with effect from a date to be appointed.

[32] 2009 c. 25.

*Under section 51 of the Criminal Justice Act 2003, on an application or on its own initiative, the court can allow a witness who is in the United Kingdom, but outside the building in which the proceedings are held, to give evidence by live link. The court must be satisfied that that is in the interests of the efficient or effective administration of justice.*

*If a witness is eligible for the assistance of a special measures direction (as to which, see the note above), the court can allow the witness to give evidence by live link under sections 19 and 24 of the 1999 Act[33]. See rules 18.8 to 18.13.]*

### Intermediary for a defendant

*In order to ensure the defendant's effective participation in his or her trial the court has an inherent power to appoint an intermediary to facilitate that participation, including during the giving of evidence by the defendant.*

CRIMINAL PRACTICE DIRECTIONS   PART 18   MEASURES TO ASSIST A WITNESS OR DEFENDANT TO GIVE EVIDENCE OR OTHERWISE PARTICIPATE

#### CPD V Evidence 18A: Measures to Assist a Witness or Defendant to give Evidence

**CPD.18A**

18A.1   For special measures applications, the procedures at CrimPR Part 18 should be followed. However, assisting a vulnerable witness to give evidence is not merely a matter of ordering the appropriate measure. Further directions about vulnerable people in the courts, ground rules hearings and intermediaries are given in paragraphs I 3D to 3G.

18A.2   Special measures need not be considered or ordered in isolation. The needs of the individual witness should be ascertained, and a combination of special measures may be appropriate. For example, if a witness who is to give evidence by live link wishes, screens can be used to shield the live link screen from the defendant and the public, as would occur if screens were being used for a witness giving evidence in the court room.

#### CPD V Evidence 18B: Witnesses giving Evidence by Live Link

**CPD.18B**

18B.1   A special measures direction for the witness to give evidence by live link may also provide for a specified person to accompany the witness (CrimPR 18.10(f)). In determining who this should be, the court must have regard to the wishes of the witness. The presence of a supporter is designed to provide emotional support to the witness, helping reduce the witness's anxiety and stress and contributing to the ability to give best evidence. It is preferable for the direction to be made well before the trial begins and to ensure that the designated person is available on the day of the witness's testimony so as to provide certainty for the witness.

18B.2   An increased degree of flexibility is appropriate as to who can act as supporter. This can be anyone known to and trusted by the witness who is not a party to the proceedings and has no detailed knowledge of the evidence in the case. The supporter may be a member of the Witness Service but need not be an usher or court official. Someone else may be appropriate.

18B.3   The usher should continue to be available both to assist the witness and the witness supporter, and to ensure that the court's requirements are properly complied with in the live link room.

18B.4   In order to be able to express an informed view about special measures, the witness is entitled to practise speaking using the live link (and to see screens in place). Simply being shown the room and equipment is inadequate for this purpose.

18B.5   If, with the agreement of the court, the witness has chosen not to give evidence by live link but to do so in the court room, it may still be appropriate for a witness supporter to be selected in the same way, and for the supporter to sit alongside the witness while the witness is giving evidence.

#### CPD V Evidence 18C: Visually Recorded Interviews: Memory Refreshing and Watching at a Different Time from the Trial Court

**CPD.18C**

18C.1   Witnesses are entitled to refresh their memory from their statement or visually recorded interview. The court should enquire at the PTPH or other case management hearing about arrangements for memory refreshing. The witness's first viewing of the visually recorded interview can be distressing or distracting. It should not be seen for the first time immediately before giving evidence. Depending upon the age and vulnerability of the witness several competing issues have to be considered and it may be that the assistance of the intermediary is needed to establish exactly how memory refreshing should be managed.

*Criminal Procedure Rules and Criminal Practice Directions*

---

[33]  1999 c. 23; section 24 was amended by paragraph 385 of Schedule 8 to, and Schedule 10 to, the Courts Act 2003 (c. 39) and section 102(1) of the Coroners and Justice Act 2009 (c. 25).

18C.2 If the interview is ruled inadmissible, the court must decide what constitutes an acceptable alternative method of memory refreshing.

18C.3 Decisions about how, when and where refreshing should take place should be court-led and made on a case-by-case basis in respect of each witness. General principles to be addressed include:

    i.   the venue for viewing. The delicate balance between combining the court familiarisation visit and watching the DVD, and having them on two separate occasions, needs to be considered in respect of each witness as combining the two may lead to 'information overload'. Refreshing need not necessarily take place within the court building but may be done, for example, at the police ABE suite;

    ii.  requiring that any viewing is monitored by a person (usually the officer in the case) who will report to the court about anything said by the witness;

    iii. whether it is necessary for the witness to see the DVD more than once for the purpose of refreshing. The court will need to ask the advice of the intermediary, if any, with respect to this;

    iv. arrangements, if the witness will not watch the DVD at the same time as the trial bench or judge and jury, for the witness to watch it before attending to be cross examined, (depending upon their ability to retain information this may be the day before).

18C.4 There is no legal requirement that the witness should watch the interview at the same time as the trial bench or jury. Increasingly, this is arranged to occur at a different time, with the advantages that breaks can be taken as needed without disrupting the trial, and cross-examination starts while the witness is fresh. An intermediary may be present to facilitate communication but should not act as the independent person designated to take a note and report to the court if anything is said.

18C.5 Where the viewing takes place at a different time from that of the trial bench or jury, the witness is sworn (or promises) just before cross-examination and, unless the judge otherwise directs:

    (a) it is good practice for the witness to be asked by the prosecutor, (or the judge/magistrate if they so direct), in appropriate language if, and when, he or she has watched the recording of the interview;

    (b) if, in watching the recording of the interview or otherwise the witness has indicated that there is something he or she wishes to correct or to add then it is good practice for the prosecutor (or the judge/magistrate if they so direct) to deal with that before cross-examination provided that proper notice has been given to the defence.

## CPD V Evidence 18D: Witness Anonymity Orders

**CPD.18D**

18D.1 This direction supplements CrimPR 18.18 to 18.22, which governs the procedure to be followed on an application for a witness anonymity order. The court's power to make such an order is conferred by the Coroners and Justice Act 2009 (in this section, 'the Act'); section 87 of the Act provides specific relevant powers and obligations.

18D.2 As the Court of Appeal stated in *R v Mayers and Others* [2008] EWCA Crim 2989, [2009] 1 WLR 1915, [2009] 1 Cr App R 30 and emphasised again in *R v Donovan and Kafunda* [2012] EWCA Crim 2749, unreported, 'a witness anonymity order is to be regarded as a special measure of the last practicable resort': Lord Chief Justice, Lord Judge. In making such an application, the prosecution's obligations of disclosure 'go much further than the ordinary duties of disclosure' (*R v Mayers*); reference should be made to the Judicial Protocol on Disclosure, see paragraph IV 15A.1.

*Case management*

18D.3 Where such an application is proposed, with the parties' active assistance the court should set a realistic timetable, in accordance with the duties imposed by CrimPR 3.2 and 3.3. Where possible, the trial judge should determine the application, and any hearing should be attended by the parties' trial advocates.

*Service of evidence and disclosure of prosecution material pending an application*

18D.4 Where the prosecutor proposes an application for a witness anonymity order, it is not necessary for that application to have been determined before the proposed evidence is served. In most cases, an early indication of what that evidence will be if an order is made will be consistent with a party's duties under CrimPR 1.2 and 3.3. The prosecutor should serve with the other prosecution evidence a witness statement setting out the proposed evidence, redacted in such a way as to prevent disclosure of the witness' identity, as permitted by section 87(4) of the Act. Likewise the prosecutor should serve with other prosecution material disclosed under the Criminal Procedure and Investigations Act 1996 any such material appertaining to the witness, similarly redacted.

*The application*

**18D.5**    An application for a witness anonymity order should be made as early as possible and within the period for which CrimPR 18.3 provides. The application, and any hearing of it, must comply with the requirements of that rule and with those of rule 18.19. In accordance with CrimPR 1.2 and 3.3, the applicant must provide the court with all available information relevant to the considerations to which the Act requires a court to have regard.

*Response to the application*

**18D.6**    A party upon whom an application for a witness anonymity order is served must serve a response in accordance with CrimPR 18.22. That period may be extended or shortened in the court's discretion: CrimPR 18.5.

**18D.7**    To avoid the risk of injustice, a respondent, whether the Prosecution or a defendant, must actively assist the court. If not already done, a respondent defendant should serve a defence statement under section 5 or 6 of the Criminal Procedure and Investigations Act 1996, so that the court is fully informed of what is in issue. When a defendant makes an application for a witness anonymity order the prosecutor should consider the continuing duty to disclose material under section 7A of the Criminal Procedure and Investigations Act 1996; therefore a prosecutor's response should include confirmation that that duty has been considered. Great care should be taken to ensure that nothing disclosed contains anything that might reveal the witness' identity. A respondent prosecutor should provide the court with all available information relevant to the considerations to which the Act requires a court to have regard, whether or not that information falls to be disclosed under the 1996 Act.

*Determination of the application*

**18D.8**    All parties must have an opportunity to make oral representations to the court on an application for a witness anonymity order: section 87(6) of the Act. However, a hearing may not be needed if none is sought: CrimPR 18.18(1) (a). Where, for example, the witness is an investigator who is recognisable by the defendant but known only by an assumed name, and there is no likelihood that the witness' credibility will be in issue, then the court may indicate a provisional decision and invite representations within a defined period, usually 14 days, including representations about whether there should be a hearing. In such a case, where the parties do not object the court may make an order without a hearing. Or where the court provisionally considers an application to be misconceived, an applicant may choose to withdraw it without requiring a hearing. Where the court directs a hearing of the application then it should allow adequate time for service of the representations in response.

**18D.9**    The hearing of an application for a witness anonymity order usually should be in private: CrimPR 18.18(1)(a), and before the trial judge wherever possible. The court has power to hear a party in the absence of a defendant and that defendant's representatives: section 87(7) of the Act and rule 18.18(1)(b). In the Crown Court, a recording of the proceedings will be made, in accordance with CrimPR 5.5. The Crown Court officer must treat such a recording in the same way as the recording of an application for a public interest ruling. It must be kept in secure conditions, and the arrangements made by the Crown Court officer for any transcription must impose restrictions that correspond with those under CrimPR 5.5(2).

**18D.10**   The hearing of an application for a witness anonymity order usually should be in private: CrimPR 18.18(1)(a). The court has power to hear a party in the absence of a defendant and that defendant's representatives: section 87(7) of the Act and rule 18.18(1)(b). In the Crown Court, a recording of the proceedings will be made, in accordance with CrimPR 5.5. The Crown Court officer must treat such a recording in the same way as the recording of an application for a public interest ruling. It must be kept in secure conditions, and the arrangements made by the Crown Court officer for any transcription must impose restrictions that correspond with those under CrimPR 5.5(2).

**18D.11**   Where confidential supporting information is presented to the court before the last stage of the hearing, the court may prefer not to read that information until that last stage.

**18D.12**   The court may adjourn the hearing at any stage, and should do so if its duty under CrimPR 3.2 so requires.

**18D.13**   On a prosecutor's application, the court is likely to be assisted by the attendance of a senior investigator or other person of comparable authority who is familiar with the case.

**18D.14**   During the last stage of the hearing it is essential that the court test thoroughly the information supplied in confidence in order to satisfy itself that the conditions prescribed by the Act are met. At that stage, if the court concludes that this is the only way in which it can satisfy itself as to a relevant condition or consideration, exceptionally it may invite the applicant to present the proposed witness to be questioned by the court. Any such questioning should be carried out at such a time, and the witness brought to the court in such a way, as to prevent disclosure of his or her identity.

Criminal Procedure Rules and Criminal Practice Directions

**18D.15** The court may ask the Attorney General to appoint special counsel to assist. However, it must be kept in mind that, 'Such an appointment will always be exceptional, never automatic; a course of last and never first resort. It should not be ordered unless and until the trial judge is satisfied that no other course will adequately meet the overriding requirement of fairness to the defendant': *R v H* [2004] UKHL 3, [2004] 2 AC 134 (at paragraph 22), [2004] 2 Cr App R 10. Whether to accede to such a request is a matter for the Attorney General, and adequate time should be allowed for the consideration of such a request.

**18D.16** The Court of Appeal in *R v Mayers* 'emphasise[d] that all three conditions, A, B and C, must be met before the jurisdiction to make a witness anonymity order arises. Each is mandatory. Each is distinct.' The Court also noted that if there is more than one anonymous witness in a case any link, and the nature of any link, between the witnesses should be investigated: 'questions of possible improper collusion between them, or cross-contamination of one another, should be addressed.'

**18D.17** Following a hearing the court should announce its decision on an application for a witness anonymity order in the parties' presence and in public: CrimPR 18.4(2). The court should give such reasons as it is possible to give without revealing the witness' identity. In the Crown Court, the court will be conscious that reasons given in public may be reported and reach the jury. Consequently, the court should ensure that nothing in its decision or its reasons could undermine any warning it may give jurors under section 90(2) of the Act. A record of the reasons must be kept. In the Crown Court, the announcement of those reasons will be recorded.

**18D.18** Should the judge grant the anonymity then the following should be considered by the judge with the assistance of the court staff, so that the practical arrangements (confidentially recorded) are in place to ensure that the witness's anonymity is not compromised:

    i.   Any pre-trial visit by the anonymous witness;

    ii.   How the witness will enter and leave the court building;

    iii.  Where the witness will wait until they give evidence;

    iv.  Provision for prosecution counsel to speak to the anonymous witness at court before they give evidence;

    v.   Provision for the anonymous witness to see their statement or view their ABEs;

    vi.  How the witness will enter and leave the court room;

    vii.  Provisions to disguise the identity of the anonymous witness whilst they give evidence (voice modulation and screens);

    viii. Provisions for the anonymous witness to have any breaks required;

    ix.  Provisions to protect the anonymity of the witness in the event of an emergency such as a security alert.

*Order*

**18D.19** Where the court makes a witness anonymity order, it is essential that the measures to be taken are clearly specified in a written record of that order approved by the court and issued on its behalf. An order made in a magistrates' court must be recorded in the court register, in accordance with CrimPR 5.4.

**18D.20** Should the application for anonymity be refused, consideration will be given as to whether the witness to whom the application related can be compelled to give evidence despite any risk to their safety and what special measures could support them to give their evidence.

**18D.21** Self-evidently, the written record of the order must not disclose the identity of the witness to whom it applies. However, it is essential that there be maintained some means of establishing a clear correlation between witness and order, and especially where in the same proceedings witness anonymity orders are made in respect of more than one witness, specifying different measures in respect of each. Careful preservation of the application for the order, including the confidential part, ordinarily will suffice for this purpose.

*Discharge or variation of the order*

**18D.22** Section 91 of the Act allows the court to discharge or vary a witness anonymity order: on application, if there has been a material change of circumstances since the order was made or since any previous variation of it; or on its own initiative. CrimPR 18.21 allows the parties to apply for the variation of a pre-trial direction where circumstances have changed.

**18D.23** The court should keep under review the question of whether the conditions for making an order are met. In addition, consistently with the parties' duties under CrimPR 1.2 and 3.3, it is incumbent on each, and in particular on the applicant for the order, to keep the need for it under review.

**18D.24** Where the court considers the discharge or variation of an order, the procedure that it adopts should be appropriate to the circumstances. As a general rule, that procedure should approximate to the procedure for determining an application for an order. The court may need to hear further representations by the applicant for the order in the absence of a respondent defendant and that defendant's representatives.

*Arrangements at trial*
**18D.25** At trial the greatest possible care must be taken to ensure that nothing will compromise the witness' anonymity. Detailed arrangements may have been proposed by the applicant under CrimPR 18.19(1)(b) and directed by the court on determining the application for the order. Such arrangements must take account of the layout of the courtroom and of the means of access for the witness, for the defendant or defendants, and for members of the public. The risk of a chance encounter between the witness and someone who may recognise him or her, either then or subsequently, must be rigorously excluded. Subject to contrary direction by the trial judge, the court staff and those accompanying the witness must adopt necessary measures to ensure that the witness is neither seen nor heard by anyone whose observation would, or might, render nugatory the court's order. Further HMCTS guidance for court staff can be found in Guidance for Criminal Courts for England and Wales for Anonymous/Protected Witnesses.

*Retention of confidential material*
**18D.26** If retained by the court, confidential material must be stored in secure conditions by the court officer. Alternatively, subject to such directions as the court may give, such material may be committed to the safe keeping of the applicant or any other appropriate person in exercise of the powers conferred by CrimPR 18.6. If the material is released to any such person, the court should ensure that it will be available to the court at trial.

**CPD V Evidence 18E: Use of s. 28 Youth Justice and Criminal Evidence Act 1999; Pre-recording of**   **CPD.18E**
**Cross-examination and Re-examination for Witnesses Captured by s. 16 YJCEA 1999**
**18E.1** When Section 28 of the Youth Justice and Criminal Evidence Act 1999 (s.28 YJCEA 1999) has been bought into force for a particular Crown Court a witness will be eligible for special measures under that section by virtue of section 16 of the Act (age or incapacity) or section 17 (fear or distress about testifying, or in proceedings for a sexual or other specified offence), to the extent provided by the relevant commencement order. A list of those orders, with links, appears at https://www.legislation.gov.uk/ukpga/1999/23/section/28
**18E.2** Applications for special measures directions are governed by Part 18 of the Criminal Procedure Rules and careful attention should be paid to the court's case management powers and the obligations on the parties. In addition to these paragraphs of these Practice Directions, paragraphs I 3D (Vulnerable people in the courts), I 3E (about ground rules hearings), I 3F (Intermediaries) V 18A (about special measures generally) and V 18C (about video recorded interviews) contain relevant guidance.
**18E.3** Other guidance applicable primarily to the parties but of which courts should be aware includes:

  (i)   the Protocol between the National Police Chiefs' Council, the Crown Prosecution Service and Her Majesty's Courts & Tribunals Service to expedite cases involving witnesses under 10 years;
  (ii)  Achieving Best Evidence in criminal proceedings;
  (iii) the Attorney General's Guidelines on Disclosure;
  (iv)  the 2013 Protocol and Good Practice Model on Disclosure of information in cases of alleged child abuse and linked criminal and care directions hearings;
  (v)   the Advocates Gateway Toolkits;
  (vi)  the Inns of Court College of Advocacy training document Advocacy and the vulnerable: 20 principles of questioning.

**18E.4** Advocates should also refer to the annex to this practice direction which contains further detailed guidance on ground rules hearings where the witness is eligible for assistance under section 16 of the 1999 Act
**18E.5** Witnesses eligible for special measures under s.28 YJCEA 1999 should be identified promptly by the police. If it will not cause undesirable delay, a representative of the Crown Prosecution Service should give prior approval before the police discuss, with the witness or with the witness' parent or carer, special measures available and the witness' needs, such that the most appropriate package of special measures can be identified. This may include use of a Registered Intermediary.

**18E.6** For timetabling of the case, it is imperative that the investigators and prosecutor commence the disclosure process at the start of the investigation. The Attorney-General's Guidelines: Disclosure for Investigators, Prosecutors and Defence Practitioners must be followed, and if applicable, the *2013 Protocol and Good Practice Model on Disclosure of information in cases of alleged child abuse and linked criminal and care directions.*

**18E.7** From the point of grant of the s.28 YJCEA 1999 special measures application, timescales provided by section 8.6 of A protocol between the Association of Chief Police Officers, the Crown Prosecution Service and Her Majesty's Courts and Tribunals Service to expedite cases involving witnesses under 10 years will cease to apply and the case should be managed in accordance with the timescales established in this practice direction.

**18E.8** Local Implementation Teams (LITs) should be established with all relevant agencies represented by someone of sufficient seniority. Their task will be to monitor the operation of the scheme and compliance with this practice direction and other relevant protocols. LITs should encourage all appropriate agencies to endorse and follow both the Protocol and the Good Practice Model. LITs should monitor compliance and issues should initially be raised at the LITs

### The first hearing in the magistrates' court

**18E.9** The prosecutor must formally notify the court and the defence at the first hearing (or as soon as possible thereafter if eligibility only becomes apparent following the first hearing)
   (a) that the case is eligible for special measures under s.28 YJCEA 1999; and
   (b) whether or not the prosecutor intends to apply for such a direction in the Crown Court

**18E.10** This practice direction applies only where the defendant indicates a not guilty plea or does not indicate a plea, and the case is sent for trial in the Crown Court.

**18E.11** In any case that is sent to the Crown Court for trial in which the prosecution has notified the court of its intention to make an application for special measures under s.28 of the YJCEA 1999 the timetable is that as established by the Better Case Management initiative. The PTPH should be listed within 28 days of the date of sending from the magistrates' court.

### Before the Plea and Trial Preparation Hearing in the Crown Court

**18E.12** A transcript of the ABE interview and the application for special measures, including under s.28 YJCEA 1999, must be served on the Court and defence at least 5 business days prior to the PTPH. The report of any Registered Intermediary addressing the issue must be served with the application for special measures.

**18E.13** Any defence representations about the application for special measures must be served before the PTPH.

**18E.14** An application for a witness summons to obtain material held by a third party, should be served in advance of the PTPH and determined at that hearing, or as soon as reasonably practicable thereafter. The timetable should accommodate any consequent hearings or applications, but it is imperative parties are prompt to obtain third party disclosure material. The prosecution must make the court and the defence aware of any difficulty as soon as it arises.

### At the Plea and Trial Preparation Hearing

**18E.15** The Resident Judge may have appointed a judicial lead from the salaried judiciary at the court centre who will be responsible for monitoring and supervising the scheme. The Plea and Trial Preparation Hearing (PTPH) must be conducted by a salaried judge.

**18E.16** The judge may hear submissions from the advocates and will rule on the application for special measures.

**18E.17** The judge will need to consider:
   • whether any of the special measures, or a combination of them, would be likely to improve the quality of the witness's evidence, and if so
   • which of the special measures, or a combination of them would be likely to maximise, so far as practicable, the quality of evidence given by the witness.

**18E.18** The judge should bear in mind all the circumstances of the case, including any views expressed by the witness and whether the measure or measures might tend to inhibit such evidence being effectively tested.

**18E.19** The judge should pay careful regard to whether a section 28 special measures direction will in fact materially advance the date for the cross-examination and re-examination, so as to maximise, along with any other measures, the quality of the witness's evidence. This will involve detailed consideration of when the section 28 recording and the trial are likely to occur. This in turn will depend, amongst other things, on any waiting list to use the recording equipment, the likely length of the section 28 hearing and the availability of the judge, the advocates, the witness and a suitable courtroom.

18E.20   Furthermore, if there have already been delays, for instance because of a lack of resources to facilitate the timely prerecording of the ABE interview (the examination-in-chief), that additionally is a matter to which the judge should have regard when viewing the situation overall and deciding whether the section 28 special measure will improve and maximise the quality of the evidence.

18E.21   Against that background, the judge should determine which, if any, of the measures, or combination of them, would be likely to maximise so far as practicable the quality of the witness's evidence. It may be necessary for the judge to revisit the decision in this context in the light of changed circumstances.

18E.22   If the application is refused (see the assumptions to be applied by the courts in s.21 and s.22 of the YJCEA 1999), this practice direction ceases to apply.

18E.23   If the application is granted, the judge should make orders and give directions for preparation for the recorded cross-examination and re-examination hearing and advance preparation for the trial, including for any outstanding disclosure of unused material. The correct and timely application of the Criminal Procedure and Investigations Act 1996 ('CPIA 1996') will be vital and close attention should be paid to the *2013 Protocol and Good Practice Model on Disclosure* (November 2013) and the Attorney-General's Guidelines: Disclosure for Investigators, Prosecutors and Defence Practitioners, as referred to above.

18E.24   The orders made are likely to include:

i.   Service of the prosecution evidence within 50 days of sending;

ii.   Directions for service of defence witness requirements;

iii.   Service of initial disclosure; under the CPIA 1996, as soon as reasonably practical; in this context, this should be interpreted as being simultaneous with the service of the prosecution evidence, i.e. within 50 days of sending for both bail and custody cases. This will be within 3 weeks of the PTPH;

iv.   Orders on disclosure material held by a third party;

v.   Service of the defence statement; under the CPIA 1996, this must be served within 28 days of the prosecutor serving or purporting to serve initial disclosure;

vi.   Any editing of the ABE interview;

vii.   It will be for the judge to decide whether a ground rules hearing is necessary. If one is to take place, depending on the circumstances of the case, this should be listed either at a convenient date prior to the recorded cross-examination and re-examination hearing or it should take place immediately prior to the recording of the cross-examination and re-examination (see CPD General matters 3E: Ground rules hearings to plan questioning of a vulnerable witness or defendant);

viii.   Service of the Ground Rules Hearing Form by the defence advocate;

ix.   Making arrangements for the witness to refresh his or her memory by viewing the recorded examination-in-chief ('ABE interview'), see CPD Evidence 18C: Visually recorded interviews: memory refreshing and watching at a different time from the jury;

x.   Making arrangements for the recorded cross-examination and re-examination hearing under s.28, including fixing a date, time and location;

xi.   Other special measures;

xii.   Directions for any further directions hearing whether at the conclusion of the recorded cross-examination and re-examination hearing or subsequently;

xiii.   Provision by the prosecution of the paginated jury bundle, if possible, in advance of the s.28 hearing;

xiv.   Fixing a date for trial.

18E.25   The timetable should ensure the prosecution evidence and initial disclosure are served swiftly. The ground rules hearing, if one is ordered, will usually be soon as is feasible after the deadline for service of the defence statement. Time must be afforded for any further disclosure of unused material following service of the defence statement and for determination of any application under s.8 of the CPIA 1996. Subject to judicial discretion applications for extensions of time for service of disclosure by either party should generally be refused.

18E.26   Where the defendant may be unfit to plead, a timetable for s.28 should usually still be set, taking into account extra time needed for the obtaining of medical reports, save in cases where it is indicated that it is unlikely that there would be a trial if the defendant is found fit.

18E.27   As far as possible, without diminishing the defendant's right to a fair trial, the timing and duration of the recorded cross-examination should take into account the needs of the witness.

18E.28   The needs of other witnesses should not be neglected. Witness and intermediary availability dates should be available for the PTPH.

*Prior to ground rules hearing and hearing under section 28*

**18E.29**   It is imperative parties abide by orders made at the PTPH, including the completion and service of the Ground Rules Hearing Form by the defence advocate. Delays or failures must be reported to the judge as soon as they arise; this is the responsibility of each legal representative. If ordered, the lead lawyer for the prosecution and defence must provide a weekly update to the court, detailing the progress and any difficulties or delays in complying with orders. The court may order a further case management hearing if necessary.

**18E.30**   Any applications under s.100 of the Criminal Justice Act 2003 ('CJA 2003') (non-defendant's bad character) or under s.41 of the YJCEA 1999 (evidence or cross-examination about complainants sexual behaviour) or any other application which may affect the cross-examination must be made promptly, and responses submitted in time for the judge to rule on the application at the ground rules hearing. Parts 21 and 22 of the Rules apply to applications under s.100 and s.41 respectively.

**18E.31**   The witness' court familiarisation visit should take place. When the witness is under 18 or it is otherwise appropriate, there should be an opportunity to practice on the live link/recording facilities. The witness must have the opportunity to view his or her ABE interview to refresh the witness' memory. It may or may not be appropriate for this to take place on the day of the court visit: CPD Evidence 18C must be followed.

**18E.32**   If the court decides that the case is suitable for the witness to give evidence from a remote site then a familiarisation visit should take place at that site. If a ground rules hearing is ordered, the judge and advocates should consider appropriate arrangements for them to talk to the witness before the cross examination hearing.

**18E.33**   Applications to vary or discharge a special measures declaration must comply with CrimPR 18.11. The rule requires the application to be made as soon as reasonably practicable after becoming aware of the grounds for doing so.

*Ground rules hearing*

**18E.34**   Advocates should master the toolkits available through The Advocate's Gateway. The toolkits have potential relevance to applications where the witness is eligible for assistance under either s.16 or s.17 YJCEA 1999. These provide guidance on questioning a vulnerable witness, see CPD General matters 3D and the annex to this practice direction and the Inns of Court College of Advocacy ("ICCA") 20 Principles of Questioning.

**18E.35**   Any appointed Registered Intermediary must attend the ground rules hearing, see CrimPR 3.9(2).

**18E.36**   Depending on the circumstances of the case, the judge may order that the defence advocate who appeared at the ground rules is to conduct the recorded cross-examination (see listing and allocation below).

**18E.37**   Topics for discussion and agreement at the ground rules hearing will depend on the individual needs of the witness, and an intermediary may provide advance indications. CPD General matters 3E must be followed. Topics that require discussion, depending on the circumstances of the case, include:

     i.    the overall length of cross-examination;

     ii.    cross-examination by a single advocate in a multi-handed case;

     iii.    any restrictions on the advocate's usual duty to 'put the defence case'.

**18E.38**   It may be helpful to discuss at this stage how any limitations on questioning will be explained to the jury.

**18E.39**   If a ground rules hearing is ordered (whether or not on a date in advance of the recorded cross-examination and re-examination), this may provide a convenient opportunity for the judge to:

     i.    rule on any application under s.100 of the CJA 2003 or s.41 of the YJCEA 1999, or other applications that may affect the cross-examination;

     ii.    decide how the witness may view exhibits or documents;

     iii.    review progress in complying with orders made at the preliminary hearing and make any necessary orders.

*Recording of cross-examination and re-examination: hearing under s.28*

18E.40  At the hearing, the witness will be cross-examined and re-examined, if required, via the live link from the court room to the witness suite (unless provision has been made for the use of a remote link) and the examination will be recorded. It is the responsibility of the designated court clerk to ensure in advance that all of the equipment is working and to contact the provider's Service Desk if support is required. Any other special measures must be in place and any intermediary or supporter should sit in the live link room with the witness. The intermediary's role is transparent and therefore must be visible and audible to the judge and advocates at the cross-examination and in the subsequent replaying.

18E.41  The judge, advocates and parties, including the defendant will usually assemble in the court room for the hearing. In some cases the judge and advocates may be in the witness suite with the witness, for example when questioning a very young child or where the witness has a particular communication need. The court will decide this on a case-by-case basis. The defendant should be able to communicate with his or her representatives and should be able to hear the witness via the live link and see the proceedings: s.28 (2). Whether the witness is screened or not will depend on the other special measures ordered, for example screens may have been ordered under s.23 YJCEA 1999.

18E.42  On the admission of the public or media to the hearing, please see below.

18E.43  At the conclusion of the hearing, the judge will issue further orders, such as for the editing of the recorded cross-examination and may set a timetable for progress.

18E.44  Under s.28(4) YJCEA 1999, the judge, on application of any parties or on the court's own motion may direct that the recorded examination is not admitted into evidence, despite any previous direction. Such direction must be given promptly, preferably immediately after the conclusion of the examination.

18E.45  Without exception, editing of the ABE interview/examination-in-chief or recorded cross-examination is precluded without an order of the court.

18E.46  The ability to record simultaneously from a court and a witness room and to play back the recording at trial will be provided in all Crown Courts as an additional facility within the existing Justice Video Service (JVS). Courts will book recording slots with the Service Desk who will launch the recording at the scheduled time when the court is ready. Recordings will be stored in a secure data centre with backup and resiliency, for authorised access.

*After the recording*

18E.47  Following the recording the judge should review compliance with orders and progress towards preparation for trial, make any further orders necessary and confirm the date of the trial. Any further orders made by the judge should be recorded and uploaded onto the relevant section of the DCS.

18E.48  If the defendant enters a guilty plea, the judge should proceed towards sentence, making any appropriate orders, such as for a Pre-Sentence Report and setting a date for sentencing. Any reduction for a guilty plea shall reflect the day of the recorded cross-examination as the first day of trial; the Sentencing Council guideline on guilty plea reductions should be applied.

*Preparation for trial*

18E.49  Parties must notify the court promptly if any difficulties arise or any orders are not complied with. The court may order a further case management hearing (FCMH).

18E.50  In accordance with orders, either after recorded cross-examination or at the FCMH, necessary editing of the ABE interview/examination-in-chief and/or the recorded cross-examination must be done only on the order of the court. Any editing must be done promptly.

18E.51  Recorded cross-examinations and re-examinations will be stored securely by the service provider so as to be accessible to the advocates and the court. It will not usually be necessary to obtain a transcript of the recorded cross-examination, but if it is difficult to comprehend, a transcript should be obtained and served. The ground rules hearing form outlines questions to the witness that might be completed electronically by the judge during cross-examination forming a contemporaneous note of the hearing, served on the parties as an agreed record.

18E.52  Editing, authorised by the judge, is to be submitted by the court to the Service Desk, who produce an edited copy. The master and all edited copy versions are retained in the secure data centre from where they can be accessed. Courts book playback timeslots with the Service Desk for the trial date. The court may authorise parties to view playback at JVS endpoints, by submitting a request form to the Service Desk. Access for those so authorised is via the Quickcode (recording ID) and a security PIN (password) on the courtroom touch panel or remote control.

18E.53   No further cross-examination or re-examination of the witness may take place unless the criteria in section 28(6) are satisfied and the judge makes a further special measures direction under section 28(5). Any such further examination must be recorded via live link as described above.

18E.54   Section 28(6) of the YJCEA 1999 provides as follows:

(6)   *The court may only give such a further direction if it appears to the court—*

(a)   *that the proposed cross-examination is sought by a party to the proceedings as a result of that party having become aware, since the time when the original recording was made in pursuance of subsection (1), of a matter which that party could not with reasonable diligence have ascertained by then, or*

(b)   *that for any other reason it is in the interests of justice to give the further direction.*

18E.55   Any application under section 28(5) must be in writing and be served on the court and the prosecution at least 20 business days before the date of trial. The application must specify:

i.     the topics on which further cross-examination is sought;

ii.    the material or matter of which the defence has become aware since the original recording;

iii.   why it was not possible for the defence to have obtained the material or ascertained the matter earlier; and

iv.    the expected impact on the issues before the court at trial.

18E.56   The prosecution should respond in writing within 5 business days of the application. The judge may determine the application on the papers or order a hearing. Any further cross-examination ordered must be recorded via live link in advance of the trial and served on the court and the parties. These timescales may be abridged for good reason on application to the judge.

*Trial*

18E.57   In accordance with the judge's directions, the ABE interview/examination-in-chief and the recorded cross-examination and re-examination, edited as directed, should be played to the jury at the appropriate point within the trial.

18E.58   The jury should not usually receive transcripts of the recordings, and if they do these should be removed from the jury as soon as the recording has been played, see CPD Trial 26L.2.

18E.59   If the matter was not addressed at the ground rules hearing, the judge should discuss with the advocates how any limitations on questioning should be explained to the jury before summing-up. If not dealt with at the ground rules hearing, this should usually occur at the commencement of the trial. The judge will need to consider when to give a direction to the jury in this context, which is likely to be necessary before the recording is played.

*After conclusion of trial*

18E.60   Immediately after the trial, the ABE interview/examination-in-chief and the recorded cross-examination and re-examination should be stored securely on the cloud.

*Listing and allocation*

18E.61   **Advocates:** Depending on the circumstances of the case, the judge may order that the defence advocate who appeared at the ground rules hearing must conduct the recorded cross-examination. When such an order is made, the judge and list office will make whatever reasonable arrangements are feasible to achieve this, assisted by the Resident Judge when necessary. Although continuity of representation is to be encouraged, it is not mandatory for the advocate who conducted the section 28 cross-examination to represent the defendant at trial.

18E.62   When the timetable for the case is being set, advocates must have their up to date availability with them (in so far as is possible). It has been ordered that the defence advocate who appeared at the ground rules hearing must conduct the recorded cross-examination, an advocate who is part-heard in another trial and is in difficulties in attending the s.28 hearing must inform the judges conducting the respective proceedings as soon as practicable. The judges shall resolve the conflict as regards the advocate's availability, taking into consideration the circumstances of the cases and the interests of justice (referring the issue, if necessary, to the Resident Judge(s)).

18E.63   Depending on the circumstances of the case, the Resident Judge or the nominated lead judge may order that the ground rules hearing and the s. 28 YJCEA 1999 hearing are to be listed before the same judge. Once the s.28 hearing has taken place, any judge, in accordance with CPD XIII Listing E, including recorders, can deal with the trial.

**18E.64**   **Listing:** Section 28 hearings should be listed at a time determined by the list officer, or as directed by the judge or Resident Judge, bearing in mind the circumstances of the witness as well the availability of the judge, the advocates and a courtroom with the relevant equipment, including the ability to record the evidence. Ground rules hearings, if they are listed in advance of the day when the recorded cross-examination and re-examination is to occur, may be held at any time, including towards the end of the court day, to accommodate the advocates and intermediary (if there is one) and to minimise disruption to other trials.

*Public, including media access, and reporting restrictions*

**18E.65**   Open justice is an essential principle of the common law. However, certain automatic statutory restrictions may apply, and the judge may consider it appropriate in the specific circumstances of a case to make an order applying discretionary restrictions. CPD I General Matters 6B must be followed and the templates published by the Judicial College (available on LMS) should be used. The parties to the proceedings, and interested parties such as the media, should have the opportunity to make representations before an order is made.

**18E.66**   The statutory powers most likely to be available to the judge are listed below. The judge should consider the specific statutory requirements necessary for the making of the particular order carefully, and the order made must be in writing.

    a)   Provisions to exclude the public from hearings:

        i.   Section 37 of the Children and Young Persons Act 1933, applicable to witnesses under 18;

        ii.   Section 25 of the YJCEA 1999, applicable to the evidence of a witness where the proceedings relate to a sexual offence or an offence under section 1 or 2 of the Modern Slavery Act 2015, or it appears to the court that there are reasonable grounds for believing that any person other than the accused has sought, or will seek, to intimidate the witness in connection with testifying in the proceedings.

    b)   Automatic reporting restrictions:

        i.   Section 1 of the Sexual Offences (Amendment) Act 1992, applicable to the complainant in any sex offence case.

    c)   Discretionary reporting restrictions:

        i.   Section 45 of the YJCEA 1999, applicable to under 18s concerned in criminal proceedings;

        ii.   Section 46 of the YJCEA 1999, applicable to an adult witness whose evidence would be diminished by fear or distress.

    d)   Postponement of fair and accurate reports under section 4(2) of the Contempt of Court Act 1981.

**18E.67**   Note that public access to information held by the court is now the subject of CrimPR 5.7 to 5.10 and CPD General matters 5B that must be followed.

**Annex for section 28 ground rules hearings at the Crown Court when dealing with witnesses under s.16 YJCEA 1999**

*Introduction*

1.   This annex is designed to assist all advocates in their preparation for cross-examination of vulnerable witnesses.

2.   Adherence to the principles below will avoid interruption during the pre-recorded cross-examination and reduce any ordered editing.

3.   Issues concerning the vulnerable witness and the nature of the cross-examination will be addressed by the judge at the Ground Rules Hearing (GRH).

4.   In appropriate cases and in particular where the witness is of very young years or suffers from a disability or disorder it is expected that the advocate will have prepared his or her cross-examination in writing for consideration by the court.

5.   It is thus incumbent on the Defence to ensure that full instructions have been taken prior to the GRH.

*Required preparation prior to the GRH*

6.   All advocates should be familiar with the relevant toolkits, available through **The Advocates Gateway** which provide guidance on questioning a vulnerable witness. A synopsis of this guidance, which advocates should have read prior to any GRH, is included in this annex.

*Attendance at, and procedure during, the GRH*

7. In preparation for trial, courts must take every reasonable step to facilitate the participation of witnesses and defendants CPR 3.8(4) (d). The court should order that the defendant attends the GRH.

8. The defence advocate must complete and submit the Ground Rules Hearing form by the time and date ordered at the PTPH.

9. The hearing facilitates the judge's duty to control questioning if and when necessary.

10. The hearing enables the court to ensure its process is adapted to enable the witness to give his or her best evidence whilst ensuring the defendant's right to a fair trial is not diminished. Accordingly the ground rules and the nature of the questioning of the witness by the advocate (and limitations imposed if necessary in accordance with principles above) will be discussed.

11. Prior to the hearing it is necessary for both advocates and the judge to have viewed the ABE evidence.

12. The judge will state what ground rules will apply. The advocates must comply with them.

13. Any intermediary must attend the GRH. It is the responsibility of those instructing the intermediary to ensure this.

14. The judge may have ordered that the defendant's advocate attending the hearing is to be the same advocate who will be conducting the recorded cross-examination (and the subsequent trial, if any).

15. Any intermediary for the witness should only be warned for the GRH and the section 28 hearing they are assisting with. An Intermediary should not be instructed unless available to attend the GRH and the section 28 hearings ordered by the court (if listed on separate days).

16. Topics for discussion and agreement at the GRH will depend on the individual needs of the witness. CPD I General Matters 3E must be followed.

17. Topics of discussion at the hearing will include the length of cross-examination and any restrictions on the advocate's usual duty to 'put the defence case'. As was made plain by the Vice President of the Court of Appeal Criminal Division in *Regina v Lubemba and Pooley* 2014 EWCA Crim 2064, advocates cannot insist upon any supposed right 'to put one's case' or previous inconsistent statements to a vulnerable witness. If there is a right to 'put one's case' it must be modified for young or vulnerable witnesses. It is perfectly possible to ensure the jury are made aware of the defence case and of significant inconsistencies without intimidation or distressing a witness. It is expected that all advocates will be familiar with and have read this case.

18. At the GRH counsel need to agree with the judge how and when the matters referred to in paragraph 11 will be explained to the jury. This explanation will normally be done by the judge, but may exceptionally, and only with the permission of the judge, be explained by counsel. If there is no agreement the judge will rule on it.

19. A Section 28 Defence GRH form should be completed as far as possible prior to attendance at the GRH before the judge.

20. Rulings will be made on any application under section 100 of the CJA 2003 or section 41 of the YCEA 1999, and on any other application that may affect the conduct of the cross examination. Any ruling will be included in the trial practice note.

21. A review will take place of the progress made by the parties in complying with the orders made at the PTPH and the court will make any other necessary orders.

22. Additional information can be found in the Inns of Court College of Advocacy training document 'Advocacy and the vulnerable: 20 principles of questioning'. This document is part of a suite of training materials available to assist advocates in dealing with questioning vulnerable victims in the criminal justice system.

*Court of Appeal guidance on questioning children of tender years and witnesses who are vulnerable as a result of mental incapacity*

In a series of decisions the Court of Appeal has made it clear that there has to be a different and fresh approach to the cross-examination of, in particular, children of tender years, and witnesses who are vulnerable as a result of mental incapacity. The following propositions have support in decisions on appeal: (*R v B 2010 EWCA Crim 4*; *R v F 2013 EWCA Crim 424*; *Wills v R 2011 EWCA Crim 1938*; *R v Edwards 2011 EWCA Crim 3028*; *R v Watts 2010 EWCA Crim 1824*; *R v W and M 2010 EWCA Crim 1926*)

'The reality of questioning children of tender years is that direct challenge that he or she is wrong or lying could lead to confusion and, worse, to capitulation which the child does not, in reality, accept.

Capitulation is not a consequence of unreliability but a function of the youngster's age. Experience has shown that young children are scared of disagreeing with a mature adult whom they do not wish to confront.

It is common, in the trial of an adult, to hear, once the nursery slopes of cross-examination have been skied, the assertion "you were never punched or kicked, as you have suggested, were you?"

It was precisely that approach which the Court is anxious to avoid. Such an approach risks confusion in the minds of the witness whose evidence was bound to take centre stage, and it is difficult to see how it can be helpful. We struggle to understand how the defendant's right to a fair trial was in any way compromised simply because Mr X was not allowed to ask the question "Simon did not punch you in the way you suggest?"

The overriding objective. The Criminal Procedure Rules objective is that criminal cases be dealt with justly. Dealing with a criminal case justly includes dealing with the case efficiently and expeditiously in ways that take account of the gravity of the offence alleged and the complexity of what is in issue.

In our collective experience the age of a witness is not determinative of his or her ability to give truthful and accurate evidence. Like adults some children will provide truthful and accurate testimony, and some will not. However children are not miniature adults, but children, and to be treated for what they are, not what they will, in the years ahead, grow to be.

There is undoubtedly a danger of a child witness wishing simply to please.

There is undoubtedly a danger of a child witness assenting to what is put rather than disagreeing during the questioning process in an endeavour to bring that process to a speedier conclusion.

It is particularly important in the case of a child witness to keep a question short and simple, and even more important than it is with an adult witness to avoid questions which are rolled up and contain, inadvertently two or three questions at once. It is generally recognised that, particularly with child witnesses, short and untagged questions are best at eliciting the evidence. By untagged we mean questions that do not contain a statement of the answer which is sought. That said, when it comes to directly contradicting a particular statement and inviting the witness to face a directly contradictory suggestion, it may often be difficult to examine otherwise.

No doubt if a way can be found of engaging the witness to tell the story, and the content then differs from what had been said before, that will be a yet better indication that the original account is wrong. But that is difficult to achieve and indeed may itself have the disadvantage of prolonging the child's time giving evidence. Even then there may be no guarantee as to which account is the more reliable.

Most of the questions which produced the answers which were chiefly relied upon, unlike many others, constituted the putting of direct suggestions with an indication of the answer "this happened didn't it?" Or "this didn't happen, did it?" The consequence of that is that it can be very difficult to tell whether the child is truly changing her account or simply taking the line of least resistance.

At the same time the right of the defendant to a fair trial must be undiminished. When the issue is whether the child is lying or mistaken, when claiming that the defendant behaved indecently towards him or her, it should not be over problematic for the advocate to formulate short, simple questions, which put the essential elements of the defendant's case to the witness, and fully ventilate before the jury the areas of evidence which bear on the child's credibility.

Aspects of evidence which undermine or are believed to undermine the child's credibility must, of course, be revealed to the jury. However it is not necessarily appropriate for them to form the subject matter of detailed cross-examination of the child, and the advocate may have to forego much of the kind of contemporary cross-examination which consists of no more than comment on matters which will be before the jury, in any event, from different sources.

Notwithstanding some of the difficulties; when all is said and done, the witness whose cross-examination is in contemplation is a child, sometimes very young, and it should not take very lengthy cross examination to demonstrate, when it is the case, that the child may indeed be fabricating, or fantasising, or imagining, or reciting a well-rehearsed untruthful script, learned by rote; or simply just suggestible, or contaminated by or in collusion with others to make false allegations, or making assertions in language which is beyond his or her level of comprehension; and are therefore likely to be derived from another source. Comment on the evidence, including comment on evidence which may bear adversely on the credibility of the child, should be addressed after the child has finished giving evidence. Clear limitations have to be imposed on the cross-examination of vulnerable young complainants.'

CRIMINAL PROCEDURE RULES    PART 19    EXPERT EVIDENCE

**R19.1**    **When this Part applies**

**19.1**   (1)   This Part applies where a party wants to introduce expert opinion evidence.

(2)   A reference to an 'expert' in this Part is a reference to a person who is required to give or prepare expert evidence for the purpose of criminal proceedings, including evidence required to determine fitness to plead or for the purpose of sentencing.

(3)   Where evidence that is introduced as evidence of fact within a witness' direct knowledge includes expert opinion the court may direct that the requirements of rules 19.2 (Expert's duty to the court) and 19.3 (Introduction of expert evidence) apply, to the extent and with such adaptations as the court directs.

*[Note. Expert medical evidence may be required to determine fitness to plead under section 4 of the Criminal Procedure (Insanity) Act 1964[1]. It may be required also under section 11 of the Powers of Criminal Courts (Sentencing) Act 2000[2], under Part III of the Mental Health Act 1983[3] or under Part 12 of the Criminal Justice Act 2003[4]. Those Acts contain requirements about the qualification of medical experts.]*

**R19.2**    **Expert's duty to the court**

**19.2**   (1)   An expert must help the court to achieve the overriding objective —

(a)   by giving opinion which is—
  (i)   objective and unbiased, and
  (ii)   within the expert's area or areas of expertise; and

(b)   by actively assisting the court in fulfilling its duty of case management under rule 3.2, in particular by—
  (i)   complying with directions made by the court, and
  (iii)   at once informing the court of any significant failure (by the expert or another) to take any step required by such a direction.

(2)   This duty overrides any obligation to the person from whom the expert receives instructions or by whom the expert is paid.

(3)   This duty includes obligations—

(a)   to define the expert's area or areas of expertise—
  (i)   in the expert's report, and
  (ii)   when giving evidence in person;

(b)   when giving evidence in person, to draw the court's attention to any question to which the answer would be outside the expert's area or areas of expertise;

(c)   inform all parties and the court if the expert's opinion changes from that contained in a report served as evidence or given in a statement; and

(d)   to disclose to the party for whom the expert's evidence is commissioned anything—
  (i)   of which the expert is aware, and
  (ii)   of which that party, if aware of it, would be required to give notice under rule 19.3(3)(c).

*[Note. The Practice Direction lists examples of matters that should be disclosed under this rule and rule 19.3(3)(c).]*

**R19.3**    **Introduction of expert evidence**

**19.3**   (1)   A party who wants another party to admit as fact a summary of an expert's conclusions must serve that summary—

(a)   on the court officer and on each party from whom that admission is sought; and

(b)   as soon as practicable after the defendant whom it affects pleads not guilty.

(2)   A party on whom such a summary is served must—

(a)   serve a response stating—
  (i)   which, if any, of the expert's conclusions are admitted as fact, and
  (ii)   where a conclusion is not admitted, what are the disputed issues concerning that conclusion; and

(b)   serve the response—
  (i)   on the court officer and on the party who served the summary, and
  (ii)   as soon as practicable, and in any event not more than 10 business days after service of the summary.

---

[1]   1964 c. 84; section 4 was substituted, together with section 4A, for section 4 as originally enacted, by section 2 of the Criminal Procedure (Insanity and Unfitness to Plead) Act 1991 (c. 25), and amended by section 22 of the Domestic Violence, Crime and Victims Act 2004 (c. 28).

[2]   2000 c. 6.

[3]   1983 c. 20.

[4]   2003 c. 44.

(3) A party who wants to introduce expert evidence otherwise than as admitted fact must—

    (a) serve a report by the expert which complies with rule 19.4 (Content of expert's report) on—

        (i) the court officer, and

        (ii) each other party;

    (b) serve the report as soon as practicable, and in any event with any application in support of which that party relies on that evidence;

    (c) serve with the report—

        (i) notice of anything of which the party serving it is aware which might reasonably be thought capable of undermining the reliability of the expert's opinion, or detracting from the credibility or impartiality of the expert, and

        (ii) an explanation of how facts stated in the report are admissible as evidence if that is not explained by the report;

    (d) if another party so requires, give that party a copy of, or a reasonable opportunity to inspect—

        (i) a record of any examination, measurement, test or experiment on which the expert's findings and opinion are based, or that were carried out in the course of reaching those findings and opinion, and

        (ii) anything on which any such examination, measurement, test or experiment was carried out.

(4) Unless the parties otherwise agree or the court directs, a party may not—

    (a) introduce expert evidence if that party has not complied with paragraph (3); or

    (b) introduce in evidence an expert report if the expert does not give evidence in person.

*[Note. The Practice Direction sets out a form of notice for use in connection with this rule.*

*A party who accepts another party's expert's conclusions may admit them as fact under section 10 of the Criminal Justice Act 1967[5].*

*Under section 81 of the Police and Criminal Evidence Act 1984[6], and under section 20(3) of the Criminal Procedure and Investigations Act 1996[7], Criminal Procedure Rules may require the disclosure of expert evidence before it is introduced as part of a party's case and prohibit its introduction without the court's permission, if it was not disclosed as required.*

*Evidence of facts which are material to the opinions expressed in an expert report, or upon which those opinions are based, may be admissible if (i) they are within the expert witness' own direct knowledge, or (ii) as hearsay evidence within the meaning of section 114 of the Criminal Justice Act 2003[8]: see also rule 19.4(b), (c), (d) and (e). Evidence of examinations etc. on which an expert relies may be admissible under section 127 of the 2003 Act[9]. Part 20 contains rules about the introduction of hearsay evidence under other provisions of that Act.*

*Under section 30 of the Criminal Justice Act 1988[10], an expert report is admissible in evidence whether or not the person who made it gives oral evidence, but if that person does not give oral evidence then the report is admissible only with the court's permission.]*

### Content of expert's report

**R19.4**

**19.4** Where rule 19.3(3) applies, an expert's report must—

    (a) give details of the expert's qualifications, relevant experience and accreditation;

    (b) give details of any literature or other information which the expert has relied on in making the report;

    (c) contain a statement setting out the substance of all facts given to the expert which are material to the opinions expressed in the report, or upon which those opinions are based;

    (d) make clear which of the facts stated in the report are within the expert's own knowledge;

    (e) where the expert has based an opinion or inference on a representation of fact or opinion made by another person for the purposes of criminal proceedings (for example, as to the outcome of an examination, measurement, test or experiment)—

        (i) identify the person who made that representation to the expert,

        (ii) give the qualifications, relevant experience and any accreditation of that person, and

[5] 1967 c. 80.

[6] 1984 c. 60; section 81 was amended by section 109(1) of, and paragraph 286 of Schedule 8 to, the Courts Act 2003 (c. 39).

[7] 1996 c. 25; section 20(3) was amended by section 109(1) of, and paragraph 378 of Schedule 8 to, the Courts Act 2003 (c. 39).

[8] 2003 c. 44

[9] 2003 c. 44; section 127 was amended by article 3 of, and paragraphs 45 and 50 of the Schedule to, S.I. 2004/2035.

[10] 1988 c. 33; section 30 was amended by section 47 of, and paragraph 32 of Schedule 1 to, the Criminal Procedure and Investigations Act 1996 (c. 25) and paragraph 60 of Schedule 3 and Schedule 37 to the Criminal Justice Act 2003 (c. 44).

(iii) certify that that person had personal knowledge of the matters stated in that representation;

(f) where there is a range of opinion on the matters dealt with in the report—
(i) summarise the range of opinion, and
(ii) give reasons for the expert's own opinion;

(g) if the expert is not able to give an opinion without qualification, state the qualification;

(h) include such information as the court may need to decide whether the expert's opinion is sufficiently reliable to be admissible as evidence;

(i) contain a summary of the conclusions reached;

(j) contain a statement that the expert understands an expert's duty to the court, and has complied and will continue to comply with that duty; and

(k) contain the same declaration of truth as a witness statement.

*[Note. Part 16 contains rules about written witness statements. Declarations of truth in witness statements are required by section 9 of the Criminal Justice Act 1967[11].]*

**R19.5**    **Expert to be informed of service of report**

19.5   A party who serves on another party or on the court a report by an expert must, at once, inform that expert of that fact.

**R19.6**    **Pre-hearing discussion of expert evidence**

19.6   (1) This rule applies where more than one party wants to introduce expert evidence.

(2) The court may direct the experts to—
(a) discuss the expert issues in the proceedings; and
(b) prepare a statement for the court of the matters on which they agree and disagree, giving their reasons.

(3) Except for that statement, the content of that discussion must not be referred to without the court's permission.

(4) A party may not introduce expert evidence without the court's permission if the expert has not complied with a direction under this rule.

*[Note. At a pre-trial hearing, a court may make binding rulings about the admissibility of evidence and about questions of law under section 9 of the Criminal Justice Act 1987[12]; sections 31 and 40 of the Criminal Procedure and Investigations Act 1996[13]; and section 8A of the Magistrates' Courts Act 1980[14].]*

**R19.7**    **Court's power to direct that evidence is to be given by a single joint expert**

19.7   (1) Where more than one defendant wants to introduce expert evidence on an issue at trial, the court may direct that the evidence on that issue is to be given by one expert only.

(2) Where the co-defendants cannot agree who should be the expert, the court may—
(a) select the expert from a list prepared or identified by them; or
(b) direct that the expert be selected in another way.

---

[11] 1967 c. 80; section 9 was amended by section 56 of, and paragraph 49 of Schedule 8 to, the Courts Act 1971 (c. 23), section 168 of, and paragraph 6 of Schedule 9 to, the Criminal Justice and Public Order Act 1994 (c. 33), section 69 of the Criminal Procedure and Investigations Act 1996 (c. 25), regulation 9 of, and paragraph 4 of Schedule 5 to, S.I. 2001/1090, paragraph 43 of Schedule 3 and Part 4 of Schedule 37 to the Criminal Justice Act 2003 (c. 44), section 26 of, and paragraph 7 of Schedule 2 to, the Armed Forces Act 2011 (c. 18) and section 80 of the Deregulation Act 2015 (c. 20). It is further amended by section 72 of, and paragraph 55 of Schedule 5 to, the Children and Young Persons Act 1969 (c. 54) and section 65 of, and paragraph 1 of Schedule 4 to, the Courts Act 2003 (c. 39), with effect from dates to be appointed.

[12] 1987 c. 38; section 9 was amended by section 170 of, and Schedule 16 to, the Criminal Justice Act 1988 (c. 33), section 6 of the Criminal Justice Act 1993 (c. 36), sections 72, 74 and 80 of, and paragraph 3 of Schedule 3 and Schedule 5 to, the Criminal Procedure and Investigations Act 1996 (c. 25), sections 45 and 310 of, and paragraphs 18, 52 and 54 of Schedule 36 and Part 3 of Schedule 37 to, the Criminal Justice Act 2003 (c. 44), article 3 of, and paragraphs 21 and 23 of S.I. 2004/2035, section 59 of, and paragraph 1 of Schedule 11 to, the Constitutional Reform Act 2005 (c. 4) and Part 10 of Schedule 10 to the Protection of Freedoms Act 2012 (c. 9). The amendment made by section 45 of the Criminal Justice Act 2003 (c. 44) is in force for certain purposes; for remaining purposes it has effect from a date to be appointed.

[13] 1996 c. 25; section 31 was amended by sections 310, 331 and 332 of, and paragraphs 20, 36, 65 and 67 of Schedule 36 and Schedule 37 to, the Criminal Justice Act 2003 (c. 44).

[14] 1980 c. 43; section 8A was inserted by section 45 of, and Schedule 3 to, the Courts Act 2003 (c. 39) and amended by SI 2006/2493 and paragraphs 12 and 14 of Schedule 5 to the Legal Aid, Sentencing and Punishment of Offenders Act 2012 (c. 10).

**Instructions to a single joint expert**                                        **R19.8**

**19.8** (1) Where the court gives a direction under rule 19.7 for a single joint expert to be used, each of the co-defendants may give instructions to the expert.

(2) A co-defendant who gives instructions to the expert must, at the same time, send a copy of the instructions to each other co-defendant.

(3) The court may give directions about—
  (a) the payment of the expert's fees and expenses; and
  (b) any examination, measurement, test or experiment which the expert wishes to carry out.

(4) The court may, before an expert is instructed, limit the amount that can be paid by way of fees and expenses to the expert.

(5) Unless the court otherwise directs, the instructing co-defendants are jointly and severally liable for the payment of the expert's fees and expenses.

**Application to withhold information from another party**                         **R19.9**

**19.9** (1) This rule applies where—
  (a) a party introduces expert evidence under rule 19.3(3);
  (b) the evidence omits information which it otherwise might include because the party introducing it thinks that that information ought not be revealed to another party; and
  (c) the party introducing the evidence wants the court to decide whether it would be in the public interest to withhold that information.

(2) The party who wants to introduce the evidence must—
  (a) apply for such a decision; and
  (b) serve the application on—
    (i) the court officer, and
    (ii) the other party, but only to the extent that serving it would not reveal what the applicant thinks ought to be withheld.

(3) The application must—
  (a) identify the information;
  (b) explain why the applicant thinks that it would be in the public interest to withhold it; and
  (c) omit from the part of the application that is served on the other party anything that would reveal what the applicant thinks ought to be withheld.

(4) Where the applicant serves only part of the application on the other party, the applicant must—
  (a) mark the other part, to show that it is only for the court; and
  (b) in that other part, explain why the applicant has withheld it from the other party.

(5) The court may—
  (a) direct the applicant to serve on the other party any part of the application which has been withheld; and
  (b) determine the application at a hearing or without a hearing.

(6) Any hearing of an application to which this rule applies—
  (a) must be in private, unless the court otherwise directs; and
  (b) if the court so directs, may be, wholly or in part, in the absence of the party from whom information has been withheld.

(7) At any hearing of an application to which this rule applies—
  (a) the general rule is that the court must consider, in the following sequence—
    (i) representations first by the applicant and then by the other party, in both parties' presence, and then
    (ii) further representations by the applicant, in the absence of the party from whom information has been withheld; but
  (b) the court may direct other arrangements for the hearing.

**Court's power to vary requirements under this Part**                            **R19.10**

**19.10** (1) The court may extend (even after it has expired) a time limit under this Part.

(2) A party who wants an extension of time must—
  (a) apply when serving the report, summary or notice for which it is required; and
  (b) explain the delay.

CRIMINAL PRACTICE DIRECTIONS   PART 19   EXPERT EVIDENCE

**CPD.19A**   **CPD V Evidence 19A: Expert Evidence**

19A.1   Expert opinion evidence is admissible in criminal proceedings at common law if, in summary, (i) it is relevant to a matter in issue in the proceedings; (ii) it is needed to provide the court with information likely to be outside the court's own knowledge and experience; and (iii) the witness is competent to give that opinion.

19A.2   Legislation relevant to the introduction and admissibility of such evidence includes section 30 of the Criminal Justice Act 1988, which provides that an expert report shall be admissible as evidence in criminal proceedings whether or not the person making it gives oral evidence, but that if he or she does not give oral evidence then the report is admissible only with the leave of the court; and CrimPR Part 19, which in exercise of the powers conferred by section 81 of the Police and Criminal Evidence Act 1984 and section 20 of the Criminal Procedure and Investigations Act 1996 requires the service of expert evidence in advance of trial in the terms required by those rules.

19A.3   In the Law Commission report entitled 'Expert Evidence in Criminal Proceedings in England and Wales', report number 325, published in March, 2011, the Commission recommended a statutory test for the admissibility of expert evidence. However, in its response the government declined to legislate. The common law, therefore, remains the source of the criteria by reference to which the court must assess the admissibility and weight of such evidence; and CrimPR 19.4 lists those matters with which an expert's report must deal, so that the court can conduct an adequate such assessment.

19A.4   In its judgment in *R v Dlugosz and Others* [2013] EWCA Crim 2, the Court of Appeal observed (at paragraph 11): 'It is essential to recall the principle which is applicable, namely in determining the issue of admissibility, the court must be satisfied that there is a sufficiently reliable scientific basis for the evidence to be admitted. If there is then the court leaves the opposing views to be tested before the jury.' Nothing at common law precludes assessment by the court of the reliability of an expert opinion by reference to substantially similar factors to those the Law Commission recommended as conditions of admissibility, and courts are encouraged actively to enquire into such factors.

19A.5   Therefore factors which the court may take into account in determining the reliability of expert opinion, and especially of expert scientific opinion, include:

(a)   the extent and quality of the data on which the expert's opinion is based, and the validity of the methods by which they were obtained;

(b)   if the expert's opinion relies on an inference from any findings, whether the opinion properly explains how safe or unsafe the inference is (whether by reference to statistical significance or in other appropriate terms);

(c)   if the expert's opinion relies on the results of the use of any method (for instance, a test, measurement or survey), whether the opinion takes proper account of matters, such as the degree of precision or margin of uncertainty, affecting the accuracy or reliability of those results;

(d)   the extent to which any material upon which the expert's opinion is based has been reviewed by others with relevant expertise (for instance, in peer-reviewed publications), and the views of those others on that material;

(e)   the extent to which the expert's opinion is based on material falling outside the expert's own field of expertise;

(f)   the completeness of the information which was available to the expert, and whether the expert took account of all relevant information in arriving at the opinion (including information as to the context of any facts to which the opinion relates);

(g)   if there is a range of expert opinion on the matter in question, where in the range the expert's own opinion lies and whether the expert's preference has been properly explained; and

(h)   whether the expert's methods followed established practice in the field and, if they did not, whether the reason for the divergence has been properly explained.

19A.6   In addition, in considering reliability, and especially the reliability of expert scientific opinion, the court should be astute to identify potential flaws in such opinion which detract from its reliability, such as:

(a)   being based on a hypothesis which has not been subjected to sufficient scrutiny (including, where appropriate, experimental or other testing), or which has failed to stand up to scrutiny;

(b)   being based on an unjustifiable assumption;

(c)   being based on flawed data;

(d)   relying on an examination, technique, method or process which was not properly carried out or applied, or was not appropriate for use in the particular case; or

(e)   relying on an inference or conclusion which has not been properly reached.

19A.7  To assist in the assessment described above, CrimPR 19.3(3)(c) requires a party who introduces expert evidence to give notice of anything of which that party is aware which might reasonably be thought capable of undermining the reliability of the expert's opinion, or detracting from the credibility or impartiality of the expert; and CrimPR 19.2(3)(d) requires the expert to disclose to that party any such matter of which the expert is aware. Examples of matters that should be disclosed pursuant to those rules include (this is not a comprehensive list), both in relation to the expert and in relation to any corporation or other body with which the expert works, as an employee or in any other capacity:

(a) any fee arrangement under which the amount or payment of the expert's fees is in any way dependent on the outcome of the case (see also the declaration required by paragraph 19B.1 of these directions);

(b) any conflict of interest of any kind, other than a potential conflict disclosed in the expert's report (see also the declaration required by paragraph 19B.1 of these directions);

(c) adverse judicial comment;

(d) any case in which an appeal has been allowed by reason of a deficiency in the expert's evidence;

(e) any adverse finding, disciplinary proceedings or other criticism by a professional, regulatory or registration body or authority, including the Forensic Science Regulator;

(f) any such adverse finding or disciplinary proceedings against, or other such criticism of, others associated with the corporation or other body with which the expert works which calls into question the quality of that corporation's or body's work generally;

(g) conviction of a criminal offence in circumstances that suggest:

   (i) a lack of respect for, or understanding of, the interests of the criminal justice system (for example, perjury; acts perverting or tending to pervert the course of public justice),

   (ii) dishonesty (for example, theft or fraud), or

   (iii) a lack of personal integrity (for example, corruption or a sexual offence);

(h) lack of an accreditation or other commitment to prescribed standards where that might be expected;

(i) a history of failure or poor performance in quality or proficiency assessments;

(j) a history of lax or inadequate scientific methods;

(k) a history of failure to observe recognised standards in the expert's area of expertise;

(l) a history of failure to adhere to the standards expected of an expert witness in the criminal justice system.

19A.8  In a case in which an expert, or a corporation or body with which the expert works, has been criticised without a full investigation, for example by adverse comment in the course of a judgment, it would be reasonable to expect those criticised to supply information about the conduct and conclusions of any independent investigation into the incident, and to explain what steps, if any, have been taken to address the criticism.

19A.9  The rules require disclosure of that of which the expert, or the party who introduces the expert evidence, is aware. The rules do not require persistent or disproportionate enquiry, and courts will recognise that there may be occasions on which neither the expert nor the party has been made aware of criticism. Nevertheless, where matters ostensibly within the scope of the disclosure obligations come to the attention of the court without their disclosure by the party who introduces the evidence then that party, and the expert, should expect a searching examination of the circumstances by the court; and, subject to what emerges, the court may exercise its power under section 81 of the Police and Criminal Evidence Act 1984 or section 20 of the Criminal Procedure and Investigations Act 1996 to exclude the expert evidence.

**CPD V Evidence 19B: Statements of Understanding and Declarations of Truth in Expert Reports**

19B.1  The statement and declaration required by CrimPR 19.4(j), (k) should be in the following terms, or in terms substantially the same as these:

'I (name) DECLARE THAT:

1. I understand that my duty is to help the court to achieve the overriding objective by giving independent assistance by way of objective, unbiased opinion on matters within my expertise, both in preparing reports and giving oral evidence. I understand that this duty overrides any obligation to the party by whom I am engaged or the person who has paid or is liable to pay me. I confirm that I have complied with and will continue to comply with that duty.

2. I confirm that I have not entered into any arrangement where the amount or payment of my fees is in any way dependent on the outcome of the case.

**CPD.19B**

3.  I know of no conflict of interest of any kind, other than any which I have disclosed in my report.
4.  I do not consider that any interest which I have disclosed affects my suitability as an expert witness on any issues on which I have given evidence.
5.  I will advise the party by whom I am instructed if, between the date of my report and the trial, there is any change in circumstances which affect my answers to points 3 and 4 above.
6.  I have shown the sources of all information I have used.
7.  I have exercised reasonable care and skill in order to be accurate and complete in preparing this report.
8.  I have endeavoured to include in my report those matters, of which I have knowledge or of which I have been made aware, that might adversely affect the validity of my opinion. I have clearly stated any qualifications to my opinion.
9.  I have not, without forming an independent view, included or excluded anything which has been suggested to me by others including my instructing lawyers.
10. I will notify those instructing me immediately and confirm in writing if for any reason my existing report requires any correction or qualification.
11. I understand that:
    (a)  my report will form the evidence to be given under oath or affirmation;
    (b)  the court may at any stage direct a discussion to take place between experts;
    (c)  the court may direct that, following a discussion between the experts, a statement should be prepared showing those issues which are agreed and those issues which are not agreed, together with the reasons;
    (d)  I may be required to attend court to be cross-examined on my report by a cross-examiner assisted by an expert.
    (e)  I am likely to be the subject of public adverse criticism by the judge if the Court concludes that I have not taken reasonable care in trying to meet the standards set out above.
12. I have read Part 19 of the Criminal Procedure Rules and I have complied with its requirements.
13. I confirm that I have acted in accordance with the code of practice or conduct for experts of my discipline, namely [*identify the code*].
14. [For Experts instructed by the Prosecution only] I confirm that I have read guidance contained in a booklet known as *Disclosure: Experts' Evidence and Unused Material* which details my role and documents my responsibilities, in relation to revelation as an expert witness. I have followed the guidance and recognise the continuing nature of my responsibilities of disclosure. In accordance with my duties of disclosure, as documented in the guidance booklet, I confirm that:
    (a)  I have complied with my duties to record, retain and reveal material in accordance with the Criminal Procedure and Investigations Act 1996, as amended;
    (b)  I have compiled an Index of all material. I will ensure that the Index is updated in the event I am provided with or generate additional material;
    (c)  in the event my opinion changes on any material issue, I will inform the investigating officer, as soon as reasonably practicable and give reasons.

    I confirm that the contents of this report are true to the best of my knowledge and belief and that I make this report knowing that, if it is tendered in evidence, I would be liable to prosecution if I have wilfully stated anything which I know to be false or that I do not believe to be true.'

### CPD V Evidence 19C: Pre-Hearing Discussion of Expert Evidence

CPD.19C    19C.1.  To assist the court in the preparation of the case for trial, parties must consider, with their experts, at an early stage, whether there is likely to be any useful purpose in holding an experts' discussion and, if so, when. Under CrimPR 19.6 such pre-trial discussions are not compulsory unless directed by the court. However, such a direction is listed in the magistrates' courts Preparation for Effective Trial form and in the Crown Court Plea and Trial Preparation Hearing form as one to be given by default, and therefore the court can be expected to give such a direction in every case unless persuaded otherwise. Those standard directions include a timetable to which the parties must adhere unless it is varied.

**19C.2.** The purpose of discussions between experts is to agree and narrow issues and in particular to identify:

(a) the extent of the agreement between them;

(b) the points of and short reasons for any disagreement;

(c) action, if any, which may be taken to resolve any outstanding points of disagreement; and

(d) any further material issues not raised and the extent to which these issues are agreed.

**19C.3.** Where the experts are to meet, that meeting conveniently may be conducted by telephone conference or live link; and experts' meetings always should be conducted by those means where that will avoid unnecessary delay and expense.

**19C.4.** Where the experts are to meet, the parties must discuss and if possible agree whether an agenda is necessary, and if so attempt to agree one that helps the experts to focus on the issues which need to be discussed. The agenda must not be in the form of leading questions or hostile in tone. The experts may not be required to avoid reaching agreement, or to defer reaching agreement, on any matter within the experts' competence.

**19C.5.** If the legal representatives do attend:

(a) they should not normally intervene in the discussion, except to answer questions put to them by the experts or to advise on the law; and

(b) the experts may if they so wish hold part of their discussions in the absence of the legal representatives.

**19C.6.** A statement must be prepared by the experts dealing with paragraphs 19C.2(a)–(d) above. Individual copies of the statements must be signed or otherwise authenticated by the experts, in manuscript or by electronic means, at the conclusion of the discussion, or as soon thereafter as practicable, and in any event within 5 business days. Copies of the statements must be provided to the parties no later than 10 business days after signing.

**19C.7.** Experts must give their own opinions to assist the court and do not require the authority of the parties to sign a joint statement. The joint statement should include a brief re-statement that the experts recognise their duties, which should be in the following terms, or in terms substantially the same as these:

'We each DECLARE THAT:

1.   We individually here re-state the Expert's Declaration contained in our respective reports that we understand our overriding duties to the court, have complied with them and will continue to do so.

2.   We have neither jointly nor individually been instructed to, nor has it been suggested that we should, avoid reaching agreement, or defer reaching agreement, on any matter within our competence.'

**19C.8.** If an expert significantly alters an opinion, the joint statement must include a note or addendum by that expert explaining the change of opinion.

CRIMINAL PROCEDURE RULES    PART 20    HEARSAY EVIDENCE

**When this Part applies**                                                          **R20.1**

**20.1**    This Part applies in a magistrates' court and in the Crown Court where a party wants to introduce hearsay evidence, within the meaning of section 114 of the Criminal Justice Act 2003[1]

*[Note. Under section 114 of the Criminal Justice Act 2003, a statement not made in oral evidence is admissible as evidence of any matter stated if—*

*(a)   a statutory provision makes it admissible;*

*(b)   a rule of law preserved by section 118 makes it admissible;*

*(c)   the parties agree to it being admissible; or*

*(d)   it is in the interests of justice for it to be admissible.*

*Under section 115 of the Act—*

*(a)   a "statement" means any representation of fact or opinion, by any means, and includes a representation in pictorial form; and*

*(b)   a "matter stated" is something stated by someone with the apparent purpose of—*

*(c)   causing another person to believe it, or*

*(d)   causing another person, or a machine, to act or operate on the basis that the matter is as stated.]*

Criminal Procedure Rules and Criminal Practice Directions

---

[1]  2003 c. 44.

**R20.2**    **Notice to introduce hearsay evidence**

20.2  (1)  This rule applies where a party wants to introduce hearsay evidence for admission under any of the following sections of the Criminal Justice Act 2003—

(a)  section 114(1)(d) (evidence admissible in the interests of justice);

(b)  section 116 (evidence where a witness is unavailable);

(c)  section 117(1)(c)[2] (evidence in a statement prepared for the purposes of criminal proceedings);

(d)  section 121 (multiple hearsay).

(2)  That party must—

(a)  serve notice on—

(i)  the court officer, and

(ii)  each other party;

(b)  in the notice—

(i)  identify the evidence that is hearsay,

(ii)  set out any facts on which that party relies to make the evidence admissible,

(iii)  explain how that party will prove those facts if another party disputes them, and

(iv)  explain why the evidence is admissible; and

(c)  attach to the notice any statement or other document containing the evidence that has not already been served.

(3)  A prosecutor who wants to introduce such evidence must serve the notice not more than—

(a)  20 business days after the defendant pleads not guilty, in a magistrates' court; or

(b)  10 business days after the defendant pleads not guilty, in the Crown Court.

(4)  A defendant who wants to introduce such evidence must serve the notice as soon as reasonably practicable.

(5)  A party entitled to receive a notice under this rule may waive that entitlement by so informing—

(a)  the party who would have served it; and

(b)  the court.

*[Note. The Practice Direction sets out a form of notice for use in connection with this rule.*

*The sections of the Criminal Justice Act 2003 listed in this rule set out the conditions on which hearsay evidence may be admitted under them.*

*If notice is not given as this rule requires, then under section 132(5) of the 2003 Act—*

*(a)  the evidence is not admissible without the court's permission;*

*(b)  if the court gives permission, it may draw such inferences as appear proper from the failure to give notice; and*

*(c)  the court may take the failure into account in exercising its powers to order costs.*

*This rule does not require notice of hearsay evidence that is admissible under any of the following sections of the 2003 Act—*

*(a)  section 117 (business and other documents), otherwise than as required by rule 20.2(1)(c);*

*(b)  section 118 (preservation of certain common law categories of admissibility);*

*(c)  section 119 (inconsistent statements);*

*(d)  section 120[3] (other previous statements of witness); or*

*(e)  section 127[4] (expert evidence: preparatory work): but see Part 19 for the procedure where a party wants to introduce such evidence.]*

**R20.3**    **Opposing the introduction of hearsay evidence**

20.3  (1)  This rule applies where a party objects to the introduction of hearsay evidence.

(2)  That party must—

(a)  apply to the court to determine the objection;

(b)  serve the application on—

---

[2]  2003 c. 44; section 117 was amended by regulation 4 of, and paragraph 8 of Schedule 3 to, S.I. 2017/730 and section 10 of the Crime (Overseas Production Orders) Act 2019 (c. 5).

[3]  2003 c. 44; section 120 was amended by sections 112 and 178 of, and Schedule 23 to, the Coroners and Justice Act 2009 (c. 25).

[4]  2003 c. 44; section 127 was amended by article 3 of, and paragraphs 45 and 50 of the Schedule to, S.I. 2004/2035.

        (i)   the court officer, and

        (ii)  each other party;

    (c)  serve the application as soon as reasonably practicable, and in any event not more than 10 business days after—

        (i)   service of notice to introduce the evidence under rule 20.2,

        (ii)  service of the evidence to which that party objects, if no notice is required by that rule, or

        (iii) the defendant pleads not guilty

        whichever of those events happens last; and

    (d)  in the application, explain—

        (i)   which, if any, facts set out in a notice under rule 20.2 that party disputes,

        (ii)  why the evidence is not admissible, and

        (iii) any other objection to the evidence.

(3)  The court—

    (a)  may determine an application—

        (i)   at a hearing, in public or in private, or

        (ii)  without a hearing;

    (b)  must not determine the application unless the party who served the notice—

        (i)   is present, or

        (ii)  has had a reasonable opportunity to respond;

    (c)  may adjourn the application; and

    (d)  may discharge or vary a determination where it can do so under—

        (i)   section 8B of the Magistrates' Courts Act 1980[5] (ruling at pre-trial hearing in a magistrates' court), or

        (ii)  section 9 of the Criminal Justice Act 1987[6], or section 31 or 40 of the Criminal Procedure and Investigations Act 1996[7] (ruling at preparatory or other pre-trial hearing in the Crown Court).

## Unopposed hearsay evidence

**R20.4**

20.4  (1)  This rule applies where—

    (a)  a party has served notice to introduce hearsay evidence under rule 20.2; and

    (b)  no other party has applied to the court to determine an objection to the introduction of the evidence.

    (2)  The court must treat the evidence as if it were admissible by agreement.

*[Note. Under section 132(4) of the Criminal Justice Act 2003, rules may provide that evidence is to be treated as admissible by agreement of the parties if notice to introduce that evidence has not been opposed.]*

## Court's power to vary requirements under this Part

**R20.5**

20.5  (1)  The court may—

    (a)  shorten or extend (even after it has expired) a time limit under this Part;

    (b)  allow an application or notice to be in a different form to one set out in the Practice Direction, or to be made or given orally; and

    (c)  dispense with the requirement for notice to introduce hearsay evidence.

    (2)  A party who wants an extension of time must—

    (a)  apply when serving the application or notice for which it is needed; and

    (b)  explain the delay.

---

[5] 1980 c. 43; section 8B was inserted by section 45 of, and Schedule 3 to, the Courts Act 2003 (c. 39) and amended by paragraph 51 of Schedule 3, and Part 4 of Schedule 37, to the Criminal Justice Act 2003 (c. 44).

[6] 1987 c. 38; section 9 was amended by section 170 of, and Schedule 16 to, the Criminal Justice Act 1988 (c. 33), section 6 of the Criminal Justice Act 1993 (c. 36), sections 72, 74 and 80 of, and paragraph 3 of Schedule 3 and Schedule 5 to, the Criminal Procedure and Investigations Act 1996 (c. 25), sections 45 and 310 of, and paragraphs 18, 52 and 54 of Schedule 36 and Part 3 of Schedule 37 to, the Criminal Justice Act 2003 (c. 44), article 3 of, and paragraphs 21 and 23 of S.I. 2004/2035, section 59 of, and paragraph 1 of Schedule 11 to, the Constitutional Reform Act 2005 (c. 4) and Part 10 of Schedule 10 to the Protection of Freedoms Act 2012 (c. 9). The amendment made by section 45 of the Criminal Justice Act 2003 (c. 44) is in force for certain purposes; for remaining purposes it has effect from a date to be appointed.

[7] 1996 c. 25; section 31 was amended by sections 310, 331 and 332 of, and paragraphs 20, 36, 65 and 67 of Schedule 36 and Schedule 37 to, the Criminal Justice Act 2003 (c. 44).

CRIMINAL PROCEDURE RULES    PART 21    EVIDENCE OF BAD CHARACTER

**R21.1**    **When this Part applies**

**21.1**    This Part applies in a magistrates' court and in the Crown Court where a party wants to introduce evidence of bad character within the meaning of section 98 of the Criminal Justice Act 2003[1]

*[Note. Under section 98 of the Criminal Justice Act 2003, evidence of a person's bad character means evidence of, or of a disposition towards, misconduct on that person's part, other than evidence that—*

*(a)  has to do with the alleged facts of the offence; or*

*(b)  is evidence of misconduct in connection with the investigation or prosecution.*

*Under section 100(1) of the Criminal Justice Act 2003, evidence of a non-defendant's bad character is admissible if—*

*(a)  it is important explanatory evidence;*

*(b)  it has substantial probative value in relation to a matter which—*

    *(i)  is a matter in issue in the proceedings, and*

    *(ii)  is of substantial importance in the context of the case as a whole; or*

*(c)  all parties to the proceedings agree to the evidence being admissible.*

*The section explains requirements (a) and (b). Unless the parties agree to the evidence being admissible, it may not be introduced without the court's permission.*

*Under section 101(1) of the Criminal Justice Act 2003, evidence of a defendant's bad character is admissible if—*

*(a)  all parties to the proceedings agree to the evidence being admissible;*

*(b)  the evidence is introduced by the defendant, or is given in answer to a question asked by the defendant in cross-examination which was intended to elicit that evidence;*

*(c)  it is important explanatory evidence;*

*(d)  it is relevant to an important matter in issue between the defendant and the prosecution;*

*(e)  it has substantial probative value in relation to an important matter in issue between the defendant and a co-defendant;*

*(f)  it is evidence to correct a false impression given by the defendant; or*

*(g)  the defendant has made an attack on another person's character.*

*Sections 102 to 106 of the Act supplement those requirements. The court must not admit evidence under (d) or (g) if, on an application by the defendant, the court concludes that to do so would be unfair.]*

**R21.2**    **Content of application or notice**

**21.2**    (1)  A party who wants to introduce evidence of bad character must—

    (a)  make an application under rule 21.3, where it is evidence of a non-defendant's bad character;

    (b)  give notice under rule 21.4, where it is evidence of a defendant's bad character.

  (2)  An application or notice must—

    (a)  set out the facts of the misconduct on which that party relies,

    (b)  explain how that party will prove those facts (whether by certificate of conviction, other official record, or other evidence), if another party disputes them, and

    (c)  explain why the evidence is admissible.

*[Note. The Practice Direction sets out forms of application and notice for use in connection with rules 21.3 and 21.4.*

*The fact that a person was convicted of an offence may be proved under—*

*(a)  section 73 of the Police and Criminal Evidence Act 1984[2] (conviction in the United Kingdom); or*

*(b)  section 7 of the Evidence Act 1851[3] (conviction outside the United Kingdom).*

*See also sections 117 and 118 of the Criminal Justice Act 2003 (admissibility of evidence contained in business and other documents).*

*Under section 10 of the Criminal Justice Act 1967[4], a party may admit a matter of fact.]*

---

[1]  2003 c. 44.
[2]  1984 c. 60; section 73 was amended by section 90(1) of, and paragraphs 125 and 128 of Schedule 13 to, the Access to Justice Act 1999 (c. 22) and paragraph 285 of Schedule 8 to, the Courts Act 2003 (c. 39).
[3]  1851 c. 99.
[4]  1967 c. 80.

**Application to introduce evidence of a non-defendant's bad character**    **R21.3**

21.3  (1)  This rule applies where a party wants to introduce evidence of the bad character of a person other than the defendant.

(2)  That party must serve an application to do so on—

(a)  the court officer; and

(b)  each other party.

(3)  The applicant must serve the application—

(a)  as soon as reasonably practicable; and in any event

(b)  not more than 10 business days after the prosecutor discloses material on which the application is based (if the prosecutor is not the applicant).

(4)  A party who objects to the introduction of the evidence must—

(a)  serve notice on—

(i)  the court officer, and

(ii)  each other party

not more than 10 business days after service of the application; and

(b)  in the notice explain, as applicable—

(i)  which, if any, facts of the misconduct set out in the application that party disputes,

(ii)  what, if any, facts of the misconduct that party admits instead,

(iii)  why the evidence is not admissible, and

(iv)  any other objection to the application.

(5)  The court—

(a)  may determine an application—

(i)  at a hearing, in public or in private, or

(ii)  without a hearing;

(b)  must not determine the application unless each party other than the applicant—

(i)  is present, or

(ii)  has had at least 10 business days in which to serve a notice of objection;

(c)  may adjourn the application; and

(d)  may discharge or vary a determination where it can do so under—

(i)  section 8B of the Magistrates' Courts Act 1980[5] (ruling at pre-trial hearing in a magistrates' court), or

(ii)  section 9 of the Criminal Justice Act 1987[6], or section 31 or 40 of the Criminal Procedure and Investigations Act 1996[7] (ruling at preparatory or other pre-trial hearing in the Crown Court).

*[Note. The Practice Direction sets out a form of application for use in connection with this rule.*

*See also rule 21.5 (reasons for decisions must be given in public).]*

**Notice to introduce evidence of a defendant's bad character**    **R21.4**

21.4  (1)  This rule applies where a party wants to introduce evidence of a defendant's bad character.

(2)  A prosecutor or co-defendant who wants to introduce such evidence must serve notice on—

(a)  the court officer; and

(b)  each other party.

(3)  A prosecutor must serve any such notice not more than—

(a)  20 business days after the defendant pleads not guilty, in a magistrates' court; or

(b)  10 business days after the defendant pleads not guilty, in the Crown Court.

(4)  A co-defendant who wants to introduce such evidence must serve the notice—

(a)  as soon as reasonably practicable; and in any event

(b)  not more than 10 business days after the prosecutor discloses material on which the notice is based.

(5)  A party who objects to the introduction of the evidence identified by such a notice must—

(a)  apply to the court to determine the objection;

---

[5]  1980 c. 43; section 8B was inserted by section 45 of, and Schedule 3 to, the Courts Act 2003 (c. 39) and amended by paragraph 51 of Schedule 3, and Part 4 of Schedule 37, to the Criminal Justice Act 2003 (c. 44).

[6]  1987 c. 38; section 9 was amended by section 170 of, and Schedule 16 to, the Criminal Justice Act 1988 (c. 33), section 6 of the Criminal Justice Act 1993 (c. 36), sections 72, 74 and 80 of, and paragraph 3 of Schedule 3 and Schedule 5 to, the Criminal Procedure and Investigations Act 1996 (c. 25), sections 45 and 310 of, and paragraphs 18, 52 and 54 of Schedule 36 and Part 3 of Schedule 37 to, the Criminal Justice Act 2003 (c. 44), article 3 of, and paragraphs 21 and 23 of S.I. 2004/2035, section 59 of, and paragraph 1 of Schedule 11 to, the Constitutional Reform Act 2005 (c. 4) and Part 10 of Schedule 10 to the Protection of Freedoms Act 2012 (c. 9). The amendment made by section 45 of the Criminal Justice Act 2003 (c. 44) is in force for certain purposes; for remaining purposes it has effect from a date to be appointed.

[7]  1996 c. 25; section 31 was amended by sections 310, 331 and 332 of, and paragraphs 20, 36, 65 and 67 of Schedule 36 and Schedule 37 to, the Criminal Justice Act 2003 (c. 44).

       (b)  serve the application on—
          (i)   the court officer, and
          (ii)  each other party
          not more than 10 business days after service of the notice; and
       (c)  in the application explain, as applicable—
          (i)   which, if any, facts of the misconduct set out in the notice that party disputes,
          (ii)  what, if any, facts of the misconduct that party admits instead,
          (iii) why the evidence is not admissible,
          (iv) why it would be unfair to admit the evidence, and
          (v)  any other objection to the notice.
  (6)  The court—
       (a)  may determine such an application—
          (i)   at a hearing, in public or in private, or
          (ii)  without a hearing;
       (b)  must not determine the application unless the party who served the notice—
          (i)   is present, or
          (ii)  has had a reasonable opportunity to respond;
       (c)  may adjourn the application; and
       (d)  may discharge or vary a determination where it can do so under—
          (i)   section 8B of the Magistrates' Courts Act 1980 (ruling at pre-trial hearing in a magistrates' court), or
          (ii)  section 9 of the Criminal Justice Act 1987, or section 31 or 40 of the Criminal Procedure and Investigations Act 1996 (ruling at preparatory or other pre-trial hearing in the Crown Court).
  (7)  A party entitled to receive such a notice may waive that entitlement by so informing—
       (a)  the party who would have served it; and
       (b)  the court.
  (8)  A defendant who wants to introduce evidence of his or her own bad character must—
       (a)  give notice, in writing or orally—
          (i)   as soon as reasonably practicable, and in any event
          (ii)  before the evidence is introduced, either by the defendant or in reply to a question asked by the defendant of another party's witness in order to obtain that evidence; and
       (b)  in the Crown Court, at the same time give notice (in writing, or orally) of any direction about the defendant's character that the defendant wants the court to give the jury under rule 25.14 (Directions to the jury and taking the verdict).

*[Note. The Practice Direction sets out a form of notice for use in connection with this rule.*

*See also rule 21.5 (reasons for decisions must be given in public).*

*If notice is not given as this rule requires, then under section 111(4) of the Criminal Justice Act 2003 the court may take the failure into account in exercising its powers to order costs.]*

## R21.5   Reasons for decisions

    **21.5**   The court must announce at a hearing in public (but in the absence of the jury, if there is one) the reasons for a decision—
       (a)  to admit evidence as evidence of bad character, or to refuse to do so; or
       (b)  to direct an acquittal or a retrial under section 107 of the Criminal Justice Act 2003.

*[Note. See section 110 of the Criminal Justice Act 2003.]*

## R21.6   Court's power to vary requirements under this Part

    **21.6**  (1)  The court may—
       (a)  shorten or extend (even after it has expired) a time limit under this Part;
       (b)  allow an application or notice to be in a different form to one set out in the Practice Direction, or to be made or given orally; and
       (c)  dispense with a requirement for notice to introduce evidence of a defendant's bad character.
    (2)  A party who wants an extension of time must—
       (a)  apply when serving the application or notice for which it is needed; and
       (b)  explain the delay.

CRIMINAL PRACTICE DIRECTIONS   PART 21   EVIDENCE OF BAD CHARACTER

## CPD V Evidence 21A: Spent Convictions

CPD.21A

21A.1   The effect of section 4(1) of the Rehabilitation of Offenders Act 1974 is that a person who has become a rehabilitated person for the purpose of the Act in respect of a conviction (known as a 'spent' conviction) shall be treated for all purposes in law as a person who has not committed, or been charged with or prosecuted for, or convicted of or sentenced for, the offence or offences which were the subject of that conviction.

21A.2   Section 4(1) of the 1974 Act does not apply, however, to evidence given in criminal proceedings: section 7(2)(a). During the trial of a criminal charge, reference to previous convictions (and therefore to spent convictions) can arise in a number of ways. The most common is when a bad character application is made under the Criminal Justice Act 2003. When considering bad character applications under the 2003 Act, regard should always be had to the general principles of the Rehabilitation of Offenders Act 1974.

21A.3   On conviction, the court must be provided with a statement of the defendant's record for the purposes of sentence. The record supplied should contain all previous convictions, but those which are spent should, so far as practicable, be marked as such. No one should refer in open court to a spent conviction without the authority of the judge, which authority should not be given unless the interests of justice so require. When passing sentence the judge should make no reference to a spent conviction unless it is necessary to do so for the purpose of explaining the sentence to be passed.

CRIMINAL PROCEDURE RULES   PART 22   EVIDENCE OF A COMPLAINANT'S
PREVIOUS SEXUAL BEHAVIOUR

## When this Part applies

R22.1

22.1   This Part applies in a magistrates' court and in the Crown Court where—
  (i)  section 41 of the Youth Justice and Criminal Evidence Act 1999[1] prohibits the introduction of evidence or cross-examination about any sexual behaviour of the complainant of a sexual offence, and
  (ii)  despite that prohibition, a defendant wants to introduce such evidence or to cross-examine a witness about such behaviour.

*[Note. Section 41 of the Youth Justice and Criminal Evidence Act 1999 prohibits evidence or cross-examination about the sexual behaviour of a complainant of a sexual offence, subject to exceptions.*

*See also—*

  *(a)  section 42 of the 1999 Act[2], which among other things defines 'sexual behaviour' and 'sexual offence';*
  *(b)  section 34, which prohibits cross-examination by a defendant in person of the complainant of a sexual offence (Part 23 contains relevant rules).]*

## Exercise of court's powers

R22.2

22.2   The court—
  (a)  must determine an application under rule 22.4 (Application for permission to introduce evidence or cross-examine)—
    (i)  at a hearing in private, and
    (ii)  in the absence of the complainant;
  (b)  must not determine the application unless—
    (i)  each party other than the applicant is present, or has had at least 10 business days in which to make representations, and
    (ii)  the court is satisfied that it has been able to take adequate account of the complainant's rights;
  (c)  may adjourn the application; and
  (d)  may discharge or vary a determination where it can do so under—
    (i)  section 8B of the Magistrates' Courts Act 1980[3] (ruling at pre-trial hearing in a magistrates' court), or

---

[1]  1999 c. 23.
[2]  1999 c. 23; section 42 was amended by paragraph 73 of Schedule 3 and Schedule 37 to the Criminal Justice Act 2003 (c. 44).
[3]  1980 c. 43; section 8B was inserted by section 45 of, and Schedule 3 to, the Courts Act 2003 (c. 39) and amended by paragraph 51 of Schedule 3, and Part 4 of Schedule 37, to the Criminal Justice Act 2003 (c. 44).

(ii) section 9 of the Criminal Justice Act 1987[4], or section 31 or 40 of the Criminal Procedure and Investigations Act 1996[5] (ruling at preparatory or other pre-trial hearing in the Crown Court).

*[Note. See also section 43 of the Youth Justice and Criminal Evidence Act 1999[6], which among other things requires an application under section 41 of the Act to be heard in private and in the absence of the complainant.*

*At a pre-trial hearing a court may make binding rulings about the admissibility of evidence and about questions of law under sections 31 and 40 of the Criminal Procedure and Investigations Act 1996[7] and section 8A of the Magistrates' Courts Act 1980[8].]*

### R22.3 Decisions and reasons

22.3 (1) A prosecutor who wants to introduce the evidence of a complainant in respect of whom the court allows the introduction of evidence or cross-examination about any sexual behaviour must—

(a) inform the complainant of the court's decision as soon as reasonably practicable; and

(b) explain to the complainant any arrangements that as a result will be made for him or her to give evidence.

(2) The court must—

(a) promptly determine an application; and

(b) allow the prosecutor sufficient time to comply with the requirements of—

(i) paragraph (1), and

(ii) the code of practice issued under section 32 of the Domestic Violence, Crime and Victims Act 2004[9].

(3) The court must announce at a hearing in public—

(a) the reasons for a decision to allow or refuse an application under rule 22.4; and

(b) if it allows such an application, the extent to which evidence may be introduced or questions asked.

*[Note. Under section 43 of the Youth Justice and Criminal Evidence Act 1999—*

*(a) the reasons for the court's decision on an application must be given in open court; and*

*(b) the court must state in open court the extent to which evidence may be introduced or questions asked.]*

### R22.4 Application for permission to introduce evidence or cross-examine

22.4. (1) A defendant who wants to introduce evidence or cross-examine a witness about any sexual behaviour of the complainant must—

(a) serve an application for permission to do so on—

(i) the court officer, and

(ii) each other party; and

(b) serve the application—

(i) as soon as reasonably practicable after becoming aware of the grounds for doing so, and in any event

---

[4] 1987 c. 38; section 9 was amended by section 170 of, and Schedule 16 to, the Criminal Justice Act 1988 (c. 33), section 6 of the Criminal Justice Act 1993 (c. 36), sections 72, 74 and 80 of, and paragraph 3 of Schedule 3 and Schedule 5 to, the Criminal Procedure and Investigations Act 1996 (c. 25), sections 45 and 310 of, and paragraphs 18, 52 and 54 of Schedule 36 and Part 3 of Schedule 37 to, the Criminal Justice Act 2003 (c. 44), article 3 of, and paragraphs 21 and 23 of S.I. 2004/2035, section 59 of, and paragraph 1 of Schedule 11 to, the Constitutional Reform Act 2005 (c. 4) and Part 10 of Schedule 10 to the Protection of Freedoms Act 2012 (c. 9). The amendment made by section 45 of the Criminal Justice Act 2003 (c. 44) is in force for certain purposes; for remaining purposes it has effect from a date to be appointed.
[5] 1996 c. 25; section 31 was amended by sections 310, 331 and 332 of, and paragraphs 20, 36, 65 and 67 of Schedule 36 and Schedule 37 to, the Criminal Justice Act 2003 (c. 44).
[6] 1999 c. 23; section 43(3) was amended by section 109(1) of, and paragraph 384(g) of Schedule 8 to, the Courts Act 2003 (c. 39).
[7] 1996 c. 25; section 31 was amended by sections 310, 331 and 332 of, and paragraphs 20, 36, 65 and 67 of Schedule 36 and Schedule 37 to, the Criminal Justice Act 2003 (c. 44).
[8] 1980 c. 43; section 8A was inserted by section 45 of, and Schedule 3 to, the Courts Act 2003 (c. 39) and amended by SI 2006/2493 and paragraphs 12 and 14 of Schedule 5 to the Legal Aid, Sentencing and Punishment of Offenders Act 2012 (c. 10).
[9] 2004 c. 28; section 32 was amended by article 8 of, and paragraph 10 of the Schedule to, S.I. 2007/2128.

(ii)   not more than 10 business days after the prosecutor discloses material on which the application is based.
(2)   The application must—
   (a)   identify the issue to which the defendant says the complainant's sexual behaviour is relevant;
   (b)   give particulars of—
      (i)   any evidence that the defendant wants to introduce, and
      (ii)   any questions that the defendant wants to ask;
   (c)   identify the exception to the prohibition in section 41 of the Youth Justice and Criminal Evidence Act 1999 on which the defendant relies; and
   (d)   give the name and date of birth of any witness whose evidence about the complainant's sexual behaviour the defendant wants to introduce.

### Application containing information withheld from another party      R22.5

22.5. (1)   This rule applies where—
   (a)   an applicant serves an application under rule 22.4 (Application for permission to introduce evidence or cross-examine); and
   (b)   the application includes information that the applicant thinks ought not be revealed to another party.
(2)   The applicant must—
   (a)   omit that information from the part of the application that is served on that other party;
   (b)   mark the other part to show that, unless the court otherwise directs, it is only for the court; and
   (c)   in that other part, explain why the applicant has withheld that information from that other party.
(3)   If the court so directs, the hearing of an application to which this rule applies may be, wholly or in part, in the absence of a party from whom information has been withheld.
(4)   At the hearing of an application to which this rule applies—
   (a)   the general rule is that the court must consider, in the following sequence—
      (i)   representations first by the applicant and then by each other party, in all the parties' presence, and then
      (ii)   further representations by the applicant, in the absence of a party from whom information has been withheld; but
   (b)   the court may direct other arrangements for the hearing.

*[Note. See section 43(3)(c) of the Youth Justice and Criminal Evidence Act 1999.]*

### Representations in response      R22.6

22.6. (1)   This rule applies where a party wants to make representations about—
   (a)   an application under rule 22.4 (Application for permission to introduce evidence or cross-examine); or
   (b)   a proposed variation or discharge of a decision allowing such an application.
(2)   Such a party must—
   (a)   serve the representations on—
      (i)   the court officer, and
      (ii)   each other party; and
   (b)   do so not more than 10 business days after, as applicable—
      (i)   service of the application, or
      (ii)   notice of the proposal to vary or discharge.
(3)   Where representations include information that the person making them thinks ought not be revealed to another party, that person must—
   (a)   omit that information from the representations served on that other party;
   (b)   mark the information to show that, unless the court otherwise directs, it is only for the court; and
   (c)   with that information include an explanation of why it has been withheld from that other party.
(4)   Representations against an application under rule 22.4 must explain the grounds of objection.
(5)   Representations against the variation or discharge of a decision must explain why it should not be varied or discharged.

### Special measures, etc. for a witness      R22.7

22.7 (1)   This rule applies where the court allows an application under rule 22.4 (Application for permission to introduce evidence or cross-examine).

(2) Despite the time limits in rule 18.4 (Making an application for a direction or order)—

    (a) a party may apply for a special measures direction or for the variation of an existing special measures direction not more than 10 business days after the court's decision; and

    (b) the court may shorten the time for opposing that application.

(3) Where the court allows the cross-examination of a witness, the court must give directions for the appropriate treatment and questioning of that witness in accordance with rule 3.8(6) and (7) (setting ground rules for the conduct of questioning).

*[Note. Special measures to improve the quality of evidence given by certain witnesses may be directed by the court under section 19 of the Youth Justice and Criminal Evidence Act 1999 and varied under section 20[10]. An application for a special measures direction may be made by a party under Part 18 or the court may make a direction on its own initiative. Rule 18.13(2) sets the usual time limit (10 business days) for opposing a special measures application.]*

**R22.8**    **Court's power to vary requirements under this Part**

**22.8.**    The court may shorten or extend (even after it has expired) a time limit under this Part.

CRIMINAL PRACTICE DIRECTIONS    PART 22    EVIDENCE OF A COMPLAINANT'S PREVIOUS SEXUAL BEHAVIOUR

**CPD.22A**    **CPD V Evidence 22A: Use of Ground Rules Hearing when Dealing with S.41 Youth Justice and Criminal Evidence Act 1999 (YJCEA 1999) Evidence of Complainant's Previous Sexual Behaviour**

*The Application*

**22A.1**   When a defendant wishes to introduce evidence, or cross-examine about the previous sexual behaviour of the complainant, then it is imperative that the timetable and procedure as laid down in the Criminal Procedure Rules Part 22 is followed. The application must be submitted in writing as soon as reasonably practicable and not more than 14 days after the prosecutor has disclosed material on which the application is based. Should the prosecution wish to make any representations then these should be served on the court and other parties not more than 14 days after receiving the application.

**22A.2**   The application must clearly state the issue to which the defendant says the complainant's sexual behaviour is relevant and the reasons why it should be admitted. It must outline the evidence which the defendant wants to introduce and articulate the questions which it is proposed should be asked. The application must identify the statutory exception to the prohibition in section 41 YJCEA 1999 on which the defendant relies and give the name and date of birth of any witness whose evidence about the complainant's sexual behaviour the defendant wants to introduce.

*The Hearing*

**22A.3**   When determining the application, the judge should examine the questions with the usual level of scrutiny expected at a ground rules hearing. For each question that it is sought to put to a witness, or evidence it is sought to adduce, the defence should identify clearly for the judge the suggested relevance it has to an issue in the case. In order for the judge to rule on which evidence can be adduced or questions put, the defence must set out individual questions for the judge; merely identifying a topic is not sufficient for this type of application. The judge should make it clear that if the application is granted then no other questions on this topic will be allowed to be asked, unless with the express permission of the court.

**22A.4**   The application should be dealt with in private and in the absence of the complainant, but the judge must state in open court, without the jury or complainant present, the reasons for the decision, and if leave is granted, the extent of the questions or evidence that is allowed.

*Late applications*

**22A.5**   Late applications should be considered with particular scrutiny especially if there is a suggestion of tactical thinking behind the timing of the application and/or when the application is based on material that has been available for some time. If consideration of a late application has the potential to disrupt the timetabling of witnesses, then the judge will need to take account of the potential impact of delay upon a witness who is due to give evidence. If necessary, the judge may defer consideration of any such application until later in the trial.

**22A.6**   By analogy, following the approach adopted by the Court of Appeal in *R v Musone* [2007] 1 WLR 2467, the trial judge is entitled to refuse the application where (s)he is satisfied that the applicant is seeking to manipulate the court process so as to prevent the respondent from being able to

---

[10]   1999 c. 23; section 20(6) was amended by paragraph 384(a) of Schedule 8 to the Courts Act 2003 (c. 39).

prepare an adequate response. This may be the only remedy available to the court to ensure that the fairness of the trial is upheld and will be particularly relevant when the application is made on the day of trial.

**22A.7**   Where the application has been granted in good time before the trial, the complainant is entitled to be made aware that such evidence is part of the defence case.

*At the trial*

**22A.8**   Advocates should be reminded that the questioning must be conducted in an appropriate manner. Any aggressive, repetitive and oppressive questioning will be stopped by the judge. Judges should intervene and stop any attempts to refer to evidence that might have been adduced under section 41, but for which no leave has been given and/or should have formed the basis of a section 41 application, but did not do so. When evidence about the complainant's previous sexual behaviour is referred to without an application, the judge may be required to consider whether the impact of that happening is so prejudicial to the overall fairness of the trial that the trial should be stopped and a re-trial should be ordered, should the impact not be capable of being ameliorated by way of jury direction.

CRIMINAL PROCEDURE RULES   PART 23   RESTRICTION ON
CROSS-EXAMINATION BY A DEFENDANT

**General rules**

**When this Part applies**                                                                            R23.1

**23.1**   This Part applies where—
  (a)  a defendant may not cross-examine in person a witness because of section 34 or section 35 of the Youth Justice and Criminal Evidence Act 1999[1] (Complainants in proceedings for sexual offences; Child complainants and other child witnesses); or
  (b)  the court can prohibit a defendant from cross-examining in person a witness under section 36 of that Act[2] (Direction prohibiting accused from cross-examining particular witness).

*[Note. Under section 34 of the Youth Justice and Criminal Evidence Act 1999, no defendant charged with a sexual offence may cross-examine in person a witness who is the complainant, either—*

  *(a)  in connection with that offence; or*
  *(b)  in connection with any other offence (of whatever nature) with which that defendant is charged in the proceedings.*

*Under section 35 of the 1999 Act, no defendant charged with an offence listed in that section may cross-examine in person a protected witness, either—*

  *(a)  in connection with that offence; or*
  *(b)  in connection with any other offence (of whatever nature) with which that defendant is charged in the proceedings.*

*A 'protected witness' is one who—*

  *(a)  either is the complainant or is alleged to have been a witness to the commission of the offence; and*
  *(b)  either is a child, within the meaning of section 35, or is due to be cross-examined after giving evidence in chief—*
    *(i)   by means of a video recording made when the witness was a child, or*
    *(ii)  in any other way when the witness was a child.*

*Under section 36 of the 1999 Act, where neither section 34 nor section 35 applies the court may give a direction prohibiting the defendant from cross-examining, or further cross-examining, in person a witness, on application by the prosecutor or on the court's own initiative. See also rules 23.3 to 23.7.]*

**Appointment of advocate to cross-examine witness**                                                 R23.2

**23.2**   (1)   This rule applies where a defendant may not cross-examine in person a witness in consequence of—
    (a)  the prohibition imposed by section 34 or section 35 of the Youth Justice and Criminal Evidence Act 1999; or
    (b)  a prohibition imposed by the court under section 36 of the 1999 Act.

---

[1]  1999 c. 23; section 35 was amended by sections 139 and 140 of, and paragraph 41 of Schedule 6 and Schedule 7 to, the Sexual Offences Act 2003 (c. 42), section 148 of, and paragraphs 35 and 36 of Schedule 26 to, the Criminal Justice and Immigration Act 2008 (c. 4) and section 105 of the Coroners and Justice Act 2009 (c. 25).
[2]  1999 c. 23.

(2) The court must, as soon as practicable, explain in terms the defendant can understand (with help, if necessary)—

(a) the prohibition and its effect;

(b) that if the defendant will not be represented by a lawyer with a right of audience in the court for the purposes of the case then the defendant is entitled to arrange for such a lawyer to cross-examine the witness on his or her behalf;

(c) that the defendant must notify the court officer of the identity of any such lawyer, with details of how to contact that person, by no later than a date set by the court; and

(d) that if the defendant does not want to make such arrangements, or if the defendant gives no such notice by that date, then—

(i) the court must decide whether it is necessary in the interests of justice to appoint such a lawyer to cross-examine the witness in the defendant's interests, and

(ii) if the court decides that that is necessary, the court will appoint a lawyer chosen by the court who will not be responsible to the defendant.

(3) Having given those explanations, the court must—

(a) ask whether the defendant wants to arrange for a lawyer to cross-examine the witness, and set a date by when the defendant must notify the court officer of the identity of that lawyer if the answer to that question is 'yes'; and

(b) if the answer to that question is 'no', or if by the date set the defendant has given no such notice—

(i) decide whether it is necessary in the interests of justice for the witness to be cross-examined by an advocate appointed to represent the defendant's interests, and

(ii) if the court decides that that is necessary, give directions for the appointment of such an advocate.

(4) The court may give the explanations and ask the questions required by this rule—

(a) at a hearing, in public or in private; or

(b) without a hearing, by written notice to the defendant.

(5) The court may extend (even after it has expired) the time limit that it sets under paragraph (3)(a)—

(a) on application by the defendant; or

(b) on its own initiative.

(6) Paragraphs (7), (8), (9) and (10) apply where the court appoints an advocate.

(7) The directions that the court gives under paragraph (3)(b)(ii) must provide for the supply to the advocate of a copy of—

(a) all material served by one party on the other, whether before or after the advocate's appointment, to which applies—

(i) Part 8 (Initial details of the prosecution case),

(ii) in the Crown Court, rule 3.19 (service of prosecution evidence in a case sent for trial),

(iii) Part 16 (Written witness statements),

(iv) Part 19 (Expert evidence),

(v) Part 20 (Hearsay evidence),

(vi) Part 21 (Evidence of bad character), or

(vii) Part 22 (Evidence of a complainant's previous sexual behaviour);

(b) any material disclosed, given or served, whether before or after the advocate's appointment, which is—

(i) prosecution material disclosed to the defendant under section 3 (Initial duty of prosecutor to disclose) or section 7A (Continuing duty of prosecutor to disclose) of the Criminal Procedure and Investigations Act 1996[3],

(ii) a defence statement given by the defendant under section 5 (Compulsory disclosure by accused) or section 6 (Voluntary disclosure by accused) of the 1996 Act[4],

(iii) a defence witness notice given by the defendant under section 6C of that Act[5] (Notification of intention to call defence witnesses), or

---

[3] 1996 c. 25; section 3 was amended by section 82 of, and paragraph 7 of Schedule 4 to, the Regulation of Investigatory Powers Act 2000 (c. 23), section 32 of, and paragraphs 20 and 21 of Schedule 36 to, the Criminal Justice Act 2003 (c. 44) and section 271 of, and paragraph 39 of Schedule 10 to, the Investigatory Powers Act 2016 (c. 25). Section 7A was inserted by section 37 of the Criminal Justice Act 2003 (c. 44) and was amended by section 271 of, and paragraph 39 of Schedule 10 to, the Investigatory Powers Act 2016 (c. 25).

[4] 1996 c. 25; section 5 was amended by section 119 of, and paragraph 126 of Schedule 8 to, the Crime and Disorder Act 1998 (c. 37), in respect of certain proceedings only, and by section 33 of, and paragraph 66 of Schedule 3, paragraphs 20 and 23 of Schedule 36 and Parts 3 and 4 of Schedule 37 to, the Criminal Justice Act 2003 (c. 44). Section 6 was amended by paragraphs 20 and 24 of Schedule 36 and Part 3 of Schedule 37 to the Criminal Justice Act 2003 (c. 44).) For transitional provisions and savings see paragraph (2) of Schedule 2 to S.I. 2005/950.

[5] 1996 c. 25; section 6C was inserted by section 34 of the Criminal Justice Act 2003 (c. 44).

(iv) an application by the defendant under section 8 of that Act[6] (Application by accused for disclosure);

(c) any case management questionnaire prepared for the purposes of the trial or, as the case may be, the appeal; and

(d) all case management directions given by the court for the purposes of the trial or the appeal.

(8) Where the defendant has given a defence statement—

(a) section 8(2) of the Criminal Procedure and Investigations Act 1996 is modified to allow the advocate, as well as the defendant, to apply for an order for prosecution disclosure under that subsection if the advocate has reasonable cause to believe that there is prosecution material concerning the witness which is required by section 7A of the Act to be disclosed to the defendant and has not been; and

(b) rule 15.5 (Defendant's application for prosecution disclosure) applies to an application by the advocate as it does to an application by the defendant.

(9) Before receiving evidence the court must establish, with the active assistance of the parties and of the advocate, and in the absence of any jury in the Crown Court—

(a) what issues will be the subject of the advocate's cross-examination; and

(b) whether the court's permission is required for any proposed question, for example where Part 21 or Part 22 applies.

(10) The appointment terminates at the conclusion of the cross-examination of the witness.

*[Note. See section 38 of the Youth Justice and Criminal Evidence Act 1999[7]. Under section 38(8) the references in that section to a 'legal representative' are to a representative who is an advocate within the meaning of rule 2.2.*

*Under section 38(7) of the 1999 Act, where the court appoints an advocate Criminal Procedure Rules may apply with modifications any of the provisions of Part I of the Criminal Procedure and Investigations Act 1996. A summary of the disclosure requirements of the 1996 Act is at the end of Part 15 (Disclosure). Under section 5 of that Act, in the Crown Court the defendant must give a defence statement. Under section 6, in a magistrates' court the defendant may give such a statement but need not do so. Under section 6C, in the Crown Court and in magistrates' courts the defendant must give a defence witness notice indicating whether he or she intends to call any witnesses (other than him or herself) and, if so, identifying them. Under section 8 a defendant may apply for prosecution disclosure only if the defendant has given a defence statement.]*

### Application to prohibit cross-examination

**Exercise of court's powers**                                                                  **R23.3**

**23.3** (1) The court may decide whether to impose or discharge a prohibition against cross-examination under section 36 of the Youth Justice and Criminal Evidence Act 1999—

(a) at a hearing, in public or in private, or without a hearing; and

(b) in a party's absence, if that party—

(i) applied for the prohibition or discharge, or

(ii) has had at least 10 business days in which to make representations.

(2) The court must announce, at a hearing in public before the witness gives evidence, the reasons for a decision—

(a) to impose or discharge such a prohibition; or

(b) to refuse to do so.

*[Note. See section 37 of the Youth Justice and Criminal Evidence Act 1999[8].]*

**Application to prohibit cross-examination**                                                    **R23.4**

**23.4** (1) This rule applies where under section 36 of the Youth Justice and Criminal Evidence Act 1999 the prosecutor wants the court to prohibit the cross-examination of a witness by a defendant in person.

(2) The prosecutor must—

(a) apply in writing, as soon as reasonably practicable after becoming aware of the grounds for doing so; and

(b) serve the application on—

(i) the court officer,

(ii) the defendant who is the subject of the application, and

(iii) any other defendant, unless the court otherwise directs.

---

[6] 1996 c. 25; section 8 was amended by section 82 of, and paragraph 7 of Schedule 4 to, the Regulation of Investigatory Powers Act 2000 (c. 23), section 38 of the Criminal Justice Act 2003 (c. 44) and section 271 of, and paragraph 39 of Schedule 10 to, the Investigatory Powers Act 2016 (c. 25).
[7] 1999 c. 23; section 38 was amended by section 109 of, and paragraph 384(f) of Schedule 8 to, the Courts Act 2003 (c. 39).
[8] 1999 c. 23; section 37 was amended by section 109 of, and paragraph 384(e) of Schedule 8 to, the Courts Act 2003 (c. 39).

(3)　The application must—

(a)　report any views that the witness has expressed about whether he or she is content to be cross-examined by the defendant in person;

(b)　identify—

(i)　the nature of the questions likely to be asked, having regard to the issues in the case,

(ii)　any relevant behaviour of the defendant at any stage of the case, generally and in relation to the witness,

(iii)　any relationship, of any nature, between the witness and the defendant,

(iv)　any other defendant in the case who is subject to such a prohibition in respect of the witness, and

(v)　any special measures direction made in respect of the witness, or for which an application has been made;

(c)　explain why the quality of evidence given by the witness on cross-examination—

(i)　is likely to be diminished if no such prohibition is imposed, and

(ii)　would be likely to be improved if it were imposed; and

(d)　explain why it would not be contrary to the interests of justice to impose the prohibition.

*[Note. The Practice Direction sets out a form of application for use in connection with this rule.]*

**R23.5　Application to discharge prohibition imposed by the court**

**23.5**　(1)　A party who wants the court to discharge a prohibition against cross-examination which the court imposed under section 36 of the Youth Justice and Criminal Evidence Act 1999 must—

(a)　apply in writing, as soon as reasonably practicable after becoming aware of the grounds for doing so; and

(b)　serve the application on—

(i)　the court officer, and

(ii)　each other party.

(2)　The applicant must—

(a)　explain what material circumstances have changed since the prohibition was imposed; and

(b)　ask for a hearing, if the applicant wants one, and explain why it is needed.

*[Note. Under section 37 of the Youth Justice and Criminal Evidence Act 1999, the court can discharge a prohibition against cross-examination which it has imposed—*

*(a)　on application, if there has been a material change of circumstances; or*

*(b)　on its own initiative.]*

**R23.6　Application containing information withheld from another party**

**23.6**　(1)　This rule applies where—

(a)　an applicant serves an application for the court to impose a prohibition against cross-examination, or for the discharge of such a prohibition; and

(b)　the application includes information that the applicant thinks ought not be revealed to another party.

(2)　The applicant must—

(a)　omit that information from the part of the application that is served on that other party;

(b)　mark the other part to show that, unless the court otherwise directs, it is only for the court; and

(c)　in that other part, explain why the applicant has withheld that information from that other party.

(3)　Any hearing of an application to which this rule applies—

(a)　must be in private, unless the court otherwise directs; and

(b)　if the court so directs, may be, wholly or in part, in the absence of a party from whom information has been withheld.

(4)　At any hearing of an application to which this rule applies—

(a)　the general rule is that the court must consider, in the following sequence—

(i)　representations first by the applicant and then by each other party, in all the parties' presence, and then

(ii)　further representations by the applicant, in the absence of a party from whom information has been withheld; but

(b)　the court may direct other arrangements for the hearing.

*[Note. See section 37 of the Youth Justice and Criminal Evidence Act 1999.]*

ensure that they are in a position properly to conduct the cross examination. Their duties might include therefore applications to admit bad character of the witness and or applications for disclosure of material relevant to the cross examination. That is as far as one can go. All these matters must be entirely fact specific. The important thing to note is that the section 38 advocate must ensure that s/he performs his/her duties in accordance with the words of the statute. It means also that their appointment comes to an end, under section 38, at the conclusion of the cross examination, save to the extent that the court otherwise determines. Technically the lawyer no longer has a role in the proceedings thereafter. However, if the lawyer is prepared to stay and assist the defendant on a pro bono basis, I see nothing in the Act and no logical reason why the court should oblige them to leave. The advocate may well prove beneficial to the efficient and fair resolution of the proceedings. The aim of the legislation as I have said is simply to stop the accused cross examining the witness. It is not to prevent the person appointed to cross examine from playing any other part in the trial.'

**23A.9**    Advocates will be alert to, and courts should keep in mind, the extent of the remuneration available to a cross-examination advocate, in assessing the amount of which the court has only a limited role: see section 19(3) of the Prosecution of Offences Act 1985, which empowers the Lord Chancellor to make regulations authorising payments out of central funds 'to cover the proper fee or costs of a legal representative appointed under section 38(4) of the Youth Justice and Criminal Evidence Act 1999 and any expenses properly incurred in providing such a person with evidence or other material in connection with his appointment', and also sections 19(3ZA) and 20(1A)(d) of the 1985 Act and the Costs in Criminal Cases (General) Regulations 1986, as amended.

**23A.10**    Advocates and courts must be alert, too, to the possibility that were an advocate to agree to represent a defendant generally at trial, for no payment save that to which such regulations entitled him or her, then the statutory condition precedent for the appointment might be removed and the appointment in consequence withdrawn.

CRIMINAL PROCEDURE RULES    PART 24    TRIAL AND SENTENCE IN A MAGISTRATES' COURT

**When this Part applies**                                                                                         **R24.1**

**24.1**    (1)    This Part applies in a magistrates' court where the court tries a case or the defendant pleads guilty.

(2)    Where the defendant is under 18, in this Part—

(a)    a reference to convicting the defendant includes a reference to finding the defendant guilty of an offence; and

(b)    a reference to sentence includes a reference to an order made on a finding of guilt.

*[Note. A magistrates' court's powers to try an allegation of an offence are contained in section 2 of the Magistrates' Courts Act 1980[1]. In relation to a defendant under 18, they are contained in sections 45, 46 and 48 of the Children and Young Persons Act 1933[2].*

*See also section 18 of the Children and Young Persons Act 1963[3]), section 47 of the Crime and Disorder Act 1998[4] and section 27 of the Sentencing Act 2020[5].*

---

[1] 1980 c. 43; section 2 was substituted by section 44 of the Courts Act 2003 (c. 39) and amended by section 41 of, and paragraph 51 of Schedule 3 to, the Criminal Justice 2003 (c. 44).

[2] 1933 c. 12; section 45 was substituted by section 50 of the Courts Act 2003 (c. 39) and amended by section 15 of, and paragraph 20 of Schedule 4 to, the Constitutional Reform Act 2005 (c. 4); section 46 was amended by section 46 of, and Schedule 7 to, the Justices of the Peace Act 1949 (c. 101), section 72 of, and paragraph 4 of Schedule 5 to, the Children and Young Persons Act 1969 (c. 54), section 154 of, and paragraph 6 of Schedule 7 to, the Magistrates' Courts Act 1980 (c. 43), sections 68 and 100 of, and paragraph 1 of Schedule 8 and paragraph 40 of Schedule 11 to, the Criminal Justice Act 1991 (c. 53) and section 109 of, and paragraph 74 of Schedule 8 to, the Courts Act 2003 (c. 39); and section 48 was amended by section 79 of, and Schedule 9 to, the Criminal Justice Act 1948 (c. 58), section 132 of, and Schedule 6 to, the Magistrates' Courts Act 1952 (c. 55), section 64 of, and paragraph 12 of Schedule 3 and Schedule 5 to, the Children and Young Persons Act 1963 (c. 37), sections 72, 79 and 83 of, and Schedules 6, 9 and 10 to, the Children and Young Persons Act 1969 (c. 54), sections 68 and 100 of, and paragraph 1 of Schedule 8 and paragraph 40 of Schedule 11 to, the Criminal Justice Act 1991 (c. 53), section 106 of, and Schedule 15 to, the Access to Justice Act 1999 (c. 22) and section 109 of, and paragraph 75 of Schedule 8 to, the Courts Act 2003 (c. 39).

[3] 1963 c. 37; section 18 was amended by section 100 of, and paragraph 40 of Schedule 11 to, the Criminal Justice Act 1991 (c. 53) and section 168 of, and paragraph 5 of Schedule 9 to, the Criminal Justice and Public Order Act 1994 (c. 33).

[4] 1998 c. 37; section 47 was amended by section 165 of, and Schedule 12 to, the Powers of Criminal Courts (Sentencing) Act 2000 (c. 6), section 332 of, and Schedule 37 to, the Criminal Justice Act 2003 (c. 44) and article 2 of, and paragraph 59 of the Schedule to S.I. 2005/886.

[5] 2020 c. 17.

*The exercise of the court's powers is affected by—*

    (a) *the classification of the offence (and the general rule, subject to exceptions, is that a magistrates' court must try—*

        (i) *an offence classified as one that can be tried only in a magistrates' court (in other legislation, described as triable only summarily), and*

        (ii) *an offence classified as one that can be tried either in a magistrates' court or in the Crown Court (in other legislation, described as triable either way) that has been allocated for trial in a magistrates' court); and*

    (b) *the defendant's age (and the general rule, subject to exceptions, is that an allegation of an offence against a defendant under 18 must be tried in a magistrates' court sitting as a youth court, irrespective of the classification of the offence and without allocation for trial there).*

*Under sections 10, 14, 27A, 121 and 148 of the Magistrates' Courts Act 1980[6] and the Justices of the Peace Rules 2016[7], the court—*

    (a) *must comprise at least two but not more than three justices, or a District Judge (Magistrates' Courts) (but a single member can adjourn the hearing);*

    (b) *must not include any member who adjudicated at a hearing to which rule 44.2 applies (defendant's declaration of no knowledge of hearing);*

    (c) *when reaching a verdict, must not include any member who was absent from any part of the hearing;*

    (d) *when passing sentence, need not include any of the members who reached the verdict (but may do so).*

*Under section 16A of the Magistrates' Courts Act 1980[8], the court may comprise a single justice where—*

    (a) *the offence charged is a summary offence not punishable with imprisonment;*

    (b) *the defendant was at least 18 years old when charged;*

    (c) *the court is satisfied that specified documents giving notice of the procedure under that section and containing other specified information have been served on the defendant; and*

    (d) *the defendant has not served notice of an intention to plead not guilty, or of a desire not to be tried in accordance with that section.*

*Under section 45 of the Children and Young Persons Act 1933[9] and under the Justices of the Peace Rules 2016, where the court is a youth court comprising justices each member must be authorised to sit as a member of that youth court.*

*Under section 150 of the Magistrates' Courts Act 1980[10], where two or more justices are present one may act on behalf of all.*

*Section 59 of the Children and Young Persons Act 1933[11] requires that—*

    (a) *the expressions 'conviction' and 'sentence' must not be used by a magistrates' court dealing with a defendant under 18; and*

    (b) *a reference in legislation to a defendant who is convicted, to a conviction, or to a sentence, must be read as including a reference to a defendant who is found guilty of an offence, a finding of guilt, or an order made on a finding of guilt, respectively.*

*Under section 14 of the Magistrates' Courts Act 1980, proceedings which begin with a summons or requisition will become void if the defendant, at any time during or after the trial, makes a statutory declaration that he or she did not know of them until a date after the trial began. See rule 44.2.*

---

[6] 1980 c. 43; section 10 was amended by section 59 of, and paragraph 1 of Schedule 9 to, the Criminal Justice Act 1982 (c. 48), section 68 of, and paragraph 6 of Schedule 8 to, the Criminal Justice Act 1991 (c. 53) and section 47 of the Crime and Disorder Act 1998 (c. 37). Section 14 was amended by section 109 of, and paragraph 205 of Schedule 8 to, the Courts Act 2003 (c. 39). Section 27A was inserted by section 46 of the Courts Act 2003 (c. 39). Section 121 was amended by section 61 of the Criminal Justice Act 1988 (c. 33), section 92 of, and paragraph 8 of Schedule 11 to, the Children Act 1989 (c. 41), section 109 of, and paragraph 237 of Schedule 8 and Schedule 10 to, the Courts Act 2003 (c. 39). Section 148 was amended by section 109 of, and paragraph 248 of Schedule 8 to, the Courts Act 2003 (c. 39).

[7] S.I. 2016/709.

[8] 1980 c. 43; section 16A was inserted by section 48 of the Criminal Justice and Courts Act 2015 (c. 2).

[9] 1933 c. 12; section 45 was substituted by section 50 of the Courts Act 2003 (c. 39) and amended by section 15 of, and paragraph 20 of Schedule 4 to, the Constitutional Reform Act 2005 (c. 4).

[10] 1980 c. 43; section 150 has been amended but none is relevant to the note to this rule.

[11] 1933 c. 12; section 59 was amended by sections 79 and 83 of, and Schedules 9 and 10 to, the Criminal Justice Act 1948 (c. 58) and section 18 of the Costs in Criminal Cases Act 1952 (c. 48).

*Under section 142 of the Magistrates' Courts Act 1980—*

    *(a) where a defendant is convicted by a magistrates' court, the court may order that the case should be heard again by different justices; and*

    *(b) the court may vary or rescind an order which it has made when dealing with a convicted defendant,*

*if in either case it appears to the court to be in the interests of justice to do so. See rule 44.3.*

*See also Part 32 (Breach, revocation and amendment of community and other orders). Rule 32.4 (Procedure on application by responsible officer) applies rules in this Part to the procedure with which that rule deals.]*

## General rules

**24.2** (1) Where this Part applies—

    (a) the general rule is that the hearing must be in public; but

    (b) the court may exercise any power it has to—

        (i) impose reporting restrictions,

        (ii) withhold information from the public, or

        (iii) order a hearing in private; and

    (c) unless the court otherwise directs, only the following may attend a hearing in a youth court—

        (i) the parties and their legal representatives,

        (ii) a defendant's parents, guardian or other supporting adult,

        (iii) a witness,

        (iv) anyone else directly concerned in the case, and

        (v) a representative of a news-gathering or reporting organisation.

    (2) Unless already done, the justices' legal adviser or the court must—

    (a) read the allegation of the offence to the defendant;

    (b) explain, in terms the defendant can understand (with help, if necessary)—

        (i) the allegation, and

        (ii) what the procedure at the hearing will be;

    (c) ask whether the defendant has been advised about the potential effect on sentence of a guilty plea;

    (d) ask whether the defendant pleads guilty or not guilty; and

    (e) take the defendant's plea.

    (3) The court may adjourn the hearing—

    (a) at any stage, to the same or to another magistrates' court; or

    (b) to a youth court, where the court is not itself a youth court and the defendant is under 18.

    (4) Paragraphs (1) and (2) of this rule do not apply where the court tries a case under rule 24.9 (Single justice procedure: special rules).

*[Note. See sections 10, 16A, 27A, 29 and 121 of the Magistrates' Courts Act 1980[12] and sections 46 and 47 of the Children and Young Persons Act 1933.*

*Where the case has been allocated for trial in a magistrates' court, part of the procedure under rule 24.2(2) will have taken place.*

*Part 6 contains rules about reporting, etc. restrictions. For a list of the court's powers to impose reporting and access restrictions, see the note to rule 6.1.*

*Under section 34A of the Children and Young Persons Act 1933[13], the court—*

    *(a) may require the defendant's parents or guardian to attend court with the defendant, where the defendant is under 18; and*

    *(b) must do so, where the defendant is under 16, unless satisfied that that would be unreasonable.*

*Part 7 contains rules about (among other things) the issue of a summons to a parent or guardian.*

*Part 46 (Representatives) contains rules allowing a parent, guardian or other supporting adult to help a defendant under 18.]*

---

[12] 1980 c. 43; section 29 was amended by sections 68 and 100 of, and paragraph 6 of Schedule 8 and paragraph 40 of Schedule 11 to, the Criminal Justice Act 1991 (c. 53), section 168 of, and paragraph 41 of Schedule 10 to, the Criminal Justice and Public Order Act 1994 (c. 33) and section 41 of, and paragraph 51 of Schedule 3 to, the Criminal Justice Act 2003 (c. 44). Section 16A was inserted by section 48 of the Criminal Justice and Courts Act 2015 (c. 2).

[13] 1933 c. 12; section 34A was inserted by section 56 of the Criminal Justice Act 1991 (c. 53) and amended by section 107 of, and paragraph 1 of Schedule 5 to, the Local Government Act 2000 (c. 22).

**R24.3** **Procedure on plea of not guilty**

**24.3** (1) This rule applies—

    (a) if the defendant has—

        (i) entered a plea of not guilty, or

        (ii) not entered a plea; or

    (b) if, in either case, it appears to the court that there may be grounds for making a hospital order without convicting the defendant.

(2) If a not guilty plea was taken on a previous occasion, the justices' legal adviser or the court must ask the defendant to confirm that plea.

(3) In the following sequence—

    (a) the prosecutor may summarise the prosecution case, concisely identifying the relevant law, outlining the facts and indicating the matters likely to be in dispute;

    (b) to help the members of the court to understand the case and resolve any issue in it, the court may invite the defendant concisely to identify what is in issue;

    (c) the prosecutor must introduce the evidence on which the prosecution case relies;

    (d) at the conclusion of the prosecution case, on the defendant's application or on its own initiative, the court—

        (i) may acquit on the ground that the prosecution evidence is insufficient for any reasonable court properly to convict, but

        (ii) must not do so unless the prosecutor has had an opportunity to make representations;

    (e) the justices' legal adviser or the court must explain, in terms the defendant can understand (with help, if necessary)—

        (i) the right to give evidence, and

        (ii) the potential effect of not doing so at all, or of refusing to answer a question while doing so;

    (f) the defendant may introduce evidence;

    (g) a party may introduce further evidence if it is then admissible (for example, because it is in rebuttal of evidence already introduced);

    (h) the prosecutor may make final representations in support of the prosecution case, where—

        (i) the defendant is represented by a legal representative, or

        (ii) whether represented or not, the defendant has introduced evidence other than his or her own; and

    (i) the defendant may make final representations in support of the defence case.

(4) Where a party wants to introduce evidence or make representations after that party's opportunity to do so under paragraph (3), the court—

    (a) may refuse to receive any such evidence or representations; and

    (b) must not receive any such evidence or representations after it has announced its verdict.

(5) If the court—

    (a) convicts the defendant; or

    (b) makes a hospital order instead of doing so,

    it must give sufficient reasons to explain its decision.

(6) If the court acquits the defendant, it may—

    (a) give an explanation of its decision; and

    (b) exercise any power it has to make—

        (i) a behaviour order,

        (ii) a costs order.

*[Note. See section 9 of the Magistrates' Courts Act 1980[14].*

*Under section 37(3) of the Mental Health Act 1983[15], if the court is satisfied that the defendant did the act or made the omission alleged, then it may make a hospital order without convicting the defendant.*

*Under section 35 of the Criminal Justice and Public Order Act 1994[16], the court may draw such inferences as appear proper from a defendant's failure to give evidence, or refusal without good cause to answer a question while doing so. The procedure set out in rule 24.3(3)(e) is prescribed by that section.*

*The admissibility of evidence that a party introduces is governed by rules of evidence.*

---

[14] 1980 c. 43.

[15] 1983 c. 20; section 37(3) was amended by sections 1 and 55 of, and paragraphs 1 and 7 of Schedule 1 and Schedule 11 to, the Mental Health Act 2007 (c. 12). 37(3) was amended by sections 1 and 55 of, and paragraphs 1 and 7 of Schedule 1 and Schedule 11 to, the Mental Health Act 2007 (c. 12).

[16] 1994 c. 33; section 35 was amended by sections 35 and 120 of, and Schedule 10 to, the Crime and Disorder Act 1998 (c. 37). The Criminal Justice Act 2003 (c. 44) amendment to section 35 is not relevant to procedure in magistrates' courts.

*Section 2 of the Criminal Procedure Act 1865[17] and section 3 of the Criminal Evidence Act 1898[18] restrict the circumstances in which the prosecutor may make final representations without the court's permission.*

*See rule 24.11 for the procedure if the court convicts the defendant.*

*Part 31 contains rules about behaviour orders.]*

### Evidence of a witness in person

**R24.4**

24.4 (1) This rule applies where a party wants to introduce evidence by calling a witness to give that evidence in person.

(2) Unless the court otherwise directs—
  (a) a witness waiting to give evidence must not wait inside the courtroom, unless that witness is—
    (i) a party, or
    (ii) an expert witness;
  (b) a witness who gives evidence in the courtroom must do so from the place provided for that purpose; and
  (c) a witness' address must not be announced unless it is relevant to an issue in the case.

(3) Before the witness gives evidence—
  (a) the party who introduces the witness' evidence must explain how that evidence is admissible, unless it is only evidence of fact within the witness' direct knowledge; and
  (b) the witness must take an oath or affirm, unless other legislation otherwise provides.

(4) In the following sequence—
  (a) the party who calls a witness must ask questions in examination-in-chief;
  (b) every other party may ask questions in cross-examination; and
  (c) the party who called the witness may ask questions in re-examination.

(5) If other legislation so permits, at any time while giving evidence a witness may refer to a record of that witness' recollection of events.

(6) The justices' legal adviser or the court may—
  (a) ask a witness questions; and in particular
  (b) where the defendant is not represented, ask any question necessary in the defendant's interests.

*[Note. Section 53 of the Youth Justice and Criminal Evidence Act 1999[19] provides that everyone is competent to give evidence in criminal proceedings unless unable to understand questions put or give intelligible answers. See also section 1 of the Criminal Evidence Act 1898[20].*

*Part 19 contains rules about the introduction of evidence of expert opinion. Part 20 contains rules about the introduction of hearsay evidence.*

*Sections 1, 3, 5 and 6 of the Oaths Act 1978[21] provide for the taking of oaths and the making of affirmations, and for the words that must be used. Section 28 of the Children and Young Persons Act 1963[22] provides that in a youth court, and where a witness in any court is under 18, an oath must include the words 'I promise' in place of the words 'I swear'. Under sections 55 and 56 of the Youth Justice and Criminal Evidence Act 1999, a person may give evidence without taking an oath, or making an affirmation, where that person (i) is under 14 or (ii) has an insufficient appreciation of the solemnity of the occasion and of the particular responsibility to tell the truth which is involved in taking an oath.*

*The questions that may be put to a witness—*

  *(a) by a party are governed by rules of evidence, for example—*
    *(i) the rule that a question must be relevant to what is in issue,*
    *(ii) the rule that the party who calls a witness must not ask that witness a leading question about what is in dispute, and*
    *(iii) the rule that a party who calls a witness may contradict that witness only in limited circumstances (see section 3 of the Criminal Procedure Act 1865)[23];*

---

[17] 1865 c. 18; section 2 was amended by section 10(2) of, and Part III of Schedule 3 to, the Criminal Law Act 1967 (c. 58).
[18] 1898 c. 36; section 3 was amended by section 1(2) of the Criminal Procedure (Right of Reply) Act 1964 (c. 34).
[19] 1999 c. 23.
[20] 1898 c. 36; section 1 was amended by section 1 of the Criminal Evidence Act 1979 (c. 16), section 78 of, and Schedule 16 to, the Criminal Justice Act 1982 (c. 48), sections 80(9) and 119(2) of, and Schedule 7 to, the Police and Criminal Evidence Act 1984 (c. 60), sections 31 and 168 of, and paragraph 2 of Schedule 10, and Schedule 11 to, the Criminal Justice and Public Order Act 1994 (c. 33), section 67 of, and paragraph 1 of Schedule 4, and Schedule 6 to, the Youth Justice and Criminal Evidence Act 1999 (c. 23) and sections 331 and 332 of, and paragraph 80 of Schedule 36, and Part 5 of Schedule 37 to, the Criminal Justice Act 2003 (c. 44).
[21] 1978 c. 19.
[22] 1963 c. 37; section 28 was amended by section 2 of the Oaths Act 1978 (c. 19) and section 100 of, and paragraph 40 of Schedule 11 to, the Criminal Justice Act 1991 (c. 53).
[23] 1865 c. 18.

(ii) any previous conviction listed in the defendant's driving record, where the offence is under the Road Traffic Regulation Act 1984[32], the Road Traffic Act 1988[33], the Road Traffic (Consequential Provisions) Act 1988[34] or the Road Traffic (Driver Licensing and Information Systems) Act 1989[35],

(iii) any other information about the defendant, relevant to sentence, of which the prosecutor served notice under paragraph (1), and

(iv) any representations and any other information served by the defendant under paragraph (4)

and rule 24.11(3) to (9) inclusive must be read accordingly;

(b) unless the court otherwise directs, the prosecutor need not attend; and

(c) the court may accept such a guilty plea and pass sentence in the defendant's absence.

(7) With the defendant's agreement, the court may deal with the case in the same way as under paragraph (6) where the defendant is present and—

(a) has served a notice of guilty plea under paragraph (4); or

(b) pleads guilty there and then.

*[Note. The procedure set out in this rule is prescribed by sections 12 and 12A of the Magistrates' Courts Act 1980[36]. Under section 12(1)(a), the Secretary of State can specify offences to which the procedure will not apply. None has been specified.*

*Under section 1 of the Magistrates' Courts Act 1980[37] a justice of the peace may issue a summons requiring a defendant to attend court to answer an allegation of an offence. Under section 29 of the Criminal Justice Act 2003[38] a prosecutor authorised under that section may issue a written charge alleging an offence and a requisition requiring a defendant to attend court. Part 7 contains relevant rules.*

*See also rule 24.11(10)(a) under which the court must adjourn where the defendant is absent before passing a custodial sentence or imposing a disqualification.*

*For the court's power, where this rule applies, to take account of a previous conviction listed in a defendant's driving record, see section 13(3A) of the Road Traffic Offenders Act 1988[39].*

*The Practice Direction sets out forms of notice for use in connection with this rule.]*

**R24.9**   **Single justice procedure: special rules**

**24.9**   (1) This rule applies where—

(a) the offence alleged—

(i) can be tried only in a magistrates' court, and

(ii) is not one punishable with imprisonment;

(b) the defendant is at least 18 years old;

(c) the prosecutor has served on the defendant—

(i) a written charge,

(ii) the material listed in paragraph (2) on which the prosecutor relies to set out the facts of the offence,

(iii) the material listed in paragraph (3) on which the prosecutor relies to provide the court with information relevant to sentence,

(iv) a notice that the procedure set out in this rule applies,

---

[32] 1984 c. 27.

[33] 1988 c. 52.

[34] 1988 c. 54.

[35] 1989 c. 22.

[36] 1980 c. 43; section 12 was amended by section 45 of, and paragraph 1 of Schedule 5 to, the Criminal Justice and Public Order Act 1994 (c. 33), section 1 of the Magistrates' Courts (Procedure) Act 1998 (c. 15), section 109 of, and paragraph 203 of Schedule 8 to, the Courts Act 2003 (c. 39), section 308 of, and Part 12 of Schedule 37 to, the Criminal Justice Act 2003 (c. 44) and section 81 of the Deregulation Act 2015 (c. 20). Section 12A was inserted by section 45 of, and paragraph 2 of Schedule 5 to, the Criminal Justice and Public Order Act 1994 (c. 33) and amended by section 109 of, and paragraph 204 of Schedule 8 to, the Courts Act 2003 (c. 39).

[37] 1980 c. 43; section 1 was amended by section 68 of, and paragraph 6 of Schedule 8 to, the Criminal Justice Act 1991 (c. 53), sections 43 and 109 of, and Schedule 10 to, the Courts Act 2003 (c. 39), section 31 of, and paragraph 12 of Schedule 7 to, the Criminal Justice Act 2003 (c. 44) and section 153 of the Police Reform and Social Responsibility Act 2011. It is further amended by paragraphs 7 and 8 of Schedule 36 to, the Criminal Justice Act 2003 (c. 44), with effect from a date to be appointed.

[38] 2003 c. 44; section 29 has been brought into force for certain purposes only (see S.I. 2007/1999, 2008/1424, 2009/2879, 2010/3005, 2011/2188, 2012/825 and 2014/633). It was amended by section 50 of, and paragraph 130 of Schedule 4 to, the Commissioners for Revenue and Customs Act 2005 (c. 11), section 59 of, and paragraph 196 of Schedule 4 to, the Serious Organised Crime and Police Act 2005 (c. 15), section 15 of, and paragraph 187 of Schedule 8 to, the Crime and Courts Act 2013 (c. 22), S.I. 2014/834 and section 46 of the Criminal Justice and Courts Act 2015 (c. 2).

[39] 1988 c. 53; section 13(3A) was inserted by section 2 of the Magistrates' Courts (Procedure) Act 1998 (c. 15).

      (v)  a notice for the defendant's use if the defendant wants to plead guilty,

      (vi)  a notice for the defendant's use if the defendant wants to plead guilty but wants the case dealt with at a hearing by a court comprising more than one justice, and

      (vii) a notice for the defendant's use if the defendant wants to plead not guilty; and

  (d)  the prosecutor has served on the court officer—

      (i)  copies of those documents, and

      (ii)  a certificate of service of those documents on the defendant.

(2)  The material that the prosecutor must serve to set out the facts of the offence is—

  (a)  a summary of the evidence on which the prosecution case is based;

  (b)  any—

      (i)  written witness statement to which Part 16 (Written witness statements) applies, or

      (ii)  document or extract setting out facts; or

  (c)  any combination of such a summary, statement, document or extract.

(3)  The material that the prosecutor must serve to provide information relevant to sentence is—

  (a)  details of any previous conviction of the defendant which the prosecutor considers relevant, other than any conviction listed in the defendant's driving record;

  (b)  if applicable, a notice that the defendant's driving record will be made available to the court; and

  (c)  a notice containing or describing any other information about the defendant, relevant to sentence, which will be made available to the court.

(4)  Not more than 15 business days after service on the defendant of the documents listed in paragraph (1)(c)—

  (a)  a defendant who wants to plead guilty must serve a notice to that effect on the court officer and include with that notice—

      (i)  any representations that the defendant wants the court to consider, and

      (ii)  a statement of the defendant's assets and other financial circumstances;

  (b)  a defendant who wants to plead guilty but wants the case dealt with at a hearing by a court comprising more than one justice must serve a notice to that effect on the court officer; and

  (c)  a defendant who wants to plead not guilty must serve a notice to that effect on the court officer.

(5)  If within 15 business days of service on the defendant of the documents listed in paragraph (1)(c) the defendant serves a notice to plead guilty under paragraph (4)(a)—

  (a)  the court officer must arrange for the court to deal with the case in accordance with that notice; and

  (b)  the time for service of any other notice under paragraph (4) expires at once.

(6)  If within 15 business days of service on the defendant of the documents listed in paragraph (1)(c) the defendant wants to withdraw a notice which he or she has served under paragraph (4)(b) (notice to plead guilty at a hearing) or under paragraph (4)(c) (notice to plead not guilty), the defendant must—

  (a)  serve notice of that withdrawal on the court officer; and

  (b)  serve any substitute notice under paragraph (4).

(7)  Paragraph (8) applies where by the date of trial the defendant has not—

  (a)  served notice under paragraph (4)(b) or (c) of wanting to plead guilty at a hearing, or wanting to plead not guilty; or

  (b)  given notice to that effect under section 16B(2) of the Magistrates' Courts Act 1980[40].

(8)  Where this paragraph applies—

  (a)  the court may try the case in the parties' absence and without a hearing;

  (b)  the court may accept any guilty plea of which the defendant has given notice under paragraph (4)(a); and

  (c)  to establish the facts of the offence and other information about the defendant relevant to sentence, the court may take account only of—

      (i)  information contained in a document served by the prosecutor under paragraph (1),

      (ii)  any previous conviction listed in the defendant's driving record, where the offence is under the Road Traffic Regulation Act 1984, the Road Traffic Act 1988, the Road Traffic (Consequential Provisions) Act 1988 or the Road Traffic (Driver Licensing and Information Systems) Act 1989,

      (iii) any other information about the defendant, relevant to sentence, of which the prosecutor served notice under paragraph (1), and

---

[40]  1980 c. 43; section 16B was inserted by section 48 of the Criminal Justice and Courts Act 2015 (c. 2).

       (iv) any representations and any other information served by the defendant under paragraph (4)(a)

and rule 24.11(3) to (9) inclusive must be read accordingly.

(9) Paragraph (10) applies where—

    (a) the defendant serves on the court officer a notice under paragraph (4)(b) or (c); or

    (b) the court which tries the defendant under paragraph (8) adjourns the trial for the defendant to attend a hearing by a court comprising more than one justice.

(10) Where this paragraph applies, the court must exercise its power to issue a summons and—

    (a) the rules in Part 7 apply (Starting a prosecution in a magistrates' court) as if the prosecutor had just served an application for a summons to be issued in the same terms as the written charge;

    (b) the rules in Part 8 (Initial details of the prosecution case) apply as if the documents served by the prosecutor under paragraph (1) had been served under that Part; and

    (c) except for rule 24.8 (Written guilty plea: special rules) and this rule, the rules in this Part apply.

*[Note. The procedure set out in this rule is prescribed by sections 16A to 16D of the Magistrates' Courts Act 1980[41] and section 29 of the Criminal Justice Act 2003[42]. Under section 16A of the 1980 Act, the court may comprise a single justice. Under section 29 of the 2003 Act, a prosecutor authorised under that section may issue a written charge alleging an offence and a single justice procedure notice. Part 7 contains relevant rules.*

*Under section 1 of the Magistrates' Courts Act 1980[43]) a justice of the peace may issue a summons requiring a defendant to attend court to answer an allegation of an offence. Under sections 16C and 16D of the 1980 Act, a justice may issue a summons requiring a defendant to attend court in the circumstances listed in rule 24.9(9).*

*For the court's power, where this rule applies, to take account of—*

    *(a) information contained or described in a document served by the prosecutor under rule 24.9(1), see section 16F of the Magistrates' Courts Act 1980[44];*

    *(b) a previous conviction listed in a defendant's driving record, see section 13(3A) of the Road Traffic Offenders Act 1988[45].*

*The Practice Direction sets out forms of notice for use in connection with this rule.]*

**R24.10**    **Application to withdraw a guilty plea**

**24.10** (1) This rule applies where the defendant wants to withdraw a guilty plea.

(2) The defendant must apply to do so—

    (a) as soon as practicable after becoming aware of the reasons for doing so; and

    (b) before sentence.

(3) Unless the court otherwise directs, the application must be in writing and the defendant must serve it on—

    (a) the court officer; and

    (b) the prosecutor.

(4) The application must—

    (a) explain why it would be unjust not to allow the defendant to withdraw the guilty plea;

    (b) identify—

        (i) any witness that the defendant wants to call, and

        (ii) any other proposed evidence; and

    (c) say whether the defendant waives legal professional privilege, giving any relevant name and date.

---

[41] 1980 c. 43; sections 16A to 16D were inserted by section 48 of the Criminal Justice and Courts Act 2015 (c. 2).

[42] 2003 c. 44; section 29 has been brought into force for certain purposes only (see S.I. 2007/1999, 2008/1424, 2009/2879, 2010/3005, 2011/2188, 2012/825 and 2014/633). It was amended by section 50 of, and paragraph 130 of Schedule 4 to, the Commissioners for Revenue and Customs Act 2005 (c. 11), section 59 of, and paragraph 196 of Schedule 4 to, the Serious Organised Crime and Police Act 2005 (c. 15), section 15 of, and paragraph 187 of Schedule 8 to, the Crime and Courts Act 2013 (c. 22), S.I. 2014/834 and section 46 of the Criminal Justice and Courts Act 2015 (c. 2).

[43] 1980 c. 43; section 1 was amended by section 68 of, and paragraph 6 of Schedule 8 to, the Criminal Justice Act 1991 (c. 53), sections 43 and 109 of, and Schedule 10 to, the Courts Act 2003 (c. 39), section 31 of, and paragraph 12 of Schedule 7 to, the Criminal Justice Act 2003 (c. 44) and section 153 of the Police Reform and Social Responsibility Act 2011. It is further amended by paragraphs 7 and 8 of Schedule 36 to, the Criminal Justice Act 2003 (c. 44), with effect from a date to be appointed.

[44] 1980 c. 43; section 16F was inserted by section 48 of the Criminal Justice and Courts Act 2015 (c. 2).

[45] 1988 c. 53; section 13(3A) was inserted by section 2 of the Magistrates' Courts (Procedure) Act 1998 (c. 15).

**Procedure if the court convicts**                                                R24.11

24.11 (1)  This rule applies if the court convicts the defendant.

   (2)  The court—

   (a)  may exercise its power to require—

      (i)   a statement of the defendant's financial circumstances,

      (ii)  a pre-sentence report; and

   (b)  may (and in some circumstances must) remit the defendant to a youth court for sentence where—

      (i)   the defendant is under 18, and

      (ii)  the convicting court is not itself a youth court.

   (3)  The prosecutor must—

   (a)  summarise the prosecution case, if the sentencing court has not heard evidence;

   (b)  identify any offence to be taken into consideration in sentencing;

   (c)  provide information relevant to sentence, including any statement of the effect of the offence on the victim, the victim's family and others; and

   (d)  where it is likely to assist the court, identify any other matter relevant to sentence, including—

      (i)   the legislation applicable,

      (ii)  any sentencing guidelines, or guideline cases,

      (iii) aggravating and mitigating features affecting the defendant's culpability and the harm which the offence caused, was intended to cause or might forseeably have caused, and

      (iv)  the effect of such of the information listed in paragraph (2)(a) as the court may need to take into account.

   (4)  The defendant must provide details of financial circumstances—

   (a)  in any form required by the court officer;

   (b)  by any date directed by the court or by the court officer.

   (5)  Where the defendant pleads guilty but wants to be sentenced on a different basis to that disclosed by the prosecution case—

   (a)  the defendant must set out that basis in writing, identifying what is in dispute;

   (b)  the court may invite the parties to make representations about whether the dispute is material to sentence; and

   (c)  if the court decides that it is a material dispute, the court must—

      (i)   invite such further representations or evidence as it may require, and

      (ii)  decide the dispute.

   (6)  Where the court has power to order the endorsement of the defendant's driving record, or power to order the defendant to be disqualified from driving—

   (a)  if other legislation so permits, a defendant who wants the court not to exercise that power must introduce the evidence or information on which the defendant relies;

   (b)  the prosecutor may introduce evidence; and

   (c)  the parties may make representations about that evidence or information.

   (7)  Before the court passes sentence—

   (a)  the court must—

      (i)   give the defendant an opportunity to make representations and introduce evidence relevant to sentence, and

      (ii)  where the defendant is under 18, give the defendant's parents, guardian or other supporting adult, if present, such an opportunity as well; and

   (b)  the justices' legal adviser or the court must elicit any further information relevant to sentence that the court may require.

   (8)  If the court requires more information, it may exercise its power to adjourn the hearing for not more than—

   (a)  3 weeks at a time, if the defendant will be in custody; or

   (b)  4 weeks at a time.

   (9)  When the court has taken into account all the evidence, information and any report available, the court must—

   (a)  subject to paragraph (10), as a general rule, pass sentence there and then;

Criminal Procedure Rules and Criminal Practice Directions

(b) the provisions listed in section 24 of the 2020 Act (including section 70 of the Proceeds of Crime Act 2002[55]); and

(c) paragraph 11 of Schedule 16 to the 2020 Act.

*See section 70(5) of the Proceeds of Crime Act 2002 for the court's power to make the statement to which this rule refers.*

*See also rules 9.15 (Committal for sentence of offence related to an offence sent for trial) and 28.8 (Sentencing, etc. after committal to the Crown Court). The note to rule 28.8 summarises the statutory provisions that apply.]*

**R24.12** **Procedure where a party is absent**

**24.12** (1) This rule—

(a) applies where a party is absent; but

(b) does not apply where—

(i) the defendant has served a notice of guilty plea under rule 24.8 (Written guilty plea: special rules), or

(ii) the court tries a case under rule 24.9 (Single justice procedure: special rules).

(2) Where the prosecutor is absent, the court may—

(a) if it has received evidence, deal with the case as if the prosecutor were present; and

(b) in any other case—

(i) enquire into the reasons for the prosecutor's absence, and

(ii) if satisfied there is no good reason, exercise its power to dismiss the allegation.

(3) Where the defendant is absent the general rule is that the court must proceed as if the defendant were present, and had pleaded not guilty (unless a plea already has been taken) but the general rule—

(a) does not apply if the defendant is under 18;

(b) is subject to the court being satisfied that—

(i) any summons or requisition was served on the defendant a reasonable time before the hearing, or

(ii) in a case in which the hearing has been adjourned, the defendant had reasonable notice of where and when it would resume; and

(c) is subject also to rule 24.11(10)(a) (restrictions on passing sentence in the defendant's absence).

(4) Where the defendant is absent, the court—

(a) must exercise its power to issue a warrant for the defendant's arrest and detention in the terms required by rule 13.3(3) (Terms of a warrant for detention or imprisonment), if it passes a custodial sentence; and

(b) may exercise its power to issue a warrant for the defendant's arrest in any other case, if it does not apply the general rule in paragraph (3) of this rule about proceeding in the defendant's absence.

*[Note. See sections 11, 15 and 16 of the Magistrates' Courts Act 1980[56].]*

*Under section 27 of the 1980 Act, where a magistrates' court dismisses an allegation of an offence classified as one that can be tried either in a magistrates' court or in the Crown Court (in other legislation, described as triable either way), that dismissal has the same effect as an acquittal in the Crown Court.*

*Under section 11 of the 1980 Act, the court may pass a custodial sentence in the defendant's absence if the case started with the defendant's arrest and charge (and not with a summons or requisition). Section 11(3A) requires that, in that event, the defendant must be brought before the court before being taken to a prison or other institution to begin serving that sentence: see also rule 13.3. Under section 7(1) of the Bail Act 1976[57], the court has power to issue a warrant for the arrest of a defendant released on bail who has failed to attend court when due to do so.*

---

[55] 2002 c. 29; section 70 was amended by section 41 of, and paragraph 75 of Schedule 3 to, the Criminal Justice Act 2003 (c. 44), section 410 of, and paragraphs 181 and 195 of Schedule 24 to, the Sentencing Act 2020 (c. 17) and section 46 of, and paragraph 19 of Schedule 13 to, the Counter-Terrorism and Sentencing Act 2021 (c. 11).

[56] 1980 c. 43; section 14 was amended by section 109 of, and paragraph 205 of Schedule 8 to, the Courts Act 2003 (c. 39).

[57] 1976 c. 63.

*Under section 13 of the 1980 Act[58], the court has power to issue a warrant for the arrest of an absent defendant, instead of proceeding, where—*

> *(1) the case started with—*
>
> > *(a) the defendant's arrest and charge, or*
> >
> > *(b) a summons or requisition, if—*
> >
> > > *(i) the court is satisfied that that summons or requisition was served on the defendant a reasonable time before the hearing, or*
> > >
> > > *(ii) the defendant was present when the hearing was arranged; and*
>
> *(2) the offence is punishable with imprisonment; or*
>
> *(3) the defendant has been convicted and the court considers imposing a disqualification.]*

### Provision of documents for the court

**R24.13**

**24.13** (1) A party who introduces a document in evidence, or who otherwise uses a document in presenting that party's case, must provide a copy for—

> (a) each other party;
>
> (b) any witness that party wants to refer to that document;
>
> (c) the court; and
>
> (d) the justices' legal adviser.

(2) Unless the court otherwise directs, on application or on its own initiative, the court officer must provide for the court—

> (a) any copy received under paragraph (1) before the hearing begins; and
>
> (b) a copy of the court officer's record of—
>
> > (i) information supplied by each party for the purposes of case management, including any revision of information previously supplied,
> >
> > (ii) each pre-trial direction for the management of the case,
> >
> > (iii) any pre-trial decision to admit evidence,
> >
> > (iv) any pre-trial direction about the giving of evidence, and
> >
> > (v) any admission to which rule 24.6 applies.

(3) Where rule 24.8 (Written guilty plea: special rules) applies, the court officer must provide for the court—

> (a) each document served by the prosecutor under rule 24.8(1)(d);
>
> (b) the defendant's driving record, where the offence is under the Road Traffic Regulation Act 1984[59], the Road Traffic Act 1988[60], the Road Traffic (Consequential Provisions) Act 1988[61] or the Road Traffic (Driver Licensing and Information Systems) Act 1989[62];
>
> (c) any other information about the defendant, relevant to sentence, of which the prosecutor served notice under rule 24.8(1); and
>
> (d) the notice of guilty plea and any representations and other information served by the defendant under rule 24.8(4).

(4) Where the court tries a case under rule 24.9 (Single justice procedure: special rules), the court officer must provide for the court—

> (a) each document served by the prosecutor under rule 24.9(1)(d);
>
> (b) the defendant's driving record, where the offence is under the Road Traffic Regulation Act 1984, the Road Traffic Act 1988, the Road Traffic (Consequential Provisions) Act 1988 or the Road Traffic (Driver Licensing and Information Systems) Act 1989;
>
> (c) any other information about the defendant, relevant to sentence, of which the prosecutor served notice under rule 24.9(1); and
>
> (d) any notice, representations and other information served by the defendant under rule 29.9(4)(a).

---

[58] 1980 c. 43; section 13 was amended by section 45 of, and paragraph 3 of Schedule 5 to, the Criminal Justice and Public Order Act 1994 (c. 33), section 48 of the Criminal Procedure and Investigations Act 1996 (c. 25), section 3 of the Magistrates' Courts (Procedure) Act 1998 (c. 15), sections 31 and 332 of, and Part 12 of Schedule 37 to, the Criminal Justice Act 2003 (c. 44) and sections 54 and 149 of, and Part 4 of Schedule 28 to, the Criminal Justice and Immigration Act 2008 (c. 4).

[59] 1984 c. 27.

[60] 1988 c. 52.

[61] 1988 c. 54.

[62] 1989 c. 22.

*Criminal Procedure Rules and Criminal Practice Directions*

*[Note. A written witness statement to which Part 16 applies may only be introduced in evidence if there has been no objection within the time limit to which rule 16.4 refers.*

*An expert report to which Part 19 applies may only be introduced in evidence if it has been served in accordance with rule 19.3.*

*See also rule 20.3 for the procedure where a party objects to the introduction of hearsay evidence, including such evidence in a document, and rules 21.3 and 21.4 for the procedure where a party objects to the introduction of evidence of bad character.*

*A direction about the giving of evidence may be made on an application to which Part 18 applies (Measures to assist a witness or defendant to give evidence).]*

**R24.14**  **Duty of justices' legal adviser**

24.14 (1)  A justices' legal adviser must attend the court and carry out the duties listed in this rule, as applicable, unless the court—
  (a)  includes a District Judge (Magistrates' Courts); and
  (b)  otherwise directs.
(2)  A justices' legal adviser must—
  (a)  before the hearing begins, by reference to what is provided for the court under rule 24.13 (Provision of documents for the court) draw the court's attention to—
    (i)  what the prosecutor alleges,
    (ii)  what the parties say is agreed,
    (iii)  what the parties say is in dispute, and
    (iv)  what the parties say about how each expects to present the case, especially where that may affect its duration and timetabling;
  (b)  whenever necessary, give the court legal advice and—
    (i)  if necessary, attend the members of the court outside the courtroom to give such advice, but
    (ii)  inform the parties (if present) of any such advice given outside the courtroom; and
  (c)  assist the court, where appropriate, in the formulation of its reasons and the recording of those reasons.
(3)  A justices' legal adviser must—
  (a)  assist an unrepresented defendant; and
  (b)  assist the court by—
    (i)  making a note of the substance of any oral evidence or representations, to help the court recall that information,
    (ii)  if the court rules inadmissible part of a written statement introduced in evidence, marking that statement in such a way as to make that clear,
    (iii)  ensuring that an adequate record is kept of the court's decisions and the reasons for them, and
    (iv)  making any announcement, other than of the verdict or sentence.
(4)  Where the defendant has served a notice of guilty plea to which rule 24.8 (Written guilty plea: special rules) applies, a justices' legal adviser must—
  (a)  unless the court otherwise directs, if any member of the public, including any reporter, is present, read aloud to the court—
    (i)  the material on which the prosecutor relies to set out the facts of the offence and to provide information relevant to sentence (or summarise any written statement included in that material, if the court so directs), and
    (ii)  any written representations by the defendant; and
  (b)  otherwise, draw the court's attention to—
    (i)  what the prosecutor alleges, and any significant features of the material listed in paragraph (4)(a)(i), and
    (ii)  any written representations by the defendant.
(5)  Where the court tries a case under rule 24.9 (Single justice procedure: special rules), a justices' legal adviser must draw the court's attention to—
  (a)  what the prosecutor alleges, and any significant features of the material on which the prosecutor relies to prove the alleged offence and to provide information relevant to sentence; and
  (b)  any representations served by the defendant.

*[Note. Section 28 of the Courts Act 2003[63] provides for the functions of a justices' legal adviser. See also sections 12 and 16A of the Magistrates' Courts Act 1980[64].*

*Under section 12(7ZA) of the 1980 Act[65], Criminal Procedure Rules may specify which of the documents listed in section 12(7) of that Act[66], if any, must be read aloud, and may require them to be read aloud only in circumstances specified in the rules.]*

### Duty of court officer and custodian                                    R24.15

24.15 (1)  The court officer must—

    (a)  serve on each party notice of where and when an adjourned hearing will resume, unless—

        (i)  the party was present when that was arranged,

        (ii)  the defendant has served a notice of guilty plea to which rule 24.8 (Written guilty plea: special rules) applies, and the adjournment is for not more than 4 weeks, or

        (iii)  the court tries a case under rule 24.9 (Single justice procedure: special rules), and the adjourned trial will resume under that rule;

    (b)  if the reason for the adjournment was to postpone sentence, include that reason in any such notice to the defendant;

    (c)  unless the court otherwise directs, make available to the parties any written report to which rule 24.11 (Procedure if the court convicts) applies;

    (d)  where the court has ordered a defendant to provide information under section 25 of the Road Traffic Offenders Act 1988[67], serve on the defendant notice of that order unless the defendant was present when it was made;

    (e)  serve on the prosecutor—

        (i)  any notice of guilty plea to which rule 24.8 (Written guilty plea: special rules) applies, and

        (ii)  any declaration served under rule 44.2 (Statutory declaration of ignorance of proceedings) that the defendant did not know about the case;

    (f)  serve on the prosecutor notice of any hearing date arranged in consequence of such a declaration, unless—

        (i)  the prosecutor was present when that was arranged, or

        (ii)  the court otherwise directs;

    (g)  serve on the prosecutor—

        (i)  notice of any hearing date arranged in consequence of the issue of a summons under rule 24.9 (Single justice procedure: special rules), and in that event

        (ii)  any notice served by the defendant under rule 24.9(2)(b) or (c);

    (h)  record the court's reasons for not proceeding in the defendant's absence where rule 24.12(3)(a) applies; and

    (i)  give the court such other assistance as it requires.

  (2)  Where the court passes a sentence of immediate imprisonment or detention, or orders a suspended sentence of imprisonment to take effect, by this rule—

    (a)  the court requires the defendant to provide, in writing or orally, his or her nationality; and

    (b)  the custodian must obtain that information and record it

*[Note. See sections 10, 11 and 12 of the Magistrates' Courts Act 1980[68].*

*Under section 25 of the Road Traffic Offenders Act 1988, where the court does not know a defendant's sex or date of birth, then on convicting the defendant of an offence involving obligatory or discretionary disqualification, the court must order the defendant to provide that information.*

*Under Part 5, the magistrates' court officer must record details of a case and of the court's decisions.]*

---

[63] 2003 c. 39; section 28 was amended by section 15 of, and paragraphs 308 and 327 of Schedule 4 to, the Constitutional Reform Act 2005 (c. 4).

[64] 1980 c. 43; section 12 was amended by section 45 of, and paragraph 1 of Schedule 5 to, the Criminal Justice and Public Order Act 1994 (c. 33), section 1 of the Magistrates' Courts (Procedure) Act 1998 (c. 15), section 109 of, and paragraph 203 of Schedule 8 to, the Courts Act 2003 (c. 39), section 308 of, and Part 12 of Schedule 37 to, the Criminal Justice Act 2003 (c. 44) and section 81 of the Deregulation Act 2015 (c. 20). Section 16A was inserted by section 48 of the Criminal Justice and Courts Act 2015 (c. 2).

[65] 1980 c. 43; section 12(7ZA) was inserted by section 81 of the Deregulation Act 2015 (c. 20).

[66] 1980 c. 43; section 12(7) was amended by section 81 of the Deregulation Act 2015 (c. 20).

[67] 1988 c. 53; section 25 was amended by section 90 of, and paragraphs 140 and 142 of Schedule 13 to, the Access to Justice Act 1999 (c. 22), section 165 of, and paragraph 118 of Schedule 9 to, the Powers of Criminal Courts (Sentencing) Act 2000 (c. 6) and section 109 of, and paragraph 311 of Schedule 8 to, the Courts Act 2003 (c. 39).

[68] 1980 c. 43; section 10 was amended by section 59 of, and paragraph 1 of Schedule 9 to, the Criminal Justice Act 1982 (c. 48), section 68 of, and paragraph 6 of Schedule 8 to, the Criminal Justice Act 1991 (c. 53) and section 47 of the Crime and Disorder Act 1998 (c. 37).

*Under section 86A of the Courts Act 2003[69], Criminal Procedure Rules must specify stages of proceedings at which the court must require the information to which rule 24.15(2) refers. A person commits an offence if, without reasonable excuse, that person fails to comply with such a requirement, whether by providing false or incomplete information or by providing no information.]*

CRIMINAL PRACTICE DIRECTIONS   PART 24   TRIAL AND SENTENCE IN A
MAGISTRATES' COURT

**CPD.24A**  **CPD VI Trial 24A: Role of the Justices' Clerk/Legal Adviser**

24A.1    The role of the justices' clerk/legal adviser is a unique one, which carries with it independence from direction when undertaking a judicial function and when advising magistrates. These functions must be carried out in accordance with the Bangalore Principles of Judicial Conduct (judicial independence, impartiality, integrity, propriety, ensuring fair treatment and competence and diligence). More specifically, duties must be discharged in accordance with the relevant professional Code of Conduct and the Legal Adviser Competence Framework.

24A.2    A justices' clerk is responsible for:
(a)   the legal advice tendered to the justices within the area;
(b)   the performance of any of the functions set out below by any member of his staff acting as justices' legal adviser;
(c)   ensuring that competent advice is available to justices when the justices' clerk is not personally present in court; and
(d)   ensuring that advice given at all stages of proceedings and powers exercised (including those delegated to justices' legal advisers) take into account the court's duty to deal with cases justly and actively to manage the case.

24A.3    Where a person other than the justices' clerk (a justices' legal adviser), who is authorised to do so, performs any of the functions referred to in this direction, he or she will have the same duties, powers and responsibilities as the justices' clerk. The justices' legal adviser may consult the justices' clerk, or other person authorised by the justices' clerk for that purpose, before tendering advice to the bench. If the justices' clerk or that person gives any advice directly to the bench, he or she should give the parties or their advocates an opportunity of repeating any relevant submissions, prior to the advice being given.

24A.4    When exercising judicial powers, a justices' clerk or legal adviser is acting in exactly the same capacity as a magistrate. The justices' clerk may delegate powers to a justices' legal adviser in accordance with the relevant statutory authority. The scheme of delegation must be clear and in writing, so that all justices' legal advisers are certain of the extent of their powers. Once a power is delegated, judicial discretion in an individual case lies with the justices' legal adviser exercising the power. When exercise of a power does not require the consent of the parties, a justices' clerk or legal adviser may deal with and decide a contested issue or may refer that issue to the court.

24A.5    It shall be the responsibility of the justices' clerk or legal adviser to provide the justices with any advice they require to perform their functions justly, whether or not the advice has been requested, on:
(a)   questions of law;
(b)   questions of mixed law and fact;
(c)   matters of practice and procedure;
(d)   the process to be followed at sentence and the matters to be taken into account, together with the range of penalties and ancillary orders available, in accordance with the relevant sentencing guidelines;
(e)   any relevant decisions of the superior courts or other guidelines;
(f)   the appropriate decision-making structure to be applied in any given case; and
(g)   other issues relevant to the matter before the court.

24A.6    In addition to advising the justices, it shall be the justices' legal adviser's responsibility to assist the court, where appropriate, as to the formulation of reasons and the recording of those reasons.

24A.7    The justices' legal adviser has a duty to assist an unrepresented defendant, see CrimPR 9.4(3)(a), 14.3(2)(a) and 24.15(3)(a), in particular when the court is making a decision on allocation, bail, at trial and on sentence.

---

[69] 2003 c. 39; section 86A was inserted by section 162 of the Policing and Crime Act 2016 (c. 3).

24A.8    Where the court must determine allocation, the legal adviser may deal with any aspect of the allocation hearing save for the decision on allocation, indication of sentence and sentence.

24A.9    When a defendant acting in person indicates a guilty plea, the legal adviser must explain the procedure and inform the defendant of their right to address the court on the facts and to provide details of their personal circumstances in order that the court can decide the appropriate sentence.

24A.10    When a defendant indicates a not guilty plea but has not completed the relevant sections of the Magistrates' Courts Trial Preparation Form, the legal adviser must either ensure that the Form is completed or, in appropriate cases, assist the court to obtain and record the essential information on the form.

24A.11    Immediately prior to the commencement of a trial, the legal adviser must summarise for the court the agreed and disputed issues, together with the way in which the parties propose to present their cases. If this is done by way of pre-court briefing, it should be confirmed in court or agreed with the parties.

24A.12    A justices' clerk or legal adviser must not play any part in making findings of fact, but may assist the bench by reminding them of the evidence, using any notes of the proceedings for this purpose, and clarifying the issues which are agreed and those which are to be determined.

24A.13    A justices' clerk or legal adviser may ask questions of witnesses and the parties in order to clarify the evidence and any issues in the case. A legal adviser has a duty to ensure that every case is conducted justly.

24A.14    When advising the justices, the justices' clerk or legal adviser, whether or not previously in court, should:
(a)    ensure that he is aware of the relevant facts; and
(b)    provide the parties with an opportunity to respond to any advice given.

24A.15    At any time, justices are entitled to receive advice to assist them in discharging their responsibilities. If they are in any doubt as to the evidence which has been given, they should seek the aid of their legal adviser, referring to his notes as appropriate. This should ordinarily be done in open court. Where the justices request their adviser to join them in the retiring room, this request should be made in the presence of the parties in court. Any legal advice given to the justices other than in open court should be clearly stated to be provisional; and the adviser should subsequently repeat the substance of the advice in open court and give the parties the opportunity to make any representations they wish on that provisional advice. The legal adviser should then state in open court whether the provisional advice is confirmed or, if it is varied, the nature of the variation.

24A.16    The legal adviser is under a duty to assist unrepresented parties, whether defendants or not, to present their case, but must do so without appearing to become an advocate for the party concerned. The legal adviser should also ensure that members of the court are aware of obligations under the Victims' Code.

24A.17    The role of legal advisers in fine default proceedings, or any other proceedings for the enforcement of financial orders, obligations or penalties, is to assist the court. They must not act in an adversarial or partisan manner, such as by attempting to establish wilful refusal or neglect or any other type of culpable behaviour, to offer an opinion on the facts, or to urge a particular course of action upon the justices. The expectation is that a legal adviser will ask questions of the defaulter to elicit information which the justices will require to make an adjudication, such as the explanation for the default. A legal adviser may also advise the justices as to the options open to them in dealing with the case.

24A.18    The performance of a legal adviser is subject to regular appraisal. For that purpose the appraiser may be present in the justices' retiring room. The content of the appraisal is confidential, but the fact that an appraisal has taken place, and the presence of the appraiser in the retiring room, should be briefly explained in open court.

**CPD VI Trial 24B: Identification for the Court of the Issues in the Case**    **CPD.24B**

24B.1    CrimPR 3.11(a) requires the court, with the active assistance of the parties, to establish what are the disputed issues in order to manage the trial. To that end, the purpose of the prosecutor's summary of the prosecution case is to explain briefly, in the prosecutor's own terms, what the case is about, including any relevant legislation or case law relevant to the particular case. It will not usually be necessary, or helpful, to present a detailed account of all the prosecution evidence due to be introduced.

**24B.2**　CrimPR 24.3(3)(b) provides for a defendant, or his or her advocate, immediately after the prosecution opening to set out the issues in the defendant's own terms, if invited to do so by the court. The purpose of any such identification of issues is to provide the court with focus as to what it is likely to be called upon to decide, so that the members of the court will be alert to those issues from the outset and can evaluate the prosecution evidence that they hear accordingly.

**24B.3**　The parties should keep in mind that, in most cases, the members of the court already will be aware of what has been declared to be in issue. The court will have access to any written admissions and to information supplied for the purposes of case management: CrimPR 24.13(2). The court's legal adviser will have drawn the court's attention to what is alleged and to what is understood to be in dispute: CrimPR 24.15(2). If a party has nothing of substance to add to that, then he or she should say so. The requirement to be concise will be enforced and the exchange with the court properly may be confined to enquiry and confirmation that the court's understanding of those allegations and issues is correct. Nevertheless, for the defendant to be offered an opportunity to identify issues at this stage may assist even if all he or she wishes to announce, or confirm, is that the prosecution is being put to proof.

**24B.4**　The identification of issues at the case management stage will have been made without the risk that they would be used at trial as statements of the defendant admissible in evidence against the defendant, provided the advocate follows the letter and the spirit of the Criminal Procedure Rules. The court may take the view that a party is not acting in the spirit of the Criminal Procedure Rules in seeking to ambush the other party or raising late and technical legal arguments that were not previously raised as issues. No party that seeks to ambush the other at trial should derive an advantage from such a course of action. The court may also take the view that a defendant is not acting in the spirit of the Criminal Procedure Rules if he or she refuses to identify the issues and puts the prosecutor to proof at the case management stage. In both such circumstances the court may limit the proceedings on the day of trial in accordance with CrimPR 3.11(d). In addition any significant divergence from the issues identified at case management at this late stage may well result in the exercise of the court's powers under CrimPR 3.5(6), the powers to impose sanctions.

**CPD.24C**　**CPD VI Trial 24C: Trial Adjournment in Magistrates' Courts**

**24C.1**　Courts are entitled to expect the parties and other participants to adhere to CrimPR 1.2 (The duty of the participants in a criminal case) and to prepare accordingly for the trial to proceed on the date arranged. The court will expect communication between the parties and with the court regarding any issues which are likely to affect the effectiveness of any trial: CrimPR 3.2(2)(b)-(e). In particular, any revision of the information provided in the preparation for effective trial form must be reported to the court and each other party well in advance of the trial, not at trial or shortly before; and in considering any application to adjourn a trial the court will regard as especially significant any failure in this respect. Any communication should clearly identify the issue and any direction sought. and should require reference to a legal adviser or case progression officer. The parties and other participants are entitled to expect the court and its staff to adhere to CrimPR 1.3 (The application by the court of the overriding objective) and to conduct its business accordingly. If relevant Criminal Procedure Rules, Criminal Practice Directions and judicial directions for trial preparation are followed, an effective trial on the date arranged will be the result.

**24C.2**　In some circumstances during preparation for trial it will become apparent to a party that a trial will not be required. It is in the interests of victims, witnesses, defendants, the court and legal representatives that these decisions are made at the earliest opportunity and that the other party, or parties, and the court are notified immediately. The requirements for an application to vacate a trial fixture are set out at paragraphs 24C.30 to 24C.32 beneath.

**24C.3**　Where a defendant who previously has pleaded not guilty decides to enter a guilty plea, notice of that decision, and the basis of plea, should be given to the prosecution and court as soon as possible so that a decision can be taken about the need for witnesses to attend (but caution should be exercised before the witnesses' attendance is dispensed with, and usually it will be advisable to set a date for the plea to be taken in advance of the date already set for trial). The sooner that notice of such a plea is given, the greater the reduction in sentence the defendant can expect. The court will expect an explanation for the change of plea to assess the level of credit to be applied.

24C.4   Where a party is unable to comply with a direction within the time set by the court, and that failure will have implications for preparation by another party or for the likelihood of the trial proceeding within the time allocated, the party concerned should advise each other party and the court immediately of the failure and of the anticipated date for compliance: CrimPR 1.2(1)(c) and 3.10(2)(d). Parties are encouraged to communicate with each other to agree alternative dates consistent with maintaining the trial fixture: CrimPR 3.7.

## Application to adjourn on day of trial

### General principles

24C.5   The court is entitled to expect that trials will start on time with all case management issues dealt with in advance of the trial date. Early engagement between the parties and communication with the court should mean that it is rare for applications to adjourn trials to be made on the day of trial, except in circumstances that could not have been foreseen. However, there will be occasions on which, on the day set for trial, the court is invited without prior warning to adjourn to another day in consequence of an event or events said to make it unjust to proceed as planned; and in some circumstances it may have been necessary to arrange to hear a contested application to adjourn a trial on the very date on which that trial is due to begin (though before making such arrangements the court should have kept in mind the need to make time available for other cases, too, where the time available for the trial will be abbreviated by the time required to hear the application to adjourn it).

24C.6   Section 10 of the Magistrates' Courts Act 1980 confers a discretionary power to adjourn, and see also CrimPR 24.2(3). The following directions codify and restate procedural principles established in a long line of judgments of the senior courts, to some of which they refer. Therefore these directions supersede those judgments and it is to these directions that magistrates' courts must refer in the first instance.

24C.7   The starting point is that the trial should proceed. The basic approach was explained by Gross LJ in *Director of Public Prosecutions v Petrie* [2015] EWHC 48 (Admin):

'... *successive initiatives ... have repeatedly exhorted the magistracy and District Bench to case manage robustly and to resist the granting of adjournments. Although there are of course instances where the interests of justice require the grant of an adjournment, this should be a course of last rather than first resort – and after other alternatives have been considered. ... It is essential that parties to proceedings in a magistrates' court should proceed on the basis of a need to get matters right first time; any suggestion of a culture readily permitting an opportunity to correct failures of preparation should be firmly dispelled.*'

24C.8   A magistrates' court may keep in mind that, if appropriate, the court's decision may be re-opened (see CrimPR 24.18), and that avenues of appeal by way of rehearing or of review are open to the parties, including in a case in which it is later discovered that the court has acted on a material mistake of fact (see *R (Director of Public Prosecutions) v Sunderland Magistrates' Court, R (Kharaghan) v City of London Magistrates' Court* [2018] EWHC 229 (Admin)). The court should not be deterred from a prompt and robust determination therefore. Only if there are compelling reasons for doing so will the High Court interfere with the court's exercise of its discretion.

24C.9   In general, the relevant principles relating to trial adjournment are these:
- the court's duty is to deal justly with the case, which includes doing justice between the parties.
- the court must have regard to the need for expedition. Delay is generally inimical to the interests of justice and brings the criminal justice system into disrepute. Proceedings in a magistrates' court should be simple and speedy.
- applications for adjournments should be rigorously scrutinised and the court must have a clear reason for adjourning. To do this, the court must review the history of the case.
- where the prosecutor asks for an adjournment the court must consider not only the interest of the defendant in getting the matter dealt with without delay but also the public interest in ensuring that criminal charges are adjudicated upon thoroughly, with the guilty convicted as well as the innocent acquitted.
- with a more serious charge the public interest that there be a trial will carry greater weight. It is, however, reasonable for the court to expect that parties should have given especially careful attention to the preparation of trials involving serious offences or where the trial has significant implications for victims or witnesses.

Criminal Procedure Rules and Criminal Practice Directions

- where the defendant asks for an adjournment the court must consider whether he or she will be able to present the defence fully without and, if not, the extent to which his or her ability to do so is compromised.
- the court must consider the consequences of an adjournment and its impact on the ability of witnesses and defendants accurately to recall events.
- the impact of adjournment on other cases. The relisting of one case almost inevitably delays or displaces the hearing of others. The length of the hearing and the extent of delay in other cases will need to be considered.

*The relevance of fault*

24C.10   As the starting point is that the trial should proceed, a consequence of doing so without adjournment may be that the prosecutor is unable to prove the prosecution case, or that the defendant is unable to explore an issue. That may be a just consequence of inadequate preparation. Even in the absence of fault on the part of either party it may not be in the interests of justice to adjourn, notwithstanding that an imperfect trial may be the result.

24C.11   The reason why the adjournment is required should be examined and if it arises through the fault of the applicant for that adjournment then that weighs against its grant, carrying weight in accordance with the gravity of the fault. For the purposes of this paragraph, the prosecutor and those who investigated the case usually should be treated as one.

24C.12   If the applicant was at fault, was it serious? A fault will be serious if the relevant act or omission has been repeated, especially where it has caused a previous adjournment, or where there is no reasonable explanation for that act or omission. The more serious the default, the less willing the court will be to adjourn.

24C.13   Where a party has been at fault, did the other party, if aware of it, draw attention to that fault promptly and explicitly? CrimPR 1.2(1)(c) imposes a collective responsibility on participants promptly to draw attention to a significant failure to take a required procedural step. CrimPR 3.10(2)(d) requires each party promptly to inform the court and the other parties of anything that may affect the date or duration of the trial or significantly affect the progress of the case in any other way. If no such action has been taken by a party who could have done so then the court may look less favourably on any application by that same party to adjourn, and especially if that application reasonably might have been made before the trial date.

*Length of adjournment*

24C.14   Were an adjournment granted, for how long would it need to be? The shorter the necessary adjournment, the less objectionable it will be – although much will depend on the ability of the court to accommodate it without undue impact on other cases. Courts must make every effort to make the adjournment as short as possible, for example by using time vacated by another trial or by conducting the hearing at another court house. In some cases it may be possible to achieve a just outcome by a short adjournment to later on the same day.

24C.15   If the reason for the application to adjourn is that the applicant party seeks more time in which to raise or explore an issue, has that party reasonable grounds for its late identification despite the requirements of CrimPR 3.3(1) read with 3.2(2) (early identification of issues)? In the absence of such grounds, that failure will constitute a fault for the purposes of these directions.

**Particular grounds of applications to adjourn trials**

24C.16   The following paragraphs identify some particular factors which may need to be taken into account in addition to those identified in paragraphs 24C.5 – 24C15.

*Absence of defendant*

24C.17   If a defendant has attained the age of 18 years, the court shall proceed in his absence unless it appears to the court to be contrary to the interests of justice to do so: section 11 of the Magistrates' Courts Act 1980. In marked contrast to the position in the Crown Court, in magistrates' courts proceeding in the absence of a defendant is the default position where the defendant is aware of the date of trial and no acceptable reason is offered for that absence. The court is not obliged to investigate if no reason is offered. In assessing where the interests of justice lie the court will take into account all factors, including such reasons for absence as may be offered; the reliability of the information supplied in support of those reasons; the date on which the reasons for absence became known to the defendant; and what action the defendant thereafter took in response. Where the defendant provides a medical note to excuse his or her non-attendance the court must consider 5C of these Practice Directions (issue of medical certificates) and give reasons if deciding to proceed notwithstanding.

**24C.18**  If the court does not proceed to trial in the absence of the defendant it is required by the 1980 Act to give its reasons, which must be specific to the case: section 11(7), and see also CrimPR 24.16(h).

**24C.19**  Where a defendant is under 18, there is no presumption that the court should proceed in absence. In deciding whether it is in the interests of justice to proceed the court should take into account:
- that trial in absence can and sometimes does result in acquittal and that it is in nobody's interests to delay an acquittal;
- that if convicted the defendant can ask that the conviction be re-opened in the interests of justice, for example if absence was involuntary;
- that if convicted the defendant has a right to a rehearing on appeal to the Crown Court;
- the age, vulnerability, or experience of the defendant;
- whether a parent or guardian is present, whether a parent or guardian ordinarily would be required to attend and whether such a person has attended a previous hearing;
- the interests of any co-defendant in the case proceeding;
- the interests of witnesses who have attended, including the age of any such witness;
- the nature of the evidence and whether memories of relevant evidence are liable to fade;
- how soon an adjourned trial can be accommodated in the court list.

When proceeding in absence or adjourning the court must give its reasons.

*Absence of witness*

**24C.20**  Where the court is asked to adjourn because a witness has failed to attend, the court must:
- rigorously investigate the steps taken to secure that witness' attendance, the reasons given for absence and the likelihood of the witness attending should the case be adjourned;
- consider the relevance of the witness to the case, and whether the witness' statement can be agreed or admitted, in whole or part, as hearsay, including under section 114(1)(d) of the Criminal Justice Act 2003;
- in the case of a defence witness, consider whether proper notice has been given of the intention to call that witness;
- consider whether an absent witness can be heard later in the trial;
- where other witnesses have attended and the court has determined that the absent witness is required, consider hearing those witnesses who are present and adjourning the case part-heard, provided the next hearing can be held conveniently in a matter of days or weeks, not months, to avoid having to recall all the witnesses.

*Failure to serve evidence in time*

**24C.21**  It should rarely be the case that an application to adjourn based on a failure to serve evidence is made on the day of trial. The court is entitled to expect that evidence will have been served in good time and in accordance with the directions of the court. The court should consider whether the party who complains of the failure had drawn attention to it: CrimPR 1.2(1)(c) and 3.10(2)(d), and see paragraphs 24C.10 – 24C.13 above.

**24C.22**  The court must conduct a rigorous inquiry into the nature of the evidence and must consider whether any of what is sought has been served, and if so when; the volume and the significance of what is sought; and the time likely to be needed for its consideration. In particular, the court must satisfy itself that any material still sought is relevant and that the party seeking it has a right to it. In some circumstances a failure to serve evidence can be addressed by refusing to admit it instead of by adjourning the trial to allow it to be served: see *R v Boardman* [2015] EWCA Crim 175; [2015] 1 Cr. App. R. 33; [2015] Crim. L.R. 451.

*Failure to comply with disclosure obligations*

**24C.23**  The parties' disclosure obligations arise from the Criminal Procedure and Investigations Act 1996. The procedure to comply with those duties is set out at CrimPR Part 15. Disclosure is not a trial issue. It should have been resolved by the parties complying with their statutory obligations and with the Rules in advance of the trial.

**24C.24**  Where a defendant complains of a prosecution failure to disclose material that ought to have been disclosed the court must first establish whether either party is applying for an adjournment as a result. If an adjournment is sought, the court should consider whether the matter can be resolved by the giving of disclosure immediately. If it cannot, the court should consider whether the parties have complied with their obligations under CrimPR 3.3 and under the provisions listed in paragraph 24C.1 above, and should consider the relevance of fault.

**24C.25**  If the prosecutor has complied or purported to comply with his or her initial disclosure obligations, no further material is disclosable and consequently no application to adjourn should be entertained unless the defendant has served a defence statement in accordance with section 6 of the Criminal Procedure and Investigations Act 1996 and CrimPR 15.4.

24C.26  If the defendant has served a defence statement and asks for further disclosure, in consequence of the prosecutor's allegedly inadequate response or in consequence of a failure to respond at all, the court has no power to entertain an application for that further disclosure unless it is made pursuant to section 8 of the Criminal Procedure and Investigations Act 1996 and CrimPR 15.5. The court should consider hearing such an application immediately, provided that there is sufficient time available for the application itself and then for the defence to consider any material disclosed in consequence of it.

### Managing trials within available court time

24C.27  Where there is a risk of a trials being adjourned for lack of court time the court or legal adviser must assess the priority to be assigned to each trial listed for hearing that day based on the needs of the parties, whether the case has been adjourned before and the seriousness of the offence; giving priority to any cases in which the defendant is in custody by reason only of a trial due to be heard that day. Where more than one court is sitting to deal with trials, liaison between courtrooms should occur to determine the potential for all listed trials to be heard through movement of cases. Where a case is moved from one courtroom to another and as a result is assigned to a different advocate, the court must allow the fresh advocate adequate time in which to prepare. Courts should always begin a trial by reviewing the need for witnesses and the timetable set during pre-trial case management. The court will be slow to adjourn a trial until it is clear that all other trials assessed as having an equal or higher priority for hearing that day will be effective.

24C.28  The court is entitled to expect that parties will present their case within the time set during pre-trial case management. In entertaining additional applications for which no time has been allowed the court must keep in mind the expectation that the trial will be completed within the allocated time with minimal impact on other cases.

24C.29  While it is preferable to complete a trial on the date allocated, there will be occasions on which it is appropriate to adjourn part-heard, particularly where it is possible to hear the majority of witnesses. If necessary future listings will be moved to accommodate the hearing.

### *Applications to vacate trials*

24C.30  To make the best use of the court's and the parties' time it is expected that applications to vacate trials will be made promptly and in writing, in advance of the date of trial. Any application should be served on each other party at the same time as it is served on the court. As a general rule, such an application will be dealt with outside the courtroom under CrimPR 3.5. An application to vacate a trial will be considered in accordance with the same principles as those identified in paragraphs 24C.5 – 24C.26 of these Directions.

24C.31  Given the binding nature of any decision on an application to vacate and refix a trial, absent a change of circumstances, it is incumbent on the parties to provide full and accurate information to the court to enable it to assess where the interests of justice lie: see *R (on the application of F and another) v Knowsley Magistrates Court* [2006] EWHC 695 (Admin); *R (Jones) v South East Surrey Local Justice Area* [2010] EWHC 916 (Admin), (2010) 174 JP 342; *DPP v Woods* [2017] EWHC 1070 (Admin). Any application should, as a minimum, include (as should, as appropriate, any response):

- the reason for the application;
- a chronology of the case, recording the dates of compliance with any directions and of communication between the parties;
- an assessment of the interests of justice, addressing the factors identified in these Practice Directions and indicating the likely effect should the court conclude that the trial should proceed on the date fixed;
- any restrictions on the future availability of witnesses;
- any likely changes to the number of witnesses or the way in which the evidence will be presented and any impact on the trial time estimate.

24C.32  On receipt of an application each other party should serve that party's response on the court and on the applicant within 2 business days unless the court otherwise directs. Any request for the matter to be determined at a hearing should be served with the application to vacate the trial or with the response to that application, as the case may be, together with the reasons for that request, to enable the court to decide whether a hearing is needed.

## CRIMINAL PROCEDURE RULES   PART 25   TRIAL AND SENTENCE IN THE CROWN COURT

*[Note. Part 3 contains rules about case management that apply during preparation for trial and at trial. The rules in this Part must be read in conjunction with those rules.]*

### When this Part applies

**R25.1**

**25.1**   This Part applies in the Crown Court where the court tries a case or the defendant pleads guilty.

*[Note. The Crown Court's powers to try an allegation of an offence are contained in sections 45 and 46 of the Senior Courts Act 1981[1].*

*The exercise of the court's powers is affected by—*

> *(a)  the classification of the offence (and the general rule, subject to exceptions, is that the Crown Court must try—*
> > *(i)  an offence classified as one that can be tried only in the Crown Court (in other legislation, described as triable only on indictment), and*
> > *(ii)  an offence classified as one that can be tried either in a magistrates' court or in the Crown Court (in other legislation, described as triable either way) that has been allocated for trial in the Crown Court); and*
> *(b)  the defendant's age (and the general rule is that an allegation of an offence against a defendant under 18 must be tried in a magistrates' court sitting as a youth court, irrespective of the classification of the offence and without allocation for trial there, unless the offence is—*
> > *(i)  one of homicide,*
> > *(ii)  one for which a convicted adult could be imprisoned for 14 years or more,*
> > *(iii)  one of certain specified offences involving firearms, or*
> > *(iv)  one of certain specified sexual offences).*

*See sections 17 and 24 of the Magistrates' Courts Act 1980[2]) and section 51A of the Crime and Disorder Act 1998[3].*

*Under section 34A of the Children and Young Persons Act 1933[4], the court—*

> *(a)  may require the defendant's parents or guardian to attend court with the defendant, where the defendant is under 18; and*
> *(b)  must do so, where the defendant is under 16,*

*unless satisfied that that would be unreasonable. Part 46 (Representatives) contains rules allowing a parent, guardian or other supporting adult to help a defendant under 18.]*

### General powers and requirements

**R25.2**

**25.2**   (1)  Where this Part applies, the general rule is that—

> (a)  the trial must be in public, but that is subject to the court's power to—
> > (i)  impose a restriction on reporting what takes place at a public hearing, or public access to what otherwise would be a public hearing,
> > (ii)  withhold information from the public during a public hearing, or
> > (iii)  order a trial in private;
> (b)  the court must not proceed if the defendant is absent, unless the court is satisfied that—
> > (i)  the defendant has waived the right to attend, and
> > (ii)  the trial will be fair despite the defendant's absence; and
> (c)  the court must not sentence the defendant to imprisonment or detention unless—
> > (i)  the defendant has a legal representative,

---

[1]  1981 c. 54.

[2]  1980 c. 43; section 24 was amended by paragraph 47 of Schedule 14 to the Criminal Justice Act 1982 (c. 48), sections 17, 68 and 101 of, and paragraph 6 of Schedule 8 and Schedule 13 to, the Criminal Justice Act 1991 (c. 53), paragraph 40 of Schedule 10, and Schedule 11, to the Criminal Justice and Public Order Act 1994 (c. 33), sections 47 and 119 of, and paragraph 40 of Schedule 8, to the Crime and Disorder Act 1998 (c. 37), paragraph 64 of Schedule 9 to the Powers of Criminal Courts (Sentencing) Act 2000 (c. 6), section 42 of, and paragraphs 1 and 9 of Schedule 3, and Part 4 of Schedule 37, to the Criminal Justice Act 2003 (c. 44) and sections 49 and 65 of, and paragraph 1 of Schedule 1 and Schedule 5 to, the Violent Crime Reduction Act 2006 (c. 38).

[3]  1998 c. 37; section 51A was inserted by paragraphs 15 and 18 of Schedule 3 to the Criminal Justice Act 2003 (c. 44) and amended by section 49 of, and paragraph 5 of Schedule 1 to, the Violent Crime Reduction Act 2006 (c. 38) and paragraph 6 of Schedule 21 to the Legal Aid, Sentencing and Punishment of Offenders Act 2012 (c. 10).

[4]  1933 c. 12; section 34A was inserted by section 56 of the Criminal Justice Act 1991 (c. 53) and amended by section 107 of, and paragraph 1 of Schedule 5 to, the Local Government Act 2000 (c. 22).

(ii)   the defendant has been sentenced to imprisonment or detention on a previous occasion in the United Kingdom, or

(iii)   the defendant could have been represented under legal aid but is not because section 226(7), (8) of the Sentencing Act 2020[5] applies to him or her.

(2)   Before proceeding to trial the court must—

   (a)   obtain the prosecutor's confirmation, in writing or orally, that the indictment on which the defendant is about to be tried sets out—

      (i)   a statement of each offence that the prosecutor wants the court to try, and

      (ii)   such particulars of the conduct constituting the commission of each such offence as the prosecutor relies upon to make clear what is alleged;

   (b)   ensure that the defendant is correctly identified by that indictment;

   (c)   satisfy itself that there has been explained to the defendant, in terms the defendant can understand (with help, if necessary), each allegation in that indictment against him or her; and

   (d)   invite any objection to the terms or validity of that indictment.

(3)   The court may adjourn the trial at any stage.

*See section 226(7), (8) of the Sentencing Act 2020, which applies to a defendant if—*

   *(a)   representation was made available to the defendant for the purposes of the proceedings under Part 1 of the Legal Aid, Sentencing and Punishment of Offenders Act 2012 but was withdrawn because of the defendant's conduct or because it appeared that the defendant's financial resources were such that he or she was not eligible for such representation;*

   *(b)   the defendant applied for such representation and the application was refused because it appeared that the defendant's financial resources were such that he or she was not eligible for such representation; or*

   *(c)   having been informed of the right to apply for such representation and having had the opportunity to do so, the defendant refused or failed to apply.*

*Part 6 contains rules about reporting, etc. restrictions. For a list of the court's powers to impose reporting and access restrictions, see the note to rule 6.1.*

*Part 10 contains rules about the content and service of indictments. Under section 2(6ZA) of the Administration of Justice (Miscellaneous Provisions) Act 1933[6], no objection to the indictment may be taken after the trial commences by reason of any failure to observe those rules.]*

**R25.3**    **Application for ruling on procedure, evidence or other question of law**

   **25.3**   (1)   This rule applies to an application—

      (a)   about—

         (i)   case management, or any other question of procedure, or

         (ii)   the introduction or admissibility of evidence, or any other question of law; and

      (b)   that has not been determined before the trial begins.

     (2)   The application is subject to any other rule that applies to it (for example, as to the time and form in which the application must be made).

     (3)   Unless the court otherwise directs, the application must be made, and the court's decision announced, in the absence of the jury (if there is one).

*[Note. See also rule 3.21 (Pre-trial hearings in the Crown Court: general rules).]*

**R25.4**    **Procedure on plea of guilty**

   **25.4**   (1)   This rule applies if—

      (a)   the defendant pleads guilty to an offence; and

      (b)   the court is satisfied that the plea represents a clear acknowledgement of guilt.

     (2)   The court need not receive evidence unless rule 25.16(4) applies (determination of facts for sentencing).

*[Note. See also rule 3.32 (Arraigning the defendant on the indictment).]*

**R25.5**    **Application to vacate a guilty plea**

   **25.5**   (1)   This rule applies where a party wants the court to vacate a guilty plea.

     (2)   Such a party must—

      (a)   apply in writing—

         (i)   as soon as practicable after becoming aware of the grounds for doing so, and

---

[5]   2020 c. 17.
[6]   1933 c. 36; section 2(6ZA) was inserted by section 116 of the Coroners and Justice Act 2009 (c. 25).

        (ii) in any event, before the final disposal of the case, by sentence or otherwise; and

  (b) serve the application on—

        (i) the court officer, and

        (ii) the prosecutor.

(3) Unless the court otherwise directs, the application must—

  (a) explain why it would be unjust for the guilty plea to remain unchanged;

  (b) indicate what, if any, evidence the applicant wishes to call;

  (c) identify any proposed witness; and

  (d) indicate whether legal professional privilege is waived, specifying any material name and date.

**Selecting the jury**          **R25.6**

**25.6** (1) This rule—

  (a) applies where—

        (i) the defendant pleads not guilty,

        (ii) the defendant declines to enter a plea and the court treats that as a not guilty plea, or

        (iii) the court determines that the defendant is not fit to be tried; but

  (b) does not apply where—

        (i) the court orders a trial without a jury because of a danger of jury tampering or where jury tampering appears to have taken place, or

        (ii) the court tries without a jury counts on an indictment after a trial of sample counts with a jury.

(2) The court must select a jury to try the case from the panel, or part of the panel, of jurors summoned by the Lord Chancellor to attend at that time and place.

(3) Where it appears that too few jurors to constitute a jury will be available from among those so summoned, the court—

  (a) may exercise its own power to summon others in the court room, or in the vicinity, up to the number likely to be required, and add their names to the panel summoned by the Lord Chancellor; but

  (b) must inform the parties, if they are absent when the court exercises that power.

(4) The court must select the jury by drawing at random each juror's name from among those so summoned and—

  (a) announcing each name so drawn; or

  (b) announcing an identifying number assigned by the court officer to that person, where the court is satisfied that that is necessary.

(5) If too few jurors to constitute a jury are available from the panel after all their names have been drawn, the court may—

  (a) exercise its own power to summon others in the court room, or in the vicinity, up to the number required; and

  (b) announce—

        (i) the name of each person so summoned, or

        (ii) an identifying number assigned by the court officer to that person, where the court is satisfied that that is necessary.

(6) The jury the court selects—

  (a) must comprise no fewer than 12 jurors; and

  (b) may comprise as many as 14 jurors to begin with, where the court expects the trial to last for more than 4 weeks.

(7) Where the court selects a jury comprising more than 12 jurors, the court must explain to them that—

  (a) the purpose of selecting more than 12 jurors to begin with is to fill any vacancy or vacancies caused by the discharge of any of the first 12 before the prosecution evidence begins;

  (b) any such vacancy or vacancies will be filled by the extra jurors in order of their selection from the panel;

  (c) the court will discharge any extra juror or jurors remaining by no later than the beginning of the prosecution evidence; and

  (d) any juror who is discharged for that reason then will be available to be selected for service on another jury, during the period for which that juror has been summoned.

(8) Each of the 12 or more jurors the court selects—

  (a) must take an oath or affirm; and

  (b) becomes a full jury member until discharged.

(9) The oath or affirmation must be in these terms, or in any corresponding terms that the juror declares to be binding on him or her—

Criminal Procedure Rules and Criminal Practice Directions

'I swear by Almighty God [*or* I do solemnly, sincerely and truly declare and affirm] that I will faithfully try the defendant and give a true verdict according to the evidence.'

*[Note. See sections 2, 5, 6, and 11 of the Juries Act 1974[7]. See also rule 38.7 (Discharging jurors).*

*Under sections 44 and 46 of the Criminal Justice Act 2003[8], the court may try a case without a jury where there is a danger of jury tampering, or where jury tampering appears to have taken place. Under section 17 of the Domestic Violence, Crime and Victims Act 2004[9], the court may try sample counts with a jury and other counts without a jury. Part 3 (preparation for trial in the Crown Court) contains rules about an application for such a trial.*

*Sections 1, 3, 4, 5 and 6 of the Oaths Act 1978[10] provide for the taking of oaths and the making of affirmations, and for the words that must be used.*

*Part 26 contains other rules about jurors.]*

**R25.7**  **Discharging jurors**

    **25.7** (1) The court may exercise its power to discharge a juror at any time—
         (a) after the juror completes the oath or affirmation; and
         (b) before the court discharges the jury.
       (2) No later than the beginning of the prosecution evidence, if the jury then comprises more than 12 jurors the court must discharge any in excess of 12 in reverse order of their selection from the panel.
       (3) The court may exercise its power to discharge the jury at any time—
         (a) after each juror has completed the oath or affirmation; and
         (b) before the jury has delivered its verdict on each offence charged in the indictment.
       (4) The court must exercise its power to discharge the jury when, in respect of each offence charged in the indictment, either—
         (a) the jury has delivered its verdict on that offence; or
         (b) the court has discharged the jury from reaching a verdict.

*[Note. See sections 16 and 18 of the Juries Act 1974[11].]*

**R25.8**  **Objecting to jurors**

    **25.8** (1) A party who objects to the panel of jurors must serve notice explaining the objection on the court officer and on the other party before the first juror's name or number is drawn.
       (2) A party who objects to the selection of an individual juror must—
         (a) tell the court of the objection—
             (i) after the juror's name or number is announced, and
             (ii) before the juror completes the oath or affirmation; and
         (b) explain the objection.
       (3) A prosecutor who exercises the prosecution right without giving reasons to prevent the court selecting an individual juror must announce the exercise of that right before the juror completes the oath or affirmation.
       (4) The court must determine an objection under paragraph (1) or (2)—
         (a) at a hearing, in public or in private; and
         (b) in the absence of the jurors, unless the court otherwise directs.

*[Note. See section 29 of the Juries Act 1825[12] and section 12 of the Juries Act 1974[13].]*

---

[7] 1974 c. 23; section 2 was amended by section 61 of the Administration of Justice Act 1982 (c. 53) and Part 10 of Schedule 37 to the Criminal Justice Act 2003 (c. 44). Section 5 was amended by section 15 of, and paragraphs 77 and 78 of Schedule 4 to, the Constitutional Reform Act 2005 (c. 4). Section 6 was amended by paragraph 45 of Schedule 15 to the Criminal Justice Act 1988 (c. 33). Section 11 was amended by section 58 of, and paragraph 8 of Schedule 10 and Schedule 11 to, the Domestic Violence, Crime and Victims Act 2004 (c. 28).

[8] 2003 c. 44.

[9] 2004 c. 28.

[10] 1978 c. 19.

[11] 1974 c. 23; section 16 was amended by sections 121 and 170 of, and Schedule 16 to, the Criminal Justice Act 1988 (c. 33).

[12] 1825 c. 50; section 29 was amended by section 40 of, and paragraph 3 of Schedule 4 to, the Courts Act 1971 (c. 23). There are other amendments not relevant to this rule.

[13] 1974 c. 23; section 12 was amended by section 170 of, and Schedule 16 to, the Criminal Justice Act 1988 (c. 33).

**Procedure on plea of not guilty**

25.9  (1)  This rule applies where—

    (a)  the defendant pleads not guilty; or

    (b)  the defendant declines to enter a plea and the court treats that as a not guilty plea.

  (2)  In the following sequence—

    (a)  where there is a jury, the court must—

      (i)  inform the jurors of each offence charged in the indictment to which the defendant pleads not guilty, and

      (ii)  explain to the jurors that it is their duty, after hearing the evidence, to decide whether the defendant is guilty or not guilty of each offence;

    (b)  the prosecutor may summarise the prosecution case, concisely outlining the facts and the matters likely to be in dispute;

    (c)  where there is a jury, to help the jurors to understand the case and resolve any issue in it the court may—

      (i)  invite the defendant concisely to identify what is in issue, if necessary in terms approved by the court, and

      (ii)  if the defendant declines to do so, direct that the jurors be given a copy of any defence statement served under rule 15.4 (Defence disclosure), edited if necessary to exclude any reference to inappropriate matters or to matters evidence of which would not be admissible;

    (d)  the prosecutor must introduce the evidence on which the prosecution case relies;

    (e)  subject to paragraph (3), at the end of the prosecution evidence, on the defendant's application or on its own initiative, the court—

      (i)  may direct the jury (if there is one) to acquit on the ground that the prosecution evidence is insufficient for any reasonable court properly to convict, but

      (ii)  must not do so unless the prosecutor has had an opportunity to make representations;

    (f)  subject to paragraph (4), at the end of the prosecution evidence, the court must ask whether the defendant intends to give evidence in person and, if the answer is 'no', then the court must satisfy itself that there has been explained to the defendant, in terms the defendant can understand (with help, if necessary)—

      (i)  the right to give evidence in person, and

      (ii)  that if the defendant does not give evidence in person, or refuses to answer a question while giving evidence, the court may draw such inferences as seem proper;

    (g)  the defendant may summarise the defence case, if he or she intends to call at least one witness other than him or herself to give evidence in person about the facts of the case;

    (h)  in this order (or in a different order, if the court so directs) the defendant may—

      (i)  give evidence in person,

      (ii)  call another witness, or witnesses, to give evidence in person, and

      (iii)  introduce any other evidence;

    (i)  a party may introduce further evidence if it is then admissible (for example, because it is in rebuttal of evidence already introduced);

    (j)  the prosecutor may make final representations, where—

      (i)  the defendant has a legal representative,

      (ii)  the defendant has called at least one witness, other than the defendant him or herself, to give evidence in person about the facts of the case, or

      (iii)  the court so permits; and

    (k)  the defendant may make final representations.

  (3)  Paragraph (2)(e) does not apply in relation to a charge of murder, manslaughter, attempted murder, or causing harm contrary to section 18 or 20 of the Offences against the Person Act 1861[14] until the court has heard all the evidence (including any defence evidence), where the defendant is charged with—

    (a)  any of those offences; and

    (b)  an offence of causing or allowing a child or vulnerable adult to die or to suffer serious physical harm, contrary to section 5 of the Domestic Violence, Crime and Victims Act 2004[15].

---

[14]  1861 c. 100; section 18 was amended by the Statute Law Revision Act 1892 (c. 19), the Statute Law Revision (No 2) Act 1893 (c. 54) and section 10 of, and Part III of Schedule 3 to, the Criminal Law Act 1967 (c. 58). Section 20 was amended by the Statute Law Revision Act 1892 (c. 19).

[15]  2004 c. 28; section 5 was amended by section 1 of the Domestic Violence, Crime and Victims (Amendment) Act 2012 (c. 4).

(4)  Paragraph (2)(f) does not apply where it appears to the court that, taking account of all the circumstances, the defendant's physical or mental condition makes it undesirable for the defendant to give evidence in person.

(5)  Where there is more than one defendant, this rule applies to each in the order their names appear in the indictment, or in an order directed by the court.

(6)  Unless the jury (if there is one) has retired to consider its verdict, the court may allow a party to introduce evidence, or make representations, after that party's opportunity to do so under paragraph (2).

(7)  Unless the jury has already reached a verdict on a count, the court may exercise its power to—
   (a)  discharge the jury from reaching a verdict on that count;
   (b)  direct the jury to acquit the defendant on that count; or
   (c)  invite the jury to convict the defendant, if the defendant pleads guilty to the offence charged by that count.

*[Note. See also rule 3.32 (Arraigning the defendant on the indictment).*

*Under section 6E of the Criminal Procedure and Investigations Act 1996[16], the court may make the direction for which rule 25.9(2)(c)(ii) provides, on application or on the court's own initiative.*

*The admissibility of evidence that a party introduces is governed by rules of evidence.*

*Under section 35 of the Criminal Justice and Public Order Act 1994[17], the court may draw such inferences as appear proper from a defendant's failure to give evidence, or refusal without good cause to answer a question while doing so. The procedure set out in rule 25.9(2)(f) and (4) is prescribed by that section.*

*Section 2 of the Criminal Evidence Act 1898[18] restricts the circumstances in which the defendant may summarise the defence case before introducing evidence.*

*Section 79 of the Police and Criminal Evidence Act 1984[19] requires a defendant who wishes to give evidence in person to do so before calling any other witness, unless the court otherwise permits.*

*Section 2 of the Criminal Procedure Act 1865[20] and section 3 of the Criminal Evidence Act 1898[21] restrict the circumstances in which the prosecutor may make final representations without the court's permission. See also section 1 of the Criminal Procedure (Right of Reply) Act 1964[22].*

*The procedure set out in rule 25.9(3) is prescribed by sections 6 and 6A of the Domestic Violence, Crime and Victims Act 2004[23].*

*Under section 17 of the Criminal Justice Act 1967[24], the court may direct the jury to acquit where the prosecutor offers no evidence.*

*See rule 25.14 for the procedure on taking the verdict and rule 25.16 for the procedure if the court convicts the defendant.]*

**R25.10**   **Defendant unfit to plead**

**25.10** (1)  This rule applies where—
   (a)  it appears to the court, on application or on its own initiative, that the defendant may not be fit to be tried; and
   (b)  the defendant has not by then been acquitted of each offence charged by the indictment.

(2)  The court—
   (a)  must exercise its power to decide, without a jury, whether the defendant is fit to be tried; but
   (b)  may postpone the exercise of that power until immediately before the opening of the defence case.

(3)  Where the court determines that the defendant is not fit to be tried—

---

[16]  1996 c. 25; section 6E was inserted by section 36 of the Criminal Justice Act 2003 (c. 44).
[17]  1994 c. 33; section 35 was amended by sections 35 and 120 of, and Schedule 10 to, the Crime and Disorder Act 1998 (c. 37) and paragraphs 62 and 63 of Schedule 36 to the Criminal Justice Act 2003 (c. 44).
[18]  1898 c. 36.
[19]  1984 c. 60.
[20]  1865 c. 18; section 2 was amended by section 10(2) of, and Part III of Schedule 3 to, the Criminal Law Act 1967 (c. 58).
[21]  1898 c. 36; section 3 was amended by section 1(2) of the Criminal Procedure (Right of Reply) Act 1964 (c. 34).
[22]  1964 c. 34; section 1 was amended by section 1 of, and the Schedule to, the Statute Law (Repeals) Act 1974 (c. 22).
[23]  2004 c. 28; section 6 was amended by section 3 of, and paragraphs 7 and 8 of the Schedule to, the Domestic Violence, Crime and Victims (Amendment) Act 2012 (c. 4) and section 6A was inserted by section 2 of that Act.
[24]  1967 c. 80; section 17 was amended by paragraph 42 of Schedule 36 to the Criminal Justice Act 2003 (c. 44).

(a) the court must exercise its power to appoint a person to put the case for the defence, taking account of all the circumstances and in particular—

    (i) the willingness and suitability (including the qualifications and experience) of that person,

    (ii) the nature and complexity of the case,

    (iii) any advantage of continuity of representation, and

    (iv) the defendant's wishes and needs;

(b) the court must select a jury, if none has been selected yet; and

(c) rule 25.9 (Procedure on plea of not guilty) applies, if the steps it lists have not already been taken, except that—

    (i) everything which that rule requires to be done by the defendant may be done instead by the person appointed to put the case for the defence,

    (ii) under rule 25.9(2)(a), the court must explain to the jurors that their duty is to decide whether or not the defendant did the act or made the omission charged as an offence, not whether the defendant is guilty of that offence, and

    (iii) rule 25.9(2)(e) does not apply (warning of consequences of defendant not giving evidence).

*[Note. See sections 4 and 4A of the Criminal Procedure (Insanity) Act 1964[25].*

*Under section 4 of the 1964 Act, the court must not determine the defendant's fitness to be tried except on the evidence of two or more registered medical practitioners, at least one of whom is approved as having special experience in the diagnosis or treatment of mental disorder. Under section 4A, if satisfied that the defendant did the act or made the omission charged as an offence the jury must make a finding to that effect, and if not so satisfied must acquit the defendant.]*

### Evidence of a witness in person                                              R25.11

**25.11** (1) This rule applies where a party wants to introduce evidence by calling a witness to give that evidence in person.

(2) Unless the court otherwise directs—

    (a) a witness waiting to give evidence must not wait inside the courtroom, unless that witness is—

        (i) a party, or

        (ii) an expert witness;

    (b) a witness who gives evidence in the courtroom must do so from the place provided for that purpose; and

    (c) a witness' address—

        (i) must not be given in public unless the address is relevant to an issue in the case, and

        (ii) may be given in writing to the court, parties and jury.

(3) Before the witness gives evidence—

    (a) the party who introduces the witness' evidence must explain how that evidence is admissible, unless it is only evidence of fact within the witness' direct knowledge; and

    (b) the witness must take an oath or affirm, unless other legislation otherwise provides.

(4) In the following sequence—

    (a) the party who calls a witness may ask questions in examination-in-chief;

    (b) if the witness gives evidence for the prosecution—

        (i) the defendant, if there is only one, may ask questions in cross-examination, or

        (ii) subject to the court's directions, each defendant, if there is more than one, may ask such questions, in the order their names appear in the indictment or as directed by the court;

    (c) if the witness gives evidence for a defendant—

        (i) subject to the court's directions, each other defendant, if there is more than one, may ask questions in cross-examination, in the order their names appear in the indictment or as directed by the court, and

        (ii) the prosecutor may ask such questions; and

    (d) the party who called the witness may ask questions in re-examination arising out of any cross-examination.

(5) If other legislation so permits, at any time while giving evidence a witness may refer to a record of that witness' recollection of events.

(6) The court may—

    (a) ask a witness questions; and in particular

    (b) where the defendant is not represented, ask a witness any question necessary in the defendant's interests.

---

[25] 1964 c. 84; sections 4 and 4A were substituted for section 4 as originally enacted by section 2 of the Criminal Procedure (Insanity and Unfitness to Plead) Act 1991 (c. 25), and amended by section 22 of the Domestic Violence, Crime and Victims Act 2004 (c. 28).

*[Note. Section 53 of the Youth Justice and Criminal Evidence Act 1999[26] provides that everyone is competent to give evidence in criminal proceedings unless unable to understand questions put or give intelligible answers. See also section 1 of the Criminal Evidence Act 1898[27].*

*Part 19 contains rules about the introduction of evidence of expert opinion. Part 20 contains rules about the introduction of hearsay evidence.*

*Sections 1, 3, 5 and 6 of the Oaths Act 1978[28] provide for the taking of oaths and the making of affirmations, and for the words that must be used. Section 28 of the Children and Young Persons Act 1963[29] provides that in a youth court, and where a witness in any court is under 18, an oath must include the words 'I promise' in place of the words 'I swear'. Under sections 55 and 56 of the Youth Justice and Criminal Evidence Act 1999, a person may give evidence without taking an oath, or making an affirmation, where that person (i) is under 14 or (ii) has an insufficient appreciation of the solemnity of the occasion and of the particular responsibility to tell the truth which is involved in taking an oath.*

*The questions that may be put to a witness—*

*(a) by a party are governed by rules of evidence, for example—*
    *(i) the rule that a question must be relevant to what is in issue,*
    *(ii) the rule that the party who calls a witness must not ask that witness a leading question about what is in dispute, and*
    *(iii) the rule that a party who calls a witness may contradict that witness only in limited circumstances (see section 3 of the Criminal Procedure Act 1865)[30];*
*(b) by the court are in its discretion, but that is subject to—*
    *(i) rules of evidence, and*
    *(ii) rule 1.3 (the application by the court of the overriding objective).*

*Under sections 34, 35 and 36 of the Youth Justice and Criminal Evidence Act 1999[31], a defendant who is not represented may not cross-examine a witness where—*

*(a) the defendant is charged with a sexual offence against the witness;*
*(b) the defendant is charged with a sexual offence, or one of certain other offences, and the witness is a child; or*
*(c) the court prohibits the defendant from cross-examining the witness.*

*Part 23 contains rules relevant to restrictions on cross-examination.*

*Under section 139 of the Criminal Justice Act 2003[32], a witness may refresh his or her memory by referring to a record made earlier, either contained in a document made or verified by the witness, or in the transcript of a sound recording, if—*

*(a) the witness states that it records his or her recollection of events at that earlier time; and*
*(b) that recollection is likely to have been significantly better when the record was made than by the time the witness gives evidence in person.*

*In some circumstances, a witness may give evidence in accordance with special measures directed by the court under section 19 of the Youth Justice and Criminal Evidence Act 1999[33], or by live link under section 32 of the Criminal Justice Act 1988[34] or section 51 of the Criminal Justice Act 2003. Part 18 contains relevant rules.]*

---

[26] 1999 c. 23.

[27] 1898 c. 36; section 1 was amended by section 1 of the Criminal Evidence Act 1979 (c. 16), section 78 of, and Schedule 16 to, the Criminal Justice Act 1982 (c. 48), sections 80(9) and 119(2) of, and Schedule 7 to, the Police and Criminal Evidence Act 1984 (c. 60), sections 31 and 168 of, and paragraph 2 of Schedule 10, and Schedule 11 to, the Criminal Justice and Public Order Act 1994 (c. 33), section 67 of, and paragraph 1 of Schedule 4, and Schedule 6 to, the Youth Justice and Criminal Evidence Act 1999 (c. 23) and sections 331 and 332 of, and paragraph 80 of Schedule 36, and Part 5 of Schedule 37 to, the Criminal Justice Act 2003 (c. 44).

[28] 1978 c. 19.

[29] 1963 c. 37; section 28 was amended by section 2 of the Oaths Act 1978 (c. 19) and section 100 of, and paragraph 40 of Schedule 11 to, the Criminal Justice Act 1991 (c. 53).

[30] 1865 c. 18.

[31] 1999 c. 23; section 35 was amended by sections 139 and 140 of, and paragraph 41 of Schedule 6 and Schedule 7 to, the Sexual Offences Act 2003 (c. 42) and section 148 of, and paragraphs 35 and 36 of Schedule 26 to, the Criminal Justice and Immigration Act 2008 (c. 4).

[32] 2003 c. 44.

[33] 1999 c. 23.

[34] 1988 c. 33; section 32 was amended by section 55 of the Criminal Justice Act 1991 (c. 53), section 29 of, and paragraph 16 of Schedule 2 to, the Criminal Appeal Act 1995 (c. 35), section 62 of the Criminal Procedure and Investigations Act 1996 (c. 25), section 67 of, and Schedule 6 and paragraph 3 of Schedule 7 to, the Youth Justice and Criminal Evidence Act 1999 (c. 23) and paragraphs 24 and 26 of the Schedule to S.I. 2004/2035.

### Evidence of a witness in writing

**25.12** (1) This rule applies where a party wants to introduce in evidence the written statement of a witness to which applies—
- (a) Part 16 (Written witness statements);
- (b) Part 19 (Expert evidence); or
- (c) Part 20 (Hearsay evidence).

(2) That party must explain how the evidence is admissible unless it is—
- (a) evidence of fact within the direct knowledge of the person who made the written statement served under rule 16.4 (Written witness statement in evidence);
- (b) contained in an expert's report served under rule 19.3 (Introduction of expert evidence); or
- (c) identified as hearsay in a notice served under rule 20.2 (Notice to introduce hearsay evidence).

(3) If the court admits such evidence each relevant part of the statement must be read or summarised aloud, unless the court otherwise directs.

*[Note. See Parts 16, 19 and 20, and the other legislation to which those Parts apply. The admissibility of evidence that a party introduces is governed by rules of evidence.*

*A written witness statement to which Part 16 applies may only be introduced in evidence if there has been no objection within the time limit to which rule 16.4 refers.*

*An expert report to which Part 19 applies may only be introduced in evidence if it has been served in accordance with rule 19.3.*

*Rule 20.3 provides for opposing the introduction of hearsay evidence, including such evidence in a document.*

*Where a witness gives evidence in person, a previous written statement by that witness may be admissible as evidence under section 119 (Inconsistent statements) or under section 120 (Other previous statements of witnesses) of the Criminal Justice Act 2003.]*

### Evidence by admission

R25.13

**25.13** (1) This rule applies where—
- (a) a party introduces in evidence a fact admitted by another party; or
- (b) parties jointly admit a fact.

(2) Unless the court otherwise directs, a written record must be made of the admission.

*[Note. See section 10 of the Criminal Justice Act 1967[35]. The admissibility of evidence that a party introduces is governed by rules of evidence.]*

### Directions to the jury and taking the verdict

R25.14

**25.14** (1) This rule applies where there is a jury.

(2) The court must give the jury directions about the relevant law at any time at which to do so will assist jurors to evaluate the evidence.

(3) After following the sequence in rule 25.9 (Procedure on plea of not guilty), the court must—
- (a) to help the jury to come to a verdict—
  - (i) give jurors directions about the relevant law, and
  - (ii) summarise for them, to such extent as is necessary, the evidence relevant to the issues they must decide;
- (b) give those directions orally and, as a general rule, in writing as well;
- (c) direct the jury to retire to consider its verdict;
- (d) if necessary, recall the jury
  - (i) to answer jurors' questions, or
  - (ii) to give directions, or further directions, about considering and delivering its verdict or verdicts, including, if appropriate, directions about reaching a verdict by a majority;
- (e) in a case in which the jury is required to return a single verdict—
  - (i) recall the jury (unless already recalled) when it informs the court that it has reached its verdict, and
  - (ii) direct the delivery of that verdict there and then;
- (f) in a case in which the jury is required to return two or more verdicts—
  - (i) recall the jury (unless already recalled) when it informs the court that it has reached a verdict or verdicts, and
  - (ii) ask the jury whether its members all agree on every verdict required;
- (g) if the answer to that question is 'yes', direct the delivery of each of those verdicts there and then; and

---

[35] 1967 c. 80.

    (h)  if the answer to that question is 'no'—
        (i)  direct the delivery there and then of any unanimous verdict that has been reached, or
        (ii)  postpone the taking of any such verdict while the jury considers each other verdict required.

(4)  Directions to the jury under paragraph (3)(a) may include questions that the court invites jurors to answer in coming to a verdict.

(5)  The court may give the jury other assistance in writing.

(6)  When the court directs the jury to deliver its verdict or verdicts, the court must ask the foreman chosen by the jury, in respect of each count—
    (a)  whether the jury has reached a verdict on which all the jurors agree;
    (b)  if so, whether that verdict is guilty or not guilty;
    (c)  if not, where the jury has deliberated for at least 2 hours and if the court decides to invite a majority verdict, then—
        (i)  whether at least 10 (of 11 or 12 jurors), or 9 (of 10 jurors), agreed on a verdict,
        (ii)  if so, is that verdict guilty or not guilty, and
        (iii)  if (and only if) such a verdict is guilty, how many jurors agreed to that verdict and how many disagreed.

(7)  Where evidence has been given that the defendant was insane, so as not to be responsible for the act or omission charged as the offence, then under paragraph (5)(b) the court must ask whether the jury's verdict is guilty, not guilty, or not guilty by reason of insanity.

*[Note. Under section 17 of the Juries Act 1974[36], the court may accept the verdict of a majority, as long as the jury has had at least 2 hours for deliberation.*

*Under section 6 of the Criminal Law Act 1967, the jury may convict a defendant of an offence other than one charged by the indictment if that offence is proved by the evidence.*

*The verdict to which rule 25.14(6) refers is provided for by section 2 of the Trial of Lunatics Act 1883[37]. The evidence required before such a verdict may be reached is prescribed by section 1 of the Criminal Procedure (Insanity and Unfitness to Plead) Act 1991[38].]*

**R25.15**    **Conviction or acquittal without a jury**

**25.15** (1)  This rule applies where—
    (a)  the court tries the case without a jury; and
    (b)  after following the sequence in rule 25.9 (Procedure on plea of not guilty).

(2)  In respect of each count, the court must give reasons for its decision to convict or acquit.

*[Note. Under sections 44 and 46 of the Criminal Justice Act 2003[39], the court may try a case without a jury where there is a danger of jury tampering, or where jury tampering appears to have taken place. Under section 17 of the Domestic Violence, Crime and Victims Act 2004[40], the court may try sample counts with a jury and other counts without a jury. Part 3 (preparation for trial in the Crown Court) contains rules about an application for such a trial.]*

**R25.16**    **Procedure if the court convicts**

**25.16** (1)  This rule applies where, in respect of any count in the indictment—
    (a)  the defendant pleads guilty; or
    (b)  the court convicts the defendant.

(2)  The court may exercise its power—
    (a)  if the defendant is an individual—
        (i)  to require a pre-sentence report,
        (ii)  to commission a medical report,
        (iii)  to require a statement of the defendant's assets and other financial circumstances;
    (b)  if the defendant is a corporation, to require such information as the court directs about the defendant's corporate structure and financial resources;
    (c)  to adjourn sentence pending—
        (i)  receipt of any such report, statement or information,
        (ii)  the verdict in a related case.

(3)  The prosecutor must—
    (a)  summarise the prosecution case, if the sentencing court has not heard evidence;

---

[36]  1974 c. 23.
[37]  1883 c. 38; section 2 was amended by section 17 of, and Schedule 2 to, the Criminal Lunatics Act 1884 (c. 64) and sections 1 and 8 of the Criminal Procedure (Insanity) Act 1964 (c. 84).
[38]  1991 c. 25.
[39]  2003 c. 44.
[40]  2004 c. 28.

      (b)  identify in writing any offence that the prosecutor proposes should be taken into consideration in sentencing;

      (c)  provide information relevant to sentence, including—

         (i)  any previous conviction of the defendant, and the circumstances where relevant,

         (ii)  any statement of the effect of the offence on the victim, the victim's family or others; and

      (d)  identify any other matter relevant to sentence, including—

         (i)  the legislation applicable,

         (ii)  any sentencing guidelines, or guideline cases,

         (iii)  aggravating and mitigating features affecting the defendant's culpability and the harm which the offence caused, was intended to cause or might foreseeably have caused, and

         (iv)  the effect of such of the information listed in paragraph (2) as the court may need to take into account.

(4)  Where the defendant pleads guilty, the court may give directions for determining the facts on the basis of which sentence must be passed if—

      (a)  the defendant wants to be sentenced on a basis agreed with the prosecutor; or

      (b)  in the absence of such agreement, the defendant wants to be sentenced on the basis of different facts to those disclosed by the prosecution case.

(5)  Where the court has power to order the endorsement of the defendant's driving record, or power to order the defendant to be disqualified from driving—

      (a)  if other legislation so permits, a defendant who wants the court not to exercise that power must introduce the evidence or information on which the defendant relies;

      (b)  the prosecutor may introduce evidence; and

      (c)  the parties may make representations about that evidence or information.

(6)  Before passing sentence—

      (a)  the court must give the defendant an opportunity to make representations and introduce evidence relevant to sentence;

      (b)  where the defendant is under 18, the court may give the defendant's parents, guardian or other supporting adult, if present, such an opportunity as well; and

      (c)  if the court requires more information, it may exercise its power to adjourn the hearing.

(7)  When the court has taken into account all the evidence, information and any report available, the court must—

      (a)  as a general rule, pass sentence at the earliest opportunity;

      (b)  when passing sentence—

         (i)  explain the reasons,

         (ii)  explain to the defendant its effect, the consequences of failing to comply with any order or pay any fine, and any power that the court has to vary or review the sentence, unless the defendant is absent or the defendant's ill-health or disorderly conduct makes such an explanation impracticable, and

         (iii)  give any such explanation in terms the defendant, if present, can understand (with help, if necessary); and

      (c)  deal with confiscation, costs and any behaviour order.

(8)  The general rule is subject to the court's power to defer sentence for up to 6 months.

*[Note. See sections 31, 52, 59, 63, 124, 125 and 126 of the Sentencing Act 2020[41].*

*Under sections 57D and 57E of the Crime and Disorder Act 1998[42], the court may require a defendant to attend a sentencing hearing by live link.*

*Under section 30 of the Sentencing Act 2020, the general rule (subject to exceptions) is that the court must obtain and consider a pre-sentence report—*

    *(a)  where it is considering a custodial sentence or a community sentence;*

    *(b)  where it thinks the defendant may pose a significant risk of causing serious harm to the public by further offending.*

*Under section 32(3) of the Sentencing Act 2020, where the court obtains a written pre-sentence report about a defendant who is under 18, it may direct that information in it must be withheld, if it would be likely to create a risk of significant harm to the defendant.*

*Rule 28.8 of these Rules applies to commissions for medical reports.*

---

[41]  2020 c.17.

[42]  1998 c. 37; sections 57A to 57E were substituted for section 57 as originally enacted by section 45 of the Police and Justice Act 2006 (c. 48), and amended by sections 106, 109 and 178 of, and Part 3 of Schedule 23 to, the Coroners and Justice Act 2009 (c. 25). Section 57A was further amended by paragraphs 36 and 39 of Schedule 12 to the Legal Aid, Sentencing and Punishment of Offenders Act 2012 (c. 10).

*Under section 35 of the Sentencing Act 2020, the court may require a defendant who is an individual to provide a statement of assets and other financial circumstances if the defendant is convicted.*

*Under section 20A of the Criminal Justice Act 1991[43], it is an offence for a defendant knowingly or recklessly to make a false or incomplete statement of assets or other financial circumstances, or to fail to provide such a statement, in response to a request by a court officer on behalf of the court.*

*The Sentencing Council may issue sentencing guidelines under section 120 of the Coroners and Justice Act 2009[44].*

*For the circumstances in which a court may (and, in some cases, must) order the endorsement of a defendant's driving record, or the disqualification of a defendant from driving, see sections 34, 35 and 44 of the Road Traffic Offenders Act 1988[45]. Under that legislation, in some circumstances the court has discretion not to make such an order. See also rule 29.1.*

*The evidence that may be introduced is subject to rules of evidence.*

*In addition to the specific powers to which this rule applies, the court has a general power to adjourn a trial: see rule 25.2.*

*Part 28 contains rules about sentencing procedure in special cases. Part 31 contains rules about behaviour orders. Part 33 contains rules about confiscation and related orders. Part 45 contains rules about costs.*

*Under section 3 of the Sentencing Act 2020, if (among other things) the defendant consents, the court may defer sentence for up to 6 months, for the purpose of allowing it to take account of the defendant's conduct after conviction, or any change in the defendant's circumstances.]*

**R25.17**    **Provision of documents for the court**

25.17 (1)   Unless the court otherwise directs, a party who introduces a document in evidence, or who otherwise uses a document in presenting that party's case, must provide a copy for—

     (a)   each other party;

     (b)   any witness that party wants to refer to the document; and

     (c)   the court.

    (2)   If the court so directs, a party who introduces or uses a document for such a purpose must provide a copy for the jury.

    (3)   Unless the court otherwise directs, on application or on its own initiative, the court officer must provide for the court—

     (a)   any copy received under paragraph (1) before the trial begins; and

     (b)   a copy of the court officer's record of—

        (i)   information supplied by each party for the purposes of case management, including any revision of information previously supplied,

        (ii)   each pre-trial direction for the management of the case,

        (iii)   any pre-trial decision to admit evidence,

        (iv)   any pre-trial direction about the giving of evidence, and

        (v)   any admission to which rule 25.13 (Evidence by admission) applies; and

     (c)   any other document served on the court officer for the use of the court.

**R25.18**    **Duty of court officer and custodian**

25.18 (1)   The court officer must—

     (a)   serve on each party notice of where and when an adjourned hearing will resume, unless that party was present when that was arranged;

     (b)   if the reason for the adjournment was to postpone sentence, include that reason in any such notice to the defendant;

---

[43]   1991 c. 53; section 20A was inserted by section 168 of, and paragraph 43 of Schedule 9 to, the Criminal Justice and Public Order Act 1994 (c. 33) and amended by sections 95 and 109 of, and paragraph 350 of Schedule 8 to, the Courts Act 2003 (c. 39) and section 44 of, and paragraph 26 of Schedule 16 to, the Crime and Courts Act 2013 (c. 22).

[44]   2009 c. 25.

[45]   1988 c. 53; section 34 was amended by section 29 of the Road Traffic Act 1991 (c. 40), section 3 of the Aggravated Vehicle-Taking Act 1992 (c. 11), section 165 of, and paragraph 121 of Schedule 9 to, the Powers of Criminal Courts (Sentencing) Act 2000 (c. 6), sections 56 and 107 of, and Schedule 8 to, the Police Reform Act 2002 (c. 30), section 25 of the Road Safety Act 2006 (c. 49), article 2 of S.I. 2007/3480, paragraphs 2 and 5 of Schedule 27 to the Legal Aid, Sentencing and Punishment of Offenders Act 2012 (c. 10), section 56 of, and paragraphs 9 and 12 of Schedule 22 to, the Crime and Courts Act 2013 (c. 22) and section 177 of, and paragraph 90 of Schedule 21 to, the Coroners and Justice Act 2009 (c. 25). Section 35 was amended by section 48 of, and paragraph 95 of Schedule 4 to, the Road Traffic Act 1991 (c. 40), section 165 of, and paragraph 122 of Schedule 9 to, the Powers of Criminal Courts (Sentencing) Act 2000 (c. 6) and section 177 of, and 90 of Schedule 21 to, the Coroners and Justice Act 2009 (c. 25). Section 44 was amended by regulations 2 and 3 of, and paragraph 10 of Schedule 2 to, S.I. 1990/144 and sections 9, 10 and 59 of, and Schedule 7 to, the Road Safety Act 2006 (c. 49).

    (c)   unless the court otherwise directs, make available to the parties any written report to which rule 25.16(2) applies (pre-sentence and medical reports);

    (d)   where the court has ordered a defendant to provide information under section 25 of the Road Traffic Offenders Act 1988[46], serve on the defendant notice of that order unless the defendant was present when it was made;

    (e)   give the court such other assistance as it requires, including—

        (i)   selecting jurors from the panel summoned by the Lord Chancellor, under rule 25.6 (Selecting the jury),

        (ii)   taking the oaths or affirmations of jurors and witnesses, under rules 25.6 and 25.11 (Evidence of a witness in person),

        (iii)   informing the jurors of the offence or offences charged in the indictment, and of their duty, under rule 25.9 (Procedure on plea of not guilty),

        (iv)   recording the date and time at which the court gives the jury oral directions under rule 25.14(2) (directions about the law),

        (v)   recording the date and time at which the court gives the jury any written directions, questions or other assistance under rule 25.14(4), and

        (vi)   asking the jury foreman to deliver the verdict, under rule 25.14(5).

**(2)**    Where the court passes a sentence of immediate imprisonment or detention, or orders a suspended sentence of imprisonment to take effect, by this rule—

    (a)   the court requires the defendant to provide, in writing or orally, his or her nationality; and

    (b)   the custodian must obtain that information and record it

*[Note. See also section 82 of the Senior Courts Act 1981[47] (Duties of officers of Crown Court).*

*Under Part 5, the court officer must—*

*    (a)   record details of a case and of the court's decisions; and*

*    (b)   give public notice of specified details about a trial, including by such arrangements as the Lord Chancellor directs.*

*Under section 25 of the Road Traffic Offenders Act 1988, where the court does not know a defendant's sex or date of birth, then on convicting the defendant of an offence involving obligatory or discretionary disqualification, the court must order the defendant to provide that information.*

*Under section 86A of the Courts Act 2003, Criminal Procedure Rules must specify stages of proceedings at which the court must require the information to which rule 25.18(2) refers. A person commits an offence if, without reasonable excuse, that person fails to comply with such a requirement, whether by providing false or incomplete information or by providing no information.]*

---

CRIMINAL PRACTICE DIRECTIONS    PART 25    TRIAL AND SENTENCE IN THE CROWN COURT

### CPD VI Trial 25A: Identification for the Jury of the Issues in the Case

**CPD.25A**

**25A.1**    CrimPR 3.11(a) requires the court, with the active assistance of the parties, to establish what are the disputed issues in order to manage the trial. To that end, prosecution opening speeches are invaluable. They set out for the jury the principal issues in the trial, and the evidence which is to be introduced in support of the prosecution case. They should clarify, not obfuscate. The purpose of the prosecution opening is to help the jury understand what the case concerns, not necessarily to present a detailed account of all the prosecution evidence due to be introduced.

**25A.2**    CrimPR 25.9(2)(c) provides for a defendant, or his or her advocate, to set out the issues in the defendant's own terms (subject to superintendence by the court), immediately after the prosecution opening. Any such identification of issues at this stage is not to be treated as a substitute for or extension of the summary of the defence case which can be given later, under CrimPR 25.9(2)(g). Its purpose is to provide the jury with focus as to the issues that they are likely to be called upon to decide, so that jurors will be alert to those issues from the outset and can evaluate the prosecution evidence that they hear accordingly. For that purpose, the defendant is not confined to what is included in the defence statement (though any divergence from the defence statement will expose the defendant to adverse comment or inference), and for the defendant to

---

[46] 1988 c. 53; section 25 was amended by section 90 of, and paragraphs 140 and 142 of Schedule 13 to, the Access to Justice Act 1999 (c. 22), section 165 of, and paragraph 118 of Schedule 9 to, the Powers of Criminal Courts (Sentencing) Act 2000 (c. 6) and section 109 of, and paragraph 311 of Schedule 8 to, the Courts Act 2003 (c. 39).

[47] 1981 c. 54; section 82 was amended by section 15 of, and paragraphs 114 and 135 of Schedule 4 to, the Constitutional Reform Act 2005 (c. 4) and sections 116 and 178 of, and Part 3 of Schedule 3 to, the Coroners and Justice Act 2009 (c. 25).

take the opportunity at this stage to identify the issues may assist even if all he or she wishes to announce is that the prosecution is being put to proof.

**25A.3**  To identify the issues for the jury at this stage also provides an opportunity for the judge to give appropriate directions about the law; for example, as to what features of the prosecution evidence they should look out for in a case in which what is in issue is the identification of the defendant by an eye-witness. Giving such directions at the outset is another means by which the jury can be helped to focus on the significant features of the evidence, in the interests of a fair and effective trial.

**25A.4**  A defendant is not entitled to identify issues at this stage by addressing the jury unless the court invites him or her to do so. Given the advantages described above, usually the court should extend such an invitation but there may be circumstances in which, in the court's judgment, it furthers the overriding objective not to do so. Potential reasons for denying the defendant the opportunity at this stage to address the jury about the issues include (i) that the case is such that the issues are apparent; (ii) that the prosecutor has given a fair, accurate and comprehensive account of the issues in opening, rendering repetition superfluous; and (iii) where the defendant is not represented, that there is a risk of the defendant, at this early stage, inflicting injustice on him or herself by making assertions to the jury to such an extent, or in such a manner, as is unfairly detrimental to his or her subsequent standing.

**25A.5**  Whether or not there is to be a defence identification of issues, and, if there is, in what manner and in what terms it is to be presented to the jury, are questions that must be resolved in the absence of the jury and that should be addressed at the opening of the trial.

**25A.6**  Even if invited to identify the issues by addressing the jury, the defendant is not obliged to accept the invitation. However, where the court decides that it is important for the jury to be made aware of what the defendant has declared to be in issue in the defence statement then the court may require the jury to be supplied with copies of the defence statement, edited at the court's direction if necessary, in accordance with section 6E(4) of the Criminal Procedure and Investigations Act 1996.

## CPD.25B        CPD VI Trial 25B: Trial Adjournment in the Crown Court

**25B.1**  A defendant has a right, in general, to be present and to be represented at his trial. However, a defendant may choose not to exercise those rights, such as by voluntarily absenting himself and failing to instruct his lawyers adequately so that they can represent him.

**25B.2**  The court has a discretion as to whether a trial should take place or continue in the defendant's absence and must exercise its discretion with due regard for the interests of justice. The overriding concern must be to ensure that such a trial is as fair as circumstances permit and leads to a just outcome. If the defendant's absence is due to involuntary illness or incapacity it would very rarely be right to exercise the discretion in favour of commencing or continuing the trial.

**25B.3**  Proceeding in the absence of a defendant is a step which ought normally to be taken only if it is unavoidable. The court must exercise its discretion as to whether a trial should take place or continue in the defendant's absence with the utmost care and caution. Due regard should be had to the judgment of Lord Bingham in *R v Jones (Anthony William)* [2002] UKHL 5, [2003] 1 A.C. 1, [2002] 2 Cr. App. R. 9. Circumstances to be taken into account before proceeding include:

i)   the conduct of the defendant,
ii)   the disadvantage to the defendant,
iii)   the public interest, taking account of the inconvenience and hardship to witnesses, and especially to any complainant, of a delay; if the witnesses have attended court and are ready to give evidence, that will weigh in favour of continuing with the trial,
iv)   the effect of any delay,
v)   whether the attendance of the defendant could be secured at a later hearing, and
vii)   the likely outcome if the defendant is found guilty.

Even if the defendant is voluntarily absent, it is still generally desirable that he or she is represented.

CRIMINAL PROCEDURE RULES   PART 26   JURORS

## R26.1        Appeal against officer's refusal to excuse or postpone jury service

**26.1**  (1)  This rule applies where a person summoned for jury service in the Crown Court, the High Court or the county court wants to appeal against a refusal by an officer on the Lord Chancellor's behalf—

(a)  to excuse that person from such service; or
(b)  to postpone the date on which that person is required to attend for such service.

(2)  The appellant must appeal to the court to which the appellant has been summoned.

(3) The appellant must—
    (a) apply in writing, as soon as reasonably practicable; and
    (b) serve the application on the court officer.

(4) The application must—
    (a) attach a copy of—
      (i) the jury summons, and
      (ii) the refusal to excuse or postpone which is under appeal; and
    (b) explain why the court should excuse the appellant from jury service, or postpone its date, as appropriate.

(5) The court to which the appeal is made—
    (a) may extend the time for appealing, and may allow the appeal to be made orally;
    (b) may determine the appeal at a hearing in public or in private, or without a hearing;
    (c) may adjourn any hearing of the appeal; but
    (d) must not determine an appeal unless the appellant has had a reasonable opportunity to make representations in person.

*[Note. See sections 9 and 9A of the Juries Act 1974[1].*

*Where a person summoned for jury service—*

    *(a) fails to attend as required; or*
    *(b) after attending as required, when selected under rule 25.6—*
      *(i) is not available, or*
      *(ii) is unfit for jury service by reason of drink or drugs*

*that conduct may be punished as if it were a contempt of court. See section 20 of the Juries Act 1974 and rules 48.5 to 48.8 (contempt of court). The maximum penalty which the court can impose is a fine of £1,000.]*

### Excusal from jury service by court
**R26.2**

**26.2** At any time before a juror completes the oath or affirmation, the court may exercise its power to excuse him or her from jury service for lack of capacity to act effectively as a juror because of an insufficient understanding of English—
    (a) on the court's own initiative, or where the court officer refers the juror to the court; and
    (b) after enquiry of the juror.

*[Note. See section 10 of the Juries Act 1974[2].]*

### Provision of information for jurors
**R26.3**

**26.3** The court officer must arrange for each juror to receive—
    (a) by such means as the Lord Chancellor directs, general information about jury service and about a juror's responsibilities;
    (b) written notice of the prohibitions against—
      (i) research by a juror into the case,
      (ii) disclosure by a juror of any such research to another juror during the trial,
      (iii) conduct by a juror which suggests that that juror intends to try the case otherwise than on the evidence, and
      (iv) disclosure by a juror of the deliberations of the jury; and
    (c) written warning that breach of those prohibitions is an offence, for which the penalty is imprisonment or a fine or both, and may be a contempt of court.

*[Note. See sections 20A, 20B, 20C and 20D of the Juries Act 1974[3].*

*The Practice Direction sets out a form of notice for use in connection with this rule.]*

### Assessment of juror's availability for long trial, etc.
**R26.4**

**26.4** (1) The court may invite each member of a panel of jurors to provide such information, by such means and at such a time as the court directs, about—
    (a) that juror's availability to try a case expected to last for longer than the juror had expected to serve; and

[1] 1974 c. 23; section 9 was amended by paragraphs 1, 3, 4, 5 and 6 of Schedule 33, and Part 10 of Schedule 37, to the Criminal Justice Act 2003 (c. 44) and paragraph 172 of Schedule 8 to the Courts Act 2003 (c. 39). Section 9A was inserted by section 120 of the Criminal Justice Act 1988 (c. 33) and amended by paragraphs 1, 7, 8, 9, 10 and 11 of Schedule 33 to the Criminal Justice Act 2003 (c. 44) and paragraph 172 of Schedule 8 to the Courts Act 2003 (c. 39).
[2] 1974 c. 23; section 10 was amended by section 168 of, and Schedule 11 to, the Criminal Justice and Public Order Act 1994 (c. 33) and sections 65 and 109 of, and paragraph 4 of Schedule 4 and Schedule 10 to, the Courts Act 2003 (c. 39).
[3] 1974 c. 23; sections 20A, 20B, 20C and 20D were inserted by sections 71, 72, 73 and 74 respectively of the Criminal Justice and Courts Act 2015 (c. 2).

    (b) any association of that juror with, or any knowledge by that juror of—
        (i) a party or witness, or
        (ii) any other person, or any place, of significance to the case.

(2) Where jurors provide information under this rule, the court may postpone the selection of the jury to try a case to allow each juror an opportunity to review and amend that information before that selection.

(3) Using that information, the court may exercise its power to excuse a juror from selection as a member of the jury to try a case, but the court must not—
    (a) excuse a juror without allowing the parties an opportunity to make representations; or
    (b) refuse to excuse a juror without allowing that juror such an opportunity.

**R26.5**   **Surrender of electronic communication devices by jurors**

**26.5** (1) This rule applies where the court can order the members of a jury to surrender for a specified period any electronic communication devices that they possess.

(2) The court may make such an order—
    (a) on application; or
    (b) on its own initiative.

(3) A party who wants the court to make such an order must—
    (a) apply as soon as reasonably practicable;
    (b) notify each other party;
    (c) specify for what period any device should be surrendered; and
    (d) explain why—
        (i) the proposed order is necessary or expedient in the interest of justice, and
        (ii) the terms of the proposed order are a proportionate means of safeguarding those interests.

*[Note. See section 15A of the Juries Act 1974[4].]*

---

CRIMINAL PRACTICE DIRECTIONS     PART 26     JURORS

**CPD.26A**   **CPD VI Trial 26A: Juries: introduction**

**26A.1** Jury service is an important public duty which individual members of the public are chosen at random to undertake. As the Court has acknowledged: 'Jury service is not easy; it never has been. It involves a major civic responsibility' (*R v Thompson* [2010] EWCA Crim 1623, [9] per Lord Judge CJ, [2011] 1 WLR 200, [2010] 2 Cr App R 27).

*Provision of information to prospective jurors*

**26A.2** HMCTS provide every person summoned as a juror with information about the role and responsibilities of a juror. Prospective jurors are provided with a pamphlet, 'Your Guide to Jury Service', and may also view the film 'Your Role as a Juror' online at any time on the Ministry of Justice YouTube site www.youtube.com/watch?v=JP7slp-X9Pc. There is also information at https://www.gov.uk/jury-service/overview

**CPD.26B**   **CPD VI Trial 26B: Juries: Preliminary Matters Arising before Jury Service Commences**

**26B.1** The effect of section 321 of the Criminal Justice Act 2003 was to remove certain categories of persons from those previously ineligible for jury service (the judiciary and others concerned with the administration of justice) and certain other categories ceased to be eligible for excusal as of right, (such as members of Parliament and medical professionals). The normal presumption is that everyone, unless ineligible or disqualified, will be required to serve when summoned to do so.

*Excusal and deferral*

**26B.2** The jury summoning officer is empowered to defer or excuse individuals in appropriate circumstances and in accordance with the HMCTS *Guidance for summoning officers when considering deferral and excusal applications* (2009): https://assets.publishing.service.gov.uk/government/uploads/system/uploads/attachment_data/file/228867/9780108508400.pdf

*Appeals from officer's refusal to excuse or postpone jury service*

**26B.3** CrimPR 26.1 governs the procedure for a person's appeal against a summoning officer's decision in relation to excusal or deferral of jury service.

*Provision of information at court*

**26B.4** The court officer is expected to provide relevant further information to jurors on their arrival in the court centre.

---

[4] 1974 c. 23; section 15A was inserted by section 69 of the Criminal Justice and Courts Act 2015 (c. 2).

## CPD VI Trial 26C: Juries: Eligibility                                     **CPD.26C**

*English language ability*

**26C.1**   Under the Juries Act 1974 section 10, a person summoned for jury service who applies for excusal on the grounds of insufficient understanding of English may, where necessary, be brought before the judge.

**26C.2**   The court may exercise its power to excuse any person from jury service for lack of capacity to act effectively as a juror because of an insufficient understanding of English.

**26C.3**   The judge has the discretion to stand down jurors who are not competent to serve by reason of a personal disability: *R v Mason* [1981] QB 881, (1980) 71 Cr App R 157; *R v Jalil* [2008] EWCA Crim 2910, [2009] 2 Cr App R (S.) 40.

*Jurors with professional and public service commitments*

**26C.4**   The legislative change in the Criminal Justice Act 2003 means that more individuals are eligible to serve as jurors, including those previously excused as of right or ineligible. Judges need to be vigilant to the need to exercise their discretion to adjourn a trial, excuse or discharge a juror should the need arise.

**26C.5**   Whether or not an application has already been made to the jury summoning officer for deferral or excusal, it is also open to the person summoned to apply to the court to be excused. Such applications must be considered with common sense and according to the interests of justice. An explanation should be required for an application being much later than necessary.

*Serving police officers, prison officers or employees of prosecuting agencies*

**26C.6**   A judge should always be made aware at the stage of jury selection if any juror in waiting is in these categories. The juror summons warns jurors in these categories that they will need to alert court staff.

**26C.7**   In the case of police officers an inquiry by the judge will have to be made to assess whether a police officer may serve as a juror. Regard should be had to: whether evidence from the police is in dispute in the case and the extent to which that dispute involves allegations made against the police; whether the potential juror knows or has worked with the officers involved in the case; whether the potential juror has served or continues to serve in the same police units within the force as those dealing with the investigation of the case or is likely to have a shared local service background with police witnesses in a trial.

**26C.8**   In the case of a serving prison officer summoned to a court, the judge will need to inquire whether the individual is employed at a prison linked to that court or is likely to have special knowledge of any person involved in a trial.

**26C.9**   The judge will need to ensure that employees of prosecuting authorities do not serve on a trial prosecuted by the prosecuting authority by which they are employed. They can serve on a trial prosecuted by another prosecuting authority: *R v Abdroikov* [2007] UKHL 37, [2007] 1 WLR 2679, [2008] 1 Cr App R 21; *Hanif v UK* [2011] ECHR 2247, (2012) 55 EHRR 16; *R v L* [2011] EWCA Crim 65, [2011] 1 Cr App R 27. Similarly, a serving police officer can serve where there is no particular link between the court and the station where the police officer serves.

**26C.10** Potential jurors falling into these categories should be excused from jury service unless there is a suitable alternative court/trial to which they can be transferred.

## CPD VI Trial 26D: Juries: Precautionary Measures before Swearing            **CPD.26D**

**26D.1**   There should be a consultation with the advocates as to the questions, if any, it may be appropriate to ask potential jurors. Topics to be considered include:
   a.   the availability of jurors for the duration of a trial that is likely to run beyond the usual period for which jurors are summoned;
   b.   whether any juror knows the defendant or parties to the case;
   c.   whether potential jurors are so familiar with any locations that feature in the case that they may have, or come to have, access to information not in evidence;
   d.   in cases where there has been any significant local or national publicity, whether any questions should be asked of potential jurors.

**26D.2**   Judges should however exercise caution. At common law a judge has a residual discretion to discharge a particular juror who ought not to be serving, but this discretion can only be exercised to prevent an individual juror who is not competent from serving. It does not include a discretion to discharge a jury drawn from particular sections of the community or otherwise to influence the overall composition of the jury. However, if there is a risk that there is widespread local knowledge of the defendant or a witness in a particular case, the judge may, after hearing submissions from the advocates, decide to exclude jurors from particular areas to avoid the risk of jurors having or acquiring personal knowledge of the defendant or a witness.

*Length of trial*

26D.3   Where the length of the trial is estimated to be significantly longer than the normal period of jury service, it is good practice for the trial judge to enquire whether the potential jurors on the jury panel foresee any difficulties with the length and if the judge is satisfied that the jurors' concerns are justified, he may say that they are not required for that particular jury. This does not mean that the judge must excuse the juror from sitting at that court altogether, as it may well be possible for the juror to sit on a shorter trial at the same court.

*Juror with potential connection to the case or parties*

26D.4   Where a juror appears on a jury panel, it will be appropriate for a judge to excuse the juror from that particular case where the potential juror is personally concerned with the facts of the particular case, or is closely connected with a prospective witness. Judges need to exercise due caution as noted above.

**CPD.26E**    **CPD VI Trial 26E: Juries: Swearing in Jurors**

*Swearing Jury for trial*

26E.1   All jurors shall be sworn or affirm. All jurors shall take the oath or affirmation in open court in the presence of one another. If, as a result of the juror's delivery of the oath or affirmation, a judge has concerns that a juror has such difficulties with language comprehension or reading ability that might affect that juror's capacity to undertake his or her duties, bearing in mind the likely evidence in the trial, the judge should make appropriate inquiry of that juror.

*Form of oath or affirmation*

26E.2   Each juror should have the opportunity to indicate to the court the Holy Book on which he or she wishes to swear. The precise wording will depend on his or her faith as indicated to the court.

26E.3   Any person who prefers to affirm shall be permitted to make a solemn affirmation instead. The wording of the affirmation is: 'I do solemnly, sincerely and truly declare and affirm that I will faithfully try the defendant and give a true verdict according to the evidence'.

**CPD.26F**    **CPD VI Trial 26F: Juries: Ensuring an effective jury panel**

*Adequacy of numbers*

26F.1   By section 6 of the Juries Act 1974, if it appears to the court that a jury to try any issue before the court will be, or probably will be, incomplete, the court may, if the court thinks fit, require any persons who are in, or in the vicinity of, the court, to be summoned (without any written notice) for jury service up to the number needed (after allowing for any who may not be qualified under section 1 of the Act, and for excusals and challenges) to make up a full jury.

**CPD.26G**    **CPD VI Trial 26G: Juries: Preliminary Instructions to Jurors**

26G.1   After the jury has been sworn and the defendant has been put in charge the judge will want to give directions to the jury on a number of matters.

26G.2   Jurors can be expected to follow the instructions diligently. As the Privy Council stated in *Taylor* [2013] UKPC 8, [2013] 1 WLR 1144:

> The assumption must be that the jury understood and followed the direction that they were given: … the experience of trial judges is that juries perform their duty according to law. … [T]he law proceeds on the footing that the jury, acting in accordance with the instructions given to them by the trial judge, will render a true verdict in accordance with the evidence. To conclude otherwise would be to underrate the integrity of the system of trial by jury and the effect on the jury of the instructions by the trial judge.

*At the start of the trial*

26G.3   Trial judges should instruct the jury on general matters which will include the time estimate for the trial and normal sitting hours. The jury will always need clear guidance on the following:
  i.   The need to try the case only on the evidence and remain faithful to their oath or affirmation;
  ii.   The prohibition on internet searches for matters related to the trial, issues arising or the parties;
  iii.   The importance of not discussing any aspect of the case with anyone outside their own number or allowing anyone to talk to them about it, whether directly, by telephone, through internet facilities such as Facebook or Twitter or in any other way;
  iv.   The importance of taking no account of any media reports about the case;
  v.   The collective responsibility of the jury. As the Lord Chief Justice made clear in *R v Thompson and Others* [2010] EWCA Crim 1623, [2011] 1 WLR 200, [2010] 2 Cr App R 27:
  [T]here is a collective responsibility for ensuring that the conduct of each member is consistent with the jury oath and that the directions of the trial judge about the

discharge of their responsibilities are followed.... The collective responsibility of the jury for its own conduct must be regarded as an integral part of the trial itself.

vi.    The need to bring any concerns, including concerns about the conduct of other jurors, to the attention of the judge at the time, and not to wait until the case is concluded. The point should be made that, unless that is done while the case is continuing, it may not be possible to deal with the problem at all.

*Subsequent reminder of the jury instructions*

26G.4    Judges should consider reminding jurors of these instructions as appropriate at the end of each day and in particular when they separate after retirement.

26G.5    Following the judge's direction to the jury, each member of the jury must be provided with a copy of the notice 'Your Legal Responsibilities as a Juror'. This notice outlines what is required of the juror during and after their time on the jury. It is not a substitute for the judge's direction, but is designed to reinforce what the judge has outlined in the direction. The court clerk should ensure a record is made of service of the notice. Jurors are advised to keep their copy of the notice with their summons and at the end of the trial, they are allowed to retain it for future information.

## CPD VI Trial 26H: Juries: Discharge of a juror for personal reasons    CPD.26H

26H.1    Where a juror unexpectedly finds him or herself in difficult professional or personal circumstances during the course of the trial, the juror should be encouraged to raise such problems with the trial judge. This might apply, for example, to a parent whose childcare arrangements unexpectedly fail, or a worker who is engaged in the provision of services the need for which can be critical, or a Member of Parliament who has deferred their jury service to an apparently more convenient time, but is unexpectedly called back to work for a very important reason. Such difficulties would normally be raised through a jury note in the normal manner.

26H.2    In such circumstances, the judge must exercise his or her discretion according to the interests of justice and the requirements of each individual case. The judge must decide for him or herself whether the juror has presented a sufficient reason to interfere with the course of the trial. If the juror has presented a sufficient reason, in longer trials it may well be possible to adjourn for a short period in order to allow the juror to overcome the difficulty.

26H.3    In shorter cases, it may be more appropriate to discharge the juror and to continue the trial with a reduced number of jurors. The power to do this is implicit in section 16(1) of the Juries Act 1974. In unusual cases (such as an unexpected emergency arising overnight) a juror need not be discharged in open court. The good administration of justice depends on the co-operation of jurors, who perform an essential public service. All such applications should be dealt with sensitively and sympathetically and the trial judge should always seek to meet the interests of justice without unduly inconveniencing any juror.

## CPD VI Trial 26J: Juries: Views    CPD.26J

26J.1    In each case in which it is necessary for the jury to view a location, the judge should produce ground rules for the view, after discussion with the advocates. The rules should contain details of what the jury will be shown and in what order and who, if anyone, will be permitted to speak and what will be said. The rules should also make provision for the jury to ask questions and receive a response from the judge, following submissions from the advocates, while the view is taking place.

## CPD VI Trial 26K: Juries: Directions, Written Materials and Summing Up    CPD.26K

*Overview*

26K.1    Sir Brian Leveson's *Review of Efficiency in Criminal Proceedings 2015* contained recommendations to improve the efficiency of jury trials including:
- Early provision of appropriate directions;
- Provision of a written route to verdict;
- Provision of a split summing up (a summing up delivered in two parts – the first part prior to the closing speeches and the second part afterwards); and
- Streamlining the summing up to help the jury focus on the issues.
    The purpose of this practice direction, and the associated criminal procedure rules, is to give effect to these recommendations.

*Record-keeping*

26K.2    Full and accurate record-keeping is essential to enable the Registrar of Criminal Appeals to obtain transcripts in the event of an application or appeal to the Court of Appeal (Criminal Division).

**26K.3** A court officer is required to record the date and time at which the court provides directions and written materials (CrimPR 25.18(e)(iv)–(v)).

**26K.4** The judge should ensure that a court officer (such as a court clerk or usher) is present in court to record the information listed in paragraph 26K.5.

**26K.5** A court officer should clearly record the:
- Date, time and subject of submissions and rulings relating to directions and written materials;
- Date, time and subject of directions and written materials provided prior to the summing up; and
- Date and time of the summing up, including both parts of a split summing up.

**26K.6** A court officer should retain a copy of written materials on the court file or database.

**26K.7** The parties should also record the information listed in paragraph 26K.5 and retain a copy of written materials. Where relevant to a subsequent application or appeal to the Court of Appeal (Criminal Division), the information listed in paragraph 26K.5 should be provided in the notice of appeal, and any written materials should be identified.

*Early provision of appropriate directions*

**26K.8** The court is required to provide directions about the relevant law at any time that will assist the jury to evaluate the evidence (CrimPR 25.14(2)). The judge may provide an early direction prior to any evidence being called, prior to the evidence to which it relates or shortly thereafter.

**26K.9** Where the judge decides it will assist the jury in:
- their approach to the evidence; and / or
- evaluating the evidence as they hear it
an early direction should be provided.

**26K.10** For example:
- Where identification is in issue, an early *Turnbull* direction is likely to assist the jury in approaching the evidence with the requisite caution; and by having the relevant considerations in mind when listening to the evidence.
- Where special measures are to be used and / or ground rules will restrict the manner and scope of questioning, an early explanation may assist the jury in their approach to the evidence.
- An early direction may also assist the jury, by having the relevant approach, considerations and / or test in mind, when listening to:
  - Expert witnesses; and
  - Evidence of bad character;
  - Hearsay;
  - Interviews of co-defendants; and
  - Evidence involving legal concepts such as knowledge, dishonesty, consent, recklessness, conspiracy, joint enterprise, attempt, self-defence, excessive force, voluntary intoxication and duress.

*Written route to verdict*

**26K.11** A route to verdict, which poses a series of questions that lead the jury to the appropriate verdict, may be provided by the court (CrimPR 25.14(3)(b)). Each question should tailor the law to the issues and evidence in the case.

**26K.12** Save where the case is so straightforward that it would be superfluous to do so, the judge should provide a written route to verdict. It may be presented (on paper or digitally) in the form of text, bullet points, a flowchart or other graphic.

*Other written materials*

**26K.13** Where the judge decides it will assist the jury, written materials should be provided. They may be presented (on paper or digitally) in the form of text, bullet points, a table, a flowchart or other graphic.

**26K.14** For example, written materials may assist the jury in relation to a complex direction or where the case involves:
- A complex chronology;
- Competing expert evidence; or
- Differing descriptions of a suspect.

**26K.15** Such written materials may be prepared by the judge or the parties at the direction of the judge. Where prepared by the parties at the direction of the judge, they will be subject to the judge's approval.

*Split summing up and provision of appropriate directions prior to closing speeches*

26K.16   Where the judge decides it will assist the jury when listening to the closing speeches, a split summing up should be provided. For example, the provision of appropriate directions prior to the closing speeches may avoid repetitious explanations of the law by the advocates.

26K.17   By way of illustration, such directions may include:
- Functions of the judge and jury;
- Burden and standard of proof;
- Separate consideration of counts;
- Separate consideration of defendants;
- Elements of offence(s);
- Defence(s);
- Route to verdict;
- Circumstantial evidence; and
- Inferences from silence.

*Closing speeches*

26K.18   The advocates closing speeches should be consistent with any directions and route to verdict already provided by the judge.

*Summing up*

26K.19   Prior to beginning or resuming the summing up at the conclusion of the closing speeches, the judge should briefly list (without repeating) any directions provided earlier in the trial. The purpose of this requirement is to provide a definitive account of all directions for the benefit of the Registrar of Criminal Appeals and the Court of Appeal (Criminal Division), in the event of an application or appeal.

26K.20   The court is required to summarise the evidence relevant to the issues to such extent as is necessary (CrimPR 25.14(3)(a)).

26K.21   To assist the jury to focus on the issues during retirement, save where the case is so straightforward that it would be superfluous to do so, the judge should provide:
- A reminder of the issues;
- A summary of the nature of the evidence relating to each issue;
- A balanced account of the points raised by the parties; and
- Any outstanding directions.

It is not necessary for the judge to recount all relevant evidence or to rehearse all of the significant points raised by the parties.

26K.22   At the conclusion of the summing up, the judge should provide final directions to the jury on the need:
- For unanimity (in respect of each count and defendant, where relevant);
- To dismiss any thoughts of majority verdicts until further direction; and
- To select a juror to chair their discussions and speak on their behalf to the court.

## CPD VI Trial 26L: Juries: Jury access to exhibits and evidence in retirement

26L.1   At the end of the summing up it is also important that the judge informs the jury that any exhibits they wish to have will be made available to them.

26L.2   Judges should invite submissions from the advocates as to what material the jury should retire with and what material before them should be removed, such as the transcript of an ABE interview (which should usually be removed from the jury as soon as the recording has been played.)

26L.3   Judges will also need to inform the jury of the opportunity to view certain audio, DVD or CCTV evidence that has been played (excluding, for example ABE interviews). If possible, it may be appropriate for the jury to be able to view any such material in the jury room alone, such as on a sterile laptop, so that they can discuss it freely; this will be a matter for the judge's discretion, following discussion with counsel.

## CPD VI Trial 26M: Juries: Jury Irregularities

26M.1   This practice direction replaces the protocol regarding jury irregularities issued by the President of the Queen's Bench Division in November 2012, and the subsequent practice direction, in light of sections 20A to 20D of the Juries Act 1974 and the associated repeal of section 8 of the Contempt of Court Act 1981 (confidentiality of jury's deliberations).
It applies to juries sworn on or after 13 April 2015.

CPD.26L

CPD.26M

Criminal Procedure Rules and Criminal Practice Directions

**26M.2**   A jury irregularity is anything that may prevent one or more jurors from remaining faithful to their oath or affirmation to 'faithfully try the defendant and give a true verdict according to the evidence.' Jury irregularities take many forms. Some are clear-cut such as a juror conducting research about the case or an attempt to suborn or intimidate a juror. Others are less clear-cut — for example, when there is potential bias or friction between jurors.

**26M.3**   A jury irregularity may involve contempt of court and / or the commission of an offence by or in relation to a juror.

**26M.4**   Under the previous version of this practice direction, the Crown Court required approval from the Vice-President of the Court of Appeal (Criminal Division) (CACD) prior to providing a juror's details to the police for the purposes of an investigation into a jury irregularity. Such approval is no longer required. Provision of a juror's details to the police is now a matter for the Crown Court.

*Jury Irregularity During Trial*

**26M.5**   A jury irregularity that comes to light during a trial may impact on the conduct of the trial. It may also involve contempt of court and / or the commission of an offence by or in relation to a juror. **The primary concern of the judge should be the impact on the trial.**

**26M.6**   A jury irregularity should be drawn to the attention of the judge in the absence of the jury as soon as it becomes known.

**26M.7**   **When the judge becomes aware of a jury irregularity, the judge should follow the procedure set out below:**
    **STEP 1:**   **Consider isolating juror(s)**
    **STEP 2:**   **Consult with advocates**
    **STEP 3:**   **Consider appropriate provisional measures (which may include surrender / seizure of electronic communications devices and taking defendant into custody)**
    **STEP 4:**   **Seek to establish basic facts of jury irregularity**
    **STEP 5:**   **Further consult with advocates**
    **STEP 6:**   **Decide what to do in relation to conduct of trial**
    **STEP 7:**   **Consider ancillary matters (contempt in face of court and / or commission of criminal offence)**

**STEP 1: CONSIDER ISOLATING JUROR(S)**

**26M.8**   The judge should consider whether the juror(s) concerned should be isolated from the rest of the jury, particularly if the juror(s) may have conducted research about the case.

**26M.9**   If two or more jurors are concerned, the judge should consider whether they should also be isolated from each other, particularly if one juror has made an accusation against another.

**STEP 2: CONSULT WITH ADVOCATES**

**26M.10**   The judge should consult with the advocates and invite submissions about appropriate provisional measures (Step 3) and how to go about establishing the basic facts of the jury irregularity (Step 4).

**26M.11**   The consultation should be conducted
    — in open court;
    — in the presence of the defendant; and
    — with all parties represented
**unless there is good reason not to do so.**

**26M.12**   If the jury irregularity involves a suspicion about the conduct of the defendant or another party, there may be good reason for the consultation to take place in the absence of the defendant or the other party. There may also be good reason for it to take place in private. If so, the proper location is in the court room, with DARTS recording, rather than in the judge's room.

**26M.13**   If the jury irregularity relates to the jury's deliberations, the judge should warn all those present that it is an offence to disclose, solicit or obtain information about a jury's deliberations (section 20D(1) of the Juries Act 1974 — see 26M.35 to 26M.38 regarding the offence and exceptions). This would include disclosing information about the jury's deliberations divulged in court during consultation with the advocates (Step 2 and Step 5) or when seeking to establish the basic facts of the jury irregularity (Step 4). The judge should emphasise that the advocates, court staff and those in the public gallery would commit the offence by explaining to another what is said in court about the jury's deliberations.

**STEP 3: CONSIDER APPROPRIATE PROVISIONAL MEASURES**

**26M.14**   **The judge should consider appropriate provisional measures which may include surrender / seizure of electronic communications devices and taking the defendant into custody.**

## Surrender / seizure of electronic communications devices

26M.15  The judge should consider whether to make an order under section 15A(1) of the Juries Act 1974 requiring the juror(s) concerned to surrender electronic communications devices, such as mobile telephones or smart phones.

26M.16  Having made an order for surrender, the judge may require a court security officer to search a juror to determine whether the juror has complied with the order. Section 54A of the Courts Act 2003 contains the court security officer's powers of search and seizure.

26M.17  Section 15A(5) of the Juries Act 1974 provides that it is contempt of court for a juror to fail to surrender an electronic communications device in accordance with an order for surrender (see paragraphs 26M.29 to 26M.30 regarding the procedure for dealing with such a contempt).

26M.18  Any electronic communications device surrendered or seized under these provisions should be kept safe by the court until returned to the juror or handed to the police as evidence.

## Taking defendant into custody

26M.19  If the defendant is on bail, and the jury irregularity involves a suspicion about the defendant's conduct, the judge should consider taking the defendant into custody. If that suspicion involves an attempt to suborn or intimidate a juror, the defendant should be taken into custody.

### STEP 4: SEEK TO ESTABLISH BASIC FACTS OF JURY IRREGULARITY

26M.20  The judge should seek to establish the basic facts of the jury irregularity for the purpose of determining how to proceed in relation to the conduct of the trial. The judge's enquiries may involve having the juror(s) concerned write a note of explanation and / or questioning the juror(s). The judge may enquire whether the juror(s) feel able to continue and remain faithful to their oath or affirmation. If there is questioning, each juror should be questioned separately, in the absence of the rest of the jury, unless there is good reason not to do so.

26M.21  In accordance with paragraphs 26M.10 to 26M.13, the enquiries should be conducted in open court; in the presence of the defendant; and with all parties represented unless there is good reason not to do so.

### STEP 5: FURTHER CONSULT WITH ADVOCATES

26M.22  The judge should further consult with the advocates and invite submissions about how to proceed in relation to the conduct of the trial and what should be said to the jury (Step 6).

26M.23  In accordance with paragraphs 26M.10 to 26M.13, the consultation should be conducted in open court; in the presence of the defendant; and with all parties represented unless there is good reason not to do so.

### STEP 6: DECIDE WHAT TO DO IN RELATION TO CONDUCT OF TRIAL

26M.24  When deciding how to proceed, the judge may take time to reflect.

26M.25  Considerations may include the stage the trial has reached. The judge should be alert to attempts by the defendant or others to thwart the trial. In cases of potential bias, the judge should consider whether a fair minded and informed observer would conclude that there was a real possibility that the juror(s) or jury would be biased (*Porter v Magill* [2001] UKHL 67, [2002] 2 AC 357).

26M.26  **In relation to the conduct of the trial, there are three possibilities:**

1. *Take no action and continue with the trial*
   If so, the judge should consider what, if anything, to say to the jury. For example, the judge may reassure the jury nothing untoward has happened or remind them their verdict is a decision of the whole jury and that they should try to work together. Anything said should be tailored to the circumstances of the case.

2. *Discharge the juror(s) concerned and continue with the trial*
   If so, the judge should consider what to say to the discharged juror(s) and the jurors who remain. All jurors should be warned not to discuss what has happened.

3. *Discharge the whole jury*
   If so, the judge should consider what to say to the jury and they should be warned not to discuss what has happened.
   If the judge is satisfied that jury tampering has taken place, depending on the circumstances, the judge may continue the trial without a jury (section 46(3) of the Criminal Justice Act 2003) or order a new trial without a jury (section 46(5) of the Criminal Justice Act 2003). Alternatively, the judge may re-list the trial. If there is a real and present danger of jury tampering in the new trial, the prosecution may apply for a trial without a jury (section 44 of the Criminal Justice Act 2003).

STEP 7: CONSIDER ANCILLARY MATTERS

**26M.27** **A jury irregularity may also involve contempt in the face of the court and / or the commission of a criminal offence. The possibilities include the following:**
— Contempt in the face of the court by a juror
— An offence by a juror or a non-juror under the Juries Act 1974
Offences that may be committed by jurors are researching the case, sharing research, engaging in prohibited conduct or disclosing information about the jury's deliberations (sections 20A to 20D of the Juries Act 1974). Non-jurors may commit the offence of disclosing, soliciting or obtaining information about the jury's deliberations (section 20D of the Juries Act 1974).
— **An offence by juror or a non-juror other than under the Juries Act 1974** A juror may commit an offence such as assault or theft. A non-juror may commit an offence in relation to a juror such as attempting to pervert the course of justice — for example, if the defendant or another attempts to suborn or intimidate a juror.

### Contempt in the face of the court by a juror

**26M.28** If a juror commits contempt in the face of the court, the juror's conduct may also constitute an offence. If so, the judge should decide whether to deal with the juror summarily under the procedure for contempt in the face of the court or refer the matter to the Attorney General's Office or the police (see paragraphs 26M.31 and 26M.33).

**26M.29** In the case of a *minor and clear* contempt in the face of the court, the judge may deal with the juror summarily. The judge should follow the procedure in CrimPR 48.5 to 48.8. The judge should also have regard to the practice direction regarding contempt of court issued in March 2015 (Practice Direction: Committal for Contempt of Court — Open Court), which emphasises the principle of open justice in relation to proceedings for contempt before all courts.

**26M.30** If a juror fails to comply with an order for surrender of an electronic communications device (see paragraphs 26M.15 to 26M.18), the judge should deal with the juror summarily following the procedure for contempt in the face of the court.

### Offence by a juror or non-juror under the Juries Act 1974

**26M.31** If it appears that an offence under the Juries Act 1974 may have been committed by a juror or non-juror (and the matter has not been dealt with summarily under the procedure for contempt in the face of the court), **the judge** should contact the Attorney General's Office to consider a police investigation, setting out the position neutrally. The officer in the case should not be asked to investigate.
Contact details for the Attorney General's Office are set out at the end of this practice direction.

**26M.32** If relevant to an investigation, any electronic communications device surrendered or seized pursuant to an order for surrender should be passed to the police as soon as practicable.

### Offence by a juror or non-juror other than under the Juries Act 1974

**26M.33** If it appears that an offence, other than an offence under the Juries Act 1974, may have been committed by a juror or non-juror (and the matter has not been dealt with summarily under the procedure for contempt in the face of the court), **the judge or a member of court staff** should contact the police setting out the position neutrally. The officer in the case should not be asked to investigate.

**26M.34** If relevant to an investigation, any electronic communications device surrendered or seized pursuant to an order for surrender should be passed to the police as soon as practicable.

*Other matters to consider*

### Jury deliberations

**26M.35** **In light of the offence of disclosing, soliciting or obtaining information about a jury's deliberations (section 20D(1) of the Juries Act 1974), great care is required if a jury irregularity relates to the jury's deliberations.**

**26M.36** *During the trial,* there are exceptions to this offence that enable the judge (and only the judge) to:
— Seek to establish the basic facts of a jury irregularity involving the jury's deliberations (Step 4); and
— Disclose information about the jury's deliberations to the Attorney General's Office if it appears that an offence may have been committed (Step 7).

**26M.37** With regard to seeking to establish the basic facts of a jury irregularity involving the jury's deliberations (Step 4), it is to be noted that during the trial it is not an offence for the judge to disclose, solicit or obtain information about the jury's deliberations for the purposes of dealing with the case (sections 20E(2)(a) and 20G(1) of the Juries Act 1974).

26M.38 With regard to disclosing information about the jury's deliberations to the Attorney General's Office if it appears that an offence may have been committed (Step 7), it is to be noted that during the trial:
— It is not an offence for the judge to disclose information about the jury's deliberations for the purposes of an investigation by a relevant investigator into whether an offence or contempt of court has been committed by or in relation to a juror (section 20E(2)(b) of the Juries Act 1974); and
— A relevant investigator means a police force or the Attorney General (section 20E(5) of the Juries Act 1974).

### Minimum number of jurors

26M.39 If it is decided to discharge one or more jurors (Step 6), a minimum of nine jurors must remain if the trial is to continue (section 16(1) of the Juries Act 1974).

### Preparation of statement by judge

26M.40 If a jury irregularity occurs, and the trial continues, the judge should have regard to the remarks of Lord Hope in *R v Connors and Mirza* [2004] UKHL 2 at [127] and [128], [2004] 1 AC 1118, [2004] 2 Cr App R 8 and consider whether to prepare a statement that could be used in an application for leave to appeal or an appeal relating to the jury irregularity.

*Jury Irregularity After Jury Discharged*

26M.41 A jury irregularity that comes to light after the jury has been discharged may involve the commission of an offence by or in relation to a juror. It may also provide a ground of appeal.
26M.42 A jury irregularity after the jury has been discharged may come to the attention of the:
— **Trial judge or court**
— **Registrar of Criminal Appeals (the Registrar)**
— **Prosecution**
— **Defence**

### Role of the trial judge or court

26M.43 The judge has no jurisdiction in relation to a jury irregularity that comes to light after the jury has been discharged (*R v Thompson and others* [2010] EWCA Crim 1623, [2011] 1 WLR 200, [2010] 2 Cr App R 27A). The jury will be deemed to have been discharged when all verdicts on all defendants have been delivered or when the jury has been discharged from giving all verdicts on all defendants.
26M.44 The judge will be *functus officio* in relation to a jury irregularity that comes to light during an adjournment between verdict and sentence. The judge should proceed to sentence unless there is good reason not to do so.
26M.45 In practice, a jury irregularity often comes to light when the judge or court receives a communication from a former juror.
26M.46 If a jury irregularity comes to the attention of a judge or court after the jury has been discharged, and regardless of the result of the trial, the judge or a member of court staff should contact the Registrar setting out the position neutrally. Any communication from a former juror should be forwarded to the Registrar.
Contact details for the Registrar are set out at the end of this practice direction.

### Role of the Registrar

26M.47 If a jury irregularity comes to the attention of the Registrar after the jury has been discharged, and regardless of the result of the trial, the Registrar should consider if it appears that an offence may have been committed by or in relation to a juror. The Registrar should also consider if there may be a ground of appeal.
26M.48 When deciding how to proceed, particularly in relation to a communication from a former juror, the Registrar may seek the direction of the Vice-President of the Court of Appeal (Criminal Division) (CACD) or another judge of the CACD in accordance with instructions from the Vice-President.
26M.49 If it appears that an offence may have been committed by or in relation to a juror, the Registrar should contact the Private Office of the Director of Public Prosecutions to consider a police investigation.
26M.50 If there may be a ground of appeal, the Registrar should inform the defence.
26M.51 If a communication from a former juror is not of legal significance, the Registrar should respond explaining that no action is required. An example of such a communication is if it is restricted to a general complaint about the verdict from a dissenting juror or an expression of doubt or second thoughts.

Criminal Procedure Rules and Criminal Practice Directions

**Role of the prosecution**

26M.52 If a jury irregularity comes to the attention of the prosecution after the jury has been discharged, which may provide a ground of appeal, they should notify the defence in accordance with their duties to act fairly and assist in the administration of justice (*R v Makin* [2004] EWCA Crim 1607, 148 SJLB 821).

**Role of the defence**

26M.53 If a jury irregularity comes to the attention of the defence after the jury has been discharged, which provides an arguable ground of appeal, an application for leave to appeal may be made.

*Other matters to consider*

**Jury deliberations**

26M.54 **In light of the offence of disclosing, soliciting or obtaining information about a jury's deliberations (section 20D(1) of the Juries Act 1974), great care is required if a jury irregularity relates to the jury's deliberations.**

26M.55 *After the jury has been discharged*, there are exceptions to this offence that enable a judge, a member of court staff, the Registrar, the prosecution and the defence to disclose information about the jury's deliberations if it appears that an offence may have been committed by or in relation to a juror or if there may be a ground of appeal.

26M.56 For example, it is to be noted that:
— After the jury has been discharged, it is not an offence for a person to disclose information about the jury's deliberations to defined persons if the person reasonably believes that an offence or contempt of court may have been committed by or in relation to a juror or the conduct of a juror may provide grounds of appeal (section 20F(1) (2) of the Juries Act 1974).
— The defined persons to whom such information may be disclosed are a member of a police force, a judge of the CACD, the Registrar of Criminal Appeals (the Registrar), a judge where the trial took place or a member of court staff where the trial took place who would reasonably be expected to disclose the information only to one of the aforementioned defined persons (section 20F(2) of the Juries Act 1974).
— After the jury has been discharged, it is not an offence for a judge of the CACD or the Registrar to disclose information about the jury's deliberations for the purposes of an investigation by a relevant investigator into whether an offence or contempt of court has been committed by or in relation to a juror or the conduct of a juror may provide grounds of appeal (section 20F(4) of the Juries Act 1974).
— A relevant investigator means a police force, the Attorney General, the Criminal Cases Review Commission (CCRC) or the Crown Prosecution Service (section 20F(10) of the Juries Act 1974).

**Investigation by the Criminal Cases Review Commission (CCRC)**

26M.57 If an application for leave to appeal, or an appeal, includes a ground of appeal relating to a jury irregularity, the Registrar may refer the case to the Full Court to decide whether to direct the CCRC to conduct an investigation under section 23A of the Criminal Appeal Act 1968.

26M.58 If the Court directs the CCRC to conduct an investigation, directions should be given as to the scope of the investigation.

**Contact Details**

**Attorney General's Office**

Contempt.SharedMailbox@attorneygeneral.gsi.gov.uk
Telephone: 020 7271 2492

**The Registrar**

penny.donnelly@hmcts.x.gsi.gov.uk (Secretary) or
criminalappealoffice.generaloffice@hmcts.gsi.gov.uk
Telephone: 020 7947 6103 (Secretary) or 020 7947 6011

**CPD.26N**

**CPD VI Trial 26N: Open Justice**

26N.1 There must be freedom of access between advocate and judge. Any discussion must, however, be between the judge and the advocates on both sides. If an advocate is instructed by a solicitor who is in court, he or she, too, should be allowed to attend the discussion. This freedom of access is important because there may be matters calling for communication or discussion of such a nature that the advocate cannot, in the client's interest, mention them in open court, e.g. the advocate, by way of mitigation, may wish to tell the judge that reliable medical evidence shows that the defendant is suffering from a terminal illness and may not have long to live. It is imperative that, so far as possible, justice must be administered in open court. Advocates should, therefore, only ask to see the judge when it is felt to be really necessary. The judge must be careful only to treat such communications as private where, in the interests of justice, this is necessary. Where any such discussion takes place it should be recorded, preferably by audio recording.

## CPD VI Trial 26P: Defendant's Right to Give or Not to Give Evidence

26P.1    At the conclusion of the evidence for the prosecution, section 35(2) of the Criminal Justice and Public Order Act 1994 requires the court to satisfy itself that the defendant is aware that the stage has been reached at which evidence can be given for the defence and that the defendant's failure to give evidence, or if he does so his failure to answer questions, without a good reason, may lead to inferences being drawn against him.

*If the defendant is legally represented*

26P.2    After the close of the prosecution case, if the defendant's representative requests a brief adjournment to advise his client on this issue the request should, ordinarily, be granted. When appropriate the judge should, in the presence of the jury, inquire of the representative in these terms:

> *'Have you advised your client that the stage has now been reached at which he may give evidence and, if he chooses not to do so or, having been sworn, without good cause refuses to answer any question, the jury may draw such inferences as appear proper from his failure to do so?'*

26P.3    If the representative replies to the judge that the defendant has been so advised, then the case shall proceed. If counsel replies that the defendant has not been so advised, then the judge shall direct the representative to advise his client of the consequences and should adjourn briefly for this purpose, before proceeding further.

*If the defendant is not legally represented*

26P.4    If the defendant is not represented, the judge shall, at the conclusion of the evidence for the prosecution, in the absence of the jury, indicate what he will say to him in the presence of the jury and ask if he understands and whether he would like a brief adjournment to consider his position.

26P.5    When appropriate, and in the presence of the jury, the judge should say to the defendant:

> *'Now is your chance to give evidence if you choose to do so. If you do give evidence it will be on oath [or affirmation], and you will be cross-examined like any other witness. If you do not give evidence the jury may hold it against you. If you do give evidence but refuse without good reason to answer the questions the jury may, as I have just explained, hold that against you. Do you now intend to give evidence?'*

## CPD VI Trial 26Q: Majority Verdicts

26Q.1    It is very important that all those trying indictable offences should, so far as possible, adopt a uniform practice when complying with section 17 of the Juries Act 1974, both in directing the jury in summing-up and also in receiving the verdict or giving further directions after retirement. So far as the summing-up is concerned, it is inadvisable for the judge, and indeed for advocates, to attempt an explanation of the section for fear that the jury will be confused. Before the jury retires, however, the judge should direct the jury in some such words as the following:

> *'As you may know, the law permits me, in certain circumstances, to accept a verdict which is not the verdict of you all. Those circumstances have not as yet arisen, so that when you retire I must ask you to reach a verdict upon which each one of you is agreed. Should, however, the time come when it is possible for me to accept a majority verdict, I will give you a further direction.'*

26Q.2    Thereafter, the practice should be as follows:
Should the jury return before two hours and ten minutes has elapsed since the last member of the jury left the jury box to go to the jury room (or such longer time as the judge thinks reasonable) (see section 17(4)), they should be asked:
(a) 'Have you reached a verdict upon which you are all agreed? Please answer "Yes" or "No".';
(b) (i) If unanimous, 'What is your verdict?';
    (ii) If not unanimous, the jury should be sent out again for further deliberation, with a further direction to arrive if possible at a unanimous verdict.

26Q.3    Should the jury return (whether for the first time or subsequently) or be sent for after the two hours and ten minutes (or the longer period) has elapsed, questions (a) and (b)(i) in the paragraph above should be put to them and, if it appears that they are not unanimous, they should be asked to retire once more and told they should continue to endeavour to reach a unanimous verdict but that, if they cannot, the judge will accept a majority verdict as in section 17(1).

**26Q.4**   When the jury finally return, they should be asked:
- (a) 'Have at least ten (or nine as the case may be) of you agreed on your verdict?';
- (b) If 'Yes', 'What is your verdict? Please only answer "Guilty" or "Not Guilty".';
- (c) (i)   If 'Not Guilty', accept the verdict without more ado;
  - (ii)   If 'Guilty', 'Is that the verdict of you all, or by a majority?';
- (d) If 'Guilty' by a majority, 'How many of you agreed to the verdict and how many dissented?'

**26Q.5**   At whatever stage the jury return, before question (a) is asked, the senior officer of the court present shall state in open court, for each period when the jury was out of court for the purpose of considering their verdict(s), the time at which the last member of the jury left the jury box to go to the jury room and the time of their return to the jury box; and will additionally state in open court the total of such periods.

**26Q.6**   The reason why section 17(3) is confined to a majority verdict of 'Guilty', and for the somewhat complicated procedure set out above, is to prevent it being known that a verdict of 'Not Guilty' is a majority verdict. If the final direction continues to require the jury to arrive, if possible, at a unanimous verdict and the verdict is received as specified, it will not be known for certain that the acquittal is not unanimous.

**26Q.7**   Where there are several counts (or alternative verdicts) left to the jury the above practice will, of course, need to be adapted to the circumstances. The procedure will have to be repeated in respect of each count (or alternative verdict), the verdict being accepted in those cases where the jury are unanimous and the further direction being given in cases in which they are not unanimous. The judge may exercise discretion in deciding when to record the unanimous verdict; the circumstances of the case may dictate that it is more desirable to give the majority direction before the recording of any unanimous verdicts. If so, then instead of being asked about each count in turn, the jury should be asked 'Have you reached verdicts upon which you are all agreed in respect of all defendants and/or all counts?'.

**26Q.8**   Should the jury in the end be unable to agree on a verdict by the required majority, the judge in his discretion will either ask them to deliberate further, or discharge them.

**26Q.9**   Section 17 will, of course, apply also to verdicts other than 'Guilty' or 'Not Guilty', e.g. to special verdicts under the Criminal Procedure (Insanity) Act 1964, following a finding by the judge that the defendant is unfit to be tried, and special verdicts on findings of fact. Accordingly, in such cases the questions to jurors will have to be suitably adjusted.

CRIMINAL PROCEDURE RULES   PART 27   RETRIAL AFTER ACQUITTAL

### General

**R27.1**   **When this Part applies**

**27.1**   (1)   Rule 27.2 applies where, under section 54 of the Criminal Procedure and Investigations Act 1996[1], the Crown Court or a magistrates' court can certify for the High Court that interference or intimidation has been involved in proceedings leading to an acquittal.

       (2)   Rules 27.3 to 27.7 apply where, under section 77 of the Criminal Justice Act 2003[2], the Court of Appeal can—
- (a) quash an acquittal for a serious offence and order a defendant to be retried; or
- (b) order that an acquittal outside the United Kingdom is no bar to the defendant being tried in England and Wales,

       if there is new and compelling evidence and it is in the interests of justice to make the order.

### Application for certificate to allow order for retrial

**R27.2**   **Application for certificate**

**27.2**   (1)   This rule applies where—
- (a) a defendant has been acquitted of an offence;
- (b) a person has been convicted of one of the following offences involving interference with or intimidation of a juror or a witness (or potential witness) in any proceedings which led to the defendant's acquittal—
  - (i) perverting the course of justice,
  - (ii) intimidation etc. of witnesses, jurors and others under section 51(1) of the Criminal Justice and Public Order Act 1994[3], or

---

[1] 1996 c. 25.
[2] 2003 c. 44.
[3] 1994 c. 33; section 51 was amended by section 29 of, and paragraph 19 of Schedule 2 to, the Criminal Appeal Act 1995 (c. 35), section 67 of, and paragraphs 21 and 22 of Schedule 4 to, the Youth Justice and Criminal Evidence Act 1999 (c. 23), paragraphs 62 and 64 of Schedule 36 to the Criminal Justice Act 2003 (c. 44), section 45 of, and paragraph 36 of Schedule 17

(iii) aiding, abetting, counselling, procuring, suborning or inciting another person to commit an offence under section 1 of the Perjury Act 1911[4]; and

(c) the prosecutor wants the court by which that person was convicted to certify for the High Court that there is a real possibility that, but for the interference or intimidation, the defendant would not have been acquitted.

(2) The prosecutor must—

(a) apply in writing as soon as practicable after that person's conviction; and

(b) serve the application on—

(i)   the court officer, and

(ii)  the defendant who was acquitted, if the court so directs.

(3) The application must—

(a) give details, with relevant facts and dates, of—

(i)   the conviction for interference or intimidation, and

(ii)  the defendant's acquittal; and

(b) explain—

(i)   why there is a real possibility that, but for the interference or intimidation, the defendant would not have been acquitted, and

(ii)  why it would not be contrary to the interests of justice to prosecute the defendant again for the offence of which he or she was acquitted, despite any lapse of time or other reason.

(4) The court may—

(a) extend the time limit under paragraph (2);

(b) allow an application to be in a different form to one set out in the Practice Direction, or to be made orally; and

(c) determine an application under this rule—

(i)   at a hearing, in private or in public; or

(ii)  without a hearing.

(5) If the court gives a certificate, the court officer must serve it on—

(a) the prosecutor; and

(b) the defendant who was acquitted.

*[Note: See Section 54 of the Criminal Procedure and Investigations Act 1996 (Acquittals tainted by intimidation, etc.).*

*For the procedure on application to the High Court, see rules 77.6 to 77.15 of the Civil Procedure Rules 1998[5].]*

### Application to Court of Appeal to quash acquittal and order retrial

**Application for reporting restriction pending application for order for retrial**                    **R27.3**

27.3  (1) This rule applies where—

(a) no application has been made under rule 27.4 (Application for order for retrial);

(b) an investigation by officers has begun into an offence with a view to an application under that rule; and

(c) the Director of Public Prosecutions wants the Court of Appeal to make, vary or remove an order for a reporting restriction under section 82 of the Criminal Justice Act 2003 (Restrictions on publication in the interests of justice).

(2) The Director must—

(a) apply in writing; and

(b) serve the application on—

(i)   the Registrar, and

(ii)  the defendant, unless the court otherwise directs.

(3) The application must, as appropriate—

(a) explain why the Director wants the court to direct that it need not be served on the defendant until the application under rule 27.4 is served;

(b) specify the proposed terms of the order, and for how long it should last;

(c) explain why an order in the terms proposed is necessary; and

(d) explain why an order should be varied or removed.

to, the Crime and Courts Act 2013 (c. 22) and section 50 of, and paragraph 14 of Schedule 11 to, the Criminal Justice and Courts Act 2015 (c. 2). It is further amended by paragraph 11 of Schedule 36 to the Criminal Justice Act 2003 (c. 44), with effect from a date to be appointed.

[4] 1911 c.6.
[5] S.I. 1998/3132; rules 77.6 to 77.15 were inserted by S.I. 2010/1953.

*Under section 89 of the 2003 Act, where the prosecutor has made an application to the Court of Appeal under rule 27.4—*

> (a) *if the defendant is in custody, the Crown Court must decide whether to remand him or her in custody to be brought before the Court of Appeal or to grant bail for that purpose; or*
> (b) *if the defendant is not in custody, and if the prosecutor so applies, the Crown Court may either issue a summons for the defendant to attend the Court of Appeal or issue a warrant for the defendant's arrest.]*

**R27.7**   **Application of other rules about procedure in the Court of Appeal**

27.7   On an application under rule 27.4 (Application for order for retrial)—
   (a) the rules in Part 36 (Appeal to the Court of Appeal: general rules) apply with the necessary modifications;
   (b) rules 39.8, 39.9 and 39.10 (bail and bail conditions in the Court of Appeal) apply as if the references in those rules to appeal included references to an application under rule 27.4; and
   (c) rule 39.14 (Renewal or setting aside of order for retrial) applies as if the reference to section 7 of the Criminal Appeal Act 1968[14] were a reference to section 84 of the Criminal Justice Act 2003[15] (Retrial).

*[Note. See also the notes to the rules listed in this rule.*

*For the powers of the Court of Appeal that may be exercised by one judge of that court or by the Registrar, and for the right to renew an application for directions to a judge or to the Court of Appeal, see the Criminal Justice Act 2003 (Retrial for Serious Offences) Order 2005[16] and rule 36.5 (Renewing an application refused by a judge or the Registrar).*

*For rules governing applications for reporting restrictions, see Part 6. For rules governing proceedings in the Crown Court about bail, see Part 14.]*

CRIMINAL PRACTICE DIRECTIONS: SENTENCING

**CPD.VII.A**   **CPD VII Sentencing A: Pleas of Guilty in the Crown Court**

**A.1**   Prosecutors and Prosecution Advocates should be familiar with and follow the Attorney-General's Guidelines on the Acceptance of Pleas and the Prosecutor's Role in the Sentencing Exercise.

**CPD.VII.B**   **CPD VII Sentencing B: Determining the Factual Basis of Sentence**

*Where a guilty plea is offered to less than the whole indictment and the prosecution is minded to accept pleas tendered to some counts or to lesser alternative counts.*

**B.1**   In some cases, defendants wishing to plead guilty will simply plead guilty to all charges on the basis of the facts as alleged and opened by the prosecution, with no dispute as to the factual basis or the extent of offending. Alternatively a defendant may plead guilty to some of the charges brought; in such a case, the judge will consider whether that plea represents a proper plea on the basis of the facts set out by the papers.

**B.2**   Where the prosecution advocate is considering whether to accept a plea to a lesser charge, the advocate may invite the judge to approve the proposed course of action. In such circumstances, the advocate must abide by the decision of the judge.

**B.3**   If the prosecution advocate does not invite the judge to approve the acceptance by the prosecution of a lesser charge, it is open to the judge to express his or her dissent with the course proposed and invite the advocate to reconsider the matter with those instructing him or her.

**B.4**   In any proceedings where the judge is of the opinion that the course proposed by the advocate may lead to serious injustice, the proceedings may be adjourned to allow the following procedure to be followed:
   (a) as a preliminary step, the prosecution advocate must discuss the judge's observations with the Chief Crown Prosecutor or the senior prosecutor of the relevant prosecuting authority as appropriate, in an attempt to resolve the issue;
   (b) where the issue remains unresolved, the Director of Public Prosecutions or the Director of the relevant prosecuting authority should be consulted;
   (c) in extreme circumstances the judge may decline to proceed with the case until the prosecuting authority has consulted with the Attorney General, as may be appropriate.

---

[14]   1968 c. 19; section 7 was amended by sections 43 and 170 of, and Schedule 16 to, the Criminal Justice Act 1988 (c. 33) and paragraph 44 of Schedule 36 to the Criminal Justice Act 2003 (c. 44).
[15]   2003 c. 44.
[16]   2003 S.I. 2005/679.

**B.5** Prior to entering a plea of guilty, a defendant may seek an indication of sentence under the procedure set out in *R v Goodyear* [2005] EWCA Crim 888, [2005] 1 WLR 2532, [2005] 2 Cr App R 20; see below.

*Where a guilty plea is offered on a limited basis*

**B.6** A defendant may put forward a plea of guilty without accepting all of the facts as alleged by the prosecution. The basis of plea offered may seek to limit the facts or the extent of the offending for which the defendant is to be sentenced. Depending on the view taken by the prosecution, and the content of the offered basis, the case will fall into one of the following categories:

(a) a plea of guilty upon a basis of plea agreed by the prosecution and defence;

(b) a plea of guilty on a basis signed by the defendant but in respect of which there is no or only partial agreement by the prosecution;

(c) a plea of guilty on a basis that contains within it matters that are purely mitigation and which do not amount to a contradiction of the prosecution case; or

(d) in cases involving serious or complex fraud, a plea of guilty upon a basis of plea agreed by the prosecution and defence accompanied by joint submissions as to sentence.

*(a) A plea of guilty upon a basis of plea agreed by the prosecution and defence*

**B.7** The prosecution may reach an agreement with the defendant as to the factual basis on which the defendant will plead guilty, often known as an 'agreed basis of plea'. It is always subject to the approval of the court, which will consider whether it adequately and appropriately reflects the evidence as disclosed on the papers, whether it is fair and whether it is in the interests of justice.

**B.8** *R v Underwood* [2004] EWCA Crim 2256, [2005] 1 Cr App R 13, [2005] 1 Cr App R (S) 90 outlines the principles to be applied where the defendant admits that he or she is guilty, but disputes the basis of offending alleged by the prosecution:

(a) The prosecution may accept and agree the defendant's account of the disputed facts or reject it in its entirety, or in part. If the prosecution accepts the defendant's basis of plea, it must ensure that the basis of plea is factually accurate and enables the sentencing judge to impose a sentence appropriate to reflect the justice of the case;

(b) In resolving any disputed factual matters, the prosecution must consider its primary duty to the court and must not agree with or acquiesce in an agreement which contains material factual disputes;

(c) If the prosecution does accept the defendant's basis of plea, it must be reduced to writing, be signed by advocates for both sides, and made available to the judge prior to the prosecution's opening;

(d) An agreed basis of plea that has been reached between the parties should not contain matters which are in dispute and any aspects upon which there is not agreement should be clearly identified;

(e) On occasion, the prosecution may lack the evidence positively to dispute the defendant's account, for example, where the defendant asserts a matter outside the knowledge of the prosecution. Simply because the prosecution does not have evidence to contradict the defendant's assertions does not mean those assertions should be agreed. In such a case, the prosecution should test the defendant's evidence and submissions by requesting a *Newton* hearing (*R v Newton* (1982) 77 Cr App R 13, (1982) 4 Cr App R (S) 388), following the procedure set out below;

(f) If it is not possible for the parties to resolve a factual dispute when attempting to reach a plea agreement under this part, it is the responsibility of the prosecution to consider whether the matter should proceed to trial, or to invite the court to hold a *Newton* hearing as necessary.

**B.9** *R v Underwood* emphasises that, whether or not pleas have been 'agreed', the judge is not bound by any such agreement and is entitled of his or her own motion to insist that any evidence relevant to the facts in dispute (or upon which the judge requires further evidence for whatever reason) should be called. Any view formed by the prosecution on a proposed basis of plea is deemed to be conditional on the judge's acceptance of the basis of plea.

**B.10** A judge is not entitled to reject a defendant's basis of plea absent a *Newton* hearing unless it is determined by the court that the basis is manifestly false and as such does not merit examination by way of the calling of evidence or alternatively the defendant declines the opportunity to engage in the process of the *Newton* hearing whether by giving evidence on his own behalf or otherwise.

*(b) A plea of guilty on a basis signed by the defendant but in respect of which there is no or only partial agreement by the prosecution*

**B.11** Where the defendant pleads guilty, but disputes the basis of offending alleged by the prosecution and agreement as to that has not been reached, the following procedure should be followed:

(a) The defendant's basis of plea must be set out in writing, identifying what is in dispute and must be signed by the defendant;

(b) The prosecution must respond in writing setting out their alternative contentions and indicating whether or not they submit that a *Newton* hearing is necessary;

(c) The court may invite the parties to make representations about whether the dispute is material to sentence; and

(d) If the court decides that it is a material dispute, the court will invite such further representations or evidence as it may require and resolve the dispute in accordance with the principles set out in *R v Newton*.

**B.12** Where the disputed issue arises from facts which are within the exclusive knowledge of the defendant and the defendant is willing to give evidence in support of his case, the defence advocate should be prepared to call the defendant. If the defendant is not willing to testify, and subject to any explanation which may be given, the judge may draw such inferences as appear appropriate.

**B.13** The decision whether or not a *Newton* hearing is required is one for the judge. Once the decision has been taken that there will be a *Newton* hearing, evidence is called by the parties in the usual way and the criminal burden and standard of proof applies. Whatever view has been taken by the prosecution, the prosecutor should not leave the questioning to the judge, but should assist the court by exploring the issues which the court wishes to have explored. The rules of evidence should be followed as during a trial, and the judge should direct himself appropriately as the tribunal of fact. Paragraphs 6 to 10 of *Underwood* provide additional guidance regarding the *Newton* hearing procedure.

*(c)  A plea of guilty on a basis that contains within it matters that are purely mitigation and which do not amount to a contradiction of the prosecution case*

**B.14** A basis of plea should not normally set out matters of mitigation but there may be circumstances where it is convenient and sensible for the document outlining a basis to deal with facts closely aligned to the circumstances of the offending which amount to mitigation and which may need to be resolved prior to sentence. The resolution of these matters does not amount to a *Newton* hearing properly so defined and in so far as facts fall to be established the defence will have to discharge the civil burden in order to do so. The scope of the evidence required to resolve issues that are purely matters of mitigation is for the court to determine.

*(d)  Cases involving serious fraud — a plea of guilty upon a basis of plea agreed by the prosecution and defence accompanied by joint submissions as to sentence*

**B.15** This section applies when the prosecution and the defendant(s) to a matter before the Crown Court involving allegations of serious or complex fraud have agreed a basis of plea and seek to make submissions to the court regarding sentence.

**B.16** Guidance for prosecutors regarding the operation of this procedure is set out in the 'Attorney General's Guidelines on Plea Discussions in Cases of Serious or Complex Fraud', which came into force on 5 May 2009 and is referred to in this direction as the 'Attorney General's Plea Discussion Guidelines'.

**B.17** In this part—

(a) 'a plea agreement' means a written basis of plea agreed between the prosecution and defendant(s) in accordance with the principles set out in *R v Underwood*, supported by admissible documentary evidence or admissions under section 10 of the Criminal Justice Act 1967;

(b) 'a sentencing submission' means sentencing submissions made jointly by the prosecution and defence as to the appropriate sentencing authorities and applicable sentencing range in the relevant sentencing guideline relating to the plea agreement;

(c) 'serious or complex fraud' includes, but is not limited to, allegations of fraud where two or more of the following are present:

(i) the amount obtained or intended to be obtained exceeded £500,000;

(ii) there is a significant international dimension;

(iii) the case requires specialised knowledge of financial, commercial, fiscal or regulatory matters such as the operation of markets, banking systems, trusts or tax regimes;

(iv) the case involves allegations of fraudulent activity against numerous victims;

(v) the case involves an allegation of substantial and significant fraud on a public body;

(vi) the case is likely to be of widespread public concern;

(vii) the alleged misconduct endangered the economic well-being of the United Kingdom, for example by undermining confidence in financial markets.

*Procedure*

**B.18**  The procedure regarding agreed bases of plea outlined above, applies with equal rigour to the acceptance of pleas under this procedure. However, because under this procedure the parties will have been discussing the plea agreement and the charges from a much earlier stage, it is vital that the judge is fully informed of all relevant background to the discussions, charges and the eventual basis of plea.

**B.19**  Where the defendant has not yet appeared before the Crown Court, the prosecutor must send full details of the plea agreement and sentencing submission(s) to the court, at least 7 days in advance of the defendant's first appearance. Where the defendant has already appeared before the Crown Court, the prosecutor must notify the court as soon as is reasonably practicable that a plea agreement and sentencing submissions under the Attorney General's Plea Discussion Guidelines are to be submitted. The court should set a date for the matter to be heard, and the prosecutor must send full details of the plea agreement and sentencing submission(s) to the court as soon as practicable, or in accordance with the directions of the court.

**B.20**  The provision to the judge of full details of the plea agreement requires sufficient information to be provided to allow the judge to understand the facts of the case and the history of the plea discussions, to assess whether the plea agreement is fair and in the interests of justice, and to decide the appropriate sentence. This will include, but is not limited to:

(i)   the plea agreement;

(ii)  the sentencing submission(s);

(iii) all of the material provided by the prosecution to the defendant in the course of the plea discussions;

(iv)  relevant material provided by the defendant, for example documents relating to personal mitigation; and

(v)   the minutes of any meetings between the parties and any correspondence generated in the plea discussions.

The parties should be prepared to provide additional material at the request of the court.

**B.21**  The court should at all times have regard to the length of time that has elapsed since the date of the occurrence of the events giving rise to the plea discussions, the time taken to interview the defendant, the date of charge and the prospective trial date (if the matter were to proceed to trial) so as to ensure that its consideration of the plea agreement and sentencing submissions does not cause any unnecessary further delay.

*Status of plea agreement and joint sentencing submissions*

**B.22**  Where a plea agreement and joint sentencing submissions are submitted, it remains entirely a matter for the court to decide how to deal with the case. The judge retains the absolute discretion to refuse to accept the plea agreement and to sentence otherwise than in accordance with the sentencing submissions made under the Attorney General's Plea Discussion Guidelines.

**B.23**  Sentencing submissions should draw the court's attention to any applicable range in any relevant guideline, and to any ancillary orders that may be applicable. Sentencing submissions should not include a specific sentence or agreed range other than the ranges set out in sentencing guidelines or authorities.

**B.24**  Prior to pleading guilty in accordance with the plea agreement, the defendant(s) may apply to the court for an indication of the likely maximum sentence under the procedure set out below (a '*Goodyear* indication').

**B.25**  In the event that the judge indicates a sentence or passes a sentence which is not within the submissions made on sentencing, the plea agreement remains binding.

**B.26**  If the defendant does not plead guilty in accordance with the plea agreement, or if a defendant who has pleaded guilty in accordance with a plea agreement, successfully applies to withdraw his plea under CrimPR 25.5, the signed plea agreement may be treated as confession evidence, and may be used against the defendant at a later stage in these or any other proceedings. Any credit for a timely guilty plea may be lost. The court may exercise its discretion under section 78 of the Police and Criminal Evidence Act 1984 to exclude any such evidence if it appears to the court that, having regard to all the circumstances, including the circumstances in which the evidence was obtained, the admission of the evidence would have such an adverse effect on the fairness of the proceedings that the court ought not to admit it.

**B.27**  Where a defendant has failed to plead guilty in accordance with a plea agreement, the case is unlikely to be ready for trial immediately. The prosecution may have been commenced earlier than it otherwise would have been, in reliance upon the defendant's agreement to plead guilty. This is likely to be a relevant consideration for the court in deciding whether or not to grant an application to adjourn or stay the proceedings to allow the matter to be prepared for trial in accordance with the protocol on the 'Control and Management of Heavy Fraud and other Complex Criminal Cases', or as required.

Criminal Procedure Rules and Criminal Practice Directions

**CPD.VII.C**    **CPD VII Sentencing C: Indications of Sentence: *R v Goodyear***

C.1    Prior to pleading guilty, it is open to a defendant in the Crown Court to request from the judge an indication of the maximum sentence that would be imposed if a guilty plea were to be tendered at that stage in the proceedings, in accordance with the guidance in *R v Goodyear* [2005] EWCA Crim 888, [2005] 1 WLR 2532, [2005] 2 Cr App R 20. The defence should notify the court and the prosecution of the intention to seek an indication in advance of any hearing.

C.2    Attention is drawn to the guidance set out in paragraphs 53 and following of *R v Goodyear*. The objective of the *Goodyear* guidelines is to safeguard against the creation or appearance of judicial pressure on a defendant. Any advance indication given should be the maximum sentence if a guilty plea were to be tendered at that stage of the proceedings only; the judge should not indicate the maximum possible sentence following conviction by a jury after trial. The judge should only give a *Goodyear* indication if one is requested by the defendant, although the judge can, in an appropriate case, remind the defence advocate of the defendant's entitlement to seek an advance indication of sentence.

C.3    Whether to give a *Goodyear* indication, and whether to give reasons for a refusal, is a matter for the discretion of the judge, to be exercised in accordance with the principles outlined by the Court of Appeal in that case. Such indications should normally not be given if there is a dispute as to the basis of plea unless the judge concludes that he or she can properly deal with the case without the need for a *Newton* hearing. If there is a basis of plea agreed by the prosecution and defence, it must be reduced into writing and a copy provided to the judge. As always, any basis of plea will be subject to the approval of the court. In cases where a dispute arises, the procedure in *R v Underwood* should be followed prior to the court considering a sentence indication further, as set out above. The judge should not become involved in negotiations about the acceptance of pleas or any agreed basis of plea, nor should a request be made for an indication of the different sentences that might be imposed if various different pleas were to be offered.

C.4    There should be no prosecution opening nor should the judge hear mitigation. However, during the sentence indication process the prosecution advocate is expected to assist the court by ensuring that the court has received all of the prosecution evidence, any statement from the victim about the impact of the offence, and any relevant previous convictions. Further, where appropriate, the prosecution should provide references to the relevant statutory powers of the court, relevant sentencing guidelines and authorities, and such other assistance as the court requires.

C.5    Attention is drawn to paragraph 70(d) of *Goodyear* which emphasises that the prosecution 'should not say anything which may create the impression that the sentence indication has the support or approval of the Crown.' This prohibition against the Crown indicating its approval of a particular sentence applies in all circumstances when a defendant is being sentenced, including when joint sentencing submissions are made.

C.6    An indication, once given, is, save in exceptional circumstances (such as arose in *R v Newman* [2010] EWCA Crim 1566, [2011] 1 Cr App R (S) 68), binding on the judge who gave it, and any other judge, subject to overriding statutory obligations such as those following a finding of 'dangerousness'. In circumstances where a judge proposes to depart from a *Goodyear* indication this must only be done in a way that does not give rise to unfairness (see *Newman*). However, if the defendant does not plead guilty, the indication will not thereafter bind the court.

C.7    If the offence is a specified offence such that the defendant might be liable to an assessment of 'dangerousness' in accordance with the Criminal Justice Act 2003 it is unlikely that the necessary material for such an assessment will be available. The court can still proceed to give an indication of sentence, but should state clearly the limitations of the indication that can be given.

C.8    A *Goodyear* indication should be given in open court in the presence of the defendant but any reference to the hearing is not admissible in any subsequent trial; and reporting restrictions should normally be imposed.

**CPD.VII.D**    **CPD VII Sentencing D: Facts to be Stated on Pleas of Guilty**

D.1    To enable the press and the public to know the circumstances of an offence of which an accused has been convicted and for which he is to be sentenced, in relation to each offence to which an accused has pleaded guilty the prosecution shall state those facts in open court, before sentence is imposed.

**CPD.VII.E**    **CPD VII Sentencing E: Concurrent and Consecutive Sentences**

E.1    Where a court passes on a defendant more than one term of imprisonment, the court should state in the presence of the defendant whether the terms are to be concurrent or consecutive. Should this not be done, the court clerk should ask the court, before the defendant leaves court, to do so.

E.2    If a defendant is, at the time of sentence, already serving two or more consecutive terms of imprisonment and the court intends to increase the total period of imprisonment, it should use the expression 'consecutive to the total period of imprisonment to which you are already subject' rather than 'at the expiration of the term of imprisonment you are now serving', as the defendant may not then be serving the last of the terms to which he is already subject.

E.3    The Sentencing Council has issued a definitive guideline on Totality which should be consulted. Under section 125(1) of the Coroners and Justice Act 2009, for offences committed after 6 April 2010, the guideline must be followed unless it would be contrary to the interests of justice to do so.

## CPD VII Sentencing F: Victim Personal Statements

CPD.VII.F

F.1    Victims of crime are invited to make a statement, known as a Victim Personal Statement ('VPS'). The statement gives victims a formal opportunity to say how a crime has affected them. It may help to identify whether they have a particular need for information, support and protection. The court will take the statement into account when determining sentence. In some circumstances, it may be appropriate for relatives of a victim to make a VPS, for example where the victim has died as a result of the relevant criminal conduct. The revised Code of Practice for Victims of Crime, published on 29 October 2013 gives further information about victims' entitlements within the criminal justice system, and the duties placed on criminal justice agencies when dealing with victims of crime.

F.2    When a police officer takes a statement from a victim, the victim should be told about the scheme and given the chance to make a VPS. The decision about whether or not to make a VPS is entirely a matter for the victim; no pressure should be brought to bear on their decision, and no conclusion should be drawn if they choose not to make such a statement. A VPS or a further VPS may be made (in proper s.9 form, see below) at any time prior to the disposal of the case. It will not normally be appropriate for a VPS to be made after the disposal of the case; there may be rare occasions between sentence and appeal when a further VPS may be necessary, for example, when the victim was injured and the final prognosis was not available at the date of sentence. However, VPS after disposal should be confined to presenting up to date factual material, such as medical information, and should be used sparingly.

F.3    If the court is presented with a VPS the following approach, subject to the further guidance given by the Court of Appeal in *R v Perkins; Bennett; Hall* [2013] EWCA Crim 323, [2013] Crim LR 533, should be adopted:

   a)    The VPS and any evidence in support should be considered and taken into account by the court, prior to passing sentence.

   b)    Evidence of the effects of an offence on the victim contained in the VPS or other statement, must be in proper form, that is a witness statement made under section 9 of the Criminal Justice Act 1967 or an expert's report; and served in good time upon the defendant's solicitor or the defendant, if he or she is not represented. Except where inferences can properly be drawn from the nature of or circumstances surrounding the offence, a sentencing court must not make assumptions unsupported by evidence about the effects of an offence on the victim. The maker of a VPS may be cross-examined on its content.

   c)    At the discretion of the court, the VPS may also be read aloud or played in open court, in whole or in part, or it may be summarised. If the VPS is to be read aloud, the court should also determine who should do so. In making these decisions, the court should take account of the victim's preferences, and follow them unless there is good reason not to do so; examples of this include the inadmissibility of the content or the potentially harmful consequences for the victim or others. Court hearings should not be adjourned solely to allow the victim to attend court to read the VPS. For the purposes of CPD I General matters 5B: Access to information held by the court, a VPS that is read aloud or played in open court in whole or in part should be considered as such, and no longer treated as a confidential document.

   d)    In all cases it will be appropriate for a VPS to be referred to in the course of the sentencing hearing and/or in the sentencing remarks.

   e)    The court must pass what it judges to be the appropriate sentence having regard to the circumstances of the offence and of the offender, taking into account, so far as the court considers it appropriate, the impact on the victim. The opinions of the victim or the victim's close relatives as to what the sentence should be are therefore not relevant, unlike the consequences of the offence on them. Victims should be advised of this. If, despite the advice, opinions as to sentence are included in the statement, the court should pay no attention to them.

**CPD.VII.G**    **CPD VII Sentencing G: Families Bereaved by Homicide and other Criminal Conduct**

**G.1**    In cases in which the victim has died as a result of the relevant criminal conduct, the victim's family is not a party to the proceedings, but does have an interest in the case. Bereaved families have particular entitlements under the Code of Practice for Victims of Crime. All parties should have regard to the needs of the victim's family and ensure that the trial process does not expose bereaved families to avoidable intimidation, humiliation or distress.

**G.2**    In so far as it is compatible with family members' roles as witnesses, the court should consider the following measures:

    a) Practical arrangements being discussed with the family and made in good time before the trial, such as seating for family members in the courtroom; if appropriate, in an alternative area, away from the public gallery;

    b) Warning being given to families if the evidence on a certain day is expected to be particularly distressing;

    c) Ensuring that appropriate use is made of the scheme for Victim Personal Statements, in accordance with the paragraphs above.

**G.3**    The sentencer should consider providing a written copy of the sentencing remarks to the family after sentence has been passed. Sentencers should tend in favour of providing such a copy, unless there is good reason not to do so, and the copy should be provided as soon as is reasonably practicable after the sentencing hearing.

**CPD.VII.H**    **CPD VII Sentencing H: Community Impact Statements**

**H.1**    A community impact statement may be prepared by the police to make the court aware of particular crime trends in the local area and the impact of these on the local community.

**H.2**    Such statements must be in proper form, that is a witness statement made under section 9 of the Criminal Justice Act 1967 or an expert's report; and served in good time upon the defendant's solicitor or the defendant, if he is not represented.

**H.3**    The community impact statement and any evidence in support should be considered and taken into account by the court, prior to passing sentence. The statement should be referred to in the course of the sentencing hearing and/or in the sentencing remarks. Subject to the court's discretion, the contents of the statement may be summarised or read out in open court.

**H.4**    The court must pass what it judges to be the appropriate sentence having regard to the circumstances of the offence and of the offender, taking into account, so far as the court considers it appropriate, the impact on the local community. Opinions as to what the sentence should be are therefore not relevant. If, despite the advice, opinions as to sentence are included in the statement, the court should pay no attention to them.

**H.5**    Except where inferences can properly be drawn from the nature of or circumstances surrounding the offence, a sentencing court must not make assumptions unsupported by evidence about the effects of an offence on the local community.

**H.6**    It will not be appropriate for a Community Impact Statement to be made after disposal of the case but before an appeal.

**CPD.VII.I**    **CPD VII Sentencing I: Impact Statements for Businesses**

**I.1**    Individual victims of crime are invited to make a statement, known as a Victim Personal Statement ('VPS'), see CPD VII Sentencing F. If a victim, or one of those others affected by a crime, is a business, enterprise or other body (including a charity or public body, for example a school or hospital), of any size, a nominated representative may make an Impact Statement for Business ('ISB'). The ISB gives a formal opportunity for the court to be informed how a crime has affected a business or other body. The court will take the statement into account when determining sentence. This does not prevent individual employees from making a VPS about the impact of the same crime on them as individuals. Indeed, the ISB should be about the impact on the business or other body exclusively, and the impact on any individual included within a VPS.

**I.2**    When a police officer takes statements about the alleged offence, he or she should also inform the business or other body about the scheme. An ISB may be made to the police at that time, or the ISB template may be downloaded from www.police.uk, completed and emailed or posted to the relevant police contact. Guidance on how to complete the form is available on www.police.uk and on the CPS website. There is no obligation to make an ISB.

**I.3**    An ISB or an updated ISB may be made (in proper s.9 form, see below) at any time prior to the disposal of the case. It will not be appropriate for an ISB to be made after disposal of the case but before an appeal.

I.4     A business or other body wishing to make an ISB should consider carefully who to nominate as the representative to make the statement on its behalf. A person making an ISB on behalf of such a business or body, the nominated representative, must be authorised to do so on its behalf, either by nature of their position, such as a director or owner or a senior official, or by having been suitably authorised, such as by the owner or Board of Directors or governing body. The nominated representative must also be in a position to give admissible evidence about the impact of the crime on the business or body. This will usually be through first hand personal knowledge, or using business documents (as defined in section 117 of the Criminal Justice Act 2003). The most appropriate person will vary depending on the nature of the crime, and the size and structure of the business or other body and may for example include a manager, director, chief executive or shop owner.

I.5     If the nominated representative leaves the business before the case comes to court, he or she will usually remain the representative, as the ISB made by him or her will still provide the best evidence of the impact of the crime, and he or she could still be asked to attend court. Nominated representatives should be made aware of the on-going nature of the role at the time of making the ISB.

I.6     If necessary a further ISB may be provided to the police if there is a change in circumstances. This could be made by an alternative nominated representative. However, the new ISB will usually supplement, not replace, the original ISB and again must contain admissible evidence. The prosecutor will decide which ISB to serve on the defence as evidence, and any ISB that is not served in evidence will be included in the unused material and considered for disclosure to the defence.

I.7     The ISB must be made in proper form, that is as a witness statement made under section 9 of the Criminal Justice Act 1967 or an expert's report; and served in good time upon the defendant's solicitor or the defendant, if he or she is not represented. The maker of an ISB can be cross-examined on its content.

I.8     The ISB and any evidence in support should be considered and taken into account by the court, prior to passing sentence. The statement should be referred to in the course of the sentencing hearing and/or in the sentencing remarks. Subject to the court's discretion, the contents of the statement may be summarised or read out in open court; the views of the business or body should be taken into account in reaching a decision.

I.9     The court must pass what it judges to be the appropriate sentence having regard to the circumstances of the offence and of the offender, taking into account, so far as the court considers it appropriate, the impact on the victims and others affected, including any business or other corporate victim. Opinions as to what the sentence should be are therefore not relevant. If, despite the advice, opinions as to sentence are included in the statement, the court should pay no attention to them.

I.10    Except where inferences can properly be drawn from the nature of or circumstances surrounding the offence, a sentencing court must not make assumptions unsupported by evidence about the effects of an offence on a business or other body.

### CPD VII Sentencing J: Binding Over Orders and Conditional Discharges                    CPD.VII.J

J.1     This direction takes into account the judgments of the European Court of Human Rights in *Steel v United Kingdom* (1999) 28 EHRR 603, [1998] Crim LR 893 and in *Hashman and Harrup v United Kingdom* (2000) 30 EHRR 241, [2000] Crim LR 185. Its purpose is to give practical guidance, in the light of those two judgments, on the practice of imposing binding over orders. The direction applies to orders made under the court's common law powers, under the Justices of the Peace Act 1361, under section 1(7) of the Justices of the Peace Act 1968 and under section 115 of the Magistrates' Courts Act 1980. This direction also gives guidance concerning the court's power to bind over parents or guardians under section 150 of the Powers of Criminal Courts (Sentencing) Act 2000 and the Crown Court's power to bind over to come up for judgment. The court's power to impose a conditional discharge under section 12 of the Powers of Criminal Courts (Sentencing) Act 2000 is also covered by this direction.

*Binding over to keep the peace*

J.2     Before imposing a binding over order, the court must be satisfied so that it is sure that a breach of the peace involving violence, or an imminent threat of violence, has occurred or that there is a real risk of violence in the future. Such violence may be perpetrated by the individual who will be subject to the order or by a third party as a natural consequence of the individual's conduct.

J.3     In light of the judgment in *Hashman*, courts should no longer bind an individual over 'to be of good behaviour'. Rather than binding an individual over to 'keep the peace' in general terms, the court should identify the specific conduct or activity from which the individual must refrain.

*Written order*

J.4 When making an order binding an individual over to refrain from specified types of conduct or activities, the details of that conduct or those activities should be specified by the court in a written order, served on all relevant parties. The court should state its reasons for the making of the order, its length and the amount of the recognisance. The length of the order should be proportionate to the harm sought to be avoided and should not generally exceed 12 months.

*Evidence*

J.5 Sections 51 to 57 of the Magistrates' Courts Act 1980 set out the jurisdiction of the magistrates' court to hear an application made on complaint and the procedure which is to be followed. This includes a requirement under section 53 to hear evidence and the parties, before making any order. This practice should be applied to all cases in the magistrates' court and the Crown Court where the court is considering imposing a binding over order. The court should give the individual who would be subject to the order and the prosecutor the opportunity to make representations, both as to the making of the order and as to its terms. The court should also hear any admissible evidence the parties wish to call and which has not already been heard in the proceedings. Particularly careful consideration may be required where the individual who would be subject to the order is a witness in the proceedings.

J.6 Where there is an admission which is sufficient to found the making of a binding over order and/or the individual consents to the making of the order, the court should nevertheless hear sufficient representations and, if appropriate, evidence, to satisfy itself that an order is appropriate in all the circumstances and to be clear about the terms of the order.

J.7 Where there is an allegation of breach of a binding over order and this is contested, the court should hear representations and evidence, including oral evidence, from the parties before making a finding. If unrepresented and no opportunity has been given previously the court should give a reasonable period for the person said to have breached the binding over order to find representation.

*Burden and standard of proof*

J.8 The court should be satisfied so that it is sure of the matters complained of before a binding over order may be imposed. Where the procedure has been commenced on complaint, the burden of proof rests on the complainant. In all other circumstances, the burden of proof rests upon the prosecution.

J.9 Where there is an allegation of breach of a binding over order, the court should be satisfied on the balance of probabilities that the defendant is in breach before making any order for forfeiture of a recognisance. The burden of proof shall rest on the prosecution.

*Recognisance*

J.10 The court must be satisfied on the merits of the case that an order for binding over is appropriate and should announce that decision before considering the amount of the recognisance. If unrepresented, the individual who is made subject to the binding over order should be told he has a right of appeal from the decision.

J.11 When fixing the amount of recognisance, courts should have regard to the individual's financial resources and should hear representations from the individual or his legal representatives regarding finances.

J.12 A recognisance is made in the form of a bond giving rise to a civil debt on breach of the order.

*Refusal to enter into a recognisance*

J.13 If there is any possibility that an individual will refuse to enter a recognisance, the court should consider whether there are any appropriate alternatives to a binding over order (for example, continuing with a prosecution). Where there are no appropriate alternatives and the individual continues to refuse to enter into the recognisance, the court may commit the individual to custody. In the magistrates' court, the power to do so will derive from section 1(7) of the Justices of the Peace Act 1968 or, more rarely, from section 115(3) of the Magistrates' Courts Act 1980, and the court should state which power it is acting under; in the Crown Court, this is a common law power.

J.14 Before the court exercises a power to commit the individual to custody, the individual should be given the opportunity to see a duty solicitor or another legal representative and be represented in proceedings if the individual so wishes. Public funding should generally be granted to cover representation. In the Crown Court this rests with the Judge who may grant a Representation Order.

J.15 In the event that the individual does not take the opportunity to seek legal advice, the court shall give the individual a final opportunity to comply with the request and shall explain the consequences of a failure to do so.

*Antecedents*

**J.16**    Courts are reminded of the provisions of section 7(5) of the Rehabilitation of Offenders Act 1974 which excludes from a person's antecedents any order of the court 'with respect to any person otherwise than on a conviction'.

*Binding over to come up for judgment*

**J.17**    If the Crown Court is considering binding over an individual to come up for judgment, the court should specify any conditions with which the individual is to comply in the meantime and not specify that the individual is to be of good behaviour.

**J.18**    The Crown Court should, if the individual is unrepresented, explain the consequences of a breach of the binding over order in these circumstances.

*Binding over of parent or guardian*

**J.19**    Where a court is considering binding over a parent or guardian under section 150 of the Powers of Criminal Courts (Sentencing) Act 2000 to enter into a recognisance to take proper care of and exercise proper control over a child or young person, the court should specify the actions which the parent or guardian is to take.

*Security for good behaviour*

**J.20**    Where a court is imposing a conditional discharge under section 12 of the Powers of Criminal Courts (Sentencing) Act 2000, it has the power, under section 12(6) to make an order that a person who consents to do so give security for the good behaviour of the offender. When making such an order, the court should specify the type of conduct from which the offender is to refrain.

## CPD VII Sentencing K: Committal for Sentence

CPD.VII.K

**K.1**    CrimPR 28.10 applies when a case is committed to the Crown Court for sentence and specifies the information and documentation that must be provided by the magistrates' court. On a committal for sentence any reasons given by the magistrates for their decision should be included with the documents. All of these documents should be made available to the judge in the Crown Court if the judge requires them, in order to decide before the hearing questions of listing or representation or the like. They will also be available to the court during the hearing if it becomes necessary or desirable for the court to see what happened in the lower court.

## CPD VII Sentencing L: Imposition of Life Sentences

CPD.VII.L

**L.1**    Section 82A of the Powers of Criminal Courts (Sentencing) Act 2000 empowers a judge when passing a sentence of life imprisonment, where such a sentence is not fixed by law, to specify by order such part of the sentence ('the relevant part') as shall be served before the prisoner may require the Secretary of State to refer his case to the Parole Board. This is applicable to defendants under the age of 18 years as well as to adult defendants.

**L.2**    Thus the life sentence falls into two parts:
(a)    the relevant part, which consists of the period of detention imposed for punishment and deterrence, taking into account the seriousness of the offence; and
(b)    the remaining part of the sentence, during which the prisoner's detention will be governed by consideration of risk to the public.

**L.3**    The judge is not obliged by statute to make use of the provisions of section 82A when passing a life sentence. However, the judge should do so, save in the very exceptional case where the judge considers that the offence is so serious that detention for life is justified by the seriousness of the offence alone, irrespective of the risk to the public. In such a case, the judge should state this in open court when passing sentence.

**L.4**    In cases where the judge is to specify the relevant part of the sentence under section 82A, the judge should permit the advocate for the defendant to address the court as to the appropriate length of the relevant part. Where no relevant part is to be specified, the advocate for the defendant should be permitted to address the court as to the appropriateness of this course of action.

**L.5**    In specifying the relevant part of the sentence, the judge should have regard to the specific terms of section 82A and should indicate the reasons for reaching his decision as to the length of the relevant part.

## CPD VII Sentencing M: Mandatory Life Sentences

CPD.VII.M

**M.1**    The purpose of this section is to give practical guidance as to the procedure for passing a mandatory life sentence under section 269 and schedule 21 of the Criminal Justice Act 2003 ('the Act'). This direction also gives guidance as to the transitional arrangements under section 276 and schedule 22 of the Act. It clarifies the correct approach to looking at the practice of the Secretary of State prior to December 2002 for the purposes of schedule 22 of the Act, in the light of the judgment in *R v*

Criminal Procedure Rules and Criminal Practice Directions

*Sullivan, Gibbs, Elener and Elener* [2004] EWCA Crim 1762, [2005] 1 Cr App R 3, [2005] 1 Cr App R (S) 67.

**M.2**    Section 269 came into force on 18 December 2003. Under section 269, all courts passing a mandatory life sentence must either announce in open court the minimum term the prisoner must serve before the Parole Board can consider release on licence under the provisions of section 28 of the Crime (Sentences) Act 1997 (as amended by section 275 of the Act), or announce that the seriousness of the offence is so exceptionally high that the early release provisions should not apply at all (a 'whole life order').

**M.3**    In setting the minimum term, the court must set the term it considers appropriate taking into account the seriousness of the offence. In considering the seriousness of the offence, the court must have regard to the general principles set out in Schedule 21 of the Act as amended and any guidelines relating to offences in general which are relevant to the case and not incompatible with the provisions of Schedule 21. Although it is necessary to have regard to such guidance, it is always permissible not to apply the guidance if a judge considers there are reasons for not following it. It is always necessary to have regard to the need to do justice in the particular case. However, if a court departs from any of the starting points given in Schedule 21, the court is under a duty to state its reasons for doing so (section 270(2)(b) of the Act).

**M.4**    Schedule 21 states that the first step is to choose one of five starting points: 'whole life', 30 years, 25 years, 15 years or 12 years. Where the 15 year starting point has been chosen, judges should have in mind that this starting point encompasses a very broad range of murders. At paragraph 35 of *Sullivan*, the court found it should not be assumed that Parliament intended to raise all minimum terms that would previously have had a lower starting point, to 15 years.

**M.5**    Where the offender was 21 or over at the time of the offence, and the court takes the view that the murder is so grave that the offender ought to spend the rest of his life in prison, the appropriate starting point is a 'whole life order' (paragraph 4(1) of Schedule 21). The effect of such an order is that the early release provisions in section 28 of the Crime (Sentences) Act 1997 will not apply. Such an order should only be specified where the court considers that the seriousness of the offence (or the combination of the offence and one or more other offences associated with it) is exceptionally high. Paragraph 4(2) sets out examples of cases where it would normally be appropriate to take the 'whole life order' as the appropriate starting point.

**M.6**    Where the offender is aged 18 to 20 and commits a murder that is so serious that it would require a whole life order if committed by an offender aged 21 or over, the appropriate starting point will be 30 years. (Paragraph 5(2)(h) of Schedule 21).

**M.7**    Where a case is not so serious as to require a 'whole life order' but where the seriousness of the offence is particularly high and the offender was aged 18 or over when he committed the offence, the appropriate starting point is 30 years (paragraph 5(1) of Schedule 21). Paragraph 5(2) sets out examples of cases where a 30 year starting point would normally be appropriate (if they do not require a 'whole life order').

**M.8**    Where the offender was aged 18 or over when he committed the offence, took a knife or other weapon to the scene intending to commit any offence or have it available to use as a weapon, and used it in committing the murder, the offence is normally to be regarded as sufficiently serious for an appropriate starting point of 25 years (paragraph 5A of Schedule 21).

**M.9**    Where the offender was aged 18 or over when he committed the offence and the case does not fall within paragraph 4(1), 5(1) or 5A(1) of Schedule 21, the appropriate starting point is 15 years (see paragraph 6).

**M.10**   18 to 20 year olds are only the subject of the 30-year, 25-year and 15-year starting points.

**M.11**   The appropriate starting point when setting a sentence of detention during Her Majesty's pleasure for offenders aged under 18 when they committed the offence is always 12 years (paragraph 7 of Schedule 21).

**M.12**   The second step after choosing a starting point is to take account of any aggravating or mitigating factors which would justify a departure from the starting point. Additional aggravating factors (other than those specified in paragraphs 4(2), 5(2) and 5A) are listed at paragraph 10 of Schedule 21. Examples of mitigating factors are listed at paragraph 11 of Schedule 21. Taking into account the aggravating and mitigating features, the court may add to or subtract from the starting point to arrive at the appropriate punitive period.

**M.13**   The third step is that the court should consider the effect of section 143(2) of the Act in relation to previous convictions; section 143(3) of the Act where the offence was committed whilst the offender was on bail; and section 144 of the Act where the offender has pleaded guilty (paragraph 12 of Schedule 21). The court should then take into account what credit the offender would have received for a remand in custody under section 240 or 240ZA of the Act and/or for a remand on bail subject to a qualifying curfew condition under section 240A, but for the fact that the mandatory sentence is one of life imprisonment. Where the offender has been thus remanded in connection with the offence or a related offence, the court should have in mind that no credit will otherwise be given for this time when the prisoner is considered for early release. The appropriate time to take it into account is when setting the minimum term. The court should make any appropriate subtraction from the punitive period it would otherwise impose, in order to reach the minimum term.

M.14 Following these calculations, the court should have arrived at the appropriate minimum term to be announced in open court. As paragraph 9 of Schedule 21 makes clear, the judge retains ultimate discretion and the court may arrive at any minimum term from any starting point. The minimum term is subject to appeal by the offender under section 271 of the Act and subject to review on a reference by the Attorney-General under section 272 of the Act.

**CPD VII Sentencing N: Transitional Arrangements for Sentences where the Offence was Committed before 18 December 2003**

CPD.VII.N

N.1 Where the court is passing a sentence of mandatory life imprisonment for an offence committed before 18 December 2003, the court should take a fourth step in determining the minimum term in accordance with section 276 and Schedule 22 of the Act.

N.2 The purpose of those provisions is to ensure that the sentence does not breach the principle of non-retroactivity, by ensuring that a lower minimum term would not have been imposed for the offence when it was committed. Before setting the minimum term, the court must check whether the proposed term is greater than that which the Secretary of State would probably have notified under the practice followed by the Secretary of State before December 2002.

N.3 The decision in *Sullivan, Gibbs, Elener and Elener* [2004] EWCA Crim 1762, [2005] 1 Cr App R 3, [2005] 1 Cr App R (S) 67 gives detailed guidance as to the correct approach to this practice and judges passing mandatory life sentences where the murder was committed prior to 18 December 2003 are well advised to read that judgment before proceeding.

N.4 The practical result of that judgment is that in sentences where the murder was committed before 31 May 2002, the best guide to what would have been the practice of the Secretary of State is the letter sent to judges by Lord Bingham CJ on 10th February 1997, the relevant parts of which are set out below.

N.5 The practice of Lord Bingham, as set out in his letter of 10 February 1997, was to take 14 years as the period actually to be served for the 'average', 'normal' or 'unexceptional' murder. Examples of factors he outlined as capable, in appropriate cases, of mitigating the normal penalty were:
(1) Youth;
(2) Age (where relevant to physical capacity on release or the likelihood of the defendant dying in prison);
(3) [Intellectual disability or mental disorder];
(4) Provocation (in a non-technical sense), or an excessive response to a personal threat;
(5) The absence of an intention to kill;
(6) Spontaneity and lack of premeditation (beyond that necessary to constitute the offence: e.g., a sudden response to family pressure or to prolonged and eventually insupportable stress);
(7) Mercy killing;
(8) A plea of guilty, or hard evidence of remorse or contrition.

N.6 Lord Bingham then listed the following factors as likely to call for a sentence more severe than the norm:
(1) Evidence of planned, professional, revenge or contract killing;
(2) The killing of a child or a very old or otherwise vulnerable victim;
(3) Evidence of sadism, gratuitous violence, or sexual maltreatment, humiliation or degradation before the killing;
(4) Killing for gain (in the course of burglary, robbery, blackmail, insurance fraud, etc.);
(5) Multiple killings;
(6) The killing of a witness, or potential witness, to defeat the ends of justice;
(7) The killing of those doing their public duty (policemen, prison officers, postmasters, firemen, judges, etc.);
(8) Terrorist or politically motivated killings;
(9) The use of firearms or other dangerous weapons, whether carried for defensive or offensive reasons;
(10) A substantial record of serious violence;
(11) Macabre attempts to dismember or conceal the body.

N.7 Lord Bingham further stated that the fact that a defendant was under the influence of drink or drugs at the time of the killing is so common he would be inclined to treat it as neutral. But in the not unfamiliar case in which a couple, inflamed by drink, indulge in a violent quarrel in which one dies, often against a background of longstanding drunken violence, then he would tend to recommend a term somewhat below the norm.

**N.8**   Lord Bingham went on to say that given the intent necessary for proof of murder, the consequences of taking life and the understandable reaction of relatives to the deceased, a substantial term will almost always be called for, save perhaps in a truly venial case of mercy killing. While a recommendation of a punitive term longer than, say, 30 years will be very rare indeed, there should not be any upper limit. Some crimes will certainly call for terms very well in excess of the norm.

**N.9**   For the purposes of sentences where the murder was committed after 31 May 2002 and before 18 December 2003, the judge should apply the Practice Statement handed down on 31 May 2002 reproduced at paragraphs N.10 to N.20 below.

**N.10**  This Statement replaces the previous single normal tariff of 14 years by substituting a higher and a normal starting point of respectively 16 (comparable to 32 years) and 12 years (comparable to 24 years). These starting points have then to be increased or reduced because of aggravating or mitigating factors such as those referred to below. It is emphasised that they are no more than starting points.

*The normal starting point of 12 years*

**N.11**  Cases falling within this starting point will normally involve the killing of an adult victim, arising from a quarrel or loss of temper between two people known to each other. It will not have the characteristics referred to in paragraph N.13. Exceptionally, the starting point may be reduced because of the sort of circumstances described in the next paragraph.

**N.12**  The normal starting point can be reduced because the murder is one where the offender's culpability is significantly reduced, for example, because:

(a)  the case came close to the borderline between murder and manslaughter; or

(b)  the offender suffered from mental disorder, or from a mental disability which lowered the degree of his criminal responsibility for the killing, although not affording a defence of diminished responsibility; or

(c)  the offender was provoked (in a non-technical sense) such as by prolonged and eventually unsupportable stress; or

(d)  the case involved an over-reaction in self-defence; or

(e)  the offence was a mercy killing.

These factors could justify a reduction to 8/9 years (equivalent to 16/18 years).

*The higher starting point of 15/16 years*

**N.13**  The higher starting point will apply to cases where the offender's culpability was exceptionally high, or the victim was in a particularly vulnerable position. Such cases will be characterised by a feature which makes the crime especially serious, such as:

(a)  the killing was 'professional' or a contract killing;

(b)  the killing was politically motivated;

(c)  the killing was done for gain (in the course of a burglary, robbery etc.);

(d)  the killing was intended to defeat the ends of justice (as in the killing of a witness or potential witness);

(e)  the victim was providing a public service;

(f)  the victim was a child or was otherwise vulnerable;

(g)  the killing was racially aggravated;

(h)  the victim was deliberately targeted because of his or her religion or sexual orientation;

(i)  there was evidence of sadism, gratuitous violence or sexual maltreatment, humiliation or degradation of the victim before the killing;

(j)  extensive and/or multiple injuries were inflicted on the victim before death;

(k)  the offender committed multiple murders.

*Variation of the starting point*

**N.14**  Whichever starting point is selected in a particular case, it may be appropriate for the trial judge to vary the starting point upwards or downwards, to take account of aggravating or mitigating factors, which relate to either the offence or the offender, in the particular case.

**N.15**  Aggravating factors relating to the offence can include:

(a)  the fact that the killing was planned;

(b)  the use of a firearm;

(c)  arming with a weapon in advance;

(d)  concealment of the body, destruction of the crime scene and/or dismemberment of the body;

(e)  particularly in domestic violence cases, the fact that the murder was the culmination of cruel and violent behaviour by the offender over a period of time.

**N.16**  Aggravating factors relating to the offender will include the offender's previous record and failures to respond to previous sentences, to the extent that this is relevant to culpability rather than to risk.

**N.17**  Mitigating factors relating to the offence will include:

(a) an intention to cause grievous bodily harm, rather than to kill;

(b) spontaneity and lack of pre-meditation.

N.18 Mitigating factors relating to the offender may include:

(a) the offender's age;

(b) clear evidence of remorse or contrition;

(c) a timely plea of guilty.

*Very serious cases*

N.19 A substantial upward adjustment may be appropriate in the most serious cases, for example, those involving a substantial number of murders, or if there are several factors identified as attracting the higher starting point present. In suitable cases, the result might even be a minimum term of 30 years (equivalent to 60 years) which would offer little or no hope of the offender's eventual release. In cases of exceptional gravity, the judge, rather than setting a whole life minimum term, can state that there is no minimum period which could properly be set in that particular case.

N.20 Among the categories of case referred to in paragraph N.13, some offences may be especially grave. These include cases in which the victim was performing his duties as a prison officer at the time of the crime, or the offence was a terrorist or sexual or sadistic murder, or involved a young child. In such a case, a term of 20 years and upwards could be appropriate.

N.21 In following this guidance, judges should bear in mind the conclusion of the Court in *Sullivan* that the general effect of both these statements is the same. While Lord Bingham does not identify as many starting points, it is open to the judge to come to exactly the same decision irrespective of which was followed. Both pieces of guidance give the judge a considerable degree of discretion.

## CPD VII Sentencing P: Procedure for Announcing the Minimum Term in Open Court

CPD.VII.P

P.1 Having gone through the three or four steps outlined above, the court is then under a duty, under section 270 of the Act, to state in open court, in ordinary language, its reasons for deciding on the minimum term or for passing a whole life order.

P.2 In order to comply with this duty, the court should state clearly the minimum term it has determined. In doing so, it should state which of the starting points it has chosen and its reasons for doing so. Where the court has departed from that starting point due to mitigating or aggravating features, it must state the reasons for that departure and any aggravating or mitigating features which have led to that departure. At that point, the court should also declare how much, if any, time is being deducted for time spent in custody and/or on bail subject to a qualifying curfew condition. The court must then explain that the minimum term is the minimum amount of time the prisoner will spend in prison, from the date of sentence, before the Parole Board can order early release. If it remains necessary for the protection of the public, the prisoner will continue to be detained after that date. The court should also state that where the prisoner has served the minimum term and the Parole Board has decided to direct release, the prisoner will remain on licence for the rest of his life and may be recalled to prison at any time.

P.3 Where the offender was 21 or over when he committed the offence and the court considers that the seriousness of the offence is so exceptionally high that a 'whole life order' is appropriate, the court should state clearly its reasons for reaching this conclusion. It should also explain that the early release provisions will not apply.

## CPD VII Sentencing Q: Financial, Etc. Information Required for Sentencing

CPD.VII.Q

Q.1 These directions supplement CrimPR 24.11 and 25.16, which set out the procedure to be followed where a defendant pleads guilty, or is convicted, and is to be sentenced. They are not concerned exclusively with corporate defendants, or with offences of an environmental, public health, health and safety or other regulatory character, but the guidance which they contain is likely to be of particular significance in such cases.

Q.2 The rules set out the prosecutor's responsibilities in all cases. Where the offence is of a character, or is against a prohibition, with which the sentencing court is unlikely to be familiar, those responsibilities are commensurately more onerous. The court is entitled to the greatest possible assistance in identifying information relevant to sentencing.

Q.3 In such a case, save where the circumstances are very straightforward, it is likely that justice will best be served by the submission of the required information in writing: see *R v Friskies Petcare (UK) Ltd* [2000] 2 Cr App R (S) 401. Though it is the prosecutor's responsibility to the court to prepare any such document, if the defendant pleads guilty, or indicates a guilty plea, then it is very highly desirable that such sentencing information should be agreed between the parties and jointly submitted. If agreement cannot be reached in all particulars, then the nature and extent of the disagreement should be indicated. If the court concludes that what is in issue is material to sentence, then it will give directions for resolution of the dispute, whether by hearing oral evidence or by other means. In every case, when passing sentence the sentencing court must make clear on

Criminal Procedure Rules and Criminal Practice Directions

what basis sentence is passed: in fairness to the defendant, and for the information of any other person, or court, who needs or wishes to understand the reasons for sentence.

**Q.4** If so directed by or on behalf of the court, a defendant must supply accurate information about financial circumstances. In fixing the amount of any fine the court must take into account, amongst other considerations, the financial circumstances of the offender (whether an individual or other person) as they are known or as they appear to be. Before fixing the amount of fine when the defendant is an individual, the court must inquire into his financial circumstances. Where the defendant is an individual the court may make a financial circumstances order in respect of him. This means an order in which the court requires an individual to provide a statement as to his financial means, within a specified time. It is an offence, punishable with imprisonment, to fail to comply with such an order or for knowingly/recklessly furnishing a false statement or knowingly failing to disclose a material fact. The provisions of section 20A Criminal Justice Act 1991 apply to any person (thereby including a corporate organisation) and place the offender under a statutory duty to provide the court with a statement as to his financial means in response to an official request. There are offences for non-compliance, false statements or non-disclosure. It is for the court to decide how much information is required, having regard to relevant sentencing guidelines or guideline cases. However, by reference to those same guidelines and cases the parties should anticipate what the court will require, and prepare accordingly. In complex cases, and in cases involving a corporate defendant, the information required will be more extensive than in others. In the case of a corporate defendant, that information usually will include details of the defendant's corporate structure; annual profit and loss accounts, or extracts; annual balance sheets, or extracts; details of shareholders' receipts; and details of the remuneration of directors or other officers.

**Q.5** In *R v F Howe and Son (Engineers) Ltd* [1999] 2 Cr App R (S) 37 the Court of Appeal observed: 'If a defendant company wishes to make any submission to the court about its ability to pay a fine it should supply copies of its accounts and any other financial information on which it intends to rely in good time before the hearing both to the court and to the prosecution. This will give the prosecution the opportunity to assist the court should the court wish it. Usually accounts need to be considered with some care to avoid reaching a superficial and perhaps erroneous conclusion. Where accounts or other financial information are deliberately not supplied the court will be entitled to conclude that the company is in a position to pay any financial penalty it is minded to impose. Where the relevant information is provided late it may be desirable for sentence to be adjourned, if necessary at the defendant's expense, so as to avoid the risk of the court taking what it is told at face value and imposing an inadequate penalty.'

**Q.6** In the case of an individual, the court is likewise entitled to conclude that the defendant is able to pay any fine imposed unless the defendant has supplied financial information to the contrary. It is the defendant's responsibility to disclose to the court such information relevant to his or her financial position as will enable it to assess what he or she reasonably can afford to pay. If necessary, the court may compel the disclosure of an individual defendant's financial circumstances. In the absence of such disclosure, or where the court is not satisfied that it has been given sufficient reliable information, the court will be entitled to draw reasonable inferences as to the offender's means from evidence it has heard and from all the circumstances of the case.

**CPD.VII.R** ## CPD VII Sentencing R: Medical Reports for Sentencing Purposes

*General observations*

**R.1** CrimPR 24.11 and 25.16 concern standard sentencing procedures in magistrates' courts and in the Crown Court respectively. CrimPR 28.8 deals with the obtaining of medical reports for sentencing purposes.

**R.2** Rule 28.8 governs the procedure to be followed where a report is commissioned at the instigation of the court. It is not a substitute for the prompt commissioning of a report or reports by a defendant or defendant's representatives where expert medical opinion is material to the defence case. In particular, the defendant's representatives may wish to obtain a medical report or reports wholly independently of the court. Nothing in these directions, therefore, should be read as discouraging the commissioning of a medical report before the case comes before the court, where such a report is expected to be material and where it is possible promptly to commission it. However, where such a report has been commissioned then if that report has not been received in time for sentencing and if the court agrees that it seems likely to be material, then the court should set a timetable for the reception of that report and should give directions for progress to be reviewed at intervals, adopting the timetable set out in these directions with such adaptations as are needed.

**R.3** In assessing the likely materiality of an expert medical report for sentencing purposes the court will be assisted by the parties' representations; by the views expressed in any pre-sentence report that may have been prepared; and by the views of practitioners in local criminal justice mental health services, whose assistance is available to the court under local liaison arrangements.

**R.4**  Where the court requires the assistance of such a report then it is essential that there should be (i) absolute clarity about who is expected to do what, by when, and at whose expense; and (ii) judicial directions for progress with that report to be monitored and reviewed at prescribed intervals, following a timetable set by the court which culminates in the consideration of the report at a hearing. This is especially important where the report in question is a psychiatric assessment of the defendant for the preparation of which specific expertise may be required which is not readily available and because in some circumstances a second such assessment, by another medical practitioner, may be required.

*Timetable for the commissioning, preparation and consideration of a report or reports*

**R.5**  CrimPR 28.8 requires the court to set a timetable appropriate to the case for the preparation and reception of a report. In doing so the court will take account of such representations and other information that it receives, including information about the anticipated availability and workload of practitioners with the appropriate expertise. However, the timetable ought not be a protracted one. It is essential to keep in mind the importance of maintaining progress: in recognition of the defendant's rights and with respect for the interests of victims and witnesses, as required by CrimPR Part 1 (the overriding objective). In a magistrates' court account must be taken, too, of section 11 of the Powers of Criminal Courts (Sentencing) Act 2000, which limits the duration of each remand pending the preparation of a report to 3 weeks, where the defendant is to be in custody, and to 4 weeks if the defendant is to be on bail.

**R.6**  Subject, therefore, to contrary judicial direction the timetable set by the court should require:
  (a)  the convening of a hearing to consider the report no more than 6 – 8 weeks after the court makes its request;
  (b)  the prompt identification of an appropriate medical practitioner or practitioners, if not already identified by the court, and the despatch of a commission or commissions accordingly, within 2 business days of the court's decision to request a report;
  (c)  acknowledgement of a commission by its recipient, and acceptance or rejection of that commission, within 5 business days of its receipt;
  (d)  enquiries by court staff to confirm that the commission has been received, and to ascertain the action being taken in response, in the event that no acknowledgement is received within 10 business days of its despatch;
  (e)  delivery of the report within 5 weeks of the despatch of the commission;
  (f)  enquiries into progress by court staff in the event that no report is received within 5 weeks of the despatch of the commission.

**R.7**  The hearing that is convened for the court to consider the report, at 6 – 8 weeks after the court requests that report, should not be adjourned before it takes place save in exceptional circumstances and then only by explicit judicial direction the reasons for which must be recorded. If by the time of that hearing the report is available, as usually should be the case, then at that hearing the court can be expected to determine the issue in respect of which the report was commissioned and pass sentence. If by that time, exceptionally, the report is not available then the court should take the opportunity provided by that hearing to enquire into the reasons, give such directions as are appropriate, and if necessary adjourn the hearing to a fixed date for further consideration then. Where it is known in advance of that hearing that the report will not be available in time, the hearing may be conducted by live link or telephone: subject, in the defendant's case, to the same considerations as are identified at paragraph I.3N.6 of these Practice Directions. However, it rarely will be appropriate to dispense altogether with that hearing, or to make enquiries and give further directions without any hearing at all, in view of the arrangements for monitoring and review that the court already will have directed and which, by definition therefore, thus far will have failed to secure the report's timely delivery.

**R.8**  Where a requirement of the timetable set by the court is not met, or where on enquiry by court staff it appears that the timetable is unlikely to be met, and in any instance in which a medical practitioner who accepts a commission asks for more time, then court staff should not themselves adjust the timetable or accede to such a request but instead should seek directions from an appropriate judicial authority. Subject to local judicial direction, that will be, in the Crown Court, the judge assigned to the case or the resident judge and, in a magistrates' court, a District Judge (Magistrates' Courts) or justice of the peace assigned to the case, or the Justices' Clerk, an assistant clerk or other senior legal adviser. Even if the timetable is adjusted in consequence:
  (a)  the hearing convened to consider the report (that is, the hearing set for no more than 6 – 8 weeks after the court made its request) rarely should be adjourned before it takes place: see paragraph R.13 above;
  (b)  directions should be given for court staff henceforth to make regular enquiries into progress, at intervals of not more than 2 weeks, and to report the outcome to an appropriate judicial authority who will decide what further directions, if any, to give.

*Criminal Procedure Rules and Criminal Practice Directions*

**R.9** Any adjournment of a hearing convened to consider the report should be to a specific date: the hearing should not be adjourned generally, or to a date to be set in due course. The adjournment of such a hearing should not be for more than a further 6 – 8 weeks save in the most exceptional circumstances; and no more than one adjournment of the hearing should be allowed without obtaining written or oral representations from the commissioned medical practitioner explaining the reasons for the delay.

*Commissioning a report*

**R.10** Guidance entitled 'Good practice guidance: commissioning, administering and producing psychiatric reports for sentencing' prepared for and published by the Ministry of Justice and HM Courts and Tribunals Service in September 2010 contains material that will assist court staff and those who are asked to prepare such reports:

http://www.ohrn.nhs.uk/resource/policy/GoodPracticeGuidePsychReports.pdf

That guidance includes standard forms of letters of instruction and other documents.

**R.11** CrimPR 28.8 requires the commissioner of a report to explain why the court seeks the report and to include relevant information about the circumstances. The HMCTS Guidance contains forms for judicial use in the instruction of court staff, and guidance to court staff on the preparation of letters of instruction, where a report is required for sentencing purposes. Where a report is requested in a case involving manslaughter by reason of diminished responsibility, the report writer should have regard to the Sentencing Council's guideline on Manslaughter by reason of Diminished Responsibility. This should assist the report writer in providing the most helpful assessment to enable the court to determine the level of diminution involved in the case.

**R.12** The commission should invite a practitioner who is unable to accept it promptly to nominate a suitably qualified substitute, if possible, and to transfer the commission to that person, reporting the transfer when acknowledging the court officer's letter. It is entirely appropriate for the commission to draw the recipient's attention to CrimPR 1.2 (the duty of the participants in a criminal case) and to CrimPR 19.2(1)(b) (the obligation of an expert witness to comply with directions made by a court and at once to inform the court of any significant failure, by the expert or another, to take any step required by such a direction).

**R.13** Where the relevant legislation requires a second psychiatric assessment by a second medical practitioner, and where no commission already has been addressed to a second such practitioner, the commission may invite the person to whom it is addressed to nominate a suitably qualified second person and to pass a copy of the commission to that person forthwith.

*Funding arrangements*

**R.14** Where a medical report has been, or is to be, commissioned by a party then that party is responsible for arranging payment of the fees incurred, even though the report is intended for the court's use. That must be made clear in that party's commission.

**R.15** Where a medical report is requested by the court and commissioned by a party or by court staff at the court's direction then the commission must include (i) confirmation that the fees will be paid by HMCTS, (ii) details of how, and to whom, to submit an invoice or claim for fees, and (iii) notice of the prescribed rates of fees and of any legislative or other criteria applicable to the calculation of the fees that may be paid.

*Remand in custody*

**R.16** Where the defendant who is to be examined will be remanded in custody then notice that directions have been given for a medical report or reports to be prepared must be included in the information given to the defendant's custodian, to ensure that the preparation of the report or reports can be facilitated. This is especially important where bail is withheld on the ground that it would be otherwise impracticable to complete the required report, and in particular where that is the only ground for withholding bail.

**CPD.VII.S** **CPD VII Sentencing S: Variation of Sentence**

**S.1** Under section 142 of the Magistrates' Courts Act 1980, in some circumstances a magistrates' court may vary or rescind a sentence or other order that it has imposed or made if that appears to be in the interests of justice. Under section 155 of the Powers of Criminal Courts (Sentencing) Act 2000 the Crown Court may vary or rescind a sentence or order which it has imposed or made, within a period of 56 days beginning with the date of that sentence or order, or beginning with the date of another defendant's acquittal or sentencing in some circumstances (see CrimPR 28.4(1)(b)).

**S.2** CrimPR 28.4(2) allows the court to exercise those powers at a hearing, in public or in private, or without a hearing. However, rule 28.4(4) confines the court's discretion to dispense with a hearing by requiring the defendant's presence, necessarily at a hearing, unless the variation is one proposed by the defendant, or the effect of the variation is such that the defendant is no more severely dealt with under the sentence as varied than before; or, if neither of those conditions is satisfied, where a hearing has been convened at which the defendant has had an opportunity to make representations, whether or not he or she in fact attends. Moreover, rule 28.4 requires service on the other party of any application to vary a sentence or order, in response to which that other party may wish to make such representations as general principles of law require to be heard. It follows that the circumstances in which a variation of sentence properly may be made without a hearing, consistently with the rule, will be confined to cases in which neither party objects to what is proposed and in which the consequences for the defendant of the variation will be neutral or benign.

S.3    In such a case usually there will be no other objection to the making of the variation without a hearing. Even in such a case, however, the court retains a discretion to convene a hearing, in the exercise of which discretion due regard must be had to the overriding objective and to the importance of dealing with criminal cases in public, in accordance with the principle of open justice. The application of that latter principle was described in *R v Cox* [2019] EWCA Crim 71; [2019] 4 WLR 88 at paragraphs 18–19 in these terms:

> 'As stated in cases such as *R v Pinkerton* [2017] 1 Cr App R(S) 47 at [8] (a case where there in fact was a downward adjustment of a concurrent custodial sentence which did not impact on the overall sentence) such alterations should be done openly "so that justice may be seen to be done". Likewise, in *R v Warren* [2017] 2 Cr App R(S) 5, the general desirability of re-sentencing taking place in the presence of the defendant and in court was stressed. Accordingly, whilst it is easy to understand the attractions of administrative convenience … and particularly perhaps where the sentencing judge is not a full-time judge based at a particular court centre, those administrative attractions should not be permitted routinely to prevail over the delivery of open justice.'

In reaching its decision the court therefore will take into account each of the relevant factors listed in CrimPR 1.1, and will be astute to distinguish between, on the one hand, the completion of details or the correction of errors of a quasi-administrative character and, on the other, a variation of sentence in which the determination will be a matter of legitimate public interest.

S.4    In any event, the making of the decision and the reasons for that decision always must be announced at a public hearing, even if only briefly and even if the parties are absent on that occasion: CrimPR 28.4(2)(b). While the decision itself must be made, and the reasons for that decision formulated, by the sentencing court itself (section 142(1) of the 1980 Act; section 155(4) of the 2000 Act), the public announcement may be made by a differently constituted court if it would be impracticable for the sentencing court to sit in public for the purpose within a reasonable time.

CRIMINAL PROCEDURE RULES    PART 28    SENTENCING PROCEDURES IN SPECIAL CASES AND
ON COMMITTAL FOR SENTENCE, ETC.

*[Note. See also—*

*(a)    Part 24, which contains rules about the general procedure on sentencing in a magistrates' court;*
*(b)    Part 25, which contains rules about the general procedure on sentencing in the Crown Court;*
*(c)    Part 29 (Road traffic penalties);*
*(d)    Part 30 (Enforcement of fines and other orders for payment); and*
*(e)    Part 32 (Breach, revocation and amendment of community and other orders).]*

**Reasons for not following usual sentencing requirements**    **R28.1**

28.1    (1)    This rule applies where the court decides—
      (a)    not to follow a relevant sentencing guideline;
      (b)    not to make, where it could—
         (i)    a reparation order (unless it passes a custodial or community sentence),
         (ii)   a compensation order,
         (iii)  a slavery and trafficking reparation order, or
         (iv)   a travel restriction order;
      (c)    not to order, where it could—
         (i)    that a suspended sentence of imprisonment is to take effect,
         (ii)   the endorsement of the defendant's driving record, or
         (iii)  the defendant's disqualification from driving, for the usual minimum period or at all;
      (d)    to pass a lesser sentence than it otherwise would have passed because the defendant has assisted, or has agreed to assist, an investigator or prosecutor in relation to an offence.
    (2)    The court must explain why it has so decided, when it explains the sentence that it has passed.

(3) Where paragraph (1)(d) applies, the court must arrange for such an explanation to be given to the defendant and to the prosecutor in writing, if the court thinks that it would not be in the public interest to explain in public.

*[Note. See sections 52, 54 and 55 of the Sentencing Act 2020[1]; section 8(7) of the Modern Slavery Act 2015[2]; section 33(2) of the Criminal Justice and Police Act 2001[3]; paragraph 14(1) of Schedule 16 to the 2020 Act; section 47(1) of the Road Traffic Offenders Act 1988[4]; and section 74 of the 2020 Act.*

*For the duty to explain the sentence the court has passed, see section 52(1) of the 2020 Act and rules 24.119 (procedure where a magistrates' court convicts) and 25.16(7) (procedure where the Crown Court convicts).*

*Under section 59 of the 2020 Act, the court when sentencing must follow any relevant sentencing guideline unless satisfied that to do so would be contrary to the interests of justice.*

*For the circumstances in which the court may make—*

  *(a)  a reparation or compensation order, see sections 110 and 134 of the 2020 Act[5];*
  *(b)  a slavery and trafficking reparation order, see section 8 of the 2015 Act;*
  *(c)  a travel restriction order against a defendant convicted of drug trafficking, see sections 33 and 34 of the 2001 Act[6].]*

**R28.2   Notice of requirements of suspended sentence and community, etc. orders**

28.2  (1)  This rule applies where the court—
        (a)  makes a suspended sentence order;
        (b)  imposes a requirement under—
              (i)   a community order,
              (ii)  a youth rehabilitation order, or
              (iii) a suspended sentence order; or
        (c)  orders the defendant to attend meetings with a supervisor.
      (2)  The court officer must notify—
        (a)  the defendant of—
              (i)   the length of the sentence suspended by a suspended sentence order, and
              (ii)  the period of the suspension;
        (b)  the defendant and, where the defendant is under 14, an appropriate adult, of—
              (i)   any requirement or requirements imposed, and
              (ii)  the identity of any responsible officer or supervisor, and the means by which that person may be contacted;
        (c)  any responsible officer or supervisor, and, where the defendant is under 14, the appropriate qualifying officer (if that is not the responsible officer), of—
              (i)   the defendant's name, address and telephone number (if available),
              (ii)  the offence or offences of which the defendant was convicted, and
              (iii) the requirement or requirements imposed; and
        (d)  the person affected, where the court imposes a requirement—
              (i)   for the protection of that person from the defendant, or
              (ii)  requiring the defendant to reside with that person.
      (3)  If the court imposes an electronic monitoring requirement, the monitor of which is not the responsible officer, the court officer must—
        (a)  notify the defendant and, where the defendant is under 16, an appropriate adult, of the monitor's identity, and the means by which the monitor may be contacted; and
        (b)  notify the monitor of—
              (i)   the defendant's name, address and telephone number (if available),
              (ii)  the offence or offences of which the defendant was convicted,
              (iii) the place or places at which the defendant's presence must be monitored,
              (iv)  the period or periods during which the defendant's presence there must be monitored, and
              (v)   the identity of the responsible officer, and the means by which that officer may be contacted.

---

[1] 2020 c. 17.
[2] 2015 c. 30.
[3] 2001 c. 16.
[4] 1988 c. 53.
[5] 2009 c. 25; section 125 was repealed by section 413 of, and Schedule 28 to, the Sentencing Act 2020 (c. 17).
[6] 2001 c. 16; section 33 was amended by sections 39(3) and 39(4) of the Identity Cards Act 2006 (c. 15).

*[Note. See sections 212(2) and 298(2) of the Sentencing Act 2020[7]; section 190(2) of the 2020 Act[8]; and section 1A(7) of the Street Offences Act 1959[9].*

*For the circumstances in which the court may—*

    (a) *make a suspended sentence order, see sections 264, 277, 286 and 288 of the 2020 Act[10];*

    (b) *make a community order (defined by section 200 of the 2020 Act), or a youth rehabilitation order (defined by section 173(1) of that Act), and for the identity and duties of responsible officers and qualifying officers, see generally Chapters 1 and 2 of Part 9 of the 2020 Act;*

    (c) *order the defendant to attend meetings with a supervisor, see section 1(2A) of the Street Offences Act 1959[11].*

*Under 174, 201 or 287 of the 2020 Act[12], the court may impose an electronic monitoring requirement to secure the monitoring of the defendant's compliance with certain other requirements (for example, a curfew or an exclusion).]*

### Notification requirements R28.3

**28.3** (1) This rule applies where, on a conviction, sentence or order, legislation requires the defendant—

    (a) to notify information to the police; or;

    (b) to be included in a barred list.

  (2) The court must tell the defendant that such requirements apply, and under what legislation.

*[Note. For the circumstances in which a defendant is required to notify information to the police, see—*

    (a) *Part 2 of, and Schedule 3 to, the Sexual Offences Act 2003([13]) (notification for the period specified by section 82 of the Act([14]) after conviction, etc. of an offence listed in Schedule 3 and committed in the circumstances specified in that Schedule);*

    (b) *Part 4 of the Counter Terrorism Act 2008[15] (notification after conviction of a specified offence of, or connected with, terrorism, for which a specified sentence is imposed).*

*For the circumstances in which a defendant will be included in a barred list, see paragraphs 1, 2, 7, 8 and 24 of Schedule 3 to the Safeguarding Vulnerable Groups Act 2006[16]. See also paragraph 25 of that Schedule[17].*

*These requirements are not part of the court's sentence.]*

### Variation of sentence R28.4

**28.4** (1) This rule—

    (a) applies where a magistrates' court or the Crown Court can vary or rescind a sentence or order, other than an order to which rule 44.3 applies (Setting aside a conviction or varying a costs etc. order); and

    (b) authorises the Crown Court, in addition to its other powers, to do so within the period of 56 days beginning with another defendant's acquittal or sentencing where—

        (i) defendants are tried separately in the Crown Court on the same or related facts alleged in one or more indictments, and

        (ii) one is sentenced before another is acquitted or sentenced.

  (2) The court—

    (a) may exercise its power—

        (i) on application by a party, or on its own initiative,

        (ii) at a hearing, in public or in private, or without a hearing; and

    (b) must announce, at a hearing in public—

---

[7] 2003 c. 44; section 219 was repealed by section 413 of, and Schedule 28 to, the Sentencing Act 2020 (c. 17).

[8] 2008 c. 4.

[9] 1959 c. 57; section 1A was inserted by section 17(1) and (3) of the Policing and Crime Act 2009 (c. 26).

[10] 2008 c. 4; Schedule 1 was repealed by section 413 of, and Schedule 28 to, the Sentencing Act 2020 (c. 17).

[11] 1959 c. 57; section 1(2A) was inserted by section 17(1) and (3) of the Policing and Crime Act 2009 (c. 26).

[12] 2008 c. 4.

[13] 2003 c. 42; Schedule 3 was amended by article 2 of S.I. 2007/296, section 63(2) of, and paragraph 63 of Schedule 6 to, the Serious Crimes Act 2007 (c. 27), section 148(1) of, and paragraphs 53 and 58 of Schedule 26 to, the Criminal Justice and Immigration Act 2008 (c. 4) and section 177(1) of, and paragraph 62 of Schedule 21 to, the Coroners and Justice Act 2009 (c. 25). Other amendments to Schedule 3 are not relevant to these Rules.

[14] 2003 c. 42; section 82 was amended by section 57 of the Violent Crime Reduction Act 2006 (c. 38).

[15] 2008 c. 28.

[16] 2006 c. 47; paragraphs 1, 2, 7 and 8 of Schedule 3 were amended by sections 81 and 89 of the Policing and Crime Act 2009 (c. 26). Paragraph 24 was amended by article 2 of S.I. 2008/3050.

[17] 2006 c. 47; paragraph 25 of Schedule 3 was amended by article 3 of S.I. 2008/3050 and section 81 of the Policing and Crime Act 2009 (c. 26).

Criminal Procedure Rules and Criminal Practice Directions

          (i)   a decision to vary or rescind a sentence or order, or to refuse to do so, and

          (ii)  the reasons for that decision.

(3)  A party who wants the court to exercise that power must—

    (a)  apply in writing as soon as reasonably practicable after—

       (i)   the sentence or order that that party wants the court to vary or rescind, or

       (ii)  where paragraph (1)(b) applies, the other defendant's acquittal or sentencing;

    (b)  serve the application on—

       (i)   the court officer, and

       (ii)  each other party; and

    (c)  in the application—

       (i)   explain why the sentence should be varied or rescinded,

       (ii)  specify the variation that the applicant proposes, and

      (iii)  if the application is late, explain why.

(4)  The court must not exercise its power in the defendant's absence unless—

    (a)  the court makes a variation—

       (i)   which is proposed by the defendant, or

       (ii)  the effect of which is that the defendant is no more severely dealt with under the sentence as varied than before; or

    (b)  the defendant has had an opportunity to make representations at a hearing (whether or not the defendant in fact attends).

(5)  The court may—

    (a)  extend (even after it has expired) the time limit under paragraph (3), unless the court's power to vary or rescind the sentence cannot be exercised; and

    (b)  allow an application to be made orally.

(6)  For the purposes of the announcement required by paragraph (2)(b), the court need not comprise the same member or members as the court by which the decision to be announced was made.

*[Note. Under section 142 of the Magistrates' Courts Act 1980[18], in some cases a magistrates' court can vary or rescind a sentence or other order that it has imposed or made, if that appears to be in the interests of justice. The power cannot be exercised if the Crown Court or the High Court has determined an appeal about that sentence or order. See also rule 44.3 (Setting aside a conviction or varying a costs etc. order), which governs the exercise by a magistrates' court of the power conferred by section 142 of the 1980 Act in the circumstances to which that rule applies.*

*Under section 385 of the Sentencing Act 2020, the Crown Court can vary or rescind a sentence or other order that it has imposed or made. The power cannot be exercised—*

    *(a)  after the period of 56 days beginning with the sentence or order (but see the note below); or*

    *(b)  if an appeal or application for permission to appeal against that sentence or order has been determined.*

*Under section 385(7) of that Act, Criminal Procedure Rules can extend that period of 56 days where another defendant is tried separately in the Crown Court on the same or related facts alleged in one or more indictments.]*

**R28.5**   **Application to vary or discharge a compensation, etc. order**

    **28.5**  (1)  This rule applies where on application by the defendant a magistrates' court can vary or discharge—

       (a)  a compensation order; or

       (b)  a slavery and trafficking reparation order.

     (2)  A defendant who wants the court to exercise that power must—

       (a)  apply in writing as soon as practicable after becoming aware of the grounds for doing so;

       (b)  serve the application on the magistrates' court officer;

       (c)  where the order was made in the Crown Court, serve a copy of the application on the Crown Court officer; and

       (d)  in the application, specify the order that the defendant wants the court to vary or discharge and explain (as applicable)—

          (i)   what civil court finding shows that the injury, loss or damage was less than it had appeared to be when the order was made,

          (ii)  in what circumstances the person for whose benefit the order was made has recovered the property for the loss of which it was made,

---

[18]  1980 c. 43; section 142 was amended by sections 26 and 29 of, and Schedule 3 to, the Criminal Appeal Act 1995 (c. 35).

(iii) why a confiscation order, unlawful profit order or slavery and trafficking reparation order makes the defendant now unable to pay compensation or reparation in full, or

(iv) in what circumstances the defendant's means have been reduced substantially and unexpectedly, and why they seem unlikely to increase for a considerable period.

(3) The court officer must serve a copy of the application on the person for whose benefit the order was made.

(4) The court must not vary or discharge the order unless—

(a) the defendant, and the person for whose benefit it was made, each has had an opportunity to make representations at a hearing (whether or not either in fact attends); and

(b) where the order was made in the Crown Court, the Crown Court has notified its consent.

*[Note. For the circumstances in which—*

*(a) the court may make a compensation order, see section 133 of the Sentencing Act 2020;*

*(b) the court may make a slavery and trafficking reparation order, see section 8 of the Modern Slavery Act 2015[19];*

*(c) a magistrates' court with power to enforce such an order may vary or discharge it under the 2020 Act, see section 143. (Under section 143(3), where the order was made in the Crown Court, the magistrates' court must first obtain the Crown Court's consent.)]*

### Application to remove, revoke or suspend a disqualification or restriction          R28.6

**28.6** (1) This rule applies where, on application by the defendant, the court can remove, revoke or suspend a disqualification or restriction included in a sentence (except a disqualification from driving).

(2) A defendant who wants the court to exercise such a power must—

(a) apply in writing, no earlier than the date on which the court can exercise the power;

(b) serve the application on the court officer; and

(c) in the application—

(i) specify the disqualification or restriction, and

(ii) explain why the defendant wants the court to remove, revoke or suspend it.

(3) The court officer must serve a copy of the application on the chief officer of police for the local justice area.

*[Note. Part 29 contains rules about disqualification from driving. See in particular rule 29.2.*

*Part 34 (Appeal to the Crown Court) and Part 35 (Appeal to the High Court by case stated) contain rules about applications to suspend disqualifications pending appeal.*

*For the circumstances in which the court may—*

*(a) remove a disqualification from keeping a dog, see section 4(6) of the Dangerous Dogs Act 1991[20]. The court may not consider an application made within 1 year of the disqualification; or, after that, within 1 year of any previous application that was refused.*

*(b) revoke or suspend a travel restriction order against a defendant convicted of drug trafficking, see section 35 of the Criminal Justice and Police Act 2001[21]). The court may not consider an application made within 2 years of the disqualification, in any case; or, after that, before a specified period has expired.]*

### Application for a restitution order by the victim of a theft                        R28.7

**28.7** (1) This rule applies where, on application by the victim of a theft, the court can order a defendant to give that person goods obtained with the proceeds of goods stolen in that theft.

(2) A person who wants the court to exercise that power if the defendant is convicted must—

(a) apply in writing as soon as practicable (without waiting for the verdict);

(b) serve the application on the court officer; and

(c) in the application—

(i) identify the goods, and

(ii) explain why the applicant is entitled to them.

(3) The court officer must serve a copy of the application on each party.

(4) The court must not determine the application unless the applicant and each party has had an opportunity to make representations at a hearing (whether or not each in fact attends).

(5) The court may—

---

[19] 2015 c. 30.
[20] 1991 c. 65; section 4(6) was amended by section 109(1) of, and paragraph 353 of Schedule 8 to, the Courts Act 2003 (c. 39).
[21] 2001 c. 16; section 35 was amended by sections 39(3) of the Identity Cards Act 2006 (c. 15).

(a)  extend (even after it has expired) the time limit under paragraph (2); and

(b)  allow an application to be made orally.

*[Note. For the circumstances in which the court may order—*

(a)  *the return of stolen goods, see section 147 of the Sentencing Act 2020[22];*

(b)  *the defendant to give the victim of the theft goods that are not themselves the stolen goods but which represent their proceeds, see section 147(1)(b) of the 2020 Act.]*

**R28.8**  **Directions for commissioning medical reports for sentencing purposes**

**28.8**  (1)  This rule applies where for sentencing purposes the court requires—

(a)  a medical examination of the defendant and a report; or

(b)  information about the arrangements that could be made for the defendant where the court is considering—

(i)  a hospital order, or

(ii)  a guardianship order.

(2)  The court must—

(a)  identify each issue in respect of which the court requires expert medical opinion and the legislation applicable;

(b)  specify the nature of the expertise likely to be required for giving such opinion;

(c)  identify each party or participant by whom a commission for such opinion must be prepared, who may be—

(i)  a party (or party's representative) acting on that party's own behalf,

(ii)  a party (or party's representative) acting on behalf of the court, or

(iii)  the court officer acting on behalf of the court;

(d)  where there are available to the court arrangements with the National Health Service under which an assessment of a defendant's mental health may be prepared, give such directions as are needed under those arrangements for obtaining the expert report or reports required;

(e)  where no such arrangements are available to the court, or they will not be used, give directions for the preparation of a commission or commissions for an expert report or expert reports, including—

(i)  such directions as can be made about supplying the expert or experts with the defendant's medical records,

(ii)  directions about the other information, about the defendant and about the offence or offences alleged to have been committed by the defendant, which is to be supplied to each expert, and

(iii)  directions about the arrangements that will apply for the payment of each expert;

(f)  set a timetable providing for—

(i)  the date by which a commission is to be delivered to each expert,

(ii)  the date by which any failure to accept a commission is to be reported to the court,

(iii)  the date or dates by which progress in the preparation of a report or reports is to be reviewed by the court officer, and

(iv)  the date by which each report commissioned is to be received by the court; and

(g)  identify the person (each person, if more than one) to whom a copy of a report is to be supplied, and by whom.

(3)  A commission addressed to an expert must—

(a)  identify each issue in respect of which the court requires expert medical opinion and the legislation applicable;

(b)  include—

(i)  the information required by the court to be supplied to the expert,

(ii)  details of the timetable set by the court, and

(iii)  details of the arrangements that will apply for the payment of the expert;

(c)  identify the person (each person, if more than one) to whom a copy of the expert's report is to be supplied; and

(d)  request confirmation that the expert from whom the opinion is sought—

(i)  accepts the commission, and

(ii)  will adhere to the timetable.

*[Note. See also rule 3.10 (directions for commissioning medical reports in connection with fitness to participate in the trial, etc.).*

*For sentencing purposes the court may request a medical examination of the defendant and a report under—*

---

[22]  2020 c. 17.

**R29.5**    **Application for declaration about a course or programme certificate decision**

29.5  (1)  This rule applies where the court can declare unjustified—

    (a)  a course provider's failure or refusal to give a certificate of the defendant's satisfactory completion of an approved course; or

    (b)  a programme provider's giving of a certificate of the defendant's failure fully to participate in an approved programme.

 (2)  A defendant who wants the court to exercise that power must—

    (a)  apply in writing, not more than 20 business days after—

      (i)  the date by which the defendant was required to complete the course, or

      (ii)  the giving of the certificate of failure fully to participate in the programme;

    (b)  serve the application on the court officer; and

    (c)  in the application, specify the course or programme and explain (as applicable)—

      (i)  that the course provider has failed to give a certificate,

      (ii)  where the course provider has refused to give a certificate, why the defendant disagrees with the reasons for that decision, or

      (iii)  where the programme provider has given a certificate, why the defendant disagrees with the reasons for that decision.

 (3)  The court officer must serve a copy of the application on the course or programme provider.

 (4)  The court must not determine the application unless the defendant, and the course or programme provider, each has had an opportunity to make representations at a hearing (whether or not either in fact attends).

*[Note. For the circumstances in which the court may reduce a road traffic penalty on condition that the defendant attend an approved course, or take part in an approved programme, see sections 30A, 34A and 34D of the Road Traffic Offenders Act 1988[17].*

*Under sections 30B, 34B and 34E of the 1988 Act[18], the court that made the order, or the defendant's local magistrates' court, on application by the defendant may review a course or programme provider's decision that the defendant has not completed the course satisfactorily, or has not participated fully in the programme.]*

**R29.6**    **Appeal against recognition of foreign driving disqualification**

29.6  (1)  This rule applies where—

    (a)  a Minister gives a disqualification notice under section 57 of the Crime (International Co-operation) Act 2003[19]; and

    (b)  the person to whom it is given wants to appeal under section 59 of the Act[20] to a magistrates' court.

 (2)  That person ('the appellant') must serve an appeal notice on—

    (a)  the court officer, at a magistrates' court in the local justice area in which the appellant lives; and

    (b)  the Minister, at the address given in the disqualification notice.

 (3)  The appellant must serve the appeal notice within the period for which section 59 of the 2003 Act provides.

 (4)  The appeal notice must—

    (a)  attach a copy of the disqualification notice;

    (b)  explain which of the conditions in section 56 of the 2003 Act[21] is not met, and why section 57 of the Act therefore does not apply; and

---

[17] 1988 c. 53; section 30A is inserted by section 34(1) and (3) of the Road Safety Act 2006 (c. 49), with effect from a date to be appointed. Section 34A was inserted by section 30 of the Road Traffic Act 1991 (c. 40). It is amended by section 177(1) and (2) of, and paragraphs 30 and 90(1) and (3) of Schedule 21 and paragraphs 30 and 31 of Schedule 22 to, the Coroners and Justice Act 2009 (c. 25), with effect from a date to be appointed. Section 34D is inserted by section 15(1) of the Road Safety Act 2006 (c. 49), with effect from a date to be appointed. It is amended by section 177(1) of, and paragraph 90(1) and (5) of Schedule 21 to, the Coroners and Justice Act 2009 (c. 25), with effect from a date to be appointed.

[18] 1988 c. 53; section 30B is inserted by section 34(1) and (3) of the Road Safety Act 2006 (c. 49), with effect from a date to be appointed. Section 34B was inserted by section 30 of the Road Traffic Act 1991 (c. 40) and amended by paragraphs 140, 145 and 146 of Schedule 13 and Part V of Schedule 15 to, the Access to Justice Act 1999 (c. 22). Section 34B is substituted by section 35 of the Road Safety Act 2006 (c. 49), with effect from a date to be appointed. Section 34E is inserted by section 15(1) of the Road Safety Act 2006 (c. 49), with effect from a date to be appointed.

[19] 2003 c. 32; section 57 is in force in relation only to an offence of which an offender has been convicted in Ireland. For remaining purposes, it will come into force on a date to be appointed.

[20] 2003 c. 32; section 59 is in force in relation only to an offence of which an offender has been convicted in Ireland. For remaining purposes, it will come into force on a date to be appointed. Section 59 was amended by article 2 of, and paragraph 97 of the Schedule to, S.I. 2005/886.

[21] 2003 c. 32; section 56 is in force in relation only to an offence of which an offender has been convicted in Ireland. For remaining purposes, it will come into force on a date to be appointed.

Criminal Procedure Rules and Criminal Practice Directions

   (b)  where paragraph (1)(a)(ii) applies (disqualification under section 35)—

       (i)  that the court must order the defendant to be disqualified from driving for a minimum of 6 months (or 1 or 2 years, as the case may be, according to the defendant's driving record), unless, having regard to all the circumstances, the court decides to order disqualification for a shorter period, or not to order disqualification at all, and

     (ii)  that circumstances of which the court cannot take account in making its decision are any that make the offence not a serious one; hardship (other than exceptional hardship); and any that during the last 3 years already have been taken into account by a court when ordering disqualification for less than the usual minimum period, or not at all, for repeated driving offences;

   (c)  where paragraph (1)(a)(iii) applies (obligatory endorsement), that the court must order the endorsement of the defendant's driving record unless the court decides that there are special reasons not to do so; and

   (d)  in every case, as applicable—

       (i)  that the court already has received representations from the defendant about whether any such special reasons or mitigating circumstances apply and will take account of them, or

     (ii)  that the defendant may make such representations now, on oath or affirmation.

(3)  Unless the court already has received such representations from the defendant, before it applies rule 24.11 (magistrates' court procedure if the court convicts) or rule 25.16 (Crown Court procedure if the court convicts), as the case may be, the court must—

   (a)  ask whether the defendant wants to make any such representations; and

   (b)  if the answer to that question is 'yes', require the defendant to take an oath or affirm and make them.

*[Note. For the circumstances in which the court—*

   *(a)  may, and in some cases must, order disqualification from driving under the Road Traffic Offenders Act 1988, see sections 26, 34, 35 and 36 of that Act[4];*

   *(b)  may, for some reasons or in some circumstances, abbreviate or dispense with a period of disqualification otherwise required by the 1988 Act, see sections 34(1) and 35(1), (4) of that Act;*

   *(c)  must usually order endorsement, see sections 9, 44 and 96 of, and Schedule 2 to, the 1988 Act.*

*For the circumstances in which the period of a disqualification from driving must or may be extended where the court also imposes a custodial sentence, see sections 35A and 35B of the 1988 Act[5].*

*For the circumstances in which the period of a disqualification from driving will be reduced if the defendant completes an approved driving course, see section 34A of the 1988 Act[6].]*

### Application to remove a disqualification from driving       **R29.2**

**29.2**  (1)  This rule applies where, on application by the defendant, the court can remove a disqualification from driving.

      (2)  A defendant who wants the court to exercise that power must—

       (a)  apply in writing, no earlier than the date on which the court can exercise the power;

       (b)  serve the application on the court officer; and

       (c)  in the application—

---

[4]  1988 c. 53; section 26 was substituted by section 25 of the Road Traffic Act 1991 (c. 40) and amended by paragraph 119 of Schedule 9 to the Powers of Criminal Courts (Sentencing) Act 2000 (c. 6), paragraphs 140 and 143 of Schedule 13 to the Access to Justice Act 1999 (c. 22), paragraph 2 of Schedule 2 to S.I. 1996/1974, paragraph 312 of Schedule 8 to the Courts Act 2003 (c. 39), paragraphs 32 and 34 of Schedule 5 to the Crime (International Co-operation) Act 2003 (c. 32) and sections 10 and 59 of, and paragraphs 30 and 32 of Schedule 3 and Schedule 7 to, the Road Safety Act 2006 (c. 49). Section 36 was substituted by section 32 of the Road Traffic Act 1991 (c. 40) and amended by paragraph 3 of Schedule 2 to S.I. 1996/1974, article 3 of S. I. 1998/1917, section 9(6) of, and paragraphs 2 and 7 of Schedule 7 to, the Road Safety Act 2006 (c. 49) and paragraphs 2 and 6 of Schedule 27 to the Legal Aid, Sentencing and Punishment of Offenders Act 2012 (c. 10). It is further amended by sections 10, 37 and 59 of, and paragraphs 30 and 39 of Schedule 3, and Schedule 7 to, the Road Safety Act 2006 (c. 49), with effect from a date to be appointed.

[5]  1988 c. 53; sections 35A and 35B were inserted by section 137 of, and paragraph 2 of Schedule 16 to, the Coroners and Justice Act 2009 (c. 25). Section 35A was amended by sections 89, 111 and 126 of, and paragraph 5 of Schedule 10, paragraph 1 of Schedule 14 and paragraph 4 of Schedule 21 to, the Legal Aid, Sentencing and Punishment of Offenders Act 2012 (c. 10) and sections 6 and 30 of, and paragraph 11 of Schedule 1 to, the Criminal Justice and Courts Act 2015 (c. 2).

[6]  1988 c. 53; section 34A was inserted by section 30 of the Road Traffic Act 1991 (c. 40). It was substituted by section 35 of the Road Safety Act 2006 (c. 49) for certain purposes, and for remaining purposes with effect from a date to be appointed. It is amended by section 177 of, and paragraphs 30 and 90 of Schedule 21 and paragraphs 30 and 31 of Schedule 22 to, the Coroners and Justice Act 2009 (c. 25), with effect from a date to be appointed.

*in which event the Crown Court may deal with the defendant only in a way in which the magistrates' court could have done.*

*Under section 23 of the 2020 Act (Power of Crown Court on committal for sentence under section 20), where the defendant is committed for sentence under section 20 of the Act the Crown Court may deal with the defendant only in a way in which the magistrates' court could have done except in relation to any suspended sentence committed under that section, in respect of which the Crown Court may exercise its usual powers on dealing with such a breach.*

*For other powers of a magistrates' court to commit a defendant to the Crown Court for sentence or otherwise to deal with the defendant, see—*

    (a) *the provisions listed in section 24 of the 2020 Act (Further powers to commit offender to the Crown Court to be dealt with); and*

    (b) *paragraph 11(2) of Schedule 16 to the 2020 Act, under which a magistrates' court may commit the defendant to the Crown Court to be dealt with there if the magistrates' court convicts the defendant of an offence during the operational period of a suspended sentence order made by the Crown Court.*

*The provisions listed in section 24 of the 2020 Act include section 70 of the Proceeds of Crime Act 2002[49] . Under that section, if a magistrates' court commits a defendant to the Crown Court so that a confiscation order can be considered then the court also may commit the defendant to the Crown Court to be dealt with there for any other offence of which the defendant has been convicted and with which the magistrates' court otherwise could deal. Under section 71 of the 2002 Act, the Crown Court may deal with the defendant in any way in which it could have done if the defendant had been convicted in that court, unless the magistrates' court did not make the statement to which section 70(5) refers. See also rule 24.11(10)(e), which refers to that statement.]*

CRIMINAL PROCEDURE RULES    PART 29 ROAD TRAFFIC PENALTIES

*[Note. Part 24 contains rules about the general procedure on sentencing in a magistrates' court. Part 25 contains corresponding rules for the Crown Court.]*

**R29.1**    **Representations about obligatory disqualification or endorsement**

    **29.1**    (1)   This rule applies—

        (a)   where the court—

            (i)   convicts the defendant of an offence involving obligatory disqualification from driving and section 34(1) of the Road Traffic Offenders Act 1988[1] (Disqualification for certain offences) applies,

            (ii)   convicts the defendant of an offence where section 35 of the 1988 Act[2] (Disqualification for repeated offences) applies, or

            (iii)   convicts the defendant of an offence involving obligatory endorsement of the defendant's driving record and section 44 of the 1988 Act[3] (Orders for endorsement) applies;

        (b)   unless the defendant is absent.

      (2)   The court must explain, in terms the defendant can understand (with help, if necessary)—

        (a)   where paragraph (1)(a)(i) applies (obligatory disqualification under section 34)—

            (i)   that the court must order the defendant to be disqualified from driving for a minimum of 12 months (or 2 or 3 years, as the case may be, according to the offence and the defendant's driving record), unless the court decides that there are special reasons to order disqualification for a shorter period, or not to order disqualification at all, and

            (ii)   if applicable, that the period of disqualification will be reduced by at least 3 months if, by no later than 2 months before the end of the reduced period, the defendant completes an approved driving course;

---

[49] 2002 c. 29; section 70 was amended by section 41 of, and paragraph 75 of Schedule 3 to, the Criminal Justice Act 2003 (c. 44), section 410 of, and paragraphs 181 and 195 of Schedule 24 to, the Sentencing Act 2020 (c. 17) and section 46 of, and paragraph 19 of Schedule 13 to, the Counter-Terrorism and Sentencing Act 2021 (c. 11).

[1] 1988 c. 53; section 34 was amended by section 29 of the Road Traffic Act 1991 (c. 40), section 3 of the Aggravated Vehicle-Taking Act 1992 (c. 11), section 165 of, and paragraph 121 of Schedule 9 to, the Powers of Criminal Courts (Sentencing) Act 2000 (c. 6), sections 56 and 107 of, and Schedule 8 to, the Police Reform Act 2002 (c. 30), section 25 of the Road Safety Act 2006 (c. 49), article 2 of S.I. 2007/3480, paragraphs 2 and 5 of Schedule 27 to the Legal Aid, Sentencing and Punishment of Offenders Act 2012 (c. 10), section 56 of, and paragraphs 9 and 12 of Schedule 22 to, the Crime and Courts Act 2013 (c. 22) and section 177 of, and paragraph 90 of Schedule 21 to, the Coroners and Justice Act 2009 (c. 25).

[2] 2005 c. 15.

[3] 2005 c. 15; section 74 was amended by article 13 of, and paragraphs 1 and 19 of Schedule 15 to, S.I. 2010/976.

convicted is one to which section 16 refers (offences punishable with imprisonment for 14 years or more and certain sexual offences), and the court is of the opinion that the offence of which the defendant has been convicted, or the combination of that offence and one or more offences associated with it, was such that the Crown Court should have the power to impose a sentence of detention under section 250 of the Act;

(c)  section 16A of the 2020 Act[44] (Committal for sentence of young offenders on summary trial of certain terrorist offences) where the defendant is under 18, the offence of which the defendant has been convicted is one within section 252A of the Act[45] (terrorism offences attracting special sentence for offenders of particular concern) and the court is of the opinion that the offence of which the defendant has been convicted, or the combination of that offence and one or more offences associated with it, was such that the Crown Court should have the power to impose a sentence of detention for more than 2 years under section 252A;

(d)  section 18 of the 2020 Act (Committal for sentence on indication of guilty plea to offence triable either way: adult offenders) where the defendant is over 18 and the court has sent the defendant to the Crown Court for trial for a related offence;

(e)  section 19 of the 2020 Act (Committal for sentence on indication of guilty plea by child with related offences) where the defendant is under 18, the court has sent the defendant to the Crown Court for trial for a related offence, and the offence of which the defendant has been convicted is one to which section 19 refers (offences punishable with imprisonment for 14 years or more and certain sexual offences); or

(f)  section 20 of the 2020 Act (Committal in certain cases where offender committed in respect of another offence) where the court commits the defendant to the Crown Court for sentence for an offence under any of sections 14 to 19 of the Act, or under one of the other provisions to which section 20 refers, and—

(i)  if that offence is an indictable offence, then the court may also commit the defendant for sentence for any other offence, or

(ii)  if that offence is a summary offence, then the court may also commit the defendant for sentence for any other offence of which the court itself has convicted the defendant and which is punishable with imprisonment or disqualification from driving, and for any suspended sentence with which the committing court could deal.

A magistrates' court must commit a convicted defendant to the Crown Court for sentence under—

(a)  section 15 of the Sentencing Act 2020[46] (Committal for sentence of dangerous adult offenders) where the defendant is over 18, the offence of which the defendant has been convicted is one to which section 15 refers, and the court is of the opinion that an extended sentence of detention or imprisonment would be available in relation to the offence; or

(b)  section 17 of the 2020 Act[47] (Committal for sentence of dangerous young offenders) where the defendant is under 18, the offence of which the defendant has been convicted is one to which section 17 refers, and the court is of the opinion that an extended sentence of detention would be available in relation to the offence.

Under sections 21 and 22 of the Sentencing Act 2020[48] (Power of Crown Court on committal for sentence of offender under section 14, 15 or 18; Power of Crown Court on committal for sentence of person under 18 under section 16, 16A, 17 or 19), where the defendant is committed for sentence under any of sections 14 to 19 of that Act the Crown Court may deal with the defendant in any way in which it could have done if the defendant had been convicted in that court, unless—

(a)  the defendant was committed for sentence under section 18 or 19;

(b)  the magistrates' court did not state the opinion to which either section 18(4) or 19(3), whichever applies, refers (see also rule 9.15 (Committal for sentence for offence related to an offence sent for trial)); and

(c)  the defendant is not convicted in the Crown Court of any offence for which the magistrates' court sent the defendant for trial,

[44]  2020 c. 17; section 16A was inserted by section 46 of, and paragraph 26 of Schedule 13 to, the Counter-Terrorism and Sentencing Act 2021 (c. 11).
[45]  2020 c. 17; section 252A was inserted by section 22 of the Counter-Terrorism and Sentencing Act 2021 (c. 11).
[46]  2020 c. 17; section 15 was amended by section 46 of, and paragraph 11 of Schedule 13 to, the Counter-Terrorism and Sentencing Act 2021 (c. 11).
[47]  2020 c. 17; section 17 was amended by section 46 of, and paragraph 26 of Schedule 13 to, the Counter-Terrorism and Sentencing Act 2021 (c. 11).
[48]  2020 c. 17; section 22 was amended by section 46 of, and paragraph 26 of Schedule 13 to, the Counter-Terrorism and Sentencing Act 2021 (c. 11).

Criminal Procedure Rules and Criminal Practice Directions

        (i)   the court officer, and

        (ii)  the defendant; and

   (c)  in the application—

        (i)   explain why the sentence should be reduced, or increased, as appropriate, and

        (ii)  identify any other matter relevant to the court's decision, including any sentencing guideline or guideline case.

(3)  The general rule is that the application must be determined by the judge who passed the sentence, unless that judge is unavailable.

(4)  The court must not determine the application in the defendant's absence unless the defendant has had an opportunity to make representations at a hearing (whether or not the defendant in fact attends).

*[Note. Under section 73 of the Serious Organised Crime and Police Act 2005[42], the Crown Court may pass a lesser sentence than it otherwise would have passed because the defendant has assisted, or has agreed to assist, an investigator or prosecutor in relation to an offence.*

*Under sections 387 and 388 of the 2020 Act, where the Crown Court has sentenced a defendant a prosecutor may apply to the court—*

   *(a)  to reduce the sentence, if the defendant subsequently assists, or agrees to assist, in the investigation or prosecution of an offence; or*

   *(b)  to increase a reduced sentence to that which the court otherwise would have passed, if the defendant agreed to give such assistance but subsequently has knowingly failed to do so.*

*Such an application may be made only where the defendant is still serving the sentence and the prosecutor thinks it is in the interests of justice to apply.]*

## R28.12   Sentencing, etc. after committal to the Crown Court

28.12  (1)  This rule applies where a magistrates' court commits the defendant to the Crown Court—

   (a)  for sentence; or

   (b)  to be dealt with under other powers available to the Crown Court after a defendant's conviction.

(2)  Rule 25.16 (Trial and sentence in the Crown Court; Procedure if the court convicts) applies as if the defendant had been convicted in the Crown Court.

(3)  As well as supplying the information required for sentencing purposes by rule 25.16(3), the prosecutor must identify any offence in respect of which the Crown Court cannot deal with the defendant in a way in which it could have done if the defendant had been convicted in the Crown Court, including—

   (a)  an offence—

        (i)   committed for sentence under section 18 or 19, as the case may be, of the Sentencing Act 2020[44], and

        (ii)  in respect of which the magistrates' court did not state the opinion to which section 18(4) or 19(3) of that Act refers;

   (b)  an offence committed for sentence under section 20 of the 2020 Act; and

   (c)  an offence—

        (i)   committed to the Crown Court under section 70 of the Proceeds of Crime Act 2002, and

        (ii)  in respect of which the magistrates' court did not make the statement to which section 70(5) of that Act refers.

*[Note. A magistrates' court may commit a convicted defendant to the Crown Court for sentence under—*

   *(a)  section 14 of the Sentencing Act 2020 (Committal for sentence on summary trial of offence triable either way: adults and corporations) where the defendant is over 18 or is a corporation, the offence is one triable either way and the court is of the opinion that the offence of which the defendant has been convicted, or the combination of that offence and one or more offences associated with it, was so serious that the Crown Court should have the power to deal with the defendant in any way that that court could have done if the defendant had been convicted there;*

   *(b)  section 16 of the 2020 Act (Committal for sentence of young offenders on summary trial of certain serious offences) where the defendant is under 18, the offence of which the defendant has been*

---

[42] 2020 c. 17.

[43] 2020 c. 17; section 19 was amended by section 46 of, and paragraph 26 of Schedule 13 to, the Counter-Terrorism and Sentencing Act 2021 (c. 11).

Criminal Procedure Rules and Criminal Practice Directions

      (iv)   note of evidence,

      (v)    statement or other document introduced in evidence,

      (vi)   medical or other report,

      (vii)  representation order or application for such order,

      (viii) interim driving disqualification; and

      (ix)   statement by the court for the purposes of section 70(5) of the Proceeds of Crime Act 2002[35]

   (b)  where paragraph (1)(b) or (c) applies, arrange—

      (i)    the transmission from the convicting to the other court of notice of the convicting court's order, and

      (ii)   the recording of that order at the other court;

   (c)  in every case, notify the defendant and, where the defendant is under 14, an appropriate adult, of the location of the other court.

*[Note. For the circumstances in which—*

   *(a)  a magistrates' court may (and, in some cases, must) commit the defendant to the Crown Court for sentence, see rules 9.15 (Committal for sentence of offence related to an offence sent for trial), 24.11 (Procedure if the court convicts) and 28.12 (Sentencing, etc. after committal to the Crown Court) (the note to rule 28.12 summarises the statutory provisions that apply);*

   *(b)  a magistrates' court may adjourn the case to another magistrates' court for sentence, see section 10 of the Magistrates' Courts Act 1980[36] and section 28 of the Sentencing Act 2020[37];*

   *(c)  a magistrates' court or the Crown Court may (and, in some cases, must) adjourn the case to a youth court for sentence, see sections 25 and 26 of the 2020 Act;*

   *(d)  a youth court may adjourn the case to a magistrates' court for sentence, see section 27 of the 2020 Act;*

   *(e)  a magistrates' court may transfer a fine to be enforced to another court, see sections 89 and 90 of the 1980 Act[40].*

*For the court's powers where it convicts a defendant who is subject to a deferred sentence, a conditional discharge, or a suspended sentence of imprisonment, imposed by another court, see section 10 of, and Schedules 2 and 16 to, the 2020 Act.*

*Under section 132 of the 2020 Act, a fine imposed or other sum ordered to be paid in the Crown Court is enforceable by a magistrates' court specified in the order, or from which the case was committed or sent to the Crown Court.*

*See also sections 212(4), 298(4) and 190(4) of the 2020 Act; and section 1A(9) of the Street Offences Act 1959[41].]*

**Application to review sentence because of assistance given or withheld**      **R28.11**

**28.11** (1) This rule applies where the Crown Court can reduce or increase a sentence on application by a prosecutor in a case in which—

   (a)  since being sentenced, the defendant has assisted, or has agreed to assist, an investigator or prosecutor in relation to an offence; or

   (b)  since receiving a reduced sentence for agreeing to give such assistance, the defendant has failed to do so.

   (2) A prosecutor who wants the court to exercise that power must—

   (a)  apply in writing as soon as practicable after becoming aware of the grounds for doing so;

   (b)  serve the application on—

---

[35] 2002 c. 29; section 70 was amended by section 41 of, and paragraph 75 of Schedule 3 to, the Criminal Justice Act 2003 (c. 44), section 410 of, and paragraphs 181 and 195 of Schedule 24 to, the Sentencing Act 2020 (c. 17) and section 46 of, and paragraph 19 of Schedule 13 to, the Counter-Terrorism and Sentencing Act 2021 (c. 11).

[36] 1980 c. 43; section 10 was amended by section 59 of, and paragraph 1 of Schedule 9 to, the Criminal Justice Act 1982 (c. 48), section 68 of, and paragraph 6 of Schedule 8 to, the Criminal Justice Act 1991 (c. 53) and section 47 of the Crime and Disorder Act 1998 (c. 37).

[37] 2020 c. 17.

[40] 1980 c. 43; section 89 was amended by section 47 of the Criminal Justice and Public Order Act 1994 (c. 33), paragraphs 95 and 107 of Schedule 13 to the Access to Justice Act 1999 (c. 22), paragraph 225 of Schedule 8 to the Courts Act 2003 (c. 39) and articles 46 and 49 of S.I. 2006/1737. Section 90 was amended by section 47(2) of the Criminal Justice and Public Order Act 1994 (c. 33), paragraph 226 of Schedule 8 to the Courts Act 2003 (c. 39) and articles 46 and 50 of S.I. 2006/1737.

[41] 1959 c. 57; section 1A was inserted by section 17(1) and (3) of the Policing and Crime Act 2009 (c. 26).

*Payments to medical practitioners for reports and for giving evidence are governed by section 19(3) of the Prosecution of Offences Act 1985[31] and by the Costs in Criminal Cases (General) Regulations 1986[32], regulation 17 (Determination of rates or scales of allowances payable out of central funds), regulation 20 (Expert witnesses, etc.) and regulation 25 (Written medical reports). The rates and scales of allowances payable under those Regulations are determined by the Lord Chancellor.]*

**R28.9**    **Information to be supplied on committal to custody or admission to hospital or guardianship**

28.9  (1)  This rule applies where the court—

    (a)  orders the defendant's committal to custody on withholding bail or on sentencing;

    (b)  orders the defendant's detention and treatment in hospital; or

    (c)  makes a guardianship order.

  (2)  Where paragraph (1)(a) applies, unless the court otherwise directs the court officer must, as soon as practicable, serve on or make available to the custodian any psychiatric, psychological or other medical report about the defendant received by the court for the purposes of the case.

  (3)  Where paragraph (1)(b) or (c) applies, unless the court otherwise directs the court officer must, as soon as practicable, serve on or make available to (as applicable) the hospital or the guardian—

    (a)  a record of the court's order;

    (b)  such information as the court has received that appears likely to assist in treating or otherwise dealing with the defendant, including information about—

      (i)  the defendant's mental condition,

      (ii)  the defendant's other circumstances, and

      (iii)  the circumstances of the offence.

*[Note. Rule 13.3 provides for the terms of a warrant for detention or imprisonment. Rule 13.4 provides for the information that such a warrant must contain.*

*For the circumstances in which the court may order the defendant's detention and treatment in hospital, see sections 35, 36, 37, 38 and 44 of the Mental Health Act 1983[33]. For the circumstances in which the court may make a guardianship order, see the same section 37.]*

**R28.10**    **Information to be supplied on committal for sentence, etc.**

28.10 (1)  This rule applies where a magistrates' court or the Crown Court convicts the defendant and—

    (a)  commits or adjourns the case to another court—

      (i)  for sentence, or

      (ii)  for the defendant to be dealt with for breach of a deferred sentence, a conditional discharge, or a suspended sentence of imprisonment, imposed by that other court;

    (b)  deals with a deferred sentence, a conditional discharge, or a suspended sentence of imprisonment, imposed by another court; or

    (c)  makes an order that another court is, or may be, required to enforce.

  (2)  Unless the convicting court otherwise directs, the court officer must, as soon as practicable—

    (a)  where paragraph (1)(a) applies, arrange the transmission from the convicting to the other court of a record of any relevant—

      (i)  certificate of conviction,

      (ii)  magistrates' court register entry,

      (iii)  decision about bail, for the purposes of section 5 of the Bail Act 1976[34],

[31] 1985 c. 23; section 19(3) was amended by section 166 of the Criminal Justice Act 1988 (c. 33), section 7 of, and paragraph 8 of Schedule 3 to, the Criminal Procedure (Insanity and Unfitness to Plead) Act 1991 (c. 25), sections 40 and 67 of, and paragraph 4 of Schedule 7 to, the Youth Justice and Criminal Evidence Act 1999 (c. 23), section 165 of, and paragraph 99 of Schedule 9 to, the Powers of Criminal Courts (Sentencing) Act 2000 (c. 6) and section 378 of, and paragraph 107 of Schedule 16 to, the Armed Forces Act 2006 (c. 52).

[32] S.I. 1986/1335; regulation 17 was amended by regulations 2 and 13 of S.I. 2008/2448, regulation 20 was amended by regulations 2 and 14 of S.I. 2008/2448 and by regulations 4 and 7 of S.I. 2012/1804, and regulation 25 was amended by regulations 2 and 10 of S.I. 2009/2720.

[33] 1983 c. 20; section 44 was amended by sections 10, 40 and 55 of, and Part 8 of Schedule 11 to, the Mental Health Act 2007 (c. 12).

[34] 1976 c. 63; section 5 was amended by section 65 of, and Schedule 12 to, the Criminal Law Act 1977 (c. 45), section 60 of the Criminal Justice Act 1982 (c. 48), paragraph 1 of Schedule 3 to the Criminal Justice and Public Order Act 1994 (c. 33), paragraph 53 of Schedule 9 to the Powers of Criminal Courts (Sentencing) Act 2000 (c. 6), section 129(1) of the Criminal Justice and Police Act 2001 (c. 16), paragraph 182 of Schedule 8 to the Courts Act 2003 (c. 39), paragraph 48 of Schedule 3, paragraphs 1 and 2 of Schedule 36, and Parts 2, 4 and 12 of Schedule 37 to the Criminal Justice Act 2003 (c. 44) and section 208 of, and paragraphs 33 and 35 of Schedule 21 to, the Legal Services Act 2007 (c. 27).

(a)  *section 35 of the Mental Health Act 1983[23], under which the court may order the defendant's detention in hospital to obtain a medical report;*

(b)  *section 36 of the 1983 Act[24], under which the Crown Court may order the defendant's detention in hospital instead of in custody pending trial or sentence;*

(c)  *section 37 of the 1983 Act[25], under which the court may order the defendant's detention and treatment in hospital, or make a guardianship order, instead of disposing of the case in another way (section 37(3) allows a magistrates' court to make such an order without convicting the defendant if satisfied that the defendant did the act or made the omission charged);*

(d)  *section 38 of the 1983 Act[26], under which the court may order the defendant's temporary detention and treatment in hospital instead of disposing of the case in another way;*

(e)  *section 232 of the Sentencing Act 2020[27], under which the court must usually obtain and consider a medical report before passing a custodial sentence if the defendant is, or appears to be, mentally disordered;*

(f)  *paragraphs 16 and 17 of Schedule 9 to the 2020 Act[28] (in the case of a defendant aged 18 or over), or paragraphs 28 and 29 of Schedule 6 to that Act (in the case of a defendant who is under 18), under which the court may impose a mental health treatment requirement.*

*For the purposes of the legislation listed in (b), (c) and (d) above, the court requires the written or oral evidence of at least two registered medical practitioners, at least one of whom is approved as having special experience in the diagnosis or treatment of mental disorder. For the purposes of (a), (e) and (f), the court requires the evidence of one medical practitioner so approved.*

*Under section 11 of the Powers of Criminal Courts (Sentencing) Act 2000[29], a magistrates' court may adjourn a trial to obtain medical reports.*

*Part 19 (Expert evidence) contains rules about the content of expert medical reports.*

*For the authorities from whom the court may require information about hospital treatment or guardianship, see sections 39 and 39A of the 1983 Act[30].*

*The Practice Direction includes a timetable for the commissioning and preparation of a report or reports which the court may adopt with such adjustments as the court directs.*

---

[23]  1983 c. 20; section 35 was amended by sections 1(4) and 10(1) and (2) of, and paragraphs 1 and 5 of Schedule 1 to, the Mental Health Act 2007 (c. 12) and section 208(1) of, and paragraphs 53 and 54 of Schedule 21 to, the Legal Services Act 2007 (c. 29).

[24]  1983 c. 20; section 36 was amended by sections 1(4), 5(1) and (2) and 10(1) and (3) of, and paragraphs 1 and 6 of Schedule 1 to, the Mental Health Act 2007 (c. 12) and section 208(1) of, and paragraphs 53 and 55 of Schedule 21 to, the Legal Services Act 2007 (c. 29).

[25]  1983 c. 20; section 37 was amended by sections 55 and 56 of, and paragraph 12 of Schedule 4 and Schedule 6 to, the Crime (Sentences) Act 1997 (c. 43), section 67 of, and paragraph 11 of Schedule 4 to, the Youth Justice and Criminal Evidence Act 1999 (c. 23), paragraph 90 of Schedule 9 to the Powers of Criminal Courts (Sentencing) Act 2000 (c. 6), section 304 of, and paragraphs 37 and 38 of Schedule 32 to, the Criminal Justice Act 2003 (c. 44), sections 49 and 65 of, and paragraph 2 of Schedule 1 and Schedule 5 to, the Violent Crime Reduction Act 2006 (c. 38), sections 1, 4, 10, 55 and paragraphs 1 and 7 of Schedule 1, and Part 1 of Schedule 11 to, the Mental Health Act 2007 (c. 12), sections 6 and 149 of, and paragraph 30 of Schedule 4, and Schedule 28 to, the Criminal Justice and Immigration Act 2008 (c. 4), sections 122 and 142 of, and paragraph 1 of Schedule 19 and paragraph 2 of Schedule 26 to, the Legal Aid, Sentencing and Punishment of Offenders Act 2012 (c. 10) and section 28 of, and paragraph 1 of Schedule 5 to, the Criminal Justice and Courts Act 2015 (c. 2). It is further amended by section 148 of, and paragraph 8 of Schedule 26 to, the Criminal Justice and Immigration Act 2008 (c. 4) with effect from a date to be appointed.

[26]  1983 c. 20; section 38 was amended by section 49(1) of the Crime (Sentences) Act 1997 (c. 43), sections 1(4) and 10(1) and (5) of, and paragraphs 1 and 8 of Schedule 1 to, the Mental Health Act 2007 (c. 12) and section 208(1) of, and paragraphs 53 and 56 of Schedule 21 to, the Legal Services Act 2007 (c. 29).

[27]  2020 c. 17.

[28]  2003 c. 44; section 207 was amended by article 4(2) of, and paragraph 7 of Schedule 5 to, S.I. 2009/1182, article 14(a) and (b) of, and Part 1 of Schedule 5 to, S.I. 2010/813, section 72 of the Health and Social Care Act 2012 (c. 7), section 73 of the Legal Aid, Sentencing and Punishment of Offenders Act 2012 (c. 10) and section 62 of, and paragraph 48 of Schedule 5 to, the Children and Social Work Act 2017 (c. 16).

[29]  2000 c. 6.

[30]  1983 c. 20; section 39 was amended by sections 2(1) and 5(1) of, and paragraph 107 of Schedule 1 and Schedule 3 to, the Health Authorities Act 1995 (c. 17), section 2(5) of, and paragraphs 42 and 46 of Schedule 2 to, the National Health Service Reform and Health Care Professions Act 2002 (c. 17), section 31(1) and (2) of the Mental Health Act 2007 (c. 12), article 3 of, and paragraph 13 of the Schedule to, S.I. 2007/961 and section 55 of, and paragraphs 24 and 28 of Schedule 5 to, the Health and Social Care Act 2012 (c. 7). Section 39A was inserted by section 27(1) of the Criminal Justice Act 1991 (c. 53).

(c) include any application to suspend the disqualification, under section 60 of the Act[22].

(5) The Minister may serve a respondent's notice, and must do so if—

    (a) the Minister wants to make representations to the court; or

    (b) the court so directs.

(6) The Minister must—

    (a) unless the court otherwise directs, serve any such respondent's notice not more than 14 days after—

        (i) the appellant serves the appeal notice, or

        (ii) a direction to do so; and

    (b) in any such respondent's notice—

        (i) identify the grounds of opposition on which the Minister relies,

        (ii) summarise any relevant facts not already included in the disqualification and appeal notices, and

        (iii) identify any other document that the Minister thinks the court will need to decide the appeal (and serve any such document with the notice).

(7) Where the court determines an appeal, the general rule is that it must do so at a hearing (which must be in public, unless the court otherwise directs).

(8) The court officer must serve on the Minister—

    (a) notice of the outcome of the appeal;

    (b) notice of any suspension of the disqualification; and

    (c) the appellant's driving licence, if surrendered to the court officer.

*[Note. Section 56 of the Crime (International Co-operation) Act 2003 sets out the conditions for recognition in the United Kingdom of a foreign driving disqualification, and provides that section 57 of the Act applies where they are met. Under section 57, the appropriate Minister may, and in some cases must, give the person concerned notice that he or she is disqualified in the UK, too, and for what period.*

*Under section 59 of the 2003 Act, that person may appeal to a magistrates' court. If the court is satisfied that section 57 of the Act does not apply in that person's case, the court must allow the appeal and notify the Minister. Otherwise, it must dismiss the appeal.*

*The time limit for appeal under section 59 of the 2003 Act is the end of the period of 21 days beginning with the day on which the Minister gives the notice under section 57. That period may be neither extended nor shortened.*

*Under section 60 of the 2003 Act, the court may suspend the disqualification, on such terms as it thinks fit.*

*Under section 63 of the 2003 Act[23], it is an offence for a person to whom the Minister gives a notice under section 57 not to surrender any licence that he or she holds, within the same period as for an appeal.]*

CRIMINAL PROCEDURE RULES    PART 30    ENFORCEMENT OF FINES
AND OTHER ORDERS FOR PAYMENT

*[Note. Part 13 contains rules about warrants for arrest, detention or imprisonment, including such warrants issued for failure to pay fines, etc.*

*Part 24 contains rules about the procedure on sentencing in a magistrates' court.*

*Part 28 contains rules about the exercise of a magistrates' court's powers to enforce an order made by another court.]*

**When this Part applies**                                                                                        **R30.1**

**30.1** (1) This Part applies where a magistrates' court can enforce payment of—

    (a) a fine, or a sum that legislation requires the court to treat as a fine; or

    (b) any other sum that a court has ordered to be paid—

        (i) on a conviction, or

        (ii) on the forfeiture of a surety.

---

[22] 2003 c. 32; section 60 is in force in relation only to an offence of which an offender has been convicted in Ireland. For remaining purposes, it will come into force on a date to be appointed. Section 60 was amended by section 40(4) of, and paragraph 79 of Schedule 9 to, the Constitutional Reform Act 2005 (c. 4).

[23] 2003 c. 32; section 63 is in force in relation only to an offence of which an offender has been convicted in Ireland. For remaining purposes, it will come into force on a date to be appointed. It was amended by sections 10(12) and 59 of, and paragraphs 74 and 75 of Schedule 3, and Schedule 7 to, the Road Safety Act 2006 (c. 49).

(2) Rules 30.7 to 30.9 apply where the court, or a fines officer, issues a warrant for an enforcement agent to take control of a defendant's goods and sell them, using the procedure in Schedule 12 to the Tribunals, Courts and Enforcement Act 2007[1].

(3) In this Part—

(a) 'defendant' means anyone liable to pay a sum to which this Part applies;

(b) 'payment terms' means by when, and by what (if any) instalments, such a sum must be paid.

*[Note. For the means by which a magistrates' court may enforce payment, see—*

*(a) Part 3 of the Magistrates' Courts Act 1980[2]; and*

*(b) Schedule 5 to the Courts Act 2003[3] and the Fines Collection Regulations 2006[4].*

*Under that Schedule and those Regulations, some enforcement powers may be exercised by a fines officer.*

*See also section 62 of, and Schedule 12 to, the Tribunals, Courts and Enforcement Act 2007. In that Act, a warrant to which this Part applies is described as 'a warrant of control'.]*

**R30.2    Exercise of court's powers**

30.2    The court must not exercise its enforcement powers unless—

(a) the court officer has served on the defendant any collection order or other notice of—

(i) the obligation to pay,

(ii) the payment terms, and

(iii) how and where the defendant must pay; and

(b) the defendant has failed to comply with the payment terms.

*[Note. See section 76 of the Magistrates' Courts Act 1980[5]; and paragraphs 12 and 13 of Schedule 5 to the Courts Act 2003[6].]*

**R30.3    Duty to give receipt**

30.3    (1) This rule applies where the defendant makes a payment to—

(a) the court officer specified in an order or notice served under rule 30.2;

(b) another court officer;

(c) any—

(i) custodian of the defendant,

(ii) supervisor appointed to encourage the defendant to pay, or

(iii) responsible officer appointed under a community sentence or a suspended sentence of imprisonment; or

(d) a person executing a warrant to which rule 13.6 (warrants for arrest, detention or imprisonment that cease to have effect on payment) or this Part applies.

(2) The person receiving the payment must—

(a) give the defendant a receipt unless the method of payment generates an independent record (for example, a bank record); and

(b) as soon as practicable transmit the payment to the court officer specified in an order or notice served under rule 30.2, if the recipient is not that court officer.

*[Note. For the effect of payment to a person executing a warrant to which rule 13.6 applies, see that rule and sections 79[7] and 125(1)[8] of the Magistrates' Courts Act 1980.*

---

[1] 2007 c. 15.

[2] 1980 c. 43.

[3] 2003 c. 39; Schedule 5 was amended by articles 2, 4, 6, 7 and 8 of S.I. 2006/1737, section 62 of, and paragraphs 148 and 149 of Schedule 13 to, the Tribunals, Courts and Enforcement Act 2007 (c. 15), section 80 of the Criminal Justice and Immigration Act 2008 (c. 4), section 88 of the Legal Aid, Sentencing and Punishment of Offenders Act 2012 (c. 10), section 10 of, and paragraphs 24 and 27 of the Schedule to, the Prevention of Social Housing Fraud Act 2013 (c. 3), section 27 of the Crime and Courts Act 2013 (c. 22) and section 56 of the Criminal Justice and Courts Act 2015 (c. 2). It is further amended by section 26 of the Crime and Courts Act 2013 (c. 22) and paragraph 23 of Schedule 5 to the Modern Slavery Act 2015 (c. 30), with effect from dates to be appointed.

[4] S.I. 2006/501.

[5] 1980 c. 43; section 76 was amended by section 7 of the Maintenance Enforcement Act 1991 (c. 17), section 78 of, and Schedule 16 to, the Criminal Justice Act 1982 (c. 48), and section 62(3) of, and paragraphs 45 and 46 of Schedule 13 to, the Tribunals, Courts and Enforcement Act 2007 (c. 15).

[6] 2003 c. 39; paragraph 13 was amended by articles 2, 4 and 15 of S.I. 2006/1737.

[7] 1980 c. 43; section 79 was amended by paragraph 219 of Schedule 8 to the Courts Act 2003 (c. 39) and section 62 of, and paragraphs 45, 47 and 48 of Schedule 13 to, the Tribunals, Courts and Enforcement Act 2007 (c. 15).

[8] 1980 c. 43; section 125 was amended by section 33 of the Police and Criminal Evidence Act 1984 (c. 60), section 65(1) of the Criminal Justice Act 1988 (c. 33), sections 95(1), 97(4) and 106 of, and Part V of Schedule 15 and Table (8) to, the Access to Justice Act 1999 (c. 22), section 109(1) of, and paragraph 238 of Schedule 8 to, the Courts Act 2003 (c. 39) and sections 62(3), 86 and 146 of and paragraphs 45 and 57 of Schedule 23 to, the Tribunals, Courts and Enforcement Act 2007 (c. 15).

*For the circumstances in which the court may appoint a person to supervise payment, see section 88 of the 1980 Act[9].]*

### Appeal against decision of fines officer                                          R30.4

30.4  (1)  This rule applies where—

    (a)  a collection order is in force;

    (b)  a fines officer makes a decision under one of these paragraphs of Schedule 5 to the Courts Act 2003—

       (i)   paragraph 22 (Application to fines officer for variation of order or attachment of earnings order, etc.),

       (ii)  paragraph 31[10] (Application to fines officer for variation of reserve terms), or

       (iii) paragraph 37[11] (Functions of fines officer in relation to defaulters: referral or further steps notice); and

    (c)  the defendant wants to appeal against that decision.

  (2)  Unless the court otherwise directs, the defendant must—

    (a)  appeal in writing not more than 10 business days after the decision;

    (b)  serve the appeal on the court officer; and

    (c)  in the appeal—

       (i)   explain why a different decision should be made, and

       (ii)  specify the decision that the defendant proposes.

  (3)  Where the court determines an appeal the general rule is that it must do so at a hearing.

*[Note. Under paragraph 12 of Schedule 5 to the Courts Act 2003, where a collection order is in force the court's powers to deal with the defendant's liability to pay the sum for which that order was made are subject to the provisions of that Schedule and to fines collection regulations.*

*For the circumstances in which a defendant may appeal against a decision to which this rule applies, see paragraphs 23, 32 and 37(9) of Schedule 5 to the 2003 Act[12]. The time limit for appeal is prescribed by those paragraphs. It may be neither extended nor shortened.]*

### Application to reduce a fine, vary payment terms or remit a courts charge          R30.5

30.5  (1)  This rule applies where—

    (a)  no collection order is in force; and the defendant wants the court to—

       (i)   reduce the amount of a fine, or

       (ii)  vary payment terms; or

    (b)  the defendant, a fines officer or an enforcement agent wants the court to remit a criminal courts charge.

  (2)  Unless the court otherwise directs, such a defendant, fines officer or enforcement agent must—

    (a)  apply in writing;

    (b)  serve the application on the court officer;

    (c)  if the application is to reduce a fine or vary payment terms, explain—

       (i)   what relevant circumstances have not yet been considered by the court, and

       (ii)  why the fine should be reduced, or the payment terms varied; and

    (d)  if the application is to remit a criminal courts charge, explain—

       (i)   how the circumstances meet the time limits and other conditions in section 50 of the Sentencing Act 2020[13], and

       (ii)  why the charge should be remitted.

  (3)  The court may determine an application—

    (a)  at a hearing, which may be in public or in private; or

    (b)  without a hearing.

---

[9]  1980 c. 43; section 88 was amended by paragraph 53 of Schedule 14 to the Criminal Justice Act 1982 (c. 48), paragraph 68 of Schedule 9 to the Powers of Criminal Courts (Sentencing) Act 2000 (c. 6) and section 62 of, and paragraphs 45 and 54 of Schedule 13 to, the Tribunals, Courts and Enforcement Act 2007 (c. 15). It is further amended by paragraphs 58 and 64 of Schedule 7 to the Criminal Justice and Court Services Act 2000 (c. 43) with effect from a date to be appointed.

[10]  2003 c. 39; paragraph 31 was amended by articles 2, 4 and 20 of S.I. 2006/1737.

[11]  2003 c. 39; paragraph 37 was amended by articles 2, 4 and 25(a) and (b) of S.I. 2006/1737.

[12]  2003 c. 39; paragraph 32 was amended by articles 2, 4 and 24(b) of S.I. 2006/1737.

[13]  2020 c. 17.

*[Note. See sections 75, 85 and 85A of the Magistrates' Courts Act 1980[14], sections 50 and 127 of the Sentencing Act 2020[15].*

*Under section 46 of the 2020 Act , a court must, at the times listed in sections 44 and 45 of that Act, order a defendant convicted of an offence to pay a charge in respect of relevant court costs. Under section 50 of the Act, a magistrates' court may remit the whole or part of such a charge, but—*

*(a) the court may do so only if it is satisfied that—*

    *(i) the defendant has taken all reasonable steps to pay the charge, having regard to his or her personal circumstances, or*

    *(ii) collection and enforcement of the charge is impracticable;*

*(b) the court may not do so at a time when the defendant is in prison; and*

*(c) the court may not do so unless the periods specified by regulations under section 21E all have expired.]*

**R30.6    Claim to avoid fine after penalty notice**

30.6  (1) This rule applies where—

    (a) a chief officer of police serves on the magistrates' court officer a certificate registering, for enforcement as a fine, a sum payable by a defendant after failure to comply with a penalty notice; and

    (b) the court or a fines officer enforces the fine.

  (2) A defendant who claims not to be the person to whom the penalty notice was issued must, unless the court otherwise directs—

    (a) make that claim in writing; and

    (b) serve it on the court officer.

  (3) The court officer must—

    (a) notify the chief officer of police by whom the certificate was registered; and

    (b) refer the case to the court.

  (4) Where such a claim is made—

    (a) the general rule is that the court must adjourn the enforcement for 28 days and fix a hearing; but

    (b) the court may make a different order.

  (5) At any such hearing, the chief officer of police must introduce any evidence to contradict the defendant's claim.

*[Note. See section 10 of the Criminal Justice and Police Act 2001[16].*

*For the circumstances in which a sum may be registered for enforcement as a fine after failure to comply with a penalty notice, see sections 8 and 9 of the 2001 Act[17].]*

**R30.7    Information to be included in a warrant of control**

30.7  (1) A warrant must identify—

    (a) each person to whom it is directed;

    (b) the defendant against whom it was issued;

    (c) the sum for which it was issued and the reason that sum is owed;

    (d) the court or fines officer who issued it, unless that is otherwise recorded by the court officer; and

    (e) the court office for the court or fines officer who issued it.

  (2) A person to whom a warrant is directed must record on it the date and time at which it is received.

  (3) A warrant that contains an error is not invalid, as long as—

---

[14]  1980 c. 43; section 75 was amended by section 11 of, and paragraph 6 of Schedule 2 to, the Maintenance Enforcement Act 1991 (c. 17). Section 85 was substituted by section 61 of the Criminal Justice Act 1988 (c. 33) and amended by section 55 of, and paragraph 10(2) of Schedule 4 to, the Crime (Sentences) Act 1997 (c. 43), section 109(1) of, and paragraph 222 of Schedule 8 to, the Courts Act 2003 (c. 39) and section 179 of the Anti-social Behaviour, Crime and Policing Act 2014 (c. 12). It is further amended by paragraphs 25 and 28 of Schedule 32 to the Criminal Justice Act 2003 (c. 44) and section 26 of the Crime and Courts Act 2013 (c. 22), with effect from dates to be appointed. Section 85A was inserted by section 51(1) of the Criminal Justice Act 1982 (c. 48).

[15]  2020 c. 17.

[16]  2001 c. 16; section 10 was amended by paragraphs 1 and 10 of Schedule 23 to the Legal Aid, Sentencing and Punishment of Offenders Act 2012 (c. 10).

[17]  2001 c. 16; section 8 was amended by section 109(1) of, and paragraph 399 of Schedule 8 to, the Courts Act 2003 (c. 39). Section 9 was amended by section 109(1) of, and paragraph 400(1) (2) (3) and (4) of Schedule 8 to, the Courts Act 2003 (c. 39).

(a)  it was issued in respect of a lawful decision by the court or fines officer; and

(b)  it contains enough information to identify that decision.

*[Note. See sections 78 and 125ZA of the Magistrates' Courts Act 1980[18].]*

**Warrant of control: application by enforcement agent for extension of time, etc.**    **R30.8**

30.8   (1)  This rule applies where an enforcement agent wants the court to exercise a power under Schedule 12 to the Tribunals, Courts and Enforcement Act 2007[19], or under regulations made under that Schedule, to—

(a)  shorten or extend a time limit;

(b)  give the agent authority to—

(i)  enter premises which the agent would not otherwise have authority to enter,

(ii)  enter or remain on premises at a time at which the agent would not otherwise have authority to be there,

(iii)  use reasonable force, in circumstances in which the agent would not otherwise have authority to use such force,

(iv)  sell goods by a method which the agent would not otherwise have authority to use, or

(v)  recover disbursements which the agent would not otherwise have authority to recover;

(c)  specify the manner in which goods which have not been sold must be disposed of.

(2)  Such an enforcement agent must—

(a)  apply in writing;

(b)  serve the application on the court officer; and

(c)  pay any fee prescribed.

(3)  The application must—

(a)  identify the power that the agent wants the court to exercise;

(b)  explain how the conditions for the exercise of that power are satisfied, including any condition that requires the agent to give another person notice of the application;

(c)  specify those persons, if any, to whom the agent has given notice in accordance with such a condition; and

(d)  propose the terms of the order that the agent wants the court to make.

(4)  A person to whom the enforcement agent has given notice of an application and who wants to make representations to the court must—

(a)  serve the representations on—

(i)  the court officer,

(ii)  the enforcement agent, and

(iii)  any other person to whom the enforcement agent gave notice;

(b)  do so as soon as reasonably practicable and in any event within such period as the court directs; and

(c)  in the representations, propose the terms of the order that that person wants the court to make, and explain why.

(5)  The court—

(a)  must not determine an application unless any person to whom the enforcement agent gave notice—

(i)  is present, or

(ii)  has had a reasonable opportunity to respond; but

(b)  subject to that, may determine an application—

(i)  at a hearing, which must be in private unless the court otherwise directs, or

(ii)  without a hearing.

*[Note. See paragraphs 8, 15, 20, 21, 25, 31, 32 and 41 of Schedule 12 to the Tribunals, Courts and Enforcement Act 2007[20], regulations 6, 9, 13, 22, 25, 28, 29, 41 and 47 of the Taking Control of Goods Regulations 2013[21] and regulation 10 of the Taking Control of Goods (Fees) Regulations 2014[22]. Under paragraph 41 of that Schedule and regulation 41 of the 2013 Regulations, on an application for authority to sell*

---

[18]  1980 c. 43; section 78 was amended by sections 37 and 46 of the Criminal Justice Act 1982 (c. 48) and paragraph 219 of Schedule 8 to, the Courts Act 2003 (c. 39). Section 125ZA was inserted by section 68 of the Tribunals, Courts and Enforcement Act 2007 (c. 15).

[19]  2007 c. 15

[20]  2007 c. 15. Paragraph 31 of Schedule 12 was amended by section 25(1), (5) of the Crime and Courts Act 2013 (c. 22). Paragraphs 60 and 66 of Schedule 12 were amended by paragraph 52 of Schedule 9 to the Crime and Courts Act 2013 (c. 22).

[21]  S.I. 2013/1894.

[22]  S.I. 2014/1.

*goods otherwise than by public auction the enforcement agent must give notice to a creditor of the defendant in the circumstances described in those provisions.]*

**R30.9   Warrant of control: application to resolve dispute**

30.9   (1)   This rule applies where a defendant's goods are sold using the procedure in Schedule 12 to the Tribunals, Courts and Enforcement Act 2007 and there is a dispute about—

(a)   what share of the proceeds of those goods should be paid by the enforcement agent to a co-owner; or

(b)   the fees or disbursements sought or recovered by the enforcement agent out of the proceeds.

(2)   An enforcement agent, a defendant or a co-owner who wants the court to resolve the dispute must—

(a)   apply in writing as soon as practicable after becoming aware of the grounds for doing so;

(b)   serve the application on—

(i)   the court officer,

(ii)   each other party to the dispute, and

(iii)   any other co-owner; and

(c)   pay any fee prescribed.

(3)   The application must—

(a)   identify the warrant of control;

(b)   specify the goods sold, the proceeds, and the fees and disbursements sought or recovered by the enforcement agent;

(c)   identify the power that the applicant wants the court to exercise;

(d)   specify the persons served with the application;

(e)   explain the circumstances of the dispute; and

(f)   propose the terms of the order that the applicant wants the court to make.

(4)   A person served with an application who wants to make representations to the court must—

(a)   serve the representations on—

(i)   the court officer,

(ii)   the applicant, and

(iii)   any other person on whom the application was served;

(b)   do so as soon as reasonably practicable and in any event within such period as the court directs; and

(c)   in the representations, propose the terms of the order that that person wants the court to make, and explain why.

(5)   The court—

(a)   must determine an application at a hearing, which must be in private unless the court otherwise directs;

(b)   must not determine an application unless each party—

(i)   is present, or

(ii)   has had a reasonable opportunity to attend.

*[Note. See paragraph 50 of Schedule 12 to the Tribunals, Courts and Enforcement Act 2007[23], and regulations 15 and 16 of the Taking Control of Goods (Fees) Regulations 2014[24].]*

Criminal Procedure Rules     Part 31     Behaviour Orders

*[Note. See Part 3 for the court's general powers to consider an application and to give directions.]*

**R31.1   When this Part applies**

31.1   (1)   This Part applies where a magistrates' court or the Crown Court can make, vary, renew, discharge or revoke a civil order—

(a)   as well as, or instead of, passing a sentence, or in any other circumstances in which other legislation allows the court to make such an order; and

(b)   that requires someone to do, or not do, something

(2)   A reference to a 'behaviour order' in this Part is a reference to any such order.

(3)   A reference to 'hearsay evidence' in this Part is a reference to evidence consisting of hearsay within the meaning of section 1(2) of the Civil Evidence Act 1995[1].

*[Note. In the circumstances set out in the Acts listed, the court can make a behaviour order—*

[23]   2007 c. 15.
[24]   S.I. 2014/1.
[1]   1995 c. 38.

(a)  on conviction, under—
    (i)  section 14A of the Football Spectators Act 1989[2] (football banning orders),
    (ii)  section 360 of the Sentencing Act 2020[3] (restraining orders),
    (iii)  sections 1C and 1D of the Crime and Disorder Act 1998[4] (anti-social behaviour orders and interim anti-social behaviour orders),
    (iv)  section 366 of the 2020 Act (parenting orders),
    (v)  section 345 of the 2020 Act (sexual harm prevention orders),
    (vi)  section 19 or 21 of the Serious Crime Act 2007[5] (serious crime prevention orders),
    (vii)  section 331 of the 2020 Act (criminal behaviour orders),
    (viii)  section 14 of the Modern Slavery Act 2015[6] (slavery and trafficking prevention orders),
    (ix)  section 19 of the Psychoactive Substances Act 2016[7] (prohibition orders),
    (x)  section 20 of the Immigration Act 2016[8] (labour market enforcement orders),
    (xi)  section 19 of the Offensive Weapons Act 2019[9] (knife crime prevention orders);
(b)  on acquittal, under section 5A of the Protection from Harassment Act 1997[10] (restraining orders on acquittal);
(c)  on the making of a finding of not guilty by reason of insanity, or a finding of disability, under section 14 of the Modern Slavery Act 2015 (slavery and trafficking prevention orders); and
(d)  in proceedings for a genital mutilation offence, under paragraph 3 of Schedule 2 to the Female Genital Mutilation Act 2003[11] (female genital mutilation protection orders).

Section 1(2) of the Civil Evidence Act 1995 defines hearsay as meaning 'a statement made otherwise than by a person while giving oral evidence in the proceedings which is tendered as evidence of the matters stated'. Section 13 of that Act defines a statement as meaning 'any representation of fact or opinion, however made'.]

**Behaviour orders: general rules**                                           R31.2

31.2  (1)  The court must not make a behaviour order unless the person to whom it is directed has had an opportunity—
    (a)  to consider—
        (i)  what order is proposed and why, and
        (ii)  the evidence in support; and
    (b)  to make representations at a hearing (whether or not that person in fact attends).
    (2)  That restriction does not apply to making an interim behaviour order, but unless other legislation otherwise provides such an order has no effect unless the person to whom it is directed—
    (a)  is present when it is made; or
    (b)  is handed a document recording the order not more than 5 business days after it is made
    (3)  Where the court decides not to make, where it could—
    (a)  a football banning order; or
    (b)  a parenting order, after a person under 16 is convicted of an offence,
    the court must announce, at a hearing in public, the reasons for its decision.

[Note. The Acts listed in the note to rule 31.1 impose requirements specific to each different type of behaviour order. Not all allow the court to make an interim behaviour order.

See section 14A(3) of the Football Spectators Act 1989[12], and section 366 of the Sentencing Act 2020.]

---

[2]  1989 c. 37; section 14A was amended by section 1 of, and paragraphs 1 and 2 of Schedule 1 to, the Football (Disorder) Act 2000 (c. 25), section 86(5) of the Anti-Social Behaviour Act 2003 (c. 38), section 139(10) of the Serious Organised Crime and Police Act 2005 (c. 15) and sections 52(2) and 65 of, and paragraphs 1 and 2 of Schedule 3 and Schedule 5 to, the Violent Crime Reduction Act 2006 (c. 38).

[3]  2020 c. 17.

[4]  1998 c. 37; section 1C was inserted by section 64 of the Police Reform Act 2002 (c. 30) and amended by sections 83 and 86 of the Anti-social Behaviour Act 2003 (c. 38), sections 139, 140, 141 and 174 of, and Part 2 of Schedule 17 to, the Serious Organised Crime and Police Act 2005 (c. 15) and sections 123 and 124 of the Criminal Justice and Immigration Act 2008 (c. 4). Section 1D was inserted by section 65 of the Police Reform Act 2002 (c. 30) and amended by section 139 of the Serious Organised Crime and Police Act 2005 (c. 15). Each section was repealed on 20th October, 2014, by section 181 of, and paragraph 24 of Schedule 11 to, the Anti-social Behaviour, Crime and Policing Act 2014 (c. 12), subject to the saving provisions of section 33 of that Act.

[5]  2007 c. 27; section 21 was amended by section 48 of the Serious Crime Act 2015 (c. 9).

[6]  2015 c. 30.

[7]  2016 c. 2.

[8]  2016 c. 19.

[9]  2019 c. 17; section 19 comes into force on a date to be appointed.

[10]  1997 c. 40; section 5A was inserted by section 12(5) of the Domestic Violence, Crime and Victims Act 2004 (c. 28).

[11]  2003 c. 31; Schedule 2 was inserted by section 73 of the Serious Crime Act 2015 (c. 9).

[12]  1989 c. 37; section 14A was substituted, together with sections 14 and 14B-14J, for the existing sections 14-17, by section 1 of, and paragraphs 1 and 2 of Schedule 1 to, the Football (Disorder) Act 2000 (c. 25).

**R31.3**    **Application for behaviour order and notice of terms of proposed order: special rules**

**31.3**   (1)   This rule applies where—

     (a)   a prosecutor wants the court to make one of the following orders if the defendant is convicted—

         (i)   an anti-social behaviour order (but this rule does not apply to an application for an interim anti-social behaviour order),

         (ii)   a serious crime prevention order,

         (iii)   a criminal behaviour order,

         (iv)   a prohibition order; or

         (v)   a knife crime prevention order;

     (b)   a prosecutor proposes, on the prosecutor's initiative or at the court's request, a sexual harm prevention order if the defendant is convicted; or

     (c)   a prosecutor proposes a restraining order whether the defendant is convicted or acquitted.

   (2)   Where paragraph (1)(a) applies (order on application), the prosecutor must serve a notice of intention to apply for such an order on—

     (a)   the court officer;

     (b)   the defendant against whom the prosecutor wants the court to make the order; and

     (c)   any person on whom the order would be likely to have a significant adverse effect, as soon as practicable (without waiting for the verdict).

   (3)   A notice under paragraph (2) must—

     (a)   summarise the relevant facts;

     (b)   identify the evidence on which the prosecutor relies in support;

     (c)   attach any written statement that the prosecutor has not already served; and

     (d)   specify the order that the prosecutor wants the court to make.

   (4)   A defendant served with a notice under paragraph (2) must—

     (a)   serve notice of any evidence on which the defendant relies on—

         (i)   the court officer, and

         (ii)   the prosecutor,

         as soon as practicable (without waiting for the verdict); and

     (b)   in the notice, identify that evidence and attach any written statement that has not already been served.

   (5)   Where paragraph (1)(b) applies (sexual harm prevention order proposed), the prosecutor must—

     (a)   serve a draft order on the court officer and on the defendant not less than 2 business days before the hearing at which the order may be made; and

     (b)   in the draft order specify those prohibitions which the prosecutor proposes as necessary for the purpose of—

         (i)   protecting the public or any particular members of the public from sexual harm from the defendant, or

         (ii)   protecting children or vulnerable adults generally, or any particular children or vulnerable adults, from sexual harm from the defendant outside the United Kingdom.

   (6)   Where paragraph (1)(c) applies (restraining order proposed), the prosecutor must—

     (a)   serve a draft order on the court officer and on the defendant as soon as practicable (without waiting for the verdict); and

     (b)   in the draft order specify—

         (i)   those prohibitions which, if the defendant is convicted, the prosecutor proposes for the purpose of protecting a person from conduct which amounts to harassment or will cause fear of violence, or

         (ii)   those prohibitions which, if the defendant is acquitted, the prosecutor proposes as necessary to protect a person from harassment by the defendant.

   (7)   Where the prosecutor wants the court to make an anti-social behaviour order, a criminal behaviour order or a prohibition order, the rules about special measures directions in Part 18 (Measures to assist a witness or defendant to give evidence) apply, but—

     (a)   the prosecutor must apply when serving a notice under paragraph (2); and

     (b)   the time limits in rule 18.4(a) do not apply.

*[Note. The Practice Direction sets out a form of notice for use in connection with this rule.*

*The orders listed in rule 31.3(1)(a) may be made on application by the prosecutor. The orders to which rule 31.3(1)(b) and (c) apply require no application and may be made on the court's own initiative. Under section 8 of the Serious Crime Act 2007 a serious crime prevention order may be made only on an application by the Director of Public Prosecutions or the Director of the Serious Fraud Office. See also paragraphs 2, 7 and 13 of Schedule 2 to the 2007 Act.*

*Under section 1I of the Crime and Disorder Act 1998[13], on an application for an anti-social behaviour order the court may give a special measures direction under the Youth Justice and Criminal Evidence Act 1999. Under section 340 of the Sentencing Act 2020[14] the court may give such a direction on an application for a criminal behaviour order, and under section 33 of the Psychoactive Substances Act 2016[15] the court may do so in proceedings for a prohibition order.*

*If a party relies on hearsay evidence, see also rules 31.6, 31.7, and 31.8.]*

**Evidence to assist the court: special rules**                                    R31.4

31.4  (1)  This rule applies where the court can make on its own initiative—
  (a)  a football banning order;
  (b)  a restraining order; or
  (c)  an anti-social behaviour order.
(2)  A party who wants the court to take account of evidence not already introduced must—
  (a)  serve notice on—
    (i)  the court officer, and
    (ii)  every other party,
    as soon as practicable (without waiting for the verdict); and
  (b)  in the notice, identify that evidence; and
  (c)  attach any written statement containing such evidence.

*[Note. If a party relies on hearsay evidence, see also rules 31.6, 31.7, and 31.8.]*

**Application to vary, renew, discharge or revoke behaviour order**                 R31.5

31.5  (1)  The court may vary, renew, discharge or revoke a behaviour order if—
  (a)  the legislation under which it is made allows the court to do so; and
  (b)  one of the following applies—
    (i)  the prosecutor,
    (ii)  the person to whom the order is directed,
    (iii) any other person protected or affected by the order,
    (iv)  the relevant authority or responsible officer,
    (v)  the relevant Chief Officer of Police,
    (vi)  the Director of Public Prosecutions, or
    (vii) the Director of the Serious Fraud Office.
(2)  A person applying under this rule must—
  (a)  apply in writing as soon as practicable after becoming aware of the grounds for doing so, explaining—
    (i)  what material circumstances have changed, if any, since the order was made, and
    (ii)  why the order should be varied, renewed, discharged or revoked, by reference to the legislation under which it was made;
  (b)  in every case, serve the application on—
    (i)  the court officer, and
    (ii)  the prosecutor (unless the prosecutor is the person applying under this rule);
  (c)  unless the order was a restraining order, serve the application on, as appropriate—
    (i)  the person to whom the order was directed, and
    (ii)  any other person protected or affected by the order; and
  (d)  serve the application on any other person if the court so directs
(3)  A party who wants the court to take account of any particular evidence before making its decision must, as soon as practicable—
  (a)  in every case, serve notice on—
    (i)  the court officer, and
    (ii)  the prosecutor (unless the prosecutor is the party serving the notice);
  (b)  unless the order was a restraining order, serve the notice on, as appropriate—
    (i)  the person to whom the order was directed, and
    (ii)  any other person protected or affected by the order;
  (c)  serve the notice on any other person if the court so directs; and
  (d)  in that notice identify the evidence and attach any written statement that has not already been served,
(4)  The court may decide an application under this rule—

[13] 1998 c. 37; section 1I was inserted by section 143 of the Serious Organised Crime and Police Act 2005 (c. 15) and amended by paragraph 72 of Schedule 21 and Part 3 of Schedule 23 to the Coroners and Justice Act 2009 (c. 25).
[14] 2014 c. 12.
[15] 2020 c. 17.

(a) at a hearing, in public or in private; or

(b) without a hearing, if the legislation under which the order was made so allows.

(5) But the court must not—

    (a) dismiss an application under this rule unless the applicant has had an opportunity to make representations at a hearing (whether or not the applicant in fact attends); or

    (b) allow an application under this rule unless everyone required to be served, by this rule or by the court, has had at least 10 business days in which to make representations, including representations about whether there should be a hearing if none is otherwise required.

(6) The court officer must—

    (a) if the order was a restraining order, serve the application under this rule on—

        (i) as appropriate, the person to whom the order was directed and any other person protected or affected by the order, and

        (ii) the relevant Chief Officer of Police;

    (b) serve the application on any other person if the court so directs;

    (c) serve any notice of evidence received by the court officer under paragraph (3) on—

        (i) each person, if any, on whom the court officer serves the application under this rule, and

        (ii) any other person if the court so directs; and

    (d) give notice of any hearing to—

        (i) the applicant, and

        (ii) any person required to be served, by this rule or by the court.

*[Note. The legislation that gives the court power to make a behaviour order may limit the circumstances in which it may be varied, renewed, discharged or revoked and may require a hearing. Under section 22E of the Serious Crime Act 2007[16], where a person already subject to a serious crime prevention order is charged with a serious offence or with an offence of failing to comply with the order, the court may vary the order so that it continues in effect until that prosecution concludes.*

*Under section 26 of the Offensive Weapons Act 2019[17], where the court has made a knife crime prevention order the court may require the applicant and the defendant to attend one or more review hearings to consider whether the order should be varied or discharged. Where a requirement or prohibition imposed by the knife crime prevention order is to have effect after the end of one year from the date the order is made, the court must convene such a review on a specified date within the last 4 weeks of that year.*

*If a party relies on hearsay evidence, see also rules 31.6, 31.7 and 31.8.]*

**R31.6**    **Notice of hearsay evidence**

**31.6**   (1) A party who wants to introduce hearsay evidence must—

    (a) serve notice on—

        (i) the court officer, and

        (ii) every other party directly affected; and

    (b) in that notice—

        (i) explain that it is a notice of hearsay evidence,

        (ii) identify that evidence,

        (iii) identify the person who made the statement which is hearsay, or explain why if that person is not identified, and

        (iv) explain why that person will not be called to give oral evidence.

(2) A party may serve one notice under this rule in respect of more than one notice and more than one witness.

*[Note. For the time within which to serve a notice of hearsay evidence, see rule 31.3(2) to (4), rule 31.4(2) and rule 31.5(3). See also the requirement in section 2 of the Civil Evidence Act 1995 for reasonable and practicable notice of a proposal to introduce hearsay evidence.*

*Rules 31.6, 31.7 and 31.8 broadly correspond with rules 3, 4 and 5 of the Magistrates' Courts (Hearsay Evidence in Civil Proceedings) Rules 1999[18], which apply in civil proceedings in magistrates' courts. Rule 3 of the 1999 Rules however includes a time limit, which may be varied by the court, or a justices' legal adviser, of 21 days before the date fixed for the hearing, for service of a hearsay notice.]*

---

[16] 2007 c. 27; section 22E was inserted by section 49 of the Serious Crime Act 2015 (c. 9).

[17] 2019 c. 17; section 26 comes into force on a date to be appointed.

[18] S.I. 1999/681, amended by S.I. 2005/617.

**Cross-examination of maker of hearsay statement** R31.7

31.7 (1) This rule applies where a party wants the court's permission to cross-examine a person who made a statement which another party wants to introduce as hearsay.

(2) The party who wants to cross-examine that person must—

(a) apply in writing, with reasons, not more than 5 business days after service of the notice of hearsay evidence; and

(b) serve the application on—

(i) the court officer,

(ii) the party who served the hearsay evidence notice, and

(iii) every party on whom the hearsay evidence notice was served.

(3) The court may decide an application under this rule with or without a hearing.

(4) But the court must not—

(a) dismiss an application under this rule unless the applicant has had an opportunity to make representations at a hearing (whether or not the applicant in fact attends); or

(b) allow an application under this rule unless everyone served with the application has had at least 5 business days in which to make representations, including representations about whether there should be a hearing.

*[Note. See also section 3 of the Civil Evidence Act 1995.]*

**Credibility and consistency of maker of hearsay statement** R31.8

31.8 (1) This rule applies where a party wants to challenge the credibility or consistency of a person who made a statement which another party wants to introduce as hearsay.

(2) The party who wants to challenge the credibility or consistency of that person must—

(a) serve notice of intention to do so on—

(i) the court officer, and

(ii) the party who served the notice of hearsay evidence

not more than 5 business days after service of that hearsay evidence notice; and

(b) in the notice, identify any statement or other material on which that party relies.

(3) The party who served the hearsay notice—

(a) may call that person to give oral evidence instead; and

(b) if so, must serve notice of intention to do so on—

(i) the court officer, and

(ii) every party on whom the hearsay notice was served

not more than 5 business days after service of the notice under paragraph (2).

*[Note. Section 5(2) of the Civil Evidence Act 1995 describes the procedure for challenging the credibility of the maker of a statement of which hearsay evidence is introduced. See also section 6 of that Act. The 1995 Act does not allow the introduction of evidence of a previous inconsistent statement otherwise than in accordance with sections 5, 6 and 7 of the Criminal Procedure Act 1865[19].]*

**Court's power to vary requirements under this Part** R31.9

31.9 Unless other legislation otherwise provides, the court may—

(a) shorten a time limit or extend it (even after it has expired);

(b) allow a notice or application to be given in a different form, or presented orally. And

(c) dispense with a requirement for service (even after service was required).

CRIMINAL PROCEDURE RULES    PART 32    BREACH, REVOCATION AND AMENDMENT OF
COMMUNITY AND OTHER ORDERS

**When this Part applies** R32.1

32.1 This Part applies where—

(a) the person responsible for a defendant's compliance with an order to which applies—

(i) Schedule 5, 7, 10 or 16 to the Sentencing Act 2020[1], or

(ii) the Schedule to the Street Offences Act 1959[2],

wants the court to deal with that defendant for failure to comply;

---

[19] 1865 c. 18; section 6 was amended by section 10 of the Decimal Currency Act 1969 (c. 19), section 90 of, and paragraph 3 of Schedule 13 to, the Access to Justice Act 1999 (c. 22), section 109 of, and paragraph 47 of Schedule 8 to, the Courts Act 2003 (c. 39) and paragraph 79 of Schedule 36 and Schedule 37 to the Criminal Justice Act 2003 (c. 44). It is further amended by section 119 of, and Schedule 7 to, the Police and Criminal Evidence Act 1984 (c. 60), with effect from a date to be appointed.

[1] 2020 c. 17.

[2] 1959 c. 57; Schedule: Orders under section 1(2A) was inserted by section 17(1) and (4) of the Policing and Crime Act 2009 (c. 26).

(b) one of the following wants the court to exercise any power it has to revoke or amend such an order—
    (i)   the responsible officer or supervisor,
    (ii)  the defendant, or
    (iii) where the legislation allows, a person affected by the order; or
(c) the court considers exercising on its own initiative any power it has to revoke or amend such an order.

*[Note. In the Sentencing Act 2020—*

    *(a) Schedule 5 deals with the breach, revocation and amendment of reparation orders;*
    *(b) Schedule 7 deals with the breach, revocation and amendment of youth rehabilitation orders;*
    *(c) Schedule 10 deals with the breach, revocation and amendment of community orders; and*
    *(d) Schedule 16 deals with the breach or amendment of suspended sentence orders, and the effect of a further conviction.]*

## R32.2   Application by responsible officer or supervisor

32.2  (1)  This rule applies where—
    (a) the responsible officer or supervisor wants the court to—
        (i)   deal with a defendant for failure to comply with an order to which this Part applies, or
        (ii)  revoke or amend such an order; or
    (b) the court considers exercising on its own initiative any power it has to—
        (i)   revoke or amend such an order, and
        (ii)  summon the defendant to attend for that purpose.
(2)  Rules 7.2 to 7.4, which deal, among other things, with starting a prosecution in a magistrates' court, apply—
    (a) as if—
        (i)   a reference in those rules to an allegation of an offence included a reference to an allegation of failure to comply with an order to which this Part applies, and
        (ii)  a reference to the prosecutor included a reference to the responsible officer or supervisor; and
    (b) with the necessary consequential modifications.

## R32.3   Application by defendant or person affected

32.3  (1)  This rule applies where—
    (a) the defendant wants the court to exercise any power it has to revoke or amend an order to which this Part applies; or
    (b) where the legislation allows, a person affected by such an order wants the court to exercise any such power.
(2)  That defendant, or person affected, must—
    (a) apply in writing, explaining why the order should be revoked or amended; and
    (b) serve the application on—
        (i)   the court officer,
        (ii)  the responsible officer or supervisor, and
        (iii) as appropriate, the defendant or the person affected.

## R32.4   Procedure on application by responsible officer or supervisor

32.4  (1)  Except for rules 24.8 (Written guilty plea; special rules) and 24.9 (Single justice procedure: special rules), the rules in Part 24, which deal with the procedure at a trial in a magistrates' court, apply—
    (a) as if—
        (i)   a reference in those rules to an allegation of an offence included a reference to an allegation of failure to comply with an order to which this Part applies,
        (ii)  a reference to the court's verdict included a reference to the court's decision to revoke or amend such an order, or to exercise any other power it has to deal with the defendant, and
        (iii) a reference to the court's sentence included a reference to the exercise of any such power; and
    (b) with the necessary consequential modifications.
(2)  The court officer must serve on each party any order revoking or amending an order to which this Part applies.

CRIMINAL PROCEDURE RULES    PART 33    CONFISCATION AND RELATED PROCEEDINGS

## General rules

### Interpretation
R33.1

**33.1** In this Part: words and expressions used have the same meaning as in Part 2 of the Proceeds of Crime Act 2002 and:

'document' means anything in which information of any description is recorded;

'hearsay evidence' means evidence consisting of hearsay within the meaning of section 1(2) of the Civil Evidence Act 1995[1];

'restraint proceedings' means proceedings under sections 42 and 58(2) and (3) of the Proceeds of Crime Act 2002[2];

'receivership proceedings' means proceedings under sections 48, 49, 50, 51, 54(4), 59(2) and (3), 62 and 63 of the 2002 Act[3];

'witness statement' means a written statement signed by a person which contains the evidence, and only that evidence, which that person would be allowed to give orally.

### Calculation of time
R33.2

**33.2** (1) This rule shows how to calculate any period of time for doing any act which is specified by this Part for the purposes of any proceedings under Part 2 of the Proceeds of Crime Act 2002 or by an order of the Crown Court in restraint proceedings or receivership proceedings.

(2) A period of time expressed as a number of days shall be computed as clear days.

(3) In this rule 'clear days' means that in computing the number of days—

    (a) the day on which the period begins; and

    (b) if the end of the period is defined by reference to an event, the day on which that event occurs,

    are not included.

(4) Where the specified period is 5 days or less and includes a day which is not a business day that day does not count.

### Court office closed
R33.3

**33.3** When the period specified by this Part, or by an order of the Crown Court under Part 2 of the Proceeds of Crime Act 2002, for doing any act at the court office falls on a day on which the office is closed, that act shall be in time if done on the next day on which the court office is open.

### Application for registration of Scottish or Northern Ireland order
R33.4

**33.4** (1) This rule applies to an application for registration of an order under article 6 of the Proceeds of Crime Act 2002 (Enforcement in different parts of the United Kingdom) Order 2002[4].

(2) The application may be made without notice.

(3) The application must be in writing and may be supported by a witness statement which must—

    (a) exhibit the order or a certified copy of the order; and

    (b) to the best of the witness's ability, give full details of the realisable property located in England and Wales in respect of which the order was made and specify the person holding that realisable property.

(4) If the court registers the order, the applicant must serve notice of the registration on—

    (a) any person who holds realisable property to which the order applies; and

    (b) any other person whom the applicant knows to be affected by the order.

(5) The permission of the Crown Court under rule 33.10 (Service outside the jurisdiction) is not required to serve the notice outside England and Wales.

### Application to vary or set aside registration
R33.5

**33.5** (1) An application to vary or set aside registration of an order under article 6 of the Proceeds of Crime Act 2002 (Enforcement in different parts of the United Kingdom) Order 2002 may be made to the Crown Court by—

    (a) any person who holds realisable property to which the order applies; and

    (b) any other person affected by the order.

---

[1] 1995 c. 38.

[2] 2002 c. 29; section 42 was amended by sections 74(2) and 92 of, and paragraphs 1 and 23 of Schedule 8, and Schedule 14 to, the Serious Crime Act 2007 (c. 27). Section 58(2) was amended by section 62(3) of, and paragraphs 142 and 143 of Schedule 13 to, the Tribunals, Courts and Enforcement Act 2007 (c. 15).

[3] 2002 c. 29; sections 49, 62 and 63 were amended by sections 74 and 82(1) of, and paragraphs 1, 29 and 30 of Schedule 8 to, the Serious Crime Act (c. 27). Section 59(2) was amended by section 62(3) of, and paragraphs 142 and 144 of Schedule 13 to, the Tribunals, Courts and Enforcement Act 2007 (c. 15).

[4] S.I. 2002/3133.

(2) The application must be in writing and may be supported by a witness statement.

(3) The application and any witness statement must be lodged with the Crown Court.

(4) The application must be served on the person who applied for registration at least 7 days before the date fixed by the court for hearing the application, unless the Crown Court specifies a shorter period.

(5) No property in England and Wales may be realised in pursuance of the order before the Crown Court has decided the application.

### R33.6　Register of orders

33.6 (1) The Crown Court must keep, under the direction of the Lord Chancellor, a register of the orders registered under article 6 of the Proceeds of Crime Act 2002 (Enforcement in different parts of the United Kingdom) Order 2002.

(2) The register must include details of any variation or setting aside of a registration under rule 33.5 and of any execution issued on a registered order.

(3) If the person who applied for registration of an order which is subsequently registered notifies the Crown Court that the court which made the order has varied or discharged the order, details of the variation or discharge, as the case may be, must be entered in the register.

### R33.7　Statements of truth

33.7 (1) Any witness statement required to be served by this Part must be verified by a statement of truth contained in the witness statement.

(2) A statement of truth is a declaration by the person making the witness statement to the effect that the witness statement is true to the best of his knowledge and belief and that he made the statement knowing that, if it were tendered in evidence, he would be liable to prosecution if he wilfully stated in it anything which he knew to be false or did not believe to be true.

(3) The statement of truth must be signed by the person making the witness statement.

(4) If the person making the witness statement fails to verify the witness statement by a statement of truth, the Crown Court may direct that it shall not be admissible as evidence.

### R33.8　Use of witness statements for other purposes

33.8 (1) Except as provided by this rule, a witness statement served in proceedings under Part 2 of the Proceeds of Crime Act 2002 may be used only for the purpose of the proceedings in which it is served.

(2) Paragraph (1) does not apply if and to the extent that—

(a) the witness gives consent in writing to some other use of it;

(b) the Crown Court gives permission for some other use; or

(c) the witness statement has been put in evidence at a hearing held in public.

### R33.9　Service of documents

33.9 (1) Rule 49.1 (Notice required to accompany process served outside the United Kingdom and translations) shall not apply in restraint proceedings and receivership proceedings.

(2) An order made in restraint proceedings or receivership proceedings may be enforced against the defendant or any other person affected by it notwithstanding that service of a copy of the order has not been effected in accordance with Part 4 if the Crown Court is satisfied that the person had notice of the order by being present when the order was made.

### R33.10　Service outside the jurisdiction

33.10 (1) Where this Part requires a document to be served on someone who is outside England and Wales, it may be served outside England and Wales with the permission of the Crown Court.

(2) Where a document is to be served outside England and Wales it may be served by any method permitted by the law of the country in which it is to be served.

(3) Nothing in this rule or in any court order shall authorise or require any person to do anything in the country where the document is to be served which is against the law of that country.

(4) Where this Part requires a document to be served a certain period of time before the date of a hearing and the recipient does not appear at the hearing, the hearing must not take place unless the Crown Court is satisfied that the document has been duly served.

### R33.11　Certificates of service

33.11 (1) Where this Part requires that the applicant for an order in restraint proceedings or receivership proceedings serve a document on another person, the applicant must lodge a certificate of service with the Crown Court within 7 days of service of the document.

(2) The certificate must state—

(a) the method of service;

(b) the date of service; and

(c) if the document is served under rule 4.9 (Service by another method), such other information as the court may require when making the order permitting service by that method.

(3) Where a document is to be served by the Crown Court in restraint proceedings and receivership proceedings and the court is unable to serve it, the court must send a notice of non-service stating the method attempted to the party who requested service.

### External requests and orders                                                    R33.12

33.12 (1) The rules in this Part and in Part 42 (Appeal to the Court of Appeal in confiscation and related proceedings) apply with the necessary modifications to proceedings under the Proceeds of Crime Act 2002 (External Requests and Orders) Order 2005[5] in the same way that they apply to corresponding proceedings under Part 2 of the Proceeds of Crime Act 2002[6].

(2) This table shows how provisions of the 2005 Order correspond with provisions of the 2002 Act.

| Article of the Proceeds of Crime Act 2002 (External Requests and Orders) Order 2005 | Section of the Proceeds of Crime Act 2002 |
|---|---|
| 8 | 41 |
| 9 | 42 |
| 10 | 43 |
| 11 | 44 |
| 15 | 48 |
| 16 | 49 |
| 17 | 58 |
| 23 | 31 |
| 27 | 50 |
| 28 | 51 |
| 41 | 62 |
| 42 | 63 |
| 44 | 65 |
| 45 | 66 |

### Confiscation proceedings

### Statements in connection with confiscation orders                                R33.13

33.13 (1) This rule applies where—
    (a) the court can make a confiscation order; and
    (b) the prosecutor asks the court to make such an order, or the court decides to make such an order on its own initiative.

(2) Within such periods as the court directs—
    (a) if the court so orders, the defendant must give such information, in such manner, as the court directs;
    (b) the prosecutor must serve a statement of information relevant to confiscation on the court officer and the defendant; and
    (c) if the court so directs—
        (i) the defendant must serve a response notice on the court officer and the prosecutor, and
        (ii) the parties must identify what is in dispute.

(3) Where it appears to the court that a person other than the defendant holds, or may hold, an interest in property held by the defendant which property is likely to be realised or otherwise used to satisfy a confiscation order—
    (a) the court must not determine the extent of the defendant's interest in that property unless that other person has had a reasonable opportunity to make representations; and
    (b) the court may order that other person to give such information, in such manner and within such a period, as the court directs.

(4) The court may—

---

[5] S.I. 2005/3181.
[6] 2002 c. 29.

Criminal Procedure Rules and Criminal Practice Directions

     (a)   shorten or extend a time limit which it has set;

     (b)   vary, discharge or supplement an order which it has made; and

     (c)   postpone confiscation proceedings without a hearing.

(5)  A prosecutor's statement of information must—

     (a)   identify the maker of the statement and show its date;

     (b)   identify the defendant in respect of whom it is served;

     (c)   specify the conviction which gives the court power to make the confiscation order, or each conviction if more than one;

     (d)   if the prosecutor believes the defendant to have a criminal lifestyle, include such matters as the prosecutor believes to be relevant in connection with deciding—

        (i)   whether the defendant has such a lifestyle,

        (ii)   whether the defendant has benefited from his or her general criminal conduct,

        (iii)  the defendant's benefit from that conduct, and

        (iv)  whether the court should or should not make such assumptions about the defendant's property as legislation permits;

     (e)   if the prosecutor does not believe the defendant to have a criminal lifestyle, include such matters as the prosecutor believes to be relevant in connection with deciding—

        (i)   whether the defendant has benefited from his or her particular criminal conduct, and

        (ii)  the defendant's benefit from that conduct; and

     (f)   in any case, include such matters as the prosecutor believes to be relevant in connection with deciding—

        (i)   whether to make a determination about the extent of the defendant's interest in property in which another person holds, or may hold, an interest, and

        (ii)  what determination to make, if the court decides to make one.

(6)  A defendant's response notice must—

     (a)   indicate the extent to which the defendant accepts the allegations made in the prosecutor's statement of information; and

     (b)   so far as the defendant does not accept an allegation, give particulars of any matters on which the defendant relies, in any manner directed by the court.

(7)  The court must satisfy itself that there has been explained to the defendant, in terms the defendant can understand (with help, if necessary)—

     (a)   that if the defendant accepts to any extent an allegation in a prosecutor's statement of information, then the court may treat that as conclusive for the purposes of deciding whether the defendant has benefited from general or particular criminal conduct, and if so by how much;

     (b)   that if the defendant fails in any respect to comply with a direction to serve a response notice, then the court may treat that as acceptance of each allegation to which the defendant has not replied, except the allegation that the defendant has benefited from general or particular criminal conduct; and

     (c)   that if the defendant fails without reasonable excuse to comply with an order to give information, then the court may draw such inference as it believes is appropriate.

*[Note. Under section 6 of the Proceeds of Crime Act 2002[7], where a defendant is convicted of an offence the Crown Court must (with some exceptions)—*

    *(a)   decide whether the defendant has 'a criminal lifestyle', within the meaning of the Act, or has benefited from particular criminal conduct;*

    *(b)   decide the 'recoverable amount', within the meaning of the Act; and*

    *(c)   make a confiscation order requiring the defendant to pay that amount.*

*Under section 14 of the 2002 Act[8], unless exceptional circumstances apply the court may postpone confiscation proceedings for a maximum of 2 years from the date of conviction, or until the end of a period of 3 months following the determination of an appeal by the defendant against conviction, if that is later.*

---

[7]  2002 c. 29; section 6 was amended by paragraph 75 of Schedule 3 to the Criminal Justice Act 2003 (c. 44), section 74(2) of, and paragraphs 1 and 2 of Schedule 8 to, the Serious Crime Act 2007 (c. 27) and section 10 of, and paragraphs 11 and 12 of the Schedule to, the Prevention of Social Housing Fraud Act 2013 (c. 3).

[8]  2002 c. 29; section 14 was amended by section 74(2) of, and paragraphs 1 and 4 of Schedule 8 to, the Serious Crime Act 2007 (c. 27).

*Under section 16 of the 2002 Act[9], where the Crown Court is considering confiscation the prosecutor must give the court a statement of information which the prosecutor believes to be relevant to what the court must decide, within such period as the court directs. Under section 17 of the Act[10], where the prosecutor gives such a statement the court may order the defendant to respond and, if the defendant does not do so, then the court may treat the defendant as accepting the prosecutor's allegations. Under section 18[11], for the purpose of obtaining information to help it in carrying out its functions the court may at any time order the defendant to give it information specified in the order and, if the defendant does not do so, then the court may draw such inference as it believes appropriate. Under section 18A[12], for the purpose of obtaining information to help it to determine the extent of the defendant's interest in property the court may at any time order a person who the court thinks may hold an interest in that property to give it information specified in the order and, if that person does not do so, then the court may draw such inference as it believes appropriate.*

*Under section 27 of the 2002 Act[13], special provisions apply where the defendant absconds.*

*Under section 97 of the Serious Organised Crime and Police Act 2005[14], the Secretary of State may by order provide for confiscation orders to be made by magistrates' courts.]*

## Application for compliance order                                                   R33.14

**33.14** (1)  This rule applies where—

    (a)  the prosecutor wants the court to make a compliance order after a confiscation order has been made;

    (b)  the prosecutor or a person affected by a compliance order wants the court to vary or discharge the order.

(2)  Such a prosecutor or person must—

    (a)  apply in writing; and

    (b)  serve the application on—

        (i)  the court officer, and

        (ii)  as appropriate, the prosecutor and any person who is affected by the compliance order (or who would be affected if it were made), unless the court otherwise directs.

(3)  The application must—

    (a)  specify—

        (i)  the confiscation order, and

        (ii)  the compliance order, if it is an application to vary or discharge that order;

    (b)  if it is an application for a compliance order—

        (i)  specify each measure that the prosecutor proposes to ensure that the confiscation order is effective, including in particular any restriction or prohibition on the defendant's travel outside the United Kingdom, and

        (ii)  explain why each such measure is appropriate;

    (c)  if it is an application to vary or discharge a compliance order, as appropriate—

        (i)  specify any proposed variation, and

        (ii)  explain why it is appropriate for the order to be varied or discharged;

    (d)  attach any material on which the applicant relies;

    (e)  propose the terms of the order; and

    (f)  ask for a hearing, if the applicant wants one, and explain why it is needed.

(4)  A person who wants to make representations about the application must—

    (a)  serve the representations on—

        (i)  the court officer, and

        (ii)  the applicant;

    (b)  do so as soon as reasonably practicable after service of the application;

    (c)  attach any material on which that person relies; and

    (d)  ask for a hearing, if that person wants one, and explain why it is needed.

(5)  The court—

---

[9]  2002 c. 29; section 16 was amended by section 74(2) of, and paragraphs 1 and 5 of Schedule 8 to, the Serious Crime Act 2007 (c. 27) and section 2 of the Serious Crime Act 2015 (c. 9).

[10]  2002 c. 29; section 17 was amended by section 74(2) of, and paragraphs 1 and 6 of Schedule 8 to, the Serious Crime Act 2007 (c. 27).

[11]  2002 c. 29; section 18 was amended by section 74(2) of, and paragraphs 1 and 7 of Schedule 8 to, the Serious Crime Act 2007 (c. 27).

[12]  2002 c. 29; section 18A was inserted by section 2 of the Serious Crime Act 2015 (c. 9).

[13]  2002 c. 29; section 27 was amended by paragraph 75 of Schedule 3 to the Criminal Justice Act 2003 (c. 44) and section 74 of, and paragraphs 1 and 14 of Schedule 8 to, the Serious Crime Act 2007 (c. 27).

[14]  2005 c. 15; section 97 was amended by S.I. 2010/976.

(f) state the amount which the bank or building society is required to pay to the court officer under the payment order;

(g) give the name and address of the court officer to whom payment is to be made; and

(h) require the bank or building society to make payment within a period of 7 days beginning on the day on which the payment order is made, unless it appears to the court that a longer or shorter period would be appropriate in the particular circumstances.

(2) In this rule 'confiscation order' has the meaning given to it by section 88(6) of the Proceeds of Crime Act 2002.

**R33.25**  **Application to realise seized property**

33.25 (1) This rule applies where—

(a) property is held by a defendant against whom a confiscation order has been made;

(b) the property has been seized by or produced to an officer; and

(c) an officer who is entitled to apply wants a magistrates' court—

(i) to make an order under section 67A of the Proceeds of Crime Act 2002[27] authorising the realisation of the property towards satisfaction of the confiscation order, or

(ii) to determine any storage, insurance or realisation costs in respect of the property which may be recovered under section 67B of the 2002 Act[28].

(2) Such an officer must—

(a) apply in writing; and

(b) serve the application on—

(i) the court officer, and

(ii) any person whom the applicant believes would be affected by an order.

(3) The application must—

(a) specify the property;

(b) explain—

(i) the applicant's entitlement to apply,

(ii) how the proposed realisation meets the conditions prescribed by section 67A of the 2002 Act, and

(iii) how any storage, etc. costs have been calculated;

(c) attach any material on which the applicant relies; and

(d) propose the terms of the order.

(4) The court may—

(a) determine the application at a hearing, or without a hearing;

(b) consider an application made orally instead of in writing; and

(c) consider an application which has not been served on a person likely to be affected by an order.

(5) If the court authorises the realisation of the property, the applicant must—

(a) notify any person affected by the order who was absent when it was made; and

(b) serve on the court officer a list of those so notified.

*[Note. Under section 67A of the Proceeds of Crime Act 2002, one of the officers listed in section 41A of the Act may apply to a magistrates' court for authority to realise property seized by such an officer if—*

*(a) a confiscation order has been made against the owner of the property;*

*(b) no receiver has been appointed in relation to that property; and*

*(c) any period allowed for payment of the confiscation order has expired.*

*Under section 67B of the 2002 Act, if a magistrates' court makes an order under section 67A then on the same or a subsequent occasion the court may determine an amount which may be recovered by the applicant in respect of reasonable costs incurred in storing or insuring the property, or realising it.]*

**R33.26**  **Appeal about decision on application to realise seized property**

33.26 (1) This rule applies where on an application under rule 33.25 for an order authorising the realisation of property—

(a) a magistrates' court decides not to make such an order and an officer who is entitled to apply wants to appeal against that decision to the Crown Court, under section 67C(1) of the Proceeds of Crime Act 2002[29];

---

[27] 2002 c. 29; section 67A was inserted by section 58 of the Policing and Crime Act 2009 (c. 26) and amended by section 14 of the Serious Crime Act 2015 (c. 9).

[28] 2002 c. 29; section 67B was inserted by section 58 of the Policing and Crime Act 2009 (c. 26).

[29] 2002 c. 29; section 67C was inserted by section 58 of the Policing and Crime Act 2009 (c. 26).

(b) a magistrates' court makes such an order and a person who is affected by that decision, other than the defendant against whom the confiscation order was made, wants to appeal against it to the Crown Court, under section 67C(2) of the 2002 Act; or

(c) a magistrates' court makes a decision about storage, etc. costs and an officer who is entitled to apply wants to appeal against that decision to the Crown Court, under section 67C(4) of the 2002 Act.

(2) The appellant must serve an appeal notice—

(a) on the Crown Court officer and on any other party; and

(b) not more than 21 days after the magistrates' court's decision, or, if applicable, service of notice under rule 33.25(5).

(3) The appeal notice must—

(a) specify the decision under appeal;

(b) where paragraph (1)(a) applies, explain why the property should be realised;

(c) in any other case, propose the order that the appellant wants the court to make, and explain why.

(4) Rule 34.11 (Constitution of the Crown Court) applies on such an appeal.

*[Note. Under section 67C of the Proceeds of Crime Act 2002, an officer entitled to apply for an order under section 67A or 67B of that Act (authority to realise seized property towards satisfaction of a confiscation order; determination of storage, etc. costs) may appeal against a refusal to make an order, or against a costs determination; and a person affected by an order, other than the owner, may appeal against the order.]*

**Application for direction about surplus proceeds**                                   **R33.27**

**33.27** (1) This rule applies where—

(a) on an application under rule 33.25, a magistrates' court has made an order authorising an officer to realise property;

(b) an officer so authorised holds proceeds of that realisation;

(c) the confiscation order has been fully paid; and

(d) the officer, or a person who had or has an interest in the property represented by the proceeds, wants a magistrates' court or the Crown Court to determine under section 67D of the Proceeds of Crime Act 2002[30]—

(i) to whom the remaining proceeds should be paid, and

(ii) in what amount or amounts.

(2) Such a person must—

(a) apply in writing; and

(b) serve the application on—

(i) the court officer, and

(ii) as appropriate, the officer holding the proceeds, or any person to whom such proceeds might be paid.

(3) The application must—

(a) specify the property which was realised;

(b) explain the applicant's entitlement to apply;

(c) describe the distribution proposed by the applicant and explain why that is proposed;

(d) attach any material on which the applicant relies; and

(e) ask for a hearing, if the applicant wants one, and explain why it is needed.

(4) A person who wants to make representations about the application must—

(a) serve the representations on—

(i) the court officer,

(ii) the applicant, and

(iii) any other person to whom proceeds might be paid;

(b) do so as soon as reasonably practicable after service of the application;

(c) attach any material on which that person relies; and

(d) ask for a hearing, if that person wants one, and explain why it is needed.

(5) The court—

(a) must not determine the application unless the applicant and each person on whom it was served—

(i) is present, or

(ii) has had an opportunity to attend or to make representations; but

(b) subject to that, may determine the application—

(i) at a hearing (which must be in private unless the court otherwise directs), or without a hearing,

(ii) in the absence of any party to the application.

---

[30] 2002 c. 29; section 67D was inserted by section 58 of the Policing and Crime Act 2009 (c. 26).

*[Note. Under section 67D of the Proceeds of Crime Act 2002, a magistrates' court or the Crown Court may determine to whom, and in what proportions, any surplus proceeds of realisation must be distributed. Once a magistrates' court has made such a determination, the Crown Court may not do so, and vice versa.]*

### Seizure and detention proceedings

**R33.28**     **Application for approval to seize property or to search**

33.28 (1) This rule applies where an officer who is entitled to apply wants the approval of a magistrates' court, under section 47G of the Proceeds of Crime Act 2002[31]—

    (a) to seize property, under section 47C of that Act[32]; or

    (b) to search premises or a person or vehicle for property to be seized, under section 47D, 47E or 47F of that Act[33].

(2) Such an officer must—

    (a) apply in writing; and

    (b) serve the application on the court officer.

(3) The application must—

    (a) explain—

        (i) the applicant's entitlement to apply, and

        (ii) how the proposed seizure meets the conditions prescribed by sections 47B, 47C and, if applicable, 47D, 47E or 47F of the 2002 Act[34];

    (b) if applicable, specify any premises, person or vehicle to be searched;

    (c) attach any material on which the applicant relies; and

    (d) propose the terms in which the applicant wants the court to give its approval.

(4) The court—

    (a) must determine the application—

        (i) at a hearing, which must be in private unless the court otherwise directs, and

        (ii) in the applicant's presence; but

    (b) may consider an application made orally instead of in writing.

*[Note. Under section 47C of the Proceeds of Crime Act 2002, if any of the conditions listed in section 47B of the Act are met then one of the officers listed in section 47A may seize property other than cash or exempt property, as defined in the section, if that officer has reasonable grounds for suspecting that—*

*    (a) the property may otherwise be made unavailable for satisfying any confiscation order that has been or may be made against a defendant; or*

*    (b) the value of the property may otherwise be diminished as a result of conduct by the defendant or any other person.*

*Under sections 47D, 47E and 47F of the 2002 Act, such an officer may search premises, a person or a vehicle, respectively, for such property, on the conditions listed in those sections.*

*By sections 47C(6), 47D(2), 47E(4), 47F(6) and 47G of the 2002 Act, such an officer may seize property, and may search for it, only with the approval of a magistrates' court or, if that is impracticable, the approval of a senior officer (as defined by section 47G), unless in the circumstances it is not practicable to obtain the approval of either.]*

**R33.29**     **Application to extend detention period**

33.29 (1) This rule applies where an officer who is entitled to apply, or the prosecutor, wants a magistrates' court to make an order, under section 47M of the Proceeds of Crime Act 2002[35], extending the period for which seized property may be detained.

(2) Such an officer or prosecutor must—

    (a) apply in writing; and

    (b) serve the application on—

        (i) the court officer, and

        (ii) any person whom the applicant believes would be affected by an order.

(3) The application must—

---

[31] 2002 c. 29; section 47G was inserted by section 55 of the Policing and Crime Act 2009 (c. 26) and amended by section 55 of, and paragraphs 14 and 17 of Schedule 21 to, the Crime and Courts Act 2013 (c. 22) and section 13 of the Serious Crime Act 2015 (c. 9).

[32] 2002 c. 29; section 47C was inserted by section 55 of the Policing and Crime Act 2009 (c. 26) and amended by section 55 of, and paragraphs 14 and 16 of Schedule 21 to, the Crime and Courts Act 2013

[33] 2002 c. 29; sections 47D, 47E and 47F were inserted by section 55 of the Policing and Crime Act 2009 (c. 26).

[34] 2002 c. 29; section 47B was inserted by section 55 of the Policing and Crime Act 2009 (c. 26) and amended by section 13 of the Serious Crime Act 2015 (c. 9).

[35] 2002 c. 29; section 47M was inserted by section 55 of the Policing and Crime Act 2009 (c. 26) and amended by section 55 of, and paragraphs 14 and 18 of Schedule 21 to, the Crime and Courts Act 2013 (c. 22).

      (a) specify—
          (i) the property to be detained, and
          (ii) whether the applicant wants it to be detained for a specified period or indefinitely;
      (b) explain—
          (i) the applicant's entitlement to apply, and
          (ii) how the proposed detention meets the conditions prescribed by section 47M of the 2002 Act;
      (c) attach any material on which the applicant relies; and
      (d) propose the terms of the order.
  (4) The court—
      (a) must determine the application—
          (i) at a hearing, which must be in private unless the court otherwise directs, and
          (ii) in the applicant's presence; but
      (b) may—
          (i) consider an application made orally instead of in writing,
          (ii) require service of the application on the court officer after it has been heard, instead of before.
  (5) If the court extends the period for which the property may be detained, the applicant must—
      (a) notify any person affected by the order who was absent when it was made; and
      (b) serve on the court officer a list of those so notified.

*[Note. Under section 47M of the Proceeds of Crime Act 2002, one of the officers listed in that section, or the prosecutor, may apply to a magistrates' court for an order extending the period of 48 hours for which, under section 47J of the Act[36], property seized under section 47C may be detained.*

*On an application to which this rule applies, hearsay evidence within the meaning of section 1(2) of the Civil Evidence Act 1995 is admissible: see section 47Q of the 2002 Act[37].]*

### Application to vary or discharge order for extended detention       R33.30

**33.30** (1) This rule applies where an officer who is entitled to apply, the prosecutor, or a person affected by an order to which rule 33.29 applies, wants a magistrates' court to vary or discharge that order, under section 47N of the Proceeds of Crime Act 2002[38].
  (2) Such a person must—
      (a) apply in writing; and
      (b) serve the application on—
          (i) the court officer, and
          (ii) as appropriate, the applicant for the order, or any person affected by the order.
  (3) The application must—
      (a) specify the order and the property detained;
      (b) explain—
          (i) the applicant's entitlement to apply,
          (ii) why it is appropriate for the order to be varied or discharged,
          (iii) if applicable, on what grounds the court must discharge the order;
      (c) attach any material on which the applicant relies;
      (d) if applicable, propose the terms of any variation; and
      (e) ask for a hearing, if the applicant wants one, and explain why it is needed.
  (4) A person who wants to make representations about the application must—
      (a) serve the representations on—
          (i) the court officer, and
          (ii) the applicant;
      (b) do so as soon as reasonably practicable after service of the application;
      (c) attach any material on which that person relies; and
      (d) ask for a hearing, if that person wants one, and explain why it is needed.
  (5) The court—
      (a) must not determine the application unless the applicant and each person on whom it was served—
          (i) is present, or
          (ii) has had an opportunity to attend or to make representations; but
      (b) subject to that, may determine the application—

---

[36] 2002 c. 29; section 47J was inserted by section 55 of the Policing and Crime Act 2009 (c. 26).
[37] 2002 c. 29; section 47Q was inserted by section 55 of the Policing and Crime Act 2009 (c. 26).
[38] 2002 c. 29; section 47N was inserted by section 55 of the Policing and Crime Act 2009 (c. 26).

(i)   at a hearing (which must be in private unless the court otherwise directs), or without a hearing,

(ii)  in the absence of any party to the application.

*[Note. Under section 47N of the Proceeds of Crime Act 2002, one of the officers listed in section 47M of the Act, the prosecutor, or a person affected by an order under section 47M, may apply to a magistrates' court for the order to be varied or discharged. Section 47N(3) lists the circumstances in which the court must discharge such an order.*

*On an application to which this rule applies, hearsay evidence within the meaning of section 1(2) of the Civil Evidence Act 1995 is admissible: see section 47Q of the 2002 Act.]*

### R33.31  Appeal about property detention decision

**33.31** (1)  This rule applies where—

(a)  on an application under rule 33.29 for an order extending the period for which property may be detained—

(i)   a magistrates' court decides not to make such an order, and

(ii)  an officer who is entitled to apply for such an order, or the prosecutor, wants to appeal against that decision to the Crown Court under section 47O(1) of the Proceeds of Crime Act 2002[39];

(b)  on an application under rule 33.30 to vary or discharge an order under rule 33.29—

(i)   a magistrates' court determines the application, and

(ii)  a person who is entitled to apply under that rule wants to appeal against that decision to the Crown Court under section 47O(2) of the 2002 Act.

(2)  The appellant must serve an appeal notice—

(a)  on the Crown Court officer and on any other party; and

(b)  not more than 21 days after the magistrates' court's decision, or, if applicable, service of notice under rule 33.29(5).

(3)  The appeal notice must—

(a)  specify the decision under appeal;

(b)  where paragraph (1)(a) applies, explain why the detention period should be extended;

(c)  where paragraph (1)(b) applies, propose the order that the appellant wants the court to make, and explain why.

(4)  Rule 34.11 (Constitution of the Crown Court) applies on such an appeal.

*[Note. Under section 47O of the Proceeds of Crime Act 2002, one of those entitled to apply for an order under section 47M of that Act (extension of detention of property) may appeal against a refusal to make an order, and one of those entitled to apply for the variation or discharge of such an order, under section 47N of that Act, may appeal against the decision on such an application.*

*On an appeal to which this rule applies, hearsay evidence within the meaning of section 1(2) of the Civil Evidence Act 1995 is admissible: see section 47Q of the 2002 Act.]*

### Restraint and receivership proceedings: rules that apply generally

### R33.32  Taking control of goods and forfeiture

**33.32** (1)  This rule applies to applications under sections 58(2) and (3) and 59(2) and (3) of the Proceeds of Crime Act 2002[40] for leave of the Crown Court to take control of goods or levy distress against property, or to exercise a right of forfeiture by peaceable re-entry in relation to a tenancy, in circumstances where the property or tenancy is the subject of a restraint order or a receiver has been appointed in respect of the property or tenancy.

(2)  The application must be made in writing to the Crown Court.

(3)  The application must be served on—

(a)  the person who applied for the restraint order or the order appointing the receiver; and

(b)  any receiver appointed in respect of the property or tenancy,

at least 7 days before the date fixed by the court for hearing the application, unless the Crown Court specifies a shorter period.

### R33.33  Joining of applications

**33.33** An application for the appointment of a management receiver or enforcement receiver under rule 33.56 may be joined with—

---

[39]  2002 c. 29; section 47O was inserted by section 55 of the Policing and Crime Act 2009 (c. 26).
[40]  2002 c. 29; section 58(2) was amended by section 62(3) of, and paragraphs 142 and 143 of Schedule 13 of the Tribunals, Courts and Enforcement Act 2007 (c. 15).

(a)  an application for a restraint order under rule 33.51; and

(b)  an application for the conferral of powers on the receiver under rule 33.57.

### Applications to be dealt with in writing                                    R33.34

33.34 Applications in restraint proceedings and receivership proceedings are to be dealt with without a hearing, unless the Crown Court orders otherwise.

### Business in chambers                                                          R33.35

33.35 Restraint proceedings and receivership proceedings may be heard in chambers.

### Power of court to control evidence                                            R33.36

33.36 (1)  When hearing restraint proceedings and receivership proceedings, the Crown Court may control the evidence by giving directions as to—

(a)  the issues on which it requires evidence;

(b)  the nature of the evidence which it requires to decide those issues; and

(c)  the way in which the evidence is to be placed before the court.

(2)  The court may use its power under this rule to exclude evidence that would otherwise be admissible.

(3)  The court may limit cross-examination in restraint proceedings and receivership proceedings.

### Evidence of witnesses                                                         R33.37

33.37 (1)  The general rule is that, unless the Crown Court orders otherwise, any fact which needs to be proved in restraint proceedings or receivership proceedings by the evidence of a witness is to be proved by their evidence in writing.

(2)  Where evidence is to be given in writing under this rule, any party may apply to the Crown Court for permission to cross-examine the person giving the evidence.

(3)  If the Crown Court gives permission under paragraph (2) but the person in question does not attend as required by the order, his evidence may not be used unless the court gives permission.

### Witness summons                                                               R33.38

33.38 (1)  Any party to restraint proceedings or receivership proceedings may apply to the Crown Court to issue a witness summons requiring a witness to—

(a)  attend court to give evidence; or

(b)  produce documents to the court.

(2)  Rule 17.3 (Application for summons, warrant or order: general rules) applies to an application under this rule as it applies to an application under section 2 of the Criminal Procedure (Attendance of Witnesses) Act 1965[41].

### Hearsay evidence                                                              R33.39

33.39 Section 2(1) of the Civil Evidence Act 1995[42] (duty to give notice of intention to rely on hearsay evidence) does not apply to evidence in restraint proceedings and receivership proceedings.

### Disclosure and inspection of documents                                        R33.40

33.40 (1)  This rule applies where, in the course of restraint proceedings or receivership proceedings, an issue arises as to whether property is realisable property.

(2)  The Crown Court may make an order for disclosure of documents.

(3)  Part 31 of the Civil Procedure Rules 1998[43] as amended from time to time shall have effect as if the proceedings were proceedings in the High Court.

### Court documents                                                               R33.41

33.41 (1)  Any order which the Crown Court issues in restraint proceedings or receivership proceedings must—

(a)  state the name and judicial title of the person who made it;

(b)  bear the date on which it is made; and

(c)  be sealed by the Crown Court.

(2)  The Crown Court may place the seal on the order—

(a)  by hand; or

(b)  by printing a facsimile of the seal on the order whether electronically or otherwise.

---

[41]  1965 c. 69; section 2 was substituted, together with sections 2 A to 2E, by section 66 of the Criminal Procedure and Investigations Act 1996 (c. 25) and amended by section 119 of, and paragraph 8 of Schedule 8 to, the Crime and Disorder Act 1998 (c. 37), section 109 of, and paragraph 126 of Schedule 8 to, the Courts Act 2003 (c. 39), paragraph 42 of Schedule 3 and Part 4 of Schedule 37 to the Criminal Justice Act 2003 (c. 44), section 169 of the Serious Organised Crime and Police Act 2005 (c. 15) and paragraph 33 of Schedule 17 to the Crime and Courts Act 2013 (c. 22).

[42]  1995 c. 38.

[43]  S.I. 1998/3132; amending instruments relevant to this Part are S.I. 2000/221 and 2001/4015.

(3) A document purporting to bear the court's seal shall be admissible in evidence without further proof.

**R33.42  Consent orders**

33.42 (1) This rule applies where all the parties to restraint proceedings or receivership proceedings agree the terms in which an order should be made.

(2) Any party may apply for a judgment or order in the terms agreed.

(3) The Crown Court may deal with an application under paragraph (2) without a hearing.

(4) Where this rule applies—

(a) the order which is agreed by the parties must be drawn up in the terms agreed;

(b) it must be expressed as being 'By Consent'; and

(c) it must be signed by the legal representative acting for each of the parties to whom the order relates or by the party if he is a litigant in person.

(5) Where an application is made under this rule, then the requirements of any other rule as to the procedure for making an application do not apply.

**R33.43  Slips and omissions**

33.43 (1) The Crown Court may at any time correct an accidental slip or omission in an order made in restraint proceedings or receivership proceedings.

(2) A party may apply for a correction without notice.

**R33.44  Supply of documents from court records**

33.44 (1) No document relating to restraint proceedings or receivership proceedings may be supplied from the records of the Crown Court for any person to inspect or copy unless the Crown Court grants permission.

(2) An application for permission under paragraph (1) must be made on notice to the parties to the proceedings.

**R33.45  Disclosure of documents in criminal proceedings**

33.45 (1) This rule applies where—

(a) proceedings for an offence have been started in the Crown Court and the defendant has not been either convicted or acquitted on all counts; and

(b) an application for a restraint order under section 42(1) of the Proceeds of Crime Act 2002 has been made.

(2) The judge presiding at the proceedings for the offence may be supplied from the records of the Crown Court with documents relating to restraint proceedings and any receivership proceedings.

(3) Such documents must not otherwise be disclosed in the proceedings for the offence.

**R33.46  Preparation of documents**

33.46 (1) Every order in restraint proceedings or receivership proceedings must be drawn up by the Crown Court unless—

(a) the Crown Court orders a party to draw it up;

(b) a party, with the permission of the Crown Court, agrees to draw it up; or

(c) the order is made by consent under rule 33.42.

(2) The Crown Court may direct that—

(a) an order drawn up by a party must be checked by the Crown Court before it is sealed; or

(b) before an order is drawn up by the Crown Court, the parties must lodge an agreed statement of its terms.

(3) Where an order is to be drawn up by a party—

(a) he must lodge it with the Crown Court no later than 7 days after the date on which the court ordered or permitted him to draw it up so that it can be sealed by the Crown Court; and

(b) if he fails to lodge it within that period, any other party may draw it up and lodge it.

(4) Nothing in this rule shall require the Crown Court to accept a document which is illegible, has not been duly authorised, or is unsatisfactory for some other similar reason.

**R33.47  Order for costs**

33.47 (1) This rule authorises the Crown Court, in addition to its other powers, to order a party to pay another party's costs in restraint or receivership proceedings.

(2) The court may make such an order—

(a) on application by the party who incurred the costs; or

(b) on its own initiative.

(3) A party who wants the court to make such an order must apply—

(a)  during the proceedings; or

(b)  as soon as practicable following the conclusion of the proceedings, and in any event within 28 days of that conclusion.

(4)  Where the court is deciding whether to make such an order it has discretion as to—

(a)  whether costs are payable by one party to another;

(b)  the amount of those costs; and

(c)  when they are to be paid.

(5)  If the court decides to make an order about costs—

(a)  the general rule is that the unsuccessful party must be ordered to pay the costs of the successful party; but

(b)  the court may make a different order.

(6)  In deciding what order (if any) to make about costs, the court must have regard to all of the circumstances, including—

(a)  the conduct of all the parties; and

(b)  whether a party has succeeded on part of an application, even if he has not been wholly successful.

(7)  The orders which the court may make include an order that a party must pay—

(a)  a proportion of another party's costs;

(b)  a stated amount in respect of another party's costs;

(c)  costs from or until a certain date only;

(d)  costs incurred before proceedings have begun;

(e)  costs relating to particular steps taken in the proceedings;

(f)  costs relating only to a distinct part of the proceedings; and

(g)  interest on costs from or until a certain date, including a date before the making of an order.

(8)  Where the court would otherwise consider making an order under paragraph (7)(f), it must instead, if practicable, make an order under paragraph (7)(a) or (c).

(9)  Where the court has ordered a party to pay costs, it may order an amount to be paid on account before the costs are assessed.

(10) The court may extend the time limit under paragraph (3)(b) even after it has expired

*[Note. See section 52 of the Senior Courts Act 1981[44].]*

**Assessment of costs**    **R33.48**

**33.48** (1)  Where the Crown Court has made an order for costs in restraint proceedings or receivership proceedings it may either—

(a)  make an assessment of the costs itself; or

(b)  order assessment of the costs under rule 45.11.

(2)  In either case, the Crown Court or the assessing authority, as the case may be, must—

(a)  only allow costs which are proportionate to the matters in issue; and

(b)  resolve any doubt which it may have as to whether the costs were reasonably incurred or reasonable and proportionate in favour of the paying party.

(3)  The Crown Court or the assessing authority, as the case may be, is to have regard to all the circumstances in deciding whether costs were proportionately or reasonably incurred or proportionate and reasonable in amount.

(4)  In particular, the Crown Court or the assessing authority must give effect to any orders which have already been made.

(5)  The Crown Court or the assessing authority must also have regard to—

(a)  the conduct of all the parties, including in particular, conduct before, as well as during, the proceedings;

(b)  the amount or value of the property involved;

(c)  the importance of the matter to all the parties;

(d)  the particular complexity of the matter or the difficulty or novelty of the questions raised;

(e)  the skill, effort, specialised knowledge and responsibility involved;

(f)  the time spent on the application; and

(g)  the place where and the circumstances in which work or any part of it was done.

---

[44]  1981 c. 54; section 52 was amended by section 31 of, and Part II of Schedule 1 to, the Prosecution of Offences Act 1985 (c. 23), section 4 of the Courts and Legal Services Act 1990 (c. 41), article 3 and paragraphs 11 and 12(a) of the Schedule to S.I. 2004/2035 and section 59 of, and paragraph 26 of Schedule 11 to, the Constitutional Reform Act 2005 (c. 4). The Act's title was amended by section 59(5) of, and paragraph 1 of Schedule 11 to, the Constitutional Reform Act 2005 (c. 4).

**R33.49    Time for complying with an order for costs**

**33.49** A party to restraint proceedings or receivership proceedings must comply with an order for the payment of costs within 14 days of—

    (a)  the date of the order if it states the amount of those costs;

    (b)  if the amount of those costs is decided later under rule 45.11, the date of the assessing authority's decision; or

    (c)  in either case, such later date as the Crown Court may specify.

**R33.50    Application of costs rules**

**33.50** Rules 33.47, 33.48 and 33.49 do not apply to the assessment of costs in proceedings to the extent that section 11 of the Access to Justice Act 1999[45] applies and provisions made under that Act make different provision.

*Restraint proceedings*

**R33.51    Application for restraint order or ancillary order**

**33.51** (1)  This rule applies where the prosecutor, or an accredited financial investigator, makes an application under section 42 of the Proceeds of Crime Act 2002[46] for—

    (a)  a restraint order, under section 41(1) of the 2002 Act; or

    (b)  an ancillary order, under section 41(7) of that Act, for the purpose of ensuring that a restraint order is effective.

    (2)  The application may be made without notice if the application is urgent or if there are reasonable grounds for believing that giving notice would cause the dissipation of realisable property which is the subject of the application.

    (3)  An application for a restraint order must be in writing and supported by a witness statement which must—

        (a)  give the grounds for the application;

        (b)  to the best of the witness' ability, give full details of the realisable property in respect of which the applicant is seeking the order and specify the person holding that realisable property;

        (c)  include the proposed terms of the order.

    (4)  An application for an ancillary order must be in writing and supported by a witness statement which must—

        (a)  give the grounds for, and full details of, the application;

        (b)  include, if appropriate—

            (i)  any request for an order for disclosure of documents to which rule 33.40 applies (Disclosure and inspection of documents),

            (ii)  the identity of any person whom the applicant wants the court to examine about the extent or whereabouts of realisable property,

            (iii)  a list of the main questions that the applicant wants to ask any such person, and

            (iv)  a list of any documents to which the applicant wants to refer such a person; and

        (c)  include the proposed terms of the order.

    (5)  An application for a restraint order and an application for an ancillary order may (but need not) be made at the same time and contained in the same documents.

    (6)  An application by an accredited financial investigator must include a statement that, under section 68 of the 2002 Act[47], the applicant has authority to apply.

**R33.52    Restraint and ancillary orders**

**33.52** (1)  The Crown Court may make a restraint order subject to exceptions, including, but not limited to, exceptions for reasonable living expenses and reasonable legal expenses, and for the purpose of enabling any person to carry on any trade, business or occupation.

    (2)  But the Crown Court must not make an exception for legal expenses where this is prohibited by section 41(4) of the Proceeds of Crime Act 2002.

    (3)  An exception to a restraint order may be made subject to conditions.

    (4)  The Crown Court must not require the applicant for a restraint order to give any undertaking relating to damages sustained as a result of the restraint order by a person who is prohibited from dealing with realisable property by the restraint order.

---

[45]  1999 c. 22; section 11 was repealed by section 39 of, and paragraph 51 of Schedule 5 to, the Legal Aid, Sentencing and Punishment of Offenders Act 2012 (c. 10) with saving and transitional provisions made by regulations 6, 7 and 8 of S.I. 2013/534.

[46]  2002 c. 29; section 42 was amended by sections 74(2) and 92 of, and paragraphs 1 and 23 of Schedule 8, and Schedule 14 to, the Serious Crime Act 2007 (c. 27) and section 12 of the Serious Crime Act 2015 (c. 9).

[47]  2002 c. 29; section 68 was amended by section 50 of the Commissioners for Revenue and Customs Act 2005 (c. 11).

(5)  The Crown Court may require the applicant for a restraint order to give an undertaking to pay the reasonable expenses of any person, other than a person who is prohibited from dealing with realisable property by the restraint order, which are incurred in complying with the restraint order.

(6)  An order must include a statement that disobedience of the order, either by a person to whom the order is addressed, or by another person, may be contempt of court and the order must include details of the possible consequences of being held in contempt of court.

(7)  Unless the Crown Court otherwise directs, an order made without notice has effect until the court makes an order varying or discharging it.

(8)  The applicant for an order must—

    (a)  serve copies of the order and of the witness statement made in support of the application on the defendant and any person who is prohibited by the order from dealing with realisable property; and

    (b)  notify any person whom the applicant knows to be affected by the order of its terms.

**Application for discharge or variation of restraint or ancillary order by a person affected by the order**      **R33.53**

33.53 (1)  This rule applies where a person affected by a restraint order makes an application to the Crown Court under section 42(3) of the Proceeds of Crime Act 2002 to discharge or vary the restraint order or any ancillary order made under section 41(7) of the Act.

(2)  The application must be in writing and may be supported by a witness statement.

(3)  The application and any witness statement must be lodged with the Crown Court.

(4)  The application and any witness statement must be served on the person who applied for the restraint order and any person who is prohibited from dealing with realisable property by the restraint order (if he is not the person making the application) at least 2 days before the date fixed by the court for hearing the application, unless the Crown Court specifies a shorter period.

**Application for variation of restraint or ancillary order by the person who applied for the order**      **R33.54**

33.54 (1)  This rule applies where the applicant for a restraint order makes an application under section 42(3) of the Proceeds of Crime Act 2002 to the Crown Court to vary the restraint order or any ancillary order made under section 41(7) of the 2002 Act (including where the court has already made a restraint order and the applicant is seeking to vary the order in order to restrain further realisable property).

(2)  The application may be made without notice if the application is urgent or if there are reasonable grounds for believing that giving notice would cause the dissipation of realisable property which is the subject of the application.

(3)  The application must be in writing and must be supported by a witness statement which must—

    (a)  give the grounds for the application;

    (b)  where the application is for the inclusion of further realisable property in a restraint order give full details, to the best of the witness's ability, of the realisable property in respect of which the applicant is seeking the order and specify the person holding that realisable property;

    (c)  where the application is to vary an ancillary order, include, if appropriate—

        (i)  any request for an order for disclosure of documents to which rule 33.40 applies (Disclosure and inspection of documents),

        (ii)  the identity of any person whom the applicant wants the court to examine about the extent or whereabouts of realisable property,

        (iii)  a list of the main questions that the applicant wants to ask any such person, and

        (iv)  a list of any documents to which the applicant wants to refer such a person; and

    (d)  include the proposed terms of the variation.

(4)  An application by an accredited financial investigator must include a statement that, under section 68 of the 2002 Act, the applicant has authority to apply.

(5)  The application and witness statement must be lodged with the Crown Court.

(6)  Except where, under paragraph (2), notice of the application is not required to be served, the application and witness statement must be served on any person who is prohibited from dealing with realisable property by the restraint order at least 2 days before the date fixed by the court for hearing the application, unless the Crown Court specifies a shorter period.

(7)  If the court makes an order for the variation of a restraint or ancillary order, the applicant must serve copies of the order and of the witness statement made in support of the application on—

    (a)  the defendant;

(b) any person who is prohibited from dealing with realisable property by the restraint order (whether before or after the variation); and

(c) any other person whom the applicant knows to be affected by the order.

**R33.55 Application for discharge of restraint or ancillary order by the person who applied for the order**

33.55 (1) This rule applies where the applicant for a restraint order makes an application under section 42(3) of the Proceeds of Crime Act 2002 to discharge the order or any ancillary order made under section 41(7) of the 2002 Act.

(2) The application may be made without notice.

(3) The application must be in writing and must state the grounds for the application.

(4) If the court makes an order for the discharge of a restraint or ancillary order, the applicant must serve copies of the order on—

(a) the defendant;

(b) any person who is prohibited from dealing with realisable property by the restraint order (whether before or after the discharge); and

(c) any other person whom the applicant knows to be affected by the order.

### Receivership proceedings

**R33.56 Application for appointment of a management or an enforcement receiver**

33.56 (1) This rule applies to an application for the appointment of a management receiver under section 48(1) of the Proceeds of Crime Act 2002[48] and an application for the appointment of an enforcement receiver under section 50(1) of the 2002 Act.

(2) The application may be made without notice if—

(a) the application is joined with an application for a restraint order under rule 33.51 (Application for restraint order or ancillary order);

(b) the application is urgent; or

(c) there are reasonable grounds for believing that giving notice would cause the dissipation of realisable property which is the subject of the application.

(3) The application must be in writing and must be supported by a witness statement which must—

(a) give the grounds for the application;

(b) give full details of the proposed receiver;

(c) to the best of the witness' ability, give full details of the realisable property in respect of which the applicant is seeking the order and specify the person holding that realisable property;

(d) where the application is made by an accredited financial investigator, include a statement that, under section 68 of the 2002 Act, the applicant has authority to apply; and

(e) if the proposed receiver is not a person falling within section 55(8) of the 2002 Act[49] and the applicant is asking the court to allow the receiver to act—

(i) without giving security, or

(ii) before he has given security or satisfied the court that he has security in place,

explain the reasons why that is necessary.

(4) Where the application is for the appointment of an enforcement receiver, the applicant must provide the Crown Court with a copy of the confiscation order made against the defendant.

(5) The application and witness statement must be lodged with the Crown Court.

(6) Except where, under paragraph (2), notice of the application is not required to be served, the application and witness statement must be lodged with the Crown Court and served on—

(a) the defendant;

(b) any person who holds realisable property to which the application relates; and

(c) any other person whom the applicant knows to be affected by the application,

at least 7 days before the date fixed by the court for hearing the application, unless the Crown Court specifies a shorter period.

(7) If the court makes an order for the appointment of a receiver, the applicant must serve copies of the order and of the witness statement made in support of the application on—

(a) the defendant;

(b) any person who holds realisable property to which the order applies; and

(c) any other person whom the applicant knows to be affected by the order.

---

[48] 2002 c. 29.
[49] 2002 c. 29; section 55(8) was amended by section 51(1) and (2) of the Policing and Crime Act 2009 (c. 26).

**Application for conferral of powers on a management receiver or an enforcement receiver**  **R33.57**

33.57 (1) This rule applies to an application for the conferral of powers on a management receiver under section 49(1) of the Proceeds of Crime Act 2002 or an enforcement receiver under section 51(1) of the 2002 Act.

(2) The application may be made without notice if the application is to give the receiver power to take possession of property and—

    (a) the application is joined with an application for a restraint order under rule 33.51 (Application for restraint order or ancillary order);

    (b) the application is urgent; or

    (c) there are reasonable grounds for believing that giving notice would cause the dissipation of the property which is the subject of the application.

(3) The application must be made in writing and supported by a witness statement which must—

    (a) give the grounds for the application;

    (b) give full details of the realisable property in respect of which the applicant is seeking the order and specify the person holding that realisable property;

    (c) where the application is made by an accredited financial investigator, include a statement that, under section 68 of the 2002 Act, the applicant has authority to apply; and

    (d) where the application is for power to start, carry on or defend legal proceedings in respect of the property, explain—

        (i) what proceedings are concerned, in what court, and

        (ii) what powers the receiver will ask that court to exercise.

(4) Where the application is for the conferral of powers on an enforcement receiver, the applicant must provide the Crown Court with a copy of the confiscation order made against the defendant.

(5) The application and witness statement must be lodged with the Crown Court.

(6) Except where, under paragraph (2), notice of the application is not required to be served, the application and witness statement must be served on—

    (a) the defendant;

    (b) any person who holds realisable property in respect of which a receiver has been appointed or in respect of which an application for a receiver has been made;

    (c) any other person whom the applicant knows to be affected by the application; and

    (d) the receiver (if one has already been appointed),

at least 7 days before the date fixed by the court for hearing the application, unless the Crown Court specifies a shorter period.

(7) If the court makes an order for the conferral of powers on a receiver, the applicant must serve copies of the order on—

    (a) the defendant;

    (b) any person who holds realisable property in respect of which the receiver has been appointed; and

    (c) any other person whom the applicant knows to be affected by the order.

**Applications for discharge or variation of receivership orders, and applications for other orders**  **R33.58**

33.58 (1) This rule applies to applications under section 62(3) of the Proceeds of Crime Act 2002 for orders (by persons affected by the action of receivers) and applications under section 63(1) of the 2002 Act[50] for the discharge or variation of orders relating to receivers.

(2) The application must be made in writing and lodged with the Crown Court.

(3) The application must be served on the following persons (except where they are the person making the application)—

    (a) the person who applied for appointment of the receiver;

    (b) the defendant;

    (c) any person who holds realisable property in respect of which the receiver has been appointed;

    (d) the receiver; and

    (e) any other person whom the applicant knows to be affected by the application,

at least 7 days before the date fixed by the court for hearing the application, unless the Crown Court specifies a shorter period.

(4) If the court makes an order for the discharge or variation of an order relating to a receiver under section 63(2) of the 2002 Act, the applicant must serve copies of the order on any persons whom he knows to be affected by the order.

---

[50] 2002 c. 29; section 63(1) was amended by section 74(2) of, and paragraphs 1 and 30 of Schedule 8 to, the Serious Crime Act 2007 (c. 27).

**R33.59**    **Sums in the hands of receivers**

**33.59** (1)   This rule applies where the amount payable under a confiscation order has been fully paid and any sums remain in the hands of an enforcement receiver.

(2)   The receiver must make an application to the Crown Court for directions as to the distribution of the sums in his hands.

(3)   The application and any evidence which the receiver intends to rely on in support of the application must be served on—

(a)   the defendant; and

(b)   any other person who held (or holds) interests in any property realised by the receiver,

at least 7 days before the date fixed by the court for hearing the application, unless the Crown Court specifies a shorter period.

(4)   If any of the provisions listed in paragraph (5) (provisions as to the vesting of funds in a trustee in bankruptcy) apply, then the Crown Court must make a declaration to that effect.

(5)   These are the provisions—

(a)   section 82 of the Bankruptcy (Scotland) Act 2016[51];

(b)   section 306B of the Insolvency Act 1986[52]; and

(c)   article 279B of the Insolvency (Northern Ireland) Order 1989[53].

**R33.60**    **Security**

**33.60** (1)   This rule applies where the Crown Court appoints a receiver under section 48 or 50 of the Proceeds of Crime Act 2002 and the receiver is not a person falling within section 55(8) of the 2002 Act[54] (and it is immaterial whether the receiver is a permanent or temporary member of staff or on secondment from elsewhere).

(2)   The Crown Court may direct that before the receiver begins to act, or within a specified time, he must either—

(a)   give such security as the Crown Court may determine; or

(b)   file with the Crown Court and serve on all parties to any receivership proceedings evidence that he already has in force sufficient security,

to cover his liability for his acts and omissions as a receiver.

(3)   The Crown Court may terminate the appointment of a receiver if he fails to—

(a)   give the security; or

(b)   satisfy the court as to the security he has in force,

by the date specified.

**R33.61**    **Remuneration**

**33.61** (1)   This rule applies where the Crown Court appoints a receiver under section 48 or 50 of the Proceeds of Crime Act 2002 and the receiver is not a person falling within section 55(8) of the 2002 Act (and it is immaterial whether the receiver is a permanent or temporary member of staff or on secondment from elsewhere).

(2)   The receiver may only charge for his services if the Crown Court—

(a)   so directs; and

(b)   specifies the basis on which the receiver is to be remunerated.

(3)   Unless the Crown Court orders otherwise, in determining the remuneration of the receiver, the Crown Court shall award such sum as is reasonable and proportionate in all the circumstances and which takes into account—

(a)   the time properly given by him and his staff to the receivership;

(b)   the complexity of the receivership;

(c)   any responsibility of an exceptional kind or degree which falls on the receiver in consequence of the receivership;

(d)   the effectiveness with which the receiver appears to be carrying out, or to have carried out, his duties; and

(e)   the value and nature of the subject matter of the receivership.

(4)   The Crown Court may refer the determination of a receiver's remuneration to be ascertained by the taxing authority of the Crown Court and rules 45.11 (Assessment and re-assessment) to 45.14 (Application for an extension of time) shall have effect as if the taxing authority was ascertaining costs.

---

[51]   2016 asp 21.

[52]   1986 c. 45; section 306B was inserted by section 456 of, and paragraphs 1 and 16 of Schedule 11 to, the Proceeds of Crime Act 2002 (c. 29).

[53]   S.I. 1989/2405 (N.I. 19); article 279B was inserted by section 456 of, and paragraph 20(3) of Schedule 11 to, the Proceeds of Crime Act 2002 (c. 29).

[54]   2002 c. 29; section 55(8) was amended by section 51(1) and (2) of the Policing and Crime Act 2009 (c. 26).

(5)  A receiver appointed under section 48 of the 2002 Act is to receive his remuneration by realising property in respect of which he is appointed, in accordance with section 49(2)(d) of the 2002 Act.

(6)  A receiver appointed under section 50 of the 2002 Act is to receive his remuneration by applying to the magistrates' court officer for payment under section 55(4)(b) of the 2002 Act[55].

### Accounts                                                                                    R33.62

33.62  (1)  The Crown Court may order a receiver appointed under section 48 or 50 of the Proceeds of Crime Act 2002 to prepare and serve accounts.

(2)  A party to receivership proceedings served with such accounts may apply for an order permitting him to inspect any document in the possession of the receiver relevant to those accounts.

(3)  Any party to receivership proceedings may, within 14 days of being served with the accounts, serve notice on the receiver—

(a)  specifying any item in the accounts to which he objects;

(b)  giving the reason for such objection; and

(c)  requiring the receiver within 14 days of receipt of the notice, either—

(i)  to notify all the parties who were served with the accounts that he accepts the objection, or

(ii)  if he does not accept the objection, to apply for an examination of the accounts in relation to the contested item.

(4)  When the receiver applies for the examination of the accounts he must at the same time lodge with the Crown Court—

(a)  the accounts; and

(b)  a copy of the notice served on him under this section of the rule.

(5)  If the receiver fails to comply with paragraph (3)(c) of this rule, any party to receivership proceedings may apply to the Crown Court for an examination of the accounts in relation to the contested item.

(6)  At the conclusion of its examination of the accounts the court must certify the result.

### Non-compliance by receiver                                                                  R33.63

33.63  (1)  If a receiver appointed under section 48 or 50 of the Proceeds of Crime Act 2002 fails to comply with any rule, practice direction or direction of the Crown Court, the Crown Court may order him to attend a hearing to explain his non-compliance.

(2)  At the hearing, the Crown Court may make any order it considers appropriate, including—

(a)  terminating the appointment of the receiver;

(b)  reducing the receiver's remuneration or disallowing it altogether; and

(c)  ordering the receiver to pay the costs of any party.

### Proceedings under the Criminal Justice Act 1988 and the Drug Trafficking Act 1994

*[Note. The relevant provisions of the 1988 and 1994 Acts were repealed on 24th March 2003, but they continue to have effect in respect of proceedings for offences committed before that date.]*

### Statements, etc. relevant to making confiscation orders                                     R33.64

33.64  (1)  Where a prosecutor or defendant—

(a)  serves on the magistrates' court officer any statement or other document under section 73 of the Criminal Justice Act 1988[56] in any proceedings in respect of an offence listed in Schedule 4 to that Act; or

(b)  serves on the Crown Court officer any statement or other document under section 11 of the Drug Trafficking Act 1994[57] or section 73 of the 1988 Act in any proceedings in respect of a drug trafficking offence or in respect of an offence to which Part VI of the 1988 Act applies,

that party must serve a copy as soon as practicable on the defendant or the prosecutor, as the case may be.

---

[55]  2002 c. 29; section 55(4)(b) was amended by paragraph 408 of Schedule 8 to, the Courts Act 2003 (c. 39).

[56]  1988 c. 33; section 73 and Schedule 4 were repealed, with savings, by paragraphs 1 and 17 of Schedule 11 and Schedule 12 to, the Proceeds of Crime Act 2002 (c. 29).

[57]  1994 c. 37; section 11 was repealed, with savings, by paragraphs 1 and 25 of Schedule 11 and Schedule 12 to, the Proceeds of Crime Act 2002 (c. 29).

(2) Any statement tendered by the prosecutor to the magistrates' court under section 73 of the 1988 Act or to the Crown Court under section 11(1) of the 1994 Act or section 73(1A) of the 1988 Act must include the following particulars—

  (a) the name of the defendant;

  (b) the name of the person by whom the statement is made and the date on which it was made;

  (c) where the statement is not tendered immediately after the defendant has been convicted, the date on which and the place where the relevant conviction occurred; and

  (d) such information known to the prosecutor as is relevant to the determination as to whether or not the defendant has benefited from drug trafficking or relevant criminal conduct and to the assessment of the value of any proceeds of drug trafficking or, as the case may be, benefit from relevant criminal conduct.

(3) Where, in accordance with section 11(7) of the 1994 Act or section 73(1C) of the 1988 Act, the defendant indicates in writing the extent to which he or she accepts any allegation contained within the prosecutor's statement, the defendant must serve a copy of that reply on the court officer.

(4) Expressions used in this rule have the same meanings as in the 1994 Act or, where appropriate, the 1988 Act.

**R33.65** **Postponed determinations**

**33.65** (1) Where an application is made by the defendant or the prosecutor—

  (a) to a magistrates' court under section 72A(5)(a) of the Criminal Justice Act 1988[58] asking the court to exercise its powers under section 72A(4) of that Act; or

  (b) to the Crown Court under section 3(5)(a) of the Drug Trafficking Act 1994[59] asking the Court to exercise its powers under section 3(4) of that Act, or under section 72A(5)(a) of the 1988 Act asking the court to exercise its powers under section 72A(4) of the 1988 Act,

the application must be in writing and the applicant must serve a copy on the prosecutor or the defendant, as the case may be.

(2) A party served with a copy of an application under paragraph (1) must, within 28 days of the date of service, notify the applicant and the court officer, in writing, whether or not that party opposes the application, giving reasons for any opposition.

(3) After the expiry of the period referred to in paragraph (2), the court may determine an application under paragraph (1) —

  (a) without a hearing; or

  (b) at a hearing at which the parties may be represented.

**R33.66** **Confiscation orders—revised assessments**

**33.66** (1) Where the prosecutor makes an application under section 13, 14 or 15 of the Drug Trafficking Act 1994[60] or section 74A, 74B or 74C of the Criminal Justice Act 1988[61], the application must be in writing and a copy must be served on the defendant.

(2) The application must include the following particulars—

  (a) the name of the defendant;

  (b) the date on which and the place where any relevant conviction occurred;

  (c) the date on which and the place where any relevant confiscation order was made or, as the case may be, varied;

  (d) the grounds on which the application is made; and

  (e) an indication of the evidence available to support the application.

---

[58] 1988 c. 33; section 72A was inserted by section 28 of the Criminal Justice Act 1993 (c. 36) and repealed, with savings, by sections 456 and 457 of, and paragraphs 1 and 17 of Schedule 11, and Schedule 12 to, the Proceeds of Crime Act 2002 (c. 29).

[59] 1994 c. 37; section 3 was repealed, with savings, by paragraphs 1 and 25 of Schedule 11 and Schedule 12 to, the Proceeds of Crime Act 2002 (c. 29).

[60] 1994 c. 37; sections 13, 14 and 15 were repealed, with savings, by paragraphs 1 and 25 of Schedule 11 and Schedule 12 to, the Proceeds of Crime Act 2002 (c. 29).

[61] 1988 c. 33; sections 74A, 74B and 74C were inserted by the Proceeds of Crime Act 1995 (c. 11), sections 5, 6 and 7 respectively, and repealed, with savings by paragraphs 1 and 17 of Schedule 11 and Schedule 12 to, the Proceeds of Crime Act 2002 (c. 29).

**Application to the Crown Court to discharge or vary order to make material available**       R33.67

33.67 (1)  Where an order under section 93H of the Criminal Justice Act 1988[62] (order to make material
        available) or section 55 of the Drug Trafficking Act 1994[63] (order to make material available)
        has been made by the Crown Court, any person affected by it may apply in writing to the court
        officer for the order to be discharged or varied, and on hearing such an application the court
        may discharge the order or make such variations to it as the court thinks fit.

(2)  Subject to paragraph (3), where a person proposes to make an application under paragraph (1)
        for the discharge or variation of an order, that person must give a copy of the application, not
        later than 48 hours before the making of the application—

        (a)  to a constable at the police station specified in the order; or

        (b)  to the office of the appropriate officer who made the application, as specified in the order,
        in either case together with a notice indicating the time and place at which the application for
        discharge or variation is to be made.

(3)  The court may direct that paragraph (2) need not be complied with if satisfied that the person
        making the application has good reason to seek a discharge or variation of the order as soon as
        possible and it is not practicable to comply with that paragraph.

(4)  In this rule:
        'constable' includes a person commissioned by the Commissioners for Her Majesty's Revenue
            and Customs;
        'police station' includes a place for the time being occupied by Her Majesty's Revenue and
            Customs.

**Application to the Crown Court for increase in term of imprisonment in default of payment**       R33.68

33.68 (1)  This rule applies to applications made, or that have effect as made, to the Crown Court under
        section 10 of the Drug Trafficking Act 1994[64] and section 75A of the Criminal Justice Act
        1988[65] (interest on sums unpaid under confiscation orders).

(2)  Notice of an application to which this rule applies to increase the term of imprisonment or
        detention fixed in default of payment of a confiscation order by a person ('the defendant') must
        be made by the prosecutor in writing to the court officer.

(3)  A notice under paragraph (2) shall—

        (a)  state the name and address of the defendant;

        (b)  specify the grounds for the application;

        (c)  give details of the enforcement measures taken, if any; and

        (d)  include a copy of the confiscation order.

(4)  On receiving a notice under paragraph (2), the court officer must—

        (a)  forthwith send to the defendant and the magistrates' court required to enforce payment of
        the confiscation order under section 140(1) of the Powers of Criminal Courts (Sentenc-
        ing) Act 2000[66], a copy of the said notice; and

        (b)  notify in writing the applicant and the defendant of the date, time and place appointed for
        the hearing of the application.

(5)  Where the Crown Court makes an order pursuant to an application mentioned in paragraph (1)
        above, the court officer must send forthwith a copy of the order—

        (a)  to the applicant;

        (b)  to the defendant;

        (c)  where the defendant is at the time of the making of the order in custody, to the person
        having custody of him or her; and

        (d)  to the magistrates' court mentioned in paragraph (4)(a).

---

[62]  1988 c. 33; section 93H was inserted by section 11 of the Proceeds of Crime Act 1995 (c. 11) and repealed, with savings,
by paragraphs 1 and 17 of Schedule 11 and Schedule 12 to, the Proceeds of Crime Act 2002 (c. 29).
[63]  1994 c. 37; section 55 was amended by paragraphs 1 and 25 of Schedule 11 and Schedule 12 to, the Proceeds of Crime Act
2002 (c. 29) and by paragraph 364 of Schedule 8 to the Courts Act 2003 (c. 39).
[64]  1994 c. 37; section 10 was repealed, with savings, by paragraphs 1 and 25 of Schedule 11 and Schedule 12 to, the Proceeds
of Crime Act 2002 (c. 29).
[65]  1988 c. 33; section 75A was inserted by section 9 of the Proceeds of Crime Act 1995 (c. 11) and repealed, with savings, by
paragraphs 1 and 17 of Schedule 11 and Schedule 12 to, the Proceeds of Crime Act 2002 (c. 29).
[66]  2000 c. 6; section 140 was amended by paragraphs 74 of Schedule 3 and Part 4 of Schedule 37 to the Criminal Justice Act
2003 (c. 44) and section 40(4) of, and paragraph 69 of Schedule 9 to, the Constitutional Reform Act 2005 (c. 4). It is further
amended by sections 74 and 75 of, and paragraphs 160 and 194 of Schedule 8 to, the Criminal Justice and Court Services Act
2000 (c. 43) with effect from a date to be appointed.

**R33.69**  **Drug trafficking—compensation on acquittal in the Crown Court**

**33.69** Where the Crown Court cancels a confiscation order under section 22(2) of the Drug Trafficking Act 1994[67], the Crown Court officer must serve notice to that effect on the High Court officer and on the court officer of the magistrates' court which has responsibility for enforcing the order.

### Contempt proceedings

**R33.70**  **Application to punish for contempt of court**

**33.70** (1) This rule applies where a person is accused of disobeying—

   (a)  a compliance order made for the purpose of ensuring that a confiscation order is effective;

   (b)  a restraint order; or

   (c)  an ancillary order made for the purpose of ensuring that a restraint order is effective.

   (2)  An applicant who wants the Crown Court to exercise its power to punish that person for contempt of court must comply with the rules in Part 48 (Contempt of court).

*[Note. The Crown Court has inherent power to punish for contempt of court a person who disobeys its order: see section 45 of the Senior Courts Act 1981[68].]*

CRIMINAL PROCEDURE RULES   PART 34   APPEAL TO THE CROWN COURT

**R34.1**  **When this Part applies**

**34.1** (1) This Part applies where—

   (a)  a defendant wants to appeal under—

      (i)   section 108 of the Magistrates' Courts Act 1980[1],

      (ii)  section 45 of the Mental Health Act 1983[2],

      (iii) section 42 of the Counter Terrorism Act 2008[3];

      (iv)  paragraph 10 of Schedule 5, paragraph 6(11) or 21(6) of Schedule 7, or paragraph 10(11), 14(8) or 23(6) of Schedule 10 to the Sentencing Act 2020[4];

   (b)  the Criminal Cases Review Commission refers a defendant's case to the Crown Court under section 11 of the Criminal Appeal Act 1995[5]

   (c)  a prosecutor wants to appeal under—

      (i)   section 14A(5A) of the Football Spectators Act 1989[6], or

      (ii)  section 147(3) of the Customs and Excise Management Act 1979[7]; or

   (d)  a person wants to appeal under—

      (i)   section 1 of the Magistrates' Courts (Appeals from Binding Over Orders) Act 1956[8],

      (ii)  section 12(5) of the Contempt of Court Act 1981[9],

      (iii) regulation 3C or 3H of the Costs in Criminal Cases (General) Regulations 1986[10],

---

[67]  1994 c. 37; section 22 was repealed, with savings, by paragraphs 1 and 25 of Schedule 11 and Schedule 12 to, the Proceeds of Crime Act 2002 (c. 29).

[68]  1981 c. 54. The Act's title was amended by section 59(5) of, and paragraph 1 of Schedule 11 to, the Constitutional Reform Act 2005 (c. 4).

[1]  1980 c. 43; section 108 was amended by sections 66(2) and 78 of, and Schedule 16 to, the Criminal Justice Act 1982 (c. 48), section 23(3) of the Football Spectators Act 1989 (c. 37), section 101(2) of, and Schedule 13 to, the Criminal Justice Act 1991 (c. 53), sections 119 and 120(2) of, and paragraph 43 of Schedule 8 and Schedule 10 to, the Crime and Disorder Act 1998 (c. 37), section 7(2) of the Football (Offences and Disorder) Act 1999 (c. 21), section 165(1) of, and paragraph 71 of Schedule 9 to, the Powers of Criminal Courts (Sentencing) Act 2000 (c. 6), section 1 of, and Schedule 3 to, the Football (Disorder) Act 2000 (c. 25), section 58(1) of, and paragraph 10 of Schedule 10 to, the Domestic Violence, Crime and Victims Act 2004 (c. 28), section 52(2) of, and paragraph 14 of Schedule 3 to, the Violent Crime Reduction Act 2006 (c. 38) and section 64 of, and paragraph 10 of Schedule 3 to, the Animal Welfare Act 2006 (c. 45).

[2]  1983 c. 20.

[3]  2008 c. 28.

[4]  2020 c. 17.

[5]  1995 c. 35.

[6]  1989 c. 37; section 14A(5A) was inserted by section 52 of, and paragraphs 1 and 3 of Schedule 3 to, the Violent Crime Reduction Act 2006 (c. 38).

[7]  1979 c. 2.

[8]  1956 c. 44; section 1 was amended by Part 1 of Schedule 7 to, the Criminal Justice Act 1967 (c. 80), Part 1 of Schedule 9 to, the Courts Act 1971 (c. 23) and Schedule 9 to, the Magistrates' Courts Act 1980 (c. 43).

[9]  1981 c. 49; section 12(5) was amended by section 165(1) of, and paragraph 83 of Schedule 9 to, the Powers of Criminal Courts (Sentencing) Act 2000 (c. 6).

[10]  S.I. 1986/1335; regulation 3C was inserted by regulation 2 of The Costs in Criminal Cases (General) (Amendment) Regulations 1991 (SI 1991/789) and amended by regulation 5 of The Costs in Criminal Cases (General) (Amendment) Regulations 2004 (SI 2004/2408). Regulation 3H was inserted by regulation 7 of The Costs in Criminal Cases (General) (Amendment) Regulations 2004 (S.I. 2004/2408).

    (iv)  section 22 of the Football Spectators Act 1989[11],

    (v)   section 10 of the Crime and Disorder Act 1998[12];

    (vi)  section 28(5)(b) of the Offensive Weapons Act 2019[13], or

    (vii) section 366(9) of the Sentencing Act 2020.

(2)  A reference to an 'appellant' in this Part is a reference to such a party or person.

*[Note. An appeal to the Crown Court is by way of re-hearing: see section 79(3) of the Senior Courts Act 1981[14]. For the powers of the Crown Court on an appeal, see section 48 of that Act.*

*A defendant may appeal from a magistrates' court to the Crown Court—*

    *(a)  under section 108 of the Magistrates' Courts Act 1980, against sentence after a guilty plea and after a not guilty plea against conviction, against a finding of guilt or against sentence;*

    *(b)  under section 45 of the Mental Health Act 1983, where the magistrates' court makes a hospital order or guardianship order without convicting the defendant;*

    *(c)  under paragraph 10 of Schedule 5, paragraph 6(11) or 21(6) of Schedule 7, or paragraph 10(11), 14(8) or 23(6) of Schedule 10 to the Sentencing Act 2020, where the magistrates' court—*

        *(i)   deals with the defendant for breach of a reparation order, a youth rehabilitation order or a community order,*

        *(ii)  except in some circumstances, amends a reparation order, or*

        *(iii) except in some circumstances, deals with an application to revoke a reparation order or a community order.*

    *(d)  under section 42 of the Counter Terrorism Act 2008, where the magistrates' court decides that an offence has a terrorist connection.*

*See section 13 of the Criminal Appeal Act 1995[15] for the circumstances in which the Criminal Cases Review Commission may refer a conviction or sentence to the Crown Court.*

*Under section 14A(5A) of the Football Spectators Act 1989, a prosecutor may appeal to the Crown Court against a failure by a magistrates' court to make a football banning order.*

*Under section 147(3) of the Customs and Excise Management Act 1979, a prosecutor may appeal to the Crown Court against any decision of a magistrates' court in proceedings for an offence under any Act relating to customs or excise.*

*Under section 1 of the Magistrates' Courts (Appeals from Binding Over Orders) Act 1956, a person bound over to keep the peace or be of good behaviour by a magistrates' court may appeal to the Crown Court.*

*Under section 12(5) of the Contempt of Court Act 1981, a person detained, committed to custody or fined by a magistrates' court for insulting a member of the court or another participant in the case, or for interrupting the proceedings, may appeal to the Crown Court.*

*Under regulation 3C of the Costs in Criminal Cases (General) Regulations 1986, a legal representative against whom a magistrates' court makes a wasted costs order under section 19A of the Prosecution of Offences Act 1985 and regulation 3B may appeal against that order to the Crown Court.*

*Under regulation 3H of the Costs in Criminal Cases (General) Regulations 1986, a third party against whom a magistrates' court makes a costs order under section 19B of the Prosecution of Offences Act 1985 and regulation 3F may appeal against that order to the Crown Court.*

*Under section 22 of the Football Spectators Act 1989, any person aggrieved by the decision of a magistrates' court making a football banning order may appeal to the Crown Court.*

*Under section 10 of the Crime and Disorder Act 1998 or under section 366(9) of the Sentencing Act 2020, a person in respect of whom a magistrates' court makes a parenting order may appeal against that order to the Crown Court.*

---

[11]  1989 c. 37; section 22 was amended by section 5 of the Football (Offences and Disorder) Act 1999 (c. 21), section 1 of, and paragraphs 9 – 11 and 17 of Schedule 2 to, the Football (Disorder) Act 2000 (c. 25) and section 109(1) and (3) of, and paragraph 335 of Schedule 8, and Schedule 10 to, the Courts Act 2003 (c. 39).

[12]  1998 c. 37; section 10 was amended by section 15 of, and paragraphs 276 and 277 of Schedule 4 to, the Constitutional Reform Act 2005 (c. 4), section 41 of the Crime and Security Act 2010 (c. 17) and section 17 of, and paragraph 52 of Schedule 9 to, the Crime and Courts Act 2013 (c. 22).

[13]  2019 c. 17; section 28 comes into force on a date to be appointed.

[14]  1981 c. 54. The Act's title was amended by section 59(5) of, and paragraph 1 of Schedule 11 to, the Constitutional Reform Act 2005 (c. 4).

[15]  1995 c. 35; section 13 was amended by section 321 of, and paragraph 3 of Schedule 11 to, the Armed Forces Act 2006 (c.52).

*Under section 28(5)(b) of the Offensive Weapons Act 2019 an applicant to a magistrates' court for the variation, renewal or discharge of a knife crime prevention order made by that court, or a respondent to such an application, may appeal to the Crown Court against the decision of the magistrates' court.]*

**R34.2**   **Service of appeal and respondent's notices**

**34.2**   (1)   An appellant must serve an appeal notice on—

(a)   the magistrates' court officer; and

(b)   every other party.

(2)   The appellant must serve the appeal notice—

(a)   as soon after the decision appealed against as the appellant wants; but

(b)   not more than 15 business days after—

(i)   sentence or the date sentence is deferred or the date of committal for sentence, whichever is earlier, if the appeal is against conviction or against a finding of guilt,

(ii)   sentence, if the appeal is against sentence, or

(iii)   the order or failure to make an order about which the appellant wants to appeal, in any other case.

(3)   The appellant must serve with the appeal notice any application for the following, with reasons—

(a)   an extension of the time limit under this rule, if the appeal notice is late;

(b)   bail pending appeal, if the appellant is in custody; or

(c)   the suspension of any disqualification imposed or order made in the case, where the magistrates' court or the Crown Court can order such a suspension pending appeal.

(4)   Where both the magistrates' court and the Crown Court can grant bail or suspend a disqualification or order pending appeal, an application must indicate by which court the appellant wants the application determined.

(5)   Where the appeal is against conviction or against a finding of guilt, unless the respondent agrees that the court should allow the appeal—

(a)   the respondent must serve a respondent's notice on—

(i)   the Crown Court officer; and

(ii)   the appellant; and

(b)   the respondent must serve that notice not more than 15 business days after service of the appeal notice.

*[Note. Under sections 4 and 5 of the Sentencing Act 2020[16], a magistrates' court may defer passing sentence for up to 6 months.*

*Under section 113 of the Magistrates' Courts Act 1980[17], the magistrates' court may grant an appellant bail pending appeal. Under section 81(1)(b) of the Senior Courts Act 1981[18], the Crown Court also may do so. See also rule 14.7.*

*Under section 39 of the Road Traffic Offenders Act 1988[19], a court which has made an order disqualifying a person from driving may suspend the disqualification pending appeal. Under section 40 of the 1988 Act[20], the appeal court may do so. See also rule 29.2.*

*Under section 129 of the Licensing Act 2003[21], a court which has made an order to forfeit or suspend a personal licence issued under that Act may suspend the order pending appeal. Under section 130 of the 2003 Act[22], the appeal court may do so.]*

**R34.3**   **Form of appeal and respondent's notices**

**34.3**   (1)   The appeal notice must—

(a)   specify—

(i)   the conviction or finding of guilt,

(ii)   the sentence, or

(iii)   the order, or the failure to make an order

---

[16]   2020 c. 17.

[17]   1980 c. 43; section 113 was amended by section 168 of, and paragraph 44 of Schedule 10 to, the Criminal Justice and Public Order Act 1994 (c. 33) and section 165 of, and paragraph 72 of Schedule 9 to, the Powers of Criminal Courts (Sentencing) Act 2000 (c. 6).

[18]   1981 c.54.

[19]   1988 c. 53.

[20]   1988 c. 53; section 40 was amended by sections 40 and 59 of, and paragraph 50 of Schedule 9 and paragraph 1 of Schedule 11 to, the Constitutional Reform Act 2005 (c.4).

[21]   2003 c. 17.

[22]   2003 c. 17; section 130 was amended by sections 40 and 59 of, and paragraph 78 of Schedule 9 and paragraph 1 of Schedule 11 to, the Constitutional Reform Act 2005 (c. 4).

about which the appellant wants to appeal;

(b) summarise the issues;

(c) in an appeal against conviction or against a finding of guilt, to the best of the appellant's ability and to assist the court in fulfilling its duty under rule 3.2 (the court's duty of case management)—

    (i) identify the witnesses who gave oral evidence in the magistrates' court,

    (ii) identify the witnesses who gave written evidence in the magistrates' court,

    (iii) identify the prosecution witnesses whom the appellant will want to question if they are called to give oral evidence in the Crown Court,

    (iv) identify the likely defence witnesses,

    (v) give notice of any special arrangements or other measures that the appellant thinks are needed for witnesses,

    (vi) explain whether the issues in the Crown Court differ from the issues in the magistrates' court, and if so how, and

    (vii) say how long the trial lasted in the magistrates' court and how long the appeal is likely to last in the Crown Court;

(d) in an appeal against a sentence, order or failure to make an order—

    (i) identify any circumstances, report or other information of which the appellant wants the court to take account, and

    (ii) explain the significance of those circumstances or that information to what is in issue;

(e) in an appeal against a finding that the appellant insulted someone or interrupted proceedings in the magistrates' court, attach—

    (i) the magistrates' court's written findings of fact, and

    (ii) the appellant's response to those findings;

(f) say whether the appellant has asked the magistrates' court to reconsider the case; and

(g) include a list of those on whom the appellant has served the appeal notice.

(2) A respondent's notice must—

(a) give the date on which the respondent was served with the appeal notice; and

(b) to assist the court in fulfilling its duty under rule 3.2—

    (i) identify the witnesses who gave oral evidence in the magistrates' court,

    (ii) identify the witnesses who gave written evidence in the magistrates' court,

    (iii) identify the prosecution witnesses whom the respondent intends to call to give oral evidence in the Crown Court,

    (iv) give notice of any special arrangements or other measures that the respondent thinks are needed for witnesses,

    (v) explain whether the issues in the Crown Court differ from the issues in the magistrates' court, and if so how, and

    (vi) say how long the trial lasted in the magistrates' court and how long the appeal is likely to last in the Crown Court.

(3) Paragraph (4) applies in an appeal against conviction or against a finding of guilt where in the magistrates' court a party to the appeal—

(a) introduced in evidence material to which applies—

    (i) Part 16 (Written witness statements),

    (ii) Part 19 (Expert evidence),

    (iii) Part 20 (Hearsay evidence),

    (iv) Part 21 (Evidence of bad character), or

    (v) Part 22 (Evidence of a complainant's previous sexual behaviour); or

(b) made an application to which applies—

    (i) Part 17 (Witness summonses, warrants and orders),

    (ii) Part 18 (Measures to assist a witness or defendant to give evidence), or

    (iii) Part 23 (Restriction on cross-examination by a defendant).

(4) If such a party wants to reintroduce that material or to renew that application in the Crown Court that party must include a notice to that effect in the appeal or respondent's notice, as the case may be.

*[Note. The Practice Direction sets out forms of appeal and respondent's notices for use in connection with this rule.*

*In some cases, a magistrates' court can reconsider a conviction, sentence or other order and make a fresh decision. See section 142 of the Magistrates' Courts Act 1980[23].*

*See also rule 3.13 (Conduct of a trial or an appeal).]*

---

[23] 1980 c. 43; section 142 was amended by sections 26 and 29 of, and Schedule 3 to, the Criminal Appeal Act 1995 (c. 35).

**R34.4    Duty of magistrates' court officer**

**34.4**  (1)  The magistrates' court officer must—

(a)  arrange for the magistrates' court to hear as soon as practicable any application to that court under rule 34.2(3)(c) (suspension of disqualification or order pending appeal); and

(b)  as soon as practicable notify the Crown Court officer of the service of the appeal notice and make available to that officer—

(i)  the appeal notice and any accompanying application served by the appellant,

(ii)  details of the parties including their addresses, and

(iii)  a copy of each magistrates' court register entry relating to the decision under appeal and to any application for bail or for the suspension of a disqualification or order pending appeal.

(2)  Where the appeal is against conviction or against a finding of guilt, the magistrates' court officer must make available to the Crown Court officer as soon as practicable—

(a)  all material served on the magistrate's court officer to which applies—

(i)  Part 8 (Initial details of the prosecution case),

(ii)  Part 16 (Written witness statements),

(iii)  Part 17 (Witness summonses, warrants and orders),

(iv)  Part 18 (Measures to assist a witness or defendant to give evidence),

(v)  Part 19 (Expert evidence),

(vi)  Part 20 (Hearsay evidence),

(vii)  Part 21 (Evidence of bad character),

(viii)  Part 22 (Evidence of a complainant's previous sexual behaviour), or

(ix)  Part 23 (Restriction on cross-examination by a defendant);

(b)  any case management questionnaire prepared for the purposes of the trial;

(c)  all case management directions given by the magistrates' court for the purposes of the trial; and

(d)  any other document, object or information for which the Crown Court officer asks.

(3)  Where the appeal is against sentence, the magistrates' court officer must make available to the Crown Court officer as soon as practicable any report received for the purposes of sentencing.

(4)  Unless the magistrates' court otherwise directs, the magistrates' court officer—

(a)  must keep any document or object exhibited in the proceedings in the magistrates' court, or arrange for it to be kept by some other appropriate person, until at least—

(i)  6 weeks after the conclusion of those proceedings, or

(ii)  the conclusion of any proceedings in the Crown Court that begin within that 6 weeks; but

(b)  need not keep such a document if—

(i)  the document that was exhibited is a copy of a document retained by the party who produced it, and

(ii)  what was in evidence in the magistrates' court was the content of that document.

*[Note. See also section 133 of the Criminal Justice Act 2003[24] (Proof of statements in documents).]*

**R34.5    Duty of person keeping exhibit**

**34.5**  A person who, under arrangements made by the magistrates' court officer, keeps a document or object exhibited in the proceedings in the magistrates' court must—

(a)  keep that exhibit until—

(i)  6 weeks after the conclusion of those proceedings, or

(ii)  the conclusion of any proceedings in the Crown Court that begin within that 6 weeks, unless the magistrates' court or the Crown Court otherwise directs; and

(b)  provide the Crown Court with any such document or object for which the Crown Court officer asks, within such period as the Crown Court officer may require.

**R34.6    Reference by the Criminal Cases Review Commission**

**34.6**  (1)  The Crown Court officer must, as soon as practicable, serve a reference by the Criminal Cases Review Commission on—

(a)  the appellant;

(b)  every other party; and

(c)  the magistrates' court officer.

(2)  The appellant may serve an appeal notice on—

(a)  the Crown Court officer; and

(b)  every other party,

not more than 15 business days later.

---

[24] 2003 c. 44.

(3)  The Crown Court must treat the reference as the appeal notice if the appellant does not serve an appeal notice.

**Preparation for appeal**                                                                R34.7

34.7  (1)  The Crown Court may conduct a preparation for appeal hearing (and if necessary more than one such hearing) where—
  (a)  it is necessary to conduct such a hearing in order to give directions for the effective determination of the appeal; or
  (b)  such a hearing is required to set ground rules for the conduct of the questioning of a witness or appellant.
(2)  Where under rule 34.3(4) a party gives notice to reintroduce material or to renew an application first introduced or made in the magistrates' court—
  (a)  no other notice or application to the same effect otherwise required by these Rules need be served; and
  (b)  any objection served by the other party in the magistrates' court is treated as renewed unless within 15 business days that party serves notice withdrawing it.
(3)  Paragraphs (4) and (5) apply where—
  (a)  the appeal is against conviction or against a finding of guilt;
  (b)  a party wants to introduce material or make an application under a Part of these Rules listed in rule 34.3(3); and
  (c)  that party gives no notice of reintroduction or renewal under rule 34.3(4) (whether because the conditions for giving such a notice are not met or for any other reason).
(4)  Such a party must serve the material, notice or application required by that Part not more than 21 days after service of the appeal notice.
(5)  Subject to paragraph (4), the requirements of that Part apply (for example, as to the form in which a notice must be given or an application made and as to the time and form in which such a notice or application may be opposed).

**Hearings and decisions**                                                                R34.8

34.8  (1)  The Crown Court as a general rule must hear in public an appeal or reference to which this part applies, but—
  (a)  may order any hearing to be in private; and
  (b)  where a hearing is about a public interest ruling, must hold that hearing in private.
(2)  The Crown Court officer must give as much notice as reasonably practicable of every hearing to—
  (a)  the parties;
  (b)  any party's custodian; and
  (c)  any other person whom the Crown Court requires to be notified.
(3)  The Crown Court officer must serve every decision on—
  (a)  the parties;
  (b)  any other person whom the Crown Court requires to be served; and
  (c)  the magistrates' court officer and any party's custodian, where the decision determines an appeal.
(4)  But where a hearing or decision is about a public interest ruling, the Crown Court officer must not—
  (a)  give notice of that hearing to; or
  (b)  serve that decision on,
  anyone other than the prosecutor who applied for that ruling, unless the court otherwise directs.

*[Note. See also Part 15 (Disclosure).]*

**Abandoning an appeal**                                                                  R34.9

34.9  (1)  The appellant—
  (a)  may abandon an appeal without the Crown Court's permission, by serving a notice of abandonment on—
      (i)   the magistrates' court officer,
      (ii)  the Crown Court officer, and
      (iii) every other party
      before the hearing of the appeal begins; but

Criminal Procedure Rules and Criminal Practice Directions

      (b)   after the hearing of the appeal begins, may only abandon the appeal with the Crown Court's permission.

(2)   A notice of abandonment must be signed by or on behalf of the appellant.

(3)   Where an appellant who is on bail pending appeal abandons an appeal—

      (a)   the appellant must surrender to custody as directed by the magistrates' court officer; and

      (b)   any conditions of bail apply until then.

*[Note. The Practice Direction sets out a form of notice of abandonment for use in connection with this rule.*

*Where an appellant abandons an appeal to the Crown Court, both the Crown Court and the magistrates' court have power to make a costs order against that appellant in favour of the respondent: see section 52 of the Senior Courts Act 1981[25] and section 109 of the Magistrates' Courts Act 1980[26]. Part 45 contains rules about costs on abandoning an appeal.]*

**R34.10**    **Court's power to vary requirements under this Part**

34.10 The Crown Court may—

    (a)   shorten or extend (even after it has expired) a time limit under this Part;

    (b)   allow an appellant to vary an appeal notice that that appellant has served;

    (c)   direct that an appeal notice be served on any person; and

    (d)   allow an appeal notice or a notice of abandonment to be in a different form to one set out in the Practice Direction, or to be presented orally.

**R34.11**    **Constitution of the Crown Court**

34.11 (1)   On the hearing of an appeal the general rule is that—

    (a)   the Crown Court must comprise—

        (i)   a judge of the High Court, a Circuit judge, a Recorder or a qualifying judge advocate, and

        (ii)   no less than two and no more than four justices of the peace, none of whom took part in the decision under appeal; and

    (b)   if the appeal is from a youth court, each justice of the peace must be qualified to sit as a member of a youth court.

(2)   Despite the general rule—

    (a)   the Crown Court may include only one justice of the peace if—

        (i)   the presiding judge decides that otherwise the start of the appeal hearing will be delayed unreasonably, or

        (ii)   one or more of the justices of the peace who started hearing the appeal is absent; and

    (b)   the Crown Court may comprise only a judge of the High Court, a Circuit judge, a Recorder or a qualifying judge advocate if—

        (i)   the appeal is against conviction, under section 108 of the Magistrates' Courts Act 1980[27], and

        (ii)   the respondent agrees that the court should allow the appeal, under section 48(2) of the Senior Courts Act 1981[28].

(3)   Before the hearing of an appeal begins and after that hearing ends—

    (a)   the Crown Court may comprise only a judge of the High Court, a Circuit judge, a Recorder or a qualifying judge advocate; and

---

[25] 1981 c. 54; section 52 was amended by section 31(5) of, and Part II of Schedule 1 to, the Prosecution of Offences Act 1985 (c. 23), section 4 of the Courts and Legal Services Act 1990 (c. 41), article 3 of, and paragraphs 11 and 12(a) of the Schedule to, S.I. 2004/2035, and section 59(5) of, and paragraph 26(1) and (2) of Schedule 11 to, the Constitutional Reform Act 2005 (c. 4). The Act's title was amended by section 59(5) of, and paragraph 1 of Schedule 11 to, the Constitutional Reform Act 2005 (c. 4).

[26] 1980 c. 43; section 109(2) was amended by section 109(1) of, and paragraph 234 of Schedule 8 to, the Courts Act 2003 (c. 39).

[27] 1980 c. 43; section 108 was amended by sections 66(2) and 78 of, and Schedule 16 to, the Criminal Justice Act 1982 (c. 48), section 23(3) of the Football Spectators Act 1989 (c. 37), section 101(2) of, and Schedule 13 to, the Criminal Justice Act 1991 (c. 53), sections 119 and 120(2) of, and paragraph 43 of Schedule 8 and Schedule 10 to, the Crime and Disorder Act 1998 (c. 37), section 7(2) of the Football (Offences and Disorder) Act 1999 (c. 21), section 165(1) of, and paragraph 71 of Schedule 9 to, the Powers of Criminal Courts (Sentencing) Act 2000 (c. 6), section 1 of, and Schedule 3 to, the Football (Disorder) Act 2000 (c. 25), section 58(1) of, and paragraph 10 of Schedule 10 to, the Domestic Violence, Crime and Victims Act 2004 (c. 28), section 52(2) of, and paragraph 14 of Schedule 3 to, the Violent Crime Reduction Act 2006 (c. 38), section 64 of, and paragraph 10 of Schedule 3 to, the Animal Welfare Act 2006 (c. 45) and section 54 of, and paragraphs 2 and 4 of Schedule 12 to, the Criminal Justice and Courts Act 2015 (c. 2).

[28] 1981 c. 54; section 48(2) was amended by section 156 of the Criminal Justice Act 1988 (c. 33).

(b)  so constituted, the court may, among other things, exercise the powers to which apply—

    (i)  the rules in this Part and in Part 3 (Case management), and

    (ii)  rule 35.2 (stating a case for the opinion of the High Court, or refusing to do so).

*[Note. See sections 73 and 74 of the Senior Courts Act 1981[29] (which allow rules of court to provide for the constitution of the Crown Court in proceedings on appeal), section 45 of the Children and Young Persons Act 1933[30] and section 9 of the Courts Act 2003[31]. Under section 8(1A) of the Senior Courts Act 1981[32], a qualifying judge advocate may not exercise the jurisdiction of the Crown Court on an appeal from a youth court.]*

CRIMINAL PRACTICE DIRECTIONS    PART 34    APPEAL TO THE CROWN COURT

**CPD IX Appeal 34A: Appeals to the Crown Court**                                      **CPD.34A**

34A.1  On an appeal against conviction CrimPR 34.3 requires the appellant and respondent to supply information needed for the effective case management of the appeal, but allows the Crown Court to relieve the appellant – not the respondent – of that obligation, in whole or part.

34A.2  The court is most likely to exercise that discretion in an appellant's favour where he or she is not represented and is unable, without assistance, to provide reliable such information. The notes to the standard form of appeal notice invite the appellant to answer the relevant questions in that form to the extent that he or she is able, explaining that while the appellant may not be able to answer all those questions nevertheless any answers that can be given will assist in making arrangements for the hearing of the appeal. Where an appellant uses the prescribed form of easy read appeal notice the court usually should assume that the appellant will not be able to supply case management information, and that form contains no questions corresponding with those in the standard appeal notice. In such a case relevant information will be supplied by the respondent in the respondent's notice and may be gleaned from material obtained from magistrates' court records by Crown Court staff.

**CPD IX Appeal 34B: Appeal to the Crown Court: Information from the Magistrates' Court**    **CPD.34B**

34B.1  CrimPR 34.4 applies when a defendant appeals to the Crown Court against conviction or sentence and specifies the information and documentation that must be made available by the magistrates' court.

34B.2  In all cases magistrates' court staff must ensure that Crown Court staff are notified of the appeal as soon as practicable: CrimPR 34.4(2)(b). In most cases Crown Court staff will be able to obtain the other information required by CrimPR 34.4(3) or (4) by direct access to the electronic records created by magistrates' court staff. However, if such access is not available then alternative arrangements must be made for the transfer of such information to Crown Court staff by electronic means. Paper copies of documents should be created and sent only as a last resort.

34B.3  On an appeal against conviction, the reasons given by the magistrates for their decision should not be included with the documents; the appeal hearing is not a review of the magistrates' court's decision but a re-hearing. There is no requirement for the Notice of Appeal form to be redacted in any way; the judge and magistrates presiding over the rehearing will base their decision on the evidence presented during the re-hearing itself.

34B.4  On an appeal solely against sentence, the magistrates' court's reasons and factual finding leading to the finding of guilt should be included, but any reasons for the sentence imposed should be omitted as the Crown Court will be conducting a fresh sentencing exercise. Whilst reasons for the sentence imposed are not necessary for the re-hearing, the Notice of Appeal form may include references to the sentence that is being appealed. There is no requirement to redact this before the form is given to the judge and magistrates hearing the appeal.

---

[29]  1981 c. 54; section 73 was amended by article 3 of, and paragraphs 11 and 12 of the Schedule to, S.I. 2004/2035 and section 26 of, and paragraph 2 of Schedule 2 to, the Armed Forces Act 2011 (c. 18). Section 74 was amended by sections 79 and 106 of, and Table (4) of Part V of Schedule 15 to, the Access to Justice Act 1999 (c. 22), article 3 of, and paragraphs 11 and 12 of the Schedule to S.I. 2004/2035, section 15 of, and paragraphs 114 and 133 of Schedule 4 to, the Constitutional Reform Act 2005 (c. 4) and section 26 of, and paragraph 3 of Schedule 2 to, the Armed Forces Act 2011 (c. 18). The Act's title was amended by section 59(5) of, and paragraph 1 of Schedule 11 to, the Constitutional Reform Act 2005 (c. 4).

[30]  1933 c. 12; section 45 was substituted by section 50 of the Courts Act 2003 (c. 39) and amended by section 15 of, and paragraph 20 of Schedule 4 to, the Constitutional Reform Act 2005 (c. 4).

[31]  2003 c. 39.

[32]  1981 c. 54; section 8(1A) was inserted by paragraph 1 of Schedule 2 to the Armed Forces Act 2011 (c. 18).

Criminal Procedure Rules    Part 35    Appeal to the High Court by Case Stated

## R35.1    When this Part applies

35.1    This Part applies where a person wants to appeal to the High Court by case stated—

(a)    under section 111 of the Magistrates' Courts Act 1980, against a decision of a magistrates' court; or

(b)    under section 28 of the Senior Courts Act 1981, against a decision of the Crown Court.

*[Note. Under section 111 of the Magistrates' Courts Act 1980, 'any person who was a party to any proceeding before a magistrates' court or is aggrieved by the conviction, order, determination or other proceeding of the court may question the proceeding on the ground that it is wrong in law or is in excess of jurisdiction by applying to the justices composing the court to state a case for the opinion of the High Court on the question of law or jurisdiction involved'.*

*Under section 28 of the Senior Courts Act 1981, 'any order, judgment or other decision of the Crown Court may be questioned by any party to the proceedings, on the ground that it is wrong in law or is in excess of jurisdiction, by applying to the Crown Court to have a case stated by that court for the opinion of the High Court.'*

*Under section 28A of the 1981 Act[1], the High Court may 'reverse, affirm or amend the determination in respect of which the case has been stated; or remit the matter to the magistrates' court, or the Crown Court, with the opinion of the High Court, and may make such other order ... as it thinks fit.' Under that section, the High Court also may send the case back for amendment, if it thinks fit.]*

## R35.2    Application to state a case

35.2    (1)    A party who wants the court to state a case for the opinion of the High Court must—

(a)    apply in writing, not more than 21 days after the decision against which the applicant wants to appeal; and

(b)    serve the application on—

(i)    the court officer, and

(ii)    each other party.

(2)    The application must—

(a)    specify the decision in issue;

(b)    specify the proposed question or questions of law or jurisdiction on which the opinion of the High Court will be asked;

(c)    indicate the proposed grounds of appeal; and

(d)    include or attach any application for the following, with reasons—

(i)    if the application is to the Crown Court, an extension of time within which to apply to state a case,

(ii)    bail pending appeal, or

(iii)    the suspension of any disqualification imposed in the case, where the court can order such a suspension pending appeal.

(3)    A party who wants to make representations about the application must—

(a)    serve the representations on—

(i)    the court officer, and

(ii)    each other party; and

(b)    do so not more than 10 business days after service of the application.

(4)    The court may determine the application without a hearing.

(5)    If the court decides not to state a case, the court officer must serve on each party—

(a)    notice of that decision; and

(b)    the court's written reasons for that decision, if not more than 15 business days later the applicant asks for those reasons.

*[Note. The time limit for applying to a magistrates' court to state a case is prescribed by section 111(2) of the Magistrates' Courts Act 1980. It may be neither extended nor shortened.*

*Under section 113 of the Magistrates' Courts Act 1980[2], the magistrates' court may grant an appellant bail pending appeal. Under section 81(1)(d) of the Senior Courts Act 1981[3], the Crown Court may do so. See also rule 14.7.]*

---

[1]    1981 c. 54; section 28A was inserted by section 1 of, and paragraph 9 of Schedule 2 to, the Statute Law (Repeals) Act 1993 (c. 50), and amended by section 61 of the Access to Justice Act 1999 (c. 22) and section 40 of, and paragraph 36 of Schedule 9 to, the Constitutional Reform Act 2005 (c. 4).

[2]    1980 c. 43; section 113 was amended by section 168 of, and paragraph 44 of Schedule 10 to, the Criminal Justice and Public Order Act 1994 (c. 33) and section 165 of, and paragraph 72 of Schedule 9 to, the Powers of Criminal Courts (Sentencing) Act 2000 (c. 6).

[3]    1981 c.54.

*Where Part 34 (Appeal to the Crown Court) applies, an application to which this rule applies may be determined by a judge of the High Court, a Circuit judge, a Recorder or a qualifying judge advocate without justices of the peace: see rule 34.11 (Constitution of the Crown Court).*

*Under section 39 of the Road Traffic Offenders Act 1988[4], a court which has made an order disqualifying a person from driving may suspend the disqualification pending appeal. See also rule 29.2.*

*The Practice Direction sets out a form of application for use in connection with this rule.]*

**Preparation of case stated**                                                                        **R35.3**

35.3  (1)  This rule applies where the court decides to state a case for the opinion of the High Court.

   (2)  The court officer must serve on each party notice of—
      (a)  the decision to state a case, and
      (b)  any recognizance ordered by the court.

   (3)  Unless the court otherwise directs, not more than 15 business days after the court's decision to state a case—
      (a)  in a magistrates' court, the court officer must serve a draft case on each party; or
      (b)  in the Crown Court, the applicant must serve a draft case on the court officer and each other party.

   (4)  The draft case must—
      (a)  specify the decision in issue;
      (b)  specify the question(s) of law or jurisdiction on which the opinion of the High Court will be asked;
      (c)  include a succinct summary of—
         (i)  the nature and history of the proceedings,
         (ii)  the court's relevant findings of fact, and
         (iii)  the relevant contentions of the parties; and
      (d)  if a question is whether there was sufficient evidence on which the court reasonably could reach a finding of fact—
         (i)  specify that finding, and
         (ii)  include a summary of the evidence on which the court reached that finding.

   (5)  Except to the extent that paragraph (4)(d) requires, the draft case must not include an account of the evidence received by the court.

   (6)  A party who wants to make representations about the content of the draft case, or to propose a revised draft, must—
      (a)  serve the representations, or revised draft, on—
         (i)  the court officer, and
         (ii)  each other party; and
      (b)  do so not more than 15 business days after service of the draft case.

   (7)  The court must state the case not more than 15 business days after the time for service of representations under paragraph (6) has expired.

   (8)  A case stated for the opinion of the High Court must—
      (a)  comply with paragraphs (4) and (5); and
      (b)  identify—
         (i)  the court that stated it, and
         (ii)  the court office for that court.

   (9)  The court officer must serve the case stated on each party.

*[Note. Under section 114 of the Magistrates' Courts Act 1980[5], a magistrates' court need not state a case until the person who applied for it has entered into a recognizance to appeal promptly to the High Court. The Crown Court has a corresponding inherent power.*

*Under section 121(6) of the 1980 Act, the magistrates' court which states a case need not include all the members of the court which took the decision questioned.*

*For the procedure on appeal to the High Court, see Part 52 of the Civil Procedure Rules 1998[6] and the associated Practice Direction.]*

---

[4]  1988 c. 53.
[5]  1980 c. 43; section 114 was amended by section 90 of, and paragraphs 95 and 113 of Schedule 13 to, the Access to Justice Act 1999 (c. 22) and section 109 of, and paragraph 235 of Schedule 8 to, the Courts Act 2003 (c. 39).
[6]  S.I. 1998/3132; Part 52 was inserted by S.I. 2000/221 and amended by paragraph 1 of Schedule 11 to the Constitutional Reform Act 2005 (c. 4) and S.I. 2003/2113, 2003/3361, 2006/3435, 2007/2204 and 2009/2092.

**R35.4**    **Duty of justices' legal adviser**

35.4   (1)   This rule applies—
    (a)   only in a magistrates' court; and
    (b)   unless the court—
        (i)   includes a District Judge (Magistrates' Courts), and
        (ii)   otherwise directs.
  (2)   A justices' legal adviser must—
    (a)   give the court legal advice; and
    (b)   if the court so requires, assist it by—
        (i)   preparing and amending the draft case, and
        (ii)   completing the case stated.

**R35.5**    **Court's power to vary requirements under this Part**

35.5   (1)   The court may shorten or extend (even after it has expired) a time limit under this Part.
  (2)   A person who wants an extension of time must—
    (a)   apply when serving the application, representations or draft case for which it is needed; and
    (b)   explain the delay.

*[Note. See also rule 35.2(2)(d)(i) and the note to rule 35.2.]*

CRIMINAL PROCEDURE RULES    PART 36    APPEAL TO THE COURT
OF APPEAL: GENERAL RULES

**R36.1**    **When this Part applies**

36.1   (1)   This Part applies to all the applications, appeals and references to the Court of Appeal to which Parts 37, 38, 39, 40, 41 and 43 apply.
  (2)   In this Part and in those, unless the context makes it clear that something different is meant, 'court' means the Court of Appeal or any judge of that court.

*[Note. See rule 2.2 for the usual meaning of 'court'.*

*Under section 53 of the Senior Courts Act 1981[1], the criminal division of the Court of Appeal exercises jurisdiction in the appeals and references to which Parts 37, 38, 39, 40 and 41 apply.*

*Under section 55 of that Act[2], the Court of Appeal must include at least two judges, and for some purposes at least three.*

*For the powers of the Court of Appeal that may be exercised by one judge of that court or by the Registrar, see sections 31, 31A, 31B, 31C and 44 of the Criminal Appeal Act 1968[3]; section 49 of the Criminal Justice Act 2003[4]; the Criminal Justice Act 2003 (Mandatory Life Sentences: Appeals in Transitional Cases) Order 2005[5]; the Serious*

---

[1]  1981 c. 54. The Act's title was amended by section 59(5) of, and paragraph 1 of Schedule 11 to, the Constitutional Reform Act 2005 (c. 4).
[2]  1981 c. 54; section 55 was amended by section 170 of, and paragraph 80 of Schedule 15 to, the Criminal Justice Act 1988 (c. 33), section 52 of the Criminal Justice and Public Order Act 1994 (c. 33) and section 58 of the Domestic Violence, Crime and Victims Act 2004 (c. 28). It is further amended by section 40 of, and paragraph 36 of Schedule 9 to, the Constitutional Reform Act 2005 (c. 4).
[3]  1968 c. 19; section 31 was amended by section 21 of, and Schedule 2 to, the Costs in Criminal Cases Act 1973 (c. 14), section 24 of, and paragraph 10 of Schedule 6 to, the Road Traffic Act 1974 (c. 50), section 29 of the Criminal Justice Act 1982 (c. 48), section 170 of, and paragraphs 20, 29 and 30 of Schedule 15 to, the Criminal Justice Act 1988 (c. 33), section 4 of, and paragraph 4 of Schedule 3 to, the Road Traffic (Consequential Provisions) Act 1988 (c. 54), section 198 of, and paragraphs 38 and 40 of Schedule 6 to, the Licensing Act 2003 (c. 17), section 87 of the Courts Act 2003 (c. 39), paragraphs 86, 87 and 88 of Schedule 36 to the Criminal Justice Act 2003 (c. 44), section 48 of the Police and Justice Act 2006 (c. 48), section 47 of, and paragraphs 1, 9 and 11 of Schedule 8 to, the Criminal Justice and Immigration Act 2008 (c. 4) and section 177 of, and paragraph 69 of Schedule 21 to, the Coroners and Justice Act 2009 (c. 25). It is further amended by section 67 of, and paragraph 4 of Schedule 4 to, the Youth Justice and Criminal Evidence Act 1999 (c. 23), with effect from a date to be appointed. Section 31A was inserted by section 6 of the Criminal Appeal Act 1995 (c. 35) and amended by sections 87 and 109 of, and Schedule 10 to, the Courts Act 2003 (c. 39) and section 331 of, and paragraphs 86 and 88 of Schedule 36 to, the Criminal Justice Act 2003 (c. 44). Section 31B was inserted by section 87 of the Courts Act 2003 (c. 39). Section 31C was inserted by section 87 of the Courts Act 2003 (c. 39) and amended by sections 47 and 149 of, and paragraphs 1 and 12 of Schedule 8 and part 3 of Schedule 28 to, the Criminal Justice and Immigration Act 2008 (c. 4). Section 44 was amended by section 24(2) of, and paragraph 11 of Schedule 6 to, the Road Traffic Act 1974 (c. 50), section 170(1) of, and paragraphs 20 and 31 of the Criminal Justice Act 1988 (c. 33), section 4 of, and paragraph 4(2) of the Road Traffic (Consequential Provisions) Act 1988 (c. 54) and section 198(1), and paragraphs 38 and 41 of Schedule 6 to, the Licensing Act 2003 (c. 17).
[4]  2003 c. 44.
[5]  S.I. 2005/2798.

*Organised Crime and Police Act 2005 (Appeals under section 74) Order 2006[6]; the Serious Crime Act 2007 (Appeals under Section 24) Order 2008[7]; and the power conferred by section 53(4) of the 1981 Act.]*

### Case management in the Court of Appeal

36.2 (1) The court and the parties have the same duties and powers as under Part 3 (Case management).

(2) The Registrar—

(a) must fulfil the duty of active case management under rule 3.2; and

(b) in fulfilling that duty may exercise any of the powers of case management under—

(i) rule 3.5 (the court's general powers of case management),

(ii) rule 3.12(3) (requiring a certificate of readiness), and

(iii) rule 3.13 (requiring a party to identify intentions and anticipated requirements) subject to the directions of the court.

(3) The Registrar must nominate a case progression officer under rule 3.4.

### Power to vary requirements

36.3 The court or the Registrar may—

(a) shorten a time limit or extend it (even after it has expired) unless that is inconsistent with other legislation;

(b) allow a party to vary any notice that that party has served;

(c) direct that a notice or application be served on any person; and

(d) allow a notice or application to be in a different form, or presented orally.

*[Note. The time limit for serving an appeal notice—*

*(a) under section 18 of the Criminal Appeal Act 1968[8] on an appeal against conviction or sentence, and*

*(b) under section 18A of that Act[9] on an appeal against a finding of contempt of court*

*may be extended but not shortened: see rule 39.2.*

*The time limit for serving an application for permission to refer a sentencing case under section 36 of the Criminal Justice Act 1988[10] may be neither extended nor shortened: see rule 41.2(4).*

*The time limits in rule 43.2 for applying to the Court of Appeal for permission to appeal or refer a case to the Supreme Court may be extended or shortened only as explained in the note to that rule.]*

### Application for extension of time

36.4 A person who wants an extension of time within which to serve a notice or make an application must—

(a) apply for that extension of time when serving that notice or making that application; and

(b) give the reasons for the application for an extension of time.

### Renewing an application refused by a judge or the Registrar

36.5 (1) This rule applies where a party with the right to do so wants to renew—

(a) to a judge of the Court of Appeal an application refused by the Registrar; or

(b) to the Court of Appeal an application refused by a judge of that court.

(2) That party must—

(a) renew the application in the form set out in the Practice Direction, signed by or on behalf of the applicant; and

(b) serve the renewed application on the Registrar not more than 10 business days after—

(i) the refusal of the application that the applicant wants to renew; or

(ii) the Registrar serves that refusal on the applicant, if the applicant was not present in person or by live link when the original application was refused.

---

[6] S.I. 2006/2135.

[7] S.I. 2008/1863.

[8] 1968 c. 19.

[9] 1968 c. 19; section 18A was inserted by section 170 of, and paragraphs 20 and 25 of Schedule 15 to, the Criminal Justice Act 1988 (c. 33).

[10] 1988 c. 33; section 36 was amended by section 272 of, and paragraphs 45 and 46 of Schedule 32 and paragraph 96 of Schedule 36 to, the Criminal Justice Act 2003 (c. 44), sections 49 and 65 of, and paragraph 3 of Schedule 1 and Schedule 5 to, the Violent Crime Reduction Act 2006 (c. 38), section 40 of, and paragraph 48 of Schedule 9 to, the Constitutional Reform Act 2005 (c. 4), sections 46, 148 and 149 of, and paragraphs 22 and 23 of Schedule 26 and Part 3 of Schedule 28 to, the Criminal Justice and Immigration Act 2008 (c. 4), paragraph 2 of Schedule 19 and paragraphs 4 and 5 of Schedule 26 to the Legal Aid, Sentencing and Punishment of Offenders Act 2012 (c. 10) and section 28 of, and paragraph 2 of Schedule 5 to, the Criminal Justice and Courts Act 2015 (c. 2). It is further amended by section 46 of the Criminal Justice and Immigration Act 2008 (c. 4) with effect from a date to be appointed.

*[Note. The time limit of 10 business days under this rule is reduced to 5 business days where Parts 37, 38 or 40 apply: see rules 37.7, 38.10 and 40.7.*

*For the right to renew an application to a judge or to the Court of Appeal, see sections 31(3), 31C and 44 of the Criminal Appeal Act 1968, the Criminal Justice Act 2003 (Mandatory Life Sentences: Appeals in Transitional Cases) Order 2005[11], the Serious Organised Crime and Police Act 2005 (Appeals under section 74) Order 2006[12] and the Serious Crime Act 2007 (Appeals under Section 24) Order 2008.*

*A party has no right under section 31C of the 1968 Act to renew to the Court of Appeal an application for procedural directions refused by a judge, but in some circumstances a case management direction might be varied: see rule 3.6.*

*If an applicant does not renew an application that a judge has refused, including an application for permission to appeal, the Registrar will treat it as if it had been refused by the Court of Appeal.*

*Under section 22 of the Criminal Appeal Act 1968[13], the Court of Appeal may direct that an appellant who is in custody is to attend a hearing by live link.]*

**R36.6**    **Hearings**

36.6   (1)   The general rule is that the Court of Appeal must hear in public—
        (a)   an application, including an application for permission to appeal; and
        (b)   an appeal or reference,
       but it may order any hearing to be in private.
     (2)   Where a hearing is about a public interest ruling, that hearing must be in private unless the court otherwise directs.
     (3)   Where the appellant wants to appeal against an order restricting public access to a trial, the court—
        (a)   may decide without a hearing—
           (i)   an application, including an application for permission to appeal, and
           (ii)   an appeal; but
        (b)   must announce its decision on such an appeal at a hearing in public.
     (4)   Where the appellant wants to appeal or to refer a case to the Supreme Court, the court—
        (a)   may decide without a hearing an application—
           (i)   for permission to appeal or to refer a sentencing case, or
           (ii)   to refer a point of law; but
        (b)   must announce its decision on such an application at a hearing in public.
     (5)   Where a party wants the court to reopen the determination of an appeal—
        (a)   the court—
           (i)   must decide the application without a hearing, as a general rule, but
           (ii)   may decide the application at a hearing; and
        (b)   need not announce its decision on such an application at a hearing in public.
     (6)   A judge of the Court of Appeal and the Registrar may exercise any of their powers—
        (a)   at a hearing in public or in private; or
        (b)   without a hearing.

*[Note. For the procedure on an appeal against an order restricting public access to a trial, see Part 40.*

*For the procedure on an application to reopen the determination of an appeal, see rule 36.15.]*

**R36.7**    **Notice of hearings and decisions**

36.7   (1)   The Registrar must give as much notice as reasonably practicable of every hearing to—
        (a)   the parties;
        (b)   any party's custodian;
        (c)   any other person whom the court requires to be notified; and
        (d)   the Crown Court officer, where Parts 37, 38 or 40 apply.
     (2)   The Registrar must serve every decision on—
        (a)   the parties;
        (b)   any other person whom the court requires to be served; and
        (c)   the Crown Court officer and any party's custodian, where the decision determines an appeal or application for permission to appeal.
     (3)   But where a hearing or decision is about a public interest ruling, the Registrar must not—
        (a)   give notice of that hearing to; or

---

[11]   S.I. 2005/2798.
[12]   S.I. 2006/2135.
[13]   1968 c. 19; section 22 was amended by section 48 of the Police and Justice Act 2006 (c. 48).

(b)  serve that decision on,

anyone other than the prosecutor who applied for that ruling, unless the court otherwise directs.

## Duty of Crown Court officer

**R36.8**

**36.8**  (1)  The Crown Court officer must—

(a)  where electronic arrangements have been made to receive and store information and documents for the Crown Court, as soon as practicable ensure that all such material is available to the Registrar in accordance with those arrangements; and

(b)  provide the Registrar with any document, object or information for which the Registrar asks, within such period as the Registrar may require.

(2)  Where someone may appeal to the Court of Appeal, the Crown Court officer must keep any document or object exhibited in the proceedings in the Crown Court, or arrange for it to be kept by some other appropriate person, until—

(a)  6 weeks after the conclusion of those proceedings; or

(b)  the conclusion of any appeal proceedings that begin within that 6 weeks,

unless the court, the Registrar or the Crown Court otherwise directs.

(3)  Where Part 37 applies (Appeal to the Court of Appeal against ruling at preparatory hearing), the Crown Court officer must as soon as practicable serve on the appellant a transcript or note of—

(a)  each order or ruling against which the appellant wants to appeal; and

(b)  the decision by the Crown Court judge on any application for permission to appeal.

(4)  Where Part 38 applies (Appeal to the Court of Appeal against ruling adverse to prosecution), the Crown Court officer must as soon as practicable serve on the appellant a transcript or note of—

(a)  each ruling against which the appellant wants to appeal;

(b)  the decision by the Crown Court judge on any application for permission to appeal; and

(c)  the decision by the Crown Court judge on any request to expedite the appeal.

(5)  Where Part 39 applies (Appeal to the Court of Appeal about conviction or sentence), the Crown Court officer must as soon as practicable serve on or make available to the Registrar—

(a)  any Crown Court judge's certificate that the case is fit for appeal;

(b)  the decision on any application at the Crown Court centre for bail pending appeal;

(c)  such of the Crown Court case papers as the Registrar requires; and

(d)  such transcript of the Crown Court proceedings as the Registrar requires.

(6)  Where Part 40 applies (Appeal to the Court of Appeal about reporting or public access) and an order is made restricting public access to a trial, the Crown Court officer must—

(a)  immediately notify the Registrar of that order, if the appellant has given advance notice of intention to appeal; and

(b)  as soon as practicable provide the applicant for that order with a transcript or note of the application.

*[Note. See also section 87(4) of the Senior Courts Act 1981[14] and rules 5.5 (Recording and transcription of proceedings in the Crown Court), 36.9 (duty of person transcribing record of proceedings in the Crown Court) and 36.10 (Duty of person keeping exhibit).]*

## Duty of person transcribing proceedings in the Crown Court

**R36.9**

**36.9**  A person who transcribes a recording of proceedings in the Crown Court under arrangements made by the Crown Court officer must provide the Registrar with any transcript for which the Registrar asks, within such period as the Registrar may require.

*[Note. See also section 32 of the Criminal Appeal Act 1968[15] and rule 5.5 (Recording and transcription of proceedings in the Crown Court).]*

## Duty of person keeping exhibit

**R36.10**

**36.10**  A person who under arrangements made by the Crown Court officer keeps a document or object exhibited in the proceedings in the Crown Court must—

(a)  keep that exhibit until—

(i)  6 weeks after the conclusion of the Crown Court proceedings, or

(ii)  the conclusion of any appeal proceedings that begin within that 6 weeks,

unless the court, the Registrar or the Crown Court otherwise directs; and

Criminal Procedure Rules and Criminal Practice Directions

---

[14]  1981 c. 54; section 87(4) was amended by articles 2 and 3 of, and paragraphs 11 and 17 of the Schedule to, S.I. 2004/2035.
[15]  1968 c. 19.

(b) provide the Registrar with any such document or object for which the Registrar asks, within such period as the Registrar may require.

*[Note. See also rule 36.8(2) (Duty of Crown Court officer).]*

**R36.11**    **Registrar's duty to provide copy documents for appeal or reference**

36.11 Unless the court otherwise directs, for the purposes of an appeal or reference—
- (a) the Registrar must—
  - (i) provide a party with a copy of any document or transcript held by the Registrar for such purposes, or
  - (ii) allow a party to inspect such a document or transcript,
  - on payment by that party of any charge fixed by the Treasury; but
- (b) the Registrar must not provide a copy or allow the inspection of—
  - (i) a document provided only for the court and the Registrar, or
  - (ii) a transcript of a public interest ruling or of an application for such a ruling.

*[Note. Section 21 of the Criminal Appeal Act 1968 requires the Registrar to collect, prepare and provide documents needed by the court.]*

**R36.12**    **Declaration of incompatibility with a Convention right**

36.12 (1) This rule applies where a party—
- (a) wants the court to make a declaration of incompatibility with a Convention right under section 4 of the Human Rights Act 1998[16]; or
- (b) raises an issue that the Registrar thinks may lead the court to make such a declaration.

(2) The Registrar must serve notice on—
- (a) the relevant person named in the list published under section 17(1) of the Crown Proceedings Act 1947[17]; or
- (b) the Treasury Solicitor, if it is not clear who is the relevant person.

(3) That notice must include or attach details of—
- (a) the legislation affected and the Convention right concerned;
- (b) the parties to the appeal; and
- (c) any other information or document that the Registrar thinks relevant.

(4) A person who has a right under the 1998 Act to become a party to the appeal must—
- (a) serve notice on—
  - (i) the Registrar, and
  - (ii) the other parties,
  - if that person wants to exercise that right; and
- (b) in that notice—
  - (i) indicate the conclusion that that person invites the court to reach on the question of incompatibility, and
  - (ii) identify each ground for that invitation, concisely outlining the arguments in support.

(5) The court must not make a declaration of incompatibility—
- (a) less than 15 business days after the Registrar serves notice under paragraph (2); and
- (b) without giving any person who serves a notice under paragraph (4) an opportunity to make representations at a hearing.

**R36.13**    **Abandoning an appeal**

36.13 (1) This rule applies where an appellant wants to—
- (a) abandon—
  - (i) an application to the court for permission to appeal, or
  - (ii) an appeal; or
- (b) reinstate such an application or appeal after abandoning it.

(2) The appellant—
- (a) may abandon such an application or appeal without the court's permission by serving a notice of abandonment on—

---

[16] 1998 c. 42; section 4 was amended by section 40 of, and paragraph 66 of Schedule 9 to, the Constitutional Reform Act 2005 (c. 4) and section 67 of, and paragraph 43 of Schedule 6 to, the Mental Capacity Act 2005 (c. 9).

[17] 1987 c. 38; section 9 was amended by section 170 of, and Schedule 16 to, the Criminal Justice Act 1988 (c. 33), section 6 of the Criminal Justice Act 1993 (c. 36), sections 72, 74 and 80 of, and paragraph 3 of Schedule 3 and Schedule 5 to, the Criminal Procedure and Investigations Act 1996 (c. 25), sections 45 and 310 of, and paragraphs 18, 52 and 54 of Schedule 36 and Part 3 of Schedule 37 to, the Criminal Justice Act 2003 (c. 44), article 3 of, and paragraphs 21 and 23 of S.I. 2004/2035, section 59 of, and paragraph 1 of Schedule 11 to, the Constitutional Reform Act 2005 (c. 4) and Part 10 of Schedule 10 to the Protection of Freedoms Act 2012 (c. 9). The amendment made by section 45 of the Criminal Justice Act 2003 (c. 44) is in force for certain purposes; for remaining purposes it has effect from a date to be appointed.

(i) the Registrar, and

(ii) any respondent

before any hearing of the application or appeal; but

(b) at any such hearing, may only abandon that application or appeal with the court's permission.

(3) A notice of abandonment must be in the form set out in the Practice Direction, signed by or on behalf of the appellant.

(4) On receiving a notice of abandonment the Registrar must—

(a) date it;

(b) serve a dated copy on—

(i) the appellant,

(ii) the appellant's custodian, if any,

(iii) the Crown Court officer, and

(iv) any other person on whom the appellant or the Registrar served the appeal notice; and

(c) treat the application or appeal as if it had been refused or dismissed by the Court of Appeal.

(5) An appellant who wants to reinstate an application or appeal after abandoning it must—

(a) apply in writing, with reasons; and

(b) serve the application on the Registrar.

*[Note. The Court of Appeal has power only in exceptional circumstances to allow an appellant to reinstate an application or appeal that has been abandoned.]*

**Grounds of appeal and opposition**                                          R36.14

**36.14** (1) If the court gives permission to appeal then unless the court otherwise directs the decision indicates that—

(a) the appellant has permission to appeal on every ground identified by the appeal notice; and

(b) the court finds reasonably arguable each ground on which the appellant has permission to appeal.

(2) If the court gives permission to appeal but not on every ground identified by the appeal notice the decision indicates that—

(a) at the hearing of the appeal the court will not consider representations that address any ground thus excluded from argument; and

(b) an appellant who wants to rely on such an excluded ground needs the court's permission to do so.

(3) An appellant who wants to rely at the hearing of an appeal on a ground of appeal excluded from argument by a judge of the Court of Appeal when giving permission to appeal must—

(a) apply for permission to do so, with reasons, and identify each such ground;

(b) serve the application on—

(i) the Registrar, and

(ii) any respondent; and

(c) serve the application not more than 10 business days after—

(i) the giving of permission to appeal, or

(ii) the Registrar serves notice of that decision on the applicant, if the applicant was not present in person or by live link when permission to appeal was given.

(4) Paragraph (5) applies where one of the following Parts applies—

(a) Part 37 (Appeal to the Court of Appeal against ruling at preparatory hearing);

(b) Part 38 (Appeal to the Court of Appeal against ruling adverse to prosecution);

(c) Part 39 (Appeal to the Court of Appeal about conviction or sentence); or

(d) Part 40 (Appeal to the Court of Appeal about reporting or public access restriction).

(5) An appellant who wants to rely on a ground of appeal not identified by the appeal notice must—

(a) apply for permission to do so and identify each such ground;

(b) in respect of each such ground—

(i) explain why it was not included in the appeal notice, and

(ii) where Part 39 applies, comply with rule 39.3(2);

(c) serve the application on—

(i) the Registrar, and

(ii) any respondent; and

(d) serve the application—

(i) as soon as reasonably practicable, and in any event

(ii) at the same time as serving any renewed application for permission to appeal which relies on that ground.

(6) Paragraph (7) applies where a party wants to abandon—

(a) a ground of appeal on which that party has permission to appeal; or

(b) a ground of opposition identified in a respondent's notice.

(7) Such a party must serve notice on—

(a) the Registrar; and

(b) each other party,

before any hearing at which that ground will be considered by the court.

*[Note. In some legislation, including the Criminal Appeal Act 1968, permission to appeal is described as 'leave to appeal'.*

*Under rule 36.5 (Renewing an application refused by a judge or the Registrar), if permission to appeal is refused the application for such permission may be renewed within the time limit (10 business days) set by that rule.]*

**R36.15    Reopening the determination of an appeal**

**36.15** (1) This rule applies where—

(a) a party wants the court to reopen a decision which determines an appeal or reference to which this Part applies (including a decision on an application for permission to appeal or refer); or

(b) the Registrar refers such a decision to the court for the court to consider reopening it.

(2) Such a party must—

(a) apply in writing for permission to reopen that decision, as soon as practicable after becoming aware of the grounds for doing so; and

(b) serve the application on the Registrar.

(3) The application must—

(a) specify the decision which the applicant wants the court to reopen; and

(b) explain—

(i) why it is necessary for the court to reopen that decision in order to avoid real injustice,

(ii) how the circumstances are exceptional and make it appropriate to reopen the decision notwithstanding the rights and interests of other participants and the importance of finality,

(iii) why there is no alternative effective remedy among any potentially available, and

(iv) any delay in making the application.

(4) The Registrar—

(a) may invite a party's representations on—

(i) an application to reopen a decision, or

(ii) a decision that the Registrar has referred, or intends to refer, to the court; and

(b) must do so if the court so directs.

(5) A party invited to make representations must serve them on the Registrar within such period as the Registrar directs.

(6) The court must not reopen a decision to which this rule applies unless each other party has had an opportunity to make representations.

*[Note. The Court of Appeal has power only in exceptional circumstances to reopen a decision to which this rule applies.]*

CRIMINAL PROCEDURE RULES    PART 37    APPEAL TO THE COURT OF APPEAL
AGAINST RULING AT PREPARATORY HEARING

**R37.1    When this Part applies**

**37.1** (1) This Part applies where a party wants to appeal under—

(a) section 9(11) of the Criminal Justice Act 1987[1] or section 35(1) of the Criminal Procedure and Investigations Act 1996[2]; or

(b) section 47(1) of the Criminal Justice Act 2003[3].

(2) A reference to an 'appellant' in this Part is a reference to such a party.

---

[1] 1947 c. 44; section 17 was amended by article 3(2) of S.I. 1968/1656.

[2] 1996 c. 25; section 35(1) was amended by section 45 of the Criminal Justice Act 2003 (c. 44). The amendment is in force for certain purposes, for remaining purposes it has effect from a date to be appointed. Section 35 was also amended by paragraphs 65 and 69 of Schedule 36 to the Criminal Justice Act 2003 (c. 44) and section 59 of, and paragraph 1 of Schedule 11 to, the Constitutional Reform Act 2005 (c. 4) and Part 10 of Schedule 10 to the Protection of Freedoms Act 2012 (c. 9).

[3] 2003 c. 44.

*[Note. Under section 9(11) of the Criminal Justice Act 1987 (which applies to serious or complex fraud cases) and under section 35(1) of the Criminal Procedure and Investigations Act 1996 (which applies to other complex, serious or long cases) a party may appeal to the Court of Appeal against an order made at a preparatory hearing in the Crown Court.*

*Under section 47(1) of the Criminal Justice Act 2003 a party may appeal to the Court of Appeal against an order in the Crown Court that because of jury tampering a trial will continue without a jury or that there will be a new trial without a jury.*

*Part 3 contains rules about preparatory hearings.*

*The rules in Part 36 (Appeal to the Court of Appeal: general rules) also apply where this Part applies.]*

## Service of appeal notice                                                                       R37.2

37.2  (1)  An appellant must serve an appeal notice on—
    (a)  the Crown Court officer;
    (b)  the Registrar; and
    (c)  every party directly affected by the order or ruling against which the appellant wants to appeal.
  (2)  The appellant must serve the appeal notice not more than 5 business days after—
    (a)  the order or ruling against which the appellant wants to appeal; or
    (b)  the Crown Court judge gives or refuses permission to appeal.

## Form of appeal notice                                                                          R37.3

37.3  (1)  An appeal notice must be in the form set out in the Practice Direction.
  (2)  The appeal notice must—
    (a)  specify each order or ruling against which the appellant wants to appeal;
    (b)  identify each ground of appeal on which the appellant relies, numbering them consecutively (if there is more than one) and concisely outlining each argument in support;
    (c)  summarise the relevant facts;
    (d)  identify any relevant authorities;
    (e)  include or attach any application for the following, with reasons—
      (i)  permission to appeal, if the appellant needs the court's permission,
      (ii)  an extension of time within which to serve the appeal notice, or
      (iii)  a direction to attend in person a hearing that the appellant could attend by live link, if the appellant is in custody;
    (f)  include a list of those on whom the appellant has served the appeal notice;
    (g)  attach—
      (i)  a transcript or note of each order or ruling against which the appellant wants to appeal,
      (ii)  all relevant skeleton arguments considered by the Crown Court judge,
      (iii)  any written application for permission to appeal that the appellant made to the Crown Court judge,
      (iv)  a transcript or note of the decision by the Crown Court judge on any application for permission to appeal, and
      (v)  any other document or thing that the appellant thinks the court will need to decide the appeal and include or attach an electronic link to each such document that has been made available to the Registrar under rule 36.8(1)(a) (Duty of Crown Court officer); and
    (h)  include or attach—
      (i)  an electronic copy of any authority identified under paragraph (2)(d), or
      (ii)  if two or more such authorities are identified, electronic copies of each together in a single electronic document.

*[Note. An appellant needs the court's permission to appeal in every case to which this Part applies unless the Crown Court judge gives permission.]*

## Crown Court judge's permission to appeal                                                        R37.4

37.4  (1)  An appellant who wants the Crown Court judge to give permission to appeal must—
    (a)  apply orally, with reasons, immediately after the order or ruling against which the appellant wants to appeal; or
    (b)  apply in writing and serve the application on—
      (i)  the Crown Court officer, and
      (ii)  every party directly affected by the order or ruling
    not more than 2 business days after that order or ruling.
  (2)  A written application must include the same information (with the necessary adaptations) as an appeal notice.

*[Note. For the Crown Court judge's power to give permission to appeal, see section 9(11) of the Criminal Justice Act 1987, section 35(1) of the Criminal Procedure and Investigations Act 1996 and section 47(2) of the Criminal Justice Act 2003.]*

**R37.5** **Respondent's notice**

37.5 (1) A party on whom an appellant serves an appeal notice may serve a respondent's notice, and must do so if—

(a) that party wants to make representations to the court; or

(b) the court so directs.

(2) Such a party must serve the respondent's notice on—

(a) the appellant;

(b) the Crown Court officer;

(c) the Registrar; and

(d) any other party on whom the appellant served the appeal notice.

(3) Such a party must serve the respondent's notice not more than 5 business days after—

(a) the appellant serves the appeal notice; or

(b) a direction to do so.

(4) The respondent's notice must be in the form set out in the Practice Direction.

(5) The respondent's notice must—

(a) give the date on which the respondent was served with the appeal notice;

(b) identify each ground of opposition on which the respondent relies, numbering them consecutively (if there is more than one), concisely outlining each argument in support and identifying the ground of appeal to which each relates;

(c) summarise any relevant facts not already summarised in the appeal notice;

(d) identify any relevant authorities;

(e) include or attach any application for the following, with reasons—

(i) an extension of time within which to serve the respondent's notice, or

(ii) a direction to attend in person any hearing that the respondent could attend by live link, if the respondent is in custody;

(f) identify any other document or thing that the respondent thinks the court will need to decide the appeal and include or attach an electronic link to each such document that has been made available to the Registrar under rule 36.8(1)(a) (Duty of Crown Court officer); and

(g) include or attach—

(i) an electronic copy of any authority identified under paragraph (5)(d), or

(ii) if two or more such authorities are identified, electronic copies of each together in a single electronic document

**R37.6** **Powers of Court of Appeal judge**

37.6 A judge of the Court of Appeal may give permission to appeal as well as exercising the powers given by other legislation (including these Rules).

*[Note. See section 31 of the Criminal Appeal Act 1968[4] and section 49 of the Criminal Justice Act 2003[5].]*

**R37.7** **Renewing applications**

37.7 Rule 36.5 (Renewing an application refused by a judge or the Registrar) applies with a time limit of 5 business days.

**R37.8** **Right to attend hearing**

37.8 (1) A party who is in custody has a right to attend a hearing in public.

(2) The court or the Registrar may direct that such a party is to attend a hearing by live link.

*[Note. See rule 36.6 (Hearings).]*

---

[4] 1968 c. 19; section 31 was amended by section 21 of, and Schedule 2 to, the Costs in Criminal Cases Act 1973 (c. 14), section 24 of, and paragraph 10 of Schedule 6 to, the Road Traffic Act 1974 (c. 50), section 29 of the Criminal Justice Act 1982 (c. 48), section 170 of, and paragraphs 20, 29 and 30 of Schedule 15 to, the Criminal Justice Act 1988 (c. 33), section 4 of, and paragraph 4 of Schedule 3 to, the Road Traffic (Consequential Provisions) Act 1988 (c. 54), section 198 of, and paragraphs 38 and 40 of Schedule 6 to, the Licensing Act 2003 (c. 17), section 87 of the Courts Act 2003 (c. 39), paragraphs 86, 87 and 88 of Schedule 36 to the Criminal Justice Act 2003 (c. 44), section 48 of the Police and Justice Act 2006 (c. 48), section 47 of, and paragraphs 1, 9 and 11 of Schedule 8 to, the Criminal Justice and Immigration Act 2008 (c. 4) and section 177 of, and paragraph 69 of Schedule 21 to, the Coroners and Justice Act 2009 (c. 25). It is further amended by section 67 of, and paragraph 4 of Schedule 4 to, the Youth Justice and Criminal Evidence Act 1999 (c. 23), with effect from a date to be appointed.

[5] 2003 c. 44.

CRIMINAL PROCEDURE RULES    PART 38    APPEAL TO THE COURT OF APPEAL
AGAINST RULING ADVERSE TO PROSECUTION

**When this Part applies**                                                      R38.1

**38.1** (1) This Part applies where a prosecutor wants to appeal under section 58(2) of the Criminal Justice Act 2003[1].

(2) A reference to an 'appellant' in this Part is a reference to such a prosecutor.

*[Note. Under section 58(2) of the Criminal Justice Act 2003 a prosecutor may appeal to the Court of Appeal against a ruling in the Crown Court. See also sections 57 and 59 to 61 of the 2003 Act.*

*The rules in Part 36 (Appeal to the Court of Appeal: general rules) also apply where this Part applies.]*

**Decision to appeal**                                                          R38.2

**38.2** (1) An appellant must tell the Crown Court judge of any decision to appeal—

(a) immediately after the ruling against which the appellant wants to appeal; or

(b) on the expiry of the time to decide whether to appeal allowed under paragraph (2).

(2) If an appellant wants time to decide whether to appeal—

(a) the appellant must ask the Crown Court judge immediately after the ruling; and

(b) the general rule is that the judge must not require the appellant to decide there and then but instead must allow until the next business day.

*[Note. If the ruling against which the appellant wants to appeal is a ruling that there is no case to answer, the appellant may appeal against earlier rulings as well: see section 58(7) of the Criminal Justice Act 2003.*

*Under section 58(8) of the 2003 Act the appellant must agree that a defendant directly affected by the ruling must be acquitted if the appellant (a) does not get permission to appeal or (b) abandons the appeal.*

*The Crown Court judge may give permission to appeal and may expedite the appeal: see rules 38.5 and 38.6.]*

**Service of appeal notice**                                                    R38.3

**38.3** (1) An appellant must serve an appeal notice on—

(a) the Crown Court officer;

(b) the Registrar; and

(c) every defendant directly affected by the ruling against which the appellant wants to appeal.

(2) The appellant must serve the appeal notice not later than—

(a) the next business day after telling the Crown Court judge of the decision to appeal, if the judge expedites the appeal; or

(b) 5 business days after telling the Crown Court judge of that decision, if the judge does not expedite the appeal.

*[Note. If the ruling against which the appellant wants to appeal is a public interest ruling, see rule 38.8.]*

**Form of appeal notice**                                                       R38.4

**38.4** (1) An appeal notice must be in the form set out in the Practice Direction.

(2) The appeal notice must—

(a) specify each ruling against which the appellant wants to appeal;

(b) identify each ground of appeal on which the appellant relies, numbering them consecutively (if there is more than one) and concisely outlining each argument in support;

(c) summarise the relevant facts;

(d) identify any relevant authorities;

(e) include or attach any application for the following, with reasons—

(i) permission to appeal, if the appellant needs the court's permission,

(ii) an extension of time within which to serve the appeal notice,

(iii) expedition of the appeal, or revocation of a direction expediting the appeal;

(f) include a list of those on whom the appellant has served the appeal notice;

(g) attach—

(i) a transcript or note of each ruling against which the appellant wants to appeal,

(ii) all relevant skeleton arguments considered by the Crown Court judge,

(iii) any written application for permission to appeal that the appellant made to the Crown Court judge,

(iv) a transcript or note of the decision by the Crown Court judge on any application for permission to appeal,

---

[1] 2003 c. 44.

        (v)   a transcript or note of the decision by the Crown Court judge on any request to expedite the appeal, and

        (vi)  any other document or thing that the appellant thinks the court will need to decide the appeal and include or attach an electronic link to each such document that has been made available to the Registrar under rule 36.8(1)(a) (Duty of Crown Court officer);

  (h)  include or attach—

        (i)   an electronic copy of any authority identified under paragraph (5)(d), or

        (ii)  if two or more such authorities are identified, electronic copies of each together in a single electronic document

  (i)  include or attach—

        (i)   an electronic copy of any authority identified under paragraph (2)(d), or

        (ii)  if two or more such authorities are identified, electronic copies of each together in a single electronic document; and

  (j)  attach a form of respondent's notice for any defendant served with the appeal notice to complete if that defendant wants to do so.

*[Note. An appellant needs the court's permission to appeal unless the Crown Court judge gives permission: see section 57(4) of the Criminal Justice Act 2003. For 'respondent's notice' see rule 38.7.]*

**R38.5   Crown Court judge's permission to appeal**

**38.5**  (1)  An appellant who wants the Crown Court judge to give permission to appeal must—

    (a)  apply orally, with reasons, immediately after the ruling against which the appellant wants to appeal; or

    (b)  apply in writing and serve the application on—

        (i)   the Crown Court officer, and

        (ii)  every defendant directly affected by the ruling

    on the expiry of the time allowed under rule 38.2 to decide whether to appeal.

  (2)  A written application must include the same information (with the necessary adaptations) as an appeal notice.

  (3)  The Crown Court judge must allow every defendant directly affected by the ruling an opportunity to make representations.

  (4)  The general rule is that the Crown Court judge must decide whether or not to give permission to appeal on the day that the application for permission is made.

*[Note. For the Crown Court judge's power to give permission to appeal, see section 57(4) of the Criminal Justice Act 2003.*

*Rule 38.5(3) does not apply where the appellant wants to appeal against a public interest ruling: see rule 38.8(5).]*

**R38.6   Expediting an appeal**

**38.6**  (1)  An appellant who wants the Crown Court judge to expedite an appeal must ask, giving reasons, on telling the judge of the decision to appeal.

  (2)  The Crown Court judge must allow every defendant directly affected by the ruling an opportunity to make representations.

  (3)  The Crown Court judge may revoke a direction expediting the appeal unless the appellant has served the appeal notice.

*[Note. For the Crown Court judge's power to expedite the appeal, see section 59 of the Criminal Justice Act 2003.*

*Rule 38.6(2) does not apply where the appellant wants to appeal against a public interest ruling: see rule 38.8(5).]*

**R38.7   Respondent's notice**

**38.7**  (1)  A defendant on whom an appellant serves an appeal notice may serve a respondent's notice, and must do so if—

    (a)  the defendant wants to make representations to the court; or

    (b)  the court so directs.

  (2)  Such a defendant must serve the respondent's notice on—

    (a)  the appellant;

    (b)  the Crown Court officer;

    (c)  the Registrar; and

    (d)  any other defendant on whom the appellant served the appeal notice.

  (3)  Such a defendant must serve the respondent's notice—

    (a)  not later than the next business day after—

> (i)   the appellant serves the appeal notice, or
> (ii)  a direction to do so
> if the Crown Court judge expedites the appeal; or
> (b)  not more than 5 business days after—
> (i)   the appellant serves the appeal notice, or
> (ii)  a direction to do so
> if the Crown Court judge does not expedite the appeal.

(4)  The respondent's notice must be in the form set out in the Practice Direction.

(5)  The respondent's notice must—
  (a)  give the date on which the respondent was served with the appeal notice;
  (b)  identify each ground of opposition on which the respondent relies, numbering them consecutively (if there is more than one), concisely outlining each argument in support and identifying the ground of appeal to which each relates;
  (c)  summarise any relevant facts not already summarised in the appeal notice;
  (d)  identify any relevant authorities;
  (e)  include or attach any application for the following, with reasons—
    (i)   an extension of time within which to serve the respondent's notice, or
    (ii)  a direction to attend in person any hearing that the respondent could attend by live link, if the respondent is in custody; and
  (f)  identify any other document or thing that the respondent thinks the court will need to decide the appeal.

### Public interest ruling

**R38.8**

**38.8** (1)  This rule applies where the appellant wants to appeal against a public interest ruling.

(2)  The appellant must not serve on any defendant directly affected by the ruling—
  (a)  any written application to the Crown Court judge for permission to appeal; or
  (b)  an appeal notice,
  if the appellant thinks that to do so in effect would reveal something that the appellant thinks ought not be disclosed.

(3)  The appellant must not include in an appeal notice—
  (a)  the material that was the subject of the ruling; or
  (b)  any indication of what sort of material it is,
  if the appellant thinks that to do so in effect would reveal something that the appellant thinks ought not be disclosed.

(4)  The appellant must serve on the Registrar with the appeal notice an annex—
  (a)  marked to show that its contents are only for the court and the Registrar;
  (b)  containing whatever the appellant has omitted from the appeal notice, with reasons; and
  (c)  if relevant, explaining why the appellant has not served the appeal notice.

(5)  Rules 38.5(3) and 38.6(2) do not apply.

*[Note. Rules 38.5(3) and 38.6(2) require the Crown Court judge to allow a defendant to make representations about (i) giving permission to appeal and (ii) expediting an appeal.]*

### Powers of Court of Appeal judge

**R38.9**

**38.9**  A judge of the Court of Appeal may—
  (a)  give permission to appeal;
  (b)  revoke a Crown Court judge's direction expediting an appeal; and
  (c)  where an appellant abandons an appeal, order a defendant's acquittal, his release from custody and the payment of his costs,
as well as exercising the powers given by other legislation (including these Rules).

### Renewing applications

**R38.10**

**38.10**  Rule 36.5 (Renewing an application refused by a judge or the Registrar) applies with a time limit of 5 business days.

### Right to attend hearing

**R38.11**

**38.11** (1)  A respondent who is in custody has a right to attend a hearing in public.

(2)  The court or the Registrar may direct that such a respondent is to attend a hearing by live link.

*[Note. See rule 36.6 (Hearings).]*

Criminal Procedure Rules and Criminal Practice Directions

CRIMINAL PROCEDURE RULES    PART 39    APPEAL TO THE COURT OF
APPEAL ABOUT CONVICTION OR SENTENCE

**R39.1**    **When this Part applies**

**39.1**  (1)  This Part applies where—

     (a)  a defendant wants to appeal under—

         (i)  Part 1 of the Criminal Appeal Act 1968[1],

         (ii)  section 274(3) of the Criminal Justice Act 2003[2],

         (iii)  paragraph 14 of Schedule 22 to the Criminal Justice Act 2003[3], or

         (iv)  section 42 of the Counter-Terrorism Act 2008[4];

     (b)  the Criminal Cases Review Commission refers a case to the Court of Appeal under section 9 of the Criminal Appeal Act 1995[5];

     (c)  a prosecutor wants to appeal to the Court of Appeal under section 14A(5A) of the Football Spectators Act 1989[6];

     (d)  a party wants to appeal under section 389 of the Sentencing Act 2020[7];

     (e)  a person found in contempt of court wants to appeal under section 13 of the Administration of Justice Act 1960[8] and section 18A of the Criminal Appeal Act 1968[9]; or

     (f)  a person wants to appeal to the Court of Appeal under—

         (i)  section 24 of the Serious Crime Act 2007[10],

         (ii)  section 28(5)(a) of the Offensive Weapons Act 2019[11], or

         (iii)  regulation 3C or 3H of the Costs in Criminal Cases (General) Regulations 1986[12].

 (2)  A reference to an 'appellant' in this Part is a reference to such a party or person.

*[Note. Under Part 1 (sections 1 to 32) of the Criminal Appeal Act 1968, a defendant may appeal against—*

     *(a)  a conviction (section 1 of the 1968 Act[13]);*

     *(b)  a sentence (sections 9 and 10 of the 1968 Act[14]);*

     *(c)  a verdict of not guilty by reason of insanity (section 12 of the 1968 Act);*

---

[1]  1968 c. 19.

[2]  2003 c. 44; section 274 was amended by section 40 of, and paragraph 82 of Schedule 9 to, the Constitutional Reform Act 2005 (c. 4).

[3]  2003 c. 44; paragraph 14 of Schedule 22 was amended by section 40 of, and paragraph 82 of Schedule 9 and paragraph 1 of Schedule 11 to, the Constitutional Reform Act 2005 (c. 4).

[4]  2008 c. 28.

[5]  1995 c. 35; section 9 was amended by section 58 of, and paragraph 31 of Schedule 10 to, the Domestic Violence, Crime and Victims Act 2004 (c. 28).

[6]  1989 c. 37; section 14A(5A) was inserted by section 52 of, and paragraphs 1 and 3 of Schedule 3 to, the Violent Crime Reduction Act 2006 (c. 38).

[7]  2020 c. 17.

[8]  1960 c. 65; section 13 was amended paragraph 40 of Schedule 8 to, the Courts Act 1971 (c. 23), Schedule 5 to, the Criminal Appeal Act 1968 (c. 19), paragraph 36 of Schedule 7 to, the Magistrates' Courts Act 1980 (c. 43), Schedule 7 to, the Supreme Court Act 1981 (c. 54), paragraph 25 of Schedule 2 to, the County Courts Act 1984 (c. 28), Schedule 15 to, the Access to Justice Act 1999 (c. 22), paragraph 13 of Schedule 9 to the Constitutional Reform Act 2005 (c. 4) and paragraph 45 of Schedule 16 to, the Armed Forces Act 2006 (c. 52).

[9]  1968 c. 19; section 18A was inserted by section 170 of, and paragraphs 20 and 25 of Schedule 15 to, the Criminal Justice Act 1988 (c. 33).

[10]  2007 c. 27.

[11]  2019 c. 17; section 28 comes into force on a date to be appointed.

[12]  S.I. 1986/1335; regulation 3C was inserted by regulation 2 of The Costs in Criminal Cases (General) (Amendment) Regulations 1991 (SI 1991/789) and amended by regulation 5 of The Costs in Criminal Cases (General) (Amendment) Regulations 2004 (SI 2004/2408). Regulation 3H was inserted by regulation 7 of The Costs in Criminal Cases (General) (Amendment) Regulations 2004 (SI 2004/2408).

[13]  1968 c. 19; section 1 was amended by section 154 of, and paragraph 71 of Schedule 7 to, the Magistrates' Courts Act 1980 (c. 43), paragraph 44 of Schedule 3 to the Criminal Justice Act 2003 (c. 44), section 1 of the Criminal Appeal Act 1995 (c. 35) and section 47 of, and paragraphs 1 and 2 of Schedule 8 to, the Criminal Justice and Immigration Act 2008 (c. 4).

[14]  1968 c. 19; section 9 was amended by section 170 of, and paragraph 21 of Schedule 15 to, the Criminal Justice Act 1988 (c. 33), section 119 of, and paragraph 12 of Schedule 8 to, the Crime and Disorder Act 1998 (c. 37), section 58 of the Access to Justice Act 1999 (c. 22) and section 271 of, and paragraph 44 of Schedule 3 and Schedule 37 to, the Criminal Justice Act 2003 (c. 44). Section 10 was amended by section 56 of, and paragraph 57 of Schedule 8 to, the Courts Act 1971 (c. 23), section 77 of, and paragraph 23 of Schedule 14 to, the Criminal Justice Act 1982 (c. 48), section 170 of, and paragraphs 20 and 22 of Schedule 15 and Schedule 16 to, the Criminal Justice Act 1988 (c. 33), section 100 of, and paragraph 3 of Schedule 11 to, the Criminal Justice Act 1991 (c. 53), sections 119 and 120 of, and paragraph 13 of Schedule 8 and Schedule 10 to, the Crime and Disorder Act 1998 (c. 37), section 58 of the Access to Justice Act 1999 (c. 22), section 67 of, and paragraph 4 of Schedule 4 and Schedule 6 to, the Youth Justice and Criminal Evidence Act 1999 (c. 23), sections 304, 319 and 322 of, and paragraphs 7 and 8 of Schedule 32 and Schedule 37 to, the Criminal Justice Act 2003 (c. 44) and section 6(2) of, and paragraph 4 of Schedule 4 to, the Criminal Justice and Immigration Act 2008 (c. 4).

(d) *a finding of disability or a finding that the defendant did the act or made the omission charged as an offence (section 15 of the 1968 Act*[15]*;*

(e) *a hospital order, interim hospital order or supervision order under section 5 or 5A of the Criminal Procedure (Insanity) Act 1964*[16] *(section 16A of the 1968 Act*[17]*).*

*See section 50 of the 1968 Act*[18] *for the meaning of 'sentence'.*

*Under section 274(3) of the 2003 Act, a defendant sentenced to life imprisonment outside the United Kingdom, and transferred to serve the sentence in England and Wales, may appeal against the minimum term fixed by a High Court judge under section 321 of the 2020 Act or under section 269 of the 2003 Act.*

*Under paragraph 14 of Schedule 22 to the Criminal Justice Act 2003 a defendant sentenced to life imprisonment may appeal against the minimum term fixed on review by a High Court judge in certain cases.*

*Under section 42 of the Counter Terrorism Act 2008 a defendant may appeal against a decision of the Crown Court that an offence has a terrorist connection.*

*See section 13 of the Criminal Appeal Act 1995*[19] *for the circumstances in which the Criminal Cases Review Commission may refer a conviction, sentence, verdict or finding to the Court of Appeal.*

*Under section 14A(5A) of the Football Spectators Act 1989 a prosecutor may appeal against a failure by the Crown Court to make a football banning order.*

*Under section 389 of the 2020 Act a prosecutor or defendant may appeal against a review by a Crown Court judge of a sentence that was reduced because the defendant assisted the investigator or prosecutor.*

*Under section 13 of the Administration of Justice Act 1960 a person in respect of whom an order or decision is made by the Crown Court in the exercise of its jurisdiction to punish for contempt of court may appeal to the Court of Appeal.*

*Under section 24 of the Serious Crime Act 2007 a person who is the subject of a serious crime prevention order, or the relevant applicant authority, may appeal to the Court of Appeal against a decision of the Crown Court in relation to that order. In addition, any person who was given an opportunity to make representations in the proceedings by virtue of section 9(4) of the Act may appeal to the Court of Appeal against a decision of the Crown Court to make, vary or not vary a serious crime prevention order.*

*Under section 28(5)(a) of the Offensive Weapons Act 2019 an applicant to the Crown Court for the variation, renewal or discharge of a knife crime prevention order made by that court, or a respondent to such an application, may appeal to the Court of Appeal against the decision of the Crown Court.*

*Under regulation 3C of the Costs in Criminal Cases (General) Regulations 1986, a legal representative against whom the Crown Court makes a wasted costs order under section 19A of the Prosecution of Offences Act 1985*[20] *and regulation 3B may appeal against that order to the Court of Appeal.*

*Under regulation 3H of the Costs in Criminal Cases (General) Regulations 1986, a third party against whom the Crown Court makes a costs order under section 19B of the Prosecution of Offences Act 1985*[21] *and regulation 3F may appeal against that order to the Court of Appeal.*

*The rules in Part 36 (Appeal to the Court of Appeal: general rules) also apply where this Part applies.]*

---

[15]   1968 c. 19; section 15 was amended by section 7 of, and paragraph 2 of Schedule 3 to, the Criminal Procedure (Insanity and Unfitness to Plead) Act 1991 (c. 25), section 1 of the Criminal Appeal Act 1995 (c. 35) and section 58 of, and paragraph 4 of Schedule 10 to, the Domestic Violence, Crime and Victims Act 2004 (c. 28) and section 47 of, and paragraphs 1 and 5 of Schedule 8 to, the Criminal Justice and Immigration Act 2008 (c. 4).

[16]   1964 c. 84; section 5 was substituted, and section 5A inserted, by section 24 of the Domestic Violence, Crime and Victims Act 2004 (c. 28). Section 5A was amended by section 15 of the Mental Health Act 2007 (c. 12).

[17]   1968 c. 19; section 16A was inserted by section 25 of the Domestic Violence, Crime and Victims Act 2004 (c. 28).

[18]   1968 c. 19; section 50 was amended by section 66 of the Criminal Justice Act 1982 (c. 48), sections 100 and 101 of, and paragraph 4 of Schedule 11 and Schedule 13 to, the Criminal Justice Act 1991 (c. 53), section 79 of, and Schedule 5 to, the Criminal Justice Act 1993 (c. 36), section 65 of, and Schedule 1 to, the Drug Trafficking Act 1994 (c. 37), section 7 of the Football (Offences and Disorder) Act 1999 (c. 21), section 24 of, and paragraph 3 of Schedule 4 to, the Access to Justice Act 1999 (c. 22), section 165 of, and paragraph 30 of Schedule 9 to, the Powers of Criminal Courts (Sentencing) Act 2000 (c. 6), section 1 of, and Schedule 3 to, the Football (Disorder) Act 2000 (c. 25), section 456 of, and paragraphs 1 and 4 of Schedule 11 to, the Proceeds of Crime Act 2002 (c. 43), section 198 of, and paragraphs 38 and 42 of Schedule 6 to, the Licensing Act 2003 (c. 17), section 52 of, and paragraph 14 of Schedule 3 to, the Violent Crime Reduction Act 2006 (c. 38), paragraph 3 of Schedule 5 to the Legal Aid, Sentencing and Punishment of Offenders Act 2012 (c. 10) and section 85 of, and paragraph 3 of Schedule 4 to, the Serious Crime Act 2015 (c. 9). It is further amended by section 55 of, and paragraph 6 of Schedule 4 to, the Crime (Sentences) Act 1997 (c. 43), with effect from a date to be appointed.

[19]   1995 c. 35; section 13 was amended by section 321 of, and paragraph 3 of Schedule 11 to, the Armed Forces Act 2006 (c. 52).

[20]   1985 c. 23; section 19A was inserted by section 111 of the Courts and Legal Services Act 1990 (c. 41).

[21]   1985 c. 23; section 19B was inserted by section 93 of the Courts Act 2003 (c. 39).

**R39.2**  **Service of appeal notice**

39.2  (1)  The appellant must serve an appeal notice on the Registrar—
      (a)  not more than 28 days after—
          (i)  the conviction, verdict, or finding,
          (ii)  the sentence,
          (iii)  the order (subject to paragraph (b)), or the failure to make an order, or
          (iv)  the minimum term review decision under section 274(3) of, or paragraph 14 of Schedule 22 to, the Criminal Justice Act 2003
        about which the appellant wants to appeal;
      (b)  not more than 15 business days after the order in a case in which the appellant appeals against a wasted or third party costs order; and
      (c)  not more than 20 business days after the Registrar serves notice that the Criminal Cases Review Commission has referred a conviction to the court.
    (2)  Unless the appeal notice includes grounds of appeal prepared by the person who was appointed to put the case for the defence under rule 25.10 (Defendant unfit to plead), paragraphs (3), (4) and (5) of this rule apply where the appeal is about—
      (a)  a finding of disability under section 4 of the Criminal Procedure (Insanity) Act 1964[22],
      (b)  a finding under section 4A of the 1964 Act that the defendant did the act or made the omission charged as an offence; or
      (c)  a hospital order, interim hospital order or supervision order made under section 5 or 5A of the 1964 Act[23];
    (3)  The Registrar must refer the appeal notice to a judge of the Court of Appeal for the judge to give or refuse to give procedural directions under section 31B of the Criminal Appeal Act 1968[24].
    (4)  The judge may—
      (a)  give such procedural directions as the case requires where the appeal notice includes grounds of appeal that the judge considers reasonably arguable; or
      (b)  refuse to give such directions, in any other case.
    (5)  Such procedural directions may include—
      (a)  a direction for the appointment of a person to put the case for the appellant on appeal;
      (b)  a direction to commission medical evidence; and
      (c)  a direction for the reference of the case to the judge again to give, or to refuse to give, further directions.

*[Note. The time limit for serving an appeal notice (a) on an appeal under Part 1 of the Criminal Appeal Act 1968 and (b) on an appeal against a finding of contempt of court is prescribed by sections 18 and 18A of the Criminal Appeal Act 1968. It may be extended, but not shortened.*

*For service of a reference by the Criminal Cases Review Commission, see rule 39.5.*

*[Under section 31C of the 1968 Act[25] a party has no right to renew to the Court of Appeal an application for procedural directions refused by a judge.]*

**R39.3**  **Form of appeal notice**

39.3  (1)  An appeal notice must—
      (a)  specify—
          (i)  the conviction, verdict, or finding,
          (ii)  the sentence, or
          (iii)  the order, or the failure to make an order about which the appellant wants to appeal;
      (b)  identify each ground of appeal on which the appellant relies (and see paragraph (2));
      (c)  identify the transcript that the appellant thinks the court will need, if the appellant wants to appeal against a conviction;
      (d)  identify the relevant sentencing powers of the Crown Court, if sentence is in issue;
      (e)  include or attach any application for the following, with reasons—
          (i)  permission to appeal, if the appellant needs the court's permission,
          (ii)  an extension of time within which to serve the appeal notice,

---

[22] 1964 c. 84; section 4 was substituted, together with section 4A, for section 4 as originally enacted, by section 2 of the Criminal Procedure (Insanity and Unfitness to Plead) Act 1991 (c. 25), and amended by section 22 of the Domestic Violence, Crime and Victims Act 2004 (c. 28).

[23] 1964 c. 84; section 5 was substituted, and section 5A inserted, by section 24 of the Domestic Violence, Crime and Victims Act 2004 (c. 28). Section 5A was amended by section 15 of the Mental Health Act 2007 (c. 12).

[24] 1968 c. 19; section 31B was inserted by section 87 of the Courts Act 2003 (c. 39).

[25] 1968 c. 19; section 31C was inserted by section 87 of the Courts Act 2003 (c. 39) and amended by sections 47 and 149 of, and paragraphs 1 and 12 of Schedule 8 and part 3 of Schedule 28 to, the Criminal Justice and Immigration Act 2008 (c. 4).

Criminal Procedure Rules and Criminal Practice Directions

     (iii) bail pending appeal,

     (iv) a direction to attend in person a hearing that the appellant could attend by live link, if the appellant is in custody,

     (v) the introduction of evidence, including hearsay evidence and evidence of bad character,

     (vi) an order requiring a witness to attend court,

     (vii) a direction for special measures for a witness,

     (viii)a direction for special measures for the giving of evidence by the appellant, or

     (ix) the suspension of any disqualification imposed, or order made, in the case, where the Court of Appeal can order such a suspension pending appeal;

  (f) identify any other document or thing that the appellant thinks the court will need to decide the appeal and include or attach an electronic link to each such document that has been made available to the Registrar under rule 36.8(1)(a) (Duty of Crown Court officer); and

  (g) include or attach—

     (i) an electronic copy of any authority identified by the grounds of appeal (see paragraph (2)(f)), or

     (ii) if two or more such authorities are identified, electronic copies of each together in a single electronic document.

(2) The grounds of appeal must—

  (a) include in no more than the first two pages a summary of the grounds that makes what then follows easy to understand;

  (b) in each ground of appeal identify the event or decision to which that ground relates;

  (c) in each ground of appeal summarise the facts relevant to that ground, but only to the extent necessary to make clear what is in issue;

  (d) concisely outline each argument in support of each ground;

  (e) number each ground consecutively, if there is more than one;

  (f) identify any relevant authority and—

     (i) state the proposition of law that the authority demonstrates, and

     (ii) identify the parts of the authority that support that proposition; and

  (a) where the Criminal Cases Review Commission refers a case to the court, explain how each ground of appeal relates (if it does) to the reasons for the reference.

*[Note. The Practice Direction sets out forms of appeal notice for use in connection with this rule.*

*In some legislation, including the Criminal Appeal Act 1968, permission to appeal is described as 'leave to appeal'.*

*An appellant needs the court's permission to appeal in every case to which this Part applies, except where—*

  *(a) the Criminal Cases Review Commission refers the case;*

  *(b) the appellant appeals against—*

     *(i) an order or decision made in the exercise of jurisdiction to punish for contempt of court, or*

     *(ii) a wasted or third party costs order; or*

  *(c) the Crown Court judge certifies under sections 1(2)(a), 11(1A), 12(b), 15(2)(b) or 16A(2)(b) of the Criminal Appeal Act 1968[26]), under section 81(1B) of the Senior Courts Act 1981[27], under section 14A(5B) of the Football Spectators Act 1989[28], or under section 24(4) of the Serious Crime Act 2007, that a case is fit for appeal.*

*A judge of the Court of Appeal may give permission to appeal under section 31 of the Criminal Appeal Act 1968[29].*

[26] 1968 c. 19; section 11(1A) was inserted by section 29 of the Criminal Justice Act 1982 (c. 48) and amended by section 47 of, and paragraphs 1 and 3 of Schedule 8 to, the Criminal Justice and Immigration Act 2008 (c. 4).

[27] 1981 c. 54; section 81(1B) was inserted by sections 29 and 60 of the Criminal Justice Act 1982 (c. 48). The Act's title was amended by section 59(5) of, and paragraph 1 of Schedule 11 to, the Constitutional Reform Act 2005 (c. 4).

[28] 1989 c. 37; section 14A(5B) was inserted by section 52 of, and paragraphs 1 and 3 of Schedule 3 to, the Violent Crime Reduction Act 2006 (c. 38).

[29] 1968 c. 19; section 31 was amended by section 21 of, and Schedule 2 to, the Costs in Criminal Cases Act 1973 (c. 14), section 24 of, and paragraph 10 of Schedule 6 to, the Road Traffic Act 1974 (c. 50), section 29 of the Criminal Justice Act 1982 (c. 48), section 170 of, and paragraphs 20, 29 and 30 of Schedule 15 to, the Criminal Justice Act 1988 (c. 33), section 4 of, and paragraph 4 of Schedule 3 to, the Road Traffic (Consequential Provisions) Act 1988 (c. 54), section 198 of, and paragraphs 38 and 40 of Schedule 6 to, the Licensing Act 2003 (c. 17), section 87 of the Courts Act 2003 (c. 39), paragraphs 86, 87 and 88 of Schedule 36 to the Criminal Justice Act 2003 (c. 44), section 48 of the Police and Justice Act 2006 (c. 48), section 47 of, and paragraphs 1, 9 and 11 of Schedule 8 to, the Criminal Justice and Immigration Act 2008 (c. 4) and section 177 of, and paragraph 69 of Schedule 21 to, the Coroners and Justice Act 2009 (c. 25). It is further amended by section 67 of, and paragraph 4 of Schedule 4 to, the Youth Justice and Criminal Evidence Act 1999 (c. 23), with effect from a date to be appointed.

*See also rules 39.7 (Introducing evidence) and 39.8 (Application for bail, or to suspend a disqualification or order, pending appeal or retrial).]*

**R39.4** **Crown Court judge's certificate that case is fit for appeal**

39.4 (1) An appellant who wants the Crown Court judge to certify that a case is fit for appeal must either—

    (a) apply orally, with reasons, immediately after there occurs—

        (i) the conviction, verdict, or finding,

        (ii) the sentence, or

        (iii) the order, or the failure to make an order

        about which the appellant wants to appeal; or

    (b) apply in writing and serve the application on the Crown Court officer not more than 10 business days after that occurred.

    (2) A written application must include the same information (with the necessary adaptations) as an appeal notice.

*[Note. The Crown Court judge may certify that a case is fit for appeal under sections 1(2)(b), 11(1A), 12(b), 15(2)(b) or 16A(2)(b) of the Criminal Appeal Act 1968, under section 81(1B) of the Senior Courts Act 1981, under section 14A(5B) of the Football Spectators Act 1989 or under section 24(4) of the Serious Crime Act 2007.*

*See also rule 39.2 (service of appeal notice required in all cases).]*

**R39.5** **Reference by Criminal Cases Review Commission**

39.5 (1) The Registrar must serve on the appellant a reference by the Criminal Cases Review Commission.

    (2) The court must treat that reference as the appeal notice if the appellant does not serve such a notice under rule 39.2.

**R39.6** **Respondent's notice**

39.6 (1) The Registrar—

    (a) may serve an appeal notice on any party directly affected by the appeal; and

    (b) must do so if the Criminal Cases Review Commission refers a conviction, verdict, finding or sentence to the court.

    (2) Such a party may serve a respondent's notice, and must do so if—

    (a) that party wants to make representations to the court; or

    (b) the court or the Registrar so directs.

    (3) Such a party must serve the respondent's notice on—

    (a) the appellant;

    (b) the Registrar; and

    (c) any other party on whom the Registrar served the appeal notice.

    (4) Such a party must serve the respondent's notice—

    (a) not more than 10 business days after the Registrar serves—

        (i) the appeal notice, or

        (ii) a direction to do so; or

    (b) not more than 20 business days after the Registrar serves notice that the Commission has referred a conviction.

    (5) The respondent's notice must be in the form set out in the Practice Direction.

    (6) The respondent's notice must—

    (a) give the date on which the respondent was served with the appeal notice;

    (b) identify each ground of opposition on which the respondent relies, numbering them consecutively (if there is more than one), concisely outlining each argument in support and identifying the ground of appeal to which each relates;

    (c) identify the relevant sentencing powers of the Crown Court, if sentence is in issue;

    (d) summarise any relevant facts not already summarised in the appeal notice;

    (e) identify any relevant authorities;

    (f) include or attach any application for the following, with reasons—

        (i) an extension of time within which to serve the respondent's notice,

        (ii) bail pending appeal,

        (iii) a direction to attend in person a hearing that the respondent could attend by live link, if the respondent is in custody,

        (iv) the introduction of evidence, including hearsay evidence and evidence of bad character,

        (v) an order requiring a witness to attend court, or

        (vi) a direction for special measures for a witness;

(g) identify any other document or thing that the respondent thinks the court will need to decide the appeal and include or attach an electronic link to each such document that has been made available to the Registrar under rule 36.8(1)(a) (Duty of Crown Court officer); and

(h) include or attach—

    (i) an electronic copy of any authority identified under paragraph (6)(e), or

    (ii) if two or more such authorities are identified, electronic copies of each together in a single electronic document.

*[Note. The Practice Direction sets out the circumstances in which the Registrar usually will serve a defendant's appeal notice on the prosecutor.*

*See also rule 39.7 (Introducing evidence).]*

## Introducing evidence

39.7 (1) The following Parts apply with such adaptations as the court or the Registrar may direct—

(a) Part 16 (Written witness statements);

(b) Part 18 (Measures to assist a witness or defendant to give evidence);

(c) Part 19 (Expert evidence);

(d) Part 20 (Hearsay evidence);

(e) Part 21 (Evidence of bad character); and

(f) Part 22 (Evidence of a complainant's previous sexual behaviour).

(2) But the general rule is that—

(a) a respondent who opposes an appellant's application or notice to which one of those Parts applies must do so in the respondent's notice, with reasons;

(b) an appellant who opposes a respondent's application or notice to which one of those Parts applies must serve notice, with reasons, on—

    (i) the Registrar, and

    (ii) the respondent

    not more than 10 business days after service of the respondent's notice; and

(c) the court or the Registrar may give directions with or without a hearing.

(3) A party who wants the court to order the production of a document, exhibit or other thing connected with the proceedings must—

(a) identify that item; and

(b) explain—

    (i) how it is connected with the proceedings,

    (ii) why its production is necessary for the determination of the case, and

    (iii) to whom it should be produced (the court, appellant or respondent, or any two or more of them).

(4) A party who wants the court to order a witness to attend to be questioned must—

(a) identify the proposed witness;

(b) explain—

    (i) what evidence the proposed witness can give,

    (ii) why that evidence is capable of belief,

    (iii) if applicable, why that evidence may provide a ground for allowing the appeal,

    (iv) on what basis that evidence would have been admissible in the case which is the subject of the application for permission to appeal or appeal, and

    (v) why that evidence was not introduced in that case; and

(c) where the court can exercise a power to which Part 18 (Measures to assist a witness or defendant to give evidence) applies, provide any information that the court may need to assess—

    (i) the measure or measures likely to maximise so far as practicable the quality of the witness' evidence, and

    (ii) the witness' own views.

(5) Where the court orders a witness to attend to be questioned, the witness must attend the hearing of the application for permission to appeal or of the appeal, as applicable, unless the court otherwise directs.

(6) Where the court orders a witness to attend to be questioned before an examiner on the court's behalf, the court must identify the examiner and may give directions about—

(a) the time and place, or times and places, at which that questioning must be carried out;

(b) the manner in which that questioning must be carried out, in particular as to—

    (i) the service of any report, statement or questionnaire in preparation for the questioning,

    (ii) the sequence in which the parties may ask questions, and

          (iii) if more than one witness is to be questioned, the sequence in which those witnesses may be questioned; and

     (c) the manner in which, and when, a record of the questioning must be submitted to the court.

(7) Where the court orders the questioning of a witness before an examiner, the court may delegate to that examiner the giving of directions under paragraph (6)(a), (b) and (c).

*[Note. An application to introduce evidence or for directions about evidence must be included in, or attached to, an appeal notice or a respondent's notice: see rules 39.3(1)(e)(v), (vi) and 39.6(6)(f)(iv), (v).*

*Under section 23 of the Criminal Appeal Act 1968[30], the Court of Appeal may order the production of a document, exhibit or other thing, may order a witness to attend to be examined before the court and may allow the introduction of evidence that was not introduced at trial. Under section 23(4), if it thinks it necessary or expedient in the interests of justice the court may order the examination of a witness to be conducted before any judge, court officer or other person, and allow the admission of a record of that examination as evidence before the court.]*

**R39.8**   **Application for bail, or to suspend a disqualification or order, pending appeal or retrial**

**39.8**   (1) This rule applies where—

     (a) a party wants to make an application to the court about bail pending appeal or retrial; or

     (b) an appellant wants to apply to the court to suspend a disqualification or order pending appeal.

(2) That party must serve an application in the form set out in the Practice Direction on—

     (a) the Registrar, unless the application is with the appeal notice; and

     (b) the other party.

(3) The court must not decide such an application without giving the other party an opportunity to make representations, including, in the case of a bail application, representations about any condition or surety proposed by the applicant.

*[Note. See section 19 of the Criminal Appeal Act 1968[31], and section 3(8) of the Bail Act 1976[32] An application about bail or about the conditions of bail may be made either by an appellant or respondent.*

*Under section 81(1) of the Senior Courts Act 1981[33], a Crown Court judge may grant bail pending appeal only (a) if that judge gives a certificate that the case is fit for appeal (see rule 39.4) and (b) not more than 28 days after the conviction or sentence against which the appellant wants to appeal.*

*Under section 39 of the Road Traffic Offenders Act 1988[34], a court which has made an order disqualifying a person from driving may suspend the disqualification pending appeal. Under section 40 of the 1988 Act[35], the appeal court may do so. See also rule 29.2.*

*Under section 129 of the Licensing Act 2003[36], a court which has made an order to forfeit or suspend a personal licence issued under that Act may suspend the order pending appeal. Under section 130 of the 2003 Act[37], the appeal court may do so.]*

---

[30] 1968 c. 19; section 23 was amended by sections 4 and 29 of, and paragraph 4 of Schedule 2 to, the Criminal Appeal Act 1995 (c. 35), section 48 of the Police and Justice Act 2006 (c. 48) and section 47 of, and paragraphs 1 and 10 of Schedule 8 to, the Criminal Justice and Immigration Act 2008 (c. 4).

[31] 1968 c. 19; section 19 was substituted by section 29 of the Criminal Justice Act 1982 (c. 48) and was amended by section 170 of, and paragraphs 20 and 26 of Schedule 15 to, the Criminal Justice Act 1988 (c. 33), section 168 of, and paragraph 22 of Schedule 10 to, the Criminal Justice and Public Order Act 1994 (c. 33) and section 59 of, and paragraph 1 of Schedule 11 to, the Constitutional Reform Act 2005 (c. 4).

[32] 1976 c. 63; section 3(8) was amended by section 65 of, and Schedule 12 to, the Criminal Law Act 1977 (c. 45) and paragraph 48 of Schedule 3 to the Criminal Justice Act 2003 (c. 44).

[33] 1981 c. 54; section 81(1) was amended by sections 29 and 60 of the Criminal Justice Act 1982 (c. 48), section 15 of, and paragraph 2 of Schedule 12 to, the Criminal Justice Act 1987 (c. 38), section 168 of, and paragraph 19 of Schedule 9 and paragraph 48 of Schedule 10 to, the Criminal Justice and Public Order Act 1994 (c. 33), section 119 of, and paragraph 48 of Schedule 8 and Schedule 10 to, the Crime and Disorder Act 1998 (c. 37), section 165 of, and paragraph 87 of Schedule 9 and Schedule 12 to, the Powers of Criminal Courts (Sentencing) Act 2000 (c. 6), paragraph 54 of Schedule 3, paragraph 4 of Schedule 36 and Part 4 of Schedule 37 to the Criminal Justice Act 2003 (c. 44), articles 2 and 6 of S.I. 2004/1033 and section 177(1) of, and paragraph 76 of Schedule 21 to, the Coroners and Justice Act 2009 (c. 25).

[34] 1988 c. 53.

[35] 1988 c. 53; section 40 was amended by sections 40 and 59 of, and paragraph 50 of Schedule 9 and paragraph 1 of Schedule 11 to, the Constitutional Reform Act 2005 (c.4).

[36] 2003 c. 17.

[37] 2003 c. 17; section 130 was amended by sections 40 and 59 of, and paragraph 78 of Schedule 9 and paragraph 1 of Schedule 11 to, the Constitutional Reform Act 2005 (c. 4).

**Conditions of bail pending appeal or retrial**

**39.9** (1) This rule applies where the court grants a party bail pending appeal or retrial subject to any condition that must be met before that party is released.

(2) The court may direct how such a condition must be met.

(3) The Registrar must serve a certificate in the form set out in the Practice Direction recording any such condition and direction on—

(a) that party;

(b) that party's custodian; and

(c) any other person directly affected by any such direction.

(4) A person directly affected by any such direction need not comply with it until the Registrar serves that person with that certificate.

(5) Unless the court otherwise directs, if any such condition or direction requires someone to enter into a recognizance it must be—

(a) in the form set out in the Practice Direction and signed before—

(i) the Registrar,

(ii) the custodian, or

(iii) someone acting with the authority of the Registrar or custodian;

(b) copied immediately to the person who enters into it; and

(c) served immediately by the Registrar on the appellant's custodian or vice versa, as appropriate.

(6) Unless the court otherwise directs, if any such condition or direction requires someone to make a payment, surrender a document or take some other step—

(a) that payment, document or step must be made, surrendered or taken to or before—

(i) the Registrar,

(ii) the custodian, or

(iii) someone acting with the authority of the Registrar or custodian; and

(b) the Registrar or the custodian, as appropriate, must serve immediately on the other a statement that the payment, document or step has been made, surrendered or taken, as appropriate.

(7) The custodian must release the appellant where it appears that any condition ordered by the court has been met.

(8) For the purposes of section 5 of the Bail Act 1976[38] (record of decision about bail), the Registrar must keep a copy of—

(a) any certificate served under paragraph (3);

(b) a notice of hearing given under rule 36.7(1); and

(c) a notice of the court's decision served under rule 36.7(2).

(9) Where the court grants bail pending retrial the Registrar must serve on the Crown Court officer copies of the documents kept under paragraph (8).

**Forfeiture of a recognizance given as a condition of bail**

**39.10** (1) This rule applies where—

(a) the court grants a party bail pending appeal or retrial; and

(b) the bail is subject to a condition that that party provides a surety to guarantee that he will surrender to custody as required; but

(c) that party does not surrender to custody as required.

(2) The Registrar must serve notice on—

(a) the surety; and

(b) the prosecutor,

of the hearing at which the court may order the forfeiture of the recognizance given by that surety.

(3) The court must not forfeit a surety's recognizance—

(a) less than 5 business days after the Registrar serves notice under paragraph (2); and

(b) without giving the surety an opportunity to make representations at a hearing.

---

[38] 1976 c. 63; section 5 was amended by section 65 of, and Schedule 12 to, the Criminal Law Act 1977 (c. 45), section 60 of the Criminal Justice Act 1982 (c. 48), paragraph 1 of Schedule 3 to the Criminal Justice and Public Order Act 1994 (c. 33), paragraph 53 of Schedule 9 to the Powers of Criminal Courts (Sentencing) Act 2000 (c. 6), section 129(1) of the Criminal Justice and Police Act 2001 (c. 16), paragraph 182 of Schedule 8 to the Courts Act 2003 (c. 39), paragraph 48 of Schedule 3, paragraphs 1 and 2 of Schedule 36, and Parts 2, 4 and 12 of Schedule 37 to the Criminal Justice Act 2003 (c. 44) and section 208 of, and paragraphs 33 and 35 of Schedule 21 to, the Legal Services Act 2007 (c. 27).

*[Note. If the purpose for which a recognizance is entered is not fulfilled, that recognizance may be forfeited by the court. If the court forfeits a surety's recognizance, the sum promised by that person is then payable to the Crown.]*

**R39.11**     **Right to attend hearing**

    39.11 A party who is in custody has a right to attend a hearing in public unless—

    (a) it is a hearing preliminary or incidental to an appeal, including the hearing of an application for permission to appeal;

    (b) it is the hearing of an appeal and the court directs that—

        (i) the appeal involves a question of law alone, and

        (ii) for that reason the appellant has no permission to attend; or

    (c) that party is in custody in consequence of—

        (i) a verdict of not guilty by reason of insanity, or

        (ii) a finding of disability.

*[Note. See rule 36.6 (Hearings) and section 22 of the Criminal Appeal Act 1968[39]. There are corresponding provisions in the Criminal Justice Act 2003 (Mandatory Life Sentences: Appeals in Transitional Cases) Order 2005[40], the Serious Organised Crime and Police Act 2005 (Appeals under section 74) Order 2006[41] and the Serious Crime Act 2007 (Appeals under Section 24) Order 2008[42]. Under section 22 of the 1968 Act and corresponding provisions in those Orders, the court may direct that an appellant who is in custody is to attend a hearing by live link.]*

**R39.12**     **Power to vary determination of appeal against sentence**

    39.12 (1) This rule applies where the court decides an appeal affecting sentence in a party's absence.

    (2) The court may vary such a decision if it did not take account of something relevant because that party was absent.

    (3) A party who wants the court to vary such a decision must—

        (a) apply in writing, with reasons; and

        (b) serve the application on the Registrar not more than 5 business days after—

            (i) the decision, if that party was represented at the appeal hearing, or

            (ii) the Registrar serves the decision, if that party was not represented at that hearing.

*[Note. Section 22(3) of the Criminal Appeal Act 1968 allows the court to sentence in an appellant's absence. There are corresponding provisions in the Criminal Justice Act 2003 (Mandatory Life Sentences: Appeals in Transitional Cases) Order 2005 and in the Serious Organised Crime and Police Act 2005 (Appeals under Section 74) Order 2006.]*

**R39.13**     **Directions about re-admission to hospital on dismissal of appeal**

    39.13 (1) This rule applies where—

    (a) an appellant subject to—

        (i) an order under section 37(1) of the Mental Health Act 1983[43] (detention in hospital on conviction), or

        (ii) an order under section 5(2) of the Criminal Procedure (Insanity) Act 1964[44] (detention in hospital on finding of insanity or disability)

        has been released on bail pending appeal; and

    (b) the court—

        (i) refuses permission to appeal,

        (ii) dismisses the appeal, or

        (iii) affirms the order under appeal.

    (2) The court must give appropriate directions for the appellant's—

        (a) re-admission to hospital; and

        (b) if necessary, temporary detention pending re-admission.

---

[39] 1968 c. 19; section 22 was amended by section 48 of the Police and Justice Act 2006 (c. 48).
[40] S.I. 2005/2798.
[41] S.I. 2006/2135.
[42] S.I. 2008/1863.
[43] 1983 c. 20; section 37(1) was amended by section 55 of, and paragraph 12 of Schedule 4 to, the Crime (Sentences) Act 1997 (c. 43) and section 304 of, and paragraphs 37 and 38 of Schedule 32 to, the Criminal Justice Act 2003 (c. 44).
[44] 1964 c. 84.

**Renewal or setting aside of order for retrial**                                                   R39.14

**39.14** (1)  This rule applies where—

    (a)  a prosecutor wants a defendant to be arraigned more than 2 months after the court ordered a retrial under section 7 of the Criminal Appeal Act 1968[45]; or

    (b)  a defendant wants such an order set aside after 2 months have passed since it was made.

  (2)  That party must apply in writing, with reasons, and serve the application on—

    (a)  the Registrar;

    (b)  the other party.

*[Note. Section 8(1) and (1A) of the Criminal Appeal Act 1968[46] set out the criteria for making an order on an application to which this rule applies.]*

CRIMINAL PRACTICE DIRECTIONS    PART 39    APPEAL TO THE COURT OF APPEAL
ABOUT CONVICTION OR SENTENCE

**CPD IX Appeal 39A: Appeals Against Conviction and Sentence — The Provision of Notice**     CPD.39A
**to the Prosecution**

**39A.1**  When an appeal notice served under CrimPR 39.2 is received by the Registrar of Criminal Appeals, the Registrar will notify the relevant prosecution authority, giving the case name, reference number and the trial or sentencing court.

**39A.2**  If the court or the Registrar directs, or invites, the prosecution authority to serve a respondent's notice under CrimPR 39.6, prior to the consideration of leave, the Registrar will also at that time serve on the prosecution authority the appeal notice containing the grounds of appeal and the transcripts, if available. If the prosecution authority is not directed or invited to serve a respondent's notice but wishes to do so, the authority should request the grounds of appeal and any existing transcript from the Criminal Appeal Office. Any respondent's notice received prior to the consideration of leave will be made available to the single judge.

**39A.3**  The Registrar of Criminal Appeals will notify the relevant prosecution authority in the event that:

    (a)  leave to appeal against conviction or sentence is granted by the single Judge; or

    (b)  the single Judge or the Registrar refers an application for leave to appeal against conviction or sentence to the Full Court for determination; or

    (c)  there is to be a renewed application for leave to appeal against sentence only.

If the prosecution authority has not yet been served with the appeal notice and transcript, the Registrar will serve these with the notification, and if leave is granted, the Registrar will also serve the authority with the comments of the single judge.

**39A.4**  The prosecution should notify the Registrar without delay if they wish to be represented at the hearing. The prosecution should note that the Registrar will not delay listing to await a response from the Prosecution as to whether they wish to attend. Prosecutors should note that occasionally, for example, where the single Judge fixes a hearing date at short notice, the case may be listed very quickly.

**39A.5**  If the prosecution wishes to be represented at any hearing, the notification should include details of Counsel instructed and a time estimate. An application by the prosecution to remove a case from the list for Counsel's convenience, or to allow further preparation time, will rarely be granted.

**39A.6**  There may be occasions when the Court of Appeal Criminal Division will grant leave to appeal to an unrepresented applicant and proceed forthwith with the appeal in the absence of the appellant and Counsel. The prosecution should not attend any hearing at which the appellant is unrepresented. *Nasteska v The former Yugoslav Republic of Macedonia (Application No.23152/05)* As a Court of Review, the Court of Appeal Criminal Division would expect the prosecution to have raised any specific matters of relevance with the sentencing Judge in the first instance.

---

[45]  1968 c.19; section 7 was amended by sections 43 and 170 of, and Schedule 16 to, the Criminal Justice Act 1988 (c. 33) and section 331 of, and paragraph 44 of Schedule 36 to, the Criminal Justice Act 2003 (c. 44).

[46]  1968 c.19; section 8(1) was amended by section 56 of, and Part IV of Schedule 11 to, the Courts Act 1971 (c. 23) and section 43 of the Criminal Justice Act 1988 (c. 33). Section 8(1A) was inserted by section 43(4) of the Criminal Justice Act 1988 (c. 33).

**39A.7** Where there is a renewed application for leave to appeal against a sentence imposed for an offence involving a fatality, the Crown Prosecution Service has indicated that it wishes to be represented at all sentence appeals in order to ensure that they are in a position, if appropriate, to make representations as to the impact of the offence upon the victim and their family. In those circumstances, if the court is minded to grant the application for leave to appeal the court should consider adjourning the hearing of the appeal to allow prosecution counsel to attend and for the victim's family to be notified and attend if they so wish.

CPD.39B

## CPD IX Appeal 39B: Listing of Appeals against Conviction and Sentence in the Court of Appeal Criminal Division (CACD)

**39B.1** Arrangements for the fixing of dates for the hearing of appeals will be made by the Criminal Appeal Office Listing Officer, under the superintendence of the Registrar of Criminal Appeals who may give such directions as he deems necessary.

**39B.2** Where possible, regard will be had to an advocate's existing commitments. However, in relation to the listing of appeals, the Court of Appeal takes precedence over all lower courts, including the Crown Court. Wherever practicable, a lower court will have regard to this principle when making arrangements to release an advocate to appear in the Court of Appeal. In case of difficulty the lower court should communicate with the Registrar. In general an advocate's commitment in a lower court will not be regarded as a good reason for failing to accept a date proposed for a hearing in the Court of Appeal.

**39B.3** Similarly when the Registrar directs that an appellant should appear by video link, the prison must give precedence to video-links to the Court of Appeal over video-links to the lower courts, including the Crown Court.

**39B.4** The copy of the Criminal Appeal Office summary provided to advocates will contain the summary writer's time estimate for the whole hearing including delivery of judgment. It will also contain a time estimate for the judges' reading time of the core material. The Listing Officer will rely on those estimates, unless the advocate for the appellant or the Crown provides different time estimates to the Listing Officer, in writing, within 7 days of the receipt of the summary by the advocate. Where the time estimates are considered by an advocate to be inadequate, or where the estimates have been altered because, for example, a ground of appeal has been abandoned, it is the duty of the advocate to inform the Court promptly, in which event the Registrar will reconsider the time estimates and inform the parties accordingly.

**39B.5** The following target times are set for the hearing of appeals. Target times will run from the receipt of the appeal by the Listing Officer, as being ready for hearing.

**39B.6**

| Nature of Appeal: | From Receipt by Listing Officer to Fixing of Hearing Date: | From Fixing of Hearing Date to Hearing: | Total Time From Receipt by Listing Officer to Hearing: |
|---|---|---|---|
| Sentence Appeal | 14 days | 14 days | 28 days |
| Conviction Appeal | 21 days | 42 days | 63 days |
| Conviction Appeal where witness to attend | 28 days | 52 days | 80 days |

**39B.7** Where legal vacations impinge, these periods may be extended. Where expedition is required, the Registrar may direct that these periods be abridged.

**39B.8** 'Appeal' includes an application for leave to appeal which requires an oral hearing.

CPD.39C

## CPD IX Appeal 39C: Appeal Notices Containing Grounds of Appeal

**39C.1** The requirements for the service of notices of appeal and the time limits for doing so are as set out in CrimPR Part 39. The Court must be provided with an appeal notice as a single document which sets out the grounds of appeal. Advocates should not provide the Court with an advice addressed to lay or professional clients. Any appeal notice or grounds of appeal served on the Court will usually be provided to the respondent.

**39C.2** Advocates should not settle grounds unless they consider that they are properly arguable. Grounds should be carefully drafted; the court is not assisted by grounds of appeal which are not properly set out and particularised in accordance with CrimPR 39.3. The grounds must:

i.   be concise; and

ii.  be presented in A4 page size and portrait orientation, in not less than 12 point font and in 1.5 line spacing.

Appellants and advocates should keep in mind the powers of the court and the Registrar to return for revision, within a directed period, grounds that do not comply with the rule or with these directions, including grounds that are so prolix or diffuse as to render them incomprehensible. They should keep in mind also the court's powers to refuse permission to appeal on any ground that is so poorly presented as to render it unarguable and thus to exclude it from consideration by the court: see CrimPR 36.14. Should leave to amend the grounds be granted, it is most unlikely that further grounds will be entertained.

**39C.3**  Where the appellant wants to appeal against conviction, transcripts must be identified in accordance with CrimPR 39.3(1)(c). This includes specifying the date and time of transcripts in the notice of appeal. Accordingly, the date and time of the summing up should be provided, including both parts of a split summing-up. Where relevant, the date and time of additional transcripts (such as rulings or early directions) should be provided. Similarly, any relevant written materials (such as route to verdict) should be identified.

**39C.4**  Where the appellant wants to rely on a ground of appeal that is not identified by the appeal notice, an application under CrimPR 36.14(5) is required. In *R v James and Others* [2018] EWCA Crim 285 the Court of Appeal identified as follows the considerations that obtain and the criteria that the court will apply on any such application:

(a)  as a general rule all the grounds of appeal that an appellant wishes to advance should be lodged with the appeal notice, subject to their being perfected on receipt of transcripts from the Registrar.

(b)  the application for permission to appeal under section 31 of the Criminal Appeal Act 1968 is an important stage in the process. It may not be treated lightly or its determination in effect ignored merely because fresh representatives would have done or argued things differently to their predecessors. Fresh grounds advanced by fresh representatives must be particularly cogent.

(c)  as well as addressing the factors material to the determination of an application for an extension of time within which to renew an application for permission to appeal, if that is required, on an application under CrimPR 36.14(5) the appellant or his or her representatives must address directly the factors which the court is likely to consider relevant when deciding whether to allow the substitution or addition of grounds of appeal. Those factors include (but this list is not exhaustive):

(i)   the extent of the delay in advancing the fresh ground or grounds;

(ii)  the reasons for that delay;

(iii) whether the facts or issues the subject of the fresh ground were known to the appellant's representatives when they advised on appeal;

(iv)  the interests of justice and the overriding objective in Part 1 of the Criminal Procedure Rules.

(d)  on the assumption that an appellant will have received advice on appeal from his or her trial advocate, who will have settled the grounds of appeal in the original appeal notice or who will have advised that there are no reasonably arguable grounds to challenge the safety of the conviction:

(i)   fresh representatives should comply with the duty of due diligence explained in *McCook* [2014] EWCA Crim 734. Waiver of privilege by the appellant is very likely to be required.

(ii)  once the trial lawyers have responded, the fresh representatives should again consider with great care their duty to the court and whether the proposed fresh grounds should be advanced as reasonably arguable and particularly cogent.

(iii) the Registrar will obtain, before the determination of the application under CrimPR 36.14(5), transcripts relevant to the fresh grounds and, where required, a respondents' notice relating to the fresh grounds.

(e)  while an application under CrimPR 36.14(5) will not require "exceptional leave", and hence the demonstration of substantial injustice should it not be granted, the hurdle for the applicant is a high one nonetheless. Representatives should remind themselves of the provisions of paragraph 39C.2 above.

(f) permission to renew out of time an application for permission to appeal is not given unless the applicant can persuade the court that very good reasons exist. If that application to renew out of time is accompanied by an application to vary the grounds of appeal, the hurdle will be higher still.

(g) any application to substitute or add grounds will be considered by a fully constituted court and at a hearing, not on the papers.

(h) on any renewal of an application for permission to appeal accompanied by an application under CrimPR 36.14(5), if the court refuses those applications it has the power to make a loss of time order or an order for costs in line with *R v Gray and Others* [2014] EWCA Crim 2372. By analogy with *R v Kirk* [2015] EWCA Crim 1764 (where the court refused an extension of time) the court has the power to order payment of the costs of obtaining the respondent's notice and any additional transcripts.

### Direct Lodgement

39C.5 With effect from 1st October 2018, Forms NG and Grounds of Appeal which are covered by Part 39 of the Criminal Procedure Rules (appeal to the Court of Appeal about conviction or sentence) are to be lodged directly with the Criminal Appeal Office and not with the Crown Court where the appellant was convicted or sentenced. This Practice Direction must be read alongside the detailed guidance notes that have been produced to accompany the new forms. They are available: https://www.justice.gov.uk/courts/procedure-rules/criminal/forms

From this date the Crown Court will no longer accept Forms NG and will return them to the sender. Forms NG and Grounds of Appeal should only be lodged once. They should, where possible, be lodged by email. Applications should not be lodged directly onto the Digital Case System. Applications must be lodged at the following address: criminalappealoffice. applications@hmcts.x.gsi.gov.uk

If you do not have access to an email account, you should post Form NG and the Grounds of Appeal to:

The Registrar, Criminal Appeal Office, Royal Courts of Justice, Strand, London WC2A 2LL.

Once an application has been effectively lodged, the Registrar will confirm receipt within 7 days.

### Service

39C.6 Legal representatives should make sure they provide their secure email address for the purposes of correspondence and service of document. The date of service for new applications lodged by email will be the day on which it is sent, if that day is a business day and if sent no later than 2:30pm on that day, otherwise the date of service will be on the next business day after it was sent.

### Completing the Form NG

39C.7 All applications must be compliant with the relevant Criminal Procedure Rules, particularly those in Part 39. A separate Form NG should be completed for each substantive application which is being made. Each application (conviction, sentence and confiscation order) has its own Form NG and must be drafted and lodged as a stand-alone application.

**CPD.39D**    ## CPD IX Appeal 39D: Respondents' Notices

39D.1 The requirements for the service of respondents' notices and the time limits for doing so are as set out in Part 39 of the Criminal Procedure Rules. Any respondent's notice served should be in accordance with Rule 39.6. The Court does not require a response to the respondent's notice.

**CPD.39E**    ## CPD IX Appeal 39E: Loss of Time

39E.1 Both the Court and the single judge have power, in their discretion, under the Criminal Appeal Act 1968 sections 29 and 31, to direct that part of the time during which an applicant is in custody after lodging his notice of application for leave to appeal should not count towards sentence. When leave to appeal has been refused by the single judge, it is necessary to consider the reasons given by the single judge before making a decision whether to renew the application. Where an application devoid of merit has been refused by the single judge he may indicate that the Full Court should consider making a direction for loss of time on renewal of the application. However, the Full Court may make such a direction whether or not such an indication has been given by the single judge.

39E.2   The case of *R v Gray and Others* [2014] EWCA Crim 2372 makes clear 'that unmeritorious renewal applications took up a wholly disproportionate amount of staff and judicial resources in preparation and hearing time. They also wasted significant sums of public money… . The more time the Court of Appeal Office and the judges spent on unmeritorious applications, the longer the waiting times were likely to be… . The only means the court has of discouraging unmeritorious applications which waste precious time and resources is by using the powers given to us by Parliament in the Criminal Appeal Act 1968 and the Prosecution of Offenders Act 1985.'

39E.3   Further, applicants and counsel are reminded of the warning given by the Court of Appeal in *R v Hart and Others* [2006] EWCA Crim 3239, [2007] 1 Cr. App. R. 31, [2007] 2 Cr. App. R. (S.) 34 and should 'heed the fact that this court is prepared to exercise its power … . The mere fact that counsel has advised that there are grounds of appeal will not always be a sufficient answer to the question as to whether or not an application has indeed been brought which was totally without merit.'

39E.4   Where the Single Judge has not indicated that the Full Court should consider making a Loss of Time Order because the defendant has already been released, the case of *R v Terence Nolan* [2017] EWCA Crim 2449 indicates that the Single Judge should consider what, if any, costs have been incurred by the Registrar and the Prosecution and should make directions accordingly. Reference should be made to the relevant Costs Division of the Criminal Practice Direction.

## CPD IX Appeal 39F: Skeleton Arguments

**CPD.39F**

39F.1   Advocates should always ensure that the court, and any other party as appropriate, has a single document containing all of the points that are to be argued. The appeal notice must comply with the requirements of CrimPR 39.3. In cases of an appeal against conviction, advocates must serve a skeleton argument when the appeal notice does not sufficiently outline the grounds of the appeal, particularly in cases where a complex or novel point of law has been raised. In an appeal against sentence it may be helpful for an advocate to serve a skeleton argument when a complex issue is raised.

39F.2   The appellant's skeleton argument, if any, must be served no later than 21 days before the hearing date, and the respondent's skeleton argument, if any, no later than 14 days before the hearing date, unless otherwise directed by the Court.

39F.3   Paragraphs XII D.17 to D.23 of these Practice Directions set out the general requirements for skeleton arguments. A skeleton argument, if provided, should contain a numbered list of the points the advocate intends to argue, grouped under each ground of appeal, and stated in no more than one or two sentences. It should be as succinct as possible. Advocates should ensure that the correct Criminal Appeal Office number and the date on which the document was served appear at the beginning of any document and that their names are at the end.

39F.4   A skeleton argument must comply with the requirements of these Practice Directions and, if applicable, of the court. The Criminal Appeal Office may refuse to accept service of a document that fails to comply and instead return that document to the advocate for amendment.

## CPD IX Appeal 39G: Criminal Appeal Office Summaries

**CPD.39G**

39G.1   To assist the Court, the Criminal Appeal Office prepares summaries of the cases coming before it. These are entirely objective and do not contain any advice about how the Court should deal with the case or any view about its merits. They consist of two Parts.

39G.2   Part I, which is provided to all of the advocates in the case, generally contains:
(a)   particulars of the proceedings in the Crown Court, including representation and details of any co-accused;
(b)   particulars of the proceedings in the Court of Appeal (Criminal Division);
(c)   the facts of the case, as drawn from the transcripts, appeal notice, respondent's notice, witness statements and/or the exhibits;
(d)   the submissions and rulings, summing up and sentencing remarks.

39G.3   The contents of the summary are a matter for the professional judgment of the writer, but an advocate wishing to suggest any significant alteration to Part I should write to the Registrar of Criminal Appeals. If the Registrar does not agree, the summary and the letter will be put to the Court for decision. The Court will not generally be willing to hear oral argument about the content of the summary.

39G.4   Advocates may show Part I of the summary to their professional or lay clients (but to no one else) if they believe it would help to check facts or formulate arguments, but summaries are not to be copied or reproduced without the permission of the Criminal Appeal Office; permission for this will not normally be given in cases involving children, or sexual offences, or where the Crown Court has made an order restricting reporting.

39G.5 Unless a judge of the High Court or the Registrar of Criminal Appeals gives a direction to the contrary, in any particular case involving material of an explicitly salacious or sadistic nature, Part I will also be supplied to appellants who seek to represent themselves before the Full Court, or who renew to the full court their applications for leave to appeal against conviction or sentence.

39G.6 Part II, which is supplied to the Court alone, contains:
   (a) a summary of the grounds of appeal; and
   (b) in appeals against sentence (and applications for such leave), summaries of the antecedent histories of the parties and of any relevant pre-sentence, medical or other reports.

39G.7 All of the source material is provided to the Court and advocates are able to draw attention to anything in it which may be of particular relevance.

**CPD.39H**    **CPD IX Appeal 39H: Criminal Appeal Office Bundles & Indexes for Full Court Hearings**

39H.1 To assist the full Court, the Criminal Appeal Office will, in most instances, prepare indexed bundles containing the documents and material which the Registrar considers necessary to understand and determine the appeal for each member of the constitution.

39H.2 The Registrar will not provide bundles where a party or the parties have been directed to prepare and lodge indexed bundles, or where an advocate has lodged indexed bundles of their own volition. Where an appellant who is not privately represented is directed to lodge indexed bundles, a Representation Order will usually be granted by the Court or the Registrar for this purpose.

39H.3 Where bundles are prepared by the Criminal Appeal Office, a copy of the index will be provided to the appellant, or if the appellant is represented, to the advocate. If the advocate or appellant considers that there is additional material which it is necessary to include in the bundle, they must notify the Registrar of this in writing.

39H.4 Where indexed bundles are lodged in response to a direction to do so, or of an advocate's own volition, unless otherwise directed, four copies of the indexed bundle should be lodged with the Registrar in good time before the hearing and in accordance with any direction as to the time by which they should be lodged. The bundles should contain only documents and material which are necessary for the proper understanding of, and determination of, the issues involved in the appeal. The index and order of documents/material in the bundles should follow the order of the Registrar's template *Index to Judge's Bundles* available from the Registrar on request.

CRIMINAL PROCEDURE RULES    PART 40    APPEAL TO THE COURT OF APPEAL ABOUT REPORTING OR PUBLIC ACCESS RESTRICTION

**R40.1**    **When this Part applies**

40.1 (1) This Part applies where a person directly affected by an order to which section 159(1) of the Criminal Justice Act 1988[1] applies wants to appeal against that order.

   (2) A reference to an 'appellant' in this Part is a reference to such a party.

*[Note. Section 159(1) of the Criminal Justice Act 1988 gives a 'person aggrieved' (in this Part described as a person directly affected) a right of appeal to the Court of Appeal against a Crown Court judge's order—*

   *(a) under section 4 or 11 of the Contempt of Court Act 1981[2];*
   *(b) under section 58(7) of the Criminal Procedure and Investigations Act 1996[3];*
   *(c) restricting public access to any part of a trial for reasons of national security or for the protection of a witness or other person; or*
   *(d) restricting the reporting of any part of a trial.*

*See also Part 6 (Reporting, etc. restrictions) and Part 18 (Measures to assist a witness or defendant to give evidence).*

*The rules in Part 36 (Appeal to the Court of Appeal: general rules) also apply where this Part applies.]*

**R40.2**    **Service of appeal notice**

40.2 (1) An appellant must serve an appeal notice on—
   (a) the Crown Court officer;
   (b) the Registrar;

---

[1] 1988 c. 33; section 159(1) was amended by section 61 of the Criminal Procedure and Investigations Act 1996 (c. 25).
[2] 1981 c. 49; section 4 was amended by section 57 of the Criminal Procedure and Investigations Act 1996 (c. 25), section 16 of, and Schedule 2 to, the Defamation Act 1996 (c. 31), paragraph 53 of Schedule 3 to the Criminal Justice Act 2003 (c. 44) and the Statute Law (Repeals) Act 2004 (c. 14).
[3] 1996 c. 25.

(c) the parties; and

(d) any other person directly affected by the order against which the appellant wants to appeal.

(2) The appellant must serve the appeal notice not later than—

(a) the next business day after an order restricting public access to the trial; or

(b) 10 business days after an order restricting reporting of the trial.

### Form of appeal notice

40.3 (1) An appeal notice must be in the form set out in the Practice Direction.

(2) The appeal notice must—

(a) specify the order against which the appellant wants to appeal;

(b) identify each ground of appeal on which the appellant relies, numbering them consecutively (if there is more than one) and concisely outlining each argument in support;

(c) summarise the relevant facts;

(d) identify any relevant authorities;

(e) include or attach, with reasons—

(i) an application for permission to appeal,

(ii) any application for an extension of time within which to serve the appeal notice,

(iii) any application for a direction to attend in person a hearing that the appellant could attend by live link, if the appellant is in custody,

(iv) any application for permission to introduce evidence, and

(v) a list of those on whom the appellant has served the appeal notice;

(f) attach any document or thing that the appellant thinks the court will need to decide the appeal and include or attach an electronic link to each such document that has been made available to the Registrar under rule 36.8(1)(a) (Duty of Crown Court officer); and

(g) include or attach—

(i) an electronic copy of any authority identified under paragraph (2)(d), or

(ii) if two or more such authorities are identified, electronic copies of each together in a single electronic document.

*[Note. An appellant needs the court's permission to appeal in every case to which this Part applies.*

*A Court of Appeal judge may give permission to appeal under section 31(2B) of the Criminal Appeal Act 1968[4].]*

### Advance notice of appeal against order restricting public access

40.4 (1) This rule applies where the appellant wants to appeal against an order restricting public access to a trial.

(2) The appellant may serve advance written notice of intention to appeal against any such order that may be made.

(3) The appellant must serve any such advance notice—

(a) on—

(i) the Crown Court officer,

(ii) the Registrar,

(iii) the parties, and

(iv) any other person who will be directly affected by the order against which the appellant intends to appeal, if it is made; and

(b) not more than 5 business days after the Crown Court officer displays notice of the application for the order.

(4) The advance notice must include the same information (with the necessary adaptations) as an appeal notice.

(5) The court must treat that advance notice as the appeal notice if the order is made.

### Duty of applicant for order restricting public access

40.5 (1) This rule applies where the appellant wants to appeal against an order restricting public access to a trial.

(2) The party who applied for the order must serve on the Registrar—

(a) a transcript or note of the application for the order; and

(b) any other document or thing that that party thinks the court will need to decide the appeal.

R40.3

R40.4

R40.5

---

[4] 1968 c. 19; section 31(2B) was inserted by section 170 of, and paragraphs 20 and 30 of Schedule 15 to, the Criminal Justice Act 1988 (c. 33).

(3) That party must serve that transcript or note and any such other document or thing as soon as practicable after—

    (a) the appellant serves the appeal notice; or

    (b) the order, where the appellant served advance notice of intention to appeal.

**R40.6**    **Respondent's notice on appeal against reporting restriction**

**40.6**  (1) This rule applies where the appellant wants to appeal against an order restricting the reporting of a trial.

  (2) A person on whom an appellant serves an appeal notice may serve a respondent's notice, and must do so if—

    (a) that person wants to make representations to the court; or

    (b) the court so directs.

  (3) Such a person must serve the respondent's notice on—

    (a) the appellant;

    (b) the Crown Court officer;

    (c) the Registrar;

    (d) the parties; and

    (e) any other person on whom the appellant served the appeal notice.

  (4) Such a person must serve the respondent's notice not more than 3 business days after—

    (a) the appellant serves the appeal notice; or

    (b) a direction to do so.

  (5) The respondent's notice must be in the form set out in the Practice Direction.

  (6) The respondent's notice must—

    (a) give the date on which the respondent was served with the appeal notice;

    (b) identify each ground of opposition on which the respondent relies, numbering them consecutively (if there is more than one), concisely outlining each argument in support and identifying the ground of appeal to which each relates;

    (c) summarise any relevant facts not already summarised in the appeal notice;

    (d) identify any relevant authorities;

    (e) include or attach any application for the following, with reasons—

      (i) an extension of time within which to serve the respondent's notice,

      (ii) a direction to attend in person any hearing that the respondent could attend by live link, if the respondent is in custody,

      (iii) permission to introduce evidence;

    (f) identify any other document or thing that the respondent thinks the court will need to decide the appeal and include or attach an electronic link to each such document that has been made available to the Registrar under rule 36.8(1)(a) (Duty of Crown Court officer); and

    (g) include or attach—

      (i) an electronic copy of any authority identified under paragraph (6)(d), or

      (ii) if two or more such authorities are identified, electronic copies of each together in a single electronic document.

**R40.7**    **Renewing applications**

**40.7**   Rule 36.5 (Renewing an application refused by a judge or the Registrar) applies with a time limit of 5 business days.

**R40.8**    **Right to introduce evidence**

**40.8**   No person may introduce evidence without the court's permission.

*[Note. Section 159(4) of the Criminal Justice Act 1988 entitles the parties to give evidence, subject to procedure rules.]*

**R40.9**    **Right to attend hearing**

**40.9**  (1) A party who is in custody has a right to attend a hearing in public of an appeal against an order restricting the reporting of a trial.

  (2) The court or the Registrar may direct that such a party is to attend a hearing by live link.

*[Note. See rule 36.6 (Hearings). The court may decide an application and an appeal without a hearing where the appellant wants to appeal against an order restricting public access to a trial: rule 36.6(3).]*

CRIMINAL PROCEDURE RULES    PART 41    REFERENCE TO THE COURT OF APPEAL OF POINT
OF LAW OR UNDULY LENIENT SENTENCING

### When this Part applies

**41.1**  This Part applies where the Attorney General wants to—

    (a)  refer a point of law to the Court of Appeal under section 36 of the Criminal Justice Act 1972[1];
or

    (b)  refer a sentencing case to the Court of Appeal under section 36 of the Criminal Justice Act 1988[2].

*[Note. Under section 36 of the Criminal Justice Act 1972, where a defendant is acquitted in the Crown Court the Attorney General may refer to the Court of Appeal a point of law in the case.*

*Under section 36 of the Criminal Justice Act 1988, if the Attorney General thinks the sentencing of a defendant in the Crown Court is unduly lenient he may refer the case to the Court of Appeal: but only if the sentence is one to which Part IV of the 1988 Act applies, and only if the Court of Appeal gives permission. See also section 35 of the 1988 Act[3] and the Criminal Justice Act 1988 (Reviews of Sentencing) Order 2006[4].*

*The rules in Part 36 (Appeal to the Court of Appeal: general rules) also apply where this Part applies.]*

### Service of notice of reference and application for permission

**41.2.**  (1)  The Attorney General must serve any notice of reference and any application for permission to
refer a sentencing case on—

    (a)  the Registrar; and

    (b)  the defendant.

  (2)  Where the Attorney General refers a point of law—

    (a)  the Attorney must give the Registrar details of—

      (i)  the defendant affected,

      (ii)  the date and place of the relevant Crown Court decision, and

      (iii)  the relevant verdict and sentencing; and

    (b)  the Attorney must give the defendant notice that—

      (i)  the outcome of the reference will not make any difference to the outcome of the trial,
and

      (ii)  the defendant may serve a respondent's notice.

  (3)  Where the Attorney General applies for permission to refer a sentencing case, the Attorney
must give the defendant notice that—

    (a)  the outcome of the reference may make a difference to that sentencing, and in particular
may result in a more severe sentence; and

    (b)  the defendant may serve a respondent's notice.

  (4)  The Attorney General must serve an application for permission to refer a sentencing case on
the Registrar not more than 28 days after the last of the sentences in that case.

*[Note. The time limit for serving an application for permission to refer a sentencing case is prescribed by paragraph 1 of Schedule 3 to the Criminal Justice Act 1988[5]. It may be neither extended nor shortened.]*

### Form of notice of reference and application for permission

**41.3**  (1)  A notice of reference and an application for permission to refer a sentencing case must give the
year and number of that reference or that case.

  (2)  A notice of reference of a point of law must—

    (a)  specify the point of law in issue and indicate the opinion that the Attorney General invites
the court to give;

---

[1]  1972 c. 71; section 36 was amended by section 31 of, and paragraph 8 of Schedule 1 to, the Prosecution of Offences Act 1985 (c. 23) and section 40 of, and paragraph 23 of Schedule 9 to, the Constitutional Reform Act 2005 (c. 4).

[2]  1988 c. 33; section 36 was amended by section 272 of, and paragraphs 45 and 46 of Schedule 32 and paragraph 96 of Schedule 36 to, the Criminal Justice Act 2003 (c. 44), sections 49 and 65 of, and paragraph 3 of Schedule 1 and Schedule 5 to, the Violent Crime Reduction Act 2006 (c. 38), section 40 of, and paragraph 48 of Schedule 9 to, the Constitutional Reform Act 2005 (c. 4), sections 46, 148 and 149 of, and paragraphs 22 and 23 of Schedule 26 and Part 3 of Schedule 28 to, the Criminal Justice and Immigration Act 2008 (c. 4), paragraph 2 of Schedule 19 and paragraphs 4 and 5 of Schedule 26 to the Legal Aid, Sentencing and Punishment of Offenders Act 2012 (c. 10) and section 28 of, and paragraph 2 of Schedule 5 to, the Criminal Justice and Courts Act 2015 (c. 2). It is further amended by section 46 of the Criminal Justice and Immigration Act 2008 (c. 4) with effect from a date to be appointed.

[3]  1988 c. 33; section 35(3) was amended by section 168 of, and paragraph 34 of Schedule 9 to, the Criminal Justice and Public Order Act 1994 (c. 33).

[4]  S.I. 2006/1116.

[5]  1988 c. 33.

Criminal Procedure Rules and Criminal Practice Directions

(b) identify each ground for that invitation, numbering them consecutively (if there is more than one) and concisely outlining each argument in support;

(c) exclude any reference to the defendant's name and any other reference that may identify the defendant;

(d) summarise the relevant facts; and

(e) identify any relevant authorities.

(3) An application for permission to refer a sentencing case must—

(a) give details of—

(i) the defendant affected,

(ii) the date and place of the relevant Crown Court decision, and

(iii) the relevant verdict and sentencing;

(b) explain why that sentencing appears to the Attorney General unduly lenient, concisely outlining each argument in support; and

(c) include the application for permission to refer the case to the court.

(4) A notice of reference of a sentencing case must—

(a) include the same details and explanation as the application for permission to refer the case;

(b) summarise the relevant facts; and

(c) identify any relevant authorities.

(5) Where the court gives the Attorney General permission to refer a sentencing case, it may treat the application for permission as the notice of reference.

(6) A notice of reference must include or attach—

(a) an electronic link to each material document that has been made available to the Registrar under rule 36.8(1)(a) (Duty of Crown Court officer); and

(b) an electronic copy of any authority identified under paragraph (2)(e) or (4)(c), or if two or more such authorities are identified then electronic copies of each together in a single electronic document.

**R41.4**   **Respondent's notice**

41.4   (1) A defendant on whom the Attorney General serves a notice of reference or an application for permission to refer a sentencing case may serve a respondent's notice, and must do so if—

(a) the defendant wants to make representations to the court; or

(b) the court so directs.

(2) Such a defendant must serve the respondent's notice on—

(a) the Attorney General; and

(b) the Registrar.

(3) Such a defendant must serve the respondent's notice—

(a) where the Attorney General refers a point of law, not more than 20 business days after—

(i) the Attorney serves the reference, or

(ii) a direction to do so; or

(b) where the Attorney General applies for permission to refer a sentencing case, not more than 10 business days after—

(i) the Attorney serves the application, or

(ii) a direction to do so.

(4) Where the Attorney General refers a point of law, the respondent's notice must—

(a) give the date on which the respondent was served with the notice of reference;

(b) identify each ground of opposition on which the respondent relies, numbering them consecutively (if there is more than one), concisely outlining each argument in support and identifying the Attorney General's ground or reason to which each relates;

(c) summarise any relevant facts not already summarised in the reference;

(d) identify any relevant authorities; and

(e) include or attach any application for the following, with reasons—

(i) an extension of time within which to serve the respondent's notice,

(ii) permission to attend a hearing that the respondent does not have a right to attend, or

(iii) a direction to attend in person a hearing that the respondent could attend by live link, if the respondent is in custody.

(5) Where the Attorney General applies for permission to refer a sentencing case, the respondent's notice must—

(a) give the date on which the respondent was served with the application;

(b) say if the respondent wants to make representations at the hearing of the application or reference; and

(c) include or attach any application for the following, with reasons—

(i) an extension of time within which to serve the respondent's notice,

(ii) permission to attend a hearing that the respondent does not have a right to attend, or

(iii) a direction to attend in person a hearing that the respondent could attend by live link, if the respondent is in custody.

(6) A respondent's notice must include or attach—

    (a) an electronic link to each material document that has been made available to the Registrar under rule 36.8(1)(a) (Duty of Crown Court officer); and

    (b) an electronic copy of any authority identified under paragraph (4)(d), or if two or more such authorities are identified then electronic copies of each together in a single electronic document.

### Variation or withdrawal of notice of reference or application for permission     R41.5

41.5 (1) This rule applies where the Attorney General wants to vary or withdraw—

    (a) a notice of reference; or

    (b) an application for permission to refer a sentencing case.

(2) The Attorney General—

    (a) may vary or withdraw the notice or application without the court's permission by serving notice on—

       (i) the Registrar, and

       (ii) the defendant

    before any hearing of the reference or application; but

    (b) at any such hearing, may only vary or withdraw that notice or application with the court's permission.

### Right to attend hearing     R41.6

41.6 (1) A respondent who is in custody has a right to attend a hearing in public unless it is a hearing preliminary or incidental to a reference, including the hearing of an application for permission to refer a sentencing case.

(2) The court or the Registrar may direct that such a respondent is to attend a hearing by live link.

*[Note. See rule 36.6 (Hearings) and paragraphs 6 and 7 of Schedule 3 to the Criminal Justice Act 1988. Under paragraph 8 of that Schedule, the Court of Appeal may sentence in the absence of a defendant whose sentencing is referred.]*

### Anonymity of defendant on reference of point of law     R41.7

41.7 Where the Attorney General refers a point of law, the court must not allow anyone to identify the defendant during the proceedings unless the defendant gives permission.

CRIMINAL PROCEDURE RULES    PART 42    APPEAL TO THE COURT OF APPEAL IN
CONFISCATION AND RELATED PROCEEDINGS

### General rules

### Extension of time     R42.1

42.1 (1) An application to extend the time limit for giving notice of application for permission to appeal under Part 2 of the Proceeds of Crime Act 2002[1] must—

    (a) be included in the notice of appeal; and

    (b) state the grounds for the application.

(2) The parties may not agree to extend any date or time limit set by this Part or by the Proceeds of Crime Act 2002 (Appeals under Part 2) Order 2003[2].

### Other applications     R42.2

42.2 Rules 39.3(2)(h) (Form of appeal notice) applies in relation to an application—

    (a) by a party to an appeal under Part 2 of the Proceeds of Crime Act 2002 that, under article 7 of the Proceeds of Crime Act 2002 (Appeals under Part 2) Order 2003, a witness be ordered to attend or that the evidence of a witness be received by the Court of Appeal; or

    (b) by the defendant to be given permission by the court to be present at proceedings for which permission is required under article 6 of the 2003 Order,

as it applies in relation to applications under Part I of the Criminal Appeal Act 1968[3] and the form in which rules 39.3 requires notice to be given may be modified as necessary.

[1] 2002 c. 29.
[2] S.I. 2003/82.
[3] 1968 c. 19.

Criminal Procedure Rules and Criminal Practice Directions

**R42.3**    **Examination of witness by court**

42.3   Rule 36.7 (Notice of hearings and decisions) applies in relation to an order of the court under article 7 of the Proceeds of Crime Act 2002 (Appeals under Part 2) Order 2003 to require a personto attend for examination as it applies in relation to such an order of the court under Part I of the Criminal Appeal Act 1968.

**R42.4**    **Supply of documentary and other exhibits**

42.4   Rule 36.11 (Registrar's duty to provide copy documents for appeal or reference) applies in relation to an appellant or respondent under Part 2 of the Proceeds of Crime Act 2002 as it applies in relation to an appellant and respondent under Part I of the Criminal Appeal Act 1968.

**R42.5**    **Registrar's power to require information from court of trial**

42.5   The Registrar may require the Crown Court to provide the Court of Appeal with any assistance or information which it requires for the purposes of exercising its jurisdiction under Part 2 of the Proceeds of Crime Act 2002, the Proceeds of Crime Act 2002 (Appeals under Part 2) Order 2003 or this Part.

**R42.6**    **Hearing by single judge**

42.6   Rule 36.6(6) (Hearings) applies in relation to a judge exercising any of the powers referred to in article 8 of the Proceeds of Crime Act 2002 (Appeals under Part 2) Order 2003[4] or the powers in rules 42.12(3) and (4) (Respondent's notice), 42.15(2) (Notice of appeal) and 42.16(6) (Respondent's notice), as it applies in relation to a judge exercising the powers referred to in section 31(2) of the Criminal Appeal Act 1968[5].

**R42.7**    **Determination by full court**

42.7   Rule 36.5 (Renewing an application refused by a judge or the Registrar) applies where a single judge has refused an application by a party to exercise in that party's favour any of the powers listed in article 8 of the Proceeds of Crime Act 2002 (Appeals under Part 2) Order 2003, or the power in rule 42.12(3) or (4) as it applies where the judge has refused to exercise the powers referred to in section 31(2) of the Criminal Appeal Act 1968.

**R42.8**    **Notice of determination and renewal of application for permission to appeal**

42.8   (1) Paragraphs (2) and (3) of this rule apply where a single judge or the Court of Appeal has determined an application or appeal under the Proceeds of Crime Act 2002 (Appeals under Part 2) Order 2003 or under Part 2 of the Proceeds of Crime Act 2002.

     (2) The Registrar must, as soon as practicable, serve notice of the determination on all of the parties to the proceedings.

     (3) Where a single judge or the Court of Appeal has disposed of an application for permission to appeal or an appeal under section 31 of the 2002 Act[6], the Registrar must also, as soon as practicable, serve the order on the Crown Court officer and the court officer for the magistrates' court responsible for enforcing any confiscation order which the Crown Court has made (the 'enforcing court').

     (4) Paragraphs (5) and (6) of this rule apply where—

         (a) a single judge has refused an application for permission to appeal under section 31 of the 2002 Act[7], and

         (b) the appellant renews that application, in time or with an application to extend the time within which to renew.

     (5) The Registrar must, as soon as practicable, notify the court officer for the enforcing court, if any, of the service of that renewed application.

     (6) Unless a single judge, the Court of Appeal or the enforcing court otherwise directs, pending disposal of the renewed application the court officer for the enforcing court must withhold the payment of any sum not yet paid—

---

[4] S.I. 2003/82.

[5] 1968 c. 19; section 31(2) was amended by section 21 of, and Schedule 2 to, the Costs in Criminal Cases Act 1973 (c. 14), section 29 of the Criminal Justice Act 1982 (c. 48), section 170 of, and paragraphs 20 and 29 of Schedule 15 to, the Criminal Justice Act 1988 (c. 33), section 87 of the Courts Act 2003 (c. 39) and section 48 of the Police and Justice Act 2006 (c. 48).

[6] 2002 c. 29; section 31 was amended by section 74 of, and paragraphs 1 and 16 of Schedule 8 to, the Serious Crime Act 2007 (c. 27).

[7] 2002 c. 29; section 31 was amended by section 74 of, and paragraphs 1 and 16 of Schedule 8 to, the Serious Crime Act 2007 (c. 27) and sections 3 and 85 of, and paragraph 27 of Schedule 4 to, the Serious Crime Act 2015 (c. 9).

(a)   which under section 13(6) of the 2002 Act[8] was directed to be paid out of sums recovered under a confiscation order, and

(b)   the payment of which is suspended pending appeal.

*[Note. See also rule 42.11 (Notice of appeal) under which (i) the Registrar must notify the court officer for the enforcing court of the service of a notice of appeal, and (ii) that court officer must notify any person whose entitlement to payment of a sum is suspended by that appeal.*

*Under section 13 of the Proceeds of Crime Act 2002, if the Crown Court makes a confiscation order and one or more priority orders, as defined in that section, against the same defendant in the same proceedings then in some circumstances the court must direct that part or all of the priority order must be paid out of sums recovered under the confiscation order.*

*A compensation order under section 134 of the Sentencing Act 2020[9] is such a priority order. Under section 141(1) of the 2020 Act, a person in whose favour a compensation order is made is not entitled to receive the amount due until there is no further possibility of the order being varied or set aside on appeal (disregarding any power to grant leave to appeal out of time). Under section 141(2) of the 2020 Act, Criminal Procedure Rules may make provision about the way in which the enforcing court is to deal with money paid in satisfaction of a compensation order where the entitlement of the person in whose favour it was made is suspended.]*

### Record of proceedings and transcripts                                                      R42.9

42.9   Rule 5.5 (Recording and transcription of proceedings in the Crown Court) and rule 36.9 (Duty of person transcribing proceedings in the Crown Court) apply in relation to proceedings in respect of which an appeal lies to the Court of Appeal under Part 2 of the Proceeds of Crime Act 2002 as they apply in relation to proceedings in respect of which an appeal lies to the Court of Appeal under Part I of the Criminal Appeal Act 1968.

### Appeal to the Supreme Court                                                                 R42.10

42.10 (1)   An application to the Court of Appeal for permission to appeal to the Supreme Court under Part 2 of the Proceeds of Crime Act 2002 must be made—

(a)   orally after the decision of the Court of Appeal from which an appeal lies to the Supreme Court; or

(b)   in the form set out in the Practice Direction, in accordance with article 12 of the Proceeds of Crime Act 2002 (Appeals under Part 2) Order 2003 and served on the Registrar.

(2)   The application may be abandoned at any time before it is heard by the Court of Appeal by serving notice in writing on the Registrar.

(3)   Rule 36.6(6) (Hearings) applies in relation to a single judge exercising any of the powers referred to in article 15 of the 2003 Order, as it applies in relation to a single judge exercising the powers referred to in section 31(2) of the Criminal Appeal Act 1968.

(4)   Rules 36.5 (Renewing an application refused by a judge or the Registrar) applies where a single judge has refused an application by a party to exercise in that party's favour any of the powers listed in article 15 of the 2003 Order as they apply where the judge has refused to exercise the powers referred to in section 31(2) of the 1968 Act.

(5)   The form in which rule 36.5(2) requires an application to be made may be modified as necessary.

### Confiscation: appeal by prosecutor or person with interest in property

### Notice of appeal                                                                            R42.11

42.11 (1)   Where an appellant wishes to apply to the Court of Appeal for permission to appeal under section 31 of the Proceeds of Crime Act 2002[10], the appellant must serve a notice of appeal in the form set out in the Practice Direction on—

(a)   the Crown Court officer;

(b)   the defendant;

(c)   the prosecutor, if the prosecutor is not the appellant; and

---

[8]   2002 c. 29; section 13 was amended by section 54 of, and paragraph 11 of Schedule 12 to, the Criminal Justice and Courts Act 2015 (c. 2), section 6 of the Serious Crime Act 2015 (c. 9), section 410 of, and paragraph 182 of Schedule 24 to, the Sentencing Act 2020 (c. 17) and section 39 of, and paragraph 7 of Schedule 3 to, the Counter-Terrorism and Sentencing Act 2021 (c. 11).

[9]   2020 c. 17.

[10]   2002 c. 29; section 31 was amended by section 74 of, and paragraphs 1 and 16 of Schedule 8 to, the Serious Crime Act 2007 (c. 27) and section 3 of the Serious Crime Act 2015 (c. 9).

(d) any person who the appellant thinks is or may be someone—
  (i) holding an interest in property in which the Crown Court determined the extent of the defendant's interest under section 10A of the 2002 Act[11], and
  (ii) who is neither the defendant nor the appellant.

(2) When a notice of appeal is served on a respondent defendant, or other person under paragraph (1)(d), it must be accompanied by a respondent's notice in the form set out in the Practice Direction for the respondent to complete and a notice which—
  (a) informs the respondent that the result of an appeal could be that the Court of Appeal would increase a confiscation order already imposed, make a confiscation order itself or direct the Crown Court to hold another confiscation hearing;
  (b) informs the respondent of any right under article 6 of the Proceeds of Crime Act 2002 (Appeals under Part 2) Order 2003[12] to be present at the hearing of the appeal, although in custody;
  (c) invites the respondent to serve any notice on the Registrar —
    (i) to apply to the Court of Appeal for permission to be present at proceedings for which such permission is required under article 6 of the 2003 Order, or
    (ii) to present any argument to the Court of Appeal on the hearing of the application or, if permission is given, the appeal, and whether the respondent wishes to present it in person or by means of a legal representative;
  (d) draws to the respondent's attention the effect of rule 42.4 (Supply of documentary and other exhibits); and
  (e) advises the respondent to consult a solicitor as soon as possible.

(3) The appellant must provide the Crown Court officer with a certificate of service stating that the appellant has served the notice of appeal on each respondent or explaining why it has not been possible to do so.

(4) The Crown Court officer must, as soon as practicable—
  (a) notify the Registrar of the service of the notice of appeal;
  (b) make available to the Registrar—
    (i) the notice of appeal and any accompanying application served by the appellant,
    (ii) details of the parties including their addresses, and
    (iii) details of the court officer for the magistrates' court responsible for enforcing any confiscation order which the Crown Court has made (the 'enforcing court').

(5) The Registrar must, as soon as practicable, notify the court officer for the enforcing court, if any, of the service of the notice of appeal.

(6) Where a person is entitled to receive a sum directed to be paid out of sums recovered under a confiscation order, the court officer for the enforcing court must, as soon as practicable, notify each such person of—
  (a) the appeal,
  (b) any suspension of that person's entitlement pending appeal, and
  (c) any power for the Court of Appeal to vary or set aside that person's entitlement on appeal.

*[Note. See section 13 of the Proceeds of Crime Act 2002 and sections 134 and 141 of the Sentencing Act 2020. See also rule 42.8 (Notice of determination and renewal of application for permission to appeal) and the note to that rule.]*

**R42.12    Respondent's notice**

42.12 (1) This rule applies where a respondent is served with a notice of appeal under rule 42.11.

(2) If the respondent wishes to oppose the application for permission to appeal, the respondent must, not more than 10 business days after service of the notice of appeal, serve on the Registrar and on the appellant a notice in the form set out in the Practice Direction—
  (a) stating the date on which the notice of appeal was served;
  (b) summarising the respondent's response to the arguments of the appellant; and
  (c) specifying the authorities which the respondent intends to cite.

(3) The time for giving notice under this rule may be extended by the Registrar, a single judge or by the Court of Appeal.

(4) Where the Registrar refuses an application under paragraph (3) for the extension of time, the respondent is entitled to have the application determined by a single judge.

(5) Where a single judge refuses an application under paragraph (3) or (4) for the extension of time, the respondent is entitled to have the application determined by the Court of Appeal.

---

[11] 2002 c. 29; section 10A was inserted by section 1 of the Serious Crime Act 2015 (c. 9).
[12] S.I. 2003/82.

### Amendment and abandonment of appeal                                                                              R42.13

**42.13** (1) The appellant may amend a notice of appeal served under rule 42.11 or abandon an appeal under section 31 of the Proceeds of Crime Act 2002—

   (a) without the permission of the court at any time before the Court of Appeal has begun hearing the appeal; and

   (b) with the permission of the court after the Court of Appeal has begun hearing the appeal, by serving notice in writing on the Registrar.

   (2) Where the appellant serves a notice abandoning an appeal under paragraph (1), the appellant must send a copy of it to—

   (a) each respondent served with the notice of appeal;

   (b) the Crown Court officer; and

   (c) the court officer for the magistrates' court responsible for enforcing any confiscation order which the Crown Court has made.

   (3) Where the appellant serves a notice amending a notice of appeal under paragraph (1), the appellant must send a copy of it to each respondent served with the notice of appeal.

   (4) Where an appeal is abandoned under paragraph (1), the application for permission to appeal or appeal must be treated, for the purposes of section 85 of the 2002 Act (Conclusion of proceedings), as having been refused or dismissed by the Court of Appeal.

### Appeal about compliance, restraint or receivership order

### Permission to appeal                                                                                             R42.14

**42.14** (1) Permission to appeal to the Court of Appeal under section 13B, section 43 or section 65 of the Proceeds of Crime Act 2002[13] may only be given where—

   (a) the Court of Appeal considers that the appeal would have a real prospect of success; or

   (b) there is some other compelling reason why the appeal should be heard.

   (2) An order giving permission to appeal may limit the issues to be heard and be made subject to conditions.

### Notice of appeal                                                                                                 R42.15

**42.15** (1) Where an appellant wishes to apply to the Court of Appeal for permission to appeal under section 13B, 43 or 65 of the Proceeds of Crime Act 2002 Act, the appellant must serve a notice of appeal in the form set out in the Practice Direction on the Crown Court officer.

   (2) Unless the Registrar, a single judge or the Court of Appeal directs otherwise, the appellant must serve the notice of appeal, accompanied by a respondent's notice in the form set out in the Practice Direction for the respondent to complete, on—

   (a) each respondent;

   (b) any person who holds realisable property to which the appeal relates; and

   (c) any other person affected by the appeal

   as soon as practicable and in any event not later than 5 business days after the notice of appeal is served on the Crown Court officer.

   (3) The appellant must serve the following documents with the notice of appeal—

   (a) four additional copies of the notice of appeal for the Court of Appeal;

   (b) four copies of any skeleton argument;

   (c) one sealed copy and four unsealed copies of any order being appealed;

   (d) four copies of any witness statement or affidavit in support of the application for permission to appeal;

   (e) four copies of a suitable record of the reasons for judgment of the Crown Court; and

   (f) four copies of the bundle of documents used in the Crown Court proceedings from which the appeal lies.

   (4) Where it is not possible to serve all of the documents referred to in paragraph (3), the appellant must indicate which documents have not yet been served and the reasons why they are not currently available.

   (5) The appellant must provide the Crown Court officer with a certificate of service stating that the notice of appeal has been served on each respondent in accordance with paragraph (2) and including full details of each respondent or explaining why it has not been possible to effect service.

---

[13] 2002 c. 29; section 65 was amended by section 74 of, and paragraphs 1 and 32 of Schedule 8 to, the Serious Crime Act 2007 (c. 27). Section 13B was inserted by section 7 of the Serious Crime Act 2015 (c. 9).

**R42.16**　**Respondent's notice**

42.16 (1)　This rule applies to an appeal under section 13B, 43 or 65 of the Proceeds of Crime Act 2002.

(2)　A respondent may serve a respondent's notice on the Registrar.

(3)　A respondent who—

(a)　is seeking permission to appeal from the Court of Appeal; or

(b)　wishes to ask the Court of Appeal to uphold the decision of the Crown Court for reasons different from or additional to those given by the Crown Court,

must serve a respondent's notice on the Registrar.

(4)　A respondent's notice must be in the form set out in the Practice Direction and where the respondent seeks permission to appeal to the Court of Appeal it must be requested in the respondent's notice.

(5)　A respondent's notice must be served on the Registrar not later than 10 business days after—

(a)　the date the respondent is served with notification that the Court of Appeal has given the appellant permission to appeal; or

(b)　the date the respondent is served with notification that the application for permission to appeal and the appeal itself are to be heard together.

(6)　Unless the Registrar, a single judge or the Court of Appeal directs otherwise, the respondent serving a respondent's notice must serve the notice on the appellant and any other respondent—

(a)　as soon as practicable; and

(b)　in any event not later than 5 business days,

after it is served on the Registrar.

**R42.17**　**Amendment and abandonment of appeal**

42.17 (1)　The appellant may amend a notice of appeal served under rule 42.15 or abandon an appeal under section 13B, 43 or 65 of the Proceeds of Crime Act 2002—

(a)　without the permission of the court at any time before the Court of Appeal has begun hearing the appeal; and

(b)　with the permission of the court after the Court of Appeal has begun hearing the appeal,

by serving notice in writing on the Registrar.

(2)　Where the appellant serves a notice under paragraph (1), the appellant must send a copy of it to each respondent.

**R42.18**　**Stay**

42.18　Unless the Court of Appeal or the Crown Court orders otherwise, an appeal under section 13B, 43 or 65 of the Proceeds of Crime Act 2002 does not operate as a stay of any order or decision of the Crown Court.

**R42.19**　**Striking out appeal notices and setting aside or imposing conditions on permission to appeal**

42.19 (1)　The Court of Appeal may—

(a)　strike out the whole or part of a notice of appeal served under rule 42.15; or

(b)　impose or vary conditions upon which an appeal under section 13B, 43 or 65 of the Proceeds of Crime Act 2002 may be brought.

(2)　The Court of Appeal may only exercise its powers under paragraph (1) where there is a compelling reason for doing so.

(3)　Where a party is present at the hearing at which permission to appeal was given, that party may not subsequently apply for an order that the Court of Appeal exercise its powers under paragraph (1)(b).

**R42.20**　**Hearing of appeals**

42.20 (1)　This rule applies to appeals under section 13B, 43 or 65 of the Proceeds of Crime Act 2002.

(2)　Every appeal must be limited to a review of the decision of the Crown Court unless the Court of Appeal considers that in the circumstances of an individual appeal it would be in the interests of justice to hold a re-hearing.

(3)　The Court of Appeal may allow an appeal where the decision of the Crown Court was—

(a)　wrong; or

(b)　unjust because of a serious procedural or other irregularity in the proceedings in the Crown Court.

(4)　The Court of Appeal may draw any inference of fact which it considers justified on the evidence.

(5)　At the hearing of the appeal a party may not rely on a matter not contained in that party's notice of appeal unless the Court of Appeal gives permission.

CRIMINAL PROCEDURE RULES    PART 43    APPEAL OR REFERENCE TO THE SUPREME COURT

**When this Part applies**    R43.1

43.1  (1)  This Part applies where—

    (a)  a party wants to appeal to the Supreme Court after—

        (i)  an application to the Court of Appeal to which Part 27 applies (Retrial following acquittal), or

        (ii)  an appeal to the Court of Appeal to which applies Part 37 (Appeal to the Court of Appeal against ruling at preparatory hearing), Part 38 (Appeal to the Court of Appeal against ruling adverse to prosecution), or Part 39 (Appeal to the Court of Appeal about conviction or sentence); or

    (b)  a party wants to refer a case to the Supreme Court after a reference to the Court of Appeal to which Part 41 applies (Reference to the Court of Appeal of point of law or unduly lenient sentencing).

    (2)  A reference to an 'appellant' in this Part is a reference to such a party.

*[Note. Under section 33 of the Criminal Appeal Act 1968[1], a party may appeal to the Supreme Court from a decision of the Court of Appeal on—*

    *(a)  an application to the court under section 76 of the Criminal Justice Act 2003[2] (prosecutor's application for retrial after acquittal for serious offence). See also Part 27.*

    *(b)  an appeal to the court under—*

        *(i)  section 9 of the Criminal Justice Act 1987[3] or section 35 of the Criminal Procedure and Investigations Act 1996[4] (appeal against order at preparatory hearing). See also Part 37.*

        *(ii)  section 47 of the Criminal Justice Act 2003[5] (appeal against order for non-jury trial after jury tampering.) See also Part 37.*

        *(iii)  Part 9 of the Criminal Justice Act 2003[6] (prosecutor's appeal against adverse ruling). See also Part 38.*

        *(iv)  Part 1 of the Criminal Appeal Act 1968[7] (defendant's appeal against conviction, sentence, etc.). See also Part 39.*

*Under section 13 of the Administration of Justice Act 1960[8], a person found to be in contempt of court may appeal to the Supreme Court from a decision of the Court of Appeal on an appeal to the court under that section. See also Part 39.*

*Under article 12 of the Criminal Justice Act 2003 (Mandatory Life Sentence: Appeals in Transitional Cases) Order 2005[9], a party may appeal to the Supreme Court from a decision of the Court of Appeal on an appeal*

---

[1]  1968 c. 19; section 33 was amended by section 152 of, and Schedule 5 to, the Supreme Court Act 1981 (c. 54), section 15 of, and paragraph 3 of Schedule 2 to, the Criminal Justice Act 1987 (c. 38), section 36(1)(a) of the Criminal Procedure and Investigations Act 1996 (c. 25), section 456 of, and paragraphs 1 and 4 of Schedule 11 to, the Proceeds of Crime Act 2002 (c. 29), sections 47, 68 and 81 of the Criminal Justice Act 2003 (c. 44), by section 40 of, and paragraph 16 of Schedule 9 to, the Constitutional Reform Act 2005 (c. 4) and sections 74 and 92 of, and paragraph 144 of Schedule 8, and Schedule 14 to, the Serious Crime Act 2007 (c. 27).

[2]  2003 c. 44.

[3]  1987 c. 38; section 9 was amended by section 170 of, and Schedule 16 to, the Criminal Justice Act 1988 (c. 33), section 6 of the Criminal Justice Act 1993 (c. 36), sections 72, 74 and 80 of, and paragraph 3 of Schedule 3 and Schedule 5 to, the Criminal Procedure and Investigations Act 1996 (c. 25), sections 45 and 310 of, and paragraphs 18, 52 and 54 of Schedule 36 and Part 3 of Schedule 37 to, the Criminal Justice Act 2003 (c. 44), article 3 of, and paragraphs 21 and 23 of S.I. 2004/2035, section 59 of, and paragraph 1 of Schedule 11 to, the Constitutional Reform Act 2005 (c. 4) and Part 10 of Schedule 10 to the Protection of Freedoms Act 2012 (c. 9). The amendment made by section 45 of the Criminal Justice Act 2003 (c. 44) is in force for certain purposes; for remaining purposes it has effect from a date to be appointed.

[4]  1996 c. 25; section 35(1) was amended by section 45 of the Criminal Justice Act 2003 (c. 44). The amendment is in force for certain purposes, for remaining purposes it has effect from a date to be appointed. Section 35 was also amended by paragraphs 65 and 69 of Schedule 36 to the Criminal Justice Act 2003 (c. 44) and section 59 of, and paragraph 1 of Schedule 11 to, the Constitutional Reform Act 2005 (c. 4) and Part 10 of Schedule 10 to the Protection of Freedoms Act 2012 (c. 9).

[5]  2003 c. 44; section 47 was amended by section 59(5) of, and paragraph 1(2) of Schedule 11 to, the Constitutional Reform Act 2005 (c. 4).

[6]  2003 c. 44.

[7]  1968 c. 19.

[8]  1960 c. 65; section 13 was amended paragraph 40 of Schedule 8 to, the Courts Act 1971 (c. 23), Schedule 5 to, the Criminal Appeal Act 1968 (c. 19), paragraph 36 of Schedule 7 to, the Magistrates' Courts Act 1980 (c. 43), Schedule 7 to, the Supreme Court Act 1981 (c. 54), paragraph 25 of Schedule 2 to, the County Courts Act 1984 (c. 28), Schedule 15 to, the Access to Justice Act 1999 (c. 22), paragraph 13 of Schedule 9 to the Constitutional Reform Act 2005 (c. 4) and paragraph 45 of Schedule 16 to, the Armed Forces Act 2006 (c. 52).

[9]  S.I. 2005/2798.

*to the court under paragraph 14 of Schedule 22 to the Criminal Justice Act 2003[10] (appeal against minimum term review decision). See also Part 39.*

*Under article 15 of the Serious Organised Crime and Police Act 2005 (Appeals under Section 74) Order 2006[11], a party may appeal to the Supreme Court from a decision of the Court of Appeal on an appeal to the court under section 74 of the Serious Organised Crime and Police Act 2005[12] (appeal against sentence review decision). See also Part 39.*

*Under section 24 of the Serious Crime Act 2007[13], a party may appeal to the Supreme Court from a decision of the Court of Appeal on an appeal to that court under that section (appeal about a serious crime prevention order). See also Part 39.*

*Under section 36(3) of the Criminal Justice Act 1972[14], the Court of Appeal may refer to the Supreme Court a point of law referred by the Attorney General to the court. See also Part 41.*

*Under section 36(5) of the Criminal Justice Act 1988[15], a party may refer to the Supreme Court a sentencing decision referred by the Attorney General to the court. See also Part 41.*

*Under section 33(3) of the Criminal Appeal Act 1968, there is no appeal to the Supreme Court—*

    *(a) from a decision of the Court of Appeal on an appeal under section 14A(5A) of the Football Spectators Act 1989[16] (prosecutor's appeal against failure to make football banning order). See Part 39.*

    *(b) from a decision of the Court of Appeal on an appeal under section 159(1) of the Criminal Justice Act 1988[17] (appeal about reporting or public access restriction). See Part 40.*

*The rules in Part 36 (Appeal to the Court of Appeal: general rules) also apply where this Part applies.]*

**R43.2**    **Application for permission or reference**

**43.2** (1) An appellant must—

    (a) apply orally to the Court of Appeal—

        (i) for permission to appeal or to refer a sentencing case, or

        (ii) to refer a point of law

        immediately after the court gives the reasons for its decision; or

    (b) apply in writing and serve the application on the Registrar and every other party not more than—

        (i) 14 days after the court gives the reasons for its decision if that decision was on a sentencing reference to which Part 41 applies (Attorney General's reference of sentencing case), or

        (ii) 28 days after the court gives those reasons in any other case.

    (2) An application for permission to appeal or to refer a sentencing case must—

    (a) identify the point of law of general public importance that the appellant wants the court to certify is involved in the decision; and

    (b) give reasons why—

        (i) that point of law ought to be considered by the Supreme Court, and

        (ii) the court ought to give permission to appeal.

    (3) An application to refer a point of law must give reasons why that point ought to be considered by the Supreme Court.

    (4) An application must include or attach any application for the following, with reasons—

    (a) an extension of time within which to make the application for permission or for a reference;

---

[10] 2003 c. 44; paragraph 14 of Schedule 22 was amended by section 40 of, and paragraph 82 of Schedule 9 and paragraph 1 of Schedule 11 to, the Constitutional Reform Act 2005 (c. 4).

[11] S.I. 2006/2135.

[12] 2005 c. 15.

[13] 2007 c. 27.

[14] 1972 c. 71; section 36(3) was amended by section 40 of, and paragraph 23 of Schedule 9 to, the Constitutional Reform Act 2005 (c. 4).

[15] 1988 c. 33; section 36(5) was amended by section 40(4) of, and paragraph 48(1) and (2) of Schedule 9 to, the Constitutional Reform Act 2005 (c. 4).

[16] 1989 c. 37; section 14A(5A) was inserted by section 52 of, and paragraphs 1 and 3 of Schedule 3 to, the Violent Crime Reduction Act 2006 (c. 38).

[17] 1988 c. 33; section 159(1) was amended by section 61 of the Criminal Procedure and Investigations Act 1996 (c. 25).

(v)     where the Court of Appeal decides a prosecutor's appeal under Part 37 (Appeal to the Court of Appeal against ruling at preparatory hearing) or Part 38 (Appeal to the Court of Appeal against ruling adverse to prosecution),

(vi)     where the Court of Appeal decides a reference by the Attorney General under Part 41 (Reference to the Court of Appeal of point of law or unduly lenient sentence),

(vii)     where the Court of Appeal decides an appeal by someone other than the defendant about a serious crime prevention order, or

(viii)     where the defendant is discharged under Part 1 or 2 of the Extradition Act 2003;

*(See section 16 of the Prosecution of Offences Act 1985 and regulation 14 of the Costs in Criminal Cases (General) Regulations 1986[36]; section 36(5) of the Criminal Justice Act 1972 and paragraph 11 of Schedule 3 to the Criminal Justice Act 1988; article 14 of the Serious Crime Act 2007 (Appeals under Section 24) Order 2008; and sections 61 and 134 of the Extradition Act 2003.)*

(b)     for a private prosecutor, in proceedings in respect of an offence that must or may be tried in the Crown Court;

*(See section 17 of the Prosecution of Offences Act 1985 and regulation 14 of the Costs in Criminal Cases (General) Regulations 1986.)*

(c)     for a person adversely affected by a serious crime prevention order, where the Court of Appeal—

    (i)    allows an appeal by that person about that order, or

    (ii)   decides an appeal about that order by someone else.

*(See article 14 of the Serious Crime Act 2007 (Appeals under Section 24) Order 2008.)*

*Where the court makes an order for the payment of a defendant's costs out of central funds—*

(a)     the general rule is that the order may not require the payment of any amount in respect of fees payable to a legal representative, or disbursements paid by a legal representative (including expert witness costs), but if the defendant is an individual then an order may require payment of such an amount in a case—

    (i)     in a magistrates' court, including in an extradition case,

    (ii)    in the Crown Court, on appeal from a magistrates' court,

    (iii)   in the Crown Court, where the defendant has been sent for trial, the High Court gives permission to serve a draft indictment or the Court of Appeal orders a retrial and the defendant has been found financially ineligible for legal aid, or

    (iv)   in the Court of Appeal, on an appeal against a verdict of not guilty by reason of insanity, or against a finding under the Criminal Procedure (Insanity) Act 1964[37], or on an appeal under section 16A of the Criminal Appeal Act 1968[38] (appeal against order made in cases of insanity or unfitness to plead); and

(b)     any such amount may not exceed an amount specified by regulations made by the Lord Chancellor.

*(See section 16A of the Prosecution of Offences Act 1985[39], sections 62A, 62B, 135A and 135B of the Extradition Act 2003[40] and regulations 4A and 7 of the Costs in Criminal Cases (General) Regulations 1986[41].)]*

### Payment of costs by one party to another

**R45.5**    **Costs on conviction and sentence, etc.**

45.5    (1)   This rule applies where the court can order a defendant to pay the prosecutor's costs if the defendant is—

    (a)   convicted or found guilty;

    (b)   dealt with in the Crown Court after committal for sentence there;

    (c)   dealt with for breach of a sentence; or

    (d)   in an extradition case—

       (i)   ordered to be extradited, under Part 1 of the Extradition Act 2003,

---

[36] S.I. 1986/1335; regulation 14 was amended by regulations 2 and 11 of S.I. 2008/2448.

[37] 1964 c. 84.

[38] 1968 c. 19; section 16A was inserted by section 25 of the Domestic Violence, Crime and Victims Act 2004 (c. 28).

[39] 1985 c. 23; section 16A was inserted by paragraphs 1 and 3 and Part 4 of Schedule 7 to the Legal Aid, Sentencing and Punishment of Offenders Act 2012 (c. 10).

[40] 2003 c. 41; sections 62A and 62B were inserted by paragraphs 12 and 15 and Part 4 of Schedule 7 to the Legal Aid, Sentencing and Punishment of Offenders Act 2012 (c. 10) and sections 135A and 135B were inserted by paragraphs 12 and 18 and Part 4 of that Schedule.

[41] S.I. 1986/1335; regulation 4A was inserted by regulations 4 and 5 of S.I. 2012/1804. Regulation 7 was substituted by regulations 4 and 6 of S.I. 2012/1804 and amended by S.I. 2013/2830.

    (m) *section 14H(5) of the Football Spectators Act 1989, for the payment by a defendant of another person's costs on an application to terminate a football banning order (see rule 45.7);*

    (n) *section 4(7) of the Dangerous Dogs Act 1991, for the payment by a defendant of another person's costs on an application to terminate a disqualification for having custody of a dog (see rule 45.7);*

    (o) *article 14 of the Serious Crime Act 2007 (Appeals under Section 24) Order 2008[20], corresponding with section 16 of the Prosecution of Offences Act 1985 (see rule 45.4);*

    (p) *article 15 of the Serious Crime Act 2007 (Appeals under Section 24) Order 2008, corresponding with section 18 of the Prosecution of Offences Act 1985 (see rule 45.6);*

    (q) *article 16 of the Serious Crime Act 2007 (Appeals under Section 24) Order 2008, corresponding with an order under section 19(1) of the 1985 Act (see rule 45.8);*

    (r) *article 17 of the Serious Crime Act 2007 (Appeals under Section 24) Order 2008, corresponding with an order under section 19A of the 1985 Act (see rule 45.9);*

    (s) *article 18 of the Serious Crime Act 2007 (Appeals under Section 24) Order 2008, corresponding with an order under section 19B of the 1985 Act (see rule 45.10);*

    (t) *section 60 or 133 of the Extradition Act 2003 (costs where extradition ordered) for the payment by a defendant of another person's costs (see rule 45.4); or*

    (u) *section 61 or 134 of the Extradition Act 2003[21] (costs where discharge ordered) for the payment out of central funds of a defendant's costs (see rule 45.4).*

*See also the Criminal Costs Practice Direction.*

*Part 39 (Appeal to the Court of Appeal about conviction or sentence) contains rules about appeals against costs orders made in the Crown Court under the legislation listed in (c) above.*

*Part 34 (Appeal to the Crown Court) and Part 39 (Appeal to the Court of Appeal about conviction or sentence) contain rules about appeals against costs orders made under the legislation listed in (e) and (f) above.*

*As to costs in restraint or receivership proceedings under Part 2 of the Proceeds of Crime Act 2002[22], see rules 33.47 to 33.50.*

*A costs order can be enforced—*

    (a) *against a defendant, under section 41(1) or (3) of the Administration of Justice Act 1970[23];*

    (b) *against a prosecutor, under section 41(2) or (3) of the Administration of Justice Act 1970;*

    (c) *against a representative, under regulation 3D of the Costs in Criminal Cases (General) Regulations 1986[24] or article 18 of the Serious Crime Act 2007 (Appeals under Section 24) Order 2008;*

    (d) *against a non-party, under regulation 3I of the Costs in Criminal Cases (General) Regulations 1986[25] or article 31 of the Serious Crime Act 2007 (Appeals under Section 24) Order 2008[26].*

*See also section 58, section 150(1) and Part III of the Magistrates' Courts Act 1980[27] and Schedule 5 to the Courts Act 2003[28].]*

## Costs orders: general rules                                                      R45.2

45.2  (1) The court must not make an order about costs unless each party and any other person directly affected—

    (a) is present; or

    (b) has had an opportunity—

        (i) to attend, or

        (ii) to make representations.

---

[20] S.I. 2008/1863.

[21] 2003 c. 41; sections 61 and 134 were amended by paragraphs 12, 13 and 16 and Part 4 of Schedule 7 to the Legal Aid, Sentencing and Punishment of Offenders Act 2012 (c. 10).

[22] 2002 c. 29.

[23] 1970 c. 31; section 41(3) was amended by section 62 of, and paragraph 35 of Schedule 13 to the Tribunals, Courts and Enforcement Act 2007 (c. 15) and section 17 of, and paragraph 52 of Schedule 9 to, the Crime and Courts Act 2013 (c. 22).

[24] S.I. 1986/1335; regulation 3D was inserted by article 2 of S.I. 1991/789 and amended by regulation 6 of S.I. 2004/2408.

[25] S.I. 1986/1335; regulation 3I was inserted by regulation 7 of S.I. 2004/2408.

[26] S.I. 2008/1863.

[27] 1980 c. 43; section 58 was amended by section 33 of, and paragraph 80 of Schedule 2 to, the Family Law Reform Act 1987 (c. 42); a relevant amendment was made to section 150(1) by paragraph 250 of Schedule 8, and Schedule 10 to, the Courts Act 2003 (c. 39).

[28] 2003 c. 39; Schedule 5 was amended by articles 2, 4, 6, 7 and 8 of S.I. 2006/1737, section 62 of, and paragraphs 148 and 149 of Schedule 13 to, the Tribunals, Courts and Enforcement Act 2007 (c. 15), section 80 of the Criminal Justice and Immigration Act 2008 (c. 4), section 88 of the Legal Aid, Sentencing and Punishment of Offenders Act 2012 (c. 10), section 10 of, and paragraphs 24 and 27 of the Schedule to, the Prevention of Social Housing Fraud Act 2013 (c. 3), section 27 of the Crime and Courts Act 2013 (c. 22) and section 56 of the Criminal Justice and Courts Act 2015 (c. 2). It is further amended by section 26 of the Crime and Courts Act 2013 (c. 22) and paragraph 23 of Schedule 5 to the Modern Slavery Act 2015 (c. 30), with effect from dates to be appointed.

      (b)  the disbursements paid by a legal representative; and

      (c)  any other expenses incurred in connection with the case.

*[Note. A costs order can be made under—*

     *(a)  section 16 of the Prosecution of Offences Act 1985[13] (defence costs), for the payment out of central funds of a defendant's costs (see rule 45.4);*

     *(b)  section 17 of the Prosecution of Offences Act 1985[14] (prosecution costs), for the payment out of central funds of a private prosecutor's costs (see rule 45.4);*

     *(c)  section 18 of the Prosecution of Offences Act 1985[15] (award of costs against accused), for the payment by a defendant of another person's costs (see rules 45.5 and 45.6);*

     *(d)  section 19(1) of the Prosecution of Offences Act 1985[16] and regulation 3 of the Costs in Criminal Cases (General) Regulations 1986, for the payment by a party of another party's costs incurred as a result of an unnecessary or improper act or omission by or on behalf of the first party (see rule 45.8);*

     *(e)  section 19A of the Prosecution of Offences Act 1985[17] (costs against legal representatives, etc.)—*

         *(i)  for the payment by a legal representative of a party's costs incurred as a result of an improper, unreasonable or negligent act or omission by or on behalf of the representative, or*

         *(ii)  disallowing the payment to that representative of such costs (see rule 45.9);*

     *(f)  section 19B of the Prosecution of Offences Act 1985[18] (provision for award of costs against third parties) and regulation 3F of the Costs in Criminal Cases (General) Regulations 1986[19], for the payment by a person who is not a party of a party's costs where there has been serious misconduct by the non-party (see rule 45.10);*

     *(g)  section 109 of the Magistrates' Courts Act 1980, section 52 of the Senior Courts Act 1981 and rule 45.6, for the payment by an appellant of a respondent's costs on abandoning an appeal to the Crown Court (see rule 45.6);*

     *(h)  section 52 of the Senior Courts Act 1981 and—*

         *(i)  rule 45.6, for the payment by a party of another party's costs on an appeal to the Crown Court in any case not covered by (c) or (g),*

         *(ii)  rule 45.7, for the payment by a party of another party's costs on an application to the Crown Court about the breach or variation of a deferred prosecution agreement, or on an application to lift the suspension of a prosecution after breach of such an agreement;*

     *(i)  section 8 of the Bankers Books Evidence Act 1879, for the payment of costs by a party or by the bank against which an application for an order is made (see rule 45.7);*

     *(j)  section 2C(8) of the Criminal Procedure (Attendance of Witnesses) Act 1965, for the payment by the applicant for a witness summons of the costs of a party who applies successfully under rule 17.7 to have it withdrawn (see rule 45.7);*

     *(k)  section 36(5) of the Criminal Justice Act 1972 or Schedule 3, paragraph 11, of the Criminal Justice Act 1988, for the payment out of central funds of a defendant's costs on a reference by the Attorney General of—*

         *(i)  a point of law, or*

         *(ii)  an unduly lenient sentence*
           *(see rule 45.4);*

     *(l)  section 159(5) of the Criminal Justice Act 1988, for the payment by a person of another person's costs on an appeal about a reporting or public access restriction (see rule 45.6);*

---

[13] 1985 c. 23; section 16 was amended by section 15 of, and paragraphs 14 and 15 of Schedule 2 to, the Criminal Justice Act 1987 (c. 38), section 150 of, and paragraph 103 of Schedule 15 to, the Criminal Justice Act 1988 (c. 33), section 7 of, and paragraph 7 of Schedule 3 to, the Criminal Procedure (Insanity and Unfitness to Plead) Act 1991 (c. 25), sections 69 and 312 of, and paragraph 57 of Schedule 3, and Part 4 of Schedule 37, to the Criminal Justice Act 2003 (c. 44), section 58 of, and Schedule 11 to, the Domestic Violence, Crime and Victims Act 2004 (c. 28), section 40 of, and paragraph 23 of Schedule 9 to, the Constitutional Reform Act 2005 (c. 4) and paragraphs 1 and 2 and Part 4 of Schedule 7 to the Legal Aid, Sentencing and Punishment of Offenders Act 2012 (c. 10).

[14] 1985 c. 23; section 17 was amended by section 40 of, and paragraph 41 of Schedule 9 to, the Constitutional Reform Act 2005 (c. 4) and paragraphs 1 and 4 and Part 4 of Schedule 7 to the Legal Aid, Sentencing and Punishment of Offenders Act 2012 (c. 10).

[15] 1985 c. 23; section 18 was amended by section 15 of, and paragraph 16 of Schedule 2 to, the Criminal Justice Act 1987 (c. 38), section 168 of, and paragraph 26 of Schedule 9 to, the Criminal Justice and Public Order Act 1994 (c. 33), sections 69 and 312 of the Criminal Justice Act 2003 (c. 44) and section 40 of, and paragraph 41 of Schedule 9 to, the Constitutional Reform Act 2005 (c. 4).

[16] 1985 c. 23.

[17] 1985 c. 23; section 19A was inserted by section 111 of the Courts and Legal Services Act 1990 (c. 41).

[18] 1985 c. 23; section 19B was inserted by section 93 of the Courts Act 2003 (c. 39).

[19] S.I. 1986/1335; regulation 3F was inserted by regulation 7 of S.I. 2004/2408 and amended by regulations 2 and 5 of S.I. 2008/2448.

Kirchberg
L-2925 Luxemburg

**44A.3** There is no prescribed form for use but the following details must be included in the back sheet to the order:
    i.   Solicitor's full address;
    ii.  Solicitor's and Court references;
    iii. Solicitor's e-mail address.

**44A.4** The European Court of Justice regularly updates its Recommendation to national courts and tribunals in relation to the initiation of preliminary ruling proceedings. The current Recommendation is 2012/C 338/01: eurlex.europa.eu/LexUriServ/LexUriServ.do?uri=OJ:C:2012:338:000 1:0006:EN:PDF

**44A.5** The referring court may request the Court of Justice of the European Union to apply its urgent preliminary ruling procedure where the referring court's proceedings relate to a person in custody. For further information see Council Decision 2008/79/EC [2008] OJ L24/42: http://eurlex. europa.eu/LexUriServ/LexUriServ.do?uri=OJ:L:2008:024:0042:0043:EN:PDF

**44A.6** Any such request must be made in a document separate from the order or in a covering letter and must set out:
    iv.  The matters of fact and law which establish the urgency;
    v.   The reasons why the urgent preliminary ruling procedure applies; and
    vi.  In so far as possible, the court's view on the answer to the question referred to the Court of Justice of the European Union for a preliminary ruling.

**44A.7** Any request to apply the urgent preliminary ruling procedure should be filed with the Senior Master as described above.

## CRIMINAL PROCEDURE RULES    PART 45    COSTS
### General rules

**When this Part applies**                                 **R45.1**

**45.1**  (1)   This Part applies where the court can make an order about costs under—
    (a)  Part II of the Prosecution of Offences Act 1985[1] and Part II, IIA or IIB of The Costs in Criminal Cases (General) Regulations 1986[2];
    (b)  section 109 of the Magistrates' Courts Act 1980[3];
    (c)  section 52 of the Senior Courts Act 1981[4] and rule 45.6 or rule 45.7;
    (d)  section 8 of the Bankers Books Evidence Act 1879[5];
    (e)  section 2C(8) of the Criminal Procedure (Attendance of Witnesses) Act 1965[6];
    (f)  section 36(5) of the Criminal Justice Act 1972[7];
    (g)  section 159(5) and Schedule 3, paragraph 11, of the Criminal Justice Act 1988[8];
    (h)  section 14H(5) of the Football Spectators Act 1989[9];
    (i)  section 4(7) of the Dangerous Dogs Act 1991[10];
    (j)  Part 3 of the Serious Crime Act 2007 (Appeals under Section 24) Order 2008[11]; or
    (k)  Part 1 or 2 of the Extradition Act 2003[12].
 (2)   In this Part, 'costs' means—
    (a)  the fees payable to a legal representative;

---

[1] 1985 c. 23.
[2] S.I. 1986/1335.
[3] 1980 c. 43; section 109(2) was amended by section 109 of, and paragraph 234 of Schedule 8 to, the Courts Act 2003 (c. 39).
[4] 1981 c. 54. The Act's title was amended by section 59(5) of, and paragraph 1 of Schedule 11 to, the Constitutional Reform Act 2005 (c. 4).
[5] 1879 c. 11.
[6] 1965 c. 69; section 2C was substituted with section 2, 2A, 2B, 2D and 2E, for the existing section 2 by section 66(1) and (2) of the Criminal Procedure and Investigations Act 1996 (c. 25).
[7] 1972 c. 71; section 36(5) was amended by section 40 of, and paragraph 23 of Schedule 9 to, the Constitutional Reform Act 2005 (c. 4).
[8] 1988 c. 33; paragraph 11 of Schedule 3 was amended by section 40 of, and paragraph 48 of Schedule 9 to, the Constitutional Reform Act 2005 (c. 4) and paragraph 11 and Part 4 of Schedule 7 to the Legal Aid, Sentencing and Punishment of Offenders Act 2012 (c. 10).
[9] 1989 c. 37; section 14H was substituted, together with sections 14, 14A-14G and 14J, for existing sections 14-17, by section 1 of, and paragraphs 1 and 2 of Schedule 1 to, the Football (Disorder) Act 2000 (c. 25).
[10] 1991 c. 65.
[11] S.I. 2008/1863.
[12] 2003 c. 41.

(b) vary or rescind—
  (i) a costs order, or
  (ii) an order to which Part 31 applies (Behaviour orders).
(2) The court may exercise its power—
  (a) on application by a party, or on its own initiative; and
  (b) at a hearing, in public or in private, or without a hearing.
(3) The court must not exercise its power in a party's absence unless—
  (a) the court makes a decision proposed by that party;
  (b) the court makes a decision to which that party has agreed in writing; or
  (c) that party has had an opportunity to make representations at a hearing (whether or not that party in fact attends).
(4) A party who wants the court to exercise its power must—
  (a) apply in writing as soon as reasonably practicable after the conviction or order that that party wants the court to set aside, vary or rescind;
  (b) serve the application on—
    (i) the court officer, and
    (ii) each other party; and
  (c) in the application—
    (i) explain why, as appropriate, the conviction should be set aside, or the order varied or rescinded,
    (ii) specify any variation of the order that the applicant proposes,
    (iii) identify any witness that the defendant wants to call, and any other proposed evidence,
    (iv) say whether the defendant waives legal professional privilege, giving any relevant name and date, and
    (v) if the application is late, explain why.
(5) The court may—
  (a) extend (even after it has expired) the time limit under paragraph (4), unless the court's power to set aside the conviction, or vary the order, can no longer be exercised; and
  (b) allow an application to be made orally.

*[Note. Under section 142 of the Magistrates' Courts Act 1980—*

  *(a) where a defendant is convicted by a magistrates' court, the court may order that the case should be heard again by different justices; and*
  *(b) the court may vary or rescind an order which it has made when dealing with a convicted defendant,*

*if in either case it appears to the court to be in the interests of justice to do so.*

*The power cannot be exercised if the Crown Court or the High Court has determined an appeal about that conviction or order.*

*See also rule 28.4 (Variation of sentence), which applies to an application under section 142 of the 1980 Act to vary or rescind a sentence.]*

## CRIMINAL PRACTICE DIRECTIONS    PART 44    REQUEST TO THE EUROPEAN COURT FOR A PRELIMINARY RULING

**CPD.44A**    **CPD IX Appeal 44A: References to the European Court of Justice**

44A.1    Further to rule 44.3 of the Criminal Procedure Rules, the order containing the reference shall be filed with the Senior Master of the Queen's Bench Division of the High Court for onward transmission to the Court of Justice of the European Union. The order should be marked for the attention of Mrs Isaac and sent to the Senior Master:
  c/o Queen's Bench Division Associates Dept
  Room WG03
  Royal Courts of Justice
  Strand
  London
  WC2A 2LL

44A.2    There is no longer a requirement that the relevant court file be sent to the Senior Master. The parties should ensure that all appropriate documentation is sent directly to the European Court at the following address:
  The Registrar
  Court of Justice of the European Union

     (ii)  a notice under rule 24.9(4)(b) (notice of intention to plead guilty at a hearing before a court comprising more than one justice), or

     (iii)  a notice under rule 24.9(4)(c) (notice of intention to plead not guilty).

(3)  The court may extend that time limit, even after it has expired—

    (a)  at a hearing, in public or in private; or

    (b)  without a hearing.

(4)  Where the defendant serves such a declaration, in time or with an extension of time in which to do so, and the case began with a summons or requisition—

    (a)  the court must treat the summons or requisition and all subsequent proceedings as void (but not the application for the summons or the written charge with which the case began);

    (b)  if the defendant is present when the declaration is served, the rules in Part 24 (Trial and sentence in a magistrates' court) apply as if the defendant had been required to attend the court on that occasion; and

    (c)  if the defendant is absent when the declaration is served—

     (i)  the rules in Part 7 apply (Starting a prosecution in a magistrates' court) as if the prosecutor had just served an application for a summons in the same terms as the original application or written charge;

     (ii)  the court may exercise its power to issue a summons in accordance with those rules; and

     (iii)  except for rule 24.8 (Written guilty plea: special rules), the rules in Part 24 then apply.

(5)  Where the defendant serves such a declaration, in time or with an extension of time in which to do so, and the case began with a single justice procedure notice—

    (a)  the court must treat the single justice procedure notice and all subsequent proceedings as void (but not the written charge with which the case began);

    (b)  rule 24.9 (Single justice procedure: special rules) applies as if the defendant had served the notice required by paragraph (2)(b) of this rule within the time allowed by rule 24.9(4); and

    (c)  where that notice is under rule 24.9(4)(b) (notice of intention to plead guilty at a hearing before a court comprising more than one justice) or under rule 24.9(4)(c) (notice of intention to plead not guilty), then—

     (i)  if the defendant is present when the declaration is served, the rules in this Part apply as if the defendant had been required to attend the court on that occasion, or

     (ii)  if the defendant is absent when the declaration is served, paragraph (6) of this rule applies.

(6)  Where this paragraph applies, the court must exercise its power to issue a summons and—

    (a)  the rules in Part 7 apply (Starting a prosecution in a magistrates' court) as if the prosecutor had just served an application for a summons in the same terms as the written charge;

    (b)  except for rule 24.8 (Written guilty plea: special rules) and rule 24.9 (Single justice procedure: special rules), the rules in Part 24 apply.

(7)  A court officer may take the statutory declaration to which this rule refers if that officer—

    (a)  is a justices' legal adviser; or

    (b)  is nominated for the purpose by such a legal adviser.

*[Note. Under sections 14 and 16E of the Magistrates' Courts Act 1980, proceedings which begin with a summons, requisition or single justice procedure notice will become void if the defendant, at any time during or after the trial, makes a statutory declaration that he or she did not know of them until a date after the trial began.*

*Under section 14(3) or section 16E(9) of the 1980 Act, the court which decides whether or not to extend the time limit for serving a declaration under this rule may comprise a single justice.*

*Section 2 of the Commissioners for Oaths Act 1889[4] allows rules that regulate the procedure of a court to authorise the taking of a statutory declaration by an officer of that court.*

*The Practice Direction sets out a form of declaration for use in connection with this rule.]*

### Setting aside a conviction or varying a costs, etc. order                   R44.3

**44.3**  (1)  This rule applies where under section 142 of the Magistrates' Courts Act 1980[5], the court can—

    (a)  set aside a conviction, or

---

[4] 1889 c. 10; section 2 was amended by section 59 of, and paragraph 15 of Schedule 11 to, the Constitutional Reform Act 2005 (c. 4).

[5] 1980 c. 43; section 142 was amended by sections 26 and 29 of, and Schedule 3 to, the Criminal Appeal Act 1995 (c. 35).

**R43.3**    **Determination of detention pending appeal, etc.**

**43.3**    On an application for permission to appeal, the Court of Appeal must—

(a)    decide whether to order the detention of a defendant who would have been liable to be detained but for the decision of the court; and

(b)    determine any application for—

(i)    bail pending appeal,

(ii)    permission to attend any hearing in the Supreme Court, or

(iii)    a representation order.

*[Note. For the liability of a defendant to be detained pending a prosecutor's appeal to the Supreme Court and afterwards, see—*

*(a)    section 37 of the Criminal Appeal Act 1968[25];*

*(b)    article 19 of the Serious Organised Crime and Police Act 2005 (Appeals under Section 74) Order 2006[26].*

*For the grant of legal aid for proceedings in the Supreme Court, see sections 14, 16 and 19 of the Legal Aid, Sentencing and Punishment of Offenders Act 2012[27].]*

**R43.4**    **Bail pending appeal**

**43.4**    Rules 39.8 (Application for bail pending appeal or retrial), 39.9 (Conditions of bail pending appeal or re-trial) and 39.10 (Forfeiture of a recognizance given as a condition of bail) apply.

CRIMINAL PROCEDURE RULES    PART 44    REOPENING A CASE IN A MAGISTRATES' COURT

**R44.1**    **When this Part applies**

**44.1**    (1)

(a)    under section 14 or section 16E of the Magistrates' Courts Act 1980[1], the defendant makes a statutory declaration of not having found out about the case until after the trial began; or

(b)    under section 142 of the 1980 Act[2], the court can—

(i)    set aside a conviction, or

(ii)    vary or rescind a costs order, or an order to which Part 31 applies (Behaviour orders).

**R44.2**    **Statutory declaration of ignorance of proceedings**

**44.2**    (1)    This rule applies where—

(a)    the case started with—

(i)    an application for a summons,

(ii)    a written charge and requisition, or

(iii)    a written charge and single justice procedure notice; and

(b)    under section 14 or section 16E of the Magistrates' Courts Act 1980[3], the defendant makes a statutory declaration of not having found out about the case until after the trial began.

(2)    The defendant must—

(a)    serve such a declaration on the court officer —

(i)    not more than 21 days after the date of finding out about the case, or

(ii)    with an explanation for the delay, if serving it more than 21 days after that date; and

(b)    serve with the declaration one of the following, as appropriate, if the case began with a written charge and single justice procedure notice—

(i)    a notice under rule 24.9(4)(a) (notice of guilty plea), with any representations that the defendant wants the court to consider and a statement of the defendant's assets and other financial circumstances, as required by that rule,

---

[25]  1968 c. 19; section 37 was amended by section 65(1) of, and paragraph 39 of Schedule 3 to, the Mental Health (Amendment) Act 1982 (c. 51), section 148 of, and paragraph 23 of Schedule 4 to, the Mental Health Act 1983 (c. 20), section 58(1) of, and paragraph 5 of Schedule 10 to, the Domestic Violence, Crime and Victims Act 2004 (c. 28), section 40 of, and paragraph 16 of Schedule 9 to, the Constitutional Reform Act 2005 (c. 4) and section 47 of, and paragraphs 1 and 13 of Schedule 8 to, the Criminal Justice and Immigration Act 2008 (c. 4).

[26]  S.I. 2006/2135.

[27]  2012 c. 10.

[1]  1980 c. 43; section 14 was amended by section 109 of, and paragraph 205 of Schedule 8 to, the Courts Act 2003 (c. 39). Section 16E was inserted by section 48 of the Criminal Justice and Courts Act 2015 (c. 2).

[2]  1980 c. 43; section 142 was amended by sections 26 and 29 of, and Schedule 3 to, the Criminal Appeal Act 1995 (c. 35).

[3]  1980 c. 43; section 14 was amended by section 109 of, and paragraph 205 of Schedule 8 to, the Courts Act 2003 (c. 39). Section 16E was inserted by section 48 of the Criminal Justice and Courts Act 2015 (c. 2).

(b)  bail pending appeal; or

(c)  permission to attend any hearing in the Supreme Court, if the appellant is in custody.

(5)  A written application must be in the form set out in the Practice Direction.

*[Note. In some legislation, including the Criminal Appeal Act 1968, permission to appeal is described as 'leave to appeal'.*

*Under the provisions listed in the note to rule 43.1, except section 36(3) of the Criminal Justice Act 1972 (Attorney General's reference of point of law), an appellant needs permission to appeal or to refer a sentencing case. Under those provisions, the Court of Appeal must not give permission unless it first certifies that—*

*(a)  a point of law of general public importance is involved in the decision, and*

*(b)  it appears to the court that the point is one which the Supreme Court ought to consider.*

*If the Court of Appeal gives such a certificate but refuses permission, an appellant may apply for such permission to the Supreme Court.*

*Under section 36(3) of the Criminal Justice Act 1972 an appellant needs no such permission. The Court of Appeal may refer the point of law to the Supreme Court, or may refuse to do so.*

*For the power of the court or the Registrar to shorten or extend a time limit, see rule 36.3. The time limit in this rule—*

*(a)  for applying for permission to appeal under section 33 of the Criminal Appeal Act 1968 (28 days) is prescribed by section 34 of that Act[18]. That time limit may be extended but not shortened by the court. But it may be extended on an application by a prosecutor only after an application to which Part 27 applies (Retrial after acquittal).*

*(b)  for applying for permission to refer a case under section 36(5) of the Criminal Justice Act 1988 (Attorney General's reference of sentencing decision: 14 days) is prescribed by paragraph 4 of Schedule 3 to that Act. That time limit may be neither extended nor shortened.*

*(c)  for applying for permission to appeal under article 12 of the Criminal Justice Act 2003 (Mandatory Life Sentence: Appeals in Transitional Cases) Order 2005 (28 days) is prescribed by article 13 of that Order. That time limit may be extended but not shortened.*

*(d)  for applying for permission to appeal under article 15 of the Serious Organised Crime and Police Act 2005 (Appeals under Section 74) Order 2006 (28 days) is prescribed by article 16 of that Order. That time limit may be extended but not shortened.*

*For the power of the Court of Appeal to grant bail pending appeal to the Supreme Court, see—*

*(a)  section 36 of the Criminal Appeal Act 1968[19];*

*(b)  article 18 of the Serious Organised Crime and Police Act 2005 (Appeals under Section 74) Order 2006[20].*

*For the right of an appellant in custody to attend a hearing in the Supreme Court, see—*

*(a)  section 38 of the Criminal Appeal Act 1968[21];*

*(b)  paragraph 9 of Schedule 3 to the Criminal Justice Act 1988[22];*

*(c)  article 15 of the Criminal Justice Act 2003 (Mandatory Life Sentences: Appeals in Transitional Cases) Order 2005[23];*

*(d)  article 20 of the Serious Organised Crime and Police Act 2005 (Appeals under Section 74) Order 2006[24].]*

---

[18]  1968 c. 19; section 34 was amended by section 88 of the Courts Act 2003 (c. 39), section 81 of the Criminal Justice Act 2003 (c. 44), and section 40(4) of, and paragraph 16 of Schedule 9 to, the Constitutional Reform Act 2005 (c. 4).

[19]  1968 c. 19; section 36 was amended by section 12 of, and paragraph 43 of Schedule 2 to, the Bail Act 1976 (c. 63), section 15 of, and paragraph 4 of Schedule 2 to, the Criminal Justice Act 1987 (c. 38), section 168 of, and paragraph 23 of Schedule 10 to, the Criminal Justice and Public Order Act 1994 (c. 33), section 36 of the Criminal Procedure and Investigations Act 1996 (c. 25), sections 47 and 68 of the Criminal Justice Act 2003 (c. 44) and section 40 of, and paragraph 16 of Schedule 9 to, the Constitutional Reform Act 2005 (c. 4).

[20]  S.I. 2006/2135.

[21]  1968 c. 19; section 38 was amended by section 81 of the Criminal Justice Act 2003 (c. 44), and section 40(4) of, and paragraph 16 of Schedule 9 to, the Constitutional Reform Act 2005 (c. 4).

[22]  1988 c. 33; paragraph 9 of Schedule 3 was amended by section 40 of, and paragraph 48 of Schedule 9 to, the Constitutional Reform Act 2005 (c. 4).

[23]  S.I. 2005/2798.

[24]  S.I. 2006/2135.

(ii) sent for extradition to the Secretary of State, under Part 2 of that Act, or

(iii) unsuccessful on an appeal by the defendant to the High Court, or on an application by the defendant for permission to appeal from the High Court to the Supreme Court.

(2) The court may make an order—

    (a) on application by the prosecutor; or

    (b) on its own initiative.

(3) Where the prosecutor wants the court to make an order—

    (a) the prosecutor must—

        (i) apply as soon as practicable, and

        (ii) specify the amount claimed; and

    (b) the general rule is that the court must make an order if it is satisfied that the defendant can pay;

(4) A defendant who wants to oppose an order must make representations as soon as practicable.

(5) If the court makes an order, it must assess the amount itself.

*[Note. See—*

    *(a)  rule 45.2;*

    *(b)  section 18 of the Prosecution of Offences Act 1985[42] and regulation 14 of the Costs in Criminal Cases (General) Regulations 1986; and*

    *(c)  sections 60 and 133 of the Extradition Act 2003.*

*Under section 18(4) and (5) of the 1985 Act, if a magistrates' court—*

    *(a)  imposes a fine, a penalty, forfeiture or compensation that does not exceed £5—*

        *(i)  the general rule is that the court will not make a costs order against the defendant, but*

        *(ii)  the court may do so;*

    *(b)  fines a defendant under 18, no costs order against the defendant may be for more than the fine.*

*Part 39 (Appeal to the Court of Appeal about conviction or sentence) contains rules about appeal against a Crown Court costs order to which this rule applies.]*

### Costs on appeal                                                                R45.6

45.6 (1) This rule—

    (a) applies where a magistrates' court, the Crown Court or the Court of Appeal can order a party to pay another person's costs on an appeal, or an application for permission to appeal; and

    (b) authorises the Crown Court, in addition to its other powers, to order a party to pay another party's costs on an appeal to that court, except on an appeal under—

        (i) section 108 of the Magistrates' Courts Act 1980[43], or

        (ii) section 45 of the Mental Health Act 1983[44].

(2) In this rule, costs include—

    (a) costs incurred in the court that made the decision under appeal; and

    (b) costs met by legal aid.

(3) The court may make an order—

    (a) on application by the person who incurred the costs; or

    (b) on its own initiative.

(4) A person who wants the court to make an order must—

    (a) apply as soon as practicable;

    (b) notify each other party;

    (c) specify—

        (i) the amount claimed, and

---

[42] 1985 c. 23; section 18 was amended by section 15 of, and paragraph 16 of Schedule 2 to, the Criminal Justice Act 1987 (c. 38), section 168 of, and paragraph 26 of Schedule 9 to, the Criminal Justice and Public Order Act 1994 (c. 33), sections 69 and 312 of the Criminal Justice Act 2003 (c. 44) and section 40 of, and paragraph 41 of Schedule 9 to, the Constitutional Reform Act 2005 (c. 4).

[43] 1980 c. 43; section 108 was amended by sections 66(2) and 78 of, and Schedule 16 to, the Criminal Justice Act 1982 (c. 48), section 23(3) of the Football Spectators Act 1989 (c. 37), section 101(2) of, and Schedule 13 to, the Criminal Justice Act 1991 (c. 53), sections 119 and 120(2) of, and paragraph 43 of Schedule 8 and Schedule 10 to, the Crime and Disorder Act 1998 (c. 37), section 7(2) of the Football (Offences and Disorder) Act 1999 (c. 21), section 165(1) of, and paragraph 71 of Schedule 9 to, the Powers of Criminal Courts (Sentencing) Act 2000 (c. 6), section 1 of, and Schedule 3 to, the Football (Disorder) Act 2000 (c. 25), section 58(1) of, and paragraph 10 of Schedule 10 to, the Domestic Violence, Crime and Victims Act 2004 (c. 28), section 52(2) of, and paragraph 14 of Schedule 3 to, the Violent Crime Reduction Act 2006 (c. 38) and section 64 of, and paragraph 10 of Schedule 3 to, the Animal Welfare Act 2006 (c. 45).

[44] 1983 c. 20.

            (ii)  against whom; and

     (d)  where an appellant abandons an appeal to the Crown Court by serving a notice of abandonment—

            (i)  apply in writing not more than 10 business days later, and

            (ii)  serve the application on the appellant and on the Crown Court officer.

(5)  A party who wants to oppose an order must—

     (a)  make representations as soon as practicable; and

     (b)  where the application was under paragraph (4)(d), serve representations on the applicant, and on the Crown Court officer, not more than 5 business days after it was served.

(6)  Where the application was under paragraph (4)(d), the Crown Court officer may—

     (a)  submit it to the Crown Court; or

     (b)  serve it on the magistrates' court officer, for submission to the magistrates' court.

(7)  If the court makes an order, it may direct an assessment under rule 45.11, or assess the amount itself where—

     (a)  the appellant abandons an appeal to the Crown Court;

     (b)  the Crown Court decides an appeal, except an appeal under—

            (i)  section 108 of the Magistrates' Courts Act 1980, or

            (ii)  section 45 of the Mental Health Act 1983; or

     (c)  the Court of Appeal decides an appeal to which Part 40 applies (Appeal to the Court of Appeal about reporting or public access restriction).

(8)  If the court makes an order in any other case, it must assess the amount itself.

*[Note. See also rule 45.2.*

*A magistrates' court can order an appellant to pay a respondent's costs on abandoning an appeal to the Crown Court.*

*The Crown Court can order—*

     *(a)  the defendant to pay the prosecutor's costs on dismissing a defendant's appeal—*

            *(i)  against conviction or sentence, under section 108 of the Magistrates' Courts Act 1980, or*

            *(ii)  where the magistrates' court makes a hospital order or guardianship order without convicting the defendant, under section 45 of the Mental Health Act 1983; and*

     *(b)  one party to pay another party's costs on deciding any other appeal to which Part 34 (Appeal to the Crown Court) applies.*

*The Court of Appeal can order—*

     *(a)  the defendant to pay another person's costs on dismissing a defendant's appeal or application to which Part 37 (Appeal to the Court of Appeal against ruling at preparatory hearing), Part 39 (Appeal to the Court of Appeal about conviction or sentence) or Part 43 (Appeal or reference to the Supreme Court) applies;*

     *(b)  the defendant to pay another person's costs on allowing a prosecutor's appeal to which Part 38 (Appeal to the Court of Appeal against ruling adverse to the prosecution) applies;*

     *(c)  the appellant to pay another person's costs on dismissing an appeal or application by a person affected by a serious crime prevention order;*

     *(d)  one party to pay another party's costs on deciding an appeal to which Part 40 (Appeal to the Court of Appeal about reporting or public access restriction) applies.*

*See section 109 of the Magistrates' Courts Act 1980[45]; section 52 of the Senior Courts Act 1981[46] (which allows rules of court to authorise the Crown Court to order costs); section 18 of the Prosecution of Offences Act 1985; section 159(5) of the Criminal Justice Act 1988[47]; and article 15 of the Serious Crime Act 2007 (Appeals under Section 24) Order 2008[48].]*

**R45.7**   **Costs on an application**

**45.7**  (1)  This rule—

     (a)  applies where the court can order a party to pay another person's costs in a case in which—

            (i)  the court decides an application for the production in evidence of a copy of a bank record,

---

[45] 1980 c. 43; section 109(2) was amended by section 109 of, and paragraph 234 of Schedule 8 to, the Courts Act 2003 (c. 39).

[46] 1981 c. 54. The Act's title was amended by section 59(5) of, and paragraph 1 of Schedule 11 to, the Constitutional Reform Act 2005 (c. 4).

[47] 1988 c. 33.

[48] S.I. 2008/1863.

     (ii) a magistrates' court or the Crown Court decides an application to terminate a football banning order,

     (iii) a magistrates' court or the Crown Court decides an application to terminate a disqualification for having custody of a dog,

     (iv) the Crown Court allows an application to withdraw a witness summons, or

     (v) the Crown Court decides an application relating to a deferred prosecution agreement under rule 11.5 (breach), rule 11.6 (variation) or rule 11.7 (lifting suspension of prosecution); and

   (b) authorises the Crown Court, in addition to its other powers, to order a party to pay another party's costs on an application to that court under rule 11.5, 11.6 or 11.7.

(2) The court may make an order—

   (a) on application by the person who incurred the costs; or

   (b) on its own initiative.

(3) A person who wants the court to make an order must—

   (a) apply as soon as practicable;

   (b) notify each other party; and

   (c) specify—

     (i) the amount claimed, and

     (ii) against whom.

(4) A party who wants to oppose an order must make representations as soon as practicable.

(5) If the court makes an order, it may direct an assessment under rule 45.11, or assess the amount itself.

*[Note. See—*

   *(a) rule 45.2;*

   *(b) section 8 of the Bankers Books Evidence Act 1879[49];*

   *(c) section 14H(5) of the Football Spectators Act 1989[50];*

   *(d) section 2C(8) of the Criminal Procedure (Attendance of Witnesses) Act 1965[51]; and*

   *(e) section 4(7) of the Dangerous Dogs Act 1991[52].*

*Section 52 of the Senior Courts Act 1981 allows rules of court to authorise the Crown Court to order costs.]*

### Costs resulting from unnecessary or improper act, etc.                    R45.8

**45.8** (1) This rule applies where the court can order a party to pay another party's costs incurred as a result of an unnecessary or improper act or omission by or on behalf of the first party.

(2) In this rule, costs include costs met by legal aid.

(3) The court may make an order—

   (a) on application by the party who incurred such costs; or

   (b) on its own initiative.

(4) A party who wants the court to make an order must—

   (a) apply in writing as soon as practicable after becoming aware of the grounds for doing so and in any event no later than the end of the case;

   (b) serve the application on—

     (i) the court officer (or, in the Court of Appeal, the Registrar), and

     (ii) each other party; and

   (c) in that application specify—

     (i) the party by whom costs should be paid,

     (ii) the relevant act or omission,

     (iii) the reasons why that act or omission meets the criteria for making an order,

     (iv) the amount claimed, and

     (v) those on whom the application has been served.

(5) Where the court considers making an order on its own initiative, it must—

   (a) identify the party against whom it proposes making the order; and

   (b) specify—

     (i) the relevant act or omission,

     (ii) the reasons why that act or omission meets the criteria for making an order, and

     (iii) with the assistance of the party who incurred the costs, the amount involved.

Criminal Procedure Rules and Criminal Practice Directions

---

[49] 1879 c. 11.

[50] 1989 c. 37; section 14H was substituted, together with sections 14, 14A-14G and 14J, for existing sections 14-17, by section 1 of, and paragraphs 1 and 2 of Schedule 1 to, the Football (Disorder) Act 2000 (c. 25).

[51] 1965 c. 69; section 2C was substituted with section 2, 2A, 2B, 2D and 2E, for the existing section 2 by section 66(1) and (2) of the Criminal Procedure and Investigations Act 1996 (c. 25).

[52] 1991 c. 65.

(6) A party who wants to oppose an order must—

    (a) make representations as soon as practicable; and

    (b) in reply to an application, serve representations on the applicant and on the court officer (or Registrar) not more than 5 business days after it was served.

(7) If the court makes an order, it must assess the amount itself.

(8) To help assess the amount, the court may direct an enquiry by—

    (a) the Lord Chancellor, where the assessment is by a magistrates' court or by the Crown Court; or

    (b) the Registrar, where the assessment is by the Court of Appeal.

(9) In deciding whether to direct such an enquiry, the court must have regard to all the circumstances including—

    (a) any agreement between the parties about the amount to be paid;

    (b) the amount likely to be allowed;

    (c) the delay and expense that may be incurred in the conduct of the enquiry; and

    (d) the particular complexity of the assessment, or the difficulty or novelty of any aspect of the assessment.

(10) If the court directs such an enquiry—

    (a) paragraphs (3) to (8) inclusive of rule 45.11 (Assessment and re-assessment) apply as if that enquiry were an assessment under that rule (but rules 45.12 (Appeal to a costs judge) and 45.13 (Appeal to a High Court judge) do not apply);

    (b) the authority that carries out the enquiry must serve its conclusions on the court officer as soon as reasonably practicable after following that procedure; and

    (c) the court must then assess the amount to be paid.

*[Note. See—*

    *(a) rule 45.2;*

    *(b) section 19(1) of the Prosecution of Offences Act 1985[53] and regulation 3 of the Costs in Criminal Cases (General) Regulations 1986[54]; and*

    *(c) article 16 of the Serious Crime Act 2007 (Appeals under Section 24) Order 2008[55].*

*Under section 19(1), (2) of the 1985 Act and regulation 3(1) of the 1986 Regulations, the court's power to make a costs order to which this rule applies can only be exercised during the proceedings.*

*Under regulation 3(5) of the 1986 Regulations, if a magistrates' court fines a defendant under 17, no costs order to which this rule applies may be for more than the fine.*

*The Criminal Costs Practice Direction sets out a form of application for use in connection with this rule.]*

### Other costs orders

**R45.9**    **Costs against a legal representative**

**45.9** (1) This rule applies where—

    (a) a party has incurred costs—

        (i) as a result of an improper, unreasonable or negligent act or omission by a legal or other representative or representative's employee, or

        (ii) which it has become unreasonable for that party to have to pay because of such an act or omission occurring after those costs were incurred; and

    (b) the court can—

        (i) order the representative responsible to pay such costs, or

        (ii) prohibit the payment of costs to that representative.

(2) In this rule, costs include costs met by legal aid.

(3) The court may make an order—

    (a) on application by the party who incurred such costs; or

    (b) on its own initiative.

(4) A party who wants the court to make an order must—

    (a) apply in writing as soon as practicable after becoming aware of the grounds for doing so and in any event no later than the end of the case;

    (b) serve the application on—

        (i) the court officer (or, in the Court of Appeal, the Registrar),

        (ii) the representative responsible,

---

[53] 1985 c. 23.

[54] S.I. 1986/1335; regulation 3 was amended by regulations 2 and 3 of S.I. 2008/2448.

[55] S.I. 2008/1863.

        (iii) each other party, and

        (iv) any other person directly affected; and

   (c) in that application specify—

        (i)   the representative responsible,

        (ii)  the relevant act or omission,

        (iii) the reasons why that act or omission meets the criteria for making an order,

        (iv) the amount claimed, and

        (v)  those on whom the application has been served.

(5) Where the court considers making an order on its own initiative, it must—

   (a) identify the representative against whom it proposes making that order; and

   (b) specify—

        (i)   the relevant act or omission,

        (ii)  the reasons why that act or omission meets the criteria for making an order, and

        (iii) with the assistance of the party who incurred the costs, the amount involved.

(6) A representative who wants to oppose an order must—

   (a) make representations as soon as practicable; and

   (b) in reply to an application, serve representations on the applicant and on the court officer (or Registrar) not more than 5 business days after it was served.

(7) If the court makes an order—

   (a) the general rule is that it must do so without waiting until the end of the case, but it may postpone making the order; and

   (b) it must assess the amount itself.

(8) To help assess the amount, the court may direct an enquiry by—

   (a) the Lord Chancellor, where the assessment is by a magistrates' court or by the Crown Court; or

   (b) the Registrar, where the assessment is by the Court of Appeal.

(9) In deciding whether to direct such an enquiry, the court must have regard to all the circumstances including—

   (a) any agreement between the parties about the amount to be paid;

   (b) the amount likely to be allowed;

   (c) the delay and expense that may be incurred in the conduct of the enquiry; and

   (d) the particular complexity of the assessment, or the difficulty or novelty of any aspect of the assessment.

(10) If the court directs such an enquiry—

   (a) paragraphs (3) to (8) inclusive of rule 45.11 (Assessment and re-assessment) apply as if that enquiry were an assessment under that rule (but rules 45.12 (Appeal to a costs judge) and 45.13 (Appeal to a High Court judge) do not apply);

   (b) the authority that carries out the enquiry must serve its conclusions on the court officer as soon as reasonably practicable after following that procedure; and

   (c) the court must then assess the amount to be paid.

(11) Instead of making an order, the court may make adverse observations about the representative's conduct for use in an assessment where—

   (a) a party's costs are—

        (i)   to be met by legal aid, or

        (ii)  to be paid out of central funds; or

   (b) there is to be an assessment under rule 45.11.

*[Note. See—*

   *(a) rule 45.2;*

   *(b) section 19A of the Prosecution of Offences Act 1985[56];*

   *(c) article 17 of the Serious Crime Act 2007 (Appeals under Section 24) Order 2008[57].*

*Under section 19A(1) of the 1985 Act, the court's power to make a costs order to which this rule applies can only be exercised during the proceedings.*

*The Criminal Costs Practice Direction sets out a form of application for use in connection with this rule.*

*Part 34 (Appeal to the Crown Court) and Part 39 (Appeal to the Court of Appeal about conviction or sentence) contain rules about appeals against a costs order to which this rule applies.]*

---

[56] 1985 c. 23; section 19A was inserted by section 111 of the Courts and Legal Services Act 1990 (c. 41).
[57] S.I. 2008/1863.

**R45.10** **Costs against a third party**

**45.10** (1) This rule applies where—

    (a) there has been serious misconduct by a person who is not a party; and

    (b) the court can order that person to pay a party's costs.

  (2) In this rule, costs include costs met by legal aid.

  (3) The court may make an order—

    (a) on application by the party who incurred the costs; or

    (b) on its own initiative.

  (4) A party who wants the court to make an order must—

    (a) apply in writing as soon as practicable after becoming aware of the grounds for doing so;

    (b) serve the application on—

      (i) the court officer (or, in the Court of Appeal, the Registrar),

      (ii) the person responsible,

      (iii) each other party, and

      (iv) any other person directly affected; and

    (c) in that application specify—

      (i) the person responsible,

      (ii) the relevant misconduct,

      (iii) the reasons why the criteria for making an order are met,

      (iv) the amount claimed, and

      (v) those on whom the application has been served.

  (5) Where the court considers making an order on its own initiative, it must—

    (a) identify the person against whom it proposes making that order; and

    (b) specify—

      (i) the relevant misconduct,

      (ii) the reasons why the criteria for making an order are met, and

      (iii) with the assistance of the party who incurred the costs, the amount involved.

  (6) A person who wants to oppose an order must—

    (a) make representations as soon as practicable; and

    (b) in reply to an application, serve representations on the applicant and on the court officer (or Registrar) not more than 5 business days after it was served.

  (7) If the court makes an order—

    (a) the general rule is that it must do so at the end of the case, but it may do so earlier; and

    (b) it must assess the amount itself.

  (8) To help assess the amount, the court may direct an enquiry by—

    (a) the Lord Chancellor, where the assessment is by a magistrates' court or by the Crown Court; or

    (b) the Registrar, where the assessment is by the Court of Appeal.

  (9) In deciding whether to direct such an enquiry, the court must have regard to all the circumstances including—

    (a) any agreement between the parties about the amount to be paid;

    (b) the amount likely to be allowed;

    (c) the delay and expense that may be incurred in the conduct of the enquiry; and

    (d) the particular complexity of the assessment, or the difficulty or novelty of any aspect of the assessment.

  (10) If the court directs such an enquiry—

    (a) paragraphs (3) to (8) inclusive of rule 45.11 (Assessment and re-assessment) apply as if that enquiry were an assessment under that rule (but rules 45.12 (Appeal to a costs judge) and 45.13 (Appeal to a High Court judge) do not apply);

    (b) the authority that carries out the enquiry must serve its conclusions on the court officer as soon as reasonably practicable after following that procedure; and

    (c) the court must then assess the amount to be paid.

*[Note. See—*

    *(a) rule 45.2;*

    *(b) section 19B of the Prosecution of Offences Act 1985 and regulation 3F of the Costs in Criminal Cases (General) Regulations 1986; and*

    *(c) article 18 of the Serious Crime Act 2007 (Appeals under Section 24) Order 2008.*

*The Criminal Costs Practice Direction sets out a form of application for use in connection with this rule.*

*Part 34 (Appeal to the Crown Court) and Part 39 (Appeal to the Court of Appeal about conviction or sentence) contain rules about appeals against a costs order to which this rule applies.]*

### Assessment and re-assessment

45.11 (1) This rule applies where the court directs an assessment under—

    (a) rule 33.48 (Confiscation and related proceedings—restraint and receivership proceedings; rules that apply generally — assessment of costs);

    (b) rule 45.6 (Costs on appeal); or

    (c) rule 45.7 (Costs on an application).

  (2) The assessment must be carried out by the relevant assessing authority, namely—

    (a) the Lord Chancellor, where the direction was given by a magistrates' court or by the Crown Court; or

    (b) the Registrar, where the direction was given by the Court of Appeal.

  (3) The party in whose favour the court made the costs order ('the applicant') must—

    (a) apply for an assessment—

      (i) in writing, in any form required by the assessing authority, and

      (ii) not more than 3 months after the costs order; and

    (b) serve the application on—

      (i) the assessing authority, and

      (ii) the party against whom the court made the costs order ('the respondent').

  (4) The applicant must—

    (a) summarise the work done;

    (b) specify—

      (i) each item of work done, giving the date, time taken and amount claimed,

      (ii) any disbursements or expenses, including the fees of any advocate, and

      (iii) any circumstances of which the applicant wants the assessing authority to take particular account; and

    (c) supply—

      (i) receipts or other evidence of the amount claimed, and

      (ii) any other information or document for which the assessing authority asks, within such period as that authority may require.

  (5) A respondent who wants to make representations about the amount claimed must—

    (a) do so in writing; and

    (b) serve the representations on the assessing authority, and on the applicant, not more than 15 business days after service of the application.

  (6) The assessing authority must—

    (a) if it seems likely to help with the assessment, obtain any other information or document;

    (b) resolve in favour of the respondent any doubt about what should be allowed; and

    (c) serve the assessment on the parties.

  (7) Where either party wants the amount allowed to be re-assessed—

    (a) that party must—

      (i) apply to the assessing authority, in writing and in any form required by that authority,

      (ii) serve the application on the assessing authority, and on the other party, not more than 15 business days after service of the assessment,

      (iii) explain the objections to the assessment,

      (iv) supply any additional supporting information or document, and

      (v) ask for a hearing, if that party wants one;

    (b) a party who wants to make representations about an application for re-assessment must—

      (i) do so in writing,

      (ii) serve the representations on the assessing authority, and on the other party, not more than 15 business days after service of the application, and

      (iii) ask for a hearing, if that party wants one; and

    (c) the assessing authority—

      (i) must arrange a hearing, in public or in private, if either party asks for one,

      (ii) subject to that, may re-assess the amount allowed with or without a hearing,

      (iii) must re-assess the amount allowed on the initial assessment, taking into account the reasons for disagreement with that amount and any other representations,

      (iv) may maintain, increase or decrease the amount allowed on the assessment,

      (v) must serve the re-assessment on the parties, and

      (vi) must serve reasons on the parties, if not more than 15 business days later either party asks for such reasons.

  (8) A time limit under this rule may be extended even after it has expired—

    (a) by the assessing authority, or

    (b) by the Senior Costs Judge, if the assessing authority declines to do so.

**R45.12**   **Appeal to a costs judge**

45.12 (1) This rule applies where—

(a) the assessing authority has re-assessed the amount allowed under rule 45.11; and

(b) either party wants to appeal against that amount.

(2) That party must—

(a) serve an appeal notice on—

(i) the Senior Costs Judge,

(ii) the other party, and

(iii) the assessing authority

not more than 15 business days after service of the written reasons for the re-assessment;

(b) explain the objections to the re-assessment;

(c) serve on the Senior Costs Judge with the appeal notice—

(i) the applications for assessment and re-assessment,

(ii) any other information or document considered by the assessing authority,

(iii) the assessing authority's written reasons for the re-assessment, and

(iv) any other information or document for which a costs judge asks, within such period as the judge may require; and

(d) ask for a hearing, if that party wants one.

(3) A party who wants to make representations about an appeal must—

(a) serve representations in writing on—

(i) the Senior Costs Judge, and

(ii) the applicant

not more than 15 business days after service of the appeal notice; and

(b) ask for a hearing, if that party wants one.

(4) Unless a costs judge otherwise directs, the parties may rely only on—

(a) the objections to the amount allowed on the initial assessment; and

(b) any other representations and material considered by the assessing authority.

(5) A costs judge—

(a) must arrange a hearing, in public or in private, if either party asks for one;

(b) subject to that, may determine an appeal with or without a hearing;

(c) may—

(i) consult the assessing authority,

(ii) consult the court which made the costs order, and

(iii) obtain any other information or document;

(d) must reconsider the amount allowed by the assessing authority, taking into account the objections to the re-assessment and any other representations;

(e) may maintain, increase or decrease the amount allowed on the re-assessment;

(f) may provide for the costs incurred by either party to the appeal; and

(g) must serve reasons for the decision on—

(i) the parties, and

(ii) the assessing authority.

(6) A costs judge may extend a time limit under this rule, even after it has expired.

*[Note. The Criminal Costs Practice Direction sets out a form for use in connection with this rule.]*

**R45.13**   **Appeal to a High Court judge**

45.13 (1) This rule applies where—

(a) a costs judge has determined an appeal under rule 45.12; and

(b) either party wants to appeal against the amount allowed.

(2) A party who wants to appeal—

(a) may do so only if a costs judge certifies that a point of principle of general importance was involved in the decision on the review; and

(b) must apply in writing for such a certificate and serve the application on—

(i) the costs judge, and

(ii) the other party

not more than 15 business days after service of the decision on the review.

(3) That party must—

(a) appeal to a judge of the High Court attached to the Queen's Bench Division as if it were an appeal from the decision of a master under Part 52 of the Civil Procedure Rules 1998[58]; and

[58] S.I. 1998/3132.

(b)   serve the appeal not more than 15 business days after service of the costs judge's certificate under paragraph (2).

(4)   A High Court judge—

(a)   may extend a time limit under this rule even after it has expired;

(b)   has the same powers and duties as a costs judge under rule 45.12; and

(c)   may hear the appeal with one or more assessors.

*[Note. See also section 70 of the Senior Courts Act 1981[59].]*

### Application for an extension of time                                                    R45.14

**45.14**  A party who wants an extension of time under rule 45.11, 45.12 or 45.13 must—

(a)   apply in writing;

(b)   explain the delay; and

(c)   attach the application, representations or appeal for which the extension of time is needed.

---

CRIMINAL PRACTICE DIRECTIONS   PART 45   COSTS

**CPD X CrimPR Part 45 Costs**                                                             CPD.45

Reference should be made to the Practice Direction (Costs in Criminal Proceedings) 2015.

---

CRIMINAL PROCEDURE RULES   PART 46   REPRESENTATIVES

### Functions of representatives and supporters                                            R46.1

**46.1**  (1)  Under these Rules, anything that a party may or must do may be done—

(a)   by a legal representative on that party's behalf;

(b)   by a person with the corporation's written authority, where that corporation is a defendant; or

(c)   with the help of a parent, guardian or other suitable supporting adult where that party is a defendant—

(i)   who is under 18, or

(ii)   whose understanding of what the case involves is limited

unless other legislation (including a rule) otherwise requires.

(2)  A member, officer or employee of a prosecutor may, on the prosecutor's behalf—

(a)   serve on the magistrates' court officer, or present to a magistrates' court, an application for a summons or warrant under section 1 of the Magistrates' Courts Act 1980[1]; or

(b)   issue a written charge and requisition, or single justice procedure notice, under section 29 of the Criminal Justice Act 2003[2].

*[Note. See also section 122 of the Magistrates' Courts Act 1980[3]. A party's legal representative must be entitled to act as such under section 13 of the Legal Services Act 2007[4].*

*Section 33(6) of the Criminal Justice Act 1925[5], section 46 of the Magistrates' Courts Act 1980[6] and Schedule 3 to that Act[7] provide for the representation of a corporation.*

---

[59]   1981 c. 54. The Act's title was amended by section 59(5) of, and paragraph 1 of Schedule 11 to, the Constitutional Reform Act 2005 (c. 4).

[1]   1980 c. 43; section 1 was amended by section 68 of, and paragraph 6 of Schedule 8 to, the Criminal Justice Act 1991 (c. 53), sections 43 and 109 of, and Schedule 10 to, the Courts Act 2003 (c. 39), section 31 of, and paragraph 12 of Schedule 7 to, the Criminal Justice Act 2003 (c. 44) and section 153 of the Police Reform and Social Responsibility Act 2011. It is further amended by paragraphs 7 and 8 of Schedule 36 to, the Criminal Justice Act 2003 (c. 44), with effect from a date to be appointed.

[2]   2003 c. 44; section 29 has been brought into force for certain purposes only (see S.I. 2007/1999, S.I. 2008/1424 and S.I. 2009/2879). It was amended by section 50 of, and paragraph 130 of Schedule 4 to, the Commissioners for Revenue and Customs Act 2005 (c. 11) and section 59 of, and paragraph 196 of Schedule 4 to, the Serious Organised Crime and Police Act 2005 (c. 15).

[3]   1980 c. 43; section 122 was amended by section 125(3) of, and paragraph 25 of Schedule 18 to, the Courts and Legal Services Act 1990 (c. 41).

[4]   2007 c. 29.

[5]   1925 c. 86.

[6]   1980 c. 43.

[7]   1980 c. 43; Schedule 3 was amended by sections 25(2) and 101(2) of, and Schedule 13 to, the Criminal Justice Act 1991 (c. 53), section 47 of, and paragraph 13 of Schedule 1 to, the Criminal Procedure and Investigations Act 1996 (c. 25) (in relation to proceedings begun on or after 1 April 1997) and paragraph 51 of Schedule 3, and Part 4 of Schedule 37, to the Criminal Justice Act 2003 (c. 44).

*Sections 3 and 6 of the Prosecution of Offences Act 1985[8] make provision about the institution of prosecutions.*

*Section 223 of the Local Government Act 1972[9] allows a member or officer of a local authority on that authority's behalf to prosecute or defend a case before a magistrates' court, and to appear in and to conduct any proceedings before a magistrates' court.*

*Part 7 contains rules about starting a prosecution.]*

**R46.2**    **Notice of appointment, etc. of legal representative: general rules**

46.2    (1)    This rule applies—
    (a)    in relation to—
        (i)    a party who does not have legal aid for the purposes of a case, and
        (ii)    a party to an extradition case in the High Court, whether that party has legal aid or not;
    (b)    where such a party—
        (i)    appoints a legal representative for the purposes of the case, or
        (ii)    dismisses such a representative, with or without appointing another; and
    (c)    where a legal representative for such a party withdraws from the case.
    (2)    Where paragraph (1)(b) applies, that party must give notice of the appointment or dismissal to—
    (a)    the court officer;
    (b)    each other party; and
    (c)    where applicable, the legal representative who has been dismissed,
    as soon as practicable and in any event within 5 business days.
    (3)    Where paragraph (1)(c) applies, that legal representative must—
    (a)    as soon as practicable give notice to—
        (i)    the court officer,
        (ii)    the party whom he or she has represented, and
        (iii)    each other party; and
    (b)    where that legal representative has represented the defendant in an extradition case in the High Court, include with the notice—
        (i)    confirmation that the defendant has notice of when and where the appeal hearing will take place and of the need to attend, if the defendant is on bail,
        (ii)    details sufficient to locate the defendant, including details of the custodian and of the defendant's date of birth and custody reference, if the defendant is in custody, and
        (iii)    details of any arrangements likely to be required by the defendant to facilitate his or her participation in consequence of the representative's withdrawal, including arrangements for interpretation.
    (4)    Any such notice—
    (a)    may be given orally if—
        (i)    it is given at a hearing, and
        (ii)    it specifies no restriction under paragraph (5)(b) (restricted scope of appointment); but
    (b)    must be in writing in any other case

---

[8]    1985 c. 23; section 3 was amended by section 15 of, and paragraph 13 of Schedule 2 to, the Criminal Justice Act 1987 (c. 38), paragraph 39 of Schedule 7 to the Police Act 1996 (c. 16), section 134 of, and paragraph 48 of Schedule 9 to, the Police Act 1997 (c. 50), section 164 of the Immigration and Asylum Act 1999 (c. 33), paragraph 10 of Schedule 7 to the Police Reform Act 2002 (c. 30), sections 86 and 92 of, and Schedule 3 to, the Anti-social Behaviour Act 2003 (c. 38), section 190 of the Extradition Act 2003 (c. 41), section 7 of the Asylum and Immigration (Treatment of Claimants, etc) Act 2004 (c. 19), section 40 of, and paragraph 41 of Schedule 9 to, the Constitutional Reform Act 2005 (c. 4), sections 59, 140 and 174 of, and paragraph 47 of Schedule 4 and Part 2 of Schedule 17 to, the Serious Organised Crime and Police Act 2005 (c. 15), sections 7, 8 and 52 of, and paragraph 15 of Schedule 3 to, the Violent Crime Reduction Act 2006 (c. 38), section 74 of, and paragraph 149 of Schedule 8 to, the Serious Crime Act 2007 (c. 27), paragraph 171 of Schedule 16 to the Police Reform and Social Responsibility Act 2011 (c. 13), section 15 of, and paragraph 30 of Schedule 8 to, the Crime and Courts Act 2013 (c. 22) and article 3 of, and paragraphs 1 and 2 of the Schedule to, S.I. 2014/834.

[9]    1972 c. 70; section 223 was amended by paragraph 9 of Schedule 3 to the Solicitors Act 1974 (c. 47), section 134 of, and Schedule 10 to, the Police Act 1977 (c. 50), section 84 of, and paragraph 21 of Schedule 14 to, the Local Government Act 1985 (c. 51), section 237 of, and Schedule 13 to, the Education Reform Act 1988 (c. 40), section 120 of, and paragraph 17 of Schedule 22 and Schedule 24 to, the Environment Act 1995 (c. 25), paragraph 1 of Schedule 7 to the Police Act 1996 (c. 16), paragraphs 1 and 13 of Schedule 13 to the Local Government and Public Involvement in Health Act 2007 (c. 28), section 208 of, and paragraph 28 of Schedule 21 to, the Legal Services Act 2007 (c. 29), paragraphs 10 and 24 of Schedule 6 to the Local Democracy, Economic Development and Construction Act 2009 (c. 20), paragraphs 100 and 109 of Schedule 16 to the Police Reform and Social Responsibility Act 2011 (c. 13) and article 2 of, and paragraphs 1 and 2 of the Schedule to, S.I. 2001/3719.

(5) A notice of the appointment of a legal representative—
  (a) must identify—
    (i) the legal representative who has been appointed, with details of how to contact that representative, and
    (ii) all those to whom the notice is given;
  (b) may specify a restriction, or restrictions, on the purpose or duration of the appointment; and
  (c) if it specifies any such restriction, may nonetheless provide that documents may continue to be served on the represented party at the representative's address until—
    (i) further notice is given under this rule, or
    (ii) that party obtains legal aid for the purposes of the case.
(6) A legal representative who is dismissed by a party or who withdraws from representing a party must, as soon as practicable, make available to that party such documents in the representative's possession as have been served on that party.

### Application to change legal representative: legal aid                           R46.3

46.3 (1) This rule applies in a magistrates' court, the Crown Court and the Court of Appeal.—
  (a) in relation to a party who has legal aid for the purposes of a case; and
  (b) where such a party wants to select a legal representative in place of the representative named in the legal aid representation order.
(2) Such a party must—
  (a) apply in writing as soon as practicable after becoming aware of the grounds for doing so; and
  (b) serve the application on—
    (i) the court officer, and
    (ii) the legal representative named in the legal aid representation order.
(3) The application must—
  (a) explain what the case is about, including what offences are alleged, what stage it has reached and what is likely to be in issue at trial;
  (b) explain how and why the applicant chose the legal representative named in the legal aid representation order;
  (c) if an advocate other than that representative has been instructed for the applicant, explain whether the applicant wishes to replace that advocate;
  (d) explain, giving relevant facts and dates—
    (i) in what way, in the applicant's opinion, there has been a breakdown in the relationship between the applicant and the current representative such that neither the individual representing the applicant nor any colleague of his or hers any longer can provide effective representation, or
    (ii) what other compelling reason, in the applicant's opinion, means that neither the individual representing the applicant nor any colleague of his or hers any longer can provide effective representation;
  (e) give details of any previous application by the applicant to replace the legal representative named in the legal aid representation order;
  (f) state whether the applicant—
    (i) waives the legal professional privilege attaching to the applicant's communications with the current representative, to the extent required to allow that representative to respond to the matters set out in the application, or
    (ii) declines to waive that privilege and acknowledges that the court may draw such inferences as it thinks fit in consequence;
  (g) explain how and why the applicant has chosen the proposed new representative;
  (h) include or attach a statement by the proposed new representative which—
    (i) confirms that that representative is eligible and willing to conduct the case for the applicant,
    (ii) confirms that that representative can and will meet the current timetable for the case, including any hearing date or dates that have been set, if the application succeeds, and
    (iii) explains what, if any, dealings that representative has had with the applicant before the present case; and
  (i) ask for a hearing, if the applicant wants one, and explain why it is needed.
(4) The legal representative named in the legal aid representation order must—
  (a) respond in writing no more than 5 business days after service of the application; and
  (b) serve the response on—
    (i) the court officer,
    (ii) the applicant, and
    (iii) the proposed new representative.

(5)    The response must—

     (a)   explain which, if any, of the matters set out in the application the current representative disputes;

     (b)   explain, as appropriate, giving relevant facts and dates—

         (i)   whether, and if so in what way, in the current representative's opinion, there has been a breakdown in the relationship with the applicant such that neither the individual representing the applicant nor any colleague of his or hers any longer can provide effective representation,

         (ii)   whether, in the current representative's opinion, there is some other compelling reason why neither the individual representing the applicant nor any colleague of his or hers any longer can provide effective representation, and if so what reason,

         (iii)   whether the current representative considers there to be a duty to withdraw from the case in accordance with professional rules of conduct, and if so the nature of that duty, and

         (iv)   whether the current representative no longer is able to represent the applicant through circumstances outside the representative's control, and if so the particular circumstances that render the representative unable to do so;

     (c)   explain what, if any, dealings the current representative had had with the applicant before the present case; and

     (d)   ask for a hearing, if the current representative wants one, and explain why it is needed.

(6)    The court may determine the application—

     (a)   without a hearing, as a general rule; or

     (b)   at a hearing, which must be in private unless the court otherwise directs.

(7)    Unless the court otherwise directs, any hearing must be in the absence of each other party and each other party's representative and advocate (if any).

(8)    If the court allows the application, as soon as practicable—

     (a)   the current representative must make available to the new representative such documents in the current representative's possession as have been served on the applicant party; and

     (b)   the new representative must serve notice of appointment on each other party.

(9)    Paragraph (10) applies where—

     (a)   the court refuses the application;

     (b)   in response to that decision—

         (i)   the applicant declines further representation by the current representative or asks for legal aid to be withdrawn, or

         (ii)   the current representative declines further to represent the applicant; and

     (c)   the court in consequence withdraws the applicant's legal aid.

(10)   The court officer must serve notice of the withdrawal of legal aid on—

     (a)   the applicant; and

     (b)   the current representative.

*[Note. Under sections 16 and 19 of the Legal Aid, Sentencing and Punishment of Offenders Act 2012[10] and Part 2 of the Criminal Legal Aid (Determinations by a Court and Choice of Representative) Regulations 2013[11], a court before which criminal proceedings take place may determine whether an individual qualifies for legal aid representation in accordance with the 2012 Act.*

*Under regulation 13 of the 2013 Regulations, in relation to any proceedings involving co-defendants a represented person must select a representative who is also instructed by a co-defendant unless there is, or there is likely to be, a conflict of interest between the two defendants.*

*Under regulation 14 of the 2013 Regulations, once a representative has been selected the person who is represented has no right to select another in the place of the first unless the court so decides, in the circumstances set out in the regulation.*

*Under regulation 9 of the 2013 Regulations, if a represented person declines to accept representation on the terms offered or requests that legal aid representation is withdrawn, or if the current representative declines to continue to represent that person, the court may withdraw legal aid.*

*See also regulation 11 of the 2013 Regulations, which requires that an application under regulation 14 (among others) must be made by the represented person, must be in writing and must specify the grounds.*

*The Practice Direction sets out forms of application and response for use in connection with this rule.]*

---

[10]   2012 c. 10.
[11]   S.I. 2013/614.

CRIMINAL PROCEDURE RULES   PART 47   INVESTIGATION ORDERS AND WARRANTS
### Section 1:  general rules

**When this Part applies**                                                    R47.1

47.1   This Part applies to the exercise of the powers listed in each of rules 47.4, 47.24, 47.35, 47.42, 47.46, 47.51, 47.54, 47.59, and 47.63

**Meaning of 'court', 'applicant' and 'respondent'**                          R47.2

47.2   In this Part—
- (a) a reference to the 'court' includes a reference to any justice of the peace or judge who can exercise a power to which this Part applies;
- (b) 'applicant' means a person who, or an authority which, can apply for an order or warrant to which this Part applies; and
- (c) 'respondent' means any person—
  - (i) against whom such an order is sought or made, or
  - (ii) on whom an application for such an order is served.

**Documents served on the court officer**                                     R47.3

47.3   (1)   Unless the court otherwise directs—
- (a) the court officer—
  - (i) may keep a written application, or arrange for the whole or any part to be kept by some other appropriate person, including the applicant, subject to any conditions that the court may impose, and
  - (ii) must arrange for any separate document to which rule 47.26(4) refers (information that the applicant thinks should be kept confidential) to be retained by the applicant, subject to any such condition; and
- (b) a person who, under such arrangements, keeps an application or retains such a document must return it to the court if and when the court officer so requires.

(2)   Where the court makes an order when the court office is closed, the applicant must, not more than 72 hours later, serve on the court officer—
- (a) a copy of the order; and
- (b) any written material that was submitted to the court.

(3)   Where the court issues a warrant—
- (a) the applicant must return it to the court officer as soon as practicable after it has been executed, and in any event not more than 3 months after it was issued (unless other legislation otherwise provides); and
- (b) the court officer must—
  - (i) keep the warrant for 12 months after its return, and
  - (ii) during that period, make it available for inspection by the occupier of the premises to which it relates, if that occupier asks to inspect it.

*[Note. See section 16(10) of the Police and Criminal Evidence Act 1984[1].]*

### Section 2:  investigation orders

**When this Section applies**                                                 R47.4

47.4   This Section applies where—
- (a) a Circuit judge can make, vary or discharge an order for the production of, or for giving access to, material under paragraph 4 of Schedule 1 to the Police and Criminal Evidence Act 1984[2], other than material that consists of or includes journalistic material;
- (b) for the purposes of a terrorist investigation, a Circuit judge can make, vary or discharge—
  - (i) an order for the production of, or for giving access to, material, or for a statement of its location, under paragraphs 5 and 10 of Schedule 5 to the Terrorism Act 2000[3], or
  - (ii) an explanation order, under paragraphs 10 and 13 of Schedule 5 to the 2000 Act[4], or

---

[1]  1984 c. 60; section 16(10) was substituted by section 114 of the Serious Organised Crime and Police Act 2005 (c. 15).
[2]  1984 c. 60; paragraph 4 of Schedule 1 was amended by section 65 of, and paragraph 6 of Schedule 4 to, the Courts Act 2003 (c. 39).
[3]  2000 c. 11; paragraph 5 of Schedule 5 is amended by section 65 of, and paragraph 9 of Schedule 4 to, the Courts Act 2003 (c. 39), with effect from a date to be appointed. Paragraph 10 of Schedule 5 was amended by section 109(1) of, and paragraph 389 of Schedule 8 to, the Courts Act 2003 (c. 39) and it is further amended by section 65 of, and paragraph 9 of Schedule 4 to, the Courts Act 2003 (c. 39), with effect from a date to be appointed.
[4]  2000 c. 11; paragraph 13 of Schedule 5 was amended by section 65 of, and paragraph 9 of Schedule 4 to, the Courts Act 2003 (c. 39) and section 41(3)(d) of the Criminal Finances Act 2017 (c. 22).

Criminal Procedure Rules and Criminal Practice Directions

(iii) a customer information order, under paragraphs 1 and 4 of Schedule 6 to the 2000 Act[5];

(c) for the purposes of—

(i) a terrorist investigation, a Circuit judge can make, and the Crown Court can vary or discharge, an account monitoring order, under paragraphs 2 and 4 of Schedule 6A to the 2000 Act[6], or

(ii) a terrorist financing investigation, a judge entitled to exercise the jurisdiction of the Crown Court can make, and the Crown Court can vary or discharge, a disclosure order, under paragraphs 9 and 14 of Schedule 5A to the 2000 Act[7];

(d) for the purposes of an investigation to which Part 8 of the Proceeds of Crime Act 2002[8] or the Proceeds of Crime Act 2002 (External Investigations) Order 2014[9] applies, a Crown Court judge can make, and the Crown Court can vary or discharge—

(i) a production order, under sections 345 and 351 of the 2002 Act[10] or under articles 6 and 12 of the 2014 Order,

(ii) an order to grant entry, under sections 347 and 351 of the 2002 Act or under articles 8 and 12 of the 2014 Order,

(iii) a disclosure order, under sections 357 and 362 of the 2002 Act[11] or under articles 16 and 21 of the 2014 Order,

(iv) a customer information order, under sections 363 and 369 of the 2002 Act[12] or under articles 22 and 28 of the 2014 Order, or

(v) an account monitoring order, under sections 370, 373 and 375 of the 2002[13] Act or under articles 29, 32 and 34 of the 2014 Order;

(e) in connection with an extradition request, a Circuit judge can make an order for the production of, or for giving access to, material under section 157 of the Extradition Act 2003[14].

(f) a magistrates' court can make a further information order under section 22B of the Terrorism Act 2000[15] in connection with—

---

[5] 2000 c. 11; paragraph 1 of Schedule 6 was amended by section 3 of, and paragraph 6 of Schedule 2 to, the Anti-terrorism, Crime and Security Act 2001 (c. 24). Paragraph 4 of Schedule 6 was amended by section 109(1) of, and paragraph 390 of Schedule 8 to, the Courts Act 2003 (c. 39).

[6] 2000 c. 11; Schedule 6A was inserted by section 3 of, and paragraph 1(1) and (3) of Part 1 of Schedule 2 to, the Anti-terrorism, Crime and Security Act 2001 (c. 24). Paragraph 4 was amended by section 41(5)(c) of the Criminal Finances Act 2017 (c. 22).

[7] 2000 c. 11; Schedule 5A was inserted by Schedule 2 to the Criminal Finances Act 2017 (c. 22).

[8] 2002 c. 29.

[9] S.I. 2014/1893.

[10] 2002 c. 29; section 345 was amended by section 75 of the Serious Crime Act 2007 (c. 27), section 169 of, and paragraphs 1 and 6 of Schedule 19 to, the Coroners and Justice Act 2009 (c. 25) and section 49 of, and paragraphs 1 and 4 of Schedule 19 to, the Crime and Courts Act 2013 (c. 22). Section 351 was amended by sections 74 and 77 of, and paragraphs 103 and 104 of Schedule 8 and paragraphs 1 and 6 of Schedule 10 to, the Serious Crime Act 2007 (c. 27), section 169 of, and paragraphs 1 and 9 of Schedule 19 to, the Coroners and Justice Act 2009 (c. 25), sections 66 and 112 of, and Part 5 of Schedule 8 to, the Policing and Crime Act 2009 (c. 26), sections 15 and 55 of, and paragraphs 108 and 136 of Schedule 8 and paragraphs 14 and 30 of Schedule 21 to, the Crime and Courts Act 2013 (c.22) and section 224 of, and paragraphs 1 and 11 of Schedule 48 to, the Finance Act 2013 (c. 29).

[11] 2002 c. 29; section 357 was amended by sections 74 and 77 of, and paragraphs 103 and 108 of Schedule 8 and paragraphs 1 and 10 of Schedule 10 to, the Serious Crime Act 2007 (c. 27), section 169 of, and paragraphs 1 and 13 of Schedule 19 to, the Coroners and Justice Act 2009 (c. 25), sections 15, 49 and 55 of, and paragraphs 108 and 139 of Schedule 8, paragraphs 1 and 8 of Schedule 19 and paragraphs 14 and 34 of Schedule 21 to, the Crime and Courts Act 2013 (c. 22) and article 3 of, and paragraphs 19 and 27 of Schedule 2 to, SI 2014/834. Section 362 was amended by section 74 of, and paragraphs 103 and 110 of Schedule 8 to, the Serious Crime Act 2007 (c. 27), section 169 of, and paragraphs 1 and 15 of Schedule 19 to, the Coroners and Justice Act 2009 (c. 25) and section 15 of, and paragraphs 108 and 140 of Schedule 8 to, the Crime and Courts Act 2013 (c. 22).

[12] 2002 c. 29; section 363 was amended by section 77 of, and paragraphs 1 and 11 of Schedule 10 to, the Serious Crime Act 2007 (c. 27), section 169 of, and paragraphs 1 and 16 of Schedule 19 to, the Coroners and Justice Act 2009 (c. 25) and section 49 of, and paragraphs 1 and 10 of Schedule 19 to, the Crime and Courts Act 2013 (c. 22). Section 369 was amended by section 74 of, and paragraphs 103 and 111 of Schedule 8 to, the Serious Crime Act 2007 (c. 27), sections 15 and 55 of, and paragraphs 108 and 141 of Schedule 8, and paragraphs 14 and 35 of Schedule 21 to, the Crime and Courts Act 2013 (c. 22) and section 224 of, and paragraphs 1 and 14 of Schedule 48 to, the Finance Act 2013 (c. 29).

[13] 2002 c. 29; section 370 was amended by section 77 of, and paragraphs 1 and 12 of Schedule 10 to, the Serious Crime Act 2007 (c. 27), section 169 of, and paragraphs 1 and 17 of Schedule 19 to, the Coroners and Justice Act 2009 (c. 25) and section 49 of, and paragraphs 1 and 12 of Schedule 19 to, the Crime and Courts Act 2013 (c. 22). Section 375 was amended by section 74 of, and paragraphs 103 and 112 of Schedule 8 to, the Serious Crime Act 2007 (c. 27), sections 15 and 55 of, and paragraphs 108 and 142 of Schedule 8 and paragraphs 14 and 36 of Schedule 21 to, the Crime and Courts Act 2013 (c. 22) and section 224 of, and paragraphs 1 and 15 of Schedule 48 to, the Finance Act 2013 (c. 29).

[14] 2003 c. 41; section 157 was amended by section 174 of the Anti-social Behaviour, Crime and Policing Act 2014 (c. 12).

[15] 2000 c. 11; section 22B was inserted by section 37 of the Criminal Finances Act 2017 (c. 22).

(i) an investigation into whether a person is involved in the commission of an offence under any of sections 15 to 18 of the 2000 Act[16],

(ii) determining whether such an investigation should be started, or

(iii) identifying terrorist property or its movement or use; and

(g) a magistrates' court can make a further information order under section 339ZH of the Proceeds of Crime Act 2002[17] in connection with—

(i) an investigation into whether a person is engaged in money laundering,

(ii) determining whether such an investigation should be started, or

(iii) an investigation into money laundering by an authority in a country outside the United Kingdom.

[Note. In outline, the orders to which these rules apply are—

(a) under the Police and Criminal Evidence Act 1984, a production order requiring a person to produce or give access to material, other than material that consists of or includes journalistic material;

(b) for the purposes of a terrorist investigation under the Terrorism Act 2000—

(i) an order requiring a person to produce, give access to, or state the location of material,

(ii) an explanation order, requiring a person to explain material obtained under a production, etc. order,

(iii) a customer information order, requiring a financial institution to provide information about an account holder,

(iv) an account monitoring order, requiring a financial institution to provide specified information, for a specified period, about an account held at that institution;

(c) for the purposes of a terrorist financing investigation under the Terrorism Act 2000, a disclosure order, requiring a person to provide information or documents, or to answer questions;

(d) for the purposes of an investigation to which Part 8 of the Proceeds of Crime Act 2002 or the Proceeds of Crime Act 2002 (External Investigations) Order 2014 applies—

(i) a production order, requiring a person to produce or give access to material,

(ii) an order to grant entry, requiring a person to allow entry to premises so that a production order can be enforced,

(iii) a disclosure order, requiring a person to provide information or documents, or to answer questions,

(iv) a customer information order, requiring a financial institution to provide information about an account holder,

(v) an account monitoring order, requiring a financial institution to provide specified information, for a specified period, about an account held at that institution;

(e) in connection with extradition proceedings, a production order requiring a person to produce or give access to material;

(f) under the Terrorism Act 2000, a further information order requiring a person to provide information related to a matter arising from a disclosure under section 21A of that Act[18] (Failure to disclose: regulated sector) or under the law of a country outside the United Kingdom which corresponds with Part III of that Act (Terrorist property);

(g) under the Proceeds of Crime Act 2002, a further information order requiring a person to provide information related to a matter arising from a disclosure under Part 7 of that Act (Money laundering) or under the law of a country outside the United Kingdom which corresponds with that Part of that Act.

These rules do not apply to an application for a production order under the Police and Criminal Evidence Act 1984 requiring a person to produce or give access to journalistic material: see paragraph 15A of Schedule 1 to the Act[19].

For all the relevant terms under which these orders can be made, see the provisions listed in rule 47.4.

Under section 8 of the Senior Courts Act 1981[20], a High Court judge, a Circuit judge, a Recorder, a qualifying judge advocate and a District Judge (Magistrates' Courts) each may act as a Crown Court judge.

---

[16] 2000 c. 11; section 17A was inserted by section 42 of the Counter-Terrorism and Security Act 2015 (c. 6).

[17] 2002 c. 29; section 339ZH was inserted by section 12 of the Criminal Finances Act 2017 (c. 22).

[18] 2000 c. 11; section 21A was inserted by section 3 of, and paragraph 5 of Schedule 2 to, the Anti-terrorism, Crime and Security Act 2001 (c. 24) and amended by regulation 2 of, and paragraphs 1 and 3 of Schedule 1 to, S.I. 2007/3398, section 59 of, and paragraphs 125 and 128 of, the Serious Organised Crime and Police Act 2005 (c. 15) and section 15 of, and paragraphs 67 and 72 of Schedule 8 to, the Crime and Courts Act 2013 (c. 22).

[19] 1984 c. 60; paragraph 15A of Schedule 1 was inserted by section 82 of the Deregulation Act 2015 (c. 20).

[20] 1981 c. 54; section 8 was amended by sections 65 and 109 of, and paragraph 259 of Schedule 8 to, the Courts Act 2003 (c. 39) and paragraph 1 of Schedule 2 to the Armed Forces Act 2011 (c. 18). The 1981 Act's title was amended by section 59(5) of, and paragraph 1 of Schedule 11 to, the Constitutional Reform Act 2005 (c. 4).

*When the relevant provisions of the Courts Act 2003 come into force, a District Judge (Magistrates' Courts) will have the same powers as a Circuit judge under the Police and Criminal Evidence Act 1984 and under the Terrorism Act 2000.*

*Under section 66 of the Courts Act 2003[21], in criminal cases a High Court judge, a Circuit judge, a Recorder and a qualifying judge advocate each has the powers of a justice of the peace who is a District Judge (Magistrates' Courts).*

*By section 341 of the Proceeds of Crime Act 2002[22], an investigation under Part 8 of the Act may be—*

    (a) *an investigation into (i) whether a person has benefited from criminal conduct, (ii) the extent or whereabouts of such benefit, (iii) the available amount in respect of that person, or (iv) the extent or whereabouts of realisable property available for satisfying a confiscation order made in respect of that person ('a confiscation investigation');*

    (b) *an investigation into whether a person has committed a money laundering offence ('a money laundering investigation');*

    (c) *an investigation into whether property is recoverable property or associated property (as defined by section 316 of the 2002 Act[23]), or into who holds the property or its extent or whereabouts ('a civil recovery investigation');*

    (d) *an investigation into the derivation of cash detained under the 2002 Act, or into whether such cash is intended to be used in unlawful conduct ('a detained cash investigation');*

    (e) *an investigation into the derivation of property detained under the 2002 Act, or into whether such property is intended to be used in unlawful conduct ('a detained property investigation');*

    (f) *an investigation into the derivation of money held in an account in relation to which an account freezing order made under the 2002 Act has effect, or into whether such money is intended to be used in unlawful conduct ('a frozen funds investigation');*

    (g) *an investigation for the purposes of Part 7 of the Coroners and Justice Act 2009[24] (criminal memoirs, etc.) into whether a person is a qualifying offender or has obtained exploitation proceeds from a relevant offence, or into the value of any benefits derived by such a person from such an offence or the amount available ('an exploitation proceeds investigation').*

*Under section 343 of the Proceeds of Crime Act 2002[25]—*

    (a) *any Crown Court judge may make an order to which this Section applies for the purposes of a confiscation investigation, a money laundering investigation, a detained cash investigation, a detained property investigation or a frozen funds investigation;*

    (b) *only a High Court judge may make such an order for the purposes of a civil recovery investigation or an exploitation proceeds investigation (and these rules do not apply to an application to such a judge in such a case).*

*As well as governing procedure on an application to the Crown Court, under the following provisions rules may govern the procedure on an application to an individual judge—*

    (a) *paragraph 15A of Schedule 1 to the Police and Criminal Evidence Act 1984;*

    (b) *paragraph 10 of Schedule 5, paragraph 14 of Schedule 5A, paragraph 4 of Schedule 6 and paragraph 5 of Schedule 6A to the Terrorism Act 2000; and*

    (c) *sections 351, 362, 369, 375 and 446 of the Proceeds of Crime Act 2002.]*

**R47.5**    **Exercise of court's powers**

    **47.5**  (1) Subject to paragraphs (2), (3) and (4), the court may determine an application for an order, or to vary or discharge an order—

        (a) at a hearing (which must be in private unless the court otherwise directs), or without a hearing; and

---

[21] 2003 c. 39; section 66 was amended by paragraph 6 of Schedule 2 to the Armed Forces Act 2011 (c. 18) and sections 17 and 21 of, and paragraphs 83 and 90 of Schedule 10 and paragraph 4 of Schedule 14 to, the Crime and Courts Act 2013 (c. 22).

[22] 2002 c. 29; section 341 was amended by section 75 of the Serious Crime Act 2007 (c. 27), section 169 of, and paragraphs 1 and 2 of Schedule 19 to, the Coroners and Justice Act 2009 (c. 25) and section 112 of, and paragraphs 99 and 110 of Schedule 7 to, the Policing and Crime Act 2009 (c. 26), section 49 of, and paragraphs 1, 2, 24 and 25 of Schedule 19 to, the Crime and Courts Act 2013 (c.22) and sections 38 and 85 of, and paragraph 55 of Schedule 4 to, the Serious Crime Act 2015 (c. 9).

[23] 2002 c. 29; section 316 was amended by paragraph 78 of Schedule 36 to the Criminal Justice Act 2003 (c. 44), section 109 of, and paragraphs 4 and 22 of Schedule 6 to, the Serious Organised Crime and Police Act 2005 (c. 15), section 74 of, and paragraphs 85 and 91 of Schedule 8 to, the Serious Crime Act 2007 (c. 27), article 12 of, and paragraphs 47 and 65 of Schedule 14 to, S.I. 2010/976, sections 15 and 48 of, and paragraphs 108 and 121 of Schedule 8 to, the Crime and Courts Act 2013 (c. 22), article 3 of, and paragraphs 19 and 25 of Schedule 2 to, SI 2014/834, section 85 of, and paragraph 54 of Schedule 4 to, the Serious Crime Act 2015 (c. 9) and article 8 of SI 2015/798.

[24] 2009 c. 25.

[25] 2002 c. 29; section 343 was amended by section 77 of, and paragraphs 1 and 3 of Schedule 10 to, the Serious Crime Act 2007 (c. 27), section 169 of, and paragraphs 1 and 4 of Schedule 19 to, the Coroners and Justice Act 2009 (c. 25) and sections 66 and 112 of, and Part 5 of Schedule 8 to, the Policing and Crime Act 2009 (c. 26).

(b)  in the absence of—
    (i)   the applicant,
    (ii)  any respondent
    (iii) any other person affected by the order.

(2)  The court must not determine such an application in the applicant's absence if—
  (a)  the applicant asks for a hearing; or
  (b)  it appears to the court that—
    (i)   the proposed order may infringe legal privilege, within the meaning of section 10 of the Police and Criminal Evidence Act 1984[26], section 348 or 361 of the Proceeds of Crime Act 2002[27] or article 9 of the Proceeds of Crime Act 2002 (External Investigations) Order 2014[28],
    (ii)  the proposed order may require the production of excluded material, within the meaning of section 11 of the 1984 Act, or
    (iii) for any other reason the application is so complex or serious as to require the court to hear the applicant.

(3)  The court must not determine such an application in the absence of any respondent or other person affected, unless—
  (a)  the absentee has had at least 2 business days in which to make representations; or
  (b)  the court is satisfied that—
    (i)   the applicant cannot identify or contact the absentee,
    (ii)  it would prejudice the investigation if the absentee were present,
    (iii) it would prejudice the investigation to adjourn or postpone the application so as to allow the absentee to attend, or
    (iv)  the absentee has waived the opportunity to attend.

(4)  The court must not determine such an application in the absence of any respondent who, if the order sought by the applicant were made, would be required to produce or give access to journalistic material, unless that respondent has waived the opportunity to attend.

(5)  The court officer must arrange for the court to hear such an application no sooner than 2 business days after it was served, unless—
  (a)  the court directs that no hearing need be arranged; or
  (b)  the court gives other directions for the hearing.

(6)  The court must not determine an application unless satisfied that sufficient time has been allowed for it.

(7)  If the court so directs, the parties to an application may attend a hearing by live link or telephone.

(8)  The court must not make, vary or discharge an order unless the applicant states, in writing or orally, that to the best of the applicant's knowledge and belief—
  (a)  the application discloses all the information that is material to what the court must decide; and
  (b)  the content of the application is true.

(9)  Where the statement required by paragraph (8) is made orally—
  (a)  the statement must be on oath or affirmation, unless the court otherwise directs; and
  (b)  the court must arrange for a record of the making of the statement.

(10) The court may—
  (a)  shorten or extend (even after it has expired) a time limit under this Section;
  (b)  dispense with a requirement for service under this Section (even after service was required); and
  (c)  consider an application made orally instead of in writing.

(11) A person who wants an extension of time must—
  (a)  apply when serving the application for which it is needed; and
  (b)  explain the delay.

## Application for order: general rules    R47.6

**47.6**  (1) This rule applies to each application for an order to which this Section applies.

(2)  The applicant must—
  (a)  apply in writing and serve the application on the court officer;
  (b)  demonstrate that the applicant is entitled to apply, for example as a constable or under legislation that applies to other officers;

---

[26]  1984 c. 60.
[27]  2002 c. 29; section 361 was amended by section 74 of, and paragraphs 103 and 109 of Schedule 8 to, the Serious Crime Act 2007 (c. 27).
[28]  S.I. 2014/1893.

Criminal Procedure Rules and Criminal Practice Directions

(c) give the court an estimate of how long the court should allow—
  (i) to read the application and prepare for any hearing, and
  (ii) for any hearing of the application;
(d) attach a draft order in the terms proposed by the applicant;
(e) serve notice of the application on the respondent if any, unless the court otherwise directs; and
(f) serve the application on any respondent to such extent, if any, as the court directs.
(3) A notice served on a respondent must—
  (a) specify the material or information in respect of which the application is made; and
  (b) identify—
    (i) the power that the applicant invites the court to exercise, and
    (ii) the conditions for the exercise of that power which the applicant asks the court to find are met.
(4) The applicant must serve any order made on a respondent.

**R47.7  Application containing information withheld from a respondent or other person**

47.7 (1) This rule applies where an application includes information that the applicant thinks ought to be revealed only to the court.
(2) The application must—
  (a) identify that information; and
  (b) explain why that information ought not to be served on a respondent or other person.
(3) At a hearing of an application to which this rule applies—
  (a) the general rule is that the court must consider, in the following sequence—
    (i) representations first by the applicant and then by the respondent if any and any other person, in the presence of them all, and then
    (ii) further representations by the applicant, in the others' absence; but
  (b) the court may direct other arrangements for the hearing.

**R47.8  Application to vary or discharge an order**

47.8 (1) This rule applies where one of the following wants the court to vary or discharge an order to which a rule in this Section refers—
  (a) an applicant;
  (b) a respondent; or
  (c) a person affected by the order.
(2) That applicant, respondent or person affected must—
  (a) apply in writing as soon as practicable after becoming aware of the grounds for doing so;
  (b) serve the application on—
    (i) the court officer, and
    (ii) the respondent, applicant, or any person known to be affected, as applicable;
  (c) explain why it is appropriate for the order to be varied or discharged;
  (d) propose the terms of any variation; and
  (e) ask for a hearing, if one is wanted, and explain why it is needed.

**R47.9  Application to punish for contempt of court**

47.9 (1) This rule applies where a person is accused of disobeying—
  (a) a production order made under paragraph 4 of Schedule 1 to the Police and Criminal Evidence Act 1984;
  (b) a production etc. order made under paragraph 5 of Schedule 5 to the Terrorism Act 2000;
  (c) an explanation order made under paragraph 13 of that Schedule;
  (d) an account monitoring order made under paragraph 2 of Schedule 6A to that Act;
  (e) a production order made under section 345 of the Proceeds of Crime Act 2002 or article 6 of the Proceeds of Crime Act 2002 (External Investigations) Order 2014;
  (f) an account monitoring order made under section 370 of the 2002 Act or article 29 of the 2014 Order; or
  (g) a production order made under section 157 of the Extradition Act 2003.
(2) An applicant who wants the court to exercise its power to punish that person for contempt of court must comply with the rules in Part 48 (Contempt of court).

*[Note. The Crown Court has power to punish for contempt of court a person who disobeys its order. See paragraphs 10(1) and 13(5) of Schedule 5, and paragraph 6(1) of Schedule 6A, to the Terrorism Act 2000; sections 351(7) and 375(6) of the Proceeds of Crime Act 2002 and articles 12(6) and 34(5) of the Proceeds of Crime Act 2002 (External Investigations) Order 2014; and section 45 of the Senior Courts Act 1981[29].*

[29] 1981 c. 54. The Act's title was amended by section 59(5) of, and paragraph 1 of Schedule 11 to, the Constitutional Reform Act 2005 (c. 4).

*A Circuit judge has power to punish a person who disobeys a production order under the Police and Criminal Evidence Act 1984 as if that were a contempt of the Crown Court: see paragraph 15 of Schedule 1 to the Act[30].*

*Disobedience to an explanation order, to a disclosure order or to a customer information order under the Terrorism Act 2000 is an offence: see paragraph 14 of Schedule 5, paragraph 11 of Schedule 5A and paragraph 1(3) of Schedule 6, to the Act.*

*Disobedience to a disclosure order or to a customer information order under the Proceeds of Crime Act 2002 or under the Proceeds of Crime Act 2002 (External Investigations) Order 2014 is an offence: see sections 359 and 366 of the Act and articles 18 and 25 of the Order. Under section 342 of the Act[31] and under article 5 of the Order, subject to the exceptions for which those provide it is an offence to make a disclosure likely to prejudice an investigation or to interfere with documents relevant to it.*

*If a person fails to comply with a further information order under the Terrorism Act 2000 or under the Proceeds of Crime Act 2002 the magistrates' court may order that person to pay an amount not exceeding £5,000, which order may be enforced as if the sum due had been adjudged to be paid by a conviction: see section 22B(8), (9) of the Terrorism Act 2000[32] and section 339ZH((8), (9) of the Proceeds of Crime Act 2002[33].]*

### Orders under the Police and Criminal Evidence Act 1984

**Application for a production order under the Police and Criminal Evidence Act 1984**    **R47.10**

**47.10** (1)  This rule applies where an applicant wants the court to make an order to which rule 47.4(a) refers.

(2)  As well as complying with rule 47.6 (Application for order: general rules), the application must, in every case—

(a)  specify the offence under investigation (and see paragraph (3)(a));

(b)  describe the material sought;

(c)  identify the respondent;

(d)  specify the premises on which the material is believed to be, or explain why it is not reasonably practicable to do so;

(e)  explain the grounds for believing that the material is on the premises specified, or (if applicable) on unspecified premises of the respondent;

(f)  specify the set of access conditions on which the applicant relies (and see paragraphs (3) and (4)); and

(g)  propose—

(i)  the terms of the order, and

(ii)  the period within which it should take effect.

(3)  Where the applicant relies on paragraph 2 of Schedule 1 to the Police and Criminal Evidence Act 1984[34] ('the first set of access conditions': general power to gain access to special procedure material), the application must—

(a)  specify the indictable offence under investigation;

(b)  explain the grounds for believing that the offence has been committed;

(c)  explain the grounds for believing that the material sought—

(i)  is likely to be of substantial value to the investigation (whether by itself, or together with other material),

(ii)  is likely to be admissible evidence at trial for the offence under investigation, and

(iii)  does not consist of or include items subject to legal privilege or excluded material;

(d)  explain what other methods of obtaining the material—

(i)  have been tried without success, or

(ii)  have not been tried because they appeared bound to fail; and

(e)  explain why it is in the public interest for the respondent to produce the material, having regard to—

(i)  the benefit likely to accrue to the investigation if the material is obtained, and

(ii)  the circumstances under which the respondent holds the material.

[30]  1984 c. 60; paragraph 15 of Schedule 1 was amended by section 65 of, and paragraph 6 of Schedule 4 to, the Courts Act 2003 (c. 39).

[31]  2002 c. 29; section 342 was amended by section 77 of, and paragraphs 1 and 2 of Schedule 10 to, the Serious Crime Act 2007 (c. 27), regulation 3 of, and paragraphs 1 and 8 of Schedule 2 to, S.I. 2007/3398 and section 169 of, and paragraphs 1 and 3 of Schedule 19 to, the Coroners and Justice Act 2009 (c. 25).

[32]  2000 c. 11; section 22B was inserted by section 37 of the Criminal Finances Act 2017 (c. 22).

[33]  2002 c. 29; section 339ZH was inserted by section 12 of the Criminal Finances Act 2017 (c. 22).

[34]  1984 c. 60; paragraph 2 of Schedule 1 was amended by sections 111 and 113 of, and paragraph 43 of Schedule 7 to, the Serious Organised Crime and Police Act 2005 (c. 15).

(4) Where the applicant relies on paragraph 3 of Schedule 1 to the Police and Criminal Evidence Act 1984[35] ('the second set of access conditions': use of search warrant power to gain access to excluded or special procedure material), the application must—

   (a) state the legislation under which a search warrant could have been issued, had the material sought not been excluded or special procedure material (in this paragraph, described as 'the main search power');

   (b) include or attach the terms of the main search power;

   (c) explain how the circumstances would have satisfied any criteria prescribed by the main search power for the issue of a search warrant; and

   (d) explain why the issue of such a search warrant would have been appropriate.

*[Note. See paragraphs 1 to 4 of Schedule 1 to the Police and Criminal Evidence Act 1984[36]. The applicant for an order must be a constable. Sections 10, 11 and 14 of the 1984 Act[37] define 'items subject to legal privilege', 'excluded material' and 'special procedure material'. The period within which an order takes effect must be specified in the order and, unless the court considers a longer period appropriate, must be 7 days from the date of the order.*

*See also the code of practice for searches of premises by police officers and the seizure of property found by police officers on persons or premises issued under section 66 of the Police and Criminal Evidence Act 1984[38].*

*The Practice Direction sets out forms of application, notice and order for use in connection with this rule.]*

### Orders under the Terrorism Act 2000

**R47.11** **Application for an order under the Terrorism Act 2000**

**47.11** (1) This rule applies where an applicant wants the court to make one of the orders to which rule 47.4(b) and (c) refers.

   (2) As well as complying with rule 47.6 (Application for order: general rules), the application must—

   (a) specify the offence under investigation;

   (b) explain how the investigation constitutes a terrorist investigation or terrorist financing investigation, as appropriate, within the meaning of the Terrorism Act 2000;[39]

   (c) identify any respondent; and

   (d) give the information required by whichever of rules 47.12 to 47.16 applies.

**R47.12** **Content of application for a production etc. order under the Terrorism Act 2000**

**47.12** (1) As well as complying with rules 47.6 and 47.11, an applicant who wants the court to make an order for the production of, or for giving access to, material, or for a statement of its location, must—

   (a) describe that material;

   (b) explain why the applicant thinks the material is—

     (i) in the respondent's possession, custody or power, or

     (ii) expected to come into existence and then to be in the respondent's possession, custody or power within 28 days of the order;

   (c) explain how the material constitutes or contains excluded material or special procedure material;

   (d) confirm that none of the material is expected to be subject to legal privilege;

   (e) explain why the material is likely to be of substantial value to the investigation;

   (f) explain why it is in the public interest for the material to be produced, or for the applicant to be given access to it, having regard to—

     (i) the benefit likely to accrue to the investigation if it is obtained, and

     (ii) the circumstances in which the respondent has the material, or is expected to have it; and

---

[35] 1984 c. 60; paragraph 3 of Schedule 1 was amended by section 113 of the Serious Organised Crime and Police Act 2005 (c. 15).

[36] 1984 c. 60; paragraphs 1 and 4 of Schedule 1 were amended by section 65 of, and paragraph 6 of Schedule 4 to, the Courts Act 2003 (c. 39).

[37] 1984 c. 60; section 14 was amended by section 1177 of, and paragraph 193 of Schedule 1 to, the Corporation Tax Act 2010 (c. 4).

[38] 1984 c. 60; section 66 was amended by section 57 of the Criminal Justice and Court Services Act 2000 (c. 43), sections 110 and 174 of, and Schedule 17 to, the Serious Organised Crime and Police Act 2005 (c. 15) and section 115 of, and paragraph 21 of Schedule 9 to, the Protection of Freedoms Act 2012 (c. 9).

[39] 2000 c. 11.

(g)   propose—
    (i)   the terms of the order, and
    (ii)   the period within which it should take effect.
(2)   An applicant who wants the court to make an order to grant entry in aid of a production order must—
    (a)   specify the premises to which entry is sought;
    (b)   explain why the order is needed; and
    (c)   propose the terms of the order.

*[Note. See paragraphs 5 to 9 of Schedule 5 to the Terrorism Act 2000[40]. The applicant for a production, etc. order must be an 'appropriate officer' as defined by paragraph 5(6) of that Schedule. Where the applicant is a counter-terrorism financial investigator the application must be for the purposes of an investigation relating to 'terrorist property' as defined by section 14 of the 2000 Act. Under paragraphs 5 and 7 of Schedule 5 to that Act a production order may require a specified person—*

*(a)   to produce to an appropriate officer within a specified period for seizure and retention any material which that person has in his or her possession, custody or power and to which the application relates; to give an appropriate officer access to any such material within a specified period; and to state to the best of that person's knowledge and belief the location of material to which the application relates if it is not in, and it will not come into, his or her possession, custody or power within the period specified; or*

*(b)   where such material is expected to come into existence within the period of 28 days beginning with the date of the order, to notify a named appropriate officer as soon as is reasonably practicable after any material to which the application relates comes into that person's possession, custody or power, and then to produce that material to an appropriate officer; to give an appropriate officer access to it; and to state to the best of that person's knowledge and belief the location of material to which the application relates if it is not in, and it will not come into, his or her possession, custody or power within that period of 28 days.*

*Under paragraph 4 of Schedule 5 to the 2000 Act, 'legal privilege', 'excluded material' and 'special procedure material' mean the same as under sections 10, 11 and 14 of the Police and Criminal Evidence Act 1984.*

*The period within which an order takes effect must be specified in the order and, unless the court otherwise directs, must be—*

*(a)   where the respondent already has the material, 7 days from the date of the order; or*
*(b)   where the respondent is expected to have the material within 28 days, 7 days from the date the respondent notifies the applicant of its receipt.*

*The Practice Direction sets out forms of application, notice and order for use in connection with this rule.]*

**Content of application for a disclosure order or further information order under the Terrorism Act 2000**    **R47.13**

**47.13** (1)   As well as complying with rules 47.6 and 47.11, an applicant who wants the court to make a disclosure order must—
    (a)   explain why the applicant thinks that—
      (i)   a person has committed an offence under any of sections 15 to 18 of the Terrorism Act 2000[41], or
      (ii)   property described in the application is terrorist property within the meaning of section 14 of the 2000 Act[42];
    (b)   describe in general terms the information that the applicant wants a person to provide;
    (c)   confirm that none of the information is—
      (i)   expected to be subject to legal privilege, or
      (ii)   excluded material;
    (d)   explain why the information is likely to be of substantial value to the investigation;
    (e)   explain why it is in the public interest for the information to be provided, having regard to the benefit likely to accrue to the investigation if it is obtained; and
    (f)   propose the terms of the order.
(2)   As well as complying with rule 47.6, an applicant who wants the court to make a further information order must—

---

[40]   2000 c. 11; paragraphs 5, 6 and 7 of Schedule 5 were amended by section 65 of, and paragraph 9 of Schedule 4 to, the Courts Act 2003 (c. 39) and section 41 of the Criminal Finances Act 2017 (c. 22).
[41]   2000 c. 11; section 17A was inserted by section 42 of the Counter-Terrorism and Security Act 2015 (c. 6).
[42]   2000 c. 11.

(a) identify the respondent from whom the information is sought and explain—

    (i) whether the respondent is the person who made the disclosure to which the information relates or is otherwise carrying on a business in the regulated sector within the meaning of Part 1 of Schedule 3A to the 2000 Act[43], and

    (ii) why the applicant thinks that the information is in the possession, or under the control, of the respondent;

(b) specify or describe the information that the applicant wants the respondent to provide;

(c) where the information sought relates to a disclosure of information by someone under section 21A of the 2000 Act[44] (Failure to disclose: regulated sector), explain—

    (i) how the information sought relates to a matter arising from that disclosure,

    (ii) how the information would assist in investigating whether a person is involved in the commission of an offence under any of sections 15 to 18 of that Act[45], or in determining whether an investigation of that kind should be started, or in identifying terrorist property or its movement or use, and

    (iii) why it is reasonable in all the circumstances for the information to be provided;

(d) where the information sought relates to a disclosure made under a requirement of the law of a country outside the United Kingdom which corresponds with Part III of the 2000 Act (Terrorist property), and an authority in that country which investigates offences corresponding with sections 15 to 18 of that Act has asked the National Crime Agency for information in connection with that disclosure, explain—

    (i) how the information sought relates to a matter arising from that disclosure,

    (ii) why the information is likely to be of substantial value to the authority that made the request in determining any matter in connection with the disclosure, and

    (iii) why it is reasonable in all the circumstances for the information to be provided;

(e) confirm that none of the information is expected to be subject to legal privilege; and

(f) propose the terms of the order, including—

    (i) how the respondent must provide the information required, and

    (ii) the date by which the information must be provided.

(3) Rule 47.8 (Application to vary or discharge an order) does not apply to a further information order.

(4) Paragraph (5) applies where a party to an application for a further information order wants to appeal to the Crown Court from the decision of the magistrates' court.

(5) The appellant must—

(a) serve an appeal notice—

    (i) on the Crown Court officer and on the other party,

    (ii) not more than 15 business days after the magistrates' court's decision; and

(b) in the appeal notice, explain, as appropriate, why the Crown Court should (as the case may be) make, discharge or vary a further information order.

(6) Rule 34.11 (Constitution of the Crown Court) applies on such an appeal.

*[Note. See sections 22B, 22D and 22E of, and Schedule 5A to, the Terrorism Act 2000[46].*

*Under paragraph 9(6) of Schedule 5A to the 2000 Act the applicant for a disclosure order must be an 'appropriate officer', as defined by paragraph 5, who is, or who is authorised to apply by, a police officer of at least the rank of superintendent.*

*Under section 22B(12) of the 2000 Act the applicant for a further information order must be 'a law enforcement officer', as defined by section 22B(14), who is, or who is authorised to apply by, a 'senior law enforcement officer', defined by section 22B(14) as a police officer of at least the rank of superintendent, the Director General of the National Crime Agency or an officer of that Agency authorised by the Director General for that purpose.*

---

[43] 2000 c. 11; Part 1 of Schedule 3A was inserted by section 3 of, and paragraph 5 of Schedule 2 to, the Anti-terrorism, Crime and Security Act 2001 (c. 24), substituted by article 2 of S.I. 2007/3288 and amended by articles 3 and 6 of, and paragraph 25 of Schedule 1 to, S.I. 2008/948, sections 183 and 237 of, and paragraph 1 of Schedule 18 and Part 29 of Schedule 25 to, the Localism Act 2011 (c. 20), regulation 79 of, and paragraph 3 of Schedule 4 to, S.I. 2011/99, article 2 of S.I. 2011/2701, article 2 of S.I. 2012/2299, article 2 of S.I. 2012/1534, regulation 46 of, and paragraph 40 of Schedule 2 to, S.I. 2013/3115, section 151 of, and paragraph 73 of Schedule 4 to, the Co-operative and Community Benefit Societies Act 2014 (c. 14), regulation 59 of, and paragraph 21 of Schedule 1 to, S.I. 2015/575, regulation 12 of S.I. 2016/680, regulation 2 of, and paragraph 11 of the Schedule to, S.I. 2017/80, regulation 109 of, and paragraph 4 of Schedule 7 to, S.I. 2017/692 and regulation 50 of, and paragraph 6 of Schedule 4 to, S.I. 2017/701.

[44] 2000 c. 11; section 21A was inserted by section 3 of, and paragraph 5 of Schedule 2 to, the Anti-terrorism, Crime and Security Act 2001 (c. 24) and amended by regulation 2 of, and paragraphs 1 and 3 of Schedule 1 to, S.I. 2007/3398, section 59 of, and paragraphs 125 and 128 of, the Serious Organised Crime and Police Act 2005 (c. 15) and section 15 of, and paragraphs 67 and 72 of Schedule 8 to, the Crime and Courts Act 2013 (c. 22).

[45] 2000 c. 11; section 17A was inserted by section 42 of the Counter-Terrorism and Security Act 2015 (c. 6).

[46] 2000 c. 11; sections 22B, 22D and 22E were inserted by section 37 to the Criminal Finances Act 2017 (c. 22). Schedule 5A was inserted by Schedule 2 to the Criminal Finances Act 2017 (c. 22).

*Section 14 of the 2000 Act[47] defines terrorist property as money or other property which is likely to be used for the purposes of terrorism; proceeds of the commission of terrorism; and proceeds of acts carried out for the purposes of terrorism. Sections 15 to 18 of the Act create offences of fund raising for the purposes of terrorism; use or possession of property for the purposes of terrorism; funding terrorism; making an insurance payment in response to a terrorist demand; and facilitating the retention or control of terrorist property.*

*A disclosure order can require a lawyer to provide a client's name and address.*

*Under section 21A of the 2000 Act[48] a person engaged in a business in the regulated sector commits an offence where the conditions listed in that section are met and that person does not disclose, in the manner required by that section, knowledge or a suspicion that another person has committed or attempted to commit an offence under any of sections 15 to 18 in Part III of the Act. Part III of the Act also contains other disclosure provisions.*

*The Practice Direction sets out forms of application, notice and order for use in connection with this rule.]*

### Content of application for an explanation order under the Terrorism Act 2000     R47.14

**47.14**   As well as complying with rules 47.6 and 47.11, an applicant who wants the court to make an explanation order must—
   (a)   identify the material that the applicant wants the respondent to explain;
   (b)   confirm that the explanation is not expected to infringe legal privilege; and
   (c)   propose the terms of the order.

*[Note. See paragraph 13 of Schedule 5 to the Terrorism Act 2000[49]. The applicant for an explanation order may be a constable or, where the application concerns material produced to a counter-terrorism financial investigator, such an investigator.*

*An explanation order can require a lawyer to provide a client's name and address.*

*The Practice Direction sets out forms of application, notice and order for use in connection with this rule.]*

### Content of application for a customer information order under the Terrorism Act 2000     R47.15

**47.15**   As well as complying with rules 47.6 and 47.11, an applicant who wants the court to make a customer information order must—
   (a)   explain why it is desirable for the purposes of the investigation to trace property said to be terrorist property within the meaning of the Terrorism Act 2000;
   (b)   explain why the order will enhance the effectiveness of the investigation; and
   (c)   propose the terms of the order.

*[Note. See Schedule 6 to the Terrorism Act 2000. The applicant for a customer information order must be a police officer of at least the rank of superintendent.*

*'Customer information' is defined by paragraph 7 of Schedule 6 to the 2000 Act. 'Terrorist property' is defined by section 14 of the Act.*

*The Practice Direction sets out forms of application, notice and order for use in connection with this rule.]*

### Content of application for an account monitoring order under the Terrorism Act 2000     R47.16

**47.16**   As well as complying with rules 47.6 and 47.11, an applicant who wants the court to make an account monitoring order must—
   (a)   specify—
      (i)   the information sought,
      (ii)   the period during which the applicant wants the respondent to provide that information (to a maximum of 90 days), and
      (iii)   where, when and in what manner the applicant wants the respondent to provide that information;
   (b)   explain why it is desirable for the purposes of the investigation to trace property said to be terrorist property within the meaning of the Terrorism Act 2000;
   (c)   explain why the order will enhance the effectiveness of the investigation; and
   (d)   propose the terms of the order.

---

[47] 2000 c. 11.
[48] 2000 c. 11; section 21A was inserted by section 3 of, and paragraph 5 of Schedule 2 to, the Anti-terrorism, Crime and Security Act 2001 (c. 24) and amended by regulation 2 of, and paragraphs 1 and 3 of Schedule 1 to, S.I. 2007/3398, section 59 of, and paragraphs 125 and 128 of, the Serious Organised Crime and Police Act 2005 (c. 15) and section 15 of, and paragraphs 67 and 72 of Schedule 8 to, the Crime and Courts Act 2013 (c. 22).
[49] 2000 c. 11; paragraph 13 of Schedule 5 was amended by section 65 of, and paragraph 9 of Schedule 4 to, the Courts Act 2003 (c. 39) and section 41(3)(d) of the Criminal Finances Act 2017 (c. 22).

*[Note. See Schedule 6A to the Terrorism Act 2000[50]. The applicant for an account monitoring order may be a police officer or a counter-terrorism financial investigator.*

*'Terrorist property' is defined by section 14 of the Act.*

*The Practice Direction sets out forms of application, notice and order for use in connection with this rule.]*

### Orders under the Proceeds of Crime Act 2002

**R47.17**    **Application for an order under the Proceeds of Crime Act 2002**

47.17 (1)   This rule applies where an applicant wants the court to make one of the orders to which rule 47.4(d) refers.

    (2)   As well as complying with rule 47.6 (Application for order: general rules), the application must—

      (a)   identify—

        (i)   any respondent, and

        (ii)   the person or property the subject of the investigation;

      (b)   in the case of an investigation in the United Kingdom, explain why the applicant thinks that—

        (i)   the person under investigation has benefited from criminal conduct, in the case of a confiscation investigation, or committed a money laundering offence, in the case of a money laundering investigation, or

        (ii)   in the case of a detained cash investigation, a detained property investigation or a frozen funds investigation, the cash or property involved, or the money held in the frozen account, was obtained through unlawful conduct or is intended to be used in unlawful conduct;

      (c)   in the case of an investigation outside the United Kingdom, explain why the applicant thinks that—

        (i)   there is an investigation by an overseas authority which relates to a criminal investigation or to criminal proceedings (including proceedings to remove the benefit of a person's criminal conduct following that person's conviction), and

        (ii)   the investigation is into whether property has been obtained as a result of or in connection with criminal conduct, or into the extent or whereabouts of such property; and

      (d)   give the additional information required by whichever of rules 47.18 to 47.22 applies.

*[Note. See also the code of practice for those exercising functions as officers and investigators issued under section 377 of the 2002 Act[51], and the code of practice for prosecutors and others issued under section 377A of that Act[52].]*

**R47.18**    **Content of application for a production order under the Proceeds of Crime Act 2002**

47.18 As well as complying with rules 47.6 and 47.17, an applicant who wants the court to make an order for the production of, or for giving access to, material, must—

    (a)   describe that material;

    (b)   explain why the applicant thinks the material is in the respondent's possession or control;

    (c)   confirm that none of the material is—

      (i)   expected to be subject to legal privilege, or

      (ii)   excluded material;

    (d)   explain why the material is likely to be of substantial value to the investigation;

    (e)   explain why it is in the public interest for the material to be produced, or for the applicant to be given access to it, having regard to—

      (i)   the benefit likely to accrue to the investigation if it is obtained, and

      (ii)   the circumstances in which the respondent has the material; and

    (f)   propose—

      (i)   the terms of the order, and

      (ii)   the period within which it should take effect, if 7 days from the date of the order would not be appropriate.

---

[50]   2000 c. 11; Schedule 6A was inserted by section 3 of, and paragraph 1(1) and (3) of Part 1 to, the Anti-terrorism, Crime and Security Act 2001 (c. 24) and amended by section 41(1), (5) of the Criminal Finances Act 2017 (c. 22).

[51]   2002 c. 29; section 377 was amended by section 74 of, and paragraphs 103 and 114 of Schedule 8 to, the Serious Crime Act 2007 (c. 27), article 12 of, and paragraphs 47 and 67 of Schedule 14 to, SI 2010/976, sections 15 and 55 of, and paragraphs 108 and 143 of Schedule 8 and paragraphs 14 and 37 of Schedule 21 to, the Crime and Courts Act 2013 (c. 22) and section 224 of, and paragraphs 1 and 17 of Schedule 48 to, the Finance Act 2013 (c. 29).

[52]   2002 c. 29; section 377A was inserted by section 74 of, and paragraphs 103 and 115 of Schedule 8 to, the Serious Crime Act 2007 (c. 27) and amended by article 3 of, and paragraphs 19 and 28 of Schedule 2 to, SI 2014/834.

*[Note. See sections 345 to 350 of the Proceeds of Crime Act 2002[53] and articles 6 to 11 of the Proceeds of Crime Act 2002 (External Investigations) Order 2014[54]. Under those provisions—*

*(a) 'excluded material' means the same as under section 11 of the Police and Criminal Evidence Act 1984; and*

*(b) 'legal privilege' is defined by section 348 of the 2002 Act.*

*A Crown Court judge may make a production order for the purposes of a confiscation investigation, a money laundering investigation, a detained cash investigation, a detained property investigation or a frozen funds investigation.*

*The applicant for a production order must be an 'appropriate officer' as defined by section 378(1), (4) and (5) of the 2002 Act[55] and article 2(1) of the 2014 Order.*

*The Practice Direction sets out forms of application, notice and order for use in connection with this rule.]*

**Content of application for an order to grant entry under the Proceeds of Crime Act 2002**     **R47.19**

**47.19** An applicant who wants the court to make an order to grant entry in aid of a production order must—

(a) specify the premises to which entry is sought;

(b) explain why the order is needed; and

(c) propose the terms of the order.

*[Note. See section 347 of the Proceeds of Crime Act 2002 and article 8 of the Proceeds of Crime Act 2002 (External Investigations) Order 2014. The applicant for an order to grant entry must be an 'appropriate officer' as defined by section 378(1), (4) and (5) of the Act and article 2(1) of the 2014 Order.]*

**Content of application for a disclosure order or further information order under the**     **R47.20**
**Proceeds of Crime Act 2002**

**47.20** (1) As well as complying with rules 47.6 and 47.17, an applicant who wants the court to make a disclosure order must—

(a) describe in general terms the information that the applicant wants a person to provide;

(b) confirm that none of the information is—

(i) expected to be subject to legal privilege, or

(ii) excluded material;

(c) explain why the information is likely to be of substantial value to the investigation;

(d) explain why it is in the public interest for the information to be provided, having regard to the benefit likely to accrue to the investigation if it is obtained; and

(e) propose the terms of the order.

(2) As well as complying with rule 47.6, an applicant who wants the court to make a further information order must—

(a) identify the respondent from whom the information is sought and explain—

(i) whether the respondent is the person who made the disclosure to which the information relates or is otherwise carrying on a business in the regulated sector within the meaning of Part 1 of Schedule 9 to the Proceeds of Crime Act 2002[56], and

(ii) why the applicant thinks that the information is in the possession, or under the control, of the respondent;

[53] 2002 c. 29; sections 345 and 346 were amended by section 75 of the Serious Crime Act 2007 (c. 27), section 169 of, and paragraphs 1, 6 and 7 of Schedule 19 to, the Coroners and Justice Act 2009 (c. 25) and section 49 of, and paragraphs 1, 4 and 5 of Schedule 19 to, the Crime and Courts Act 2013 (c. 22). Section 350 was amended by section 77 of, and paragraphs 1 and 5 of Schedule 10 to, the Serious Crime Act 2007 (c. 27), section 169 of, and paragraphs 1 and 8 of Schedule 19 to, the Coroners and Justice Act 2009 (c. 25) and sections 66 and 112 of, and Schedule 8 to, the Policing and Crime Act 2009 (c. 26).
[54] S.I. 2014/1893.
[55] 2002 c. 29; section 378 was amended by section 59 of, and paragraphs 168 and 175 of Schedule 4 to, the Serious Organised Crime and Police Act 2005 (c. 15), sections 74, 77 and 80 of, and paragraphs 103 and 116 of Schedule 8 and paragraphs 1 and 13 of Schedule 10 to, the Serious Crime Act 2007 (c. 27), sections 15, 49 and 55 of, and paragraphs 108 and 144 of Schedule 8 and paragraphs 1, 24, 27, 29 and 30 of Schedule 19 to, the Crime and Courts Act 2013 (c. 22) and section 224 of, and paragraphs 1 and 18 of Schedule 48 to, the Finance Act 2013 (c. 29).
[56] 2002 c. 29; Part 1 of Schedule 9 was substituted by articles 2 and 3 of S.I. 2007/3287 and amended by sections 183 and 237 of, and paragraph 2 of Schedule 18 and Part 29 of Schedule 25 to, the Localism Act 2011 (c. 20), regulation 79 of, and paragraph 3 of Schedule 4 to, S.I. 2011/99, article 3 of S.I. 2011/2701, article 3 of S.I. 2012/1534, article 3 of S.I. 2012/2299, regulation 46 of, and paragraph 41 of Schedule 2 to, S.I. 2013/3115, section 151 of, and paragraph 81 of Schedule 4 to, the Co-operative and Community Benefit Societies Act 2014 (c. 14), regulation 59 of, and paragraph 23 of Schedule 1 to, S.I. 2015/575, regulation 14 of S.I. 2016/680, regulation 2 of, and paragraph 13 of the Schedule to, S.I. 2017/80, regulation 109 of, and paragraph 6 of Schedule 7 to, S.I. 2017/692 and regulation 50 of, and paragraph 7 of Schedule 4 to, S.I. 2017/701.

      (b)  specify or describe the information that the applicant wants the respondent to provide;

      (c)  where the information sought relates to a disclosure of information under Part 7 of the Proceeds of Crime Act 2002 (Money laundering), explain—

         (i)  how the information sought relates to a matter arising from that disclosure,

        (ii)  how the information would assist in investigating whether a person is engaged in money laundering or in determining whether an investigation of that kind should be started, and

       (iii)  why it is reasonable in all the circumstances for the information to be provided;

      (d)  where the information sought relates to a disclosure made under a requirement of the law of a country outside the United Kingdom which corresponds with Part 7 of the 2002 Act, and an authority in that country which investigates money laundering has asked the National Crime Agency for information in connection with that disclosure, explain—

         (i)  how the information sought relates to a matter arising from that disclosure,

        (ii)  why the information is likely to be of substantial value to the authority that made the request in determining any matter in connection with the disclosure, and

       (iii)  why it is reasonable in all the circumstances for the information to be provided;

      (e)  confirm that none of the information is expected to be subject to legal privilege; and

      (f)  propose the terms of the order, including—

         (i)  how the respondent must provide the information required, and

        (ii)  the date by which the information must be provided.

(3)  Rule 47.8 (Application to vary or discharge an order) does not apply to a further information order.

(4)  Paragraph (5) applies where a party to an application for a further information order wants to appeal to the Crown Court from the decision of the magistrates' court.

(5)  The appellant must—

      (a)  serve an appeal notice on the Crown Court officer and on the other party not more than 15 business days after the magistrates' court's decision; and

      (b)  in the appeal notice, explain, as appropriate, why the Crown Court should (as the case may be) make, discharge or vary a further information order.

(6)  Rule 34.11 (Constitution of the Crown Court) applies on such an appeal.

*[Note. See sections 339ZH, 339ZJ, 339ZK, 357, 358 and 361 of the Proceeds of Crime Act 2002[57] and articles 16, 17 and 20 of the Proceeds of Crime Act 2002 (External Investigations) Order 2014[58].*

*Where the 2002 Act applies, a Crown Court judge may make a disclosure order for the purposes of a confiscation investigation or a money laundering investigation.*

*The applicant for a disclosure order must be a 'relevant authority' as defined by section 357(7) of the 2002 Act, or an 'appropriate officer' as defined by article 2(1) of the 2014 Order where the Order applies. Under section 362(6) of the Act[59], a relevant authority who under section 357(7) is an 'appropriate officer' (as defined by section 378(1), (4) and (5)[60]) may apply only if that person is, or is authorised to do so by, a 'senior appropriate officer' (as defined by section 378(2)).*

---

[57] 2002 c. 29; sections 339ZH, 339ZJ and 339ZK were inserted by section 12 of the Criminal Finances Act 2017 (c. 22). Section 357 was amended by sections 74 and 77 of, and paragraphs 103 and 108 of Schedule 8 and paragraphs 1 and 10 of Schedule 10 to, the Serious Crime Act 2007 (c. 27), section 169 of, and paragraphs 1 and 13 of Schedule 19 to, the Coroners and Justice Act 2009 (c. 25), sections 15, 49 and 55 of, and paragraphs 108 and 139 of Schedule 8, paragraphs 1 and 8 of Schedule 19 and paragraphs 14 and 34 of Schedule 21 to, the Crime and Courts Act 2013 (c. 22) and article 3 of, and paragraphs 19 and 27 of Schedule 2 to, SI 2014/834 and section 7(2) of, and paragraph 51 of Schedule 5 to, the Criminal Finances Act 2017 (c. 22). Section 358 was amended by section 169 of, and paragraphs 1 and 14 of Schedule 19 to, the Coroners and Justice Act 2009 (c. 25), section 49(a) of, and paragraphs 1 and 9 of Schedule 19 to, the Crime and Courts Act 2013 (c. 22) and section 7(3) of the Criminal Finances Act 2017 (c. 22). Section 361 was amended by section 74 of, and paragraphs 103 and 109 of Schedule 8 to, the Serious Crime Act 2007 (c. 27).

[58] S.I. 2014/1893.

[59] 2002 c. 29; section 362 was amended by section 74 of, and paragraphs 103 and 110 of Schedule 8 to, the Serious Crime Act 2007 (c. 27), section 169 of, and paragraphs 1 and 15 of Schedule 19 to, the Coroners and Justice Act 2009 (c. 25) and section 15 of, and paragraphs 108 and 140 of Schedule 8 to, the Crime and Courts Act 2013 (c. 22). It is further amended by section 7(4) of the Criminal Finances Act 2017 (c. 22), with effect from a date to be appointed.

[60] 2002 c. 29; section 378 was amended by section 59 of, and paragraphs 168 and 175 of Schedule 4 to, the Serious Organised Crime and Police Act 2005 (c. 15), sections 74, 77 and 80 of, and paragraphs 103 and 116 of Schedule 8 and paragraphs 1 and 13 of Schedule 10 to, the Serious Crime Act 2007 (c. 27), sections 15, 49 and 55 of, and paragraphs 108 and 144 of Schedule 8 and paragraphs 1, 24, 27, 29 and 30 of Schedule 19 to, the Crime and Courts Act 2013 (c. 22) and section 224 of, and paragraphs 1 and 18 of Schedule 48 to, the Finance Act 2013 (c. 29). It is further amended by paragraph 25 of Schedule 1, and paragraph 59 of Schedule 5, to the Criminal Finances Act 2017 (c. 22), with effect from dates to be appointed.

*Under section 339ZH(1), (12) the applicant for a further information order must be the Director General of the National Crime Agency or an officer of that Agency authorised by the Director General for that purpose.*

*A disclosure order can require a lawyer to provide a client's name and address.*

*Under sections 330, 331 and 332 in Part 7 of the 2002 Act[61] a person engaged in a business in the regulated sector commits an offence where the conditions listed in any of those sections are met and that person does not disclose, in the manner required by the relevant section, knowledge or a suspicion that another person is engaged in money laundering.*

*The Practice Direction sets out forms of application, notice and order for use in connection with this rule.]*

**Content of application for a customer information order under the Proceeds of Crime Act 2002**    **R47.21**

47.21 As well as complying with rules 47.6 and 47.17, an applicant who wants the court to make a customer information order must—
   (a) explain why customer information about the person under investigation is likely to be of substantial value to that investigation;
   (b) explain why it is in the public interest for the information to be provided, having regard to the benefit likely to accrue to the investigation if it is obtained; and
   (c) propose the terms of the order.

*[Note. See sections 363, 364, 365 and 368 of the Proceeds of Crime Act 2002[62] and articles 22, 23, 24 and 27 of the Proceeds of Crime Act 2002 (External Investigations) Order 2014.*

*A Crown Court judge may make a customer information order for the purposes of a confiscation investigation or a money laundering investigation.*

*The applicant for a customer information order must be an 'appropriate officer' as defined by section 378(1), (4) and (5) of the 2002 Act and article 2(1) of the 2014 Order.*

*'Customer information' is defined by section 364 of the 2002 Act and article 2(1) of the 2014 Order.*

*The Practice Direction sets out forms of application, notice and order for use in connection with this rule.]*

**Content of application for an account monitoring order under the Proceeds of Crime Act 2002**    **R47.22**

47.22 As well as complying with rules 47.6 and 47.17, an applicant who wants the court to make an account monitoring order for the provision of account information must—
   (a) specify—
      (i) the information sought,
      (ii) the period during which the applicant wants the respondent to provide that information (to a maximum of 90 days), and
      (iii) when and in what manner the applicant wants the respondent to provide that information;
   (b) explain why the information is likely to be of substantial value to the investigation;
   (c) explain why it is in the public interest for the information to be provided, having regard to the benefit likely to accrue to the investigation if it is obtained; and
   (d) propose the terms of the order.

*[Note. See sections 370, 371 and 374 of the Proceeds of Crime Act 2002[63] and articles 29, 30 and 33 of the Proceeds of Crime Act 2002 (External Investigations) Order 2014.*

---

[61] 2002 c. 29; section 330 was amended by sections 102, 104, 105, 106 and 174 of, and Schedule 17 to, the Serious Organised Crime and Police Act 2005 (c. 15), article 2 of S.I. 2006/308, regulation 3 of, and paragraphs 1 and 2 of Schedule 2 to, S.I. 2007/3398 and section 15 of, and paragraphs 108 and 129 of Schedule 8 to, the Crime and Courts Act 2013 (c. 22). Section 331 was amended by sections 102 and 104 of the Serious Organised Crime and Police Act 2005 (c. 15) and section 15 of, and paragraphs 108 and 130 of Schedule 8 to, the Crime and Courts Act 2013 (c. 22). Section 332 was amended by sections 102 and 104 of the Serious Organised Crime and Police Act 2005 (c. 15) and section 15 of, and paragraphs 108 and 131 of Schedule 8 to, the Crime and Courts Act 2013 (c. 22).

[62] 2002 c. 29; section 363 was amended by section 77 of, and paragraphs 1 and 11 of Schedule 10 to, the Serious Crime Act 2007 (c. 27), section 169 of, and paragraphs 1 and 16 of Schedule 19 to, the Coroners and Justice Act 2009 (c. 25) and section 49 of, and paragraphs 1 and 10 of Schedule 19 to, the Crime and Courts Act 2013 (c. 22). Section 364 was amended by section 107 of the Serious Organised Crime and Police Act 2005 (c. 27) and article 2(1) of and paragraph 196 of Schedule 1 to, S.I. 2009/1941.

[63] 2002 c. 29; section 370 was amended by section 77 of, and paragraphs 1 and 12 of Schedule 10 to, the Serious Crime Act 2007 (c. 27), section 169 of, and paragraphs 1 and 17 of Schedule 19 to, the Coroners and Justice Act 2009 (c. 25) and section 49 of, and paragraphs 1 and 12 of Schedule 19 to, the Crime and Courts Act 2013 (c. 22).

*Where the 2002 Act applies, a Crown Court judge may make an account monitoring order for the purposes of a confiscation investigation, a money laundering investigation, a detained cash investigation, a detained property investigation or a frozen funds investigation.*

*The applicant for an account monitoring order must be an 'appropriate officer' as defined by section 378(1), (4) and (5) of the 2002 Act and article 2(1) of the 2014 Order.*

*'Account information' is defined by section 370 of the 2002 Act and article 29(3) of the 2014 Order.*

*The Practice Direction sets out forms of application, notice and order for use in connection with this rule.]*

### Orders under the Extradition Act 2003

**R47.23**   **Application for a production order under the Extradition Act 2003**

47.23 (1)   This rule applies where an applicant wants the court to make an order to which rule 47.4(e) refers.

(2)   As well as complying with rule 47.6 (Application for order: general rules), the application must—

(a)   identify the person whose extradition is sought;

(b)   specify the extradition offence of which that person is accused;

(c)   identify the respondent; and

(d)   describe the special procedure or excluded material sought.

(3)   In relation to the person whose extradition is sought, the application must explain the grounds for believing that—

(a)   that person has committed the offence for which extradition is sought;

(b)   that offence is an extradition offence; and

(c)   that person is in the United Kingdom or is on the way to the United Kingdom.

(4)   In relation to the material sought, the application must—

(a)   specify the premises on which the material is believed to be;

(b)   explain the grounds for believing that—

(i)   the material is on those premises,

(ii)   the material consists of or includes special procedure or excluded material, and

(iii)   the material would be likely to be admissible evidence at a trial in England and Wales for the offence for which extradition is sought;

(c)   explain what other methods of obtaining the material—

(i)   have been tried without success, or

(ii)   have not been tried because they appeared bound to fail; and

(d)   explain why it is in the public interest for the respondent to produce or give access to the material.

(5)   The application must propose—

(a)   the terms of the order, and

(b)   the period within which it should take effect.

*[Note. See sections 157 and 158 of the Extradition Act 2003[64]. Under those provisions—*

(c)   *'special procedure material' means the same as under section 14 of the Police and Criminal Evidence Act 1984; and*

(d)   *'excluded material' means the same as under section 11 of the 1984 Act.*

*The applicant for a production order must be a constable.*

*The period within which an order takes effect must be specified in the order and, unless the court considers a longer period appropriate, must be 7 days from the date of the order.]*

### Section 3: investigation warrants

**R47.24**   **When this Section applies**

47.24 This Section applies where—

(a)   a justice of the peace can issue a warrant under—

(i)   section 8 of the Police and Criminal Evidence Act 1984[65] or,

(ii)   section 2 of the Criminal Justice Act 1987[66];

(b)   a Circuit judge can issue a warrant under—

---

[64] 2003 c. 41; section 157 was amended by section 174 of the Anti-social Behaviour, Crime and Policing Act 2014 (c. 12).
[65] 1984 c. 60; section 8 was amended by paragraph 80 of Schedule 14 to the Immigration and Asylum Act 1999 (c. 33), sections 111, 113 and 114 of, and paragraph 43 of Schedule 7 to, the Serious Organised Crime and Police Act 2005 (c. 15) and section 86 of the Finance Act 2007 (c. 11).
[66] 1987 c. 38; section 2 was amended by sections 143 and 170 of, and paragraph 113 of Schedule 15 to, the Criminal Justice Act 1988 (c. 33), section 164 of the Criminal Justice and Public Order Act 1994 (c. 33), paragraph 20 of Schedule 3 to the

(i)    paragraph 12 of Schedule 1 to the Police and Criminal Evidence Act 1984[67],

(ii)    paragraph 11 of Schedule 5 to the Terrorism Act 2000[68], or

(iii)    section 160 of the Extradition Act 2003[69];

(c)    a Crown Court judge can issue a warrant under—

(i)    section 352 of the Proceeds of Crime Act 2002[70], or

(ii)    article 13 of the Proceeds of Crime Act 2002 (External Investigations) Order 2014[71]; and

(d)    a court to which these Rules apply can issue a warrant to search for and seize articles or persons under a power not listed in paragraphs (a), (b) or (c).

*[Note. In outline, the warrants to which these rules apply are—*

*(a)    under the Police and Criminal Evidence Act 1984, a warrant authorising entry to, and the search of, premises for material, articles or persons;*

*(b)    under the Criminal Justice Act 1987, a warrant authorising entry to, and the search of, premises for documents sought by the Director of the Serious Fraud Office;*

*(c)    under the Terrorism Act 2000, a warrant authorising entry to, and the search of, premises for material sought for the purposes of a terrorist investigation;*

*(d)    under the Proceeds of Crime Act 2002 or under the Proceeds of Crime Act 2002 (External Investigations) Order 2014, a warrant authorising entry to, and the search of, premises for material sought for the purposes of a confiscation investigation, a money laundering investigation, a detained cash investigation or an external investigation;*

*(e)    under the Extradition Act 2003, a warrant authorising entry to, and the search of, premises for material sought in connection with the prosecution of a person whose extradition has been requested;*

*(f)    under other Acts, comparable warrants.*

*For all the relevant terms under which such warrants can be issued, see the provisions listed in this rule.*

*Under section 8 of the Senior Courts Act 1981[72], a High Court judge, a Circuit judge, a Recorder, a qualifying judge advocate and a District Judge (Magistrates' Courts) each may act as a Crown Court judge.*

*When the relevant provisions of the Courts Act 2003 come into force, a District Judge (Magistrates' Courts) will have the same powers as a Circuit judge under the Police and Criminal Evidence Act 1984 and under the Terrorism Act 2000.*

*Under section 66 of the Courts Act 2003[73], in criminal cases a High Court judge, a Circuit judge, a Recorder and a qualifying judge advocate each has the powers of a justice of the peace who is a District Judge (Magistrates' Courts).*

*As well as governing procedure on an application to a magistrates' court or the Crown Court, under the following provisions rules may govern the procedure on an application to an individual Circuit or Crown Court judge—*

*(a)    paragraph 15A of Schedule 1 to the Police and Criminal Evidence Act 1984[74];*

*(b)    paragraph 11 of Schedule 5 to the Terrorism Act 2000;*

*(c)    section 352 of the Proceeds of Crime Act 2002; and*

*(d)    section 160 of the Extradition Act 2003.]*

Youth Justice and Criminal Evidence Act 1999 (c. 23), paragraph 23 of Schedule 2 to the Criminal Justice and Police Act 2001 (c. 16), paragraphs 11 and 12 of Schedule 5 to the Crime (International Co-operation) Act 2003 (c. 32) and section 12 of, and paragraphs 11, 12 and 13 of Schedule 1 to, the Criminal Justice Act 2003 (c. 44).

[67]    1984 c. 60; paragraph 12 of Schedule 1 was amended by section 65 of, and paragraph 6 of Schedule 4 to, the Courts Act 2003 (c. 39) and section 113 of the Serious Organised Crime and Police Act 2005 (c. 15).

[68]    2000 c. 11; paragraph 11 of Schedule 5 was amended by section 26 of the Terrorism Act 2006 (c. 11) and section 82 of the Deregulation Act 2015 (c. 20). It is further amended by section 65 of, and paragraph 9 of Schedule 4 to, the Courts Act 2003 (c. 39), with effect from a date to be appointed.

[69]    2003 c. 41; section 160 was amended by section 174 of the Anti-social Behaviour, Crime and Policing Act 2014 (c. 12).

[70]    2002 c. 29; section 352 was amended by sections 74, 76, 77 and 80 of, and paragraphs 103 and 105 of Schedule 8 and paragraphs 1 and 7 of Schedule 10 to, the Serious Crime Act 2007 (c. 27), section 169 of, and paragraphs 1 and 10 of Schedule 19 to, the Coroners and Justice Act 2009 (c. 25), sections 15, 49 and 55 of, and paragraphs 108 and 137 of Schedule 8, paragraphs 1 and 6 of Schedule 19 and paragraphs 14 and 31 of Schedule 21 to, the Crime and Courts Act 2013 (c. 22), section 224 of, and paragraphs 1 and 12 of Schedule 48 to, the Finance Act 2013 (c. 29), article 3 of, and paragraphs 19 and 26 of Schedule 2 to, SI 2014/834 and section 82 of the Deregulation Act 2015 (c. 20).

[71]    S.I. 2014/1893.

[72]    1981 c. 54; section 8 was amended by sections 65 and 109 of, and paragraph 259 of Schedule 8 to, the Courts Act 2003 (c. 39) and paragraph 1 of Schedule 2 to the Armed Forces Act 2011 (c. 18). The 1981 Act's title was amended by section 59(5) of, and paragraph 1 of Schedule 11 to, the Constitutional Reform Act 2005 (c. 4).

[73]    2003 c. 39; section 66 was amended by paragraph 6 of Schedule 2 to the Armed Forces Act 2011 (c. 18) and sections 17 and 21 of, and paragraphs 83 and 90 of Schedule 10 and paragraph 4 of Schedule 14 to, the Crime and Courts Act 2013 (c. 22).

[74]    1984 c. 60; paragraph 15A of Schedule 1 was inserted by section 82 of the Deregulation Act 2015 (c. 20).

*For a list of the types of investigation under Part 8 of the Proceeds of Crime Act 2002 and a list of the powers of judges in respect of each type, see the note to rule 47.4 (Section 2: Investigation orders; When this Section applies.]*

**R47.25**    **Exercise of court's powers**

47.25 (1)   The court must determine an application for a warrant—

     (a)   at a hearing, which must be in private unless the court otherwise directs;

     (b)   in the presence of the applicant; and

     (c)   in the absence of any person affected by the warrant, including any person in occupation or control of premises which the applicant wants to search.

(2)   If the court so directs, the applicant may attend the hearing by live link or telephone.

(3)   The court must not determine an application unless satisfied that sufficient time has been allowed for it.

(4)   The court must not determine an application unless the applicant confirms, on oath or affirmation, that to the best of the applicant's knowledge and belief—

     (a)   the application discloses all the information that is material to what the court must decide, including any circumstances that might reasonably be considered capable of undermining any of the grounds of the application; and

     (b)   the content of the application is true.

(5)   If the court requires the applicant to answer a question about an application—

     (a)   the applicant's answer must be on oath or affirmation;

     (b)   the court must arrange for a record of the gist of the question and reply; and

     (c)   if the applicant cannot answer to the court's satisfaction, the court may—

         (i)   specify the information the court requires, and

         (ii)   give directions for the presentation of any renewed application.

(6)   If the court considers information to which rule 47.26(4) refers (information that the applicant thinks should be kept confidential), the court must so record

(7)   Unless to do so would be inconsistent with other legislation, on an application the court may issue—

     (a)   a warrant in respect of specified premises;

     (b)   a warrant in respect of all premises occupied or controlled by a specified person;

     (c)   a warrant in respect of all premises occupied or controlled by a specified person which specifies some of those premises; or

     (d)   more than one warrant—

         (i)   each one in respect of premises specified in the warrant,

         (ii)   each one in respect of all premises occupied or controlled by a person specified in the warrant (whether or not such a warrant also specifies any of those premises), or

         (iii)   at least one in respect of specified premises and at least one in respect of all premises occupied or controlled by a specified person (whether or not such a warrant also specifies any of those premises).

(8)   Paragraph (9) applies—

     (a)   only in a magistrates' court; and

     (b)   unless the court—

         (i)   includes a District Judge (Magistrates' Courts), and

         (ii)   otherwise directs.

(9)   A justices' legal adviser must—

     (a)   give the court legal advice; and

     (b)   assist the court by completing the preparation of any warrant to be issued.

*[Note. See section 15 of the Police and Criminal Evidence Act 1984[75] and section 2(4) of the Criminal Justice Act 1987[76]. Not all the powers to which the rules in this Section apply permit the issue of a warrant in respect of all premises occupied or controlled by a specified person: see, for example, rule 47.32 (Application for warrant under section 352 of the Proceeds of Crime Act 2002).]*

**R47.26**    **Application for warrant: general rules**

47.26 (1)   This rule applies to each application to which this Section applies.

(2)   The applicant must—

     (a)   apply in writing;

     (b)   serve the application on—

         (i)   the court officer, or

         (ii)   if the court office is closed, the court;

---

[75]   1984 c. 60; section 15 was amended by sections 113 and 114 of the Serious Organised Crime and Police Act 2005 (c. 15) and article 7 of S.I. 2005/3496.

[76]   1987 c. 38.

(c) demonstrate that the applicant is entitled to apply, for example as a constable or under legislation that applies to other officers;

(d) give the court an estimate of how long the court should allow—
   (i) to read and prepare for the application, and
   (ii) for the hearing of the application; and

(e) tell the court when the applicant expects any warrant issued to be executed.

(3) The application must disclose anything known or reported to the applicant that might reasonably be considered capable of undermining any of the grounds of the application.

(4) Where the application includes information that the applicant thinks should not be supplied under rule 5.7 (Supply to a party of information or documents from records or case materials) to a person affected by a warrant, where the application includes information that the applicant thinks should be kept confidential—
   (a) set out that information in a separate document, marked accordingly; and
   (b) in that document, explain why the applicant thinks that that information ought not to be supplied to anyone other than the court.

(5) The application must include—
   (a) a declaration by the applicant that to the best of the applicant's knowledge and belief—
      (i) the application discloses all the information that is material to what the court must decide, including anything that might reasonably be considered capable of undermining any of the grounds of the application, and
      (ii) the content of the application is true; and
   (b) a declaration by an officer senior to the applicant that the senior officer has reviewed and authorised the application.

(6) The application must attach a draft warrant or warrants in the terms proposed by the applicant.

## Information to be included in a warrant                                    R47.27

47.27 (1) A warrant must identify—
   (a) the person or description of persons by whom it may be executed;
   (b) any person who may accompany a person executing the warrant;
   (c) so far as practicable—
      (i) the material, documents, articles or persons to be sought, and
      (ii) any information to be sought which may be stored electronically;
   (d) the legislation under which it was issued;
   (e) the name of the applicant;
   (f) the court that issued it, unless that is otherwise recorded by the court officer;
   (g) the court office for the court that issued it; and
   (h) the date on which it was issued.

(2) A warrant must specify—
   (a) either—
      (i) the premises to be searched, where the application was for authority to search specified premises, or
      (ii) the person in occupation or control of premises to be searched, where the application was for authority to search any premises occupied or controlled by that person; and
   (b) the number of occasions on which specified premises may be searched, if more than one.

(3) A warrant must include, by signature, initial, or otherwise, an indication that it has been approved by the court that issued it.

(4) Where a warrant comprises more than a single page, each page must include such an indication.

(5) A copy of a warrant must include a prominent certificate that it is such a copy.

*[Note. See sections 15 and 16 of the Police and Criminal Evidence Act 1984[77]. Not all the powers to which the rules in this Section apply permit the issue of a warrant in respect of all premises occupied or controlled by a specified person: see, for example, rule 47.32 (Application for warrant under section 352 of the Proceeds of Crime Act 2002).]*

## Application for warrant under section 8 of the Police and Criminal Evidence Act 1984      R47.28

47.28 (1) This rule applies where an applicant wants a magistrates' court to issue a warrant or warrants under section 8 of the Police and Criminal Evidence Act 1984[78].

[77] 1984 c. 60; section 16 was amended by paragraph 281 of Schedule 8 to the Courts Act 2003 (c. 39), section 2 of the Criminal Justice Act 2003 (c. 44), sections 113 and 114 of the Serious Organised Crime and Police Act 2005 (c. 15) and article 8 of S.I. 2005/3496.
[78] 1984 c. 60; section 8 was amended by paragraph 80 of Schedule 14 to the Immigration and Asylum Act 1999 (c. 33), sections 111, 113 and 114 of, and paragraph 43 of Schedule 7 to, the Serious Organised Crime and Police Act 2005 (c. 15) and section 86 of the Finance Act 2007 (c. 11).

(2) As well as complying with rule 47.26, the application must—

  (a) specify the offence under investigation (and see paragraph (3));

  (b) so far as practicable, identify the material sought (and see paragraph (4));

  (c) specify the premises to be searched (and see paragraphs (5) and (6));

  (d) state whether the applicant wants the premises to be searched on more than one occasion (and see paragraph (7)); and

  (e) state whether the applicant wants other persons to accompany the officers executing the warrant or warrants (and see paragraph (8)).

(3) In relation to the offence under investigation, the application must—

  (a) state whether that offence is—

    (i) an indictable offence, or

    (ii) a relevant offence as defined in section 28D of the Immigration Act 1971[79]; and

  (b) explain the grounds for believing that the offence has been committed.

(4) In relation to the material sought, the application must—

  (a) explain the grounds for believing that that material—

    (i) is likely to be of substantial value to the investigation (whether by itself, or together with other material),

    (ii) is likely to be admissible evidence at trial for the offence under investigation, and

    (iii) does not consist of or include items subject to legal privilege, excluded material or special procedure material; and

  (b) if that material may be stored in an electronic device or devices—

    (i) so far as practicable, describe each device or kind of device sought, and

    (ii) explain the grounds for believing that the material may be stored there.

(5) In relation to premises which the applicant wants to be searched and can specify, the application must—

  (a) specify each set of premises;

  (b) in respect of each set of premises, explain the grounds for believing that material sought is on those premises; and

  (c) in respect of each set of premises, explain the grounds for believing that—

    (i) it is not practicable to communicate with any person entitled to grant entry to the premises,

    (ii) it is practicable to communicate with such a person but it is not practicable to communicate with any person entitled to grant access to the material sought,

    (iii) entry to the premises will not be granted unless a warrant is produced, or

    (iv) the purpose of a search may be frustrated or seriously prejudiced unless a constable arriving at the premises can secure immediate entry to them.

(6) In relation to premises which the applicant wants to be searched but at least some of which the applicant cannot specify, the application must—

  (a) explain the grounds for believing that—

    (i) because of the particulars of the offence under investigation it is necessary to search any premises occupied or controlled by a specified person, and

    (ii) it is not reasonably practicable to specify all the premises which that person occupies or controls which might need to be searched;

  (b) specify as many sets of premises as is reasonably practicable;

  (c) in respect of each set of premises, whether specified or not, explain the grounds for believing that material sought is on those premises; and

  (d) in respect of each specified set of premises, explain the grounds for believing that—

    (i) it is not practicable to communicate with any person entitled to grant entry to the premises,

    (ii) it is practicable to communicate with such a person but it is not practicable to communicate with any person entitled to grant access to the material sought,

    (iii) entry to the premises will not be granted unless a warrant is produced, or

    (iv) the purpose of a search may be frustrated or seriously prejudiced unless a constable arriving at the premises can secure immediate entry to them.

(7) In relation to any set of premises which the applicant wants to be searched on more than one occasion, the application must—

  (a) explain why it is necessary to search on more than one occasion in order to achieve the purpose for which the applicant wants the court to issue the warrant; and

  (b) specify any proposed maximum number of occasions.

---

[79] 1971 c. 77; section 28D was inserted by section 131 of the Immigration and Asylum Act 1999 (c. 33) and amended by sections 144 and 150 of the Nationality, Immigration and Asylum Act 2002 (c. 41).

(8) In relation to any set of premises which the applicant wants to be searched by the officers executing the warrant with other persons authorised by the court, the application must—

    (a) identify those other persons, by function or description; and

    (b) explain why those persons are required.

*[Note. Under section 8 of the Police and Criminal Evidence Act 1984, where there are reasonable grounds for believing that an indictable offence has been committed a constable may apply to a justice of the peace for a warrant authorising a search for evidence on specified premises, or on the premises of a specified person. Under section 8(6) of the 1984 Act, section 8 applies also in relation to relevant offences as defined in section 28D(4) of the Immigration Act 1971 (some of which are not indictable offences).*

*Under section 23 of the 1984 Act[80], 'premises' includes any place, and in particular any vehicle, vessel, aircraft or hovercraft, any offshore installation, any renewable energy installation and any tent or moveable structure.*

*Under section 16(3) of the 1984 Act[81], entry and search under a warrant must be within 3 months from the date of its issue.*

*See also the code of practice for the search of premises issued under section 66 of the 1984 Act[82].*

*The Practice Direction sets out forms of application and warrant for use in connection with this rule.]*

## Application for warrant under section 2 of the Criminal Justice Act 1987      R47.29

47.29 (1) This rule applies where an applicant wants a magistrates' court to issue a warrant or warrants under section 2 of the Criminal Justice Act 1987[83].

    (2) As well as complying with rule 47.26, the application must—

        (a) describe the investigation being conducted by the Director of the Serious Fraud Office and include—

            (i) an explanation of what is alleged and why, and

            (ii) a chronology of relevant events;

        (b) specify the document, documents or description of documents sought by the applicant (and see paragraphs (3) and (4)); and

        (c) specify the premises which the applicant wants to be searched (and see paragraph (5)).

    (3) In relation to each document or description of documents sought, the application must—

        (a) explain the grounds for believing that each such document—

            (i) relates to a matter relevant to the investigation, and

            (ii) could not be withheld from disclosure or production on grounds of legal professional privilege;

        (b) explain the grounds for believing that—

            (i) a person has failed to comply with a notice by the Director to produce the document or documents,

            (ii) it is not practicable to serve such a notice, or

            (iii) the service of such a notice might seriously impede the investigation; and

        (c) if the document or documents may be stored in an electronic device or devices—

            (i) so far as practicable, describe each device or kind of device sought, and

            (ii) explain the grounds for believing that the document or documents may be stored there.

    (4) In relation to any document or description of documents which the applicant wants to be preserved but not seized under a warrant, the application must—

        (a) specify the steps for which the applicant wants the court's authority in order to preserve and prevent interference with the document or documents; and

        (b) explain why such steps are necessary.

    (5) In respect of each set of premises which the applicant wants to be searched, the application must explain the grounds for believing that a document or description of documents sought by the applicant is on those premises.

    (6) If the court so directs, the applicant must make available to the court material on which is based the information given under paragraph (2).

[80] 1984 c. 60; section 23 was amended by sections 103 and 197 of, and Part 1 of Schedule 23 to, the Energy Act 2004 (c. 20).

[81] 1984 c. 60; section 16(3) was amended by section 114 of the Serious Organised Crime and Police Act 2005 (c. 15).

[82] 1984 c. 60; section 66 was amended by section 57 of the Criminal Justice and Court Services Act 2000 (c. 43), sections 110 and 174 of, and Schedule 17 to, the Serious Organised Crime and Police Act 2005 (c. 15) and section 115 of, and paragraph 21 of Schedule 9 to, the Protection of Freedoms Act 2012 (c. 9).

[83] 1987 c. 38; section 2 was amended by sections 143 and 170 of, and paragraph 113 of Schedule 15 to, the Criminal Justice Act 1988 (c. 33), section 164 of the Criminal Justice and Public Order Act 1994 (c. 33), paragraph 20 of Schedule 3 to the Youth Justice and Criminal Evidence Act 1999 (c. 23), paragraph 23 of Schedule 2 to the Criminal Justice and Police Act 2001 (c. 16), paragraphs 11 and 12 of Schedule 5 to the Crime (International Co-operation) Act 2003 (c. 32) and section 12 of, and paragraphs 11, 12 and 13 of Schedule 1 to, the Criminal Justice Act 2003 (c. 44).

*[Note. Under section 2 of the Criminal Justice Act 1987, where the Director of the Serious Fraud Office is investigating a case of serious or complex fraud a member of that Office may apply to a justice of the peace for a warrant authorising a search of specified premises for documents relating to any matter relevant to the investigation. Under section 66 of the Courts Act 2003[84], a Circuit judge can exercise the power to issue a warrant.*

*Under section 16(3) of the Police and Criminal Evidence Act 1984, entry and search under a warrant must be within 3 months from the date of its issue.*

*The Practice Direction sets out forms of application and warrant for use in connection with this rule.]*

**R47.30** **Application for warrant under paragraph 12 of Schedule 1 to the Police and Criminal Evidence Act 1984**

47.30 (1) This rule applies where an applicant wants a Circuit judge to issue a warrant or warrants under paragraph 12 of Schedule 1 to the Police and Criminal Evidence Act 1984[85].

(2) As well as complying with rule 47.26, the application must—

(a) specify the offence under investigation (and see paragraph (3)(a));

(b) specify the set of access conditions on which the applicant relies (and see paragraphs (3) and (4));

(c) so far as practicable, identify the material sought and if that material may be stored in an electronic device or devices—

(i) so far as practicable, describe each device or kind of device sought, and

(ii) explain the grounds for believing that the material may be stored there;

(d) specify the premises to be searched (and see paragraphs (6) and (7)); and

(e) state whether the applicant wants other persons to accompany the officers executing the warrant or warrants (and see paragraph (8)).

(3) Where the applicant relies on paragraph 2 of Schedule 1 to the Police and Criminal Evidence Act 1984[86] ('the first set of access conditions': general power to gain access to special procedure material), the application must—

(a) specify the indictable offence under investigation;

(b) explain the grounds for believing that the offence has been committed;

(c) explain the grounds for believing that the material sought—

(i) is likely to be of substantial value to the investigation (whether by itself, or together with other material),

(ii) is likely to be admissible evidence at trial for the offence under investigation, and

(iii) does not consist of or include items subject to legal privilege or excluded material;

(d) explain what other methods of obtaining the material—

(i) have been tried without success, or

(ii) have not been tried because they appeared bound to fail; and

(e) explain why it is in the public interest to obtain the material, having regard to—

(i) the benefit likely to accrue to the investigation if the material is obtained, and

(ii) the circumstances under which the material is held.

(4) Where the applicant relies on paragraph 3 of Schedule 1 to the Police and Criminal Evidence Act 1984[87] ('the second set of access conditions': use of search warrant power to gain access to excluded or special procedure material), the application must—

(a) state the legislation under which a search warrant could have been issued, had the material sought not been excluded or special procedure material (in this paragraph, described as 'the main search power');

(b) include or attach the terms of the main search power;

(c) explain how the circumstances would have satisfied any criteria prescribed by the main search power for the issue of a search warrant; and

(d) explain why the issue of such a search warrant would have been appropriate.

(5) Where the applicant relies on the second set of access conditions and on an assertion that a production order made under paragraph 4 of Schedule 1 to the 1984 Act[88] in respect of the material sought has not been complied with—

---

[84] 2003 c. 39; section 66 was amended by paragraph 6 of Schedule 2 to the Armed Forces Act 2011 (c. 18) and sections 17 and 21 of, and paragraphs 83 and 90 of Schedule 10 and paragraph 4 of Schedule 14 to, the Crime and Courts Act 2013 (c. 22).

[85] 1984 c. 60; paragraph 12 of Schedule 1 was amended by section 65 of, and paragraph 6 of Schedule 4 to, the Courts Act 2003 (c. 39) and section 113 of the Serious Organised Crime and Police Act 2005 (c. 15).

[86] 1984 c. 60; paragraph 2 of Schedule 1 was amended by sections 111 and 113 of, and paragraph 43 of Schedule 7 to, the Serious Organised Crime and Police Act 2005 (c. 15).

[87] 1984 c. 60; paragraph 3 of Schedule 1 was amended by section 113 of the Serious Organised Crime and Police Act 2005 (c. 15).

[88] 1984 c. 60; paragraph 4 of Schedule 1 was amended by section 65 of, and paragraph 6 of Schedule 4 to, the Courts Act 2003 (c. 39).

(a) the application must—
    (i) identify that order and describe its terms, and
    (ii) specify the date on which it was served; but
(b) the application need not comply with paragraphs (6) or (7).

(6) In relation to premises which the applicant wants to be searched and can specify, the application must (unless paragraph (5) applies)—
    (a) specify each set of premises;
    (b) in respect of each set of premises, explain the grounds for believing that material sought is on those premises; and
    (c) in respect of each set of premises, explain the grounds for believing that—
        (i) it is not practicable to communicate with any person entitled to grant entry to the premises,
        (ii) it is practicable to communicate with such a person but it is not practicable to communicate with any person entitled to grant access to the material sought,
        (iii) the material sought contains information which is subject to a restriction on disclosure or an obligation of secrecy contained in an enactment and is likely to be disclosed in breach of the restriction or obligation if a warrant is not issued, or
        (iv) service of notice of an application for a production order under paragraph 4 of Schedule 1 to the 1984 Act may seriously prejudice the investigation.

(7) In relation to premises which the applicant wants to be searched but at least some of which the applicant cannot specify, the application must (unless paragraph (5) applies)—
    (a) explain the grounds for believing that—
        (i) because of the particulars of the offence under investigation it is necessary to search any premises occupied or controlled by a specified person, and
        (ii) it is not reasonably practicable to specify all the premises which that person occupies or controls which might need to be searched;
    (b) specify as many sets of premises as is reasonably practicable;
    (c) in respect of each set of premises, whether specified or not, explain the grounds for believing that material sought is on those premises; and
    (d) in respect of each specified set of premises, explain the grounds for believing that—
        (i) it is not practicable to communicate with any person entitled to grant entry to the premises,
        (ii) it is practicable to communicate with such a person but it is not practicable to communicate with any person entitled to grant access to the material sought,
        (iii) the material sought contains information which is subject to a restriction on disclosure or an obligation of secrecy contained in an enactment and is likely to be disclosed in breach of the restriction or obligation if a warrant is not issued, or
        (iv) service of notice of an application for a production order under paragraph 4 of Schedule 1 to the 1984 Act may seriously prejudice the investigation.

(8) In relation to any set of premises which the applicant wants to be searched by the officers executing the warrant with other persons authorised by the court, the application must—
    (a) identify those other persons, by function or description; and
    (b) explain why those persons are required.

*[Note. Under paragraph 12 of Schedule 1 to the Police and Criminal Evidenced Act 1984, where the conditions listed in that paragraph and, if applicable, in paragraphs 12A and 14 of that Schedule[89] are fulfilled a constable may apply to a Circuit judge for a warrant authorising a search for evidence consisting of special procedure material or, in some cases, excluded material on specified premises or on the premises of a specified person.*

*Under section 16(3) of the 1984 Act[90], entry and search under a warrant must be within 3 months from the date of its issue.*

*See also the code of practice for the search of premises issued under section 66 of the 1984 Act.*

*The Practice Direction sets out forms of application and warrant for use in connection with this rule.]*

---

[89] 1984 c. 60; paragraph 12A of Schedule 1 was inserted by section 113 of the Serious Organised Crime and Police Act 2005 (c. 15). Paragraph 14 of Schedule 1 was amended by sections 113 and 174 of, and Schedule 17 to, the Serious Organised Crime and Police Act 2005 (c. 15).

[90] 1984 c. 60; section 16(3) was amended by section 114 of the Serious Organised Crime and Police Act 2005 (c. 15).

**R47.31**　**Application for warrant under paragraph 11 of Schedule 5 to the Terrorism Act 2000**

**47.31** (1)　This rule applies where an applicant wants a Circuit judge to issue a warrant or warrants under paragraph 11 of Schedule 5 to the Terrorism Act 2000[91].

(2)　As well as complying with rule 47.26, the application must—

(a)　specify the offence under investigation;

(b)　explain how the investigation constitutes a terrorist investigation within the meaning of the Terrorism Act 2000;

(c)　so far as practicable, identify the material sought (see also paragraph (4)) and if that material may be stored in an electronic device or devices—

(i)　so far as practicable, describe each device or kind of device sought, and

(ii)　explain the grounds for believing that the material may be stored there;

(d)　specify the premises to be searched (and see paragraph (5)); and

(e)　state whether the applicant wants other persons to accompany the officers executing the warrant or warrants (and see paragraph (6)).

(3)　Where the applicant relies on an assertion that a production order made under paragraph 5 of Schedule 5 to the 2000 Act[92] in respect of material on the premises has not been complied with—

(a)　the application must—

(i)　identify that order and describe its terms, and

(ii)　specify the date on which it was served; but

(b)　the application need not comply with paragraphs (4) or (5)(b).

(4)　In relation to the material sought, unless paragraph (3) applies the application must explain the grounds for believing that—

(a)　the material consists of or includes excluded material or special procedure material but does not include items subject to legal privilege;

(b)　the material is likely to be of substantial value to a terrorist investigation (whether by itself, or together with other material); and

(c)　it is not appropriate to make an order under paragraph 5 of Schedule 11 to the 2000 Act in relation to the material because—

(i)　it is not practicable to communicate with any person entitled to produce the material,

(ii)　it is not practicable to communicate with any person entitled to grant access to the material or entitled to grant entry to premises to which the application for the warrant relates, or

(iii)　a terrorist investigation may be seriously prejudiced unless a constable can secure immediate access to the material.

(5)　In relation to the premises which the applicant wants to be searched, the application must—

(a)　specify—

(i)　where paragraph (3) applies, the respondent and any premises to which the production order referred, or

(ii)　in any other case, one or more sets of premises, or any premises occupied or controlled by a specified person (which may include one or more specified sets of premises);

(b)　unless paragraph (3) applies, in relation to premises which the applicant wants to be searched but cannot specify, explain why—

(i)　it is necessary to search any premises occupied or controlled by the specified person, and

(ii)　it is not reasonably practicable to specify all the premises which that person occupies or controls which might need to be searched; and

(c)　explain the grounds for believing that material sought is on those premises.

(6)　In relation to any set of premises which the applicant wants to be searched by the officers executing the warrant with other persons authorised by the court, the application must—

(a)　identify those other persons, by function or description; and

(b)　explain why those persons are required.

---

[91]　2000 c. 11; paragraph 11 of Schedule 5 was amended by section 26 of the Terrorism Act 2006 (c. 11) and section 82 of the Deregulation Act 2015 (c. 20). It is further amended by section 65 of, and paragraph 9 of Schedule 4 to, the Courts Act 2003 (c. 39), with effect from a date to be appointed.
[92]　2000 c. 11; paragraph 5 of Schedule 5 is amended by section 65 of, and paragraph 9 of Schedule 4 to, the Courts Act 2003 (c. 39), with effect from a date to be appointed.

*[Note. Under paragraph 11 of Schedule 5 to the Terrorism Act 2000, where the conditions listed in that paragraph and in paragraph 12 of that Schedule[93] are fulfilled a constable may apply to a Circuit judge for a warrant authorising a search for material consisting of excluded material or special procedure material on specified premises or on the premises of a specified person.*

*Under section 16(3) of the 1984 Act, entry and search under a warrant must be within 3 months from the date of its issue.*

*See also the code of practice for the search of premises issued under section 66 of the 1984 Act.*

*The Practice Direction sets out forms of application and warrant for use in connection with this rule.]*

## Application for warrant under section 352 of the Proceeds of Crime Act 2002      R47.32

**47.32** (1) This rule applies where an applicant wants a Crown Court judge to issue a warrant or warrants under—

    (a) section 352 of the Proceeds of Crime Act 2002[94]; or

    (b) article 13 of the Proceeds of Crime Act 2002 (External Investigations) Order 2014[95].

(2) As well as complying with rule 47.26, the application must—

    (a) explain whether the investigation is a confiscation investigation, a money laundering investigation, a detained cash investigation, a detained property investigation, a frozen funds investigation or an external investigation;

    (b) in the case of an investigation in the United Kingdom, explain why the applicant suspects that—

        (i) the person under investigation has benefited from criminal conduct, in the case of a confiscation investigation, or committed a money laundering offence, in the case of a money laundering investigation, or

        (ii) in the case of a detained cash investigation, a detained property investigation or a frozen funds investigation, the cash or property involved, or the money held in the frozen account, was obtained through unlawful conduct or is intended to be used in unlawful conduct;

    (c) in the case of an investigation outside the United Kingdom, explain why the applicant believes that—

        (i) there is an investigation by an overseas authority which relates to a criminal investigation or to criminal proceedings (including proceedings to remove the benefit of a person's criminal conduct following that person's conviction), and

        (ii) the investigation is into whether property has been obtained as a result of or in connection with criminal conduct, or into the extent or whereabouts of such property;

    (d) indicate what material is sought (and see paragraphs (4) and (5));

    (e) specify the premises to be searched (and see paragraph (6)); and

    (f) state whether the applicant wants other persons to accompany the officers executing the warrant or warrants (and see paragraph (7)).

(3) Where the applicant relies on an assertion that a production order made under sections 345 and 351 of the 2002 Act[96] or under articles 6 and 12 of the 2014 Order has not been complied with—

    (a) the application must—

        (i) identify that order and describe its terms,

        (ii) specify the date on which it was served, and

---

[93] 2000 c. 11; paragraph 12 of Schedule 5 was amended by Section 26 of the Terrorism Act 2006 (c. 11). It is further amended by section 65 of, and paragraph 9 of Schedule 4 to, the Courts Act 2003 (c. 39), with effect from a date to be appointed.

[94] 2002 c. 29; section 352 was amended by sections 74, 76, 77 and 80 of, and paragraphs 103 and 105 of Schedule 8 and paragraphs 1 and 7 of Schedule 10 to, the Serious Crime Act 2007 (c. 27), section 169 of, and paragraphs 1 and 10 of Schedule 19 to, the Coroners and Justice Act 2009 (c. 25), sections 15, 49 and 55 of, and paragraphs 108 and 137 of Schedule 8, paragraphs 1 and 6 of Schedule 19 and paragraphs 14 and 31 of Schedule 21 to, the Crime and Courts Act 2013 (c. 22), section 224 of, and paragraphs 1 and 12 of Schedule 48 to, the Finance Act 2013 (c. 29), article 3 of, and paragraphs 19 and 26 of Schedule 2 to, SI 2014/834 and section 82 of the Deregulation Act 2015 (c. 20).

[95] S.I. 2014/1893.

[96] 2002 c. 29; section 345 was amended by section 75 of the Serious Crime Act 2007 (c. 27), section 169 of, and paragraphs 1 and 6 of Schedule 19 to, the Coroners and Justice Act 2009 (c. 25) and section 49 of, and paragraphs 1 and 4 of Schedule 19 to, the Crime and Courts Act 2013 (c. 22). Section 351 was amended by sections 74 and 77 of, and paragraphs 103 and 104 of Schedule 8 and paragraphs 1 and 6 of Schedule 10 to, the Serious Crime Act 2007 (c. 27), section 169 of, and paragraphs 1 and 9 of Schedule 19 to, the Coroners and Justice Act 2009 (c. 25), sections 66 and 112 of, and Part 5 of Schedule 8 to, the Policing and Crime Act 2009 (c. 26), sections 15 and 55 of, and paragraphs 108 and 136 of Schedule 8 and paragraphs 14 and 30 of Schedule 21 to, the Crime and Courts Act 2013 (c.22) and section 224 of, and paragraphs 1 and 11 of Schedule 48 to, the Finance Act 2013 (c. 29).

(iii) explain the grounds for believing that the material in respect of which the order was made is on the premises specified in the application for the warrant; but

(b) the application need not comply with paragraphs (4) or (5).

(4) Unless paragraph (3) applies, in relation to the material sought the application must—

(a) specify the material and if that material may be stored in an electronic device or devices—

    (i) so far as practicable, describe each device or kind of device sought, and

    (ii) explain the grounds for believing that the material may be stored there;

(b) give a general description of the material and explain the grounds for believing that it relates to the person, cash, property or money under investigation and—

    (i) in the case of a confiscation investigation, relates to the question whether that person has benefited from criminal conduct, or to any question about the extent or whereabouts of that benefit,

    (ii) in the case of a money laundering investigation, relates to the question whether that person has committed a money laundering offence,

    (iii) in the case of a detained cash investigation, a detained property investigation or a frozen funds investigation into the derivation of cash, property or money, relates to the question whether that cash, property or money is recoverable property,

    (iv) in the case of a detained cash investigation, a detained property investigation or a frozen funds investigation into the intended use of cash, property or money, relates to the question whether that cash, property or money is intended by any person to be used in unlawful conduct, or

    (v) in the case of an investigation outside the United Kingdom, relates to that investigation.

(5) Unless paragraph (3) applies, in relation to the material sought the application must explain also the grounds for believing that—

(a) the material consists of or includes special procedure material but does not include excluded material or privileged material;

(b) the material is likely to be of substantial value to the investigation (whether by itself, or together with other material); and

(c) it is in the public interest for the material to be obtained, having regard to—

    (i) other potential sources of information, and

    (ii) the benefit likely to accrue to the investigation if the material is obtained.

(6) In relation to the premises which the applicant wants to be searched, unless paragraph (3) applies the application must—

(a) explain the grounds for believing that material sought is on those premises;

(b) if the application specifies the material sought, explain the grounds for believing that it is not appropriate to make a production order under sections 345 and 351 of the 2002 Act or under articles 6 and 12 of the 2014 Order because—

    (i) it is not practicable to communicate with any person against whom the production order could be made,

    (ii) it is not practicable to communicate with any person who would be required to comply with an order to grant entry to the premises, or

    (iii) the investigation might be seriously prejudiced unless an appropriate person is able to secure immediate access to the material; and

(c) if the application gives a general description of the material sought, explain the grounds for believing that—

    (i) it is not practicable to communicate with any person entitled to grant entry to the premises,

    (ii) entry to the premises will not be granted unless a warrant is produced, or

    (iii) the investigation might be seriously prejudiced unless an appropriate person arriving at the premises is able to secure immediate access to them.

(7) In relation to any set of premises which the applicant wants to be searched by those executing the warrant with other persons authorised by the court, the application must—

(a) identify those other persons, by function or description; and

(b) explain why those persons are required.

*[Note. Under section 352 of the Proceeds of Crime Act 2002 where there is a confiscation investigation, a money laundering investigation, a detained cash investigation, a detained property investigation or a frozen funds investigation, an 'appropriate officer' within the meaning of that section may apply to a Crown Court judge for a warrant authorising a search for special procedure material on specified premises, on the conditions listed in that section and in section 353 of the Act[97].*

---

*Under article 13 of the Proceeds of Crime Act 2002 (External Investigations) Order 2014, where there is an external investigation an 'appropriate officer' within the meaning of that article may apply to a Crown Court judge for a warrant authorising a search for special procedure material on specified premises, on the conditions listed in that article and in article 14 of the Order.*

*Under section 16(3) of the 1984 Act[98], as applied by article 3 of the Proceeds of Crime Act 2002 (Application of Police and Criminal Evidence Act 1984) Order 2015[99], entry and search under a warrant must be within 3 months from the date of its issue.*

*See also the code of practice for the search of premises issued under section 66 of the 1984 Act.*

*The Practice Direction sets out forms of application and warrant for use in connection with this rule.]*

**Application for warrant under section 160 of the Extradition Act 2003**    **R47.33**

47.33 (1)   This rule applies where an applicant wants a Circuit judge to issue a warrant or warrants under section 160 of the Extradition Act 2003[100].

(2)   As well as complying with rule 47.26, the application must—
    (a)   identify the person whose extradition is sought (and see paragraph (3));
    (b)   specify the extradition offence of which that person is accused;
    (c)   specify the material, or description of material, sought (and see paragraph (4)); and
    (d)   specify the premises to be searched (and see paragraph (5)).

(3)   In relation to the person whose extradition is sought, the application must explain the grounds for believing that—
    (a)   that person has committed the offence for which extradition is sought;
    (b)   that offence is an extradition offence; and
    (c)   that person is in the United Kingdom or is on the way to the United Kingdom.

(4)   In relation to the material sought, the application must—
    (a)   explain the grounds for believing that—
        (i)   the material consists of or includes special procedure or excluded material, and
        (ii)   the material would be likely to be admissible evidence at a trial in England and Wales for the offence for which extradition is sought; and
    (b)   if that material may be stored in an electronic device or devices—
        (i)   so far as practicable, describe each device or kind of device sought, and
        (ii)   explain the grounds for believing that the material may be stored there.

(5)   In relation to the premises which the applicant wants to search, the application must explain the grounds for believing that—
    (a)   material sought is on those premises; and
    (b)   one or more of the following conditions is satisfied, namely—
        (i)   it is not practicable to communicate with any person entitled to grant entry to the premises,
        (ii)   it is practicable to communicate with such a person but it is not practicable to communicate with any person entitled to grant access to the material sought, or
        (iii)   the material contains information which is subject to a restriction on disclosure or an obligation of secrecy contained in an enactment and is likely to be disclosed in breach of the restriction or obligation if a warrant is not issued.

(6)   In relation to any set of premises which the applicant wants to be searched by the officers executing the warrant with other persons authorised by the court, the application must—
    (a)   identify those other persons, by function or description; and
    (b)   explain why those persons are required.

*[Note. Under section 160 of the Extradition Act 2003, where a person's extradition is sought a constable may apply to a Circuit judge for a warrant authorising a search for special procedure material or excluded material on specified premises, on the conditions listed in that section.*

*Under section 16(3) of the 1984 Act, entry and search under a warrant must be within 3 months from the date of its issue.*

*See also the code of practice for the search of premises issued under section 66 of the 1984 Act.]*

---

19 to, the Coroners and Justice Act 2009 (c. 25), sections 15, 49 and 55 of, and paragraphs 108 and 138 of Schedule 8, paragraphs 1 and 7 of Schedule 19 and paragraphs 14 and 32 of Schedule 21 to, the Crime and Courts Act 2013 (c. 22), section 224 of, and paragraphs 1 and 13 of Schedule 48 to, the Finance Act 2013 (c. 29) and section 38 of the Serious Crime Act 2015 (c. 9) and paragraph 48 of Schedule 5 to the Criminal Finances Act 2017 (c. 22).

[98]   1984 c. 60; section 16(3) was amended by section 114 of the Serious Organised Crime and Police Act 2005 (c. 15).
[99]   S.I. 2015/759.
[100]   2003 c. 41; section 160 was amended by section 174 of the Anti-social Behaviour, Crime and Policing Act 2014 (c. 12).

**R47.34** **Application for warrant under any other power**

**47.34** (1) This rule applies—

    (a) where an applicant wants a court to issue a warrant or warrants under a power (in this rule, 'the relevant search power') to which rule 47.24(d) (other powers) refers; but

    (b) subject to any inconsistent provision in legislation that applies to the relevant search power.

(2) As well as complying with rule 47.26, the application must—

    (a) demonstrate the applicant's entitlement to apply;

    (b) identify the relevant search power (and see paragraph (3));

    (c) so far as practicable, identify the articles or persons sought (see also paragraph (4)) and if such an article may be stored in an electronic device or devices—

        (i) so far as practicable, describe each device or kind of device sought, and

        (ii) explain the grounds for believing that the article may be stored there;

    (d) specify the premises to be searched (and see paragraphs (5) and (6));

    (e) state whether the applicant wants the premises to be searched on more than one occasion, if the relevant search power allows (and see paragraph (7)); and

    (f) state whether the applicant wants other persons to accompany the officers executing the warrant or warrants, if the relevant search power allows (and see paragraph (8)).

(3) The application must—

    (a) include or attach the terms of the relevant search power; and

    (b) explain how the circumstances satisfy the criteria prescribed by that power for making the application.

(4) In relation to the articles or persons sought, the application must explain how they satisfy the criteria prescribed by the relevant search power about such articles or persons.

(5) In relation to premises which the applicant wants to be searched and can specify, the application must—

    (a) specify each set of premises; and

    (b) in respect of each, explain how the circumstances satisfy any criteria prescribed by the relevant search power—

        (i) for asserting that the articles or persons sought are on those premises, and

        (ii) for asserting that the court can exercise its power to authorise the search of those particular premises.

(6) In relation to premises which the applicant wants to be searched but at least some of which the applicant cannot specify, the application must—

    (a) explain how the relevant search power allows the court to authorise such searching;

    (b) specify the person who occupies or controls such premises;

    (c) specify as many sets of such premises as is reasonably practicable;

    (d) explain why—

        (i) it is necessary to search more premises than those specified, and

        (ii) it is not reasonably practicable to specify all the premises which the applicant wants to be searched;

    (e) in respect of each set of premises, whether specified or not, explain how the circumstances satisfy any criteria prescribed by the relevant search power for asserting that the articles or persons sought are on those premises; and

    (f) in respect of each specified set of premises, explain how the circumstances satisfy any criteria prescribed by the relevant search power for asserting that the court can exercise its power to authorise the search of those premises.

(7) In relation to any set of premises which the applicant wants to be searched on more than one occasion, the application must—

    (a) explain how the relevant search power allows the court to authorise such searching;

    (b) explain why the applicant wants the premises to be searched more than once; and

    (c) specify any proposed maximum number of occasions.

(8) In relation to any set of premises which the applicant wants to be searched by the officers executing the warrant with other persons authorised by the court, the application must—

    (a) identify those other persons, by function or description; and

    (b) explain why those persons are required.

*[Note. See, among other provisions, sections 15 and 16 of the Police and Criminal Evidence Act 1984[101], which apply to an application by a constable under any Act for a warrant authorising the search of specified premises, or the search of premises of a specified person, and to the execution of such a warrant. Unless other legislation*

---

[101] 1984 c. 60; section 15 was amended by sections 113 and 114 of the Serious Organised Crime and Police Act 2005 (c. 15) and article 7 of S.I. 2005/3496. Section 16 was amended by paragraph 281 of Schedule 8 to the Courts Act 2003 (c. 39),

*otherwise provides, under section 16(3) of the 1984 Act entry and search under a warrant must be within 3 months from the date of its issue.*

*The Practice Direction sets out forms of application and warrant for use in connection with this rule.]*

### Section 4:  orders for the retention or return of property

**When this Section applies**                                                                                 **R47.35**

47.35 (1)  This Section applies where—

    (a)  under section 1 of the Police (Property) Act 1897[102], a magistrates' court can—

        (i)  order the return to the owner of property which has come into the possession of the police or the National Crime Agency in connection with an investigation of a suspected offence, or

        (ii)  make such order with respect to such property as the court thinks just, where the owner cannot be ascertained; and

    (b)  a Crown Court judge can—

        (i)  order the return of seized property under section 59(4) of the Criminal Justice and Police Act 2001[103], or

        (ii)  order the examination, retention, separation or return of seized property under section 59(5) of the Act.

    (2)  In this Section, a reference to a person with 'a relevant interest' in seized property means someone from whom the property was seized, or someone with a proprietary interest in the property, or someone who had custody or control of it immediately before it was seized.

**Exercise of court's powers**                                                                                **R47.36**

47.36 (1)  The court may determine an application for an order—

    (a)  at a hearing (which must be in private unless the court otherwise directs), or without a hearing; and

    (b)  in a party's absence, if that party—

        (i)  applied for the order, or

        (ii)  has had at least 10 business days in which to make representations.

    (2)  The court officer must arrange for the court to hear such an application no sooner than 10 business days after it was served, unless—

    (a)  the court directs that no hearing need be arranged; or

    (b)  the court gives other directions for the hearing.

    (3)  If the court so directs, the parties to an application may attend a hearing by live link or telephone.

    (4)  The court may—

    (a)  shorten or extend (even after it has expired) a time limit under this Section;

    (b)  dispense with a requirement for service under this Section (even after service was required); and

    (c)  consider an application made orally instead of in writing.

    (5)  A person who wants an extension of time must—

    (a)  apply when serving the application or representations for which it is needed; and

    (b)  explain the delay.

**Application for an order under section 1 of the Police (Property) Act 1897**                          **R47.37**

47.37 (1)  This rule applies where an applicant wants the court to make an order to which rule 47.35(1)(a) refers.

    (2)  The applicant must apply in writing and serve the application on—

    (a)  the court officer; and

    (b)  as appropriate—

        (i)  the officer who has the property,

        (ii)  any person who appears to be its owner.

    (3)  The application must—

    (a)  explain the applicant's interest in the property (either as a person who claims to be its owner or as an officer into whose possession the property has come);

    (b)  specify the direction that the applicant wants the court to make, and explain why; and

    (c)  include or attach a list of those on whom the applicant has served the application.

---

section 2 of the Criminal Justice Act 2003 (c. 44), sections 113 and 114 of the Serious Organised Crime and Police Act 2005 (c. 15) and article 8 of S.I. 2005/3496.

[102]  1897 c. 30; section 1 was amended by sections 33 and 36 of, and Part III of Schedule 3 to, the Theft Act 1968 (c. 60), section 58 of the Criminal Justice Act 1972 (c. 71), section 192 of, and Part I of Schedule 5 to, the Consumer Credit Act 1974 (c. 39), the Statute Law (Repeals) Act 1989 (c. 43) and section 4 of the Police (Property) Act 1997 (c. 30).

[103]  2001 c. 16.

*[Note. Under section 1 of the Police (Property) Act 1897, the owner of property which has come into the possession of the police or the National Crime Agency in connection with the investigation of a suspected offence can apply to a magistrates' court for an order for its delivery to the claimant.]*

**R47.38**    **Application for an order under section 59 of the Criminal Justice and Police Act 2001**

47.38 (1) This rule applies where an applicant wants the court to make an order to which rule 47.35(1)(b) refers.

(2) The applicant must apply in writing and serve the application on—

(a) the court officer; and

(b) as appropriate—

(i) the person who for the time being has the seized property,

(ii) each person whom the applicant knows or believes to have a relevant interest in the property.

(3) In each case, the application must—

(a) explain the applicant's interest in the property (either as a person with a relevant interest, or as possessor of the property in consequence of its seizure, as appropriate);

(b) explain the circumstances of the seizure of the property and identify the power that was exercised to seize it (or which the person seizing it purported to exercise, as appropriate); and

(c) include or attach a list of those on whom the applicant has served the application.

(4) On an application for an order for the return of property under section 59(4) of the Criminal Justice and Police Act 2001, the application must explain why any one or more of these applies—

(a) there was no power to make the seizure;

(b) the property seized is, or contains, an item subject to legal privilege which is not an item that can be retained lawfully in the circumstances listed in section 54(2) of the Act[104];

(c) the property seized is, or contains, excluded or special procedure material which is not material that can be retained lawfully in the circumstances listed in sections 55 and 56 of the Act; or

(d) the property seized is, or contains, something taken from premises under section 50 of the Act, or from a person under section 51 of the Act, in the circumstances listed in those sections and which cannot lawfully be retained on the conditions listed in the Act.

(5) On an application for an order for the examination, retention, separation or return of property under section 59(5) of the 2001 Act, the application must—

(a) specify the direction that the applicant wants the court to make, and explain why;

(b) if applicable, specify each requirement of section 53(2) of the Act (examination and return of property) which is not being complied with; and

(c) if applicable, explain why the retention of the property by the person who now has it would be justified on the grounds that, even if it were returned, it would immediately become appropriate for that person to get it back under—

(i) a warrant for its seizure, or

(ii) a production order made under paragraph 4 of Schedule 1 to the Police and Criminal Evidence Act 1984[105], section 20BA of the Taxes Management Act 1970[106] or paragraph 5 of Schedule 5 to the Terrorism Act 2000[107].

*[Note. Under section 59 of the Criminal Justice and Police Act 2001, a person with a 'relevant interest' (see rule 47.35(2)) in seized property can apply in the circumstances listed in the Act to a Crown Court judge for an order for its return. A person who has the property in consequence of its seizure can apply for an order authorising its retention. Either can apply for an order relating to the examination of the property.]*

**R47.39**    **Application containing information withheld from another party**

47.39 (1) This rule applies where—

(a) an applicant serves an application to which rule 47.37 (Application for an order under section 1 of the Police (Property) Act 1897) or rule 47.38 (Application for an order under section 59 of the Criminal Justice and Police Act 2001) applies; and

---

[104] 2001 c. 16; section 55 was amended by sections 456 and 457 of, and paragraphs 1 and 40 of Schedule 11 and Schedule 12 to, the Proceeds of Crime Act 2002 (c. 29). Section 56 was amended by article 364 of SI 2001/3649, section 12 of, and paragraph 14 of Schedule 1 to, the Criminal Justice Act 2003 (c. 44) and article 2 of, and paragraph 189 of Schedule 1 to, S.I. 2009/1941.

[105] 1984 c. 60; paragraph 4 of Schedule 1 was amended by section 65 of, and paragraph 6 of Schedule 4 to, the Courts Act 2003 (c. 39).

[106] 1970 c. 9; section 20BA was inserted by section 149 of the Finance Act 2000 (c. 17).

[107] 2000 c. 11; paragraph 5 of Schedule 5 is amended by section 65 of, and paragraph 9 of Schedule 4 to, the Courts Act 2003 (c. 39), with effect from a date to be appointed.

      (b) the application includes information that the applicant thinks ought not be revealed to another party.

(2) The applicant must—

      (a) omit that information from the part of the application that is served on that other party;

      (b) mark the other part to show that, unless the court otherwise directs, it is only for the court; and

      (c) in that other part, explain why the applicant has withheld that information from that other party.

(3) If the court so directs, any hearing of an application to which this rule applies may be, wholly or in part, in the absence of a party from whom information has been withheld.

(4) At any hearing of an application to which this rule applies—

      (a) the general rule is that the court must consider, in the following sequence—

         (i) representations first by the applicant and then by each other party, in all the parties' presence, and then

         (ii) further representations by the applicant, in the absence of a party from whom information has been withheld; but

      (b) the court may direct other arrangements for the hearing.

## Representations in response                                                                      R47.40

47.40 (1) This rule applies where a person wants to make representations about an application under rule 47.37 or rule 47.38.

(2) Such a person must—

      (a) serve the representations on—

         (i) the court officer, and

         (ii) the applicant and any other party to the application;

      (b) do so not more than 10 business days after service of the application; and

      (c) ask for a hearing, if that person wants one.

(3) Representations in opposition to an application must explain why the grounds on which the applicant relies are not met.

(4) Where representations include information that the person making them thinks ought not be revealed to another party, that person must—

      (a) omit that information from the representations served on that other party;

      (b) mark the information to show that, unless the court otherwise directs, it is only for the court; and

      (c) with that information include an explanation of why it has been withheld from that other party.

## Application to punish for contempt of court                                                      R47.41

47.41 (1) This rule applies where a person is accused of disobeying an order under section 59 of the Criminal Justice and Police Act 2001.

(2) A person who wants the court to exercise its power to punish that person for contempt of court must comply with the rules in Part 48 (Contempt of court).

*[Note. A Crown Court judge has power to punish a person who disobeys an order under section 59 of the 2001 Act as if that were a contempt of the Crown Court: see section 59(9) of the Act.]*

### Section 5: orders for the retention of fingerprints, etc.

## When this Section applies                                                                        R47.42

47.42 This Section applies where—

      (a) a District Judge (Magistrates' Court) can make an order under—

         (i) section 63F(7) or 63R(6) of the Police and Criminal Evidence Act 1984[108], or

         (ii) paragraph 20B(5) or 20G(6) of Schedule 8 to the Terrorism Act 2000[109]; and

      (b) the Crown Court can determine an appeal under—

         (i) section 63F(10) of the Police and Criminal Evidence Act 1984, or

         (ii) paragraph 20B(8) of Schedule 8 to the Terrorism Act 2000.

*[Note. Under the Police and Criminal Evidence Act 1984 or under the Terrorism Act 2000, an order may be made extending the period during which fingerprints, DNA profiles or samples may be retained by the police.]*

---

[108] 1984 c. 60; section 63D was inserted by section 1 of the Protection of Freedoms Act 2012 (c. 9). Section 63R was inserted by section 14 of that Act.

[109] 2000 c. 11; paragraph 20B of Schedule 8 was inserted by section 19 of, and paragraph 1 of Schedule 1 to, the Protection of Freedoms Act 2012 (c. 9) (for certain purposes, and for remaining purposes with effect from a date to be appointed) and amended by section 181 of, and paragraph 125 of Schedule 11 to, the Anti-social Behaviour, Crime and Policing Act 2014 (c. 12). Paragraph 20G of Schedule 8 was inserted by section 19 of, and paragraph 1 of Schedule 1 to, the Protection of Freedoms Act 2012 (c. 9) for certain purposes, and for remaining purposes with effect from a date to be appointed.

**R47.43**   **Exercise of court's powers**

**47.43** (1) The court must determine an application under rule 47.44, and an appeal under rule 47.45—
    (a) at a hearing, which must be in private unless the court otherwise directs; and
    (b) in the presence of the applicant or appellant.

  (2) The court must not determine such an application or appeal unless any person served under those rules—
    (a) is present; or
    (b) has had an opportunity—
      (i) to attend, or
      (ii) to make representations.

**R47.44**   **Application to extend retention period**

**47.44** (1) This rule applies where a magistrates' court can make an order extending the period for which there may be retained material consisting of—
    (a) fingerprints taken from a person—
      (i) under a power conferred by Part V of the Police and Criminal Evidence Act 1984[110],
      (ii) with that person's consent, in connection with the investigation of an offence by the police, or
      (iii) under a power conferred by Schedule 8 to the Terrorism Act 2000[111] in relation to a person detained under section 41 of that Act;
    (b) a DNA profile derived from a DNA sample so taken; or
    (c) a sample so taken.

  (2) A chief officer of police who wants the court to make such an order must—
    (a) apply in writing—
      (i) within the period of 3 months ending on the last day of the retention period, where the application relates to fingerprints or a DNA profile, or
      (ii) before the expiry of the retention period, where the application relates to a sample;
    (b) in the application—
      (i) identify the material,
      (ii) state when the retention period expires,
      (iii) give details of any previous such application relating to the material, and
      (iv) outline the circumstances in which the material was acquired;
    (c) serve the application on the court officer, in every case; and
    (d) serve the application on the person from whom the material was taken, where—
      (i) the application relates to fingerprints or a DNA profile, or
      (ii) the application is for the renewal of an order extending the retention period for a sample.

  (3) An application to extend the retention period for fingerprints or a DNA profile must explain why that period should be extended.

  (4) An application to extend the retention period for a sample must explain why, having regard to the nature and complexity of other material that is evidence in relation to the offence, the sample is likely to be needed in any proceedings for the offence for the purposes of—
    (a) disclosure to, or use by, a defendant; or
    (b) responding to any challenge by a defendant in respect of the admissibility of material that is evidence on which the prosecution proposes to rely.

  (5) On an application to extend the retention period for fingerprints or a DNA profile, the applicant must serve notice of the court's decision on any respondent where—
    (a) the court makes the order sought; and
    (b) the respondent was absent when it was made.

*[Note. See rule 47.42(a). The powers to which rule 47.44 applies may be exercised only by a District Judge (Magistrates' Courts).*

*The time limits for making an application under this rule are prescribed by sections 63F(8) and 63R(8) of the Police and Criminal Evidence Act 1984[112], and by paragraphs 20B(6) and 20G(8) of Schedule 8 to the Terrorism Act 2000[113]. They may be neither extended nor shortened.*

---

[110] 1984 c. 60.

[111] 2000 c. 11.

[112] 1984 c. 60; section 63F was inserted by section 3 of the Protection of Freedoms Act 2012 (c. 9). Section 63R was inserted by section 14 of that Act.

[113] 2000 c. 11; paragraph 20B of Schedule 8 was inserted by section 19 of, and paragraph 1 of Schedule 1 to, the Protection of Freedoms Act 2012 (c. 9) (for certain purposes, and for remaining purposes with effect from a date to be appointed) and amended by section 181 of, and paragraph 125 of Schedule 11 to, the Anti-social Behaviour, Crime and Policing Act 2014 (c.

*Sections 63D and 63R of the 1984 Act[114], and paragraphs 20A and 20G of Schedule 8 to the 2000 Act[115], provide for the circumstances in which there must be destroyed the material to which this rule applies.*

*Section 63F of the 1984 Act, and paragraph 20B of Schedule 8 to the 2000 Act, provide for the circumstances in which fingerprints and DNA profiles may be retained instead of being destroyed. Under section 63F(7) and paragraph 20B(5), a chief officer of police to whom those provisions apply may apply for an order extending the statutory retention period of 3 years by up to another 2 years.*

*Section 63R of the 1984 Act and paragraph 20G of Schedule 8 to the 2000 Act provide for the circumstances in which samples taken from a person may be retained instead of being destroyed. Under section 63R(6) of the 1984 Act and paragraph 20G(6) of Schedule 8 to the 2000 Act, a chief officer of police to whom those provisions apply may apply for an order to retain a sample for up to 12 months after the date on which it would otherwise have to be destroyed. Under section 63R(9) and paragraph 20G(9), such an order may be renewed, on one or more occasions, for a further period of not more than 12 months from the end of the period when the order would otherwise cease to have effect.]*

### Appeal                                                                            R47.45

**47.45** (1)  This rule applies where, under rule 47.44, a magistrates' court determines an application relating to fingerprints or a DNA profile and—

    (a)  the person from whom the material was taken wants to appeal to the Crown Court against an order extending the retention period; or

    (b)  a chief officer of police wants to appeal to the Crown Court against a refusal to make such an order.

  (2)  The appellant must—

    (a)  serve an appeal notice—

      (i)  on the Crown Court officer and on the other party, and

      (ii)  not more than 15 business days after the magistrates' court's decision, or, if applicable, service of notice under rule 47.44(5); and

    (b)  in the appeal notice, explain, as appropriate, why the retention period should, or should not, be extended.

  (3)  Rule 34.11 (Constitution of the Crown Court) applies on such an appeal.

*[Note. Under section 63F(10) of the Police and Criminal Evidence Act 1984, and under paragraph 20B(8) of Schedule 8 to the Terrorism Act 2000, the person from whom fingerprints were taken, or from whom a DNA profile derives, may appeal to the Crown Court against an order extending the retention period; and a chief officer of police may appeal to the Crown Court against the refusal of such an order.]*

### Section 6: investigation anonymity orders under the Coroners and Justice Act 2009

#### When this Section applies                                                        R47.46

**47.46** This Section applies where—

    (a)  a justice of the peace can make or discharge an investigation anonymity order, under sections 76 and 80(1) of the Coroners and Justice Act 2009[116]; and

    (b)  a Crown Court judge can determine an appeal against—

      (i)  a refusal of such an order, under section 79 of the 2009 Act, or

      (ii)  a decision on an application to discharge such an order, under section 80(6) of the 2009 Act.

*[Note. Under the Coroners and Justice Act 2009, an investigation anonymity order may be made prohibiting the disclosure of information that identifies, or might identify, a specified person as someone who is, or was, willing to assist the investigation of an offence of murder or manslaughter caused by a gun or knife.]*

#### Exercise of court's powers                                                       R47.47

**47.47** (1)  The court may determine an application for an investigation anonymity order, and any appeal against the refusal of such an order—

    (a)  at a hearing (which must be in private unless the court otherwise directs); or

    (b)  without a hearing.

  (2)  The court must determine an application to discharge an investigation anonymity order, and any appeal against the decision on such an application—

    (a)  at a hearing (which must be in private unless the court otherwise directs); and

---

12). Paragraph 20G of Schedule 8 was inserted by section 19 of, and paragraph 1 of Schedule 1 to, the Protection of Freedoms Act 2012 (c. 9) for certain purposes, and for remaining purposes with effect from a date to be appointed.

[114] 1984 c. 60; section 63D was inserted by section 1 of the Protection of Freedoms Act 2012 (c. 9).

[115] 2000 c. 11; paragraph 20A of Schedule 8 was inserted by section 19 of, and paragraph 1 of Schedule 1 to, the Protection of Freedoms Act 2012 (c. 9) for certain purposes, and for remaining purposes with effect from a date to be appointed.

[116] 2009 c. 25.

    (b) in the presence of the person specified in the order, unless—
        (i) that person applied for the discharge of the order,
        (ii) that person has had an opportunity to make representations, or
        (iii) the court is satisfied that it is not reasonably practicable to communicate with that person.
  (3) The court may consider an application or an appeal made orally instead of in writing.

**R47.48**    **Application for an investigation anonymity order**

**47.48** (1) This rule applies where an applicant wants a magistrates' court to make an investigation anonymity order.
  (2) The applicant must—
    (a) apply in writing;
    (b) serve the application on the court officer;
    (c) identify the person to be specified in the order, unless—
        (i) the applicant wants the court to determine the application at a hearing, or
        (ii) the court otherwise directs;
    (d) explain how the proposed order meets the conditions prescribed by section 78 of the Coroners and Justice Act 2009[117];
    (e) say if the applicant intends to appeal should the court refuse the order;
    (f) attach any material on which the applicant relies; and
    (g) propose the terms of the order.
  (3) At any hearing of the application, the applicant must—
    (a) identify to the court the person to be specified in the order, unless—
        (i) the applicant has done so already, or
        (ii) the court otherwise directs; and
    (b) unless the applicant has done so already, inform the court if the applicant intends to appeal should the court refuse the order.

*[Note. See section 77 of the Coroners and Justice Act 2009.]*

**R47.49**    **Application to discharge an investigation anonymity order**

**47.49** (1) This rule applies where one of the following wants a magistrates' court to discharge an investigation anonymity order—
    (a) an applicant; or
    (b) the person specified in the order.
  (2) That applicant or the specified person must—
    (a) apply in writing as soon as practicable after becoming aware of the grounds for doing so;
    (b) serve the application on—
        (i) the court officer, and as applicable
        (ii) the applicant for the order, and
        (iii) the specified person;
    (c) explain—
        (i) what material circumstances have changed since the order was made, or since any previous application was made to discharge it, and
        (ii) why it is appropriate for the order to be discharged; and
    (d) attach—
        (i) a copy of the order, and
        (ii) any material on which the applicant relies.
  (3) A party must inform the court if that party intends to appeal should the court discharge the order.

*[Note. See section 80 of the Coroners and Justice Act 2009.]*

**R47.50**    **Appeal**

**47.50** (1) This rule applies where one of the following ('the appellant') wants to appeal to the Crown Court—
    (a) the applicant for an investigation anonymity order, where a magistrates' court has refused to make the order; or
    (b) a party to an application to discharge such an order, where a magistrates' court has decided that application.
  (2) The appellant must—
    (a) serve on the Crown Court officer a copy of the application to the magistrates' court; and
    (b) where the appeal concerns a discharge decision, notify each other party,
  not more than 15 business days after the decision against which the appellant wants to appeal.

---

[117] 2009 c. 25.

(3)  The Crown Court must hear the appeal without justices of the peace.

*[Note. See sections 79 and 80(6) of the Coroners and Justice Act 2009, and section 74 of the Senior Courts Act 1981[118].]*

### Section 7:  investigation approval orders under the Regulation of Investigatory Powers Act 2000

When this Section applies                                                                                          **R47.51**

47.51 This Section applies where a justice of the peace can make an order approving—

    (a)  the grant or renewal of an authorisation, or the giving or renewal of a notice, under section 23A of the Regulation of Investigatory Powers Act 2000[119]; and

    (b)  the grant or renewal of an authorisation under section 32A of the 2000 Act[120].

*[Note. Under the Regulation of Investigatory Powers Act 2000, an order may be made approving a local authority officer's authorisation for the obtaining of information about the use of postal or telecommunications services, or for the use of surveillance or of a 'covert human intelligence source'.]*

Exercise of court's powers                                                                                          **R47.52**

47.52 (1)  Rule 47.5 (Investigation orders; Exercise of court's powers) applies, subject to sections 23B(2) and 32B(2) of the Regulation of Investigatory Powers Act 2000[121].

    (2)  Where a magistrates' court refuses to approve the grant, giving or renewal of an authorisation or notice, the court must not exercise its power to quash that authorisation or notice unless the applicant has had at least 2 business days from the date of the refusal in which to make representations.

*[Note. Under sections 23B(2) and 32B(2) of the Regulation of Investigatory Powers Act 2000, the applicant is not required to give notice of an application to any person to whom the authorisation or notice relates, or to such a person's legal representatives. See also sections 23B(3) and 32B(3) of the 2000 Act.]*

Application for approval for authorisation or notice                                                                 **R47.53**

47.53 (1)  This rule applies where an applicant wants a magistrates' court to make an order approving—

    (a)  under sections 23A and 23B of the Regulation of Investigatory Powers Act 2000[122]—

      (i)  an authorisation to obtain or disclose communications data, under section 22(3) of the 2000 Act[123], or

      (ii)  a notice that requires a postal or telecommunications operator if need be to obtain, and in any case to disclose, communications data, under section 22(4) of the 2000 Act; or

    (b)  under sections 32A and 32B of the Regulation of Investigatory Powers Act 2000[124], an authorisation for—

      (i)  the carrying out of directed surveillance, under section 28 of the 2000 Act, or

      (ii)  the conduct or use of a covert human intelligence source, under section 29 of the 2000 Act[125].

    (2)  The applicant must—

    (a)  apply in writing and serve the application on the court officer;

    (b)  attach the authorisation or notice which the applicant wants the court to approve;

    (c)  attach such other material (if any) on which the applicant relies to satisfy the court—

      (i)  as required by section 23A(3) and (4) of the 2000 Act, in relation to communications data,

      (ii)  as required by section 32A(3) and (4) of the 2000 Act, in relation to directed surveillance, or

      (iii)  as required by section 32A(5) and (6), and, if relevant, section 43(6A), of the 2000 Act[126], in relation to a covert human intelligence source; and

---

[118] 1981 c. 54; section 74 was amended by sections 79 and 106 of, and Table (4) of Part V of Schedule 15 to, the Access to Justice Act 1999 (c. 22), article 3 of, and paragraphs 11 and 12 of the Schedule to S.I. 2004/2035 and section 15 of, and paragraphs 114 and 133 of Schedule 4 to, the Constitutional Reform Act 2005 (c. 4). The Act's title was amended by section 59(5) of, and paragraph 1 of Schedule 11 to, the Constitutional Reform Act 2005 (c. 4).

[119] 2000 c. 23; section 23A was inserted by section 37 of the Protection of Freedoms Act 2012 (c. 9).

[120] 2000 c. 23; section 32A was inserted by section 38 of the Protection of Freedoms Act 2012 (c. 9).

[121] 2000 c. 23; section 23B was inserted by section 37 and section 32B by section 38 of the Protection of Freedoms Act 2012 (c. 9).

[122] 2000 c. 23; sections 23A and 23B were inserted by section 37 of the Protection of Freedoms Act 2012 (c. 9).

[123] 2000 c. 23; section 22 was amended by section 112 of, and paragraphs 12 and 13 of Schedule 7 to, the Policing and Crime Act 2009 (c. 26).

[124] 2000 c. 23; sections 32A and 32B were inserted by section 38 of the Protection of Freedoms Act 2012 (c. 9).

[125] 2000 c. 23; section 29 was amended by section 8 of the Policing and Crime Act 2009 (c. 26).

[126] 2000 c. 23; section 43(6A) was inserted by section 38 of the Protection of Freedoms Act 2012 (c. 9).

(d) propose the terms of the order.

*[Note. See also rule 47.5, under which the court may—*

*(a) exercise its powers in the parties' absence; and*

*(b) consider an application made orally.*

*Under section 23A(3) to (5) of the Regulation of Investigatory Powers Act 2000, on an application for an order approving an authorisation or notice concerning communications data (as defined in section 21 of the Act[127]), the court must be satisfied that—*

*(a) the person who granted or renewed the authorisation, or who gave or renewed the notice, was entitled to do so;*

*(b) the grant, giving or renewal met any prescribed restrictions or conditions;*

*(c) at the time the authorisation or notice was granted, given or renewed, as the case may be, there were reasonable grounds for believing that to obtain or disclose the data described in the authorisation or notice was—*

*(i) necessary, for the purpose of preventing or detecting crime or preventing disorder, and*

*(ii) proportionate to what was sought to be achieved by doing so; and*

*(d) there remain reasonable grounds for believing those things, at the time the court considers the application.*

*The Regulation of Investigatory Powers (Communications Data) Order 2010[128] specifies the persons who are entitled to grant, give or renew an authorisation or notice concerning such data, and for what purpose each may do so.*

*Under section 32A(3) and (4) of the Regulation of Investigatory Powers Act 2000, on an application for an order approving an authorisation concerning directed surveillance (as defined in section 26 of the Act[129]), the court must be satisfied that—*

*(a) the person who granted the authorisation was entitled to do so;*

*(b) the grant met any prescribed restrictions or conditions;*

*(c) at the time the authorisation was granted there were reasonable grounds for believing that the surveillance described in the authorisation was—*

*(i) necessary, for the purpose of preventing or detecting crime or preventing disorder, and*

*(ii) proportionate to what was sought to be achieved by it; and*

*(d) there remain reasonable grounds for believing those things, at the time the court considers the application.*

*Under section 32A(5) and (6) of the Regulation of Investigatory Powers Act 2000, on an application for an order approving an authorisation of the conduct or use of a covert human intelligence source (as defined in section 26 of the Act), the court must be satisfied that—*

*(a) the person who granted the authorisation was entitled to do so;*

*(b) the grant met any prescribed restrictions or conditions;*

*(c) at the time the authorisation was granted there were reasonable grounds for believing that the conduct or use of a covert human intelligence source described in the authorisation was—*

*(i) necessary, for the purpose of preventing or detecting crime or preventing disorder, and*

*(ii) proportionate to what was sought to be achieved by it; and*

*(d) there remain reasonable grounds for believing those things, at the time the court considers the application.*

*Under section 43(6A) of the 2000 Act, on an application to approve the renewal of such an authorisation the court in addition must—*

*(a) be satisfied that, since the grant or latest renewal of the authorisation, a review has been carried out of the use made of the source, of the tasks given to him or her and of the information obtained; and*

*(b) consider the results of that review.*

*The Regulation of Investigatory Powers (Directed Surveillance and Covert Human Intelligence Sources) Order 2010[130] specifies the persons who are entitled to grant an authorisation concerning such surveillance or such a source, and for what purpose each may do so.*

---

[127] 2000 c. 23; section 21 was amended by section 88 of, and paragraphs 5 and 7 of Schedule 12 to, the Serious Crime Act 2007 (c. 27).

[128] S.I. 2010/480.

[129] 2000 c. 23; section 26 was amended by section 406 of, and paragraph 161 of Schedule 17 to, the Communications Act 2003 (c. 21).

[130] S.I. 2010/521.

*Under sections 23B(2) and 32B(2) of the 2000 Act, the applicant is not required to give notice of an application to any person to whom the authorisation or notice relates, or to such a person's legal representatives.]*

### Section 8: orders for access to documents, etc. under the Criminal Appeal Act 1995

**When this Section applies**                                                                         **R47.54**

47.54 This Section applies where the Crown Court can order a person to give the Criminal Cases Review Commission access to a document or other material under section 18A of the Criminal Appeal Act 1995[131].

*[Note. Under section 18A of the Criminal Appeal Act 1995, on an application by the Criminal Cases Review Commission the court may order that the Commission be given access to a document or material in a person's possession or control if the court thinks that that document or material may assist the Commission in the exercise of any of their functions.]*

**Exercise of court's powers**                                                                        **R47.55**

47.55 (1) Subject to paragraphs (2), (3) and (4), the court may determine an application by the Criminal Cases Review Commission for an order—
    (a) at a hearing (which must be in private unless the court otherwise directs), or without a hearing; and
    (b) in the absence of—
        (i) the Commission,
        (ii) the respondent, and
        (iii) any other person affected by the order.
    (2) The court must not determine such an application in the Commission's absence if—
    (a) the Commission asks for a hearing; or
    (b) it appears to the court that the application is so complex or serious as to require the court to hear the Commission.
    (3) The court must not determine such an application in the absence of any respondent or other person affected, unless—
    (a) the absentee has had at least 2 business days in which to make representations; or
    (b) the court is satisfied that—
        (i) the Commission cannot identify or contact the absentee,
        (ii) it would prejudice the exercise of the Commission's functions to adjourn or postpone the application so as to allow the absentee to attend, or
        (iii) the absentee has waived the opportunity to attend.
    (4) The court must not determine such an application in the absence of any respondent who, if the order sought by the Commission were made, would be required to produce or give access to journalistic material, unless that respondent has waived the opportunity to attend.
    (5) The court officer must arrange for the court to hear such an application no sooner than 2 business days after it was served, unless—
    (a) the court directs that no hearing need be arranged; or
    (b) the court gives other directions for the hearing.
    (6) The court must not determine an application unless satisfied that sufficient time has been allowed for it.
    (7) If the court so directs, the parties to an application may attend a hearing by live link or telephone.
    (8) The court must not make an order unless an officer of the Commission states, in writing or orally, that to the best of that officer's knowledge and belief—
    (a) the application discloses all the information that is material to what the court must decide; and
    (b) the content of the application is true.
    (9) Where the statement required by paragraph (8) is made orally—
    (a) the statement must be on oath or affirmation, unless the court otherwise directs; and
    (b) the court must arrange for a record of the making of the statement.
    (10) The court may shorten or extend (even after it has expired) a time limit under this Section.

**Application for an order for access**                                                                **R47.56**

47.56 (1) Where the Criminal Cases Review Commission wants the court to make an order for access to a document or other material, the Commission must—
    (a) apply in writing and serve the application on the court officer;
    (b) give the court an estimate of how long the court should allow—
        (i) to read the application and prepare for any hearing, and

---

[131] 1995 c. 35; section 18A was inserted by section 1 of the Criminal Cases Review Commission (Information) Act 2016 (c. 17).

(ii)   for any hearing of the application;

(c)   attach a draft order in the terms proposed by the Commission; and

(d)   serve the application and draft order on the respondent.

(2)   The application must—

    (a)   identify the respondent;

    (b)   describe the document, or documents, or other material sought;

    (c)   explain the reasons for thinking that—

        (i)   what is sought is in the respondent's possession or control, and

        (ii)   access to what is sought may assist the Commission in the exercise of any of their functions; and

    (d)   explain the Commission's proposals for—

        (i)   the manner in which the respondent should give access, and

        (ii)   the period within which the order should take effect.

(3)   The Commission must serve any order made on the respondent.

*[Note. Under section 18A(3) of the Criminal Appeal Act 1995, the court may give directions for the manner in which access to a document or other material must be given, and may direct that the Commission must be allowed to take away such a document or material, or to make copies. Under section 18A(4) of the Act, the court may direct that the respondent must not destroy, damage or alter a document or other material before the direction is withdrawn by the court.]*

**R47.57**   **Application containing information withheld from a respondent or other person**

**47.57** (1)   This rule applies where—

    (a)   the Criminal Cases Review Commission serves an application under rule 47.56 (Application for an order for access); and

    (b)   the application includes information that the Commission thinks ought not be revealed to a recipient.

(2)   The Commission must—

    (a)   omit that information from the part of the application that is served on that recipient;

    (b)   mark the other part, to show that it is only for the court; and

    (c)   in that other part, explain why the Commission has withheld it from that recipient.

(3)   A hearing of an application to which this rule applies may take place, wholly or in part, in the absence of that recipient and any other person.

(4)   At a hearing of an application to which this rule applies—

    (a)   the general rule is that the court must consider, in the following sequence—

        (i)   representations first by the Commission and then by the other parties, in the presence of them all, and then

        (ii)   further representations by the Commission, in the others' absence; but

    (b)   the court may direct other arrangements for the hearing.

**R47.58**   **Application to punish for contempt of court**

**47.58** (1)   This rule applies where a person is accused of disobeying an order for access made under section 18A of the Criminal Appeal Act 1995.

(2)   An applicant who wants the court to exercise its power to punish that person for contempt of court must comply with the rules in Part 48 (Contempt of court).

*[Note. The Crown Court has power to punish for contempt of court a person who disobeys its order. See section 45 of the Senior Courts Act 1981[132].]*

### Section 9: order for the extension of a moratorium period under the Proceeds of Crime Act 2002

**R47.59**   **When this Section applies**

**47.59** (1)   This Section applies where the Crown Court can extend a moratorium period under section 336A of the Proceeds of Crime Act 2002[133].

(2)   In this Section, 'respondent' means, as well as a person within the meaning of rule 47.2(c), an 'interested person' within the meaning of section 336D of the 2002 Act[134].

---

[132]   1981 c. 54. The Act's title was amended by section 59(5) of, and paragraph 1 of Schedule 11 to, the Constitutional Reform Act 2005 (c. 4).

[133]   2002 c. 29; section 336A was inserted by section 10 of the Criminal Finances Act 2017 (c. 22).

[134]   2002 c. 29; section 336D was inserted by section 10 of the Criminal Finances Act 2017 (c. 22).

*[Note. Under section 336A of the Proceeds of Crime Act 2002, the Crown Court may extend a moratorium period under section 335 or section 336 of the Act[135] by up to 31 days beginning with the day after the day on which the period otherwise would end.*

*Under sections 335 and 336 of the 2002 Act, a moratorium period is the period of 31 days starting with the day on which consent to the doing of an act is refused by a constable, a customs officer or the Director General of the National Crime Agency. The act to which those sections refer is one that would be an offence under section 327, 328 or 329 of the 2002 Act (money laundering offences) but for the making of a disclosure within the meaning of section 338 to such an officer in relation to that act. On the expiry of the moratorium period the person who made the disclosure will be treated as having the relevant officer's consent to the doing of the act and so will commit no offence by doing it.*

*The Crown Court may extend a moratorium period more than once, but the total period of extension may not exceed 186 days beginning with the day after the day on which the first 31 day period ended.*

*Under section 336D(3) of the 2002 Act, 'interested person' means the person who made the disclosure and any other person who appears to the person making an application under rule 47.61 to have an interest in the property that is the subject of that disclosure.]*

## Exercise of court's powers                                      R47.60

**47.60** (1) The court may determine an application to which rule 47.61 (Application for extension of moratorium period) applies—

    (a) at a hearing (which must be in private unless the court otherwise directs), or without a hearing; and

    (b) in the absence of—

        (i) the applicant, and

        (ii) a respondent.

(2) The court must not determine such an application in the applicant's absence if the applicant asks for a hearing.

(3) The court must not determine such an application in the absence of a respondent unless—

    (a) the absentee has had at least 2 business days in which to make representations; or

    (b) the court is satisfied that—

        (i) the applicant cannot identify or contact the absentee,

        (ii) it would prejudice the investigation if the absentee were present,

        (iii) it would prejudice the investigation to adjourn or postpone the application so as to allow the absentee to attend, or

        (iv) the absentee has waived the opportunity to attend.

(4) The court officer must arrange for the court to hear such an application no sooner than 2 business days after notice of the application was served, unless—

    (a) the court directs that no hearing need be arranged; or

    (b) the court gives other directions for the hearing.

(5) If the court so directs, the parties to an application may attend a hearing by live link or telephone.

(6) The court must not extend a moratorium period unless the applicant states, in writing or orally, that to the best of the applicant's knowledge and belief—

    (a) the application discloses all the information that is material to what the court must decide; and

    (b) the content of the application is true.

(7) Where the statement required by paragraph (6) is made orally—

    (a) the statement must be on oath or affirmation, unless the court otherwise directs; and

    (b) the court must arrange for a record of the making of the statement.

(8) The court may—

    (a) shorten or extend (even after it has expired) a time limit imposed by this rule;

    (b) dispense with a requirement for service under this Section (even after service was required); and

    (c) consider an application made orally instead of in writing.

---

[135] 2002 c. 29; section 335 was amended by section 10 of the Criminal Finances Act 2017 (c. 22). Section 336 was amended by paragraphs 168 and 173 of Schedule 4 to the Serious Organised Crime and Police Act 2005 (c. 15), paragraphs 108 and 133 of Schedule 8 to the Crime and Courts Act 2013 (c .22) and section 10 of the Criminal Finances Act 2017 (c. 22).

**R47.61**    **Application for extension of moratorium period**

**47.61** (1) This rule applies where an applicant wants the court to extend a moratorium period.

     (2) The applicant must—

         (a) apply in writing before the date on which the moratorium period otherwise would end;

         (b) demonstrate that the applicant is entitled to apply as a senior officer within the meaning of section 336D of the Proceeds of Crime Act 2002;

         (c) serve the application on the court officer;

         (d) serve notice on each respondent that an application has been made; and

         (e) serve the application on each respondent to such extent, if any, as the court directs.

     (3) The application must specify—

         (a) the disclosure in respect of which the application is made;

         (b) the date on which the moratorium period began;

         (c) the date and period of any previous extension of that period; and

         (d) the date on which that period is due to end.

     (4) The application must—

         (a) describe the investigation being carried out in relation to that disclosure; and

         (b) explain the grounds for believing that—

             (i) the investigation is being conducted diligently and expeditiously,

             (ii) further time is needed for conducting the investigation, and

             (iii) it would be reasonable in all the circumstances for the moratorium period to be extended.

     (5) A respondent who objects to the application must—

         (a) serve notice of the objection on—

             (i) the court officer, and

             (ii) the applicant,

         not more than 2 business days after service of notice of the application; and

         (b) in that notice explain the grounds of the objection.

     (6) The applicant must serve any order made on each respondent.

*[Note. The Practice Direction sets out forms of application and notice of objection for use in connection with this rule.*

*Under section 336D of the Proceeds of Crime Act 2002, 'senior officer' means the Director General of the National Crime Agency or an authorised officer of that Agency, a police officer of at least the rank of inspector, an officer of HM Revenue and Customs or an immigration officer of equivalent rank, a senior member of the Financial Conduct Authority, the Director of the Serious Fraud Office or an authorised member of that Office, or an accredited financial investigator.*

*The time limit for making an application is prescribed by section 336A(3) of the Proceeds of Crime Act 2002. It may be neither extended nor shortened. Under section 336B(2) of the Act[136] the court must determine the application as soon as reasonably practicable. Under section 336C[137], where an application is made and not determined before the moratorium period otherwise would expire then that period is extended until (i) the application is determined, or (ii) the expiry of 31 days beginning with the day after the day on which that period expired, whichever occurs first.]*

**R47.62**    **Application containing information withheld from a respondent**

**47.62** (1) This rule applies where an application to extend a moratorium period includes an application to withhold information from a respondent.

     (2) The applicant must—

         (a) omit that information from any part of the application that is served on the respondent;

         (b) mark the other part to show that, unless the court otherwise directs, it is only for the court; and

         (c) in that other part, explain the grounds for believing that the disclosure of that information would have one or more of the following results—

             (i) evidence of an offence would be interfered with or harmed,

             (ii) the gathering of information about the possible commission of an offence would be interfered with,

---

[136] 2002 c. 29; section 336B was inserted by section 10 of the Criminal Finances Act 2017 (c. 22).
[137] 2002 c. 29; section 336C was inserted by section 10 of the Criminal Finances Act 2017 (c. 22).

       (iii)  a person would be interfered with or physically injured,

       (iv)  the recovery of property under this Act would be hindered, or

       (v)  national security would be put at risk.

(3)  At any hearing of an application to which this rule applies—

    (a)  the court must first determine the application to withhold information, in the respondent's absence and that of any legal representative of the respondent; and

    (b)  if the court allows the application to withhold information, then in the following sequence—

       (i)  the court must consider representations first by the applicant and then by the respondent, in the presence of both, and

       (ii)  the court may consider further representations by the applicant in the respondent's absence and that of any legal representative of the respondent.

(4)  If the court refuses an application to withhold information from the respondent, the applicant may withdraw the application to extend the moratorium period.

*[Note. See section 336B of the Proceeds of Crime Act 2002.]*

## Section 10: orders for access to electronic data under the Crime (Overseas Production Orders) Act 2019

**When this Section applies**                                            **R47.63**

**47.63** (1)  This Section applies where the Crown Court can make an overseas production order under section 1 of the Crime (Overseas Production Orders) Act 2019.[138]

    (2)  In this Section, a reference to a person affected by such an order includes a person by whom or on whose behalf there is stored any journalistic data specified or described in the application for that order.

*[Note. Under section 1 of the Crime (Overseas Production Orders) Act 2019, on an application by an appropriate officer (defined by section 2 of the Act) a Crown Court judge may order a person (in these rules, 'the respondent') to produce or give access to electronic data (by section 3, 'data stored electronically'), other than excepted such data, where, among other criteria listed in sections 1 and 4 of the Act, the judge is satisfied that—*

    *(a)  there are reasonable grounds for believing that—*

       *(i)  an indictable offence has been committed and proceedings in respect of the offence have been instituted or the offence is being investigated, or*

       *(ii)  the order is sought for the purposes of a terrorist investigation within the meaning of the Terrorism Act 2000; and*

    *(b)  there are reasonable grounds for believing that the respondent operates in, or is based in, a country or territory outside the United Kingdom which is a party to, or which participates in, a designated international co-operation arrangement.*

*Section 3 of the 2019 Act defines 'excepted electronic data' as data stored electronically that is (a) an item subject to legal privilege, or (b) a personal record within the meaning of section 3(7) (medical, etc. records) which (i) was created in circumstances giving rise to a continuing obligation of confidence to an individual who can be identified from that record, or (ii) is held subject to a restriction on disclosure, or an obligation of secrecy, contained in an enactment. Where the respondent against whom an overseas production order is sought is a telecommunications operator, within the meaning of the Investigatory Powers Act 2016, 'excepted electronic data' also includes communications data within the meaning of the 2016 Act. Where the investigation in aid of which an overseas production order is sought is a terrorist investigation other than a terrorist financing investigation within the meaning of the Terrorism Act 2000, 'excepted electronic data' does not include a confidential personal record.*

*Section 12 of the Act defines 'journalistic data' as electronic data that (a) was created or acquired for the purposes of journalism and (b) is stored by or on behalf of a person who created or acquired it for those purposes.]*

**Exercise of court's powers**                                           **R47.64**

**47.64** (1)  Subject to paragraphs (2), (3) and (4), the court may determine an application under rule 47.68 for an overseas production order, or an application under rule 47.69 to vary or revoke an order—

    (a)  at a hearing (which must be in private unless the court otherwise directs), or without a hearing; and

    (b)  in the absence of—

---

[138]  2019 c. 5.

      (i)  the applicant,

      (ii)  the respondent, and

      (iii)  any other person affected by the order.

(2)  The court must not determine such an application in the applicant's absence if—

    (a)  the applicant asks for a hearing; or

    (b)  it appears to the court that—

      (i)  the proposed order may require the production of excepted electronic data, within the meaning of section 3 of the Crime (Overseas Production Orders) Act 2019, or

      (ii)  for any other reason the application is so complex or serious as to require the court to hear the applicant.

(3)  The court must not determine such an application in the absence of any respondent or other person affected unless—

    (a)  the absentee has had at least 2 business days in which to make representations; or

    (b)  the court is satisfied that—

      (i)  the applicant cannot identify or contact the absentee,

      (ii)  it would prejudice the investigation if the absentee were present,

      (iii)  where journalistic data is sought, it would prejudice the investigation of another indictable offence or another terrorist investigation if the absentee were present,

      (iv)  it would prejudice the investigation to adjourn or postpone the application so as to allow the absentee to attend, or

      (v)  the absentee has waived the opportunity to attend.

(4)  The court must not determine such an application in the absence of any respondent who, if the order sought by the applicant were made, would be required to produce or give access to journalistic data, unless that respondent has waived the opportunity to attend.

(5)  The court officer must arrange for the court to hear such an application no sooner than 2 business days after notice of the application was served, unless—

    (a)  the court directs that no hearing need be arranged; or

    (b)  the court gives other directions for the hearing.

(6)  The court must not determine an application unless satisfied that sufficient time has been allowed for it.

(7)  If the court so directs, the parties to an application may attend a hearing by live link or telephone.

(8)  The court must not make, vary or revoke an order unless the applicant states, in writing or orally, that to the best of the applicant's knowledge and belief—

    (a)  the application discloses all the information that is material to what the court must decide; and

    (b)  the content of the application is true.

(9)  Where the statement required by paragraph (8) is made orally—

    (a)  the statement must be on oath or affirmation, unless the court otherwise directs; and

    (b)  the court must arrange for a record of the making of the statement.

(10)  The court may—

    (a)  shorten or extend (even after it has expired) a time limit under this Section;

    (b)  dispense with a requirement for service under this Section (even after service was required); and

    (c)  consider an application made orally instead of in writing.

(11)  A person who wants an extension of time must—

    (a)  apply when serving the application for which it is needed; and

    (b)  explain the delay.

## R47.65  Application for order

47.65 (1)  An applicant who wants the court to make an overseas production order must—

    (a)  apply in writing and serve the application on the court officer;

    (b)  demonstrate that the applicant is entitled to apply;

    (c)  give the court an estimate of how long the court should allow—

      (i)  to read the application and prepare for any hearing, and

      (ii)  for any hearing of the application;

    (d)  attach a draft order in the terms proposed by the applicant;

    (e)  serve notice of the application on the respondent and on any other person affected by the order, unless the court otherwise directs; and

(f) serve the application on the respondent and on any such other person to such extent, if any, as the court directs.

(2) A notice served on the respondent and on any other person affected by the order must—

(a) specify or describe the electronic data in respect of which the application is made; and

(b) identify—

(i) the power that the applicant invites the court to exercise, and

(ii) the conditions for the exercise of that power which the applicant asks the court to find are met.

(3) The application must—

(a) specify the designated international co-operation arrangement by reference to which the application is made;

(b) identify the respondent;

(c) explain the grounds for believing that the respondent operates in, or is based in, a country or territory outside the United Kingdom which is a party to, or participates in, that designated international co-operation arrangement;

(d) specify or describe the electronic data in respect of which the order is sought;

(e) explain the grounds for believing that the electronic data sought does not consist of or include excepted electronic data;

(f) briefly describe the investigation for the purposes of which the electronic data is sought and explain—

(i) the grounds for believing that an indictable offence has been committed which is under investigation or in respect of which proceedings have begun, or

(ii) how the investigation constitutes a terrorist investigation within the meaning of the Terrorism Act 2000;

(g) explain the grounds for believing that the respondent has possession or control of all or part of the electronic data sought;

(h) explain the grounds for believing that the electronic data sought is likely to be of substantial value to the investigation, or to the proceedings (as the case may be), whether by itself or together with other material;

(i) where paragraph (3)(f)(i) applies, explain the grounds for believing that all or part of the electronic data sought is likely to be relevant evidence in respect of the offence concerned;

(j) explain the grounds for believing that it is in the public interest for the respondent to produce or give access to the electronic data sought, having regard to—

(i) the benefit likely to accrue to the investigation, or to the proceedings (as the case may be), if that data is obtained, and

(ii) the circumstances under which the respondent has possession or control of any of that data;

(k) specify—

(i) the person, or the description of person, to whom the applicant wants the court to order that electronic data must be produced or made accessible, and

(ii) the period by the end of which the applicant wants the court to order that that electronic data must be produced or made accessible (which must be a period of 7 days beginning with the day on which the order is served on the respondent, unless the court otherwise directs); and

(l) where the applicant wants the court to include a non-disclosure requirement in the order—

(i) explain why such a requirement would be appropriate, and

(ii) specify or describe when the applicant wants that requirement, if ordered, to expire.

(4) In the event that an overseas production order is made, the applicant must serve the order on the Secretary of State for service on the respondent.

(5) Where notice of the application was served on a respondent, in the event that the application is dismissed or abandoned the applicant must—

(a) promptly so notify that respondent; and

(b) where the application is dismissed, promptly inform that respondent if the court none-theless orders that for a period that respondent must not—

(i) conceal, destroy, alter or dispose of any of the electronic data specified or described in the application, or

(ii) disclose the making of the application or its contents to any person.

*[Note. See sections 1, 2, 4 and 5 of the Crime (Overseas Production Orders) Act 2019.*

*Under section 8 of the 2019 Act, an overseas production order may include a non-disclosure requirement obliging the respondent not to disclose the making of the order or its contents to any person except with the court's permission or with the written permission of the applicant (or an equivalent appropriate officer).*

*Under section 9 of the Act, an overseas production order may be served only by the Secretary of State.*

*Under section 12 of the Act, if there are reasonable grounds for believing that the electronic data specified or described in the application consists of or includes journalistic data then unless the judge otherwise directs notice of the application must be served on (a) the person against whom the overseas production order is sought and (b) if different, the person by whom, or on whose behalf, the journalistic data is stored. The criteria for making such a direction correspond with those listed in rule 47.64(3)(b).*

*Under section 13 of the Act, following service of notice of an application for an overseas production order the respondent must not conceal, destroy, alter or dispose of any of the electronic data specified or described in the application, or disclose the making of the application or its contents to any person, except with the court's permission or with the written permission of the applicant (or an equivalent appropriate officer). Those obligations are superseded if an order is made. If the application is abandoned or dismissed, those obligations cease unless, in the event of dismissal, the court otherwise orders.*

*Section 14 of the Act provides for the means of service of notices and orders.*

*The Practice Direction sets out forms of application, notice and order for use in connection with this rule.]*

**R47.66**     **Application to vary or revoke an order**

47.66 (1)   The orders to which this rule applies are—
    (a)  an overseas production order;
    (b)  an order under section 8(4) of the Crime (Overseas Production Orders) Act 2019 maintaining an unexpired non-disclosure requirement;
    (c)  an order under section 13(3) of the 2019 Act maintaining a duty not to conceal, destroy, alter or dispose of electronic data, and not to disclose the making or content of an application for an overseas production order; and
    (d)  an order under section 13(4)(b) of the Act maintaining a duty not to conceal, destroy, alter or dispose of electronic data.

(2)   This rule applies where one of the following wants the court to vary, to further vary or to revoke an order listed in paragraph (1)—
    (a)  the applicant for that order, or an equivalent appropriate officer;
    (b)  the respondent;
    (c)  another person affected by the order; or
    (d)  the Secretary of State.

(3)   The applicant for the variation or revocation must—
    (a)  apply in writing as soon as practicable after becoming aware of the grounds for doing so;
    (b)  serve the application on—
        (i)   the court officer, and
        (ii)  as applicable, the applicant for the order, the respondent, any other person known to be affected and the Secretary of State; and
    (c)  ask for a hearing, if one is wanted, and explain why it is needed.

(4)   Where the applicant wants the court to vary, or further vary, an overseas production order, the application must—
    (a)  specify or describe the electronic data in respect of which the varied order is sought (which may include electronic data not specified or described in the original order);
    (b)  satisfy or, as the case may be, continue to satisfy, the requirements of rule 47.65(3)(a) and (c) to (i) (which may be done by reference to the original application); and
    (c)  meet the requirements of rule 47.65(3)(j).

(5)   Where the applicant wants the court to revoke an overseas production order, the application must—
    (a)  explain why revocation is appropriate;
    (b)  if the applicant wants the court, despite revocation, to maintain the requirement that for a period the respondent must not conceal, destroy, alter or dispose of any of the electronic data specified or described in the order—
        (i)   explain why it would be appropriate to maintain that requirement, and
        (ii)  specify or describe when the applicant wants that requirement, if maintained, to expire; and

    (c)   if the order includes an unexpired non-disclosure requirement that the applicant wants the court, despite revocation, to maintain—
        (i)   explain why it would be appropriate to maintain that requirement, and
        (ii)  specify or describe when the applicant wants that requirement, if maintained, to expire.

(6)   Where the applicant wants the court to vary, to further vary or to revoke an order under section 8(4), section 13(3) or section 13(4)(b) of the 2019 Act the application must—
    (a)   explain—
        (i)   what material circumstances have changed since the order was made, and
        (ii)  why the order should be varied or revoked, as the case may be, as a result; and
    (b)   if applicable, specify the variation proposed.

*[Note. See sections 7, 11(1) and 18(2) of the Crime (Overseas Production Orders) Act 2019.*

*Under section 8(4) of the 2019 Act, where the court revokes an overseas production order which includes an unexpired non-disclosure requirement the court may order that the respondent is to remain subject to that requirement for a defined period.*

*Under section 13(3) of the Act, where the court dismisses an application for an overseas production order then the duty under section 13(1)(a) not to conceal, destroy, alter or dispose of any of the electronic data specified or described in the application, and under section 13(1)(b) not to disclose the making of the application or its contents to any person except with the court's permission or with the written permission of the applicant (or an equivalent appropriate officer), ceases to apply unless the court orders that a person served with notice of the application is to remain subject to that duty for a defined period.*

*Under section 13(4)(b) of the Act, where the court revokes an overseas production order before it is served then the duty under section 13(1)(a) not to conceal, destroy, alter or dispose of any of the electronic data specified or described in the application for the order ceases to apply unless the court orders that a person served with notice of the application is to remain subject to that duty for a defined period.]*

### Application containing information withheld from a respondent or other person      R47.67

47.67  (1)   This rule applies where an application under rule 47.65 or 47.66 includes information that the applicant thinks ought to be revealed only to the court.
      (2)   The application must—
         (a)   identify that information; and
         (b)   explain why that information ought not to be served on the respondent or another person.
      (3)   At a hearing of an application to which this rule applies—
         (a)   the general rule is that the court must consider, in the following sequence—
            (i)   representations first by the applicant and then by the respondent and any other person, in the presence of them all, and then
            (ii)  further representations by the applicant, in the others' absence; but
         (b)   the court may direct other arrangements for the hearing.

### Application to punish for contempt of court      R47.68

47.68  (1)   This rule applies where a person is accused of disobeying an order made by the court under the Crime (Overseas Production Orders) Act 2019.
      (2)   An applicant who wants the court to exercise its power to punish that person for contempt of court must comply with the rules in Part 48 (Contempt of court).

*[Note. The Crown Court has power to punish for contempt of court a person who disobeys its order: see section 45 of the Senior Courts Act 1981[139]. Under section 11(4) of the Crime (Overseas Production Orders) Act 2019, an order made by a judge under the Act has effect as if it were an order of the Crown Court.]*

---

[139] 1981 c. 54. The Act's title was amended by section 59(5) of, and paragraph 1 of Schedule 11 to, the Constitutional Reform Act 2005 (c. 4).

Criminal Procedure Rules and Criminal Practice Directions

**CPD.47A**    **CPD XI Other Proceedings 47A: Investigation Orders and Warrants**

47A.1    Powers of entry, search and seizure, and powers to obtain banking and other confidential information, are among the most intrusive that investigators can exercise. Every application must be carefully scrutinised with close attention paid to what the relevant statutory provision requires of the applicant and to what it permits. CrimPR Part 47 must be followed, and the prescribed forms (retaining the Notes for Guidance section) must be used. These are designed to prompt applicants, and the courts, to deal with all of the relevant criteria.

47A.2    The issuing of a warrant or the making of such an order is never to be treated as a formality and it is therefore essential that the judge or magistrate considering the application is given, and must take, sufficient time for the purpose. The prescribed forms require the applicant to provide a time estimate, and listing officers and justices' legal advisers should take account of these.

47A.3    Applicants for orders and warrants owe the court duties of candour and truthfulness. On any application made without notice to the respondent, and so on all applications for search warrants, the duty of frank and complete disclosure is especially onerous. The applicant must draw the court's attention to any information that is unfavourable to the application. The existence of unfavourable information will not necessarily lead to the application being refused; it will be a matter for the court what weight to place on each piece of information. As Hughes LJ made clear in *Re Stanford International Limited*[1] 'In effect a prosecutor seeking an *ex parte* order must put on his defence hat and ask himself what, if he was representing the defendant or a third party with a relevant interest, he would be saying to the judge, and, having answered that question, that is what he must tell the judge'. This is, as Aitkins LJ recognised, 'a heavy burden but a vital safeguard. Full details must be given[2].'

47A.4    Where an applicant supplements an application with additional oral or written information, on questioning by the court or otherwise, it is essential that the court keeps an adequate record. What is needed will depend upon the circumstances. The Rules require that a record of the 'gist' be retained. The purpose of such a record is to allow the sufficiency of the court's reasons for its decision subsequently to be assessed. The gravity of such decisions requires that their exercise should be susceptible to scrutiny and to explanation by reference to all of the information that was taken into account.

47A.5    The forms that accompany CrimPR Part 47 provide for the most frequently encountered applications. The included Notes for Guidance summarise for the applicant and the court the relevant criteria for making and considering an application. However, there are some hundreds of powers of entry, search and seizure, supplied by a corresponding number of legislative provisions. In any criminal matter, if there is no form designed for the particular warrant or order sought, the forms should still be used, as far as is practicable, and adapted as necessary. The applicant should pay particular attention to the specific legislative requirements for the granting of such an application to ensure that the court has all of the necessary information, and, if the court might be unfamiliar with the legislation, should provide a copy of the relevant provisions. Applicants must comply with the duties of candour and truthfulness, and include in their application the declarations required by the Rules and must make disclosure of any unfavourable information to the court.

**CPD.47B**    **CPD XI Other Proceedings 47B: Investigation Orders and Warrants in the Crown Court**

47B.1    This section covers applications made under:
  (i)    Schedule 1 Police and Criminal Evidence Act 1984 (PACE);
  (ii)   Section 2 Criminal Justice Act 1987;
  (iii)  Drug Trafficking Act 1994;
  (iv)   Part 8 of the Proceeds of Crime Act 2002;
  (v)    Section 5 Coroners and Justice Act 2009;
  (vi)   Terrorism Act 2000.

It does NOT cover applications under the Extradition Act 2003.

**Crown Court Centres**

47B.2    Investigators must give careful consideration to which Crown Court centre is most appropriate to hear the application. In all cases, the application must explain the rationale for choosing the particular court centre. Relevant considerations will usually be:

---

[1] [2010] EWCA Civ 137 at para 159.
[2] *R (On the Application of S, F and L) v Chief Constable of the British Transport Police and Southwark Crown Court* [2013] EWHC 2189 (Admin) at [45 (d)].

*[Note. By reason of sections 15 and 45 of the Senior Courts Act 1981[1], the Court of Appeal and the Crown Court each has an inherent power to suspend imprisonment for contempt of court, on conditions, or for a period, or both.]*

**Application to discharge an order for imprisonment**    **R48.4**

**48.4** (1)  This rule applies where the court can discharge an order for a respondent's imprisonment for contempt of court.

(2)  A respondent who wants the court to discharge such an order must—

(a)  apply in writing, unless the court otherwise directs, and serve any written application on—

(i)  the court officer, and

(ii)  any applicant under rule 48.9 on whose application the respondent was imprisoned;

(b)  in the application—

(i)  explain why it is appropriate for the order for imprisonment to be discharged, and

(ii)  give details of any appeal, and its outcome; and

(c)  ask for a hearing, if the respondent wants one.

*[Note. By reason of sections 15 and 45 of the Senior Courts Act 1981, the Court of Appeal and the Crown Court each has an inherent power to discharge an order for a respondent's imprisonment for contempt of court in failing to comply with a court order.*

*Under section 97(4) of the Magistrates' Courts Act 1980[2], a magistrates' court can discharge an order for imprisonment if the respondent gives evidence.*

*Under section 12(4) of the Contempt of Court Act 1981[3], a magistrates' court can discharge an order for imprisonment made under that section.]*

### Contempt of court by obstruction, disruption, etc.

**Initial procedure on obstruction, disruption etc.**    **R48.5**

**48.5** (1)  This rule applies where the court observes, or someone reports to the court—

(a)  in the Court of Appeal or the Crown Court, obstructive, disruptive, insulting or intimidating conduct, in the courtroom or in its vicinity, or otherwise immediately affecting the proceedings;

(b)  in the Crown Court, a contravention of—

(i)  section 3 of the Criminal Procedure (Attendance of Witnesses) Act 1965[4] (disobeying a witness summons); or

(ii)  section 20 of the Juries Act 1974[5] (disobeying a jury summons);

(c)  in a magistrates' court, a contravention of—

(i)  section 97(4) of the Magistrates' Courts Act 1980 (refusing to give evidence), or

(ii)  section 12 of the Contempt of Court Act 1981[6] (insulting or interrupting the court, etc.);

(d)  a contravention of section 9 of the Contempt of Court Act 1981[7] (without the court's permission, recording the proceedings, etc.); or

(e)  any other conduct with which the court can deal as, or as if it were, a criminal contempt of court, except failure to surrender to bail under section 6 of the Bail Act 1976[8].

---

[1]  1981 c. 54.

[2]  1980 c. 43; section 97(4) was amended by sections 13 and 14 of, and paragraph 7 of Schedule 2 to, the Contempt of Court Act 1981 (c. 47) and section 17 of, and paragraph 6 of Schedule 3 and Part I of Schedule 4 to, the Criminal Justice Act 1991 (c. 53).

[3]  1981 c. 49.

[4]  1965 c. 69; section 3 was amended by section 56 of, and Part IV of Schedule 11 to, the Courts Act 1971 (c. 23) and sections 65 and 66 of the Criminal Procedure and Investigations Act 1996 (c. 25).

[5]  1974 c. 23; section 20 was amended by sections 37, 38 and 46 of the Criminal Justice Act 1982 (c. 48), section 170(1) of, and paragraph 46 of Schedule 15 to, the Criminal Justice Act 1988 (c. 33), paragraph 28 of Schedule 10 to, the Criminal Justice and Public Order Act 1994 (c. 33) and paragraphs 1 and 14 of Schedule 33 to, the Criminal Justice Act 2003 (c. 44).

[6]  1981 c. 49; section 12 was amended by section 78 of, and Schedule 16 to, the Criminal Justice Act 1982 (c. 48), section 17(3) of, and Part I of Schedule 4 to, the Criminal Justice Act 1991 (c. 53); section 65(3) and (4) of, and paragraph 6(4) of Schedule 3 to, the Criminal Justice Act 1993 (c. 36) and section 165 of, and paragraph 83 of Schedule 9 to, the Powers of Criminal Courts (Sentencing) Act 2000 (c. 6).

[7]  1981 c. 49.

[8]  1976 c. 63; section 6 was amended by sections 37, 38 and 46 of the Criminal Justice Act 1982 (c. 48), section 109 of, and paragraph 184 of Schedule 8 to, the Courts Act 2003 (c. 39) and section 15 of, and paragraph 48(1), (4) of Schedule 3 to, the Criminal Justice Act 2003 (c. 44).

(2) Unless the respondent's behaviour makes it impracticable to do so, the court must—
- (a) explain, in terms the respondent can understand (with help, if necessary)—
  - (i) the conduct that is in question,
  - (ii) that the court can impose imprisonment, or a fine, or both, for such conduct,
  - (iii) (where relevant) that the court has power to order the respondent's immediate temporary detention, if in the court's opinion that is required,
  - (iv) that the respondent may explain the conduct,
  - (v) that the respondent may apologise, if he or she so wishes, and that this may persuade the court to take no further action, and
  - (vi) that the respondent may take legal advice; and
- (b) allow the respondent a reasonable opportunity to reflect, take advice, explain and, if he or she so wishes, apologise.

(3) The court may then—
- (a) take no further action in respect of that conduct;
- (b) enquire into the conduct there and then; or
- (c) postpone that enquiry (if a magistrates' court, only until later the same day).

*[Note. The conduct to which this rule applies is sometimes described as 'criminal' contempt of court.*

*By reason of sections 15 and 45 of the Senior Courts Act 1981, the Court of Appeal and the Crown Court each has an inherent power to imprison (for a maximum of 2 years), or fine (to an unlimited amount), or both, a respondent for contempt of court for the conduct listed in paragraph (1)(a), (b), (d) or (e). See also section 14 of the Contempt of Court Act 1981[9].*

*Under section 97(4) of the Magistrates' Courts Act 1980, and under sections 12 and 14 of the Contempt of Court Act 1981, a magistrates' court can imprison (for a maximum of 1 month), or fine (to a maximum of £2,500), or both, a respondent who contravenes a provision listed in paragraph (1)(c) or (d). Section 12(1) of the 1981 Act allows the court to deal with any person who—*

- *(a) wilfully insults the justice or justices, any witness before or officer of the court or any solicitor or counsel having business in the court, during his or their sitting or attendance in court or in going to or returning from the court; or*
- *(b) wilfully interrupts the proceedings of the court or otherwise misbehaves in court.*

*Under section 89 of the Powers of Criminal Courts (Sentencing) Act 2000[10], no respondent who is under 21 may be imprisoned for contempt of court. Under section 108 of that Act[11], a respondent who is at least 18 but under 21 may be detained if the court is of the opinion that no other method of dealing with him or her is appropriate. Under section 14(2A) of the Contempt of Court Act 1981[12], a respondent who is under 17 may not be ordered to attend an attendance centre.*

---

[9] 1981 c. 49; section 14 was amended by sections 77 and 78 of, and paragraph 60 of Schedule 14 and Schedule 16 to, the Criminal Justice Act 1982 (c. 48), section 65 of, and paragraphs 59 and 60 of Schedule 3 to, the Mental Health (Amendment) Act 1982 (c. 51), section 148 of, and paragraph 57 of Schedule 4 to, the Mental Health Act 1983 (c. 20), section 1 of the County Courts (Penalties for Contempt) Act 1983 (c. 45), section 17 of, and Parts 1 and V of Schedule 4 to, the Criminal Justice Act 1991 (c. 53), section 65 of, and paragraph 6 of Schedule 3 to, the Criminal Justice Act 1993 (c. 36), section 165 of, and paragraph 84 of Schedule 9 to, the Powers of Criminal Courts (Sentencing) Act 2000 (c. 6), section 1 of, and paragraph 19 of Schedule 1 to, the Mental Health Act 2007 (c. 12) and section 17 of, and paragraph 52 of Schedule 9 and paragraph 53 of Schedule 10 to, the Crime and Courts Act 2013 (c. 22). It is further amended by sections 6 and 149 of, and paragraph 25 of Schedule 4 and Part 1 of Schedule 28 to, the Criminal Justice and Immigration Act 2008 (c. 4), with effect from a date to be appointed.

[10] 2000 c. 6; section 89 was amended by paragraph 74 of Schedule 3, and Part 4 of Schedule 37, to the Criminal Justice Act 2003 (c. 44). It is further amended by section 74 of, and paragraphs 160 and 180 of Schedule 7 to, the Criminal Justice and Court Services Act 2000 (c. 43) with effect from a date to be appointed.

[11] 2000 c. 6; section 108 is repealed by sections 74 and 75 of, and paragraphs 160 and 188 of Schedule 7 and Schedule 8 to, the Criminal Justice and Court Services Act 2000 (c. 43), with effect from a date to be appointed.

[12] 1981 c. 49; section 14 was amended by section 65(1) of, and paragraphs 59 and 60 of Schedule 3 to, the Mental Health (Amendment) Act 1982 (c. 51), section 148 of, and paragraph 57 of Schedule 4 to, the Mental Health Act 1983 (c. 20), section 17(3) of, and Parts 1 and V of Schedule 4 to, the Criminal Justice Act 1991 (c. 53), section 65(3) and (4) of, and paragraph 6(5) of Schedule 3 to, the Criminal Justice Act 1993 (c. 36), section 165(1) of, and paragraph 84 of Schedule 9 to, the Powers of Criminal Courts (Sentencing) Act 2000 (c. 6), section 1(4) of, and paragraph 19 of Schedule 1 to, the Mental Health Act 2007 (c. 12) and section 17 of, and paragraph 52 of Schedule 9 and paragraph 53 of Schedule 10 to, the Crime and Courts Act 2013 (c. 22). It is further amended by sections 6(2) and 149 of, and paragraph 25 of Schedule 4 and Part 1 of Schedule 28 to, the Criminal Justice and Immigration Act 2008 (c. 4), with effect from a date to be appointed.

*Under section 258 of the Criminal Justice Act 2003[13], a respondent who is imprisoned for contempt of court must be released unconditionally after serving half the term.*

*Under sections 14, 15 and 16 of the Legal Aid, Sentencing and Punishment of Offenders Act 2012[14], the respondent may receive advice and representation in "proceedings for contempt committed, or alleged to have been committed, by an individual in the face of the court".*

*By reason of sections 15 and 45 of the Senior Courts Act 1981, the Court of Appeal and the Crown Court each has an inherent power temporarily to detain a respondent, for example to restore order, when dealing with obstructive, disruptive, insulting or intimidating conduct. Under section 12(2) of the Contempt of Court Act 1981[15], a magistrates' court can temporarily detain a respondent until later the same day on a contravention of that section.*

*Part 14 contains rules about bail.]*

### Review after temporary detention                                        R48.6

**48.6** (1) This rule applies in a case in which the court has ordered the respondent's immediate temporary detention for conduct to which rule 48.5 applies.

(2) The court must review the case—
   (a) if a magistrates' court, later the same day; or
   (b) in the Court of Appeal or the Crown Court, no later than the next business day.

(3) On the review, the court must—
   (a) unless the respondent is absent, repeat the explanations required by rule 48.5(2)(a); and
   (b) allow the respondent a reasonable opportunity to reflect, take advice, explain and, if he or she so wishes, apologise.

(4) The court may then—
   (a) take no further action in respect of the conduct;
   (b) if a magistrates' court, enquire into the conduct there and then; or
   (c) if the Court of Appeal or the Crown Court—
      (i) enquire into the conduct there and then, or
      (ii) postpone the enquiry, and order the respondent's release from such detention in the meantime.

### Postponement of enquiry                                                  R48.7

**48.7** (1) This rule applies where the Court of Appeal or the Crown Court postpones the enquiry.

(2) The court must arrange for the preparation of a written statement containing such particulars of the conduct in question as to make clear what the respondent appears to have done.

(3) The court officer must serve on the respondent—
   (a) that written statement;
   (b) notice of where and when the postponed enquiry will take place; and
   (c) a notice that—
      (i) reminds the respondent that the court can impose imprisonment, or a fine, or both, for contempt of court, and
      (ii) warns the respondent that the court may pursue the postponed enquiry in the respondent's absence, if the respondent does not attend.

### Procedure on enquiry                                                     R48.8

**48.8** (1) At an enquiry, the court must—
   (a) ensure that the respondent understands (with help, if necessary) what is alleged, if the enquiry has been postponed from a previous occasion;
   (b) explain what the procedure at the enquiry will be; and
   (c) ask whether the respondent admits the conduct in question.

(2) If the respondent admits the conduct, the court need not receive evidence.

(3) If the respondent does not admit the conduct, the court must consider—
   (a) any statement served under rule 48.7;
   (b) any other evidence of the conduct;
   (c) any evidence introduced by the respondent; and
   (d) any representations by the respondent about the conduct.

(4) If the respondent admits the conduct, or the court finds it proved, the court must—

---

[13] 2003 c. 44; section 258 was amended by article 3 of S.I. 2005/643, section 34 of the Police and Justice Act 2006 (c. 4) and sections 117 and 121 of, and paragraphs 1 and 5 of Schedule 17 and paragraphs 1 and 8 of Schedule 20 to, the Legal Aid, Sentencing and Punishment of Offenders Act 2012 (c. 10).
[14] 2012 c. 10.
[15] 1981 c. 49; section 12(2) was amended by Part 1 of Schedule 4 to the Criminal Justice Act 1991 (c. 53).

   (a) before imposing any punishment for contempt of court, give the respondent an opportunity to make representations relevant to punishment;

   (b) explain, in terms the respondent can understand (with help, if necessary)—

      (i) the reasons for its decision, including its findings of fact, and

      (ii) the punishment it imposes, and its effect; and

   (c) if a magistrates' court, arrange for the preparation of a written record of those findings.

(5) The court that conducts an enquiry—

   (a) need not include the same member or members as the court that observed the conduct; but

   (b) may do so, unless that would be unfair to the respondent.

### Contempt of court by failure to comply with court order, etc.

**R48.9**    **Initial procedure on failure to comply with court order, etc.**

**48.9**  (1) This rule applies where—

   (a) a party, or other person directly affected, alleges—

      (i) in the Crown Court, a failure to comply with an order to which applies rule 33.70 (compliance order, restraint order or ancillary order), rule 47.9 (certain investigation orders under the Police and Criminal Evidence Act 1984[16], the Terrorism Act 2000[17], the Proceeds of Crime Act 2002[18], the Proceeds of Crime Act 2002 (External Investigations) Order 2014[19] and the Extradition Act 2003[20]), rule 47.41 (order for retention or return of property under section 59 of the Criminal Justice and Police Act 2001[21]) or rule 47.58 (order for access under section 18A of the Criminal Appeal Act 1995[22]),

      (ii) in the Court of Appeal or the Crown Court, any other conduct with which that court can deal as a civil contempt of court, or

      (iii) in the Crown Court or a magistrates' court, unauthorised use of disclosed prosecution material under section 17 of the Criminal Procedure and Investigations Act 1996[23]; or

   (b) the court deals on its own initiative with conduct to which paragraph (1)(a) applies.

(2) Such a party or person must—

   (a) apply in writing and serve the application on the court officer; and

   (b) serve on the respondent—

      (i) the application, and

      (ii) notice of where and when the court will consider the allegation (not less than 10 business days after service).

(3) The application must—

   (a) identify the respondent;

   (b) explain that it is an application for the respondent to be dealt with for contempt of court;

   (c) contain such particulars of the conduct in question as to make clear what is alleged against the respondent; and

   (d) include a notice warning the respondent that the court—

      (i) can impose imprisonment, or a fine, or both, for contempt of court, and

      (ii) may deal with the application in the respondent's absence, if the respondent does not attend the hearing.

(4) A court which acts on its own initiative under paragraph (1)(b) must—

   (a) arrange for the preparation of a written statement containing the same information as an application; and

   (b) arrange for the service on the respondent of—

      (i) that written statement, and

      (ii) notice of where and when the court will consider the allegation (not less than 10 business days after service).

*[Note. The conduct to which this rule applies is sometimes described as 'civil' contempt of court.*

---

[16] 1984 c. 60.

[17] 2000 c. 11.

[18] 2002 c. 29.

[19] S.I. 2014/1893.

[20] 2003 c. 41.

[21] 2001 c. 16; section 59 was amended by section 82 of the Deregulation Act 2015 (c. 20).

[22] 1995 c. 35; section 18A was inserted by section 1 of the Criminal Cases Review Commission (Information) Act 2016 (c. 17).

[23] 1996 c. 25; section 17 was amended by section 331 of, and paragraphs 20 and 33 of Schedule 36 to, the Criminal Justice Act 2003 (c. 44).

*By reason of section 45 of the Senior Courts Act 1981[24], the Crown Court has an inherent power to imprison (for a maximum of 2 years), or fine (to an unlimited amount), or both, a respondent for conduct in contempt of court by failing to comply with a court order or an undertaking given to the court.*

*Under section 18 of the Criminal Procedure and Investigations Act 1996—[25]*

> *(a)  the Crown Court can imprison (for a maximum of 2 years), or fine (to an unlimited amount), or both;*
>
> *(b)  a magistrates' court can imprison (for a maximum of 6 months), or fine (to a maximum of £5,000), or both,*

*a person who uses disclosed prosecution material in contravention of section 17 of that Act. See also rule 15.8.*

*Under section 89 of the Powers of Criminal Courts (Sentencing) Act 2000, no respondent who is under 21 may be imprisoned for contempt of court. Under section 108 of that Act, a respondent who is at least 18 but under 21 may be detained if the court is of the opinion that no other method of dealing with him or her is appropriate. Under section 14(2A) of the Contempt of Court Act 1981, a respondent who is under 17 may not be ordered to attend an attendance centre.*

*Under section 258 of the Criminal Justice Act 2003, a respondent who is imprisoned for contempt of court must be released unconditionally after serving half the term.*

*The Practice Direction sets out a form of application for use in connection with this rule.*

*The rules in Part 4 require that an application under this rule must be served by handing it to the person accused of contempt of court unless the court otherwise directs.]*

### Procedure on hearing                                                    R48.10

48.10 (1)  At the hearing of an allegation under rule 48.9, the court must—
      (a)  ensure that the respondent understands (with help, if necessary) what is alleged;
      (b)  explain what the procedure at the hearing will be; and
      (c)  ask whether the respondent admits the conduct in question.
  (2)  If the respondent admits the conduct, the court need not receive evidence.
  (3)  If the respondent does not admit the conduct, the court must consider—
      (a)  the application or written statement served under rule 48.9;
      (b)  any other evidence of the conduct;
      (c)  any evidence introduced by the respondent; and
      (d)  any representations by the respondent about the conduct.
  (4)  If the respondent admits the conduct, or the court finds it proved, the court must—
      (a)  before imposing any punishment for contempt of court, give the respondent an opportunity to make representations relevant to punishment;
      (b)  explain, in terms the respondent can understand (with help, if necessary)—
         (i)   the reasons for its decision, including its findings of fact, and
         (ii)  the punishment it imposes, and its effect; and
      (c)  in a magistrates' court, arrange for the preparation of a written record of those findings.

### Introduction of written witness statement or other hearsay               R48.11

48.11 (1)  Where rule 48.9 applies, an applicant or respondent who wants to introduce in evidence the written statement of a witness, or other hearsay, must—
      (a)  serve a copy of the statement, or notice of other hearsay, on—
         (i)   the court officer, and
         (ii)  the other party; and
      (b)  serve the copy or notice—
         (i)   when serving the application under rule 48.9, in the case of an applicant, or
         (ii)  not more than 5 business days after service of that application or of the court's written statement, in the case of the respondent.
  (2)  Such service is notice of that party's intention to introduce in evidence that written witness statement, or other hearsay, unless that party otherwise indicates when serving it.
  (3)  A party entitled to receive such notice may waive that entitlement.

Criminal Procedure Rules and Criminal Practice Directions

---

[24]  1981 c. 54.
[25]  1996 c. 25.

*[Note. On an application under rule 48.9, hearsay evidence is admissible under the Civil Evidence Act 1995. Section 1(2) of the 1995 Act[26] defines hearsay as meaning 'a statement made otherwise than by a person while giving oral evidence in the proceedings which is tendered as evidence of the matters stated'. Section 13 of the Act[27] defines a statement as meaning 'any representation of fact or opinion, however made'.*

*Under section 2 of the 1995 Act[28], a party who wants to introduce hearsay in evidence must give reasonable and practicable notice, in accordance with procedure rules, unless the recipient waives that requirement.]*

**R48.12   Content of written witness statement**

48.12 (1)   This rule applies to a written witness statement served under rule 48.11.

(2)   Such a written witness statement must contain a declaration by the person making it that it is true to the best of that person's knowledge and belief.

*[Note. By reason of sections 15 and 45 of the Senior Courts Act 1981[29], the Court of Appeal and the Crown Court each has an inherent power to imprison (for a maximum of 2 years), or fine (to an unlimited amount), or both, for contempt of court a person who, in a written witness statement to which this rule applies, makes, or causes to be made, a false statement without an honest belief in its truth. See also section 14 of the Contempt of Court Act 1981[30].]*

**R48.13   Content of notice of other hearsay**

48.13 (1)   This rule applies to a notice of hearsay, other than a written witness statement, served under rule 48.11.

(2)   Such a notice must—

(a)   set out the evidence, or attach the document that contains it; and

(b)   identify the person who made the statement that is hearsay.

**R48.14   Cross-examination of maker of written witness statement or other hearsay**

48.14 (1)   This rule applies where a party wants the court's permission to cross-examine a person who made a statement which another party wants to introduce as hearsay.

(2)   The party who wants to cross-examine that person must—

(a)   apply in writing, with reasons; and

(b)   serve the application on—

(i)   the court officer, and

(ii)   the party who served the hearsay.

(3)   A respondent who wants to cross-examine such a person must apply to do so not more than 5 business days after service of the hearsay by the applicant.

(4)   An applicant who wants to cross-examine such a person must apply to do so not more than 3 business days after service of the hearsay by the respondent.

(5)   The court—

(a)   may decide an application under this rule without a hearing; but

(b)   must not dismiss such an application unless the person making it has had an opportunity to make representations at a hearing.

*[Note. See also section 3 of the Civil Evidence Act 1995[31].]*

**R48.15   Credibility and consistency of maker of written witness statement or other hearsay**

48.15 (1)   This rule applies where a party wants to challenge the credibility or consistency of a person who made a statement which another party wants to introduce as hearsay.

(2)   The party who wants to challenge the credibility or consistency of that person must—

(a)   serve notice of intention to do so on—

---

[26]   1995 c. 38.
[27]   1995 c. 38.
[28]   1995 c. 38.
[29]   1981 c. 54.
[30]   1981 c. 49; section 14 was amended by sections 77 and 78 of, and paragraph 60 of Schedule 14 and Schedule 16 to, the Criminal Justice Act 1982 (c. 48), section 65 of, and paragraphs 59 and 60 of Schedule 3 to, the Mental Health (Amendment) Act 1982 (c. 51), section 148 of, and paragraph 57 of Schedule 4 to, the Mental Health Act 1983 (c. 20), section 1 of the County Courts (Penalties for Contempt) Act 1983 (c. 45), section 17 of, and Parts 1 and V of Schedule 4 to, the Criminal Justice Act 1991 (c. 53), section 65 of, and paragraph 6 of Schedule 3 to, the Criminal Justice Act 1993 (c. 36), section 165 of, and paragraph 84 of Schedule 9 to, the Powers of Criminal Courts (Sentencing) Act 2000 (c. 6), section 1 of, and paragraph 19 of Schedule 1 to, the Mental Health Act 2007 (c. 12) and section 17 of, and paragraph 52 of Schedule 9 and paragraph 53 of Schedule 10 to, the Crime and Courts Act 2013 (c. 22). It is further amended by sections 6 and 149 of, and paragraph 25 of Schedule 4 and Part 1 of Schedule 28 to, the Criminal Justice and Immigration Act 2008 (c. 4), with effect from a date to be appointed.
[31]   1995 c. 38.

       (i)   the court officer, and

       (ii)   the party who served the hearsay; and

    (b)   in it, identify any statement or other material on which that party relies.

  (3)   A respondent who wants to challenge such a person's credibility or consistency must serve such a notice not more than 5 business days after service of the hearsay by the applicant.

  (4)   An applicant who wants to challenge such a person's credibility or consistency must serve such a notice not more than 3 business days after service of the hearsay by the respondent.

  (5)   The party who served the hearsay—

    (a)   may call that person to give oral evidence instead; and

    (b)   if so, must serve notice of intention to do so on—

       (i)   the court officer, and

       (ii)   the other party

      as soon as practicable after service of the notice under paragraph (2).

*[Note. Section 5(2) of the Civil Evidence Act 1995[32] describes the procedure for challenging the credibility of the maker of a statement of which hearsay evidence is introduced. See also section 6 of that Act[33].*

*The 1995 Act does not allow the introduction of evidence of a previous inconsistent statement otherwise than in accordance with sections 5, 6 and 7 of the Criminal Procedure Act 1865[34].]*

### Magistrates' courts' powers to adjourn, etc.

**R48.16**

**48.16** (1)   This rule applies where a magistrates' court deals with unauthorised disclosure of prosecution material under sections 17 and 18 of the Criminal Procedure and Investigations Act 1996[35].

  (2)   The sections of the Magistrates' Courts Act 1980 listed in paragraph (3) apply as if in those sections—

    (a)   'complaint' and 'summons' each referred to an application or written statement under rule 48.9;

    (b)   'complainant' meant an applicant; and

    (c)   'defendant' meant the respondent.

  (3)   Those sections are—

    (a)   section 51[36] (issue of summons on complaint);

    (b)   section 54[37] (adjournment);

    (c)   section 55[38] (non-appearance of defendant);

    (d)   section 97(1)[39] Superscript footnote number (summons to witness);

    (e)   section 121(1)[40] (constitution and place of sitting of court); and

    (f)   section 123[41] (defect in process).

  (4)   Section 127 of the 1980 Act[42] (limitation of time) does not apply.

*[Note. Under section 19(3) of the Criminal Procedure and Investigations Act 1996[43], Criminal Procedure Rules may contain provisions equivalent to those contained in Schedule 3 to the Contempt of Court Act 1981[44] (which allows magistrates' courts in cases of contempt of court to use certain powers such courts possess in other cases).]*

### Court's power to vary requirements

**R48.17**

**48.17** (1)   The court may shorten or extend (even after it has expired) a time limit under rule 48.11, 48.14 or 48.15.

---

[32]  1995 c. 38.

[33]  1995 c. 38.

[34]  1865 c. 18; section 6 was amended by section 10 of the Decimal Currency Act 1969 (c. 19), section 90 of, and paragraph 3 of Schedule 13 to, the Access to Justice Act 1999 (c. 22), section 109 of, and paragraph 47 of Schedule 8 to, the Courts Act 2003 (c. 39) and paragraph 79 of Schedule 36 and Schedule 37 to the Criminal Justice Act 2003 (c. 44). It is further amended by section 119 of, and Schedule 7 to, the Police and Criminal Evidence Act 1984 (c. 60), with effect from a date to be appointed.

[35]  1996 c. 25; section 17 was amended by section 331 of, and paragraphs 20 and 33 of Schedule 36 to, the Criminal Justice Act 2003 (c. 44).

[36]  1980 c. 43; section 51 was substituted by section 47(1) of the Courts Act 2003 (c. 39).

[37]  1980 c. 43.

[38]  1980 c. 43.

[39]  1980 c. 43; section 97(1) was substituted by section 169(2) of the Serious Organised Crime and Police Act 2005 (c. 15).

[40]  1980 c. 43.

[41]  1980 c. 43.

[42]  1980 c. 43.

[43]  1996 c. 25; section 19(3) was amended by section 109 of, and paragraph 377 of Schedule 8 to, the Courts Act 2003 (c. 39) and section 15 of, and paragraph 251 of Schedule 4 to, the Constitutional Reform Act 2005 (c. 4).

[44]  1981 c. 49; Schedule 3 has been amended but the amendment is not relevant to this rule.

(2) A person who wants an extension of time must—
 (a) apply when serving the statement, notice or application for which it is needed; and
 (b) explain the delay.

CRIMINAL PRACTICE DIRECTIONS    PART 48    CONTEMPT OF COURT

**CPD.48A**   **CPD XI Other proceedings 48A: Contempt in the Face of the Magistrates' Court**

*General*

**48A.1** The procedure to be followed in cases of contempt of court is given in CrimPR Part 48. The magistrates' courts' power to deal with contempt in the face of the court is contained within section 12 of the Contempt of Court Act 1981. Magistrates' courts also have the power to punish a witness who refuses to be sworn or give evidence under section 97(4) of the Magistrates' Courts Act 1980.

*Contempt consisting of wilfully insulting anyone specified in section 12 or interrupting proceedings*

**48A.2** In the majority of cases, an apology and a promise as to future conduct should be sufficient for the court to order a person's release. However, there are likely to be certain cases where the nature and seriousness of the misconduct requires the court to consider using its powers, under section 12(2) of the Contempt of Court Act 1981, either to fine or to order the person's committal to custody.

*Imposing a penalty for contempt*

**48A.3** The court should allow the person a further opportunity to apologise for his or her contempt, and should follow the procedure at CrimPR 48.8(4). The court should consider whether it is appropriate to release the person or whether it must exercise its powers to fine the person or to commit the person to custody under section 12(2) of the 1981 Act. In deciding how to deal with the person, the court should have regard to the period for which he or she has been detained, whether the conduct was admitted and the seriousness of the contempt. Any period of committal to custody should be for the shortest period of time commensurate with the interests of preserving good order in the administration of justice.

CRIMINAL PROCEDURE RULES    PART 49    INTERNATIONAL CO-OPERATION

**R49.1**   **Notice required to accompany process served outside the United Kingdom and translations**

**49.1** (1) The notice which by virtue of section 3(4)(b) of the Crime (International Co-operation) Act 2003[1] (general requirements for service of process) must accompany any process served outside the United Kingdom must give the information specified in paragraphs (2) and (4) below.

 (2) The notice must—
  (a) state that the person required by the process to appear as a party or attend as a witness can obtain information about his rights in connection therewith from the relevant authority; and
  (b) give the particulars specified in paragraph (4) about that authority.

 (3) The relevant authority where the process is served—
  (a) at the request of the prosecuting authority, is that authority; or
  (b) at the request of the defendant or the prosecutor in the case of a private prosecution, is the court by which the process is served.

 (4) The particulars referred to in paragraph (2) are—
  (a) the name and address of the relevant authority, together with its telephone and fax numbers and e-mail address; and
  (b) the name of a person at the relevant authority who can provide the information referred to in paragraph (2)(a), together with his telephone and fax numbers and e-mail address.

 (5) The magistrates' court or Crown Court officer must send, together with any process served outside the United Kingdom—
  (a) any translation which is provided under section 3(3)(b) of the 2003 Act; and
  (b) any translation of the information required to be given by this rule which is provided to him.

 (6) In this rule 'process' has the same meaning as in section 51(3) of the 2003 Act.

---

[1] 2003 c. 32.

**Proof of service outside the United Kingdom**                                          **R49.2**

**49.2** (1) A statement in a certificate given by or on behalf of the Secretary of State—

(a) that process has been served on any person under section 4(1) of the Crime (International Co-operation) Act 2003 (service of process otherwise than by post);

(b) of the manner in which service was effected; and

(c) of the date on which process was served;

shall be admissible as evidence of any facts so stated.

(2) In this rule 'process' has the same meaning as in section 51(3) of the 2003 Act.

**Supply of copy of notice of request for assistance abroad**                            **R49.3**

**49.3** Where a request for assistance under section 7 of the Crime (International Co-operation) Act 2003 is made by a justice of the peace or a judge exercising the jurisdiction of the Crown Court and is sent in accordance with section 8(1) of the 2003 Act, the magistrates' court or Crown Court officer shall send a copy of the letter of request to the Secretary of State as soon as practicable after the request has been made.

**Persons entitled to appear and take part in proceedings before a nominated court,**     **R49.4**
**and exclusion of the public**

**49.4** A court nominated under section 15(1) of the Crime (International Co-operation) Act 2003 (nominating a court to receive evidence) may—

(a) determine who may appear or take part in the proceedings under Schedule 1 to the 2003 Act before the court and whether a party to the proceedings is entitled to be legally represented; and

(b) direct that the public be excluded from those proceedings if it thinks it necessary to do so in the interests of justice.

**Record of proceedings to receive evidence before a nominated court**                    **R49.5**

**49.5** (1) Where a court is nominated under section 15(1) of the Crime (International Co-operation) Act 2003 the magistrates' court or Crown Court officer shall enter in an overseas record—

(a) details of the request in respect of which the notice under section 15(1) of the 2003 Act was given;

(b) the date on which, and place at which, the proceedings under Schedule 1 to the 2003 Act in respect of that request took place;

(c) the name of any witness who gave evidence at the proceedings in question;

(d) the name of any person who took part in the proceedings as a legal representative or an interpreter;

(e) whether a witness was required to give evidence on oath or (by virtue of section 5 of the Oaths Act 1978[2]) after making a solemn affirmation; and

(f) whether the opportunity to cross-examine any witness was refused.

(2) When the court gives the evidence received by it under paragraph 6(1) of Schedule 1 to the 2003 Act to the court or authority that made the request or to the territorial authority for forwarding to the court or authority that made the request, the magistrates' court or Crown Court officer shall send to the court, authority or territorial authority (as the case may be) a copy of an extract of so much of the overseas record as relates to the proceedings in respect of that request.

*[Note. As to the keeping of an overseas record, see rule 49.9.]*

**Interpreter for the purposes of proceedings involving a television or telephone link**   **R49.6**

**49.6** (1) This rule applies where a court is nominated under section 30(3) (hearing witnesses in the UK through television links) or section 31(4) (hearing witnesses in the UK by telephone) of the Crime (International Co-operation) Act 2003.

(2) Where it appears to the justices' legal adviser or the Crown Court officer that the witness to be heard in the proceedings under Part 1 or 2 of Schedule 2 to the 2003 Act ('the relevant proceedings') is likely to give evidence in a language other than English, he shall make arrangements for an interpreter to be present at the proceedings to translate what is said into English.

(3) Where it appears to the justices' legal adviser or the Crown Court officer that the witness to be heard in the relevant proceedings is likely to give evidence in a language other than that in which the proceedings of the court referred to in section 30(1) or, as the case may be, 31(1) of the 2003 Act ('the external court') will be conducted, he shall make arrangements for an

---

[2] 1978 c. 19.

interpreter to be present at the relevant proceedings to translate what is said into the language in which the proceedings of the external court will be conducted.

   (4)   Where the evidence in the relevant proceedings is either given in a language other than English or is not translated into English by an interpreter, the court shall adjourn the proceedings until such time as an interpreter can be present to provide a translation into English.

   (5)   Where a court in Wales understands Welsh—

      (a)   paragraph (2) does not apply where it appears to the justices' legal adviser or Crown Court officer that the witness in question is likely to give evidence in Welsh;

      (b)   paragraph (4) does not apply where the evidence is given in Welsh; and

      (c)   any translation which is provided pursuant to paragraph (2) or (4) may be into Welsh instead of English.

## R49.7   Record of television link hearing before a nominated court

**49.7**   (1)   This rule applies where a court is nominated under section 30(3) of the Crime (International Co-operation) Act 2003.

   (2)   The magistrates' court or Crown Court officer shall enter in an overseas record—

      (a)   details of the request in respect of which the notice under section 30(3) of the 2003 Act was given;

      (b)   the date on which, and place at which, the proceedings under Part 1 of Schedule 2 to that Act in respect of that request took place;

      (c)   the technical conditions, such as the type of equipment used, under which the proceedings took place;

      (d)   the name of the witness who gave evidence;

      (e)   the name of any person who took part in the proceedings as a legal representative or an interpreter; and

      (f)   the language in which the evidence was given.

   (3)   As soon as practicable after the proceedings under Part 1 of Schedule 2 to the 2003 Act took place, the magistrates' court or Crown Court officer shall send to the external authority that made the request a copy of an extract of so much of the overseas record as relates to the proceedings in respect of that request.

*[Note. As to the keeping of an overseas record, see rule 49.9.]*

## R49.8   Record of telephone link hearing before a nominated court

**49.8**   (1)   This rule applies where a court is nominated under section 31(4) of the Crime (International Co-operation) Act 2003.

   (2)   The magistrates' court or Crown Court officer shall enter in an overseas record—

      (a)   details of the request in respect of which the notice under section 31(4) of the 2003 Act was given;

      (b)   the date, time and place at which the proceedings under Part 2 of Schedule 2 to the 2003 Act took place;

      (c)   the name of the witness who gave evidence;

      (d)   the name of any interpreter who acted at the proceedings; and

      (e)   the language in which the evidence was given.

*[Note. As to the keeping of an overseas record, see rule 49.9.]*

## R49.9   Overseas record

**49.9**   (1)   The overseas records of a magistrates' court shall be part of the register (within the meaning of section 150(1) of the Magistrates' Courts Act 1980[3]).

   (2)   The overseas records of any court shall not be open to inspection by any person except—

      (a)   as authorised by the Secretary of State; or

      (b)   with the leave of the court.

*[Note. As to the making of court records, see rule 5.4.]*

## R49.10   Overseas freezing orders

**49.10**   (1)   This rule applies where a court is nominated under section 21(1) of the Crime (International Co-operation) Act 2003[4] to give effect to an overseas freezing order.

   (2)   Where the Secretary of State serves a copy of such an order on the court officer—

      (a)   the general rule is that the court must consider the order no later than the next business day; but

---

[3] 1980 c. 43; a relevant amendment was made to section 150(1) by paragraph 250 of Schedule 8, and Schedule 10 to, the Courts Act 2003 (c. 39).

[4] 2003 c. 32.

(b) exceptionally, the court may consider the order later than that, though not more than 5 business days after service.

(3) The court must not consider the order unless—

    (a) it is satisfied that the chief officer of police for the area in which the evidence is situated has had notice of the order; and

    (b) that chief officer of police has had an opportunity to make representations, at a hearing if that officer wants.

(4) The court may consider the order—

    (a) without a hearing; or

    (b) at a hearing, in public or in private.

*[Note. Under sections 20, 21 and 22 of the Crime (International Co-operation) Act 2003, a court nominated by the Secretary of State must consider an order, made by a court or other authority in a country outside the United Kingdom, the purpose of which is to protect evidence in the United Kingdom which may be used in proceedings or an investigation in that other country pending the transfer of that evidence to that country. The court may decide not to give effect to such an order only if—*

    *(a) were the person whose conduct is in question to be charged with the offence to which the order relates, a previous conviction or acquittal would entitle that person to be discharged; or*

    *(b) giving effect to the order would be incompatible with a Convention right, within the meaning of the Human Rights Act 1998.]*

## Overseas forfeiture orders          R49.11

49.11 (1) This rule applies where—

    (a) the Crown Court can—

        (i) make a restraint order under article 5 of the Criminal Justice (International Co-operation) Act 1990 (Enforcement of Overseas Forfeiture Orders) Order 2005[5], or

        (ii) give effect to an external forfeiture order under article 19 of that Order;

    (b) the Director of Public Prosecutions or the Director of the Serious Fraud Office receives—

        (i) a request for the restraint of property to which article 3 of the 2005 Order applies, or

        (ii) a request to give effect to an external forfeiture order to which article 15 of the Order applies; and

    (c) the Director wants the Crown Court to—

        (i) make such a restraint order, or

        (ii) give effect to such a forfeiture order.

(2) The Director must—

    (a) apply in writing;

    (b) serve the application on the court officer; and

    (c) serve the application on the defendant and on any other person affected by the order, unless the court is satisfied that—

        (i) the application is urgent, or

        (ii) there are reasonable grounds for believing that to give notice of the application would cause the dissipation of the property which is the subject of the application.

(3) The application must—

    (a) identify the property the subject of the application;

    (b) identify the person who is or who may become the subject of such a forfeiture order;

    (c) explain how the requirements of the 2005 Order are satisfied, as the case may be—

        (i) for making a restraint order, or

        (ii) for giving effect to a forfeiture order;

    (d) where the application is to give effect to a forfeiture order, include an application to appoint the Director as the enforcement authority; and

    (e) propose the terms of the Crown Court order.

(4) If the court allows the application, it must—

    (a) where it decides to make a restraint order—

        (i) specify the property the subject of the order,

        (ii) specify the person or persons who are prohibited from dealing with that property,

        (iii) specify any exception to that prohibition, and

        (iv) include any ancillary order that the court believes is appropriate to ensure that the restraint order is effective; and

    (b) where it decides to give effect to a forfeiture order, exercise its power to—

        (i) direct the registration of the order as an order of the Crown Court,

---

[5] S.I. 2005/3180.

Criminal Procedure Rules and Criminal Practice Directions

          (ii) give directions for notice of the order to be given to any person affected by it, and

          (iii) appoint the applicant Director as the enforcement authority.

(5) Paragraph (6) applies where a person affected by an order, or the Director, wants the court to vary or discharge a restraint order or cancel the registration of a forfeiture order.

(6) Such a person must—

    (a) apply in writing as soon as practicable after becoming aware of the grounds for doing so;

    (b) serve the application on the court officer and, as applicable—

        (i) the other party, and

        (ii) any other person who will or may be affected;

    (c) explain why it is appropriate, as the case may be—

        (i) for the restraint order to be varied or discharged, or

        (ii) for the registration of the forfeiture order to be cancelled;

    (d) propose the terms of any variation; and

    (e) ask for a hearing, if one is wanted, and explain why it is needed.

(7) The court may—

    (a) consider an application

        (i) at a hearing, which must be in private unless the court otherwise directs, or

        (ii) without a hearing; and

    (b) allow an application to be made orally.

*[Note. Under article 19 of the Criminal Justice (International Co-operation) Act 1990 (Enforcement of Overseas Forfeiture Orders) Order 2005, on the application of the Director of Public Prosecutions or the Director of the Serious Fraud Office the Crown Court may give effect to an order made by a court in a country outside the United Kingdom for the forfeiture and destruction, or other disposal, of any property in respect of which an offence has been committed in that country, or which was used or intended for use in connection with the commission of such an offence (described in the Order as an 'external forfeiture order').*

*Under article 5 of the 2005 Order, on the application of the Director of Public Prosecutions or the Director of the Serious Fraud Office the Crown Court may make a restraint order prohibiting any specified person from dealing with property, for the purpose of facilitating the enforcement of such a forfeiture order which has yet to be made.]*

CRIMINAL PROCEDURE RULES    PART 50    EXTRADITION

**Section 1: general rules**

**R50.1**    **When this Part applies**

**50.1**    (1) This Part applies to extradition under Part 1 or Part 2 of the Extradition Act 2003[1].

(2) Section 2 of this Part applies to proceedings in a magistrates' court, and in that Section—

    (a) rules 50.3 to 50.7, 50.15 and 50.16 apply to extradition under Part 1 of the Act;

    (b) rules 50.3, 50.4 and 50.8 to 50.16 apply to extradition under Part 2 of the Act.

(3) Section 3 of this Part applies where—

    (a) a party wants to appeal to the High Court against an order by the magistrates' court or by the Secretary of State; and

    (b) a party to an appeal to the High Court wants to appeal further to the Supreme Court under—

        (i) section 32 of the Act (appeal under Part 1 of the Act), or

        (ii) section 114 of the Act (appeal under Part 2 of the Act).

(4) Section 4 of this Part applies to proceedings in a magistrates' court under—

    (a) sections 54 and 55 of the Act (Request for consent to other offence being dealt with; Questions for decision at consent hearing); and

    (b) sections 56 and 57 of the Act (Request for consent to further extradition to category 1 territory; Questions for decision at consent hearing).

(5) In this Part, and for the purposes of this Part in other rules—

    (a) 'magistrates' court' means a District Judge (Magistrates' Courts) exercising the powers to which Section 2 of this Part applies;

    (b) 'presenting officer' means an officer of the National Crime Agency, a police officer, a prosecutor or other person representing an authority or territory seeking the extradition of a defendant; and

    (c) 'defendant' means a person arrested under Part 1 or Part 2 of the Extradition Act 2003.

*[Note. The Extradition Act 2003 provides for the extradition of a person accused or convicted of a crime to the territory within which that person is accused, was convicted or is to serve a sentence.*

---

[1] 2003 c. 41.

*Under Part 1 of the Act (sections 1 to 68), the magistrates' court may give effect to a warrant for arrest issued by an authority in a territory designated for the purposes of that Part.*

*Under Part 2 of the Act (sections 69 to 141), the magistrates' court and the Secretary of State may give effect to a request for extradition made under a treaty between the United Kingdom and the requesting territory.*

*Under sections 67 and 139 of the Extradition Act 2003[2], a District Judge (Magistrates' Courts) must be designated for the purposes of the Act to exercise the powers to which Section 2 of this Part applies.*

*There are rights of appeal to the High Court from decisions of the magistrates' court and of the Secretary of State: see Section 3 of this Part.]*

**Further objective in extradition proceedings**                                    **R50.2**

**50.2**   When exercising a power to which this Part applies, as well as furthering the overriding objective, in accordance with rule 1.3, the court must have regard to the importance of—
   (a)   mutual confidence and recognition between judicial authorities in the United Kingdom and in requesting territories; and
   (b)   the conduct of extradition proceedings in accordance with international obligations, including obligations to deal swiftly with extradition requests.

### Section 2:  extradition proceedings in a magistrates' court

**Exercise of magistrates' court's powers**                                          **R50.3**

**50.3**   (1)   The general rule is that the magistrates' court must exercise its powers at a hearing in public, but—
   (a)   that is subject to any power the court has to—
      (i)   impose reporting restrictions,
      (ii)   withhold information from the public, or
      (iii)   order a hearing in private; and
   (b)   despite the general rule the court may, without a hearing—
      (i)   give any directions to which rule 50.4 applies (Case management in the magistrates' court and duty of court officer), or
      (ii)   determine an application which these Rules allow to be determined by a magistrates' court without a hearing in a case to which this Part does not apply.
   (2)   If the court so directs, a party may attend by live link any hearing except an extradition hearing under rule 50.6 or 50.13.
   (3)   Where the defendant is absent from a hearing—
   (a)   the general rule is that the court must proceed as if the defendant—
      (i)   were present, and
      (ii)   opposed extradition on any ground of which the court has been made aware;
   (b)   the general rule does not apply if the defendant is under 18;
   (c)   the general rule is subject to the court being satisfied that—
      (i)   the defendant had reasonable notice of where and when the hearing would take place,
      (ii)   the defendant has been made aware that the hearing might proceed in his or her absence, and
      (iii)   there is no good reason for the defendant's absence; and
   (d)   the general rule does not apply but the court may exercise its powers in the defendant's absence where—
      (i)   the court discharges the defendant,
      (ii)   the defendant is represented and the defendant's presence is impracticable by reason of his or her ill health or disorderly conduct, or
      (iii)   on an application under rule 50.32 (Application for consent to deal with another offence or for consent to further extradition), the defendant is represented or the defendant's presence is impracticable by reason of his or her detention in the territory to which he or she has been extradited.
   (4)   The court may exercise its power to adjourn—
   (a)   if either party asks, or on its own initiative; and
   (b)   in particular—
      (i)   to allow there to be obtained information that the court requires,
      (ii)   following a provisional arrest under Part 1 of the Extradition Act 2003, pending receipt of the warrant,

---

[2] 2003 c. 41; sections 67 and 139 were amended by section 15 of, and paragraphs 352 and 353 of Schedule 4 to, the Constitutional Reform Act 2005 (c. 4) and section 42 of, and paragraph 15 of Schedule 13 to, the Police and Justice Act 2006 (c. 48).

       (iii)   following a provisional arrest with a warrant under Part 2 of the Act, pending receipt of the extradition request,

       (iv)   following a provisional arrest without a warrant under Part 2 of the Act, pending receipt of evidence or information required by the court,

       (v)   if the court is informed that the defendant is serving a custodial sentence in the United Kingdom,

       (vi)   if it appears to the court that the defendant is not fit to be extradited, unless the court discharges the defendant for that reason,

       (vii)   where a court dealing with a warrant to which Part 1 of the Act applies is informed that another such warrant has been received in the United Kingdom,

       (viii)   where a court dealing with a warrant to which Part 1 of the Act applies is informed of a request for the temporary transfer of the defendant to the territory to which the defendant's extradition is sought, or a request for the defendant to speak to the authorities of that territory, or

       (ix)   during a hearing to which rule 50.32 applies (Application for consent to deal with another offence or for consent to further extradition).

(5)   The court must exercise its power to adjourn if informed that the defendant has been charged with an offence in the United Kingdom.

(6)   The general rule is that, before exercising a power to which this Part applies, the court must give each party an opportunity to make representations, unless that party is absent without good reason.

(7)   The court may—

      (a)   shorten a time limit or extend it (even after it has expired), unless that is inconsistent with other legislation;

      (b)   direct that a notice or application be served on any person; and

      (c)   allow a notice or application to be in a different form to one set out in the Practice Direction, or to be presented orally.

(8)   A party who wants an extension of time within which to serve a notice or make an application must—

      (a)   apply for that extension of time when serving that notice or making that application; and

      (b)   give the reasons for the application for an extension of time.

*[Note. See sections 8A, 8B, 9, 21B, 22, 23, 25 and 44 of the Extradition Act 2003[3] (powers in relation to extradition under Part 1 of the Act) and sections 76A, 76B, 77, 88, 89 and 91 of the Act[4] (powers in relation to extradition under Part 2 of the Act). Under sections 9 and 77 of the Act, at the extradition hearing the court has the same powers (as nearly as may be) as a magistrates' court would have if the proceedings were the summary trial of an allegation against the defendant: see also rule 24.12(3) (Trial and sentence in a magistrates' court; procedure where the defendant is absent).*

*Under sections 206A to 206C of the 2003 Act[5], the court may require a defendant to attend by live link a preliminary hearing to which rule 50.5, 50.9 or 50.11 applies, any hearing for the purposes of rule 50.12 and the hearing to which rule 50.32 applies.*

*Part 6 contains rules about reporting and access restrictions.*

*Part 14 contains rules about bail. Rules 14.2(3) and 14.7(7)(c) allow an application to be determined without a hearing in the circumstances to which those rules apply.*

*The principal time limits are prescribed by the Extradition Act 2003: see rule 50.16.]*

**R50.4**   **Case management in the magistrates' court and duty of court officer**

50.4   (1)   The magistrates' court and the parties have the same duties and powers as under Part 3 (Case management), subject to—

      (a)   rule 50.2 (Special objective in extradition proceedings); and

---

[3] 2003 c. 41; sections 8A and 8B were inserted by section 69 of the Policing and Crime Act 2009 (c. 26). Sections 9 and 44 were amended by paragraph 16 of Schedule 13 to the Police and Justice Act 2006 (c. 48). Section 21B was inserted by section 159 of the Anti-social Behaviour, Crime and Policing Act 2014 (c. 12). Section 22 was amended by section 71 of the Policing and Crime Act 2009 (c. 26). Section 23 was amended by paragraph 7 of Schedule 13 to the Police and Justice Act 2006 (c. 48) and section 71 of the Policing and Crime Act 2009 (c. 26).

[4] 2003 c. 41; sections 76A and 76B were inserted by section 70 of the Policing and Crime Act 2009 (c. 26). Section 77 was amended by paragraph 16 of Schedule 13 to the Police and Justice Act 2006 (c. 48). Section 88 was amended by section 71 of the Policing and Crime Act 2009 (c. 26). Section 89 was amended by paragraph 7 of Schedule 13 to the Police and Justice Act 2006 (c. 48) and section 71 of the Policing and Crime Act 2009 (c. 26).

[5] 2003 c. 41; sections 206A, 206B and 206C were inserted by section 78 of the Policing and Crime Act 2009 (c. 26).

(b) paragraph (2) of this rule.

(2) Rule 3.6 (Application to vary a direction) does not apply to a decision to extradite or discharge.

(3) Where this rule applies, active case management by the court includes—

    (a) if the court requires information from the authorities in the requesting territory—

        (i) nominating a court officer, the designated authority which certified the arrest warrant where Part 1 of the Extradition Act 2003 Act applies, a party or other person to convey that request to those authorities, and

        (ii) in a case in which the terms of that request need to be prepared in accordance with directions by the court, giving such directions accordingly; and

    (b) giving such directions as are required where, under section 21B of the Extradition Act 2003[6], the parties agree—

        (i) to the temporary transfer of the defendant to the requesting territory, or

        (ii) that the defendant should speak with representatives of an authority in that territory.

(4) Where this rule applies, active assistance by the parties includes—

    (a) applying for any direction needed as soon as reasonably practicable; and

    (b) concisely explaining the reasons for any application for the court to direct—

        (i) the preparation of a request to which paragraph (3)(a) applies, or

        (ii) the making of arrangements to which paragraph (3)(b) applies.

(5) Where this rule applies, active assistance by the presenting officer includes—

    (a) taking reasonable steps to ensure that the defendant will be able to understand (with help, if necessary)—

        (i) what is alleged by the warrant, if Part 1 of the 2003 Act applies, or

        (ii) the content of the extradition request, if Part 2 of the Act applies; and

    (b) providing in writing identification of the equivalent offence or offences under the law of England and Wales for the conduct being relied on if—

        (i) this is raised for the defence as an issue and the court considers it necessary to identify the equivalent offence or offences in writing, or

        (ii) the defendant is not represented.

(6) The court officer must—

    (a) as soon as practicable, serve notice of the court's decision to extradite or discharge—

        (i) on the defendant,

        (ii) on the designated authority which certified the arrest warrant, where Part 1 of the 2003 Act applies, and

        (iii) on the Secretary of State, where Part 2 of the Act applies; and

    (b) give the court such assistance as it requires.

*[Note. Part 3 contains rules about case management which apply at an extradition hearing and during preparation for that hearing. This rule must be read in conjunction with those rules.*

*Under section 21B of the Extradition Act 2003 (Request for temporary transfer etc.), where Part 1 of the Act applies, and in the circumstances described in that section, the parties may agree to the defendant's temporary transfer to the requesting territory, or may agree that the defendant will speak to representatives of an investigating, prosecuting or judicial authority in that territory. On the making by a party of a request to such effect the court must if necessary adjourn the proceedings for 7 days while the other party considers it. If the parties then agree to proceed with the proposed transfer or discussion the court must adjourn the proceedings for however long seems necessary.]*

### Extradition under Part 1 of the Extradition Act 2003

**Preliminary hearing after arrest**　　　　　　　　　　　　　　　　　　　　　　**R50.5**

50.5 (1) This rule applies where the defendant is first brought before the court after—

    (a) arrest under a warrant to which Part 1 of the Extradition Act 2003 applies; or

    (b) provisional arrest under Part 1 of the Act.

(2) The presenting officer must—

    (a) serve on the court officer—

        (i) the arrest warrant, and

        (ii) a certificate, given by the authority designated by the Secretary of State, that the warrant was issued by an authority having the function of issuing such warrants in the territory to which the defendant's extradition is sought; or

    (b) apply at once for an extension of time within which to serve that warrant and that certificate.

(3) An application under paragraph (2)(b) must—

---

[6] 2003 c. 41; section 21B was inserted by section 159 of the Anti-social Behaviour, Crime and Policing Act 2014 (c. 12).

Criminal Procedure Rules and Criminal Practice Directions

  (a) explain why the requirement to serve the warrant and certificate at once could not reasonably be complied with; and

  (b) include—

   (i) any written material in support of that explanation, and

   (ii) representations about bail pending service of those documents.

(4) When the presenting officer serves the warrant and certificate, in the following sequence the court must—

  (a) decide whether the defendant is the person in respect of whom the warrant was issued;

  (b) explain, in terms the defendant can understand (with help, if necessary)—

   (i) the allegation made in the warrant, and

   (ii) that the defendant may consent to extradition, and how that may be done and with what effect;

  (c) give directions for an extradition hearing to begin—

   (i) no more than 21 days after the defendant's arrest, or

   (ii) if either party so applies, at such a later date as the court decides is in the interests of justice;

  (d) consider any ancillary application, including an application about bail pending the extradition hearing; and

  (e) give such directions as are required for the preparation and conduct of the extradition hearing.

*[Note. See sections 4, 6, 7 and 8 of the Extradition Act 2003[7].*

*Under section 6 of the Act, following a provisional arrest pending receipt of a warrant the defendant must be brought before the court within 48 hours, and the warrant and certificate must be served within that same period. If they are not so served, the court may extend the time for service by a further 48 hours.*

*Under section 45 of the Act[8], a defendant's consent to extradition must be given before the court, must be recorded in writing, and is irrevocable. Consent may not be given unless the defendant has a legal representative with him or her when giving consent, or the defendant has failed or refused to apply for legal aid, or legal aid has been refused or withdrawn.*

*Part 14 contains rules about bail.]*

## R50.6   Extradition hearing

50.6 (1) This rule applies at the extradition hearing arranged by the court under rule 50.5.

(2) In the following sequence, the court must decide—

  (a) whether the offence specified in the warrant is an extradition offence;

  (b) whether a bar to extradition applies, namely—

   (i)  the rule against double jeopardy,

   (ii)  absence of prosecution decision,

   (iii)  extraneous considerations,

   (iv)  the passage of time,

   (v)  the defendant's age,

   (vi)  speciality,

   (vii)  earlier extradition or transfer to the United Kingdom, or

   (viii) forum;

  (c) where the warrant alleges that the defendant is unlawfully at large after conviction, whether conviction was in the defendant's presence and if not—

   (i) whether the defendant was absent deliberately, and

   (ii) if the defendant was not absent deliberately, whether the defendant would be entitled to a retrial (or to a review of the conviction, amounting to a retrial);

  (d) whether extradition would be—

   (i) compatible with the defendant's human rights, and

   (ii) proportionate;

  (e) whether it would be unjust or oppressive to extradite the defendant because of his or her physical or mental condition;

---

[7] 2003 c. 41; section 6 was amended by section 77 of the Policing and Crime Act 2009 (c. 26). Section 7 was amended by paragraph 16 of Schedule 13 to the Police and Justice Act 2006 (c. 48) and section 77 of the Policing and Crime Act 2009 (c. 26). Section 8 was amended by paragraph 16 of Schedule 13 to the Police and Justice Act 2006 (c. 48) and section 155 of the Anti-social Behaviour, Crime and Policing Act 2014 (c. 12).

[8] 2003 c. 41; section 45 was amended by paragraphs 62 and 63 of Schedule 5 to the Legal Aid, Sentencing and Punishment of Offenders Act 2012 (c. 10) and section 163 of the Anti-social Behaviour, Crime and Policing Act 2014 (c. 12).

(f) after deciding each of (a) to (e) above, before progressing to the next, whether to order the defendant's discharge, and

(g) whether to order the temporary transfer of the defendant to the territory to which the defendant's extradition is sought.

(3) If the court discharges the defendant, the court must consider any ancillary application, including an application about—

(a) reporting restrictions; or

(b) costs.

(4) If the court does not discharge the defendant, the court must—

(a) exercise its power to order the defendant's extradition;

(b) explain, in terms the defendant can understand (with help, if necessary), that the defendant may appeal to the High Court within the next 7 days; and

(c) consider any ancillary application, including an application about—

(i) bail pending extradition,

(ii) reporting restrictions, or

(iii) costs.

(5) If the court orders the defendant's extradition, the court must order its postponement where—

(a) the defendant has been charged with an offence in the United Kingdom; or

(b) the defendant has been sentenced to imprisonment or detention in the United Kingdom.

*[Note. See sections 10, 11, 20, 21, 21B, 25, 26, 36A, 36B, 64 and 65 of the Extradition Act 2003[9].*

*Part 6 contains rules about reporting restrictions. Part 45 contains rules about costs.]*

**Discharge where warrant withdrawn**                                                      **R50.7**

**50.7** (1) This rule applies where the authority that certified the warrant gives the court officer notice that the warrant has been withdrawn—

(a) after the start of the hearing under rule 50.5; and

(b) before the court orders the defendant's extradition or discharge.

(2) The court must exercise its power to discharge the defendant.

*[Note. See section 41 of the Extradition Act 2003.]*

### Extradition under Part 2 of the Extradition Act 2003

**Issue of arrest warrant**                                                                **R50.8**

**50.8** (1) This rule applies where the Secretary of State serves on the court officer—

(a) an extradition request to which Part 2 of the Extradition Act 2003 applies;

(b) a certificate given by the Secretary of State that the request was received in the way approved for the request; and

(c) a copy of any Order in Council which applies to the request.

(2) In the following sequence, the court must decide—

(a) whether the offence in respect of which extradition is requested is an extradition offence; and

(b) whether there is sufficient evidence, or (where the Secretary of State has so ordered, for this purpose) information, to justify the issue of a warrant of arrest.

(3) The court may issue an arrest warrant—

(a) without giving the parties an opportunity to make representations; and

(b) without a hearing, or at a hearing in public or in private.

*[Note. See sections 70, 71, 137 and 138 of the Extradition Act 2003[10].]*

**Preliminary hearing after arrest**                                                       **R50.9**

**50.9** (1) This rule applies where a defendant is first brought before the court after arrest under a warrant to which rule 50.8 applies.

(2) In the following sequence, the court must—

---

[9] 2003 c. 41; section 11 was amended by paragraphs 3 and 4 of Schedule 13 to the Police and Justice Act 2006 (c. 48), paragraphs 1 and 2 of Schedule 20 to the Crime and Courts Act 2013 (c. 22) and sections 156, 157, 158 and 181 of, and paragraph 104 of Schedule 11 to, the Anti-social Behaviour, Crime and Policing Act 2014 (c. 12). Section 21 was amended by paragraph 16 of Schedule 13 to the Police and Justice Act 2006 (c. 48). Section 21B was inserted by section 159 of the Anti-social Behaviour, Crime and Policing Act 2014 (c. 12), section 26 was amended by section 160 of that Act, sections 36A and 36B were inserted by section 161 of that Act and sections 64 and 65 were substituted by section 164 of that Act.

[10] 2003 c. 41; section 70 was amended by paragraphs 1 and 17 of Schedule 13 to the Police and Justice Act 2006 (c. 48). Section 71 was amended by paragraph 202 of Schedule 16 to the Armed Forces Act 2006 (c. 52). Section 137 was amended by sections 164 and 181 of, and paragraph 117 of Schedule 11 to, the Anti-social Behaviour, Crime and Policing Act 2014 (c. 12). Section 138 was amended by sections 164 and 181 of, and paragraph 118 of Schedule 11 to, the 2014 Act.

  (a) explain, in terms the defendant can understand (with help, if necessary)—
      (i)   the content of the extradition request, and
      (ii)  that the defendant may consent to extradition, and how that may be done and with what effect;
  (b) arrange for an extradition hearing to begin—
      (i)   no more than 2 months later, or
      (ii)  if either party so applies, at such a later date as the court decides is in the interests of justice;
  (c) consider any ancillary application, including an application about bail pending the extradition hearing; and
  (d) give any direction as is appropriate to the needs of the case about the introduction of evidence at the extradition hearing.

*[Note. See sections 72 and 75 of the Extradition Act 2003[11].*

*Under section 127 of the 2003 Act[12] a defendant's consent to extradition must be given before the court, must be recorded in writing, and is irrevocable. Consent may not be given unless the defendant has a legal representative with him or her when giving consent, or the defendant has failed or refused to apply for legal aid, or legal aid has been refused or withdrawn.*

*Part 14 contains rules about bail.]*

**R50.10    Issue of provisional arrest warrant**

**50.10** (1) This rule applies where a presenting officer wants a justice of the peace to issue a provisional arrest warrant under Part 2 of the Extradition Act 2003, pending receipt of an extradition request.
  (2) The presenting officer must—
      (a) serve an application for a warrant on the court officer; and
      (b) verify that application on oath or affirmation.
  (3) In the following sequence, the justice must decide—
      (a) whether the alleged offence is an extradition offence; and
      (b) whether there is sufficient evidence, or (where the Secretary of State has so ordered, for this purpose) information, to justify the issue of a warrant of arrest.

*[Note. See sections 73, 137 and 138 of the Extradition Act 2003[13].]*

**R50.11    Preliminary hearing after provisional arrest**

**50.11** (1) This rule applies where a defendant is first brought before the court after arrest—
      (a) under a provisional arrest warrant to which rule 50.10 applies; or
      (b) under section 74A of the Extradition Act 2003[14], without a warrant.
  (2) Where paragraph (1)(b) applies the court must first—
      (a) on the basis of such evidence or information as is produced to the court, decide whether a warrant to which rule 50.10 applies would be issued if the defendant were not already under arrest; and
      (b) if no such warrant would be issued, order the defendant's discharge.
  (3) Unless the court orders the defendant's discharge under paragraph (2), the court must—
      (a) explain, in terms the defendant can understand (with help, if necessary)—
          (i)   the allegation in respect of which the defendant has been arrested, and
          (ii)  that the defendant may consent to extradition, and how that may be done and with what effect; and
      (b) consider any ancillary application, including an application about bail pending receipt of the extradition request.

---

[11] 2003 c. 41; section 72 was amended by paragraph 16 of Schedule 13 to the Police and Justice Act 2006 (c. 48).
[12] 2003 c. 41; section 127 was amended by paragraphs 62 and 64 of Schedule 5 to the Legal Aid, Sentencing and Punishment of Offenders Act 2012 (c. 10).
[13] 2003 c. 41; section 73 was amended by paragraph 203 of Schedule 16 to the Armed Forces Act 2006 (c. 52). Section 137 was amended by sections 164 and 181 of, and paragraph 117 of Schedule 11 to, the Anti-social Behaviour, Crime and Policing Act 2014 (c. 12). Section 138 was amended by sections 164 and 181 of, and paragraph 118 of Schedule 11 to, the 2014 Act.
[14] 2003 c. 41; section 74A was inserted by paragraphs 1 and 2 of the Schedule to the Extradition (Provisional Arrest) Act 2020 (c. 18).

*[Note. See sections 74, 74A, 74B, 74C, 74D and 74E of the Extradition Act 2003[15]. Under section 127 of the Act, a defendant's consent to extradition must be given before the court, must be recorded in writing, and is irrevocable. Consent may not be given unless the defendant has a legal representative with him or her when giving consent, or the defendant has failed or refused to apply for legal aid, or legal aid has been refused or withdrawn.]*

### Arrangement of extradition hearing after provisional arrest                    R50.12

**50.12** (1) This rule applies when the Secretary of State serves on the court officer—
    (a) a request for extradition in respect of which a defendant has been arrested—
        (i) under a provisional arrest warrant to which rule 50.10 applies, or
        (ii) under section 74A of the Extradition Act 2003, without a warrant;
    (b) a certificate given by the Secretary of State that the request was received in the way approved for the request; and
    (c) a copy of any Order in Council which applies to the request.
  (2) Unless a time limit for service of the request has expired, the court must—
    (a) give directions for an extradition hearing to begin—
        (i) no more than 2 months after service of the request, or
        (ii) if either party so applies, at such a later date as the court decides is in the interests of justice;
    (b) consider any ancillary application, including an application about bail pending the extradition hearing; and
    (c) give such directions as are required for the preparation and conduct of the extradition hearing.

*[Note. See section 76 of the Extradition Act 2003.]*

### Extradition hearing                                                            R50.13

**50.13** (1) This rule applies at the extradition hearing directed under rule 50.9 or rule 50.12.
  (2) In the following sequence, the court must decide—
    (a) whether the documents served on the court officer by the Secretary of State include—
        (i) those listed in rule 50.8(1) or rule 50.12(1), as the case may be,
        (ii) particulars of the person whose extradition is requested,
        (iii) particulars of the offence specified in the request, and
        (iv) as the case may be, a warrant for the defendant's arrest, or a certificate of the defendant's conviction and (if applicable) sentence, issued in the requesting territory;
    (b) whether the defendant is the person whose extradition is requested;
    (c) whether the offence specified in the request is an extradition offence;
    (d) whether the documents served on the court officer by the Secretary of State have been served also on the defendant;
    (e) whether a bar to extradition applies, namely—
        (i) the rule against double jeopardy,
        (ii) extraneous considerations,
        (iii) the passage of time,
        (iv) hostage-taking considerations, or
        (v) forum;
    (f) where the request accuses the defendant of an offence, whether there is evidence which would be sufficient to make a case requiring an answer by the defendant if the extradition proceedings were a trial (unless the Secretary of State has otherwise ordered, for this purpose);
    (g) where the request accuses the defendant of being unlawfully at large after conviction, whether the defendant was—
        (i) convicted in his or her presence, or
        (ii) absent deliberately;
    (h) where the request accuses the defendant of being unlawfully at large after conviction, and the defendant was absent but not deliberately—
        (i) whether the defendant would be entitled to a retrial (or to a review of the conviction amounting to a retrial), and
        (ii) if so, whether there is evidence which would be sufficient to make a case requiring an answer by the defendant if the extradition proceedings were a trial (unless the Secretary of State has otherwise ordered, for this purpose);
    (i) whether extradition would be compatible with the defendant's human rights;

Criminal Procedure Rules and Criminal Practice Directions

---

[15] 2003 c. 41; sections 74B, 74C, 74D and 74E were inserted by paragraphs 1 and 2 of the Schedule to the Extradition (Provisional Arrest) Act 2020 (c. 18).

        (j)   whether it would be unjust or oppressive to extradite the defendant because of his or her physical or mental condition; and

        (k)   after deciding each of (a) to (j) above, before progressing to the next, whether to order the defendant's discharge.

    (3)  If the court discharges the defendant, the court must consider any ancillary application, including an application about—

        (a)  reporting restrictions; or

        (b)  costs.

    (4)  If the court does not discharge the defendant, the court must—

        (a)  exercise its power to send the case to the Secretary of State to decide whether to extradite the defendant;

        (b)  explain, in terms the defendant can understand (with help, if necessary), that—

           (i)    the defendant may appeal to the High Court not more than 14 days after being informed of the Secretary of State's decision, and

          (ii)   any such appeal brought before the Secretary of State's decision has been made will not be heard until after that decision; and

        (c)  consider any ancillary application, including an application about—

           (i)    bail pending extradition,

          (ii)   reporting restrictions, or

         (iii)  costs.

    (5)  If the Secretary of State orders the defendant's extradition, the court must order its postponement where—

        (a)  the defendant has been charged with an offence in the United Kingdom; or

        (b)  the defendant has been sentenced to imprisonment or detention in the United Kingdom.

*[Note. See sections 78, 79, 84, 85, 86, 87, 91, 92, 137 and 138 of the Extradition Act 2003[16].*

*Part 6 contains rules about reporting restrictions. Part 45 contains rules about costs.]*

**R50.14**   **Discharge where extradition request withdrawn**

    **50.14** (1)  This rule applies where the Secretary of State gives the court officer notice that the extradition request has been withdrawn—

        (a)  after the start of the hearing under rule 50.9 or 50.11; and

        (b)  before the court—

           (i)    sends the case to the Secretary of State to decide whether to extradite the defendant, or

          (ii)   discharges the defendant.

    (2)  The court must exercise its power to discharge the defendant.

*[Note. See section 122 of the Extradition Act 2003.]*

### Evidence at extradition hearing

**R50.15**   **Introduction of additional evidence**

    **50.15** (1)  Where a party wants to introduce evidence at an extradition hearing under the law that would apply if that hearing were a trial, the relevant Part of these Rules applies with such adaptations as the court directs.

    (2)  If the court admits as evidence the written statement of a witness—

        (a)  each relevant part of the statement must be read or summarised aloud; or

        (b)  the court must read the statement and its gist must be summarised aloud.

    (3)  If a party introduces in evidence a fact admitted by another party, or the parties jointly admit a fact, a written record must be made of the admission.

*[Note. The admissibility of evidence that a party introduces is governed by rules of evidence.*

*Under section 202 of the Extradition Act 2003[17], the court may receive in evidence—*

    *(a)   a warrant to which Part 1 of the Act applies;*

    *(b)   any other document issued in a territory to which Part 1 of the Act applies, if the document is authenticated as required by the Act;*

---

[16] 2003 c. 41; section 79 was amended by paragraphs 4 and 5 of Schedule 20 to the Crime and Courts Act 2013 (c. 22). Section 103 was amended by section 160 of the Anti-social Behaviour, Crime and Policing Act 2014 (c. 12). Section 118A and 118B were inserted by section 161 of the 2014 Act. Section 137 was amended by sections 164 and 181 of, and paragraph 117 of Schedule 11 to, the 2014 Act. Section 138 was amended by sections 164 and 181 of, and paragraph 118 of Schedule 11 to, the 2014 Act.

[17] 2003 c. 41; section 202 was amended by paragraph 26 of Schedule 13 to the Police and Justice Act 2006 (c. 48).

(c)    a document issued in a territory to which Part 2 of the Act applies, if the document is authenticated as required by the Act.

Under sections 84 and 86 of the Act, which apply to evidence, if required, at an extradition hearing to which Part 2 of the Act applies, the court may accept as evidence of a fact a statement by a person in a document if oral evidence by that person of that fact would be admissible, and the statement was made to a police officer, or to someone else responsible for investigating offences or charging offenders.

Under section 205 of the Act, section 9 (proof by written witness statement) and section 10 (proof by formal admission) of the Criminal Justice Act 1967[18] apply to extradition proceedings as they apply in relation to proceedings for an offence.]

### Discharge after failure to comply with a time limit

**Defendant's application to be discharged**                                                      R50.16

50.16 (1)    This rule applies where a defendant wants to be discharged—
    (a)    because of a failure—
        (i)    to give the defendant a copy of any warrant under which the defendant is arrested as soon as practicable after arrest,
        (ii)    to bring the defendant before the court as soon as practicable after arrest under a warrant,
        (iii)    to bring the defendant before the court no more than 48 hours after provisional arrest under Part 1 of the Extradition Act 2003;
        (iv)    to give the defendant a copy of any certificate enabling provisional arrest without a warrant under section 74A of the 2003 Act as soon as practicable after arrest, or
        (v)    to bring the defendant before the court as soon as practicable after arrest under that section;
    (b)    because of a defect in a certificate enabling arrest without a warrant under section 74A of the 2003 Act;
    (c)    because there were no reasonable grounds on which there could have been issued a certificate enabling arrest without a warrant under section 74A of the 2003 Act;
    (d)    following the expiry of a time limit for—
        (i)    service of a warrant to which Part 1 of the 2003 Act applies, after provisional arrest under that Part of the Act (48 hours, under section 6 of the Act[19], unless the court otherwise directs),
        (ii)    service of an extradition request to which Part 2 of the Act applies, after provisional arrest under that Part of the Act (45 days, under section 74 of the Act[20], unless the Secretary of State has otherwise ordered for this purpose),
        (iii)    receipt of an undertaking that the defendant will be returned to complete a sentence in the United Kingdom, where the court required such an undertaking (21 days, under section 37 of the Act[21]),
        (iv)    making an extradition order, after the defendant has consented to extradition under Part 1 of the Act (10 days, under section 46 of the Act[22]),
        (v)    extradition, where an extradition order has been made under Part 1 of the Act and any appeal by the defendant has failed (10 days, under sections 35, 36 and 47 of the Act[23], unless the court otherwise directs),
        (vi)    extradition, where an extradition order has been made under Part 2 of the Act and any appeal by the defendant has failed (28 days, under sections 117 and 118 of the Act[24]),

---

[18]    1967 c. 80; section 9 was amended by section 56 of, and paragraph 49 of Schedule 8 to, the Courts Act 1971 (c. 23), section 168 of, and paragraph 6 of Schedule 9 to, the Criminal Justice and Public Order Act 1994 (c. 33), section 69 of the Criminal Procedure and Investigations Act 1996 (c. 25), regulation 9 of, and paragraph 4 of Schedule 5 to, S.I. 2001/1090, paragraph 43 of Schedule 3 and Part 4 of Schedule 37 to the Criminal Justice Act 2003 (c. 44), section 26 of, and paragraph 7 of Schedule 2 to, the Armed Forces Act 2011 (c. 18) and section 80 of the Deregulation Act 2015 (c. 20). It is further amended by section 72 of, and paragraph 55 of Schedule 5 to, the Children and Young Persons Act 1969 (c. 54) and section 65 of, and paragraph 1 of Schedule 4 to, the Courts Act 2003 (c. 39), with effect from dates to be appointed.
[19]    2003 c. 41; section 6 was amended by section 77 of the Policing and Crime Act 2009 (c. 26).
[20]    2003 c. 41; section 74 was amended by paragraph 16 of Schedule 13 to the Police and Justice Act 2006 (c. 48).
[21]    2003 c. 41; section 37 was amended by paragraphs 9 and 10 of Schedule 13 to the Police and Justice Act 2006 (c. 48).
[22]    2003 c. 41; section 46 was amended by paragraph 16 of Schedule 13 to the Police and Justice Act 2006 (c. 48).
[23]    2003 c. 41; section 35 was amended by paragraph 9 of Schedule 13 to the Police and Justice Act 2006 (c. 48). Section 36 was amended by section 40 of, and paragraph 81 of Schedule 9 to, the Constitutional Reform Act 2005 (c. 4).
[24]    2003 c. 41; section 118 was amended by section 40 of, and paragraph 81 of Schedule 9 to, the Constitutional Reform Act 2005 (c. 4).

Criminal Procedure Rules and Criminal Practice Directions

   (vii) the resumption of extradition proceedings, where those proceedings were adjourned pending disposal of another extradition claim which has concluded (21 days, under section 180 of the Act),

   (viii) extradition, where extradition has been deferred pending the disposal of another extradition claim which has concluded (21 days, under section 181 of the Act), or

   (ix) re-extradition, where the defendant has been returned to the United Kingdom to serve a sentence before serving a sentence overseas (as soon as practicable, under section 187 of the Act[25]); or

  (e) because an extradition hearing does not begin on the date arranged by the court.

 (2) Unless the court otherwise directs—

  (a) such a defendant must apply in writing and serve the application on—

   (i) the magistrates' court officer,

   (ii) the High Court officer, where paragraph (1)(d)(v) applies, and

   (iii) the prosecutor;

  (b) the application must explain the grounds on which it is made; and

  (c) the court officer must arrange a hearing as soon as practicable, and in any event no later than the second business day after an application is served.

*[Note. See sections 4(4) & (5), 6(6) & (7), 8(7) & (8)[26], 35(5), 36(8), 37(7), 46(8)[27], 47(4), 72(5) & (6), 74(5), (6) & (10), 74D(10), 75(4),76(5), 117(3), 118(7), 180(4) & (5), 181(4) & (5) and 187(3) of the Extradition Act 2003.]*

### Section 3: appeal to the High Court

*[Note. Under Part 1 of the Extradition Act 2003—*

 *(a) a defendant may appeal to the High Court against an order for extradition made by the magistrates' court; and*

 *(b) the authority requesting the defendant's extradition may appeal to the High Court against an order for the defendant's discharge,*

*(see sections 26 and 28 of the Act[28].*

*Under Part 2 of the 2003 Act—*

 *(a) a defendant may appeal to the High Court against an order by the magistrates' court sending a case to the Secretary of State for a decision whether to extradite the defendant;*

 *(b) a defendant may appeal to the High Court against an order for extradition made by the Secretary of State; and*

 *(c) the territory requesting the defendant's extradition may appeal to the High Court against an order for the defendant's discharge by the magistrates' court or by the Secretary of State,*

*(see sections 103, 105, 108 and 110 of the Act[29].*

*In each case the appellant needs the High Court's permission to appeal (in the 2003 Act, described as 'leave to appeal').]*

**R50.17** **Exercise of the High Court's powers**

 50.17 (1) The general rule is that the High Court must exercise its powers at a hearing in public, but—

  (a) that is subject to any power the court has to—

   (i) impose reporting restrictions,

   (ii) withhold information from the public, or

   (iii) order a hearing in private;

  (b) despite the general rule, the court may determine without a hearing—

   (i) an application for the court to consider out of time an application for permission to appeal to the High Court,

   (ii) an application for permission to appeal to the High Court (but a renewed such application must be determined at a hearing),

   (iii) an application for permission to appeal from the High Court to the Supreme Court,

---

[25] 2003 c. 41; section 187 was amended by paragraph 15 of Schedule 13 to the Police and Justice Act 2006 (c. 48).

[26] 2003 c. 41; section 8 was amended by paragraph 16 of Schedule 13 to the Police and Justice Act 2006 (c. 48).

[27] 2003 c. 41; section 46 was amended by paragraph 16 of Schedule 13 to the Police and Justice Act 2006 (c. 48).

[28] 2003 c. 41; sections 26 and 28 were amended by section 160 of the Anti-social Behaviour, Crime and Policing Act 2014 (c. 12).

[29] 2003 c. 41; section 108 was amended by paragraphs 10 and 12 of Schedule 20 to the Crime and Courts Act 2013 (c. 22). Section 108 was further amended, and sections 103, 105 and 110 were amended, by section 160 of the Anti-social Behaviour, Crime and Policing Act 2014 (c. 12).

        (iv) an application for permission to reopen a decision under rule 50.27 (Reopening the determination of an appeal), or

        (v) an application concerning bail; and

    (c) despite the general rule the court may, without a hearing—

        (i) give case management directions,

        (ii) reject a notice or application and, if applicable, dismiss an application for permission to appeal, where rule 50.31 (Payment of High Court fees) applies and the party who served the notice or application fails to comply with that rule, or

        (iii) make a determination to which the parties have agreed in writing.

(2) If the High Court so directs, a party may attend a hearing by live link.

(3) The general rule is that where the High Court exercises its powers at a hearing it may do so only if the defendant attends, in person or by live link, but, despite the general rule, the court may exercise its powers in the defendant's absence if—

    (a) the defendant waives the right to attend;

    (b) subject to any appeal to the Supreme Court, the result of the court's order would be the discharge of the defendant; or

    (c) the defendant is represented and—

        (i) the defendant is in custody, or

        (ii) the defendant's presence is impracticable by reason of his or her ill health or disorderly conduct.

(4) If the High Court gives permission to appeal to the High Court—

    (a) unless the court otherwise directs, the decision indicates that the appellant has permission to appeal on every ground identified by the appeal notice;

    (b) unless the court otherwise directs, the decision indicates that the court finds reasonably arguable each ground on which the appellant has permission to appeal; and

    (c) the court must give such directions as are required for the preparation and conduct of the appeal, including a direction as to whether the appeal must be heard by a single judge of the High Court or by a divisional court.

(5) If the High Court decides without a hearing an application for permission to appeal from the High Court to the Supreme Court, the High Court must announce its decision at a hearing in public.

(6) The High Court may—

    (a) shorten a time limit or extend it (even after it has expired), unless that is inconsistent with other legislation;

    (b) allow or require a party to vary or supplement a notice that that party has served;

    (c) direct that a notice or application be served on any person; and

    (d) allow a notice or application to be in a different form to one set out in the Practice Direction, or to be presented orally.

(7) A party who wants an extension of time within which to serve a notice or make an application must—

    (a) apply for that extension of time when serving that notice or making that application; and

    (b) give the reasons for the application for an extension of time.

*[Note. The time limits for serving an appeal notice are prescribed by the Extradition Act 2003: see rule 50.19.]*

### Case management in the High Court

                                                                     **R50.18**

50.18 (1) The High Court and the parties have the same duties and powers as under Part 3 (Case management), subject to—

    (a) rule 50.2 (Special objective in extradition proceedings); and

    (b) paragraph (3) of this rule.

(2) A master of the High Court, a deputy master, or a court officer nominated for the purpose by the Lord Chief Justice—

    (a) must fulfil the duty of active case management under rule 3.2, and in fulfilling that duty may exercise any of the powers of case management under—

        (i) rule 3.5 (the court's general powers of case management),

        (ii) rule 3.12(3) (requiring a certificate of readiness), and

        (iii) rule 3.13 (requiring a party to identify intentions and anticipated requirements) subject to the directions of a judge of the High Court; and

    (b) must nominate a case progression officer under rule 3.4.

(3) Rule 3.6 (Application to vary a direction) does not apply to a decision to give or to refuse—

    (a) permission to appeal; or

    (b) permission to reopen a decision under rule 50.27 (Reopening the determination of an appeal).

Criminal Procedure Rules and Criminal Practice Directions

**R50.19**   Service of appeal notice

**50.19** (1) A party who wants to appeal to the High Court must serve an appeal notice on—

    (a) in every case—

        (i) the High Court officer,

        (ii) the other party, and

        (iii) the Director of Public Prosecutions, unless the Director already has the conduct of the proceedings;

    (b) the designated authority which certified the arrest warrant, where Part 1 of the Extradition Act 2003 applies; and

    (c) the Secretary of State, where the appeal is against—

        (i) an order by the Secretary of State, or

        (ii) an order by the magistrates' court sending a case to the Secretary of State.

(2) A defendant who wants to appeal must serve the appeal notice—

    (a) not more than 7 days after the day on which the magistrates' court makes an order for the defendant's extradition, starting with that day, where that order is under Part 1 of the Extradition Act 2003; or

    (b) not more than 14 days after the day on which the Secretary of State informs the defendant of the Secretary of State's decision, starting with that day, where under Part 2 of the Act—

        (i) the magistrates' court sends the case to the Secretary of State for a decision whether to extradite the defendant, or

        (ii) the Secretary of State orders the defendant's extradition.

(3) An authority or territory seeking the defendant's extradition which wants to appeal against an order for the defendant's discharge must serve the appeal notice—

    (a) not more than 7 days after the day on which the magistrates' court makes that order, starting with that day, if the order is under Part 1 of the Extradition Act 2003;

    (b) not more than 14 days after the day on which the magistrates' court makes that order, starting with that day, if the order is under Part 2 of the Act; or

    (c) not more than 14 days after the day on which the Secretary of State informs the territory's representative of the Secretary of State's order, starting with that day, where the order is under Part 2 of the Act.

*[Note. See sections 26, 28, 103, 105, 108 and 110 of the Extradition Act 2003[30]. The time limits for serving an appeal notice are prescribed by those sections. They may be neither shortened nor extended, but—*

    *(a)  if a defendant applies out of time for permission to appeal to the High Court the court must not for that reason refuse to consider the application if the defendant did everything reasonably possible to ensure that the notice was given as soon as it could be; and*

    *(b)  a defendant may apply out of time for permission to appeal to the High Court on human rights grounds against an order for extradition made by the Secretary of State.*

*Under section 3 of the Prosecution of Offences Act 1985[31], the Director of Public Prosecutions may conduct extradition proceedings (but need not do so).]*

**R50.20**   Form of appeal notice

**50.20** (1) An appeal notice constitutes—

    (a) an application to the High Court for permission to appeal to that court; and

    (b) an appeal to that court, if the court gives permission.

(2) An appeal notice must be in writing.

---

[30]  2003 c. 41; section 108 was amended by paragraphs 10 and 12 of Schedule 20 to the Crime and Courts Act 2013 (c. 22). Section 108 was further amended, and sections 26, 28, 103, 105 and 110 were amended, by section 160 of the Anti-social Behaviour, Crime and Policing Act 2014 (c. 12).

[31]  1985 c. 23; section 3 was amended by section 15 of, and paragraph 13 of Schedule 2 to, the Criminal Justice Act 1987 (c. 38), paragraph 39 of Schedule 7 to the Police Act 1996 (c. 16), section 134 of, and paragraph 48 of Schedule 9 to, the Police Act 1997 (c. 50), section 164 of the Immigration and Asylum Act 1999 (c. 33), paragraph 10 of Schedule 7 to the Police Reform Act 2002 (c. 30), sections 86 and 92 of, and Schedule 3 to, the Anti-social Behaviour Act 2003 (c. 38), section 190 of the Extradition Act 2003 (c. 41), section 7 of the Asylum and Immigration (Treatment of Claimants, etc) Act 2004 (c. 19), section 40 of, and paragraph 41 of Schedule 9 to, the Constitutional Reform Act 2005 (c. 4), sections 59, 140 and 174 of, and paragraph 47 of Schedule 4 and Part 2 of Schedule 17 to, the Serious Organised Crime and Police Act 2005 (c. 15), sections 7, 8 and 52 of, and paragraph 15 of Schedule 3 to, the Violent Crime Reduction Act 2006 (c. 38), section 74 of, and paragraph 149 of Schedule 8 to, the Serious Crime Act 2007 (c. 27), paragraph 171 of Schedule 16 to the Police Reform and Social Responsibility Act 2011 (c. 13), section 15 of, and paragraph 30 of Schedule 8 to, the Crime and Courts Act 2013 (c. 22) and article 3 of, and paragraphs 1 and 2 of the Schedule to, S.I. 2014/834.

(3) In every case, the appeal notice must—
  (a) specify—
    (i) the date of the defendant's arrest under Part 1 or Part 2 of the Extradition Act 2003, and
    (ii) the decision about which the appellant wants to appeal, including the date of that decision;
  (b) identify each ground of appeal on which the appellant relies;
  (c) summarise the relevant facts;
  (d) identify any document or other material that the appellant thinks the court will need to decide the appeal; and
  (e) include or attach a list of those on whom the appellant has served the appeal notice.
(4) If a defendant serves an appeal notice after the expiry of the time limit specified in rule 50.19 (Service of appeal notice)—
  (a) the notice must—
    (i) explain what the defendant did to ensure that it was served as soon as it could be, and
    (ii) include or attach such evidence as the defendant relies upon to support that explanation; and
  (b) where the appeal is on human rights grounds against an order for extradition made by the Secretary of State, the notice must explain why—
    (i) the appeal is necessary to avoid real injustice, and
    (ii) the circumstances are exceptional and make it appropriate to consider the appeal.
(5) Unless the High Court otherwise directs, the appellant may amend the appeal notice—
  (a) by serving on those listed in rule 50.19(1) the appeal notice as so amended; and
  (b) not more than 10 business days after service of the appeal notice.
(6) Where the appeal is against an order by the magistrates' court—
  (a) if the grounds of appeal are that the magistrates' court ought to have decided differently a question of fact or law at the extradition hearing, the appeal notice must—
    (i) identify that question,
    (ii) explain what decision the magistrates' court should have made, and why, and
    (iii) explain why the magistrates' court would have been required not to make the order under appeal, if that question had been decided differently; and
  (b) if the grounds of appeal are that there is an issue which was not raised at the extradition hearing, or that evidence is available which was not available at the extradition hearing, the appeal notice must—
    (i) identify that issue or evidence,
    (ii) explain why it was not then raised or available,
    (iii) explain why that issue or evidence would have resulted in the magistrates' court deciding a question differently at the extradition hearing, and
    (iv) explain why, if the court had decided that question differently, the court would have been required not to make the order it made.
(7) Where the appeal is against an order by the Secretary of State—
  (a) if the grounds of appeal are that the Secretary of State ought to have decided differently a question of fact or law, the appeal notice must—
    (i) identify that question,
    (ii) explain what decision the Secretary of State should have made, and why, and
    (iii) explain why the Secretary of State would have been required not to make the order under appeal, if that question had been decided differently; and
  (b) if the grounds of appeal are that there is an issue which was not raised when the case was being considered by the Secretary of State, or that information is available which was not then available, the appeal notice must—
    (i) identify that issue or information,
    (ii) explain why it was not then raised or available,
    (iii) explain why that issue or information would have resulted in the Secretary of State deciding a question differently, and
    (iv) explain why, if the Secretary of State had decided that question differently, the order under appeal would not have been made.

*[Note. The Practice Direction sets out a form of appeal notice for use in connection with this rule.]*

**R50.21**     **Respondent's notice**

50.21 (1) A party on whom an appellant serves an appeal notice under rule 50.19 may serve a respondent's notice, and must do so if—

     (a) that party wants to make representations to the High Court; or

     (b) the court so directs.

(2) Such a party must serve any such notice on—

     (a) the High Court officer;

     (b) the appellant;

     (c) the Director of Public Prosecutions, unless the Director already has the conduct of the proceedings; and

     (d) any other person on whom the appellant served the appeal notice.

(3) Such a party must serve any such notice, as appropriate—

     (a) not more than 10 business days after—

         (i) service on that party of an amended appeal notice under rule 50.20(5) (Form of appeal notice), or

         (ii) the expiry of the time for service of any such amended appeal notice

     whichever of those events happens first; and

     (b) not more than 5 business days after service on that party of—

         (i) an appellant's notice renewing an application for permission to appeal, or

         (ii) a direction to serve a respondent's notice.

(4) A respondent's notice must—

     (a) give the date or dates on which the respondent was served with, as appropriate—

         (i) the appeal notice,

         (ii) the appellant's notice renewing the application for permission to appeal, or

         (iii) the direction to serve a respondent's notice;

     (b) identify each ground of opposition on which the respondent relies and the ground of appeal to which each such ground of opposition relates;

     (c) summarise any relevant facts not already summarised in the appeal notice; and

     (d) identify any document or other material that the respondent thinks the court will need to decide the appeal.

*[Note. Under rule 50.17, the High Court may extend or shorten the time limit under this rule.]*

**R50.22**     **Renewing an application for permission to appeal, restoring excluded grounds, etc.**

50.22 (1) This rule—

     (a) applies where the High Court—

         (i) refuses permission to appeal to the High Court, or

         (ii) gives permission to appeal to the High Court but not on every ground identified by the appeal notice; but

     (b) does not apply where—

         (i) a defendant applies out of time for permission to appeal to the High Court, and

         (ii) the court for that reason refuses to consider that application.

(2) Unless the court refuses permission to appeal at a hearing, the appellant may renew the application for permission by serving notice on—

     (a) the High Court officer;

     (b) the respondent; and

     (c) any other person on whom the appellant served the appeal notice,

     not more than 5 business days after service of notice of the court's decision on the appellant.

(3) If the court refuses permission to appeal, the renewal notice must explain the grounds for the renewal.

(4) If the court gives permission to appeal but not on every ground identified by the appeal notice the decision indicates that—

     (a) at the hearing of the appeal the court will not consider representations that address any ground thus excluded from argument; and

     (b) an appellant who wants to rely on such an excluded ground needs the court's permission to do so.

(5) An appellant who wants to rely at the hearing of an appeal on a ground of appeal excluded from argument must—

     (a) apply in writing, with reasons, and identify each such ground;

     (b) serve the application on—

        (i)   the High Court officer, and

        (ii)  the respondent; and

    (c)  serve the application not more than 5 business days after—

        (i)   the giving of permission to appeal, or

        (ii)  the High Court officer serves notice of that decision on the applicant, if the applicant was not present in person or by live link when permission to appeal was given.

(6)  Paragraph (7) applies where a party wants to abandon—

    (a)  a ground of appeal on which that party has permission to appeal; or

    (b)  a ground of opposition identified in a respondent's notice.

(7)  Such a party must serve notice on—

    (a)  the High Court officer; and

    (b)  each other party,

before any hearing at which that ground will be considered by the court.

*[Note. Under rule 50.17 (Exercise of the High Court's powers), the High Court may extend or shorten the time limits under this rule.*

*Rule 50.19 (Service of appeal notice) and the note to that rule set out the time limits for appeal.]*

**Appeal hearing**                                                                      **R50.23**

**50.23** (1)  Unless the High Court otherwise directs, where the appeal to the High Court is under Part 1 of the Extradition Act 2003 the hearing of the appeal must begin no more than 40 days after the defendant's arrest.

(2)  Unless the High Court otherwise directs, where the appeal to the High Court is under Part 2 of the 2003 Act the hearing of the appeal must begin no more than 76 days after the later of—

    (a)  service of the appeal notice; or

    (b)  the day on which the Secretary of State informs the defendant of the Secretary of State's order, in a case in which—

        (i)   the appeal is by the defendant against an order by the magistrates' court sending the case to the Secretary of State, and

        (ii)  the appeal notice is served before the Secretary of State decides whether the defendant should be extradited.

(3)  If the effect of the decision of the High Court on the appeal is that the defendant is to be extradited—

    (a)  the High Court must consider any ancillary application, including an application about—

        (i)   bail pending extradition,

        (ii)  reporting restrictions, or

        (iii) costs; and

    (b)  the High Court is the appropriate court to order a postponement of the defendant's extradition where—

        (i)   the defendant has been charged with an offence in the United Kingdom, or

        (ii)  the defendant has been sentenced to imprisonment or detention in the United Kingdom.

(4)  If the effect of the decision of the High Court on the appeal is that the defendant is discharged, the High Court must consider any ancillary application, including an application about—

    (a)  reporting restrictions; or

    (b)  costs.

*[Note. Under sections 31 and 113 of the Extradition Act 2003[32], if the appeal hearing does not begin within the period prescribed by this rule or ordered by the High Court the appeal must be taken to have been dismissed by decision of the High Court.*

*Under section 103 of the Extradition Act 2003[33], a defendant's appeal against an order by the magistrates' court sending the case to the Secretary of State must not be heard until after the Secretary of State has decided whether to order the defendant's extradition.*

*Part 6 contains rules about reporting restrictions. Part 45 contains rules about costs.]*

---

[32]  2003 c. 41.

[33]  2003 c. 41; section 103 was amended by section 160 of the Anti-social Behaviour, Crime and Policing Act 2014 (c. 12).

*See sections 36A, 36B, 118A and 118B Extradition Act 2003[34]. Where there is an appeal against an order for extradition, rules may provide that the appeal court may exercise the power under those sections to postpone the extradition.]*

**R50.24**    **Early termination of appeal: order by consent, etc.**

50.24 (1) This rule applies where—

    (a) an appellant has served an appeal notice under rule 50.19; and

    (b) the High Court—

        (i) has not determined the application for permission to appeal, or

        (ii) where the court has given permission to appeal, has not determined the appeal.

  (2) Where the warrant or extradition request with which the appeal is concerned is withdrawn—

    (a) the party or person so informing the court must serve on the High Court officer—

        (i) notice to that effect by the authority or territory requesting the defendant's extradition,

        (ii) details of how much of the warrant or extradition request remains outstanding, if any, and of any other warrant or extradition request outstanding in respect of the defendant,

        (iii) details of any bail condition to which the defendant is subject, if the defendant is on bail, and

        (iv) details sufficient to locate the defendant, including details of the custodian and of the defendant's date of birth and custody reference, if the defendant is in custody; and

    (b) paragraph (5) applies but only to the extent that the parties want the court to deal with an ancillary matter.

  (3) Where a defendant with whose discharge the appeal is concerned consents to extradition, paragraph (5) applies but only to the extent that the parties want the court to—

    (a) give directions for that consent to be given to the magistrates' court or to the Secretary of State, as the case may be; or

    (b) deal with an ancillary matter.

  (4) Paragraph (5) applies where the parties want the court to make a decision on which they are agreed—

    (a) determining the application for permission to appeal or the appeal, as the case may be;

    (b) specifying the date on which that application or appeal is to be treated as discontinued; and

    (c) determining an ancillary matter, including costs, if applicable.

  (5) The parties must serve on the High Court officer, in one or more documents—

    (a) a draft order in the terms proposed;

    (b) evidence of each party's agreement to those terms; and

    (c) concise reasons for the request that the court make the proposed order.

*[Note. Under sections 42 and 124 of the Extradition Act 2003[35], where an appeal is pending in the High Court and the court is informed that the relevant warrant or extradition request has been withdrawn the court must—*

    *(a) order the defendant's discharge and quash the extradition order or decision, where the defendant has appealed against extradition;*

    *(b) dismiss the application for permission to appeal or the appeal, as the case may be, where the authority or territory requesting the defendant's extradition has appealed against the defendant's discharge.*

*Under sections 45 and 127 of the 2003 Act[36], a defendant in respect of whom no extradition order or decision has been made may give consent to extradition in the magistrates' court, or may give such consent to the Secretary of State if the case has been sent there.*

---

[34] 2003 c. 41; sections 36A, 36B, 118A and 118B were inserted by section 161 of the Anti-social Behaviour, Crime and Policing Act 2014 (c. 12).

[35] 2003 c. 41; sections 42 and 124 were amended by article 3 of S.I. 2015/992.

[36] 2003 c. 41; sections 45 was amended by section 39 of, and paragraphs 62 and 63 of Schedule 5 to, the Legal Aid, Sentencing and Punishment of Offenders Act 2012 (c. 10) and section 163 of the Anti-social Behaviour, Crime and Policing Act 2014 (c. 12). Section 127 was amended by section 39 of, and paragraphs 62 and 64 of Schedule 5 to, the Legal Aid, Sentencing and Punishment of Offenders Act 2012 (c. 10).

*Where the effect of the High Court's decision is that the defendant is to be extradited, sections 36 and 118 of the Act[37] set time limits for extradition after the end of the case.*

*Part 45 contains rules about costs.]*

**Application for permission to appeal to the Supreme Court**                    **R50.25**

50.25 (1) This rule applies where a party to an appeal to the High Court wants to appeal to the Supreme Court.

   (2) Such a party must—
      (a) apply orally to the High Court for permission to appeal immediately after the court's decision; or
      (b) apply in writing and serve the application on the High Court officer and every other party not more than 14 days after that decision.

   (3) Such a party must—
      (a) identify the point of law of general public importance that the appellant wants the High Court to certify is involved in the decision;
      (b) serve on the High Court officer a statement of that point of law; and
      (c) give reasons why—
         (i) that point of law ought to be considered by the Supreme Court, and
         (ii) the High Court ought to give permission to appeal.

   (4) As well as complying with paragraph (3), a defendant's application for permission to appeal to the Supreme Court must include or attach any application for the following, with reasons—
      (a) bail pending appeal; or
      (b) permission to attend any hearing in the Supreme Court, if the appellant is in custody.

*[Note. See sections 32 and 114 of the Extradition Act 2003[38]. Those sections prescribe the time limit for serving an application for permission to appeal to the Supreme Court. It may be neither shortened nor extended.]*

**Determination of detention pending appeal to the Supreme Court against discharge**          **R50.26**

50.26 On an application for permission to appeal to the Supreme Court against a decision of the High Court which, but for that appeal, would have resulted in the defendant's discharge, the High Court must—
   (a) decide whether to order the detention of the defendant; and
   (b) determine any application for—
      (i) bail pending appeal,
      (ii) permission to attend any hearing in the Supreme Court, or
      (iii) a representation order.

*[Note. See sections 33A and 115A of the Extradition Act 2003[39].*

*For the grant of legal aid for proceedings in the Supreme Court, see sections 14, 16 and 19 of the Legal Aid, Sentencing and Punishment of Offenders Act 2012[40].]*

**Reopening the determination of an appeal**                              **R50.27**

50.27 (1) This rule applies where a party wants the High Court to reopen a decision of that court which determines an appeal or an application for permission to appeal.

   (2) Such a party must—
      (a) apply in writing for permission to reopen that decision, as soon as practicable after becoming aware of the grounds for doing so; and
      (b) serve the application on the High Court officer and every other party.

   (3) The application must—
      (a) specify the decision which the applicant wants the court to reopen; and
      (b) give reasons why—
         (i) it is necessary for the court to reopen that decision in order to avoid real injustice,
         (ii) the circumstances are exceptional and make it appropriate to reopen the decision, and
         (iii) there is no alternative effective remedy.

---

[37] 2003 c. 41; sections 36 and 118 were amended by section 40 of, and paragraph 81 of Schedule 9 to, the Constitutional Reform Act 2005 (c. 4).
[38] 2003 c. 41; sections 32 and 114 were amended by paragraph 81 of Schedule 9 to the Constitutional Reform Act 2005 (c. 4) and section 42 of, and paragraph 8 of Schedule 13 to, the Police and Justice Act 2006 (c. 48).
[39] 2003 c. 41; sections 33A and 115A were inserted by section 42 of, and paragraphs 8 and 35 of Schedule 13 to, the Police and Justice Act 2006 (c. 48).
[40] 2012 c. 10.

(4) The court must not give permission to reopen a decision unless each other party has had an opportunity to make representations.

**R50.28** **Declaration of incompatibility with a Convention right**

50.28 (1) This rule applies where a party—

    (a) wants the High Court to make a declaration of incompatibility with a Convention right under section 4 of the Human Rights Act 1998[41]; or

    (b) raises an issue that appears to the High Court may lead to the court making such a declaration.

(2) If the High Court so directs, the High Court officer must serve notice on—

    (a) the relevant person named in the list published under section 17(1) of the Crown Proceedings Act 1947[42]; or

    (b) the Treasury Solicitor, if it is not clear who is the relevant person.

(3) That notice must include or attach details of—

    (a) the legislation affected and the Convention right concerned;

    (b) the parties to the appeal; and

    (c) any other information or document that the High Court thinks relevant.

(4) A person who has a right under the 1998 Act to become a party to the appeal must—

    (a) serve notice on—

        (i) the High Court officer, and

        (ii) the other parties,

    if that person wants to exercise that right; and

    (b) in that notice—

        (i) indicate the conclusion that that person invites the High Court to reach on the question of incompatibility, and

        (ii) identify each ground for that invitation, concisely outlining the arguments in support.

(5) The High Court must not make a declaration of incompatibility—

    (a) less than 15 business days after the High Court officer serves notice under paragraph (2); and

    (b) without giving any person who serves a notice under paragraph (4) an opportunity to make representations at a hearing.

**R50.29** **Duties of court officers**

50.29 (1) The magistrates' court officer must—

    (a) keep any document or object exhibited in the proceedings in the magistrates' court, or arrange for it to be kept by some other appropriate person, until—

        (i) 6 weeks after the conclusion of those proceedings, or

        (ii) the conclusion of any proceedings in the High Court that begin within that 6 weeks;

    (b) provide the High Court with any document, object or information for which the High Court officer asks, within such period as the High Court officer may require; and

    (c) arrange for the magistrates' court to hear as soon as practicable any application to that court for bail pending appeal.

(2) A person who, under arrangements made by the magistrates' court officer, keeps a document or object exhibited in the proceedings in the magistrates' court must—

    (a) keep that exhibit until—

        (i) 6 weeks after the conclusion of those proceedings, or

        (ii) the conclusion of any proceedings in the High Court that begin within that 6 weeks, unless the magistrates' court or the High Court otherwise directs; and

    (b) provide the High Court with any such document or object for which the High Court officer asks, within such period as the High Court officer may require.

(3) The High Court officer must—

    (a) give as much notice as reasonably practicable of each hearing to—

        (i) the parties,

        (ii) the defendant's custodian, if any, and

        (iii) any other person whom the High Court requires to be notified;

    (b) serve a record of each order or direction of the High Court on—

        (i) the parties,

        (ii) any other person whom the High Court requires to be notified;

---

[41] 1998 c. 42; section 4 was amended by section 40 of, and paragraph 66 of Schedule 9 to, the Constitutional Reform Act 2005 (c. 4) and section 67 of, and paragraph 43 of Schedule 6 to, the Mental Capacity Act 2005 (c. 9).
[42] 1947 c. 44; section 17 was amended by article 3(2) of S.I. 1968/1656.

(c) if the High Court's decision determines an appeal or application for permission to appeal, serve a record of that decision on—

    (i) the defendant's custodian, if any,

    (ii) the magistrates' court officer, and

    (iii) the designated authority which certified the arrest warrant, where Part 1 of the Extradition Act 2003 applies;

(d) where rule 50.24 applies (Early termination of appeal: order by consent, etc.), arrange for the High Court to consider the document or documents served under that rule; and

(e) treat the appeal as if it had been dismissed by the High Court where—

    (i) the hearing of the appeal does not begin within the period required by rule 50.23 (Appeal hearing) or ordered by the High Court, or

    (ii) on an appeal by a requesting territory under section 105 of the Extradition Act 2003[43], the High Court directs the magistrates' court to decide a question again and the magistrates' court comes to the same conclusion as it had done before.

*[Note. See section 106 of the Extradition Act 2003[44].]*

**Constitution of the High Court**                                  **R50.30**

**50.30** (1) A master of the High Court or a deputy master, may exercise any power of the High Court to which the rules in this Section apply, except the power to—

    (a) give or refuse permission to appeal;

    (b) determine an appeal;

    (c) reopen a decision which determines an appeal or an application for permission to appeal;

    (d) grant or withhold bail; or

    (e) impose or vary a condition of bail.

(2) Despite paragraph (1), such a master or deputy master may exercise one of the powers listed in paragraph (1)(a), (b), (d) or (e) if making a decision to which the parties have agreed in writing.

(3) A renewed application for permission to appeal to the High Court may be determined by—

    (a) a single judge of the High Court other than the judge who first refused permission, or

    (b) a divisional court.

(4) An appeal may be determined by—

    (a) a single judge of the High Court; or

    (b) a divisional court.

*[Note. See sections 19 and 66 of the Senior Courts Act 1981[45].]*

**Payment of High Court fees**                                      **R50.31**

**50.31** (1) This rule applies where a party serves on the High Court officer a notice or application in respect of which a court fee is payable under legislation that requires the payment of such a fee.

(2) Such a party must pay the fee, or satisfy the conditions for any remission of the fee, when so serving the notice or application.

(3) If such a party fails to comply with paragraph (2), then unless the High Court otherwise directs—

    (a) the High Court officer must serve on that party a notice requiring payment of the fee due, or satisfaction of the conditions for any remission of that fee, within a period specified in the notice;

    (b) that party must comply with such a requirement; and

    (c) until the expiry of the period specified in the notice, the High Court must not exercise its power—

        (i) to reject the notice or application in respect of which the fee is payable, or

        (ii) to dismiss an application for permission to appeal, in consequence of rejecting an appeal notice.

[43] 2003 c. 41; section 105 was amended by section 160 of the Anti-social Behaviour, Crime and Policing Act 2014 (c. 12).

[44] 2003 c. 41; section 106 was amended by section 42 of, and paragraph 8 of Schedule 13 to, the Police and Justice Act 2006 (c. 48).

[45] 1981 c. 54.

*Criminal Procedure Rules and Criminal Practice Directions*

*[Note. Section 92 of the Courts Act 2003[46] and the Civil Proceedings Fees Order 2008[47] require the payment of High Court fees in cases to which this Section of this Part applies. Article 5 and Schedule 2 to the 2008 Order provide for the remission of such fees in some cases.]*

### Section 4: post-extradition proceedings

**R50.32**   **Application for consent to deal with another offence or for consent to further extradition**

**50.32** (1)   This rule applies where—
   (a)   a defendant has been extradited to a territory under Part 1 of the Extradition Act 2003[48];
      and
   (b)   the court officer receives from the authority designated by the Secretary of State a request for the court's consent to—
      (i)   the defendant being dealt with in that territory for an offence other than one in respect of which the extradition there took place, or
      (ii)   the defendant's further extradition from there to another such territory for an offence.
   (2)   The presenting officer must serve on the court officer—
      (a)   the request; and
      (b)   a certificate given by the designated authority that the request was made by a judicial authority with the function of making such requests in the territory to which the defendant was extradited.
   (3)   The court must—
      (a)   give directions for service by a party or other person on the defendant of notice that the request for consent has been received, unless satisfied that it would not be practicable for such notice to be served;
      (b)   give directions for a hearing to consider the request to begin—
         (i)   no more than 21 days after the request was received by the designated authority, or
         (ii)   at such a later date as the court decides is in the interests of justice; and
      (c)   give such directions as are required for the preparation and conduct of that hearing.
   (4)   At the hearing directed under paragraph (3), in the following sequence the court must decide—
      (a)   whether the consent requested is required, having regard to—
         (i)   any opportunity given for the defendant to leave the requesting territory after extradition which the defendant did not take within 45 days of arrival there,
         (ii)   if the defendant did not take such an opportunity, any requirements for consent imposed by the law of the requesting territory or by arrangements between that territory and the United Kingdom where the request is for consent to deal with the defendant in that territory for another offence, and
         (iii)   if the defendant did not take such an opportunity, any requirements for consent imposed by arrangements between the requesting territory and the United Kingdom where the request is for consent to extradite the defendant to another territory for an offence; and
      (b)   if such consent is required, then—
         (i)   whether the offence in respect of which consent is requested is an extradition offence, and
         (ii)   if it is, whether the court would order the defendant's extradition under sections 11 to 25 of the Extradition Act 2003 (bars to extradition and other considerations) were the defendant in the United Kingdom and the court was considering extradition for that offence.
   (5)   The court must give directions for notice of its decision to be conveyed to the authority which made the request.
   (6)   Rules 50.3 (Exercise of magistrates' court's powers) and 50.4 (Case management in the magistrates' court and duty of court officer) apply on an application under this rule.

*[Note. See sections 54, 55, 56 and 57 of the Extradition Act 2003[49].]*

---

[46]   2003 c. 39; section 92 was amended by sections 15 and 59 of, and paragraphs 308 and 345 of Schedule 4 and paragraph 4 of Schedule 11 to, the Constitutional Reform Act 2005 (c. 4) and section 17 of, and paragraph 40 of Schedule 9 and paragraphs 83 and 95 of Schedule 10 to, the Crime and Courts Act 2013.
[47]   S. I. 2008/1053; amended by S.I. 2013/1410, 2013/2302, 2014/874.
[48]   2003 c. 41.
[49]   2003 c. 41.

CRIMINAL PRACTICE DIRECTIONS    PART 50    EXTRADITION

**CPD XI Other Proceedings 50A: Extradition: General Matters and Management of the Appeal**        **CPD.50A**

*General matters: expedition at all times*

**50A.1**    Compliance with these directions is essential to ensure that extradition proceedings are dealt with expeditiously, both in accordance with the spirit of the Council Framework Decision of 13 June 2002 on the European Arrest Warrant and surrender procedures between Member States and the United Kingdom's other treaty obligations. It is of the utmost importance that orders which provide directions for the proper management and progress of cases are obeyed so that the parties can fulfil their duty to assist the court in furthering the overriding objective and in making efficient use of judicial resources. To that end:

(i)    the court may, and usually should, give case management directions, which may be based on a model, but adapted to the needs of the individual case, requiring the parties to supply case management information, consistently with the overriding objective of the Criminal Procedure Rules and compatibly with the parties' entitlement to legal professional and litigation privilege;

(ii)    a defendant whose extradition is requested must expect to be required to identify what he or she intends to put in issue so that directions can be given to achieve a single, comprehensive and effective extradition hearing at the earliest possible date;

(iii)    where the issues are such that further information from the requesting authority or state is needed then it is essential that the request is formulated clearly and in good time, in terms to which the parties can expect to contribute but which terms must be approved by the court, in order that those to whom the request is addressed will be able to understand what is sought, and why, and so can respond promptly;

(iv)    where such a request or other document, including a formal notice to the defendant of a post-extradition consent request, requires transmission to an authority or other person in a requesting state or other place outside the UK, it is essential that clear and realistic directions for the transmission are given, identifying who is to be responsible and to what timetable, having regard to the capacity of the proposed courier. Once given, such directions must be promptly complied with and the court at once informed if difficulties are encountered.

(v)    any skeleton argument must comply with the requirements of these Practice Directions and, if applicable, of the court. (Paragraphs XII D.17 to D.23 set out the general requirements for skeleton arguments. Paragraphs XI 50E.1 to 50E.7 set out some special requirements that apply in an extradition appeal to the High Court.)

*General guidance under s. 2(7A) Extradition Act 2003 (as amended by the Anti-Social Behaviour, Crime and Policing Act 2014)*

**50A.2**    When proceeding under section 21A of the Act and considering under subsection (3)(a) of the Act the seriousness of the conduct alleged to constitute the extradition offence, the judge will determine the issue on the facts of each case as set out in the warrant, subject to the guidance in paragraph 50A.3 below.

**50A.3**    In any case where the conduct alleged to constitute the offence falls into one of the categories in the table at paragraph 50A.5 below, unless there are exceptional circumstances, the judge should generally determine that extradition would be disproportionate. It would follow under the terms of s. 21A(4)(b) of the Act that the judge must order the person's discharge.

**50A.4**    The exceptional circumstances referred to above in paragraph 50A.3 will include:

i.    Vulnerable victim

ii.    Crime committed against someone because of their disability, gender-identity, race, religion or belief, or sexual orientation

iii.    Significant premeditation

iv.    Multiple counts

v.    Extradition also sought for another offence

vi.    Previous offending history

**50A.5** The table is as follows:

| Category of offence | Examples |
|---|---|
| Minor **theft** — (not robbery/ burglary or theft from the person) | Where the theft is of a low monetary value and there is a low impact on the victim or indirect harm to others, for example:<br>(a) Theft of an item of food from a supermarket<br>(b) Theft of a small amount of scrap metal from company premises<br>(c) Theft of a very small sum of money |
| Minor financial offences (**forgery, fraud** and **tax** offences) | Where the sums involved are small and there is a low impact on the victim and / or low indirect harm to others, for example:<br>(a) Failure to file a tax return or invoices on time<br>(b) Making a false statement in a tax return<br>(c) Dishonestly applying for a tax refund<br>(d) Obtaining a bank loan using a forged or falsified document<br>(e) Non-payment of child maintenance |
| Minor **road traffic, driving** and related offences | Where no injury, loss or damage was incurred to any person or property, for example:<br>(a) Driving whilst using a mobile phone<br>(b) Use of a bicycle whilst intoxicated |
| Minor **public order** offences | Where there is no suggestion the person started the trouble, and the offending behaviour was for example:<br>(a) Non-threatening verbal abuse of a law enforcement officer or government official<br>(b) Shouting or causing a disturbance, without threats<br>(c) Quarrelling in the street, without threats |
| Minor **criminal damage**, (other than by fire) | For example, breaking a window |
| **Possession of controlled substance** (other than one with a high capacity for harm such as heroin, cocaine, LSD or crystal meth) | Where it was possession of a very small quantity and intended for personal use |

CPD.50B **CPD XI Other Proceedings 50B Management of the Appeal to the High Court**

**50B.1** Applications for permission to appeal to the High Court under the Extradition Act 2003 must be started in the Administrative Court of the Queen's Bench Division at the Royal Courts of Justice in London.

**50.B.2** A Lord Justice of Appeal appointed by the Lord Chief Justice will have responsibility to assist the President of the Queen's Bench Division with overall supervision of extradition appeals.

*Definitions*

**50B.3** Where appropriate 'appeal' includes 'application for permission to appeal'.

**50B.4** 'EAW' means European Arrest Warrant.

**50B.5** A 'nominated legal officer of the court' is a court officer assigned to the Administrative Court Office who is a barrister or solicitor and who has been nominated for the purpose by the Lord Chief Justice under CrimPR 50.18 and 50.30.

*Forms*

**50B.6** The forms are to be used in the High Court, in accordance with the CrimPR 50.19, 50.20, 50.21 and 50.22.

**50B.7** The forms may be amended or withdrawn from time to time, or new forms added, under the authority of the Lord Chief Justice: see CrimPD I 5A.

*Management of the Appeal*

**50B.8**   Where it is not possible for the High Court to begin to hear the appeal in accordance with time limits contained in Crim PR 50.23(1) and (2), the Court may extend the time limit if it believes it to be in the interests of justice to do so and may do so even after the time limit has expired.

**50B.9**   The power to extend those time limits may be exercised by a Lord Justice of Appeal, a Single Judge of the High Court, a Master of the Administrative Court or a nominated legal officer of the court.

**50B.10**   Case Management directions setting down a timetable may be imposed upon the parties by a Lord Justice of Appeal, a Single Judge of the High Court, a Master of the Administrative Court or a nominated legal officer of the court. For the court's constitution and relevant powers and duties see section 4 of the Senior Courts Act 1981 and CrimPR 50.18 and 50.30.

*Listing of Oral, Renewal Hearings and Substantive Hearings*

**50B.11**   Arrangements for the fixing of dates for hearings will be made by a Listing Officer of the Administrative Court under the direction of the Judge with overall responsibility for supervision of extradition appeals.

**50B.12**   A Lord Justice of Appeal, a Single Judge of the High Court, a Master of the Administrative Court or a nominated legal officer of the court may give such directions to the Listing Officer as they deem necessary with regard to the fixing of dates, including as to whether cases in the same/related proceedings or raising the same or similar issues should be heard together or consecutively under the duty imposed by Crim PR 1.1(2)(e). Parties must alert the nominated legal officer of the court for the need for such directions.

**50B.13**   Save in exceptional circumstances, regard will not be given to an advocate's existing commitments. This is in accordance with the spirit of the legislation that extradition matters should be dealt with expeditiously. Extradition matters are generally not so complex that an alternative advocate cannot be instructed.

**50B.14**   If a party disagrees with the time estimate given by the Court, they must inform the Listing Office within 5 business days of the notification of the listing and they must provide a time estimate of their own.

*Expedited appeals*

**50B.15**   The Court may direct that the hearing of an appeal be expedited.

**50B.16**   The Court will deal with requests for an expedited appeal without a hearing. Requests for expedition must be made in writing, either within the appeal notice, or by application notice, clearly marked with the Administrative Court reference number, which must be lodged with the Administrative Court Office or emailed to the appropriate email address: administrativecourt office.crimex@hmcts.x.gsi.gov.uk and notice must be given to the other parties.

**50B.17**   Any requests for an expedited appeal made to an out of hours Judge must be accompanied by:
 i)   A detailed chronology;
 ii)  Reasons why the application could not be made within Court hours;
 iii) Any Orders or Judgments made in the proceedings.

*Amendment to Notices*

**50B.18**   Amendment to Notice of Appeal requiring permission
 (i)   Subject to Crim PR 50.20(5), an appeal notice may not be amended without the permission of the Court: CrimPR 50.17(6)(b);
 (ii)  An application for permission to amend made before permission to appeal has been considered will be determined without a hearing;
 (iii) An application for permission to amend after permission to appeal has been granted and any submissions in opposition will normally be dealt with at the hearing unless there is any risk that the hearing may have to be adjourned. If there is any risk that the application to amend may lead the other party to seek time to answer the proposed amendment, the application must be made as soon as practicable and well in advance of the hearing. A failure to make immediate applications for such an amendment is likely to result in refusal.
 (iv)  Legal representatives or the appellant, if acting in person, must
   a.   Inform the Court at the time they make the application if the existing time estimate is affected by the proposed amendment; and
   b.   Attempt to agree any revised time estimate no later than 5 business days after service of the application.
 (v)   where the appellant wishes to restore grounds of appeal excluded on the grant of permission to appeal, the procedure is governed by CrimPR 50.22.

**50B.19**    Amendment to Respondent's Notice

     (i)   A respondent's notice may not be amended without the permission of the Court: CrimPR 50.17(6)(b);

     (ii)   An application for permission to amend made before permission to appeal has been considered will be determined without a hearing.

     (iii)   An application for permission to amend after permission to appeal has been granted and any submissions in opposition will normally be dealt with at the hearing unless there is any risk that the hearing may have to be adjourned. If there is any risk that the application to amend may require the other party to seek time to answer the proposed amendment, the application must be made as soon as practicable and well in advance of the hearing. A failure to make immediate applications for such an amendment is likely to result in refusal.

     (iv)   Legal representatives or the appellant, if acting in person, must

         a.   Inform the Court at the time they make the application if the existing time estimate is affected by the proposed amendment; and

         b.   Attempt to agree any revised time estimate no later than 5 business days after service of the application.

*Use of Live-Links*

**50B.20**    When a party acting in person is in custody, the Court office will request the institution to use live-link for attendance at any oral or renewal hearing or substantive appeal. The institution must give precedence to all such applications in the High Court over live-links to the lower courts, including the Crown Court.

*Interpreters*

**50B.21**    It is the responsibility of the Court Listing Officer to ensure the attendance of an accredited interpreter when an unrepresented party in extradition proceedings is acting in person and does not understand or speak English.

**50B.22**    Where a party who does not understand or speak English is legally represented it is the responsibility of his/her solicitors to instruct an interpreter if required for any hearing in extradition proceedings.

*Disposing of applications and appeals by way of consent*

**50B.23**    CrimPR 50.24 governs the submission of Consent Orders and lists the essential requirements for such orders. Any Consent Order, the effect of which will be to allow extradition to proceed, must specify the date on which the appeal proceedings are to be treated as discontinued, for the purposes of section 36 or 118, as the case may be, of the Extradition Act 2003: whether that is to be the date on which the order is made or some later date. A Consent Order may be approved by a Lord Justice of Appeal, a Single Judge of the High Court or, under CrimPR 50.30(2), a nominated legal officer of the court. The order may, but need not, be pronounced in open court: CrimPR 50.17(1)(c)(iii). Once approved, the order will be sent to the parties and to any other person as required by CrimPR 50.29(3)(b), (c).

**50B.24**    A consent order to allow an appeal brought under s.28 of the Extradition Act 2003 must provide —

     (i)   for the quashing of the decision of the District Judge in Westminster Magistrates' Court discharging the Requested Person;

     (ii)   for the matter to be remitted to the District Judge to hold fresh extradition proceedings;

     (iii)   for any ancillary matter, such as bail or costs.

**50B.25**    A consent order to allow an appeal brought under s.110 of the Extradition Act 2003 must provide —

     (i)   for the quashing of the decision of the Secretary of State for the Home Department not to order extradition;

     (ii)   for the matter to be remitted to the Secretary of State to make a fresh decision on whether or not to order extradition;

     (iii)   for any ancillary matter, such as bail or costs.

**50B.26**    (a)   a Consent Order is intended to dispose of an application for permission to appeal which has not yet been considered by the court, the order must make clear by what means that will be achieved, bearing in mind that an application for permission which is refused without a hearing can be renewed under CrimPR 50.22(2). If the parties intend to exclude the possibility of renewal the order should declare either (i) that the time limit under rule 50.22(2) is reduced to nil, or (ii) permission to appeal is given and the appeal determined on the other terms of the order.

     (b)   one of the parties is a child or protected party, the documents served under CrimPR 50.24(5) must include an opinion from the advocate acting on behalf of the child or protected party and, in the case of a protected party, any relevant documents prepared for the Court of Protection.

*Fees*

**50B.27**   Applications to extend representation orders do not attract any fee.

**50B.28**   Fees are payable for all other applications in accordance with the current Fees Order.

**CPD XI Other Proceedings 50C: Extradition: Representation Orders**

**50C.1**   Representation orders may be granted by a Lord Justice of Appeal, a Single Judge of the High Court, a Master of the Administrative Court or a nominated legal officer of the court upon a properly completed CRM14 being lodged with the Court. A representation order will cover junior advocate and solicitors for the preparation of the Notice of Appeal to determination of the appeal.

**50C.2**   Applications to extend representation orders may be granted by a Lord Justice of Appeal, a Single Judge of the High Court, a Master of the Administrative Court or a nominated Court Officer who may direct a case management hearing before a Lord Justice of Appeal, a Single Judge, or a Master of the Administrative Court. Since these applications do not attract a fee, parties may lodge them with the Court by attaching them to an email addressed to the nominated legal officer of the court.

**50C.3**   Applications to extend representation orders to cover the instruction of Queen's Counsel to appear either alone or with junior advocate must be made in writing, either by letter or application notice, clearly marked with the Administrative Court reference number, which must be lodged with the Administrative Court Office or emailed to the appropriate email address: administrativecourtoffice.crimex@hmcts.x.gsi.gov.uk.

The request must:

(i)    identify the substantial novel or complex issues of law or fact in the case;

(ii)   explain why these may only be adequately presented by a Queen's Counsel;

(iii)  state whether a Queen's Counsel has been instructed on behalf of the respondent;

(iv)   explain any delay in making the request;

(v)    be supported by advice from junior advocate or Queen's Counsel.

**50C.4**   Applications for prior authority to cover the cost of obtaining expert evidence must be made in writing, either by letter, clearly marked with the Administrative Court reference number, which must be sent or emailed to the Administrative Court Office.

The request must:

(i)    confirm that the evidence sought has not been considered in any previous appeals determined by the appellate courts;

(ii)   explain why the evidence was not called at the extradition hearing in Westminster Magistrates' Court and what evidence can be produced to support that;

(iii)  explain why the new evidence would have resulted in the District Judge deciding a question at the extradition hearing differently and whether, if so, the District Judge would have been required to make a different order as to discharge of the requested person;

(iv)   explain why the evidence was not raised when the case was being considered by the Secretary of State for the Home Department or information was available that was not available at that time;

(v)    explain why the new evidence would have resulted in the Secretary of State deciding a question differently, and if the question had been decided differently, the Secretary of State would not have ordered the person's extradition;

(vi)   state when the need for the new evidence first became known;

(vii)  explain any delay in making the request;

(viii) explain what relevant factual, as opposed to expert evidence, is being given by whom to create the factual basis for the expert's opinion;

(ix)   explain why this particular area of expertise is relevant: for example why a child psychologist should be appointed as opposed to a social worker;

(x)    state whether the requested person has capacity;

(xi)   set out a full breakdown of all costs involved including any VAT or other tax payable, including alternative quotes or explaining why none are available;

(xii)  provide a list of all previous extensions of the representation order and the approval of expenditure to date;

(xiii) provide a timetable for the production of the evidence and its anticipated effect on the time estimate and hearing date;

(xiv)  set out the level of compliance to date with any directions order.

**50C.5**   Experts must have direct personal experience of and proven expertise in the issue on which a report is sought; it is only if they do have such experience and it is relevant, that they can give evidence of what they have observed.

**50C.6** Where an order is granted to extend a representation order to obtain further evidence it will still be necessary for the party seeking to rely on the new evidence to satisfy the Court hearing the application for permission or the substantive appeal that the evidence obtained should be admitted having regard to sections 27(4) and 29(4) of the Extradition Act 2003 and the judgment in *Szombathely City Court v Fenyvesi* [2009] EWHC 231 (Admin).

**50C.7** Applications to extend representation for the translation of documents must be made in writing, either by letter, clearly marked with the Administrative Court reference number, which must be sent to Administrative Court Office, The Royal Courts of Justice, Strand, London, WC2A 2LL or emailed to the appropriate email address: administrativecourtoffice.crimex@hmcts.x.gsi.gov.uk
The request should:

(i) explain the importance of the document for which a translation is being sought and the justification for obtaining it;

(ii) explain what it is believed the contents of the document is and the issues it will assist the court to address in hearing the appeal;

(iii) confirm that the evidence sought has not been considered in any previous appeals determined by the appellate courts;

(iv) confirm that the evidence sought was not called at the extradition hearing in the Westminster Magistrates' Court;

(v) explain why the evidence sought would have resulted in the District Judge deciding a question at the extradition hearing differently and whether, if so, the District Judge would have been required to make a different order as to discharge of the requested person;

(vi) confirm that the new evidence was not raised when the case was being considered by the Secretary of State for the Home Department;

(vii) explain why the new evidence sought would have resulted in the Secretary of State deciding a question differently, and if the question had been decided differently, the Secretary of State would not have ordered the person's extradition;

(viii) confirm when the need for the new evidence first became known;

(ix) explain any delay in making the request;

(x) explain fully the evidential basis for incurring the expenditure;

(xi) explain why the appellant cannot produce the evidence himself or herself in the form of a statement of truth;

(xii) set out a full breakdown of all costs involved including any VAT or other tax payable and the Legal Aid Agency contractual rates;

(xiii) provide a list of all previous extensions of the representation order and the expenditure to date.

**50C.8** Where an order is made to extend representation to cover the cost of the translation of documents it will still be necessary for the party seeking to rely on the documents as evidence to satisfy the Court that it should be admitted at the hearing of the appeal having regard to sections 27(4) and 29(4) of the Extradition Act 2003 and the judgment in *Szombathely City Court v Fenyvesi* [2009] EWHC 231 (Admin).

**CPD.50D**

## CPD XI Other Proceedings 50D: Extradition: Applications, etc

*Extension or abridgement of time*

**50D.1** (i) Any party who seeks extension or abridgment of time for the service of documents, evidence or skeleton arguments must apply to the High Court on the appropriate form and pay the appropriate fee.

(ii) Applications for extension or abridgment of time may be determined by a Lord Justice of Appeal, a Single Judge of the High Court, a Master of the Administrative Court or a nominated legal officer of the court.

(iii) Applications for extension of time must include a witness statement setting out the reasons for non-compliance with any previous order and the proposed timetable for compliance.

(iv) Any application made to an out of hours Judge must be accompanied with:
a. A detailed chronology;
b. Reasons why the application could not be made within Court hours;
c. Any Orders or Judgments made in the proceedings

*Representatives*

**50D.2** CrimPR Part 46 applies.

**50D.3**   Where under CrimPR 46.2(1)(c) a legal representative withdraws from the case then that representative should satisfy him or herself that the defendant is aware of the time and date of the appeal hearing and of the need to attend, by live link if the court has so directed. If the legal representative has any reason to doubt that the defendant is so aware then he or she should promptly notify the Administrative Court Office.

*Application to adjourn*

**50D.4**   Where a hearing date has been fixed, any application to vacate the hearing must be made on the appropriate form. A fee is required for the application if it is made within 14 days of the hearing date. The application must:
  (i)   explain the reasons why an application is being made to vacate the hearing;
  (ii)  detail the views of the other parties to the appeal;
  (iii) include a draft order with the application notice.

**50D.5**   If the parties both seek an adjournment then the application must be submitted for consideration by a Lord Justice of Appeal, a Single Judge of the High Court or a Master of the Administrative Court. Exceptional circumstances must be shown if a date for the hearing has been fixed or the adjournment will result in material delay to the determination of the appeal.

**50D.6**   An application to adjourn following a compromise agreement must be supported by evidence justifying exceptional circumstances and why it is in compliance with the overriding objective.

*Variation of directions*

**50D.7**   Where parties are unable to comply with any order of the court they must apply promptly to vary directions before deadlines for compliance have expired and seek further directions. An application to vary directions attracts a fee and the application notice, to be submitted on the appropriate form, must:
  (i)   provide full and proper explanations for why the current and existing directions have not been complied with;
  (ii)  detail the views of the other parties to the appeal;
  (iii) include a draft order setting out in full the timetable and directions as varied i.e. a superseding order which stands alone.

**50D.8**   A failure to make the application prior to the expiry of the date specified in the order will generally result in the refusal of the application unless good reasons are shown.

*Application to certify a point of law of general public importance*

**50D.9**   Where an application is made under CrimPR 50.25(2)(b) the application must be made on the appropriate form accompanied by the relevant fee.

**50D.10**  Any response to the application must be made within 10 business days.

**50D.11**  Where an application to certify is granted but permission to appeal to the Supreme Court is refused, it shall be for those representing the Requested Person to apply for an extension of the Representation Order to cover proceedings in the Supreme Court, if so advised.

**50D.12**  The representation order may be extended by a Lord Justice of Appeal, a Single Judge of the High Court, a Master of the Administrative Court or a nominated legal officer of the court.

**50D.13**  The result of the application to certify a point of law of general public importance and permission to appeal to the Supreme Court may be notified in advance to the legal representatives but legal representatives must not communicate it to the Requested Person until 1 hour before the pronouncement is made in open court.

**50D.14**  There shall be no public announcement of the result until after it has been formally pronounced.

*Application to reopen the determination of an appeal*

**50D.15**  An application under CrimPR 50.27 to reopen an appeal must be referred to the court that determined the appeal, but may if circumstances require be considered by a judge or judges other than those who determined the original appeal.

*Application to extend required period for removal pursuant to section 36 of the Extradition Act 2003*

**50D.16**  Where an application is made for an extension of the required period within which to extradite a Requested Person it must be accompanied by:
  (i)   a witness statement explaining why it is not possible to remove the Requested Person within the required period and the proposed timetable for removal;
  (ii)  a draft order.

**50D.17**  The application to extend time may be made before or after the expiry of the required period for extradition, but the court will scrutinise with particular care an application made after its expiry.

50D.18   Where extensions of time are sought for the same reason in respect of a number of Requested Persons who are due to be extradited at the same time, a single application may be made to the court listing each of the Requested Persons for whom an extension is sought.

50D.19   The application may be determined by a Lord Justice of Appeal, a Single Judge of the High Court, a Master of the Administrative listing those persons may be granted.

*Application for directions ancillary to a discharge pursuant to section 42 or 124 of the Extradition Act 2003*

50D.20   Where the High Court is informed that the warrant or extradition request has been withdrawn then unless ancillary matters are dealt with by Consent Order an application notice must be issued seeking any such directions. The notice of discharge of a Requested Person must be accompanied by:

     (i)   the notification by the requesting state that the EAW has been withdrawn together with a translation of the same;

     (ii)   a witness statement containing:

         a.   details of whether the withdrawn EAW is the only EAW outstanding in respect of the Requested Person;

         b.   details of other EAWs outstanding in respect of the Requested Person and the stage which the proceedings have reached;

         c.   whether only part of the EAW has been withdrawn;

         d.   details of any bail conditions;

         e.   details of any institution in which the Requested Person is being detained, the Requested Person's prison number and date of birth.

50D.21   The order for discharge may be made by a Lord Justice of Appeal, a Single Judge of the High Court, a Master of the Administrative Court or a nominated legal officer of the court.

50D.22   It is the responsibility of the High Court to serve the approved order on the appropriate institution and Westminster Magistrates' Court.

## CPD.50E    CPD XI Other Proceedings 50E: Extradition: Court Papers

*Skeleton arguments*

50E.1   The Court on granting permission to appeal or directing an oral hearing for permission to appeal will give directions as to the filing of skeleton arguments. Strict compliance is required with all time limits.

50E.2   A skeleton argument must:

     (a)   not normally exceed 25 pages (excluding front sheets and back sheets) and be concise;

     (b)   be printed on A4 paper in not less than 12 point font and 1.5 line spacing;

     (c)   define the issues in the appeal;

     (d)   be set out in numbered paragraphs;

     (e)   be cross-referenced to any relevant document in the bundle;

     (f)   be self-contained and not incorporate by reference material from previous skeleton arguments;

     (g)   not include extensive quotations from documents or authorities.

50E.3   Where it is necessary to refer to an authority, the skeleton argument must

     (a)   state the proposition of law the authority demonstrates; and

     (b)   identify but not quote the parts of the authority that support the proposition.

50E.4   If more than one authority is cited in support of a given proposition, the skeleton argument must briefly state why.

50E.5   A chronology of relevant events will be necessary in most appeals.

50E.6   Where a skeleton argument has been prepared in respect of an application for permission to appeal, the same skeleton argument may be relied upon in the appeal upon notice being given to the Court or a replacement skeleton may be lodged not less than 10 business days before the hearing of the appeal.

50E.7   At the hearing the Court may refuse to hear argument on a point not included in a skeleton argument filed within the prescribed time.

*Bundles*

50E.8   The bundle for the hearing should be agreed by the parties save where the Requested Person is acting in person. In those circumstances the Court expects the Requesting State to prepare the bundle.

50E.9   The bundle must be paginated and indexed.

50E.10 Subject to any order made by the Court, the following documents must be included in the appeal bundle:
(i) a copy of the appellant's notice;
(ii) a copy of any respondent's notice;
(iii) a copy of any appellant's or respondent's skeleton argument;
(iv) a copy of the order under appeal;
(v) a copy of any order made by the Court in the exercise of its case management powers;
(vi) any judgment of the Court made in a previous appeal involving the party or parties which is relevant to the present proceedings.
(vii) where the bundle of papers reaches more than 200 pages, the parties should agree a core appeal bundle which must contain (i)–(vi) above.

50E.11 The Bundle should only contain relevant documents and must not include duplicate documents.

50E.12 Bundles lodged with the Court will not be returned to the parties but will be destroyed in the confidential waste system at the conclusion of the proceedings and without further notification.

## CPD XI Other Proceedings 50F: Extradition: Consequences of Non Compliance with Directions CPD.50F

50F.1 Failure to comply with these directions will lead to applications for permission and appeals being dealt with on the material available to the Court at the time when the decision is made.

50F.2 Judges dealing with extradition appeals will seek full and proper explanations for any breaches of the rules and the provisions of this Practice Direction.

50F.3 If no good explanation can be given immediately by counsel or solicitors, the senior partner or the departmental head responsible is likely to be called to court to explain any failure to comply with a court order. Where counsel or solicitors fail to obey orders of the Court and are unable to provide proper and sufficient reasons for their disobedience they may anticipate the matter being formally referred to the President of the Queen's Bench Division with a recommendation that the counsel or solicitors involved be reported to their professional bodies.

50F.4 The court may also refuse to admit any material or any evidence not filed in compliance with the order for Directions or outside a time limit specified by the court.

50F.5 A failure to comply with the time limits or other requirements for skeleton arguments will have the consequences specified in 50E.7.

## CRIMINAL PRACTICE DIRECTIONS: GENERAL APPLICATION

## CPD XII General Application A: Court Dress CPD.XII.A

A.1 In magistrates' courts, advocates appear without robes or wigs. In all other courts, Queen's Counsel wear a short wig and a silk (or stuff) gown over a court coat with bands, junior counsel wear a short wig and stuff gown with bands. Solicitors and other advocates authorised under the Courts and Legal Services Act 1990 wear a black solicitor's gown with bands; they may wear short wigs in circumstances where they would be worn by Queen's Counsel or junior counsel.

A.2 High Court Judges hearing criminal cases may wear the winter criminal robe year-round. However, scarlet summer robes may be worn.

## CPD XII General Application B: Modes of Address and Titles of Judges and Magistrates CPD.XII.B

*Modes of Address*
B.1 The following judges, when sitting in court, should be addressed as 'My Lord' or 'My Lady', as the case may be, whatever their personal status:
(a) Judges of the Court of Appeal and of the High Court;
(b) any Circuit Judge sitting as a judge of the Court of Appeal (Criminal Division) or the High Court under section 9(1) of the Senior Courts Act 1981;
(c) any judge sitting at the Central Criminal Court;
(d) any Senior Circuit Judge who is an Honorary Recorder.

B.2 Subject to the paragraph above, Circuit Judges, qualifying judge advocates, Recorders and Deputy Circuit Judges should be addressed as 'Your Honour' when sitting in court.
District Judges (Magistrates' Courts) should be addressed as 'Sir [or Madam]' or 'Judge' when sitting in Court.
Magistrates in court should be addressed through the Chairperson as 'Sir [or Madam]' or collectively as 'Your Worships'.

*Description*

**B.3**   In cause lists, forms and orders members of the judiciary should be described as follows:
(a)   Circuit Judges, as 'His [or Her] Honour Judge A'.
When the judge is sitting as a judge of the High Court under section 9(1) of the Senior Courts Act 1981, the words 'sitting as a judge of the High Court' should be added;
(b)   Recorders, as 'Mr [or Mrs, Ms or Miss] Recorder B'.
This style is appropriate irrespective of any honour or title which the recorder might possess, but if in any case it is desired to include an honour or title, the alternative description, 'Sir CD, Recorder' or 'The Lord D, Recorder' may be used;
(c)   Deputy Circuit Judges, as 'His [or Her] Honour EF, sitting as a Deputy Circuit Judge';
(d)   qualifying judge advocates, as 'His [or Her] Honour GH, sitting as a qualifying judge advocate.';
(e)   District Judges (Magistrates' Courts), as 'District Judge (Magistrates' Courts) J'.

**CPD.XII.C**   **CPD XII General Application C: Availability of Judgments Given in the Court of Appeal and the High Court**

**C.1**   For cases in the High Court, reference should be made to Practice Direction 40E, the supplementary Practice Direction to the Civil Procedure Rules Part 40.

**C.2**   For cases in the Court of Appeal (Criminal Division), the following provisions apply.

*Availability of reserved judgments before handing down, corrections and applications consequential on judgment*

**C.3**   Where judgment is to be reserved the Presiding Judge may, at the conclusion of the hearing, invite the views of the parties' legal representatives as to the arrangements to be made for the handing down of the judgment.

**C.4**   Unless the court directs otherwise, the following provisions apply where the Presiding Judge is satisfied that the judgment will attract no special degree of confidentiality or sensitivity.

**C.5**   The court will provide a copy of the draft judgment to the parties' legal representatives about three working days before handing down, or at such other time as the court may direct. Every page of every judgment which is made available in this way will be marked 'Unapproved judgment: No permission is granted to copy or use in court.' The draft is supplied in confidence and on the conditions that:
(a)   neither the draft judgment nor its substance will be disclosed to any other person or used in the public domain; and
(b)   no action will be taken (other than internally) in response to the draft judgment, before the judgment is handed down.

**C.6**   Unless the parties' legal representatives are told otherwise when the draft judgment is circulated, any proposed corrections to the draft judgment should be sent to the clerk of the judge who prepared the draft (or to the associate, if the judge has no clerk) with a copy to any other party's legal representatives, by 12 noon on the day before judgment is handed down.

**C.7**   If, having considered the draft judgment, the prosecution will be applying to the Court for a retrial or either party wishes to make any other application consequent on the judgment, the judge's clerk should be informed with a time estimate for the application by 12 noon on the day before judgment is handed down. This will enable the court to make appropriate listing arrangements and notify advocates to attend if the court so requires. There is no fee payable to advocates who attend the hand down hearing if not required to do so by the court. If either party is considering applying to the Court to certify a point for appeal to the Supreme Court, it would assist if the judge's clerk could be informed at the same time, although this is not obligatory as under section 34 of the Criminal Appeal Act 1968, the time limit for such applications is 28 days.

*Communication to the parties including the defendant or the victim*

**C.8**   The contents are not to be communicated to the parties, including to the defendant, respondent or the victim (defined as a person entitled to receive services under the Code of Practice for Victims of Crime) until two hours before the listed time for pronouncement of judgment.

**C.9**   Judges may permit more information about the result of a case to be communicated on a confidential basis to the parties including to the defendant, respondent or the victim at an earlier stage if good reason is shown for making such a direction.

**C.10**   If, for any reason, the parties' legal representatives have special grounds for seeking a relaxation of the usual condition restricting disclosure to the parties, a request for relaxation of the condition may be made informally through the judge's clerk (or through the associate, if the judge has no clerk).

**C.11**   If the parties or their legal representatives are in any doubt about the persons to whom copies of the draft judgment may be distributed they should enquire of the judge or Presiding Judge.

C.12 Any breach of the obligations or restrictions in this section or failure to take reasonable steps to ensure compliance may be treated as contempt of court.

*Restrictions on disclosure or reporting*

C.13 Anyone who is supplied with a copy of the handed-down judgment, or who reads it in court, will be bound by any direction which the court may have given in a child case under section 39 of the Children and Young Persons Act 1933 or section 45 or 45A of the Youth Justice and Criminal Evidence Act 1999, or any other form of restriction on disclosure, or reporting, of information in the judgment.

C.14 Copies of the approved judgment can be ordered from the official shorthand writers, on payment of the appropriate fee. Judgments identified as of legal or public interest will generally be made available on the website managed by BAILLI: http://www.bailii.org/

**CPD XII General Application D: Citation of Authority and Provision of Copies of Judgments to the Court**    **CPD.XII.D**

D.1 This Practice Direction applies to all criminal matters before the Court of Appeal (Criminal Division), the Crown Court and the magistrates' courts. In relation to those matters only, Practice Direction (Citation of Authorities) [2012] 1 WLR 780 is hereby revoked.

*Citation of authority*

D.2 In *R v Erskine; R v Williams* [2009] EWCA Crim 1425, [2010] 1 WLR 183, (2009) 2 Cr App R 29 the Lord Chief Justice stated:

    75. The essential starting point, relevant to any appeal against conviction or sentence, is that, adapting the well known aphorism of Viscount Falkland in 1641: if it is not necessary to refer to a previous decision of the court, it is necessary not to refer to it. Similarly, if it is not necessary to include a previous decision in the bundle of authorities, it is necessary to exclude it. That approach will be rigidly enforced.

    76. It follows that when the advocate is considering what authority, if any, to cite for a proposition, only an authority which establishes the principle should be cited. Reference should not be made to authorities which do no more than either (a) illustrate the principle or (b) restate it.

    78. Advocates must expect to be required to justify the citation of each authority relied on or included in the bundle. The court is most unlikely to be prepared to look at an authority which does no more than illustrate or restate an established proposition.

    80. . . .In particular, in sentencing appeals, where a definitive Sentencing Guidelines Council guideline is available there will rarely be any advantage in citing an authority reached before the issue of the guideline, and authorities after its issue which do not refer to it will rarely be of assistance. In any event, where the authority does no more than uphold a sentence imposed at the Crown Court, the advocate must be ready to explain how it can assist the court to decide that a sentence is manifestly excessive or wrong in principle.

D.3 Advocates should only cite cases when it is necessary to do so; when the case identifies or represents a principle or the development of a principle. In sentencing appeals, other cases are rarely helpful, providing only an illustration, and this is especially true if there is a sentencing guideline. Unreported cases should only be cited in exceptional circumstances, and the advocate must expect to explain why such a case has been cited.

D.4 Advocates should not assume that because a case cited to the court is not referred to in the judgment the court has not considered it; it is more likely that the court was not assisted by it.

D.5 When an authority is to be cited, whether in written or oral submissions, the advocate should always provide the neutral citation followed by the law report reference.

D.6 The following practice should be followed:

    i)   Where a judgment is reported in the Official Law Reports (A.C., Q.B., Ch., Fam.) published by the Incorporated Council of Law Reporting for England and Wales or the Criminal Appeal Reports or the Criminal Appeal Reports (Sentencing) one of those two series of reports must be cited; either is equally acceptable. However, where a judgment is reported in the Criminal Appeal Reports or the Criminal Appeal Reports (Sentencing) that reference must be given in addition to any other reference. Other series of reports and official transcripts of judgment may only be used when a case is not reported, or not yet reported, in the Official Law Reports or the Criminal Appeal Reports or the Criminal Appeal Reports (Sentencing).

    ii)  If a judgment is not reported in the Official Law Reports, the Criminal Appeal Reports or the Criminal Appeal Reports (Sentencing), but it is reported in an authoritative series of reports which contains a headnote and is made by individuals holding a Senior Courts qualification (for the purposes of section 115 of the Courts and Legal Services Act 1990), that report should be cited.

    iii) Where a judgment is not reported in any of the reports referred to above, but is reported in other reports, they may be cited.

Criminal Procedure Rules and Criminal Practice Directions

iv)  Where a judgment has not been reported, reference may be made to the official transcript if that is available, not the handed-down text of the judgment, as this may have been subject to late revision after the text was handed down. Official transcripts may be obtained from, for instance, BAILLI (http://www.bailii.org/).

**D.7**   In the majority of cases, it is expected that all references will be to the Official Law Reports and the Criminal Appeal Reports or the Criminal Appeal Reports (Sentencing); it will be rare for there to be a need to refer to any other reports. An unreported case should not be cited unless it contains a relevant statement of legal principle not found in reported authority, and it is expected that this will only occur in exceptional circumstances.

*Provision of copies of judgments to the Court*

**D.8**   The paragraphs below specify whether or not copies should be provided to the court. Authorities should not be included for propositions not in dispute. If more than one authority is to be provided, the copies should be presented in paginated and tagged bundles.

**D.9**   If required, copies of judgments should be provided either by way of a photocopy of the published report or by way of a copy of a reproduction of the judgment in electronic form that has been authorised by the publisher of the relevant series, but in any event:

i)   the report must be presented to the court in an easily legible form (a 12-point font is preferred but a 10 or 11-point font is acceptable); and

ii)  the advocate presenting the report must be satisfied that it has not been reproduced in a garbled form from the data source.

In any case of doubt the court will rely on the printed text of the report (unless the editor of the report has certified that an electronic version is more accurate because it corrects an error contained in an earlier printed text of the report).

**D.10**  If such a copy is unavailable, a printed transcript such as from BAILLI may be included.

*Provision of copies to the Court of Appeal (Criminal Division)*

**D.11**  Advocates must provide to the Registrar of Criminal Appeals, with their appeal notice, respondent's notice or skeleton argument, a list of authorities upon which they wish to rely in their written or oral submissions. The list of authorities should contain the name of the applicant, appellant or respondent and the Criminal Appeal Office number where known. The list should include reference to the relevant paragraph numbers in each authority. An updated list can be provided if a new authority is issued, or in response to a respondent's notice or skeleton argument. From time to time, the Registrar may issue guidance as to the style or content of lists of authorities, including a suggested format; this guidance should be followed by all parties. The latest guidance is available from the Criminal Appeal Office.

**D.12**  If the case cited is reported in the Official Law Reports, the Criminal Appeal Reports or the Criminal Appeal Reports (Sentencing), the law report reference must be given after the neutral citation, and the relevant paragraphs listed, but copies should not be provided to the court.

**D.13**  If, exceptionally, reference is made to a case that is not reported in the Official Law Reports, the Criminal Appeal Reports or the Criminal Appeal Reports (Sentencing), three copies must be provided to the Registrar with the list of authorities and the relevant appeal notice or respondent's notice (or skeleton argument, if provided). The relevant passages of the authorities should be marked or sidelined.

*Provision of copies to the Crown Court and the magistrates' courts*

**D.14**  When the court is considering routine applications, it may be sufficient for the court to be referred to the applicable legislation or to one of the practitioner texts. However, it is the responsibility of the advocate to ensure that the court is provided with the material that it needs properly to consider any matter.

**D.15**  If it would assist the court to consider any authority, the directions at paragraphs D.2 to D.7 above relating to citation will apply and a list of authorities should be provided.

**D.16**  Copies should be provided by the party seeking to rely upon the authority in accordance with CrimPR 24.13. This Rule is applicable in the magistrates' courts, and in relation to the provision of authorities, should also be followed in the Crown Court since courts often do not hold library stock (see CrimPR 25.17). Advocates should comply with paragraphs D.8 to D.10 relating to the provision of copies to the court.

**D.17**  The court may give directions for the preparation of skeleton arguments. Such directions will provide for the time within which skeleton arguments must be served and for the issues which they must address. Such directions may provide for the number of pages, or the number of words, to which a skeleton argument is to be confined. Any such directions displace the following to the extent of any inconsistency. Subject to that, however, a skeleton argument must:

i.   not normally exceed 15 pages (excluding front sheets and back sheets) and be concise;

    ii.   be presented in A4 page size and portrait orientation, in not less than 12 point font and in 1.5 line spacing;

    iii.  define the issues;

    iv.  be set out in numbered paragraphs;

    v.   be cross-referenced to any relevant document in any bundle prepared for the court;

    vi.  be self-contained and not incorporate by reference material from previous skeleton arguments;

    vii. not include extensive quotations from documents or authorities.

**D.18** Where it is necessary to refer to an authority, the skeleton argument must:

    i.   state the proposition of law the authority demonstrates; and

    ii.   identify but not quote the parts of the authority that support the proposition.

**D.19** If more than one authority is cited in support of a given proposition, the skeleton argument must briefly state why.

**D.20** A chronology of relevant events will be necessary in most cases.

**D.21** There are directions at paragraphs I 3C.3 and 3C.4 of these Practice Directions that apply to the service of skeleton arguments in support of, and in opposition to, an application to stay an indictment on the grounds of abuse of process; and directions at paragraphs IX 39F.1 to 39F.3 that apply to the service of skeleton arguments in the Court of Appeal. Where a skeleton argument has been prepared in respect of an application for permission to appeal, the same skeleton argument may be relied upon in the appeal upon notice being given to the court, or a replacement skeleton may be served to the timetable set out in those paragraphs.

**D.22** At the hearing the court may refuse to hear argument on a point unless it is included in a skeleton argument which (i) is served within the required time, and (ii) complies with the requirements of these Practice Directions (as varied, if applicable, by direction of the court). Any application for a variation, or further variation, of those requirements must give reasons, and such an application must accompany any skeleton argument that does not comply.

**D.23** In *R v James, R v Selby* [2016] EWCA Crim 1639; [2017] Crim.L.R. 228 the Court of Appeal observed (at paragraphs 52 to 54):

'Legal documents of unnecessary and too often of excessive length offer very little assistance to the court. In *Tombstone Ltd v Raja* [2008] EWCA Civ 1441, [2009] 1 WLR 1143 Mummery LJ said:

"Practitioners … are well advised to note the risk of the court's negative reaction to unnecessarily long written submissions. The skeleton argument procedure was introduced to assist the court, as well as the parties, by improving preparations for, and the efficiency of, adversarial oral hearings, which remain central to this court's public role… . An unintended and unfortunate side effect of the growth in written advocacy… has been that too many practitioners, at increased cost to their clients and diminishing assistance to the court, burden their opponents and the court with written briefs."

He might have penned those remarks had he been sitting in these two cases, and many more, in this Division.

In *Standard Bank PLC v Via Mat International* [2013] EWCA Civ 490, [2013] 2 All ER (Comm) 1222 the excessive length of court documents prompted:

"It is important that both practitioners and their clients understand that skeleton arguments are not intended to serve as vehicles for extended advocacy and that in general a short, concise skeleton is both more helpful to the court and more likely to be persuasive than a longer document which seeks to develop every point which the advocate would wish to make in oral argument."

No area of law is exempt from the requirement to produce careful and concise documents: *Tchenquiz v Director of the Serious Fraud Office* [2014] EWCA Civ 1333, [2015] 1 WLR 838, paragraph 10.'

**CPD XII General application E: Preparation of Judgments: Neutral Citation**    **CPD.XII.E**

**E.1** Since 11 January 2001 every judgment of the Court of Appeal, and of the Administrative Court, and since 14 January 2002 every judgment of the High Court, has been prepared and issued as approved with single spacing, paragraph numbering (in the margins) and no page numbers. In courts with more than one judge, the paragraph numbering continues sequentially through each judgment and does not start again at the beginning of each judgment. Indented paragraphs are not numbered. A unique reference number is given to each judgment. For judgments of the Court of Appeal, this number is given by the official shorthand writers, Merrill Legal Solutions (Tel: 020 7421 4000 ext.4036). For judgments of the High Court, it is provided by the Courts Recording and Transcription Unit at the Royal Courts of Justice. Such a number will also be furnished, on request to the Courts Recording and Transcription Unit, Royal Courts of Justice, Strand, London WC2A 2LL (Tel: 020 7947 7820), (e-mail: rcj.cratu@hmcts.gsi.gov.uk) for High Court judgments delivered outside London.

E.2    Each Court of Appeal judgment starts with the year, followed by EW (for England and Wales), then CA (for Court of Appeal), followed by Civ or Crim and finally the sequential number. For example, '*Smith v Jones* [2001] EWCA Civ 10'.

E.3    In the High Court, represented by HC, the number comes before the divisional abbreviation and, unlike Court of Appeal judgments, the latter is bracketed: (Ch), (Pat), (QB), (Admin), (Comm), (Admlty), (TCC) or (Fam), as appropriate. For example, '[2002] EWHC 123 (Fam)', or '[2002] EWHC 124 (QB)', or '[2002] EWHC 125 (Ch)'.

E.4    This 'neutral citation', as it is called, is the official number attributed to the judgment and must always be used at least once when the judgment is cited in a later judgment. Once the judgment is reported, this neutral citation appears in front of the familiar citation from the law reports series. Thus: '*Smith v Jones* [2001] EWCA Civ 10; [2001] QB 124; [2001] 2 All ER 364', etc.

E.5    Paragraph numbers are referred to in square brackets. When citing a paragraph from a High Court judgment, it is unnecessary to include the descriptive word in brackets: (Admin), (QB), or whatever. When citing a paragraph from a Court of Appeal judgment, however, 'Civ' or 'Crim' is included. If it is desired to cite more than one paragraph of a judgment, each numbered paragraph should be enclosed with a square bracket. Thus paragraph 59 in *Green v White* [2002] EWHC 124 (QB) would be cited: '*Green v White* [2002] EWHC 124 at [59]'; paragraphs 30 – 35 in *Smith v Jones* would be '*Smith v Jones* [2001] EWCA Civ 10 at [30] – [35]'; similarly, where a number of paragraphs are cited: '*Smith v Jones* [2001] EWCA Civ 10 at [30], [35] and [40 – 43]'.

E.6    If a judgment is cited more than once in a later judgment, it is helpful if only one abbreviation is used, e.g., '*Smith v Jones*' or '*Smith's case*', but preferably not both (in the same judgment).

**CPD.XII.F**    **CPD XII General application F: Citation of Hansard**

F.1    Where any party intends to refer to the reports of Parliamentary proceedings as reported in the Official Reports of either House of Parliament ('Hansard') in support of any such argument as is permitted by the decisions in *Pepper v Hart* [1993] AC 593 and *Pickstone v Freemans PLC* [1989] AC 66, or otherwise, he must, unless the court otherwise directs, serve upon all other parties and the court copies of any such extract, together with a brief summary of the argument intended to be based upon such extract. No other report of Parliamentary proceedings may be cited.

F.2    Unless the court otherwise directs, service of the extract and summary of the argument shall be effected not less than 5 clear working days before the first day of the hearing, whether or not it has a fixed date. Advocates must keep themselves informed as to the state of the lists where no fixed date has been given. Service on the court shall be effected by sending three copies to the Registrar of Criminal Appeals, Royal Courts of Justice, Strand, London, WC2A 2LL or to the court manager of the relevant Crown Court centre, as appropriate. If any party fails to do so, the court may make such order (relating to costs or otherwise) as is, in all the circumstances, appropriate.

CRIMINAL PRACTICE DIRECTIONS LISTING

**CPD.XIII.A**    **CPD XIII Listing A: Judicial Responsibility for Listing and Key Principles**

*Listing as a judicial responsibility and function*

A.1    Listing is a judicial responsibility and function. The purpose is to ensure that all cases are brought to a hearing or trial in accordance with the interests of justice, that the resources available for criminal justice are deployed as effectively as possible, and that cases are heard by an appropriate judge or bench with the minimum of delay.

A.2    The agreement reached between the Lord Chief Justice and the Secretary of State for Constitutional Affairs and Lord Chancellor set out in a statement to the House of Lords on 26 January 2004 ('the Concordat'), states that judges, working with HMCTS, are responsible for deciding on the assignment of cases to particular courts and the listing of those cases before particular judges. Therefore:

(a)    The Presiding Judges of each circuit have the overall responsibility for listing at all courts, Crown and magistrates', on their circuit;

(b)    Subject to the supervision of the Presiding Judges, the Resident Judge at each Crown Court has the general responsibility within his or her court centre for the allocation of criminal judicial work, to ensure the just and efficient despatch of the business of the court or group of courts. This includes overseeing the deployment of allocated judges at the court or group, including the distribution of work between all the judges allocated to that court. A Resident Judge must appoint a deputy or deputies to exercise his or her functions when he or she is absent from his or her court centre. See also paragraph A.5: Discharge of judicial responsibilities;

(c)    The listing officer in the Crown Court is responsible for carrying out the day-to-day operation of listing practice under the direction of the Resident Judge. The listing officer at each Crown Court centre has one of the most important functions at that Crown Court and makes a vital contribution to the efficient running of that Crown Court and to the efficient operation of the administration of criminal justice;

(d) In the magistrates' courts, the Judicial Business Group, subject to the supervision of the Presiding Judges of the circuit, is responsible for determining the listing practice in that area. The day-to-day operation of that listing practice is the responsibility of the justices' clerk with the assistance of the listing officer.

*Key principles of listing*

A.3 When setting the listing practice, the Resident Judge or the Judicial Business Group should take into account principles a-j:

(a) Ensure the timely trial of cases and resolution of other issues (such as confiscation) so that justice is not delayed. The following factors are relevant:

   i. In general, each case should be tried within as short a time of its arrival in the court as is consistent with the interests of justice, the needs of victims and witnesses, and with the proper and timely preparation by the prosecution and defence of their cases in accordance with the directions and timetable set;

   ii. Priority should be accorded to the trial of young defendants, and cases where there are vulnerable or young witnesses. In *R v Barker* [2010] EWCA Crim 4, the Lord Chief Justice highlighted 'the importance to the trial and investigative process of keeping any delay in a case involving a child complainant to an irreducible minimum';

   iii. Custody time limits (CTLs) should be observed, see CPD XIII Listing F;

   iv. Every effort must be made to avoid delay in cases in which the defendant is on bail;

(b) Ensure that in the magistrates' court unless impracticable, non-custody anticipated guilty plea cases are listed 14 days after charge, and non-custody anticipated not guilty pleas are listed 28 days after charge;

(c) Provide, when possible, for certainty and/or as much advance notice as possible, of the trial date; and take all reasonable steps to ensure that the trial date remains fixed;

(d) Ensure that a judge or bench with any necessary authorisation and of appropriate experience is available to try each case and, wherever desirable and practicable, there is judicial continuity, including in relation to post-trial hearings;

(e) Strike an appropriate balance in the use of resources, by taking account of:

   i. The efficient deployment of the judiciary in the Crown Court and the magistrates' courts taking into account relevant sitting requirements for magistrates. See CPD XIII Annex 1 for information to support judicial deployment in the magistrates' courts;

   ii. The proper use of the courtrooms available at the court;

   iii. The provision in long and/or complex cases for adequate reading time for the judiciary;

   iv. The facilities in the available courtrooms, including the security needs (such as a secure dock), size and equipment, such as video and live link facilities;

   v. The proper use of those who attend the Crown Court as jurors;

   vi. The availability of legal advisers in the magistrates' courts;

   vii. The need to return those sentenced to custody as soon as possible after the sentence is passed, and to facilitate the efficient operation of the prison escort contract;

(f) Provide where practicable:

   i. the defendant and the prosecution with the advocate of their choice where this does not result in any delay to the trial of the case; and,

   ii. for the efficient deployment of advocates, lawyers and associate prosecutors of the Crown Prosecution Service, and other prosecuting authorities, and of the resources available to the independent legal profession, for example by trying to group certain cases together;

(g) Meet the need for special security measures for category A and other high-risk defendants;

(h) Ensure that proper time (including judicial reading time) is afforded to hearings in which the court is exercising powers that impact on the rights of individuals, such as applications for investigative orders or warrants;

(i) Consider the significance of ancillary proceedings, such as confiscation hearings, and the need to deal with such hearings promptly and, where possible, for such hearings to be conducted by the trial judge;

(j) Provide for government initiatives or projects approved by the Lord Chief Justice.

A.4 Although the listing practice at each Crown Court centre and magistrates' court will take these principles into account, the listing practice adopted will vary from court to court depending particularly on the number of courtrooms and the facilities available, the location and the workload, its volume and type.

*Discharge of judicial responsibilities*

**A.5**  The Resident Judge of each court is responsible for:

i.  ensuring that good practice is implemented throughout the court, such that all hearings commence on time;

ii.  ensuring that the causes of trials that do not proceed on the date originally fixed are examined to see if there is any systemic issue;

iii.  monitoring the general performance of the court and the listing practices;

iv.  monitoring the timeliness of cases and reporting any cases of serious concern to the Presiding Judge;

v.  maintaining and reviewing annually a list of Recorders, qualifying judge advocates and Deputy Circuit Judges authorised to hear appeals from the magistrates' courts unless such a list is maintained by the Presiding Judge.

**A.6**  The Judicial Business Group for each clerkship subject to the overall jurisdiction of the Presiding Judge is responsible for:

i.  monitoring the workload and anticipated changes which may impact on listing policies;

ii.  ensuring that any listing practice meets the needs of the system as a whole.

**CPD.XIII.B    CPD XIII Listing B: Classification**

**B.1**  The classification structure outlined below is solely for the purposes of trial in the Crown Court. The structure has been devised to accommodate practical administrative functions and is not intended to reflect a hierarchy of the offences therein.

Offences are classified as follows:

Class 1: A:

i.  Murder;

ii.  Attempted Murder;

iii.  Manslaughter;

iv.  Infanticide;

v.  Child destruction (section 1(1) of the Infant Life (Preservation) Act 1929);

vi.  Abortion (section 58 of the Offences against the Person Act 1861);

vii.  Assisting a suicide;

viii.  Cases including section 5 of the Domestic Violence, Crime and Victims Act 2004, as amended (if a fatality has resulted);

ix.  Soliciting, inciting, encouraging or assisting, attempting or conspiring to commit any of the above offences or assisting an offender having committed such an offence.

Class 1: B:

i.  Genocide;

ii.  Torture, hostage-taking and offences under the War Crimes Act 1991;

iii.  Offences under ss. 51 and 52 International Criminal Courts Act 2001;

iv.  An offence under section 1 of the Geneva Conventions Act 1957;

v.  Terrorism offences (where offence charged is indictable only and took place during an act of terrorism or for the purposes of terrorism as defined in s.1 of the Terrorism Act 2000);

vi.  Piracy, under the Merchant Shipping and Maritime Security Act 1997;

vii.  Treason;

viii.  An offence under the Official Secrets Acts;

ix.  Incitement to disaffection;

x.  Soliciting, inciting, encouraging or assisting, attempting or conspiring to commit any of the above offences or assisting an offender having committed such an offence.

Class 1: C:

i.  Prison mutiny, under the Prison Security Act 1992;

ii.  Riot in the course of serious civil disturbance;

iii.  Serious gang related crime resulting in the possession or discharge of firearms, particularly including a campaign of firebombing or extortion, especially when accompanied by allegations of drug trafficking on a commercial scale;

iv.  Complex sexual offence cases in which there are many complainants (often under age, in care or otherwise particularly vulnerable) and/or many defendants who are alleged to have systematically groomed and abused them, often over a long period of time;

v.  Cases involving people trafficking for sexual, labour or other exploitation and cases of human servitude;

vi.  Soliciting, inciting, encouraging or assisting, attempting or conspiring to commit any of the above offences or assisting an offender having committed such an offence.

Class 1: D:
i. Causing death by dangerous driving;
ii. Causing death by careless driving;
iii. Causing death by unlicensed, disqualified or uninsured driving;
iv. Any Health and Safety case resulting in a fatality or permanent serious disability;
v. Any other case resulting in a fatality or permanent serious disability;
vi. Soliciting, inciting, encouraging or assisting, attempting or conspiring to commit any of the above offences or assisting an offender having committed such an offence.

Class 2: A
i. Arson with intent to endanger life or reckless as to whether life was endangered;
ii. Cases in which explosives, firearms or imitation firearms are used or carried or possessed;
iii. Kidnapping or false imprisonment (without intention to commit a sexual offence but charged on the same indictment as a serious offence of violence such as under section 18 or section 20 of the Offences Against the Person Act 1861);
iv. Cases in which the defendant is a police officer, member of the legal profession or a high profile or public figure;
v. Cases in which the complainant or an important witness is a high profile or public figure;
vi. Riot otherwise than in the course of serious civil disturbance;
vii. Child cruelty;
viii. Cases including section 5 of the Domestic Violence, Crime and Victims Act 2004, as amended (if no fatality has resulted);
ix. Soliciting, inciting, encouraging or assisting, attempting or conspiring to commit any of the above offences or assisting an offender having committed such an offence.

Class 2: B
i. Any sexual offence, with the exception of those included in Class 1C;
ii. Kidnapping or false imprisonment (with intention to commit a sexual offence or charged on the same indictment as a sexual offence);
iii. Soliciting, inciting, encouraging or assisting, attempting or conspiring to commit any of the above offences or assisting an offender having committed such an offence.

Class 2: C:
i. Serious, complex fraud;
ii. Serious and/or complex money laundering;
iii. Serious and/or complex bribery;
iv. Corruption;
v. Complex cases in which the defendant is a corporation (including cases for sentence as well as for trial);
vi. Any case in which the defendant is a corporation with a turnover in excess of £1bn (including cases for sentence as well as for trial);
vii. Soliciting, inciting, encouraging or assisting, attempting or conspiring to commit any of the above offences or assisting an offender having committed such an offence.

Class 3: All other offences not listed in the classes above.

*Deferred Prosecution Agreements*
B.2 Cases coming before the court under section 45 [of] and Schedule 17 [to] the Crime and Courts Act 2013 must be referred to the President of the Queen's Bench Division who will allocate the matter to a judge from a list of judges approved by the Lord Chief Justice. Only the allocated judge may thereafter hear any matter or make any decision in relation to that case.

*Criminal Cases Review Commission*
B.3 Where the CCRC refers a case upon conviction from the magistrates' courts to the Crown Court, this shall be dealt with at a Crown Court centre designated by the Senior Presiding Judge.

**CPD XIII Listing C: Referral of Cases in the Crown Court to the Resident Judge and to the Presiding Judges**
C.1 This Practice Direction specifies:
    (a) cases which must be referred to a Presiding Judge for release; and
    (b) cases which must be referred to the Resident Judge before being assigned to a judge, Recorder or qualifying judge advocate to hear.

**CPD.XIII.C**

Criminal Procedure Rules and Criminal Practice Directions

It is applicable to all Crown Courts, but its application may be modified by the Senior Presiding Judge or the Presiding Judges, with the approval of the Senior Presiding Judge, through the provision of further specific guidance to Resident Judges in relation to the allocation and management of the work at their court.

C.2    This Practice Direction does not prescribe the way in which the Resident Judge gives directions as to listing policy to the listing officer; its purpose is to ensure that there is appropriate judicial control over the listing of cases. However, the Resident Judge must arrange with the listing officers a satisfactory means of ensuring that all cases listed at their court are listed before judges, Recorders or qualifying judge advocates of suitable seniority and experience, subject to the requirements of this Practice Direction. The Resident Judge should ensure that listing officers are made aware of the contents and importance of this Practice Direction, and that listing officers develop satisfactory procedures for referral of cases to him or her.

C.3    In order to assist the Resident Judge and the listing officer, all cases sent to the Crown Court should where possible include a brief case summary prepared by the prosecution. The prosecutor should ensure that any factors that make the case complex, or would lead it to be referred to the Resident Judge or a Presiding Judge are highlighted. The defence may also send submissions to the court, again highlighting any areas of complexity or any other factors that might assist in the case being allocated to an appropriate judge.

*Cases in the Crown Court to be referred to the Resident Judge*

C.4    All cases in Class 1A, 1B, 1C, 1D, 2A and 2C must be referred to the Resident Judge as must any case which appears to raise particularly complex, sensitive or serious issues.

C.5    Resident Judges should give guidance to the judges and staff of their respective courts as to which Class 2B cases should be referred to them following consultation with the Senior Presiding Judge. This will include any cases that may be referred to the Presiding Judge, see below. Class 2B cases to be referred to the Resident Judge are likely to be identified by the list officer, or by the judge at the first hearing in the Crown Court. Any appeal against conviction and/or sentence from a Youth Court involving a Class 2B case must be brought to the attention of the Resident Judge as soon as practicable. Where not provided with the appeal papers, the list officer must obtain a full summary of the prosecution case so as to allow an informed allocation decision to be made.

C.6    Once a case has been referred to the Resident Judge, the Resident Judge should refer the case to the Presiding Judge, following the guidance below, or allocate the case to an appropriate category of judge, and if possible to a named judge.

*Cases in the Crown Court to be referred to a Presiding Judge*

C.7    All cases in Class 1A, 1B and 1C must be referred by the Resident Judge to a Presiding Judge, as must a case in any class which is:

    i.    An usually grave or complex case or one in which a novel and important point of law is to be raised;

    ii.   A case where it is alleged that the defendant caused more than 1 fatality;

    iii.  A non-fatal case of baby shaking where serious injury resulted;

    iv.  A case where the defendant is a police officer, or a member of the legal profession or a high profile figure;

    v.   A case which for any reason is likely to attract exceptional media attention;

    vi.  A case where a large organisation or corporation may, if convicted, be ordered to pay a very large fine;

    vii. Any case likely to last more than three months.

C.8    Resident Judges are encouraged to refer any other case if they think it is appropriate to do so.

C.9    Presiding Judges and Resident Judges should agree a system for the referral of cases to the Presiding Judge, ideally by electronic means. The system agreed should include provision for the Resident Judge to provide the Presiding Judge with a brief summary of the case, a clear recommendation by the Resident Judge about the judges available to try the case and any other comments. A written record of the decision and brief reasons for it must be made and retained.

C.10  Once a case has been referred to the Presiding Judge, the Presiding Judge may retain the case for trial by a High Court Judge, or release the case back to the Resident Judge, either for trial by a named judge, or for trial by an identified category of judges, to be allocated by the Resident Judge.

**CPD.XIII.D**    **CPD XIII Listing D: Authorisation of Judges**

D.1    Judges must be authorised by the Lord Chief Justice before they may hear certain types of case.

D.2    Judges (other than High Court Judges) to hear Class 1A cases must be authorised to hear such cases. Any judge previously granted a 'Class 1' or 'murder' authorisation is authorised to hear Class 1A cases. Judges previously granted an 'attempted murder' (including soliciting, incitement or conspiracy thereof) authorisation can only deal with these cases within Class 1A.

D.3 Judges (other than High Court Judges) to hear sexual offences cases in Class 1C or any case within Class 2B must be authorised to hear such cases. Any judge previously granted a 'Class 2' or 'serious sex offences' authorisation is authorised to hear sexual offences cases in Class 1C or 2B. It is a condition of the authorisation that it does not take effect until the judge has attended the relevant Judicial College course; the Resident Judge should check in the case of newly authorised judges that they have attended the course. Judges who have been previously authorised to try such cases should make every effort to ensure their training is up-to-date and maintained by attending the Serious Sexual Offences Seminar at least once every three years. See CPD XIII Annex 2 for guidance in dealing with sexual offences in the youth court.

D.4 Cases in the magistrates' courts involving the imposition of very large fines

    i.   Where a defendant appears before a magistrates' court for an either way offence, to which CPD XIII Annex 3 applies the case must be dealt with by a DJ (MC) who has been authorised to deal with such cases by the Chief Magistrate.

    ii.  The authorised DJ (MC) must first consider whether such cases should be allocated to the Crown Court or, where the defendant pleads guilty, committed for sentence under s. 3 Powers of [Criminal] Courts (Sentenc[ing]) Act 2000, and must do so when the DJ (MC) considers the offence or combination of offences so serious that the Crown Court should deal with the defendant had they been convicted on indictment.

    iii. If an authorised DJ (MC) decides not to commit such a case the reasons must be recorded in writing to be entered onto the court register.

### CPD XIII Listing E: Allocation of Business within the Crown Court

CPD.XIII.E

E.1 Cases in Class 1A may only be tried by:

    i.   a High Court Judge, or

    ii.  a Circuit Judge, or Deputy High Court Judge, authorised to try such cases and provided that the Presiding Judge has released the case for trial by such a judge; or

    iii. a Deputy Circuit Judge to whom the case has been specifically released by the Presiding Judge.

E.2 Cases in Class 1B may only be tried by:

    i.   a High Court Judge, or

    ii.  a Circuit Judge, or a Deputy High Court Judge, provided that the Presiding Judge has released the case for trial by such a judge; or

    iii. a Deputy Circuit Judge to whom the case has been specifically released by the Presiding Judge.

E.3 Cases in Class 1C may only be tried by:

    i.   a High Court Judge, or

    ii.  a Circuit Judge, or a Deputy High Court Judge, or Deputy Circuit Judge, authorised to try such cases (if the case requires the judge to be authorised to hear sexual offences cases), provided that the Presiding Judge has released the case for trial by such a judge, or, if the case is a sexual offence, the Presiding Judge has assigned the case to that named judge.

    See also CPD XIII Listing C.10.

E.4 Cases in Class 1D and 2A may be tried by:

    i.   a High Court Judge, or

    ii.  a Circuit Judge, or Deputy High Court Judge, or Deputy Circuit Judge, or a Recorder or a qualifying judge advocate, provided that either the Presiding Judge has released the case or the Resident Judge has allocated the case for trial by such a judge; with the exception that Class 2A i) cases may not be tried by a Recorder or qualifying judge advocate.

E.5 Cases in Class 2B may be tried by:

    i.   a High Court Judge, or

    ii.  a Circuit Judge, or Deputy High Court Judge, or Deputy Circuit Judge, or a Recorder or a qualifying judge advocate, authorised to try such cases and provided that either the Presiding Judge has released the case or the Resident Judge has allocated the case for trial by such a judge.

E.6 Cases in Class 2C may be tried by:

    i.   a High Court Judge, or

    ii.  a Circuit Judge, or Deputy High Court Judge, or Deputy Circuit Judge, or a Recorder or a qualifying judge advocate, with suitable experience (for example, with company accounts or other financial information) and provided that either the Presiding Judge has released the case or the Resident Judge has allocated the case for trial by such a judge.

E.7 Cases in Classes 1D, 2A and 2C will usually be tried by a Circuit Judge.

E.8 Cases in Class 3 may be tried by a High Court Judge, or a Circuit Judge, a Deputy Circuit Judge, a Recorder or a qualifying judge advocate. A case in Class 3 shall not be listed for trial by a High Court Judge except with the consent of a Presiding Judge.

E.9 If a case has been allocated to a judge, Recorder or qualifying judge advocate, the preliminary hearing should be conducted by the allocated judge if practicable, and if not, if possible by a judge

Criminal Procedure Rules and Criminal Practice Directions

of at least equivalent standing. PCMHs should only be heard by Recorders or qualifying judge advocates with the approval of the Resident Judge.

E.10    For cases in Class 1A, 1B or 1C, or any case that has been referred to the Presiding Judge, the preliminary hearing and PCMH must be conducted by a High Court Judge; by a Circuit Judge; or by a judge authorised by the Presiding Judges to conduct such hearings. In the event of a guilty plea before such an authorised judge, the case will be adjourned for sentencing and will immediately be referred to the Presiding Judge who may retain the case for sentence by a High Court Judge, or release the case back to the Resident Judge, either for sentence by a named judge, or for sentence by an identified category of judges, to be allocated by the Resident Judge.

E.11    Appeals from decisions of magistrates' courts shall be heard by:
i.    a Resident Judge, or
ii.    a Circuit Judge, nominated by the Resident Judge, or
iii.    a Recorder or qualifying judge advocate or a Deputy Circuit Judge listed by the Presiding Judge to hear such appeals; or, if there is no such list nominated by the Resident Judge to hear such appeals;
iv.    and, no less than two and no more than four justices of the peace, none of whom took part in the decision under appeal;
v.    where no Circuit Judge or Recorder or qualifying judge advocate satisfying the requirements above is available, by a Circuit Judge, Recorder, qualifying judge advocate or Deputy Circuit Judge selected by the Resident Judge to hear a specific case or cases listed on a specific day.

E.12    Appeals from the youth court in relation to sexual offences shall be heard by:
i.    A Resident Judge or;
ii.    a Circuit Judge nominated by the Resident Judge who is authorised under D.3 to hear sexual offences in Class 1C or Class 2B;
iii.    and no less than two and no more than four justices of the peace, none of whom took part in the decision under appeal. The justices of the peace must have undertaken specific training to deal with youth matters.
iv.    No appeal against conviction and/or sentence from a Youth Court involving a Class 1C or Class 2B offence shall be heard by a Recorder save with the express permission of the Presiding Judge of the Circuit.

E.13    Allocation or committal for sentence following breach (such as a matter in which a community order has been made, or a suspended sentence passed), should, where possible, be listed before the judge who originally dealt with the matter or, if not, before a judge of the same or higher level.

E.14    Applications for removal of a driving disqualification should be made to the location of the Crown Court where the order of disqualification was made. Where possible, the matter should be listed before the judge who originally dealt with the matter or, if not, before a judge of the same or higher level.

**CPD.XIII.F**    **CPD XIII Listing F: Listing of Trials, Custody Time Limits and Transfer of Cases**

*Estimates of trial length*

F.1    Under the regime set out in the Criminal Procedure Rules, the parties will be expected to provide an accurate estimate of the length of trial at the hearing where the case is to be managed based on a detailed estimate of the time to be taken with each witness to be called, and accurate information about the availability of witnesses.

F.2    At the hearing the judge will ask the prosecution to clarify any custody time limit ('CTL') dates. The court clerk must ensure the CTL date is marked clearly on the court file or electronic file. When a case is subject to a CTL all efforts must be made at the first hearing to list the case within the CTL and the judge should seek to ensure this. Further guidance on listing CTL cases can be found below.

*Cases that should usually have fixed trial dates*

F.3    The cases where fixtures should be given will be set out in the listing practice applicable at the court, but should usually include the following:
i.    Cases in classes 1A, 1B, 1C, 2B and 2C;
ii.    Cases involving vulnerable and intimidated witnesses (including domestic violence cases), whether or not special measures have been ordered by the court;
iii.    Cases where the witnesses are under 18 or have to come from overseas;
iv.    Cases estimated to last more than a certain time — the period chosen will depend on the size of the centre and the available judges;
v.    Cases where a previous fixed hearing has not been effective;
vi.    Re-trials; and,
vii.    Cases involving expert witnesses.

*Custody Time Limits*

F.4 Every effort must be made to list cases for trial within the CTL limits set by Parliament. The guiding principles are:

    i. At the first hearing in the Crown Court, prosecution will inform the court when the CTL lapses.

    ii. All efforts must be made to list the case within the CTL. The CTL may only be extended in accordance with s. 22 Prosecution of Offences Act 1985 and the Prosecution of Offences (Custody Time Limits) Regulations 1987.

    iii. If suitable, given priority and listed on a date not less than 2 weeks before the CTL expires, the case may be placed in a warned list.

    iv. The CTL must be kept under continual review by the parties, HMCTS and the Resident Judge.

    v. If the CTL is at risk of being exceeded, an additional hearing should take place and should be listed before the Resident Judge or trial judge or other judge nominated by the Resident Judge.

    vi. An application to extend the CTL in any case listed outside the CTL must be considered by the court whether or not it was listed with the express consent of the defence.

    vii. Any application to extend CTLs must be considered as a matter of urgency. The reasons for needing the extension must be ascertained and fully explained to the court.

    viii. Where courtroom or judge availability is an issue, the court must itself list the case to consider the extension of any CTL. The Delivery Director of the circuit must provide a statement setting out in detail what has been done to try to accommodate the case within the CTL.

    ix. Where courtroom or judge availability is not in issue, but all parties and the court agree that the case will not be ready for trial before the expiration of the CTL, a date may be fixed outside the CTL. This may be done without prejudice to any application to extend the CTLs or with the express consent of the defence; this must be noted on the papers.

F.5 As legal argument may delay the swearing in of a jury, it is desirable to extend the CTL to a date later than the first day of the trial.

*Re-trials ordered by the Court of Appeal*

F.6 The Crown Court must comply with the directions of the Court of Appeal and cannot vary those directions without reference to the Court of Appeal.

F.7 In cases where a retrial is ordered by the Court of Appeal the CTL is 112 days starting from the date that the new indictment is preferred i.e. from the date that the indictment is delivered to the Crown Court. Court centres should check that CREST has calculated the dates correctly and that it has not used 182 days on cases that have previously been 'sent'.

*Changes to the date of fixed cases*

F.8 Once a trial date or window is fixed, it should not be vacated or moved without good reason. Under the Criminal Procedure Rules, parties are expected to be ready by the trial date.

F.9 The listing officer may, in circumstances determined by the Resident Judge, agree to the movement of the trial to a date to which the defence and prosecution both consent, provided the timely hearing of the case is not delayed. The prosecution will be expected to have consulted the witnesses before agreeing to any change.

F.10 In all other circumstances, requests to adjourn or vacate fixtures or trial windows must be referred to the Resident Judge for his or her personal attention; the Resident Judge may delegate the decision to a named deputy.

*Transferring cases to another court*

F.11 Transfer between courts on the same circuit must be agreed by the Resident Judges of each court, subject to guidance from the Presiding Judges of the circuit.

F.12 Transfer of trials between circuits must be agreed between the Presiding Judges and Delivery Directors of the respective circuits.

F.13 Transfers may be agreed either in specific cases or in accordance with general principles agreed between those cited above.

## CPD XIII Listing G: Listing of Hearings other than Trials

CPD.XIII.G

G.1 In addition to trials, the court's listing practice will have to provide court time for shorter matters, such as those listed below. These hearings are important, often either for setting the necessary case management framework for the proper and efficient preparation of cases for trial, or for determining matters that affect the rights of individuals. They must be afforded the appropriate level of resource that they require to be considered properly, and this may include judicial reading time as well as an appropriate length of hearing.

G.2 The applicant is responsible for notifying the court, and the other party if appropriate, and ensuring that the papers are served in good time, including a time estimate for judicial reading time and for the hearing. The applicant must endeavour to complete the application within the time estimate provided unless there are exceptional circumstances.

**G.3**    Hearings other than trials include the following:

     i.     Applications for search warrants and Production Orders, sufficient reading time must be provided, see G.8 below;

     ii.    Bail applications;

     iii.   Applications to vacate or adjourn hearings;

     iv.   Applications for dismissal of charges;

     v.     Preparation for trial hearings, plea and trial preparation hearings, and other pre-trial case management hearings;

     vi.   Applications for disclosure of further unused material under section 8 of CPIA 1996;

     vii.   Case progression or case management hearings;

     viii. Applications in respect of sentence indications not sought at the PTPH;

     ix.   Sentences;

     x.     Civil applications under the Anti-Social Behaviour, Crime and Policing Act 2014;

     xi.   Breach proceedings (and see paragraph G.12 beneath);"

     xii.   Appeals from the magistrates' court: it is essential in all cases where witnesses are likely to be needed on the appeal to check availability before a date is fixed (and see paragraphs G.13 to G.15 beneath);

     xiii. Appeals from the youth court: where the case involves a Class 2B offence then a directions hearing will be required before the re-hearing to consider special measures, ground rules and appropriate adjustments for the hearing of the trial.

**G.4**    Short hearings should not generally be listed before a judge such that they may delay the start or continuation of a trial at the Crown Court. It is envisaged that any such short hearing will be completed by 10.30am or start after 4.30pm.

**G.5**    Each Crown Court equipped with a video link with a prison must have in place arrangements for the conduct of PCMHs, other pre-trial hearings and sentencing hearings by video link.

*Notifying sureties of hearing dates*

**G.6**    Where a surety has entered into a recognizance in the magistrates' court in respect of a case allocated or sent to the Crown Court and where the bail order or recognizance refers to attendance at the first hearing in the Crown Court, the defendant should be reminded by the listing officer that the surety should attend the first hearing in the Crown Court in order to provide further recognizance. If attendance is not arranged, the defendant may be remanded in custody pending the recognisance being provided.

**G.7**    The Court should also notify sureties of the dates of the hearing at the Crown Court at which the defendant is ordered to appear in as far in advance as possible: see the observations of Parker LJ in *R v Crown Court at Reading ex p. Bello* [1992] 3 All ER 353.

*Applications for Production Orders and Search Warrants*

**G.8**    The use of production orders and search warrants involve the use of intrusive state powers that affect the rights and liberties of individuals. It is the responsibility of the court to ensure that those powers are not abused. To do so, the court must be presented with a properly completed application, on the appropriate form, which includes a summary of the investigation to provide the context for the order, a clear explanation of how the statutory requirements are fulfilled, and full and frank disclosure of anything that might undermine the basis for the application. Further directions on the proper making and consideration of such applications will be provided by Practice Direction. However, the complexity of the application must be taken into account in listing it such that the judge is afforded appropriate reading time and the hearing is given sufficient time for the issues to be considered thoroughly, and a short judgment given.

*Confiscation and Related Hearings*

**G.9**    Applications for restraint orders should be determined by the Resident Judge, or a judge nominated by the Resident Judge, at the Crown Court location at which they are lodged.

**G.10**   In order to prevent possible dissipation of assets of significant value, applications under the Proceeds of Crime Act 2002 should be considered urgent when lists are being fixed. In order to prevent potential prejudice, applications for the variation and discharge of orders, for the appointment of receivers, and applications to punish alleged breaches of orders as a contempt of court should similarly be treated as urgent and listed expeditiously.

*Confiscation Hearings*

**G.11**   It is important that confiscation hearings take place in good time after the defendant is convicted or sentenced.

**Breach proceedings**

G.12  As a general rule, proceedings to which CrimPR Part 32 applies (breach of community and other orders) should be brought in the court, and in case of the Crown Court at the Crown Court centre, at which the sentence was imposed, or in the magistrates' court at which the breach of a Crown Court order ordinarily would be dealt with. An exception to that general rule should be made, however, to reflect the application of CrimPR Part 1, the overriding objective, and the key listing principles at A above, where the defendant's home is significantly closer to another court with jurisdiction to determine the proceedings, in which case those proceedings should be brought in that court. If the court in which the breach proceedings are brought was not the sentencing court, or the magistrates' court for the Crown Court centre at which the sentence was passed, then the authority by which the proceedings are instituted must explain the reasons for choosing it. Any dispute over the proper venue for should be determined by the relevant Presiding Judges.

**Appeals from magistrates' courts**

G.13  As a general rule, the hearing in the Crown Court of an appeal to which CrimPR Part 34 applies (appeal against conviction or sentence from a magistrates' court) should take place at the Crown Court centre to which that magistrates' court ordinarily sends cases for trial or commits for sentence. This general rule applies irrespective of the location of the magistrates' court at which the case first began, if that was not the court at which the defendant was convicted, or sentenced, or both, because the reasons that led to the case being dealt with at a different magistrates' court may apply equally to the hearing of the appeal.

G.14  There are two exceptions to that general rule, however, each of which reflects the application of CrimPR Part 1, the overriding objective, and the key listing principles at A above. First, if on an appeal against conviction witnesses are required to give evidence in person then the appeal should be heard at the Crown Court centre which is the most conveniently situated for the majority of those witnesses. This exception is likely to apply where the defendant's conviction and sentence have been imposed at a magistrates' court distant from the place at which the offence occurred, perhaps because the defendant had failed to attend a hearing at the court for that area and subsequently was arrested for breach of bail and convicted and sentenced at another court. The information required of the parties to the appeal by CrimPR 34.3 and by the associated appeal forms will be essential to determining the most appropriate venue for the appeal. Second, where the appeal is against sentence only, or if, exceptionally, on an appeal against conviction no witnesses are required to give evidence in person, then then the appeal should be heard at the Crown Court centre which is the closest to the defendant's home. This exception is likely to apply where the defendant has been convicted and sentenced at a magistrates' court for the area in which the offence occurred but at a distance from the defendant's usual or present residence. This exception must not, however, be allowed to operate to the disadvantage of any victim of the offence who is expected to attend the sentencing in the Crown Court.

G.15  Once an appeal is submitted to the Crown Court, arrangements for its hearing, at that or at another Crown Court centre if appropriate, must be made by Crown Court staff under the direction of the Resident judge or Resident judges concerned. Any dispute over the proper venue for the appeal should be determined by the relevant Presiding Judges.

## CPD XIII Annex 1: General Principles for the Deployment of the Judiciary in the Magistrates' Court

**CPD.XIII.x1**

This distils the full deployment guidance issued in November 2012. The relevant sections dealing specifically with the allocation of work within the magistrates' court have been incorporated into this Practice Direction. It does not seek to replace the guidance in its entirety.

*Presumptions*

1. The presumptions which follow are intended to provide an acceptable and flexible framework establishing the deployment of the DJ (MC)s and magistrates. The system must be capable of adaptation to meet particular needs, whether of locality or caseload. In any event, the presumptions which follow are illustrative not exhaustive.

2. DJ(MC)s should generally (not invariably) be deployed in accordance with the following presumptions ('the Presumptions'):
   (a)  Cases involving complex points of law and evidence.
   (b)  Cases involving complex procedural issues.
   (c)  Long cases (included on grounds of practicality).
   (d)  Interlinked cases (given the need for consistency, together with their likely complexity and novelty).
   (e)  Cases for which armed police officers are required in court, such as high end firearms cases.

Criminal Procedure Rules and Criminal Practice Directions

(f) A share of the more routine business of the Court, including case management and pre-trial reviews, (for a variety of reasons, including the need for DJ(MC)s to have competence in all areas of work and the desirability of an equitable division of work between magistrates and DJ(MC)s, subject always to the interests of the administration of justice).

(g) Where appropriate, in supporting the training of magistrates.

(h) Occasionally, in mixed benches of DJ(MC)s and magistrates (with a particular view both to improving the case management skills of magistrates and to improving the culture of collegiality).

(i) In the short term tackling of particular local backlogs ('backlog busting'), sometimes in combination with magistrates from the local or (with the SPJ's approval) adjoining benches.

3. In accordance with current arrangements certain classes of cases necessarily require DJ(MC)s and have therefore been excluded from the above presumptions; these are as follows:
   (a) Extradition;
   (b) Terrorism;
   (c) Prison Adjudications;
   (d) Sex cases in the Youth Court as per Annex 2;
   (e) Cases where the defendant is likely to be sentenced to a very large fine, see Annex 3;
   (f) The Special Jurisdiction of the Chief Magistrate.

4. In formulating the Presumptions, the following considerations have been taken into account:
   (a) The listing of cases is here, as elsewhere, a judicial function, see CPD XIII A.1. In the magistrates' courts the Judicial Business Group, subject to the supervision of the Presiding Judges of the circuit, is responsible for determining the day to day listing practice in that area. The day-to-day operation of that listing practice is the responsibility of the justices' clerk with the assistance of the listing officer.
   (b) Equally, providing the training of magistrates is a responsibility of justices' clerks.
   (c) It is best not to treat 'high profile' cases as a separate category but to consider their listing in the light of the principles and presumptions. The circumstances surrounding high profile cases do not permit ready generalisation, save that they are likely to require especially sensitive handling. Listing decisions involving such cases will often benefit from good communication at a local level between the justices' clerk, the DJ (MC) and the Bench Chairman.

   Account must be taken of the need to maintain the competences of all members of the judiciary sitting in the magistrates' court.

5. The Special Jurisdiction of the Senior District Judge (Chief Magistrate) concerns cases which fall into the following categories:
   i. cases with a terrorism connection;
   ii. cases involving war crimes and crimes against humanity;
   iii. matters affecting state security;
   iv. cases brought under the Official Secrets Act;
   v. offences involving royalty or parliament;
   vi. offences involving diplomats;
   vii. corruption of public officials;
   viii. police officers charged with serious offences;
   ix. cases of unusual sensitivity.

6. Where cases fall within the category of the Special Jurisdiction they must be heard by:-
   i. the Senior District Judge (or if not available);
   ii. the Deputy Senior District Judge (or if not available);
   iii. a District Judge approved by the Senior District Judge or his/her deputy for the particular case.

7. Where a doubt may exist as to whether or not a case falls within the Special Jurisdiction, reference should always be made to the Senior District Judge or to the Deputy Senior District Judge for clarification.

**CPD.XIII.x2**  **CPD XIII Annex 2: Sexual Offences in the Youth Court**

*Introduction*

1. This annex sets out the procedure to be applied in the Youth Court in all cases involving allegations of sexual offences which are capable of being sent for trial at the Crown Court under the grave crime provisions.

2. This applies to all cases involving such charges, irrespective of the gravity of the allegation, the age of the defendant and / or the antecedent history of the defendant[1].

---

[1] So, for example, every allegation of sexual touching, under s3 of the Sexual Offences Act 2003, is covered by this protocol.

3. This does not alter the test[2] that the Youth Court must apply when determining whether a case is a 'grave crime'.

4. In the Crown Court, cases involving allegations of sexual offences frequently involve complex and sensitive issues and only those Circuit Judges and Recorders who have been specifically authorised and who have attended the appropriate Judicial College course may try this type of work.

5. A number of District Judges (Magistrates' Courts) have now undertaken training in dealing with these difficult cases and have been specifically authorised to hear cases involving serious sexual offences which fall short of requiring to be sent to the Crown Court ('an authorised DJ(MC)'). As such, a procedure similar to that of the Crown Court will now apply to allegations of sexual offences in the Youth Court.

*Procedure*

6. The determination of venue in the Youth Court is governed by section 51 Crime and Disorder Act 1998, which provides that the youth must be tried summarily unless charged with such a grave crime that long term detention is a realistic possibility[3], or that one of the other exceptions to this presumption arises.

7. Wherever possible such cases should be listed before an authorised DJ(MC), to decide whether the case falls within the grave crime provisions and should therefore be sent for trial. If jurisdiction is retained and the allegation involves actual, or attempted, penetrative activity, the case must be tried by an authorised DJ(MC). In all other cases, the authorised DJ(MC) must consider whether the case is so serious and / or complex that it must be tried by an authorised DJ(MC), or whether the case can be heard by any DJ(MC) or any Youth Court Bench.

8. If it is not practicable for an authorised DJ(MC) to determine venue, any DJ(MC) or any Youth Court Bench may consider that issue. If jurisdiction is retained, appropriate directions may be given but the case papers, including a detailed case summary and a note of any representations made by the parties, must be sent to an authorised DJ(MC) to consider. As soon as possible the authorised DJ(MC) must decide whether the case must be tried by an authorised DJ(MC) or whether the case is suitable to be heard by any DJ(MC) or any Youth Court Bench; however, if the case involves actual, or alleged, penetrative activity, the trial must be heard by an authorised DJ(MC).

9. Once an authorised DJ(MC) has decided that the case is one which must be tried by an authorised DJ(MC), and in all cases involving actual or alleged penetrative activity, all further procedural hearings should, so far as practicable, be heard by an authorised DJ(MC).

*Cases remitted for sentence*

10. All cases which are remitted for sentence from the Crown Court to the Youth Court should be listed for sentence before an authorised DJ(MC).

*Arrangements for an authorised DJ(MC) to be appointed*

11. Where a case is to be tried by an authorised DJ(MC) but no such Judge is available, the Bench Legal Adviser should contact the Chief Magistrates Office for an authorised DJ(MC) to be assigned.

## CPD XIII Annex 3: Cases Involving Very Large Fines in the Magistrates' Court

**CPD.XIII.x3**

1. This Annex applies when s. 85 Legal Aid, Sentencing and Punishment of Offenders Act 2012 comes into force and the magistrates' court has the power to impose a maximum fine of any amount.

2. An authorised DJ(MC) must deal with any allocation decision, trial and sentencing hearing in the following types of cases which are triable either way:

   a) Cases involving death or significant, life changing injury or a high risk of death or significant, life-changing injury;

   b) Cases involving substantial environmental damage or polluting material of a dangerous nature;

   c) Cases where major adverse effect on human health or quality of life, animal health or flora has resulted;

   d) Cases where major costs through clean up, site restoration or animal rehabilitation have been incurred;

   e) Cases where the defendant corporation has a turnover in excess of £10 million but does not exceed £250 million, and has acted in a deliberate, reckless or negligent manner;

---

[2] Set out in the Sentencing Guidelines Council's definitive guideline, entitled 'Overarching Principles — Sentencing Youths' Published by the Sentencing Guidelines Council in November 2009.

[3] Section 24(1) of the Magistrates Court Act 1980

  f) Cases where the defendant corporation has a turnover in excess of £250 million;

  g) Cases where the court will be expected to analyse complex company accounts;

  h) High profile cases or ones of an exceptionally sensitive nature.

3. The prosecution agency must notify the justices' clerk where practicable of any case of the type mentioned in paragraph 2 of this Annex, no less than 7 days before the first hearing to ensure that an authorised DJ(MC) is available at the first hearing.

4. The justices' clerk shall contact the Office of the Chief Magistrate to ensure that an authorised DJ(MC) can be assigned to deal with such a case if there is not such a person available in the courthouse.

5. Where an authorised DJ(MC) is not appointed at the first hearing the court shall adjourn the case. The court shall ask the accused for an indication of his plea, but shall not allocate the case nor, if the accused indicates a guilty plea, sentence him, commit him for sentence, ask for a pre-sentence report or give any indication as to likely sentence that will be imposed. The justices' clerk shall ensure an authorised DJ(MC) is appointed for the following hearing.

6. When dealing with sentence, section 3 of the Powers of Criminal Courts (Sentenc[ing]) Act 2000 can be invoked where, despite the magistrates' court having maximum fine powers available to it, the offence or combination of offences make it so serious that the Crown Court should deal with it as though the person had been convicted on indictment.

7. An authorised DJ(MC) should consider allocating the case to the Crown Court or committing the accused for sentence.

**CPD.XIII.x4** **CPD XIII Annex 4: Application This annex replaces the Protocol on the case management of Terrorism Cases issued in December 2006 by the President of the Queen's Bench Division**

1. This annex applies to 'terrorism cases'. For the purposes of this annex a case is a 'terrorism case' where:

 (a) one of the offences charged against any of the defendants is indictable only and it is alleged by the prosecution that there is evidence that it took place during an act of terrorism or for the purposes of terrorism as defined in s1 of the Terrorist Act 2000. This may include, but is not limited to:

  (i) murder;

  (ii) manslaughter;

  (iii) an offence under section 18 of the Offences against the Person Act 1861 (wounding with intent);

  (iv) an offence under section 23 or 24 of that Act (administering poison etc);

  (v) an offence under section 28 or 29 of that Act (explosives);

  (vi) an offence under section 2, 3 or 5 of the Explosive Substances Act 1883 (causing explosions);

  (vii) an offence under section 1(2) of the Criminal Damage Act 1971 (endangering life by damaging property);

  (viii) an offence under section 1 of the Biological Weapons Act 1974 (biological weapons);

  (ix) an offence under section 2 of the Chemical Weapons Act 1996 (chemical weapons);

  (x) an offence under section 56 of the Terrorism Act 2000 (directing a terrorist organisation);

  (xi) an offence under section 59 of that Act (inciting terrorism overseas);

  (xii) offences under (v), (vii) and (viii) above given jurisdiction by virtue of section 62 of that Act (terrorist bombing overseas); and

  (xiii) an offence under section 5 of the Terrorism Act 2006 (preparation of terrorism acts).

 (b) one of the offences charged is indictable only and includes an allegation by the prosecution of serious fraud that took place during an act of terrorism or for the purposes of terrorism as defined in s1 of the Terrorist Act 2000 and the prosecutor gives a notice under section 51B of the Crime and Disorder Act 1998 (Notices in serious or complex fraud cases);

 (c) one of the offences charged is indictable only, which includes an allegation that a defendant conspired, incited or attempted to commit an offence under sub paragraphs (1)(a) or (b) above; or

 (d) it is a case (which can be indictable only or triable either way) that a judge of the terrorism cases list (see paragraph 2(a) below) considers should be a terrorism case. In deciding whether a case not covered by subparagraphs (1)(a), (b) or (c) above should be a terrorism case, the judge may hear representations from the Crown Prosecution Service.

*The terrorism cases list*

2. (a) All terrorism cases, wherever they originate in England and Wales, will be managed in a list known as the 'terrorism cases list' by such judges of the High Court as are nominated by the President of the Queen's Bench Division.

(b) Such cases will be tried, unless otherwise directed by the President of the Queen's Bench Division, by a judge of the High Court as nominated by the President of the Queen's Bench Division.

3. The judges managing the terrorism cases referred to in paragraph 2(a) will be supported by the London and South Eastern Regional Co-ordinator's Office (the 'Regional Co-ordinator's Office'). An official of that office or an individual nominated by that office will act as the case progression officer for cases in that list for the purposes of CrimPR 3.4.

*Procedure after charge*

4. Immediately after a person has been charged in a terrorism case, anywhere in England and Wales, a representative of the Crown Prosecution Service will notify the person on the 24 hour rota for special jurisdiction matters at Westminster Magistrates' Court of the following information:
    (a) the full name of each defendant and the name of his solicitor of other legal representative, if known;
    (b) the charges laid;
    (c) the name and contact details of the Crown Prosecutor with responsibility for the case, if known; and
    (d) confirmation that the case is a terrorism case.

5. The person on the 24-hour rota will then ensure that all terrorism cases wherever they are charged in England and Wales are listed before the Chief Magistrate or other District Judge designated under the Terrorism Act 2000. Unless the Chief Magistrate or other District Judge designated under the Terrorism Act 2000 directs otherwise, the first appearance of all defendants accused of terrorism offences will be listed at Westminster Magistrates' Court.

6. In order to comply with section 46 of the Police and Criminal Evidence Act 1984, if a defendant in a terrorism case is charged at a police station within the local justice area in which Westminster Magistrates' Court is situated, the defendant must be brought before Westminster Magistrates' Court as soon as is practicable and in any event not later than the first sitting after he is charged with the offence. If a defendant in a terrorism case is charged in a police station outside the local justice area in which Westminster Magistrates' Court is situated, unless the Chief Magistrate or other designated judge directs otherwise, the defendant must be removed to that area as soon as is practicable. He must then be brought before Westminster Magistrates' Court as soon as is practicable after his arrival in the area and in any event not later than the first sitting of Westminster Magistrates' Court after his arrival in that area.

7. As soon as is practicable after charge a representative of the Crown Prosecution Service will also provide the Regional Listing Co-ordinator's Office with the information listed in paragraph 4 above.

8. The Regional Co-ordinator's Office will then ensure that the Chief Magistrate and the Legal Aid Agency have the same information.

*Cases to be sent to the Crown Court under section 51 of the Crime and Disorder Act 1998*

9. The court should ordinarily direct that the plea and trial preparation hearing should take place about 14 days after charge.

10. The sending magistrates' court should contact the Regional Listing Co-ordinator's Office who will be responsible for notifying the magistrates' court as to the relevant Crown Court to which to send the case.

11. In all terrorism cases, the magistrates' court case progression form for cases sent to the Crown Court under section 51 of the Crime and Disorder Act 1998 should not be used. Instead of the automatic directions set out in that form, the magistrates' court shall make the following directions to facilitate the preliminary hearing at the Crown Court:
    (a) three days prior to the preliminary hearing in the terrorism cases list, the prosecution must serve upon each defendant and the Regional Listing co-ordinator:
        (i) a preliminary summary of the case;
        (ii) the names of those who are to represent the prosecution, if known;
        (iii) an estimate of the length of the trial;
        (iv) a suggested provisional timetable which should generally include:
            • the general nature of further enquiries being made by the prosecution,
            • the time needed for the completion of such enquiries,
            • the time required by the prosecution to review the case,
            • a timetable for the phased service of the evidence,
            • the time for the provision by the Attorney General for his consent if necessary,
            • the time for service of the detailed defence case statement,
            • the date for the case management hearing, and
            • the estimated trial date;

(v) a preliminary statement of the possible disclosure issues setting out the nature and scale of the problem, including the amount of unused material, the manner in which the prosecution seeks to deal with these matters and a suggested timetable for discharging their statutory duty; and

(vi) any information relating to bail and custody time limits.

(b) one day prior to the preliminary hearing in the terrorist cases list, each defendant must serve in writing on the Regional Listing Co-ordinator and the prosecution:

(i) the proposed representation;

(ii) observations on the timetable; and

(iii) an indication of plea and the general nature of the defence.

*Cases to be sent to the Crown Court after the prosecutor gives notice under section 51B of the Crime and Disorder Act 1998*

12. If a terrorism case is to be sent to the Crown Court after the prosecutor gives a notice under section 51B of the Crime and Disorder Act 1998 the magistrates' court should proceed as in paragraphs 9-11 above.

13. When a terrorism case is so sent or transferred the case will go into the terrorism list and be managed by a judge as described in paragraph 2(a) above.

*The plea and trial preparation hearing at the Crown Court*

14. At the plea and trial preparation hearing, the judge will determine whether the case is one to remain in the terrorism list and if so, give directions setting the provisional timetable.

15. The Legal Aid Agency must attend the hearing by an authorised officer to assist the court.

*Use of video links*

16. Unless a judge otherwise directs, all Crown Court hearings prior to the trial will be conducted by video link for all defendants in custody.

*Security*

17. The police service and the prison service will provide the Regional Listing Co-ordinator's Office with an initial joint assessment of the security risks associated with any court appearance by the defendants within 14 days of charge. Any subsequent changes in circumstances or the assessment of risk which have the potential to impact upon the choice of trial venue will be notified to the Regional Listing Co-ordinator's Office immediately.

**CPD.XIII.x5**    **CPD XIII Annex 5: Management of cases from the organised crime division of the Crown Prosecution Service This annex replaces the guidance issued by the Senior Presiding Judge in January 2014**

1. The Organised Crime Division (OCD) of the CPS is responsible for prosecution of cases from the National Crime Agency (NCA). Typically, these cases involve more than one defendant, are voluminous and raise complex and specialised issues of law. It is recognised that if not closely managed, such cases have the potential to cost vast amounts of public money and take longer than necessary.

2. This annex applies to all cases handled by the OCD.

*Designated court centres*

3. Subject to the overriding discretion of the Presiding Judges of the circuit, OCD cases should normally be heard at Designated Court Centres (DCC). The process of designating court centres for this purpose has taken into account geographical factors and the size, security and facilities of those court centres. The designated court centres are:

(a) Northern Circuit: Manchester, Liverpool and Preston.

(b) North Eastern Circuit: Leeds, Newcastle and Sheffield.

(c) Western Circuit: Bristol and Winchester.

(d) South Eastern Circuit (not including London): Reading, Luton, Chelmsford, Ipswich, Maidstone, Lewes and Hove.

(e) South Eastern Circuit (London only): Southwark, Blackfriars, Kingston, Woolwich, Croydon and the Central Criminal Court.

(f) Midland Circuit: Birmingham, Leicester and Nottingham.

(g) Wales Circuit: Cardiff, Swansea and Mold.

*Selection of designated court centres*

4. If arrests are made in different parts of the country and the OCD seeks to have all defendants tried by one Crown Court, the OCD will, at the earliest opportunity, write to the relevant court cluster manager with a recommendation as to the appropriate designated

court centre, requesting that the decision be made by the relevant Presiding Judges. In the event that the designated court centre within one region is unable to accommodate a case, for example, as a result of a custody time limit expiry date, consideration may be given to transferring the case to a DCC in another region with the consent of the relevant Presiding Judges.

5. There will be a single point of contact person at the OCD for each HMCTS region, to assist listing co-ordinators.

6. The single contact person for each HMCTS region will be the relevant Cluster Manager, with the exception of the South Eastern Circuit, where the appropriate person will be the Regional Listing Co-ordinator.

*Designation of the trial judge*

7. The trial judge will be assigned by the Presiding Judge at the earliest opportunity, and in accordance with CPD XIII Listing E: Allocation of Business within the Crown Court. Where the trial judge is unable to continue with the case, all further pre-trial hearings should be by a single judge until a replacement has been assigned.

*Procedure after charge*

8. Within 24 hours of the laying of a charge, a representative of the OCD will notify the relevant Cluster Manager of the following information to enable an agreement to be reached between that Cluster Manager and the reviewing CPS lawyer before the first appearance as to the DCC to which the case should be sent:
   (a) the full name of each defendant and the name of his legal representatives, if known;
   (b) the charges laid; and
   (c) the name and contact details of the Crown Prosecutor with responsibility for the case.

*Exceptions*

9. Where it is not possible to have a case dealt with at a DCC, the OCD should liaise closely with the relevant Cluster Manager and the Presiding Judges to ensure that the cases are sent to the most appropriate court centre. This will, among other things, take into account the location of the likely source of the case, convenience of the witnesses, travelling distance for OCD staff and facilities at the court centres.

10. In the event that it is allocated to a non-designated court centre, the OCD should be permitted to make representations in writing to the Presiding Judges within 14 days as to why the venue is not suitable. The Presiding Judges will consider the reasons and, if necessary, hold a hearing. The CPS may renew their request at any stage where further reasons come to light that may affect the original decision on venue.

11. Nothing in this annex should be taken to remove the right of the defence to make representations as to the venue.

Criminal Procedure Rules and Criminal Practice Directions

# SENTENCING GUIDELINES

# Sentencing Guidelines

This is an edited version of the sentencing guidelines, both those originally issued by the Sentencing Guidelines Council and those issued by the Sentencing Council for England and Wales which are now published direct to the Sentencing Council website: https://www.sentencingcouncil.org.uk/. By virtue of the Coroners and Justice Act 2009 (Commencement No. 4, Transitional and Saving Provisions) Order 2010 (SI 2010 No. 816), art. 7, guidelines issued by the SGC 'are to be treated as guidelines issued by the Sentencing Council'. For more on the status of guidelines and the duty of courts to follow them, see **E1.4** in the main work.

### Crown Court and Magistrates' Court

The Sentencing Council produces sentencing guidelines for use in the Magistrates' Court and the Crown Court. The Overarching Guidelines are common to both. This section includes all of the Crown Court offence guidelines by offence type and many of these are also triable either way. For those offence guidelines which are included solely in the Magistrates' Court Sentencing Guidelines see **SG10**.

### The application of sentencing principles during the Covid-19 emergency

On 23 June 2020 the Sentencing Council issued a statement on Covid-19 and the impact on conditions in prisons and the potentially heavier impact of custodial sentences on offenders and their families. The statement noted that well-established sentencing principles are familiar to judges and magistrates and were reaffirmed by the Lord Chief Justice when giving the judgment of the Court of Appeal in *Manning* [2020] EWCA Crim 592, [2020] 4 WLR 77, and that the purpose of the statement was to help to clarify the position for those less familiar with the principles or not involved in the criminal justice system.

In *Manning*, the Lord Chief Justice observed (at [41]) that the impact of the Covid-19 emergency on prisons is well-known, and continued as follows:

> The current conditions in prisons represent a factor which can properly be taken into account in deciding whether to suspend a sentence. In accordance with established principles, any court will take into account the likely impact of a custodial sentence upon an offender and, where appropriate, upon others as well. Judges and magistrates can, therefore, and in our judgment should, keep in mind that the impact of a custodial sentence is likely to be heavier during the current emergency than it would otherwise be. Those in custody are, for example, confined to their cells for much longer periods than would otherwise be the case—currently, 23 hours a day. They are unable to receive visits. Both they and their families are likely to be anxious about the risk of the transmission of Covid-19.
> 42. Applying ordinary principles, where a court is satisfied that a custodial sentence must be imposed, the likely impact of that sentence continues to be relevant to the further decisions as to its necessary length and whether it can be suspended. Moreover, sentencers can and should also bear in mind the Reduction in Sentence Guideline. That makes clear that a guilty plea may result in a different type of sentence or enable a magistrates' court to retain jurisdiction, rather than committing for sentence.

Throughout the sentencing process, and in considering all the circumstances of the individual case, the court must bear in mind the practical realities of the effects of the current health emergency. The court should consider whether increased weight should be given to mitigating factors, and should keep in mind that the impact of immediate imprisonment is likely to be particularly heavy for some groups of offenders or their families.

In addition, when applying the *Reduction in sentence for a guilty plea* guideline, the court must consider the exceptions in that guideline. The exceptions include whether there were particular circumstances affecting the defendant's ability to understand the allegations or to receive the advice necessary before pleading guilty, or where the defendant pleads guilty to, and is then convicted of, a different offence from that originally charged. In making these considerations, the court must keep in mind the practical difficulties of defendants accessing legal advice during the present emergency.

This work uses 'SG1-1', 'SG1-2' (etc.) paragraph numbers as a cross-referencing aid for readers. The guidelines as provided by the Sentencing Council are not individually numbered and are presented as a group of Overarching Guidelines and a collection of individual offence guidelines associated with an offence type.

The following table lists the sentencing guidelines by type, the Effective From dates, and the paragraph at which the guidelines can be located:

| Overarching Guidelines | SG Effective From Date | BCP Paragraph |
|---|---|---|
| Allocation | 01 March 2016 | SG1 |
| Domestic Abuse | 24 May 2018 | SG6 |
| General Guideline: Overarching Principles | 01 October 2019 | SG2 |
| Imposition of Community and Custodial Sentences | 01 February 2017 | SG9 |
| Offences Taken Into Consideration | 11 June 2012 | SG3 |
| Reduction in Sentence for a Guilty Plea (First Hearing on or after 1 June 2017) | 01 June 2017 | SG5 |
| Sentencing Children and Young People | 01 June 2017 | SG8 |
| Sentencing Offenders with Mental Disorders, Developmental Disorders, or Neurological Impairments | 01 October 2020 | SG7 |
| Totality | 11 June 2012 | SG4 |

| Magistrates' Court Sentencing Guidelines | | SG10 |
|---|---|---|
| **Offences on indictment or triable either way** | | |

| Offence Type | Number of Guidelines | SG Effective From Date | BCP Paragraph |
|---|---|---|---|
| Arson and Criminal Damage | 7 | 01 October 2019 | SG11 |
| Assault Offences | 8 | 01 July 2021 | SG12 |
| Attempted Murder | 1 | 27 July 2009 | SG13 |
| Bladed Articles and Offensive Weapons | 11 including one related to Sentencing Children and Young People | 01 June 2018 | SG14 |
| Breach Offences | 15 | 01 October 2018 | SG15 |
| Burglary Offences | 4 including one related to Theft | 16 January 2012 | SG19 |
| Causing Death by Driving | 4 | 15 July 2008 | SG22 |
| Child Cruelty | 4 | 01 January 2019 | SG20 |
| Dangerous Dog Offences | 3 | 01 July 2016 | SG21 |
| Drug Offences | 8 | 01 April 2021 | SG23 |
| Environmental Offences | 12 | 01 July 2014 | SG24 |
| Fraud, Bribery, and Money Laundering Offences | 19 | 01 October 2014 | SG26 |
| Health and Safety Offences | 5 | 01 February 2016 | SG28 |
| Intimidatory Offences | 7 | 01 October 2018 | SG27 |
| Manslaughter | 4 | 01 November 2018 | SG25 |
| Public Order | 6 | 01 January 2020 | SG29 |
| Robbery Offences | 4 including one related to Sentencing Children and Young People | 01 April 2016 | SG30 |
| Sexual Offences | 54 including 4 related to Sentencing Children and Young People | 01 April 2014 | SG31 |
| Terrorism Offences | 17 | 27 April 2018 | SG32 |
| Theft Offences | 5 including one related to Burglary | 01 February 2016 | SG33 |
| Firearms Offences | 9 | 01 January 2021; 01 January 2022 (Importation) | SG34 |
| Trade mark, unauthorised use of | 2 | 01 October 2021 | SG35 |

| Offence Type | Number of Guidelines | SG Effective From Date | BCP Paragraph |
|---|---|---|---|
| Slavery, servitude and forced or compulsory labour/Human trafficking | 3 | 01 October 2021 | SG36 |

The following table of offences lists all of the offence specific guidelines in alphabetical order indicating where the standard steps apply.

| Guideline | Assistance to prosecution step | Guilty plea step | Reasons step | Time on bail step |
|---|---|---|---|---|
| Abstracting electricity | 3 | 4 | 7 | 8 |
| Abuse of position of trust: sexual activity in the presence of a child/Abuse of position of trust: causing a child to watch a sexual act | 3 | 4 | 8 | 9 |
| Abuse of position of trust: sexual activity with a child/Abuse of position of trust: causing or inciting a child to engage in sexual activity | 3 | 4 | 8 | 9 |
| Administering a substance with intent | 3 | 4 | 8 | 9 |
| Affray | 3 | 4 | 8 | 9 |
| Aggravated burglary | 3 | 4 | 8 | 9 |
| Alcohol sale offences (Revised 2017) | 3 | 4 | 7 | n/a |
| Animal cruelty (Revised 2017) | 3 | 4 | 7 | 8 |
| Arranging or facilitating the commission of a child sex offence | n/a | n/a | n/a | n/a |
| Arson (criminal damage by fire) | 3 | 4 | 8 | 9 |
| Arson/criminal damage with intent to endanger life or reckless as to whether life endangered | 3 | 4 | 8 | 9 |
| Assault by penetration | 3 | 4 | 8 | 9 |
| Assault occasioning actual bodily harm/Racially or religiously aggravated ABH | n/a | 5 | 9 | 10 |
| Assault of a child under 13 by penetration | 3 | 4 | 8 | 9 |
| Assaults on emergency workers — see SG12-7 Common assault / Racially or religiously aggravated common assault/ Common assault on emergency worker | | | | |
| Assault with intent to resist arrest | 3 | 4 | 8 | 9 |
| Attempted murder | 3 | 4 | 9 | n/a |
| Benefit Fraud | 3 | 4 | 7 | 8 |
| Bladed articles and offensive weapons – possession | 4 | 5 | 8 | 9 |
| Bladed articles and offensive weapons – threats | 4 | 5 | 8 | 9 |
| Bladed articles and offensive weapons (possession and threats) – children and young people | n/a | 4 | n/a | n/a |
| Brakes defective | n/a | n/a | n/a | n/a |
| Brakes defective (over 3.5 tonnes) | n/a | n/a | n/a | n/a |
| Breach of a community order | n/a | n/a | n/a | n/a |
| Breach of a criminal behaviour order | 3 | 4 | 7 | 8 |
| Breach of a protective order (restraining and non-molestation orders) | 3 | 4 | 7 | 8 |
| Breach of a sexual harm prevention order | 3 | 4 | 7 | 8 |
| Breach of a suspended sentence order | n/a | n/a | n/a | n/a |

| Guideline | Assistance to prosecution step | Guilty plea step | Reasons step | Time on bail step |
|---|---|---|---|---|
| Breach of disqualification from acting as a director | 3 | 4 | 7 | 8 |
| Breach of disqualification from keeping an animal | 3 | 4 | 7 | 8 |
| Breach of post-sentence supervision | n/a | n/a | n/a | n/a |
| Breach of supervision default order | n/a | n/a | n/a | n/a |
| Breach of a Slavery and Trafficking Prevention Order/Breach of a Slavery and Trafficking Risk Order | n/a | n/a | n/a | n/a |
| Breach offences (other) | n/a | n/a | n/a | n/a |
| Bribery | 3 | 4 | 7 | 8 |
| Care workers: sexual activity in the presence of a person with a mental disorder/Care workers: causing a person with a mental disorder to watch a sexual act | 3 | 4 | 8 | 9 |
| Care workers: sexual activity with a person with a mental disorder/Care workers: causing or inciting sexual activity | 3 | 4 | 8 | 9 |
| Careless Driving (drive without due care and attention) (Revised 2017) | 3 | 4 | 7 | n/a |
| Carrying a firearm in a public place | 4 | 5 | 8 | 9 |
| Causing a person to engage in sexual activity without consent | 3 | 4 | 8 | 9 |
| Causing death by careless driving when under the influence of drink or drugs, etc | n/a | n/a | n/a | n/a |
| Causing death by careless or inconsiderate driving | n/a | n/a | n/a | n/a |
| Causing death by dangerous driving | n/a | n/a | n/a | n/a |
| Causing death by driving: unlicensed, disqualified or uninsured drivers | n/a | n/a | n/a | n/a |
| Causing grievous bodily harm with intent to do grievous bodily harm/Wounding with intent to do GBH | 3 | 4 | 8 | 9 |
| Causing or allowing a child to suffer serious physical harm/Causing or allowing a child to die | 3 | 4 | 9 | 10 |
| Causing or inciting a child under 13 to engage in sexual activity | 3 | 4 | 8 | 9 |
| Causing or inciting prostitution for gain/Controlling prostitution for gain | 3 | 4 | 8 | 9 |
| Causing or inciting sexual exploitation of a child/Controlling a child in relation to sexual exploitation/Arranging or facilitating sexual exploitation of a child | 3 | 4 | 8 | 9 |
| Child sex offences committed by children or young persons (sections 9–12) (offender under 18)/Sexual activity with a child family member (offender under 18)/Inciting a child family member to engage in sexual activity (offender under 18) | n/a | n/a | n/a | n/a |
| Collection of terrorist information | 3 | 4 | 7 | 8 |
| Committing an offence with intent to commit a human trafficking offence | n/a | n/a | n/a | n/a |

| Guideline | Assistance to prosecution step | Guilty plea step | Reasons step | Time on bail step |
|---|---|---|---|---|
| Committing an offence with intent to commit a sexual offence / Common assault on emergency worker | n/a | n/a | n/a | n/a |
| Common assault/Racially or religiously aggravated common assault | 4 | 5 | 9 | 10 |
| Communication network offences (Revised 2017) | 3 | 4 | 7 | 8 |
| Condition of vehicle/accessories/equipment involving danger of injury – buses/goods vehicles | n/a | n/a | n/a | n/a |
| Condition of vehicle/accessories/equipment involving danger of injury | n/a | n/a | n/a | n/a |
| Controlling or coercive behaviour in an intimate or family relationship | 3 | 4 | 7 | 8 |
| Corporate manslaughter | 5 | 6 | 9 | n/a |
| Corporate offenders: fraud, bribery and money laundering | 6 | 7 | 10 | n/a |
| Criminal damage (other than by fire) value exceeding £5,000/Racially or religiously aggravated criminal damage | 3 | 4 | 7 | 8 |
| Criminal damage (other than by fire) value not exceeding £5,000/Racially or religiously aggravated criminal damage | 3 | 4 | 7 | 8 |
| Cruelty to a child – assault and ill treatment, abandonment, neglect and failure to protect | 3 | 4 | 9 | 10 |
| Dangerous driving | n/a | n/a | n/a | n/a |
| Dangerous parking | n/a | n/a | n/a | n/a |
| Disclosing private sexual images | 3 | 4 | 7 | 8 |
| Disorderly behaviour with intent to cause harassment, alarm or distress/Racially or religiously aggravated disorderly behaviour with intent to cause harassment, alarm or distress | 3 | 4 | 8 | 9 |
| Disorderly behaviour/Racially or religiously aggravated disorderly behaviour | 3 | 4 | 7 | 8 |
| Domestic burglary | 3 | 4 | 8 | 9 |
| Drive in reverse or wrong way on motorway | n/a | n/a | n/a | n/a |
| Drive in reverse or wrong way on slip road | n/a | n/a | n/a | n/a |
| Drive off carriageway (central reservation or hard shoulder) | n/a | n/a | n/a | n/a |
| Drive otherwise than in accordance with licence | n/a | n/a | n/a | n/a |
| Drive otherwise than in accordance with licence (where could be covered) | n/a | n/a | n/a | n/a |
| Drive whilst disqualified (Revised 2017) | 3 | 4 | 7 | 8 |
| Drug driving (guidance only) | n/a | n/a | n/a | n/a |
| Drug offences involving newer and less common drugs | n/a | n/a | n/a | n/a |
| Drugs – class A – fail to attend/remain for initial assessment | 3 | 4 | 7 | n/a |
| Drugs – class A – fail/refuse to provide a sample | 3 | 4 | 7 | n/a |

| Guideline | Assistance to prosecution step | Guilty plea step | Reasons step | Time on bail step |
|---|---|---|---|---|
| Drunk and disorderly in a public place (Revised 2017) | 3 | 4 | 7 | n/a |
| Encouragement of terrorism | 3 | 4 | 7 | 8 |
| Engaging in sexual activity in the presence of a child/Causing a child to watch a sexual act | 3 | 4 | 8 | 9 |
| Engaging in sexual activity in the presence of a person with mental disorder impeding choice/Causing a person, with mental disorder impeding choice, to watch a sexual act | 3 | 4 | 8 | 9 |
| Engaging in sexual activity in the presence procured by inducement, threat or deception, of a person with mental disorder/Causing a person with a mental disorder to watch a sexual act by inducement, threat or deception | 3 | 4 | 8 | 9 |
| Environmental offences (other) | n/a | n/a | n/a | n/a |
| Exceed permitted driving time/periods of duty | n/a | n/a | n/a | n/a |
| Excess Alcohol (drive/attempt to drive) (Revised 2017) | 3 | 4 | 7 | 8 |
| Excess Alcohol (in charge) (Revised 2017) | 3 | 4 | 7 | 8 |
| Exhaust defective | n/a | n/a | n/a | n/a |
| Exhaust emission | n/a | n/a | n/a | n/a |
| Explosive substances (terrorism only) | 3 | 4 | 9 | 10 |
| Exposure | 3 | 4 | 8 | 9 |
| Fail to comply with notification requirements | 3 | 4 | 7 | 8 |
| Fail to comply with police constable directing traffic | n/a | n/a | n/a | n/a |
| Fail to comply with traffic sign (e.g. give way sign, keep left sign, temporary signs) | n/a | n/a | n/a | n/a |
| Fail to comply with traffic sign (e.g. red traffic light, stop sign, double white lines, no entry sign) | n/a | n/a | n/a | n/a |
| Fail to co-operate with preliminary (roadside) breath test | n/a | n/a | n/a | n/a |
| Fail to give information of driver's identity as required | n/a | n/a | n/a | n/a |
| Fail to keep/return written record sheets | n/a | n/a | n/a | n/a |
| Fail to notify change of ownership to DVLA | n/a | n/a | n/a | n/a |
| Fail to produce insurance certificate | n/a | n/a | n/a | n/a |
| Fail to produce test certificate | n/a | n/a | n/a | n/a |
| Fail to provide specimen for analysis (drive/attempt to drive) (Revised 2017) | 3 | 4 | 7 | 8 |
| Fail to provide specimen for analysis (in charge) (Revised 2017) | 3 | 4 | 7 | 8 |
| Fail to stop when required by police constable | n/a | n/a | n/a | n/a |
| Fail to stop/report road accident (Revised 2017) | 3 | 4 | 7 | 8 |
| Fail to use appropriate child car seat | n/a | n/a | n/a | n/a |
| Failing to protect girl from risk of genital mutilation | 3 | 4 | 8 | 9 |

| Guideline | Assistance to prosecution step | Guilty plea step | Reasons step | Time on bail step |
|---|---|---|---|---|
| Failure to disclose information about acts of terrorism | 3 | 4 | 8 | 9 |
| Failure to surrender to bail | 3 | 4 | 7 | 8 |
| Falsify or alter records with intent to deceive | n/a | n/a | n/a | n/a |
| Firearm, carrying in a public place | n/a | n/a | n/a | n/a |
| Firearms – importation | 3 | 4 | 7 | 8 |
| Firearms – possession by person prohibited | 3 | 4 | 7 | 8 |
| Firearms – possession of a prohibited weapon | 4 | 5 | 8 | 9 |
| Firearms – possession with intent – other offences | 4 | 5 | 9 | 10 |
| Firearms – possession with intent to cause fear to violence | 4 | 5 | 9 | 10 |
| Firearms – possession with intent endanger life | 4 | 5 | 9 | 10 |
| Firearms – possession without certificate | 3 | 4 | 7 | 8 |
| Firearms – Transfer and manufacture | 4 | 5 | 8 | 9 |
| Football related offences (Revised 2017) | 3 | 4 | 7 | n/a |
| Fraud | 3 | 4 | 7 | 8 |
| Fraudulent evasion of a prohibition by bringing into or taking out of the UK a controlled drug | 4 | 5 | 8 | 9 |
| Funding terrorism | 3 | 4 | 8 | 9 |
| Going equipped for theft or burglary | 3 | 4 | 7 | 8 |
| Gross negligence manslaughter | 3 | 4 | 8 | 9 |
| Handling stolen goods | 3 | 4 | 7 | 8 |
| Harassment (fear of violence)/Stalking (fear of violence)/Racially or religiously aggravated harassment (fear of violence)/stalking (fear of violence) | 3 | 4 | 8 | 9 |
| Harassment/Stalking/Racially or religiously aggravated harassment/stalking | 3 | 4 | 7 | 8 |
| Identity documents – possess false/another's/improperly obtained | Removed as the offence has been repealed | | | |
| Importing or exporting a psychoactive substance | 3 | 4 | 7 | 8 |
| Individuals: Breach of duty of employer towards employees and non-employees/Breach of duty of self-employed to others/Breach of duty of employees at work/Breach of Health and Safety regulations/Secondary liability | 4 | 5 | 8 | 9 |
| Individuals: Breach of food safety and food hygiene regulations | 4 | 5 | 8 | 9 |
| Individuals: Trade mark, unauthorised use of etc. | 3 | 4 | 7 | 8 |
| Individuals: Unauthorised or harmful deposit, treatment or disposal etc of waste/Illegal discharges to air, land and water | 7 | 8 | 11 | 12 |
| Inducement, threat or deception to procure sexual activity with a person with a mental disorder/Causing a person with a mental disorder to engage in or agree to engage in sexual activity by inducement, threat or deception | 3 | 4 | 8 | 9 |

| Guideline | Assistance to prosecution step | Guilty plea step | Reasons step | Time on bail step |
|---|---|---|---|---|
| Inflicting grievous bodily harm/Unlawful wounding/Racially or religiously aggravated GBH/Unlawful wounding | 4 | 5 | 9 | 10 |
| Keeping a brothel used for prostitution | 3 | 4 | 7 | 8 |
| Learner driver or excluded vehicle | n/a | n/a | n/a | n/a |
| Lights defective | n/a | n/a | n/a | n/a |
| Make U turn on motorway | n/a | n/a | n/a | n/a |
| Making Off Without Payment | 3 | 4 | 7 | 8 |
| Manslaughter by reason of diminished responsibility | 6 | 7 | 10 | 11 |
| Manslaughter by reason of loss of control | 3 | 4 | 8 | 9 |
| Meeting a child following sexual grooming | 3 | 4 | 8 | 9 |
| Money laundering | 3 | 4 | 7 | 8 |
| Motoring offences appropriate for imposition of fine or discharge | n/a | n/a | n/a | n/a |
| No excise licence | n/a | n/a | n/a | n/a |
| No goods vehicle plating certificate | n/a | n/a | n/a | n/a |
| No goods vehicle test certificate | n/a | n/a | n/a | n/a |
| No insurance (Revised 2017) | 3 | 4 | 7 | n/a |
| No operators licence | n/a | n/a | n/a | n/a |
| No test certificate | n/a | n/a | n/a | n/a |
| Non-domestic burglary | 3 | 4 | 8 | 9 |
| Number of passengers or way carried involving danger of injury | n/a | n/a | n/a | n/a |
| Number of passengers or way carried involving danger of injury (over 3.5 tonnes) | n/a | n/a | n/a | n/a |
| Obstruct/resist a police constable in execution of duty (Revised 2017) | 3 | 4 | 7 | n/a |
| Organisations: Breach of duty of employer towards employees and non-employees/Breach of duty of self-employed to others/Breach of Health and Safety regulations | 5 | 6 | 9 | n/a |
| Organisations: Breach of food safety and food hygiene regulations | 5 | 6 | 9 | n/a |
| Organisations: Trade mark, unauthorised use of etc. | 6 | 7 | 10 | n/a |
| Organisations: Unauthorised or harmful deposit, treatment or disposal etc of waste/Illegal discharges to air, land and water | 8 | 9 | 12 | n/a |
| Overloading/exceeding axle weight | n/a | n/a | n/a | n/a |
| Overloading/exceeding axle weight (over 3.5 tonnes) | n/a | n/a | n/a | n/a |
| Owner or person in charge of a dog dangerously out of control in any place in England or Wales (whether or not a public place) | 3 | 4 | 7 | 8 |
| Owner or person in charge of a dog dangerously out of control in any place in England or Wales (whether or not a public place) where a person is injured | 3 | 4 | 7 | 8 |

| Guideline | Assistance to prosecution step | Guilty plea step | Reasons step | Time on bail step |
|---|---|---|---|---|
| Owner or person in charge of a dog dangerously out of control in any place in England or Wales (whether or not a public place) where an assistance dog is injured or killed | 3 | 4 | 7 | 8 |
| Owner or person in charge of a dog dangerously out of control in any place in England or Wales (whether or not a public place) where death is caused | 3 | 4 | 7 | 8 |
| Paying for the sexual services of a child | 3 | 4 | 8 | 9 |
| Pelican/zebra crossing contravention | n/a | n/a | n/a | n/a |
| Permitting premises to be used | 4 | 5 | 8 | 9 |
| Position or manner in which load secured (not involving danger) | n/a | n/a | n/a | n/a |
| Position or manner in which load secured (not involving danger) (over 3.5 tonnes) | n/a | n/a | n/a | n/a |
| Possession for terrorist purposes | 3 | 4 | 9 | 10 |
| Possession of a controlled drug | 3 | 4 | 7 | 8 |
| Possession of a prohibited dog/Breeding, selling, exchanging or advertising a prohibited dog | 3 | 4 | 7 | 8 |
| Possession of articles for use in frauds/Making or supplying articles for use in frauds | 3 | 4 | 7 | 8 |
| Possession of indecent photograph of child/ Indecent photographs of children | 3 | 4 | 8 | 9 |
| Preparation of terrorist acts | 3 | 4 | 9 | 10 |
| Producing a psychoactive substance | 3 | 4 | 7 | 8 |
| Production of a controlled drug/Cultivation of cannabis plant | 4 | 5 | 8 | 9 |
| Proscribed organisations – membership | 3 | 4 | 7 | 8 |
| Proscribed organisations – support | 3 | 4 | 7 | 8 |
| Racial hatred offences/Hatred against persons on religious grounds or grounds of sexual orientation | 3 | 4 | 7 | 8 |
| Railway fare evasion (Revised 2017) | 3 | 4 | 7 | n/a |
| Rape | 3 | 4 | 8 | 9 |
| Rape of a child under 13 | 3 | 4 | 8 | 9 |
| Revenue fraud | 3 | 4 | 7 | 8 |
| Riot | 3 | 4 | 8 | 9 |
| Robbery – dwelling | 3 | 4 | 8 | 9 |
| Robbery – professionally planned commercial | 3 | 4 | 8 | 9 |
| Robbery – Sentencing children and young people | n/a | see next tab | n/a | n/a |
| Robbery – street and less sophisticated commercial | 3 | 4 | 8 | 9 |
| School non-attendance (Revised 2017) | 3 | 4 | 7 | n/a |
| Seat belt offences | n/a | n/a | n/a | n/a |
| Sex with an adult relative: penetration/Sex with an adult relative: consenting to penetration | 3 | 4 | 8 | 9 |
| Sexual activity in a public lavatory | 3 | 4 | 7 | n/a |

| Guideline | Assistance to prosecution step | Guilty plea step | Reasons step | Time on bail step |
|---|---|---|---|---|
| Sexual activity with a child family member/ Inciting a child family member to engage in sexual activity | 3 | 4 | 8 | 9 |
| Sexual activity with a child/Causing or inciting a child to engage in sexual activity | 3 | 4 | 8 | 9 |
| Sexual activity with a person with a mental disorder impeding choice/Causing or inciting a person, with a mental disorder impeding choice, to engage in sexual activity | 3 | 4 | 8 | 9 |
| Sexual assault | 3 | 4 | 8 | 9 |
| Sexual assault of a child under 13 | 3 | 4 | 8 | 9 |
| Sexual offences – historic | n/a | n/a | n/a | n/a |
| Sexual offences – Sentencing children and young people | n/a | see next tab | n/a | n/a |
| Slavery, servitude and forced or compulsory labour | 3 | 4 | 8 | 9 |
| Speed limiter not used or incorrectly calibrated | n/a | n/a | n/a | n/a |
| Speeding (Revised 2017) | 3 | 4 | 7 | n/a |
| Steering defective | n/a | n/a | n/a | n/a |
| Steering defective (over 3.5 tonnes) | n/a | n/a | n/a | n/a |
| Stop on hard shoulder | n/a | n/a | n/a | n/a |
| Supplying or offering to supply a controlled drug/Possession of a controlled drug with intent to supply it to another | 4 | 5 | 8 | 9 |
| Tachograph not used/not working | n/a | n/a | n/a | n/a |
| Taxi touting/soliciting for hire (Revised 2017) | 3 | 4 | 7 | n/a |
| Terrorism offences | n/a | n/a | n/a | n/a |
| Theft – general | 3 | 4 | 7 | 8 |
| Theft from a shop or stall | 3 | 4 | 7 | 8 |
| Threatening behaviour – fear or provocation of violence/Racially or religiously aggravated threatening behaviour – fear or provocation of violence | 3 | 4 | 8 | 9 |
| Threats to destroy or damage property | 3 | 4 | 7 | 8 |
| Threats to kill | 3 | 4 | 8 | 9 |
| Trafficking people for sexual exploitation | 3 | 4 | 8 | 9 |
| Trespass with intent to commit a sexual offence | 3 | 4 | 8 | 9 |
| TV licence payment evasion (Revised 2017) | 3 | 4 | 7 | n/a |
| Tyres defective | n/a | n/a | n/a | n/a |
| Tyres defective – buses/goods vehicles | n/a | n/a | n/a | n/a |
| Unfit through drink or drugs (drive/attempt to drive) (Revised 2017) | 3 | 4 | 7 | 8 |
| Unfit through drink or drugs (in charge) (Revised 2017) | 3 | 4 | 7 | 8 |
| Unlawful act manslaughter | 3 | 4 | 8 | 9 |
| Use of mobile telephone | n/a | n/a | n/a | n/a |

| Guideline | Assistance to prosecution step | Guilty plea step | Reasons step | Time on bail step |
|---|---|---|---|---|
| Vehicle in prohibited lane | n/a | n/a | n/a | n/a |
| Vehicle interference (Revised 2017) | 3 | 4 | 7 | 8 |
| Vehicle licence/registration fraud | n/a | n/a | n/a | n/a |
| Vehicle taking (aggravated). Damage caused to property other than the vehicle in accident or damage caused to vehicle | n/a | n/a | n/a | n/a |
| Vehicle taking (aggravated). Dangerous driving or accident causing injury | n/a | n/a | n/a | n/a |
| Vehicle taking, without consent (Revised 2017) | 3 | 4 | 7 | 8 |
| Violent disorder | 3 | 4 | 8 | 9 |
| Voyeurism | 3 | 4 | 8 | 9 |
| Walk on motorway, slip road or hard shoulder | n/a | n/a | n/a | n/a |
| Weight, position or distribution of load or manner in which load secured involving danger of injury | n/a | n/a | n/a | n/a |
| Weight, position or distribution of load or manner in which load secured involving danger of injury (over 3.5 tonnes) | n/a | n/a | n/a | n/a |
| Witness intimidation | n/a | n/a | n/a | n/a |

## EQUAL TREATMENT BENCH BOOK                                          SG0-3

Guideline users should be aware that the *Equal Treatment Bench Book* covers important aspects of fair treatment and disparity of outcomes for different groups in the criminal justice system. It provides guidance which sentencers are encouraged to take into account wherever applicable, to ensure that there is fairness for all involved in court proceedings.

## APPLICABILITY                                                       SG0-4

In accordance with section 120 of the Coroners and Justice Act 2009, the Sentencing Council issues this definitive guideline. It applies to all offenders aged 18 and older, who are sentenced on or after the effective date of this guideline, regardless of the date of the offence.*

Section 59(1) of the Sentencing Code provides that:

Every court –

1. must, in sentencing an offender, follow any sentencing guidelines which are relevant to the offender's case, and
2. must, in exercising any other function relating to the sentencing of offenders, follow any sentencing guidelines which are relevant to the exercise of the function,
unless the court is satisfied that it would be contrary to the interests of justice to do so."

This guideline applies only to offenders aged 18 and older. General principles to be considered in the sentencing of children and young people are in the Sentencing Council definitive guideline, Overarching Principles — Sentencing Children and Young People.

* The maximum sentence that applies to an offence is the maximum that applied at the date of the offence.

## FOLLOWING THESE GUIDELINES                                         SG0-5

When sentencing an offender, every court is under a statutory obligation to follow any relevant sentencing guideline unless it would be contrary to the interests of justice to do so (Sentencing Code, s.59(1)). If a court imposes a sentence outside the range indicated in an offence specific guideline, it is obliged to state its reasons for doing so (Sentencing Code, s.52(6)).

**When to use these guidelines**

- These guidelines apply to sentencing in a magistrates' court whatever the composition of the court. They cover offences for which sentences are frequently imposed in a magistrates' court when dealing with adult offenders.
- They also apply to allocation (mode of trial) decisions. When dealing with an either way offence for which there is no plea or an indication of a not guilty plea, these guidelines will be relevant to the allocation decision and should be consulted at this stage to assess the likely sentence. Reference should be made to the Allocation guideline.
- These guidelines apply also to the Crown Court when dealing with appeals against sentences imposed in a magistrates' court and when sentencing for summary only offences.

The offence guidelines include two structures: pre-Sentencing Council guidelines (created by the Sentencing Guidelines Council) and Sentencing Council guidelines.

**SG0-6** USING PRE-SENTENCING COUNCIL GUIDELINES

This section explains the key decisions involved in the sentencing process for SGC guidelines.

**1. Assess offence seriousness (culpability and harm)**

Offence seriousness is the starting point for sentencing under the Sentencing Code. The court's assessment of offence seriousness will:

- determine which of the sentencing thresholds has been crossed;
- indicate whether a custodial, community or other sentence is the most appropriate;
- be the key factor in deciding the length of a custodial sentence, the onerousness of requirements to be incorporated in a community sentence and the amount of any fine imposed.

When considering the seriousness of any offence, the court must consider the offender's culpability in committing the offence and any harm which the offence caused, was intended to cause, or might foreseeably have caused (Sentencing Code, s.63). In using these guidelines, this assessment should be approached in two stages.

**2. Offence seriousness (culpability and harm)**

*A. Identify the appropriate starting point*

The guidelines set out examples of the nature of activity which may constitute the offence, progressing from less to more serious conduct, and provide a starting point based on a **first time offender pleading not guilty**. The guidelines also specify a sentencing range for each example of activity. Within the guidelines, a first time offender is a person who does not have a conviction which, by virtue of section 65 of the Sentencing Code, must be treated as an aggravating factor.

Sentencers should begin by considering which of the examples of offence activity corresponds most closely to the circumstances of the particular case in order to identify the appropriate starting point:

- where the starting point is a fine, this is indicated as band A, B or C;
- where the community sentence threshold is passed, the guideline sets out whether the starting point should be a low, medium or high level community order. For more information, see Imposition of Community and Custodial Sentences;
- where the starting point is a custodial sentence, see Imposition of Community and Custodial Sentence.

The Council's definitive guideline Overarching Principles: Seriousness, published 16 December 2004, identified four levels of culpability for sentencing purposes (intention, recklessness, knowledge and negligence). The starting points in the individual offence guidelines assume that culpability is at the highest level applicable to the offence (often, but not always, intention). Where a lower level of culpability is present, this should be taken into account.

*B. Consider the effect of aggravating and mitigating factors*

Once the starting point has been identified, the court can add to or reduce this to reflect any aggravating or mitigating factors that impact on the culpability of the offender and/or harm caused by the offence to reach a provisional sentence. Any factors contained in the description of the activity used to reach the starting point must not be counted again. The range is the bracket into which the provisional sentence will normally fall after having regard to factors which aggravate or mitigate the seriousness of the offence. However:

- the court is not precluded from going outside the range where the facts justify it;
- previous convictions which aggravate the seriousness of the current offence may take the provisional sentence beyond the range, especially where there are significant other aggravating factors present.

In addition, where an offender is being sentenced for multiple offences, the court's assessment of the totality of the offending may result in a sentence above the range indicated for the individual offences, including a sentence of a different type. See the definitive guideline on Totality for more information. The guidelines identify aggravating and mitigating factors which may be particularly relevant to each individual offence. These include some factors drawn from the general list of aggravating and mitigating factors in the Council's definitive guideline (see 'seriousness' link above). In each case, sentencers should have regard to the full list, which includes the factors that, by statute, make an offence more serious:

- offence committed while on bail for other offences;
- offence was racially or religiously aggravated;
- offence was motivated by, or demonstrates, hostility based on the victim's sexual orientation (or presumed sexual orientation);
- offence was motivated by, or demonstrates, hostility based on the victim being (or being presumed to be) transgender;
- offence was motivated by, or demonstrates, hostility based on the victim's disability (or presumed disability);
- offender has previous convictions that the court considers can reasonably be treated as aggravating factors having regard to their relevance to the current offence and the time that has elapsed since conviction.

While the lists in the offence guidelines and other material referenced above, aim to identify the most common aggravating and mitigating factors, they are not intended to be exhaustive. Sentencers should always consider whether there are any other factors that make the offence more or less serious.

### 3. Form a preliminary view of the appropriate sentence, then consider offender mitigation

When the court has reached a provisional sentence based on its assessment of offence seriousness, it should take into account matters of offender mitigation. The issue of remorse should be taken into account at this point along with other mitigating features such as admissions to the police in interview.

### 4. Consider a reduction for a guilty plea

*Reduction in sentence for a guilty plea, where first hearing is on or after 1 June 2017*

[See SG5-3]

*Reduction in sentence for a guilty plea, where first hearing is before 1 June 2017*

The Council guideline Reduction in Sentence for a Guilty Plea, revised 2007, states that the punitive elements of the sentence should be reduced to recognise an offender's guilty plea. The reduction has no impact on sentencing decisions in relation to ancillary orders, including disqualification. The level of the reduction should reflect the stage at which the offender indicated a willingness to admit guilt and will be gauged on a sliding scale, ranging from a recommended one third (where the guilty plea was entered at the first reasonable opportunity), reducing to a recommended one quarter (where a trial date has been set) and to a recommended one tenth (for a guilty plea entered at the 'door of the court' or after the trial has begun). There is a presumption that the recommended reduction will be given unless there are good reasons for a lower amount. The application of the reduction may affect the type, as well as the severity, of the sentence. It may also take the sentence below the range in some cases. The court must state that it has reduced a sentence to reflect a guilty plea (Sentencing Code, s.52(7)). It should usually indicate what the sentence would have been if there had been no reduction as a result of the plea.

### 5. Consider ancillary orders, including compensation

Ancillary orders of particular relevance to individual offences are identified in the relevant guidelines. The court must always consider making a compensation order where the offending has resulted in personal injury, loss or damage. The court is required to give reasons if it decides not to make such an order (Sentencing Code, s.55).

- Ancillary orders – Magistrates' Court
- Ancillary orders – Crown Court Compendium, Part II Sentencing, S7

### 6. Decide sentence Give reasons

Review the total sentence to ensure that it is proportional to the offending behaviour and properly balanced. Sentencers must state reasons for the sentence passed in every case, including for any ancillary orders imposed (Sentencing Code, s.52). It is particularly important to identify any aggravating or mitigating factors, or matters of offender mitigation, that have resulted in a sentence more or less severe than the suggested starting point. If a court imposes a sentence of a different kind or outside the range indicated in the guidelines, it must state its reasons for doing so (Sentencing Code, s.52(6)). The court should also give its reasons for not making an order that has been canvassed before it or that it might have been expected to make.

# USING SENTENCING COUNCIL GUIDELINES

This section of the user guide explains the key decisions involved in the sentencing process for Sentencing Council guidelines.

### STEP ONE: Determining the offence category

The decision making process includes a two-step approach to assessing seriousness. The first step is to determine the offence category by means of an assessment of the offender's culpability and the harm caused, or intended, by reference only to the factors set out at step one in each guideline. The contents are tailored for each offence and comprise the principal factual elements of the offence.

### STEP TWO: Starting point and category range

The guidelines provide a starting point which applies to all offenders irrespective of plea or previous convictions. The guidelines also specify a category range for each offence category. The guidelines provide non-exhaustive lists of aggravating and mitigating factors relating to the context of the offence and to the offender. Sentencers should identify whether any combination of these, or other relevant factors, should result in an upward or downward adjustment from the starting point. In some cases, it may be appropriate to move outside the identified category range when reaching a provisional sentence.

This short video shows you how to use the expanded explanations in step two (start at 01:40). *https://youtu.be/CbYmouIMefU*

### FURTHER STEPS

Having reached a provisional sentence, there are a number of further steps within the guidelines. These steps are clearly set out within each guideline and are tailored specifically for each offence in order to ensure that only the most appropriate guidance is included within each offence specific guideline. The further steps include:

* reduction for assistance to the prosecution;
* reduction for guilty pleas (the court should take account of any potential reduction for a guilty plea in accordance with section 73 of the Sentencing Code and the guideline for Reduction in Sentence for a Guilty Plea [see **SG5-12**]);
* where an offender is being sentenced for multiple offences – the court's assessment of the totality of the offending may result in a sentence above the range indicated for the individual offences, including a sentence of a different type (for more information, refer to the Totality guideline);
* compensation orders and/or ancillary orders appropriate to the case (Magistrates' court ancillary orders; Crown Court Compendium, Part II Sentencing, s.7);
* reasons for, and explain the effect of, the sentence.

Where there is no guideline for an offence, refer to the General guideline [See **SG-2**].

# EXPANDED EXPLANATIONS IN GUIDELINES

The General guideline for sentencing offences that do not have a specific sentencing guideline, published by the Sentencing Council, came into force on 1 October 2019.

A set of expanded explanations are effective from the same day. These are now embedded in all existing offence specific guidelines. They add extra information to aggravating and mitigating factors to make it easier for courts to maintain consistency and transparency when sentencing. The expanded explanations will not change the factors in guidelines.

The expanded explanations are included at SG2-17.

# PART 1   ALLOCATION

DETERMINING WHETHER CASES SHOULD BE DEALT WITH BY A                **SG1-1**
MAGISTRATES' COURT OR THE CROWN COURT

**Effective from:** 01 March 2016

**Venue for trial**

**It is important to ensure that all cases are tried at the appropriate level.**

1. In general, either way offences should be tried summarily unless:
   - the outcome would clearly be a sentence in excess of the court's powers for the offence(s) concerned after taking into account personal mitigation and any potential reduction for a guilty plea; or
   - for reasons of unusual legal, procedural or factual complexity, the case should be tried in the Crown Court. This exception may apply in cases where a very substantial fine is the likely sentence. Other circumstances where this exception will apply are likely to be rare and case specific; the court will rely on the submissions of the parties to identify relevant cases.
2. In cases with no factual or legal complications the court should bear in mind its **power to commit for sentence after a trial** and **may retain jurisdiction** notwithstanding that the likely sentence might exceed its powers.
3. Cases may be tried summarily even where the defendant is subject to a Crown Court Suspended Sentence Order or Community Order.[1]
4. All parties should be asked by the court to make representations as to whether the case is suitable for summary trial. The court should refer to definitive guidelines (if any) to assess the likely sentence for the offence in the light of the facts alleged by the prosecution case, taking into account all aspects of the case including those advanced by the defence, including any personal mitigation to which the defence wish to refer.

**Where the court decides that the case is suitable to be dealt with in the magistrates' court, it must warn the defendant that all sentencing options remain open and, if the defendant consents to summary trial and is convicted by the court or pleads guilty, the defendant may be committed to the Crown Court for sentence.**

**Committal for sentence**

There is ordinarily no statutory restriction on committing an either way case for sentence following conviction. The general power of the magistrates' court to commit to the Crown Court for sentence after a finding that a case is suitable for summary trial and/or conviction continues to be available where the court is of the opinion 'that the offence or the combination of the offence and one or more offences associated with it was so serious that the Crown Court should have the power to deal with the offender in any way it could deal with him if he had been convicted on indictment'.[2]

However, where the court proceeds to the summary trial of certain offences relating to criminal damage, upon conviction there is no power to commit to the Crown Court for sentence.[3]

The court should refer to any definitive guideline to arrive at the appropriate sentence taking into account all of the circumstances of the case including personal mitigation and the appropriate guilty plea reduction.

In borderline cases the court should consider obtaining a pre-sentence report before deciding whether to commit to the Crown Court for sentence.

Where the offending is so serious that the court is of the opinion that the Crown Court should have the power to deal with the offender, the case should be committed to the Crown Court for sentence even if a community order may be the appropriate sentence (this will allow the Crown Court to deal with any breach of a community order, if that is the sentence passed).

**Children and young people jointly charged with adults – interests of justice test**

The proper venue for the trial of any child or young person is normally the youth court. Subject to statutory restrictions, that remains the case where a child or young person is charged jointly with an adult.

This guideline does not provide information on the complex statutory framework for dealing with a youth jointly charged with an adult …

---

[1] The power to commit the case to the Crown Court to be dealt with under para.11(2) of Schedule 16 or para. 24 of Schedule 10 to the Sentencing Code can be exercised if the defendant is convicted.

[2] Sentencing Code s.14

[3] Magistrates' Courts Act 1980, s.3(4) and s.22

The following guidance must be applied in those cases where the interests of justice test falls to be considered:

1. If the adult is sent for trial to the Crown Court, the court should conclude that the child or young person must be tried separately in the youth court unless it is in the interests of justice for the child or young person and the adult to be tried jointly.
2. Examples of factors that should be considered when deciding whether it is in the interests of justice to send the child or young person to the Crown Court (rather than having a trial in the youth court) include:
   - whether separate trials will cause injustice to witnesses or to the case as a whole (consideration should be given to the provisions of sections 27 and 28 of the Youth Justice and Criminal Evidence Act 1999);
   - the age of the child or young person: the younger they are, the greater the desirability that they be tried in the youth court;
   - the age gap between the child or young person and the adult: a substantial gap in age militates in favour of the child or young person being tried in the youth court;
   - the lack of maturity of the child or young person;
   - the relative culpability of the child or young person compared with the adult and whether the alleged role played by the child or young person was minor;
   - the lack of previous convictions on the part of the child or young person.
3. The court should bear in mind that the youth court now has a general power to commit for sentence following conviction pursuant to Section 16 of the Sentencing Code. In appropriate cases this will permit the same court to sentence adults and child or young persons who have been tried separately.

**Statutory framework**

[Omitted. Sets out the MCA 1980, s. 19(1) to (4) (see **D6.21**) and the CAJA 2009, s. 125(1) (see **SG19-1**).]

# PART 2   GENERAL GUIDELINE: OVERARCHING PRINCIPLES

APPLICABILITY

[For the standard text on applicability see **SG0-4**]

**Effective from:** 01 October 2019

- For sentencing offences for which there is no offence specific sentencing guideline, and
- For use in conjunction with offence specific sentencing guidelines

APPLICABILITY                                                      **SG2-2**

Accompanying the General guideline are a set of expanded explanations which were effective from the same day. These are now embedded in all existing offence specific guidelines. They add extra information to aggravating and mitigating factors to make it easier for courts to maintain consistency and transparency when sentencing. The expanded explanations will not change the factors in guidelines.

The expanded explanations are included in this Part at **SG2-17** following the General guideline.

**STEP 1  Reaching a provisional sentence**                        **SG2-3**

a)   Where there is no definitive sentencing guideline for the offence, to arrive at a provisional sentence the court should take account of all of the following (if they apply):
- the statutory maximum sentence (and if appropriate minimum sentence) for the offence;
- sentencing judgments of the Court of Appeal (Criminal Division) for the offence; and
- definitive sentencing guidelines for analogous offences.

The court will be assisted by the parties in identifying the above.

For the avoidance of doubt the court should **not** take account of any draft sentencing guidelines.

When considering definitive guidelines for analogous offences the court must apply these carefully, making adjustments for any differences in the statutory maximum sentence and in the elements of the offence. This will not be a merely arithmetical exercise.

b)   Where possible the court should follow the stepped approach of sentencing guidelines to arrive at the sentence.

**The seriousness of the offence is assessed by considering:**

- the culpability [see **SG2-18**] of the offender

and
- the **harm** [see **SG2-19**] caused by the offending.

c)   The initial assessment of harm and culpability should take no account of plea or previous convictions.

> The court should consider which of the five purposes of sentencing (below) it is seeking to achieve through the sentence that is imposed. More than one purpose might be relevant and the importance of each must be weighed against the particular offence and offender characteristics when determining sentence.
> - The punishment of offenders
> - The reduction of crime (including its reduction by deterrence)
> - The reform and rehabilitation of offenders
> - The protection of the public
> - The making of reparation by offenders to persons affected by their offences

**STEP 2  Aggravating and mitigating factors**                      **SG2-4**

Once a provisional sentence is arrived at the court should take into account factors that may make the offence more serious and factors which may reduce seriousness or reflect personal mitigation.

- Identify whether a combination of these or other relevant factors should result in any upward or downward adjustment from the sentence arrived at so far.
- It is for the sentencing court to determine how much weight should be assigned to the aggravating and mitigating factors taking into account all of the circumstances of the offence and the offender.
- Not all factors that apply will necessarily influence the sentence.

- When sentencing an offence for which a **fixed penalty notice** was available the reason why the offender did not take advantage of the fixed penalty will be a relevant consideration. [see SG2-20]
- If considering a fine – see information on fine band ranges below.
- If considering a community or custodial sentence refer also to the Imposition of community and custodial sentences definitive guideline [See SG9-2 for community orders and SG9-3 for custodial sentences] – see information on community orders and custodial sentences below.

**SG2-5**   Fines

| Fines | Starting point | Range |
|---|---|---|
| Fine Band A | 50% of relevant weekly income | 25 – 75% of relevant weekly income |
| Fine Band B | 100% of relevant weekly income | 75 – 125% of relevant weekly income |
| Fine Band C | 150% of relevant weekly income | 125 – 175% of relevant weekly income |
| Fine Band D | 250% of relevant weekly income | 200 – 300% of relevant weekly income |
| Fine Band E | 400% of relevant weekly income | 300 – 500% of relevant weekly income |
| Fine Band F | 600% of relevant weekly income | 500 – 700% of relevant weekly income |

- The court should determine the appropriate level of fine in accordance with this guideline and section 125 of the Sentencing Code, which requires that the fine must reflect the seriousness of the offence and that the court must take into account the financial circumstances of the offender.
- Where possible, if a financial penalty is imposed, it should remove any economic benefit the offender has derived through the commission of the offence including:
  o   avoided costs;
  o   operating savings;
  o   any gain made as a direct result of the offence.
- The fine should meet, in a fair and proportionate way, the objectives of punishment, deterrence and the removal of gain derived through the commission of the offence; **it should not be cheaper to offend than to comply with the law.**
- In considering economic benefit, the court should avoid double recovery.
- Where the means of the offender are limited, priority should be given to compensation (where applicable) over payment of any other financial penalty.
- Where it is not possible to calculate or estimate the economic benefit, the court may wish to draw on information from the enforcing authorities about the general costs of operating within the law.
- When sentencing **organisations** the fine must be sufficiently substantial to have a real economic impact which will bring home to both management and shareholders the need to comply with the law. The court should ensure that the effect of the fine (particularly if it will result in closure of the business) is proportionate to the gravity of the offence.
- Obtaining financial information: It is for the offender to disclose to the court such data relevant to their financial position as will enable it to assess what they can reasonably afford to pay. If necessary, the court may compel the disclosure of an individual offender's financial circumstances pursuant to section 35 of the Sentencing Code. In the absence of such disclosure, or where the court is not satisfied that it has been given sufficient reliable information, the court will be entitled to draw reasonable inferences as to the offender's means from evidence it has heard and from all the circumstances of the case. In setting a fine, the court may conclude that the offender is able to pay any fine imposed unless the offender has supplied financial information to the contrary.

**SG2-6**   Community Orders and Custodial Sentences

[For the imposition of community orders, including the community orders table, see Imposition of Community and Custodial Sentences at **SG9-2.**

For the imposition of custodial sentences see Imposition of Community and Custodial Sentences at **SG9-3.**]

**Factors increasing seriousness**

(Factors are not listed in any particular order and are not exhaustive)

*Statutory aggravating factors*

- Previous convictions [See **SG2-21**], having regard to a) the **nature** of the offence to which the conviction relates and its **relevance** to the current offence; and b) the **time** that has elapsed since the conviction
- Offence committed whilst on bail [See **SG2-22**],
- Offence motivated by, or demonstrating hostility based on any of the following characteristics or presumed characteristics of the victim: religion, race, disability, sexual orientation, or transgender identity [See **SG2-23**],
- Offence was committed against an emergency worker acting in the exercise of functions as such a worker [See **SG2-24**],

*Other aggravating factors*

- Commission of offence whilst under the influence of alcohol or drugs [See **SG2-25**],
- Offence was committed as part of a group [See **SG2-26**],
- Offence involved use or threat of a weapon [See **SG2-27**],
- Planning of an offence [See **SG2-28**],
- Commission of the offence for financial gain [See **SG2-29**],
- High level of profit from the offence [See **SG2-30**],
- Abuse of trust or dominant position [See **SG2-31**],
- Restraint, detention or additional degradation of the victim [See **SG2-32**],
- Vulnerable victim [See **SG2-33**],
- Victim was providing a public service or performing a public duty at the time of the offence [See **SG2-34**],
- Other(s) put at risk of harm by the offending [See **SG2-35**],
- Offence committed in the presence of other(s) (especially children) [See **SG2-36**],
- Actions after the event including but not limited to attempts to cover up/conceal evidence [See **SG2-37**],
- Blame wrongly placed on other(s) [See **SG2-38**],
- Failure to respond to warnings or concerns expressed by others about the offender's behaviour [See **SG2-39**],
- Offence committed on licence or while subject to court order(s) [See **SG2-40**],
- Offence committed in custody [See **SG2-41**],
- Offences taken into consideration [See **SG2-42**],
- Offence committed in a domestic context [See **SG2-43**],
- Offence committed in a terrorist context [See **SG2-44**],
- Location and/or timing of offence [See **SG2-45**],
- Established evidence of community/wider impact [See **SG2-46**],
- Prevalence [See **SG2-47**],

**Factors reducing seriousness or reflecting personal mitigation**

(Factors are not listed in any particular order and are not exhaustive)

- No previous convictions or no relevant/recent convictions [See **SG2-48**],
- Good character and/or exemplary conduct [See **SG2-49**],
- Remorse [See **SG2-50**],
- Self-reporting [See **SG2-51**],
- Cooperation with the investigation/ early admissions [See **SG2-52**],
- Little or no planning [See **SG2-53**],
- The offender was in a lesser or subordinate role if acting with others/performed limited role under direction [See **SG2-54**],
- Involved through coercion, intimidation or exploitation [See **SG2-55**],
- Limited awareness or understanding of the offence [See **SG2-56**],
- Little or no financial gain [See **SG2-57**],
- Delay since apprehension [See **SG2-58**],
- Activity originally legitimate [See **SG2-59**],
- Age and/or lack of maturity [See **SG2-60**],

Sentencing Guidelines

> - Sole or primary carer for dependent relatives [See **SG2-61**],
> - Physical disability or serious medical condition requiring urgent, intensive or long-term treatment [See **SG2-62**],
> - Mental disorder or learning disability [See **SG2-63**],
> - Determination and/or demonstration of steps having been taken to address addiction or offending behaviour [See **SG2-64**],

**SG2-9**     **STEP 3 Consider any factors which indicate a reduction for assistance to the prosecution**

The court should take into account section 74 of the Sentencing Code (reduction in sentence for assistance to prosecution) and any other rule of law by virtue of which an offender may receive a discounted sentence in consequence of assistance given (or offered) to the prosecutor or investigator.

**SG2-10**    **STEP 4 Reduction for guilty pleas**

The court should take account of any potential reduction for a guilty plea in accordance with section 73 of the Sentencing Code and the guideline for Reduction in Sentence for a Guilty Plea [see **SG5-1–SG5-12**].

**SG2-11**    **STEP 5 Dangerousness**

**Where the offence is listed in Schedule 15, Schedule 18 and/or Schedule 19 of the Criminal Justice Act 2003**

The court should consider:

1) whether having regard to the criteria contained in Chapter 6 of Part 10 of the Sentencing Code it would be appropriate to impose an extended sentence (sections 266 and 279) and

2) whether having regard to sections 273 and 283 of the Sentencing Code it would be appropriate to impose a life sentence.

When sentencing offenders to a life sentence under these provisions, the notional determinate sentence should be used as the basis for the setting of a minimum term.

**SG2-12**    **STEP 6 Special custodial sentence for certain offenders of particular concern**

Where the offence is listed in Schedule 13 of the Sentencing Code and the court does not impose a sentence of imprisonment for life or an extended sentence, but does impose a period of imprisonment, the term of the sentence must be equal to the aggregate of the appropriate custodial term and a further period of 1 year for which the offender is to be subject to a licence (sections 265 and 278 of the Sentencing Code).

See the **Crown Court Compendium, Part II Sentencing S4-3** for further details.

**SG2-13**    **STEP 7 Totality principle**

If sentencing an offender for more than one offence, or where the offender is already serving a sentence, consider whether the total sentence is just and proportionate to the overall offending behaviour in accordance with the Offences Taken into Consideration [see **SG3**] and **Totality** [see **SG4**] guidelines.

**SG2-14**    **STEP 8 Compensation and ancillary orders**

In all cases the court should consider whether to make compensation and/or other ancillary orders.

Where the offence involves a firearm, an imitation firearm or an offensive weapon the court may consider the criteria in section 19 of the Serious Crime Act 2007 for the imposition of a Serious Crime Prevention Order.

- **Ancillary orders – Magistrates' Court** [SG10-5]
- **Ancillary orders – Crown Court Compendium, Part II Sentencing, S7**

**SG2-15**    **STEP 9 Reasons**

Section 52 of the Sentencing Code imposes a duty to give reasons for, and explain the effect of, the sentence.

**SG2-16**    **STEP 10 Consideration for time spent on bail (tagged curfew)**

The court must consider whether to give credit for time spent on bail in accordance with section 240A of the Criminal Justice Act 2003 and section 325 of the Sentencing Code.

**SG2-17**    **Expanded explanations**

**Effective date:** October 1 2019

The following section sets out the text of the expanded explanations which accompany the General guideline. These are now embedded in all existing offence specific guidelines. They add extra information to aggravating and mitigating factors to make it easier for courts to maintain consistency and transparency when sentencing. The expanded explanations will not change the factors in guidelines.

**Care should be taken to avoid double counting factors including those already taken into account in assessing culpability or harm or those inherent in the offence**

### Culpability

SG2-18

**Culpability** is assessed with reference to the offender's role, level of intention and/or premeditation and the extent and sophistication of planning.

- The court should balance these factors to reach a fair assessment of the offender's overall culpability in all the circumstances of the case and the offender.
- The mere presence of a factor that is inherent in the offence should not be used in assessing culpability.
- Deliberate or gratuitous violence or damage to property, over and above what is needed to carry out the offence will normally indicate a higher level of culpability.
- For offences where there is no requirement for the offender to have any level of intention, recklessness, negligence, dishonesty, knowledge, understanding or foresight for the offence to be made out, the range of culpability **may** be inferred from the circumstances of the offence as follows:

| Highest level | Deliberate – intentional act or omission |
|---|---|
| ⇓ | Reckless – acted or failed to act regardless of the foreseeable risk |
|  | Negligent – failed to take steps to guard against the act or omission |
| Lowest level | Low/no culpability – act or omission with none of the above features |

- For offences that require some level of culpability (eg intention, recklessness or knowledge) to be made out, the range of culpability will be narrower. Relevant factors **may** typically include but are not limited to:

| Highest level | High level of planning/sophistication/leading role |
|---|---|
| ⇓ | Some planning/significant role |
| Lowest level | Little or no planning/minor role |

- These models of assessing culpability will not be applicable to all offences.

### Harm

SG2-19

**Harm** – which the offence caused, was intended to cause or might foreseeably have caused

- There may be primary and secondary victims of an offence and, depending on the offence, victims may include one or more individuals, a community, the general public, the state, the environment and/or animal(s). In some cases there may not be an identifiable victim.
- An assessment of harm should generally reflect the overall impact of the offence upon the victim(s) and may include direct harm (including physical injury, psychological harm and financial loss) and consequential harm.
- When considering the value of property lost or damaged the court should also take account of any sentimental value to the victim(s) and any disruption caused to a victim's life, activities or business.
- When considering harm to animals or the environment relevant considerations will include the impact on rare or endangered species or sensitive locations, and any suffering caused.
- Where harm was intended but no harm or a lower level of harm resulted – the sentence will normally be assessed with reference to the level of harm intended.
- Where the harm caused is greater than that intended – the sentence will normally be assessed with reference to the level of harm suffered by the victim.
- Dealing with a risk of harm involves consideration of both the likelihood of harm occurring and the extent of it if it does.
- Risk of harm is less serious than the same actual harm. Where the offence has caused risk of harm but no (or less) actual harm the normal approach is to move down to the next category of harm. This may not be appropriate if either the likelihood or extent of potential harm is particularly high.
- A Victim Personal Statement (VPS) or other impact statement may assist the court in assessing harm, but the absence of a VPS or other impact statement should not be taken to indicate the absence of harm.
- The court should balance these characteristics to reach a fair assessment of harm in the context of the circumstances of the offence.

Sentencing Guidelines

| Highest level | Very serious harm caused to individual victim(s) or to wider public/environment etc |
|---|---|
| ⇓ | Serious harm caused OR high risk of very serious harm |
| | Significant harm caused OR high risk of serious harm |
| Lowest level | Low/no harm caused OR high risk significant harm |

The table should be used in conjunction with the notes above and may not be applicable to all offences.

**SG2-20** **Fixed Penalty Notice**

**Penalty notices** may be issued as an alternative to prosecution in respect of a range of offences. An admission of guilt is not a prerequisite to issuing a penalty notice. An offender who is issued with a penalty notice may nevertheless be prosecuted for the offence if he or she:

- asks to be tried for the offence; or
- fails to pay the penalty within the period stipulated in the notice and the prosecutor decides to proceed with charges.

In some cases of non-payment, the penalty is automatically registered and enforceable as a fine without need for recourse to the courts. This procedure applies to penalty notices for disorder and fixed penalty notices issued in respect of certain road traffic offences but not to fixed penalty notices issued for most other criminal offences.

When sentencing in cases in which a penalty notice was available:

- the fact that the offender did not take advantage of the penalty (whether that was by requesting a hearing or failing to pay within the specified timeframe) does not increase the seriousness of the offence and must not be regarded as an aggravating factor. The appropriate sentence must be determined in accordance with the sentencing principles set out in this guideline (including the amount of any fine, which must take an offender's financial circumstances into account), disregarding the availability of the penalty. In some cases this may result in a fine that is lower than the fixed penalty.
- where a penalty notice could not be offered or taken up for reasons unconnected with the offence itself, such as administrative difficulties outside the control of the offender, the starting point should be a fine equivalent to the amount of the penalty and no order of costs should be imposed. The offender should not be disadvantaged by the unavailability of the penalty notice in these circumstances.

Where an offender has had previous penalty notice(s), the fact that an offender has previously been issued with a penalty notice does not increase the seriousness of the current offence and must not be regarded as an aggravating factor. It may, however, properly influence the court's assessment of the offender's suitability for a particular sentence, so long as it remains within the limits established by the seriousness of the current offence.

**SG2-21** **Previous convictions**

*Guidance on the use of previous convictions*

The following guidance should be considered when seeking to determine the degree to which previous convictions should aggravate sentence:

Section 143 of the Criminal Justice Act 2003 states that:

> In considering the seriousness of an offence ("the current offence") committed by an offender who has one or more previous convictions, the court must treat each previous conviction as an aggravating factor if (in the case of that conviction) the court considers that it can reasonably be so treated having regard, in particular, to—
> (a) the nature of the offence to which the conviction relates and its relevance to the current offence, and
> (b) the time that has elapsed since the conviction.

1. Previous convictions are considered at step two in the Council's offence-specific guidelines.
2. The primary significance of previous convictions (including convictions in other jurisdictions) is the extent to which they indicate trends in offending behaviour and possibly the offender's response to earlier sentences.
3. Previous convictions are normally **relevant** to the current offence when they are of a similar type.
4. Previous convictions of a type different from the current offence **may** be relevant where they are an indication of persistent offending or escalation and/or a failure to comply with previous court orders.
5. Numerous and frequent previous convictions might indicate an underlying problem (for example, an addiction) that could be addressed more effectively in the community and will not necessarily indicate that a custodial sentence is necessary.
6. If the offender received a non-custodial disposal for the previous offence, a court should not necessarily move to a custodial sentence for the fresh offence.

7. In cases involving significant persistent offending, the community and custody thresholds may be crossed even though the current offence normally warrants a lesser sentence. If a custodial sentence is imposed it should be proportionate and kept to the necessary minimum.

8. The aggravating effect of relevant previous convictions reduces with the passage of time; **older convictions are less relevant** to the offender's culpability for the current offence and less likely to be predictive of future offending.

9. Where the previous offence is particularly old it will normally have little relevance for the current sentencing exercise.

10. The court should consider the time gap since the previous conviction and the reason for it. Where there has been a significant gap between previous and current convictions or a reduction in the frequency of offending this may indicate that the offender has made attempts to desist from offending in which case the aggravating effect of the previous offending will diminish.

11. Where the current offence is significantly less serious than the previous conviction (suggesting a decline in the gravity of offending), the previous conviction may carry less weight.

12. When considering the totality of previous offending a court should take a rounded view of the previous crimes and not simply aggregate the individual offences.

13. Where information is available on the context of previous offending this may assist the court in assessing the relevance of that prior offending to the current offence.

### Offence committed whilst on bail                                                                                        SG2-22

Section 64 of the Sentencing Code states:

> In considering the seriousness of any offence committed while the offender was on bail, the court must —
> (a) treat the fact that it was committed in those circumstances as an aggravating factor and
> (b) state in open court that the offence is so aggravated.

### Offence motivated by, or demonstrating hostility based on any of the following characteristics   SG2-23
### or presumed characteristics of the victim: religion, race, disability, sexual orientation, or
### transgender identity

See below for the statutory provisions.

- **Note the requirement for the court to state that the offence has been aggravated by the relevant hostility.**
- **Where the element of hostility is core to the offending, the aggravation will be higher than where it plays a lesser role.**

*Increase in sentences for racial or religious aggravation*

Section 66 of the Sentencing Code states:

> Hostility
>
> (1) This section applies where a court is considering the seriousness of an offence which is aggravated by—
>     (a) racial hostility,
>     (b) religious hostility,
>     (c) hostility related to disability,
>     (d) hostility related to sexual orientation, or
>     (e) hostility related to transgender identity.
> This is subject to subsection (3).
> (2) The court—
>     (a) must treat the fact that the offence is aggravated by hostility of any of those types as an aggravating factor, and
>     (b) must state in open court that the offence is so aggravated.
> (3) So far as it relates to racial and religious hostility, this section does not apply in relation to an offence under sections 29 to 32 of the Crime and Disorder Act 1998 (racially or religiously aggravated offences).
> (4) For the purposes of this section, an offence is aggravated by hostility of one of the kinds mentioned in subsection (1) if—
>     (a) at the time of committing the offence, or immediately before or after doing so, the offender demonstrated towards the victim of the offence hostility based on—
>         (i) the victim's membership (or presumed membership) of a racial group,
>         (ii) the victim's membership (or presumed membership) of a religious group,
>         (iii) a disability (or presumed disability) of the victim,
>         (iv) the sexual orientation (or presumed sexual orientation) of the victim, or (as the case may be)
>         (v) the victim being (or being presumed to be) transgender, or
>     (b) the offence was motivated (wholly or partly) by—
>         (i) hostility towards members of a racial group based on their membership of that group,
>         (ii) hostility towards members of a religious group based on their membership of that group,
>         (iii) hostility towards persons who have a disability or a particular disability,
>         (iv) hostility towards persons who are of a particular sexual orientation, or (as the case may be)
>         (v) hostility towards persons who are transgender.

(5) For the purposes of paragraphs (a) and (b) of subsection (4), it is immaterial whether or not the offender's hostility is also based, to any extent, on any other factor not mentioned in that paragraph.

(6) In this section—

    (a) references to a racial group are to a group of persons defined by reference to race, colour, nationality (including citizenship) or ethnic or national origins;

    (b) references to a religious group are to a group of persons defined by reference to religious belief or lack of religious belief;

    (c) "membership" in relation to a racial or religious group, includes association with members of that group;

    (d) "disability" means any physical or mental impairment;

    (e) references to being transgender include references to being transsexual, or undergoing, proposing to undergo or having undergone a process or part of a process of gender reassignment;

    (f) "presumed" means presumed by the offender.

**SG2-24** **Offence was committed against an emergency worker acting in the exercise of functions as such a worker**

See below for the statutory provisions.

- **Note the requirement for the court to state that the offence has been so aggravated.**
- **Note this statutory factor only applies to certain violent or sexual offences as listed below.**
- **For other offences the factor 'Victim was providing a public service or performing a public duty at the time of the offence' can be applied where relevant.**

The Sentencing Code states:

67 Assaults on emergency workers

(1) This section applies where a court is considering the seriousness of an offence listed in subsection (3).

(2) If the offence was committed against an emergency worker acting in the exercise of functions as such a worker, the court—

    (a) must treat that fact as an aggravating factor, and

    (b) must state in open court that the offence is so aggravated.

(3) The offences referred to in subsection (1) are—

    (a) an offence under any of the following provisions of the Offences against the Person Act 1861—

        (i) section 16 (threats to kill);

        (ii) section 18 (wounding with intent to cause grievous bodily harm);

        (iii) section 20 (malicious wounding);

        (iv) section 23 (administering poison etc);

        (v) section 28 (causing bodily injury by explosives);

        (vi) section 29 (using explosives etc with intent to do grievous bodily harm);

        (vii) section 47 (assault occasioning actual bodily harm);

    (b) an offence under section 3 of the Sexual Offences Act 2003 (sexual assault);

    (c) manslaughter;

    (d) kidnapping;

    (e) an inchoate offence in relation to any of the preceding offences.

(4) For the purposes of subsection (2) the circumstances in which an offence is to be taken as committed against a person acting in the exercise of functions as an emergency worker include circumstances where the offence takes place at a time when the person is not at work but is carrying out functions which, if done in work time, would have been in the exercise of functions as an emergency worker.

(5) In this section—

"ancillary offence", in relation to an offence, means any of the following—

    (a) aiding, abetting, counselling or procuring the commission of the offence;

    (b) an offence under Part 2 of the Serious Crime Act 2007 (encouraging or assisting crime) in relation to the offence;

    (c) attempting or conspiring to commit the offence;

"emergency worker" has the meaning given by section 3.

(6) Nothing in this section prevents a court from treating the fact mentioned in subsection (1)(b) as an aggravating factor in relation to offences not listed in subsection (3).

(7) This section applies only in relation to offences committed on or after the day it comes into force.

**Meaning of "emergency worker"**

68 Emergency workers for the purposes of section 67

(1) In section 67, "emergency worker" means—

    (a) a constable;

    (b) a person (other than a constable) who has the powers of a constable or is otherwise employed for police purposes or is engaged to provide services for police purposes;

    (c) a National Crime Agency officer;

    (d) a prison officer;

    (e) a person (other than a prison officer) employed or engaged to carry out functions in a custodial institution of a corresponding kind to those carried out by a prison officer;

   (f)  a prisoner custody officer, so far as relating to the exercise of escort functions;

   (g)  a custody officer, so far as relating to the exercise of escort functions;

   (h)  a person employed for the purposes of providing, or engaged to provide, fire services or fire and rescue services;

   (i)  a person employed for the purposes of providing, or engaged to provide, search services or rescue services (or both);

   (j)  a person employed for the purposes of providing, or engaged to provide—

      (i)  NHS health services, or

      (ii)  services in the support of the provision of NHS health services, and whose general activities in doing so involve face to face interaction with individuals receiving the services or with other members of the public.

(2)  It is immaterial for the purposes of subsection (1) whether the employment or engagement is paid or unpaid.

(3)  In this section—

"custodial institution" means any of the following—

      (a)  a prison;

      (b)  a young offender institution, secure training centre or secure college;

      (c)  a removal centre, a short-term holding facility or pre-departure accommodation, as defined by section 147 of the Immigration and Asylum Act 1999;

      (d)  services custody premises, as defined by section 300(7) of the Armed Forces Act 2006;

"custody officer" has the meaning given by section 12(3) of the Criminal Justice and Public Order Act 1994;

"escort functions"—

      (a)  in the case of a prisoner custody officer, means the functions specified in section 80(1) of the Criminal Justice Act 1991;

      (b)  in the case of a custody officer, means the functions specified in paragraph 1 of Schedule 1 to the Criminal Justice and Public Order Act 1994;

"NHS health services" means any kind of health services provided as part of the health service continued under section 1(1) of the National Health Service Act 2006 and under section 1(1) of the National Health Service (Wales) Act 2006;

"prisoner custody officer" has the meaning given by section 89(1) of the Criminal Justice Act 1991.

## Commission of offence whilst under the influence of alcohol or drugs      SG2-25

The fact that an offender is **voluntarily** intoxicated at the time of the offence will tend to increase the seriousness of the offence provided that the intoxication has **contributed to the offending**.

This applies regardless of whether the offender is under the influence of legal or illegal substance(s).

In the case of a person addicted to drugs or alcohol the intoxication may be considered not to be voluntary, but the court should have regard to the extent to which the offender has sought help or engaged with any assistance which has been offered or made available in dealing with the addiction.

An offender who has voluntarily consumed drugs and/or alcohol must accept the consequences of the behaviour that results, even if it is out of character.

## Offence was committed as part of a group      SG2-26

The mere membership of a group (two or more persons) should not be used to increase the sentence, but where the **offence was committed as part** of a group this will normally make it more serious because:

- the **harm** caused (both physical or psychological) or the potential for harm may be greater and/or
- the **culpability** of the offender may be higher (the role of the offender within the group will be a relevant consideration).

Culpability based on role in group offending could range from:

- Higher culpability indicated by a leading role in the group and/or the involvement by the offender of others through coercion, intimidation or exploitation, to
- Lower culpability indicated by a lesser or subordinate role under direction and/or involvement of the offender through coercion, intimidation or exploitation.

Courts should be alert to factors that suggest that an offender may have been the subject of coercion, intimidation or exploitation (including as a result of domestic abuse, trafficking or modern slavery) which the offender may find difficult to articulate, and where appropriate ask for this to be addressed in a PSR.

Where the offending is part of an organised criminal network, this will make it more serious, and the role of the offender in the organisation will also be relevant.

When sentencing young adult offenders (typically aged 18–25), consideration should also be given to the guidance on the mitigating factor relating to age and/or lack of maturity when considering the significance of group offending.

**SG2-27** **Offence involved use or threat of a weapon**
- A 'weapon' can take many forms
- The use or production of a weapon has relevance
  - o to the **culpability** of the offender where it indicates planning or intention to cause harm; and
  - o to the **harm** caused (both physical or psychological) or the potential for harm.
- Relevant considerations will include:
  - o the dangerousness of the weapon;
  - o whether the offender brought the weapon to the scene, or just used what was available on impulse;
  - o whether the offender made or adapted something for use as a weapon;
  - o the context in which the weapon was threatened, used or produced.

When sentencing young adult offenders (typically aged 18–25), consideration should also be given to the guidance on the mitigating factor relating to age and/or lack of maturity when assessing the relevance of this factor to culpability.

**SG2-28** **Planning of an offence**
- Evidence of planning normally indicates a higher level of intention and pre-meditation which increases the level of culpability.
- Planning may be inferred from the scale and sophistication of the offending and/or the role of the offender.
- The greater the degree of planning the greater the culpability.

**SG2-29** **Commission of the offence for financial gain**
- Where an offence (which is not one which by its nature is an acquisitive offence) has been committed wholly or in part for financial gain or the avoidance of cost, this will increase the seriousness.
- Where the offending is committed in a commercial context for financial gain or the avoidance of costs, this will normally indicate a higher level of culpability.
  - o examples would include, but are not limited to, dealing in unlawful goods, failing to disclose relevant matters to an authority or regulator, failing to comply with a regulation or failing to obtain the necessary licence or permission in order to avoid costs.
  - o offending of this type can undermine legitimate businesses.
- See the guidance on fines if considering a financial penalty.

**SG2-30** **High level of profit from the offence**
- A high level of profit is likely to indicate:
  - o high culpability in terms of planning and
  - o a high level of harm in terms of loss caused to victims or the undermining of legitimate businesses
- In most situations a high level of gain will be a factor taken into account at step one – care should be taken to avoid double counting.
- See the guidance on fines if considering a financial penalty.

**SG2-31** **Abuse of trust or dominant position**
- A close examination of the facts is necessary and a clear justification should be given if abuse of trust is to be found.
- In order for an abuse of trust to make an offence more serious the relationship between the offender and victim(s) must be one that would give rise to the offender having a significant level of responsibility towards the victim(s) on which the victim(s) would be entitled to rely.
- Abuse of trust may occur in many factual situations. Examples may include relationships such as teacher and pupil, parent and child, employer and employee, professional adviser and client, or carer (whether paid or unpaid) and dependant. It may also include ad hoc situations such as a late-night taxi driver and a lone passenger. These examples are not exhaustive and do not necessarily indicate that abuse of trust is present.
- Additionally an offence may be made more serious where an offender has abused their position to facilitate and/or conceal offending.
- Where an offender has been given an inappropriate level of responsibility, abuse of trust is unlikely to apply.

**SG2-32** **Restraint, detention or additional degradation of the victim**
Where an offender deliberately causes **additional** harm to a victim over and above that which is an essential element of the offence – this will increase seriousness. Examples may include, but are not limited to, posts of images on social media designed to cause additional distress to the victim.

Where any such actions are the subject of separate charges, this should be taken into account when assessing totality.

When sentencing young adult offenders (typically aged 18–25), consideration should also be given to the guidance on the mitigating factor relating to age and/or lack of maturity when considering the significance of this factor.

### Vulnerable victim                                                                                                    SG2-33

- An offence is more serious if the victim is vulnerable because of personal circumstances such as (but not limited to) age, illness or disability (unless the vulnerability of the victim is an element of the offence).
- Other factors such as the victim being isolated, incapacitated through drink or being in an unfamiliar situation **may** lead to a court considering that the offence is more serious.
- The extent to which any vulnerability may impact on the sentence is a matter for the court to weigh up in each case.
- Culpability will be increased if the offender **targeted** a victim because of an actual or perceived vulnerability.
- Culpability will be increased if the victim is made vulnerable by the actions of the offender (such as a victim who has been intimidated or isolated by the offender).
- Culpability is increased if an offender persisted in the offending once it was obvious that the victim was vulnerable (for example continuing to attack an injured victim).
- The level of harm (physical, psychological or financial) is likely to be increased if the victim is vulnerable.

### Victim was providing a public service or performing a public duty at the time of the offence          SG2-34

This reflects:

- the fact that people in public facing roles are more exposed to the possibility of harm and consequently more vulnerable and/or
- the fact that someone is working in the public interest merits the additional protection of the courts.

This applies whether the victim is a public or private employee or acting in a voluntary capacity.

Care should be taken to avoid double counting where the statutory aggravating factor relating to emergency workers applies.

### Other(s) put at risk of harm by the offending                                                        SG2-35

- Where there is risk of harm to other(s) not taken in account at step one and not subject to a separate charge, this makes the offence more serious.
- Dealing with a risk of harm involves consideration of both the likelihood of harm occurring and the extent of it if it does.

Where any such risk of harm is the subject of separate charges, this should be taken into account when assessing totality.

When sentencing young adult offenders (typically aged 18–25), consideration should also be given to the guidance on the mitigating factor relating to age and/or lack of maturity when considering the significance of this factor.

### Offence committed in the presence of other(s) (especially children)                                   SG2-36A

- This reflects the psychological harm that may be caused to those who witnessed the offence.
- The presence of one or more children may in some situations make the primary victim more vulnerable – for example an adult may be less able to resist the offender if concerned about the safety or welfare of children present.
- When sentencing young adult offenders (typically aged 18–25), consideration should also be given to the guidance on the mitigating factor relating to age and/or lack of maturity when considering the significance of this factor.

### Offence committed in the presence of others, especially children and/or non-users                     SG2-36B

[This variant of the extended explanation is used in relation to supplying or possessing controlled drugs.]

- Where there is risk of harm to other(s) not taken in account at step one and not subject to a separate charge, this makes the offence more serious.
- Dealing with a risk of harm involves consideration of both the likelihood of harm occurring and the extent of it if it does.

Where any such risk of harm is the subject of separate charges, this should be taken into account when assessing totality.

When sentencing young adult offenders (typically aged 18–25), consideration should also be given to the guidance on the mitigating factor relating to age and/or lack of maturity when considering the significance of this factor.

**SG2-50**   **Remorse**

The court will need to be satisfied that the offender is genuinely remorseful for the offending behaviour in order to reduce the sentence (separate from any guilty plea reduction).

Lack of remorse should never be treated as an aggravating factor.

**SG2-51**   **Self-reporting**

Where an offender has self-reported to the authorities, particularly in circumstances where the offence may otherwise have gone undetected, this should reduce the sentence (separate from any guilty plea reduction).

**SG2-52**   **Cooperation with the investigation/early admissions**

Assisting or cooperating with the investigation and/or making pre-court admissions may ease the effect on victims and witnesses and save valuable police time justifying a reduction in sentence (separate from any guilty plea reduction).

**SG2-53**   **Little or no planning**

Where an offender has committed the offence with little or no prior thought, this is likely to indicate a lower level of culpability and therefore justify a reduction in sentence.

**However,** impulsive acts of unprovoked violence or other types of offending may indicate a propensity to behave in a manner that would not normally justify a reduction in sentence.

**SG2-54**   **The offender was in a lesser or subordinate role if acting with others/performed limited role under direction**

Whereas acting as part of a group may make an offence more serious, if the offender's role was minor this may indicate lower culpability and justify a reduction in sentence.

**SG2-55**   **Involved through coercion, intimidation or exploitation**
- Where this applies it will reduce the culpability of the offender.
- This factor may be of particular relevance where the offender has been the victim of domestic abuse, trafficking or modern slavery, but may also apply in other contexts.
- Courts should be alert to factors that suggest that an offender may have been the subject of coercion, intimidation or exploitation which the offender may find difficult to articulate, and where appropriate ask for this to be addressed in a PSR.

**SG2-56**   **Limited awareness or understanding of the offence**

The factor may apply to reduce the culpability

- of an offender acting alone who has not appreciated the seriousness of the offence **or**
- of an offender who is acting with others and does not appreciate the extent of the overall offending.

If the offender had genuinely failed to understand or appreciate the seriousness of the offence, the sentence may be reduced from that which would have applied if the offender had understood the full extent of the offence and the likely harm that would be caused.

Where an offender lacks capacity to understand the full extent of the offending see the guidance under 'Mental disorder or learning disability'.

**SG2-57**   **Little or no financial gain**

Where an offence (which is not one which by its nature is an acquisitive offence) is committed in a context where financial gain could arise, the culpability of the offender may be reduced where it can be shown that the offender **did not seek to gain financially** from the conduct and did not in fact do so.

**SG2-58**   **Delay since apprehension**

Where there has been an unreasonable delay in proceedings since apprehension which is not the fault of the offender, the court may take this into account by reducing the sentence **if this has had a detrimental effect on the offender.**

Note: No fault should attach to an offender for not admitting an offence and/or putting the prosecution to proof of its case.

**SG2-59**   **Activity originally legitimate**

Where the offending arose from an activity which was originally legitimate, but became unlawful (for example because of a change in the offender's circumstances or a change in regulations), this **may** indicate lower culpability and thereby a reduction in sentence.

This factor will not apply where the offender has used a legitimate activity to mask a criminal activity.

**Age and/or lack of maturity**

Age and/or lack of maturity can affect:

- the offender's responsibility for the offence and
- the effect of the sentence on the offender.

Either or both of these considerations may justify a reduction in the sentence.

The emotional and developmental age of an offender is of at least equal importance to their chronological age (if not greater).

In particular young adults (typically aged 18–25) are still developing neurologically and consequently may be less able to:

- evaluate the consequences of their actions
- limit impulsivity
- limit risk taking

Young adults are likely to be susceptible to peer pressure and are more likely to take risks or behave impulsively when in company with their peers.

Immaturity can also result from atypical brain development. Environment plays a role in neurological development and factors such as adverse childhood experiences including deprivation and/or abuse may affect development.

An immature offender may find it particularly difficult to cope with custody and therefore may be more susceptible to self-harm in custody.

An immature offender may find it particularly difficult to cope with the requirements of a community order without appropriate support.

There is a greater capacity for change in immature offenders and they may be receptive to opportunities to address their offending behaviour and change their conduct.

Many young people who offend either stop committing crime, or begin a process of stopping, in their late teens and early twenties. Therefore a young adult's previous convictions may not be indicative of a tendency for further offending.

Where the offender is a care leaver the court should enquire as to any effect a sentence may have on the offender's ability to make use of support from the local authority. (Young adult care leavers are entitled to time limited support. Leaving care services may change at the age of 21 and cease at the age of 25, unless the young adult is in education at that point.) See also the Sentencing Children and Young People Guideline ([**SG8** at] paragraphs 1.16 and 1.17).

Where an offender has turned 18 between the commission of the offence and conviction the court should take as its starting point the sentence likely to have been imposed on the date at which the offence was committed, but applying the purposes of sentencing adult offenders. See also the Sentencing Children and Young People Guideline ([**SG8** at] paragraphs 6.1 to 6.3).

When considering a custodial or community sentence for a young adult the National Probation Service should address these issues in a PSR.

**Sole or primary carer for dependent relatives**

This factor is particularly relevant where an offender is on the cusp of custody or where the suitability of a community order is being considered. See also the Imposition of community and custodial sentences guideline.

For offenders on the cusp of custody, imprisonment should not be imposed where there would be an impact on dependants which would make a custodial sentence disproportionate to achieving the aims of sentencing.

Where custody is unavoidable consideration of the impact on dependants may be relevant to the length of the sentence imposed and whether the sentence can be suspended.

For more serious offences where a substantial period of custody is appropriate, this factor will carry less weight.

When imposing a community sentence on an offender with primary caring responsibilities the effect on dependants must be considered in determining suitable requirements.

In addition when sentencing an offender who is pregnant relevant considerations may include:

- any effect of the sentence on the health of the offender and
- any effect of the sentence on the unborn child

The court should ensure that it has all relevant information about dependent children before deciding on sentence.

When an immediate custodial sentence is necessary, the court must consider whether proper arrangements have been made for the care of any dependent children and if necessary consider adjourning sentence for this to be done.

When considering a community or custodial sentence for an offender who has, or may have, caring responsibilities the court should ask the National Probation Service to address these issues in a PSR.

Useful information can be found in the *Equal Treatment Bench Book* (see in particular Chapter 6 paragraphs 94–100).

**SG2-62    Physical disability or serious medical condition requiring urgent, intensive or long-term treatment**

- The court can take account of physical disability or a serious medical condition by way of mitigation as a reason for reducing the length of the sentence, either on the ground of the greater impact which imprisonment will have on the offender, or as a matter of generally expressed mercy in the individual circumstances of the case.
- However, such a condition, even when it is difficult to treat in prison, will not automatically entitle the offender to a lesser sentence than would otherwise be appropriate.
- There will always be a need to balance issues personal to an offender against the gravity of the offending (including the harm done to victims), and the public interest in imposing appropriate punishment for serious offending.
- A terminal prognosis is not in itself a reason to reduce the sentence even further. The court must impose a sentence that properly meets the aims of sentencing even if it will carry the clear prospect that the offender will die in custody. The prospect of death in the near future will be a matter considered by the prison authorities and the Secretary of State under the early release on compassionate grounds procedure (ERCG).
- But, an offender's knowledge that he will likely face the prospect of death in prison, subject only to the ERCG provisions, is a factor that can be considered by the sentencing judge when determining the sentence that it would be just to impose.

**SG2-63    Mental disorder or learning disability**

Mental disorders and learning disabilities are different things, although an individual may suffer from both. A **learning disability** is a permanent condition developing in childhood, whereas **mental illness** (or a mental health problem) can develop at any time, and is not necessarily permanent; people can get better and resolve mental health problems with help and treatment.

In the context of sentencing a broad interpretation of the terms 'mental disorder' and 'learning disabilities' should be adopted to include:

- Offenders with an intellectual impairment (low IQ);
- Offenders with a cognitive impairment such as (but not limited to) dyslexia, attention deficit hyperactivity disorder (ADHD);
- Offenders with an autistic spectrum disorder (ASD) including Asperger's syndrome;
- Offenders with a personality disorder;
- Offenders with a mental illness.

Offenders may have a combination of the above conditions.

Sentencers should be alert to the fact that not all mental disorders or learning disabilities are visible or obvious.

A mental disorder or learning disability can affect both:

1. the offender's responsibility for the offence and
2. the impact of the sentence on the offender.

The court will be assisted by a PSR and, where appropriate, medical reports (including from court mental health teams) in assessing:

1. the degree to which a mental disorder or learning disability has reduced the offender's responsibility for the offence. This may be because the condition had an impact on the offender's ability to understand the consequences of their actions, to limit impulsivity and/or to exercise self-control.
    - a relevant factor will be the degree to which a mental disorder or learning disability has been exacerbated by the actions of the offender (for example by the **voluntary** abuse of drugs or alcohol or by **voluntarily** failing to follow medical advice);

- in considering the extent to which the offender's actions were voluntary, the extent to which a mental disorder or learning disability has an impact on the offender's ability to exercise self-control or to engage with medical services will be a relevant consideration.

2. any effect of the mental disorder or learning disability on the impact of the sentence on the offender; a mental disorder or learning disability may make it more difficult for the offender to cope with custody or comply with a community order.

**Determination and/or demonstration of steps having been taken to address addiction or offending behaviour**   **SG2-64**

Where offending is driven by or closely associated with drug or alcohol abuse (for example stealing to feed a habit, or committing acts of disorder or violence whilst drunk) a commitment to address the underlying issue may justify a reduction in sentence. This will be particularly relevant where the court is considering whether to impose a sentence that focuses on rehabilitation.

Similarly, a commitment to address other underlying issues that may influence the offender's behaviour may justify the imposition of a sentence that focusses on rehabilitation.

The court will be assisted by a PSR in making this assessment.

Sentencing Guidelines

# PART 3   OFFENCES TAKEN INTO CONSIDERATION

Effective from: 11 June 2012

**SG3-1**                                    APPLICABILITY

[For the standard text on applicability see SG0-4]

**SG3-2**   **General principles**

When sentencing an offender who requests offences to be taken into consideration (TICs), courts should pass a total sentence which reflects *all* the offending behaviour. The sentence must be just and proportionate and must not exceed the statutory maximum for the conviction offence.

**SG3-3**   **Offences to be taken into consideration**

The court has discretion as to whether or not to take TICs into account. In exercising its discretion the court should take into account that TICs are capable of reflecting the offender's overall criminality. The court is likely to consider that the fact that the offender has assisted the police (particularly if the offences would not otherwise have been detected) and avoided the need for further proceedings demonstrates a genuine determination by the offender to 'wipe the slate clean'.[4]

It is generally **undesirable** for TICs to be accepted in the following circumstances:

- where the TIC is likely to attract a greater sentence than the conviction offence;
- where it is in the public interest that the TIC should be the subject of a separate charge;
- where the offender would avoid a prohibition, ancillary order or similar consequence which it would have been desirable to impose on conviction. For example:
- where the TIC attracts mandatory disqualification or endorsement and the offence(s) for which the defendant is to be sentenced do not;
- where the TIC constitutes a breach of an earlier sentence;[5]
- where the TIC is a specified offence for the purposes of section 306 of the Sentencing Code, but the conviction offence is non-specified; or
- where the TIC is not founded on the same facts or evidence or part of a series of offences of the same or similar character (unless the court is satisfied that it is in the interests of justice to do so).

**SG3-4**   **Jurisdiction**

The magistrates' court cannot take into consideration an indictable only offence.

The Crown Court can take into account summary only offences provided the TICs are founded on the same facts or evidence as the indictable charge, or are part of a series of offences of the same or similar character as the indictable conviction offence.[6]

**SG3-5**   **Procedural safeguards**

A court should generally only take offences into consideration if the following procedural provisions have been satisfied:

- the police or prosecuting authorities have prepared a schedule of offences (TIC schedule) that they consider suitable to be taken into consideration. The TIC schedule should set out the nature of each offence, the date of the offence(s), relevant detail about the offence(s) (including, for example, monetary values of items) and any other brief details that the court should be aware of;
- a copy of the TIC schedule must be provided to the defendant and his representative (if he has one) before the sentence hearing. The defendant should sign the TIC schedule to provisionally admit the offences;
- at the sentence hearing, the court should ask the defendant in open court whether he admits each of the offences on the TIC schedule and whether he wishes to have them taken into consideration;[7]
- if there is any doubt about the admission of a particular offence, it should not be accepted as a TIC. Special care should be taken with vulnerable and/or unrepresented defendants;

---

[4] Per Lord Chief Justice, *R v Miles* [2006] EWCA Crim 256
[5] *R v Webb* (1953) 37 Cr App 82
[6] Criminal Justice Act 1988, s. 40
[7] *Anderson v DPP* [1978] AC 964

- if the defendant is committed to the Crown Court for sentence, this procedure must take place again at the Crown Court even if the defendant has agreed to the schedule in the magistrates' court.

## Application                                                                             SG3-6

The sentence imposed on an offender should, in most circumstances, be increased to reflect the fact that other offences have been taken into consideration. The court should:

1. Determine the sentencing starting point for the conviction offence, referring to the relevant definitive sentencing guidelines. No regard should be had to the presence of TICs at this stage.
2. Consider whether there are any aggravating or mitigating factors that justify an upward or downward adjustment from the starting point.

The presence of TICs should generally be treated as an aggravating feature that justifies an upward adjustment from the starting point. Where there is a large number of TICs, it may be appropriate to move outside the category range, although this must be considered in the context of the case and subject to the principle of totality. The court is limited to the statutory maximum for the conviction offence.

3. Continue through the sentencing process including:
   - consider whether the frank admission of a number of offences is an indication of a defendant's remorse or determination and/or demonstration of steps taken to address addiction or offending behaviour;
   - any reduction for a guilty plea should be applied to the overall sentence;
   - the principle of totality;
   - when considering ancillary orders these can be considered in relation to any or all of the TICs, specifically:
   - compensation orders[8]—in the magistrate[s'] court the total compensation cannot exceed the limit for the conviction offence;
   - restitution orders.[9]

---

[8] s. 139 Sentencing Code
[9] s. 148 Sentencing Code

# PART 4   TOTALITY

**Effective from:** 11 June 2012

**SG4-1**                                    APPLICABILITY

[For the standard text on applicability see SG0-4]

**SG4-2   General principles**

The principle of totality comprises two elements:

1. All courts, when sentencing for more than a single offence, should pass a total sentence which reflects all the offending behaviour before it and is just and proportionate. This is so whether the sentences are structured as concurrent or consecutive. Therefore, concurrent sentences will ordinarily be longer than a single sentence for a single offence.
2. It is usually impossible to arrive at a just and proportionate sentence for multiple offending simply by adding together notional single sentences. It is necessary to address the offending behaviour, together with the factors personal to the offender as a whole.

**SG4-3   Concurrent/consecutive sentences**

There is no inflexible rule governing whether sentences should be structured as concurrent or consecutive components. The overriding principle is that the overall sentence must be just and proportionate.

**SG4-4   General approach (as applied to Determinate Custodial Sentences)**

1. **Consider the sentence for each individual offence, referring to the relevant sentencing guidelines.**
2. **Determine whether the case calls for concurrent or consecutive sentences.**

**Concurrent sentences will ordinarily be appropriate where:**

a) **offences arise out of the same incident or facts.**

*Examples include:*

- a single incident of dangerous driving resulting in injuries to multiple victims;[10]
- robbery with a weapon where the weapon offence is ancillary to the robbery and is not distinct and independent of it;[11]
- fraud and associated forgery;
- separate counts of supplying different types of drugs of the same class as part of the same transaction.

b) **there is a series of offences of the same or similar kind, especially when committed against the same person.**

*Examples include:*

- repetitive small thefts from the *same* person, such as by an employee;
- repetitive benefit frauds of the same kind, committed in each payment period.

Where concurrent sentences are to be passed the sentence should reflect the overall criminality involved. The sentence should be appropriately aggravated by the presence of the associated offences.

*Examples include:*

- a single incident of dangerous driving resulting in injuries to multiple victims where there are separate charges relating to each victim. The sentences should generally be passed concurrently, but each sentence should be aggravated to take into account the harm caused;
- repetitive fraud or theft, where charged as a series of small frauds/thefts, would be properly considered in relation to the total amount of money obtained and the period of time over which the offending took place. The sentences should generally be passed concurrently, each one reflecting the overall seriousness;
- robbery with a weapon where the weapon offence is ancillary to the robbery and is not distinct and independent of it. The principal sentence for the robbery should properly reflect the presence of the weapon. The court must avoid double-counting and may deem it preferable for the possession of the weapon's offence to run concurrently to avoid the appearance of under-sentencing in respect of the robbery.[12]

---

[10] *R v Lawrence* (1989) 11 Cr App R (S) 580
[11] *R v Poulton and Celaire* [2002] EWCA Crim 2487; *Attorney General's Reference No 21 & 22 of 2003* [2003] EWCA Crim 3089
[12] *Attorney General's Reference Nos 21 & 22 of 2003*

Consecutive sentences will ordinarily be appropriate where:

a)  **offences arise out of unrelated facts or incidents.**

*Examples include:*

- where the offender commits a theft on one occasion and a common assault against a different victim on a separate occasion;
- an attempt to pervert the course of justice in respect of another offence also charged;[13]
- a Bail Act offence;[14]
- any offence committed within the prison context;
- offences that are unrelated because whilst they were committed simultaneously they are distinct and there is an aggravating element that requires separate recognition, for example:
    o  an assault on a constable committed to try to evade arrest for another offence also charged;[15]
    o  where the defendant is convicted of drug dealing and possession of a firearm offence. The firearm offence is not the essence or the intrinsic part of the drugs offence and requires separate recognition;[16]
    o  where the defendant is convicted of threats to kill in the context of an indecent assault on the same occasion, the threats to kill could be distinguished as a separate element.[17]

b)  **offences that are of the same or similar kind but where the overall criminality will not sufficiently be reflected by concurrent sentences.**

*Examples include:*

- where offences committed against *different* people, such as repeated thefts involving attacks on several different shop assistants;[18]
- where offences of domestic violence or sexual offences are committed against the *same* individual.

c)  **one or more offence(s) qualifies for a statutory minimum sentence and concurrent sentences would improperly undermine that minimum**[19]

However it is not permissible to impose consecutive sentences for offences committed at the same time in order to evade the statutory maximum penalty.[20]

Where consecutive sentences are to be passed add up the sentences for each offence and consider if the aggregate length is just and appropriate.

If the aggregate length is not just and proportionate the court should consider how to reach a just and proportionate sentence. There are a number of ways in which this could be achieved.

*Examples include:*

- when sentencing for similar offence types or offences of a similar level of severity the court can consider:
    o  whether all of the offences can be proportionately reduced (with particular reference to the category ranges within the sentencing guidelines) and passed consecutively;
    o  whether, despite their similarity, a most serious principal offence can be identified and the other sentences can all be proportionately reduced (with particular reference to the category ranges within sentencing guidelines) and passed consecutively in order that the sentence for the lead offence can be clearly identified.
- when sentencing for two or more offences of differing levels of seriousness the court can consider:
    o  whether some offences are of such low seriousness in the context of the most serious offence(s) that they can be recorded as 'no separate penalty' (for example technical breaches or minor driving offences not involving mandatory disqualification);
    o  whether some of the offences are of lesser seriousness and are unrelated to the most serious offence(s), that they can be ordered to run concurrently so that the sentence for the most serious offence(s) can be clearly identified.

3.  **Test the overall sentence(s) against the requirement that they be just and proportionate.**
4.  **Consider whether the sentence is structured in a way that will be best understood by all concerned with it.**

---

[13]  *Attorney General's Reference No 1 of 1990* (1990) 12 Cr App R (S) 245
[14]  *R v Millen* (1980) 2 Cr App R (S) 357
[15]  *R v Kastercum* (1972) 56 Cr App R 298
[16]  *R v Poulton and Celaire* [2002] EWCA Crim 2487; *Attorney General's Reference Nos 21 & 22 of 2003* [2003] EWCA Crim 3089
[17]  *R v Fletcher* [2002] 2 CAR (S) 127
[18]  *R v Jamieson & Jamieson* [2008] EWCA Crim 2761
[19]  *R v Raza* (2010) 1 Cr App R (S) 56
[20]  *R v Ralphs* [2009] EWCA Crim 2555

Sentencing Guidelines

Specific applications — Custodial sentences

SG4-5                          EXISTING DETERMINATE SENTENCE, WHERE
                          DETERMINATE SENTENCE TO BE PASSED

| Circumstance | Approach |
|---|---|
| **Offender serving a determinate sentence** (offence(s) committed before original sentence imposed) | Consider what the sentence length would have been if the court had dealt with the offences at the same time and ensure that the totality of the sentence is just and proportionate in all the circumstances. If it is not, an adjustment should be made to the sentence imposed for the latest offence. |
| **Offender serving a determinate sentence** (offence(s) committed after original sentence imposed) | Generally the sentence will be consecutive as it will have arisen out of an unrelated incident. The court must have regard to the totality of the offender's criminality when passing the second sentence, to ensure that the total sentence to be served is just and proportionate. Where a prisoner commits acts of violence in prison, any reduction for totality is likely to be minimal.[21] |
| **Offender serving a determinate sentence but released from custody** | The new sentence should start on the day it is imposed: s.225 Sentencing Code prohibits a sentence of imprisonment running consecutively to a sentence from which a prisoner has been released. The sentence for the new offence will take into account the aggravating feature that it was committed on licence. However, it must be commensurate with the new offence and cannot be artificially inflated with a view to ensuring that the offender serves a period in custody additional to the recall period (which will be an unknown quantity in most cases);[22] this is so even if the new sentence will, in consequence, add nothing to the period actually served. |
| **Offender sentenced to a determinate term and subject to an existing suspended sentence order** | Where an offender commits an additional offence during the operational period of a suspended sentence and the court orders the suspended sentence to be activated, the additional sentence will generally be consecutive to the activated suspended sentence, as it will arise out of unrelated facts. |

SG4-6                         EXTENDED SENTENCES FOR PUBLIC PROTECTION

| Circumstance | Approach |
|---|---|
| **Extended sentences—using multiple offences to calculate the requisite determinate term** | In the case of extended sentences imposed under the Sentencing Code, providing there is at least one specified offence, the threshold requirement under s.267 or s.280 of the Sentencing Code is reached if the total determinate sentence for all offences (specified or not) would be four years or more. The extended sentence should be passed either for one specified offence or concurrently on a number of them. Ordinarily either a concurrent determinate sentence or no separate penalty will be appropriate to the remaining offences.[23] |
| | The extension period is such as the court considers necessary for the purpose of protecting members of the public from serious harm caused by the offender committing further specified offences.[24] The extension period must not exceed five years (or eight for a sexual offence). The whole aggregate term must not exceed the statutory maximum. The custodial period must be adjusted for totality in the same way as determinate sentences would be. The extension period is measured by the need for protection and therefore does not require adjustment. |

[21] *R v Ali* (1998) 2 Cr App R 123
[22] *R v Costello* [2010] EWCA Crim 371
[23] *R v Pinnell* [2010] EWCA Crim 2848
[24] *R v Cornelius* [2002] EWCA Crim 138

| Circumstance | Approach |
| --- | --- |
| Imposing multiple indeterminate sentences on the same occasion and using multiple offences to calculate the minimum term for an indeterminate sentence | Indeterminate sentences should start on the date of their imposition and so should generally be ordered to run concurrently. If the life sentence provisions in sections 272–274 or sections 283–285 of the Sentencing Code apply then:<br>a) first assess the notional determinate term for all offences (specified or otherwise), adjusting for totality in the usual way;[25]<br>b) ascertain whether any relevant sentence condition is met; and<br>c) the indeterminate sentence should generally be passed concurrently on all offences to which it can apply, but there may be some circumstances in which it suffices to pass it on a single such offence. |
| Indeterminate sentence (where the offender is already serving an existing determinate sentence) | It is generally undesirable to order an indeterminate sentence to be served consecutively to any other period of imprisonment on the basis that indeterminate sentences should start on their imposition.[26] The court should instead order the sentence to run concurrently but can adjust the minimum term for the new offence to reflect half of any period still remaining to be served under the existing sentence (to take account of the early release provisions for determinate sentences). The court should then review the minimum term to ensure that the total sentence is just and proportionate. |
| Indeterminate sentence (where the offender is already serving an existing indeterminate sentence) | It is generally undesirable to order an indeterminate sentence to be served consecutively to any other period of imprisonment on the basis that indeterminate sentences should start on their imposition. However, where necessary the court can order an indeterminate sentence to run consecutively to an indeterminate sentence passed on an earlier occasion.[27] The second sentence will commence on the expiration of the minimum term of the original sentence and the offender will become eligible for a parole review after serving both minimum terms.[28] The court should consider the length of the aggregate minimum terms that must be served before the offender will be eligible for consideration by the Parole Board. If this is not just and proportionate, the court can adjust the minimum term. |
| Ordering a determinate sentence to run consecutively to an indeterminate sentence | The court can order a determinate sentence to run consecutively to an indeterminate sentence. The determinate sentence will commence on the expiry of the minimum term of the indeterminate sentence and the offender will become eligible for a parole review after serving half of the determinate sentence.[29]<br>The court should consider the total sentence that the offender will serve before becoming eligible for consideration for release. If this is not just and proportionate, the court can reduce the length of the determinate sentence, or alternatively, can order the second sentence to be served concurrently. |

---

[25]  *R v Rahuel Delucca* [2010] EWCA Crim 710
[26]  *R v O'Brien* [2006] EWCA Crim 1741
[27]  *R v Hills* [2008] EWCA Crim 1871; *R v Ashes* [2007] EWCA Crim 1848
[28]  Crime (Sentences) Act 1997, s. 28(1B)
[29]  ibid, s. 28

**SG4-8**                SPECIFIC APPLICATIONS — NON-CUSTODIAL SENTENCES

### Multiple Fines for Non-Imprisonable Offences

| Circumstance | Approach |
|---|---|
| Offender convicted of more than one offence where a fine is appropriate | The total fine is inevitably cumulative.<br>The court should determine the fine for each individual offence based on the seriousness of the offence[30] and taking into account the circumstances of the case including the financial circumstances of the offender so far as they are known, or appear, to the court.[31]<br><br>The court should add up the fines for each offence and consider if they are just and proportionate.<br>If the aggregate total is not just and proportionate the court should consider how to reach a just and proportionate fine. There are a number of ways in which this can be achieved.<br>*For example:*<br>• where an offender is to be fined for two or more offences that arose out of the same incident or where there are multiple offences of a repetitive kind, especially when committed against the same person, it will often be appropriate to impose for the most serious offence a fine which reflects the totality of the offending where this can be achieved within the maximum penalty for that offence. No separate penalty should be imposed for the other offences;<br>• where an offender is to be fined for two or more offences that arose out of different incidents, it will often be appropriate to impose a separate fine for each of the offences. The court should add up the fines for each offence and consider if they are just and proportionate. If the aggregate amount is not just and proportionate the court should consider whether all of the fines can be proportionately reduced. Separate fines should then be passed.<br>Where separate fines are passed, the court must be careful to ensure that there is no double-counting.[32]<br>Where compensation is being ordered, that will need to be attributed to the relevant offence as will any necessary ancillary orders. |
| Multiple offences attracting fines — crossing the community threshold | If the offences being dealt with are all imprisonable, then the community threshold can be crossed by reason of multiple offending, when it would not be crossed for a single offence.[33] However, if the offences are non-imprisonable (e.g. driving without insurance) the threshold cannot be crossed.[34] |

**SG4-9**                FINES IN COMBINATION WITH OTHER SENTENCES

| Circumstance | Approach |
|---|---|
| A fine may be imposed in addition to any other penalty for the same offence except: | • a hospital order;<br>• a discharge;<br>• a sentence fixed by law (minimum sentences, EPP, IPP);<br>• a minimum term imposed under s. 313 or s. 314 of the Sentencing Code;<br>• a life sentence imposed under s. 274 or s. 285 Sentencing Code or a sentence of detention for life for an offender under 18 under s. 258 Sentencing Code. |

---

[30] s.125(1) Sentencing Code
[31] s.125(2) Sentencing Code
[32] *R v Pointon* [2008] EWCA Crim 513
[33] s.204(2) Sentencing Code
[34] s.202 Sentencing Code restricts the power to make a community order by limiting it to cases where the offence is punishable with imprisonment

| Circumstance | Approach |
|---|---|
| Fines and determinate custodial sentences | A fine should not generally be imposed in combination with a custodial sentence because of the effect of imprisonment on the means of the defendant. However, exceptionally, it may be appropriate to impose a fine in addition to a custodial sentence where:<br>• the sentence is suspended;<br>• a confiscation order is not contemplated; **and**<br>• there is no obvious victim to whom compensation can be awarded; **and**<br>• the offender has, or will have, resources from which a fine can be paid.[35] |

COMMUNITY ORDERS                                      SG4-10

| Circumstance | Approach |
|---|---|
| Multiple offences attracting community orders—crossing the custody threshold | If the offences are all imprisonable and none of the individual sentences merit a custodial sentence, the custody threshold can be crossed by reason of multiple offending.[36] If the custody threshold has been passed, the court should refer to the offence ranges in sentencing guidelines for the offences and to the general principles. |
| Multiple offences, where one offence would merit immediate custody and one offence would merit a community order | A community order should not be ordered to run consecutively to or concurrently with a custodial sentence. Instead the court should generally impose one custodial sentence that is aggravated appropriately by the presence of the associated offence(s). The alternative option is to impose no separate penalty for the offence of lesser seriousness. |
| Offender convicted of more than one offence where a community order is appropriate | A community order is a composite package rather than an accumulation of sentences attached to individual counts. The court should generally impose a single community order that reflects the overall criminality of the offending behaviour. Where it is necessary to impose more than one community order, these should be ordered to run concurrently and for ease of administration, each of the orders should be identical. |
| Offender convicted of an offence while serving a community order | The power to deal with the offender depends on his being convicted whilst the order is still in force;[37] it does not arise where the order has expired, even if the additional offence was committed whilst it was still current.<br>If an offender, in respect of whom a community order made by a magistrates' court is in force, is convicted by a magistrates' court of an additional offence, the magistrates' court should ordinarily revoke the previous community order and sentence afresh for both the original and the additional offence.<br>Where an offender, in respect of whom a community order made by a Crown Court is in force, is convicted by a magistrates' court, the magistrates' court may, and ordinarily should, commit the offender to the Crown Court, in order to allow the Crown Court to re-sentence for the original offence and the additional offence.<br>The sentencing court should consider the overall seriousness of the offending behaviour taking into account the additional offence and the original offence. The court should consider whether the combination of associated offences is sufficiently serious to justify a custodial sentence.<br>If the court does not consider that custody is necessary, it should impose a single community order that reflects the overall totality of criminality. The court must take into account the extent to which the offender complied with the requirements of the previous order. |

[35] [This footnote refers to guidance that has been superseded.]
[36] s.204(2) Sentencing Code
[37] Paragraphs 22 and 25 of Schedule 10 to the Sentencing Code

SG4-11

## Disqualifications from Driving

| Circumstance | Approach |
|---|---|
| Offender convicted of two or more obligatory disqualification offences (s. 34(1) Road Traffic Offender Act 1988) | The court must impose an order of disqualification for each offence unless for special reasons it does not disqualify the offender.[38] <br> All orders of disqualification imposed by the court on the same date take effect immediately and cannot be ordered to run consecutively to one another. <br> The court should take into account all offences when determining the disqualification periods and should generally impose like periods for each offence. |
| Offender convicted of two or more offences involving either: <br> a) discretionary disqualification and obligatory endorsement from driving; or <br> b) obligatory disqualification but the court for special reasons does not disqualify the offender and the penalty points to be taken into account number 12 or more (ss. 28 and 35 Road Traffic Offender Act 1988) | Where an offender is convicted on the same occasion of more than one offence to which s. 35(1) Road Traffic Offender Act 1988 applies, only one disqualification shall be imposed on him.[39] However, the court must take into account all offences when determining the disqualification period. For the purposes of appeal, any disqualification imposed shall be treated as an order made on conviction of each of the offences.[40] |
| Other combinations involving two or more offences involving discretionary disqualification | As orders of disqualification take effect immediately, it is generally desirable for the court to impose a single disqualification order that reflects the overall criminality of the offending behaviour. |

SG4-12

## Compensation Orders

| Circumstance | Approach |
|---|---|
| Global compensation orders | The court should not fix a global compensation figure unless the offences were committed against the same victim.[41] Where there are competing claims for limited funds, the total compensation available should normally be apportioned on a pro rata basis.[42] |
| | The court may combine a compensation order with any other form of order. |
| Compensation orders and fines | Priority is given to the imposition of a compensation order over a fine.[43] This does not affect sentences other than fines. This means that the fine should be reduced or, if necessary, dispensed with altogether, to enable the compensation to be paid. |
| Compensation orders and confiscation orders | A compensation order can be combined with a confiscation order where the amount that may be realised is sufficient. If such an order is made, priority should be given to compensation.[44] |

---

[38] Road Traffic Offender Act 1988, s. 34(1) <br>
[39] ibid, s. 34(3) <br>
[40] ibid <br>
[41] s.135(4) Sentencing Code <br>
[42] *R v Mitchell* [2001] Crim LR 239 <br>
[43] s.134(2) Sentencing Code <br>
[44] *R v Warton* [1976] Crim LR 520

| Circumstance | Approach |
|---|---|
| **Compensation orders and community orders** | A compensation order can be combined with a community order. |
| **Compensation orders and suspended sentence orders** | A compensation order can be combined with a suspended sentence order.[45] |
| **Compensation orders and custody** | A compensation order can be combined with a sentence of immediate custody where the offender is clearly able to pay or has good prospects of employment on his release from custody. |

Sentencing Guidelines

---

[45] *R v Miller* [1976] Crim LR 694

# PART 5    REDUCTION IN SENTENCE
# FOR A GUILTY PLEA

**SG5-1**    **Effective from:** 01 June 2017

(For cases where the first hearing was before 1 June 2017 refer to the earlier guideline [See **SG5-12**])

Section 73 of the Sentencing Code provides:

(1) In determining what sentence to pass on an offender who has pleaded guilty to an offence[46] in proceedings before that court or another court, a court must take into account:
  (a) the stage in the proceedings for the offence at which the offender indicated his intention to plead guilty, and
  (b) the circumstances in which this indication was given.

Nothing in this guideline affects the duty of the parties to progress cases (including the service of material) and identify any issues in dispute in compliance with the Criminal Procedure Rules and Criminal Practice Directions.

**SG5-2**    **A. Applicability of Guideline**

[For the standard text on applicability see **SG0-4**.]

**SG5-3**    **B. Key Principles**

**The purpose of this guideline is to encourage those who are going to plead guilty to do so as early in the court process as possible. Nothing in the guideline should be used to put pressure on a defendant to plead guilty.**

Although a guilty person is entitled not to admit the offence and to put the prosecution to proof of its case, an acceptance of guilt:

a) normally reduces the impact of the crime upon victims;
b) saves victims and witnesses from having to testify; and
c) is in the public interest in that it saves public time and money on investigations and trials.

A guilty plea produces greater benefits the earlier the plea is indicated. In order to maximise the above benefits and to provide an incentive to those who are guilty to indicate a guilty plea as early as possible, this guideline makes a clear distinction between a reduction in the sentence available at the first stage of the proceedings and a reduction in the sentence available at a later stage of the proceedings.

The purpose of reducing the sentence for a guilty plea is to yield the benefits described above. The guilty plea should be considered by the court to be independent of the offender's personal mitigation.

- Factors such as admissions at interview, co-operation with the investigation and demonstrations of remorse should **not** be taken into account in determining the level of reduction. Rather, they should be considered separately and prior to any guilty plea reduction, as potential mitigating factors.
- The benefits apply regardless of the strength of the evidence against an offender. The strength of the evidence should **not** be taken into account when determining the level of reduction.
- The guideline applies only to the punitive elements of the sentence and has no impact on ancillary orders including orders of disqualification from driving.

**SG5-4**    **C. The Approach**

**Stage 1:** Determine the appropriate sentence for the offence(s) in accordance with any offence specific sentencing guideline.
**Stage 2:** Determine the level of reduction for a guilty plea in accordance with this guideline.
**Stage 3:** State the amount of that reduction.
**Stage 4:** Apply the reduction to the appropriate sentence.
**Stage 5:** Follow any further steps in the offence specific guideline to determine the final sentence.

**SG5-5**    **D. Determining the Level of Reduction**

**The maximum level of reduction in sentence for a guilty plea is one-third**

**D1. Plea indicated at the first stage of the proceedings**

---

[46] 'Offence' includes breach of an order where this constitutes a separate criminal offence but not breach of terms of a sentence or licence.

Where a guilty plea is indicated at the first stage of proceedings a reduction of **one-third** should be made (subject to the exceptions in section F). The first stage will normally be the first hearing at which a plea or indication of plea is sought and recorded by the court.[47]

**D2. Plea indicated after the first stage of proceedings – maximum one quarter – sliding scale of reduction thereafter**

After the first stage of the proceedings the maximum level of reduction is **one-quarter** (subject to the exceptions in section F).

The reduction should be decreased from **one-quarter** to a maximum of **one-tenth** on the first day of trial having regard to the time when the guilty plea is first indicated to the court relative to the progress of the case and the trial date (subject to the exceptions in section F). The reduction should normally be decreased further, even to zero, if the guilty plea is entered during the course of the trial.

For the purposes of this guideline a trial will be deemed to have started when pre-recorded cross-examination has begun.

**E.   Applying the Reduction**                                                                                  SG5-6

**E1.   Imposing one type of sentence rather than another**

The reduction in sentence for a guilty plea can be taken into account by imposing one type of sentence rather than another; for example:

- by reducing a custodial sentence to a community sentence, or
- by reducing a community sentence to a fine.

Where a court has imposed one sentence rather than another to reflect the guilty plea there should normally be no further reduction on account of the guilty plea. Where, however, the less severe type of sentence is justified by other factors, the appropriate reduction for the plea should be applied in the normal way.

**E2.   More than one summary offence**

When dealing with more than one summary offence, the aggregate sentence is limited to a maximum of six months. Allowing for a reduction for each guilty plea, consecutive sentences might result in the imposition of the maximum six month sentence. Where this is the case, the court **may** make a modest *additional* reduction to the *overall* sentence to reflect the benefits derived from the guilty pleas.

**E3.   Keeping an either way case in the magistrates' court to reflect a guilty plea**

Reducing a custodial sentence to reflect a guilty plea may enable a magistrates' court to retain jurisdiction of an either way offence rather than committing the case for sentence to the Crown Court.

In such cases a magistrates' court should apply the appropriate reduction to the sentence for the offence(s) arrived at in accordance with any offence specific sentencing guideline and if the resulting sentence is then within its jurisdiction it should go on to sentence.

**F.   Exceptions**                                                                                              SG5-7

**F1.   Further information, assistance or advice necessary before indicating plea**

Where the sentencing court is satisfied that there were particular circumstances which significantly reduced the defendant's ability to understand what was alleged or otherwise made it unreasonable to expect the defendant to indicate a guilty plea **sooner than was done**, a reduction of one-third should still be made.

In considering whether this exception applies, sentencers should distinguish between cases in which it is necessary to receive advice and/or have sight of evidence in order to understand whether the defendant is in fact and law guilty of the offence(s) charged, and cases in which a defendant merely delays guilty plea(s) in order to assess the strength of the prosecution evidence and the prospects of conviction or acquittal.

**F2.   Newton Hearings and special reasons hearings**

In circumstances where an offender's version of events is rejected at a Newton hearing[48] or special reasons hearing[49], the reduction which would have been available at the stage of proceedings the plea was indicated

---

[47] In cases where (in accordance with the Criminal Procedure Rules) a defendant is given the opportunity to enter a guilty plea without attending a court hearing, doing so within the required time limits will constitute a plea at the first stage of proceedings.

[48] A Newton hearing is held when an offender pleads guilty but disputes the case as put forward by the prosecution and the dispute would make a difference to the sentence. The judge will normally hear evidence from witnesses to decide which version of the disputed facts to base the sentence on.

[49] A special reasons hearing occurs when an offender is convicted of an offence carrying mandatory licence endorsement or disqualification from driving and seeks to persuade the court that there are extenuating circumstances relating to the offence

should normally be halved. Where witnesses are called during such a hearing, it may be appropriate further to decrease the reduction.

### F3. Offender convicted of a lesser or different offence

If an offender is convicted of a lesser or different offence from that originally charged, and has earlier made an unequivocal indication of a guilty plea to this lesser or different offence to the prosecution and the court, the court should give the level of reduction that is appropriate to the stage in the proceedings at which this indication of plea (to the lesser or different offence) was made taking into account any other of these exceptions that apply. In the Crown Court where the offered plea is a permissible alternative on the indictment as charged, the offender will not be treated as having made an unequivocal indication unless the offender has entered that plea.

### F4. Minimum sentence under section 311 of the Sentencing Code for certain offences involving firearms that are prohibited weapons

There can be no reduction for a guilty plea if the effect of doing so would be to reduce the length of sentence below the required minimum term.

### F5. Minimum sentences under sections 312, 313, 314 and 315 of the Sentencing Code for persons aged 18 or over

In circumstances where:

- an *appropriate* custodial sentence of at least six months falls to be imposed (under section 312 or 315 of the Sentencing Code) on a person aged 18 or over who has been convicted under sections 1 or 1A of the Prevention of Crime Act 1953; or sections 139, 139AA or 139A of the Criminal Justice Act 1988 (certain possession of knives or offensive weapon offences) **or**
- a minimum sentence falls to be imposed under section 313 (third class A drug trafficking offence) or section 314 (third domestic burglary) of the Sentencing Code, the court may impose any sentence in accordance with this guideline which is not less than **80 per cent** of the *appropriate* custodial period.[50]

**SG5-8**  ## G.  Mandatory Life Sentences For Murder

Murder is the most serious criminal offence and the sentence prescribed is different from all other sentences. By law, the sentence for murder is imprisonment (detention) for life and an offender will remain subject to the sentence for the rest of his life.

Given the special characteristic of the offence of murder and the unique statutory provision in Schedule 21 of the Sentencing Code of starting points for the minimum term to be served by an offender, careful consideration has to be given to the extent of any reduction for a guilty plea and to the need to ensure that the minimum term properly reflects the seriousness of the offence. Whilst the general principles continue to apply (both that a guilty plea should be encouraged and that the extent of any reduction should reduce if the indication of plea is later than the first stage of the proceedings) the process of determining the level of reduction will be different.

### Determining the level of reduction

Whereas a court should consider the fact that an offender has pleaded guilty to murder when deciding whether it is appropriate to order a whole life term, where a court determines that there should be a whole life minimum term, there will be no reduction for a guilty plea.

In other circumstances:

- the court will weigh carefully the overall length of the minimum term taking into account other reductions for which the offender may be eligible so as to avoid a combination leading to an inappropriately short sentence;
- where it is appropriate to reduce the minimum term having regard to a plea of guilty, the reduction will not exceed one-sixth and will never exceed five years;
- the maximum reduction of one-sixth or five years (whichever is less) should only be given when a guilty plea has been indicated at the first stage of the proceedings. Lesser reductions should be given for guilty pleas after that point, with a maximum of one-twentieth being given for a guilty plea on the day of trial.

The exceptions outlined at F1 and F2 above, apply to murder cases.

---

that the court should take into account by reducing or avoiding endorsement or disqualification. This may involve calling witnesses to give evidence.

[50] In accordance with s.73(3) and (4) of the Sentencing Code

**Appendix 1**

**Flowchart illustrating reductions for either way offences** (offences that can be tried in a magistrates' court or the Crown Court)

This flowchart is provided as an illustration of the operation of the guideline as at 1 June 2017.

It does not form part of the guideline.

The reductions and timings are subject to the exceptions set out in the guideline

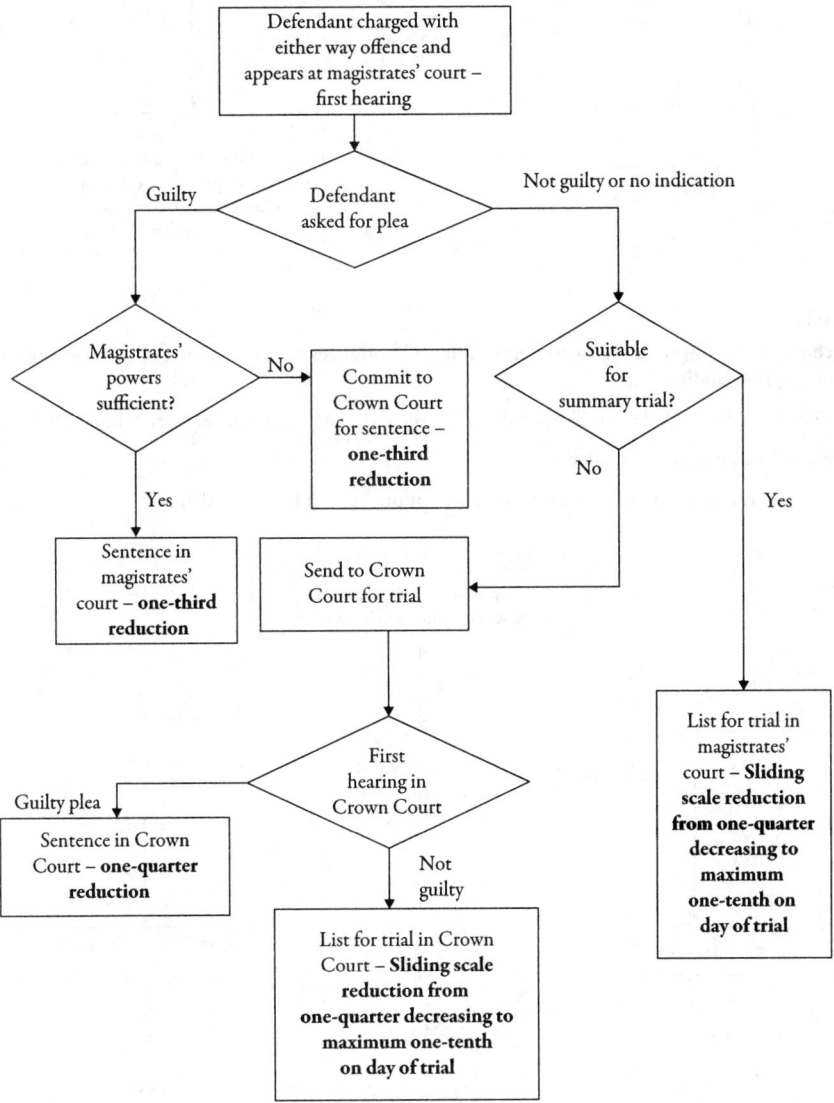

**Appendix 2**

**Flowchart illustrating reductions for summary only offences** (offences that can be tried only in a magistrates' court)

This flowchart is provided as an illustration of the operation of the guideline as at 1 June 2017.

It does not form part of the guideline.

The reductions and timings are subject to the exceptions set out in the guideline

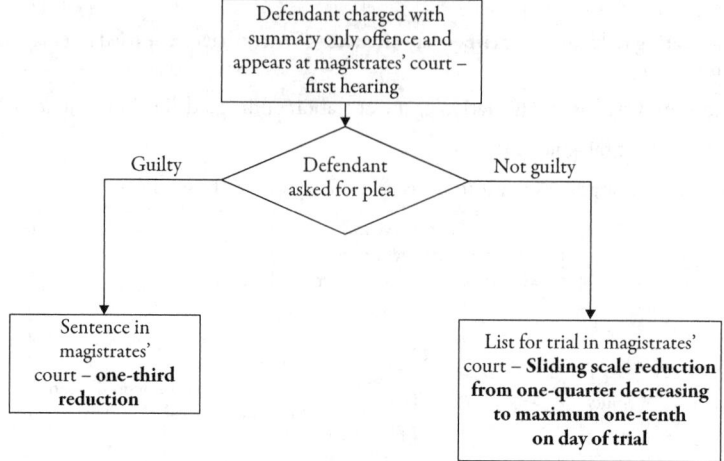

**SG5-11** **Appendix 3**

**Flowchart illustrating reductions for indictable only offences** (offences that can be tried only in the Crown Court excluding murder)

This flowchart is provided as an illustration of the operation of the guideline as at 1 June 2017.

It does not form part of the guideline.

The reductions and timings are subject to the exceptions set out in the guideline

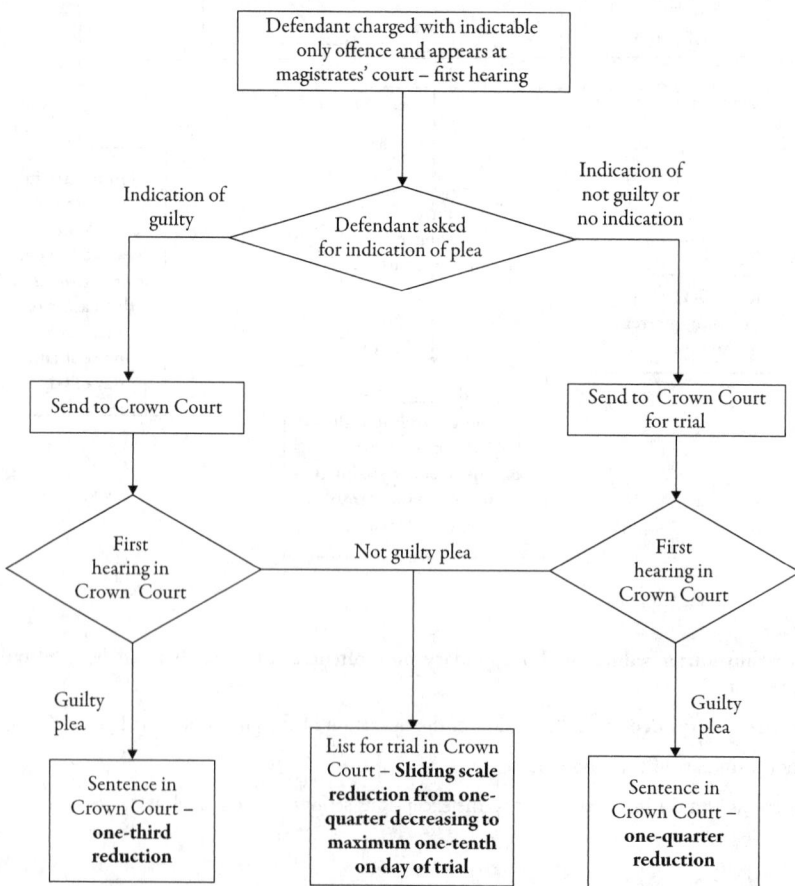

Note: this guideline has not been updated in line with the Sentencing Code

**Effective from:** 23 July 2007

**Statutory provisions**

Section 144 Criminal Justice Act 2003 provides:

(1) In determining what sentence to pass on an offender who has pleaded guilty to an offence in proceedings before that or another court, a court must take into account:
  (a) the stage in the proceedings for the offence at which the offender indicated his intention to plead guilty, and
  (b) the circumstances in which this indication was given.

(2) In the case of an offence the sentence for which falls to be imposed under subsection (2) of section 110 or 111 of the Sentencing Act, nothing in that subsection prevents the court, after taking into account any matter referred to in subsection (1) of this section, from imposing any sentence which is not less than 80 per cent of that specified in that subsection.

Section 174(2) Criminal Justice Act 2003 provides:

(2) In complying with subsection (1)(a), the court must:
  (a) ……..
  (b) ……..
  (c) ……..
  (d) where as a result of taking into account any matter referred to in section 144(1), the court imposes a punishment on the offender which is less severe than the punishment it would otherwise have imposed, state that fact, …
  (e) ……..

1.1 This guideline applies whether a case is dealt with in a magistrates' court or in the Crown Court and whenever practicable in the youth court (taking into account legislative restrictions such as those relevant to the length of Detention and Training orders).

1.2 The application of this guideline to sentencers when arriving at the appropriate minimum term for the offence of murder, see Application to Sentencing for Murder.

**Statement of purpose**

2.1 When imposing a custodial sentence, statute requires that a court must impose the shortest term that is commensurate with the seriousness of the offence(s).[51] Similarly, when imposing a community order, the restrictions on liberty must be commensurate with the seriousness of the offence(s).[52] Once that decision is made, a court is required to give consideration to the reduction for any guilty plea. As a result, the final sentence after the reduction for a guilty plea will be less than the seriousness of the offence requires.

2.2 A reduction in sentence is appropriate because a guilty plea avoids the need for a trial (thus enabling other cases to be disposed of more expeditiously), shortens the gap between charge and sentence, saves considerable cost, and, in the case of an early plea, saves victims and witnesses from the concern about having to give evidence. The reduction principle derives from the need for the effective administration of justice and not as an aspect of mitigation.

2.3 Where a sentencer is in doubt as to whether a custodial sentence is appropriate, the reduction attributable to a guilty plea will be a relevant consideration. Where this is amongst the factors leading to the imposition of a non-custodial sentence, there will be no need to apply a further reduction on account of the guilty plea. A similar approach is appropriate where the reduction for a guilty plea is amongst the factors leading to the imposition of a financial penalty or discharge instead of a community order.

2.4 When deciding the most appropriate length of sentence, the sentencer should address separately the issue of remorse, together with any other mitigating features, before calculating the reduction for the guilty plea. Similarly, assistance to the prosecuting or enforcement authorities is a separate issue which may attract a reduction in sentence under other procedures; care will need to be taken to ensure that there is no "double counting".

2.5 The implications of other offences that an offender has asked to be taken into consideration should be reflected in the sentence before the reduction for guilty plea has been applied.

---

[51] Criminal Justice Act 2003, s.153(2)
[52] Criminal Justice Act 2003, s.148(2)

2.6 A reduction in sentence should only be applied to the **punitive elements** of a penalty.[53] The guilty plea reduction has **no** impact on sentencing decisions in relation to ancillary orders, including orders of disqualification from driving.

### Application of the reduction principle

3.1 Recommended approach

| The court decides sentence for the offence(s) taking into account aggravating and mitigating factors and any other offences that have been formally admitted (TICs). |
|---|
| ⇓ |
| The court selects the amount of the reduction by reference to the sliding scale. |
| ⇓ |
| The court applies the reduction. |
| ⇓ |
| When pronouncing sentence the court should usually state what the sentence would have been if there had been no reduction as a result of the guilty plea |

### Determining the level of reduction

4.1 The level of reduction should be **a proportion of the total sentence** imposed, with the proportion calculated by reference to the circumstances in which the guilty plea was indicated, in particular the stage in the proceedings. The greatest reduction will be given where the plea was indicated at the "first reasonable opportunity".

4.2 Save where section 144(2) of the 2003 Act applies,[54] the level of the reduction will be gauged on a **sliding scale** ranging from a recommended one third (where the guilty plea was entered at the first reasonable opportunity in relation to the offence for which sentence is being imposed), reducing to a recommended **one quarter** (where a trial date has been set) and to a recommended **one tenth** (for a guilty plea entered at the 'door of the court' or after the trial has begun). See diagram below.

4.3 The level of reduction should reflect the stage at which the offender indicated a **willingness to admit guilt** to the offence for which he is eventually sentenced:

1. the largest recommended reduction will not normally be given unless the offender indicated willingness to admit guilt at the **first reasonable opportunity**; when this occurs will vary from case to case (see illustrative examples);
2. where the admission of guilt comes later than the first reasonable opportunity, the reduction for guilty plea will normally be less than one third;
3. where the plea of guilty comes very late, it is still appropriate to give some reduction;
4. if after pleading guilty there is a Newton hearing and the offender's version of the circumstances of the offence is rejected, this should be taken into account in determining the level of reduction;
5. if the not guilty plea was entered and maintained for tactical reasons (such as to retain privileges whilst on remand), a late guilty plea should attract very little, if any, discount.

| In each category, there is a presumption that the recommended reduction will be given unless there are good reasons for a lower amount. | | |
|---|---|---|
| First reasonable opportunity | After a trial date is set | Door of the court/after trial has begun |
| Recommended 1/3 | Recommended 1/4 | Recommended 1/10 |

### Withholding a reduction

*On the basis of dangerousness*

5.1 Where a sentence for a "dangerous offender" is imposed under the provisions in the Criminal Justice Act 2003, whether the sentence requires the calculation of a minimum term or is an extended sentence, the approach will be the same as for any other determinate sentence (see also **section G** below).[55]

---

[53] Where a court imposes an indeterminate sentence for public protection, the reduction principle applies in the normal way to the determination of the minimum term (see On the basis of dangerousness and Application to other Indeterminate Sentences) but release from custody requires the authorisation of the Parole Board once that minimum term has been served.

[54] See Statutory Provisions.

[55] There will be some cases arising from offences committed before the commencement of the relevant provisions of the Criminal Justice Act 2003 in which a court will determine that a longer than commensurate, extended, or indeterminate sentence is required for the protection of the public. In such a case, the minimum custodial term (but not the protection of public element of the sentence) should be reduced to reflect the plea.

*Where the prosecution case is overwhelming*

5.2   The purpose of giving credit is to encourage those who are guilty to plead at the earliest opportunity. Any defendant is entitled to put the prosecution to proof and so every defendant who is guilty should be encouraged to indicate that guilt at the first reasonable opportunity.

5.3   Where the prosecution case is overwhelming, it may not be appropriate to give the full reduction that would otherwise be given. Whilst there is a presumption in favour of the full reduction being given where a plea has been indicated at the first reasonable opportunity, the fact that the prosecution case is overwhelming without relying on admissions from the defendant may be a reason justifying departure from the guideline.

5.4   Where a court is satisfied that a lower reduction should be given for this reason, a recommended reduction of 20% is likely to be appropriate where the guilty plea was indicated at the first reasonable opportunity.

5.5   A court departing from a guideline must state the reasons for doing so.[56]

*Where the maximum penalty for the offence is thought to be too low*

5.6   The sentencer is bound to sentence for the offence with which the offender has been charged, and to which he has pleaded guilty. The sentencer cannot remedy perceived defects (for example an inadequate charge or maximum penalty) by refusal of the appropriate discount.

*Where jurisdictional issues arise*

*(i)   Where sentencing powers are limited to 6 months imprisonment despite multiple offences*

5.7   When the total sentence for both or all of the offences is 6 months imprisonment, a court may determine to impose consecutive sentences which, even allowing for a reduction for a guilty plea where appropriate on each offence, would still result in the imposition of the maximum sentence available. In such circumstances, in order to achieve the purpose for which the reduction principle has been established,[57] some modest allowance should normally be given against the total sentence for the entry of a guilty plea.

*(ii)   Where a maximum sentence might still be imposed*

5.8   Despite a guilty plea being entered which would normally attract a reduction in sentence, a magistrates' court may impose a sentence of imprisonment of 6 months for a single either-way offence where, but for the plea, that offence would have been committed to the Crown Court for sentence.

5.9   Similarly, a detention and training order of 24 months may be imposed on an offender aged under 18 if the offence is one which would but for the plea have attracted a sentence of long-term detention in excess of 24 months under the Powers of Criminal Courts (Sentencing) Act 2000, section 91.

**Application to sentencing for murder**

6.1   Murder has always been regarded as the most serious criminal offence and the sentence prescribed is different from other sentences. By law, the sentence for murder is imprisonment (detention) for life and an offender will remain subject to the sentence for the rest of his/her life.

6.2   The decision whether to release the offender from custody during this sentence will be taken by the Parole Board which will consider whether it is safe to release the offender on licence. The court that imposes the sentence is required by law to set a minimum term that has to be served before the Parole Board may start to consider whether to authorise release on licence. If an offender is released, the licence continues for the rest of the offender's life and recall to prison is possible at any time.

6.3   Uniquely, Parliament has set starting points[58] (based on the circumstances of the killing) which a court will apply when it fixes the minimum term. Parliament has further prescribed that, having identified the appropriate starting point, the court must then consider whether to increase or reduce it in the light of aggravating or mitigating factors, some of which are listed in statute. Finally, Parliament specifically provides[59] that the obligation to have regard to any guilty plea applies to the fixing of the minimum term, by making the same statutory provisions that apply to other offences apply to murder without limiting the courts discretion (as it did with other sentences under the Powers of Criminal Courts (Sentencing) Act 2000).

6.4   There are important differences between the usual fixed term sentence and the minimum term set following the imposition of the mandatory life sentence for murder. The most significant of these, from the sentencer's point of view, is that a reduction for a plea of guilty in the case of murder will

---

[56]   Criminal Justice Act 2003, s.174(2)(a)
[57]   See Statement of Purpose.
[58]   Criminal Justice Act 2003, schedule 21
[59]   Criminal Justice Act 2003, schedule 1 para 12(c)

have double the effect on time served in custody when compared with a determinate sentence. This is because a determinate sentence will provide (in most circumstances) for the release of the offender[60] on licence halfway through the total sentence whereas in the case of murder a minimum term is the period in custody before consideration is given by the Parole Board to whether release is appropriate.

6.5 Given this difference, the special characteristic of the offence of murder and the unique statutory provision of starting points, careful consideration will need to be given to the extent of any reduction and to the need to ensure that the minimum term properly reflects the seriousness of the offence. Whilst the general principles continue to apply (both that a guilty plea should be encouraged and that the extent of any reduction should reduce if the indication of plea is later than the first reasonable opportunity), the process of determining the level of reduction will be different.

### 6.6 Approach

1. Where a court determines that there should be a whole life minimum term, there will be no reduction for a guilty plea.
2. In other circumstances:
3. a. the court will weigh carefully the overall length of the minimum term taking into account other reductions for which the offender may be eligible so as to avoid a combination leading to an inappropriately short sentence;
   b. where it is appropriate to reduce the minimum term having regard to a plea of guilty, the reduction will not exceed one sixth and will never exceed 5 years;
   c. the sliding scale will apply so that, where it is appropriate to reduce the minimum term on account of a guilty plea, the recommended reduction (one sixth or five years whichever is the less) is only available where there has been an indication of willingness to plead guilty at the first reasonable opportunity, with a recommended 5% for a late guilty plea;
   d. the court should then review the sentence to ensure that the minimum term accurately reflects the seriousness of the offence taking account of the statutory starting point, all aggravating and mitigating factors and any guilty plea entered.

### Application to other indeterminate sentences

7.1 There are other circumstances in which an indeterminate sentence will be imposed. This may be a discretionary life sentence or imprisonment for public protection.

7.2 As with the mandatory life sentence imposed following conviction for murder, the court will be obliged to fix a minimum term to be served before the Parole Board is able to consider whether the offender can be safely released.

7.3 However, the process by which that minimum term is fixed is different from that followed in relation to the mandatory life sentence and requires the court first to determine what the equivalent determinate sentence would have been. Accordingly, the approach to the calculation of the reduction for any guilty plea should follow the process and scale adopted in relation to determinate sentences, as set out in Determining the level of reduction.

### First reasonable opportunity

1. The critical time for determining the reduction for a guilty plea is the first reasonable opportunity for the defendant to have indicated a willingness to plead guilty. This opportunity will vary with a wide range of factors and the court will need to make a judgement on the particular facts of the case before it.
2. The key principle is that the purpose of giving a reduction is to recognise the benefits that come from a guilty plea not only for those directly involved in the case in question but also in enabling courts more quickly to deal with other outstanding cases.
3. This Annex seeks to help courts to adopt a consistent approach by giving examples of circumstances where a determination will have to be made:
   (a) the first reasonable opportunity may be the first time that a defendant appears before the court and has the opportunity to plead guilty;
   (b) but the court may consider that it would be reasonable to have expected an indication of willingness even earlier, perhaps whilst under interview;

**Note:** For a) and b) to apply, the court will need to be satisfied that the defendant (and any legal adviser) would have had sufficient information about the allegations

   (c) where an offence triable either way is committed to the Crown Court for trial and the defendant pleads guilty at the first hearing in that Court, the reduction will be less than if there had been an indication of a guilty plea given to the magistrates' court (recommended reduction of one third) but more than if the plea had been entered after a trial date had been set (recommended reduction of one quarter), and is likely to be in the region of 30%;

---

[60] In accordance with the provisions of the Criminal Justice Act 2003.

(d) where an offence is triable only on indictment, it may well be that the first reasonable opportunity would have been during the police station stage; where that is not the case, the first reasonable opportunity is likely to be at the first hearing in the Crown Court;

(e) where a defendant is convicted after pleading guilty to an alternative (lesser) charge to that to which he/she had originally pleaded not guilty, the extent of any reduction will be determined by the stage at which the defendant first formally indicated to the court willingness to plead guilty to the lesser charge, and the reason why that lesser charge was proceeded with in preference to the original charge.

# PART 6    DOMESTIC ABUSE

**Effective from:** 24 May 2018

**SG6-1**                                    APPLICABILITY

[For the standard text on applicability see **SG0-4**]

**SG6-2**    *Scope of the guideline*

1.  This guideline identifies the principles relevant to the sentencing of cases involving domestic abuse. Domestic abuse is a general term describing a range of violent and/or controlling or coercive behaviour.

2.  This guideline applies (but is not limited) to cases which fall within the statutory definition of domestic abuse as defined by Part 1 of the Domestic Abuse Act 2021. In summary domestic abuse is defined for the purposes of that Act as:

    Behaviour (whether a single act or a course of conduct) consisting of one or more of:
    - physical or sexual abuse;
    - violent or threatening behaviour;
    - controlling or coercive behaviour;
    - economic abuse (any behaviour that has a substantial adverse effect on the victim's ability to acquire, use or maintain money or other property, or obtain goods or services);
    - psychological, emotional or other abuse

    between those aged 16 or over:
    - who are, or have been married to or civil partners of each other;
    - who have agreed to marry or enter into a civil partnership agreement one another (whether or not the agreement has been terminated);
    - who are, or have been, in an intimate personal relationship with each other;
    - who each have, or have had, a parental relationship in relation to the same child; or
    - who are relatives.

    This definition applies whether the behaviour is directed to the victim or directed at another person (for example, the victim's child). A victim of domestic abuse can include a child who sees or hears, or experiences the effects of, the abuse, and is related to the primary victim or offender.

3.  For the purposes of this guideline domestic abuse also includes so-called 'honour' based abuse, female genital mutilation (FGM) and forced marriage.

4.  The principles in this guideline will also apply to persons living in the same household whose relationship, though not precisely within the categories described in para 2 above, involves a similar expectation of mutual trust and security.

5.  Controlling behaviour is a range of acts designed to make a person subordinate and/or dependent by isolating them from sources of support, exploiting their resources and capabilities for personal gain, depriving them of the means needed for independence, resistance and escape and/or regulating their everyday behaviour.

6.  Coercive behaviour is an act or pattern of acts of assault, threats, humiliation (whether public or private) and intimidation or other abuse that is used to harm, punish, or frighten the victim. Abuse may take place through person to person contact, or through other methods, including but not limited to, telephone calls, text, email, social networking sites or use of GPS tracking devices.

7.  Care should be taken to avoid stereotypical assumptions regarding domestic abuse. Irrespective of gender, domestic abuse occurs amongst people of all ethnicities, sexualities, ages, disabilities, religion or beliefs, immigration status or socio-economic backgrounds. Domestic abuse can occur between family members as well as between intimate partners.

8.  Many different criminal offences can involve domestic abuse and, where they do, the court should ensure that the sentence reflects that an offence has been committed within this context.

**SG6-3**    *Assessing seriousness*

7.  The domestic context of the offending behaviour makes the offending more serious because it represents a violation of the trust and security that normally exists between people in an intimate or family relationship. Additionally, there may be a continuing threat to the victim's safety, and in the worst cases a threat to their life or the lives of others around them.

8.  Domestic abuse offences are regarded as particularly serious within the criminal justice system. Domestic abuse is likely to become increasingly frequent and more serious the longer it continues, and may result in death. Domestic abuse can inflict lasting trauma on victims and their extended families,

especially children and young people who either witness the abuse or are aware of it having occurred. Domestic abuse is rarely a one-off incident and it is the cumulative and interlinked physical, psychological, sexual, emotional or financial abuse that has a particularly damaging effect on the victims and those around them.

9. Cases in which the victim has withdrawn from the prosecution do not indicate a lack of seriousness and no inference should be made regarding the lack of involvement of the victim in a case.

### Aggravating and mitigating factors

SG6-4

The following list of non-exhaustive aggravating and mitigating factors are of **particular relevance to offences committed in a domestic context**, and should be considered alongside offence specific factors.

#### Aggravating Factors

- Abuse of trust and abuse of power
- Victim is particularly vulnerable (*all victims of domestic abuse are potentially vulnerable due to the nature of the abuse, but some victims of domestic abuse may be more vulnerable than others, and not all vulnerabilities are immediately apparent*)
- Steps taken to prevent the victim reporting an incident
- Steps taken to prevent the victim obtaining assistance
- Victim forced to leave home, or steps have to be taken to exclude the offender from the home to ensure the victim's safety
- Impact on children (children can be adversely impacted by both direct and indirect exposure to domestic abuse)
- Using contact arrangements with a child to instigate an offence
- A proven history of violence or threats by the offender in a domestic context
- A history of disobedience to court orders (*such as, but not limited to, Domestic Violence Protection Orders, non-molestation orders, restraining orders*)

#### Mitigating Factors

- Positive good character – *as a general principle of sentencing, a court will take account of an offender's positive good character. However, it is recognised that one of the factors that can allow domestic abuse to continue unnoticed for lengthy periods is the ability of the perpetrator to have a public and a private face. In respect of offences committed within a domestic context, an offender's good character in relation to conduct outside these offences should generally be of no relevance where there is a proven pattern of behaviour*
- Evidence of genuine recognition of the need for change, and evidence of obtaining help or treatment to effect that change

### Other factors influencing sentence

SG6-5

The following points of principle should be considered by a court when imposing sentence for any offences committed in a domestic context:

10. A sentence imposed for an offence committed within a domestic context should be determined by the seriousness of the offence, not by **any** expressed wishes of the victim. There are a number of reasons why it may be particularly important that this principle is observed within this context:
    - The court is sentencing on behalf of the wider public
    - No victim is responsible for the sentence imposed
    - There is a risk that a plea for mercy made by a victim will be induced by threats made by, or by a fear of, the offender
    - The risk of such threats will be increased if it is generally believed that the severity of the sentence may be affected by the wishes of the victim.

11. Provocation is no mitigation to an offence within a domestic context, except in rare circumstances.

12. The offender or the victim may ask the court to consider the interests of any children by imposing a less severe sentence. The court should consider not only the effect on the children if the relationship is disrupted but also the likely effect of any further incidents of domestic abuse. The court should take great care with such requests, as the sentence should primarily be determined by the seriousness of the offence.

13. Offences involving serious violence, or where the emotional/psychological harm caused is severe, will warrant a custodial sentence in the majority of cases.

14. Some offences will be specified offences for the purposes of the dangerous offender provisions.[61] In such circumstances, consideration will need to be given to whether there is significant risk of serious harm to members of the public by the commission of further specified offences. The 'public' includes family members and if this test is met, the court will be required to impose a life sentence, or an extended sentence in appropriate cases.

---

[61] Criminal Justice Act 2003 (as amended) sections 224, 229

15. Passing the custody threshold does not mean that a custodial sentence should be deemed inevitable. Where the custody threshold is only just crossed, the court will wish to consider whether the better option is instead to impose a community order, including a requirement to attend an accredited domestic abuse programme or domestic abuse specific intervention. Such an option will normally only be appropriate where the court is satisfied that the offender genuinely intends to reform his or her behaviour and that there is a real prospect of rehabilitation being successful.

16. The court should also consider whether it is appropriate to make a restraining order, and if doing so, should ensure that it has all relevant up to date information. The court may also wish to consider making other orders, such as a European protection order, sexual harm prevention order, criminal behaviour order (this is not an exhaustive list). Further details for restraining orders are set out below.

**SG6-6**    *Restraining order*

17. Where an offender is convicted of any offence, the court may make a restraining order (Sentencing Code, sections 359 and 360).

18. Orders can be made on the initiative of the court; the views of the victim should be sought, but their consent is not required.

19. The order may prohibit the offender from doing anything for the purpose of protecting the victim of the offence, or any other person mentioned in the order, from further conduct which amounts to harassment or will cause a fear of violence.

20. If the parties are to continue or resume a relationship, courts may consider a prohibition within the restraining order not to molest the victim (as opposed to a prohibition on contacting the victim).

21. The order may have effect for a specified period or until further order.

22. A court before which a person is acquitted of an offence may make a restraining order if the court considers that it is necessary to protect a person from harassment by the defendant (Protection from Harassment Act 1997, section 5A).

**SG6-7**    *Victim personal statements*

23. The absence of a Victim Personal Statement (VPS) should not be taken to indicate the absence of harm. A court should consider, where available, a VPS which will help it assess the immediate and possible long-term effects of the offence on the victim (and any children, where relevant) as well as the harm caused, whether physical or psychological.

# PART 7   SENTENCING OFFENDERS WITH MENTAL DISORDERS, DEVELOPMENTAL DISORDERS, OR NEUROLOGICAL IMPAIRMENTS

**Effective from:** 01 October 2020

APPLICABILITY                                                         **SG7-1**

[For the standard text on applicability see **SG0-4**]

SECTION ONE: GENERAL APPROACH                                        **SG7-2**

1. This guideline applies when sentencing offenders who at the time of the offence and/or at the time of sentencing have any mental disorder, neurological impairment or developmental disorder, such as those listed within **Annex A**.
2. The fact that an offender has an impairment or disorder[62] should always be considered by the court but will not necessarily have an impact on sentencing.
3. There are a wide range of mental disorders, neurological impairments and developmental disorders and the level of any impairment will vary between individuals. Accordingly, in assessing whether the impairment or disorder has any impact on sentencing, the approach to sentencing should be individualistic and focused on the issues in the case.
4. Sentencers should note the following:
   - some mental disorders can fluctuate and an offender's state during proceedings may not be representative of their condition at the time the offence was committed,
   - care should be taken to avoid making assumptions. Many mental disorders, neurological impairments or developmental disorders are not easily recognisable,
   - no adverse inference should necessarily be drawn if an offender had not previously either been formally diagnosed or willing to disclose an impairment or disorder,
   - offenders may be unaware or unwilling to accept they have an impairment or disorder and may fear stigmatisation if they disclose it,
   - it is not uncommon for people to have a number of different impairments and disorders. This is known as 'co-morbidity',
   - drug and/or alcohol dependence can be a factor, and may mask an underlying disorder,
   - difficulties of definition and classification in this field are common. There may be differences of expert opinion and diagnosis in relation to the offender or it may be that no specific disorder can be identified,
   - a formal diagnosis is not always required, and
   - where a formal diagnosis is required, a report by a suitably qualified expert will be necessary.
5. It is important that courts are aware of relevant cultural, ethnicity and gender considerations of offenders within a mental health context. This is because a range of evidence suggests that people from BAME communities may be more likely to experience stigma attached to being labelled as having a mental health concern, may be more likely to have experienced difficulty in accessing mental health services and in acknowledging a disorder and seeking help, may be more likely to enter the mental health services via the courts or the police rather than primary care and are more likely to be treated under a section of the MHA. In addition, female offenders are more likely to have underlying mental health needs and the impact therefore on females from BAME communities in particular is likely to be higher, given the intersection between gender and race. Moreover, refugees and asylum seekers may be more likely to experience mental health problems than the general population. Further information can be found at Chapters six and eight of the *Equal Treatment Bench Book*.
6. In any case where the offender is or appears to be suffering from a mental disorder at the date of sentencing, the court must obtain and consider a medical report before passing a custodial sentence other than one fixed by law, unless, in the circumstances of the case, the court considers that it is unnecessary (s.232 Sentencing Code). A report may be unnecessary if existing, reliable and up to date information is available. If considering making a hospital or interim order, the court can request information about a patient from the local health services (s.39 of the MHA). Further information about s.232 and requests for reports can be found at **Annex B** of this document.
7. Where a custodial sentence is passed the court should forward psychiatric, psychological, or other medical reports to the prison along with any other information relevant to the offender's physical and

---

[62] For ease, the guideline does not necessarily list all impairments and disorders each time in the guidance, but refers to 'impairments or disorders', but this should be taken to include all relevant impairments and disorders including those listed in Annex A.

     mental health, in accordance with rule 28.9 of the Criminal Procedure Rules. This will ensure that the prison has appropriate information about the offender's condition and can ensure their welfare.

8.   Courts should always be alive to the impact of an impairment or disorder on an offender's ability to understand and participate in proceedings. Courts should ensure that offenders understand their sentence and what will happen if they reoffend and/ or breach the terms of their licence or supervision. Courts should also ensure that any ancillary orders, such as restraining orders, are capable of being understood and fulfilled by the offender. Courts should therefore put the key points in a clear and straightforward way. Clarity of explanation is also important for victims in order that they too can understand the sentence. Further information can be found at Chapter four of the *Equal Treatment Bench Book*.

**SG7-3**                       Section two: Assessing culpability

9.   Culpability may be reduced if an offender was at the time of the offence suffering from an impairment or disorder (or combination of impairments or disorders) such as those listed in **Annex A.**

10.   The sentencer should make an initial assessment of culpability in accordance with any relevant offence-specific guideline, and should then consider whether culpability was reduced by reason of the impairment or disorder.

11.   Culpability will only be reduced if there is sufficient connection between the offender's impairment or disorder and the offending behaviour.

12.   In some cases, the impairment or disorder may mean that culpability is significantly reduced. In other cases, the impairment or disorder may have no relevance to culpability. A careful analysis of all the circumstances of the case and all relevant materials is therefore required.

13.   The sentencer, who will be in possession of all relevant information, is in the best position to make the assessment of culpability. Where relevant expert evidence is put forward, it must always be considered and will often be very valuable. However, it is the duty of the sentencer to make their own decision, and the court is not bound to follow expert opinion if there are compelling reasons to set it aside.

14.   The sentencer must state clearly their assessment of whether the offender's culpability was reduced and, if it was, the reasons for and extent of that reduction. The sentencer must also state, where appropriate, their reasons for not following an expert opinion.

15.   Courts may find the following questions a useful starting point. They are not exhaustive, and they are not a check list as the range of offenders, impairments and disorders is wide.
   - **At the time of the offence did the offender's impairment or disorder impair their ability:**
     - o   to exercise appropriate judgement,
     - o   to make rational choices,
     - o   to understand the nature and consequences of their actions?
   - At the time of the offence, did the offender's impairment or disorder cause them to behave in a disinhibited way?
   - Are there other factors related to the offender's impairment or disorder which reduce culpability?
   - **Medication.** Where an offender was failing to take medication prescribed to them at the time of the offence, the court will need to consider the extent to which that failure was wilful or arose as a result of the offender's lack of insight into their impairment or disorder,
   - **"Self-medication".** Where an offender made their impairment or disorder worse by "self-medicating" with alcohol or non-prescribed or illicit drugs at the time of the offence, the court will need to consider the extent to which the offender was aware that would be the effect,
   - **Insight.** Courts need to be cautious before concluding that just because an offender has some insight into their impairment or disorder and/or insight into the importance of taking their medication, that insight automatically increases the culpability for the offence. Any insight, and its effect on culpability, is a matter of degree for the court to assess.

**SG7-4**                      Section three: Determining the sentence

16. **General principles.**
   - Impairments or disorders experienced by the offender are factors which sentencers are required to consider at Step 1 (where the impairment or disorder is linked to the offence) or at Step 2 (where it is not linked to the offence) when considering the stepped approach set out in offence-specific guidelines,
   - Impairments or disorders may be relevant to the decision about the type of sentence imposed, in particular a disposal under powers contained in the MHA,

- Impairments or disorders may be relevant to an assessment of whether the offender is dangerous as that term is defined for sentencing purposes in Chapter 6 of Part 10 of the Sentencing Code.

17. **Fines/discharge.** Many offences committed by an offender with an impairment or disorder may not require any therapeutic intervention or the offence may be so minor that the appropriate disposal is a fine or discharge.

18. **Community orders.** When passing a community order (only available if the offence is imprisonable), it will be important to ensure that the conditions of any order are bespoke to the offender, taking account of any practical barriers to compliance that their condition or disorder may create. Community orders can fulfil all the purposes of sentencing and consideration should be given to all of the options for community orders, including Mental Health Treatment Requirements (MHTR), Rehabilitation Requirement (RAR), Alcohol Treatment Requirement (ATR), and Drug Rehabilitation Requirement (DRR) in light of what is available locally. A MHTR with either an ATR and or a DRR can be made for offenders with dual diagnosis. A RAR can offer targeted work with the individual and may be more appropriate than a MHTR.

19. MHTRs provide a useful option for offenders who would not otherwise qualify for treatment under the MHA. For offenders with mental health issues, such orders may result in reductions in offending compared with short custodial sentences. Where the offender's culpability is reduced by their mental state and/or the public interest is served by ensuring they receive appropriate treatment, a MHTR may be more appropriate than custody. Even where the custody threshold is crossed, a community order with a MHTR may be a proper alternative to a short or moderate custodial sentence. A community order with a MHTR may be appropriate where the offence is not serious enough to cross the custody threshold. A MHTR is not suitable for an offender who is unlikely to comply with the treatment, for example if they have a chaotic lifestyle. See the Imposition of Community and Custodial Sentences definitive guideline.

20. **Drug and alcohol treatment orders.** Where the offender is dependent on or has a propensity to misuse drugs or alcohol and there is sufficient prospect of success, a community order with a DRR or an ATR may be a proper alternative to a short or moderate custodial sentence. Courts should be mindful that where an offender has failed to comply with a DRR or ATR in the past, that does not necessarily mean that they will fail now. Courts will need a thorough assessment about the offender's current motivation and ability to tackle their addiction in a pre-sentence report or addendum report provided by the alcohol or drug treatment order provider.

21. With all community orders, at least one requirement must be imposed for the purpose of punishment and/or a fine in addition to the community order – unless there are exceptional circumstances relating to the offence or the offender that would make it unjust in all the circumstances to do so. It is a matter for the court to decide which requirements amount to punishment in each case.

22. **Custodial sentences.** Where an offender is on the cusp of custody or detention, the court may consider that the impairment or disorder may make a custodial sentence disproportionate to achieving the aims of sentencing and that the public are better protected and crime reduced by a rehabilitative approach. Where custody or detention is unavoidable, consideration of the impact on the offender of the impairment or disorder may be relevant to the length of sentence and to the issue of whether any sentence may be suspended. This is because an offender's impairment or disorder may mean that a custodial sentence weighs more heavily on them and/or because custody can exacerbate the effects of impairments or disorders. In accordance with the principles applicable in cases of physical ill-health, impairments or disorders can only be taken into account in a limited way so far as the impact of custody is concerned. Nonetheless, the court must have regard both to any additional impact of a custodial sentence on the offender because of an impairment or disorder, and to any personal mitigation to which their impairment or disorder is relevant.

23. **Mental health disposals. Further detailed information about disposals specific to mental health can be found at Annex C.** Decisions as to the various mental health sentences are always fact specific and in some cases no mental health disposal may be appropriate. The court will need to weigh up a number of factors, which may include, but are not limited to:
- The nature of the offence for which the offender is being sentenced,
- The offender's antecedents,
- The offender's behaviour when unwell,
- The offender's insight into their condition,
- The offender's level of compliance with any previous treatment and medication,
- The speed at which risk factors may escalate,
- The need to protect the public. In deciding on a sentence, courts should also carefully consider the criteria for and regime on release. It should not be assumed that one order is better than another, or that one order offers greater protection to the public than another. Careful analysis of all the facts is required in each case, including what is practically available, before deciding on the

appropriate disposal. The graver the offence, and the greater the risk to the public on release of the offender, the greater the emphasis the court must place upon the protection of the public and the release regime,

- Other protective factors that are available.

24. **S.37- Hospital order and guardianship orders.**
   a. A hospital order provides for the offender to be detained in hospital for treatment. A guardianship order places the offender under the guardianship of the local social services authority or a person approved by the authority, usually in the community,
   b. If the offender has been convicted in the Crown Court, and is aged 21 or over, before making a hospital order, (with or without a restriction order) the court must consider if it would be more appropriate to pass a sentence of imprisonment with a hospital and limitation direction under s.45A. If a hospital order is made, the court must give reasons as to why the sentence has no penal element,
   c. The criteria for making such orders and the release regimes are set out in **Annex C.**

25. **S.41-Restriction order.**
   a. Where a hospital order is made, the Crown Court may make a restriction order if it appears to the court that it is necessary to do so for the protection of the public from serious harm, having regard to the nature of the offence, the antecedents of the offender and the risk of their committing further offences if set at large,
   b. In summary, a restriction order lasts indefinitely and means that only the Secretary of State (SoS) (and in certain circumstances the tribunal) can permit the offender to leave, transfer to another hospital, and be discharged from hospital,
   c. The criteria for making such orders and their effect are set out in **Annex C.**

26. **S.45A- Imprisonment with hospital direction and limitation direction.**
   a. These orders are only available where an offender aged 21 or over has been convicted of an offence before the Crown Court,
   b. These orders are sometimes referred to as 'hybrid orders'. If the criteria are met for a hospital order, with or without a s.41 restriction order, the court must consider if it would be more appropriate to pass a sentence of imprisonment with a direction that the offender is detained in hospital rather than prison. This is a hospital direction. This must be accompanied with a limitation direction which means that the offender is subject to the special restrictions of a s.41 order. This is known as a limitation direction,
   c. The court will need to consider the different release regimes under s.37/s.41 order and a s.45A order. The court's conclusion as to which regime will better protect the public will depend on a careful assessment of the facts in an individual case,
   d. The criteria for making such directions and the release regimes are set out in **Annex C.**

27. **Secretary of State transfer powers.**
   If a sentenced prisoner becomes mentally unwell, prisons can ask the SoS to give permission to transfer the prisoner to hospital, s.47 MHA. The SoS can add a restriction direction to this transfer, s.49 MHA, which has the same effect as a restriction under s.41 MHA.

28. **Treatment outside of the NHS**
   In all cases where the court is considering a mental health disposal, the court must be satisfied that treatment is available and will continue to be available and funded for the duration of the order. If the treatment proposed is not within a NHS hospital, courts should take particular care to confirm the proposed hospital/treatment centre has the appropriate level of security and specialist staff able to address the offending behaviour in addition to treating the mental disorder. Courts should always be very cautious before passing a hospital order or mental health treatment order in any case in which the cost of the treatment would be met from non NHS funds. This may result in wholly inadequate safeguarding processes. It should also be noted that probation will not monitor privately funded mental health treatment requirements.

**This information provided in Annex A below is correct as of the date of the guideline coming into force on 01/10/2020. It does not form part of the guideline.**

SG7-5      Annex A – main classes of mental disorders and presenting features

(This information is only intended as general assistance to sentencers in understanding common impairments and mental disorders.)

Mental disorder is a catch-all term for illnesses and developmental disorders. Mental disorder is a collection of symptoms (the person's experiences) and signs (features that may be observed by an outside observer). For categorisation as a disorder, these problems should be associated with distress and/or interference with personal functions.

Sentencers may see references to DSM/ICD[63] classification systems in reports. This section is not concerned with classifications systems which aim to provide lists of recognised mental disorders and their symptoms.

Broadly the concept of *illness* is used for disorders which start after a sustained period – often a lifetime – of health or average/normal psychological function e.g. schizophrenia, depression.

*Developmental disorders* are conditions which may be apparent at birth, but always have early enough onset that the individual never quite fitted within the average behavioural range. Behaviour has three main components – thinking (cognitions), feeling (emotions, affect) and actions. Autism, generalised or specific intellectual (learning) disabilities, and personality disorders are examples.

*Other disorders* which may be relevant in court lie at the interface between psychiatry and neurology. Epilepsy in its various forms is an example, Acquired Brain Injury (ABI) is another example. ABI is an injury caused to the brain since birth, most often as a result of trauma, tumour, stroke, illness or infection.

**Brief descriptions of some of the more common disorders likely to be relevant in court**

*Psychotic illnesses*

These affect cognitions, emotional capacities and actions.

There are two main groups – those which are associated with more generalised illness or bodily problems, often called 'delirium', and those which are not – often referred to as 'primary psychosis', which include schizophrenia and bipolar disorders.

*Delirium* is likely to present with some impairment in consciousness. It may occur as an acute phase of a dementing process, but also with serious infections or generalised problems with bodily functions, such as hormonal disturbances. Delirium may also occur in the context of drug (including alcohol) taking or withdrawal from such substances.

People may misinterpret sensory input in any of its main forms (sight, hearing, smell, taste, touch), thus having 'illusions'; their sensory experiences may be so disturbed that they see or hear or smell or taste or feel things which are not there at all to the external observer (hallucinations). Their thinking may be disturbed in its own right, or following from these perceptual problems, such that they have pathological beliefs (delusions).

Delirium is likely to resolve as the underlying condition is treated.

*Schizophrenia and bipolar disorders* are disorders in which consciousness is unimpaired, but sensory (illusions, hallucinations) and cognitive (delusions, formal thought disorder) disturbances occur.

In *schizophrenia*, serious disturbances of emotion also occur in which the person either cannot experience or express emotions accurately, or both, and may be unaware of the difficulty. Terms like – 'incongruous affect', when the emotional experience or expression is the opposite from what a healthy observer might expect for the situation, or 'flattened affect', when the person seems to have little or no emotion at all, are quite common. Tests for empathy may show that this is reduced.

People may also present with 'formal thought disorder' – when the form of thought, and thus speech is hard to follow and may include nonsensical, made-up words. Hallucinations most commonly take the form of 'third person hallucinations' when the person hears others talking about them, but when no-one is doing so.

Delusions are beliefs which, in full form, are wholly impervious to reason, generally, but not always based on a false premise. Persecutory/paranoid delusions are probably the most common. Passivity delusions – when the individual 'knows' that his/her thoughts, feelings or actions are controlled by another person or an external system – may be particularly associated with violence. If hypochondriacal delusions occur, they tend to be bizarre and may be dangerous – for example a belief in a machine causing all the problems implanted in his/her eye. Many aspects of schizophrenia are treatable, but 'cure' is unlikely and deterioration over years quite common. Nevertheless, people with the condition can attain a good quality of life and safety if a full range of relevant treatments can be sustained.

*Delusional disorder* is sometimes diagnosed when the only abnormality appears to be the presence of a single delusion and can be easily missed. Apart from the impact of the *delusion* or its ramifications, functioning is not markedly impaired, and behaviour is not obviously bizarre or odd.

*Bipolar illness* – also referred to by the older, now less used term 'manic depression' – is characterised by repeated episodes of depression (low mood and low activity levels) and (hypo)mania (high mood and high

---

Sentencing Guidelines

activity levels). Psychotic symptoms are not invariably present at either extreme, but depressive psychotic symptoms include hypochondriacal delusions of a kind that the person believes his/her body is rotting away, or delusions of catastrophe; suicidal ideas are common and the rare situation of family killings with suicide of the perpetrator may occur in such states. In a manic phase, the individual may have grandiose or omnipotent delusions, accompanied by reckless and/or disinhibited acts.

*Unipolar affective illnesses* – people may have recurrent depressions or recurrent manic episodes, but not both.

*Schizoaffective illness* looks like a hybrid of schizophrenia and bipolar disorder; it may not be a distinct disorder.

### Non-psychotic illnesses

These include depression (seriously low mood and perhaps suicide related behaviours, but without delusions) and anxiety disorders. The latter include a range of conditions; the more common include phobic disorders (people recognise that their fear is not well founded in fact, but experience fear anyway which may interfere with their everyday life), obsessive compulsive disorders (again, the fear recognised for what it is, but still thoughts and fears intrude and maybe rituals must be performed), panic attacks and post-traumatic stress disorders [PTSD].

**PTSD** can only be diagnosed if it follows a seriously traumatic event which happened directly to the person, which the person witnessed it as it happened to others and/or had to deal with the aftermath (emergency service workers may be as vulnerable as the general population), or which the person learned about soon afterwards but it affected someone very close to him/her. Generally, the scale of the event is taken to be life-threatening or life-changing and/or that the person affected unquestionably thought it so. Guidance is that the condition must emerge within six months of this – it may not be immediately apparent. It is important to have evidence that the condition did follow the event. Most people will get some of the symptoms or signs in such circumstances; guidance is that these may be collectively regarded as a disorder if they persist to a degree that they are disruptive to the individual's usual lifestyle for over a month. There are people who have experienced multiple traumas and the presenting features may therefore represent a worsening/exacerbation of PTSD which started after a previous event rather than a completely new presentation.

As well as mental and physiological symptoms and signs (like racing heartbeat, tight chest, uncomfortable sensations in the gut), and of anxiety, and often some depressive features, typical features are:

- extremely distressing intrusions of memories or experiences of the event which disrupt waking life (flashback memories) and/or sleep (nightmares), dissociative reactions (if the surroundings are perceived as unreal this is called 'derealisation'. If the person him-or herself feels detached, outside him/herself and/or more as an observer of self than a real person this is called 'depersonalisation'), when the individual is not very aware of his/her real surroundings but living again in the trauma; sometimes specific real experiences may trigger this (for example if an assailant had been wearing a particular perfume/aftershave chance contact with a perfectly harmless person who happens to use the same may trigger a flashback and reaction more appropriate to the traumatic experience than the reality,
- persistent, active avoidance of any reminders of the trauma – including unwillingness to talk about it, inability to read documents relating to it,
- persistent negative feelings about self and others; many have no concept of a future,
- alterations in arousal – so, irritability, reckless behaviour, being over-watchful, problems with concentrating, exaggerated 'startle responses' to actually non-threatening events, various difficulties with sleep.

### Substance use disorders

Substance use disorders arise when the individual no longer has significant personal control over intake and/or s/he has signs and symptoms of secondary disease. Substances of abuse affect the nervous system, often altering its activity so that the experience of the consumer is that when they do not have the substance they have very unpleasant symptoms or signs ranging from intense anxiety through to psychotic symptoms (withdrawal symptoms/signs), and so they have to keep taking the substance in order to feel almost normal. Secondary disease may affect any part of the body, although most commonly those areas that process the substances – like the gut or the liver – and the brain.

### Developmental disorders

*Intellectual disability [ID] (learning disability)* – names for these conditions keep changing over time in a constant effort to reduce stigma. Problems may be generalised (probably most relevant in court) or specific – for example relating to a particular language function. As the labels suggest, the core problem is cognitive – those affected may have a lower than average ability to learn at all and to acquire language. Inevitably, this is an over-simplification as there are often problems with emotions and actions too, and it is hard to distinguish the extent to which these are part of the primary condition and the extent to which they follow from difficulties in learning. A tested 'intelligence quotient' (IQ) is often used to indicate severity – mild, moderate, severe. Average intelligence is taken as 80–120. A person with severe generalised intellectual disability mental will have a tested IQ under 35, and cannot live independently. In varying degrees those with moderate (IQ 35–49), mild (IQ 50–69) or borderline ID (IQ 70–80) can live independently, but are particularly vulnerable if they enter the criminal justice system.

*Autism and autistic spectrum disorder* (the latter sometimes referred to as Asperger's syndrome, but this term is now discouraged) are pervasive developmental disorders generally affecting people throughout life. It is estimated that about 1% of people in the UK are affected. Intelligence may be impaired as well, but is often not.

Given that these are spectrum conditions, although people diagnosed as being autistic or as being on the autistic spectrum may share certain characteristics, everyone will be different and it is important to note that there is considerable variation in how people are affected. Simply being 'on the spectrum' is not necessarily a disorder at all. As the opening comments to this Annex notes, to qualify as a disorder the state or condition has to interfere in some way in the capacities of the person with it; this may be with their mood and wellbeing and/or it may be with their ability to function in society and/or as they would wish. This statement could be applied to almost any disorder, but it is particularly pertinent to developmental conditions.

Many people with autism or on the autistic spectrum show highly developed logical thinking and show strengths in problem solving. Some have extraordinary but atypical abilities, for example of memory. Terms like 'high functioning' and 'low functioning' autism have been used but are unhelpful. It is better to document and recognise the mix of abilities and difficulties in each individual. As understanding of some of the more specific underlying mechanisms in their development grows, identification of such disorders is increasingly being made for the first time in adulthood.

There may also be possible problems with language, which may include interpreting words or phrases very literally and having difficulty with vague or ambiguous questions or instructions or 'unwritten rules'. Other features may include difficulty in dealing with unexpected or sudden change, hypothetical thinking and making a decision about something which has not yet happened or intuitive thinking, which may rely in part on identifying emotional cues. Some people may be hypersensitive to stimuli including light, noise, temperature or touch.

The use of 'Autism' as a term has varied over time. The American DSM-5 no longer uses the term autism at all. It is still used in the UK and is generally used by psychiatrists to indicate the most pervasive and extreme incapacity to understand or empathise with others, to show any emotional reciprocity and to develop or maintain relationships. Generally, in such cases, the individual seeks 'sameness' and may be inflexible in routines or repeated, simple actions. If these are interrupted, extreme anxiety and/or aggression may follow. However, as stated earlier, there is considerable variation in how people are affected. In less formal usage, the term 'autism' may be used to cover a broader range of behaviours exhibited by less intrusive or pronounced character traits. This paragraph therefore notes some of the behaviours that can be seen within the autistic spectrum, it is not to say that everyone with autism will display these behaviours.

'Autism'/autistic behaviours were once seen as one of the core sets of features of schizophrenia and may still be referred to in this context. The underlying neurological/brain difficulties may well be similar in some respects, but these are distinct conditions. Most people with autism/autistic spectrum disorders do not become psychotic.

*Attentional deficit hyperactivity disorder [ADHD]* is similarly apparent from a very early age, although may not be completely recognised until the individual starts school. It is not uncommonly associated with other developmental disorders, but also occurs alone, when it is characterised by profound difficulties in concentrating in ordinary social situations or on tasks (many can focus on computer based activities) and very high levels of physical activity. Children are seen as 'disruptive' and can easily be made worse under conventional behavioural control efforts. As with all developmental disorders, it may persist into adult life.

*Conduct disorders*, if unresolved, are the childhood precursors of personality disorders. Emphasis is on repeated patterns of extreme dissocial, aggressive or defiant behaviours, persistent through childhood, which cannot be completely explained by one of the other developmental disorders.

*Personality disorders.* The personality is not considered to be fully formed until adulthood, so, by definition these are conditions which can affect only adults. Although adulthood is often taken as 18 years old, there isn't a set time threshold when the brain and physiology is one day that of a child and the next of an adult. For a diagnosis of personality disorder, there must be evidence of continuity with problems such as conduct disorder throughout childhood and adolescence. Similar conditions may arise in adulthood after, say, brain injury or disease, but this would be *personality change*.

Specific personality disorder labels are generally descriptive, following from their most prominent characteristics. Treatment needs mean that is probably most helpful to think of the personality disorder clusters rather than specific disorders – thus:

Cluster A – the paranoid, eccentric, schizoid

Cluster B – the emotionally unstable, histrionic, narcissistic, antisocial

Cluster C – the anxious, avoidant, obsessional (anankastic), dependent

'Psychopathic disorder' is not a recognised diagnosis; its use should be avoided as pejorative and unscientific. 'Psychopathy' is similarly not a diagnosis, but rather a term that has been introduced to indicate whether a person had crossed a threshold on one of a number of possible psychopathy scales. Generally, these scales measure two things – the extent to which antisocial behaviours are widespread and have been repeated through the life course, and the extent to which the individual has capacity for empathy.

Both these elements have, correctly, been used as indicators of risks or repetition of unwanted behaviours. It is obvious that established behaviour patterns are likely to continue unless deliberately disrupted; on the other hand, it is always easier to tell if progress has been made when a previously repeated behaviour ceases over a substantial period of time under a range of circumstances.

If empathy is severely impaired – for example the capacity to recognise distress in others and make appropriate use of that information – this may severely impair capacity to desist from harming others.

Risk of harm to self is very high among people with personality disorder.

### The dementias

Dementia follows from brain damage. Each aspect of behaviour may be affected. The most obvious is the cluster of cognitive problems, with forgetfulness, difficulties in following a train of thought and making judgements prominent. There are commonly also directly related emotional problems, as the brain can no longer control emotions, and also secondary emotional problems when the person retains insight and is aware of progressively losing his or her mental abilities. Capacity for control of actions may also be impaired, resulting in what is often referred to as 'disinhibited behaviour'.

Evidence for dementia will come in several forms – the clinical examination, which should include asking the affected person about his/her experiences and for a history of the development of the condition; for obvious reasons it is more than usually important to get a history from relatives and friends too. People with dementia may retain the capacity to give a long and fascinating account of their problems which has little basis in reality (referred to as confabulation).

Simple tests of memory and other cognitive functions may be enough for basic diagnosis and to help the court, but it is generally best to map cognitive functions with detailed psychological testing, and there may be some very specific deficits which are relevant in court – for example difficulties in recognising people or experience of perceptual distortions. Brain imaging techniques may have particular value in verifying the nature and extent of the brain damage underpinning the problems.

The dementias are progressive. People may be helped to manage their difficulties, sometimes the progress may be slowed, and sometimes worsening of some aspects of the condition may render other aspects less problematic or risky, but these are not conditions from which people recover.

The most common dementias are a function of unhealthy aging. There has been an increase in offending among older people, so these are conditions increasingly likely to be seen in the courts. A few of the dementias, usually those with early onset, have a clear genetic cause; there is evidence that there is a genetic contribution to most.

**Alzheimer's disease/dementia** is among the commonest given a name. The pattern of destruction of brain tissue is more-or-less specific to this dementia, and there is a genetic component to it. Where the genetic component is strong, onset may be at a younger age (50, occasionally younger) but more typically onset is around 65–70. The characteristics are more-or-less as described above. Variations in presentation often indicate which parts of the brain are most affected at any particular time, but this is a generalised condition.

One of the more difficult dementias to recognise in relation to offending is fronto-temporal dementia (referring to the lobes of the brain most affected). Compared with other dementias, memory is spared for longer, but behavioural problems may be prominent. It is also less common than Alzheimer's or dementia of old age, and more often missed. It should be considered if a well socialised person becomes aggressive or antisocial for the first time in later adulthood (onset generally 45–65).

Dementias may also, however, follow from brain damage from external causes, for example a serious head injury, in relation to other disorders affecting the whole body, like diabetes, or from having taken noxious substances – especially excessive alcohol, but a range of other drugs too.

### Acquired brain injury (ABI)

ABI is an injury to the brain which has occurred since birth. Causes include: tumour, stroke, haemorrhage, encephalitis, carbon monoxide poisoning, hypoxic injury or trauma. Principal causes of trauma resulting in ABI are falls, road traffic collisions, workplace injuries, violent assault and sporting injuries. Even after a minor head injury, brain function can be impaired temporarily (concussion). Effects include headaches, dizziness, fatigue, depression, irritability and memory problems, lasting for weeks, months or even years.

Survivors of more severe brain injury are likely to have long term problems affecting their personality, relationships and ability to live independently. Issues can be compounded as the effects of ABI are often hidden and may fluctuate. The cognitive, psychological, emotional and behavioural effects of brain injury can be difficult to detect by those without specialist training.

### Multi-morbidity and comorbidity (dual diagnosis)

These terms are often used interchangeably to mean that the individual has more than one disorder although, strictly, comorbidity means that the conditions arose simultaneously. This is a very common situation among people who have a disorder of mental health. It is generally very hard to disentangle which disorder came first or whether they arose simultaneously. Psychiatrists and other clinicians still sometimes use the term 'dual diagnosis'. The term 'dual diagnosis' was invented to describe people who had a psychosis and a substance use disorder, but sometimes people use it for other pairs of disorders (e.g. psychosis and personality disorder) and, in practice, it is quite usual for people who come to court and have more than one disorder to have several – so a psychotic illness *and* more than one substance use disorder *and* a personality disorder *and* sometimes also a learning disability.

Where focus is on psychosis and substance use disorder, it is not clear that it matters clinically, except insofar as the idea that a psychotic condition is 'drug induced' may, in the context of scarce service resources, be used to deny services. In addition to having several mental disorders – for example schizophrenia, personality disorder, cannabis use disorder and reactive depression – an individual is likely to be multiply disadvantaged socially – for example homeless or disconnected from family – and some clinicians will include these social disadvantages in the sum of comorbidities. They are certainly relevant to outcomes.

### Glossary of most commonly prescribed drugs[64]

#### Commonly used oral anti-psychotic medicines

- amisulpride
- aripiprazole
- chlorpromazine
- haloperidol
- olanzapine
- quetiapine
- risperidone
- clozapine

#### Commonly used anti-depressants

- citalopram
- dapoxetine
- escitalopram
- fluoxetine
- fluvoxamine
- paroxetine
- sertraline
- vortioxetine
- duloxetine
- venlafaxine
- mirtazapine

#### Commonly used medicines to treat bi-polar disorder

- lithium

---

[64] Note that some drugs can be prescribed for a number of different conditions, e.g paroxetine and sertraline can be used to treat both PTSD and depression

Sentencing Guidelines

*Commonly used medicines to treat ADHD*
- methylphenidate
- dexamphetamine
- lisdexamfetamine

*Commonly used medicines to treat PTSD*
- paroxetine
- sertraline

*Commonly used medicines to treat dementia*
- donepezil
- rivastigmine
- galantamine

*Commonly used medicines to treat addiction*
- naltrexone
- methadone

**SG7-6**                    ANNEX B – REPORTS

**This information provided below is correct as of the date of the guideline coming into force on 01/10/2020. It does not form part of the guideline.**

Courts should refer to the form '*Directions for Commissioning a Psychiatric or other medical report for sentencing purposes*', rule 28.8, regarding commissioning a medical report.

Courts may find it helpful to consider including a request for information (via ticking the 'any other matter' box on the form) on the following issues:

- how the condition relates to the offences committed,
- the level of impairment due to the condition at the time of the offence and currently,
- if there has been a failure of compliance (e.g. not attending appointments, failing to take prescribed medication) what is thought to be driving that behaviour,
- if a particular disposal is recommended, the expected length of time that might be required for treatment, and details of the regime on release/post release supervision,
- any communication difficulties and/or requirement for an intermediary.

Further information on requests for reports can be found within the Criminal Practice Directions (I General Matters 3P Commissioning Medical Reports [see **CPD.3P**] and VII Medical Reports for Sentencing Purposes R [see **CPD.VII.R**]).

When requested by clinicians wanting to undertake an inpatient assessment, for offences punishable with imprisonment, courts may wish to consider making an interim hospital order (s.38 MHA). Before making a s.38 order the court should ensure that the statutory requirements are satisfied.

Where appropriate, assessments can also be made in the community.

**Additional requirements in case of offender suffering from mental disorder (s.232 Sentencing Code)**

(1) This section applies where—
    (a) the offender is or appears to be suffering from a mental disorder, and
    (b) the court passes a custodial sentence other than one fixed by law ("the sentence").
(2) Before passing the sentence, the court must obtain and consider a medical report unless, in the circumstances of the case, it considers that it is unnecessary to obtain a medical report.
(3) Before passing the sentence, the court must consider—
    (a) (any information before it which relates to the offender's mental condition (whether given in a medical report, a pre-sentence report or otherwise), and
    (b) (the likely effect of such a sentence on that condition and on any treatment which may be available for it.
(4) If the court did not obtain a medical report where required to do so by this section, the sentence is not invalidated by the fact that it did not do so.
(5) Any court, on an appeal against the sentence, must—
    (a) obtain a medical report if none was obtained by the court below, and
    (b) consider any such report obtained by it or by that court.
(6) In this section—
    "medical report" means a report as to an offender's mental condition made or submitted orally or in writing by a registered medical practitioner who is approved for the purposes of section 12 of the Mental Health Act 1983—
    (a) by the Secretary of State, or

(b) by another person by virtue of section 12ZA or 12ZB of that Act, as having special experience in the diagnosis or treatment of mental disorder;

"mental disorder" has the same meaning as in the Mental Health Act 1983.

(7) Nothing in this section is to be taken to limit—

(a) the pre-sentence report requirements (see section 30), or

(b) any requirement for a court to take into account all information that is available to it about the circumstances of any offence, including any aggravating or mitigating factors.

Annex C – Sentencing disposals: criteria and release provisions                SG7-7

**This information provided below is correct as of the date of the guideline coming into force on 01/10/2020. It does not form part of the guideline.**

Sentencing Guidelines

| Mental Health Treatment Requirement (Schedule 9 part 9 Sentencing Code) (can only be imposed as part of a community order or suspended sentence order) | |
|---|---|
| **May be made by:** | A magistrates' court or the Crown Court |
| **In respect of an offender who is:** | Convicted of an offence punishable with imprisonment. |
| **If the court is satisfied** | That the mental condition of the offender is such as requires and may be susceptible to treatment but does not warrant detention under a hospital order.<br>The treatment required must be such one of the following kinds of treatment as may be specified in the relevant order—<br>(a) in-patient treatment in a care home, an independent hospital or a hospital within the meaning of the Mental Health Act 1983, but not in hospital premises where high security psychiatric services are provided;<br>(b) treatment as a non-resident patient at such institution or place as may be specified in the order;<br>(c) treatment by or under the direction of such registered medical practitioner or registered psychologist (or both);<br>during a particular period or particular periods, but the nature of the treatment is not to be specified in the order. |
| **And the court is satisfied** | That arrangements have been or can be made for the treatment to be specified in the order and that the offender has expressed a willingness to comply with the requirement. |

| Hospital order (s. 37 MHA 1983) | | |
|---|---|---|
| **May be made by:** | A magistrates' court or the Crown Court | |
| **In respect of a person who is:** | *Where made by a magistrates' court:* | *Where made by the Crown Court:* |
| | Convicted by that court of an offence punishable on summary conviction with imprisonment,<br>or<br>* Charged before that court with such an offence but who has not been convicted or whose case has not proceeded to trial, if the court is satisfied that the person did the act or made the omission charged. | Convicted before that court for an offence punishable with imprisonment (other than murder). |
| **If the court is satisfied** | On the written or oral evidence of two doctors, at least one of whom must be approved under section 12, that<br>• the offender is suffering from mental disorder of a nature or degree which makes it appropriate for the offender to be detained in a hospital for medical treatment, and<br>• appropriate medical treatment is available. | |
| **And the court is of the opinion** | Having regard to all the circumstances, including the nature of the offence and the character and antecedents of the offender, and to the other available methods of dealing with the offender, that a hospital order is the most suitable method of dealing with the case. | |
| **And it is also satisfied** | On the written or oral evidence of the approved clinician who would have overall responsibility for the offender's case, or of some other person representing the managers of the relevant hospital, that arrangements have been made for the offender to be admitted to that hospital within the period of 28 days starting with the day of the order. | |

*This guideline does not deal with orders other than on conviction.

- These orders are an alternative to punishment. Under s.57(3) of the Sentencing Code, the five statutory purposes of sentencing in s.57(2) do not apply when making a hospital order (with or without restriction), an interim hospital order or a limitation direction,
- A hospital order or guardianship order can only be made where the criteria are met **at the time of sentence**, irrespective of the condition at the date of the offence,
- Hospital orders and guardianship orders are not available to treat substance use disorders and addictions, s.1(3) MHA,
- When making a hospital order, the court will need to consider if a restriction order is necessary. The magistrates' court does not have the power to make a restriction order but, if it considers it is appropriate to make a s.37 order upon conviction (but not where there has been a finding of having done the act or omission) and a s.41 restriction order may be appropriate, it can commit to the Crown court, even for a summary only offence, s.43 (see below),
- When making a hospital order, the court cannot pass a sentence of imprisonment, a community order, a youth rehabilitation order or a referral order or impose a fine. The court may make any other order which it has the power to make, such as a compensation order.

| Restriction Order (s.41 MHA 1983) | |
|---|---|
| A restriction order (s.41) may be imposed by the Crown Court where a hospital order has been made and: | |
| If | At least one of the doctors whose evidence is taken into account by the Court before deciding to give the hospital order has given evidence orally. |
| And, having regard to | • the nature of the offence; <br> • the antecedents of the offender; and <br> • the risk of the offender committing further offences if set at large. |
| The Court thinks | It necessary for the protection of the public from serious harm for the person to be subject to the special restrictions which flow from a restriction order. |

- A restriction order should not be passed simply to mark the seriousness of the offence,
- Where the court is considering if it is necessary to make a restriction order to protect the public from serious harm, the harm need not be limited to personal injury nor need it relate to the public in general, but it does not include harm to the offender. The risk need not be linked only to the offence for which the offender is being sentenced. A comparatively minor offence, where other factors are present, may lead the court to conclude that there is a risk of serious harm,
- The parties must be given an opportunity to address the court before making a restriction order,
- A restriction order can be passed where neither psychiatrist recommends such an order, as the court is not bound by expert evidence, though it will wish to have careful regard to it,
- In some cases the treating psychiatrist may prefer not to give evidence or provide a report in case it compromises treatment.

| Imprisonment with Hospital Direction and Limitation Direction (s.45A MHA 1983) | |
|---|---|
| May be given by: | The Crown Court |
| In respect of a person who is | Aged 21 or over and convicted before that court of an offence punishable with imprisonment (other than murder). |
| If the court is satisfied | On the written or oral evidence of two doctors, at least one of whom must be approved under section 12, and at least one of whom must have given evidence orally, that: <br> • the offender is suffering from mental disorder of a nature or degree which makes it appropriate for the offender to be detained in a hospital for medical treatment, and <br> • appropriate medical treatment is available. |
| And the Court | Has first considered making a hospital order under section 37, but has decided instead to impose a sentence of imprisonment. |
| And it is also satisfied | On the written or oral evidence of the approved clinician who would have overall responsibility for the offender's case or of some other person representing the managers of the relevant hospital, that arrangements have been made for the offender to be admitted to that hospital within the 28 days starting with the day of the order. |

- If a penal element is appropriate, taking account of the level of culpability and the seriousness of the offence, and the mental disorder can be dealt with by directions under s.45A, then the judge should make such directions,

- The court will need to hear evidence about the different release regimes under s. 37/s.41 orders and a s. 45A order from the medical witness. Once the order is made the release provision cannot be altered. There will be cases where the protection of the public via a restriction order will outweigh the importance of a penal element and other cases where greater public protection is provided by a hybrid order.

| Committal to the Crown Court (s.43 MHA 1983) | |
|---|---|
| A magistrates' court may commit a person to the Crown Court with a view to a restriction order if (s. 43(1)) | |
| The person | Is aged 14 or over, and<br>Has been **convicted**\* by the court of an offence punishable on summary conviction by imprisonment. |
| And | The court could make a hospital order under section 37 |
| But having regard to | The nature of the offence,<br>The antecedents of the offender, and<br>The risk of the offender committing further offences if set at large. |
| The court considers | That if a hospital order is made, a restriction order should also be made. |

\*Note: there is no power to commit to the Crown Court for a restriction order where a magistrates' court has made a finding that a defendant has done the act/made the omission charged under s. 37(3) MHA.

The Crown Court is required to inquire into the circumstances of the patient's case and either:

- to make a hospital order (with or without a restriction order), as if the offender had been convicted before the Crown Court, rather than by the magistrates' court, or
- to deal with the offender in some other way the magistrates' court would have been able to originally.

| Guardianship order (s. 37 MHA 1983) | | |
|---|---|---|
| May be made by | a magistrates' court or the Crown Court | |
| In respect of a person who is aged 16 or over and who is | where made by a magistrates' court | where made by the Crown Court |
| | convicted by that court of an offence punishable (in the case of an adult) on summary conviction with custody<br>or<br>\* charged before (but not convicted by) that court with such an offence, if the court is satisfied that the person did the act or made the omission charged. | convicted before that court for an offence punishable with imprisonment (other than murder). |
| If the court is satisfied | on the written or oral evidence of two doctors, at least one of whom must be approved under section 12, that the offender is 16 or over, and has a mental disorder of a nature or degree which warrants the offender's reception into guardianship under the Act. | |
| And the court is of the opinion | having regard to all the circumstances including the nature of the offence and the character and antecedents of the offender, and to the other available methods of dealing with the offender, that a guardianship order is the most suitable method of dealing with the case. | |
| And it is also satisfied | that the local social services authority or proposed private guardian is willing to receive the offender into guardianship. | |

\*This guideline does not deal with orders other than on conviction

Guardianship enables patients to receive care outside hospital where it cannot be provided without the use of compulsory powers. The Act allows for people ('patients') to be placed under the guardianship of a guardian. The guardian may be a local social services authority, or an individual ('a private guardian'), such as a relative of the patient, who is approved by a local authority. Guardians have three specific powers: residence, attendance and access.

- The *residence power* allows guardians to require patients to live at a specified place,
- The *attendance power* lets guardians require the patient to attend specified places at specified times for medical treatment, occupation, education or training. This might include a day centre, or a hospital, surgery or clinic,
- The *access power* means guardians may require access to the patient to be given at the place where the patient is living, to any doctor, approved mental health professional, or other specified person. This power could be used, for example, to ensure that patients do not neglect themselves.

**Effect of hospital orders, restriction orders and 'hybrid orders' and their release provisions:**

1. References to 'the tribunal' are references to the First Tier Tribunal (Mental Health) for England, and the Mental Health Review Tribunal for Wales.

2. **Hospital Orders**
   a. A hospital order initially lasts for six months, but can be renewed for a further six months, and then a for a year at a time, s. 20,
   b. A hospital order can be discharged by the responsible clinician or manager of the responsible hospital or the patient's nearest relative (subject to certain safeguards in s.25), s. 23,
   c. The responsible clinician can discharge the patient under a community treatment order, which makes the patient liable to recall to hospital, s. 17A-17E,
   d. After six months, the patient, or their nearest relative, can apply to the tribunal for discharge, s.69. If no application has been made by the patient, or their nearest relative, then the hospital managers must refer the case to the tribunal, and must also refer the case to the tribunal if it has been more than three years since the case was last considered by the tribunal, s.68. The SoS can refer the patient to the tribunal at any time, s. 67,
   e. Powers of the Tribunal:
      i. The tribunal shall direct the release of the patient, immediately or on a future date, if it is not satisfied that, s. 72(1)(b)(i) & (ii):
         1. the criteria for a hospital order are met; or
         2. it is necessary for the health or safety of the patient or for the protection of other persons that he should receive treatment or that appropriate medical treatment is available for him,
      ii. The tribunal has powers to discharge a community patient, s. 72(1)(c),
      iii. The tribunal may recommend that the responsible clinician consider whether to make a community treatment order, but cannot make any such order itself, and may further consider the case if the responsible clinician does not make such an order, s. 72(3A).

3. **Restriction Orders**
   a. When a restriction order is made, both the restriction order and the hospital order last indefinitely and do not need to be renewed,
   b. The patient cannot be granted leave of absence or transferred to another hospital or discharged without the consent of the SoS, s. 41(3)(c),
   c. If the restriction order ceases, the hospital order can still remain in force, s. 42(5),
   d. Powers of the SoS:
      i. If satisfied that a restriction order is no longer required for the protection of the public from serious harm, the SoS can direct the restriction order ceases to have effect and the patient is held as if subject to a hospital order, s. 42(1),
      ii. The SoS can discharge the patient from hospital absolutely or subject to conditions. If the patient is discharged absolutely, he ceases to be detained under the hospital order, s. 42(2),
      iii. If the patient has been conditionally discharged, the SoS may recall the patient at any time, s. 42(3),
      iv. If a patient has been conditionally discharged, and the restriction order ceases to have effect, the patient is deemed to have been absolutely discharged, s. 42(4),
   e. Restricted patients can make applications to the relevant tribunals, s. 70,
   f. The SoS may refer a restricted patient to the relevant tribunal at any time, s. 71(1). Such a referral shall be made if the patient's case has not been considered within the last three years, s. 71(2),
   g. In any tribunal proceedings, the SoS becomes a party,
   h. Powers of the Tribunal:
      i. If the tribunal is not satisfied that the criteria for a hospital order are still met, and is satisfied that it is not appropriate for the patient to remain liable to recall for further treatment, the tribunal shall direct the absolute discharge of the patient, and the hospital order and the restriction order cease, s. 73(1) & (3),
      ii. If the tribunal is not satisfied that the criteria for a hospital order are still met but considers that it is appropriate for the patient to remain liable to recall to hospital for further treatment, the tribunal shall direct the conditional discharge of the patient, s. 73(2). If the patient is conditionally discharged, they must comply with any conditions imposed by the tribunal or the SoS and are liable to recall by the SoS, s. 73(4). If the patient has not been recalled and the restriction order ceases, the patient is deemed to have been absolutely discharged from both the restriction order and the hospital order, s. 73(6).

4. **Hybrid Orders**
   a. Hybrid Orders are generally made in cases where a long determinate or indeterminate sentence is being imposed,
   b. Under s. 45A, where the period of imprisonment is determinate, if the defendant's health improves so that his responsible clinician or the Tribunal notifies the Secretary of State (SoS) that

he no longer requires treatment in hospital under the MHA, the SoS will generally remit the patient to prison under s. 50(1) of the MHA to serve the rest of his sentence. On arrival in prison, the s. 45A order would cease to have effect: the offender would continue to serve his prison sentence and his release from that sentence would be in accordance with the usual provisions. However, if there has been no improvement at the automatic release date, the limitation direction aspect of s. 45A falls away. At that point, the patient remains in hospital but is treated as though they are subject to an unrestricted hospital order so that the point at which he is discharged from hospital is a matter for the clinicians, with no input from the SoS,

c.  Where the period of imprisonment is indeterminate, if a s. 45A patient's health improves such that his responsible clinician or the Tribunal notifies the SoS that he no longer requires treatment in hospital under the MHA, the SoS will generally remit the patient to prison under s. 50(1) MHA. On arrival in prison, the s.45A order would cease to have any effect whatsoever. Release would be considered by the Parole Board in the usual way. If a s.45A patient has passed their tariff date and the Tribunal then notified the SoS that he is ready for conditional discharge, the SoS could notify the Tribunal that he should be so discharged (s. 74(2)). In that case, the offender would be subject to mental health supervision and recall in the usual way. However, the SoS would, in practice, refer the offender to the Parole Board.

# PART 8   SENTENCING CHILDREN AND YOUNG PEOPLE: OVERARCHING PRINCIPLES AND OFFENCE SPECIFIC GUIDELINES FOR SEXUAL OFFENCES AND ROBBERY

**Effective from:** 01 June 2017

**SG8-1**                                    APPLICABILITY

[For the standard text on applicability see **SG0-4**]

**SG8-2**                              GUILTY PLEA SECTION ONLY

Section 73 of the Sentencing Code provides:

> (1) *This section applies where a court is determining what sentence to pass on an offender who has pleaded guilty to an offence in proceedings before that or another court.*[65]
>
> (2) *The court must take into account the following matters—*
>
> > (a) *the stage in the proceedings for the offence at which the offender indicated the intention to plead guilty, and*
> >
> > (b) *the circumstances in which the indication was given.*

This section of the guideline applies regardless of the date of the offence to all children or young people where the **first hearing** is on or after 1 June 2017. It applies equally in youth courts, magistrates' courts and the Crown Court.

**SG8-3**       OVERARCHING PRINCIPLES — SENTENCING CHILDREN AND YOUNG PEOPLE

### SECTION ONE: General approach

### Sentencing principles

1.1    When sentencing children or young people (those aged under 18 at the date of the finding of guilt) a court must[66] have regard to:
- the principal aim of the youth justice system (to prevent offending by children and young people);[67] and
- the welfare of the child or young person.[68]

1.2    While the seriousness of the offence will be the starting point, the approach to sentencing should be individualistic and focused on the child or young person, as opposed to offence focused. For a child or young person the sentence should focus on rehabilitation where possible. A court should also consider the effect the sentence is likely to have on the child or young person (both positive and negative) as well as any underlying factors contributing to the offending behaviour.

1.3    Domestic and international laws dictate that a custodial sentence should always be a measure of last resort for children and young people and statute provides that a custodial sentence may only be imposed when the offence is so serious that no other sanction is appropriate (see section six for more information on custodial sentences).

1.4    It is important to avoid 'criminalising' children and young people unnecessarily; the primary purpose of the youth justice system is to encourage children and young people to take responsibility for their own actions and promote re-integration into society rather than to punish. Restorative justice disposals may be of particular value for children and young people as they can encourage them to take responsibility for their actions and understand the impact their offence may have had on others.

1.5    It is important to bear in mind any factors that may diminish the culpability of a child or young person. Children and young people are not fully developed and they have not attained full maturity. As such, this can impact on their decision making and risk taking behaviour. It is important to consider the extent to which the child or young person has been acting impulsively and whether their conduct has been affected by inexperience, emotional volatility or negative influences. They may not fully appreciate the effect their actions can have on other people and may not be capable of fully understanding the distress and pain they cause to the victims of their crimes. Children and young people are also likely to be susceptible to peer pressure and other external

---

[65] Offence' includes breach of an order where this constitutes a separate criminal offence but not breach of terms of a sentence or licence.

[66] This section does not apply when imposing a mandatory life sentence, when imposing a statutory minimum custodial sentence, when imposing detention for life under the dangerous offender provisions or when making certain orders under the Mental Health Act 1983.

[67] s.37(1) Crime and Disorder Act 1998

[68] s.44(1) Children and Young Persons Act 1933

influences and changes taking place during adolescence can lead to experimentation, resulting in criminal behaviour. When considering a child or young person's age their emotional and developmental age is of at least equal importance to their chronological age (if not greater).

1.6    For these reasons, children and young people are likely to benefit from being given an opportunity to address their behaviour and may be receptive to changing their conduct. They should, if possible, be given the opportunity to learn from their mistakes without undue penalisation or stigma, especially as a court sanction might have a significant effect on the prospects and opportunities of the child or young person and hinder their re-integration into society.

1.7    Offending by a child or young person is often a phase which passes fairly rapidly and so the sentence should not result in the alienation of the child or young person from society if that can be avoided.

1.8    The impact of punishment is likely to be felt more heavily by a child or young person in comparison to an adult as any sentence will seem longer due to their young age. In addition penal interventions may interfere with a child or young person's education and this should be considered by a court at sentencing.

1.9    Any restriction on liberty must be commensurate with the seriousness of the offence. In considering the seriousness of any offence, the court must consider the child or young person's culpability in committing the offence and any harm which the offence caused, was intended to cause or might foreseeably have caused.[69]

1.10   Section 57 of the Sentencing Code sets out the purposes of sentencing for offenders under 18. Those purposes of sentencing include; the punishment of offenders; the reform and rehabilitation of offenders; and, the protection of the public, and the making of reparation by offenders to persons affected by their offences. This differs from the purposes of sentencing an adult as it does not include the additional consideration; the reduction of crime (including its reduction by deterrence).

**For more information on assessing the seriousness of the offence see section four.**

**Welfare**

1.11   The statutory obligation to have regard to the welfare of a child or young person includes the obligation to secure proper provision for education and training,[70] to remove the child or young person from undesirable surroundings where appropriate[71] and the need to choose the best option for the child or young person taking account of the circumstances of the offence.

1.12   **In having regard to the welfare of the child or young person, a court should ensure that it is alert to:**
- **any mental health problems or learning difficulties/disabilities;**
- **any experiences of brain injury or traumatic life experience (including exposure to drug and alcohol abuse) and the developmental impact this may have had;**
- **any speech and language difficulties and the effect this may have on the ability of the child or young person (or any accompanying adult) to communicate with the court, to understand the sanction imposed or to fulfil the obligations resulting from that sanction;**
- **the vulnerability of children and young people to self harm, particularly within a** custodial environment; and
- **the effect on children and young people of experiences of loss and neglect and/or abuse.**

1.13   Factors regularly present in the background of children and young people that come before the court include deprived homes, poor parental employment records, low educational attainment, early experience of offending by other family members, experience of abuse and/or neglect, negative influences from peer associates and the misuse of drugs and/or alcohol.

1.14   The court should always seek to ensure that it has access to information about how best to identify and respond to these factors and, where necessary, that a proper assessment has taken place in order to enable the most appropriate sentence to be imposed.

1.15   The court should consider the reasons why, on some occasions, a child or young person may conduct themselves inappropriately in court (e.g. due to nervousness, a lack of understanding of the system, a belief that they will be discriminated against, peer pressure to behave in a certain way because of others present, a lack of maturity etc) and take this into account.

---

[69] s.63 Sentencing Code
[70] s. 44 Children and Young Persons Act 1933
[71] ibid

1.16 Evidence shows that looked after children and young people are over-represented in the criminal justice system.[72] When dealing with a child or young person who is looked after the court should also bear in mind the additional complex vulnerabilities that are likely to be present in their background. For example, looked after children and young people may have no or little contact with their family and/or friends, they may have special educational needs and/or emotional and behavioural problems, they may be heavily exposed to peers who have committed crime and they are likely to have accessed the care system as a result of abuse, neglect or parental absence due to bereavement, imprisonment or desertion. The court should also bear in mind that the level of parental-type support that a looked after child or young person receives throughout the criminal justice process may vary, and may be limited. For example, while parents are required to attend court hearings, this is not the case for social workers responsible for looked after children and young people. In some instances a looked after child or young person (including those placed in foster homes and independent accommodation, as well as in care homes) may be before the court for a low level offence that the police would not have been involved in, if it had occurred in an ordinary family setting.

1.17 For looked after children and young people who have committed an offence that crosses the custody threshold sentencers will need to consider any impact a custodial sentence may have on their leaving care rights and whether this impact is proportionate to the seriousness of the offence. For other young people who are in the process of leaving care or have recently left care then sentencers should bear in mind any effect this often difficult transition may have had on the young person's behaviour.

1.18 There is also evidence to suggest that black and minority ethnic children and young people are over-represented in the youth justice system.[73] The factors contributing to this are complex. One factor is that a significant proportion of looked after children and young people are from a black and minority ethnic background.[74] A further factor may be the experience of such children and young people in terms of discrimination and negative experiences of authority. When having regard to the welfare of the child or young person to be sentenced, the particular factors which arise in the case of black and minority ethnic children and young people need to be taken into account.

1.19 The requirement to have regard to the welfare of a child or young person is subject to the obligation to impose only those restrictions on liberty that are commensurate with the seriousness of the offence; accordingly, a court should not impose greater restrictions because of other factors in the child or young person's life.

1.20 When considering a child or young person who may be particularly vulnerable, sentencers should consider which available disposal is best able to support the child or young person and which disposals could potentially exacerbate any underlying issues. This is particularly important when considering custodial sentences as there are concerns about the effect on vulnerable children and young people of being in closed conditions, with significant risks of self harm, including suicide.

1.21 The vulnerability factors that are often present in the background of children and young people should also be considered in light of the offending behaviour itself. Although they do not alone cause offending behaviour – there are many children and young people who have experienced these circumstances but do not commit crime – there is a correlation and any response to criminal activity amongst children and young people will need to recognise the presence of such factors in order to be effective.

**These principles do not undermine the fact that the sentence should reflect the seriousness of the offence. Further guidance on assessing the seriousness of an offence can be found at section four.**

SG8-4 SECTION TWO: Allocation
(See also the allocation charts below when reading this section.)

2.1 **Subject to the exceptions noted below, cases involving children and young people should be tried in the youth court.** It is the court which is best designed to meet their specific needs. A trial in the Crown Court with the inevitably greater formality and greatly increased number of people

---

[72] Department for Education (2014) Outcomes for Children Looked After by Local Authorities in England, as at 31 March 2014. Statistical First Release 49/2014. [accessed via: https://www.gov.uk/government/statistics/outcomes-for-children-looked-after-by-local-authorities]

[73] https://assets.publishing.service.gov.uk/government/uploads/system/uploads/attachment_data/file/63 9261/bame-disproportionality-in-the-cjs.pdf

[74] https://www.gov.uk/government/statistics/children-looked-after-in-england-including-adoption-2015-to-2016 (National table, figure B1)

involved (including a jury and the public) should be reserved for the most serious cases.[75] The welfare principles in this guideline apply to all cases, including those tried or sentenced in the Crown Court.

**This section covers the exceptions to this requirement.**[76]

2.2   A child or young person must always appear in the Crown Court for trial if:
- charged with homicide;
- charged with a firearms offence subject to a mandatory minimum sentence of three years (and is over 16 years of age at the time of the offence); or
- notice has been given to the court (under section 51B or 51C of the Crime and Disorder Act 1998) in a serious or complex fraud or child case.

### Dangerousness

2.3   A case should be sent to the Crown Court for trial if the offence charged is a specified offence[77] **and** it seems to the court that if found guilty the child or young person would meet the criteria for a sentence under the dangerous offender provisions.

2.4   A sentence under the dangerous offender provisions can only be imposed if:
- the child or young person is found guilty of a specified violent or sexual offence; **and**
- the court is of the opinion that there is a significant risk to the public of serious harm caused by the child or young person committing further specified offences; **and**
- a custodial term of at least four years would be imposed for the offence.

2.5   A 'significant risk' is more than a mere possibility of occurrence. The assessment of dangerousness should take into account all the available information relating to the circumstances of the offence and **may** also take into account any information regarding previous patterns of behavior relating to this offence and any other relevant information relating to the child or young person. In making this assessment it will be essential to obtain a pre-sentence report.

2.6   Children and young people may change and develop within a shorter time than adults and this factor, along with their level of maturity, may be highly relevant when assessing probable future conduct and whether it may cause a significant risk of serious harm.[78]

2.7   In anything but the most serious cases it may be impossible for the court to form a view as to whether the child or young person would meet the criteria of the dangerous offender provisions without greater knowledge of the circumstances of the offence and the child or young person. In those circumstances jurisdiction for the case should be retained in the youth court. If, following a guilty plea or a finding of guilt, the dangerousness criteria appear to be met then the child or young person should be committed **for sentence**.

### Grave crimes

2.8   Where a child or young person is before the court for an offence to which section 250 Sentencing Code applies and the court considers that it ought to be possible to sentence them to more than two years' detention if found guilty of the offence, then they should be sent to the Crown Court. The test to be applied by the court is whether there is a **real prospect** that a sentence in excess of two years' detention will be imposed.

2.9   An offence comes within section 250 where:
- it is punishable with 14 years' imprisonment or more for an adult (but is not a sentence fixed by law);
- it is an offence of sexual assault, a child sex offence committed by a child or young person, sexual activity with a child family member or inciting a child family member to engage in sexual activity; or
- it is one of a number of specified offences in relation to firearms, ammunition and weapons which are subject to a minimum term but, in respect of which, a court has found exceptional circumstances justifying a lesser sentence.

2.10   Before deciding whether to send the case to the Crown Court or retain jurisdiction in the youth court, the court should hear submissions from the prosecution and defence. As there is now a power to commit grave crimes for sentence[79] the court should no longer take the prosecution case at its highest when deciding whether to retain jurisdiction.[80] In most cases it is likely to be

[75] R on the application of H, A and O v Southampton Youth Court [2004] EWHC 2912 Admin
[76] s. 24 Magistrates' Courts Act 1980
[77] As listed in Schedule 18 Sentencing Code
[78] R v Lang [2005] EWCA Crim 2864, [2006] 1 WLR 2509
[79] s.16 Sentencing Code
[80] R (DPP) v South Tyneside Youth Court [2015] EWHC 1455 (Admin)

impossible to decide whether there is a real prospect that a sentence in excess of two years' detention will be imposed without knowing more about the facts of the case and the circumstances of the child or young person. In those circumstances the youth court should retain jurisdiction and commit for sentence if it is of the view, having heard more about the facts and the circumstances of the child or young person, that its powers of sentence are insufficient.

**Where the court decides that the case is suitable to be dealt with in the youth court it must warn the child or young person that all available sentencing options remain open and, if found guilty, the child or young person may be committed to the Crown Court for sentence.**

**Children and young people should only be sent for trial or committed for sentence to the Crown Court when charged with or found guilty of an offence of such gravity that a custodial sentence substantially exceeding two years is a realistic possibility. For children aged 10 or 11, and children/young people aged 12–14 who are not persistent offenders, the court should take into account the normal prohibition on imposing custodial sentences.**

### Charged alongside an adult

2.11 The proper venue for the trial of any child or young person is normally the youth court. Subject to statutory restrictions, that remains the case where a child or young person is jointly charged with an adult. If the adult is sent for trial to the Crown Court, the court should conclude that the child or young person must be tried separately in the youth court unless it is in the interests of justice for the child or young person and the adult to be tried jointly.

2.12 Examples of factors that should be considered when deciding whether to send the child or young person to the Crown Court (rather than having a trial in the youth court) include:
- whether separate trials will cause injustice to witnesses or to the case as a whole (consideration should be given to the provisions of sections 27 and 28 of the Youth Justice and Criminal Evidence Act 1999);
- the age of the child or young person; the younger the child or young person, the greater the desirability that the child or young person be tried in the youth court;
- the age gap between the child or young person and the adult; a substantial gap in age militates in favour of the child or young person being tried in the youth court;
- the lack of maturity of the child or young person;
- the relative culpability of the child or young person compared with the adult and whether the alleged role played by the child or young person was minor; and/or
- the lack of previous findings of guilt on the part of the child or young person.

2.13 The court should bear in mind that the youth court now has a general power to commit for sentence (as discussed at paragraph 2.9); in appropriate cases this will permit a sentence to be imposed by the same court on adults and children and young people who have been tried separately.

2.14 The court should follow the plea before venue procedure (see flowcharts on pages 11–13) prior to considering whether it is in the interests of justice for the child or young person and the adult to be tried jointly.

### Remittal from the Crown Court for sentence

2.15 If a child or young person is found guilty before the Crown Court of an offence other than homicide the court must remit the case to the youth court, unless it would be undesirable to do so.[81] In considering whether remittal is undesirable a court should balance the need for expertise in the sentencing of children and young people with the benefits of the sentence being imposed by the court which determined guilt.

2.16 Particular attention should be given to children and young people who are appearing before the Crown Court only because they have been charged with an adult offender; referral orders are generally not available in the Crown Court but may be the most appropriate sentence.

---

[81] s.25 Sentencing Code

**Child or young person charged alone or with other children and young people**
(This is intended to be a reference tool only; for full guidance on allocation, particularly for grave crimes, please see [above])

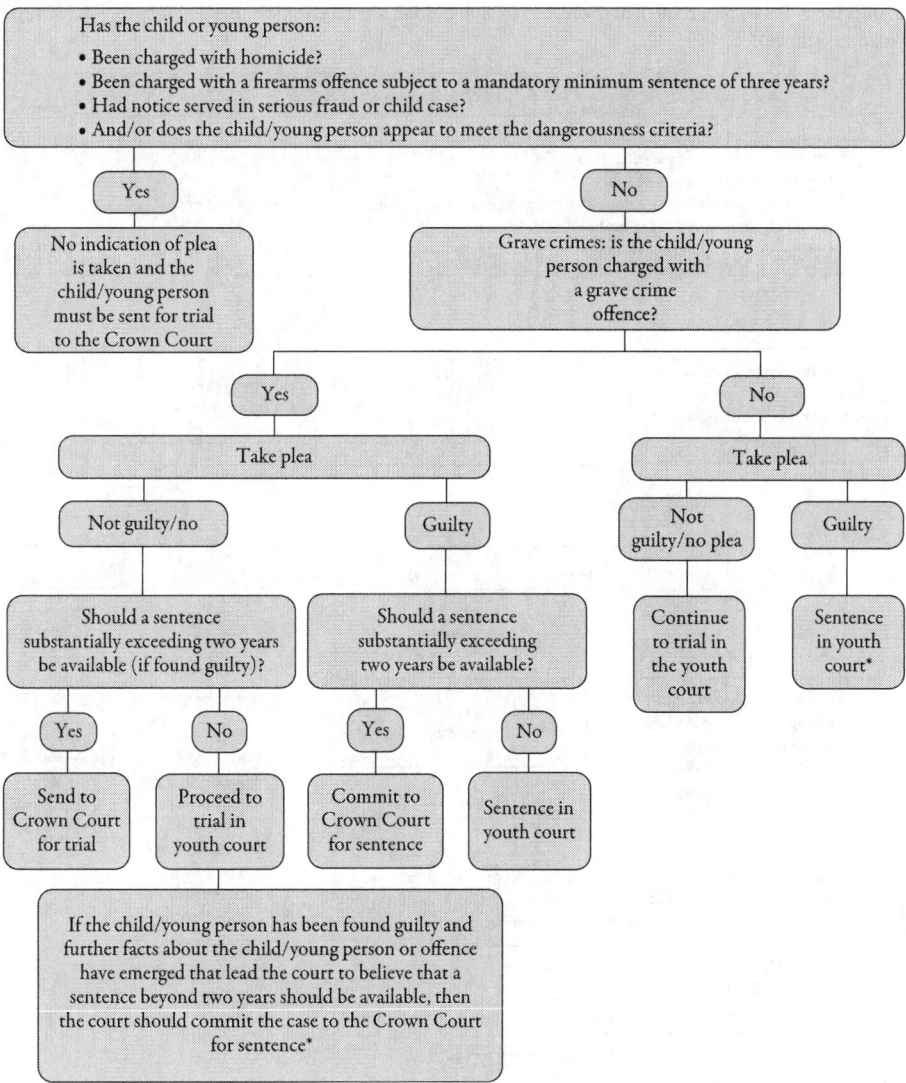

* If the dangerousness provisions appear to be satisfied the court must commit for sentence

**Child or young person and adult charged as co-defendants where the adult is charged with an indictable only offence (or an offence where notice is given to the court under s. 51B or s. 51C Crime & Disorder Act 1998)**

(This is intended to be a reference tool only; for full guidance on allocation, particularly for grave crimes, please see [above])

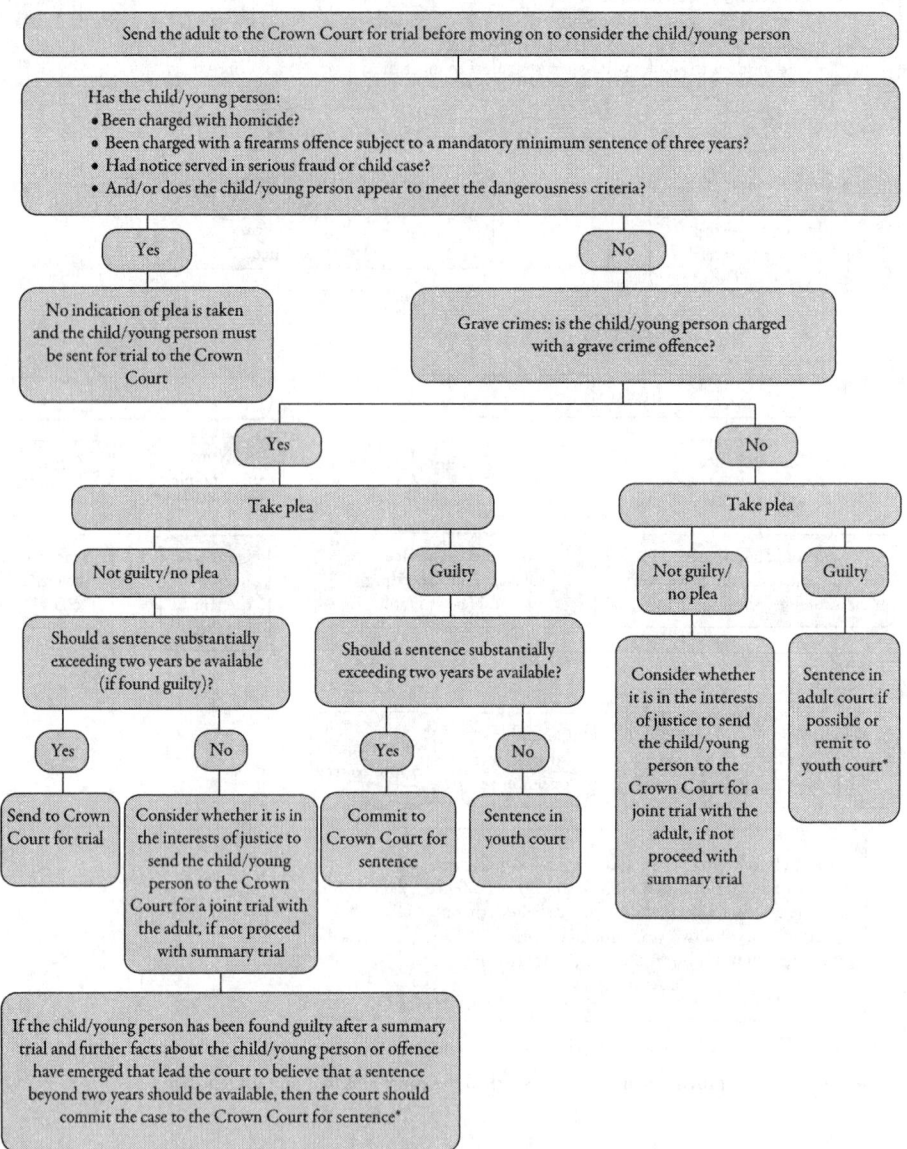

Send the adult to the Crown Court for trial before moving on to consider the child/young person

Has the child/young person:
- Been charged with homicide?
- Been charged with a firearms offence subject to a mandatory minimum sentence of three years?
- Had notice served in serious fraud or child case?
- And/or does the child/young person appear to meet the dangerousness criteria?

**Yes** → No indication of plea is taken and the child/young person must be sent for trial to the Crown Court

**No** → Grave crimes: is the child/young person charged with a grave crime offence?

**Yes** → Take plea

- **Not guilty/no plea** → Should a sentence substantially exceeding two years be available (if found guilty)?
  - **Yes** → Send to Crown Court for trial
  - **No** → Consider whether it is in the interests of justice to send the child/young person to the Crown Court for a joint trial with the adult, if not proceed with summary trial

- **Guilty** → Should a sentence substantially exceeding two years be available?
  - **Yes** → Commit to Crown Court for sentence
  - **No** → Sentence in youth court

**No** → Take plea

- **Not guilty/ no plea** → Consider whether it is in the interests of justice to send the child/young person to the Crown Court for a joint trial with the adult, if not proceed with summary trial

- **Guilty** → Sentence in adult court if possible or remit to youth court*

If the child/young person has been found guilty after a summary trial and further facts about the child/young person or offence have emerged that lead the court to believe that a sentence beyond two years should be available, then the court should commit the case to the Crown Court for sentence*

\* If the dangerousness provisions appear to be satisfied the court must commit for sentence

**Child or young person and adult charged as co-defendants where the adult is charged with either way offence**

(This is intended to be a reference tool only; for full guidance on allocation, particularly for grave crimes, please see [above].)

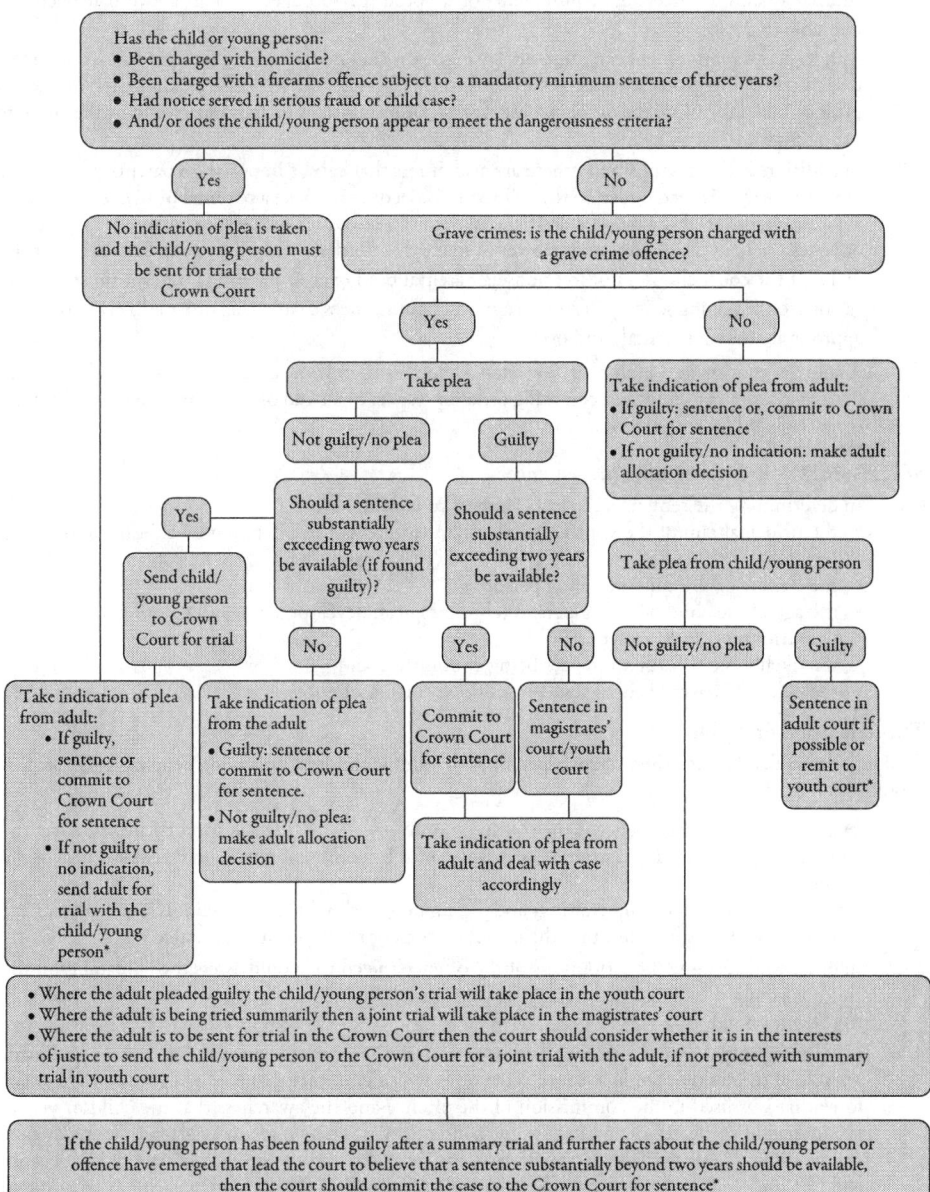

Has the child or young person:
- Been charged with homicide?
- Been charged with a firearms offence subject to a mandatory minimum sentence of three years?
- Had notice served in serious fraud or child case?
- And/or does the child/young person appear to meet the dangerousness criteria?

**Yes**

No indication of plea is taken and the child/young person must be sent for trial to the Crown Court

**No**

Grave crimes: is the child/young person charged with a grave crime offence?

**Yes**

Take plea

Not guilty/no plea

Should a sentence substantially exceeding two years be available (if found guilty)?

**Yes**

Send child/young person to Crown Court for trial

**No**

Guilty

Should a sentence substantially exceeding two years be available?

**Yes**

Commit to Crown Court for sentence

**No**

Sentence in magistrates' court/youth court

Take indication of plea from adult and deal with case accordingly

**No**

Take indication of plea from adult:
- If guilty: sentence or, commit to Crown Court for sentence
- If not guilty/no indication: make adult allocation decision

Take plea from child/young person

Not guilty/no plea

Guilty

Sentence in adult court if possible or remit to youth court*

Take indication of plea from adult:
- If guilty, sentence or commit to Crown Court for sentence
- If not guilty or no indication, send adult for trial with the child/young person*

Take indication of plea from the adult
- Guilty: sentence or commit to Crown Court for sentence.
- Not guilty/no plea: make adult allocation decision

- Where the adult pleaded guilty the child/young person's trial will take place in the youth court
- Where the adult is being tried summarily then a joint trial will take place in the magistrates' court
- Where the adult is to be sent for trial in the Crown Court then the court should consider whether it is in the interests of justice to send the child/young person to the Crown Court for a joint trial with the adult, if not proceed with summary trial in youth court

If the child/young person has been found guilty after a summary trial and further facts about the child/young person or offence have emerged that lead the court to believe that a sentence substantially beyond two years should be available, then the court should commit the case to the Crown Court for sentence*

* If the dangerousness provisions appear to be satisfied the court must commit for sentence

Sentencing Guidelines

**SG8-5**    **SECTION THREE: Parental responsibilities**

3.1    For any child or young person aged under 16 appearing before court there is a statutory requirement that parents/guardians attend during all stages of proceedings, unless the court is satisfied that this would be unreasonable having regard to the circumstances of the case.[82] The court may also enforce this requirement for a young person aged 16 and above if it deems it desirable to do so.

3.2    Although this requirement can cause a delay in the case before the court it is important it is adhered to. If a court does find exception to proceed in the absence of a responsible adult then extra care must be taken to ensure the outcomes are clearly communicated to and understood by the child or young person.

3.3    In addition to this responsibility there are also orders that can be imposed on parents. If the child or young person is aged under 16 then the court has a duty to make a **parental bind over** or impose a **parenting order**, if it would be desirable in the interest of preventing the commission of further offences.[83] There is a discretionary power to make these orders where the young person is aged 16 or 17. If the court chooses not to impose a parental bind over or parenting order it must state its reasons for not doing so in open court. In most circumstances a parenting order is likely to be more appropriate than a parental bind over.

3.4    A court cannot make a bind over alongside a referral order. If the court makes a referral order the duty on the court to impose a parenting order in respect of a child or young person under 16 years old is replaced by a discretion.[84]

**SG8-6**    **SECTION FOUR: Determining the sentence**

4.1    In determining the sentence, the key elements to consider are:
- the principal aim of the youth justice system (to prevent re-offending by children and young people);
- the welfare of the child or young person;
- the age of the child or young person (chronological, developmental and emotional);
- the seriousness of the offence;
- the likelihood of further offences being committed; and
- the extent of harm likely to result from those further offences.

**The seriousness of the offence**

(This applies to all offences; when offence specific guidance for children and young people is available this should be referred to.)

4.2    The seriousness of the offence is the starting point for determining the appropriate sentence; the sentence imposed and any restriction on liberty must be commensurate with the seriousness of the offence.

4.3    The approach to sentencing children and young people should always be individualistic and the court should always have in mind the principal aims of the youth justice system.

4.4    In order to determine the seriousness of the offence the court should assess the culpability of the child or young person and the harm that was caused, intended to be caused or could foreseeably have been caused.

4.5    In assessing **culpability** the court will wish to consider the extent to which the offence was planned, the role of the child or young person (if the offence was committed as part of a group), the level of force that was used in the commission of the offence and the awareness that the child or young person had of their actions and its possible consequences. There is an expectation that in general a child or young person will be dealt with less severely than an adult offender. In part, this is because children and young people are unlikely to have the same experience and capacity as an adult to understand the effect of their actions on other people or to appreciate the pain and distress caused and because a child or young person may be less able to resist temptation, especially where peer pressure is exerted. Children and young people are inherently more vulnerable than adults due to their age and the court will need to consider any mental health problems and/or learning disabilities they may have, as well as their emotional and developmental age. Any external factors that may have affected the child or young person's behaviour should be taken into account.

---

[82] s.34A Children and Young Persons Act 1933
[83] s.376 and s.366 Sentencing Code
[84] s.366(3) Sentencing Code

4.6   In assessing **harm** the court should consider the level of physical and psychological harm caused to the victim, the degree of any loss caused to the victim and the extent of any damage caused to property. (This assessment should also include a consideration of any harm that was intended to be caused or could foreseeably have been caused in the committal of the offence.)

4.7   The court should also consider any aggravating or mitigating factors that may increase or reduce the overall seriousness of the offence. **If any of these factors are included in the definition of the committed offence they should not be taken into account when considering the relative seriousness of the offence before the court.**

| **Aggravating factors** |
| --- |
| *Statutory aggravating factors:* |
| Previous findings of guilt, having regard to a) the **nature** of the offence to which the finding of guilt relates and its **relevance** to the current offence; and b) the **time** that has elapsed since the finding of guilt |
| Offence committed whilst on bail |
| Offence motivated by, or demonstrating hostility based on any of the following characteristics or presumed characteristics of the victim: religion, race, disability, sexual orientation or transgender identity |
| *Other aggravating factors (non-exhaustive):* |
| Steps taken to prevent the victim reporting or obtaining assistance |
| Steps taken to prevent the victim from assisting or supporting the prosecution |
| Victim is particularly vulnerable due to factors including but not limited to age, mental or physical disability |
| Restraint, detention or additional degradation of the victim |
| Prolonged nature of offence |
| Attempts to conceal/dispose of evidence |
| Established evidence of community/wider impact |
| Failure to comply with current court orders |
| Attempt to conceal identity |
| Involvement of others through peer pressure, bullying, coercion or manipulation |
| Commission of offence whilst under the influence of alcohol or drugs |
| History of antagonising or bullying the victim |
| Deliberate humiliation of victim, including but not limited to filming of the offence, deliberately committing the offence before a group of peers with the intention of causing additional distress or circulating details/photos/videos etc of the offence on social media or within peer groups |
| **Factors reducing seriousness or reflecting personal mitigation (non-exhaustive)** |
| No previous findings of guilt **or** no relevant/recent findings of guilt |
| Remorse, particularly where evidenced by voluntary reparation to the victim |
| Good character and/or exemplary conduct |
| Unstable upbringing including but not limited to: <br> • time spent looked after <br> • lack of familial presence or support <br> • disrupted experiences in accommodation or education <br> • exposure to drug/alcohol abuse, familial criminal behaviour or domestic abuse <br> • victim of neglect or abuse, or exposure to neglect or abuse of others <br> • experiences of trauma or loss |
| Participated in offence due to bullying, peer pressure, coercion or manipulation |
| Limited understanding of effect on victim |
| Serious medical condition requiring urgent, intensive or long-term treatment |
| Communication or learning disabilities or mental health concerns |
| In education, work or training |
| Particularly young or immature child or young person (where it affects their responsibility) |
| Determination and/or demonstration of steps taken to address addiction or offending behaviour |

Sentencing Guidelines

### Age and maturity of the child or young person

4.8    There is a statutory presumption that no child under the age of 10 can be guilty of an offence.[85]

4.9    With a child or young person, the consideration of age requires a different approach to that which would be adopted in relation to the age of an adult. Even within the category of child or young person the response of a court to an offence is likely to be very different depending on whether the child or young person is at the lower end of the age bracket, in the middle or towards the top end.

4.10   Although chronological age dictates in some instances what sentence can be imposed (see section six for more information) the developmental and emotional age of the child or young person should always be considered and it is of at least equal importance as their chronological age. It is important to consider whether the child or young person has the necessary maturity to appreciate fully the consequences of their conduct, the extent to which the child or young person has been acting on an impulsive basis and whether their conduct has been affected by inexperience, emotional volatility or negative influences.

**SG8-7    SECTION FIVE: Guilty plea**

This section of the guideline applies regardless of the date of the offence to all children or young people where the **first hearing** is on or after 1 June 2017. It applies equally in youth courts, magistrates' courts and the Crown Court.

### Key principles

5.1    The purpose of this section of the guideline is to encourage those who are going to plead guilty to do so as early in the court process as possible. Nothing in this section should be used to put pressure on a child or young person to plead guilty.

5.2    Although a guilty person is entitled not to admit the offence and to put the prosecution to proof of its case, an acceptance of guilt:

1.  normally reduces the impact of the crime upon victims;
2.  saves victims and witnesses from having to testify; and
3.  is in the public interest in that it saves public time and money on investigations and trials.

5.3    A guilty plea produces greater benefits the earlier the plea is made. In order to maximise the above benefits and to provide an incentive to those who are guilty to indicate a guilty plea as early as possible, this section of the guideline makes a clear distinction between a reduction in the sentence available at the first stage of the proceedings and a reduction in the sentence available at a later stage of the proceedings.

5.4    The purpose of reducing the sentence for a guilty plea is to yield the benefits described above and the guilty plea should be considered by the court to be independent of the child or young person's mitigation.

- Factors such as admissions at interview, co-operation with the investigation and demonstrations of remorse should **not** be taken into account in determining the level of reduction. Rather, they should be considered separately and prior to any guilty plea reduction, as potential mitigating factors.
- The benefits apply regardless of the strength of the evidence against a child or young person. The strength of the evidence should **not** be taken into account when determining the level of reduction.
- This section applies only to the punitive elements of the sentence and has no impact on ancillary orders including orders of disqualification from driving.

### The approach

**Stage 1**: Determine the appropriate sentence for the offence(s) in accordance with any offence specific sentencing guideline or using this *Overarching Principles* guideline.
**Stage 2**: Determine the level of reduction for a guilty plea in accordance with this guideline.
**Stage 3**: State the amount of that reduction.
**Stage 4**: Apply the reduction to the appropriate sentence.
**Stage 5**: Follow any further steps in the offence specific guideline to determine the final sentence.

**Nothing in this guideline affects the duty of the parties to progress cases (including the service of material) and identify any issues in dispute in compliance with the Criminal Procedure Rules and Criminal Practice Directions.**

---

[85]  s. 50 Children and Young Persons Act 1933

### Determining the level of reduction

**The maximum level of reduction for a guilty plea is one-third.**

#### 5.5   Plea indicated at the first stage of the proceedings

Where a guilty plea is indicated at the first stage of proceedings a reduction of **one-third** should be made (subject to the exceptions below). The first stage will normally be the first hearing in the magistrates' or youth court at which a plea is sought and recorded by the court.[86]

#### 5.6   Plea indicated after the first stage of proceedings – maximum one quarter – sliding scale of reduction thereafter

After the first stage of the proceedings the maximum level of reduction is **one-quarter** (subject to the exceptions below).

5.7   The reduction should be decreased from **one-quarter** to a maximum of **one-tenth** on the first day of trial having regard to the time when the guilty plea is first indicated relative to the progress of the case and the trial date (subject to the exceptions below). The reduction should normally be decreased further, even to zero, if the guilty plea is entered during the course of the trial.

5.8   For the purposes of this guideline a trial will be deemed to have started when pre-recorded cross-examination has begun.

### Applying the reduction

#### Detention and training orders

5.9   A detention and training order (DTO) can only be imposed for the periods prescribed – 4, 6, 8, 10, 12, 18 or 24 months. If the reduction in sentence for a guilty plea results in a sentence that falls between two prescribed periods the court must impose the lesser of those two periods.

This may result in a reduction greater than a third, in order that the full reduction is given and a lawful sentence imposed.

#### Imposing one type of sentence rather than another

5.10   The reduction in sentence for a guilty plea can be taken into account by imposing one type of sentence rather than another, for example:

- by reducing a custodial sentence to a community sentence; or
- by reducing a community sentence to a different means of disposal.

Alternatively the court could reduce the length or severity of any punitive requirements attached to a community sentence.

5.11   The court must always have regard to the principal aim of the youth justice system, which is to prevent offending by children and young people. It is, therefore, important that the court ensures that any sentence imposed is an effective disposal.

5.12   Where a court has imposed one sentence rather than another to reflect the guilty plea there should normally be no further reduction on account of the guilty plea. Where, however, the less severe type of sentence is justified by other factors, the appropriate reduction for the plea should be applied in the normal way.

#### More than one summary offence

5.13   When dealing with more than one summary offence, the aggregate sentence is limited to a maximum of six months. Allowing for a reduction for each guilty plea, consecutive sentences might result in the imposition of the maximum six month sentence. Where this is the case, the court **may** make a modest *additional* reduction to the overall sentence to reflect the benefits derived from the guilty plea.

#### Sentencing up to 24 months DTO for offences committed by children and young people

5.14   A DTO of up to 24 months may be imposed on a child or young person if the offence is one which, but for the plea, would have attracted a sentence of detention in excess of 24 months under section 250 of the Sentencing Code.

---

[86] In cases where (in accordance with the Criminal Procedure Rules) a child/young person is given the opportunity to enter a guilty plea without attending a court hearing, doing so within the required time limits will constitute a plea at the first stage of proceedings.

Sentencing Guidelines

## Exceptions

### Referral order

5.15　As a referral order is a sentence that is only available upon pleading guilty there should be no further reduction of the sentence to reflect the guilty plea.

### Further information, assistance or advice necessary before indicating plea

5.16　Where the sentencing court is satisfied that there were particular circumstances which significantly reduced the child or young person's ability to understand what was alleged, or otherwise made it unreasonable to expect the child or young person to indicate a guilty plea **sooner than was done**, a reduction of one-third should still be made.

5.17　In considering whether this exception applies, sentencers should distinguish between cases in which it is necessary to receive advice and/or have sight of evidence in order to understand whether the child or young person is, in fact and law, guilty of the offence(s) charged, and cases in which a child or young person merely delays guilty plea(s) in order to assess the strength of the prosecution evidence and the prospects of a finding of guilt or acquittal.

### Newton hearings and special reasons hearings

5.18　In circumstances where a child or young person's version of events is rejected at a Newton hearing[87] or special reasons hearing,[88] the reduction which would have been available at the stage of proceedings the plea was indicated should normally be halved. Where witnesses are called during such a hearing, it may be appropriate further to decrease the reduction.

### Child or young person found guilty of a lesser or different offence

5.19　If a child or young person is found guilty of a lesser or different offence from that originally charged, and has earlier made an unequivocal indication of a guilty plea to this lesser or different offence to the prosecution and the court, the court should give the level of reduction that is appropriate to the stage in the proceedings at which this indication of plea (to the lesser or different offence) was made taking into account any other of these exceptions that apply. In the Crown Court where the offered plea is a permissible alternative on the indictment as charged, the child or young person will not be treated as having made an unequivocal indication unless the defendant has entered that plea.

### Minimum sentence under section 51A of the Firearms Act 1968

5.20　There can be no reduction for a guilty plea if the effect of doing so would be to reduce the length of sentence below the required minimum term.

### Appropriate custodial sentences for young persons aged at least 16 but under 18 when found guilty under the Prevention of Crime Act 1953 and Criminal Justice Act 1988

5.21　In circumstances where an appropriate custodial sentence of a DTO of at least four months falls to be imposed on a young person who is aged at least 16 but under 18, who has been found guilty under sections 1 or 1A of the Prevention of Crime Act 1953; or section 139, 139AA or 139A of the Criminal Justice Act 1988 (certain possession of knives or offensive weapon offences) the court may impose any sentence that it considers appropriate, having taken into consideration the general principles set out above.

### Mandatory life sentences for murder

5.22　Murder is the most serious criminal offence and the sentence prescribed is different from all other sentences. By law, the sentence for murder is detention for life and the child or young person will remain subject to the sentence for the rest of their life.

5.23　Given the special characteristic of the offence of murder and the unique statutory provision in Schedule 21 of the Sentencing Code of starting points for the minimum term to be served by a child or young person, careful consideration has to be given to the extent of any reduction for a guilty plea and to the need to ensure that the minimum term properly reflects the seriousness of the offence.

---

[87] A Newton hearing is held when a child/young person pleads guilty but disputes the case as put forward by the prosecution and the dispute would make a difference to the sentence. The judge will normally hear evidence from witnesses to decide which version of the disputed facts to base the sentence on.

[88] A special reasons hearing occurs when a child/young person is found guilty of an offence carrying a mandatory licence endorsement or disqualification from driving and seeks to persuade the court that there are extenuating circumstances relating to the offence that the court should take into account by reducing or avoiding endorsement or disqualification. This may involve calling witnesses to give evidence.

5.24   Whilst the general principles continue to apply (both that a guilty plea should be encouraged and that the extent of any reduction should reduce if the indication of plea is later than the first stage of the proceedings) the process of determining the level of reduction will be different.

### Determining the level of reduction

5.25   In other circumstances:
- the court will weigh carefully the overall length of the minimum term taking into account other reductions for which the child or young person may be eligible so as to avoid a combination leading to an inappropriately short sentence;
- where it is appropriate to reduce the minimum term having regard to a plea of guilty, the reduction will not exceed one-sixth and will never exceed five years; and
- the maximum reduction of one-sixth or five years (whichever is less) should only be given when a guilty plea has been indicated at the first stage of the proceedings. Lesser reductions should be given for guilty pleas after that point, with a maximum of one-twentieth being given for a guilty plea on the day of trial.

The exceptions outlined at 5.16–5.18 apply to murder cases.

### SECTION SIX: Available sentences

SG8-8

### Crossing a significant age threshold between commission of offence and sentence

6.1   There will be occasions when an increase in the age of a child or young person will result in the maximum sentence on the date of the *finding of guilt* being greater than that available on the date on which the offence was *committed* (primarily turning 12, 15 or 18 years old).

6.2   In such situations the court should take as its starting point the sentence likely to have been imposed on the date at which the offence was committed. This includes young people who attain the age of 18 between the *commission* and *the finding of guilt of the offence* [89] but when this occurs the purpose of sentencing adult offenders[90] has to be taken into account, which is:
- the punishment of offenders;
- the reduction of crime (including its reduction by deterrence);
- the reform and rehabilitation of offenders;
- the protection of the public; and
- the making of reparation by offenders to persons affected by their offences.

6.3   When any significant age threshold is passed it will rarely be appropriate that a more severe sentence than the maximum that the court could have imposed at the time the offence was committed should be imposed. However, a sentence at or close to that maximum may be appropriate.

### Persistent offenders

6.4   Some sentences can only be imposed on children and young people if they are deemed a persistent offender. A child or young person **must** be classed as such for one of the following to be imposed:
- a youth rehabilitation order (YRO) with intensive supervision and surveillance when aged under 15;
- a YRO with fostering when aged under 15; and
- a detention and training order (DTO) when aged 12–14.

6.5   The term persistent offender is not defined in statute but has been considered by the Court of Appeal. In general it is expected that the child or young person would have had previous contact with authority as a result of criminal behaviour. This includes previous findings of guilt as well as admissions of guilt such as restorative justice disposals and conditional cautions.

6.6   A child or young person who has committed one previous offence cannot reasonably be classed as a persistent offender, and a child or young person who has committed two or more previous offences should not necessarily be assumed to be one. To determine if the behavior is persistent the nature of the previous offences and the lapse of time between the offences would need to be considered.[91]

6.7   If there have been three findings of guilt in the past 12 months for imprisonable offences of a comparable nature (or the child or young person has been made the subject of orders as detailed above in relation to an imprisonable offence) then the court could certainly justify classing the child or young person as a persistent offender.

6.8   When a child or young person is being sentenced in a single appearance for a series of separate, comparable offences committed over a short space of time then the court could justifiably consider the child or young person to be a persistent offender, despite the fact that there may be no previous

---

[89]  *R v Ghafoor* [2002] EWCA Crim 1857, [2003] 1 Cr App R (S) 428
[90]  s.57 Sentencing Code
[91]  *R v M* [2008] EWCA Crim 3329

findings of guilt.[92] In these cases the court should consider whether the child or young person has had prior opportunity to address their offending behavior before imposing one of the optional sentences available for persistent offenders only; if the court determines that the child or young person has not had an opportunity to address their behaviour and believes that an alternative sentence has a reasonable prospect of preventing re-offending then this alternative sentence should be imposed.

6.9 The court may also wish to consider any evidence of a reduction in the level of offending when taking into account previous offending behaviour. Children and young people may be unlikely to desist from committing crime in a clear cut manner but there may be changes in patterns of criminal behaviour (e.g. committing fewer and/or less serious offences or there being longer lengths of time between offences) that indicate that the child or young person is attempting to desist from crime.

6.10 Even where a child or young person is found to be a persistent offender, a court is not obliged to impose one of the optional sentences. The approach should still be individualistic and all other considerations still apply. **Custodial sentences must be a last resort for all children and young people** and there is an expectation that they will be particularly rare for children and young people aged 14 or under.

**Sentences available by age:**

| Sentence | Age of child or young person | | | Rehabilitation period |
|---|---|---|---|---|
| | 10–11 | 12–14 | 15–17 | |
| Absolute or conditional discharge or reparation order | ✓ | ✓ | ✓ | Absolute discharge and reparation: spent on day of sentence Conditional discharge: spent on last day of the period of discharge |
| Financial order | ✓ | ✓ | ✓ | Spent 6 months after the finding of guilt |
| Referral order | ✓ | ✓ | ✓ | Spent on day of completion |
| Youth rehabilitation order (YRO) | ✓ | ✓ | ✓ | Spent 6 months after the last day the order is to have effect |
| YRO with intensive supervision and surveillance or fostering | x | ✓ For persistent offenders **only** | ✓ | Spent 6 months after the last day the order is to have effect |
| Detention and training order | x | ✓ For persistent offenders **only** | ✓ | 6 months or under: spent 18 months after the sentence is completed (including supervision period) More than 6 months: spent 24 months after the sentence is completed (including supervision period) |
| s. 250 Sentencing Code detention (grave crime) | ✓ | ✓ | ✓ | More than 6 months – 30 months: spent 24 months after sentence completed (including licence period) More than 30 months – 48 months: spent 42 months after sentence completed (including licence period) More than 48 months: never spent |
| Extended sentence of detention[*] | ✓ | ✓ | ✓ | Never spent |

* If found guilty of a specified violent or sexual offence and the court is of the opinion that there is a significant risk to the public of serious harm caused by the child or young person committing further specified offences.

6.11 Some sentences have longer rehabilitation periods than others, for example referral orders are spent on the last day on which the order is to have effect.[93] Sentences can also have varying impacts on the future of children and young people; for example absolute or conditional discharges are not deemed to be treated as convictions other than for the purposes of criminal proceedings[94] and therefore may have a lesser impact on the child or young person's future prospects than other

[92] *R v S* [2000] 1 Cr App R (S) 18
[93] s.139 Legal Aid, Sentencing and Punishment of Offenders Act 2012
[94] s.82 Sentencing Code

sentences. The length of the rehabilitation periods and any likely effects on the child or young person's future prospects should be taken into account when considering if the sentence is commensurate to the seriousness of the offence.

### Breaches and the commission of further offences during the period of an order

6.12   If a child or young person is found guilty of breaching an order, or commits a further offence during the period of an order, the court will have various options available depending upon the nature of the order (**see Appendix one**). The primary aim of the court should be to encourage compliance and seek to support the rehabilitation of the child or young person.

### Absolute or conditional discharge and reparation orders

6.13   An absolute discharge is appropriate in the least serious cases when, despite a finding of guilt, the court considers that no punishment should be imposed.

6.14   A conditional discharge is appropriate when, despite a finding of guilt, the offence is not serious enough to warrant an immediate punishment. The fixed period of conditional discharge must not exceed three years. Unless exceptional circumstances are found, a conditional discharge cannot be imposed if the child or young person has received one of the following in the previous 24 months: two or more cautions; or a conditional caution followed by a caution.[95]

6.15   A reparation order can require a child or young person to make reparation to the victim of the offence, where a victim wishes it, or to the community as a whole. Before making an order the court must consider a written report from a relevant authority, e.g. a youth offending team (YOT), and the order must be commensurate with the seriousness of the offence.

6.16   If the court has the power to make a reparation order but chooses not to do so, it must give its reasons.

### Financial order

6.17   The court may impose a fine for any offence (unless the criteria for a mandatory referral order are met). In accordance with statutory requirements, where financial orders are being considered, priority must be given to compensation orders and, when an order for costs is to be made alongside a fine, the amount of the cost must not exceed the amount of the fine. If the child or young person is under 16 then the court has a duty to order parents or guardians to pay the fine; if the young person is 16 or over this duty is discretionary. In practice, many children and young people will have limited financial resources and the court will need to determine whether imposing a fine will be the most effective disposal.

6.18   A court should bear in mind that children and young people may have money that is specifically required for travel costs to school, college or apprenticeships and lunch expenses.

### Referral orders

6.19   A referral order is the mandatory sentence in a youth court or magistrates' court for most children and young people who have committed an offence for the first time and have pleaded guilty to an imprisonable offence. Exceptions are for offences where a sentence is fixed by law or if the court deems a custodial sentence, an absolute or conditional discharge or a hospital order to be more appropriate.

6.20   A discretionary referral order can also be imposed for any offence where there has been a plea of guilty regardless of previous offending history. It should be remembered that they are not community orders and in general terms may be regarded as orders which fall between community disposals and fines. However, bearing in mind that the principal aim of the youth justice system is to prevent children and young people offending, second or subsequent referral orders should be considered in those cases where:

(a)   the offence is not serious enough for a YRO but the child or young person does appear to require some intervention OR

(b)   the offence is serious enough for a YRO but it is felt that a referral order would be the best way to prevent further offending (as an example, this may be because the child or young person has responded well in the past to such an order and the offence now before the court is dissimilar to that for which a referral order was previously imposed).

Referral orders are the main sentence for delivering restorative justice and all panel members are trained Restorative Conference Facilitators; as such they can be an effective sentence in encouraging children and young people to take responsibility for their actions and understand the effect their offence may have had on their victim.

6.21   In cases where children or young people have offended for the first time and have pleaded guilty to committing an offence which is on the cusp of the custody threshold, YOTs should be encouraged

---

[95]   s. 66ZB Crime and Disorder Act 1998

to convene a Youth Offender Panel prior to sentence (sometimes referred to as a 'pseudo-panel' or 'pre-panel') where the child or young person is asked to attend before a panel and agree an intensive contract. If that contract is placed before the sentencing youth court, the court can then decide whether it is sufficient to move below custody on this occasion. The proposed contract is not something the court can alter in any way; the court will still have to make a decision between referral order and custody but can do so on the basis that if it makes a referral order it can have confidence in what that will entail in the particular case.

6.22    The court determines the length of the order but a Referral Order Panel determines the requirements of the order.

| Offence seriousness | Suggested length of referral order |
| --- | --- |
| Low | • 3–5 months |
| Medium | • 5–7 months |
| High | • 7–9 months |
| Very high | • 10–12 months |

The YOT may propose certain requirements and the length of these requirements may not correspond to the above table; if the court feels these requirements will best achieve the aims of the youth justice system then they may still be imposed.

### Youth rehabilitation orders (YRO)

6.23    A YRO is a community sentence within which a court may include one or more requirements designed to provide for punishment, protection of the public, reducing re-offending and reparation.

6.24    When imposing a YRO, the court must fix a period within which the requirements of the order are to be completed; this must not be more than three years from the date on which the order comes into effect.

6.25    The offence must be 'serious enough' in order to impose a YRO, but it does not need to be an imprisonable offence. Even if an offence is deemed 'serious enough' the court is not obliged to make a YRO.

6.26    The requirements included within the order (and the subsequent restriction on liberty) and the length of the order must be proportionate to the seriousness of the offence and suitable for the child or young person. The court should take care to ensure that the requirements imposed are not too onerous so as to make breach of the order almost inevitable.

6.27    The available requirements within a YRO are:
   • activity requirement (maximum 90 days);
   • supervision requirement;
   • unpaid work requirement (between 40 and 240 hours);*
   • programme requirement;
   • attendance centre requirement (maximum 12 hours for children aged 10–13, between 12 and 24 hours for young people aged 14 or 15 and between 12 and 36 hours for young people aged 16 or over (all ages refer to age at date of the finding of guilt));
   • prohibited activity requirement;
   • curfew requirement (maximum 12 months and between 2 and 16 hours a day);
   • exclusion requirement (maximum 3 months);
   • electronic monitoring requirement;
   • residence requirement;*
   • local authority residence requirement (maximum 6 months but not for any period after young person attains age of 18);
   • fostering requirement (maximum 12 months but not for any period after young person attains age of 18);**
   • mental health treatment requirement;
   • drug treatment requirement (with or without drug testing);
   • intoxicating substance requirement;
   • education requirement; and
   • intensive supervision and surveillance requirement.**

* These requirements are only available for young people aged 16 or 17 years old on the date of the finding of guilt.

** These requirements can only be imposed if the offence is an imprisonable one AND the custody threshold has been passed. For children and young people aged under 15 they must be deemed a persistent offender.

**Many of the above requirements have additional restrictions. Always consult your legal adviser before imposing a YRO.**

6.28   When determining the nature and extent of the requirements the court should primarily consider the likelihood of the child or young person re-offending and the risk of the child or young person causing serious harm. A higher risk of re-offending does not in itself justify a greater restriction on liberty than is warranted by the seriousness of the offence; any requirements should still be commensurate with the seriousness of the offence and regard must still be had for the welfare of the child or young person.

6.29   The YOT will assess this as part of their report and recommend an intervention level to the court for consideration. It is possible for the court to ask the YOT to consider a particular requirement.

|  | Child or Young person profile | Requirements of order[96] |
|---|---|---|
| Standard | Low likelihood of re-offending **and** a low risk of serious harm | Primarily seek to repair harm caused through, for example:<br>• reparation;<br>• unpaid work;<br>• supervision; and/or<br>• attendance centre. |
| Enhanced | Medium likelihood of re-offending **or** a medium risk of serious harm | Seek to repair harm caused and to enable help or change through, for example:<br>• supervision;<br>• reparation;<br>• requirement to address behaviour e.g. drug treatment, offending behaviour programme, education programme; and/or<br>• a combination of the above. |
| Intensive | High likelihood of re-offending **or** a very high risk of serious harm | Seek to ensure the control of and enable help or change for the child or young person through, for example:<br>• supervision;<br>• reparation;<br>• requirement to address behaviour;<br>• requirement to monitor or restrict movement, e.g. prohibited activity, curfew, exclusion or electronic monitoring; and/or<br>• a combination of the above. |

6.30   If a child or young person is assessed as presenting a high risk of re-offending or of causing serious harm but the offence that was committed is of relatively low seriousness then the appropriate requirements are likely to be primarily rehabilitative or for the protection of the public.

6.31   Likewise if a child or young person is assessed as presenting a low risk of re-offending or of causing serious harm but the offence was of relatively high seriousness then the appropriate requirements are likely to be primarily punitive.

**Orders with intensive supervision and surveillance or with fostering**

6.32   An intensive supervision and surveillance requirement and a fostering requirement are both community alternatives to custody.

6.33   The offence must be punishable by imprisonment, cross the custody threshold and a custodial sentence must be merited before one of these requirements can be imposed.

6.34   An order of this nature may only be imposed on a child or young person aged below 15 (at the time of the finding of guilt) if they are a persistent offender.

**With intensive supervision and surveillance:**

6.35   An order of this nature must include an extended activity requirement of between 90 and 180 days, a supervision requirement and a curfew requirement. Where appropriate, a YRO with intensive supervision and surveillance may also include additional requirements (other than a fostering requirement), although the order as a whole must comply with the obligation that the requirements must be those most suitable for the child or young person and that any restrictions on liberty are commensurate with the seriousness of the offence.

---

[96] The examples provided here are not exclusive; the YOT will make recommendations based upon their assessment of the young offender which may vary from some of the examples given.

6.36    When imposing such an order, the court must ensure that the requirements are not so onerous as to make the likelihood of breach almost inevitable.

### With fostering:

6.37    Where a fostering requirement is included within a YRO, it will require the child or young person to reside with a local authority foster parent for a specified period that must not exceed 12 months.

6.38    In order to impose this requirement the court must be satisfied that the behaviour which constituted the offence was due to a significant extent to the circumstances in which the child or young person was living, and that the imposition of fostering requirement would assist in the child or young person's rehabilitation. It is likely that other rights will be engaged (such as those under Article 8 of the European Convention on Human Rights)[97] and any interference with such rights must be proportionate.

6.39    The court must consult the child or young person's parent or guardian (unless impracticable) and the local authority before including this requirement. It can only be included if the child or young person was legally represented in court when consideration was being given to imposing such a requirement unless the child or young person, having had the opportunity to do so, did not apply for representation or that right was withdrawn because of the child or young person's conduct. **This requirement may be included only where the court has been notified that arrangements are available in the area of the relevant authority.**

6.40    A YRO with a fostering requirement must include a supervision requirement and can include other requirements when appropriate (except an intensive supervision and surveillance requirement). The order as a whole must comply with the obligation that the requirements must be those most suitable for the child or young person and that any restrictions on liberty are commensurate with the seriousness of the offence.

6.41    It is unlikely that the statutory criteria[98] will be met in many cases; where they are met and the court is considering making an order, care should be taken to ensure that there is a well developed plan for the care and support of the child or young person throughout the period of the order and following conclusion of the order. The court will need to be provided with sufficient information, including proposals for education and training during the order and plans for the child or young person on completion of the order.

### Custodial sentences

**A custodial sentence should always be used as a last resort. If offence specific guidelines for children and young people are available then the court should consult them in the first instance to assess whether custody is the most appropriate disposal.**

The available custodial sentences for children and young people are:

| Youth Court | Crown Court |
| --- | --- |
| • 4 months;<br>• 6 months;<br>• 8 months;<br>• 10 months;<br>• 12 months;<br>• 18 months; or<br>• 24 months. | • Detention and training order (the same periods are available as in the youth court)<br>• Long-term detention (under section 250 Sentencing Code)<br>• Extended sentence of detention or detention for life (if dangerousness criteria are met)<br>• Detention at Her Majesty's pleasure (for offences of murder) |

6.42    Under both domestic and international law, a custodial sentence must only be imposed as a **'measure of last resort;'** statute provides that such a sentence may be imposed only where an offence is 'so serious that neither a fine alone nor a community sentence can be justified'.[99] If a custodial sentence is imposed, a court must state its reasons for being satisfied that the offence is so serious that no other sanction would be appropriate and, in particular, why a YRO with intensive supervision and surveillance or fostering could not be justified.

6.43    The term of a custodial sentence must be the shortest commensurate with the seriousness of the offence; any case that warrants a DTO of less than four months must result in a non-custodial sentence. The court should take account of the circumstances, age and maturity of the child or young person.

6.44    In determining whether an offence has crossed the custody threshold the court will need to assess the seriousness of the offence, in particular the level of harm that was caused, or was likely to have

---

[97]  Right to respect for family and private life
[98]  See paragraphs 5.28–5.30
[99]  s.230 Sentencing Code

been caused, by the offence. The risk of serious harm in the future must also be assessed. The pre-sentence report will assess this criterion and must be considered before a custodial sentence is imposed. A custodial sentence is most likely to be unavoidable where it is necessary to protect the public from serious harm.

6.45   Only if the court is satisfied that the offence crosses the custody threshold, and that no other sentence is appropriate, the court may, as a preliminary consideration, consult the equivalent adult guideline in order to decide upon the appropriate length of the sentence.

6.46   When considering the relevant adult guideline, the court **may** feel it appropriate to apply a sentence broadly within the region of half to two thirds of the adult sentence for those aged 15–17 and allow a greater reduction for those aged under 15. This is only a rough guide and must not be applied mechanistically. In most cases when considering the appropriate reduction from the adult sentence the **emotional and developmental age and maturity of the child or young person is of at least equal importance as their chronological age**.

6.47   The individual factors relating to the offence and the child or young person are of the greatest importance and may present good reason to impose a sentence outside of this range. The court should bear in mind the negative effects a short custodial sentence can have; short sentences disrupt education and/or training and family relationships and support which are crucial stabilising factors to prevent re-offending.

6.48   There is an expectation that custodial sentences will be particularly rare for a child or young person aged 14 or under. If custody is imposed, it should be for a shorter length of time than that which a young person aged 15–17 would receive if found guilty of the same offence. For a child or young person aged 14 or under the sentence should normally be imposed in a youth court (except in cases of homicide or when the dangerous offender criteria are met).

6.49   The welfare of the child or young person must be considered when imposing any sentence but is especially important when a custodial sentence is being considered. A custodial sentence could have a significant effect on the prospects and opportunities of the child or young person and a child or young person is likely to be more susceptible than an adult to the contaminating influences that can be expected within a custodial setting. There is a high reconviction rate for children and young people that have had custodial sentences and there have been many studies profiling the effect on vulnerable children and young people, particularly the risk of self harm and suicide and so it is of utmost importance that custody is a last resort.

### Detention and training order (DTO)

6.50   A court can only impose a DTO if the child or young person is legally represented unless they have refused to apply for legal aid or it has been withdrawn as a result of their conduct.

6.51   If it is determined that the offence is of such seriousness that a custodial sentence is unavoidable then the length of this sentence must be considered on an individual basis. The court must take into account the chronological age of the child or young person, as well as their maturity, emotional and developmental age and other relevant factors, such as their mental health or any learning disabilities.

6.52   A DTO cannot be imposed on any child under the age of 12 at the time of the finding of guilt and is only applicable to children aged 12–14 if they are deemed to be a persistent offender. (See section on persistent offenders on page 22.)

6.53   A DTO can be made only for the periods prescribed – 4, 6, 8, 10, 12, 18 or 24 months. Any time spent on remand in custody or on bail subject to a qualifying curfew condition should be taken into account when calculating the length of the order. The accepted approach is to double the time spent on remand before deciding the appropriate period of detention, in order to ensure that the regime is in line with that applied to adult offenders.[100] After doubling the time spent on remand the court should then adopt the nearest prescribed period available for a DTO.

### Long-term detention

6.54   A child or young person may be sentenced by the Crown Court to long-term detention under section 250 Sentencing Code if found guilty of a grave crime and neither a community order nor a DTO is suitable.

6.55   These cases may be sent for trial to the Crown Court or committed for sentence only[101] (see section two for further information).

6.56   It is possible that, following a guilty plea, a two year detention order may be appropriate as opposed to a sentence of long term detention (under section 250 Sentencing Code), to account for the reduction.

---

[100]   *R v Eagles* [2006] EWCA Crim 2368
[101]   s.16 Sentencing Code

**Dangerous offenders**

6.57    If a child or young person is found to be a dangerous offender they can be sentenced to **extended detention** or **detention for life**.

6.58    A sentence of extended detention may be imposed only where the appropriate custodial term would be 4 years or more. The extension period must not exceed 5 years in the case of a specified violent offence and 8 years in the case of a specified sexual offence. The term of the extended sentence of detention must not exceed the maximum term of imprisonment for an adult offender convicted of that offence.

6.59    A sentence of detention for life should be used as a last resort when an extended sentence is not able to provide the level of public protection that is necessary. In order to determine this, the court should consider the following factors in the order given:
- the seriousness of the offence;
- the child or young person's previous findings of guilt;
- the level of danger posed to the public and whether there is a reliable estimate of the length of time the child or young person will remain a danger; and
- the alternative sentences available.

The court is required to set a minimum term which must be served in custody before parole can be considered.

**Detention at Her Majesty's pleasure**

6.60    This is the mandatory sentence for any child or young person found guilty of committing a murder. The starting point for the minimum term is 12 years.

**SG8-9**    APPENDIX: Breach of orders

**Breach of a conditional discharge**

7.1     If a child or young person commits an offence during the period of conditional discharge then the court has the power to re-sentence the original offence. The child or young person should be dealt with on the basis of their age when convicted (if different from their current age) and the court can deal with the original offence(s) in any way which it could have if the child or young person had just been found guilty.

7.2     There is no requirement to re-sentence; if a court deems it appropriate to do so they can sentence the child or young person for the new offence and leave the conditional discharge in place. If the order was made by the Crown Court then the youth court can commit the child or young person in custody or release them on bail until they can be brought or appear before the Crown Court. The court shall also send to the Crown Court a memorandum of conviction.

7.3     If the offender is convicted of committing a new offence after attaining the age of 18 but during the period of a conditional discharge made by a youth court then they may be re-sentenced for the original offence by the convicting adult magistrates' court. If the adult magistrates' court decides to take no action then the youth court that imposed the conditional discharge may summon the offender for the breach to be dealt with.

**Breach of a reparation order**

7.4     If it is proved to the appropriate court that the child or young person has failed to comply with any requirement of a reparation order that is currently in force then the court can:
- order the child or young person to pay a fine not exceeding £1,000; or
- revoke the order and re-sentence the child or young person using the range of sentencing options that are currently available. However the sentence imposed must be one that could be imposed on a child or young person who was the age that the offender was when in fact convicted.

If re-sentencing the child or young person the court must take into account the extent to which the child or young person has complied with the requirements of this order.

7.5     If the order was made by the Crown Court then the youth court can commit the child or young person in custody or release them on bail until they can be brought or appear before the Crown Court.

7.6     The child or young person or a Youth Offending Team (YOT) officer can also apply for the order to be revoked or amended. There is no power to re-sentence in this situation as the child or young person has not been found to be in breach of requirements.

**Breach of a referral order (referral back to court)**

7.7     If a child or young person is found to have breached the conditions of their referral order the court can revoke the referral order and re-sentence the child or young person using the range of sentencing options (other than a referral order) that are currently available. However the sentence imposed must be one that could be imposed on a child or young person who was the age that the offender was when in fact convicted. If the court chooses not to revoke the referral order then it is possible to:

- allow the referral order to continue with the existing contract;
- extend the length of the referral order up to a maximum of 12 months (in total); or
- impose a fine up to a maximum of £2,500.

7.8   If an offender has attained the age of 18 by the first court hearing then breach proceedings must be dealt with by the adult magistrates' court.

### Commission of further offences whilst on a referral order

7.9   The court has the power to extend a referral order in respect of additional or further offences. This applies to not only a first referral order but also to any subsequent referral orders. Any period of extension must not exceed the total 12 month limit for a referral order.

7.10   If the court chooses not to extend the existing referral order or impose a discharge they have the power to impose a new referral order (where the discretionary referral order conditions are satisfied) in respect of the new offences only. This order can remain or run alongside the new order or the court may direct that the contract under the new order is not to take effect until the earlier order is revoked or discharged. Alternatively, the court may impose an absolute or conditional discharge.

7.11   If the court sentences in any other way they have a discretionary power to revoke the referral order. Where an order is revoked, if it appears to be in the interests of justice, the court may deal with the original offence(s) using the range of sentencing options (other than a referral order) that are currently available. However the sentence imposed must be one that could be imposed on a child or young person who was the age that the offender was when in fact convicted. Where the referral contract has taken effect, the court shall have regard to the extent of the child or young person's compliance with the terms of the contract.

### Breach of a youth rehabilitation order (YRO)

7.12   Where a child or young person is in breach of a YRO the following options are available to the court:

- take no action and allow the order to continue in its original form;
- impose a fine (up to £2,500) (and allow the order to continue in its original form);
- amend the terms of the order; or
- revoke the order and re-sentence the child or young person.

7.13   If the terms of the order are amended the new requirements must be capable of being complied with before the expiry of the overall period. The court may impose any requirement that is currently available (provided the requirement is available to a child or young person who is the age that the offender was at the time in fact convicted) and this may be in addition to, or in substitution for, any requirements contained in the order. If the YRO did not contain an unpaid work requirement and the court includes such a requirement using this power, the minimum period of unpaid work is 20 hours; this will give greater flexibility when responding to less serious breaches or where there are significant other requirements to be complied with.

7.14   A court may not amend the terms of a YRO that did not include an extended activity requirement or a fostering requirement by inserting them at this stage; should these requirements be considered appropriate following breach, the child or young person must be re-sentenced and the original YRO revoked.

7.15   A court must ensure that it has sufficient information to enable it to understand why the order has been breached and should be satisfied that the YOT and other local authority services have taken all steps necessary to ensure that the child or young person has been given appropriate opportunity and the support necessary for compliance. This is particularly important if the court is considering imposing a custodial sentence as a result of the breach.

7.16   Where the failure arises primarily from non-compliance with reporting or other similar obligations and a sanction is necessary, the most appropriate response is likely to be the inclusion of (or increase in) a primarily punitive requirement such as the curfew requirement, unpaid work, the exclusion requirement and the prohibited activity requirement or the imposition of a fine. However, continuing failure to comply with the order is likely to lead to revocation of the order and re-sentencing for the original offence.

7.17   Where the child or young person has 'wilfully and persistently' failed to comply with the order, and the court proposes to sentence again for the offence(s) in respect of which the order was made, additional powers are available.

A child or young person will almost certainly be considered to have 'wilfully and persistently' breached a YRO where there have been three breaches that have demonstrated a lack of willingness to comply with the order that have resulted in an appearance before court.

7.18    The additional powers available to the court when re-sentencing a child or young person who has 'wilfully and persistently' breached their order are:
- the making of a YRO with intensive supervision and surveillance even though the offence is non-imprisonable;
- a custodial sentence if the YRO that is breached is one with an intensive supervision and surveillance requirement, which was imposed for an offence that was imprisonable; and
- the imposition of a DTO for four months for breach of a YRO with intensive supervision and surveillance which was imposed following wilful and persistent breach of an order made for a non-imprisonable offence.

The primary objective when sentencing for breach of a YRO is to ensure that the child or young person completes the requirements imposed by the court.

7.19    If an offender has attained the age of 18 by the first court hearing then breach proceedings must be dealt with by the adult magistrates' court. If the court chooses to revoke the order then its powers are limited to those available to the court at the time of the original sentence.

### Commission of further offences during a YRO

7.20    If a child or young person commits an offence whilst subject to a YRO the court can impose any sentence for the new matter, but can only impose a new YRO if they revoke the existing order. Where the court revokes the original order they may re-sentence that matter at the same time as sentencing the new offence.

### Breach of a detention and training order (DTO)

7.21    If a child or young person is found to have breached a supervision requirement after release from custody then the court may:
- impose a further period of custody of up to three months or the length of time from the date the breach was committed until the end of the order, **whichever is shorter;**
- impose a further period of supervision of up to three months or the length of time from the date the breach was committed until the end of the order, **whichever is shorter;**
- impose a fine of up to £1,000; or
- take no action.

Even if the offender has attained the age of 18 proceedings for breach of the supervision requirements must be dealt with in the youth court.

### Commission of further offences during a DTO

7.22    If a child or young person is found guilty of a further imprisonable offence committed during the currency of the order then the court can impose a further period of detention. This period of detention cannot exceed the period between the date of the new offence and the date of when the original order would have expired.

7.23    This period can be served consecutively or concurrently with any sentence imposed for the new offence and this period should not be taken into account when determining the appropriate length of the sentence for the new offence.

**SG8-10**                     Sexual Offences Guideline

Sentencing a child or young person for sexual offences involves a number of different considerations from adults. The primary difference is the age and level of maturity. Children and young people are less emotionally developed than adults; offending can arise through inappropriate sexual experimentation; gang or peer group pressure to engage in sexual activity; or a lack of understanding regarding consent, exploitation, coercion and appropriate sexual behaviour.

Below is a non-exhaustive list of factors that illustrate the type of background factors that may have played a part in leading a child or young person to commit an offence of this kind.

- Victim of neglect or abuse (sexual, physical or emotional) or has witnessed the neglect or abuse of another.
- Exposure to pornography or materials which are age inappropriate.
- Involvement in gangs.
- Associated with child sexual exploitation.
- Unstable living or educational arrangements.
- Communication or learning disabilities or mental health concerns.

- Part of a peer group, school or neighbourhood where harmful sexual norms and attitudes go unchallenged.
- A trigger event such as the death of a close relative or a family breakdown.

> This guideline should be read alongside the Overarching Principles – Sentencing Children and Young People definitive guideline which provides comprehensive guidance on the sentencing principles and welfare considerations that the court should have in mind when sentencing children and young people.

The first step in determining the sentence is to assess the seriousness of the offence. This assessment is made by considering the nature of the offence and any aggravating and mitigating factors relating to the offence itself. **The fact that a sentence threshold is crossed does not necessarily mean that that sentence should be imposed.**

### STEP 1  Offence Seriousness – Nature of the offence

The boxes below give **examples** of the type of culpability and harm factors that may indicate that a particular threshold of sentence has been crossed.

| A non-custodial sentence* may be the most suitable disposal where one or more of the following factors apply: |
| --- |
| Any form of non-penetrative sexual activity |
| Any form of sexual activity (including penetration) without coercion, exploitation or pressure except where there is a significant disparity in age or maturity |
| Minimal psychological or physical harm caused to the victim |

| A custodial sentence or youth rehabilitation order with intensive supervision and surveillance* or fostering* may be justified where one or more of the following factors apply: |
| --- |
| Any penetrative activity involving coercion, exploitation or pressure |
| Use or threats of violence against the victim or someone known to the victim |
| Prolonged detention/sustained incident |
| Severe psychological or physical harm caused to the victim |

\* Where the child or young person appears in the magistrates' court, and the conditions for a compulsory referral order apply, a referral order must be imposed unless the court is considering imposing a discharge, hospital order or custody.

### STEP 2  Offence Seriousness – Aggravating and mitigating factors

To complete the assessment of seriousness the court should consider the aggravating and mitigating factors relevant to the offence.

| Aggravating factors |
| --- |
| *Statutory aggravating factors:* |
| Previous findings of guilt, having regard to a) the **nature** of the offence to which the finding of guilt relates and its relevance to the current offence; and b) the time that has elapsed since the finding of guilt |
| Offence committed whilst on bail |
| Offence motivated by, or demonstrating hostility based on any of the following characteristics or presumed |
| characteristics of the victim: religion, race, disability, sexual orientation or transgender identity |
| *Other aggravating factors (non-exhaustive):* |
| Significant degree of planning |
| Child or young person acts together with others to commit the offence |
| Use of alcohol/drugs on victim to facilitate the offence |
| Abuse of trust |
| Deliberate humiliation of victim, including but not limited to filming of the offence, deliberately committing the offence before a group of peers with the intention of causing additional distress or circulating details/photos/videos etc of the offence on social media or within peer groups |
| Grooming |
| Significant disparity of age between the child or young person and the victim (measured chronologically or with reference to level of maturity) (where not taken into account at step one) |
| Victim is particularly vulnerable due to factors including but not limited to age, mental or physical disability |

Sentencing Guidelines

| Any steps taken to prevent reporting the incident/seeking assistance |
| --- |
| Pregnancy or STI as a consequence of offence |
| Blackmail |
| Use of weapon |
| **Mitigating factors (non-exhaustive)** |
| No previous findings of guilt **or** no relevant/recent findings of guilt |
| Good character and/or exemplary conduct |
| Participated in offence due to bullying, peer pressure, coercion or manipulation |
| Genuine belief that activity was lawful |

## STEP 3  Personal mitigation

Having assessed the offence seriousness, the court should then consider the mitigation personal to the child or young person to determine whether a custodial sentence or a community sentence is necessary. The effect of personal mitigation may reduce what would otherwise be a custodial sentence to a non-custodial one, or a community sentence to a different means of disposal.

| **Personal mitigating factors (non-exhaustive)** |
| --- |
| Particularly young or immature child or young person (where it affects their responsibility) |
| Communication or learning disabilities or mental health concerns |
| Unstable upbringing including but not limited to:- |
| • time spent looked after |
| • lack of familial presence or support |
| • disrupted experiences in accommodation or education |
| • exposure to drug/alcohol abuse, familial criminal behaviour or domestic abuse |
| • exposure by others to pornography or sexually explicit materials |
| • victim of neglect or abuse, or exposure to neglect or abuse of others |
| • experiences of trauma or loss |
| Determination and/or demonstration of steps taken to address offending behaviour |
| Strong prospect of rehabilitation |
| Child or young person in education, training or employment |

## STEP 4  Reduction for guilty plea

The court should take account of any potential reduction for a guilty plea in accordance with section 73 of the Sentencing Code and part one, section five of the *Overarching Principles – Sentencing Children and Young People* definitive guideline.

The reduction in sentence for a guilty plea can be taken into account by imposing one type of sentence rather than another; for example:

•  by reducing a custodial sentence to a community sentence; or
•  by reducing a community sentence to a different means of disposal.

Alternatively the court could reduce the length or severity of any punitive requirements attached to a community sentence.

See the *Overarching Principles – Sentencing Children and Young People* definitive guideline for details of other available sentences including Referral Orders and Reparation Orders.

## STEP 5  Review the sentence

The court must now review the sentence to ensure it is the most appropriate one for the child or young person. This will include an assessment of the likelihood of reoffending and the risk of causing serious harm. A report from the Youth Offending Team may assist.

See the *Overarching Principles – Sentencing Children and Young People* definitive guideline for comprehensive guidance on the sentencing principles and welfare considerations that the court should have in mind when sentencing children and young people, and for the full range of the sentences available to the court.

## Referral Orders

In cases where children or young people have offended for the first time and have pleaded guilty to committing an offence which is on the cusp of the custody threshold, YOTs should be encouraged to convene a Youth Offender Panel prior to sentence (sometimes referred to as a 'pseudo-panel' or 'pre-panel') where the child or young person is asked to attend before a panel and agree an intensive contract. If that contract is placed before the sentencing youth court, the court can then decide whether it is sufficient to move below custody on this occasion. The proposed contract is not something the court can alter in any way; the court will still have to make a decision between referral order and custody but can do so on the basis that if it makes a referral order it can have confidence in what that will entail in the particular case.

The court determines the length of the order but a Referral Order Panel determines the requirements of the order.

| Offence seriousness | Suggested length of referral order |
| --- | --- |
| Low | • 3–5 months |
| Medium | • 5–7 months |
| High | • 7–9 months |
| Very high | • 10–12 months |

The YOT may propose certain requirements and the length of these requirements may not correspond to the above table; if the court feels these requirements will best achieve the aims of the youth justice system then they may still be imposed.

## Youth Rehabilitation Order (YRO)

The following table sets out the different levels of intensity that are available under a Youth Rehabilitation Order. The level of intensity and the content of the order will depend upon the court's assessment of seriousness.

| Requirements of order | | |
| --- | --- | --- |
| Standard | Low likelihood of re-offending **and** a low risk of serious harm | Primarily seek to repair harm caused through, for example: <br>• reparation; <br>• unpaid work; <br>• supervision; and/or <br>• attendance centre. |
| Enhanced | Medium likelihood of re-offending **or** a medium risk of serious harm | Seek to repair harm caused and to enable help or change through, for example: <br>• supervision; <br>• reparation; <br>• requirement to address behaviour e.g. drug treatment, offending behaviour programme, education programme; and/or <br>• a combination of the above. |
| Intensive | High likelihood of re-offending **or** a very high risk of serious harm | Seek to ensure the control of and enable help or change for the child or young person through, for example: <br>• supervision; <br>• reparation; <br>• requirement to address behaviour; <br>• requirement to monitor or restrict movement, e.g. prohibited activity, curfew, exclusion or electronic monitoring; and/or <br>• a combination of the above. |

### YRO with Intensive Supervision and Surveillance (ISS) or YRO with Fostering

A YRO with an ISS or fostering requirement can only be imposed where the court is of the opinion that the offence has crossed the custody threshold and custody is merited.

The YRO with ISS includes an extended activity requirement, a supervision requirement and curfew. The YRO with fostering requires the child or young person to reside with a local authority foster parent for a specified period of up to 12 months.

**Custodial Sentences**

If a custodial sentence is imposed, the court must state its reasons for being satisfied that the offence is so serious that no other sanction would be appropriate and, in particular, why a YRO with ISS or fostering could not be justified.

Where a custodial sentence is **unavoidable** the length of custody imposed must be the shortest commensurate with the seriousness of the offence. The court may want to consider the equivalent adult guideline in order to determine the appropriate length of the sentence.

If considering the adult guideline, the court may feel it appropriate to apply a sentence broadly within the region of half to two thirds of the appropriate adult sentence for those aged 15–17 and allow a greater reduction for those aged under 15. This is only a rough guide and must not be applied mechanically. The individual factors relating to the offence and the child or young person are of the greatest importance and may present good reason to impose a sentence outside of this range.

**SG8-11**                                  Robbery Guideline

This guideline should be read alongside the *Overarching Principles – Sentencing Children and Young People* definitive guideline which provides comprehensive guidance on the sentencing principles and welfare considerations that the court should have in mind when sentencing children and young people.

The first step in determining the sentence is to assess the seriousness of the offence. This assessment is made by considering the nature of the offence and any aggravating and mitigating factors relating to the offence itself. **The fact that a sentence threshold is crossed does not necessarily mean that that sentence should be imposed.**

**STEP 1  Offence Seriousness – Nature of the offence**

The boxes below give **examples** of the type of culpability and harm factors that may indicate that a particular threshold of sentence has been crossed.

| A non-custodial sentence* may be the most suitable disposal where one or more of the following factors apply: |
| --- |
| Threat or use of minimal force |
| Little or no physical or psychological harm caused to the victim |
| Involved through coercion, intimidation or exploitation |

| A custodial sentence or youth rehabilitation order with intensive supervision and surveillance* or fostering* may be justified where one or more of the following factors apply: |
| --- |
| Use of very significant force |
| Threat or use of a bladed article, firearm or imitation firearm (where produced) |
| Significant physical or psychological harm caused to the victim |

\* Where the child or young person appears in the magistrates' court, and the conditions for a compulsory referral order apply, a referral order must be imposed unless the court is considering imposing a discharge, hospital order or custody.

**STEP 2  Offence Seriousness – Aggravating and mitigating factors**

To complete the assessment of seriousness the court should consider the aggravating and mitigating factors relevant to the offence.

| Aggravating factors |
| --- |
| *Statutory aggravating factors:* |
| Previous findings of guilt, having regard to a) the **nature** of the offence to which the finding of guilt relates and its **relevance** to the current offence; and b) the **time** that has elapsed since the finding of guilt |
| Offence committed whilst on bail |
| Offence motivated by, or demonstrating hostility based on any of the following characteristics or presumed characteristics of the victim: religion, race, disability, sexual orientation or transgender identity |

| *Other aggravating factors (non-exhaustive):* |
|---|
| Significant degree of planning |
| Deliberate humiliation of victim, including but not limited to filming of the offence, deliberately committing the offence before a group of peers with the intention of causing additional distress or circulating details/photos/videos etc of the offence on social media or within peer groups |
| Threat or use of a weapon other than a bladed article, firearm or imitation firearm (whether produced or not) |
| Threat to use a bladed article, firearm or imitation firearm (not produced) |
| Victim is particularly vulnerable due to factors including but not limited to age, mental or physical disability |
| A leading role where offending is part of a group |
| Attempt to conceal identity (for example, wearing a balaclava or hood) |
| Any steps taken to prevent reporting the incident/seeking assistance |
| High value goods or sums targeted or obtained (includes economic, personal or sentimental) |
| Restraint, detention or additional degradation of the victim |
| **Mitigating factors (non-exhaustive)** |
| No previous findings of guilt **or** no relevant/recent findings of guilt |
| Good character and/or exemplary conduct |
| Participated in offence due to bullying, peer pressure, coercion or manipulation |
| Remorse, particularly where evidenced by voluntary reparation to the victim |
| Little or no planning |

## STEP 3  Personal mitigation

Having assessed the offence seriousness, the court should then consider the mitigation personal to the child or young person to determine whether a custodial sentence or a community sentence is necessary. The effect of personal mitigation may reduce what would otherwise be a custodial sentence to a non-custodial one, or a community sentence to a different means of disposal.

| **Personal mitigating factors (non-exhaustive)** |
|---|
| Particularly young or immature child or young person (where it affects their responsibility) |
| Communication or learning disabilities or mental health concerns |
| Unstable upbringing including but not limited to: |
| • time spent looked after |
| • lack of familial presence or support |
| • disrupted experiences in accommodation or education |
| • exposure to drug/alcohol abuse, familial criminal behaviour or domestic abuse |
| • victim of neglect or abuse, or exposure to neglect or abuse of others |
| • experiences of trauma or loss |
| Determination and/or demonstration of steps taken to address offending behaviour |
| Child or young person in education, training or employment |

## STEP 4  Reduction for guilty plea

The court should take account of any potential reduction for a guilty plea in accordance with section 73 of the Sentencing Code and part one, section five of the *Overarching Principles – Sentencing Children and Young People* definitive guideline.

The reduction in sentence for a guilty plea can be taken into account by imposing one type of sentence rather than another; for example:

- by reducing a custodial sentence to a community sentence; or
- by reducing a community sentence to a different means of disposal.

Alternatively the court could reduce the length or severity of any punitive requirements attached to a community sentence.

Sentencing Guidelines

See the *Overarching Principles – Sentencing Children and Young People* definitive guideline for details of other available sentences including Referral Orders and Reparation Orders.

### STEP 5  Review the sentence

The court must now review the sentence to ensure it is the most appropriate one for the child or young person. This will include an assessment of the likelihood of reoffending and the risk of causing serious harm. A report from the Youth Offending Team may assist.

See the *Overarching Principles – Sentencing Children and Young People* definitive guideline for comprehensive guidance on the sentencing principles and welfare considerations that the court should have in mind when sentencing children and young people, and for the full range of the sentences available to the court.

### Referral Orders

In cases where children or young people have offended for the first time and have pleaded guilty to committing an offence which is on the cusp of the custody threshold, YOTs should be encouraged to convene a Youth Offender Panel prior to sentence (sometimes referred to as a 'pseudo-panel' or 'pre-panel') where the child or young person is asked to attend before a panel and agree an intensive contract. If that contract is placed before the sentencing youth court, the court can then decide whether it is sufficient to move below custody on this occasion. The proposed contract is not something the court can alter in any way; the court will still have to make a decision between referral order and custody but can do so on the basis that if it makes a referral order it can have confidence in what that will entail in the particular case. The court determines the length of the order but a Referral Order Panel determines the requirements of the order.

| Offence seriousness | Suggested length of referral order |
|---------------------|-------------------------------------|
| Low | • 3–5 months |
| Medium | • 5–7 months |
| High | • 7–9 months |
| Very high | • 10–12 months |

The YOT may propose certain requirements and the length of these requirements may not correspond to the above table; if the court feels these requirements will best achieve the aims of the youth justice system then they may still be imposed.

### Youth Rehabilitation Order (YRO)

The following table sets out the different levels of intensity that are available under a YRO. The level of intensity and the content of the order will depend upon the court's assessment of seriousness.

| Requirements of order | | |
|------------------------|---|---|
| Standard | Low likelihood of re-offending **and** a low risk of serious harm | Primarily seek to repair harm caused through, for example:<br>• reparation;<br>• unpaid work;<br>• supervision; and/or<br>• attendance centre. |
| Enhanced | Medium likelihood of re-offending **or** a medium risk of serious harm | Seek to repair harm caused and to enable help or change through, for example:<br>• supervision;<br>• reparation;<br>• requirement to address behaviour e.g. drug treatment, offending behaviour programme, education programme; and/or<br>• a combination of the above. |

| Requirements of order | | |
|---|---|---|
| Intensive | High likelihood of re-offending **or** a very high risk of serious harm | Seek to ensure the control of and enable help or change for the child or young person through, for example:<br>• supervision;<br>• reparation;<br>• requirement to address behaviour;<br>• requirement to monitor or restrict movement, e.g. prohibited activity, curfew, exclusion or electronic monitoring; and/or<br>• a combination of the above. |

### YRO with Intensive Supervision and Surveillance (ISS) or YRO with fostering

A YRO with an ISS or fostering requirement can only be imposed where the court is of the opinion that the offence has crossed the custody threshold, and custody is merited.

The YRO with ISS includes an extended activity requirement, a supervision requirement and curfew.

The YRO with fostering requires the child or young person to reside with a local authority foster parent for a specified period of up to 12 months.

### Custodial Sentences

If a custodial sentence is imposed, the court must state its reasons for being satisfied that the offence is so serious that no other sanction would be appropriate and, in particular, why a YRO with ISS or fostering could not be justified.

Where a custodial sentence is **unavoidable** the length of custody imposed must be the shortest commensurate with the seriousness of the offence. The court may want to consider the equivalent adult guideline in order to determine the appropriate length of the sentence.

If considering the adult guideline, the court may feel it appropriate to apply a sentence broadly within the region of half to two thirds of the appropriate adult sentence for those aged 15–17 and allow a greater reduction for those aged under 15. This is only a rough guide and must not be applied mechanistically. The individual factors relating to the offence and the child or young person are of the greatest importance and may present good reason to impose a sentence outside of this range.

# PART 9    IMPOSITION OF COMMUNITY AND CUSTODIAL SENTENCES

**Effective from:** 01 February 2017

**SG9-1**                                                    APPLICABILITY

[For the standard text on applicability see **SG0-4**]

**SG9-2**                                        IMPOSITION OF COMMUNITY ORDERS

### General Principles

Community orders can fulfil all of the purposes of sentencing. In particular, they can have the effect of restricting the offender's liberty while providing punishment in the community, rehabilitation for the offender, and/or ensuring that the offender engages in reparative activities.

A community order must not be imposed unless the offence is 'serious enough to warrant the making of such an order'.[102] Where an offender is being sentenced for a non-imprisonable offence, there is no power to make a community order.[103]

Sentencers must consider all available disposals at the time of sentence; even where the threshold for a community sentence has been passed, a fine or discharge may be an appropriate penalty. In particular, a Band D fine may be an appropriate alternative to a community order.

The court must ensure that the restriction on the offender's liberty is commensurate with the seriousness of the offence[104] and that the requirements imposed are the most suitable for the offender.[105]

Sentences should not necessarily escalate from one community order range to the next on each sentencing occasion. The decision as to the appropriate range of community order should be based upon the seriousness of the new offence(s) (which will take into account any previous convictions).

Save in exceptional circumstances at least one requirement must be imposed for the purpose of punishment and/or a fine imposed in addition to the community order.[106] It is a matter for the court to decide which requirements amount to a punishment in each case.

### Community Order Levels

The seriousness of the offence should be the initial factor in determining which requirements to include in a community order. Offence-specific guidelines refer to three sentencing levels within the community order band based on offence seriousness (low, medium and high).

The culpability and harm present in the offence(s) should be considered to identify which of the three sentencing levels within the community order band (low, medium and high) is appropriate.

See below for **non-exhaustive** examples of requirements that might be appropriate in each.

At least one requirement **MUST** be imposed for the purpose of punishment and/or a fine imposed in addition to the community order unless there are exceptional circumstances which relate to the offence or the offender that would make it unjust in all the circumstances to do so.[107]

A full list of requirements, including those aimed at offender rehabilitation, is available below.

| Low | Medium | High |
|-----|--------|------|
| Offences only just cross community order threshold, where the seriousness of the offence or the nature of the offender's record means that a discharge or fine is inappropriate | Offences that obviously fall within the community order band | Offences only just fall below the custody threshold or the custody threshold is crossed but a community order is more appropriate |

---

[102] s.204(2) Sentencing Code
[103] s.202(1)(b) Sentencing Code
[104] s.208(6) Sentencing Code
[105] s.208(3) Sentencing Code
[106] s.208(10) and (11) Sentencing Code
[107] s.208(10) and (11) Sentencing Code

| Low | Medium | High |
|---|---|---|
| In general, only one requirement will be appropriate and the length may be curtailed if additional requirements are necessary | | More intensive sentences which combine two or more requirements may be appropriate |
| Suitable requirements might include:<br>• Any appropriate rehabilitative requirement(s)<br>• 40–80 hours of unpaid work<br>• Curfew requirement within the lowest range (for example up to 16 hours per day for a few weeks)<br>• Exclusion requirement, for a few months<br>• Prohibited activity requirement<br>• Attendance centre requirement (where available) | Suitable requirements might include:<br>• Any appropriate rehabilitative requirement(s)<br>• Greater number of hours of unpaid work (for example 80–150 hours)<br>• Curfew requirement within the middle range (for example up to 16 hours for 2–3 months)<br>• Exclusion requirement lasting in the region of 6 months<br>• Prohibited activity requirement | Suitable requirements might include:<br>• Any appropriate rehabilitative requirement(s)<br>• 150–300 hours of unpaid work<br>• Curfew requirement within the middle range (for example up to 16 hours for 2–3 months)<br>• Exclusion order lasting in the region of 12 months |
| * If order does not contain a punitive requirement, suggested fine levels are indicated below: | | |
| BAND A FINE | BAND B FINE | BAND C FINE |

### Specific considerations in determining requirements

i) Where two or more requirements are included, they must be compatible with one another and must not be excessive.

ii) Any requirement must not conflict with an offender's religious beliefs or with the requirements of any other court order to which they may be subject. Interference with an offender's attendance at work or educational establishment should also be avoided.

iii) The particular requirements imposed must be suitable for the individual offender and will be influenced by a range of factors, including:
- the stated purpose(s) of the sentence;
- the risk of re-offending;
- the ability of the offender to comply;
- the availability of the requirements in the local area.

### Requirements

Community orders consist of one or more of the following requirements:

- **unpaid work requirement** (40–300 hours to be completed within 12 months)
- **rehabilitation activity requirement** (RAR's provide flexibility for responsible officers in managing an offender's rehabilitation post sentence. The court does not prescribe the activities to be included but will specify the maximum number of activity days the offender must complete. The responsible officer will decide the activities to be undertaken. Where appropriate this requirement should be made in addition to, and not in place of, other requirements. Sentencers should ensure the activity length of a RAR is suitable and proportionate).
- **programme requirement** (specify the number of days)
- **prohibited activity requirement** (must consult National Probation Service)
- **curfew requirement** (2–16 hours in any 24 hours; maximum term 12 months; must consider those likely to be affected; see note on electronic monitoring below)
- **exclusion requirement** (from a specified place/places; maximum period 2 years: may be continuous or only during specified periods; see note on electronic monitoring below)
- **residence requirement** (to reside at a place specified or as directed by the responsible officer)
- **foreign travel prohibition requirement** (not to exceed 12 months)
- **mental health treatment requirement** (may be residential/non-residential; must be by/under the direction of a registered medical practitioner or chartered psychologist. The court must be satisfied: (a) that the mental condition of the offender is such as requires and may be susceptible to treatment but is not such as to warrant the making of a hospital or guardianship order; (b) that arrangements for treatment have been made; (c) that the offender has expressed willingness to comply).

- **drug rehabilitation requirement** (the court must be satisfied that the offender is dependent on or has a propensity to misuse drugs which requires or is susceptible to treatment. The offender must consent to the order. Treatment can be residential or non-residential, and reviews must be attended by the offender (subject to application for amendment) at intervals of not less than a month (discretionary on requirements of up to 12 months, mandatory on requirements of over 12 months))
- **alcohol treatment requirement** (residential or non-residential; must have offender's consent; court must be satisfied that the offender is dependent on alcohol and that the dependency is susceptible to treatment)
- **alcohol abstinence and monitoring requirement** (where available)
- **attendance centre requirement** (12–36 hours) (Only available for offenders under 25 when convicted)

### Pre-sentence reports

In many cases, a pre-sentence report will be pivotal in helping the court decide whether to impose a community order and, if so, whether particular requirements or combinations of requirements are suitable for an individual offender. Whenever the court reaches the provisional view that a community order may be appropriate, it should request a pre-sentence report (whether written or verbal) unless the court is of the opinion that a report is unnecessary in all the circumstances of the case. It may be helpful to indicate to the National Probation Service the court's preliminary opinion as to which of the three sentencing ranges is relevant and the purpose(s) of sentencing that the package of requirements is expected to fulfil. Ideally a pre-sentence report should be completed on the same day to avoid adjourning the case. If an adjournment cannot be avoided, the information should be provided to the National Probation Service in written form and a copy retained on the court file for the benefit of the sentencing court. **However, the court must make clear to the offender that all sentencing options remain open including, in appropriate cases, committal for sentence to the Crown Court.**

### Electronic monitoring

The court must impose an electronic monitoring requirement where it makes a community order with a curfew or exclusion requirement save where:[108]

- there is a person (other than the offender) without whose co-operation it will not be practicable to secure the monitoring and that person does not consent;[109] and/or
- electronic monitoring is unavailable and/or impractical;[110] and/or
- in the particular circumstances of the case, it considers it inappropriate to do so.[111]

The court may impose electronic monitoring in all other cases. Electronic monitoring should be used with the primary purpose of promoting and monitoring compliance with other requirements, in circumstances where the punishment of the offender and/or the need to safeguard the public and prevent re-offending are the most important concerns.

**SG9-3**

## IMPOSITION OF CUSTODIAL SENTENCES

The approach to the imposition of a custodial sentence should be as follows:

### 1) Has the custody threshold been passed?

- A custodial sentence must not be imposed unless the offence or the combination of the offence and one or more offences associated with it was so serious that neither a fine alone nor a community sentence can be justified for the offence.
- There is no general definition of where the custody threshold lies. The circumstances of the individual offence and the factors assessed by offence-specific guidelines will determine whether an offence is so serious that neither a fine alone nor a community sentence can be justified. Where no offence specific guideline is available to determine seriousness, the harm caused by the offence, the culpability of the offender and any previous convictions will be relevant to the assessment.
- The clear intention of the threshold test is to reserve prison as a punishment for the most serious offences.

### 2) Is it unavoidable that a sentence of imprisonment be imposed?

- Passing the custody threshold does not mean that a custodial sentence should be deemed inevitable. Custody should not be imposed where a community order could provide sufficient restriction on an offender's liberty (by way of punishment) while addressing the rehabilitation of the offender to prevent future crime.

---

[108] Sch. 9 paras. 10 and 12 Sentencing Code
[109] Sch. 9 para. 33 Sentencing Code
[110] Sch. 9 para. 34 Sentencing Code
[111] Sch. 9 paras. 10 and 12 Sentencing Code

- For offenders on the cusp of custody, imprisonment should not be imposed where there would be an impact on dependants which would make a custodial sentence disproportionate to achieving the aims of sentencing.

### 3)  What is the shortest term commensurate with the seriousness of the offence?

- In considering this the court must NOT consider any licence or post sentence supervision requirements which may subsequently be imposed upon the offender's release.

### 4)  Can the sentence be suspended?

- A suspended sentence **MUST NOT** be imposed as a more severe form of community order. A **suspended sentence is a custodial sentence. Sentencers should be clear that they would impose an immediate custodial sentence if the power to suspend were not available.** If not, a non-custodial sentence should be imposed.

The following factors should be weighed in considering whether it is possible to suspend the sentence:

| Factors indicating that it would not be appropriate to suspend a custodial sentence | Factors indicating that it may be appropriate to suspend a custodial sentence |
|---|---|
| Offender presents a risk/danger to the public | Realistic prospect of rehabilitation |
| Appropriate punishment can only be achieved by immediate custody | Strong personal mitigation |
| History of poor compliance with court orders | Immediate custody will result in significant harmful impact upon others |

The imposition of a custodial sentence is both punishment and a deterrent. To ensure that the overall terms of the suspended sentence are commensurate with offence seriousness, care must be taken to ensure requirements imposed are not excessive. A court wishing to impose onerous or intensive requirements should reconsider whether a community sentence might be more appropriate.

**Pre-sentence report**

Whenever the court reaches the provisional view that:

- the custody threshold has been passed; and, if so
- the length of imprisonment which represents the shortest term commensurate with the seriousness of the offence;

the court should obtain a pre-sentence report, whether verbal or written, unless the court considers a report to be unnecessary. Ideally a pre-sentence report should be completed on the same day to avoid adjourning the case.

**Magistrates:** Consult your legal adviser before deciding to sentence to custody without a pre-sentence report.

SUSPENDED SENTENCES: GENERAL GUIDANCE     **SG9-4**

i)   The guidance regarding pre-sentence reports applies if suspending custody.
ii)  If the court imposes a term of imprisonment of between 14 days and 2 years (subject to magistrates' courts sentencing powers), it may suspend the sentence for between 6 months and 2 years (the 'operational period'). The time for which a sentence is suspended should reflect the length of the sentence; up to 12 months might normally be appropriate for a suspended sentence of up to 6 months.
iii) Where the court imposes two or more sentences to be served consecutively, the court may suspend the sentence where the aggregate of the terms is between 14 days and 2 years (subject to magistrates' courts sentencing powers).
iv)  When the court suspends a sentence, it may impose one or more requirements for the offender to undertake in the community. The requirements are identical to those available for community orders above.
v)   A custodial sentence that is suspended should be for the same term that would have applied if the sentence was to be served immediately.

# Sentencing Decision Flowchart

## SENTENCING

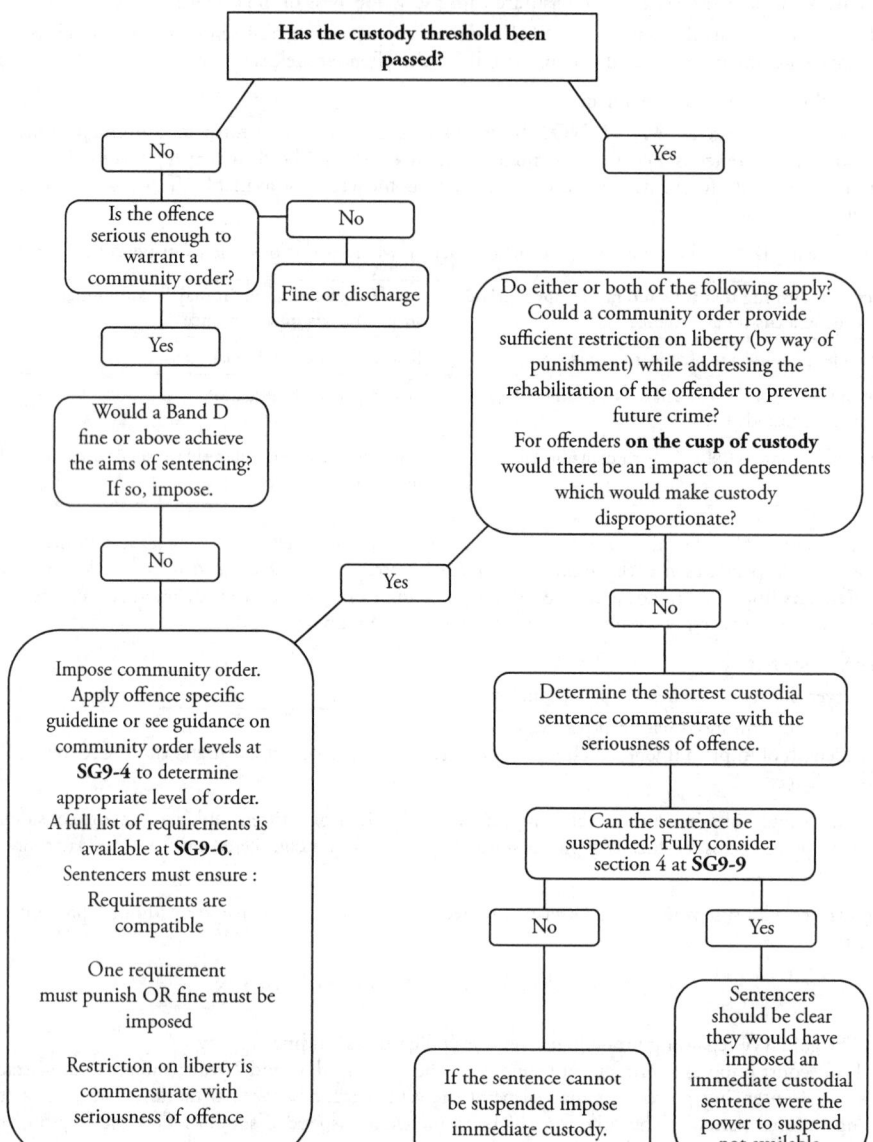

# PART 10   MAGISTRATES' COURT SENTENCING GUIDELINES

This Part sets out the Explanatory Materials for the Magistrates' Court Sentencing Guidelines followed by the offence guidelines which are specific to the Magistrates' Court.

Following these guidelines                                   **SG10-1**

**Following these guidelines**

When sentencing an offender, every court is under a statutory obligation to follow any relevant sentencing guideline unless it would be contrary to the interests of justice to do so (Sentencing Code, s.59(1)). If a court imposes a sentence outside the range indicated in an offence specific guideline, it is obliged to state its reasons for doing so (Sentencing Code, s.52(6)).

**When to use these guidelines**

These guidelines apply to sentencing in a magistrates' court whatever the composition of the court. They cover offences for which sentences are frequently imposed in a magistrates' court when dealing with adult offenders.

They also apply to allocation (mode of trial) decisions. When dealing with an either way offence for which there is no plea or an indication of a not guilty plea, these guidelines will be relevant to the allocation decision and should be consulted at this stage to assess the likely sentence. Reference should be made to the allocation guideline. [See **SG1**]

These guidelines apply also to the Crown Court when dealing with appeals against sentences imposed in a magistrates' court and when sentencing for summary only offences.

Using pre-Sentencing Council guidelines                         **SG10-2**

The offence guidelines include two structures: pre-Sentencing Council guidelines (issued by the Sentencing Guidelines Council) before 2010 and Sentencing Council guidelines issued from 2011 onwards.

**Using pre-Sentencing Council guidelines (guidelines issued before 2010)**
This section explains the key decisions involved in the sentencing process for SGC guidelines.

*1. Assess offence seriousness (culpability and harm)*
Offence seriousness is the starting point for sentencing under the Sentencing Code. The court's assessment of offence seriousness will:

- determine which of the sentencing thresholds has been crossed;
- indicate whether a custodial, community or other sentence is the most appropriate;
- be the key factor in deciding the length of a custodial sentence, the onerousness of requirements to be incorporated in a community sentence and the amount of any fine imposed.

When considering the seriousness of any offence, the court must consider the offender's culpability in committing the offence and any harm which the offence caused, was intended to cause, or might foreseeably have caused (Sentencing Code, s. 63). In using these guidelines, this assessment should be approached in two stages.

*2. Offence seriousness (culpability and harm)*
*A. Identify the appropriate starting point*
The guidelines set out examples of the nature of activity which may constitute the offence, progressing from less to more serious conduct, and provide a starting point based on a **first time offender pleading not guilty.** The guidelines also specify a sentencing range for each example of activity. Within the guidelines, a first time offender is a person who does not have a conviction which, by virtue of section 65 of the Sentencing Code, must be treated as an aggravating factor.

Sentencers should begin by considering which of the examples of offence activity corresponds most closely to the circumstances of the particular case in order to identify the appropriate starting point:

- where the starting point is a fine, this is indicated as band A, B or C. For more information, see the approach to assessing fines;

- where the community sentence threshold is passed, the guideline sets out whether the starting point should be a low, medium or high level community order. For more information, see community order ranges;
- where the starting point is a custodial sentence, see custodial sentences.

The Council's definitive guideline *Overarching Principles: Seriousness*, published 16 December 2004, identifies four levels of culpability for sentencing purposes (intention, recklessness, knowledge and negligence). The starting points in the individual offence guidelines assume that culpability is at the highest level applicable to the offence (often, but not always, intention). Where a lower level of culpability is present, this should be taken into account.

### 2. Offence seriousness (culpability and harm)

#### B. Consider the effect of aggravating and mitigating factors

Once the starting point has been identified, the court can add to or reduce this to reflect any aggravating or mitigating factors that impact on the culpability of the offender and/or harm caused by the offence to reach a provisional sentence. Any factors contained in the description of the activity used to reach the starting point must not be counted again. The range is the bracket into which the provisional sentence will normally fall after having regard to factors which aggravate or mitigate the seriousness of the offence. However:

- the court is not precluded from going outside the range where the facts justify it;
- previous convictions which aggravate the seriousness of the current offence may take the provisional sentence beyond the range, especially where there are significant other aggravating factors present.

In addition, where an offender is being sentenced for multiple offences, the court's assessment of the totality of the offending may result in a sentence above the range indicated for the individual offences, including a sentence of a different type. See the definitive guidelines on *Offences Taken into Consideration* [**SG3**] and *Totality* [**SG4**] for more information. The guidelines identify aggravating and mitigating factors which may be particularly relevant to each individual offence. These include some factors drawn from the general list of aggravating and mitigating factors in the Council's definitive guideline (see 'seriousness' link above). In each case, sentencers should have regard to the full list, which includes the factors that, by statute, make an offence more serious:

- offence committed while on bail for other offences;
- offence was racially or religiously aggravated;
- offence was motivated by, or demonstrates, hostility based on the victim's sexual orientation (or presumed sexual orientation);
- offence was motivated by, or demonstrates, hostility based on the victim being (or being presumed to be) transgender;
- offence was motivated by, or demonstrates, hostility based on the victim's disability (or presumed disability);
- offender has previous convictions that the court considers can reasonably be treated as aggravating factors having regard to their relevance to the current offence and the time that has elapsed since conviction.

While the lists in the offence guidelines and other material referenced above, aim to identify the most common aggravating and mitigating factors, they are not intended to be exhaustive. Sentencers should always consider whether there are any other factors that make the offence more or less serious.

### 3. Form a preliminary view of the appropriate sentence, then consider offender mitigation

When the court has reached a provisional sentence based on its assessment of offence seriousness, it should take into account matters of offender mitigation. The Council guideline *Overarching Principles: Seriousness* states that the issue of remorse should be taken into account at this point along with other mitigating features such as admissions to the police in interview.

### 4. Consider a reduction for a guilty plea

*Reduction in sentence for a guilty plea, where first hearing is on or after 1 June 2017*

Key principles [See **SG5**]

#### For cases where the first hearing is before 1 June 2017

The Council guideline *Reduction in Sentence for a Guilty Plea*, revised 2007, states that the punitive elements of the sentence should be reduced to recognise an offender's guilty plea. The reduction has no impact on sentencing decisions in relation to ancillary orders, including disqualification. The level of the reduction should reflect the stage at which the offender indicated a willingness to admit guilt and will be gauged on a sliding scale, ranging from a recommended one third (where the guilty plea was entered at the first reasonable opportunity), reducing to a recommended one quarter (where a trial date has been set) and to a recommended one tenth (for a guilty plea entered at the 'door of the court' or after the trial has begun). There is a presumption that the recommended reduction will be given unless there are good reasons for a lower amount. The application of the reduction may affect the type, as well as the severity, of the sentence. It may also take the sentence below the range in some cases. The court must state that it has reduced a sentence to reflect a guilty plea (Sentencing Code, s. 52(7)). It should usually indicate what the sentence would have been if there had been no reduction as a result of the plea.

### 5. Consider ancillary orders, including compensation

Ancillary orders of particular relevance to individual offences are identified in the relevant guidelines. The court must always consider making a compensation order where the offending has resulted in personal injury, loss or damage. The court is required to give reasons if it decides not to make such an order (Sentencing Code, s. 55).

[See the Sentencing Council Explanatory Materials for Ancillary Orders in the Magistrates' Courts and the Crown Court Compendium, Part II Sentencing, S7; Ancillary Orders]

### 6. Decide sentence Give reasons

Review the total sentence to ensure that it is proportional to the offending behaviour and properly balanced. Sentencers must state reasons for the sentence passed in every case, including for any ancillary orders imposed (Sentencing Code, s. 52). It is particularly important to identify any aggravating or mitigating factors, or matters of offender mitigation, that have resulted in a sentence more or less severe than the suggested starting point. If a court imposes a sentence of a different kind or outside the range indicated in the guidelines, it must state its reasons for doing so (Sentencing Code, s. 52(6)). The court should also give its reasons for not making an order that has been canvassed before it or that it might have been expected to make.

### Using Sentencing Council guidelines                        SG10-3

The offence guidelines include two structures: pre-Sentencing Council guidelines (issued by the Sentencing Guidelines Council) before 2010 and Sentencing Council guidelines issued from 2011 onwards.

### Using Sentencing Council guidelines (guidelines effective from 2011 onwards)

*This section of the user guide explains the key decisions involved in the sentencing process for Sentencing Council guidelines.*

### STEP ONE:  Determining the offence category

The decision making process includes a two-step approach to assessing seriousness. The first step is to determine the offence category by means of an assessment of the offender's culpability and the harm caused, or intended, by reference only to the factors set out at step one in each guideline. The contents are tailored for each offence and comprise the principal factual elements of the offence.

### STEP TWO:  Starting point and category range

The guidelines provide a starting point which applies to all offenders irrespective of plea or previous convictions. The guidelines also specify a category range for each offence category. The guidelines provide non-exhaustive lists of aggravating and mitigating factors relating to the context of the offence and to the offender. Sentencers should identify whether any combination of these, or other relevant factors, should result in an upward or downward adjustment from the starting point. In some cases, it may be appropriate to move outside the identified category range when reaching a provisional sentence.

### FURTHER STEPS

Having reached a provisional sentence, there are a number of further steps within the guidelines. These steps are clearly set out within each guideline and are tailored specifically for each offence in order to ensure that only the most appropriate guidance is included within each offence specific guideline. The further steps include:

- reduction for assistance to the prosecution;
- reduction for guilty pleas (the court should take account of any potential reduction for a guilty plea in accordance with section 73 of the Sentencing Code and the guideline for Reduction in Sentence for a Guilty Plea [SG5-1–SG5-12];
- where an offender is being sentenced for multiple offences – the court's assessment of the totality of the offending may result in a sentence above the range indicated for the individual offences, including a sentence of a different type (for more information, refer to the *Totality* guideline [see **SG4**]);
- compensation orders and/or ancillary orders appropriate to the case; and
- give reasons for, and explain the effect of, the sentence.

Where there is no guideline for an offence, refer to the General Guideline [see SG2].

**SG10-4**                    LIST OF AGGRAVATING AND MITIGATING FACTORS

Taken from Sentencing Guidelines Council Guideline Overarching Principles: Seriousness.

The lists below bring together the most important aggravating and mitigating features with potential application to more than one offence or class of offences. They include some factors which are integral features of certain offences; in such cases, the presence of the aggravating factor is already reflected in the penalty for the offence and cannot be used as justification for increasing the sentence further. The lists are not intended to be comprehensive and the factors are not listed in any particular order of priority. If two or more of the factors listed describe the same feature care needs to be taken to avoid "double counting".

### Aggravating factors
*Factors indicating higher culpability:*
- offence committed whilst on bail for other offences;
- failure to respond to previous sentences;
- offence was racially or religiously aggravated;
- offence motivated by, or demonstrating, hostility to the victim based on his or her sexual orientation (or presumed sexual orientation);
- offence motivated by, or demonstrating, hostility based on the victim's disability (or presumed disability);
- previous conviction(s), particularly where a pattern of repeat offending is disclosed;
- planning of an offence;
- an intention to commit more serious harm than actually resulted from the offence;
- offenders operating in groups or gangs;
- 'professional' offending;
- commission of the offence for financial gain (where this is not inherent in the offence itself);
- high level of profit from the offence;
- an attempt to conceal or dispose of evidence;
- failure to respond to warnings or concerns expressed by others about the offender's behaviour;
- offence committed whilst on licence;
- offence motivated by hostility towards a minority group, or a member or members of it;
- deliberate targeting of vulnerable victim(s);
- commission of an offence while under the influence of alcohol or drugs;
- use of a weapon to frighten or injure victim;
- deliberate and gratuitous violence or damage to property, over and above what is needed to carry out the offence;
- abuse of power;
- abuse of a position of trust.

*Factors indicating a more than usually serious degree of harm:*
- multiple victims;
- an especially serious physical or psychological effect on the victim, even if unintended;
- a sustained assault or repeated assaults on the same victim;
- victim is particularly vulnerable;
- location of the offence (for example, in an isolated place);
- offence is committed against those working in the public sector or providing a service to the public;
- presence of others for example, relatives, especially children or partner of the victim;
- additional degradation of the victim (for example, taking photographs of a victim as part of a sexual offence);
- in property offences, high value (including sentimental value) of property to the victim, or substantial consequential loss (for example, where the theft of equipment causes serious disruption to a victim's life or business).

### Mitigating factors
*Factors indicating lower culpability:*
- a greater degree of provocation than normally expected;
- mental illness or disability;
- youth or age, where it affects the responsibility of the individual defendant;
- the fact that the offender played only a minor role in the offence.

**Offender mitigation**

- genuine remorse;
- admissions to police in interview;
- ready co-operation with authorities.

ANCILLARY ORDERS                                                   SG10-5

### 1. Introduction to ancillary orders

1. There are several ancillary orders available in a magistrates' court which should be considered in appropriate cases. Annex A lists the offences in respect of which certain orders are available [not reproduced]. The individual offence guidelines above also identify ancillary orders particularly likely to be relevant to the offence. In all cases, consult your legal adviser regarding available orders and their specific requirements and effects.
2. Ancillary orders should be taken into account when assessing whether the overall penalty is commensurate with offence seriousness.

### 2. Anti-social behaviour orders                                              SG10-6

These have now been replaced by Criminal Behaviour Orders (see below)

### 3. Binding over orders                                                       SG10-7

The court has the power to bind an individual over to keep the peace.[112]

The order is designed to prevent future misconduct and requires the individual to promise to pay a specified sum if the terms of the order are breached. Exercise of the power does not depend upon conviction.

Guidance on the making of binding over orders is set out in [CPD VII, Sentencing J: see **CPD.VII.J**]. Key principles include:

(1) before imposing the order, the court must be satisfied so that it is sure that a breach of the peace involving violence or an imminent threat of violence has occurred, or that there is a real risk of violence in the future. The court should hear evidence and the parties before making any order;
(2) the court should state its reasons for making the order;
(3) the order should identify the specific conduct or activity from which the individual must refrain, the length of the order and the amount of the recognisance;
(4) the length of the order should be proportionate to the harm sought to be avoided and should not generally exceed 12 months;
(5) when fixing the amount of the recognisance, the court should have regard to the individual's financial resources.

### 4. Confiscation orders                                                       SG10-8

Confiscation orders under the Proceeds of Crime Act 2002 may only be made by the Crown Court.

An offender convicted of an offence in a magistrates' court must be committed to the Crown Court where this is requested by the prosecution with a view to a confiscation order being considered.[113]

If the committal is made in respect of an either way offence, the court must state whether it would have committed the offender to the Crown Court for sentencing had the issue of a confiscation order not arisen.

### 5. Criminal Behaviour Orders                                                 SG10-9

A Criminal Behaviour Order (CBO) is an order which is available on conviction for any criminal offence by any criminal court, introduced by the Anti-social Behaviour, Crime and Policing Act 2014 (ABCPA 2014, s.22) with effect from 20 October 2014. It replaces the former powers of the court to make orders such as an ASBO or a drinking banning order on conviction. The statutory provisions relating to CBOs are now contained in Chapter 1 of Part 11 of the Sentencing Code.

A CBO is an order designed to tackle the most serious and persistent anti-social individuals where their behaviour has brought them before a criminal court. The anti-social behaviour to be addressed does not need to be connected to the criminal behaviour, or activity which led to the conviction. However, if there is no link the court will need to reflect on the reasons for making the order.

---

[112] Justices of the Peace Act 1361, Magistrates' Court Act 1980, s. 115
[113] Proceeds of Crime Act 2002, s. 70

A CBO can deal with a wide range of anti-social behaviours following the offender's conviction, for example threatening violence against others in the community, or persistently being drunk and aggressive in public. However, the order should not be designed to stop reasonable, trivial or benign behaviours that have not caused, or are not likely to cause anti-social behaviour.

Any application will be made by the prosecution (Sentencing Code, s.331(1)(b)).[114] The majority of applications will therefore be made by the CPS, either at their own initiative, or at the request of the police. However, it may also be applied for by local councils, providing they are the prosecuting authority in the case. *The court cannot make a CBO of its own volition.*

A CBO may only be made against an offender when they have been sentenced to at least a conditional discharge for the substantive offence.[115] *A CBO cannot be made where the offender has been given an absolute discharge.*

The court may only make a CBO if:

1. It is satisfied that the offender has engaged in behaviour that caused or was likely to cause harassment, alarm or distress to any person,[116] and
2. It considers that making the order will help in preventing the offender from engaging in such behaviour.[117]

*For the first condition, the burden of proof on the prosecution is to the criminal standard.* (There is no test of necessity as with ASBOs.)

A CBO may:

1. Prohibit the offender from doing anything described in the order ('a prohibition'), and/or
2. Require the offender to do anything described in the order ('a requirement').[118]

However, any prohibitions and/or requirements must, so far as practicable, avoid any interference with times an offender would normally work, attend school or other educational establishment and any conflict with any other court order.[119]

If the order requires the offender to do anything, then the order must specify the individual or organisation that is responsible for supervising compliance with the requirement (Sentencing Code, s.333(1)) and must hear from them about both the suitability and enforceability of a requirement, before including it in the CBO.[120]

The order must be proportionate and reasonable. It will be for the court to decide the measures which are most appropriate and available to tackle the underlying cause of the anti-social behaviour.

The order should be tailored to the specific needs of each perpetrator.

When deciding whether or not to make a CBO, the court is entitled to consider evidence submitted by the prosecution and by the offender.[121] It does not matter whether the evidence would have been admissible, or has been heard as part of the criminal proceedings in which the offender was convicted,[122] but it should be relevant to the test to be applied to the making of the order (i.e. that the offender has engaged in behaviour that caused, or was likely to cause, harassment, alarm or distress to any person, and that the court considers that making the order will assist in preventing the offender from engaging in such behaviour). This evidence could include hearsay or bad character evidence. Special measures are available for witnesses who are vulnerable and intimidated witnesses in accordance with the Youth Justice and Criminal Evidence Act 1999.[123]

A CBO takes effect on the day it is made,[124] unless the offender is already subject to an existing CBO, in which case it may take effect on the day in which the previous order expires.[125] The order must

---

[114] Sentencing Code, s.331(1)(b)
[115] Sentencing Code, s.331(3)
[116] Sentencing Code, s.331(2)(a)
[117] Sentencing Code, s.331(2)(b)
[118] Sentencing Code, s.330
[119] Sentencing Code, s.331(4)
[120] Sentencing Code, s.331(2)
[121] Sentencing Code, s.332(1)
[122] Sentencing Code, s.332(2)
[123] Sentencing Code, s.340
[124] Sentencing Code, s.334(1)
[125] Sentencing Code, s.334(2)

specify the period for which it has effect.[126] In the case of an adult, the order must be for a fixed period of not less than two years or it may be an indefinite period, so that it is made until further order.[127] An order may specify different periods for which particular prohibitions or requirements have effect within the order.[128]

The court can impose an *interim order* in cases where the offender is convicted but the court is adjourning the hearing of the application for a CBO,[129] before or after sentence for the offence. The offender need not be sentenced to be made subject to an interim order.[130] The court can make an interim order if the court thinks it is just to do so. An interim order can be made until final hearing or further order.[131] When making an interim order the court has the same powers as if it were making a final order.[132]

It is likely that the hearing for a CBO will take place at the same time as the sentencing for the criminal case. For adult offenders, there is no formal consultation requirement. However, in order to ensure that applications are made appropriately and efficiently, there is an expectation that any relevant agencies will have been consulted so that the prosecution have the relevant information to decide whether to make an order or not and if so, in what terms. The prosecution should be prepared to deal with an application on the date of hearing.

The court may deal with the application for a CBO at the same time as it imposes sentence for the offence. Alternatively, the court may sentence the offender for the criminal offence and adjourn the application for a CBO to a later date.[133] However, the court cannot hear an application once sentence has taken place, unless the application was made by the prosecution before sentence was concluded, as an application cannot be made retrospectively.

If the offender does not appear at an adjourned hearing for a CBO, the court may further adjourn the proceedings, issue a warrant for the offender's arrest, or hear the proceedings in the offender's absence.[134] To issue a warrant for the offender's arrest, the court must be satisfied that the offender has been given adequate notice of the time and place for the hearing.[135] To proceed in the offender's absence, the court must be satisfied that the offender has been given adequate notice of the time and place for the hearing and been told if they do not attend, the court may hear the application in their absence.[136]

Further guidance is provided by the Home Office in *Anti-social Behaviour, Crime and Policing Act 2014: Reform of anti-social behaviour powers; Statutory guidance for frontline professionals.* July 2014.[137]

### 6. Deprivation of ownership of animal                                      SG10-10

Where an offender convicted of one of the following offences under the Animal Welfare Act 2006 is the owner of an animal in relation to which the offence is committed, the court may make an order depriving him or her of ownership of the animal and for its disposal:[138]

(1) causing unnecessary suffering (s.4);
(2) mutilation (s.5);
(3) docking of dogs' tails (ss.6(1) and 6(2));
(4) fighting etc. (s.8);
(5) breach of duty to ensure welfare (s.9);
(6) breach of disqualification order (s.36(9)).

The court is required to give reasons if it decides not to make such an order.

Deprivation of ownership may be ordered instead of or in addition to dealing with the offender in any other way.

---

[126] Sentencing Code, s.334(3)
[127] Sentencing Code, s.334(5)
[128] Sentencing Code, s.335(1)
[129] Sentencing Code, s.335(2)
[130] Sentencing Code, s.335(3)
[131] Sentencing Code, s.335(2)
[132] Sentencing Code, s.335(4)
[133] Sentencing Code, s.332(3)
[134] Sentencing Code, s.332(4)
[135] Sentencing Code, s.332(5)
[136] Sentencing Code, s.332(6)
[137] www.gov.uk/government/uploads/system/uploads/attachment_data/file/332839/StatutoryGuidanceFrontline.pdf
[138] Animal Welfare Act 2006, s.33

**SG10-11**  **7. Deprivation orders**

The court has the power to deprive an offender of property used for the purpose of committing or facilitating the commission of an offence, whether or not it deals with the offender in any other way.

Before making the order, the court must have regard to the value of the property and the likely financial and other effects on the offender.

Without limiting the circumstances in which the court may exercise the power, a vehicle is deemed to have been used for the purpose of committing the offence where the offence is punishable by imprisonment and consists of:

1. driving, attempting to drive, or being in charge of a motor vehicle;
2. failing to provide a specimen; or
3. failing to stop and/or report an accident

**SG10-12**  **8. Destruction orders and contingent destruction orders for dogs**

See Step 6 of the relevant guideline for dangerous dog offences:

- Breeding, selling, exchanging or advertising a prohibited dog, Dangerous Dogs Act 1991, s.1(7)
- Owner or person in charge of a dog dangerously out of control in any place in England and Wales (whether or not a public place), Dangerous Dogs Act 1991, s.3(1)
- Owner or person in charge of a dog dangerously out of control in any place in England and Wales (whether or not a public place) where a person is injured, Dangerous Dogs Act 1991, s.3(1)
- Owner or person in charge of a dog dangerously out of control in any place in England and Wales (whether or not a public place) where an assistance dog is injured or killed, Dangerous Dogs Act 1991, s.3(1)
- Owner or person in charge of a dog dangerously out of control in any place in England and Wales (whether or not a public place) where death is caused, Dangerous Dogs Act 1991, s.3(1)
- Possession of a prohibited dog, Dangerous Dogs Act 1991, s.1(7)

**SG10-13**  **9. Disqualification from driving — general power**

- The court may disqualify any person convicted of an offence from driving for such period as it thinks fit.[139] This may be instead of or in addition to dealing with the offender in any other way.
- The section does not require the offence to be connected to the use of a vehicle. The Court of Appeal has held that the power is available as part of the overall punitive element of a sentence, and the only restrictions on the exercise of the power are those in the statutory provision.[140]

**SG10-14**  **10. Disqualification from ownership of animals**

Where an offender is convicted of one of the following offences under the Animal Welfare Act 2006, the court may disqualify him or her from owning or keeping animals, dealing in animals, and/or transporting animals:[141]

(1) causing unnecessary suffering (s.4);
(2) mutilation (s.5);
(3) docking of dogs' tails (ss.6(1) and 6(2));
(4) administration of poisons etc. (s.7);
(5) fighting etc. (s.8);
(6) breach of duty to ensure welfare (s.9);
(7) breach of licensing or registration requirements (s.13(6));
(8) breach of disqualification order (s.36(9)).

The court is required to give reasons if it decides not to make such an order.

The court may specify a period during which an offender may not apply for termination of the order under section 43 of the Animal Welfare Act 2006; if no period is specified, an offender may not apply for termination of the order until one year after the order was made.

Disqualification may be imposed instead of or in addition to dealing with the offender in any other way.

---

[139] Sentencing Code s.163
[140] *R v Cliff* [2004] EWCA Crim 3139
[141] ibid, s.34

### 11.  Disqualification of company directors

SG10-15

The Company Directors Disqualification Act 1986 empowers the court to disqualify an offender from being a director or taking part in the promotion, formation or management of a company for up to five years.

An order may be made in two situations:

(1)   where an offender has been convicted of an indictable offence in connection with the promotion, formation, management, liquidation or striking off of a company;[142] or

(2)   where an offender has been convicted of an offence involving a failure to file documents with, or give notice to, the registrar of companies. If the offence is triable only summarily, disqualification can be ordered only where the offender has been the subject of three default orders or convictions in the preceding five years.[143]

### 12.  Drinking banning orders

SG10-16

These have now been replaced by Criminal Behaviour Orders. [See **SG10-9**]

### 13.  Exclusion orders

SG10-17

The court may make an exclusion order where an offender has been convicted of an offence committed on licensed premises involving the use or threat of violence.

The order prohibits the offender from entering *specified* licensed premises without the consent of the licensee. The term of the order must be between three months and two years.

### 14.  Football banning orders

SG10-18

The court must make a football banning order where an offender has been convicted of a relevant offence and it is satisfied that there are reasonable grounds to believe that making a banning order would help to prevent violence or disorder.[144] If the court is not so satisfied, it must state that fact and give its reasons.

Relevant offences are those set out in schedule 1 [to] the Football Spectators Act 1989 …

The order requires the offender to report to a police station within five days, may require the offender to surrender his or her passport, and may impose requirements on the offender in relation to any regulated football matches.

Where the order is imposed in addition to a sentence of immediate imprisonment, the term of the order must be between six and ten years. In other cases, the term of the order must be between three and five years.

### 15.  Forfeiture and destruction of drugs

SG10-19

Where an offender is convicted of an offence under the Misuse of Drugs Act 1971, the court may order forfeiture and destruction of anything shown to the satisfaction of the court to relate to the offence.[145]

### 16.  Forfeiture and destruction of goods bearing unauthorised trade mark

SG10-20

Where the court is satisfied that an offence under section 92 of the Trade Marks Act 1994 has been committed, it must (on the application of a person who has come into possession of the goods in connection with the investigation or prosecution of the offence) order forfeiture of the goods.[146]

If it considers it appropriate, instead of ordering destruction of the goods, the court may direct that they be released to a specified person on condition that the offending sign is erased, removed or obliterated.

### 17.  Forfeiture and destruction of weapons orders

SG10-21

A court convicting a person of possession of an offensive weapon may make an order for the forfeiture or disposal of the weapon (Prevention of Crime Act 1953, s. 1(2))

See also deprivation orders [at **SG10-11**].

---

[142]  Company Directors Disqualification Act 1988, s.2
[143]  ibid, s.5
[144]  Football Spectators Act 1989, s.14A
[145]  Misuse of Drugs Act 1971, s.27(1)
[146]  Trade Marks Act 1994, s.97

Sentencing Guidelines

**SG10-22**    **18. Forfeiture or suspension of liquor licence**

Where an offender who holds a personal licence to supply alcohol is charged with a 'relevant offence', he or she is required to produce the licence to the court, or inform the court of its existence, no later than his or her first appearance.[147]

'Relevant offences' are listed in schedule 4 [to] the Licensing Act 2003 …

Where the offender is convicted, the court may order forfeiture of the licence or suspend it for up to six months.[148] When deciding whether to order forfeiture or suspension, the court may take account of the offender's previous convictions for 'relevant offences'.[149]

Whether or not forfeiture or suspension is ordered, the court is required to notify the licensing authority of the offender's conviction and the sentence imposed.

**SG10-23**    **19. Parenting orders**

The court may make a parenting order where an offender has been convicted of an offence under section 444 of the Education Act 1996 (failing to secure regular attendance at school) and the court is satisfied that the order would be desirable in the interests of preventing the commission of any further offence under that section.[150]

The order may impose such requirements that the court considers desirable in the interests of preventing the commission of a further offence under section 444.

A requirement to attend a counselling or guidance programme may be included only if the offender has been the subject of a parenting order on a previous occasion.

The term of the order must not exceed 12 months.

**SG10-24**    **20. Restitution orders**

Where goods have been stolen and an offender is convicted of any offence with reference to theft of those goods, the court may make a restitution order.[151]

The court may:

(1)    order anyone in possession or control of the stolen goods to restore them to the victim;
(2)    on the application of the victim, order that goods directly or indirectly representing the stolen goods (as being the proceeds of any disposal or realisation of the stolen goods) be transferred to the victim; or
(3)    order that a sum not exceeding the value of the stolen goods be paid to the victim out of any money taken out of the offender's possession on his or her apprehension.

**SG10-25**    **21. Restraining orders**

Where an offender is convicted of any offence, the court may make a restraining order.[152]

The order may prohibit the offender from doing anything for the purpose of protecting the victim of the offence, or any other person mentioned in the order, from further conduct which amounts to harassment or will cause a fear of violence.

The order may have effect for a specified period or until further order.

A court before which a person is *acquitted* of an offence may make a restraining order if the court considers that it is necessary to protect a person from harassment by the defendant.[153] *Consult your legal adviser for guidance.*

**SG10-26**    **22. Sexual harm prevention orders**

Sexual Harm Prevention Orders (SHPO) can be made in relation to a person who has been convicted of an offence listed in either Schedule 3 or Schedule 5 to the Sexual Offences Act 2003 either in the UK or overseas (further details below). This includes offenders whose convictions pre-date the commencement of the 2003 Act (Part 11 Chapter 2 of the Sentencing Code).

---

[147]  Licensing Act 2003, s.128(1)
[148]  ibid, s.129(2)
[149]  ibid, s.129(3)
[150]  Sentencing Code, s.369
[151]  Sentencing Code, s.148
[152]  Sentencing Code, s.360
[153]  Protection from Harassment Act 1997, s.5A

A SHPO can also be made where a person is found not guilty by reason of insanity or found to be under a disability and to have done the act charged, or cautioned etc. for an offence listed in either Schedule 3 or Schedule 5 to the Sexual Offences Act 2003.[154]

No application is necessary for the court to make a SHPO at the point of sentence although the prosecutor may wish to invite the court to consider making an order in appropriate cases. The court may ask pre-sentence report writers to consider the suitability of a SHPO on a non-prejudicial basis.

In order to make a SHPO, the court must be satisfied that the offender presents a risk of sexual harm to the public (or particular members of the public) and that an order is necessary to protect against this risk. The details of the offence are likely to be a key factor in the court's decision, together with the offender's previous convictions and the assessment of risk presented by the national probation service in any pre-sentence report. The court may take into consideration the range of other options available to it in respect of protecting the public. The court may want to consider:

1.  would an order minimise the risk of harm to the public or to any particular members of the public?
2.  is it proportionate?
3.  can it be policed effectively?

The only prohibitions which can be imposed by a SHPO are those which are necessary for the purpose of protecting the public from sexual harm from the defendant. These can, however, be wide ranging. An order may, for example, prohibit someone from undertaking certain forms of employment such as acting as a home tutor to children. It may also prohibit the offender from engaging in particular activities on the internet. The decision of the Court of Appeal in *R v Smith and Others* [2011] EWCA Crim 1772 reinforces the need for the terms of a SHPO to be tailored to the exact requirements of the case. SHPOs may be used to limit and manage internet use by an offender, where it is considered proportionate and necessary to do so. The behaviour prohibited by the order might well be considered unproblematic if exhibited by another member of the public — it is the offender's previous offending behaviour and subsequent demonstration that they may pose a risk of further such behaviour, which will make them eligible for an order.

The order may include only negative prohibitions; there is no power to impose positive obligations. The order may have effect for a fixed period (not less than five years) or until further order. *Consult your legal adviser for guidance.*

### 23.  Sexual offences prevention orders                                                                SG10-27

These have now been replaced by Sexual Harm Prevention Orders. [See **SG10-26**] A Sexual Offences Prevention Order may only be made if the order was applied for before 8 March 2015. *Consult your legal adviser for guidance.*

### 24.  Automatic orders on conviction for sexual offences                                                SG10-28

The following requirements or provisions are **not** part of the sentence imposed by the court but apply automatically by operation of law. The role of the court is to inform the offender of the applicable requirements and/or prohibition.

**Notification requirements** [Sections 80 to 88 and Schedule 3 of the Sexual Offences Act 2003] A relevant offender automatically becomes subject to notification requirements, obliging him to notify the police of specified information for a specified period. The court should inform the offender accordingly. The operation of the notification requirement is **not** a relevant consideration in determining the sentence for the offence.

**Protection for children and vulnerable adults** [Section 2 and Schedule 3 of the Safeguarding Vulnerable Groups Act 2006; Safeguarding Vulnerable Groups Act 2006 (Prescribed Criteria and Miscellaneous Provisions) Regulations 2009 (SI 2009/37) (as amended)] A statutory scheme pursuant to which offenders *will* or *may* be barred from regulated activity relating to children or vulnerable adults, with or without the right to make representations, depending on the offence. The court should inform the offender accordingly.

### Additional note: Availability of ancillary orders                                                    SG10-29

The lists below identify offences covered in the MCSG for which particular ancillary orders are available.

**In all cases, consult your legal adviser regarding available orders and their specific requirements and effects**

---

[154] SOA 2003, s.103A

*Football banning orders – Football Spectators Act 1989, s.14A*

Available on conviction of a 'relevant offence', listed in schedule 1 to the Football Spectators Act 1989. These include:

- possession of alcohol or being drunk while entering/trying to enter ground – Sporting Events (Control of Alcohol etc) Act 1985, s.2;
- disorderly behaviour – Public Order Act 1986, s.5 – committed: (a) during a period relevant to a football match (see below) at any premises while the offender was at, or was entering or leaving or trying to enter or leave, the premises; (b) on a journey to or from a football match and the court makes a declaration that the offence related to football matches; or (c) during a period relevant to a football match (see below) and the court makes a declaration that the offence related to that match;
- any offence involving the use or threat of violence towards another person committed: (a) during a period relevant to a football match (see below) at any premises while the offender was at, or was entering or leaving or trying to enter or leave, the premises; (b) on a journey to or from a football match and the court makes a declaration that the offence related to football matches; or (c) during a period relevant to a football match (see below) and the court makes a declaration that the offence related to that match;
- any offence involving the use or threat of violence towards property committed: (a) during a period relevant to a football match (see below)at any premises while the offender was at, or was entering or leaving or trying to enter or leave, the premises; (b) on a journey to or from a football match and the court makes a declaration that the offence related to football matches; or (c) during a period relevant to a football match (see below) and the court makes a declaration that the offence related to that match;
- any offence involving the use, carrying or possession of an offensive weapon or firearm committed: (a) during a period relevant to a football match (see below) at any premises while the offender was at, or was entering or leaving or trying to enter or leave, the premises; (b) on a journey to or from a football match and the court makes a declaration that the offence related to football matches; or (c) during a period relevant to a football match (see below) and the court makes a declaration that the offence related to that match;
- drunk and disorderly – Criminal Justice Act 1967, s.91(1) – committed on a journey to or from a football match and the court makes a declaration that the offence related to football matches;
- driving/attempting to drive when unfit through drink or drugs – Road Traffic Act 1988, s.4 – committed on a journey to or from a football match and the court makes a declaration that the offence related to football matches;
- in charge of a vehicle when unfit through drink or drugs – Road Traffic Act 1988, s.4 – committed on a journey to or from a football match and the court makes a declaration that the offence related to football matches;
- driving/attempting to drive with excess alcohol – Road Traffic Act 1988, s.5 – committed on a journey to or from a football match and the court makes a declaration that the offence related to football matches;
- in charge of a vehicle with excess alcohol – Road Traffic Act 1988, s.5 – committed on a journey to or from a football match and the court makes a declaration that the offence related to football matches;
- any offence under the Football (Offences) Act 1991;
- unauthorised sale of tickets – Criminal Justice and Public Order Act 1994, s.166.

The following periods are 'relevant' to a football match (Football Spectators Act 1989, Sch.1 para.4):

(a) the period beginning:
   i.   24 hours before the start of the match; or
   ii.  24 hours before the time at which it is advertised to start;
   which ever is the earliest, and ending 24 hours after the end of the match;
(b) where a match advertised to start at a particular time on a particular day is postponed to a later day, or does not take place, the period in the advertised day beginning 24 hours before and ending 24 hours after that time.

*Forfeiture or suspension of personal liquor licence – Licensing Act 2003, s.129*

Available on conviction of a 'relevant offence', listed in schedule 4 to the Licensing Act 2003.

These include:

- an offence under the Licensing Act 2003;
- an offence under the Firearms Act 1968;
- theft – Theft Act 1968, s.1;
- burglary – Theft Act 1968, s.9;
- abstracting electricity – Theft Act 1968, s.13;
- handling stolen goods – Theft Act 1968, s.22;

- going equipped for theft – Theft Act 1968, s.25;
- production of a controlled drug – Misuse of Drugs Act 1971, s.4(2);
- supply of a controlled drug – Misuse of Drugs Act 1971, s.4(3);
- possession of a controlled drug with intent to supply – Misuse of Drugs Act 1971, s.5(3);
- evasion of duty – Customs and Excise Management Act 1979, s.170 (excluding s.170(1)(a));
- driving/attempting to drive when unfit through drink or drugs – Road Traffic Act 1988, s.4;
- in charge of a vehicle when unfit through drink or drugs – Road Traffic Act 1988, s.4;
- driving/attempting to drive with excess alcohol – Road Traffic Act 1988, s.5;
- in charge of a vehicle with excess alcohol – Road Traffic Act 1988, s.5;
- unauthorised use of trade mark where the goods in question are or include alcohol – Trade Marks Act 1994, ss.92(1) and 92(2);
- sexual assault – Sexual Offences Act 2003, s.3;
- exploitation of prostitution – Sexual Offences Act 2003, ss.52 and 53;
- exposure – Sexual Offences Act 2003, s.66;
- voyeurism – Sexual Offences Act 2003, s.67;
- a violent offence, being any offence which leads, or is intended or likely to lead, to death or to physical injury.

### Sexual Harm Prevention Orders

Available in respect of an offence listed in schedule 3 or 5 to the Sexual Offences Act 2003.

These include:

- possession of indecent photograph of a child – Criminal Justice Act 1988, s.160;
- sexual assault – Sexual Offences Act 2003, s.3;
- exposure – Sexual Offences Act 2003, s.66;
- voyeurism – Sexual Offences Act 2003, s.67;
- threats to kill – Offences against the Person Act 1861, s.16;
- wounding/causing grievous bodily harm – Offences against the Person Act 1861, s.20;
- assault with intent to resist arrest – Offences against the Person Act 1861, s.38;
- assault occasioning actual bodily harm – Offences against the Person Act 1861, s.47;
- burglary with intent to inflict grievous bodily harm or to do unlawful damage to a building/anything within it – Theft Act 1968, s.9;
- arson – Criminal Damage Act 1971, s.1;
- violent disorder – Public Order Act 1986, s.2;
- affray – Public Order Act 1986, s.3;
- harassment – conduct causing fear of violence – Protection from Harassment Act 1994, s.4;
- racially or religiously aggravated wounding/causing grievous bodily harm – Crime and Disorder Act 1998, s.29;
- racially or religiously aggravated assault occasioning actual bodily harm – Crime and Disorder Act 1998, s.29;
- racially or religiously aggravated common assault – Crime and Disorder Act 1998, s.29;
- racially or religiously aggravated threatening behaviour – Crime and Disorder Act 1998, s.31(1)(a);
- racially or religiously aggravated disorderly behaviour with intent to cause harassment, alarm or distress – Crime and Disorder Act 1998, s.31(1)(b);
- exploitation of prostitution – Sexual Offences Act 2003, ss.52 and 53.

Section 344(2) of the Sentencing Code provides that any conditions in Sch.3 SOA 2003 relating to the age of the offender or the victim, or the sentence imposed on the offender may be disregarded in making a Sexual Harm Prevention Order.

## COMMUNITY ORDERS                                                              SG10-30

[See Imposition of community and custodial sentences guideline at **SG9-2**.]

## CUSTODIAL SENTENCES                                                           SG10-31

[See Imposition of community and custodial sentences guideline at **SG9-3**.]

**SG10-32**

DEFERRED SENTENCES

The court is empowered to defer passing sentence for up to six months.[155] The court may impose any conditions during the period of deferment that it considers appropriate. These could be specific requirements as set out in the provisions for community sentences, restorative justice activities[156] or requirements that are drawn more widely.[157] The purpose of deferment is to enable the court to have regard to the offender's conduct after conviction or any change in his or her circumstances, including the extent to which the offender has complied with any requirements imposed by the court.

The following conditions must be satisfied before sentence can be deferred:[158]

1. the offender must consent (and in the case of restorative justice activities the other participants must consent);
2. the offender must undertake to comply with requirements imposed by the court; and
3. the court must be satisfied that deferment is in the interests of justice.

Deferred sentences will be appropriate in very limited circumstances:

- deferred sentences will be appropriate in very limited circumstances;
- deferred sentences are likely to be relevant predominantly in a small group of cases close to either the community or custodial sentence threshold where, should the offender be prepared to adapt his behaviour in a way clearly specified by the sentencer, the court may be prepared to impose a lesser sentence;
- sentencers should impose specific and measurable conditions that do not involve a serious restriction on liberty;
- the court should give a clear indication of the type of sentence it would have imposed if it had decided not to defer;
- the court should also ensure that the offender understands the consequences of failure to comply with the court's wishes during the deferment period.

If the offender fails to comply with any requirement imposed in connection with the deferment, or commits another offence, he or she can be brought back to court before the end of the deferment period and the court can proceed to sentence.

**SG10-33**

FINES AND FINANCIAL ORDERS
APPROACH TO THE ASSESSMENT OF FINES

**SG10-34**   **1. Introduction**

The amount of a fine must reflect the *seriousness* of the offence.[159]

The court must also take into account the *financial circumstances* of the offender; this applies whether it has the effect of increasing or reducing the fine.[160]

The aim is for the fine to have an equal impact on offenders with different financial circumstances; it should be a hardship but should not force the offender below a reasonable 'subsistence' level. Normally a fine should be of an amount that is capable of being paid within 12 months though there may be exceptions to this.

The guidance below aims to establish a clear, consistent and principled approach to the assessment of fines that will apply fairly in the majority of cases. However, it is impossible to anticipate every situation that may be encountered and in each case the court will need to exercise its judgement to ensure that the fine properly reflects the *seriousness of the offence* and takes into account the *financial circumstances* of the offender.

---

[155] Sentencing Code, s.5
[156] ibid, s. 1ZA(3)
[157] Sentencing Code, s.3
[158] Sentencing Code, s.5
[159] Sentencing Code, s.125(1)
[160] Sentencing Code, s.125(2) and (3)

## 2. Fine bands

For the purpose of the offence guidelines, a fine is based on one of three bands (A, B or C). The selection of the relevant fine band, and the position of the individual offence within that band, is determined by the seriousness of the offence. In some cases fine bands D–F may be used even where the community or custody threshold have been passed.

| Fines | Starting point | Range |
|---|---|---|
| Fine Band A | 50% of relevant weekly income | 25–75% of relevant weekly income |
| Fine Band B | 100% of relevant weekly income | 75–125% of relevant weekly income |
| Fine Band C | 150% of relevant weekly income | 125–175% of relevant weekly income |
| Fine Band D | 250% of relevant weekly income | 200–300% of relevant weekly income |
| Fine Band E | 400% of relevant weekly income | 300–500% of relevant weekly income |
| Fine Band F | 600% of relevant weekly income | 500–700% of relevant weekly income |

For an explanation of the meaning of starting point and range, both generally and in relation to fines, refer to either the guide to using pre-Sentencing Council guidelines [See **SG10-2**] or the guide to using Sentencing Council guidelines [**SG10-3**].

## 3. Definition of relevant weekly income

The *seriousness* of an offence determines the choice of fine band and the position of the offence within the range for that band. The offender's *financial circumstances* are taken into account by expressing that position as a proportion of the offender's *relevant weekly income*.
Where

- an offender is in receipt of income from employment or is self-employed *and*
- that income is *more than £120 per week* after deduction of tax and national insurance (or equivalent where the offender is self-employed), the actual income is the *relevant weekly income*.

Where

- an offender's only source of income is state benefit (including where there is relatively low additional income as permitted by the benefit regulations) or
- the offender is in receipt of income from employment or is self-employed but the amount of income after deduction of tax and national insurance is *£120 or less*, the *relevant weekly income is deemed to be £110*.

Additional information about the basis for this approach is set out [at **SG10-38**].

In calculating relevant weekly income, no account should be taken of tax credits, housing benefit, child benefit or similar.

### No reliable information

Where an offender has failed to provide information, or the court is not satisfied that it has been given sufficient reliable information, it is entitled to make such determination as it thinks fit regarding the financial circumstances of the offender.[161] Any determination should be clearly stated on the court records for use in any subsequent variation or enforcement proceedings. In such cases, a record should also be made of the applicable fine band and the court's assessment of the position of the offence within that band based on the seriousness of the offence.

Where there is no information on which a determination can be made, the court should proceed on the basis of an *assumed relevant weekly income of £440*. This is derived from national median pre-tax earnings; a gross figure is used as, in the absence of financial information from the offender, it is not possible to calculate appropriate deductions.[162]

Where there is some information that tends to suggest a significantly lower or higher income than the recommended £440 default sum, the court should make a determination based on that information.

---

[161] Sentencing Code, s.126

[162] This figure is a projected estimate based upon the 2012–13 Survey of Personal Incomes using economic assumptions consistent with the Office for Budget Responsibility's March 2015 economic and fiscal outlook. The latest actual figure is for 2012–13, when median pre-tax income was £404 per week (https://www.gov.uk/government/statistics/shares-of-total-income-before-and-after-tax-and-income-tax-for-percentile-groups).

A court is empowered to remit a fine in whole or part if the offender subsequently provides information as to means.[163] The assessment of offence seriousness and, therefore, the appropriate fine band and the position of the offence within that band is not affected by the provision of this information.

**SG10-37**    **4. Assessment of financial circumstances**

While the initial consideration for the assessment of a fine is the offender's relevant weekly income, the court is required to take account of the offender's *financial circumstances* including assets more broadly. Guidance on important parts of this assessment is set out below.

An offender's financial circumstances may have the effect of increasing or reducing the amount of the fine; however, they are not relevant to the assessment of offence seriousness. They should be considered separately from the selection of the appropriate fine band and the court's assessment of the position of the offence within the range for that band.

*Out of the ordinary expenses*

In deciding the proportions of relevant weekly income that are the starting points and ranges for each fine band, account has been taken of reasonable living expenses. Accordingly, no further allowance should normally be made for these. In addition, no allowance should normally be made where the offender has dependants.

Outgoings will be relevant to the amount of the fine only where the expenditure is *out of the ordinary* and *substantially* reduces the ability to pay a financial penalty so that the requirement to pay a fine based on the standard approach would lead to *undue* hardship.

*Unusually low outgoings*

Where the offender's living expenses are substantially lower than would normally be expected, it may be appropriate to adjust the amount of the fine to reflect this. This may apply, for example, where an offender does not make any financial contribution towards his or her living costs.

*Savings*

Where an offender has savings these will not normally be relevant to the assessment of the amount of a fine although they may influence the decision on time to pay.

However, where an offender has little or no income but has substantial savings, the court may consider it appropriate to adjust the amount of the fine to reflect this.

*Household has more than one source of income*

Where the household of which the offender is a part has more than one source of income, the fine should normally be based on the income of the offender alone.

However, where the offender's part of the income is very small (or the offender is wholly dependent on the income of another), the court may have regard to the extent of the household's income and assets which will be available to meet any fine imposed on the offender.[164]

*Potential earning capacity*

Where there is reason to believe that an offender's potential earning capacity is greater than his or her current income, the court may wish to adjust the amount of the fine to reflect this.[165] This may apply, for example, where an unemployed offender states an expectation to gain paid employment within a short time. The basis for the calculation of fine should be recorded in order to ensure that there is a clear record for use in variation or enforcement proceedings.

*High income offenders*

Where the offender is in receipt of very high income, a fine based on a proportion of relevant weekly income may be disproportionately high when compared with the seriousness of the offence. In such cases, the court should adjust the fine to an appropriate level; as a general indication, in most cases the fine for a first time offender pleading not guilty should not exceed 75% of the maximum fine. In the case of fines which are unlimited the court should decide the appropriate level with the guidance of the legal adviser.

---

[163] Sentencing Code, s.127
[164] *R v Engen* [2004] EWCA Crim 1536 (CA)
[165] *R v Little* (unreported) 14 April 1976 (CA)

### 5. Approach to offenders on low income

SG10-38

An offender whose primary source of income is state benefit will generally receive a base level of benefit (e.g. job seekers' allowance, a relevant disability benefit or income support) and may also be eligible for supplementary benefits depending on his or her individual circumstances (such as child tax credits, housing benefit, council tax benefit and similar). In some cases these benefits may have been replaced by Universal Credit.

If relevant weekly income were defined as the amount of benefit received, this would usually result in higher fines being imposed on offenders with a higher level of need; in most circumstances that would not properly balance the seriousness of the offence with the financial circumstances of the offender. While it might be possible to exclude from the calculation any allowance above the basic entitlement of a single person, that could be complicated and time consuming.

Similar issues can arise where an offender is in receipt of a low earned income since this may trigger eligibility for means related benefits such as working tax credits and housing benefit depending on the particular circumstances. It will not always be possible to determine with any confidence whether such a person's financial circumstances are significantly different from those of a person whose primary source of income is state benefit.

For these reasons, a simpler and fairer approach to cases involving offenders in receipt of low income (whether primarily earned or as a result of benefit) is to identify an amount that is deemed to represent the offender's relevant weekly income.

While a precise calculation is neither possible nor desirable, it is considered that an amount that is approximately half-way between the base rate for job seekers' allowance and the net weekly income of an adult earning the minimum wage for 30 hours per week represents a starting point that is both realistic and appropriate; this is currently £120.[166] The calculation is based on a 30 hour working week in recognition of the fact that many of those on minimum wage do not work a full 37 hour week and that lower minimum wage rates apply to younger people.

It is expected that this figure will remain in use until 31 March 2015. Future revisions of the guideline will update the amount in accordance with current benefit and minimum wage levels.

### 6. Offence committed for 'commercial' purposes

SG10-39

Some offences are committed with the intention of gaining a significant commercial benefit. These often occur where, in order to carry out an activity lawfully, a person has to comply with certain processes which may be expensive. They include, for example, 'taxi-touting' (where unauthorised persons seek to operate as taxi drivers) and 'fly-tipping' (where the cost of lawful disposal is considerable).

In some of these cases, a fine based on the standard approach set out above may not reflect the level of financial gain achieved or sought through the offending. Accordingly:

a.  where the offender has generated income or avoided expenditure to a level that can be calculated or estimated, the court may wish to consider that amount when determining the financial penalty;

b.  where it is not possible to calculate or estimate that amount, the court may wish to draw on information from the enforcing authorities about the general costs of operating within the law.

### 7. Offence committed by an organisation

SG10-40

Where an offence is committed by an organisation, guidance on fines can be found in the environmental offences guideline [see **SG24**].

See the Criminal Practice Direction CPD XIII Listing Annex 3 [see **CPD.XIII.x3**] for directions on dealing with cases involving very large fines in the magistrates' court.[167]

### 8. Reduction for a guilty plea

SG10-41

Where a guilty plea has been entered, the amount of the fine should be reduced by the appropriate proportion. Courts should refer to the guideline for Reduction in Sentence for a Guilty Plea [**SG5-1–SG5-12**].

---

[166] With effect from 1 October 2014, the minimum wage is £6.50 per hour for an adult aged 21 or over. Based on a 30 hour week, this equates to approximately £189 after deductions for tax and national insurance. To ensure equivalence of approach, the level of job seekers' allowance for a single person aged 18 to 24 has been used for the purpose of calculating the mid point; this is currently £57.90.

[167] https://www.justice.gov.uk/courts/procedure-rules/criminal/rulesmenu-2015

**SG10-42    9.  Maximum Fines**

A fine must not exceed the statutory limit. Where this is expressed in terms of a 'level', the maxima are:

| Level 1 | £200 |
|---------|------|
| Level 2 | £500 |
| Level 3 | £1,000 |
| Level 4 | £2,500 |
| Level 5 | unlimited[168] |

See the Criminal Practice Direction XIII Listing Annex 3 [see **CPD.XIII.x3**] for directions on dealing with cases involving very large fines in the magistrates' court.

**SG10-43    10.  Multiple offences**

Where an offender is to be fined for two or more offences that arose out of the same incident, it will often be appropriate to impose on the most serious offence a fine which reflects the totality of the offending where this can be achieved within the maximum penalty for that offence. 'No separate penalty' should be imposed for the other offences.

Where compensation is being ordered, that will need to be attributed to the relevant offence as will any necessary ancillary orders.

**SG10-44    11.  Imposition of fines with custodial sentences**

A fine and a custodial sentence may be imposed for the same offence although there will be few circumstances in which this is appropriate, particularly where the custodial sentence is to be served immediately. One example might be where an offender has profited financially from an offence but there is no obvious victim to whom compensation can be awarded. Combining these sentences is most likely to be appropriate only where the custodial sentence is short and/or the offender clearly has, or will have, the means to pay.

Care must be taken to ensure that the overall sentence is proportionate to the seriousness of the offence and that better off offenders are not able to 'buy themselves out of custody'.

*[Notes to consult legal adviser]*

**SG10-45    12.  Payment**

A fine is payable in full on the day on which it is imposed. The offender should always be asked for immediate payment when present in court and some payment on the day should be required wherever possible.

Where that is not possible, the court may, in certain circumstances,[169] require the offender to be detained. More commonly, a court will allow payments to be made over a period set by the court:

a. if periodic payments are allowed, the fine should normally be payable within a maximum of 12 months;
b. compensation should normally be payable within 12 months. However, in exceptional circumstances it may be appropriate to allow it to be paid over a period of up to 3 years.

Where fine bands D, E and F apply (see paragraph 5 above), it may be appropriate for the fine to be of an amount that is larger than can be repaid within 12 months. In such cases, the fine should normally be payable within a maximum of 18 months (band D) or 2 years (bands E and F).

When allowing payment by **instalments payments should be set at a realistic rate taking into account the offender's disposable** income. The following approach may be useful:

---

[168]  For offences committed after 13 March 2015. For offences committed before that date the level 5 maximum is £5,000.
[169]  See section 82 of the Magistrates' Court Act for restrictions on the power to impose imprisonment on default.

| Net weekly income | Starting point for weekly payment |
|---|---|
| £60 | £5 |
| £120 | £10 |
| £200 | £25 |
| £250 | £30 |
| £300 | £50 |
| £400 | £80 |

If the offender has dependants or larger than usual commitments, the weekly payment is likely to be decreased.

The payment terms must be included in any **collection order** made in respect of the amount imposed; see below.

### 13. Collection orders                                                                 SG10-46

The Courts Act 2003 created a fines collection scheme which provides for greater administrative enforcement of fines. Consult your legal adviser for further guidance.

#### *Attachment of earnings orders/applications for benefit deductions*

Unless it would be impracticable or inappropriate to do so, the court must make an attachment of earnings or (AEO) or application for benefit deductions (ABD) whenever:

- compensation is imposed;[170] or
- the court concludes that the offender is an existing defaulter and that the existing default cannot be disregarded.[171]

In other cases, the court may make an AEO or ABD with the offender's consent.[172]

The court must make a collection order in every case in which a fine or compensation order is imposed unless this would be impracticable or inappropriate.[173] The collection order must state:

- the amount of the sum due, including the amount of any fine, compensation order or other sum;
- whether the court considers the offender to be an existing defaulter;
- whether an AEO or ABD has been made and information about the effect of the order;
- if the court has not made an AEO or ABD, the payment terms;
- if an AEO or ABD has been made, the reserve terms (i.e. the payment terms that will apply if the AEO or ABD fails). It will often be appropriate to set a reserve term of payment in full within 14 days.

COMPENSATION                                                    SG10-47

### 1. Introduction to compensation

1. The court *must* consider making a compensation order in any case where personal injury, loss or damage has resulted from the offence. It can either be a sentence in its own right or an ancillary order. The court must give reasons if it decides not to order compensation.[174]
2. There is no statutory limit on the amount of compensation that may be imposed in respect of offences for an offender aged 18 or over. Compensation may also be ordered in respect of offences taken into consideration.[175]
3. Where the personal injury, loss or damage arises from a road accident, a compensation order may be made only if there is a conviction for an offence under the Theft Act 1968, or the offender is uninsured and the Motor Insurers' Bureau will not cover the loss.
4. Subject to consideration of the victim's views (see paragraph 6 below), the court must order compensation wherever possible and should not have regard to the availability of other sources such as civil litigation or the Criminal Injuries Compensation Scheme. Any amount paid by an offender under a compensation order will generally be deducted from a subsequent civil award or payment under the Scheme to avoid double compensation.

---

[170] Courts Act 2003, sch.5, para.7A
[171] ibid, para.8
[172] ibid, para.9
[173] ibid, para.12
[174] Sentencing Code, s.55
[175] Sentencing Code, s.139

5.  Compensation may be ordered for such amount as the court considers appropriate having regard to any evidence and any representations made by the offender or prosecutor. The court must also take into account the offender's means (see also paragraphs 9–11 below).
6.  Compensation should benefit, not inflict further harm on, the victim. Any financial recompense from the offender may cause distress. A victim may or may not want compensation from the offender and assumptions should not be made either way. The victim's views are properly obtained through sensitive discussion by the police or witness care unit, when it can be explained that the offender's ability to pay will ultimately determine whether, and how much, compensation is ordered and whether the compensation will be paid in one lump sum or by instalments. If the victim does not want compensation, this should be made known to the court and respected.
7.  In cases where it is difficult to ascertain the full amount of the loss suffered by the victim, consideration should be given to making a compensation order for an amount representing the agreed or likely loss. Where relevant information is not immediately available, it may be appropriate to grant an adjournment for it to be obtained.
8.  The court should consider two types of loss:
    •  financial loss sustained as a result of the offence such as the cost of repairing damage or, in case of injury, any loss of earnings or medical expenses;
    •  pain and suffering caused by the injury (including terror, shock or distress) and any loss of facility. This should be assessed in light of all factors that appear to the court to be relevant, including any medical evidence, the victim's age and personal circumstances.
9.  Once the court has formed a preliminary view of the appropriate level of compensation, it must have regard to the means of the offender so far as they are known. Where the offender has little money, the order may have to be scaled down or additional time allowed to pay; the court may allow compensation to be paid over a period of up to three years in appropriate cases.
10. The fact that a custodial sentence is imposed does not, in itself, make it inappropriate to order compensation; however, it may be relevant to whether the offender has the means to satisfy the order. [*Note to consult legal adviser*].
11. Where the court considers that it would be appropriate to impose a fine and a compensation order but the offender has insufficient means to pay both, priority should be given to compensation. Compensation also takes priority over the victim surcharge where the offender's means are an issue.

## 2.  Suggested starting points for physical and mental injuries

The tables below suggest starting points for compensating physical and mental injuries commonly encountered in a magistrates' court. They have been developed to be consistent with the approach in the Criminal Injuries Compensation Authority tariff (revised 2012). The CICA tariff makes no award for minor injuries which result in short term disability; the suggested starting points for these injuries are adapted from an earlier tariff.

| Physical Injury | | |
| --- | --- | --- |
| Type of injury | Description | Suggested Starting point |
| Graze | Depending on size | Up to £75 |
| Bruise | Depending on size | Up to £100 |
| Cut: no permanent scar | Depending on size and whether stitched | £100–300 |
| Black eye | | £125 |
| Eye | Blurred or double vision lasting up to 6 weeks<br>Blurred or double vision lasting for 6 to 13 weeks<br>Blurred or double vision lasting for more than 13 weeks (recovery expected) | £500<br>£1,000<br>£1,500 |
| Brain | Concussion lasting one week | £1,500 |
| Nose | Undisplaced fracture of nasal bone<br>Displaced fracture requiring manipulation<br>Deviated nasal septum requiring septoplasty | £1,000<br>£2,000<br>£2,000 |
| Loss of non-front tooth<br>Loss of front tooth | Depending on cosmetic effect | £750 per tooth<br>£1,500 per tooth |

**Physical Injury**

| Type of injury | Description | Suggested Starting point |
|---|---|---|
| Facial scar | Minor disfigurement (permanent) | £1,000 |
| Arm | Fractured humerus, radius, ulna (substantial recovery) | £1,500 |
| Shoulder | Dislocated (substantial recovery) | £900 |
| Wrist | Dislocated/fractured—including scaphoid fracture (substantial recovery)<br>Fractured—colles type (substantial recovery) | £2,400<br>£2,400 |
| Sprained wrist, ankle | Disabling for up to 6 weeks<br>Disabling for 6 to 13 weeks<br>Disabling for more than 13 weeks | £500<br>£800<br>£1,000 |
| [431] Finger | Fractured finger other than index finger (substantial recovery)<br>Fractured index finger (substantial recovery)<br>Fractured thumb (substantial recovery) | £300<br>£1,200<br>£1,750 |
| Leg | Fractured fibula (substantial recovery)<br>Fractured femur, tibia (substantial recovery) | £1,000<br>£1,800 |
| Abdomen | Injury requiring laparotomy | £1,800 |
| **Mental injury** | | |
| Temporary mental anxiety (including terror, shock, distress), not medically verified | | £500 |
| Disabling mental anxiety, lasting more than 6 weeks, medically verified* | | £1,000 |
| Disability mental illness, lasting up to 28 weeks, confirmed by psychiatric diagnosis* | | £1,500 |

*mental injury is disabling if it has a substantial adverse effect on a person's ability to carry out normal day-to-day activities for the time specified (e.g. impaired work or school performance or effects on social relationships or sexual dysfunction).

**Physical and sexual injury**

The following table, which is also based on the Criminal Injuries Compensation Authority tariff, sets out suggested starting points for compensating physical and sexual abuse. It will be rare for cases involving this type of harm to be dealt with in a magistrates' court and it will be important to *consult your legal adviser for guidance in these situations*.

| Type of injury | Description | Suggested starting point |
|---|---|---|
| Physical abuse of adult | Intermittent physical assaults resulting in accumulation of healed wounds, burns or scalds, but with no appreciable disfigurement | £2,000 |
| Physical abuse of child | Isolated or intermittent assault(s) resulting in weals, hair pulled from scalp etc.<br>Intermittent physical assaults resulting in accumulation of healed wounds, burns or scalds, but with no appreciable disfigurement | £1,000<br>£1,000 |
| Sexual abuse of adult | Non-penetrative indecent physical acts over clothing<br>Non-penetrative indecent act(s) under clothing | £1,000<br>£2,000 |
| Sexual abuse of child (under 18) | Non-penetrative indecent physical act(s) over clothing<br>Non-penetrative frequent assaults over clothing or non-penetrative indecent act under clothing<br>Repetitive indecent acts under clothing | £1,000<br>£1,500 or 2,000<br>£3,300 |

PROSECUTION COSTS                                                            **SG10-48**

Where an offender is convicted of an offence, the court has discretion to make such order as to costs as it considers just and reasonable.[176]

---

[176] Prosecution of Offences Act 1985, s.18

The Court of Appeal has given the following guidance:[177]

i)   an order for costs should never exceed the sum which, having regard to the offender's means and any other financial order imposed, he or she is able to pay and which it is reasonable to order him or her to pay;

ii)  an order for costs should never exceed the sum which the prosecutor actually and reasonably incurred;

iii) the purpose of the order is to compensate the prosecutor. Where the conduct of the defence has put the prosecutor to avoidable expense, the offender may be ordered to pay some or all of that sum to the prosecutor but the offender must not be punished for exercising the right to defend himself or herself;

iv)  the costs ordered to be paid should not be grossly disproportionate to any fine imposed for the offence. This principle was affirmed in *BPS Advertising Limited v London Borough of Barnet*[178] in which the Court held that, while there is no question of an arithmetical relationship, the question of costs should be viewed in the context of the maximum penalty considered by Parliament to be appropriate for the seriousness of the offence;

v)   if the combined total of the proposed fine and the costs sought by the prosecutor exceeds the sum which the offender could reasonably be ordered to pay, the costs order should be reduced rather than the fine;

vi)  it is for the offender to provide details of his or her financial position so as to enable the court to assess what he or she can reasonably afford to pay. If the offender fails to do so, the court is entitled to draw reasonable inferences as to means from all the circumstances of the case;

vii) if the court proposes to make any financial order against the offender, it must give him or her fair opportunity to adduce any relevant financial information and to make appropriate submissions.

Where the prosecutor is the Crown Prosecution Service, prosecution costs exclude the costs of the investigation, which are met by the police. In non-CPS cases where the costs of the investigation are incurred by the prosecutor a costs award may cover the costs of investigation as well as prosecution.[179]

However, where the investigation was carried out as part of a council officer's routine duties, for which he or she would have been paid in the normal way, this is a relevant factor to be taken into account when deciding the appropriate amount of any costs order.[180]

Where the court wishes to impose costs in addition to a fine, compensation and/or the victim surcharge but the offender has insufficient resources to pay the total amount, the order of priority is:

i)   compensation;
ii)  victim surcharge;
iii) fine;
iv)  costs.

**SG10-49**                                  SURCHARGE

When sentencing for offences committed on or after 1 October 2012 a magistrates' court must order the surcharge in the following ways (Criminal Justice Act 2003, s.161A; CJA 2003 (Surcharge) Order 2012; CJA 2003 (Surcharge) (Amendment) Order 2016, CJA 2003 (Surcharge) (Amendment) Order 2019 and CJA 2003 (Surcharge) (Amendment) Order 2020). This is a mandatory requirement set out in section 42 of the Sentencing Code. Courts can reduce the amount of the surcharge (if necessary to nil) if – and only if – an offender cannot pay both the surcharge and one or more of the following orders:

• compensation order,

• unlawful profit order,

• slavery and trafficking reparation order.

If a defendant can afford to make payment in addition to one or more of those orders, the court **must** impose a surcharge, rather than another financial order such as costs.

---

[177]  *R v Northallerton Magistrates' Court, ex parte Dove* [2000] 1 Cr App R (S) 136 (CA)
[178]  [2006] EWCA 3335 (Admin) QBD
[179]  Further guidance is provided in the Criminal Costs Practice Direction and the Criminal Procedure Rules Part 76 [See Criminal Procedure Rules on Costs R45] see https://www.justice.gov.uk/courts/procedure-rules/criminal/rulesmenu-2015
[180]  ibid

**Offenders aged 18 and older at the date of the offence**

| Disposal type | One or more offence(s) committed before 8 April 2016 | One or more offence(s) committed before 28 June 2019 | All offence(s) committed on or after 28 June 2019 |
|---|---|---|---|
| Conditional discharge | £15 | £20 | £21 |
| Fine | 10 per cent of the fine value | | |
| | £20 minimum and £120 maximum (rounded up or down to the nearest pound) | £30 minimum and £170 maximum (rounded up or down to the nearest pound) | £32 minimum and £181 maximum (rounded up or down to the nearest pound) |
| Community sentence | £60 | £85 | £90 |
| Suspended sentence order | £80 (six months or less) | £115 (six months or less) | £122 (six months or less) |
| Immediate custody | *£80 (six months or less) | £115 (six months or less) | £122 (six months or less) |

**Offenders aged under 18 at the date of the offence**

| Disposal type | One or more offence(s) committed before 8 April 2016 | One or more offence(s) committed before 28 June 2019 | All offence(s) committed on or after 28 June 2019 |
|---|---|---|---|
| Conditional discharge | £10 | £15 | £16 |
| Fine, Youth Rehabilitation Order, Community Order, Referral Order | £15 | £20 | £21 |
| Suspended sentence order | £20 | £30 | £32 |
| Immediate custody | *£20 | £30 | £32 |

* When sentencing an offender to immediate custody for a single offence committed before 1 September 2014 or more than one offence, at least one of which was committed before 1 September 2014, no surcharge is payable.

**Person who is not an individual (for example, a company or other legal person)**

| Disposal type | One or more offence(s) committed before 8 April 2016 | One or more offence(s) committed before 28 June 2019 | All offence(s) committed on or after 28 June 2019 |
|---|---|---|---|
| Conditional discharge | £15 | £20 | £21 |
| Fine | 10 per cent of the fine value with a £20 minimum and a £120 maximum (rounded up or down to the nearest pound) | 10 per cent of the fine value with a £30 minimum and a £170 maximum (rounded up or down to the nearest pound) | 10 per cent of the fine value with a £32 minimum and a £181 maximum (rounded up or down to the nearest pound) |

Where an offender is dealt with in different ways only one surcharge (whichever attracts the higher sum) will be paid. Where there is more than one fine ordered, then the surcharge for the highest individual fine is assessed, NOT the total of all fines ordered. Where a custodial sentence is imposed the surcharge is based upon the longest individual sentence, NOT the aggregate term imposed.

Where the court dealing with an offender for more than one offence and at least one offence was committed when the offender was under 18, the surcharge should be ordered at the rate for under 18s (Criminal Justice Act 2003 (Surcharge) Order 2012 art. 5(3)).

There is no victim surcharge payable when compensation is ordered as a sentence (as opposed to ancillary order).

The surcharge is not payable where the court is dealing with breach of a community order, suspended sentence order or conditional discharge.

Sentencing Guidelines

However, where the court deals with an offender for an offence and at the same time deals with one or more of the following:

- breach of a community order (whether by re-sentencing for the original offence or imposing a fine or more onerous requirements),
- breach of a suspended sentence (whether by activating the sentence in full or part or imposing a fine or amending the order), or
- re-sentence following breach of a conditional discharge (but not when simply allowing a conditional discharge to continue)

the surcharge for the new offence must be calculated by reference to the date that the earliest offence (including any offence for which the sentence has been breached) was committed.

Where the offender has the means to pay the financial impositions of the court, there should be no reduction in compensation or fines whenever the surcharge is ordered. However, when the court:

- orders the offender to pay both a surcharge and compensation, but the offender is unable to pay both, the court must reduce the amount of the surcharge (if necessary to nil) (Sentencing Code, s.42(3)); or
- orders the offender to pay both a fine and a surcharge, the court may only reduce the fine to the extent that the offender is unable to pay both (Sentencing Code, s.125(4)).

Where the offender does not have sufficient means to pay the total financial penalty considered appropriate by the court, the order of priority is:

- compensation
- surcharge
- fine
- costs.

When sentencing for one or more offences any one of which was committed **after 1 April 2007 but before 1 October 2012**, a surcharge is payable only if the offender is dealt with by way of a fine, at a flat rate of £15 (Criminal Justice Act 2003 (Surcharge) Order 2012 art. 7(2)).

**SG10-50**                                     HATE CRIME[181]

### 1. Racial or religious aggravation—statutory provisions

Sections 29 to 32 of the Crime and Disorder Act 1998 create specific racially or religiously aggravated offences, which have higher maximum penalties than the non-aggravated versions of those offences. The individual offence guidelines indicate whether there is a specifically aggravated form of the offence.

An offence is racially or religiously aggravated for the purposes of sections 29–32 of the Act if the offender demonstrates hostility towards the victim based on his or her membership (or presumed membership) of a racial or religious group, or if the offence is (wholly or partly) motivated by racial or religious hostility.

For all other offences, section 66 of the Sentencing Code provides that the court must regard racial or religious aggravation as an aggravating factor.

The court should not treat an offence as racially or religiously aggravated for the purposes of section 66 where a racially or religiously aggravated form of the offence was charged but resulted in an acquittal. The court should not normally treat an offence as racially or religiously aggravated if a racially or religiously aggravated form of the offence was available but was not charged. *Consult your legal adviser for further guidance in these situations.*

### 2. Aggravation related to disability, sexual orientation or transgender identity—statutory provisions

Under section 66 of the Sentencing Code, the court must treat as an aggravating factor the fact that:

- an offender demonstrated hostility towards the victim based on his or her disability, sexual orientation or transgender identity (or presumed disability, sexual orientation or transgender identity); or
- the offence was (wholly or partly) motivated by hostility towards persons who have a particular disability, who are of a particular sexual orientation or who are transgender.

### 3. Approach to sentencing

A court should not conclude that offending involved aggravation related to race, religion, disability, sexual orientation or transgender identity without first putting the offender on notice and allowing him or her to challenge the allegation.

---

[181] In respect of the guidance in paragraphs 5–9 below, courts must treat transgender identity as an aggravating factor under s. 146 of the Criminal Justice Act 2003 only upon implementation of s. 65 of the Legal Aid, Sentencing and Punishment of Offenders Act 2012.

When sentencing any offence where such aggravation is found to be present, the following approach should be followed. This applies both to the specific racially or religiously aggravated offences under the Crime and Disorder Act 1998 and to offences which are regarded as aggravated under section 66 of the Sentencing Code:

- sentencers should first determine the appropriate sentence, leaving aside the element of aggravation related to race, religion, disability, sexual orientation or transgender identity but taking into account all other aggravating or mitigating factors;
- the sentence should then be increased to take account of the aggravation related to race, religion, disability, sexual orientation or transgender identity;
- the increase may mean that a more onerous penalty of the same type is appropriate, or that the threshold for a more severe type of sentence is passed;
- the sentencer must state in open court that the offence was aggravated by reason of race, religion, disability, sexual orientation or transgender identity;
- the sentencer should state what the sentence would have been without that element of aggravation.

The extent to which the sentence is increased will depend on the seriousness of the aggravation. The following factors could be taken as indicating a high level of aggravation:

*Offender's intention*

- The element of aggravation based on race, religion, disability, sexual orientation or transgender identity was planned
- The offence was part of a pattern of offending by the offender
- The offender was a member of, or was associated with, a group promoting hostility based on race, religion, disability, sexual orientation or transgender identity
- The incident was deliberately set up to be offensive or humiliating to the victim or to the group of which the victim is a member

**Impact on the victim or others**

- The offence was committed in the victim's home
- The victim was providing a service to the public
- The timing or location of the offence was calculated to maximise the harm or distress it caused
- The expressions of hostility were repeated or prolonged
- The offence caused fear and distress throughout a local community or more widely
- The offence caused particular distress to the victim and/or the victim's family.

At the lower end of the scale, the aggravation may be regarded as less serious if:

- It was limited in scope or duration
- The offence was not motivated by hostility on the basis of race, religion, disability, sexual orientation or transgender identity, and the element of hostility or abuse was minor or incidental

In these guidelines, the specific racially or religiously aggravated offences under the Crime and Disorder Act 1998 are addressed on the same page as the 'basic offence'; the starting points and ranges indicated on the guideline relate to the 'basic' (i.e. non-aggravated) offence. The increase for the element of racial or religious aggravation may result in a sentence above the range; **this will not constitute a departure from the guideline for which reasons must be given.**

Out of Court Disposals                                **SG10-51**

### 1. Introduction to out of court disposals

There are several alternatives to formal charges available to police and CPS when dealing with adults, including cannabis and khat warnings, penalty notices for disorder, community resolution, simple cautions and conditional cautions.

Local authorities and other land managers can also issue fixed penalty notices as an alternative to prosecution for certain environmental and other anti-social behaviour offences.

Enforcing authorities may set the amount of fixed penalties for anti-social behaviour up to a statutory maximum of £100.

Enforcing authorities set their own level of fixed penalty for environmental offences, within the ranges specified in the Environmental Offences (Fixed Penalties) (England) Regulation 2017. A statutory default penalty amount may also apply if the enforcing authority has not specified a local fixed penalty amount.

To encourage prompt payment, enforcing authorities may offer recipients a reduction in the penalty if paid within 14 days. The minimum discounted penalty for environmental offences is also set out in the relevant legislation.

Sentencing Guidelines

## 2. Cannabis or khat warning

A cannabis or khat warning may be given where the offender is found in possession of a small amount of cannabis or khat consistent with personal use and the offender admits the elements of the offence. The drug is confiscated and a record of the warning will be made on local systems. The warning is not a conviction and should not be regarded as an aggravating factor when sentencing for subsequent offences.

## 3. Simple caution

A simple caution may be issued where there is evidence that the offender has committed an offence, the offender admits to the offence, and the offender agrees to being given the caution.

When sentencing an offender who has received a simple caution on a previous occasion:

- the simple caution is not a previous conviction and, therefore, is not a statutory aggravating factor;
- however, the caution will form part of the offender's criminal record and if the caution is recent and is relevant to the current offence it may be considered to be an aggravating factor.

## 4. Conditional caution

A conditional caution[182] requires an offender to comply with conditions, as an alternative to prosecution. The conditions that can be attached must be rehabilitative, reparative and/or a financial penalty. (If the offender is a 'relevant foreign offender' — that is someone without permission to enter or stay in the UK, conditions can be offered that have the object of effecting departure from and preventing return to the UK.) Before the caution can be given, the offender must admit the offence and consent to the conditions. When sentencing an offender who has received a conditional caution in respect of an earlier offence:

- a conditional caution is not a previous conviction and, therefore, is not a statutory aggravating factor;
- however, if the conditional caution is recent and is relevant to the current offence it may be considered to be an aggravating factor;
- the offender's response to the caution may properly influence the court's assessment of the offender's suitability for a particular sentence, so long as it remains within the limits established by the seriousness of the current offence.

### Approach to sentencing for offence for which offender was cautioned but failed to comply with conditions

If the offender fails, without reasonable cause, to comply with the conditional caution, he or she may be prosecuted for the original offence. When sentencing in such a case:

- the offender's non-compliance with the conditional caution does not increase the seriousness of the original offence and must not be regarded as an aggravating factor;
- the offender's non-compliance may be relevant to selection of the type of sentence. For example, it may indicate that it is inappropriate to include certain requirements as part of a community order. The circumstances of the offender's failure to satisfy the conditions, and any partial compliance, will be relevant to this assessment.

## 5. Penalty notices—fixed penalty notices and penalty notices for disorder

Penalty notices may be issued as an alternative to prosecution in respect of a range of offences. Unlike conditional cautions, an admission of guilt is not a prerequisite to issuing a penalty notice.

An offender who is issued with a penalty notice may nevertheless be prosecuted for the offence if he or she:

- asks to be tried for the offence;
- fails to pay the penalty within the period stipulated in the notice and the prosecutor decides to proceed with charges.[183]

When sentencing in cases in which a penalty notice was available:

- the fact that the offender did not take advantage of the penalty (whether that was by requesting a hearing or failing to pay within the specified timeframe) does not increase the seriousness of the offence and must not be regarded as an aggravating factor. The appropriate sentence must be determined in accordance with the sentencing principles set out above (including the amount of any fine, which must take an offender's financial circumstances into account), disregarding the availability of the penalty;
- where a penalty notice was not offered or taken up for reasons unconnected with the offence itself, such as administrative difficulties outside the control of the offender, the starting point should be a fine equivalent to the amount of the penalty and no order of costs should be imposed. The offender should

---

[182]  Criminal Justice Act 2003, s.22

[183]  In some cases of non-payment, the penalty is automatically registered and enforceable as a fine without need for recourse to the courts. This procedure applies to penalty notices for disorder and fixed penalty notices issued in respect of certain road traffic offences but not to fixed penalty notices issued for most other criminal offences.

not be disadvantaged by the unavailability of the penalty notice in these circumstances. Please refer to the list of offences for which penalty notices are available, and the amount of the penalty.

Where an offender has had previous penalty notice(s), the fact that an offender has previously been issued with a penalty notice does not increase the seriousness of the current offence and must not be regarded as an aggravating factor. It may, however, properly influence the court's assessment of the offender's suitability for a particular sentence, so long as it remains within the limits established by the seriousness of the current offence.

### 6. Community resolution

Community resolution is an informal non-statutory disposal used for dealing with less serious crime and anti-social behaviour where the offender accepts responsibility. The views of the victim (where there is one) are taken into account in reaching an informal agreement between the parties which can involve restorative justice techniques.

When sentencing an offender who has received a community resolution for an earlier offence:

• A community resolution is not a conviction and is therefore not a statutory aggravating factor, but if recent and relevant to the offence it may be considered to be an aggravating factor.

### 7. Offences for which penalty notices are available

The tables below list the offences for which penalty notices are available and the amount of penalty. **Consult your legal adviser for further guidance.**

Penalty notices for disorder

| Offence | Legislation | Amount |
| --- | --- | --- |
| Criminal damage (where damage under £500 in value, and not normally where damage over £300) | Criminal Damage Act 1971, s.1 | £90 |
| Disorderly behaviour | Public Order Act 1986, s.5 | £90 |
| Drunk and disorderly | Criminal Justice Act 1967, s.91 | £90 |
| Sale of alcohol to drunk person on relevant premises (not including off-licenses) | Licensing Act 2003, s.141 | £90 |
| Sale of alcohol to person under 18 (staff only; licensees should be subject of a summons) | Licensing Act 2003, s.146 | £90 |
| Theft from a shop (where goods under £200 in value, and not normally where goods over £100) | Theft Act 1968, s.1 | £90 |

Fixed penalty notices

| Offence | Legislation | Amount | Penalty points |
| --- | --- | --- | --- |
| Brakes, steering or tyres defective | Road Traffic Act 1988, s.41A | £200 | 3 |
| Breach of other construction and use requirements | Road Traffic Act 1988, s.42 | £100 or £200 | – |
| Careless driving | Road Traffic Act 1988, s.3 | £100 | 3 |
| Driving other than in accordance with licence | Road Traffic Act 1988, s.87(1) | £100 | 3 |
| Failing to comply with police officer signal | Road Traffic Act 1988, s.35 | £100 | 3 |
| Failing to comply with traffic sign | Road Traffic Act 1988, s.36 | £100 | 3 |
| Failing to supply details of driver's identity | Road Traffic Act 1988, s.172 | £200 | 6 |
| No insurance | Road Traffic Act 1988, s.143 | £300 | 6 |
| No test certificate | Road Traffic Act 1988, s.47 | £100 | – |
| Overloading/exceeding axle weight | Road Traffic Act 1988, s.41B | £100 to £300 | – |
| Pelican/zebra crossing contravention | Road Traffic Regulation Act 1984, s.25(5) | £100 | 3 |

| Offence | Legislation | Amount | Penalty points |
|---|---|---|---|
| Railway fare evasion (where penalty notice scheme in operation by train operator) | Railways (Penalty Fares) Regulations 1994 | £20 or twice the full single fare to next stop, whichever is greater | – |
| Seat belt offences £100 | Road Traffic Act 1988, s.14 and s.15(2) or 15(4) | £100 | – |
| School non-attendance | Education Act 1996, s.444(1) | £60 if paid within 21 days; £120 if paid within 28 days | – |
| Speeding | Road Traffic Regulation Act 1984, s.89(1) | £100 | 3 |
| Using hand-held mobile phone while driving | Road Traffic Act 1988, s.41D | From 1 March 2017 £200 | 6 |
| Using vehicle in dangerous condition | Road Traffic Act 1988, s.40A | £100 | 3 |

### Fixed Penalty Notices – Environmental and anti-social behaviour offences

| Offence | Legislation | Statutory range for fixed penalty | Minimum discounted penalty | Default penalty |
|---|---|---|---|---|
| Littering | Environmental Protection Act 1990, s.88 | £50 – £150 | £50 | £100 |
| Graffiti | Anti-social behaviour Act 2003, s.43 | £50 – £150 | £50 | £100 |
| Fly-posting | Anti-social behaviour Act 2003, s.43 | £50 – £150 | £50 | £100 |
| Unauthorised distribution of free literature on designated land | Environmental Protection Act 1990, s.88 | £50 – £150 | £50 | £100 |
| Alarm noise: failure to nominate key-holder or to notify local authority of key-holder's details | Clean Neighbourhoods and Environment Act 2005, s.73 | £50 – £80 | £50 | £75 |
| Nuisance parking | Clean Neighbourhoods and Environment Act 2005, s.6 | £100 | £60 | £100 |
| Abandoning a vehicle | Clean Neighbourhoods and Environment Act 2005, s.10 | £200 | £120 | £200 |
| Fly-tipping | Unauthorised Deposit of Waste (Fixed Penalties) Regulations 2016 | £150 – £400 | £120 | £200 |
| Household waste duty of care | Environmental Protection Act 1990, s.34ZA | £150 – £400 | £120 | £200 |
| Failure to produce a waste transfer note | Environmental Protection Act 1990, s.34A | £300 | £180 | £300 |
| Industrial and commercial waste receptacle offences | Environmental Protection Act 1990, s.47ZA | £75 – £110 | £60 | £100 |
| Noise exceeding permitted level – domestic premises | Noise Act 1996, s.8 | £75 – £110 | £60 | £100 |

| Offence | Legislation | Statutory range for fixed penalty | Minimum discounted penalty | Default penalty |
|---|---|---|---|---|
| Noise exceeding permitted level – licensed premises | Noise Act 1996, s.8 | £500 | £500 – no discount allowed | £500 |
| Breach of a Public Spaces Protection Order | Anti-social Behaviour, Crime and Policing Act 2014, s68 | Up to £100 | No statutory minimum | n/a |
| Breach of a Community Protection Notice | Anti-social Behaviour, Crime and Policing Act 2014, s52 | Up to £100 | No statutory minimum | n/a |

### OFFENCES COMMITTED IN A DOMESTIC CONTEXT

**SG10-52**

[See Overarching Principles: Domestic Abuse at **SG6**]

### ROAD TRAFFIC OFFENCES – DISQUALIFICATION

**SG10-53**

#### 1. Obligatory disqualification

Some offences carry obligatory disqualification for a minimum of 12 months.[184] The minimum period is automatically increased where there have been certain previous convictions and disqualifications.

An offender must be disqualified for at least two years if he or she has been disqualified two or more times for a period of at least 56 days in the three years preceding the commission of the offence.[185] The following disqualifications are to be disregarded for the purposes of this provision:

- interim disqualification;
- disqualification where vehicle used for the purpose of crime;
- disqualification for stealing or taking a vehicle or going equipped to steal or take a vehicle.

An offender must be disqualified for *at least three years* if he or she is convicted of one of the following offences *and* has within the ten years preceding the commission of the offence been convicted of any of these offences:[186]

- causing death by careless driving when under the influence of drink or drugs;
- driving or attempting to drive while unfit;
- driving or attempting to drive with excess alcohol;
- failing to provide a specimen (drive/attempting to drive).

The individual offence guidelines above indicate whether disqualification is mandatory for the offence and the applicable minimum period. Consult your legal adviser for further guidance.

#### 2. Special Reasons

The period of disqualification may be reduced or avoided if there are special reasons.[187] These must relate to the offence; circumstances peculiar to the offender cannot constitute special reasons.[188] The Court of Appeal has established that, to constitute a special reason, a matter must:[189]

- be a mitigating or extenuating circumstance;
- not amount in law to a defence to the charge;
- be directly connected with the commission of the offence;
- be one which the court ought properly to take into consideration when imposing sentence.

*Consult your legal adviser for further guidance on special reasons applications.*

#### 3. 'Totting up' disqualification

Disqualification for a *minimum* of six months must be ordered if an offender incurs 12 penalty points or more within a three-year period.[190] The minimum period may be automatically increased if the offender

---

[184] Road Traffic Offenders Act 1988, s.34
[185] ibid, s.34(4)
[186] ibid, s.34(3)
[187] ibid, s.34(1)
[188] *Whittal v Kirby* [1946] 2 All ER 552 (CA)
[189] *R v Wickens* (1958) 42 Cr App R 436 (CA)
[190] Road Traffic Offenders Act 1988, s.35

has been disqualified within the preceding three years. Totting up disqualifications, unlike other disqualifications, erase all penalty points.

The period of a totting up disqualification can be reduced or avoided for exceptional hardship or other mitigating circumstances. No account is to be taken of hardship that is not exceptional hardship or circumstances alleged to make the offence not serious. Any circumstances taken into account in the preceding three years to reduce or avoid a totting disqualification must be disregarded.[191]

*Consult your legal adviser for further guidance on exceptional hardship applications.*

### 4. Discretionary disqualification

Whenever an offender is convicted of an endorsable offence or of taking a vehicle without consent, the court has a discretionary power to disqualify instead of imposing penalty points. The individual offence guidelines above indicate whether the offence is endorsable and the number or range of penalty points it carries.

The number of variable points or the period of disqualification should reflect the seriousness of the offence. Some of the individual offence guidelines above include penalty points and/or periods of disqualification in the sentence starting points and ranges; however, the court is not precluded from sentencing outside the range where the facts justify it. Where a disqualification is for less than 56 days, there are some differences in effect compared with disqualification for a longer period; in particular, the licence will automatically come back into effect at the end of the disqualification period (instead of requiring application by the driver) and the disqualification is not taken into account for the purpose of increasing subsequent obligatory periods of disqualification.[192]

In some cases in which the court is considering discretionary disqualification the offender may already have sufficient penalty points on his or her licence that he or she would be liable to a 'totting up' disqualification if further points were imposed. In these circumstances, the court should impose penalty points rather than discretionary disqualification so that the minimum totting up disqualification period applies (see paragraph 6 above).

### 5. Disqualification until a test is passed

Where an offender is convicted of dangerous driving, the court must order disqualification until an extended driving test is passed.

The court has discretion to disqualify until a test is passed where an offender is convicted of any endorsable offence.[193] Where disqualification is obligatory, the extended test applies. In other cases, it will be the ordinary test.

An offender disqualified as a 'totter' under the penalty points provisions may also be ordered to re-take a driving test; in this case, the extended test applies.

The discretion to order a re-test is likely to be exercised where there is evidence of inexperience, incompetence or infirmity, or the disqualification period is lengthy (that is, the offender is going to be 'off the road' for a considerable time).

### 6. Reduced period of disqualification for completion of rehabilitation course

Where an offender is disqualified for 12 months or more in respect of an alcohol-related driving offence, the court may order that the period of disqualification will be reduced if the offender satisfactorily completes an approved rehabilitation course.[194]

Before offering an offender the opportunity to attend a course, the court must be satisfied that an approved course is available and must inform the offender of the effect of the order, the fees that the offender is required to pay, and when he or she must pay them.

The court should also explain that the offender may be required to satisfy the Secretary of State that he or she does not have a drink problem and is fit to drive before the offender's licence will be returned at the end of the disqualification period.[195]

In general, a court should consider offering the opportunity to attend a course to all offenders convicted of a relevant offence for the first time. The court should be willing to consider offering an offender the opportunity to attend a second course where it considers there are good reasons. It will not usually be appropriate to give an offender the opportunity to attend a third course.

---

[191] ibid
[192] ibid, ss.34(4), 35(2), 37(1A)
[193] ibid, s.36(4)
[194] Road Traffic Act 1988
[195] Road Traffic Offenders Act 1988, s.34A

The reduction must be at least three months but cannot be more than one quarter of the total period of disqualification:

- a period of 12 months disqualification must be reduced to nine months;
- in other cases, a reduction of one week should be made for every month of the disqualification so that, for example, a disqualification of 24 months will be reduced by 24 weeks.

When it makes the order, the court must specify a date for completion of the course which is at least two months before the end of the reduced period of disqualification.

### 7. Disqualification in the offender's absence

When considering disqualification in absence the starting point should be that disqualification in absence should be imposed if there is no reason to believe the defendant is not aware of the proceedings, and after the statutory notice has been served pursuant to section 11(4) of the Magistrates' Courts Act 1980 where appropriate. Disqualification should not be imposed in absence where there is evidence that the defendant has an acceptable reason for not attending or where there are reasons to believe it would be contrary to the interests of justice to do so.

### 8. New drivers

Drivers who incur six points or more during the two-year probationary period after passing the driving test will have their licence revoked automatically by the Secretary of State; they will be able to drive only after application for a provisional licence pending the passing of a further test.[196]

An offender liable for an endorsement which will cause the licence to be revoked under the new drivers' provisions may ask the court to disqualify rather than impose points. This will avoid the requirement to take a further test. Generally, this would be inappropriate since it would circumvent the clear intention of Parliament.

### 9. Extension period of disqualification from driving where a custodial sentence is also imposed

Where a court imposes disqualification in addition to a custodial sentence or a detention and training order, the court must extend the disqualification period by one half of the custodial sentence or detention or training order to take into account the period the offender will spend in custody. This will avoid a driving ban expiring, or being significantly diminished, during the period the offender is in custody (s.35a Criminal Justice and Courts Act, 2015). Periods of time spent on remand or subject to an electronically monitored curfew do Where a rehabilitation course is completed, any extension period is disregarded when reducing the ban.

For example where a court imposes a 6 month custodial sentence and a disqualification period of 12 months, the ban will be extended to 15 months. Where a rehabilitation course is completed, the reduction will remain at a maximum of 3 months.

VICTIMS

SG10-54

### 1. Victim Personal Statements

A victim personal statement (VPS) gives victims a formal opportunity to say how a crime has affected them. Where the victim has chosen to make such a statement, a court should consider and take it into account prior to passing sentence.

[CPD VII, Sentencing F: see **CPD.VII.F**] emphasises that:

- evidence of the effects of an offence on the victim must be in the form of a witness statement under section 9 of the Criminal Justice Act 1967 or an expert's report;
- the statement must be served on the defence prior to sentence;
- except where inferences can properly be drawn from the nature of or circumstances surrounding the offence, the court must not make assumptions unsupported by evidence about the effects of an offence on the victim;
- at the discretion of the court the VPS may also be read aloud in whole or in part or it may be summarised. If it is to be read aloud the court should also determine who should do so. In making these decisions the court should take into account the victim's preferences, and follow them unless there is a good reason not to do so (for example, inadmissible or potentially harmful content). Court hearings should not be adjourned solely to allow the victim to attend court to read the VPS;
- the court must pass what it judges to be the appropriate sentence having regard to the circumstances of the offence and the offender, taking into account, so far as the court considers it appropriate, the consequences to the victim;

---

[196]  Road Traffic (New Drivers) Act 1995

- the opinions of the victim or the victim's close relatives as to what the sentence should be are not relevant.

See also the guidance on compensation [at **SG10-47**] particularly with reference to the victim's views as to any compensation order that may be imposed.

**2. Prevalence and community impact statements**

Taken from the Sentencing Guidelines Council's definitive guideline *Overarching Principles: Seriousness*.

The seriousness of an individual case should be judged on its own dimensions of harm and culpability rather than as part of a collective social harm.

However, there may be exceptional local circumstances that arise which may lead a court to decide that prevalence should influence sentencing levels. The pivotal issue in such cases will be the harm being caused to the community. It is essential that sentencers both have supporting evidence from an external source (for example a community impact statement compiled by the police) to justify claims that a particular crime is prevalent in their area and are satisfied that there is a compelling need to treat the offence more seriously than elsewhere. A community impact statement is a document providing information to the court about the impact of offences on the community.

The key factor in determining whether sentencing levels should be enhanced in response to prevalence will be the level of harm being caused in the locality. Enhanced sentences should be exceptional and in response to exceptional circumstances. Sentencers must sentence within the sentencing guidelines once the prevalence has been addressed.

**SG10-55**                                    OFFENCES

The offences set out in this part cover those offences in the Magistrates' Court Sentencing Guidelines which are not covered in the Overarching Guidelines [See **SG1** to **SG9**] and the Crown Court offence guidelines [Set out by offence type from **SG11** to **SG33**]

The following table lists those offence guidelines applicable to the Magistrates' Court and the paragraph reference for their location in this Supplement.

| Magistrates' Court Sentencing Guidelines | | |
|---|---|---|
| Offence | Offence Type | Supplement Reference |
| Abstracting electricity | Theft Offences | SG33 |
| Abuse of position of trust: causing a child to watch a sexual act | Sexual Offences | SG31 |
| Abuse of position of trust: causing or inciting a child to engage in sexual activity | Sexual Offences | SG31 |
| Abuse of position of trust: sexual activity in the presence of a child/ Abuse of position of trust: causing a child to watch a sexual act | Sexual Offences | SG31 |
| Abuse of position of trust: sexual activity with a child/ Abuse of position of trust: causing or inciting a child to engage in sexual activity | Sexual Offences | SG31 |
| Administering a substance with intent | Sexual Offences | SG31 |
| Affray | Public Order | SG29 |
| Alcohol sale offences (Revised 2017) | Magistrates' Court | SG10-56 |
| Animal cruelty (Revised 2017) | Magistrates' Court | SG10-57 |
| Arranging or facilitating sexual exploitation of a child | Sexual Offences | SG31 |
| Arranging or facilitating the commission of a child sex offence | Sexual Offences | SG31 |
| Arson (criminal damage by fire) | Arson and Criminal Damage | SG11-2 |
| Assault occasioning actual bodily harm/Racially or religiously aggravated ABH | Assault Offences | SG12-4 |

| Magistrates' Court Sentencing Guidelines | | |
| --- | --- | --- |
| Assault on a police constable in execution of his duty | Assault Offences | SG12-6 |
| Assault with intent to resist arrest | Assault Offences | SG12-5 |
| Benefit fraud | Fraud, Bribery and Money Laundering Offences | SG26 |
| Bladed articles and offensive weapons – possession | Bladed Articles and Offensive Weapons | SG14-2 |
| Bladed articles and offensive weapons – threats | Bladed Articles and Offensive Weapons | SG14-3 |
| Bladed articles and offensive weapons (possession and threats) – children and young people | Bladed Articles and Offensive Weapons | SG14-4 |
| Brakes defective | Magistrates' Court | SG10-58 |
| Brakes defective (over 3.5 tonnes) | Magistrates' Court | SG10-59 |
| Breach of a community order | Breach Offences | SG15-2 |
| Breach of a criminal behaviour order | Breach Offences | SG15-7 |
| Breach of a foreign travel order | Breach Offences | SG15-8 |
| Breach of a protective order (restraining and non-molestation orders) | Breach Offences | SG15-6 |
| Breach of a sexual harm prevention order | Breach Offences | SG15-8 |
| Breach of a sexual offences prevention order | Breach Offences | SG15-8 |
| Breach of a slavery and trafficking prevention order/breach of a slavery and trafficking risk order | Modern Slavery Offences | SG36-4 |
| Breach of a suspended sentence order | Breach Offences | SG15-3 |
| Breach of an anti-social behaviour order | Breach Offences | SG15-13 |
| Breach of disqualification from acting as a director | Breach Offences | SG15-10 |
| Breach of disqualification from keeping an animal | Breach Offences | SG15-11 |
| Breach of post-sentence supervision | Breach Offences | SG15-4 |
| Breach of supervision default order | Breach Offences | SG15-4 |
| Breach offences (other) | Breach Offences | SG15-12 |
| Breeding, selling, exchanging or advertising a prohibited dog | Magistrates' Court | SG10-127 |
| Bribery | Fraud, Bribery and Money Laundering Offences | SG26 |
| Bribery: Being bribed | Fraud, Bribery and Money Laundering Offences | SG26 |
| Bribery: Bribery of foreign public officials | Fraud, Bribery and Money Laundering Offences | SG26 |
| Bribery: Bribing another person | Fraud, Bribery and Money Laundering Offences | SG26 |
| Care workers: causing a person with a mental disorder to watch a sexual act | Sexual Offences | SG31 |
| Care workers: causing or inciting sexual activity | Sexual Offences | SG31 |
| Care workers: sexual activity in the presence of a person with a mental disorder/ Care workers: causing a person with a mental disorder to watch a sexual act | Sexual Offences | SG31 |

| Magistrates' Court Sentencing Guidelines | | |
|---|---|---|
| Care workers: sexual activity with a person with a mental disorder/ Care workers: causing or inciting sexual activity | Sexual Offences | SG31 |
| Carrying a firearm in a public place | Firearms Offences | SG34-2 |
| Careless driving (drive without due care and attention) (Revised 2017) | Magistrates' Court | SG10-60 |
| Causing a child to watch a sexual act | Sexual Offences | SG31 |
| Causing a person to engage in sexual activity without consent | Sexual Offences | SG31 |
| Causing a person with a mental disorder to engage in or agree to engage in sexual activity by inducement, threat or deception | Sexual Offences | SG31 |
| Causing a person with a mental disorder to watch a sexual act by inducement, threat or deception | Sexual Offences | SG31 |
| Causing a person, with mental disorder impeding choice, to watch a sexual act | Sexual Offences | SG31 |
| Causing death by careless or inconsiderate driving | Causing Death by Driving | SG22 |
| Causing death by driving: unlicensed, disqualified or uninsured drivers | Causing Death by Driving | SG22 |
| Causing or inciting a child to engage in sexual activity | Sexual Offences | SG31 |
| Causing or inciting a child under 13 to engage in sexual activity | Sexual Offences | SG31 |
| Causing or inciting a person, with a mental disorder impeding choice, to engage in sexual activity | Sexual Offences | SG31 |
| Causing or inciting prostitution for gain/ Controlling prostitution for gain | Sexual Offences | SG31 |
| Causing or inciting sexual exploitation of a child/ Controlling a child in relation to sexual exploitation/ Arranging or facilitating sexual exploitation of a child | Sexual Offences | SG31 |
| Child sex offences committed by children or young persons (sections 9–12) (offender under 18)/ Sexual activity with a child family member (offender under 18)/ Inciting a child family member to engage in sexual activity (offender under 18) | Sexual Offences | SG31 |
| Collection of terrorist information | Terrorism Offences | SG32 |
| Committing an offence with intent to commit a sexual offence | Sexual Offences | SG31 |
| Committing offence with intent to commit a human trafficking offence | Modern Slavery Offences | SG36-3 |
| Common assault/Racially or religiously aggravated common assault | Assault Offences | SG12-7 |
| Communication network offences (Revised 2017) | Magistrates' Court | SG10-61 |
| Condition of vehicle/ accessories/ equipment involving danger of injury – buses/goods vehicles | Magistrates' Court | SG10-62 |
| Condition of vehicle/accessories/equipment involving danger of injury | Magistrates' Court | SG10-63 |
| Controlling a child in relation to sexual exploitation | Sexual Offences | SG31 |
| Controlling or coercive behaviour in an intimate or family relationship | Intimidatory Offences | SG27 |

| Magistrates' Court Sentencing Guidelines | | |
|---|---|---|
| Controlling prostitution for gain | Sexual Offences | SG31 |
| Corporate offenders (bribery) | Fraud, Bribery and Money Laundering Offences | SG26 |
| Corporate offenders (fraud) | Fraud, Bribery and Money Laundering Offences | SG26 |
| Corporate offenders (fraud): Cheat the public revenue | Fraud, Bribery and Money Laundering Offences | SG26 |
| Corporate offenders (fraud): Conspiracy to defraud | Fraud, Bribery and Money Laundering Offences | SG26 |
| Corporate offenders (money laundering) | Fraud, Bribery and Money Laundering Offences | SG26 |
| Corporate offenders: fraud, bribery and money laundering | Fraud, Bribery and Money Laundering Offences | SG26-8 |
| Criminal damage (other than by fire) value exceeding £5,000/ Racially or religiously aggravated criminal damage | Arson and Criminal Damage | SG11-3 |
| Criminal damage (other than by fire) value not exceeding £5,000/ Racially or religiously aggravated criminal damage | Arson and Criminal Damage | SG11-5 |
| Cruelty to a child – assault and ill treatment, abandonment, neglect, and failure to protect | Child Cruelty | SG20-2 |
| Cultivation of cannabis plant | Drug Offences | SG23 |
| Dangerous driving | Magistrates Court | SG10-64 |
| Dangerous parking | Magistrates' Court | SG10-65 |
| Disclosing private sexual images | Sexual Offences | SG27-4 |
| Disorderly behaviour/ Racially or religiously aggravated disorderly behaviour | Magistrates' Court | SG10-66 |
| Disorderly behaviour with intent to cause harassment, alarm or distress/ Racially or religiously aggravated disorderly behaviour with intent to cause harassment, alarm or distress | Public Order Offences | SG29-3 |
| Domestic burglary | Burglary Offences | SG19-3 |
| Drive in reverse or wrong way on motorway | Magistrates' Court | SG10-67 |
| Drive in reverse or wrong way on slip road | Magistrates' Court | SG10-68 |
| Drive off carriageway (central reservation or hard shoulder) | Magistrates' Court | SG10-69 |
| Drive otherwise than in accordance with licence | Magistrates' Court | SG10-70 |
| Drive otherwise than in accordance with licence (where could be covered) | Magistrates' Court | SG10-71 |
| Drive whilst disqualified (Revised 2017) | Magistrates' Court | SG10-72 |
| Drug driving (guidance only) | Magistrates' Court | SG10-73 |
| Drugs – class A – fail to attend/remain for initial assessment | Magistrates' Court | SG10-74 |
| Drugs – class A – fail/refuse to provide a sample | Magistrates' Court | SG10-75 |
| Drunk and disorderly in a public place (Revised 2017) | Magistrates' Court | SG10-76 |
| Exceed permitted driving time/periods of duty | Magistrates' Court | SG10-78 |
| Excess Alcohol (drive/attempt to drive) (Revised 2017) | Magistrates' Court | SG10-79 |
| Excess Alcohol (in charge) (Revised 2017) | Magistrates' Court | SG10-80 |
| Exhaust defective | Magistrates' Court | SG10-81 |

| Magistrates' Court Sentencing Guidelines | | |
|---|---|---|
| Exhaust emission | Magistrates' Court | SG10-82 |
| Exposure | Sexual Offences | SG31-30 |
| Fail to co-operate with preliminary (roadside) breath test | Magistrates Court | SG10-83 |
| Fail to comply with notification requirements | Breach Offences | SG15-9 |
| Fail to comply with police constable directing traffic | Magistrates' Court | SG10-84 |
| Fail to comply with traffic sign (e.g. give way sign, keep left sign, temporary signs) | Magistrates' Court | SG10-85 |
| Fail to comply with traffic sign (e.g. red traffic light, stop sign, double white lines, no entry sign) | Magistrates' Court | SG10-86 |
| Fail to give information of driver's identity as required | Magistrates' Court | SG10-87 |
| Fail to keep/ return written record sheets | Magistrates' Court | SG10-88 |
| Fail to notify change of ownership to DVLA | Magistrates' Court | SG10-89 |
| Fail to produce insurance certificate | Magistrates' Court | SG10-90 |
| Fail to produce test certificate | Magistrates' Court | SG10-91 |
| Fail to provide specimen for analysis (drive/ attempt to drive) (Revised 2017) | Magistrates' Court | SG10-92 |
| Fail to provide specimen for analysis (in charge) (Revised 2017) | Magistrates' Court | SG10-93 |
| Fail to stop when required by police constable | Magistrates' Court | SG10-94 |
| Fail to stop/report road accident (Revised 2017) | Magistrates' Court | SG10-95 |
| Fail to use appropriate child car seat | Magistrates' Court | SG10-96 |
| Failure to disclose information about acts of terrorism | Terrorism Offences | SG32 |
| Failure to surrender to bail | Breach Offences | SG15-5 |
| Falsify or alter records with intent to deceive | Magistrates' Court | SG10-97 |
| Firearms – possession by person prohibited | Firearms Offences | SG34-3 |
| Firearms – possession of prohibited weapon | Firearms Offences | SG34-4 |
| Firearms – possession with intent to endanger life | Firearms Offences | SG34-7 |
| Firearms – possession without certificate | Firearms Offences | SG34-8 |
| Firearms – importation | Firearms Offences | SG34-10 |
| Football related offences (Revised 2017)/p | Magistrates' Court | SG10-99 |
| Fraud | Fraud, Bribery and Money Laundering Offences | SG26 |
| Fraudulent evasion of a prohibition by bringing into or taking out of the UK a controlled drug | Drug Offences | SG23 |
| Funding terrorism | Terrorism Offences | SG32 |
| Funding terrorism – funding arrangements | Terrorism Offences | SG32 |
| Funding terrorism – fundraising | Terrorism Offences | SG32 |
| Funding terrorism – money laundering | Terrorism Offences | SG32 |
| Funding terrorism – use and possession | Terrorism Offences | SG32 |
| Going equipped for theft or burglary | Burglary Offences: Theft Offences | SG19 |
| Handling stolen goods | Theft Offences | SG33 |

| Magistrates' Court Sentencing Guidelines | | |
|---|---|---|
| Harassment (fear of violence)/ Stalking (fear of violence)/ Racially or religiously aggravated harassment (fear of violence)/stalking (fear of violence) | Intimidatory Offences | SG27 |
| Harassment/ Stalking/ Racially or religiously aggravated harassment/stalking | Intimidatory Offences | SG27 |
| Identity documents – possess false/ another's/ improperly obtained | Removed as the offence has been repealed | |
| Importing or Exporting a Psychoactive Substance | Drug Offences | SG23-7 |
| Inciting a child family member to engage in sexual activity | Sexual Offences | SG31 |
| Inciting a child family member to engage in sexual activity (offender under 18) | Sexual Offences | SG31 |
| Indecent photographs of children | Sexual Offences | SG31 |
| Individuals: Breach of an abatement notice | Magistrates' Court | SG10-101 |
| Individuals: Breach of duty of care | Environmental Offences | SG24 |
| Individuals: Breach of duty of employer towards employees and non-employees/ Breach of duty of self-employed to others/ Breach of duty of employees at work/ Breach of Health and Safety regulations/ Secondary liability | Health and Safety Offences | SG28 |
| Individuals: Breach of food safety and food hygiene regulations | Health and Safety Offences | SG28 |
| Individuals: Illegal discharges to air, land and water | Environmental Offences | SG24 |
| Individuals: Restrictions on use of public sewers | Environmental Offences | SG24 |
| Individuals: Transfrontier shipment of waste | Environmental Offences | SG24 |
| Individuals: Transporting controlled waste without registering | Environmental Offences | SG24 |
| Individuals: Unauthorised or harmful deposit, treatment or disposal etc of waste/ Illegal discharges to air, land and water | Environmental Offences | SG24 |
| Inducement, threat or deception to procure sexual activity with a person with a mental disorder/ Causing a person with a mental disorder to engage in or agree to engage in sexual activity by inducement, threat or deception | Sexual Offences | SG31 |
| Inflicting grievous bodily harm/ Unlawful wounding/ Racially or religiously aggravated GBH/ Unlawful wounding | Assault Offences | SG12-8 |
| Keeping a brothel used for prostitution | Sexual Offences | SG31 |
| Learner driver or excluded vehicle | Magistrates' Court | SG10-102 |
| Lights defective | Magistrates' Court | SG10-103 |
| Make U turn on motorway | Magistrates' Court | SG10-104 |
| Making off without payment | Theft Offences | SG33 |
| Making or supplying articles for use in frauds | Fraud, Bribery and Money Laundering Offences | SG26 |
| Meeting a child following sexual grooming | Sexual Offences | SG31 |
| Money laundering | Fraud, Bribery and Money Laundering Offences | SG26 |
| Money laundering: acquisition, use and possession of criminal property | Fraud, Bribery and Money Laundering Offences | SG26 |

Sentencing Guidelines

| Magistrates' Court Sentencing Guidelines | | |
|---|---|---|
| Money laundering: concealing/ disguising/ converting/ transferring/ removing criminal property from England and Wales | Fraud, Bribery and Money Laundering Offences | SG26 |
| Money laundering: entering into arrangements concerning criminal property | Fraud, Bribery and Money Laundering Offences | SG26 |
| Motoring offences appropriate for imposition of fine or discharge | Magistrates' Court | SG10-105 |
| No excise licence | Magistrates' Court | SG10-111 |
| No goods vehicle plating certificate | Magistrates' Court | SG10-112 |
| No goods vehicle test certificate | Magistrates' Court | SG10-113 |
| No insurance (Revised 2017) | Magistrates' Court | SG10-114 |
| No operators licence | Magistrates' Court | SG10-115 |
| No test certificate | Magistrates' Court | SG10-116 |
| Non-domestic burglary | Burglary Offences | SG19-4 |
| Number of passengers or way carried involving danger of injury | Magistrates' Court | SG10-117 |
| Number of passengers or way carried involving danger of injury (over 3.5 tonnes) | Magistrates' Court | SG10-118 |
| Obstruct/ resist a police constable in execution of duty (Revised 2017) | Magistrates' Court | SG10-119 |
| Organisations: Breach of an abatement notice | Magistrates' Court | SG10-120 |
| Organisations: Breach of duty of care | Environmental Offences | SG24 |
| Organisations: Breach of duty of employer towards employees and non-employees/ Breach of duty of self-employed to others/ Breach of Health and Safety regulations | Health and Safety Offences | SG28 |
| Organisations: Breach of food safety and food hygiene regulations | Health and Safety Offences | SG28 |
| Organisations: Illegal discharges to air, land and water | Environmental Offences | SG24 |
| Organisations: Restrictions on use of public sewers | Environmental Offences | SG24 |
| Organisations: Transfrontier shipment of waste | Environmental Offences | SG24 |
| Organisations: Unauthorised or harmful deposit, treatment or disposal etc of waste/ Illegal discharges to air, land and water | Environmental Offences | SG24 |
| Overloading/ exceeding axle weight | Magistrates' Court | SG10-121 |
| Overloading/ exceeding axle weight (over 3.5 tonnes) | Magistrates' Court | SG10-122 |
| Owner or person in charge of a dog dangerously out of control in any place in England or Wales (whether or not a public place) | Magistrates' Court | SG10-123 |
| Owner or person in charge of a dog dangerously out of control in any place in England or Wales (whether or not a public place) where a person is injured | Dangerous Dog Offences | SG21 |
| Owner or person in charge of a dog dangerously out of control in any place in England or Wales (whether or not a public place) where an assistance dog is injured or killed | Dangerous Dog Offences | SG21 |
| Owner or person in charge of a dog dangerously out of control in any place in England or Wales (whether or not a public place) where death is caused | Dangerous Dog Offences | SG21 |

| Magistrates' Court Sentencing Guidelines | | |
|---|---|---|
| Paying for the sexual services of a child | Sexual Offences | SG31 |
| Pelican/ zebra crossing contravention | Magistrates' Court | SG10-124 |
| Permitting premises to be used | Drug Offences | SG23-5 |
| Position or manner in which load secured (not involving danger) | Magistrates' Court | SG10-125 |
| Position or manner in which load secured (not involving danger) (over 3.5 tonnes) | Magistrates' Court | SG10-126 |
| Possession for terrorist purposes | Terrorism Offences | SG32 |
| Possession of a controlled drug | Drug Offences | SG23 |
| Possession of a controlled drug with intent to supply it to another | Drug Offences | SG23 |
| Possession of a prohibited dog/ Breeding, selling, exchanging or advertising a prohibited dog | Magistrates' Court | SG10-127 |
| Possession of an article with blade/point in a public place | Bladed Articles and Offensive Weapons | SG14-2 |
| Possession of an article with blade/point on school premises | Bladed Articles and Offensive Weapons | SG14-2 |
| Possession of an offensive weapon in a public place | Bladed Articles and Offensive Weapons | SG14-2 |
| Possession of an offensive weapon on school premises | Bladed Articles and Offensive Weapons | SG14-2 |
| Possession of articles for use in frauds/ Making or supplying articles for use in frauds | Fraud, Bribery and Money Laundering Offences | SG26 |
| Possession of indecent photograph of child/ Indecent photographs of children | Sexual Offences | SG31 |
| Producing a Psychoactive Substance | Drug Offences | SG23-8 |
| Production of a controlled drug/ Cultivation of cannabis plant | Drug Offences | SG23 |
| Proscribed organisations – membership | Terrorism Offences | SG32 |
| Proscribed organisations – support | Terrorism Offences | SG32 |
| Racial hatred offences/ Hatred against persons on religious grounds or grounds of sexual orientation | Public Order | SG29-4 |
| Railway fare evasion (Revised 2017) | Magistrates' Court | SG10-128 |
| Revenue fraud | Fraud, Bribery and Money Laundering Offences | SG26 |
| Robbery – Sentencing children and young people | Robbery Offences | SG30 |
| School non-attendance (Revised 2017) | Magistrates' Court | SG10-129 |
| Seat belt offences | Magistrates' Court | SG10-130 |
| Sex with an adult relative: consenting to penetration | Sexual Offences | SG31 |
| Sex with an adult relative: penetration/ Sex with an adult relative: consenting to penetration | Sexual Offences | SG31 |
| Sexual activity in a public lavatory | Magistrates' Court | SG10-131 |
| Sexual activity with a child family member (offender under 18) | Sexual Offences | SG31 |
| Sexual activity with a child family member/ Inciting a child family member to engage in sexual activity | Sexual Offences | SG31 |
| Sexual activity with a child/ Causing or inciting a child to engage in sexual activity | Sexual Offences | SG31 |

Sentencing Guidelines

**CULPABILITY demonstrated by one or more of the following:**

### Factors indicating higher culpability

- No attempt made to establish age
- Sale for consumption by group of intoxicated persons
- Sale intended for consumption by a child or young person
- Offender in management position (or equivalent)
- Evidence of failure to police the sale of alcohol

### Factors indicating lower culpability

- Offender deceived by false identification
- Evidence of substantial effort to police the sale of alcohol
- Offender acting under direction

**HARM demonstrated by one or more of the following:**

### Factors indicating greater harm

- Supply to younger child/children
- Supply causes or contributes to antisocial behaviour
- Large quantity of alcohol supplied

### Factors indicating lesser harm

- All other cases

## STEP 2 Starting point and category range

Having determined the category at step one, the court should use the starting point to reach a sentence within the appropriate category range in the table below. The starting point applies to all offenders irrespective of plea or previous convictions.

| Offence Category | Starting Point | Range |
|---|---|---|
| **Category 1** | Band C fine | Band B fine – Band C fine |
| **Category 2** | Band B fine | Band A fine – Band C fine |
| **Category 3** | Band A fine | Conditional discharge – Band B fine |

Note: refer to fines for **offence committed for 'commercial' purposes**

### Fines

[See **SG10-35** for band ranges]

### Factors increasing or reducing seriousness

The court should then consider adjustment for any aggravating or mitigating factors. The following is a **non-exhaustive** list of additional factual elements providing the context of the offence and factors relating to the offender. Identify whether any combination of these, or other relevant factors, should result in an upward or downward adjustment from the sentence arrived at so far.

### Factors increasing seriousness

*Statutory aggravating factors:*

- Previous convictions, having regard to a) the **nature** of the offence to which the conviction relates and its **relevance** to the current offence; and b) the **time** that has elapsed since the conviction
- Offence committed whilst on bail
- Offence motivated by, or demonstrating hostility based on any of the following characteristics or presumed characteristics of the victim: religion, race, disability, sexual orientation or transgender identity

*Other aggravating factors:*

- Failure to comply with current court orders
- Offence committed on licence or post sentence supervision

### Factors reducing seriousness or reflecting personal mitigation

- No previous convictions **or** no relevant/recent convictions
- Offence committed as the result of substantial intimidation

**STEP 3   Consider any factors which indicate a reduction, such as assistance to the prosecution**

The court should take into account section 74 of the Sentencing Code (reduction in sentence for assistance to prosecution) and any other rule of law by virtue of which an offender may receive a discounted sentence in consequence of assistance given (or offered) to the prosecutor or investigator.

**STEP 4   Reduction for guilty pleas**

The court should take account of any potential reduction for a guilty plea in accordance with section 73 of the Sentencing Code and the guideline for Reduction in Sentence for a Guilty Plea [**SG5-1–SG5-12**].

**STEP 5   Totality principle**

If sentencing an offender for more than one offence, or where the offender is already serving a sentence, consider whether the total sentence is just and proportionate to the overall offending behaviour in accordance with the *Totality* guideline [see **SG4**].

**STEP 6   Compensation and ancillary orders**

In all cases, the court should consider whether to make compensation [see **SG10-47**] and/or other ancillary orders including deprivation and/or forfeiture or suspension of personal liquor licence [See **SG10-5**].

Where the offence has resulted in personal injury, loss or damage the court must give reasons if it decides not to order compensation (Sentencing Code, s.55).

[See the Sentencing Council Explanatory Materials for Ancillary Orders in the Magistrates' Courts at SG10-5 and the Crown Court Compendium, Part II Sentencing, S7; Ancillary Orders]

**STEP 7   Reasons**

Section 52 of the Sentencing Code imposes a duty to give reasons for, and explain the effect of, the sentence.

ANIMAL CRUELTY - INTERIM GUIDANCE                        **SG10-57**

*Animal Welfare Act 2006*

**Effective from:** guidance only

**Interim guidance - offences committed on or after 29 June 2021.**

The maximum penalty for the following offences increased from six months to five years from 29 June 2021:

- Causing unnecessary suffering (section 4, Animal Welfare Act 2006);
- Carrying out a non-exempted mutilation (section 5, Animal Welfare Act 2006);
- Docking the tail of a dog except where permitted (section 6(1) and 6(2), Animal Welfare Act 2006;
- Administering a poison to an animal (section 7, Animal Welfare Act 2006); and
- Involvement in an animal fight (section 8, Animal Welfare Act 2006).

The offences listed above committed on or after 29 June 2021 will be triable either way (they can be dealt with in magistrates' courts or the Crown Court).

Currently offences contrary to section 4 (causing unnecessary suffering) and section 8 (involvement in an animal fight) are covered by a Sentencing Council guideline.

The guideline also applies to offences contrary to section 9 (breach of duty of person responsible for animal to ensure welfare) - the maximum sentence for the section 9 offence remains six months' custody and the guideline therefore remains in force for that offence.

The Sentencing Council will develop and consult on a revised guideline for the offences with a five-year maximum. Until that revised guideline is available, courts may continue to refer to the existing guideline [below] to assist in the assessment of the level of seriousness of a case, but the sentence table will be of limited use in determining the sentence.

Information from the passage of the legislation in Parliament indicates that the increase in the maximum sentence was designed to provide for higher penalties for the most serious offences. It was not intended to increase significantly the number of offenders who receive custodial sentences.

If considering a community or custodial sentence, courts must follow the Imposition guideline [see SG9-1].

## ANIMAL CRUELTY (REVISED 2017)

*Animal Welfare Act 2006, s.4 (unnecessary suffering), s. 8 (fighting etc), s. 9*
*(breach of duty of person responsible for animal to ensure welfare)*

**Effective from:** 24 April 2017

Triable only summarily
Maximum: Unlimited fine and/or 6 months
Offence range: Band A fine–26 weeks' custody

**Note:** For offences under section 4 (unnecessary suffering) and section 8 (fighting etc) committed on or after 29 June 2021 the maximum penalty is five years' custody. The sentence levels in this guideline are therefore unlikely to apply to these offences and very serious cases should be committed to the Crown Court for sentence. See the interim guidance [above].

### STEP 1 Determining the offence category

The court should determine culpability and harm caused with reference **only** to the factors below. Where an offence does not fall squarely into a category, individual factors may require a degree of weighting before making an overall assessment and determining the appropriate offence category.

**CULPABILITY demonstrated by one or more of the following:**

*Factors indicating high culpability*

- Deliberate or gratuitous attempt to cause suffering
- Prolonged or deliberate ill treatment or neglect
- Ill treatment in a commercial context
- A leading role in illegal activity

*Factors indicating medium culpability*

- All cases not falling into high or low culpability

*Factors indicating low culpability*

- Well intentioned but incompetent care
- Mental disorder or learning disability, where linked to the commission of the offence

**HARM demonstrated by one or more of the following:**

*Factors indicating greater harm*

- Death or serious injury/harm to animal
- High level of suffering caused

*Factors indicating lesser harm*

- All other cases

### STEP 2 Starting point and category range

Having determined the category at step one, the court should use the corresponding starting point to reach a sentence within the category range below. The starting point applies to all offenders irrespective of plea or previous convictions.

A case of particular gravity, reflected by multiple features of culpability in step one, could merit upward adjustment from the starting point before further adjustment for aggravating or mitigating features, set out below.

|  | High culpability | Medium culpability | Low culpability |
|---|---|---|---|
| **Greater harm** | **Starting point** 18 weeks' custody | **Starting point** Medium level community order | **Starting point** Band C fine |
|  | **Category range** 12–26 weeks' custody | **Category range** Low level community order – High level community order | **Category range** Band B fine – Low level community order |
| **Lesser harm** | **Starting point** High level community order | **Starting point** Low level community order | **Starting point** Band B fine |
|  | **Category range** Low level community order – 12 weeks' custody | **Category range** Band C fine – Medium level community order | **Category range** Band A fine – B and C fine |

## Fines

[See **SG10-35** for band ranges]

## Community Orders and Custodial Sentences

[For the imposition of community orders, including the community orders table, see Imposition of Community and Custodial Sentences at **SG9-2**. For the imposition of custodial sentences see Imposition of Community and Custodial Sentences at **SG9-3**.]

### Factors increasing or reducing seriousness

The court should then consider further adjustment for any aggravating or mitigating factors. The following is a **non-exhaustive** list of additional factual elements providing the context of the offence and factors relating to the offender. Identify whether any combination of these, or other relevant factors, should result in an upward or downward adjustment from the sentence arrived at so far.

### Factors increasing seriousness

*Statutory aggravating factors:*

- Previous convictions, having regard to a) the **nature** of the offence to which the conviction relates and its **relevance** to the current offence; and b) the **time** that has elapsed since the conviction
- Offence committed whilst on bail
- Offence motivated by, or demonstrating hostility based on any of the following characteristics or presumed characteristics of the owner/keeper of the animal: religion, race, disability, sexual orientation or transgender identity

*Other aggravating factors:*

- Distress caused to owner where not responsible for the offence
- Failure to comply with current court orders
- Offence committed on licence or post sentence supervision
- Use of weapon
- Allowing person of insufficient experience or training to have care of animal(s)
- Use of technology to publicise or promote cruelty
- Ignores warning/professional advice/declines to obtain professional advice
- Use of another animal to inflict death or injury
- Offender in position of responsibility
- Animal requires significant intervention to recover
- Animal being used in public service or as an assistance dog

### Factors reducing seriousness or reflecting personal mitigation

- No previous convictions **or** no relevant/recent convictions
- Remorse
- Good character and/or exemplary conduct
- Serious medical condition requiring urgent, intensive or long-term treatment
- Age and/or lack of maturity where it affects the responsibility of the offender
- Mental disorder or learning disability, where not linked to the commission of the offence
- Sole or primary carer for dependent relatives
- Offender has been given an inappropriate level of trust or responsibility
- Voluntary surrender of animals to authorities
- Cooperation with the investigation
- Isolated incident

### STEP 3  Consider any factors which indicate a reduction, such as assistance to the prosecution

The court should take into account section 74 of the Sentencing Code (reduction in sentence for assistance to prosecution) and any other rule of law by virtue of which an offender may receive a discounted sentence in consequence of assistance given (or offered) to the prosecutor or investigator.

### STEP 4  Reduction for guilty pleas

The court should take account of any potential reduction for a guilty plea in accordance with section 73 of the Sentencing Code and the guideline for Reduction in Sentence for a Guilty Plea [**SG5-1–SG5-12**].

### STEP 5  Totality principle

If sentencing an offender for more than one offence, or where the offender is already serving a sentence, consider whether the total sentence is just and proportionate to the overall offending behaviour in accordance with the *Totality* guideline. [See **SG4**]

Where the offence has resulted in personal injury, loss or damage the court must give reasons if it decides not to order compensation (Sentencing Code, s.55).

[See the Sentencing Council Explanatory Materials for Ancillary Orders in the Magistrates' Courts at SG10-5]

**STEP 7  Reasons**

Section 52 of the Sentencing Code imposes a duty to give reasons for, and explain the effect of, the sentence.

**SG10-61**                    COMMUNICATION NETWORK OFFENCES (REVISED 2017)

*Communications Act 2003, ss. 127(1) and 127(2)*

**Effective from:** 24 April 2017

Triable only summarily
Maximum: Unlimited fine and/or 6 months
Offence range: Band A fine–15 weeks' custody

**STEP 1  Determining the offence category**

The Court should determine the offence category using the table below.

| Category 1 | Higher culpability and greater harm |
| Category 2 | Higher culpability and lesser harm or lower culpability and greater harm |
| Category 3 | Lower culpability and lesser harm |

The court should determine the offender's culpability and the harm caused with reference **only** to the factors below. Where an offence does not fall squarely into a category, individual factors may require a degree of weighting before making an overall assessment and determining the appropriate offence category.

**CULPABILITY demonstrated by one or more of the following:**

*Factors indicating higher culpability*

- Targeting of a vulnerable victim
- Targeting offending (in terms of timing or location) to maximise effect
- Use of threats (including blackmail)
- Threat to disclose intimate material or sexually explicit images
- Campaign demonstrated by multiple calls and/or wide distribution
- False calls to emergency services
- Offence motivated by, or demonstrating, hostility based on any of the following characteristics or presumed characteristics of the victim(s): religion, race, disability, sexual orientation or transgender identity

*Factors indicating lower culpability*

- All other cases

**HARM demonstrated by one or more of the following:**

*Factors indicating greater harm*

- Substantial distress or fear to victim(s) **or** moderate impact on several victims
- Major disruption

*Factors indicating lesser harm*

- All other cases

**STEP 2  Starting point and category range**

Having determined the category at step one, the court should use the corresponding starting point to reach a sentence within the category range in the table below. The starting point applies to all offenders irrespective of plea or previous convictions.

| Offence Category | Starting Point | Range |
| --- | --- | --- |
| Category 1 | 9 weeks' custody | High level community order – 15 weeks' custody |
| Category 2 | Medium level community order | Low level community order – High level community order |
| Category 3 | Band B fine | Band A fine – Band C fine |

**Fines**

[See **SG10-35** for band ranges]

**Community Orders and Custodial Sentences**

[For the imposition of community orders, including the community orders table, see Imposition of Community and Custodial Sentences at **SG9-2**. For the imposition of custodial sentences see Imposition of Community and Custodial Sentences at **SG9-3**.]

**Factors increasing or reducing seriousness**

The court should then consider adjustment for any aggravating or mitigating factors. The following is a **non-exhaustive** list of additional factual elements providing the context of the offence and factors relating to the offender. Identify whether any combination of these, or other relevant factors, should result in an upward or downward adjustment from the sentence arrived at so far.

**Factors increasing seriousness**

*Statutory aggravating factors*

- Previous convictions, having regard to a) the **nature** of the offence to which the conviction relates and its **relevance** to the current offence; and b) the **time** that has elapsed since the conviction
- Offence committed whilst on bail

*Other aggravating factors*

- Failure to comply with current court orders including restraining order
- Offence committed on licence or post sentence supervision
- Offence committed whilst subject to sex offender notification requirements
- Offence linked to domestic abuse
- Abuse of trust
- Targeting emergency services (where not taken into account at step one)

**Factors reducing seriousness or reflecting personal mitigation**

- No previous convictions **or** no relevant/recent convictions
- Remorse
- Good character and/or exemplary conduct
- Isolated incident
- Age and/or lack of maturity where it affects the responsibility of the offender
- Mental disorder or learning disability
- Sole or primary carer for dependent relatives
- Limited awareness or understanding of the offence

**STEP 3   Consider any factors which indicate a reduction, such as assistance to the prosecution**

The court should take into account section 74 of the Sentencing Code (reduction in sentence for assistance to prosecution) and any other rule of law by virtue of which an offender may receive a discounted sentence in consequence of assistance given (or offered) to the prosecutor or investigator.

**STEP 4   Reduction for guilty pleas**

The court should take account of any potential reduction for a guilty plea in accordance with section 73 of the Sentencing Code and the guideline for Reduction in Sentence for a Guilty Plea [**SG5-1–SG5-12**].

**STEP 5   Totality principle**

If sentencing an offender for more than one offence, or where the offender is already serving a sentence, consider whether the total sentence is just and proportionate to the overall offending behaviour in accordance with the *Totality* guideline. [See **SG4**]

**STEP 6   Compensation and ancillary orders**

In all cases, the court should consider whether to make compensation [See **SG10-47**] and/or other ancillary orders including restraining orders.

Where the offence has resulted in personal injury, loss or damage the court must give reasons if it decides not to order compensation (Sentencing Code, s.55).

[See the Sentencing Council Explanatory Materials for Ancillary Orders in the Magistrates' Courts at **SG10-5**]

**STEP 7   Reasons**

Section 52 of the Sentencing Code imposes a duty to give reasons for, and explain the effect of, the sentence.

Sentencing Guidelines

**STEP 8  Consideration for time spent on bail (tagged curfew)**

The court must consider whether to give credit for time spent on bail in accordance with section 240A of the Criminal Justice Act 2003 and section 325 of the Sentencing Code.

SG10-62       CONDITION OF VEHICLE/ACCESSORIES/EQUIPMENT INVOLVING DANGER OF INJURY — BUSES/GOODS VEHICLES

*Road Traffic Act 1988, s. 40A*

**Effective from:** 04 August 2008

**Part 5: Offences re buses/goods vehicles over 3.5 tonnes (GVW)**

* The guidelines for these offences differentiate between three types of offender: driver; owner-driver; and owner-company. **For owner-driver, the starting point is the same as for driver; however, the court should consider an uplift of at least 25 per cent.**

** In all cases, take safety, damage to roads and commercial gain into account. Refer to guidance where offence committed for 'commercial' purposes.

**Maximum fines**

A fine must not exceed the statutory limit. Where this is expressed in terms of a 'level', the maxima are:

| | |
|---|---|
| Level 1 | £200 |
| Level 2 | £500 |
| Level 3 | £1,000 |
| Level 4 | £2,500 |
| Level 5 | Unlimited |

| Offence | Maximum | Points | Starting point | Special considerations |
|---|---|---|---|---|
| No goods vehicle plating certificate | L3 | – | A (driver) A* (owner-driver) B (owner-company) | |
| No goods vehicle test certificate | L4 | – | B (driver) B* (owner-driver) C (owner-company) | |
| Brakes defective | L5 | 3 | B (driver) B* (owner-driver) C (owner-company) | |
| Steering defective | L5 | 3 | B (driver) B* (owner-driver) C (owner-company) | |
| Tyres defective | L5 | 3 | B (driver) B* (owner-driver) C (owner-company) | Fine is for each single tyre (but ordinarily only one set of points apply where several offences committed on the same occasion) |
| Exhaust emission | L4 | – | B (driver) B* (owner-driver) C (owner-company) | |
| Condition of vehicle/ accessories/ equipment involving danger of injury (Road Traffic Act 1988, s.40A) | L5 | 3 | B (driver) B* (owner-driver) C (owner-company) | Must disqualify for at least six months if offender has one or more previous convictions for same offence within three years |

| Offence | Maximum | Points | Starting point | Special considerations |
|---|---|---|---|---|
| Number of passengers or way carried involving danger of injury (Road Traffic Act 1988, s.40A) | L5 | 3 | B (driver) B* (owner-driver) C (owner-company) | Must disqualify for at least six months if offender has one or more previous convictions for same offence within three years |
| Weight, position or distribution of load or manner in which load secured involving danger of injury (Road Traffic Act 1988, s.40A) | L5 | 3 | B (driver) B* (owner-driver) C (owner-company) | Must disqualify for at least six months if offender has one or more previous convictions for same offence within three years |
| Position or manner in which load secured (not involving danger) (Road Traffic Act 1988, s.42) | L4 | – | B (driver) B* (owner-driver) C (owner-company) | |
| Overloading/ exceeding axle weight | L5 | – | B (driver) B* (owner-driver) C (owner-company) | Starting points cater for cases where the overload is up to and including 10 per cent. Thereafter, 10 per cent should be added to the penalty for each additional one per cent of overload. Penalty per axle. |
| No operators licence | L4 (PSV) L5 (Goods) | – | B (driver) B* (owner-driver) C (owner-company) | |
| Speed limiter not used or incorrectly calibrated | L4 | – | B (driver) B* (owner-driver) C (owner-company) | |
| Tachograph not used/not working | L5 | – | B (driver) B* (owner-driver) C (owner-company) | |
| Exceed permitted driving time/ periods of duty | L4 | – | B (driver) B* (owner-driver) C (owner-company) | |
| Fail to keep/return written record sheets | L4 | – | B (driver) B* (owner-driver) C (owner-company) | |
| Falsify or alter records with intent to deceive | L5/2 years | – | B (driver) B* (owner-driver) C (owner-company) | Either way offence |

**Fines**

[See **SG10-35** for band ranges]

CONDITION OF VEHICLE/ACCESSORIES/EQUIPMENT INVOLVING    **SG10-63**
DANGER OF INJURY — BUSES/GOODS VEHICLES

[See Motoring offences appropriate for imposition of fine or discharge, Part Two: Offences concerning the vehicle **SG10-107**.]

**SG10-64**                    DANGEROUS DRIVING

*Road Traffic Act 1988, s. 2*

Triable either way
Triable either way
Maximum: 2 years' custody

- Must endorse and disqualify for *at least* 12 months. Must order extended re-test
- Must disqualify for *at least* 2 years if offender has had two or more disqualifications for periods of 56 days or more in preceding 3 years. If there is a delay in sentencing after conviction, consider interim disqualification

**Offence seriousness (culpability and harm)**

*A.  Identify the appropriate starting point*

Starting points based on first time offender pleading not guilty

| Examples of nature of activity | Starting point | Range |
|---|---|---|
| Single incident where little or no damage or risk of personal injury | Medium level community order | Low level community order–high level community order  Disqualify 12–15 months |
| Incident(s) involving excessive speed or showing off, especially on busy roads or in built-up area; OR Single incident where little or no damage or risk of personal injury but offender was disqualified driver | 12 weeks' custody | High level community order–26 weeks' custody  Disqualify 15–24 months |
| Prolonged bad driving involving deliberate disregard for safety of others; OR Incident(s) involving excessive speed or showing off, especially on busy roads or in built-up area, by disqualified driver; OR Driving as described in box above while being pursued by police | Crown Court | Crown Court |

**Community Orders and Custodial Sentences**

[For the imposition of community orders, including the community orders table, see Imposition of Community and Custodial Sentences at **SG9-2**. For the imposition of custodial sentences see Imposition of Community and Custodial Sentences at **SG9-3**.]

*B.  Consider the effect of aggravating and mitigating factors (other than those within examples above)*

Common aggravating and mitigating factors are identified [elsewhere]—the following may be particularly relevant but these lists are not exhaustive

| Factors indicating higher culpability | Factors indicating lower culpability |
|---|---|
| 1.  Disregarding warnings of others | 1.  Genuine emergency |
| 2.  Evidence of alcohol or drugs | 2.  Speed not excessive |
| 3.  Carrying out other tasks while driving | 3.  Offence due to inexperience rather than irresponsibility of driver |
| 4.  Carrying passengers or heavy load | |
| 5.  Tiredness | |
| 6.  Aggressive driving, such as driving much too close to vehicle in front, racing, inappropriate attempts to overtake, or cutting in after overtaking | |
| 7.  Driving when knowingly suffering from a medical condition which significantly impairs the offender's driving skills | |
| 8.  Driving a poorly maintained or dangerously loaded vehicle, especially where motivated by commercial concerns | |
| **Factors indicating greater degree of harm** | |
| 1.  Injury to others | |
| 2.  Damage to other vehicles or property | |

**Common aggravating and mitigating factors**

[See **SG10-4**]

**Form a preliminary view of the appropriate sentence, then consider offender mitigation**

*Offender mitigation*

- Genuine remorse
- Admissions to police in interview
- Ready co-operation with authorities

**Consider a reduction for a guilty plea**

- Reduction in Sentence for a Guilty Plea (where first hearing is on or after 1 June 2017 [see **SG5-1**], or first hearing before 1 June 2017 [see **SG5-12**]).

**Consider ancillary orders, including compensation and deprivation of property**

View guidance on available ancillary orders and compensation.

Where the offence has resulted in personal injury, loss or damage the court must give reasons if it decides not to order compensation (Sentencing Code, s.55).

- Ancillary orders – Magistrates' Court [see **SG10-5**]

**Decide sentence**

**Give reasons**

<br>

DANGEROUS PARKING    **SG10-65**

[See Motoring offences appropriate for imposition of fine or discharge, Part Three: Offences concerning use of vehicle **SG10-108**.]

DISORDERLY BEHAVIOUR/RACIALLY OR RELIGIOUSLY AGGRAVATED DISORDERLY BEHAVIOUR    **SG10-66**

*Crime and Disorder Act 1998, s. 31(1)(c), Public Order Act 1986, s.5*

**Effective from:** 01 January 2020

**Disorderly behaviour, Public Order Act 1986, s.5**

Triable only summarily
Maximum: Level 3 fine
Offence range: Discharge – Fine

**Racially or religiously aggravated disorderly behaviour, Crime and Disorder Act 1998, s.31(1)(c)**

Triable only summarily
Maximum: Level 4 fine

**STEP 1  Determining the offence category**

The court should determine the offence category with reference **only** to the factors listed in the tables below. In order to determine the category the court should assess **culpability** and **harm.**

**Culpability demonstrated by one or more of the following:**

*A – High culpability*

Targeting of individual(s) by a group

- Sustained incident
- Use of force
- Substantial disturbance

*B – Lesser culpability*

- All other cases

**Harm**

The court should consider the factors set out below to determine the level of harm that has been caused or was intended to be caused to the victim.

*Category 1*

- Serious distress or alarm caused
- Distress or alarm caused to multiple persons present

*Category 2*

- All other cases

## STEP 2 Starting point and category range

Having determined the category at step one, the court should use the corresponding starting point to reach a sentence within the category range below. The starting point applies to all offenders irrespective of plea or previous convictions.

| Harm | Culpability | |
|---|---|---|
| | A | B |
| Category 1 | **Starting point**<br>Band C fine | **Starting point**<br>Band B fine |
| | **Category range**<br>Band B – Band C fine | **Category range**<br>Band A – Band C fine |
| Category 2 | **Starting point**<br>Band B fine | **Starting point**<br>Band A fine |
| | **Category range**<br>Band A – Band C fine | **Category range**<br>Discharge – Band B fine |

### Fines
[See **SG10-35** for band ranges]

### Factors increasing or reducing seriousness

The table below contains a **non-exhaustive** list of additional factual elements providing the context of the offence and factors relating to the offender. Identify whether any combination of these, or other relevant factors, should result in an upward or downward adjustment from the sentence arrived at so far.

### Factors increasing seriousness

*Statutory aggravating factors:*
- Previous convictions, having regard to a) the **nature** of the offence to which the conviction relates and its **relevance** to the current offence; and b) the **time** that has elapsed since the conviction
- Offence committed whilst on bail
- Offence motivated by, or demonstrating hostility based on any of the following characteristics or presumed characteristics of the victim: disability, sexual orientation or transgender identity

*Other aggravating factors:*
- Planning
- Offence committed against those working in the public sector or providing a service to the public
- Commission of offence whilst under the influence of alcohol/drugs
- Vulnerable persons or children present
- Victim is targeted due to a vulnerability (or a perceived vulnerability)
- History of antagonising the victim
- Victim(s) had no opportunity to escape situation (eg: offence occurred on public transport)
- Offence committed whilst on licence or post sentence supervision
- Failure to comply with current court orders

### Factors reducing seriousness or reflecting personal mitigation
- No previous convictions **or** no relevant/recent convictions
- Remorse
- Good character and/or exemplary conduct
- Age and/or lack of maturity
- Mental disorder or learning disability
- Sole or primary carer for dependent relatives

### Racially or religiously aggravated offences only
*Summary only offence. Maximum sentence for the aggravated offence is level 4 fine.*

**SG10-67** DRIVE IN REVERSE OR WRONG WAY ON MOTORWAY

[See Motoring offences appropriate for imposition of fine or discharge, Part Four: Motorway Offences SG10-109.]

DRIVE IN REVERSE OR WRONG WAY ON SLIP ROAD                      **SG10-68**

[See Motoring offences appropriate for imposition of fine or discharge, Part Four: Motorway Offences SG10-109.]

DRIVE OFF CARRIAGEWAY (CENTRAL RESERVATION OR HARD SHOULDER)    **SG10-69**

[See Motoring offences appropriate for imposition of fine or discharge, Part Four: Motorway Offences SG10-109.]

DRIVE OTHERWISE THAN IN ACCORDANCE WITH LICENCE                 **SG10-70**

[See Motoring offences appropriate for imposition of fine or discharge, Part One: Offences concerning the driver SG10-106.]

DRIVE OTHERWISE THAN IN ACCORDANCE WITH LICENCE                 **SG10-71**
(WHERE COULD BE COVERED)

[See Motoring offences appropriate for imposition of fine or discharge, Part One: Offences concerning the driver SG10-106.]

DRIVE WHILST DISQUALIFIED (REVISED 2017)                        **SG10-72**

*Road Traffic Act 1988, s.103*

**Effective from:** 24 April 2017

Triable only summarily
Maximum: Unlimited fine and/or 6 months
Offence range: Band C fine–26 weeks' custody

**STEP 1   Determining the offence category**
The Court should determine the offence category using the table below.

| Category 1 | Higher culpability **and** greater harm |
| Category 2 | Higher culpability **and** lesser harm **or** lower culpability **and** greater harm |
| Category 3 | Lower culpability **and** lesser harm |

The court should determine the offender's culpability and the harm caused with reference **only** to the factors below. Where an offence does not fall squarely into a category, individual factors may require a degree of weighting before making an overall assessment and determining the appropriate offence category.

**CULPABILITY demonstrated by one or more of the following:**
**Factors indicating higher culpability**
• Driving shortly after disqualification imposed
• Vehicle obtained during disqualification period
• Driving for reward

**Factors indicating lower culpability**
• All other cases

**HARM demonstrated by one or more of the following:**
*Factors indicating greater harm*
• Significant distance driven
• Evidence of associated bad driving

*Factors indicating lesser harm*
• All other cases

**STEP 2   Starting point and category range**
Having determined the category at step one, the court should use the appropriate starting point to reach a sentence within the category range in the table below. The starting point applies to all offenders irrespective of plea or previous convictions.

| Level of seriousness | Starting Point | Range | Penalty points/ disqualification |
|---|---|---|---|
| Category 1 | 12 weeks' custody | High Level community order – 26 weeks' custody | Disqualify for 12–18 months beyond expiry of current ban (Extend if imposing immediate custody) |
| Category 2 | High level community order | Medium level community order – 12 weeks' custody | Disqualify for 6–12 months beyond expiry of current ban (Extend if imposing immediate custody) |
| Category 3 | Low level community order | Band C fine – Medium level community order | Disqualify for 3–6 months beyond expiry of current ban OR 6 points |

- **Must endorse and may disqualify. If no disqualification impose 6 points**
- **Extend disqualification if imposing immediate custody**

### Fines

[See **SG10-35** for band ranges]

### Community Orders and Custodial Sentences

[For the imposition of community orders, including the community orders table, see Imposition of Community and Custodial Sentences at **SG9-2**. For the imposition of custodial sentences see Imposition of Community and Custodial Sentences at **SG9-3**.]

### Factors increasing or reducing seriousness

The court should then consider further adjustment for any aggravating or mitigating factors. The following is a **non-exhaustive** list of additional factual elements providing the context of the offence and factors relating to the offender. Identify whether any combination of these, or other relevant factors, should result in an upward or downward adjustment from the sentence arrived at so far.

### Factors increasing seriousness

*Statutory aggravating factors:*

- Previous convictions, having regard to
  a) the **nature** of the offence to which the conviction relates and its **relevance** to the current offence; and
  b) the **time** that has elapsed since the conviction.

**Note** An offender convicted of this offence will always have at least one relevant previous conviction for the offence that resulted in disqualification. The starting points and ranges take this into account; any other previous convictions should be considered in the usual way.

- Offence committed whilst on bail

*Other aggravating factors:*

- Failure to comply with current court orders (not including the current order for disqualification)
- Offence committed on licence or post sentence supervision
- Carrying passengers
- Giving false details

### Factors reducing seriousness or reflecting personal mitigation

- No previous convictions **or** no relevant/recent convictions
- Good character and/or exemplary conduct
- Remorse
- Genuine emergency established
- Age and/or lack of maturity where it affects the responsibility of the offender
- Serious medical condition requiring urgent, intensive or long-term treatment
- Sole or primary carer for dependent relatives

### STEP 3  Consider any factors which indicate a reduction, such as assistance to the prosecution

The court should take into account section 74 of the Sentencing Code (reduction in sentence for assistance to prosecution) and any other rule of law by virtue of which an offender may receive a discounted sentence in consequence of assistance given (or offered) to the prosecutor or investigator.

### STEP 4  Reduction for guilty pleas

The court should take account of any potential reduction for a guilty plea in accordance with section 73 of the Sentencing Code and the guideline for Reduction in Sentence for a Guilty Plea [SG5-1–SG5-12].

### STEP 5  Totality principle

If sentencing an offender for more than one offence, or where the offender is already serving a sentence, consider whether the total sentence is just and proportionate to the overall offending behaviour in accordance with the *Totality* guideline. [See SG4]

### STEP 6  Compensation and ancillary orders

In all cases, the court should consider whether to make compensation and/or other ancillary orders including disqualification from driving [See SG10-5].

Where the offence has resulted in personal injury, loss or damage the court must give reasons if it decides not to order compensation (Sentencing Code, s.55).

### STEP 7  Reasons

Section 52 of the Sentencing Code imposes a duty to give reasons for, and explain the effect of, the sentence.

### STEP 8  Consideration for time spent on bail (tagged curfew)

The court must consider whether to give credit for time spent on bail in accordance with section 240A of the Criminal Justice Act 2003 and section 325 of the Sentencing Code.

## DRUG DRIVING (GUIDANCE ONLY)                                    SG10-73

Since the new offence came into force in March 2015 the Sentencing Council has received a large number of requests for a sentencing guideline. It has been brought to our attention that there are concerns with sentencing in this area and a risk of inconsistent practices developing.

The new offence is a strict liability offence, which is committed once the specified limit for any of 17 specified controlled drugs is exceeded. The 17 drugs include both illegal drugs and drugs that may be medically prescribed.

The limits for illegal drugs are set in line with a zero tolerance approach but ruling out accidental exposure. The limits for drugs that may be medically prescribed are set in line with a road safety risk-based approach, at levels above the normal concentrations found with therapeutic use. This is different from the approach taken when setting the limit for alcohol, where the limit was set at a level where the effect of the alcohol would be expected to have impaired a person's driving ability. For these reasons it would be wrong to rely on the *Driving with Excess Alcohol* guideline when sentencing an offence under this legislation.

### Guidance Only

At present there is insufficient reliable data available from the Department for Transport upon which the Sentencing Council can devise a full guideline. For that reason, and given the number of requests for guidance that have been received, the Sentencing Council has devised the attached guidance to assist sentencers.

It is important to note that **this guidance does not carry the same authority as a sentencing guideline**, and sentencers are not obliged to follow it. However, it is hoped that the majority of sentencers will find it useful in assisting them to deal with these cases.

The Sentencing Council will, in due course produce a guideline with the assistance of evidence and data gathered by the Department for Transport. Any new guideline will be made subject to public consultation before it is finalised.

### Background

The Crime and Courts Act 2013 inserted a new section 5A into the Road Traffic Act 1988 (RTA), which makes it an offence to drive, attempt to drive, or be in charge of a motor vehicle with a concentration of a specified controlled drug in the body above the specified limit. The offence came into force on 2 March 2015.

**Driving or Attempting to Drive**

> Triable only summarily:
>
> Maximum: Unlimited fine and/or 6 months
>
> - Must endorse and disqualify for at least 12 months
> - Must disqualify for at least 2 years if offender has had two or more disqualifications for periods of 56 days or more in preceding 3 years – refer to disqualification guidance and consult your legal adviser for further guidance
> - Must disqualify for at least 3 years if offender has been convicted of a relevant offence in preceding 10 years – consult your legal adviser for further guidance
>
> If there is a delay in sentencing after conviction, consider interim disqualification

As a guide, where an offence of driving or attempting to drive has been committed and there are no factors that increase seriousness the Court should consider a starting point of a **Band C fine** [For band ranges, see **SG10-35**], and a disqualification in the region of 12–22 months. See below for the list of factors that increase seriousness 0. Please note this is an exhaustive list and only factors that appear in the list should be considered.

Where there are factors that increase seriousness the Court should consider increasing the sentence on the basis of the level of seriousness.

The community order threshold is likely to be crossed where there is evidence of one or more factors that increase seriousness. The Court should also consider imposing a disqualification in the region of 23–28 months.

**Factors increasing or reducing seriousness**

The **custody** threshold is likely to be crossed where there is evidence of one or more factors that increase seriousness and one or more aggravating factors. The Court should also consider imposing a disqualification in the region of 29–36 months.

Having determined a starting point, the Court should consider additional factors that may make the offence more or less serious.

**Factors that increase seriousness (this is an exhaustive list)**
- Evidence of another specified drug[197] or of alcohol in the body
- Evidence of an unacceptable standard of driving
- Driving (or in charge of) an LGV, HGV or PSV
- Driving (or in charge of) a vehicle driven for hire or reward

**Aggravating and mitigating factors (these are non-exhaustive lists)**
*Aggravating factors*
- Previous convictions having regard to a) the **nature** of the offence to which the conviction relates and its **relevance** to the current offence; and b) the **time** that has elapsed since the conviction
- Location e.g. near school
- Carrying passengers
- High level of traffic or pedestrians in the vicinity
- Poor road or weather conditions

*Mitigating factors*
- No previous convictions or no relevant/recent convictions
- Remorse
- Good character and/or exemplary conduct
- Age and/or lack of maturity where it affects the responsibility of the offender
- Mental disorder or learning disability
- Sole or primary carer for dependent relatives
- Very short distance driven
- Genuine emergency established

---

[197] For these purposes, cocaine and benzoylecgonine (BZE) shall be treated as one drug as they both occur in the body as a result of cocaine use rather than poly-drug use. Similarly 6-Monoacteylmorphine and Morphine shall be treated as one drug as they both occur in the body as a result of heroin use. Finally, Diazepam and Temazepam shall be treated as one drug as they also both occur in the body as a result of Temazepam use.

**In charge**

> Triable only summarily
> Maximum: Level 4 fine and/or 3 months
> Must endorse and may disqualify. If no disqualification, impose 10 points

As a guide, where an offence of being in charge has been committed but there are no factors that increase seriousness the Court should consider a starting point of a Band B fine, and endorsing the licence with 10 penalty points. The list of factors that increase seriousness appears below. Please note this is an exhaustive list and only factors that appear in the list should be considered.

Where there are factors that increase seriousness, the Court should consider increasing the sentence on the basis of the level of seriousness.

The community order threshold is likely to be crossed where there is evidence of one or more factors that increase seriousness and one or more aggravating factors (see below). The Court should also consider imposing a disqualification.

Where there is evidence of one or more factors that increase seriousness and a greater number of aggravating factors (see below) the Court may consider it appropriate to impose a short custodial sentence of up to 12 weeks. The Court should also consider imposing a disqualification.

Having determined a starting point, the Court should consider additional factors that may make the offence more or less serious. A non-exhaustive list of aggravating and mitigating factors is set out below.

**Factors that increase seriousness (this is an exhaustive list)**
- Evidence of another specified drug[198] or of alcohol in the body
- Evidence of an unacceptable standard of driving
- Driving (or in charge of) an LGV, HGV or PSV
- Driving (or in charge of) a vehicle driven for hire or reward

**Aggravating and mitigating factors (these are non-exhaustive lists)**

*Aggravating factors*
- Previous convictions having regard to a) the nature of the offence to which the conviction relates and its relevance to the current offence; and b) the time that has elapsed since the conviction
- Location e.g. near school
- Carrying passengers
- High level of traffic or pedestrians in the vicinity
- Poor road or weather conditions

*Mitigating Factors*
- No previous convictions or no relevant/recent convictions
- Remorse
- Good character and/or exemplary conduct
- Age and/or lack of maturity where it affects the responsibility of the offender
- Mental disorder or learning disability
- Sole or primary carer for dependent relatives
- Very short distance driven
- Genuine emergency established

### Drugs—Class A—Fail to Attend/Remain for Initial Assessment   SG10-74

*Drugs Act 2005, s.12*

**Effective from:** 24 April 2017

Triable only summarily
Maximum: Level 4 fine and/or 3 months
Offence range: Band A fine–High level community order

---

[198] For these purposes, cocaine and benzoylecgonine (BZE) shall be treated as one drug as they both occur in the body as a result of cocaine use rather than poly-drug use. Similarly, 6-Monoacteylmorphine and Morphine shall be treated as one drug as they both occur in the body as a result of heroin use. Finally, Diazepam and Temazepam shall be treated as one drug as they also both occur in the body as a result of Temazepam use.

## STEP 1  Determining the offence category

The Court should determine the offence category using the table below.

| Category 1 | Higher culpability **and** greater harm |
|---|---|
| Category 2 | Higher culpability **and** lesser harm **or** lower culpability **and** greater harm |
| Category 3 | Lower culpability **and** lesser harm |

The court should determine the offender's culpability and the harm caused with reference **only** to the factors below. Where an offence does not fall squarely into a category, individual factors may require a degree of weighting before making an overall assessment and determining the appropriate offence category.

### CULPABILITY demonstrated by one or more of the following:

**Factor indicating higher culpability**

- Deliberate failure to attend/remain

**Factor indicating lower culpability**

- All other cases

### HARM demonstrated by one or more of the following:

**Factor indicating greater harm**

- Aggressive, abusive or disruptive behaviour

**Factor indicating lesser harm**

- All other cases

## STEP 2  Starting point and category range

Having determined the category at step one, the court should use the corresponding starting point to reach a sentence within the category range in the table below. The starting point applies to all offenders irrespective of plea or previous convictions.

| Offence Category | Starting Point | Range |
|---|---|---|
| Category 1 | Medium level community order | Low level community order – High level community order |
| Category 2 | Band C fine | Band B fine – Low level community order |
| Category 3 | Band B fine | Band A fine – Band C fine |

### Fines

[See **SG10-35** for band ranges]

### Community Orders

[For the imposition of community orders, including the community orders table, see Imposition of Community and Custodial Sentences at **SG9-2**.]

### Factors increasing or reducing seriousness

The court should then consider further adjustment for any aggravating or mitigating factors. The following is a **non-exhaustive** list of additional factual elements providing the context of the offence and factors relating to the offender. Identify whether any combination of these, or other relevant factors, should result in an upward or downward adjustment from the sentence arrived at so far.

### Factors increasing seriousness

*Statutory aggravating factors:*

- Previous convictions, having regard to a) the **nature** of the offence to which the conviction relates and its **relevance** to the current offence; and b) the **time** that has elapsed since the conviction
- Offence committed whilst on bail
- Offence motivated by, or demonstrating hostility based on any of the following characteristics or presumed characteristics of the victim: religion, race, disability, sexual orientation or transgender identity

*Other aggravating factors:*

- Failure to comply with current court orders
- Offence committed on licence or post sentence supervision
- Offender's actions result in a waste of resources

**Factors reducing seriousness or reflecting personal mitigation**

- No previous convictions or no relevant/recent convictions
- Remorse
- Good character and/or exemplary conduct
- Serious medical condition requiring urgent, intensive or long-term treatment
- Age and/or lack of maturity where it affects the responsibility of the offender
- Mental disorder or learning disability
- Sole or primary carer for dependent relatives
- Determination and/or demonstration of steps having been taken to address addiction or offending behaviour
- Attempts made to re-arrange appointments

**STEP 3   Consider any factors which indicate a reduction, such as assistance to the prosecution**

The court should take into account section 74 of the Sentencing Code (reduction in sentence for assistance to prosecution) and any other rule of law by virtue of which an offender may receive a discounted sentence in consequence of assistance given (or offered) to the prosecutor or investigator.

**STEP 4   Reduction for guilty pleas**

The court should take account of any potential reduction for a guilty plea in accordance with section 73 of the Sentencing Code and the guideline for Reduction in Sentence for a Guilty Plea [**SG5-1–SG5-12**].

**STEP 5   Totality principle**

If sentencing an offender for more than one offence, or where the offender is already serving a sentence, consider whether the total sentence is just and proportionate to the overall offending behaviour in accordance with the *Totality* guideline. [See **SG4**]

**STEP 6   Consider ancillary orders**

In all cases, the court should consider whether to make compensation and/or other ancillary orders. [See **SG10-5**]

Where the offence has resulted in personal injury, loss or damage the court must give reasons if it decides not to order compensation (Sentencing Code, s.55).

**STEP 7   Reasons**

Section 52 of the Sentencing Code imposes a duty to give reasons for, and explain the effect of, the sentence.

DRUGS—CLASS A—FAIL/REFUSE TO PROVIDE A SAMPLE                    **SG10-75**

*Police and Criminal Evidence Act 1984, s.63B*

**Effective from:** 24 April 2017

Triable only summarily
Maximum: Level 4 fine and/or 3 months
Offence range: Band A fine–High level community order

**STEP 1   Determining the offence category**

The Court should determine the offence category using the table below.

| Category 1 | Higher culpability **and** greater harm |
|---|---|
| Category 2 | Higher culpability **and** lesser harm **or** lower culpability **and** greater harm |
| Category 3 | Lower culpability **and** lesser harm |

The court should determine the offender's culpability and the harm caused with reference **only** to the factors below. Where an offence does not fall squarely into a category, individual factors may require a degree of weighting before making an overall assessment and determining the appropriate offence category.

**CULPABILITY demonstrated by one or more of the following:**

**Factors indicating higher culpability**

- Deliberate refusal

**Factors indicating lower culpability**

- All other cases

**HARM demonstrated by one or more of the following:**

**Factors indicating greater harm**

- Aggressive, abusive or disruptive behaviour

**Factors indicating lesser harm**

- All other cases

### STEP 2 Starting point and category range

Having determined the category at step one, the court should use the starting point to reach a sentence within the appropriate category range in the table below. The starting point applies to all offenders irrespective of plea or previous convictions.

| Offence Category | Starting Point | Range |
|---|---|---|
| Category 1 | Medium level community order | Low level community order – High level community order |
| Category 2 | Band C fine | Band B fine – Low level community order |
| Category 3 | Band B fine | Band A fine – Band C fine |

**Fines**

[See **SG10-35** for band ranges]

**Community Orders**

[For the imposition of community orders, including the community orders table, see Imposition of Community and Custodial Sentences at **SG9-2.**]

**Factors increasing or reducing seriousness** The court should then consider adjustment for any aggravating or mitigating factors. The following is a **non-exhaustive** list of additional factual elements providing the context of the offence and factors relating to the offender. Identify whether any combination of these, or other relevant factors, should result in an upward or downward adjustment from the sentence arrived at so far.

**Factors increasing seriousness**

*Statutory aggravating factors:*

- Previous convictions, having regard to a) the **nature** of the offence to which the conviction relates and its **relevance** to the current offence; and b) the **time** that has elapsed since the conviction
- Offence committed whilst on bail
- Offence motivated by, or demonstrating hostility based on any of the following characteristics or presumed characteristics of the victim: religion, race, disability, sexual orientation or transgender identity

*Other aggravating factors:*

- Failure to comply with current court orders
- Offence committed on licence or post sentence supervision
- Offender's actions result in a waste of resources

**Factors reducing seriousness or reflecting personal mitigation**

- No previous convictions **or** no relevant/recent convictions
- Remorse
- Good character and/or exemplary conduct
- Serious medical condition requiring urgent, intensive or long-term treatment
- Age and/or lack of maturity where it affects the responsibility of the offender
- Mental disorder or learning disability
- Sole or primary carer for dependent relatives
- Determination and/or demonstration of steps having been taken to address addiction or offending behaviour

### STEP 3 Consider any factors which indicate a reduction, such as assistance to the prosecution

The court should take into account section 74 of the Sentencing Code (reduction in sentence for assistance to prosecution) and any other rule of law by virtue of which an offender may receive a discounted sentence in consequence of assistance given (or offered) to the prosecutor or investigator.

### STEP 4 Reduction for guilty pleas

The court should take account of any potential reduction for a guilty plea in accordance with section 73 of the Sentencing Code and the guideline for Reduction in Sentence for a Guilty Plea [**SG5-1–SG5-12**].

**STEP 5  Totality principle**

If sentencing an offender for more than one offence, or where the offender is already serving a sentence, consider whether the total sentence is just and proportionate to the overall offending behaviour in accordance with the *Totality* guideline. [See **SG4**]

**STEP 6  Consider ancillary orders**

In all cases, the court should consider whether to make **compensation** and/or other ancillary orders. [See **SG10-5**]

Where the offence has resulted in personal injury, loss or damage the court must give reasons if it decides not to order compensation (Sentencing Code, s.55).

**STEP 7  Reasons**

Section 52 of the Sentencing Code imposes a duty to give reasons for, and explain the effect of, the sentence.

DRUNK AND DISORDERLY IN A PUBLIC PLACE (REVISED 2017)        **SG10-76**

*Criminal Justice Act 1967, s.91*

**Effective from:** 24 April 2017

Triable only summarily
Maximum: Level 3 fine
Offence range: Conditional discharge–Band C fine

**STEPS 1 and 2  Determining the offence seriousness**

The starting point applies to all offenders irrespective of plea or previous convictions.

| Starting Point | Range |
|---|---|
| Band A fine | Conditional discharge – Band C fine |

**Fines**

[See **SG10-35** for band ranges]

**Factors increasing or reducing seriousness**

The court should then consider adjustment for any aggravating or mitigating factors. The following is a **non-exhaustive** list of additional factual elements providing the context of the offence and factors relating to the offender. Identify whether any combination of these, or other relevant factors, should result in an upward or downward adjustment from the sentence arrived at so far.

**Factors increasing seriousness**

*Statutory aggravating factors:*

- Previous convictions, having regard to
  a) the **nature** of the offence to which the conviction relates and its **relevance** to the current offence; and
  b) the **time** that has elapsed since the conviction
- Offence committed whilst on bail
- Offence motivated by, or demonstrating hostility based on any of the following characteristics or presumed characteristics of the victim: religion, race, disability, sexual orientation or transgender identity

*Other aggravating factors:*

- Substantial disturbance caused
- Offence ties up disproportionate police resource
- Disregard of earlier warning regarding conduct
- Failure to comply with current court orders
- Offence committed on licence or post sentence supervision
- Location of the offence
- Timing of the offence
- Offence committed against those working in the public sector or providing a service to the public
- Presence of others including, especially children or vulnerable people

**Factors reducing seriousness or reflecting personal mitigation**

- Minimal disturbance caused
- No previous convictions **or** no relevant/recent convictions
- Remorse
- Good character and/or exemplary conduct
- Age and/or lack of maturity where it affects the responsibility of the offender
- Mental disorder or learning disability

### STEP 3  Consider any factors which indicate a reduction, such as assistance to the prosecution

The court should take into account section 74 of the Sentencing Code (reduction in sentence for assistance to prosecution) and any other rule of law by virtue of which an offender may receive a discounted sentence in consequence of assistance given (or offered) to the prosecutor or investigator.

### STEP 4  Reduction for guilty pleas

The court should take account of any potential reduction for a guilty plea in accordance with section 73 of the Sentencing Code and the guideline for Reduction in Sentence for a Guilty Plea [**SG5-1–SG5-12**].

### STEP 5  Totality principle

If sentencing an offender for more than one offence, or where the offender is already serving a sentence, consider whether the total sentence is just and proportionate to the overall offending behaviour in accordance with the *Totality* guideline. [See **SG4**]

### STEP 6  Compensation and ancillary orders

In all cases, the court should consider whether to make compensation and/or other ancillary orders, including a football banning order (where appropriate). [See **SG10-5**]

Where the offence has resulted in personal injury, loss or damage the court must give reasons if it decides not to order compensation (Sentencing Code, s.55).

### STEP 7  Reasons

Section 52 of the Sentencing Code imposes a duty to give reasons for, and explain the effect of, the sentence.

**SG10-77**                  Environmental Offences (other)

**Effective from:** 01 July 2014

**[For environmental offences in the Crown Court Sentencing Guidelines see SG24]**

**Other environmental offences**

In addition to the offences for which there are detailed guidelines under the Environmental Permitting (England and Wales) Regulations 2010 and 2016 (regulations 12 and 38 (1), (2) and (3)),

- Unauthorised or harmful deposit, treatment or disposal etc of waste (individuals) and Illegal discharges to air, land and water (individuals);
- Unauthorised or harmful deposit, treatment or disposal etc of waste (organisations) and Illegal discharges to air, land and water (organisations)

there are other relevant and analogous environmental offences. The court should refer to the sentencing approach in steps one to three and five and six of the guidelines, adjusting the starting points and ranges bearing in mind the statutory maxima for those offences.

An indicative list of such offences is set out below.

| Offence | Mode of trial | Statutory maxima |
|---|---|---|
| Section 1 Control of Pollution (Amendment) Act 1989 – transporting controlled waste without registering | Triable summarily only | Unlimited fine |
| Section 34 Environmental Protection Act 1990 – breach of duty of care | Triable either way | When tried on indictment: unlimited fine<br><br>When tried summarily: unlimited fine |

| Offence | Mode of trial | Statutory maxima |
|---|---|---|
| Section 80 Environmental Protection Act 1990 – breach of an abatement notice | Triable summarily only | Where the offence is committed on industrial, trade or business premises: unlimited fine<br><br>Where the offence is committed on non-industrial etc premises: unlimited fine with a further fine of an amount equal to one-tenth of that level for each day on which the offence continues after the conviction |
| Section 111 Water Industry Act 1991 – restrictions on use of public sewers | Triable either way | When tried on indictment: imprisonment for a term not exceeding two years or a fine or both<br><br>When tried summarily: a fine not exceeding the statutory maximum and a further fine not exceeding £50 for each day on which the offence continues after conviction |
| Offences under the Transfrontier Shipment of Waste Regulations 2007 | Triable either way | When tried on indictment: a fine or two years imprisonment or both<br><br>When tried summarily: a fine not exceeding the statutory maximum or three months' imprisonment or both |

Sentencing Guidelines

## EXCEED PERMITTED DRIVING TIME/PERIODS OF DUTY    SG10-78

[See Motoring offences appropriate for imposition of fine or discharge, Part Five: Offences re buses/goods vehicles over 3.5 tonnes (GVW) SG10-110.]

## EXCESS ALCOHOL (DRIVE/ATTEMPT TO DRIVE) (REVISED 2017)    SG10-79

*Road Traffic Act 1988, s.5(1)(a)*

**Effective from:** 24 April 2017

Triable only summarily
Maximum: Unlimited fine and/or 6 months
Offence range: Band B fine–26 weeks' custody

**STEPS 1 and 2  Determining the offence seriousness**
- Must endorse and disqualify for at least 12 months
- Must disqualify for at least 2 years if offender has had two or more disqualifications for periods of 56 days or more in preceding 3 years – refer to disqualification guidance and consult your legal adviser for further guidance
- Must disqualify for at least 3 years if offender has been convicted of a relevant offence in preceding 10 years – consult your legal adviser for further guidance
- Extend disqualification if imposing immediate custody

**If there is a delay in sentencing after conviction, consider interim disqualification.**

The starting point applies to all offenders irrespective of plea or previous convictions.

| Level of alcohol | | | Starting point | Range | Disqualification | Disqual. 2nd offence in 10 years – see note above |
|---|---|---|---|---|---|---|
| Breath (µg) | Blood (mg) | Urine (mg) | | | | |
| 120–150 and above | 276–345 and above | 367–459 and above | 12 weeks' custody | High level community order – 26 weeks' custody | 29–36 months (Extend if imposing immediate custody) | 36–60 months |

| Level of alcohol | | | Starting point | Range | Disqualification | Disqual. 2nd offence in 10 years – see note above |
|---|---|---|---|---|---|---|
| Breath (µg) | Blood (mg) | Urine (mg) | | | | |
| 90–119 | 207–275 | 275–366 | Medium level community order | Low level community order – High level community order | 23–28 months | **36–52 months** |
| 60–89 | 138–206 | 184–274 | Band C Fine | Band C Fine – Low level community order | 17–22 months | **36–46 months** |
| 36–59 | 81–137 | 108–183 | Band C Fine | Band B Fine – Band C fine | 12–16 months | **36–40 months** |

Note: when considering the guidance regarding the length of disqualification in the case of a second offence, the period to be imposed in any individual case will depend on an assessment of all the relevant circumstances, including the length of time since the earlier ban was imposed and the gravity of the current offence but disqualification must be for at least three years.

### Fines
[See **SG10-35** for band ranges]

### Community Orders and Custodial Sentences
[For the imposition of community orders, including the community orders table, see Imposition of Community and Custodial Sentences at **SG9-2**. For the imposition of custodial sentences see Imposition of Community and Custodial Sentences at **SG9-3**.]

### Factors increasing or reducing seriousness
The court should then consider further adjustment for any aggravating or mitigating factors. The following is a **non-exhaustive** list of additional factual elements providing the context of the offence and factors relating to the offender. Identify whether any combination of these, or other relevant factors, should result in an upward or downward adjustment from the sentence arrived at so far.

### Factors increasing seriousness
*Statutory aggravating factors:*
- Previous convictions, having regard to a) the **nature** of the offence to which the conviction relates and its **relevance** to the current offence; and b) the **time** that has elapsed since the conviction
- Offence committed whilst on bail

*Other aggravating factors:*
- Failure to comply with current court orders
- Offence committed on licence or post sentence supervision
- LGV, HGV, PSV etc
- Poor road or weather conditions
- Carrying passengers
- Driving for hire or reward
- Evidence of unacceptable standard of driving
- Involved in accident
- High level of traffic or pedestrians in the vicinity

### Factors reducing seriousness or reflecting personal mitigation
- No previous convictions **or** no relevant/recent convictions
- Genuine emergency established*
- Spiked drinks*
- Very short distance driven*
- Remorse

- Good character and/or exemplary conduct
- Serious medical condition requiring urgent, intensive or long-term treatment
- Age and/or lack of maturity where it affects the responsibility of the offender
- Mental disorder or learning disability
- Sole or primary carer for dependent relatives

* even where not amounting to special reasons

### STEP 3  Consider any factors which indicate a reduction, such as assistance to the prosecution

The court should take into account section 74 of the Sentencing Code (reduction in sentence for assistance to prosecution) and any other rule of law by virtue of which an offender may receive a discounted sentence in consequence of assistance given (or offered) to the prosecutor or investigator.

### STEP 4  Reduction for guilty pleas

The court should take account of any potential reduction for a guilty plea in accordance with section 73 of the Sentencing Code and the guideline for Reduction in Sentence for a Guilty Plea [SG5-1–SG5-12].

### STEP 5  Totality principle

If sentencing an offender for more than one offence, or where the offender is already serving a sentence, consider whether the total sentence is just and proportionate to the overall offending behaviour in accordance with the *Totality* guideline. [See **SG4**]

### STEP 6  Compensation and ancillary orders

In all cases, the court should consider whether to make **compensation** and/or other **ancillary orders** including offering a drink/drive rehabilitation course, deprivation, and /or forfeiture or suspension of personal liquor licence. [See **SG10-5**]

Where the offence has resulted in personal injury, loss or damage the court must give reasons if it decides not to order compensation (Sentencing Code, s.55).

### STEP 7  Reasons

Section 52 of the Sentencing Code imposes a duty to give reasons for, and explain the effect of, the sentence.

### STEP 8  Consideration for time spent on bail (tagged curfew)

The court must consider whether to give credit for time spent on bail in accordance with section 240A of the Criminal Justice Act 2003 and section 325 of the Sentencing Code.

Excess Alcohol (In Charge) (Revised 2017)                         **SG10-80**

*Road Traffic Act 1988, s.5(1)(b)*

**Effective from:** 24 April 2017

Triable only summarily
Maximum: Level 4 fine and/or 3 months
Offence range: Band A fine–6 weeks' custody

### STEPS 1 and 2  Determining the offence seriousness

- **Must endorse and may disqualify. If no disqualification impose 10 points**
- **Extend any disqualification if imposing immediate custody**

The starting point applies to all offenders irrespective of plea or previous convictions.

| Level of alcohol | | | Starting point | Range | Disqualification/ Points |
|---|---|---|---|---|---|
| Breath (µg) | Blood (mg) | Urine (mg) | | | |
| 120–150 and above | 276–345 and above | 367–459 and above | Medium level community order | Low level community order – 6 weeks' custody | Disqualify 6–12 months (Extend if imposing immediate custody) |
| 90–119 | 207–275 | 275–366 | Band C fine | Band C Fine – Medium level community order | Consider disqualification up to 6 months OR 10 points |

| Level of alcohol | | | Starting point | Range | Disqualification/ Points |
|---|---|---|---|---|---|
| Breath (µg) | Blood (mg) | Urine (mg) | | | |
| 60–89 | 138–206 | 184–274 | Band B fine | Band B fine – Band C fine | Consider disqualification **OR** 10 points |
| 36–59 | 81–137 | 108–183 | Band B fine | Band A fine – Band B fine | 10 points |

### Fines

[See **SG10-35** for band ranges]

### Community Orders and Custodial Sentences

[For the imposition of community orders, including the community orders table, see Imposition of Community and Custodial Sentences at **SG9-2**. For the imposition of custodial sentences see Imposition of Community and Custodial Sentences at **SG9-3**.]

### Factors increasing or reducing seriousness

The court should then consider further adjustment for any aggravating or mitigating factors. The following is a **non-exhaustive** list of additional factual elements providing the context of the offence and factors relating to the offender. Identify whether any combination of these, or other relevant factors, should result in an upward or downward adjustment from the sentence arrived at so far.

### Factors increasing seriousness

*Statutory aggravating factors:*

- Previous convictions, having regard to a) the **nature** of the offence to which the conviction relates and its **relevance** to the current offence; and b) the **time** that has elapsed since the conviction
- Offence committed whilst on bail

*Other aggravating factors:*

- Failure to comply with current court orders
- Offence committed on licence or post sentence supervision
- In charge of LGV, HGV, PSV etc
- High likelihood of driving
- Offering to drive for hire or reward

### Factors reducing seriousness or reflecting personal mitigation

- No previous convictions **or** no relevant/recent convictions
- Low likelihood of driving
- Spiked drinks[*]
- Remorse
- Good character and/or exemplary conduct
- Serious medical condition requiring urgent, intensive or long-term treatment
- Age and/or lack of maturity where it affects the responsibility of the offender
- Mental disorder or learning disability
- Sole or primary carer for dependent relatives

[*] even where not amounting to special reasons

### STEP 3 Consider any factors which indicate a reduction, such as assistance to the prosecution

The court should take into account section 74 of the Sentencing Code (reduction in sentence for assistance to prosecution) and any other rule of law by virtue of which an offender may receive a discounted sentence in consequence of assistance given (or offered) to the prosecutor or investigator.

### STEP 4 Reduction for guilty pleas

The court should take account of any potential reduction for a guilty plea in accordance with section 73 of the Sentencing Code and the guideline for Reduction in Sentence for a Guilty Plea [**SG5-1–SG5-12**].

### STEP 5 Totality principle

If sentencing an offender for more than one offence, or where the offender is already serving a sentence, consider whether the total sentence is just and proportionate to the overall offending behaviour in accordance with the *Totality* guideline. [See **SG4**]

**STEP 6  Compensation and ancillary orders**

In all cases, the court should consider whether to make **compensation** and/or other **ancillary orders** including offering a **drink/drive rehabilitation course**, **deprivation**, and/or **forfeiture or suspension of personal liquor licence**. [See **SG10-5**]

Where the offence has resulted in personal injury, loss or damage the court must give reasons if it decides not to order compensation (Sentencing Code, s.55).

**STEP 7  Reasons**

Section 52 of the Sentencing Code imposes a duty to give reasons for, and explain the effect of, the sentence.

**STEP 8  Consideration for time spent on bail (tagged curfew)**

The court must consider whether to give credit for time spent on bail in accordance with section 240A of the Criminal Justice Act 2003 and section 325 of the Sentencing Code.

EXHAUST DEFECTIVE                                                     **SG10-81**

[See Motoring offences appropriate for imposition of fine or discharge, Part Two: Offences concerning the vehicle **SG10-107**.]

EXHAUST EMISSION                                                      **SG10-82**

[See Motoring offences appropriate for imposition of fine or discharge, Part Five: Offences re buses/goods vehicles over 3.5 tonnes (GVW) **SG10-110**.]

FAIL TO CO-OPERATE WITH PRELIMINARY (ROADSIDE) BREATH TEST           **SG10-83**

[See Motoring offences appropriate for imposition of fine or discharge, Part One: Offences concerning the driver **SG10-106**.]

FAIL TO COMPLY WITH POLICE CONSTABLE DIRECTING TRAFFIC               **SG10-84**

[See Motoring offences appropriate for imposition of fine or discharge, Part Three: Offences concerning use of vehicle **SG10-108**.]

FAIL TO COMPLY WITH TRAFFIC SIGN                                     **SG10-85**
(E.G. GIVE WAY SIGN, KEEP LEFT SIGN, TEMPORARY SIGNS)

[See Motoring offences appropriate for imposition of fine or discharge, Part Three: Offences concerning use of vehicle **SG10-108**.]

FAIL TO COMPLY WITH TRAFFIC SIGN                                     **SG10-86**
(E.G. RED TRAFFIC LIGHT, STOP SIGN, DOUBLE WHITE LINES, NO ENTRY SIGN)

[See Motoring offences appropriate for imposition of fine or discharge, Part Three: Offences concerning use of vehicle **SG10-108**.]

FAIL TO GIVE INFORMATION OF DRIVER'S IDENTITY AS REQUIRED            **SG10-87**

[See Motoring offences appropriate for imposition of fine or discharge, Part One: Offences concerning the driver **SG10-106**.]

FAIL TO KEEP/RETURN WRITTEN RECORD SHEETS                            **SG10-88**

[See Motoring offences appropriate for imposition of fine or discharge, Part Five: Offences re buses/goods vehicles over 3.5 tonnes (GVW) **SG10-110**.]

FAIL TO NOTIFY CHANGE OF OWNERSHIP TO DVLA                           **SG10-89**

[See Motoring offences appropriate for imposition of fine or discharge, Part Two: Offences concerning the vehicle **SG10-107**.]

Sentencing Guidelines

**SG10-90**

## FAIL TO PRODUCE INSURANCE CERTIFICATE

[See Motoring offences appropriate for imposition of fine or discharge, Part One: Offences concerning the driver **SG10-106**.]

**SG10-91**

## FAIL TO PRODUCE TEST CERTIFICATE

[See Motoring offences appropriate for imposition of fine or discharge, Part One: Offences concerning the driver **SG10-106**.]

**SG10-92**

## FAIL TO PROVIDE SPECIMEN FOR ANALYSIS
## (DRIVE/ATTEMPT TO DRIVE) (REVISED 2017)

*Road Traffic Act 1988, s.7(6)*

**Effective from:** 24 April 2017

Triable only summarily
Maximum: Unlimited fine and/or 6 months
Offence range: Band B fine–26 weeks' custody

### STEP 1 Determining the offence category

The Court should determine the offence category using the table below.

| Category 1 | Higher culpability **and** greater harm |
| Category 2 | Higher culpability **and** lesser harm **or** lower culpability **and** greater harm |
| Category 3 | Lower culpability **and** lesser harm |

The court should determine the offender's culpability and the harm caused with reference **only** to the factors below. Where an offence does not fall squarely into a category, individual factors may require a degree of weighting before making an overall assessment and determining the appropriate offence category.

**CULPABILITY demonstrated by one or more of the following:**

**Factors indicating higher culpability**

• Deliberate refusal/ failure

**Factors indicating lower culpability**

• All other cases

**HARM demonstrated by one or more of the following:**

**Factors indicating greater harm**

• High level of impairment

**Factors indicating lesser harm**

• All other cases

### STEP 2 Starting point and category range

Having determined the category at step one, the court should use the appropriate starting point to reach a sentence within the category range in the table below.

• **Must endorse and disqualify for at least 12 months**
• **Must disqualify for at least 2 years if offender has had two or more disqualifications for periods of 56 days or more in preceding 3 years – refer to the disqualification guidance and consult your legal adviser for further guidance**
• **Must disqualify for at least 3 years if offender has been convicted of a relevant offence in preceding 10 years – consult your legal adviser for further guidance**
• **Extend disqualification if imposing immediate custody**

**If there is a delay in sentencing after conviction, consider interim disqualification.**

The starting point applies to all offenders irrespective of plea or previous convictions.

| Level of seriousness | Starting point | Range | Disqualification | Disqual. 2nd offence in 10 years |
|---|---|---|---|---|
| Category 1 | 12 weeks' custody | High level community order – 26 weeks' custody | 29–36 months (Extend if imposing immediate custody) | 36–60 months (Extend if imposing immediate custody |
| Category 2 | Medium level community order | Low level community order – High level community order | 17–28 months | 36–52 months |
| Category 3 | Band C fine | Band B fine – Low level community order | 12–16 months | 36–40 months |

Note: when considering the guidance regarding the length of disqualification in the case of a second offence, the period to be imposed in any individual case will depend on an assessment of all the relevant circumstances, including the length of time since the earlier ban was imposed and the gravity of the current offence but disqualification must be for at least three years.

### Fines

[See **SG10-35** for band ranges]

### *Community Orders and Custodial Sentences*

[For the imposition of community orders, including the community orders table, see Imposition of Community and Custodial Sentences at **SG9-2**. For the imposition of custodial sentences see Imposition of Community and Custodial Sentences at **SG9-3**.]

### Factors increasing or reducing seriousness

The court should then consider further adjustment for any aggravating or mitigating factors. The following is a **non-exhaustive** list of additional factual elements providing the context of the offence and factors relating to the offender. Identify whether any combination of these, or other relevant factors, should result in an upward or downward adjustment from the sentence arrived at so far.

### Factors increasing seriousness

*Statutory aggravating factors:*
- Previous convictions, having regard to
  a) the **nature** of the offence to which the conviction relates and its **relevance** to the current offence; and
  b) the **time** that has elapsed since the co
- Offence committed whilst on bail

*Other aggravating factors:*
- Failure to comply with current court orders
- Offence committed on licence or post sentence supervision
- LGV, HGV PSV etc.
- Poor road or weather conditions
- Carrying passengers
- Driving for hire or reward
- Evidence of unacceptable standard of driving
- Involved in accident
- High level of traffic or pedestrians in the vicinity

### Factors reducing seriousness or reflecting personal mitigation

- No previous convictions or no relevant/recent convictions
- Remorse
- Good character and/or exemplary conduct
- Serious medical condition requiring urgent, intensive or long-term treatment
- Age and/or lack of maturity where it affects the responsibility of the offender
- Mental disorder or learning disability
- Sole or primary carer for dependent relatives

### STEP 3  Consider any factors which indicate a reduction, such as assistance to the prosecution

The court should take into account section 74 of the Sentencing Code (reduction in sentence for assistance to prosecution) and any other rule of law by virtue of which an offender may receive a discounted sentence in consequence of assistance given (or offered) to the prosecutor or investigator.

Sentencing Guidelines

### STEP 4  Reduction for guilty pleas

The court should take account of any potential reduction for a guilty plea in accordance with section 73 of the Sentencing Code and the guideline for Reduction in Sentence for a Guilty Plea [SG5-1–SG5-12].

### STEP 5  Totality principle

If sentencing an offender for more than one offence, or where the offender is already serving a sentence, consider whether the total sentence is just and proportionate to the overall offending behaviour in accordance with the *Totality* guideline. [See SG4]

### STEP 6  Consider ancillary orders

In all cases, the court should consider whether to make **compensation** and/or other **ancillary orders** including offering a **drink/drive rehabilitation course**. [See SG10-5 for Ancillary Orders]

Where the offence has resulted in personal injury, loss or damage the court must give reasons if it decides not to order compensation (Sentencing Code, s.55).

### STEP 7  Reasons

Section 52 of the Sentencing Code imposes a duty to give reasons for, and explain the effect of, the sentence.

### STEP 8  Consideration for time spent on bail (tagged curfew)

The court must consider whether to give credit for time spent on bail in accordance with section 240A of the Criminal Justice Act 2003 and section 325 of the Sentencing Code.

SG10-93                  FAIL TO PROVIDE SPECIMEN FOR ANALYSIS (IN CHARGE)

*Road Traffic Act 1988, s. 7(6)*

**Effective from:** 24 April 2017

Triable only summarily
Maximum: Level 4 fine and/or 3 months
Offence range: Band B fine–6 weeks' custody

### STEP 1  Determining the offence category

The Court should determine the offence category using the table below.

| Category 1 | Higher culpability **and** greater harm |
| Category 2 | Higher culpability **and** lesser harm **or** lower culpability **and** greater harm |
| Category 3 | Lower culpability **and** lesser harm |

The court should determine the offender's culpability and the harm caused with reference **only** to the factors below. Where an offence does not fall squarely into a category, individual factors may require a degree of weighting before making an overall assessment and determining the appropriate offence category.

**CULPABILITY demonstrated by one or more of the following:**

**Factors indicating higher culpability**
• Deliberate refusal/ failure

**Factors indicating lower culpability**
• Honestly held belief but unreasonable excuse
• Genuine attempt to comply
• All other cases

**HARM demonstrated by one or more of the following:**

**Factors indicating greater harm**
• High level of impairment

**Factors indicating lesser harm**
• All other cases

### STEP 2  Starting point and category range

Having determined the category at step one, the court should use the corresponding starting point to reach a sentence within the category range below.

- Must endorse and may disqualify. If no disqualification impose 10 points
- Extend any disqualification if imposing immediate custody

The starting point applies to all offenders irrespective of plea or previous convictions.

| Level of seriousness | Starting Point | Range | Disqualification/points |
|---|---|---|---|
| Category 1 | Medium level community order | Low level community order – 6 weeks' custody | Disqualify 6–12 months (Extend if imposing immediate custody) |
| Category 2 | Band C fine | Band C fine – Medium level community order | Disqualify up to 6 months **OR** 10 points |
| Category 3 | Band B fine | Band B fine | 10 points |

### Fines

[See **SG10-35** for band ranges]

### Community Orders and Custodial Sentences

[For the imposition of community orders, including the community orders table, see Imposition of Community and Custodial Sentences at **SG9-2**. For the imposition of custodial sentences see Imposition of Community and Custodial Sentences at **SG9-3**.]

### Factors increasing or reducing seriousness

The court should then consider further adjustment for any aggravating or mitigating factors. The following is a **non-exhaustive** list of additional factual elements providing the context of the offence and factors relating to the offender. Identify whether any combination of these, or other relevant factors, should result in an upward or downward adjustment from the sentence arrived at so far.

### Factors increasing seriousness

*Statutory aggravating factors:*

- Previous convictions, having regard to
  a) the **nature** of the offence to which the conviction relates and its **relevance** to the current offence; and
  b) the **time** that has elapsed since the conviction
- Offence committed whilst on bail

*Other aggravating factors:*

- High likelihood of driving
- Failure to comply with current court orders
- Offence committed on licence or post sentence supervision
- In charge of LGV, HGV, PSV etc.
- Offering to drive for hire or reward

### Factors reducing seriousness or reflecting personal mitigation

- No previous convictions **or** no relevant/recent convictions
- Remorse
- Good character and/or exemplary conduct
- Serious medical condition requiring urgent, intensive or long-term treatment
- Age and/or lack of maturity where it affects the responsibility of the offender
- Mental disorder or learning disability
- Sole or primary carer for dependent relatives

### STEP 3   Consider any factors which indicate a reduction, such as assistance to the prosecution

The court should take into account section 74 of the Sentencing Code (reduction in sentence for assistance to prosecution) and any other rule of law by virtue of which an offender may receive a discounted sentence in consequence of assistance given (or offered) to the prosecutor or investigator.

### STEP 4   Reduction for guilty pleas

The court should take account of any potential reduction for a guilty plea in accordance with section 73 of the Sentencing Code and the guideline for Reduction in Sentence for a Guilty Plea [**SG5-1–SG5-12**].

### STEP 5   Totality principle

If sentencing an offender for more than one offence, or where the offender is already serving a sentence, consider whether the total sentence is just and proportionate to the overall offending behaviour in accordance with the *Totality* guideline. [See **SG4**]

### STEP 6 Compensation and ancillary orders

In all cases, the court should consider whether to make **compensation** and/or other **ancillary orders** including offering a **drink/drive rehabilitation course, deprivation,** and/or **forfeiture or suspension of personal liquor licence.** [See **SG10-5** for Ancillary Orders]

Where the offence has resulted in personal injury, loss or damage the court must give reasons if it decides not to order compensation (Sentencing Code, s.55).

### STEP 7 Reasons

Section 52 of the Sentencing Code imposes a duty to give reasons for, and explain the effect of, the sentence.

### STEP 8 Consideration for time spent on bail (tagged curfew)

The court must consider whether to give credit for time spent on bail in accordance with section 240A of the Criminal Justice Act 2003 and section 325 of the Sentencing Code.

**SG10-94**                    FAIL TO STOP WHEN REQUIRED BY POLICE CONSTABLE

[See Motoring offences appropriate for imposition of fine or discharge, Part Three: Offences concerning use of vehicle **SG10-108.**]

**SG10-95**             FAIL TO STOP/REPORT ROAD ACCIDENT (REVISED 2017)

*Road Traffic Act 1988, s.170(4)*

**Effective from:** 24 April 2017

Triable only summarily
Maximum: Unlimited fine and/or 6 months
Offence range: Band A fine–26 weeks' custody

### STEP 1 Determining the offence category

The Court should determine the offence category using the table below.

| Category 1 | Higher culpability **and** greater harm |
| --- | --- |
| Category 2 | Higher culpability **and** lesser harm **or** lower culpability **and** greater harm |
| Category 3 | Lower culpability **and** lesser harm |

The court should determine the offender's culpability and the harm caused with reference **only** to the factors below. Where an offence does not fall squarely into a category, individual factors may require a degree of weighting before making an overall assessment and determining the appropriate offence category.

**CULPABILITY demonstrated by one or more of the following:**

**Factors indicating higher culpability**

• Offence committed in circumstances where a request for a sample of breath, blood or urine would have been made had the offender stopped
• Offence committed by offender seeking to avoid arrest for another offence
• Offender knew or suspected that personal injury caused and/or left injured party at scene
• Giving false details

**Factors indicating lower culpability**

• All other cases

**HARM demonstrated by one or more of the following:**

**Factors indicating greater harm**

• Injury caused
• Significant damage

**Factors indicating lesser harm**

• All other cases

### STEP 2 Starting point and category range

Having determined the category at step one, the court should use the appropriate starting point to reach a sentence within the category range in the table below. The starting point applies to all offenders irrespective of plea or previous convictions.

- Must endorse and may disqualify. If no disqualification impose 3–9 points
- Extend disqualification if imposing immediate custody

| Level of seriousness | Starting Point | Range | Disqualification/points |
| --- | --- | --- | --- |
| Category 1 | High level community order | Low level community order – 26 weeks' custody | Disqualify 6–12 months **OR** 9–10 points (Extend if imposing immediate custody) |
| Category 2 | Band C fine | Band B fine – Medium level community order | Disqualify up to 6 months **OR** 7–8 points |
| Category 3 | Band B fine | Band A fine – Band C fine | 5–6 points |

### Fines

[See **SG10-35** for band ranges]

### Community Orders and Custodial Sentences

[For the imposition of community orders, including the community orders table, see Imposition of Community and Custodial Sentences at **SG9-2**. For the imposition of custodial sentences see Imposition of Community and Custodial Sentences at **SG9-3**.]

### Factors increasing or reducing seriousness

The court should then consider further adjustment for any aggravating or mitigating factors. The following is a **non-exhaustive** list of additional factual elements providing the context of the offence and factors relating to the offender. Identify whether any combination of these, or other relevant factors, should result in an upward or downward adjustment from the sentence arrived at so far.

### Factors increasing seriousness

*Statutory aggravating factors:*

- Previous convictions, having regard to
  a) the **nature** of the offence to which the conviction relates and its **relevance** to the current offence; and
  b) the **time** that has elapsed since the conviction.
- Offence committed whilst on bail

*Other aggravating factors:*

- Little or no attempt made to comply with duty
- Evidence of bad driving
- Failure to comply with current court orders
- Offence committed on licence or post sentence supervision

### Factors reducing seriousness or reflecting personal mitigation

- No previous convictions **or** no relevant/recent convictions
- Remorse
- Good character and/or exemplary conduct
- Reasonably believed identity known
- Genuine fear of retribution
- Significant attempt made to comply with duty
- Serious medical condition requiring urgent, intensive or long-term treatment
- Age and/or lack of maturity where it affects the responsibility of the offender
- Mental disorder or learning disability
- Sole or primary carer for dependent relatives

### STEP 3  Consider any factors which indicate a reduction, such as assistance to the prosecution

The court should take into account section 74 of the Sentencing Code (reduction in sentence for assistance to prosecution) and any other rule of law by virtue of which an offender may receive a discounted sentence in consequence of assistance given (or offered) to the prosecutor or investigator.

### STEP 4  Reduction for guilty pleas

The court should take account of any potential reduction for a guilty plea in accordance with section 73 of the Sentencing Code and the guideline for Reduction in Sentence for a Guilty Plea [**SG5-1–SG5-12**].

### STEP 5  Totality principle

If sentencing an offender for more than one offence, or where the offender is already serving a sentence, consider whether the total sentence is just and proportionate to the overall offending behaviour in accordance with the *Totality* guideline. [See **SG4**]

**STEP 6  Compensation and ancillary orders**

In all cases, the court should consider whether to make **compensation** and/or other ancillary orders, including **disqualification from driving** and **deprivation of a vehicle**. [See **SG10-5** for Ancillary Orders]

Where the offence has resulted in personal injury, loss or damage the court must give reasons if it decides not to order compensation (Sentencing Code, s.55).

**STEP 7  Reasons**

Section 52 of the Sentencing Code imposes a duty to give reasons for, and explain the effect of, the sentence.

**STEP 8  Consideration for time spent on bail (tagged curfew)**

The court must consider whether to give credit for time spent on bail in accordance with section 240A of the Criminal Justice Act 2003 and section 325 of the Sentencing Code.

**SG10-96**                FAIL TO USE APPROPRIATE CHILD CAR SEAT

[See Motoring offences appropriate for imposition of fine or discharge, Part Three: Offences concerning use of vehicle **SG10-108**.]

**SG10-97**         FALSIFY OR ALTER RECORDS WITH INTENT TO DECEIVE

[See Motoring offences appropriate for imposition of fine or discharge, Part Five: Offences re buses/goods vehicles over 3.5 tonnes (GVW) **SG10-110**.]

**SG10-98**             FIREARM, CARRYING IN PUBLIC PLACE

Omitted — see **SG34-2**

**SG10-99**                  FOOTBALL RELATED OFFENCES

*Criminal Justice and Public Order Act 1994: s.166 (unauthorised sale or attempted sale of tickets); Football Offences Act 1991: s.2 (throwing missile); s.3 (indecent or racist chanting); s.4 (going onto prohibited areas); Sporting Events (Control of Alcohol etc.) Act 1985: s.2(1) (possession of alcohol whilst entering or trying to enter ground); s.2(2) (being drunk in, or whilst trying to enter, ground).*

**Effective from:** 24 April 2017

Triable only summarily
Maximum:
Level 2 fine (being drunk in ground)
Level 3 fine (throwing missile; indecent or racist chanting; going onto prohibited areas) Unlimited fine (unauthorised sale of tickets)
Level 3 fine and/or 3 months (possession of alcohol)
Offence range:
Conditional discharge–High level community order (possession of alcohol)
Conditional discharge–Band C fine (all other offences)

**STEP 1  Determining the offence category**

The Court should determine the offence category using the table below.

| Category 1 | Higher culpability **and** greater harm |
| Category 2 | Higher culpability **and** lesser harm **or** lower culpability **and** greater harm |
| Category 3 | Lower culpability **and** lesser harm |

The court should determine the offender's culpability and the harm caused with reference **only** to the factors below. Where an offence does not fall squarely into a category, individual factors may require a degree of weighting before making an overall assessment and determining the appropriate offence category.

**CULPABILITY demonstrated by one or more of the following:**

**Factors indicating higher culpability**

- Deliberate or flagrant action
- Disregard of warnings
- Commercial operation
- Inciting others

- (Possession of) Large quantity of alcohol
- Targeted abuse

## Factors indicating lower culpability

- All other cases

## HARM demonstrated by one or more of the following:

### Factor indicating greater harm

- Distress or alarm caused
- Actual injury or risk of injury
- Significant financial loss to others

### Factors indicating lesser harm

- All other cases

## STEP 2   Starting point and category range

Having determined the category at step one, the court should use the starting point to reach a sentence within the appropriate category range in the table below. The starting point applies to all offenders irrespective of plea or previous convictions.

| Offence Category | Starting Point | Range |
| --- | --- | --- |
| Category 1 | Band C fine | Band C fine |
| Category 2 | Band B fine | Band A fine – Band C fine |
| Category 3 | Band A fine | Conditional discharge – Band B fine |

### Possession of alcohol only

| Offence Category | Starting Point | Range |
| --- | --- | --- |
| Category 1 | Band C fine | Band C fine – High level community order |
| Category 2 | Band B fine | Band A fine – B and C fine |
| Category 3 | Band A fine | Conditional discharge – Band B fine |

### Fines

[See **SG10-35** for band ranges]

### Community Orders

[For the imposition of community orders, including the community orders table, see Imposition of Community and Custodial Sentences at **SG9-2**.]

### Factors increasing or reducing seriousness

The court should then consider adjustment for any aggravating or mitigating factors. The following is a **non-exhaustive** list of additional factual elements providing the context of the offence and factors relating to the offender. Identify whether any combination of these, or other relevant factors, should result in an upward or downward adjustment from the sentence arrived at so far.

### Factors increasing seriousness

*Statutory aggravating factors:*

- Previous convictions, having regard to
  a) the **nature** of the offence to which the conviction relates and its **relevance** to the current offence; and
  b) the **time** that has elapsed since the conviction
- Offence committed whilst on bail
- Offence motivated by, or demonstrating hostility based on any of the following characteristics or presumed characteristics: religion, race, disability, sexual orientation or transgender identity

*Other aggravating factors:*

- Presence of children
- Offence committed on licence or post sentence supervision

**Factors reducing seriousness or reflecting personal mitigation**

- Remorse
- Admissions to police in interview
- Ready co-operation with authorities
- Minimal disturbance caused
- No previous convictions **or** no relevant/recent convictions
- Good character and/or exemplary conduct
- Age and/or lack of maturity where it affects the responsibility of the offender
- Mental disorder or learning disability

**STEP 3  Consider any factors which indicate a reduction, such as assistance to the prosecution**

The court should take into account section 74 of the Sentencing Code (reduction in sentence for assistance to prosecution) and any other rule of law by virtue of which an offender may receive a discounted sentence in consequence of assistance given (or offered) to the prosecutor or investigator.

**STEP 4  Reduction for guilty pleas**

The court should take account of any potential reduction for a guilty plea in accordance with section 73 of the Sentencing Code and the guideline for Reduction in Sentence for a Guilty Plea [**SG5-1–SG5-12**].

**STEP 5  Totality principle**

If sentencing an offender for more than one offence, or where the offender is already serving a sentence, consider whether the total sentence is just and proportionate to the overall offending behaviour in accordance with the *Totality* guideline. [See **SG4**]

**STEP 6  Compensation and ancillary orders**

In all cases, the court should consider whether to make **compensation** and/or other **ancillary orders**, including a **football banning order**. [See **SG10-5** for Ancillary Orders]

Where the offence has resulted in personal injury, loss or damage the court must give reasons if it decides not to order compensation (Sentencing Code, s.55).

**STEP 7  Reasons**

Section 52 of the Sentencing Code imposes a duty to give reasons for, and explain the effect of, the sentence.

**SG10-100**     IDENTITY DOCUMENTS — POSSESS FALSE /ANOTHER'S/IMPROPERLY OBTAINED

[Removed as this offence has been repealed.]

**SG10-101**                INDIVIDUALS: BREACH OF AN ABATEMENT NOTICE

[See Environmental Offences (Other) at **SG10-77**]

**SG10-102**                LEARNER DRIVER OR EXCLUDED VEHICLE

[See Motoring offences appropriate for imposition of fine or discharge, Part Four: Motorway Offences **SG10-109**.]

**SG10-103**                       LIGHTS DEFECTIVE

[See Motoring offences appropriate for imposition of fine or discharge, Part Two: Offences concerning the vehicle **SG10-107**.]

**SG10-104**                   MAKE U TURN ON MOTORWAY

[See Motoring offences appropriate for imposition of fine or discharge, Part Four: Motorway Offences **SG10-109**]

**SG10-105**     MOTORING OFFENCES APPROPRIATE FOR IMPOSITION OF FINE OR DISCHARGE

**Effective from:** 04 August 2008

The Motoring Offences guidelines consist of five Parts.

**Maximum fines**

A fine must not exceed the statutory limit. Where this is expressed in terms of a 'level', the maxima are:

| Level 1 | £200 |
|---------|------|
| Level 2 | £500 |
| Level 3 | £1,000 |
| Level 4 | £2,500 |
| Level 5 | Unlimited |

**Fines**

[See **SG10-35** for band ranges]

### MOTORING OFFENCES APPROPRIATE FOR IMPOSITION OF FINE OR DISCHARGE, PART ONE: OFFENCES CONCERNING THE DRIVER

**SG10-106**

| Offence | Maximum | Points | Starting point | Special considerations |
|---------|---------|--------|----------------|------------------------|
| Fail to co-operate with preliminary (roadside) breath test | L3 | 4 | B | |
| Fail to give information of driver's identity as required | L3 | 6 | C | For limited companies, endorsement is not available; a fine is the only available penalty |
| Fail to produce insurance certificate | L4 | – | A | Fine per offence, not per document |
| Fail to produce test certificate | L3 | – | A | |
| Drive otherwise than in accordance with licence (where could be covered) | L3 | – | A | |
| Drive otherwise than in accordance with licence | L3 | 3–6 | A | Aggravating factor if no licence ever held |

### MOTORING OFFENCES APPROPRIATE FOR IMPOSITION OF FINE OR DISCHARGE, PART TWO: OFFENCES CONCERNING THE VEHICLE

**SG10-107**

\* The guidelines for some of the offences below differentiate between three types of offender when the offence is committed in the course of business: driver, owner-driver and owner-company. **For owner-driver, the starting point is the same as for driver; however, the court should consider an uplift of at least 25%.**

| Offence | Maximum | Points | Starting point | Special considerations |
|---------|---------|--------|----------------|------------------------|
| No excise licence | L3 or 5 times annual duty, whichever is greater | – | A (1–3 months unpaid) B (4–6 months unpaid) C (7–12 months unpaid) | Add duty lost |
| Fail to notify change of ownership to DVLA | L3 | – | A | If offence committed in course of business: A (driver) A\* (owner-driver) B (owner-company) |

Sentencing Guidelines

| Offence | Maximum | Points | Starting point | Special considerations |
|---|---|---|---|---|
| No test certificate | L3 | – | A | If offence committed in course of business: A (driver) A* (owner-driver) B (owner-company) |
| Brakes defective | L4 | 3 | B | If offence committed in course of business: B (driver) B* (owner-driver) C (owner-company) L5 if goods vehicle—see Part 5 below |
| Steering defective | L4 | 3 | B | If offence committed in course of business: B (driver) B* (owner-driver) C (owner-company) L5 if goods vehicle—see Part 5 below |
| Tyres defective | L4 | 3 | B | If offence committed in course of business: B (driver) B* (owner-driver) C (owner-company) L5 if goods vehicle—see Part 5 below Penalty per tyre |
| Condition of vehicle/accessories/Equipment involving danger of injury (Road Traffic Act 1988, s.40A) | L4 | 3 | B | Must disqualify for at least 6 months if offender has one or more previous convictions for same offence within three years If offence committed in course of business: B (driver) B* (owner-driver) C (owner-company) L5 if goods vehicle—see Part 5 below |
| Exhaust defective | L3 | – | A | If offence committed in course of business: A (driver) A* (owner-driver) B (owner-company) |
| Lights defective | L3 | – | A | If offence committed in course of business: A (driver) A* (owner-driver) B (owner-company) |

**SG10-108**

MOTORING OFFENCES APPROPRIATE FOR
IMPOSITION OF FINE OR DISCHARGE, PART THREE:
OFFENCES CONCERNING USE OF VEHICLE

*The guidelines for some of the offences below differentiate between three types of offender when the offence is committed in the course of business: driver, owner-driver and owner-company. **For owner-driver, the starting point is the same as for driver; however, the court should consider an uplift of at least 25%.**

| Offence | Maximum | Points | Starting point | Special considerations |
|---|---|---|---|---|
| Weight, position or distribution of load or manner in which load secured involving danger of injury (Road Traffic Act 1988, s.40A) | L4 | 3 | B | Must disqualify for at least 6 months if offender has one or more previous convictions for same offence within three years. If offence committed in course of business: A (driver) A* (owner-driver) B (owner-company) L5 if goods vehicle—see Part 5 below |
| Number of passengers or way carried involving danger of injury (Road Traffic Act 1988, s.40A) | L4 | 3 | B | If offence committed in course of business: A (driver) A* (owner-driver) B (owner-company) L5 if goods vehicle—see Part 5 below |
| Position or manner in which load secured (not involving danger) (Road Traffic Act 1988, s.42) | L3 | – | A | L4 if goods vehicle—see Part 5 below |

| Offence | Maximum | Points | Starting point | Special considerations |
|---|---|---|---|---|
| Overloading/ exceeding axle weight | L5 | – | A | Starting point caters for cases where the overload is up to and including 10%. Thereafter, 10% should be added to the penalty for each additional 1% of overload Penalty per axle If offence committed in course of business: A (driver) A* (owner-driver) B (owner-company) If goods vehicle—see Part 5 below |
| Dangerous parking | L3 | 3 | A | |
| Pelican/zebra crossing contravention | L3 | 3 | A | |
| Fail to comply with traffic sign (e.g. red traffic light, stop sign, double white lines, no entry sign) | L3 | 3 | A | |
| Fail to comply with traffic sign (e.g. give way sign, keep left sign, temporary signs) | L3 | – | A | |
| Fail to comply with police constable directing traffic | L3 | 3 | A | |
| Fail to stop when required by police constable | L5 (mechanically propelled vehicle) L3 (cycle) | – | B | |
| Use of mobile telephone | L3 | 3 | A | |
| Seat belt offences | L2 (adult or child in front) L2 (child in rear) | – | A | |
| Fail to use appropriate child car seat | L2 | – | A | |

MOTORING OFFENCES APPROPRIATE FOR
IMPOSITION OF FINE OR DISCHARGE:
PART 4: MOTORWAY OFFENCES

SG10-109

| Offence | Maximum | Points | Starting point | Special considerations |
|---|---|---|---|---|
| Drive in reverse or wrong way on slip road | L4 | 3 | B | |
| Drive in reverse or wrong way on motorway | L4 | 3 | C | |
| Drive off carriageway (central reservation or hard shoulder) | L4 | 3 | B | |
| Make U turn | L4 | 3 | C | |
| Learner driver or excluded vehicle | L4 | 3 | B | |
| Stop on hard shoulder | L4 | – | A | |
| Vehicle in prohibited lane | L4 | 3 | A | |
| Walk on motorway, slip road or hard shoulder | L4 | – | A | |

**SG10-110**    PART 5: OFFENCES RE BUSES/GOODS VEHICLES OVER 3.5 TONNES (GVW)

<sup>*</sup> The guidelines for these offences differentiate between three types of offender: driver; owner-driver; and owner-company. **For owner-driver, the starting point is the same as for driver; however, the court should consider an uplift of at least 25%.**

<sup>**</sup> In all cases, take safety, damage to roads and commercial gain into account. Refer [below] for approach to fines for 'commercially motivated' offences.

| Offence | Maximum | Points | Starting point | Special considerations |
|---|---|---|---|---|
| No goods vehicle plating certificate | L3 | – | A (driver)<br>A* (owner-driver)<br>B (owner-company) | |
| No goods vehicle test certificate | L4 | – | B (driver)<br>B* (owner-driver)<br>C (owner-company) | |
| Brakes defective | L5 | 3 | B (driver)<br>B* (owner-driver)<br>C (owner-company) | |
| Steering defective | L5 | 3 | B (driver)<br>B* (owner-driver)<br>C (owner-company) | |
| Tyres defective | L5 | 3 | B (driver)<br>B* (owner-driver)<br>C (owner-company) | Fine is for each single tyre (but ordinarily only one set of points apply where several offences committed on the same occasion) |
| Exhaust emission | L4 | – | B (driver)<br>B* (owner-driver)<br>C (owner-company) | |
| Condition of vehicle/accessories/equipment involving danger of injury (Road Traffic Act 1988, s.40A) | L5 | 3 | B (driver)<br>B* (owner-driver)<br>C (owner-company) | Must disqualify for at least 6 months if offender has one or more previous convictions for same offence within three years |
| Number of passengers or way carried involving danger of injury (Road Traffic Act 1988, s.40A) | L5 | 3 | B (driver)<br>B* (owner-driver)<br>C (owner-company) | Must disqualify for at least 6 months if offender has one or more previous convictions for same offence within three years |
| Weight, position or distribution of load or manner in which load secured involving danger of injury (Road Traffic Act 1988, s.40A) | L5 | 3 | B (driver)<br>B* (owner-driver)<br>C (owner-company) | Must disqualify for at least 6 months if offender has one or more previous convictions for same offence within three years |
| Position or manner in which load secured (not involving danger) (Road Traffic Act 1988, s.42) | L4 | – | B (driver)<br>B* (owner-driver)<br>C (owner-company) | |
| Overloading/exceeding axle weight | L5 | – | B (driver)<br>B* (owner-driver)<br>C (owner-company) | Starting points cater for cases where the overload is up to and including 10%. Thereafter, 10% should be added to the penalty for each additional 1% of overload Penalty per axle |
| No operator's licence | L4 (PSV)<br>L5<br>(Goods) | – | B (driver)<br>B* (owner-driver)<br>C (owner-company) | |
| Speed limiter not used or incorrectly calibrated | L4 | – | B (driver)<br>B* (owner-driver)<br>C (owner-company) | |

| Offence | Maximum | Points | Starting point | Special considerations |
|---|---|---|---|---|
| Tachograph not used/not working | L5 | – | B (driver)<br>B* (owner-driver)<br>C (owner-company) | |
| Exceed permitted driving time/periods of duty | L4 | – | B (driver)<br>B* (owner-driver)<br>C (owner-company) | |
| Fail to keep/return written record sheets | L4 | – | B (driver)<br>B* (owner-driver)<br>C (owner-company) | |
| Falsify or alter records with intent to deceive | L5/2 years | – | B (driver)<br>B* (owner-driver)<br>C (owner-company) | Either way offence |

## No Excise Licence

SG10-111

[See Motoring offences appropriate for imposition of fine or discharge, Part Two: Offences concerning the vehicle **SG10-107**.]

## No Goods Vehicle Plating Certificate

SG10-112

[See Motoring offences appropriate for imposition of fine or discharge, Part Five: Offences re buses/goods vehicles over 3.5 tonnes (GVW) **SG10-110**.]

## No Goods Vehicle Test Certificate

SG10-113

[See Motoring offences appropriate for imposition of fine or discharge, Part Five: Offences re buses/goods vehicles over 3.5 tonnes (GVW) **SG10-110**.]

## No Insurance (Revised 2017)

SG10-114

*Road Traffic Act 1988, s.143*

**Effective from:** 24 April 2017

Triable only summarily
Maximum: Unlimited fine
Offence range: Band B–Band C fine

### STEP 1   Determining the offence category

The Court should determine the offence category using the table below.

| Category 1 | Higher culpability **and** greater harm |
|---|---|
| Category 2 | Higher culpability **and** lesser harm or lower culpability and greater harm |
| Category 3 | Lower culpability **and** lesser harm |

The court should determine the offender's culpability and the harm caused with reference **only** to the factors below. Where an offence does not fall squarely into a category, individual factors may require a degree of weighting before making an overall assessment and determining the appropriate offence category.

### CULPABILITY demonstrated by one or more of the following:

#### Factors indicating higher culpability

- Never passed test
- Gave false details
- Driving LGV, HGV, PSV etc
- Driving for hire or reward
- Evidence of sustained uninsured use

#### Factors indicating lower culpability

- All other cases

### HARM demonstrated by one or more of the following:

#### Factors indicating greater harm

- Involved in accident where injury caused
- Involved in accident where damage caused

**Factors indicating lesser harm**

- All other cases

## STEP 2 Starting point and category range

Having determined the category at step one, the court should use the appropriate starting point to reach a sentence within the category range in the table below. The starting point applies to all offenders irrespective of plea or previous convictions.

| Level of seriousness | Starting Point | Range | Disqualification/points |
|---|---|---|---|
| Category 1 | Band C fine | Band C fine | Disqualify 6–12 months |
| Category 2 | Band C fine | Band C fine | Consider disqualification for up to 6 months OR 8 points |
| Category 3 | Band C fine | Band B fine – Band C fine | 6–8 points |

• **Must endorse and may disqualify. If no disqualification impose 6–8 points**

**Fines**

[See **SG10-35** for band ranges]

**Factors increasing or reducing seriousness**

The court should then consider further adjustment for any aggravating or mitigating factors. The following is a **non-exhaustive** list of additional factual elements providing the context of the offence and factors relating to the offender. Identify whether any combination of these, or other relevant factors, should result in an upward or downward adjustment from the sentence arrived at so far.

**Factors increasing seriousness**

*Statutory aggravating factors:*

- Previous convictions, having regard to
  a) the **nature** of the offence to which the conviction relates and its **relevance** to the current offence; and
  b) the **time** that has elapsed since the conviction
- Offence committed whilst on bail

*Other aggravating factors:*

- Failure to comply with current court orders
- Offence committed on licence or post sentence supervision

**Factors reducing seriousness or reflecting personal mitigation**

- No previous convictions **or** no relevant/recent convictions
- Remorse
- Good character and/or exemplary conduct
- Responsibility for providing insurance rests with another (where not amounting to a defence)
- Genuine misunderstanding
- Recent failure to renew or failure to transfer vehicle details where insurance was in existence
- Vehicle not being driven

## STEP 3 Consider any factors which indicate a reduction, such as assistance to the prosecution

The court should take into account section 74 of the Sentencing Code (reduction in sentence for assistance to prosecution) and any other rule of law by virtue of which an offender may receive a discounted sentence in consequence of assistance given (or offered) to the prosecutor or investigator.

## STEP 4 Reduction for guilty pleas

The court should take account of any potential reduction for a guilty plea in accordance with section 73 of the Sentencing Code and the guideline for Reduction in Sentence for a Guilty Plea [**SG5-1–SG5-12**].

## STEP 5 Totality principle

If sentencing an offender for more than one offence, or where the offender is already serving a sentence, consider whether the total sentence is just and proportionate to the overall offending behaviour in accordance with the *Totality* guideline. [See **SG4**]

## STEP 6 Compensation and ancillary orders

In all cases, the court should consider whether to make **compensation** and/or other **ancillary orders**. [See **SG10-5** for ancillary orders]

Where the offence has resulted in personal injury, loss or damage the court must give reasons if it decides not to order compensation (Sentencing Code, s.55).

**STEP 7   Reasons**

Section 52 of the Sentencing Code imposes a duty to give reasons for, and explain the effect of, the sentence.

### No Operators Licence                                                    **SG10-115**

[See Motoring offences appropriate for imposition of fine or discharge, Part Five: Offences re buses/goods vehicles over 3.5 tonnes (GVW) **SG10-110**.]

### No Test Certificate                                                     **SG10-116**

[See Motoring offences appropriate for imposition of fine or discharge, Part Two: Offences concerning the vehicle **SG10-107**.]

### Number of Passengers or Way Carried Involving Danger of Injury     **SG10-117**

[See Motoring offences appropriate for imposition of fine or discharge, Part Three: Offences concerning use of vehicle **SG10-108**.]

### Number of passengers or way carried involving danger of injury (over 3.5 tonnes)    **SG10-118**

[See Motoring offences appropriate for imposition of fine or discharge, Part Five: Offences re buses/goods vehicles over 3.5 tonnes (GVW) **SG10-110**.]

### Obstruct/Resist a Police Constable in Execution of Duty (Revised 2017)   **SG10-119**

*Police Act 1996, s.89(2)*

**Effective from:** 24 April 2017

Triable only summarily
Maximum: Level 3 fine and/or one month
Offence range: Conditional Discharge–Medium level community order

**STEP 1   Determining the offence category**

The Court should determine the offence category using the table below.

| Category 1 | Higher culpability **and** greater harm |
| Category 2 | Higher culpability **and** lesser harm **or** lower culpability **and** greater harm |
| Category 3 | Lower culpability **and** lesser harm |

The court should determine the offender's culpability and the harm caused with reference **only** to the factors below. Where an offence does not fall squarely into a category, individual factors may require a degree of weighting before making an overall assessment and determining the appropriate offence category.

**CULPABILITY demonstrated by one or more of the following:**

**Factors indicating higher culpability**
- Deliberate obstruction or interference
- Use of force, aggression or intimidation
- Group action

**Factors indicating lower culpability**
- All other cases

**HARM demonstrated by one or more of the following:**
**Factors indicating greater harm**
- Offender's actions significantly increase risk to officer or other(s)
- Offender's actions result in a suspect avoiding arrest
- Offender's actions result in a significant waste of resources

**Factors indicating lesser harm**

• All other cases

### STEP 2  Starting point and category range

Having determined the category at step one, the court should use the corresponding starting point to reach a sentence within the category range below. The starting point applies to all offenders irrespective of plea or previous convictions.

| Offence Category | Starting Point | Range |
|---|---|---|
| Category 1 | Low level community order | Band C fine – Medium level community order |
| Category 2 | Band B fine | Band A fine – Band C fine |
| Category 3 | Band A fine | Conditional discharge – Band B fine |

**Fines**

[See **SG10-35** for band ranges]

**Community Orders**

[For the imposition of community orders, including the community orders table, see Imposition of Community and Custodial Sentences at **SG9-2.**]

**Factors increasing or reducing seriousness**

The court should then consider adjustment for any aggravating or mitigating factors. The following is a **non-exhaustive** list of additional factual elements providing the context of the offence and factors relating to the offender. Identify whether any combination of these, or other relevant factors, should result in an upward or downward adjustment from the sentence arrived at so far.

**Factors increasing seriousness**

*Statutory aggravating factors:*

• Previous convictions, having regard to
  a) the **nature** of the offence to which the conviction **relates** and its relevance to the current offence; and
  b) the **time** that has elapsed since the conviction
• Offence committed whilst on bail
• Offence motivated by, or demonstrating hostility based on any of the following characteristics or presumed characteristics of the victim: religion, race, disability, sexual orientation or transgender identity

*Other aggravating factors:*

• Failure to comply with current court orders
• Offence committed on licence or post sentence supervision
• Blame wrongly placed on others
• Injury caused to an officer/another
• Giving false details

**Factors reducing seriousness or reflecting personal mitigation**

• No previous convictions **or** no relevant/recent convictions
• Remorse
• Brief incident
• Acting under direction or coercion of another
• Genuinely held belief if coming to the aid of another, that the other was suffering severe medical difficulty
• Good character and/or exemplary conduct
• Serious medical condition requiring urgent, intensive or long-term treatment
• Age and/or lack of maturity where it affects the responsibility of the offender
• Mental disorder or learning disability
• Sole or primary carer for dependent relatives

### STEP 3  Consider any factors which indicate a reduction, such as assistance to the prosecution

The court should take into account section 74 of the Sentencing Code (reduction in sentence for assistance to prosecution) and any other rule of law by virtue of which an offender may receive a discounted sentence in consequence of assistance given (or offered) to the prosecutor or investigator.

## STEP 4  Reduction for guilty pleas

The court should take account of any potential reduction for a guilty plea in accordance with section 73 of the Sentencing Code and the guideline for Reduction in Sentence for a Guilty Plea [**SG5-1–SG5-12**].

## STEP 5  Totality principle

If sentencing an offender for more than one offence, or where the offender is already serving a sentence, consider whether the total sentence is just and proportionate to the overall offending behaviour in accordance with the *Totality* guideline. [See **SG4**]

## STEP 6  Compensation and ancillary orders

In all cases, the court should consider whether to make **compensation** and/or other **ancillary orders**. [See **SG10-5** for ancillary orders].

Where the offence has resulted in personal injury, loss or damage the court must give reasons if it decides not to order compensation (Sentencing Code, s.55).

## STEP 7  Reasons

Section 52 of the Sentencing Code imposes a duty to give reasons for, and explain the effect of, the sentence.

### ORGANISATIONS: BREACH OF AN ABATEMENT NOTICE                SG10-120

[See Environmental Offences – Other at **SG10-77**]

### OVERLOADING/EXCEEDING AXLE WEIGHT                            SG10-121

[See Motoring offences appropriate for imposition of fine or discharge, Part Three: Offences concerning use of vehicle **SG10-108**.]

### OVERLOADING/EXCEEDING AXLE WEIGHT (OVER 3.5 TONNES)          SG10-122

[See Motoring offences appropriate for imposition of fine or discharge, Part Five: Offences re buses/goods vehicles over 3.5 tonnes (GVW) **SG10-110**.]

### OWNER OR PERSON IN CHARGE OF A DOG                           SG10-123
### DANGEROUSLY OUT OF CONTROL IN ANY PLACE IN ENGLAND OR WALES
### (WHETHER OR NOT A PUBLIC PLACE)

*Dangerous Dogs Act 1991, s.3(1)*

**Effective from:** 01 July 2016

Triable only summarily
Maximum: 6 months' custody
Offence range: Discharge – 6 months' custody

## STEP 1 Determining the offence category

In order to determine the category the court should assess **culpability** and **harm**. The court should determine the offence category with reference only to the factors in the tables below.

The level of culpability is determined by weighing up all the factors of the case. **Where there are characteristics present which fall under different levels of culpability, the court should balance these characteristics to reach a fair assessment of the offender's culpability.**

### Culpability demonstrated by one or more of the following

*A – Higher culpability*

- Dog used as a weapon or to intimidate people
- Dog known to be prohibited
- Dog trained to be aggressive
- Offender disqualified from owning a dog, or failed to respond to official warnings, or to comply with orders concerning the dog

*B – Lower culpability*

- Attempts made to regain control of the dog and/or intervene
- Provocation of dog without fault of the offender
- Evidence of safety or control measures having been taken
- Incident could not have reasonably been foreseen by the offender
- Momentary lapse of control/attention

Where the court makes a destruction order, it **may** appoint a person to undertake destruction and order the offender to pay what it determines to be the reasonable expenses of destroying the dog and keeping it pending its destruction.

**Fit and proper person**

In determining whether a person is a fit and proper person to be in charge of a dog the following non-exhaustive factors may be relevant:

- any relevant previous convictions, cautions or penalty notices;
- the nature and suitability of the premises that the dog is to be kept at by the person;
- where the police have released the dog pending the court's decision whether the person has breached conditions imposed by the police; and
- any relevant previous breaches of court orders.

[For Ancillary orders in the Magistrates' Court see **SG10-5**]

**STEP 7 Reasons**

Section 52 of the Sentencing Code imposes a duty to give reasons for, and explain the effect of, the sentence.

**STEP 8 Consideration for time spent on bail (tagged curfew)**

The court must consider whether to give credit for time spent on bail in accordance with section 240A of the Criminal Justice Act 2003 and section 325 of the Sentencing Code.

**SG10-124**                      PELICAN/ZEBRA CROSSING CONTRAVENTION

[See Motoring offences appropriate for imposition of fine or discharge, Part Three: Offences concerning use of vehicle **SG10-108**.]

**SG10-125**    POSITION OR MANNER IN WHICH LOAD SECURED (NOT INVOLVING DANGER)

[See Motoring offences appropriate for imposition of fine or discharge, Part Three: Offences concerning use of vehicle **SG10-108**.]

**SG10-126**              POSITION OR MANNER IN WHICH LOAD SECURED
                      (NOT INVOLVING DANGER) (OVER 3.5 TONNES)

[See Motoring offences appropriate for imposition of fine or discharge, Part Five: Offences re buses/goods vehicles over 3.5 tonnes (GVW) **SG10-110**.]

**SG10-127**    POSSESSION OF A PROHIBITED DOG/BREEDING, SELLING, EXCHANGING OR
                      ADVERTISING A PROHIBITED DOG

*Dangerous Dogs Act 1991, s.1(7)*

**Effective from:** 01 July 2016

**Possession of a prohibited dog**, Dangerous Dogs Act 1991 (section 1(7))
**Breeding, selling, exchanging or advertising a prohibited dog**, Dangerous Dogs Act 1991 (section 1(7))
Triable only summarily
Maximum: 6 months' custody
Offence range: Discharge – 6 months' custody

**STEP 1 Determining the offence category**

In order to determine the category the court should assess **culpability** and **harm**. The court should determine the offence category with reference only to the factors in the tables below.

The level of culpability is determined by weighing up all the factors of the case. **Where there are characteristics present which fall under different levels of culpability, the court should balance these characteristics to reach a fair assessment of the offender's culpability.**

**Culpability demonstrated by one or more of the following**

*A – Higher culpability*

- Possessing a dog known to be prohibited
- Breeding from a dog known to be prohibited
- Selling, exchanging or advertising a dog known to be prohibited
- Offence committed for gain
- Dog used to threaten or intimidate

- Permitting fighting
- Training and/or possession of paraphernalia for dog fighting

*B – Lower culpability*

- All other cases

## Harm

The level of harm is assessed by weighing up all the factors of the case.

### Greater harm

- High risk to the public and/or animals

### Lesser harm

- Low risk to the public and/or animals

### STEP 2  Starting point and category range

Having determined the category at step one, the court should use the starting point to reach a sentence within the appropriate category range in the table below. The starting point applies to all offenders irrespective of plea or previous convictions.

| | Culpability | |
|---|---|---|
| Harm | **A** | **B** |
| Greater harm | **Starting point**<br>Medium level community order | **Starting point**<br>Band B fine |
| | **Category range**<br>Band C fine – 6 months' custody | **Category range**<br>Band A fine – Low level community order |
| Lesser harm | **Starting point**<br>Band C fine | **Starting point**<br>Band A fine |
| | **Category range**<br>Band B fine – Medium level community order | **Category range**<br>Discharge – Band B fine |

### Fines

[See **SG10-35** for band ranges]

### Community Orders and Custodial Sentences

[For the imposition of community orders, including the community orders table, see Imposition of Community and Custodial Sentences at **SG9-2**. For the imposition of custodial sentences see Imposition of Community and Custodial Sentences at **SG9-3**.]

### Factors increasing or reducing seriousness

The court should then consider any adjustment for any aggravating or mitigating factors. Below is a **non-exhaustive** list of additional factual elements providing the context of the offence and factors relating to the offender. Identify whether any combination of these, or other relevant factors, should result in an upward or downward adjustment from the starting point.

### Factors increasing seriousness

*Statutory aggravating factors*

- Previous convictions, having regard to
  a)  the **nature** of the offence to which the conviction relates and its **relevance** to the current offence; and
  b)  the **time** that has elapsed since the conviction
- Offence committed whilst on bail

*Other aggravating factors*

- Presence of children or others who are vulnerable because of personal circumstances
- Ill treatment or failure to ensure welfare needs of the dog (where connected to the offence and where not charged separately)
- Established evidence of community/wider impact
- Failure to comply with current court orders
- Offence committed on licence or post sentence supervision
- Offences taken into consideration

**Factors reducing seriousness or reflecting personal mitigation**

- No previous convictions **or** no relevant/recent convictions
- Unaware that dog was prohibited type despite reasonable efforts to identify type
- Evidence of safety or control measures having been taken by owner
- Prosecution results from owner notification
- Evidence of responsible ownership
- Remorse
- Good character and/or exemplary conduct
- Serious medical condition requiring urgent, intensive or long-term treatment
- Age and/or lack of maturity where it affects the responsibility of the offender
- Mental disorder or learning disability
- Sole or primary carer for dependent relatives
- Determination and/or demonstration of steps having been taken to address offending behaviour
- Lapse of time since the offence where this is not the fault of the offender

### STEP 3  Consider any other factors which indicate a reduction, such as assistance to the prosecution

The court should take into account section 74 of the Sentencing Code (reduction in sentence for assistance to prosecution) and any other rule of law by virtue of which an offender may receive a discounted sentence in consequence of assistance given (or offered) to the prosecutor or investigator.

### STEP 4  Reduction for guilty pleas

The court should take account of any potential reduction for a guilty plea in accordance with section 73 of the Sentencing Code and the guideline for Reduction in Sentence for a Guilty Plea [SG5-1–SG5-12].

### STEP 5  Totality principle

If sentencing an offender for more than one offence, or where the offender is already serving a sentence, consider whether the total sentence is just and proportionate to the overall offending behaviour in accordance with the *Totality* guideline [see **SG4**].

### STEP 6  Compensation and ancillary orders

The court should consider compensation orders in all cases where personal injury, loss or damage has resulted from the offence. The court must give reasons if it decides not to award compensation in such cases (Sentencing Code s.55).

**Compensation order**

The court should consider compensation orders in all cases where personal injury, loss or damage has resulted from the offence. The court must give reasons if it decides not to award compensation in such cases.

**Other ancillary orders available include**

*Disqualification from having a dog*

The court **may** disqualify the offender from having custody of a dog for such period as it thinks fit. The test the court should consider is whether the offender is a fit and proper person to have custody of a dog.

*Destruction order/contingent destruction order*

In any case where the offender is not the owner of the dog, the owner must be given an opportunity to be present and make representations to the court. The court **shall** make a destruction order unless the court is satisfied that the dog would not constitute a danger to public safety. In reaching a decision, the court should consider the relevant circumstances which **must** include:

- the temperament of the dog and its past behaviour;
- whether the owner of the dog, or the person for the time being in charge of it is a fit and proper person to be in charge of the dog;

and **may** include:

- other relevant circumstances.

If the court is satisfied that the dog would not constitute a danger to public safety, it **shall** make a contingent destruction order requiring that the dog be exempted from the prohibition on possession or custody within the requisite period. Where the court makes a destruction order, it **may** appoint a person to undertake destruction and order the offender to pay what it determines to be the reasonable expenses of destroying the dog and keeping it pending its destruction.

**Fit and proper person**

In determining whether a person is a fit and proper person to be in charge of a dog the following non-exhaustive factors may be relevant:

- any relevant previous convictions, cautions or penalty notices;
- the nature and suitability of the premises that the dog is to be kept at by the person;
- where the police have released the dog pending the court's decision whether the person has breached conditions imposed by the police; and
- any relevant previous breaches of court orders.

Note: the court must be satisfied that the person who is assessed by the court as a fit and proper person can demonstrate that they are the owner or the person ordinarily in charge of that dog at the time the court is considering whether the dog is a danger to public safety. Someone who has previously not been in charge of the dog should not be considered for this assessment because it is an offence under the Dangerous Dogs Act 1991 to make a gift of a prohibited dog.

[See Ancillary orders – Magistrates' Court, **SG10-5**]

### STEP 7  Reasons

Section 52 of the Sentencing Code imposes a duty to give reasons for, and explain the effect of, the sentence.

### STEP 8  Consideration for time spent on bail (tagged curfew)

The court must consider whether to give credit for time spent on bail in accordance with section 240A of the Criminal Justice Act 2003 and section 325 of the Sentencing Code.

Railway Fare Evasion (Revised 2017)

**SG10-128**

*Regulation of Railways Act 1889, s.5(3) (travelling on railway without paying fare,*
*with intent to avoid payment); s.5(1) (failing to produce ticket)*

Sentencing Guidelines

**Effective from:** 24 April 2017

Triable only summarily
Maximum:
Level 2 fine (s.5(1) failing to produce ticket)
Level 3 fine and/or 3 months (s.5(3) travelling on railway with intent to avoid payment)

Offence range:
Conditional Discharge–Band C fine (s.5(1))
Conditional Discharge–Low level community order (s.5(3))

### STEP 1  Determining the offence category

The Court should determine the offence category using the table below.

| Category 1 | Higher culpability **and** greater harm |
| --- | --- |
| Category 2 | Higher culpability **and** lesser harm **or** lower culpability **and** greater harm |
| Category 3 | Lower culpability **and** lesser harm |

The court should determine the offender's culpability and the harm caused with reference **only** to the factors below. Where an offence does not fall squarely into a category, individual factors may require a degree of weighting before making an overall assessment and determining the appropriate offence category.

**CULPABILITY demonstrated by one or more of the following:**

**Factors indicating higher culpability**

- Aggressive, abusive or disruptive behaviour

**Factors indicating lower culpability**

- All other cases

**HARM demonstrated by one or more of the following:**

**Factors indicating greater harm**

- High revenue loss

**Factors indicating lesser harm**

- All other cases

## STEP 2  Starting point and category range

Having determined the category at step one, the court should use the corresponding starting point to reach a sentence within the category range below. The starting point applies to all offenders irrespective of plea or previous convictions.

### Travelling on railway without paying fare, with intent

| Offence Category | Starting Point | Range |
|---|---|---|
| Category 1 | Band C fine | Band B fine – Low level community order |
| Category 2 | Band B fine | Band A fine – Band C fine |
| Category 3 | Band A fine | Conditional discharge – Band B fine |

### Failing to produce a ticket

| Offence Category | Starting Point | Range |
|---|---|---|
| Category 1 | Band B fine | Band B fine – Band C fine |
| Category 2 | Band A fine | Band A fine – Band B fine |
| Category 3 | Band A fine | Conditional discharge – Band B fine |

### Fines

[See **SG10-35** for band ranges]

### Community Orders

[For the imposition of community orders, including the community orders table, see Imposition of Community and Custodial Sentences at **SG9-2**.]

### Factors increasing or reducing seriousness

The court should then consider adjustment for any aggravating or mitigating factors. The following is a **non-exhaustive** list of additional factual elements providing the context of the offence and factors relating to the offender. Identify whether any combination of these, or other relevant factors, should result in an upward or downward adjustment from the sentence arrived at so far.

### Factors increasing seriousness

*Statutory aggravating factors:*

- Previous convictions, having regard to
  a) the **nature** of the offence to which the conviction relates and its **relevance** to the current offence; and
  b) the **time** that has elapsed since the conviction
- Offence committed whilst on bail
- Offence motivated by, or demonstrating hostility based on any of the following characteristics or presumed characteristics of the victim: religion, race, disability, sexual orientation or transgender identity

*Other aggravating factors:*

- Offender has avoided paying any of the fare
- Offender produces incorrect ticket or document to pass as legitimate fare payer
- Failure to comply with current court orders
- Abuse to staff
- Offence committed on licence or post sentence supervision

### Factors reducing seriousness or reflecting personal mitigation

- No previous convictions **or** no relevant/recent convictions
- Remorse
- Good character and/or exemplary conduct
- Serious medical condition requiring urgent, intensive or long-term treatment
- Age and/or lack of maturity where it affects the responsibility of the offender
- Mental disorder or learning disability
- Sole or primary carer for dependent relatives

**STEP 3  Consider any factors which indicate a reduction, such as assistance to the prosecution**

The court should take into account section 74 of the Sentencing Code (reduction in sentence for assistance to prosecution) and any other rule of law by virtue of which an offender may receive a discounted sentence in consequence of assistance given (or offered) to the prosecutor or investigator.

**STEP 4  Reduction for guilty pleas**

The court should take account of any potential reduction for a guilty plea in accordance with section 73 of the Sentencing Code and the guideline for Reduction in Sentence for a Guilty Plea [**SG5-1–SG5-12**].

**STEP 5  Totality principle**

If sentencing an offender for more than one offence, or where the offender is already serving a sentence, consider whether the total sentence is just and proportionate to the overall offending behaviour in accordance with the *Totality* guideline. [See **SG4**]

**STEP 6  Compensation and ancillary orders**

In all cases, the court should consider whether to make **compensation** and/or other **ancillary orders**. [See **SG10-5** for ancillary orders.]

Where the offence has resulted in personal injury, loss or damage the court must give reasons if it decides not to order compensation (Sentencing Code, s.55).

**STEP 7  Reasons**

Section 52 of the Sentencing Code imposes a duty to give reasons for, and explain the effect of, the sentence.

School Non-attendance (Revised 2017)

**SG10-129**

*Education Act 1996, s.444(1) (parent fails to secure regular attendance at school of registered pupil);
s.444(1A) (Parent knowingly fails to secure regular attendance at school of registered pupil)*

**Effective from: 24 April 2017**

Triable only summarily
Maximum:
Level 3 fine (s.444(1) parent fails to secure regular attendance at school);
Level 4 fine and/or 3 months (s.444(1A) parent knowingly fails to secure regular attendance at school)
Offence range:
Conditional discharge–Band C fine (s.444(1))
Band A fine–High level community order (s.444(1A))

**STEP 1  Determining the offence seriousness**

The Court should determine the offence category using the table below.

| Category 1 | Higher culpability **and** greater harm |
|---|---|
| Category 2 | Higher culpability **and** lesser harm **or** lower culpability **and** greater harm |
| Category 3 | Lower culpability **and** lesser harm |

The court should determine the offender's culpability and the harm caused with reference only to the factors below. Where an offence does not fall squarely into a category, individual factors may require a degree of weighting before making an overall assessment and determining the appropriate offence category.

**CULPABILITY demonstrated by one or more of the following:**

**Factors indicating higher culpability**

- Refusal/failure to engage with guidance and support offered
- Threats to teachers and/or officials
- Parent encouraging non attendance

**Factors indicating lower culpability**

- Genuine efforts to ensure attendance
- Parent concerned by child's allegations of bullying
- Parent put in fear of violence and/or threats from the child

**HARM demonstrated by one or more of the following:**

**Factors indicating greater harm**

- Significant and lengthy period of education missed
- Adverse influence on other children of the family

**Factors indicating lesser harm**

- All other cases

## STEP 2 Starting point and category range

Having determined the category at step one, the court should use the corresponding starting point to reach a sentence within the category range below. The starting point applies to all offenders irrespective of plea or previous convictions.

**s.444(1A) (Parent knowingly fails to secure regular attendance at school of registered pupil)**

| Offence Category | Starting Point | Range |
|---|---|---|
| Category 1 | Medium level community order | Low level community order – High level community order |
| Category 2 | Band C fine | Band B fine – Low level community order |
| Category 3 | Band B fine | Band A fine – Band C fine |

**s.444(1) (parent fails to secure regular attendance at school of registered pupil)**

| Offence Category | Starting Point | Range |
|---|---|---|
| Category 1 | Band C fine | Band B fine – Band C fine |
| Category 2 | Band B fine | Band A fine – Band B fine |
| Category 3 | Band A fine | Conditional Discharge – Band B fine |

**Fines**

[See **SG10-35** for band ranges]

**Community Orders and Custodial Sentences**

[For the imposition of community orders, including the community orders table, see Imposition of Community and Custodial Sentences at **SG9-2.**]

**Factors increasing or reducing seriousness**

The court should then consider adjustment for any aggravating or mitigating factors. The following is a **non-exhaustive** list of additional factual elements providing the context of the offence and factors relating to the offender. Identify whether any combination of these, or other relevant factors, should result in an upward or downward adjustment from the sentence arrived at so far.

**Factors increasing seriousness**

*Statutory aggravating factors:*

- Previous convictions, having regard to
  a) the **nature** of the offence to which the conviction relates and its **relevance** to the current offence; and
  b) the **time** that has elapsed since the conviction
- Offence committed whilst on bail

*Other aggravating factors:*

- Failure to comply with current court orders
- Offence committed on licence or post sentence supervision

**Factors reducing seriousness or reflecting personal mitigation**

- No previous convictions **or** no relevant/recent convictions
- Remorse
- Good character and/or exemplary conduct
- Serious medical condition requiring urgent, intensive or long-term treatment
- Age and/or lack of maturity where it affects the responsibility of the offender
- Mental disorder or learning disability (of offender)
- Parent unaware of child's whereabouts
- Previously good attendance

## STEP 3 Consider any factors which indicate a reduction, such as assistance to the prosecution

The court should take into account section 74 of the Sentencing Code (reduction in sentence for assistance to prosecution) and any other rule of law by virtue of which an offender may receive a discounted sentence in consequence of assistance given (or offered) to the prosecutor or investigator.

### STEP 4   Reduction for guilty pleas

The court should take account of any potential reduction for a guilty plea in accordance with section 73 of the Sentencing Code and the guideline for Reduction in Sentence for a Guilty Plea [**SG5-1–SG5-12**].

### STEP 5   Totality principle

If sentencing an offender for more than one offence, or where the offender is already serving a sentence, consider whether the total sentence is just and proportionate to the overall offending behaviour in accordance with the *Totality* guideline. [See **SG4**.]

### STEP 6   Compensation and ancillary orders

In all cases, the court should consider whether to make **compensation** and/or other **ancillary orders** including **parenting orders**. [See **SG10-5** for ancillary orders.]

Where the offence has resulted in personal injury, loss or damage the court must give reasons if it decides not to order compensation (Sentencing Code, s.55)

### STEP 7   Reasons

Section 52 of the Sentencing Code imposes a duty to give reasons for, and explain the effect of, the sentence.

SEAT BELT OFFENCES

SG10-130

[See Motoring offences appropriate for imposition of fine or discharge, Part Three: Offences concerning use of vehicle **SG10-108**.]

SEXUAL ACTIVITY IN A PUBLIC LAVATORY

SG10-131

*Sexual Offences Act 2003, s.71*

**Effective from:** 24 April 2017

Triable only summarily
Maximum: Unlimited fine and/or 6 months
Offence range: Band A fine–High level community order

### STEP 1   Determining the offence category

The Court should determine the offence category using the table below.

| Category 1 | Higher culpability **and** greater harm |
|------------|------------------------------------------|
| Category 2 | Higher culpability **and** lesser harm **or** lower culpability **and** greater harm |
| Category 3 | Lower culpability **and** lesser harm |

The court should determine the offender's culpability and the harm caused with reference **only** to the factors below. Where an offence does not fall squarely into a category, individual factors may require a degree of weighting before making an overall assessment and determining the appropriate offence category.

**CULPABILITY demonstrated by one or more of the following:**

**Factors indicating higher culpability**

- Intimidating behaviour/threats of violence to member(s) of the public
- Blatant behaviour

**Factors indicating lower culpability**

- All other cases

**HARM demonstrated by one or more of the following:**

**Factors indicating greater harm**

- Distress suffered by members of the public
- Children or young persons present

**Factors indicating lesser harm**

- All other cases

### STEP 2   Starting point and category range

Having determined the category at step one, the court should use the starting point to reach a sentence within the appropriate category range in the table below. The starting point applies to all offenders irrespective of plea or previous convictions.

Sentencing Guidelines

| Offence Category | Starting Point | Range |
|---|---|---|
| **Category 1** | Low level community order | Band C fine – High level community order |
| **Category 2** | Band C fine | Band B fine – Low level community order |
| **Category 3** | Band B fine | Band A fine – Band C fine |

Persistent offending of this nature may justify an upward adjustment outside the category range and may cross the community threshold even though the offence otherwise warrants a lesser sentence.

### Fines

[See **SG10-35** for band ranges]

### Community Orders

[For the imposition of community orders, including the community orders table, see Imposition of Community and Custodial Sentences at **SG9-2**.]

### Factors increasing or reducing seriousness

The court should then consider adjustment for any aggravating or mitigating factors. The following is a **non-exhaustive** list of additional factual elements providing the context of the offence and factors relating to the offender. Identify whether any combination of these, or other relevant factors, should result in an upward or downward adjustment from the sentence arrived at so far.

### Factors increasing seriousness

*Statutory aggravating factors:*

- Previous convictions, having regard to
  a) the **nature** of the offence to which the conviction relates and its **relevance** to the current offence; and
  b) the **time** that has elapsed since the conviction
- Offence committed whilst on bail

*Other aggravating factors:*

- Failure to comply with current court orders
- Offence committed on licence or post sentence supervision
- Offences taken into consideration
- Location
- Presence of children
- Established evidence of community/wider impact

### Factors reducing seriousness or reflecting personal mitigation

- No previous convictions **or** no relevant/recent convictions
- Remorse
- Good character and/or exemplary conduct
- Serious medical condition requiring urgent, intensive or long-term treatment
- Age and/or lack of maturity where it affects the responsibility of the offender
- Mental disorder or learning disability

### STEP 3  Consider any factors which indicate a reduction, such as assistance to the prosecution

The court should take into account section 74 of the Sentencing Code (reduction in sentence for assistance to prosecution) and any other rule of law by virtue of which an offender may receive a discounted sentence in consequence of assistance given (or offered) to the prosecutor or investigator.

### STEP 4  Reduction for guilty pleas

The court should take account of any potential reduction for a guilty plea in accordance with section 73 of the Sentencing Code and the guideline for Reduction in Sentence for a Guilty Plea [**SG5-1–SG5-12**].

### STEP 5  Totality principle

If sentencing an offender for more than one offence, or where the offender is already serving a sentence, consider whether the total sentence is just and proportionate to the overall offending behaviour in accordance with the *Totality* guideline. [See **SG4**]

### STEP 6  Compensation and ancillary orders

In all cases, the court should consider whether to make **compensation** and/or other **ancillary orders**. [See **SG10-5** for ancillary orders.]

## STEP 7  Reasons

Section 52 of the Sentencing Code imposes a duty to give reasons for, and explain the effect of, the sentence.

### Speed Limiter Not Used or Incorrectly Calibrated           SG10-132

[See Motoring offences appropriate for imposition of fine or discharge, Part Five: Offences re buses/goods vehicles over 3.5 tonnes (GVW) **SG10-110**.]

### Speeding (Revised 2017)           SG10-133

*Road Traffic Regulation Act 1984, s.89(1)*

**Effective from:** 24 April 2017

Triable only summarily
Maximum: Level 3 fine (level 4 if motorway)
Offence range: Band A fine–Band C fine

### STEPS 1 and 2  Determining the offence seriousness

The starting point applies to all offenders irrespective of plea or previous convictions.

| Speed limit (mph) | Recorded speed (mph) | | |
|---|---|---|---|
| 20 | 41 and above | 31–40 | 21–30 |
| 30 | 51 and above | 41–50 | 31–40 |
| 40 | 66 and above | 56–65 | 41–55 |
| 50 | 76 and above | 66–75 | 51–65 |
| 60 | 91 and above | 81–90 | 61–80 |
| 70 | 101 and above | 91–100 | 71–90 |
| Sentencing range | Band C fine | Band B fine | Band A fine |
| Points/disqualification | Disqualify 7–56 days **OR** 6 points | Disqualify 7–28 days **OR** 4–6 points | 3 points |

- **Must endorse and may disqualify. If no disqualification impose 3–6 points**
- **Where an offender is driving grossly in excess of the speed limit the court should consider a disqualification in excess of 56 days.**

### Fines

[See **SG10-35** for band ranges]

### Factors increasing or reducing seriousness

The court should then consider further adjustment for any aggravating or mitigating factors. The following is a **non-exhaustive** list of additional factual elements providing the context of the offence and factors relating to the offender. Identify whether any combination of these, or other relevant factors, should result in an upward or downward adjustment from the sentence arrived at so far.

### Factors increasing seriousness

*Statutory aggravating factors:*
- Previous convictions, having regard to
  a) the **nature** of the offence to which the conviction relates and its **relevance** to the current offence; and
  b) the **time** that has elapsed since the conviction
- Offence committed whilst on bail

*Other aggravating factors:*
- Offence committed on licence or post sentence supervision
- Poor road or weather conditions
- Driving LGV, HGV, PSV etc.
- Towing caravan/trailer
- Carrying passengers or heavy load
- Driving for hire or reward
- Evidence of unacceptable standard of driving over and above speed
- Location e.g. near school
- High level of traffic or pedestrians in the vicinity

**Factors reducing seriousness or reflecting personal mitigation**
- No previous convictions **or** no relevant/recent convictions
- Good character and/or exemplary conduct
- Genuine emergency established

### STEP 3 Consider any factors which indicate a reduction, such as assistance to the prosecution

The court should take into account section 74 of the Sentencing Code (reduction in sentence for assistance to prosecution) and any other rule of law by virtue of which an offender may receive a discounted sentence in consequence of assistance given (or offered) to the prosecutor or investigator.

### STEP 4 Reduction for guilty pleas

The court should take account of any potential reduction for a guilty plea in accordance with section 73 of the Sentencing Code and the guideline for Reduction in Sentence for a Guilty Plea [SG5-1–SG5-12].

### STEP 5 Totality principle

If sentencing an offender for more than one offence, or where the offender is already serving a sentence, consider whether the total sentence is just and proportionate to the overall offending behaviour in accordance with the *Totality* guideline. [See SG4]

### STEP 6 Compensation and ancillary orders

In all cases, the court should consider whether to make **compensation** and/or other **ancillary orders**. [See SG10-5 for ancillary orders]

Where the offence has resulted in personal injury, loss or damage the court must give reasons if it decides not to order compensation (Sentencing Code, s.55).

### STEP 7 Reasons

Section 52 of the Sentencing Code imposes a duty to give reasons for, and explain the effect of, the sentence.

SG10-134                              STEERING DEFECTIVE

[See Motoring offences appropriate for imposition of fine or discharge, Part Two: Offences concerning the vehicle SG10-107.]

SG10-135                 STEERING DEFECTIVE (OVER 3.5 TONNES)

[See Motoring offences appropriate for imposition of fine or discharge, Part Five: Offences re buses/goods vehicles over 3.5 tonnes (GVW) SG10-110.]

SG10-136                       STOP ON HARD SHOULDER

[See Motoring offences appropriate for imposition of fine or discharge, Part Four: Motorway Offences SG10-109]

SG10-137               TACHOGRAPH NOT USED/NOT WORKING

[See Motoring offences appropriate for imposition of fine or discharge, Part Five: Offences re buses/goods vehicles over 3.5 tonnes (GVW) SG10-110.]

SG10-138                 TAXI TOUTING/SOLICITING FOR HIRE

*Criminal Justice and Public Order Act 1994, s.167*

**Effective from:** 24 April 2017

Triable only summarily
Maximum: Level 4 fine
Offence range: Conditional Discharge–Band C fine

### STEP 1 Determining the offence category

The Court should determine the offence category using the table below.

| Category 1 | Higher culpability **and** greater harm |
| Category 2 | Higher culpability **and** lesser harm **or** lower culpability **and** greater harm |
| Category 3 | Lower culpability **and** lesser harm |

The court should determine the offender's culpability and the harm caused with reference **only** to the factors below. Where an offence does not fall squarely into a category, individual factors may require a degree of weighting before making an overall assessment and determining the appropriate offence category.

## CULPABILITY demonstrated by one or more of the following:

### Factors indicating higher culpability

- Targeting of vulnerable/unsuspecting victim(s) (including tourists)
- Commercial business/large scale operation
- Offender not licensed to drive
- Positive step(s) taken to deceive

### Factors indicating lower culpability

- All other cases

## HARM demonstrated by one or more of the following:

### Factors indicating greater harm

- Passenger safety compromised by vehicle condition
- Passenger(s) overcharged

### Factors indicating lesser harm

- All other cases

## STEP 2   Starting point and category range

Having determined the category at step one, the court should use the starting point to reach a sentence within the appropriate category range in the table below. The starting point applies to all offenders irrespective of plea or previous convictions.

| Offence Category | Starting Point | Range |
|---|---|---|
| Category 1 | Band C fine | Band B fine – Band C fine and disqualification 6–12 months |
| Category 2 | Band B fine | Band A fine – Band B fine and consider disqualification 3–6 months |
| Category 3 | Band A fine | Conditional discharge – Band A fine and consider disqualification 1–3 months |

Note: refer to fines for **offence committed for 'commercial' purposes**

### Fines

[See **SG10-35** for band ranges]

### Factors increasing or reducing seriousness

The court should then consider adjustment for any aggravating or mitigating factors. The following is a **non-exhaustive** list of additional factual elements providing the context of the offence and factors relating to the offender. Identify whether any combination of these, or other relevant factors, should result in an upward or downward adjustment from the sentence arrived at so far.

### Factors increasing seriousness

*Statutory aggravating factors:*
- Previous convictions, having regard to
  a)  the **nature** of the offence to which the conviction relates and its **relevance** to the current offence; and
  b)  the **time** that has elapsed since the conviction
- Offence committed whilst on bail

*Other aggravating factors:*
- Failure to comply with current court orders
- Offence committed on licence or post sentence supervision
- PHV licence refused/ ineligible

### Factors reducing seriousness or reflecting personal mitigation

- No previous convictions **or** no relevant/recent convictions
- Remorse
- Good character and/or exemplary conduct
- Mental disorder or learning disability
- Sole or primary carer for dependent relatives

**STEP 3  Consider any factors which indicate a reduction, such as assistance to the prosecution**

The court should take into account section 74 of the Sentencing Code (reduction in sentence for assistance to prosecution) and any other rule of law by virtue of which an offender may receive a discounted sentence in consequence of assistance given (or offered) to the prosecutor or investigator.

**STEP 4  Reduction for guilty pleas**

The court should take account of any potential reduction for a guilty plea in accordance with section 73 of the Sentencing Code and the guideline for Reduction in Sentence for a Guilty Plea [**SG5-1–SG5-12**].

**STEP 5  Totality principle**

If sentencing an offender for more than one offence, or where the offender is already serving a sentence, consider whether the total sentence is just and proportionate to the overall offending behaviour in accordance with the *Totality* guideline. [See **SG4**]

**STEP 6  Compensation and ancillary orders**

In all cases, the court should consider whether to make **compensation** and/or other **ancillary orders**, including **disqualification from driving** and the **deprivation of a vehicle**. [See **SG10-5** for ancillary orders].

Where the offence has resulted in personal injury, loss or damage the court must give reasons if it decides not to order compensation (Sentencing Code, s.55).

**STEP 7  Reasons**

Section 52 of the Sentencing Code imposes a duty to give reasons for, and explain the effect of, the sentence.

**SG10-139**  See SG35-1–SG35-3

**SG10-140**                TV LICENCE PAYMENT EVASION (REVISED 2017)

*Communications Act 2003, s.363*

**Effective from:** 24 April 2017

Triable only summarily
Maximum: Level 3 fine
Offence range: Band A fine–Band B fine

**STEP 1  Determining the offence category**

The Court should determine the offence category using the table below.

| Category 1 | Higher culpability **and** greater harm |
|---|---|
| Category 2 | Higher culpability **and** lesser harm **or** lower culpability **and** greater harm |
| Category 3 | Lower culpability **and** lesser harm |

The court should determine the offender's culpability and the harm caused with reference **only** to the factors below. Where an offence does not fall squarely into a category, individual factors may require a degree of weighting before making an overall assessment and determining the appropriate offence category.

**CULPABILITY demonstrated by one or more of the following:**

**Factors indicating higher culpability**

- No attempt to obtain TV Licence
- Had additional subscription television service
- Attempts made to evade detection

**Factors indicating lower culpability**

- Accidental oversight or belief licence held (eg failure of financial arrangement)
- Confusion of responsibility
- Licence immediately obtained
- Significant efforts made to be licensed

**HARM demonstrated by one or more of the following:**

**Factor indicating greater harm**

- Prolonged period without TV licence (over 6 months unlicensed use)

**Factors indicating lesser harm**

- Short period without television licence (under 6 months unlicensed use)

### STEP 2  Starting point and category range

Having determined the category at step one, the court should use the starting point to reach a sentence within the appropriate category range in the table below. The starting point applies to all offenders irrespective of plea or previous convictions.

| Offence Category | Starting Point | Range |
|---|---|---|
| Category 1 | Band B fine | Band B fine |
| Category 2 | Band B fine | Band A fine – Band B fine |
| Category 3 | Band A fine | Conditional discharge – Band A fine |

**Fines**

[See **SG10-35** for band ranges]

**Factors increasing or reducing seriousness**

The court should then consider adjustment for any aggravating or mitigating factors. The following is a **non-exhaustive** list of additional factual elements providing the context of the offence and factors relating to the offender. Identify whether any combination of these, or other relevant factors, should result in an upward or downward adjustment from the sentence arrived at so far.

**Factors increasing seriousness**

*Statutory aggravating factors:*

- Previous convictions, having regard to
  a) the **nature** of the offence to which the conviction relates and its **relevance** to the current offence; and
  b) the **time** that has elapsed since the conviction
- Offence committed whilst on bail

*Other aggravating factors:*

- Failure to comply with current court orders
- Offence committed on licence or post sentence supervision

**Factors reducing seriousness or reflecting personal mitigation**

- No previous convictions **or** no relevant/recent convictions
- Remorse, especially if evidenced by immediate purchase of television licence
- Good character and/or exemplary conduct
- Age and/or lack of maturity where it affects the responsibility of the offender
- Mental disorder or learning disability
- Offender experiencing significant financial hardship at time of offence due to **exceptional** circumstances

### STEP 3  Consider any factors which indicate a reduction, such as assistance to the prosecution

The court should take into account section 74 of the Sentencing Code (reduction in sentence for assistance to prosecution) and any other rule of law by virtue of which an offender may receive a discounted sentence in consequence of assistance given (or offered) to the prosecutor or investigator.

### STEP 4  Reduction for guilty pleas

The court should take account of any potential reduction for a guilty plea in accordance with section 73 of the Sentencing Code and the guideline for Reduction in Sentence for a Guilty Plea [**SG5-1–SG5-12**].

### STEP 5  Totality principle

If sentencing an offender for more than one offence, or where the offender is already serving a sentence, consider whether the total sentence is just and proportionate to the overall offending behaviour in accordance with the *Totality* guideline. [See **SG4**].

### STEP 6  Compensation and ancillary orders

In all cases, the court should consider whether to make **compensation** and/or other **ancillary orders**. [See **SG10-5** for ancillary orders].

Where the offence has resulted in personal injury, loss or damage the court must give reasons if it decides not to order compensation (Sentencing Code, s.55).

**STEP 7  Reasons**

Section 52 of the Sentencing Code imposes a duty to give reasons for, and explain the effect of, the sentence.

**SG10-141**
## TYRES DEFECTIVE

[See Motoring offences appropriate for imposition of fine or discharge, Part Two: Offences concerning the vehicle **SG10-107**.]

**SG10-142**
## TYRES DEFECTIVE – BUSES/GOODS VEHICLES

[See Motoring offences appropriate for imposition of fine or discharge, Part Five: Offences re buses/goods vehicles over 3.5 tonnes (GVW) **SG10-110**.]

**SG10-143**
## UNFIT THROUGH DRINK OR DRUGS (DRIVE/ATTEMPT TO DRIVE) (REVISED 2017)

*Road Traffic Act 1988, s.4(1)*

**Effective from:** 24 April 2017

Triable only summarily
Maximum: Unlimited fine and/or 6 months
Offence range: Band B fine–26 weeks' custody

**STEP 1  Determining the offence category**
The Court should determine the offence category using the table below.

| Category 1 | Higher culpability **and** greater harm |
|------------|------------------------------------------|
| Category 2 | Higher culpability **and** lesser harm **or** lower culpability **and** greater harm |
| Category 3 | Lower culpability **and** lesser harm |

The court should determine the offender's culpability and the harm caused with reference **only** to the factors below. Where an offence does not fall squarely into a category, individual factors may require a degree of weighting before making an overall assessment and determining the appropriate offence category.

**CULPABILITY demonstrated by one or more of the following:**

**Factors indicating higher culpability**
- Driving LGV, HGV or PSV etc.
- Driving for hire or reward

**Factors indicating lower culpability**
- All other cases

**HARM demonstrated by one or more of the following:**

**Factors indicating greater harm**
- High level of impairment

**Factors indicating lesser harm**
- All other cases

**STEP 2  Starting point and category range**
Having determined the category at step one, the court should use the appropriate starting point to reach a sentence within the category range in the table below.
- **Must endorse and disqualify for at least 12 months**
- **Must disqualify for at least 2 years if offender has had two or more disqualifications for periods of 56 days or more in preceding 3 years – refer to the disqualification guidance and consult your legal adviser for further guidance**
- **Must disqualify for at least 3 years if offender has been convicted of a relevant offence in preceding 10 years – consult your legal adviser for further guidance**
- **Extend disqualification if imposing immediate custody**

**If there is a delay in sentencing after conviction, consider interim disqualification.**

The starting point applies to all offenders irrespective of plea or previous convictions

| Level of seriousness | Starting point | Range | Disqualification | Disqual. 2nd offence in 10 years |
|---|---|---|---|---|
| Category 1 | 12 weeks' custody | High level community order – 26 weeks' custody | 29–36 months (Extend if imposing immediate custody) | 36–60 months (Extend if imposing immediate custody |
| Category 2 | Medium level community order | Low level community order – High level community order | 17–28 months | 36–52 months |
| Category 3 | Band C fine | Band B fine – Low level community order | 12–16 months | 36–40 months |

Note: when considering the guidance regarding the length of disqualification in the case of a second offence, the period to be imposed in any individual case will depend on an assessment of all the relevant circumstances, including the length of time since the earlier ban was imposed and the gravity of the current offence but disqualification must be for at least three years.

### Fines

[See **SG10-35** for band ranges]

### Community Orders and Custodial Sentences

[For the imposition of community orders, including the community orders table, see Imposition of Community and Custodial Sentences at **SG9-2**. For the imposition of custodial sentences see Imposition of Community and Custodial Sentences at **SG9-3**.]

### Factors increasing or reducing seriousness

The court should then consider further adjustment for any aggravating or mitigating factors. The following is a **non-exhaustive** list of additional factual elements providing the context of the offence and factors relating to the offender. Identify whether any combination of these, or other relevant factors, should result in an upward or downward adjustment from the sentence arrived at so far.

### Factors increasing seriousness

*Statutory aggravating factors:*

- Previous convictions, having regard to
  a) the **nature** of the offence to which the conviction relates and its **relevance** to the current offence; and
  b) the **time** that has elapsed since the conviction
- Offence committed whilst on bail

*Other aggravating factors:*

- Failure to comply with current court orders
- Offence committed on licence or post sentence supervision
- Poor road or weather conditions
- Evidence of unacceptable standard of driving
- Involved in accident
- Carrying passengers
- High level of traffic or pedestrians in the vicinity

### Factors reducing seriousness or reflecting personal mitigation

- No previous convictions **or** no relevant/recent convictions
- Remorse
- Good character and/or exemplary conduct
- Serious medical condition requiring urgent, intensive or long-term treatment
- Age and/or lack of maturity where it affects the responsibility of the offender
- Mental disorder or learning disability
- Sole or primary carer for dependent relatives

### STEP 3  Consider any factors which indicate a reduction, such as assistance to the prosecution

The court should take into account section 74 of the Sentencing Code (reduction in sentence for assistance to prosecution) and any other rule of law by virtue of which an offender may receive a discounted sentence in consequence of assistance given (or offered) to the prosecutor or investigator.

### STEP 4  Reduction for guilty pleas

The court should take account of any potential reduction for a guilty plea in accordance with section 73 of the Sentencing Code and the guideline for Reduction in Sentence for a Guilty Plea [**SG5-1–SG5-12**].

Sentencing Guidelines

### STEP 5 Totality principle

If sentencing an offender for more than one offence, or where the offender is already serving a sentence, consider whether the total sentence is just and proportionate to the overall offending behaviour in accordance with the *Totality* guideline. [See **SG4**]

### STEP 6 Compensation and ancillary orders

In all cases, the court should consider whether to make **compensation** and/or other **ancillary orders** including offering a **drink/drive rehabilitation course**, **deprivation**, and/or **forfeiture or suspension of personal liquor licence**. [See **SG10-5** for ancillary orders]

Where the offence has resulted in personal injury, loss or damage the court must give reasons if it decides not to order compensation (Sentencing Code, s.55).

### STEP 7 Reasons

Section 52 of the Sentencing Code imposes a duty to give reasons for, and explain the effect of, the sentence.

### STEP 8 Consideration for time spent on bail (tagged curfew)

The court must consider whether to give credit for time spent on bail in accordance with section 240A of the Criminal Justice Act 2003 and section 325 of the Sentencing Code.

**SG10-144**

## UNFIT THROUGH DRINK OR DRUGS (IN CHARGE) (REVISED 2017)

*Road Traffic Act 1988, s.4(2)*

**Effective from:** 24 April 2017

Triable only summarily
Maximum: Level 4 fine and/or 3 months
Offence range: Band B fine–12 weeks' custody

### STEP 1 Determining the offence category

The Court should determine the offence category using the table below.

| Category 1 | Higher culpability **and** greater harm |
|---|---|
| Category 2 | Higher culpability **and** lesser harm **or** lower culpability **and** greater harm |
| Category 3 | Lower culpability **and** lesser harm |

The court should determine the offender's culpability and the harm caused with reference **only** to the factors below. Where an offence does not fall squarely into a category, individual factors may require a degree of weighting before making an overall assessment and determining the appropriate offence category.

**CULPABILITY demonstrated by one or more of the following:**

**Factors indicating higher culpability**
- High likelihood of driving
- In charge of LGV, HGV or PSV etc.
- Offering to drive for hire or reward

**Factors indicating lower culpability**
- All other cases

**HARM demonstrated by one or more of the following:**

**Factors indicating greater harm**
- High level of impairment

**Factors indicating lesser harm**
- All other cases

### STEP 2 Starting point and category range

Having determined the category at step one, the court should use the appropriate starting point to reach a sentence within the category range in the table below.
- **Must endorse and may disqualify. If no disqualification impose 10 points**
- **Extend disqualification if imposing immediate custody**

The starting point applies to all offenders irrespective of plea or previous convictions.

| Level of seriousness | Starting Point | Range | Disqualification/points |
|---|---|---|---|
| Category 1 | High level community order | Medium level community order – 12 weeks' custody | Consider disqualification (extend if imposing immediate custody) OR 10 points |
| Category 2 | Band C fine | Band B fine – Medium level community order | Consider disqualification OR 10 points |
| Category 3 | Band B fine | Band B fine | 10 points |

## Fines

[See **SG10-35** for band ranges]

### Community Orders and Custodial Sentences

[For the imposition of community orders, including the community orders table, see Imposition of Community and Custodial Sentences at **SG9-2**. For the imposition of custodial sentences see Imposition of Community and Custodial Sentences at **SG9-3**.]

### Factors increasing or reducing seriousness

The court should then consider further adjustment for any aggravating or mitigating factors. The following is a **non-exhaustive** list of additional factual elements providing the context of the offence and factors relating to the offender. Identify whether any combination of these, or other relevant factors, should result in an upward or downward adjustment from the sentence arrived at so far.

### Factors increasing seriousness

*Statutory aggravating factors:*

- Previous convictions, having regard to
  a)   the **nature** of the offence to which the conviction relates and its **relevance** to the current offence; and
  b)   the **time** that has elapsed since the conviction
- Offence committed whilst on bail

*Other aggravating factors:*

- Failure to comply with current court orders
- Offence committed on licence or post sentence supervision

### Factors reducing seriousness or reflecting personal mitigation

- No previous convictions **or** no relevant/recent convictions
- Remorse
- Good character and/or exemplary conduct
- Serious medical condition requiring urgent, intensive or long-term treatment
- Age and/or lack of maturity where it affects the responsibility of the offender
- Mental disorder or learning disability
- Sole or primary carer for dependent relatives

### STEP 3   Consider any factors which indicate a reduction, such as assistance to the prosecution

The court should take into account section 74 of the Sentencing Code (reduction in sentence for assistance to prosecution) and any other rule of law by virtue of which an offender may receive a discounted sentence in consequence of assistance given (or offered) to the prosecutor or investigator.

### STEP 4   Reduction for guilty pleas

The court should take account of any potential reduction for a guilty plea in accordance with section 73 of the Sentencing Code and the guideline for Reduction in Sentence for a Guilty Plea [**SG5-1–SG5-12**].

### STEP 5   Totality principle

If sentencing an offender for more than one offence, or where the offender is already serving a sentence, consider whether the total sentence is just and proportionate to the overall offending behaviour in accordance with the *Totality* guideline. [See **SG4**]

### STEP 6   Compensation and ancillary orders

In all cases, the court should consider whether to make **compensation** and/or other **ancillary orders** including offering a **drink/drive rehabilitation course, deprivation**, and/or **forfeiture or suspension of personal liquor licence**. [See **SG10-5** for ancillary orders].

Where the offence has resulted in personal injury, loss or damage the court must give reasons if it decides not to order compensation (Sentencing Code, s.55).

**STEP 7  Reasons**

Section 52 of the Sentencing Code imposes a duty to give reasons for, and explain the effect of, the sentence.

**STEP 8  Consideration for time spent on bail (tagged curfew)**

The court must consider whether to give credit for time spent on bail in accordance with section 240A of the Criminal Justice Act 2003 and section 325 of the Sentencing Code.

**SG10-145**                    USE OF MOBILE TELEPHONE

[See Motoring offences appropriate for imposition of fine or discharge, Part Two: Offences concerning the vehicle **SG10-107**.]

**SG10-146**                    VEHICLE IN PROHIBITED LANE

[See Motoring offences appropriate for imposition of fine or discharge, Part Four: Motorway Offences **SG10-109**]

**SG10-147**            VEHICLE INTERFERENCE (REVISED 2017)

*Criminal Attempts Act 1981, s.9*

**Effective from:** 24 April 2017

Triable only summarily
Maximum: Level 4 fine and/or 3 months
Offence range: Band A fine–12 weeks' custody

**STEP 1  Determining the offence category**

The Court should determine the offence category using the table below.

| Category 1 | Higher culpability **and** greater harm |
| Category 2 | Higher culpability **and** lesser harm **or** lower culpability **and** greater harm |
| Category 3 | Lower culpability **and** lesser harm |

The court should determine the offender's culpability and the harm caused with reference **only** to the factors below. Where an offence does not fall squarely into a category, individual factors may require a degree of weighting before making an overall assessment and determining the appropriate offence category.

**CULPABILITY demonstrated by one or more of the following:**

**Factors indicating higher culpability**

* Leading role where offending is part of a group activity
* Targeting of particular vehicles and/or contents
* Planning

**Factors indicating lower culpability**

* All other cases

**HARM demonstrated by one or more of the following:**

**Factors indicating greater harm**

* Damage caused significant financial loss, inconvenience or distress to victim
* Vehicle left in a dangerous condition

**Factors indicating lesser harm**

* All other cases

**STEP 2  Starting point and category range**

Having determined the category at step one, the court should use the corresponding starting point to reach a sentence within the category range in the table below. The starting point applies to all offenders irrespective of plea or previous convictions.

| Offence Category | Starting Point | Range |
| --- | --- | --- |
| Category 1 | High level community order | Medium level community order – 12 weeks' custody |
| Category 2 | Medium level community order | Band C fine – High level community order |
| Category 3 | Band C fine | Band A fine – Low level community order |

[See **SG10-35** for band ranges]

## Community Orders and Custodial Sentences

[For the imposition of community orders, including the community orders table, see Imposition of Community and Custodial Sentences at **SG9-2**. For the imposition of custodial sentences see Imposition of Community and Custodial Sentences at **SG9-3**.]

### Factors increasing or reducing seriousness

The court should then consider adjustment for any aggravating or mitigating factors. The following is a **non-exhaustive** list of additional factual elements providing the context of the offence and factors relating to the offender. Identify whether any combination of these, or other relevant factors, should result in an upward or downward adjustment from the sentence arrived at so far.

### Factors increasing seriousness

*Statutory aggravating factors:*

- Previous convictions, having regard to
    a)  the **nature** of the offence to which the conviction relates and its **relevance** to the current offence; and
    b)  the **time** that has elapsed since the conviction
- Offence committed whilst on bail

*Other aggravating factors:*

- Failure to comply with current court orders
- Offence committed on licence or post sentence supervision
- Part of a spree
- Offence against emergency services vehicle

### Factors reducing seriousness or reflecting personal mitigation

- No previous convictions **or** no relevant/recent convictions
- Good character and/or exemplary conduct
- Age and/or lack of maturity where it affects the responsibility of the offender
- Mental disorder or learning disability
- Sole or primary carer for dependent relatives

## STEP 3   Consider any factors which indicate a reduction, such as assistance to the prosecution

The court should take into account section 74 of the Sentencing Code (reduction in sentence for assistance to prosecution) and any other rule of law by virtue of which an offender may receive a discounted sentence in consequence of assistance given (or offered) to the prosecutor or investigator.

## STEP 4   Reduction for guilty pleas

The court should take account of any potential reduction for a guilty plea in accordance with section 73 of the Sentencing Code and the guideline for Reduction in Sentence for a Guilty Plea [**SG5-1–SG5-12**].

## STEP 5   Totality principle

If sentencing an offender for more than one offence, or where the offender is already serving a sentence, consider whether the total sentence is just and proportionate to the overall offending behaviour in accordance with the *Totality* guideline. [See **SG4**]

## STEP 6   Compensation and ancillary orders

In all cases, the court should consider whether to make **compensation** and/or other **ancillary orders**, including **disqualification from driving.** [See SG10-5 for ancillary orders.]

Where the offence has resulted in personal injury, loss or damage the court must give reasons if it decides not to order compensation (Sentencing Code, s.55).

## STEP 7   Reasons

Section 52 of the Sentencing Code imposes a duty to give reasons for, and explain the effect of, the sentence.

## STEP 8   Consideration for time spent on bail (tagged curfew)

The court must consider whether to give credit for time spent on bail in accordance with section 240A of the Criminal Justice Act 2003 and section 325 of the Sentencing Code.

VEHICLE LICENCE/REGISTRATION FRAUD

*Vehicle Excise and Registration Act 1994, s.44*

**Effective from:** 04 August 2008

Triable either way
Maximum when tried summarily: Level 5 fine
Maximum when tried on indictment: 2 years

**Offence seriousness (culpability and harm)**

*A. Identify the appropriate starting point*

Starting points based on first time offender pleading not guilty

| Examples of nature of activity | Starting point | Range |
|---|---|---|
| Use of unaltered licence from another vehicle | Band B fine | Band B fine |
| Forged licence bought for own use, or forged/altered for own use | Band C fine | Band C fine |
| Use of number plates from another vehicle; or Licence/number plates forged or altered for sale to another | High level community order (in Crown Court) | Medium level community order–Crown Court (Note: community order and custody available only in Crown Court) |

**Fines**

[See **SG10-35** for band ranges]

*B. Consider the effect of aggravating and mitigating factors (other than those within examples above)*

| Factors indicating higher culpability | Factors indicating lower culpability |
|---|---|
| 1. LGV, PSV, taxi etc.<br>2. Long-term fraudulent use<br><br>**Factors indicating greater degree of harm**<br>1. High financial gain<br>2. Innocent victim deceived<br>3. Legitimate owner inconvenienced | 1. Licence/registration mark from another vehicle owned by defendant<br>2. Short-term use |

**Common aggravating and mitigating factors**

[See **SG10-4** for the standard list of common aggravating and mitigating factors.]

**Form a preliminary view of the appropriate sentence, then consider offender mitigation**

Offender mitigation

* Genuine remorse
* Admissions to police in interview
* Ready co-operation with authorities

**Consider a reduction for a guilty plea**

* Reduction in Sentence for a Guilty Plea (where first hearing is on or after 1 June 2017 [see **SG5-1**], or first hearing before 1 June 2017 [see **SG5-12**]).

**Consider ancillary orders, including compensation**

View guidance on available ancillary orders and compensation.

Where the offence has resulted in personal injury, loss or damage the court must give reasons if it decides not to order compensation (Sentencing Code, s.55).

[For ancillary orders in the Magistrates' Court see **SG10-5**.]

**Consider disqualification from driving and deprivation of property (including vehicle)**

**Decide sentence**

**Give reasons**

VEHICLE TAKING (AGGRAVATED)                                    **SG10-149**
DAMAGE CAUSED TO PROPERTY OTHER THAN THE VEHICLE IN
ACCIDENT OR DAMAGE CAUSED TO THE VEHICLE

*Theft Act 1968, s.12A(2)(c) and (d)*

**Effective from:** 04 August 2008

Triable either way (triable only summarily if damage under £5,000)
Maximum: 2 years' custody; 14 years if accident caused death

**Note:** this guideline does not take account of the increase in magistrates' courts' sentencing powers for either way offences committed on or after 2 May 2022

• Must endorse and disqualify for at least 12 months
• Must disqualify for *at least* 2 years if offender has had two or more disqualifications for periods of 56 days or more in preceding 3 years — see explanatory material on obligatory disqualification [Note to seek legal advice]

If there is a delay in sentencing after conviction, consider interim disqualification

**Offence seriousness (culpability and harm)**

*A. Identify the appropriate starting point*

Starting points based on first time offender pleading not guilty

| Examples of nature of activity | Starting point | Range |
|---|---|---|
| Exceeding authorised use of e.g. employer's or relative's vehicle; retention of hire car beyond return date; minor damage to taken vehicle | Medium level community order | Low level community order–high level community order |
| Greater damage to taken vehicle and/or moderate damage to another vehicle and/or property | High level community order | Medium level community order–12 weeks' custody |
| Vehicle taken as part of burglary or from private premises; severe damage | 18 weeks' custody | 12–26 weeks' custody (Crown Court if damage over £5,000) |

**Community Orders and Custodial Sentences**

[For the imposition of community orders, including the community orders table, see Imposition of Community and Custodial Sentences at **SG9-2**. For the imposition of custodial sentences see Imposition of Community and Custodial Sentences at **SG9-3**.]

*B. Consider the effect of aggravating and mitigating factors (other than those within examples above)*

The following may be particularly relevant but these lists are not exhaustive

| Factors indicating higher culpability | Factors indicating lower culpability |
|---|---|
| 1. Vehicle deliberately damaged/destroyed<br>2. Offender under influence of alcohol/drugs<br><br>**Factors indicating greater degree of harm**<br>1. Passenger(s) carried<br>2. Vehicle belonging to elderly or disabled person<br>3. Emergency services vehicle<br>4. Medium to large goods vehicle<br>5. Damage caused in moving traffic accident | 1. Misunderstanding with owner<br>2. Damage resulting from actions of another (where this does not provide a defence) |

**Common aggravating and mitigating factors**

[See **SG10-4** for the list of common aggravating and mitigating factors]

**Form a preliminary view of the appropriate sentence, then consider offender mitigation**

**Offender mitigation**

• Genuine remorse
• Admissions to police in interview
• Ready co-operation with authorities

**Consider a reduction for a guilty plea**

- Reduction in Sentence for a Guilty Plea (where first hearing is on or after 1 June 2017 [see **SG5-1**], or first hearing before 1 June 2017 [see **SG5-12**]).

**Consider ancillary orders, including compensation**

View guidance on available ancillary orders and compensation.

Where the offence has resulted in personal injury, loss or damage the court must give reasons if it decides not to order compensation (Sentencing Code, s.55).

- Ancillary orders – Magistrates' Court [see **SG10-5**]

**Decide sentence**

**Give reasons**

**SG10-150**

VEHICLE TAKING (AGGRAVATED)
DANGEROUS DRIVING OR ACCIDENT CAUSING INJURY

*Theft Act 1968, ss.12A(2)(a) and (b)*

**Effective from:** 04 August 2008

Triable either way
Maximum when tried summarily: Level 5 fine and/or 6 months
Maximum when tried on indictment: 2 years; 14 years if accident caused death

**Note:** this guideline does not take account of the increase in magistrates' courts' sentencing powers for either way offences committed on or after 2 May 2022

- Must endorse and disqualify for at least 12 months
- Must disqualify for *at least* 2 years if offender has had two or more disqualifications for periods of 56 days or more in preceding 3 years – refer to explanatory material on obligatory disqualification [Note to take legal advice]

If there is a delay in sentencing after conviction, consider interim disqualification

**Offence seriousness (culpability and harm)**

*A. Identify the appropriate starting point*

Starting points based on first time offender pleading not guilty

| Examples of nature of activity | Starting point | Range |
|---|---|---|
| Taken vehicle involved in single incident of bad driving where little or no damage or risk of personal injury | High level community order | Medium level community order–12 weeks' custody |
| Taken vehicle involved in incident(s) involving excessive speed or showing off, especially on busy roads or in built-up area | 18 weeks' custody | 12–26 weeks' custody |
| Taken vehicle involved in prolonged bad driving involving deliberate disregard for safety of others | Crown Court | Crown Court |

**Community Orders and Custodial Sentences**

[For the imposition of community orders, including the community orders table, see Imposition of Community and Custodial Sentences at **SG9-2**. For the imposition of custodial sentences see Imposition of Community and Custodial Sentences at **SG9-3**.]

*B. Consider the effect of aggravating and mitigating factors (other than those within examples above)*

Common aggravating and mitigating factors are identified [elsewhere]—the following may be particularly relevant but these lists are not exhaustive

| Factors indicating higher culpability | Factors indicating greater degree of harm |
|---|---|
| 1. Disregarding warnings of others<br>2. Evidence of alcohol or drugs<br>3. Carrying out other tasks while driving<br>4. Carrying passengers or heavy load<br>5. Tiredness<br>6. Trying to avoid arrest<br>7. Aggressive driving, such as driving much too close to vehicle in front, inappropriate attempts to over-take, or cutting in after overtaking | 1. Injury to others<br>2. Damage to other vehicles or property |

### Common aggravating and mitigating factors

[See **SG10-4** for a list of common aggravating and mitigating factors]

### Factors increasing or reducing seriousness

### Aggravating factors

*Factors indicating higher culpability:*

- Offence committed whilst on bail for other offences
- Failure to respond to previous sentences
- Offence was racially or religiously aggravated
- Offence motivated by, or demonstrating, hostility to the victim based on his or her sexual orientation (or presumed sexual orientation)
- Offence motivated by, or demonstrating, hostility based on the victim's disability (or presumed disability)
- Previous conviction(s), particularly where a pattern of repeat offending is disclosed
- Planning of an offence
- An intention to commit more serious harm than actually resulted from the offence
- Offenders operating in groups or gangs
- 'Professional' offending
- Commission of the offence for financial gain (where this is not inherent in the offence itself)
- High level of profit from the offence
- An attempt to conceal or dispose of evidence
- Failure to respond to warnings or concerns expressed by others about the offender's behaviour
- Offence committed whilst on licence
- Offence motivated by hostility towards a minority group, or a member or members of it
- Deliberate targeting of vulnerable victim(s)
- Commission of an offence while under the influence of alcohol or drugs
- Use of a weapon to frighten or injure victim
- Deliberate and gratuitous violence or damage to property, over and above what is needed to carry out the offence
- Abuse of power
- Abuse of a position of trust

*Factors indicating a more than usually serious degree of harm:*

- Multiple victims
- An especially serious physical or psychological effect on the victim, even if unintended
- A sustained assault or repeated assaults on the same victim
- Victim is particularly vulnerable
- Location of the offence (for example, in an isolated place)
- Offence is committed against those working in the public sector or providing a service to the public
- Presence of others e.g. relatives, especially children or partner of the victim
- Additional degradation of the victim (e.g. taking photographs of a victim as part of a sexual offence)
- In property offences, high value (including sentimental value) of property to the victim, or substantial consequential loss (e.g. where the theft of equipment causes serious disruption to a victim's life or business)

### Mitigating factors
*Factors indicating lower culpability:*

- A greater degree of provocation than normally expected
- Mental illness or disability
- Youth or age, where it affects the responsibility of the individual defendant
- The fact that the offender played only a minor role in the offence

**Form a preliminary view of the appropriate sentence, then consider offender mitigation**

*Offender mitigation*

- Genuine remorse
- Admissions to police in interview
- Ready co-operation with authorities

**Consider a reduction for a guilty plea**

- Reduction in Sentence for a Guilty Plea (where first hearing is on or after 1 June 2017 [see **SG5-1**], or first hearing before 1 June 2017 [see **SG5-12**]).

**Consider ancillary orders, including compensation**

View guidance on available ancillary orders and compensation.

Where the offence has resulted in personal injury, loss or damage the court must give reasons if it decides not to order compensation (Sentencing Code, s.55).

[For ancillary orders in the Magistrates' Court see **SG10-5**]

**Decide sentence**

**Give reasons**

**SG10-151**
                            Vehicle Taking, Without Consent (Revised 2017)

*Theft Act 1968, s.12*

**Effective from:** 24 April 2017

Triable only summarily
Maximum: Unlimited fine and/or 6 months
Offence range: Band B fine–26 weeks' custody

### STEP 1  Determining the offence category

The Court should determine the offence category using the table below.

| Category 1 | Higher culpability **and** greater harm |
| --- | --- |
| Category 2 | Higher culpability **and** lesser harm **or** lower culpability **and** greater harm |
| Category 3 | Lower culpability **and** lesser harm |

The court should determine the offender's culpability and the harm caused with reference only to the factors below. Where an offence does not fall squarely into a category, individual factors may require a degree of weighting before making an overall assessment and determining the appropriate offence category.

**CULPABILITY demonstrated by one or more of the following:**

**Factors indicating higher culpability**

- A leading role where offending is part of a group activity
- Involvement of others through coercion, intimidation or exploitation
- Sophisticated nature of offence/significant planning
- Abuse of position of power or trust or responsibility
- Commission of offence in association with or to further other criminal activity

**Factors indicating lower culpability**

- Performed limited function under direction
- Involved through coercion, intimidation or exploitation
- Limited awareness or understanding of offence
- Exceeding authorised use of e.g. employer's or relative's vehicle
- Retention of hire car for short period beyond return date

**HARM demonstrated by one or more of the following: Factors indicating greater harm**

- Vehicle later burnt
- Vehicle belonging to elderly/disabled person
- Emergency services vehicle
- Medium to large goods vehicle
- Passengers carried
- Damage to lock/ignition
- Vehicle taken from private premises

**Factors indicating lesser harm**

- All other cases

## STEP 2  Starting point and category range

Having determined the category at step one, the court should use the appropriate starting point to reach a sentence within the category range in the table below. The starting point applies to all offenders irrespective of plea or previous convictions.

| Level of seriousness | Starting Point | Range | Disqualification |
|---|---|---|---|
| Category 1 | High level community order | Medium level community order – 26 weeks' custody | Consider disqualification 9 to 12 months (Extend if imposing immediate custody) |
| Category 2 | Medium level community order | Low level community order – High level community order | Consider disqualification 5 to 8 months |
| Category 3 | Low level community order | Band B fine – Medium level community order | Consider disqualification |

• **Extend any disqualification if imposing immediate cusody [See SG10-53]**

**Fines**

[See **SG10-35** for band ranges]

**Community Orders and Custodial Sentences**

[For the imposition of community orders, including the community orders table, see Imposition of Community and Custodial Sentences at **SG9-2**. For the imposition of custodial sentences see Imposition of Community and Custodial Sentences at **SG9-3**.]

**Factors increasing or reducing seriousness**

The court should then consider further adjustment for any aggravating or mitigating factors. The following is a **non-exhaustive** list of additional factual elements providing the context of the offence and factors relating to the offender. Identify whether any combination of these, or other relevant factors, should result in an upward or downward adjustment from the sentence arrived at so far.

**Factors increasing seriousness**

*Statutory aggravating factors:*

- Previous convictions, having regard to a) the nature of the offence to which the conviction relates and its relevance to the current offence; and b) the time that has elapsed since the conviction
- Offence committed whilst on bail

*Other aggravating factors:*

- Failure to comply with current court orders
- Offence committed on licence or post sentence supervision

**Factors reducing seriousness or reflecting personal mitigation**

- No previous convictions or no relevant/recent convictions
- Remorse
- Good character and/or exemplary conduct
- Age and/or lack of maturity where it affects the responsibility of the offender
- Mental disorder or learning disability
- Sole or primary carer for dependent relatives
- Co-operation with the investigation

## STEP 3  Consider any factors which indicate a reduction, such as assistance to the prosecution

The court should take into account section 74 of the Sentencing Code (reduction in sentence for assistance to prosecution) and any other rule of law by virtue of which an offender may receive a discounted sentence in consequence of assistance given (or offered) to the prosecutor or investigator.

## STEP 4  Reduction for guilty pleas

The court should take account of any potential reduction for a guilty plea in accordance with section 73 of the Sentencing Code and the guideline for Reduction in Sentence for a Guilty Plea [**SG5-1–SG5-12**].

*Sentencing Guidelines*

**STEP 5 Totality principle**

If sentencing an offender for more than one offence, or where the offender is already serving a sentence, consider whether the total sentence is just and proportionate to the overall offending behaviour in accordance with the *Totality* guideline. [See **SG4**]

**STEP 6 Compensation and ancillary orders**

In all cases, the court should consider whether to make **compensation** and/or other **ancillary orders**, including **disqualification from driving**. [See **SG10-4** for information on ancillary orders.]

Where the offence has resulted in personal injury, loss or damage the court must give reasons if it decides not to order compensation (Sentencing Code, s.55)

**STEP 7 Reasons**

Section 52 of the Sentencing Code imposes a duty to give reasons for, and explain the effect of, the sentence.

**STEP 8 Consideration for time spent on bail (tagged curfew)**

The court must consider whether to give credit for time spent on bail in accordance with section 240A of the Criminal Justice Act 2003 and section 325 of the Sentencing Code.

**SG10-152**

WALK ON MOTORWAY, SLIP ROAD OR HARD SHOULDER

[See Motoring offences appropriate for imposition of fine or discharge, Part Four: Motorway Offences **SG10-109**]

**SG10-153**

WEIGHT, POSITION OR DISTRIBUTION OF LOAD OR
MANNER IN WHICH LOAD SECURED INVOLVING DANGER OF INJURY

[See Motoring offences appropriate for imposition of fine or discharge, Part Three: Offences concerning use of vehicle **SG10-108**.]

**SG10-154**

WEIGHT, POSITION OR DISTRIBUTION OF LOAD OR MANNER IN
WHICH LOAD SECURED INVOLVING DANGER OF INJURY
(OVER 3.5 TONNES)

[See Motoring offences appropriate for imposition of fine or discharge, Part Five: Offences re buses/goods vehicles over 3.5 tonnes (GVW) **SG10-110**.]

**SG10-155**

WITNESS INTIMIDATION

*Criminal Justice and Public Order Act 1994, s.51*

**Effective from:** 04 August 2008

Triable either way
Maximum: 5 years' custody

**Note:** this guideline does not take account of the increase in magistrates' courts' sentencing powers for either way offences committed on or after 2 May 2022

Where offence committed in domestic context, refer [below] for guidance

**Offence seriousness (culpability and harm)**

*A. Identify the appropriate starting point*

Starting points based on first time offender pleading not guilty

| Examples of nature of activity | Starting point | Range |
|---|---|---|
| Sudden outburst in chance encounter | 6 weeks' custody | Medium level community order–18 weeks' custody |
| Conduct amounting to a threat; staring at, approaching or following witnesses; talking about the case; trying to alter or stop evidence | 18 weeks' custody | 12 weeks' custody–Crown Court |
| Threats of violence to witnesses and/or their families; deliberately seeking out witnesses | Crown Court | Crown Court |

## Community Orders and Custodial Sentences

[For the imposition of community orders, including the community orders table, see Imposition of Community and Custodial Sentences at **SG9-2**. For the imposition of custodial sentences see Imposition of Community and Custodial Sentences at **SG9-3**.]

*B.  Consider the effect of aggravating and mitigating factors (other than those within examples above)*

The following may be particularly relevant but these lists are not exhaustive

### Factors indicating higher culpability

- Breach of bail conditions
- Offender involves others

### Factors indicating greater degree of harm

- Detrimental impact on administration of justice
- Contact made at or in vicinity of victim's home

### Common aggravating and mitigating factors

[Common aggravating and mitigating factors are set out at **SG10-4**.]

### Form a preliminary view of the appropriate sentence, then consider offender mitigation

*Offender mitigation*

- Genuine remorse
- Admissions to police in interview
- Ready co-operation with authorities

### Consider a reduction for a guilty plea

- Reduction in Sentence for a Guilty Plea (where first hearing is on or after 1 June 2017 [see **SG5-1**], or first hearing before 1 June 2017 [see **SG5-12**])

### Consider ancillary orders, including compensation

View guidance on available ancillary orders and compensation.

Where the offence has resulted in personal injury, loss or damage the court must give reasons if it decides not to order compensation (Sentencing Code, s.55).

- Ancillary orders – Magistrates' Court [see **SG10-5**]

### Decide sentence
### Give reasons

## ENVIRONMENTAL/HEALTH AND SAFETY OFFENCES                    **SG10-156**

[Omitted.]

# PART 11   ARSON AND CRIMINAL DAMAGE

**SG11-1**

APPLICABILITY

[For the standard text on applicability see **SG0-4**.]

**SG11-2**

ARSON (CRIMINAL DAMAGE BY FIRE)

**Effective from:** 01 October 2019

*Criminal Damage Act 1971, s.1(1) and (3)*

This is a Schedule 19 offence for the purposes of sections 274 and section 285 (required life sentence for offence carrying life sentence) of the Sentencing Code.

Triable either way
Maximum: Life imprisonment
Offence range: Discharge – 8 years' custody

Where offence committed in domestic context, refer to **Overarching principles – domestic abuse** [SG5-1–SG5-8]*

* The maximum sentence that applies to an offence is the maximum that applied at the date of the offence.

Courts should consider requesting a report from: liaison and diversion services, a medical practitioner, or where it is necessary, ordering a psychiatric report, to ascertain both whether the offence is linked to a mental disorder or learning disability (to assist in the assessment of culpability) and whether any mental health disposal should be considered.

### STEP 1 Determining the offence category

The court should determine the offence category with reference only to the factors in the tables below. In order to determine the category the court should assess **culpability** and **harm**.

The level of **culpability** is determined by weighing up all the factors of the case. **Where there are characteristics present which fall under different levels of culpability, the court should balance these characteristics to reach a fair assessment of the offender's culpability.**

| Culpability demonstrated by one or more of the following |
| --- |
| A – **High culpability** |
| • High degree of planning or premeditation<br>• Revenge attack<br>• Use of accelerant<br>• Intention to cause very serious damage to property<br>• Intention to create a high risk of injury to persons |
| B – **Medium culpability** |
| • Some planning<br>• Recklessness as to whether very serious damage caused to property<br>• Recklessness as to whether serious injury caused to persons<br>• Other cases that fall between categories A and C because:<br>  o Factors are present in A and C which balance each other out **and/or**<br>  o The offender's culpability falls between the factors described in A and C |
| C – **Lesser culpability** |
| • Little or no planning; offence committed on impulse<br>• Recklessness as to whether some damage to property caused<br>• Offender's responsibility substantially reduced by mental disorder or learning disability<br>• Involved through coercion, intimidation or exploitation |

| Harm | |
|---|---|
| The level of harm is assessed by weighing up all the factors of the case. | |
| Category 1 | • Serious physical and/or psychological harm caused<br>• Serious consequential economic or social impact of offence<br>• High value of damage caused |
| Category 2 | • Harm that falls between categories 1 and 3 |
| Category 3 | • No or minimal physical and/or psychological harm caused<br>• Low value of damage caused |

## STEP 2  Starting point and category range

Having determined the category at step one, the court should use the corresponding starting point to reach a sentence within the category range below. The starting point applies to all offenders irrespective of plea or previous convictions.

Where the offender is dependent on or has a propensity to misuse drugs or alcohol, which is linked to the offending, a community order with a drug rehabilitation requirement under Part 10, or an alcohol treatment requirement under under Part 11, of Schedule 9 of the Sentencing Code may be a proper alternative to a short or moderate custodial sentence.

Where the offender suffers from a medical condition that is susceptible to treatment but does not warrant detention under a hospital order, a community order with a mental health treatment requirement under Part 9 of Schedule 9 of the Sentencing Code may be a proper alternative to a short or moderate custodial sentence.

**In exceptional cases within category 1A, sentences of above 8 years may be appropriate.**

| Harm | Culpability | | |
|---|---|---|---|
| | **A** | **B** | **C** |
| Category 1 | **Starting point**<br>4 years' custody | **Starting point**<br>1 year 6 months' custody | **Starting point**<br>9 months' custody |
| | **Category range**<br>2 – 8 years' custody | **Category range**<br>9 months – 3 years' custody | **Category range**<br>6 months – 1 year 6 months' custody |
| Category 2 | **Starting point**<br>2 years' custody | **Starting point**<br>9 months' custody | **Starting point**<br>High level community order |
| | **Category range**<br>1 – 4 years' custody | **Category range**<br>6 months – 1 year 6 months' custody | **Category range**<br>Medium level community order – 9 months' custody |
| Category 3 | **Starting point**<br>1 year's custody | **Starting point**<br>High level community order | **Starting point**<br>Low level community order |
| | **Category range**<br>6 months – 2 years' custody | **Category range**<br>Medium level Community order – 9 months' custody | **Category range**<br>Discharge – High level community order |

### Community Orders and Custodial Sentences

[For the imposition of community orders and custodial sentences see **SG9**.]

### Factors increasing or reducing seriousness

The court should then consider any adjustment for any aggravating or mitigating factors. Below is a **non-exhaustive** list of additional factual elements providing the context of the offence and factors relating to the offender.

Identify whether any combination of these, or other relevant factors, should result in an upward or downward adjustment from the starting point.

| Factors increasing seriousness |
| --- |
| *Statutory aggravating factors* |
| • Previous convictions, having regard to a) the **nature** of the offence to which the conviction relates and its **relevance** to the current offence; and b) the **time** that has elapsed since the conviction<br>• Offence committed whilst on bail<br>• Offence motivated by, or demonstrating hostility based on any of the following characteristics or presumed characteristics of the victim: religion, race, disability, sexual orientation, or transgender identity |
| *Other aggravating factors* |
| • Commission of offence whilst under the influence of alcohol or drugs<br>• Offence committed for financial gain<br>• Offence committed to conceal other offences<br>• Victim is particularly vulnerable<br>• Offence committed within a domestic context<br>• Fire set in or near a public amenity<br>• Damage caused to heritage and/or cultural assets<br>• Significant impact on emergency services or resources<br>• Established evidence of community/wider impact<br>• Failure to comply with current court orders<br>• Offence committed on licence or post sentence supervision<br>• Offences taken into consideration |
| **Factors reducing seriousness or reflecting personal mitigation** |
| • No previous convictions **or** no relevant/recent convictions<br>• Steps taken to minimise the effect of the fire or summon assistance<br>• Remorse<br>• Good character and/or exemplary conduct<br>• Serious medical condition requiring urgent, intensive or long-term treatment<br>• Age and/or lack of maturity<br>• Mental disorder or learning disability (where not taken into account at step one)<br>• Sole or primary carer for dependent relatives<br>• Determination and/or demonstration of steps having been taken to address addiction or offending behaviour |

### STEP 3  Consider any factors which indicate a reduction, such as assistance to the prosecution

The court should take into account section 74 of the Sentencing Code (reduction in sentence for assistance to prosecution) and any other rule of law by virtue of which an offender may receive a discounted sentence in consequence of assistance given (or offered) to the prosecutor or investigator.

### STEP 4  Reduction for guilty pleas

The court should take account of any potential reduction for a guilty plea in accordance with section 73 of the Sentencing Code and the guideline for Reduction in Sentence for a Guilty Plea [**SG5-1–SG5-12**].

### STEP 5  Dangerousness

The court should consider whether having regard to the criteria contained in Chapter 6 of Part 10 of the Sentencing Code it would be appropriate to impose a life sentence (sections 274 and 285) or an extended sentence (sections 266 and 279). When sentencing offenders to a life sentence under these provisions the notional determinate sentence should be used as the basis for the setting of a minimum term.

### STEP 6  Totality principle

If sentencing an offender for more than one offence, or where the offender is already serving a sentence, consider whether the total sentence is just and proportionate to the overall offending behaviour in accordance with the *Totality* guideline [see **SG4**].

### STEP 7  Compensation and ancillary orders

In all cases, the court must consider whether to make a **compensation order** [see **SG10-47**] and/or other ancillary orders.

*Compensation order*

The court should consider compensation orders in all cases where personal injury, loss or damage has resulted from the offence. The court must give reasons if it decides not to award compensation in such cases (Sentencing Code, s.55).

**STEP 8  Reasons**

Section 52 of the Sentencing Code imposes a duty to give reasons for, and explain the effect of, the sentence.

**STEP 9  Consideration for time spent on bail (tagged curfew)**

The court must consider whether to give credit for time spent on bail in accordance with section 240A of the Criminal Justice Act 2003 and section 325 of the Sentencing Code.

CRIMINAL DAMAGE (OTHER THAN BY FIRE) VALUE EXCEEDING £5,000/   **SG11-3**
RACIALLY OR RELIGIOUSLY AGGRAVATED CRIMINAL DAMAGE

*Crime and Disorder Act 1998, s.30, Criminal Damage Act 1971, s.1(1)*

**Effective from:** 01 October 2019

**Criminal damage (other than by fire) value exceeding £5,000**, Criminal Damage Act 1971, s.1(1)

Triable either way
Maximum: 10 years' custody
Offence range: Discharge – 4 years' custody

---

**Note:**

Where an offence of criminal damage is added to the indictment at the Crown Court (having not been charged before) the statutory maximum sentence is 10 years' custody regardless of the value of the damage. In such cases where the value does not exceed £5,000 regard should also be had to the not exceeding £5000 guideline.

---

**Racially or religiously aggravated criminal damage**, Crime and Disorder Act 1998, s.30

Triable either way
Maximum: 14 years' custody

Where offence committed in domestic context, refer to **Overarching principles – domestic abuse** [see **SG6**].

For racially or religiously aggravated offences the category of the offence should be identified with reference to the factors below, and the sentence increased in accordance with the guidance at Step 3.

**STEP 1  Determining the offence category**

The court should determine the offence category with reference only to the factors in the tables below. In order to determine the category the court should assess **culpability** and **harm**.

The level of **culpability** is determined by weighing up all the factors of the case. **Where there are characteristics present which fall under different levels of culpability, the court should balance these characteristics to reach a fair assessment of the offender's culpability.**

| Culpability demonstrated by one or more of the following |
| --- |
| A – **High culpability** |
| • High degree of planning or premeditation<br>• Revenge attack<br>• Intention to cause very serious damage to property<br>• Intention to create a high risk of injury to persons |
| B – **Medium culpability** |
| • Some planning<br>• Recklessness as to whether very serious damage caused to property<br>• Recklessness as to whether serious injury caused to persons<br>• Other cases that fall between categories A and C because:<br>  o Factors are present in A and C which balance each other out **and/or**<br>  o The offender's culpability falls between the factors described in A and C |
| C – **Lesser culpability** |
| • Little or no planning; offence committed on impulse<br>• Recklessness as to whether some damage to property caused<br>• Offender's responsibility substantially reduced by mental disorder or learning disability<br>• Involved through coercion, intimidation or exploitation |

Sentencing Guidelines

| Harm | |
|---|---|
| The level of harm is assessed by weighing up all the factors of the case. | |
| Category 1 | • Serious distress caused<br>• Serious consequential economic or social impact of offence<br>• High value of damage |
| Category 2 | • Harm that falls between categories 1 and 3 |
| Category 3 | • No or minimal distress caused<br>• Low value damage |

### STEP 2  Starting point and category range

Having determined the category at step one, the court should use the corresponding starting point to reach a sentence within the category range below. The starting point applies to all offenders irrespective of plea or previous convictions.

Where the offender is dependent on or has a propensity to misuse drugs or alcohol, which is linked to the offending, a community order with a drug rehabilitation requirement under under Part 10, or an alcohol treatment requirement under under Part 11, of Schedule 9 of the Sentencing Code may be a proper alternative to a short or moderate custodial sentence.

Where the offender suffers from a medical condition that is susceptible to treatment but does not warrant detention under a hospital order, a community order with a mental health treatment requirement under Part 9 of Schedule 9 of the Sentencing Code may be a proper alternative to a short or moderate custodial sentence.

**Maximum: 10 years' custody (basic offence)**

| | Culpability | | |
|---|---|---|---|
| **Harm** | **A** | **B** | **C** |
| Category 1 | **Starting point**<br>1 year 6 months' custody | **Starting point**<br>6 months' custody | **Starting point**<br>High level community order |
| | **Category range**<br>6 months – 4 years' custody | **Category range**<br>High level community order – 1 year 6 months' custody | **Category range**<br>Medium level community order – 9 months' custody |
| Category 2 | **Starting point**<br>6 months' custody | **Starting point**<br>High level community order | **Starting point**<br>Low level community order |
| | **Category range**<br>High level community order – 1 year 6 months' custody | **Category range**<br>Medium level community order – 9 months' custody | **Category range**<br>Band C fine – High level community order |
| Category 3 | **Starting point**<br>High level community order | **Starting point**<br>Low level community order | **Starting point**<br>Band B fine |
| | **Category range**<br>Medium level community order – 9 months' custody | **Category range**<br>Band C fine – High level community order | **Category range**<br>Discharge – Low level community order |

For band ranges, see **SG10-129.**

### Community Orders and Custodial Sentences

[For the imposition of community orders and custodial sentences see **SG9**.]

### Additional factors affecting seriousness

The court should then consider any adjustment for any aggravating or mitigating factors. Below is a **non-exhaustive** list of additional factual elements providing the context of the offence and factors relating to the offender.

Identify whether any combination of these, or other relevant factors, should result in an upward or downward adjustment from the starting point.

**Factors increasing seriousness**

*Statutory aggravating factors*

- Previous convictions, having regard to a) the **nature** of the offence to which the conviction relates and its **relevance** to the current offence; and b) the **time** that has elapsed since the conviction
- Offence committed whilst on bail
- Offence motivated by, or demonstrating hostility based on any of the following characteristics or presumed characteristics of the victim: disability, sexual orientation, or transgender identity

*Other aggravating factors*

- Damaged items of great value to the victim (whether economic, commercial, sentimental or personal value)
- Commission of offence whilst under the influence of alcohol or drugs
- Victim is particularly vulnerable
- Offence committed in a domestic context
- Damage caused to heritage and/or cultural assets
- Significant impact on emergency services or resources
- Established evidence of community/wider impact
- Failure to comply with current court orders
- Offence committed on licence or post sentence supervision
- Offences taken into consideration

**Factors reducing seriousness or reflecting personal mitigation**

- No previous convictions or no relevant/recent convictions
- Remorse
- Good character and/or exemplary conduct
- Serious medical condition requiring urgent, intensive or long-term treatment
- Age and/or lack of maturity
- Mental disorder or learning disability (where not taken into account at step one)
- Sole or primary carer for dependent relatives
- Determination and/or demonstration of steps having been taken to address addiction or offending behaviour

**STEP 3   Aggravated offences**                                                          SG11-4

*Racially or religiously aggravated criminal damage offences only*

Having determined the category of the basic offence to identify the sentence of a non-aggravated offence, the court should now consider the level of racial or religious aggravation involved and apply an appropriate uplift to the sentence in accordance with the guidance below. The following is a list of factors which the court should consider to determine the level of aggravation. Where there are characteristics present which fall under different levels of aggravation, the court should balance these to reach a fair assessment of the level of aggravation present in the offence.

**Maximum sentence for the aggravated offence on indictment is 14 years' custody (maximum for the basic offence is 10 years' custody)**

Care should be taken to avoid double counting factors already taken into account in assessing the level of harm at step one

| High level of racial or religious aggravation | Sentence uplift |
| --- | --- |
| Racial or religious aggravation was the predominant motivation for the offence.<br>Offender was a member of, or was associated with, a group promoting hostility based on race or religion.<br>Aggravated nature of the offence caused severe distress to the victim or the victim's family (**over and above the distress already considered at step one**).<br>Aggravated nature of the offence caused serious fear and distress throughout local community or more widely. | Increase the length of custodial sentence if already considered for the basic offence or consider a custodial sentence, if not already considered for the basic offence. |

*Sentencing Guidelines*

| Medium level of racial or religious aggravation | Sentence uplift |
|---|---|
| Racial or religious aggravation formed a significant proportion of the offence as a whole.<br>Aggravated nature of the offence caused some distress to the victim or the victim's family (**over and above the distress already considered at step one**).<br>Aggravated nature of the offence caused some fear and distress throughout local community or more widely. | Consider a significantly more onerous penalty of the same type or consider a more severe type of sentence than for the basic offence. |
| Low level of racial or religious aggravation | Sentence uplift |
| Aggravated element formed a minimal part of the offence as a whole.<br>Aggravated nature of the offence caused minimal or no distress to the victim or the victim's family (**over and above the distress already considered at step one**). | Consider a more onerous penalty of the same type identified for the basic offence. |

Magistrates may find that, although the appropriate sentence for the basic offence would be within their powers, the appropriate increase for the aggravated offence would result in a sentence in excess of their powers. If so, they must commit for sentence to the Crown Court.

The sentencer should state in open court that the offence was aggravated by reason of race or religion, and should also state what the sentence would have been without that element of aggravation.

### STEP 4  Consider any factors which indicate a reduction, such as assistance to the prosecution

The court should take into account section 74 of the Sentencing Code (reduction in sentence for assistance to prosecution) and any other rule of law by virtue of which an offender may receive a discounted sentence in consequence of assistance given (or offered) to the prosecutor or investigator.

### STEP 5  Reduction for guilty pleas

The court should take account of any potential reduction for a guilty plea in accordance with section 73 of the Sentencing Code and the Reduction in Sentence for a Guilty Plea guideline.

### STEP 6  Totality principle

If sentencing an offender for more than one offence, or where the offender is already serving a sentence, consider whether the total sentence is just and proportionate to the overall offending behaviour in accordance with the Totality guideline [**SG4**].

### STEP 7  Compensation and ancillary orders

In all cases, the court must consider whether to make a compensation order and/or other ancillary orders.

*Compensation order*

The court should consider compensation orders in all cases where personal injury, loss or damage has resulted from the offence. The court must give reasons if it decides not to award compensation in such cases (Sentencing Code, s.55).

### STEP 8  Reasons

Section 52 of the Sentencing Code imposes a duty to give reasons for, and explain the effect of, the sentence.

### STEP 9  Consideration for time spent on bail (tagged curfew)

The court must consider whether to give credit for time spent on bail in accordance with section 240A of the Criminal Justice Act 2003 and section 325 of the Sentencing Code.

**SG11-5**     Criminal Damage (Other than by fire) Value not Exceeding £5,000/ Racially or Religiously Aggravated Criminal Damage

*Crime and Disorder Act 1998, s.30, Criminal Damage Act 1971, s.1(1)*

**Effective from:** 01 October 2019

**Criminal damage (other than by fire) value not exceeding £5,000**, Criminal Damage Act 1971, s.1(1)

Triable only summarily
Maximum: Level 4 fine and/or 3 months' custody
Offence range: Discharge – 3 months' custody

Note:

Where an offence of criminal damage is added to the indictment at the Crown Court (having not been charged before) the statutory maximum sentence is 10 years' custody regardless of the value of the damage. In such cases where the value does not exceed £5,000, the exceeding £5,000 guideline should be used but regard should also be had to this guideline.

**Racially or religiously aggravated criminal damage**, Crime and Disorder Act 1998, s.30

Triable either way
Maximum: 14 years' custody

Where offence committed in domestic context, refer to **Overarching principles – domestic abuse** [see **SG6**].

For racially or religiously aggravated offences the category of the offence should be identified with reference to the factors below, and the sentence increased in accordance with the guidance at Step 3

## STEP 1  Determining the offence category

The court should determine the offence category with reference only to the factors in the tables below. In order to determine the category the court should assess **culpability** and **harm.**

The level of **culpability** is determined by weighing up all the factors of the case. **Where there are characteristics present which fall under different levels of culpability, the court should balance these characteristics to reach a fair assessment of the offender's culpability.**

| Culpability demonstrated by one or more of the following: |
| --- |
| A – **High culpability**<br><br>• High degree of planning or premeditation<br>• Revenge attack<br>• Intention to cause very serious damage to property<br>• Intention to create a high risk of injury to persons |
| B – **Medium culpability**<br><br>• Some planning<br>• Recklessness as to whether very serious damage caused to property<br>• Recklessness as to whether serious injury caused to persons<br>• Other cases that fall between categories A and C because:<br>  o Factors are present in A and C which balance each other out **and/or**<br>  o The offender's culpability falls between the factors described in A and C |
| C – **Lesser culpability**<br><br>• Little or no planning; offence committed on impulse<br>• Recklessness as to whether some damage to property caused<br>• Offender's responsibility substantially reduced by mental disorder or learning disability<br>• Involved through coercion, intimidation or exploitation |

| Harm | |
| --- | --- |
| The level of harm is assessed by weighing up all the factors of the case. | |
| Category 1 | • Serious distress caused<br>• Serious consequential economic or social impact of offence<br>• High value of damage |
| Category 2 | • All other cases |

## STEP 2  Starting point and category range

Having determined the category at step one, the court should use the corresponding starting point to reach a sentence within the category range below. The starting point applies to all offenders irrespective of plea or previous convictions.

Where the offender is dependent on or has a propensity to misuse drugs or alcohol, which is linked to the offending, a community order with a drug rehabilitation requirement under under part 10, or an alcohol treatment requirement under under Part 11, of Schedule 9 of the Sentencing Code may be a proper alternative to a short or moderate custodial sentence.

Where the offender suffers from a medical condition that is susceptible to treatment but does not warrant detention under a hospital order, a community order with a mental health treatment requirement under Part 9 of Schedule 9 of the Sentencing Code may be a proper alternative to a short or moderate custodial sentence.

**Maximum Level 4 fine and/or 3 months custody (basic offence)**

| Harm | Culpability | | |
|---|---|---|---|
| | A | B | C |
| Category 1 | **Starting point**<br>High level community order | **Starting point**<br>Low level community order | **Starting point**<br>Band B fine |
| | **Category range**<br>Medium level community order – 3 months' custody | **Category range**<br>Band C fine – High level community order | **Category range**<br>Discharge – Low level community order |
| Category 2 | **Starting point**<br>Low level community order | **Starting point**<br>Band B fine | **Starting point**<br>Band A fine |
| | **Category range**<br>Band C fine – High level community order | **Category range**<br>Discharge – Low level community order | **Category range**<br>Discharge – Band B fine |

### Fines

[For the standard schedule of fines see **SG2-5**.]

### Community Orders and Custodial Sentences

[For the imposition of community orders and custodial sentences see **SG9**.]

The court should then consider any adjustment for any aggravating or mitigating factors. Below is a **non-exhaustive** list of additional factual elements providing the context of the offence and factors relating to the offender.

Identify whether any combination of these, or other relevant factors, should result in an upward or downward adjustment from the starting point.

### Factors increasing seriousness

*Statutory aggravating factors*

- Previous convictions, having regard to
  a) the **nature** of the offence to which the conviction relates and its **relevance** to the current offence; and
  b) the **time** that has elapsed since the conviction
- Offence committed whilst on bail
- Offence motivated by, or demonstrating hostility based on any of the following characteristics or presumed characteristics of the victim: disability, sexual orientation, or transgender identity

*Other aggravating factors*

- Damaged items of great value to the victim (whether economic, commercial, sentimental or personal value)
- Commission of offence whilst under the influence of alcohol or drugs
- Victim is particularly vulnerable
- Offence committed within a domestic context
- Damage caused to heritage and/or cultural assets
- Significant impact on emergency services or resources
- Established evidence of community/wider impact
- Failure to comply with current court orders
- Offence committed on licence or post sentence supervision
- Offences taken into consideration

### Factors reducing seriousness or reflecting personal mitigation

- No previous convictions **or** no relevant/recent convictions
- Remorse
- Good character and/or exemplary conduct
- Serious medical condition requiring urgent, intensive or long-term treatment
- Age and/or lack of maturity

- Mental Disorder or learning disability (where not taken into account at step one)
- Sole or primary carer for dependent relative
- Determination and/or demonstration of steps having been taken to address addiction or offending behaviour

## STEP 3  Aggravated offences

*Racially or Religiously Aggravated Criminal Damage Offences Only*

Having determined the category of the basic offence to identify the sentence of a non-aggravated offence, the court should now consider the level of racial or religious aggravation involved and apply an appropriate uplift to the sentence in accordance with the guidance below. The following is a list of factors which the court should consider to determine the level of aggravation. Where there are characteristics present which fall under different levels of aggravation, the court should balance these to reach a fair assessment of the level of aggravation present in the offence.

**Maximum sentence for the aggravated offence on indictment is 14 years' custody (maximum for the basic offence is 10 years' custody).**

Care should be taken to avoid double counting factors already taken into account in assessing the level of harm at step one.

| High level of racial or religious aggravation | Sentence uplift. |
| --- | --- |
| Racial or religious aggravation was the predominant motivation for the offence.<br>Offender was a member of, or was associated with, a group promoting hostility based on race or religion.<br>Aggravated nature of the offence caused severe distress to the victim or the victim's family (**over and above the distress already considered at step one**).<br>Aggravated nature of the offence caused serious fear and distress throughout local community or more widely. | Increase the length of custodial sentence if already considered for the basic offence or consider a custodial sentence, if not already considered for the basic offence. |
| **Medium level of racial or religious aggravation** | **Sentence uplift** |
| Racial or religious aggravation formed a significant proportion of the offence as a whole.<br>Aggravated nature of the offence caused some distress to the victim or the victim's family (**over and above the distress already considered at step one**).<br>Aggravated nature of the offence caused some fear and distress throughout local community or more widely. | Consider a significantly more onerous penalty of the same type **or consider** a more severe type of sentence than for the basic offence. |
| **Low level of racial or religious aggravation** | **Sentence uplift** |
| Aggravated element formed a minimal part of the offence as a whole.<br>Aggravated nature of the offence caused minimal or no distress to the victim or the victim's family (**over and above the distress already considered at step one**). | Consider a more onerous penalty of the same type identified for the basic offence. |

Magistrates may find that, although the appropriate sentence for the basic offence would be within their powers, the appropriate increase for the aggravated offence would result in a sentence in excess of their powers. If so, they must commit for sentence to the Crown Court.

The sentencer should state in open court that the offence was aggravated by reason of race or religion, and should also state what the sentence would have been without that element of aggravation.

## STEP 4  Consider any factors which indicate a reduction, such as assistance to the prosecution

The court should take into account section 74 of the Sentencing Code (reduction in sentence for assistance to prosecution) and any other rule of law by virtue of which an offender may receive a discounted sentence in consequence of assistance given (or offered) to the prosecutor or investigator.

## STEP 5  Reduction for guilty pleas

The court should take account of any potential reduction for a guilty plea in accordance with section 73 of the Sentencing Code and the guideline for Reduction in Sentence for a Guilty Plea [SG5-1–SG5-12].

Sentencing Guidelines

**STEP 6  Totality principle**

If sentencing an offender for more than one offence, or where the offender is already serving a sentence, consider whether the total sentence is just and proportionate to the overall offending behaviour in accordance with the *Totality* guideline [see **SG4**].

**STEP 7  Compensation and ancillary orders**

In all cases, the court must consider whether to make a compensation order and/or other ancillary orders.

*Compensation order*

The court should consider compensation orders in all cases where personal injury, loss or damage has resulted from the offence.

The court must give reasons if it decides not to award compensation in such cases (Sentencing Code, s.55).

**STEP 8  Reasons**

Section 52 of the Sentencing Code imposes a duty to give reasons for, and explain the effect of, the sentence.

**STEP 9  Consideration for time spent on bail (tagged curfew)**

The court must consider whether to give credit for time spent on bail in accordance with section 240A of the Criminal Justice Act 2003 and section 325 of the Sentencing Code.

**SG11-7**            Arson/Criminal Damage with Intent to Endanger Life or
                            Reckless as to Whether Life Endangered

*Criminal Damage Act 1971, s.1(2)*

**Effective from:** 01 October 2019

This is a Schedule 19 offence for the purposes of sections 274 and section 285 (required life sentence for offence carrying life sentence) of the Sentencing Code. This is a specified offence for the purposes of sections 266 and 279 (extended sentence for certain violent, sexual or terrorism offences) of the Sentencing Code.

Triable only on indictment
Maximum: Life imprisonment
Offence range: High level community order – 12 years' custody

Where offence committed in domestic context, refer to **Overarching principles – domestic abuse** [see **SG6**].

**STEP 1  Determining the offence category**

The court should determine the offence category with reference only to the factors in the tables below. In order to determine the category the court should assess **culpability** and **harm.**

| Within this guideline culpability is fixed: culpability A is for intent, culpability B is for recklessness. | |
| --- | --- |
| Culpability A | • Offender intended to endanger life |
| Culpability B | • Offender was reckless as to whether life was endangered |

| Harm |
| --- |
| The level of harm is assessed by weighing up all the factors of the case. |
| **Category 1**<br>• Very serious physical and/or psychological harm caused<br>• High risk of very serious physical and/or psychological harm<br>• Serious consequential economic or social impact of offence caused<br>• Very high value of damage caused |
| **Category 2**<br>• Significant physical and/or psychological harm caused<br>• Significant risk of serious physical and/or psychological harm<br>• Significant value of damage caused<br>• All other harm that falls between categories 1 and 3 |

> **Category 3**
> * No or minimal physical and/or psychological harm caused
> * Low risk of serious physical and/or psychological harm
> * Low value of damage caused

### STEP 2  Starting point and category range

Having determined the category at step one, the court should use the corresponding starting point to reach a sentence within the category range below. The starting point applies to all offenders irrespective of plea or previous convictions.

Where the offender is dependent on or has a propensity to misuse drugs or alcohol, which is linked to the offending, a community order with a drug rehabilitation requirement under under Part 10, or an alcohol treatment requirement under under Part 11, of Schedule 9 of the Sentencing Code may be a proper alternative to a short or moderate custodial sentence.

Where the offender suffers from a medical condition that is susceptible to treatment but does not warrant detention under a hospital order, a community order with a mental health treatment requirement under Part 9 of Schedule 9 of the Sentencing Code may be a proper alternative to a short or moderate custodial sentence.

**In exceptional cases within category 1A, sentences of above 12 years may be appropriate.**

| Harm | Culpability | |
|---|---|---|
| | **A** | **B** |
| Category 1 | **Starting point**<br>8 years' custody | **Starting point**<br>6 years' custody |
| | **Category range**<br>5 years – 12 years' custody | **Category range**<br>4 years – 10 years' custody |
| Category 2 | **Starting point**<br>6 years' custody | **Starting point**<br>4 years' custody |
| | **Category range**<br>4 – 8 years' custody | **Category range**<br>2 – 6 years' custody |
| Category 3 | **Starting point**<br>2 years' custody | **Starting point**<br>1 year's custody |
| | **Category range**<br>6 months – 4 years' custody | **Category range**<br>High level community order – 2 years 6 months' custody |

### Community Orders and Custodial Sentences

[For information on Community Orders, and Custodial Sentences see **SG9**.]

The court should then consider any adjustment for any aggravating or mitigating factors. Below is a **non-exhaustive** list of additional factual elements providing the context of the offence and factors relating to the offender.

Identify whether any combination of these, or other relevant factors, should result in an upward or downward adjustment from the starting point.

Care should be taken to avoid double counting factors already taken into account in assessing the level of harm at step one

### Additional factors affecting seriousness

#### Factors increasing seriousness

*Statutory aggravating factors*

* Previous convictions, having regard to a) the **nature** of the offence to which the conviction relates and its **relevance** to the current offence; and b) the **time** that has elapsed since the conviction
* Offence committed whilst on bail
* Offence motivated by, or demonstrating hostility based on any of the following characteristics or presumed characteristics of the victim: religion, race, disability, sexual orientation, or transgender identity

*Other aggravating factors*
- Commission of offence whilst under the influence of alcohol or drugs
- Revenge attack
- Significant degree of planning or premeditation
- Use of accelerant
- Fire set in or near a public amenity
- Victim is particularly vulnerable
- Offence committed within a domestic context
- Damage caused to heritage and/or cultural assets
- Multiple people endangered
- Significant impact on emergency services or resources
- Established evidence of community/wider impact
- Failure to comply with current court orders
- Offence committed on licence or post sentence supervision
- Offences taken into consideration

**Factors reducing seriousness or reflecting personal mitigation**
- No previous convictions or no relevant/recent convictions
- Offender's responsibility substantially reduced by mental disorder or learning disability
- Lack of premeditation
- Involved through coercion, intimidation or exploitation
- Remorse
- Good character and/or exemplary conduct
- Serious medical condition requiring urgent, intensive or long-term treatment
- Age and/or lack of maturity
- Sole or primary carer for dependent relatives
- Determination and/or demonstration of steps having been taken to address addiction or offending behaviour

### STEP 3  Consider any factors which indicate a reduction, such as assistance to the prosecution

The court should take into account section 74 of the Sentencing Code (reduction in sentence for assistance to prosecution) and any other rule of law by virtue of which an offender may receive a discounted sentence in consequence of assistance given (or offered) to the prosecutor or investigator.

### STEP 4  Reduction for guilty pleas

The court should take account of any potential reduction for a guilty plea in accordance with section 73 of the Sentencing Code and the guideline for Reduction in Sentence for a Guilty Plea [**SG5-1–SG5-12**].

### STEP 5  Dangerousness

The court should consider whether having regard to the criteria contained in Chapter 6 of Part 10 of the Sentencing Code it would be appropriate to impose a life sentence (sections 274 and 285) or an extended sentence (sections 266 and 279). When sentencing offenders to a life sentence under these provisions the notional determinate sentence should be used as the basis for the setting of a minimum term.

### STEP 6  Totality principle

If sentencing an offender for more than one offence, or where the offender is already serving a sentence, consider whether the total sentence is just and proportionate to the overall offending behaviour in accordance with the *Totality* guideline [see **SG4**.]

### STEP 7  Compensation and ancillary orders

In all cases, the court must consider whether to make a **compensation order** and/or other **ancillary orders**.

*Compensation order*

The court should consider compensation orders in all cases where personal injury, loss or damage has resulted from the offence. The court must give reasons if it decides not to award compensation in such cases.

### STEP 8  Reasons

Section 52 of the Sentencing Code imposes a duty to give reasons for, and explain the effect of, the sentence.

**STEP 9  Consideration for time spent on bail (tagged curfew)**

The court must consider whether to give credit for time spent on bail in accordance with section 240A of the Criminal Justice Act 2003 and section 325 of the Sentencing Code.

THREATS TO DESTROY OR DAMAGE PROPERTY                    **SG11-8**

*Criminal Damage Act 1971, s.2*

**Effective from:** 01 October 2019

Triable either way
Maximum: 10 years' custody
Offence range: Discharge – 4 years' custody

Where offence committed in domestic context, refer to **Overarching principles – domestic abuse.** [SG6].

In cases of threats to cause damage by fire, courts should consider requesting a report from: liaison and diversion services, a medical practitioner, or where it is necessary, ordering a psychiatric report, to ascertain both whether the offence is linked to a mental disorder or learning disability (to assist in the assessment of culpability) and whether any mental health disposal should be considered.

**STEP 1  Determining the offence category**

The court should determine the offence category with reference only to the factors in the tables below. In order to determine the category the court should assess **culpability** and **harm.**

The level of **culpability** is determined by weighing up all the factors of the case. **Where there are characteristics present which fall under different levels of culpability, the court should balance these characteristics to reach a fair assessment of the offender's culpability.**

| Culpability demonstrated by one or more of the following |
| --- |
| **A – High culpability**<br>• Significant planning or premeditation<br>• Offence motivated by revenge<br>• Offence committed to intimidate, coerce or control<br>• Threat to burn or bomb property |
| **B – Medium culpability**<br>Cases that fall between categories A and C because:<br>• Factors are present in A and C which balance each other out **and/or**<br>• The offender's culpability falls between the factors described in A and C |
| **C – Lesser culpability**<br>• Little or no planning; offence committed on impulse<br>• Offender's responsibility substantially reduced by mental disorder or learning disability<br>• Involved through coercion, intimidation or exploitation |

| Harm | |
| --- | --- |
| The level of harm is assessed by weighing up all the factors of the case. | |
| Category 1 | • Serious distress caused to the victim<br>• Serious disruption/inconvenience caused to others<br>• High level of consequential financial harm and inconvenience caused to the victim |
| Category 2 | • Harm that falls between categories 1 and 3 |
| Category 3 | • No or minimal distress caused to the victim |

Where the offender is dependent on or has a propensity to misuse drugs or alcohol, which is linked to the offending, a community order with a drug rehabilitation requirement under under Part 10, or an alcohol treatment requirement under under Part 11, of Schedule 9 of the Sentencing Code may be a proper alternative to a short or moderate custodial sentence.

Where the offender suffers from a medical condition that is susceptible to treatment but does not warrant detention under a hospital order, a community order with a mental health treatment requirement under Part 9 of Schedule 9 of the Sentencing Code may be a proper alternative to a short or moderate custodial sentence.

**STEP 2  Starting point and category range**

Having determined the category at step one, the court should use the corresponding starting point to reach a sentence within the category range below. The starting point applies to all offenders irrespective of plea or previous convictions.

| Harm | Culpability | | |
|---|---|---|---|
| | **A** | **B** | **C** |
| **Category 1** | **Starting point** 1 year 6 months' custody | **Starting point** 6 months' custody | **Starting point** High level community order |
| | **Category range** 6 months – 4 years' custody | **Category range** High level community order – 1 year 6 months' custody | **Category range** Medium level community order – 9 months' custody |
| **Category 2** | **Starting point** 6 months' custody | **Starting point** High level community order | **Starting point** Low level community order |
| | **Category range** High level community order – 1 year 6 months' custody | **Category range** Medium level community order – 9 months' custody | **Category range** Band C fine – High level community order |
| **Category 3** | **Starting point** High level community order | **Starting point** Low level community order | **Starting point** Band B fine |
| | **Category range** Medium level community order – 9 months' custody | **Category range** Band C fine – High level community order | **Category range** Discharge – Low level community order |

**Fines**

[For the standard schedule of fines see **SG2-5**.]

**Community Orders and Custodial Sentences**

[See Imposition of Community and Custodial Sentences at **SG9**.]

**Factors increasing or reducing seriousness**

The court should then consider any adjustment for any aggravating or mitigating factors. Below is a **non-exhaustive** list of additional factual elements providing the context of the offence and factors relating to the offender.

Identify whether any combination of these, or other relevant factors, should result in an upward or downward adjustment from the starting point.

**Factors increasing seriousness**

*Statutory aggravating factors*

- Previous convictions, having regard to
  - a) the **nature** of the offence to which the conviction relates and its **relevance** to the current offence; and
  - b) the **time** that has elapsed since the conviction
- Offence committed whilst on bail
- Offence motivated by, or demonstrating hostility based on any of the following characteristics or presumed characteristics of the victim: religion, race, disability, sexual orientation, or transgender identity

*Other aggravating factors*

- Commission of offence whilst under the influence of alcohol or drugs
- Victim is particularly vulnerable
- Offence committed in a domestic context
- Threats made in the presence of children
- Considerable damage threatened
- Damage threatened to heritage and/or cultural assets
- Established evidence of community/wider impact
- Failure to comply with current court orders

- Offence committed on licence or post sentence supervision
- Offences taken into consideration

**Factors reducing seriousness or reflecting personal mitigation**

- No previous convictions **or** no relevant/recent convictions
- Remorse
- Good character and/or exemplary conduct
- Serious medical condition requiring urgent, intensive or long-term treatment
- Age and/or lack of maturity
- Mental disorder or learning disability (where not taken into account at step one)
- Sole or primary carer for dependent relatives
- Determination and/or demonstration of steps having been taken to address addiction or offending behaviour

### STEP 3  Consider any factors which indicate a reduction, such as assistance to the prosecution

The court should take into account section 74 of the Sentencing Code (reduction in sentence for assistance to prosecution) and any other rule of law by virtue of which an offender may receive a discounted sentence in consequence of assistance given (or offered) to the prosecutor or investigator.

### STEP 4  Reduction for guilty pleas

The court should take account of any potential reduction for a guilty plea in accordance with section 73 of the Sentencing Code and the guideline for Reduction in Sentence for a Guilty Plea [SG5-1–SG5-12].

### STEP 5  Totality principle

If sentencing an offender for more than one offence, or where the offender is already serving a sentence, consider whether the total sentence is just and proportionate to the overall offending behaviour in accordance with the *Totality* guideline [see SG4].

### STEP 6  Compensation and ancillary orders

In all cases, the court must consider whether to make a **compensation order** and/or other **ancillary orders**.

*Compensation order*

The court should consider compensation orders in all cases where personal injury, loss or damage has resulted from the offence.

The court must give reasons if it decides not to award compensation in such cases (Sentencing Code, s.55).

### STEP 7  Reasons

Section 52 of the Sentencing Code imposes a duty to give reasons for, and explain the effect of, the sentence.

### STEP 8  Consideration for time spent on bail (tagged curfew)

The court must consider whether to give credit for time spent on bail in accordance with section 240A of the Criminal Justice Act 2003 and section 325 of the Sentencing Code.

Sentencing Guidelines

# PART 12   ASSAULT OFFENCES

**Effective from:** 01 July 2021

**SG12-1**

APPLICABILITY

[For the standard text on applicability see **SG0-4.**]

**SG12-2**

ASSAULT OCCASIONING ACTUAL BODILY HARM / RACIALLY OR
RELIGIOUSLY AGGRAVATED ABH

*Crime and Disorder Act 1998, s. 29, Offences against the Person Act 1861, s. 47*

**Effective from:** 01 July 2021

**Assault occasioning actual bodily harm,** Offences against the Person Act 1861 (section 47)

**Racially or religiously aggravated ABH,** Crime and Disorder Act 1998 (section 29)

Triable either way

**Section 47**
Maximum: 5 years' custody

Offence range: Fine – 4 years' custody

**Section 29**
Maximum: 7 years' custody

These are specified offences for the purposes of sections 266 and 279 (extended sentence for certain violent, sexual or terrorism offences) of the Sentencing Code.

**STEP 1   Determining the offence category**

The court should determine the offence category with reference **only** to the factors listed in the tables below. In order to determine the category the court should assess **culpability** and **harm.**

**Culpability**

The level of culpability is determined by weighing all the factors of the case. Where there are characteristics present which fall under different levels of culpability, the court should balance these characteristics giving appropriate weight to relevant factors to reach a fair assessment of the offender's culpability.

*A – High culpability*
- Significant degree of planning or premeditation
- Victim obviously vulnerable due to age, personal characteristics or circumstances
- Use of a highly dangerous weapon or weapon equivalent*
- Strangulation/suffocation/asphyxiation
- Leading role in group activity
- Prolonged/persistent assault

*B – Medium culpability*
- Use of a weapon or weapon equivalent which does not fall within category A
- Lesser role in group activity
- Cases falling between category A or C because:
    - Factors in both high and lesser categories are present which balance each other out; and/or
    - The offender's culpability falls between the factors as described in high and lesser culpability

*C – Lesser culpability*
- No weapon used
- Excessive self defence
- Impulsive/spontaneous and short-lived assault
- Mental disorder or learning disability, where linked to the commission of the offence

* A highly dangerous weapon can include weapons such as knives and firearms. Highly dangerous weapon equivalents can include corrosive substances (such as acid), whose dangerous nature must be substantially above and beyond the legislative definition of an offensive weapon which is; *'any article made or adapted for use for causing injury, or is intended by the person having it with him for such use'.* The court must determine whether the weapon or weapon equivalent is highly dangerous on the facts and circumstances of the case.

## Harm

*Category 1*
• Serious physical injury or serious psychological harm and/or substantial impact upon victim

*Category 2*
• Harm falling between categories 1 and 3

*Category 3*
• Some level of physical injury or psychological harm with limited impact upon victim

### STEP 2   Starting point and category range

Having determined the category, the court should use the corresponding starting points to reach a sentence within the category range below. The starting point applies to all offenders irrespective of plea or previous convictions. A case of particular gravity, reflected by multiple features of culpability in step one, could merit upward adjustment from the starting point before further adjustment for aggravating or mitigating features, set out below.

Sentencers should be aware that there is evidence of a disparity in sentence outcomes for this offence which indicates that a higher proportion of Black and Mixed ethnicity offenders receive an immediate custodial sentence than White, Asian and Chinese or Other ethnicity offenders. There may be many reasons for these differences, but in order to apply the guidelines fairly sentencers may find useful information and guidance at Chapter 8 paragraphs 185 to 193 of the Equal Treatment Bench Book.

| Harm | Culpability | | |
|---|---|---|---|
| | **A** | **B** | **C** |
| Harm 1 | **Starting point** 2 years 6 months' custody | **Starting point** 1 year 6 months' custody | **Starting point** 36 weeks' custody |
| | **Category range** 1 year 6 months' – 4 years' custody | **Category range** 36 weeks' – 2 years 6 months' custody | **Category range** High level community order – 1 year 6 months' custody |
| Harm 2 | **Starting point** 1 year 6 months' custody | **Starting point** 36 weeks' custody | **Starting point** High level community order |
| | **Category range** 36 weeks' – 2 years 6 months' custody | **Category range** High level community order – 1 year 6 months' custody | **Category range** Low level community order – 36 weeks' custody |
| Harm 3 | **Starting point** 36 weeks' custody | **Starting point** High level community order | **Starting point** Medium level community order |
| | **Category range** High level community order – 1 year 6 months' custody | **Category range** Low level community order – 36 weeks' custody | **Category range** Band B fine – 26 weeks' custody |

## Fines

[For the standard schedule of fines see **SG2-5**.]

## Community Orders and Custodial Sentences

[For the imposition of community orders, including the community orders table, see Imposition of Community and Custodial Sentences at **SG9-2**.

For the imposition of custodial sentences see Imposition of Community and Custodial Sentences at **SG9-3**.]

The table below contains a non-exhaustive list of additional factual elements providing the context of the offence and factors relating to the offender. Identify whether any combination of these, or other relevant factors, should result in an upward or downward adjustment from the starting point. In some cases, having considered these factors, it may be appropriate to move outside the identified category range.

**Factors increasing seriousness**

*Statutory aggravating factors:*

- Previous convictions, having regard to
  a) the **nature** of the offence to which the conviction relates and its **relevance** to the current offence; and
  b) the **time** that has elapsed since the conviction
- Offence committed whilst on bail
- Offence motivated by, or demonstrating hostility based on any of the following characteristics or presumed characteristics of the victim: disability, sexual orientation or transgender identity
- Offence was committed against an emergency worker acting in the exercise of functions as such a worker

*Other aggravating factors:*

- Deliberate spitting or coughing
- Offence committed against those working in the public sector or providing a service to the public or against a person coming to the assistance of an emergency worker
- Offence committed in prison (where not taken into account as a statutory aggravating factor)
- Offence committed in a domestic context
- History of violence or abuse towards victim by offender
- Presence of children
- Gratuitous degradation of victim
- Abuse of power and/or position of trust
- Any steps taken to prevent the victim reporting an incident, obtaining assistance and/or from assisting or supporting the prosecution
- Commission of offence whilst under the influence of alcohol/drugs
- Offence committed whilst on licence or subject to post sentence supervision
- Failure to comply with current court orders

**Factors reducing seriousness or reflecting personal mitigation**

- No previous convictions or no relevant/recent convictions
- Remorse
- Good character and/or exemplary conduct
- Significant degree of provocation
- History of significant violence or abuse towards the offender by the victim
- Age and/or lack of maturity
- Mental disorder or learning disability, where not linked to the commission of the offence
- Sole or primary carer for dependent relative(s)
- Determination and/or demonstration of steps taken to address addiction or offending behaviour
- Serious medical conditions requiring urgent, intensive or long-term treatment

## STEP 3    Aggravated offences

### Section 29 Racially or Religiously Aggravated Offences Only

Having determined the category of the basic offence to identify the sentence of a non-aggravated offence, the court should now consider the level of racial or religious aggravation involved and apply an appropriate uplift to the sentence in accordance with the guidance below. The following is a list of factors which the court should consider to determine the level of aggravation. Where there are characteristics present which fall under different levels of aggravation, the court should balance these to reach a fair assessment of the level of aggravation present in the offence.

**Maximum sentence for the aggravated offence on indictment is 7 years' custody (maximum when tried summarily is 6 months' custody)**

Care should be taken to avoid double counting factors already taken into account in assessing the level of harm at step one

| High Level of Racial or Religious Aggravation | Sentence Uplift |
|---|---|
| • Racial or religious aggravation was the predominant motivation for the offence.<br>• Offender was a member of, or was associated with, a group promoting hostility based on race or religion.<br>• Aggravated nature of the offence caused severe distress to the victim or the victim's family (over and above the distress already considered at step one).<br>• Aggravated nature of the offence caused serious fear and distress throughout local community or more widely. | Increase the length of custodial sentence if already considered for the basic offence or consider a custodial sentence, if not already considered for the basic offence. |
| **Medium Level of Racial or Religious Aggravation** | **Sentence Uplift** |
| • Racial or religious aggravation formed a significant proportion of the offence as a whole.<br>• Aggravated nature of the offence caused some distress to the victim or the victim's family (over and above the distress already considered at step one).<br>• Aggravated nature of the offence caused some fear and distress throughout local community or more widely. | Consider a significantly more onerous penalty of the same type or consider a more severe type of sentence than for the basic offence. |
| **Low Level of Racial or Religious Aggravation** | **Sentence Uplift** |
| • Aggravated element formed a minimal part of the offence as a whole.<br>• Aggravated nature of the offence caused minimal or no distress to the victim or the victim's family (over and above the distress already considered at step one). | Consider a more onerous penalty of the same type identified for the basic offence. |

Magistrates may find that, although the appropriate sentence for the basic offence would be within their powers, the appropriate increase for the aggravated offence would result in a sentence in excess of their powers. If so, they must commit for sentence to the Crown Court.

**The sentencer should state in open court that the offence was aggravated by reason of race or religion, and should also state what the sentence would have been without that element of aggravation.**

**STEP 4   Consider any other factors which indicate a reduction, such as assistance to the prosecution**

The court should take into account section 74 of the Sentencing Code (reduction in sentence for assistance to prosecution) and any other rule of law by virtue of which an offender may receive a discounted sentence in consequence of assistance given (or offered) to the prosecutor or investigator.

**STEP 5   Reduction for guilty pleas**

The court should take account of any potential reduction for a guilty plea in accordance with section 73 of the Sentencing Code and the Reduction in Sentence for a Guilty Plea guideline.

**STEP 6   Dangerousness**

The court should consider whether having regard to the criteria contained in Chapter 6 of Part 10 of the Sentencing Code it would be appropriate to impose an extended sentence (sections 266 and 279).

**STEP 7   Totality principle**

If sentencing an offender for more than one offence, or where the offender is already serving a sentence, consider whether the total sentence is just and proportionate to the offending behaviour. See Totality guideline [see **SG4**].

**STEP 8   Compensation and ancillary orders**

In all cases, the court should consider whether to make compensation and/or other ancillary orders. The court must give reasons if it decides not to order compensation (Sentencing Code, s. 55).

• Ancillary orders – Magistrates' Court
• Ancillary orders – Crown Court Compendium

**STEP 9   Reasons**

Section 52 of the Sentencing Code imposes a duty to give reasons for, and explain the effect of, the sentence.

**STEP 10   Consideration for time spent on bail (tagged curfew)**

The court must consider whether to give credit for time spent on bail in accordance with section 240A of the Criminal Justice Act 2003 and section 325 of the Sentencing Code.

**SG 12-3**                   Assault with Intent to Resist Arrest

*Offences against the Person Act 1861, s. 38*

**Effective from:** 01 July 2021

Triable either way
Maximum: 2 years' custody
Offence Range: Fine –1 year 3 months' custody

This is a specified offence for the purposes of sections 266 and 279 (extended sentence for certain violent, sexual or terrorism offences) of the Sentencing Code.

**STEP 1   Determining the offence category**

The court should determine the offence category with reference **only** to the factors listed in the tables below. In order to determine the category the court should assess **culpability** and **harm.**

**Culpability**

The level of culpability is determined by weighing all the factors of the case. Where there are characteristics present which fall under different levels of culpability, the court should balance these characteristics to reach a fair assessment of the offender's culpability.

*A – High culpability*
- Intention to cause fear of serious harm, including disease transmission
- Victim obviously vulnerable due to age, personal characteristics or circumstances
- Prolonged/persistent assault
- Use of substantial force
- Threatened or actual use of weapon or weapon equivalent*
- Strangulation/suffocation/asphyxiation
- Leading role in group activity

*B – Lesser culpability*
- Lesser role in group activity
- Mental disorder or learning disability, where linked to the commission of the offence
- All other cases not captured by category A factors

* Examples of a weapon equivalent can include but are not limited to: a shod foot, use of acid, use of animal in commission of offence.

**Harm**

In assessing the level of harm, consideration should be given to:

- the number of injuries
- severity of injury and pain suffered and
- the duration or longevity of any psychological harm or distress caused.

*Category 1*
- More than minor physical or psychological harm/distress

*Category 2*
- Minor physical or psychological harm/distress

*Category 3*
- No/very low level of physical harm and/or distress

**STEP 2   Starting point and category range**

Having determined the category, the court should use the corresponding starting points to reach a sentence within the category range below. The starting point applies to all offenders irrespective of plea or previous convictions. A case of particular gravity, reflected by multiple features of culpability in step one, could merit upward adjustment from the starting point before further adjustment for aggravating or mitigating features, set out below.

Sentencers should be aware that there is evidence of a disparity in sentence outcomes for this offence which indicates that a higher proportion of Black and Mixed ethnicity offenders receive an immediate custodial sentence than White, Asian and Chinese or Other ethnicity offenders. There may be many reasons for these differences, but in order to apply the guidelines fairly sentencers may find useful information and guidance at Chapter 8 paragraphs 185 to 193 of the Equal Treatment Bench Book.

| Harm | Culpability | |
|---|---|---|
| | **A** | **B** |
| Harm 1 | **Starting point**<br>36 weeks' custody | **Starting point**<br>26 weeks' custody |
| | **Category range**<br>26 weeks' custody – 1 year 3 months'<br>custody | **Category range**<br>High level community order –<br>36 weeks' custody |
| Harm 2 | **Starting point**<br>26 weeks' custody | **Starting point**<br>High level community order |
| | **Category range**<br>High level community order – 36 weeks'<br>custody | **Category range**<br>Low level community order – 26 weeks'<br>custody |
| Harm 3 | **Starting point**<br>High level community order | **Starting point**<br>Medium level community order |
| | *Category range*<br>Low level community order – 26 weeks'<br>custody | **Category range**<br>Band B fine – High level community order |

**Fines**

[For the standard schedule of fines see SG2-5.]

**Community Orders and Custodial Sentences**

[For the imposition of community orders, including the community orders table, see Imposition of Community and Custodial Sentences at SG9-2.

For the imposition of custodial sentences see Imposition of Community and Custodial Sentences at SG9-3.]

The table below contains a non-exhaustive list of additional factual elements providing the context of the offence and factors relating to the offender. Identify whether any combination of these, or other relevant factors, should result in an upward or downward adjustment from the starting point. In some cases, having considered these factors, it may be appropriate to move outside the identified category range.

**Factors increasing seriousness**

*Statutory aggravating factors:*

- Previous convictions, having regard to
  a) the **nature** of the offence to which the conviction relates and its **relevance** to the current offence; and
  b) the **time** that has elapsed since the conviction
- Offence committed whilst on bail
- Offence motivated by, or demonstrating hostility based on any of the following characteristics or presumed characteristics of the victim: race, religion, disability, sexual orientation or transgender identity

*Other aggravating factors:*

- Deliberate spitting or coughing (where not taken into account at step one)
- Biting
- Presence of children
- Gratuitous degradation of victim
- Any steps taken to prevent the victim reporting an incident, obtaining assistance and/or from assisting or supporting the prosecution
- Commission of offence whilst under the influence of alcohol/drugs
- Offence committed whilst on licence or subject to post sentence supervision
- Failure to comply with current court orders

**Factors reducing seriousness or reflecting personal mitigation**

- No previous convictions or no relevant/recent convictions
- Remorse
- Good character and/or exemplary conduct
- Age and/or lack of maturity
- Mental disorder or learning disability, where not linked to the commission of the offence
- Sole or primary carer for dependent relative(s)
- Determination and/or demonstration of steps taken to address addiction or offending behaviour
- Serious medical conditions requiring urgent, intensive or long-term treatment

### STEP 3  Consider any other factors which indicate a reduction, such as assistance to the prosecution

The court should take into account section 74 of the Sentencing Code (reduction in sentence for assistance to prosecution) and any other rule of law by virtue of which an offender may receive a discounted sentence in consequence of assistance given (or offered) to the prosecutor or investigator.

### STEP 4  Reduction for guilty pleas

The court should take account of any potential reduction for a guilty plea in accordance with section 73 of the Sentencing Code and the Reduction in Sentence for a Guilty Plea guideline.

### STEP 5  Dangerousness

The court should consider whether having regard to the criteria contained in Chapter 6 of Part 10 of the Sentencing Code it would be appropriate to impose an extended sentence (sections 266 and 279).

### STEP 6  Totality principle

If sentencing an offender for more than one offence, or where the offender is already serving a sentence, consider whether the total sentence is just and proportionate to the offending behaviour. See Totality guideline [see **SG4**].

### STEP 7  Compensation and ancillary orders

In all cases, the court should consider whether to make compensation and/or other ancillary orders. The court must give reasons if it decides not to order compensation (Sentencing Code, s. 55).

- Ancillary orders – Magistrates' Court
- Ancillary orders – Crown Court Compendium

### STEP 8  Reasons

Section 52 of the Sentencing Code imposes a duty to give reasons for, and explain the effect of, the sentence.

### STEP 9  Consideration for time spent on bail (tagged curfew)

The court must consider whether to give credit for time spent on bail in accordance with section 240A of the Criminal Justice Act 2003 and section 325 of the Sentencing Code.

**SG12-4**
ASSAULTS ON EMERGENCY WORKERS

See **SG12-7**

**SG12-5**
ATTEMPTED MURDER

*Criminal Attempts Act 1981, s. 1(1)*

**Effective from:** 01 July 2021

Triable only on indictment
Maximum: Life imprisonment
Offence range: 3 – 40 years' custody

This is a Schedule 19 offence for the purposes of sections 274 and 285 (required life sentence for offence carrying life sentence) of the Sentencing Code.

For offences committed on or after 3 December 2012, this is an offence listed in Part 1 of Schedule 15 for the purposes of sections 273 and 283 (life sentence for second listed offence) of the Sentencing Code.

This is a specified offence for the purposes of sections 266 and 279 (extended sentence for certain violent, sexual or terrorism offences) of the Sentencing Code.

Where the offence has a terrorist connection this is an offence listed in Schedule 13 for the purposes of sections 265 and 278 (required special sentence for certain offenders of particular concern) of the Sentencing Code.

## STEP 1   Determining the offence category

The characteristics below are indications of the level of culpability that may attach to the offender's conduct. Where there are characteristics present which fall into both higher and lower categories, the court must carefully weigh those characteristics to reach a fair assessment of the category which best reflects the offender's overall culpability in all the circumstances of the case. The court may then adjust the starting point for that category to reflect the presence of characteristics from another category.

Culpability demonstrated by one or more of the following:

### A – Very high culpability

- Abduction of the victim with intent to murder
- Attempted murder of a child
- Offence motivated by or involves sexual or sadistic conduct
- Offence involves the use of a firearm or explosive or fire
- Offence committed for financial gain
- Attempted murder of a police officer or prison officer in the course of their duty
- Offence committed for the purpose of advancing a political, religious, racial or ideological cause
- Offence intended to obstruct or interfere with the course of justice
- Offence motivated by racial or religious hostility or hostility related to victim's sexual orientation, disability or transgender identity

### B – High culpability

- Offender took a knife or other weapon to the scene intending to commit any offence or have it available to use as a weapon, and used that knife or other weapon in committing the offence
- Planning or premeditation of murder

### C – Medium culpability

- Use of weapon not in category A or B
- Lack of premeditation/spontaneous attempt to kill

### D – Lesser culpability

- Excessive self defence
- Offender acted in response to prolonged or extreme violence or abuse by victim
- Offender's responsibility substantially reduced by mental disorder or learning disability
- Genuine belief by the offender that the offence was an act of mercy

### Harm

#### Category 1

- Injury results in physical or psychological harm resulting in lifelong dependency on third party care or medical treatment
- Offence results in a permanent, irreversible injury or psychological condition which has a substantial and long term effect on the victim's ability to carry out their normal day to day activities or on their ability to work

#### Category 2

- Serious physical or psychological harm not in category 1

#### Category 3

- All other cases

## STEP 2   Starting point and category range

Having determined the category, the court should use the corresponding starting points to reach a sentence within the category range below before further adjustment for aggravating or mitigating features, set out below.

Sentencers should be aware that there is evidence of a disparity in sentence outcomes for this offence which indicates that for Black and Asian offenders custodial sentence lengths have on average been longer than for White offenders. There may be many reasons for these differences, but in order to apply the guidelines fairly sentencers may find useful information and guidance at Chapter 8 paragraphs 185 to 193 of the Equal Treatment Bench Book.

For offences involving an extreme nature of one or more very high or high culpability factors a sentence higher than the offence range or an extended or life sentence may be appropriate. Extended and life sentences are dealt with at Step 5 of the guideline.

| Harm | Culpability | | | |
|---|---|---|---|---|
| | **A** | **B** | **C** | **D** |
| Harm 1 | **Starting point** 35 years' custody | **Starting point** 30 years' custody | **Starting point** 25 years' custody | **Starting point** 14 years' custody |
| | **Category range** 30 – 40 years' custody | **Category range** 25 – 35 years' custody | **Category range** 20 – 30 years' custody | **Category range** 10 – 20 years' custody |
| Harm 2 | **Starting point** 30 years' custody | **Starting point** 25 years' custody | **Starting point** 20 years' custody | **Starting point** 8 years' custody |
| | **Category range** 25 – 35 years' custody | **Category range** 20 – 30 years' custody | **Category range** 15 – 25 years' custody | **Category range** 5 – 12 years' custody |
| Harm 3 | **Starting point** 25 years' custody | **Starting point** 20 years' custody | **Starting point** 10 years' custody | **Starting point** 5 years' custody |
| | **Category range** 20 – 30 years' custody | **Category range** 15 – 25 years' custody | **Category range** 7 – 15 years' custody | **Category range** 3 – 6 years' custody |

> *Note:*
>
> Note: The table is for a single offence against a single victim. Where another offence or offences arise out of the same incident or facts, concurrent sentences **reflecting the overall criminality** of offending will ordinarily be appropriate: please refer to the *Totality* guideline and step 7 of this guideline.

**Custodial Sentences**

[For the imposition of custodial sentences see Imposition of Community and Custodial Sentences at SG9-3.]

The table below contains a non-exhaustive list of additional factual elements providing the context of the offence and factors relating to the offender. Identify whether any combination of these, or other relevant factors, should result in an upward or downward adjustment from the starting point. In some cases, having considered these factors, it may be appropriate to move outside the identified category range.

**Factors increasing seriousness**

*Statutory aggravating factors:*
- Previous convictions, having regard to
  a) the **nature** of the offence to which the conviction relates and its **relevance** to the current offence; and
  b) the **time** that has elapsed since the convictionOffence committed whilst on bail
- Offence demonstrating hostility based on any of the following characteristics or presumed characteristics of the victim: religion, race, disability, sexual orientation, or transgender identity

*Other aggravating factors:*
- Offence committed against those working in the public sector or providing a service to the public
- Offence committed in prison
- Offence committed in a domestic context
- History of violence or abuse towards victim by offender (where not taken into account at step one)
- Abuse of power and/or position of trust
- Gratuitous degradation of victim
- Others put at risk of harm by the offence
- Use of duress or threats against another person to facilitate the commission of the offence
- Actions after the event (including but not limited to attempts to cover up/conceal evidence)
- Steps taken to prevent the victim from seeking or receiving medical assistance

- Commission of offence whilst under the influence of alcohol/drugs
- Offence committed whilst on licence or subject to post sentence supervision
- Failure to comply with current court orders

**Factors reducing seriousness or reflecting personal mitigation**

- No previous convictions or no relevant/recent convictions
- Significant degree of provocation (including due to prolonged and/or excessive stress linked to circumstances of offence)
- History of significant violence or abuse towards the offender by the victim (where not taken into account at step one)
- Attempt by offender to give assistance/summon help when the attempted murder failed
- Remorse
- Good character and/or exemplary conduct
- Age and/or lack of maturity
- Mental disorder or learning disability, where not linked to the commission of the offence (where not taken into account at step one)
- Sole or primary carer for dependent relative(s)
- Serious medical conditions requiring urgent, intensive or long-term treatment

**STEP 3    Consider any other factors which indicate a reduction, such as assistance to the prosecution**

The court should take into account section 74 of the Sentencing Code (reduction in sentence for assistance to prosecution) and any other rule of law by virtue of which an offender may receive a discounted sentence in consequence of assistance given (or offered) to the prosecutor or investigator.

**STEP 4    Reduction for guilty pleas**

The court should take account of any potential reduction for a guilty plea in accordance with section 73 of the Sentencing Code and the Reduction in Sentence for a Guilty Plea guideline.

**STEP 5    Dangerousness**

The court should consider:

1) whether having regard to the criteria contained in Chapter 6 of Part 10 of the Sentencing Code it would be appropriate to impose a life sentence (sections 274 and 285)
2) whether having regard to sections 273 and 283 of the Sentencing Code it would be appropriate to impose a life sentence
3) whether having regard to the criteria contained in Chapter 6 of Part 10 of the Sentencing Code it would be appropriate to impose an extended sentence (sections 266 and 279)

When sentencing offenders to a life sentence under these provisions, the notional determinate sentence should be used as the basis for the setting of a minimum term.

**STEP 6    Required special sentence for certain offenders of particular concern**

Where the offence has a terrorist connection and satisfies the criteria in section 278 of the Sentencing Code and the court does not impose a sentence of imprisonment for life or an extended sentence, but does impose a period of imprisonment, the term of the sentence must be equal to the aggregate of the appropriate custodial term and a further period of 1 year for which the offender is to be subject to a licence (sections 265 and 278 of the Sentencing Code).

**STEP 7    Totality principle**

If sentencing an offender for more than one offence, or where the offender is already serving a sentence, consider whether the total sentence is just and proportionate to the offending behaviour. See Totality guideline [see **SG4**].

**STEP 8    Compensation and ancillary orders**

In all cases, the court should consider whether to make compensation and/or other ancillary orders. The court must give reasons if it decides not to order compensation (Sentencing Code, s. 55).

- Ancillary orders – Crown Court Compendium

**STEP 9    Reasons**

Section 52 of the Sentencing Code imposes a duty to give reasons for, and explain the effect of, the sentence.

CAUSING GRIEVOUS BODILY HARM WITH INTENT TO DO GRIEVOUS BODILY
HARM/WOUNDING WITH INTENT TO DO GBH

*Offences against the Person Act 1861, s. 18*

**Effective from:** 01 July 2021

Triable only on indictment
Maximum: Life imprisonment
Offence range: 2 – 16 years' custody

This is a Schedule 19 offence for the purposes of sections 274 and 285 (required life sentence for offence carrying life sentence) of the Sentencing Code.

For offences committed on or after 3 December 2012, this is an offence listed in Part 1 of Schedule 15 for the purposes of sections 273 and 283 (life sentence for second listed offence) of the Sentencing Code.

This is a specified offence for the purposes of sections 266 and 279 (extended sentence for certain violent, sexual or terrorism offences) of the Sentencing Code.

**STEP 1    Determining the offence category**

The court should determine the offence category with reference **only** to the factors listed in the tables below. In order to determine the category the court should assess **culpability** and **harm.**

**Culpability**

The level of culpability is determined by weighing all the factors of the case. Where there are characteristics present which fall under different levels of culpability, the court should balance these characteristics giving appropriate weight to relevant factors to reach a fair assessment of the offender's culpability.

*A – High culpability*
• Significant degree of planning or premeditation
• Victim obviously vulnerable due to age, personal characteristics or circumstances
• Use of a highly dangerous weapon or weapon equivalent*
• Strangulation/suffocation/asphyxiation
• Leading role in group activity
• Prolonged/persistent assault
• Revenge

*B – Medium culpability*
• Use of a weapon or weapon equivalent which does not fall within category A
• Lesser role in group activity
• Cases falling between category high and low culpability because:
    • Factors in both high and lesser categories are present which balance each other out; **and/or**
    • The offender's culpability falls between the factors as described in high and lesser culpability

*C – Lesser culpability*
• No weapon used
• Excessive self defence
• Offender acted in response to prolonged or extreme violence or abuse by victim
• Mental disorder or learning disability, where linked to the commission of the offence

* A highly dangerous weapon can include weapons such as knives and firearms. Highly dangerous weapon equivalents can include corrosive substances (such as acid), whose dangerous nature must be substantially above and beyond the legislative definition of an offensive weapon which is; *'any article made or adapted for use for causing injury, or is intended by the person having it with him for such use'.* The court must determine whether the weapon or weapon equivalent is highly dangerous on the facts and circumstances of the case.

**Harm**

All cases will involve 'really serious harm', which can be physical or psychological, or wounding. The court should assess the level of harm caused with reference to the impact on the victim

*Category 1*
• Particularly grave or life-threatening injury caused
• Injury results in physical or psychological harm resulting in lifelong dependency on third party care or medical treatment

- Offence results in a permanent, irreversible injury or psychological condition which has a substantial and long term effect on the victim's ability to carry out their normal day to day activities or on their ability to work

## Category 2
- Grave injury
- Offence results in a permanent, irreversible injury or condition not falling within category 1

## Category 3
- All other cases of really serious harm
- All other cases of wounding

### STEP 2   Starting point and category range

Having determined the category, the court should use the corresponding starting points to reach a sentence within the category range below. The starting point applies to all offenders irrespective of plea or previous convictions. A case of particular gravity, reflected by multiple features of culpability in step one, could merit upward adjustment from the starting point before further adjustment for aggravating or mitigating features, set out below.

Sentencers should be aware that there is evidence of a disparity in sentence outcomes for this offence which indicates that for Black and Asian offenders immediate custodial sentence lengths have on average been longer than for White, Mixed and Chinese or Other ethnicity offenders. There may be many reasons for these differences, but in order to apply the guidelines fairly sentencers may find useful information and guidance at Chapter 8 paragraphs 185 to 193 of the Equal Treatment Bench Book.

**For category A1 offences the extreme nature of one or more high culpability factors or the extreme impact caused by a combination of high culpability factors may attract a sentence higher than the category range**

| Harm | Culpability | | |
|---|---|---|---|
| | **A** | **B** | **C** |
| Category 1 | **Starting point** 12 years' custody | **Starting point** 7 years' custody | **Starting point** 5 years' custody |
| | **Category range** 10 – 16 years' custody | **Category range** 6 – 10 years' custody | **Category range** 4 – 7 years' custody |
| Category 2 | **Starting point** 7 years' custody | **Starting point** 5 years' custody | **Starting point** 4 years' custody |
| | **Category range** 6 – 10 years' custody | **Category range** 4 – 7 years' custody | **Category range** 3 – 6 years' custody |
| Category 3 | **Starting point** 5 years' custody | **Starting point** 4 years' custody | **Starting point** 3 years' custody |
| | **Category range** 4 –7 years' custody | **Category range** 3 – 6 years' custody | **Category range** 2 – 4 years' custody |

### Custodial Sentences

For the imposition of custodial sentences see Imposition of Community and Custodial Sentences at SG9-3.

The table below contains a non-exhaustive list of additional factual elements providing the context of the offence and factors relating to the offender. Identify whether any combination of these, or other relevant factors, should result in an upward or downward adjustment from the starting point. In some cases, having considered these factors, it may be appropriate to move outside the identified category range.

### Factors increasing seriousness

*Statutory aggravating factors:*
- Previous convictions,  having regard to
  a)  the **nature** of the offence to which the conviction relates and its **relevance** to the current offence; and
  b)  the **time** that has elapsed since the conviction
- Offence committed whilst on bail
- Offence motivated by, or demonstrating hostility based on any of the following characteristics or presumed characteristics of the victim: race, religion, disability, sexual orientation or transgender identity

- Offence was committed against an emergency worker acting in the exercise of functions as such a worker

*Other aggravating factors:*

- Offence committed against those working in the public sector or providing a service to the public or against a person coming to the assistance of an emergency worker
- Offence committed in prison (where not taken into account as a statutory aggravating factor)
- Offence committed in a domestic context
- History of violence or abuse towards victim by offender (where not taken into account at step one)
- Presence of children
- Gratuitous degradation of victim
- Abuse of power and/or position of trust
- Any steps taken to prevent the victim reporting an incident, obtaining assistance and/or from assisting or supporting the prosecution
- Commission of offence whilst under the influence of alcohol/drugs
- Offence committed whilst on licence or subject to post sentence supervision
- Failure to comply with current court orders

**Factors reducing seriousness or reflecting personal mitigation**

- No previous convictions or no relevant/recent convictions
- Remorse
- Good character and/or exemplary conduct
- Significant degree of provocation
- History of significant violence or abuse towards the offender by the victim (where not taken into account at step one)
- Age and/or lack of maturity
- Mental disorder or learning disability, where not linked to the commission of the offence
- Sole or primary carer for dependent relative(s)
- Determination and/or demonstration of steps taken to address addiction or offending behaviour
- Serious medical conditions requiring urgent, intensive or long-term treatment

**STEP 3   Consider any other factors which indicate a reduction, such as assistance to the prosecution**

The court should take into account section 74 of the Sentencing Code (reduction in sentence for assistance to prosecution) and any other rule of law by virtue of which an offender may receive a discounted sentence in consequence of assistance given (or offered) to the prosecutor or investigator.

**STEP 4   Reduction for guilty pleas**

The court should take account of any potential reduction for a guilty plea in accordance with section 73 of the Sentencing Code and the Reduction in Sentence for a Guilty Plea guideline.

**STEP 5   Dangerousness**

The court should consider:

1) whether having regard to the criteria contained in Chapter 6 of Part 10 of the Sentencing Code it would be appropriate to impose a life sentence (sections 274 and 285)
2) whether having regard to sections 273 and 283 of the Sentencing Code it would be appropriate to impose a life sentence.
3) whether having regard to the criteria contained in Chapter 6 of Part 10 of the Sentencing Code it would be appropriate to impose an extended sentence (sections 266 and 279)

When sentencing offenders to a life sentence under these provisions, the notional determinate sentence should be used as the basis for the setting of a minimum term.

**STEP 6   Totality principle**

If sentencing an offender for more than one offence, or where the offender is already serving a sentence, consider whether the total sentence is just and proportionate to the offending behaviour. See Totality guideline [see **SG4**].

**STEP 7   Compensation and ancillary orders**

In all cases, the court should consider whether to make compensation and/or other ancillary orders. The court must give reasons if it decides not to order compensation (Sentencing Code, s. 55).

- Ancillary orders – Crown Court Compendium

**STEP 8    Reasons**

Section 52 of the Sentencing Code imposes a duty to give reasons for, and explain the effect of, the sentence.

**STEP 9    Consideration for time spent on bail (tagged curfew)**

The court must consider whether to give credit for time spent on bail in accordance with section 240A of the Criminal Justice Act 2003 and section 325 of the Sentencing Code.

**STEP 10    Consideration for time spent on bail (tagged curfew)**

The court must consider whether to give credit for time spent on bail in accordance with section 240A of the Criminal Justice Act 2003 and section 325 of the Sentencing Code.

COMMON ASSAULT/RACIALLY OR RELIGIOUSLY AGGRAVATED COMMON           **SG12-7**
ASSAULT/COMMON ASSAULT ON EMERGENCY WORKER

*Assaults on Emergency Workers (Offences) Act 2018, s. 1, Crime and Disorder*
*Act 1998, s. 29, Criminal Justice Act 1988, s. 39*

**Effective from:** 01 July 2021

**Common Assault**, Criminal Justice Act 1988 (section 39)
**Racially/religiously aggravated common assault**, Crime and Disorder Act 1998 (section 29)

**Assaults on emergency workers,** Assaults on Emergency Workers (Offences) Act 2018 (section 1)

**Section 39**
Triable only summarily
Maximum: 6 months' custody

Offence range: Discharge – 26 weeks' custody

**Racially or religiously aggravated offence – Section 29**
Triable either way
Maximum: 2 years' custody

**Offence committed against an emergency worker – Section 1**
Triable either way
Maximum: 1 year's custody

Racially or religiously aggravated common assault is a specified offence for the purposes of sections 266 and 279 (extended sentence for certain violent, sexual or terrorism offences) of the Sentencing Code.

**STEP 1    Determining the offence category**

The court should determine the offence category with reference **only** to the factors listed in the tables below. In order to determine the category the court should assess **culpability** and **harm**.

**Culpability**

The level of culpability is determined by weighing all the factors of the case. **Where there are characteristics present which fall under different levels of culpability, the court should balance these characteristics to reach a fair assessment of the offender's culpability.**

*A – High culpability*

- Intention to cause fear of serious harm, including disease transmission
- Victim obviously vulnerable due to age, personal characteristics or circumstances
- Prolonged/ persistent assault
- Use of substantial force
- Strangulation/ suffocation/ asphyxiation
- Threatened or actual use of weapon or weapon equivalent*
- Leading role in group activity

*B – Lesser culpability*

- Lesser role in group activity
- Mental disorder or learning disability, where linked to the commission of the offence
- Excessive self defence
- All other cases not captured by category A factors

*Examples of a weapon equivalent can include but are not limited to: a shod foot, use of acid, use of animal in commission of offence.

## Harm

In assessing the level of harm, consideration should be given to:

- the number of injuries
- severity of injury and pain suffered
- duration or longevity of any psychological harm or distress caused

### Category 1

- More than minor physical or psychological harm/distress

### Category 2

- Minor physical or psychological harm/distress

### Category 3

- No/very low level of physical harm and/or distress

## STEP 2   Starting point and category range

Having determined the category, the court should use the corresponding starting points to reach a sentence within the category range below. The starting point applies to all offenders irrespective of plea or previous convictions. A case of particular gravity, reflected by multiple features of culpability in step one, could merit upward adjustment from the starting point before further adjustment for aggravating or mitigating features, set out below.

| Harm | Culpability | |
|---|---|---|
| | **A** | **B** |
| Harm 1 | **Starting point**<br>High level community order | **Starting point**<br>Medium level community order |
| | **Category range**<br>Low level community order – 26 weeks' custody | **Category range**<br>Low level community order – 16 weeks' custody |
| Harm 2 | **Starting point**<br>Medium level community order | **Starting point**<br>Low level community order |
| | **Category range**<br>Low level community order – 16 weeks' custody | **Category range**<br>Band C fine – High level community order |
| Harm 3 | **Starting point**<br>Low level community order | **Starting point**<br>Band C fine |
| | **Category range**<br>Band C fine – High level community order | **Category range**<br>Discharge – Low level community order |

## Fines

[For the standard schedule of fines see SG2-5.]

## Community Orders and Custodial Sentences

[For the imposition of community orders, including the community orders table, see Imposition of Community and Custodial Sentences at SG9-2.

For the imposition of custodial sentences see Imposition of Community and Custodial Sentences at SG9-3.]

The table below contains a non-exhaustive list of additional factual elements providing the context of the offence and factors relating to the offender. Identify whether any combination of these, or other relevant factors, should result in an upward or downward adjustment from the starting point. In some cases, having considered these factors, it may be appropriate to move outside the identified category range.

**Factors increasing seriousness**

*Statutory aggravating factors:*

- Previous convictions , having regard to
  a) the **nature** of the offence to which the conviction relates and its **relevance** to the current offence; and
  b) the **time** that has elapsed since the conviction
- Offence committed whilst on bail
- Offence motivated by, or demonstrating hostility based on any of the following characteristics or presumed characteristics of the victim: disability, sexual orientation or transgender identity

*Other aggravating factors:*

- Deliberate spitting or coughing (where not taken into account at step one)
- Biting
- Offence committed against those working in the public sector or providing a service to the public or against a person coming to the assistance of an emergency worker
- Offence committed in prison
- Presence of children
- Offence committed in a domestic context
- Gratuitous degradation of victim
- Abuse of power and/or position of trust
- Any steps taken to prevent the victim reporting an incident, obtaining assistance and/or from assisting or supporting the prosecution
- Commission of offence whilst under the influence of alcohol/drugs
- Offence committed whilst on licence or subject to post sentence supervision
- Failure to comply with current court orders

**Factors reducing seriousness or reflecting personal mitigation**

- No previous convictions or no relevant/recent convictions
- Remorse
- Good character and/or exemplary conduct
- Significant degree of provocation
- Age and/or lack of maturity
- Mental disorder or learning disability, where not linked to the commission of the offence
- Sole or primary carer for dependent relative(s)
- Determination and/or demonstration of steps taken to address addiction or offending behaviour
- Serious medical conditions requiring urgent, intensive or long-term treatment

## STEP 3    Aggravated offences

**Racially or Religiously Aggravated Offences**

Having determined the category of the basic offence to identify the sentence of a non-aggravated offence, the court should now consider the level of racial or religious aggravation involved and apply an appropriate uplift to the sentence in accordance with the guidance below. The following is a list of factors which the court should consider to determine the level of aggravation. Where there are characteristics present which fall under different levels of aggravation, the court should balance these to reach a fair assessment of the level of aggravation present in the offence.

Maximum sentence for the racially or religiously aggravated offence is 2 years' custody

Maximum sentence for the aggravated offence of assault on an emergency worker is 1 year's custody

Care should be taken to avoid double counting factors already taken into account in assessing the level of harm at step one

Sentencing Guidelines

| High Level of Racial or Religious Aggravation | Sentence Uplift |
|---|---|
| • Racial or religious aggravation was the predominant motivation for the offence.<br>• Offender was a member of, or was associated with, a group promoting hostility based on race or religion.<br>• Aggravated nature of the offence caused severe distress to the victim or the victim's family (over and above the distress already considered at step one).<br>• Aggravated nature of the offence caused serious fear and distress throughout local community or more widely. | Increase the length of custodial sentence if already considered for the basic offence or consider a custodial sentence, if not already considered for the basic offence. |
| **Medium Level of Racial or Religious Aggravation** | **Sentence Uplift** |
| • Racial or religious aggravation formed a significant proportion of the offence as a whole.<br>• Aggravated nature of the offence caused some distress to the victim or the victim's family (over and above the distress already considered at step one).<br>• Aggravated nature of the offence caused some fear and distress throughout local community or more widely. | Consider a significantly more onerous penalty of the same type or consider a more severe type of sentence than for the basic offence. |
| **Low Level of Racial or Religious Aggravation** | **Sentence Uplift** |
| • Aggravated element formed a minimal part of the offence as a whole.<br>• Aggravated nature of the offence caused minimal or no distress to the victim or the victim's family (over and above the distress already considered at step one). | Consider a more onerous penalty of the same type identified for the basic offence. |

Magistrates may find that, although the appropriate sentence for the basic offence would be within their powers, the appropriate increase for the aggravated offence would result in a sentence in excess of their powers. If so, they must commit for sentence to the Crown Court.

**The sentencer should state in open court that the offence was aggravated by reason of race or religion, and should also state what the sentence would have been without that element of aggravation.**

## ASSAULT ON EMERGENCY WORKER AGGRAVATED OFFENCES

**Maximum sentence for the aggravated offence on indictment is 1 year's custody (maximum when tried summarily is 6 months' custody)**

Having determined the category of the basic offence to identify the sentence of a non-aggravated offence, the court should now apply an appropriate uplift to the sentence in accordance with the guidance below. **The uplifted sentence may considerably exceed the basic offence category range.**

| Category A1 | Increase the length of custodial sentence if already considered for the basic offence or consider a custodial sentence, if not already considered for the basic offence. |
|---|---|
| Category A2 or B1 | Consider a significantly more onerous penalty of the same type or consider a more severe type of sentence than for the basic offence. |
| Category A3 or B2 or B3 | Consider a more onerous penalty of the same type identified for the basic offence. |

Magistrates may find that, although the appropriate sentence for the basic offence would be within their powers, the appropriate increase for the aggravated offence would result in a sentence in excess of their powers. If so, they must commit for sentence to the Crown Court.

**The sentencer should state in open court that the offence was aggravated by reason of the victim being an emergency worker, and should also state what the sentence would have been without that element of aggravation.**

**STEP 4   Consider any other factors which indicate a reduction, such as assistance to the prosecution**

The court should take into account section 74 of the Sentencing Code (reduction in sentence for assistance to prosecution) and any other rule of law by virtue of which an offender may receive a discounted sentence in consequence of assistance given (or offered) to the prosecutor or investigator.

**STEP 5   Reduction for guilty pleas**

The court should take account of any potential reduction for a guilty plea in accordance with section 73 of the Sentencing Code and the Reduction in Sentence for a Guilty Plea guideline.

**STEP 6   Dangerousness**

Racially or religiously aggravated common assault is a specified offence. The court should consider whether having regard to the criteria contained in Chapter 6 of Part 10 of the Sentencing Code it would be appropriate to impose an extended sentence (sections 266 and 279).

**STEP 7   Totality principle**

If sentencing an offender for more than one offence, or where the offender is already serving a sentence, consider whether the total sentence is just and proportionate to the offending behaviour. See Totality guideline [see **SG4**].

**STEP 8   Compensation and ancillary orders**

In all cases, the court should consider whether to make compensation and/or other ancillary orders. The court must give reasons if it decides not to order compensation (Sentencing Code, s. 55).

- Ancillary orders – Magistrates' Court
- Ancillary orders – Crown Court Compendium

**STEP 9   Reasons**

Section 52 of the Sentencing Code imposes a duty to give reasons for, and explain the effect of, the sentence.

**STEP 10   Consideration for time spent on bail (tagged curfew)**

The court must consider whether to give credit for time spent on bail in accordance with section 240A of the Criminal Justice Act 2003 and section 325 of the Sentencing Code.

INFLICTING GRIEVOUS BODILY HARM/UNLAWFUL WOUNDING/RACIALLY OR        **SG12-8**
RELIGIOUSLY AGGRAVATED GBH/UNLAWFUL WOUNDING/RACIALLY OR
RELIGIOUSLY AGGRAVATED UNLAWFUL WOUNDING

*Crime and Disorder Act 1998, s. 29, Offences against the Person Act 1861, s. 20*

**Effective from:** 01 July 2021

**Inflicting grievous bodily harm/unlawful wounding,** Offences against the Person Act 1861 (section 20)

**Racially or religiously aggravated GBH/unlawful wounding,** Crime and Disorder Act 1998 (section 29)

Triable either way

**Section 20**
Maximum: 5 years' custody

Offence range: Community order – 4 years 6 months' custody

**Section 29**
Maximum: 7 years' custody

These are specified offences for the purposes of sections 266 and 279 (extended sentence for certain violent, sexual or terrorism offences) of the Sentencing Code.

**STEP 1 – Determining the offence category**

The court should determine the offence category with reference **only** to the factors listed in the tables below. In order to determine the category the court should assess **culpability** and **harm.**

**Culpability**

The level of culpability is determined by weighing all the factors of the case. Where there are characteristics present which fall under different levels of culpability, the court should balance these characteristics giving appropriate weight to relevant factors to reach a fair assessment of the offender's culpability.

## A – High culpability

- Significant degree of planning or premeditation
- Victim obviously vulnerable due to age, personal characteristics or circumstances
- Use of a highly dangerous weapon or weapon equivalent*
- Strangulation/suffocation/asphyxiation
- Leading role in group activity
- Prolonged/persistent assault

## B – Medium culpability

- Use of a weapon or weapon equivalent which does not fall within category A
- Lesser role in group activity
- Cases falling between category A or C because:
  - Factors in both high and lesser categories are present which balance each other out; and/or
  - The offender's culpability falls between the factors as described in high and lesser culpability

## C – Lesser culpability

- No weapon used
- Excessive self defence
- Impulsive/spontaneous and short-lived assault
- Mental disorder or learning disability, where linked to the commission of the offence

* A highly dangerous weapon can include weapons such as knives and firearms. Highly dangerous weapon equivalents can include corrosive substances (such as acid), whose dangerous nature must be substantially above and beyond the legislative definition of an offensive weapon which is; *'any article made or adapted for use for causing injury, or is intended by the person having it with him for such use'*. The court must determine whether the weapon or weapon equivalent is highly dangerous on the facts and circumstances of the case.

### Harm

All cases will involve 'really serious harm', which can be physical or psychological, or wounding. The court should assess the level of harm caused with reference to the impact on the victim

### Category 1

- Particularly grave and/or life-threatening injury caused
- Injury results in physical or psychological harm resulting in lifelong dependency on third party care or medical treatment
- Offence results in a permanent, irreversible injury or condition which has a substantial and long term effect on the victim's ability to carry out their normal day to day activities or on their ability to work

### Category 2

- Grave injury
- Offence results in a permanent, irreversible injury or condition not falling within category 1

### Category 3

- All other cases of really serious harm
- All other cases of wounding

### STEP 2   Starting point and category range

Having determined the category, the court should use the corresponding starting points to reach a sentence within the category range below. The starting point applies to all offenders irrespective of plea or previous convictions. A case of particular gravity, reflected by multiple features of culpability in step one, could merit upward adjustment from the starting point before further adjustment for aggravating or mitigating features, set out below.

Sentencers should be aware that there is evidence of a disparity in sentence outcomes for this offence which indicates that a higher proportion of Black, Mixed and Chinese or Other ethnicity offenders receive an immediate custodial sentence than White and Asian offenders. There may be many reasons for these differences, but in order to apply the guidelines fairly sentencers may find useful information and guidance at Chapter 8 paragraphs 185 to 193 of the Equal Treatment Bench Book.

| Harm | Culpability | | |
|---|---|---|---|
| | **A** | **B** | **C** |
| Harm 1 | **Starting point**<br>4 years' custody | **Starting point**<br>3 years' custody | **Starting point**<br>2 years' custody |
| | **Category range**<br>3 years – 4 years 6<br>months' custody | **Category range**<br>2 – 4 years' custody | **Category range**<br>1 – 3 years' custody |
| Harm 2 | **Starting point**<br>3 years' custody | **Starting point**<br>2 years' custody | **Starting point**<br>1 year's custody |
| | **Category range**<br>2 – 4 years' custody | **Category range**<br>1 – 3 years' custody | **Category range**<br>High level community<br>order – 2 years' custody |
| Harm 3 | **Starting point**<br>2 years' custody | **Starting point**<br>1 year's custody | **Starting point**<br>26 weeks' custody |
| | **Category range**<br>1 – 3 years' custody | **Category range**<br>High level community order – 2<br>years' custody | **Category range**<br>Medium level community<br>order – 1 year's custody |

**Community Orders and Custodial Sentences**

[For the imposition of community orders, including the community orders table, see Imposition of Community and Custodial Sentences at **SG9-2**.

For the imposition of custodial sentences see Imposition of Community and Custodial Sentences at **SG9-3**.]

The table below contains a non-exhaustive list of additional factual elements providing the context of the offence and factors relating to the offender. Identify whether any combination of these, or other relevant factors, should result in an upward or downward adjustment from the starting point. In some cases, having considered these factors, it may be appropriate to move outside the identified category range.

**Factors increasing seriousness**

*Statutory aggravating factors:*
- Previous convictions, having regard to
  a)  the **nature** of the offence to which the conviction relates and its **relevance** to the current offence; and
  b)  the **time** that has elapsed since the conviction
- Offence committed whilst on bail
- Offence motivated by, or demonstrating hostility based on any of the following characteristics or presumed characteristics of the victim: disability, sexual orientation or transgender identity
- Offence was committed against an emergency worker acting in the exercise of functions as such a worker

*Other aggravating factors:*
- Offence committed against those working in the public sector or providing a service to the public or against a person coming to the assistance of an emergency worker
- Offence committed in prison (where not taken into account as a statutory aggravating factor)
- Offence committed in a domestic context
- History of violence or abuse towards victim by offender
- Presence of children
- Gratuitous degradation of victim
- Abuse of power and/or position of trust
- Any steps taken to prevent the victim reporting an incident, obtaining assistance and/or from assisting or supporting the prosecution
- Commission of offence whilst under the influence of alcohol/drugs
- Offence committed whilst on licence or post sentence supervision
- Failure to comply with current court orders

**Factors reducing seriousness or reflecting personal mitigation**
- No previous convictions or no relevant/recent convictions
- Remorse
- Good character and/or exemplary conduct

- Significant degree of provocation
- History of significant violence or abuse towards the offender by the victim
- Age and/or lack of maturity
- Mental disorder or learning disability, where not linked to the commission of the offence
- Sole or primary carer for dependent relative(s)
- Determination and/or demonstration of steps taken to address addiction or offending behaviour
- Serious medical conditions requiring urgent, intensive or long-term treatment

### STEP 3   Aggravated offences

### Section 29 Racially or Religiously Aggravated Offences Only

Having determined the category of the basic offence to identify the sentence of a non-aggravated offence, the court should now consider the level of racial or religious aggravation involved and apply an appropriate uplift to the sentence in accordance with the guidance below. The following is a list of factors which the court should consider to determine the level of aggravation. Where there are characteristics present which fall under different levels of aggravation, the court should balance these to reach a fair assessment of the level of aggravation present in the offence.

**Maximum sentence for the aggravated offence on indictment is 7 years' custody (maximum when tried summarily is 6 months' custody)**

Care should be taken to avoid double counting factors already taken into account in assessing the level of harm at step one

| High Level of Racial or Religious Aggravation | Sentence Uplift |
|---|---|
| • Racial or religious aggravation was the predominant motivation for the offence.<br>• Offender was a member of, or was associated with, a group promoting hostility based on race or religion.<br>• Aggravated nature of the offence caused severe distress to the victim or the victim's family (over and above the distress already considered at step one).<br>• Aggravated nature of the offence caused serious fear and distress throughout local community or more widely. | Increase the length of custodial sentence if already considered for the basic offence or consider a custodial sentence, if not already considered for the basic offence. |
| Medium Level of Racial or Religious Aggravation | Sentence Uplift |
| • Racial or religious aggravation formed a significant proportion of the offence as a whole.<br>• Aggravated nature of the offence caused some distress to the victim or the victim's family (over and above the distress already considered at step one).<br>• Aggravated nature of the offence caused some fear and distress throughout local community or more widely. | Consider a significantly more onerous penalty of the same type or consider a more severe type of sentence than for the basic offence. |
| Low Level of Racial or Religious Aggravation | Sentence Uplift |
| • Aggravated element formed a minimal part of the offence as a whole.<br>• Aggravated nature of the offence caused minimal or no distress to the victim or the victim's family (over and above the distress already considered at step one). | Consider a more onerous penalty of the same type identified for the basic offence. |

Magistrates may find that, although the appropriate sentence for the basic offence would be within their powers, the appropriate increase for the aggravated offence would result in a sentence in excess of their powers. If so, they must commit for sentence to the Crown Court.

**The sentencer should state in open court that the offence was aggravated by reason of race or religion, and should also state what the sentence would have been without that element of aggravation.**

### STEP 4   Consider any other factors which indicate a reduction, such as assistance to the prosecution

The court should take into account section 74 of the Sentencing Code (reduction in sentence for assistance to prosecution) and any other rule of law by virtue of which an offender may receive a discounted sentence in consequence of assistance given (or offered) to the prosecutor or investigator.

**STEP 5    Reduction for guilty pleas**

The court should take account of any potential reduction for a guilty plea in accordance with section 73 of the Sentencing Code and the Reduction in Sentence for a Guilty Plea guideline.

**STEP 6    Dangerousness**

These are specified violent offences. The court should consider whether having regard to the criteria contained in Chapter 6 of Part 10 of the Sentencing Code it would be appropriate to impose an extended sentence (sections 266 and 279).

**STEP 7    Totality principle**

If sentencing an offender for more than one offence, or where the offender is already serving a sentence, consider whether the total sentence is just and proportionate to the offending behaviour. See Totality guideline [see **SG4**].

**STEP 8    Compensation and ancillary orders**

In all cases, the court should consider whether to make compensation and/or other ancillary orders. The court must give reasons if it decides not to order compensation (Sentencing Code, s. 55).

- Ancillary orders – Magistrates' Court
- Ancillary orders – Crown Court Compendium

**STEP 9    Reasons**

Section 52 of the Sentencing Code imposes a duty to give reasons for, and explain the effect of, the sentence.

**STEP 10    Consideration for time spent on bail (tagged curfew)**

The court must consider whether to give credit for time spent on bail in accordance with section 240A of the Criminal Justice Act 2003 and section 325 of the Sentencing Code.

Sentencing Guidelines

# PART 13    ATTEMPTED MURDER

**Effective from:** 17 July 2009

*Criminal Attempts Act 1981, s.1(1)*

Triable on indictment
Maximum: Life imprisonment

This is a Schedule 19 offence for the purposes of sections 274 and section 285 (required life sentence for offence carrying life sentence) of the Sentencing Code. For offences committed on or after 3 December 2012, this is an offence listed in Part 1 of Schedule 15 for the purposes of sections 273 and 283 (life sentence for second listed offence) of the Sentencing Code.

This is a specified offence for the purposes of sections 266 and 279 (extended sentence for certain violent, sexual or terrorism offences) of the Sentencing Code.

**SG13-1**    [For the standard text on applicability see **SG0-04**]

**SG13-2**                       ATTEMPTED MURDER

### Key Factors

This is a Schedule 19 offence for the purposes of sections 274 and section 285 (required life sentence for offence carrying life sentence) of the Sentencing Code.

For offences committed on or after 3 December 2012, this is an offence listed in Part 1 of Schedule 15 for the purposes of sections 273 and 283 (life sentence for second listed offence) of the Sentencing Code.

This is a specified offence for the purposes of sections 266 and 279 (extended sentence for certain violent, sexual or terrorism offences) of the Sentencing Code.

The starting points and ranges are based upon a first time adult offender convicted after a trial. They will be relevant when imposing a determinate sentence and when fixing any minimum term that may be necessary. When setting the minimum term to be served within an indeterminate sentence, in accordance with normal practice that term will usually be half the equivalent determinate sentence.

Attempted murder requires an intention to kill. Accordingly, an offender convicted of this offence will have demonstrated a high level of culpability. Even so, the precise level of culpability will vary in line with the circumstances of the offence and whether the offence was planned or spontaneous. The use of a weapon may influence this assessment.

The level of injury or harm sustained by the victim as well as any harm that the offence was intended to cause or might foreseeably have caused, must be taken into account and reflected in the sentence imposed.

The degree of harm will vary greatly. Where there is low harm and high culpability, culpability is more significant. Even in cases where a low level of injury (or no injury) has been caused, an offence of attempted murder will be extremely serious.

The most serious offences will include those which encompass the factors set out in Schedule 21 to the Sentencing Code, paragraphs 2 and 3 that, had the offence been murder, would make the seriousness of the offence "exceptionally high" or "particularly high".

The particular facts of the offence will identify the appropriate level. In all cases, the aggravating and mitigating factors that will influence the identification of the provisional sentence within the range follow those set out in schedule 21 with suitable adjustments. This guideline is not intended to provide for an offence found to be based on a genuine belief that the murder would have been an act of mercy.

When assessing the seriousness of an offence, the court should also refer to the list of general aggravating and mitigating factors in the Council guideline on Seriousness. Care should be taken to ensure there is no double counting where an essential element of the offence charged might, in other circumstances, be an aggravating factor.

#### OFFENCE SERIOUSNESS (CULPABILITY AND HARM)

**A.**   Identify the appropriate starting point
Starting points based on first time offender aged 18 or over pleading not guilty.

| Nature of offence | Starting point | Range |
|---|---|---|
| **Level 1** The most serious offences including those which (if the charge had been murder) would come within para.2 or para.3 of Schedule 21 of the Sentencing Code<br>• Serious and long term physical or psychological harm<br>• Some physical or psychological harm<br>• Little or no physical or psychological harm | • 30 years' custody<br>• 20 years' custody<br>• 15 years' custody | • 27–35 years' custody<br>• 17–25 years' custody<br>• 12–20 years' custody |
| **Level 2** Other planned attempt to kill<br>• Serious and long term physical or psychological harm<br>• Some physical or psychological harm<br>• Little or no physical or psychological harm | • 20 years' custody<br>• 15 years' custody<br>• 10 years' custody | • 17–25 years' custody<br>• 12–20 years' custody<br>• 7–15 years' custody |
| **Level 3** Other spontaneous attempt to kill<br>• Serious and long term physical or psychological harm<br>• Some physical or psychological harm<br>• Little or no physical or psychological harm | • 15 years' custody<br>• 12 years' custody<br>• 9 years' custody | • 12–20 years' custody<br>• 9–17 years' custody<br>• 6–14 years' custody |

The presence of one or more aggravating features will indicate a more severe sentence within the suggested range and, if the aggravating feature(s) are exceptionally serious, the case will move up to the next level.

**Custodial Sentences**

Sentencing flowcharts are available at Imposition of Community and Custodial Sentences definitive guideline. [See **SG9**]

The approach to the imposition of a custodial sentence should be as follows:

1) **Has the custody threshold been passed?**
   - A custodial sentence must not be imposed unless the offence or the combination of the offence and one or more offences associated with it was so serious that neither a fine alone nor a community sentence can be justified for the offence.
   - There is no general definition of where the custody threshold lies. The circumstances of the individual offence and the factors assessed by offence-specific guidelines will determine whether an offence is so serious that neither a fine alone nor a community sentence can be justified. Where no offence specific guideline is available to determine seriousness, the harm caused by the offence, the culpability of the offender and any previous convictions will be relevant to the assessment.
   - The clear intention of the threshold test is to reserve prison as a punishment for the most serious offences.
2) **Is it unavoidable that a sentence of imprisonment be imposed?**
   - Passing the custody threshold does not mean that a custodial sentence should be deemed inevitable. Custody should not be imposed where a community order could provide sufficient restriction on an offender's liberty (by way of punishment) while addressing the rehabilitation of the offender to prevent future crime.
   - For offenders on the cusp of custody, imprisonment should not be imposed where there would be an impact on dependants which would make a custodial sentence disproportionate to achieving the aims of sentencing.
3) **What is the shortest term commensurate with the seriousness of the offence?**
   - In considering this the court must NOT consider any licence or post sentence supervision requirements which may subsequently be imposed upon the offender's release.
4) **Can the sentence be suspended?**
   - A suspended sentence **MUST NOT** be imposed as a more severe form of community order. A suspended sentence is a custodial sentence. **Sentencers should be clear that they would impose an immediate custodial sentence if the power to suspend were not available.** If not, a non-custodial sentence should be imposed.

The following factors should be weighed in considering whether it is possible to suspend the sentence:

| Factors indicating that it would <u>not</u> be appropriate to suspend a custodial sentence | Factors indicating that it may be appropriate to suspend a custodial sentence |
|---|---|
| Offender presents a risk/danger to the public | Realistic prospect of rehabilitation |
| Appropriate punishment can only be achieved by immediate custody | Strong personal mitigation |
| History of poor compliance with court orders | Immediate custody will result in significant harmful impact upon others |

The imposition of a custodial sentence is both punishment and a deterrent. To ensure that the overall terms of the suspended sentence are commensurate with offence seriousness, care must be taken to ensure requirements imposed are not excessive. A court wishing to impose onerous or intensive requirements should reconsider whether a community sentence might be more appropriate.

### Pre-sentence report

Whenever the court reaches the provisional view that:

- the custody threshold has been passed; and, if so
- the length of imprisonment which represents the shortest term commensurate with the seriousness of the offence;

the court should obtain a pre-sentence report, whether verbal or written, **unless** the court considers a report to be unnecessary. Ideally a pre-sentence report should be completed on the same day to avoid adjourning the case.

**Magistrates:** Consult your legal adviser before deciding to sentence to custody without a pre-sentence report.

### Suspended Sentences: General Guidance

i) The guidance regarding pre-sentence reports applies if suspending custody.
ii) If the court imposes a term of imprisonment of between 14 days and 2 years (subject to magistrates' courts sentencing powers), it may suspend the sentence for between 6 months and 2 years (the 'operational period'). The time for which a sentence is suspended should reflect the length of the sentence; up to 12 months might normally be appropriate for a suspended sentence of up to 6 months.
iii) Where the court imposes two or more sentences to be served consecutively, the court may suspend the sentence where the aggregate of the terms is between 14 days and 2 years (subject to magistrates' courts sentencing powers).
iv) When the court suspends a sentence, it may impose one or more requirements for the offender to undertake in the community. The requirements are identical to those available for community orders, see the guideline on Imposition of Community and Custodial Sentences.
v) A custodial sentence that is suspended should be for the same term that would have applied if the sentence was to be served immediately.

### B. Consider the effect of aggravating and mitigating factors (other than those within examples above)

The following may be particularly relevant but **these lists are not exhaustive**

### Specific aggravating factors

*Factors indicating higher culpability*

a. the fact that the victim was particularly vulnerable, for example, because of age or disability
b. mental or physical suffering inflicted on the victim
c. the abuse of a position of trust
d. the use of duress or threats against another person to facilitate the commission of the offence
e. the fact that the victim was providing a public service or performing a public duty

### Specific mitigating factors

*Factors indicating lesser culpability*

a. the fact that the offender suffered from any mental disorder or mental disability which lowered his degree of culpability
b. the fact that the offender was provoked (for example, by prolonged stress)
c. the fact that the offender acted to any extent in self-defence
d. the age of the offender

### Common aggravating and mitigating factors

Taken from Sentencing Guidelines Council Guideline Overarching Principles: Seriousness [see SG2].

### Aggravating factors

*Factors indicating higher culpability*

- Offence committed whilst on bail for other offences
- Failure to respond to previous sentences
- Offence was racially or religiously aggravated
- Offence motivated by, or demonstrating, hostility to the victim based on his or her sexual orientation (or presumed sexual orientation)
- Offence motivated by, or demonstrating, hostility based on the victim's disability (or presumed disability)
- Previous conviction(s), particularly where a pattern of repeat offending is disclosed

- Planning of an offence
- An intention to commit more serious harm than actually resulted from the offence
- Offenders operating in groups or gangs
- 'Professional' offending
- Commission of the offence for financial gain (where this is not inherent in the offence itself)
- High level of profit from the offence
- An attempt to conceal or dispose of evidence
- Failure to respond to warnings or concerns expressed by others about the offender's behaviour
- Offence committed whilst on licence
- Offence motivated by hostility towards a minority group, or a member or members of it
- Deliberate targeting of vulnerable victim(s)
- Commission of an offence while under the influence of alcohol or drugs
- Use of a weapon to frighten or injure victim
- Deliberate and gratuitous violence or damage to property, over and above what is needed to carry out the offence
- Abuse of power
- Abuse of a position of trust

*Factors indicating a more than usually serious degree of harm*

- Multiple victims
- An especially serious physical or psychological effect on the victim, even if unintended
- A sustained assault or repeated assaults on the same victim
- Victim is particularly vulnerable
- Location of the offence (for example, in an isolated place)
- Offence is committed against those working in the public sector or providing a service to the public
- Presence of others e.g. relatives, especially children or partner of the victim
- Additional degradation of the victim (e.g. taking photographs of a victim as part of a sexual offence)
- In property offences, high value (including sentimental value) of property to the victim, or substantial consequential loss (e.g. where the theft of equipment causes serious disruption to a victim's life or business)

**Mitigating factors**

*Factors indicating lower culpability*

- A greater degree of provocation than normally expected
- Mental illness or disability
- Youth or age, where it affects the responsibility of the individual defendant
- The fact that the offender played only a minor role in the offence

**Form a preliminary view of the appropriate sentence, then consider offender mitigation**

*Offender mitigation*

- Genuine remorse
- Admissions to police in interview
- Ready co-operation with authorities

**Consider a reduction for a guilty plea**

- Reduction in Sentence for a Guilty Plea (where first hearing is on or after 1 June 2017 [see **SG5-1**], or first hearing before 1 June 2017 [see **SG5-12**]).

**Decide sentence**

**Give reasons**

# PART 14    BLADED ARTICLES AND OFFENSIVE WEAPONS

**Effective from:** 01 June 2018

**SG14-1** APPLICABILITY

[For the standard text on applicability see **SG0-04**.]

**SG14-2** BLADED ARTICLES AND OFFENSIVE WEAPONS – POSSESSION

**Possession of an offensive weapon in a public place**
Prevention of Crime Act 1953 (section 1(1))

**Possession of an article with blade/point in a public place**
Criminal Justice Act 1988 (section 139(1))

**Possession of an offensive weapon on school premises**
Criminal Justice Act 1988 (section 139A(2))

**Possession of an article with blade/point on school premises**
Criminal Justice Act 1988 (section 139A(1))

**Unauthorised possession in prison of a knife or offensive weapon**
Prison Act 1952 (section 40CA)

Triable either way

Maximum: 4 years' custody

Offence range: Fine–2 years 6 months' custody

This guideline applies only to offenders aged 18 and older.

This offence is subject to statutory minimum sentencing provisions.

See step 3 for further details.

**STEP 1   Determining the offence category**

The court should determine the offence category with reference only to the factors listed in the tables below. In order to determine the category, the court should assess **culpability** and **harm**.

The court should weigh all the factors set out below in determining the offender's culpability.

**Where there are characteristics present which fall under different levels of culpability, the court should balance these characteristics to reach a fair assessment of the offender's culpability.**

| **Culpability** demonstrated by one or more of the following: | |
| --- | --- |
| A | <ul><li>Possession of a bladed article</li><li>Possession of a highly dangerous weapon*</li><li>Offence motivated by, or demonstrating hostility based on any of the following characteristics or presumed characteristics of the victim: religion, race, disability, sexual orientation or transgender identity</li></ul> |
| B | <ul><li>Possession of weapon (other than a bladed article or a highly dangerous weapon) – used to threaten or cause fear</li></ul> |
| C | <ul><li>Possession of weapon (other than a bladed article or a highly dangerous weapon) – not used to threaten or cause fear</li></ul> |
| D | <ul><li>Possession of weapon falls just short of reasonable excuse</li></ul> |

* NB an offensive weapon is defined in legislation as 'any article made or adapted for use for causing injury, or is intended by the person having it with him for such use'. A highly dangerous weapon is, therefore, a weapon, including a corrosive substance (such as acid), whose dangerous nature must be substantially above and beyond this. The court must determine whether the weapon is highly dangerous on the facts and circumstances of the case.

| Harm | |
|---|---|
| The court should consider the factors set out below to determine the level of harm that has been caused or was risked | |
| Category 1 | • Offence committed at a school or other place where vulnerable people are likely to be present<br>• Offence committed in prison<br>• Offence committed in circumstances where there is a risk of serious disorder<br>• Serious alarm/distress |
| Category 2 | • All other cases |

## STEP 2  Starting point and category range

Having determined the category at step one, the court should use the corresponding starting point to reach a sentence within the category range below. The starting point applies to all offenders irrespective of plea or previous convictions. A case of particular gravity, reflected by multiple features of culpability or harm in step one, could merit upward adjustment from the starting point before further adjustment for aggravating or mitigating features, set out below.

| Harm | Culpability | | | |
|---|---|---|---|---|
| | A | B | C | D |
| Category 1 | Starting point<br>1 year 6 months' custody | Starting point<br>9 months' custody | Starting point<br>3 months' custody | Starting point<br>High level community order |
| | Category range<br>1–2 years 6 months' custody | Category range<br>6 months'–1 year 6 months' custody | Category range<br>High level community order–6 months' custody | Category range<br>Medium level community order–3 months' custody |
| Category 2 | Starting point<br>6 months' custody | Starting point<br>High level community order | Starting point<br>Medium level community order | Starting point<br>Low level community order |
| | Category range<br>3 months'–1 year's custody | Category range<br>Medium level community order–6 months' custody | Category range<br>Low level community order–High level community order | Category range<br>Band C fine–Medium level community order |

### Fines

[For the standard schedule of fines see **SG2-5**.]

### Community Orders and Custodial Sentences

[For the imposition of community orders, including the community orders table, see Imposition of Community and Custodial Sentences at **SG9-2**. For the imposition of custodial sentences see Imposition of Community and Custodial Sentences at **SG9-3**.]

### Factors increasing or reducing seriousness

The table below contains a non-exhaustive list of additional factual elements providing the context of the offence and factors relating to the offender. Identify whether any combination of these, or other relevant factors, should result in an upward or downward adjustment from the sentence arrived at so far. In particular, relevant recent convictions are likely to result in an upward adjustment. In some cases, having considered these factors, it may be appropriate to move outside the identified category range.

### Factors increasing seriousness

*Statutory aggravating factors*

• Previous convictions, having regard to
  a) the **nature** of the offence to which the conviction relates and its **relevance** to the current offence; and
  b) the **time** that has elapsed since the conviction (unless the convictions will be relevant for the purposes of the statutory minimum sentencing provisions – see step three)
• Offence committed whilst on bail

*Other aggravating factors*

- Offence was committed as part of a group or gang
- Attempts to conceal identity
- Commission of offence whilst under the influence of alcohol or drugs
- Attempts to conceal/dispose of evidence
- Failure to comply with current court orders
- Offence committed on licence or post sentence supervision
- Offences taken into consideration
- Failure to respond to warnings about behaviour

**Factors reducing seriousness or reflecting personal mitigation**

- No previous convictions **or** no relevant/recent convictions
- Good character and/or exemplary conduct
- Serious medical condition requiring urgent, intensive or long-term treatment
- Age and/or lack of maturity where it affects the responsibility of the offender
- Mental disorder or learning disability
- Sole or primary carer for dependent relatives
- Co-operation with the police

### STEP 3  Minimum Terms – second or further relevant offence

When sentencing the offences of:

- possession of an offensive weapon in a public place;
- possession of an article with a blade/point in a public place;
- possession of an offensive weapon on school premises; and
- possession of an article with blade/point on school premises

a court must impose a sentence of at least 6 months' imprisonment where this is a second or further relevant offence **unless the court is of the opinion that there are particular circumstances relating to the offence, the previous offence or the offender which make it unjust to do so in all the circumstances.**

A 'relevant offence' includes those offences listed above and the following offences:

- threatening with an offensive weapon in a public place;
- threatening with an article with a blade/point in a public place;
- threatening with an article with a blade/point on school premises; and
- threatening with an offensive weapon on school premises.

### Unjust in all of the circumstances

In considering whether a statutory minimum sentence would be 'unjust in all of the circumstances' the court must have regard to the particular circumstances of the offence and the offender. If the circumstances of the offence, the previous offence or the offender make it unjust to impose the statutory minimum sentence then the court **must impose either a shorter custodial sentence than the statutory minimum provides or an alternative sentence.**

### The offence

Having reached this stage of the guideline the court should have made a provisional assessment of the seriousness of the current offence. In addition, the court must consider the seriousness of the previous offence(s) and the period of time that has elapsed between offences. Where the seriousness of the combined offences is such that it falls far below the custody threshold, or where there has been a significant period of time between the offences, the court may consider it unjust to impose the statutory minimum sentence.

### The offender

The court should consider the following factors to determine whether it would be unjust to impose the statutory minimum sentence;

- any strong personal mitigation;
- whether there is a realistic prospect of rehabilitation;
- whether custody will result in significant impact on others.

### STEP 4  Consider any factors which indicate a reduction for assistance to the prosecution

The court should take into account section 74 of the Sentencing Code (reduction in sentence for assistance to prosecution) and any other rule of law by virtue of which an offender may receive a discounted sentence in consequence of assistance given (or offered) to the prosecutor or investigator.

**STEP 5   Reduction for guilty pleas**

The court should take account of any potential reduction for a guilty plea in accordance with section 73 of the Sentencing Code and the guideline for Reduction in Sentence for a Guilty Plea [**SG5-1–SG5-12**].

Where a statutory minimum sentence has been imposed, the court must ensure that any reduction for a guilty plea does not reduce the sentence to less than 80 per cent of the statutory minimum.

**STEP 6   Totality principle**

If sentencing an offender for more than one offence, or where the offender is already serving a sentence, consider whether the total sentence is just and proportionate to the overall offending behaviour in accordance with the *Totality* guideline [see **SG4**].

**STEP 7   Ancillary orders**

In all cases the court should consider whether to make ancillary orders.

**STEP 8   Reasons**

Section 52 of the Sentencing Code imposes a duty to give reasons for, and explain the effect of, the sentence.

**STEP 9   Consideration for time spent on bail**

The court must consider whether to give credit for time spent on bail in accordance with section 240A of the Criminal Justice Act 2003 and section 325 of the Sentencing Code.

BLADED ARTICLES AND OFFENSIVE WEAPONS – THREATS      **SG14-3**

**Threatening with an offensive weapon in a public place**

Prevention of Crime Act 1953 (section 1A)

**Threatening with an article with blade/point in a public place**

Criminal Justice Act 1988 (section 139AA(1))

**Threatening with an article with blade/point or offensive weapon on school premises**

Criminal Justice Act 1988 (section 139AA(1))
Triable either way
Maximum: 4 years' custody
Offence range: 6 months' custody–3 years' custody

**This offence is subject to statutory minimum sentencing provisions.**

**See STEP 3 for further details.**

**STEP 1   Determining the offence category**

The court should determine the offence category with reference **only** to the factors listed in the tables below. In order to determine the category, the court should assess **culpability** and **harm**.

The court should weigh all the factors set out below in determining the offender's culpability.

**Where there are characteristics present which fall under different levels of culpability, the court should balance these characteristics to reach a fair assessment of the offender's culpability.**

| Culpability demonstrated by one or more of the following: | |
| --- | --- |
| **A – Higher culpability:** | • Offence committed using a bladed article<br>• Offence committed using a highly dangerous weapon*<br>• Offence motivated by, or demonstrating hostility based on any of the following characteristics ore presumed characteristics of the victim: religion, race, disability, sexual orientation or transgender identity<br>• Significant degree of planning or premeditation |
| **B – Lower culpability:** | • All other cases |

\* NB an offensive weapon is defined in legislation as 'any article made or adapted for use for causing injury, or is intended by the person having it with him for such use'. A highly dangerous weapon is, therefore, a weapon, including a corrosive substance (such as acid), whose dangerous nature must be substantially above and beyond this. The court must determine whether the weapon is highly dangerous on the facts and circumstances of the case

| Harm | |
|---|---|
| The court should consider the factors set out below to determine the level of harm that has been caused or was intended to be caused to the victim. | |
| Category 1 | • Offence committed at a school or other place where vulnerable people are likely to be present<br>• Offence committed in prison<br>• Offence committed in circumstances where there is a risk of serious disorder<br>• Serious alarm/distress caused to the victim<br>• Prolonged incident |
| Category 2 | • All other cases |

## STEP 2  Starting point and category range

Having determined the category at step one, the court should use the corresponding starting point to reach a sentence within the category range below. The starting point applies to all offenders irrespective of plea or previous convictions. A case of particular gravity, reflected by multiple features of culpability or harm in step one, could merit upward adjustment from the starting point before further adjustment for aggravating or mitigating features, set out below.

| | Culpability | |
|---|---|---|
| Harm | A | B |
| Category 1 | **Starting point**<br>2 years' custody | **Starting point**<br>1 year 6 months' custody |
| | **Category range**<br>1 year 6 months'–3 years' custody | **Category range**<br>1–2 years' custody |
| Category 2 | **Starting point**<br>15 months' custody | **Starting point**<br>6 months' custody |
| | **Category range**<br>9 months'–2 years' custody | **Category range**<br>6 months'–1 year 6 months' custody |

### Custodial Sentences

[For the imposition of custodial sentences see Imposition of Community and Custodial Sentences at SG9-3.]

### Factors increasing or reducing seriousness

The table below contains a **non-exhaustive** list of additional factual elements providing the context of the offence and factors relating to the offender. Identify whether any combination of these, or other relevant factors, should result in an upward or downward adjustment from the sentence arrived at so far. In particular, relevant recent convictions are likely to result in an upward adjustment. In some cases, having considered these factors, it may be appropriate to move outside the identified category range.

### Factors increasing seriousness

*Statutory aggravating factors*

- Previous convictions, having regard to
  a) the **nature** of the offence to which the conviction relates and its **relevance** to the current offence; and
  b) the **time** that has elapsed since the conviction
- Offence committed whilst on bail

*Other aggravating factors*

- Victim is targeted due to a vulnerability (or a perceived vulnerability)
- Offence was committed as part of a group or gang
- Attempts to conceal identity
- Commission of offence whilst under the influence of alcohol or drugs
- Attempts to conceal/dispose of evidence
- Offence committed against those working in the public sector or providing a service to the public
- Steps taken to prevent the victim reporting or obtaining assistance and/or from assisting or supporting the prosecution
- Failure to comply with current court orders
- Offence committed on licence or post sentence supervision

- Offences taken into consideration
- Failure to respond to warnings about behaviour

**Factors reducing seriousness or reflecting personal mitigation**

- No previous convictions **or** no relevant/recent convictions
- Good character and/or exemplary conduct
- Serious medical condition requiring urgent, intensive or long-term treatment
- Age and/or lack of maturity where it affects the responsibility of the offender
- Mental disorder or learning disability (where not linked to the commission of the offence)
- Little or no planning
- Sole or primary carer for dependent relatives
- Co-operation with the police

## STEP 3  Minimum Terms

When sentencing these offences a court must impose a sentence of at least 6 months imprisonment unless the court is of the opinion that there are particular circumstances relating to the offence or the offender which make it unjust to do so in all the circumstances.

### Unjust in all of the circumstances

In considering whether a statutory minimum sentence would be 'unjust in all of the circumstances' the court must have regard to the particular circumstances of the offence and the offender. If the circumstances of the offence or the offender make it unjust to impose the statutory minimum sentence then the court **must impose either a shorter custodial sentence than the statutory minimum provides or an alternative sentence.**

### The offence

Having reached this stage of the guideline the court should have made a provisional assessment of the seriousness of the offence. Where the court has determined that the offence seriousness falls far below the custodial threshold the court may consider it unjust to impose the statutory minimum sentence.

### The offender

The court should consider the following factors to determine whether it would be unjust to impose the statutory minimum sentence;

- any strong personal mitigation;
- whether there is a realistic prospect of rehabilitation;
- whether custody will result in significant impact on others.

## STEP 4  Consider any factors which indicate a reduction for assistance to the prosecution

The court should take into account section 74 of the Sentencing Code (reduction in sentence for assistance to prosecution) and any other rule of law by virtue of which an offender may receive a discounted sentence in consequence of assistance given (or offered) to the prosecutor or investigator.

## STEP 5  Reduction for guilty pleas

The court should take account of any potential reduction for a guilty plea in accordance with section 73 of the Sentencing Code and the guideline for Reduction in Sentence for a Guilty Plea [**SG5-1–SG5-12**].

Where a statutory minimum sentence has been imposed, the court must ensure that any reduction for a guilty plea does not reduce the sentence to less than 80 per cent of the statutory minimum.

## STEP 6  Totality principle

If sentencing an offender for more than one offence, or where the offender is already serving a sentence, consider whether the total sentence is just and proportionate to the overall offending behaviour in accordance with the *Totality* guideline [see **SG4**].

## STEP 7  Ancillary orders

In all cases the court should consider whether to make ancillary orders.

## STEP 8  Reasons

Section 52 of the Sentencing Code imposes a duty to give reasons for, and explain the effect of, the sentence.

## STEP 9  Consideration for time spent on bail

The court must consider whether to give credit for time spent on bail in accordance with section 240A of the Criminal Justice Act 2003 and section 325 of the Sentencing Code.

    BLADED ARTICLES AND OFFENSIVE WEAPONS (POSSESSION AND THREATS) – CHILDREN AND YOUNG PEOPLE

This guideline should be read alongside the *Overarching Principles- Sentencing Children and Young People* definitive guideline which provides comprehensive guidance on the sentencing principles and welfare considerations that the court should have in mind when sentencing children and young people.

**The offence is subject to statutory minimum sentencing provisions. See Step 5 for further details.**

The first step in determining the sentence is to assess the seriousness of the offence. This assessment is made by considering the nature of the offence and any aggravating and mitigating factors relating to the offence itself. **The fact that a sentence threshold is crossed does not necessarily mean that that sentence should be imposed.**

### STEP 1   Offence seriousness – nature of the offence

The boxes below give examples of the type of culpability and harm factors that may indicate that a particular threshold of sentence has been crossed.

| A non-custodial sentence* may be the most suitable disposal where one or more of the following factors apply: |
| --- |
| Possession of weapon falls just short of reasonable excuse |
| No/minimal risk of weapon being used to threaten or cause harm |
| Fleeting incident and no/minimal distress |

| A custodial sentence or youth rehabilitation order with intensive supervision and surveillance* or fostering* may be justified where one or more of the following factors apply: |
| --- |
| Possession of a bladed article whether produced or not |
| Possession of a highly dangerous weapon† whether produced or not |
| Offence motivated by, or demonstrating hostility based on any of the following characteristics or presumed characteristics of the victim: religion, race, disability, sexual orientation or transgender identity |
| Prolonged incident and serious alarm/distress |
| Offence committed at a school or other place where vulnerable people may be present |

\* Where the child or young person appears in the magistrates' court, and the conditions for a compulsory referral order apply, a referral order must be imposed unless the court is considering imposing a discharge, hospital order or custody.

† NB an offensive weapon is defined in legislation as 'any article made or adapted for use for causing injury, or is intended by the person having it with him for such use'. A highly dangerous weapon is, therefore, a weapon, including a corrosive substance (such as acid), whose dangerous nature must be substantially above and beyond this. The court must determine whether the weapon is highly dangerous on the facts and circumstances of the case.

### STEP 2   Offence seriousness – aggravating and mitigating factors

To complete the assessment of seriousness the court should consider the aggravating and mitigating factors relevant to the offence.

| Aggravating factors |
| --- |
| *Statutory aggravating factors:*<br>Previous findings of guilt, having regard to a) the **nature** of the offence to which the finding of guilt relates and its **relevance** to the current offence; and b) the **time** that has elapsed since the finding of guilt (unless the convictions will be relevant for the purposes of the statutory minimum sentencing provisions – see step five) |
| Offence committed whilst on bail<br>*Other aggravating factors (non-exhaustive):*<br>Significant degree of planning /premeditation<br>Deliberate humiliation of victim, including but not limited to filming of the offence, deliberately committing the offence before a group of peers with the intent of causing additional distress or circulating details/photos/videos etc of the offence on social media or within peer groups<br>Victim is particularly vulnerable due to factors including but not limited to age, mental or physical disability<br>Offence was committed as part of a group or gang<br>Attempts to conceal identity<br>Steps taken to prevent reporting the incident/seeking assistance<br>Commission of offence whilst under the influence of alcohol or drugs<br>Offence committed against those working in the public sector or providing a service to the public |

| Mitigating factors (non-exhaustive) |
| --- |
| No findings of guilt **or** no relevant/recent findings of guilt<br>Good character and/or exemplary conduct<br>Participated in offence due to bullying, peer pressure, coercion or manipulation<br>Little or no planning<br>Co-operation with the police |

## STEP 3  Personal mitigation

Having assessed the offence seriousness the court should then consider the mitigation personal to the child or young person to determine whether a custodial sentence or a community sentence is necessary. The effect of personal mitigation may reduce what would otherwise be a custodial sentence to a non-custodial one or a community sentence to a different means of disposal.

| Personal mitigating factors (non-exhaustive) |
| --- |
| Particularly young or immature child or young person (where it affects their responsibility)<br>Communication or learning disabilities or mental health concerns<br>Unstable upbringing including but not limited to:-<br>• time spent looked after<br>• lack of familial presence or support<br>• disrupted experiences in accommodation or education<br>• exposure to drug/alcohol abuse, familial criminal behaviour or domestic abuse<br>• victim of neglect or abuse, or exposure to neglect or abuse of others<br>• experiences of trauma or loss<br>Determination and/or demonstration of steps taken to address offending behaviour<br>Child or young person in education, training or employment |

## STEP 4  Reduction for guilty pleas

The court should take account of any potential reduction for a guilty plea in accordance with section 73 of the Sentencing Code and the guideline for Reduction in Sentence for a Guilty Plea [**SG5-1–SG5-12**].

The reduction in sentence for a guilty plea can be taken into account by imposing one type of sentence rather than another; for example:

• by reducing a custodial sentence to a community sentence, or
• by reducing a community sentence to a different means of disposal.

Alternatively the court could reduce the length or severity of any punitive requirements attached to a community sentence.

See the Overarching Principles – Sentencing Children and Young People definitive guideline for details of other available sentences including Referral Orders and Reparation Orders.

## STEP 5  Statutory minimum sentencing provisions

The following provisions apply to those young people who were aged 16 or over on the date of the offence[199]

### Threatening with Bladed Articles or Offensive Weapons

When sentencing these offences a court must impose a sentence of at least 4 months Detention and Training Order unless the court is of the opinion that there are particular circumstances relating to the offence, the previous offence or the young person which make it unjust to do so in all the circumstances.

### Possession of Bladed Articles or Offensive Weapons

When sentencing the offences of:

• possession of an offensive weapon in a public place;
• possession of an article with a blade/point in a public place;
• possession of an offensive weapon on school premises; and
• possession of an article with blade/point on school premises a court must impose a sentence of at least 4 months' Detention and Training Order where this is a second or further relevant offence unless the court is of the opinion that there are particular circumstances relating to the offence, any previous relevant offence or the young person which make it unjust to do so in all the circumstances.

A 'relevant offence' includes those offences listed above and the following offences:

---

[199] The age of the young person at the date of the earlier offence(s) is irrelevant.

Sentencing Guidelines

If considering the adult guideline, the court may feel it appropriate to apply a sentence broadly within the region of half to two thirds of the appropriate adult sentence for those aged 15–17 and allow a greater reduction for those aged under 15. This is only a rough guide and must not be applied mechanistically. The individual factors relating to the offence and the child or young person are of the greatest importance and may present good reason to impose a sentence outside of this range.

# PART 15   BREACH OFFENCES

**Effective from:** 01 October 2018

APPLICABILITY                                                SG15-1

[For the standard text on applicability see **SG0-4**]

BREACH OF A COMMUNITY ORDER                                **SG15-2**

*Sentencing Code, Sch. 10*

## Breach of community order by failing to comply with requirements

The court must take into account the extent to which the offender has complied with the requirements of the community order when imposing a penalty.

In assessing the level of compliance with the order the court should consider:

i)   the overall attitude and engagement with the order as well as the proportion of elements completed;
ii)  the impact of any completed or partially completed requirements on the offender's behaviour;
iii) the proximity of breach to imposition of order; and
iv)  evidence of circumstances or offender characteristics, such as disability, mental health issues or learning difficulties which have impeded offender's compliance with the order.

| Overall compliance with order | Penalty |
|---|---|
| Wilful and persistent non-compliance | Revoke the order and re-sentence imposing custodial sentence (even where the offence seriousness did not originally merit custody) |
| Low level of compliance | Revoke the order and re-sentence original offence **OR** Add curfew requirement 20–30 days* **OR** 30–50 hours additional unpaid work/extend length of order/ add additional requirement(s) **OR** Band C fine |
| Medium level of compliance | Revoke the order and resentence original offence **OR** Add curfew requirement 10–20 days* **OR** 20–30 hours additional unpaid work/extend length of order/ add additional requirement(s) **OR** Band B fine |
| High level of compliance | Add curfew requirement 6–10 days* **OR** 10–20 hours additional unpaid work/extend length of order/ add additional requirement(s) **OR** Band A fine |

* curfew days do not have to be consecutive and may be distributed over particular periods, for example at weekends, as the court deems appropriate. The period of the curfew should not exceed the duration of the community order and cannot be for longer than 12 months.

### Fines

[For the standard schedule of fines see **SG2-5**.]

### Community Orders and Custodial Sentences

[For the imposition of community orders, including the community orders table, see Imposition of Community and Custodial Sentences at **SG9-2**. For the imposition of custodial sentences see Imposition of Community and Custodial Sentences at **SG9-3**.]

### Technical guidance

a) If imposing more onerous requirements the length of the order may be extended up to 3 years or six months longer than the previous length, whichever is longer (but only once).

b) If imposing unpaid work as a more onerous requirement and an unpaid work requirement was not previously included, the minimum number of hours that can be imposed is 20.

c) The maximum fine that can be imposed is £2,500.

d) If re-sentencing, a suspended sentence **MUST NOT** be imposed as a more severe alternative to a community order. A suspended sentence may only be imposed if it is fully intended that the offender serve a custodial sentence in accordance with the Imposition of Community and Custodial Sentences guideline.

e) Where a magistrates' court is dealing with a breach of a community order imposed by the Crown Court, the magistrates' court may impose a fine or more onerous requirements; otherwise it may commit the offender to custody, or release the offender on bail, until the offender can be brought or appear before the Crown Court.

### Powers of the court following a subsequent conviction

A conviction for a further offence does not constitute a breach of a community order. However, in such a situation, the court should consider the following guidance from the *Totality* guideline [see **SG4**]:

### Offender convicted of an offence while serving a community order

The power to deal with the offender depends on his being convicted whilst the order is still in force; it does not arise where the order has expired, even if the additional offence was committed whilst it was still current.

If an offender, in respect of whom a community order made by a magistrates' court is in force, is convicted by a magistrates' court of an additional offence, the magistrates' court should ordinarily revoke the previous community order and sentence afresh for both the original and the additional offence.

Where an offender, in respect of whom a community order made by a Crown Court is in force, is convicted by a magistrates' court, the magistrates' court may, and ordinarily should, commit the offender to the Crown Court, in order to allow the Crown Court to re-sentence for the original offence and the additional offence.

The sentencing court should consider the overall seriousness of the offending behaviour taking into account the additional offence and the original offence. The court should consider whether the combination of associated offences is sufficiently serious to justify a custodial sentence.

If the court does not consider that custody is necessary, it should impose a single community order that reflects the overall totality of criminality. The court must take into account the extent to which the offender complied with the requirements of the previous order.

**SG15-3**
## BREACH OF A SUSPENDED SENTENCE ORDER

*Sentencing Code, Sch. 16*

### 1) Conviction for further offence committed during operational period of order

The court must activate the custodial sentence unless it would be unjust in all the circumstances to do so. The predominant factor in determining whether activation is unjust relates to the level of compliance with the suspended sentence order and the facts/nature of any new offence. **These factors are already provided for in the penalties below which are determined by the nature of the new offence and level of compliance, but permit a reduction to the custodial term for relevant completed or partially completed requirements where appropriate.**

The facts/nature of the new offence is the primary consideration in assessing the action to be taken on the breach.

Where the breach is in the second or third category below, the prior level of compliance is also relevant. In assessing the level of compliance with the order the court should consider:

i) the overall attitude and engagement with the order as well as the proportion of elements completed;

ii) the impact of any completed or partially completed requirements on the offender's behaviour;

iii) the proximity of breach to imposition of order; and

iv) evidence of circumstances or offender characteristics, such as disability, mental health issues or learning difficulties which have impeded offender's compliance with the order.

| Breach involves | Penalty |
|---|---|
| Multiple and/or more serious new offence(s) committed | Full activation of original custodial term |
| New offence similar in type and gravity to offence for which suspended sentence order imposed and:<br>a) No/low level of compliance with suspended sentence order<br>OR<br>b) Medium or High level of compliance with suspended sentence order | Full activation of original custodial term<br>Activate sentence but apply appropriate reduction* to original custodial term taking into consideration any unpaid work or curfew requirements completed |
| New offence less serious than original offence but requires a custodial sentence and:<br>a) No/low level of compliance with suspended sentence order<br>OR<br>b) Medium or high level of compliance with suspended sentence order | Full activation of original custodial term<br>Activate sentence but apply appropriate reduction* to original custodial term taking into consideration any unpaid work or curfew requirements completed |
| New offence does not require custodial sentence | Activate sentence but apply reduction* to original custodial term taking into consideration any unpaid work or curfew requirements completed<br>OR<br>Impose more onerous requirement(s) and/or extend supervision period and/ or extend operational period and/or impose fine |

\* It is for the court dealing with the breach to identify the appropriate proportionate reduction depending on the extent of any compliance with the requirements specified

**Fines**
[For the standard schedule of fines see **SG2-5**.]

**Community Orders and Custodial Sentences**
[For the imposition of community orders, including the community orders table, see Imposition of Community and Custodial Sentences at **SG9-2**. For the imposition of custodial sentences see Imposition of Community and Custodial Sentences at **SG9-3**.]

*Unjust in all the circumstances*
The court dealing with the breach should remember that the court imposing the original sentence determined that a custodial sentence was appropriate in the original case.

In determining if there are other factors which would cause activation to be unjust, the court may consider all factors including:

* any strong personal mitigation;
* whether there is a realistic prospect of rehabilitation;
* whether immediate custody will result in significant impact on others.

Only new and exceptional factors/circumstances not present at the time the suspended sentence order was imposed should be taken into account.

In cases where the court considers that it would be unjust to order the custodial sentence to take effect, it must state its reasons and it must deal with the offender in one of the following ways:

(a)   impose a fine not exceeding £2,500; OR
(b)   extend the operational period (to a maximum of two years from date of original sentence); OR
(c)   if the SSO imposes community requirements, do one or more of:
    (i)   impose more onerous community requirements;
    (ii)   extend the supervision period (to a maximum of two years from date of original sentence);
    (iii)   extend the operational period (to a maximum of two years from date of original sentence).

**2)   Failure to comply with a community requirement during the supervision period of the order**
The court must activate the custodial sentence unless it would be unjust in all the circumstances to do so. The predominant factor in determining whether activation is unjust relates to the level of compliance with the suspended sentence order. This factor is already provided for in the penalties below which are determined by the level of compliance, but permit a reduction to the custodial term for relevant completed or partially completed requirements where appropriate.

The court must take into account the extent to which the offender has complied with the suspended sentence order when imposing a sentence.

In assessing the level of compliance with the order the court should consider:

i)   the overall attitude and engagement with the order as well as the proportion of elements completed;
ii)  the impact of any completed or partially completed requirements on the offender's behaviour; and
iii) the proximity of breach to imposition of order; and
iv) evidence of circumstances or offender characteristics, such as disability, mental health issues or learning difficulties which have impeded offender's compliance with the order.

| Breach involves | Penalty |
| --- | --- |
| No/low level of compliance | Full activation of original custodial term |
| Medium level of compliance | Activate sentence but apply reduction* to original custodial term taking into consideration any unpaid work or curfew requirements completed |
| High level of compliance | Activate sentence but apply reduction* to original custodial term taking into consideration any unpaid work or curfew requirements completed <br> **OR** <br> Impose more onerous requirement(s) and/or extend supervision period and/ or extend operational period and/or impose fine |

* It is for the court dealing with the breach to identify the appropriate proportionate reduction depending on the extent of any compliance with the requirements specified

### Unjust in all the circumstances

The court dealing with the breach should remember that the court imposing the original sentence determined that a custodial sentence was appropriate in the original case.

In determining if there are other factors which would cause activation to be unjust, the court may consider all factors including:

- any strong personal mitigation;
- whether there is a realistic prospect of rehabilitation;
- whether immediate custody will result in significant impact on others.

Only new and exceptional factors/circumstances not present at the time the suspended sentence order was imposed should be taken into account.

In cases where the court considers that it would be unjust to order the custodial sentence to take effect, it must state its reasons and it must deal with the offender in one of the following ways:

(a) impose a fine not exceeding £2,500; **OR**
(b) extend the operational period (to a maximum of two years from date of original sentence); **OR**
(c) if the SSO imposes community requirements, do one or more of:
    (i)   impose more onerous community requirements;
    (ii)  extend the supervision period (to a maximum of two years from date of original sentence);
    (iii) extend the operational period (to a maximum of two years from date of original sentence).

**SG15-4**       BREACH OF POST-SENTENCE SUPERVISION

*Criminal Justice Act 2003 (section 256AC and Schedule 19A)*

**Effective from:** 01 October 2018

### Breach of post-sentence supervision

Where the court determines a penalty is appropriate for a breach of a post sentence supervision requirement it must take into account the extent to which the offender has complied with all of the requirements of the post-sentence supervision or supervision default order when imposing a penalty.

In assessing the level of compliance with the order the court should consider:

i)   the offender's overall attitude and engagement with the order as well as the proportion of elements completed;
ii)  the impact of any completed or partially completed requirements on the offender's behaviour;
iii) the proximity of the breach to the imposition of the order; and
iv) evidence of circumstances or offender characteristics, such as disability, mental health issues or learning difficulties which have impeded offender's compliance with the order.

| Level of Compliance | Penalty |
|---|---|
| Low | Up to 7 days' committal to custody<br>**OR**<br>Supervision default order in range of 30–40 hours unpaid work<br>**OR**<br>8–12 hour curfew for minimum of 20 days |
| Medium | Supervision default order in range of 20–30 hours unpaid work<br>**OR**<br>4–8 hour curfew for minimum of 20 days<br>**OR**<br>Band B fine |
| High | Band A fine |

**Breach of supervision default order**

| Level of Compliance | Penalty |
|---|---|
| Low | Revoke supervision default order and order up to 14 days' committal to custody |
| Medium | Revoke supervision default order and impose new order in range of 40–60 hours unpaid work<br>**OR**<br>8–16 hour curfew for minimum of 20 days |
| High | Band B fine |

**Fines**

[For the standard schedule of fines see **SG2-5.**]

**Community Orders and Custodial Sentences**

[For the imposition of community orders, including the community orders table, see Imposition of Community and Custodial Sentences at **SG9-2.** For the imposition of custodial sentences see Imposition of Community and Custodial Sentences at **SG9-3.**]

i)   A supervision default order must include either:

an unpaid work requirement of between 20 hours–60 hours
**OR**
a curfew requirement for between 2–16 hours for a minimum of 20 days and no longer than the end of the post sentence supervision period.

ii)   The maximum fine which can be imposed is £1,000.

FAILURE TO SURRENDER TO BAIL                                           **SG15-5**

*Bail Act 1976 (section 6)*

Triable either way
Maximum: 12 months' custody
Offence range: Discharge–26 weeks' custody

**STEP 1   Determining the offence category**

The court should determine the offence category with reference only to the factors listed in the tables below. In order to determine the category the court should assess **culpability** and **harm**.

| Culpability | |
|---|---|
| A | Failure to surrender represents deliberate attempt to evade or delay justice |
| B | Cases falling between categories A and C |
| C | Reason for failure to surrender just short of reasonable cause |

**Harm**

The level of **harm** is determined by weighing up all the factors of the case to determine the harm that has been caused or was intended to be caused.

Sentencing Guidelines

| Category 1 | Failure to attend Crown Court hearing results in substantial delay and/or interference with the administration of justice |
| Category 2 | Failure to attend magistrates' court hearing results in substantial delay and/or interference with the administration of justice* |
| Category 3 | Cases in either the magistrates' court or Crown Court not in categories 1 and 2 |

\* In particularly serious cases where the failure to attend is in the magistrates' court and the consequences of the delay have a severe impact on victim(s) and /or witness(es) <u>warranting a sentence outside of the powers of the magistrates' court</u>, the case should be committed to the Crown Court pursuant to section 6(6)(a) of the Bail Act 1976 and the Crown Court should sentence the case according to the range in Category A1.

### STEP 2 Starting point and category range

Having determined the category at step one, the court should use the corresponding starting point to reach a sentence within the category range from the appropriate sentence table below. The starting point applies to all offenders irrespective of plea or previous convictions.

**Where a custodial sentence is available within the category range and the substantive offence attracts a custodial sentence, a consecutive custodial sentence should normally be imposed for the failure to surrender offence.**

| Harm | Culpability | | |
|---|---|---|---|
| | **A** | **B** | **C** |
| Category 1 | **Starting point** 6 weeks' custody **Category range** 28 days'–26 weeks' custody[1] | **Starting point** 21 days' custody **Category range** High level community order*–13 weeks' custody | **Starting point** Medium level community order* **Category range** Low level community order*–6 weeks' custody |
| Category 2 | **Starting point** 21 days' custody **Category range** High level community order*–13 weeks' custody | **Starting point** Medium level community order* **Category range** Band B fine–6 weeks' custody | **Starting point** Band B fine **Category range** Band A fine–Low level community order* |
| Category 3 | **Starting point** 14 days' custody **Category range** Low level community order*–6 weeks' custody | **Starting point** Band C fine **Category range** Band A fine–Medium level community order* | **Starting point** Band A fine **Category range** Discharge–Band B fine |

Maximum sentence in magistrates' court – 3 months' imprisonment
Maximum sentence in Crown Court – 12 months' imprisonment
\* To include a curfew and/or unpaid work requirement only
[1] In A1 cases which are particularly serious and where the consequences of the delay have a severe impact on victim(s) and /or witness(es), a sentence in excess of the specified range may be appropriate.

### Fines

[For the standard schedule of fines see **SG2-5**.]

### Community Orders and Custodial Sentences

[For the imposition of community orders, including the community orders table, see Imposition of Community and Custodial Sentences at **SG9-2**. For the imposition of custodial sentences see Imposition of Community and Custodial Sentences at **SG9-3**.]

### Additional Factors Affecting Seriousness

The table below contains a **non-exhaustive** list of additional factual elements providing the context of the offence and factors relating to the offender. Identify whether any combination of these, or other relevant factors, should result in an upward or downward adjustment from the starting point. In some cases, having considered these factors, it may be appropriate to move outside the identified category range.

### Factors increasing seriousness

*Statutory aggravating factor*

- Previous convictions, having regard to
  a) the nature of the offence to which the conviction relates and its relevance to the current offence; and
  b) the time that has elapsed since the conviction

*Other aggravating factors*
- History of breach of court orders or police bail
- Distress to victim(s) and /or witness(es)
- Offence committed on licence or while subject to post sentence supervision

**Factors reducing seriousness or reflecting personal mitigation**
- Genuine misunderstanding of bail or requirements
- Prompt voluntary surrender
- Sole or primary carer for dependent relatives

### STEP 3  Consider any factors which indicate a reduction for assistance to the prosecution

The court should take into account section 74 of the Sentencing Code (reduction in sentence for assistance to prosecution) and any other rule of law by virtue of which an offender may receive a discounted sentence in consequence of assistance given (or offered) to the prosecutor or investigator.

### STEP 4  Reduction for guilty pleas

The court should take account of any potential reduction for a guilty plea in accordance with section 73 of the Sentencing Code and the guideline for Reduction in Sentence for a Guilty Plea [SG5-1–SG5-12].

### STEP 5  Totality principle

If sentencing an offender for more than one offence, or where the offender is already serving a sentence, consider whether the total sentence is just and proportionate to the overall offending behaviour in accordance with the *Totality* guideline. [See **SG4**]

### STEP 6  Ancillary orders

In all cases the court should consider whether to make **compensation** [See **SG10-47**] and/or ancillary orders.

Where the offence has resulted in personal injury, loss or damage the court must give reasons if it decides not to order compensation (Sentencing Code, s.55).

[See the Sentencing Council Explanatory Materials for Ancillary Orders in the Magistrates' Courts at **SG10-5** and the Crown Court Compendium, Part II Sentencing, S7; Ancillary Orders]

Note: when dealing with a breach of a sexual harm prevention order, the court has no standalone power to make a fresh order or to vary the order.

The court only has the power to vary an order if an application is made in accordance with section 103E of the Sexual Offences Act 2003 or section 350 of the Sentencing Code.

The court only has the power to make an order in the circumstances set out in section 103A of the Sexual Offences Act 2003 or section 345 of the Sentencing Code.

### STEP 7  Reasons

Section 52 of the Sentencing Code imposes a duty to give reasons for, and explain the effect of, the sentence.

### STEP 8  Consideration for time spent on bail (tagged curfew)

The court must consider whether to give credit for time spent on bail in accordance with section 240A of the Criminal Justice Act 2003 and section 325 of the Sentencing Code.

## BREACH OF A PROTECTIVE ORDER (RESTRAINING AND NON-MOLESTATION ORDERS)                                    SG15-6

*Family Law Act 1996, s.42A (breach of non-molestation order), Protection from Harassment Act 1997, s.5A, Sentencing Code, s.363 (restraining orders)*

Effective from: 01 October 2018

Triable either way
Maximum: 5 years' custody
Offence range: Fine–4 years' custody

### STEP 1  Determining the offence category

The court should determine the offence category with reference only to the factors listed in the tables below. In order to determine the category the court should assess **culpability** and **harm**.

Sentencing Guidelines

### Culpability

In assessing culpability, the court should consider the intention and motivation of the offender in committing any breach.

| A | • Very serious and/or persistent breach |
|---|---|
| B | • Deliberate breach falling between A and C |
| C | • Minor breach<br>• Breach just short of reasonable excuse |

### Harm

The level of harm is determined by weighing up all the factors of the case to determine the harm that has been caused or was intended to be caused.

| Category 1 | Breach causes **very** serious harm or distress |
|---|---|
| Category 2 | Cases falling between categories 1 and 3 |
| Category 3 | Breach causes little or no harm or distress* |

\* where a breach is committed in the context of a background of domestic abuse, the sentencer should take care not to underestimate the harm which may be present in a breach

### STEP 2  Starting point and category range

Having determined the category at step one, the court should use the corresponding starting point to reach a sentence within the category range from the appropriate sentence table below. The starting point applies to all offenders irrespective of plea or previous convictions.

| Harm | Culpability | | |
|---|---|---|---|
| | A | B | C |
| Category 1 | **Starting point**<br>2 years' custody<br>**Category range**<br>1–4 years' custody | **Starting point**<br>1 year's custody<br>**Category range**<br>High level community order–2 years' custody | **Starting point**<br>12 weeks' custody<br>**Category range**<br>Medium level community order–1 year's custody |
| Category 2 | **Starting point**<br>1 year's custody<br>**Category range**<br>High level community order–2 years' custody | **Starting point**<br>12 weeks' custody<br>**Category range**<br>Medium level community order–1 year's custody | **Starting point**<br>High level community order<br>**Category range**<br>Low level community order–26 weeks' custody |
| Category 3 | **Starting point**<br>12 weeks' custody<br>**Category range**<br>Medium level community order–1 year's custody | **Starting point**<br>High level community order<br>**Category range**<br>Low level community order–26 weeks' custody | **Starting point**<br>Low level community order<br>**Category range**<br>Band B fine–High level community order |

The table above refers to single offences. Where there are multiple offences consecutive sentences may be appropriate – please refer to the *Totality* guideline [see SG-4].

### Additional Factors Affecting Seriousness

The table below contains a non-exhaustive list of additional factual elements providing the context of the offence and factors relating to the offender. Identify whether any combination of these, or other relevant factors, should result in an upward or downward adjustment from the starting point. In some cases, having considered these factors, it may be appropriate to move outside the identified category range.

| A | • Very serious and/or persistent breach |
|---|---|
| B | • Deliberate breach falling between A and C |
| C | • Minor breach<br>• Breach just short of reasonable excuse |

| Category 1 | Breach causes very serious harm or distress |
|------------|---------------------------------------------|
| Category 2 | Cases falling between categories 1 and 3 |
| Category 3 | Breach causes little or no harm or distress |

### Factors increasing seriousness

*Statutory aggravating factors*

- Previous convictions, having regard to
  - a) the **nature** of the offence to which the conviction relates and its **relevance** to the current offence; and
  - b) the **time** that has elapsed since the conviction
- Offence committed whilst on bail

*Other aggravating factors*

- Breach committed shortly after order made
- History of disobedience to court orders (where not already taken into account as a previous conviction)
- Breach involves a further offence (where not separately prosecuted)
- Using contact arrangements with a child/children to instigate offence and/or proven history of violence or threats by offender
- Breach results in victim or protected person being forced to leave their home
- Impact upon children or family members
- Victim or protected subject of order breached is particularly vulnerable
- Offender takes steps to prevent victim or subject harmed by breach from reporting an incident or seeking assistance
- Offence committed on licence or while subject to post sentence supervision

### Factors reducing seriousness or reflecting personal mitigation

- Breach committed after long period of compliance
- Prompt voluntary surrender/admission of breach or failure
- Age and/or lack of maturity where it affects the responsibility of the offender
- Mental disorder or learning disability where linked to the commission of the offence
- Sole or primary carer for dependent relatives
- Contact not initiated by offender – a careful examination of all the circumstances is required before weight is given to this factor

### STEPS 3 to 8

[These are in the same terms as those applicable to failure to surrender to bail: see **SG15-10** *et seq.*]

BREACH OF A CRIMINAL BEHAVIOUR ORDER        **SG15-7**
(ALSO APPLICABLE TO BREACH OF AN ANTI-SOCIAL BEHAVIOUR ORDER)

*Sentencing Code, s.339*

Triable either way
Maximum: 5 years' custody
Offence range: Fine–4 years' custody

### STEP 1   Determining the offence category

The court should determine the offence category with reference only to the factors listed in the tables below. In order to determine the category the court should assess **culpability** and **harm**.

### Culpability

In assessing culpability, the court should consider the intention and motivation of the offender in committing any breach.

| A | • Very serious and/or persistent breach |
|---|------------------------------------------|
| B | • Deliberate breach falling between A and C |
| C | • Minor breach<br>• Breach just short of reasonable excuse |

### Harm

The level of harm is determined by weighing up all the factors of the case to determine the harm that has been caused or was at risk of being caused.

In assessing any risk of harm posed by the breach, consideration should be given to the original offence(s) or activity for which the order was imposed and the circumstances in which the breach arose.

| Category 1 | • Breach causes very serious harm or distress<br>• Breach demonstrates a continuing risk of serious criminal and/or anti-social behaviour |
|---|---|
| Category 2 | • Cases falling between categories 1 and 3 |
| Category 3 | • Breach causes little or no harm or distress<br>• Breach demonstrates a continuing risk of minor criminal and/or anti-social behaviour |

## STEP 2 Starting point and category range

Having determined the category at step one, the court should use the corresponding starting point to reach a sentence within the category range from the appropriate sentence table below. The starting point applies to all offenders irrespective of plea or previous convictions.

| Harm | Culpability | | |
|---|---|---|---|
| | **A** | **B** | **C** |
| Category 1 | **Starting point**<br>2 years' custody | **Starting point**<br>1 year's custody | **Starting point**<br>12 weeks' custody |
| | **Category range**<br>1–4 years' custody | **Category range**<br>High level community order–2 years' custody | **Category range**<br>Medium level community order–1 year's custody |
| Category 2 | **Starting point**<br>1 year's custody | **Starting point**<br>12 weeks' custody | **Starting point**<br>High level community order |
| | **Category range**<br>High level community order–2 years' custody | **Category range**<br>Medium level community order–1 year's custody | **Category range**<br>Low level community order–26 weeks' custody |
| Category 3 | **Starting point**<br>12 weeks' custody | **Starting point**<br>High level community order | **Starting point**<br>Low level community order |
| | **Category range**<br>Medium level community order–1 year's custody | **Category range**<br>Low level community order–26 weeks' custody | **Category range**<br>Band B fine–High level community order |

**NOTE:** A Conditional Discharge **MAY NOT** be imposed for breach of a criminal behaviour order.

### Fines

[For the standard schedule of fines see **SG2-5**.]

### Community Orders and Custodial Sentences

[For the imposition of community orders, including the community orders table, see Imposition of Community and Custodial Sentences at SG9-2. For the imposition of custodial sentences see Imposition of Community and Custodial Sentences at SG9-3.]

### Factors increasing or reducing seriousness

The table below contains a **non-exhaustive** list of additional factual elements providing the context of the offence and factors relating to the offender. Identify whether any combination of these, or other relevant factors, should result in an upward or downward adjustment from the starting point. In some cases, having considered these factors, it may be appropriate to move outside the identified category range.

### Factors increasing seriousness

*Statutory aggravating factors*

• Previous convictions, having regard to
  a) the **nature** of the offence to which the conviction relates and its **relevance** to the current offence; and
  b) the time that has elapsed since the conviction
• Offence committed whilst on bail

*Other aggravating factors*
- Offence is a further breach, following earlier breach proceedings
- Breach committed shortly after order made
- History of disobedience of court orders or orders imposed by local authorities
- Breach constitutes a further offence (where not separately prosecuted)
- Targeting of a person the order was made to protect or a witness in the original proceedings
- Victim or protected subject of order breached is particularly vulnerable due to age, disability, culture, religion, language, or other factors
- Offence committed on licence or while subject to post sentence supervision

**Factors reducing seriousness or reflecting personal mitigation**
- Genuine misunderstanding of terms of order
- Breach committed after long period of compliance
- Prompt voluntary surrender/admission of breach or failure
- Age and/or lack of maturity where it affects the responsibility of the offender
- Mental disorder or learning disability
- Sole or primary carer for dependent relatives

## STEPS 3 to 8
[These are in the same terms as those applicable to failure to surrender to bail: see **SG15-5**.]

BREACH OF A SEXUAL HARM PREVENTION ORDER            **SG15-8**
(ALSO APPLICABLE TO BREACH OF A SEXUAL OFFENCES
PREVENTION ORDER AND TO BREACH OF A FOREIGN TRAVEL ORDER)

*Sentencing Code, s. 354, Sexual Offences Act 2003, s. 103I*

Triable either way
Maximum: 5 years' custody
Offence range Fine–4 years and 6 months' custody

## STEP 1  Determining the offence category
The court should determine the offence category with reference only to the factors listed in the tables below. In order to determine the category the court should assess **culpability** and **harm**.

**Culpability**

In assessing culpability, the court should consider the **intention** and **motivation** of the offender in committing any breach.

| A | • Very serious and/or persistent breach |
|---|---|
| B | • Deliberate breach falling between A and C |
| C | • Minor breach<br>• Breach just short of reasonable excuse |

**Harm**

The level of **harm** is determined by weighing up all the factors of the case to determine the harm that has been caused or was at risk of being caused.

In assessing any risk of harm posed by the breach, consideration should be given to the original offence(s) or activity for which the order was imposed and the circumstances in which the breach arose.

| Category 1 | Breach causes or risks **very** serious harm or distress |
|---|---|
| Category 2 | Cases falling between categories 1 and 3 |
| Category 3 | Breach causes or risks little or no harm or distress |

## STEP 2  Starting point and category range
Having determined the category at step one, the court should use the corresponding starting point to reach a sentence within the category range from the appropriate sentence table below. The starting point applies to all offenders irrespective of plea or previous convictions.

| Harm | Culpability | | |
|---|---|---|---|
| | **A** | **B** | **C** |
| Category 1 | **Starting point** 3 years' custody **Category range** 2–4 years 6 months' custody | **Starting point** 2 years' custody **Category range** 36 weeks–3 years' custody | **Starting point** 1 year's custody **Category range** High level community order–2 years' custody |
| Category 2 | **Starting point** 2 years' custody **Category range** 36 weeks–3 years' custody | **Starting point** 1 year's custody **Category range** High level community order–2 years' custody | **Starting point** High level community order **Category range** Medium level community order–26 weeks' custody |
| Category 3 | **Starting point** 1 year's custody **Category range** High level community order–2 years' custody | **Starting point** 26 weeks' custody **Category range** Medium level community order–36 weeks' custody | **Starting point** Medium level community order **Category range** Band B fine–High level community order |

### Fines

[For the standard schedule of fines see **SG2-5**.]

### Community Orders and Custodial Sentences

[For the imposition of community orders, including the community orders table, see Imposition of Community and Custodial Sentences at **SG9-2**. For the imposition of custodial sentences see Imposition of Community and Custodial Sentences at **SG9-3**.]

### Factors increasing or reducing seriousness

The table below contains a **non-exhaustive** list of additional factual elements providing the context of the offence and factors relating to the offender. Identify whether any combination of these, or other relevant factors, should result in an upward or downward adjustment from the starting point. In some cases, having considered these factors, it may be appropriate to move outside the identified category range.

### Factors increasing seriousness

*Statutory aggravating factors*

- Previous convictions, having regard to
    a) the nature of the offence to which the conviction relates and its relevance to the current offence; and
    b) the time that has elapsed since the conviction
- Offence committed whilst on bail

*Other aggravating factors*

- Breach committed immediately or shortly after order made
- History of disobedience of court orders (where not already taken into account as a previous conviction)
- Breach involves a further offence (where not separately prosecuted)
- Targeting of particular individual the order was made to protect
- Victim or protected subject of order is particularly vulnerable
- Offender takes steps to prevent victim or subject harmed by breach from reporting an incident or seeking assistance
- Offence committed on licence or while subject to post sentence supervision

### Factors reducing seriousness or reflecting personal mitigation

- Breach committed after long period of compliance
- Prompt voluntary surrender/admission of breach
- Age and/or lack of maturity where it affects the responsibility of the offender
- Mental disorder or learning disability where linked to the commission of the offence
- Sole or primary carer for dependent relatives

### STEPS 3 to 8

[These are in the same terms as those applicable to failure to surrender to bail: see **SG15-5**.]

*Sexual Offences Act 2003 (section 91)*

Triable either way
Maximum: 5 years' custody
Offence range: Fine–4 years' custody

## STEP 1  Determining the offence category

The court should determine the offence category with reference only to the factors listed in the tables below. In order to determine the category the court should assess **culpability** and **harm**.

### Culpability

In assessing culpability, the court should consider the **intention** and **motivation** of the offender in committing any breach.

| A | • Determined attempts to avoid detection<br>• Long period of non compliance |
|---|---|
| B | • Deliberate failure to comply with requirement |
| C | • Minor breach<br>• Breach just short of reasonable excuse |

### Harm

The level of **harm** is determined by weighing up all the factors of the case to determine the harm that has been caused or was at risk of being caused.

In assessing any risk of harm posed by the breach, consideration should be given to the original offence(s) or activity for which the order was imposed and the circumstances in which the breach arose.

| Category 1 | Breach causes or risks very serious harm or distress |
|---|---|
| Category 2 | Cases falling between categories 1 and 3 |
| Category 3 | Breach causes or risks little or no harm or distress |

## STEP 2  Starting point and category range

Having determined the category at step one, the court should use the corresponding starting point to reach a sentence within the category range from the appropriate sentence table below. The starting point applies to all offenders irrespective of plea or previous convictions.

| Harm | Culpability | | |
|---|---|---|---|
| | **A** | **B** | **C** |
| Category 1 | **Starting point**<br>2 years' custody<br>**Category range**<br>1 year's–4 years' custody | **Starting point**<br>1 year's custody<br>**Category range**<br>26 weeks'–2 years' custody | **Starting point**<br>36 weeks' custody<br>**Category range**<br>26 weeks'–1 year 6 months' custody |
| Category 2 | **Starting point**<br>1 year's custody<br>**Category range**<br>26 weeks'–2 years' custody | **Starting point**<br>36 weeks' custody<br>**Category range**<br>26 weeks'–1 year 6 months' custody | **Starting point**<br>High level community order<br>**Category range**<br>Medium level community order–36 weeks' custody |
| Category 3 | **Starting point**<br>36 weeks' custody<br>**Category range**<br>26 weeks'–1 year 6 months' custody | **Starting point**<br>High level community order<br>**Category range**<br>Medium level community order–36 weeks' custody | **Starting point**<br>Low level community order<br>**Category range**<br>Band B fine–Medium level community order |

### Fines

[For the standard schedule of fines see **SG2-5**.]

**Factors reducing seriousness or reflecting personal mitigation**

- Breach not motivated by personal gain
- Breach committed after long period of compliance
- Genuine misunderstanding of terms of disqualification
- Evidence of voluntary reparation/compensation made to those suffering loss
- Breach activity minimal or committed for short duration
- Age and/or lack of maturity where it affects the responsibility of the offender
- Mental disorder or learning disability where linked to the commission of the offence
- Sole or primary carer for dependent relatives

## STEPS 3 to 8

[These are in the same terms as those applicable to failure to surrender to bail: see **SG15-5** *et seq.*]

**SG15-11**            BREACH OF DISQUALIFICATION FROM KEEPING AN ANIMAL

*Animal Welfare Act 2006 (section 34(9))*

Triable only summarily
Maximum: 6 months' custody
Offence range: Discharge–26 weeks' custody

## STEP 1  Determining the offence category

The court should determine the offence category with reference only to the factors listed in the tables below. In order to determine the category the court should assess **culpability** and **harm**.

**Culpability**

| A | Serious and/or persistent breach |
|---|---|
| B | All other cases |

**Harm**

The level of **harm** is determined by weighing up all the factors of the case to determine the harm that has been caused or was at risk of being caused.

In assessing any risk of harm posed by the breach, consideration should be given to the original offence(s) or activity for which the order was imposed and the circumstances in which the breach arose.

| Category 1 | • Breach causes or risks death or very serious harm or suffering to animal(s)<br>• Breach results in risk of or actual serious harm to individual(s) |
|---|---|
| Category 2 | • Cases falling between categories 1 and 3 |
| Category 3 | • Breach causes or risks little or no harm or suffering to animal(s)<br>• Breach results in very low risk of or little or no harm to individual(s) |

## STEP 2  Starting point and category range

Having determined the category at step one, the court should use the corresponding starting point to reach a sentence within the category range from the appropriate sentence table below. The starting point applies to all offenders irrespective of plea or previous convictions. The court should then consider further adjustment within the category range for aggravating or mitigating features.

| Harm | Culpability | |
| | A | B |
|---|---|---|
| Category 1 | **Starting point**<br>16 weeks' custody<br>**Category range**<br>6 weeks'–26 weeks' custody | **Starting point**<br>8 weeks' custody<br>**Category range**<br>Medium level community order–16 weeks' custody |
| Category 2 | **Starting point**<br>8 weeks' custody<br>**Category range**<br>Medium level community order–16 weeks' custody | **Starting point**<br>Medium level community order<br>**Category range**<br>Band C Fine–High level community order |

| Harm | Culpability | |
|------|-------------|---|
| | **A** | **B** |
| Category 3 | **Starting point**<br>Medium level community order<br>**Category range**<br>Band C Fine–High level community order | **Starting point**<br>Band A Fine<br>**Category range**<br>Discharge–Band B Fine |

### Fines
[For the standard schedule of fines see **SG2-5**.]

### Community Orders and Custodial Sentences
[For the imposition of community orders, including the community orders table, see Imposition of Community and Custodial Sentences at **SG9-2**. For the imposition of custodial sentences see Imposition of Community and Custodial Sentences at **SG9-3**.]

### Factors increasing or reducing seriousness
The table below contains a **non-exhaustive** list of additional factual elements providing the context of the offence and factors relating to the offender. Identify whether any combination of these, or other relevant factors, should result in an upward or downward adjustment from the starting point. In some cases, having considered these factors, it may be appropriate to move outside the identified category range.

### Factors increasing seriousness
*Statutory aggravating factors*
- Previous convictions, having regard to
  a) the nature of the offence to which the conviction relates and its relevance to the current offence; and
  b) the time that has elapsed since the conviction
- Offence committed whilst on bail

*Other aggravating factors*
- Breach committed immediately or shortly after order made
- History of disobedience to court orders
- Breach conducted in commercial context
- Breach involves deceit regarding ownership of/responsibility for animal
- Harm risked or caused to multiple animals (where not taken into account at step one)
- Offence committed on licence or while subject to post sentence supervision

### Factors reducing seriousness or reflecting personal mitigation
- Breach committed after long period of compliance
- Genuine misunderstanding of terms of order
- Prompt voluntary surrender/admission of breach or failure
- Age and/or lack of maturity where it affects the responsibility of the offender
- Mental disorder or learning disability where linked to the commission of the offence
- Sole or primary carer for dependent relatives

### STEPS 3 to 8
[These are in the same terms as those applicable to failure to surrender to bail: see **SG15-5**.]

## OTHER BREACH OFFENCES                                        **SG15-12**

Where an offence is not covered by a sentencing guideline a court is also entitled to use, and may be assisted by, a guideline for an analogous offence subject to differences in the elements of the offences and the statutory maxima.

In sentencing the breach offences below, the court should refer to the sentencing approach in step one of the guideline for breach of a criminal behaviour order [see **SG15-7**] to determine culpability and harm, and determine an appropriate sentence bearing in mind the maximum penalty for the offence.

| Offence | Mode of Trial | Maximum Sentence |
|---|---|---|
| Breach of football banning order (section 14J Football Spectators Act 1989 | Triable summarily only | A person guilty of an offence under this section is liable on summary conviction to imprisonment for a term not exceeding six months, or a fine not exceeding level 5 on the standard scale, or both. |
| Failure to comply with dispersal order Part 3 Anti-social Behaviour, Crime and Policing Act 2014 (Requires a person committing, or likely to commit ASB to leave an area for up to 48 hours.) | Triable summarily only | A person guilty of an offence under subsection (1) (Failure to move on) is liable on summary conviction— to imprisonment for a period not exceeding 3 months, or to a fine not exceeding level 4 on the standard scale. A person guilty of an offence under subsection (3) (Failure to hand over items) is liable on summary conviction to a fine not exceeding level 2 on the standard scale. |
| Community protection notice Part 4, Chapter 1 Anti-social Behaviour, Crime and Policing Act 2014 (Stops a person, business or organisation committing ASB which spoils the community's quality of life.) | Triable summarily only | A person guilty of an offence under this section is liable on summary conviction - to a fine not exceeding level 4 on the standard scale, in the case of an individual; or an unlimited fine in the case of a body (If dealt with by way of fixed penalty, a fixed penalty notice of up to £100.) |
| Breach of public spaces protection order Part 4, Chapter 2 Anti-social Behaviour, Crime and Policing Act 2014 (Stops people committing ASB in a particular public place.) | Triable summarily only | A person guilty of an offence under this section is liable on summary conviction to a fine not exceeding level 3 on the standard scale. (If dealt with by way of fixed penalty, a fixed penalty notice of up to £100.) |
| Closure Power Part 4, Chapter 3 Anti-social Behaviour, Crime and Policing Act 2014 (Allows the police or local council to close premises where ASB is being committed, or is likely to be committed.) | Triable summarily only | A person guilty of obstructing a person acting under section 79 or 85(1) is liable on summary conviction— (a) to imprisonment for a period not exceeding 3 months, or (b) to a fine A person who is guilty of remaining on or entering premises in contravention of a closure order is liable on summary conviction— (a) to imprisonment for a period not exceeding 6 months, or (b) to a fine, or to both. |

# PART 16   BAIL, FAIL TO SURRENDER TO

[Failure to Surrender to Bail is now included in Breach Offences at **SG15-12**.]

# PART 17    ANTI-SOCIAL BEHAVIOUR ORDERS, BREACH OF

[Breach of a Criminal Behaviour order is now at SG15-13.]

# PART 18   PROTECTIVE ORDER, BREACH OF

[Breach of a Protective Order is now at **SG15-6.**]

# PART 19   BURGLARY OFFENCES

APPLICABILITY

[For the standard text on applicability see **SG0-4**.]

AGGRAVATED BURGLARY

*Theft Act 1968 (section 10)*

**Effective from:** 16 January 2012

Triable only on indictment
Maximum: Life imprisonment
Offence range: 1–13 years' custody

This is a Schedule 19 offence for the purposes of sections 274 and 285 (required life sentence for offence carrying life sentence) of the Sentencing Code.

This is a specified offence for the purposes of sections 266 and 279 (extended sentence for certain violent, sexual or terrorism offences) of the Sentencing Code.

## STEP 1  Determining the offence category

The court should determine the offence category using the table below.

| Category 1 | Greater harm **and** higher culpability |
| --- | --- |
| Category 2 | Greater harm **and** lower culpability **or** lesser harm **and** higher culpability |
| Category 3 | Lesser harm **and** lower culpability |

The court should determine culpability and harm caused or intended, by reference only to the factors below, which comprise the principal factual elements of the offence. Where an offence does not fall squarely into a category, individual factors may require a degree of weighting before making an overall assessment and determining the appropriate offence category.

### Harm

*Factors indicating greater harm*

- Theft of/damage to property causing a significant degree of loss to the victim (whether economic, commercial, sentimental or personal value)
- Soiling, ransacking or vandalism of property
- Victim at home or on the premises (or returns) while offender present
- Significant physical or psychological injury or other significant trauma to the victim
- Violence used or threatened against victim, particularly involving a weapon
- Context of general public disorder

*Factors indicating lesser harm*

- No physical or psychological injury or other significant trauma to the victim
- No violence used or threatened and a weapon is not produced

### Culpability

*Factors indicating higher culpability*

- Victim or premises deliberately targeted (for example, due to vulnerability or hostility based on disability, race, sexual orientation)
- A significant degree of planning or organisation
- Equipped for burglary (for example, implements carried and/or use of vehicle)
- Weapon present on entry
- Member of a group or gang

**Factors indicating lower culpability**

- Offender exploited by others
- Mental disorder or learning disability, where linked to the commission of the offence

## STEP 2  Starting point and category range

Having determined the category, the court should use the corresponding starting points to reach a sentence within the category range below. The starting point applies to all offenders irrespective of plea or previous convictions. A case of particular gravity, reflected by multiple features of culpability or harm in step 1, could merit upward adjustment from the starting point before further adjustment for aggravating or mitigating features.

| Offence Category | Starting Point (*Applicable to all offenders*) | Category Range (*Applicable to all offenders*) |
|---|---|---|
| Category 1 | 10 years' custody | 9–13 years' custody |
| Category 2 | 6 years' custody | 4–9 years' custody |
| Category 3 | 2 years' custody | 1–4 years' custody |

[For the Guidelines relating to Custodial Sentences see **SG9-3**.]

### Factors increasing or reducing seriousness

The table below contains a **non-exhaustive** list of additional factual elements providing the context of the offence and factors relating to the offender. Identify whether any combination of these, or other relevant factors, should result in an upward or downward adjustment from the starting point. **In particular, relevant recent convictions are likely to result in an upward adjustment.** In some cases, having considered these factors, it may be appropriate to move outside the identified category range.

| Factors increasing seriousness | Factors reducing seriousness or reflecting personal mitigation |
|---|---|
| *Statutory aggravating factors:* Previous convictions, having regard to a) the nature of the offence to which the conviction relates and its relevance to the current offence; and b) the time that has elapsed since the conviction Offence committed whilst on bail | Subordinate role in a group or gang Injuries caused recklessly Nothing stolen or only property of very low value to the victim (whether economic, commercial, sentimental or personal) Offender has made voluntary reparation to the victim No previous convictions or no relevant/recent convictions Remorse Good character and/or exemplary conduct Determination, and/or demonstration of steps taken to address addiction or offending behaviour Serious medical conditions requiring urgent, intensive or long-term treatment Age and/or lack of maturity where it affects the responsibility of the offender Lapse of time since the offence where this is not the fault of the offender Mental disorder or learning disability, where not linked to the commission of the offence Sole or primary carer for dependent relatives |
| *Other aggravating factors include:* Child at home (or returns home) when offence committed Offence committed at night Abuse of power and/or position of trust Gratuitous degradation of victim Any steps taken to prevent the victim reporting the incident or obtaining assistance and/or from assisting or supporting the prosecution Victim compelled to leave their home (in particular victims of domestic violence) Established evidence of community impact Commission of offence whilst under the influence of alcohol or drugs Failure to comply with current court orders Offence committed whilst on licence Offences Taken Into Consideration (TICs) | |

### STEP 3  Consider any factors which indicate a reduction, such as assistance to the prosecution

The court should take into account section 74 of the Sentencing Code (reduction in sentence for assistance to prosecution) and any other rule of law by virtue of which an offender may receive a discounted sentence in consequence of assistance given (or offered) to the prosecutor or investigator.

### STEP 4  Reduction for guilty pleas

The court should take account of any potential reduction for a guilty plea in accordance with section 73 of the Sentencing Code and the guideline for Reduction in Sentence for a Guilty Plea (where first hearing is on or after 1 June 2017 [see **SG5-1**], or first hearing before 1 June 2017 [see **SG5-12**]).

### STEP 5  Dangerousness

The court should consider whether having regard to the criteria contained in Chapter 6 of Part 10 of the Sentencing Code it would be appropriate to impose a life sentence (sections 274 and 285) or an extended sentence (sections 266 and 279). When sentencing offenders to a life sentence under these provisions the notional determinate sentence should be used as the basis for the setting of a minimum term.

**STEP 6  Totality principle**

If sentencing an offender for more than one offence, or where the offender is already serving a sentence, consider whether the total sentence is just and proportionate to the offending behaviour. See the *Totality* guideline [see **SG4**].

**STEP 7  Compensation and ancillary orders**

In all cases, courts should consider whether to make compensation and/or other ancillary orders. Where the offence has resulted in personal injury, loss or damage the court must give reasons if it decides not to order compensation (Sentencing Code, s.55).

[See Ancillary orders – Crown Court Compendium, Part II Sentencing, S7.]

**STEP 8  Reasons**

Section 52 of the Sentencing Code imposes a duty to give reasons for, and explain the effect of, the sentence.

**STEP 9  Consideration for time spent on bail (tagged curfew)**

The court must consider whether to give credit for time spent on bail in accordance with section 240A of the Criminal Justice Act 2003 and section 325 of the Sentencing Code.

**SG19-3**                                    DOMESTIC BURGLARY

*Theft Act 1968 (section 9)*

**Effective from:** 16 January 2012

Triable either way (except as noted below)
Maximum when tried summarily: Level 5 fine and/or 26 weeks' custody
Maximum when tried on indictment: 14 years' custody

Offence range: Community order–6 years' custody

This is a specified offence for the purposes of sections 266 and 279 (extended sentence for certain violent, sexual or terrorism offences) of the Sentencing Code if it was committed with intent to:

    (a)  inflict grievous bodily harm on a person, or
    (b)  do unlawful damage to a building or anything in it.

This offence is indictable only where:

    (a)  it is a burglary comprising the commission of, or an intention to commit, an offence which is triable only on indictment; or
    (b)  any person in the dwelling was subjected to violence or the threat of violence; or
    (c)  if the defendant were convicted, it would be a third qualifying conviction for domestic burglary.

Where sentencing an offender for a qualifying third domestic burglary, the Court must apply section 314 of the Sentencing Code and impose a custodial term of at least three years, unless it is satisfied that there are particular circumstances which relate to any of the offences or to the offender which would make it unjust to do so.

**STEP 1  Determining the offence category**

The court should determine the offence category using the table below.

| Category 1 | Greater harm **and** higher culpability |
|---|---|
| Category 2 | Greater harm **and** lower culpability **or** lesser harm **and** higher culpability |
| Category 3 | Lesser harm **and** lower culpability |

The court should determine culpability and harm caused or intended, by reference **only** to the factors below, which comprise the principal factual elements of the offence. Where an offence does not fall squarely into a category, individual factors may require a degree of weighting before making an overall assessment and determining the appropriate offence category.

**Harm**

*Factors indicating greater harm*

- Theft of/damage to property causing a significant degree of loss to the victim (whether economic, sentimental or personal value)
- Soiling, ransacking or vandalism of property

- Occupier at home (or returns home) while offender present
- Trauma to the victim, beyond the normal inevitable consequence of intrusion and theft
- Violence used or threatened against victim
- Context of general public disorder

*Factors indicating lesser harm*

- Nothing stolen or only property of very low value to the victim (whether economic, sentimental or personal)
- Limited damage or disturbance to property

## Culpability

*Factors indicating higher culpability*

- Victim or premises deliberately targeted (for example, due to vulnerability or hostility based on disability, race, sexual orientation)
- A significant degree of planning or organisation
- Knife or other weapon carried (where not charged separately)
- Equipped for burglary (for example, implements carried and/or use of vehicle)
- Member of a group or gang

*Factors indicating lower culpability*

- Offence committed on impulse, with limited intrusion into property
- Offender exploited by others
- Mental disorder or learning disability, where linked to the commission of the offence

## STEP 2  Starting point and category range

Having determined the category, the court should use the corresponding starting points to reach a sentence within the category range below. The starting point applies to all offenders irrespective of plea or previous convictions.

Where the offender is dependent on or has a propensity to misuse drugs and there is sufficient prospect of success, a community order with a drug rehabilitation requirement under Part 10 of Schedule 9 of the Sentencing Code may be a proper alternative to a short or moderate custodial sentence.

A case of particular gravity, reflected by multiple features of culpability or harm in step 1, could merit upward adjustment from the starting point before further adjustment for aggravating or mitigating features, set out below.

| Offence Category | Starting Point *(Applicable to all offenders)* | Category Range *(Applicable to all Offenders)* |
|---|---|---|
| Category 1 | 3 years' custody | 2–6 years' custody |
| Category 2 | 1 year's custody | High level community order–2 years' custody |
| Category 3 | High level Community Order | Low level community order–26 weeks' custody |

### Community Orders and Custodial Sentences

[For the imposition of community orders, including the community orders table, see Imposition of Community and Custodial Sentences at **SG9-2**. For the imposition of custodial sentences see Imposition of Community and Custodial Sentences at **SG9-3**.]

### Factors increasing or reducing seriousness

The table below contains a non-exhaustive list of additional factual elements providing the context of the offence and factors relating to the offender. Identify whether any combination of these, or other relevant factors, should result in an upward or downward adjustment from the starting point. **In particular, relevant recent convictions are likely to result in an upward adjustment**. In some cases, having considered these factors, it may be appropriate to move outside the identified category range.

When sentencing **category 2 or 3** offences, the court should also consider the custody threshold as follows:

- Has the custody threshold been passed?
- If so, is it unavoidable that a custodial sentence be imposed?
- If so, can that sentence be suspended?

| Factors increasing seriousness | Factors reducing seriousness or reflecting personal mitigation |
|---|---|
| *Statutory aggravating factors*: Previous convictions, having regard to a) the nature of the offence to which the conviction relates and its relevance to the current offence; and b) the time that has elapsed since the conviction[*] <br> Offence committed whilst on bail <br><br> *Other aggravating factors include*: <br> Child at home (or returns home) when offence committed <br> Offence committed at night <br> Gratuitous degradation of the victim <br> Any steps taken to prevent the victim reporting the incident or obtaining assistance and/or from assisting or supporting the prosecution <br> Victim compelled to leave their home (in particular victims of domestic violence) <br> Established evidence of community impact <br> Commission of offence whilst under the influence of alcohol or drugs <br> Failure to comply with current court orders <br> Offence committed whilst on licence <br> Offences Taken Into Consideration (TICs) | Offender has made voluntary reparation to the victim <br> Subordinate role in a group or gang <br> No previous convictions or no relevant/recent convictions <br> Remorse <br> Good character and/or exemplary conduct <br> Determination, and/or demonstration of steps taken to address addiction or offending behaviour <br> Serious medical conditions requiring urgent, intensive or long-term treatment <br> Age and/or lack of maturity where it affects the responsibility of the offender <br> Lapse of time since the offence where this is not the fault of the offender <br> Mental disorder or learning disability, where not linked to the commission of the offence <br> Sole or primary carer for dependent relatives |

\* Where sentencing an offender for a qualifying **third domestic burglary**, the Court must apply section 314 of the Sentencing Code and impose a custodial term of at least three years, unless it is satisfied that there are particular circumstances which relate to any of the offences or to the offender which would make it unjust to do so.

## STEP 3  Consider any factors which indicate a reduction, such as assistance to the prosecution

The court should take into account any rule of law by virtue of which an offender may receive a discounted sentence in consequence of assistance given (or offered) to the prosecutor or investigator.

## STEP 4  Reduction for guilty pleas

The court should take account of any potential reduction for a guilty plea in accordance with section 73 of the Sentencing Code and the guideline for Reduction in Sentence for a Guilty Plea [**SG5-1–SG5-12**].

*Where a minimum sentence is imposed under section 314 of the Sentencing Code, the sentence must not be less than 80 percent of the appropriate custodial period after any reduction for a guilty plea.*

## STEP 5  Dangerousness

A burglary offence under section 9 Theft Act 1968 is a serious specified offence within the meaning of chapter 5 of the Criminal Justice Act 2003 if it was committed with the intent to (a) inflict grievous bodily harm on a person, or (b) do unlawful damage to a building or anything in it. The court should consider whether having regard to the criteria contained in Chapter 6 of Part 10 of the Sentencing Code it would be appropriate to impose an extended sentence (sections 266 and 279).

## STEP 6  Totality principle

If sentencing an offender for more than one offence, or where the offender is already serving a sentence, consider whether the total sentence is just and proportionate to the offending behaviour. See the *Totality* guideline [see **SG4**].

## STEP 7  Compensation and ancillary orders

In all cases, courts should consider whether to make compensation and/or other ancillary orders.

Where the offence has resulted in personal injury, loss or damage the court must give reasons if it decides not to order compensation (Sentencing Code, s.55).

[See Ancillary orders – Magistrates' Court; Ancillary orders – Crown Court Compendium, Part II Sentencing, S7]

## STEP 8  Reasons

Section 52 of the Sentencing Code imposes a duty to give reasons for, and explain the effect of, the sentence.

## STEP 9  Consideration for time spent on bail (tagged curfew)

The court must consider whether to give credit for time spent on bail in accordance with section 240A of the Criminal Justice Act 2003 and section 325 of the Sentencing Code.

NON-DOMESTIC BURGLARY                                    **SG19-4**

*Theft Act 1968 (section 9)*

**Effective from:** 16 January 2012

Triable either way (except as noted below)
Maximum when tried summarily: Level 5 fine and/or 26 weeks' custody
Maximum when tried on indictment: 10 years' custody
Offence range: Fine–5 years' custody

This is a specified offence for the purposes of sections 266 and 279 (extended sentence for certain violent, sexual or terrorism offences) of the Sentencing Code if it was committed with intent to:

(a)  inflict grievous bodily harm on a person, or
(b)  do unlawful damage to a building or anything in it.

This offence is **indictable only** where it is a burglary comprising the commission of, or an intention to commit, an offence which is triable only on indictment.

## STEP 1  Determining the offence category

The court should determine the offence category using the table below.

| Category 1 | Greater harm **and** higher culpability |
| Category 2 | Greater harm **and** lower culpability **or** lesser harm **and** higher culpability |
| Category 3 | Lesser harm **and** lower culpability |

The court should determine culpability and harm caused or intended, by reference only to the factors below, which comprise the principal factual elements of the offence. Where an offence does not fall squarely into a category, individual factors may require a degree of weighting before making an overall assessment and determining the appropriate offence category.

### Harm

*Factors indicating greater harm*

- Theft of/damage to property causing a significant degree of loss to the victim (whether economic, commercial or personal value)
- Soiling, ransacking or vandalism of property
- Victim on the premises (or returns) while offender present
- Trauma to the victim, beyond the normal inevitable consequence of intrusion and theft
- Violence used or threatened against victim
- Context of general public disorder

*Factors indicating lesser harm*

- Nothing stolen or only property of very low value to the victim (whether economic, commercial or personal)
- Limited damage or disturbance to property

### Culpability

*Factors indicating higher culpability*

- Premises or victim deliberately targeted (to include pharmacy or doctor's surgery and targeting due to vulnerability of victim or hostility based on disability, race, sexual orientation and so forth)
- A significant degree of planning or organisation
- Knife or other weapon carried (where not charged separately)
- Equipped for burglary (for example, implements carried and/or use of vehicle)
- Member of a group or gang

*Factors indicating lower culpability*

- Offence committed on impulse, with limited intrusion into property
- Offender exploited by others
- Mental disorder or learning disability, where linked to the commission of the offence

## STEP 2  Starting point and category range

Having determined the category, the court should use the corresponding starting points to reach a sentence within the category range below. The starting point applies to all offenders irrespective of plea or previous convictions.

Where the defendant is dependent on or has a propensity to misuse drugs and there is sufficient prospect of success, a community order with a drug rehabilitation requirement under section 209 of the Criminal Justice Act 2003 may be a proper alternative to a short or moderate custodial sentence.

A case of particular gravity, reflected by multiple features of culpability or harm in step 1, could merit upward adjustment from the starting point before further adjustment for aggravating or mitigating features, set out below.

| Offence Category | Starting Point<br>*(Applicable to all offenders)* | Category Range<br>*(Applicable to all Offenders)* |
|---|---|---|
| Category 1 | 2 years' custody | 1–5 years' custody |
| Category 2 | 18 weeks' custody | Low level community order–51 weeks' custody |
| Category 3 | Medium level community order | Band B fine–18 weeks' custody |

### Fines
[For the standard schedule of fines see SG2-5.]

### Community Orders and Custodial Sentences
[For the imposition of community orders, including the community orders table, see Imposition of Community and Custodial Sentences at SG9-2. For the imposition of custodial sentences see Imposition of Community and Custodial Sentences at SG9-3.]

### Factors increasing or reducing seriousness
The table below contains a non-exhaustive list of additional factual elements providing the context of the offence and factors relating to the offender. Identify whether any combination of these, or other relevant factors, should result in an upward or downward adjustment from the starting point. **In particular, relevant recent convictions are likely to result in an upward adjustment.** In some cases, having considered these factors, it may be appropriate to move outside the identified category range.

When sentencing **category 2 or 3** offences, the court should also consider the custody threshold as follows:

- Has the custody threshold been passed?
- If so, is it unavoidable that a custodial sentence be imposed?
- If so, can that sentence be suspended?

When sentencing **category 3** offences, the court should also consider the community order threshold as follows:

- Has the community order threshold been passed?

### Factors increasing seriousness
*Statutory aggravating factors*
- Previous convictions, having regard to
  a)  the nature of the offence to which the conviction relates and its relevance to the current offence; and
  b)  the time that has elapsed since the conviction
- Offence committed whilst on bail

*Other aggravating factors include*
- Offence committed at night, particularly where staff present or likely to be present
- Abuse of a position of trust
- Gratuitous degradation of the victim
- Any steps taken to prevent the victim reporting an incident, obtaining assistance and/or from assisting or supporting the prosecution
- Established evidence of community impact
- Commission of offence whilst under the influence of alcohol or drugs
- Failure to comply with current court orders
- Offence committed on licence or post sentence supervision
- Offences taken into consideration (TICs)

### Factors reducing seriousness or reflecting personal mitigation
- Offender has made voluntary reparation to the victim
- Subordinate role in a group or gang
- No previous convictions **or** no relevant/recent convictions
- Remorse

- Good character and/or exemplary conduct
- Determination and/or demonstration of steps taken to address addiction or offending behaviour
- Serious medical conditions requiring urgent, intensive or long-term treatment
- Age and/or lack of maturity where it affects the responsibility of the offender
- Lapse of time since the offence where this is not the fault of the offender
- Mental disorder or learning disability, where not linked to the commission of the offence
- Sole or primary carer for dependent relatives

### STEP 3  Consider any other factors which indicate a reduction, such as assistance to the prosecution

The court should take into account any rule of law by virtue of which an offender may receive a discounted sentence in consequence of assistance given (or offered) to the prosecutor or investigator.

### STEP 4  Reduction for guilty pleas

The court should take account of any potential reduction for a guilty plea in accordance with section 73 of the Sentencing Code and the guideline for Reduction in Sentence for a Guilty Plea [SG5-1–SG5-12].

### STEP 5  Dangerousness

A burglary offence under section 9 Theft Act 1968 is a serious specified offence if it was committed with the intent to

(a) inflict grievous bodily harm on a person, or
(b) do unlawful damage to a building or anything in it.

The court should consider whether having regard to the criteria contained in Chapter 6 of Part 10 of the Sentencing Code it would be appropriate to impose an extended sentence (sections 266 and 279).

### STEP 6  Totality principle

If sentencing an offender for more than one offence, or where the offender is already serving a sentence, consider whether the total sentence is just and proportionate to the offending behaviour. See the *Totality* guideline [see **SG4**].

### STEP 7  Compensation and ancillary orders

In all cases, courts should consider whether to make compensation and/or other ancillary orders.

Where the offence has resulted in personal injury, loss or damage the court must give reasons if it decides not to order compensation (Sentencing Code, s.55).

[See Ancillary orders – Magistrates' Court; Ancillary orders – Crown Court Compendium, Part II Sentencing, S7]

### STEP 8  Reasons

Section 52 of the Sentencing Code imposes a duty to give reasons for, and explain the effect of, the sentence.

### STEP 9  Consideration for time spent on bail (tagged curfew)

The court must consider whether to give credit for time spent on bail in accordance with section 240A of the Criminal Justice Act 2003 and section 325 of the Sentencing Code.

*Sentencing Guidelines*

# PART 20    CHILD CRUELTY

**SG20-1**

APPLICABILITY

[For the standard text on applicability see **SG0-4**]

**SG20-2**     CRUELTY TO A CHILD – ASSAULT AND ILL TREATMENT, ABANDONMENT,
NEGLECT, AND FAILURE TO PROTECT

*Children and Young Persons Act 1933 (section 1(1))*

**Effective from:** 01 January 2019

Triable either way
Maximum: 10 years' custody
Offence range: Community order–8 years' custody

This is a specified offence for the purposes of sections 266 and 279 (extended sentence for certain violent, sexual or terrorism offences) of the Sentencing Code.

**STEP 1   Determining the offence category**

The court should determine the offence category with reference **only** to the factors listed in the tables below. In order to determine the category the court should assess **culpability** and **harm**.

The court should weigh all the factors set out below in determining the offender's culpability.

**Where there are characteristics present which fall under different levels of culpability, the court should balance these characteristics to reach a fair assessment of the offender's culpability.**

**Culpability demonstrated by one or more of the following**

*A   High culpability*

- Prolonged and/or multiple incidents of serious cruelty, including serious neglect
- Gratuitous degradation of victim and/or sadistic behaviour
- Use of very significant force
- Use of a weapon
- Deliberate disregard for the welfare of the victim
- Failure to take any steps to protect the victim from offences in which the above factors are present
- Offender with professional responsibility for the victim (where linked to the commission of the offence)

*B   Medium culpability*

- Use of significant force
- Prolonged and/or multiple incidents of cruelty, including neglect
- Limited steps taken to protect victim in cases with category A factors present
- Other cases falling between A and C because:
  - ° Factors in both high and lesser categories are present which balance each other out; and/or
  - ° The offender's culpability falls between the factors as described in high and lesser culpability

*C   Lesser culpability*

- Offender's responsibility substantially reduced by mental disorder or learning disability or lack of maturity
- Offender is victim of domestic abuse, including coercion and/or intimidation (where linked to the commission of the offence)
- Steps taken to protect victim but fell just short of what could reasonably be expected
- Momentary or brief lapse in judgement including in cases of neglect
- Use of some force or failure to protect the victim from an incident involving some force
- Low level of neglect

**Harm**

The court should consider the factors set out below to determine the level of harm that has been caused or was intended to be caused to the victim.

## Psychological, developmental or emotional harm

A finding that the psychological, developmental or emotional harm is **serious** may be based on a clinical diagnosis but the court may make such a finding based on other evidence from or on behalf of the victim that serious psychological, developmental or emotional harm exists. It is important to be clear that the absence of such a finding does **not** imply that the psychological, developmental or emotional harm suffered by the victim is minor or trivial.

*Category 1*
- Serious psychological, developmental, and/or emotional harm
- Serious physical harm (including illnesses contracted due to neglect)

*Category 2*

Cases falling between categories 1 and 3

- A high likelihood of category 1 harm being caused

*Category 3*
- Little or no psychological, developmental, and/or emotional harm
- Little or no physical harm

## STEP 2  Starting point and category range

Having determined the category at step one, the court should use the corresponding starting point to reach a sentence within the category range below. The starting point applies to all offenders irrespective of plea or previous convictions.

**Where a case does not fall squarely within a category, adjustment from the starting point may be required before adjustment for aggravating or mitigating features.**

| Harm | Culpability | | |
|---|---|---|---|
| | A | B | C |
| Category 1 | **Starting point**<br>6 years' custody | **Starting point**<br>3 years' custody | **Starting point**<br>1 year's custody |
| | **Category range**<br>4–8 years' custody | **Category range**<br>2–6 years' custody | **Category range**<br>High level community order–2 years 6 months' custody |
| Category 2 | **Starting point**<br>3 years' custody | **Starting point**<br>1 year's custody | **Starting point**<br>High level community order |
| | **Category range**<br>2–6 years' custody | **Category range**<br>High level community order–2 years 6 months' custody | **Category range**<br>Medium level community order–1 year's custody |
| Category 3 | **Starting point**<br>1 year's custody | **Starting point**<br>High level community order | **Starting point**<br>Medium level community order |
| | **Category range**<br>High level community order–2 years 6 months' custody | **Category range**<br>Medium level community order–1 year's custody | **Category range**<br>Low level community order–6 months' custody |

## Community Orders and Custodial Sentences

[For information on Community Orders, and Custodial Sentences see **SG9**.]

## Factors increasing or reducing seriousness

The table below contains a **non-exhaustive** list of additional factual elements providing the context of the offence and factors relating to the offender. Identify whether any combination of these, or other relevant factors, should result in an upward or downward adjustment from the sentence arrived at so far. In particular, relevant recent convictions are likely to result in an upward adjustment. In some cases, having considered these factors, it may be appropriate to move outside the identified category range.

**Factors increasing seriousness**

*Statutory aggravating factors*

- Previous convictions, having regard to a) the **nature** of the offence to which the conviction relates and its **relevance** to the current offence; and b) the **time** that has elapsed since the conviction
- Offence committed whilst on bail

*Other aggravating factors*

- Failure to seek medical help (where not taken into account at step one)
- Commission of offence whilst under the influence of alcohol or drugs
- Deliberate concealment and/or covering up of the offence
- Blame wrongly placed on others
- Failure to respond to interventions or warnings about behaviour
- Threats to prevent reporting of the offence
- Failure to comply with current court orders
- Offence committed on licence or post sentence supervision
- Offences taken into consideration
- Offence committed in the presence of another child

**Factors reducing seriousness or reflecting personal mitigation**

- No previous convictions **or** no relevant/recent convictions
- Remorse
- Determination and demonstration of steps having been taken to address addiction or offending behaviour, including co-operation with agencies working for the welfare of the victim
- Sole or primary carer for dependent relatives (**see step five for further guidance on parental responsibilities**)
- Good character and/or exemplary conduct (where previous good character/exemplary conduct has been used to facilitate or conceal the offence, this should not normally constitute mitigation and such conduct may constitute aggravation)
- Serious medical condition requiring urgent, intensive or long-term treatment
- Mental disorder, learning disability or lack of maturity (where not taken into account at step one)
- Co-operation with the investigation

### STEP 3 Consider any factors which indicate a reduction for assistance to the prosecution

The court should take into account section 74 of the Sentencing Code (reduction in sentence for assistance to prosecution) and any other rule of law by virtue of which an offender may receive a discounted sentence in consequence of assistance given (or offered) to the prosecutor or investigator.

### STEP 4 Reduction for guilty pleas

The court should take account of any potential reduction for a guilty plea in accordance with section 73 of the Sentencing Code and the guideline for Reduction in Sentence for a Guilty Plea [SG5-1–SG5-12].

### STEP 5 Parental responsibilities of sole or primary carers

In the majority of child cruelty cases the offender will have parental responsibility for the victim.

When considering whether to impose custody the court should step back and review whether this sentence will be in the best interests of the victim (as well as other children in the offender's care). This must be balanced with the seriousness of the offence and all sentencing options remain open to the court but careful consideration should be given to the effect that a custodial sentence could have on the family life of the victim and whether this is proportionate to the seriousness of the offence. This may be of particular relevance in lower culpability cases or where the offender has otherwise been a loving and capable parent/carer.

Where custody is unavoidable consideration of the impact on the offender's children may be relevant to the length of the sentence imposed. For more serious offences where a substantial period of custody is appropriate, this consideration will carry less weight.

### STEP 6 Dangerousness

The court should consider whether having regard to the criteria contained in Chapter 6 of Part 10 of the Sentencing Code it would be appropriate to impose an extended sentence (sections 266 and 279).

### STEP 7 Totality principle

If sentencing an offender for more than one offence, or where the offender is already serving a sentence, consider whether the total sentence is just and proportionate to the overall offending behaviour in accordance with the *Totality* guideline [see SG4].

STEP 8  Ancillary orders

- In all cases the court should consider whether to make ancillary orders. See Ancillary orders – Magistrates' Court [**SG10-5**]; Crown Court Compendium, Part II Sentencing, S7; Ancillary Orders]

STEP 9  Reasons

Section 52 of the Sentencing Code imposes a duty to give reasons for, and explain the effect of, the sentence.

STEP 10  Consideration for time spent on bail (tagged curfew)

The court must consider whether to give credit for time spent on bail in accordance with section 240A of the Criminal Justice Act 2003 and section 325 of the Sentencing Code.

## CAUSING OR ALLOWING A CHILD TO SUFFER SERIOUS PHYSICAL HARM/CAUSING OR ALLOWING A CHILD TO DIE

**SG20-3**

*Domestic Violence, Crime and Victims Act 2004 (section 5)*

Effective from: 01 January 2019

**Causing or allowing a child to suffer serious physical harm**
Indictable only
Maximum: 10 years' custody
Offence range: Community order–9 years' custody

**Causing or allowing a child to die**
Indictable only
Maximum: 14 years' custody
Offence range: 1 year's custody–14 years' custody

These are specified offences for the purposes of sections 266 and 279 (extended sentence for certain violent, sexual or terrorism offences) of the Sentencing Code.

This guideline applies only when the victim of the offence is aged 15 or under.

STEP 1  Determining the offence category

The court should determine the offence category with reference **only** to the factors listed in the tables below. In order to determine the category, the court should assess **culpability** and **harm**.

The court should weigh all the factors set out below in determining the offender's culpability.

**Where there are characteristics present which fall under different levels of culpability, the court should balance these characteristics to reach a fair assessment of the offender's culpability.**

**Culpability demonstrated by one or more of the following**

*A  High culpability*

- Prolonged and/or multiple incidents of serious cruelty, including serious neglect
- Gratuitous degradation of victim and/or sadistic behaviour
- Use of very significant force
- Use of a weapon
- Deliberate disregard for the welfare of the victim
- Failure to take any steps to protect the victim from offences in which the above factors are present
- Offender with professional responsibility for the victim (where linked to the commission of the offence)

*B  Medium culpability*

- Use of significant force
- Prolonged and/or multiple incidents of cruelty, including neglect
- Limited steps taken to protect victim in cases with category A factors present
- Other cases falling between A and C because:
  - Factors in both high and lesser categories are present which balance each other out; and/or
  - The offender's culpability falls between the factors as described in high and lesser culpability

*C  Lesser culpability*

- Offender's responsibility substantially reduced by mental disorder or learning disability or lack of maturity
- Offender is victim of domestic abuse, including coercion and/or intimidation (where linked to the commission of the offence)
- Steps taken to protect victim but fell just short of what could reasonably be expected

- Momentary or brief lapse in judgement including in cases of neglect
- Use of some force or failure to protect the victim from an incident involving some force
- Low level of neglect

## Harm

The court should consider the factors set out below to determine the level of harm that has been caused or was intended to be caused to the victim.

### Psychological, developmental or emotional harm

A finding that the psychological, developmental or emotional harm is **serious** may be based on a clinical diagnosis but the court may make such a finding based on other evidence from or on behalf of the victim that serious psychological, developmental or emotional harm exists. It is important to be clear that the absence of such a finding does **not** imply that the psychological/developmental harm suffered by the victim is minor or trivial.

### Category 1

- Death

### Category 2

- Serious physical harm which has a substantial and/or long term effect
- Serious psychological, developmental and/or emotional harm
- Significantly reduced life expectancy
- A progressive, permanent or irreversible condition

### Category 3

- Serious physical harm that does not fall into category 2

## STEP 2  Starting point and category range

Having determined the category at step one, the court should use the corresponding starting point to reach a sentence within the category range below. The starting point applies to all offenders irrespective of plea or previous convictions.

Where a case does not fall squarely within a category, adjustment from the starting point may be required before adjustment for aggravating or mitigating features.

| Harm | Culpability | | |
|---|---|---|---|
| | **A** | **B** | **C** |
| Category 1 | **Starting point**<br>9 years' custody | **Starting point**<br>5 years' custody | **Starting point**<br>2 years' custody |
| | **Category range**<br>7–14 years' custody | **Category range**<br>3–8 years' custody | **Category range**<br>1–4 years' custody |
| Category 2 | **Starting point**<br>7 years' custody | **Starting point**<br>3 years' custody | **Starting point**<br>1 year 6 months' custody |
| | **Category range**<br>5–9 years' custody | **Category range**<br>1 year 6 months–6 years' custody | **Category range**<br>6 months–3 years' custody |
| Category 3 | **Starting point**<br>3 years' custody | **Starting point**<br>1 year 6 months' custody | **Starting point**<br>9 months' custody |
| | **Category range**<br>1 year 6 months–6 years' custody | **Category range**<br>6 months–3 years' custody | **Category range**<br>High level community order–2 years' custody |

[For information on Community Orders, and Custodial Sentences see **SG9**.]

### Factors increasing or reducing seriousness

The table below contains a **non-exhaustive** list of additional factual elements providing the context of the offence and factors relating to the offender. Identify whether any combination of these, or other relevant factors, should result in an upward or downward adjustment from the sentence arrived at so far. In particular, relevant recent convictions are likely to result in an upward adjustment. In some cases, having considered these factors, it may be appropriate to move outside the identified category range.

**Factors increasing seriousness**

*Statutory aggravating factors*
- Previous convictions, having regard to
  a) the **nature** of the offence to which the conviction relates and its **relevance** to the current offence; and
  b) the **time** that has elapsed since the conviction
- Offence committed whilst on bail

*Other aggravating factors*
- Failure to seek medical help (where not taken into account at step one)
- Prolonged suffering prior to death
- Commission of offence whilst under the influence of alcohol or drugs
- Deliberate concealment and/or covering up of the offence
- Blame wrongly placed on others
- Failure to respond to interventions or warnings about behaviour
- Threats to prevent reporting of the offence
- Failure to comply with current court orders
- Offence committed on licence or post sentence supervision
- Offences taken into consideration
- Offence committed in the presence of another child

**Factors reducing seriousness or reflecting personal mitigation**
- No previous convictions **or** no relevant/recent convictions
- Remorse
- Determination and demonstration of steps having been taken to address addiction or offending behaviour, including co-operation with agencies working for the welfare of the victim
- Sole or primary carer for dependent relatives (**see step five for further guidance on parental responsibilities**)
- Good character and/or exemplary conduct (where previous good character/exemplary conduct has been used to facilitate or conceal the offence, this should not normally constitute mitigation and such conduct may constitute aggravation)
- Serious medical condition requiring urgent, intensive or long-term treatment
- Mental disorder, learning disability or lack of maturity (where not taken into account at step one)
- Co-operation with the investigation

### STEP 3  Consider any factors which indicate a reduction for assistance to the prosecution

The court should take into account section 74 of the Sentencing Code (reduction in sentence for assistance to prosecution) and any other rule of law by virtue of which an offender may receive a discounted sentence in consequence of assistance given (or offered) to the prosecutor or investigator.

### STEP 4  Reduction for guilty pleas

The court should take account of any potential reduction for a guilty plea in accordance with section 73 of the Sentencing Code and the guideline for Reduction in Sentence for a Guilty Plea [**SG5-1–SG5-12**].

### STEP 5  Parental responsibilities of sole or primary carers

In the majority of child cruelty cases the offender will have parental responsibility for the victim.

When considering whether to impose custody the court should step back and review whether this sentence will be in the best interests of the victim (as well as other children in the offender's care). This must be balanced with the seriousness of the offence and all sentencing options remain open to the court but careful consideration should be given to the effect that a custodial sentence could have on the family life of the victim and whether this is proportionate to the seriousness of the offence. This may be of particular relevance in lower culpability cases or where the offender has otherwise been a loving and capable parent/carer.

Where custody is unavoidable consideration of the impact on the offender's children may be relevant to the length of the sentence imposed. For more serious offences where a substantial period of custody is appropriate, this consideration will carry less weight.

### STEP 6  Dangerousness

The court should consider whether having regard to the criteria contained in Chapter 6 of Part 10 of the Sentencing Code it would be appropriate to impose an extended sentence (sections 266 and 279).

### STEP 7 Totality principle

If sentencing an offender for more than one offence, or where the offender is already serving a sentence, consider whether the total sentence is just and proportionate to the overall offending behaviour in accordance with the *Totality* guideline [see **SG4**].

### STEP 8 Ancillary orders

In all cases the court should consider whether to make ancillary orders. [See the Crown Court Compendium, Part II Sentencing, S7; Ancillary Orders.]

### STEP 9 Reasons

Section 52 of the Sentencing Code imposes a duty to give reasons for, and explain the effect of, the sentence.

### STEP 10 Consideration for time spent on bail (tagged curfew)

The court must consider whether to give credit for time spent on bail in accordance with section 240A of the Criminal Justice Act 2003 and section 325 of the Sentencing Code.

**SG20-4**

## FAILING TO PROTECT GIRL FROM RISK OF GENITAL MUTILATION

*Female Genital Mutilation Act 2003 (section 3A)*

**Effective from:** 01 January 2019

Indictable only
Maximum: 7 years' custody
Offence range: Community order–6 years' custody

### STEP 1 Determining the offence category

The court should determine the offence category with reference **only** to the factors listed in the tables below. In order to determine the category, the court should assess **culpability** and **harm**.

The court should weigh all the factors set out below in determining the offender's culpability.

**Where there are characteristics present which fall under different levels of culpability, the court should balance these characteristics to reach a fair assessment of the offender's culpability.**

**Culpability demonstrated by one or more of the following**

*A High culpability*

- Child was the subject of an FGM Protection Order
- Failure to respond to interventions or warnings including, but not limited to, those from medical professionals/social services
- Involving others through coercion, intimidation or exploitation
- Failure to take any steps to protect the victim from the FGM offence

*B Medium culpability*

- Limited steps taken to protect the victim from the FGM offence
- Other cases falling between A and C because:
  ° Factors in both high and lesser categories are present which balance each other out; and/or
  ° The offender's culpability falls between the factors as described in high and lesser culpability

*C Lesser culpability*

- Steps taken to protect the victim but fell just short of what could reasonably be expected
- Offender is victim of domestic abuse (where linked to commission of the offence)
- Offender subjected to coercion, intimidation or exploitation
- Offender's responsibility substantially reduced by mental disorder or learning disability

**Harm**

The court should consider the factors set out below to determine the level of harm that has been caused to the victim.

*Psychological harm*

A finding that the psychological harm is serious may be based on a clinical diagnosis but the court may make such a finding based on other evidence from or on behalf of the victim that serious psychological harm exists. It is important to be clear that the absence of such a finding does not imply that the harm suffered by the victim is minor or trivial.

*Category 1*
- Serious physical or psychological harm which has a substantial or long-term effect

*Category 2*
- Harm which does not fall into category 1

### STEP 2  Starting point and category range

Having determined the category at step one, the court should use the corresponding starting point to reach a sentence within the category range below. The starting point applies to all offenders irrespective of plea or previous convictions.

**Where a case does not fall squarely within a category, adjustment from the starting point may be required before adjustment for aggravating or mitigating features.**

| Harm | Culpability | | |
|---|---|---|---|
| | **A** | **B** | **C** |
| Category 1 | **Starting point**<br>5 years' custody | **Starting point**<br>3 years' custody | **Starting point**<br>1 year's custody |
| | **Category range**<br>3–6 years' custody | **Category range**<br>2–4 years' custody | **Category range**<br>High level community order–3 years' custody |
| Category 2 | **Starting point**<br>3 years' custody | **Starting point**<br>1 year's custody | **Starting point**<br>High level community order |
| | **Category range**<br>2–4 years' custody | **Category range**<br>High level community order–2 years' custody | **Category range**<br>Low level community order–1 year's custody |

[For information on Community Orders, and Custodial Sentences see **SG9**.]

**Factors increasing or reducing seriousness**

The table below contains a **non-exhaustive** list of additional factual elements providing the context of the offence and factors relating to the offender. Identify whether any combination of these, or other relevant factors, should result in an upward or downward adjustment from the sentence arrived at so far. In particular, relevant recent convictions are likely to result in an upward adjustment. In some cases, having considered these factors, it may be appropriate to move outside the identified category range.

**Factors increasing seriousness**

*Statutory aggravating factors*
- Previous convictions, having regard to
  a) the nature of the offence to which the conviction relates and its relevance to the current offence; and
  b) the time that has elapsed since the conviction
- Offence committed whilst on bail

*Other aggravating factors*
- Failure to seek medical help when necessary
- Deliberate concealment and/or covering up of the offence
- Blame wrongly placed on others
- Threats to prevent reporting of the offence
- Failure to comply with current court orders (where not taken into account at step one)
- Offence committed on licence or post sentence supervision
- Offences taken into consideration

**Factors reducing seriousness or reflecting personal mitigation**
- No previous convictions or no relevant/recent convictions
- Remorse
- Offender particularly isolated with limited access to support
- Appropriate medical care sought for victim
- Sole or primary carer for dependent relatives (**see step five for further guidance on parental responsibilities**)
- Good character and/or exemplary conduct
- Serious medical condition requiring urgent, intensive or long-term treatment
- Age and/or lack of maturity

*Sentencing Guidelines*

- Mental disorder or learning disability (where not taken into account at step one)
- Co-operation with the investigation

### STEP 3 Consider any factors which indicate a reduction for assistance to the prosecution

The court should take into account section 74 of the Sentencing Code (reduction in sentence for assistance to prosecution) and any other rule of law by virtue of which an offender may receive a discounted sentence in consequence of assistance given (or offered) to the prosecutor or investigator.

### STEP 4 Reduction for guilty pleas

The court should take account of any potential reduction for a guilty plea in accordance with section 73 of the Sentencing Code and the guideline for Reduction in Sentence for a Guilty Plea [SG5-1–SG5-12].

### STEP 5 Parental responsibilities of sole or primary carers

In the majority of child cruelty cases the offender will have parental responsibility for the victim.

When considering whether to impose custody the court should step back and review whether this sentence will be in the best interests of the victim (as well as other children in the offender's care). This must be balanced with the seriousness of the offence and all sentencing options remain open to the court but careful consideration should be given to the effect that a custodial sentence could have on the family life of the victim and whether this is proportionate to the seriousness of the offence. This may be of particular relevance in lower culpability cases or where the offender has otherwise been a loving and capable parent/carer.

Where custody is unavoidable consideration of the impact on the offender's children may be relevant to the length of the sentence imposed. For more serious offences where a substantial period of custody is appropriate, this consideration will carry less weight.

### STEP 6 Totality principle

If sentencing an offender for more than one offence, or where the offender is already serving a sentence, consider whether the total sentence is just and proportionate to the overall offending behaviour in accordance with the *Totality* guideline [see SG4].

### STEP 7 Ancillary orders

In all cases the court should consider whether to make ancillary orders. [See the Crown Court Compendium, Part II Sentencing, S7; Ancillary Orders.]

### STEP 8 Reasons

Section 52 of the Sentencing Code imposes a duty to give reasons for, and explain the effect of, the sentence.

### STEP 9 Consideration for time spent on bail (tagged curfew)

The court must consider whether to give credit for time spent on bail in accordance with section 240A of the Criminal Justice Act 2003 and section 325 of the Sentencing Code.

# PART 21   DANGEROUS DOG OFFENCES

[For the standard text on applicability see **SG0-4**.]

OWNER OR PERSON IN CHARGE OF A DOG DANGEROUSLY OUT OF CONTROL IN    SG21-2
ANY PLACE IN ENGLAND OR WALES (WHETHER OR NOT A PUBLIC PLACE) WHERE
DEATH IS CAUSED

*Dangerous Dogs Act 1991 (section 3(1))*

**Effective from:** 01 July 2016

Triable either way
Maximum: 14 years' custody
Offence range: High level community order–14 years' custody

## STEP 1  Determining the offence category

In order to determine the category the court should assess **culpability** and **harm**. The court should determine the offence category with reference only to the factors in the tables below.

The level of culpability is determined by weighing up all the factors of the case. **Where there are characteristics present which fall under different levels of culpability, the court should balance these characteristics to reach a fair assessment of the offender's culpability.**

**Culpability demonstrated by one or more of the following**

*A – High culpability*

- Dog used as a weapon or to intimidate people
- Dog known to be prohibited
- Dog trained to be aggressive
- Offender disqualified from owning a dog, or failed to respond to official warnings, or to comply with orders concerning the dog

*B – Medium culpability*

All other cases where characteristics for categories A or C are not present, and in particular:

- Failure to respond to warnings or concerns expressed by others about the dog's behaviour
- Failure to act on prior knowledge of the dog's aggressive behaviour
- Lack of safety or control measures taken in situations where an incident could reasonably have been foreseen
- Failure to intervene in the incident (where it would have been reasonable to do so)
- Ill treatment or failure to ensure welfare needs of the dog (where connected to the offence and where not charged separately)

*C – Lesser culpability*

- Attempts made to regain control of the dog and/or intervene
- Provocation of the dog without fault of the offender
- Evidence of safety or control measures having been taken
- Incident could not have reasonably been foreseen by the offender
- Momentary lapse of control/attention

## Harm

There is no variation in the level of harm caused, as by definition the harm involved in an offence where a death is caused is always of the utmost seriousness.

## STEP 2  Starting point and category range

Having determined the category at step one, the court should use the corresponding starting points to reach a sentence within the category range below. The starting point applies to all offenders irrespective of plea or previous convictions.

Sentencing Guidelines

| High culpability | Starting point<br>8 years' custody | Category range<br>6–14 years' custody |
|---|---|---|
| Medium culpability | Starting point<br>4 years' custody | Category range<br>2–7 years' custody |
| Lesser culpability | Starting point<br>1 year's custody | Category range<br>High level community order–2 years' custody |

[For information on Community Orders and Custodial Sentences see SG9.]

**The table is for single offences. Concurrent sentences reflecting the overall criminality of offending will ordinarily be appropriate where offences arise out of the same incident or facts: please refer to the *Totality* guideline** [see SG4].

### Factors increasing or reducing seriousness

The court should then consider any adjustment for any aggravating or mitigating factors. The following is a **non-exhaustive** list of additional factual elements providing the context of the offence and factors relating to the offender.

Identify whether any combination of these, or other relevant factors, should result in an upward or downward adjustment from the starting point.

### Factors increasing seriousness

*Statutory aggravating factors*

- Previous convictions, having regard to
  a) the **nature** of the offence to which the conviction relates and its **relevance** to the current offence; and
  b) the **time** that has elapsed since the conviction
- Offence committed whilst on bail
- Offence motivated by, or demonstrating hostility based on any of the following characteristics or presumed characteristics of the victim: religion, race, disability, sexual orientation or transgender identity

*Other aggravating factors*

- Victim is a child or otherwise vulnerable because of personal circumstances
- Location of the offence
- Sustained or repeated attack
- Significant ongoing effect on witness(es) to the attack
- Serious injury caused to others (where not charged separately)
- Significant practical and financial effects of offence on relatives/carers
- Allowing person insufficiently experienced or trained, to be in charge of the dog
- Lack or loss of control of dog due to influence of alcohol or drugs
- Offence committed against those working in the public sector or providing a service to the public
- Injury to other animals
- Established evidence of community/wider impact
- Failure to comply with current court orders (except where taken into account in assessing culpability)
- Offence committed on licence or post sentence supervision
- Offences taken into consideration

### Factors reducing seriousness or reflecting personal mitigation

- No previous convictions **or** no relevant/recent convictions
- Isolated incident
- No previous complaints against, or incidents involving the dog
- Evidence of responsible ownership
- Remorse
- Good character and/or exemplary conduct
- Serious medical condition requiring urgent, intensive or long-term treatment
- Age and/or lack of maturity where it affects the responsibility of the offender
- Mental disorder or learning disability
- Sole or primary carer for dependent relatives
- Determination and/or demonstration of steps having been taken to address offending behaviour

**STEP 3  Consider any factors which indicate a reduction, such as assistance to the prosecution**

The court should take into account section 74 of the Sentencing Code (reduction in sentence for assistance to prosecution) and any other rule of law by virtue of which an offender may receive a discounted sentence in consequence of assistance given (or offered) to the prosecutor or investigator.

**STEP 4  Reduction for guilty pleas**

The court should take account of any potential reduction for a guilty plea in accordance with section 44 of the Criminal Justice Act 2003 and the guideline for Reduction in Sentence for a Guilty Plea (where first hearing is on or after 1 June 2017 [see **SG5-1**], or first hearing before 1 June 2017 [see **SG5-12**]).

**STEP 5  Totality principle**

If sentencing an offender for more than one offence, or where the offender is already serving a sentence, consider whether the total sentence is just and proportionate to the overall offending behaviour in accordance with the *Totality* guideline [see **SG4**].

**STEP 6  Compensation and ancillary orders**

In all cases, the court should consider whether to make a compensation order and/or other ancillary orders.

*Compensation order*

The court should consider compensation orders in all cases where personal injury, loss or damage has resulted from the offence.

The court must give reasons if it decides not to award compensation in such cases (Sentencing Code, s.55).

**Other ancillary orders available include:**

*Disqualification from having a dog*

The court **may** disqualify the offender from having custody of a dog. The test the court should consider is whether the offender is a fit and proper person to have custody of a dog.

*Destruction order/contingent destruction order*

In any case where the offender is not the owner of the dog, the owner must be given an opportunity to be present and make representations to the court.

If the dog is a prohibited dog refer to the guideline for possession of a prohibited dog in relation to destruction/contingent destruction orders. The court **shall** make a destruction order unless the court is satisfied that the dog would not constitute a danger to public safety.

In reaching a decision, the court should consider the relevant circumstances which **must** include:

- the temperament of the dog and its past behaviour;
- whether the owner of the dog, or the person for the time being in charge of it is a fit and proper person to be in charge of the dog;

and **may** include:

- other relevant circumstances.

If the court is satisfied that the dog would not constitute a danger to public safety and the dog is not prohibited, it **may** make a contingent destruction order requiring the dog to be kept under proper control. A contingent destruction order may specify the measures to be taken by the owner for keeping the dog under proper control, which include:

- muzzling;
- keeping on a lead;
- neutering in appropriate cases; and
- excluding it from a specified place.

Where the court makes a destruction order, it **may** appoint a person to undertake destruction and order the offender to pay what it determines to be the reasonable expenses of destroying the dog and of keeping it pending its destruction.

*Fit and proper person*

In determining whether a person is a fit and proper person to be in charge of a dog the following non-exhaustive factors may be relevant:

- any relevant previous convictions, cautions or penalty notices;
- the nature and suitability of the premises that the dog is to be kept at by the person;

*Sentencing Guidelines*

- where the police have released the dog pending the court's decision whether the person has breached conditions imposed by the police; and
- any relevant previous breaches of court orders.

[See the Ancillary Orders – Magistrates' Court [at **SG10-5**] and the Crown Court Compendium, Part II Sentencing, S7; Ancillary Orders.]

### STEP 7 Reasons

Section 52 of the Sentencing Code imposes a duty to give reasons for, and explain the effect of, the sentence.

### STEP 8 Consideration for time spent on bail (tagged curfew)

The court must consider whether to give credit for time spent on bail in accordance with section 240A of the Criminal Justice Act 2003 and section 325 of the Sentencing Code.

**SG21-3**  OWNER OR PERSON IN CHARGE OF A DOG DANGEROUSLY OUT OF CONTROL IN ANY PLACE IN ENGLAND OR WALES (WHETHER OR NOT A PUBLIC PLACE) WHERE A PERSON IS INJURED

*Dangerous Dogs Act 1991 (section 3(1))*

**Effective from:** 01 July 2016

Triable either way
Maximum: 5 years' custody
Offence range: Discharge–4 years' custody

### STEP 1 Determining the offence category

In order to determine the category the court should assess **culpability** and **harm**. The court should determine the offence category with reference only to the factors in the tables below.

The level of culpability is determined by weighing up all the factors of the case. **Where there are characteristics present which fall under different levels of culpability, the court should balance these characteristics to reach a fair assessment of the offender's culpability.**

**Culpability demonstrated by one or more of the following**

*A – High culpability*

- Dog used as a weapon or to intimidate people
- Dog known to be prohibited
- Dog trained to be aggressive
- Failure to respond to official warnings or to comply with orders concerning the dog
- Offender disqualified from owning a dog, or failed to respond to official warnings, or to comply with orders concerning the dog

*B – Medium culpability*

All other cases where characteristics for categories A or C are not present, and in particular:

- Failure to respond to warnings or concerns expressed by others about the dog's behaviour
- Failure to act on prior knowledge of the dog's aggressive behaviour
- Lack of safety or control measures taken in situations where an incident could reasonably have been foreseen
- Failure to intervene in the incident (where it would have been reasonable to do so)
- Ill treatment or failure to ensure welfare needs of the dog (where connected to the offence and where not charged separately)

*C – Lesser culpability*

- Attempts made to regain control of the dog and/or intervene
- Provocation of the dog without fault of the offender
- Evidence of safety or control measures having been taken
- Incident could not have reasonably been foreseen by the offender
- Momentary lapse of control/attention

## Harm

The level of harm is assessed by weighing up all the factors of the case.

| Category 1 | Serious injury (which includes disease transmission) Serious psychological harm |
| --- | --- |
| Category 2 | Harm that falls between categories 1 and 3 |
| Category 3 | Minor injury and no significant psychological harm |

## STEP 2  Starting point and category range

Having determined the category at step one, the court should use the corresponding starting points to reach a sentence within the category range below. The starting point applies to all offenders irrespective of plea or previous convictions.

| Harm | Culpability | | |
| --- | --- | --- | --- |
| | A | B | C |
| Category 1 | Starting point 3 years' custody | Starting point 1 year 6 months' custody | Starting point High level community order |
| | Category range 2 years 6 months'–4 years' custody | Category range 6 months'–2 years 6 months' custody | Category range Medium level community order–6 months' custody |
| Category 2 | Starting point 2 years' custody | Starting point 6 months' custody | Starting point Band C fine |
| | Category range 1 year–3 years' custody | Category range Medium level community order–1 year's custody | Category range Band B fine–High level community order |
| Category 3 | Starting point 6 months' custody | Starting point Low level community | Starting point Band B fine order |
| | Category range High level community order–1 year 6 months' custody | Category range Band C fine–6 months' custody | Category range Discharge–Band C fine |

## Fines

[For the standard schedule of fines see **SG2-5**.]

## Community Orders and Custodial Sentences

[For the imposition of community orders, including the community orders table, see Imposition of Community and Custodial Sentences at **SG9-2**. For the imposition of custodial sentences see Imposition of Community and Custodial Sentences at **SG9-3**.]

**The table is for single offences. Concurrent sentences reflecting the overall criminality of offending will ordinarily be appropriate where offences arise out of the same incident or facts: please refer to the** *Totality* **guideline** [see **SG4**].

## Factors increasing or reducing seriousness

The court should then consider any adjustment for any aggravating or mitigating factors. The following is a **non-exhaustive** list of additional factual elements providing the context of the offence and factors relating to the offender.

Identify whether any combination of these, or other relevant factors, should result in an upward or downward adjustment from the starting point.

## Factors increasing seriousness

*Statutory aggravating factors*

- Previous convictions, having regard to
  a) the **nature** of the offence to which the conviction relates and its **relevance** to the current offence; and
  b) the **time** that has elapsed since the conviction
- Offence committed whilst on bail

- Offence motivated by, or demonstrating hostility based on any of the following characteristics or presumed characteristics of the victim: religion, race, disability, sexual orientation or transgender identity

### Other aggravating factors

- Victim is a child or otherwise vulnerable because of personal circumstances
- Location of the offence
- Sustained or repeated attack
- Significant ongoing effect on witness(es) to the attack
- Serious injury caused to others (where not charged separately)
- Significant practical and financial effects of offence on relatives/carers
- Allowing person insufficiently experienced or trained, to be in charge of the dog
- Lack or loss of control of dog due to influence of alcohol or drugs
- Offence committed against those working in the public sector or providing a service to the public
- Injury to other animals
- Established evidence of community/wider impact
- Failure to comply with current court orders (except where taken into account in assessing culpability)
- Offence committed on licence or post sentence supervision
- Offences taken into consideration

### Factors reducing seriousness or reflecting personal mitigation

- No previous convictions **or** no relevant/recent convictions
- Isolated incident
- No previous complaints against, or incidents involving the dog
- Evidence of responsible ownership
- Remorse
- Good character and/or exemplary conduct
- Serious medical condition requiring urgent, intensive or long-term treatment
- Age and/or lack of maturity where it affects the responsibility of the offender
- Mental disorder or learning disability
- Sole or primary carer for dependent relatives
- Determination and/or demonstration of steps having been taken to address offending behaviour

[Steps 3 to 8 are identical to those applicable where death is caused [see **SG21-2**]].

**SG21-4**     OWNER OR PERSON IN CHARGE OF A DOG DANGEROUSLY OUT OF CONTROL
IN ANY PLACE IN ENGLAND OR WALES (WHETHER OR NOT A PUBLIC PLACE)
WHERE AN ASSISTANCE DOG IS INJURED OR KILLED

*Dangerous Dogs Act 1991 (section 3(1))*

**Effective from:** 01 July 2016

Triable either way
Maximum: 3 years' custody
Offence range: Discharge–2 years' 6 months' custody

### STEP 1   Determining the offence category

In order to determine the category the court should assess **culpability** and **harm**. The court should determine the offence category with reference only to the factors in the tables below.

The level of culpability is determined by weighing up all the factors of the case. **Where there are characteristics present which fall under different levels of culpability, the court should balance these characteristics to reach a fair assessment of the offender's culpability.**

### Culpability demonstrated by one or more of the following

*A – High culpability*

- Dog used as a weapon or to intimidate people or dogs
- Dog known to be prohibited
- Dog trained to be aggressive
- Offender disqualified from owning a dog, or failed to respond to official warnings, or to comply with orders concerning the dog
- Offence motivated by, or demonstrating hostility to the victim (assisted person) based on the victim's disability (or presumed disability)

*B – Medium culpability*

All other cases where characteristics for categories A or C are not present, and in particular:

- Failure to respond to warnings or concerns expressed by others about the dog's behaviour
- Failure to act on prior knowledge of the dog's aggressive behaviour
- Lack of safety or control measures taken in situations where an incident could reasonably have been foreseen
- Failure to intervene in the incident (where it would have been reasonable to do so)
- Ill treatment or failure to ensure welfare needs of the dog (where connected to the offence and where not charged separately)

*C – Lesser culpability*

- Attempts made to regain control of the dog and/or intervene
- Provocation of the dog without fault of the offender
- Evidence of safety or control measures having been taken
- Incident could not have reasonably been foreseen by the offender
- Momentary lapse of control/attention

**Harm**

The level of **harm** is assessed by weighing up all the factors of the case.

| Category 1 | Fatality or serious injury to an assistance dog and/or |
|------------|---------------------------------------------------------|
|            | Serious impact on the assisted person (whether psychological or other harm caused by the offence) |
| Category 2 | Harm that falls between categories 1 and 3 |
| Category 3 | Minor injury to assistance dog and impact of the offence on the assisted person is limited |

**STEP 2   Starting point and category range**

Having determined the category at step one, the court should use the corresponding starting point to reach a sentence within the category range below. The starting point applies to all offenders irrespective of plea or previous convictions.

| Harm | Culpability | | |
|------|-------------|------|------|
|      | A | B | C |
| Category 1 | **Starting point** 2 years' custody | **Starting point** 9 months' custody | **Starting point** Medium level community order |
|            | **Category range** 1 year–2 years 6 months' custody | **Category range** Medium level community order–1 year's custody | **Category range** Low level community order–High level community order |
| Category 2 | **Starting point** 1 years' custody | **Starting point** High level community order | **Starting point** Band B fine |
|            | **Category range** 6 months'–1 year 6 months' custody | **Category range** Low level community order–6 months' custody | **Category range** Band A fine–Low level community order |
| Category range 3 | **Starting point** High level community order | **Starting point** Band C fine | **Starting point** Band A fine |
|                  | **Category range** Medium level community order–6 months' custody | **Category range** Band B fine–High level community order | **Category range** Discharge–Band B fine |

**Factors increasing or reducing seriousness**

The court should then consider any adjustment for any aggravating or mitigating factors. The following is a **non-exhaustive** list of additional factual elements providing the context of the offence and factors relating to the offender.

Identify whether any combination of these, or other relevant factors, should result in an upward or downward adjustment from the starting point.

**Factors increasing seriousness**

*Statutory aggravating factors*

- Previous convictions having regard to
  a) the **nature** of the offence to which the conviction relates and its **relevance** to the current offence; and
  b) the **time** that has elapsed since the conviction
- Offence committed whilst on bail
- Offence motivated by, or demonstrating hostility based on any of the following characteristics or presumed characteristics of the victim: religion, race, sexual orientation or transgender identity

*Other aggravating factors*

- Location of the offence
- Sustained or repeated attack
- Significant ongoing effect on witness(es) to the attack
- Allowing person insufficiently experienced or trained, to be in charge of the dog
- Lack or loss of control of the dog due to influence of alcohol or drugs
- Offence committed against those working in the public sector or providing a service to the public
- Injury to other animals
- Cost of retraining an assistance dog
- Established evidence of community/wider impact
- Failure to comply with current court orders (except where taken into account in assessing culpability)
- Offence committed on licence or post sentence supervision
- Offences taken into consideration

**Factors reducing seriousness or reflecting personal mitigation**

- No previous convictions **or** no relevant/recent convictions
- Isolated incident
- No previous complaints against, or incidents involving the dog
- Evidence of responsible ownership
- Remorse
- Good character and/or exemplary conduct
- Serious medical condition requiring urgent, intensive or long-term treatment
- Age and/or lack of maturity where it affects the responsibility of the offender
- Mental disorder or learning disability
- Sole or primary carer for dependent relatives
- Determination and/or demonstration of steps having been taken to address offending behaviour

[Steps 3 to 8 are identical to those applicable where death is caused [see **SG21-2**].]

**SG21-5**          Owner or Person in Charge of a Dog Dangerously
                    Out of Control in any Place in England or Wales
                         (whether or not a Public Place)

                         *Dangerous Dogs Act 1991 (section 3(1))*

**Effective from:** 01 July 2016

Triable only summarily
Maximum: 6 months' custody
Offence range: Discharge–6 months' custody

**STEP 1 Determining the offence category**

In order to determine the category the court should assess **culpability** and **harm**. The court should determine the offence category with reference only to the factors in the tables below.

The level of culpability is determined by weighing up all the factors of the case. **Where there are characteristics present which fall under different levels of culpability, the court should balance these characteristics to reach a fair assessment of the offender's culpability.**

**Culpability demonstrated by one or more of the following**

| A – Higher culpability |
| --- |
| Dog used as a weapon or to intimidate people |
| Dog known to be prohibited |
| Dog trained to be aggressive |
| Offender disqualified from owning a dog, or failed to respond to official warnings, or to comply with orders concerning the dog |

| B – Lower culpability |
| --- |
| Attempts made to regain control of the dog and/or intervene |
| Provocation of dog without fault of the offender |
| Evidence of safety or control measures having been taken |
| Incident could not have reasonably been foreseen by the offender |
| Momentary lapse of control/attention |

### Harm

The level of harm is assessed by weighing up all the factors of the case.

| Greater harm | Presence of children or others who are vulnerable because of personal circumstances |
| --- | --- |
| | Injury to other animals |
| Lesser harm | Low risk to the public |

### STEP 2  Starting point and category range

Having determined the category at step one, the court should use the corresponding starting point to reach a sentence within the category range below. The starting point applies to all offenders irrespective of plea or previous convictions.

| Harm | Culpability | |
| --- | --- | --- |
| | **A** | **B** |
| Greater harm | **Starting point**<br>Medium level community order | **Starting point**<br>Band B fine |
| | **Category range**<br>Band C fine–6 months' custody | **Category range**<br>Band A fine–Band C fine |
| Lesser harm | **Starting point**<br>Band C fine | **Starting point**<br>Band A fine |
| | **Category range**<br>Band B fine–Low level community order | **Category range**<br>Discharge–Band B fine |

### Fines

[For the standard schedule of fines see **SG2-5**.]

### Community Orders and Custodial Sentences

[For the imposition of community orders, including the community orders table, see Imposition of Community and Custodial Sentences at **SG9-2**. For the imposition of custodial sentences see Imposition of Community and Custodial Sentences at **SG9-3**.]

### Factors increasing or reducing seriousness

The court should then consider any adjustment for any aggravating or mitigating factors. The following is a **non-exhaustive** list of additional factual elements providing the context of the offence and factors relating to the offender.

Identify whether any combination of these, or other relevant factors, should result in an upward or downward adjustment from the starting point.

### Factors increasing seriousness

*Statutory aggravating factors*

- Previous convictions, having regard to
  a) the **nature** of the offence to which the conviction relates and its **relevance** to the current offence; and
  b) the **time** that has elapsed since the conviction

- Offence committed whilst on bail
- Offence motivated by, or demonstrating hostility based on any of the following characteristics or presumed characteristics of the victim: religion, race, disability, sexual orientation or transgender identity

*Other aggravating factors*

- Victim is a child or otherwise vulnerable because of personal circumstances
- Location of the offence
- Sustained or repeated attack
- Significant ongoing effect on witness(es) to the attack
- Serious injury caused to others (where not charged separately)
- Significant practical and financial effects of offence on relatives/carers
- Allowing person insufficiently experienced or trained, to be in charge of the dog
- Lack or loss of control of dog due to influence of alcohol or drugs
- Offence committed against those working in the public sector or providing a service to the public
- Injury to other animals
- Established evidence of community/wider impact
- Failure to comply with current court orders (except where taken into account in assessing culpability)
- Offence committed on licence or post sentence supervision
- Offences taken into consideration

**Factors reducing seriousness or reflecting personal mitigation**

- No previous convictions **or** no relevant/recent convictions
- Isolated incident
- No previous complaints against, or incidents involving the dog
- Evidence of responsible ownership
- Remorse
- Good character and/or exemplary conduct
- Serious medical condition requiring urgent, intensive or long-term treatment
- Age and/or lack of maturity where it affects the responsibility of the offender
- Mental disorder or learning disability
- Sole or primary carer for dependent relatives
- Determination and/or demonstration of steps having been taken to address offending behaviour

[Steps 3 to 8 are similar to those applicable where death or injury is caused following an attack by a dog [see **SG21-2**]. However, in Step 6, instead of the duty on the court to make a destruction order unless it is satisfied that the dog would not constitute a danger to public safety the requirement is as follows:

If the dog is not prohibited and the court is satisfied that the dog would constitute a danger to public safety the court **may** make a destruction order.

**SG21-6**                        POSSESSION OF A PROHIBITED DOG

*Dangerous Dogs Act 1991 (section 1(7))*

BREEDING, SELLING, EXCHANGING OR ADVERTISING A PROHIBITED DOG

*Dangerous Dogs Act 1991 (section 1(7))*

**Effective from:** 01 July 2016

Triable only summarily
Maximum: 6 months' custody
Offence range: Discharge–6 months' custody

**STEP 1 Determining the offence category**

In order to determine the category the court should assess **culpability** and **harm**. The court should determine the offence category with reference only to the factors in the tables below.

The level of culpability is determined by weighing up all the factors of the case. **Where there are characteristics present which fall under different levels of culpability, the court should balance these characteristics to reach a fair assessment of the offender's culpability.**

**Culpability demonstrated by one or more of the following**

| **A – Higher culpability:** |
| --- |
| Possessing a dog known to be prohibited |
| Breeding from a dog known to be prohibited |
| Selling, exchanging or advertising a dog known to be prohibited |
| Offence committed for gain |
| Dog used to threaten or intimidate |
| Permitting fighting |
| Training and/or possession of paraphernalia for dog fighting |
| **B – Lower culpability:** |
| All other cases |

## Harm

The level of harm is assessed by weighing up all the factors of the case.

| Greater harm | High risk to the public and/or animals |
| --- | --- |
| Lesser harm | Low risk to the public and/or animals |

## STEP 2  Starting point and category range

Having determined the category at step one, the court should use the corresponding starting point to reach a sentence within the category range below. The starting point applies to all offenders irrespective of plea or previous convictions.

| Harm | Culpability | |
| --- | --- | --- |
| | A | B |
| Greater harm | **Starting point**<br>Medium level community order | **Starting point**<br>Band B fine |
| | **Category range**<br>Band C fine–6 months' custody | **Category range**<br>Band A fine–Low level community order |
| Lesser harm | **Starting point**<br>Band C fine | **Starting point**<br>Band A fine |
| | **Category range**<br>Band B fine–Medium level community order | **Category range**<br>Discharge–Band B fine |

## Factors increasing or reducing seriousness

The court should then consider any adjustment for any aggravating or mitigating factors. The following is a **non-exhaustive** list of additional factual elements providing the context of the offence and factors relating to the offender.

Identify whether any combination of these, or other relevant factors, should result in an upward or downward adjustment from the starting point.

### Factors increasing seriousness

*Statutory aggravating factors*

- Previous convictions, having regard to
  a) the **nature** of the offence to which the conviction relates and its **relevance** to the current offence; and
  b) the **time** that has elapsed since the conviction
- Offence committed whilst on bail

*Other aggravating factors*

- Presence of children or others who are vulnerable because of personal circumstances
- Ill treatment or failure to ensure welfare needs of the dog (where connected to the offence and where not charged separately)
- Established evidence of community/wider impact
- Failure to comply with current court orders
- Offence committed on licence
- Offences taken into consideration

**Factors reducing seriousness or reflecting personal mitigation**

- No previous convictions or no relevant/recent convictions
- Unaware that dog was prohibited type despite reasonable efforts to identify type
- Evidence of safety or control measures having been taken by owner
- Prosecution results from owner notification
- Evidence of responsible ownership
- Remorse
- Good character and/or exemplary conduct
- Serious medical condition requiring urgent, intensive or long-term treatment
- Age and/or lack of maturity where it affects the responsibility of the offender
- Mental disorder or learning disability
- Sole or primary carer for dependent relatives
- Determination and/or demonstration of steps having been taken to address offending behaviour
- Lapse of time since the offence where this is not the fault of the offender

[Steps 3 to 5, 7 and 8 are identical to those applicable where death or injury is caused by virtue of an attack by a dog [see **SG21-2**]. [Step 6 is set out below.]

## STEP 6  Compensation and ancillary orders

In all cases, the court must consider whether to make a compensation order and/or other ancillary orders.

*Compensation order*

The court should consider compensation orders in all cases where personal injury, loss or damage has resulted from the offence. The court must give reasons if it decides not to award compensation in such cases.

**Other ancillary orders available include:**

*Disqualification from having a dog*

The court may disqualify the offender from having custody of a dog for such period as it thinks fit. The test the court should consider is whether the offender is a fit and proper person to have custody of a dog.

*Destruction order/contingent destruction order*

In any case where the offender is not the owner of the dog, the owner must be given an opportunity to be present and make representations to the court.

The court **shall** make a destruction order unless the court is satisfied that the dog would not constitute a danger to public safety.

In reaching a decision, the court should consider the relevant circumstances which **must** include:

- the temperament of the dog and its past behaviour;
- whether the owner of the dog, or the person for the time being in charge of it is a fit and proper person to be in charge of the dog;

and **may** include:

- other relevant circumstances.

If the court is satisfied that the dog would not constitute a danger to public safety, it **shall** make a contingent destruction order requiring that the dog be exempted from the prohibition on possession or custody within the requisite period.

Where the court makes a destruction order, it **may** appoint a person to undertake destruction and order the offender to pay what it determines to be the reasonable expenses of destroying the dog and keeping it pending its destruction.

*Fit and proper person*

In determining whether a person is a fit and proper person to be in charge of a dog the following non-exhaustive factors may be relevant:

- any relevant previous convictions, cautions or penalty notices;
- the nature and suitability of the premises that the dog is to be kept at by the person;
- where the police have released the dog pending the court's decision whether the person has breached conditions imposed by the police; and
- any relevant previous breaches of court orders.

Note: the court must be satisfied that the person who is assessed by the court as a fit and proper person can demonstrate that they are the owner or the person ordinarily in charge of that dog at the time the court is considering whether the dog is a danger to public safety. Someone who has previously not been in charge of the dog should not be considered for this assessment because it is an offence under the Dangerous Dogs Act 1991 to make a gift of a prohibited dog.

# PART 22   CAUSING DEATH BY DRIVING

**SG22-1**

[For the standard text on applicability see **SG0-4**.]

**SG22-2**

CAUSING DEATH BY DANGEROUS DRIVING

*Road Traffic Act 1988, s.1*

**Effective from:** 04 August 2008

Triable on indictment
Maximum penalty: 14 years' imprisonment; minimum disqualification of 2 years with compulsory extended re-test

This is a specified offence for the purposes of sections 266 and 279 (extended sentence for certain violent, sexual or terrorism offences) of the Sentencing Code.

**Key factors**

The following guideline applies to a 'first-time offender' aged 18 or over convicted after trial who has not been assessed as a dangerous offender requiring a sentence under 266 and 279 (extended sentence for certain violent, sexual or terrorism offences) of the Sentencing Code.

When assessing the seriousness of any offence, the court must always refer to the full list of aggravating and mitigating factors in the Council guideline on Seriousness [now replaced by the General guideline: see **SG2**] as well as those set out in the guideline table as being particularly relevant to this type of offending behaviour.

**Levels of seriousness**

The 3 levels are distinguished by factors related predominantly to the standard of driving; the general description of the degree of risk is complemented by examples of the type of bad driving arising. The presence of aggravating factors or combinations of a small number of determinants of seriousness will increase the starting point within the range. Where there is a larger group of determinants of seriousness and/or aggravating factors, this may justify moving the starting point to the next level.

**Level 1** – The most serious offences encompassing driving that involved a deliberate decision to ignore (or a flagrant disregard for) the rules of the road and an apparent disregard for the great danger being caused to others. Such offences are likely to be characterised by:

* A prolonged, persistent and deliberate course of very bad driving AND/OR
* Consumption of substantial amounts of alcohol or drugs leading to gross impairment AND/OR
* A group of determinants of seriousness which in isolation or smaller number would place the offence in level 2

Level 1 is that for which the increase in maximum penalty was aimed primarily. Where an offence involves both of the determinants of seriousness identified, particularly if accompanied by aggravating factors such as multiple deaths or injuries, or a very bad driving record, this may move an offence towards the top of the sentencing range.

**Level 2** – This is driving that created a substantial risk of danger and is likely to be characterised by:

* Greatly excessive speed, racing or competitive driving against another driver OR
* Gross avoidable distraction such as reading or composing text messages over a period of time OR
* Driving whilst ability to drive is impaired as a result of consumption of alcohol or drugs, failing to take prescribed medication or as a result of a known medical condition OR
* A group of determinants of seriousness which in isolation or smaller number would place the offence in level 3

**Level 3** – This is driving that created a significant risk of danger and is likely to be characterised by:

* Driving above the speed limit/at a speed that is inappropriate for the prevailing conditions OR
* Driving when knowingly deprived of adequate sleep or rest or knowing that the vehicle has a dangerous defect or is poorly maintained or is dangerously loaded OR
* A brief but obvious danger arising from a seriously dangerous manoeuvre OR
* Driving whilst avoidably distracted OR
* Failing to have proper regard to vulnerable road users

The starting point and range overlap with Level 2 is to allow the breadth of discretion necessary to accommodate circumstances where there are significant aggravating factors.

**Personal mitigation**

Sentencers should take into account relevant matters of personal mitigation; in particular:

*Good driving record*

This is not a factor that automatically should be treated as a mitigating factor, especially now that the presence of previous convictions is a statutory aggravating factor. However, any evidence to show that an offender has previously been an exemplary driver, for example having driven an ambulance, police vehicle, bus, taxi or similar vehicle conscientiously and without incident for many years, is a fact that the courts may well wish to take into account by way of personal mitigation. This is likely to have even greater effect where the driver is driving on public duty (for example, on ambulance, fire services or police duties) and was responding to an emergency.

*Giving assistance at the scene*

There may be many reasons why an offender does not offer help to the victims at the scene—the offender may be injured, traumatised by shock, afraid of causing further injury or simply have no idea what action to take—and it would be inappropriate to assess the offence as more serious on this ground (and so increase the level of sentence). However, where an offender gave direct, positive, assistance to victim(s) at the scene of a collision, this should be regarded as personal mitigation.

*Remorse*

Whilst it can be expected that anyone who has caused death by driving would be expected to feel remorseful, this cannot undermine its importance for sentencing purposes. Remorse is identified as personal mitigation in the Council guideline [see Overarching Principles at **SG2**] and the Council can see no reason for it to be treated differently for this group of offences. It is for the court to determine whether an expression of remorse is genuine; where it is, this should be taken into account as personal mitigation.

**Assessing seriousness**

This guideline applies to the four guidelines for *causing death by dangerous driving, causing death by driving under the influence of alcohol or drugs, causing death by careless driving and causing death by driving: unlicensed, disqualified or uninsured drivers.*

*Determinants of seriousness*

There are five factors that may be regarded as determinants of offence seriousness, each of which can be demonstrated in a number of ways. Common examples of each of the determinants are set out below and key issues are discussed below: see, Alcohol/drugs, Avoidable distractions, Vulnerable road users.

**Examples of the determinants**

**Awareness of risk**

- a prolonged, persistent and deliberate course of very bad driving

**Effect of alcohol or drugs**

- consumption of alcohol above the legal limit
- consumption of alcohol at or below the legal limit where this impaired the offender's ability to drive
- failure to supply a specimen for analysis
- consumption of illegal drugs, where this impaired the offender's ability to drive
- consumption of legal drugs or medication where this impaired the offender's ability to drive (including legal medication known to cause drowsiness) where the driver knew, or should have known, about the likelihood of impairment

**Inappropriate speed of vehicle**

- greatly excessive speed; racing; competitive driving against another vehicle
- driving above the speed limit
- driving at a speed that is inappropriate for the prevailing road or weather conditions
- driving a PSV, HGV or other goods vehicle at a speed that is inappropriate either because of the nature of the vehicle or its load, especially when carrying passengers

**Seriously culpable behaviour of offender**

- aggressive driving (such as driving much too close to the vehicle in front, persistent inappropriate attempts to overtake, or cutting in after overtaking)
- driving while using a hand-held mobile phone
- driving whilst the driver's attention is avoidably distracted, for example by reading or adjusting the controls of electronic equipment such as a radio, hands-free mobile phone or satellite navigation equipment

- driving when knowingly suffering from a medical or physical condition that significantly impairs the offender's driving skills, including failure to take prescribed medication
- driving when knowingly deprived of adequate sleep or rest, especially where commercial concerns had a bearing on the commission of the offence
- driving a poorly maintained or dangerously loaded vehicle, especially where commercial concerns had a bearing on the commission of the offence

**Victim**

- failing to have proper regard to vulnerable road users

**Issues relating to the determinants of seriousness are considered below**

*Alcohol/drugs*

For those offences where the presence of alcohol or drugs is not an element of the offence, where there is sufficient evidence of driving impairment attributable to alcohol or drugs, the consumption of alcohol or drugs prior to driving will make an offence more serious. Where the drugs were legally purchased or prescribed, the offence will only be regarded as more serious if the offender knew or should have known that the drugs were likely to impair driving ability.

Unless inherent in the offence or charged separately, failure to provide a specimen for analysis (or to allow a blood specimen taken without consent to be analysed) should be regarded as a determinant of offence seriousness.

Where it is established to the satisfaction of the court that an offender had consumed alcohol or drugs unwittingly before driving, that may be regarded as a mitigating factor. However, consideration should be given to the circumstances in which the offender decided to drive or continue to drive when driving ability was impaired.

*Avoidable distractions*

A distinction has been drawn between **ordinary** avoidable distractions and those that are more significant because they divert the attention of the driver for longer periods or to a greater extent; in this guideline these are referred to as a **gross** avoidable distraction. The guideline for causing death by dangerous driving provides for a gross avoidable distraction to place the offence in a higher level of seriousness.

Any avoidable distraction will make an offence more serious but the degree to which an offender's driving will be impaired will vary. Where the reaction to the distraction is significant, it may be the factor that determines whether the offence is based on **dangerous** driving or on **careless** driving; in those circumstances, care must be taken to avoid 'double counting'.

Using a hand-held mobile phone when driving is, in itself, an unlawful act; the fact that an offender was avoidably distracted by using a hand-held mobile phone when a causing death by driving offence was committed will always make an offence more serious. Reading or composing text messages **over a period of time** will be a **gross** avoidable distraction and is likely to result in an offence of causing death by dangerous driving being in a higher level of seriousness.

Where it is proved that an offender was briefly distracted by reading a text message or adjusting a hands-free set or its controls at the time of the collision, this would be on a par with consulting a map or adjusting a radio or satellite navigation equipment, activities that would be considered an avoidable distraction.

*Vulnerable road users*

Cyclists, motorbike riders, horse riders, pedestrians and those working in the road are vulnerable road users and a driver is expected to take extra care when driving near them. Driving too close to a bike or horse; allowing a vehicle to mount the pavement; driving into a cycle lane; and driving without the care needed in the vicinity of a pedestrian crossing, hospital, school or residential home, are all examples of factors that should be taken into account when determining the seriousness of an offence. 'Actions of others' below for the approach where the actions of another person contributed to the collision.

The fact that the victim of a causing death by driving offence was a particularly vulnerable road user is a factor that should be taken into account when determining the seriousness of an offence.

**Aggravating and mitigating factors**

*More than one person killed*

The seriousness of any offence included in these guidelines will generally be greater where more than one person is killed since it is inevitable that the degree of harm will be greater. In relation to the assessment of culpability, whilst there will be circumstances in which a driver could reasonably anticipate the possible death of more than one person (for example, the driver of a vehicle with passengers (whether that is a bus, taxi or private car) or a person driving badly in an area where there are many people), there will be many circumstances where the driver could not anticipate the number of people who would be killed.

The greater obligation on those responsible for driving other people is not an element essential to the quality of the driving and so has not been included amongst the determinants of seriousness that affect the choice of sentencing range. In practical terms, separate charges are likely to be brought in relation to each death caused. Although concurrent sentences are likely to be imposed (in recognition of the fact that the charges relate to one episode of offending behaviour), each individual sentence is likely to be higher because the offence is aggravated by the fact that more than one death has been caused.

Where more than one person is killed, that will aggravate the seriousness of the offence because of the increase in harm. Where the number of people killed is high **and** that was reasonably foreseeable, the number of deaths is likely to provide sufficient justification for moving an offence into the next highest sentencing band.

### Effect on offender

Injury to the offender may be a mitigating factor when the offender has suffered very serious injuries. In most circumstances, the weighting it is given will be dictated by the circumstances of the offence and the effect should bear a direct relationship to the extent to which the offender's driving was at fault—the greater the fault, the less the effect on mitigation; this distinction will be of particular relevance where an offence did not involve any fault in the offender's standard of driving.

Where one or more of the victims was in a close personal or family relationship with the offender, this may be a mitigating factor. In line with the approach where the offender is very seriously injured, the degree to which the relationship influences the sentence should be linked to offender culpability in relation to the commission of the offence; mitigation for this reason is likely to have less effect where the culpability of the driver is particularly high.

### Actions of others

Where the actions of the victim or a third party contributed to the commission of an offence, this should be acknowledged and taken into account as a mitigating factor.

### Offender's age/lack of driving experience

The Council guideline Overarching Principles: Seriousness [now replaced by the General guidelines; see **SG2**] includes a generic mitigating factor 'youth or age, where it affects the responsibility of the individual defendant' [now 'Age and/or lack of maturity']. There is a great deal of difference between recklessness or irresponsibility—which may be due to youth—and inexperience in dealing with prevailing conditions or an unexpected or unusual situation that presents itself—which may be present regardless of the age of the offender. The fact that an offender's lack of driving experience contributed to the commission of an offence should be treated as a mitigating factor; in this regard, the age of the offender is not relevant.

### Personal mitigation

[See Key factors, above, for personal mitigation factors: **good driving record**, and **conduct after the offence** represented by **giving assistance at the scene** and **remorse**.]

### Summary

Evidence that an offender is normally a careful and conscientious driver, giving direct, positive assistance to a victim and genuine remorse may be taken into account as personal mitigation and may justify a reduction in sentence.

### 1.  Identify dangerous offenders

Offences under s.1 of the Road Traffic Act 1988 are specified offences for the purposes of sections 266 and 279 (extended sentence for certain violent, sexual or terrorism offences) of the Sentencing Code. The court must determine having regard to the criteria contained in Chapter 6 of Part 10 of the Sentencing Code whether there is a significant risk of serious harm by the commission of a further specified offence.

### 2.  Identify the appropriate starting point

Identify the level or description that most nearly matches the particular facts of the offence for which sentence is being imposed.

Starting points based on first time offender pleading not guilty

| Nature of offence | Starting point | Sentencing range |
|---|---|---|
| **Level 1**<br>The most serious offences encompassing driving that involved a deliberate decision to ignore (or a flagrant disregard for) the rules of the road and an apparent disregard for the great danger being caused to others | 8 years' custody | 7–14 years' custody |
| **Level 2**<br>Driving that created a **substantial** risk of danger | 5 years' custody | 4–7 years' custody |
| **Level 3**<br>Driving that created a **significant** risk of danger<br>*(Where the driving is markedly less culpable than for this level, reference should be made to the starting point and range for the most serious level of causing death by careless driving)* | 3 years' custody | 2–5 years' custody |

**Custodial Sentences**

For the imposition of custodial sentences see Imposition of Community and Custodial Sentences [at SG9-3].

**3. Consider relevant aggravating factors, both general and those specific to the type of the offence**

This may result in a sentence level being identified that is higher than the suggested starting point, sometimes substantially so

*Additional aggravating factors*
- Previous convictions for motoring offences, particularly offences that involve bad driving or the consumption of excessive alcohol or drugs before driving
- More than one person killed as a result of the offence
- Serious injury to one or more victims, in addition to the death(s)
- Disregard of warnings
- Other offences committed at the same time, such as driving other than in accordance with the terms of a valid licence; driving while disqualified; driving without insurance; taking a vehicle without consent; driving a stolen vehicle
- The offender's irresponsible behaviour such as failing to stop, falsely claiming that one of the victims was responsible for the collision, or trying to throw the victim off the car by swerving in order to escape
- Driving off in an attempt to avoid detection or apprehension

**4. Consider mitigating factors and person mitigation**

There may be general or offence specific mitigating factors and matters of personal mitigation which could result in a sentence that is lower than the suggested starting point (possibly substantially so), or a sentence of a different type.

*Additional mitigating factors*
- Alcohol or drugs consumed unwittingly
- Offender was seriously injured in the collision
- The victim was a close friend or relative
- Actions of the victim or a third party contributed significantly to the likelihood of a collision occurring and/or death resulting
- The offender's lack of driving experience contributed to the commission of the offence
- The driving was in response to a proven and genuine emergency falling short of a defence

*Common aggravating and mitigating factors*

[See **SG2** for the standard factors under seriousness in the Guideline Overarching Principles.]

**5. Reduction for a guilty plea**

The court will then apply any reduction for a guilty plea following the approach set out in the Council's guideline, Reduction in Sentence for a Guilty Plea (where first hearing is on or after 1 June 2017 [see **SG5-1**], or first hearing before 1 June 2017 [see **SG5-12**])

**6. Consider ancillary orders**

The court should consider whether ancillary orders are appropriate or necessary.

[See the Crown Court Compendium, Part II Sentencing, s7; Ancillary Orders]

### 7.  The totality principle

The court should review the total sentence to ensure that it is proportionate to the offending behaviour and properly balanced. See *Totality* guideline [at **SG4**].

### 8.  Reasons

When a court moves from the suggested starting points and sentencing ranges identified in the guidelines, it should explain its reasons for doing so.

CAUSING DEATH BY CARELESS DRIVING WHEN UNDER THE INFLUENCE OF       **SG22-3**
DRINK OR DRUGS OR HAVING FAILED EITHER TO PROVIDE A SPECIMEN
FOR ANALYSIS OR TO PERMIT ANALYSIS OF A BLOOD SAMPLE

*Road Traffic Act 1988 (section 3A)*

**Effective from:** 15 July 2008

**Maximum penalty:** 14 years' imprisonment; minimum disqualification of 2 years with compulsory extended re-test

This is a specified offence for the purposes of sections 266 and 279 (extended sentence for certain violent, sexual or terrorism offences) of the Sentencing Code.

**Key factors**

The following guideline applies to a 'first-time offender' aged 18 or over convicted after trial who has not been assessed as a dangerous offender requiring a sentence under sections 266 and 279 (extended sentence for certain violent, sexual or terrorism offences) of the Sentencing Code.

When assessing the seriousness of any offence, the court must always refer to the full list of aggravating and mitigating factors in the Council guideline on Seriousness[200] [now replaced by the General guideline: see SG2] as well as those set out in the adjacent table as being particularly relevant to this type of offending behaviour.

This offence can be committed through:

- being unfit to drive through drink or drugs;
- having consumed so much alcohol as to be over the prescribed limit;
- failing without reasonable excuse to provide a specimen for analysis within the timescale allowed; or
- failing without reasonable excuse to permit the analysis of a blood sample taken when incapable of giving consent.

In comparison with causing death by dangerous driving, the level of culpability in the actual manner of driving is lower but that culpability is increased in all cases by the fact that the offender has driven after consuming drugs or an excessive amount of alcohol. Accordingly, there is considerable parity in the levels of seriousness with the deliberate decision to drive after consuming alcohol or drugs aggravating the careless standard of driving onto a par with dangerous driving.

The fact that the offender was under the influence of drink or drugs is an inherent element of this offence:

- For those offences where the presence of alcohol or drugs is not an element of the offence, where there is sufficient evidence of driving impairment attributable to alcohol or drugs, the consumption of alcohol or drugs prior to driving will make an offence more serious. Where the drugs were legally purchased or prescribed, the offence will only be regarded as more serious if the offender knew or should have known that the drugs were likely to impair driving ability.
- Unless inherent in the offence or charged separately, failure to provide a specimen for analysis (or to allow a blood specimen taken without consent to be analysed) should be regarded as a determinant of offence seriousness.
- Where it is established to the satisfaction of the court that an offender had consumed alcohol or drugs unwittingly before driving, that may be regarded as a mitigating factor. However, consideration should be given to the circumstances in which the offender decided to drive or continue to drive when driving ability was impaired.

The guideline is based both on the level of alcohol or drug consumption and on the degree of carelessness.

The increase in sentence is more marked where there is an increase in the level of intoxication than where there is an increase in the degree of carelessness reflecting the 14 year imprisonment maximum for this offence compared with a 5 year maximum for causing death by careless or inconsiderate driving alone.

---

[200] https://www.sentencingcouncil.org.uk/publications/item/offences-taken-into-consideration-and-totality-definitive-guideline/

A refusal to supply a specimen for analysis may be a calculated step by an offender to avoid prosecution for driving when having consumed in excess of the prescribed amount of alcohol, with a view to seeking to persuade the court that the amount consumed was relatively small. A court is entitled to draw adverse inferences from a refusal to supply a specimen without reasonable excuse and should treat with caution any attempt to persuade the court that only a limited amount of alcohol had been consumed.[201] The three levels of seriousness where the offence has been committed in this way derive from the classification in the Magistrates' Court Sentencing Guidelines.

*Personal mitigation*

[The personal mitigation factors are the same as for Causing Death by Dangerous Driving. See **SG22-2** for these personal mitigation factors: **good driving record**, and **conduct after the offence** represented by **giving assistance at the scene** and **remorse**.]

*Assessing seriousness*

This information applies to the four guidelines for *causing death by dangerous driving, causing death by driving under the influence of alcohol or drugs, causing death by careless driving* and *causing death by driving: unlicensed, disqualified or uninsured drivers.*

[The factors are set out in the guideline for Causing Death By Dangerous Driving. See **SG22-2**.]

### 1.  Identify dangerous offenders

Offences under s.3A of the Road Traffic Act 1988 are specified offences for the purposes of sections 266 and 279 (extended sentence for certain violent, sexual or terrorism offences) of the Sentencing Code. The court must determine having regard to the criteria contained in Chapter 6 of Part 10 of the Sentencing Code whether there is a significant risk of serious harm by the commission of a further specified offence.

### 2.  Identify the appropriate starting point

Identify the level or description that most nearly matches the particular facts of the offence for which sentence is being imposed.

Starting points based on first time offender pleading not guilty

| The legal limit of alcohol is 35 µg breath (80 mg in blood and 107 mg in urine) | Careless/inconsiderate driving arising from momentary inattention with no aggravating factors | Other cases of careless/ inconsiderate driving | Careless/inconsiderate driving falling not far short of dangerousness |
|---|---|---|---|
| 71 µor above of alcohol/ high quantity of drugs OR deliberate non-provision of specimen where evidence of serious impairment | **Starting point:** 6 years' custody **Sentencing range:** 5–10 years' custody | **Starting point:** 7 years' custody **Sentencing range:** 6–12 years' custody | **Starting point:** 8 years' custody **Sentencing range:** 7–14 years' custody |
| 51–70 µg of alcohol/ moderate quantity of drugs OR deliberate non-provision of specimen | **Starting point:** 4 years' custody **Sentencing range:** 3–7 years' custody | **Starting point:** 5 years' custody **Sentencing range:** 4–8 years' custody | **Starting point:** 6 years' custody **Sentencing range:** 5–9 years' custody |
| 35–50 µg of alcohol/ minimum quantity of drugs OR test refused because of honestly held but unreasonable belief | **Starting point:** 18 months' custody **Sentencing range:** 26 weeks'–4 years' custody | **Starting point:** 3 years' custody **Sentencing range:** 2–5 years' custody | **Starting point:** 4 years' custody **Sentencing range:** 3–6 years' custody |

**Custodial Sentences**

For the imposition of custodial sentences see Imposition of Community and Custodial Sentences at SG9-3.

### 3.  Consider relevant aggravating factors, both general and those specific to the type of the offence

This may result in a sentence level being identified that is higher than the suggested starting point, sometimes substantially so

---

[201] *Overarching Principles: Seriousness*, published 16 December 2004, www.sentencing-guidelines.gov.uk

*Additional aggravating factors*

- Other offences committed at the same time, such as driving other than in accordance with the terms of a valid licence; driving while disqualified; driving without insurance; taking a vehicle without consent; driving a stolen vehicle
- Previous convictions for motoring offences, particularly offences that involve bad driving or the consumption of excessive alcohol before driving
- More than one person was killed as a result of the offence
- Serious injury to one or more persons in addition to the death(s)
- Irresponsible behaviour such as failing to stop or falsely claiming that one of the victims was responsible for the collision

### 4.   Consider mitigating factors and personal mitigation

There may be general or offence specific mitigating factors and matters of personal mitigation which could result in a sentence that is lower than the suggested starting point (possibly substantially so), or a sentence of a different type.

*Additional mitigating factors*

- Alcohol or drugs consumed unwittingly
- Offender was seriously injured in the collision
- The victim was a close friend or relative
- The actions of the victim or a third party contributed significantly to the likelihood of a collision occurring and/or death resulting
- The driving was in response to a proven and genuine emergency falling short of a defence

*Common aggravating and mitigating factors*

[See SG2 for the standard factors under seriousness in the Guideline Overarching Principles.]

### 5.   Reduction for a guilty plea

The court will then apply any reduction for a guilty plea following the approach set out in the Council's guideline, Reduction in Sentence for a Guilty Plea (where first hearing is on or after 1 June 2017 [see SG5-1], or first hearing before 1 June 2017 [see **SG5-12**]).

### 6.   Consider ancillary orders

The court should consider whether ancillary orders are appropriate or necessary.

[See the Crown Court Compendium, Part II Sentencing, S7; Ancillary Orders]

### 7.   The totality principle

The court should review the total sentence to ensure that it is proportionate to the offending behaviour and properly balanced. See *Totality* guideline [at **SG4**].

### 8.   Reasons

When a court moves from the suggested starting points and sentencing ranges identified in the guidelines, it should explain its reasons for doing so.

## CAUSING DEATH BY CARELESS OR INCONSIDERATE DRIVING    SG22-4

*Road Traffic Act 1988 (section 2B)*

**Effective from:** 04 August 2008

Triable either way
Maximum: 5 years' custody

### Key factors

The following guideline applies to a 'first-time offender' aged 18 or over convicted after trial.

When assessing the seriousness of any offence, the court must always refer to the full list of aggravating and mitigating factors in the Council guideline on Seriousness [now replaced by the General guideline] as well as those set out in the guideline as being particularly relevant to this type of offending behaviour.

Disqualification of the offender from driving and endorsement of the offender's driving licence are mandatory, and the offence carries between 3 and 11 penalty points when the court finds special reasons for not imposing disqualification. There is a discretionary power to order an extended driving test where a person is convicted of this offence.

Since the maximum sentence has been set at 5 years imprisonment, the sentence ranges are generally lower for this offence than for the offences of causing death by dangerous driving or causing death by careless driving under the influence, for which the maximum sentence is 14 years imprisonment. However, it is unavoidable that some cases will be on the borderline between dangerous and careless driving, or may involve a number of factors that significantly increase the seriousness of an offence. As a result, the guideline for this offence identifies three levels of seriousness, the range for the highest of which overlaps with ranges for the lowest level of seriousness for causing death by dangerous driving.

The three levels of seriousness are defined by the degree of carelessness involved in the standard of driving. The most serious level for this offence is where the offender's driving fell not that far short of dangerous. The least serious group of offences relates to those cases where the level of culpability is low – for example in a case involving an offender who misjudges the speed of another vehicle, or turns without seeing an oncoming vehicle because of restricted visibility. Other cases will fall into the intermediate level.

The starting point for the most serious offence of causing death by careless driving is lower than that for the least serious offence of causing death by dangerous driving in recognition of the different standards of driving behaviour. However, the range still leaves scope, within the 5 year maximum, to impose longer sentences where the case is particularly serious.

Where the level of carelessness is low and there are no aggravating factors, even the fact that death was caused is not sufficient to justify a prison sentence.

A fine is unlikely to be an appropriate sentence for this offence; where a non-custodial sentence is considered appropriate, this should be a community order. The nature of the requirements will be determined by the purpose identified by the court as of primary importance. Requirements most likely to be relevant include unpaid work requirement, activity requirement, programme requirement and curfew requirement.

*Personal mitigation*

[The personal mitigation factors are the same as for Causing Death by Dangerous Driving. See **SG22-2** for these personal mitigation factors: **good driving record**, and conduct after the offence represented by **giving assistance at the scene** and **remorse**.]

*Assessing seriousness*

This information applies to the four guidelines for *causing death by dangerous driving, causing death by driving under the influence of alcohol or drugs, causing death by careless driving* and *causing death by driving: unlicensed, disqualified or uninsured drivers.*

[The factors are set out in the guideline for Causing Death by Dangerous Driving. See **SG22-2**.]

**1. Identify the appropriate starting point**

Identify the level or description that most nearly matches the particular facts of the offence for which sentence is being imposed.

Starting points based on first time offender pleading not guilty

| Nature of offence | Starting point | Sentencing range |
|---|---|---|
| Careless or inconsiderate driving falling not far short of dangerous driving | 15 months' custody | 36 weeks'–3 years' custody |
| Other cases of careless or inconsiderate driving | 36 weeks' custody | Community order (HIGH)–2 years' custody |
| Careless or inconsiderate driving arising from momentary inattention with no aggravating factors | Community order (MEDIUM) | Community order (LOW)–Community order (HIGH) |

**Community Orders and Custodial Sentences**

For the imposition of community orders, including the community orders table, see Imposition of Community and Custodial Sentences at **SG9-2**.

For the imposition of custodial sentences see Imposition of Community and Custodial Sentences at **SG9-3**.

**2.   Consider relevant aggravating factors, both general and those specific to the type of the offence**

This may result in a sentence level being identified that is higher than the suggested starting point, sometimes substantially so.

*Additional aggravating factors*

- Other offences committed at the same time, such as driving other than in accordance with the terms of a valid licence; driving while disqualified; driving without insurance; taking a vehicle without consent; driving a stolen vehicle
- Previous convictions for motoring offences, particularly offences that involve bad driving
- More than one person was killed as a result of the offence
- Serious injury to one or more persons in addition to the death(s)
- Irresponsible behaviour, such as failing to stop or falsely claiming that one of the victims was responsible for the collision

**3.   Consider mitigating factors and person mitigation**

There may be general or offence specific mitigating factors and matters of personal mitigation which could result in a sentence that is lower than the suggested starting point (possibly substantially so), or a sentence of a different type.

*Additional mitigating factors*

- Offender was seriously injured in the collision
- The victim was a close friend or relative
- Actions of the victim or a third party contributed to the commission of the offence
- The offender's lack of driving experience contributed significantly to the likelihood of a collision occurring and/or death resulting
- The driving was in response to a proven and genuine emergency falling short of a defence

*Common aggravating and mitigating factors*

[See **SG2** for the standard factors under seriousness in the Guideline Overarching Principles.]

**4.   Reduction for a guilty plea**

The court will then apply any reduction for a guilty plea following the approach set out in the Council's guideline, Reduction in Sentence for a Guilty Plea (where first hearing is on or after 1 June 2017 [see **SG5-1**], or first hearing before 1 June 2017 [see **SG5-12**]).

**5.   Consider ancillary orders**

The court should consider whether ancillary orders are appropriate or necessary.

[See the Crown Court Compendium, Part II Sentencing, s7; Ancillary Orders]

**6.   The totality principle**

The court should review the total sentence to ensure that it is proportionate to the offending behaviour and properly balanced. See *Totality* guideline [at **SG4**].

**7.   Reasons**

When a court moves from the suggested starting points and sentencing ranges identified in the guidelines, it should explain its reasons for doing so.

CAUSING DEATH BY DRIVING: UNLICENSED, DISQUALIFIED                **SG22-5**
OR UNINSURED DRIVERS

*Road Traffic Act 1988 (section 3ZB)*

**Effective from:** 04 August 2008

Triable either way
Maximum: 2 years' custody

**NOTE:** the maximum sentence for **causing death by disqualified driving** is now **10 years** (section 3ZC Road Traffic Act 1988 – with effect from 13 April 2015). The sentence levels in this guideline are therefore unlikely to apply to this offence.

## Key factors

The following guideline applies to a 'first-time offender' aged 18 or over convicted after trial. An offender convicted of causing death by driving whilst disqualified will always have at least one relevant previous conviction for the offence that resulted in the disqualification. The starting point and range take this into account; any other previous convictions should be considered in the usual way.

When assessing the seriousness of any offence, the court must always refer to the full list of aggravating and mitigating factors in the Council guideline on Seriousness [now replaced by the General guideline: see SG2] as well as those set out in the guideline as being particularly relevant to this type of offending behaviour.

Disqualification of the offender from driving and endorsement of the offender's driving licence are mandatory, and the offence carries between 3 and 11 penalty points when the court finds special reasons for not imposing disqualification. There is a discretionary power to order an extended driving test where a person is convicted of this offence.

Culpability arises from the offender driving a vehicle on a road or other public place when, by law, not allowed to do so; the offence does not require proof of any fault in the standard of driving. [But see *R v Hughes* [2013] UKSC 56.]

Being uninsured, unlicensed or disqualified are the only determinants of seriousness for this offence, as there are no factors relating to the standard of driving. The list of aggravating factors identified is slightly different as the emphasis is on the decision to drive by an offender who is not permitted by law to do so.

In some cases, the extreme circumstances that led an offender to drive whilst unlicensed, disqualified or uninsured may result in a successful defence of 'duress of circumstances'. In less extreme circumstances, where the decision to drive was brought about by a genuine and proven emergency, that may mitigate offence seriousness and so it is included as an additional mitigating factor.

A driver may hold a reasonable belief in relation to the validity of insurance (for example having just missed a renewal date or relied on a third party to make an application) and also the validity of a licence (for example incorrectly believing that a licence covered a particular category of vehicle). In light of this, an additional mitigating factor covers those situations where an offender genuinely believed that there was valid insurance or a valid licence.

### Personal mitigation

[The personal mitigation factors are the same as for Causing Death by Dangerous Driving. See SG22-2 for these personal mitigation factors: **good driving record**, and conduct after the offence represented by **giving assistance at the scene** and **remorse**.]

### Assessing seriousness

This information applies to the four guidelines for *causing death by dangerous driving, causing death by driving under the influence of alcohol or drugs, causing death by careless driving* and *causing death by driving: unlicensed, disqualified or uninsured drivers*.

[The factors are set out in the guideline for Causing Death by Dangerous Driving. See SG22-2.]

### 1. Identify dangerous offenders

Offences under s.3ZC of the Road Traffic Act 1988 (causing death by disqualified driving) are specified offences for the purposes of sections 266 and 279 (extended sentence for certain violent, sexual or terrorism offences) of the Sentencing Code. The court must determine having regard to the criteria contained in Chapter 6 of Part 10 of the Sentencing Code whether there is a significant risk of serious harm by the commission of a further specified offence.

### 2. Identify the appropriate starting point

Identify the level or description that most nearly matches the particular facts of the offence for which sentence is being imposed.

Starting points based on first time offender pleading not guilty

| Nature of offence | Starting point | Sentencing range |
|---|---|---|
| The offender was disqualified from driving **OR** The offender was unlicensed or uninsured plus 2 or more aggravating factors from the list below | 12 months' custody | 36 weeks'–2 years' custody |
| The offender was unlicensed or uninsured plus at least 1 aggravating factor from the list below | 26 weeks' custody | Community order (HIGH)– 36 weeks' custody |
| The offender was unlicensed or uninsured—no aggravating factors | Community order (MEDIUM) | Community order (LOW)–Community order (HIGH) |

### Community Orders and Custodial Sentences

For the imposition of community orders, including the community orders table, see Imposition of Community and Custodial Sentences at **SG9-2**.

For the imposition of custodial sentences see Imposition of Community and Custodial Sentences at **SG9-3**.

**3.   Consider relevant aggravating factors, both general and those specific to the type of the offence**

This may result in a sentence level being identified that is higher than the suggested starting point, sometimes substantially so.

*Additional aggravating factors*

• Previous convictions for motoring offences, whether involving bad driving or involving an offence of the same kind that forms part of the present conviction (ie unlicensed, disqualified or uninsured driving)
• More than one person was killed as a result of the offence
• Serious injury to one or more persons in addition to the death(s)
• Disregard of warnings
• Irresponsible behaviour such as failing to stop or falsely claiming that someone else was driving

**4.   Consider mitigating factors and person mitigation**

There may be general or offence specific mitigating factors and matters of personal mitigation which could result in a sentence that is lower than the suggested starting point (possibly substantially so), or a sentence of a different type.

*Additional mitigating factors*

• The decision to drive was brought about by a proven and genuine emergency falling short of a defence
• The offender genuinely believed that he or she was insured or licensed to drive
• The offender was seriously injured as a result of the collision
• The victim was a close friend or relative

*Common aggravating and mitigating factors*

[See **SG2** for the standard factors under seriousness in the Guideline Overarching Principles.]

**5.   Reduction for a guilty plea**

The court will then apply any reduction for a guilty plea following the approach set out in the Council's guideline, Reduction in Sentence for a Guilty Plea (where first hearing is on or after 1 June 2017 [see **SG5-1**], or first hearing before 1 June 2017 [see **SG5-12**]).

**6.   Consider ancillary orders**

The court should consider whether ancillary orders are appropriate or necessary.

[See the Crown Court Compendium, Part II Sentencing, s7; Ancillary Orders]

**7.   The totality principle**

The court should review the total sentence to ensure that it is proportionate to the offending behaviour and properly balanced. See *Totality* guideline [at **SG4**].

**8.   Reasons**

When a court moves from the suggested starting points and sentencing ranges identified in the guidelines, it should explain its reasons for doing so.

# PART 23   DRUG OFFENCES

## APPLICABILITY

[For the standard text on applicability see **SG0-4**.]

## FRAUDULENT EVASION OF A PROHIBITION BY BRINGING INTO OR TAKING OUT OF THE UK A CONTROLLED DRUG

*Misuse of Drugs Act 1971, s.3; Customs and Excise Management Act 1979, s.170(2)*

**Effective from:** 01 April 2021

Triable either way unless the defendant could receive the minimum sentence of seven years for a third drug trafficking offence under section 313 of the Sentencing Code in which case the offence is triable only on indictment.

**Class A**
Maximum: Life imprisonment

Offence range: Band A fine – 16 years' custody

**Class B**
Maximum: 14 years' custody and/or unlimited fine

Offence range: Discharge – 10 years' custody

**Class C**
Maximum: 14 years' custody and/or unlimited fine

Offence range: Discharge – 8 years' custody

This offence is subject to statutory minimum sentencing provisions.

See Step 3 for further details.

**STEP 1   Determine the offence category**

The court should determine the offender's culpability (role) and the harm caused (quantity) with reference only to the factors listed in the tables below.

In assessing culpability, the sentencer should weigh up all the factors of the case to determine role. Where there are characteristics present which fall under different role categories, or where the level of the offender's role is affected by the scale of the operation, the court should balance these characteristics to reach a fair assessment of the offender's culpability.

**Culpability demonstrated by the offender's role**

One or more of these characteristics may demonstrate the offender's role. These lists are not exhaustive.

*Leading role*

- Directing or organising buying and selling on a commercial scale
- Substantial links to, and influence on, others in a chain
- Close links to original source
- Expectation of substantial financial or other advantage
- Uses business as cover
- Abuses a position of trust or responsibility

*Significant role*

- Operational or management function within a chain
- Involves others in the operation whether by pressure, influence, intimidation or reward
- Expectation of significant financial or other advantage, (save where this advantage is limited to meeting the offender's own habit) whether or not operating alone
- Some awareness and understanding of scale of operation

*Lesser role*

- Performs a limited function under direction
- Engaged by pressure, coercion, intimidation, grooming and/ or control
- Involvement through naivety, immaturity or exploitation
- No influence on those above in a chain
- Very little, if any, awareness or understanding of the scale of operation

- If own operation, solely for own use (considering reasonableness of account in all the circumstances)
- Expectation of limited, if any, financial or other advantage (including meeting the offender's own habit)

## Harm

In assessing harm, quantity is determined by the weight of the product.

## Category of harm

Indicative quantities of some common drugs, upon which the starting point is to be based, are given in the table below. Where a drug (such as fentanyl or its agonists) is not listed in the table below, sentencers should expect to be provided with expert evidence to assist in determining the potency of the particular drug and in equating the quantity in the case with the quantities set out in the guidelines in terms of the harm caused. There will often be no precise calculation possible, but courts are reminded that in cases of particularly potent drugs, even very small quantities may be held to be equivalent to large quantities of the drugs listed.

### Category 1

- Heroin, cocaine – 5kg
- Ecstasy – 7,000 tablets*
- MDMA – 5kg
- LSD – 250,000 squares
- Amphetamine – 20kg
- Cannabis – 200kg
- Ketamine – 5kg
- Synthetic cannabinoid receptor agonists (for example 'spice') – very large quantity indicative of an industrial scale operation

### Category 2

- Heroin, cocaine – 1kg
- Ecstasy – 1,300 tablets*
- MDMA – 1kg
- LSD – 25,000 squares
- Amphetamine – 4kg
- Cannabis – 40kg
- Ketamine – 1kg
- Synthetic cannabinoid receptor agonists (for example 'spice') – large quantity indicative of a commercial operation

### Category 3

- Heroin, cocaine – 150g
- Ecstasy –200 tablets*
- MDMA – 150g
- LSD – 2,500 squares
- Amphetamine – 750g
- Cannabis – 6kg
- Ketamine – 150g
- Synthetic cannabinoid receptor agonists (for example 'spice') – smaller quantity between categories 2 and 4

### Category 4

- Heroin, cocaine – 5g
- Ecstasy – 13 tablets*
- MDMA – 5g
- LSD – 170 squares
- Amphetamine – 20g
- Cannabis – 100g
- Ketamine – 5g
- Synthetic cannabinoid receptor agonists (for example 'spice') – very small quantity

* Ecstasy tablet quantities based on a typical quantity of 150mg MDMA per tablet[1]

Sentencing Guidelines

## STEP 2　Starting point and category range

Having determined the category at step one, the court should use the corresponding starting point to reach a sentence within the category range below. The starting point applies to all offenders irrespective of plea or previous convictions. A case of particular gravity, reflected by multiple features of culpability or harm in step one, could merit upward adjustment from the starting point before further adjustment for aggravating or mitigating features, set out below.

Where the operation is on the most serious and commercial scale, involving a quantity of drugs significantly higher than category 1, sentences of 20 years and above may be appropriate, depending on the offender's role.

Where the defendant is dependent on or has a propensity to misuse drugs and there is sufficient prospect of success, a community order with a drug rehabilitation requirement under part 10 of Schedule 9 of the Sentencing Code can be a proper alternative to a short or moderate length custodial sentence.

**Sentencers should be aware that there is evidence of a disparity in sentence outcomes for this offence which indicates that a higher proportion of Black, Asian and Other ethnicity offenders receive an immediate custodial sentence than White offenders. There may be many reasons for these differences, but in order to apply the guidelines fairly sentencers may find useful information and guidance at Chapter 8 paragraphs 185 to 193 of the Equal Treatment Bench Book.**

| CLASS A | Leading Role | Significant Role | Lesser Role |
|---|---|---|---|
| Category 1 | **Starting point** 14 years' custody | **Starting point** 10 years' custody | **Starting point** 8 years' custody |
| | **Category range** 12 – 16 years' custody | **Category range** 9 – 12 years' custody | **Category range** 6 – 9 years' custody |
| Category 2 | **Starting point** 11 years' custody | **Starting point** 8 years' custody | **Starting point** 6 years' custody |
| | **Category range** 9 – 13 years' custody | **Category range** 6 years 6 months' – 10 years' custody | **Category range** 5 – 7 years' custody |
| Category 3 | **Starting point** 8 years 6 months' custody | **Starting point** 6 years' custody | **Starting point** 3 years' custody |
| | **Category range** 6 years 6 months' – 10 years' custody | **Category range** 5 – 7 years' custody | **Category range** 18 months' – 5 years' custody |
| Category 4 | **Starting point** 5 years' custody | **Starting point** 3 years' custody | **Starting point** Low level community order |
| | **Category range** 4 years 6 months' – 7 years 6 months' custody | **Category range** 18 months' – 5 years' custody | **Category range** Band A fine – 18 months' custody |

| CLASS B | Leading Role | Significant Role | Lesser Role |
|---|---|---|---|
| Category 1 | **Starting point** 8 years' custody | **Starting point** 5 years 6 months' custody | **Starting point** 4 years' custody |
| | **Category range** 7 – 10 years' custody | **Category range** 5 – 7 years' custody | **Category range** 2 years 6 months' – 5 years' custody |
| Category 2 | **Starting point** 6 years' custody | **Starting point** 4 years' custody | **Starting point** 2 years' custody |
| | **Category range** 4 years 6 months' – 8 years' custody | **Category range** 2 years 6 months' – 5 years' custody | **Category range** 18 months' – 3 years' custody |

| CLASS B | Leading Role | Significant Role | Lesser Role |
|---|---|---|---|
| Category 3 | **Starting point** 4 years' custody | **Starting point** 2 years' custody | **Starting point** 9 months' custody |
| | **Category range** 2 years 6 months' – 5 years' custody | **Category range** 18 months' – 3 years' custody | **Category range** 12 weeks' – 18 months' custody |
| Category 4 | **Starting point** 18 months' custody | **Starting point** High level community order | **Starting point** Band C fine |
| | **Category range** 26 weeks' – 3 years' custody | **Category range** Medium level community order – 9 months' custody | **Category range** Discharge – 26 weeks' custody |

| CLASS C | Leading Role | Significant Role | Lesser Role |
|---|---|---|---|
| Category 1 | **Starting point** 5 years' custody | **Starting point** 3 years' custody | **Starting point** 18 months' custody |
| | **Category range** 4 – 8 years' custody | **Category range** 2 – 5 years' custody | **Category range** 1 – 3 years' custody |
| Category 2 | **Starting point** 3 years 6 months' custody | **Starting point** 18 months' custody | **Starting point** 26 weeks' custody |
| | **Category range** 2 – 5 years' custody | **Category range** 1 – 3 years' custody | **Category range** 12 weeks' – 18 months' custody |
| Category 3 | **Starting point** 18 months' custody | **Starting point** 26 weeks' custody | **Starting point** High level community order |
| | **Category range** 1 – 3 years' custody | **Category range** 12 weeks' – 18 months' custody | **Category range** Medium level community order – 26 weeks' custody |
| Category 4 | **Starting point** 9 months' custody | **Starting point** High level community order | **Starting point** Band B fine |
| | **Category range** High level community order – 2 years' custody | **Category range** Medium level community order – 12 weeks' custody | **Category range** Discharge – High level community order |

*Sentencing Guidelines*

### Fines

[For the standard schedule of fines see **SG2-5**.]

### Community Orders and Custodial Sentences

[For the imposition of community orders, including the community orders table, see Imposition of Community and Custodial Sentences at **SG9-2**.

For the imposition of custodial sentences see Imposition of Community and Custodial Sentences at **SG9-3**.]

### Factors increasing seriousness

*Statutory aggravating factors*

- Previous convictions [see **SG2-21**] having regard to
  a)  nature of the offence to which conviction relates and relevance to current offence; and
  b)  time elapsed since conviction
- Offence committed on bail [see **SG2-22**]

*Other aggravating factors*

- Offender used or permitted a person under 18 to deliver a controlled drug to a third person
- Exploitation of children and/or vulnerable persons to assist in drug-related activity
- Involving an innocent agent in the commission of the offence
- Exposure of drug user to the risk of serious harm over and above that expected by the user, for example, through the method of production or subsequent adulteration of the drug
- Exposure of those involved in drug dealing to the risk of serious harm, for example through method of transporting drugs
- Exposure of third parties to the risk of serious harm, for example, through the location of the drug-related activity
- Use of sophisticated methods or technologies in order to avoid or impede detection
- Presence of weapons, where not charged separately
- Use of violence (where not charged as separate offence or taken into account at step one)
- Failure to comply with current court orders
- Offence committed on licence or post sentence supervision

**Factors reducing seriousness or reflecting personal mitigation**

- Involvement due to pressure, intimidation or coercion falling short of duress, except where already taken into account at step one
- Importation only of drug to which offender addicted and quantity consistent with personal use
- Mistaken belief of the offender regarding the type of drug, taking into account the reasonableness of such belief in all the circumstances
- Isolated incident
- No previous convictions or no relevant or recent convictions
- Remorse
- Good character and/or exemplary conduct
- Determination and/or demonstration of steps having been taken to address addiction or offending behaviour
- Serious medical conditions requiring urgent, intensive or long-term treatment
- Age and/or lack of maturity where it affects the responsibility of the offender
- Mental disorder or learning disability
- Sole or primary carer for dependent relatives
- Offender's vulnerability was exploited

## STEP 3   Minimum Terms

For class A cases, section 313 of the Sentencing Code provides that a court should impose an appropriate custodial sentence of at least seven years for a third class **A** trafficking offence except where the court is of the opinion that there are particular circumstances which (a) relate to any of the offences or to the offender; and (b) would make it unjust to do so in all the circumstances.

**Unjust in all of the circumstances**

In considering whether a statutory minimum sentence would be 'unjust in all of the circumstances' the court must have regard to the particular circumstances of the offence and the offender. If the circumstances of the offence, the previous offences or the offender make it unjust to impose the statutory minimum sentence then the court **must impose either a shorter custodial sentence than the statutory minimum provides or an alternative sentence.**

**The offence**

Having reached this stage of the guideline the court should have made a provisional assessment of the seriousness of the current offence. In addition, the court must consider the seriousness of the previous offences and the period of time that has elapsed between offences. Where the seriousness of the combined offences is such that it falls below the custody threshold, or where there has been a significant period of time between the offences, the court may consider it unjust to impose the statutory minimum sentence.

**The offender**

The court should consider the following factors to determine whether it would be unjust to impose the statutory minimum sentence;

- any strong personal mitigation;
- whether there is a realistic prospect of rehabilitation;
- whether custody will result in significant impact on others.

**STEP 4    Consider any factors which indicate a reduction, such as assistance to the prosecution**

The court should take into account section 74 of the Sentencing Code (assistance by defendants: reduction or review of sentence) and any other rule of law by virtue of which an offender may receive a discounted sentence in consequence of assistance given (or offered) to the prosecutor or investigator.

**STEP 5    Reduction for guilty pleas**

The court should take account of any potential reduction for a guilty plea in accordance with section 73 of the Sentencing Code and the and the Reduction in Sentence for a Guilty Plea guideline [see **SG5-1–SG5-12**].

In circumstances where an appropriate custodial sentence of 7 years falls to be imposed under section 313 of the Sentencing Code (third Class A drug trafficking offences), the court may impose any sentence in accordance with this guideline which is not less than 80 per cent of the appropriate custodial period.

**STEP 6    Totality principle**

If sentencing an offender for more than one offence, or where the offender is already serving a sentence, consider whether the total sentence is just and proportionate to the offending behaviour. See Totality guideline [see **SG4**].

**STEP 7    Confiscation and ancillary orders**

Confiscation orders under the Proceeds of Crime Act 2002 may only be made by the Crown Court. The Crown Court must proceed with a view to making a confiscation order if it is asked to do so by the prosecutor or if the Crown Court believes it is appropriate for it to do so.

Where, following conviction in a magistrates' court, the prosecutor applies for the offender to be committed to the Crown Court with a view to a confiscation order being considered, the magistrates' court must commit the offender to the Crown Court to be sentenced there (section 70 of the Proceeds of Crime Act 2002). This applies to summary only and either-way offences.

Where, but for the prosecutor's application under s.70, the magistrates' court would have committed the offender for sentence to the Crown Court anyway it must say so. Otherwise the powers of sentence of the Crown Court will be limited to those of the magistrates' court.

Confiscation must be dealt with before, and taken into account when assessing, any other fine or financial order (except compensation).

(See Proceeds of Crime Act 2002 sections 6 and 13).

The court should also consider whether to make ancillary orders.

**STEP 8    Reasons**

Section 52 of the Sentencing Code imposes a duty to give reasons for, and explain the effect of, the sentence.

**STEP 9    Consideration for time spent on bail**

The court must consider whether to give credit for time spent on bail in accordance with section 240A of the Criminal Justice Act 2003 and section 325 of the Sentencing Code.

[1] NB. In the earlier guidelines, published in 2012, ecstasy tablet quantities were based on a typical quantity of 100mg MDMA per tablet

SUPPLYING OR OFFERING TO SUPPLY A CONTROLLED DRUG/POSSESSION OF A      **SG23-3**
CONTROLLED DRUG WITH INTENT TO SUPPLY IT TO ANOTHER

*Misuse of Drugs Act 1971 s.4(3), Misuse of Drugs Act 1971, s.5(3)*

**Effective from:** 01 April 2021

**Supplying or offering to supply a controlled drug**, Misuse of Drugs Act 1971 (section 4(3))

**Possession of a controlled drug with intent to supply it to another**, Misuse of Drugs Act 1971 (section 5(3))

Triable either way unless the defendant could receive the minimum sentence of seven years for a third drug trafficking offence under section 313 of the Sentencing Code in which case the offence is triable only on indictment.

**Class A**
Maximum: Life imprisonment

Offence range: High level community order – 16 years' custody

**Class B**

Maximum: 14 years' custody and/or unlimited fine

Offence range: Band B fine – 10 years' custody

**Class C**

Maximum: 14 years' custody and/or unlimited fine

Offence range: Band A – 8 years' custody

This offence is subject to statutory minimum sentencing provisions.

See Step 3 for further details.

**STEP 1    Determine the offence category**

The court should determine the offender's culpability (role) and the harm caused (quantity) with reference to the tables below.

In assessing culpability, the sentencer should weigh up all the factors of the case to determine role. Where there are characteristics present which fall under different role categories, or where the level of the offender's role is affected by the scale of the operation, the court should balance these characteristics to reach a fair assessment of the offender's culpability.

**Culpability demonstrated by the offender's role**

One or more of these characteristics may demonstrate the offender's role. These lists are not exhaustive.

*Leading role*
- Directing or organising buying and selling on a commercial scale
- Substantial links to, and influence on, others in a chain
- Close links to original source
- Expectation of substantial financial or other advantage
- Uses business as cover
- Abuses a position of trust or responsibility

*Significant role*
- Operational or management function within a chain
- Involves others in the operation whether by pressure, influence, intimidation or reward
- Expectation of significant financial or other advantage (save where this advantage is limited to meeting the offender's own habit), whether or not operating alone
- Some awareness and understanding of scale of operation

*Lesser role*
- Performs a limited function under direction
- Engaged by pressure, coercion, intimidation, grooming and/or control
- Involvement through naivety, immaturity or exploitation
- No influence on those above in a chain
- Very little, if any, awareness or understanding of the scale of operation
- Expectation of limited, if any, financial or other advantage (including meeting the offender's own habit)

**Harm**

In assessing harm, quantity is determined by the weight of the product. Where the offence is supply directly to users (including street dealing or supply in custodial institutions), the quantity of product is less indicative of the harm caused and therefore the starting point is not solely based on quantity. The court should consider all offences involving supplying directly to users as at least category 3 harm, and make an adjustment from the starting point within that category considering the quantity of drugs in the particular case.

Indicative quantities of the most common drugs, upon which the starting point is to be based) are given in the table below. Where a drug (such as fentanyl or its agonists) is not listed in the table below, sentencers should expect to be provided with expert evidence to assist in determining the potency of the particular drug and in equating the quantity in the case with the quantities set out in the guidelines in terms of the harm caused. There will often be no precise calculation possible, but courts are reminded that in cases of particularly potent drugs, even very small quantities may be held to be equivalent to large quantities of the drugs listed.

*Category 1*
- Heroin, cocaine – 5kg
- Ecstasy – 7,000 tablets*
- MDMA – 5kg
- LSD – 250,000 squares
- Amphetamine – 20kg
- Cannabis – 200kg
- Ketamine – 5kg
- Synthetic cannabinoid receptor agonists (for example 'spice') – very large quantity indicative of an industrial scale operation

*Category 2*
- Heroin, cocaine – 1kg
- Ecstasy – 1,300 tablets*
- MDMA – 1kg
- LSD – 25,000 squares
- Amphetamine – 4kg
- Cannabis – 40kg
- Ketamine – 1kg
- Synthetic cannabinoid receptor agonists (for example 'spice') – large quantity indicative of a commercial operation

*Category 3*
Selling directly to users

OR

Supply of drugs in a custodial institution

OR

- Heroin, cocaine – 150g
- Ecstasy – 200 tablets*
- MDMA – 150g
- LSD – 2,500 squares
- Amphetamine – 750g
- Cannabis – 6kg
- Ketamine – 150g
- Synthetic cannabinoid receptor agonists (for example 'spice') – smaller quantity between categories 2 and 4

*Category 4*
- Heroin, cocaine – 5g
- Ecstasy – 13 tablets*
- MDMA – 5g
- LSD – 170 squares
- Amphetamine – 20g
- Cannabis – 100g
- Ketamine – 5g
- Synthetic cannabinoid receptor agonists (for example 'spice') – very small quantity

Note – where the offence is selling directly to users or supply in a custodial institution the starting point is not based on quantity – go to category 3

*Ecstasy tablet quantities based on a typical quantity of 150mg MDMA per tablet[1]

STEP 2    **Starting point and category range**

Having determined the category at step one, the court should use the corresponding starting point to reach a sentence within the category range below. The starting point applies to all offenders irrespective of plea or previous convictions. A case of particular gravity, reflected by multiple features of culpability or harm in step one, could merit upward adjustment from the starting point before further adjustment for aggravating or mitigating features, set out below.

Where the operation is on the most serious and commercial scale, involving a quantity of drugs significantly higher than category 1, sentences of 20 years and above may be appropriate, depending on the offender's role.

Sentencers should be aware that there is evidence of a disparity in sentence outcomes for this offence which indicates that a higher proportion of Black, Asian and Other ethnicity offenders receive an immediate custodial sentence than White offenders and that for Asian offenders custodial sentence lengths have on average been longer than for White offenders. There may be many reasons for these differences, but in order to apply the guidelines fairly sentencers may find useful information and guidance at Chapter 8 paragraphs 123 to 129 of the Equal Treatment Bench Book.

| CLASS A | Leading Role | Significant Role | Lesser Role |
|---|---|---|---|
| Category 1 | **Starting point**<br>14 years' custody | **Starting point**<br>10 years' custody | **Starting point**<br>7 years' custody |
| | **Category range**<br>12 – 16 years' custody | **Category range**<br>9 – 12 years' custody | **Category range**<br>6 – 9 years' custody |
| Category 2 | **Starting point**<br>11 years' custody | **Starting point**<br>8 years' custody | **Starting point**<br>5 years' custody |
| | **Category range**<br>9 – 13 years' custody | **Category range**<br>6 years 6 months' –<br>10 years' custody | **Category range**<br>3 years 6 months' –<br>7 years' custody |
| Category 3 | **Starting point**<br>8 years 6 months'<br>custody | **Starting point**<br>4 years 6 months'<br>custody | **Starting point**<br>3 years' custody |
| | **Category range**<br>6 years 6 months' –<br>10 years' custody | **Category range**<br>3 years 6 months' –<br>7 years' custody | **Category range**<br>2 – 4 years 6 months'<br>custody |
| Category 4 | **Starting point**<br>5 years 6 months'<br>custody | **Starting point**<br>3 years 6 months'<br>custody | **Starting point**<br>18 months' custody |
| | **Category range**<br>4 years 6 months' –<br>7 years 6 months'<br>custody | **Category range**<br>2 – 5 years' custody | **Category range**<br>High level community<br>order – 3 years' custody |

| CLASS B | Leading Role | Significant Role | Lesser Role |
|---|---|---|---|
| Category 1 | **Starting point**<br>8 years' custody | **Starting point**<br>5 years 6 months'<br>custody | **Starting point**<br>3 years' custody |
| | **Category range**<br>7 – 10 years' custody | **Category range**<br>5 – 7 years' custody | **Category range**<br>2 years 6 months' –<br>5 years' custody |
| Category 2 | **Starting point**<br>6 years' custody | **Starting point**<br>4 years' custody | **Starting point**<br>1 year's custody |
| | **Category range**<br>4 years 6 months' –<br>8 years' custody | **Category range**<br>2 years 6 months' –<br>5 years' custody | **Category range**<br>26 weeks' – 3 years'<br>custody |
| Category 3 | **Starting point**<br>4 years' custody | **Starting point**<br>1 year's custody | **Starting point**<br>High level community<br>order |
| | **Category range**<br>2 years 6 months' –<br>5 years' custody | **Category range**<br>26 weeks' – 3 years'<br>custody | **Category range**<br>Low level community<br>order – 26 weeks'<br>custody |
| Category 4 | **Starting point**<br>18 months' custody | **Starting point**<br>High level community<br>order | **Starting point**<br>Low level community<br>order |
| | **Category range**<br>26 weeks' – 3 years'<br>custody | **Category range**<br>Medium level<br>community order – 26<br>weeks' custody | **Category range**<br>Band B fine – Medium<br>level community order |

| CLASS C | Leading Role | Significant Role | Lesser Role |
|---------|--------------|------------------|-------------|
| Category 1 | **Starting point** 5 years' custody | **Starting point** 3 years' custody | **Starting point** 18 months' custody |
|  | **Category range** 4 – 8 years' custody | **Category range** 2 – 5 years' custody | **Category range** 1 – 3 years' custody |
| Category 2 | **Starting point** 3 years 6 months' custody | **Starting point** 18 months' custody | **Starting point** 26 weeks' custody |
|  | **Category range** 2 – 5 years' custody | **Category range** 1 – 3 years' custody | **Category range** 12 weeks' – 18 months' custody |
| Category 3 | **Starting point** 18 months' custody | **Starting point** 26 weeks' custody | **Starting point** High level community order |
|  | **Category range** 1 – 3 years' custody | **Category range** 12 weeks' – 18 months' custody | **Category range** Low level community order – 12 weeks' custody |
| Category 4 | **Starting point** 26 weeks' custody | **Starting point** High level community order | **Starting point** Low level community order |
|  | **Category range** High level community order – 18 months' custody | **Category range** Low level community order – 12 weeks' custody | **Category range** Band A fine – Medium level community order |

Sentencing Guidelines

**Fines**

[For the standard schedule of fines see **SG2-5**.]

**Community Orders and Custodial Sentences**

[For the imposition of community orders, including the community orders table, see Imposition of Community and Custodial Sentences at **SG9-2**.

For the imposition of custodial sentences see Imposition of Community and Custodial Sentences at **SG9-3**.]

The table below contains a non-exhaustive list of additional factual elements providing the context of the offence and factors relating to the offender. Identify whether any combination of these, or other relevant factors, should result in and upward or downward adjustment from the starting point. In some cases, having considered these factors, it may be appropriate to move outside the identified category range.

There may be exceptional local circumstances that arise which may lead a court to decide that prevalence of drug offending should influence sentencing levels. The pivotal issue in such cases will be the harm caused to the community.

It is essential that the court before taking account of prevalence:

- has supporting evidence from an external source, for example, Community Impact Statements, to justify claims that drug offending is prevalent in their area, and is causing particular harm in that community; and
- is satisfied that there is a compelling need to treat the offence more seriously than elsewhere.

**Factors increasing seriousness**

*Statutory aggravating factors*

- Previous convictions [see **SG2-21**] having regard to
  a)  nature of the offence to which conviction relates and relevance to current offence; and
  b)  time elapsed since conviction
- Offender used or permitted a person under 18 to deliver a controlled drug to a third person
- Offender 18 or over supplies or offers to supply a drug on, or in the vicinity of, school premises either when school in use as such or at a time between one hour before and one hour after they are to be used.
- Offence committed on bail [see **SG2-22**]

*Other aggravating factors include*

- Exploitation of children and/or vulnerable persons to assist in drug-related activity
- Exercising control over the home of another person for drug-related activity
- Targeting of any premises where children or other vulnerable persons are likely to be present
- Exposure of drug user to the risk of serious harm over and above that expected by the user, for example, through the method of production or subsequent adulteration of the drug
- Exposure of those involved in drug dealing to the risk of serious harm, for example through method of transporting drugs
- Exposure of third parties to the risk of serious harm, for example, through the location of the drug-related activity
- Attempts to conceal or dispose of evidence, where not charged separately
- Presence of others, especially children and/or non-users
- Presence of weapons, where not charged separately
- Use of violence (where not charged as separate offence or taken into account at step one)
- Failure to comply with current court orders
- Offending took place in prison (unless already taken into consideration at step 1)
- Offender was supplying or involved in the supply of drugs into prison
- Offence committed on licence or post sentence supervision
- Established evidence of community impact
- Use of sophisticated methods or technologies in order to avoid or impede detection

**Factors reducing seriousness or reflecting personal mitigation**

- Involvement due to pressure, intimidation or coercion falling short of duress, except where already taken into account at step one
- Supply only of drug to which offender addicted
- Mistaken belief of the offender regarding the type of drug, taking into account the reasonableness of such belief in all the circumstances
- Isolated incident
- No previous convictions or no relevant or recent convictions
- Remorse
- Good character and/or exemplary conduct
- Determination and/or demonstration of steps having been taken to address addiction or offending behaviour
- Serious medical conditions requiring urgent, intensive or long-term treatment
- Age and/or lack of maturity where it affects the responsibility of the offender
- Mental disorder or learning disability
- Sole or primary carer for dependent relatives
- Offender's vulnerability was exploited

**STEP 3   Minimum Terms**

For class A cases, section 313 of the Sentencing Code provides that a court should impose an appropriate custodial sentence of at least seven years for a third class A trafficking offence except where the court is of the opinion that there are particular circumstances which (a) relate to any of the offences or to the offender; and (b) would make it unjust to do so in all the circumstances.

**Unjust in all of the circumstances**

In considering whether a statutory minimum sentence would be 'unjust in all of the circumstances' the court must have regard to the particular circumstances of the offence and the offender. If the circumstances of the offence, the previous offences or the offender make it unjust to impose the statutory minimum sentence then the court must impose either a shorter custodial sentence than the statutory minimum provides or an alternative sentence.

**The offence**

Having reached this stage of the guideline the court should have made a provisional assessment of the seriousness of the current offence. In addition, the court must consider the seriousness of the previous offences and the period of time that has elapsed between offences. Where the seriousness of the combined offences is such that it falls below the custody threshold, or where there has been a significant period of time between the offences, the court may consider it unjust to impose the statutory minimum sentence.

**The offender**

The court should consider the following factors to determine whether it would be unjust to impose the statutory minimum sentence;

- any strong personal mitigation;

- whether there is a realistic prospect of rehabilitation;
- whether custody will result in significant impact on others.

### STEP 4   Consider any factors which indicate a reduction, such as assistance to the prosecution

The court should take into account section 74 of the Sentencing Code (assistance by defendants: reduction or review of sentence) and any other rule of law by virtue of which an offender may receive a discounted sentence in consequence of assistance given (or offered) to the prosecutor or investigator.

### STEP 5   Reduction for guilty pleas

The court should take account of any potential reduction for a guilty plea in accordance with section 73 of the Sentencing Code and the Reduction in Sentence for a Guilty Plea guideline [see **SG5-1–SG5-12**].

In circumstances where an appropriate custodial sentence of 7 years falls to be imposed under section 313 of the Sentencing Code (third Class A drug trafficking offences), the court may impose any sentence in accordance with this guideline which is not less than 80 per cent of the appropriate custodial period.

### STEP 6   Totality principle

If sentencing an offender for more than one offence, or where the offender is already serving a sentence, consider whether the total sentence is just and proportionate to the offending behaviour. See Totality guideline [see **SG4**].

### STEP 7   Confiscation and ancillary orders

Confiscation orders under the Proceeds of Crime Act 2002 may only be made by the Crown Court. The Crown Court must proceed with a view to making a confiscation order if it is asked to do so by the prosecutor or if the Crown Court believes it is appropriate for it to do so.

Where, following conviction in a magistrates' court, the prosecutor applies for the offender to be committed to the Crown Court with a view to a confiscation order being considered, the magistrates' court must commit the offender to the Crown Court to be sentenced there (section 70 of the Proceeds of Crime Act 2002). This applies to summary only and either-way offences.

Where, but for the prosecutor's application under s.70, the magistrates' court would have committed the offender for sentence to the Crown Court anyway it must say so. Otherwise the powers of sentence of the Crown Court will be limited to those of the magistrates' court.

Confiscation must be dealt with before, and taken into account when assessing, any other fine or financial order (except compensation).

(See Proceeds of Crime Act 2002 sections 6 and 13)

The court should also consider whether to make ancillary orders.

### STEP 8   Reasons

Section 52 of the Sentencing Code imposes a duty to give reasons for, and explain the effect of, the sentence.

### STEP 9   Consideration for time spent on bail

The court must consider whether to give credit for time spent on bail in accordance with section 240A of the Criminal Justice Act 2003 and section 325 of the Sentencing Code.

[1] NB. In the earlier guidelines, published in 2012, ecstasy tablet quantities were based on a typical quantity of 100mg MDMA per tablet

PRODUCTION OF A CONTROLLED DRUG/CULTIVATION OF CANNABIS PLANT      **SG23-4**

*Misuse of Drugs Act 1971, s.4(2)(a) or (b), Misuse of Drugs Act 1971, s.6(2)*

**Effective from:** 01 April 2021

**Production of a controlled drug**, Misuse of Drugs Act 1971 (section 4(2)(a) or (b))

**Cultivation of cannabis plant**, Misuse of Drugs Act 1971 (section 6(2))

Triable either way unless the defendant could receive the minimum sentence of seven years for a third drug trafficking offence under section 313 of the Sentencing Code in which case the offence is triable only on indictment.

### Production of a controlled drug

**Class A**
Maximum: Life imprisonment

Offence range: High level community order – 16 years' custody

**Class B**

Maximum: 14 years' custody and/or unlimited fine

Offence range: Band B fine – 10 years' custody

**Class C**

Maximum: 14 years' custody and/or unlimited fine

Offence range: Discharge – 8 years' custody

**Cultivation of cannabis plant** Maximum: 14 years' custody

Offence range: Band A fine – 8 years' custody

This offence is subject to statutory minimum sentencing provisions.

See Step 3 for further details.

## STEP 1    Determine the offence category

The court should determine the offender's culpability (role) and the harm caused (output or potential output) with reference to the tables below.

In assessing culpability, the sentencer should weigh up all the factors of the case to determine role. Where there are characteristics present which fall under different role categories, or where the level of the offender's role is affected by the scale of the operation, the court should balance these characteristics to reach a fair assessment of the offender's culpability.

### Culpability demonstrated by the offender's role

One or more of these characteristics may demonstrate the offender's role. These lists are not exhaustive.

*Leading role*
- Directing or organising production/cultivation on a commercial scale
- Substantial links to, and influence on, others in a chain
- Close links to original source
- Expectation of substantial financial or other advantage
- Uses business as cover
- Abuses a position of trust or responsibility

*Significant role*
- Operational or management function within a chain
- Involves others in the operation whether by pressure, influence, intimidation or reward
- Expectation of significant financial or other advantage (save where this advantage is limited to meeting the offender's own habit), whether or not operating alone
- Some awareness and understanding of scale of operation

*Lesser role*
- Performs a limited function under direction
- Engaged by pressure, coercion, intimidation, grooming and/or control
- Involvement through naivety, immaturity or exploitation
- No influence on those above in a chain
- Very little, if any, awareness or understanding of the scale of operation
- If own operation, solely for own use (considering reasonableness of account in all the circumstances)
- Expectation of limited, if any, financial advantage, (including meeting the offender's own habit)

### Harm

In assessing harm, output or potential output are determined by the weight of the product or number of plants/scale of operation. Indicative output or potential output, upon which the starting point is to be based, is given in the table below. Where a drug (such as fentanyl or its agonists) is not listed in the table below, sentencers should expect to be provided with expert evidence to assist in determining the potency of the particular drug and in equating the quantity in the case with the quantities set out in the guidelines in terms of the harm caused. There will often be no precise calculation possible, but courts are reminded that in cases of particularly potent drugs, even very small quantities may be held to be equivalent to large quantities of the drugs listed.

*Category 1*
- Heroin, cocaine – 5kg
- Ecstasy – 7,000 tablets*
- MDMA – 5kg
- LSD – 250,000 squares

- Amphetamine – 20kg
- Cannabis – operation capable of producing industrial quantities for commercial use
- Ketamine – 5kg
- Synthetic cannabinoid receptor agonists (for example 'spice') – very large quantity indicative of an industrial scale operation

*Category 2*
- Heroin, cocaine – 1kg
- Ecstasy – 1,300 tablets*
- MDMA – 1kg
- LSD – 25,000 squares
- Amphetamine – 4kg
- Cannabis – operation capable of producing significant quantities for commercial use
- Ketamine – 1kg
- Synthetic cannabinoid receptor agonists (for example 'spice') – large quantity indicative of a commercial operation

*Category 3*
- Heroin, cocaine – 150g
- Ecstasy – 200 tablets (see note below)
- MDMA – 150g
- LSD – 2,500 squares
- Amphetamine – 750g
- Cannabis – 20 plants**
- Ketamine – 150g
- Synthetic cannabinoid receptor agonists (for example 'spice') – smaller quantity between categories 2 and 4

*Category 4*
- Heroin, cocaine – 5g
- Ecstasy – 13 tablets*
- MDMA – 5g
- LSD – 170 squares
- Amphetamine – 20g
- Cannabis – 7 plants**
- Ketamine – 5g
- Synthetic cannabinoid receptor agonists (for example 'spice') – very small quantity

*Ecstasy tablet quantities based on a typical quantity of 150mg MDMA per tablet[1]

**with an assumed yield of 55g per plant

STEP 2    **Starting point and category range**

Having determined the category at step one, the court should use the corresponding starting point to reach a sentence within the category range below. The starting point applies to all offenders irrespective of plea or previous convictions. A case of particular gravity, reflected by multiple features of culpability or harm in step one, could merit upward adjustment from the starting point before further adjustment for aggravating or mitigating features, set out below.

Where the operation is on the most serious and commercial scale, involving a quantity of drugs significantly higher than category 1, sentences of 20 years and above may be appropriate, depending on the offender's role.

Sentencers should be aware that there is evidence of a disparity in sentence outcomes for this offence which indicates that a higher proportion of Asian and Other ethnicity offenders receive an immediate custodial sentence than Black and White offenders. There may be many reasons for these differences, but in order to apply the guidelines fairly sentencers may find useful information and guidance at Chapter 8 paragraphs 185 to 193 of the Equal Treatment Bench Book.

| CLASS A | Leading Role | Significant Role | Lesser Role |
|---|---|---|---|
| Category 1 | **Starting point**<br>14 years' custody | **Starting point**<br>10 years' custody | **Starting point**<br>7 years' custody |
|  | **Category range**<br>12 – 16 years' custody | **Category range**<br>9 – 12 years' custody | **Category range**<br>6 – 9 years' custody |

- Failure to comply with current court orders
- Offence committed on licence or post sentence supervision
- Offending took place in prison (unless already taken into consideration at step 1)
- Established evidence of community impact
- Use of sophisticated methods or technologies in order to avoid or impede detection

### Factors reducing seriousness or reflecting personal mitigation

- Involvement due to pressure, intimidation or coercion falling short of duress, except where already taken into account at step one
- Isolated incident
- No previous convictions or no relevant or recent convictions
- Offender's vulnerability was exploited
- Remorse
- Good character and/or exemplary conduct
- Determination and/or demonstration of steps having been taken to address addiction or offending behaviour
- Serious medical conditions requiring urgent, intensive or long-term treatment
- Age and/or lack of maturity where it affects the responsibility of the offender
- Mental disorder or learning disability
- Sole or primary carer for dependent relatives

### STEP 3   Minimum Terms

For class A cases, section 313 of the Sentencing Code provides that a court should impose an appropriate custodial sentence of at least seven years for a third class A trafficking offence except where the court is of the opinion that there are particular circumstances which (a) relate to any of the offences or to the offender; and (b) would make it unjust to do so in all the circumstances.

### Unjust in all of the circumstances

In considering whether a statutory minimum sentence would be 'unjust in all of the circumstances' the court must have regard to the particular circumstances of the offence and the offender. If the circumstances of the offence, the previous offences or the offender make it unjust to impose the statutory minimum sentence then the court **must impose either a shorter custodial sentence than the statutory minimum provides or an alternative sentence.**

### The offence

Having reached this stage of the guideline the court should have made a provisional assessment of the seriousness of the current offence. In addition, the court must consider the seriousness of the previous offences and the period of time that has elapsed between offences. Where the seriousness of the combined offences is such that it falls below the custody threshold, or where there has been a significant period of time between the offences, the court may consider it unjust to impose the statutory minimum sentence.

### The offender

The court should consider the following factors to determine whether it would be unjust to impose the statutory minimum sentence;

- any strong personal mitigation;
- whether there is a realistic prospect of rehabilitation;
- whether custody will result in significant impact on others.

### STEP 4   Consider any factors which indicate a reduction, such as assistance to the prosecution

The court should take into account section 74 of the Sentencing Code (assistance by defendants: reduction or review of sentence) and any other rule of law by virtue of which an offender may receive a discounted sentence in consequence of assistance given (or offered) to the prosecutor or investigator.

### STEP 5   Reduction for guilty pleas

The court should take account of any potential reduction for a guilty plea in accordance with section 73 of the Sentencing Code and the Reduction in Sentence for a Guilty Plea guideline [see **SG5-1–SG5-12**]. In circumstances where an appropriate custodial sentence of 7 years falls to be imposed under section 313 of the Sentencing Code (third Class A drug trafficking offences), the court may impose any sentence in accordance with this guideline which is not less than **80 per cent** of the **appropriate** custodial period.

### STEP 6   Totality principle

If sentencing an offender for more than one offence, or where the offender is already serving a sentence, consider whether the total sentence is just and proportionate to the offending behaviour. See Totality guideline [see **SG4**].

## STEP 7   Confiscation and ancillary orders

Confiscation orders under the Proceeds of Crime Act 2002 may only be made by the Crown Court. The Crown Court must proceed with a view to making a confiscation order if it is asked to do so by the prosecutor or if the Crown Court believes it is appropriate for it to do so.

Where, following conviction in a magistrates' court, the prosecutor applies for the offender to be committed to the Crown Court with a view to a confiscation order being considered, the magistrates' court must commit the offender to the Crown Court to be sentenced there (section 70 of the Proceeds of Crime Act 2002). This applies to summary only and either-way offences.

Where, but for the prosecutor's application under s.70, the magistrates' court would have committed the offender for sentence to the Crown Court anyway it must say so. Otherwise the powers of sentence of the Crown Court will be limited to those of the magistrates' court.

Confiscation must be dealt with before, and taken into account when assessing, any other fine or financial order (except compensation).

(See Proceeds of Crime Act 2002 sections 6 and 13)

The court should also consider whether to make ancillary orders.

## STEP 8   Reasons

Section 52 of the Sentencing Code imposes a duty to give reasons for, and explain the effect of, the sentence.

## STEP 9   Consideration for time spent on bail

The court must consider whether to give credit for time spent on bail in accordance with section 240A of the Criminal Justice Act 2003 and section 325 of the Sentencing Code.

[1] NB. In the earlier guidelines, published in 2012, ecstasy tablet quantities were based on a typical quantity of 100mg MDMA per tablet

### PERMITTING PREMISES TO BE USED                                           SG23-5

*Misuse of Drugs Act 1971, s.8*

**Effective from:** 01 April 2021

Triable either way unless the defendant could receive the minimum sentence of seven years for a third drug trafficking offence under section 313 of the Sentencing Code in which case the offence is triable only on indictment.

## Class A

Maximum: 14 years' custody

Offence range: Low level community order – 4 years' custody

## Class B

Maximum: 14 years' custody

Offence range: Band A fine – 18 months' custody

## Class C

Maximum: 14 years' custody

Offence range: Discharge – 26 weeks' custody

This offence is subject to statutory minimum sentencing provisions.

See Step 3 for further details.

## STEP 1   Determining the offence category

The court should determine the offence category with reference only to the factors listed in the tables below. In order to determine the category, the court should assess culpability and harm.

## Culpability

Where there are characteristics present which fall under different levels of culpability, the court should balance these characteristics to reach a fair assessment of the offender's culpability.

## A – Higher culpability

- Participates in the exploitation of a child or vulnerable person including one who is also involved in the drugs operation
- Permits premises to be used primarily for drug activity
- Permits use in expectation of substantial financial gain
- Uses legitimate business premises to aid and/or conceal illegal activity

## B – Lower culpability

- Permits use for limited or no financial gain
- No active role in drug activity taking place
- Involved due to intimidation or coercion
- Offender's vulnerability has been exploited

### Harm

Where there are characteristics present which fall under different levels of harm, the court should balance these characteristics to reach a fair assessment of the harm caused or likely to be caused

### Category 1

- Regular drug-related activity and/or premises used for drug activity over a long period
- Higher quantity of drugs (substantially higher than the quantities given for Category 2)

### Category 2

- Infrequent drug-related activity and/or premises used for drug activity over a short period
- Lower quantity of drugs

Indicative quantities

### STEP 2    Starting point and category range

Having determined the category, the court should use the corresponding starting points to reach a sentence within the category range below. The starting point applies to all offenders irrespective of plea or previous convictions. A case of particular gravity, reflected by multiple features of culpability in step one, could merit upward adjustment from the starting point before further adjustment for aggravating or mitigating features, set out below.

| CLASS A | Culpability | |
|---|---|---|
| | A | B |
| Harm 1 | **Starting point**<br>2 years 6 months' custody | **Starting point**<br>36 weeks' custody |
| | **Category range**<br>18 months' – 4 years' custody | **Category range**<br>High level community order –<br>18 months' custody |
| Harm 2 | **Starting point**<br>36 weeks' custody | **Starting point**<br>Medium level community order |
| | **Category range**<br>High level community order –<br>18 months' custody | **Category range**<br>Low level community order – High level<br>community order |

| CLASS B | Culpability | |
|---|---|---|
| | A | B |
| Harm 1 | **Starting point**<br>1 year's custody | **Starting point**<br>High level community order |
| | **Category range**<br>26 weeks' – 18 months' custody | **Category range**<br>Low level community order – 26 weeks'<br>custody |
| Harm 2 | **Starting point**<br>High level community order | **Starting point**<br>Band C fine |
| | **Category range**<br>Low level community order – 26 weeks'<br>custody | **Category range**<br>Band A fine – Low level community<br>order |

| CLASS C | Culpability | |
|---|---|---|
| | **A** | **B** |
| Harm 1 | **Starting point**<br>12 weeks' custody | **Starting point**<br>Low level community order |
| | **Category range**<br>High level community order – 26 weeks' custody* | **Category range**<br>Band C fine – High level community order |
| Harm 2 | **Starting point**<br>Low level community order | **Starting point**<br>Band A fine |
| | **Category range**<br>Band C fine – High level community order | **Category range**<br>Discharge – Low level community order |

\* When tried summarily, the maximum penalty is 12 weeks' custody.

**Fines**

[For the standard schedule of fines see **SG2-5**.]

**Community Orders and Custodial Sentences**

[For the imposition of community orders, including the community orders table, see Imposition of Community and Custodial Sentences at **SG9-2**.

For the imposition of custodial sentences see Imposition of Community and Custodial Sentences at **SG9-3**.]

Where the defendant is dependent on or has a propensity to misuse drugs and there is sufficient prospect of success, a community order with a drug rehabilitation requirement under part 10 of Schedule 9 of the Sentencing Code can be a proper alternative to a short or moderate length custodial sentence.

The table below contains a non-exhaustive list of additional factual elements providing the context of the offence and factors relating to the offender. Identify whether any combination of these, or other relevant factors, should result in an upward or downward adjustment from the starting point. In some cases, having considered these factors, it may be appropriate to move outside the identified category range.

**Factors increasing seriousness**

*Statutory aggravating factors*

- Previous convictions [see **SG2-21**], having regard to
  a) the **nature** of the offence to which the conviction relates and its **relevance** to the current offence; and
  b) the **time** that has elapsed since the conviction
- Offence committed whilst on bail [see **SG2-22**]
- Offence motivated by, or demonstrating hostility based on any of the following characteristics of the victim: disability, sexual orientation or gender identity

*Other aggravating factors*

- Premises adapted to facilitate drug activity
- Location of premises, for example proximity to school
- Attempts to conceal or dispose of evidence, where not charged separately
- Presence of others, especially children and/or non-users
- Presence of weapons, where not charged separately
- Failure to comply with current court orders
- Other offences taken into consideration (TICs)
- Offence committed whilst on licence or subject to post sentence supervision

**Factors reducing seriousness or reflecting personal mitigation**

- No previous convictions or no relevant/recent convictions
- Remorse
- Good character and/or exemplary conduct
- Involved due to naivety
- Isolated incident
- Determination and/or demonstration of steps having been taken to address addiction or offending behaviour
- Serious medical conditions requiring urgent, intensive or long-term treatment
- Age and/or lack of maturity where it affects the responsibility of the offender

- Mental disorder or learning disability
- Sole or primary carer for dependent relative(s)

### STEP 3   Minimum Terms

For class A cases, section 313 of the Sentencing Code provides that a court should impose an appropriate custodial sentence of at least seven years for a third class A trafficking offence except where the court is of the opinion that there are particular circumstances which (a) relate to any of the offences or to the offender; and (b) would make it unjust to do so in all the circumstances.

### Unjust in all of the circumstances

In considering whether a statutory minimum sentence would be 'unjust in all of the circumstances' the court must have regard to the particular circumstances of the offence and the offender. If the circumstances of the offence, the previous offences or the offender make it unjust to impose the statutory minimum sentence then the court must impose either a shorter custodial sentence than the statutory minimum provides or an alternative sentence.

### The offence

Having reached this stage of the guideline the court should have made a provisional assessment of the seriousness of the current offence. In addition, the court must consider the seriousness of the previous offences and the period of time that has elapsed between offences. Where the seriousness of the combined offences is such that it falls below the custody threshold, or where there has been a significant period of time between the offences, the court may consider it unjust to impose the statutory minimum sentence.

### The offender

The court should consider the following factors to determine whether it would be unjust to impose the statutory minimum sentence;

any strong personal mitigation;

whether there is a realistic prospect of rehabilitation;

whether custody will result in significant impact on others.

### STEP 4   Consider any factors which indicate a reduction, such as assistance to the prosecution

The court should take into account section 74 of the Sentencing Code (assistance by defendants: reduction or review of sentence) and any other rule of law by virtue of which an offender may receive a discounted sentence in consequence of assistance given (or offered) to the prosecutor or investigator.

### STEP 5   Reduction for guilty pleas

The court should take account of any potential reduction for a guilty plea in accordance with section 73 of the Sentencing Code and the Reduction in Sentence for a Guilty Plea guideline [see **SG5-1–SG5-12**].

In circumstances where an appropriate custodial sentence of 7 years falls to be imposed under section 313 of the Sentencing Code, the court may impose any sentence in accordance with this guideline which is not less than **80 per cent** of the **appropriate** custodial period.

### STEP 6   Totality principle

If sentencing an offender for more than one offence, or where the offender is already serving a sentence, consider whether the total sentence is just and proportionate to the offending behaviour. See Totality guideline [see **SG4**].

### STEP 7   Confiscation and ancillary orders

Confiscation orders under the Proceeds of Crime Act 2002 may only be made by the Crown Court. The Crown Court must proceed with a view to making a confiscation order if it is asked to do so by the prosecutor or if the Crown Court believes it is appropriate for it to do so.

Where, following conviction in a magistrates' court, the prosecutor applies for the offender to be committed to the Crown Court with a view to a confiscation order being considered, the magistrates' court must commit the offender to the Crown Court to be sentenced there (section 70 of the Proceeds of Crime Act 2002). This applies to summary only and either-way offences.

Where, but for the prosecutor's application under s.70, the magistrates' court would have committed the offender for sentence to the Crown Court anyway it must say so. Otherwise the powers of sentence of the Crown Court will be limited to those of the magistrates' court.

Confiscation must be dealt with before, and taken into account when assessing, any other fine or financial order (except compensation).

(See Proceeds of Crime Act 2002 sections 6 and 13)

The court should also consider whether to make ancillary orders.

## STEP 8   Reasons

Section 52 of the Sentencing Code imposes a duty to give reasons for, and explain the effect of, the sentence.

## STEP 9   Consideration for time spent on bail

The court must consider whether to give credit for time spent on bail in accordance with section 240A of the Criminal Justice Act 2003 and section 325 of the Sentencing Code.

POSSESSION OF A CONTROLLED DRUG                    **SG23-6**

*Misuse of Drugs Act 1971, s.5(2)*

**Effective from:** 01 April 2021

Triable either way

**Class A**

Maximum: 7 years' custody
Offence range: Fine – 51 weeks' custody

**Class B**

Maximum: 5 years' custody
Offence range: Discharge – 26 weeks' custody

**Class C**

Maximum: 2 years' custody
Offence range: Discharge – Medium community order

## STEP 1   Determining the offence category

The court should identify the offence category based on the class of drug involved.

| Category 1 | Class A drug |
|------------|--------------|
| Category 2 | Class B drug |
| Category 3 | Class C drug |

## STEP 2   Starting point and category range

Having determined the category at step one, the court should use the corresponding starting point to reach a sentence within the category range below. The starting point applies to all offenders irrespective of plea or previous convictions. A case of particular gravity, reflected by multiple features of culpability or harm in step one, could merit upward adjustment from the starting point before further adjustment for aggravating or mitigating features, set out below.

| Offence category | Starting Point<br>*(applicable to all offenders)* | Category Range<br>*(applicable to all offenders)* |
|------------------|----------------------------------------------------|----------------------------------------------------|
| Category 1 (class A) | Band C fine | Band A fine – 51 weeks' custody |
| Category 2 (class B) | Band B fine | Discharge – 26 weeks' custody* |
| Category 3 (class C) | Band A fine | Discharge – Medium level community order* |

\* When heard summarily, the maximum penalty is 12 weeks' custody

**Fines**

[For the standard schedule of fines see **SG2-5**.]

**Community Orders and Custodial Sentences**

[For the imposition of community orders, including the community orders table, see Imposition of Community and Custodial Sentences at **SG9-2**.

For the imposition of custodial sentences see Imposition of Community and Custodial Sentences at **SG9-3**.]

The table below contains a non-exhaustive list of additional factual elements providing the context of the offence and factors relating to the offender. Identify whether any combination of these, or other relevant factors, should result in an upward or downward adjustment from the starting point.

In particular, possession of drugs in prison is likely to result in an upward adjustment. In some cases, having considered these factors, it may be appropriate to move outside the identified category range.

**Factors increasing seriousness**

*Statutory aggravating factors*

- Previous convictions [see **SG2-21**], having regard to
  a)  nature of the offence to which conviction relates and relevance to current offence; and
  b)  time elapsed since conviction
- Offence committed on bail [see **SG2-22**]

*Other aggravating factors*

- Possession of drug in prison
- Presence of others, especially children and/or non-users
- Possession of drug in a school or licensed premises
- Large quantity*
- Failure to comply with current court orders
- Offence committed on licence
- Attempts to conceal or dispose of evidence, where not charged separately
- Established evidence of community impact

**Factors reducing seriousness or reflecting personal mitigation**

- No previous convictions or no relevant or recent convictions
- Remorse
- Good character and/or exemplary conduct
- Small quantity*
- Offender is using cannabis to help with a diagnosed medical condition
- Determination and/or demonstration of steps having been taken to address addiction or offending behaviour
- Serious medical conditions requiring urgent, intensive or long-term treatment
- Isolated incident
- Age and/or lack of maturity where it affects the responsibility of the offender
- Mental disorder or learning disability
- Sole or primary carer for dependent relatives

*Whether a quantity is high or low will depend on the nature and potency of the drug.

## STEP 3    Consider any factors which indicate a reduction, such as assistance to the prosecution

The court should take into account section 74 of the Sentencing Code (assistance by defendants: reduction or review of sentence) and any other rule of law by virtue of which an offender may receive a discounted sentence in consequence of assistance given (or offered) to the prosecutor or investigator.

## STEP 4    Reduction for guilty pleas

The court should take account of any potential reduction for a guilty plea in accordance with section 73 of the Sentencing Code and the Reduction in Sentence for a Guilty Plea guideline [see **SG5-1–SG5-12**].

## STEP 5    Totality principle

If sentencing an offender for more than one offence, or where the offender is already serving a sentence, consider whether the total sentence is just and proportionate to the offending behaviour. See Totality guideline [see **SG4**].

## STEP 6    Ancillary orders

Confiscation orders under the Proceeds of Crime Act 2002 may only be made by the Crown Court. The Crown Court must proceed with a view to making a confiscation order if it is asked to do so by the prosecutor or if the Crown Court believes it is appropriate for it to do so.

Where, following conviction in a magistrates' court, the prosecutor applies for the offender to be committed to the Crown Court with a view to a confiscation order being considered, the magistrates' court must commit the offender to the Crown Court to be sentenced there (section 70 of the Proceeds of Crime Act 2002). This applies to summary only and either-way offences.

Where, but for the prosecutor's application under s.70, the magistrates' court would have committed the offender for sentence to the Crown Court anyway it must say so. Otherwise the powers of sentence of the Crown Court will be limited to those of the magistrates' court.

Confiscation must be dealt with before, and taken into account when assessing, any other fine or financial order (except compensation).

# Producing a Psychoactive Substance

*Psychoactive Substances Act 2016, s.4*

**Effective from:** 01 April 2021

Triable either way

Maximum: 7 years' custody

Offence range: Band B Fine – 6 years' custody

## STEP 1 Determining the offence category

The court should determine the offender's culpability (role) and the harm caused (output or potential output) with reference to the tables below.

In assessing culpability, the sentencer should weigh up all the factors of the case to determine role. Where there are characteristics present which fall under different role categories, or where the level of the offender's role is affected by the scale of the operation, the court should balance these characteristics to reach a fair assessment of the offender's culpability.

**Culpability demonstrated by the offender's role**

One or more of these characteristics may demonstrate the offender's role. These lists are not exhaustive.

*Leading role*

- Directing or organising production on a commercial scale
- Substantial links to, and influence on, others in a chain
- Close links to original source
- Expectation of substantial financial or other advantage
- Uses business as cover
- Abuses a position of trust or responsibility

*Significant role*

- Operational or management function within a chain
- Involves others in the operation whether by pressure, influence, intimidation or reward
- Expectation of significant financial or other advantage (save where this advantage is limited to meeting the offender's own habit), whether or not operating alone
- Some awareness and understanding of scale of operation

*Lesser role*

- Performs a limited function under direction
- Engaged by pressure, coercion, intimidation, grooming and/or control
- Involvement through naivety, immaturity or exploitation
- No influence on those above in a chain
- Very little, if any, awareness or understanding of the scale of operation
- Expectation of limited, if any, financial advantage, (including meeting the offender's own habit)
- If own operation, solely for own use (considering reasonableness of account in all the circumstances)

**Harm**

In assessing harm, the sentencer should consider the factors below. Where there are characteristics present which fall under different harm categories the court should balance these characteristics to reach a fair assessment of harm.

Where evidence is available as to the potential effects of the substance and harm likely to be caused by those effects, the court should consider whether this affects the category of harm. Where the harm is very great, or very small, this may lead the court to move the starting point for the offence up or down within the category, or to place the offence in a higher or lower category than that indicated by the other factors listed.

*Category 1*

- Large quantity indicative of industrial scale operation

*Category 2*

- Quantity indicative of smaller-scale commercial operation

*Category 3*

- Very small quantity

*Other aggravating factors include*

- Exploitation of children and/or vulnerable persons to assist in the offending
- Involving an innocent agent in the commission of the offence
- Targeting of any premises where children or other vulnerable persons are likely to be present
- Exposure of psychoactive substance user to the risk of serious harm over and above that expected by the user, for example, through the method of production or subsequent adulteration of the substance
- Exposure of those involved in dealing in the psychoactive substance to the risk of serious harm, for example through method of transporting the substance
- Exposure of third parties to the risk of serious harm
- Attempts to conceal or dispose of evidence, where not charged separately
- Presence of weapons, where not charged separately
- Use of violence (where not charged as separate offence or taken into account at step one)
- Failure to comply with current court orders
- Offence committed on licence or post sentence supervision
- Use of sophisticated methods or technologies in order to avoid or impede detection

**Factors reducing seriousness or reflecting personal mitigation**

- Involvement due to pressure, intimidation or coercion falling short of duress, except where already taken into account at step one.
- Importation only of psychoactive substance to which offender addicted and of quantity consistent with personal use
- Mistaken belief of the offender regarding the type of substance, taking into account the reasonableness of such belief in all the circumstances
- Isolated incident
- No previous convictions or no relevant or recent convictions
- Remorse
- Good character and/or exemplary conduct
- Determination and/or demonstration of steps having been taken to address addiction or offending behaviour
- Serious medical conditions requiring urgent, intensive or long-term treatment
- Age and/or lack of maturity where it affects the responsibility of the offender
- Mental disorder or learning disability
- Sole or primary carer for dependent relatives
- Offender's vulnerability was exploited

**STEP 3   Consider any factors which indicate a reduction, such as assistance to the prosecution**

The court should take into account section 74 of the Sentencing Code (assistance by defendants: reduction or review of sentence) and any other rule of law by virtue of which an offender may receive a discounted sentence in consequence of assistance given (or offered) to the prosecutor or investigator.

**STEP 4   Reduction for guilty pleas**

The court should take account of any potential reduction for a guilty plea in accordance with section 73 of the Sentencing Code and the Reduction in Sentence for a Guilty Plea guideline [see **SG5-1–SG5-12**].

**STEP 5   Totality principle**

If sentencing an offender for more than one offence, or where the offender is already serving a sentence, consider whether the total sentence is just and proportionate to the offending behaviour. See Totality guideline [see **SG4**].

**STEP 6   Confiscation and ancillary orders**

In all cases, the court is required to consider confiscation where the Crown invokes the process or where the court considers it appropriate. It should also consider whether to make ancillary orders.

**STEP 7   Reasons**

Section 52 of the Sentencing Code imposes a duty to give reasons for, and explain the effect of, the sentence.

**STEP 8   Consideration for time spent on bail**

The court must consider whether to give credit for time spent on bail in accordance with section 240A of the Criminal Justice Act 2003 and section 325 of the Sentencing Code.

Where evidence is available as to the potential effects of the substance and harm likely to be caused by those effects, the court should consider whether this affects the category of harm. Where the harm is very great, or very small, this may lead the court to move the starting point for the offence up or down within the category, or to place the offence in a higher or lower category than that indicated by the other factors listed.

### Category 1
• Large quantity indicative of commercial-scale operation

### Category 2
• Quantity indicative of smaller-scale commercial operation

### Category 3
• Very small quantity

### STEP 2  Starting point and category range

Having determined the category at step one, the court should use the corresponding starting point to reach a sentence within the category range below. The starting point applies to all offenders irrespective of plea or previous convictions. A case of particular gravity, reflected by multiple features of culpability or harm in step one, could merit upward adjustment from the starting point before further adjustment for aggravating or mitigating features, set out below.

|  | Leading Role | Significant Role | Lesser Role |
|---|---|---|---|
| Category 1 | **Starting point**<br>4 years' custody | **Starting point**<br>2 years' custody | **Starting point**<br>1 year's custody |
|  | **Category range**<br>3 – 6 years' custody | **Category range**<br>1 – 3 years' 6 months' custody | **Category range**<br>26 weeks' – 2 years' custody |
| Category 2 | **Starting point**<br>2 years' custody | **Starting point**<br>1 year's custody | **Starting point**<br>High level community order |
|  | **Category range**<br>1 – 3 years' 6 months' custody | **Category range**<br>26 weeks' – 2 years' custody | **Category range**<br>Low level community order – 26 weeks' custody |
| Category 3 | **Starting point**<br>1 year's custody | **Starting point**<br>High level community order | **Starting point**<br>Band B fine |
|  | **Category range**<br>26 weeks' – 2 years' custody | **Category range**<br>Low level community order – 26 weeks' custody | **Category range**<br>Discharge – High level community order |

### Fines
[For the standard schedule of fines see **SG2-5**.]

### Community Orders and Custodial Sentences
[For the imposition of community orders, including the community orders table, see Imposition of Community and Custodial Sentences at **SG9-2**.

For the imposition of custodial sentences see Imposition of Community and Custodial Sentences at **SG9-3**.]

The table below contains a **non-exhaustive** list of additional factual elements providing the context of the offence and factors relating to the offender. Identify whether any combination of these, or other relevant factors, should result in and upward or downward adjustment from the starting point. In some cases, having considered these factors, it may be appropriate to move outside the identified category range.

### Factors increasing seriousness
#### Statutory aggravating factors
• Previous convictions [see **SG2-21**], having regard to
   a)  nature of the offence to which conviction relates and relevance to current offence; and
   b)  time elapsed since conviction
• Offence committed on bail [see **SG2-22**]

(See Proceeds of Crime Act 2002 sections 6 and 13).

The court should also consider whether to make ancillary orders.

### STEP 7   Reasons

Section 52 of the Sentencing Code imposes a duty to give reasons for, and explain the effect of, the sentence.

### STEP 8   Consideration for time spent on bail

The court must consider whether to give credit for time spent on bail in accordance with section 240A of the Criminal Justice Act 2003 and section 325 of the Sentencing Code.

## IMPORTING OR EXPORTING A PSYCHOACTIVE SUBSTANCE                                SG23-7

*Psychoactive Substances Act 2016, s.8*

**Effective from:** 01 April 2021

Triable either way

Maximum: 7 years' custody

Offence range: Discharge – 6 years' custody

### STEP 1   Determine the offence category

The court should determine the offender's culpability (role) and the harm caused (quantity) with reference to the tables below.

In assessing culpability, the sentencer should weigh up all the factors of the case to determine role. Where there are characteristics present which fall under different role categories, or where the level of the offender's role is affected by the scale of the operation, the court should balance these characteristics to reach a fair assessment of the offender's culpability.

**Culpability demonstrated by the offender's role**

One or more of these characteristics may demonstrate the offender's role. These lists are not exhaustive.

*Leading role*

- Directing or organising buying and selling on a commercial scale
- Substantial links to, and influence on, others in a chain
- Close links to original source
- Expectation of substantial financial or other advantage
- Uses business as cover
- Abuses a position of trust or responsibility

*Significant role*

- Operational or management function within a chain
- Involves others in the operation whether by pressure, influence, intimidation or reward
- Expectation of significant financial or other advantage, (save where this advantage is limited to meeting the offender's own habit) whether or not operating alone
- Some awareness and understanding of scale of operation

*Lesser role*

- Performs a limited function under direction
- Engaged by pressure, coercion, intimidation, grooming and/ or control
- Involvement through naivety, immaturity or exploitation
- No influence on those above in a chain
- Very little, if any, awareness or understanding of the scale of operation
- If own operation, solely for own use (considering reasonableness of account in all the circumstances)
- Expectation of limited, if any, financial or other advantage (including meeting the offender's own habit)

**Harm**

In assessing harm, the sentencer should consider the factors below. Where there are characteristics present which fall under different harm categories the court should balance these characteristics to reach a fair assessment of harm.

## STEP 2   Starting point and category range

Having determined the category at step one, the court should use the corresponding starting point to reach a sentence within the category range below. The starting point applies to all offenders irrespective of plea or previous convictions. A case of particular gravity, reflected by multiple features of culpability or harm in step one, could merit upward adjustment from the starting point before further adjustment for aggravating or mitigating features, set out below.

|  | Leading Role | Significant Role | Lesser Role |
|---|---|---|---|
| Category 1 | **Starting point** 4 years' custody | **Starting point** 2 years' custody | **Starting point** 1 year's custody |
|  | **Category range** 3 – 6 years' custody | **Category range** 1 – 3 years' 6 months' custody | **Category range** 26 weeks' – 2 years' custody |
| Category 2 | **Starting point** 2 years' custody | **Starting point** 1 year's custody | **Starting point** High level community order |
|  | **Category range** 1 – 3 years' 6 months' custody | **Category range** 26 weeks' – 2 years' custody | **Category range** Low level community order – 26 weeks' custody |
| Category 3 | **Starting point** 1 year's custody | **Starting point** High level community order | **Starting point** Low level community order |
|  | **Category range** 26 weeks' – 2 years' custody | **Category range** Low level community order – 26 weeks' custody | **Category range** Band B fine – Medium level community order |

### Fines

[For the standard schedule of fines see SG2-5.]

### Community Orders and Custodial Sentences

[For the imposition of community orders, including the community orders table, see Imposition of Community and Custodial Sentences at SG9-2.

For the imposition of custodial sentences see Imposition of Community and Custodial Sentences at SG9-3.]

The table below contains a non-exhaustive list of additional factual elements providing the context of the offence and factors relating to the offender. Identify whether any combination of these, or other relevant factors, should result in and upward or downward adjustment from the starting point. In some cases, having considered these factors, it may be appropriate to move outside the identified category range.

### Factors increasing seriousness

*Statutory aggravating factors*

- Previous convictions [see SG2-21], having regard to
  a) nature of the offence to which condition relates and relevance to current offence; and
  b) time elapsed since conviction
- Offence committed on bail [see SG2-22]

*Other aggravating factors include*

- Exploitation of children and/or vulnerable persons to assist in the offending
- Exercising control over the home of another person for the purposes of the offending
- Nature of any likely supply
- Level of any profit element
- Use of premises accompanied by unlawful access to electricity/other utility supply of others, where not charged separately
- Ongoing/large scale operation as evidenced by presence and nature of specialist equipment
- Exposure of psychoactive substance user to the risk of serious harm over and above that expected by the user, for example, through the method of production or subsequent adulteration of the substance
- Exposure of those involved in producing the psychoactive substances to the risk of serious harm, for example through method of production
- Exposure of third parties to the risk of serious harm
- Attempts to conceal or dispose of evidence, where not charged separately

Sentencing Guidelines

- Presence of others, especially children and/or non-users
- Presence of weapons, where not charged separately
- Use of violence (where not charged as separate offence or taken into account at step one)
- Failure to comply with current court orders
- Offence committed on licence or post sentence supervision
- Offending took place in prison (unless already taken into consideration at step 1)
- Established evidence of community impact
- Use of sophisticated methods or technologies in order to avoid or impede detection

**Factors reducing seriousness or reflecting personal mitigation**

- Involvement due to pressure, intimidation or coercion falling short of duress, except where already taken into account at step one.
- Isolated incident
- No previous convictions or no relevant or recent convictions
- Offender's vulnerability was exploited
- Remorse
- Good character and/or exemplary conduct
- Determination and/or demonstration of steps having been taken to address addiction or offending behaviour
- Serious medical conditions requiring urgent, intensive or long-term treatment
- Age and/or lack of maturity where it affects the responsibility of the offender
- Mental disorder or learning disability
- Sole or primary carer for dependent relatives

**STEP 3  Consider any factors which indicate a reduction, such as assistance to the prosecution**

The court should take into account section 74 of the Sentencing Code (assistance by defendants: reduction or review of sentence) and any other rule of law by virtue of which an offender may receive a discounted sentence in consequence of assistance given (or offered) to the prosecutor or investigator.

**STEP 4  Reduction for guilty pleas**

The court should take account of any potential reduction for a guilty plea in accordance with section 73 of the Sentencing Code and the Reduction in Sentence for a Guilty Plea guideline [see **SG5-1–SG5-12**].

**STEP 5  Totality principle**

If sentencing an offender for more than one offence, or where the offender is already serving a sentence, consider whether the total sentence is just and proportionate to the offending behaviour. See Totality guideline [see **SG4**].

**STEP 6  Ancillary orders**

In all cases, the court should consider whether to make ancillary orders.

**STEP 7  Reasons**

Section 52 of the Sentencing Code imposes a duty to give reasons for, and explain the effect of, the sentence.

**STEP 8  Consideration for time spent on bail**

The court must consider whether to give credit for time spent on bail in accordance with section 240A of the Criminal Justice Act 2003 and section 325 of the Sentencing Code.

**SG23-9**      SUPPLYING, OR OFFERING TO SUPPLY, A PSYCHOACTIVE SUBSTANCE/POSSESSION OF PSYCHOACTIVE SUBSTANCE WITH INTENT TO SUPPLY

*Psychoactive Substances Act 2016, s.5(1) or 5(2), Psychoactive Substances Act 2016, s.7(1)*

**Effective from:** 01 April 2021

**Supplying, or offering to supply, a psychoactive substance,** Psychoactive Substances Act 2016 (sections 5(1) or 5(2))

**Possession of psychoactive substance with intent to supply,** Psychoactive Substances Act 2016 (section 7(1))

Maximum: 7 years' custody

Offence range: Band B Fine – 6 years' custody

**STEP 1  Determine the offence category**

The court should determine the offender's culpability (role) and the harm caused with reference to the tables below.

In assessing culpability, the sentencer should weigh up all the factors of the case to determine role. Where there are characteristics present which fall under different role categories, **or where the level of the offender's role is affected by the scale of the operation,** the court should balance these characteristics to reach a fair assessment of the offender's culpability.

**Culpability demonstrated by the offender's role**

One or more of these characteristics may demonstrate the offender's role. These lists are not exhaustive.

*Leading role*

• Directing or organising buying and selling on a commercial scale
• Substantial links to, and influence on, others in a chain
• Close links to original source
• Expectation of substantial financial or other advantage
• Uses business as cover
• Abuses a position of trust or responsibility

*Significant role*

• Operational or management function within a chain
• Involves others in the operation whether by pressure, influence, intimidation or reward
• Expectation of significant financial or other advantage (save where this advantage is limited to meeting the offender's own habit), whether or not operating alone
• Some awareness and understanding of scale of operation

*Lesser role*

• Performs a limited function under direction
• Engaged by pressure, coercion, intimidation, grooming and/or control
• Involvement through naivety, immaturity or exploitation
• No influence on those above in a chain
• Very little, if any, awareness or understanding of the scale of operation
• Expectation of limited, if any, financial or other advantage (including meeting the offender's own habit)

**Harm**

In assessing harm, the sentencer should consider the factors below. Where there are characteristics present which fall under different harm categories the court should balance these characteristics to reach a fair assessment of harm.

Where evidence is available as to the potential effects of the substance and harm likely to be caused by those effects, the court should consider whether this affects the category of harm. Where the harm is very great, or very small, this may lead the court to move the starting point for the offence up or down within the category, or to place the offence in a higher or lower category than that indicated by the other factors listed.

*Category 1*

• Large quantity indicative of commercial-scale operation
• Supply in a custodial institution

*Category 2*

• Supply directly to users

*Category 3*

• Very small quantity

**STEP 2  Starting point and category range**

Having determined the category at step one, the court should use the corresponding starting point to reach a sentence within the category range below. The starting point applies to all offenders irrespective of plea or previous convictions. A case of particular gravity, reflected by multiple features of culpability or harm in step one, could merit upward adjustment from the starting point before further adjustment for aggravating or mitigating features, set out below.

Sentencing Guidelines

|  | Leading Role | Significant Role | Lesser Role |
|---|---|---|---|
| Category 1 | **Starting point**<br>4 years' custody | **Starting point**<br>2 years' custody | **Starting point**<br>1 year's custody |
|  | **Category range**<br>3 – 6 years' custody | **Category range**<br>1 – 3 years' 6 months' custody | **Category range**<br>26 weeks' – 2 years' custody |
| Category 2 | **Starting point**<br>2 years' custody | **Starting point**<br>1 year's custody | **Starting point**<br>High level community order |
|  | **Category range**<br>1 – 3 years' 6 months' custody | **Category range**<br>26 weeks' – 2 years' custody | **Category range**<br>Low level community order – 26 weeks' custody |
| Category 3 | **Starting point**<br>1 year's custody | **Starting point**<br>High level community order | **Starting point**<br>Low level community order |
|  | **Category range**<br>26 weeks' – 2 years' custody | **Category range**<br>Low level community order – 26 weeks' custody | **Category range**<br>Band B fine – Medium level community order |

**Fines**

[For the standard schedule of fines see **SG2-5**.]

**Community Orders and Custodial Sentences**

[For the imposition of community orders, including the community orders table, see Imposition of Community and Custodial Sentences at **SG9-2**.

For the imposition of custodial sentences see Imposition of Community and Custodial Sentences at **SG9-3**.]

The table below contains a non-exhaustive list of additional factual elements providing the context of the offence and factors relating to the offender. Identify whether any combination of these, or other relevant factors, should result in and upward or downward adjustment from the starting point. In some cases, having considered these factors, it may be appropriate to move outside the identified category range.

**Factors increasing seriousness**

*Statutory aggravating factors*

- Previous convictions [see **SG2-21**], having regard to a) nature of the offence to which conviction relates and relevance to current offence; and b) time elapsed since conviction
- In connection with the offence, the offender used a courier who, at the time of the commission of the offence, was aged under 18 (except where taken into account at Step 1)
- The offence was committed on or in the vicinity of school premises at a relevant time
- The offence was committed in a custodial institution
- Offence committed on bail [see **SG2-22**]

*Other aggravating factors include*

- Exploitation of children and/or vulnerable persons to assist in the offending
- Exercising control over the home of another person for the purposes of the offending
- Targeting of any premises where children or other vulnerable persons are likely to be present
- Exposure of psychoactive substance user to the risk of serious harm over and above that expected by the user, for example, through the method of production or subsequent adulteration of the substance
- Exposure of those involved in dealing in the psychoactive substance to the risk of serious harm, for example through method of transporting the substance
- Exposure of third parties to the risk of serious harm
- Attempts to conceal or dispose of evidence, where not charged separately
- Presence of others, especially children and/or non-users
- Presence of weapons, where not charged separately
- Use of violence (where not charged as separate offence or taken into account at step one)
- Failure to comply with current court orders
- Offending took place in prison (unless already taken into consideration at step 1)
- Offender was supplying or involved in the supply of psychoactive substances into prison

- Offence committed on licence or post sentence supervision
- Established evidence of community impact
- Use of sophisticated methods or technologies in order to avoid or impede detection

There may be exceptional local circumstances that arise which may lead a court to decide that prevalence of psychoactive substance offending should influence sentencing levels. The pivotal issue in such cases will be the harm caused to the community.

It is essential that the court before taking account of prevalence:

- has supporting evidence from an external source, for example, Community Impact Statements, to justify claims that psychoactive substance offending is prevalent in their area, and is causing particular harm in that community; and
- is satisfied that there is a compelling need to treat the offence more seriously than elsewhere.

**Factors reducing seriousness or reflecting personal mitigation**

- Involvement due to pressure, intimidation or coercion falling short of duress, except where already taken into account at step one
- Supply only of psychoactive substance to which offender addicted
- Mistaken belief of the offender regarding the type of substance, taking into account the reasonableness of such belief in all the circumstances
- Isolated incident
- No previous convictions or no relevant or recent convictions
- Remorse
- Good character and/or exemplary conduct
- Determination and/or demonstration of steps having been taken to address addiction or offending behaviour
- Serious medical conditions requiring urgent, intensive or long-term treatment
- Age and/or lack of maturity where it affects the responsibility of the offender
- Mental disorder or learning disability
- Sole or primary carer for dependent relatives
- Offender's vulnerability was exploited

### STEP 3   Consider any factors which indicate a reduction, such as assistance to the prosecution

The court should take into account section 74 of the Sentencing Code (assistance by defendants: reduction or review of sentence) and any other rule of law by virtue of which an offender may receive a discounted sentence in consequence of assistance given (or offered) to the prosecutor or investigator.

### STEP 4   Reduction for guilty pleas

The court should take account of any potential reduction for a guilty plea in accordance with section 73 of the Sentencing Code and the Reduction in Sentence for a Guilty Plea guideline [see **SG5-1–SG5-12**].

### STEP 5   Totality principle

If sentencing an offender for more than one offence, or where the offender is already serving a sentence, consider whether the total sentence is just and proportionate to the offending behaviour. See Totality guideline [see **SG4**].

### STEP 6   Confiscation and ancillary orders

Confiscation orders under the Proceeds of Crime Act 2002 may only be made by the Crown Court. The Crown Court must proceed with a view to making a confiscation order if it is asked to do so by the prosecutor or if the Crown Court believes it is appropriate for it to do so.

Where, following conviction in a magistrates' court, the prosecutor applies for the offender to be committed to the Crown Court with a view to a confiscation order being considered, the magistrates' court must commit the offender to the Crown Court to be sentenced there (section 70 of the Proceeds of Crime Act 2002). This applies to summary only and either-way offences.

Where, but for the prosecutor's application under s.70, the magistrates' court would have committed the offender for sentence to the Crown Court anyway it must say so. Otherwise the powers of sentence of the Crown Court will be limited to those of the magistrates' court.

Confiscation must be dealt with before, and taken into account when assessing, any other fine or financial order (except compensation).

(See Proceeds of Crime Act 2002 sections 6 and 13)

The court should also consider whether to make ancillary orders.

**STEP 7 Reasons**

Section 52 of the Sentencing Code imposes a duty to give reasons for, and explain the effect of, the sentence.

**STEP 8 Consideration for time spent on bail**

The court must consider whether to give credit for time spent on bail in accordance with section 240A of the Criminal Justice Act 2003 and section 325 of the Sentencing Code.

# PART 24   ENVIRONMENTAL OFFENCES

[For other environmental offences covered by the Magistrates' Court Sentencing Guidelines see SG10-77]

APPLICABILITY SG24-1

[For the standard text on applicability see **SG0-4.**]

ORGANISATIONS: UNAUTHORISED OR HARMFUL DEPOSIT, TREATMENT OR DISPOSAL ETC. OF WASTE ILLEGAL DISCHARGES TO AIR, LAND AND WATER SG24-2

*Environmental Permitting (England and Wales) Regulations 2010 , regulations 12 and 38(1), (2) and (3),*
*Environmental Permitting (England and Wales) Regulations 2016, regulations 12 and 38(1), (2) and (3),*
*Environmental Protection Act 1990, s.33*

**Effective from:** 01 July 2014

Also relevant, with adjustments, to certain related offences (see [**SG24-4**])

Triable either way
Maximum: when tried on indictment: unlimited fine: when tried summarily: £50,000 fine
Offence range: £100 fine–£3 million fine

**Use this guideline when the offender is an organisation. If the offender is an individual, please refer to the guideline for individuals.**

**Confiscation**

Committal to the Crown Court for sentence is mandatory if confiscation (see step two) is to be considered: Proceeds of Crime Act 2002 section 70. In such cases magistrates should state whether they would otherwise have committed for sentence.

Financial orders must be considered in this order: (1) compensation, (2) confiscation, and (3) fine (see Proceeds of Crime Act 2002 section 13).

Also relevant, with adjustments, to certain related offences [see Environmental Offences (Other) at SG24-4].

**STEP 1  Compensation**

The court must consider making a compensation order requiring the offender to pay compensation for any personal injury, loss or damage resulting from the offence in such an amount as the court considers appropriate, having regard to the evidence and to the means of the offender.

Where the means of the offender are limited, priority should be given to the payment of compensation over payment of any other financial penalty.

Reasons should be given if a compensation order is not made. (See sections 55 and 133 to 135 of the Sentencing Code)

**STEP 2  Confiscation**

Confiscation orders under the Proceeds of Crime Act 2002 may only be made by the Crown Court. The Crown Court must proceed with a view to making a confiscation order if it is asked to do so by the prosecutor or if the Crown Court believes it is appropriate for it to do so.

Where, following conviction in a magistrates' court, the prosecutor applies for the offender to be committed to the Crown Court with a view to a confiscation order being considered, the magistrates' court must commit the offender to the Crown Court to be sentenced there (section 70 of the Proceeds of Crime Act 2002). This applies to summary only and either-way offences.

Where, but for the prosecutor's application under s.70, the magistrates' court would have committed the offender for sentence to the Crown Court anyway it must say so. Otherwise the powers of sentence of the Crown Court will be limited to those of the magistrates' court.

Confiscation must be dealt with before, and taken into account when assessing, any other fine or financial order (except compensation).

(See Proceeds of Crime Act 2002 sections 6 and 13)

Sentencing Guidelines

## STEP 3 Determining the offence category

The court should determine the offence category using only the culpability and harm factors in the tables below. The culpability and harm categories are on a sliding scale; there is inevitable overlap between the factors described in adjacent categories. Where an offence does not fall squarely into a category, individual factors may require a degree of weighting before making an overall assessment and determining the appropriate offence category.

Dealing with a **risk of harm** involves consideration of both the likelihood of harm occurring and the extent of it if it does. Risk of harm is less serious than the same actual harm. Where the offence has caused risk of harm but no (or less) actual harm the normal approach is to move down to the next category of harm. This may not be appropriate if either the likelihood or extent of potential harm is particularly high.

| Culpability | Harm | |
|---|---|---|
| **Deliberate**<br>Intentional breach of or flagrant disregard for the law by person(s) whose position of responsibility in the organisation is such that their acts/omissions can properly be attributed to the organisation;<br>**OR**<br>deliberate failure by organisation to put in place and to enforce such systems as could reasonably be expected in all the circumstances to avoid commission of the offence. | Category 1 | • Polluting material of a dangerous nature, for example, hazardous chemicals or sharp objects<br>• Major adverse effect or damage to air or water quality, amenity value, or property<br>• Polluting material was noxious, widespread or pervasive with long-lasting effects on human health or quality of life, animal health or flora<br>• Major costs incurred through clean-up, site restoration or animal rehabilitation<br>• Major interference with, prevention or undermining of other lawful activities or regulatory regime due to offence |
| **Reckless**<br>Actual foresight of, or wilful blindness to, risk of offending but risk nevertheless taken by person(s) whose position of responsibility in the organisation is such that their acts/omissions can properly be attributed to the organisation;<br>**OR**<br>reckless failure by organisation to put in place and to enforce such systems as could reasonably be expected in all the circumstances to avoid commission of the offence. | Category 2 | • Significant adverse effect or damage to air or water quality, amenity value, or property<br>• Significant adverse effect on human health or quality of life, animal health or flora<br>• Significant costs incurred through clean-up, site restoration or animal rehabilitation<br>• Significant interference with or undermining of other lawful activities or regulatory regime due to offence<br>• Risk of category 1 harm |
| **Negligent**<br>Failure by the organisation as a whole to take reasonable care to put in place and enforce proper systems for avoiding commission of the offence. | Category 3 | • Minor, localised adverse effect or damage to air or water quality, amenity value, or property<br>• Minor adverse effect on human health or quality of life, animal health or flora<br>• Low costs incurred through clean-up, site restoration or animal rehabilitation<br>• Limited interference with or undermining of other lawful activities or regulatory regime due to offence<br>• Risk of category 2 harm |
| **Low or no culpability**<br>Offence committed with little or no fault on the part of the organisation as a whole, for example by accident or the act of a rogue employee and despite the presence and due enforcement of all reasonably required preventive measures, or where such proper preventive measures were unforeseeably overcome by exceptional events. | Category 4 | • Risk of category 3 harm |

## STEP 4   Starting point and category range

Having determined the category, the court should refer to the tables [below]. There are four tables of starting points and ranges: one for large organisations, one for medium organisations, one for small organisations and one for micro-organisations. The court should refer to the table that relates to the size of the offending organisation.

The court should use the corresponding starting point to reach a sentence within the category range. The court should then consider further adjustment within the category range for aggravating and mitigating features, set out below.

### General principles to follow in setting a fine

The court should determine the appropriate level of fine in accordance with section 125 of the Sentencing Code, which requires that the fine must reflect the seriousness of the offence and requires the court to take into account the financial circumstances of the offender.

The level of fine should reflect the extent to which the offender fell below the required standard. The fine should meet, in a fair and proportionate way, the objectives of punishment, deterrence and the removal of gain derived through the commission of the offence; it should not be cheaper to offend than to take the appropriate precautions.

### Obtaining financial information

Offenders which are companies, partnerships or bodies delivering a public or charitable service, are expected to provide comprehensive accounts for the last three years, to enable the court to make an accurate assessment of its financial status. In the absence of such disclosure, or where the court is not satisfied that it has been given sufficient reliable information, the court will be entitled to draw reasonable inferences as to the offender's means from evidence it has heard and from all the circumstances of the case.

Normally, only information relating to the organisation before the court will be relevant, unless it is demonstrated to the court that the resources of a linked organisation are available and can properly be taken into account.

1. *For companies*: annual accounts. Particular attention should be paid to turnover; profit before tax; directors' remuneration, loan accounts and pension provision; and assets as disclosed by the balance sheet. Most companies are required to file audited accounts at Companies House. **Failure to produce relevant recent accounts on request may properly lead to the conclusion that the company can pay any appropriate fine.**

2. *For partnerships*: annual accounts. Particular attention should be paid to turnover; profit before tax; partners' drawings, loan accounts and pension provision; assets as above. Limited Liability Partnerships (LLPs) may be required to file audited accounts with Companies House. **If adequate accounts are not produced on request, see paragraph 1.**

3. *For local authorities, fire authorities and similar public bodies*: the Annual Revenue Budget ('ARB') is the equivalent of turnover and the best indication of the size of the defendant organisation. It is unlikely to be necessary to analyse specific expenditure or reserves (where relevant) unless inappropriate expenditure is suggested.

4. *For health trusts*: the independent regulator of NHS Foundation Trusts is Monitor. It publishes quarterly reports and annual figures for the financial strength and stability of trusts from which the annual income can be seen, available via **www.monitor-nhsft.gov.uk**. Detailed analysis of expenditure or reserves is unlikely to be called for.

5. *For charities*: it will be appropriate to inspect annual audited accounts. Detailed analysis of expenditure or reserves is unlikely to be called for unless there is a suggestion of unusual or unnecessary expenditure.

At step four, the court will be required to focus on the organisation's annual turnover or equivalent to reach a starting point for a fine. At step six, the court may be required to refer to the other financial factors listed above to ensure that the proposed fine is proportionate.

---

**Very large organisations**

Where a defendant company's turnover or equivalent very greatly exceeds the threshold for large companies, it may be necessary to move outside the suggested range to achieve a proportionate sentence.

---

**Large** — Turnover or equivalent: £50 million and over.

| Large | Starting Point | Range |
|---|---|---|
| **Deliberate** | | |
| Category 1 | £1,000,000 | £450,000–£3,000,000 |
| Category 2 | £500,000 | £180,000–£1,250,000 |
| Category 3 | £180,000 | £100,000–£450,000 |
| Category 4 | £100,000 | £55,000–£250,000 |
| **Reckless** | | |
| Category 1 | £550,000 | £250,000–£1,500,000 |
| Category 2 | £250,000 | £100,000–£650,000 |
| Category 3 | £100,000 | £60,000–£250,000 |
| Category 4 | £60,000 | £35,000–£160,000 |
| **Negligent** | | |
| Category 1 | £300,000 | £140,000–£750,000 |
| Category 2 | £140,000 | £60,000–£350,000 |
| Category 3 | £60,000 | £35,000–£150,000 |
| Category 4 | £35,000 | £22,000–£100,000 |
| **Low / No culpability** | | |
| Category 1 | £50,000 | £25,000–£130,000 |
| Category 2 | £25,000 | £14,000–£70,000 |
| Category 3 | £14,000 | £10,000–£40,000 |
| Category 4 | £10,000 | £7,000–£25,000 |

**Medium** — Turnover or equivalent: between £10 million and £50 million.

| Medium | Starting Point | Range |
|---|---|---|
| **Deliberate** | | |
| Category 1 | £400,000 | £170,000–£1,000,000 |
| Category 2 | £170,000 | £70,000–£450,000 |
| Category 3 | £70,000 | £40,000–£180,000 |
| Category 4 | £40,000 | £22,000–£100,000 |
| **Reckless** | | |
| Category 1 | £220,000 | £100,000–£500,000 |
| Category 2 | £100,000 | £40,000–£250,000 |
| Category 3 | £40,000 | £24,000–£100,000 |
| Category 4 | £24,000 | £14,000–£60,000 |
| **Negligent** | | |
| Category 1 | £120,000 | £55,000–£300,000 |
| Category 2 | £55,000 | £25,000–£140,000 |
| Category 3 | £25,000 | £14,000–£60,000 |
| Category 4 | £14,000 | £8,000–£35,000 |

| Medium | Starting Point | Range |
|---|---|---|
| **Low / No culpability** | | |
| Category 1 | £20,000 | £10,000–£50,000 |
| Category 2 | £10,000 | £5,500–£25,000 |
| Category 3 | £5,000 | £3,500–£14,000 |
| Category 4 | £3,000 | £2,500–£10,000 |

**Small** — Turnover or equivalent: between £2 million and £10 million.

| Small | Starting Point | Range |
|---|---|---|
| **Deliberate** | | |
| Category 1 | £100,000 | £45,000–£400,000 |
| Category 2 | £45,000 | £17,000–£170,000 |
| Category 3 | £17,000 | £10,000–£70,000 |
| Category 4 | £10,000 | £5,000–£40,000 |
| **Reckless** | | |
| Category 1 | £55,000 | £24,000–£220,000 |
| Category 2 | £24,000 | £10,000–£100,000 |
| Category 3 | £10,000 | £5,000–£40,000 |
| Category 4 | £5,000 | £3,000–£24,000 |
| **Negligent** | | |
| Category 1 | £30,000 | £13,000–£120,000 |
| Category 2 | £13,000 | £6,000–£55,000 |
| Category 3 | £6,000 | £3,000–£23,000 |
| Category 4 | £3,000 | £1,500–£14,000 |
| **Low / No culpability** | | |
| Category 1 | £5,000 | £2,500–£20,000 |
| Category 2 | £2,500 | £1,000–£10,000 |
| Category 3 | £1,000 | £700–£5,000 |
| Category 4 | £700 | £400–£3,500 |

**Micro** — Turnover or equivalent: not more than £2 million.

| Micro | Starting Point | Range |
|---|---|---|
| **Deliberate** | | |
| Category 1 | £50,000 | £9,000–£95,000 |
| Category 2 | £22,000 | £3,000–£45,000 |
| Category 3 | £9,000 | £2,000–£17,000 |
| Category 4 | £5,000 | £1,000–£10,000 |
| **Reckless** | | |
| Category 1 | £30,000 | £3,000–£55,000 |
| Category 2 | £12,000 | £1,500–£24,000 |
| Category 3 | £5,000 | £1,000–£10,000 |
| Category 4 | £3,000 | £500–£5,500 |

| Micro | Starting Point | Range |
|---|---|---|
| **Negligent** | | |
| Category 1 | £15,000 | £1,500–£30,000 |
| Category 2 | £6,500 | £1,000–£13,000 |
| Category 3 | £2,500 | £500–£5,500 |
| Category 4 | £1,400 | £350–£3,000 |
| **Low / No culpability** | | |
| Category 1 | £2,500 | £500–£5,000 |
| Category 2 | £1,000 | £350–£2,400 |
| Category 3 | £400 | £175–£1,000 |
| Category 4 | £200 | £100–£700 |

**Factors increasing or reducing seriousness**

The table below contains a **non-exhaustive** list of factual elements providing the context of the offence and factors relating to the offender. Identify whether any combination of these, or other relevant factors, should result in an upward or downward adjustment from the starting point. **In particular, relevant recent convictions and/or a history of non-compliance are likely to result in a substantial upward adjustment.** In some cases, having considered these factors, it may be appropriate to move outside the identified category range.

**Factors increasing seriousness**

*Statutory aggravating factors*

- Previous convictions, having regard to
  a) the nature of the offence to which the conviction relates and its relevance to the current offence; and
  b) the time that has elapsed since the conviction

*Other aggravating factors include*

- History of non-compliance with warnings by regulator
- Location of the offence, for example, near housing, schools, livestock or environmentally sensitive sites
- Repeated incidents of offending or offending over an extended period of time, where not charged separately
- Deliberate concealment of illegal nature of activity
- Ignoring risks identified by employees or others
- Established evidence of wider/community impact
- Breach of any order
- Offence committed for financial gain
- Obstruction of justice

**Factors reducing seriousness or reflecting mitigation**

- No previous convictions **or** no relevant/recent convictions
- Evidence of steps taken to remedy problem
- Remorse
- Compensation paid voluntarily to remedy harm caused
- One-off event not commercially motivated
- Little or no financial gain
- Effective compliance and ethics programme
- Self-reporting, co-operation and acceptance of responsibility
- Good character and/or exemplary conduct

**STEPS 5 to 7**

The court should now 'step back' and, using the factors set out in steps five, six and seven, review whether the sentence as a whole meets, in a fair way, the objectives of punishment, deterrence and removal of gain derived through the commission of the offence. At steps five to seven, the court may increase or reduce the proposed fine reached at step four, if necessary moving outside the range.

**STEP 5 Ensure that the combination of financial orders (compensation, confiscation if appropriate, and fine) removes any economic benefit derived from the offending**

The court should remove any economic benefit the offender has derived through the commission of the offence including:

- avoided costs;
- operating savings;
- any gain made as a direct result of the offence.

Where the offender is fined, the amount of economic benefit derived from the offence should normally be added to the fine arrived at in step four. If a confiscation order is made, in considering economic benefit, the court should avoid double recovery.

Economic benefit will not always be an identifiable feature of a case. For example, in some water pollution cases there may be strict liability but very little obvious gain. However, even in these cases there may be some avoidance of cost, for example alarms not installed and maintained, inadequate funding or security measures not installed. Any costs avoided will be considered as economic benefit.

Where it is not possible to calculate or estimate the economic benefit, the court may wish to draw on information from the enforcing authorities about the general costs of operating within the law.

**STEP 6  Check whether the proposed fine based on turnover is proportionate to the means of the offender**

**The combination of financial orders must be sufficiently substantial to have a real economic impact which will bring home to both management and shareholders the need to improve regulatory compliance. Whether the fine will have the effect of putting the offender out of business will be relevant; in some bad cases this may be an acceptable consequence.**

It will be necessary to examine the financial circumstances of the organisation in the round. If an organisation has a small profit margin relative to its turnover, downward adjustment may be needed. If it has a large profit margin, upward adjustment may be needed.

**In considering the ability of the offending organisation to pay any financial penalty, the court can take into account the power to allow time for payment or to order that the amount be paid in instalments.**

**STEP 7  Consider other factors that may warrant adjustment of the proposed fine**

The court should consider any further factors that are relevant to ensuring that the proposed fine is proportionate having regard to the means of the offender and the seriousness of the offence.

**Where the fine will fall on public or charitable bodies, the fine should normally be substantially reduced if the offending organisation is able to demonstrate the proposed fine would have a significant impact on the provision of their services.**

The non-exhaustive list below contains additional factual elements the court should consider in deciding whether an increase or reduction to the proposed fine is required:

- fine impairs offender's ability to make restitution to victims;
- impact of fine on offender's ability to improve conditions in the organisation to comply with the law;
- impact of fine on employment of staff, service users, customers and local economy.

**STEP 8  Consider any factors which indicate a reduction, such as assistance to the prosecution**

The court should take into account section 74 of the Sentencing Code (reduction in sentence for assistance to prosecution) and any other rule of law by virtue of which an offender may receive a discounted sentence in consequence of assistance given (or offered) to the prosecutor or investigator.

**STEP 9  Reduction for guilty pleas**

The court should take account of any potential reduction for a guilty plea in accordance with section 73 of the Sentencing Code and the guideline for Reduction in Sentence for a Guilty Plea [**SG5-1–SG5-12**].

**STEP 10  Ancillary orders**

In all cases, the court must consider whether to make ancillary orders. These may include:

**Forfeiture of vehicle**

The court may order the forfeiture of a vehicle used in or for the purposes of the commission of the offence in accordance with section 33C of the Environmental Protection Act 1990.

**Deprivation of property**

Where section 33C of the Environmental Protection Act 1990 does not apply, the court may order the offender be deprived of property used to commit crime or intended for that purpose in accordance with section 143 of the Powers of Criminal Courts (Sentencing) Act 2000. In considering whether to make an order under section 143, the court must have regard to the value of the property and the likely effects on the offender of making the order taken together with any other order the court makes.

### Remediation

Where an offender is convicted of an offence under regulation 38(1), (2) or (3) of the Environmental Permitting (England and Wales) Regulations 2010, a court may order the offender to take steps to remedy the cause of the offence within a specified period in accordance with regulation 44 of the Environmental Permitting (England and Wales) Regulations 2010.

### STEP 11 Totality principle

If sentencing an offender for more than one offence, or where the offender is already serving a sentence, consider whether the total sentence is just and proportionate to the offending behaviour. See *Totality* guideline [at **SG4**].

### STEP 12 Reasons

Section 52 of the Sentencing Code imposes a duty to give reasons for, and explain the effect of, the sentence.

### Other environmental offences

In sentencing other relevant and analogous environmental offences, the court should refer to the sentencing approach in steps one to three and five to seven of the guideline, **adjusting the starting points and ranges bearing in mind the statutory maxima** for those offences.

[See Environmental Offences (Other) at **SG24-4**.]

**SG24-3**     INDIVIDUALS: UNAUTHORISED OR HARMFUL DEPOSIT, TREATMENT OR DISPOSAL ETC. OF WASTE/ILLEGAL DISCHARGES TO AIR, LAND AND WATER

*Environmental Protection Act 1990, s. 33, Environmental Permitting (England and Wales) Regulations 2010, regulations 12 and 38(1), (2) and (3), Environmental Permitting (England and Wales) Regulations 2016, regulations 12 and 38(1), (2) and (3)*
**Effective from:** 01 July 2014

Also relevant, with adjustments, to certain related offences [See Environmental Offences (Other) at **SG24-4**.]

Triable either way

Maximum: 5 years' custody

Offence range: conditional discharge–3 years' custody

Use this guideline when the offender is an individual. If the offender is an organisation, please refer to the guideline for organisations.

### Confiscation

Committal to the Crown Court for sentence is mandatory if confiscation (see step two) is to be considered: Proceeds of Crime Act 2002 section 70. In such cases magistrates should state whether they would otherwise have committed for sentence.

If a fine is imposed, the financial orders must be considered in this order:

(1) compensation,
(2) confiscation, and
(3) fine (see Proceeds of Crime Act 2002 section 13).

### STEP 1 Compensation

The court must consider making a compensation order requiring the offender to pay compensation for any personal injury, loss or damage resulting from the offence in such an amount as the court considers appropriate, having regard to the evidence and to the means of the offender.

Where the means of the offender are limited, priority should be given to the payment of compensation over payment of any other financial penalty.

Reasons should be given if a compensation order is not made.

(See sections 55 and 133 to 135 of the Sentencing Code)

**STEP 2  Confiscation (Crown Court only)**

Confiscation orders under the Proceeds of Crime Act 2002 may only be made by the Crown Court. The Crown Court must proceed with a view to making a confiscation order if it is asked to do so by the prosecutor or if the Crown Court believes it is appropriate for it to do so.

Where, following conviction in a magistrates' court, the prosecutor applies for the offender to be committed to the Crown Court with a view to a confiscation order being considered, the magistrates' court must commit the offender to the Crown Court to be sentenced there (section 70 of the Proceeds of Crime Act 2002). This applies to summary only and either-way offences.

Where, but for the prosecutor's application under s.70, the magistrates' court would have committed the offender for sentence to the Crown Court anyway it must say so. Otherwise the powers of sentence of the Crown Court will be limited to those of the magistrates' court.

Confiscation must be dealt with before, and taken into account when assessing, any other fine or financial order (except compensation).

(See Proceeds of Crime Act 2002 sections 6 and 13)

**STEP 3  Determining the offence category**

The court should determine the offence category using only the culpability and harm factors in the tables below. The culpability and harm categories are on a sliding scale; there is inevitable overlap between the factors described in adjacent categories. Where an offence does not fall squarely into a category, individual factors may require a degree of weighting before making an overall assessment and determining the appropriate offence category.

Dealing with a **risk of harm** involves consideration of both the likelihood of harm occurring and the extent of it if it does. Risk of harm is less serious than the same actual harm. Where the offence has caused risk of harm but no (or less) actual harm the normal approach is to move down to the next category of harm. This may not be appropriate if either the likelihood or extent of potential harm is particularly high.

| Culpability | Harm | |
|---|---|---|
| **Deliberate** Where the offender intentionally breached, or flagrantly disregarded, the law **Reckless** Actual foresight of, or wilful blindness to, risk of offending but risk nevertheless taken **Negligent** Offence committed through act or omission which a person exercising reasonable care would not commit | Category 1 | • Polluting material of a dangerous nature, for example, hazardous chemicals or sharp objects<br>• Major adverse effect or damage to air or water quality, amenity value, or property<br>• Polluting material was noxious, widespread or pervasive with long-lasting effects on human health or quality of life, animal health, or flora<br>• Major costs incurred through clean-up, site restoration or animal rehabilitation<br>• Major interference with, prevention or undermining of other lawful activities or regulatory regime due to offence |
| **Low or no culpability** Offence committed with little or no fault, for example by genuine accident despite the presence of proper preventive measures, or where such proper preventive measures were unforeseeably overcome by exceptional events | Category 2 | • Significant adverse effect or damage to air or water quality, amenity value, or property<br>• Significant adverse effect on human health or quality of life, animal health or flora<br>• Significant costs incurred through clean-up, site restoration or animal rehabilitation<br>• Significant interference with or undermining of other lawful activities or regulatory regime due to offence<br>• Risk of category 1 harm |
| | Category 3 | • Minor, localised adverse effect or damage to air or water quality, amenity value, or property<br>• Minor adverse effect on human health or quality of life, animal health or flora<br>• Low costs incurred through clean-up, site restoration or animal rehabilitation<br>• Limited interference with or undermining of other lawful activities or regulatory regime due to offence<br>• Risk of category 2 harm |
| | Category 4 | • Risk of category 3 harm |

## STEP 4  Starting point and category range

Having determined the category, the court should refer to the starting points [not reproduced here] to reach a sentence within the category range. The court should then consider further adjustment within the category range for aggravating and mitigating features, [not reproduced here].

### General principles to follow in setting a fine

The court should determine the appropriate level of fine in accordance with section 125 of the Sentencing Code, which requires that the fine must reflect the seriousness of the offence and requires the court to take into account the financial circumstances of the offender.

The level of fine should reflect the extent to which the offender fell below the required standard. The fine should meet, in a fair and proportionate way, the objectives of punishment, deterrence and the removal of gain derived through the commission of the offence; it should not be cheaper to offend than to take the appropriate precautions.

### Obtaining financial information

In setting a fine, the court may conclude that the offender is able to pay any fine imposed unless the offender has supplied any financial information to the contrary. It is for the offender to disclose to the court such data relevant to their financial position as will enable it to assess what they can reasonably afford to pay. If necessary, the court may compel the disclosure of an individual offender's financial circumstances pursuant to section 35 of the Sentencing Code. **In the absence of such disclosure, or where the court is not satisfied that it has been given sufficient reliable information, the court will be entitled to draw reasonable inferences as to the offender's means from evidence it has heard and from all the circumstances of the case.**

### Starting points and ranges

Where the range includes a potential sentence of custody, the court should consider the custody threshold as follows:

- Has the custody threshold been passed?
- If so, is it unavoidable that a custodial sentence be imposed?
- If so, can that sentence be suspended?

Where the range includes a potential sentence of a community order, the court should consider the community order threshold as follows:

- Has the community order threshold been passed?

**However, even where the community order threshold has been passed, a fine will normally be the most appropriate disposal.** Where confiscation is not applied for, consider, if wishing to remove any economic benefit derived through the commission of the offence, combining a fine with a community order.

| Offence category | Starting Point | Range |
|---|---|---|
| **Deliberate** | | |
| Category 1 | 18 months' custody | 1–3 years' custody |
| Category 2 | 1 year's custody | 26 weeks'–18 months' custody |
| Category 3 | Band F fine | Band E fine or medium level community order– 26 weeks' custody |
| Category 4 | Band E fine | Band D fine or low level community order–B and E fine |
| **Reckless** | | |
| Category 1 | 26 weeks' custody | Band F fine or high level community order–12 months' custody |
| Category 2 | Band F fine | Band E fine or medium level community order– 26 weeks' custody |
| Category 3 | Band E fine | Band D fine or low level community order–Band E fine |
| Category 4 | Band D fine | Band C fine–Band D fine |
| **Negligent** | | |
| Category 1 | Band F fine | Band E fine or medium level community order– 26 weeks' custody |
| Category 2 | Band E fine | Band D fine or low level community order–Band E fine |
| Category 3 | Band D fine | Band C fine–Band D fine |
| Category 4 | Band C fine | Band B fine–Band C fine |

| Offence category | Starting Point | Range |
|---|---|---|
| Low / No culpability | | |
| Category 1 | Band D fine | Band C fine–Band D fine |
| Category 2 | Band C fine | Band B fine–Band C fine |
| Category 3 | Band B fine | Band A fine–Band B fine |
| Category 4 | Band A fine | Conditional discharge–Band A fine |

### Fines

[For the standard schedule of fines see **SG2-5**.]

### Community Orders and Custodial Sentences

[For the imposition of community orders, including the community orders table, see Imposition of Community and Custodial Sentences at **SG9-2**. For the imposition of custodial sentences see Imposition of Community and Custodial Sentences at **SG9-3**.]

#### Factors increasing or reducing seriousness

The table below contains a **non-exhaustive** list of factual elements providing the context of the offence and factors relating to the offender. Identify whether any combination of these, or other relevant factors, should result in an upward or downward adjustment from the starting point. **In particular, relevant recent convictions and/or a history of non-compliance are likely to result in a substantial upward adjustment.** In some cases, having considered these factors, it may be appropriate to move outside the identified category range.

#### Factors increasing seriousness

### Statutory aggravating factors

- Previous convictions, having regard to
  a)   the nature of the offence to which the conviction relates and its relevance to the current offence; and
  b)   the time that has elapsed since the conviction
- Offence committed whilst on bail

### Other aggravating factors include

- History of non-compliance with warnings by regulator
- Location of the offence, for example, near housing, schools, livestock or environmentally sensitive sites
- Repeated incidents of offending or offending over an extended period of time, where not charged separately
- Deliberate concealment of illegal nature of activity
- Ignoring risks identified by employees or others
- Established evidence of wider/community impact
- Breach of any order
- Offence committed for financial gain
- Obstruction of justice
- Offence committed on licence or post sentence supervision

### Factors reducing seriousness or reflecting personal mitigation

- No previous convictions **or** no relevant/recent convictions
- Remorse
- Compensation paid voluntarily to remedy harm caused
- Evidence of steps taken to remedy problem
- One-off event not commercially motivated
- Little or no financial gain
- Self-reporting, co-operation and acceptance of responsibility
- Good character and/or exemplary conduct
- Mental disorder or learning disability, where linked to the commission of the offence
- Serious medical conditions requiring urgent, intensive or long-term treatment
- Age and/or lack of maturity where it affects the responsibility of the offender
- Sole or primary carer for dependent relatives

## STEPS 5 and 6

Where the sentence is or includes a fine, the court should 'step back' and, using the factors set out in steps five and six, **review whether the sentence as a whole meets, in a fair way, the objectives of punishment, deterrence and removal of gain derived through the commission of the offence.** At steps five and six, the court may increase or reduce the proposed fine reached at step four, if necessary moving outside the range.

### STEP 5 Ensure that the combination of financial orders (compensation, confiscation if appropriate, and fine) removes any economic benefit derived from the offending

The court should remove any economic benefit the offender has derived through the commission of the offence including:

- avoided costs;
- operating savings;
- any gain made as a direct result of the offence.

Where the offender is fined, the amount of economic benefit derived from the offence should normally be added to the fine arrived at in step four. If a confiscation order is made, in considering economic benefit, the court should avoid double recovery.

Economic benefit will not always be an identifiable feature of a case. For example, in some water pollution cases there may be strict liability but very little obvious gain. However, even in these cases there may be some avoidance of cost, for example alarms not installed and maintained, inadequate funding or security measures not installed. Any costs avoided will be considered as economic benefit.

Where it is not possible to calculate or estimate the economic benefit derived from the offence, the court may wish to draw on information from the enforcing authorities about the general costs of operating within the law.

### STEP 6 Consider other factors that may warrant adjustment of the proposed fine

The court should consider any further factors that are relevant to ensuring that the proposed fine is proportionate having regard to the means of the offender and the seriousness of the offence.

The **non-exhaustive** list below contains additional factual elements the court should consider in deciding whether an increase or reduction to the proposed fine is required:

- fine impairs offender's ability to make restitution to victims;
- impact of fine on offender's ability to improve conditions to comply with the law;
- impact of fine on employment of staff, service users, customers and local economy.

### STEP 7 Consider any factors which indicate a reduction, such as assistance to the prosecution

The court should take into account section 74 of the Sentencing Code (reduction in sentence for assistance to prosecution) and any other rule of law by virtue of which an offender may receive a discounted sentence in consequence of assistance given (or offered) to the prosecutor or investigator.

### STEP 8 Reduction for guilty pleas

The court should take account of any potential reduction for a guilty plea in accordance with section 73 of the Sentencing Code and the guideline for Reduction in Sentence for a Guilty Plea [SG5-1–SG5-12].

### STEP 9 Ancillary orders

In all cases, the court must consider whether to make ancillary orders. These may include:

#### Disqualification of director

An offender may be disqualified from being a director of a company in accordance with section 2 of the Company Directors Disqualification Act 1986. The maximum period of disqualification is 15 years (Crown Court) or 5 years (magistrates' court).

#### Disqualification from driving

The Crown Court may order disqualification from driving where it is satisfied that a motor vehicle was used (by the offender or by anyone else) for the purpose of committing, or facilitating the commission of, the offence (section 164 of the Sentencing Code).

The court may disqualify an offender from driving on conviction for any offence either in addition to any other sentence or instead of any other sentence (section 163 of the Sentencing Code).

The court should inform the offender of its intention to disqualify and hear representations.

**Forfeiture of vehicle**

The court may order the forfeiture of a vehicle used in or for the purposes of the commission of the offence in accordance with section 33C of the Environmental Protection Act 1990.

**Deprivation of property**

Where section 33C of the Environmental Protection Act 1990 does not apply, the court may order the offender to be deprived of property used to commit crime or intended for that purpose in accordance with section 153 of the Sentencing Code. In considering whether to make an order under section 153, the court must have regard to the value of the property and the likely effects on the offender of making the order taken together with any other order the court makes (section 155 of the Sentencing Code).

**Remediation**

Where an offender is convicted of an offence under regulation 38(1), (2) or (3) of the Environmental Permitting (England and Wales) Regulations 2010, a court may order the offender to take steps to remedy the cause of the offence within a specified period in accordance with regulation 44 of the Environmental Permitting (England and Wales) Regulations 2010.

**STEP 10  Totality principle**

If sentencing an offender for more than one offence, or where the offender is already serving a sentence, consider whether the total sentence is just and proportionate to the offending behaviour. See *Totality* guideline [at **SG4**].

**STEP 11  Reasons**

Section 52 of the Sentencing Code imposes a duty to give reasons for, and explain the effect of, the sentence.

**STEP 12  Consideration for time spent on bail (tagged curfew)**

The court must consider whether to give credit for time spent on bail in accordance with section 240A of the Criminal Justice Act 2003 and section 325 of the Sentencing Code.

**Other environmental offences**

In sentencing other relevant and analogous environmental offences, the court should refer to the sentencing approach in steps one to three and five and six of the guideline, **adjusting the starting points and ranges bearing in mind the statutory maxima** for those offences.

[See Environmental Offences (Other) at **SG24-4**.]

ENVIRONMENTAL OFFENCES (OTHER)                                          **SG24-4**

*Environmental Permitting (England and Wales) Regulations 2010 and 2016*

**Effective from:** 01 July 2014

In addition to the offences for which there are detailed guidelines under the Environmental Protection Act 1990 (section 33) and the Environmental Permitting (England and Wales) Regulations 2010 (regulations 12 and 38(1), (2) and (3)),

- Unauthorised or harmful deposit, treatment or disposal etc of waste (individuals) and Illegal discharges to air, land and water (individuals);
- Unauthorised or harmful deposit, treatment or disposal etc of waste (organisations) and Illegal discharges to air, land and water (organisations)

there are other relevant and analogous environmental offences. The court should refer to the sentencing approach in steps one to three and five and six of the guidelines, adjusting the starting points and ranges bearing in mind the statutory maxima for those offences.

An indicative list of such offences is set out below.

[For other environmental offences covered by the Magistrates' Court Sentencing Guidelines see **SG10-77**.]

| Offence | Mode of trial | Statutory maxima |
|---|---|---|
| Section 1 Control of Pollution (Amendment) Act 1989 – transporting controlled waste without registering | Triable summarily only | Unlimited fine |

| Offence | Mode of trial | Statutory maxima |
|---------|---------------|------------------|
| Section 34 Environmental Protection Act 1990 – breach of duty of care | Triable either way | When tried on indictment: unlimited fine <br> When tried summarily: unlimited fine |
| Section 80 Environmental Protection Act 1990 – breach of an abatement notice | Triable summarily only | Where the offence is committed on industrial, trade or business premises: unlimited fine <br> Where the offence is committed on non-industrial etc premises: unlimited fine with a further fine of an amount equal to one-tenth of that level for each day on which the offence continues after the conviction |
| Section 111 Water Industry Act 1991 – restrictions on use of public sewers | Triable either way | When tried on indictment: imprisonment for a term not exceeding two years or a fine or both <br> When tried summarily: a fine not exceeding the statutory maximum and a further fine not exceeding £50 for each day on which the offence continues after conviction |
| Offences under the Transfrontier Shipment of Waste Regulations 2007 | Triable either way | When tried on indictment: a fine or two years imprisonment or both <br> When tried summarily: a fine not exceeding the statutory maximum or three months' imprisonment or both |

# PART 25   MANSLAUGHTER

[For the standard text on applicability see **SG0-4**.]

When sentencing organisations for the offence of corporate manslaughter refer to the Sentencing Council Corporate Manslaughter definitive guideline [see **SG28**].

**Structure, ranges and starting points**

For the purposes of section 60 of the Sentencing Code the guideline specifies offence ranges – the range of sentences appropriate for each type of offence. Within each offence, the Council has specified a number of categories which reflect varying degrees of seriousness. The offence range is split into category ranges – sentences appropriate for each level of seriousness. The Council has also identified a starting point within each category.

Starting points define the position within a category range from which to start calculating the provisional sentence. The court should consider further features of the offence or the offender that warrant adjustment of the sentence within the range, including the aggravating and mitigating factors set out at step two. Starting points and ranges apply to all offenders, whether they have pleaded guilty or been convicted after trial.

Credit for a guilty plea is taken into consideration only at step four (step seven for manslaughter by reason of diminished responsibility) in the decision making process, after the appropriate sentence has been identified.

*Common law*

**Effective from:** 01 November 2018

Triable only on indictment
Maximum: Life imprisonment
Offence range: 1–24 years' custody

This is a Schedule 19 offence for the purposes of sections 274 and section 285 (required life sentence for offence carrying life sentence) of the Sentencing Code.

For offences committed on or after 3 December 2012, this is an offence listed in Part 1 of Schedule 15 for the purposes of sections 273 and 283 (life sentence for second listed offence) of the Sentencing Code.

This is a specified offence for the purposes of sections 266 and 279 (extended sentence for certain violent, sexual or terrorism offences) of the Sentencing Code.

The type of manslaughter (and thereby the appropriate guideline) should have been identified prior to sentence. If there is any dispute or uncertainty about the type of manslaughter that applies the judge should give clear reasons for the basis of sentence.

**STEP 1  Determining the offence category**

**Culpability**

- The characteristics set out below are indications of the level of culpability that may attach to the offender's conduct; the court should balance these characteristics to reach a fair assessment of the offender's overall culpability in the context of the circumstances of the offence.
- The court should avoid an overly mechanistic application of these factors.

| A – Very high culpability | Very high culpability **may** be indicated by:<br>• the extreme character of one or more culpability B factors and /or<br>• a combination of culpability B factors |
|---|---|
| B – Factors indicating high culpability | Death was caused in the course of an unlawful act which involved an intention by the offender to cause harm falling just short of GBH |
| | Death was caused in the course of an unlawful act which carried a high risk of death or GBH which was or ought to have been obvious to the offender |
| | Death was caused in the course of committing or escaping from a serious offence in which the offender played more than a minor role |
| | Concealment, destruction, defilement or dismemberment of the body (where not separately charged) |
| C – Factors indicating medium culpability | Cases falling between high and lower **including but not limited to**<br>• where death was caused in the course of an unlawful act which involved an intention by the offender to cause harm (or recklessness as to whether harm would be caused) that falls between high and lower culpability<br>• where death was caused in the course of committing or escaping from a less serious offence but in which the offender played more than a minor role |
| D – Factors indicating lower culpability | Death was caused in the course of an unlawful act<br>• which was in defence of self or other(s) (where not amounting to a defence) OR<br>• where there was no intention by the offender to cause any harm **and** no obvious risk of anything more than minor harm OR<br>• in which the offender played a minor role |
| | The offender's responsibility was substantially reduced by mental disorder, learning disability or lack of maturity |

### Harm

For all cases of manslaughter the harm caused will inevitably be of the utmost seriousness. The loss of life is taken into account in the sentencing levels at step two.

### STEP 2  Starting point and category range

Having determined the category at step one, the court should use the corresponding starting point to reach a sentence within the category range below. The starting point applies to all offenders irrespective of plea or previous convictions.

• **Where a case does not fall squarely within a category, adjustment from the starting point may be required before adjustment for aggravating or mitigating features.**

| Culpability | | | |
|---|---|---|---|
| A | B | C | D |
| Starting point 18 years' custody | Starting point 12 years' custody | Starting point 6 years' custody | Starting point 2 years' custody |
| Category range 11–24 years' custody | Category range 8–16 years' custody | Category range 3–9 years' custody | Category range 1–4 years' custody |

Note: The table is for a single offence of manslaughter resulting in a single fatality. Where another offence or offences arise out of the same incident or facts, concurrent sentences **reflecting the overall criminality** of offending will ordinarily be appropriate: please refer to the *Offences Taken into Consideration* and *Totality* guidelines [see **SG3** and **SG4** respectively] and step six of this guideline.

### Factors increasing or reducing seriousness

There follows a **non-exhaustive** list of additional elements providing the context of the offence and factors relating to the offender. Identify whether a combination of these or other relevant factors should result in any upward or downward adjustment from the sentence arrived at so far.

**Care should be taken to avoid double counting factors already taken into account in assessing culpability**

**Factors increasing seriousness**

*Statutory aggravating factors*

- Previous convictions, having regard to
  a) the **nature** of the offence to which the conviction relates and its relevance to the current offence; and
  b) the **time** that has elapsed since the conviction (See step five for a consideration of dangerousness)
- Offence committed whilst on bail
- Offence motivated by, or demonstrating hostility based on any of the following characteristics or presumed characteristics of the victim: religion, race, disability, sexual orientation or transgender identity
- Offence was committed against an emergency worker acting in the exercise of functions as such a worker

*Other aggravating factors*

- History of violence or abuse towards victim by offender
- Involvement of other(s) through coercion, intimidation or exploitation
- Significant mental or physical suffering caused to the deceased
- Victim particularly vulnerable due to age or disability
- Victim was providing a public service or performing a public duty at the time of the offence
- Commission of offence whilst under the influence of alcohol or drugs
- Persistence of violence
- Offence involved use of a weapon
- Other(s) put at risk of harm by the offending
- Leading role in group
- Death occurred in the context of an offence which was planned or premeditated
- Offence committed in the presence of children
- Actions after the event (including but not limited to attempts to cover up/conceal evidence)
- Blame wrongly placed on other(s)
- Abuse of a position of trust
- Offence committed on licence or post sentence supervision or while subject to court order(s)

**Factors reducing seriousness or reflecting personal mitigation**

- No previous convictions **or** no relevant/recent convictions
- Remorse
- Attempts to assist the victim
- History of significant violence or abuse towards the offender by the victim
- Lack of premeditation
- Good character and/or exemplary conduct
- Serious medical conditions requiring urgent, intensive or long-term treatment
- Mental disorder or learning disability
- Age and/or lack of maturity
- Sole or primary carer for dependent relatives

**STEP 3   Consider any factors which indicate a reduction for assistance to the prosecution**

The court should take into account section 74 of the Sentencing Code (reduction in sentence for assistance to prosecution) and any other rule of law by virtue of which an offender may receive a discounted sentence in consequence of assistance given (or offered) to the prosecutor or investigator.

**STEP 4   Reduction for guilty pleas**

The court should take account of any potential reduction for a guilty plea in accordance with section 73 of the Sentencing Code and the guideline for Reduction in Sentence for a Guilty Plea [**SG5-1–SG5-12**].

**STEP 5   Dangerousness**

The court should consider:

1) whether having regard to the criteria contained in Chapter 6 of Part 10 of the Sentencing Code it would be appropriate to impose a life sentence (sections 274 and 285);
2) whether having regard to sections 273 and 283 of the Sentencing Code it would be appropriate to impose a life sentence;
3) whether having regard to the criteria contained in Chapter 6 of Part 10 of the Sentencing Code it would be appropriate to impose an extended sentence (sections 266 and 279).

When sentencing offenders to a life sentence under these provisions, the notional determinate sentence should be used as the basis for the setting of a minimum term.

**STEP 6 Totality principle**

If sentencing an offender for more than one offence, or where the offender is already serving a sentence, consider whether the total sentence is just and proportionate to the overall offending behaviour in accordance with the *Totality* guideline. [See **SG4**.]

**STEP 7 Compensation and ancillary orders**

In all cases the court should consider whether to make compensation and/or other ancillary orders.

**STEP 8 Reasons**

Section 52 of the Sentencing Code imposes a duty to give reasons for, and explain the effect of, the sentence.

**STEP 9 Consideration for time spent on bail (tagged curfew)**

The court must consider whether to give credit for time spent on bail in accordance with section 240A of the Criminal Justice Act 2003 and section 325 of the Sentencing Code.

**SG25-3**

## Gross Negligence Manslaughter

*Common law*

Triable only on indictment
Maximum: Life imprisonment
Offence range: 1–18 years' custody

This is a Schedule 19 offence for the purposes of sections 274 and 285 (required life sentence for offence carrying life sentence) of the Sentencing Code.

For offences committed on or after 3 December 2012, this is an offence listed in Part 1 of Schedule 15 for the purposes of sections 273 and 283 (life sentence for second listed offence) of the Sentencing Code.

This is a specified offence for the purposes of sections 266 and 279 (extended sentence for certain violent, sexual or terrorism offences) of the Sentencing Code.

The type of manslaughter (and thereby the appropriate guideline) should have been identified prior to sentence. If there is any dispute or uncertainty about the type of manslaughter that applies the judge should give clear reasons for the basis of sentence.

**STEP 1 Determining the offence category**

**Culpability**

- The characteristics set out below are indications of the level of culpability that may attach to the offender's conduct; the court should balance these characteristics to reach a fair assessment of the offender's overall culpability in the context of the circumstances of the offence.
- The court should avoid an overly mechanistic application of these factors particularly in cases to which they do not readily apply.

| A – Very high culpability | Very high culpability **may** be indicated by:<br>• the extreme character of one or more culpability B factors and /or<br>• a combination of culpability B factors |
|---|---|
| B – Factors indicating high culpability | The offender continued or repeated the negligent conduct in the face of the obvious suffering caused to the deceased by that conduct |
| | The negligent conduct was in the context of other serious criminality |
| | The offence was particularly serious because the offender showed a blatant disregard for a very high risk of death resulting from the negligent conduct |
| | The negligent conduct was motivated by financial gain (or avoidance of cost) |
| | The offender was in a leading role if acting with others in the offending |
| | Concealment, destruction, defilement or dismemberment of the body (where not separately charged) |
| C – Factors indicating medium culpability | Cases falling between high and lower because<br>• factors are present in high and lower which balance each other out **and/or**<br>• the offender's culpability falls between the factors as described in high and lower |

| D – Factors indicating lower culpability | The negligent conduct was a lapse in the offender's otherwise satisfactory standard of care |
|---|---|
| | The offender was in a lesser or subordinate role if acting with others in the offending |
| | The offender's responsibility was substantially reduced by mental disorder, learning disability or lack of maturity |

## Harm

For all cases of manslaughter the harm caused will inevitably be of the utmost seriousness. The loss of life is taken into account in the sentencing levels at step two.

## STEP 2  Starting point and category range

Having determined the category at step one, the court should use the corresponding starting point to reach a sentence within the category range below. The starting point applies to all offenders irrespective of plea or previous convictions.

- Where a case does not fall squarely within a category, adjustment from the starting point may be required before adjustment for aggravating or mitigating features.

| Culpability | | | |
|---|---|---|---|
| A | B | C | D |
| Starting point 12 years' custody | Starting point 8 years' custody | Starting point 4 years' custody | Starting point 2 years' custody |
| Category range 10–18 years' custody | Category range 6–12 years' custody | Category range 3–7 years' custody | Category range 1–4 years' custody |

## Custodial Sentences

[For the imposition of custodial sentences see Imposition of Community and Custodial Sentences at SG9-3.]

**Where the offender's acts or omissions would also constitute another offence, the sentencer should have regard to any guideline relevant to the other offence to ensure that the sentence for manslaughter does not fall below what would be imposed under that guideline.**

Note: The table is for a single offence of manslaughter resulting in a single fatality. Where another offence or offences arise out of the same incident or facts, concurrent sentences **reflecting the overall criminality** of offending will ordinarily be appropriate: please refer to the *Offences Taken into Consideration* and *Totality* guidelines [see **SG3** and **SG4** respectively] and step six of this guideline.

## Factors increasing or reducing seriousness

There follows a **non-exhaustive** list of additional elements providing the context of the offence and factors relating to the offender. Identify whether a combination of these or other relevant factors should result in any upward or downward adjustment from the sentence arrived at so far.

**Care should be taken to avoid double counting factors already taken into account in assessing culpability**

## Factors increasing seriousness

*Statutory aggravating factors*
- Previous convictions, having regard to
  a) the nature of the offence to which the conviction relates and its relevance to the current offence; and
  b) the time that has elapsed since the conviction (See step five for a consideration of dangerousness)
- Offence committed whilst on bail
- Offence motivated by, or demonstrating hostility based on any of the following characteristics or presumed characteristics of the victim: religion, race, disability, sexual orientation or transgender identity

*Other aggravating factors*
- History of violence or abuse towards victim by offender
- Involvement of others through coercion, intimidation or exploitation
- Significant mental or physical suffering caused to the deceased
- Offender ignored previous warnings

- Commission of offence whilst under the influence of alcohol or drugs
- Offence involved use of a weapon
- Other(s) put at risk of harm by the offending
- Actions after the event (including but not limited to attempts to cover up/conceal evidence)
- Investigation has been hindered and/or other(s) have suffered as a result of being falsely blamed by the offender
- Offence committed on licence or post sentence supervision or while subject to court order(s)

**Factors reducing seriousness or reflecting personal mitigation**

- No previous convictions or no relevant/recent convictions
- Remorse
- Attempts to assist the victim
- Self-reporting and/or co-operation with the investigation
- For reasons beyond the offender's control, the offender lacked the necessary expertise, equipment, support or training which contributed to the negligent conduct
- For reasons beyond the offender's control, the offender was subject to stress or pressure (including from competing or complex demands) which related to and contributed to the negligent conduct
- For reasons beyond the offender's control, the negligent conduct occurred in circumstances where there was reduced scope for exercising usual care and competence
- The negligent conduct was compounded by the actions or omissions of others beyond the offender's control
- Good character and/or exemplary conduct
- Serious medical conditions requiring urgent, intensive or long-term treatment
- Mental disorder or learning disability
- Age and/or lack of maturity
- Sole or primary carer for dependent relatives

**STEP 3  Consider any factors which indicate a reduction for assistance to the prosecution**

The court should take into account section 74 of the Sentencing Code (reduction in sentence for assistance to prosecution) and any other rule of law by virtue of which an offender may receive a discounted sentence in consequence of assistance given (or offered) to the prosecutor or investigator.

**STEP 4  Reduction for guilty pleas**

The court should take account of any potential reduction for a guilty plea in accordance with section 73 of the Sentencing Code and the guideline for Reduction in Sentence for a Guilty Plea [**SG5-1–SG5-12**].

**STEP 5  Dangerousness**

The court should consider:

1) whether having regard to the criteria contained in Chapter 6 of Part 10 of the Sentencing Code it would be appropriate to impose a life sentence (sections 274 and 285);
2) whether having regard to sections 273 and 283 of the Sentencing Code it would be appropriate to impose a life sentence;
3) whether having regard to the criteria contained in Chapter 6 of Part 10 of the Sentencing Code it would be appropriate to impose an extended sentence (sections 266 and 279).

When sentencing offenders to a life sentence under these provisions, the notional determinate sentence should be used as the basis for the setting of a minimum term.

**STEP 6  Totality principle**

If sentencing an offender for more than one offence, or where the offender is already serving a sentence, consider whether the total sentence is just and proportionate to the overall offending behaviour in accordance with the *Totality* guideline. [See **SG4**.]

**STEP 7  Compensation and ancillary orders**

In all cases the court should consider whether to make compensation and/or other ancillary orders.

In appropriate cases an offender may be disqualified from being a director of a company in accordance with section 2 of the Company Directors Disqualification Act 1986. The maximum period of disqualification is 15 years.

**STEP 8  Reasons**

Section 52 of the Sentencing Code imposes a duty to give reasons for, and explain the effect of, the sentence.

**STEP 9  Consideration for time spent on bail (tagged curfew)**

The court must consider whether to give credit for time spent on bail in accordance with section 240A of the Criminal Justice Act 2003 and section 325 of the Sentencing Code.

MANSLAUGHTER BY REASON OF LOSS OF CONTROL                    **SG25-4**

*Common Law and Coroners and Justice Act 2009 (sections 54 and 55)*

**Effective from:** 01 November 2018

Triable only on indictment
Maximum: Life imprisonment
Offence range: 3–20 years' custody

This is a Schedule 19 offence for the purposes of sections 274 and 285 (required life sentence for offence carrying life sentence) of the Sentencing Code.

For offences committed on or after 3 December 2012, this is an offence listed in Part 1 of Schedule 15 for the purposes of sections 273 and 283 (life sentence for second listed offence) of the Sentencing Code.

This is a specified offence for the purposes of sections 266 and 279 (extended sentence for certain violent, sexual or terrorism offences) of the Sentencing Code.

The type of manslaughter (and thereby the appropriate guideline) should have been identified prior to sentence. If there is any dispute or uncertainty about the type of manslaughter that applies the judge should give clear reasons for the basis of sentence.

**STEP 1  Determining the offence category**

**Culpability**

- The characteristics set out below are indications of the level of culpability that may attach to the offender's conduct; the court should balance these characteristics to reach a fair assessment of the offender's overall culpability in the context of the circumstances of the offence.
- The court should avoid an overly mechanistic application of these factors.

| A – High culpability | • Planning of criminal activity (including the carrying of a weapon) **before** the loss of control<br>• Offence committed in the context of other serious criminal activity<br>• Use of a firearm (whether or not taken to the scene)<br>• Loss of self-control in circumstances which only just met the criteria for a qualifying trigger<br>• Concealment, destruction, defilement or dismemberment of the body (where not separately charged) |
|---|---|
| B – Medium culpability | Cases falling between high and lower because:<br>• factors are present in high and lower which balance each other out **and/or**<br>• the offender's culpability falls between the factors as described in high and lower |
| C – Lower culpability | • Qualifying trigger represented a very high degree of provocation |

**Harm**

For all cases of manslaughter the harm caused will inevitably be of the utmost seriousness. The loss of life is taken into account in the sentencing levels at step two.

**STEP 2  Starting point and category range**

Having determined the category at step one, the court should use the corresponding starting point to reach a sentence within the category range below. The starting point applies to all offenders irrespective of plea or previous convictions.

- Where a case does not fall squarely within a category, adjustment from the starting point may be required before adjustment for aggravating or mitigating features

Sentencing Guidelines

| Culpability | | |
|---|---|---|
| A | B | C |
| **Starting point**<br>14 years' custody | **Starting point**<br>8 years' custody | **Starting point**<br>5 years' custody |
| **Category range**<br>10–20 years' custody | **Category range**<br>5–12 years' custody | **Category range**<br>3–6 years' custody |

### Custodial Sentences

[For the imposition of custodial sentences see Imposition of Community and Custodial Sentences at SG9-3.]

Note: The table is for a single offence of manslaughter resulting in a single fatality. Where another offence or offences arise out of the same incident or facts, concurrent sentences **reflecting the overall criminality** of offending will ordinarily be appropriate: please refer to the *Offences Taken into Consideration* and *Totality* guidelines [see **SG3** and **SG4** respectively] and step six of this guideline

### Factors increasing and reducing seriousness

Below is a **non-exhaustive** list of additional elements providing the context of the offence and factors relating to the offender. Identify whether a combination of these or other relevant factors should result in any upward or downward adjustment from the sentence arrived at so far.

Care should be taken to avoid double counting factors already taken into account in assessing culpability or in the finding of a qualifying trigger

### Factors increasing seriousness

*Statutory aggravating factors*

- Previous convictions, having regard to
  - a) the **nature** of the offence to which the conviction relates and its **relevance** to the current offence; and
  - b) the **time** that has elapsed since the conviction (See step five for a consideration of dangerousness)
- Offence committed whilst on bail
- Offence motivated by, or demonstrating hostility based on any of the following characteristics or presumed characteristics of the victim: religion, race, disability, sexual orientation or transgender identity
- Offence was committed against an emergency worker acting in the exercise of functions as such a worker

*Other aggravating factors*

- History of violence or abuse towards victim by offender
- Involvement of other(s) through coercion, intimidation or exploitation
- Significant mental or physical suffering caused to the deceased
- Victim was providing a public service or performing a public duty at the time of the offence
- Commission of offence whilst under the influence of alcohol or drugs
- Persistence of violence
- Offence involved use of a weapon
- Other(s) put at risk of harm by the offending
- Actions after the event (including but not limited to attempts to cover up/ conceal evidence)
- Offence committed on licence or post sentence supervision or while subject to court order(s)

### Factors reducing seriousness or reflecting personal mitigation

- No previous convictions **or** no relevant/recent convictions
- Remorse
- Intention to cause serious bodily harm rather than to kill
- History of significant violence or abuse towards the offender by the victim
- Violence initiated by the victim
- Serious medical conditions requiring urgent, intensive or long-term treatment
- Mental disorder or learning disability
- Age and/or lack of maturity
- Sole or primary carer for dependent relatives

The court should take into account section 74 of the Sentencing Code (reduction in sentence for assistance to prosecution) and any other rule of law by virtue of which an offender may receive a discounted sentence in consequence of assistance given (or offered) to the prosecutor or investigator.

**STEP 4  Reduction for guilty pleas**

The court should take account of any potential reduction for a guilty plea in accordance with section 73 of the Sentencing Code and the guideline for Reduction in Sentence for a Guilty Plea [**SG5-1–SG5-12**].

**STEP 5  Dangerousness**

The court should consider:

1) whether having regard to the criteria contained in Chapter 6 of Part 10 of the Sentencing Code it would be appropriate to impose a life sentence (sections 274 and 285);
2) whether having regard to sections 273 and 283 of the Sentencing Code it would be appropriate to impose a life sentence;
3) whether having regard to the criteria contained in Chapter 6 of Part 10 of the Sentencing Code it would be appropriate to impose an extended sentence (sections 266 and 279).

When sentencing offenders to a life sentence under these provisions, the notional determinate sentence should be used as the basis for the setting of a minimum term.

**STEP 6  Totality principle**

If sentencing an offender for more than one offence, or where the offender is already serving a sentence, consider whether the total sentence is just and proportionate to the overall offending behaviour in accordance with the *Totality* guideline. [See **SG4**]

**STEP 7  Compensation and ancillary orders**

In all cases the court should consider whether to make compensation and/or other ancillary orders.

**STEP 8  Reasons**

Section 52 of the Sentencing Code imposes a duty to give reasons for, and explain the effect of, the sentence.

**STEP 9  Consideration for time spent on bail (tagged curfew)**

The court must consider whether to give credit for time spent on bail in accordance with section 240A of the Criminal Justice Act 2003 and section 325 of the Sentencing Code.

MANSLAUGHTER BY REASON OF DIMINISHED RESPONSIBILITY                **SG25-5**

*Common Law and Homicide Act 1957 (section 2)*

**Effective from:** 01 November 2018

Triable only on indictment
Maximum: Life imprisonment
Offence range: 3–40 years' custody

This is a Schedule 19 offence for the purposes of sections 274 and 285 (required life sentence for offence carrying life sentence) of the Sentencing Code.

For offences committed on or after 3 December 2012, this is an offence listed in Part 1 of Schedule 15 for the purposes of sections 273 and 283 (life sentence for second listed offence) of the Sentencing Code.

This is a specified offence for the purposes of sections 266 and 279 (extended sentence for certain violent, sexual or terrorism offences) of the Sentencing Code.

The type of manslaughter (and thereby the appropriate guideline) should have been identified prior to sentence. If there is any dispute or uncertainty about the type of manslaughter that applies the judge should give clear reasons for the basis of sentence.

**STEP 1  Assessing the degree of responsibility retained: high, medium or lower**

- A conviction for manslaughter by reason of diminished responsibility necessarily means that the offender's ability to understand the nature of the conduct, form a rational judgment and/or exercise self-control was substantially impaired.
- The court should determine what level of responsibility the offender **retained:**
  - High;
  - Medium; or
  - Lower
- The court should consider the extent to which the offender's responsibility was diminished by the mental disorder **at the time of the offence** with reference to the medical evidence and all the relevant information available to the court.
- The degree to which the offender's actions or omissions contributed to the seriousness of the mental disorder at the time of the offence may be a relevant consideration. For example:

- where an offender exacerbates the mental disorder by voluntarily abusing drugs or alcohol or by voluntarily failing to seek or follow medical advice this may increase responsibility. In considering the extent to which the offender's behaviour was voluntary, the extent to which a mental disorder has an impact on the offender's ability to exercise self-control or to engage with medical services will be relevant.
- The degree to which the mental disorder was undiagnosed and/or untreated may be a relevant consideration. For example:
  - where an offender has sought help but not received appropriate treatment this may reduce responsibility.

### Harm

For all cases of manslaughter the harm caused will inevitably be of the utmost seriousness. The loss of life is taken into account in the sentencing levels at step two.

### STEP 2 Starting point and category range

Having determined the level of responsibility retained at step one, the court should use the corresponding starting point to reach a sentence within the category range below. The starting point applies to all offenders irrespective of plea or previous convictions.

| Level of responsibility retained | | |
| --- | --- | --- |
| High | Medium | Lower |
| Starting point 24 years' custody | Starting point 15 years' custody | Starting point 7 year's custody |
| Category range 15–40 years' custody | Category range 10–25 years' custody | Category range 3–12 years' custody |

Note: The table is for a single offence of manslaughter resulting in a single fatality. Where another offence or offences arise out of the same incident or facts concurrent sentences **reflecting the overall criminality** of offending will ordinarily be appropriate: please refer to the *Offences Taken into Consideration* and *Totality* guidelines [see **SG3** and **SG4** respectively] and step eight of this guideline.

### Additional factors affecting seriousness

Below is a **non-exhaustive** list of additional factual elements providing the context of the offence and factors relating to the offender. Identify whether a combination of these or other relevant factors should result in any upward or downward adjustment from the sentence arrived at so far.

Care should be taken to avoid double counting factors already taken into account in assessing the level of responsibility retained

### Factors increasing seriousness

*Statutory aggravating factors*
- Previous convictions, having regard to
  a) the nature of the offence to which the conviction relates and its relevance to the current offence; and
  b) the time that has elapsed since the conviction (See step three for a consideration of dangerousness)
- Offence committed whilst on bail
- Offence motivated by, or demonstrating hostility based on any of the following characteristics or presumed characteristics of the victim: religion, race, disability, sexual orientation or transgender identity
- Offence was committed against an emergency worker acting in the exercise of functions as such a worker

*Other aggravating factors*
- History of violence or abuse towards victim by offender
- Involvement of other(s) through coercion, intimidation or exploitation
- Significant mental or physical suffering caused to the deceased
- Victim particularly vulnerable due to age or disability
- Victim was providing a public service or performing a public duty at the time of the offence
- Commission of offence whilst under the influence of alcohol or drugs (the extent to which a mental disorder has an effect on offender's ability to make informed judgments or exercise self-control will be a relevant consideration in deciding how much weight to attach to this factor)
- A significant degree of planning or premeditation
- Offence involved use of a weapon

- Other(s) put at risk of harm by the offending
- Actions after the event (including but not limited to attempts to cover up/conceal evidence)
- Concealment, destruction, defilement or dismemberment of the body
- Blame wrongly placed on other(s)
- Offence committed on licence or post sentence supervision or while subject to court order(s)

**Factors reducing seriousness or reflecting personal mitigation**

- No previous convictions **or** no relevant/recent convictions
- Remorse
- Intention to cause serious bodily harm rather than to kill
- History of significant violence or abuse towards the offender by the victim
- Lack of premeditation
- The offender acted in self-defence or in fear of violence (where not amounting to a defence)
- The offender made genuine and sustained attempts to seek help for the mental disorder
- Belief by the offender that the killing was an act of mercy
- Good character and/or exemplary conduct
- Serious medical conditions requiring urgent, intensive or long-term treatment
- Age and/or lack of maturity
- Sole or primary carer for dependent relatives

### STEP 3  Consideration of dangerousness

The court should then go on to consider:

1) whether having regard to the criteria contained in Chapter 6 of Part 10 of the Sentencing Code it would be appropriate to impose a life sentence (sections 274 and 285)
2) whether having regard to sections 273 and 283 of the Sentencing Code it would be appropriate to impose a life sentence.
3) whether having regard to the criteria contained in Chapter 6 of Part 10 of the Sentencing Code it would be appropriate to impose an extended sentence (sections 266 and 279)

When sentencing offenders to a life sentence under these provisions, the notional determinate sentence should be used as the basis for the setting of a minimum term.

### STEP 4  Consideration of mental health disposals (Mental Health Act 1983)

**Where:**

(i)    the evidence of medical practitioners suggests that the offender is currently suffering from a mental disorder,
(ii)   treatment is available, and
(iii)  the court considers that a hospital order (with or without a restriction) may be an appropriate way of dealing with the case,

the court should consider **all sentencing options** including a section 45A direction and consider the importance of a penal element in the sentence taking into account the level of responsibility assessed at step one.

#### Section 45A hospital and limitation direction

a.    Before a hospital order is made under section 37 (with or without a restriction order under section 41), consider whether the mental disorder can appropriately be dealt with by custody with a hospital and limitation direction under section 45A. In deciding whether a section 45A direction is appropriate the court should bear in mind that the limitation direction will cease to have effect at the automatic release date of a determinate sentence.
b.    If a penal element is appropriate and the mental disorder can appropriately be dealt with by a direction under section 45A, then the judge should make such a direction. (Not available for a person under the age of 21 at the time of conviction).

#### Section 37 hospital order and section 41 restriction order

c.    If a section 45A direction is not appropriate the court must then consider (assuming the conditions in section 37(2)(a) are satisfied) whether the matters referred to in section 37(2)(b) would make a hospital order (with or without a restriction order under section 41) the most suitable disposal. The court should explain why a penal element is not appropriate.

### STEP 5  IN ALL CASES Consider factors that may warrant an adjustment to the sentence

Cases of manslaughter by reason of diminished responsibility vary considerably on the facts of the offence and on the circumstances of the offender.

- The court should review whether the sentence as a whole meets the objectives of punishment, rehabilitation and protection of the public in a fair and proportionate way.
- Relevant factors will include the psychiatric evidence and the regime on release.
- An adjustment may require a departure from the sentence range identified at step two above.

### STEP 6  Consider any factors which indicate a reduction for assistance to the prosecution

The court should take into account section 74 of the Sentencing Code (reduction in sentence for assistance to prosecution) and any other rule of law by virtue of which an offender may receive a discounted sentence in consequence of assistance given (or offered) to the prosecutor or investigator.

### STEP 7  Reduction for guilty pleas

The court should take account of any potential reduction for a guilty plea in accordance with section 73 of the Sentencing Code and the guideline for Reduction in Sentence for a Guilty Plea [SG5-1–SG5-12].

### STEP 8  Totality principle

If sentencing an offender for more than one offence, or where the offender is already serving a sentence, consider whether the total sentence is just and proportionate to the overall offending behaviour in accordance with the *Totality* guideline [at **SG4**].

### STEP 9  Compensation and ancillary orders

In all cases the court should consider whether to make compensation and/or other ancillary orders.

### STEP 10  Reasons

Section 52 of the Sentencing Code imposes a duty to give reasons for, and explain the effect of, the sentence.

### STEP 11  Consideration for time spent on bail (tagged curfew)

The court must consider whether to give credit for time spent on bail in accordance with section 240A of the Criminal Justice Act 2003 and section 325 of the Sentencing Code.

# PART 26   FRAUD, BRIBERY AND MONEY LAUNDERING OFFENCES

[For the standard text on applicability see **SG0-4**.]

*Common law, Fraud Act 2006, s.1, Theft Act 1968, s.17*

**Effective from:** 01 October 2014

**Fraud by false representation, fraud by failing to disclose information, fraud by abuse of position**, Fraud Act 2006 (section 1)
Triable either way

**Conspiracy to defraud**, Common Law
Triable on indictment only
Maximum: 10 years' custody
Offence range: Discharge–8 years' custody

**False accounting**, Theft Act 1968 (section 17)
Triable either way
Maximum: 7 years' custody
Offence range: Discharge–6 years and 6 months' custody

## STEP 1   Determining the offence category

The court should determine the offence category with reference to the tables below. In order to determine the category the court should assess **culpability** and **harm**.

| Culpability |
| --- |
| The level of culpability is **determined by weighing up all the factors of the case to determine the offender's role and the extent to which the offending was planned and the sophistication with which it was carried out.** |

| Culpability demonstrated by one or more of the following: |
| --- |
| **A — High culpability** |
| A leading role where offending is part of a group activity |
| Involvement of others through pressure, influence |
| Abuse of position of power or trust or responsibility |
| Sophisticated nature of offence/significant planning |
| Fraudulent activity conducted over sustained period of time |
| Large number of victims |
| Deliberately targeting victim on basis of vulnerability |
| **B — Medium culpability** |
| Other cases where characteristics for categories A or C are not present<br>–   Factors are present in A and C which balance each other out and/or<br>–   The offender's culpability falls between the factors as described in A and C |
| A significant role where offending is part of a group activity |
| **C — Lesser culpability** |
| Involved through coercion, intimidation or exploitation |
| Not motivated by personal gain |
| Peripheral role in organised fraud |
| Opportunistic 'one-off' offence; very little or no planning |
| Limited awareness or understanding of the extent of fraudulent activity |

**Where there are characteristics present which fall under different levels of culpability, the court should balance these characteristics to reach a fair assessment of the offender's culpability.**

**Harm**

> **Harm** is initially assessed by the actual, intended or risked loss as may arise from the offence.

The values in the table below are to be used for **actual** or **intended** loss only.

Intended loss relates to offences where circumstances prevent the actual loss that is intended to be caused by the fraudulent activity.

**Risk of loss** (for instance in mortgage frauds) involves consideration of both the likelihood of harm occurring and the extent of it if it does. Risk of loss is less serious than actual or intended loss. Where the offence has caused risk of loss but no (or much less) actual loss the normal approach is to move down to the corresponding point in the next category. This may not be appropriate if either the likelihood or extent of risked loss is particularly high.

**Harm A — Loss caused or intended**

| Category 1 | £500,000 or more | Starting point based on £1 million |
|---|---|---|
| Category 2 | £100,000–£500,000 **or** Risk of category 1 harm | Starting point based on £300,000 |
| Category 3 | £20,000–£100,000 **or** Risk of category 2 harm | Starting point based on £50,000 |
| Category 4 | £5,000–£20,000 **or** Risk of category 3 harm | Starting point based on £12,500 |
| Category 5 | Less than £5,000 **or** Risk of category 4 harm | Starting point based on £2,500 |
| **Risk of category 5 harm, move down the range within the category** | | |

| **Harm B — Victim impact demonstrated by one or more of the following:** |
|---|
| The court should then take into account the level of harm caused to the victim(s) or others to determine whether it warrants the sentence being moved up to the corresponding point in the next category or further up the range of the initial category. |
| **High impact** — move up a category; if in category 1 move up the range |
| Serious detrimental effect on the victim whether financial or otherwise, for example substantial damage to credit rating |
| Victim particularly vulnerable (due to factors including but not limited to their age, financial circumstances, mental capacity) |
| **Medium impact** — move upwards within the category range |
| Considerable detrimental effect on the victim whether financial or otherwise |
| **Lesser impact** — no adjustment |
| Some detrimental impact on victim, whether financial or otherwise |

## STEP 2 Starting point and category range

Having determined the category at step one, the court should use the appropriate starting point (as adjusted in accordance with step one above) to reach a sentence within the category range in the table below. The starting point applies to all offenders irrespective of plea or previous convictions.

Where the value is larger or smaller than the amount on which the starting point is based, this should lead to upward or downward adjustment as appropriate.

Where the value greatly exceeds the amount of the starting point in category 1, it may be appropriate to move outside the identified range.

**TABLE 1  Section 1 Fraud Act 2006 conspiracy to defraud**
Maximum: 10 years' custody

|  | Culpability | | |
|---|---|---|---|
| Harm | A | B | C |
| **Category 1**<br>£500,000 or more<br><br>Starting point based on<br>£1 million | **Starting point**<br>7 years' custody<br><br>**Category range**<br>5–8 years' custody | **Starting point**<br>5 years' custody<br><br>**Category range**<br>3–6 years' custody | **Starting point**<br>3 years' custody<br><br>**Category range**<br>18 months'–4 years'<br>custody |
| **Category 2**<br>£100,000–£500,000<br><br>Starting point based<br>on £300,000 | **Starting point**<br>5 years' custody<br><br>**Category range**<br>3–6 years' custody | **Starting point**<br>3 years' custody<br><br>**Category range**<br>18 months'–4 years'<br>custody | **Starting point**<br>18 months' custody<br><br>**Category range**<br>26 weeks'–3 years'<br>custody |
| **Category 3**<br>£20,000–£100,000<br><br>Starting point based on<br>£50,000 | **Starting point**<br>3 years' custody<br><br>**Category range**<br>18 months'–4 years'<br>custody | **Starting point**<br>18 months' custody<br><br>**Category range**<br>26 weeks'–3 years'<br>custody | **Starting point**<br>26 weeks' custody<br><br>**Category range**<br>Medium level<br>community order–1<br>year's custody |
| **Category 4**<br>£5,000–£20,000<br><br><br>Starting point based<br>on £12,500 | **Starting point**<br>18 months' custody<br><br><br>**Category range**<br>26 weeks'–3 years'<br>custody | **Starting point**<br>26 weeks' custody<br><br><br>**Category range**<br>Medium level<br>community order–<br>1 year's custody | **Starting point**<br>Medium level<br>community order<br><br>**Category range**<br>Band B fine–<br>High level community<br>order |
| **Category 5**<br>Less than £5,000<br><br><br>Starting point based<br>on £2,500 | **Starting point**<br>36 weeks' custody<br><br><br>**Category range**<br>High level community<br>order–1 year's custody | **Starting point**<br>Medium level<br>community order<br><br>**Category range**<br>Band B fine–26 weeks'<br>custody | **Starting point**<br>Band B fine<br><br><br>**Category range**<br>Discharge–Medium<br>level<br>community order |

**TABLE 2  Section 17 Theft Act 1968: False Accounting**
Maximum: 7 years' custody

|  | Culpability | | |
|---|---|---|---|
| Harm | A | B | C |
| **Category 1**<br>£500,000 or more<br><br>Starting point based on<br>£1 million | **Starting point**<br>5 years 6 months'<br>custody<br><br>**Category range**<br>4 years'–6 years 6<br>months' custody | **Starting point**<br>4 years' custody<br><br><br>**Category range**<br>2 years 6 months'–5<br>years' custody | **Starting point**<br>2 years 6 months'<br>custody<br><br>**Category range**<br>15 months'–3 years 6<br>months' custody |
| **Category 2**<br>£100,000–£500,000<br><br>Starting point based on<br>£300,000 | **Starting point**<br>4 years' custody<br><br><br>**Category range**<br>2 years 6 months'–5<br>years' custody | **Starting point**<br>2 years 6 months'<br>custody<br><br>**Category range**<br>15 months'–3 years 6<br>months' custody | **Starting point**<br>15 months' custody<br><br><br>**Category range**<br>26 weeks'–2 years 6<br>months' custody |

|  | Culpability | | |
|---|---|---|---|
| Harm | A | B | C |
| Category 3<br>£20,000–£100,000<br><br>Starting point based on £50,000 | **Starting point**<br>2 years 6 months' custody<br><br>**Category range**<br>15 months'–3 years 6 months' custody | **Starting point**<br>15 months' custody<br><br>**Category range**<br>High level community order–2 years 6 months' custody | **Starting point**<br>High level community order<br><br>**Category range**<br>Low level community order–36 weeks' custody |
| Category 4<br>£5,000–£20,000<br><br>Starting point based on £12,500 | **Starting point**<br>15 months' custody<br><br>**Category range**<br>High level community order–2 years 6 months' custody | **Starting point**<br>High level community order<br><br>**Category range**<br>Low level community order–36 weeks' custody | **Starting point**<br>Low level community order<br><br>**Category range**<br>Band B fine–Medium level community order |
| Category 5<br>Less than £5,000<br><br>Starting point based on £2,500 | **Starting point**<br>26 weeks' custody<br><br>**Category range**<br>Medium level community order–36 weeks' custody | **Starting point**<br>Low level community order<br><br>**Category range** Band B fine–Medium level community order | **Starting point**<br>Band B fine<br><br>**Category range**<br>Discharge–Low level community order |

**Fines**

[For the standard schedule of fines see **SG2-5**.]

**Community Orders and Custodial Sentences**

[For the imposition of community orders, including the community orders table, see Imposition of Community and Custodial Sentences at **SG9-2**. For the imposition of custodial sentences see Imposition of Community and Custodial Sentences at **SG9-3**.]

**Factors increasing or reducing seriousness**

The table below contains a non-exhaustive list of additional factual elements providing the context of the offence and factors relating to the offender.

Identify whether any combination of these or other relevant factors should result in an upward or downward adjustment from the sentence arrived at so far.

Consecutive sentences for multiple offences may be appropriate where large sums are involved.

**Factors increasing seriousness**

*Statutory aggravating factors*
- Previous convictions, having regard to
  a) the nature of the offence to which the conviction relates and its relevance to the current offence; and
  b) the time that has elapsed since the conviction
- Offence committed whilst on bail

*Other aggravating factors*
- Steps taken to prevent the victim reporting or obtaining assistance and/ or from assisting or supporting the prosecution
- Attempts to conceal/dispose of evidence
- Established evidence of community/wider impact
- Failure to comply with current court orders
- Offence committed on licence or post sentence supervision
- Offences taken into consideration
- Failure to respond to warnings about behaviour
- Offences committed across borders
- Blame wrongly placed on others

**Factors reducing seriousness or reflecting personal mitigation**

• No previous convictions or no relevant/recent convictions
• Remorse
• Good character and/or exemplary conduct
• Little or no prospect of success
• Serious medical conditions requiring urgent, intensive or long-term treatment
• Age and/ or lack of maturity where it affects the responsibility of the offender
• Lapse of time since apprehension where this does not arise from the conduct of the offender
• Mental disorder or learning disability
• Sole or primary carer for dependent relatives
• Offender co-operated with investigation, made early admissions and/or voluntarily reported offending
• Determination and/or demonstration of steps taken to address addiction or offending behaviour
• Activity originally legitimate

**STEP 3  Consider any factors which indicate a reduction, such as assistance to the prosecution**

The court should take into account section 74 of the Sentencing Code (reduction in sentence for assistance to prosecution) and any other rule of law by virtue of which an offender may receive a discounted sentence in consequence of assistance given (or offered) to the prosecutor or investigator.

**STEP 4  Reduction for guilty pleas**

The court should take account of any potential reduction for a guilty plea in accordance with section 73 of the Sentencing Code and the guideline for Reduction in Sentence for a Guilty Plea [**SG5-1–SG5-12**].

**STEP 5  Totality principle**

If sentencing an offender for more than one offence, or where the offender is already serving a sentence, consider whether the total sentence is just and proportionate to the overall offending behaviour. See *Totality* guideline [at **SG4**].

**STEP 6  Confiscation, compensation and ancillary orders**

Confiscation orders under the Proceeds of Crime Act 2002 may only be made by the Crown Court. The Crown Court must proceed with a view to making a confiscation order if it is asked to do so by the prosecutor or if the Crown Court believes it is appropriate for it to do so.

Where, following conviction in a magistrates' court, the prosecutor applies for the offender to be committed to the Crown Court with a view to a confiscation order being considered, the magistrates' court must commit the offender to the Crown Court to be sentenced there (section 70 of the Proceeds of Crime Act 2002). This applies to summary only and either-way offences.

Where, but for the prosecutor's application under s.70, the magistrates' court would have committed the offender for sentence to the Crown Court anyway it must say so. Otherwise the powers of sentence of the Crown Court will be limited to those of the magistrates' court.

Confiscation must be dealt with before, and taken into account when assessing, any other fine or financial order (except compensation).

(See Proceeds of Crime Act 2002 sections 6 and 13)

Where the offence has resulted in loss or damage the court must consider whether to make a compensation order. The court must give reasons if it decides not to award compensation in such cases (Sentencing Code, s.55).

If the court makes both a confiscation order and an order for compensation and the court believes the offender will not have sufficient means to satisfy both orders in full, the court must direct that the compensation be paid out of sums recovered under the confiscation order (section 13 of the Proceeds of Crime Act 2002).

[See the Sentencing Council Explanatory Materials for Ancillary Orders in the Magistrates' Courts at **SG10-5** and the Crown Court Compendium, Part II Sentencing, S7; Ancillary Orders]

**STEP 7  Reasons**

Section 52 of the Sentencing Code imposes a duty to give reasons for, and explain the effect of, the sentence.

**STEP 8  Consideration for time spent on bail (tagged curfew)**

The court must consider whether to give credit for time spent on bail in accordance with section 240A of the Criminal Justice Act 2003 and section 325 of the Sentencing Code.

POSSESSION OF ARTICLES FOR USE IN FRAUDS/MAKING OR SUPPLYING ARTICLES FOR USE IN FRAUDS

*Fraud Act 2006, s.6, Fraud Act 2006, s.7*

**Effective from:** 01 October 2014

### Possession of articles for use in frauds

Fraud Act 2006 (section 6)
Triable either way
Maximum: 5 years' custody
Offence range: Band A fine–3 years' custody

### Making or supplying articles for use in frauds

Fraud Act 2006 (section 7)
Triable either way
Maximum: 10 years' custody
Offence range: Band C fine–7 years' custody

### STEP 1 Determining the offence category

The court should determine the offence category with reference to the tables below. In order to determine the category the court should assess **culpability** and **harm**.

### Culpability

The level of culpability is determined by weighing up all the factors of the case to determine the offender's role and the extent to which the offending was planned and the sophistication with which it was carried out.

| Culpability demonstrated by one or more of the following: |
| --- |
| **A — High culpability** |
| A leading role where offending is part of a group activity |
| Involvement of others through pressure, influence |
| Abuse of position of power or trust or responsibility |
| Sophisticated nature of offence/significant planning |
| Fraudulent activity conducted over sustained period of time |
| Articles deliberately designed to target victims on basis of vulnerability |
| **B — Medium culpability** |
| Other cases where characteristics for categories A or C are not present |
| A significant role where offending is part of a group activity |
| **C — Lesser culpability** |
| Performed limited function under direction |
| Involved through coercion, intimidation or exploitation |
| Not motivated by personal gain |
| Opportunistic 'one-off' offence; very little or no planning |
| Limited awareness or understanding of extent of fraudulent activity |

**Where there are characteristics present which fall under different levels of culpability, the court should balance these characteristics to reach a fair assessment of the offender's culpability.**

| Harm |
| --- |
| This guideline refers to preparatory offences where no substantive fraud has been committed. The level of harm is determined by weighing up all the factors of the case to determine the harm that would be caused if the article(s) were used to commit a substantive offence. |

| Greater harm |
| --- |
| Large number of articles created/supplied/in possession |
| Article(s) have potential to facilitate fraudulent acts affecting large number of victims |
| Article(s) have potential to facilitate fraudulent acts involving significant sums |
| Use of third party identities |
| Offender making considerable gain as result of the offence |
| **Lesser harm** |
| All other offences |

### STEP 2  Starting point and category range

Having determined the category at step one, the court should use the appropriate starting point to reach a sentence within the category range in the table below. The starting point applies to all offenders irrespective of plea or previous convictions.

**TABLE 1  Section 6 Fraud Act 2006: Possessing articles for use in fraud**
Maximum: 5 years' custody

| Harm | Culpability | | |
| --- | --- | --- | --- |
| | A | B | C |
| Greater | **Starting point** 18 months' custody | **Starting point** 36 weeks' custody | **Starting point** High level community order |
| | **Category range** 36 weeks' custody– 3 years' custody | **Category range** High level community order–2 years' custody | **Category range** Medium level community order–26 weeks' custody |
| Lesser | **Starting point** 26 weeks' custody | **Starting point** Medium level community order | **Starting point** Band B fine |
| | Category range High level community order–18 months' custody | Category range Low level community order–26 weeks' custody | Category range Band A fine–Medium level community order |

**TABLE 2  Section 7 Fraud Act 2006: Making or adapting or supplying articles for use in fraud**
Maximum: 10 years' custody

| Harm | Culpability | | |
| --- | --- | --- | --- |
| | A | B | C |
| Greater | **Starting point** 4 years 6 months' custody | **Starting point** 2 years 6 months' custody | **Starting point** 1 year's custody |
| | **Category range** 3–7 years' custody | **Category range** 18 months'–5 years' custody | **Category range** High level community order–3 years' custody |
| Lesser | **Starting point** 2 years' custody | **Starting point** 36 weeks' custody | **Starting point** Medium level community order |
| | **Category range** 26 weeks'–4 years' custody | **Category range** Low level community order–2 years' custody | **Category range** Band C fine–26 weeks' custody |

### Fines

[For the standard schedule of fines see **SG2-5.**]

### Community Orders and Custodial Sentences

[For the imposition of community orders, including the community orders table, see Imposition of Community and Custodial Sentences at **SG9-2.** For the imposition of custodial sentences see Imposition of Community and Custodial Sentences at **SG9-3.**]

Sentencing Guidelines

**Factors increasing or reducing seriousness**

The table below contains a non-exhaustive list of additional factual elements providing the context of the offence and factors relating to the offender.

Identify whether any combination of these or other relevant factors should result in an upward or downward adjustment from the starting point

**Consecutive sentences for multiple offences may be appropriate where large sums are involved.**

**Factors increasing seriousness**

*Statutory aggravating factors*

- Previous convictions, having regard to
  a) the nature of the offence to which the conviction relates and its relevance to the current offence; and
  b) the time that has elapsed since the conviction
- Offence committed whilst on bail

*Other aggravating factors*

- Steps taken to prevent the victim reporting or obtaining assistance and/or from assisting or supporting the prosecution
- Attempts to conceal/dispose of evidence
- Established evidence of community/wider impact
- Failure to comply with current court orders
- Offence committed on licence or post sentence supervision
- Offences taken into consideration
- Failure to respond to warnings about behaviour
- Offences committed across borders
- Blame wrongly placed on others

**STEPS 3 to 8**

[These are identical to those set out in the Fraud guideline at **SG26-2.**]

**SG26-4**                            REVENUE FRAUD

*Common law, Customs and Excise Management Act 1979 (sections 50, 170 and 170B),*
*Fraud Act 2006, s.1, Taxes Management Act 1970 (section 106A), Theft Act 1968, s.17,*
*Value Added Tax Act 1994 (section 72)*

**Effective from:** 01 October 2014

Fraud: Conspiracy to defraud, common law

Triable on indictment only
Maximum: 10 years' custody
Offence range: Low level community order–8 years' custody

Fraud, Fraud Act 2006 (section 1)

Triable either way
Maximum: 10 years' custody
Offence range: Low level community order–8 years' custody

False accounting, Theft Act 1968 (section 17)

Fraudulent evasion of VAT; False statement for VAT purposes; Conduct amounting to an offence, Value Added Tax Act 1994 (section 72)

Fraudulent evasion of income tax, Taxes Management Act 1970 (section 106A)

**Fraudulent evasion of excise duty; Improper importation of goods, Customs and Excise Management Act 1979 (sections 50, 170 and 170B)**
Triable either way
Maximum: 7 years' custody
Offence range: Band C fine–6 years and 6 months' custody

**Fraud: Cheat the public revenue (common law)**
Triable on indictment only
Maximum: Life imprisonment
Offence range: 3–17 years' custody

**STEP 1  Determining the offence category**

The court should determine the offence category with reference to the tables below. In order to determine the category the court should assess **culpability** and **harm**. The level of culpability is determined by weighing up all the factors of the case to determine the offender's role and the extent to which the offending was planned and the sophistication with which it was carried out.

## CULPABILITY

Demonstrated by one or more of the following:

*A – High culpability*
- A leading role where offending is part of a group activity
- Involvement of others through pressure/influence
- Abuse of position of power or trust or responsibility
- Sophisticated nature of offence/significant planning
- Fraudulent activity conducted over sustained period of time

*B – Medium culpability*
- A significant role where offending is part of a group activity
- Other cases that fall between categories A or C because:
  o  Factors are present in A and C which balance each other out **and/or**
  o  The offender's culpability falls between the factors as described in A and C

*C – Lesser culpability*
- Involved through coercion, intimidation or exploitation
- Not motivated by personal gain
- Opportunistic 'one-off' offence; very little or no planning
- Performed limited function under direction
- Limited awareness or understanding of extent of fraudulent activity

**Where there are characteristics present which fall under different levels of culpability, the court should balance these characteristics to reach a fair assessment of the offender's culpability**

Harm

| Harm – Gain/intended gain to offender or loss/intended loss to HMRC | | |
|---|---|---|
| Category 1 | £50 million or more | Starting point based on £1 million |
| Category 2 | £10 million-£50 million | Starting point based on £30 million |
| Category 3 | £2 million-£10 million | Starting point based on £5 million |
| Category 4 | £500,000-£2 million | Starting point based on £1 million |
| Category 5 | £100,000-£500,000 | Starting point based on £300,000 |
| Category 6 | £20,000-£100,000 | Starting point based on £50,000 |
| Category 7 | Less than £20,000 | Starting point based on £12,500 |

**STEP 2  Starting point and category range**

Having determined the category at step one, the court should use the appropriate starting point to reach a sentence within the category range in the table below. The starting point applies to all offenders irrespective of plea or previous convictions.

Where the value is larger or smaller than the amount on which the starting point is based, this should lead to upward or downward adjustment as appropriate.

**Where the value greatly exceeds the amount of the starting point in category 1, it may be appropriate to move outside the identified range.**

**Table 1  Section 1 Fraud Act 2006: Conspiracy to defraud (common law)**

Maximum: 10 years' custody

For offences where the value of the fraud is over £2 million refer to the corresponding category in Table 3 subject to the maximum sentence of 10 years for this offence.

| Harm | Culpability | | |
|---|---|---|---|
| | A | B | C |
| Category 4 £500,000–£2 million<br><br>Starting point based on £1 million | **Starting point** 7 years' custody<br><br>**Category range** 5–8 years' custody | **Starting point** 5 years' custody<br><br>**Category range** 3–6 years' custody | **Starting point** 3 years' custody<br><br>**Category range** 18 months'–4 years' custody |
| Category 5 £100,000–£500,000<br><br>Starting point based on £300,000 | **Starting point** 5 years' custody<br><br>**Category range** 3–6 years' custody | **Starting point** 3 years' custody<br><br>**Category range** 18 months'–4 years' custody | **Starting point** 18 months' custody<br><br>**Category range** 26 weeks'–3 years' custody |
| Category 6 £20,000–£100,000<br><br>Starting point based on £50,000 | **Starting point** 3 years' custody<br><br>**Category range** 18 months'–4 years' custody | **Starting point** 18 months' custody<br><br>**Category range** 26 weeks'–3 years' custody | **Starting point** 26 weeks' custody<br><br>**Category range** Medium level community order–1 year's custody |
| Category 7 Less than £20,000<br><br>Starting point based on £12,500 | **Starting point** 18 months' custody<br><br>**Category range** 36 weeks'–3 years' custody | **Starting point** 36 weeks' custody<br><br>**Category range** Medium level community order–18 months' custody | **Starting point** Medium level community order<br><br>**Category range** Low level community order–High level community order |

**TABLE 2  Section 17 Theft Act 1968: False Accounting**

Section 72(1) Value Added Tax Act 1994: Fraudulent evasion of VAT

Section 72(3) Valued Added Tax Act 1994: False statement for VAT purposes

Section 72(8) Value Added Tax Act 1994: Conduct amounting to an offence

Section 106(a) Taxes Management Act 1970: Fraudulent evasion of income tax

Section 170(1)(a)(i), (ii), (b), 170(2)(a), 170B Customs and Excise Management Act 1979: Fraudulent evasion of excise duty

Section 50(1)(a), (2) Customs and Excise Management Act 1979: Improper importation of goods

Maximum: 7 years' custody

**TABLE 2:  Revenue Fraud – other revenue fraud offences**

| Harm | Culpability | | |
|---|---|---|---|
| | A | B | C |
| Category 4 £500,000–£2 million<br><br>Starting point based on £1 million | **Starting point** 5 years 6 months' custody<br><br>**Category range** 4 years'–6 years 6 months' custody | **Starting point** 4 years' custody<br><br>**Category range** 2 years 6 months'–5 years' custody | **Starting point** 2 years 6 months' custody<br><br>**Category range** 15 months'–3 years 6 months' custody |

| Harm | Culpability | | |
|---|---|---|---|
| | A | B | C |
| Category 5<br>£100,000–£500,000<br><br>Starting point based on £300,000 | **Starting point**<br>4 years' custody<br><br>**Category range**<br>2 years 6 months'–5 years' custody | **Starting point**<br>2 years 6 months' custody<br><br>**Category range**<br>15 months'–3 years 6 months' custody | **Starting point**<br>15 months' custody<br><br>**Category range**<br>26 weeks'–2 years 6 months' custody |
| Category 6<br>£20,000–£100,000<br><br>Starting point based on £50,000 | **Starting point**<br>2 years 6 months' custody<br><br>**Category range**<br>15 months'–3 years 6 months' custody | **Starting point**<br>15 months' custody<br><br>**Category range**<br>High level community order–2 years 6 months' custody | **Starting point**<br>High level community order<br><br>**Category range**<br>Low level community order–36 weeks' custody |
| Category 7<br>Less than £20,000<br><br>Starting point based on £12,500 | **Starting point**<br>15 months' custody<br><br>**Category range**<br>26 weeks'–2 years 6 months' custody | **Starting point**<br>26 weeks' custody<br><br>**Category range**<br>Medium level community order–15 months' custody | **Starting point**<br>Medium level community order<br><br>**Category range**<br>Band C fine–High level community order |

## TABLE 3  Cheat the Revenue (common law)

Maximum: Life imprisonment

Where the offending is on the most serious scale, involving sums significantly higher than the starting point in category 1, sentences of 15 years and above may be appropriate depending on the role of the offender. In cases involving sums below £2 million the court should refer to Table 1.

**Table 3:**  Revenue Fraud – Cheat the revenue

| Harm | Culpability | | |
|---|---|---|---|
| | A | B | C |
| Category 1<br>£50 million or more<br><br>Starting point based on £80 million | **Starting point**<br>12 years' custody<br><br>**Category range**<br>10–17 years' custody | **Starting point**<br>8 years' custody<br><br>**Category range**<br>7–12 years' custody | **Starting point**<br>6 years' custody<br><br>**Category range**<br>4–8 years' custody |
| Category 2<br>£10 million–£50 million<br><br>Starting point based on £30 million | **Starting point**<br>10 years' custody<br><br>**Category range**<br>8–13 years' custody | **Starting point**<br>7 years' custody<br><br>**Category range**<br>5–9 years' custody | **Starting point**<br>5 years' custody<br><br>**Category range**<br>3–6 years' custody |
| Category 3<br>£2 million–£10 million<br><br>Starting point based on £5 million | **Starting point**<br>8 years' custody<br><br>**Category range**<br>6–10 years' custody | **Starting point**<br>6 years' custody<br><br>**Category range**<br>4–7 years' custody | **Starting point**<br>4 years' custody<br><br>**Category range**<br>3–5 years' custody |

## Fines

[For the standard schedule of fines see **SG2-5**.]

## Community Orders and Custodial Sentences

[For the imposition of community orders, including the community orders table, see Imposition of Community and Custodial Sentences at **SG9-2**. For the imposition of custodial sentences see Imposition of Community and Custodial Sentences at **SG9-3**.]

**Factors increasing or reducing seriousness**

The table below contains a non-exhaustive list of additional factual elements providing the context of the offence and factors relating to the offender.

Identify whether any combination of these or other relevant factors should result in any further upward or downward adjustment from the starting point.

**Consecutive sentences for multiple offences may be appropriate where large sums are involved.**

**Factors increasing seriousness**

*Statutory aggravating factors*

- Previous convictions, having regard to
   a)   the nature of the offence to which the conviction relates and its relevance to the current offence; and
   b)   the time that has elapsed since the conviction
- Offence committed whilst on bail

*Other aggravating factors*

- Involves multiple frauds
- Number of false declarations
- Attempts to conceal/dispose of evidence
- Failure to comply with current court orders
- Offence committed on licence or post sentence supervision
- Offences taken into consideration
- Failure to respond to warnings about behaviour
- Blame wrongly placed on others
- Damage to third party (for example as a result of identity theft)
- Dealing with goods with an additional health risk
- Disposing of goods to underage purchasers

**Factors reducing seriousness or reflecting personal mitigation**

- No previous convictions **or** no relevant/recent convictions
- Remorse
- Good character and/or exemplary conduct
- Little or no prospect of success
- Serious medical condition requiring urgent, intensive or long term treatment
- Age and/or lack of maturity where it affects the responsibility of the offender
- Lapse of time since apprehension where this does not arise from the conduct of the offender
- Mental disorder or learning disability
- Sole or primary carer for dependent relatives
- Offender co-operated with investigation, made early admissions and/or voluntarily reported offending
- Determination and/or demonstration of steps having been taken to address addiction or offending behaviour
- Activity originally legitimate

**STEPS 3 to 8**

[These are identical to those set out in the Fraud guideline at **SG26-2**]

**SG26-5**                                  Benefit Fraud

*Common law, Fraud Act 2006, s.1, Social Security Administration Act 1992, s.111A, Social Security Administration Act 1992, s.112, Tax Credits Act 2002, s.35, Theft Act 1968, s.17*

**Effective from:** 01 October 2014

**Dishonest representations for obtaining benefit etc**

Social Security Administration Act 1992 (section 111A)

**Tax Credit fraud**

Tax Credits Act 2002 (section 35)

**False accounting**

Theft Act 1968 (section 17)
Triable either way
Maximum: 7 years' custody
Offence range: Discharge–6 years 6 months' custody

**False representations for obtaining benefit etc**

Social Security Administration Act 1992 (section 112)
Triable summarily only
Maximum: Level 5 fine and/or 3 months' custody
Offence range: Discharge–12 weeks' custody

**Fraud by false representation, fraud by failing to disclose information, fraud by abuse of position**

Fraud Act 2006 (section 1)
Triable either way

**Conspiracy to defraud**

Common law
Triable on indictment only
Maximum: 10 years' custody
Offence range: Discharge–8 years' custody

### STEP 1   Determining the offence category

The court should determine the offence category with reference to the tables below. In order to determine the category the court should assess **culpability** and **harm**. The level of **culpability** is determined by weighing up all the factors of the case to determine the offender's role and the extent to which the offending was planned and the sophistication with which it was carried out.

### CULPABILITY

Demonstrated by one or more of the following:

*A – High culpability*

- A leading role where offending is part of a group activity
- Involvement of others through pressure/influence
- Abuse of position of power or trust or responsibility
- Sophisticated nature of offence/significant planning

*B – Medium culpability*

- Claim not fraudulent from the outset
- A significant role where offending is part of a group activity
- Other cases that fall between categories A or C because:
  - o   Factors are present in A and C which balance each other out **and/or**
  - o   The offender's culpability falls between the factors as described in A and C

*C – Lesser culpability*

- Involved through coercion, intimidation or exploitation
- Performed limited function under direction

**Where there are characteristics present which fall under different levels of culpability, the court should balance these characteristics to reach a fair assessment of the offender's culpability.**

Harm

| Harm – Amount obtained or intended to be obtained | | |
|---|---|---|
| Category 1 | £500,000–£2 million | Starting point based on £1 million |
| Category 2 | £100,000–£500,000 | Starting point based on £300,000 |
| Category 3 | £50,000–£100,000 | Starting point based on £75,000 |
| Category 4 | £10,000–£50,000 | Starting point based on £30,000 |
| Category 5 | £2,500–£10,000 | Starting point based on £5,000 |
| Category 6 | Less than £2,500 | Starting point based on £1,000 |

### STEP 2   Starting point and category range

Having determined the category at step one, the court should use the appropriate starting point to reach a sentence within the category range in the table below. The starting point applies to all offenders irrespective of plea or previous convictions.

Where the value is larger or smaller than the amount on which the starting point is based, this should lead to upward or downward adjustment as appropriate.

Where the value greatly exceeds the amount of the starting point in category 1, it may be appropriate to move outside the identified range.

**TABLE 1 Section 111A Social Security Administration Act 1992: Dishonest representations to obtain benefit etc**

Section 35 Tax Credits Act 2002: Tax Credit fraud
Section 17 Theft Act 1968: False accounting
Maximum: 7 years' custody

| | Culpability | | |
|---|---|---|---|
| **Harm** | **A** | **B** | **C** |
| **Category 1**<br>£500,000 or more<br><br>Starting point based on £1 million | **Starting point**<br>5 years 6 months' custody<br><br>**Category range**<br>4 years'–6 years 6 months' custody | **Starting point**<br>4 years' custody<br><br>**Category range**<br>2 years 6 months'– 5 years' custody | **Starting point**<br>2 years 6 months' custody<br><br>**Category range**<br>15 months'–3 years 6 months' custody |
| **Category 2**<br>£100,000–£500,000<br><br>Starting point based on £300,000 | **Starting point**<br>4 years' custody<br><br>**Category range**<br>2 years 6 months'– 5 years' custody | **Starting point**<br>2 years 6 months' custody<br><br>**Category range**<br>15 months'–3 years 6 months' custody | **Starting point**<br>1 year's custody<br><br>**Category range**<br>26 weeks'–2 years 6 months' custody |
| **Category 3**<br>£50,000–£100,000<br><br>Starting point based on £75,000 | **Starting point**<br>2 years 6 months' custody<br><br>**Category range**<br>2 years'–3 years 6 months' custody | **Starting point**<br>1 year's custody<br><br>**Category range**<br>26 weeks'–2 years 6 months' custody | **Starting point**<br>26 weeks' custody<br><br>**Category range**<br>High level community order–36 weeks' custody |
| **Category 4**<br>£10,000–£50,000<br><br>Starting point based on £30,000 | **Starting point**<br>18 months' custody<br><br>**Category range**<br>36 weeks'–2 years 6 months' custody | **Starting point**<br>36 weeks' custody<br><br>**Category range**<br>Medium level community order–21 months' custody | **Starting point**<br>Medium level community order<br><br>**Category range**<br>Low level community order–26 weeks' custody |
| **Category 5**<br>£2,500–£10,000<br><br>Starting point based on £5,000 | **Starting point**<br>36 weeks' custody<br><br>**Category range**<br>Medium level community order–18 months' custody | **Starting point**<br>Medium level community order<br><br>**Category range**<br>Low level community order–26 weeks' custody | **Starting point**<br>Low level community order<br><br>**Category range**<br>Band B fine–Medium level community order |
| **Category 6**<br>Less than £2,500<br><br>Starting point based on £1,000 | **Starting point**<br>Medium level community order<br><br>**Category range**<br>Low level community order–26 weeks' custody | **Starting point**<br>Low level community order<br><br>**Category range**<br>Band A fine–Medium level community order | **Starting point**<br>Band A fine<br><br>**Category range**<br>Discharge–Band B fine |

**TABLE 2  Section 112 Social Security Administration Act 1992: False representations for obtaining benefit etc**

Maximum: Level 5 fine and/or 3 months' custody

| Harm | Culpability | | |
|---|---|---|---|
| | A | B | C |
| **Category 5**<br><br>Above £2,500<br><br>Starting point based on £5,000 | **Starting point**<br>High level community order<br><br>**Category range**<br>Medium level community order–12 weeks' custody | **Starting point**<br>Medium level community order<br><br>**Category range**<br>Band B fine–High level community order | **Starting point**<br>Low level community order<br><br>**Category range**<br>Band A fine–Medium level community order |
| **Category 6**<br>Less than £2,500<br><br>Starting point based on £1,000 | **Starting point**<br>Medium level community order<br><br>**Category range**<br>Low level community order–High level community order | **Starting point**<br>Band B fine<br><br>**Category range**<br>Band A fine–Band C fine | **Starting point**<br>Band A fine<br><br>**Category range**<br>Discharge–Band B fine |

**TABLE 3  Section 1 Fraud Act 2006**

Conspiracy to defraud (common law)

Maximum: 10 years' custody

| Harm | Culpability | | |
|---|---|---|---|
| | A | B | C |
| **Category 1**<br>£500,000 or more<br><br>Starting point based on £1 million | **Starting point**<br>7 years' custody<br><br>**Category range**<br>5–8 years' custody | **Starting point**<br>5 years' custody<br><br>**Category range**<br>3–6 years' custody | **Starting point**<br>3 years' custody<br><br>**Category range**<br>18 months'–4 years' custody |
| **Category 2**<br>£100,000–£500,000<br><br>Starting point based on £300,000 | **Starting point**<br>5 years' custody<br><br>**Category range**<br>3–6 years' custody | **Starting point**<br>3 years' custody<br><br>**Category range**<br>18 months'–4 years' custody | **Starting point**<br>15 months' custody<br><br>**Category range**<br>26 weeks'–3 years' custody |
| **Category 3**<br>£50,000–£100,000<br><br>Starting point based on £75,000 | **Starting point**<br>3 years' custody<br><br>**Category range**<br>2 years 6 months'–4 years' custody | **Starting point**<br>15 months' custody<br><br>**Category range**<br>36 weeks'–3 years' custody | **Starting point**<br>36 weeks' custody<br><br>**Category range**<br>26 weeks'–1 year's custody |
| **Category 4**<br>£10,000–£50,000<br><br>Starting point based on £30,000 | **Starting point**<br>21 months' custody<br><br>**Category range**<br>1 year's–3 years' custody | **Starting point**<br>1 year's custody<br><br>**Category range**<br>High level community order–2 years' custody | **Starting point**<br>High level community order<br><br>**Category range**<br>Low level community order–26 weeks' custody |
| **Category 5**<br>£2,500–£10,000<br><br>Starting point based on £5,000 | **Starting point**<br>1 year's custody<br><br>**Category range**<br>High level community order–2 years' custody | **Starting point**<br>High level community order<br><br>**Category range**<br>Low level community order–26 weeks' custody | **Starting point**<br>Medium level community order<br><br>**Category range**<br>Band C fine–High level community order |

| Harm | Culpability | | |
|------|-------------|---|---|
| | **A** | **B** | **C** |
| **Category 6**<br>Less than £2,500<br><br>Starting point based on £1,000 | **Starting point**<br>High level community order<br><br>**Category range**<br>Low level community order–26 weeks' custody | **Starting point**<br>Low level community order<br><br>**Category range**<br>Band B fine–Medium level community order | **Starting point**<br>Band B fine<br><br>**Category range**<br>Discharge–Band C fine |

## Fines

[For the standard schedule of fines see SG2-5.]

## Community Orders and Custodial Sentences

[For the imposition of community orders, including the community orders table, see Imposition of Community and Custodial Sentences at SG9-2. For the imposition of custodial sentences see Imposition of Community and Custodial Sentences at SG9-3.]

## Factors increasing or reducing seriousness

The table below contains a non-exhaustive list of additional factual elements providing the context of the offence and factors relating to the offender.

Identify whether any combination of these or other relevant factors should result in any further upward or downward adjustment from the starting point.

**Consecutive sentences for multiple offences may be appropriate where large sums are involved.**

### Factors increasing seriousness

*Statutory aggravating factors*

- Previous convictions, having regard to
  a) the nature of the offence to which the conviction relates and its relevance to the current offence; and
  b) the time that has elapsed since the conviction
- Offence committed whilst on bail

*Other aggravating factors*

- Claim fraudulent from the outset
- Proceeds of fraud funded lavish lifestyle
- Length of time over which the offending was committed
- Number of false declarations
- Attempts to conceal/dispose of evidence
- Failure to comply with current court orders
- Offence committed on licence or post sentence supervision
- Offences taken into consideration
- Failure to respond to warnings about behaviour
- Blame wrongly placed on others
- Damage to third party (for example as a result of identity theft)

### Factors reducing seriousness or reflecting personal mitigation

- No previous convictions **or** no relevant/recent convictions
- Remorse
- Good character and/or exemplary conduct
- Serious medical condition requiring urgent, intensive or long term treatment
- Legitimate entitlement to benefits not claimed
- Little or no prospect of success
- Age and/or lack of maturity where it affects the responsibility of the offender
- Lapse of time since apprehension where this does not arise from the conduct of the offender
- Mental disorder or learning disability
- Sole or primary carer for dependent relatives
- Offender co-operated with investigation, made early admissions and/or voluntarily reported offending
- Determination and/or demonstration of steps having been taken to address addiction or offending behaviour
- Offender experiencing significant financial hardship or pressure at time fraud was committed due to **exceptional** circumstances

[STEPS 3 to 5 are identical to those set out at SG26-2]

### STEP 6  Confiscation, compensation and ancillary orders

Confiscation orders under the Proceeds of Crime Act 2002 may only be made by the Crown Court. The Crown Court must proceed with a view to making a confiscation order if it is asked to do so by the prosecutor or if the Crown Court believes it is appropriate for it to do so.

Where, following conviction in a magistrates' court, the prosecutor applies for the offender to be committed to the Crown Court with a view to a confiscation order being considered, the magistrates' court must commit the offender to the Crown Court to be sentenced there (section 70 of the Proceeds of Crime Act 2002). This applies to summary only and either-way offences.

Where, but for the prosecutor's application under s.70, the magistrates' court would have committed the offender for sentence to the Crown Court anyway it must say so. Otherwise the powers of sentence of the Crown Court will be limited to those of the magistrates' court.

Confiscation must be dealt with before, and taken into account when assessing, any other fine or financial order (except compensation).

(See Proceeds of Crime Act 2002 sections 6 and 13)

Where the offence has resulted in loss or damage the court must consider whether to make a compensation order. The court must give reasons if it decides not to award compensation in such cases (Sentencing Code, s.55).

The court may also consider whether to make any ancillary orders.

[See the Sentencing Council Explanatory Materials for Ancillary Orders in the Magistrates' Courts at SG10-5 and the Crown Court Compendium, Part II Sentencing, S7; Ancillary Orders]

[Steps 7 and 8 are identical to those set out at **SG26-2**]

MONEY LAUNDERING                                                    **SG26-6**

*Proceeds of Crime Act 2002, s.327, Proceeds of Crime Act 2002, s.328,*
*Proceeds of Crime Act 2002, s.329*

**Effective from:** 01 October 2014

**Concealing/disguising/converting/transferring/removing criminal property from England & Wales**
Proceeds of Crime Act 2002 (section 327)

**Entering into arrangements concerning criminal property**
Proceeds of Crime Act 2002 (section 328)

**Acquisition, use and possession of criminal property**
Proceeds of Crime Act 2002 (section 329)

Triable either way
Maximum: 14 years' custody
Offence range: Band B fine–13 years' imprisonment

### STEP 1  Determining the offence category

The court should determine the offence category with reference to the tables below. In order to determine the category the court should assess **culpability** and **harm. The level of culpability is determined by weighing up all the factors of the case to determine the offender's role and the extent to which the offending was planned and the sophistication with which it was carried out.**

Culpability

Demonstrated by one or more of the following:

*A – High culpability*
- A leading role where offending is part of a group activity
- Involvement of others through pressure/influence
- Abuse of position of power or trust or responsibility
- Sophisticated nature of offence/significant planning
- Criminal activity conducted over sustained period of time

## B – Medium culpability

- A significant role where offending is part of a group activity
- Other cases that fall between categories A or C because:
  - o Factors are present in A and C which balance each other out **and/or**
  - o The offender's culpability falls between the factors as described in A and C

## C – Lesser culpability

- Performed limited function under direction
- Not motivated by personal gain
- Opportunistic 'one-off' offence; very little or no planning
- Limited awareness or understanding of extent of criminal activity

**Where there are characteristics present which fall under different levels of culpability, the court should balance these characteristics to reach a fair assessment of the offender's culpability.**

**Harm A – Harm is initially assessed by the value of the money laundered**

| Category 1 | £10 million or more | Starting point based on £30 million |
|---|---|---|
| Category 2 | £2 million–£10 million | Starting point based on £5 million |
| Category 3 | £500,000–£2 million | Starting point based on £1 million |
| Category 4 | £100,000–£500,000 | Starting point based on £300,000 |
| Category 5 | £10,000–£100,000 | Starting point based on £50,000 |
| Category 6 | Less than £10,000 | Starting point based on £5,000 |

**Harm B**

> Money laundering is an integral component of much serious criminality. **To complete the assessment of harm, the court should take into account the level of harm associated with the underlying offence to determine whether it warrants upward adjustment of the starting point within the range, or in appropriate cases, outside the range.** Where it is possible to identify the underlying offence, regard should be given to the relevant sentencing levels for that offence.

## STEP 2  Starting point and category range

Having determined the category at step one, the court should use the appropriate starting point (as adjusted in accordance with step one above) to reach a sentence within the category range in the table below. The starting point applies to all offenders irrespective of plea or previous convictions.

Where the value is larger or smaller than the amount on which the starting point is based, this should lead to upward or downward adjustment as appropriate.

Where the value greatly exceeds the amount of the starting point in category 1, it may be appropriate to move outside the identified range.

**Section 327 Proceeds of Crime Act 2002: Concealing/disguising/converting/transferring/removing criminal property from England & Wales**

**Section 328 Proceeds of Crime Act 2002: Entering into arrangements concerning criminal property**

**Section 329 Proceeds of Crime Act 2002: Acquisition, use and possession of criminal property**

Maximum: 14 years' custody

| Harm | Culpability | | |
|---|---|---|---|
| | **A** | **B** | **C** |
| **Category 1** £10 million or more<br><br>Starting point based on £30 million | **Starting point** 10 years' custody<br><br>**Category range** 8–13 years' custody | **Starting point** 7 years' custody<br><br>**Category range** 5–10 years' custody | **Starting point** 4 years' custody<br><br>**Category range** 3–6 years' custody |
| **Category 2** £2 million–£10 million<br><br>Starting point based on £5 million | **Starting point** 8 years' custody<br><br>**Category range** 6–9 years' custody | **Starting point** 6 years' custody<br><br>**Category range** 3 years 6 months'– 7 years' custody | **Starting point** 3 years 6 months' custody<br><br>**Category range** 2–5 years' custody |

| Harm | Culpability | | |
|------|-------------|---|---|
| | **A** | **B** | **C** |
| **Category 3**<br>£500,000–£2 million<br><br>Starting point based on<br>£1 million | **Starting point**<br>7 years' custody<br><br>**Category range**<br>5–8 years' custody | **Starting point**<br>5 years' custody<br><br>**Category range**<br>3–6 years' custody | **Starting point**<br>3 years' custody<br><br>**Category range**<br>18 months'–4 years'<br>custody |
| **Category 4**<br>£100,000–£500,000<br><br>Starting point based on<br>£300,000 | **Starting point**<br>5 years' custody<br><br>**Category range**<br>3–6 years' custody | **Starting point**<br>3 years' custody<br><br>**Category range**<br>18 months'–4 years'<br>custody | **Starting point**<br>18 months' custody<br><br>**Category range**<br>26 weeks'–3 years'<br>custody |
| **Category 5**<br>£10,000–£100,000<br><br>Starting point based on<br>£50,000 | **Starting point**<br>3 years' custody<br><br>**Category range**<br>18 months'–4 years'<br>custody | **Starting point**<br>18 months' custody<br><br>**Category range**<br>26 weeks'–3 years'<br>custody | **Starting point**<br>26 weeks' custody<br><br>**Category range**<br>Medium level<br>community order–1<br>year's custody |
| **Category 6**<br>Less than £10,000<br><br>Starting point based on<br>£5,000 | **Starting point**<br>1 year's custody<br><br>**Category range**<br>26 weeks'–2 years'<br>custody | **Starting point**<br>High level community<br>order<br><br>**Category range**<br>Low level community<br>order–1 year's custody | **Starting point**<br>Low level community<br>order<br><br>**Category range**<br>Band B fine–Medium<br>level community order |

**Fines**

[For the standard schedule of fines see **SG2-5**.]

**Community Orders and Custodial Sentences**

[For the imposition of community orders, including the community orders table, see Imposition of Community and Custodial Sentences at **SG9-2**. For the imposition of custodial sentences see Imposition of Community and Custodial Sentences at **SG9-3**.]

**Factors increasing or reducing seriousness**

The table below contains a non-exhaustive list of additional factual elements providing the context of the offence and factors relating to the offender.

Identify whether any combination of these or other relevant factors should result in an upward or downward adjustment of the sentence arrived at thus far.

**Consecutive sentences for multiple offences may be appropriate where large sums are involved.**

**Factors increasing seriousness**

*Statutory aggravating factors*

- Previous convictions, having regard to
  a)  the nature of the offence to which the conviction relates and its relevance to the current offence; and
  b)  the time that has elapsed since the conviction
- Offence committed whilst on bail

*Other aggravating factors*

- Attempts to conceal/dispose of evidence
- Established evidence of community/wider impact
- Failure to comply with current court orders
- Offence committed on licence or post sentence supervision
- Offences taken into consideration
- Failure to respond to warnings about behaviour
- Offences committed across borders
- Blame wrongly placed on others
- Damage to third party for example loss of employment to legitimate employees

**Factors reducing seriousness or reflecting personal mitigation**
- No previous convictions **or** no relevant/recent convictions
- Remorse
- Little or no prospect of success
- Good character and/or exemplary conduct
- Serious medical conditions requiring urgent, intensive or long-term treatment
- Age and/or lack of maturity where it affects the responsibility of the offender
- Lapse of time since apprehension where this does not arise from the conduct of the offender
- Mental disorder or learning disability
- Sole or primary carer for dependent relatives
- Offender co-operated with investigation, made early admissions and/or voluntarily reported offending
- Determination and/or demonstration of steps having been taken to address addiction or offending behaviour
- Activity originally legitimate

**STEPS 3 to 8**
[These are identical to those set out at **SG26-2.**]

**SG26-7**                                    BRIBERY

*Bribery Act 2010, s.1, Bribery Act 2010, s.2, Bribery Act 2010, s.6*

**Effective from:** 01 October 2014

**Bribing another person**
Bribery Act 2010 (section 1)

**Being bribed**
Bribery Act 2010 (section 2)

**Bribery of foreign public officials**
Bribery Act 2010 (section 6)

Triable either way
Maximum: 10 years' custody
Offence range: Discharge–8 years' custody

**STEP 1  Determining the offence category**

The court should determine the offence category with reference to the tables below. In order to determine the category the court should assess **culpability** and **harm**.

**The level of culpability is determined by weighing up all the factors of the case to determine the offender's role and the extent to which the offending was planned and the sophistication with which it was carried out.**

**Culpability**

Demonstrated by one or more of the following;

*A – High culpability*
- A leading role where offending is part of a group activity
- Involvement of others through pressure, influence
- Abuse of position of significant power or trust or responsibility
- Intended corruption (directly or indirectly) of a senior official performing a public function
- Intended corruption (directly or indirectly) of a law enforcement officer
- Sophisticated nature of offence/significant planning
- Offending conducted over sustained period of time
- Motivated by expectation of substantial financial, commercial or political gain

*B – Medium culpability*
- A significant role where offending is part of a group activity
- Other cases that fall between categories A or C because:
  - o  Factors are present in A and C which balance each other out **and/or**
  - o  The offender's culpability falls between the factors as described in A and C

*C – Lesser culpability*
- Involved through coercion, intimidation or exploitation
- Not motivated by personal gain
- Peripheral role in organised activity
- Opportunistic 'one-off' offence; very little or no planning
- Limited awareness or understanding of extent of corrupt activity

**Where there are characteristics present which fall under different levels of culpability, the court should balance these characteristics to reach a fair assessment of the offender's culpability.**

**Harm is assessed in relation to any impact caused by the offending (whether to identifiable victims or in a wider context) and the actual or intended gain to the offender.**

**Harm**

Demonstrated by one or more of the following factors:

*Category 1*
- Serious detrimental effect on individuals (for example by provision of substandard goods or services resulting from the corrupt behaviour)
- Serious environmental impact
- Serious undermining of the proper function of local or national government, business or public services
- Substantial actual or intended financial gain to offender or another or loss caused to others

*Category 2*
- Significant detrimental effect on individuals
- Significant environmental impact
- Significant undermining of the proper function of local or national government, business or public services
- Significant actual or intended financial gain to offender or another or loss caused to others
- Risk of category 1 harm

*Category 3*
- Limited detrimental impact on individuals, the environment, government, business or public services
- Risk of category 2 harm

*Category 4*
- Risk of category 3 harm

**Risk of harm** involves consideration of both the likelihood of harm occurring and the extent of it if it does. Risk of harm is less serious than the same actual harm. Where the offence has caused risk of harm but no (or much less) actual harm, the normal approach is to move to the next category of harm down. This may not be appropriate if either the likelihood or extent of potential harm is particularly high.

**STEP 2   Starting point and category range**
Having determined the category at step one, the court should use the corresponding starting point to reach a sentence within the category range below. The starting point applies to all offenders irrespective of plea or previous convictions.

**Section 1 Bribery Act 2010: Bribing another person**

**Section 2 Bribery Act 2010: Being bribed**

**Section 6 Bribery Act 2010: Bribery of foreign public officials**

Maximum: 10 years' custody

| Harm | Culpability | | |
|------|------|------|------|
|  | **A** | **B** | **C** |
| Category 1 | **Starting point** 7 years' custody | **Starting point** 5 years' custody | **Starting point** 3 years' custody |
|  | **Category range** 5–8 years' custody | **Category range** 3–6 years' custody | **Category range** 18 months'–4 years' custody |

*Sentencing Guidelines*

| Harm | Culpability | | |
|---|---|---|---|
| | **A** | **B** | **C** |
| Category 2 | **Starting point** 5 years' custody | **Starting point** 3 years' custody | **Starting point** 18 months' custody |
| | **Category range** 3–6 years' custody | **Category range** 18 months'–4 years' custody | **Category range** 26 weeks'–3 years' custody |
| Category 3 | **Starting point** 3 years' custody | **Starting point** 18 months' custody | **Starting point** 26 weeks' custody |
| | **Category range** 18 months'–4 years' custody | **Category range** 26 weeks'–3 years' custody | **Category range** Medium level community order–1 year's custody |
| Category 4 | **Starting point** 18 months' custody | **Starting point** 26 weeks' custody | **Starting point** Medium level community order |
| | **Category range** 26 weeks'–3 years' custody | **Category range** Medium level community order–1 year's custody | **Category range** Band B fine–High level community order |

**Fines**

[For the standard schedule of fines see **SG2-5**.]

**Community Orders and Custodial Sentences**

[For the imposition of community orders, including the community orders table, see Imposition of Community and Custodial Sentences at **SG9-2**. For the imposition of custodial sentences see Imposition of Community and Custodial Sentences at **SG9-3**.]

**Additional factors affecting seriousness**

The table below contains a non-exhaustive list of additional factual elements providing the context of the offence and factors relating to the offender.

Identify whether any combination of these or other relevant factors should result in an upward or downward adjustment from the starting point.

Consecutive sentences for multiple offences may be appropriate where large sums are involved.

**Factors increasing seriousness**

*Statutory aggravating factors*

- Previous convictions, having regard to a) the nature of the offence to which the conviction relates and its relevance to the current offence; and b) the time that has elapsed since the conviction
- Offence committed whilst on bail

*Other aggravating factors*

- Steps taken to prevent victims reporting or obtaining assistance and/or from assisting or supporting the prosecution
- Attempts to conceal/dispose of evidence
- Established evidence of community/wider impact
- Failure to comply with current court orders
- Offence committed on licence or post sentence supervision
- Offences taken into consideration
- Failure to respond to warnings about behaviour
- Offences committed across borders
- Blame wrongly placed on others
- Pressure exerted on another party
- Offence committed to facilitate other criminal activity

**Factors reducing seriousness or reflecting personal mitigation**

- No previous convictions **or** no relevant/recent convictions
- Remorse

- Good character and/or exemplary conduct
- Little or no prospect of success
- Serious medical conditions requiring urgent, intensive or long-term treatment
- Age and/or lack of maturity where it affects the responsibility of the offender
- Lapse of time since apprehension where this does not arise from the conduct of the offender
- Mental disorder or learning disability
- Sole or primary carer for dependent relatives
- Offender co-operated with investigation, made early admissions and/or voluntarily reported offending

## STEPS 3 to 8

[STEPS 3 TO 5 ARE IDENTICAL TO THOSE SET OUT AT **SG26-2**]

### STEP 6   Confiscation, compensation and ancillary orders

Confiscation orders under the Proceeds of Crime Act 2002 may only be made by the Crown Court. The Crown Court must proceed with a view to making a confiscation order if it is asked to do so by the prosecutor or if the Crown Court believes it is appropriate for it to do so.

Where, following conviction in a magistrates' court, the prosecutor applies for the offender to be committed to the Crown Court with a view to a confiscation order being considered, the magistrates' court must commit the offender to the Crown Court to be sentenced there (section 70 of the Proceeds of Crime Act 2002). This applies to summary only and either-way offences.

Where, but for the prosecutor's application under s.70, the magistrates' court would have committed the offender for sentence to the Crown Court anyway it must say so. Otherwise the powers of sentence of the Crown Court will be limited to those of the magistrates' court.

Confiscation must be dealt with before, and taken into account when assessing, any other fine or financial order (except compensation).

(See Proceeds of Crime Act 2002 sections 6 and 13)

Where the offence has resulted in loss or damage the court must consider whether to make a compensation order and must give reasons if it decides not to order compensation (Sentencing Code s.55).

CORPORATE OFFENDERS: FRAUD, BRIBERY, AND MONEY LAUNDERING          **SG26-8**

*Bribery Act 2010, s.1, Bribery Act 2010, s.2, Bribery Act 2010, s.6, Bribery Act 2010, s.7,*
*Common law, Customs and Excise Management Act 1979 s.170, Fraud Act 2006, s.1,*
*Fraud Act 2006, s.6, Fraud Act 2006, s.7, Proceeds of Crime Act 2002, s.327,*
*Proceeds of Crime Act 2002, s.328, Proceeds of Crime Act 2002, s.329, Theft Act 1968, s.17,*
*Value Added Tax Act 1994 s.72*

**Effective from:** 01 October 2014

### Fraud

Conspiracy to defraud (common law)
Cheat the public revenue (common law)
Triable only on indictment
Fraud Act 2006 (sections 1, 6 and 7)
Theft Act 1968 (section 17)
Value Added Tax Act 1994 (section 72)
Customs and Excise Management Act 1979 (section 170)
Triable either way

### Bribery

Bribery Act 2010 (sections 1, 2 and 6)
Triable either way
Bribery Act 2010 (section 7)
Triable only on indictment

### Money laundering

Proceeds of Crime Act 2002 (sections 327, 328 and 329)
Triable either way
Maximum: Unlimited fine

Most cases of corporate offending in this area are likely to merit allocation for trial to the Crown Court.

Committal for sentence is mandatory if confiscation (see step two) is to be considered. (Proceeds of Crime Act 2002 section 70).

## STEP 1 Compensation

The court must consider making a compensation order requiring the offender to pay compensation for any personal injury, loss or damage resulting from the offence in such an amount as the court considers appropriate, having regard to the evidence and to the means of the offender.

Where the means of the offender are limited, priority should be given to the payment of compensation over payment of any other financial penalty.

Reasons should be given if a compensation order is not made.

(See sections 55 and 133 to 135 of the Sentencing Code)

## STEP 2 Confiscation

Confiscation orders under the Proceeds of Crime Act 2002 may only be made by the Crown Court. The Crown Court must proceed with a view to making a confiscation order if it is asked to do so by the prosecutor or if the Crown Court believes it is appropriate for it to do so.

Where, following conviction in a magistrates' court, the prosecutor applies for the offender to be committed to the Crown Court with a view to a confiscation order being considered, the magistrates' court must commit the offender to the Crown Court to be sentenced there (section 70 of the Proceeds of Crime Act 2002). This applies to summary only and either-way offences.

Where, but for the prosecutor's application under s.70, the magistrates' court would have committed the offender for sentence to the Crown Court anyway it must say so. Otherwise the powers of sentence of the Crown Court will be limited to those of the magistrates' court.

Confiscation must be dealt with before, and taken into account when assessing, any other fine or financial order (except compensation).

(See Proceeds of Crime Act 2002 sections 6 and 13)

## STEP 3 Determining the offence category

The sentencer should weigh up all the factors of the case to determine culpability. **Where there are characteristics present which fall under different categories, the court should balance these characteristics to reach a fair assessment of the offender's culpability.**

### Culpability

**Demonstrated by the offending corporation's role and motivation**
May be demonstrated by one or more of the following non-exhaustive characteristics:

*A – High culpability*
- Corporation plays a leading role in organised, planned unlawful activity (whether acting alone or with others)
- Wilful obstruction of detection (for example destruction of evidence, misleading investigators, suborning employees)
- Involving others through pressure or coercion (for example employees or suppliers)
- Targeting of vulnerable victims or a large number of victims
- Corruption of local or national government officials or ministers
- Corruption of officials performing a law enforcement role
- Abuse of dominant market position or position of trust or responsibility
- Offending committed over a sustained period of time
- Culture of wilful disregard of commission of offences by employees or agents with no effort to put effective systems in place (section 7 Bribery Act only)

*B – Medium culpability*
- Corporation plays a significant role in unlawful activity organised by others
- Activity not unlawful from the outset
- Corporation reckless in making false statement (section 72 VAT Act 1994)
- Other cases that fall between categories A or C because:
  - o Factors are present in A and C which balance each other out **and/or**
  - o The offending corporation's culpability falls between the factors as described in A and C

*C – Lesser culpability*
- Corporation plays a minor, peripheral role in unlawful activity organised by others
- Some effort made to put bribery prevention measures in place but insufficient to amount to a defence (section 7 Bribery Act only)
- Involvement through coercion, intimidation or exploitation

## Harm

Harm is represented by a financial sum calculated by reference to the table below
**Amount obtained or intended to be obtained (or loss avoided or intended to be avoided)**

### Fraud

For offences of fraud, conspiracy to defraud, cheating the Revenue and fraudulent evasion of duty or VAT, harm will normally be the actual or intended gross gain to the offender.

### Bribery

For offences under the Bribery Act the appropriate figure will normally be the gross profit from the contract obtained, retained or sought as a result of the offending. An alternative measure for offences under section 7 may be the likely cost avoided by failing to put in place appropriate measures to prevent bribery.

### Money laundering

For offences of money laundering the appropriate figure will normally be the amount laundered or, alternatively, the likely cost avoided by failing to put in place an effective anti-money laundering programme if this is higher.

### General

Where the actual or intended gain cannot be established, the appropriate measure will be the amount that the court considers was likely to be achieved in all the circumstances.

In the absence of sufficient evidence of the amount that was likely to be obtained, 10–20 per cent of the relevant revenue (for instance between 10 and 20 per cent of the worldwide revenue derived from the product or business area to which the offence relates for the period of the offending) **may** be an appropriate measure.

There may be large cases of fraud or bribery in which the true harm is to commerce or markets generally. That may justify adopting a harm figure beyond the normal measures here set out.

## STEP 4  Starting point and category range

Having determined the culpability level at step three, the court should use the table below to determine the starting point within the category range below. The starting point applies to all offenders irrespective of plea or previous convictions.

The harm figure at step three is multiplied by the relevant percentage figure representing culpability.

|  | Culpability Level | | |
|---|---|---|---|
|  | A | B | C |
| Harm figure multiplier | Starting point 300% | Starting point 200% | Starting point 100% |
|  | Category range 250% to 400% | Category range 100% to 300% | Category range 20% to 150% |

## Additional factors affecting seriousness

Having determined the appropriate starting point, the court should then consider adjustment within the category range for aggravating or mitigating features. In some cases, having considered these factors, it may be appropriate to move outside the identified category range. (See below for a **non-exhaustive** list of aggravating and mitigating factors.)

## Factors increasing seriousness

- Previous relevant convictions or subject to previous relevant civil or regulatory enforcement action
- Corporation or subsidiary set up to commit fraudulent activity
- Fraudulent activity endemic within corporation
- Attempts made to conceal misconduct
- Substantial harm (whether financial or otherwise) suffered by victims of offending or by third parties affected by offending
- Risk of harm greater than actual or intended harm (for example in banking/credit fraud)
- Substantial harm caused to integrity or confidence of markets
- Substantial harm caused to integrity of local or national governments
- Serious nature of underlying criminal activity (money laundering offences)
- Offence committed across borders or jurisdictions

**Factors reducing seriousness or reflecting mitigation**

- No previous relevant convictions or previous relevant civil or regulatory enforcement action
- Victims voluntarily reimbursed/compensated
- No actual loss to victims
- Corporation co-operated with investigation, made early admissions and/or voluntarily reported offending
- Offending committed under previous director(s)/manager(s)
- Little or no actual gain to corporation from offending

**General principles to follow in setting a fine**

The court should determine the appropriate level of fine in accordance with section 125 of the Sentencing Code, which requires that the fine must reflect the seriousness of the offence and requires the court to take into account the financial circumstances of the offender.

**Obtaining financial information**

*Companies and bodies delivering public or charitable services*

Where the offender is a company or a body which delivers a public or charitable service, it is expected to provide comprehensive accounts for the last three years, to enable the court to make an accurate assessment of its financial status. In the absence of such disclosure, or where the court is not satisfied that it has been given sufficient reliable information, the court will be entitled to draw reasonable inferences as to the offender's means from evidence it has heard and from all the circumstances of the case.

1. *For companies*: annual accounts. Particular attention should be paid to turnover; profit before tax; directors' remuneration, loan accounts and pension provision; and assets as disclosed by the balance sheet. Most companies are required to file audited accounts at Companies House. Failure to produce relevant recent accounts on request may properly lead to the conclusion that the company can pay any appropriate fine.

2. *For partnerships*: annual accounts. Particular attention should be paid to turnover; profit before tax; partners' drawings, loan accounts and pension provision; assets as above. Limited liability partnerships (LLPs) may be required to file audited accounts with Companies House. If adequate accounts are not produced on request, see paragraph 1.

3. *For local authorities, fire authorities and similar public bodies*: the Annual Revenue Budget ('ARB') is the equivalent of turnover and the best indication of the size of the defendant organisation. It is unlikely to be necessary to analyse specific expenditure or reserves unless inappropriate expenditure is suggested.

4. *For health trusts*: the independent regulator of NHS Foundation Trusts is Monitor. It publishes quarterly reports and annual figures for the financial strength and stability of trusts from which the annual income can be seen, available via www.monitor-nhsft.gov.uk. Detailed analysis of expenditure or reserves is unlikely to be called for.

5. *For charities*: it will be appropriate to inspect annual audited accounts. Detailed analysis of expenditure or reserves is unlikely to be called for unless there is a suggestion of unusual or unnecessary expenditure.

**STEP 5  Adjustment of fine**

Having arrived at a fine level, the court should consider whether there are any further factors which indicate an adjustment in the level of the fine. The court should 'step back' and consider the overall effect of its orders. The combination of orders made, compensation, confiscation and fine ought to achieve:

- the removal of all gain
- appropriate additional punishment, and
- deterrence

The fine may be adjusted to ensure that these objectives are met in a fair way. The court should consider any further factors relevant to the setting of the level of the fine to ensure that the fine is proportionate, having regard to the size and financial position of the offending organisation and the seriousness of the offence.

The fine must be substantial enough to have a real economic impact which will bring home to both management and shareholders the need to operate within the law. Whether the fine will have the effect of putting the offender out of business will be relevant; in some bad cases this may be an acceptable consequence.

In considering the ability of the offending organisation to pay any financial penalty the court can take into account the power to allow time for payment or to order that the amount be paid in instalments.

The court should consider whether the level of fine would otherwise cause unacceptable harm to third parties. In doing so the court should bear in mind that the payment of any compensation determined at step one should take priority over the payment of any fine.

The table below contains a **non-exhaustive** list of additional factual elements for the court to consider. The Court should identify whether any combination of these, or other relevant factors, should result in a proportionate increase or reduction in the level of fine.

### Factors to consider in adjusting the level of fine
- Fine fulfils the objectives of punishment, deterrence and removal of gain
- The value, worth or available means of the offender
- Fine impairs offender's ability to make restitution to victims
- Impact of fine on offender's ability to implement effective compliance programmes
- Impact of fine on employment of staff, service users, customers and local economy (but not shareholders)
- Impact of fine on performance of public or charitable function

### STEP 6   Consider any factors which would indicate a reduction, such as assistance to the prosecution
The court should take into account section 74 of the Sentencing Code (reduction in sentence for assistance to prosecution) and any other rule of law by virtue of which an offender may receive a discounted sentence in consequence of assistance given (or offered) to the prosecutor or investigator.

### STEP 7   Reduction for guilty pleas
The court should take account of any potential reduction for a guilty plea in accordance with section 73 of the Sentencing Code and the guideline for Reduction in Sentence for a Guilty Plea [**SG5-1–SG5-12**].

### STEP 8   Ancillary orders
In all cases the court must consider whether to make any ancillary orders. [See the Sentencing Council Explanatory Materials for Ancillary Orders in the Magistrates' Courts at **SG10-5** and the Crown Court Compendium, Part II Sentencing, S7; Ancillary Orders]

### STEP 9   Totality principle
If sentencing an offender for more than one offence, consider whether the total sentence is just and proportionate to the offending behaviour. See *Totality* guideline [at **SG4**].

### STEP 10   Reasons
Section 52 of the Sentencing Code imposes a duty to give reasons for, and explain the effect of, the sentence.

# PART 27   INTIMIDATORY OFFENCES

**SG27-1**

APPLICABILITY

[For the standard text on applicability see **SG0-4**.]

**SG27-2**

HARASSMENT (FEAR OF VIOLENCE)/STALKING (FEAR OF VIOLENCE)/
RACIALLY OR RELIGIOUSLY AGGRAVATED HARASSMENT (FEAR OF VIOLENCE)/
STALKING (FEAR OF VIOLENCE)

*Crime and Disorder Act 1998, s.31(1)(b), Protection from Harassment Act 1997, s.4,
Protection from Harassment Act 1997, s.4A*

**Effective from:** 01 October 2018

**Harassment (putting people in fear of violence), Protection from Harassment Act 1997, s.4**

**Stalking (involving fear of violence or serious alarm or distress), Protection from Harassment Act 1997, s.4A**

Triable either way
Maximum: 10 years' custody
Offence range: Fine–8 years' custody

Section 4 and section 4A are specified offences for the purposes of sections 266 and 279 (extended sentence for certain violent, sexual or terrorism offences) of the Sentencing Code.

**Racially or religiously aggravated stalking (involving fear of violence or serious alarm or distress), Crime and Disorder Act 1998, s.32(1)(b)**

Triable either way
Maximum: 14 years' custody

Where offence committed in a domestic context, also refer to Overarching Principles – Domestic Abuse. [see **SG6**].

For racially or religiously aggravated offences the category of the offence should be identified with reference to the factors below, and the sentence increased in accordance with the guidance at Step 3

## STEP 1  Determining the offence category

The court should determine the offence category with reference only to the factors in the tables below. In order to determine the category the court should assess **culpability** and **harm**.

The level of **culpability** is determined by weighing up all the factors of the case. **Where there are characteristics present which fall under different levels of culpability, the court should balance these characteristics to reach a fair assessment of the offender's culpability.**

**Culpability**

Demonstrated by one or more of the following:

| A | Very high culpability — the extreme nature of one or more culpability B factors or the extreme culpability indicated by a combination of culpability B factors may elevate to category A. |
|---|---|
| B | High culpability:<br>• Conduct intended to maximise fear or distress<br>• High degree of planning and/or sophisticated offence<br>• Persistent action over a prolonged period<br>• Offence motivated by, or demonstrating, hostility based on any of the following characteristics or presumed characteristics of the victim: age, sex, disability, sexual orientation or transgender identity |
| C | Medium culpability:<br>Cases that fall between categories B and D, and in particular:<br>• Conduct intended to cause some fear or distress<br>• Some planning<br>• Scope and duration of offence that falls between categories B and D |

| D | Lesser culpability: |
|---|---|
|   | • Offender's responsibility substantially reduced by mental disorder or learning disability<br>• Conduct unlikely to cause significant fear or distress<br>• Little or no planning<br>• Offence was limited in scope and duration |

## Harm

Demonstrated by one or more of the following:

| Category 1 | • Very serious distress caused to the victim<br>• Significant psychological harm caused to the victim<br>• Victim caused to make considerable changes to lifestyle to avoid contact |
|---|---|
| Category 2 | Harm that falls between categories 1 and 3, and in particular:<br>• Some distress caused to the victim<br>• Some psychological harm caused to the victim<br>• Victim caused to make some changes to lifestyle to avoid contact |
| Category 3 | • Limited distress or harm caused to the victim |

## STEP 2  Starting point and category range

Having determined the category at step one, the court should use the corresponding starting point to reach a sentence within the category range below. The starting point applies to all offenders irrespective of plea or previous convictions.

**Sentencers should consider whether to ask for psychiatric reports in order to assist in the appropriate sentencing (hospital orders, or mental health treatment requirements) of certain offenders to whom this consideration may be relevant.**

**Maximum: 10 years' custody (basic offence)**

| Harm | Culpability | | | |
|---|---|---|---|---|
|  | A | B | C | D |
| Category 1 | Starting point<br>5 years' custody | Starting point<br>2 years 6 months' custody | Starting point<br>36 weeks' custody | Starting point<br>12 weeks' custody |
|  | Category range<br>3 years 6 months'–8 years' custody | Category range<br>1–4 years' custody | Category range<br>12 weeks–1 year 6 months' custody | Category range<br>High level community order–36 weeks' custody |
| Category 2 | Starting point<br>2 years 6 months' custody | Starting point<br>36 weeks' custody | Starting point<br>12 weeks' custody | Starting point<br>High level community order |
|  | Category range<br>1–4 years' custody | Category range<br>12 weeks'–1 year 6 months' custody | Category range<br>High level community order–36 weeks' custody | Category range<br>Low level community order–12 weeks' custody |
| Category 3 | Starting point<br>36 weeks' custody | Starting point<br>12 weeks' custody | Starting point<br>High level community order | Starting point<br>Low level community order |
|  | Category range<br>12 weeks'–1 year 6 months' custody | Category range<br>High level community order–36 weeks' custody | Category range<br>Low level community order–12 weeks' custody | Category range<br>Band C fine–High level community order |

### Fines

[For the standard schedule of fines see SG2-5.]

### Community Orders and Custodial Sentences

[For the imposition of community orders, including the community orders table, see Imposition of Community and Custodial Sentences at SG9-2. For the imposition of custodial sentences see Imposition of Community and Custodial Sentences at SG9-3.]

### Factors increasing or reducing seriousness

The court should then consider any adjustment for any aggravating or mitigating factors. Below is a **non-exhaustive** list of additional factual elements providing the context of the offence and factors relating to the offender.

Identify whether any combination of these, or other relevant factors, should result in an upward or downward adjustment from the starting point.

### Factors increasing seriousness

*Statutory aggravating factors*

- Previous convictions, having regard to
  a)  the nature of the offence to which the conviction relates and its relevance to the current offence; and
  b)  the time that has elapsed since the conviction
- Offence committed whilst on bail

*Other aggravating factors*

- Using a position of trust to facilitate the offence
- Victim is particularly vulnerable (not all vulnerabilities are immediately apparent)
- Grossly violent or offensive material sent
- Impact of offence on others, particularly children
- Exploiting contact arrangements with a child to commit an offence
- Offence committed against those working in the public sector or providing a service to the public
- Failure to comply with current court orders
- Offence committed on licence or post sentence supervision
- Offences taken into consideration

### Factors reducing seriousness or reflecting personal mitigation

- No previous convictions **or** no relevant/recent convictions
- Remorse
- Good character and/or exemplary conduct
- Serious medical conditions requiring urgent, intensive or long-term treatment
- Age and/or lack of maturity
- Mental disorder or learning disability (where not taken into account at step one)
- Sole or primary carer for dependent relatives
- Determination and/or demonstration of steps having been taken to address offending behaviour

### STEP 3  Aggravated offences

### Racially or religiously aggravated harassment/stalking offences only

Having determined the category of the basic offence to identify the sentence of a non-aggravated offence, the court should now consider the level of racial or religious aggravation involved and apply an appropriate uplift to the sentence in accordance with the guidance below. The following is a list of factors which the court should consider to determine the level of aggravation. Where there are characteristics present which fall under different levels of aggravation, the court should balance these to reach a fair assessment of the level of aggravation present in the offence.

**Maximum sentence for the aggravated offence on indictment is 14 years' custody (maximum for the basic offence is 10 years' custody)**

| High Level of Racial or Religious Aggravation | Sentence Uplift |
|---|---|
| • Racial or religious aggravation was the predominant motivation for the offence. <br> • Offender was a member of, or was associated with, a group promoting hostility based on race or religion (where linked to the commission of the offence). <br> • Aggravated nature of the offence caused severe distress to the victim or the victim's family (over and above the distress already considered at step one). <br> • Aggravated nature of the offence caused serious fear and distress throughout local community or more widely. | Increase the length of custodial sentence if already considered for the basic offence or consider a custodial sentence, if not already considered for the basic offence. |
| Medium Level of Racial or Religious Aggravation | Sentence Uplift |
| • Racial or religious aggravation formed a significant proportion of the offence as a whole. <br> • Aggravated nature of the offence caused some distress to the victim or the victim's family (over and above the distress already considered at step one). <br> • Aggravated nature of the offence caused some fear and distress throughout local community or more widely. | Consider a significantly more onerous penalty of the same type or consider a more severe type of sentence than for the basic offence. |
| Low Level of Racial or Religious Aggravation | Sentence Uplift |
| • Aggravated element formed a minimal part of the offence as a whole. <br> • Aggravated nature of the offence caused minimal or no distress to the victim or the victim's family (over and above the distress already considered at step one). | Consider a more onerous penalty of the same type identified for the basic offence. |

Magistrates may find that, although the appropriate sentence for the basic offence would be within their powers, the appropriate increase for the aggravated offence would result in a sentence in excess of their powers. If so, they must commit for sentence to the Crown Court.

**The sentencer should state in open court that the offence was aggravated by reason of race or religion, and should also state what the sentence would have been without that element of aggravation.**

### STEP 4   Consider any factors which indicate a reduction for assistance to the prosecution

The court should take into account section 74 of the Sentencing Code (reduction in sentence for assistance to prosecution) and any other rule of law by virtue of which an offender may receive a discounted sentence in consequence of assistance given (or offered) to the prosecutor or investigator.

### STEP 5   Reduction for guilty pleas

The court should take account of any potential reduction for a guilty plea in accordance with section 73 of the Sentencing Code and the guideline for Reduction in Sentence for a Guilty Plea [**SG5-1–SG5-12**].

### STEP 6   Dangerousness

The court should consider whether having regard to the criteria contained in Chapter 6 of Part 10 of the Sentencing Code it would be appropriate to impose an extended sentence (sections 266 and 279).

### STEP 7   Totality principle

If sentencing an offender for more than one offence, or where the offender is already serving a sentence, consider whether the total sentence is just and proportionate to the overall offending behaviour in accordance with the *Totality* guideline. [See **SG4**]

### STEP 8   Compensation and ancillary orders

In all cases, the court must consider whether to make a compensation order and/or other ancillary orders.

*Compensation order*

The court should consider compensation orders in all cases where personal injury, loss or damage has resulted from the offence. The court must give reasons if it decides not to award compensation in such cases (Sentencing Code, s.55).

**Other ancillary orders available include:**

*Restraining order*

Where an offender is convicted of any offence, the court may make a restraining order (section 360 of the Sentencing Code).

The order may prohibit the offender from doing anything for the purpose of protecting the victim of the offence, or any other person mentioned in the order, from further conduct which amounts to harassment or will cause a fear of violence.

The order may have effect for a specified period or until further order.

[See the Sentencing Council Explanatory Materials for Ancillary Orders in the Magistrates' Courts at **SG10-5** and the Crown Court Compendium, Part II Sentencing, S7; Ancillary Orders]

**STEP 9  Reasons**

Section 52 of the Sentencing Code imposes a duty to give reasons for, and explain the effect of, the sentence.

**STEP 10  Consideration for time spent on bail (tagged curfew)**

The court must consider whether to give credit for time spent on bail in accordance with section 240A of the Criminal Justice Act 2003 and section 325 of the Sentencing Code.

**SG27-3**            HARASSMENT/STALKING/RACIALLY OR RELIGIOUSLY
                 AGGRAVATED HARASSMENT/STALKING

*Crime and Disorder Act 1998, s.31(1)(a), Protection from Harassment Act 1997, s.2, Protection from Harassment Act 1997, s.2A*

**Effective from:** 01 October 2018

**Harassment**, Protection from Harassment Act 1997, s.2
**Stalking**, Protection from Harassment Act 1997, s.2A

Triable only summarily
Maximum: 6 months' custody
Offence range: Discharge–26 weeks' custody

**Racially or religiously aggravated harassment**, Crime and Disorder Act 1998, s.32(1)(a)

**Racially or religiously aggravated stalking**, Crime and Disorder Act 1998, s.32(1)(a)

Triable either way
Maximum: 2 years' custody

Where offence committed in a domestic context, also refer to Overarching Principles: Domestic Abuse. [See **SG6**.]

For racially or religiously aggravated offences the category of the offence should be identified with reference to the factors below, and the sentence increased in accordance with the guidance at Step 3

**STEP 1  Determining the offence category**

The court should determine the offence category with reference only to the factors in the tables below. In order to determine the category the court should assess **culpability** and **harm**.

The level of **culpability** is determined by weighing up all the factors of the case. **Where there are characteristics present which fall under different levels of culpability, the court should balance these characteristics to reach a fair assessment of the offender's culpability.**

**Culpability demonstrated by one or more of the following:**

| A | **High culpability:**<br>• Conduct intended to maximise fear or distress<br>• High degree of planning and/or sophisticated offence<br>• Persistent action over a prolonged period<br>• Threat of serious violence<br>• Offence motivated by, or demonstrating hostility based on any of the following characteristics or presumed characteristics of the victim: age, sex, disability, sexual orientation or transgender identity |
|---|---|
| B | **Medium culpability:**<br>Cases that fall between categories A and C, in particular:<br>• Conduct intended to cause some fear or distress<br>• Some planning<br>• Threat of some violence<br>• Scope and duration of offence that falls between categories A and C |

| C | Lesser culpability: |
|---|---|
| | • Offender's responsibility substantially reduced by mental disorder or learning disability |
| | • Little or no planning |
| | • Offence was limited in scope and duration |

## Harm

**The level of harm is assessed by weighing up all the factors of the case.**

| Category 1 | • Very serious distress caused to the victim |
|---|---|
| | • Significant psychological harm caused to the victim |
| | • Victim caused to make considerable changes to lifestyle to avoid contact |
| Category 2 | Harm that falls between categories 1 and 3, and in particular: |
| | • Some distress caused to the victim |
| | • Some psychological harm caused to the victim |
| | • Victim caused to make some changes to lifestyle to avoid contact |
| Category 3 | • Limited distress or harm caused to the victim |

### STEP 2  Starting point and category range

Having determined the category at step one, the court should use the corresponding starting point to reach a sentence within the category range below. The starting point applies to all offenders irrespective of plea or previous convictions.

**Maximum 6 months' custody (basic offence)**

| Harm | Culpability | | |
|---|---|---|---|
| | **A** | **B** | **C** |
| Category 1 | **Starting point** 12 weeks' custody | **Starting point** High level community order | **Starting point** Medium level community order |
| | **Category range** High level community order–26 weeks' custody | **Category range** Medium level community order–16 weeks' custody | **Category range** Low level community order–12 weeks' custody |
| Category 2 | **Starting point** High level community order | **Starting point** Medium level community order | **Starting point** Low level community order |
| | **Category range** Medium level community order–16 weeks' custody | **Category range** Low level community order–12 weeks' custody | **Category range** Band B fine–Medium level community order |
| Category 3 | **Starting point** Medium level community order | **Starting point** Low level community order | **Starting point** Band B fine |
| | **Category range** Low level community order–12 weeks' custody | **Category range** Band B fine–Medium level community order | **Category range** Discharge–Low level community order |

### Fines

[For the standard schedule of fines see **SG2-5**.]

### Community Orders and Custodial Sentences

[For the imposition of community orders, including the community orders table, see Imposition of Community and Custodial Sentences at **SG9-2**. For the imposition of custodial sentences see Imposition of Community and Custodial Sentences at **SG9-3**.]

### Factors increasing or reducing seriousness

The court should then consider any adjustment for any aggravating or mitigating factors. Below is a **non-exhaustive** list of additional factual elements providing the context of the offence and factors relating to the offender.

Identify whether any combination of these, or other relevant factors, should result in an upward or downward adjustment from the starting point.

**Factors increasing seriousness**

*Statutory aggravating factors*

- Previous convictions, having regard to
  a) the nature of the offence to which the conviction relates and its relevance to the current offence; and
  b) the time that has elapsed since the conviction
- Offence committed whilst on bail

*Other aggravating factors*

- Using a position of trust to facilitate the offence
- Victim is particularly vulnerable (not all vulnerabilities are immediately apparent)
- Grossly violent or offensive material sent
- Impact of offence on others, particularly children
- Exploiting contact arrangements with a child to commit the offence
- Offence committed against those working in the public sector or providing a service to the public
- Failure to comply with current court orders
- Offence committed on licence or post sentence supervision
- Offences taken into consideration

**Factors reducing seriousness or reflecting personal mitigation**

- No previous convictions **or** no relevant/recent convictions
- Remorse
- Good character and/or exemplary conduct
- Serious medical condition requiring urgent, intensive or long-term treatment
- Age and/or lack of maturity
- Mental disorder or learning disability (where not taken into account at step one)
- Sole or primary carer for dependent relatives
- Determination and/or demonstration of steps having been taken to address offending behaviour

## STEP 3  Aggravated offences

**Racially or religiously aggravated harassment/ stalking offences only**

Having determined the category of the basic offence to identify the sentence of a non-aggravated offence, the court should now consider the level of racial or religious aggravation involved and apply an appropriate uplift to the sentence in accordance with the guidance below. The following is a list of factors which the court should consider to determine the level of aggravation. Where there are characteristics present which fall under different levels of aggravation, the court should balance these to reach a fair assessment of the level of aggravation present in the offence.

## STEP 4  Consider any factors which indicate a reduction for assistance to the prosecution

The court should take into account section 74 of the Sentencing Code (reduction in sentence for assistance to prosecution) and any other rule of law by virtue of which an offender may receive a discounted sentence in consequence of assistance given (or offered) to the prosecutor or investigator.

## STEP 5  Reduction for guilty pleas

The court should take account of any potential reduction for a guilty plea in accordance with section 73 of the Sentencing Code and the guideline for Reduction in Sentence for a Guilty Plea [**SG5-1–SG5-12**].

## STEP 6  Totality principle

If sentencing an offender for more than one offence, or where the offender is already serving a sentence, consider whether the total sentence is just and proportionate to the overall offending behaviour in accordance with the *Totality* guideline. [See **SG4**]

## STEP 7  Compensation and ancillary orders

The court should consider compensation orders in all cases where personal injury, loss or damage has resulted from the offence.

*Compensation order*

The court should consider compensation orders in all cases where personal injury, loss or damage has resulted from the offence. The court must give reasons if it decides not to award compensation in such cases.

**Other ancillary orders available include:**

*Restraining order*

Where an offender is convicted of any offence, the court may make a restraining order (section 360 of the Sentencing Code).

The order may prohibit the offender from doing anything for the purpose of protecting the victim of the offence, or any other person mentioned in the order, from further conduct which amounts to harassment or will cause a fear of violence.

The order may have effect for a specified period or until further order.

[See the Sentencing Council Explanatory Materials for Ancillary Orders in the Magistrates' Courts at **SG10-5** and the Crown Court Compendium, Part II Sentencing, S7; Ancillary Orders]

**STEP 8   Reasons**

Section 52 of the Sentencing Code imposes a duty to give reasons for, and explain the effect of, the sentence.

**STEP 9   Consideration for time spent on bail (tagged curfew)**

The court must consider whether to give credit for time spent on bail in accordance with section 240A of the Criminal Justice Act 2003 and section 325 of the Sentencing Code.

### DISCLOSING PRIVATE SEXUAL IMAGES                                              **SG27-4**

*Criminal Justice and Courts Act 2015 (section 33)*

**Effective from:** 01 October 2018

Triable either way
Maximum: 2 years' custody
Offence range: Discharge–1 year 6 months' custody

Where offence committed in a domestic context, also refer to the *Overarching principles: Domestic abuse* guideline. [See **SG6**]

**STEP 1   Determining the offence category**

The court should determine the offence category with reference only to the factors in the tables below. In order to determine the category the court should assess **culpability** and **harm**.

The level of **culpability** is determined by weighing up all the factors of the case. **Where there are characteristics present which fall under different levels of culpability, the court should balance these characteristics to reach a fair assessment of the offender's culpability.**

**Culpability demonstrated by one or more of the following:**

| A – Higher culpability | • Conduct intended to maximise distress and/or humiliation<br>• Images circulated widely/publically<br>• Significant planning and/or sophisticated offence<br>• Repeated efforts to keep images available for viewing |
|---|---|
| B – Medium culpability | • Some planning<br>• Scope and duration that falls between categories A and C<br>• All other cases that fall between categories A and C |
| C – Lesser culpability | • Offender's responsibility substantially reduced by mental disorder or learning disability<br>• Little or no planning<br>• Conduct intended to cause limited distress and/or humiliation<br>• Offence was limited in scope and duration |

**Harm**

The level of harm is assessed by weighing up all the factors of the case.

| Category 1 | • Very serious distress caused to the victim<br>• Significant psychological harm caused to the victim<br>• Offence has a considerable practical impact on the victim |
|---|---|

| Category 2 | Harm that falls between categories 1 and 3, and in particular:<br>• Some distress caused to the victim<br>• Some psychological harm caused to the victim<br>• Offence has some practical impact on the victim |
| Category 3 | • Limited distress or harm caused to the victim |

## STEP 2  Starting point and category range

Having determined the category at step one, the court should use the corresponding starting point to reach a sentence within the category range below. The starting point applies to all offenders irrespective of plea or previous convictions.

| Harm | Culpability | | |
| --- | --- | --- | --- |
| | **A** | **B** | **C** |
| Category 1 | **Starting point**<br>1 year's custody | **Starting point**<br>26 weeks' custody | **Starting point**<br>12 weeks' custody |
| | **Category range**<br>26 weeks'–1 year 6 months' custody | **Category range**<br>12 weeks'–1 year's custody | **Category range**<br>High level community order–26 weeks' custody |
| Category 2 | **Starting point**<br>26 weeks' custody | **Starting point**<br>12 weeks' custody | **Starting point**<br>High level community order |
| | **Category range**<br>12 weeks'–1 year's custody | **Category range**<br>High level community order–26 weeks' custody | **Category range**<br>Low level community order–12 weeks' custody |
| Category 3 | **Starting point**<br>12 weeks' custody | **Starting point**<br>High level community order | **Starting point**<br>Low level community order |
| | **Category range**<br>High level community order–26 weeks' custody | **Category range**<br>Low level community order–12 weeks' custody | **Category range**<br>Discharge–High level community order |

### Community Orders and Custodial Sentences

[For the imposition of community orders, including the community orders table, see Imposition of Community and Custodial Sentences at **SG9-2**. For the imposition of custodial sentences see Imposition of Community and Custodial Sentences at **SG9-3**.]

### Factors increasing or reducing seriousness

The court should then consider any adjustment for any aggravating or mitigating factors. Below is a **non-exhaustive** list of additional factual elements providing the context of the offence and factors relating to the offender.

Identify whether any combination of these, or other relevant factors, should result in an upward or downward adjustment from the starting point.

### Factors increasing seriousness

*Statutory aggravating factors*

• Previous convictions, having regard to a) the **nature** of the offence to which the conviction relates and its **relevance** to the current offence; and b) the **time** that has elapsed since the conviction
• Offence committed whilst on bail
• Offence motivated by, or demonstrating hostility based on any of the following characteristics or presumed characteristics of the victim: religion, race, disability, sexual orientation, or transgender identity

*Other aggravating factors*

• Impact of offence on others, particularly children
• Victim is particularly vulnerable (not all vulnerabilities are immediately apparent)
• Failure to comply with current court orders
• Offence committed on licence or post sentence supervision
• Offences taken into consideration

**Factors reducing seriousness or reflecting personal mitigation**

- No previous convictions **or** no relevant/recent convictions
- Offender took steps to limit circulation of images
- Remorse
- Good character and/or exemplary conduct
- Serious medical condition requiring urgent, intensive or long-term treatment
- Age and/or lack of maturity
- Mental disorder or learning disability (where not taken into account at step one)
- Sole or primary carer for dependent relatives
- Determination and/or demonstration of steps having been taken to address offending behaviour

## STEPS 3 to 8

[These are in the same terms as those applicable to Harassment: Protection from Harassment Act 1997 (section 2) and Stalking: Protection from Harassment Act 1997 (section 2A): see **SG27-3**.]

CONTROLLING OR COERCIVE BEHAVIOUR IN AN INTIMATE OR FAMILY           **SG27-5**
RELATIONSHIP

**Effective from:** 01 October 2018

*Serious Crime Act 2015 (section 76)*

Triable either way
Maximum: 5 years' custody
Offence range: Community order–4 years' custody

Where offence committed in a domestic context, also refer to the *Overarching principles: Domestic abuse* guideline. [See **SG6**]

## STEP 1   Determining the offence category

The court should determine the offence category with reference only to the factors in the tables below. In order to determine the category the court should assess **culpability** and **harm**.

The level of **culpability** is determined by weighing up all the factors of the case. **Where there are characteristics present which fall under different levels of culpability, the court should balance these characteristics to reach a fair assessment of the offender's culpability.**

**Culpability demonstrated by one or more of the following:**

| A – Higher culpability | <ul><li>Conduct intended to maximise fear or distress</li><li>Persistent action over a prolonged period</li><li>Use of multiple methods of controlling or coercive behaviour</li><li>Sophisticated offence</li><li>Conduct intended to humiliate and degrade the victim</li></ul> |
|---|---|
| B – Medium culpability | <ul><li>Conduct intended to cause some fear or distress</li><li>Scope and duration of offence that falls between categories A and C</li><li>All other cases that fall between categories A and C</li></ul> |
| C – Lesser culpability | <ul><li>Offender's responsibility substantially reduced by mental disorder or learning disability</li><li>Offence was limited in scope and duration</li></ul> |

### Harm

The level of harm is assessed by weighing up all the factors of the case.

| Category 1 | <ul><li>Fear of violence on many occasions</li><li>Very serious alarm or distress which has a substantial adverse effect on the victim</li><li>Significant psychological harm</li></ul> |
|---|---|
| Category 2 | <ul><li>Fear of violence on at least two occasions</li><li>Serious alarm or distress which has a substantial adverse effect on the victim</li></ul> |

## STEP 2   Starting point and category range

Having determined the category at step one, the court should use the corresponding starting point to reach a sentence within the category range below. The starting point applies to all offenders irrespective of plea or previous convictions.

| Harm | Culpability | | |
|---|---|---|---|
| | **A** | **B** | **C** |
| Category 1 | **Starting point**<br>2 years 6 months'<br>custody | **Starting point**<br>1 year's custody | Starting point<br>26 weeks' custody |
| | **Category range**<br>1–4 years' custody | **Category range**<br>26 weeks'–2 years 6<br>months' custody | **Category range**<br>High level community<br>order–1 year's custody |
| Category 2 | **Starting point**<br>1 year's custody | **Starting point**<br>26 weeks' custody | **Starting point**<br>Medium level<br>community order |
| | **Category range**<br>26 weeks'–2 years 6<br>months' custody | **Category range**<br>High level community<br>order–1 year's custody | **Category range**<br>Low level community<br>order–26 weeks' custody |

## Community Orders and Custodial Sentences

[For the imposition of community orders, including the community orders table, see Imposition of Community and Custodial Sentences at **SG9-2**. For the imposition of custodial sentences see Imposition of Community and Custodial Sentences at **SG9-3**.]

## Factors increasing or reducing seriousness

The court should then consider any adjustment for any aggravating or mitigating factors. Below is a **non-exhaustive** list of additional factual elements providing the context of the offence and factors relating to the offender.

Identify whether any combination of these, or other relevant factors, should result in an upward or downward adjustment from the starting point

## Factors increasing seriousness

*Statutory aggravating factors*

- Previous convictions, having regard to a) the **nature** of the offence to which the conviction relates and its **relevance** to the current offence; and b) the **time** that has elapsed since the conviction
- Offence committed whilst on bail
- Offence motivated by, or demonstrating hostility based on any of the following characteristics or presumed characteristics of the victim: religion, race, disability, sexual orientation, or transgender identity

*Other aggravating factors*

- Steps taken to prevent the victim reporting an incident
- Steps taken to prevent the victim obtaining assistance
- A proven history of violence or threats by the offender in a domestic context
- Impact of offence on others particularly children
- Exploiting contact arrangements with a child to commit the offence
- Victim is particularly vulnerable (not all vulnerabilities are immediately apparent)
- Victim left in debt, destitute or homeless
- Failure to comply with current court orders
- Offence committed on licence or post sentence supervision
- Offences taken into consideration

## Factors reducing seriousness or reflecting personal mitigation

- No previous convictions **or** no relevant/recent convictions
- Remorse
- Good character and/or exemplary conduct
- Serious medical condition requiring urgent, intensive or long-term treatment
- Age and/or lack of maturity
- Mental disorder or learning disability (where not taken into account at step one)
- Sole or primary carer for dependent relatives
- Determination and/or demonstration of steps having been taken to address offending behaviour

## STEPS 3 to 5

[These are in the same terms as those applicable to Harassment: Protection from Harassment Act 1997 (section 2) and Stalking: Protection from Harassment Act 1997 (section 2A): see **SG27-3**.]

### STEP 6  Compensation and ancillary orders

In all cases, the court must consider whether to make a compensation order and/or other ancillary orders.

### Compensation order

The court should consider compensation orders in all cases where personal injury, loss or damage has resulted from the offence. The court must give reasons if it decides not to award compensation in such cases (Sentencing Code, s.55).

### STEPS 7 and 8

[These are in the same terms as those applicable to Harassment: Protection from Harassment Act 1997 (section 2) and Stalking: Protection from Harassment Act 1997 (section 2A): see **SG27-3**.]

THREATS TO KILL                                               **SG27-6**

*Offences Against the Person Act 1861 (section 16)*

**Effective from:** 01 October 2018

Triable either way
Maximum: 10 years' custody
Offence range: Community order–7 years' custody

This is a specified offence for the purposes of sections 266 and 279 (extended sentence for certain violent, sexual or terrorism offences) of the Sentencing Code.

Where offence committed in a domestic context, also refer to the *Overarching principles: Domestic abuse* guideline [see **SG6**].

### STEP 1  Determining the offence category

The court should determine the offence category with reference only to the factors in the tables below. In order to determine the category the court should assess **culpability** and **harm**.

The level of **culpability** is determined by weighing up all the factors of the case. **Where there are characteristics present which fall under different levels of culpability, the court should balance these characteristics to reach a fair assessment of the offender's culpability.**

**Culpability demonstrated by one or more of the following:**

| A – Higher culpability | • Significant planning and/or sophisticated offence<br>• Visible weapon<br>• Threat(s) made in the presence of children<br>• History of and/or campaign of violence towards the victim<br>• Threat(s) with significant violence |
|---|---|
| B – Medium culpability | **Cases that fall between categories A and C because:**<br>• Factors are present in A and C which balance each other out and/or<br>• The offender's culpability falls between the factors described in A and C |
| C – Lesser culpability | • Offender's responsibility substantially reduced by mental disorder or learning disability<br>• Offence was limited in scope and duration |

### Harm

The level of harm is assessed by weighing up all the factors of the case.

| Category 1 | • Very serious distress caused to the victim<br>• Significant psychological harm caused to the victim<br>• Offence has a considerable practical impact on the victim |
|---|---|
| Category 2 | **Harm that falls between categories 1 and 3, and in particular:**<br>• Some distress caused to the victim<br>• Some psychological harm caused to the victim<br>• Offence has some practical impact on the victim |
| Category 3 | • Little or no distress or harm caused to the victim |

## STEP 2  Starting point and category range

Having determined the category at step one, the court should use the corresponding starting point to reach a sentence within the category range below. The starting point applies to all offenders irrespective of plea or previous convictions.

| Harm | Culpability | | |
|---|---|---|---|
| | A | B | C |
| Category 1 | **Starting point**<br>4 years' custody | **Starting point**<br>2 years' custody | **Starting point**<br>1 year's custody |
| | **Category range**<br>2–7 years' custody | **Category range**<br>1–4 years' custody | **Category range**<br>26 weeks'–2 years 6 months' custody |
| Category 2 | **Starting point**<br>2 years' custody | **Starting point**<br>1 year's custody | **Starting point**<br>26 weeks' custody |
| | **Category range**<br>1–4 years' custody | **Category range**<br>26 weeks'–2 years 6 months' custody | **Category range**<br>High level community order–1 year's custody |
| Category 3 | **Starting point**<br>1 year's custody | **Starting point**<br>26 weeks' custody | **Starting point**<br>Medium level community order |
| | **Category range**<br>26 weeks'–2 years 6 months' custody | **Category range**<br>High level community order–1 year's custody | **Category range**<br>Low level community order–High level community order |

**Community Orders and Custodial Sentences**

[For the imposition of community orders, including the community orders table, see Imposition of Community and Custodial Sentences at **SG9-2**. For the imposition of custodial sentences see Imposition of Community and Custodial Sentences at **SG9-3**.]

**Factors increasing or reducing seriousness**

The court should then consider any adjustment for any aggravating or mitigating factors. Below is a **non-exhaustive** list of additional factual elements providing the context of the offence and factors relating to the offender.

Identify whether any combination of these, or other relevant factors, should result in an upward or downward adjustment from the starting point

**Factors increasing seriousness**

*Statutory aggravating factors*

- Previous convictions, having regard to
  a) the nature of the offence to which the conviction relates and its relevance to the current offence; and
  b) the time that has elapsed since the conviction
- Offence committed whilst on bail
- Offence motivated by, or demonstrating hostility based on any of the following characteristics or presumed characteristics of the victim: religion, race, disability, sexual orientation, or transgender identity
- Offence was committed against an emergency worker acting in the exercise of functions as such a worker

*Other aggravating factors*

- Offence committed against those working in the public sector or providing a service to the public
- Impact of offence on others, particularly children
- Victim is particularly vulnerable (not all vulnerabilities are immediately apparent)
- Failure to comply with current court orders
- Offence committed on licence or post sentence supervision
- Offences taken into consideration

**Factors reducing seriousness or reflecting personal mitigation**

- No previous convictions **or** no relevant/recent convictions
- Remorse
- Good character and/or exemplary conduct

- Serious medical condition requiring urgent, intensive or long-term treatment
- Age and/or lack of maturity
- Mental disorder or learning disability (where not taken into account at step one)
- Sole or primary carer for dependent relatives
- Determination and/or demonstration of steps having been taken to address offending behaviour

**STEP 3   Consider any factors which indicate a reduction, such as assistance to the prosecution**

The court should take into account section 74 of the Sentencing Code (reduction in sentence for assistance to prosecution) and any other rule of law by virtue of which an offender may receive a discounted sentence in consequence of assistance given (or offered) to the prosecutor or investigator.

**STEP 4   Reduction for guilty pleas**

The court should take account of any potential reduction for a guilty plea in accordance with section 73 of the Sentencing Code and the guideline for Reduction in Sentence for a Guilty Plea [SG5-1–SG5-12].

**STEP 5   Dangerousness**

The court should consider whether having regard to the criteria contained in Chapter 6 of Part 10 of the Sentencing Code it would be appropriate to impose an extended sentence (sections 266 and 279).

**STEP 6   Totality principle**

If sentencing an offender for more than one offence, or where the offender is already serving a sentence, consider whether the total sentence is just and proportionate to the overall offending behaviour in accordance with the *Totality* guideline. [See **SG4**]

**STEP 7   Compensation and ancillary orders**

**Compensation order**

The court should consider compensation orders in all cases where personal injury, loss or damage has resulted from the offence.

The court must give reasons if it decides not to award compensation in such cases.

*Compensation order*

The court should consider compensation orders in all cases where personal injury, loss or damage has resulted from the offence. The court must give reasons if it decides not to award compensation in such cases.

**Other ancillary orders available include:**

*Restraining order*

Where an offender is convicted of any offence, the court may make a restraining order (section 360 of the Sentencing Code).

The order may prohibit the offender from doing anything for the purpose of protecting the victim of the offence, or any other person mentioned in the order, from further conduct which amounts to harassment or will cause a fear of violence.

The order may have effect for a specified period or until further order.

[See the Sentencing Council Explanatory Materials for Ancillary Orders in the Magistrates' Courts at **SG10-5** and the Crown Court Compendium, Part II Sentencing, S7; Ancillary Orders]

**STEP 8   Reasons**

Section 52 of the Sentencing Code imposes a duty to give reasons for, and explain the effect of, the sentence.

**STEP 9**

The court must consider whether to give credit for time spent on bail in accordance with section 240A of the Criminal Justice Act 2003 and section 325 of the Sentencing Code.

Sentencing Guidelines

# PART 28   HEALTH AND SAFETY OFFENCES

**SG28-1**

APPLICABILITY

[For the standard text on applicability see **SG0-4**.]

**SG28-2**

CORPORATE MANSLAUGHTER

*Corporate Manslaughter and Corporate Homicide Act 2007 (section 1)*

**Effective from:** 01 February 2016

Triable only on indictment
Maximum: unlimited fine
Offence range: £180,000 fine–£20 million fine

## STEP 1  Determining the seriousness of the offence

By definition, the **harm** and **culpability** involved in corporate manslaughter will be very serious. Every case will involve death and corporate fault at a high level. The court should assess factors affecting the seriousness of the offence within this context by asking:

*(a) How foreseeable was serious injury?*

Usually, the more foreseeable a serious injury was, the graver the offence. Failure to heed warnings or advice from the authorities, employees or others or to respond appropriately to 'near misses' arising in similar circumstances may be factors indicating greater foreseeability of serious injury.

*(b) How far short of the appropriate standard did the offender fall?*

Where an offender falls far short of the appropriate standard, the level of culpability is likely to be high. Lack of adherence to recognised standards in the industry or the inadequacy of training, supervision and reporting arrangements may be relevant factors to consider.

*(c) How common is this kind of breach in this organisation?*

How widespread was the non-compliance? Was it isolated in extent or, for example, indicative of a systematic departure from good practice across the offender's operations or representative of systemic failings? Widespread non-compliance is likely to indicate a more serious offence.

*(d) Was there more than one death, or a high risk of further deaths, or serious personal injury in addition to death?*

The greater the number of deaths, very serious personal injuries or people put at high risk of death, the more serious the offence.

- **Offence Category A:** Where answers to questions (a)–(d) indicate a high level of harm or culpability within the context of offence.
- **Offence Category B:** Where answers to questions (a)–(d) indicate a lower level of culpability.

## STEP 2  Starting point and category range

Having determined the offence category, the court should identify the relevant table for the offender from the tables below. There are tables for different sized organisations.

**At step two**, the court is required to focus on the organisation's annual turnover or equivalent to reach a starting point for a fine. The court should then consider further adjustment within the category range for aggravating and mitigating features.

**At step three**, the court may be required to refer to other financial factors listed below to ensure that the proposed fine is proportionate.

**Obtaining financial information**

The offender is expected to provide comprehensive accounts for the last three years, to enable the court to make an accurate assessment of its financial status. In the absence of such disclosure, or where the court is not satisfied that it has been given sufficient reliable information, the court will be entitled to draw reasonable inferences as to the offender's means from evidence it has heard and from all the circumstances of the case, **which may include the inference that the offender can pay any fine.**

Normally, only information relating to the organisation before the court will be relevant, unless it is demonstrated to the court that the resources of a linked organisation are available and can properly be taken into account.

1. **For companies:** annual accounts. Particular attention should be paid to turnover; profit before tax; directors' remuneration, loan accounts and pension provision; and assets as disclosed by the balance sheet. Most companies are required to file audited accounts at Companies House. **Failure to produce relevant recent accounts on request may properly lead to the conclusion that the company can pay any appropriate fine.**

2. **For partnerships:** annual accounts. Particular attention should be paid to turnover; profit before tax; partners' drawings, loan accounts and pension provision; assets as above. Limited liability partnerships (LLPs) may be required to file audited accounts with Companies House. **If adequate accounts are not produced on request, see paragraph 1.**

3. **For local authorities, fire authorities and similar public bodies:** the Annual Revenue Budget ('ARB') is the equivalent of turnover and the best indication of the size of the organisation. It is unlikely to be necessary to analyse specific expenditure or reserves (where relevant) unless inappropriate expenditure is suggested.

4. **For health trusts:** the independent regulator of NHS Foundation Trusts is Monitor. It publishes quarterly reports and annual figures for the financial strength and stability of trusts from which the annual income can be seen, available via **www.monitor-nhsft.gov.uk**. Detailed analysis of expenditure or reserves is unlikely to be called for.

5. **For charities:** it will be appropriate to inspect annual audited accounts. Detailed analysis of expenditure or reserves is unlikely to be called for unless there is a suggestion of unusual or unnecessary expenditure.

### Very large organisation

Where an offending organisation's turnover or equivalent very greatly exceeds the threshold for large organisations, it may be necessary to move outside the suggested range to achieve a proportionate sentence.

### Large organisation

Turnover more than £50 million

| Offence category | Starting point | Category range |
|---|---|---|
| A | £7,500,000 | £4,800,000–£20,000,000 |
| B | £5,000,000 | £3,000,000–£12,500,000 |

### Medium organisation

Turnover £10 million to £50 million

| Offence category | Starting point | Category range |
|---|---|---|
| A | £3,000,000 | £1,800,000–£7,500,000 |
| B | £2,000,000 | £1,200,000–£5,000,000 |

### Small organisation

Turnover £10 million to £50 million

| Offence category | Starting point | Category range |
|---|---|---|
| A | £800,000 | £540,000–£2,800,000 |
| B | £540,000 | £350,000–£2,000,000 |

### Micro organisation

Turnover up to £2 million

| Offence category | Starting point | Category range |
|---|---|---|
| A | £450,000 | £270,000–£800,000 |
| B | £300,000 | £180,000–£540,000 |

### Additional Factors Affecting Seriousness

The table below contains a **non-exhaustive** list of factual elements providing the context of the offence and factors relating to the offender. Identify whether any combination of these, or other relevant factors, should result in an upward or downward adjustment from the starting point.

### Factors increasing seriousness

*Statutory aggravating factors*

- Previous convictions, having regard to
  a) the nature of the offence to which the conviction relates and its relevance to the current offence; and
  b) the time that has elapsed since the conviction [see **SG2-21**]

*Other aggravating factors*

- Cost-cutting at the expense of safety
- Deliberate concealment of illegal nature of activity
- Breach of any court order
- Obstruction of justice [see **SG2-37**]
- Poor health and safety record
- Falsification of documentation or licences
- Deliberate failure to obtain or comply with relevant licences in order to avoid scrutiny by authorities
- Offender exploited vulnerable victims [see **SG2-33**]

### Factors reducing seriousness or reflecting mitigation

- No previous convictions **or** no relevant/recent convictions [see **SG2-48**]
- Evidence of steps taken to remedy problem
- High level of co-operation with the investigation, beyond that which will always be expected [see **SG2-52**]
- Good health and safety record
- Effective health and safety procedures in place
- Self-reporting, co-operation and acceptance of responsibility [see **SG2-51**]
- Other events beyond the responsibility of the offender contributed to the death (**however**, actions of victims are unlikely to be considered contributory events. Offenders are required to protect workers or others who are neglectful of their own safety in a way which is reasonably foreseeable)

### STEPS 3 and 4

The court should 'step back', review and, if necessary, adjust the initial fine based on turnover to **ensure that it fulfils the objectives of sentencing** for these offences. The court may adjust the fine upwards or downwards, including outside the range.

### STEP 3   Check whether the proposed fine based on turnover is proportionate to the overall means of the offender

*General principles to follow in setting a fine*

The court should finalise the appropriate level of fine in accordance with section 125 of the Sentencing Code, which requires that the fine must reflect the seriousness of the offence and requires the court to take into account the financial circumstances of the offender.

Fines cannot and do not attempt to value a human life in money. The fine should meet the objectives of punishment, the reduction of offending through deterrence and removal of gain derived through the commission of the offence. The fine **must be sufficiently substantial to have a real economic impact which will bring home to management and shareholders the need to achieve a safe environment for workers and members of the public affected by their activities.**

*Review of the fine based on turnover*

The court should 'step back', review and, if necessary, adjust the initial fine reached at step two to **ensure that it fulfils the general principles** set out above. The court may adjust the fine upwards or downwards including outside of the range.

The court should examine the financial circumstances of the offender in the round to assess the economic realities of the organisation and the most efficacious way of giving effect to the purposes of sentencing.

In finalising the sentence, the court should have regard to the following factors:

- The profitability of an organisation will be a relevant factor. If an organisation has a small profit margin relative to its turnover, downward adjustment may be needed. If it has a large profit margin, upward adjustment may be needed.
- Any quantifiable economic benefit derived from the offence, including through avoided costs or operating savings, should normally be added to the fine arrived at in step two. Where this is not readily available, the court may draw on information available from enforcing authorities and others about general costs of operating within the law.
- Whether the fine will have the effect of putting the offender out of business will be relevant; in some cases this may be an acceptable consequence.

In considering the ability of the offending organisation to pay any financial penalty, the court can take into account the **power to allow time for payment or to order that the amount be paid in instalments,** if necessary over a number of years.

## STEP 4  Consider other factors that may warrant adjustment of the proposed fine

The court should consider any wider impacts of the fine within the organisation or on innocent third parties; such as (but not limited to):

- impact of the fine on offender's ability to improve conditions in the organisation to comply with the law;
- impact of the fine on employment of staff, service users, customers and local economy (but not shareholders or directors).

Where the fine will fall on public or charitable bodies, the fine should normally be substantially reduced if the offending organisation is able to demonstrate the proposed fine would have a significant impact on the provision of their services.

## STEP 5  Consider any factors which indicate a reduction, such as assistance to the prosecution

The court should take into account section 74 of the Sentencing Code (reduction in sentence for assistance to prosecution) and any other rule of law by virtue of which an offender may receive a discounted sentence in consequence of assistance given (or offered) to the prosecutor or investigator.

## STEP 6  Reduction for guilty pleas

The court should take account of any potential reduction for a guilty plea in accordance with section 73 of the Sentencing Code and the guideline for Reduction in Sentence for a Guilty Plea [SG5-1–SG5-12].

## STEP 7  Compensation and ancillary orders

In all cases, the court must consider whether to make ancillary orders. These may include:

### Publicity Orders (Section 10 Corporate Manslaughter and Corporate Homicide Act 2007)

A publicity order should ordinarily be imposed in a case of corporate manslaughter. It may require publication in a specified manner of:

a)  the fact of conviction;
b)  specified particulars of the offence;
c)  the amount of any fine;
d)  the terms of any remedial order.

The object of a publicity order is deterrence and punishment.

(i)   The order should specify with particularity the matters to be published in accordance with section 10(1). Special care should be taken with the terms of the particulars of the offence committed.
(ii)  The order should normally specify the place where public announcement is to be made, and consideration should be given to indicating the size of any notice or advertisement required. It should ordinarily contain a provision designed to ensure that the conviction becomes known to shareholders in the case of companies and local people in the case of public bodies. Consideration should be given to requiring a statement on the offender's website. A newspaper announcement may be unnecessary if the proceedings are certain to receive news coverage in any event, but if an order requires publication in a newspaper it should specify the paper, the form of announcement to be made and the number of insertions required.
(iii) The prosecution should provide the court in advance of the sentencing hearing, and should serve on the offender, a draft of the form of order suggested and the judge should personally endorse the final form of the order.
(iv)  Consideration should be given to stipulating in the order that any comment placed by the offender alongside the required announcement should be separated from it and clearly identified as such.

A publicity order is part of the penalty. Any exceptional cost of compliance should be considered in fixing the fine. It is not, however, necessary to fix the fine first and then deduct the cost of compliance.

### Remediation (Section 9 Corporate Manslaughter and Corporate Homicide Act 2007)

An offender ought by the time of sentencing to have remedied any specific failings involved in the offence and if it has not, will be deprived of significant mitigation.

If, however, it has not, a remedial order should be considered if it can be made sufficiently specific to be enforceable. The prosecution is required by section 9(2) Corporate Manslaughter and Corporate Homicide Act 2007 to give notice of the form of any such order sought, which can only be made on its application. The judge should personally endorse the final form of such an order.

Sentencing Guidelines

The cost of compliance with such an order should not ordinarily be taken into account in fixing the fine; the order requires only what should already have been done.

### Compensation

Where the offence has resulted in loss or damage, the court must consider whether to make a compensation order and must give reasons if it decides not to order compensation (Sentencing Code, s.55). The assessment of compensation in cases involving death or serious injury will usually be complex and will ordinarily be covered by insurance. In the great majority of cases the court should conclude that compensation should be dealt with in the civil courts, and should say that no order is made for that reason. If compensation is awarded, priority should be given to the payment of compensation over payment of any other financial penalty where the means of the offender are limited.

Where the offender does not have sufficient means to pay the total financial penalty considered appropriate by the court, compensation and fine take priority over prosecution costs.

[See the Crown Court Compendium, Part II Sentencing, S7; Ancillary Orders]

### STEP 8   Totality principle

If sentencing an offender for more than one offence, consider whether the total sentence is just and proportionate to the offending behaviour in accordance with the *Totality* guideline [see **SG4**].

### STEP 9   Reasons

Section 52 of the Sentencing Code imposes a duty to give reasons for, and explain the effect of, the sentence.

**SG28-3**

## INDIVIDUALS: BREACH OF DUTY OF EMPLOYER TOWARDS EMPLOYEES AND NON-EMPLOYEES/BREACH OF DUTY OF SELF-EMPLOYED TO OTHERS/BREACH OF DUTY OF EMPLOYEES AT WORK/BREACH OF HEALTH AND SAFETY REGULATIONS/SECONDARY LIABILITY

*Health and Safety at Work Act 1974 (section 33(1)(a) for breaches of sections 2, 3 and 7, Health and Safety at Work Act 1974 (section 33(1)(c)), Health and Safety at Work Act 1974 (sections 36 and 37(1) for breaches of sections 2 and 3 and section 33(1)(c)*

**Effective from:** 01 February 2016

Triable either way
Maximum: 2 years' custody
Offence range: Conditional discharge–2 years' custody

### STEP 1   Determining the offence category

The court should determine the offence category using only the culpability and harm factors in the lists below.

### Culpability

Where there are factors present in the case that fall in different categories of culpability, the court should balance these factors to reach a fair assessment of the offender's culpability.

**Very high**

• Where the offender intentionally breached, or flagrantly disregarded, the law

**High**

• Actual foresight of, or wilful blindness to, risk of offending but risk nevertheless taken

**Medium**

• Offence committed through act or omission which a person exercising reasonable care would not commit

**Low**

Offence committed with little fault, for example, because:

• significant efforts were made to address the risk although they were inadequate on this occasion
• there was no warning/circumstance indicating a risk to health and safety
• failings were minor and occurred as an isolated incident

### Harm

Health and safety offences are concerned with failures to manage risks to health and safety and do not require proof that the offence caused any actual harm. **The offence is in creating a risk of harm.**

1) Use the table below to identify an initial harm category based on the **risk of harm created by the offence**. The assessment of harm requires a consideration of **both**: – the seriousness of the harm risked (A, B or C) by the offender's breach; **and** – the likelihood of that harm arising (high, medium or low).

| | Seriousness of harm risked | | |
|---|---|---|---|
| | Level A<br>• Death<br>• Physical or mental impairment resulting in lifelong dependency on third party care for basic needs<br>• Significantly reduced life expectancy | Level B<br>• Physical or mental impairment, not amounting to Level A, which has a substantial and long-term effect on the sufferer's ability to carry out normal day-to-day activities or on their ability to return to work<br>• A progressive, permanent or irreversible condition | Level C<br>• All other cases not falling within Level A or Level B |
| High likelihood of harm | Harm category 1 | Harm category 2 | Harm category 3 |
| Medium likelihood of harm | Harm category 2 | Harm category 3 | Harm category 4 |
| Low likelihood of harm | Harm category 3 | Harm category 4 | Harm category 4 (start towards bottom of range) |

2) Next, the court must consider if the following factors apply. These two factors should be considered in the round in assigning the final harm category.
   i) **Whether the offence exposed a number of workers or members of the public to the risk of harm.** The greater the number of people, the greater the risk of harm.
   ii) **Whether the offence was a significant cause of actual harm.** Consider whether the offender's breach was a **significant cause*** of actual harm and the extent to which other factors contributed to the harm caused. Actions of victims are unlikely to be considered contributory events for sentencing purposes. Offenders are required to protect workers or others who may be neglectful of their own safety in a way that is reasonably foreseeable.

If one or both of these factors apply the court must consider either moving up a harm category or substantially moving up within the category range at step two overleaf. If already in harm category 1 and wishing to move higher, move up from the starting point at step two overleaf. The court should not move up a harm category if actual harm was caused but to a lesser degree than the harm that was risked, as identified on the scale of seriousness above.

*A significant cause is one which more than minimally, negligibly or trivially contributed to the outcome. It does not have to be the sole or principal cause.*

## Obtaining financial information
[See the coverage in the General Guideline – Overarching Principles at **SG2-5**.]

## Starting points and ranges
Where the range includes a potential sentence of custody, the court should consider the custody threshold as follows:

- has the custody threshold been passed?
- if so, is it unavoidable that a custodial sentence be imposed?
- if so, can that sentence be suspended?

Where the range includes a potential sentence of a community order, the court should consider the community order threshold as follows:

- has the community order threshold been passed?

Even where the community order threshold has been passed, a fine will normally be the most appropriate disposal where the offence was committed for economic benefit. Or, if wishing to remove economic benefit derived through the commission of the offence, consider combining a fine with a community order.

| | Starting point | Category range |
|---|---|---|
| **Very high culpability** | | |
| Harm category 1 | 18 months' custody | 1–2 years' custody |
| Harm category 2 | 1 year's custody | 26 weeks'–18 months' custody |
| Harm category 3 | 26 weeks' custody | Band F fine or high level community order–1 year's custody |
| Harm category 4 | Band F fine | Band E fine–26 weeks' custody |
| **High culpability** | | |
| Harm category 1 | 1 year's custody | 26 weeks'–18 months' custody |
| Harm category 2 | 26 weeks' custody | Band F fine or high level community order–1 year's custody |
| Harm category 3 | Band F fine | Band E fine or medium level community order–26 weeks' custody |
| Harm category 4 | Band E fine | Band D fine–Band E fine |
| **Medium culpability** | | |
| Harm category 1 | 26 weeks' custody | Band F fine or high level community order–1 year's custody |
| Harm category 2 | Band F fine | Band E fine or medium level community order–26 weeks' custody |
| Harm category 3 | Band E fine | Band D fine or low level community order–Band E fine |
| Harm category 4 | Band D fine | Band C fine–Band D fine |
| **Low culpability** | | |
| Harm category 1 | Band F fine | Band E fine or medium level community order–26 weeks' custody |
| Harm category 2 | Band D fine | Band C fine–Band D fine |
| Harm category 3 | Band C fine | Band B fine–Band C fine |
| Harm category 4 | Band A fine | Conditional discharge–Band A fine |

### Fines
[For the standard schedule of fines see **SG2-5**.]

### Community Orders and Custodial Sentences
[For the imposition of community orders, including the community orders table, see Imposition of Community and Custodial Sentences at **SG9-2**. For the imposition of custodial sentences see Imposition of Community and Custodial Sentences at **SG9-3**.]

### Factors increasing or reducing seriousness

### Factors increasing seriousness

*Statutory aggravating factors*
- Previous convictions, having regard to
  a) the nature of the offence to which the conviction relates and its relevance to the current offence; and
  b) the time that has elapsed since the conviction
- Offence committed whilst on bail

*Other aggravating factors include*
- Cost-cutting at the expense of safety
- Deliberate concealment of illegal nature of activity
- Breach of any court order
- Obstruction of justice

- Poor health and safety record
- Falsification of documentation or licences
- Deliberate failure to obtain or comply with relevant licences in order to avoid scrutiny by authorities
- Targeting vulnerable victims

### Factors reducing seriousness or reflecting personal mitigation

- No previous convictions **or** no relevant/recent convictions
- Evidence of steps taken voluntarily to remedy problem
- High level of co-operation with the investigation, beyond that which will always be expected
- Good health and safety record
- Effective health and safety procedures in place
- Self-reporting, co-operation and acceptance of responsibility
- Good character and/or exemplary conduct
- Inappropriate degree of trust or responsibility
- Mental disorder or learning disability, where linked to the commission of the offence
- Serious medical conditions requiring urgent, intensive or long term treatment
- Age and/or lack of maturity where it affects the responsibility of the offender
- Sole or primary carer for dependent relatives

### STEP 3   Review any financial element of the sentence

Where the sentence is or includes a fine, the court should 'step back' and, using the factors set out below, review whether the sentence as a whole meets the objectives of sentencing for these offences. The court may increase or reduce the proposed fine reached at step two, if necessary moving outside of the range.

#### General principles to follow in setting a fine

The court should finalise the appropriate level of fine in accordance with section 125 of the Sentencing Code, which requires that the fine must reflect the seriousness of the offence and that the court must take into account the financial circumstances of the offender.

The level of fine should reflect the extent to which the offender fell below the required standard. The fine should meet, in a fair and proportionate way, the objectives of punishment, deterrence and the removal of gain derived through the commission of the offence; it should not be cheaper to offend than to take the appropriate precautions.

#### Review of the fine

Where the court proposes to impose a fine it should 'step back', review and, if necessary, adjust the initial fine reached at step two to **ensure that it fulfils the general principles** set out above.

Any quantifiable economic benefit derived from the offence, including through avoided costs or operating savings, should normally be added to the fine arrived at in step two. Where this is not readily available, the court may draw on information available from enforcing authorities and others about the general costs of operating within the law.

In finalising the sentence, the court should have regard to the following factors relating to the wider impacts of the fine on innocent third parties; such as (but not limited to):

- impact of the fine on offender's ability to comply with the law;
- impact of the fine on employment of staff, service users, customers and local economy.

### STEP 4   Consider any factors which indicate a reduction, such as assistance to the prosecution

The court should take into account section 74 of the Sentencing Code (reduction in sentence for assistance to prosecution) and any other rule of law by virtue of which an offender may receive a discounted sentence in consequence of assistance given (or offered) to the prosecutor or investigator.

### STEP 5   Reduction for guilty pleas

The court should take account of any potential reduction for a guilty plea in accordance with section 73 of the Sentencing Code and the guideline for Reduction in Sentence for a Guilty Plea [**SG5-1–SG5-12**].

### STEP 6   Compensation and ancillary orders

In all cases, the court must consider whether to make ancillary orders. These may include:

#### Disqualification of director

An offender may be disqualified from being a director of a company in accordance with section 2 of the Company Directors Disqualification Act 1986. The maximum period of disqualification is 15 years (Crown Court) or 5 years (magistrates' court).

*Remediation*

Under section 42(1) of the Health and Safety at Work Act 1974, the court may impose a remedial order in addition to or instead of imposing any punishment on the offender.

An offender ought by the time of sentencing to have remedied any specific failings involved in the offence and if not, will be deprived of significant mitigation.

The cost of compliance with such an order should not ordinarily be taken into account in fixing the fine; the order requires only what should already have been done.

*Forfeiture*

Where the offence involves the acquisition or possession of an explosive article or substance, section 42(4) enables the court to order forfeiture of the explosive.

*Compensation*

Where the offence has resulted in personal injury, loss or damage, the court must consider whether to make a compensation order and must give reasons if it decides not to order compensation (Sentencing Code, s.55). The assessment of compensation in cases involving death or serious injury will usually be complex and will ordinarily be covered by insurance. In the great majority of cases the court should conclude that compensation should be dealt with in the civil courts, and should say that no order is made for that reason. If compensation is awarded, priority should be given to the payment of compensation over payment of any other financial penalty where the means of the offender are limited. Where the offender does not have sufficient means to pay the total financial penalty considered appropriate by the court, compensation and fine take priority over prosecution costs.
[See the Sentencing Council Explanatory Materials for Ancillary Orders in the Magistrates' Courts and the Crown Court Compendium, Part II Sentencing, S7; Ancillary Orders.]

### STEP 7  Totality principle

If sentencing an offender for more than one offence, or where the offender is already serving a sentence, consider whether the total sentence is just and proportionate to the offending behaviour in accordance with the *Totality* guideline [see **SG4**].

### STEP 8  Reasons

Section 52 of the Sentencing Code imposes a duty to give reasons for, and explain the effect of, the sentence.

### STEP 9  Consideration for time spent on bail (tagged curfew)

The court must consider whether to give credit for time spent on bail in accordance with section 240A of the Criminal Justice Act 2003 and section 325 of the Sentencing Code.

**SG28-4**         INDIVIDUALS: BREACH OF FOOD SAFETY AND FOOD HYGIENE REGULATIONS

*Food Hygiene (Wales) Regulations 2006 (regulation 17(1)), Food Safety and Hygiene (England) Regulations 2013 (regulation 19(1)), The General Food Regulations 2004 (regulation 4)*

**Effective from:** 01 February 2016

Triable either way
Maximum:
- when tried on indictment, unlimited fine and/or 2 years' custody
- when tried summarily: unlimited fine
For offences under The General Food Regulations, the maximum when tried summarily is an unlimited fine **and/or 6 months' custody**

Offence range: Conditional discharge – 18 months' custody

### STEP 1  Determining the offence category

The court should determine the offence category using only the culpability and harm factors in the lists below. Where an offence does not fall squarely into a category, individual factors may require a degree of weighting to make an overall assessment.

**Culpability**
*Very high*
Where the offender intentionally breached, or flagrantly disregarded, the law

*High*
Actual foresight of, or wilful blindness to, risk of offending but risk nevertheless taken

*Medium*

Offence committed through act or omission which a person exercising reasonable care would not commit

*Low*

Offence committed with little fault, for example, because:

- significant efforts were made to address the risk although they were inadequate on this occasion
- there was no warning/circumstance indicating a risk to food safety
- failings were minor and occurred as an isolated incident

## Harm

The list below contains factors relating to both actual harm and risk of harm. Dealing with a risk of harm involves consideration of both the likelihood of harm occurring and the extent of it if it does.

*Category 1*

- Serious adverse effect(s) on individual(s) and/or having a widespread impact
- High risk of an adverse effect on individual(s) – including where supply was to persons that are vulnerable

*Category 2*

- Adverse effect on individual(s) (not amounting to Category 1)
- Medium risk of an adverse effect on individual(s) or low risk of serious adverse effect
- Regulator and/or legitimate industry substantially undermined by offender's activities
- Relevant authorities unable to trace products in order to investigate risks to health, or are otherwise inhibited in identifying or addressing risks to health
- Consumer misled regarding food's compliance with religious or personal beliefs

*Category 3*

- Low risk of an adverse effect on individual(s)
- Public misled about the specific food consumed, but little or no risk of actual adverse effect on individual(s)

## STEP 2 Starting point and category range

Having determined the category, the court should refer to the starting points in the table below to reach a sentence within the category range. The court should then consider further adjustment within the category range for aggravating and mitigating features, set out below.

### Obtaining financial information

*Starting points and ranges*

Where the range includes a potential sentence of custody, the court should consider the custody threshold as follows:

- has the custody threshold been passed?
- if so, is it unavoidable that a custodial sentence be imposed?
- if so, can that sentence be suspended?

Where the range includes a potential sentence of a community order, the court should consider the community order threshold as follows:

- has the community order threshold been passed?

**Even where the community order threshold has been passed, a fine will normally be the most appropriate disposal.** Or, consider, if wishing to remove economic benefit derived through the commission of the offence, combining a fine with a community order.

|  | Starting point | Range |
|---|---|---|
| **Very high culpability** | | |
| Harm category 1 | 9 months' custody | Band F fine–18 months' custody |
| Harm category 2 | Band F fine | Band E fine–9 months' custody |
| Harm category 3 | Band E fine | Band D fine–26 weeks' custody |
| **High culpability** | | |
| Harm category 1 | Band F fine | Band E fine–9 months' custody |
| Harm category 2 | Band E fine | Band D fine–26 weeks' custody |

|                    | Starting point | Range |
|--------------------|----------------|-------|
| Harm category 3    | Band D fine    | Band C fine–Band E fine |
| **Medium culpability** |            |       |
| Harm category 1    | Band E fine    | Band D fine–Band F fine |
| Harm category 2    | Band D fine    | Band C fine–Band E fine |
| Harm category 3    | Band C fine    | Band B fine–Band C fine |
| **Low culpability** |               |       |
| Harm category 1    | Band C fine    | Band B fine–Band C fine |
| Harm category 2    | Band B fine    | Band A fine–Band B fine |
| Harm category 3    | Band A fine    | Conditional discharge–Band A fine |

### Fines

[For the standard schedule of fines see **SG2-5**.]

### Custodial Sentences

[For the imposition of custodial sentences see Imposition of Community and Custodial Sentences at **SG9-3**.]

**Note on statutory maxima on summary conviction.** For offences under *regulation 19(1) Food Safety and Hygiene (England) Regulations 2013* and *regulation 17(1) Food Hygiene (Wales) Regulations 2006*, the maximum sentence magistrates may pass on summary conviction is an unlimited fine; therefore for these offences, magistrates may not pass a community order. *Regulation 4* of *The General Food Regulations 2004* is in force in Wales but not in England. For offences under *regulation 4*, the maximum sentence on summary conviction is 6 months' custody and/or an unlimited fine.

### Factors increasing or reducing seriousness

You will see below a **non-exhaustive** list of factual elements providing the context of the offence and factors relating to the offender. Identify whether any combination of these, or other relevant factors, should result in an upward or downward adjustment from the starting point. **In particular, relevant recent convictions are likely to result in a substantial upward adjustment.** In some cases, having considered these factors, it may be appropriate to move outside the identified category range.

### Factors increasing seriousness

*Statutory aggravating factors*
- Previous convictions, having regard to a) the nature of the offence to which the conviction relates and its relevance to the current offence; and b) the time that has elapsed since the conviction
- Offence committed whilst on bail

*Other aggravating factors include:*
- Motivated by financial gain
- Deliberate concealment of illegal nature of activity
- Established evidence of wider/community impact
- Breach of any court order
- Obstruction of justice
- Poor food safety or hygiene record
- Refusal of free advice or training

### Factors reducing seriousness or reflecting personal mitigation

- No previous convictions **or** no relevant/recent convictions
- Steps voluntarily taken to remedy problem
- High level of co-operation with the investigation, beyond that which will always be expected
- Good food safety/hygiene record
- Self-reporting, co-operation and acceptance of responsibility
- Good character and/or exemplary conduct
- Mental disorder or learning disability, where linked to the commission of the offence
- Serious medical conditions requiring urgent, intensive or long-term treatment
- Age and/or lack of maturity where it affects the responsibility of the offender
- Sole or primary carer for dependent relatives

## STEP 3 to STEP 6

[These are the same as the Steps for the guideline on Individuals: Breach of Duty of Employer Towards Employees and Non-Employees at **SG28-3**.]

## STEP 6   Compensation and ancillary orders

### Ancillary orders

In all cases the court must consider whether to make ancillary orders. These may include:

#### Hygiene Prohibition Order

These orders are available under both the Food Safety and Hygiene (England) Regulations 2013 and the Food Hygiene (Wales) Regulations 2006.

If the court is satisfied that the health risk condition in Regulation 7(2) is fulfilled it **shall** impose the appropriate prohibition order in Regulation 7(3).

Where a food business operator is convicted of an offence under the Regulations and the court thinks it proper to do so in all the circumstances of the case, the court **may** impose a prohibition on the operator pursuant to Regulation 7(4). An order under Regulation 7(4) is not limited to cases where there is an immediate risk to public health; the court might conclude that there is such a risk of some future breach of the regulations or the facts of any particular offence or combination of offences may alone justify the imposition of a Hygiene Prohibition Order. In deciding whether to impose an order the court will want to consider the history of convictions or a failure to heed warnings or advice in deciding whether an order is proportionate to the facts of the case. Deterrence may also be an important consideration.

#### Disqualification of director

An offender may be disqualified from being a director of a company in accordance with section 2 of the Company Directors Disqualification Act 1986. The maximum period of disqualification is 15 years (Crown Court) or 5 years (magistrates' court).

#### Compensation

Where the offence results in personal injury, loss or damage the court must consider whether to make a compensation order and must give reasons if it decides not to order compensation (Sentencing Code, s.55). If compensation is awarded, priority should be given to the payment of compensation over payment of any other financial penalty where the means of the offender are limited. Where the offender does not have sufficient means to pay the total financial penalty considered appropriate by the court, compensation and fine take priority over prosecution costs

- Ancillary orders – Magistrates' Court [see **SG10-5**]
- Ancillary orders – Crown Court Compendium, Part II Sentencing, S7

## STEP 7   Totality principle

If sentencing an offender for more than one offence, or where the offender is already serving a sentence, consider whether the total sentence is just and proportionate to the offending behaviour in accordance with *Totality* guideline [see **SG4**].

Where the offender is convicted of more than one offence where a fine is appropriate, the court should consider the Totality guideline.

The total fine is inevitably cumulative.

The court should determine the fine for each individual offence based on the seriousness of the offence and taking into account the circumstances of the case including the financial circumstances of the offender so far as they are known, or appear, to the court.

The court should add up the fines for each offence and consider if they are just and proportionate.

If the aggregate total is not just and proportionate the court should consider how to reach a just and proportionate fine. There are a number of ways in which this can be achieved.

For example:

- where an offender is to be fined for two or more offences that arose out of the same incident or where there are multiple offences of a repetitive kind, especially when committed against the same person, it will often be appropriate to impose for the most serious offence a fine which reflects the totality of the offending where this can be achieved within the maximum penalty for that offence. No separate penalty should be imposed for the other offences;

- where an offender is to be fined for two or more offences that arose out of different incidents, it will often be appropriate to impose a separate fine for each of the offences. The court should add up the fines for each offence and consider if they are just and proportionate. If the aggregate amount is not just and proportionate the court should consider whether all of the fines can be proportionately reduced. Separate fines should then be passed.

Where separate fines are passed, the court must be careful to ensure that there is no double-counting.

Where compensation is being ordered, that will need to be attributed to the relevant offence as will any necessary ancillary orders.

### STEP 8　Reasons

Section 52 of the Sentencing Code imposes a duty to give reasons for, and explain the effect of, the sentence.

### STEP 9　Consideration for time spent on bail (tagged curfew)

The court must consider whether to give credit for time spent on bail in accordance with section 240A of the Criminal Justice Act 2003 and section 325 of the Sentencing Code.

## SG28-5　ORGANISATIONS: BREACH OF DUTY OF EMPLOYER TOWARDS EMPLOYEES AND NON-EMPLOYEES/BREACH OF DUTY OF SELF-EMPLOYED TO OTHERS/ BREACH OF HEALTH AND SAFETY REGULATIONS

*Health and Safety at Work Act 1974 (section 33(1)(a) for breaches of sections 2, 3 and 7, Health and Safety at Work Act 1974 (section 33(1)(c)),*

**Effective from:** 01 February 2016

Triable either way
Maximum:
- when tried on indictment: unlimited fine
- when tried summarily: unlimited fine
Offence range: £50 fine – £10 million fine

### STEP 1　Determining the offence category

The court should determine the offence category using only the culpability and harm factors in the lists below.

### Culpability

Where there are factors present in the case that fall in different categories of culpability, the court should balance these factors to reach a fair assessment of the offender's culpability.

*Very high*
- Deliberate breach of or flagrant disregard for the law

*High*
- Offender fell far short of the appropriate standard for example, by:
  - failing to put in place measures that are recognised standards in the industry;
  - ignoring concerns raised by employees or others;
  - failing to make appropriate changes following prior incident(s) exposing risks to health and safety;
  - allowing breaches to subsist over a long period of time.
- Serious and/or systemic failure within the organisation to address risks to health and safety

*Medium*
- Offender fell short of the appropriate standard in a manner that falls between descriptions in 'high' and 'low' culpability categories
- Systems were in place but these were not sufficiently adhered to or implemented

*Low*
- Offender did not fall far short of the appropriate standard; for example, because:
  - significant efforts were made to address the risk although they were inadequate on this occasion;
  - there was no warning/circumstance indicating a risk to health and safety
- Failings were minor and occurred as an isolated incident

## Harm

Health and safety offences are concerned with failures to manage risks to health and safety and do not require proof that the offence caused any actual harm. **The offence is in creating a risk of harm.**

1) Use the table below to identify an initial harm category based on the **risk of harm created by the offence**. The assessment of harm requires a consideration of **both**: – the seriousness of the harm risked (A, B or C) by the offender's breach; **and** – the likelihood of that harm arising (high, medium or low).

| Seriousness of harm risked | | | |
|---|---|---|---|
| | **Level A**<br>• Death<br>• Physical or mental impairment resulting in lifelong dependency on third party care for basic needs<br>• Significantly reduced life expectancy | **Level B**<br>• Physical or mental impairment, not amounting to Level A, which has a substantial and long-term effect on the sufferer's ability to carry out normal day-to-day activities or on their ability to return to work<br>• A progressive, permanent or irreversible condition | **Level C**<br>• All other cases not falling within Level A or Level B |
| **High likelihood of harm** | Harm category 1 | Harm category 2 | Harm category 3 |
| **Medium likelihood of harm** | Harm category 2 | Harm category 3 | Harm category 4 |
| **Low likelihood of harm** | Harm category 3 | Harm category 4 | Harm category 4 (start towards bottom of range) |

2) **Next, the court must consider if the following factors apply. These two factors should be considered in the round in assigning the final harm category.**
   i) **Whether the offence exposed a number of workers or members of the public to the risk of harm.** The greater the number of people, the greater the risk of harm.
   ii) **Whether the offence was a significant cause of actual harm.** Consider whether the offender's breach was a **significant cause\*** of actual harm and the extent to which other factors contributed to the harm caused. Actions of victims are unlikely to be considered contributory events for sentencing purposes. Offenders are required to protect workers or others who may be neglectful of their own safety in a way which is reasonably foreseeable.

If one or both of these factors apply the court must consider either moving up a harm category or substantially moving up within the category range at step two overleaf. If already in harm category 1 and wishing to move higher, move up from the starting point at step two on the following pages. The court should not move up a harm category if actual harm was caused but to a lesser degree than the harm that was risked, as identified on the scale of seriousness above.

*\* A significant cause is one which more than minimally, negligibly or trivially contributed to the outcome. It does not have to be the sole or principal cause.*

## STEP 2  Starting point and category range

Having determined the offence category, the court should identify the relevant table for the offender on the following pages. There are tables for different sized organisations.

**At step two**, the court is required to focus on the organisation's annual turnover or equivalent to reach a starting point for a fine. The court should then consider further adjustment within the category range for aggravating and mitigating features.

**At step three**, the court may be required to refer to other financial factors listed below to ensure that the proposed fine is proportionate.

*Obtaining financial information*

[See the coverage in the General Guideline – Overarching Principles at **SG2-5**.]

Sentencing Guidelines

*Very large organisation*

Where an offending organisation's turnover or equivalent very greatly exceeds the threshold for large organisations, it may be necessary to move outside the suggested range to achieve a proportionate sentence.

**Large – Turnover or equivalent: £50 million and over**

| Large | Starting Point | Range |
| --- | --- | --- |
| **Very high culpability** | | |
| Harm category 1 | £4,000,000 | £2,600,000–£10,000,000 |
| Harm category 2 | £2,000,000 | £1,000,000–£5,250,000 |
| Harm category 3 | £1,000,000 | £500,000–£2,700,000 |
| Harm category 4 | £500,000 | £240,000–£1,300,000 |
| **High culpability** | | |
| Harm category 1 | £2,400,000 | £1,500,000–£6,000,000 |
| Harm category 2 | £1,100,000 | £550,000–£2,900,000 |
| Harm category 3 | £540,000 | £250,000–£1,450,000 |
| Harm category 4 | £240,000 | £120,000–£700,000 |
| **Medium culpability** | | |
| Harm category 1 | £1,300,000 | £800,000–£3,250,000 |
| Harm category 2 | £600,000 | £300,000–£1,500,000 |
| Harm category 3 | £300,000 | £130,000–£750,000 |
| Harm category 4 | £130,000 | £50,000–£350,000 |
| **Low culpability** | | |
| Harm category 1 | £300,000 | £180,000–£700,000 |
| Harm category 2 | £100,000 | £35,000–£250,000 |
| Harm category 3 | £35,000 | £10,000–£140,000 |
| Harm category 4 | £10,000 | £3,000–£60,000 |

**Medium – Turnover or equivalent: between £10 million and £50 million**

| Medium | Starting Point | Range |
| --- | --- | --- |
| **Very high culpability** | | |
| Harm category 1 | £1,600,000 | £1,000,000–£4,000,000 |
| Harm category 2 | £800,000 | £400,000–£2,000,000 |
| Harm category 3 | £400,000 | £180,000–£1,000,000 |
| Harm category 4 | £190,000 | £90,000–£500,000 |
| **High culpability** | | |
| Harm category 1 | £950,000 | £600,000–£2,500,000 |
| Harm category 2 | £450,000 | £220,000–£1,200,000 |
| Harm category 3 | £210,000 | £100,000–£550,000 |
| Harm category 4 | £100,000 | £50,000–£250,000 |
| **Medium culpability** | | |
| Harm category 1 | £540,000 | £300,000–£1,300,000 |
| Harm category 2 | £240,000 | £100,000–£600,000 |
| Harm category 3 | £100,000 | £50,000–£300,000 |
| Harm category 4 | £50,000 | £20,000–£130,000 |
| **Low culpability** | | |
| Harm category 1 | £130,000 | £75,000–£300,000 |

| Medium | Starting Point | Range |
|---|---|---|
| Harm category 2 | £40,000 | £14,000–£100,000 |
| Harm category 3 | £14,000 | £3,000–£60,000 |
| Harm category 4 | £3,000 | £1,000–£10,000 |

**Small – Turnover or equivalent: between £2 million and £10 million**

| Small | Starting Point | Range |
|---|---|---|
| Very high culpability | | |
| Harm category 1 | £450,000 | £300,000–£1,600,000 |
| Harm category 2 | £200,000 | £100,000–£800,000 |
| Harm category 3 | £100,000 | £50,000–£400,000 |
| Harm category 4 | £50,000 | £20,000–£190,000 |
| High culpability | | |
| Harm category 1 | £250,000 | £170,000–£1,000,000 |
| Harm category 2 | £100,000 | £50,000–£450,000 |
| Harm category 3 | £54,000 | £25,000–£210,000 |
| Harm category 4 | £24,000 | £12,000–£100,000 |
| Medium culpability | | |
| Harm category 1 | £160,000 | £100,000–£600,000 |
| Harm category 2 | £54,000 | £25,000–£230,000 |
| Harm category 3 | £24,000 | £12,000–£100,000 |
| Harm category 4 | £12,000 | £4,000–£50,000 |
| Low culpability | | |
| Harm category 1 | £45,000 | £25,000–£130,000 |
| Harm category 2 | £9,000 | £3,000–£40,000 |
| Harm category 3 | £3,000 | £700–£14,000 |
| Harm category 4 | £700 | £100–£5,000 |

**Micro – Turnover or equivalent: not more than £2 million**

| Micro | Starting Point | Range |
|---|---|---|
| Very high culpability | | |
| Harm category 1 | £250,000 | £150,000–£450,000 |
| Harm category 2 | £100,000 | £50,000–£200,000 |
| Harm category 3 | £50,000 | £25,000–£100,000 |
| Harm category 4 | £24,000 | £12,000–£50,000 |
| High culpability | | |
| Harm category 1 | £160,000 | £100,000–£250,000 |
| Harm category 2 | £54,000 | £30,000–£110,000 |
| Harm category 3 | £30,000 | £12,000–£54,000 |
| Harm category 4 | £12,000 | £5,000–£21,000 |
| Medium culpability | | |
| Harm category 1 | £100,000 | £60,000–£160,000 |
| Harm category 2 | £30,000 | £14,000–£70,000 |
| Harm category 3 | £14,000 | £6,000–£25,000 |
| Harm category 4 | £6,000 | £2,000–£12,000 |

| Micro | Starting Point | Range |
|---|---|---|
| Low culpability | | |
| Harm category 1 | £30,000 | £18,000–£60,000 |
| Harm category 2 | £5,000 | £1,000–£20,000 |
| Harm category 3 | £1,200 | £200–£7,000 |
| Harm category 4 | £200 | £50–£2,000 |

**Factors increasing or reducing seriousness**

The table below contains a **non-exhaustive** list of factual elements providing the context of the offence and factors relating to the offender. Identify whether any combination of these, or other relevant factors, should result in an upward or downward adjustment from the starting point. **In particular, relevant recent convictions are likely to result in a substantial upward adjustment.** In some cases, having considered these factors, it may be appropriate to move outside the identified category range.

**Factors increasing seriousness**

*Statutory aggravating factors*

- Previous convictions, having regard to
  a) the nature of the offence to which the conviction relates and its relevance to the current offence; and
  b) the time that has elapsed since the conviction

*Other aggravating factors include*

- Cost-cutting at the expense of safety
- Deliberate concealment of illegal nature of activity
- Breach of any court order
- Obstruction of justice
- Poor health and safety record
- Falsification of documentation or licences
- Deliberate failure to obtain or comply with relevant licences in order to avoid scrutiny by authorities
- Targeting vulnerable victims

**Factors reducing seriousness or reflecting mitigation**

- No previous convictions **or** no relevant/recent convictions
- Evidence of steps taken voluntarily to remedy problem
- High level of co-operation with the investigation, beyond that which will always be expected
- Good health and safety record
- Effective health and safety procedures in place
- Self-reporting, co-operation and acceptance of responsibility

**STEPS 3 and 4**

The court should 'step back', review and, if necessary, adjust the initial fine based on turnover to ensure that it fulfils the objectives of sentencing for these offences. The court may adjust the fine upwards or downwards, including outside the range.

**STEP 3  Check whether the proposed fine based on turnover is proportionate to the overall means of the offender**

*General principles to follow in setting a fine*

The court should finalise the appropriate level of fine in accordance with section 125 of the Sentencing Code, which requires that the fine must reflect the seriousness of the offence and that the court must take into account the financial circumstances of the offender.

The level of fine should reflect the extent to which the offender fell below the required standard. The fine should meet, in a fair and proportionate way, the objectives of punishment, deterrence and the removal of gain derived through the commission of the offence; it should not be cheaper to offend than to take the appropriate precautions.

The fine must be **sufficiently substantial to have a real economic impact which will bring home to both management and shareholders the need to comply with health and safety legislation.**

*Review of the fine based on turnover*

The court should 'step back', review and, if necessary, adjust the initial fine reached at step two to **ensure that it fulfils the general principles** set out above. The court may adjust the fine upwards or downwards including outside of the range.

The court should examine the financial circumstances of the offender in the round to assess the economic realities of the organisation and the most efficacious way of giving effect to the purposes of sentencing.

In finalising the sentence, the court should have regard to the following factors:

- The profitability of an organisation will be relevant. If an organisation has a small profit margin relative to its turnover, downward adjustment may be needed. If it has a large profit margin, upward adjustment may be needed.
- Any quantifiable economic benefit derived from the offence, including through avoided costs or operating savings, should normally be added to the fine arrived at in step two. Where this is not readily available, the court may draw on information available from enforcing authorities and others about the general costs of operating within the law.
- Whether the fine will have the effect of putting the offender out of business will be relevant; in some bad cases this may be an acceptable consequence.

In considering the ability of the offending organisation to pay any financial penalty, the court can take into account the **power to allow time for payment or to order that the amount be paid in instalments**, if necessary over a number of years.

### STEP 4  Consider other factors that may warrant adjustment of the proposed fine

The court should consider any wider impacts of the fine within the organisation or on innocent third parties; such as (but not limited to):

- the fine impairs offender's ability to make restitution to victims;
- impact of the fine on offender's ability to improve conditions in the organisation to comply with the law;
- impact of the fine on employment of staff, service users, customers and local economy (but not shareholders or directors).

Where the fine will fall on public or charitable bodies, the fine should normally be substantially reduced if the offending organisation is able to demonstrate the proposed fine would have a significant impact on the provision of its services.

### STEP 5  Consider any factors which indicate a reduction, such as assistance to the prosecution

The court should take into account section 74 of the Sentencing Code (reduction in sentence for assistance to prosecution) and any other rule of law by virtue of which an offender may receive a discounted sentence in consequence of assistance given (or offered) to the prosecutor or investigator.

### STEP 6  Reduction for guilty pleas

The court should take account of any potential reduction for a guilty plea in accordance with section 73 of the Sentencing Code and the guideline for Reduction in Sentence for a Guilty Plea [SG5-1–SG5-12].

### STEP 7  Compensation and ancillary orders

In all cases, the court must consider whether to make ancillary orders. These may include:

*Remediation*

Under section 42(1) of the Health and Safety at Work Act 1974, the court may impose a remedial order in addition to or instead of imposing any punishment on the offender.

An offender ought by the time of sentencing to have remedied any specific failings involved in the offence and if it has not, will be deprived of significant mitigation.

The cost of compliance with such an order should not ordinarily be taken into account in fixing the fine; the order requires only what should already have been done.

*Forfeiture*

Where the offence involves the acquisition or possession of an explosive article or substance, section 42(4) enables the court to order forfeiture of the explosive.

*Compensation*

Where the offence has resulted in personal injury, loss or damage, the court must consider whether to make a compensation order and must give reasons if it decides not to order compensation (Sentencing Code, s.55). The assessment of compensation in cases involving death or serious injury will usually be complex and will ordinarily be covered by insurance. In the great majority of cases the court should conclude that compensation should be dealt with in the civil courts, and should say that no order is made for that reason. If compensation is awarded, priority should be given to the payment of compensation over payment of any other financial penalty where the means of the offender are limited. Where the offender does not have sufficient means to pay the total financial penalty considered appropriate by the court, compensation and fine take priority over prosecution costs.

[See the Sentencing Council Explanatory Materials for Ancillary Orders in the Magistrates' Courts at **SG10-5** and the Crown Court Compendium, Part II Sentencing, S7; Ancillary Orders]

### STEP 8 Totality principle

If sentencing an offender for more than one offence, consider whether the total sentence is just and proportionate to the offending behaviour in accordance with the *Totality* guideline. [See **SG4**.]

### STEP 9 Reasons

Section 52 of the Sentencing Code imposes a duty to give reasons for, and explain the effect of, the sentence.

**SG28-6**    ORGANISATIONS: BREACH OF FOOD SAFETY AND FOOD HYGIENE REGULATIONS

*Food Hygiene (Wales) Regulations 2006 (regulation 17(1)), Food Safety and Hygiene (England) Regulations 2013 (regulation 19(1)), The General Food Regulations 2004 (regulation 4)*

**Effective from:** 01 February 2016

Triable either way
Maximum: when tried on indictment: unlimited fine when tried summarily: unlimited fine
Offence range: £100 fine–£3 million fine

### STEP 1 Determining the offence category

The court should determine the offence category using only the culpability and harm factors in the lists below. Where an offence does not fall squarely into a category, individual factors may require a **degree of weighting** to make an overall assessment.

### Culpability

*Very high*

• Deliberate breach of or flagrant disregard for the law

*High*

• Offender fell far short of the appropriate standard; for example, by:
  • failing to put in place measures that are recognised standards in the industry
  • ignoring concerns raised by regulators, employees or others
  • allowing breaches to subsist over a long period of time
• Serious and/or systemic failure within the organisation to address risks to health and safety

*Medium*

• Offender fell short of the appropriate standard in a manner that falls between descriptions in 'high' and 'low' culpability categories
• Systems were in place but these were not sufficiently adhered to or implemented

*Low*

• Offender did not fall far short of the appropriate standard; for example, because:
  • significant efforts were made to secure food safety although they were inadequate on this occasion
  • there was no warning/circumstance indicating a risk to food safety
• Failings were minor and occurred as an isolated incident

### Harm

The list below contains factors relating to both actual harm and risk of harm. Dealing with a **risk of harm** involves consideration of both the likelihood of harm occurring and the extent of it if it does.

*Category 1*

• Serious adverse effect(s) on individual(s) and/or having a widespread impact
• High risk of an adverse effect on individual(s) including where supply was to groups that are vulnerable

*Category 2*

• Adverse effect on individual(s) (not amounting to Category 1)
• Medium risk of an adverse effect on individual(s) or low risk of serious adverse effect
• Regulator and/or legitimate industry substantially undermined by offender's activities
• Relevant authorities unable to trace products in order to investigate risks to health, or are otherwise inhibited in identifying or addressing risks to health
• Consumer misled regarding food's compliance with religious or personal beliefs

*Category 3*

- Low risk of an adverse effect on individual(s)
- Public misled about the specific food consumed, but little or no risk of actual adverse effect on individual(s)

### STEP 2   Starting point and category range

Having determined the offence category, the court should identify the relevant table for the offender on the following pages. There are tables for different sized organisations.

**At step two**, the court is required to focus on the organisation's annual turnover or equivalent to reach a starting point for a fine. The court should then consider further adjustment within the category range for aggravating and mitigating features.

**At step three**, the court may be required to refer to other financial factors listed below to ensure that the proposed fine is proportionate.

*Obtaining financial information*

[See the coverage in the General Guideline – Overarching Principles at SG2-5.]

*Very large organisation*

Where an offending organisation's turnover or equivalent very greatly exceeds the threshold for large organisations, it may be necessary to move outside the suggested range to achieve a proportionate sentence.

Large – Turnover or equivalent: £50 million and over

| Large | Starting Point | Range |
|---|---|---|
| **Very high culpability** | | |
| Harm category 1 | £1,200,000 | £500,000–£3,000,000 |
| Harm category 2 | £500,000 | £200,000–£1,400,000 |
| Harm category 3 | £200,000 | £90,000–£500,000 |
| **High culpability** | | |
| Harm category 1 | £500,000 | £200,000–£1,400,000 |
| Harm category 2 | £230,000 | £90,000–£600,000 |
| Harm category 3 | £90,000 | £50,000–£240,000 |
| **Medium culpability** | | |
| Harm category 1 | £200,000 | £80,000–£500,000 |
| Harm category 2 | £90,000 | £35,000–£220,000 |
| Harm category 3 | £35,000 | £20,000–£100,000 |
| **Low culpability** | | |
| Harm category 1 | £35,000 | £18,000–£90,000 |
| Harm category 2 | £18,000 | £9,000–£50,000 |
| Harm category 3 | £10,000 | £6,000–£25,000 |

Medium – Turnover or equivalent: between £10 million and £50 million

| Medium | Starting Point | Range |
|---|---|---|
| **Very high culpability** | | |
| Harm category 1 | £450,000 | £200,000–£1,200,000 |
| Harm category 2 | £200,000 | £80,000–£500,000 |
| Harm category 3 | £80,000 | £40,000–£200,000 |
| **High culpability** | | |
| Harm category 1 | £200,000 | £90,000–£500,000 |
| Harm category 2 | £90,000 | £35,000–£220,000 |
| Harm category 3 | £35,000 | £18,000–£90,000 |

| Medium | Starting Point | Range |
|---|---|---|
| **Medium culpability** | | |
| Harm category 1 | £80,000 | £35,000–£190,000 |
| Harm category 2 | £35,000 | £14,000–£90,000 |
| Harm category 3 | £14,000 | £7,000–£35,000 |
| **Low culpability** | | |
| Harm category 1 | £12,000 | £7,000–£35,000 |
| Harm category 2 | £7,000 | £3,500–£18,000 |
| Harm category 3 | £3,500 | £2,000–£10,000 |

**Small – Turnover or equivalent: between £2 million and £10 million**

| Small | Starting Point | Range |
|---|---|---|
| **Very high culpability** | | |
| Harm category 1 | £120,000 | £50,000–£450,000 |
| Harm category 2 | £50,000 | £18,000–£200,000 |
| Harm category 3 | £18,000 | £9,000–£80,000 |
| **High culpability** | | |
| Harm category 1 | £50,000 | £22,000–£200,000 |
| Harm category 2 | £24,000 | £8,000–£90,000 |
| Harm category 3 | £9,000 | £4,000–£35,000 |
| **Medium culpability** | | |
| Harm category 1 | £18,000 | £7,000–£70,000 |
| Harm category 2 | £8,000 | £3,000–£35,000 |
| Harm category 3 | £3,000 | £1,500–£12,000 |
| **Low culpability** | | |
| Harm category 1 | £3,000 | £1,400–£12,000 |
| Harm category 2 | £1,400 | £700–£7,000 |
| Harm category 3 | £700 | £300–£3,000 |

**Micro – Turnover or equivalent: not more than £2 million**

| Micro | Starting Point | Range |
|---|---|---|
| **Very high culpability** | | |
| Harm category 1 | £60,000 | £25,000–£120,000 |
| Harm category 2 | £25,000 | £10,000–£50,000 |
| Harm category 3 | £10,000 | £5,000–£18,000 |
| **High culpability** | | |
| Harm category 1 | £25,000 | £10,000–£50,000 |
| Harm category 2 | £12,000 | £4,000–£22,000 |
| Harm category 3 | £4,000 | £2,000–£9,000 |
| **Medium culpability** | | |
| Harm category 1 | £10,000 | £3,000–£18,000 |
| Harm category 2 | £4,000 | £1,400–£8,000 |
| Harm category 3 | £1,400 | £700–£3,000 |

| Micro | Starting Point | Range |
|---|---|---|
| Low culpability | | |
| Harm category 1 | £1,200 | £500–£3,000 |
| Harm category 2 | £500 | £200–£1,400 |
| Harm category 3 | £200 | £100–£700 |

**Factors increasing or reducing seriousness**

You will see below a **non-exhaustive** list of factual elements providing the context of the offence and factors relating to the offender. Identify whether any combination of these, or other relevant factors, should result in an upward or downward adjustment from the starting point. **In particular, relevant recent convictions are likely to result in a substantial upward adjustment.** In some cases, having considered these factors, it may be appropriate to move outside the identified category range.

**Factors increasing seriousness**

*Statutory aggravating factors*

- Previous convictions, having regard to a) the nature of the offence to which the conviction relates and its relevance to the current offence; and b) the time that has elapsed since the conviction

*Other aggravating factors include*

- Motivated by financial gain
- Deliberate concealment of illegal nature of activity
- Established evidence of wider/community impact
- Breach of any court order
- Obstruction of justice
- Poor food safety or hygiene record
- Refusal of free advice or training

**Factors reducing seriousness or reflecting mitigation**

- No previous convictions or no relevant/recent convictions
- Steps taken voluntarily to remedy problem
- High level of co-operation with the investigation, beyond that which will always be expected
- Good food safety/hygiene record
- Self-reporting, co-operation and acceptance of responsibility

**STEPS 3 and 4**

The court should 'step back', review and, if necessary, adjust the initial fine based on turnover to **ensure that it fulfils the objectives of sentencing** for these offences. The court may adjust the fine upwards or downwards, including outside the range. Full regard should be given to the totality principle at step eight where multiple offences are involved.

**STEP 3   Check whether the proposed fine based on turnover is proportionate to the overall means of the offender**

*General principles to follow in setting a fine*

The court should finalise the fine in accordance with section 125 of the Sentencing Code, which requires that the fine must reflect the seriousness of the offence and that the court must take into account the financial circumstances of the offender.

The level of fine should reflect the extent to which the offender fell below the required standard. **The fine should meet, in a fair and proportionate way, the objectives of punishment, deterrence and the removal of gain derived through the commission of the offence;** it should not be cheaper to offend than to take the appropriate precautions.

The fine must be **sufficiently substantial to have a real economic impact which will bring home to both management and shareholders the need to operate within the law.**

*Review of the fine based on turnover*

The court should 'step back', review and, if necessary, adjust the initial fine reached at step two to **ensure that it fulfils the general principles** set out above. The court may adjust the fine upwards or downwards including outside of the range.

The court should examine the financial circumstances of the offender in the round to enable the court to assess the economic realities of the company and the most efficacious way of giving effect to the purposes of sentencing.

Sentencing Guidelines

In finalising the sentence, the court should have regard to the following factors:

- The profitability of an organisation will be relevant. If an organisation has a small profit margin relative to its turnover, downward adjustment may be needed. If it has a large profit margin, upward adjustment may be needed.
- Any quantifiable economic benefit derived from the offence, including through avoided costs or operating savings, should normally be added to the total fine arrived at in step two. Where this is not readily available, the court may draw on information available from enforcing authorities and others about the general costs of operating within the law.
- Whether the fine will have the effect of putting the offender out of business will be relevant; in some bad cases this may be an acceptable consequence.

In considering the ability of the offending organisation to pay any financial penalty, the court can take into account the **power to allow time for payment or to order that the amount be paid in instalments**, if necessary over a number of years.

### STEP 4 Consider other factors that may warrant adjustment of the proposed fine

Where the fine will fall on public or charitable bodies, the fine should normally be substantially reduced if the offending organisation is able to demonstrate the proposed fine would have a significant impact on the provision of their services.

The court should consider any wider impacts of the fine within the organisation or on innocent third parties; such as (but not limited to):

- impact of the fine on offender's ability to improve conditions in the organisation to comply with the law;
- impact of the fine on employment of staff, service users, customers and local economy (but not shareholders or directors).

### STEP 5 Consider any factors which indicate a reduction, such as assistance to the prosecution

The court should take into account section 74 of the Sentencing Code (reduction in sentence for assistance to prosecution) and any other rule of law by virtue of which an offender may receive a discounted sentence in consequence of assistance given (or offered) to the prosecutor or investigator.

### STEP 6 Reduction for guilty pleas

The court should take account of any potential reduction for a guilty plea in accordance with section 73 of the Sentencing Code and the guideline for Reduction in Sentence for a Guilty Plea [**SG5-1–SG5-12**].

### STEP 7 Compensation and ancillary orders

*Hygiene Prohibition Order*

These orders are available under both the Food Safety and Hygiene (England) Regulations 2013 and the Food Hygiene (Wales) Regulations 2006.

If the court is satisfied that the health risk condition in Regulation 7(2) is fulfilled it **shall** impose the appropriate prohibition order in Regulation 7(3).

Where a food business operator is convicted of an offence under the Regulations and the court thinks it is proper to do so in all the circumstances of the case, the court **may** impose a prohibition on the operator pursuant to Regulation 7(4). An order under Regulation 7(4) is not limited to cases where there is an immediate risk to public health; the court might conclude that there is such a risk of some future breach of the regulations or the facts of any particular offence or combination of offences may alone justify the imposition of a Hygiene Prohibition Order. In deciding whether to impose an order, the court will want to consider the history of convictions or a failure to heed warnings or advice in deciding whether an order is proportionate to the facts of the case. Deterrence may also be an important consideration.

*Compensation*

Where the offence results in personal injury, loss or damage the court must consider whether to make a compensation order and must give reasons if it decides not to order compensation (Sentencing Code, s.55).

If compensation is awarded, priority should be given to the payment of compensation over payment of any other financial penalty where the means of the offender are limited. Where the offender does not have sufficient means to pay the total financial penalty considered appropriate by the court, compensation and fine take priority over prosecution costs.

- Ancillary orders – Magistrates' Court [see **SG10-5**]
- Ancillary orders – Crown Court Compendium, Part II Sentencing, S7

## STEP 8  Totality principle

If sentencing an offender for more than one offence, consider whether the total sentence is just and proportionate to the offending behaviour in accordance with the *Totality* guideline [see **SG4**] from which the following guidance is taken:

The total fine is inevitably cumulative.

The court should determine the fine for each individual offence based on the seriousness of the offence and taking into account the circumstances of the case including the financial circumstances of the offender so far as they are known, or appear, to the court.

The court should add up the fines for each offence and consider if they are just and proportionate.

If the aggregate total is not just and proportionate the court should consider how to reach a just and proportionate fine. There are a number of ways in which this can be achieved.

*For example:*

- where an offender is to be fined for two or more offences that arose out of the same incident or where there are multiple offences of a repetitive kind, especially when committed against the same person, it will often be appropriate to impose for the most serious offence a fine which reflects the totality of the offending where this can be achieved within the maximum penalty for that offence. No separate penalty should be imposed for the other offences;
- where an offender is to be fined for two or more offences that arose out of different incidents, it will often be appropriate to impose a separate fine for each of the offences. The court should add up the fines for each offence and consider if they are just and proportionate. If the aggregate amount is not just and proportionate the court should consider whether all of the fines can be proportionately reduced. Separate fines should then be passed.

Where separate fines are passed, the court must be careful to ensure that there is no double-counting.

Where compensation is being ordered, that will need to be attributed to the relevant offence as will any necessary ancillary orders.

## STEP 9  Reasons

Section 52 of the Sentencing Code imposes a duty to give reasons for, and explain the effect of, the sentence.

# PART 29    PUBLIC ORDER OFFENCES

**SG29-1**

APPLICABILITY

[For the standard text on applicability see **SG0-4**.]

**SG29-2**

AFFRAY

*Public Order Act 1986, s.3*

**Effective from:** 01 January 2020

Triable either way
Maximum: 3 years' custody
Offence range: Fine–2 years 9 months' custody

This is a specified offence for the purposes of sections 266 and 279 (extended sentence for certain violent, sexual or terrorism offences) of the Sentencing Code.

## STEP 1 Determining the offence category

The court should determine the offence category with reference **only** to the factors listed in the tables below. In order to determine the category the court should assess **culpability** and **harm.**

**Culpability demonstrated by one or more of the following:**

| A | • Targeting of individual(s) by a group |
|---|---|
|   | • Use of a weapon to inflict violence |
|   | • Use of serious or sustained violence |
|   | • Intention to cause fear of very serious violence |
| B | • Threat of violence by any weapon (whether or not produced) |
|   | • Threat or use of violence falling between levels in categories A and C |
| C | • Threat or use of minimal violence |
|   | • The offender acted in self-defence or in fear of violence (where not amounting to a defence) |

**Harm**

**The level of harm is determined by weighing up all the factors of the case to determine the harm that has been caused or was intended to be caused.**

| Category 1 | • Serious physical injury to others |
|---|---|
|   | • Serious fear/distress caused |
| Category 2 | • Harm falling between categories 1 and 3 |
| Category 3 | • Little or no physical injury to others |
|   | • Some fear/distress caused |

## STEP 2 Starting point and category range

Having determined the category at step one, the court should use the corresponding starting point to reach a sentence within the category range from the appropriate sentence table below. The starting point applies to all offenders irrespective of plea or previous convictions.

| Harm | Culpability | | |
|------|---|---|---|
| | **A** | **B** | **C** |
| Category 1 | **Starting point** 2 years' custody | **Starting point** 1 year's custody | **Starting point** 26 weeks' custody |
| | **Category range** 1 year 6 months–2 years 9 months' custody | **Category range** 26 weeks'–1 year 6 months' custody | **Category range** Medium level community order–1 year's custody |
| Category 2 | **Starting point** 1 year's custody | **Starting point** 26 weeks' custody | **Starting point** High level community order |
| | **Category range** 26 weeks'–1 year 6 months' custody | **Category range** Medium level community order–1 year's custody | **Category range** Low level community order–9 months' custody |
| Category 3 | **Starting point** 26 weeks' custody | **Starting point** High level community order | **Starting point** Medium level community order |
| | **Category range** Medium level community order–1 year's custody | **Category range** Low level community order–36 weeks' custody | **Category range** Band C Fine–High level community order |

**Fines**

[For the standard schedule of fines see **SG2-5**.]

**Community Orders and Custodial Sentences**

[For the imposition of community orders, including the community orders table, see Imposition of Community and Custodial Sentences at **SG9-2**.

For the imposition of custodial sentences see Imposition of Community and Custodial Sentences at **SG9-3**.]

**Additional factors affecting seriousness**

**The non-exhaustive lists below include additional factual elements providing context to the offender's role in an offence and other factors relating to the offender.**

First identify factors relating to the offender's role in the offence to identify whether any combination of these should result in an upward or downward adjustment from the sentence arrived at so far.

Other relevant aggravating and mitigating factors should then be considered to determine if further adjustment to the sentence is required.

**Factors increasing seriousness**

*Statutory aggravating factors*

- Previous convictions [see **SG2-21**], having regard to
  a) the **nature** of the offence to which the conviction relates and its **relevance** to the current offence; and
  b) the **time** that has elapsed since the conviction
- Offence committed whilst on bail [see **SG2-22**]
- Offence motivated by, or demonstrating hostility based on any of the following characteristics or presumed characteristics of the victim: religion, race, disability, sexual orientation or transgender identity [see **SG2-23**]

*Other aggravating factors*

- Incident occurred in busy public area
- Leading role where offending is part of group activity [see **SG2-26**]
- Offender threw missiles/objects
- Incident occurred in victim's home
- Vulnerable persons or children present during incident [see **SG2-35**]
- Prolonged incident
- Significant impact on public resources
- Threats or violence directed towards public servants in the course of their duty [see **SG2-34**]
- Injury to service animal

- Commission of offence whilst under the influence of alcohol or drugs [see **SG2-25**]
- Large number of persons affected
- Offence committed while on licence or subject to post sentence supervision [see **SG2-40**]
- Failure to comply with current court orders [see **SG2-40**]

### Factors reducing seriousness or reflecting personal mitigation

- No previous convictions or no relevant/recent convictions [see **SG2-48**]
- Good character and/or exemplary conduct [see **SG2-49**]
- Remorse [see **SG2-50**]
- Incident short-lived
- Evidence of steps initially taken to defuse incident
- Significant degree of provocation
- Low level involvement
- Minor/peripheral role in group activity [see **SG2-54**]
- No members of public present other than those participating in violence
- Age and/or lack of maturity
- Mental disorder or learning disability [see **SG2-63**]
- Sole or primary carer for dependent relatives [see **SG2-61**]

### STEP 3 Consider any factors which indicate a reduction for assistance to the prosecution

The court should take into account section 74 of the Sentencing Code (reduction in sentence for assistance to prosecution) and any other rule of law by virtue of which an offender may receive a discounted sentence in consequence of assistance given (or offered) to the prosecutor or investigator.

### STEP 4 Reduction for guilty pleas

The court should take account of any potential reduction for a guilty plea in accordance with section 73 of the Sentencing Code and the guideline for Reduction in Sentence for a Guilty Plea [**SG5-1–SG5-12**].

### STEP 5 Dangerousness

The court should consider whether having regard to the criteria contained in Chapter 6 of Part 10 of the Sentencing Code it would be appropriate to impose an extended sentence (sections 266 and 279).

### STEP 6 Totality principle

If sentencing an offender for more than one offence, or where the offender is already serving a sentence, consider whether the total sentence is just and proportionate to the overall offending behaviour in accordance with the Totality guideline [see **SG4**].

### STEP 7 Compensation and ancillary orders

In all cases the court should consider whether to make compensation and/or other ancillary orders. Where the offence has resulted in personal injury, loss or damage the court must give reasons if it decides not to order compensation (Sentencing Code, s.55).

In particular, where the offender is convicted of a relevant offence within Schedule 1 of the Football Spectators Act 1989, the court must consider whether a Football Banning Order should be made pursuant to s14A Football Spectators Act 1989, and if not give reasons why.

[See the Sentencing Council Explanatory Materials for Ancillary Orders in the Magistrates' Courts at **SG10-5** and the Crown Court Compendium, Part II Sentencing, S7; Ancillary Orders]

### STEP 8 Reasons

Section 52 of the Sentencing Code imposes a duty to give reasons for, and explain the effect of, the sentence.

### STEP 9 Consideration for time spent on bail (tagged curfew)

The court must consider whether to give credit for time spent on bail in accordance with section 240A of the Criminal Justice Act 2003 and section 325 of the Sentencing Code.

For racially or religiously aggravated offences the category of the offence should be identified with reference to the factors below, and the sentence increased in accordance with the guidance at Step 3

**Effective from:** 01 January 2020

**Disorderly behaviour with intent to cause harassment, alarm or distress,**

Public Order Act 1986, s.4A

Triable only summarily
Maximum: 6 months' custody
Offence range: Discharge–26 weeks' custody

**Racially or religiously aggravated disorderly behaviour with intent to cause harassment, alarm or distress,**

Crime and Disorder Act 1998, s.31(1)(b)

Triable either way
Maximum: 2 years' custody

The racially or religiously aggravated offence is a specified offence for the purposes of sections 266 and 279 (extended sentence for certain violent, sexual or terrorism offences) of the Sentencing Code.

### STEP 1  Determining the Offence Category

The court should determine the offence category with reference **only** to the factors listed in the tables below. In order to determine the category the court should assess **culpability** and **harm**.

| Culpability demonstrated by one or more of the following: | |
| --- | --- |
| A – High culpability: | • Targeting of individual(s) by a group<br>• Sustained incident<br>• Use of substantial force<br>• Substantial disturbance<br>• Production of weapon<br>• Missiles thrown |
| B – Lesser culpability | • All other cases |

| Harm | |
| --- | --- |
| The court should consider the factors set out below to determine the level of harm that has been caused or was intended to be caused to the victim | |
| Category 1 | • Serious distress or alarm caused<br>• Distress or alarm caused to multiple persons present |
| Category 2 | • All other cases |

### STEP 2  Starting point and category range

Having determined the category at step one, the court should use the corresponding starting point to reach a sentence within the category range below. The starting point applies to all offenders irrespective of plea or previous convictions.

| Harm | Culpability | |
| --- | --- | --- |
| | A | B |
| Category 1 | **Starting point**<br>High level community order | **Starting point**<br>Low level community order |
| | **Category range**<br>Low level community order–26 weeks' custody | **Category range**<br>Band C fine–12 weeks' custody |

| Harm | Culpability | |
|---|---|---|
| Category 2 | **Starting point**<br>Low level community order | **Starting point**<br>Band C fine |
| | **Category range**<br>Band C Fine–12 weeks' custody | **Category range**<br>Discharge–Low level community order |

### Fines

[For the standard schedule of fines see **SG2-5**.]

### Community Orders and Custodial Sentences

[For the imposition of community orders, including the community orders table, see Imposition of Community and Custodial Sentences at **SG9-2**.

For the imposition of custodial sentences see Imposition of Community and Custodial Sentences at **SG9-3**.]

The table below contains a **non-exhaustive** list of additional factual elements providing the context of the offence and factors relating to the offender. Identify whether any combination of these, or other relevant factors, should result in an upward or downward adjustment from the sentence arrived at so far.

### Additional Factors Affecting Seriousness

### Factors increasing seriousness

*Statutory aggravating factors*

- Previous convictions [see **SG2-21**], having regard to
  a) the **nature** of the offence to which the conviction relates and its **relevance** to the current offence; and
  b) the **time** that has elapsed since the conviction
- Offence committed whilst on bail [see **SG2-22**]
- Offence motivated by, or demonstrating hostility based on any of the following characteristics or presumed characteristics of the victim: disability, sexual orientation or transgender identity [see **SG2-23**]

*Other aggravating factors*

- Planning [see **SG2-28**]
- Offence committed against those working in the public sector or providing a service to the public [see **SG2-34**]
- Leading role in group [see **SG2-26**]
- Vulnerable persons or children present [see **SG2-35**]
- Victim is targeted due to a vulnerability (or a perceived vulnerability) where not already taken into account in considering racial or religious aggravation [see **SG2-33**]
- History of antagonising the victim
- Victim(s) had no opportunity to escape situation (ie: offence occurred on public transport)
- Commission of offence whilst under the influence of alcohol or drugs [see **SG2-25**]
- Large number of persons affected
- Offence committed while on licence or subject to post sentence supervision [see **SG2-40**]
- Failure to comply with current court orders [see **SG2-40**]

### Factors reducing seriousness or reflecting personal mitigation

- Peripheral role in group activity [see **SG2-54**]
- No previous convictions or no relevant/recent convictions [see **SG2-48**]
- Remorse [see **SG2-50**]
- Good character and/or exemplary conduct [see **SG2-49**]
- Age and/or lack of maturity [see **SG2-60**]
- Mental disorder or learning disability [see **SG2-63**]
- Sole or primary carer for dependent relatives [see **SG2-61**]

### STEP 3 Aggravated offences

### Racially or religiously aggravated offences only

Having determined the category of the basic offence to identify the sentence of a non aggravated offence, the court should now consider the level of racial or religious aggravation involved and apply an appropriate uplift to the sentence in accordance with the guidance below. The following is a list of factors which the court should consider to determine the level of aggravation. Where there are characteristics present which fall under different levels of aggravation, the court should balance these to reach a fair assessment of the level of aggravation present in the offence.

**Maximum sentence for the aggravated offence is 2 years' custody**

Care should be taken to avoid double counting factors already taken into account in assessing the level of harm at step one

| High level of racial or religious aggravation | Sentence uplift |
|---|---|
| Racial or religious aggravation was the predominant motivation for the offence.<br>Offender was a member of, or was associated with, a group promoting hostility based on race or religion.<br>Aggravated nature of the offence caused severe distress to the victim or the victim's family (over and above the distress already considered at step one).<br>Aggravated nature of the offence caused serious fear and distress throughout local community or more widely. | Increase the length of custodial sentence if already considered for the basic offence or consider a custodial sentence, if not already considered for the basic offence. |
| **Medium level of racial or religious aggravation** | **Sentence uplift** |
| Racial or religious aggravation formed a significant proportion of the offence as a whole.<br>Aggravated nature of the offence caused some distress to the victim or the victim's family (over and above the distress already considered at step one).<br>Aggravated nature of the offence caused some fear and distress throughout local community or more widely. | Consider a significantly more onerous penalty of the same type or consider a more severe type of sentence than for the basic offence. |
| **Low level of racial or religious aggravation** | **Sentence uplift** |
| Aggravated element formed a minimal part of the offence as a whole.<br>Aggravated nature of the offence caused minimal or no distress to the victim or the victim's family (over and above the distress already considered at step one). | Consider a more onerous penalty of the same type identified for the basic offence. |

Magistrates may find that, although the appropriate sentence for the basic offence would be within their powers, the appropriate increase for the aggravated offence would result in a sentence in excess of their powers. If so, they must commit for sentence to the Crown Court.

**The sentencer should state in open court that the offence was aggravated by reason of race or religion, and should also state what the sentence would have been without that element of aggravation.**

### STEP 4   Consider any factors which indicate a reduction for assistance to the prosecution

The court should take into account section 74 of the Sentencing Code (reduction in sentence for assistance to prosecution) and any other rule of law by virtue of which an offender may receive a discounted sentence in consequence of assistance given (or offered) to the prosecutor or investigator.

### STEP 5   Reduction for guilty pleas

The court should take account of any potential reduction for a guilty plea in accordance with section 73 of the Sentencing Code and the guideline for Reduction in Sentence for a Guilty Plea [SG5-1–SG5-12].

### STEP 6   Dangerousness (Racially or Religiously Aggravated Offences Only)

The court should consider whether having regard to the criteria contained in Chapter 6 of Part 10 of the Sentencing Code it would be appropriate to impose an extended sentence (sections 266 and 279).

### STEP 7   Totality principle

If sentencing an offender for more than one offence, or where the offender is already serving a sentence, consider whether the total sentence is just and proportionate to the overall offending behaviour in accordance with the Totality guideline [see **SG4**].

### STEP 8   Compensation and ancillary orders

In all cases the court should consider whether to make compensation and/or other ancillary orders.

Where the offence has resulted in personal injury, loss or damage the court must give reasons if it decides not to order compensation (Sentencing Code, s.55).

In particular, where the offender is convicted of a relevant offence within Schedule 1 of the Football Spectators Act 1989, the court must consider whether a Football Banning Order should be made pursuant to s14A Football Spectators Act 1989, and if not give reasons why.

Sentencing Guidelines

[See the Sentencing Council Explanatory Materials for Ancillary Orders in the Magistrates' Courts at **SG10-5** and the Crown Court Compendium, Part II Sentencing, S7; Ancillary Orders]

**STEP 9  Reasons**

Section 52 of the Sentencing Code imposes a duty to give reasons for, and explain the effect of, the sentence.

**STEP 10  Consideration for time spent on bail (tagged curfew)**

The court must consider whether to give credit for time spent on bail in accordance with section 240A of the Criminal Justice Act 2003 and section 325 of the Sentencing Code.

**SG29-4**        RACIAL HATRED OFFENCES/HATRED AGAINST PERSONS ON RELIGIOUS
GROUNDS OR GROUNDS OF SEXUAL ORIENTATION

*Public Order Act 1986, ss.18–23, Public Order Act 1986, ss.29B–29G*

**Effective from:** 01 January 2020

**Racial hatred offences,** Public Order Act 1986, (ss.18–23)

**Hatred against persons on religious grounds or grounds of sexual orientation,** Public Order Act 1986 (ss. 29B–29G)

Triable either way
Maximum: 7 years' custody
Offence range: Community order – 6 years' custody

**STEP 1  Determining the offence category**

The court should determine the offence category with reference **only** to the factors listed in the tables below. In order to determine the category the court should assess **culpability** and **harm**.

| Culpability demonstrated by one or more of the following: | |
|---|---|
| A – High culpability | • Offender uses position of trust, authority or influence to stir up hatred<br>• Intention to incite serious violence<br>• Persistent activity |
| B – Medium culpability | • Factors in categories A and C not present |
| C – Lesser culpability | • Reckless as to whether hatred would be stirred up (applicable to racial hatred offences only) |

| Harm | |
|---|---|
| The court should consider the factors set out below to determine the level of harm that has been caused or was intended to be caused to the victim | |
| Category 1 | • Statement/publication/performance or broadcast directly encourages activity which threatens or endangers life<br>• Widespread dissemination of statement/publication/performance broadcast |
| Category 2 | • All other cases |

**STEP 2  Starting point and category range**

Having determined the category at step one, the court should use the corresponding starting point to reach a sentence within the category range below. The starting point applies to all offenders irrespective of plea or previous convictions

| Harm | | Culpability | |
|---|---|---|---|
| | A | B | C |
| Category 1 | **Starting point**<br>3 years' custody | **Starting point**<br>2 years' custody | **Starting point**<br>1 year's custody |
| | **Category range**<br>2–6 years' custody | **Category range**<br>1–4 years' custody | **Category range**<br>6 months–3 years' custody |

| Category 2 | Starting point<br>2 years' custody | Starting point<br>1 year's custody | Starting point<br>High level community<br>order |
|---|---|---|---|
| | Category range<br>1–4 years' custody | Category range<br>6 months–3 years' custody | Category range<br>Low level community<br>order–1 year's custody |

### Community Orders and Custodial Sentences

[For the imposition of community orders, including the community orders table, see Imposition of Community and Custodial Sentences at **SG9-2**.

For the imposition of custodial sentences see Imposition of Community and Custodial Sentences at **SG9-3**.]

### Additional factors affecting seriousness

The table below contains a **non-exhaustive** list of additional factual elements providing the context of the offence and factors relating to the offender. Identify whether any combination of these, or other relevant factors, should result in an upward or downward adjustment from the sentence arrived at so far.

### Factors increasing seriousness

*Statutory aggravating factors*

- Previous convictions [see SG2-21], having regard to a) the **nature** of the offence to which the conviction relates and its **relevance** to the current offence; and b) the **time** that has elapsed since the conviction
- Offence committed whilst on bail [see **SG2-22**]

*Other aggravating factors*

- Planning of event or campaign designed to stir up hatred
- Timing of incident – particularly sensitive social climate
- Vulnerable/impressionable audience
- Significant volume of publications published or disseminated (where not taken into account at Step One)
- Used multiple social media platforms to reach a wider audience (where not taken into account at Step One)
- Offence committed while on licence or subject to post sentence supervision [see **SG2-40**]
- Failure to comply with current court orders [see **SG2-40**]

### Factors reducing seriousness or reflecting personal mitigation

- Minor/peripheral role in group activity [see **SG2-54**]
- Previous good character [see **SG2-49**]
- No previous convictions or no relevant/recent convictions [see **SG2-48**]
- Offender took steps to limit dissemination (the court should examine the offender's true motive in limiting dissemination before applying this factor)
- Remorse [see **SG2-50**]
- Age and/or lack of maturity [see **SG2-60**]
- Mental disorder or learning disability [see **SG2-63**]
- Sole or primary carer for dependent relatives [see **SG2-61**]

### STEP 3  Consider any factors which indicate a reduction for assistance to the prosecution

The court should take into account section 74 of the Sentencing Code (reduction in sentence for assistance to prosecution) and any other rule of law by virtue of which an offender may receive a discounted sentence in consequence of assistance given (or offered) to the prosecutor or investigator.

### STEP 4  Reduction for guilty pleas

The court should take account of any potential reduction for a guilty plea in accordance with section 73 of the Sentencing Code and the guideline for Reduction in Sentence for a Guilty Plea [**SG5-1–SG5-12**].

### STEP 5  Totality principle

If sentencing an offender for more than one offence, or where the offender is already serving a sentence, consider whether the total sentence is just and proportionate to the overall offending behaviour in accordance with the Totality guideline [see **SG4**].

### STEP 6 Compensation and ancillary orders

In all cases, the court should consider whether to make compensation and/or other ancillary orders. Where the offence has resulted in personal injury, loss or damage the court must give reasons if it decides not to order compensation (Sentencing Code, s.55).

### STEP 7 Reasons

Section 52 of the Sentencing Code imposes a duty to give reasons for, and explain the effect of, the sentence.

### STEP 8 Consideration for time spent on bail (tagged curfew)

The court must consider whether to give credit for time spent on bail in accordance with section 240A of the Criminal Justice Act 2003 and section 325 of the Sentencing Code.

**SG29-5**

RIOT

*Public Order Act 1986, s.1*

**Effective from:** 01 January 2020

Triable only on indictment
Maximum: 10 years' custody
Offence range: 3–9 years' custody

This is a specified offence for the purposes of sections 266 and 279 (extended sentence for certain violent, sexual or terrorism offences) of the Sentencing Code.

#### Other offences committed within incidents of riot

Where sentencing other offences committed in the context of riot, the court should treat the context of the offending as a severely aggravating feature of any offence charged.

### STEP 1 Determining the offence category

The court should determine the offence category with reference **only** to the factors listed in the tables below. In order to determine the category the court should assess **culpability** and **harm.**

| Culpability | |
|---|---|
| A | • Offender used or intended to use petrol bomb or incendiary device<br>• Offender used or intended to use firearm or other highly dangerous weapon\*<br>• Offender was an instigator or carried out a leading role<br>• Offenders actions escalated level of violence and/or disorder |
| B | • Any incident of riot not including category A factors |

\* The court must determine whether the weapon is highly dangerous on the facts and circumstances of the case. The dangerous nature must be substantially above and beyond the legislative definition of an offensive weapon, which is 'any article made or adapted for use for causing injury, or is intended by the person having it with him for such use'.

| Harm | |
|---|---|
| **The level of harm is determined by weighing up all the factors of the case to determine the harm that has been caused or was intended to be caused** | |
| Category 1 | Multiple or extreme examples of the following:<br>• Incident results in serious physical injury or very serious fear and/or distress<br>• Incident causes serious disruption or severe detrimental impact to community<br>• Incident causes loss of livelihood or substantial costs to businesses<br>• Incident causes substantial costs to be incurred to public purse<br>• Incident involves attacks on police or public servants<br>• Incident results in extensive damage to property |
| Category 2 | • All other cases |

### STEP 2 Starting point and category range

Having determined the category at step one, the court should use the corresponding starting point to reach a sentence within the category range below. The starting point applies to all offenders irrespective of plea or previous convictions.

| Harm | Culpability | |
|---|---|---|
| | A | B |
| Category 1 | **Starting point**<br>7 years' custody | **Starting point**<br>6 years' custody |
| | **Category range**<br>6–9 years' custody | **Category range**<br>4–7 years' custody |
| Category 2 | **Starting point**<br>6 years' custody | **Starting point**<br>5 years' custody |
| | **Category range**<br>4–7 years' custody | **Category range**<br>3–6 years' custody |

**Custodial Sentences**

[For the imposition of custodial sentences see Imposition of Community and Custodial Sentences at SG9-3.]

**Additional factors affecting seriousness**

The **non-exhaustive** lists below include additional factual elements providing context to the offender's role in an offence and other factors relating to the offender.

First identify factors relating to the offender's role in the offence to identify whether any combination of these should result in an upward or downward adjustment from the sentence arrived at so far.

Other relevant aggravating and mitigating factors should then be considered to determine if further adjustment to the sentence is required.

**Care should be taken not to double count aggravating factors which were relevant to the culpability assessment, particularly in cases where culpability is assessed as high.**

**Factors increasing seriousness**

*Statutory aggravating factors*

- Previous convictions [see **SG2-21**], having regard to a) the **nature** of the offence to which the conviction relates and its **relevance** to the current offence; and b) the **time** that has elapsed since the conviction
- Offence committed whilst on bail [see **SG2-22**]
- Offence motivated by, or demonstrating hostility based on any of the following characteristics or presumed characteristics of the victim: disability, sexual orientation or transgender identity [see **SG2-23**]

*Other aggravating factors*

- Active and persistent participant
- Incitement of others
- Actively recruited other participants
- Offender masked or disguised to evade detection
- Incident occurred in busy public area
- Took steps to prevent emergency services from carrying out their duties
- Offender used weapon [see **SG2-27**]
- Offender threw missiles/objects
- Use of significant physical violence
- Injury to service animal
- Possession of weapon or article intended to injure
- Vulnerable persons or children present during incident [see **SG2-33**]
- Commission of offence whilst under the influence of alcohol or drugs [see **SG2-25**]
- Ignored warnings or exclusion notices [see **SG2-39**]
- Offence committed while on licence or subject to post sentence supervision [see **SG2-40**]
- Failure to comply with current court orders [see **SG2-40**]

**Factors reducing seriousness or reflecting personal mitigation**

- Low level involvement
- No previous convictions or no relevant/recent convictions [see **SG2-48**]
- Remorse [see **SG2-50**]
- Age and/or lack of maturity [see **SG2-60**]
- Mental disorder or learning disability [see **SG2-63**]
- Good character and/or exemplary conduct [see **SG2-49**]
- Sole or primary carer for dependent relatives [see **SG2-61**]

Sentencing Guidelines

### STEP 3  Consider any factors which indicate a reduction for assistance to the prosecution

The court should take into account section 74 of the Sentencing Code (reduction in sentence for assistance to prosecution) and any other rule of law by virtue of which an offender may receive a discounted sentence in consequence of assistance given (or offered) to the prosecutor or investigator.

### STEP 4  Reduction for guilty pleas

The court should take account of any potential reduction for a guilty plea in accordance with section 73 of the Sentencing Code and the guideline for Reduction in Sentence for a Guilty Plea [SG5-1–SG5-12].

### STEP 5  Dangerousness

The court should consider whether having regard to the criteria contained in Chapter 6 of Part 10 of the Sentencing Code it would be appropriate to impose an extended sentence (sections 266 and 279).

### STEP 6  Totality principle

If sentencing an offender for more than one offence, or where the offender is already serving a sentence, consider whether the total sentence is just and proportionate to the overall offending behaviour in accordance with the Totality guideline. [see SG4].

### STEP 7  Compensation and ancillary orders

In all cases the court should consider whether to make compensation and/or other ancillary orders. Where the offence has resulted in personal injury, loss or damage the court must give reasons if it decides not to order compensation (Sentencing Code, s.55).

### STEP 8  Reasons

Section 52 of the Sentencing Code imposes a duty to give reasons for, and explain the effect of, the sentence.

### STEP 9  Consideration for time spent on bail (tagged curfew)

The court must consider whether to give credit for time spent on bail in accordance with section 240A of the Criminal Justice Act 2003 and section 325 of the Sentencing Code.

**SG29-6**

## THREATENING BEHAVIOUR – FEAR OR PROVOCATION OF VIOLENCE/RACIALLY OR RELIGIOUSLY AGGRAVATED THREATENING BEHAVIOUR – FEAR OR PROVOCATION OF VIOLENCE

**Effective from:** 01 January 2020

**Threatening behaviour – fear or provocation of violence,** Public Order Act 1986, s.4

Triable only summarily
Maximum: 6 months' custody
Offence range: Discharge—26 weeks' custody

**Racially or religiously aggravated threatening behaviour – fear or provocation of violence,** Crime and Disorder Act 1998 s.31(1)(a)

Triable either way
Maximum: 2 years' custody

**The racially or religiously aggravated offence is a specified offence for the purposes of sections 266 and 279 (extended sentence for certain violent, sexual or terrorism offences) of the Sentencing Code.**

For racially or religiously aggravated offences the category of the offence should be identified with reference to the factors below, and the sentence increased in accordance with the guidance at Step 3

### STEP 1  Determining the offence category

The court should determine the offence category with reference **only** to the factors listed in the tables below. In order to determine the category the court should assess **culpability** and **harm**.

| Culpability demonstrated by one or more of the following: | |
| --- | --- |
| **A – High culpability** | • Targeting of individual(s) by a group<br>• Intention to cause fear of serious violence<br>• Sustained incident<br>• Use of substantial force<br>• Production of weapon<br>• Missiles thrown |
| **B – Lesser culpability** | • All other cases |

| Harm | |
|---|---|
| The court should consider the factors set out below to determine the level of harm that has been caused or was intended to be caused to the victim | |
| Category 1 | • Victim feared serious violence<br>• Fear of violence caused to multiple persons present<br>• Incident escalated into violence |
| Category 2 | • All other cases |

## STEP 2  Starting point and category range

Having determined the category at step one, the court should use the corresponding starting point to reach a sentence within the category range below. The starting point applies to all offenders irrespective of plea or previous convictions.

| Harm | Culpability | |
|---|---|---|
| | A | B |
| Category 1 | **Starting point**<br>High level community order | **Starting point**<br>Medium level community order |
| | **Category range**<br>Low level community order–26 weeks' custody | **Category range**<br>Band C fine–12 weeks' custody |
| Category 2 | **Starting point**<br>Medium level community order | **Starting point**<br>Low level community order |
| | **Category range**<br>Band C fine–12 weeks' custody | **Category range**<br>Discharge–Medium level community order |

### Fines

[For the standard schedule of fines see **SG2-5**.]

### Community Orders and Custodial Sentences

[For the imposition of community orders, including the community orders table, see Imposition of Community and Custodial Sentences at **SG9-2**.

For the imposition of custodial sentences see Imposition of Community and Custodial Sentences at **SG9-3**.]

### Additional factors affecting seriousness

The table below contains a **non-exhaustive** list of additional factual elements providing the context of the offence and factors relating to the offender. Identify whether any combination of these, or other relevant factors, should result in an upward or downward adjustment from the sentence arrived at so far.

### Factors increasing seriousness

*Statutory aggravating factors*
- Previous convictions [see **SG2-21**], having regard to a) the **nature** of the offence to which the conviction relates and its **relevance** to the current offence; and b) the **time** that has elapsed since the conviction
- Offence committed whilst on bail [see **SG2-22**]
- Offence motivated by, or demonstrating hostility based on any of the following characteristics or presumed characteristics of the victim: disability, sexual orientation or transgender identity [see **SG2-23**]

*Other aggravating factors*
- Planning [see **SG2-28**]
- Offence committed against those working in the public sector or providing a service to the public [see **SG2-34**]
- Leading role where offending is part of group activity [see **SG2-26**]
- Vulnerable persons or children present [see **SG2-33**]
- Victim is targeted due to a vulnerability (or a perceived vulnerability) where not already taken into account in considering racial or religious aggravation [see **SG2-33**]
- History of antagonising the victim
- Victim(s) had no opportunity to escape situation (ie: offence occurred on public transport)
- Commission of offence whilst under the influence of alcohol/drugs [see **SG2-25**]

- Offence committed while on licence or subject to post sentence supervision [see **SG2-40**]
- Failure to comply with current court orders [see **SG2-40**]

### Factors reducing seriousness or reflecting personal mitigation

- Minor/peripheral role in group activity [see **SG2-54**]
- No previous convictions or no relevant/recent convictions [see **SG2-48**]
- Remorse [see **SG2-50**]
- Good character and/or exemplary conduct [see **SG2-49**]
- Age and/or lack of maturity [see **SG2-60**]
- Mental disorder or learning disability [see **SG2-63**]
- Sole or primary carer for dependent relatives [see **SG2-61**]

### STEP 3   Aggravated offences

#### Racially or religiously aggravated criminal damage offences only

Having determined the category of the basic offence to identify the sentence of a non-aggravated offence, the court should now consider the level of racial or religious aggravation involved and apply an appropriate uplift to the sentence in accordance with the guidance below. The following is a list of factors which the court should consider to determine the level of aggravation. Where there are characteristics present which fall under different levels of aggravation, the court should balance these to reach a fair assessment of the level of aggravation present in the offence.

#### Maximum sentence for the aggravated offence is 2 years' custody

Care should be taken to avoid double counting factors already taken into account in assessing the level of harm at step one

| High level of racial or religious aggravation | Sentence uplift |
| --- | --- |
| Racial or religious aggravation was the predominant motivation for the offence. <br> Offender was a member of, or was associated with, a group promoting hostility based on race or religion. <br> Aggravated nature of the offence caused severe distress to the victim or the victim's family (over and above the distress already considered at step one). <br> Aggravated nature of the offence caused serious fear and distress throughout local community or more widely. | Increase the length of custodial sentence if already considered for the basic offence or consider a custodial sentence, if not already considered for the basic offence. |
| **Medium level of racial or religious aggravation** | **Sentence uplift** |
| Racial or religious aggravation formed a significant proportion of the offence as a whole. <br> Aggravated nature of the offence caused some distress to the victim or the victim's family (over and above the distress already considered at step one). <br> Aggravated nature of the offence caused some fear and distress throughout local community or more widely. | Consider a significantly more onerous penalty of the same type or consider a more severe type of sentence than for the basic offence. |
| **Low level of racial or religious aggravation** | **Sentence uplift** |
| Aggravated element formed a minimal part of the offence as a whole. <br> Aggravated nature of the offence caused minimal or no distress to the victim or the victim's family (over and above the distress already considered at step one). | Consider a more onerous penalty of the same type identified for the basic offence. |

Magistrates may find that, although the appropriate sentence for the basic offence would be within their powers, the appropriate increase for the aggravated offence would result in a sentence in excess of their powers. If so, they must commit for sentence to the Crown Court.

**The sentencer should state in open court that the offence was aggravated by reason of race or religion, and should also state what the sentence would have been without that element of aggravation.**

### STEP 4   Consider any factors which indicate a reduction for assistance to the prosecution

The court should take into account section 74 of the Sentencing Code (reduction in sentence for assistance to prosecution) and any other rule of law by virtue of which an offender may receive a discounted sentence in consequence of assistance given (or offered) to the prosecutor or investigator.

**STEP 5  Reduction for guilty pleas**

The court should take account of any potential reduction for a guilty plea in accordance with section 73 of the Sentencing Code and the guideline for Reduction in Sentence for a Guilty Plea [SG5-1–SG5-12].

**STEP 6  (Racially or Religously Aggravated Offences Only) Dangerousness**

The court should consider whether having regard to the criteria contained in Chapter 6 of Part 10 of the Sentencing Code it would be appropriate to impose an extended sentence (sections 266 and 279).

**STEP 7  Totality principle**

If sentencing an offender for more than one offence, or where the offender is already serving a sentence, consider whether the total sentence is just and proportionate to the overall offending behaviour in accordance with the Totality guideline [see **SG4**].

**STEP 8  Compensation and ancillary orders**

In all cases the court should consider whether to make compensation and/or other ancillary orders.

Where the offence has resulted in personal injury, loss or damage the court must give reasons if it decides not to order compensation (Sentencing Code, s.55).

In particular, where the offender is convicted of a relevant offence within Schedule 1 of the Football Spectators Act 1989, the court must consider whether a Football Banning Order should be made pursuant to s14A Football Spectators Act 1989, and if not give reasons why.

[See the Sentencing Council Explanatory Materials for Ancillary Orders in the Magistrates' Courts at **SG10-5** and the Crown Court Compendium, Part II Sentencing, S7; Ancillary Orders]

**STEP 9  Reasons**

Section 52 of the Sentencing Code imposes a duty to give reasons for, and explain the effect of, the sentence.

**STEP 10  Consideration for time spent on bail (tagged curfew)**

The court must consider whether to give credit for time spent on bail in accordance with section 240A of the Criminal Justice Act 2003 and section 325 of the Sentencing Code.

VIOLENT DISORDER                                                   **SG29-7**

*Public Order Act 1986, s.2*

**Effective from:** 01 January 2020

Triable either way
Maximum: 5 years' custody
Offence range: Community order—4 years 6 months' custody

This is a specified offence for the purposes of sections 266 and 279 (extended sentence for certain violent, sexual or terrorism offences) of the Sentencing Code.

**STEP 1  Determining the offence category**

The court should determine the offence category with reference **only** to the factors listed in the tables below. In order to determine the category the court should assess **culpability** and **harm**.

| Culpability | |
|---|---|
| A | Factors in Category B present **AND** any of:<br>• Offender used or intended to use petrol bomb or incendiary device<br>• Offender used or intended to use firearm or other highly dangerous weapon*<br>• Offender was an instigator or carried out a leading role<br>• Targeting of individual(s) by a group |
| B | • Offender participated in incident which involved widespread and/or large scale acts of violence on people and/or property<br>• Offender participated in incident involving serious acts of violence<br>• Offender participated in incident involving significant planning of unlawful activity<br>• Offender participated in incident involving persistent and/or sustained unlawful activity |
| C | • Offence involved threats of violence only<br>• Offence involved lower level of violence or activity than included in Category B |

Sentencing Guidelines

*The court must determine whether the weapon is highly dangerous on the facts and circumstances of the case. The dangerous nature must be substantially above and beyond the legislative definition of an offensive weapon, which is 'any article made or adapted for use for causing injury, or is intended by the person having it with him for such use'.

| Harm | |
|---|---|
| The level of harm is determined by weighing up all the factors of the case to determine the harm that has been caused or was intended to be caused | |
| Category 1 | • Cases involving multiple or extreme category 2 factors |
| Category 2 | • Incident results in serious physical injury or serious fear and/or distress and/or disruption<br>• Incident causes serious disruption or severe detrimental impact to community<br>• Incident causes loss of livelihood or substantial costs to businesses<br>• Incident causes substantial costs to be incurred to public purse<br>• Incident results in attacks on police or public servants<br>• Incident results in extensive damage to property |
| Category 3 | • Offence involved threats of violence only<br>• Offence involved lower level of violence or activity than included in category 2 |

## STEP 2 Starting point and category range

Having determined the category at step one, the court should use the corresponding starting point to reach a sentence within the category range from the appropriate sentence table below. The starting point applies to all offenders irrespective of plea or previous convictions.

| Harm | | Culpability | |
|---|---|---|---|
| | A | B | C |
| Category 1 | **Starting point**<br>4 years' custody | **Starting point**<br>3 years' custody | **Starting point**<br>2 years' custody |
| | **Category range**<br>3–4 years' 6 months custody | **Category range**<br>2–4 years' custody | **Category range**<br>1–3 years' custody |
| Category 2 | **Starting point**<br>3 years' custody | **Starting point**<br>2 years' custody | **Starting point**<br>1 year's custody |
| | **Category range**<br>2–4 years' custody | **Category range**<br>1–3 years' custody | **Category range**<br>High level community order–2 years' custody |
| Category 3 | **Starting point**<br>2 years' custody | **Starting point**<br>1 year's custody | **Starting point**<br>26 weeks' custody |
| | **Category range**<br>1–3 years' custody | **Category range**<br>High level community order–2 years' custody | **Category range**<br>Medium level community order–1 year's custody |

## Community Orders and Custodial Sentences

[For the imposition of community orders, including the community orders table, see Imposition of Community and Custodial Sentences at **SG9-2**.

For the imposition of custodial sentences see Imposition of Community and Custodial Sentences at **SG9-3**.]

## Additional factors affecting seriousness

The non-exhaustive lists below include additional factual elements providing context to the offender's role in an offence and other factors relating to the offender.

First identify factors relating to the offender's role in the offence to identify whether any combination of these should result in an upward or downward adjustment from the sentence arrived at so far.

Other relevant aggravating and mitigating factors should then be considered to determine if further adjustment to the sentence is required.

**Care should be taken not to double count aggravating factors which were relevant to the culpability assessment, particularly in cases where culpability is assessed as high.**

**Factors increasing seriousness**

*Statutory aggravating factors*

- Previous convictions [see **SG2-21**], having regard to a) the **nature** of the offence to which the conviction relates and its **relevance** to the current offence; and b) the **time** that has elapsed since the conviction
- Offence committed whilst on bail [see **SG2-22**]
- Offence motivated by, or demonstrating hostility based on any of the following characteristics or presumed characteristics of the victim: disability, sexual orientation or transgender identity [see **SG2-23**]

*Other aggravating factors*

- Active and persistent participant
- Incitement of others
- Offender masked or disguised to evade detection
- Incident occurred in busy public area
- Offender used weapon [see **SG2-27**]
- Offender threw missiles/objects
- Use of significant physical violence
- Injury to service animal
- Possession of weapon or article intended to injure
- Attack by animal used or threatened in commission of offence
- Incident occurred in victim's home
- Vulnerable persons or children present during incident [see **SG2-33**]
- Commission of offence whilst under the influence of alcohol or drugs [see **SG2-25**]
- Failure to comply with current court orders [see **SG2-40**]
- Offence committed while on licence or subject to post sentence supervision [see **SG2-40**]

**Factors reducing seriousness or reflecting personal mitigation**

- No previous convictions or no relevant/recent convictions [see **SG2-48**]
- Evidence of steps initially taken to defuse incident
- Low level involvement
- Minor/peripheral role
- Remorse [see **SG2-50**]
- Good character and/or exemplary conduct [see **SG2-49**]
- Sole or primary carer for dependent relatives [see **SG2-61**]
- Age and/or lack of maturity [see **SG2-60**]
- Mental disorder or learning disability [see **SG2-63**]

**STEP 3   Consider any factors which indicate a reduction for assistance to the prosecution**

The court should take into account section 74 of the Sentencing Code (reduction in sentence for assistance to prosecution) and any other rule of law by virtue of which an offender may receive a discounted sentence in consequence of assistance given (or offered) to the prosecutor or investigator.

**STEP 4   Reduction for guilty pleas**

The court should take account of any potential reduction for a guilty plea in accordance with section 73 of the Sentencing Code and the guideline for Reduction in Sentence for a Guilty Plea [**SG5-1–SG5-12**].

**STEP 5   Dangerousness**

The court should consider whether having regard to the criteria contained in Chapter 6 of Part 10 of the Sentencing Code it would be appropriate to impose an extended sentence (sections 266 and 279).

**STEP 6   Totality principle**

If sentencing an offender for more than one offence, or where the offender is already serving a sentence, consider whether the total sentence is just and proportionate to the overall offending behaviour in accordance with the Totality guideline [see **SG4**].

**STEP 7   Compensation and ancillary orders**

In all cases the court should consider whether to make compensation and/or other ancillary orders. Where the offence has resulted in personal injury, loss or damage the court must give reasons if it decides not to order compensation (Sentencing Code, s.55). In particular, where the offender is convicted of a relevant offence within Schedule 1 of the Football Spectators Act 1989, the court must consider whether a Football Banning Order should be made pursuant to s14A Football Spectators Act 1989, and if not give reasons why.

[See the Sentencing Council Explanatory Materials for Ancillary Orders in the Magistrates' Courts at **SG10-5** and the Crown Court Compendium, Part II Sentencing, S7; Ancillary Orders]

**STEP 8 Reasons**

Section 52 of the Sentencing Code imposes a duty to give reasons for, and explain the effect of, the sentence.

**STEP 9 Consideration for time spent on bail (tagged curfew)**

The court must consider whether to give credit for time spent on bail in accordance with section 240A of the Criminal Justice Act 2003 and section 325 of the Sentencing Code.

# PART 30   ROBBERY

APPLICABILITY                                    SG30-1

[For the standard text on applicability see **SG0-4**.]

ROBBERY – STREET AND LESS SOPHISTICATED COMMERCIAL          **SG30-2**

*Theft Act 1968 (section 8(1))*

**Effective from:** 01 April 2016

Triable only on indictment
Maximum: Life imprisonment
Offence range: Community order–12 years' custody

This is a Schedule 19 offence for the purposes of sections 274 and 285 (required life sentence for offence carrying life sentence) of the Sentencing Code.

For offences committed on or after 3 December 2012, where, at some time during the commission of the offence, the offender had in his or her possession a firearm or an imitation firearm within the meaning of the Firearms Act 1968, this is an offence listed in Part 1 of Schedule 15 for the purposes of sections 273 and 283 (life sentence for second listed offence) of the Sentencing Code.

This is a specified offence for the purposes of sections 266 and 279 (extended sentence for certain violent, sexual or terrorism offences) of the Sentencing Code.

**STEP 1   Determining the offence category**

The court should determine the offence category with reference **only** to the factors listed in the tables below. In order to determine the category the court should assess **culpability** and **harm**.

The court should weigh all the factors set out below in determining the offender's culpability.

**Where there are characteristics present which fall under different levels of culpability, the court should balance these characteristics to reach a fair assessment of the offender's culpability.**

| Culpability demonstrated by one or more of the following: | |
|---|---|
| A – High culpability | • Use of a weapon to inflict violence<br>• Production of a bladed article or firearm or imitation firearm to threaten violence<br>• Use of very significant force in the commission of the offence<br>• Offence motivated by, or demonstrating hostility based on any of the following characteristics or presumed characteristics of the victim: religion, race, disability, sexual orientation or transgender identity |
| B – Medium Culpability | • Production of a weapon other than a bladed article or firearm or imitation firearm to threaten violence<br>• Threat of violence by any weapon (but which is not produced)<br>• Other cases where characteristics for categories A or C are not present<br>  – Factors are present in A and C which balance each other out and/or<br>  – The offender's culpability falls between the factors as described in A and C |
| C – Lesser culpability | • Involved through coercion, intimidation or exploitation<br>• Threat or use of minimal force<br>• Mental disability or learning disability where linked to the commission of the offence |

| Harm<br>The court should consider the factors set out below to determine the level of harm that has been caused or was intended to be caused to the victim. | |
|---|---|
| Category 1 | • Serious physical and/or psychological harm caused to the victim<br>• Serious detrimental effect on the business |
| Category 2 | • Other cases where characteristics for categories 1 or 3 are not present |
| Category 3 | • No/minimal physical or psychological harm caused to the victim<br>• No/minimal detrimental effect on the business |

Sentencing Guidelines

## STEP 2  Starting point and category range

Having determined the category at step one, the court should use the corresponding starting point to reach a sentence within the category range below. The starting point applies to all offenders irrespective of plea or previous convictions. A case of particular gravity, reflected by multiple features of culpability or harm in step one, could merit upward adjustment from the starting point before further adjustment for aggravating or mitigating features, set out below.

Consecutive sentences for multiple offences may be appropriate – please refer to the *Totality* guideline [see SG4].

| Harm | Culpability | | |
|---|---|---|---|
| | A | B | C |
| Category 1 | Starting point 8 years' custody Category range 7–12 years' custody | Starting point 5 years' custody Category range 4–8 years' custody | Starting point 4 years' custody Category range 3–6 years' custody |
| Category 2 | Starting point 5 years' custody Category range 4–8 years' custody | Starting point 4 years' custody Category range 3–6 years' custody | Starting point 2 years' custody Category range 1–4 years' custody |
| Category 3 | Starting point 4 years' custody Category range 3–6 years' custody | Starting point 2 years' custody Category range 1–4 years' custody | Starting point 1 year's custody Category range High level community order–3 years' custody |

### Community Orders and Custodial Sentences

[For the imposition of community orders, including the community orders table, see Imposition of Community and Custodial Sentences at SG9-2.

For the imposition of custodial sentences see Imposition of Community and Custodial Sentences at SG9-3.]

### Additional factors affecting seriousness

The table below contains a **non-exhaustive** list of additional factual elements providing the context of the offence and factors relating to the offender. Identify whether any combination of these, or other relevant factors, should result in an upward or downward adjustment from the sentence arrived at so far. In particular, relevant recent convictions are likely to result in an upward adjustment. In some cases, having considered these factors, it may be appropriate to move outside the identified category range.

### Factors increasing seriousness

*Statutory aggravating factors*

- Previous convictions [see SG2-21], having regard to
  a)  the **nature** of the offence to which the conviction relates and its **relevance** to the current offence; and
  b)  the **time** that has elapsed since the conviction
- Offence committed whilst on bail [see SG2-22]

*Other aggravating factors*

- High value goods or sums targeted or obtained (whether economic, personal or sentimental)
- Victim is targeted due to a vulnerability (or a perceived vulnerability) [see SG2-33]
- Significant planning [see SG2-28]
- Steps taken to prevent the victim reporting or obtaining assistance and/or from assisting or supporting the prosecution [see SG2-37]
- Prolonged nature of event
- Restraint, detention or additional degradation of the victim [see SG2-32]
- A leading role where offending is part of a group activity [see SG2-26]
- Involvement of others through coercion, intimidation or exploitation
- Location of the offence (including cases where the location of the offence is the victim's residence) [see SG2-45]
- Timing of the offence [see SG2-45]
- Attempt to conceal identity (for example, wearing a balaclava or hood)
- Commission of offence whilst under the influence of alcohol or drugs [see SG2-25]

- Attempts to conceal/dispose of evidence [see **SG2-37**]
- Established evidence of community/wider impact [see **SG2-46**]
- Failure to comply with current court orders [see **SG2-40**]
- Offence committed on licence [see **SG2-40**]
- Offences taken into consideration [see **SG3**]
- Failure to respond to warnings about behaviour [see **SG2-39**]

**Factors reducing seriousness or reflecting personal mitigation**

- No previous convictions or no relevant/recent convictions [see **SG2-48**]
- Remorse, particularly where evidenced by voluntary reparation to the victim [see **SG2-50**]
- Good character and/or exemplary conduct [see **SG2-49**]
- Serious medical condition requiring urgent, intensive or long-term treatment [see **SG2-62**]
- Age and/or lack of maturity where it affects the responsibility of the offender [see **SG2-60**]
- Mental disorder or learning disability (where not linked to the commission of the offence) [see **SG2-63**]
- Little or no planning [see **SG2-53**]
- Sole or primary carer for dependent relatives [see **SG2-61**]
- Determination and/or demonstration of steps taken to address addiction or offending behaviour [see **SG2-64**]

**STEP 3  Consider any factors which indicate a reduction for assistance to the prosecution**

The court should take into account section 74 of the Sentencing Code (reduction in sentence for assistance to prosecution) and any other rule of law by virtue of which an offender may receive a discounted sentence in consequence of assistance given (or offered) to the prosecutor or investigator.

**STEP 4  Reduction for guilty pleas**

The court should take account of any potential reduction for a guilty plea in accordance with section 73 of the Sentencing Code and the guideline for Reduction in Sentence for a Guilty Plea [**SG5-1–SG5-12**].

**STEP 5  Dangerousness**

The court should consider:

1) whether having regard to the criteria contained in Chapter 6 of Part 10 of the Sentencing Code it would be appropriate to impose a life sentence (sections 274 and 285);
2) (where, at some time during the commission of the offence, the offender had in his or her possession a firearm or an imitation firearm within the meaning of the Firearms Act 1968) whether having regard to sections 273 and 283 of the Sentencing Code it would be appropriate to impose a life sentence;
3) whether having regard to the criteria contained in Chapter 6 of Part 10 of the Sentencing Code it would be appropriate to impose an extended sentence (sections 266 and 279).

When sentencing offenders to a life sentence under these provisions, the notional determinate sentence should be used as the basis for the setting of a minimum term.

**STEP 6  Totality principle**

If sentencing an offender for more than one offence, or where the offender is already serving a sentence, consider whether the total sentence is just and proportionate to the overall offending behaviour in accordance with the *Totality* guideline [see **SG4**].

**STEP 7  Compensation and ancillary orders**

In all cases the court should consider whether to make compensation and/or other ancillary orders. Where the offence has resulted in personal injury, loss or damage the court must give reasons if it decides not to order compensation (Sentencing Code, s.55).

Where the offence involves a firearm, an imitation firearm or an offensive weapon the court may consider the criteria in section 19 of the Serious Crime Act 2007 for the imposition of a Serious Crime Prevention Order.

[See the Crown Court Compendium, Part II Sentencing, S7; Ancillary Orders]

**STEP 8  Reasons**

Section 52 of the Sentencing Code imposes a duty to give reasons for, and explain the effect of, the sentence.

**STEP 9  Consideration for time spent on bail (tagged curfew)**

The court must consider whether to give credit for time spent on bail in accordance with section 240A of the Criminal Justice Act 2003 and section 325 of the Sentencing Code.

# ROBBERY – PROFESSIONALLY PLANNED COMMERCIAL

*Theft Act 1968 (section 8(1))*

**Effective from:** 01 April 2016

Triable only on indictment
Maximum: Life imprisonment
Offence range: 18 months'–20 years' custody

This is a Schedule 19 offence for the purposes of sections 274 and 285 (required life sentence for offence carrying life sentence) of the Sentencing Code.

For offences committed on or after 3 December 2012, where, at some time during the commission of the offence, the offender had in his or her possession a firearm or an imitation firearm within the meaning of the Firearms Act 1968, this is an offence listed in Part 1 of Schedule 15 for the purposes of sections 273 and 283 (life sentence for second listed offence) of the Sentencing Code.

This is a specified offence for the purposes of sections 266 and 279 (extended sentence for certain violent, sexual or terrorism offences) of the Sentencing Code.

**This guideline applies only to offenders aged 18 and older.**

**Professionally planned commercial robbery refers to robberies involving a significant degree of planning, sophistication or organisation.**

## STEP 1 Determining the offence category

The court should determine the offence category with reference **only** to the factors listed in the tables below. In order to determine the category the court should assess **culpability** and **harm**.

The court should weigh all the factors set out below in determining the offender's culpability.

**Where there are characteristics present which fall under different levels of culpability, the court should balance these characteristics to reach a fair assessment of the offender's culpability.**

| Culpability demonstrated by one or more of the following: | |
|---|---|
| **A – High culpability** | • Use of a weapon to inflict violence<br>• Production of a bladed article or firearm or imitation firearm to threaten violence<br>• Use of very significant force in the commission of the offence<br>• A leading role where offending is part of a group activity<br>• Offence motivated by, or demonstrating hostility based on any of the following characteristics or presumed characteristics of the victim: religion, race, disability, sexual orientation or transgender identity<br>• Abuse of position |
| **B – Medium culpability** | • Production of a weapon other than a bladed article or firearm or imitation firearm to threaten violence<br>• Threat of violence by any weapon (but which is not produced)<br>• Other cases that fall between categories A or C because:<br>  – Factors are present in A and C which balance each other out and/or<br>  – The offender's culpability falls between the factors as described in A and C |
| **C – Lesser culpability** | • Performed limited function under direction<br>• Involved through coercion, intimidation or exploitation<br>• Threat or use of minimal force<br>• Mental disability or learning disability where linked to the commission of the offence |

**Harm**

The level of harm is determined by weighing up all the factors of the case to determine the harm that has been caused or was intended to be caused to the victim. The victim relates both to the commercial organisation that has been robbed and any individual(s) who has suffered the use or threat of force during the commission of the offence.

| Category 1 | • Serious physical and/or psychological harm caused to the victim<br>• Serious detrimental effect on the business<br>• Very high value goods or sums targeted or obtained (whether economic, personal or sentimental) |
|---|---|
| Category 2 | • Other cases where characteristics for categories 1 or 3 are not present |
| Category 3 | • No/minimal physical or psychological harm caused to the victim<br>• No/minimal detrimental effect on the business<br>• Low value goods or sums targeted or obtained (whether economic, personal or sentimental) |

## STEP 2  Starting point and category range

Having determined the category at step one, the court should use the corresponding starting point to reach a sentence within the category range below. The starting point applies to all offenders irrespective of plea or previous convictions. A case of particular gravity, reflected by multiple features of high culpability or harm in step one, could merit upward adjustment from the starting point before further adjustment for aggravating or mitigating features, set out [below].

Consecutive sentences for multiple offences may be appropriate particularly where exceptionally high levels of harm have been caused, please refer to the *Totality* guideline [see **SG4**].

**Where multiple offences or a single conspiracy to commit multiple offences of particular severity have taken place sentences in excess of 20 years may be appropriate.**

| Harm | Culpability | | |
|---|---|---|---|
| | **A** | **B** | **C** |
| Category 1 | **Starting point**<br>16 years' custody<br>**Category range**<br>12–20 years' custody | **Starting point**<br>9 years' custody<br>**Category range**<br>7–14 years' custody | **Starting point**<br>5 years' custody<br>**Category range**<br>4–8 years' custody |
| Category 2 | **Starting point**<br>9 years' custody<br>**Category range**<br>7–14 years' custody | **Starting point**<br>5 years' custody<br>**Category range**<br>4–8 years' custody | **Starting point**<br>3 years' custody<br>**Category range**<br>2–5 years' custody |
| Category 3 | **Starting point**<br>5 years' custody<br>**Category range**<br>4–8 years' custody | **Starting point**<br>3 years' custody<br>**Category range**<br>2–5 years' custody | **Starting point**<br>2 years' custody<br>**Category range**<br>18 months'–4 years' custody |

### Custodial Sentences

[For the imposition of custodial sentences see Imposition of Community and Custodial Sentences at SG9-3.]

### Additional factors affecting seriousness

The table below contains a **non-exhaustive** list of additional factual elements providing the context of the offence and factors relating to the offender. Identify whether any combination of these, or other relevant factors, should result in an upward or downward adjustment from the sentence arrived at so far. In particular, relevant recent convictions are likely to result in an upward adjustment. In some cases, having considered these factors, it may be appropriate to move outside the identified category range.

### Factors increasing seriousness

*Statutory aggravating factors*

• Previous convictions [see **SG2-21**], having regard to
   a)  the **nature** of the offence to which the conviction relates and its **relevance** to the current offence; and
   b)  the **time** that has elapsed since the conviction

- Offence committed whilst on bail [see **SG2-22**]

*Other aggravating factors*
- Victim is targeted due to a vulnerability (or a perceived vulnerability) [see **SG2-33**]
- Steps taken to prevent the victim reporting or obtaining assistance and/or from assisting or supporting the prosecution [see **SG2-37**]
- Prolonged nature of attack
- Restraint, detention or additional degradation of the victim [see **SG2-32**]
- Involvement of others through coercion, intimidation or exploitation
- Location of the offence (including cases where the location of the offence is the victim's residence) [see **SG2-45**]
- Timing of the offence [see **SG2-45**]
- Attempt to conceal identity (for example, wearing a balaclava or hood)
- Commission of offence whilst under the influence of alcohol or drugs [see **SG2-25**]
- Attempts to conceal/dispose of evidence [see **SG2-37**]
- Established evidence of community/wider impact [see **SG2-46**]
- Failure to comply with current court orders [see **SG2-40**]
- Offence committed on licence [see **SG2-40**]
- Offences taken into consideration [see **SG3**]
- Failure to respond to warnings about behaviour [see **SG2-39**]

### Factors reducing seriousness or reflecting personal mitigation
- No previous convictions or no relevant/recent convictions [see **SG2-48**]
- Remorse, particularly where evidenced by voluntary reparation to the victim [see **SG2-50**]
- Good character and/or exemplary conduct [see **SG2-49**]
- Serious medical condition requiring urgent, intensive or long-term treatment [see **SG2-62**]
- Age and/or lack of maturity where it affects the responsibility of the offender [see **SG2-60**]
- Mental disorder or learning disability (where not linked to the commission of the offence) [see **SG2-63**]
- Sole or primary carer for dependent relatives [see **SG2-61**]
- Determination and/or demonstration of steps taken to address addiction or offending behaviour [see **SG2-64**]

### STEPS 3 to 9
[These are identical to those that apply in respect of street and less sophisticated commercial robbery: see SG30-2.]

**SG30-4**

ROBBERY — DWELLING

*Theft Act 1968 (section 8(1))*

**Effective from:** 01 April 2016

Triable only on indictment
Maximum: Life imprisonment
Offence range: 1 year's custody–16 years' custody

This is a Schedule 19 offence for the purposes of sections 274 and 285 (required life sentence for offence carrying life sentence) of the Sentencing Code.

For offences committed on or after 3 December 2012, where, at some time during the commission of the offence, the offender had in his or her possession a firearm or an imitation firearm within the meaning of the Firearms Act 1968, this is an offence listed in Part 1 of Schedule 15 for the purposes of sections 273 and 283 (life sentence for second listed offence) of the Sentencing Code.

This is a specified offence for the purposes of sections 266 and 279 (extended sentence for certain violent, sexual or terrorism offences) of the Sentencing Code.

**This guideline applies only to offenders aged 18 and older.**

### STEP 1 Determining the offence category
The court should determine the offence category with reference **only** to the factors listed in the tables below. In order to determine the category the court should assess **culpability** and **harm**.

The court should weigh all the factors set out below in determining the offender's culpability.

Where there are characteristics present which fall under different levels of culpability, the court should balance these characteristics to reach a fair assessment of the offender's culpability.

| Culpability demonstrated by one or more of the following: | |
|---|---|
| A – High culpability | • Use of a weapon to inflict violence<br>• Production of a bladed article or firearm or imitation firearm to threaten violence<br>• Use of very significant force in the commission of the offence<br>• Sophisticated organised nature of offence<br>• A leading role where offending is part of a group activity<br>• Offence motivated by, or demonstrating hostility based on any of the following characteristics or presumed characteristics of the victim: religion, race, disability, sexual orientation or transgender identity<br>• Abuse of position |
| B – Medium culpability | • Production of a weapon other than a bladed article or firearm or imitation firearm to threaten violence<br>• Threat of violence by any weapon (but which is not produced)<br>• A significant role where offending is part of a group activity<br>• Other cases that fall between categories A or C because:<br>  – Factors are present in A and C which balance each other out and/or<br>  – The offender's culpability falls between the factors as described in A and C |
| C – Lesser culpability | • Performed limited function under direction<br>• Involved through coercion, intimidation or exploitation<br>• Threat or use of minimal force<br>• Very little or no planning<br>• Mental disability or learning disability where linked to the commission of the offence |

| Harm<br>The court should weigh up all the factors set out below to determine the harm that has been caused or was intended to be caused to the victim. | |
|---|---|
| Category 1 | • Serious physical and/or psychological harm caused to the victim<br>• Very high value goods or sums targeted or obtained (whether economic, sentimental or personal)<br>• Soiling, ransacking or vandalism of property |
| Category 2 | • Other cases where characteristics for categories 1 or 3 are not present |
| Category 3 | • No/minimal physical or psychological harm caused to the victim<br>• Low value goods or sums targeted or obtained (whether economic, personal or sentimental)<br>• Limited damage or disturbance to property |

## STEP 2  Starting point and category range

Having determined the category at step one, the court should use the corresponding starting point to reach a sentence within the category range below. The starting point applies to all offenders irrespective of plea or previous convictions. A case of particular gravity, reflected by multiple features of culpability or harm in step one, could merit upward adjustment from the starting point before further adjustment for aggravating or mitigating features, set out below.

Consecutive sentences for multiple offences may be appropriate particularly where exceptionally high levels of harm have been caused – please refer to the *Totality* guideline [see **SG4**].

In a case of particular gravity, reflected by extremely serious violence, a sentence in excess of 13 years may be appropriate.

| Harm | Culpability | | |
|---|---|---|---|
| | A | B | C |
| Category 1 | **Starting point**<br>13 years' custody<br>**Category range**<br>10–16 years' custody | **Starting point**<br>8 years' custody<br>**Category range**<br>6–10 years' custody | **Starting point**<br>5 years' custody<br>**Category range**<br>4–8 years' custody |

| Harm | Culpability | | |
|---|---|---|---|
| | A | B | C |
| Category 2 | Starting point 8 years' custody Category range 6–10 years' custody | Starting point 5 years' custody Category range 4–8 years' custody | Starting point 3 years' custody Category range 2–5 years' custody |
| Category 3 | Starting point 5 years' custody Category range 4–8 years' custody | Starting point 3 years' custody Category range 2–5 years' custody | Starting point 18 months' custody Category range 1–3 years' custody |

### Custodial Sentences

[For the imposition of custodial sentences see Imposition of Community and Custodial Sentences at SG9-3.]

### Additional factors affecting seriousness

The table [below] contains a **non-exhaustive** list of additional factual elements providing the context of the offence and factors relating to the offender. Identify whether any combination of these, or other relevant factors, should result in an upward or downward adjustment from the sentence arrived at so far. In particular, relevant recent convictions are likely to result in an upward adjustment. In some cases, having considered these factors, it may be appropriate to move outside the identified category range.

### Factors increasing seriousness

*Statutory aggravating factors*

- Previous convictions [see SG2-21], having regard to
  a) the **nature** of the offence to which the conviction relates and its **relevance** to the current offence; and
  b) the **time** that has elapsed since the conviction
- Offence committed whilst on bail [see SG2-22]

*Other aggravating factors*

- Victim is targeted due to a vulnerability (or a perceived vulnerability) [see SG2-33]
- Steps taken to prevent the victim reporting or obtaining assistance and/or from assisting or supporting the prosecution [see SG2-37]
- Prolonged nature of attack
- Restraint, detention or additional degradation of the victim [see SG2-32]
- Involvement of others through coercion, intimidation or exploitation
- Timing of the offence [see SG2-45]
- Attempt to conceal identity (for example, wearing a balaclava or hood)
- Commission of offence whilst under the influence of alcohol or drugs [see SG2-25]
- Attempts to conceal/dispose of evidence [see SG2-37]
- Child or vulnerable person at home (or returns home) when offence committed [see SG2-36A]
- Victim compelled to leave their home
- Established evidence of community/wider impact [see SG2-46]
- Failure to comply with current court orders [see SG2-40]
- Offence committed on licence [see SG2-40]
- Offences taken into consideration [see SG3]
- Failure to respond to warnings about behaviour [see SG2-39]

### Factors reducing seriousness or reflecting personal mitigation

- No previous convictions or no relevant/recent convictions [see SG2-48]
- Remorse, particularly where evidenced by voluntary reparation to the victim [see SG2-50]
- Good character and/or exemplary conduct [see SG2-49]
- Serious medical condition requiring urgent, intensive or long-term treatment [see SG2-62]
- Age and/or lack of maturity where it affects the responsibility of the offender [see SG2-60]
- Mental disorder or learning disability (where not linked to the commission of the offence) [see SG2-63]
- Sole or primary carer for dependent relatives [see SG2-61]
- Determination and/or demonstration of steps taken to address addiction or offending

### STEPS 3 to 9

[These are identical to those that apply in respect of street and less sophisticated commercial robbery: see SG30-2.]

# PART 31   SEXUAL OFFENCES

**SG31-1**

APPLICABILITY

[For the standard text on applicability see **SG0-4**.]

**SG31-2**

ADDITIONAL ANCILLARY ORDERS – SEXUAL OFFENCES

**Slavery and trafficking prevention orders**

*Modern Slavery Act 2015, s.14*

A court may make a slavery and trafficking prevention order against an offender convicted of a slavery or human trafficking offence, if satisfied that:

- there is a risk the offender may commit a slavery or human trafficking offence; and
- it is necessary to make the order for the purpose of protecting persons generally, or particular persons, from the physical or psychological harm which would be likely to occur if the offender committed such an offence.

**Automatic orders on conviction**

The following requirements or provisions are not part of the sentence imposed by the court but apply automatically by operation of law. The role of the court is to inform the offender of the applicable requirements and/or prohibition.

| Requirement or provision | Statutory reference |
|---|---|
| Notification requirements<br>A relevant offender automatically becomes subject to notification requirements, obliging him to notify the police of specified information for a specified period. The court should inform the offender accordingly.<br><br>*The operation of the notification requirement is not a relevant consideration in determining the sentence for the offence.* | Sections 80 to 88 and Schedule 3 of the Sexual Offences Act 2003 |
| Protection for children and vulnerable adults<br>A statutory scheme pursuant to which offenders will or may be barred from regulated activity relating to children or vulnerable adults, with or without the right to make representations, depending on the offence. The court should inform the offender accordingly. | Section 2 and Schedule 3 of the Safeguarding Vulnerable Groups Act 2006<br>Safeguarding Vulnerable Groups Act 2006 (Prescribed Criteria and Miscellaneous Provisions) Regulations 2009 (SI 2009/37) (as amended) |

**SG31-3**

RAPE

*Sexual Offences Act 2003 (section 1)*

**Effective from:** 01 April 2014

[For rape of a child under 13, see **SG31-7**.]

Triable only on indictment
Maximum: Life imprisonment
Offence range: 4–19 years' custody

This is a Schedule 19 offence for the purposes of sections 274 and 285 (required life sentence for offence carrying life sentence) of the Sentencing Code.

For offences committed on or after 3 December 2012, this is an offence listed in Part 1 of Schedule 15 for the purposes of sections 273 and 283 (life sentence for second listed offence) of the Sentencing Code.

This is a specified offence for the purposes of sections 266 and 279 (extended sentence for certain violent, sexual or terrorism offences) of the Sentencing Code.

**STEP 1   Determining the offence category**

The court should determine which categories of harm and culpability the offence falls into by reference **only** to the tables below.

Offences may be of such severity, for example involving a campaign of rape, that sentences of 20 years and above may be appropriate.

### Harm

| Category 1 | • The extreme nature of one or more category 2 factors or the extreme impact caused by a combination of category 2 factors **may** elevate to category 1 |
|---|---|
| Category 2 | • Severe psychological or physical harm<br>• Pregnancy or STI as a consequence of offence<br>• Additional degradation/humiliation<br>• Abduction<br>• Prolonged detention/sustained incident<br>• Violence or threats of violence (beyond that which is inherent in the offence)<br>• Forced/uninvited entry into victim's home<br>• Victim is particularly vulnerable due to personal circumstances* |
| Category 3 | Factor(s) in categories 1 and 2 not present |

* For children under 13 please refer to the guideline [at **SG31-7**].

### Culpability

| A | B |
|---|---|
| • Significant degree of planning<br>• Offender acts together with others to commit the offence<br>• Use of alcohol/drugs on victim to facilitate the offence<br>• Abuse of trust<br>• Previous violence against victim<br>• Offence committed in course of burglary<br>• Recording of the offence<br>• Commercial exploitation and/or motivation<br>• Offence racially or religiously aggravated<br>• Offence motivated by, or demonstrating, hostility to the victim based on his or her sexual orientation (or presumed sexual orientation) or transgender identity (or presumed transgender identity)<br>• Offence motivated by, or demonstrating, hostility to the victim based on his or her disability (or presumed disability) | Factor(s) in category A not present |

### STEP 2   Starting point and category range

Having determined the category, the court should use the corresponding starting points to reach a sentence within the category range below. The starting point applies to all offenders irrespective of plea or previous convictions. Having determined the starting point, step two allows further adjustment for aggravating or mitigating features set out below.

A case of particular gravity, reflected by multiple features of culpability or harm in step one, could merit upward adjustment from the starting point before further adjustment for aggravating or mitigating features, set out below.

| | A | B |
|---|---|---|
| Category 1 | **Starting point**<br>15 years' custody<br>**Category range**<br>13–19 years' custody | **Starting point**<br>12 years' custody<br>**Category range**<br>10–15 years' custody |
| Category 2 | **Starting point**<br>10 years' custody<br>**Category range**<br>9–13 years' custody | **Starting point**<br>8 years' custody<br>**Category range**<br>7–9 years' custody |
| Category 3 | **Starting point**<br>7 years' custody<br>**Category range**<br>6–9 years' custody | **Starting point**<br>5 years' custody<br>**Category range**<br>4–7 years' custody |

## Custodial Sentences

[For the imposition of custodial sentences see Imposition of Community and Custodial Sentences at **SG9-3**.]

## Additional factors affecting seriousness

The table below contains a **non-exhaustive** list of additional factual elements providing the context of the offence and factors relating to the offender. Identify whether any combination of these, or other relevant factors, should result in an upward or downward adjustment from the starting point. **In particular, relevant recent convictions are likely to result in an upward adjustment.** In some cases, having considered these factors, it may be appropriate to move outside the identified category range.

## Aggravating factors

### Statutory aggravating factors

- Previous convictions, having regard to
  a) the nature of the offence to which the conviction relates and its relevance to the current offence; and
  b) the time that has elapsed since the conviction
- Offence committed whilst on bail

### Other aggravating factors

- Specific targeting of a particularly vulnerable victim
- Ejaculation (where not taken into account at step one)
- Blackmail or other threats made (where not taken into account at step one)
- Location of offence
- Timing of offence
- Use of weapon or other item to frighten or injure
- Victim compelled to leave their home (including victims of domestic violence)
- Failure to comply with current court orders
- Offence committed whilst on licence
- Exploiting contact arrangements with a child to commit an offence
- Presence of others, especially children
- Any steps taken to prevent the victim reporting an incident, obtaining assistance and/or from assisting or supporting the prosecution
- Attempts to dispose of or conceal evidence
- Commission of offence whilst under the influence of alcohol or drugs

## Mitigating factors

- No previous convictions **or** no relevant/recent convictions
- Remorse
- Previous good character and/or exemplary conduct*
- Age and/or lack of maturity where it affects the responsibility of the offender
- Mental disorder or learning disability, particularly where linked to the commission of the offence

* Previous good character/exemplary conduct is different from having no previous convictions. The more serious the offence, the less the weight which should normally be attributed to this factor. Where previous good character/exemplary conduct has been used to facilitate the offence, this mitigation should not normally be allowed and such conduct may constitute an aggravating factor.

In the context of this offence, previous good character/exemplary conduct should not normally be given any significant weight and will not normally justify a reduction in what would otherwise be the appropriate sentence.

## STEP 3   Consider any factors which indicate a reduction, such as assistance to the prosecution

The court should take into account section 74 of the Sentencing Code (reduction in sentence for assistance to prosecution) and any other rule of law by virtue of which an offender may receive a discounted sentence in consequence of assistance given (or offered) to the prosecutor or investigator.

## STEP 4   Reduction for guilty pleas

The court should take account of any potential reduction for a guilty plea in accordance with section 73 of the Sentencing Code and the guideline for Reduction in Sentence for a Guilty Plea [**SG5-1–SG5-12**].

## STEP 5   Dangerousness

The court should consider:

1) whether having regard to the criteria contained in Chapter 6 of Part 10 of the Sentencing Code it would be appropriate to impose a life sentence (sections 274 and 285);

2) whether having regard to sections 273 and 283 of the Sentencing Code it would be appropriate to impose a life sentence;

3) whether having regard to the criteria contained in Chapter 6 of Part 10 of the Sentencing Code it would be appropriate to impose an extended sentence (sections 266 and 279).

When sentencing offenders to a life sentence under these provisions, the notional determinate sentence should be used as the basis for the setting of a minimum term.

### STEP 6 Totality principle

If sentencing an offender for more than one offence, or where the offender is already serving a sentence, consider whether the total sentence is just and proportionate to the offending behaviour. See *Totality* guideline [at **SG4**].

### STEP 7 Ancillary orders

The court must consider whether to make any ancillary orders. The court must also consider what other requirements or provisions may *automatically* apply. [See the Crown Court Compendium, Part II Sentencing, S7; Ancillary Orders]

#### Additional ancillary orders – sexual offences

[See **SG31-2** for additional ancillary orders for sexual offences covering slavery and trafficking prevention orders and automatic orders on conviction.]

### STEP 8 Reasons

Section 52 of the Sentencing Code imposes a duty to give reasons for, and explain the effect of, the sentence.

### STEP 9 Consideration for time spent on bail (tagged curfew)

The court must consider whether to give credit for time spent on bail in accordance with section 240A of the Criminal Justice Act 2003 and section 325 of the Sentencing Code.

**SG31-4**

ASSAULT BY PENETRATION

*Sexual Offences Act 2003 (section 2)*

**Effective from:** 01 April 2014

Triable only on indictment
Maximum: Life imprisonment
Offence range: Community order–19 years' custody

This is a Schedule 19 offence for the purposes of sections 274 and 285 (required life sentence for offence carrying life sentence) of the Sentencing Code.

For offences committed on or after 3 December 2012, this is an offence listed in Part 1 of Schedule 15 for the purposes of sections 273 and 283 (life sentence for second listed offence) of the Sentencing Code.

This is a specified offence for the purposes of sections 266 and 279 (extended sentence for certain violent, sexual or terrorism offences) of the Sentencing Code.

### STEP 1 Determining the offence category

The court should determine which categories of harm and culpability the offence falls into by reference **only** to the tables below.

**Harm**

| Category 1 | • The extreme nature of one or more category 2 factors or the extreme impact caused by a combination of category 2 factors **may** elevate to category 1 |
|---|---|
| Category 2 | • Severe psychological or physical harm<br>• Penetration using large or dangerous object(s)<br>• Additional degradation/humiliation<br>• Abduction<br>• Prolonged detention/sustained incident<br>• Violence or threats of violence (beyond that which is inherent in the offence)<br>• Forced/uninvited entry into victim's home<br>• Victim is particularly vulnerable due to personal circumstances* |
| Category 3 | Factor(s) in categories 1 and 2 not present |

* For children under 13 please refer to the guideline [at **SG31-7**].

## Culpability

| A | B |
|---|---|
| • Significant degree of planning<br>• Offender acts together with others to commit the offence<br>• Use of alcohol/drugs on victim to facilitate the offence<br>• Abuse of trust<br>• Previous violence against victim<br>• Offence committed in course of burglary<br>• Recording of the offence<br>• Commercial exploitation and/or motivation<br>• Offence racially or religiously aggravated<br>• Offence motivated by, or demonstrating, hostility to the victim based on his or her sexual orientation (or presumed sexual orientation) or transgender identity (or presumed transgender identity)<br>• Offence motivated by, or demonstrating, hostility to the victim based on his or her disability (or presumed disability) | Factor(s) in category A not present |

### STEP 2   Starting point and category range

Having determined the category, the court should use the corresponding starting points to reach a sentence within the category range below. The starting point applies to all offenders irrespective of plea or previous convictions.

Having determined the starting point, step two allows further adjustment for aggravating or mitigating features, set out below.

A case of particular gravity, reflected by multiple features of culpability or harm in step one, could merit upward adjustment from the starting point before further adjustment for aggravating or mitigating features, set out below.

Where there is a sufficient prospect of rehabilitation, a community order with a sex offender treatment programme requirement under Part 3 of Schedule 9 of the Sentencing Code can be a proper alternative to a short or moderate length custodial sentence.

|  | A | B |
|---|---|---|
| Category 1 | **Starting point**<br>15 years' custody<br>**Category range**<br>13–19 years' custody | **Starting point**<br>12 years' custody<br>**Category range**<br>10–15 years' custody |
| Category 2 | **Starting point**<br>8 years' custody<br>**Category range**<br>5–13 years' custody | **Starting point**<br>6 years' custody<br>**Category range**<br>4–9 years' custody |
| Category 3 | **Starting point**<br>4 years' custody<br>**Category range**<br>2–6 years' custody | **Starting point**<br>2 years' custody<br>**Category range**<br>High level community order–4 years' custody |

### Community Orders and Custodial Sentences

[For the imposition of community orders, including the community orders table, see Imposition of Community and Custodial Sentences at SG9-2. For the imposition of custodial sentences see Imposition of Community and Custodial Sentences at SG9-3.]

### Factors increasing or reducing seriousness

The table below contains a **non-exhaustive** list of additional factual elements providing the context of the offence and factors relating to the offender. Identify whether any combination of these, or other relevant factors, should result in an upward or downward adjustment from the starting point. **In particular, relevant recent convictions are likely to result in an upward adjustment.** In some cases, having considered these factors, it may be appropriate to move outside the identified category range.

When sentencing appropriate **category 3** offences, the court should also consider the custody threshold as follows:

Sentencing Guidelines

- Has the custody threshold been passed?
- If so, is it unavoidable that a custodial sentence be imposed?
- If so, can that sentence be suspended?

## Aggravating factors

### Statutory aggravating factors

- Previous convictions, having regard to
  a) the nature of the offence to which the conviction relates and its relevance to the current offence; and
  b) the time that has elapsed since the conviction
- Offence committed whilst on bail

### Other aggravating factors

- Specific targeting of a particularly vulnerable victim
- Blackmail or other threats made (where not taken into account at step one)
- Location of offence
- Timing of offence
- Use of weapon or other item to frighten or injure
- Victim compelled to leave their home (including victims of domestic violence)
- Failure to comply with current court orders
- Offence committed on licence or post sentence supervision
- Exploiting contact arrangements with a child to commit an offence
- Presence of others, especially children
- Any steps taken to prevent the victim reporting an incident, obtaining assistance and/or from assisting or supporting the prosecution
- Attempts to dispose of or conceal evidence
- Commission of offence whilst under the influence of alcohol or drugs

## Mitigating factors

- No previous convictions or no relevant/recent convictions
- Remorse
- Previous good character and/or exemplary conduct*
- Age and/or lack of maturity where it affects the responsibility of the offender
- Mental disorder or learning disability, particularly where linked to the commission of the offence

* Previous good character/exemplary conduct is different from having no previous convictions. The more serious the offence, the less the weight which should normally be attributed to this factor. Where previous good character/exemplary conduct has been used to facilitate the offence, this mitigation should not normally be allowed and such conduct may constitute an aggravating factor.

In the context of this offence, previous good character/exemplary conduct should not normally be given any significant weight and will not normally justify a reduction in what would otherwise be the appropriate sentence.

## STEP 3  Consider any factors which indicate a reduction, such as assistance to the prosecution

The court should take into account section 74 of the Sentencing Code (reduction in sentence for assistance to prosecution) and any other rule of law by virtue of which an offender may receive a discounted sentence in consequence of assistance given (or offered) to the prosecutor or investigator.

## STEP 4  Reduction for guilty plea

The court should take account of any potential reduction for a guilty plea in accordance with section 73 of the Sentencing Code and the guideline for Reduction in Sentence for a Guilty Plea [SG5-1–SG5-12].

## STEP 5  Dangerousness

The court should consider:

1) whether having regard to the criteria contained in Chapter 6 of Part 10 of the Sentencing Code it would be appropriate to impose a life sentence (sections 274 and 285)
2) whether having regard to sections 273 and 283 of the Sentencing Code it would be appropriate to impose a life sentence
3) whether having regard to the criteria contained in Chapter 6 of Part 10 of the Sentencing Code it would be appropriate to impose an extended sentence (sections 266 and 279)

When sentencing offenders to a life sentence under these provisions, the notional determinate sentence should be used as the basis for the setting of a minimum term.

## STEP 6  Totality principle

If sentencing an offender for more than one offence, or where the offender is already serving a sentence, consider whether the total sentence is just and proportionate to the offending behaviour. See the *Totality* guideline [at **SG4**].

## STEP 7  Ancillary orders

The court must consider whether to make any ancillary orders. The court must also consider what other requirements or provisions may automatically apply.

[See the Crown Court Compendium, Part II Sentencing, S7; Ancillary Orders]

### Additional ancillary orders – sexual offences

[See SG31-2 for additional ancillary orders for sexual offences covering slavery and trafficking prevention orders and automatic orders on conviction.]

## STEP 8  Reasons

Section 52 of the Sentencing Code imposes a duty to give reasons for, and explain the effect of, the sentence.

## STEP 9  Consideration for time spent on bail (tagged curfew)

The court must consider whether to give credit for time spent on bail in accordance with section 240A of the Criminal Justice Act 2003 and section 325 of the Sentencing Code.

SEXUAL ASSAULT

*Sexual Offences Act 2003 (section 3)*

**SG31-5**

**Effective from:** 01 April 2014

Triable either way
Maximum: 10 years' custody
Offence range: Community order–7 years' custody

This is a specified offence for the purposes of sections 266 and 279 (extended sentence for certain violent, sexual or terrorism offences) of the Sentencing Code.

## STEP 1  Determining the offence category

The court should determine which categories of harm and culpability the offence falls into by reference **only** to the tables below.

| Harm | |
|---|---|
| Category 1 | • Severe psychological or physical harm<br>• Abduction<br>• Violence or threats of violence<br>• Forced/uninvited entry into victim's home |
| Category 2 | • Touching of naked genitalia or naked breasts<br>• Prolonged detention/sustained incident<br>• Additional degradation/humiliation<br>• Victim is particularly vulnerable due to personal circumstances[*] |
| Category 3 | Factor(s) in categories 1 and 2 not present |

[*] For children under 13 please refer to the guideline [at **SG31-9**].

| Culpability | |
|---|---|
| A | B |
| • Significant degree of planning<br>• Offender acts together with others to commit the offence<br>• Use of alcohol/drugs on victim to facilitate the offence | |

| | |
|---|---|
| • Abuse of trust<br>• Previous violence against victim<br>• Offence committed in course of burglary<br>• Recording of offence<br>• Commercial exploitation and/or motivation<br>• Offence racially or religiously aggravated<br>• Offence motivated by, or demonstrating, hostility to the victim based on his or her sexual orientation (or presumed sexual orientation) or transgender identity (or presumed transgender identity)<br>• Offence motivated by, or demonstrating, hostility to the victim based on his or her disability (or presumed disability) | Factor(s) in category A not present |

### STEP 2   Starting point and category range

Having determined the category, the court should use the corresponding starting points to reach a sentence within the category range below. The starting point applies to all offenders irrespective of plea or previous convictions. Having determined the starting point, step two allows further adjustment for aggravating or mitigating features, set out below.

A case of particular gravity, reflected by multiple features of culpability or harm in step one, could merit upward adjustment from the starting point before further adjustment for aggravating or mitigating features, set out below.

Where there is a sufficient prospect of rehabilitation, a community order with a sex offender treatment programme requirement under Part 3 of Schedule 9 of the Sentencing Code can be a proper alternative to a short or moderate length custodial sentence.

| | A | B |
|---|---|---|
| Category 1 | **Starting point**<br>4 years' custody<br>**Category range**<br>3–7 years' custody | **Starting point**<br>2 years 6 months' custody<br>**Category range**<br>2–4 years' custody |
| Category 2 | **Starting point**<br>2 years' custody<br>**Category range**<br>1–4 years' custody | **Starting point**<br>1 year's custody<br>**Category range**<br>High level community order–2 years' custody |
| Category 3 | **Starting point**<br>26 weeks' custody<br>**Category range**<br>High level community order–1 year's custody | **Starting point**<br>High level community order<br>**Category range**<br>Medium level community order–26 weeks' custody |

### Community Orders and Custodial Sentences

[For the imposition of community orders, including the community orders table, see Imposition of Community and Custodial Sentences at **SG9-2.** For the imposition of custodial sentences see Imposition of Community and Custodial Sentences at **SG9-3.**]

### Factors increasing or reducing seriousness

Below is a **non-exhaustive** list of additional factual elements providing the context of the offence and factors relating to the offender. Identify whether any combination of these, or other relevant factors, should result in an upward or downward adjustment from the starting point.

**In particular, relevant recent convictions are likely to result in an upward adjustment.** In some cases, having considered these factors, it may be appropriate to move outside the identified category range.

When sentencing appropriate **category 2 or 3 offences**, the court should also consider the custody threshold as follows:

• Has the custody threshold been passed?
• If so, is it unavoidable that a custodial sentence be imposed?
• If so, can that sentence be suspended?

**Aggravating factors**

*Statutory aggravating factors*

- Previous convictions, having regard to
  a) the nature of the offence to which the conviction relates and its relevance to the current offence; and
  b) the time that has elapsed since the conviction
- Offence committed whilst on bail
- Offence was committed against an emergency worker acting in the exercise of functions as such a worker

*Other aggravating factors*

- Specific targeting of a particularly vulnerable victim
- Blackmail or other threats made (where not taken into account at step one)
- Location of the offence
- Timing of the offence
- Use of weapon or other item to frighten or injure
- Victim compelled to leave their home (including victims of domestic violence)
- Failure to comply with current court orders
- Offence committed whilst on licence
- Exploiting contact arrangements with a child to commit an offence
- Presence of others, especially children
- Any steps taken to prevent the victim reporting an incident, obtaining assistance and/or from assisting or supporting the prosecution
- Attempts to dispose of or conceal evidence
- Commission of offence whilst under the influence of alcohol or drugs

**Mitigating factors**

- No previous convictions **or** no relevant/recent convictions
- Remorse
- Previous good character and/or exemplary conduct*
- Age and/or lack of maturity where it affects the responsibility of the offender
- Mental disorder or learning disability, particularly where linked to the commission of the offence
- Demonstration of steps taken to address offending behaviour

* Previous good character/exemplary conduct is different from having no previous convictions. The more serious the offence, the less the weight which should normally be attributed to this factor. Where previous good character/exemplary conduct has been used to facilitate the offence, this mitigation should not normally be allowed and such conduct may constitute an aggravating factor.

**STEP 3  Consider any factors which indicate a reduction, such as assistance to the prosecution**

The court should take into account section 74 of the Sentencing Code (reduction in sentence for assistance to prosecution) and any other rule of law by virtue of which an offender may receive a discounted sentence in consequence of assistance given (or offered) to the prosecutor or investigator.

**STEP 4  Reduction for guilty pleas**

The court should take account of any potential reduction for a guilty plea in accordance with section 73 of the Sentencing Code and the guideline for Reduction in Sentence for a Guilty Plea [**SG5-1–SG5-12**].

**STEP 5  Dangerousness**

The court should consider whether having regard to the criteria contained in Chapter 6 of Part 10 of the Sentencing Code it would be appropriate to impose an extended sentence (sections 266 and 279).

**STEP 6  Totality principle**

If sentencing an offender for more than one offence, or where the offender is already serving a sentence, consider whether the total sentence is just and proportionate to the offending behaviour. See *Totality* guideline [at **SG4**].

**STEP 7  Ancillary orders**

The court must consider whether to make any ancillary orders. The court must also consider what other requirements or provisions may *automatically* apply.

[For ancillary orders in the Magistrates' Court see **SG10-5**. For the Crown Court, see the Crown Court Compendium, Part II Sentencing, S7; Ancillary Orders]

**Additional ancillary orders – sexual offences**

[See **SG31-2** for additional ancillary orders for sexual offences covering slavery and trafficking prevention orders and automatic orders on conviction.]

### STEP 8 Reasons

Section 52 of the Sentencing Code imposes a duty to give reasons for, and explain the effect of, the sentence.

### STEP 9 Consideration for time spent on bail (tagged curfew)

The court must consider whether to give credit for time spent on bail in accordance with section 240A of the Criminal Justice Act 2003 and section 325 of the Sentencing Code.

**SG31-6**      CAUSING A PERSON TO ENGAGE IN SEXUAL ACTIVITY WITHOUT CONSENT

*Sexual Offences Act 2003 (section 4)*

**Effective from:** 01 April 2014

Triable only on indictment (if penetration involved), otherwise triable either way
Maximum: Life imprisonment (if penetration involved), otherwise 10 years
Offence range: Community order–7 years' custody (if no penetration involved) / 19 years' custody (if penetration involved)

Where the offence involved penetration this is a Schedule 19 offence for the purposes of sections 274 and 285 (required life sentence for offence carrying life sentence) of the Sentencing Code.

For offences involving penetration committed on or after 3 December 2012, this is an offence listed in Part 1 of Schedule 15 for the purposes of sections 273 and 283 (life sentence for second listed offence) of the Sentencing Code.

This is a specified offence for the purposes of sections 266 and 279 (extended sentence for certain violent, sexual or terrorism offences) of the Sentencing Code.

### STEP 1 Determining the offence category

The court should determine which categories of harm and culpability the offence falls into by reference **only** to the tables below.

**Harm**

| Category 1 | • The extreme nature of one or more category 2 factors or the extreme impact caused by a combination of category 2 factors **may** elevate to category 1 |
|---|---|
| Category 2 | • Severe psychological or physical harm<br>• Penetration using large or dangerous object(s)<br>• Pregnancy or STI as a consequence of offence<br>• Additional degradation/humiliation<br>• Abduction<br>• Prolonged detention/sustained incident<br>• Violence or threats of violence<br>• Forced/uninvited entry into victim's home<br>• Victim is particularly vulnerable due to personal circumstances* |
| Category 3 | Factor(s) in categories 1 and 2 not present |

*For children under 13 please refer to the guideline [at **SG31-10**].

## Culpability

| A | B |
|---|---|
| • Significant degree of planning<br>• Offender acts together with others to commit the offence<br>• Use of alcohol/drugs on victim to facilitate the offence<br>• Abuse of trust<br>• Previous violence against victim<br>• Offence committed in course of burglary<br>• Recording of the offence<br>• Commercial exploitation and/or motivation<br>• Offence racially or religiously aggravated<br>• Offence motivated by, or demonstrating, hostility to the victim based on his or her sexual orientation (or presumed sexual orientation) or transgender identity (or presumed transgender identity)<br>• Offence motivated by, or demonstrating, hostility to the victim based on his or her disability (or presumed disability) | Factor(s) in category A not present |

### STEP 2  Starting point and category range

Having determined the category, the court should use the corresponding starting points to reach a sentence within the category range below. The starting point applies to all offenders irrespective of plea or previous convictions.

Having determined the starting point, step two allows further adjustment for aggravating or mitigating features, set out below.

A case of particular gravity, reflected by multiple features of culpability or harm in step one, could merit upward adjustment from the starting point before further adjustment for aggravating or mitigating features, set out below.

Where there is a sufficient prospect of rehabilitation, a community order with a sex offender treatment programme requirement under Part 3 of Schedule 9 of the Sentencing Code can be a proper alternative to a short or moderate length custodial sentence.

### Where offence involved penetration

|  | A | B |
|---|---|---|
| Category 1 | **Starting point**<br>15 years' custody<br>**Category range**<br>13–19 years' custody | **Starting point**<br>12 years' custody<br>**Category range**<br>10–15 years' custody |
| Category 2 | **Starting point**<br>8 years' custody<br>**Category range**<br>5–13 years' custody | **Starting point**<br>6 years' custody<br>**Category range**<br>4–9 years' custody |
| Category 3 | **Starting point**<br>4 years' custody<br>**Category range**<br>2–6 years' custody | **Starting point**<br>2 years' custody<br>**Category range**<br>High level community order–4 years' custody |

### Where offence did not involve penetration

|  | A | B |
|---|---|---|
| Category 1 | **Starting point**<br>4 years' custody<br>**Category range**<br>3–7 years' custody | **Starting point**<br>2 years 6 months' custody<br>**Category range**<br>2–4 years' custody |
| Category 2 | **Starting point**<br>2 years' custody<br>**Category range**<br>1–4 years' custody | **Starting point**<br>1 year's custody<br>**Category range**<br>High level community order–2 years' custody |

Sentencing Guidelines

|  | A | B |
|---|---|---|
| Category 3 | **Starting point**<br>26 weeks' custody<br>**Category range**<br>High level community<br>order–1 year's custody | **Starting point**<br>High level community order<br>**Category range**<br>Medium level community order–26 weeks' custody |

### Community Orders and Custodial Sentences

[For the imposition of community orders, including the community orders table, see Imposition of Community and Custodial Sentences at **SG9-2**. For the imposition of custodial sentences see Imposition of Community and Custodial Sentences at **SG9-3**.]

### Factors increasing or reducing seriousness

The table below contains a **non-exhaustive** list of additional factual elements providing the context of the offence and factors relating to the offender. Identify whether any combination of these, or other relevant factors, should result in an upward or downward adjustment from the starting point. **In particular, relevant recent convictions are likely to result in an upward adjustment.** In some cases, having considered these factors, it may be appropriate to move outside the identified category range.

When sentencing appropriate **category 2 or 3** offences, the court should also consider the custody threshold as follows:

- Has the custody threshold been passed?
- If so, is it unavoidable that a custodial sentence be imposed?
- If so, can that sentence be suspended?

### Aggravating factors

*Statutory aggravating factors*

- Previous convictions, having regard to
  a) the nature of the offence to which the conviction relates and its relevance to the current offence; and
  b) the time that has elapsed since the conviction
- Offence committed whilst on bail

*Other aggravating factors*

- Specific targeting of a particularly vulnerable victim
- Ejaculation (where not taken into account at step one)
- Blackmail or other threats made (where not taken into account at step one)
- Location of offence
- Timing of offence
- Use of weapon or other item to frighten or injure
- Victim compelled to leave their home (including victims of domestic violence)
- Failure to comply with current court orders
- Offence committed whilst on licence
- Exploiting contact arrangements with a child to commit an offence
- Presence of others, especially children
- Any steps taken to prevent the victim reporting an incident, obtaining assistance and/or from assisting or supporting the prosecution
- Attempts to dispose of or conceal evidence
- Commission of offence whilst under the influence of alcohol or drugs

### Mitigating factors

- No previous convictions **or** no relevant/recent convictions
- Previous good character and or exemplary conduct*
- Remorse
- Age and/or lack of maturity where it affects the responsibility of the offender
- Mental disorder or learning disability, particularly where linked to the commission of the offence

* Previous good character/exemplary conduct is different from having no previous convictions. The more serious the offence, the less the weight which should normally be attributed to this factor. Where previous good character/exemplary conduct has been used to facilitate the offence, this mitigation should not normally be allowed and such conduct may constitute an aggravating factor.

In the context of this offence, previous good character/exemplary conduct should not normally be given any significant weight and will not normally justify a reduction in what would otherwise be the appropriate sentence.

**STEP 3  Consider any factors which indicate a reduction, such as assistance to the prosecution**

The court should take into account section 74 of the Sentencing Code (reduction in sentence for assistance to prosecution) and any other rule of law by virtue of which an offender may receive a discounted sentence in consequence of assistance given (or offered) to the prosecutor or investigator.

**STEP 4  Reduction for guilty plea**

The court should take account of any potential reduction for a guilty plea in accordance with section 73 of the Sentencing Code and the guideline for Reduction in Sentence for a Guilty Plea [SG5-1–SG5-12].

**STEP 5  Dangerousness**

The court should consider:

1) whether having regard to the criteria contained in Chapter 6 of Part 10 of the Sentencing Code it would be appropriate to impose a life sentence (sections 274 and 285);
2) whether having regard to sections 273 and 283 of the Sentencing Code it would be appropriate to impose a life sentence;
3) whether having regard to the criteria contained in Chapter 6 of Part 10 of the Sentencing Code it would be appropriate to impose an extended sentence (sections 266 and 279).

When sentencing offenders to a life sentence under these provisions, the notional determinate sentence should be used as the basis for the setting of a minimum term.

**STEP 6  Totality principle**

If sentencing an offender for more than one offence, or where the offender is already serving a sentence, consider whether the total sentence is just and proportionate to the offending behaviour. See *Totality* guideline [at **SG4**].

**STEP 7  Ancillary orders**

The court must consider whether to make any ancillary orders. The court must also consider what other requirements or provisions may automatically apply.

[For ancillary orders in the Magistrates' Court see **SG10-5**. For the Crown Court, see the Crown Court Compendium, Part II Sentencing, S7; Ancillary Orders]

**Additional ancillary orders – sexual offences**

[See **SG31-2** for additional ancillary orders for sexual offences covering slavery and trafficking prevention orders and automatic orders on conviction.]

**STEP 8  Reasons**

Section 52 of the Sentencing Code imposes a duty to give reasons for, and explain the effect of, the sentence.

**STEP 9  Consideration for time spent on bail (tagged curfew)**

The court must consider whether to give credit for time spent on bail in accordance with section 240A of the Criminal Justice Act 2003 and section 325 of the Sentencing Code.

RAPE OF A CHILD UNDER 13                                                **SG31-7**

*Sexual Offences Act 2003 (section 5)*

**Effective from:** 01 April 2014

Triable only on indictment
Maximum: Life imprisonment
Offence range: 6–19 years' custody

This is a Schedule 19 offence for the purposes of sections 274 and 285 (required life sentence for offence carrying life sentence) of the Sentencing Code.

For offences committed on or after 3 December 2012, this is an offence listed in Part 1 of Schedule 15 for the purposes of sections 273 and 283 (life sentence for second listed offence) of the Sentencing Code.

This is a specified offence for the purposes of sections 266 and 279 (extended sentence for certain violent, sexual or terrorism offences) of the Sentencing Code.

This is an offence listed in Schedule 13 for the purposes of sections 265 and 278 (required special sentence for certain offenders of particular concern) of the Sentencing Code.

### STEP 1  Determining the offence category

The court should determine which categories of harm and culpability the offence falls into by reference **only** to the tables below.

**Offences may be of such severity, for example involving a campaign of rape, that sentences of 20 years and above may be appropriate.**

When dealing with the statutory offence of rape of a child under 13, the court may be faced with a wide range of offending behaviour.

Sentencers should have particular regard to the fact that these offences are not only committed through force or fear of force but may include exploitative behaviour towards a child which should be considered to indicate high culpability.

This guideline is designed to deal with the majority of offending behaviour which deserves a significant custodial sentence; the starting points and ranges reflect the fact that such offending merits such an approach. There may also be **exceptional** cases, where a lengthy community order with a requirement to participate in a sex offender treatment programme may be the best way of changing the offender's behaviour and of protecting the public by preventing any repetition of the offence. This guideline may not be appropriate where the sentencer is satisfied that on the available evidence, and in the absence of exploitation, a young or particularly immature defendant genuinely believed, on reasonable grounds, that the victim was aged 16 or over and that they were engaging in lawful sexual activity.

Sentencers are reminded that if sentencing outside the guideline they must be satisfied that it would be contrary to the interests of justice to follow the guideline.

### Harm

| Category 1 | • The extreme nature of one or more category 2 factors or the extreme impact caused by a combination of category 2 factors **may** elevate to category 1 |
| --- | --- |
| Category 2 | • Severe psychological or physical harm<br>• Pregnancy or STI as a consequence of offence<br>• Additional degradation/humiliation<br>• Abduction<br>• Prolonged detention /sustained incident<br>• Violence or threats of violence<br>• Forced/uninvited entry into victim's home<br>• Child is particularly vulnerable due to extreme youth and/or personal circumstances |
| Category 3 | Factor(s) in categories 1 and 2 not present |

### Culpability

| A | B |
| --- | --- |
| • Significant degree of planning<br>• Offender acts together with others to commit the offence<br>• Use of alcohol/drugs on victim to facilitate the offence<br>• Grooming behaviour used against victim<br>• Abuse of trust<br>• Previous violence against victim<br>• Offence committed in course of burglary<br>• Sexual images of victim recorded, retained, solicited or shared<br>• Deliberate isolation of victim<br>• Commercial exploitation and/or motivation<br>• Offence racially or religiously aggravated<br>• Offence motivated by, or demonstrating, hostility to the victim based on his or her sexual orientation (or presumed sexual orientation) or transgender identity (or presumed transgender identity)<br>• Offence motivated by, or demonstrating, hostility to the victim based on his or her disability (or presumed disability) | Factor(s) in category A not present |

### STEP 2  Starting point and category range

Having determined the category, the court should use the corresponding starting points to reach a sentence within the category range below. The starting point applies to all offenders irrespective of plea or previous convictions. Having determined the starting point, step two allows further adjustment for aggravating or mitigating features, set out below.

A case of particular gravity, reflected by multiple features of culpability or harm in step one, could merit upward adjustment from the starting point before further adjustment for aggravating or mitigating features, set out below.

Sentencers should also note the wording set out at step one which may be applicable in exceptional cases.

|  | A | B |
|---|---|---|
| Category 1 | **Starting point**<br>16 years' custody<br>**Category range**<br>13–19 years' custody | **Starting point**<br>13 years' custody<br>**Category range**<br>11–17 years' custody |
| Category 2 | **Starting point**<br>13 years' custody<br>**Category range**<br>11–17 years' custody | **Starting point**<br>10 years' custody<br>**Category range**<br>8–13 years' custody |
| Category 3 | **Starting point**<br>10 years' custody<br>**Category range**<br>8–13 years' custody | **Starting point**<br>8 years' custody<br>**Category range**<br>6–11 years' custody |

## Custodial Sentences

[For the imposition of custodial sentences see Imposition of Community and Custodial Sentences at **SG9-3**.]

### Factors increasing or reducing seriousness

The table below contains a **non-exhaustive** list of additional factual elements providing the context of the offence and factors relating to the offender. Identify whether any combination of these, or other relevant factors, should result in an upward or downward adjustment from the starting point. **In particular, relevant recent convictions are likely to result in an upward adjustment.** In some cases, having considered these factors, it may be appropriate to move outside the identified category range.

### Aggravating factors

*Statutory aggravating factors*

- Previous convictions, having regard to
  a) the nature of the offence to which the conviction relates and its relevance to the current offence; and
  b) the time that has elapsed since the conviction
- Offence committed whilst on bail

*Other aggravating factors*

- Specific targeting of a particularly vulnerable child
- Ejaculation (where not taken into account at step one)
- Blackmail or other threats made (where not taken into account at step one)
- Location of offence
- Timing of offence
- Use of weapon or other item to frighten or injure
- Victim compelled to leave their home, school, etc
- Failure to comply with current court orders
- Offence committed whilst on licence
- Exploiting contact arrangements with a child to commit an offence
- Presence of others, especially other children
- Any steps taken to prevent the victim reporting an incident, obtaining assistance and/or from assisting or supporting the prosecution
- Attempts to dispose of or conceal evidence
- Commission of offence whilst offender under the influence of alcohol or drugs
- Victim encouraged to recruit others

### Mitigating factors

- No previous convictions **or** no relevant/recent convictions
- Remorse
- Previous good character and/or exemplary conduct*
- Age and/or lack of maturity where it affects the responsibility of the offender
- Mental disorder or learning disability, particularly where linked to the commission of the offence

\* Previous good character/exemplary conduct is different from having no previous convictions. The more serious the offence, the less the weight which should normally be attributed to this factor. Where previous good character/exemplary conduct has been used to facilitate the offence, this mitigation should not normally be allowed and such conduct may constitute an aggravating factor.

In the context of this offence, previous good character/exemplary conduct should not normally be given any significant weight and will not normally justify a reduction in what would otherwise be the appropriate sentence.

### STEP 3 Consider any factors which indicate a reduction, such as assistance to the prosecution

The court should take into account section 74 of the Sentencing Code (reduction in sentence for assistance to prosecution) and any other rule of law by virtue of which an offender may receive a discounted sentence in consequence of assistance given (or offered) to the prosecutor or investigator.

### STEP 4 Reduction for guilty pleas

The court should take account of any potential reduction for a guilty plea in accordance with section 73 of the Sentencing Code and the guideline for Reduction in Sentence for a Guilty Plea [SG5-1–SG5-12].

### STEP 5 Dangerousness

The court should consider:

1) whether having regard to the criteria contained in Chapter 6 of Part 10 of the Sentencing Code it would be appropriate to impose a life sentence (sections 274 and 285);
2) whether having regard to sections 273 and 283 of the Sentencing Code it would be appropriate to impose a life sentence;
3) whether having regard to the criteria contained in Chapter 6 of Part 10 of the Sentencing Code it would be appropriate to impose an extended sentence (sections 266 and 279).

When sentencing offenders to a life sentence under these provisions, the notional determinate sentence should be used as the basis for the setting of a minimum term.

### STEP 6 Required special sentence for certain offenders of particular concern

Where the court does not impose a sentence of imprisonment for life or an extended sentence, but does impose a period of imprisonment, the term of the sentence must be equal to the aggregate of the appropriate custodial term and a further period of 1 year for which the offender is to be subject to a licence (sections 265 and 278 of the Sentencing Code).

### STEP 7 Totality principle

If sentencing an offender for more than one offence, or where the offender is already serving a sentence, consider whether the total sentence is just and proportionate to the offending behaviour. See *Totality* guideline [at **SG4**].

### STEP 8 Ancillary orders

The court must consider whether to make any ancillary orders. The court must also consider what other requirements or provisions may *automatically* apply.

[See the Crown Court Compendium, Part II Sentencing, S7; Ancillary Orders]

#### Additional ancillary orders – sexual offences

[See SG31-2 for additional ancillary orders for sexual offences covering slavery and trafficking prevention orders and automatic orders on conviction.]

### STEP 9 Reasons

Section 52 of the Sentencing Code imposes a duty to give reasons for, and explain the effect of, the sentence.

### STEP 10 Consideration for time spent on bail (tagged curfew)

The court must consider whether to give credit for time spent on bail in accordance with section 240A of the Criminal Justice Act 2003 and section 325 of the Sentencing Code.

**SG31-8**                  ASSAULT OF A CHILD UNDER 13 BY PENETRATION

*Sexual Offences Act 2003 (section 6)*

**Effective from:** 01 April 2014

Triable only on indictment
Maximum: Life imprisonment
Offence range: 2–19 years' custody

This is a Schedule 19 offence for the purposes of sections 274 and 285 (required life sentence for offence carrying life sentence) of the Sentencing Code.

For offences committed on or after 3 December 2012, this is an offence listed in Part 1 of Schedule 15 for the purposes of sections 273 and 283 (life sentence for second listed offence) of the Sentencing Code.

This is a specified offence for the purposes of sections 266 and 279 (extended sentence for certain violent, sexual or terrorism offences) of the Sentencing Code.

This is an offence listed in Schedule 13 for the purposes of sections 265 and 278 (required special sentence for certain offenders of particular concern) of the Sentencing Code.

### STEP 1  Determining the offence category

The court should determine which categories of harm and culpability the offence falls into by reference **only** to the tables below.

### Harm

| Category 1 | The extreme nature of one or more category 2 factors or the extreme impact caused by a combination of category 2 factors **may** elevate to category 1 |
|---|---|
| Category 2 | • Severe psychological or physical harm<br>• Penetration using large or dangerous object(s)<br>• Additional degradation/humiliation<br>• Abduction<br>• Prolonged detention /sustained incident<br>• Violence or threats of violence<br>• Forced/uninvited entry into victim's home<br>• Child is particularly vulnerable due to extreme youth and/or personal circumstances |
| Category 3 | Factor(s) in categories 1 and 2 not present |

### Culpability

| A | B |
|---|---|
| • Significant degree of planning<br>• Offender acts together with others to commit the offence<br>• Use of alcohol/drugs on victim to facilitate the offence<br>• Grooming behaviour used against victim<br>• Abuse of trust<br>• Previous violence against victim<br>• Offence committed in course of burglary<br>• Sexual images of victim recorded, retained, solicited or shared<br>• Deliberate isolation of victim<br>• Commercial exploitation and/or motivation<br>• Offence racially or religiously aggravated<br>• Offence motivated by, or demonstrating, hostility to the victim based on his or her sexual orientation (or presumed sexual orientation) or transgender identity (or presumed transgender identity)<br>• Offence motivated by, or demonstrating, hostility to the victim based on his or her disability (or presumed disability) | Factor(s) in category A not present |

### STEP 2  Starting point and category range

Having determined the category, the court should use the corresponding starting points to reach a sentence within the category range below. The starting point applies to all offenders irrespective of plea or previous convictions. Having determined the starting point, step two allows further adjustment for aggravating or mitigating features, set out below.

A case of particular gravity, reflected by multiple features of culpability or harm in step one, could merit upward adjustment from the starting point before further adjustment for aggravating or mitigating features, set out below.

Sentencing Guidelines

|            | A                                                                                      | B                                                                                      |
|------------|----------------------------------------------------------------------------------------|----------------------------------------------------------------------------------------|
| Category 1 | **Starting point**<br>16 years' custody<br>**Category range**<br>13–19 years' custody  | **Starting point**<br>13 years' custody<br>**Category range**<br>11–17 years' custody  |
| Category 2 | **Starting point**<br>11 years' custody<br>**Category range**<br>7–15 years' custody   | **Starting point**<br>8 years' custody<br>**Category range**<br>5–13 years' custody    |
| Category 3 | **Starting point**<br>6 years' custody<br>**Category range**<br>4–9 years' custody     | **Starting point**<br>4 years' custody<br>**Category range**<br>2–6 years' custody     |

### Custodial Sentences

[For the imposition of custodial sentences see Imposition of Community and Custodial Sentences at **SG9-3**.]

### Factors increasing or reducing seriousness

The table below contains a **non-exhaustive** list of additional factual elements providing the context of the offence and factors relating to the offender. Identify whether any combination of these, or other relevant factors, should result in an upward or downward adjustment from the starting point. **In particular, relevant recent convictions are likely to result in an upward adjustment.** In some cases, having considered these factors, it may be appropriate to move outside the identified category range.

### Aggravating factors

#### Statutory aggravating factors
- Previous convictions, having regard to
  a)  the nature of the offence to which the conviction relates and its relevance to the current offence; and
  b)  the time that has elapsed since the conviction
- Offence committed whilst on bail

#### Other aggravating factors
- Specific targeting of a particularly vulnerable child
- Blackmail or other threats made (where not taken into account at step one)
- Location of offence
- Timing of offence
- Use of weapon or other item to frighten or injure
- Victim compelled to leave their home, school, etc.
- Failure to comply with current court orders
- Offence committed on licence or post sentence supervision
- Exploiting contact arrangements with a child to commit an offence
- Presence of others, especially other children
- Any steps taken to prevent the victim reporting an incident, obtaining assistance and/or from assisting or supporting the prosecution
- Attempts to dispose of or conceal evidence
- Commission of offence whilst under the influence of alcohol or drugs
- Victim encouraged to recruit others

### Mitigating factors
- No previous convictions **or** no relevant/recent convictions
- Remorse
- Previous good character and/or exemplary conduct*
- Age and/or lack of maturity where it affects the responsibility of the offender
- Mental disorder or learning disability, particularly where linked to the commission of the offence

* Previous good character/exemplary conduct is different from having no previous convictions. The more serious the offence, the less the weight which should normally be attributed to this factor. Where previous good character/exemplary conduct has been used to facilitate the offence, this mitigation should not normally be allowed and such conduct may constitute an aggravating factor.

In the context of this offence, previous good character/exemplary conduct should not normally be given any significant weight and will not normally justify a reduction in what would otherwise be the appropriate sentence.

**STEP 3  Consider any factors which indicate a reduction, such as assistance to the prosecution**

The court should take into account section 74 of the Sentencing Code (reduction in sentence for assistance to prosecution) and any other rule of law by virtue of which an offender may receive a discounted sentence in consequence of assistance given (or offered) to the prosecutor or investigator.

**STEP 4  Reduction for guilty plea**

The court should take account of any potential reduction for a guilty plea in accordance with section 73 of the Sentencing Code and the guideline for Reduction in Sentence for a Guilty Plea [SG5-1–SG5-12].

**STEP 5  Dangerousness**

The court should consider:

1) whether having regard to the criteria contained in Chapter 6 of Part 10 of the Sentencing Code it would be appropriate to impose a life sentence (sections 274 and 285);
2) whether having regard to sections 273 and 283 of the Sentencing Code it would be appropriate to impose a life sentence;
3) whether having regard to the criteria contained in Chapter 6 of Part 10 of the Sentencing Code it would be appropriate to impose an extended sentence (sections 266 and 279).

When sentencing offenders to a life sentence under these provisions, the notional determinate sentence should be used as the basis for the setting of a minimum term.

**STEP 6  Required special sentence for certain offenders of particular concern**

Where the court does not impose a sentence of imprisonment for life or an extended sentence, but does impose a period of imprisonment, the term of the sentence must be equal to the aggregate of the appropriate custodial term and a further period of 1 year for which the offender is to be subject to a licence (sections 265 and 278 of the Sentencing Code).

**STEP 7  Totality principle**

If sentencing an offender for more than one offence, or where the offender is already serving a sentence, consider whether the total sentence is just and proportionate to the offending behaviour. See *Totality* guideline [at **SG4**].

**STEP 8  Ancillary orders**

The court must consider whether to make any ancillary orders. The court must also consider what other requirements or provisions may *automatically* apply.

[See the Crown Court Compendium, Part II Sentencing, s7; Ancillary Orders]

**Additional ancillary orders – sexual offences**

[See **SG31-2** for additional ancillary orders for sexual offences covering slavery and trafficking prevention orders and automatic orders on conviction.]

**STEP 9  Reasons**

Section 52 of the Sentencing Code imposes a duty to give reasons for, and explain the effect of, the sentence.

**STEP 10  Consideration for time spent on bail (tagged curfew)**

The court must consider whether to give credit for time spent on bail in accordance with section 240A of the Criminal Justice Act 2003 and section 325 of the Sentencing Code.

SEXUAL ASSAULT OF A CHILD UNDER 13                                **SG31-9**

*Sexual Offences Act 2003 (section 7)*

**Effective from:** 01 April 2014

Triable either way
Maximum: 14 years' custody
Offence range: Community order–9 years' custody

For offences committed on or after 3 December 2012, this is an offence listed in Part 1 of Schedule 15 for the purposes of sections 273 and 283 (life sentence for second listed offence) of the Sentencing Code.

This is a specified offence for the purposes of sections 266 and 279 (extended sentence for certain violent, sexual or terrorism offences) of the Sentencing Code.

**STEP 1  Determining the offence category**

The court should determine which categories of harm and culpability the offence falls into by reference **only** to the tables below.

**Harm**

| Category 1 | • Severe psychological or physical harm<br>• Abduction<br>• Violence or threats of violence<br>• Forced/uninvited entry into victim's home |
| --- | --- |
| Category 2 | • Touching of naked genitalia or naked breast area<br>• Prolonged detention/sustained incident<br>• Additional degradation/humiliation<br>• Child is particularly vulnerable due to extreme youth and/or personal circumstances |
| Category 3 | Factor(s) in categories 1 and 2 not present |

**Culpability**

| A | B |
| --- | --- |
| • Significant degree of planning<br>• Offender acts together with others to commit the offence<br>• Use of alcohol/drugs on victim to facilitate the offence<br>• Grooming behaviour used against victim<br>• Abuse of trust<br>• Previous violence against victim<br>• Offence committed in course of burglary<br>• Sexual images of victim recorded, retained, solicited or shared<br>• Deliberate isolation of victim<br>• Commercial exploitation and/or motivation<br>• Offence racially or religiously aggravated<br>• Offence motivated by, or demonstrating, hostility to the victim based on his or her sexual orientation (or presumed sexual orientation) or transgender identity (or presumed transgender identity)<br>• Offence motivated by, or demonstrating, hostility to the victim based on his or her disability (or presumed disability) | Factor(s) in category A not present |

### STEP 2   Starting point and category range

Having determined the category, the court should use the corresponding starting points to reach a sentence within the category range below. The starting point applies to all offenders irrespective of plea or previous convictions. Having determined the starting point, step two allows further adjustment for aggravating or mitigating features, set out below.

A case of particular gravity, reflected by multiple features of culpability or harm in step one, could merit upward adjustment from the starting point before further adjustment for aggravating or mitigating features, set out below.

Where there is a sufficient prospect of rehabilitation, a community order with a sex offender treatment programme requirement under Part 3 of Schedule 9 of the Sentencing Code can be a proper alternative to a short or moderate length custodial sentence.

| | A | B |
| --- | --- | --- |
| Category 1 | **Starting point**<br>6 years' custody<br>**Category range**<br>4–9 years' custody | **Starting point**<br>4 years' custody<br>**Category range**<br>3–7 years' custody |
| Category 2 | **Starting point**<br>4 years' custody<br>**Category range**<br>3–7 years' custody | **Starting point**<br>2 years' custody<br>**Category range**<br>1–4 years' custody |
| Category 3 | **Starting point**<br>1 year's custody<br>**Category range**<br>26 weeks'–<br>2 years' custody | **Starting point**<br>26 weeks' custody<br>**Category range**<br>High level community order–1 year's custody |

## Community Orders and Custodial Sentences

[For the imposition of community orders, including the community orders table, see Imposition of Community and Custodial Sentences at **SG9-2**. For the imposition of custodial sentences see Imposition of Community and Custodial Sentences at **SG9-3**.]

## Factors increasing or reducing seriousness

Below is a **non-exhaustive** list of additional factual elements providing the context of the offence and factors relating to the offender. Identify whether any combination of these, or other relevant factors, should result in an upward or downward adjustment from the starting point. **In particular, relevant recent convictions are likely to result in an upward adjustment.**

In some cases, having considered these factors, it may be appropriate to move outside the identified category range.

## Aggravating factors

### Statutory aggravating factors

- Previous convictions, having regard to
  a) the nature of the offence to which the conviction relates and its relevance to the current offence; and
  b) the time that has elapsed since the conviction
- Offence committed whilst on bail

### Other aggravating factors

- Specific targeting of a particularly vulnerable child
- Blackmail or other threats made (where not taken into account at step one)
- Location of offence
- Timing of offence
- Use of weapon or other item to frighten or injure
- Victim compelled to leave their home, school, etc
- Failure to comply with current court orders
- Offence committed whilst on licence
- Exploiting contact arrangements with a child to commit an offence
- Presence of others, especially other children
- Any steps taken to prevent the victim reporting an incident, obtaining assistance and/or from assisting or supporting the prosecution
- Attempts to dispose of or conceal evidence
- Commission of offence whilst under the influence of alcohol or drugs
- Victim encouraged to recruit others

## Mitigating factors

- No previous convictions **or** no relevant/recent convictions
- Remorse
- Previous good character and/or exemplary conduct*
- Age and/or lack of maturity where it affects the responsibility of the offender
- Mental disorder or learning disability, particularly where linked to the commission of the offence

* Previous good character/exemplary conduct is different from having no previous convictions. The more serious the offence, the less the weight which should normally be attributed to this factor. Where previous good character/exemplary conduct has been used to facilitate the offence, this mitigation should not normally be allowed and such conduct may constitute an aggravating factor.

In the context of this offence, previous good character/exemplary conduct should not normally be given any significant weight and will not normally justify a reduction in what would otherwise be the appropriate sentence.

## STEP 3   Consider any factors which indicate a reduction, such as assistance to the prosecution

The court should take into account section 74 of the Sentencing Code (reduction in sentence for assistance to prosecution) and any other rule of law by virtue of which an offender may receive a discounted sentence in consequence of assistance given (or offered) to the prosecutor or investigator.

## STEP 4   Reduction for guilty pleas

The court should take account of any potential reduction for a guilty plea in accordance with section 73 of the Sentencing Code and the guideline for Reduction in Sentence for a Guilty Plea [SG5-1–SG5-12].

## STEP 5   Dangerousness

The court should consider:

1) whether having regard to the criteria contained in Chapter 6 of Part 10 of the Sentencing Code it would be appropriate to impose an extended sentence (sections 266 and 279) and

2) whether having regard to sections 273 and 283 of the Sentencing Code it would be appropriate to impose a life sentence.

When sentencing offenders to a life sentence under these provisions, the notional determinate sentence should be used as the basis for the setting of a minimum term.

### STEP 6  Totality principle

If sentencing an offender for more than one offence, or where the offender is already serving a sentence, consider whether the total sentence is just and proportionate to the offending behaviour. See *Totality* guideline [at **SG4**].

### STEP 7  Ancillary orders

The court must consider whether to make any ancillary orders. The court must also consider what other requirements or provisions may automatically apply.

[For ancillary orders in the Magistrates' Court see **SG10-5**. For the Crown Court, see the Crown Court Compendium, Part II Sentencing, S7; Ancillary Orders]

#### Additional ancillary orders – sexual offences

[See **SG31-2** for additional ancillary orders for sexual offences covering slavery and trafficking prevention orders and automatic orders on conviction.]

### STEP 8  Reasons

Section 52 of the Sentencing Code imposes a duty to give reasons for, and explain the effect of, the sentence.

### STEP 9  Consideration for time spent on bail (tagged curfew)

The court must consider whether to give credit for time spent on bail in accordance with section 240A of the Criminal Justice Act 2003 and section 325 of the Sentencing Code.

## SG31-10    CAUSING OR INCITING A CHILD UNDER 13 TO ENGAGE IN SEXUAL ACTIVITY

*Sexual Offences Act 2003 (section 8)*

Triable only on indictment (if penetration involved), otherwise triable either way
Maximum: Life imprisonment (if penetration involved), otherwise 14 years' custody
Offence range: 1–17 years' custody

Where the offence involved penetration this is a Schedule 19 offence for the purposes of sections 274 and 285 (required life sentence for offence carrying life sentence) of the Sentencing Code.

For offences involving penetration committed on or after 3 December 2012, this is an offence listed in Part 1 of Schedule 15 for the purposes of sections 273 and 283 (life sentence for second listed offence) of the Sentencing Code.

This is a specified offence for the purposes of sections 266 and 279 (extended sentence for certain violent, sexual or terrorism offences) of the Sentencing Code.

### STEP 1  Determining the offence category

The court should determine which categories of harm and culpability the offence falls into by reference **only** to the tables below.

#### Harm

| | |
|---|---|
| Category 1 | • The extreme nature of one or more category 2 factors or the extreme impact caused by a combination of category 2 factors **may** elevate to category 1 |
| Category 2 | • Severe psychological or physical harm<br>• Penetration of vagina or anus (using body or object) by, or of, victim<br>• Penile penetration of mouth by, or of, victim<br>• Additional degradation/humiliation<br>• Abduction<br>• Prolonged detention/sustained incident<br>• Violence or threats of violence<br>• Forced/uninvited entry into victim's home<br>• Child is particularly vulnerable due to extreme youth and/or personal circumstances |
| Category 3 | Factor(s) in categories 1 and 2 not present |

## Culpability

| A | B |
|---|---|
| • Significant degree of planning<br>• Offender acts together with others to commit the offence<br>• Use of alcohol/drugs on victim to facilitate the offence<br>• Grooming behaviour used against victim<br>• Abuse of trust<br>• Previous violence against victim<br>• Offence committed in course of burglary<br>• Sexual images of victim recorded, retained, solicited or shared<br>• Deliberate isolation of victim<br>• Commercial exploitation and/or motivation<br>• Offence racially or religiously aggravated<br>• Offence motivated by, or demonstrating hostility to the victim based on his or her sexual orientation (or presumed sexual orientation) or transgender identity (or presumed transgender identity)<br>• Offence motivated by, or demonstrating, hostility to the victim based on his or her disability (or presumed disability) | Factor(s) in category A not present |

### STEP 2  Starting point and category range

Having determined the category, the court should use the corresponding starting points to reach a sentence within the category range below. The starting point applies to all offenders irrespective of plea or previous convictions. Having determined the starting point, step two allows further adjustment for aggravating or mitigating features, set out below.

A case of particular gravity, reflected by multiple features of culpability or harm in step one, could merit upward adjustment from the starting point before further adjustment for aggravating or mitigating features, set out below.

| | A | B |
|---|---|---|
| Category 1 | **Starting point**<br>13 years' custody<br>**Category range**<br>11–17 years' custody | **Starting point**<br>11 years' custody<br>**Category range**<br>10–15 years' custody |
| Category 2 | **Starting point**<br>8 years' custody<br>**Category range**<br>5–10 years' custody | **Starting point**<br>6 years' custody<br>**Category range**<br>3–9 years' custody |
| Category 3 | **Starting point**<br>5 years' custody<br>**Category range**<br>3–8 years' custody | **Starting point**<br>2 years' custody<br>**Category range**<br>1–4 years' custody |

### Custodial Sentences

[For the imposition of custodial sentences see Imposition of Community and Custodial Sentences at SG9-3.]

### Factors increasing or reducing seriousness

The table below contains a **non-exhaustive** list of additional factual elements providing the context of the offence and factors relating to the offender. Identify whether any combination of these, or other relevant factors, should result in an upward or downward adjustment from the starting point. **In particular, relevant recent convictions are likely to result in an upward adjustment.** In some cases, having considered these factors, it may be appropriate to move outside the identified category range.

### Aggravating factors

*Statutory aggravating factors*

• Previous convictions, having regard to
  a) the nature of the offence to which the conviction relates and its relevance to the current offence; and
  b) the time that has elapsed since the conviction
• Offence committed whilst on bail

*Other aggravating factors*

- Specific targeting of a particularly vulnerable child
- Ejaculation (where not taken into account at step one)
- Blackmail or other threats made (where not taken into account at step one)
- Pregnancy or STI as a consequence of offence
- Location of offence
- Timing of offence
- Use of weapon or other item to frighten or injure
- Victim compelled to leave their home, school, etc
- Failure to comply with current court orders
- Offence committed whilst on licence
- Exploiting contact arrangements with a child to commit an offence
- Presence of others, especially children
- Any steps taken to prevent the victim reporting an incident, obtaining assistance and/or from assisting or supporting the prosecution
- Attempts to dispose of or conceal evidence
- Commission of offence whilst under the influence of alcohol or drugs
- Victim encouraged to recruit others

**Mitigating factors**

- No previous convictions **or** no relevant/recent convictions
- Remorse
- Previous good character and/or exemplary conduct*
- Age and/or lack of maturity where it affects the responsibility of the offender
- Mental disorder or learning disability, particularly where linked to the commission of the offence
- Sexual activity was incited but no activity took place because the offender voluntarily desisted or intervened to prevent it

* Previous good character/exemplary conduct is different from having no previous convictions. The more serious the offence, the less the weight which should normally be attributed to this factor. Where previous good character/exemplary conduct has been used to facilitate the offence, this mitigation should not normally be allowed and such conduct may constitute an aggravating factor.

In the context of this offence, previous good character/exemplary conduct should not normally be given any significant weight and will not normally justify a reduction in what would otherwise be the appropriate sentence.

### STEPS 3 to 9

[These are the same as those applicable to rape: see **SG31-3**.]

**SG31-11**                         SEXUAL ACTIVITY WITH A CHILD

*Sexual Offences Act 2003 (section 9)*

## CAUSING OR INCITING A CHILD TO ENGAGE IN SEXUAL ACTIVITY

*Sexual Offences Act 2003 (section 10)*

**Effective from:** 01 April 2014

Triable only on indictment (if penetration involved), otherwise, triable either way
Maximum: 14 years' custody
Offence range: Community order–10 years' custody

For offences committed on or after 3 December 2012, these are offences listed in Part 1 of Schedule 15 for the purposes of sections 273 and 283 (life sentence for second listed offence) of the Sentencing Code.

These are **specified offences** for the purposes of sections 266 and 279 (extended sentence for certain violent, sexual or terrorism offences) under the Sentencing Code.

**Arranging or facilitating the commission of a child offence (section 14 of the Sexual Offences Act 2003)**

The starting points and ranges in this guideline are also applicable to offences of arranging or facilitating the commission of a child offence. In such cases, the level of harm should be determined by reference to the type of activity arranged or facilitated. Sentences commensurate with the applicable starting point and range will ordinarily be appropriate. For offences involving significant commercial exploitation and/or an international element, it may, in the interests of justice, be appropriate to increase a sentence to a point above the category range. In exceptional cases, such as where a vulnerable offender performed a limited role, having been coerced or exploited by others, sentences below the starting point and range may be appropriate.

## STEP 1  Determining the offence category

The court should determine which categories of harm and culpability the offence falls into by reference **only** to the tables below.

This guideline also applies to offences committed remotely/online.

### Harm

| Category 1 | • Penetration of vagina or anus (using body or object)<br>• Penile penetration of mouth<br>In either case by, or of, the victim |
|---|---|
| Category 2 | Touching, or exposure, of naked genitalia or naked breasts by, or of, the victim |
| Category 3 | Other sexual activity |

### Culpability

| A | B |
|---|---|
| • Significant degree of planning<br>• Offender acts together with others to commit the offence<br>• Use of alcohol/drugs on victim to facilitate the offence<br>• Grooming behaviour used against victim<br>• Abuse of trust<br>• Use of threats (including blackmail)<br>• Sexual images of victim recorded, retained, solicited or shared<br>• Specific targeting of a particularly vulnerable child<br>• Offender lied about age<br>• Significant disparity in age<br>• Commercial exploitation and/or motivation<br>• Offence racially or religiously aggravated<br>• Offence motivated by, or demonstrating, hostility to the victim based on his or her sexual orientation (or presumed sexual orientation) or transgender identity (or presumed transgender identity)<br>• Offence motivated by, or demonstrating, hostility to the victim based on his or her disability (or presumed disability) | Factor(s) in category A not present |

## STEP 2  Starting point and category range

Having determined the category, the court should use the corresponding starting points to reach a sentence within the category range below. The starting point applies to all offenders irrespective of plea or previous convictions. Having determined the starting point, step two allows further adjustment for aggravating or mitigating features, set out below.

A case of particular gravity, reflected by multiple features of culpability or harm in step one, could merit upward adjustment from the starting point before further adjustment for aggravating or mitigating features, set out below.

Where there is a sufficient prospect of rehabilitation, a community order with a sex offender treatment programme requirement under Part 3 of Schedule 9 of the Sentencing Code can be a proper alternative to a short or moderate length custodial sentence.

| | A | B |
|---|---|---|
| Category 1 | **Starting point**<br>5 years' custody<br>**Category range**<br>4–10 years' custody | **Starting point**<br>1 year's custody<br>**Category range**<br>High level community order–2 years' custody |

|  | A | B |
|---|---|---|
| Category 2 | **Starting point**<br>3 years' custody<br>**Category range**<br>2–6 years' custody | **Starting point**<br>26 weeks' custody<br>**Category range**<br>High level community order–1 year's custody |
| Category 3 | **Starting point**<br>26 weeks' custody<br>**Category range**<br>High level community order–3 years' custody | **Starting point**<br>Medium level community order<br>**Category range**<br>Low level community order–High level community order |

### Community Orders and Custodial Sentences

[For the imposition of community orders, including the community orders table, see Imposition of Community and Custodial Sentences at **SG9-2**. For the imposition of custodial sentences see Imposition of Community and Custodial Sentences at **SG9-3**.]

### Factors increasing or reducing seriousness

The table below contains a **non-exhaustive** list of additional factual elements providing the context of the offence and factors relating to the offender. Identify whether any combination of these, or other relevant factors, should result in an upward or downward adjustment from the starting point. **In particular, relevant recent convictions are likely to result in an upward adjustment.** In some cases, having considered these factors, it may be appropriate to move outside the identified category range.

When sentencing appropriate **category 2 or 3 offences**, the court should also consider the custody threshold as follows:

- Has the custody threshold been passed?
- If so, is it unavoidable that a custodial sentence be imposed?
- If so, can that sentence be suspended?

### Aggravating factors
*Statutory aggravating factors*
- Previous convictions, having regard to
  - a) the nature of the offence to which the conviction relates and its relevance to the current offence; and
  - b) the time that has elapsed since the conviction
- Offence committed whilst on bail

*Other aggravating factors*
- Severe psychological or physical harm
- Ejaculation
- Pregnancy or STI as a consequence of offence
- Location of offence
- Timing of offence
- Victim compelled to leave their home, school, etc
- Failure to comply with current court orders
- Offence committed whilst on licence
- Exploiting contact arrangements with a child to commit an offence
- Presence of others, especially other children
- Any steps taken to prevent the victim reporting an incident, obtaining assistance and/or from assisting or supporting the prosecution
- Attempts to dispose of or conceal evidence
- Failure of offender to respond to previous warnings
- Commission of offence whilst under the influence of alcohol or drugs
- Victim encouraged to recruit others
- Period over which offence committed

### Mitigating factors
- No previous convictions **or** no relevant/recent convictions
- Remorse
- Previous good character and/or exemplary conduct*
- Age and/or lack of maturity where it affects the responsibility of the offender
- Mental disorder or learning disability, particularly where linked to the commission of the offence

- Sexual activity was incited but no activity took place because the offender voluntarily desisted or intervened to prevent it

\* Previous good character/exemplary conduct is different from having no previous convictions. The more serious the offence, the less the weight which should normally be attributed to this factor. Where previous good character/exemplary conduct has been used to facilitate the offence, this mitigation should not normally be allowed and such conduct may constitute an aggravating factor.

In the context of this offence, previous good character/exemplary conduct should not normally be given any significant weight and will not normally justify a reduction in what would otherwise be the appropriate sentence.

### STEPS 3 to 9
[These are the same as those applicable to Rape, see **SG31-3**.]

SEXUAL ACTIVITY WITH A CHILD FAMILY MEMBER          **SG31-12**

*Sexual Offences Act 2003 (section 25)*

INCITING A CHILD FAMILY MEMBER TO ENGAGE IN SEXUAL ACTIVITY

*Sexual Offences Act 2003 (section 26)*

**Effective from:** 01 April 2014

Triable only on indictment (if penetration involved) otherwise, triable either way
Maximum: 14 years' custody
Offence range: Community order–10 years' custody

For offences committed on or after 3 December 2012, these are offences listed in Part 1 of Schedule 15 for the purposes of sections 273 and 283 (life sentence for second listed offence) of the Sentencing Code.

These are specified offences for the purposes of sections 266 and 279 (extended sentence for certain violent, sexual or terrorism offences) of the Sentencing Code.

### STEP 1   Determining the offence category
The court should determine which categories of harm and culpability the offence falls into by reference **only** to the tables below. This offence involves those who have a family relationship with the victim and it should be assumed that the greater the abuse of trust within this relationship the more grave the offence.

**Harm**

| Category 1 | • Penetration of vagina or anus (using body or object)<br>• Penile penetration of mouth<br>In either case by, or of, the victim |
|---|---|
| Category 2 | Touching of naked genitalia or naked breasts by, or of, the victim |
| Category 3 | Other sexual activity |

**Culpability**

| A | B |
|---|---|
| • Significant degree of planning<br>• Offender acts together with others to commit the offence<br>• Use of alcohol/drugs on victim to facilitate the offence<br>• Grooming behaviour used against victim<br>• Use of threats (including blackmail)<br>• Sexual images of victim recorded, retained, solicited or shared<br>• Specific targeting of a particularly vulnerable child<br>• Significant disparity in age<br>• Commercial exploitation and/or motivation<br>• Offence racially or religiously aggravated | Factor(s) in category A not present |

| A | B |
|---|---|
| • Offence motivated by, or demonstrating, hostility to the victim based on his or her sexual orientation (or presumed sexual orientation) or transgender identity (or presumed transgender identity) <br> • Offence motivated by, or demonstrating, hostility to the victim based on his or her disability (or presumed disability) | |

## STEP 2 Starting point and category range

Having determined the category, the court should use the corresponding starting points to reach a sentence within the category range below. The starting point applies to all offenders irrespective of plea or previous convictions. Having determined the starting point, step two allows further adjustment for aggravating or mitigating features, set out below.

A case of particular gravity, reflected by multiple features of culpability or harm in step one, could merit upward adjustment from the starting point before further adjustment for aggravating or mitigating features, set out below.

Where there is a sufficient prospect of rehabilitation, a community order with a sex offender treatment programme requirement under Part 3 of Schedule 9 of the Sentencing Code can be a proper alternative to a short or moderate length custodial sentence.

| | A | B |
|---|---|---|
| Category 1 | **Starting point** <br> 6 years' custody <br> **Category range** <br> 4–10 years' custody | **Starting point** <br> 3 years 6 months' custody <br> **Category range** <br> 2 years 6 months'–5 years' custody |
| Category 2 | **Starting point** <br> 4 years' custody <br> **Category range** <br> 2–6 years' custody | **Starting point** <br> 18 months' custody <br> **Category range** <br> 26 weeks'–2 years 6 months' custody |
| Category 3 | **Starting point** <br> 1 year's custody <br> **Category range** <br> High level community order–3 years' custody | **Starting point** <br> Medium level community order <br> **Category range** <br> Low level community order–High level community order |

## Community Orders and Custodial Sentences

[For the imposition of community orders, including the community orders table, see Imposition of Community and Custodial Sentences at SG9-2. For the imposition of custodial sentences see Imposition of Community and Custodial Sentences at SG9-3.]

### Factors increasing or reducing seriousness

The table below contains a **non-exhaustive** list of additional factual elements providing the context of the offence and factors relating to the offender. Identify whether any combination of these, or other relevant factors, should result in an upward or downward adjustment from the starting point. **In particular, relevant recent convictions are likely to result in an upward adjustment.** In some cases, having considered these factors, it may be appropriate to move outside the identified category range.

When sentencing appropriate **category 3 offences**, the court should also consider the custody threshold as follows:

- Has the custody threshold been passed?
- If so, is it unavoidable that a custodial sentence be imposed?
- If so, can that sentence be suspended?

### Aggravating factors

*Statutory aggravating factors*

- Previous convictions, having regard to
  - a) the nature of the offence to which the conviction relates and its relevance to the current offence; and
  - b) the time that has elapsed since the conviction
- Offence committed whilst on bail

*Other aggravating factors*
- Severe psychological or physical harm
- Ejaculation
- Pregnancy or STI as a consequence of offence
- Location of offence
- Timing of offence
- Victim compelled to leave their home, school, etc
- Failure to comply with current court orders
- Offence committed whilst on licence
- Exploiting contact arrangements with a child to commit an offence
- Presence of others, especially other children
- Any steps taken to prevent the victim reporting an incident, obtaining assistance and/or from assisting or supporting the prosecution
- Attempts to dispose of or conceal evidence
- Failure of offender to respond to previous warnings
- Commission of offence whilst under the influence of alcohol or drugs
- Victim encouraged to recruit others
- Period over which offence committed

**Mitigating factors**
- No previous convictions **or** no relevant/recent convictions
- Remorse
- Previous good character and/or exemplary conduct*
- Age and/or lack of maturity where it affects the responsibility of the offender
- Mental disorder or learning disability, particularly where linked to the commission of the offence
- Sexual activity was incited but no activity took place because the offender voluntarily desisted or intervened to prevent it

* Previous good character/exemplary conduct is different from having no previous convictions. The more serious the offence, the less the weight which should normally be attributed to this factor. Where previous good character/exemplary conduct has been used to facilitate the offence, this mitigation should not normally be allowed and such conduct may constitute an aggravating factor.

In the context of this offence, previous good character/exemplary conduct should not normally be given any significant weight and will not normally justify a reduction in what would otherwise be the appropriate sentence.

## STEPS 3 to 9
[These are in the same terms as those applicable to Sexual Assault: see **SG31-5**.]

ENGAGING IN SEXUAL ACTIVITY IN THE PRESENCE OF A CHILD          **SG31-13**

*Sexual Offences Act 2003 (section 11)*

CAUSING A CHILD TO WATCH A SEXUAL ACT

*Sexual Offences Act 2003 (section 12)*

**Effective from:** 01 April 2014

Triable either way
Maximum: 10 years' custody
Offence range: Community order–6 years' custody

For offences committed on or after 3 December 2012, these are offences listed in Part 1 of Schedule 15 for the purposes of sections 273 and 283 (life sentence for second listed offence) of the Sentencing Code.

These are specified offences for the purposes of sections 266 and 279 (extended sentence for certain violent, sexual or terrorism offences) of the Sentencing Code.

**Arranging or facilitating the commission of a child offence (section 14 of the Sexual Offences Act 2003)**
The starting points and ranges in this guideline are also applicable to offences of arranging or facilitating the commission of a child offence. In such cases, the level of harm should be determined by reference to the type of activity arranged or facilitated. Sentences commensurate with the applicable starting point and

range will ordinarily be appropriate. For offences involving significant commercial exploitation and/or an international element, it may, in the interests of justice, be appropriate to increase sentence to a point above the category range. In exceptional cases, such as where a vulnerable offender performed a limited role, having been coerced or exploited by others, sentences below the starting point and range may be appropriate.

### STEP 1 Determining the offence category

The court should determine which categories of harm and culpability the offence falls into by reference **only** to the tables below.

**Harm**

| Category 1 | • Causing victim to view extreme pornography<br>• Causing victim to view indecent/prohibited images of children<br>• Engaging in, or causing a victim to view live, sexual activity involving sadism/violence/sexual activity with an animal/a child |
|---|---|
| Category 2 | Engaging in, or causing a victim to view images of or view live, sexual activity involving:<br>• penetration of vagina or anus (using body or object)<br>• penile penetration of the mouth<br>• masturbation |
| Category 3 | Factor(s) in categories 1 and 2 not present |

**Culpability**

| A | B |
|---|---|
| • Significant degree of planning<br>• Offender acts together with others in order to commit the offence<br>• Use of alcohol/drugs on victim to facilitate the offence<br>• Grooming behaviour used against victim<br>• Abuse of trust<br>• Use of threats (including blackmail)<br>• Specific targeting of a particularly vulnerable child<br>• Significant disparity in age<br>• Commercial exploitation and/or motivation<br>• Offence racially or religiously aggravated<br>• Offence motivated by, or demonstrating, hostility to the victim based on his or her sexual orientation (or presumed sexual orientation) or transgender identity (or presumed transgender identity)<br>• Offence motivated by, or demonstrating, hostility to the victim based on his or her disability (or presumed disability) | Factor(s) in category A not present |

### STEP 2 Starting point and category range

Having determined the category, the court should use the corresponding starting points to reach a sentence within the category range below. The starting point applies to all offenders irrespective of plea or previous convictions. Having determined the starting point, step two allows further adjustment for aggravating or mitigating features, set out below.

A case of particular gravity, reflected by multiple features of culpability or harm in step one, could merit upward adjustment from the starting point before further adjustment for aggravating or mitigating features, set out below.

Where there is a sufficient prospect of rehabilitation, a community order with a sex offender treatment programme requirement under Part 3 of Schedule 9 of the Sentencing Code can be a proper alternative to a short or moderate length custodial sentence.

|  | A | B |
|---|---|---|
|  | **Starting point**<br>4 years' custody<br>**Category range**<br>3–6 years' custody | **Starting point**<br>2 years' custody<br>**Category range**<br>1–3 years' custody |
| Category 2 | **Starting point**<br>2 years' custody<br>**Category range**<br>1–3 years' custody | **Starting point**<br>1 year's custody<br>**Category range**<br>High level community order–18 months' custody |
| Category 3 | **Starting point**<br>26 weeks' custody<br>**Category range**<br>High level community<br>order–1 year's custody | **Starting point**<br>Medium level community order<br>**Category range**<br>Low level community order–Medium level<br>community order |

## Community Orders and Custodial Sentences

[For the imposition of community orders, including the community orders table, see Imposition of Community and Custodial Sentences at **SG9-2**. For the imposition of custodial sentences see Imposition of Community and Custodial Sentences at **SG9-3**.]

### Factors increasing or reducing seriousness

The table below contains a **non-exhaustive** list of additional factual elements providing the context of the offence and factors relating to the offender. Identify whether any combination of these, or other relevant factors, should result in an upward or downward adjustment from the starting point. **In particular, relevant recent convictions are likely to result in an upward adjustment.** In some cases, having considered these factors, it may be appropriate to move outside the identified category range.

When sentencing appropriate **category 2 or 3 offences**, the court should also consider the custody threshold as follows:

- has the custody threshold been passed?
- if so, is it unavoidable that a custodial sentence be imposed?
- if so, can that sentence be suspended?

### Aggravating factors

*Statutory aggravating factors*

- Previous convictions, having regard to
  a)  the nature of the offence to which the conviction relates and its relevance to the current offence; and
  b)  the time that has elapsed since the conviction
- Offence committed whilst on bail

*Other aggravating factors*

- Location of offence
- Timing of offence
- Victim compelled to leave their home, school, etc
- Failure to comply with current court orders
- Offence committed whilst on licence
- Exploiting contact arrangements with a child to commit an offence
- Presence of others, especially other children
- Any steps taken to prevent the victim reporting an incident, obtaining assistance and/or from assisting or supporting the prosecution
- Attempts to dispose of or conceal evidence
- Failure of offender to respond to previous warnings
- Commission of offence whilst offender under the influence of alcohol or drugs
- Victim encouraged to recruit others

### Mitigating factors

- No previous convictions or no relevant/recent convictions
- Remorse
- Previous good character and/or exemplary conduct*
- Age and/or lack of maturity where it affects the responsibility of the offender
- Mental disorder or learning disability, particularly where linked to the commission of the offence
- Demonstration of steps taken to address offending behaviour

*Sentencing Guidelines*

\* Previous good character/exemplary conduct is different from having no previous convictions. The more serious the offence, the less the weight which should normally be attributed to this factor. Where previous good character/exemplary conduct has been used to facilitate the offence, this mitigation should not normally be allowed and such conduct may constitute an aggravating factor.

**STEPS 3 to 9**

[These are the same terms as those applicable to Sexual Assault: see **SG31-5**.]

**SG31-14**　Arranging or Facilitating the Commission of a Child Sex Offence

*Sexual Offences Act 2003 (section 14)*

**Effective from:** 01 April 2014

Triable either way
Maximum: 14 years' custody

For offences committed on or after 3 December 2012, these are offences listed in Part 1 of Schedule 15 for the purposes of sections 273 and 283 (life sentence for second listed offence) of the Sentencing Code.

These are specified offences for the purposes of sections 266 and 279 (extended sentence for certain violent, sexual or terrorism offences) of the Sentencing Code.

**Important—Additional guidance where no child victim exists**

On 25 January 2020 the Court of Appeal (Criminal Division) heard the cases of *R v Privett and Others*[202] which concerned the application of this guideline specifically in cases where no child victim exists. The Court of Appeal concluded that the following approach should be taken when applying this guideline (at paragraph 67; see also paragraph 72):

> The judge should, first, identify the category of harm on the basis of the sexual activity the defendant intended ('the level of harm should be determined by reference to the type of activity arranged or facilitated'), and, second, adjust the sentence in order to ensure it is 'commensurate' with, or proportionate to, the applicable starting point and range if no sexual activity had occurred (including because the victim was fictional) ('sentences commensurate with the applicable starting point and range will ordinarily be appropriate').

The Court of Appeal invited the Sentencing Council to consider whether any and, if so, what clarification of the relevant sentencing guideline is necessary, and whether further guidance can be given to sentencers.

The Sentencing Council has considered this invitation and intends to revise the guideline in due course. In the interim sentencers are advised to follow the above approach set out by the Court of Appeal.

Sentencers should refer to the guideline for the applicable, substantive offence of arranging or facilitating under sections 9 to 12: [see **SG31-14**].

- Sexual activity with a child, Sexual Offences Act 2003, section 9
- Causing or inciting a child to engage in sexual activity, Sexual Offences Act 2003, section 10
- Engaging in sexual activity in the presence of a child, Sexual Offences Act 2003, section 11
- Causing a child to watch a sexual act, Sexual Offences Act 2003, section 12

The level of harm should be determined by reference to the type of activity arranged or facilitated. Sentences commensurate with the applicable starting point and range will ordinarily be appropriate. For offences involving significant commercial exploitation and/or an international element, it may, in the interests of justice, be appropriate to increase a sentence to a point above the category range. In exceptional cases, such as where a vulnerable offender performed a limited role, having been coerced or exploited by others, sentences below the starting point and range may be appropriate.

**SG31-15**　Meeting a Child following Sexual Grooming

*Sexual Offences Act 2003 (section 15)*

**Effective from:** 01 April 2014

Triable either way
Maximum: 10 years' custody
Offence range: 1–7 years' custody

---

[202] [2020] EWCA Crim 557

For offences committed on or after 3 December 2012, this is an offence listed in Part 1 of Schedule 15 for the purposes of sections 273 and 283 (life sentence for second listed offence) of the Sentencing Code.

These are specified offences for the purposes of sections 266 and 279 (extended sentence for certain violent, sexual or terrorism offences) of the Sentencing Code.

### STEP 1  Determining the offence category

The court should determine the offence category using the table below.

| Category 1 | Raised harm **and** raised culpability |
|---|---|
| Category 2 | Raised harm **or** raised culpability |
| Category 3 | Grooming **without** raised harm or culpability factors present |

The court should determine culpability and harm caused or intended, by reference **only** to the factors below, which comprise the principal factual elements of the offence. Where an offence does not fall squarely into a category, individual factors may require a degree of weighting before making an overall assessment and determining the appropriate offence category.

Factors

| Factors indicating raised harm |
|---|
| • Continued contact despite victim's attempts to terminate contact<br>• Sexual images exchanged<br>• Victim exposed to extreme sexual content for example, extreme pornography<br>• Child is particularly vulnerable due to personal circumstances |

| Factors indicating raised culpability |
|---|
| • Offender acts together with others to commit the offence<br>• Communication indicates penetrative sexual activity is intended<br>• Offender lied about age/persona<br>• Use of threats (including blackmail), gifts or bribes<br>• Abuse of trust<br>• Specific targeting of a particularly vulnerable child<br>• Abduction/detention<br>• Commercial exploitation and/or motivation<br>• Offence racially or religiously aggravated<br>• Offence motivated by, or demonstrating, hostility to the victim based on his or her sexual orientation (or presumed sexual orientation) or transgender identity (or presumed transgender identity)<br>• Offence motivated by, or demonstrating, hostility to the victim based on his or her disability (or presumed disability) |

### STEP 2  Starting point and category range

Having determined the category, the court should use the corresponding starting points to reach a sentence within the category range below. The starting point applies to all offenders irrespective of plea or previous convictions. Having determined the starting point, step two allows further adjustment for aggravating or mitigating features, set out below.

A case of particular gravity, reflected by multiple features of culpability or harm in step one, could merit upward adjustment from the starting point before further adjustment for aggravating or mitigating features, set out below.

| Category 1 | **Starting point**<br>4 years' custody<br>**Category range**<br>3–7 years' custody |
|---|---|
| Category 2 | **Starting point**<br>2 years' custody<br>**Category range**<br>1–4 years' custody |

| Category 3 | Starting point<br>18 months' custody<br>Category range<br>1 year–2 years 6 months' custody |
|------------|-----------------------------------------------------------------------------------------------|

## Custodial Sentences

[For the imposition of custodial sentences see Imposition of Community and Custodial Sentences at SG9-3.]

## Factors increasing or reducing seriousness

The table below contains a **non-exhaustive** list of additional factual elements providing the context of the offence and factors relating to the offender. Identify whether any combination of these, or other relevant factors, should result in an upward or downward adjustment from the starting point. **In particular, relevant recent convictions are likely to result in an upward adjustment.** In some cases, having considered these factors, it may be appropriate to move outside the identified category range.

## Aggravating factors

### Statutory aggravating factors

- Previous convictions, having regard to
  a) the nature of the offence to which the conviction relates and its relevance to the current offence; and
  b) the time that has elapsed since the conviction
- Offence committed whilst on bail

### Other aggravating factors

- Failure to comply with current court orders
- Offence committed whilst on licence
- Any steps taken to prevent the victim reporting an incident, obtaining assistance and/or from assisting or supporting the prosecution
- Attempts to dispose of or conceal evidence
- Victim encouraged to recruit others

## Mitigating factors

- No previous convictions **or** no relevant/recent convictions
- Remorse
- Previous good character and/or exemplary conduct*
- Age and/or lack of maturity where it affects the responsibility of the offender
- Mental disorder or learning disability, particularly where linked to the commission of the offence
- Demonstration of steps taken to address offending behaviour

\* Previous good character/exemplary conduct is different from having no previous convictions. The more serious the offence, the less the weight which should normally be attributed to this factor. Where previous good character/exemplary conduct has been used to facilitate the offence, this mitigation should not normally be allowed and such conduct may constitute an aggravating factor.

## STEPS 3 to 9

[These are in the same terms as those applicable to Rape: see **SG31-3**.]

**SG31-16**

## ABUSE OF POSITION OF TRUST: SEXUAL ACTIVITY WITH A CHILD

*Sexual Offences Act 2003 (section 16)*

## ABUSE OF POSITION OF TRUST: CAUSING OR INCITING A CHILD TO ENGAGE IN SEXUAL ACTIVITY

*Sexual Offences Act 2003 (section 17)*

**Effective from:** 01 April 2014

Triable either way
Maximum: 5 years' custody
Offence range: Community order–2 years' custody

These are specified offences for the purposes of sections 266 and 279 (extended sentence for certain violent, sexual or terrorism offences) of the Sentencing Code.

## STEP 1  Determining the offence category

The court should determine which categories of harm and culpability the offence falls into by reference **only** to the tables below.

This guideline also applies to offences committed remotely/online.

### Harm

| Category 1 | • Penetration of vagina or anus (using body or object)<br>• Penile penetration of mouth<br>In either case by, or of, the victim |
|---|---|
| Category 2 | • Touching, or exposure, of naked genitalia or naked breasts by, or of, the victim |
| Category 3 | Factor(s) in categories 1 and 2 not present |

### Culpability

| A | B |
|---|---|
| • Significant degree of planning<br>• Offender acts together with others to commit the offence<br>• Use of alcohol/drugs on victim to facilitate the offence<br>• Grooming behaviour used against victim<br>• Use of threats (including blackmail)<br>• Sexual images of victim recorded, retained, solicited or shared<br>• Specific targeting of a particularly vulnerable child<br>• Commercial exploitation and/or motivation<br>• Offence racially or religiously aggravated<br>• Offence motivated by, or demonstrating, hostility to the victim based on his or her sexual orientation (or presumed sexual orientation) or transgender identity (or presumed transgender identity)<br>• Offence motivated by, or demonstrating, hostility to the victim based on his or her disability (or presumed disability) | Factor(s) in category A not present |

## STEP 2  Starting point and category range

Having determined the category, the court should use the corresponding starting points to reach a sentence within the category range below. The starting point applies to all offenders irrespective of plea or previous convictions. Having determined the starting point, step two allows further adjustment for aggravating or mitigating features, set out below.

A case of particular gravity, reflected by multiple features of culpability or harm in step one, could merit upward adjustment from the starting point before further adjustment for aggravating or mitigating features, set out below.

Where there is a sufficient prospect of rehabilitation, a community order with a sex offender treatment programme requirement under Part 3 of Schedule 9 of the Sentencing Code can be a proper alternative to a short or moderate length custodial sentence.

|  | A | B |
|---|---|---|
| Category 1 | **Starting point**<br>18 months' custody<br>**Category range**<br>1–2 years' custody | **Starting point**<br>1 year's custody<br>**Category range**<br>26 weeks'–18 months' custody |
| Category 2 | **Starting point**<br>1 year's custody<br>**Category range**<br>26 weeks'–18 months' custody | **Starting point**<br>26 weeks' custody<br>**Category range**<br>High level community order–1 year's custody |
| Category 3 | **Starting point**<br>26 weeks' custody<br>**Category range**<br>High level community order–1 year's custody | **Starting point**<br>Medium level community order<br>**Category range**<br>Low level community order–High level community order |

## Community Orders and Custodial Sentences

[For the imposition of community orders, including the community orders table, see Imposition of Community and Custodial Sentences at **SG9-2**. For the imposition of custodial sentences see Imposition of Community and Custodial Sentences at **SG9-3**.]

### Factors increasing or reducing seriousness

The table below contains a **non-exhaustive** list of additional factual elements providing the context of the offence and factors relating to the offender. Identify whether any combination of these, or other relevant factors, should result in an upward or downward adjustment from the starting point. **In particular, relevant recent convictions are likely to result in an upward adjustment.** In some cases, having considered these factors, it may be appropriate to move outside the identified category range.

When sentencing appropriate **category 2 or 3 offences**, the court should also consider the custody threshold as follows:

- Has the custody threshold been passed?
- If so, is it unavoidable that a custodial sentence be imposed?
- If so, can that sentence be suspended?

### Aggravating factors

#### Statutory aggravating factors

- Previous convictions, having regard to
  a) the nature of the offence to which the conviction relates and its relevance to the current offence; and
  b) the time that has elapsed since the conviction
- Offence committed whilst on bail

#### Other aggravating factors

- Ejaculation
- Pregnancy or STI as a consequence of offence
- Location of offence
- Timing of offence
- Victim compelled to leave their home, school, etc.
- Failure to comply with current court orders
- Offence committed whilst on licence
- Presence of others, especially other children
- Any steps taken to prevent the victim reporting an incident, obtaining assistance and/or from assisting or supporting the prosecution
- Attempts to dispose of or conceal evidence
- Failure of offender to respond to previous warnings
- Commission of offence whilst under the influence of alcohol or drugs
- Victim encouraged to recruit others

### Mitigating factors

- No previous convictions or no relevant/recent convictions
- Remorse
- Previous good character and/or exemplary conduct*
- Age and/or lack of maturity where it affects the responsibility of the offender
- Mental disorder or learning disability, particularly where linked to the commission of the offence
- Sexual activity was incited but no activity took place because the offender voluntarily desisted or intervened to prevent it
- Demonstration of steps taken to address offending behaviour

* Previous good character/exemplary conduct is different from having no previous convictions. The more serious the offence, the less the weight which should normally be attributed to this factor. Where previous good character/exemplary conduct has been used to facilitate the offence, this mitigation should not normally be allowed and such conduct may constitute an aggravating factor.

### STEPS 3 to 9

[These are in the same terms as those applicable to Sexual Assault: see **SG31-5**.]

ABUSE OF POSITION OF TRUST: SEXUAL ACTIVITY IN THE PRESENCE OF A CHILD   **SG31-17**

*Sexual Offences Act 2003 (section 18)*

ABUSE OF POSITION OF TRUST: CAUSING A CHILD TO WATCH A SEXUAL ACT

*Sexual Offences Act 2003 (section 19)*

**Effective from:** 01 April 2014

Triable either way
Maximum: 5 years' custody
Offence range: Community order–2 years' custody

These are specified offences for the purposes of sections 266 and 279 (extended sentence for certain violent, sexual or terrorism offences) of the Sentencing Code.

**STEP 1  Determining the offence category**

The court should determine which categories of harm and culpability the offence falls into by reference **only** to the tables below.

**Harm**

| Category 1 | • Causing victim to view extreme pornography<br>• Causing victim to view indecent/prohibited images of children<br>• Engaging in, or causing a victim to view live, sexual activity involving sadism/violence/sexual activity with an animal/a child |
|---|---|
| Category 2 | Engaging in, or causing a victim to view images of or view live, sexual activity involving:<br>• penetration of vagina or anus (using body or object)<br>• penile penetration of mouth<br>• masturbation |
| Category 3 | Factor(s) in categories 1 and 2 not present |

**Culpability**

| A | B |
|---|---|
| • Significant degree of planning<br>• Offender acts together with others to commit the offence<br>• Use of alcohol/drugs on victim to facilitate the offence<br>• Grooming behaviour used against victim<br>• Use of threats (including blackmail)<br>• Specific targeting of a particularly vulnerable child<br>• Commercial exploitation and/or motivation<br>• Offence racially or religiously aggravated<br>• Offence motivated by, or demonstrating, hostility to the victim based on his or her sexual orientation (or presumed sexual orientation) or transgender identity (or presumed transgender identity)<br>• Offence motivated by, or demonstrating, hostility to the victim based on his or her disability (or presumed disability) | Factor(s) in category A not present |

**STEP 2  Starting point and category range**

Having determined the category, the court should use the corresponding starting points to reach a sentence within the category range below. The starting point applies to all offenders irrespective of plea or previous convictions. Having determined the starting point, step two allows further adjustment for aggravating or mitigating features, set out below.

A case of particular gravity, reflected by multiple features of culpability or harm in step one, could merit upward adjustment from the starting point before further adjustment for aggravating or mitigating features, set out below.

Where there is a sufficient prospect of rehabilitation, a community order with a sex offender treatment programme requirement under Part 3 of Schedule 9 of the Sentencing Code can be a proper alternative to a short or moderate length custodial sentence.

Sentencing Guidelines

|  | **A** | **B** |
|---|---|---|
| Category 1 | **Starting point**<br>18 months' custody<br>**Category range**<br>1–2 years' custody | **Starting point**<br>1 year's custody<br>**Category range**<br>26 weeks'–18 months' custody |
| Category 2 | **Starting point**<br>1 year's custody<br>**Category range**<br>26 weeks'–18 months' custody | **Starting point**<br>26 weeks' custody<br>**Category range**<br>High level community order–1 year's custody |
| Category 3 | **Starting point**<br>26 weeks' custody<br>**Category range**<br>High level community order–1 year's custody | **Starting point**<br>Medium level community order<br>**Category range**<br>Low level community order–High level community order |

### Community Orders and Custodial Sentences

[For the imposition of community orders, including the community orders table, see Imposition of Community and Custodial Sentences at **SG9-2**. For the imposition of custodial sentences see Imposition of Community and Custodial Sentences at **SG9-3**.]

### Factors increasing or reducing seriousness

The table below contains a **non-exhaustive** list of additional factual elements providing the context of the offence and factors relating to the offender. Identify whether any combination of these, or other relevant factors, should result in an upward or downward adjustment from the starting point. **In particular, relevant recent convictions are likely to result in an upward adjustment.** In some cases, having considered these factors, it may be appropriate to move outside the identified category range.

When sentencing appropriate **category 2 or 3 offences**, the court should also consider the custody threshold as follows:

- Has the custody threshold been passed?
- If so, is it unavoidable that a custodial sentence be imposed?
- If so, can that sentence be suspended?

### Aggravating factors

*Statutory aggravating factors*

- Previous convictions, having regard to
  a) the nature of the offence to which the conviction relates and its relevance to the current offence; and
  b) the time that has elapsed since the conviction
- Offence committed whilst on bail

*Other aggravating factors*

- Location of offence
- Timing of offence
- Victim compelled to leave their home, school, etc
- Failure to comply with current court orders
- Offence committed whilst on licence
- Presence of others, especially other children
- Any steps taken to prevent the victim reporting an incident, obtaining assistance and/or from assisting or supporting the prosecution
- Attempts to dispose of or conceal evidence
- Failure of offender to respond to previous warnings
- Commission of offence whilst under the influence of alcohol or drugs
- Victim encouraged to recruit others

### Mitigating factors

- No previous convictions or no relevant/recent convictions
- Remorse
- Previous good character and/or exemplary conduct*
- Age and/or lack of maturity where it affects the responsibility of the offender
- Mental disorder or learning disability, particularly where linked to the commission of the offence
- Demonstration of steps taken to address offending behaviour

\* Previous good character/exemplary conduct is different from having no previous convictions. The more serious the offence, the less the weight which should normally be attributed to this factor. Where previous good character/exemplary conduct has been used to facilitate the offence, this mitigation should not normally be allowed and such conduct may constitute an aggravating factor.

### STEPS 3 to 9

[These are in the same terms as those applicable to Sexual Assault: see **SG31-5**.]

POSSESSION OF INDECENT PHOTOGRAPH OF CHILD          **SG31-18**

*Criminal Justice Act 1988 (section 160)*

**Effective from:** 01 April 2014

Triable either way
Maximum: 5 years' custody
Offence range: Community order–3 years' custody

INDECENT PHOTOGRAPHS OF CHILDREN

*Protection of Children Act 1978 (section 1)*

**Effective from:** 01 April 2014

Triable either way
Maximum: 10 years' custody
Offence range: Community order–9 years' custody

For section 1 offences committed on or after 3 December 2012, these are offences listed in Part 1 of Schedule 15 for the purposes of sections 273 and 283 (life sentence for second listed offence) of the Sentencing Code.

These are specified offences for the purposes of sections 266 and 279 (extended sentence for certain violent, sexual or terrorism offences) of the Sentencing Code.

### STEP 1  Determining the offence category

The court should determine the offence category using the table below.

|            | Possession | Distribution* | Production** |
|------------|------------|---------------|--------------|
| Category A | Possession of images involving penetrative sexual activity<br>Possession of images involving sexual activity with an animal or sadism | Sharing images involving penetrative sexual activity<br>Sharing images involving sexual activity with an animal or sadism | Creating images involving penetrative sexual activity<br>Creating images involving sexual activity with an animal or sadism |
| Category B | Possession of images involving non-penetrative sexual activity | Sharing of images involving non-penetrative sexual activity | Creating images involving non-penetrative sexual activity |
| Category C | Possession of other indecent images not falling within categories A or B | Sharing of other indecent images not falling within categories A or B | Creating other indecent images not falling within categories A or B |

\* Distribution includes possession with a view to distributing or sharing images.

\*\* Production includes the taking or making of any image at source for instance the original image. Making an image by simple downloading should be treated as possession for the purposes of sentencing.

**In most cases the intrinsic character of the most serious of the offending images will initially determine the appropriate category. If, however, the most serious images are unrepresentative of the offender's conduct a lower category may be appropriate. A lower category will not, however, be appropriate if the offender has produced or taken (for example photographed) images of a higher category.**

## STEP 2 Starting point and category range

Having determined the category, the court should use the corresponding starting points to reach a sentence within the category range below. The starting point applies to all offenders irrespective of plea or previous convictions. Having determined the starting point, step two allows further adjustment for aggravating or mitigating features, set out below.

Where there is a sufficient prospect of rehabilitation, a community order with a sex offender treatment programme requirement under Part 3 of Schedule 9 of the Sentencing Code can be a proper alternative to a short or moderate length custodial sentence.

|  | Possession | Distribution | Production |
|---|---|---|---|
| Category A | **Starting point**<br>1 year's custody<br>**Category range**<br>26 weeks–3 years' custody | **Starting point**<br>3 years' custody<br>**Category range**<br>2–5 years' custody | **Starting point**<br>6 years' custody<br>**Category range**<br>4–9 years' custody |
| Category B | **Starting point**<br>26 weeks' custody<br>**Category range**<br>High level community order–18 months' custody | **Starting point**<br>1 year's custody<br>**Category range**<br>26 weeks–2 years' custody | **Starting point**<br>2 years' custody<br>**Category range**<br>1–4 years' custody |
| Category C | **Starting point**<br>High level community order<br>**Category range**<br>Medium level community order–26 weeks' custody | **Starting point**<br>13 weeks' custody<br>**Category range**<br>High level community order–26 weeks' custody | **Starting point**<br>18 months' custody<br>**Category range**<br>1–3 years' custody |

## Community Orders and Custodial Sentences

[For the imposition of community orders, including the community orders table, see Imposition of Community and Custodial Sentences at SG9-2. For the imposition of custodial sentences see Imposition of Community and Custodial Sentences at SG9-3.]

## Factors increasing or reducing seriousness

Below is a **non-exhaustive** list of additional factual elements providing the context of the offence and factors relating to the offender. Identify whether any combination of these, or other relevant factors, should result in an upward or downward adjustment from the starting point. **In particular, relevant recent convictions are likely to result in an upward adjustment.** In some cases, having considered these factors, it may be appropriate to move outside the identified category range.

When sentencing appropriate **category B or C offences**, the court should also consider the custody threshold as follows:

- Has the custody threshold been passed?
- If so, is it unavoidable that a custodial sentence be imposed?
- If so, can that sentence be suspended?

## Aggravating factors

### Statutory aggravating factors

- Previous convictions, having regard to
  a) the nature of the offence to which the conviction relates and its relevance to the current offence; and
  b) the time that has elapsed since the conviction
- Offence committed whilst on bail

### Other aggravating factors

- Failure to comply with current court orders
- Offence committed whilst on licence
- Age and/or vulnerability of the child depicted*
- Discernible pain or distress suffered by child depicted
- Period over which images were possessed, distributed or produced
- High volume of images possessed, distributed or produced
- Placing images where there is the potential for a high volume of viewers
- Collection includes moving images
- Attempts to dispose of or conceal evidence
- Abuse of trust

- Child depicted known to the offender
- Active involvement in a network or process that facilitates or commissions the creation or sharing of indecent images of children
- Commercial exploitation and/or motivation
- Deliberate or systematic searching for images portraying young children, category A images or the portrayal of familial sexual abuse
- Large number of different victims
- Child depicted intoxicated or drugged

### Mitigating factors

- No previous convictions **or** no relevant/recent convictions
- Remorse
- Previous good character and/or exemplary conduct**
- Age and/or lack of maturity where it affects the responsibility of the offender
- Mental disorder or learning disability, particularly where linked to the commission of the offence
- Demonstration of steps taken to address offending behaviour

*Age and/or vulnerability of the child should be given significant weight. In cases where the actual age of the victim is difficult to determine sentencers should consider the development of the child (infant, pre-pubescent, post-pubescent)*

** *Previous good character/exemplary conduct is different from having no previous convictions. The more serious the offence, the less the weight which should normally be attributed to this factor. Where previous good character/exemplary conduct has been used to facilitate the offence, this mitigation should not normally be allowed and such conduct may constitute an aggravating factor.*

### STEPS 3 to 9

[These are the same terms as those applicable to Causing a person to engage in sexual activity without consent: see **SG31-6**.]

CAUSING OR INCITING PROSTITUTION FOR GAIN

*Sexual Offences Act 2003 (section 52)*

CONTROLLING PROSTITUTION FOR GAIN

*Sexual Offences Act 2003 (section 53)*

**SG31-19**

**Effective from:** 01 April 2014

Triable either way
Maximum: 7 years' custody
Offence range: Community order–6 years' custody

These are specified offences for the purposes of sections 266 and 279 (extended sentence for certain violent, sexual or terrorism offences) of the Sentencing Code.

### STEP 1   Determining the offence category

The court should determine which categories of harm and culpability the offence falls into by reference **only** to the tables below.

### Harm

| Category 1 | <ul><li>Abduction/detention</li><li>Violence or threats of violence</li><li>Sustained and systematic psychological abuse</li><li>Individual(s) forced or coerced to participate in unsafe/degrading sexual activity</li><li>Individual(s) forced or coerced into seeing many 'customers'</li><li>Individual(s) forced/coerced/deceived into prostitution</li></ul> |
|---|---|
| Category 2 | Factor(s) in category 1 not present |

Sentencing Guidelines

## Culpability

| A | B | C |
|---|---|---|
| • Causing, inciting or controlling prostitution on significant commercial basis<br>• Expectation of significant financial or other gain<br>• Abuse of trust<br>• Exploitation of those known to be trafficked<br>• Significant involvement in limiting the freedom of prostitute(s)<br>• Grooming of individual(s) to enter prostitution including through cultivation of a dependency on drugs or alcohol | • Close involvement with prostitute(s) for example control of finances, choice of clients, working conditions, etc (where offender's involvement is not as a result of coercion) | • Performs limited function under direction<br>• Close involvement but engaged by coercion/intimidation/exploitation |

## STEP 2  Starting point and category range

Having determined the category, the court should use the corresponding starting points to reach a sentence within the category range below. The starting point applies to all offenders irrespective of plea or previous convictions. Having determined the starting point, step two allows further adjustment for aggravating or mitigating features, set out below.

A case of particular gravity, reflected by multiple features of culpability or harm in step one, could merit upward adjustment from the starting point before further adjustment for aggravating or mitigating features, set out below.

Where there is a sufficient prospect of rehabilitation, a community order with a sex offender treatment programme requirement under Part 3 of Schedule 9 of the Sentencing Code can be a proper alternative to a short or moderate length custodial sentence.

| | A | B | C |
|---|---|---|---|
| Category 1 | **Starting point**<br>4 years' custody<br>**Category range**<br>3–6 years' custody | **Starting point**<br>2 years 6 months' custody<br>**Category range**<br>2–4 years' custody | **Starting point**<br>1 year's custody<br>**Category range**<br>26 weeks'–2 years' custody |
| Category 2 | **Starting point**<br>2 years' 6 months' custody<br>**Category range**<br>2–5 years' custody | **Starting point**<br>1 year's custody<br>**Category range**<br>High level community order–2 years' custody | **Starting point**<br>Medium level community Order<br>**Category range**<br>Low level community order–High level community order |

### Community Orders and Custodial Sentences

[For the imposition of community orders, including the community orders table, see Imposition of Community and Custodial Sentences at SG9-2. For the imposition of custodial sentences see Imposition of Community and Custodial Sentences at SG9-3.]

### Factors increasing or reducing seriousness

The table below contains a **non-exhaustive** list of additional factual elements providing the context of the offence and factors relating to the offender. Identify whether any combination of these, or other relevant factors, should result in an upward or downward adjustment from the starting point.

**In particular, relevant recent convictions are likely to result in an upward adjustment.** In some cases, having considered these factors, it may be appropriate to move outside the identified category range. When sentencing appropriate **category 2 offences**, the court should also consider the custody threshold as follows:

• Has the custody threshold been passed?
• If so, is it unavoidable that a custodial sentence be imposed?
• If so, can that sentence be suspended?

**Aggravating factors**

*Statutory aggravating factors*

- Previous convictions, having regard to
  a)  the nature of the offence to which the conviction relates and its relevance to the current offence; and
  b)  the time that has elapsed since the conviction
- Offence committed whilst on bail

*Other aggravating factors*

- Failure to comply with current court orders
- Offence committed whilst on licence
- Deliberate isolation of prostitute(s)
- Threats made to expose prostitute(s) to the authorities (for example, immigration or police), family/ friends or others
- Harm threatened against the family/friends of prostitute(s)
- Passport/identity documents removed
- Prostitute(s) prevented from seeking medical treatment
- Food withheld
- Earnings withheld/kept by offender or evidence of excessive wage reduction or debt bondage, inflated travel or living expenses or unreasonable interest rates
- Any steps taken to prevent the reporting of an incident, obtaining assistance and/or from assisting or supporting the prosecution
- Attempts to dispose of or conceal evidence
- Prostitute(s) forced or coerced into pornography
- Timescale over which operation has been run

**Mitigating factors**

- No previous convictions **or** no relevant/recent convictions
- Remorse
- Previous good character and/or exemplary conduct*
- Age and/or lack of maturity where it affects the responsibility of the offender
- Mental disorder or learning disability, particularly where linked to the commission of the offence
- Demonstration of steps taken to address offending behaviour

* Previous good character/exemplary conduct is different from having no previous convictions. The more serious the offence, the less the weight which should normally be attributed to this factor. Where previous good character/exemplary conduct has been used to facilitate the offence, this mitigation should not normally be allowed and such conduct may constitute an aggravating factor.

**STEPS 3 to 9**

[These are the same terms as those applicable to Sexual Assault: see **SG31-6**.]

KEEPING A BROTHEL USED FOR PROSTITUTION  **SG31-20**

*Sexual Offences Act 1956 (section 33A)*

**Effective from:** 01 April 2014

Triable either way
Maximum: 7 years' custody
Offence range: Community order–6 years' custody

The terms 'prostitute' and 'prostitution' are used in this guideline in accordance with the statutory language contained in the Sexual Offences Act 2003.

**STEP 1  Determining the offence category**

The court should determine which categories of harm and culpability the offence falls into by reference **only** to the tables below.

## Harm

| Category 1 | • Under 18 year olds working in brothel<br>• Abduction/detention<br>• Violence or threats of violence<br>• Sustained and systematic psychological abuse<br>• Those working in brothel forced or coerced to participate in unsafe/degrading sexual activity<br>• Those working in brothel forced or coerced into seeing many 'customers'<br>• Those working in brothel forced/coerced/deceived into prostitution<br>• Established evidence of community impact |
|---|---|
| Category 2 | Factor(s) in category 1 not present |

## Culpability

| A | B | C |
|---|---|---|
| • Keeping brothel on significant commercial basis<br>• Involvement in keeping a number of brothels<br>• Expectation of significant financial or other gain<br>• Abuse of trust<br>• Exploitation of those known to be trafficked<br>• Significant involvement in limiting freedom of those working in brothel<br>• Grooming of a person to work in the brothel including through cultivation of a dependency on drugs or alcohol | • Keeping/managing premises<br>• Close involvement with those working in brothel e.g. control of finances, choice of clients, working conditions, etc. (where offender's involvement is not as a result of coercion) | • Performs limited function under direction<br>• Close involvement but engaged by coercion/intimidation/exploitation |

## STEP 2  Starting point and category range

Having determined the category, the court should use the corresponding starting points to reach a sentence within the category range below. The starting point applies to all offenders irrespective of plea or previous convictions. Having determined the starting point, step two allows further adjustment for aggravating or mitigating features, set out below.

A case of particular gravity, reflected by multiple features of culpability or harm in step one, could merit upward adjustment from the starting point before further adjustment for aggravating or mitigating features, set out below.

Where there is a sufficient prospect of rehabilitation, a community order with a sex offender treatment programme requirement under Part 3 of Schedule 9 of the Sentencing Code can be a proper alternative to a short or moderate length custodial sentence.

| | A | B | C |
|---|---|---|---|
| Category 1 | **Starting point**<br>5 years' custody<br>**Category range**<br>3–6 years' custody | **Starting point**<br>3 years' custody<br>**Category range**<br>2–5 years' custody | **Starting point**<br>1 year's custody<br>**Category range**<br>High level community order–18 months' custody |
| Category 2 | **Starting point**<br>3 years' custody<br>**Category range**<br>2–5 years' custody | **Starting point**<br>12 months' custody<br>**Category range**<br>26 weeks'–2 years' custody | **Starting point**<br>Medium level community order<br>**Category range**<br>Low level community order–High level community order |

## Community Orders and Custodial Sentences

[For the imposition of community orders, including the community orders table, see Imposition of Community and Custodial Sentences at **SG9-2**. For the imposition of custodial sentences see Imposition of Community and Custodial Sentences at **SG9-3**.]

### Factors increasing or reducing seriousness

The table below contains a **non-exhaustive** list of additional factual elements providing the context of the offence and factors relating to the offender. Identify whether any combination of these, or other relevant factors, should result in an upward or downward adjustment from the starting point. **In particular, relevant recent convictions are likely to result in an upward adjustment.** In some cases, having considered these factors, it may be appropriate to move outside the identified category range.

When sentencing appropriate **offences**, the court should also consider the custody threshold as follows:

- Has the custody threshold been passed?
- If so, is it unavoidable that a custodial sentence be imposed?
- If so, can that sentence be suspended?

### Aggravating factors

*Statutory aggravating factors*

- Previous convictions, having regard to
  a) the nature of the offence to which the conviction relates and its relevance to the current offence; and
  b) the time that has elapsed since the conviction
- Offence committed whilst on bail

*Other aggravating factors*

- Failure to comply with current court orders
- Offence committed whilst on licence
- Deliberate isolation of those working in brothel
- Threats made to expose those working in brothel to the authorities (for example, immigration or police), family/friends or others
- Harm threatened against the family/friends of those working in brothel
- Passport/identity documents removed
- Those working in brothel prevented from seeking medical treatment
- Food withheld
- Those working in brothel passed around by offender and moved to other brothels
- Earnings of those working in brothel withheld/kept by offender or evidence of excessive wage reduction or debt bondage, inflated travel or living expenses or unreasonable interest rates
- Any steps taken to prevent those working in brothel reporting an incident, obtaining assistance and/or from assisting or supporting the prosecution
- Attempts to dispose of or conceal evidence
- Those working in brothel forced or coerced into pornography
- Timescale over which operation has been run

### Mitigating factors

- No previous convictions **or** no relevant/recent convictions
- Remorse
- Previous good character and/or exemplary conduct*
- Age and/or lack of maturity where it affects the responsibility of the offender
- Mental disorder or learning disability, particularly where linked to the commission of the offence
- Demonstration of steps taken to address offending behaviour

* Previous good character/exemplary conduct is different from having no previous convictions. The more serious the offence, the less the weight which should normally be attributed to this factor. Where previous good character/exemplary conduct has been used to facilitate the offence, this mitigation should not normally be allowed and such conduct may constitute an aggravating factor.

### STEP 3  Consider any factors which indicate a reduction, such as assistance to the prosecution

The court should take into account section 74 of the Sentencing Code (reduction in sentence for assistance to prosecution) and any other rule of law by virtue of which an offender may receive a discounted sentence in consequence of assistance given (or offered) to the prosecutor or investigator.

### STEP 4  Reduction for guilty pleas

The court should take account of any potential reduction for a guilty plea in accordance with section 73 of the Sentencing Code and the guideline for Reduction in Sentence for a Guilty Plea [SG5-1–SG5-12].

### STEP 5  Totality principle

If sentencing an offender for more than one offence, or where the offender is already serving a sentence, consider whether the total sentence is just and proportionate to the offending behaviour. See *Totality* guideline [at **SG4**].

**STEP 6  Ancillary orders**

The court must consider whether to make any ancillary orders. The court must also consider what other requirements or provisions may *automatically* apply.

[See the Sentencing Council Explanatory Materials for Ancillary Orders in the Magistrates' Courts at **SG10-5** and the Crown Court Compendium, Part II Sentencing, S7; Ancillary Orders]

**Additional ancillary orders – sexual offences**

[See **SG31-2** for additional ancillary orders for sexual offences covering slavery and trafficking prevention orders and automatic orders on conviction.]

**STEP 7  Reasons**

Section 52 of the Sentencing Code imposes a duty to give reasons for, and explain the effect of, the sentence.

**STEP 8  Consideration for time spent on bail (tagged curfew)**

The court must consider whether to give credit for time spent on bail in accordance with section 240A of the Criminal Justice Act 2003 and section 325 of the Sentencing Code.

**SG31-21**          CAUSING OR INCITING SEXUAL EXPLOITATION OF A CHILD

*Sexual Offences Act 2003 (section 48)*

CONTROLLING A CHILD IN RELATION TO SEXUAL EXPLOITATION

*Sexual Offences Act 2003 (section 49)*

ARRANGING OR FACILITATING SEXUAL EXPLOITATION OF A CHILD

*Sexual Offences Act 2003 (section 50)*

**Effective from:** 01 April 2014

Triable either way
Maximum: 14 years' custody
Offence range:
- Victim aged under 13: 1–3 years' custody
- Victim aged 13–15: 26 weeks'–1 years' custody
- Victim aged 16–17: Community order–7 years' custody

For offences committed on or after 3 December 2012, these are offences listed in Part 1 of Schedule 15 for the purposes of sections 273 and 283 (life sentence for second listed offence) of the Sentencing Code.

These are specified offences for the purposes of sections 266 and 279 (extended sentence for certain violent, sexual or terrorism offences) of the Sentencing Code.

**STEP 1  Determining the offence category**

The court should determine which categories of harm and culpability the offence falls into by reference **only** to the tables below.

For offences that involve wide scale commercial and/or international activity sentences above the category range may be appropriate.

**Harm**

| Category 1 | • Victims involved in penetrative sexual activity<br>• Abduction/detention<br>• Violence or threats of violence<br>• Sustained and systematic psychological abuse<br>• Victim(s) participated in unsafe/degrading sexual activity beyond that which is inherent in the offence<br>• Victim(s) passed around by the offender to other 'customers' and/or moved to other brothels |
|---|---|
| Category 2 | Factor(s) in category 1 not present |

## Culpability

| A | B | C |
|---|---|---|
| • Directing or organising sexual exploitation of a child on significant commercial basis<br>• Expectation of significant financial or other gain<br>• Abuse of trust<br>• Exploitation of victim(s) known to be trafficked<br>• Significant involvement in limiting the freedom of the victim(s)<br>• Grooming of a victim for sexual exploitation including through cultivation of a dependency on drugs or alcohol | • Close involvement with inciting, controlling, arranging or facilitating sexual exploitation (where offender's involvement is not as a result of coercion) | • Performs limited function under direction<br>• Close involvement but engaged by coercion/ intimidation /exploitation |

### STEP 2  Starting point and category range

Having determined the category, the court should use the corresponding starting points to reach a sentence within the category range below. The starting point applies to all offenders irrespective of plea or previous convictions. Having determined the starting point, step two allows further adjustment for aggravating or mitigating features, set out below.

A case of particular gravity, reflected by multiple features of culpability or harm in step one, could merit upward adjustment from the starting point before further adjustment for aggravating or mitigating features, set out below.

Where there is a sufficient prospect of rehabilitation, a community order with a sex offender treatment programme requirement under Part 3 of Schedule 9 of the Sentencing Code can be a proper alternative to a short or moderate length custodial sentence.

| | Age | A | B | C |
|---|---|---|---|---|
| **Category 1** | U13 | **Starting point**<br>10 years' custody<br>**Category range**<br>8–13 years' custody | **Starting point**<br>8 years' custody<br>**Category range**<br>6–11 years' custody | **Starting point**<br>5 years' custody<br>**Category range**<br>2–6 years' custody |
| | 13–15 | **Starting point**<br>8 years' custody<br>**Category range**<br>6–11 years' custody | **Starting point**<br>5 years' custody<br>**Category range**<br>4–8 years' custody | **Starting point**<br>2 years 6 months' custody<br>**Category range**<br>1–4 years' custody |
| | 16–17 | **Starting point**<br>4 years' custody<br>**Category range**<br>3–7 years' custody | **Starting point**<br>2 years' custody<br>**Category range**<br>1–4 years' custody | **Starting point**<br>1 year's custody<br>**Category range**<br>26 weeks'–2 years' custody |
| **Category 2** | U13 | **Starting point**<br>8 years' custody<br>**Category range**<br>6–11 years' custody | **Starting point**<br>6 years' custody<br>**Category range**<br>4–9 years' custody | **Starting point**<br>2 years' custody<br>**Category range**<br>1–4 years' custody |
| | 13–15 | **Starting point**<br>6 years' custody<br>**Category range**<br>4–9 years' custody | **Starting point**<br>3 years' custody<br>**Category range**<br>2–5 years' custody | **Starting point**<br>1 year's custody<br>**Category range**<br>26 weeks'–2 years' custody |
| | 16–17 | **Starting point**<br>3 years' custody<br>**Category range**<br>2–5 years' custody | **Starting point**<br>1 year's custody<br>**Category range**<br>26 weeks'–2 years' custody | **Starting point**<br>26 weeks' custody<br>**Category range**<br>High level community order–1 year's custody |

Sentencing Guidelines

## Community Orders and Custodial Sentences

[For the imposition of community orders, including the community orders table, see Imposition of Community and Custodial Sentences at **SG9-2**. For the imposition of custodial sentences see Imposition of Community and Custodial Sentences at **SG9-3**.]

## Factors increasing or reducing seriousness

The table below contains a **non-exhaustive** list of additional factual elements providing the context of the offence and factors relating to the offender. Identify whether any combination of these, or other relevant factors, should result in an upward or downward adjustment from the starting point. **In particular, relevant recent convictions are likely to result in an upward adjustment.** In some cases, having considered these factors, it may be appropriate to move outside the identified category range.

When sentencing appropriate **category 2 offences**, the court should also consider the custody threshold as follows:

- Has the custody threshold been passed?
- If so, is it unavoidable that a custodial sentence be imposed?
- If so, can that sentence be suspended?

## Aggravating factors

### Statutory aggravating factors

- Previous convictions, having regard to
  a) the nature of the offence to which the conviction relates and its relevance to the current offence; and
  b) the time that has elapsed since the conviction
- Offence committed whilst on bail

### Other aggravating factors

- Failure to comply with current court orders
- Offence committed whilst on licence
- Deliberate isolation of the victim(s)
- Vulnerability of the victim(s)
- Threats made to expose victims(s) to the authorities (for example, immigration or police), family/ friends or others
- Harm threatened against the family/friends of victim(s)
- Passport/identity documents removed
- Victim(s) prevented from seeking medical treatment
- Victim(s) prevented from attending school
- Food withheld
- Earnings withheld/kept by offender or evidence of excessive wage reduction or debt bondage, inflated travel or living expenses or unreasonable interest rates
- Any steps taken to prevent the victim reporting an incident, obtaining assistance and/or from assisting or supporting the prosecution
- Attempts to dispose of or conceal evidence
- Timescale over which the operation has been run

## Mitigating factors

- No previous convictions **or** no relevant/recent convictions
- Remorse
- Previous good character and/or exemplary conduct*
- Age and/or lack of maturity where it affects the responsibility of the offender
- Mental disorder or learning disability, particularly where linked to the commission of the offence

* Previous good character/exemplary conduct is different from having no previous convictions. The more serious the offence, the less the weight which should normally be attributed to this factor. Where previous good character/exemplary conduct has been used to facilitate the offence, this mitigation should not normally be allowed and such conduct may constitute an aggravating factor.

## STEPS 3 to 9

[These are the same terms as those applicable to Rape: see **SG31-3**.]

*Sexual Offences Act 2003 (section 47)*

**Effective from:** 01 April 2014

Triable only on indictment (if involving penetration against victim under 16)—otherwise triable either way

| Maximum: | Victim under 13 (penetrative) | Life imprisonment |
| | Victim under 13 (non-penetrative) | 14 years' custody |
| | Victim aged 13–15 | 14 years' custody |
| | Victim aged 16–17 | 7 years' custody |
| Offence range: | Victim aged 16–17 | Community order–5 years' custody |

This guideline should only be used where the victim is aged 16 or 17 years old. If the victim is under 13 please refer to the guidelines for rape of a child under 13 [see **SG31-7**], assault by penetration of a child under 13 [see **SG31-8**], sexual assault of a child under 13 [see **SG31-9**], or causing or inciting a child under 13 to engage in sexual activity [see **SG31-10**] depending on the activity involved in the offence.

If the victim is aged 13–15 please refer to the sexual activity with a child guideline [see **SG31-11**].

Where the victim is 16 or 17 years old, this is a specified offence for the purposes of sections 266 and 279 (extended sentence for certain violent, sexual or terrorism offences) of the Sentencing Code.

### STEP 1   Determining the offence category

The court should determine which categories of harm and culpability the offence falls into by reference **only** to the tables below.

This guideline should only be used where the victim was aged 16 or 17 years old.

**Harm**

| Category 1 | • Penetration of vagina or anus (using body or object) by, or of, the victim <br> • Penile penetration of mouth by, or of, the victim <br> • Violence or threats of violence <br> • Victim subjected to unsafe/degrading sexual activity (beyond that which is inherent in the offence) |
| Category 2 | • Touching of naked genitalia or naked breasts by, or of, the victim |
| Category 3 | • Other sexual activity |

**Culpability**

| A | B |
|---|---|
| • Abduction/detention <br> • Sexual images of victim recorded, retained, solicited or shared <br> • Offender acts together with others to commit the offence <br> • Use of alcohol/drugs on victim <br> • Abuse of trust <br> • Previous violence against victim <br> • Sexual images of victim recorded, retained, solicited or shared <br> • Blackmail or other threats made (including to expose victim to the authorities, family/friends or others) <br> • Offender aware that he has a sexually transmitted disease <br> • Offender aware victim has been trafficked | Factor(s) in category A not present |

### STEP 2   Starting point and category range

Having determined the category, the court should use the corresponding starting points to reach a sentence within the category range below **for victims aged 16 or 17**. The starting point applies to all offenders irrespective of plea or previous convictions. Having determined the starting point, step two allows further adjustment for aggravating or mitigating features, set out below.

A case of particular gravity, reflected by multiple features of culpability in step one, could merit upward adjustment from the starting point before further adjustment for aggravating or mitigating features, set out below.

Where there is a sufficient prospect of rehabilitation, a community order with a sex offender treatment programme requirement under Part 3 of Schedule 9 of the Sentencing Code can be a proper alternative to a short or moderate length custodial sentence.

|  | A | B |
|---|---|---|
| Category 1 | **Starting point**<br>4 years' custody<br>**Category range**<br>2–5 years' custody | **Starting point**<br>2 years' custody<br>**Category range**<br>1–4 years' custody |
| Category 2 | **Starting point**<br>3 years' custody<br>**Category range**<br>1–4 years' custody | **Starting point**<br>1 year's custody<br>**Category range**<br>26 weeks'–2 years' custody |
| Category 3 | **Starting point**<br>1 year's custody<br>**Category range**<br>26 weeks'–2 years' custody | **Starting point**<br>26 weeks' custody<br>**Category range**<br>High level community order–1 year's custody |

### Community Orders and Custodial Sentences

[For the imposition of community orders, including the community orders table, see Imposition of Community and Custodial Sentences at **SG9-2**. For the imposition of custodial sentences see Imposition of Community and Custodial Sentences at **SG9-3**.]

### Factors increasing or reducing seriousness

The table below contains a **non-exhaustive** list of additional factual elements providing the context of the offence and factors relating to the offender. Identify whether any combination of these, or other relevant factors, should result in an upward or downward adjustment from the starting point. **In particular, relevant recent convictions are likely to result in an upward adjustment.** In some cases, having considered these factors, it may be appropriate to move outside the identified category range.

When sentencing appropriate **category 3 offences**, the court should also consider the custody threshold as follows:

- Has the custody threshold been passed?
- If so, is it unavoidable that a custodial sentence be imposed?
- If so, can that sentence be suspended?

### Aggravating factors

*Statutory aggravating factors*

- Previous convictions, having regard to
  a) the nature of the offence to which the conviction relates and its relevance to the current offence; and
  b) the time that has elapsed since the conviction
- Offence committed whilst on bail

*Other aggravating factors*

- Ejaculation
- Failure to comply with current court orders
- Offence committed whilst on licence
- Any steps taken to prevent the victim reporting an incident, obtaining assistance and/or from assisting or supporting the prosecution
- Attempts to dispose of or conceal evidence

### Mitigating factors

- No previous convictions **or** no relevant/recent convictions
- Remorse
- Previous good character and/or exemplary conduct*
- Age and/or lack of maturity where it affects the responsibility of the offender
- Mental disorder or learning disability, particularly where linked to the commission of the offence
- Demonstration of steps taken to address offending behaviour

* Previous good character/exemplary conduct is different from having no previous convictions. The more serious the offence, the less the weight which should normally be attributed to this factor. Where previous good character/exemplary conduct has been used to facilitate the offence, this mitigation should not normally be allowed and such conduct may constitute an aggravating factor.

## STEPS 3 to 9

[These are in the same terms as those applicable to Rape: see **SG31-3**.]

TRAFFICKING PEOPLE FOR SEXUAL EXPLOITATION                                    **SG31-23**

*Sexual Offences Act 2003 (sections 59A)*

**Effective from:** 01 April 2014

Triable either way
Maximum: 14 years' custody
Offence range: Community order–12 years' custody

This is a specified offence for the purposes of sections 266 and 279 (extended sentence for certain violent, sexual or terrorism offences) of the Sentencing Code. The term 'prostitution' is used in this guideline in accordance with the statutory language contained in the Sexual Offences Act 2003.

**(This guideline also applies to offences, committed before 6 April 2013, of trafficking into/within/out of the UK for sexual exploitation contrary to sections 57 to 59 of the Sexual Offences Act 2003)**

**Interim explanatory guidance pending the production of a full guideline for Modern Slavery**

* Section 59A of the Sexual Offences Act 2003 (SOA) has now been repealed by Schedule 5, paragraph 5 of the Modern Slavery Act 2015 (MSA). However, section 59A SOA remains in force for those offences committed wholly or partly before 31 July 2015.

Sentencers may consider that this is an appropriate guideline to follow when sentencing cases of sexual exploitation prosecuted under section 2 of the MSA. However, it is important to note that although the either way offence in section 2 of the MSA is in some ways similar to the SOA offence the maximum penalty for the MSA offence is life imprisonment. In addition the following provisions apply to the offence under the MSA:

- This is a Schedule 19 offence for the purposes of sections 274 and 285 (required life sentence for offence carrying life sentence) of the Sentencing Code.
- For offences committed on or after 31 July 2015, this is an offence listed in Part 1 of Schedule 15 for the purposes of sections 273 and 283 (life sentence for second listed offence) of the Sentencing Code.
- This is a specified offence for the purposes of sections 266 and 279 (extended sentence for certain violent, sexual or terrorism offences) of the Sentencing Code.

Sentencers seeking to rely on this guideline when sentencing offenders under the MSA may, therefore, need to adjust the starting point and ranges bearing in mind the increased statutory maximum.

## STEP 1   Determining the offence category

The court should determine which categories of harm and culpability the offence falls into by reference **only** to the tables below.

**Harm**

| Category 1 | • Abduction/detention |
|---|---|
| | • Violence or threats of violence |
| | • Sustained and systematic psychological abuse |
| | • Victim(s) under 18 |
| | • Victim(s) forced or coerced to participate in unsafe/degrading sexual activity |
| | • Victim(s) forced/coerced into prostitution |
| | • Victim(s) tricked/deceived as to purpose of visit |
| Category 2 | Factor(s) in category 1 not present |

## Culpability

| A | B | C |
|---|---|---|
| • Directing or organising trafficking on significant commercial basis<br>• Expectation of significant financial or other gain<br>• Significant influence over others in trafficking organisation/hierarchy<br>• Abuse of trust | • Operational or management function within hierarchy<br>• Involves others in operation whether by coercion/ intimidation/exploitation or reward (and offender's involvement is not as a result of coercion) | • Performs limited function under direction<br>• Close involvement but engaged by coercion/ intimidation/exploitation |

## STEP 2 Starting point and category range

Having determined the category of harm and culpability, the court should use the corresponding starting points to reach a sentence within the category range below. The starting point applies to all offenders irrespective of plea or previous convictions. Having determined the starting point, step two allows further adjustment for aggravating or mitigating features, set out below.

A case of particular gravity, reflected by multiple features of culpability or harm in step one, could merit upward adjustment from the starting point before further adjustment for aggravating or mitigating features, set out below.

Where there is a sufficient prospect of rehabilitation, a community order with a sex offender treatment programme requirement under Part 3 of Schedule 9 of the Sentencing Code can be a proper alternative to a short or moderate length custodial sentence.

|  | A | B | C |
|---|---|---|---|
| Category 1 | Starting point<br>8 years' custody<br>Category range<br>6–2 years' custody | Starting point<br>6 years' custody<br>Category range<br>4–8 years' custody | Starting point<br>18 months' custody<br>Category range<br>26 weeks'–2 years' custody |
| Category 2 | Starting point<br>6 years' custody<br>Category range<br>4–8 years' custody | Starting point<br>4 years' custody<br>Category range<br>2–6 years' custody | Starting point<br>26 weeks' custody<br>Category range<br>High level community order–18 months' custody |

### Community Orders and Custodial Sentences

[For the imposition of community orders, including the community orders table, see Imposition of Community and Custodial Sentences at **SG9-2**. For the imposition of custodial sentences see Imposition of Community and Custodial Sentences at **SG9-3**.]

### Factors increasing or reducing seriousness

The table below contains a **non-exhaustive** list of additional factual elements providing the context of the offence and factors relating to the offender. Identify whether any combination of these, or other relevant factors, should result in an upward or downward adjustment from the starting point. **In particular, relevant recent convictions are likely to result in an upward adjustment.** In some cases, having considered these factors, it may be appropriate to move outside the identified category range.

When sentencing appropriate **category 2 offences**, the court should also consider the custody threshold as follows:

• Has the custody threshold been passed?
• If so, is it unavoidable that a custodial sentence be imposed?
• If so, can that sentence be suspended?

### Aggravating factors

#### Statutory aggravating factors

• Previous convictions, having regard to
   a) the nature of the offence to which the conviction relates and its relevance to the current offence; and
   b) the time that has elapsed since the conviction
• Offence committed whilst on bail

*Other aggravating factors*
- Failure to comply with current court orders
- Offence committed whilst on licence
- Deliberate isolation of victim(s)
- Children of victim(s) left in home country due to trafficking
- Threats made to expose victim(s) to the authorities (for example, immigration or police), family/ friends or others
- Harm threatened against the family/friends of victim
- Exploitation of victim(s) from particularly vulnerable backgrounds
- Victim(s) previously trafficked/sold/passed around
- Passport/identity documents removed
- Victim(s) prevented from seeking medical treatment
- Food withheld
- Use of drugs/alcohol or other substance to secure victim's compliance
- Earnings of victim(s) withheld/kept by offender or evidence of excessive wage reduction, debt bondage, inflated travel or living expenses, unreasonable interest rates
- Any steps taken to prevent the victim reporting an incident, obtaining assistance and/or from assisting or supporting the prosecution
- Attempts to dispose of or conceal evidence
- Timescale over which operation has been run

**Mitigating factors**
- No previous convictions or no relevant/recent convictions
- Remorse
- Previous good character and/or exemplary conduct*
- Age and/or lack of maturity where it affects the responsibility of the offender
- Mental disorder or learning disability, particularly where linked to the commission of the offence

* Previous good character/exemplary conduct is different from having no previous convictions. The more serious the offence, the less the weight which should normally be attributed to this factor. Where previous good character/exemplary conduct has been used to facilitate the offence, this mitigation should not normally be allowed and such conduct may constitute an aggravating factor.

In the context of this offence, previous good character/exemplary conduct should not normally be given any significant weight and will not normally justify a reduction in what would otherwise be the appropriate sentence.

**STEPS 3 to 9**
[These are in the same terms as those applicable to Rape: see **SG31-3**.]

SEXUAL ACTIVITY WITH A PERSON WITH A MENTAL DISORDER IMPEDING CHOICE    **SG31-24**

*Sexual Offences Act 2003 (section 30)*

CAUSING OR INCITING A PERSON, WITH A MENTAL DISORDER IMPEDING CHOICE, TO ENGAGE IN SEXUAL ACTIVITY

*Sexual Offences Act 2003 (section 31)*

**Effective from:** 01 April 2014

Triable only on indictment (if penetration involved) otherwise, triable either way
Maximum: Life imprisonment (if penetration involved) otherwise, 14 years' custody
Offence range: Community order–19 years' custody

Where the offence involved penetration these are Schedule 19 offences for the purposes of sections 274 and section 285 (required life sentence for offence carrying life sentence) of the Sentencing Code.

For offences involving penetration committed on or after 3 December 2012, these are offences listed in Part 1 of Schedule 15 for the purposes of sections 273 and 283 (life sentence for second listed offence) of the Sentencing Code.

These are specified offences for the purposes of sections 266 and 279 (extended sentence for certain violent, sexual or terrorism offences) of the Sentencing Code.

### STEP 1 Determining the offence category

The court should determine which categories of harm and culpability the offence falls into by reference **only** to the tables below.

### Harm

| Category 1 | • The extreme nature of one or more category 2 factors or the extreme impact caused by a combination of category 2 factors **may** elevate to category 1 |
|---|---|
| Category 2 | • Severe psychological or physical harm <br> • Pregnancy or STI as a consequence of offence <br> • Additional degradation/humiliation <br> • Abduction <br> • Prolonged detention /sustained incident <br> • Violence or threats of violence <br> • Forced/uninvited entry into victim's home or residence |
| Category 3 | Factor(s) in categories 1 and 2 not present |

### Culpability

| A | B |
|---|---|
| • Significant degree of planning <br> • Offender acts together with others to commit the offence <br> • Use of alcohol/drugs on victim to facilitate the offence <br> • Grooming behaviour used against victim <br> • Abuse of trust <br> • Previous violence against victim <br> • Offence committed in course of burglary <br> • Sexual images of victim recorded, retained, solicited or shared <br> • Deliberate isolation of victim <br> • Commercial exploitation and/or motivation <br> • Offence racially or religiously aggravated <br> • Offence motivated by, or demonstrating, hostility to the victim based on his or her sexual orientation (or presumed sexual orientation) or transgender identity (or presumed transgender identity) <br> • Offence motivated by, or demonstrating, hostility to the victim based on the victim's disability (or presumed disability) | Factor(s) in category A not present |

### STEP 2 Starting point and category range

Having determined the category of harm and culpability, the court should use the corresponding starting points to reach a sentence within the category range below. The starting point applies to all offenders irrespective of plea or previous convictions. Having determined the starting point, step two allows further adjustment for aggravating or mitigating features, set out below.

A case of particular gravity, reflected by multiple features of culpability or harm in step one, could merit upward adjustment from the starting point before further adjustment for aggravating or mitigating features, set out below.

Where there is a sufficient prospect of rehabilitation, a community order with a sex offender treatment programme requirement under Part 3 of Schedule 9 of the Sentencing Code can be a proper alternative to a short or moderate length custodial sentence.

### Where offence involved penetration

|  | A | B |
|---|---|---|
| Category 1 | **Starting point** <br> 16 years' custody <br> **Category range** <br> 13–19 years' custody | **Starting point** <br> 13 years' custody <br> **Category range** <br> 11–17 years' custody |
| Category 2 | **Starting point** <br> 13 years' custody <br> **Category range** <br> 11–17 years' custody | **Starting point** <br> 10 years' custody <br> **Category range** <br> 8–13 years' custody |

|              | A                                                                 | B                                                                 |
| ------------ | ----------------------------------------------------------------- | ----------------------------------------------------------------- |
| Category 3   | **Starting point**<br>10 years' custody<br>**Category range**<br>8–13 years' custody | **Starting point**<br>8 years' custody<br>**Category range**<br>6–11 years' custody |

**Where offence did not involve penetration**

|              | A                                                                 | B                                                                 |
| ------------ | ----------------------------------------------------------------- | ----------------------------------------------------------------- |
| Category 1   | **Starting point**<br>6 years' custody<br>**Category range**<br>4–9 years' custody | **Starting point**<br>4 years' custody<br>**Category range**<br>3–7 years' custody |
| Category 2   | **Starting point**<br>4 years' custody<br>**Category range**<br>3–7 years' custody | **Starting point**<br>2 years' custody<br>**Category range**<br>1–4 years' custody |
| Category 3   | **Starting point**<br>1 year's custody<br>**Category range**<br>26 weeks'–<br>2 years' custody | **Starting point**<br>26 weeks' custody<br>**Category range**<br>High level community order–<br>1 year's custody |

### Community Orders and Custodial Sentences

[For the imposition of community orders, including the community orders table, see Imposition of Community and Custodial Sentences at **SG9-2**. For the imposition of custodial sentences see Imposition of Community and Custodial Sentences at **SG9-3**.]

### Factors increasing or reducing seriousness

The table below contains a **non-exhaustive** list of additional factual elements providing the context of the offence and factors relating to the offender. Identify whether any combination of these, or other relevant factors, should result in an upward or downward adjustment from the starting point. **In particular, relevant recent convictions are likely to result in an upward adjustment.** In some cases, having considered these factors, it may be appropriate to move outside the identified category range.

When appropriate, the court should also consider the custody threshold as follows:

- Has the custody threshold been passed?
- If so, is it unavoidable that a custodial sentence be imposed?
- If so, can that sentence be suspended?

### Aggravating factors

*Statutory aggravating factors*

- Previous convictions, having regard to
  a) the nature of the offence to which the conviction relates and its relevance to the current offence; and
  b) the time that has elapsed since the conviction
- Offence committed whilst on bail

*Other aggravating factors*

- Ejaculation (where not taken into account at step one)
- Blackmail or other threats made (where not taken into account at step one)
- Location of offence
- Timing of offence
- Use of weapon or other item to frighten or injure
- Victim compelled to leave their home or institution (including victims of domestic violence)
- Failure to comply with current court orders
- Offence committed whilst on licence
- Presence of others, especially children
- Any steps taken to prevent the victim reporting an incident, obtaining assistance and/or from assisting or supporting the prosecution
- Attempts to dispose of or conceal evidence
- Commission of offence whilst under the influence of alcohol or drugs

**Mitigating factors**

- No previous convictions **or** no relevant/recent convictions
- Remorse
- Previous good character and/or exemplary conduct*
- Age and/or lack of maturity where it affects the responsibility of the offender
- Mental disorder or learning disability, particularly where linked to the commission of the offence
- Sexual activity was incited but no activity took place because the offender voluntarily desisted or intervened to prevent it

\* Previous good character/exemplary conduct is different from having no previous convictions. The more serious the offence, the less the weight which should normally be attributed to this factor. Where previous good character/exemplary conduct has been used to facilitate the offence, this mitigation should not normally be allowed and such conduct may constitute an aggravating factor.

In the context of this offence, previous good character/exemplary conduct should not normally be given any significant weight and will not normally justify a reduction in what would otherwise be the appropriate sentence.

### STEPS 3 to 9

[These are the same terms as those applicable to rape: see **SG31-3**.]

**SG31-25**    ENGAGING IN SEXUAL ACTIVITY IN THE PRESENCE OF A PERSON WITH MENTAL DISORDER IMPEDING CHOICE

*Sexual Offences Act 2003 (section 32)*

CAUSING A PERSON, WITH MENTAL DISORDER IMPEDING CHOICE, TO WATCH A SEXUAL ACT

*Sexual Offences Act 2003 (section 33)*

**Effective from:** 01 April 2014

Triable either way
Maximum: 10 years' custody
Offence range: Community order–6 years' custody

These are specified offences for the purposes of sections 266 and 279 (extended sentence for certain violent, sexual or terrorism offences) of the Sentencing Code.

### STEP 1  Determining the offence category

The court should determine which categories of harm and culpability the offence falls into by reference **only** to the tables below.

**Harm**

| Category 1 | • Causing victim to view extreme pornography<br>• Causing victim to view indecent/prohibited images of children<br>• Engaging in, or causing a victim to view live, sexual activity involving sadism/violence/sexual activity with an animal/a child |
|---|---|
| Category 2 | Engaging in, or causing a victim to view images of or view live, sexual activity involving:<br>• penetration of vagina or anus (using body or object)<br>• penile penetration of mouth<br>• masturbation |
| Category 3 | Factor(s) in categories 1 and 2 not present |

## Culpability

| A | B |
|---|---|
| • Significant degree of planning<br>• Offender acts together with others in order to commit the offence<br>• Use of alcohol/drugs on victim to facilitate the offence<br>• Grooming behaviour used against victim<br>• Abuse of trust<br>• Use of threats (including blackmail)<br>• Commercial exploitation and/or motivation<br>• Offence racially or religiously aggravated<br>• Offence motivated by, or demonstrating, hostility to the victim based on his or her sexual orientation (or presumed sexual orientation) or transgender identity (or presumed transgender identity)<br>• Offence motivated by, or demonstrating, hostility to the victim based on his or her disability (or presumed disability) | Factor(s) in category A not present |

## STEP 2  Starting point and category range

Having determined the category of harm and culpability, the court should use the corresponding starting points to reach a sentence within the category range below. The starting point applies to all offenders irrespective of plea or previous convictions.

Having determined the starting point, step two allows further adjustment for aggravating or mitigating features, set out below.

A case of particular gravity, reflected by multiple features of culpability or harm in step one, could merit upward adjustment from the starting point before further adjustment for aggravating or mitigating features, set out below.

Where there is a sufficient prospect of rehabilitation, a community order with a sex offender treatment programme requirement under Part 3 of Schedule 9 of the Sentencing Code can be a proper alternative to a short or moderate length custodial sentence.

|  | A | B |
|---|---|---|
| Category 1 | **Starting point**<br>4 years' custody<br>**Category range**<br>3–6 years' custody | **Starting point**<br>2 years' custody<br>**Category range**<br>1–3 years' custody |
| Category 2 | **Starting point**<br>2 years' custody<br>**Category range**<br>1–3 years' custody | **Starting point**<br>1 year's custody<br>**Category range**<br>High level community order–18 months' custody |
| Category 3 | **Starting point**<br>26 weeks' custody<br>**Category range**<br>High level community order–1 year's custody | **Starting point**<br>Medium level community order<br>**Category range**<br>Low level community order–Medium level community order |

## Community Orders and Custodial Sentences

[For the imposition of community orders, including the community orders table, see Imposition of Community and Custodial Sentences at **SG9-2**. For the imposition of custodial sentences see Imposition of Community and Custodial Sentences at **SG9-3**.]

### Factors increasing or reducing seriousness

The table below contains a **non-exhaustive** list of additional factual elements providing the context of the offence and factors relating to the offender. Identify whether any combination of these, or other relevant factors, should result in an upward or downward adjustment from the starting point. **In particular, relevant recent convictions are likely to result in an upward adjustment.** In some cases, having considered these factors, it may be appropriate to move outside the identified category range.

When sentencing appropriate **category 2 or 3 offences**, the court should also consider the custody threshold as follows:

- Has the custody threshold been passed?
- If so, is it unavoidable that a custodial sentence be imposed?
- If so, can that sentence be suspended?

**Aggravating factors**

*Statutory aggravating factors*

- Previous convictions, having regard to
  a) the nature of the offence to which the conviction relates and its relevance to the current offence; and
  b) the time that has elapsed since the conviction
- Offence committed whilst on bail

*Other aggravating factors*

- Location of offence
- Timing of offence
- Failure to comply with current court orders
- Offence committed whilst on licence
- Any steps taken to prevent the victim reporting an incident, obtaining assistance and/or from assisting or supporting the prosecution
- Attempts to dispose of or conceal evidence
- Commission of offence whilst under the influence of alcohol or drugs

**Mitigating factors**

- No previous convictions **or** no relevant/recent convictions
- Remorse
- Previous good character and/or exemplary conduct*
- Age and/or lack of maturity where it affects the responsibility of the offender
- Mental disorder or learning disability, particularly where linked to the commission of the offence
- Demonstration of steps taken to address offending behaviour

* Previous good character/exemplary conduct is different from having no previous convictions. The more serious the offence, the less the weight which should normally be attributed to this factor. Where previous good character/exemplary conduct has been used to facilitate the offence, this mitigation should not normally be allowed and such conduct may constitute an aggravating factor.

**STEP 3  Consider any factors which indicate a reduction, such as assistance to the prosecution**

The court should take into account section 74 of the Sentencing Code (reduction in sentence for assistance to prosecution) and any other rule of law by virtue of which an offender may receive a discounted sentence in consequence of assistance given (or offered) to the prosecutor or investigator.

**STEP 4  Reduction for guilty plea**

The court should take account of any potential reduction for a guilty plea in accordance with section 73 of the Sentencing Code and the guideline for Reduction in Sentence for a Guilty Plea [**SG5-1–SG5-12**].

**STEP 5  Dangerousness**

The court should consider whether having regard to the criteria contained in Chapter 6 of Part 10 of the Sentencing Code it would be appropriate to impose an extended sentence (sections 266 and 279).

**STEP 6  Totality principle**

If sentencing an offender for more than one offence, or where the offender is already serving a sentence, consider whether the total sentence is just and proportionate to the offending behaviour. See *Totality* guideline [at **SG4**].

**STEP 7  Ancillary orders**

The court must consider whether to make any ancillary orders. The court must also consider what other requirements or provisions may automatically apply.

[See the Crown Court Compendium, Part II Sentencing, S7; Ancillary Orders]

**Additional ancillary orders – sexual offences**

[See **SG31-2** for additional ancillary orders for sexual offences covering slavery and trafficking prevention orders and automatic orders on conviction.]

**STEP 8  Reasons**

Section 52 of the Sentencing Code imposes a duty to give reasons for, and explain the effect of, the sentence.

**STEP 9  Consideration for time spent on bail (tagged curfew)**

The court must consider whether to give credit for time spent on bail in accordance with section 240A of the Criminal Justice Act 2003 and section 325 of the Sentencing Code.

### INDUCEMENT, THREAT OR DECEPTION TO PROCURE SEXUAL ACTIVITY WITH A PERSON WITH A MENTAL DISORDER                SG31-26

*Sexual Offences Act 2003 (section 34)*

### CAUSING A PERSON WITH A MENTAL DISORDER TO ENGAGE IN OR AGREE TO ENGAGE IN SEXUAL ACTIVITY BY INDUCEMENT, THREAT OR DECEPTION

*Sexual Offences Act 2003 (section 35)*

**Effective from:** 01 April 2014

Triable only on indictment (if penetration involved); otherwise triable either way
Maximum: Life imprisonment (if penetration involved); otherwise 14 years' custody
Offence range: Community order–10 years' custody

Where the offence involved penetration these are Schedule 19 offences for the purposes of sections 274 and 285 (required life sentence for offence carrying life sentence) of the Sentencing Code.

For offences involving penetration committed on or after 3 December 2012, these are offences listed in Part 1 of Schedule 15 for the purposes of sections 273 and 283 (life sentence for second listed offence) of the Sentencing Code.

These are specified offences for the purposes of sections 266 and 279 (extended sentence for certain violent, sexual or terrorism offences) of the Sentencing Code.

**STEP 1  Determining the offence category**

The court should determine which categories of harm and culpability the offence falls into by reference **only** to the tables below.

**This guideline also applies to offences committed remotely/online.**

**Harm**

| Category 1 | • Penetration of vagina or anus (using body or object)<br>• Penile penetration of mouth<br>In either case by, or of, the victim |
| --- | --- |
| Category 2 | Touching, or exposure, of naked genitalia or naked breasts by, or of, the victim |
| Category 3 | Other sexual activity |

**Culpability**

| A | B |
| --- | --- |
| • Significant degree of planning<br>• Offender acts together with others to commit the offence<br>• Use of alcohol/drugs on victim to facilitate the offence<br>• Abuse of trust<br>• Sexual images of victim recorded, retained, solicited or shared<br>• Commercial exploitation and/or motivation<br>• Offence racially or religiously aggravated<br>• Offence motivated by, or demonstrating, hostility to the victim based on his or her sexual orientation (or presumed sexual orientation) or transgender identity (or presumed transgender identity)<br>• Offence motivated by, or demonstrating, hostility to the victim based on his or her disability (or presumed disability) | Factor(s) in category A not present |

## STEP 2 Starting point and category range

Having determined the category of harm and culpability, the court should use the corresponding starting points to reach a sentence within the category range below. The starting point applies to all offenders irrespective of plea or previous convictions. Having determined the starting point, step two allows further adjustment for aggravating or mitigating features, set out below.

A case of particular gravity, reflected by multiple features of culpability or harm in step one, could merit upward adjustment from the starting point before further adjustment for aggravating or mitigating features, set out below.

Where there is a sufficient prospect of rehabilitation, a community order with a sex offender treatment programme requirement under Part 3 of Schedule 9 of the Sentencing Code can be a proper alternative to a short or moderate length custodial sentence.

|  | A | B |
|---|---|---|
| Category 1 | **Starting point**<br>5 years' custody<br>**Category range**<br>4–10 years' custody | **Starting point**<br>1 year's custody<br>**Category range**<br>High level community order–2 years' custody |
| Category 2 | **Starting point**<br>3 years' custody<br>**Category range**<br>2–6 years' custody | **Starting point**<br>26 weeks' custody<br>**Category range**<br>High level community order–1 year's custody |
| Category 3 | **Starting point**<br>26 weeks' custody<br>**Category range**<br>High level community order–3 years' custody | **Starting point**<br>Medium level community order<br>**Category range**<br>Low level community order–High level community order |

### Community Orders and Custodial Sentences

[For the imposition of community orders, including the community orders table, see Imposition of Community and Custodial Sentences at **SG9-2**. For the imposition of custodial sentences see Imposition of Community and Custodial Sentences at **SG9-3**.]

### Factors increasing or reducing seriousness

The table below contains a **non-exhaustive** list of additional factual elements providing the context of the offence and factors relating to the offender. Identify whether any combination of these, or other relevant factors, should result in an upward or downward adjustment from the starting point. **In particular, relevant recent convictions are likely to result in an upward adjustment.** In some cases, having considered these factors, it may be appropriate to move outside the identified category range.

When sentencing appropriate **category 2 or 3 offences**, the court should also consider the custody threshold as follows:

- Has the custody threshold been passed?
- If so, is it unavoidable that a custodial sentence be imposed?
- If so, can that sentence be suspended?

### Aggravating factors

*Statutory aggravating factors*
- Previous convictions, having regard to
  a) the nature of the offence to which the conviction relates and its relevance to the current offence; and
  b) the time that has elapsed since the conviction
- Offence committed whilst on bail

*Other aggravating factors*
- Severe psychological or physical harm
- Ejaculation
- Pregnancy or STI as a consequence of offence
- Location of offence
- Timing of offence
- Victim compelled to leave their home or institution (including victims of domestic violence)

- Failure to comply with current court orders
- Offence committed whilst on licence
- Any steps taken to prevent the victim reporting an incident, obtaining assistance and/or from assisting or supporting the prosecution
- Attempts to dispose of or conceal evidence
- Commission of offence whilst under the influence of alcohol or drugs

**Mitigating factors**

- No previous convictions **or** no relevant/recent convictions
- Remorse
- Previous good character and/or exemplary conduct*
- Age and/or lack of maturity where it affects the responsibility of the offender
- Mental disorder or learning disability, particularly where linked to the commission of the offence

*Previous good character/exemplary conduct is different from having no previous convictions. The more serious the offence, the less the weight which should normally be attributed to this factor. Where previous good character/exemplary conduct has been used to facilitate the offence, this mitigation should not normally be allowed and such conduct may constitute an aggravating factor.

In the context of this offence, previous good character/exemplary conduct should not normally be given any significant weight and will not normally justify a reduction in what would otherwise be the appropriate sentence.

**STEPS 3 to 9**

[These are the same terms as those applicable to Sexual Assault: see **SG31-5**.]

### ENGAGING IN SEXUAL ACTIVITY IN THE PRESENCE, PROCURED BY INDUCEMENT, THREAT OR DECEPTION, OF A PERSON WITH A MENTAL DISORDER

**SG31-27**

*Sexual Offences Act 2003 (section 36)*

### CAUSING A PERSON WITH A MENTAL DISORDER TO WATCH A SEXUAL ACT BY INDUCEMENT, THREAT OR DECEPTION

*Sexual Offences Act 2003 (section 37)*

**Effective from:** 01 April 2014

Triable either way
Maximum: 10 years' custody
Offence range: Community order–6 years' custody

These are specified offences for the purposes of sections 266 and 279 (extended sentence for certain violent, sexual or terrorism offences) of the Sentencing Code.

**STEP 1   Determining the offence category**

The court should determine which categories of harm and culpability the offence falls into by reference **only** to the tables below.

**Harm**

| Category 1 | • Causing victim to view extreme pornography<br>• Causing victim to view indecent/prohibited images of children<br>• Engaging in, or causing a victim to view live, sexual activity involving sadism/violence/sexual activity with an animal/a child |
|---|---|
| Category 2 | Engaging in, or causing a victim to view images of or view live, sexual activity involving:<br>• penetration of vagina or anus (using body or object)<br>• penile penetration of mouth<br>• masturbation |
| Category 3 | Factor(s) in categories 1 and 2 not present |

Sentencing Guidelines

## Culpability

| A | B |
|---|---|
| • Significant degree of planning<br>• Offender acts together with others in order to commit the offence<br>• Use of alcohol/drugs on victim to facilitate the offence<br>• Abuse of trust<br>• Commercial exploitation and/or motivation<br>• Offence racially or religiously aggravated<br>• Offence motivated by, or demonstrating, hostility to the victim based on his or her sexual orientation (or presumed sexual orientation) or transgender identity (or presumed transgender identity)<br>• Offence motivated by, or demonstrating, hostility to the victim based on his or her disability (or presumed disability) | Factor(s) in category A not present |

## STEP 2  Starting point and category range

Having determined the category of harm and culpability, the court should use the corresponding starting points to reach a sentence within the category range below. The starting point applies to all offenders irrespective of plea or previous convictions. Having determined the starting point, step two allows further adjustment for aggravating or mitigating features, set out below.

A case of particular gravity, reflected by multiple features of culpability or harm in step one, could merit upward adjustment from the starting point before further adjustment for aggravating or mitigating features, set out below.

Where there is a sufficient prospect of rehabilitation, a community order with a sex offender treatment programme requirement under Part 3 of Schedule 9 of the Sentencing Code can be a proper alternative to a short or moderate length custodial sentence.

|  | A | B |
|---|---|---|
| Category 1 | **Starting point**<br>4 years' custody<br>**Category range**<br>3–6 years' custody | **Starting point**<br>2 years' custody<br>**Category range**<br>1–3 years' custody |
| Category 2 | **Starting point**<br>2 years' custody<br>**Category range**<br>1–3 years' custody | **Starting point**<br>1 year's custody<br>**Category range**<br>High level community order–18 months' custody |
| Category 3 | **Starting point**<br>26 weeks' custody<br>**Category range**<br>High level community order–1 year's custody | **Starting point**<br>Medium level community order<br>**Category range**<br>Low level community order–Medium level community order |

## Community Orders and Custodial Sentences

[For the imposition of community orders, including the community orders table, see Imposition of Community and Custodial Sentences at **SG9-2**. For the imposition of custodial sentences see Imposition of Community and Custodial Sentences at **SG9-3**.]

## Factors increasing or reducing seriousness

The table below contains a **non-exhaustive** list of additional factual elements providing the context of the offence and factors relating to the offender. Identify whether any combination of these, or other relevant factors, should result in an upward or downward adjustment from the starting point. **In particular, relevant recent convictions are likely to result in an upward adjustment.** In some cases, having considered these factors, it may be appropriate to move outside the identified category range.

When sentencing appropriate **category 2 or 3 offences**, the court should also consider the custody threshold as follows:

• Has the custody threshold been passed?
• If so, is it unavoidable that a custodial sentence be imposed?
• If so, can that sentence be suspended?

## Aggravating factors

### Statutory aggravating factors

- Previous convictions, having regard to
  - a) the nature of the offence to which the conviction relates and its relevance to the current offence; and
  - b) the time that has elapsed since the conviction
- Offence committed whilst on bail

### Other aggravating factors

- Location of offence
- Timing of offence
- Failure to comply with current court orders
- Offence committed whilst on licence
- Any steps taken to prevent the victim reporting an incident, obtaining assistance and/or from assisting or supporting the prosecution
- Attempts to dispose of or conceal evidence
- Commission of offence whilst under the influence of alcohol or drugs

## Mitigating factors

- No previous convictions **or** no relevant/recent convictions
- Remorse
- Previous good character and/or exemplary conduct*
- Age and/or lack of maturity where it affects the responsibility of the offender
- Mental disorder or learning disability, particularly where linked to the commission of the offence
- Demonstration of steps taken to address offending behaviour

* Previous good character/exemplary conduct is different from having no previous convictions. The more serious the offence, the less the weight which should normally be attributed to this factor. Where previous good character/exemplary conduct has been used to facilitate the offence, this mitigation should not normally be allowed and such conduct may constitute an aggravating factor.

## STEPS 3 to 9

[These are in the same terms as those applicable to Engaging in sexual activity in the presence of a person with mental disorder impeding choice/ Causing a person, with mental disorder impeding choice, to watch a sexual act: see **SG31-25**.]

CARE WORKERS: SEXUAL ACTIVITY WITH A PERSON WITH A MENTAL DISORDER          **SG31-28**

*Sexual Offences Act 2003 (section 38)*

CARE WORKERS: CAUSING OR INCITING SEXUAL ACTIVITY

*Sexual Offences Act 2003 (section 39)*

**Effective from:** 01 April 2014

Triable only on indictment (if penetration involved); otherwise triable either way
Maximum: 14 years' custody (if penetration involved); otherwise 10 years' custody
Offence range: Community order–10 years' custody

These are specified offences for the purposes of sections 266 and 279 (extended sentence for certain violent, sexual or terrorism offences) of the Sentencing Code.

## STEP 1  Determining the offence category

The court should determine which categories of harm and culpability the offence falls into by reference **only** to the tables below.

**This guideline also applies to offences committed remotely/online.**

**Harm**

| Category 1 | • Penetration of vagina or anus (using body or object)<br>• Penile penetration of mouth<br>In either case by, or of, the victim |
| --- | --- |
| Category 2 | • Touching, or exposure, of naked genitalia or naked breasts by, or of, the victim |
| Category 3 | Factor(s) in categories 1 and 2 not present |

*(vertical margin text)* Sentencing Guidelines

## Culpability

| A | B |
|---|---|
| • Significant degree of planning<br>• Offender acts together with others to commit the offence<br>• Use of alcohol/drugs on victim to facilitate the offence<br>• Grooming behaviour used against victim<br>• Use of threats (including blackmail)<br>• Sexual images of victim recorded, retained, solicited or shared<br>• Commercial exploitation and/or motivation<br>• Offence racially or religiously aggravated<br>• Offence motivated by, or demonstrating, hostility to the victim based on his or her sexual orientation (or presumed sexual orientation) or transgender identity (or presumed transgender identity)<br>• Offence motivated by, or demonstrating, hostility to the victim based on his or her disability (or presumed disability) | Factor(s) in category A not present |

## STEP 2  Starting point and category range

Having determined the category of harm and culpability, the court should use the corresponding starting points to reach a sentence within the category range below. The starting point applies to all offenders irrespective of plea or previous convictions. Having determined the starting point, step two allows further adjustment for aggravating or mitigating features, set out below.

A case of particular gravity, reflected by multiple features of culpability or harm in step one, could merit upward adjustment from the starting point before further adjustment for aggravating or mitigating features, set out below.

Where there is a sufficient prospect of rehabilitation, a community order with a sex offender treatment programme requirement under Part 3 of Schedule 9 of the Sentencing Code can be a proper alternative to a short or moderate length custodial sentence.

| | A | B |
|---|---|---|
| Category 1 | **Starting point**<br>5 years' custody<br>**Category range**<br>4–10 years' custody | **Starting point**<br>18 months' custody<br>**Category range**<br>1–2 years' custody |
| Category 2 | **Starting point**<br>3 year's custody<br>**Category range**<br>2–6 years' custody | **Starting point**<br>26 weeks' custody<br>**Category range**<br>Medium level community order–1 year's custody |
| Category 3 | **Starting point**<br>26 weeks' custody<br>**Category range**<br>High level community order–3 years' custody | **Starting point**<br>Medium level community order<br>**Category range**<br>Low level community order–High level community order |

## Community Orders and Custodial Sentences

[For the imposition of community orders, including the community orders table, see Imposition of Community and Custodial Sentences at SG9-2. For the imposition of custodial sentences see Imposition of Community and Custodial Sentences at SG9-3.]

### Factors increasing or reducing seriousness

The table below contains a **non-exhaustive** list of additional factual elements providing the context of the offence and factors relating to the offender. Identify whether any combination of these, or other relevant factors, should result in an upward or downward adjustment from the starting point. **In particular, relevant recent convictions are likely to result in an upward adjustment.** In some cases, having considered these factors, it may be appropriate to move outside the identified category range.

When sentencing appropriate **category 2 or 3 offences**, the court should also consider the custody threshold as follows:

- Has the custody threshold been passed?
- If so, is it unavoidable that a custodial sentence be imposed?
- If so, can that sentence be suspended?

## Aggravating factors
### Statutory aggravating factors
- Previous convictions, having regard to
    a)  the nature of the offence to which the conviction relates and its relevance to the current offence; and
    b)  the time that has elapsed since the conviction
- Offence committed whilst on bail

### Other aggravating factors
- Ejaculation
- Pregnancy or STI as a consequence of offence
- Location of offence
- Timing of offence
- Victim compelled to leave their home or institution (including victims of domestic violence)
- Failure to comply with current court orders
- Offence committed whilst on licence
- Any steps taken to prevent the victim reporting an incident, obtaining assistance and/or from assisting or supporting the prosecution
- Attempts to dispose of or conceal evidence
- Failure of offender to respond to previous warnings
- Commission of offence whilst under the influence of alcohol or drugs

## Mitigating factors
- No previous convictions **or** no relevant/recent convictions
- Remorse
- Previous good character and/or exemplary conduct*
- Age and/or lack of maturity where it affects the responsibility of the offender
- Mental disorder or learning disability, particularly where linked to the commission of the offence
- Sexual activity was incited but no activity took place because the offender voluntarily desisted or intervened to prevent it

\* Previous good character/exemplary conduct is different from having no previous convictions. The more serious the offence, the less the weight which should normally be attributed to this factor. Where previous good character/exemplary conduct has been used to facilitate the offence, this mitigation should not normally be allowed and such conduct may constitute an aggravating factor.

In the context of this offence, previous good character/exemplary conduct should not normally be given any significant weight and will not normally justify a reduction in what would otherwise be the appropriate sentence.

## STEPS 3 to 9
[These are in the same terms as those applicable to Engaging in sexual activity in the presence of a person with mental disorder impeding choice/ Causing a person, with mental disorder impeding choice, to watch a sexual act: see **SG31-25**.]

SG31-29

Care Workers: Sexual Activity in the Presence of a person
with a Mental Disorder

*Sexual Offences Act 2003 (section 40)*

Care Workers: Causing a Person with a Mental Disorder
to Watch a Sexual Act

*Sexual Offences Act 2003 (section 41)*

**Effective from:** 01 April 2014

Triable either way
Maximum: 7 years' custody
Offence range: Community order–2 years' custody

These are specified offences for the purposes of sections 266 and 279 (extended sentence for certain violent, sexual or terrorism offences) of the Sentencing Code.

## STEP 1  Determining the offence category

The court should determine which categories of harm and culpability the offence falls into by reference **only** to the tables below.

### Harm

| Category 1 | • Causing victim to view extreme pornography<br>• Causing victim to view indecent/prohibited images of children<br>• Engaging in, or causing a victim to view live, sexual activity involving sadism/violence/ sexual activity with an animal/a child |
|---|---|
| Category 2 | Engaging in, or causing a victim to view images of or view live, sexual activity involving:<br>• penetration of vagina or anus (using body or object)<br>• penile penetration of mouth<br>• masturbation |
| Category 3 | Factor(s) in categories 1 and 2 not present |

### Culpability

| A | B |
|---|---|
| • Significant degree of planning<br>• Offender acts together with others to commit the offence<br>• Use of alcohol/drugs on victim to facilitate the offence<br>• Grooming behaviour used against victim<br>• Use of threats (including blackmail)<br>• Commercial exploitation and/or motivation<br>• Offence racially or religiously aggravated<br>• Offence motivated by, or demonstrating, hostility to the victim based on his or her sexual orientation (or presumed sexual orientation) or transgender identity (or presumed transgender identity)<br>• Offence motivated by, or demonstrating, hostility to the victim based on his or her disability (or presumed disability) | Factor(s) in category A not present |

## STEP 2  Starting point and category range

Having determined the category of harm and culpability, the court should use the corresponding starting points to reach a sentence within the category range below. The starting point applies to all offenders irrespective of plea or previous convictions. Having determined the starting point, step two allows further adjustment for aggravating or mitigating features, set out below.

A case of particular gravity, reflected by multiple features of culpability or harm in step one, could merit upward adjustment from the starting point before further adjustment for aggravating or mitigating features, set out below.

Where there is a sufficient prospect of rehabilitation, a community order with a sex offender treatment programme requirement under Part 3 of Schedule 9 of the Sentencing Code can be a proper alternative to a short or moderate length custodial sentence.

|  | A | B |
|---|---|---|
| Category 1 | **Starting point**<br>18 months' custody<br>**Category range**<br>1–2 years' custody | **Starting point**<br>1 year's custody<br>**Category range**<br>26 weeks'–18 months' custody |
| Category 2 | **Starting point**<br>1 year's custody<br>**Category range**<br>26 weeks'–18 months' custody | **Starting point**<br>26 weeks' custody<br>**Category range**<br>High level community order–1 year's custody |

|              | A                                                                                                        | B                                                                                                           |
| ------------ | -------------------------------------------------------------------------------------------------------- | ----------------------------------------------------------------------------------------------------------- |
| Category 3   | **Starting point**<br>26 weeks' custody<br>**Category range**<br>High level community order–1 year's custody | **Starting point**<br>Medium level community order<br>**Category range**<br>Low level community order–High level community order |

**Community Orders and Custodial Sentences**

[For the imposition of community orders, including the community orders table, see Imposition of Community and Custodial Sentences at **SG9-2**. For the imposition of custodial sentences see Imposition of Community and Custodial Sentences at **SG9-3**.]

**Factors increasing or reducing seriousness**

The table below contains a **non-exhaustive** list of additional factual elements providing the context of the offence and factors relating to the offender. Identify whether any combination of these, or other relevant factors, should result in an upward or downward adjustment from the starting point. **In particular, relevant recent convictions are likely to result in an upward adjustment.** In some cases, having considered these factors, it may be appropriate to move outside the identified category range.

When sentencing appropriate **category 2 or 3 offences**, the court should also consider the custody threshold as follows:

- Has the custody threshold been passed?
- If so, is it unavoidable that a custodial sentence be imposed?
- If so, can that sentence be suspended?

**Aggravating factors**

*Statutory aggravating factors*

- Previous convictions, having regard to
  a) the nature of the offence to which the conviction relates and its relevance to the current offence; and
  b) the time that has elapsed since the conviction
- Offence committed whilst on bail

*Other aggravating factors*

- Location of offence
- Timing of offence
- Failure to comply with current court orders
- Offence committed whilst on licence
- Any steps taken to prevent the victim reporting an incident, obtaining assistance and/or from assisting or supporting the prosecution
- Attempts to dispose of or conceal evidence
- Failure of offender to respond to previous warnings
- Commission of offence whilst under the influence of alcohol or drugs

**Mitigating factors**

- No previous convictions **or** no relevant/recent convictions
- Remorse
- Previous good character and/or exemplary conduct*
- Age and/or lack of maturity where it affects the responsibility of the offender
- Mental disorder or learning disability, particularly where linked to the commission of the offence
- Demonstration of steps taken to address offending behaviour

* Previous good character/exemplary conduct is different from having no previous convictions. The more serious the offence, the less the weight which should normally be attributed to this factor. Where previous good character/exemplary conduct has been used to facilitate the offence, this mitigation should not normally be allowed and such conduct may constitute an aggravating factor.

In the context of this offence, previous good character/exemplary conduct should not normally be given any significant weight and will not normally justify a reduction in what would otherwise be the appropriate sentence.

Sentencing Guidelines

- Mental disorder or learning disability, particularly where linked to the commission of the offence
- Demonstration of steps taken to address offending behaviour

*Previous good character/exemplary conduct is different from having no previous convictions. The more serious the offence, the less the weight which should normally be attributed to this factor. Where previous good character/exemplary conduct has been used to facilitate the offence, this mitigation should not normally be allowed and such conduct may constitute an aggravating factor.

### STEPS 3 to 9
[These are in the same terms as those applicable to Sexual Assault: see **SG31-5**.]

**SG31-32**            SEX WITH AN ADULT RELATIVE: PENETRATION

*Sexual Offences Act 2003 (section 64)*

SEX WITH AN ADULT RELATIVE: CONSENTING TO PENETRATION

*Sexual Offences Act 2003 (section 65)*

**Effective from:** 01 April 2014

Triable either way
Maximum: 2 years' custody
Offence range: Fine–2 years' custody

These are specified offences for the purposes of sections 266 and 279 (extended sentence for certain violent, sexual or terrorism offences) of the Sentencing Code.

### STEP 1  Determining the offence category
The court should determine the offence category using the table below.

| Category 1 | Raised harm **and** raised culpability |
|---|---|
| Category 2 | Raised harm **or** raised culpability |
| Category 3 | Sex with an adult relative **without** raised harm or culpability factors present |

The court should determine culpability and harm caused or intended, by reference **only** to the factors below, which comprise the principal factual elements of the offence. Where an offence does not fall squarely into a category, individual factors may require a degree of weighting before making an overall assessment and determining the appropriate offence category.

*Factors indicating raised harm*
- Victim is particularly vulnerable due to personal circumstances
- Child conceived

*Factors indicating raised culpability*
- Grooming behaviour used against victim
- Use of threats (including blackmail)

### STEP 2  Starting point and category range
Having determined the category, the court should use the corresponding starting points to reach a sentence within the category range below. The starting point applies to all offenders irrespective of plea or previous convictions. Having determined the starting point, step two allows further adjustment for aggravating or mitigating features, set out below.

A case of particular gravity, reflected by multiple features of culpability or harm in step one, could merit upward adjustment from the starting point before further adjustment for aggravating or mitigating features, set out below.

Where there is a sufficient prospect of rehabilitation, a community order with a sex offender treatment programme requirement under Part 3 of Schedule 9 of the Sentencing Code can be a proper alternative to a short or moderate length custodial sentence.

| Category 1 | **Starting point**<br>1 year's custody<br>**Category range**<br>26 weeks'–2 years' custody |
|---|---|

| Category 2 | **Starting point**<br>High level community order<br>**Category range**<br>Medium level community order–<br>1 year's custody |
| --- | --- |
| Category 3 | **Starting point**<br>Medium level community order<br>**Category range**<br>Band A fine–High level community order |

### Fines

[See **SG10-35** for band ranges.]

### Community Orders and Custodial Sentences

[For the imposition of community orders, including the community orders table, see Imposition of Community and Custodial Sentences at **SG9-2**. For the imposition of custodial sentences see Imposition of Community and Custodial Sentences at **SG9-3**.]

### Factors increasing or reducing seriousness

The table below contains a **non-exhaustive** list of additional factual elements providing the context of the offence and factors relating to the offender. Identify whether any combination of these, or other relevant factors, should result in an upward or downward adjustment from the starting point. **In particular, relevant recent convictions are likely to result in an upward adjustment.** In some cases, having considered these factors, it may be appropriate to move outside the identified category range.

When sentencing **category 2 offences**, the court should also consider the custody threshold as follows:

- Has the custody threshold been passed?
- If so, is it unavoidable that a custodial sentence be imposed?
- If so, can that sentence be suspended?

When sentencing **category 3 offences**, the court should also consider the community order threshold as follows:

- Has the community order threshold been passed?

### Aggravating factors

#### Statutory aggravating factors

- Previous convictions, having regard to
  - a) the nature of the offence to which the conviction relates and its relevance to the current offence; and
  - b) the time that has elapsed since the conviction
- Offence committed whilst on bail

#### Other aggravating factors

- Failure to comply with current court orders
- Offence committed whilst on licence
- Failure of offender to respond to previous warnings
- Any steps taken to prevent reporting an incident, obtaining assistance and/or from assisting or supporting the prosecution
- Attempts to dispose of or conceal evidence

### Mitigating factors

- No previous convictions **or** no relevant/recent convictions
- Remorse
- Previous good character and/or exemplary conduct*
- Age and/or lack of maturity where it affects the responsibility of the offender
- Mental disorder or learning disability, particularly where linked to the commission of the offence
- Demonstration of steps taken to address offending behaviour

* Previous good character/exemplary conduct is different from having no previous convictions. The more serious the offence, the less the weight which should normally be attributed to this factor. Where previous good character/exemplary conduct has been used to facilitate the offence, this mitigation should not normally be allowed and such conduct may constitute an aggravating factor.

**STEPS 3 to 9**

[These are in the same terms as those applicable to Engaging in sexual activity in the presence of a person with mental disorder impeding choice/ Causing a person, with mental disorder impeding choice, to watch a sexual act: see **SG31-25**.]

**SG31-33**          ADMINISTERING A SUBSTANCE WITH INTENT

*Sexual Offences Act 2003 (section 61)*

**Effective from:** 01 April 2014

Triable either way
Maximum: 10 years' custody
Offence range: 1–9 years' custody

This is a specified offence for the purposes of sections 266 and 279 (extended sentence for certain violent, sexual or terrorism offences) of the Sentencing Code.

**STEP 1 Determining the offence category**

The court should determine the offence category using the table below.

| Category 1 | Raised harm **and** raised culpability |
|---|---|
| Category 2 | Raised harm **or** raised culpability |
| Category 3 | Administering a substance with intent **without** raised harm or culpability factors present |

The court should determine culpability and harm caused or intended, by reference **only** to the factors below, which comprise the principal factual elements of the offence. Where an offence does not fall squarely into a category, individual factors may require a degree of weighting before making an overall assessment and determining the appropriate offence category. Where no substantive sexual offence has been committed the main consideration for the court will be the offender's conduct as a whole including, but not exclusively, the offender's intention.

*Factors indicating raised harm*

- Severe psychological or physical harm
- Prolonged detention /sustained incident
- Additional degradation/humiliation

*Factors indicating raised culpability*

- Significant degree of planning
- Specific targeting of a particularly vulnerable victim
- Intended sexual offence carries a statutory maximum of life
- Abuse of trust
- Recording of offence
- Offender acts together with others to commit the offence
- Commercial exploitation and/or motivation
- Offence racially or religiously aggravated
- Offence motivated by, or demonstrating, hostility to the victim based on his or her sexual orientation (or presumed sexual orientation) or transgender identity (or presumed transgender identity)
- Offence motivated by, or demonstrating, hostility to the victim based on his or her disability (or presumed disability)

**STEP 2 Starting point and category range**

Having determined the category, the court should use the corresponding starting points to reach a sentence within the category range below. The starting point applies to all offenders irrespective of plea or previous convictions. Having determined the starting point, step two allows further adjustment for aggravating or mitigating features, set out below.

A case of particular gravity, reflected by multiple features of culpability or harm in step one, could merit upward adjustment from the starting point before further adjustment for aggravating or mitigating features, set out below.

| Category 1 | **Starting point**<br>6 years' custody<br>**Category range**<br>4–9 years' custody |
|---|---|

| Category 2 | **Starting point**<br>4 years' custody<br>**Category range**<br>3–7 years' custody |
|---|---|
| Category 3 | **Starting point**<br>2 years' custody<br>**Category range**<br>1–5 years' custody |

### Custodial Sentences

[For the imposition of custodial sentences see Imposition of Community and Custodial Sentences at SG9-3.]

### Factors increasing or reducing seriousness

The table below contains a **non-exhaustive** list of additional factual elements providing the context of the offence and factors relating to the offender. Identify whether any combination of these, or other relevant factors, should result in an upward or downward adjustment from the starting point. **In particular, relevant recent convictions are likely to result in an upward adjustment.** In some cases, having considered these factors, it may be appropriate to move outside the identified category range.

### Aggravating factors

*Statutory aggravating factors*

- Previous convictions, having regard to
  a) the nature of the offence to which the conviction relates and its relevance to the current offence; and
  b) the time that has elapsed since the conviction
- Offence committed whilst on bail

*Other aggravating factors*

- Location of offence
- Timing of offence
- Any steps taken to prevent reporting an incident, obtaining assistance and/or from assisting or supporting the prosecution
- Attempts to dispose of or conceal evidence
- Failure to comply with current court orders
- Offence committed whilst on licence

### Mitigating factors

- No previous convictions or no relevant/recent convictions
- Remorse
- Previous good character and/or exemplary conduct*
- Age and/or lack of maturity where it affects the responsibility of the offender
- Mental disorder or learning disability, particularly where linked to the commission of the offence
- Demonstration of steps taken to address offending behaviour

* Previous good character/exemplary conduct is different from having no previous convictions. The more serious the offence, the less the weight which should normally be attributed to this factor. Where previous good character/exemplary conduct has been used to facilitate the offence, this mitigation should not normally be allowed and such conduct may constitute an aggravating factor.

### STEPS 3 to 9

[These are in the same terms as those applicable to Sexual Assault: see **SG31-5.**]

## COMMITTING AN OFFENCE WITH INTENT TO COMMIT A SEXUAL OFFENCE        **SG31-34**

*Sexual Offences Act 2003 (section 62)*

**Effective from:** 01 April 2014

Triable only on indictment (if kidnapping or false imprisonment committed), otherwise, triable either way
Maximum: Life imprisonment (if kidnapping or false imprisonment committed), otherwise, 10 years

Where kidnapping or false imprisonment was committed this is a Schedule 19 offence for the purposes of sections 274 and 285 (required life sentence for offence carrying life sentence) of the Sentencing Code.

For offences committed by kidnapping or false imprisonment, on or after 3 December 2012, this is an offence listed in Part 1 of Schedule 15 for the purposes of sections 273 and 283 (life sentence for second listed offence) of the Sentencing Code.

This is a specified offence for the purposes of sections 266 and 279 (extended sentence for certain violent, sexual or terrorism offences) of the Sentencing Code.

The starting point and range should be commensurate with that for the preliminary offence actually committed, but with an enhancement to reflect the intention to commit a sexual offence.

The enhancement will vary depending on the nature and seriousness of the intended sexual offence, but 2 years is suggested as a suitable enhancement where the intent was to commit rape or assault by penetration.

**SG31-35**          TRESPASS WITH INTENT TO COMMIT A SEXUAL OFFENCE

*Sexual Offences Act 2003 (section 63)*

**Effective from:** 01 April 2014

Triable either way
Maximum: 10 years' custody
Offence range: 1–9 years' custody

This is a specified offence for the purposes of sections 266 and 279 (extended sentence for certain violent, sexual or terrorism offences) of the Sentencing Code.

**STEP 1  Determining the offence category**

The court should determine the offence category using the table below.

| Category 1 | Raised harm **and** raised culpability |
|---|---|
| Category 2 | Raised harm **or** raised culpability |
| Category 3 | Trespass with intent to commit a sexual offence **without** raised harm or culpability factors present |

The court should determine culpability and harm caused or intended, by reference **only** to the factors below, which comprise the principal factual elements of the offence. Where an offence does not fall squarely into a category, individual factors may require a degree of weighting before making an overall assessment and determining the appropriate offence category. Where no substantive sexual offence has been committed the main consideration for the court will be the offender's conduct as a whole including, but not exclusively, the offender's intention.

*Factors indicating raised harm*
- Prolonged detention/sustained incident
- Additional degradation/humiliation
- Offence committed in victim's home

*Factors indicating raised culpability*
- Significant degree of planning
- Specific targeting of a particularly vulnerable victim
- Intended sexual offence attracts a statutory maximum of life imprisonment
- Possession of weapon or other item to frighten or injure
- Abuse of trust
- Offender acts together with others to commit the offence
- Commercial exploitation and/or motivation
- Offence racially or religiously aggravated
- Offence motivated by, or demonstrating, hostility to the victim based on his or her sexual orientation (or presumed sexual orientation) or transgender identity (or presumed transgender identity)
- Offence motivated by, or demonstrating, hostility to the victim based on his or her disability (or presumed disability)

**STEP 2  Starting point and category range**

Having determined the category, the court should use the corresponding starting points to reach a sentence within the category range below. The starting point applies to all offenders irrespective of plea or previous convictions. Having determined the starting point, step two allows further adjustment for aggravating or mitigating features, set out below.

A case of particular gravity, reflected by multiple features of culpability or harm in step one, could merit upward adjustment from the starting point before further adjustment for aggravating or mitigating features, set out below.

| Category 1 | **Starting point** 6 years' custody **Category range** 4–9 years' custody |
| Category 2 | **Starting point** 4 years' custody **Category range** 3–7 years' custody |
| Category 3 | **Starting point** 2 years' custody **Category range** 1–5 years' custody |

### Custodial Sentences

[For the imposition of custodial sentences see Imposition of Community and Custodial Sentences at SG9-3.]

### Factors increasing or reducing seriousness

The table below contains a **non-exhaustive** list of additional factual elements providing the context of the offence and factors relating to the offender. Identify whether any combination of these, or other relevant factors, should result in an upward or downward adjustment from the starting point. **In particular, relevant recent convictions are likely to result in an upward adjustment.** In some cases, having considered these factors, it may be appropriate to move outside the identified category range.

### Aggravating factors

*Statutory aggravating factors*

- Previous convictions, having regard to
  a) the nature of the offence to which the conviction relates and its relevance to the current offence; and
  b) the time that has elapsed since the conviction
- Offence committed whilst on bail

*Other aggravating factors*

- Location of offence
- Timing of offence
- Any steps taken to prevent reporting an incident, obtaining assistance and/or from assisting or supporting the prosecution
- Attempts to dispose of or conceal evidence
- Failure to comply with current court orders
- Offence committed whilst on licence

### Mitigating factors

- No previous convictions **or** no relevant/recent convictions
- Remorse
- Previous good character and/or exemplary conduct*
- Age and/or lack of maturity where it affects the responsibility of the offender
- Mental disorder or learning disability, particularly where linked to the commission of the offence
- Demonstration of steps taken to address offending behaviour

* Previous good character/exemplary conduct is different from having no previous convictions. The more serious the offence, the less the weight which should normally be attributed to this factor. Where previous good character/exemplary conduct has been used to facilitate the offence, this mitigation should not normally be allowed and such conduct may constitute an aggravating factor.

### STEPS 3 to 9

[These are in the same terms as those applicable to Engaging in sexual activity in the presence of a person with mental disorder impeding choice/ Causing a person, with mental disorder impeding choice, to watch a sexual act: see **SG31-25**.]

**SG31-36**         CHILD SEX OFFENCES COMMITTED BY CHILDREN OR YOUNG PERSONS
                        (SECTIONS 9–12) (OFFENDER UNDER 18)

*Sexual Offences Act 2003 (section 13)*

SEXUAL ACTIVITY WITH A CHILD FAMILY MEMBER (OFFENDER UNDER 18)

*Sexual Offences Act 2003 (section 25)*

INCITING A CHILD FAMILY MEMBER TO ENGAGE IN SEXUAL ACTIVITY
(OFFENDER UNDER 18)

*Sexual Offences Act 2003 (section 26)*

**Effective from:** 01 April 2014

Triable either way
Maximum: 5 years' custody

These are 'grave crimes' for the purposes of section 249 of the Sentencing Code.

These are specified offences for the purposes of section 254 (extended sentence for certain violent, sexual or terrorism offences) of the Sentencing Code. When sentencing offenders under 18, a court must in particular follow:

* Sentencing Children and Young People: Overarching Principles [see **SG8-1**].
* Sentencing Children and Young People: Sexual Offences [see **SG8-10**].

and have regard to:

* the principal aim of the young justice system (to prevent offending by children and young people); and the welfare of young offenders.

**SG31-37**                         SEXUAL OFFENCES – HISTORIC

*Sexual Offences Act 1956 (unless otherwise stated)*

**Effective from:** see offences

**[Details of the principal offences are set out as an Annex to this guideline at SG31-38.]**

When sentencing sexual offences under the Sexual Offences Act 1956, or other legislation pre-dating the 2003 Act, the court should apply the following principles:[203]

1.  The offender must be sentenced in accordance with the sentencing regime applicable at the *date of sentence*. Under sections 57 and 63 of the Sentencing Code the court must have regard to the statutory purposes of sentencing and must base the sentencing exercise on its assessment of the seriousness of the offence.
2.  The sentence is limited to the maximum sentence available at the *date of the commission of the offence*. If the maximum sentence has been reduced, the lower maximum will be applicable.
3.  The court should have regard to any applicable sentencing guidelines for equivalent offences under the Sexual Offences Act 2003. Where the offence, if committed on the day on which the offender was convicted, would have constituted an offence contrary to section 5 or section 6 of the Sexual Offences Act 2003, sections 265 and 278 of the Sentencing Code (special custodial sentence for certain offenders of particular concern) apply.
4.  The seriousness of the offence, assessed by the culpability of the offender and the harm caused or intended, is the main consideration for the court. The court should not seek to establish the likely sentence had the offender been convicted shortly after the date of the offence.
5.  When assessing the culpability of the offender, the court should have regard to relevant culpability factors set out in any applicable guideline.
6.  The court must assess carefully the harm done to the victim based on the facts available to it, having regard to relevant harm factors set out in any applicable guideline. Consideration of the circumstances which brought the offence to light will be of importance.

---

[203] *R v H and others* [2011] EWCA Crim 2753

7. The court must consider the relevance of the passage of time carefully as it has the potential to aggravate or mitigate the seriousness of the offence. It will be an aggravating factor where the offender has continued to commit sexual offences against the victim or others or has continued to prevent the victim reporting the offence.

8. Where there is an absence of further offending over a long period of time, especially combined with evidence of good character, this may be treated by the court as a mitigating factor. However, as with offences dealt with under the Sexual Offences Act 2003, previous good character/exemplary conduct is different from having no previous convictions. The more serious the offence, the less the weight which should normally be attributed to this factor. Where previous good character/exemplary conduct has been used to facilitate the offence, this mitigation should not normally be allowed and such conduct may constitute an aggravating factor.

9. If the offender was very young and immature at the time of the offence, depending on the circumstances of the offence, this may be regarded as personal mitigation.

10. If the offender made admissions at the time of the offence that were not investigated this is likely to be regarded as personal mitigation. Even greater mitigation is available to the offender who reported himself to the police and/or made early admissions.

11. A reduction for an early guilty plea should be made in the usual manner.

ANNEX – HISTORIC OFFENCES                                    SG31-38

| Offence (Sexual Offences Act 1956 unless stated otherwise) | Effective dates | Maximum |
|---|---|---|
| **Rape and assault offences** | | |
| Rape (section 1) | 1 January 1957–30 April 2004 | Life |
| Buggery with a person or animal (section 12) | 1 January 1957–30 April 2004 (from 3 November 1994 non-consensual acts of buggery were defined as rape) | Life |
| Indecent assault on a woman (section 14) | 1 January 1957–30 April 2004 | 1 January 1957–1 July 1960: 2 years 2 July 1960–15 September 1985: 2 years or 5 years if victim under 13 and age stated on indictment 16 September 1985 onwards: 10 years |
| Indecent assault upon a man (section 15) | 1 January 1957–30 April 2004 | 10 years |
| **Offences against children** | | |
| Sexual intercourse with a girl under 13 (section 5) | 1 January 1957–30 April 2004 | Life |
| Incest by a male person (section 10) | 1 January 1957–30 April 2004 | Life if victim under 13; otherwise 7 years |
| Incest by a female person (section 11) | 1 January 1957–30 April 2004 | 7 years |
| Indecency between men (section 13) | 1 January 1957–30 April 2004 | 1 January 1957–2 November 1994: 2 years 3 November 1994 onwards: Male offender over 21 with male under age of consent: 5 years Otherwise: 2 years |
| Indecency with a child (section 1 of the Indecency with Children Act 1960) | 2 July 1960–30 April 2004 | 1 July 1960–30 September 1997: 2 years 1 October 1997 onwards: 10 years *Note: on 11 January 2001 the age definition of a child increased from 14 to 16.* |

Sentencing Guidelines

| Incitement of a girl under 16 to commit incest (section 54 of the Criminal Law Act 1977) | 8 September 1977–30 April 2004 | 2 years |
|---|---|---|
| Abuse of position of trust (section 3 of the Sexual Offences (Amendment) Act 2000) | 8 January 2001–30 April 2004 | 5 years |

**Indecent images**

| Taking indecent photographs of a child (section 1 of the Protection of Children Act 1978) | 20 August 1978–present | 20 August 1978–10 January 2001: 3 years<br>11 January 2001 onwards: 10 years |
|---|---|---|
| Possession of indecent photographs of a child (section 160 of the Criminal Justice Act 1988) | 29 September 1988–present | 29 September 1988–10 January 2001:<br>6 months<br>11 January 2001 onwards: 5 years |

**Exploitation offences**

| Procurement of woman by threats (section 2)<br>Procurement by false pretences (section 3)<br>Causing prostitution of women (section 22)<br>Procuration of girl under 21 for unlawful sexual intercourse in any part of the world (section 23)<br>Detention in a brothel (section 24)<br>Permitting a defective to use premises for intercourse (section 27)<br>Causing or encouraging prostitution (etc) of a girl under 16 (section 28)<br>Causing or encouraging prostitution of a defective (section 29) | 1 January 1957–30 April 2004 | 2 years |
|---|---|---|
| Living on earnings of prostitution (section 30)<br>Controlling a prostitute (section 31) | 1 January 1957–30 April 2004 | 1 January 1957–15 August 1959: 2 years<br>16 August 1959 onwards: 7 years |
| Trafficking into/within/out of the UK for sexual exploitation (sections 57–59 of the Sexual Offences Act 2003) | 1 May 2005–5 April 2013 | 14 years |

**Offences against those with a mental disorder**

| Intercourse with a defective (section 7)<br>Procurement of a defective (section 9) | 1 January 1957–30 April 2004 | 2 years |
|---|---|---|
| Sexual intercourse with patients (section 128 of the Mental Health Act 1956) | 1 November 1960–30 April 2004 | 2 years |

**Other offences**

| Administering drugs to obtain or facilitate intercourse (section 4) | 1 January 1957–30 April 2004 | 2 years |
|---|---|---|
| Burglary with intent to commit rape (section 9 of the Theft Act 1968) | 1 January 1969–30 April 2004 | 14 years if dwelling; otherwise 10 years |

[Note this schedule is included in the Guidelines with thanks to Sweet & Maxwell, HHJ Rook QC and Robert Ward CBE for their kind permission to reproduce parts of *Sexual Offences Law & Practice*.]

# PART 32    TERRORISM OFFENCES

[For the standard text on applicability see **SG0-4**.]

**Effective from:** 27 April 2018

**Note for offences committed on or after 29 June 2021:** Any offence which is punishable on indictment with imprisonment for more than 2 years and is not specified in Schedule A1 of the Sentencing Code may be deemed to have a terrorist connection.

Sentencing for offences not covered by offence specific terrorism guidelines but with a terrorist connection, section 69 of the Sentencing Code.

Where a court is considering the seriousness of an offence specified in Schedule 1 of the Sentencing Code, and it appears that the offence has or may have a terrorist connection, the court must determine whether that is the case. To make this determination the court may hear evidence, and must take account of any representations made by the parties.

If the court determines that the offence has a terrorist connection it must treat that fact as a statutory aggravating factor and state in open court that the offence was so aggravated.

**Notification requirements apply to these offences.**

**Offences not covered by Schedule 1 of the Sentencing Code**
Where a court is considering the seriousness of an offence not specified in Schedule 1 of the Sentencing Code, and it appears that the offence has or may have a terrorist connection, the court should determine whether that is the case by hearing evidence where necessary. If the court determines that the offence has a terrorist connection it may treat that fact as a non-statutory aggravating factor where it appears relevant and appropriate to do so.

**Notification requirements do not apply to these offences.**

**ADDITIONAL GUIDANCE**
[See **SG32-12**]

*Terrorism Act 2006 (section 5)*

**Effective from:** 27 April 2018

Triable only on indictment
Maximum: Life imprisonment
Offence range: 3 years' custody–Life Imprisonment (minimum term 40 years)

**Note for offences committed on or after 29 June 2021:** This offence is a serious terrorism offence listed in Part 1 of Schedule 17A for the purposes of sections 268B and 282B (serious terrorism sentence) and section 323 (minimum term order: other life sentences) of the Sentencing Code. Where the criteria for a serious terrorism sentence are met a minimum custodial sentence of 14 years must be imposed unless exceptional circumstances apply. In a serious terrorism case (s. 323(4) Sentencing Code) the minimum term must be at least 14 years unless exceptional circumstances apply.

These provisions have not yet been reflected in this guideline.

This is a Schedule 19 offence for the purposes of sections 274 and 285 (required life sentence for offence carrying life sentence) of the Sentencing Code.

For offences committed on or after 13 April 2015, these are offences listed in Part 1 of Schedule 15 for the purposes of sections 273 and 283 (life sentence for second listed offence) of the Sentencing Code.

This is a specified offence for the purposes of sections 266 and 279 (extended sentence for certain violent, sexual or terrorism offences) of the Sentencing Code.

This is an offence listed in Schedule 13 for the purposes of sections 265 and 278 (required special sentence for certain offenders of particular concern) of the Sentencing Code.

This guideline applies only to offenders aged 18 and older

### STEP 1 Determining the offence category

The court should determine the offence category with reference **only** to the factors listed in the tables below. In order to determine the category the court should assess **culpability** and **harm**.

The court should weigh all the factors set out below in determining the offender's culpability. **Where there are characteristics present which fall under different levels of culpability, the court should balance these characteristics to reach a fair assessment of the offender's culpability.**

**Culpability demonstrated by one or more of the following**

| A | • **Acting alone**, or in **a leading** role, in terrorist activity where preparations were complete or were so close to completion that, but for apprehension, the activity was very likely to have been carried out |
|---|---|
| B | • **Acting alone**, or in a **leading** role, in terrorist activity where preparations were advanced and, but for apprehension, the activity was likely to have been carried out<br>• **Significant** role in terrorist activity where preparations were complete or were so close to completion that, but for apprehension, the activity was very likely to have been carried out<br>• Offender has coordinated others to take part in terrorist activity, whether in the UK or abroad (where not falling within A) |
| C | • **Leading** role in terrorist activity where preparations were not far advanced<br>• **Significant** role in terrorist activity where preparations were advanced and, but for apprehension, the activity was likely to have been carried out<br>• **Lesser** role in terrorist activity where preparations were complete or were so close to completion that, but for apprehension, the activity was very likely to have been carried out<br>• Offender acquires training or skills for purpose of terrorist activity (where not falling within A or B)<br>• Acts of significant assistance or encouragement of other(s) (where not falling within A or B) |
| D | • Offender has engaged in very limited preparation for terrorist activity<br>• Act(s) of lesser assistance or encouragement of other(s)<br>• Other cases not falling within A, B or C |

| Harm<br>Harm is assessed based on the type of harm risked and the likelihood of that harm being caused.<br>When considering the likelihood of harm, the court should consider the viability of any plan. | |
|---|---|
| Category 1 | • Multiple deaths risked and very likely to be caused |
| Category 2 | • Multiple deaths risked but not very likely to be caused<br>• Any death risked and very likely to be caused |
| Category 3 | • Any death risked but not very likely to be caused<br>• Risk of widespread or serious damage to property or economic interests<br>• Risk of a substantial impact upon civic infrastructure<br>• Any other cases |

### STEP 2 Starting point and category range

Having determined the category at step one, the court should use the corresponding starting point to reach a sentence within the category range below. The starting point applies to all offenders irrespective of plea or previous convictions. A case of particular gravity, reflected by multiple features of culpability or harm in step one, could merit upward adjustment from the starting point before further adjustment for aggravating or mitigating features. **Offenders committing the most serious offences are likely to be found dangerous and so the table below includes options for life sentences. However, the court should consider the dangerousness provisions in *all* cases, having regard to the criteria contained in Chapter 6 of Part 10 of the Sentencing Code to make the appropriate determination, before imposing either a life sentence or an extended sentence. (See Step 5 below).**

The court must also consider the provisions set out in sections 265 and 278 of the Sentencing Code (required special sentence for certain offenders of particular concern). (See Step 6 below).

| Harm | Culpability | | | |
|---|---|---|---|---|
| | **A** | **B** | **C** | **D** |
| Category 1 | **Starting point** Life imprisonment – minimum term 35 years' custody | **Starting point** Life imprisonment – minimum term 25 years' custody | **Starting point** Life imprisonment – minimum term 15 years' custody | **Starting point** 15 years' custody |
| | **Category range** Life imprisonment – minimum term 30–40 years' custody | **Category range** Life imprisonment – minimum term 20–30 years' custody | **Category range** Life imprisonment – minimum term 10–20 years' custody | **Category range** 10–20 years' custody |
| Category 2 | **Starting point** Life imprisonment – minimum term 25 years | **Starting point** Life imprisonment – minimum term 15 years | **Starting point** 15 years' custody | **Starting point** 8 years' custody |
| | **Category range** Life imprisonment – minimum term 20–30 years' custody | **Category range** Life imprisonment – minimum term 10–20 years' custody | **Category range** 10–20 years' custody | **Category range** 6–10 years' custody |
| Category 3 | **Starting point** 16 years' custody | **Starting point** 12 years' custody | **Starting point** 8 years' custody | **Starting point** 4 years' custody |
| | **Category range** 12–20 years' custody | **Category range** 8–16 years' custody | **Category range** 6–10 years' custody | **Category range** 3–6 years' custody |

### Custodial Sentences

[For the imposition of custodial sentences see Imposition of Community and Custodial Sentences at SG9-3.]

### Additional factors affecting seriousness

The table below contains a **non-exhaustive** list of additional factual elements providing the context of the offence and factors relating to the offender. Identify whether any combination of these, or other relevant factors, should result in an upward or downward adjustment from the sentence arrived at so far. In particular, relevant recent convictions are likely to result in an upward adjustment. In some cases, having considered these factors, it may be appropriate to move outside the identified category range.

### Factors increasing seriousness

*Statutory aggravating factors*

- Previous convictions [see **SG2-21**], having regard to a) the **nature** of the offence to which the conviction relates and its **relevance** to the current offence; and b) the **time** that has elapsed since the conviction
- Offence committed whilst on bail [see **SG2-22**]
- Offence motivated by, or demonstrating hostility based on any of the following characteristics or presumed characteristics of the victim: religion, race, disability, sexual orientation or transgender identity [see **SG2-23**] *(When considering this factor, sentencers should bear in mind the statutory definition of terrorism in section 1 of the Terrorism Act 2000, and should be careful to avoid double counting)*

*Other aggravating factors*

- Recent and/or repeated possession or accessing of extremist material
- Communication with other extremists
- Deliberate use of encrypted communications or similar technologies to facilitate the commission of the offence and/or avoid or impede detection
- Offender attempted to disguise their identity to prevent detection
- Indoctrinated or encouraged others
- Preparation was with a view to engage in combat with UK armed forces
- Conduct in preparation includes the actual or planned commission of other offences, where not taken into account in step one
- Failure to respond to warnings [see **SG2-39**]
- Failure to comply with current court orders [see **SG2-40**]
- Offence committed on licence or Post Sentence Supervision [see **SG2-40**]
- Offence committed whilst in prison [see **SG2-41**]

Sentencing Guidelines

**Factors reducing seriousness or reflecting personal mitigation**

- No previous convictions **or** no relevant/recent convictions [see **SG2-48**]
- Good character and/or exemplary conduct [see **SG2-49**]
- Offender involved through coercion, intimidation or exploitation [see **SG2-55**]
- Clear evidence of a change of mind set prior to arrest
- Offender's responsibility substantially reduced by mental disorder or learning disability [see **SG2-63**]
- Age and/or lack of maturity where it affects the responsibility of the offender [see **SG2-60**]
- Sole or primary carer for dependent relatives [see **SG2-61**]

**STEP 3  Consider any factors which indicate a reduction, such as assistance to the prosecution**

The court should take into account section 74 of the Sentencing Code (reduction in sentence for assistance to prosecution) and any other rule of law by virtue of which an offender may receive a discounted sentence in consequence of assistance given (or offered) to the prosecutor or investigator.

**STEP 4  Reduction for guilty plea**

The court should take account of any potential reduction for a guilty plea in accordance with section 73 of the Sentencing Code and the guideline for Reduction in Sentence for a Guilty Plea [**SG5-1–SG5-12**].

**STEP 5  Dangerousness**

The court should consider:

1) whether having regard to the criteria contained in Chapter 6 of Part 10 of the Sentencing Code it would be appropriate to impose a life sentence (sections 274 and 285);
2) whether having regard to sections 273 and 283 of the Sentencing Code it would be appropriate to impose a life sentence;
3) whether having regard to the criteria contained in Chapter 6 of Part 10 of the Sentencing Code it would be appropriate to impose an extended sentence (sections 266 and 279).

When sentencing offenders to a life sentence under these provisions, the notional determinate sentence should be used as the basis for the setting of a minimum term.

**STEP 6  Required special sentence for certain offenders of particular concern**
**(sections 265 and 278 of the Sentencing Code)**

Where the court does not impose a sentence of imprisonment for life or an extended sentence, but does impose a period of imprisonment, the term of the sentence must be equal to the aggregate of the appropriate custodial term and a further period of 1 year for which the offender is to be subject to a licence.

**STEP 7  Totality principle**

If sentencing an offender for more than one offence, or where the offender is already serving a sentence, consider whether the total sentence is just and proportionate to the overall offending behaviour in accordance with the *Totality* guideline [see **SG4**].

**STEP 8  Ancillary orders**

In all cases the court should consider whether to make ancillary orders.

[See the Crown Court Compendium, Part II Sentencing, S7; Ancillary Orders]

**STEP 9  Reasons**

Section 52 of the Sentencing Code imposes a duty to give reasons for, and explain the effect of, the sentence.

**STEP 10  Consideration for time spent on bail (tagged curfew)**

The court must consider whether to give credit for time spent on bail in accordance with section 240A of the Criminal Justice Act 2003 and section 325 of the Sentencing Code.

**ADDITIONAL GUIDANCE**

[See **SG32-12**]

**SG32-4**                    EXPLOSIVE SUBSTANCES (TERRORISM ONLY)

*Explosive Substances Act 1883, s.2, Explosive Substances Act 1883, s.3*

**Effective from:** 27 April 2018

**Causing explosion likely to endanger life or property,** Explosive Substances Act 1883, s.2
**Attempt to cause explosion, or making or keeping explosive with intent to endanger life or property,**
Explosive Substances Act 1883, s.3

Triable only on indictment

Maximum: Life imprisonment

Offence range: 3 years' custody–Life Imprisonment (minimum term 40 years)

**Note for offences committed on or after 29 June 2021:** This offence is a serious terrorism offence listed in Part 1 of Schedule 17A for the purposes of sections 268B and 282B (serious terrorism sentence) and section 323 (minimum term order: other life sentences) of the Sentencing Code. Where the criteria for a serious terrorism sentence are met a minimum custodial sentence of 14 years must be imposed unless exceptional circumstances apply. In a serious terrorism case (s. 323(4) Sentencing Code) the minimum term must be at least 14 years unless exceptional circumstances apply.

These provisions have not yet been reflected in this guideline.

These are Schedule 19 offences for the purposes of sections 274 and 285 (required life sentence for offence carrying life sentence) of the Sentencing Code.

For offences committed on or after 13 April 2015, these are offences listed in Part 1 of Schedule 15 for the purposes of sections 273 and 283 (life sentence for second listed offence) of the Sentencing Code.

These are specified offences for the purposes of sections 266 and 279 (extended sentence for certain violent, sexual or terrorism offences) of the Sentencing Code.

These are offences listed in Schedule 13 for the purposes of sections 265 and 278 (required special sentence for certain offenders of particular concern) of the Sentencing Code.

## STEP 1  Determining the offence category

The court should determine the offence category with reference **only** to the factors listed in the tables below. In order to determine the category, the court should assess **culpability** and **harm**.

The court should weigh all the factors set out below in determining the offender's culpability.

**Where there are characteristics present which fall under different levels of culpability, the court should balance these characteristics to reach a fair assessment of the offender's culpability.**

**Culpability demonstrated by one or more of the following**

| A | • Offender caused an explosion or used, developed or was in possession of a viable explosive device<br>• **Acting alone**, or in a **leading** role, in terrorist activity involving explosives, where preparations were complete or were so close to completion that, but for apprehension, the activity was very likely to have been carried out |
|---|---|
| B | • Offender took significant steps towards creating an explosion or developing or obtaining a viable explosive device<br>• **Acting alone**, or in a **leading** role, in terrorist activity involving explosives where preparations were advanced and, but for apprehension, the activity was likely to have been carried out<br>• **Significant** role in terrorist activity involving explosives where preparations were complete or were so close to completion that, but for apprehension, the activity was very likely to have been carried out |
| C | • **Leading** role in terrorist activity involving explosives where preparations were not far advanced<br>• **Significant** role in terrorist activity involving explosives where preparations were advanced and, but for apprehension, the activity was likely to have been carried out<br>• **Lesser** role in terrorist activity involving explosives where preparations were complete or were so close to completion that, but for apprehension, the activity was very likely to have been carried out<br>• Act(s) of significant assistance or encouragement of other(s) involved in causing, developing or possessing an explosive device (where not falling within A or B) |
| D | • Offender took very limited steps toward creating an explosion or developing or obtaining a viable explosive device<br>• Offender has engaged in very limited preparation of terrorist activity involving explosives<br>• Act(s) of lesser assistance or encouragement of other(s)<br>• Other cases not falling within A, B or C |

### Harm
Harm is assessed based on the type of harm risked and the likelihood of that harm being caused. When considering the likelihood of harm, the court should consider the viability of any plan.

| Category 1 | • Multiple deaths risked and very likely to be caused |
|---|---|
| Category 2 | • Multiple deaths risked but not very likely to be caused<br>• Any death risked and very likely to be caused |
| Category 3 | • Any death risked but not very likely to be caused<br>• Risk of widespread or serious damage to property or economic interests<br>• Risk of a substantial impact upon civic infrastructure<br>• Any other cases |

## STEP 2 Starting point and category range

Having determined the category at step one, the court should use the corresponding starting point to reach a sentence within the category range below. The starting point applies to all offenders irrespective of plea or previous convictions. A case of particular gravity, reflected by multiple features of culpability or harm in step one, could merit upward adjustment from the starting point before further adjustment for aggravating or mitigating features, set out below. **Offenders committing the most serious offences are likely to be found dangerous and so the table below includes options for life sentences. However, the court should consider the dangerousness provisions in *all* cases, having regard to the criteria contained in Chapter 6 of Part 10 of the Sentencing Code to make the appropriate determination, before imposing either a life sentence or an extended sentence. (See Step 5 below).**

**The court must also consider the provisions set out in sections 265 and 278 of the Sentencing Code (required special sentence for certain offenders of particular concern). (See Step 6 below).**

| Harm | Culpability | | | |
|---|---|---|---|---|
| | **A** | **B** | **C** | **D** |
| Category 1 | **Starting point** Life imprisonment– minimum term 35 years' custody | **Starting point** Life imprisonment– minimum term 25 years' custody | **Starting point** Life imprisonment– minimum term 15 years' custody | **Starting point** 15 years' custody |
| | **Category range** Life imprisonment –minimum term 30–40 years' custody | **Category range** Life imprisonment –minimum term 20–30 years' custody | **Category range** Life imprisonment –minimum term 10–20 years' custody | **Category range** 10–20 years' custody |
| Category 2 | **Starting point** Life imprisonment– minimum term 25 years | **Starting point** Life imprisonment– minimum term 15 years | **Starting point** 15 years' custody | **Starting point** 8 years' custody |
| | **Category range** Life imprisonment –minimum term 20–30 years' custody | **Category range** Life imprisonment –minimum term 10–20 years' custody | **Category range** 10–20 years' custody | **Category range** 6–10 years custody |
| Category 3 | **Starting point** 16 years' custody | **Starting point** 12 years' custody | **Starting point** 8 years' custody | **Starting point** 4 years' custody |
| | **Category range** 12–20 years' custody | **Category range** 8–16 years' custody | **Category range** 6–10 years' custody | **Category range** 3–6 years' custody |

### Community Orders and Custodial Sentences

[See Imposition of Community and Custodial Sentences at SG9-3.]

### Additional factors affecting seriousness

The table below contains a **non-exhaustive** list of additional factual elements providing the context of the offence and factors relating to the offender. Identify whether any combination of these, or other relevant factors, should result in an upward or downward adjustment from the sentence arrived at so far. In particular, relevant recent convictions are likely to result in an upward adjustment. In some cases, having considered these factors, it may be appropriate to move outside the identified category range.

**Factors increasing seriousness**

*Statutory aggravating factors*

- Previous convictions [see **SG2-21**], having regard to a) the **nature** of the offence to which the conviction relates and its **relevance** to the current offence; and b) the **time** that has elapsed since the conviction
- Offence committed whilst on bail [see **SG2-22**]
- Offence motivated by, or demonstrating hostility based on any of the following characteristics or presumed characteristics of the victim: religion, race, disability, sexual orientation or transgender identity [see **SG2-23**] *(When considering this factor, sentencers should bear in mind the statutory definition of terrorism in section 1 of the Terrorism Act 2000, and should be careful to avoid double counting)*

*Other aggravating factors*

- Recent and/or repeated possession or accessing of extremist material
- Communication with other extremists
- Deliberate use of encrypted communications or similar technologies to facilitate the commission of the offence and/or avoid or impede detection
- Offender attempted to disguise their identity to prevent detection
- Indoctrinated or encouraged others
- Conduct in preparation includes the actual or planned commission of other offences, where not taken into account in step one
- Failure to respond to warnings [see **SG2-39**]
- Failure to comply with current court orders [see **SG2-40**]
- Offence committed on licence or Post Sentence Supervision [see **SG2-40**]
- Offence committed whilst in prison [see **SG2-41**]

**Factors reducing seriousness or reflecting personal mitigation**

- No previous convictions **or** no relevant/recent convictions [see **SG2-48**]
- Good character and/or exemplary conduct [see **SG2-49**]
- Offender involved through coercion, intimidation or exploitation [see **SG2-55**]
- Clear evidence of a change of mind set prior to arrest
- Offender's responsibility substantially reduced by mental disorder or learning disability [see **SG2-63**]
- Age and/or lack of maturity where it affects the responsibility of the offender [see **SG2-60**]
- Sole or primary carer for dependent relatives [see **SG2-61**]

**STEP 3   Consider any factors which indicate a reduction, such as assistance to the prosecution**

The court should take into account section 74 of the Sentencing Code (reduction in sentence for assistance to prosecution) and any other rule of law by virtue of which an offender may receive a discounted sentence in consequence of assistance given (or offered) to the prosecutor or investigator.

**STEP 4   Reduction for guilty plea**

The court should take account of any potential reduction for a guilty plea in accordance with section 73 of the Sentencing Code and the guideline for Reduction in Sentence for a Guilty Plea [**SG5-1–SG5-12**].

**STEP 5   Dangerousness**

The court should consider:

1) whether having regard to the criteria contained in Chapter 6 of Part 10 of the Sentencing Code it would be appropriate to impose a life sentence (sections 274 and 285);
2) whether having regard to sections 273 and 283 of the Sentencing Code it would be appropriate to impose a life sentence;
3) whether having regard to the criteria contained in Chapter 6 of Part 10 of the Sentencing Code it would be appropriate to impose an extended sentence (sections 266 and 279).

When sentencing offenders to a life sentence under these provisions, the notional determinate sentence should be used as the basis for the setting of a minimum term.

**STEP 6   Required special sentence for certain offenders of particular concern**

Where the court does not impose a sentence of imprisonment for life or an extended sentence, but does impose a period of imprisonment, the term of the sentence must be equal to the aggregate of the appropriate custodial term and a further period of 1 year for which the offender is to be subject to a licence (sections 265 and 278 of the Sentencing Code).

**STEP 7   Totality principle**

If sentencing an offender for more than one offence, or where the offender is already serving a sentence, consider whether the total sentence is just and proportionate to the overall offending behaviour in accordance with the *Totality* guideline [see **SG4**].

**STEP 8 Ancillary orders**

In all cases the court should consider whether to make ancillary orders.

[See the Crown Court Compendium, Part II Sentencing, S7; Ancillary Orders]

**STEP 9 Reasons**

Section 52 of the Sentencing Code imposes a duty to give reasons for, and explain the effect of, the sentence.

**STEP 10 Consideration for time spent on bail (tagged curfew)**

The court must consider whether to give credit for time spent on bail in accordance with section 240A of the Criminal Justice Act 2003 and section 325 of the Sentencing Code.

**ADDITIONAL GUIDANCE**

[See SG32-12]

SG32-5

ENCOURAGEMENT OF TERRORISM

*Terrorism Act 2006, s.1, Terrorism Act 2006, s.2*

**Effective from:** 27 April 2018

**Encouragement of terrorism,** Terrorism Act 2006, s.1
**Dissemination of terrorist publications**, Terrorism Act 2006, s.2

Triable either way
Maximum: 7 years' custody [see note below]
Offence range: High level community order–6 years' custody

Note for offences **committed** on or after **12 April 2019:**

The maximum sentence is increased to **15 years** (section 7(6) and (7) Counter-Terrorism and Border Security Act 2019). **The increase has not yet been reflected in the sentence levels in this guideline.**

These are specified offences for the purposes of sections 266 and 279 (extended sentence for certain violent, sexual or terrorism offences) of the Sentencing Code.

Note for offences **sentenced** on or after **12 April 2019:**

These are offences listed in Schedule 13 for the purposes of sections 265 and 278 (required special sentence for certain offenders of particular concern) of the Sentencing Code.

**This guideline applies only to offenders aged 18 and older**

**STEP 1 Determining the offence category**

The court should determine the offence category with reference **only** to the factors listed in the tables below. In order to determine the category, the court should assess **culpability** and **harm.**

The court should weigh all the factors set out below in determining the offender's culpability. **Where there are characteristics present which fall under different levels of culpability, the court should balance these characteristics to reach a fair assessment of the offender's culpability.**

**Culpability demonstrated by one or more of the following**

| A | • Offender in position of trust, authority or influence and abuses their position to encourage others<br>• Intended to encourage others to engage in any form of terrorist activity<br>• Intended to provide assistance to others to engage in terrorist activity |
|---|---|
| B | • Reckless as to whether others would be encouraged or assisted to engage in terrorist activity and published statement/disseminated publication widely to a large or targeted audience (if via social media this can include both open or closed groups) |
| C | • Other cases where characteristics for categories A or B are not present |

| Harm<br>The court should consider the factors set out below to determine the level of harm | |
|---|---|
| Category 1 | • Evidence that others have acted on or been assisted by the encouragement to carry out activities endangering life<br>• Statement or publication provides instruction for specific terrorist activity endangering life |

| Category 2 | • Evidence that others have acted on or been assisted by the encouragement to carry out activities not endangering life<br>• Statement or publication provides non-specific content encouraging support for terrorist activity endangering life<br>• Statement or publication provides instruction for specific terrorist activity not endangering life |
|---|---|
| Category 3 | • Statement or publication provides non-specific content encouraging support for terrorist activity not endangering life<br>• Other cases where characteristics for categories 1 or 2 are not present |

## STEP 2  Starting point and category range

Having determined the category at step one, the court should use the corresponding starting point to reach a sentence within the category range below. The starting point applies to all offenders irrespective of plea or previous convictions. A case of particular gravity, reflected by multiple features of culpability or harm in step one, could merit upward adjustment from the starting point before further adjustment for aggravating or mitigating features, set out below.

| Harm | Culpability | | |
|---|---|---|---|
| | **A** | **B** | **C** |
| Category 1 | **Starting point**<br>5 years' custody | **Starting point**<br>4 years' custody | **Starting point**<br>3 years' custody |
| | Category range<br>4–6 years' custody | Category range<br>3–5 years' custody | Category range<br>2–4 years' custody |
| Category 2 | **Starting point**<br>4 years' custody | **Starting point**<br>3 years' custody | **Starting point**<br>2 years' custody |
| | Category range<br>3–5 years' custody | Category range<br>2–4 years' custody | Category range<br>1–3 years' custody |
| Category 3 | **Starting point**<br>3 years' custody | **Starting point**<br>2 years' custody | **Starting point**<br>1 year's custody |
| | Category range<br>2–4 years' custody | Category range 1–3 years' custody | Category range High level community order–2 years' custody |

### Community Orders and Custodial Sentences

[For the imposition of community orders, including the community orders table, see Imposition of Community and Custodial Sentences at **SG9-2**. For the imposition of custodial sentences see Imposition of Community and Custodial Sentences at **SG9-3**.]

### Factors increasing or reducing seriousness

The table below contains a **non-exhaustive** list of additional factual elements providing the context of the offence and factors relating to the offender. Identify whether any combination of these, or other relevant factors, should result in an upward or downward adjustment from the sentence arrived at so far. In particular, relevant recent convictions are likely to result in an upward adjustment. In some cases, having considered these factors, it may be appropriate to move outside the identified category range.

### Factors increasing seriousness

*Statutory aggravating factors*

• Previous convictions [see **SG2-21**], having regard to a) the **nature** of the offence to which the conviction relates and its **relevance** to the current offence; and b) the **time** that has elapsed since the conviction
• Offence committed whilst on bail [see **SG2-22**]
• Offence motivated by, or demonstrating hostility based on any of the following characteristics or presumed characteristics of the victim: religion, race, disability, sexual orientation or transgender identity [see **SG2-23**] *(When considering this factor, sentencers should bear in mind the statutory definition of terrorism in section 1 of the Terrorism Act 2000, and should be careful to avoid double counting)*

*Other aggravating factors*

• Specifically targeted audience (if not considered at step 1)
• Vulnerable/impressionable audience (if not considered at step 1)
• Communication with known extremists

- Deliberate use of encrypted communications or similar technologies to facilitate the commission of the offence and/or avoid or impede detection
- Significant volume of terrorist publications published or disseminated
- Used multiple social media platforms to reach a wider audience
- Offender attempted to disguise their identity to prevent detection
- Failure to respond to warnings [see SG2-39]
- Failure to comply with current court orders [see SG2-40]
- Offence committed on licence or Post Sentence Supervision [see SG2-40]
- Offence committed whilst in prison [see SG2-41]

**Factors reducing seriousness or reflecting personal mitigation**

- No previous convictions **or** no relevant/recent convictions [see SG2-48]
- Good character and/or exemplary conduct [see SG2-49]
- Offender involved through coercion, intimidation or exploitation [see SG2-55]
- Clear evidence of a change of mind set prior to arrest
- Offender's responsibility substantially reduced by mental disorder or learning disability [see SG2-63]
- Age and/or lack of maturity where it affects the responsibility of the offender [see SG2-60]
- Sole or primary carer for dependent relatives [see SG2-61]

**STEP 3  Consider any factors which indicate a reduction for assistance to the prosecution**

The court should take into account section 74 of the Sentencing Code (reduction in sentence for assistance to prosecution) and any other rule of law by virtue of which an offender may receive a discounted sentence in consequence of assistance given (or offered) to the prosecutor or investigator.

**STEP 4  Reduction for guilty pleas**

The court should take account of any potential reduction for a guilty plea in accordance with section 73 of the Sentencing Code and the guideline for Reduction in Sentence for a Guilty Plea [SG5-1–SG5-12].

**STEP 5  Totality principle**

If sentencing an offender for more than one offence, or where the offender is already serving a sentence, consider whether the total sentence is just and proportionate to the overall offending behaviour in accordance with the *Totality* guideline [see SG4].

**STEP 6  Ancillary orders**

In all cases the court should consider whether to make ancillary orders.

[See the Sentencing Council Explanatory Materials for Ancillary Orders in the Magistrates' Courts at SG10-5 and the Crown Court Compendium, Part II Sentencing, S7; Ancillary Orders]

**STEP 7  Reasons**

Section 52 of the Sentencing Code imposes a duty to give reasons for, and explain the effect of, the sentence.

**STEP 8  Consideration for time spent on bail (tagged curfew)**

The court must consider whether to give credit for time spent on bail in accordance with section 240A of the Criminal Justice Act 2003 and section 325 of the Sentencing Code.

**ADDITIONAL GUIDANCE**
[See SG32-12]

**SG32-6**                     PROSCRIBED ORGANISATIONS – MEMBERSHIP

*Terrorism Act 2000 (section 11)*

**Effective from:** 27 April 2018

Triable either way
Maximum: 10 years' custody
Offence range: High level community order–9 years' custody

**Note for offences committed on or after 29 June 2021:** The maximum sentence is increased to 14 years (section 26 (1)(b) and (2) Counter Terrorism and Sentencing Act 2021). This increase has not yet been reflected in the sentence levels in this guideline.

This is a specified offence for the purposes of sections 266 and 279 (extended sentence for certain violent, sexual or terrorism offences) of the Sentencing Code.

Note for offences **sentenced** on or after **12 April 2019**: This is an offence listed in Schedule 13 for the purposes of sections 265 and 278 (required special sentence for certain offenders of particular concern) of the Sentencing Code.

This guideline applies only to offenders aged 18 and older

### STEP 1  Determining the offence category

The court should determine the offence category with reference **only** to the factors listed in the tables below. In order to determine the category, the court should assess **culpability** and **harm**.

The court should weigh all the factors set out below in determining the offender's culpability. **Where there are characteristics present which fall under different levels of culpability, the court should balance these characteristics to reach a fair assessment of the offender's culpability.**

**Culpability demonstrated by one or more of the following**

| A | • Prominent member of organisation |
|---|---|
| B | • Active (but not prominent) member of organisation |
| C | • All other cases |

### Harm

There is no variation in the level of harm caused. Membership of any organisation which is concerned in terrorism either through the commission, participation, preparation, promotion or encouragement of terrorism is inherently harmful.

### STEP 2  Starting point and category range

Having determined the category at step one, the court should use the corresponding starting point to reach a sentence within the category range below. The starting point applies to all offenders irrespective of plea or previous convictions. A case of particular gravity, reflected by multiple features of culpability in step one, could merit upward adjustment from the starting point before further adjustment for aggravating or mitigating features, set out below.

| Harm | Culpability | | |
|---|---|---|---|
| | A | B | C |
| Category 1 | **Starting point** 7 years' custody | **Starting point** 5 years' custody | **Starting point** 2 years' custody |
| | **Category range** 5–9 years' custody | **Category range** 3–7 years' custody | **Category range** High level community order–4 years' custody |

### Community Orders and Custodial Sentences

[For the imposition of community orders, including the community orders table, see Imposition of Community and Custodial Sentences at **SG9-2**. For the imposition of custodial sentences see Imposition of Community and Custodial Sentences at **SG9-3**.]

### Factors increasing or reducing seriousness

The table below contains a non-exhaustive list of additional factual elements providing the context of the offence and factors relating to the offender. Identify whether any combination of these, or other relevant factors, should result in an upward or downward adjustment from the sentence arrived at so far. In particular, relevant recent convictions are likely to result in an upward adjustment. In some cases, having considered these factors, it may be appropriate to move outside the identified category range.

### Factors increasing seriousness

*Statutory aggravating factors*

- Previous convictions [see **SG2-21**], having regard to a) the **nature** of the offence to which the conviction relates and its **relevance** to the current offence; and b) the **time** that has elapsed since the conviction
- Offence committed whilst on bail [see **SG2-22**]
- Offence motivated by, or demonstrating hostility based on any of the following characteristics or presumed characteristics of the victim: religion, race, disability, sexual orientation or transgender identity [see **SG2-23**] *(When considering this factor, sentencers should bear in mind the statutory definition of terrorism in section 1 of the Terrorism Act 2000, and should be careful to avoid double counting)*

*Other aggravating factors*
- Length of time over which offending was committed
- Failure to respond to warnings [see **SG2-39**]
- Failure to comply with current court orders [see **SG2-40**]
- Offence committed on licence or Post Sentence Supervision [see **SG2-40**]
- Offence committed whilst in prison [see **SG2-41**]

**Factors reducing seriousness or reflecting personal mitigation**
- Unaware that organisation was proscribed
- No previous convictions **or** no relevant/recent convictions [see **SG2-48**]
- Good character and/or exemplary conduct [see **SG2-49**]
- Offender involved through coercion, intimidation or exploitation [see **SG2-55**]
- Clear evidence of a change of mind set prior to arrest
- Offender's responsibility substantially reduced by mental disorder or learning disability [see **SG2-63**]
- Age and/or lack of maturity where it affects the responsibility of the offender [see **SG2-60**]
- Sole or primary carer for dependent relatives [see **SG2-61**]

**STEP 3  Consider any factors which indicate a reduction for assistance to the prosecution**

The court should take into account section 74 of the Sentencing Code (reduction in sentence for assistance to prosecution) and any other rule of law by virtue of which an offender may receive a discounted sentence in consequence of assistance given (or offered) to the prosecutor or investigator.

**STEP 4  Reduction for guilty pleas**

The court should take account of any potential reduction for a guilty plea in accordance with section 73 of the Sentencing Code and the guideline for Reduction in Sentence for a Guilty Plea [**SG5-1–SG5-12**].

**STEP 5  Totality principle**

If sentencing an offender for more than one offence, or where the offender is already serving a sentence, consider whether the total sentence is just and proportionate to the overall offending behaviour in accordance with the *Totality* guideline [see **SG4**].

**STEP 6  Ancillary orders**

In all cases the court should consider whether to make ancillary orders.

[See the Sentencing Council Explanatory Materials for Ancillary Orders in the Magistrates' Courts at **SG10-5** and the Crown Court Compendium, Part II Sentencing, S7; Ancillary Orders]

**STEP 7  Reasons**

Section 52 of the Sentencing Code imposes a duty to give reasons for, and explain the effect of, the sentence.

**STEP 8  Consideration for time spent on bail (tagged curfew)**

The court must consider whether to give credit for time spent on bail in accordance with section 240A of the Criminal Justice Act 2003 and section 325 of the Sentencing Code.

**ADDITIONAL GUIDANCE**
[See **SG32-12**]

**SG32-7**                    PROSCRIBED ORGANISATIONS – SUPPORT

*Terrorism Act 2000 (section 12)*

**Effective from:** 27 April 2018

Triable either way
Maximum: 10 years' custody
Offence range: High level community order–9 years' custody

**Note for offences committed on or after 29 June 2021:** The maximum sentence is increased to 14 years (section 26 (1)(b) and (2) Counter Terrorism and Sentencing Act 2021). This increase has not yet been reflected in the sentence levels in this guideline.

This is a specified offence for the purposes of sections 266 and 279 (extended sentence for certain violent, sexual or terrorism offences) of the Sentencing Code.

Note for offences **sentenced** on or after **12 April 2019**: This is an offence listed in Schedule 13 for the purposes of sections 265 and 278 (required special sentence for certain offenders of particular concern) of the Sentencing Code.

This guideline applies only to offenders aged 18 and older

## STEP 1  Determining the offence category

The court should determine the offence category with reference **only** to the factors listed in the tables below. In order to determine the category, the court should assess **culpability** and **harm**.

The court should weigh all the factors set out below in determining the offender's culpability. **Where there are characteristics present which fall under different levels of culpability, the court should balance these characteristics to reach a fair assessment of the offender's culpability.**

**Culpability demonstrated by one or more of the following**

| A | • Offender in position of trust, authority or influence and abuses their position<br>• Persistent efforts to gain widespread or significant support for organisation<br>• Encourages activities intended to cause endangerment to life |
|---|---|
| B | • Arranged or played a significant part in the arrangement of a meeting/event aimed at gaining a significant support for organisation<br>• Intended to gain widespread or significant support for organisation<br>• Encourages activities intended to cause widespread or serious damage to property, or economic interests or substantial impact upon civic infrastructure |
| C | • Lesser cases where characteristics for categories A or B are not present |

| Harm<br>The court should consider the factors set out below to determine the level of harm | |
|---|---|
| Category 1 | • Evidence that others have acted on or been assisted by the encouragement to carry out activities endangering life<br>• Significant support for the organisation gained or likely to be gained |
| Category 2 | • Evidence that others have acted on or been assisted by the encouragement to carry out activities not endangering life |
| Category 3 | • All other cases |

## STEP 2  Starting point and category range

Having determined the category at step one, the court should use the corresponding starting point to reach a sentence within the category range below. The starting point applies to all offenders irrespective of plea or previous convictions. A case of particular gravity, reflected by multiple features of culpability or harm in step one, could merit upward adjustment from the starting point before further adjustment for aggravating or mitigating features, set out below.

| Harm | Culpability | | |
|---|---|---|---|
| | A | B | C |
| Category 1 | **Starting point**<br>7 years' custody | **Starting point**<br>5 years' custody | **Starting point**<br>3 years' custody |
| | **Category range**<br>6–9 years' custody | **Category range**<br>4–6 years' custody | **Category range**<br>2–4 years' custody |
| Category 2 | **Starting point**<br>6 years' custody | **Starting point**<br>4 years' custody | **Starting point**<br>2 years' custody |
| | **Category range**<br>5–7 years' custody | **Category range**<br>3–5 years' custody | **Category range**<br>1–3 years' custody |
| Category 3 | **Starting point**<br>5 years' custody | **Starting point**<br>3 years' custody | **Starting point**<br>1 years' custody |
| | **Category range**<br>4–6 years' custody | **Category range**<br>2–4 years' custody | **Category range** High level community order–2 years' custody |

Sentencing Guidelines

### Community Orders and Custodial Sentences

[For the imposition of community orders, including the community orders table, see Imposition of Community and Custodial Sentences at **SG9-2**. For the imposition of custodial sentences see Imposition of Community and Custodial Sentences at **SG9-3**.]

### Factors increasing or reducing seriousness

The table below contains a **non-exhaustive** list of additional factual elements providing the context of the offence and factors relating to the offender. Identify whether any combination of these, or other relevant factors, should result in an upward or downward adjustment from the sentence arrived at so far. In particular, relevant recent convictions are likely to result in an upward adjustment. In some cases, having considered these factors, it may be appropriate to move outside the identified category range.

### Factors increasing seriousness

*Statutory aggravating factors*

- Previous convictions [see **SG2-21**], having regard to a) the **nature** of the offence to which the conviction relates and its **relevance** to the current offence; and b) the **time** that has elapsed since the conviction
- Offence committed whilst on bail [see **SG2-22**]
- Offence motivated by, or demonstrating hostility based on any of the following characteristics or presumed characteristics of the victim: religion, race, disability, sexual orientation or transgender identity [see **SG2-23**] *(When considering this factor, sentencers should bear in mind the statutory definition of terrorism in section 1 of the Terrorism Act 2000, and should be careful to avoid double counting)*

*Other aggravating factors*

- Vulnerable/impressionable audience
- Failure to respond to warnings [see **SG2-39**]
- Failure to comply with current court orders [see **SG2-40**]
- Offence committed on licence or Post Sentence Supervision [see **SG2-40**]
- Offence committed whilst in prison [see **SG2-41**]

### Factors reducing seriousness or reflecting personal mitigation

- No previous convictions **or** no relevant/recent convictions [see **SG2-48**]
- Good character and/or exemplary conduct [see **SG2-49**]
- Offender involved through coercion, intimidation or exploitation [see **SG2-55**]
- Clear evidence of a change of mind set prior to arrest
- Offender's responsibility substantially reduced by mental disorder or learning disability [see **SG2-63**]
- Age and/or lack of maturity where it affects the responsibility of the offender [see **SG2-60**]
- Sole or primary carer for dependent relatives [see **SG2-61**]

### STEP 3  Consider any factors which indicate a reduction for assistance to the prosecution

The court should take into account section 74 of the Sentencing Code (reduction in sentence for assistance to prosecution) and any other rule of law by virtue of which an offender may receive a discounted sentence in consequence of assistance given (or offered) to the prosecutor or investigator.

### STEP 4  Reduction for guilty pleas

The court should take account of any potential reduction for a guilty plea in accordance with section 73 of the Sentencing Code and the guideline for Reduction in Sentence for a Guilty Plea [**SG5-1–SG5-12**].

### STEP 5  Totality principle

If sentencing an offender for more than one offence, or where the offender is already serving a sentence, consider whether the total sentence is just and proportionate to the overall offending behaviour in accordance with the *Totality* guideline [see **SG4**].

### STEP 6  Ancillary orders

In all cases the court should consider whether to make ancillary orders.

[See the Sentencing Council Explanatory Materials for Ancillary Orders in the Magistrates' Courts at **SG10-5** and the Crown Court Compendium, Part II Sentencing, S7; Ancillary Orders]

### STEP 7  Reasons

Section 52 of the Sentencing Code imposes a duty to give reasons for, and explain the effect of, the sentence.

### STEP 8  Consideration for time spent on bail (tagged curfew)

The court must consider whether to give credit for time spent on bail in accordance with section 240A of the Criminal Justice Act 2003 and section 325 of the Sentencing Code.

**ADDITIONAL GUIDANCE**
[See SG32-12]

FUNDING TERRORISM                                      **SG32-8**

**Effective from:** 27 April 2018

**Fundraising**, Terrorism Act 2000, s.15

**Use and possession**, Terrorism Act 2000, s.16

**Funding arrangements**, Terrorism Act 2000, s.17

**Money laundering**, Terrorism Act 2000, s.18

Triable either way
Maximum: 14 years' custody
Offence range: High level community order–13 years' custody

These are offences listed in Schedule 13 for the purposes of sections 265 and 278 (required special sentence for certain offenders of particular concern) of the Sentencing Code.

This guideline applies only to offenders aged 18 and older

**STEP 1  Determining the offence category**

The court should determine the offence category with reference **only** to the factors listed in the tables below. In order to determine the category, the court should assess **culpability** and **harm**.

The court should weigh all the factors set out below in determining the offender's culpability.

**Where there are characteristics present which fall under different levels of culpability, the court should balance these characteristics to reach a fair assessment of the offender's culpability.**

**Culpability demonstrated by one or more of the following**

| A | <ul><li>A significant role where offending is part of a group activity</li><li>Involvement of others through pressure or influence</li><li>Abuse of position of power, trust or responsibility</li><li>Sophisticated nature of offence/significant planning</li><li>Activities took place over a sustained period of time</li></ul> |
|---|---|
| B | <ul><li>Cases whose characteristics fall between A and C</li></ul> |
| C | <ul><li>Performed limited function under direction</li><li>Very little or no planning</li></ul> |

| Harm<br>The court should consider the factors set out below to determine the level of harm | |
|---|---|
| Category 1 | <ul><li>Money or property made, or likely to make, a significant contribution to furthering terrorism</li><li>Use or provision of money or property to fund or assist activities endangering life</li></ul> |
| Category 2 | <ul><li>Use or provision of money or property to fund or assist activities which involve a risk of widespread or serious damage to property, or economic interests or substantial impact upon civic infrastructure</li><li>All other cases whose characteristics fall between 1 and 3</li></ul> |
| Category 3 | <ul><li>Money or property made, or was likely to make, a minor contribution to furthering terrorism</li></ul> |

**STEP 2  Starting point and category range**

Having determined the category at step one, the court should use the corresponding starting point to reach a sentence within the category range below. The starting point applies to all offenders irrespective of plea or previous convictions. A case of particular gravity, reflected by multiple features of culpability or harm in step one, could merit upward adjustment from the starting point before further adjustment for aggravating or mitigating features, set out below.

| Harm | Culpability | | |
|---|---|---|---|
| | **A** | **B** | **C** |
| Category 1 | **Starting point** 12 years' custody | **Starting point** 9 years' custody | **Starting point** 7 years' custody |
| | **Category range** 10–13 years' custody | **Category range** 8–10 years' custody | **Category range** 6–8 years' custody |
| Category 2 | **Starting point** 9 years' custody | **Starting point** 7 years' custody | **Starting point** 4 years' custody |
| | **Category range** 8–10 years' custody | **Category range** 6–8 years' custody | **Category range** 2–5 years' custody |
| Category 3 | **Starting point** 7 years' custody | **Starting point** 4 years' custody | **Starting point** 2 years' custody |
| | **Category range** 6–8 years' custody | **Category range** 2–5 years' custody | **Category range** High level community order–3 years' custody |

### Community Orders and Custodial Sentences

[For the imposition of community orders, including the community orders table, see Imposition of Community and Custodial Sentences at **SG9-2**. For the imposition of custodial sentences see Imposition of Community and Custodial Sentences at **SG9-3**.]

### Factors increasing or reducing seriousness

The table below contains a **non-exhaustive** list of additional factual elements providing the context of the offence and factors relating to the offender. Identify whether any combination of these, or other relevant factors, should result in an upward or downward adjustment from the sentence arrived at so far. In particular, relevant recent convictions are likely to result in an upward adjustment. In some cases, having considered these factors, it may be appropriate to move outside the identified category range.

### Factors increasing seriousness

*Statutory aggravating factors*

- Previous convictions [see **SG2-21**], having regard to a) the **nature** of the offence to which the conviction relates and its **relevance** to the current offence; and b) the **time** that has elapsed since the conviction
- Offence committed whilst on bail [see **SG2-22**]
- Offence motivated by, or demonstrating hostility based on any of the following characteristics or presumed characteristics of the victim: religion, race, disability, sexual orientation or transgender identity [see **SG2-23**] *(When considering this factor, sentencers should bear in mind the statutory definition of terrorism in section 1 of the Terrorism Act 2000, and should be careful to avoid double counting)*

*Other aggravating factors*

- Deliberate use of encrypted communications or similar technologies to facilitate the commission of the offence and/or avoid or impede detection
- Indoctrinated or encouraged others
- Use or provision of false or fraudulent identification
- Misrepresenting nature of organisation
- Failure to respond to warnings [see **SG2-39**]
- Failure to comply with current court orders [see **SG2-40**]
- Offence committed on licence or Post Sentence Supervision [see **SG2-40**]

### Factors reducing seriousness or reflecting personal mitigation

- No previous convictions **or** no relevant/recent convictions [see **SG2-48**]
- Good character and/or exemplary conduct [see **SG2-49**]
- Offender involved through coercion, intimidation or exploitation [see **SG2-55**]
- Offender's responsibility substantially reduced by mental disorder or learning disability [see **SG2-63**]
- Age and/or lack of maturity where it affects the responsibility of the offender [see **SG2-60**]
- Sole or primary carer for dependent relatives [see **SG2-61**]

### STEP 3 Consider any factors which indicate a reduction for assistance to the prosecution

The court should take into account section 74 of the Sentencing Code (reduction in sentence for assistance to prosecution) and any other rule of law by virtue of which an offender may receive a discounted sentence in consequence of assistance given (or offered) to the prosecutor or investigator.

### STEP 4  Reduction for guilty pleas

The court should take account of any potential reduction for a guilty plea in accordance with section 73 of the Sentencing Code and the guideline for Reduction in Sentence for a Guilty Plea [SG5-1–SG5-12].

### STEP 5  Required special sentence for certain offenders of particular concern

Where the court does not impose a sentence of imprisonment for life or an extended sentence, but does impose a period of imprisonment, the term of the sentence must be equal to the aggregate of the appropriate custodial term and a further period of 1 year for which the offender is to be subject to a licence (sections 265 and 278 of the Sentencing Code).

### STEP 6  Totality principle

If sentencing an offender for more than one offence, or where the offender is already serving a sentence, consider whether the total sentence is just and proportionate to the overall offending behaviour in accordance with the *Totality* guideline [see **SG4**].

### STEP 7  Ancillary orders

In all cases the court should consider whether to make ancillary orders.

[See the Sentencing Council Explanatory Materials for Ancillary Orders in the Magistrates' Courts at **SG10**-5 and the Crown Court Compendium, Part II Sentencing, S7; Ancillary Orders]

### STEP 8  Reasons

Section 52 of the Sentencing Code imposes a duty to give reasons for, and explain the effect of, the sentence.

### STEP 9  Consideration for time spent on bail (**tagged curfew**)

The court must consider whether to give credit for time spent on bail in accordance with section 240A of the Criminal Justice Act 2003 and section 325 of the Sentencing Code.

### ADDITIONAL GUIDANCE

[See **SG32-12**]

FAILURE TO DISCLOSE INFORMATION ABOUT ACTS OF TERRORISM                    **SG32-9**

*Terrorism Act 2000 (section 38B)*

**Effective from:** 27 April 2018

Triable either way
Maximum: 5 years' custody
Offence range: High level community order–4 years 6 months' custody

Note for offences **committed** on or after **12 April 2019**: The maximum sentence is increased to **10 years** (section 7(2) Counter-Terrorism and Border Security Act 2019). **The increase has not yet been reflected in the sentence levels in this guideline.**

This is an offence listed in Schedule 13 for the purposes of sections 265 and 278 (required special sentence for certain offenders of particular concern) of the Sentencing Code.

This guideline applies only to offenders aged 18 and older

### STEP 1  Determining the offence category

The court should determine the offence category with reference **only** to the factors listed in the tables below. In order to determine the category, the court should assess **culpability** and **harm**.

The court should weigh all the factors set out below in determining the offender's culpability.

**Culpability demonstrated by one or more of the following**

| A | • Information was very significant (including, but not limited to, information which could have prevented an act of terrorism |
|---|---|
| B | • Cases whose characteristics fall between A and C |
| C | • Information was of low significance |

**Harm**
The court should consider the factors set out below to determine the level of harm

| Category 1 | • Information related to terrorist activity endangering life<br>• Information related to terrorist activity intended to cause widespread or serious damage to property, or economic interest or substantial impact upon civic infrastructure |
|---|---|
| Category 2 | • All other cases |

## STEP 2 Starting point and category range

Having determined the category at step one, the court should use the corresponding starting point to reach a sentence within the category range below. The starting point applies to all offenders irrespective of plea or previous convictions. A case of particular gravity, reflected by multiple features of culpability or harm in step one, could merit upward adjustment from the starting point before further adjustment for aggravating or mitigating features, set out below.

| Harm | Culpability | | |
|---|---|---|---|
| | A | B | C |
| Category 1 | Starting point<br>4 years' custody | Starting point<br>3 years' custody | Starting point<br>2 years' custody |
| | Category range<br>3–4 years 6 months' custody | Category range<br>2–4 years' custody | Category range 6 months–3 years' custody |
| Category 2 | Starting point<br>3 years' custody | Starting point<br>2 years' custody | Starting point<br>1 years 6 months' custody |
| | Category range<br>2–4 years' custody | Category range<br>6 months–3 years' custody | Category range<br>High level community order–2 years' custody |

### Community Orders and Custodial Sentences

[For the imposition of community orders, including the community orders table, see Imposition of Community and Custodial Sentences at SG9-2. For the imposition of custodial sentences see Imposition of Community and Custodial Sentences at SG9-3.]

### Factors increasing or reducing seriousness

The table below contains a **non-exhaustive** list of additional factual elements providing the context of the offence and factors relating to the offender. Identify whether any combination of these, or other relevant factors, should result in an upward or downward adjustment from the sentence arrived at so far. In particular, relevant recent convictions are likely to result in an upward adjustment. In some cases, having considered these factors, it may be appropriate to move outside the identified category range.

### Factors increasing seriousness

### Statutory aggravating factors

- Previous convictions [see **SG2-21**], having regard to a) the **nature** of the offence to which the conviction relates and its **relevance** to the current offence; and b) the **time** that has elapsed since the conviction
- Offence committed whilst on bail [see **SG2-22**]
- Offence motivated by, or demonstrating hostility based on any of the following characteristics or presumed characteristics of the victim: religion, race, disability, sexual orientation or transgender identity [see **SG2-23**] *(When considering this factor, sentencers should bear in mind the statutory definition of terrorism in section 1 of the Terrorism Act 2000, and should be careful to avoid double counting)*

### *Other aggravating factors*

- Many lives endangered
- Length of time over which offending was committed
- Failure to respond to warnings [see **SG2-39**]
- Failure to comply with current court orders [see **SG2-40**]
- Offence committed on licence or Post Sentence Supervision [see **SG2-40**]
- Offence committed whilst in prison [see **SG2-41**]

**Factors reducing seriousness or reflecting personal mitigation**

* No previous convictions **or** no relevant/recent convictions [see **SG2-48**]
* Good character and/or exemplary conduct [see **SG2-49**]
* Offender involved through coercion, intimidation or exploitation [see **SG2-55**]
* Offender discloses information but not as soon as was reasonably practicable
* Offender's responsibility substantially reduced by mental disorder or learning disability [see **SG2-63**]
* Age and/or lack of maturity where it affects the responsibility of the offender [see **SG2-60**]
* Sole or primary carer for dependent relatives [see **SG2-61**]

**STEP 3   Consider any factors which indicate a reduction for assistance to the prosecution**

The court should take into account section 74 of the Sentencing Code (reduction in sentence for assistance to prosecution) and any other rule of law by virtue of which an offender may receive a discounted sentence in consequence of assistance given (or offered) to the prosecutor or investigator.

**STEP 4   Reduction for guilty pleas**

The court should take account of any potential reduction for a guilty plea in accordance with section 73 of the Sentencing Code and the guideline for Reduction in Sentence for a Guilty Plea [**SG5-1–SG5-12**].

**STEP 5   Required special sentence for certain offenders of particular concern**

Where the court does not impose a sentence of imprisonment for life or an extended sentence, but does impose a period of imprisonment, the term of the sentence must be equal to the aggregate of the appropriate custodial term and a further period of 1 year for which the offender is to be subject to a licence (sections 265 and 278 of the Sentencing Code).

**STEP 6   Totality principle**

If sentencing an offender for more than one offence, or where the offender is already serving a sentence, consider whether the total sentence is just and proportionate to the overall offending behaviour in accordance with the *Totality* guideline [see **SG4**].

**STEP 7   Ancillary orders**

In all cases the court should consider whether to make ancillary orders.

[See the Sentencing Council Explanatory Materials for Ancillary Orders in the Magistrates' Courts at **SG10-5** and the Crown Court Compendium, Part II Sentencing, S7; Ancillary Orders]

**STEP 8   Reasons**

Section 52 of the Sentencing Code imposes a duty to give reasons for, and explain the effect of, the sentence.

**STEP 9   Consideration for time spent on bail (tagged curfew)**

The court must consider whether to give credit for time spent on bail in accordance with section 240A of the Criminal Justice Act 2003 and section 325 of the Sentencing Code.

**ADDITIONAL GUIDANCE**

[See **SG32-12**]

POSSESSION FOR TERRORIST PURPOSES                        **SG32-10**

*Terrorism Act 2000 (section 57)*

**Effective from:** 27 April 2018

Triable either way
Maximum: 15 years' custody
Offence range: 1–14 years' custody

This is a Schedule 19 offence for the purposes of sections 274 and 285 (required life sentence for offence carrying life sentence) of the Sentencing Code.

For offences committed on or after 13 April 2015, these are offences listed in Part 1 of Schedule 15 for the purposes of sections 273 and 283 (life sentence for second listed offence) of the Sentencing Code.

This is a specified offence for the purposes of sections 266 and 279 (extended sentence for certain violent, sexual or terrorism offences) of the Sentencing Code.

This is an offence listed in Schedule 13 for the purposes of sections 265 and 278 (required special sentence for certain offenders of particular concern) of the Sentencing Code.

This guideline applies only to offenders aged 18 and older.

## STEP 1   Determining the offence category

The court should determine the offence category with reference **only** to the factors listed in the tables below. In order to determine the category, the court should assess **culpability** and **harm**.

The court should weigh all the factors set out below in determining the offender's culpability.

**Where there are characteristics present which fall under different levels of culpability, the court should balance these characteristics to reach a fair assessment of the offender's culpability.**

**Culpability demonstrated by one or more of the following**

| A | • Possession of article(s) indicates that the offender's preparations for terrorist activity are complete or almost complete<br>• Offender is a significant participant in the commission, preparation or instigation of an act of terrorism |
|---|---|
| B | • Cases whose characteristics fall between A and C |
| C | • Possession of article(s) indicates that offender has engaged in limited preparation toward terrorist activity<br>• Offender is of limited assistance or encouragement to others who are preparing for terrorist activity |

### Harm

Harm is assessed based on the type of harm risked and the likelihood of that harm being caused

| Category 1 | • Article(s) had potential to facilitate an offence endangering life **and harm is very likely to be caused** |
|---|---|
| Category 2 | • Article(s) had potential to facilitate an offence endangering life **but harm is not very likely to be caused**<br>• Article(s) had potential to facilitate an offence causing widespread or serious damage to property, or economic interest or substantial upon civic infrastructure |
| Category 3 | • All other cases |

## STEP 2   Starting point and category range

Having determined the category at step one, the court should use the corresponding starting point to reach a sentence within the category range below. The starting point applies to all offenders irrespective of plea or previous convictions. A case of particular gravity, reflected by multiple features of culpability or harm in step one, could merit upward adjustment from the starting point before further adjustment for aggravating or mitigating features, set out below.

| Harm | Culpability | | |
|---|---|---|---|
| | **A** | **B** | **C** |
| Category 1 | **Starting point**<br>12 years' custody | **Starting point**<br>7 years' custody | **Starting point**<br>4 years' custody |
| | Category range<br>9–14 years' custody | Category range<br>6–9 years' custody | Category range<br>3–6 years' custody |
| Category 2 | **Starting point**<br>8 years' custody | **Starting point**<br>6 years' custody | **Starting point**<br>3 years' custody |
| | Category range<br>7–9 years' custody | Category range<br>4–7 years' custody | Category range<br>2–4 years' custody |
| Category 3 | **Starting point**<br>6 years' custody | **Starting point**<br>4 years' custody | **Starting point**<br>2 years' custody |
| | Category range<br>4–7 years' custody | Category range<br>2–5 years' custody | Category range 1–3<br>years' custody |

### Custodial Sentences

[For the imposition of custodial sentences see Imposition of Community and Custodial Sentences at SG9-3.]

**Factors increasing or reducing seriousness**

The table below contains a non-exhaustive list of additional factual elements providing the context of the offence and factors relating to the offender. Identify whether any combination of these, or other relevant factors, should result in an upward or downward adjustment from the sentence arrived at so far. In particular, relevant recent convictions are likely to result in an upward adjustment. In some cases, having considered these factors, it may be appropriate to move outside the identified category range.

**Factors increasing seriousness**

*Statutory aggravating factors*

- Previous convictions [see **SG2-21**], having regard to a) the **nature** of the offence to which the conviction relates and its **relevance** to the current offence; and b) the **time** that has elapsed since the conviction
- Offence committed whilst on bail [see **SG2-22**]
- Offence motivated by, or demonstrating hostility based on any of the following characteristics or presumed characteristics of the victim: religion, race, disability, sexual orientation or transgender identity [see **SG2-23**] *(When considering this factor, sentencers should bear in mind the statutory definition of terrorism in section 1 of the Terrorism Act 2000, and should be careful to avoid double counting)*

*Other aggravating factors*

- Article has the potential to endanger many lives
- Length of time over which offending was committed
- Communication with other extremists
- Deliberate use of encrypted communications or similar technologies to facilitate the commission of the offence and/or avoid or impede detection
- Offender attempted to disguise their identity to prevent detection
- Indoctrinated or encouraged others
- Failure to respond to warnings [see **SG2-39**]
- Failure to comply with current court orders [see **SG2-40**]
- Offence committed on licence or Post Sentence Supervision [see **SG2-40**]
- Offence committed whilst in prison [see **SG2-41**]

**Factors reducing seriousness or reflecting personal mitigation**

- No previous convictions **or** no relevant/recent convictions [see **SG2-48**]
- Good character and/or exemplary conduct [see **SG2-49**]
- Offender involved through coercion, intimidation or exploitation [see **SG2-55**]
- Clear evidence of a change of mind set prior to arrest
- Offender's responsibility substantially reduced by mental disorder or learning disability [see **SG2-63**]
- Age and/or lack of maturity where it affects the responsibility of the offender [see **SG2-60**]
- Sole or primary carer for dependent relatives [see **SG2-61**]

**STEP 3  Consider any factors which indicate a reduction for assistance to the prosecution**

The court should take into account section 74 of the Sentencing Code (reduction in sentence for assistance to prosecution) and any other rule of law by virtue of which an offender may receive a discounted sentence in consequence of assistance given (or offered) to the prosecutor or investigator.

**STEP 4  Reduction for guilty pleas**

The court should take account of any potential reduction for a guilty plea in accordance with section 73 of the Sentencing Code and the guideline for Reduction in Sentence for a Guilty Plea [**SG5-1–SG5-12**].

**STEP 5  Dangerousness**

The court should consider:

1) whether having regard to the criteria contained in Chapter 6 of Part 10 of the Sentencing Code it would be appropriate to impose a life sentence (sections 274 and 285);
2) whether having regard to sections 273 and 283 of the Sentencing Code it would be appropriate to impose a life sentence;
3) whether having regard to the criteria contained in Chapter 6 of Part 10 of the Sentencing Code it would be appropriate to impose an extended sentence (sections 266 and 279).

When sentencing offenders to a life sentence under these provisions, the notional determinate sentence should be used as the basis for the setting of a minimum term.

**STEP 6  Required special sentence for certain offenders of particular concern (sections 265 and 278 of the Sentencing Code)**

Where the court does not impose a sentence of imprisonment for life or an extended sentence, but does impose a period of imprisonment, the term of the sentence must be equal to the aggregate of the appropriate custodial term and a further period of 1 year for which the offender is to be subject to a licence.

**STEP 7  Totality principle**

If sentencing an offender for more than one offence, or where the offender is already serving a sentence, consider whether the total sentence is just and proportionate to the overall offending behaviour in accordance with the *Totality* guideline [see **SG4**].

**STEP 8  Ancillary orders**

In all cases the court should consider whether to make ancillary orders.

[See the Sentencing Council Explanatory Materials for Ancillary Orders in the Magistrates' Courts at **SG10-5** and the Crown Court Compendium, Part II Sentencing, S7; Ancillary Orders]

**STEP 9  Reasons**

Section 52 of the Sentencing Code imposes a duty to give reasons for, and explain the effect of, the sentence.

**STEP 10  Consideration for time spent on bail (tagged curfew)**

The court must consider whether to give credit for time spent on bail in accordance with section 240A of the Criminal Justice Act 2003 and section 325 of the Sentencing Code.

**ADDITIONAL GUIDANCE**
[See SG32-12]

SG32-11                         COLLECTION OF TERRORIST INFORMATION

*Terrorism Act 2000 (section 58)*

Triable either way
Maximum: 10 years' custody
Offence range: High level community order–9 years' custody

Note for offences **committed** on or after **12 April 2019**:

The maximum sentence is increased to **15 years** (section 7(3) Counter-Terrorism and Border Security Act 2019). **The increase has not yet been reflected in the sentence levels in this guideline.**

This is a specified offence for the purposes of sections 266 and 279 (extended sentence for certain violent, sexual or terrorism offences) of the Sentencing Code.

Note for offences **sentenced** on or after **12 April 2019**:

This is an offence listed in Schedule 13 for the purposes of sections 265 and 278 (required special sentence for certain offenders of particular concern) of the Sentencing Code.

This guideline applies only to offenders aged 18 and older

**STEP 1  Determining the offence category**

The court should determine the offence category with reference **only** to the factors listed in the tables below. In order to determine the category, the court should assess **culpability** and **harm**.

The court should weigh all the factors set out below in determining the offender's culpability. **Where there are characteristics present which fall under different levels of culpability, the court should balance these characteristics to reach a fair assessment of the offender's culpability.**

**Culpability demonstrated by one or more of the following**

| A | • Offender collected, made a record of, or was in possession of information for use in a specific terrorist act |
|---|---|
| B | • Offender collected, made a record of, or was in possession of information likely to be useful to a person committing or preparing an act of terrorism and the offender had terrorist connections or motivations<br>• Offender repeatedly accessed extremist material (where not falling within A) |
| C | • Offender collected, made a record of, or was in possession of information likely to be useful to a person committing or preparing an act of terrorism but had no terrorist connections or motivations |

## Harm

Harm is assessed based on the type of harm risked and the likelihood of that harm being caused

| Category 1 | • Material provides instruction for specific terrorist activity endangering life **and harm is very likely to be caused** |
|---|---|
| Category 2 | • Material provides instruction for specific terrorist activity endangering life **but harm is not very likely to be caused**<br>• Material provides instruction for specific terrorist activity intended to cause widespread or serious damage to property, or economic interest or substantial impact upon civic infrastructure |
| Category 3 | • All other cases |

## STEP 2  Starting point and category range

Having determined the category at step one, the court should use the corresponding starting point to reach a sentence within the category range below. The starting point applies to all offenders irrespective of plea or previous convictions. A case of particular gravity, reflected by multiple features of culpability or harm in step one, could merit upward adjustment from the starting point before further adjustment for aggravating or mitigating features, set out below.

| Harm | Culpability | | |
|---|---|---|---|
| | A | B | C |
| Category 1 | **Starting point**<br>7 years' custody | **Starting point**<br>5 years' custody | **Starting point**<br>2 years' custody |
| | **Category range**<br>5–9 years' custody | **Category range**<br>3–6 years' custody | **Category range**<br>1–4 years' custody |
| Category 2 | **Starting point**<br>6 years' custody | **Starting point**<br>4 years' custody | **Starting point**<br>1 year 6 months' custody |
| | **Category range**<br>4–8 years' custody | **Category range**<br>3–5 years' custody | **Category range**<br>6 months–3 years' custody |
| Category 3 | **Starting point**<br>5 years' custody | **Starting point**<br>3 years' custody | **Starting point**<br>1 year's custody |
| | **Category range**<br>3–6 years' custody | **Category range**<br>2–5 years' custody | **Category range**<br>High level community order–2 years' custody |

## Community Orders and Custodial Sentences

[For the imposition of community orders, including the community orders table, see Imposition of Community and Custodial Sentences at **SG9-2**. For the imposition of custodial sentences see Imposition of Community and Custodial Sentences at **SG9-3**.]

## Factors increasing or reducing seriousness

The table below contains a **non-exhaustive** list of additional factual elements providing the context of the offence and factors relating to the offender. Identify whether any combination of these, or other relevant factors, should result in an upward or downward adjustment from the sentence arrived at so far. In particular, relevant recent convictions are likely to result in an upward adjustment. In some cases, having considered these factors, it may be appropriate to move outside the identified category range.

## Factors increasing seriousness

*Statutory aggravating factors*

- Previous convictions [see **SG2-21**], having regard to a) the **nature** of the offence to which the conviction relates and its **relevance** to the current offence; and b) the **time** that has elapsed since the conviction
- Offence committed whilst on bail [see **SG2-22**]
- Offence motivated by, or demonstrating hostility based on any of the following characteristics or presumed characteristics of the victim: religion, race, disability, sexual orientation or transgender identity [see **SG2-23**] *(When considering this factor, sentencers should bear in mind the statutory definition of terrorism in section 1 of the Terrorism Act 2000, and should be careful to avoid double counting)*

*Other aggravating factors*
- Significant volume of terrorist publications
- Length of time over which offending was committed
- Deliberate use of encrypted communications or similar technologies to facilitate the commission of the offence and/or avoid or impede detection
- Failure to respond to warnings [see **SG2-39**]
- Failure to comply with current court orders [see **SG2-40**]
- Offence committed on licence or Post Sentence Supervision [see **SG2-40**]
- Offence committed whilst in prison [see **SG2-41**]

**Factors reducing seriousness or reflecting personal mitigation**
- No previous convictions **or** no relevant/recent convictions [see **SG2-48**]
- Good character and/or exemplary conduct [see **SG2-49**]
- Offender involved through coercion, intimidation or exploitation [see **SG2-55**]
- Clear evidence of a change of mind set prior to arrest
- Offender's responsibility substantially reduced by mental disorder or learning disability [see **SG2-63**]
- Age and/or lack of maturity where it affects the responsibility of the offender [see **SG2-60**]
- Sole or primary carer for dependent relatives [see **SG2-61**]

**STEP 3  Consider any factors which indicate a reduction for assistance to the prosecution**

The court should take into account section 74 of the Sentencing Code (reduction in sentence for assistance to prosecution) and any other rule of law by virtue of which an offender may receive a discounted sentence in consequence of assistance given (or offered) to the prosecutor or investigator.

**STEP 4  Reduction for guilty pleas**

The court should take account of any potential reduction for a guilty plea in accordance with section 73 of the Sentencing Code and the guideline for Reduction in Sentence for a Guilty Plea [**SG5-1–SG5-12**].

**STEP 5  Totality principle**

If sentencing an offender for more than one offence, or where the offender is already serving a sentence, consider whether the total sentence is just and proportionate to the overall offending behaviour in accordance with the *Totality* guideline [see **SG4**].

**STEP 6  Ancillary orders**

In all cases the court should consider whether to make ancillary orders.

[See the Sentencing Council Explanatory Materials for Ancillary Orders in the Magistrates' Courts at **SG10-5** and the Crown Court Compendium, Part II Sentencing, S7; Ancillary Orders]

**STEP 7  Reasons**

Section 52 of the Sentencing Code imposes a duty to give reasons for, and explain the effect of, the sentence.

**STEP 8  Consideration for time spent on bail (tagged curfew)**

The court must consider whether to give credit for time spent on bail in accordance with section 240A of the Criminal Justice Act 2003 and section 325 of the Sentencing Code.

**ADDITIONAL GUIDANCE**

[See **SG32-12**]

**SG32-12**                          ADDITIONAL GUIDANCE

| ANCILLARY ORDER | STATUTORY REFERENCE |
| --- | --- |
| **Confiscation** <br> A confiscation order may be made by the Crown Court in circumstances in which the offender has obtained a financial benefit as a result of, or in connection with, his criminal conduct. | Section 6 and Schedule 2 of the Proceeds of Crime Act 2002 |
| **Forfeiture** <br> When sentencing for a funding offence (sections 15-18 Terrorism Act 2000), the court may order the forfeiture of money or property which the offender had possession or control of at the time of the offence | Section 23 to 23B Terrorism Act 2000 |

# PART 33    THEFT

[For the standard text on applicability see **SG0-4**.]

*Theft Act 1968 (section 1)*

**Effective from:** 01 February 2016

Theft from the person
Theft in a dwelling
Theft in breach of trust
Theft from a motor vehicle
Theft of a motor vehicle
Theft of a pedal bicycle
and all other section 1 Theft Act 1968 offences, excluding theft from a shop or stall [for which see
SG33-3]

Triable either way
Maximum: 7 years' custody
Offence range: Discharge–6 years' custody

## STEP 1  Determining the offence category

The court should determine the offence category with reference **only** to the factors identified in the
following tables. In order to determine the category the court should assess **culpability** and **harm**.

The level of culpability is determined by weighing up all the factors of the case to determine the offender's
role and the extent to which the offending was **planned** and the **sophistication** with which it was carried
out.

| CULPABILITY demonstrated by one or more of the following: |
| --- |
| **A — High culpability** |
| A leading role where offending is part of a group activity |
| Involvement of others through coercion, intimidation or exploitation |
| Breach of a high degree of trust or responsibility |
| Sophisticated nature of offence/significant planning |
| Theft involving intimidation or the use or threat of force |
| Deliberately targeting victim on basis of vulnerability |
| **B — Medium culpability** |
| A significant role where offending is part of a group activity |
| Some degree of planning involved |
| Breach of some degree of trust or responsibility |
| Other cases that fall between categories A or C because: |
| – Factors are present in A and C which balance each other out **and/or** |
| – The offender's culpability falls between the factors as described in A and C |
| **C — Lesser culpability** |
| Performed limited function under direction |
| Involved through coercion, intimidation or exploitation |
| Little or no planning |
| Limited awareness or understanding of offence |

**Where there are characteristics present which fall under different levels of culpability, the court should
balance these characteristics to reach a fair assessment of the offender's culpability.**

Sentencing Guidelines

## Harm

**Harm** is assessed by reference to the **financial loss** that results from the theft **and any significant additional harm** suffered by the victim or others — examples of significant additional harm may include **but are not limited to:**

| |
|---|
| Items stolen were of substantial value to the loser — regardless of monetary worth |
| High level of inconvenience caused to the victim or others |
| Consequential financial harm to victim or others |
| Emotional distress |
| Fear/loss of confidence caused by the crime |
| Risk of or actual injury to persons or damage to property |
| Impact of theft on a business |
| Damage to heritage assets |
| Disruption caused to infrastructure |

*Intended loss should be used where actual loss has been prevented.*

| | |
|---|---|
| Category 1 | Very high value goods stolen (above £100,000) **or** <br> High value with significant additional harm to the victim or others |
| Category 2 | High value goods stolen (£10,000 to £100,000) and no significant additional harm **or** <br> Medium value with significant additional harm to the victim or others |
| Category 3 | Medium value goods stolen (£500 to £10,000) **and** no significant additional harm or <br> Low value with significant additional harm to the victim or others |
| Category 4 | Low value goods stolen (up to £500) **and** <br> Little or no significant additional harm to the victim or others |

## STEP 2  Starting point and category range

Having determined the category at step one, the court should use the starting point to reach a sentence within the appropriate category range in the table below.

The starting point applies to all offenders irrespective of plea or previous convictions.

| Harm | Culpability | | |
|---|---|---|---|
| | **A** | **B** | **C** |
| **Category 1** <br> Adjustment should be made for any significant additional harm factors where very high value goods are stolen. | **Starting point** <br> 3 years 6 months' custody | **Starting point** <br> 2 years' custody | **Starting point** <br> 1 year's custody |
| | **Category range** <br> 2 years 6 months'–6 years' custody | **Category range** <br> 1–3 years–6 months' custody | **Category range** <br> 26 weeks'–2 years' custody |
| **Category 2** | **Starting point** <br> 2 years' custody | **Starting point** <br> 1 year's custody | **Starting point** <br> High level community order |
| | **Category range** <br> 1–3 years 6 months' custody | **Category range** <br> 26 weeks'–2 years' custody | **Category range** <br> Low level community order–36 weeks' custody |
| **Category 3** | **Starting point** <br> 1 year's custody | **Starting point** <br> High level community order | **Starting point** <br> Band C fine |
| | **Category range** <br> 26 weeks'–2 years' custody | **Category range** <br> Low level community order–36 weeks' custody | **Category range** <br> Band B fine–Low level community order |

| Harm | Culpability | | |
|---|---|---|---|
| | **A** | **B** | **C** |
| Category 4 | **Starting point** High level community order | **Starting point** Low level community order | **Starting point** Band B fine |
| | **Category range** Medium level community order–36 weeks' custody | **Category range** Band C fine–Medium level community order | **Category range** Discharge–Band C fine |

The table above refers to single offences. Where there are multiple offences, consecutive sentences may be appropriate: please refer to the *Totality* guideline [see **SG4**].

Where multiple offences are committed in circumstances which justify consecutive sentences, and the total amount stolen is in excess of £1 million, then an aggregate sentence in excess of 7 years may be appropriate.

### Fines
[For the standard schedule of fines see **SG2-5**.]

### Community Orders and Custodial Sentences
[For the imposition of community orders, including the community orders table, see Imposition of Community and Custodial Sentences at **SG9-2**.

For the imposition of custodial sentences see Imposition of Community and Custodial Sentences at **SG9-3**.]

Where the offender is dependent on or has a propensity to misuse drugs or alcohol and there is sufficient prospect of success, a community order with a drug rehabilitation requirement under Part 10, or an alcohol treatment requirement under Part 11, of Schedule 9 of the Sentencing Code may be a proper alternative to a short or moderate custodial sentence.

Where the offender suffers from a medical condition that is susceptible to treatment but does not warrant detention under a hospital order, a community order with a mental health treatment requirement under Part 9 of Schedule 9 of the Sentencing Code may be a proper alternative to a short or moderate custodial sentence.

### Additional factors affecting seriousness
The court should then consider further adjustment for any aggravating or mitigating factors. The following is a **non-exhaustive** list of additional factual elements providing the context of the offence and factors relating to the offender. Identify whether any combination of these, or other relevant factors, should result in an upward or downward adjustment from the sentence arrived at so far.

### Factors increasing seriousness
*Statutory aggravating factors*
• Previous convictions [see **SG2-21**], having regard to
  a)  the **nature** of the offence to which the conviction relates and its **relevance** to the current offence; and
  b)  the **time** that has elapsed since the conviction
• Offence committed whilst on bail [see **SG2-22**]
• Offence motivated by, or demonstrating hostility based on any of the following characteristics of the victim: sex, disability, sexual orientation or transgender identity [see **SG2-23**]

*Other aggravating factors*
• Stealing goods to order
• Steps taken to prevent the victim reporting or obtaining assistance and/or from assisting or supporting the prosecution [see **SG2-37**]
• Offender motivated by intention to cause harm or out of revenge
• Offence committed over sustained period of time
• Attempts to conceal/dispose of evidence [see **SG2-37**]
• Failure to comply with current court orders [see **SG2-40**]
• Offence committed on licence [see **SG2-40**]
• Offences taken into consideration [see **SG3**]
• Blame wrongly placed on others [see **SG2-38**]
• Established evidence of community/wider impact (for issues other than prevalence) [see **SG2-46**]
• Prevalence – see below

**Factors reducing seriousness or reflecting personal mitigation**

- No previous convictions or no relevant/recent convictions [see **SG2-48**]
- Remorse, particularly where evidenced by voluntary reparation to the victim [see **SG2-50**]
- Good character and/or exemplary conduct [see **SG2-49**]
- Serious medical condition requiring urgent, intensive or long-term treatment [see **SG2-62**]
- Age and/or lack of maturity where it affects the responsibility of the offender [see **SG2-60**]
- Mental disorder or learning disability (where not linked to the commission of the offence) [see **SG2-63**]
- Sole or primary carer for dependent relatives [see **SG2-61**]
- Determination and/or demonstration of steps taken to address addiction or offending behaviour [see **SG2-64**]
- Inappropriate degree of trust or responsibility

### Prevalence

There may be exceptional local circumstances that arise which may lead a court to decide that prevalence should influence sentencing levels. The pivotal issue in such cases will be the harm caused to the community. It is essential that the court before taking account of prevalence:

- has supporting evidence from an external source, for example, Community Impact Statements, to justify claims that a particular crime is prevalent in their area, and is causing particular harm in that community, and
- is satisfied that there is a compelling need to treat the offence more seriously than elsewhere.

### STEP 3 Consider any factors which indicate a reduction, such as assistance to the prosecution

The court should take into account section 74 of the Sentencing Code (reduction in sentence for assistance to prosecution) and any other rule of law by virtue of which an offender may receive a discounted sentence in consequence of assistance given (or offered) to the prosecutor or investigator.

### STEP 4 Reduction for guilty pleas

The court should take account of any potential reduction for a guilty plea in accordance with section 73 of the Sentencing Code and the guideline for Reduction in Sentence for a Guilty Plea [**SG5-1–SG5-12**].

### STEP 5 Totality principle

If sentencing an offender for more than one offence, or where the offender is already serving a sentence, consider whether the total sentence is just and proportionate to the overall offending behaviour in accordance with the *Totality* guideline [see **SG4**].

### STEP 6 Confiscation orders under the Proceeds of Crime Act 2002 may only be made by the Crown Court. The Crown Court must proceed with a view to making a confiscation order if it is asked to do so by the prosecutor or if the Crown Court believes it is appropriate for it to do so.

Where, following conviction in a magistrates' court, the prosecutor applies for the offender to be committed to the Crown Court with a view to a confiscation order being considered, the magistrates' court must commit the offender to the Crown Court to be sentenced there (section 70 of the Proceeds of Crime Act 2002). This applies to summary only and either-way offences.

Where, but for the prosecutor's application under s.70, the magistrates' court would have committed the offender for sentence to the Crown Court anyway it must say so. Otherwise the powers of sentence of the Crown Court will be limited to those of the magistrates' court.

Confiscation must be dealt with before, and taken into account when assessing, any other fine or financial order (except compensation).

(See Proceeds of Crime Act 2002 sections 6 and 13)

Where the offence has resulted in loss or damage the court must consider whether to make a compensation order and must give reasons if it decides not to order compensation (Sentencing Code, s.55).

If the court makes both a confiscation order and an order for compensation and the court believes the offender will not have sufficient means to satisfy both orders in full, the court must direct that the compensation be paid out of sums recovered under the confiscation order (section 13 of the Proceeds of Crime Act 2002).

[See the Sentencing Council Explanatory Materials for Ancillary Orders in the Magistrates' Courts at **SG10-5** and the Crown Court Compendium, Part II Sentencing, S7; Ancillary Orders]

### STEP 7 Reasons

Section 52 of the Sentencing Code imposes a duty to give reasons for, and explain the effect of, the sentence.

**STEP 8  Consideration for time spent on bail (tagged curfew)**

The court must consider whether to give credit for time spent on bail in accordance with section 240A of the Criminal Justice Act 2003 and section 325 of the Sentencing Code.

THEFT FROM A SHOP OR STALL

*Theft Act 1968 (section 1)*

SG33-3

**Effective from:** 01 February 2016

Triable either way
Maximum: 7 years' custody (except for an offence of low-value shoplifting which is treated as a summary only offence in accordance with section 22A of the Magistrates' Courts Act 1980 where the maximum is 6 months' custody).
Offence range: Discharge–3 years' custody

**STEP 1  Determining the offence category**

The court should determine the offence category with reference **only** to the factors identified in the following tables. In order to determine the category the court should assess **culpability** and **harm**.

The level of culpability is determined by weighing up all the factors of the case to determine the offender's role and the extent to which the offending was **planned** and the **sophistication** with which it was carried out.

| CULPABILITY demonstrated by one or more of the following: |
| --- |
| **A — High culpability** |
| A leading role where offending is part of a group activity |
| Involvement of others through coercion, intimidation or exploitation |
| Sophisticated nature of offence/significant planning |
| Significant use or threat of force |
| Offender subject to a banning order from the relevant store |
| Child accompanying offender is actively used to **facilitate** the offence (not merely present when offence is committed) |
| **B — Medium culpability** |
| A significant role where offending is part of a group activity |
| Some degree of planning involved |
| Limited use or threat of force |
| All other cases where characteristics for categories A or C are not present |
| **C — Lesser culpability** |
| Performed limited function under direction |
| Involved through coercion, intimidation or exploitation |
| Little or no planning |
| Mental disorder/learning disability where linked to commission of the offence |

**Where there are characteristics present which fall under different levels of culpability, the court should balance these characteristics to reach a fair assessment of the offender's culpability.**

**Harm**

**Harm** is assessed by reference to the **financial loss** that results from the theft **and any significant additional harm** suffered by the victim—examples of significant additional harm may include **but are not limited to:**

| Emotional distress |
| Damage to property |
| Effect on business |
| A greater impact on the victim due to the size or type of their business |
| A particularly vulnerable victim |

*Intended loss should be used where actual loss has been prevented.*

| Category 1 | High value goods stolen (above £1,000) **or** <br> Medium value with significant additional harm to the victim |
| Category 2 | Medium value goods stolen (£200 to £1,000) **and** no significant additional harm **or** <br> Low value with significant additional harm to the victim |
| Category 3 | Low value goods stolen (up to £200) **and** <br> Little or no significant additional harm to the victim |

### STEP 2 Starting point and category range

Having determined the category at step one, the court should use the starting point to reach a sentence within the appropriate category range in the table below.

The starting point applies to all offenders irrespective of plea or previous convictions.

| Harm | Culpability | | |
| --- | --- | --- | --- |
| | A | B | C |
| **Category 1** <br> Where the value greatly exceeds £1,000 it may be appropriate to move outside the identified range. Adjustment should be made for any significant additional harm where high value goods are stolen. | **Starting point** <br> 26 weeks' custody | **Starting point** <br> Medium level community order | **Starting point** <br> Band C fine |
| | **Category range** <br> 12 weeks'–3 years' custody | **Category range** <br> Low level community order–26 weeks' custody | **Category range** <br> Band B fine–Low level community order |
| **Category 2** | **Starting point** <br> 12 weeks' custody | **Starting point** <br> Low level community order | **Starting point** <br> Band B fine |
| | **Category range** <br> High level community order–26 weeks' custody | **Category range** <br> Band C fine–Medium level community order | **Category range** <br> Band A fine–Band C fine |
| **Category 3** | **Starting point** <br> High level community order | **Starting point** <br> Band C fine | **Starting point** <br> Band A fine |
| | **Category range** <br> Low level community order–12 weeks' custody | **Category range** <br> Band B fine–Low level community order | **Category range** <br> Discharge–Band B fine |

### Fines

[For the standard schedule of fines see **SG2-5**.]

### Community Orders and Custodial Sentences

[For the imposition of community orders, including the community orders table, see Imposition of Community and Custodial Sentences at **SG9-2**.

For the imposition of custodial sentences see Imposition of Community and Custodial Sentences at **SG9-3**.]

Consecutive sentences for multiple offences may be appropriate—please refer to the *Offences Taken Into Consideration* and *Totality* guidelines [see **SG3** and **SG4**].

Previous diversionary work with an offender does not preclude the court from considering this type of sentencing option again if appropriate.

Where the offender is dependent on or has a propensity to misuse drugs or alcohol and there is sufficient prospect of success, a community order with a drug rehabilitation requirement under Part 10, or an alcohol treatment requirement under Part 11, of Schedule 9 of the Sentencing Code may be a proper alternative to a short or moderate custodial sentence.

Where the offender suffers from a medical condition that is susceptible to treatment but does not warrant detention under a hospital order, a community order with a mental health treatment requirement under Part 9 of Schedule 9 of the Sentencing Code may be a proper alternative to a short or moderate custodial sentence.

### Additional factors affecting seriousness

The court should then consider further adjustment for any aggravating or mitigating factors. The following is a **non-exhaustive** list of additional factual elements providing the context of the offence and factors relating to the offender. Identify whether any combination of these, or other relevant factors, should result in an upward or downward adjustment from the sentence arrived at so far.

### Factors increasing seriousness

*Statutory aggravating factors*
- Previous convictions [see **SG2-21**], having regard to
   a) the **nature** of the offence to which the conviction relates and its **relevance** to the current offence; and
   b) the time that has elapsed since the conviction Relevant recent convictions **may** justify an upward adjustment, including outside the category range. In cases involving significant persistent offending, the community and custodial thresholds may be crossed even though the offence otherwise warrants a lesser sentence. Any custodial sentence must be kept to the necessary minimum
- Offence committed whilst on bail [see **SG2-22**]
- Offence motivated by, or demonstrating hostility based on any of the following characteristics of the victim: sex, disability, sexual orientation or transgender identity [see **SG2-23**]

*Other aggravating factors*
- Stealing goods to order
- Steps taken to prevent the victim reporting or obtaining assistance and/or from assisting or supporting the prosecution [see **SG2-37**]
- Attempts to conceal/dispose of evidence [see **SG2-37**]
- Offender motivated by intention to cause harm or out of revenge
- Failure to comply with current court orders [see **SG2-40**]
- Offence committed on licence [see **SG2-40**]
- Offences taken into consideration [see **SG3**]
- Established evidence of community/wider impact (for issues other than prevalence) [see **SG2-46**]
- Prevalence – see below

### Factors reducing seriousness or reflecting personal mitigation
- No previous convictions or no relevant/recent convictions [see **SG2-48**]
- Remorse, particularly where evidenced by voluntary reparation to the victim [see **SG2-50**]
- Good character and/or exemplary conduct [see **SG2-49**]
- Serious medical condition requiring urgent, intensive or long-term treatment [see **SG2-62**]
- Age and/or lack of maturity where it affects the responsibility of the offender [see **SG2-60**]
- Mental disorder or learning disability (where not linked to the commission of the offence) [see **SG2-63**]
- Sole or primary carer for dependent relatives [see **SG2-61**]
- Determination and/or demonstration of steps taken to address addiction or offending behaviour [see **SG2-64**]
- Offender experiencing **exceptional** financial hardship

### Prevalence

There may be exceptional local circumstances that arise which may lead a court to decide that prevalence should influence sentencing levels. The pivotal issue in such cases will be the harm caused to the community.

It is essential that the court before taking account of prevalence:

- has supporting evidence from an external source, for example, Community Impact Statements, to justify claims that a particular crime is prevalent in their area, and is causing particular harm in that community, and
- is satisfied that there is a compelling need to treat the offence more seriously than elsewhere.

[Steps 3 to 8 are identical to those applicable to General Theft: see **SG33-2**.]

**SG33-4**                         HANDLING STOLEN GOODS

*Theft Act 1968 (section 22)*

**Effective from:** 01 February 2016

Triable either way
Maximum: 14 years' custody
Offence range: Discharge–8 years' custody

**STEP 1 Determining the offence category**

The court should determine the offence category with reference **only** to the factors identified in the following tables. In order to determine the category the court should assess **culpability** and **harm**.

The level of culpability is determined by weighing up all the factors of the case to determine the offender's role and the extent to which the offending was **planned** and the **sophistication** with which it was carried out.

**CULPABILITY**

**Culpability demonstrated by one or more of the following**

| A — High culpability |
| --- |
| A leading role where offending is part of a group activity |
| Involvement of others through coercion, intimidation or exploitation |
| Abuse of position of power or trust or responsibility |
| Professional and sophisticated offence |
| Advance knowledge of the primary offence |
| Possession of very recently stolen goods from a domestic burglary or robbery |
| **B — Medium culpability** |
| A significant role where offending is part of a group activity |
| Offender acquires goods for resale |
| Other cases that fall between categories A or C because: |
| – Factors are present in A and C which balance each other out **and/or** |
| – The offender's culpability falls between the factors as described in A and C |
| **C — Lesser culpability** |
| Performed limited function under direction |
| Involved through coercion, intimidation or exploitation |
| Little or no planning |
| Limited awareness or understanding of offence |
| Goods acquired for offender's personal use |

**Where there are characteristics present which fall under different levels of culpability, the court should balance these characteristics to reach a fair assessment of the offender's culpability.**

**Harm**

**Harm** is assessed by reference to the **financial value** (to the loser) of the handled goods **and any significant additional harm** associated with the underlying offence on the victim or others — examples of additional harm may include **but are not limited to:**

| Property stolen from a domestic burglary or a robbery (unless this has already been taken into account in assessing culpability) |
| Items stolen were of substantial value to the loser, regardless of monetary worth |
| Metal theft causing disruption to infrastructure |
| Damage to heritage assets |

| Category 1 | Very high value goods stolen (above £100,000) **or** High value with significant additional harm to the victim or others |
| Category 2 | High value goods stolen (£10,000 to £100,000) and no significant additional harm **or** Medium value with significant additional harm to the victim or others |
| Category 3 | Medium value goods stolen (£1,000 to £10,000) and no significant additional harm **or** Low value with significant additional harm to the victim or others |
| Category 4 | Low value goods stolen (up to £1,000) **and** Little or no significant additional harm to the victim or others |

## STEP 2  Starting point and category range

Having determined the category at step one, the court should use the starting point to reach a sentence within the appropriate category range in the table below.

The starting point applies to all offenders irrespective of plea or previous convictions.

| | Culpability | | |
|---|---|---|---|
| Harm | A | B | C |
| **Category 1** Where the value greatly exceeds £100,000, it may be appropriate to move outside the identified range. Adjustment should be made for any significant additional harm where very high value stolen goods are handled | **Starting point** 5 years' custody | **Starting point** 3 years' custody | **Starting point** 1 year's custody |
| | **Category range** 3–8 years' custody | **Category range** 1 year 6 months'–4 years' custody | **Category range** 26 weeks'–1 year 6 months' custody |
| **Category 2** | **Starting point** 3 years' custody | **Starting point** 1 year's custody | **Starting point** High level community order |
| | **Category range** 1 year 6 months'–4 years' custody | **Category range** 26 weeks'–1 year 6 months' custody | **Category range** Low level community order–26 weeks' custody |
| **Category 3** | **Starting point** 1 year's custody | **Starting point** High level community order | **Starting point** Band C fine |
| | **Category range** 26 weeks'–2 years' custody | **Category range** Low level community order–26 weeks' custody | **Category range** Band B fine–Low level community order |
| **Category 4** | **Starting point** High level community order | **Starting point** Low level community order | **Starting point** Band B fine |
| | **Category range** Medium level community order–26 weeks' custody | **Category range** Band C fine–High level community order | **Category range** Discharge–Band C fine |

## Fines

[For the standard schedule of fines see **SG2-5**.]

### Community Orders and Custodial Sentences

For the imposition of community orders, including the community orders table, see Imposition of Community and Custodial Sentences at SG9-2.

[For the imposition of custodial sentences see Imposition of Community and Custodial Sentences at SG9-3.]

Consecutive sentences for multiple offences may be appropriate — please refer to the *Totality* guideline [see SG4].

### Additional factors affecting seriousness

The court should then consider further adjustment for any aggravating or mitigating factors. The following is a **non-exhaustive** list of additional factual elements providing the context of the offence and factors relating to the offender. Identify whether any combination of these, or other relevant factors, should result in an upward or downward adjustment from the starting point.

### Factors increasing seriousness

*Statutory aggravating factors*

- Previous convictions, having regard to
  a) the **nature** of the offence to which the conviction relates and its **relevance** to the current offence; and
  b) the **time** that has elapsed since the conviction [see SG2-21]
- Offence committed whilst on bail [see SG2-22]

*Other aggravating factors*

- Seriousness of the underlying offence, for example, armed robbery
- Deliberate destruction, disposal or defacing of stolen property
- Damage to a third party
- Failure to comply with current court orders [see SG2-40]
- Offence committed on licence [see SG2-40]
- Offences taken into consideration [see SG3]
- Established evidence of community/wider impact [see SG2-46]

### Factors reducing seriousness or reflecting personal mitigation

- No previous convictions or no relevant/recent convictions [see SG2-48]
- Good character and/or exemplary conduct [see SG2-49]
- Serious medical condition requiring urgent, intensive or long-term treatment [see SG2-62]
- Age and/or lack of maturity where it affects the responsibility of the offender [see SG2-60]
- Mental disorder or learning disability (where not linked to the commission of the offence) [see SG2-63]
- Sole or primary carer for dependent relatives [see SG2-61]
- Determination and/or demonstration of steps taken to address addiction or offending behaviour [see SG2-64]

[Steps 3 to 8 are identical to those applicable to General Theft: see SG33-2.]

**SG33-5**

## GOING EQUIPPED FOR THEFT OR BURGLARY

*Theft Act 1968 (section 25)*

**Effective from:** 01 February 2016

Triable either way
Maximum: 3 years' custody
Offence range: Discharge–18 months' custody

### STEP 1 Determining the offence category

The court should determine the offence category with reference **only** to the factors identified in the following tables. In order to determine the category the court should assess **culpability** and **harm**.

The level of culpability is determined by weighing up all the factors of the case to determine the offender's role and the extent to which the offending was **planned** and the **sophistication** with which it was carried out.

## CULPABILITY

### Culpability demonstrated by one or more of the following

| A — High culpability |
| --- |
| A leading role where offending is part of a group activity |
| Involvement of others through coercion, intimidation or exploitation |
| Significant steps taken to conceal identity and/or avoid detection |
| Sophisticated nature of offence/significant planning |
| Offender equipped for robbery or domestic burglary |

| B — Medium culpability |
| --- |
| A significant role where offending is part of a group activity |
| Other cases that fall between categories A or C because: |
| – Factors are present in A and C which balance each other out **and/or** |
| – The offender's culpability falls between the factors as described in A and C |

| C — Lesser culpability |
| --- |
| Involved through coercion, intimidation or exploitation |
| Limited awareness or understanding of offence |
| Little or no planning |

**Where there are characteristics present which fall under different levels of culpability, the court should balance these characteristics to reach a fair assessment of the offender's culpability.**

### Harm

This guideline refers to preparatory offences where no theft has been committed. The level of harm is determined by weighing up all the factors of the case to determine the harm that would be caused if the item(s) were used to commit a substantive offence.

### Greater harm

| Possession of item(s) which have the potential to facilitate an offence affecting a large number of victims |
| --- |
| Possession of item(s) which have the potential to facilitate an offence involving high value items |

### Lesser harm

| All other cases |
| --- |

## STEP 2  Starting point and category range

Having determined the category at step one, the court should use the starting point to reach a sentence within the appropriate category range in the table below.

The starting point applies to all offenders irrespective of plea or previous convictions.

| Harm | Culpability | | |
| --- | --- | --- | --- |
| | A | B | C |
| Greater | **Starting point**<br>1 year's custody | **Starting point**<br>18 weeks' custody | **Starting point**<br>Medium level community order |
| | **Category range**<br>26 weeks'–1 year 6 months' custody | **Category range**<br>High level community order –36 weeks' custody | **Category range**<br>Low level community order– High level community order |
| Lesser | **Starting point**<br>26 weeks' custody | **Starting point**<br>High level community order | **Starting point**<br>Band C fine |
| | **Category range**<br>12 weeks'–36 weeks' custody | **Category range**<br>Medium level community order–12 weeks' custody | **Category range**<br>Discharge–Medium level community order |

**Fines**

[For the standard schedule of fines see **SG2-5**.]

**Community Orders and Custodial Sentences**

[For the imposition of community orders, including the community orders table, see Imposition of Community and Custodial Sentences at **SG9-2**.

For the imposition of custodial sentences see Imposition of Community and Custodial Sentences at **SG9-3**.]

Consecutive sentences for multiple offences may be appropriate — please refer to the *Totality* guideline [see **SG4**]. The court should then consider further adjustment for any aggravating or mitigating factors.

**Additional factors affecting seriousness**

The following is a **non-exhaustive** list of additional factual elements providing the context of the offence and factors relating to the offender. Identify whether any combination of these, or other relevant factors, should result in an upward or downward adjustment from the starting point.

**Factors increasing seriousness**

*Statutory aggravating factors*

- Previous convictions, having regard to
  a) the **nature** of the offence to which the conviction relates and its **relevance** to the current offence; and
  b) the **time** that has elapsed since the conviction [see **SG2-21**]
- Offence committed whilst on bail [see **SG2-22**]

*Other aggravating factors*

- Attempts to conceal/dispose of evidence [see **SG2-37**]
- Established evidence of community/wider impact [see **SG2-46**]
- Failure to comply with current court orders [see **SG2-40**]
- Offence committed on licence or post sentence supervision [see **SG2-40**]
- Offences taken into consideration [see **SG3**]

**Factors reducing seriousness or reflecting personal mitigation**

- No previous convictions or no relevant/recent convictions [see **SG2-48**]
- Good character and/or exemplary conduct [see **SG2-49**]
- Serious medical condition requiring urgent, intensive or long-term treatment [see **SG2-62**]
- Age and/or lack of maturity where it affects the responsibility of the offender [see **SG2-60**]
- Mental disorder or learning disability (where not linked to the commission of the offence) [see **SG2-63**]
- Sole or primary carer for dependent relatives [see **SG2-61**]
- Determination and/or demonstration of steps taken to address addiction or offending behaviour [see **SG2-64**]

[Steps 3 to 8 are identical to those applicable to General Theft: see **SG33-2**.]

**SG33-6**                              ABSTRACTING ELECTRICITY

*Theft Act 1968 (section 13)*

**Effective from:** 01 February 2016

Triable either way
Maximum: 5 years' custody
Offence range: Discharge–1 year's custody

**STEP 1 Determining the offence category**

The court should determine the offence category with reference **only** to the factors identified in the following tables. In order to determine the category the court should assess **culpability** and **harm**.

The level of culpability is determined by weighing up all the factors of the case to determine the offender's role and the extent to which the offending was **planned** and the **sophistication** with which it was carried out.

## CULPABILITY

### Culpability demonstrated by one or more of the following

| A — High culpability |
| --- |
| A leading role where offending is part of a group activity |
| Involvement of others through coercion, intimidation or exploitation |
| Sophisticated nature of offence/significant planning |
| Abuse of position of power or trust or responsibility |
| Commission of offence in association with or to further other criminal activity |

| B — Medium culpability |
| --- |
| A significant role where offending is part of a group activity |
| Other cases that fall between categories A or C because: |
| – Factors are present in A and C which balance each other out **and/or** |
| – The offender's culpability falls between the factors as described in A and C |

| C — Lesser culpability |
| --- |
| Performed limited function under direction |
| Involved through coercion, intimidation or exploitation |
| Limited awareness or understanding of offence |

**Where there are characteristics present which fall under different levels of culpability, the court should balance these characteristics to reach a fair assessment of the offender's culpability.**

### Harm

The level of harm is assessed by weighing up all the factors of the case to determine the level of harm caused.

### Greater harm

| |
| --- |
| A significant risk of, or actual injury to persons or damage to property |
| Significant volume of electricity extracted as evidenced by length of time of offending and/or advanced type of illegal process used |

### Lesser harm

| |
| --- |
| All other cases |

### STEP 2  Starting point and category range

Having determined the category at step one, the court should use the starting point to reach a sentence within the appropriate category range in the table below.

The starting point applies to all offenders irrespective of plea or previous convictions.

| Harm | Culpability | | |
| --- | --- | --- | --- |
| | A | B | C |
| Greater | **Starting point**<br>12 weeks' custody | **Starting point**<br>Medium level<br>community order | **Starting point**<br>Band C fine |
| | **Category range**<br>High level community<br>order–1 year's custody | **Category range**<br>Low level community<br>order–12 weeks' custody | **Category range**<br>Band B fine–Low level<br>community order |

| Harm | Culpability | | |
|------|-------------|---|---|
| | A | B | C |
| Lesser | **Starting point** High level community order | **Starting point** Low level community order | **Starting point** Band A fine |
| | **Category range** Medium level community order–12 weeks' custody | **Category range** Band C fine–Medium level community order | **Category range** Discharge–Band C fine |

### Fines

[For the standard schedule of fines see SG2-5.]

### Community Orders and Custodial Sentences

[For the imposition of community orders, including the community orders table, see Imposition of Community and Custodial Sentences at **SG9-2**.

For the imposition of custodial sentences see Imposition of Community and Custodial Sentences at **SG9-3**.]

### Additional factors affecting seriousness

The court should then consider further adjustment for any aggravating or mitigating factors. The table below contains a **non-exhaustive** list of additional factual elements providing the context of the offence and factors relating to the offender.

Identify whether any combination of these, or other relevant factors, should result in an upward or downward adjustment from the starting point.

### Factors increasing seriousness

*Statutory aggravating factors*

- Previous convictions, having regard to
  a) the **nature** of the offence to which the conviction relates and its **relevance** to the current offence; and
  b) the **time** that has elapsed since the conviction [see **SG2-21**]
- Offence committed whilst on bail [see **SG2-22**]

*Other aggravating factors*

- Electricity abstracted from another person's property
- Attempts to conceal/dispose of evidence [see **SG2-37**]
- Failure to comply with current court orders [see **SG2-40**]
- Offence committed on licence [see **SG2-40**]
- Offences taken into consideration [see **SG3**]
- Blame wrongly placed on others [see **SG2-38**]
- Established evidence of community/wider impact [see **SG2-46**]

### Factors reducing seriousness or reflecting personal mitigation

- No previous convictions or no relevant/recent convictions [see **SG2-48**]
- Good character and/or exemplary conduct [see **SG2-49**]
- Serious medical condition requiring urgent, intensive or long-term treatment [see **SG2-62**]
- Age and/or lack of maturity where it affects the responsibility of the offender [see **SG2-60**]
- Mental disorder or learning disability (where not linked to the commission of the offence) [see **SG2-63**]
- Sole or primary carer for dependent relatives [see **SG2-61**]
- Determination and/or demonstration of steps taken to address addiction or offending behaviour [see **SG2-64**]

[Steps 3 to 5 are identical to those applicable to General Theft: see **SG33-2**.]

### STEP 6 Confiscation, compensation and ancillary orders

Confiscation orders under the Proceeds of Crime Act 2002 may only be made by the Crown Court. The Crown Court must proceed with a view to making a confiscation order if it is asked to do so by the prosecutor or if the Crown Court believes it is appropriate for it to do so.

Where, following conviction in a magistrates' court, the prosecutor applies for the offender to be committed to the Crown Court with a view to a confiscation order being considered, the magistrates' court must commit the offender to the Crown Court to be sentenced there (section 70 of the Proceeds of Crime Act 2002). Where, but for the prosecutor's application under s.70, the magistrates' court would have committed the offender for sentence to the Crown Court anyway it must say so. Otherwise the powers of sentence of the Crown Court will be limited to those of the magistrates' court.

Confiscation must be dealt with before, and taken into account when assessing, any other fine or financial order (except compensation).

(See Proceeds of Crime Act 2002 sections 6 and 13)

Where the offence has resulted in loss or damage the court must consider whether to make a compensation order and must give reasons if it does not do so (section 55 of the Sentencing Code).

The court should also consider whether to make ancillary orders. These may include a deprivation order or a restitution order.

[See the Sentencing Council Explanatory Materials for Ancillary Orders in the Magistrates' Courts at **SG10-5** and the Crown Court Compendium, Part II Sentencing, S7; Ancillary Orders]

[Steps 7 and 8 are identical to those applicable to General Theft: see **SG33-2.**]

MAKING OFF WITHOUT PAYMENT                                 **SG33-7**

*Theft Act 1978 (section 3)*

**Effective from:** 01 February 2016

Triable either way
Maximum: 2 years' custody
Offence range: Discharge–36 weeks' custody

**STEP 1  Determining the offence category**

The court should determine the offence category with reference **only** to the factors identified in the following tables. In order to determine the category the court should assess **culpability** and **harm**.

The level of culpability is determined by weighing up all the factors of the case to determine the offender's role and the extent to which the offending was **planned** and the **sophistication** with which it was carried out.

**CULPABILITY**

**Culpability demonstrated by one or more of the following**

| A — High culpability |
| --- |
| A leading role where offending is part of a group activity |
| Involvement of others through coercion, intimidation or exploitation |
| Sophisticated nature of offence/significant planning |
| Offence involving intimidation or the use or threat of force |
| Deliberately targeting victim on basis of vulnerability |
| **B — Medium culpability** |
| A significant role where offending is part of a group activity |
| Some degree of planning involved |
| Other cases that fall between categories A or C because: |
| – Factors are present in A and C which balance each other out **and/or** |
| – The offender's culpability falls between the factors as described in A and C |
| **C — Lesser culpability** |
| Performed limited function under direction |
| Involved through coercion, intimidation or exploitation |
| Little or no planning |
| Limited awareness or understanding of offence |

Where there are characteristics present which fall under different levels of culpability, the court should balance these characteristics to reach a fair assessment of the offender's culpability.

## Harm

**Harm** is assessed by reference to the **actual loss** that results from the offence **and any significant additional harm** suffered by the victim — examples of additional harm may include **but are not limited to:**

- A high level of inconvenience caused to the victim
- Emotional distress
- Fear/loss of confidence caused by the crime
- A greater impact on the victim due to the size or type of their business

| | |
|---|---|
| Category 1 | Goods or services obtained above £200 or<br>Goods/services up to £200 with significant additional harm to the victim |
| Category 2 | Goods or services obtained up to £200 and<br>Little or no significant additional harm to the victim |

## STEP 2  Starting point and category range

Having determined the category at step one, the court should use the starting point to reach a sentence within the appropriate category range in the table below.

The starting point applies to all offenders irrespective of plea or previous convictions.

| Harm | Culpability | | |
|---|---|---|---|
| | A | B | C |
| **Category 1**<br>Where the value greatly exceeds £200, it may be appropriate to move outside the identified range. Adjustment should be made for any significant additional harm for offences above £200. | **Starting point**<br>12 weeks' custody | **Starting point**<br>Low level community order | **Starting point**<br>Band B fine |
| | **Category range**<br>High level community order—36 weeks' custody | **Category range**<br>Band C fine—High level community order | **Category range**<br>Band A fine—Low level community order |
| **Category 2** | **Starting point**<br>Medium level community order | **Starting point**<br>Band C fine | **Starting point**<br>Band A fine |
| | **Category range**<br>Low level community order—12 weeks' custody | **Category range**<br>Band B fine—Low level community order | **Category range**<br>Discharge—Band B fine |

## Fines

[For the standard schedule of fines see **SG2-5**.]

## Community Orders and Custodial Sentences

[For the imposition of community orders, including the community orders table, see Imposition of Community and Custodial Sentences at **SG9-2**.

For the imposition of custodial sentences see Imposition of Community and Custodial Sentences at **SG9-3**.]

Consecutive sentences for multiple offences may be appropriate — please refer to the *Offences Taken Into Consideration* and *Totality* guidelines [see **SG3** and **SG4**].

## Additional factors affecting seriousness

The court should then consider further adjustment for any aggravating or mitigating factors. The following list is a **non-exhaustive** list of additional factual elements providing the context of the offence and factors relating to the offender.

Identify whether any combination of these, or other relevant factors, should result in an upward or downward adjustment from the starting point.

Factors increasing seriousness

*Statutory aggravating factors*

- Previous convictions [see **SG2-21**], having regard to
  a) the **nature** of the offence to which the conviction relates and its **relevance** to the current offence; and
  b) the **time** that has elapsed since the conviction
- Offence committed whilst on bail [see **SG2-22**]
- Offence motivated by, or demonstrating hostility based on any of the following characteristics of the victim: sex, disability, sexual orientation or transgender identity [see **SG2-23**]

*Other aggravating factors*

- Steps taken to prevent the victim reporting or obtaining assistance and/or from assisting or supporting the prosecution [see **SG2-37**]
- Attempts to conceal/dispose of evidence [see **SG2-37**]
- Failure to comply with current court orders [see **SG2-40**]
- Offence committed on licence [see **SG2-40**]
- Offences taken into consideration [see **SG3**]
- Established evidence of community/wider impact [see **SG2-46**]

Factors reducing seriousness or reflecting personal mitigation

- No previous convictions or no relevant/recent convictions [see **SG2-48**]
- Remorse, particularly where evidenced by voluntary reparation to the victim [see **SG2-50**]
- Good character and/or exemplary conduct [see **SG2-49**]
- Serious medical condition requiring urgent, intensive or long-term treatment [see **SG2-62**]
- Age and/or lack of maturity where it affects the responsibility of the offender [see **SG2-60**]
- Mental disorder or learning disability (where not linked to the commission of the offence) [see **SG2-63**]
- Sole or primary carer for dependent relatives [see **SG2-61**]
- Determination and/or demonstration of steps taken to address addiction or offending behaviour [see **SG2-64**]

[Steps 3 to 8 are identical to those applicable to General Theft: see **SG33-2**.]

ANNEX                                                                                   **SG33-8**

[The tables set out here are also set out in the Magistrates' Court Sentencing Guidelines, which include further guidance on fines and community orders: see **SG10-35** and **SG9-2**.]

# PART 34    FIREARMS OFFENCES

APPLICABILITY

[For the standard text on applicability see **SG0-4**.]

CARRYING A FIREARM IN A PUBLIC PLACE

*Firearms Act 1968, s.19*

**Effective from:** 01 January 2021

(a)  a loaded shot gun
(b)  an air weapon (whether loaded or not)
(c)  any other firearm (whether loaded or not) together with ammunition suitable for use in that firearm
(d)  an imitation firearm

Triable either way except: Indictable only if the firearm is specified in section 5(1)(a), (ab), (aba), (ac), (ad), (ae) or (af) or section 5(1A)(a) of the Firearms Act 1968

Summary only if the firearm is an air weapon

Maximum: 7 years' custody (12 months' custody for imitation firearms, 6 months' custody for an air weapon)
Offence range: Discharge–4 years' custody

**STEP 1  Determining the offence category**

The court should determine the offence category with reference **only** to the factors listed in the tables below. In order to determine the category the court should assess **culpability** and **harm.**

**Culpability – Type of weapon**

Use the table below to identify an initial culpability category based on the type of weapon only. This assessment focuses on the nature of the weapon itself only, not whether the weapon was loaded or in working order.

Where the weapon does not fall squarely in one category, the court may need to adjust the starting point in step 2.

> Type 1
> • Shotgun which has been shortened within the meaning of section 4(4)
> • Firearm which has been converted within the meaning of section 4(4)
>
> Type 2
> • All other firearms or shotguns
> • Ammunition (where not at Type 3)
>
> Type 3
> • Very small quantity of ammunition

Culpability – Other culpability factors

The court should weigh all the factors set out below in determining the offender's culpability

> **High culpability:**
> • Offender uses weapon for a criminal purpose
> • Offender intends weapon to be used for a criminal purpose, or is reckless as to whether it would be so used
>
> **Medium culpability:**
> • Weapon produced or used (where not at High culpability)
> • Weapon loaded or held with compatible ammunition (where not at High culpability)
> • Offender intends weapon to be used or is reckless as to whether it would be used (where not at High culpability)
>
> **Lower culpability:**
> • No use or intention to use
> • Possession falls just short of reasonable excuse

Where there are characteristics present which fall under different levels of culpability, the court should balance these characteristics to reach a fair assessment of the offender's culpability.

## Culpability category

Identify the final culpability category in the table below, considering both the **Type of weapon** and **Other culpability factors.**

| Other culpability factors | Type of weapon | | |
|---|---|---|---|
| | 1 | 2 | 3 |
| High | Culpability category A | Culpability category A | Culpability category B |
| Medium | Culpability category A | Culpability category B | Culpability category C |
| Lower | Culpability category B | Culpability category C | Culpability category C |

## Harm

Harm is assessed by reference to the risk of harm or disorder occurring and/or actual alarm/distress caused.

When considering the risk of harm, relevant considerations may include the location of the offence, the number and vulnerability of people exposed, especially children, and the accessibility and visibility of the weapon.

---

**Category 1**
- Serious alarm/distress caused
- High risk of death or serious physical or psychological harm
- High risk of serious disorder

**Category 2**
- All other cases falling between category 1 and category 3 because:
  - Factors in both 1 and 3 are present which balance each other out; and/or
  - The harm falls between the factors as described in 1 and 3

**Category 3**
- No/minimal alarm/distress caused
- No/minimal risk of death or serious physical or psychological harm
- No/minimal risk of serious disorder

---

Where there are characteristics present which fall under different levels of harm, the court should balance these characteristics to reach a fair assessment of the harm.

## STEP 2  Starting point and category range

Having determined the category at step 1, the court should use the corresponding starting point to reach a sentence within the category range below. The starting point applies to all offenders irrespective of plea or

The offence may be subject to a statutory minimum sentence.

See step 3 for details of the minimum sentencing provisions and the approach to be taken to consideration of exceptional circumstances.

| Harm | Culpability | | |
|---|---|---|---|
| | A | B | C |
| Category 1 | **Starting point** 2 years' custody | **Starting point** 1 year's custody | **Starting point** High level community order |
| | **Category range** 1–4 years' custody | **Category range** 6 months'–2 years' custody* | **Category range** Low level community order–1 year's custody* |

| Harm | Culpability | | |
|---|---|---|---|
| | A | B | C |
| Category 2 | **Starting point**<br>1 year's custody | **Starting point**<br>High level community order | **Starting point**<br>Medium level community order |
| | **Category range**<br>6 months'–2 years' custody | **Category range**<br>Low level community order–1 year's custody* | **Category range**<br>Band B fine–High level community order |
| Category 3 | **Starting point**<br>High level community order | **Starting point**<br>Medium level community order | **Starting point**<br>Band B fine |
| | **Category range**<br>Low level community order–1 year's custody | **Category range**<br>Band B fine–High level community order | **Category range**<br>Discharge–Band C Fine |

* Where the weapon is an imitation firearm, the maximum penalty is 12 months' custody.
* Where the weapon is an air weapon, the maximum penalty is 6 months' custody

**Fines**

[For the standard schedule of fines see **SG2-5**.]

**Community Orders and Custodial Sentences**

[For the imposition of community orders, including the community orders table, see Imposition of Community and Custodial Sentences at **SG9-2**.

For the imposition of custodial sentences see Imposition of Community and Custodial Sentences at **SG9-3**.]

The following is a **non-exhaustive** list of additional factual elements providing the context of the offence and factors relating to the offender. Identify whether any combination of these, or other relevant factors, should result in an upward or downward adjustment from the sentence arrived at so far. In some cases, having considered these factors, it may be appropriate to move outside the identified category range.

**Factors increasing seriousness**

*Statutory aggravating factors*

- Previous convictions [see **SG2-21**], having regard to
  a) the **nature** of the offence to which the conviction relates and its **relevance** to the current offence; and
  b) the **time** that has elapsed since the conviction
- Offence committed whilst on bail [see **SG2-22**]

*Other aggravating factors:*

- Firearm modified to make it more dangerous
- Steps taken to disguise firearm (where not firearm under section 5(1A)(a))
- Steps taken to make imitation firearm appear more realistic (See step 6 on totality when sentencing for more than one offence)
- Firearm/ammunition kept with multiple weapons and/or substantial quantity of ammunition (See step 6 on totality when sentencing more than one offence)
- Offence was committed as part of a group
- Abuse of position as registered firearms dealer or certificate holder
- Commission of offence whilst under the influence of alcohol or drugs
- Offender prohibited from possessing weapon or ammunition because of previous conviction (Care should be taken to avoid double counting matters taken into account when considering previous convictions. See step 6 on totality when sentencing more than one offence)
- Failure to comply with current court orders
- Offence committed on licence or post sentence supervision

**Factors reducing seriousness or reflecting personal mitigation**

- No previous convictions or no relevant/recent convictions
- Good character and/or exemplary conduct
- Firearm incomplete or incapable of being discharged (including stun gun that is not charged and not held with a functioning charger)
- No knowledge or suspicion that item possessed was firearm/ammunition

- No knowledge or suspicion that firearm/ammunition is prohibited
- Held on behalf of another through coercion, intimidation or exploitation
- Genuine mistake about whether covered by lawful authorisation
- Voluntary surrender of firearm/ammunition
- Offender co-operated with investigation and/or made early admissions
- Remorse
- Serious medical condition requiring urgent, intensive or long-term treatment
- Age and/or lack of maturity
- Mental disorder or learning disability
- Sole or primary carer for dependent relatives

### STEP 3  Minimum term and exceptional circumstances

**Minimum Term**

1. Where the minimum term provisions under section 311 and Schedule 20 of the Sentencing Code apply, a court must impose a sentence of at least five years' custody irrespective of plea **unless the court is of the opinion that there are exceptional circumstances relating to the offence or to the offender which justify its not doing so.**

*Applicability*

2. The minimum terms provisions apply when sentencing offences in respect of a firearm or ammunition specified in section 5(1)(a), (ab), (aba), (ac), (ad), (ae), (af) or (c) or section 5(1A)(a) of the Firearms Act 1968 committed on or after 6 April 2007. Note: the minimum term provisions do **not** apply to offences charged as conspiracies.
3. The minimum term applies to *all* such offences including the first offence. Where it applies the sentence cannot be reduced below the minimum term for a guilty plea (see Step 5 – Reduction for guilty pleas).
4. The minimum term of five years applies to offenders aged 18 or over **when the offence was committed**. See below for guidance when sentencing offenders aged under 18.
5. Where the minimum term applies, this should be stated expressly.

**Exceptional circumstances**

6. In considering whether there are exceptional circumstances that would justify not imposing the statutory minimum sentence, the court must have regard to:
   - the particular circumstances of the offence **and**
   - the particular circumstances of the offender.
   either of which may give rise to exceptional circumstances
7. Where the factual circumstances are disputed, the procedure should follow that of a Newton hearing: see Criminal Practice Directions VII: Sentencing B [see **CPD.VII.B**].
8. Where the issue of exceptional circumstances has been raised the court should give a clear explanation as to why those circumstances have or have not been found.

*Principles*

9. Circumstances are exceptional if the imposition of the minimum term would result in an arbitrary and disproportionate sentence.
10. The circumstances must truly be exceptional. It is important that courts do not undermine the intention of Parliament and the deterrent purpose of the minimum term provisions by too readily accepting exceptional circumstances.
11. The court should look at all of the circumstances of the case taken together. A single striking factor may amount to exceptional circumstances, or it may be the collective impact of all of the relevant circumstances.
12. The mere presence of one or more of the following should not *in itself* be regarded as exceptional:
    - One or more lower culpability factors
    - One or more mitigating factors
    - A plea of guilty

*Where exceptional circumstances are found*

13. If there are exceptional circumstances that justify not imposing the statutory minimum sentence then the court **must impose either a shorter custodial sentence than the statutory minimum provides or an alternative sentence**. Note: a guilty plea reduction applies in the normal way if the minimum term is not imposed (see Step 5 – Reduction for guilty pleas).

Sentencing Guidelines

**Sentencing offenders aged under 18 at the date of the offence**

1. Where the offender is aged 16 or 17 **when the offence was committed**, the minimum term is three years' custody. Where the offender is under 16 **when the offence was committed**, the minimum term does not apply.
2. Subject to the minimum term, where the offender is aged under 18 **at the date of conviction** the court should determine the sentence in accordance with the Sentencing Children and Young People guideline [SG8-1–SG8-11], particularly paragraphs 6.42–6.49 on custodial sentences.
3. This guidance states at paragraph 6.46: "When considering the relevant adult guideline, the court may feel it appropriate to apply a sentence broadly within the region of half to two thirds of the adult sentence for those aged 15–17 and allow a greater reduction for those aged under 15. This is only a rough guide and must not be applied mechanistically. In most cases when considering the appropriate reduction from the adult sentence the emotional and developmental age and maturity of the child or young person is of at least equal importance as their chronological age."
4. The considerations above on exceptional circumstances relating to the offence or offender apply equally when sentencing offenders aged 16 or 17 at the date of the offence.

### STEP 4  Consider any factors which indicate a reduction for assistance to the prosecution

The court should take into account section 74 of the Sentencing Code (reduction in sentence for assistance to prosecution) and any other rule of law by virtue of which an offender may receive a discounted sentence in consequence of assistance given (or offered) to the prosecutor or investigator.

### STEP 5  Reduction for guilty pleas

The court should take account of any potential reduction for a guilty plea in accordance with section 73 of the Sentencing Code and the Reduction in sentence for a guilty plea guideline [SG5-1–SG5-12].

Where a **mandatory minimum sentence** has been imposed under section 311 of the Sentencing Code, the court must ensure that any reduction for a guilty plea does not reduce the sentence to less than the mandatory minimum.

### STEP 6  Totality principle

If sentencing an offender for more than one offence, or where the offender is already serving a sentence, consider whether the total sentence is just and proportionate to the overall offending behaviour in accordance with the *Totality* guideline [see **SG4**].

### STEP 7  Ancillary orders

In all cases the court should consider whether to make ancillary orders.

### Forfeiture and destruction of firearms and cancellation of certificate

The court should consider ordering forfeiture or disposal of any firearm or ammunition and the cancellation of any firearms certificate. Section 52 of the Firearms Act 1968 provides for the forfeiture and disposal of firearms and the cancellation of firearms and shotgun certificates where a person is convicted of this offence **and** is given a custodial sentence **or** a community order containing a requirement not to possess, use or carry a firearm.

### STEP 8  Reasons

Section 52 of the Sentencing Code imposes a duty to give reasons for, and explain the effect of, the sentence.

### STEP 9  Consideration for time spent on bail

The court must consider whether to give credit for time spent on bail in accordance with section 240A of the Criminal Justice Act 2003 and section 325 of the Sentencing Code.

**SG34-3**  FIREARMS – POSSESSION BY PERSON PROHIBITED

*Firearms Act 1968, s.21(4) and (5)*

**Effective from:** 01 January 2021

**Possession of a firearm or ammunition by person with previous convictions prohibited from possessing a firearm or ammunition**

Triable either way
Maximum: 5 years' custody
Offence range: Discharge–4 years' custody

### STEP 1  Determining the offence category

The court should determine the offence category with reference **only** to the factors listed in the tables below. In order to determine the category the court should assess **culpability** and **harm**.

## Culpability – Type of weapon

Use the table below to identify an initial culpability category based on the type of weapon only. This assessment focuses on the nature of the weapon itself only, not whether the weapon was loaded or in working order.

Where the weapon or ammunition does not fall squarely in one category, the court may need to adjust the starting point in step 2.

---

**Type 1**
- Firearm or ammunition prohibited under section 5 (where not at Type 2)

**Type 2**
- Weapon prohibited under section 5(1)(b)
- Firearm, for which a certificate is required
- Shotgun for which a certificate is required
- Air weapon for which a certificate is required
- Ammunition for which a certificate is required (where not at Type 3)

**Type 3**
- Air weapon that is not prohibited and for which no certificate is required
- Antique weapon (kept as a curiosity or ornament) that is not prohibited and for which no certificate is required
- Ammunition that is not prohibited and for which no certificate is required
- Very small quantity of ammunition for which a certificate is required

---

## Culpability – Other culpability factors

The court should weigh all the factors set out below in determining the offender's culpability.

## Culpability category

Identify the final culpability category in the table below, considering both the **Type of weapon** and **Other culpability factors**.

|  | Type of weapon | | |
|---|---|---|---|
|  | 1 | 2 | 3 |
| High | Culpability category A | Culpability category A | Culpability category B |
| Medium | Culpability category A | Culpability category B | Culpability category C |
| Lower | Culpability category B | Culpability category C | Culpability category C |

## Harm

Harm is assessed by reference to the risk of harm or disorder occurring and/or actual alarm/distress caused.

When considering the risk of harm, relevant considerations may include the location of the offence, the number and vulnerability of people exposed, especially children, and the accessibility and visibility of the weapon.

---

**Category 1**
- Serious alarm/distress caused
- High risk of death or serious physical or psychological harm
- High risk of serious disorder

**Category 2**
- All other cases falling between category 1 and category 3 because:
  - Factors in both 1 and 3 are present which balance each other out; and/or
  - The harm falls between the factors as described in 1 and 3

**Category 3**
- No/minimal alarm/distress caused
- No/minimal risk of death or serious physical or psychological harm
- No/minimal risk of serious disorder

---

Where there are characteristics present which fall under different levels of harm, the court should balance these characteristics to reach a fair assessment of the harm.

Sentencing Guidelines

### STEP 2  Starting point and category range

Having determined the category at step 1, the court should use the corresponding starting point to reach a sentence within the category range below. The starting point applies to all offenders irrespective of plea or previous convictions.

| Harm | Culpability | | |
|---|---|---|---|
| | **A** | **B** | **C** |
| Category 1 | **Starting point** 3 years 6 months' custody | **Starting point** 2 years 6 months' custody | **Starting point** 1 year's custody |
| | **Category range** 2 years 6 months–4 years 6 months' custody | **Category range** 1–3 years 6 months' custody | **Category range** High level community order–2 years' custody |
| Category 2 | **Starting point** 2 years 6 months' custody | **Starting point** 1 year's custody | **Starting point** Medium level community order |
| | **Category range** 1–3 years 6 months' custody | **Category range** High level community order–2 years' custody | **Category range** Band A fine–6 months' custody |
| Category 3 | **Starting point** 1 year's custody | **Starting point** Medium level community order | **Starting point** Band A fine |
| | **Category range** High level community order–2 years' custody | **Category range** Band A fine–6 months' custody | **Category range** Discharge–Band C Fine |

**Fines**

[For the standard schedule of fines see **SG2-5**.]

**Community Orders and Custodial Sentences**

[For the imposition of community orders, including the community orders table, see Imposition of Community and Custodial Sentences at **SG9-2**.

For the imposition of custodial sentences see Imposition of Community and Custodial Sentences at **SG9-3**.]

The following is a **non-exhaustive** list of additional factual elements providing the context of the offence and factors relating to the offender. Identify whether any combination of these, or other relevant factors, should result in an upward or downward adjustment from the sentence arrived at so far. In some cases, having considered these factors, it may be appropriate to move outside the identified category range.

**Factors increasing seriousness**

*Statutory aggravating factors:*
- Previous convictions, having regard to
  a) the **nature** of the offence to which the conviction relates and its **relevance** to the current offence; and
  b) the **time** that has elapsed since the conviction
- Offence committed whilst on bail

*Other aggravating factors:*
- Firearm modified to make it more dangerous
- Steps taken to disguise firearm (where not firearm under section 5(1A)(a))
- Firearm/ammunition kept with multiple weapons and/or substantial quantity of ammunition (See step 5 on totality when sentencing more than one offence)
- Offence was committed as part of a group
- Commission of offence whilst under the influence of alcohol or drugs
- Failure to comply with current court orders
- Offence committed on licence or post sentence supervision

**Factors reducing seriousness or reflecting personal mitigation**
- No previous convictions or no relevant/recent convictions
- Good character and/or exemplary conduct
- Firearm incomplete or incapable of being discharged
- No knowledge or suspicion that item possessed was firearm/ammunition
- No knowledge or suspicion that firearm/ammunition is prohibited

- Held on behalf of another through coercion, intimidation, or exploitation
- Genuine misunderstanding about terms of prohibition
- Voluntary surrender of firearm/ammunition
- Offender co-operated with investigation and/or made early admissions
- Remorse
- Serious medical condition requiring urgent, intensive or long-term treatment
- Age and/or lack of maturity
- Mental disorder or learning disability
- Sole or primary carer for dependent relatives

### STEP 3  Consider any factors which indicate a reduction for assistance to the prosecution

The court should take into account section 74 of the Sentencing Code (reduction in sentence for assistance to prosecution) and any other rule of law by virtue of which an offender may receive a discounted sentence in consequence of assistance given (or offered) to the prosecutor or investigator.

### STEP 4  Reduction for guilty pleas

The court should take account of any potential reduction for a guilty plea in accordance with section 73 of the Sentencing Code and the Reduction in sentence for a guilty plea guideline [see **SG5-1–SG5-12**].

### STEP 5  Totality principle

If sentencing an offender for more than one offence, or where the offender is already serving a sentence, consider whether the total sentence is just and proportionate to the overall offending behaviour in accordance with the *Totality* guideline [see **SG4**].

### STEP 6  Ancillary orders

In all cases the court should consider whether to make ancillary orders.

#### Forfeiture and destruction of firearms and cancellation of certificate

The court should consider ordering forfeiture or disposal of any firearm or ammunition and the cancellation of any firearms certificate. Section 52 of the Firearms Act 1968 provides for the forfeiture and disposal of firearms and the cancellation of firearms and shotgun certificates where a person is convicted of this offence **and** is given a custodial sentence **or** a community order containing a requirement not to possess, use or carry a firearm.

### STEP 7  Reasons

Section 52 of the Sentencing Code imposes a duty to give reasons for, and explain the effect of, the sentence.

### STEP 8  Consideration for time spent on bail (tagged curfew)

The court must consider whether to give credit for time spent on bail in accordance with section 240A of the Criminal Justice Act 2003 and section 325 of the Sentencing Code.

FIREARMS – POSSESSION OF PROHIBITED WEAPON                                   **SG34-4**

*Firearms Act 1968, s.5(1), 5(1A)*

**Effective from:** 01 January 2021

**Possession, purchase or acquisition of a prohibited weapon or ammunition**

Indictable only: Section 5(1)(a), (ab), (aba), (ac), (ad), (ae), (af), (ag), (ba), (c) Section 5(1A)(a)
Triable either way: Section 5(1)(b) Section 5(1A)(b), (c), (d), (e), (f), (g)
Maximum: 10 years' custody
Offence range: Discharge–10 years' custody

### STEP 1  Determining the offence category

The court should determine the offence category with reference **only** to the factors listed in the tables below. In order to determine the category the court should assess **culpability** and **harm**.

#### Culpability – Type of weapon

Use the table below to identify an initial culpability category based on the **type of weapon** only. This assessment focuses on the nature of the weapon itself only, not whether the weapon was loaded or in working order.

Courts should take care to ensure the categorisation is appropriate for the specific weapon. Where the weapon or ammunition does not fall squarely in one category, the court may need to adjust the starting point in step 2.

References to weapon below include a component part of such a weapon.

## Type 1

Weapon that is designed or adapted to be capable of killing two or more people at the same time or in rapid succession

- This would **normally** include a weapon under:
  - section 5(1)(a)
  - section 5(1)(ab)
  - section 5(1)(aba)
  - section 5(1)(ac)
  - section 5(1)(ad)
  - section 5(1)(ae)
  - section 5(1A)(c)
  - section 5(1)(ag)
  - section 5(1)(ba)

## Type 2

All other weapons falling between Type 1 and Type 3

- This would **normally** include a weapon under:
  - section 5(1)(af)
  - section 5(1A)(a)
  (including disguised stun guns when charged under that section)

Ammunition under:

- section 5(1)(c), 5(1A)(b) and (d)–(g) (where not at Type 3)

## Type 3

Weapon that is not designed to be lethal

- This would **normally** include a weapon under:
  - section 5(1)(b)

Very small quantity of ammunition

## Culpability – Other culpability factors

The court should weigh all the factors set out below in determining the offender's culpability.

### High culpability
- Offender uses firearm/ammunition for a criminal purpose
- Offender intends firearm/ammunition to be used for a criminal purpose, or is reckless as to whether it would be so used

### Medium culpability
- Firearm/ammunition produced or used (where not at High culpability)
- Firearm loaded or held with compatible ammunition or stun gun that is charged (where not at High culpability)
- Offender intends firearm/ammunition to be used or is reckless as to whether it would be used (where not at High culpability)

### Lower culpability
- No use or intention to use

**Where there are characteristics present which fall under different levels of culpability, the court should balance these characteristics to reach a fair assessment of the offender's culpability.**

### Culpability category

Identify the final culpability category in the table below, considering both the **Type of weapon** and **Other culpability factors**.

| Other culpability factors | Type of weapon | | |
|---|---|---|---|
| | 1 | 2 | 3 |
| High | Culpability category A | Culpability category A | Culpability category B |
| Medium | Culpability category B | Culpability category B | Culpability category B |
| Lower | Culpability category B | Culpability category C | Culpability category C |

Harm

Harm is assessed by reference to the risk of harm or disorder occurring and/or actual alarm/distress caused.

When considering the risk of harm, relevant considerations may include the location of the offence, the number and vulnerability of people exposed, especially children, and the accessibility and visibility of the weapon.

---

**Category 1**
- Serious alarm/distress caused
- High risk of death or serious physical or psychological harm
- High risk of serious disorder

**Category 2**
- All other cases falling between category 1 and category 3 because:
  - Factors in both 1 and 3 are present which balance each other out; and/or
  - The harm falls between the factors as described in 1 and 3

**Category 3**
- No/minimal alarm/distress caused
- No/minimal risk of death or serious physical or psychological harm
- No/minimal risk of serious disorder

---

Where there are characteristics present which fall under different levels of harm, the court should balance these characteristics to reach a fair assessment of the harm.

Having determined the category at step 1, the court should use the corresponding starting point to reach a sentence within the category range below. The starting point applies to all offenders irrespective of plea or previous convictions.

Table 1 should be used if the offence is subject to statutory minimum sentencing provisions.

Table 2 should be used for all other cases.

See step 3 for details of the minimum sentencing provisions and the approach to be taken to consideration of exceptional circumstances.

TABLE 1: Offences subject to the statutory minimum sentence (Section 5(1)(a), (ab), (aba), (ac), (ad), (ae), (af), (c), section 5(1A)(a))

| Harm | Culpability | | |
|---|---|---|---|
| | A | B | C |
| Category 1 | Starting point 8 years' custody | Starting point 7 years' custody | Starting point 6 years' custody |
| | Category range 7–10 years' custody | Category range 6–8 years' custody | Category range 5–7 years' custody |
| Category 2 | Starting point 7 years' custody | Starting point 6 years' custody | Starting point 5 years 6 months' custody |
| | Category range 6–8 years' custody | Category range 5–7 years' custody | Category range 5–7 years' custody |
| Category 3 | Starting point 6 years' custody | Starting point 5 years 6 months' custody | Starting point 5 years' custody |
| | Category range 5–7 years' custody | Category range 5–7 years' custody | Category range 5–6 years' custody |

**TABLE 2: Offences not subject to the statutory minimum sentence**

| Harm | Culpability | | |
|---|---|---|---|
| | A | B | C |
| Category 1 | **Starting point**<br>3 years' custody | **Starting point**<br>2 years' custody | **Starting point**<br>1 year's custody |
| | **Category range**<br>2–5 years' custody | **Category range**<br>1–3 years' custody | **Category range**<br>High level community order–2 years' custody |
| Category 2 | **Starting point**<br>2 years' custody | **Starting point**<br>1 year's custody | **Starting point**<br>Medium level community order |
| | **Category range**<br>1–3 years' custody | **Category range**<br>High level community order–2 years' custody | **Category range**<br>Band C fine–High level community order |
| Category 3 | **Starting point**<br>1 year's custody | **Starting point**<br>Medium level community order | **Starting point**<br>Band C fine |
| | **Category range**<br>High level community order–2 years' custody | **Category range**<br>Band C fine–High level community order | **Category range**<br>Discharge–Low level community order |

**Fines**

[For the standard schedule of fines see **SG2-5**.]

**Community Orders and Custodial Sentences**

[For the imposition of community orders, including the community orders table, see Imposition of Community and Custodial Sentences at **SG9-2**.

For the imposition of custodial sentences see Imposition of Community and Custodial Sentences at **SG9-3**.]

The following is a **non-exhaustive** list of additional factual elements providing the context of the offence and factors relating to the offender. Identify whether any combination of these, or other relevant factors, should result in an upward or downward adjustment from the sentence arrived at so far. In some cases, having considered these factors, it may be appropriate to move outside the identified category range.

**Factors increasing seriousness**

*Statutory aggravating factors:*

- Previous convictions, having regard to
  a) the **nature** of the offence to which the conviction relates and its **relevance** to the current offence; and
  b) the **time** that has elapsed since the conviction
- Offence committed whilst on bail

*Other aggravating factors:*

- Firearm modified to make it more dangerous
- Steps taken to disguise firearm (where not firearm under section 5(1A)(a))
- Firearm/ammunition kept with multiple weapons and/or substantial quantity of ammunition (See step 6 on totality when sentencing more than one offence.)
- Offence was committed as part of a group
- Involvement by the offender of others through coercion, intimidation or exploitation
- Abuse of position as registered firearms dealer, certificate holder or other authorised user
- Commission of offence whilst under the influence of alcohol or drugs
- Offender prohibited from possessing weapon or ammunition because of previous conviction (Care should be taken to avoid double counting matters taken into account when considering previous convictions. See step 6 on totality when sentencing more than one offence.)
- Failure to comply with current court orders
- Offence committed on licence or post sentence supervision

**Factors reducing seriousness or reflecting personal mitigation**

- No previous convictions or no relevant/recent convictions
- Good character and/or exemplary conduct
- Firearm incomplete or incapable of being discharged (including stun gun that is not charged and not held with a functioning charger)
- No knowledge or suspicion that item possessed was firearm/ammunition
- No knowledge or suspicion that firearm/ammunition is prohibited
- Held on behalf of another through coercion, intimidation, or exploitation
- Voluntary surrender of firearm/ammunition
- Offender co-operated with investigation and/or made early admissions
- Remorse
- Serious medical condition requiring urgent, intensive or long-term treatment
- Age and/or lack of maturity
- Mental disorder or learning disability
- Sole or primary carer for dependent relatives

### STEP 3   Minimum term and exceptional circumstances

**Minimum term**

1. Where the minimum term provisions under section 311 and Schedule 20 of the Sentencing Code apply, a court must impose a sentence of at least five years' custody irrespective of plea **unless the court is of the opinion that there are exceptional circumstances relating to the offence or to the offender which justify its not doing so.**

*Applicability*

2. The minimum term provisions apply when sentencing an offence under the Firearms Act 1968, section 5(1)(a), (ab), (aba), (ac), (ad), (ae), (af) or (c) or section 5(1A)(a) committed on or after 22 January 2004. Note: the minimum term provisions do **not** apply to offences charged as conspiracies.
3. The minimum term applies to *all* such offences including the first offence. Where it applies the sentence cannot be reduced below the minimum term for a guilty plea (see Step 5 – Reduction for guilty pleas).
4. The minimum term of five years applies to offenders aged 18 or over **when the offence was committed.** See below for guidance when sentencing offenders aged under 18 when the offence was committed.
5. Where the minimum term applies, this should be stated expressly.

**Exceptional circumstances**

6. In considering whether there are exceptional circumstances that would justify not imposing the statutory minimum sentence, the court must have regard to:
   - the particular circumstances of the offence **and**
   - the particular circumstances of the offender
   either of which may give rise to exceptional circumstances
7. Where the factual circumstances are disputed, the procedure should follow that of a Newton hearing: see Criminal Practice Directions VII: Sentencing B.
8. Where the issue of exceptional circumstances has been raised the court should give a clear explanation as to why those circumstances have or have not been found.

*Principles*

9. Circumstances are exceptional if the imposition of the minimum term would result in an arbitrary and disproportionate sentence.
10. The circumstances must truly be exceptional. It is important that courts do not undermine the intention of Parliament and the deterrent purpose of the minimum term provisions by too readily accepting exceptional circumstances.
11. The court should look at all of the circumstances of the case taken together. A single striking factor may amount to exceptional circumstances, or it may be the collective impact of all of the relevant circumstances.
12. The mere presence of one or more of the following should not in itself be regarded as exceptional:
    - One or more lower culpability factors
    - The type of weapon or ammunition falling under type 2 or 3
    - One or more mitigating factors
    - A plea of guilty

*Where exceptional circumstances are found*

13. If there are exceptional circumstances that justify not imposing the statutory minimum sentence then the court **must impose either a shorter custodial sentence than the statutory minimum provides or an alternative sentence.** Note: a guilty plea reduction applies in the normal way if the minimum term is not imposed (see Step 5 – Reduction for guilty pleas).

14. The court may find it useful to refer to the range of sentences under culpability A of Table 2 (Offences not subject to the statutory minimum sentence) in step 2 above. The court should impose a sentence that is appropriate to the individual case.

### Sentencing offenders aged under 18 at the date of the offence

1. Where the offender is aged 16 or 17 **when the offence was committed**, the minimum term is three years' custody. Where the offender is under 16 **when the offence was committed**, the minimum term does not apply.

2. Subject to the minimum term, where the offender is aged under 18 **at the date of conviction** the court should determine the sentence in accordance with the Sentencing Children and Young People guideline [**SG8-1–SG8-11**] particularly paragraphs 6.42–6.49 on custodial sentences.

3. This guidance states at paragraph 6.46: "When considering the relevant adult guideline, the court may feel it appropriate to apply a sentence broadly within the region of half to two thirds of the adult sentence for those aged 15–17 and allow a greater reduction for those aged under 15. This is only a rough guide and must not be applied mechanistically. In most cases when considering the appropriate reduction from the adult sentence the emotional and developmental age and maturity of the child or young person is of at least equal importance as their chronological age."

4. The considerations above on exceptional circumstances relating to the offence or offender apply equally when sentencing offenders aged 16 or 17 at the date of the offence.

### STEP 4  Consider any factors which indicate a reduction for assistance to the prosecution

The court should take into account section 74 of the Sentencing Code (reduction in sentence for assistance to prosecution) and any other rule of law by virtue of which an offender may receive a discounted sentence in consequence of assistance given (or offered) to the prosecutor or investigator.

### STEP 5  Reduction for guilty pleas

The court should take account of any potential reduction for a guilty plea in accordance with section 73 of the Sentencing Code and the Reduction in Sentence for a Guilty Plea guideline [see **SG5-1–SG5-12**].

Where a **minimum sentence** has been imposed under section 311 of the Sentencing Code, the court must ensure that any reduction for a guilty plea does not reduce the sentence to less than the required minimum term.

### STEP 6  Totality principle

If sentencing an offender for more than one offence, or where the offender is already serving a sentence, consider whether the total sentence is just and proportionate to the overall offending behaviour in accordance with the *Totality* guideline [see **SG4**].

### STEP 7  Ancillary orders

In all cases the court should consider whether to make ancillary orders.

### Forfeiture and destruction of firearms and cancellation of certificate

The court should consider ordering forfeiture or disposal of any firearm or ammunition and the cancellation of any firearms certificate. Section 52 of the Firearms Act 1968 provides for the forfeiture and disposal of firearms and the cancellation of firearms and shotgun certificates where a person is convicted of this offence **and** is given a custodial sentence **or** a community order containing a requirement not to possess, use or carry a firearm.

### Serious Crime Prevention Order

The Crown Court may consider the criteria in section 19 of the Serious Crime Act 2007 for the imposition of a Serious Crime Prevention Order.

### STEP 8  Reasons

Section 52 of the Sentencing Code imposes a duty to give reasons for, and explain the effect of, the sentence.

### STEP 9  Consideration for time spent on bail (tagged curfew)

The court must consider whether to give credit for time spent on bail in accordance with section 240A of the Criminal Justice Act 2003 and section 325 of the Sentencing Code.

**Category 1**
- Severe physical harm caused
- Severe psychological harm caused

**Category 2**
- Serious physical harm
- Serious psychological harm
- High risk of death or severe physical or psychological harm
- High risk of serious disorder

**Category 3**
- Alarm/distress caused
- All other cases not falling into 1 or 2

Where there are characteristics present which fall under different levels of harm, the court should balance these characteristics to reach a fair assessment of the harm.

Where separate charges apply, for example in relation to any death or injury caused, the court should have regard to totality (see step 7).

**STEP 2 Starting point and category range**

Having determined the category at step 1, the court should use the corresponding starting point to reach a sentence within the category range below. The starting point applies to all offenders irrespective of plea or previous convictions.

This offence may be subject to a statutory minimum sentence.

See step 3 for details of the minimum sentencing provisions and the approach to be taken to consideration of exceptional circumstances.

| Harm | Culpability | | |
|---|---|---|---|
| | **A** | **B** | **C** |
| Category 1 | **Starting point** 18 years' custody | **Starting point** 14 years' custody | **Starting point** 10 years' custody |
| | **Category range** 16–22 years' custody | **Category range** 11–17 years' custody | **Category range** 8–12 years' custody |
| Category 2 | **Starting point** 14 years' custody | **Starting point** 10 years' custody | **Starting point** 7 years' custody |
| | **Category range** 11–17 years' custody | **Category range** 8–12 years' custody | **Category range** 5–9 years' custody |
| Category 3 | **Starting point** 10 years' custody | **Starting point** 7 years' custody | **Starting point** 5 years' custody |
| | **Category range** 8–12 years' custody | **Category range** 5–9 years' custody | **Category range** 4–7 years' custody |

**Custodial sentences**

**In cases involving multiple counts of serious offending, sentences above the top of the range may be justified having regard to totality (see step 7).**

The following is a **non-exhaustive** list of additional factual elements providing the context of the offence and factors relating to the offender. Identify whether any combination of these, or other relevant factors, should result in an upward or downward adjustment from the sentence arrived at so far. In some cases, having considered these factors, it may be appropriate to move outside the identified category range.

[For the imposition of custodial sentences see Imposition of Community and Custodial Sentences at SG9-3.]

*Firearms Act 1968, s.16*

**Effective from:** 01 January 2021

Indictable only
Maximum: Life imprisonment
Offence range: 4–22 years' custody

This is a Schedule 19 offence for the purposes of sections 274 and 285 (required life sentence for offence carrying life sentence) of the Sentencing Code.

For offences committed on or after 3 December 2012, this is an offence listed in Part 1 of Schedule 15 for the purposes of sections 273 and 283 (life sentence for second listed offence) of the Sentencing Code.

This is a specified offence listed in Part 1 of Schedule 18 for the purposes of sections 266 and 279 (extended sentence for certain violent, sexual or terrorism offences) of the Sentencing Code.

**STEP 1  Determining the offence category**

The court should determine the offence category with reference **only** to the factors listed in the tables below. In order to determine the category the court should assess **culpability** and **harm.**

The court should weigh all the factors set out below in determining the offender's culpability.

**Where there are characteristics present which fall under different levels of culpability, the court should balance these characteristics to reach a fair assessment of the offender's culpability.**

**Culpability demonstrated by one or more of the following:**

---

**A – High culpability:**
- Sophisticated nature of offence/significant planning
- Leading role where offending is part of a group activity
- Distribution or supply of firearms on a significant scale
- Firearm discharged
- Prolonged incident

**B – Medium culpability:**
- Significant role where offending is part of a group activity
- Some degree of planning
- Firearm loaded or held with compatible ammunition but not discharged
- Other cases falling between culpability A and C because:
  - Factors are present in A and C which balance each other out and/or
  - The offender's culpability falls between the factors as described in A and C

**C – Lower culpability:**
- Lesser role where offending is part of group activity
- Little or no planning or unsophisticated offending
- Firearm not produced or visible
- Conduct limited in scope and duration

---

**Harm**
**The court should consider the factors set out below to determine the level of harm that has been caused or was risked.**

**This step is assessed by reference to the risk of harm or disorder occurring and/or actual harm caused. When considering the risk of harm, relevant considerations may include the location of the offence, the number and vulnerability of people exposed, especially** children, and the accessibility and visibility of the weapon.

Sentencing Guidelines

> **Category 1**
> - Severe physical harm caused
> - Severe psychological harm caused
>
> **Category 2**
> - Serious physical harm caused
> - Serious psychological harm caused
> - High risk of death or severe physical or psychological harm
> - High risk of serious disorder
>
> **Category 3**
> - Alarm/distress caused
> - All other cases not falling into 1 or 2
>
> **Where there are characteristics present which fall under different levels of harm, the court should balance these characteristics to reach a fair assessment of the harm.**
>
> **Where separate charges apply, for example in relation to any death or injury caused, the court should have regard to totality (see step 7).**

### STEP 2  Starting point and category range

Having determined the category at step 1, the court should use the corresponding starting point to reach a sentence within the category range below. The starting point applies to all offenders irrespective of plea or previous convictions.

Table 1 should be used if the offence was committed using a firearm

Table 2 should be used if the offence was committed using an imitation firearm

This offence may be subject to a statutory minimum sentence.

See step 3 for details of the minimum sentencing provisions and the approach to be taken to consideration of exceptional circumstances.

### TABLE 1: Firearm

| Harm | Culpability | | |
|---|---|---|---|
| | **A** | **B** | **C** |
| Category 1 | **Starting point** 8 years' custody | **Starting point** 6 years' custody | **Starting point** 4 years' custody |
| | **Category range** 7–9 years' custody | **Category range** 4–8 years' custody | **Category range** 3–6 years' custody |
| Category 2 | **Starting point** 6 years' custody | **Starting point** 4 years' custody | **Starting point** 2 years' custody |
| | **Category range** 4–8 years' custody | **Category range** 3–6 years' custody | **Category range** 1–4 years' custody |
| Category 3 | **Starting point** 4 years' custody | **Starting point** 2 years' custody | **Starting point** 1 year 6 months' custody |
| | **Category range** 3–6 years' custody | **Category range** 1–4 years' custody | **Category range** 6 months–2 years' custody |

### TABLE 2: Imitation firearm

| Harm | Culpability | | |
|---|---|---|---|
| | **A** | **B** | **C** |
| Category 1 | **Starting point** 6 years' custody | **Starting point** 4 years' custody | **Starting point** 2 years' custody |
| | **Category range** 4–8 years' custody | **Category range** 3–6 years' custody | **Category range** 1–4 years' custody |

Sentencing Guidelines

| Harm | Culpability | | |
|---|---|---|---|
| | **A** | **B** | **C** |
| Category 2 | **Starting point** 4 years' custody | **Starting point** 2 years' custody | **Starting point** 1 year 6 months' custody |
| | **Category range** 3–6 years' custody | **Category range** 1–4 years' custody | **Category range** 6 months–2 years' custody |
| Category 3 | **Starting point** 2 years' custody | **Starting point** 1 year 6 months' custody | **Starting point** 6 months' custody |
| | **Category range** 1–4 years' custody | **Category range** 6 months–2 years' custody | **Category range** Medium level community order–1 year's custody |

### Community Orders and Custodial Sentences

[For the imposition of community orders, including the community orders table, see Imposition of Community and Custodial Sentences at **SG9-2**.

For the imposition of custodial sentences see Imposition of Community and Custodial Sentences at **SG9-3**.]

The following is a **non-exhaustive** list of additional factual elements providing the context of the offence and factors relating to the offender. Identify whether any combination of these, or other relevant factors, should result in an upward or downward adjustment from the sentence arrived at so far. In some cases, having considered these factors, it may be appropriate to move outside the identified category range.

### Factors increasing seriousness

*Statutory aggravating factors:*

- Previous convictions, having regard to a) the **nature** of the offence to which the conviction relates and its **relevance** to the current offence; and b) the **time** that has elapsed since the conviction
- Offence committed whilst on bail
- Offence motivated by, or demonstrating hostility based on any of the following characteristics or presumed characteristics of the victim: religion, race, disability, sexual orientation or transgender identity

*Other aggravating factors:*

- Firearm is prohibited under section 5 and subject to minimum term (taking care to avoid double counting with minimum term provisions)
- Firearm under section 5(1)(a) (automatic weapon)
- Firearm modified to make it more dangerous
- Steps taken to disguise firearm (where not firearm under section 5(1A)(a))
- Imitation firearm is readily convertible
- Steps taken to make imitation firearm appear more realistic (See step 7 on totality when sentencing for more than one offence.)
- Firearm/ammunition held with multiple weapons and/or substantial quantity of ammunition (See step 7 on totality when sentencing for more than one offence)
- Offence was committed as part of a group (except where already taken into account at step 1)
- Offence committed to further organised criminal activity (except where already taken into account at step 1)
- Expectation of substantial financial gain (except where already taken into account at step 1)
- Attempts to conceal or dispose of the firearm or other evidence
- Serious damage to property caused (See step 7 on totality when sentencing for more than one offence)
- Abuse of position as registered firearms dealer, certificate holder or other authorised user
- Commission of offence whilst under the influence of alcohol or drugs
- Offender prohibited from possessing weapon or ammunition because of previous conviction (Care should be taken to avoid double counting matters taken into account when considering previous convictions. See step 7 on totality when sentencing for more than one offence)
- Failure to comply with current court orders
- Offence committed on licence or post sentence supervision

**Factors reducing seriousness or reflecting personal mitigation**

- No previous convictions or no relevant/recent convictions
- Good character and/or exemplary conduct
- Firearm incomplete or incapable of being discharged (including stun gun that is not charged and not held with a functioning charger)
- Imitation firearm is unrealistic and unconvincing
- Involved through coercion, intimidation, or exploitation
- Voluntary surrender of firearm
- Offender co-operated with investigation and/or made early admissions
- Remorse
- Serious medical condition requiring urgent, intensive or long-term treatment
- Age and/or lack of maturity
- Mental disorder or learning disability
- Sole or primary carer for dependent relatives

### STEP 3  Minimum Term and exceptional circumstances

**Minimum Term**

1. Where the minimum term provisions under section 311 and Schedule 20 of the Sentencing Code apply, a court must impose a sentence of at least five years' custody irrespective of plea **unless the court is of the opinion that there are exceptional circumstances relating to the offence or to the offender which justify its not doing so.**

*Applicability*

2. The minimum terms provisions apply when sentencing offences in respect of a firearm or ammunition specified in section 5(1)(a), (ab), (aba), (ac), (ad), (ae), (af) or (c) or section 5(1A)(a) of the Firearms Act 1968 committed on or after 6 April 2007. Note: the minimum term provisions do **not** apply to offences charged as conspiracies.
3. The minimum term applies to *all* such offences including the first offence, and regardless of plea. Where it applies the sentence cannot be reduced below the minimum term for a guilty plea (see Step 5 – Reduction for guilty pleas).
4. The minimum term of five years applies to offenders aged 18 or over **when the offence was committed**. See below for guidance when sentencing offenders aged under 18 when the offence was committed.
5. Where the minimum term applies, this should be stated expressly.

**Exceptional circumstances**

6. In considering whether there are exceptional circumstances that would justify not imposing the statutory minimum sentence, the court must have regard to:
   - the particular circumstances of the offence **and**
   - the particular circumstances of the offender.
   either of which may give rise to exceptional circumstances
7. Where the factual circumstances are disputed, the procedure should follow that of a Newton hearing: see Criminal Practice Directions VII: Sentencing B [see **CPD.VII.B**].
8. Where the issue of exceptional circumstances has been raised the court should give a clear explanation as to why those circumstances have or have not been found.

*Principles*

9. Circumstances are exceptional if the imposition of the minimum term would result in an arbitrary and disproportionate sentence.
10. The circumstances must truly be exceptional. It is important that courts do not undermine the intention of Parliament and the deterrent purpose of the minimum term provisions by too readily accepting exceptional circumstances.
11. The court should look at all of the circumstances of the case taken together. A single striking factor may amount to exceptional circumstances, or it may be the collective impact of all of the relevant circumstances.
12. The mere presence of one or more of the following should not *in itself* be regarded as exceptional:
    - One or more lower culpability factors
    - One or more mitigating factors
    - A plea of guilty

Sentencing Guidelines

*Where exceptional circumstances are found*

13. If there are exceptional circumstances that justify not imposing the statutory minimum sentence then the court **must impose either a shorter custodial sentence than the statutory minimum provides or an alternative sentence.** Note: a guilty plea reduction applies in the normal way if the minimum term is not imposed (see Step 5 – Reduction for guilty pleas).

### Sentencing offenders aged under 18 at the date of the offence

1. Where the offender is aged 16 or 17 **when the offence was committed**, the minimum term is three years' custody. Where the offender is under 16 **when the offence was committed**, the minimum term does not apply.
2. Subject to the minimum term, where the offender is aged under 18 **at the date of conviction** the court should determine the sentence in accordance with the Sentencing Children and Young People guideline, [**SG8-1–SG8-11**], particularly paragraphs 6.42–6.49 on custodial sentences.
3. This guidance states at paragraph 6.46: "When considering the relevant adult guideline, the court may feel it appropriate to apply a sentence broadly within the region of half to two thirds of the adult sentence for those aged 15–17 and allow a greater reduction for those aged under 15. This is only a rough guide and must not be applied mechanistically. In most cases when considering the appropriate reduction from the adult sentence the emotional and developmental age and maturity of the child or young person is of at least equal importance as their chronological age."
4. The considerations above on exceptional circumstances relating to the offence or offender apply equally when sentencing offenders aged 16 or 17 at the date of the offence.

### STEP 4   Consider any factors which indicate a reduction for assistance to the prosecution

The court should take into account section 74 of the Sentencing Code (reduction in sentence for assistance to prosecution) and any other rule of law by virtue of which an offender may receive a discounted sentence in consequence of assistance given (or offered) to the prosecutor or investigator.

### STEP 5   Reduction for guilty pleas

The court should take account of any reduction for a guilty plea in accordance with section 73 of the Sentencing Code and the Reduction in sentence for a guilty plea guideline [see **SG5-1–SG5-12**].

Where a **minimum sentence** has been imposed under section 311 of the Sentencing Code, the court must ensure that any reduction for a guilty plea does not reduce the sentence to less than the required minimum term.

### STEP 6   Dangerousness

The court should consider whether having regard to the criteria contained in Chapter 6 of Part 10 of the Sentencing Code it would be appropriate to impose an extended sentence (sections 266 and 279).

### STEP 7   Totality principle

If sentencing an offender for more than one offence, or where the offender is already serving a sentence, consider whether the total sentence is just and proportionate to the overall offending behaviour in accordance with the *Totality* guideline [see **SG4**].

### STEP 8   Ancillary orders

In all cases the court should consider whether to make ancillary orders.

### Forfeiture and destruction of firearms and cancellation of certificate

The court should consider ordering forfeiture or disposal of any firearm or ammunition and the cancellation of any firearms certificate. Section 52 of the Firearms Act 1968 provides for the forfeiture and disposal of firearms and the cancellation of firearms and shotgun certificates where a person is convicted of this offence **and** is given a custodial sentence **or** a community order containing a requirement not to possess, use or carry a firearm.

### STEP 9   Reasons

Section 52 of the Sentencing Code imposes a duty to give reasons for, and explain the effect of, the sentence.

### STEP 10   Consideration for time spent on bail (tagged curfew)

The court must consider whether to give credit for time spent on bail in accordance with section 240A of the Criminal Justice Act 2003 and section 325 of the Sentencing Code.

**STEP 9 Reasons**

Section 52 of the Sentencing Code imposes a duty to give reasons for, and explain the effect of, the sentence.

**STEP 10 Consideration for time spent on bail (tagged curfew)**

The court must consider whether to give credit for time spent on bail in accordance with section 240A of the Criminal Justice Act 2003 and section 325 of the Sentencing Code.

**SG34-6** FIREARMS – POSSESSION WITH INTENT TO CAUSE FEAR OF VIOLENCE

*Firearms Act 1968, s.16A*

**Effective from:** 01 January 2021

**Possession of firearm or imitation firearm with intent to cause fear of violence**

Indictable only
Maximum: 10 years' custody
Offence range: Medium level community order–9 years' custody

This is a specified offence listed in Part 1 of Schedule 18 for the purposes of sections 266 and 279 (extended sentence for certain violent, sexual or terrorism offences) of the Sentencing Code.

**STEP 1 Determining the offence category**

The court should determine the offence category with reference **only** to the factors listed in the tables below. In order to determine the category the court should assess **culpability** and **harm.**

The court should weigh all the factors set out below in determining the offender's culpability.

**Where there are characteristics present which fall under different levels of culpability, the court should balance these characteristics to reach a fair assessment of the offender's culpability.**

**Culpability demonstrated by one or more of the following:**

| |
|---|
| **A – High culpability:**<br>• Intention falling just short of intent to endanger life<br>• Conduct intended to maximise fear or distress<br>• Sophisticated nature of offence/significant planning<br>• Leading role where offending is part of a group activity<br>• Firearm or imitation firearm discharged<br>• Prolonged incident |
| **B – Medium culpability:**<br>• Firearm or imitation firearm loaded or held with compatible ammunition but not discharged<br>• Significant role where offending is part of a group activity<br>• Some degree of planning<br>• Other cases falling between culpability A and C because:<br>  o Factors are present in A and C which balance each other out and/or<br>  o The offender's culpability falls between the factors as described in A and C |
| **C – Lower culpability:**<br>• No intention to cause injury to persons<br>• Lesser role where offending is part of group activity<br>• Little or no planning or unsophisticated offending<br>• Firearm or imitation firearm not produced or visible<br>• Conduct limited in scope and duration |

**Harm**

The court should consider the factors set out below to determine the level of harm that has been caused or was risked. This step is assessed by reference to the risk of harm or disorder occurring and/or actual harm caused. When considering the risk of harm, relevant considerations may include the location of the offence, the number and vulnerability of people exposed, especially children and the accessibility and visibility of the weapon.

*Where exceptional circumstances are found*

13. If there are exceptional circumstances that justify not imposing the statutory minimum sentence then the court **must impose either a shorter custodial sentence than the statutory minimum provides or an alternative sentence.** Note: a guilty plea reduction applies in the normal way if the minimum term is not imposed (see Step 5 – Reduction for guilty pleas).

### Sentencing offenders aged under 18 at the date of the offence

1. Where the offender is aged 16 or 17 **when the offence was committed**, the minimum term is three years' custody. Where the offender is under 16 **when the offence was committed**, the minimum term does not apply.

2. Subject to the minimum term, where the offender is aged under 18 **at the date of conviction** the court should determine the sentence in accordance with the Sentencing Children and Young People guideline [**SG8-1–SG8-11**], particularly paragraphs 6.42–6.49 on custodial sentences.

3. This guidance states at paragraph 6.46: "When considering the relevant adult guideline, the court may feel it appropriate to apply a sentence broadly within the region of half to two thirds of the adult sentence for those aged 15–17 and allow a greater reduction for those aged under 15. This is only a rough guide and must not be applied mechanistically. In most cases when considering the appropriate reduction from the adult sentence the emotional and developmental age and maturity of the child or young person is of at least equal importance as their chronological age."

4. The considerations above on exceptional circumstances relating to the offence or offender apply equally when sentencing offenders aged 16 or 17 at the date of the offence.

### STEP 4  Consider any factors which indicate a reduction for assistance to the prosecution

The court should take into account section 74 of the Sentencing Code (reduction in sentence for assistance to prosecution) and any other rule of law by virtue of which an offender may receive a discounted sentence in consequence of assistance given (or offered) to the prosecutor or investigator.

### STEP 5  Reduction for guilty pleas

The court should take account of any reduction for a guilty plea in accordance with section 73 of the Sentencing Code and the Reduction in sentence for a guilty plea guideline [see **SG5-1–SG5-12**].

Where a **mandatory minimum sentence** has been imposed under section 311 of the Sentencing Code, the court must ensure that any reduction for a guilty plea does not reduce the sentence to less than the mandatory minimum.

### STEP 6  Dangerousness

The court should consider:

1) whether having regard to the criteria contained in Chapter 6 of Part 10 of the Sentencing Code it would be appropriate to impose a life sentence (sections 274 and 285) or an extended sentence (sections 266 and 279) and

2) whether having regard to sections 273 and 283 of the Sentencing Code it would be appropriate to impose a life sentence.

When sentencing offenders to a life sentence under these provisions, the notional determinate sentence should be used as the basis for the setting of a minimum term.

### STEP 7  Totality principle

If sentencing an offender for more than one offence, or where the offender is already serving a sentence, consider whether the total sentence is just and proportionate to the overall offending behaviour in accordance with the *Totality* guideline [see **SG4**].

### STEP 8  Ancillary orders

In all cases the court should consider whether to make ancillary orders.

### Forfeiture and destruction of firearms and cancellation of certificate

The court should consider ordering forfeiture or disposal of any firearm or ammunition and the cancellation of any firearms certificate. Section 52 of the Firearms Act 1968 provides for the forfeiture and disposal of firearms and the cancellation of firearms and shotgun certificates where a person is convicted of this offence **and** is given a custodial sentence **or** a community order containing a requirement not to possess, use or carry a firearm.

- Firearm incomplete or incapable of being discharged (including stun gun that is not charged and not held with a functioning charger)
- Imitation firearm is unrealistic and unconvincing
- Involved through coercion, intimidation, or exploitation
- Voluntary surrender of firearm
- Offender co-operated with investigation and/or made early admissions
- Remorse
- Serious medical condition requiring urgent, intensive or long-term treatment
- Age and/or lack of maturity
- Mental disorder or learning disability
- Sole or primary carer for dependent relatives

### STEP 3 Minimum term and exceptional circumstances

### Minimum Term

1. Where the minimum term provisions under section 311 and Schedule 20 of the Sentencing Code apply, a court must impose a sentence of at least five years' custody irrespective of plea **unless the court is of the opinion that there are exceptional circumstances relating to the offence or to the offender which justify its not doing so.**

*Applicability*

2. The minimum terms provisions apply when sentencing offences in respect of a firearm or ammunition specified in section 5(1)(a), (ab), (aba), (ac), (ad), (ae), (af) or (c) or section 5(1A)(a) of the Firearms Act 1968 committed on or after 6 April 2007. Note: the minimum term provisions do **not** apply to offences charged as conspiracies.
3. The minimum term applies to *all* such offences including the first offence, and regardless of plea. Where it applies the sentence cannot be reduced below the minimum term for a guilty plea (see Step 5 – Reduction for guilty pleas).
4. The minimum term of five years applies to offenders aged 18 or over **when the offence was committed.** See below for guidance when sentencing offenders aged under 18 when the offence was committed.
5. Where the minimum term applies, this should be stated expressly.

### Exceptional circumstances

6. In considering whether there are exceptional circumstances that would justify not imposing the statutory minimum sentence, the court must have regard to:
   - the particular circumstances of the offence **and**
   - the particular circumstances of the offender.
   either of which may give rise to exceptional circumstances
7. Where the factual circumstances are disputed, the procedure should follow that of a Newton hearing: see Criminal Practice Directions VII: Sentencing B [see **CPD.VII.B**].
8. Where the issue of exceptional circumstances has been raised the court should give a clear explanation as to why those circumstances have or have not been found.

*Principles*

9. Circumstances are exceptional if the imposition of the minimum term would result in an arbitrary and disproportionate sentence.
10. The circumstances must truly be exceptional. It is important that courts do not undermine the intention of Parliament and the deterrent purpose of the minimum term provisions by too readily accepting exceptional circumstances.
11. The court should look at all of the circumstances of the case taken together. A single striking factor may amount to exceptional circumstances, or it may be the collective impact of all of the relevant circumstances.
12. The mere presence of one or more of the following should not *in itself* be regarded as exceptional:
    - One or more lower culpability factors
    - One or more mitigating factors
    - A plea of guilty

| Harm | Culpability | | |
|---|---|---|---|
| | A | B | C |
| Category 2 | **Starting point**<br>7 years' custody | **Starting point**<br>4 years' custody | **Starting point**<br>2 years' custody |
| | **Category range**<br>5–9 years' custody | **Category range**<br>2–6 years' custody | **Category range**<br>1–3 years' custody |
| Category 3 | **Starting point**<br>4 years' custody | **Starting point**<br>2 years' custody | **Starting point**<br>1 year's custody |
| | **Category range**<br>2–6 years' custody | **Category range**<br>1–3 years' custody | **Category range**<br>High level community<br>order–2 years' custody |

## Community Orders and Custodial Sentences

[For the imposition of community orders, including the community orders table, see Imposition of Community and Custodial Sentences at **SG9-2**.

For the imposition of custodial sentences see Imposition of Community and Custodial Sentences at **SG9-3**.]

The following is a **non-exhaustive** list of additional factual elements providing the context of the offence and factors relating to the offender. Identify whether any combination of these, or other relevant factors, should result in an upward or downward adjustment from the sentence arrived at so far. In some cases, having considered these factors, it may be appropriate to move outside the identified category range.

### Factors increasing seriousness

*Statutory aggravating factors:*
- Previous convictions,  having regard to
  a) the **nature** of the offence to which the conviction relates and its **relevance** to the current offence; and
  b) the **time** that has elapsed since the conviction
- Offence committed whilst on bail
- Offence motivated by, or demonstrating hostility based on any of the following characteristics or presumed characteristics of the victim: religion, race, disability, sexual orientation or transgender identity

*Other aggravating factors:*
- Firearm prohibited under section 5 and subject to minimum term (taking care to avoid double counting with minimum term provisions)
- Firearm under section 5(1)(a) (automatic weapon)
- Firearm modified to make it more dangerous
- Steps taken to disguise firearm (where not firearm under section 5(1A)(a))
- Imitation firearm is readily convertible
- Steps taken to make imitation firearm appear more realistic (See step 7 on totality when sentencing for more than one offence.)
- Firearm/ammunition held with multiple weapons and/or substantial quantity of ammunition (See step 7 on totality when sentencing for more than one offence)
- Offence was committed as part of a group (except where already taken into account at step 1)
- Offender's actions resulted in a suspect avoiding arrest
- Expectation of substantial financial gain (except where already taken into account at step 1)
- Attempts to conceal or dispose of the firearm or other evidence
- Serious damage to property caused (See step 7 on totality when sentencing for more than one offence)
- Abuse of position as registered firearms dealer, certificate holder or other authorised user
- Commission of offence whilst under the influence of alcohol or drugs
- Offender prohibited from possessing weapon or ammunition because of previous conviction (Care should be taken to avoid double counting matters taken into account when considering previous convictions. See step 7 on totality when sentencing for more than one offence.)
- Failure to comply with current court orders
- Offence committed on licence or post sentence supervision

### Factors reducing seriousness or reflecting personal mitigation
- No previous convictions or no relevant/recent convictions
- Good character and/or exemplary conduct

**Category 1**
- Severe physical harm caused
- Severe psychological harm caused

**Category 2**
- Serious physical harm caused
- Serious psychological harm caused
- High risk of death or severe physical or psychological harm
- High risk of serious disorder

**Category 3**
- Alarm/distress caused
- All other cases not falling into 1 or 2

Where there are characteristics present which fall under different levels of harm, the court should balance these characteristics to reach a fair assessment of the harm.

Where separate charges apply, for example in relation to any death or injury caused, the court should have regard to totality (see step 7).

### STEP 2 Starting point and category range

Having determined the category at step 1, the court should use the corresponding starting point to reach a sentence within the category range below. The starting point applies to all offenders irrespective of plea or previous convictions.

Table 1 should be used if the offence was committed using a firearm

Table 2 should be used if the offence was committed using an imitation firearm

This offence may be subject to a statutory minimum sentence

See step 3 for details of the minimum sentencing provisions and the approach to be taken to consideration of exceptional circumstances.

### TABLE 1: Firearm

| Harm | Culpability | | |
| --- | --- | --- | --- |
| | **A** | **B** | **C** |
| Category 1 | **Starting point** 12 years' custody | **Starting point** 9 years' custody | **Starting point** 7 years' custody |
| | **Category range** 10–16 years' custody | **Category range** 7–11 years' custody | **Category range** 5–9 years' custody |
| Category 2 | **Starting point** 9 years' custody | **Starting point** 7 years' custody | **Starting point** 4 years' custody |
| | **Category range** 7–11 years' custody | **Category range** 5–9 years' custody | **Category range** 2–6 years' custody |
| Category 3 | **Starting point** 7 years' custody | **Starting point** 4 years' custody | **Starting point** 2 years' custody |
| | **Category range** 5–9 years' custody | **Category range** 2–6 years' custody | **Category range** 1–3 years' custody |

### TABLE 2: Imitation firearm

| Harm | Culpability | | |
| --- | --- | --- | --- |
| | **A** | **B** | **C** |
| Category 1 | **Starting point** 9 years' custody | **Starting point** 7 years' custody | **Starting point** 4 years' custody |
| | **Category range** 7–11 years' custody | **Category range** 5–9 years' custody | **Category range** 2–6 years' custody |

FIREARMS – POSSESSION WITH INTENT – OTHER OFFENCES                    **SG34-5**

*Firearms Act 1968, s.17(1), Firearms Act 1968, s.17(2), Firearms Act 1968, s.18*

**Effective from:** 01 January 2021

**Use of firearm or imitation firearm to resist arrest**, Firearms Act 1968 (section 17(1))

**Possession of firearm or imitation firearm while committing a Schedule 1 offence**, Firearms Act 1968 (section 17(2))

**Carrying firearm or imitation firearm with criminal intent**, Firearms Act 1968 (section 18)

Indictable only
Maximum: Life imprisonment
Offence range: High level community order–16 years' custody

These are Schedule 19 offences for the purposes of sections 274 and 285 (required life sentence for offence carrying life sentence) of the Sentencing Code.

For offences committed on or after 3 December 2012, these are offences listed in Part 1 of Schedule 15 for the purposes of sections 273 and 283 (life sentence for second listed offence) of the Sentencing Code.

These are specified offences listed in Part 1 of Schedule 18 for the purposes of sections 266 and 279 (extended sentence for certain violent, sexual or terrorism offences) of the Sentencing Code.

STEP 1   Determining the offence category

The court should determine the offence category with reference **only** to the factors listed in the tables below. In order to determine the category the court should assess **culpability** and **harm**.

The court should weigh all the factors set out below in determining the offender's culpability.

**Where there are characteristics present which fall under different levels of culpability, the court should balance these characteristics to reach a fair assessment of the offender's culpability.**

**Culpability demonstrated by one or more of the following:**

*A – High culpability:*
• Sophisticated nature of offence/significant planning
• Leading role where offending is part of a group activity
• Firearm or imitation firearm discharged
• Prolonged incident
• Conduct intended to maximise fear or distress
• Serious nature of intended or actual associated offence

*B – Medium culpability:*
• Firearm or imitation firearm loaded or held with compatible ammunition but not discharged
• Significant role where offending is part of a group activity
• Some degree of planning
• Other cases falling between culpability A and C because:
   • Factors are present in A and C which balance each other out and/or
   • The offender's culpability falls between the factors as described in A and C

*C – Lower culpability:*
• No intention to cause injury to persons
• Lesser role where offending is part of group activity
• Little or no planning or unsophisticated offending
• Conduct limited in scope and duration
• Firearm or imitation firearm not produced or visible
• Less serious nature of intended offence

Harm
The court should consider the factors set out below to determine the level of harm that has been caused or was risked.

This step is assessed by reference to the risk of harm or disorder occurring and/or actual harm caused.

When considering the risk of harm, relevant considerations may include the number and vulnerability of people exposed, especially children, accessibility and visibility of the weapon, and the location of the offence.

Sentencing Guidelines

**Factors increasing seriousness**

*Statutory aggravating factors:*

- Previous convictions, having regard to
  a) the **nature** of the offence to which the conviction relates and its **relevance** to the current offence; and
  b) the **time** that has elapsed since the conviction
- Offence committed whilst on bail
- Offence motivated by, or demonstrating hostility based on any of the following characteristics or presumed characteristics of the victim: religion, race, disability, sexual orientation or transgender identity

*Other aggravating factors:*

- Firearm under section 5(1)(a) (automatic weapon)
- Firearm modified to make it more dangerous
- Steps taken to disguise firearm (where not firearm under section 5(1A)(a))
- Firearm/ammunition held with multiple weapons and/or substantial quantity of ammunition (See step 7 on totality when sentencing more than one offence)
- Offence was committed as part of a group (except where already taken into account at step 1)
- Offence committed to further organised criminal activity (except where already taken into account at step 1)
- Expectation of substantial financial gain (except where already taken into account at step 1)
- Attempts to conceal or dispose of the firearm or other evidence
- Serious damage to property caused (See step 7 on totality when sentencing more than one offence)
- Abuse of position as registered firearms dealer, certificate holder or other authorised user
- Commission of offence whilst under the influence of alcohol or drugs
- Offender prohibited from possessing weapon or ammunition because of previous conviction (Care should be taken to avoid double counting matters taken into account when considering previous convictions. See step 7 on totality when sentencing more than one offence)
- Failure to comply with current court orders
- Offence committed on licence or post sentence supervision

**Factors reducing seriousness or reflecting personal mitigation**

- No previous convictions or no relevant/recent convictions
- Good character and/or exemplary conduct
- Firearm incomplete or incapable of being discharged
- Firearm/ammunition not prohibited under section 5
- Involved through coercion, intimidation, or exploitation
- Voluntary surrender of firearm/ammunition
- Offender co-operated with investigation and/or made early admissions
- Remorse
- Serious medical condition requiring urgent, intensive or long-term treatment
- Age and/or lack of maturity
- Mental disorder or learning disability
- Sole or primary carer for dependent relatives

### STEP 3  Minimum Term and exceptional circumstances

**Minimum Term**

1. Where the minimum term provisions under section 311 and Schedule 20 of the Sentencing Code apply, a court must impose a sentence of at least five years' custody irrespective of plea **unless the court is of the opinion that there are exceptional circumstances relating to the offence or to the offender which justify its not doing so.**

*Applicability*

2. The minimum terms provisions apply when sentencing offences in respect of a firearm or ammunition specified in section 5(1)(a), (ab), (aba), (ac), (ad), (ae), (af) or (c) or section 5(1A)(a) of the Firearms Act 1968 committed on or after 6 April 2007. Note: the minimum term provisions do **not** apply to offences charged as conspiracies.

3. The minimum term applies to *all* such offences including the first offence, and regardless of plea. Where it applies the sentence cannot be reduced below the minimum term for a guilty plea (see Step 5 – Reduction for guilty pleas).

4. The minimum term of five years applies to offenders aged 18 or over **when the offence was committed**. See below for guidance when sentencing offenders aged under 18 when the offence was committed.

5. Where the minimum term applies, this should be stated expressly.

**Exceptional circumstances**

6. In considering whether there are exceptional circumstances that would justify not imposing the statutory minimum sentence, the court must have regard to:
   • the particular circumstances of the offence **and**
   • the particular circumstances of the offender.
   either of which may give rise to exceptional circumstances

7. Where the factual circumstances are disputed, the procedure should follow that of a Newton hearing: see Criminal Practice Directions VII: Sentencing B [see **CPD.VII.B**].

8. Where the issue of exceptional circumstances has been raised the court should give a clear explanation as to why those circumstances have or have not been found.

*Principles*

9. Circumstances are exceptional if the imposition of the minimum term would result in an arbitrary and disproportionate sentence.

10. The circumstances must truly be exceptional. It is important that courts do not undermine the intention of Parliament and the deterrent purpose of the minimum term provisions by too readily accepting exceptional circumstances.

11. The court should look at all of the circumstances of the case taken together. A single striking factor may amount to exceptional circumstances, or it may be the collective impact of all of the relevant circumstances.

12. The mere presence of one or more of the following should not *in itself* be regarded as exceptional:
   • One or more lower culpability factors
   • One or more mitigating factors
   • A plea of guilty

*Where exceptional circumstances are found*

13. If there are exceptional circumstances that justify not imposing the statutory minimum sentence then the court **must impose either a shorter custodial sentence than the statutory minimum provides or an alternative sentence.** Note: a guilty plea reduction applies in the normal way if the minimum term is not imposed (see Step 5 – Reduction for guilty pleas).

**Sentencing offenders aged under 18 at the date of the offence**

1. Where the offender is aged 16 or 17 **when the offence was committed**, the minimum term is three years' custody. Where the offender is under 16 **when the offence was committed**, the minimum term does not apply.

2. Subject to the minimum term, where the offender is aged under 18 **at the date of conviction** the court should determine the sentence in accordance with the Sentencing Children and Young People guideline [**SG8-1–SG8-11**], particularly paragraphs 6.42–6.49 on custodial sentences.

3. This guidance states at paragraph 6.46: "When considering the relevant adult guideline, the court may feel it appropriate to apply a sentence broadly within the region of half to two thirds of the adult sentence for those aged 15–17 and allow a greater reduction for those aged under 15. This is only a rough guide and must not be applied mechanistically. In most cases when considering the appropriate reduction from the adult sentence the emotional and developmental age and maturity of the child or young person is of at least equal importance as their chronological age."

4. The considerations above on exceptional circumstances relating to the offence or offender apply equally when sentencing offenders aged 16 or 17 at the date of the offence.

**STEP 4 Consider any factors which indicate a reduction for assistance to the prosecution**

The court should take into account section 74 of the Sentencing Code (reduction in sentence for assistance to prosecution) and any other rule of law by virtue of which an offender may receive a discounted sentence in consequence of assistance given (or offered) to the prosecutor or investigator.

**STEP 5 Reduction for guilty pleas**

The court should take account of any potential reduction for a guilty plea in accordance with section 73 of the Sentencing Code and the *Guilty Plea* guideline [**SG5-1–SG5-12**].

Where a **minimum sentence** has been imposed under section 311 of the Sentencing Code, the court must ensure that any reduction for a guilty plea does not reduce the sentence to less than the required minimum term.

## STEP 6  Dangerousness

The court should consider

1) whether having regard to the criteria contained in Chapter 6 of Part 10 of the Sentencing Code it would be appropriate to impose a life sentence (sections 274 and 285) or an extended sentence (sections 266 and 279) and
2) whether having regard to sections 273 and 283 of the Sentencing Code it would be appropriate to impose a life sentence.

When sentencing offenders to a life sentence under these provisions, the notional determinate sentence should be used as the basis for the setting of a minimum term.

## STEP 7  Totality principle

If sentencing an offender for more than one offence, or where the offender is already serving a sentence, consider whether the total sentence is just and proportionate to the overall offending behaviour in accordance with the *Totality* guideline [see **SG4**].

## STEP 8  Ancillary orders

In all cases the court should consider whether to make ancillary orders.

### Forfeiture and destruction of firearms and cancellation of certificate

The court should consider ordering forfeiture or disposal of any firearm or ammunition and the cancellation of any firearms certificate. Section 52 of the Firearms Act 1968 provides for the forfeiture and disposal of firearms and the cancellation of firearms and shotgun certificates where a person is convicted of this offence and is given a custodial sentence or a community order containing a requirement not to possess, use or carry a firearm.

## STEP 9  Reasons

Section 52 of the Sentencing Code imposes a duty to give reasons for, and explain the effect of, the sentence.

## STEP 10  Consideration for time spent on bail (tagged curfew)

The court must consider whether to give credit for time spent on bail in accordance with section 240A of the Criminal Justice Act 2003 and section 325 of the Sentencing Code.

FIREARMS – POSSESSION WITHOUT CERTIFICATE                              **SG34-8**

*Firearms Act 1968, s.1(1)(a), Firearms Act 1968, s.1(1)(b), Firearms Act 1968, s.2(1)*

**Effective from:** 01 January 2021

**Possession, purchase or acquisition of a firearm without a certificate**, Firearms Act 1968 (section 1(1)(a))

**Possession, purchase or acquisition of ammunition without a certificate**, Firearms Act 1968 (section 1(1)(b))

**Possession, purchase or acquisition of a shotgun without a certificate**, Firearms Act 1968 (section 2(1))

Triable either way
Maximum: 5 years' custody, or 7 years for the section 1(1) offence where it is aggravated within the meaning of section 4(4) of the Act (shortened shotgun or converted firearm)
Offence range: Discharge–4 years 6 months' custody

## STEP 1  Determining the offence category

The court should determine the offence category with reference **only** to the factors listed in the tables below. In order to determine the category the court should assess **culpability** and **harm**.

### Culpability – Type of weapon

Use the table below to identify an initial culpability category based on the **type of weapon** only. This assessment focuses on the nature of the weapon itself only, not whether the weapon was loaded or in working order.

Where the weapon or ammunition does not fall squarely in one category, the court may need to adjust the starting point in step 2.

---

**Type 1**
- Shotgun which has been shortened within the meaning of section 4(4)
- Firearm which has been converted within the meaning of section 4(4)

**Type 2**
- All other firearms or shotguns
- Ammunition (where not at Type 3)

**Type 3**
- Very small quantity of ammunition

---

### Culpability – Other culpability factors

The court should weigh all the factors set out below in determining the offender's culpability.

---

**High culpability:**
- Offender uses shotgun/firearm/ammunition for a criminal purpose
- Offender intends shotgun/firearm/ammunition to be used for a criminal purpose, or is reckless as to whether it would be so used

**Medium culpability:**
- Shotgun/firearm/ammunition produced or used (where not at High culpability)
- Shotgun/firearm loaded or held with compatible ammunition (where not at High culpability)
- Offender intends shotgun/firearm/ammunition to be used or is reckless as to whether it would be used (where not at High culpability)

**Lower culpability:**
- No use or intention to use

---

**Where there are characteristics present which fall under different levels of culpability, the court should balance these characteristics to reach a fair assessment of the offender's culpability.**

### Culpability category

Identify the final culpability category in the table below, considering both the **Type of weapon** and **Other culpability factors**.

|                            | Type of weapon        |                       |                       |
| -------------------------- | --------------------- | --------------------- | --------------------- |
| Other culpability factors  | 1                     | 2                     | 3                     |
| High                       | Culpability category A | Culpability category A | Culpability category B |
| Medium                     | Culpability category A | Culpability category B | Culpability category C |
| Lower                      | Culpability category B | Culpability category C | Culpability category C |

### Harm

This step is assessed by reference to the risk of harm or disorder occurring and/or actual alarm/distress caused. When considering the risk of harm, relevant considerations may include the location of the offence, the number and vulnerability of people exposed, especially children, and the accessibility and visibility of the weapon.

---

**Category 1**
- Serious alarm/distress caused
- High risk of death or serious physical or psychological harm
- High risk of serious disorder

**Category 2**
- All other cases falling between category 1 and category 3 because:
  - o Factors in both 1 and 3 are present which balance each other out; and/or
  - o The harm falls between the factors as described in 1 and 3

**Category 3**
- No/minimal alarm/distress caused
- No/minimal risk of death or serious physical or psychological harm
- No/minimal risk of serious disorder

Where there are characteristics present which fall under different levels of harm, the court should balance these characteristics to reach a fair assessment of the harm.

## STEP 2  Starting point and category range

Having determined the category at step 1, the court should use the corresponding starting point to reach a sentence within the category range below. The starting point applies to all offenders irrespective of plea or previous convictions.

The table below refers to offences for which the maximum sentence is five years. Where the offence is aggravated under section 4(4) (i.e. the weapon is a converted firearm or shortened shotgun), the maximum penalty is seven years and sentencers should consider increasing the sentences shown.

| Harm | Culpability | | |
|---|---|---|---|
| | A | B | C |
| Category 1 | **Starting point** 3 years 6 months' custody | **Starting point** 2 years 6 months' custody | **Starting point** 1 year's custody |
| | **Category range** 2 years 6 months'–4 years 6 months' custody | **Category range** 1–3 years 6 months' custody | **Category range** High level community order–2 years' custody |
| Category 2 | **Starting point** 2 years 6 months' custody | **Starting point** 1 year's custody | **Starting point** Medium level community order |
| | **Category range** 1–3 years 6 months' custody | **Category range** High level community order–2 years' custody | **Category range** Discharge–6 months' custody |
| Category 3 | **Starting point** 1 year's custody | **Starting point** Medium level community order | **Starting point** Band A fine |
| | **Category range** High level community order–2 years' custody | **Category range** Band A fine–6 months' custody | **Category range** Discharge–Band C Fine |

### Fines

[For the standard schedule of fines see **SG2-5**.]

### Community Orders and Custodial Sentences

[For the imposition of community orders, including the community orders table, see Imposition of Community and Custodial Sentences at **SG9-2**.

For the imposition of custodial sentences see Imposition of Community and Custodial Sentences at **SG9-3**.]

The following is a **non-exhaustive** list of additional factual elements providing the context of the offence and factors relating to the offender. Identify whether any combination of these, or other relevant factors, should result in an upward or downward adjustment from the sentence arrived at so far. In some cases, having considered these factors, it may be appropriate to move outside the identified category range.

### Factors increasing seriousness

*Statutory aggravating factors:*

- Previous convictions, having regard to a) the **nature** of the offence to which the conviction relates and its **relevance** to the current offence; and b) the **time** that has elapsed since the conviction
- Offence committed whilst on bail

*Other aggravating factors:*

- Firearm modified to make it more dangerous
- Steps taken to disguise firearm
- Firearm/ammunition kept with multiple weapons and/or substantial quantity of ammunition (See step 5 on totality when sentencing more than one offence)
- Offence was committed as part of a group
- Abuse of position as registered firearms dealer or certificate holder
- Possession continued after certificate refused or revoked
- Poor record of firearms compliance
- Commission of offence whilst under the influence of alcohol or drugs

*Sentencing Guidelines*

- Offender prohibited from possessing weapon or ammunition because of previous conviction (Care should be taken to avoid double counting matters taken into account when considering previous convictions. See step 5 on totality when sentencing more than one offence)
- Failure to comply with current court orders
- Offence committed on licence or post sentence supervision

**Factors reducing seriousness or reflecting personal mitigation**
- No previous convictions or no relevant/recent convictions
- Good character and/or exemplary conduct
- Firearm incomplete or incapable of being discharged
- No knowledge or suspicion that item possessed was firearm/ammunition
- Held on behalf of another through coercion, intimidation, or exploitation
- Steps taken to obtain certificate
- Certificate not obtained/renewed due to genuine oversight or misunderstanding
- Good record of firearms licensing compliance
- Voluntary surrender of firearm/ammunition
- Offender co-operated with investigation and/or made early admissions
- Remorse
- Serious medical condition requiring urgent, intensive or long-term treatment
- Age and/or lack of maturity
- Mental disorder or learning disability
- Sole or primary carer for dependent relatives

**STEP 3  Consider any factors which indicate a reduction for assistance to the prosecution**

The court should take into account section 74 of the Sentencing Code (reduction in sentence for assistance to prosecution) and any other rule of law by virtue of which an offender may receive a discounted sentence in consequence of assistance given (or offered) to the prosecutor or investigator.

**STEP 4  Reduction for guilty pleas**

The court should take account of any potential reduction for a guilty plea in accordance with section 73 of the Sentencing Code and the Reduction in sentence for a guilty plea guideline [see **SG5-1–SG5-12**].

**STEP 5  Totality principle**

If sentencing an offender for more than one offence, or where the offender is already serving a sentence, consider whether the total sentence is just and proportionate to the overall offending behaviour in accordance with the *Totality* guideline [see **SG4**].

**STEP 6  Ancillary orders**

In all cases the court should consider whether to make ancillary orders.

**Forfeiture and destruction of firearms and cancellation of certificate**

The court should consider ordering forfeiture or disposal of any firearm or ammunition and the cancellation of any firearms certificate. Section 52 of the Firearms Act 1968 provides for the forfeiture and disposal of firearms and the cancellation of firearms and shotgun certificates where a person is convicted of this offence **and** is given a custodial sentence **or** a community order containing a requirement not to possess, use or carry a firearm.

**Serious Crime Prevention Order**

The Crown Court may consider the criteria in section 19 of the Serious Crime Act 2007 for the imposition of a Serious Crime Prevention Order.

**STEP 7  Reasons**

Section 52 of the Sentencing Code imposes a duty to give reasons for, and explain the effect of, the sentence.

**STEP 8  Consideration for time spent on bail (tagged curfew)**

The court must consider whether to give credit for time spent on bail in accordance with section 240A of the Criminal Justice Act 2003 and section 325 of the Sentencing Code.

FIREARMS – TRANSFER AND MANUFACTURE                                    **SG34-9**

*Firearms Act 1968, s.5(2A)(a), Firearms Act 1968, s.5(2A)(b), Firearms Act 1968, s.5(2A)(c), Firearms Act 1968, s.5(2A)(d)*

**Effective from:** 01 January 2021

**Manufacture weapon or ammunition specified in section 5(1)**, Firearms Act 1968 (section 5(2A)(a))

**Sell or transfer prohibited weapon or ammunition**, Firearms Act 1968 (section 5(2A)(b))

**Possess for sale or transfer prohibited weapon or ammunition**, Firearms Act 1968 (section 5(2A)(c))

**Purchase or acquire for sale or transfer prohibited weapon or ammunition**, Firearms Act 1968 (section 5(2A)(d))

Indictable only
Maximum: Life imprisonment
Offence range: 3–28 years' custody

*Applicability*

**This offence is subject to statutory minimum sentencing provisions which are taken into account at steps 2 and 3. Sentencers should follow each step of the guideline to ensure that all relevant factors are considered.**

STEP 1   Determining the offence category

The court should determine the offence category with reference **only** to the factors listed in the tables below. In order to determine the category the court should assess **culpability** and **harm**.

The court should weigh all the factors set out below in determining the offender's culpability.

**Where there are characteristics present which fall under different levels of culpability, the court should balance these characteristics to reach a fair assessment of the offender's culpability.**

**Culpability** demonstrated by one or more of the following:

---

**Category 1**
- Large-scale commercial and/or highly sophisticated enterprise – indicators may include:
  - o Large number of prohibited weapons/ammunition involved
  - o Operation over significant time period
  - o Operation over significant geographic range
  - o Close connection to other serious criminal activity
- Evidence firearm/ammunition subsequently used to cause serious injury or death

**Category 2**
- Medium-scale enterprise and/or some degree of sophistication, including cases falling between category 1 and category 3 because:
  - o Factors in both 1 and 3 are present which balance each other out; and/or
  - o The harm falls between the factors as described in 1 and 3
- Evidence firearm/ammunition subsequently used in criminal offending (where not at category 1)

**Category 3**
- Smaller-scale and/or unsophisticated enterprise – indicators may include:
  - o Limited number of prohibited weapons/ammunition involved
  - o Operation over limited time period
  - o Operation over limited geographic range
  - o Minimal/no connection to other serious criminal activity
- Evidence firearm/ammunition not subsequently used in criminal offending

---

**Where there are characteristics present which fall under different levels of harm, the court should balance these characteristics to reach a fair assessment of the harm.**

Sentencing Guidelines

## STEP 2 Starting point and category range

Having determined the category at step 1, the court should use the corresponding starting point to reach a sentence within the category range below. The starting point applies to all offenders irrespective of plea or previous convictions.

This offence may be subject to a statutory minimum sentence

See step 3 for details of the minimum sentencing provisions and the approach to be taken to consideration of exceptional circumstances.

| Harm | Culpability | | |
| --- | --- | --- | --- |
| | A | B | C |
| Category 1 | **Starting point**<br>20 years' custody | **Starting point**<br>14 years' custody | **Starting point**<br>10 years' custody |
| | **Category range**<br>16–28 years' custody | **Category range**<br>12–18 years' custody | **Category range**<br>8–14 years' custody |
| Category 2 | **Starting point**<br>14 years' custody | **Starting point**<br>10 years' custody | **Starting point**<br>8 years' custody |
| | **Category range**<br>12–18 years' custody | **Category range**<br>8–14 years' custody | **Category range**<br>6–12 years' custody |
| Category 3 | **Starting point**<br>10 years' custody | **Starting point**<br>8 years' custody | **Starting point**<br>6 years' custody |
| | **Category range**<br>8–14 years' custody | **Category range**<br>6–12 years' custody | **Category range**<br>3–8 years' custody |

## Custodial sentences

The following is a **non-exhaustive** list of additional factual elements providing the context of the offence and factors relating to the offender. Identify whether any combination of these, or other relevant factors, should result in an upward or downward adjustment from the sentence arrived at so far. In some cases, having considered these factors, it may be appropriate to move outside the identified category range.

## Harm

**The court should consider the steps set out below to determine the level of harm caused.**

**This step is assessed by reference to the scale and nature of the enterprise and any actual harm caused, regardless of the offender's role.**

*Statutory aggravating factors:*
- Previous convictions, having regard to
  a) the **nature** of the offence to which the conviction relates and its **relevance** to the current offence; and
  b) the **time** that has elapsed since the conviction
- Offence committed whilst on bail

*Other aggravating factors:*
- Firearm under section 5(1)(a) (automatic weapon)
- Steps taken to disguise firearm (where not firearm under section 5(1A)(a))
- Compatible ammunition and/or silencer(s) supplied with firearm (See step 6 on totality when sentencing for more than one offence)
- Others put at risk of harm, including by location or method of manufacture or transfer
- Use of business as a cover
- Attempts to conceal or dispose of the firearm or other evidence
- Commission of offence whilst under the influence of alcohol or drugs
- Offender prohibited from possessing weapon or ammunition because of previous conviction (Care should be taken to avoid double counting matters taken into account when considering previous convictions. See step 6 on totality when sentencing for more than one offence)
- Failure to comply with current court orders
- Offence committed on licence or post sentence supervision

**Factors reducing seriousness or reflecting personal mitigation**

- No previous convictions or no relevant/recent convictions
- Good character and/or exemplary conduct
- Firearm/ammunition not subject to minimum term
- Firearm incomplete or incapable of being discharged (including stun gun that is not charged and not held with a functioning charger)
- Genuine belief that firearm will not be used for criminal purpose
- No knowledge or suspicion that item possessed was firearm/ammunition
- No knowledge or suspicion that firearm/ammunition is prohibited
- Voluntary surrender of firearm/ammunition
- Offender co-operated with investigation and/or made early admissions
- Remorse
- Serious medical condition requiring urgent, intensive or long-term treatment
- Age and/or lack of maturity
- Mental disorder or learning disability
- Sole or primary carer for dependent relatives

**STEP 3  Minimum term and exceptional circumstances**

**Minimum Term**

1. Where the minimum term provisions under section 311 and Schedule 20 of the Sentencing Code apply, a court must impose a sentence of at least five years' custody irrespective of plea **unless the court is of the opinion that there are exceptional circumstances relating to the offence or to the offender which justify its not doing so.**

*Applicability*

2. The minimum terms provisions apply when sentencing offences in respect of a firearm or ammunition specified in section 5(1)(a), (ab), (aba), (ac), (ad), (ae), (af) or (c) or section 5(1A)(a) of the Firearms Act 1968. Note: the minimum term provisions do **not** apply to offences charged as conspiracies.
3. The minimum term applies to *all* such offences including the first offence, and regardless of plea. Where it applies the sentence cannot be reduced below the minimum term for a guilty plea (see Step 5 – Reduction for guilty pleas).
4. The minimum term of five years applies to offenders aged 18 or over **when the offence was committed.** See below for guidance when sentencing offenders aged under 18 when the offence was committed.
5. Where the minimum term applies, this should be stated expressly.

**Exceptional circumstances**

6. In considering whether there are exceptional circumstances that would justify not imposing the statutory minimum sentence, the court must have regard to:
   - the particular circumstances of the offence **and**
   - the particular circumstances of the offender.
   either of which may give rise to exceptional circumstances
7. Where the factual circumstances are disputed, the procedure should follow that of a Newton hearing: see Criminal Practice Directions VII: Sentencing B [see **CPD.VII.B**].
8. Where the issue of exceptional circumstances has been raised the court should give a clear explanation as to why those circumstances have or have not been found.

*Principles*

9. Circumstances are exceptional if the imposition of the minimum term would result in an arbitrary and disproportionate sentence.
10. The circumstances must truly be exceptional. It is important that courts do not undermine the intention of Parliament and the deterrent purpose of the minimum term provisions by too readily accepting exceptional circumstances.
11. The court should look at all of the circumstances of the case taken together. A single striking factor may amount to exceptional circumstances, or it may be the collective impact of all of the relevant circumstances.
12. The mere presence of one or more of the following should not *in itself* be regarded as exceptional:
    - One or more lower culpability factors
    - One or more mitigating factors
    - A plea of guilty

*Where exceptional circumstances are found*

13. If there are exceptional circumstances that justify not imposing the statutory minimum sentence then the court **must impose either a shorter custodial sentence than the statutory minimum provides or an alternative sentence.** Note: a guilty plea reduction applies in the normal way if the minimum term is not imposed (see Step 5 – Reduction for guilty pleas).

### Sentencing offenders aged under 18 at the date of the offence

1. Where the offender is aged 16 or 17 **when the offence was committed**, the minimum term is three years' custody. Where the offender is under 16 **when the offence was committed**, the minimum term does not apply.
2. Subject to the minimum term, where the offender is aged under 18 **at the date of conviction** the court should determine the sentence in accordance with the Sentencing Children and Young People guideline [**SG8-1–SG8-11**], particularly paragraphs 6.42–6.49 on custodial sentences.
3. This guidance states at paragraph 6.46: "When considering the relevant adult guideline, the court may feel it appropriate to apply a sentence broadly within the region of half to two thirds of the adult sentence for those aged 15–17 and allow a greater reduction for those aged under 15. This is only a rough guide and must not be applied mechanistically. In most cases when considering the appropriate reduction from the adult sentence the emotional and developmental age and maturity of the child or young person is of at least equal importance as their chronological age."
4. The considerations above on exceptional circumstances relating to the offence or offender apply equally when sentencing offenders aged 16 or 17 at the date of the offence.

### STEP 4 Consider any factors which indicate a reduction for assistance to the prosecution

The court should take into account section 74 of the Sentencing Code (reduction in sentence for assistance to prosecution) and any other rule of law by virtue of which an offender may receive a discounted sentence in consequence of assistance given (or offered) to the prosecutor or investigator.

### STEP 5 Reduction for guilty pleas

The court should take account of any reduction for a guilty plea in accordance with section 73 of the Sentencing Code and the Reduction in sentence for a guilty plea guideline [see **SG5-1–SG5-12**].

Where a **minimum sentence** has been imposed under section 311 of the Sentencing Code, the court must ensure that any reduction for a guilty plea does not reduce the sentence to less than the required minimum term.

### STEP 6 Totality principle

If sentencing an offender for more than one offence, or where the offender is already serving a sentence, consider whether the total sentence is just and proportionate to the overall offending behaviour in accordance with the *Totality* guideline [see **SG4**].

### STEP 7 Ancillary orders

In all cases the court should consider whether to make ancillary orders.

### Forfeiture and destruction of firearms and cancellation of certificate

The court should consider ordering forfeiture or disposal of any firearm or ammunition and the cancellation of any firearms certificate. Section 52 of the Firearms Act 1968 provides for the forfeiture and disposal of firearms and the cancellation of firearms and shotgun certificates where a person is convicted of this offence **and** is given a custodial sentence **or** a community order containing a requirement not to possess, use or carry a firearm.

### Serious Crime Prevention Order

The court may consider the criteria in section 19 of the Serious Crime Act 2007 for the imposition of a Serious Crime Prevention Order.

### STEP 8 Reasons

Section 52 of the Sentencing Code imposes a duty to give reasons for, and explain the effect of, the sentence.

### STEP 9 Consideration for time spent on bail (tagged curfew)

The court must consider whether to give credit for time spent on bail in accordance with section 240A of the Criminal Justice Act 2003 and section 325 of the Sentencing Code.

*Customs and Excise Management Act 1979 (s.170(1)(b), (2), (3) and (4A)(a)),*
*Customs and Excise Management Act 1979 (s.50(3), (4) and (5A)(a))*

**Effective from:** 01 January 2022

**Improper importation of goods**

Customs and Excise Management Act 1979 (section 50(3), (4) and (5A)(a))

**Fraudulent evasion of prohibition/restriction**

Customs and Excise Management Act 1979 (section 170(1)(b), (2), (3) and (4A)(a))

Triable either way

Maximum: 7 years unless committed in Great Britain in connection with a prohibition or restriction on the importation or exportation of any weapon or ammunition that is of a kind mentioned in section 5(1)(a), (ab), (aba), (ac), (ad), (ae), (af), (ag), (ba) or (c) or (1A)(a) of the Firearms Act 1968 in which case the maximum is life imprisonment

Offence range: Fine – 28 years' custody

**STEP 1  Determining the offence category**

The court should determine the offence category with reference only to the factors listed in the tables below. In order to determine the category the court should assess culpability and harm.

**Culpability – Type of weapon**

Use the table below to identify an initial culpability category based on the type of weapon only. This assessment focuses on the nature of the weapon itself only, not whether the weapon was loaded or in working order.

Courts should take care to ensure the categorisation is appropriate for the specific weapon. Where the weapon or ammunition does not fall squarely in one category, the court may need to adjust the starting point in step 2.

References to weapon below include a component part of such a weapon.

---

**Type 1**

Weapon that is designed or adapted to be capable of killing two or more people at the same time or in rapid succession
• This would **normally** include a weapon prohibited under the following sections of the Firearms Act 1968:
  o  section 5(1)(a)
  o  section 5(1)(ab)
  o  section 5(1)(aba)
  o  section 5(1)(ac)
  o  section 5(1)(ad)
  o  section 5(1)(ae)
  o  section 5(1A)(c)
  o  section 5(1)(ag)
  o  section 5(1)(ba)

**Type 2**

All other weapons falling between Type 1 and Type 3
• This would **normally** include a weapon requiring certification or prohibited under the following sections
  of the Firearms Act 1968:
  o  section 1
  o  section 5(1)(af)
  o  section 5(1A)(a)
(including disguised stun guns when charged under that section)
Ammunition (where not at Type 3)
• This would **normally** include ammunition requiring certification or prohibited under the following sections of the Firearms Act 1968:
  o  section 1
  o  section 5(1)(c)
  o  5(1A)(b) and (d)–(g)

---

> Type 3
> Weapon that is not designed or adapted to be lethal
> • This would **normally** include a weapon under section 5(1)(b)
> Very small quantity of ammunition

### Culpability – Other culpability factors

The court should weigh all the factors set out below in determining the offender's culpability.

> **High culpability**
> • Leading role where offending is part of a group activity
> • Significant planning, including but not limited to significant steps to evade detection
> • Abuse of position of trust or responsibility, for example registered firearms dealer, customs official
> • Expectation of substantial financial or other advantage
> • Involves others through coercion, intimidation or exploitation
>
> **Medium culpability**
> • Significant role where offending is part of a group activity
> • Some degree of planning, including but not limited to some steps to evade detection
> • Expectation of significant financial or other advantage
> • Other cases falling between higher and lower culpability because:
>    o Factors are present in higher and lower which balance each other out and/or
>    o The offender's culpability falls between the factors as described in higher and lower
>
> **Lower culpability**
> • Lesser role where offending is part of a group activity, including but not limited to performing a limited function under direction
> • Involved through coercion, intimidation or exploitation
> • Little or no planning
> • Expectation of limited, if any, financial or other advantage

### Culpability category

Identify the final culpability category in the table below, considering both the Type of weapon and Other culpability factors.

|                           | Type of weapon        |                       |                       |
| ------------------------- | --------------------- | --------------------- | --------------------- |
| **Other culpability factors** | 1                 | 2                     | 3                     |
| **High**                  | Culpability category A | Culpability category B | Culpability category C |
| **Medium**                | Culpability category B | Culpability category C | Culpability category C |
| **Lower**                 | Culpability category C | Culpability category C | Culpability category D |

### Harm

Harm is assessed by reference to the scale and nature of the importation regardless of the offender's role and regardless of whether the importation was intercepted.

> **Category 1**
> • Large-scale commercial enterprise – indicators may include:
>    o Large number of firearms/ammunition involved
>    o Operation over significant time period
>    o Close connection to other serious criminal activity
>
> **Category 2**
> • Medium-scale enterprise and/or some degree of sophistication, including cases falling between category 1 and category 3 because:
>    o Factors in both 1 and 3 are present which balance each other out; and/or
>    o The harm falls between the factors as described in 1 and 3
>
> **Category 3**
> • Smaller-scale **and** unsophisticated enterprise – indicators may include:
>    o Limited number of firearms/ammunition involved
>    o Minimal/no connection to other serious criminal activity

**STEP 2  Starting point and category range**

Having determined the category at step 1, the court should use the corresponding starting point to reach a sentence within the category range below. The starting point applies to all offenders irrespective of plea or previous convictions.

Table 1 should be used if the offence is subject to a maximum life sentence

Table 2 should be used if the offence is subject to a maximum 7 year sentence

**TABLE 1: Offences subject to the statutory maximum of a life sentence (offence relates to weapon or ammunition that is of a kind mentioned in Section 5(1)(a), (ab), (aba), (ac), (ad), (ae), (af), (ag), (ba), (c), section 5(1A)(a) Firearms Act 1968)**

| Harm | Culpability | | | |
|---|---|---|---|---|
| | A | B | C | D |
| Category 1 | **Starting point** 20 years' custody | **Starting point** 14 years' custody | **Starting point** 10 years' custody | **Starting point** 6 years' custody |
| | **Category range** 16–28 years' custody | **Category range** 10–17 years' custody | **Category range** 8–12 years' custody | **Category range** 4–8 years' custody |
| Category 2 | **Starting point** 14 years' custody | **Starting point** 10 years' custody | **Starting point** 6 years' custody | **Starting point** 3 years' custody |
| | **Category range** 10–17 years' custody | **Category range** 8–12 years' custody | **Category range** 4–8 years' custody | **Category range** 2–5 years' custody |
| Category 3 | **Starting point** 10 years' custody | **Starting point** 5 years' custody | **Starting point** 3 years' custody | **Starting point** 2 years' custody |
| | **Category range** 8–12 years' custody | **Category range** 3–8 years' custody | **Category range** 2–5 years' custody | **Category range** 1–3 years' custody |

**TABLE 2: Offences subject to the statutory maximum sentence of 7 years**

| Harm | Culpability | | |
|---|---|---|---|
| | A/B | C | D |
| Category 1 | **Starting point** 5 years' custody | **Starting point** 3 years' custody | **Starting point** 2 years' custody |
| | **Category range** 4–7 years' custody | **Category range** 2–5 years' custody | **Category range** 1–3 years' custody |
| Category 2 | **Starting point** 3 years' custody | **Starting point** 2 years' custody | **Starting point** 1 year's custody |
| | **Category range** 2–5 years' custody | **Category range** 1–3 years' custody | **Category range** High level community order – 2 years' custody |
| Category 3 | **Starting point** 2 years' custody | **Starting point** 1 year's custody | **Starting point** Medium level community order |
| | **Category range** 1–3 years' custody | **Category range** High level community order – 2 years' custody | **Category range** Band C fine – High level community order |

**Fines**

[For the standard schedule of fines see **SG2-5**.]

**Community Orders and Custodial Sentences**

[For the imposition of community orders, including the community orders table, see Imposition of Community and Custodial Sentences at **SG9-2**.

For the imposition of custodial sentences see Imposition of Community and Custodial Sentences at **SG9-3**.]

Consecutive sentences for multiple offences may be appropriate — please refer to the Offences Taken Into Consideration and Totality guidelines [see **SG3** and **SG4**].

The table below contains a non-exhaustive list of additional factual elements providing the context of the offence and factors relating to the offender. Identify whether any combination of these, or other relevant factors, should result in an upward or downward adjustment from the sentence arrived at so far. In some cases, having considered these factors, it may be appropriate to move outside the identified category range.

**Factors increasing seriousness**

*Statutory aggravating factors:*

- Previous convictions, having regard to a) the **nature** of the offence to which the conviction relates and its **relevance** to the current offence; and b) the **time** that has elapsed since the conviction
- Offence committed whilst on bail

*Other aggravating factors:*

- Compatible ammunition and/or silencer(s) imported with firearm (see step 5 on totality when sentencing more than one offence)
- Others put at risk of harm by method of importation
- Offender intends firearm/ammunition to be used or is reckless as to whether it would be used
- Use of business as a cover
- Attempts to dispose of the firearm or other evidence
- Commission of offence whilst under the influence of alcohol or drugs
- Offender prohibited from possessing weapon or ammunition because of previous conviction (see step 5 on totality when sentencing more than one offence)
- Failure to comply with current court orders
- Offence committed on licence or post sentence supervision

**Factors reducing seriousness or reflecting personal mitigation**

- No previous convictions or no relevant/recent convictions
- Good character and/or exemplary conduct
- Firearm incomplete or incapable of being discharged (including stun gun that is not charged and not held with a functioning charger)
- Very small scale importation **and** very low risk of harm to others
- Genuine belief that firearm/ammunition will not be used for criminal purpose
- Offender co-operated with investigation and/or made early admissions
- Remorse
- Serious medical condition requiring urgent, intensive or long-term treatment
- Age and/or lack of maturity
- Mental disorder or learning disability
- Sole or primary carer for dependent relatives

**STEP 3  Consider any factors which indicate a reduction for assistance to the prosecution**

The court should take into account section 74 of the Sentencing Code (reduction in sentence for assistance to prosecution) and any other rule of law by virtue of which an offender may receive a discounted sentence in consequence of assistance given (or offered) to the prosecutor or investigator.

**STEP 4  Reduction for guilty pleas**

The court should take account of any reduction for a guilty plea in accordance with section 74 of the Sentencing Code and the Reduction in sentence for a guilty plea guideline [see **SG5-1–SG5-12**].

**STEP 5  Totality principle**

If sentencing an offender for more than one offence, or where the offender is already serving a sentence, consider whether the total sentence is just and proportionate to the overall offending behaviour in accordance with the Totality guideline [see SG4].

## STEP 6  Ancillary orders

In all cases the court should consider whether to make ancillary orders.

- Ancillary orders – Magistrates' Court
- Ancillary orders – Crown Court Compendium

### Forfeiture of firearms

Where the offender is convicted of an offence contrary to section 170 of the Customs and Excise Management Act 1979 the court may consider making an order for forfeiture under section 170(6).

For any offence, the court may consider making an order for deprivation under section 153 of the Sentencing Code of any property used in the commission of the offence.

### Serious Crime Prevention Order

Where the offender is convicted of an offence contrary to section 170 Customs and Excise Management Act 1979, the court may consider the criteria in section 19 of the Serious Crime Act 2007 for the imposition of a Serious Crime Prevention Order.

## STEP 7  Reasons

Section 52 of the Sentencing Code imposes a duty to give reasons for, and explain the effect of, the sentence.

## STEP 8  Consideration for time spent on bail (tagged curfew)

The court must consider whether to give credit for time spent on bail in accordance with section 240A of the Criminal Justice Act 2003 and section 325 of the Sentencing Code.

Sentencing Guidelines

# PART 35    TRADE MARK, UNAUTHORISED USE OF

**SG35-1**

APPLICABILITY

[For the standard text on applicability see **SG0-4**.]

**SG35-2**

INDIVIDUALS: TRADE MARK, UNAUTHORISED USE OF ETC.

*Trade Marks Act 1994, s.92*

**Effective from:** 01 October 2021

Triable either way
Maximum: 10 years' custody
Offence range: Discharge – 7 years' custody

Use this guideline when the offender is an individual. If the offender is an organisation, please refer to the **Organisations: Trade mark, unauthorised use of etc.** guideline [see **SG35-3**].

This guideline applies only to offenders aged 18 and older. General principles to be considered in the sentencing of children and young people are in the Sentencing Council definitive guideline, Sentencing Children and Young People: Overarching Principles and Offence Specific Guidelines for Sexual Offences and Robbery [see **SG8-1** *et seq.*].

*The maximum sentence that applies to an offence is the maximum that applied at the date of the offence.

## STEP 1   Determining the offence category

The court should determine the offence category with reference to culpability and harm.

### Culpability

The level of culpability is determined by weighing up all the factors of the case to determine the offender's **role** and the extent to which the offending was **planned** and the **sophistication** with which it was carried out.

### A – High culpability

- Sophisticated nature of offence/significant planning (examples **may** include but are not limited to: the use of multiple outlets or trading identities for the sale of counterfeit goods, the use of multiple accounts for receiving payment, the use of professional equipment to produce goods, the use of a website that mimics that of the trade mark owner or a legitimate trader, offending over a sustained period of time)
- A leading role where offending is part of a group activity
- Involvement of others through coercion, intimidation or exploitation

### B – Medium culpability

- Some degree of organisation/planning involved
- A significant role where offending is part of a group activity
- Other cases that fall between categories A or C because:
  - Factors are present in A and C which balance each other out **and/or**
  - The offender's culpability falls between the factors as described in A and C

### C – Lesser culpability

- Little or no organisation/planning
- Performed limited function under direction
- Involved through coercion, intimidation or exploitation
- Limited awareness or understanding of the offence

**Where there are characteristics present which fall under different levels of culpability, the court should balance these characteristics to reach a fair assessment of the offender's culpability.**

### Harm

The assessment of harm for this offence involves putting a monetary figure on the offending with reference to the **value of equivalent genuine goods** and assessing **any significant additional harm** suffered by the trade mark owner or purchasers/ end users of the counterfeit goods:

1. Where there is evidence of the volume of counterfeit goods sold or possessed:
   a. the monetary value should be assessed by taking the **equivalent retail value of legitimate versions** of the counterfeit goods involved in the offending
   b. Where it would be impractical to assign an equivalent retail value of legitimate versions, an estimate should be used.
2. Where there is no evidence of the volume of counterfeit goods sold or possessed:
   a. In the case of labels or packaging, harm should be assessed by taking the **equivalent retail value of legitimate goods** to which the labels or packaging could reasonably be applied, taking an average price of the relevant products.
   b. In the case of equipment or articles for the making of copies of trade marks, the court will have to make an assessment of the scale of the operation and assign an equivalent value from the table below.

**Note:** the equivalent retail value is likely to be considerably higher than the actual value of the counterfeit items and this is accounted for in the sentence levels. However, in **exceptional** cases where the equivalent retail value is grossly disproportionate to the actual value, an adjustment **may** be made.

The general harm caused to purchasers/ end users (by being provided with counterfeit goods), to legitimate businesses (through loss of business) and to the owners of the trade mark (through loss of revenue and reputational damage) is reflected in the sentence levels at step 2.

Examples of **significant additional harm** may include but are not limited to:

* Substantial damage to the legitimate business of the trade mark owner (taking into account the size of the business)
* Purchasers/ end users put at risk of physical harm from counterfeit goods

Where purchasers/ end users are put at **risk of death or serious physical harm** from counterfeit goods, harm should be **at least category 3** even if the equivalent retail value of the goods falls below £50,000.

|  | Equivalent value of legitimate goods | Starting point based on |
|---|---|---|
| Category 1 | £1 million or more **or** category 2 value with significant additional harm | £2 million |
| Category 2 | £300,000 – £1 million **or** category 3 value with significant additional harm | £600,000 |
| Category 3 | £50,000 – £300,000 **or** category 4 value with significant additional harm | £125,000 |
| Category 4 | £5,000 – £50,000 **or** category 5 value with significant additional harm | £30,000 |
| Category 5 | Less than £5,000 **and** little or no significant additional harm | £2,500 |

## STEP 2   Starting point and category range

Having determined the category at step 1, the court should use the appropriate starting point to reach a sentence within the category range in the table below. The starting point applies to all offenders irrespective of plea or previous convictions.

Where the value is larger or smaller than the amount on which the starting point is based, this should lead to upward or downward adjustment as appropriate.

For offences where the equivalent retail value is £1 million or more an upward adjustment within the category range should be made for any significant additional harm.

| Harm | Culpability | | |
|---|---|---|---|
|  | A | B | C |
| Category 1<br>£1 million or more<br>Starting point based on £2 million | **Starting point**<br>5 years' custody | **Starting point**<br>3 years' custody | **Starting point**<br>2 years' custody |
|  | **Category range**<br>3–7 years' custody | **Category range**<br>2–5 years' custody | **Category range**<br>1–3 years' custody |

Sentencing Guidelines

| Harm | Culpability | | |
|------|---------|---|---|
| | A | B | C |
| **Category 2**<br>**£300,000 – £1 million**<br>Starting point based on £600,000 | **Starting point**<br>4 years' custody | **Starting point**<br>2 years' custody | **Starting point**<br>1 year's custody |
| | **Category range**<br>2–5 years' custody | **Category range**<br>1–3 years' custody | **Category range**<br>26 weeks'–2 years' custody |
| **Category 3**<br>**£50,000–£300,000**<br>Starting point based on £125,000 | **Starting point**<br>2 years' custody | **Starting point**<br>1 year's custody | **Starting point**<br>High level community order |
| | **Category range**<br>1–3 years' custody | **Category range**<br>26 weeks'–2 years' custody | **Category range**<br>Low level community order –26 weeks' custody |
| **Category 4**<br>**£5,000 – £50,000**<br>Starting point based on £30,000 | **Starting point**<br>1 year's custody | **Starting point**<br>High level community order | **Starting point**<br>Band C fine |
| | **Category range**<br>26 weeks –2 years custody | **Category range**<br>Low level community order – 26 weeks' custody | **Category range**<br>Band B fine – Medium level community order |
| **Category 5**<br>**Less than £5,000**<br>Starting point based on £2,500 | **Starting point**<br>High level community order | **Starting point**<br>Band C fine | **Starting point**<br>Band B fine |
| | **Category range**<br>Low level community order – 26 weeks' custody | **Category range**<br>Band B fine – Medium level community order | **Category range**<br>Discharge – Band C fine |

This is an offence where it may be appropriate to combine a community order with a fine

**Fines**

[For the standard schedule of fines see **SG2-5**.]

**Community Orders and Custodial Sentences**

[For the imposition of community orders, including the community orders table, see Imposition of Community and Custodial Sentences at **SG9-2**.

For the imposition of custodial sentences see Imposition of Community and Custodial Sentences at **SG9-3**.]

**Factors increasing seriousness**

*Statutory aggravating factors*

- Previous convictions, having regard to
  a) the nature of the offence to which the conviction relates and its relevance to the current offence; and
  b) the time that has elapsed since the conviction
- Offence committed whilst on bail

*Other aggravating factors*

- Purchasers or others put at risk of harm from counterfeit items (where not taken into account at step 1)
- Expectation of substantial financial gain
- Attempts to conceal/dispose of evidence
- Attempts to conceal identity
- Failure to respond to warnings about behaviour
- Blame wrongly placed on others
- Offences taken into consideration
- Failure to comply with current court orders
- Offence committed on licence or post sentence supervision

**Factors reducing seriousness or reflecting personal mitigation**
- No previous convictions **or** no relevant/recent convictions
- Remorse
- Good character and/or exemplary conduct
- Offender co-operated with investigation, made early admissions and/or voluntarily reported offending
- Expectation of limited financial gain
- Lapse of time since apprehension where this does not arise from the conduct of the offender
- Serious medical conditions requiring urgent, intensive or long-term treatment
- Age and/or lack of maturity
- Mental disorder or learning disability
- Sole or primary carer for dependent relatives

**STEP 3   Consider any factors which indicate a reduction, such as assistance to the prosecution**

The court should take into account section 74 of the Sentencing Code (reduction in sentence for assistance to prosecution) and any other rule of law by virtue of which an offender may receive a discounted sentence in consequence of assistance given (or offered) to the prosecutor or investigator.

**STEP 4   Reduction for guilty pleas**

The court should take account of any potential reduction for a guilty plea in accordance with section 73 of the Sentencing Code and the guideline for Reduction in Sentence for a Guilty Plea [**SG5-1–SG5-12**].

**STEP 5   Totality principle**

If sentencing an offender for more than one offence, or where the offender is already serving a sentence, consider whether the total sentence is just and proportionate to the overall offending behaviour in accordance with the *Totality* guideline [see **SG4**].

**STEP 6   Confiscation, compensation and ancillary orders**

Confiscation orders under the Proceeds of Crime Act 2002 may only be made by the Crown Court. The Crown Court must proceed with a view to making a confiscation order if it is asked to do so by the prosecutor or if the Crown Court believes it is appropriate for it to do so.

Where, following conviction in a magistrates' court, the prosecutor applies for the offender to be committed to the Crown Court with a view to a confiscation order being considered, the magistrates' court must commit the offender to the Crown Court to be sentenced there (section 70 of the Proceeds of Crime Act 2002). This applies to summary only and either-way offences.

Where, but for the prosecutor's application under s.70, the magistrates' court would have committed the offender for sentence to the Crown Court anyway it must say so. Otherwise the powers of sentence of the Crown Court will be limited to those of the magistrates' court.

(Note: the valuation of counterfeit goods for the purposes of confiscation proceedings is not the same as the valuation used for the purposes of assessing harm in this sentencing guideline.)

Confiscation must be dealt with before, and taken into account when assessing, any other fine or financial order (except compensation). (See Proceeds of Crime Act 2002 sections 6 and 13)

Where the offence has resulted in loss or damage the court must consider whether to make a compensation order and must give reasons if it does not do so (section 55 of the Sentencing Code).

Where the offence has resulted in loss or damage the court must consider whether to make a **compensation order** and must give reasons if it does not do so (section 55 of the Sentencing Code).

If the court makes both a confiscation order and an order for compensation and the court believes the offender will not have sufficient means to satisfy both orders in full, the court must direct that the compensation be paid out of sums recovered under the confiscation order (section 13 of the Proceeds of Crime Act 2002).

**Forfeiture – section 97 of the Trade Marks Act 1994**

The prosecution may apply for forfeiture of goods or materials bearing a sign likely to be mistaken for a registered trademark or articles designed for making copies of such a sign. The court shall make an order for forfeiture only if it is satisfied that a relevant offence has been committed in relation to the goods, material or articles. A court may infer that such an offence has been committed in relation to any goods, material or articles if it is satisfied that such an offence has been committed in relation to goods, material or articles which are representative of them (whether by reason of being of the same design or part of the same consignment or batch or otherwise).

The court may also consider whether to make other ancillary orders. These may include a deprivation order and disqualification from acting as a company director.

- Ancillary orders – Magistrates' Court
- Ancillary orders – Crown Court Compendium, Part II Sentencing

### STEP 7 Reasons

Section 52 of the Sentencing Code imposes a duty to give reasons for, and explain the effect of, the sentence.

### STEP 8 Consideration for time spent on bail (tagged curfew)

The court must consider whether to give credit for time spent on bail in accordance with section 240A of the Criminal Justice Act 2003 and section 325 of the Sentencing Code.

**SG35-3**        ORGANISATIONS: TRADE MARK, UNAUTHORISED USE OF ETC.

*Trade Marks Act 1994, s.92*

**Effective from:** 01 October 2021

Triable either way
Maximum: Unlimited fine
Offence range: £250 fine to £450,000 fine

Use this guideline when the offender is an organisation. If the offender is an individual please refer to the **Individuals: Trade mark, unauthorised use of etc.** guideline [see **SG35-2**].

### STEP 1 Compensation

The court must consider making a compensation order requiring the offender to pay compensation for any personal injury, loss or damage resulting from the offence in such an amount as the court considers appropriate, having regard to the evidence and to the means of the offender.

Where the means of the offender are limited, priority should be given to the payment of compensation over payment of any other financial penalty.

Reasons should be given if a compensation order is not made (section 55 of the Sentencing Code)

### STEP 2 Confiscation

Confiscation orders under the Proceeds of Crime Act 2002 may only be made by the **Crown Court**. Confiscation must be considered by the Crown Court if either the prosecutor asks for it or the Crown Court thinks that it may be appropriate.

Where, following conviction in a magistrates' court, the prosecutor applies for the offender to be committed to the Crown Court with a view to a confiscation order being considered, the magistrates' court must commit the offender to the Crown Court to be sentenced there (section 70 of the Proceeds of Crime Act 2002). Where, but for the prosecutor's application under s.70, the magistrates' court would have committed the offender for sentence to the Crown Court anyway it must say so. Otherwise the powers of sentence of the Crown Court will be limited to those of the magistrates' court.

(Note: the valuation of counterfeit goods for the purposes of confiscation proceedings will not be the same as the valuation used for the purposes of assessing harm in this sentencing guideline.)

Confiscation must be dealt with before, and taken into account when assessing, any other fine or financial order (except compensation).

(See Proceeds of Crime Act 2002 sections 6 and 13)

### STEP 3 Determining the offence category

The court should determine the offence category with reference to culpability and harm.

### Culpability

The level of culpability is determined by weighing up all the factors of the case to determine the offending organisation's **role** and the extent to which the offending was **planned** and the **sophistication** with which it was carried out.

### A – High culpability

- Organisation plays a leading role in organised, planned unlawful activity whether acting alone or with others (indicators of planned activity **may** include but are not limited to: the use of multiple outlets or trading identities for the sale of counterfeit goods, the use of multiple accounts for receiving payment,

the use of professional equipment to produce goods, the use of a website that mimics that of the trade mark owner or a legitimate trader, offending over a sustained period of time)
- Involving others through pressure or coercion (for example employees or suppliers)

### B – Medium culpability
- Organisation plays a significant role in unlawful activity organised by others
- Some degree of organisation/planning involved
- Other cases that fall between categories A or C because:
  - Factors are present in A and C which balance each other out **and/or**
  - The offender's culpability falls between the factors as described in A and C

### C – Lesser culpability
- Organisation plays a minor, peripheral role in unlawful activity organised by others
- Involvement through coercion, intimidation or exploitation
- Little or no organisation/planning
- Limited awareness or understanding of the offence

**Where there are characteristics present which fall under different levels of culpability, the court should balance these characteristics to reach a fair assessment of the offender's culpability.**

### Harm
The assessment of harm for this offence involves putting a monetary figure on the offending with reference to the **value of equivalent genuine goods** and assessing **any significant additional harm** suffered by the trade mark owner or purchasers/ end users of the counterfeit goods:

1. Where there is evidence of the volume of counterfeit goods sold or possessed:
   a. The monetary value should be assessed by taking the **equivalent retail value of legitimate versions** of the counterfeit goods involved in the offending.
   b. Where it would be impractical to assign an equivalent retail value of legitimate versions, an estimate should be used.
2. Where there is no evidence of the volume of counterfeit goods sold or possessed:
   a. In the case of labels or packaging, harm should be assessed by taking the **equivalent retail value of legitimate goods** to which the labels or packaging could reasonably be applied, taking an average price of the relevant products.
   b. In the case of equipment or articles for the making of copies of trade marks, the court will have to make an assessment of the scale of the operation and assign an equivalent value from the table below.

**Note:** the equivalent retail value is likely to be considerably higher than the actual value of the counterfeit items and this is accounted for in the sentence levels. However, in **exceptional** cases where the equivalent retail value is grossly disproportionate to the actual value, an adjustment **may** be made.

The general harm caused to purchasers/ end users (by being provided with counterfeit goods), to legitimate businesses (through loss of business) and to the owners of the trade mark (through loss of revenue and reputational damage) is reflected in the sentence levels at step 4.

Examples of **significant additional harm** may include but are not limited to:

- Substantial damage to the legitimate business of the trade mark owner (taking into account the size of the business)
- Purchasers/ end users put at risk of physical harm from counterfeit goods

Where purchasers/ end users are put at **risk of death or serious physical harm** from counterfeit goods, harm should be **at least category 3** even if the equivalent retail value of the goods falls below £50,000.

|            | Equivalent value of legitimate goods | Starting point based on |
|------------|--------------------------------------|-------------------------|
| Category 1 | £1 million or more **or** category 2 value with significant additional harm | £2 million |
| Category 2 | £300,000 – £1 million **or** category 3 value with significant additional harm | £600,000 |
| Category 3 | £50,000 – £300,000 **or** category 4 value with significant additional harm | £125,000 |

| | Equivalent value of legitimate goods | Starting point based on |
|---|---|---|
| Category 4 | £5,000 – £50,000 **or** category 5 value with significant additional harm | £30,000 |
| Category 5 | Less than £5,000 **and** little or no significant additional harm | £2,500 |

### STEP 4  Starting point and category range

Having determined the category at step 3, the court should use the table below to determine the starting point within the category range below. The starting point applies to all offenders irrespective of plea or previous convictions.

Where the value is larger or smaller than the amount on which the starting point is based, this should lead to upward or downward adjustment as appropriate.

For offences where the equivalent retail value is £1 million or more an upward adjustment within the category range should be made for any significant additional harm.

**The fine levels below assume that the offending organisation has an annual turnover of not more than £2 million. In cases where turnover is higher, adjustment may need to be made at Step 5 below including outside the offence range.**

| Harm | Culpability | | |
|---|---|---|---|
| | **A** | **B** | **C** |
| Category 1<br>£1 million or more<br>Starting point based on £2 million | **Starting point**<br>£250,000 | **Starting point**<br>£100,000 | **Starting point**<br>£50,000 |
| | **Category range**<br>£150,000–£450,000 | **Category range**<br>£50,000–£200,000 | **Category range**<br>£25,000–£100,000 |
| Category 2<br>£300,000 – £1million<br>Starting point based on £600,000 | **Starting point**<br>£150,000 | **Starting point**<br>£50,000 | **Starting point**<br>£25,000 |
| | **Category range**<br>£75,000–£250,000 | **Category range**<br>£25,000–£100,000 | **Category range**<br>£15,000–£50,000 |
| Category 3<br>£50,000 – £300,000<br>Starting point based on £125,000 | **Starting point**<br>£50,000 | **Starting point**<br>£25,000 | **Starting point**<br>£10,000 |
| | **Category range**<br>£25,000–£100,000 | **Category range**<br>£15,000–£50,000 | **Category range**<br>£5,000–£25,000 |
| Category 4<br>£5,000- £50,000<br>Starting point based on £30,000 | **Starting point**<br>£25,000 | **Starting point**<br>£10,000 | **Starting point**<br>£5,000 |
| | **Category range**<br>£15,000–£50,000 | **Category range**<br>£5,000–£25,000 | **Category range**<br>£2,000–£10,000 |
| Category 5<br>Less than £5,000<br>Starting point based on £2,500 | **Starting point**<br>£10,000 | **Starting point**<br>£5,000 | **Starting point**<br>£1,000 |
| | **Category range**<br>£5,000–£25,000 | **Category range**<br>£2,000–£10,000 | **Category range**<br>£250–£5,000 |

Having determined the appropriate starting point, the court should then consider adjustment within the category range for aggravating or mitigating features. The following list is a **non-exhaustive** list of additional factual elements providing the context of the offence and factors relating to the offender. Identify whether any combination of these, or other relevant factors, should result in an upward or downward adjustment from the starting point.

### Factors increasing seriousness

- Previous relevant convictions or subject to previous relevant civil or regulatory enforcement action
- Organisation or subsidiary set up to commit counterfeiting activity
- Counterfeiting activity endemic within organisation
- Expectation of substantial financial gain
- Purchasers put at risk of harm from counterfeit items (where not taken into account at step 3)
- Attempts to conceal/dispose of evidence
- Attempts to conceal identity

- Failure to respond to warnings
- Blame wrongly placed on others

**Factors reducing seriousness or reflecting mitigation**
- No previous convictions or previous relevant civil or regulatory enforcement action
- Offender co-operated with investigation, made early admissions and/or voluntarily reported offending
- Little or no actual gain to organisation from offending
- Lapse of time since apprehension where this does not arise from the conduct of the offender

**General principles to follow in setting a fine.** The court should determine the appropriate level of fine in accordance with section 125 of the Sentencing Code, which requires that the fine must reflect the seriousness of the offence and requires the court to take into account the financial circumstances of the offender.

Obtaining financial information

**STEP 5   Adjustment of fine**

**Note the fine levels above assume that the offending organisation has an annual turnover of not more than £2 million. In cases where turnover is higher, adjustment may need to be made including outside the offence range.**

Having arrived at a fine level, the court should consider whether there are any further factors which indicate an adjustment in the level of the fine including outside the category range. The court should 'step back' and consider the overall effect of its orders. The combination of orders made, compensation, confiscation and fine ought to achieve:

- the removal of all gain
- appropriate additional punishment, and
- deterrence

The fine may be adjusted to ensure that these objectives are met in a fair way. The court should consider any further factors relevant to the setting of the level of the fine to ensure that the fine is proportionate, having regard to the size and financial position of the offending organisation and the seriousness of the offence.

The fine must be substantial enough to have a real economic impact which will bring home to both management and shareholders the need to operate within the law. Whether the fine will have the effect of putting the offender out of business will be relevant; in some bad cases this may be an acceptable consequence.

In considering the ability of the offending organisation to pay any financial penalty the court can take into account the power to allow time for payment or to order that the amount be paid in instalments.

The court should consider whether the level of fine would otherwise cause unacceptable harm to third parties. In doing so the court should bear in mind that the payment of any compensation determined at step one should take priority over the payment of any fine.

Below is a **non-exhaustive** list of additional factual elements for the court to consider.

The court should identify whether any combination of these, or other relevant factors, should result in a proportionate increase or reduction in the level of fine.

Factors to consider in adjusting the level of fine

- Fine fulfils the objectives of punishment, deterrence and removal of gain
- The value, worth or available means of the offender
- Fine impairs offender's ability to make restitution to victims
- Impact of fine on offender's ability to implement effective compliance programmes
- Impact of fine on employment of staff, service users, customers and local economy (but not shareholders)
- Impact of fine on performance of public or charitable function

**STEP 6   Consider any factors which indicate a reduction, such as assistance to the prosecution**

The court should take into account section 74 of the Sentencing Code (reduction in sentence for assistance to prosecution) and any other rule of law by virtue of which an offender may receive a discounted sentence in consequence of assistance given (or offered) to the prosecutor or investigator.

**STEP 7   Reduction for guilty pleas**

The court should take account of any potential reduction for a guilty plea in accordance with section 73 of the Sentencing Code and the guideline for Reduction in Sentence for a Guilty Plea [**SG5-1–SG5-12**].

Sentencing Guidelines

**STEP 8  Totality principle**

If sentencing an offender for more than one offence, or where the offender is already serving a sentence, consider whether the total sentence is just and proportionate to the overall offending behaviour in accordance with the *Totality* guideline [see **SG4**].

**STEP 9  Ancillary orders**

**Forfeiture – section 97 of the Trade Marks Act 1994**

The prosecution may apply for forfeiture of goods or materials bearing a sign likely to be mistaken for a registered trademark or articles designed for making copies of such a sign. The court shall make an order for forfeiture only if it is satisfied that a relevant offence has been committed in relation to the goods, material or articles. A court may infer that such an offence has been committed in relation to any goods, material or articles if it is satisfied that such an offence has been committed in relation to goods, material or articles which are representative of them (whether by reason of being of the same design or part of the same consignment or batch or otherwise).

The court may also consider whether to make other ancillary orders. These may include a deprivation order.

- Ancillary orders – Magistrates' Court
- Ancillary orders – Crown Court Compendium, Part II Sentencing

**STEP 10  Reasons**

Section 52 of the Sentencing Code imposes a duty to give reasons for, and explain the effect of, the sentence.

# PART 36   MODERN SLAVERY OFFENCES

[For the standard text on applicability see **SG0-4**]

SLAVERY, SERVITUDE AND FORCED OR
COMPULSORY LABOUR/HUMAN TRAFFICKING

**SG36-2**

*Modern Slavery Act 2015, section 1 / Modern Slavery Act 2015, section 2*

**Effective from:** 01 October 2021

Triable either way
Maximum: Life imprisonment
Offence range: High level community order – 18 years' custody

These are Schedule 19 offences for the purposes of sections 274 and 285 (required life sentence for offence carrying life sentence) of the Sentencing Code.

For offences committed on or after 3 December 2012, these are offences listed in Part 1 of Schedule 15 for the purposes of sections 273 and 283 (life sentence for second listed offence) of the Sentencing Code.

These are specified offences for the purposes of sections 266 and 279 (extended sentence for certain violent, sexual or terrorism offences) of the Criminal Justice Act 2003.

## STEP 1  Determining the offence category

### Culpability

In assessing culpability, the court should weigh up all the factors of the case, including the offender's role, to determine the appropriate level. Where there are characteristics present which fall under different categories, or where the level of the offender's role is affected by the very small scale of the operation, the court should balance these characteristics to reach a fair assessment of the offender's culpability.

### A – High Culpability

- Leading role in the offending
- Expectation of substantial financial or other material advantage
- High degree of planning/premeditation
- Use or threat of a substantial degree of physical violence towards victim(s) or their families
- Use or threat of a substantial degree of sexual violence or abuse towards victim(s) or their families

### B – Medium culpability

- Significant role in the offending
- Involves others in the offending whether by coercion, intimidation, exploitation or reward
- Expectation of significant financial or other material advantage
- Some planning/premeditation
- Use or threat of some physical violence towards victim(s) or their families
- Use or threat of some sexual violence or abuse towards victim(s) or their families
- Other threats towards victim(s) or their families
- Other cases falling between A and C because:
  - Factors in both high and lower categories are present which balance each other out and/or
  - The offender's culpability falls between the factors as described in A and C

### C – Lower culpability

- Engaged by pressure, coercion or intimidation, or has been a victim of slavery or trafficking related to this offence
- Performs limited function under direction
- Limited understanding/knowledge of the offending
- Expectation of limited or no financial or other material advantage
- Little or no planning/premeditation

### Harm

Use the factors given in the table below to identify the Harm category. If the offence involved multiple victims or took place over a significant period of time sentencers may consider moving up a harm category or moving up substantially within a category range.

The assessment of harm may be assisted by available expert evidence, but may be made on the basis of factual evidence from the victim, including evidence contained in a Victim Personal Statement (VPS). Whether a VPS provides evidence which is sufficient for a finding of serious harm depends on the circumstances of the particular case and the contents of the VPS. **However, the absence of a VPS (or other impact statement) should not be taken to indicate the absence of harm.**

Loss of personal autonomy is an inherent feature of this offending and is reflected in sentencing levels. The nature of the relationship between offender and victim in modern slavery cases may mean that the victim does not recognise themselves as such, may minimise the seriousness of their treatment, may see the perpetrator as a friend or supporter, or may choose not to give evidence through shame, regret or fear. A victim's apparent consent to their treatment should be treated with caution.

**Sentencers should therefore be careful not to assume that absence of evidence of harm from those trafficked or kept in slavery, servitude or in forced or compulsory labour indicates a lack of harm or seriousness. A close examination of all the particular circumstances will be necessary.**

### Category 1
- Exposure of victim(s) to high risk of death

A category 2 offence may also be elevated to category 1 by –

- The extreme nature of one or more factors
- The extreme impact caused by a combination of factors

### Category 2
- Serious physical harm which has a substantial and/or long-term effect
- Serious psychological harm which has a substantial and/or long-term effect
- Substantial and long-term adverse impact on the victim's daily life after the offending has ceased
- Victim(s) deceived or coerced into sexual activity

### Category 3
- Some physical harm
- Some psychological harm
- Significant financial loss/disadvantage to the victim(s)
- Exposure of victim(s) to additional risk of serious physical or psychological harm
- Other cases falling between categories 2 and 4 because:
  - Factors in both categories 2 and 4 are present which balance each other out and/or
  - The level of harm falls between the factors as described in categories 2 and 4

### Category 4
- Limited physical harm
- Limited psychological harm
- Limited financial loss/disadvantage to the victim(s)

### STEP 2 Starting point and category range

Having determined the category at step one, the court should use the corresponding starting point to reach a sentence within the category range below. The starting point applies to all offenders irrespective of plea or previous convictions.

| Harm | Culpability | | |
|------|-------------|---|---|
| | **A** | **B** | **C** |
| Category 1 | **Starting point** 14 years' custody | **Starting point** 12 years' custody | **Starting point** 8 years' custody |
| | **Category range** 10–18 years' custody | **Category range** 9–14 years' custody | **Category range** 6–10 years' custody |
| Category 2 | **Starting point** 10 years' custody | **Starting point** 8 years' custody | **Starting point** 4 years' custody |
| | **Category range** 8–12 years' custody | **Category range** 6–10 years' custody | **Category range** 3–7 years' custody |
| Category 3 | **Starting point** 8 years' custody | **Starting point** 6 years' custody | **Starting point** 2 years' custody |
| | **Category range** 6–10 years' custody | **Category range** 5–8 years' custody | **Category range** 1–4 years' custody |

| Harm | Culpability | | |
|---|---|---|---|
| Category 4 | **Starting point**<br>5 years' custody | **Starting point**<br>3 years' custody | **Starting point**<br>26 weeks' custody |
| | **Category range**<br>4–7 years' custody | **Category range**<br>1–5 years' custody | **Category range**<br>High level community<br>order – 18 months' custody |

### Community orders and custodial sentences

[For the imposition of community orders, including the community orders table, see Imposition of Community and Custodial Sentences at **SG9-2**.

For the imposition of custodial sentences see Imposition of Community and Custodial Sentences at **SG9-3**.]

Where another offence or offences arise out of the same incident or facts concurrent sentences **reflecting the overall criminality** of offending will ordinarily be appropriate: please refer to the *Totality* guideline [see **SG4**] and step six of this guideline.

Below is a **non-exhaustive** list of additional elements providing the context of the offence and factors relating to the offender. Identify whether a combination of these or other relevant factors should result in any upward or downward adjustment from the sentence arrived at so far.

**Care should be taken to avoid double counting factors already taken into account in assessing culpability**

### Factors increasing seriousness

*Statutory aggravating factors*

- Previous convictions, having regard to
  a) the **nature** of the offence to which the conviction relates and its **relevance** to the current offence; and
  b) the **time** that has elapsed since the conviction
- Offence committed whilst on bail
- Offence motivated by, or demonstrating hostility based on any of the following characteristics or presumed characteristics of the victim: religion, race, disability, sexual orientation or transgender identity

*Other aggravating factors*

- Offending took place over a long period of time (in the context of these offences, this is likely to mean months or years) where not taken into account at step 1
- Steps taken to prevent the victim reporting the offence or obtaining assistance
- Deliberate targeting of victim who is particularly vulnerable (due to age or other reason)
- Victim's passport or identity documents removed
- Gratuitous degradation of victim
- Large-scale, sophisticated and/or commercial operation (where not taken into account at step 1)
- Abuse of trust/responsibility
- Substantial measures taken to restrain the victim
- Victim forced to commit criminal offences (whether or not he/she would be able to raise a defence if charged with those offences), where not taken into account at step 1

### Factors reducing seriousness or reflecting personal mitigation

- No recent or relevant convictions
- Offender has been a victim of slavery/trafficking in circumstances unrelated to this offence
- Good character and/or exemplary conduct
- Remorse
- Sole or primary carer for dependent relatives
- Age/lack of maturity
- Mental disorder or learning disability
- Physical disability or serious medical condition requiring urgent, intensive or long-term treatment
- Offender cooperated with investigation, made early admissions and/or voluntarily reported offending

### STEP 3  Consider any factors which indicate a reduction for assistance to the prosecution

The court should take into account section 74 of the Sentencing Code (reduction in sentence for assistance to prosecution) and any other rule of law by virtue of which an offender may receive a discounted sentence in consequence of assistance given (or offered) to the prosecutor or investigator.

Sentencing Guidelines

## STEP 4  Reduction for guilty pleas

The court should take account of any potential reduction for a guilty plea in accordance with section 73 of the Sentencing Code and the guideline for Reduction in Sentence for a Guilty Plea [**SG5-1–SG5-12**].

## STEP 5  Dangerousness

The court should consider:

1) whether having regard to the criteria contained in Chapter 6 of Part 10 of the Sentencing Code it would be appropriate to impose a life sentence (sections 274 and 285);
2) whether having regard to sections 273 and 283 of the Sentencing Code it would be appropriate to impose a life sentence;
3) whether having regard to the criteria contained in Chapter 6 of Part 10 of the Sentencing Code it would be appropriate to impose an extended sentence (sections 266 and 279).

When sentencing offenders to a life sentence under these provisions, the notional determinate sentence should be used as the basis for the setting of a minimum term.

## STEP 6  Totality principle

If sentencing an offender for more than one offence, or where the offender is already serving a sentence, consider whether the total sentence is just and proportionate to the overall offending behaviour in accordance with the *Totality* guideline [see **SG4**].

## STEP 7  Ancillary orders

In all cases, the court must consider whether to make a compensation order and/or other ancillary orders. The following are most relevant in modern slavery cases:

### Slavery and trafficking prevention orders

Under section 14 of the Modern Slavery Act 2015, a court may make a slavery and trafficking prevention order against an offender convicted of a slavery or human trafficking offence, if it is satisfied that

* there is a risk that the offender may commit a slavery or human trafficking offence, and
* it is necessary to make the order for the purpose of protecting persons generally, or particular persons, from the physical or psychological harm which would be likely to occur if the offender committed such an offence.

### Confiscation

Confiscation orders under the Proceeds of Crime Act 2002 may only be made by the Crown Court. The Crown Court must proceed with a view to making a confiscation order if it is asked to do so by the prosecutor or if the Crown Court believes it is appropriate for it to do so.

Where, following conviction in a magistrates' court, the prosecutor applies for the offender to be committed to the Crown Court with a view to a confiscation order being considered, the magistrates' court must commit the offender to the Crown Court to be sentenced there (section 70 of the Proceeds of Crime Act 2002). This applies to summary only and either-way offences.

Where, but for the prosecutor's application under s.70, the magistrates' court would have committed the offender for sentence to the Crown Court anyway it must say so. Otherwise the powers of sentence of the Crown Court will be limited to those of the magistrates' court.

Confiscation must be dealt with before, and taken into account when assessing, any other fine or financial order (except compensation).

(See Proceeds of Crime Act 2002 sections 6 and 13)

### Slavery and trafficking reparation orders

Where a confiscation order has been made by the Crown Court under section 6 of the Proceeds of Crime Act 2002 the court may make a slavery and trafficking reparation order under section 8 of the 2015 Act, requiring the offender to pay compensation to the victim for any harm resulting from an offence under sections 1, 2 or 4 of that Act. In practice, the reparation will come out of the amount taken under the confiscation order. **In every eligible case, the court must consider whether to make a slavery and trafficking reparation order, and if one is not made the judge must give reasons.** However, a slavery and trafficking reparation order cannot be made if the court has made a compensation order under section 134 of the Sentencing Code.

**Restraining order**

Where an offender is convicted of any offence, the court may make a restraining order (section 360 of the Sentencing Code). The order may prohibit the offender from doing anything for the purpose of protecting the victim of the offence, or any other person mentioned in the order, from further conduct which amounts to harassment or will cause a fear of violence.

The order may have effect for a specified period or until further order.

**Forfeiture**

A court convicting someone on indictment of human trafficking under section 2 of the 2015 Act may order the forfeiture of a vehicle, ship or aircraft used or intended to be used in connection with the offence of which the person is convicted (see section 11 of the 2015 Act).

**STEP 8   Reasons**

Section 52 of the Sentencing Code imposes a duty to give reasons for, and explain the effect of, the sentence.

**STEP 9   Consideration for time spent on bail**

The court must consider whether to give credit for time spent on bail in accordance with section 240A of the Criminal Justice Act 2003 and section 325 of the Sentencing Code.

COMMITTING OFFENCE WITH INTENT TO COMMIT                                **SG36-3**
A HUMAN TRAFFICKING OFFENCE

*Modern Slavery Act 2015, s.4*

**Effective from:** 01 October 2021

Triable only on indictment (if kidnapping or false imprisonment committed),
otherwise triable either way

Maximum: Life imprisonment (if kidnapping or false imprisonment committed),
otherwise 10 years' custody

The starting point and range should be commensurate with that for the preliminary offence actually committed but with an enhancement to reflect the intention to commit a human trafficking offence. The enhancement will vary depending on the nature and seriousness of the intended trafficking offence, the seriousness of the preliminary offence, and the extent to which the offender was themselves the victim of modern slavery, pressure, coercion or intimidation, but up to 2 years' custody is suggested as a suitable enhancement. Sentencers should also take into account the totality of offending (see the *Totality* guideline [see **SG4**] in particular where the preliminary offence or other modern slavery offences are to be sentenced alongside the section 4 offence).

BREACH OF A SLAVERY AND TRAFFICKING PREVENTION                          **SG36-4**
ORDER/BREACH OF A SLAVERY AND TRAFFICKING RISK ORDER

*Modern Slavery Act 2015, s.30*

**Effective from: 01 October 2021**

Triable either way
Maximum: 5 years' imprisonment

In sentencing an offence under section 30, a court is entitled to use, and may be assisted by, a guideline for an analogous offence subject to differences in the elements of the offences and the statutory maxima. Depending on the nature of the particular slavery and trafficking risk, an analogous offence may be one or more of the following:

- Breach of a sexual harm prevention order [see **SG15-8**]
- Breach of a criminal behaviour order [see **SG15-7**]

The court will also wish to consider the General guideline [see **SG2-1** *et seq.*].

# Index